Frequently Used Symbols

β beta coefficient, a measure of an asset's systematic riskiness.
C call option value.
CAPM capital asset pricing model.
CAR cumulative average residuals.
CF cash flow; CF_t is cash flow in period *t*.
CML capital market line.
COV_{ij} covariance of the returns between assets *i* and *j*.
D dividend per share of stock; D_t is dividend per share during period *t*.
DDM dividend discount model.
DM deutschemark (German currency).
EBIT earnings before interest and taxes.
EBITDA earning before interest, taxes, depreciation, and amortization.
EMH efficient market hypothesis.
EPS earnings per share.
E(R) expected return; $E(R_t)$ is the expected return during period *t*.
F futures contract delivery price.
FV future value.
FVIF future value interest factor for a lump sum.
FVIFA future value interest factor for an annuity.
FX foreign exchange.
G geometric mean.
g growth rate in earnings, dividends, or stock prices.
h hedge ratio.
HPR holding period return.
HPY holding period yield.
I rate of inflation. E(I) is the expected rate of inflation.
k required rate of return.
£ pound (United Kingdom currency).
OAS option-adjusted spread.
P price of a share of stock or put option; P_o is the current price.
P/BV price/book value ratio.
P/E price/earnings ratio.
PPP purchasing power parity.
P/S price/sales ratio.
PV present value.
PVIF present value interest factor for a lump sum.
PVIFA present value interest factor for an annuity.
r_{ij} correlation coefficient between assets *i* and *j*.
RFR rate of return on a risk-free asset.
ROA return on assets.
ROE return on equity.
RR fraction of a firm's earnings retained rather than paid out. It is equal to (1 − D/E), where D/E is the ratio of dividends (D) to earnings (E).
SML security market line.
Σ summation sign (capital sigma).
σ standard deviation (lowercase sigma).
σ_{ij} covariance between returns for security *i* and *j*.
t tax rate.
time when used as a subscript (e.g., D_t—the dividend in year *t*).
T time to expiration.
V value of an asset; V_j is the value of asset *j*.
WACC weighted average cost of capital.
X option exercise price.
¥ yen (Japanese currency).
YTC yield to call.
YTM yield to maturity.

Investment Analysis and Portfolio Management

Sixth Edition

Investment Analysis and Portfolio Management

Sixth Edition

Frank K. Reilly
University of Notre Dame

Keith C. Brown
University of Texas at Austin

The Dryden Press
Harcourt College Publishers
Fort Worth Philadelphia San Diego New York Orlando Austin San Antonio
Toronto Montreal London Sydney Tokyo

Publisher	Mike Roche
Executive Editor	Mike Reynolds
Market Strategist	Charlie Watson
Developmental Editor	Terri House
Project Editor	Jon Davies
Art Director	Scott Baker
Production Manager	Lois West

Cover image: FPG International.

ISBN: 0-03-025809-x
Library of Congress Catalog Card Number: 99-74300

Portions of this work were published in previous editions.

Address for Domestic Orders
The Dryden Press, 6277 Sea Harbor Drive, Orlando, FL 32887-6777
800-782-4479

Address for International Orders
International Customer Service
The Dryden Press, 6277 Sea Harbor Drive, Orlando, FL 32887-6777
407-345-3800
(fax) 407-345-4060
(e-mail) hbintl@harcourtbrace.com

Address for Editorial Correspondence
The Dryden Press, 301 Commerce Street, Suite 3700, Fort Worth, TX 76102

Web Site Address
http://www.hbcollege.com

Printed in the United States of America

0 1 2 3 4 5 6 7 8   032   9 8 7 6 5 4 3 2

The Dryden Press
Harcourt College Publishers

To my best friend and wife,
Therese,
and the greatest gifts and
sources of our happiness,
Frank K. III, Charlotte, and Lauren
Clarence R. II
Therese B., and Anita
Edgar B., Michele, Kayleigh, and Madison J. T.

F. K. R.

To Sheryl, Alexander, and Andrew,
who make it all worthwhile

K. C. B.

The Dryden Press Series in Finance

Amling and Droms
Investment Fundamentals

Berry and Young
Managing Investments: A Case Approach

Besley and Brigham
Essentials of Managerial Finance
Twelfth Edition

Besley and Brigham
Principle of Finance

Boone, Kurtz, and Hearth
Planning Your Financial Future
Second Edition

Brigham, Gapenski, and Daves
Intermediate Financial Management
Sixth Edition

Brigham, Gapenski, and Ehrhardt
Financial Management: Theory and Practice
Ninth Edition

Brigham and Houston
Fundamentals of Financial Management
Eighth Edition

Brigham and Houston
Fundamentals of Financial Management: Concise
Second Edition

Brigham and Klein
2000 Cases in Financial Management: Dryden Request

Chance
An Introduction to Derivatives
Fourth Edition

Conroy
Finance Interactive

Cooley
Advances in Business Financial Management: A Collection of Readings
Second Edition

Dickerson, Campsey, and Brigham
Introduction to Financial Management
Fourth Edition

Eaker, Fabozzi, and Grant
International Corporate Finance

Gardner, Mills, and Cooperman
Managing Financial Institutions: An Asset/Liability Approach
Fourth Edition

Gitman and Joehnk
Personal Financial Planning
Eighth Edition

Greenbaum and Thakor
Contemporary Financial Intermediation

Hall
Effective Use of a Financial Calculator

Hayes and Meerschwam
Financial Institutions: Contemporary Cases in the Financial Services Industry

Hearth and Zaima
Contemporary Investments: Security and Portfolio Analysis
Second Edition

Johnson
Issues and Readings in Managerial Finance
Fourth Edition

Kidwell, Peterson, and Blackwell
Financial Institutions, Markets, and Money
Seventh Edition

Koch and MacDonald
Bank Management
Fourth Edition

Leahigh
Pocket Guide to Finance

Maness and Zietlow
Short-Term Financial Management

Mayes and Shank
Financial Analysis with Lotus 1-2-3 for Windows

Mayes and Shank
Financial Analysis with Microsoft Excel

Mayo
Financial Institutions, Investments, and Management: An Introduction
Sixth Edition

Mayo
Investments: An Introduction
Sixth Edition

Osteryoung, Newman, and Davies
Small Firm Finance: An Entrepreneurial Analysis

Reilly and Brown
Investment Analysis and Portfolio Management
Sixth Edition

Reilly and Norton
Investments
Fifth Edition

Sandburg
Discovering Your Finance Career

Seitz and Ellison
Capital Budgeting and Long-Term Financing Decisions
Third Edition

Siegel and Siegel
Futures Markets

Smith and Spudeck
Interest Rates: Principles and Applications

Stickney and Brown
Financial Reporting and Statement Analysis: A Strategic Perspective
Fourth Edition

Preface

The pleasure of authoring a textbook comes from writing about a subject that you enjoy and find exciting. As an author, you hope that you can pass on to the reader not only knowledge but also the excitement that you feel for the subject. In addition, writing about investments brings an added stimulant because the subject can affect the reader during his or her entire business career and beyond. We hope what readers derive from this course will help them enjoy better lives through managing their resources properly.

The purpose of this book is to help you learn how to manage your money so that you will derive the maximum benefit from what you earn. To accomplish this purpose, you need to learn about the investment alternatives that are available today and, what is more important, to develop a way of analyzing and thinking about investments that will remain with you in the years ahead when new and different investment opportunities become available.

Because of its dual purpose, the book mixes description and theory. The descriptive material discusses available investment instruments and considers the purpose and operation of capital markets in the United States and around the world. The theoretical portion details how you should evaluate current investments and future opportunities to develop a portfolio of investments that will satisfy your risk–return objectives.

Preparing this sixth edition has been challenging for two reasons. First, many changes have occurred in the securities markets during the last few years in terms of theory, new financial instruments, and trading practices. Second, as mentioned in prior editions, capital markets have become global. Consequently, very early in the book we present the compelling case for global investing. Subsequently, to ensure that you are prepared to function in this new global environment, almost every chapter discusses how investment practice or theory is influenced by the globalization of investments and capital markets. This completely integrated treatment is to ensure that you leave this course with a completely global mindset on investments that will serve you well in the 21st century.

Intended Market

This text is addressed to both graduate and advanced undergraduate students who are looking for an in-depth discussion of investments and portfolio management. The presentation of the material is intended to be rigorous and empirical, without being overly quantitative. A proper discussion of the modern developments in investments and portfolio theory must be rigorous. The detailed discussion of numerical empirical studies reflects the belief that it is essential for our theories to be exposed to the real world and be judged on the basis of how well they help us understand and explain reality.

Key Features of the Sixth Edition

When planning the sixth edition of *Investment Analysis and Portfolio Management,* we wanted to retain its traditional strengths and capitalize on new developments in the investments area to make it the most comprehensive investments textbook available.

First, the sixth edition maintains its unparalleled international coverage. Investing knows no borders, and although the total integration of domestic and global investment opportunities may seem to contradict the need for separate discussions of international issues, it in fact makes the need for specific information on non-U.S. markets, instruments, conventions, and techniques even more compelling. Sections of chapters that deal with international topics are designated by this icon for easy identification.

Second, today's investing environment includes derivative securities not as exotic anomalies but as standard investment instruments. We felt that *Investment Analysis and Portfolio Management* must reflect that situation. Consequently, our four chapters on derivatives have been rewritten to provide an even more intuitive, clear discussion of the different instruments, their markets, valuation, trading strategies, and general use as risk management/return enhancement tools.

The introductory derivatives chapter appears early in the book as Chapter 11 in the section on "Developments in Investment Theory." We kept this placement from the previous edition because we are still committed to the philosophy that every investments student needs to be exposed to the basics of derivative instruments, markets, and usage. Our Chapter 11 provides this overview.

For instructors who want to get into more detail on derivative pricing, valuation, and strategies, we have three separate chapters near the end of the book. Chapter 23 discusses forwards and futures contracts first, before options, because typically investors consider forward/futures positions before they turn to options to hedge risk. Chapter 24 then covers option contracts, which are variations of forwards and futures. Part 4 concludes with a chapter on swaps, warrants, convertibles, and structured notes. Chapter 25 is an in-depth discussion of these more "advanced" derivative types.

Third, Chapter 10, "Extensions and Testing of Asset Pricing Theories," follows immediately after the introductory chapter on asset pricing models. We felt that instructors who wanted to teach this chapter would do so in this order.

Fourth, we have added many new questions and problems to the end-of-chapter material, including a significant number of CFA exercises through the 1999 exam, to provide more student practice on executing computations to more sophisticated investment problems. These are designated by the CFA (CFA) icon.

WEB SITE LISTINGS To reflect the growing use of the World Wide Web as a learning tool and a source of information, each chapter contains an annotated list of the Web sites that relate to the chapter's topic. Students will want to "surf the net" using these applications to gain further insight into the practice of investments and the textbook discussions.

Major Content Changes in the Sixth Edition

The text has been thoroughly updated for currency. In addition to these time-related revisions, we have also made the following specific changes to individual chapters:

Chapter 3 Includes results of a new study of risk–return results and correlations among domestic and foreign capital market assets through 1997.

Chapter 4 Contains a new discussion and presentation showing the numerous mergers and affiliations taking place among equity markets in the United States and around the world.

Chapter 7 Includes a discussion of studies that examined the price-earnings/growth rate (PEG) ratios and how useful they are for selecting stocks. Also includes a discussion of new evidence that indicates that the prevailing monetary policy environment has had a significant impact on stock prices directly, but also influences how other variables affect stocks. Contains an expanded discussion of the implications of the EMH results for analysts and portfolio managers.

Chapter 11 Includes greatly expanded coverage of the basic payoffs and trading mechanics of forwards, futures, and options, with new examples based on actual market data. Also contains a substantially revised section on using derivatives to manage portfolio risk.

Chapter 12 Contains a discussion of a new example company—the Walgreen Company—that continues into the industry and company analysis. Also considers the effect of leases on financial risk ratios.

Chapter 13 Includes a major addition to the equity valuation section, where we consider two major approaches to equity valuation (discounted cash-flow techniques and relative valuation techniques). Subsequently, there is a specific discussion of why and when to use each of the approaches followed by a description and discussion of each of the cash-flow and relative valuation techniques.

Chapter 14 Includes a discussion of several recent studies that have found that monetary policy and the monetary environment have an impact on stock returns. Also discusses new studies that indicate that the relationship between stock returns and other variables such as size and price-to-book value are also affected by the ease or tightness of monetary policy.

Chapter 15 Contains a discussion and detailed presentation regarding the recently created Treasury Inflation Protected Securities (TIPS). Also contains an updated presentation on the issuance of high-yield bonds using 144A issues that have come to dominate the high-yield bond market.

Chapter 16 Includes bond valuation using a single discount rate and valuation using prevailing spot rates. There is an expanded discussion of option-adjusted duration that considers the duration of the noncallable bond and bonds with embedded options. The section on effective duration is dramatically modified and expanded to include effective convexity and provides detailed computations of effective duration and convexity based on a bond pricing model. We show effective duration–yield curves and effective convexity–yield curves for option-free, callable, and putable bonds. Also we introduce empirical duration that can be used for other assets including common stock. Because of some shortcomings of the "traditional" yield spread, we discuss and demonstrate how to calculate static yield spreads. Finally, there is a new discussion on option-adjusted spreads (OAS), and we present the steps involved in estimating the OAS for a specific bond.

Chapter 17 Contains the results from a recent study that demonstrates the very competitive risk-adjusted performance for various bonds compared to other capital assets during the period 1980–1997.

Chapter 18 Includes an expanded analysis of the aggregate market that follows from the presentation in Chapter 13, which introduced the two general approaches to equity valuation and the several techniques that flow from these approaches. The cash-flow techniques are employed to compute specific estimates of value for the S&P 400 Index. In addition, we compute and analyze relative valuation ratios for the market including price-to-earnings, price-to-book value, price-to-cash-flow, and price-to-sales.

Chapter 19 Contains a new discussion of the business cycle and its effect on alternative industry sectors, as well as a consideration of structural economic changes and the impact that these changes have on various industries. Again, we apply the several valuation techniques included in the two valuation approaches to the retail drugstore industry. This includes using a two-stage, free cash-flow growth model and the relative valuation ratios with comparisons to similar ratios for the aggregate market. A new appendix to the chapter discusses an article that considers how the analysis of the components of the return on assets for an industry provides insights into the competitive strategy for the industry.

Chapter 20 Includes a valuation of Walgreen Company using several present-value-of-cash-flow models including two-stage growth models. Also, examines the several relative valuation ratios for Walgreen and compares the company ratios to comparable market and industry ratios. The growth company valuation model section is reorganized to integrate value-added models, such as economic value added (EVA) and the sales franchise model with the traditional growth company models, to show how they are similar and provide insights to each other.

Chapter 22 Contains a new discussion on the merits of passive versus active asset management. Also includes extensive new sections that explain growth versus value investing, that introduce and illustrate the topic of Style Analysis, and that present Asset Allocation strategies. There is also a revised section on using derivatives with equity portfolios.

Chapter 23 Includes revised examples throughout the chapter emphasizing actual market data, and revised sections on the mechanics of futures trading and on index arbitrage.

Chapter 24 Contains an extensive new section on exotic options, plus extensive revisions to the section on the binomial option pricing model and the option strategies section. There are also revised discussions of the role volatility plays in option valuation and trading and of option trading fundamentals. Finally, an extended discussion of the Black-Scholes model in practice is included.

Chapter 25 Includes a revised discussion of the interest-rate-swap valuation, an expanded and revised discussion of convertible bonds and structured notes, and a revised section on using swaps to manage portfolio risk.

Chapter 26 Has been expanded (and retitled) to cover all forms of professional asset management, instead of just covering mutual funds. Included is an extensive new section comparing the various forms of private and public professional asset management, with examples of practices at specific firms, and a new section evaluating the benefits of mutual funds, along with new material on mutual fund objectives. There is also an extensive new section on ethics and regulation in the professional asset management industry, which includes discussions of soft dollars and compensation arrangements. Finally, the chapter contains revised examples of mutual fund structure and performance using actual market data.

Chapter 27 Includes extensive new sections on peer group comparisons, on the information ratio performance measure, and on reporting investment performance, including a discussion of time-weighted versus dollar-weighted returns and AIMR's Performance Presentation Standards. The chapter also contains updated examples of performance measurement using actual market data and a revised treatment of bond portfolio measurement.

SUPPLEMENT PACKAGE

The preparation of the sixth edition provided the opportunity to enhance the supplement products offered to instructors and students who use *Investment Analysis and Portfolio Management.* The result of this examination is a greatly improved package that provides more than just basic answers and solutions. We are indebted to the supplement writers who devoted their time, energy, and creativity to making this supplement package the best it has ever been.

THE INSTRUCTOR'S MANUAL AND TEST BANK The *Instructor's Manual and Test Bank,* written by Jeanette Diamond at the University of Nebraska at Omaha, contains a brief outline of each chapter's key concepts and equations that can be easily copied and distributed to students as a reference tool. The *Test Bank* includes an extensive set of new questions and problems and complete solutions to the testing material.

For instructors who would like to prepare their exams via computer, The Dryden Press will provide a Microsoft Word diskette with the complete *Test Bank* for easy test compilation.

THE SOLUTIONS MANUAL This separate volume, which can be purchased by students if instructors wish, contains all the answers to the end-of-chapter questions and solutions to end-of-chapter problems. Again, Jeanette Diamond was ever diligent in the preparation of these materials, ensuring the most error-free solutions possible.

LECTURE PRESENTATION SOFTWARE A comprehensive set of slides in PowerPoint are available. Each chapter has a self-contained presentation that covers all the key concepts, equations, and examples within the chapter. The files can be used as is for an innovative, interactive class presentation. Instructors who have access to Microsoft PowerPoint can modify the slides in any way they wish, adding or deleting materials to match their needs.

STUDY GUIDE A student *Study Guide,* prepared by David Leahigh of King's College, includes the following for each chapter: a reference outline of definitions and equations; a brief concept outline; extensive exercises, including true-false, fill-in-the-blank, multiple-choice, and short-answer questions; a set of problems that provide additional practice; and answers to all of these exercises. The *Study Guide* is an excellent resource for all students wanting additional information and practice.

WEB SITE A book-specific Web site contains useful downloadable ancillary and resource materials for instructors and students. You can access it at **www.harcourtcollege.com**.

The Dryden Press will provide complimentary supplements or supplement packages to those adopters qualified under our adoption policy. Please contact your sales representative to learn how you may qualify. If as an adopter or potential user you receive supplements you do not need, please return them to your sales representative or send them to:

Attn: Returns Department
Troy Warehouse
465 South Lincoln Drive
Troy, MO 63379

ACKNOWLEDGMENTS

So many people have helped us in so many ways that we hesitate to list them, fearing that we may miss someone. Accepting this risk, we will begin with the University of Notre Dame and the University of Texas at Austin because of their direct support. Also, we must thank the Bernard J. Hank Family, who have endowed the Chair that helped bring Frank Reilly back to Notre Dame and that has provided support for our work.

Reviewers for this edition were:

Robert Brooks
University of Alabama

Greg Filbeck
University of Toledo

Eric Higgins
Drexel University

Iqbal Mansur
Widener University

Murli Rajan
University of Scranton

Narendar V. Rao
Northeastern Illinois University

We were fortunate to have the following excellent reviewers for earlier editions:

John Alexander
Clemson University

Robert Angell
East Carolina University

George Aragon
Boston College

Brian Belt
University of Missouri—Kansas City

Omar M. Benkato
Ball State University

Arand Bhattacharya
University of Cincinnati

Carol Billingham
Central Michigan University

Susan Block
University of California—Santa Barbara

Gerald A. Blum
Babson College

Robert E. Brooks
University of Alabama

Robert J. Brown
Harrisburg, Pennsylvania

Charles Cao
Pennsylvania State University

Atreya Chakraborty
Brandeis University

Dosoung Choi
University of Tennessee

Robert Clark
University of Vermont

John Clinebell
University of Northern Colorado

James D'Mello
Western Michigan University

Eugene F. Drzycimski
University of Wisconsin—Oshkosh

William Dukes
Texas Tech University

John Dunkelberg
Wake Forest University

Eric Emory
Sacred Heart University

Thomas Eyssell
University of Missouri—St. Louis

James Feller
Middle Tennessee State University

Eurico Ferreira
Clemson University

Michael Ferri
John Carroll University

Joseph E. Finnerty
University of Illinois

Harry Friedman
New York University

R. H. Gilmer
University of Mississippi

Stephen Goldstein
University of South Carolina

Steven Goldstein
Robinson-Humphrey/American Express

Keshav Gupta
Oklahoma State University

Sally A. Hamilton
Santa Clara University

Ronald Hoffmeister
Arizona State University

Ron Hutchins
Eastern Michigan University

A. James Ifflander
Arizona State University

Stan Jacobs
Central Washington University

Kwang Jun
Michigan State University

Jaroslaw Komarynsky
Northern Illinois University

Danny Litt
Century Software Systems/UCLA

Miles Livingston
University of Florida

Christopher Ma
Texas Tech University

Davinder Malhotra
Philadelphia College of Textiles and Science

Stephen Mann
University of South Carolina

Iqbal Mansur
Widener University

George Mason
University of Hartford

John Matthys
DePaul University

Michael McBain
Marquette University

Dennis McConnell
University of Maine

Jeanette Medewitz
University of Nebraska—Omaha

Jacob Michaelsen
University of California—Santa Cruz

Nicholas Michas
Northern Illinois University

Thomas W. Miller Jr.
University of Missouri—Columbia

Lalatendu Misra
University of Texas—San Antonio

Michael Murray
LaCrosse, Wisconsin

Henry Oppenheimer
University of Rhode Island

John Peavy
Southern Methodist University

George Philippatos
University of Tennessee

George Pinches
University of Kansas

Rose Prasad
Central Michigan University

Laurie Prather
University of Tennessee at Chattanooga

George A. Racette
University of Oregon

Murli Rajan
University of Scranton

Steve Rich
Baylor University

Bruce Robin
Old Dominion University

James Rosenfeld
Emory University

Stanley D. Ryals
Investment Counsel, Inc.

Katrina F. Sherrerd
Association of Investment Management and Research

Shekar Shetty
University of South Dakota

Frederic Shipley
DePaul University

Douglas Southard
Virginia Polytechnic Institute

Harold Stevenson
Arizona State University

Kishore Tandon
The City University of New York—Baruch College

Donald Thompson
Georgia State University

David E. Upton
Virginia Commonwealth University

E. Theodore Veit
Rollins College

Premal Vora
King's College

Bruce Wardrep
East Carolina University

Robert Weigand
University of South Florida

Rolf Wubbels
New York University

Valuable comments and suggestions have come from former graduate students at the University of Illinois: Wenchi Kao, DePaul University, and David Wright, University of Wisconsin—Parkside. Once more, we were blessed with bright, dedicated research assistants when we needed them the most. This includes Pensiri Koomsap and Lu Sun, who have been extremely careful, dependable, and creative.

Current and former colleagues have been very helpful: Yu-Chi Chang, Rob Batallio, and Paul Schultz, University of Notre Dame; C. F. Lee, Rutgers University; and John M. Wachowicz, University of Tennessee. As always, some of the best insights and most stimulating comments continue to come during too-infrequent walks with a very good friend, Jim Gentry of the University of Illinois.

We are convinced that a professor who wants to write a book that is academically respectable, relevant, as well as realistic requires help from the "real world." We have been fortunate to develop relationships with a number of individuals (including a growing number of former students) whom we consider our contacts with reality.

We especially want to thank Robert Conway, who was the managing director of the London office of Goldman, Sachs and Company, for suggesting several years ago that it was essential to have the book reflect the rapidly evolving global market. This important advice has had a profound effect on this book over time.

The following individuals have graciously provided important insights and material:

Sharon Athey
Brown Brothers Harriman

Joseph C. Bencivenga
Bankers Trust

Lowell Benson
Robert A. Murray Partners

David G. Booth
Dimensional Fund Advisors, Inc.

Gary Brinson
UBS Brinson

Charles K. Brown
Goldman, Sachs and Company

David Chapman
University of Texas

Dwight D. Churchill
Fidelity Management and Research

Abby Joseph Cohen
Goldman, Sachs and Company

Thomas Coleman
Adler, Coleman and Company (NYSE)

Robert Conway
Goldman, Sachs and Company

Robert J. Davis
Crimson Capital Company

Robert J. Davis Jr.
Merrill Lynch Pierce Fenner and Smith

Philip Delaney Jr.
Northern Trust Bank

Sam Eisenstadt
Value Line

Frank J. Fabozzi
Journal of Portfolio Management

Paul Feldman
Goldman, Sachs and Company

Kenneth Fisher
Forbes

John J. Flanagan Jr.
Lawrence, O'Donnell, Marcus and Company

H. Gifford Fong
Gifford Fong Associates

Martin S. Fridson
Merrill Lynch Pierce Fenner and Smith

Khalid Ghayur
HSBC Asset Management Ltd.

Richard A. Grasso
New York Stock Exchange

William J. Hank
Moore Financial Corporation

Rick Hans
Walgreen Corporation

Lea B. Hansen
Greenwich Associates

W. Van Harlow
Fidelity Management and Research

John W. Jordan II
The Jordan Company

Andrew Kalotay
Kalotay Associates

Luke Knecht
RCM Capital Management

Warren N. Koontz Jr.
Loomis, Sayles and Company

Mark Kritzman
Windham Capital Management

Martin Leibowitz
TIAA-CREF

Douglas R. Lempereur
Templeton Investment Counsel, Inc.

Robert Levine
Nomura Securities

Michael Lipper
Lipper Analytical

Amy Lipton
Bankers Trust

George W. Long
Long Investment Management Ltd.

Scott Lummer
401(k) Forum

John Maginn
Mutual of Omaha

Scott Malpass
University of Notre Dame

Andras Marosi
University of Texas

Dominic Marshall
Benson Associates

Richard McCabe
Merrill Lynch Pierce Fenner and Smith

Michael McCowin
State of Wisconsin Investment Board

Terrence J. McGlinn
McGlinn Capital Markets

Janet T. Miller
Rowland and Company

Brian Moore
McDonald's Corporation

Salvator Muoio
SM Investors, LP

Robert G. Murray
First Interstate Bank of Oregon

Gabrielle Napolitano
Goldman, Sachs and Company

Ian Rossa O'Reilly
Wood Gundy, Inc.

Robert Parrino
University of Texas

Philip J. Purcell III
Morgan Stanley Dean Witter

Jack Pycik
Consultant

Chet Ragavan
Merrill Lynch Pierce Fenner and Smith

John C. Rudolf
Summit Capital Management

Stanley Ryals
Investment Counsel, Inc.

Ron Ryan
Ryan Labs, Inc.

Sean St. Clair
Lehman Brothers

Robert F. Semmens Jr.
The Beacon Group

Brian Singer
UBS Brinson

Clay Singleton
Ibbotson Associates

Donald J. Smith
Boston University

William Smith
Morgan Stanley Dean Witter

Fred H. Speece Jr.
Speece, Lewis and Thorson

William M. Stephens
Husic Capital Management

James Stork
Duff and Phelps

Kevin Terhaar
UBS Brinson

Anthony Vignola
Kidder, Peabody and Company

William M. Wadden
Stein, Roe and Farnham

Sushi Wadhwani
Goldman, Sachs and Company

Jeffrey M. Weingarten
Goldman, Sachs and Company

Ken Wiles
Fulcrum Financial Group

Robert Wilmouth
National Futures Association

Richard S. Wilson
Ryan Labs, Inc.

We continue to benefit from the help and consideration of the dedicated people who are or have been associated with the Institute of Chartered Financial Analysts, which is a part of the Association for Investment Management and Research: Jeff Beutow, Tom Bowman, Whit Broome, Bob Johnson, Bob Luck, Pete Morley, Sue Martin, Katie Sherrerd, and Donald Tuttle.

Professor Reilly would like to thank his assistant, Cheri Gray, who had the unenviable task of keeping his office and his life in some sort of order during this project. Jon Davies was the understanding project editor who put up with both of our schedules and brought the book from messy manuscript and sloppy exhibits to bound volume with incredibly good humor.

As always, our greatest gratitude is to our families—past, present, and future. Our parents gave us life and helped us understand love and how to give it. Most important are our wives who provide love, understanding, and support throughout the day and night. We thank God for our children and grandchildren who ensure that our lives are full of love, laughs, and excitement.

Frank K. Reilly
Notre Dame, Indiana

Keith C. Brown
Austin, Texas
October 1999

About the Authors

Frank K. Reilly is the Bernard J. Hank Professor of Business Administration and former dean of the College of Business Administration at the University of Notre Dame. Holding degrees from the University of Notre Dame (B.B.A.), Northwestern University (M.B.A.), and the University of Chicago (Ph.D.), Professor Reilly has taught at the University of Illinois, the University of Kansas, and the University of Wyoming in addition to the University of Notre Dame. He has several years of experience as a senior securities analyst, as well as experience in stock and bond trading. A Chartered Financial Analyst (CFA), he has been a member of the Council of Examiners, the Research Foundation, the Council on Education and Research, the Education Committee, and the CFA Grading Committee, and is currently on the Board of Trustees of the Institute of Chartered Financial Analysts. Professor Reilly has been president of the Financial Management Association, the Midwest Business Administration Association, the Eastern Finance Association, the Academy of Financial Services, and the Midwest Finance Association. He is or has been on the board of directors of the Norwest Bank of Indiana, the Investment Analysts Society of Chicago, Brinson Global Funds (chairman), Fort Dearborn Income Securities, Greenwood Trust Co., NIBCO, Inc., Battery Park Funds, Inc., Morgan Stanley Dean Witter Trust, Certified Financial Planners Board of Standards, and the Association for Investment Management and Research (immediate past chairman).

As the author of more than one hundred articles, monographs, and papers, Professor Reilly has written for numerous publications including *Journal of Finance, Journal of Financial and Quantitative Analysis, Journal of Accounting Research, Financial Management, Financial Analysts Journal, Journal of Fixed Income, Financial Review,* and *Journal of Portfolio Management.* In addition to *Investment Analysis and Portfolio Management,* Sixth Edition, Professor Reilly is the coauthor of another textbook, *Investments,* Fifth Edition (The Dryden Press, 1999), with Edgar A. Norton.

Professor Reilly was named on the list of *Outstanding Educators in America* and has received the University of Illinois Alumni Association Graduate Teaching Award, the Outstanding Educator Award from the M.B.A. class at the University of Illinois, and the Outstanding Teacher Award from the M.B.A. class at Notre Dame. He also received the C. Stewart Sheppard Award from the Association of Investment Management and Research (AIMR) for his contribution to the educational mission of the Association. He is editor of *Readings and Issues in Investments, Ethics and the Investment Industry,* and *High Yield Bonds: Analysis and Risk Assessment,* and is or has been a member of the editorial boards of *Financial Management, European Journal of Finance, Financial Review, Financial Services Review, Journal of Applied Business Research, Journal of Financial Education,* and *Quarterly Review of Economics and Business.* He is included in *Who's Who in Finance and Industry, Who's Who in America, Who's Who in American Education,* and *Who's Who in the World.*

Keith C. Brown holds the position of Allied Bancshares Centennial Fellow and Professor of Finance at the Graduate School of Business, University of Texas. He received his B.A. in Economics from San Diego State University, where he was a member of the Phi Beta Kappa, Phi Kappa Phi, and Omicron Delta Epsilon honor societies. He received his M.S. and Ph.D. in Financial Economics from the Krannert Graduate School of Management at Purdue University. Since leaving school in 1981, he has specialized in teaching Investments, Derivatives, and Capital Markets courses at the M.B.A. and Ph.D. levels and has received six awards for teaching innovation and excellence. In addition to his academic responsibilities, he is also President and Chief Operating Officer of The M.B.A. Investment Fund, L.L.C., a privately funded investment company managed by graduate students at the University of Texas.

Professor Brown has published more than 40 articles, monographs, chapters, and papers on topics ranging from asset pricing and investment strategy to financial risk management. His publications have appeared in such journals as *Journal of Finance, Journal of Financial Economics, Journal of Financial and Quantitative Analysis, Review of Economics and Statistics, Financial Analysts Journal, Financial Management, Advances in Futures and Options Research, Journal of Fixed Income, Journal of Applied Corporate Finance,* and *Journal of Portfolio Management.* In addition to his contributions to *Investment Analysis and Portfolio Management,* Sixth Edition, he is a coauthor of *Interest Rate and Currency Swaps: A Tutorial,* a textbook published in 1995 through the Association for Investment Management and Research (AIMR). He received a Graham and Dodd Award from the Financial Analysts Federation as an author of one of the best articles published by *Financial Analysts Journal* in 1990, and a Smith-Breeden Prize from the *Journal of Finance* in 1996.

In August 1988, Professor Brown received his charter from the Institute of Chartered Financial Analysts (ICFA). He has served as a member of AIMR's CFA Candidate Curriculum Committee and Education Committee, and on the CFA Examination Grading staff. For 5 years, he was the research director of the Research Foundation of the ICFA, from which position he guided the development of the research portion of the organization's worldwide educational mission. For the past several years, he has also been associate editor for *Financial Analysts Journal.* In other professional service, Professor Brown has been a regional director for the Financial Management Association and has served as the applied research track chairman for that organization's annual conference.

Professor Brown is the cofounder and senior partner of Fulcrum Financial Group, a portfolio management and investment advisory firm located in Austin, Texas, and Charlotte, North Carolina, that currently oversees portfolios holding a total of $60 million in fixed-income securities. From May 1987 to August 1988 he was based in New York as a senior consultant to the Corporate Professional Development Department at Manufacturers Hanover Trust Company. He has lectured extensively throughout the world on investment and risk management topics in the executive development programs for such companies as Chase Manhattan Bank, Chemical Bank, Lehman Brothers, Union Bank of Switzerland, Shearson, Chase Bank of Texas, The Beacon Group, Motorola, and Halliburton. He also spent 13 months as a senior planner with a California-based financial planning firm.

Contents in Brief

CONTENTS

xxiii

Investment Analysis and Portfolio Management

Sixth Edition

Part

1 The Investment Background

N
E
W
S

The chapters in this section will provide a background for your study of investments by answering the following questions:

- Why do people invest?
- How do you measure the returns and risks for alternative investments?
- What factors should you consider when you make asset allocation decisions?
- What investments are available?
- How do securities markets function?
- How and why are securities markets in the United States and around the world changing?
- What are the major uses of security market indexes?
- How can you evaluate the market behavior of common stocks and bonds?
- What factors cause differences among stock-and-bond market indexes?

In the first chapter we consider why an individual would invest, how to measure the rates of return and risk for alternative investments, and what factors determine an investor's required rate of return on an investment. The latter point will be important in subsequent analyses when we work to understand investor behavior, the markets for alternative securities, and the valuation of various investments.

Because the ultimate decision facing an investor is the makeup of his or her portfolio, Chapter 2 deals with the all-important asset allocation decision. This includes specific steps in the portfolio management process and factors that influence the makeup of an investor's portfolio over his or her life cycle.

To minimize risk, investment theory asserts the need to diversify. Chapter 3 begins our exploration of investments available to investors, by making an overpowering case for investing globally rather than limiting choices to only U.S. securities. Building on this premise, we discuss several investment instruments found in global markets. We conclude the chapter with a review of the historical rates of return and measures of risk for a number of alternative asset groups.

In Chapter 4 we examine how markets work in general, and then specifically focus on the purpose and function of primary and secondary bond and stock markets. During the 1980s and 1990s, significant changes have occurred in the operation of the securities market, including a trend toward a global market. After discussing these changes, the globalization of existing markets, and the rapid development of new capital markets around the world, we speculate about how global markets will continue to expand available investment alternatives.

Investors, market analysts, and financial theorists often gauge the behavior of securities markets by evaluating changes in various market indexes and evaluate portfolio performance by comparing a portfolio's results to an appropriate benchmark. In Chapter 5 we examine and compare a number of stock-market and bond-market indexes that can be used for these purposes for the domestic and global markets.

This initial section provides the framework for you to understand various securities, how to allocate among alternative asset classes, the markets where they are bought and sold, the indexes that reflect their performance, and how you might manage a collection of investments in a portfolio. Specific portfolio management techniques are described in later chapters.

Chapter

1 The Investment Setting

After you read this chapter, you should be able to answer the following questions:

- Why do individuals invest?
- What is an investment?
- How do investors measure the rate of return on an investment?
- How do investors measure the risk related to alternative investments?
- What factors contribute to the rates of return that investors require on alternative investments?
- What macroeconomic and microeconomic factors contribute to changes in the required rates of return for individual investments and investments in general?

This initial chapter discusses several topics basic to the subsequent chapters. We begin by defining the term *investment* and discussing the returns and risks related to investments. This leads to a presentation of how to measure the expected and historical rates of returns for an individual asset or a portfolio of assets. In addition, we consider how to measure risk not only for an individual investment, but also for an investment that is part of a portfolio.

The third section of the chapter discusses the factors that determine the required rate of return for an individual investment. The factors discussed are those that contribute to an asset's *total* risk. Because most investors have a portfolio of investments, it is necessary to consider how to measure the risk of an asset when it is a part of a large portfolio of assets. The risk that prevails when an asset is part of a portfolio is referred to as its *systematic risk.*

The final section deals with what causes *changes* in an asset's required rate of return over time. Changes occur because of both macroeconomic events that affect all investment assets and microeconomic events that affect the specific asset.

WHAT IS AN INVESTMENT?

For most of your life, you will be earning and spending money. Rarely, though, will your current money income exactly balance with your consumption desires. Sometimes you may have more money than you want to spend; at other times you may want to purchase more than you can afford. These imbalances will lead you either to borrow or to save to maximize the long-run benefits from your income.

When current income exceeds current consumption desires, people tend to save the excess. They can do any of several things with these savings. One possibility is to put the money under a mattress or bury it in the backyard until some future time when consumption desires exceed current income. When they retrieve their savings from the mattress or backyard, they have the same amount they saved.

Another possibility is that they can give up the immediate possession of these savings for a future larger amount of money that will be available for future consumption. This tradeoff of *present* consumption for a higher level of *future* consumption is the reason for saving. What you do with the savings to make them increase over time is *investment.*[1]

Those who give up immediate possession of savings (that is, defer consumption) expect to receive in the future a greater amount than they gave up. Conversely, those who consume more than their current income (that is, borrow) must be willing to pay back in the future more than they borrowed.

The rate of exchange between *future consumption* (future dollars) and *current consumption* (current dollars) is the *pure rate of interest.* Both people's willingness to pay this difference for borrowed funds and their desire to receive a surplus on their savings give rise to an interest rate referred to as the *pure time value of money.* This interest rate is established in the capital market by a comparison of the supply of excess income available (savings) to be invested and the demand for excess consumption (borrowing) at a given time. If you can exchange $100 of certain income today for $104 of certain income 1 year from today, then the pure rate of exchange on a risk-free investment (that is, the time value of money) is said to be 4 percent (104/100 − 1).

The investor who gives up $100 today expects to consume $104 of goods and services in the future. This assumes that the general price level in the economy stays the same. This price stability has rarely been the case during the past several decades when inflation rates have varied from 1.1 percent in 1986 to 13.3 percent in 1979, with an average of about 5.5 percent a year from 1970 to 1999. If investors expect a change in prices, they will require a higher rate of return to compensate for it. For example, if an investor expects a rise in prices (that is, he or she expects inflation) at the rate of 2 percent during the period of investment, he or she will increase the required interest rate by 2 percent. In our example, the investor would require $106 in the future to defer the $100 of consumption during an inflationary period (a 6 percent nominal interest rate will be required instead of 4 percent).

Further, if the future payment from the investment is not certain, the investor will demand an interest rate that exceeds the pure time value of money plus the inflation rate. The uncertainty of the payments from an investment is the *investment risk.* The additional return added to the nominal interest rate is called a *risk premium.* In our previous example, the investor would require more than $106 one year from today to compensate for the uncertainty. As an example, if the required amount were $110, $4, or 4 percent, would be considered a risk premium.

INVESTMENT DEFINED

From our discussion we can specify a formal definition of investment. Specifically, an **investment** is the current commitment of dollars for a period of time in order to derive future payments that will compensate the investor for (1) the time the funds are committed, (2) the expected rate of inflation, and (3) the uncertainty of the future payments. The "investor" can be an individual, a government, a pension fund, or a corporation. Similarly, this definition includes all types of investments, including investments by corporations in plant and equipment and investments by individuals in stocks, bonds, commodities, or real estate. This text emphasizes investments by individual investors. In all cases the investor is trading a *known* dollar amount today for some *expected* future stream of payments that will be greater than the current outlay.

---

[1]In contrast, when current income is less than current consumption desires, people borrow to make up the difference. Although we will discuss borrowing on several occasions, the major emphasis of this text is how to invest savings.

At this point, we have answered the questions about why people invest and what they want from their investments. They invest to earn a return from savings due to their deferred consumption. They want a rate of return that compensates them for the time, the expected rate of inflation, and the uncertainty of the return. This return, the investor's **required rate of return**, is discussed throughout this book. A central question of this book is how investors select investments that will give them their required rates of return.

The next section of this chapter describes how to measure the expected or historical rate of return on an investment and also how to quantify the uncertainty of expected returns. You need to understand these techniques for measuring the rate of return and the uncertainty of these returns to evaluate the suitability of a particular investment. Although our emphasis will be on financial assets, such as bonds and stocks, we will refer to other assets, such as art and antiques. Chapter 3 discusses the range of financial assets and also considers some nonfinancial assets.

MEASURES OF RETURN AND RISK

The purpose of this book is to help you understand how to choose among alternative investment assets. This selection process requires that you estimate and evaluate the expected risk–return tradeoffs for the alternative investments available. Therefore, you must understand how to measure the rate of return and the risk involved in an investment accurately. To meet this need, in this section we examine ways to quantify return and risk. The presentation will consider how to measure both *historical* and *expected* rates of return and risk.

We consider historical measures of return and risk because this book and other publications provide numerous examples of historical average rates of return and risk measures for various assets, and understanding these presentations is important. In addition, these historical results are often used by investors when attempting to estimate the *expected* rates of return and risk for an asset class.

The first measure is the historical rate of return on an individual investment over the time period the investment is held (that is, its holding period). Next, we consider how to measure the *average* historical rate of return for an individual investment over a number of time periods. The third subsection considers the average rate of return for a *portfolio* of investments.

Given the measures of historical rates of return, we will present the traditional measures of risk for a historical time series of returns (that is, the variance and standard deviation).

Following the presentation of measures of historical rates of return and risk, we turn to estimating the *expected* rate of return for an investment. Obviously, such an estimate contains a great deal of uncertainty, and we present measures of this uncertainty or risk.

Measures of Historical Rates of Return

When you are evaluating alternative investments for inclusion in your portfolio, you will often be comparing investments with widely different prices or lives. As an example, you might want to compare a $10 stock that pays no dividends to a stock selling for $150 that pays dividends of $5 a year. To properly evaluate these two investments, you must accurately compare their historical rates of returns. A proper measurement of the rates of return is the purpose of this section.

When we invest, we defer current consumption in order to add to our wealth so that we can consume more in the future. Therefore, when we talk about a return on an investment, we are concerned with the *change in wealth* resulting from this investment. This change in wealth can be either due to cash inflows, such as interest or dividends, or caused by a change in the price of the asset (positive or negative).

If you commit \$200 to an investment at the beginning of the year and you get back \$220 at the end of the year, what is your return for the period? The period during which you own an investment is called its *holding period*, and the return for that period is the **holding period return (HPR)**. In this example, the HPR is 1.10, calculated as follows:

1.1

$$\text{HPR} = \frac{\text{Ending Value of Investment}}{\text{Beginning Value of Investment}} = \frac{\$220}{\$200} = 1.10$$

This value will always be zero or greater—that is, it can never be a negative value. A value greater than 1.0 reflects an increase in your wealth, which means that you received a positive rate of return during the period. A value less than 1.0 means that you suffered a decline in wealth, which indicates that you had a negative return during the period. An HPR of zero indicates that you lost all your money.

Although HPR helps us express the change in value of an investment, investors generally evaluate returns in *percentage terms on an annual basis*. This conversion to annual percentage rates makes it easier to directly compare alternative investments that have markedly different characteristics. The first step in converting an HPR to an annual percentage rate is to derive a percentage return, referred to as the **holding period yield (HPY)**. The HPY is equal to the HPR minus 1.

1.2

$$\text{HPY} = \text{HPR} - 1$$

In our example:

$$\text{HPY} = 1.10 - 1 = 0.10 = 10\%$$

To derive an *annual* HPY, you compute an *annual* HPR and subtract 1. Annual HPR is found by:

1.3

$$\text{Annual HPR} = \text{HPR}^{1/n}$$

where:

n = number of years the investment is held

Consider an investment that cost \$250 and is worth \$350 after being held for two years:

$$\begin{aligned}\text{HPR} &= \frac{\text{Ending Value of Investment}}{\text{Beginning Value of Investment}} = \frac{\$350}{\$250}\\ &= 1.40\\ \text{Annual HPR} &= 1.40^{1/n}\\ &= 1.40^{1/2}\\ &= 1.1832\\ \text{Annual HPY} &= 1.1832 - 1 = 0.1832\\ &= 18.32\%\end{aligned}$$

In contrast, consider an investment of \$100 held for only six months that earned a return of \$12:

$$\text{HPR} = \frac{\$112}{\$100} = 1.12\ (n = 0.5)$$
$$\text{Annual HPR} = 1.12^{1/.5}$$
$$= 1.12^2$$
$$= 1.2544$$
$$\text{Annual HPY} = 1.2544 - 1 = 0.2544$$
$$= 25.44\%$$

Note that we made some implicit assumptions when converting the HPY to an annual basis. This annualized holding period yield computation assumes a constant annual yield for each year. In the two-year investment, we assumed an 18.32 percent rate of return each year, compounded. In the partial year HPR that was annualized, we assumed that the return is compounded for the whole year. That is, we assumed that the rate of return earned during the first part of the year is likewise earned on the value at the end of the first six months. The 12 percent rate of return for the initial six months compounds to 25.44 percent for the full year.[2]

Remember one final point: The ending value of the investment can be the result of a change in price for the investment alone (for example, a stock going from \$20 a share to \$22 a share), income from the investment alone, or a combination of price change and income. Ending value includes the value of everything related to the investment.

Computing Mean Historical Returns

Now that we have calculated the HPY for a single investment for a single year, we want to consider **mean rates of return** for a single investment and for a portfolio of investments. Over a number of years, a single investment will likely give high rates of return during some years and low rates of return, or possibly negative rates of return, during others. Your analysis should consider each of these returns, but you also want a summary figure that indicates this investment's typical experience, or the rate of return you should expect to receive if you owned this investment over an extended period of time. You can derive such a summary figure by computing the mean rate of return for this investment over some period of time.

Alternatively, you might want to evaluate a portfolio of investments that might include similar investments (for example, all stocks or all bonds) or a combination of investments (for example, stocks, bonds, and real estate). In this instance, you would calculate the mean rate of return for this portfolio of investments for an individual year or for a number of years.

SINGLE INVESTMENT Given a set of annual rates of return (HPYs) for an individual investment, there are two summary measures of return performance. The first is the arithmetic mean return, the second the geometric mean return. To find the **arithmetic mean (AM)**, the sum (Σ) of annual holding period yields is divided by the number of years (n) as follows:

1.4
$$\text{AM} = \Sigma\text{HPY}/n$$

where:

ΣHPY = the sum of annual holding period yields

[2] To check that you understand the calculations, determine the annual HPY for a three-year HPR of 1.50. (Answer: 14.47 percent.) Compute the annual HPY for a three-month HPR of 1.06. (Answer: 26.25 percent.)

An alternative computation, the **geometric mean (GM)**, is the *n*th root of the product of the HPRs for *n* years.

1.5

$$GM = \left[\pi HPR\right]^{1/n} - 1$$

where:

π = the product of the annual holding period returns as follows:

$$(HPR_1) \times (HPR_2) \ldots (HPR_n)$$

To illustrate these alternatives, consider an investment with the following data:

Year	Beginning Value	Ending Value	HPR	HPY
1	100.0	115.0	1.15	0.15
2	115.0	138.0	1.20	0.20
3	138.0	110.4	0.80	−0.20

$$\begin{aligned} AM &= \left[(0.15) + (0.20) + (-.020)\right]/3 \\ &= 0.15/3 \\ &= 0.05 = 5\% \end{aligned}$$

$$\begin{aligned} GM &= \left[(1.15 \times (1.20) \times (0.80)\right]^{1/3} - 1 \\ &= (1.104)^{1/3} - 1 \\ &= 1.03353 - 1 \\ &= 0.03353 = 3.353\% \end{aligned}$$

Investors are typically concerned with long-term performance when comparing alternative investments. GM is considered a superior measure of the long-term mean rate of return because it indicates the compound annual rate of return based on the ending value of the investment versus its beginning value.[3] Specifically, using the prior example, if we compounded 3.353 percent for three years, $(1.03353)^3$, we would get an ending wealth value of 1.104.

Although the arithmetic average provides a good indication of the expected rate of return for an investment during a future individual year, it is biased upward if you are attempting to measure an asset's long-term performance. This is obvious for a volatile security. Consider, for example, a security that increases in price from $50 to $100 during year 1 and drops back to $50 during year 2. The annual HPYs would be:

Year	Beginning Value	Ending Value	HPR	HPY
1	50	100	2.00	1.00
2	100	50	0.50	–0.50

[3]Note that the GM is the same whether you compute the geometric mean of the individual annual holding period yields or the annual HPY for a three-year period, comparing the ending value to the beginning value, as discussed earlier under annual HPY for a multiperiod case.

This would give an arithmetic mean rate of return of:

$$
\begin{aligned}
[(1.00) + (-0.50)]/2 &= 50/2 \\
&= 0.25 = 25\%
\end{aligned}
$$

This investment brought no change in wealth and therefore no return, yet the arithmetic mean rate of return is computed to be 25 percent.

The geometric mean rate of return would be:

$$
\begin{aligned}
(2.00 \times 0.50)^{1/2} - 1 &= (1.00)^{1/2} - 1 \\
&= 1.00 - 1 = 0\%
\end{aligned}
$$

This answer of a 0 percent rate of return accurately measures the fact that there was no change in wealth from this investment.

When rates of return are the same for all years, the geometric mean will be equal to the arithmetic mean. If the rates of return vary over the years, the geometric mean will always be lower than the arithmetic mean. The difference between the two mean values will depend on the year-to-year changes in the rates of return. Larger annual changes in the rates of return—that is, more volatility—will result in a greater difference between the alternative mean values.

An awareness of both methods of computing mean rates of return is important because published accounts of investment performance or descriptions of financial research will use both the AM and the GM as measures of average historical returns. We will also use both throughout this book. Currently most studies dealing with long-run historical rates of return include both arithmetic and geometric mean rates of return.

A PORTFOLIO OF INVESTMENTS The mean historical rate of return (HPY) for a portfolio of investments is measured as the weighted average of the HPYs for the individual investments in the portfolio, or the overall change in value of the original portfolio. The weights used in computing the averages are the relative *beginning* market values for each investment; this is referred to as *dollar-weighted* or *value-weighted* mean rate of return. This technique is demonstrated by the examples in Table 1.1. As shown, the HPY is the same (9.5 percent) whether you compute the weighted average return using the beginning market value weights or if you compute the overall change in the total value of the portfolio.

Although the analysis of historical performance is useful, selecting investments for your portfolio requires you to predict the rates of return you *expect* to prevail. The next section discusses how you would derive such estimates of expected rates of return. We recognize the great uncertainty regarding these future expectations, and we will discuss how one measures this uncertainty, which is referred to as the risk of an investment.

Calculating Expected Rates of Return

Risk is the uncertainty that an investment will earn its expected rate of return. In the examples in the prior section, we examined *realized* historical rates of return. In contrast, an investor who is evaluating a future investment alternative expects or anticipates a certain rate of return. The investor might say that he or she *expects* the investment will provide a rate of return of 10 percent, but this is actually the investor's most likely estimate, also referred to as a *point estimate*. Pressed further, the investor would probably acknowledge the uncertainty of this point estimate return and admit the possibility that, under certain conditions, the annual rate of return on this investment might go as low as −10 percent or as high as 25 percent. The point is, the specification of a larger range of possible returns from an investment reflects the investor's uncertainty regarding what the actual return will be. Therefore, a larger range of expected returns makes the investment riskier.

TABLE 1.1 **COMPUTATION OF HOLDING PERIOD YIELD FOR A PORTFOLIO**

Investment	Number of Shares	Beginning Price	Beginning Market Value	Ending Price	Ending Market Value	HPR	HPY	Market Weight	Weighted HPY
A	100,000	$10	$ 1,000,000	$12	$ 1,200,000	1.20	20%	0.05	0.01
B	200,000	20	4,000,000	21	4,200,000	1.05	5	0.20	0.01
C	500,000	30	15,000,000	33	16,500,000	1.10	10	0.75	0.075
Total			$20,000,000		$21,900,000				0.095

$$\text{HPR} = \frac{21{,}900{,}000}{20{,}000{,}000} = 1.095$$

$$\text{HPY} = 1.095 - 1 = 0.095 = 9.5\%$$

An investor determines how certain the expected rate of return on an investment is by analyzing estimates of expected returns. To do this, the investor assigns probability values to all *possible* returns. These probability values range from zero, which means no chance of the return, to one, which indicates complete certainty that the investment will provide the specified rate of return. These probabilities are typically subjective estimates based on the historical performance of the investment or similar investments modified by the investor's expectations for the future. As an example, an investor may know that about 30 percent of the time the rate of return on this particular investment was 10 percent. Using this information along with future expectations regarding the economy, one can derive an estimate of what might happen in the future.

The *expected* return from an investment is defined as:

1.6

$$\text{Expected Return} = \sum_{i=1}^{n} (\text{Probability of Return}) \times (\text{Possible Return})$$

$$E(R_i) = \left[(P_1)(R_1) + (P_2)(R_2) + (P_3)(R_3) + \ldots + (P_nR_n)\right]$$

$$E(R_i) = \sum_{i=1}^{n} (P_i)(R_i)$$

Let us begin our analysis of the effect of risk with an example of perfect certainty wherein the investor is absolutely certain of a return of 5 percent. Figure 1.1 illustrates this situation.

Perfect certainty allows only one possible return, and the probability of receiving that return is 1.0. Few investments provide certain returns. In the case of perfect certainty, there is only one value for P_iR_i:

$$E(R_i) = (1.0)(0.05) = 0.05$$

In an alternative scenario, suppose an investor believed an investment could provide several different rates of return depending on different possible economic conditions. As an example, in a strong economic environment with high corporate profits and little or no inflation, the investor might expect the rate of return on common stocks during the next year to reach as high as 20 percent. In contrast, if there is an economic decline with a higher-than-average rate of inflation, the investor might expect the rate of return on common stocks during the next year to be −20 percent. Finally, with no major change in the economic environment, the rate of return during the next year would probably approach the long-run average of 10 percent.

FIGURE 1.1 **PROBABILITY DISTRIBUTION FOR RISK-FREE INVESTMENT**

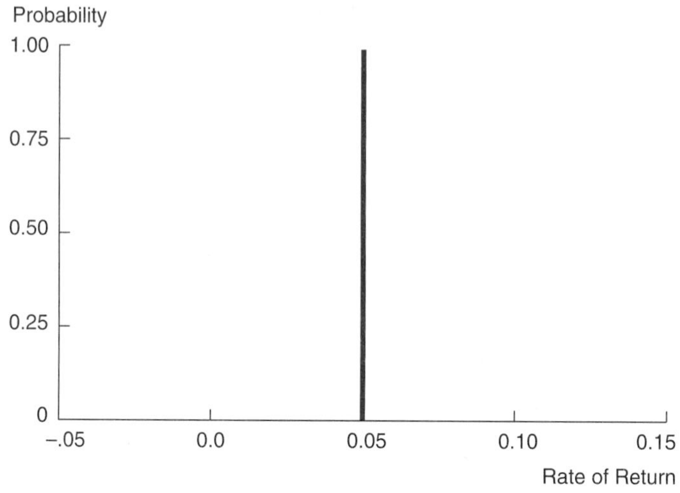
Probability
1.00
0.75
0.50
0.25
0
–.05
0.0
0.05
0.10
0.15
Rate of Return

The investor might estimate probabilities for each of these economic scenarios based on past experience and the current outlook as follows:

Economic Conditions	Probability	Rate of Return
Strong economy, no inflation	0.15	0.20
Weak economy, above-average inflation	0.15	−0.20
No major change in economy	0.70	0.10

This set of potential outcomes can be visualized as shown in Figure 1.2.

The computation of the expected rate of return [$E(R_i)$] is as follows:

$$E(R_i) = [(0.15)(0.20)] + [(0.15)(-0.20)] + [(0.70)(0.10)]$$
$$= 0.07$$

Obviously, the investor is less certain about the expected return from this investment than about the return from the prior investment with its single possible return.

A third example is an investment with 10 possible outcomes ranging from −40 percent to 50 percent with the same probability for each rate of return. A graph of this set of expectations would appear as shown in Figure 1.3.

In this case, there are numerous outcomes from a wide range of possibilities. The expected rate of return [$E(R_i)$] for this investment would be:

$$\begin{aligned} E(R_i) &= (0.10)(-0.40) + (0.10)(-0.30) + (0.10)(-0.20) + (0.10)(-0.10) + (0.10)(0.0) \\ &\quad + (0.10)(0.10) + (0.10)(0.20) + (0.10)(0.30) + (0.10)(0.40) + (0.10)(0.50) \\ &= (-0.04) + (-0.03) + (-0.02) + (-0.01) + (0.00) + (0.01) + (0.02) + (0.03) \\ &\quad + (0.04) + (0.05) \\ &= 0.05 \end{aligned}$$

FIGURE 1.2

PROBABILITY DISTRIBUTION FOR RISKY INVESTMENT WITH THREE POSSIBLE RATES OF RETURN

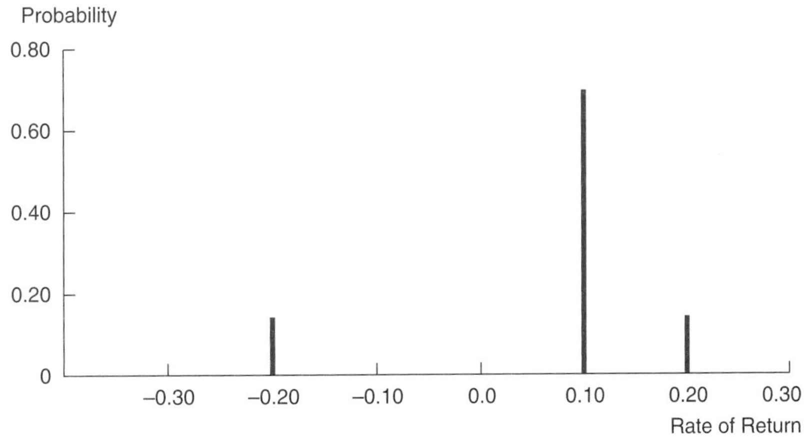
Probability
0.80
0.60
0.40
0.20
0
−0.30
−0.20
−0.10
0.0
0.10
0.20
0.30
Rate of Return

FIGURE 1.3

PROBABILITY DISTRIBUTION FOR RISKY INVESTMENT WITH 10 POSSIBLE RATES OF RETURN

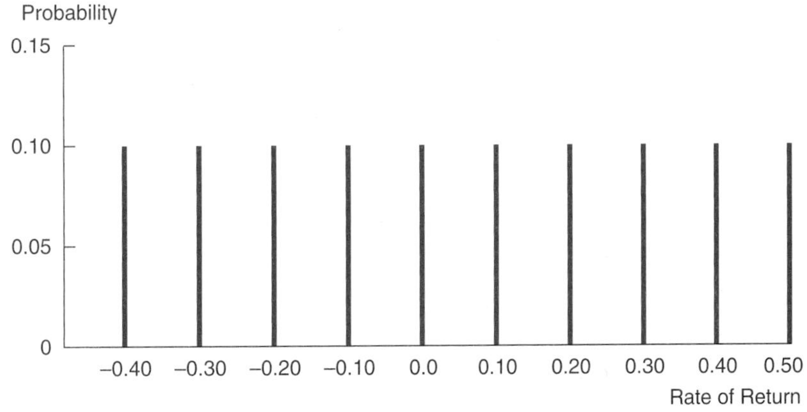
Probability
0.15
0.10
0.05
0
−0.40
−0.30
−0.20
−0.10
0.0
0.10
0.20
0.30
0.40
0.50
Rate of Return

The *expected* rate of return for this investment is the same as the certain return discussed in the first example, but in this case, the investor is highly uncertain about the *actual* rate of return. This would be considered a risky investment because of that uncertainty. We would anticipate that an investor faced with the choice between this risky investment and the certain (risk-free) case would select the certain alternative. This expectation is based on the belief that most investors are **risk averse**, which means that if everything else is the same, they will select the investment that offers greater certainty.

MEASURING THE RISK OF EXPECTED RATES OF RETURN

We have shown that we can calculate the expected rate of return and evaluate the uncertainty, or risk, of an investment by identifying the range of possible returns from that investment and assigning each possible return a weight based on the probability that it will occur. Although the graphs help us visualize the dispersion of possible returns, most investors want to quantify this dispersion using statistical techniques. These statistical measures allow you to compare the return and risk measures for alternative investments directly. Two possible measures of risk (uncertainty) have received support in theoretical work on portfolio theory: the *variance* and the *standard deviation* of the estimated distribution of expected returns.

In this section, we demonstrate how variance and standard deviation measure the dispersion of possible rates of return around the expected rate of return. We will work with the examples discussed earlier. The formula for variance is as follows:

1.7

$$\text{Variance } (\sigma^2) = \sum_{i=1}^{n} (\text{Probability}) \times \left(\begin{matrix}\text{Possible} \\ \text{Return}\end{matrix} - \begin{matrix}\text{Expected} \\ \text{Return}\end{matrix}\right)^2$$
$$= \sum_{i=1}^{n} (P_i)[R_i - E(R_i)]^2$$

VARIANCE The larger the **variance** for an expected rate of return, the greater the dispersion of expected returns and the greater the uncertainty, or risk, of the investment. The variance for the perfect-certainty example would be:

$$(\sigma^2) = \sum_{i=1}^{n} P_i[R_i - E(R_i)]^2$$
$$= 1.0(0.05 - 0.05)^2 = 1.0(0.0) = 0$$

Note that in perfect certainty, there is *no variance of return* because there is no deviation from expectations, and therefore *no risk*, or *uncertainty*. The variance for the second example would be:

$$(\sigma^2) = \sum_{i=1}^{n} P_i[R_i - E(R_i)]^2$$
$$= [(0.15)(0.20 - 0.07)^2 + (0.15)(-0.20 - 0.07)^2 + (0.70)(0.10 - 0.07)^2]$$
$$= [0.010935 + 0.002535 + 0.00063]$$
$$= 0.0141$$

STANDARD DEVIATION The **standard deviation** is the square root of the variance:

1.8

$$\text{Standard Deviation} = \sqrt{\sum_{i=1}^{n} P_i[R_i - E(R_i)]^2}$$

For the second example, the standard deviation would be:

$$\sigma = \sqrt{0.0141}$$
$$= 0.11874$$

A RELATIVE MEASURE OF RISK In some cases, an unadjusted variance or standard deviation can be misleading. If conditions are not similar—that is, if there are major differences in the expected rates of return—it is necessary to use a measure of *relative variability* to indicate risk per unit of expected return. A widely used relative measure of risk is the **coefficient of variation**, calculated as follows:

1.9

$$\begin{matrix}\text{Coefficient of} \\ \text{Variation (CV)}\end{matrix} = \frac{\text{Standard Deviation of Returns}}{\text{Expected Rate of Return}}$$
$$= \frac{\sigma_i}{E(R)}$$

The CV for the example above would be:

$$CV = \frac{0.11874}{0.07000}$$
$$= 1.696$$

This measure of relative variability and risk is used by financial analysts to compare alternative investments with widely different rates of return and standard deviations of returns. As an illustration, consider the following two investments:

	Investment A	Investment B
Expected return	0.07	0.12
Standard deviation	0.05	0.07

Comparing absolute measures of risk, investment B appears to be riskier because it has a standard deviation of 7 percent versus 5 percent for investment A. In contrast, the CV figures show that investment B has less relative variability or lower risk per unit of expected return as follows:

$$CV_A = \frac{0.05}{0.07} = 0.714$$
$$CV_B = \frac{0.07}{0.12} = 0.583$$

RISK MEASURES FOR HISTORICAL RETURNS

To measure the risk for a series of historical rates of returns, we use the same measures as for expected returns (variance and standard deviation) except that we consider the historical holding period yields (HPY) as follows:

1.10
$$\sigma_2 = \sum_{i=1}^{n}[HPY_i - E(HPY)]^2/n$$

where:

σ^2 = the variance of the series
HPY_i = the holding period yield during period i
E(HPY) = the expected value of the holding period yield that is equal to the arithmetic mean of the series
n = the number of observations

The standard deviation is the square root of the variance. Both measures indicate how much the individual observations over time deviated from the expected value of the series. An example computation is contained in the appendix to this chapter. As we will see in subsequent chapters where we present historical rates of return for alternative asset classes, presenting the standard deviation as a measure of risk for the series or asset class is fairly common.

DETERMINANTS OF REQUIRED RATES OF RETURN

In this section we continue our consideration of factors that you must consider when selecting securities for an investment portfolio. You will recall that this selection process

TABLE 1.2 **PROMISED YIELDS ON ALTERNATIVE BONDS**

Type of Bond	1992	1993	1994	1995	1996	1997	1998
U.S. government 3-month Treasury bills	3.43%	3.00%	4.25%	5.49%	5.01%	5.06%	4.78%
U.S. government long-term bonds	7.52	6.59	7.41	6.93	6.80	6.67	5.69
Aaa corporate bonds	8.14	7.77	7.97	7.59	7.37	7.27	6.53
Baa corporate bonds	8.98	7.93	8.63	7.83	8.05	7.87	7.22

Source: *Federal Reserve Bulletin,* various issues.

involves finding securities that provide a rate of return that compensates you for: (1) the time value of money during the period of investment, (2) the expected rate of inflation during the period, and (3) the risk involved.

The summation of these three components is called the *required rate of return.* This is the minimum rate of return that you should accept from an investment to compensate you for deferring consumption. Because of the importance of the required rate of return to the total investment selection process, this section contains a discussion of the three components and what influences each of them.

The analysis and estimation of the required rate of return is complicated by the behavior of market rates over time. First, a wide range of rates are available for alternative investments at any time. Second, the rates of return on specific assets change dramatically over time. Third, the difference between the rates available (that is, the spread) on different assets changes over time.

The yield data in Table 1.2 for alternative bonds demonstrates these three characteristics. First, even though all these securities have promised returns based upon bond contracts, the promised annual yields during any year differ substantially. As an example, during 1992 the average yields on alternative assets ranged from 3.43 percent on T-bills to 8.98 percent for Baa corporate bonds. Second, the changes in yields for a specific asset are shown by the three-month Treasury bill rate that went from 3.00 percent in 1993 to 5.49 percent in 1995. Third, an example of a change in the difference between yields over time (referred to as a spread) is shown by the Baa–Aaa spread.[4] The yield spread in 1993 was only 16 basis points (7.93–7.77), but the spread in 1996 was 68 basis points (8.05–7.37). (A basis point is 0.01 percent.)

Because differences in yields result from the riskiness of each investment, you must understand the risk factors that affect the required rates of return and include them in your assessment of investment opportunities. Because the required returns on all investments change over time, and because large differences separate individual investments, you need to be aware of the several components that determine the required rate of return, starting with the risk-free rate. The discussion in this chapter considers the three components of the required rate of return and briefly discusses what affects these components. The presentation in Chapter 10 on valuation theory will discuss the factors that affect these components in greater detail.

THE REAL RISK-FREE RATE

The **real risk-free rate (RRFR)** is the basic interest rate, assuming no inflation and no uncertainty about future flows. An investor in an inflation-free economy who knew with cer-

[4]Bonds are rated by rating agencies based upon the credit risk of the securities, that is, the probability of default. Aaa is the top rating Moody's (a prominent rating service) gives to bonds with almost no probability of default. (Only U.S. Treasury bonds are considered to be of higher quality.) Baa is a lower rating Moody's gives to bonds of generally high quality that have some possibility of default under adverse economic conditions.

tainty what cash flows he or she would receive at what time would demand the real risk-free rate on an investment. Earlier we called this the *pure time value of money*, because the only sacrifice the investor made was deferring the use of the money for a period of time. This real risk-free rate of interest is the price charged for the exchange between current goods and future goods.

Two factors, one subjective and one objective, influence this exchange price. The subjective factor is the time preference of individuals for the consumption of income. When individuals give up $100 of consumption this year, how much consumption do they want a year from now to compensate for that sacrifice? The strength of the human desire for current consumption influences the rate of compensation required. Time preferences vary among individuals, and the market creates a composite rate that includes the preferences of all investors. This composite rate changes gradually over time because it is influenced by all the investors in the economy, whose changes in preferences may offset one another.

The objective factor that influences the real risk-free rate is the set of investment opportunities available in the economy. The investment opportunities are determined in turn by the long-run real growth rate of the economy. A rapidly growing economy produces more and better opportunities to invest funds and experience positive rates of return. A change in the economy's long-run real growth rate causes a change in all investment opportunities and a change in the required rates of return on all investments. Just as investors supplying capital should demand a higher rate of return when growth is higher, those looking for funds to invest should be willing and able to pay a higher rate of return to use the funds for investment because of the higher growth rate. Thus, a *positive* relationship exists between the real growth rate in the economy and the RRFR.

Factors Influencing the Nominal Risk-Free Rate (NRFR)

Earlier, we observed that an investor would be willing to forgo current consumption in order to increase future consumption at a rate of exchange called the *risk-free rate of interest*. This rate of exchange was measured in real terms because the investor wanted to increase the consumption of actual goods and services rather than consuming the same amount that had come to cost more money. Therefore, when we discuss rates of interest, we need to differentiate between real rates of interest that adjust for changes in the general price level, as opposed to *nominal* rates of interest that are stated in money terms. That is, nominal rates of interest that prevail in the market are determined by real rates of interest, plus factors that will affect the nominal rate of interest, such as the expected rate of inflation and the monetary environment. It is important to understand these factors.

As noted earlier, the variables that determine the real risk-free rate change only gradually over the long term. Therefore, you might expect the required rate on a risk-free investment to be quite stable over time. As discussed in connection with Table 1.2, rates on three-month T-bills were *not* stable over the period from 1992 to 1998. This is demonstrated with additional observations in Table 1.3, which contains yields on T-bills for the period 1978 to 1998.

Investors view T-bills as a prime example of a default-free investment because the government has unlimited ability to derive income from taxes or to create money from which to pay interest. Therefore, rates on T-bills should change only gradually. In fact, the data show a highly erratic pattern. Specifically, there was an increase from about 7 percent in 1978 to more than 14 percent in 1981 before declining to less than 6 percent in 1987 and 3.33 percent in 1993. In sum, T-bill rates almost doubled in three years and then declined by almost 60 percent in six years. Clearly, the nominal rate of interest on a default-free investment is *not* stable in the long run or the short run, even though the underlying determinants of the RRFR are quite stable. The point is, two other factors influence the *nominal risk-free rate* (NRFR): (1) the relative ease or tightness in the capital markets, and (2) the expected rate of inflation.

TABLE 1.3

THREE-MONTH TREASURY BILL YIELDS AND RATES OF INFLATION

Year	3-Month T-Bills	Rate of Inflation	Year	3-Month T-bills	Rate of Inflation
1978	7.19%	7.70%	1989	8.11%	4.65%
1979	10.07	11.30	1990	7.50	6.11
1980	11.43	7.70	1991	5.38	3.06
1981	14.03	10.40	1992	3.43	2.90
1982	10.61	6.10	1993	3.33	2.75
1983	8.61	3.20	1994	4.25	2.67
1984	9.52	4.00	1995	5.49	2.54
1985	7.48	3.80	1996	5.01	3.32
1986	5.98	1.10	1997	5.06	1.70
1987	5.78	4.40	1998	4.78	1.60
1988	6.67	4.40			

Source: *Federal Reserve Bulletin,* various issues; *Economic Report of the President,* various issues.

CONDITIONS IN THE CAPITAL MARKET You will recall from prior courses in economics and finance that the purpose of capital markets is to bring together investors who want to invest savings with companies or governments who need capital to expand or to finance budget deficits. The cost of funds at any time (the interest rate) is the price that equates the current supply and demand for capital. A change in the relative ease or tightness in the capital market is a short-run phenomenon caused by a temporary disequilibrium in the supply and demand of capital.

As an example, disequilibrium could be caused by an unexpected change in monetary policy (for example, a change in the growth rate of the money supply) or fiscal policy (for example, a change in the federal deficit). Such a change in monetary policy or fiscal policy will produce a change in the NRFR of interest, but the change should be short-lived because in the longer run, the higher or lower interest rates will affect capital supply and demand. As an example, a decrease in the growth rate of the money supply (a tightening in monetary policy) will reduce the supply of capital and increase interest rates. In turn, this increase in interest rates (for example, the price of money) will cause an increase in savings and a decrease in the demand for capital by corporations or individuals. These changes in market conditions will bring rates back to the long-run equilibrium, which is based on the long-run growth rate of the economy.

EXPECTED RATE OF INFLATION Previously, it was noted that if investors expected the price level to increase during the investment period, they would require the rate of return to include compensation for the expected rate of inflation. Assume that you require a 4 percent real rate of return on a risk-free investment, but you expect prices to increase by 3 percent during the investment period. In this case, you should increase your required rate of return by this expected rate of inflation to about 7 percent [(1.04 × 1.03) − 1]. If you do not increase your required return, the $104 you receive at the end of the year will represent a real return of only 1 percent, not 4 percent. Because prices have increased by 3 percent during the year, what previously cost $100 now costs $103, so you can consume only about 1 percent more at the end of the year [($104/103) − 1]. If you had required a 7.12 percent nominal return, your real consumption could have increased by 4 percent [($107.12/103) − 1]. Therefore, an investor's nominal required rate of return on a risk-free investment should be:

1.11 $$\text{NRFR} = (1 + \text{RRFR}) \times (1 + \text{Expected Rate of Inflation}) - 1$$

Rearranging the formula, you can calculate the real risk-free rate of return on an investment as follows:

1.12
$$\text{RRFR} = \left[\frac{(1 + \text{Nominal Risk-Free Rate of Return})}{(1 + \text{Rate of Inflation})}\right] - 1$$

To see how this works, assume that the nominal return on U.S. government T-bills was 9 percent during a given year, when the rate of inflation was 5 percent. In this instance, the real risk-free rate of return on these T-bills was 3.8 percent, as follows:

$$\begin{aligned} \text{RRFR} &= [(1 + 0.09)/(1 + 0.05)] - 1 \\ &= 1.038 - 1 \\ &= 0.038 = 3.8\% \end{aligned}$$

This discussion makes it clear that the nominal rate of interest on a risk-free investment is not a good estimate of the RRFR, because the nominal rate can change dramatically in the short run in reaction to temporary ease or tightness in the capital market or because of changes in the expected rate of inflation. The significant changes in the average yield on T-bills shown in Table 1.3 were caused by the large changes in the rates of inflation during this period.

THE COMMON EFFECT All the factors discussed thus far regarding the required rate of return affect all investments equally. Whether the investment is in stocks, bonds, real estate, or machine tools, if the expected rate of inflation increases from 2 percent to 6 percent, the investor's required rate of return for *all* investments should increase by 4 percent. Similarly, if a decline in the expected real growth rate of the economy causes a decline in the RRFR of 1 percent, the required return on all investments should decline by 1 percent.

Risk Premium

A risk-free investment was defined as one for which the investor is certain of the amount and timing of the expected returns. The returns from most investments do not fit this pattern. An investor typically is not completely certain of the income to be received or when it will be received. Investments can range in uncertainty from basically risk-free securities, such as T-bills, to highly speculative investments, such as the common stock of small companies engaged in high-risk enterprises.

Most investors require higher rates of return on investments if they perceive there is any uncertainty about the expected rate of return. This increase in the required rate of return over the NRFR is the **risk premium (RP)**. Although the required risk premium represents a composite of all uncertainty, it is possible to consider several fundamental sources of uncertainty. In this section we identify and discuss briefly the major sources of uncertainty, including: (1) business risk, (2) financial risk (leverage), (3) liquidity risk, (4) exchange rate risk, and (5) country risk.

Business risk is the uncertainty of income flows caused by the nature of a firm's business. The less certain the income flows of the firm, the less certain the income flows to the investor. Therefore, the investor will demand a risk premium that is based on the uncertainty caused by the basic business of the firm. As an example, a retail food company would typically experience stable sales and earnings growth over time and would have low business risk compared to a firm in the auto industry, where sales and earnings fluctuate substantially over the business cycle, implying high business risk.

Financial risk is the uncertainty introduced by the method by which the firm finances its investments. If a firm uses only common stock to finance investments, it incurs only business risk. If a firm borrows money to finance investments, it must pay fixed financing charges (in the form of interest to creditors) prior to providing income to the common stockholders, so the uncertainty of returns to the equity investor increases. This increase in uncertainty because of fixed-cost financing is called *financial risk* or *financial leverage*, and causes an increase in the stock's risk premium.[5]

Liquidity risk is the uncertainty introduced by the secondary market for an investment.[6] When an investor acquires an asset, he or she expects that the investment will mature (as with a bond) or that it will be salable to someone else. In either case, the investor expects to be able to convert the security into cash and use the proceeds for current consumption or other investments. The more difficult it is to make this conversion, the greater the liquidity risk. An investor must consider two questions when assessing the liquidity risk of an investment: (1) How long will it take to convert the investment into cash? (2) How certain is the price to be received? Similar uncertainty faces an investor who wants to acquire an asset: How long will it take to acquire the asset? How uncertain is the price to be paid?

Uncertainty regarding how fast an investment can be bought or sold, or the existence of uncertainty about its price, increases liquidity risk. A U.S. government Treasury bill has almost no liquidity risk because it can be bought or sold in minutes at a price almost identical to the quoted price. In contrast, examples of illiquid investments include a work of art, an antique, or a parcel of real estate in a remote area. For such investments, it may require a long time to find a buyer, and the selling prices could vary substantially from expectations. Investors will increase their required rates of return to compensate for liquidity risk. Liquidity risk can be a significant consideration when investing in foreign securities depending on the country and the liquidity of its stock and bond markets.

Exchange rate risk is the uncertainty of returns to an investor who acquires securities denominated in a currency different from his or her own. The likelihood of incurring this risk is becoming greater as investors buy and sell assets around the world, as opposed to only assets within their own countries. A U.S. investor who buys Japanese stock denominated in yen must consider not only the uncertainty of the return in yen, but also any change in the exchange value of the yen relative to the U.S. dollar. That is, in addition to the foreign firm's business and financial risk and the security's liquidity risk, the investor must consider the additional uncertainty of the return on this Japanese stock when it is converted from yen to U.S. dollars.

As an example of exchange rate risk, assume that you buy 100 shares of Mitsubishi Electric at 1,050 yen when the exchange rate is 115 yen to the dollar. The dollar cost of this investment would be about $9.13 per share (1,050/115). A year later you sell the 100 shares at 1,200 yen when the exchange rate is 130 yen to the dollar. When you calculate the HPY in yen, you find the stock has increased in value by about 14 percent (1,200/1,050), but this is the HPY for a Japanese investor. A U.S. investor receives a much lower rate of return because during this period the yen has weakened relative to the dollar by about 13 percent (that is, it requires more yen to buy a dollar—130 versus 115). At the new exchange rate, the stock is worth $9.23 per share (1,200/130). Therefore, the return to you as a U.S. investor would be only about 1 percent ($9.23/$9.13) versus 14 percent for the Japanese investor. The difference in return for the Japanese investor and U.S. investor is caused by the decline in the value of the yen relative to the dollar. Clearly, the exchange rate could have gone in the other direction, the dollar weakening against the yen. In this case, as a U.S.

[5]For a discussion of financial leverage, see Eugene F. Brigham, *Fundamentals of Financial Management*, 8th ed. (Hinsdale, Ill.: The Dryden Press, 1998), 221–225.

[6]You will recall from prior courses that the overall capital market is composed of the primary market and the secondary market. Securities are initially sold in the primary market and all subsequent transactions take place in the secondary market. These concepts are discussed in Chapter 4.

investor you would have experienced the 14 percent return measured in yen, as well as a gain from the exchange rate change.

The more volatile the exchange rate between two countries, the less certain you would be regarding the exchange rate, the greater the exchange rate risk, and the larger would be the exchange rate risk premium you would require.[7]

There can also be exchange rate risk for a U.S. firm that is extensively multinational in terms of sales and components (costs). As will be discussed, this risk can generally be hedged at a cost.

Country risk, also called *political risk*, is the uncertainty of returns caused by the possibility of a major change in the political or economic environment of a country. The United States is acknowledged to have the smallest country risk in the world because its political and economic systems are the most stable. Nations with high country risk include Russia, because of the health problems of Yeltsin and the several changes in the government hierarchy and its currency during 1998, and Indonesia, where there were student demonstrations, major riots, and fires prior to the resignation of President Suharto in May 1998. In both instances the stock markets experienced significant declines surrounding these events.[8] Individuals who invest in countries that have unstable political–economic systems must add a country risk premium when determining their required rates of return.

When investing globally (which will be emphasized throughout the book), investors must consider these additional uncertainties. How liquid are the secondary markets for stocks and bonds in the country? Are any of the country's securities traded on major stock exchanges in the United States, London, Tokyo, or Germany? What will happen to exchange rates during the investment period? What is the probability of a political or economic change that will adversely affect your rate of return? Exchange rate risk and country risk differ among countries. A good measure of exchange rate risk would be the absolute variability of the exchange rate relative to a composite exchange rate. The analysis of country risk is much more subjective and must be based on the history and current environment of the country.

This discussion of risk components can be considered a security's *fundamental risk* because it deals with the intrinsic factors that should affect a security's standard deviation of returns over time. In subsequent discussion, the standard deviation of returns is referred to as a measure of the security's *total risk.*

$$\text{Risk Premium} = f(\text{Business Risk, Financial Risk, Liquidity Risk, Exchange Rate Risk, Country Risk})$$

Risk Premium and Portfolio Theory

An alternative view of risk has been derived from extensive work in portfolio theory and capital market theory by Markowitz, Sharpe, and others.[9] These theories are dealt with in greater detail in Chapters 6 and 7, but their impact on the risk premium should be mentioned

---

[7]An article that examines the pricing of exchange rate risk in the U.S. market is Philippe Jorion, "The Pricing of Exchange Rate Risk in the Stock Market," *Journal of Financial and Quantitative Analysis* 26, no. 3 (September 1991): 363–376.

[8]Carlotta Gall, "Moscow Stock Market Falls by 11.8%," *Financial Times,* 19 May 1998, 1; "Russian Contagion Hits Neighbours," *Financial Times,* 29 May 1998, 17; John Thornhill, "Russian Stocks Fall 10% over Lack of Support from IMF," *Financial Times,* 2 June 1998, 1; Robert Chote, "Indonesia Risks Further Unrest as Debt Talks Falter," *Financial Times,* 11 May 1998, 1; Sander Thoenes, " Suharto Cuts Visit as Riots Shake Jakarta," *Financial Times,* 14 May 1998, 12; Sander Thoenes, "Economy Hit As Jakarta Is Paralysed," *Financial Times,* 15 May 1998, 17.

[9]These works include Harry Markowitz, "Portfolio Selection," *Journal of Finance* 7, no. 1 (March 1952): 77–91; Harry Markowitz, *Portfolio Selection—Efficient Diversification of Investments* (New Haven, Conn.: Yale University Press, 1959); and William F. Sharpe, "Capital Asset Prices: A Theory of Market Equilibrium under Conditions of Risk," *Journal of Finance* 19, no. 3 (September 1964): 425–442.

briefly at this point. This prior work by Markowitz and Sharpe indicated that investors should use an *external market* measure of risk. Under a specified set of assumptions, all rational, profit-maximizing investors want to hold a completely diversified market portfolio of risky assets, and they borrow or lend to arrive at a risk level that is consistent with their risk preferences. Under these conditions, the relevant risk measure for an individual asset is its *comovement with the market portfolio*. This comovement, which is measured by an asset's covariance with the market portfolio, is referred to as an asset's **systematic risk**, the portion of an individual asset's total variance attributable to the variability of the total market portfolio. In addition, individual assets have variance that is unrelated to the market portfolio (that is, nonmarket variance) that is due to unique features. This nonmarket variance is called *unsystematic risk* and it is generally considered unimportant because it is eliminated in a large, diversified portfolio. Therefore, under these assumptions, *the risk premium for an individual earning asset is a function of the asset's systematic risk with the aggregate market portfolio of risky assets*. The measure of an asset's systematic risk is referred to as its *beta:*

$$\text{Risk Premium} = f(\text{Systematic Market Risk})$$

Fundamental Risk versus Systematic Risk

Some might expect a conflict between the market measure of risk (systematic risk) and the fundamental determinants of risk (business risk, and so on). A number of studies have examined the relationship between the market measure of risk (systematic risk) and accounting variables used to measure the fundamental risk factors, such as business risk, financial risk, and liquidity risk. The authors of these studies have generally concluded that *a significant relationship exists between the market measure of risk and the fundamental measures of risk*.[10] Therefore, the two measures of risk can be complementary. This consistency seems reasonable because, in a properly functioning capital market, the market measure of the risk should reflect the fundamental risk characteristics of the asset. As an example, you would expect a firm that has high business risk and financial risk to have an above average beta. At the same time, as we discuss in Chapter 7, a firm that has a high level of fundamental risk and a large standard deviation of return on stock can have a lower level of systematic risk because its variability of earnings and stock price is not related to the aggregate economy or the aggregate market. Therefore, one can specify the risk premium for an asset as:

$$\begin{aligned}\text{Risk Premium} &= f(\text{Business Risk, Financial Risk, Liquidity Risk, Exchange}\\ &\quad \text{Rate Risk, Country Risk})\\ &\quad \text{or}\\ \text{Risk Premium} &= f(\text{Systematic Market Risk})\end{aligned}$$

Summary of Required Rate of Return

The overall required rate of return on alternative investments is determined by three variables: (1) the economy's RRFR, which is influenced by the investment opportunities in the economy (that is, the long-run real growth rate); (2) variables that influence the NRFR, which include short-run ease or tightness in the capital market and the expected rate of inflation (notably, these variables, which determine the NRFR, are the same for all investments); and (3) the risk premium on the investment. In turn, this risk premium can be related to fundamental factors, including business risk, financial risk, liquidity risk, exchange rate risk, and country risk, or it can be a function of systematic market risk (beta).

---

[10]A brief review of some of the earlier studies is contained in Donald J. Thompson II, "Sources of Systematic Risk in Common Stocks," *Journal of Business* 49, no. 2 (April 1976): 173–188. There is a further discussion of specific variables in Chapter 9.

MEASURES AND SOURCES OF RISK In this chapter we have examined both measures and sources of risk arising from an investment. The *measures* of risk for an investment are:

- Variance of rates of return
- Standard deviation of rates of return
- Coefficient of variation of rates of return (standard deviation/means)
- Covariance of returns with the market portfolio (beta)

The *sources* of risk are:

- Business risk
- Financial risk
- Liquidity risk
- Exchange rate risk
- Country risk

RELATIONSHIP BETWEEN RISK AND RETURN

Previously, we showed how to measure the risk and rates of return for alternative investments, and we discussed what determines the rates of return that investors require. This section discusses the risk–return combinations that might be available at a point in time and illustrates the factors that cause *changes* in these combinations.

Figure 1.4 graphs the expected relationship between risk and return. It shows that investors increase their required rates of return as perceived risk (uncertainty) increases. The line that reflects the combination of risk and return available on alternative investments is referred to as the **security market line (SML)**. The SML reflects the risk–return combinations available for all risky assets in the capital market at a given time. Investors would select investments that are consistent with their risk preferences; some would consider only low-risk investments, whereas others welcome high-risk investments.

FIGURE 1.4 **RELATIONSHIP BETWEEN RISK AND RETURN**

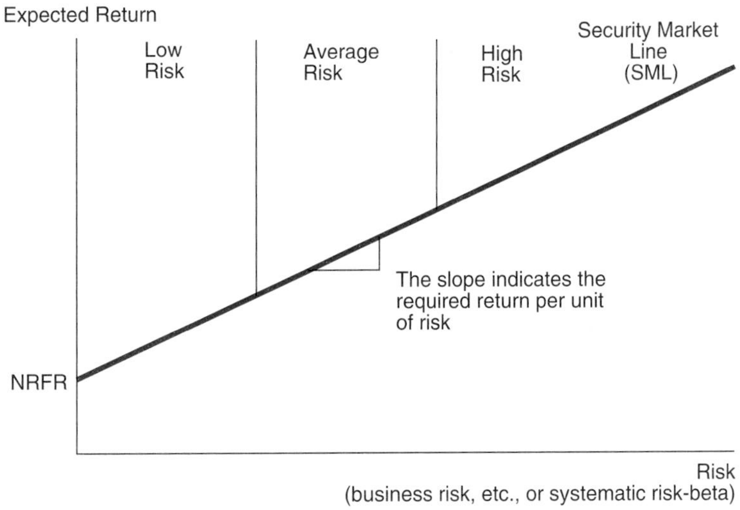
Expected Return
Low Risk
Average Risk
High Risk
Security Market Line (SML)
The slope indicates the required return per unit of risk
NRFR
Risk
(business risk, etc., or systematic risk-beta)

FIGURE 1.5

CHANGES IN THE REQUIRED RATE OF RETURN DUE TO MOVEMENTS ALONG THE SML

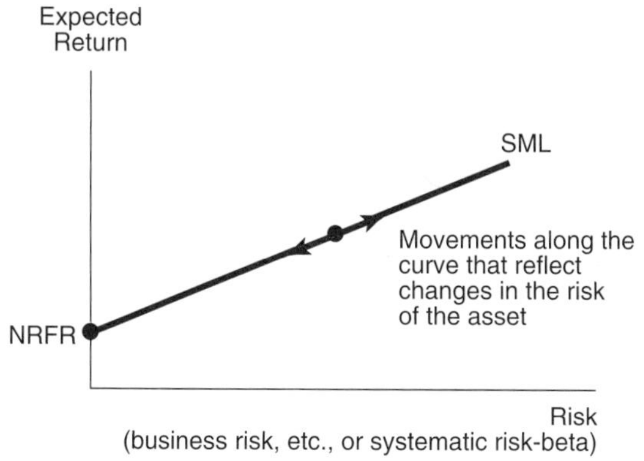
Expected
Return
SML
Movements along the
curve that reflect
changes in the risk
of the asset
NRFR
Risk
(business risk, etc., or systematic risk-beta)

Beginning with an initial security market line, three changes can occur. First, individual investments can change positions on the SML because of changes in the perceived risk of the investments. Second, the slope of the SML can change because of a change in the attitudes of investors toward risk; that is, investors can change the returns they require per unit of risk. Third, the SML can experience a parallel shift due to a change in the RRFR or the expected rate of inflation—that is, a change in the NRFR. These three possibilities are discussed in this section.

Movements Along the SML

Investors place alternative investments somewhere along the SML based on their perceptions of the risk of the investment. Obviously, if an investment's risk changes due to a change in one of its risk sources (business risk, and such), it will move along the security market line. For example, if a firm increases its financial risk by selling a large bond issue that increases its financial leverage, investors will perceive its common stock as riskier and the stock will move up the SML to a higher risk position. Investors will then require a higher rate of return. As the common stock becomes riskier, it changes its position on the SML. Any change in an asset that affects its fundamental risk factors or its market risk (that is, its beta) will cause the asset to move *along* the SML as shown in Figure 1.5. Note that the SML does not change, only the position of assets on the SML.

Changes in the Slope of the SML

The slope of the security market line indicates the return per unit of risk required by all investors. Assuming a straight line, it is possible to select any point on the SML and compute a risk premium (RP) through the equation:

1.13 $$RP_i = E(R_i) - NRFR$$

where:

RP_i = risk premium for asset i
$E(R_i)$ = the expected return for asset i
NRFR = the nominal return on a risk-free asset

If a point on the SML is identified as the portfolio that contains all the risky assets in the market (referred to as the *market portfolio*), it is possible to compute a market risk premium as follows:

FIGURE 1.6

PLOT OF MOODY'S CORPORATE BOND YIELD SPREADS (Baa–Aaa): MONTHLY 1966–1998

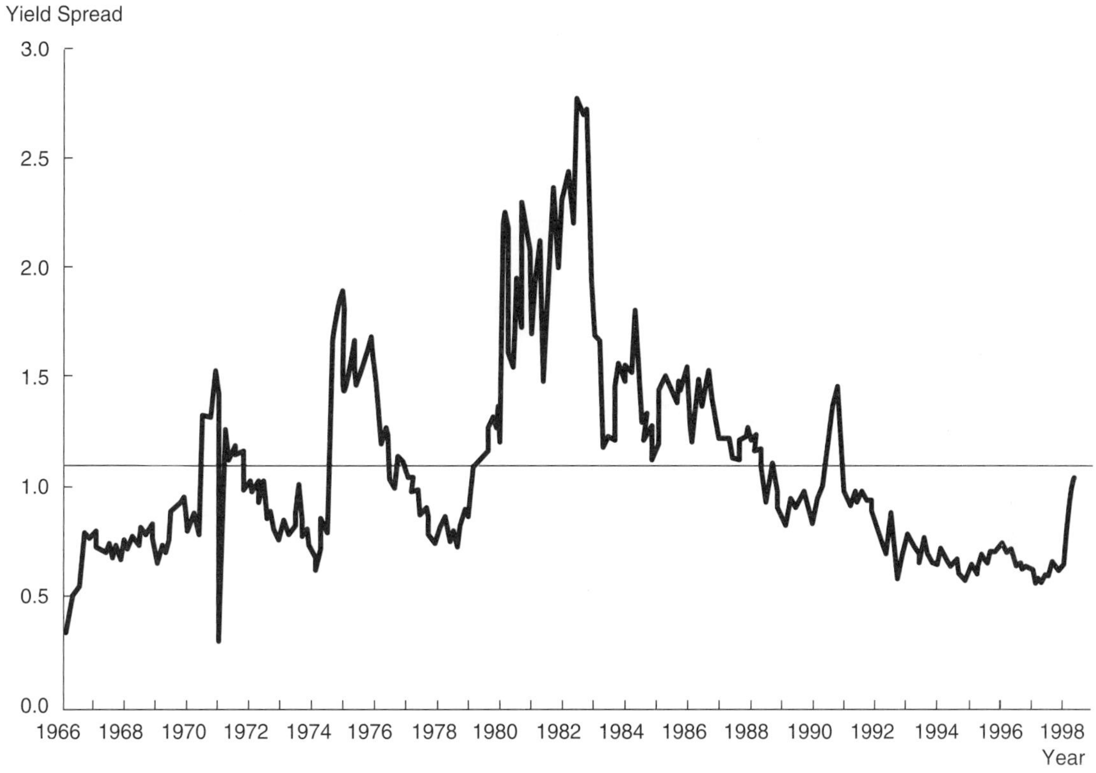
Yield Spread
3.0
2.5
2.0
1.5
1.0
0.5
0.0
1966
1968
1970
1972
1974
1976
1978
1980
1982
1984
1986
1988
1990
1992
1994
1996
1998
Year

1.14

$$RP_m = E(R_m) - NRFR$$

where:

RP_m = the risk premium on the market portfolio
$E(R_m)$ = the expected return on the market portfolio
NRFR = the nomial return on a risk-free asset

This market risk premium is *not constant* because the slope of the security market line changes over time. Although we do not understand completely what causes these changes in the slope, we do know that there are changes in the *yield* differences between assets with different levels of risk even though the inherent risk differences are relatively constant.

These differences in yields are referred to as **yield spreads**, and these yield spreads change over time. As an example, if the yield on a portfolio of Aaa-rated bonds is 7.50 percent and the yield on a portfolio of Baa-rated bonds is 9.00 percent, we would say that the yield spread is 1.50 percent. This 1.50 percent is referred to as a risk premium because the Baa-rated bond is considered to have higher credit risk—that is, greater probability of default. This Baa–Aaa yield spread is *not* constant over time. For an example of changes in a yield spread, note the substantial difference in yield spreads on Aaa-rated bonds and Baa-rated bonds shown in Figure 1.6.

FIGURE 1.7 **CHANGE IN MARKET RISK PREMIUM**

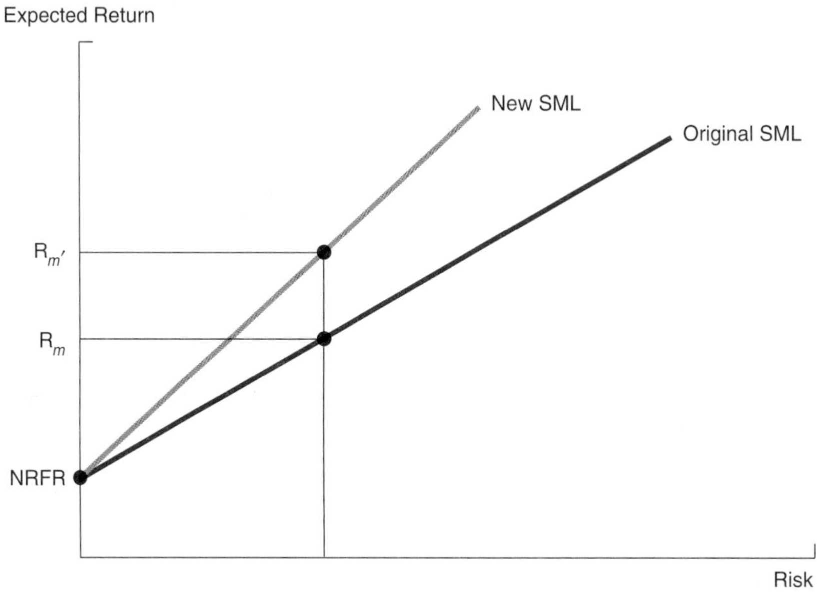
Expected Return
New SML
Original SML
Rm′
Rm
NRFR
Risk

Although the underlying risk factors for the portfolio of bonds in the Aaa-rated bond index and the Baa-rated bond index would probably not change dramatically over time, it is clear from the time-series plot in Figure 1.6 that the difference in yields (i.e., the yield spread) has experienced changes of more than 100 basis points (1 percent) in a short period of time (for example, see the yield spread increase in 1974 to 1975 and the dramatic yield spread decline in 1983 to 1984). Such a significant change in the yield spread during a period where there is no major change in the risk characteristics of Baa bonds relative to Aaa bonds would imply a change in the market risk premium. Specifically, although the risk levels of the bonds remain relatively constant, investors have changed the yield spreads they demand to accept this relatively constant difference in risk.

This change in the risk premium implies a change in the slope of the security market line. Such a change is shown in Figure 1.7. The figure assumes an increase in the market risk premium, which means an increase in the slope of the market line. Such a change in the slope of the SML (the risk premium) will affect the required rate of return for all risky assets. Irrespective of where an investment is on the original SML, its required rate of return will increase, although its individual risk characteristics remain unchanged.

CHANGES IN CAPITAL MARKET CONDITIONS OR EXPECTED INFLATION

The graph in Figure 1.8 shows what happens to the SML when there are changes in one of the following factors: (1) expected real growth in the economy, (2) capital market conditions, or (3) the expected rate of inflation. For example, an increase in expected real growth, temporary tightness in the capital market, or an increase in the expected rate of inflation will cause the SML to experience a parallel shift upward. The parallel shift occurs because changes in expected real growth or in capital market conditions, or a change in the expected rate of inflation affect all investments, no matter what their levels of risk.

FIGURE 1.8 **CAPITAL MARKET CONDITIONS, EXPECTED INFLATION, AND THE SECURITY MARKET LINE**

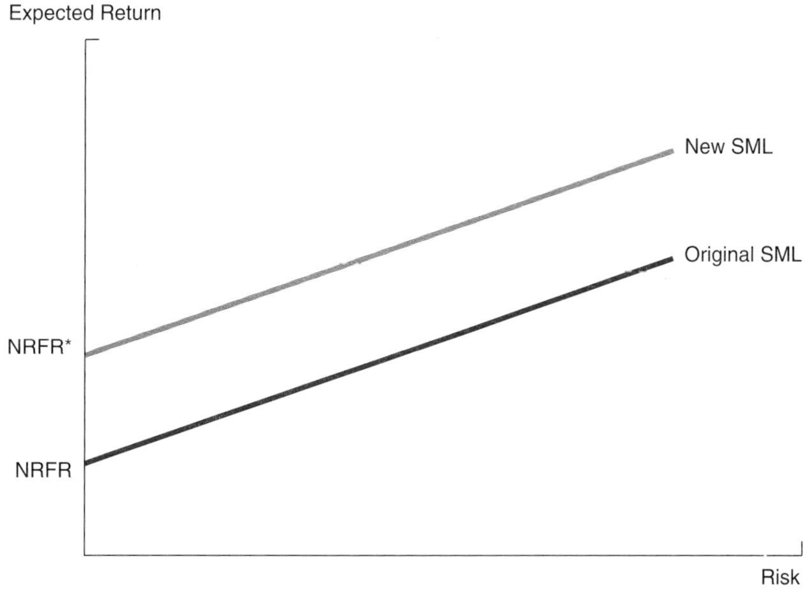
Expected Return
New SML
Original SML
NRFR*
NRFR
Risk

SUMMARY OF CHANGES IN THE REQUIRED RATE OF RETURN

The relationship between risk and the required rate of return for an investment can change in three ways:

1. A movement *along* the SML demonstrates a change in the risk characteristics of a specific investment, such as a change in its business risk, its financial risk, or its systematic risk (its beta). This change affects only the individual investment.
2. A change in the *slope* of the SML occurs in response to a change in the attitudes of investors toward risk. Such a change demonstrates that investors want either higher or lower rates of return for the same risk. This is also described as a change in the market risk premium (R_m − NRFR). A change in the risk premium will affect all risky investments.
3. A *shift* in the security market line reflects a change in expected real growth, a change in market conditions (such as ease or tightness of money), or a change in the expected rate of inflation. Again, such a change will affect all investments.

THE INTERNET *Investments Online*

There are a great many Internet sites that seek to assist the beginning or novice investor. Because they cover the basics, have helpful links to other Internet sites, and sometimes allow users to calculate items of interest (rates of return, the size of an investment necessary to meet a certain goal, and so on), these sites are useful for the experienced investor, too.

www.financenter.com Financenter has nearly everything for personal financial decisions. It includes insights about buying or selling a home or car or using a credit line, and information helpful for making insurance and investing decisions. It includes a number of "ClickClacs"—a series of calculation input screens—to help investors, both novice and experienced, answer a variety of questions, from help with the decision to

(continued)

THE INTERNET *Investments Online (cont.)*

lease or purchase a car to investment-return calculations.

www.investorama.com This site allows you to obtain information on stocks, including stock price and mutual fund quotes. It contains links to over 11,500 finance-related sites in 130 different categories. In addition, this site has links to the home pages of over 4,900 public companies, where you can obtain current company information and financial statements. For the beginner, this site has several tutorials on investing.

www.moneyadvisor.com Some financial decisions involve qualitative factors as investors or borrowers weigh one choice against another. Other decisions are more quantitative in nature, and some are a mix of both. To help you with decisions in the latter two categories, this Web site offers a calculator feature to help make decisions, such as whether to take the rebate offer or special dealer financing rates when buying a car. Other calculations and information can answer questions about loans, mortgages, insurance, taxes, and college and other saving goals. The site also includes several "just for fun" calculations. By answering several questions, you can compute your body mass ratio and compare it to the ideal; you can also estimate your life expectancy.

www.investorguide.com This is another site offering a plethora of information that is useful to both the novice and seasoned investor. It contains links to pages with market summaries, news research, and much more. It offers users a glossary of investment terms and 1,000 questions and answers on a variety of topics. Basic investment education issues are taught here, and users can learn more through links to discussion groups, investment strategies, and many other topics. There are links to a number of personal financial help pages, including sites dealing with buying a home or car, retirement, loans, and insurance. It offers links to a number of calculator functions to help users make financial decisions.

Some other sites that may be of interest:

www.finweb.com Electronic publishing, databases, working papers, links to other Web sites

www.cob.ohio-state.edu/dept/fin/osudata.htm Contains links to numerous finance sites

www.aaii.org Home page for the American Association of Individual Investors, a group dealing with investor education.

Many representatives of the financial press have Internet sites:

www.wsj.com *The Wall Street Journal*
www.ft.com *Financial Times*
www.fortune.com *Fortune* magazine
www.money.com *Money* magazine
www.forbes.com *Forbes* magazine
www.worth.com *Worth* magazine
www.barrons.com *Barron's* newspaper

Summary

The purpose of this chapter is to provide background that can be used in subsequent chapters. To achieve that goal, we covered several topics:

- We discussed why individuals save part of their income and why they decide to invest their savings. We defined *investment* as the current commitment of these savings for a period of time to derive a rate of return that compensates for the time involved, the expected rate of inflation, and the uncertainty.
- We examined ways to quantify historical return and risk to help analyze alternative investment opportunities. We considered two measures of mean return (arithmetic and geometric) and applied these to a historical series for an individual investment and to a portfolio of investments during a period of time.
- We considered the concept of uncertainty and alternative measures of risk (the variance, standard deviation, and a relative measure of risk—the coefficient of variation).
- Before discussing the determinants of the required rate of return for an investment, we noted that the estimation of the required rate of return is complicated because the rates on individual investments change over time, because there is a wide range of rates of return available on alternative investments, and because the differences between required returns on alternative investments (for example, the yield spreads) likewise change over time.

- We examined the specific factors that determine the required rate of return: (a) the real risk-free rate, which is based on the real rate of growth in the economy, (b) the nominal risk-free rate, which is influenced by capital market conditions and the expected rate of inflation, and (c) a risk premium, which is a function of fundamental factors, such as business risk, or the systematic risk of the asset relative to the market portfolio (that is, its beta).
- We discussed the risk–return combinations available on alternative investments at a point in time (illustrated by the SML) and the three factors that can cause changes in this relationship. First, a change in the inherent risk of an investment (that is, its fundamental risk or market risk) will cause a movement along the SML. Second, a change in investors' attitudes toward risk will cause a change in the required return per unit of risk—that is, a change in the market risk premium. Such a change will cause a change in the slope of the SML. Finally, a change in expected real growth, in capital market conditions, or in the expected rate of inflation will cause a parallel shift of the SML.

Based on this understanding of the investment environment, you are prepared to consider the asset allocation decision. This is the subject of Chapter 2.

Questions

1. Discuss the overall purpose people have for investing. Define investment.
2. As a student, are you saving or borrowing? Why?
3. Divide a person's life from ages 20 to 70 into 10-year segments and discuss the likely saving or borrowing patterns during each period.
4. Discuss why you would expect the saving–borrowing pattern to differ by occupation (for example, for a doctor versus a plumber).
5. *The Wall Street Journal* reported that the yield on common stocks is about 4 percent, whereas a study at the University of Chicago contends that the annual rate of return on common stocks since 1926 has averaged about 10 percent. Reconcile these statements.
6. Some financial theorists consider the variance of the distribution of expected rates of return to be a good measure of uncertainty. Discuss the reasoning behind this measure of risk and its purpose.
7. Discuss the three components of an investor's required rate of return on an investment.
8. Discuss the two major factors that determine the market nominal risk-free rate (NRFR). Explain which of these factors would be more volatile over the business cycle.
9. Briefly discuss the five fundamental factors that influence the risk premium of an investment.
10. You own stock in the Gentry Company, and you read in the financial press that a recent bond offering has raised the firm's debt/equity ratio from 35 percent to 55 percent. Discuss the effect of this change on the variability of the firm's net income stream, other factors being constant. Discuss how this change would affect your required rate of return on the common stock of the Gentry Company.
11. Draw a properly labeled graph of the security market line (SML) and indicate where you would expect the following investments to fall along that line. Discuss your reasoning.
    a. Common stock of large firms
    b. U.S. government bonds
    c. United Kingdom government bonds
    d. Low-grade corporate bonds
    e. Common stock of a Japanese firm
12. Explain why you would change your nominal required rate of return if you expected the rate of inflation to go from zero (no inflation) to 7 percent. Give an example of what would happen if you did not change your required rate of return under these conditions.
13. Assume the long-run growth rate of the economy increased by 1 percent and the expected rate of inflation increased by 4 percent. What would happen to the required rates of return on government bonds and common stocks? Show graphically how the effects of these changes would differ between these alternative investments.
14. You see in the *Wall Street Journal* that the yield spread between Baa corporate bonds and Aaa corporate bonds has gone from 350 basis points (3.5 percent) to 200 basis points (2 percent). Show graphically the effect of this change in yield spread on the SML and discuss its effect on the required rate of return for common stocks.
15. Give an example of a liquid investment and an illiquid investment. Discuss why you consider each of them to be liquid or illiquid.

Problems

1. On February 1, you bought some stock for \$34 a share and a year later you sold it for \$39 a share. During the year you received a cash dividend of \$1.50 a share. Compute your HPR and HPY on this stock investment.
2. On August 15, you purchased some stock at \$65 a share and a year later you sold it for \$61 a share. During the year, you received dividends of \$3 a share. Compute your HPR and HPY on this investment.
3. At the beginning of last year you invested \$4,000 in 80 shares of the Chang Corporation. During the year Chang paid dividends of \$5 per share. At the end of the year you sold the 80 shares for \$59 a share. Compute your total HPY on these shares and indicate how much was due to the price change and how much was due to the dividend income.
4. The rates of return computed in Problems 1, 2, and 3 are nominal rates of return. Assuming that the rate of inflation during the year was 4 percent, compute the real rates of return on these investments. Compute the real rates of return if the rate of inflation were 8 percent.
5. During the past 5 years, you owned two stocks that had the following annual rates of return:

Year	Stock T	Stock B
1	0.19	0.08
2	0.08	0.03
3	−0.12	−0.09
4	−0.03	0.02
5	0.15	0.04

   a. Compute the arithmetic mean annual rate of return for each stock. Which stock is most desirable by this measure?
   b. Compute the standard deviation of the annual rate of return for each stock. (Use Chapter 1 Appendix if necessary.) By this measure, which is the preferable stock?
   c. Compute the coefficient of variation for each stock. (Use the Chapter 1 Appendix if necessary.) By this relative measure of risk, which stock is preferable?
   d. Compute the geometric mean rate of return for each stock. Discuss the difference between the arithmetic mean return and the geometric mean return for each stock. Relate the differences in the mean returns to the standard deviation of the return for each stock.
6. You are considering acquiring shares of common stock in the Madison Beer Corporation. Your rate of return expectations are as follows:

Possible Rate of Return	Probability
−0.10	0.30
0.00	0.10
0.10	0.30
0.25	0.30

   Compute the expected return $[E(R_i)]$ on this investment.
7. A stockbroker calls you and suggests that you invest in the Anita Computer Company. After analyzing the firm's annual report and other material, you believe that the distribution of rates of return is as follows:

Possible Rate of Return	Probability
−0.60	0.05
−0.30	0.20
−0.10	0.10
0.20	0.30
0.40	0.20
0.80	0.15

Compute the expected return $[E(R_i)]$ on this stock.

8. Without any formal computations, do you consider Madison Beer in Problem 6 or Antia Computer in Problem 7 to present greater risk? Discuss your reasoning.
9. During the past year, you had a portfolio that contained U.S. government T-bills, long-term government bonds, and common stocks. The rates of return on each of them were as follows:

U.S. government T-bills	5.50%
U.S. government long-term bonds	7.50
U.S. common stocks	11.60

During the year, the consumer price index, which measures the rate of inflation, went from 160 to 172 (1982–1984 = 100). Compute the rate of inflation during this year. Compute the real rates of return on each of the investments in your portfolio based on the inflation rate.

10. You read in *Business Week* that a panel of economists has estimated that the long-run real growth rate of the U.S. economy over the next five-year period will average 3 percent. In addition, a bank newsletter estimates that the average annual rate of inflation during this five-year period will be about 4 percent. What nominal rate of return would you expect on U.S. government T-bills during this period?
11. What would your required rate of return be on common stocks if you wanted a 5 percent risk premium to own common stocks given what you know from Problem 10? If common stock investors became more risk averse, what would happen to the required rate of return on common stocks? What would be the impact on stock prices?
12. Assume that the consensus required rate of return on common stocks is 14 percent. In addition, you read in *Fortune* that the expected rate of inflation is 5 percent and the estimated long-term real growth rate of the economy is 3 percent. What interest rate would you expect on U.S. government T-bills? What is the approximate risk premium for common stocks implied by these data?

References

Fama, Eugene F., and Merton H. Miller. *The Theory of Finance*. New York: Holt, Rinehart and Winston, 1972.

Fisher, Irving. *The Theory of Interest*. New York: Macmillan, 1930; reprinted by Augustus M. Kelley, 1961.

Chapter 1 APPENDIX

COMPUTATION OF VARIANCE AND STANDARD DEVIATION

Variance and standard deviation are measures of how actual values differ from the expected values (arithmetic mean) for a given series of values. In this case, we want to measure how rates of return differ from the arithmetic mean value of a series. There are other measures of dispersion, but variance and standard deviation are the best known because they are used in statistics and probability theory. Variance is defined as:

$$\text{Variance } (\sigma^2) = \sum_{i=1}^{n} (\text{Probability})(\text{Possible Return} - \text{Expected Return})^2$$
$$= \sum_{i=1}^{n} (P_i)[R_i - E(R_i)]^2$$

Consider the following example, as discussed in the chapter:

Probability of Possible Return (P_i)	Possible Return (R_i)	P_iR_i
0.15	0.20	0.03
0.15	−0.20	−0.03
0.70	0.10	0.07
		$\Sigma = 0.07$

This gives an expected return $[E(R_i)]$ of 7 percent. The dispersion of this distribution as measured by variance is:

Probability (P_i)	Return (R_i)	$R_i - E(R_i)$	$[R_i - E(R_i)]^2$	$P_i[R_i - E(R_i)]^2$
0.15	0.20	0.13	0.0169	0.002535
0.15	−0.20	−0.27	0.0729	0.010935
0.70	0.10	0.03	0.0009	0.000630
				$\Sigma = 0.014100$

The variance (σ^2) is equal to 0.0141. The standard deviation is equal to the square root of the variance:

$$\text{Standard Deviation } (\sigma^2) = \sqrt{\sum_{i=1}^{n} P_i[R_i - E(R_i)]^2}$$

Consequently, the standard deviation for the preceding example would be:

$$\sigma_i = \sqrt{0.0141} = 0.11874$$

In this example, the standard deviation is approximately 11.87 percent. Therefore, you could describe this distribution as having an expected value of 7 percent and a standard deviation of 11.87 percent.

In many instances, you might want to compute the variance or standard deviation for a historical series in order to evaluate the past performance of the investment. Assume that you are given the following information on annual rates of return (HPY) for common stocks listed on the New York Stock Exchange (NYSE):

Year	Annual Rate of Return
19_5	0.07
19_6	0.11
19_7	−0.04
19_8	0.12
19_9	−0.06

In this case, we are not examining expected rates of return, but actual returns. Therefore, we assume equal probabilities, and the expected value (in this case the mean value, R) of the series is the sum of the individual observations in the series divided by the number of observations, or 0.04 (0.20/5). The variances and standard deviations are:

Year	R_i	$R_i - \bar{R}$	$(R_i - \bar{R})^2$	
19_5	0.07	0.03	0.0009	$\sigma^2 = 0.0286/5$
19_6	0.11	0.07	0.0049	$= 0.00572$
19_7	−0.04	−0.08	0.0064	
19_8	0.12	0.08	0.0064	$\sigma = \sqrt{0.00572}$
19_9	−0.06	−0.10	0.0110	$= 0.0756$
			$\Sigma = 0.0286$	

We can interpret the performance of NYSE common stocks during this period of time by saying that the average rate of return was 4 percent and the standard deviation of annual rates of return was 7.56 percent.

Coefficient of Variation

In some instances you might want to compare the dispersion of two different series. The variance and standard deviation are *absolute* measures of dispersion. That is, they can be influenced by the magnitude of the original numbers. To compare series with greatly different values, you need a *relative* measure of dispersion. A measure of relative dispersion is the coefficient of variation, which is defined as:

$$\text{Coefficient of Variation (CV)} = \frac{\text{Standard Deviation of Returns}}{\text{Expected Rate of Return}}$$

A larger value indicates greater dispersion relative to the arithmetic mean of the series. For the previous example, the CV would be:

$$CV_1 = \frac{0.0756}{0.0400} = 1.89$$

It is possible to compare this value to a similar figure having a markedly different distribution. As an example, assume you wanted to compare this investment to another investment that had an average rate of return of 10 percent and a standard deviation of 9 percent. The standard deviations alone tell you that the second series has greater dispersion (9 percent versus 7.56 percent) and might be considered to have higher risk. In fact, the relative dispersion for this second investment is much less.

$$CV_1 = \frac{0.0756}{0.0400} = 1.89$$

$$CV_2 = \frac{0.0900}{0.1000} = 0.90$$

Considering the relative dispersion and the total distribution, most investors would probably prefer the second investment.

PROBLEMS

1. Your rate of return expectations for the common stock of Gray Disc Company during the next year are:

Possible Rate of Return	Probability
−0.10	0.25
0.00	0.15
0.10	0.35
0.25	0.25

a. Compute the expected return [$E(R_i)$] on this investment, the variance of this return (σ^2), and its standard deviation (σ).
b. Under what conditions can the standard deviation be used to measure the relative risk of two investments?
c. Under what conditions must the coefficient of variation be used to measure the relative risk of two investments?

2. Your rate of return expectations for the stock of Kayleigh Computer Company during the next year are:

Possible Rate of Return	Probability
−0.60	0.15
−0.30	0.10
−0.10	0.05
0.20	0.40
0.40	0.20
0.80	0.10

a. Compute the expected return [$E(R_i)$] on this stock, the variance (σ^2) of this return, and its standard deviation (σ).
b. On the basis of expected return [$E(R_i)$] alone, discuss whether Gray Disc or Kayleigh Computer is preferable.
c. On the basis of standard deviation (σ) alone, discuss whether Gray Disc or Kayleigh Computer is preferable.
d. Compute the coefficients of variation (CVs) for Gray Disc and Kayleigh Computer and discuss which stock return series has the greater relative dispersion.

3. The following are annual rates of return for U.S. government T-bills and United Kingdom common stocks.

Year	U.S. Government T-Bills	United Kingdom Common Stock
19_5	.063	.150
19_6	.081	.043
19_7	.076	.374
19_8	.090	.192
19_9	.085	.106

a. Compute the arithmetic mean rate of return and standard deviation of rates of return for the two series.
b. Discuss these two alternative investments in terms of their arithmetic average rates of return, their absolute risk, and their relative risk.
c. Compute the geometric mean rate of return for each of these investments. Compare the arithmetic mean return and geometric mean return for each investment and discuss this difference between mean returns as related to the standard deviation of each series.

Chapter

2 THE ASSET ALLOCATION DECISION*

After you read this chapter, you should be able to answer the following questions:

- What is asset allocation?
- What are the four steps in the portfolio management process?
- What is the role of asset allocation in investment planning?
- Why is a policy statement important to the planning process?
- What objectives and constraints should be detailed in a policy statement?
- How and why do investment goals change over a person's lifetime and circumstances?
- Why do asset allocation strategies differ across national boundaries?

The previous chapter informed us that *risk drives return.* Therefore, the practice of investing funds and managing portfolios should focus primarily on managing risk rather than on managing returns.

This chapter examines some of the practical implications of risk management in the context of asset allocation. **Asset allocation** is the process of deciding how to distribute an investor's wealth among different countries and asset classes for investment purposes. An **asset class** is comprised of securities that have similar characteristics, attributes, and risk/return relationships. A broad asset class, such as "bonds," can be divided into smaller asset classes, such as Treasury bonds, corporate bonds, and high-yield bonds. We will see that, in the long run, the highest compounded returns will most likely accrue to those investors with larger exposures to risky assets. We will also see that although there are no shortcuts or guarantees to investment success, maintaining a reasonable and disciplined approach to investing will increase the likelihood of investment success over time.

The asset allocation decision is not an isolated choice; rather, it is a component of a portfolio management process. In this chapter we present an overview of the four-step portfolio management process. As we will see, the first step in the process is to develop an investment policy statement, or plan, that will guide all future decisions. Much of an asset allocation strategy depends on the investor's policy statement, which includes the investor's goals or objectives, constraints, and investment guidelines.

What we mean by an "investor" can range from an individual to trustees overseeing a corporation's multi-billion-dollar pension fund, a university endowment, or invested premiums for an insurance company. Regardless of who the investor is or how simple or complex the investment needs, he or she should develop a policy statement before making long-term investment decisions. Although most of our examples will be in the context of an individual investor, the concepts we introduce here—investment objectives, constraints, benchmarks, and so on—apply to any investor, individual or institutional. We'll review historical data to show the importance of the asset allocation decision and discuss the need for investor education, an important issue for individuals or companies who offer retirement or

*The authors acknowledge the collaboration of Professor Edgar Norton of Illinois State University on this chapter.

savings plans to their employees. The chapter concludes by examining asset allocation strategies across national borders to show the effect of market environment and culture on investing patterns; what is appropriate for a U.S.-based investor is not necessarily appropriate for a non–U.S.-based investor.

INDIVIDUAL INVESTOR LIFE CYCLE

Financial plans and investment needs are as different as each individual. Investment needs change over a person's life cycle. How individuals structure their financial plan should be related to their age, financial status, future plans, risk aversion characteristcs, and needs.

THE PRELIMINARIES

Before embarking on an investment program, we need to make sure other needs are satisfied. No serious investment plan should be started until a potential investor has adequate income to cover living expenses and has a safety net should the unexpected occur.

INSURANCE Life insurance should be a component of any financial plan. Life insurance protects loved ones against financial hardship should death occur before our financial goals are met. The death benefit paid by the insurance company can help pay medical bills and funeral expenses and provide cash that the family can use to maintain their lifestyle, retire debt, or invest for future needs (for example, children's education, spouse retirement). Therefore, one of the first steps in developing a financial plan is to purchase adequate life insurance coverage.

Insurance can also serve more immediate purposes, including being a means to meet long-term goals, such as retirement planning. On reaching retirement age, you can receive the cash or surrender value of your life insurance policy and use the proceeds to supplement your retirement lifestyle or for estate planning purposes.

You can choose among several basic life insurance contracts. *Term life insurance* provides only a death benefit; the premium to purchase the insurance changes every renewal period. Term insurance is the least expensive life insurance to purchase, although the premium will rise as you age to reflect the increased probability of death. *Universal* and *variable life policies,* although technically different from each other, are similar in that they each provide both a death benefit and a savings plan to the insured. The premium paid on such policies exceeds the cost to the insurance company of providing the death benefit alone; the excess premium is invested in a number of investment vehicles chosen by the insured. The policy's cash value grows over time, based on the size of the excess premium and on the performance of the underlying investment funds. Insurance companies may restrict the ability to withdraw funds from these policies before the policyholder reaches a certain age.

Insurance coverage also provides protection against other uncertainties. Health insurance helps to pay medical bills. Disability insurance provides continuing income should you become unable to work. Automobile and home (or rental) insurance provide protection against accidents and damage to cars or residences.

Although nobody ever expects to use their insurance coverage, a first step in a sound financial plan is to have adequate coverage "just in case." Lack of insurance coverage can ruin the best-planned investment program.

CASH RESERVE Emergencies, job layoffs and unforeseen expenses happen, and good investment opportunities emerge. It is important to have a cash reserve to help meet these occasions. In addition to providing a safety cushion, a cash reserve reduces the likelihood of being forced to sell investments at inopportune times to cover unexpected expenses. Most experts recommend a cash reserve equal to about six months' living expenses. Calling it a "cash" reserve does not mean the funds should be in cash; rather, the funds should be in investments you can easily convert to cash with little chance of a loss in value. Money market mutual funds and bank accounts are appropriate vehicles for the cash reserve.

Similar to the financial plan, an investor's insurance and cash reserve needs will change over his or her life. We've already mentioned how a retired person may "cash out" a life insurance policy to supplement income. The need for disability insurance declines when a person retires. In contrast, other insurance, such as supplemental Medicare coverage or nursing home insurance, may become more important.

LIFE CYCLE NET WORTH AND INVESTMENT STRATEGIES

Assuming the basic insurance and cash reserve needs are met, individuals can start a serious investment program with their savings. Because of changes in their net worth and risk tolerance, individuals' investment strategies will change over their lifetime. Below we review various phases in the investment life cycle. Although each individual's needs and preferences are different, some general traits affect most investors over the life cycle. Let's look at the four life cycle phases as shown in Figure 2.1 (the third and fourth phases are shown as concurrent).

ACCUMULATION PHASE Individuals in the early-to-middle years of their working careers are in the **accumulation phase**. As the name implies, they are attempting to accumulate assets to satisfy fairly immediate needs (for example, a down payment for a house) or longer-term goals (children's college education, retirement). Typically, their net worth is small, and debt from car loans or their own past college loans may be heavy. As a result of their typically long investment time horizon and their future earning ability, individuals in the accumulation phase are willing to make moderately high-risk investments in the hopes of making above-average nominal returns over time.

CONSOLIDATION PHASE Individuals in the **consolidation phase** are typically past the midpoint of their careers, have paid off much or all of their outstanding debts, and perhaps have paid, or have the assets to pay, their children's college bills. Earnings exceed expenses, so the excess can be invested to provide for future retirement or estate planning needs. The typical investment horizon is still long (20 to 30 years), so moderate-risk investments remain attractive. Because individuals in this phase have some concern about capital preservation, they do not want to take very large risks that may put their current nest egg in jeopardy.

SPENDING PHASE The **spending phase** typically begins when individuals retire. Living expenses are covered by social security income and income from prior investments, including employer pension plans. Because their earning years have concluded (although some retirees take part-time positions or do consulting work), they seek greater protection of their capital. At the same time, they must balance their desire to preserve the nominal value of their savings with the need to protect themselves against a decline in the *real* value of their savings due to inflation. The average 65-year-old person in the United States has a life expectancy of about 20 years. Thus, although their overall portfolio may be less risky than in the consolidation phase, they still need to have some risky growth investments, such as common stocks, for inflation (purchasing power) protection.

GIFTING PHASE The **gifting phase** is similar to, and may be concurrent with, the spending phase. In this stage, individuals believe they have sufficient income and assets to

FIGURE 2.1 **RISE AND FALL OF PERSONAL NET WORTH OVER A LIFETIME**

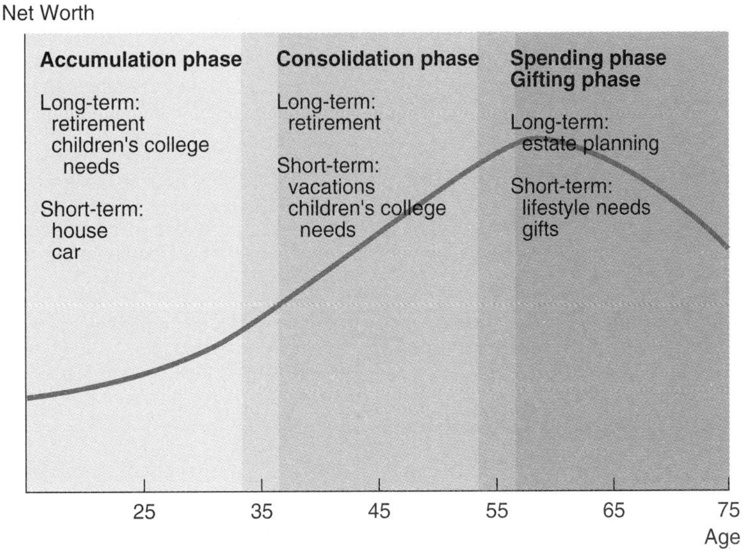
Net Worth
Accumulation phase
Long-term:
retirement
children's college needs
Short-term:
house
car
Consolidation phase
Long-term:
retirement
Short-term:
vacations
children's college needs
Spending phase
Gifting phase
Long-term:
estate planning
Short-term:
lifestyle needs
gifts
25
35
45
55
65
75
Age

cover their expenses while maintaining a reserve for uncertainties. Excess assets can be used to provide financial assistance to relatives or friends, to establish charitable trusts, or to fund trusts that provide an estate planning tool to minimize estate taxes.

LIFE CYCLE INVESTMENT GOALS

During the investment life cycle, individuals have a variety of financial goals. **Near-term, high-priority goals** are shorter-term financial objectives that individuals set to fund purchases that are personally important to them, such as accumulating funds to make a house down payment, buy a new car, or take a trip. Parents with teenage children may have a near-term, high-priority goal to accumulate funds to help pay college expenses. Because of the emotional importance of these goals and their short time horizon, high-risk investments are not usually considered suitable for achieving them.

Long-term, high-priority goals typically include some form of financial independence, such as the ability to retire at a certain age. Because of their long-term nature, higher-risk investments can be used to help meet these objectives.

Lower-priority goals are just that—it might be nice to meet these objectives, but it is not critical. Examples include the ability to purchase a new car every few years, redecorate the home with expensive furnishings, or take a long, luxurious vacation.

A well-developed policy statement considers these diverse goals over an investor's lifetime. The following sections detail the process for constructing an investment policy, creating a portfolio that is consistent with the policy and the environment, managing the portfolio, and monitoring its applicability to the investor over time.

THE PORTFOLIO MANAGEMENT PROCESS

The process of managing an investment portfolio never stops. Once the funds are initially invested according to the plan, the real work begins in monitoring and updating the status of the portfolio and the investor's needs.

FIGURE 2.2 **THE PORTFOLIO MANAGEMENT PROCESS**

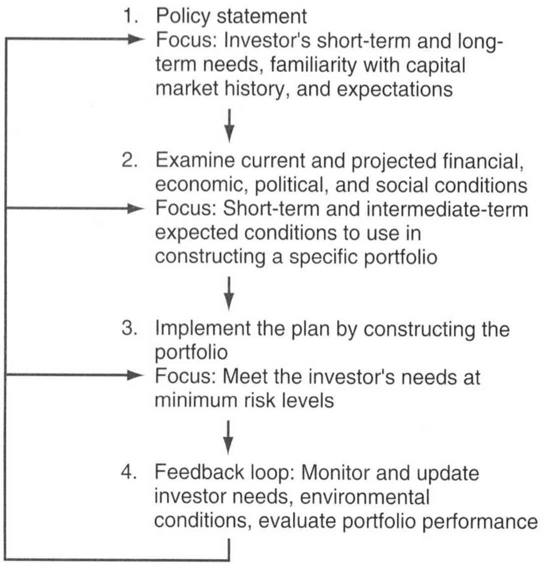
1. Policy statement
Focus: Investor's short-term and long-term needs, familiarity with capital market history, and expectations
2. Examine current and projected financial, economic, political, and social conditions
Focus: Short-term and intermediate-term expected conditions to use in constructing a specific portfolio
3. Implement the plan by constructing the portfolio
Focus: Meet the investor's needs at minimum risk levels
4. Feedback loop: Monitor and update investor needs, environmental conditions, evaluate portfolio performance

The first step in the portfolio management process, as seen in Figure 2.2, is for the investor, either alone or with the assistance of an investment advisor, to construct a **policy statement**. The policy statement is a road map; in it investors specify the types of risks they are willing to take and their investment goals and constraints. All investment decisions are based on the policy statement to ensure they are appropriate for the investor. We will examine the process of constructing a policy statement later in this chapter. Because investor needs change over time, the policy statement must be periodically reviewed and updated.

The process of investing seeks to peer into the future and determine strategies that offer the best possibility of meeting the policy statement guidelines. In the second step of the portfolio management process, the manager should study current financial and economic conditions and forecast future trends. The investor's needs, as reflected in the policy statement, and financial market expectations will jointly determine investment strategy. Economies are dynamic; they are affected by numerous industry struggles, politics, and changing demographics and social attitudes. Thus, the portfolio will require constant monitoring and updating to reflect changes in financial market expectations. We examine the process of evaluating and forecasting economic trends in Chapter 14.

The third step of the portfolio management process is to construct the portfolio. With the investor's policy statement and financial market forecasts as input, the investor and any advisors determine how to allocate available funds across different countries, asset classes, and securities. This involves constructing a portfolio that will minimize the investor's risks while meeting the needs specified in the policy statement. Financial theory frequently assists portfolio construction, as we will discuss in Part 2. Some of the practical aspects of selecting investments for inclusion in a portfolio are discussed in Parts 4 and 5.

The fourth step in the portfolio management process is the continual monitoring of the investor's needs, capital market conditions, and, when necessary, updating the policy statement. Based upon all of this, the investment strategy is modified accordingly. A component of the monitoring process is to evaluate a portfolio's performance and compare the relative results to the expectations and the requirements listed in the policy statement. The evaluation of portfolio performance is discussed in Chapter 27.

THE NEED FOR A POLICY STATEMENT

As noted above, a policy statement is a road map that guides the investment process. Constructing a policy statement is an invaluable planning tool that will help the investor understand his or her needs better as well as assist an advisor or portfolio manager in managing a client's funds. While it does not guarantee investment success, a policy statement will provide discipline for the investment process and reduce the possibility of making hasty, inappropriate decisions. There are two important reasons for constructing a policy statement: First, it helps the investor decide on realistic investment goals after learning about the financial markets and the risks of investing. Second, it creates a standard by which to judge the performance of the portfolio manager.

Understand and Articulate Realistic Investor Goals

When asked about their investment goal, people often say, "to make a lot of money," or some similar response. Such a goal has two drawbacks: First, it may not be appropriate for the investor, and second, it is too open-ended to provide guidance for specific investments and time frames. Such an objective is well suited for someone going to the racetrack or buying lottery tickets, but it is inappropriate for someone investing funds in financial and real assets.

An important purpose of writing a policy statement is to help investors understand their own needs, objectives, and investment constraints. As part of this, investors need to learn about financial markets and the risks of investing. This background will help prevent them from making inappropriate investment decisions in the future and will increase the possibility that they will satisfy their specific, measurable financial goals.

Thus, the policy statement helps the investor to specify realistic goals and become more informed about the risks and costs of investing. Market values of assets, whether they be stocks, bonds, or real estate, can fluctuate dramatically. For example, during the October 1987 crash, the Dow Jones Industrial Average (DJIA) fell more than 20 percent in one day; in October 1997 the Dow fell "only" 7 percent. A review of market history shows that it is not unusual for asset prices to decline by 10 percent to 20 percent over several months. Investors will typically focus on a single statistic, such as an 11 percent average annual rate of return on stocks, and expect the market to rise 11 percent every year. Such thinking ignores the risk of stock investing. Part of the process of developing a policy statement is for the investor to become familiar with the risks of investing, because we know that a strong positive relationship exists between risk and return.

One expert in the field recommends that investors should think about the following set of questions and explain their answers as part of the process of constructing a policy statement:

1. What are the real risks of an adverse financial outcome, especially in the short run?
2. What probable emotional reactions will I have to an adverse financial outcome?
3. How knowledgeable am I about investments and markets?

4. What other capital or income sources do I have? How important is this particular portfolio to my overall financial position?
5. What, if any, legal restrictions may affect my investment needs?
6. What, if any, unanticipated consequences of interim fluctuations in portfolio value might affect my investment policy?

Adapted from Charles D. Ellis, *Investment Policy: How to Win the Loser's Game* (Homewood, Ill.: Dow Jones–Irwin, 1985), 25–26.

In summary, constructing a policy statement is mainly the investor's responsibility. It is a process whereby investors articulate their realistic needs and goals and become familiar with financial markets and investing risks. Without this information, investors cannot adequately communicate their needs to the portfolio manager. Without this input from investors, the portfolio manager cannot construct a portfolio that will satisfy clients' needs; the result of bypassing this step will most likely be future aggravation and dissatisfaction.

Standards for Evaluating Portfolio Performance

The policy statement also assists in judging the performance of the portfolio manager. Performance cannot be judged without an objective standard; the policy statement provides that objective standard. The portfolio's performance should be compared to guidelines specified in the policy statement, not on the portfolio's overall return. For example, if an investor has a low tolerance for risky investments, the portfolio manager should not be fired simply because the portfolio does not perform as well as the risky S&P 500 stock index. Because risk drives returns, the investor's lower-risk investments, as specified in the investor's policy statement, will probably earn lower returns than if all the investor's funds were placed in the stock market.

The policy statement will typically include a **benchmark portfolio,** or comparison standard. The risk of the benchmark, and the assets included in the benchmark, should agree with the client's risk preferences and investment needs. In turn, the investment performance of the portfolio manager should be compared to this benchmark portfolio. For example, an investor who specifies low-risk investments in the policy statement should compare the portfolio manager's performance against a low-risk benchmark portfolio. Likewise, an investor seeking high-risk, high-return investments should compare the portfolio's performance against a high-risk benchmark.

Because it sets an objective performance standard, the policy statement acts as a starting point for periodic portfolio review and client communication with managers. Questions concerning portfolio performance or the manager's faithfulness to the policy can be addressed in the context of the written policy guidelines. Managers should mainly be judged by whether they consistently followed the client's policy guidelines. The portfolio manager who makes unilateral deviations from policy is not working in the best interests of the client. Therefore, even deviations that result in higher portfolio returns can and should be grounds for the manager's dismissal.

Thus, we see the importance of the client constructing the policy statement: The client must first understand his or her own needs before communicating them to the portfolio manager. In turn, the portfolio manager must implement the client's desires by following the investment guidelines. As long as policy is followed, shortfalls in performance should not be a major concern. Remember that the policy statement is designed to impose an investment discipline on the client and portfolio manager. The less knowledgeable they are, the more likely clients are to inappropriately judge the performance of the portfolio manager.

OTHER BENEFITS A sound policy statement helps to protect the client against a portfolio manager's inappropriate investments or unethical behavior. Without clear, written guidance, some managers may consider investing in high-risk investments, hoping to earn a quick return. Such actions are probably counter to the investor's specified needs and risk preferences. Though legal recourse is a possibility against such action, writing a clear and unambiguous policy statement should safeguard against such innappropriate manager behavior.

Just because one specific manager currently manages your account does not mean that person will always manage your funds. As with other positions, your portfolio manager may be promoted or dismissed or take a better job. Therefore, after a while your funds may come under the management of an individual you do not know and who does not know you. To prevent costly delays during this transition, you can ensure that the new manager "hits the ground running" with a clearly written policy statement. A policy statement should prevent delays in monitoring and rebalancing your portfolio and will help create a seamless transition from one money manager to another.

To sum up, a clearly written policy statement helps avoid future potential problems. When the client clearly specifies his or her needs and desires, the portfolio manager can more effectively construct an appropriate portfolio. The policy statement provides an objective measure for evaluating portfolio performance, helps guard against ethical lapses by the portfolio manager, and aids in the transition between money managers. Therefore, the first step before beginning any investment program, whether it is for an individual or a multibillion-dollar pension fund, is to construct a policy statement.

An appropriate policy statement should satisfactorily answer the following questions:

1. Is the policy carefully designed to meet the specific needs and objectives of this particular investor? (Cookie-cutter or one-size-fits-all policy statements are generally inappropriate.)
2. Is the policy written so clearly and explicitly that a competent stranger could manage the portfolio in conformance with the client's needs? In case of a manager transition, could the new manager use this policy statement to handle your portfolio in accordance with your needs?
3. Would the client have been able to remain committed to the policies during the capital market experiences of the past 60 to 70 years? That is, does the client fully understand investment risks and the need for a disciplined approach to the investment process?
4. Would the portfolio manager have been able to maintain the policy over the same period? (Discipline is a two-way street; we do not want the portfolio manager to change strategies because of a disappointing market.)
5. Would the policy, if implemented, have achieved the client's objectives? (Bottom line: would the policy have worked to meet the client's needs?)

Adapted from Charles D. Ellis, *Investment Policy: How to Win the Loser's Game* (Homewood, Ill.: Dow Jones–Irwin, 1985), 62.

INPUT TO THE POLICY STATEMENT

Before an investor and advisor can construct a policy statement, they need to have an open and frank exchange of information, ideas, fears, and goals. To build a framework for this information-gathering process, the client and advisor need to discuss the client's investment objectives and constraints. To illustrate this framework, we will discuss the investment objectives and constraints that may confront a "typical" 25-year-old and 65-year-old investors.

INVESTMENT OBJECTIVES

The investor's **objectives** are his or her investment goals expressed in terms of both risk and returns. The relationship between risk and returns requires that goals not be expressed only in terms of returns. Expressing goals only in terms of returns can lead to inappropriate investment practices by the portfolio manager, such as the use of high-risk investment strategies or account "churning," which involves moving quickly in and out of investments in an attempt to buy low and sell high.

For example, a person may have a stated return goal such as "double my investment in five years." Before such a statement becomes part of the policy statement, the client must become fully informed of investment risks associated with such a goal, including the possibility of loss. *A careful analysis of the client's risk tolerance should precede any discussion of return objectives.* It makes little sense for a person who is risk averse to invest funds in high-risk assets. Investment firms survey clients to gauge their risk tolerance. For example, Merrill Lynch has asked its clients to place themselves in one of the four categories in Figure 2.3. Sometimes investment magazines or books contain tests that individuals can take to help them evaluate their risk tolerance (see Figure 2.4).

Risk tolerance is more than a function of an individual's psychological makeup; it is affected by other factors, including a person's current insurance coverage and cash reserves. Risk tolerance is also affected by an individual's family situation (for example, marital status and the number and ages of children) and by age. We know that older persons generally have shorter investment time frames within which to make up any losses; they also have years of experience, including living through various market gyrations and "corrections" (a euphemism for downtrends or crashes) that younger people have not experienced or whose effect they do not fully appreciate. Risk tolerance is also influenced by one's current net worth and income expectations. All else being equal, individuals with higher incomes have a greater propensity to undertake risk, because their incomes can help cover any shortfall. Likewise, individuals with larger net worths can afford to place some assets in risky investments while the remaining assets provide a cushion against losses.

A person's return objective may be stated in terms of an absolute or a relative percentage return, but it may also be stated in terms of a general goal, such as capital preservation, current income, capital appreciation, or total return.

Capital preservation means the investors want to minimize their risk of loss, usually in real terms: They seek to maintain the purchasing power of their investment. In other words, the return needs to be no less than the rate of inflation. Generally, this is a strategy for strongly risk-averse investors or for funds soon to be needed, say, for next year's tuition payment or a down payment on a house.

Capital appreciation is an appropriate objective when the investors want the portfolio to grow in real terms over time to meet some future need. Under this strategy, growth mainly occurs through capital gains—that is, buying assets at a low price and selling them later at a higher price. This is an aggressive strategy for investors willing to take on risk to meet their objective. Generally, longer-term investors seeking to build a retirement or college education fund may have this goal.

When **current income** is the return objective, the investors want the portfolio to concentrate on generating income rather than capital gains. This strategy sometimes suits investors who want to supplement their earnings with income generated by their portfolio to meet their living expenses. Retirees may favor this objective for part of their portfolio to help generate spendable funds.

FIGURE 2.3 **RISK CATEGORIES AND SUGGESTED ASSET ALLOCATIONS FOR MERRILL LYNCH CLIENTS**

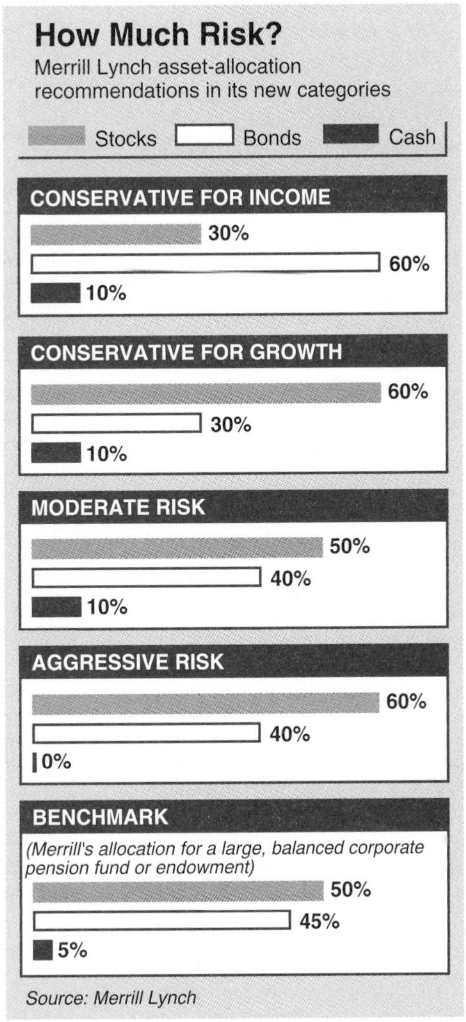
How Much Risk?
Merrill Lynch asset-allocation recommendations in its new categories
Stocks
Bonds
Cash
CONSERVATIVE FOR INCOME
30%
60%
10%
CONSERVATIVE FOR GROWTH
60%
30%
10%
MODERATE RISK
50%
40%
10%
AGGRESSIVE RISK
60%
40%
0%
BENCHMARK
(Merrill's allocation for a large, balanced corporate pension fund or endowment)
50%
45%
5%
Source: Merrill Lynch

Source: William Power, "Merrill Lynch to Ask Investors to Pick a Risk Category," *Wall Street Journal,* 2 July 1990, C1. Reprinted with permission of the *Wall Street Journal.* 1990, Dow Jones and Co., Inc. All rights reserved.

The objective for the **total return** strategy is similar to that of capital appreciation; namely, the investors want the portfolio to grow over time to meet a future need. Whereas the capital appreciation strategy seeks to do this primarily through capital gains, the total return strategy seeks to increase portfolio value by both capital gains and reinvesting current income. Because the total return strategy has both income and capital gains components, its risk exposure lies between that of the current income and capital appreciation strategies.

Investment Objective: 25-Year-Old What is an appropriate investment objective for our typical 25-year-old investor? Assume he holds a steady job, is a valued employee, has adequate insurance coverage, and has enough money in the bank to provide a cash reserve. Let's also assume that his current long-term, high-priority investment goal is to build a

FIGURE 2.4 **HOW MUCH RISK IS RIGHT FOR YOU?**

You've heard the expression "no pain, no gain"? In the investment world, the comparable phrase would be "no risk, no reward."

How you feel about risking your money will drive many of your investment decisions. The risk-comfort scale extends from very conservative (you don't want to risk losing a penny regardless of how little your money earns) to very aggressive (you're willing to risk much of your money for the possibility that it will grow tremendously). As you might guess, most investors' tolerance for risk falls somewhere in between.

If you're unsure of what your level of risk tolerance is, this quiz should help.

1. You win $300 in an office football pool. You: a) spend it on groceries b) purchase lottery tickets c) put it in a money market account d) buy some stock.
2. Two weeks after buying 100 shares of a $20 stock, the price jumps to over $30. You decide to: a) buy more stock; it's obviously a winner b) sell it and take your profits c) sell half to recoup some costs and hold the rest d) sit tight and wait for it to advance even more.
3. On days when the stock market jumps way up, you: a) wish you had invested more b) call your financial advisor and ask for recommendations c) feel glad you're not in the market because it fluctuates too much d) pay little attention.
4. You're planning a vacation trip and can either lock in a fixed room-and-meals rate of $150 per day or book standby and pay anywhere from $100 to $300 per day. You: a) take the fixed-rate deal b) talk to people who have been there about the availability of last-minute accommodations c) book standby and also arrange vacation insurance because you're leery of the tour operator d) take your chances with standby.
5. The owner of your apartment building is converting the units to condominiums. You can buy your unit for $75,000 or an option on a unit for $15,000. (Units have recently sold for close to $100,000, and prices seem to be going up.) For financing, you'll have to borrow the down payment and pay mortgage and condo fees higher than your present rent. You: a) buy your unit b) buy your unit and look for another to buy c) sell the option and arrange to rent the unit yourself d) sell the option and move out because you think the conversion will attract couples with small children.
6. You have been working three years for a rapidly growing company. As an executive, you are offered the option of buying up to 2% of company stock: 2,000 shares at $10 a share. Although the company is privately owned (its stock does not trade on the open market), its majority owner has made handsome profits selling three other businesses and intends to sell this one eventually. You: a) purchase all the shares you can and tell the owner you would invest more if allowed b) purchase all the shares c) purchase half the shares d) purchase a small amount of shares.
7. You go to a casino for the first time. You choose to play: a) quarter slot machines b) $5 minimum-bet roulette c) dollar slot machine d) $25 minimum-bet blackjack.
8. You want to take someone out for a special dinner in a city that's new to you. How do you pick a place? a) read restaurant reviews in the local newspaper b) ask co-workers if they know of a suitable place c) call the only other person you know in this city, who eats out a lot but only recently moved there d) visit the city sometime before your dinner to check out the restaurants yourself.
9. The expression that best describes your lifestyle is: a) no guts, no glory b) just do it! c) look before you leap d) all good things come to those who wait.
10. Your attitude toward money is best described as: a) a dollar saved is a dollar earned b) you've got to spend money to make money c) cash and carry only d) whenever possible, use other people's money.

SCORING SYSTEM: Score your answers this way: (1) a-1, b-4, c-2, d-3 (2) a-4, b-1, c-3, d-2 (3) a-3, b-4, c-2, d-1 (4) a-2, b-3 c-1, d-4 (5) a-3, b-4, c-2, d-1 (6) a-4, b-3, c-2, d-1 (7) a-1, b-3, c-2, d-4 (8) a-2, b-3, c-4, d-1 (9), a-4, b-3, c-2, d-1 (10) a-2, b-3,c-1, d-4.

What your total score indicates:

- 10–17: You're not willing to take chances with your money, even though it means you can't make big gains.
- 18–25: You're semi-conservative, willing to take a small chance with enough information.
- 24–32: You're semi-aggressive, willing to take chances if you think the odds of earning more are in your favor.
- 33–40: You're aggressive, looking for every opportunity to make your money grow, even though in some cases the odds may be quite long. You view money as a tool to make more money.

Source: "How Much Risk Can You Handle?" from *Feathering Your Nest. The Retirement Planner* by Lisa Berger. © 1993 Lisa Berger. Reprinted by permission of Workman Publishing Company, Inc. All Rights Reserved.

retirement fund. Depending on his risk preferences, he can select a strategy carrying moderate to high amounts of risk because the income stream from his job will probably grow over time. Further, given his young age and income growth potential, a low-risk strategy, such as capital preservation or current income, is inappropriate for his retirement fund goal; a total return or capital appreciation objective would be most appropriate. Here's a possible objective statement:

> Invest funds in a variety of moderate to higher risk investments. The average risk of the equity portfolio should exceed that of a broad stock market index, such as the NYSE stock index. Equity exposure should range from 80 percent to 95 percent of the total portfolio. Remaining funds should be invested in short- and intermediate-term notes and bonds.

Investment Objective: 65-Year-Old Assume our typical 65-year-old investor likewise has adequate insurance coverage and a cash reserve. Let's also assume she is retiring this year. This individual will want less risk exposure than the 25-year-old investor, because her earning power from employment will soon be ending; she will not be able to recover any investment losses by saving more out of her paycheck. Depending on her income from social security and a pension plan, she may need some current income from her retirement portfolio to meet living expenses. Given that she can be expected to live an average of another 20 years, she will need protection against inflation. A risk-averse investor will choose a combination of current income and capital preservation strategy; a more risk-tolerant investor will choose a combination of current income and total return in an attempt to have principal growth outpace inflation. Here's an example of such an objective statement:

> Invest in stock and bond investments to meet income needs (from bond income and stock dividends) and to provide for real growth (from equities). Fixed-income securities should comprise 60–70 percent of the total portfolio; of this, 10–20 percent should be invested in short-term securities for extra liquidity and safety. The remaining 30–40 percent of the portfolio should be invested in high-quality stocks whose risk is similar to the S&P 500 index.

More detailed analyses for our 25-year-old and our 65-year-old would make more specific assumptions about the risk tolerance of each, as well as clearly enumerate their investment goals, return objectives, the funds they have to invest at the present, and the funds they expect to invest over time.

Investment Constraints

In addition to the investment objective that sets limits on risk and return, certain other constraints also affect the investment plan. Investment constraints include liquidity needs, an investment time horizon, tax factors, legal and regulatory constraints, and unique needs and preferences.

LIQUIDITY NEEDS An asset is **liquid** if it can be quickly converted to cash at a price close to fair market value. Generally, assets are more liquid if many traders are interested in a fairly standardized product. Treasury bills are a highly liquid security; real estate and venture capital are not.

Investors may have liquidity needs that the investment plan must take into consideration. For example, although an investor may have a primary long-term goal, several near-term goals may also require available funds. Wealthy individuals with sizable tax obligations need adequate liquidity to pay their taxes without upsetting their investment plan. Some saving for retirement may need funds for shorter-term purposes, such as buying a car or a house, or making college tuition payments.

Our typical 25-year-old investor probably has little need for liquidity as he focuses on his long-term retirement fund goal. This constraint may change, however, should he face a period of unemployment or should near-term goals, such as honeymoon expenses or a house down payment, enter the picture. Should any changes occur, the investor needs to revise his policy statement and financial plans accordingly.

Our soon-to-be-retired 65-year-old investor has a greater need for liquidity. Although she may receive regular checks from her pension plan and social security, it is not likely that they will equal her working paycheck. She will want some of her portfolio in liquid securities to meet unexpected expenses or bills.

TIME HORIZON Time horizon as an investment constraint briefly entered our earlier discussion of near-term and long-term high-priority goals. A close (but not perfect) relationship exists between an investor's time horizon, liquidity needs, and ability to handle risk. Investors with long investment horizons generally require less liquidity and can tolerate greater portfolio risk: less liquidity because the funds are not usually needed for many years; greater risk tolerance because any shortfalls or losses can be overcome by returns earned in subsequent years.

Investors with shorter time horizons generally favor less-risky investments because losses are harder to overcome during a short time frame.

Because of life expectancies, our 25-year-old investor has a longer investment time horizon than our 65-year-old investor. But, as discussed earlier, this does not mean the 65-year-old should put all her money in short-term CDs; she needs the inflation protection that long-term investments, such as common stock, can provide. Still, because of the differing time horizons, the 25-year-old will probably have a greater proportion of his portfolio in equities, including stocks in small firms or international firms, than the 65-year-old.

TAX CONCERNS Investment planning is complicated by the tax code; taxes complicate the situation even more if international investments are part of the portfolio. Taxable income from interest, dividends, or rents is taxable at the investor's marginal tax rate. The marginal tax rate is the proportion of the next one dollar in income paid as taxes. Table 2.1 shows the marginal tax rates for different levels of taxable income. As of 1998, the top federal marginal tax rate was 39.6 percent. State taxes make the tax bite even higher.

Capital gains or losses arise from asset price changes. They are taxed differently than income. Income is taxed when it is received; capital gains or losses are taxed only when the asset is sold and the gain or loss is realized. **Unrealized capital gains** reflect the price appreciation of currently held assets that have *not* been sold; the tax liability on unrealized capital gains can be deferred indefinitely. Capital gains only become taxable after the asset has been sold for a price higher than its cost, or **basis**. If appreciated assets are passed on to an heir upon the investor's death, the basis of the assets is considered to be their value on the date of the holder's death. The heirs can then sell the assets and not pay capital gains tax. Capital gains taxes are paid on **realized capital gains**. The Tax Reform Act of 1997 lowered the top capital gain tax rate to 20 percent for assets held longer than 18 months.[1]

Sometimes we make a trade-off between taxes and diversification needs. If entrepreneurs concentrate much of their wealth in equity holdings of their firm, or if employees purchase substantial amounts of their employer's stock through payroll deduction plans during their working life, their portfolios may contain a large amount of unrealized capital gains. In addition, the risk position of such a portfolio may be quite high, because it is concentrated in a single company. The decision to sell some of the company stock in order to diversify the portfolio's risk by reinvesting the proceeds in other assets must be balanced against the resulting tax liability.

---

[1]Christopher Georges, "Congress Clears Tax, Budget Bills," *Wall Street Journal,* 1 August 1997, A2, A11.

TABLE 2.1

INDIVIDUAL MARGINAL TAX RATES, 1997

	Taxable Income	Tax	Percent on Excess
Married Filing Jointly	$ 0	$ 0.00	15%
	41,200	6,180.00	28
	99,600	22,532.00	31
	151,750	38,698.50	36
	271,050	81,646.50	39.6
Single	$ 0	$ 0.00	15%
	24,650	3,697.50	28
	59,750	13,525.50	31
	124,650	33,644.50	36
	271,050	86,348.50	39.6
Head of Household	$ 0	$ 0.00	15%
	33,050	4,957.50	28
	85,350	19,601.50	31
	138,200	35,985.00	36
	271,050	83,811.00	39.6
Married Filing Separately	$ 0	$ 0.00	15%
	20,600	3,090.00	28
	49,800	11,266.00	31
	75,875	19,349.25	36
	135,525	40,823.25	39.6

Some find the difference between average and marginal income tax rates confusing. The **marginal tax rate** is the part of each additional dollar in income that is paid as tax. Thus, a married person, filing jointly, with an income of $50,000 will have a marginal tax rate of 28 percent. The 28 percent marginal tax rate should be used to determine after-tax returns on investments.

The **average tax rate** is simply a person's total tax payment divided by their total income. It represents the average tax paid on each dollar the person earned. From Table 2.1, a married person, filing jointly, will pay $8,644 in tax on a $50,000 income [$6,180 plus 0.28($50,000 − $41,200)]. His or her average tax rate is $8,644/$50,000 or 17.29 percent.

Note that the average tax rate is a weighted average of the person's marginal tax rates paid on each dollar of income. The first $41,200 of income has a marginal tax rate of 15 percent; the next $8,800 has a 28 percent marginal tax rate:

$$\frac{\$41{,}200}{\$50{,}000} \times 0.15 + \frac{\$\ 8{,}800}{\$50{,}000} \times .28 = 0.1729, \text{ or the average tax rate of } 17.29\%$$

Another tax factor is that some sources of income are exempt from federal and state taxes. Interest on federal securities, such as Treasury bills, notes, and bonds, is exempt from state taxes. Interest on municipal bonds (bonds issued by a state or other local governing body) are exempt from federal taxes. Further, if the investor purchases municipal bonds issued by a local governing body of the state in which they live, the interest is usually exempt from both state and federal income tax. Thus, high-income individuals have an incentive to purchase municipal bonds to reduce their tax liabilities.

The after-tax return on a taxable investment is:

$$\text{After-Tax Return} = \text{Pre-Tax Return } (1 - \text{Marginal Tax Rate})$$

Thus, the after-tax return on a taxable investment should be compared to that on municipals before deciding which should be purchased by a tax-paying investor. Alternatively, a municipal's equivalent taxable yield can be computed. The equivalent taxable yield is what a taxable bond investment would have to offer to produce the same after-tax return as the municipal. It is given by:

$$\text{Equivalent Taxable Yield} = \frac{\text{Municipal Yield}}{1 - \text{Marginal Tax Rate}}$$

To illustrate, if an investor is in the 28 percent marginal tax bracket, a taxable investment yield of 8 percent has an after-tax yield of 8 percent $\times$ (1 $-$ 0.28), or 5.76 percent; an equivalent-risk municipal security offering a yield greater than 5.76 percent offers the investor greater after-tax returns. On the other hand, a municipal bond yielding 6 percent has an equivalent taxable yield of 6%/(1 $-$ 0.28) = 8.33%; to earn more money after taxes, an equivalent-risk taxable investment has to offer a return greater than 8.33 percent.

There are other means to reduce tax liabilities. Contributions to an IRA (individual retirement account) may qualify as a tax deduction if certain income limits are met. The investment returns of the IRA investment, including any income, are deferred until the funds are withdrawn from the account. Any funds withdrawn from an IRA are taxable as current income, regardless of whether growth in the IRA occurs as a result of capital gains, income, or both. The benefits of deferring taxes can dramatically compound over time. Figure 2.5 illustrates how \$1,000 invested in an IRA at a tax-deferred rate of 8 percent grows compared to funds invested in a taxable investment that returns (from bond income) 8 percent pre-tax. For an investor in the 28 percent bracket, this investment grows at an after-tax rate of 5.76 percent. After 30 years, the value of the tax-deferred investment is nearly twice that of the taxable investment.

Tax-deductible contributions of up to \$2,000 to a regular IRA are subject to income and other limitations. The Tax Reform Act of 1997 created the Roth IRA. The Roth IRA

FIGURE 2.5 **EFFECT OF TAX DEFERRAL ON INVESTOR WEALTH OVER TIME**

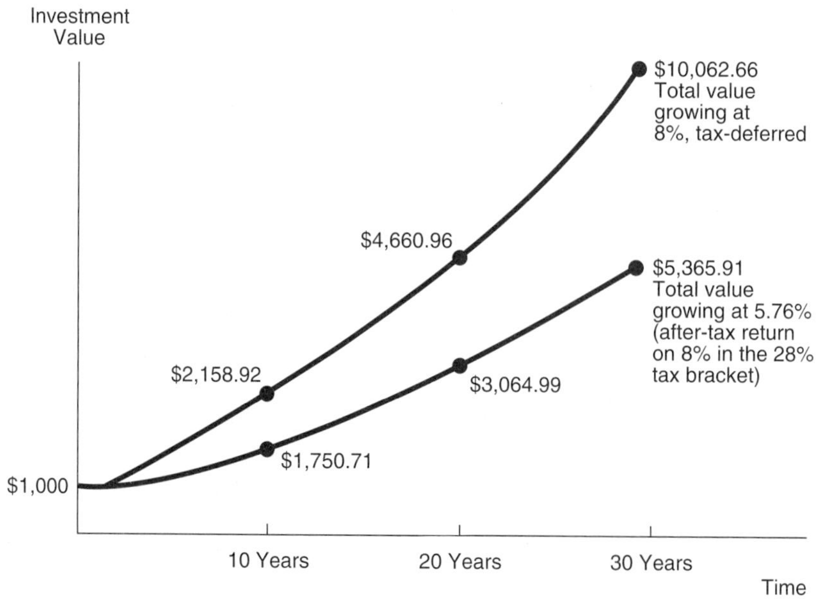
Investment Value
$10,062.66
Total value
growing at
8%, tax-deferred
$4,660.96
$5,365.91
Total value
growing at 5.76%
(after-tax return
on 8% in the 28%
tax bracket)
$2,158.92
$3,064.99
$1,750.71
$1,000
10 Years
20 Years
30 Years
Time

contribution, although not tax deductible, allows up to $2,000 to be invested each year; the returns on this investment will grow on a tax-deferred basis and can be withdrawn, tax-free, if the funds are invested for at least five years and are withdrawn after the investor reaches age 59½.[2] The Roth IRA is subject to limitations based on the investor's annual income, but the income ceiling is much higher than that for the regular IRA.

For money you intend to invest in some type of IRA, the advantage of the Roth IRA's tax-free withdrawals will outweigh the tax-deduction benefit from the regular IRA—unless you expect your tax rate when the funds are withdrawn to be substantially less than when you initially invest the funds.[3]

Tax questions can puzzle the most astute minds. For example, depending on one's situation, it may be best to hold stock in taxable rather than in tax-deferred accounts, such as IRAs, company retirement plans, and variable annuities, mainly because earnings on such tax-deferred accounts are taxed as ordinary income when the funds are withdrawn. Even if most of the growth in a tax-deferred equity investment arises from capital gains, the withdrawals will be taxed at the higher ordinary income tax rate. Stocks held in taxable accounts will likely have large capital gains tax liability over the years; thus, after the 1997 Tax Reform Act's slashing of realized capital gains tax rates, taxable equity accounts may offer better after-tax return potential than tax-deferred investments. This will not be true in all cases. The point is, any analysis must consider each investor's return, time horizon, and tax assumptions.[4]

Other tax-deferred investments include cash values of life insurance contracts that accumulate tax-free until the funds are withdrawn. Employers may offer employees 401(k) or 403(b) plans, which allow the employee to reduce taxable income by making tax-deferred investments; many times employee contributions are matched by employer donations (up to a specified limit), thus allowing the employees to double their investment with little risk!

Our typical 25-year-old investor probably is in a fairly low tax bracket, so detailed tax planning will not be a major concern, and tax-exempt income, such as that available from municipals, will also not be a concern. Nonetheless, he should still invest as much as possible into tax-deferred plans, such as an IRA or a 401(k). The drawback to such investments, however, is that early withdrawals (before age 59½) are taxable and subject to an additional 10 percent early withdrawal tax. Should the liquidity constraint of these plans be too restrictive, the young investor should probably consider total-return- or capital-appreciation-oriented mutual funds as a means to gain diversification and meet his objectives.

Our 65-year-old retiree may face a different situation. If she is in a high tax bracket prior to retiring—and therefore has sought tax-exempt income and tax-deferred investments—her situation may change shortly after retirement. Without large, regular paychecks, the need for tax-deferred investments or tax-exempt income becomes less. Taxable income may now offer higher after-tax yields than tax-exempt municipals due to the investor's lower tax bracket. Should her employer's stock be a large component of her retirement account, careful decisions must be made regarding the need to diversify versus the cost of realizing large capital gains (in her lower tax bracket).

LEGAL AND REGULATORY FACTORS As you might expect, the investment process and financial markets are highly regulated. At times, these legal and regulatory factors constrain the investment strategies of individuals and institutions.

---

[2] Earlier tax-free withdrawals are possible if the funds are to be used for educational purposes or first-time home purchases.

[3] For additional insights, see Jonathan Clements, "Jam Today or Jam Tomorrow? Roth IRA Will Show Many Investors It Pays to Wait," *Wall Street Journal,* 16 September 1997, C1.

[4] Ellen E. Schultz, "Stock Funds May Be Wrong for Your IRA," *Wall Street Journal,* 4 January 1996, C1, 21.

In our discussion about taxes, we mentioned one such constraint: Funds removed from a regular IRA account or 401(k) plan before age 59½ are taxable and subject to an additional 10 percent withdrawal penalty. You may also be familiar with the tag line in many bank CD advertisements—"substantial interest penalty upon early withdrawal." Such regulations and rules as these may make such investments unattractive for investors with substantial liquidity needs in their portfolios.

Regulations can also constrain the investment choices available to someone in a **fiduciary** role. A fiduciary, or trustee, supervises an investment portfolio of a third party, such as a trust account or discretionary account.[5] The fiduciary must make investment decisions in accordance with the owner's wishes; a properly written policy statement assists this process. In addition, trustees of a trust account must meet the "prudent man" standard, which means that they must invest and manage the funds as a prudent person would manage his or her own affairs. Notably, the prudent-man standard is based on the composition of the entire portfolio, not each individual asset in the portfolio.[6]

All investors must respect some laws, such as insider trading prohibitions. Insider trading involves the purchase and sale of securities on the basis of important information that is not publicly known. Typically, the people possessing such private or inside information are the firm's managers, who have a fiduciary duty to their shareholders. Security transactions based on access to inside information violate the fiduciary trust the shareholders have placed with management, because the managers seek personal financial gain from their privileged position as agents for the shareholders.

For our typical 25-year-old investor, legal and regulatory matters will be of little concern, with the possible exception of insider trading laws and the penalties associated with early withdrawal of funds from tax-deferred retirement accounts. Should he seek a financial advisor to assist him in constructing a financial plan, the financial advisor would have to obey the regulations pertinent to a client–advisor relationship.

Similar concerns confront our 65-year-old investor. In addition, as a retiree if she wants to do some estate planning and set up trust accounts, she should seek legal and tax advice to ensure her plans are properly implemented.

UNIQUE NEEDS AND PREFERENCES This category covers the individual concerns of each investor. Some investors may want to exclude certain investments from their portfolio solely on the basis of personal preferences. For example, they may request that no firms that manufacture or sell tobacco, alcohol, pornography, or environmentally harmful products be included in their portfolio. More than $250 billion was invested by year-end 1998 by groups and individuals using specific screening criteria for socially conscious investments.

Another example of a personal constraint is the time and expertise a person has for managing his or her portfolio. Busy executives may prefer to relax during nonworking hours and let a trusted advisor manage their investments. Retirees, on the other hand, may have the time but believe they lack the expertise to choose and monitor investments, so they may also seek professional advice.

Some of the constraints we previously discussed can also be considered as unique needs and preferences. For example, consider the businessperson with a large portion of his wealth tied up in his firm's stock. Though it may be financially prudent to sell some of the

---

[5]A discretionary account is one in which the fiduciary, many times a financial planner or stockbroker, has the authority to purchase and sell assets in the owner's portfolio without first receiving the owner's approval.

[6]As we will discuss in Chapter 8, it is sometimes wise to hold assets that are individually risky in the context of a well-diversified portfolio, even if the investor is strongly risk averse.

firm's stock and reinvest the proceeds for diversification purposes, it may be hard for the individual to approve such a strategy due to emotional ties to the firm. Further, if the stock holdings are in a private company, it may be difficult to find a buyer except if shares are sold at a discount from their fair market value.

Because each investor is unique, the implications of this final constraint differ for each person; there is no "typical" 25-year-old or 65-year-old investor. Each individual will have to communicate specific goals in a well-constructed policy statement.

Institutional investors (endowments, pension funds, and the like) also need to have investment policy statements. Factors considered by institutional investors when developing policy statements are found in the appendix.

CONSTRUCTING THE POLICY STATEMENT

A policy statement may not have separate headings for each, but should incorporate the investor's objectives (risk and return) and constraints (liquidity, time horizon, tax factors, legal and regulatory constraints, and unique needs and preferences). The policy statement allows the investor to determine what factors are personally important and should be reflected in the investment plan. To do without a policy statement is to place the success of the financial plan in jeopardy.

Surveys show that fewer than 40 percent of employees who participate in their firm's retirement savings plan have a good understanding of the value of diversification, the harmful effect of inflation on one's savings, or the relationship between risk and return. Because of this lack of investment expertise, the market for financial planning services and education is a growth industry.

Participants in employer-sponsored retirement plans have invested an average of 42 percent of their retirement funds in their employer's stock. Having so much money invested in one asset violates diversification principles. To put this in context, most mutual funds are limited to having no more than 5 percent of their assets in any one company's stock; a firm's pension plan can invest no more than 10 percent of its funds in the firm's stock. Thus, individuals are unfortunately doing what government regulations prevent many institutional investors from doing.[7] Other studies point out that the average stock allocation in retirement plans is lower than it should be to allow for growth of principal over time.

Studies of retirement plans show that Americans are not saving enough to finance their retirement years and they are not planning sufficiently for what will happen to their savings after they retire.[8] Americans are saving at about one-half the rate needed to finance their retirement. This poor savings rate, coupled with lack of diversification and lack of equity growth potential in their portfolios, can lead to disappointments in one's retirement years.

THE IMPORTANCE OF ASSET ALLOCATION

A major reason why investors develop policy statements is to determine an overall investment strategy. Though a policy statement does not indicate which specific securities to purchase and when they should be sold, it should provide guidelines as to the asset classes to

[7]Ellen R. Schultz, "Workers Put Too Much in Their Employer's Stock," *Wall Street Journal,* 13 September 1996, C1, C25.

[8]Andy Pasztor, "Middle-Aged, Elderly Have Fewer Assets Than Expected," *Wall Street Journal,* 25 July 1995, B1; Jonathan Clements, "Retirement Honing: How Much Should You Have Saved for a Comfortable Life?" *Wall Street Journal,* 28 January 1997, C1; Jonathan Clements, "Squeezing the Right Amount from a Retirement Stash," *Wall Street Journal,* 25 February 1997, C1; Jonathan Clements, "Curb Your Spending, Boost Your Saving and Watch Retirement Nest Egg Grow," *Wall Street Journal,* 2 September 1997, C1.

include and the relative proportions of the investor's funds to invest in each class. How the investor divides funds into different asset classes is the process of asset allocation. Rather than present strict percentages, asset allocation is usually expressed in ranges. This allows the investment manager some freedom, based on his or her reading of capital market trends, to invest toward the upper or lower end of the ranges. For example, suppose a policy statement requires that common stocks be 60 percent to 80 percent of the value of the portfolio and that bonds should be 20 percent to 40 percent of the portfolio's value. If a manager is particularly bullish about stocks, she will increase the allocation of stocks toward the 80 percent upper end of the equity range and decrease bonds toward the 20 percent lower end of the bond range. Should she be more optimistic about bonds, that manager may shift the allocation closer to 40 percent of the funds invested in bonds with the remainder in equities.

A review of historical data and empirical studies indicates the importance of the asset allocation decision and the investment policy statement process. In general, four decisions are made when constructing an investment strategy:

- What asset classes to consider for investment;
- What normal or policy weights to assign to each eligible asset class;
- The allowable allocation ranges based on policy weights;
- What specific securities to purchase for the portfolio.

Studies on investment performance over time have come to a surprising conclusion: 85 percent to 95 percent of overall investment returns arise from the first and second decisions, the long-term asset allocation decisions. Good stock or bond pickers may add some value to portfolio performance, but the major source of investment return and risk over time is the asset allocation decision. A well-constructed policy statement can go a long way toward ensuring that an appropriate asset allocation decision is implemented. Although our data review will focus primarily on U.S. securities, in Chapter 3 we present a strong case for global asset allocation.

Real Investment Returns after Taxes and Costs

Figure 2.6 provides additional historical perspectives on returns. It indicates how an investment of $1 would have grown over the 1926 to 1998 period and, using fairly conservative assumptions, examines how investment returns are affected by taxes and inflation.

Focusing first on stocks, funds invested in 1926 in the S&P 500 would have averaged an 11.0 percent annual return by the end of 1998. Unfortunately, this return is unrealistic because if the funds were invested over time, taxes would have to be paid and inflation would erode the real purchasing power of the invested funds.

Except for tax-exempt investors and tax-deferred accounts, annual tax payments reduce investment returns. Incorporating taxes into the analysis lowers the after-tax average annual return of a stock investment to 8.1 percent.

But the major reduction in the value of our investment is caused by inflation. The real after-tax average annual return on a stock over this time frame was only 4.9 percent, which is quite a bit less than our initial unadjusted 11.0 percent return!

This example shows the long-run impact of taxes and inflation on the real value of a stock portfolio. For bonds and bills, however, the results in Figure 2.6 show something even more surprising. After adjusting for taxes, long-term bonds barely maintained their purchasing power; T-bills *lost* value in real terms. One dollar invested in long-term government bonds in 1926 gave the investor an annual average after-tax real return of 0.4 percent. An investment in Treasury bills lost an average of 0.5 percent after taxes and inflation. Municipal bonds, because of the protection they offer from taxes, earned an average annual real return of over 2 percent during this time.

FIGURE 2.6 **THE EFFECT OF TAXES AND INFLATION ON INVESTMENT RETURNS, 1926–1998**

Compound Annual Returns: 1926—1998	Before taxes and inflation	After taxes	After taxes and inflation
Common Stocks	11.0%	8.1%	4.9%
Long-Term Govt. Bonds	5.2%	3.6%	0.4%
Treasury Bills	3.8%	2.7%	—0.5%
Municipal Bonds (est.)	6.0%	6.0%	2.9%

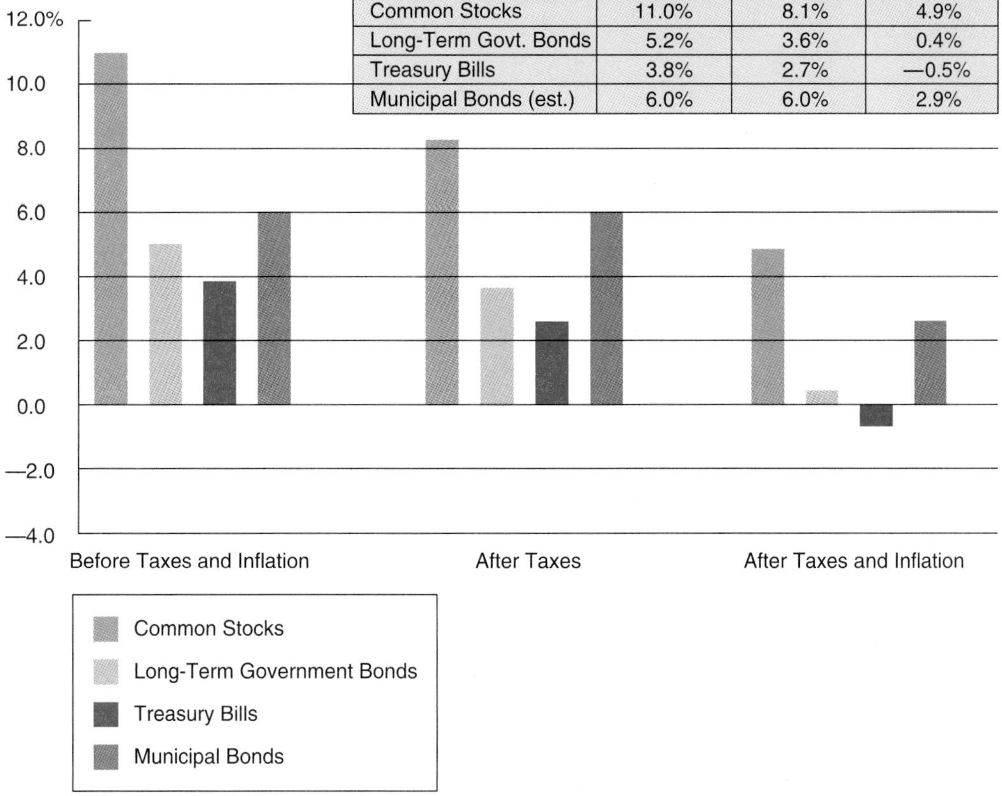
12.0%
10.0
8.0
6.0
4.0
2.0
0.0
—2.0
—4.0
Before Taxes and Inflation
After Taxes
After Taxes and Inflation
Common Stocks
Long-Term Government Bonds
Treasury Bills
Municipal Bonds

Source: *Stocks, Bonds, Bills, and Inflation,* Ibbotson Associates, Chicago, Ill., 1998, and author calculations.

This historical analysis demonstrates that, for taxable investments, the only way to maintain purchasing power over time when investing in financial assets is to invest in common stocks. An asset allocation decision for a taxable portfolio that does not include a substantial commitment to common stocks makes it difficult for the portfolio to maintain real value over time.[9]

Returns and Risks of Different Asset Classes

By focusing on returns we have ignored its partner—risk. Assets with higher long-term returns have these returns to compensate for their risk. Table 2.2 illustrates returns (unadjusted for costs and taxes) for several asset classes over time. As expected, the higher returns available from equities come at the cost of higher risk. This is precisely why investors need a policy statement and why the investor and manager must understand the capital markets and have a disciplined approach to investing. Safe Treasury bills will sometimes outperform equities, and, because of their higher risk, common stocks sometimes

[9]Of course other equity-oriented investments, such as venture capital or real estate, may also provide inflation protection after adjusting for portfolio costs and taxes. Studies of the performance of the new inflation-protected Treasury securities may show their usefulness in protecting investors from inflation as well.

TABLE 2.2 **HISTORICAL AVERAGE ANNUAL RETURNS AND RETURN VARIABILITY, 1926–1998**

	Geometric Mean	Arithmetic Mean	Standard Deviation	Distribution
Large company stocks	11.2%	13.2%	20.3%	
Small company stocks[a]	12.4	17.4	33.8	
Long-term corporate bonds	5.8	6.1	8.6	
Long-term government bonds	5.3	5.7	9.2	
Intermediate-term government bonds	5.3	5.5	5.7	
U.S. Treasury bills	3.8	3.8	3.2	
Inflation	3.1	3.2	4.5	

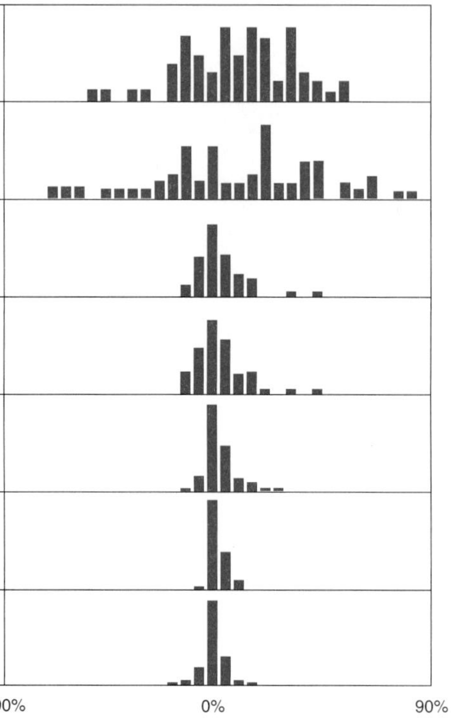
–90%
0%
90%

[a]The 1933 Small Company Stock Total Return was 142.9 percent.

Source: © *Stocks, Bonds, Bills, and Inflation 1999 Yearbook,* ™ Ibbotson Associates, Chicago. Used with permission. All rights reserved.

lose significant value. These are times when undisciplined and uneducated investors sell their stocks at a loss and vow never to invest in equities again. In contrast, these are times when disciplined investors stick to their investment plan and position their portfolio for the next bull market.[10] By holding on to their stocks and perhaps purchasing more at depressed prices, the equity portion of the portfolio will experience a substantial increase in the future.

The asset allocation decision determines to a great extent both the returns and the volatility of the portfolio. Table 2.2 indicates that stocks are riskier than bonds or T-bills. Figure 2.7 and Table 2.3 illustrate the year-by-year volatility of stock returns and show that stocks have sometimes earned returns lower than those of T-bills for extended periods of time. Sticking with an investment policy and riding out the difficult times can earn attractive long-term rates of return.[11]

One popular way to measure risk is to examine the variability of returns over time by computing a standard deviation or variance of annual rates of return for an asset class. This

[10]Newton's law of gravity seems to work two ways in financial markets. What goes up must come down; it also appears over time that what goes down may come back up. Contrarian investors and some "value" investors use this concept of reversion to the mean to try to outperform the indexes over time.

[11]The added benefits of diversification—combining different asset classes in the portfolio—may reduce overall portfolio risk without harming potential return. The topic of diversification is discussed in Chapter 8.

TABLE 2.3

OVER LONG TIME PERIODS, EQUITIES OFFER HIGHER RETURNS

Stocks far outperformed Treasury bills during the 30 years through 1997, but stocks often did worse than T-bills when held for shorter periods during those 30 years.

	Compound Annual Total Return[a]	
S&P 500 Stock Index	12.7%	
Treasury Bills	6.8	
	Length of Holding Period (calendar years)	**Percentage of Periods That Stocks Trailed Bills**
	1	37%
	5	23
	10	17
	20	0

[a]Price change plus reinvested income

Source: Author calculations. Data from *Stocks, Bonds, Bills, and Inflation,* Ibbotson Associates, Chicago, Ill., 1998.

measure indicates that stocks are risky and T-bills are not. Another intriguing measure of risk is the probability of *not* meeting your investment return objective. From this perspective, if the investor has a long time horizon, the risk of equities is small and that of T-bills is large because of their differences in expected returns.

Focusing solely on return variability as a measure of risk ignores a significant risk for income-oriented investors, such as retirees or endowment funds. "Safe," income-oriented investments, such as Treasury bills or certificates of deposit, suffer from *reinvestment risk*—that is, the risk that interim cash flows or the principal paid at maturity will be reinvested in a lower-yielding security. The year of 1992 was particularly hard on investors in "safe" T-bills, because their T-bill income fell 37 percent from 1991 levels due to lower interest rates. Table 2.4 compares the variability of income payouts from common stocks (measured by the dividends from the S&P 500), and T-bills. Over the 1926 to 1998 time frame, dividend income from stocks rose 58 times compared to 41 times for T-bills. The income from stocks fell only 11 times, while T-bill rollovers resulted in an income loss 28 times. The worst one-year drop in stock income, 39.0 percent in 1932, was not as severe as the largest decline, 76.6 percent, in T-bill income, which occurred in 1940. In addition, the growth rate of income from stocks far outpaced that of inflation and the growth of income from T-bills. During the 1926 through 1998 period, stock dividends rose more than 1,800 percent, inflation rose 700 percent, and T-bill income rose only 60 percent. When one considers the growth in principal that stocks offer, we see that "conservative," income-oriented T-bill investors are in fact exposed to substantial amounts of risk.

Asset Allocation Summary

A carefully constructed policy statement determines the types of assets that should be included in a portfolio. The asset allocation decision, not the selection of specific stocks and bonds, determines most of the portfolio's returns over time. Although seemingly risky, investors seeking capital appreciation, income, or even capital preservation over long time periods will do well to include a sizable allocation to the equity portion in their portfolio. As reviewed in this section, a strategy's risk may depend on the investor's goals and time horizon. At times, investing in T-bills may be a riskier strategy than investing in common stocks due to reinvestment risks and the risk of not meeting long-term investment return goals.

FIGURE 2.7 **EQUITY RISK: LONG-TERM AND SHORT-TERM PERSPECTIVES**

Historically, the S&P 500 has posted healthy gains . . .
Total returns, by decade, including share price gains and reinvested dividends, in percent

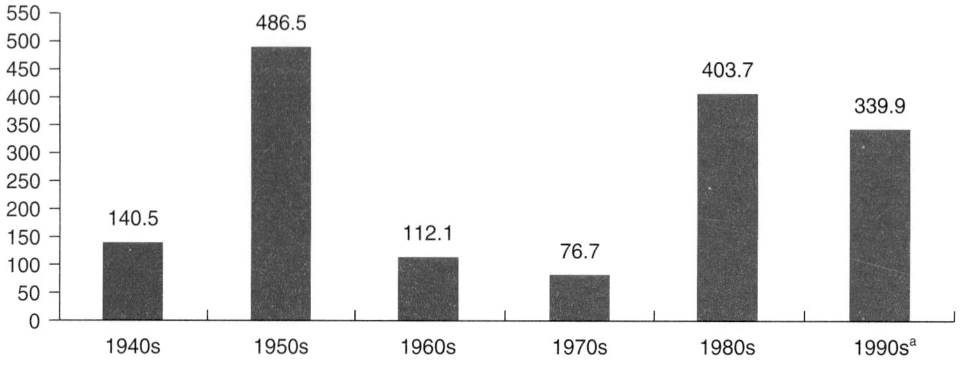
550
500
450
400
350
300
250
200
150
100
50
0
140.5
486.5
112.1
76.7
403.7
339.9
1940s
1950s
1960s
1970s
1980s
1990s[a]

[a]Through Dec 31, 1998

. . . But getting there can be rough
Annual total returns including share price gains and reinvested dividends, in percent

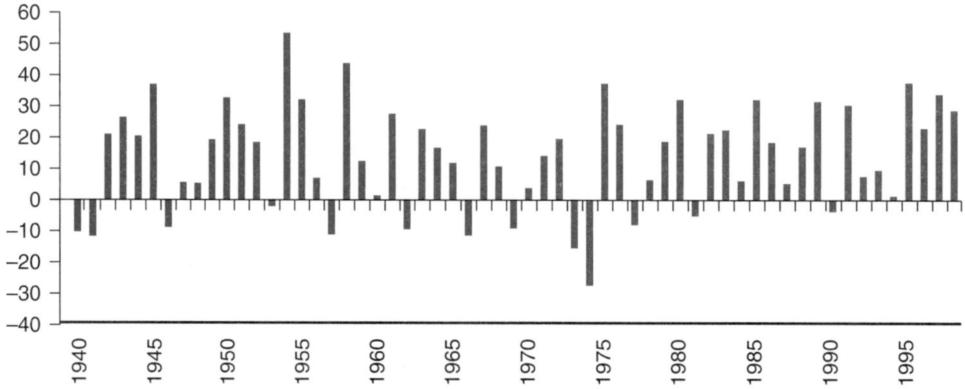
60
50
40
30
20
10
0
−10
−20
−30
−40
1940
1945
1950
1955
1960
1965
1970
1975
1980
1985
1990
1995

Sources: "Why It's Risky Not to Invest More in Stocks," *Wall Street Journal*, 11 February 1992, C1; and Ibbotson Associates, Inc. Updated by authors, using Ibbotson Associates data.

ASSET ALLOCATION AND CULTURAL DIFFERENCES

Thus far our analysis has focused on U.S. investors. Non-U.S. investors make their asset allocation decisions in much the same manner. But because they face different social, economic, political, and tax environments, their allocation decisions differ from those of U.S. investors. Figure 2.8 shows the portfolio mixes of institutional investors in the United States, the United Kingdom, Germany, and Japan. In the United States, equities (both foreign and domestic) comprise about 45 percent of invested assets. In the United Kingdom,

TABLE 2.4 **COMPARISON OF INCOME PAYOUTS FROM COMMON STOCKS AND TREASURY BILLS, 1926–1998**

During the past 71 years, stocks have been a more reliable source of income than either bonds or Treasury bills. The figures below presume that each year an investor spent all dividend and interest income kicked off by the securities, but left the capital intact.

				1926 To 1998	
	Years When Payout Rose	Years When Payout Fell	Worst One-Year Drop in Income	Change in Value of Income	Change in Value of Principal
Stocks	58	13	−39%	1,824.6%	5,152.4%
20-Year Treasury bonds	39	32	−9.5	78	−9.4
5-Year Treasury bonds	41	30	−36.9	62.4	25.7
Treasury bills	42	29	−76.6	60.9	—

Table data source: Ibbotson Associates, Inc.

Source: "T-Bill Trauma and the Meaning of Risk," *Wall Street Journal,* 12 February 1993, C1. Reprinted with permission of the *Wall Street Journal.* Updated by the authors, using Ibbotson data.

equities make up 72 percent of assets; in Germany, equities are only 11 percent of the portfolio; in Japan, equities are 24 percent of assets.

National differences can explain much of the divergent portfolio strategies. Of these four nations, the average age of the population is the highest in Germany and Japan and lowest in the United States and the United Kingdom, which helps explain the greater use of equities in the latter countries. Government privatization programs during the 1980s in the United Kingdom encouraged equity ownership among individual and institutional investors. In Germany, regulations prevent insurance firms from having more than 20 percent of their assets in equities. Both Germany and Japan have banking sectors that invest privately in firms and whose officers sit on corporate boards. Since 1960, the cost of living in the United Kingdom has increased at a rate more than 4.5 times that of Germany; this inflationary bias in the United Kingdom economy favors equities in U.K. asset allocations.

The need to invest in equities for portfolio growth is less in Germany, where workers receive generous state pensions. Germans tend to show a cultural aversion to the stock market: Many Germans are risk-averse and consider stock investing a form of gambling. Although this attitude is changing, the German stock market is rather illiquid, with only a handful of stocks accounting for 50 percent of total stock trading volume.[12]

Other OECD (Organization for Economic Cooperation and Development) countries place regulatory restrictions on institutional investors. For example, pension funds in Austria must have at least 50 percent of their assets in bank deposits or schilling-denominated bonds. Belgium limits pension funds to a minimum 15 percent investment in government bonds. Finland places a 5 percent limit on investments outside its borders by pension funds, and French pension funds must invest a minimum of 34 percent in public debt instruments.[13]

Asset allocation policy and strategy are determined in the context of an investor's objectives and constraints. Among the factors that explain differences in investor behavior across countries, however, are their political and economic environments.

---

[12]Peter Gumbel, "The Hard Sell: Getting Germans to Invest in Stocks," *Wall Street Journal,* 4 August 1995, A2.

[13]Joel Chernoff, "OECD Eyes Pension Rules," *Pensions and Investments,* 23 December 1996, 2, 34.

FIGURE 2.8 **PORTFOLIO MIXES, VARIOUS COUNTRIES, 1990–1991**

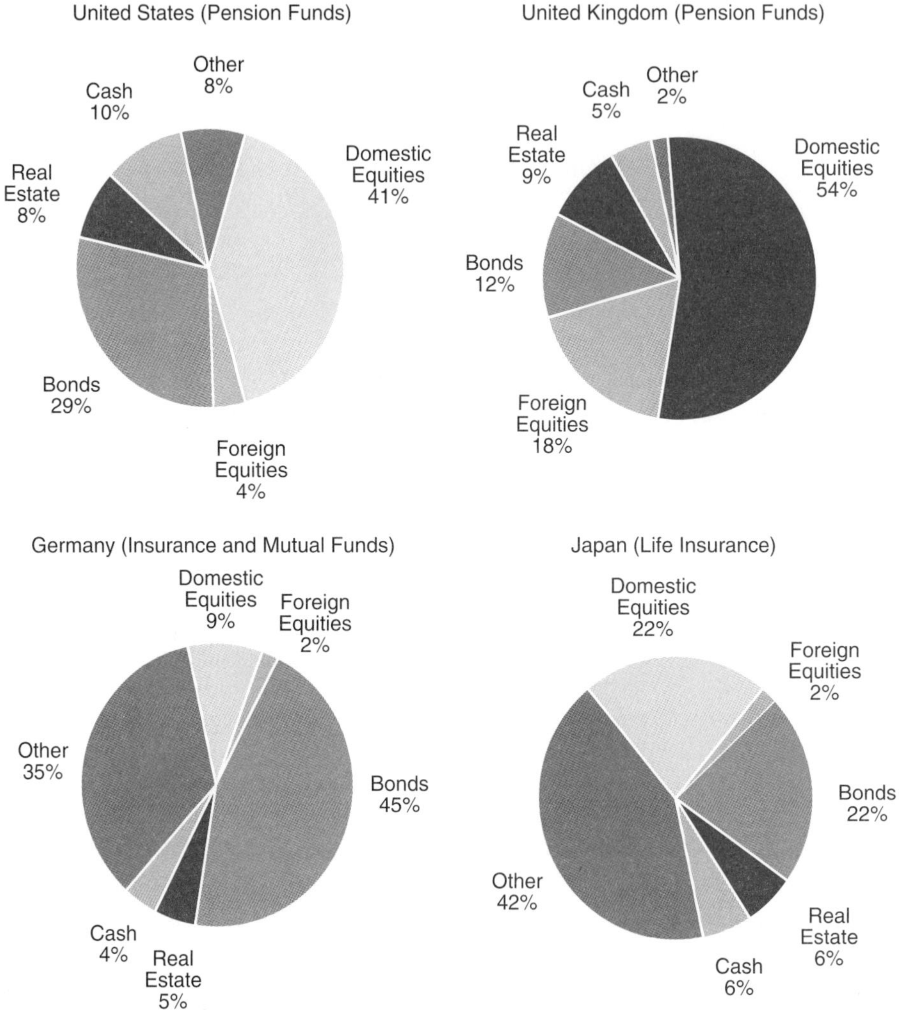
United States (Pension Funds)
Other 8%
Cash 10%
Real Estate 8%
Domestic Equities 41%
Bonds 29%
Foreign Equities 4%
United Kingdom (Pension Funds)
Other 2%
Cash 5%
Real Estate 9%
Domestic Equities 54%
Bonds 12%
Foreign Equities 18%
Germany (Insurance and Mutual Funds)
Domestic Equities 9%
Foreign Equities 2%
Other 35%
Bonds 45%
Cash 4%
Real Estate 5%
Japan (Life Insurance)
Domestic Equities 22%
Foreign Equities 2%
Bonds 22%
Other 42%
Real Estate 6%
Cash 6%

Source: Michael Howell, "Culture and Portfolio Mix—Why Brits Prefer Equities and Germans Prefer *Bunds*" Reprinted with permission, from *Investing Worldwide III:* Copyright 1992, Association for Investment Management and Research, Charlottesville, Va. All rights reserved.

THE INTERNET *Investments Online*

Many inputs go into an investment policy statement as an investor maps out his or her objectives and constraints. Some inputs and helpful information are available in the following Web sites. Many of the sites referenced in Chapter 1 contain important information and insights about asset allocation decisions, as well.

www.ssa.gov Expected retirement funds from social security can be obtained by using the Social Security Administration's Web site.

www.ibbotson.com Much of the data in this chapter's charts and tables came from Ibbotson's published sources. Many professional financial planners make use of Ibbotson's data and education resources.

THE INTERNET *Investments Online (cont.)*

www.mfea.com This is the home page of the Mutual Fund Education Alliance. It contains useful information that is relevant here and in Chapter 26, Portfolio Management Using Investment Companies. This site covers key investing concepts and has a discussion of risk versus reward. What is most relevant here is a page within the Web site: **www.mfea.com/planidx.html** presents a risk-tolerance quiz for investors.

Other interesting sites include:

www.asec.com This is the home page of the American Saving Education Council

www.cccsedu.org/home.html The home page of the Consumer Credit Counseling Service contains insights on managing and getting out of debt, money management, education issues, and a "fritter finder," which helps users find out where all their income goes.

Many professional organizations have Web sites for use by their members, those interested in seeking professional finance designations, and those interested in seeking advice from a professional financial advisor. These sites include:

www.aimr.org This is the association for Investment Management and Research home page. AIMR awards the globally recognized CFA (Chartered Financial Analyst) designation. This site provides information about the CFA designation, AIMR publications, investor education, and various Internet resources.

www.amercoll.edu This is the Web site for The American College, which is the training arm of the insurance industry. The American College offers the CLU and ChFC designations, which are typically earned by insurance professionals.

www.icfp.org The home page for the Institute for Certified Financial Planners offers features and topics of interest to financial planners, including information on earning the CFP designation and receiving the *Journal of Financial Planning.*

www.cfp-board.org The home page for the Certified Financial Planner (CFP) organization contains information for those holding the CFP mark as well as those interested in working toward earning this designation. News and information about the financial-planning profession can be found here, too.

www.napfa.org This is the home page for the National Association of Personal Financial Advisors. This is the trade group for fee-only financial planners. Fee-only planners do not sell products that pay them a commission; should they recommend a commission-generating product, they pass the commission on to the investor. This site features press releases, finding a fee-only planner in your area, a list of financial resources on the Web, and position openings in the financial-planning field.

Summary

- The chapter has reviewed the importance of developing an investment policy statement before implementing a serious investment plan. By forcing investors to examine their needs, risk tolerance, and familiarity with the capital markets, chances improve for correctly identifying appropriate investor objectives and constraints. Investment plans are enhanced by the accurate formulation of a policy statement.
- We also reviewed the importance of the asset allocation decision in determining long-run portfolio investment returns and risks. Because the asset allocation decision follows setting the objectives and constraints, it is clear that the success of the investment program depends on the first step, the construction of the policy statement.
- Investors have many opportunities to invest in both domestic and international assets. The next chapter reviews investment choices and makes a strong case for including global assets in the asset allocation decision.

Questions

1. "Young people with little wealth should not invest money in risky assets such as the stock market, because they can't afford to lose what little money they have." Do you agree or disagree with this statement? Why?

2. Your healthy 63-year-old neighbor is about to retire and comes to you for advice. From talking with her, you find out she was planning on taking all the money out of her company's retirement plan and investing it in bond mutual funds and money market funds. What advice should you give her?
3. Discuss how an individual's investment strategy may change as he or she goes through the accumulation, consolidation, spending, and gifting phases of life.
4. Why is a policy statement important?
5. Use the questionnaire in the "How much risk is right for you?" box (see p. 46) to determine your risk tolerance. Use this information to help write a policy statement for yourself.
6. Your 45-year-old uncle is 20 years away from retirement; your 35-year-old older sister is about 30 years away from retirement. How might their investment policy statements differ?
7. What information is necessary before a financial planner can assist a person in constructing an investment policy statement?
8. Use the Internet to find the home pages for some financial planning firms. What strategies do they emphasize? What do they say about their asset allocation strategy? What are their firms' emphases: value investing, international diversification, principal preservation, retirement and estate planning, and such?
9. *CFA Examination Level III (1993)*

   Mr. Franklin is 70 years of age, is in excellent health, pursues a simple but active lifestyle, and has no children. He has interest in a private company for $90 million and has decided that a medical research foundation will receive half the proceeds now; it will also be the primary beneficiary of his estate upon his death. Mr. Franklin is committed to the foundation's well-being because he believes strongly that, through it, a cure will be found for the disease that killed his wife. He now realizes that an appropriate investment policy and asset allocations are required if his goals are to be met through investment of his considerable assets. Currently, the following assets are available for use in building an appropriate portfolio:

$45.0	million cash (from sale of the private company interest, net of pending $45 million gift to the foundation)
10.0	million stocks and bonds ($5 million each)
9.0	million warehouse property (now fully leased)
1.0	million Franklin residence
$65.0	million total available assets

   a. Formulate and justify an investment policy statement setting forth the appropriate guidelines within which future investment actions should take place. Your policy statement must encompass all relevant objective and constraint considerations.
   b. Recommend and justify a long-term asset allocation that is consistent with the investment policy statement you created in Part a above. Briefly explain the key assumptions you made in generating your allocation.

Problems

1. Suppose your first job pays you $28,000 annually. What percentage should your cash reserve contain? How much life insurance should you carry if you are unmarried? If you are married with two young children?
2. What is the marginal tax rate for a couple, filing jointly, if their taxable income is $20,000? $40,000? $60,000? What is their tax bill for each of these income levels? What is the average tax rate for each of these income levels?
3. What is the marginal tax rate for a single individual if her taxable income is $20,000? $40,000? $60,000? What is her tax bill for each of these income levels? What is her average tax rate for each of these income levels?
4. a. Someone in the 36 percent tax bracket can earn 9 percent annually on her investments in a tax-exempt IRA account. What will be the value of a one-time $10,000 investment in five years? Ten years? Twenty years?

b. Suppose the above 9 percent return is taxable rather than tax-deferred and the taxes are paid annually. What will be the after-tax value of her $10,000 investment after 5, 10, and 20 years?

5. a. Someone in the 15 percent tax bracket can earn 10 percent on his investments in a tax-exempt IRA account. What will be the value of a $10,000 investment in 5 years? 10 years? 20 years?

b. Suppose the above 10 percent return is taxable rather than tax-deferred. What will be the after-tax value of his $10,000 investment after 5, 10, and 20 years?

References

Bhatia, Sanjiv, ed. *Managing Assets for Individual Investors.* Charlottesville, Va.: Association for Investment Management and Research, 1995.

Ellis, Charles D. *Investment Policy: How to Win the Loser's Game.* Homewood, Ill.: Dow Jones–Irwin, 1985.

Peavy, John. *Cases in Portfolio Management.* Charlottesville, Va.: Association for Investment Management and Research, 1990.

Peavy, John W., ed. *Investment Counsel for Private Clients.* Charlottesville, Va.: Association for Investment Management and Research, 1993.

Chapter 2 APPENDIX

OBJECTIVES AND CONSTRAINTS OF INSTITUTIONAL INVESTORS

Institutional investors manage large amounts of funds in the course of their business. They include mutual funds, pension funds, insurance firms, endowments, and banks. In this appendix we review the characteristics of various institutional investors and discuss their typical investment objectives and constraints.

Mutual Funds

A mutual fund pools together sums of money from investors, which are then invested in financial assets. Each mutual fund has its own investment objective, such as capital appreciation, high current income, or money market income. A mutual fund will state its investment objective, and investors, as part of their own investment strategies, choose the funds in which to invest. Two basic constraints face mutual funds: those created by law to protect mutual fund investors, and those that represent choices made by the mutual fund's managers. Some of these constraints will be discussed in the mutual fund's prospectus, which must be given to all prospective investors before they purchase shares in a mutual fund. Mutual funds will be discussed in more detail in Chapter 21.

Pension Funds

Pension funds are a major component of retirement planning for individuals. As of March 1997, U.S. pension assets were nearly $6.4 trillion. Basically, a firm's pension fund receives contributions from the firm, its employees, or both. The funds are invested with the purpose of giving workers either a lump-sum payment or the promise of an income stream after their retirement. **Defined benefit pension plans** promise to pay retirees a specific income stream after retirement. The size of the benefit is usually based on factors that include the worker's salary or time of service, or both. The company contributes a certain amount each year to the pension plan; the size of the contribution depends on assumptions concerning future salary increases and the rate of return to be earned on the plan's assets. Under a defined benefit plan, the company carries the risk of paying the future pension benefit to retirees; should investment performance be poor, or should the company be unable to make adequate contributions to the plan, the shortfall must be made up in future years. "Poor" investment performance means the actual return on the plan's assets fell below the assumed **actuarial rate of return**. The actuarial rate is the discount rate used to find the present value of the plan's future obligations and thus determines the size of the firm's annual contribution to the pension plan.

Defined contribution pension plans do not promise set benefits; rather, employees' benefits depend on the size of the contributions made to the pension fund and the returns earned on the fund's investments. Thus, the plan's risk is borne by the employees. Unlike a defined benefit plan, employees' retirement income is not an obligation of the firm.

A pension plan's objectives and constraints depend on whether the plan is a *defined benefit plan* or a *defined contribution plan.* We review each separately below.

DEFINED BENEFIT The plan's risk tolerance depends on the plan's funding status and its actuarial rate. For **underfunded plans** (where the present value of the fund's liabilities to employees exceeds the value of the fund's assets), a more conservative approach toward risk is taken to ensure that the funding gap is closed over time. This may entail a strategy whereby the firm makes larger plan contributions and assumes a lower actuarial rate. **Overfunded plans** (where the present value of the pension liabilities is less than the plan's assets) allow a more aggressive investment strategy in which the firm reduces its contributions and increases the risk exposure of the plan. The return objective is to meet the plan's actuarial rate of return, which is set by actuaries who estimate future pension obligations based on assumptions about future salary increases, current salaries, retirement patterns, worker life expectancies, and the firm's benefit formula. The actuarial rate also helps determine the size of the firm's plan contributions over time.

The liquidity constraint on defined benefit funds is mainly a function of the average age of employees. A younger employee base means less liquidity is needed; an older employee base generally means more liquidity is needed to pay current pension obligations to retirees. The time horizon constraint is also affected by the average age of employees, although some experts recommend using a 5- to 10-year horizon for planning purposes. Taxes are not a major concern to the plan, because pension plans are exempt from paying tax on investment returns. The major legal constraint is that the plan must be run in accordance with ERISA, the Employee Retirement and Income Security Act, and investments must satisfy the "prudent expert" standard when evaluated in the context of the overall pension plan's portfolio.

DEFINED CONTRIBUTION As the individual worker decides how his contributions to the plan are to be invested, the objectives and constraints for defined contribution plans depend on the individual. Because the worker carries the risk of inadequate retirement funding rather than the firm, defined contribution plans are generally more conservatively invested (some suggest that employees tend to be too conservative). If, however, the plan is considered more of an estate planning tool for a wealthy founder or officer of the firm, a higher risk tolerance and return objective is appropriate because most of the plan's assets will ultimately be owned by the individual's heirs.

The liquidity and time horizon needs for the plan differ depending on the average age of the employees and the degree of employee turnover within the firm. Similar to defined benefit plans, defined contribution plans are tax-exempt and are governed by the provisions of ERISA.

Endowment Funds

Endowment funds arise from contributions made to charitable or educational institutions. Rather than immediately spending the funds, the organization invests the money for the purpose of providing a future stream of income to the organization. The investment policy of an endowment fund is the result of a "tension" between the organization's need for current income and the desire to plan for a growing stream of income in the future to protect against inflation.

To meet the institution's operating budget needs, the fund's return objective is often set by adding the spending rate (the amount taken out of the funds each year) and the expected inflation rate. Funds that have more risk-tolerant trustees may have a higher spending rate than those overseen by more risk-averse trustees. Because a total return approach usually serves to meet the return objective over time, the organization is generally withdrawing both income and capital gain returns to meet budgeted needs. The risk tolerance of an endowment fund is largely affected by the collective risk tolerance of the organization's trustees.

Due to the fund's long-term time horizon, liquidity requirements are minor except for the need to spend part of the endowment each year and maintain a cash reserve for emergencies. Many endowments are tax-exempt, although income from some private foundations can be taxed at either a 1 percent or 2 percent rate. Short-term capital gains are taxable, but long-term capital gains are not. Regulatory and legal constraints arise on the state level, where most endowments are regulated. Unique needs and preferences may affect investment strategies, especially among college or religious endowments, which sometimes have strong preferences about social investing issues.

INSURANCE COMPANIES

The investment objectives and constraints for an insurance company depend on whether it is a life insurance company or a nonlife (such as a property and casualty) insurance firm.

LIFE INSURANCE COMPANIES Except for firms dealing only in term life insurance, life insurance firms collect premiums during a person's lifetime that must be invested until a death benefit is paid to the insurance contract's beneficiaries. At any time the insured can turn in her policy and receive its cash surrender value. Discussing investment policy for an insurance firm is also complicated by the insurance industry's proliferation of insurance and quasi-investment products.

Basically, an insurance company wants to earn a positive "spread," which is the difference between the rate of return on investment minus the rate of return it credits its various policyholders. This concept is similar to a defined benefit pension fund that tries to earn a rate of return in excess of its actuarial rate. If the spread is positive, the insurance firm's surplus reserve account rises; if not, the surplus account declines by an amount reflecting the negative spread. A growing surplus is an important competitive tool for life insurance companies. Attractive investment returns allow the company to advertise better policy returns than those of its competitors. A growing surplus also allows the firm to offer new products and expand insurance volume.

Because life insurance companies are quasi-trust funds for savings, fiduciary principles limit the risk tolerance of the invested funds. The National Association of Insurance Commissioners (NAIC) establishes risk categories for bonds and stocks; companies with excessive investments in higher-risk categories must set aside extra funds in a mandatory securities valuation reserve (MSVR) to protect policyholders against losses.

Insurance companies' liquidity needs have increased over the years due to increases in policy surrenders and product-mix changes. A company's time horizon depends upon its specific product mix. Life insurance policies require longer-term investments, whereas guaranteed insurance contracts (GICs) and shorter-term annuities require shorter investment time horizons.

Tax rules changed considerably for insurance firms in the 1980s. For tax purposes, investment returns are divided into two components: first, the policyholder's share, which is the return portion covering the actuarially assumed rate of return needed to fund reserves; and second, the balance that is transferred to reserves. Unlike pensions and endowments, life insurance firms pay income and capital gains taxes at the corporate tax rates on this second component of return.

Except for the NAIC, most insurance regulation is on the state level. Regulators oversee the eligible asset classes and the reserves (MSVR) necessary for each asset class, and enforce the "prudent expert" investment standard. Audits ensure that various accounting rules and investment regulations are followed.

NONLIFE INSURANCE COMPANIES Cash outflows are somewhat predictable for life insurance firms, based on their mortality tables. In contrast, the cash flows required by major accidents, disasters, and lawsuit settlements are not as predictable for nonlife insurance firms.

Due to their fiduciary responsibility to claimants, risk exposures are low to moderate. Depending on the specific company and competitive pressures, premiums may be affected both by the probability of a claim and the investment returns earned by the firm. Typically, casualty insurance firms invest their insurance reserves in bonds for safety purposes and to provide needed income to pay claims; capital and surplus funds are invested in equities for their growth potential. As with life insurers, property and casualty firms have a stronger competitive position when their surplus accounts are larger than those of their competitors. Many insurers now focus on a total return objective as a means to increase their surplus accounts over time.

Because of uncertain claim patterns, liquidity is a concern for property and casualty insurers who also want liquidity so they can switch between taxable and tax-exempt investments as their underwriting activities generate losses and profits. The time horizon for investments is typically shorter than that of life insurers, although many invest in long-term bonds to earn the higher yields available on these instruments. Investing strategy for the firm's surplus account focuses on long-term growth.

Regulation of property and casualty firms is more permissive than for life insurers. Similar to life companies, states regulate classes and quality of investments for a certain percentage of the firm's assets. But beyond this restriction, insurers can invest in many different types and qualities of instruments, except that some states limit the proportion of real estate assets.

BANKS Pension funds, endowments, and insurance firms obtain virtually free funds for investment purposes. Not so with banks. To have funds to lend, they must attract investors in a competitive interest rate environment. They compete against other banks and also against companies that offer other investment vehicles, from bonds to common stocks. A bank's success relies primarily on its ability to generate returns in excess of its funding costs.

A bank tries to maintain a positive difference between its cost of funds and its returns on assets. If banks anticipate falling interest rates, they will try to invest in longer-term assets to lock in the returns while seeking short-term deposits, whose interest cost is expected to fall over time. When banks expect rising rates they will try to lock in longer-term deposits with fixed-interest costs, while investing funds short term to capture rising interest rates. The risk of such strategies is that losses may occur should a bank incorrectly forecast the direction of interest rates. The aggressiveness of a bank's strategy will be related to the size of its capital ratio and the oversight of regulators.

Banks need substantial liquidity to meet withdrawals and loan demand. A bank has two forms of liquidity. Internal liquidity is provided by a bank's investment portfolio that includes highly liquid assets that can be sold to raise cash. A bank has external liquidity if it can borrow funds in the federal funds markets (where banks lend reserves to other banks), from the Federal Reserve Bank's discount window, or by selling certificates of deposit at attractive rates.

Banks have a short time horizon for several reasons. First, they have a strong need for liquidity. Second, because they want to maintain an adequate interest revenue–interest expense spread, they generally focus on shorter-term investments to avoid interest rate risk and to avoid getting "locked in" to a long-term revenue source. Third, because banks typically offer short-term deposit accounts (demand deposits, NOW accounts, and such), they need to match the maturity of their assets and liabilities to avoid taking undue risks.[14]

Banks are heavily regulated by numerous state and federal agencies. The Federal Reserve Board, the Comptroller of the Currency, and the Federal Deposit Insurance Corporation all oversee various components of bank operations. The Glass-Steagall Act restricts the equity investments that banks can make. Unique situations that affect each bank's investment policy depend on their size, market, and management skills in matching asset and liability sensitivity to interest rates. For example, a bank in a small community may have many customers who deposit their money with it for the sake of convenience. A bank in a more populated area will find its deposit flows are more sensitive to interest rates and competition from nearby banks.

Institutional Investor Summary

Among the great variety of institutions, each institution has its "typical" investment objectives and constraints. This discussion has given us a taste of the differences that exist among types of institutions and some of the major issues confronting them. Notably, just as with individual investors, "cookie-cutter" policy statements are inappropriate for institutional investors. The specific objectives, constraints, and investment strategies must be determined on a case-by-case basis.

---

[14]An asset/liability mismatch caused the ultimate downfall of savings and loan associations. They attracted short-term liabilities (deposit accounts) and invested in long-term assets (mortgages). When interest rates became more volatile in the early 1980s and short-term rates increased dramatically, S&Ls suffered large losses.

Chapter 3

Selecting Investments in a Global Market

After you read this chapter, you should be able to answer the following questions:

- Why should investors have a global perspective regarding their investments?
- What has happened to the relative size of U.S. and foreign stock and bond markets?
- What are the differences in the rates of return on U.S. and foreign securities markets?
- How can changes in currency exchange rates affect the returns that U.S. investors experience on foreign securities?
- Is there additional advantage to diversifying in international markets beyond the benefits of domestic diversification?
- What alternative securities are available? What are their cash flow and risk properties?
- What are the historical return and risk characteristics of the major investment instruments?
- What is the relationship among the returns for foreign and domestic investment instruments? What is the implication of these relationships for portfolio diversification?

Individuals are willing to defer current consumption for many reasons. Some save for their children's college tuition or their own; others wish to accumulate down payments for a home, car, or boat; others want to amass adequate retirement funds for the future. Whatever the reason for an investment program, the techniques we used in Chapter 1 to measure risk and return will help you evaluate alternative investments.

But what are those alternatives? Thus far, we have said little about the investment opportunities available in financial markets. In this chapter, we address this issue by surveying investment alternatives. This is essential background for making the asset allocation decision discussed in Chapter 2 and for later chapters where we analyze several individual investments, such as bonds, common stock, and other securities. It is also important when we consider how to construct and evaluate portfolios of investments.

As an investor in the 21st century, you have an array of investment choices unavailable a few decades ago. Together, the dynamism of financial markets, technological advances, and new regulations have resulted in numerous new investment instruments and expanded trading opportunities.[1] Improvements in communications and relaxation of international regulations have made it easier for investors to trade in both domestic and global markets. Telecommunications networks enable U.S. brokers to reach security exchanges in London, Tokyo, and other European and Asian cities as easily as those in New York, Chicago, and other U.S. cities. The competitive environment in the brokerage industry and the deregulation of the banking sector have made it possible for more financial institutions to

[1]For an excellent discussion of the reasons for the development of numerous financial innovations and the effect of these innovations on world capital markets, see Merton H. Miller, *Financial Innovations and Market Volatility* (Cambridge, Mass.: Blackwell Publishers, 1991).

compete for investor dollars. This has spawned investment vehicles with a variety of maturities, risk–return characteristics, and cash flow patterns. In this chapter we examine some of these choices.

As an investor, you need to understand the differences among investments so you can build a properly diversified **portfolio** that conforms to your objectives. That is, you should seek to acquire a group of investments with different patterns of returns over time. If chosen carefully, such portfolios minimize risk for a given level of return because low or negative rates of return on some investments during a period of time are offset by above-average returns on others. The goal is to build a balanced portfolio of investments with relatively stable overall rates of return. A major goal of this text is to help you understand and evaluate the risk–return characteristics of investment portfolios. An appreciation of alternative security types is the starting point for this analysis.

This chapter is divided into three main sections. As noted earlier, investors can choose securities from financial markets around the world. Therefore, in the first section we look at a combination of reasons why investors *should* include foreign as well as domestic securities in their portfolios. Taken together, these reasons provide a compelling case for global investing. We continue the investigation of where to invest in Chapter 4 when we examine securities markets around the world in more detail.

In the second section of this chapter, we discuss securities in domestic and global markets, describing their main features and cash flow patterns. From this discussion, you will see that the varying risk–return characteristics of alternative investments suit the preferences of different investors. Some securities are more appropriate for individuals, whereas others are better suited for financial institutions, such as insurance companies and pension funds.

The third and final section contains an assessment of the historical risk and return performance of several investment instruments from around the world and examines the relationship among the returns for many of these securities. An understanding of these relationships will provide further support for global investing.

THE CASE FOR GLOBAL INVESTMENTS

Twenty years ago, the bulk of investments available to individual investors consisted of stocks and bonds sold on U.S. securities markets. Now, however, a call to your broker gives you access to a wide range of securities sold throughout the world. Currently, you can purchase stock in General Motors or Toyota, U.S. Treasury bonds or Japanese government bonds, a mutual fund that invests in U.S. biotechnology companies, a global growth stock fund or a German stock fund, or options on a U.S. stock index along with innumerable other investments.

Several changes have caused this explosion of investment opportunities. For one, the growth and development of numerous foreign financial markets, such as those in Japan, the United Kingdom, and Germany, as well as in emerging markets, such as China, have made these markets accessible and viable for investors around the world. Numerous U.S. investment firms have recognized this opportunity and established and expanded facilities in these countries. This expansion was aided by major advances in telecommunications technology that made it possible to maintain constant contact with offices and financial markets around the world. In addition to the efforts by U.S. firms, foreign firms and investors undertook counterbalancing initiatives, including significent mergers of firms and security exchanges that will be discussed in Chapter 4. As a result, investors and investment firms from around the world found it desirable and possible to trade securities worldwide. Thus, investment alternatives are available from the traditional U.S. financial markets and from security markets around the world.[2]

Three interrelated reasons U.S. investors should think of constructing global investment portfolios can be summarized as follows:

1. When investors compare the absolute and relative sizes of U.S. and foreign markets for stocks and bonds, they see that ignoring foreign markets reduces their choices to less than 50 percent of available investment opportunities. Because more opportunities broaden your range of risk–return choices, it makes sense to evaluate foreign securities when selecting investments and building a portfolio.
2. The rates of return available on non-U.S. securities often have substantially exceeded those for U.S.-only securities. The higher returns on non-U.S. *equities* can be justified by the higher growth rates for the countries where they are issued. These superior results typically prevail even when the returns are risk-adjusted.
3. One of the major tenets of investment theory is that investors should diversify their portfolio. Because the relevant factor when diversifying a portfolio is low correlation between asset returns, diversification with uncorrelated foreign securities can help to substantially reduce portfolio risk.

In this section, we analyze these reasons to demonstrate the advantages to a growing role of foreign financial markets for U.S. investors and to assess the benefits and risks of trading in these markets. Notably, the reasons why global investing is appropriate for U.S. investors are generally even more compelling for non-U.S. investors.

Relative Size of U.S. Financial Markets

Prior to 1970, the securities traded in the U.S. stock and bond markets comprised about 65 percent of all the securities available in world capital markets. Therefore, a U.S. investor selecting securities strictly from U.S. markets had a fairly complete set of investments available. Under these conditions, most U.S. investors probably believed that it was not worth the time and effort to expand their investment universe to include the limited investments available in foreign markets. That situation has changed dramatically over the past 30 years. Currently, investors who ignore foreign stock and bond markets limit their investment choices substantially.

Figure 3.1 shows the breakdown of securities available in world capital markets in 1969 and 1998. Not only has the overall value of all securities increased dramatically (from \$2.3 trillion to \$58 trillion), but the composition has also changed. Concentrating on proportions of bond and equity investments, the figure shows that U.S. dollar bonds and U.S. equity securities made up 53 percent of the total value of all securities in 1969 versus 28.4 percent for the total of nondollar bonds and equity. By 1998, U.S. bonds and equities accounted for 42.3 percent of the total securities market versus 47.3 percent for nondollar bonds and stocks. These data indicate that if you consider only the stock and bond market, the U.S. proportion of this combined market has declined from 65 percent of the total in 1969 to about 47 percent in 1998.

The point is, the U.S. security markets now include a smaller proportion of the total world capital market, and it is likely that this trend will continue. The faster economic growth of many other countries compared to the United States will require foreign governments and individual companies to issue debt and equity securities to finance this growth.

[2]In this regard, see Scott E. Pardee, "Internationalization of Financial Markets," Federal Reserve Bank of Kansas City, *Economic Review* (February 1987): 3–7.

FIGURE 3.1 **TOTAL INVESTABLE CAPITAL MARKET**

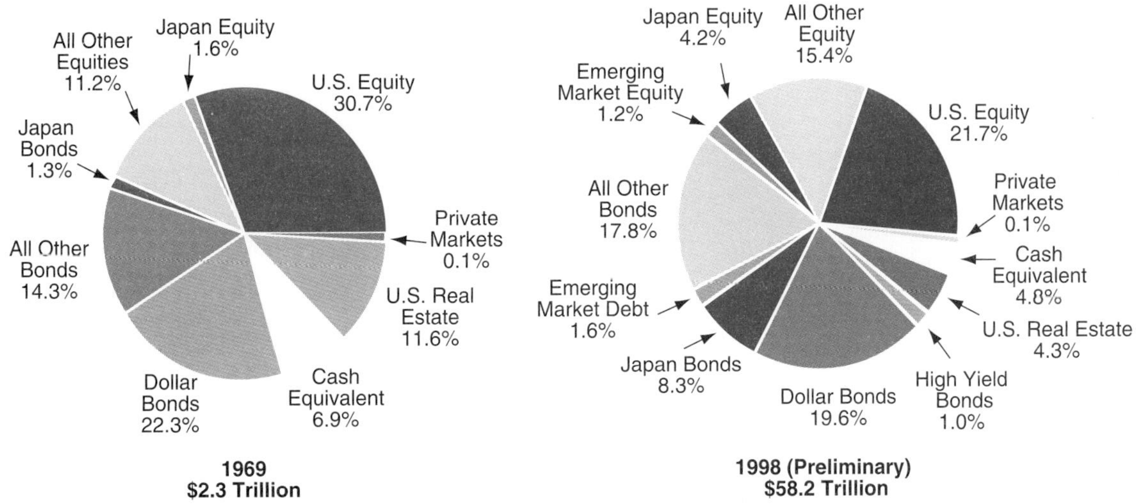
All Other Equities 11.2%
Japan Equity 1.6%
U.S. Equity 30.7%
Japan Bonds 1.3%
Private Markets 0.1%
All Other Bonds 14.3%
U.S. Real Estate 11.6%
Dollar Bonds 22.3%
Cash Equivalent 6.9%
1969
$2.3 Trillion
Japan Equity 4.2%
All Other Equity 15.4%
Emerging Market Equity 1.2%
U.S. Equity 21.7%
All Other Bonds 17.8%
Private Markets 0.1%
Cash Equivalent 4.8%
Emerging Market Debt 1.6%
U.S. Real Estate 4.3%
Japan Bonds 8.3%
High Yield Bonds 1.0%
Dollar Bonds 19.6%
1998 (Preliminary)
$58.2 Trillion

Source: Brinson Partners, Inc., Chicago, Ill.

Therefore, U.S. investors should consider investing in foreign securities because of the growing importance of these foreign securities in world capital markets. Not investing in foreign stocks and bonds means you are ignoring almost 53 percent of the securities that are available to you.

Rates of Return on U.S. and Foreign Securities

An examination of the rates of return on U.S. and foreign securities not only demonstrates that many non-U.S. securities provide superior rates of return, but also shows the impact of the exchange rate risk discussed in Chapter 1.

GLOBAL BOND MARKET RETURNS Table 3.1 reports annual compound rates of return for several major international bond markets for 1987–1996. The *domestic return* is the rate of return an investor within the country would earn. In contrast, the return in U.S. dollars is what a U.S. investor would earn after adjusting for changes in the currency exchange rates during the period.

An analysis of the domestic returns in Table 3.1 indicates that the performance of the U.S. bond market ranked fourth out of the six countries. When the impact of exchange rates is considered, the U.S. experience was the lowest out of six. The difference in performance for domestic versus U.S. dollar returns means that the exchange rate effect for a U.S. investor who invested in foreign bonds was always positive (that is, the U.S. dollar was weak) and added to the domestic performance.

As an example, the domestic return on Japanese bonds was 6.49 percent compared with the return for U.S. bonds of 8.10 percent. The Japanese foreign exchange effect was 3.20 percent, which increased the return on Japanese bonds converted to U.S. dollars to 9.90 percent, which was above the return for U.S. bonds. The point is, a U.S. investor who invested in non-U.S. bonds from several countries could experience rates of return close to or above those of U.S. investors who limited themselves to the U.S. bond market.

GLOBAL EQUITY MARKET RETURNS Table 3.2 shows the compound growth rate of prices in local currencies and in U.S. dollars for 12 major equity markets, four areas of the world, and the total world for the period from 1986 to 1998. The performance in

TABLE 3.1

INTERNATIONAL BOND MARKET COMPOUND ANNUAL RATES OF RETURN: 1987–1996

	COMPONENTS OF RETURN		
	Total Domestic Return	Total Return in U.S. $	Exchange Rate Effect
Canada	10.89	10.98	0.01
France	10.52	12.73	2.00
Germany	7.41	9.79	2.22
Japan	6.49	9.90	3.20
United Kingdom	11.30	12.91	1.45
United States	8.10	8.10	—

Source: Frank K. Reilly and David J. Wright, "Global Bond Markets: Benchmarks and Risk–Return Performance" (May 1997). Based on data from Merrill Lynch Bond Indexes.

local currency indicated that the U.S. market was ranked seventh of the total 17 countries and areas or was the seventh of 12 countries. The performance results in U.S. dollars indicate that the currency effect was positive for investors in 8 of the 11 foreign countries (the U.S. dollar was weak relative to these currencies). The currency effect only hurt the dollar returns for Australia, Canada, and Sweden. Overall, in U.S. dollar returns, the U.S. market was ranked 15th of the 17 countries and areas or 11th of 12 countries.

Like the bond market performance, these results for equity markets around the world indicate that investors who limited themselves to the U.S. market experienced rates of return below those in many other countries. This is true for comparisons that considered both domestic returns and rates of return adjusted for exchange rates.

Individual Country Risk and Return

As shown, most countries experienced higher compound returns on bonds and stocks than the United States. A natural question is whether these superior rate of return results are attributable to higher levels of risk for securities in these countries.

Table 3.3 contains the returns and risk measures for six major bond markets in local currency and U.S. dollars, along with a composite ratio of return per unit of risk. The results in local currency are similar to the rate of return results—the U.S. bond market ranked fourth of the six countries. The results when returns and risk are measured in U.S. dollars were quite different. Specifically, although the returns in U.S. dollars always increased because of the weak dollar, the risk measures typically increased dramatically (that is, the average risk for the five non-U.S. countries more than doubled, going from 5.08 percent to 11.89 percent). As a result, the returns per unit of risk for these countries declined significantly and the U.S. return/risk performance ranked first. Beyond the impact on the relative results in U.S. dollars, these significant increases in the volatility for returns of foreign stocks in U.S. dollars are evidence of the exchange rate risk discussed in Chapter 1.

Figure 3.2 contains the scatter plot of local currency equity returns (the compound growth rate of price) and risk for the 12 individual countries, four regions of the world, and the total world for 1986 to 1997. The risk measure is the standard deviation of daily returns as discussed in Chapter 1. Notably, the U.S. market experienced one of the lowest risk values. The return-to-risk position above the line of best fit indicates that the U.S. performance in local currency was tied for first out of 17, mainly because of the low measure of risk. The results in U.S. dollars in Figure 3.3 show similar risk results. Measuring return and risk in U.S. dollars, the U.S. return/risk performance is ranked third of 17. While most countries or areas experienced higher returns in U.S. dollars, similar to the bond results, the risk measures increased substantially due to the exchange rate risk.

TABLE 3.2

FT-ACTUARIES WORLD EQUITY TOTAL RETURN PERFORMANCE: GEOMETRIC AVERAGE YEARLY RETURNS IN LOCAL CURRENCY AND U.S. DOLLARS, 1986–1998

	Local Currency		U.S. Dollars	
	Percent	Rank	Percent	Rank
Australia	9.0	9	8.1	10
Canada	6.9	11	6.2	11
France	11.8	5	14.4	6
Germany	7.5	10	10.7	9
Italy	10.8	8	10.9	8
Japan	0.8	12	5.3	12
Netherlands	12.7	4	16.1	3
Spain	17.5	2	18.2	1
Sweden	17.8	1	17.2	2
Switzerland	11.0	7	14.6	4
United Kingdom	11.4	6	12.7	7
United States	14.5	3	14.5	5

TABLE 3.3

INTERNATIONAL BOND MARKET RETURN-RISK RESULTS: LOCAL CURRENCY AND U.S. DOLLARS, 1987–1996

	Local Currency			U.S. Dollars		
Country	Return	Risk	Return/Risk	Return	Risk	Return/Risk
Canada	10.89	6.58	1.66	10.98	9.08	1.21
France	10.52	4.26	2.47	12.73	10.94	1.16
Germany	7.41	3.18	2.33	9.79	11.74	0.83
Japan	6.49	4.91	1.32	9.90	14.08	0.70
United Kingdom	11.30	6.49	1.74	12.91	13.60	0.95
United States	8.10	4.77	1.70	8.10	4.77	1.70

Risk of Combined Country Investments

Thus far, we have discussed the risk and return results for individual countries. In Chapter 1, we considered the idea of combining a number of assets into a portfolio and noted that investors should create diversified portfolios to reduce the variability of the returns over time. We discussed how proper diversification reduces the variability (our measure of risk) of the portfolio because alternative investments have different patterns of returns over time. Specifically, when the rates of return on some investments are negative or below average, other investments in the portfolio will be experiencing above-average rates of return. Therefore, if a portfolio is properly diversified, it should provide a more stable rate of return for the total portfolio (that is, it will have a lower standard deviation and therefore less risk). Although we will discuss and demonstrate portfolio theory in detail in Chapter 8, we need to consider the concept at this point to fully understand the benefits of global investing.

The way to measure whether two investments will contribute to diversifying a portfolio is to compute the correlation coefficient between their rates of return over time. Correlation coefficients can range from +1.00 to −1.00. A correlation of +1.00 means that the rates of return for these two investments move exactly together. Combining investments that move

FIGURE 3.2

ANNUAL RATES OF RETURN AND RISK FOR MAJOR STOCK MARKETS IN LOCAL CURRENCY: 1986–1997

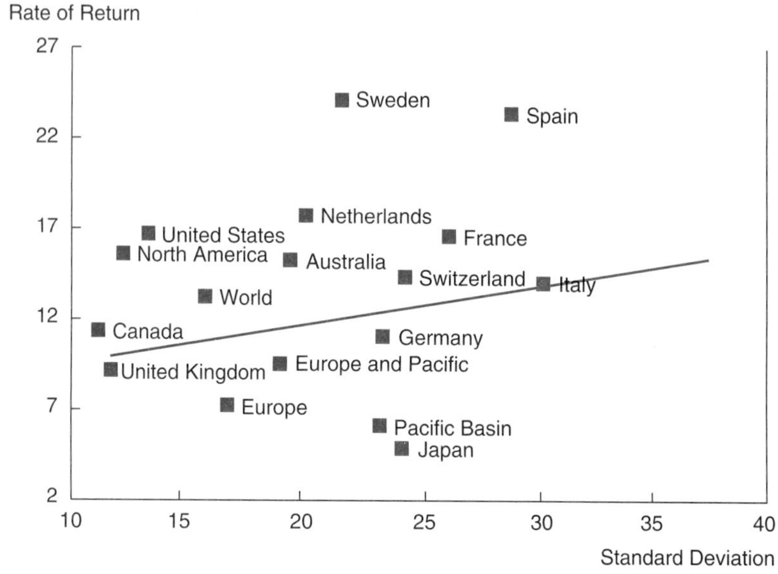
Rate of Return
27
22
17
12
7
2
Sweden
Spain
Netherlands
United States
France
North America
Australia
Switzerland
Italy
World
Canada
Germany
United Kingdom
Europe and Pacific
Europe
Pacific Basin
Japan
10
15
20
25
30
35
40
Standard Deviation

FIGURE 3.3

ANNUAL RATES OF RETURN AND RISK FOR MAJOR STOCK MARKETS IN U.S. DOLLARS: 1986–1997

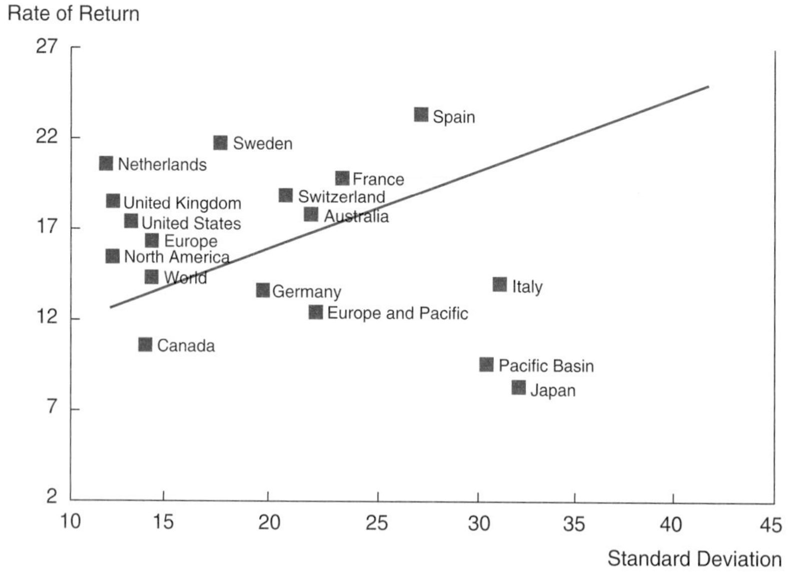
Rate of Return
27
22
17
12
7
2
Spain
Sweden
Netherlands
France
United Kingdom
Switzerland
United States
Australia
Europe
North America
World
Germany
Italy
Europe and Pacific
Canada
Pacific Basin
Japan
10
15
20
25
30
35
40
45
Standard Deviation

together in a portfolio would not help diversify the portfolio because they have identical rate-of-return patterns over time. In contrast, a correlation coefficient of −1.00 means that the rates of return for two investments move exactly opposite to each other. When one investment is experiencing above-average rates of return, the other is suffering through similar below-average rates of return. Combining two investments with large negative correlation in a portfolio would contribute much to diversification because it would stabilize the rates of return over time, reducing the standard deviation of the portfolio rates of return and hence the risk of the portfolio. Therefore, if you want to diversify your portfolio and reduce your risk, you want an investment that has either *low positive* correlation, *zero* correlation, or, ideally, *negative correlation* with the other investments in your portfolio. With this in mind, the following discussion considers the correlations of returns among U.S. bonds and stocks with the returns on foreign bonds and stocks.

GLOBAL BOND PORTFOLIO RISK Table 3.4 lists the correlation coefficients between rates of return for bonds in the United States and bonds in major foreign markets in domestic and U.S. dollar terms from 1987 to 1996. Notice that only one correlation between domestic rates of return is above 0.50. For a U.S. investor, the important correlations are between the rates of return in U.S. dollars. In this case, all the correlations between returns in U.S. dollars are substantially lower than the correlations among domestic returns and there is only one correlation above 0.32. Notably, while the individual volatilities increased substantially when returns were converted to U.S. dollars, the correlations among returns in U.S. dollars declined.

These low positive correlations among returns in U.S. dollars mean that U.S. investors have substantial opportunities for risk reduction through global diversification of bond portfolios. A U.S. investor who bought bonds in any market except Canada would substantially reduce the standard deviation of the well-diversified portfolio.

Why do these correlation coefficients for returns between U.S. bonds and those of various foreign countries differ? That is, why is the U.S.–Canada correlation 0.57 whereas the U.S.–Japan correlation is only 0.15? The answer is that the international trade patterns, economic growth, fiscal policies, and monetary policies of the countries differ. We do not have an integrated world economy, but rather a collection of economies that are related to one another in different ways. As an example, the U.S. and Canadian economies are closely related because of their geographic proximity, similar domestic economic policies, and the extensive trade between them. Each is the other's largest trading partner. In contrast, the United States has less trade with Japan and the fiscal and monetary policies of the two countries differ dramatically.

A country between these extremes is France. The United States has a significant trade relationship with France, but each has a fairly independent set of economic policies. Therefore, the U.S.–France correlation falls between those with Canada and Japan. The point is, macroeconomic differences cause the correlation of bond returns between the United States and each country to likewise differ. These differing correlations make it worthwhile to diversify with foreign bonds, and the different correlations indicate which countries will provide the greatest reduction in the standard deviation (risk) of returns for a U.S. investor.

Also, *the correlation of returns between a single pair of countries changes over time* because the factors influencing the correlations, such as international trade, economic growth,

TABLE 3.4

CORRELATION COEFFICIENTS BETWEEN RATES OF RETURN ON BONDS IN THE UNITED STATES AND MAJOR FOREIGN MARKETS: 1987–1996 (MONTHLY DATA)

	Domestic Returns	Returns in U.S. Dollars
Canada	0.72	0.57
France	0.47	0.32
Germany	0.44	0.27
Japan	0.34	0.15
United Kingdom	0.40	0.23

Source: Frank K. Reilly and David J. Wright, "Global Bond Markets: Alternative Benchmarks and Risk–Return Performance" (May 1997).

fiscal policy, and monetary policy, change over time. A change in any of these variables will produce a change in how the economies are related and in the relationship between returns on bonds. As an example, the correlation between bond returns in the United States and Japan before 1980 was quite low, reflecting limited trade and independent economic policies. During the 1980s and 1990s, international trade between the two countries increased substantially and so did the correlation between returns on bonds.

Figure 3.4 shows what happens to the risk–return tradeoff when we combine U.S. and foreign bonds. A comparison of a completely non-U.S. portfolio (100 percent foreign) and a 100 percent U.S. portfolio indicates that the non-U.S. portfolio has both a higher rate of return and a higher standard deviation of returns than the U.S. portfolio. Combining the two portfolios in different proportions provides an interesting set of points.

As we will discuss in Chapter 8, the expected rate of return is a weighted average of the two portfolios. In contrast, the risk (standard deviation) of the combination is *not* a weighted average, but also depends on the correlation between the two portfolios. In this example, the risk levels of the combined portfolios decline below those of the individual portfolios. Therefore, by adding noncorrelated foreign bonds to a portfolio of U.S. bonds, a U.S. investor is able to not only increase the expected rate of return, but also reduce the risk of a total U.S. bond portfolio.

GLOBAL EQUITY PORTFOLIO RISK The correlation of world equity markets resembles that for bonds. Table 3.5 lists the correlation coefficients between monthly

FIGURE 3.4 **RISK–RETURN TRADE-OFF FOR INTERNATIONAL BOND PORTFOLIOS**

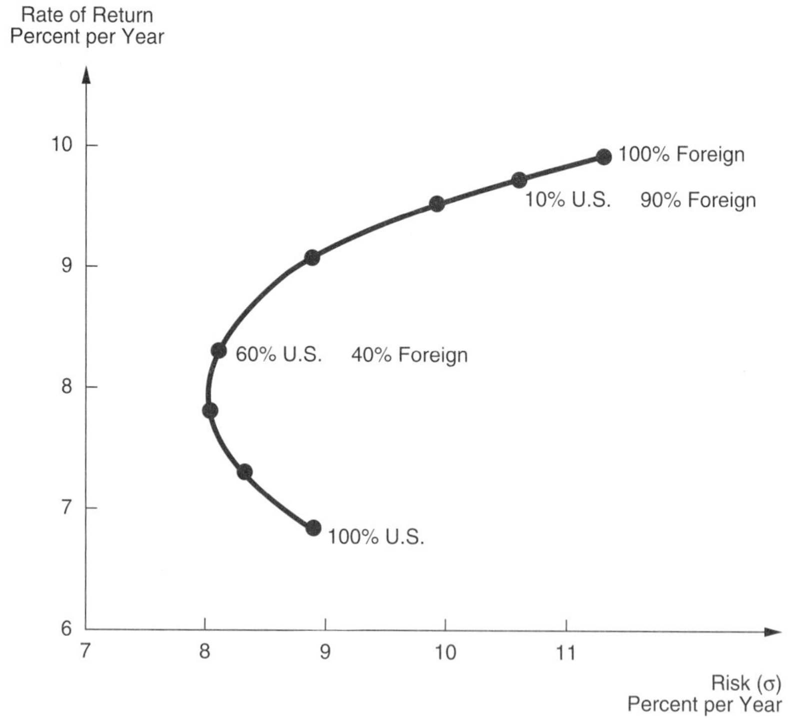
Rate of Return
Percent per Year
10
9
8
7
6
7
8
9
10
11
100% Foreign
10% U.S. 90% Foreign
60% U.S. 40% Foreign
100% U.S.
Risk (σ)
Percent per Year

Source: Kenneth Cholerton, Pierre Piergerits, and Bruno Solnik, "Why Invest in Foreign Currency Bonds?" *Journal of Portfolio Management* 12, no. 4 (summer 1986): 4–8. This copyrighted material is reprinted with permission from *Journal of Portfolio Management*, a publication of Institutional Investor, Inc., 488 Madison Avenue, New York, NY 10022.

equity returns of each country and the U.S. market (in both domestic and U.S. dollars) for the 12-year period from 1986 to 1998. Most of the correlations between local currency returns (7 of 11) topped 0.50. The correlations among rates of return adjusted for exchange rates were always lower; only 4 of the 11 correlations between U.S. dollar returns exceeded 0.50, and the average correlation was only 0.47.

These relatively small positive correlations between U.S. stocks and foreign stocks have similar implications to those derived for bonds. Investors can reduce the overall risk of their stock portfolios by including foreign stocks.

Figure 3.5 demonstrates the impact of international equity diversification. These curves demonstrate that as you increase the number of randomly selected securities in a portfolio, the standard deviation will decline due to the benefits of diversification *within your own country*. This is referred to as domestic diversification. After a certain number of securities (30 to 40), the curve will flatten out at a risk level that reflects the basic market risk for the domestic economy. The lower curve illustrates the benefits of international diversification. This curve demonstrates that adding foreign securities to a U.S. portfolio to create a global portfolio enables an investor to experience lower overall risk because the non-U.S. securities are not correlated with our economy or our stock market, allowing the investor to eliminate some of the basic market risks of the U.S. economy.

To see how this works, consider, for example, the effect of inflation and interest rates on all U.S. securities. As discussed in Chapter 1, all U.S. securities will be affected by these variables. In contrast, a Japanese stock is mainly affected by what happens in the Japanese economy and will typically not be affected by changes in U.S. variables. Thus, adding Japanese, German, and French stocks to a U.S. stock portfolio reduces the portfolio risk of the global portfolio to a level that reflects only worldwide systematic factors.

SUMMARY ON GLOBAL INVESTING At this point, we have considered the relative size of the market for non-U.S. bonds and stocks and found that it has grown in size and importance, becoming too big to ignore. We have also examined the rates of return for foreign bond and stock investments and determined that, when considering domestic results, their rates of return per unit of risk were superior to those in the U.S. market. This did not typically carry over for returns in U.S. dollars because the returns in U.S. dollars were significantly higher and this had a major impact on the return/risk results. Finally, we

TABLE 3.5

CORRELATION COEFFICIENTS BETWEEN PRICE RETURNS ON COMMON STOCKS IN THE UNITED STATES AND MAJOR FOREIGN STOCK MARKETS: 1986–1998

	Local Currency Price Returns	U.S. Dollar Price Returns
Australia	0.53	0.46
Canada	0.77	0.75
France	0.58	0.50
Germany	0.53	0.44
Italy	0.35	0.29
Japan	0.36	0.28
Netherlands	0.66	0.61
Spain	0.58	0.51
Sweden	0.49	0.48
Switzerland	0.64	0.53
United Kingdom	0.72	0.62

Source: Correlation table computed by the author using monthly FT-Actuaries return data from Goldman, Sachs & Co.

FIGURE 3.5 **RISK REDUCTION THROUGH NATIONAL AND INTERNATIONAL DIVERSIFICATION**

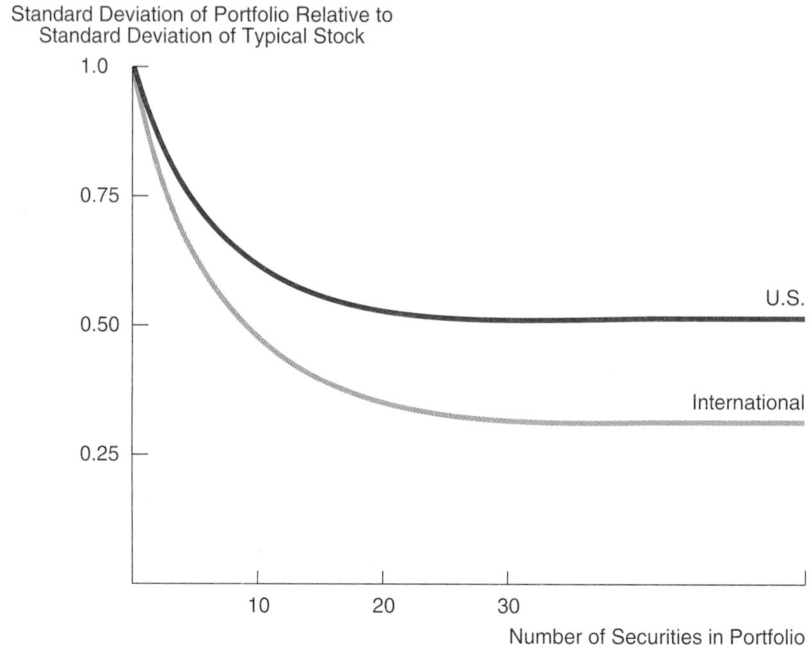
Standard Deviation of Portfolio Relative to
Standard Deviation of Typical Stock
1.0
0.75
0.50
0.25
U.S.
International
10
20
30
Number of Securities in Portfolio

Source: B. H. Solnik, "Why Not Diversify Internationally Rather Than Domestically?" *Financial Analysts Journal* (July–August 1974): 48–54. Reprinted by permission of the *Financial Analysts Journal.*

discussed constructing a portfolio of investments and the importance of diversification in reducing the variability of returns over time, which reduces the risk of the portfolio. It was noted that in order to have successful diversification, an investor should combine investments with low positive or negative correlations between rates of return. An analysis of the correlation between rates of return on U.S. and foreign bonds and stocks indicated a consistent pattern of low positive correlations. Therefore, the existence of relatively high rates of return on foreign securities combined with low correlation coefficients indicates that adding foreign stocks and bonds to a U.S. portfolio *will almost certainly reduce the risk of the portfolio and can possibly increase its average return.*

As promised, several rather compelling reasons exist for adding foreign securities to a U.S. portfolio. Therefore, developing a global investment perspective is important because such an approach has been shown to be justified, and because this current trend in the investment world will continue in the future. Implementing this new global investment perspective will not be easy because it requires an understanding of new terms, instruments (such as Eurobonds), and institutions (such as non-U.S. stock and bond markets). Still, the effort is justified because you are developing a set of skills and a way of thinking that will serve you always.

The next section presents an overview of investment alternatives from around the world, beginning with fixed-income investments and progressing through numerous alternatives.

GLOBAL INVESTMENT CHOICES

This section provides an important foundation for subsequent chapters in which we describe techniques to value individual investments and combine alternative investments into properly diversified portfolios that conform to your risk–return objectives. In this section, we briefly describe the numerous investment alternatives available and provide a brief overview of each. The purpose of this survey is to briefly introduce each of these investment alternatives so you can appreciate the full spectrum of alternatives.

The investments are divided by asset classes. Specifically, in the first subsection, we describe fixed-income investments, including bonds and preferred stocks. In the second subsection, we discuss equity investments, and the third subsection contains a discussion of special equity instruments, such as warrants and options, which have characteristics of both fixed-income and equity instruments. In subsection four, we consider futures contracts that allow for a wide range of return–risk profiles. The fifth subsection considers investment companies.

All these investments are called *financial assets* because their payoffs are in money. In contrast, *real assets,* such as real estate, are discussed in the sixth subsection. We conclude with assets that are considered *low liquidity investments* because of the relative difficulty in buying and selling them. This includes art, antiques, coins, stamps, and precious gems.

The final section of the chapter describes the historical return and risk patterns for many individual investment alternatives and the correlations among the returns for these investments. This additional background and perspective will help you evaluate individual investments in order to build a properly diversified portfolio of investments from around the world.

Fixed-Income Investments

Fixed-income investments have a contractually mandated payment schedule. Their investment contracts promise specific payments at predetermined times, although the legal force behind the promise varies and this affects their risks and required returns. At one extreme, if the issuing firm does not make its payment at the appointed time, creditors can declare the issuing firm bankrupt. In other cases (for example, income bonds), the issuing firm must make payments only if it earns profits. In yet other instances (for example, preferred stock), the issuing firm does not have to make payments unless its board of directors votes to do so.

Investors who acquire fixed-income securities (except preferred stock) are really lenders to the issuers. Specifically, you lend some amount of money, the *principal*, to the borrower. In return, the borrower promises to make periodic interest payments and to pay back the principal at the maturity of the loan.

SAVINGS ACCOUNTS You might not think of savings accounts as fixed-income investments, yet an individual who deposits funds in a savings account at a bank or savings and loan association (S&L) is really lending money to the institution and, as a result, earning a fixed payment. These investments are generally considered to be convenient, liquid, and low-risk because almost all are insured. Consequently, their rates of return are generally low compared with other alternatives. Several versions of these accounts have been developed to appeal to investors with differing objectives.

The passbook savings account has no minimum balance, and funds may be withdrawn at any time with little loss of interest. Due to its flexibility, the promised interest on passbook accounts is relatively low.

For investors with larger amounts of funds who are willing to give up liquidity, banks and S&Ls developed **certificates of deposit (CDs)**, which require minimum deposits (typically $500) and have fixed durations (usually three months, six months, one year, two years). The promised rates on CDs are higher than those for passbook savings, and the rate increases with the size and the duration of the deposit. An investor who wants to cash in a CD prior to its stated expiration date must pay a heavy penalty in the form of a much lower interest rate.

Investors with large sums of money ($10,000 or more) can invest in Treasury bills (T-bills)—short-term obligations (maturing in 3 to 12 months) of the U.S. government. To compete against T-bills, banks and S&Ls issue money market certificates, which require minimum investments of $10,000 and have minimum maturities of six months. The promised rate on these certificates fluctuates at some premium over the weekly rate on six-month T-bills. Investors can redeem these certificates only at the bank of issue, and they incur penalties if they withdraw their funds before maturity.

CAPITAL MARKET INSTRUMENTS **Capital market instruments** are fixed-income obligations that trade in the secondary market, which means you can buy and sell them to other individuals or institutions. Capital market instruments fall into four categories: (1) U.S. Treasury securities, (2) U.S. government agency securities, (3) municipal bonds, and (4) corporate bonds.

U.S. Treasury securities. All government securities issued by the U.S. Treasury are fixed-income instruments. They may be bills, notes, or bonds depending on their times to maturity. Specifically, bills mature in one year or less, notes in over one to 10 years, and bonds in more than 10 years from time of issue. U.S. government obligations are essentially free of credit risk because there is little chance of default and they are highly liquid.

U.S. government agency securities. Agency securities are sold by various agencies of the government to support specific programs, but they are not direct obligations of the Treasury. Examples of agencies that issue these bonds include the Federal National Mortgage Association (FNMA or Fannie Mae), which sells bonds and uses the proceeds to purchase mortgages from insurance companies or savings and loans; and the Federal Home Loan Bank (FHLB), which sells bonds and loans the money to its 12 banks, which in turn provide credit to savings and loans and other mortgage-granting institutions. Other agencies are the Government National Mortgage Association (GNMA or Ginnie Mae), Banks for Cooperatives, Federal Land Banks (FLBs), and the Federal Housing Administration (FHA).

Although the securities issued by federal agencies are not direct obligations of the government, they are virtually default-free because it is inconceivable that the government would allow them to default. Also they are fairly liquid. Because they are not officially guaranteed by the Treasury, they are not considered riskless. Also, because they are not as liquid as Treasury bonds, they typically provide slightly higher returns than Treasury issues.

Municipal bonds. Municipal bonds are issued by local government entities as either general obligation or revenue bonds. General obligation bonds (GOs) are backed by the full taxing power of the municipality, whereas revenue bonds pay the interest from revenue generated by specific projects (the revenue to pay the interest on sewer bonds comes from water taxes).

Municipal bonds differ from other fixed-income securities because they are tax-exempt. The interest earned from them is exempt from taxation by the federal government and by the state that issued the bond, provided the investor is a resident of that state. For this reason, municipal bonds are popular with investors in high tax brackets. For an investor having a marginal tax rate of 35 percent, a regular bond with an interest rate of 8 percent yields a net return after taxes of only 5.20 percent [$0.08 \times (1 - 0.35)$]. Such an investor would prefer a tax-free bond of equal risk with a 6 percent yield. This allows municipal bonds to offer yields that are lower than yields on comparable taxable bonds, generally by about 25 to 30 percent.

Corporate bonds. Corporate bonds are fixed-income securities issued by industrial corporations, public utility corporations, or railroads to raise funds to invest in plant, equipment, or working capital. They can be broken down by issuer, in terms of credit quality (measured by the ratings assigned by an agency on the basis of probability of default), in terms of maturity (short term, intermediate term, or long term), or based on some component of the indenture (sinking fund or call feature).

All bonds include an **indenture**, which is the legal agreement that lists the obligations of the issuer to the bondholder, including the payment schedule and features such as call provisions and sinking funds. **Call provisions** specify when a firm can issue a call for the bonds prior to their maturity, at which time current bondholders must submit the bonds to the issuing firm, which redeems them (that is, pays back the principal and a small premium). A **sinking fund** provision specifies payments the issuer must make to redeem a given percentage of the outstanding issue prior to maturity.

Corporate bonds fall into various categories based on their contractual promises to investors. They will be discussed in order of their seniority.

Senior secured bonds are the most senior bonds in a firm's capital structure and have the lowest risk of distress or default. They include various secured issues that differ based on the assets that are pledged. **Mortgage bonds** are backed by liens on specific assets, such as land and buildings. In the case of bankruptcy, the proceeds from the sale of these assets are used to pay off the mortgage bondholders. **Collateral trust bonds** are a form of mortgage bond except that the assets backing the bonds are financial assets, such as stocks, notes, and other high-quality bonds. Finally, **equipment trust certificates** are mortgage bonds that are secured by specific pieces of transportation equipment, such as locomotives and boxcars for a railroad and airplanes for an airline.

Debentures are promises to pay interest and principal, but they pledge no specific assets (referred to as *collateral*) in case the firm does not fulfill its promise. This means that the bondholder depends on the success of the borrower to make the promised payment. Debenture owners usually have first call on the firm's earnings and any assets that are not already pledged by the firm as backing for senior secured bonds. If the issuer does not make an interest payment, the debenture owners can declare the firm bankrupt and claim any unpledged assets to pay off the bonds.

Subordinated bonds are similar to debentures, but in the case of default, subordinated bondholders have claim to the assets of the firm only after the firm has satisfied the claims of all senior secured and debenture bondholders. That is, the claims of subordinated bondholders are subordinate to those of other bondholders. Within this general category of subordinated issues, you can find senior subordinated, subordinated, and junior subordinated bonds. Junior subordinated bonds have the weakest claim of all bondholders.

Income bonds stipulate interest payment schedules, but the interest is due and payable only if the issuers earn the income to make the payment by stipulated dates. If the company does not earn the required amount, it does not have to make the interest payment and it cannot be declared bankrupt. Instead, the interest payment is considered in arrears and, if subsequently earned, it must be paid off. Because the issuing firm is not legally bound to make its interest payments except when the firm earns it, an income bond is not considered as safe as a debenture or a mortgage bond, so income bonds offer higher returns to compensate investors for the added risk. Although there are a limited number of corporate income bonds, these income bonds are fairly popular with municipalities because municipal revenue bonds are basically income bonds.

Convertible bonds have the interest and principal characteristics of other bonds, with the added feature that the bondholder has the option to turn them back to the firm in exchange for its common stock. For example, a firm could issue a $1,000 face-value bond and stipulate that owners of the bond could turn the bond in to the issuing corporation and convert it into 40 shares of the firm's common stock. These bonds appeal to investors because they combine the features of a fixed-income security with the option of conversion into the common stock of the firm, should the firm prosper.

Because of their desirability, convertible bonds generally pay lower interest rates than nonconvertible debentures of comparable risk. The difference in the required interest rate increases with the growth potential of the company because this increases the value of the option to convert the bonds into common stock. These bonds are almost always subordinated to the nonconvertible debt of the firm, so they are considered to have higher credit risk and receive a lower rating from the rating firms.

An alternative to convertible bonds is a debenture with warrants attached. A **warrant** allows the bondholder to purchase the firm's common stock from the firm at a specified price for a given time period. The specified purchase price for the stock set in the warrant is typically above the price of the stock at the time the firm issues the bond but below the expected future stock price. The warrant makes the debenture more desirable, which lowers its required yield. The warrant also provides the firm with future common stock capital when the holder exercises the warrant and buys the stock from the firm.

Unlike the typical bond that pays interest every six months and its face value at maturity, a **zero coupon bond** promises no interest payments during the life of the bond but only the payment of the principal at maturity. Therefore, the purchase price of the bond is the present value of the principal payment at the required rate of return. For example, the price of a zero coupon bond that promises to pay $10,000 in five years with a required rate of return of 8 percent is $6,756. To find this, assuming semiannual compounding (which is the norm), use the present value factor for 10 periods at 4 percent, which is 0.6756.

PREFERRED STOCK Preferred stock is classified as a fixed-income security because its yearly payment is stipulated as either a coupon (for example, 5 percent of the face value) or a stated dollar amount (for example, $5 preferred). Preferred stock differs from bonds because its payment is a dividend and therefore not legally binding. For each period, the firm's board of directors must vote to pay it, similar to a common stock dividend. Even if the firm earned enough money to pay the preferred stock dividend, the board of directors could theoretically vote to withhold it. Because most preferred stock is cumulative, the unpaid dividends would accumulate to be paid in full at a later time.

Although preferred dividends are not legally binding as are the interest payments on a bond, they are considered *practically* binding because of the credit implications of a missed dividend. Because corporations can exclude 80 percent of intercompany dividends from taxable income, preferred stocks have become attractive investments for financial corporations. For example, a corporation that owns preferred stock of another firm and receives $100 in dividends can exclude 80 percent of this amount and pay taxes on only 20 percent of it ($20). Assuming a 40 percent tax rate, the tax would only be $8 or 8 percent versus 40 percent on other investment income. Due to this tax benefit, the yield on high-grade preferred stock is typically lower than that on high-grade bonds.

International Bond Investing

As noted earlier, more than half of all fixed-income securities available to U.S. investors are issued by firms in countries outside the United States. Investors identify these securities in different ways: by the country or city of the issuer (for example, United States, United Kingdom, Japan); by the location of the primary trading market (for example, United States, London); by the home country of the major buyers; and by the currency in which the securities are denominated (for example, dollars, yen, pounds sterling). We identify foreign bonds by their country of origin and include these other differences in each description.

A **Eurobond** is an international bond denominated in a currency not native to the country where it is issued. Specific kinds of Eurobonds include Eurodollar bonds, Euroyen bonds, Eurodeutschemark bonds, and Eurosterling bonds. A Eurodollar bond is denominated in U.S. dollars and sold outside the United States to non-U.S. investors. A specific example would be a U.S. dollar bond issued by General Motors and sold in London. Eurobonds are typically issued in Europe, with the major concentration in London.

Eurobonds can also be denominated in yen or deutschemarks. For example, Nippon Steel can issue Euroyen bonds for sale in London. Also, if it appears that investors are looking for foreign currency bonds, a U.S. corporation can issue a Euroyen bond in London.

Yankee bonds are sold in the United States, denominated in U.S. dollars, but issued by foreign corporations or governments.[3] This allows a U.S. citizen to buy the bond of a foreign firm or government but receive all payments in U.S. dollars, eliminating exchange rate risk.

An example would be a U.S. dollar–denominated bond issued by British Airways. Similar bonds are issued in other countries, including the Bulldog Market, which involves British sterling–denominated bonds issued in the United Kingdom by non-British firms, or the Samurai Market, which involves yen-denominated bonds issued in Japan by non-Japanese firms.

International domestic bonds are sold by an issuer within its own country in that country's currency. An example would be a bond sold by Nippon Steel in Japan denominated in yen. A U.S. investor acquiring such a bond would receive maximum diversification, but would incur exchange rate risk.

EQUITY INSTRUMENTS

This section describes several equity instruments, which differ from fixed-income securities because their returns are not contractual. As a result, you can receive returns that are much better or much worse than what you would receive on a bond. We begin with common stock, the most popular equity instrument and probably the most popular investment instrument.

Common stock represents *ownership* of a firm. Owners of the common stock of a firm share in the company's successes and problems. If, like Wal-Mart Stores, Home Depot, Microsoft, or Intel, the company prospers, the investor receives high rates of return and can become wealthy. In contrast, the investor can lose money if the firm does not do well or even goes bankrupt, as the once formidable Penn Central, W. T. Grant, and Interstate Department Stores all did. In these instances, the firm is forced to liquidate its assets and pay off all its creditors. Notably, the firm's preferred stockholders and common stock owners receive what is left. Investing in common stock entails all the advantages and disadvantages of ownership and is a relatively risky investment compared with fixed-income securities.

COMMON STOCK CLASSIFICATIONS When considering an investment in common stock, people tend to divide the vast universe of stocks into categories based on general business lines and by industry within these business lines. The division gives classifications for industrial firms, utilities, transportation firms, and financial institutions. Within each of these business lines are industries. The most diverse group—the industrial group—includes such industries as automobiles, industrial machinery, chemicals, and beverages. Utilities include electrical power companies, gas suppliers, and the water industry. Transportation includes airlines, trucking firms, and railroads.

[3]For a discussion of the growth of this market related to stocks, see Michael Siconolf, "Foreign Firms Step Up Offerings in U.S," *Wall Street Journal*, 1 June 1992, C1, C2.

Financial institutions include banks, savings and loans, insurance companies, and investment firms.

An alternative classification scheme might separate domestic (U.S.) and foreign common stocks. We avoid this division because the business line–industry breakdown is more appropriate and useful when constructing a diversified portfolio of global common stock investments. With a global capital market, the focus of analysis should include all the companies in an industry viewed in a global setting. The point is, it is not relevant whether a major chemical firm is located in the United States or Germany, just as it is not releveant whether a computer firm is located in Michigan or California. Therefore, when considering the automobile industry, it is necessary to go beyond pure U.S. auto firms like General Motors and Ford, and consider auto firms from throughout the world, such as Honda Motors, Porsche, Daimler-Chrysler, Nissan, and Fiat.

Therefore, our discussion on foreign equities concentrates on how you buy and sell these securities because this procedural information has often been a major impediment. Many investors may recognize the desirability of investing in foreign common stock because of the risk and return characteristics, but they may be intimidated by the logistics of the transaction. The purpose of the next section is to alleviate this concern by explaining the alternatives available.

ACQUIRING FOREIGN EQUITIES Currently, there are several ways to acquire foreign common stock:

1. Purchase or sale of American Depository Receipts (ADRs)
2. Purchase or sale of American shares
3. Direct purchase or sale of foreign shares listed on a U.S. or foreign stock exchange
4. Purchase or sale of international or global mutual funds

Purchase or Sale of American Depository Receipts The easiest way to acquire foreign shares directly is through **American Depository Receipts (ADRs)**. These are certificates of ownership issued by a U.S. bank that represent indirect ownership of a certain number of shares of a specific foreign firm on deposit in a bank in the firm's home country. ADRs are a convenient way to own foreign shares because the investor buys and sells them in U.S. dollars and receives all dividends in U.S. dollars. This means that the price and returns reflect both the domestic returns for the stock and the exchange rate effect. Also, the price of an ADR can reflect the fact that it represents multiple shares—for example, an ADR can be for 5 or 10 shares of the foreign stock. ADRs can be issued at the discretion of a bank based on the demand for the stock. The shareholder absorbs the additional handling costs of an ADR through higher transfer expenses, which are deducted from dividend payments.

ADRs are quite popular in the United States because of their diversification benefits.[4] By the end of 1997, 356 foreign companies had stocks listed on the New York Stock Exchange (NYSE) and 288 of these were available through ADRs, including all the stock listed from Japan, the United Kingdom, Australia, Mexico, and the Netherlands. In addition, 84 foreign firms are listed on the American Stock Exchange (AMEX) with most of the non-Canadian stocks available through ADRs.

---

[4]For evidence of this, see Dennis T. Officer and Ronald Hoffmeister, "ADRs: A Substitute for the Real Thing?" *Journal of Portfolio Management* 13, no. 2 (winter 1987): 61–65; and Mahmoud Wahab and Amit Khandwala, "Why Not Diversify Internationally with ADRs?" *Journal of Portfolio Management* 19, no. 2 (winter 1993): 75–82.

Purchase or Sale of American Shares American shares are securities issued in the United States by a transfer agent acting on behalf of a foreign firm. Because of the added effort and expense incurred by the foreign firm, a limited number of American shares are available.

Direct Purchase or Sale of Foreign Shares The most difficult and complicated foreign equity transaction takes place in the country where the firm is located because it must be carried out in the foreign currency and the shares must then be transferred to the United States. This routine can be cumbersome. A second alternative is a transaction on a foreign stock exchange outside the country where the securities originated. For example, if you acquired shares of a French auto company listed on the London Stock Exchange (LSE), the shares would be denominated in pounds and the transfer would be swift, assuming your broker has a membership on the LSE.

Finally, you could purchase foreign stocks listed on the NYSE or AMEX. This is similar to buying a U.S. stock, but only a limited number of foreign firms qualify for—and are willing to accept—the cost of listing. Still, this number is growing. At the end of 1997, more than 83 foreign firms (mostly Canadian) were directly listed on the NYSE, in addition to the firms that were available through ADRs. Also, many foreign firms are traded on the National Association of Securities Dealers Automatic Quotations (NASDAQ) system.

Purchase or Sale of International or Global Mutual Funds Numerous investment companies invest all or a portion of their funds in stocks of firms outside the United States. The alternatives range from *global funds*, which invest in both U.S. stocks and foreign stocks, to *international funds*, which invest almost wholly outside the United States. In turn, international funds can: (1) diversify across many countries, (2) concentrate in a segment of the world (for example, Europe, South America, the Pacific basin), (3) concentrate in a specific country (for example, the Japan Fund, the Germany Fund, the Italy Fund, or the Korea Fund), or (4) concentrate in types of markets (for example, emerging markets, which would include stocks from countries such as Thailand, Indonesia, India, and China). A mutual fund is a convenient path to global investing, particularly for a small investor, because the purchase or sale of one of these funds is similar to a transaction for a comparable U.S. mutual fund.[5]

SPECIAL EQUITY INSTRUMENTS: OPTIONS

In addition to common stock investments, it is also possible to invest in equity-derivative securities, which are securities that have a claim on the common stock of a firm. This would include **options**—rights to buy or sell common stock at a specified price for a stated period of time. The two kinds of option instruments are (1) warrants and (2) puts and calls.

WARRANTS As mentioned earlier, a warrant is an option issued by a corporation that gives the holder the right to acquire a firm's common stock from the company at a specified price within a designated time period. The warrant does not constitute ownership of the stock, only the option to buy the stock.

PUTS AND CALLS A **call option** is similar to a warrant because it is an option to buy the common stock of a company within a certain period at a specified price called the *striking price*. A call option differs from a warrant because it is not issued by the company but by another investor who is willing to assume the other side of the transaction. Options also are typically valid for a shorter time period than warrants. Call options are generally valid

[5]Mutual funds in general and those related to global investing will be discussed in Chapter 26.

for less than a year, whereas warrants extend more than five years. The holder of a **put option** has the right to sell a given stock at a specified price during a designated time period. Puts are useful to investors who expect a stock price to decline during the specified period or to investors who own the stock and want protection from a price decline.

Futures Contracts

Another instrument that provides an alternative to the purchase of an investment is a **futures contract**. This agreement provides for the future exchange of a particular asset at a specified delivery date (usually within nine months) in exchange for a specified payment at the time of delivery. Although the full payment is not made until the delivery date, a good faith deposit, the *margin*, is made to protect the seller. This is typically about 10 percent of the value of the contract.

The bulk of trading on the commodity exchanges is in futures contracts. The current price of the futures contract is determined by the participants' beliefs about the future for the commodity. For example, in July of a given year, a trader could speculate on the Chicago Board of Trade for wheat in September, December, March, and May of the next year. If the investor expected the price of a commodity to rise, he or she could buy a futures contract on one of the commodity exchanges for later sale. If the investor expected the price to fall, he or she could sell a futures contract on an exchange with the expectation of buying similar contracts later when the price had declined to cover the sale.

Several differences exist between investing in an asset through a futures contract and investing in the asset itself. One is the use of a small good-faith deposit, which increases the volatility of returns. Because an investor puts up only a small portion of the total value of the futures contract (10 to 15 percent), when the price of the commodity changes, the change in the total value of the contract is large compared to the amount invested. Another unique aspect is the term of the investment: Although stocks can have infinite maturities, futures contracts typically expire in less than a year.

FINANCIAL FUTURES In addition to futures contracts on commodities, a recent innovation has been the development of futures contracts on financial instruments, such as T-bills, Treasury bonds, and Eurobonds. For example, it is possible to buy or sell a futures contract that promises future delivery of $100,000 of Treasury bonds at a set price and yield. The major exchanges for financial futures are the Chicago Mercantile Exchange (CME) and the Chicago Board of Trade (CBOT). These futures contracts allow individual investors, bond portfolio managers, and corporate financial managers to protect themselves against volatile interest rates. Certain currency futures allow individual investors or portfolio managers to speculate on or to protect against changes in currency exchange rates. Finally, futures contracts pertain to stock market series, such as the S&P (Standard & Poor's) 500, the *Value Line* Index, and the Nikkei Average on the Tokyo Stock Exchange.

Investment Companies

The investment alternatives described so far are individual securities that can be acquired from a government entity, a corporation, or another individual. However, rather than directly buying an individual stock or bond issued by one of these sources, you may choose to acquire these investments indirectly by buying shares in an investment company, also called a *mutual fund*, that owns a portfolio of individual stocks, bonds, or a combination of the two. Specifically, an **investment company** sells shares in itself and uses the proceeds of this sale to acquire bonds, stocks, or other investment instruments. As a result, an investor who acquires shares in an investment company is a partial owner of the investment company's portfolio of stocks or bonds. We distinguish investment companies by the types of investment instruments they acquire. Discussions of some of the major types follow.

MONEY MARKET FUNDS **Money market funds** are investment companies that acquire high-quality, short-term investments (referred to as *money market* instruments), such as T-bills, high-grade commercial paper (public short-term loans) from various corporations, and large CDs from the major money center banks. The yields on the money market portfolios always surpass those on normal bank CDs because the investment by the money market fund is larger and the fund can commit to longer maturities than the typical individual. In addition, the returns on commercial paper are above the prime rate. The typical minimum initial investment in a money market fund is $1,000, it charges no sales commission, and minimum additions are $250 to $500. You can always withdraw funds from your money market fund without penalty (typically by writing a check on the account), and you receive interest to the day of withdrawal.

Individuals tend to use money market funds as alternatives to bank savings accounts because they are generally quite safe (although they are not insured, they typically limit their investments to high-quality, short-term investments), they provide yields above what is available on most savings accounts, and the funds are readily available. Therefore, you might use one of these funds to accumulate funds to pay tuition or for a down payment on a car. Because of relatively high yields and extreme flexibility and liquidity, the total value of these funds reached more than $1 trillion in 1998.

BOND FUNDS Bond funds generally invest in various long-term government, corporate, or municipal bonds. They differ by the type and quality of the bonds included in the portfolio as assessed by various rating services. Specifically, the bond funds range from those that invest only in risk-free government bonds and high-grade corporate bonds to those that concentrate in lower-rated corporate or municipal bonds, called *high-yield bonds* or *junk bonds*. The expected rate of return from various bond funds will differ, with the low-risk government bond funds paying the lowest returns and the high-yield bond funds expected to pay the highest returns.

COMMON STOCK FUNDS Numerous common stock funds invest to achieve stated investment objectives, which can include aggressive growth, income, precious metal investments, and international stocks. Such funds offer smaller investors the benefits of diversification and professional management. They include different investment styles, such as growth or value, and concentrate in alternative-sized firms, including small-cap, midcap, and large-capitalization stocks. To meet the diverse needs of investors, numerous funds have been created that concentrate in one industry or sector of the economy, such as chemicals, electric utilities, health, housing, and technology. These funds are diversified within a sector or an industry, but are not diversified across the total market. Investors who participate in a sector or an industry fund bear more risk than investors in a total market fund because the sector funds will tend to fluctuate more than an aggregate market fund that is diversified across all sectors. Also, international funds that invest outside the United States and global funds that invest in the United States and in other countries offer opportunities for global investing by individual investors.[6]

---

[6]For a study that examines the diversification of individual country funds, see Warren Bailey and Joseph Lim, "Evaluating the Diversification Benefits of the New Country Funds," *Journal of Portfolio Management* 18, no. 3 (spring 1992): 74–80.

BALANCED FUNDS Balanced funds invest in a combination of bonds and stocks of various sorts depending on their stated objectives.

REAL ESTATE Like commodities, most investors view real estate as an interesting and profitable investment alternative but believe that it is only available to a small group of experts with a lot of capital to invest. In reality, some feasible real estate investments require no detailed expertise or large capital commitments. We will begin by considering low-capital alternatives.

REAL ESTATE INVESTMENT TRUSTS (REITS) A **real estate investment trust** is an investment fund designed to invest in various real estate properties. It is similar to a stock or bond mutual fund, except that the money provided by the investors is invested in property and buildings rather than in stocks and bonds. There are several types of REITs.

Construction and development trusts lend the money required by builders during the initial construction of a building. Mortgage trusts provide the long-term financing for properties. Specifically, they acquire long-term mortgages on properties once construction is completed. Equity trusts own various income-producing properties, such as office buildings, shopping centers, or apartment houses. Therefore, an investor who buys shares in an equity real estate investment trust is buying part of a portfolio of income-producing properties.

REITs have experienced periods of great popularity and significant depression in line with changes in the aggregate economy and the money market. Although they are subject to cyclical risks depending on the economic environment, they offer small investors a way to participate in real estate investments.[7]

DIRECT REAL ESTATE INVESTMENT The most common type of direct real estate investment is the purchase of a home, which is the largest investment most people ever make. Today, according to the Federal Home Loan Bank, the average cost of a single family house exceeds $100,000. The purchase of a home is considered an investment because the buyer pays a sum of money either all at once or over a number of years through a mortgage. For most people, those unable to pay cash for a house, the financial commitment includes a down payment (typically 10 to 20 percent of the purchase price) and specific mortgage payments over a 20 to 30-year period that include reducing the loan's principal and paying interest on the outstanding balance. Subsequently, a homeowner hopes to sell the house for its cost plus a gain.

RAW LAND Another direct real estate investment is the purchase of raw land with the intention of selling it in the future at a profit. During the time you own the land, you have negative cash flows caused by mortgage payments, property maintenance, and taxes. An obvious risk is the possible difficulty of selling it for an uncertain price. Raw land generally has low liquidity compared to most stocks and bonds. An alternative to buying and selling the raw land is the development of the land into a housing project or a shopping mall.

LAND DEVELOPMENT Typically, land development involves buying raw land, dividing it into individual lots, and building houses on it. Alternatively, buying land and building a shopping mall would also be considered land development. This is a feasible form of investment, but requires a substantial commitment of capital, time, and expertise.

---

[7]See Eric S. Hardy, "The Ground Floor," *Forbes*, 14 August 1995, 185; and Susan E. Kuhn, "Real Estate: A Smart Alternative to Stocks," *Fortune*, 27 May 1996, 186.

Although the risks can be high because of the commitment of time and capital, the rates of return from a successful housing or commercial development can be significant.[8]

RENTAL PROPERTY Many investors with an interest in real estate investing acquire apartment buildings or houses with low down payments, with the intention of deriving enough income from the rents to pay the expenses of the structure, including the mortgage payments. For the first few years following the purchase, the investor generally has no reported income from the building because of tax-deductible expenses, including the interest component of the mortgage payment and depreciation on the structure. Subsequently, rental property provides a cash flow and an opportunity to profit from the sale of the property.[9]

Low-Liquidity Investments

Most of the investment alternatives we have described are traded on securities markets. Except for real estate, most of these securities have good liquidity. Although many investors view the investments we discuss in this section as alternatives to financial investments, financial institutions do not typically acquire them because they are considered to be fairly illiquid and have high transaction costs compared to stocks and bonds. Many of these assets are sold at auctions, causing expected prices to vary substantially. In addition, transaction costs are high because there is generally no national market for these investments, so local dealers must be compensated for the added carrying costs and the cost of searching for buyers or sellers. Given these liquidity risk considerations, many financial theorists view the following low-liquidity investments more as hobbies than investments, even though studies have indicated that some of these assets have experienced substantial rates of return.

ANTIQUES The investors who earn the greatest returns from antiques are dealers who acquire them at estate sales or auctions to refurbish and sell at a profit. If we gauge the value of antiques based on prices established at large public auctions, it appears that many serious collectors enjoy substantial rates of return. In contrast, the average investor who owns a few pieces to decorate his or her home finds such returns elusive. The high transaction costs and illiquidity of antiques may erode any profit that the individual may earn when selling these pieces. The subsequent discussion of rates of return on various assets will provide some evidence on the returns.

ART The entertainment sections of newspapers or the personal finance sections of magazines often carry stories of the results of major art auctions, such as when Van Gogh's *Irises* and *Sunflowers* sold for $59 million and $36 million, respectively.

Obviously, these examples and others indicate that some paintings have increased significantly in value and thereby generated large rates of return for their owners. However, investing in art typically requires substantial knowledge of art and the art world, a large amount of capital to acquire the work of well-known artists, patience, and an ability to absorb high transaction costs. For investors who enjoy fine art and have the resources, these can be satisfying investments, but for most small investors, this is a difficult area in

---

[8]For a review of studies that have examined returns on real estate, see William Goetzmann and Roger Ibbotson, "The Performance of Real Estate as an Asset Class," *Journal of Applied Corporate Finance* 3, no. 1 (spring 1990): 65–76; C. F. Myer and James Webb, "Return Properties of Equity REITs, Common Stocks, and Commercial Real Estate: A Comparison," *Journal of Real Estate Research* 8, no. 1 (1993): 87–106; and Stephen Ross and Randall Zisler, "Risk and Return in Real Estate," *Journal of Real Estate Financial Economics* 4, no. 2 (1991): 175–190. For an analysis of the diversification possibilities, see Susan Hudson-Wilson and Bernard L. Elbaum, "Diversification Benefits for Investors in Real Estate," *Journal of Portfolio Management* 21, no. 3 (spring 1995): 92–99.

[9]For a discussion of this alternative, see Diane Harris, "An Investment for Rent," *Money*, April 1984, 87–90.

which to get returns that compensate for the uncertainty and illiquidity. This was especially true between 1989 and 1995 when there was a bear market in art.[10]

COINS AND STAMPS Many individuals enjoy collecting coins or stamps as a hobby and as an investment. The market for coins and stamps is fragmented compared to the stock market, but it is more liquid than the market for art and antiques. Indeed, the volume of coins and stamps traded has prompted the publication of weekly and monthly price lists.[11] An investor can get a widely recognized grading specification on a coin or stamp and, once graded, a coin or stamp can usually be sold quickly through a dealer.[12] It is important to recognize that the percentage difference between the bid price the dealer will pay to buy the stamp or coin and the asking or selling price the investor must pay the dealer is going to be fairly large compared to the difference between the bid and ask prices on stocks and bonds.

DIAMONDS Diamonds can be and have been good investments during many periods. Still, investors who purchase diamonds must realize that: (1) diamonds can be highly illiquid, (2) the grading process that determines their quality is quite subjective, (3) most investment-grade gems require substantial investments, and (4) they generate no positive cash flow during the holding period until the stone is sold. In fact, during the holding period the investor must cover costs of insurance and storage. Finally, there are appraisal costs before selling.[13]

In this section, we have described the most common investment alternatives to introduce you to the range of investments available. We will discuss many of these in more detail when we consider how you evaluate them for investment purposes. You should keep in mind that new investment alternatives are constantly being created and developed. You can keep abreast of these by reading business newspapers and magazines.

In our final section, we will present some data on historical rates of return and risk measures for several of these investments to provide background on their historical return–risk performance. This should give you some insights into the returns and risk characteristics you might expect in the future.

HISTORICAL RISK/RETURNS ON ALTERNATIVE INVESTMENTS

How do investors weigh the costs and benefits of owning investments and make decisions to build portfolios that will provide the best risk–return combinations? To help individual or institutional investors answer this question, financial theorists have examined extensive

[10]For a discussion of art sold at auction, see Alexandra Peers, "With Spring Auction, Shaky Art Market Faces Flood of Less-than-Stellar Works," *Wall Street Journal*, 29 April 1992, C1, C16; and "Market Is Picture of Optimism in Flux," *Wall Street Journal*, 26 April 1996, C1.

[11]A weekly publication for coins is *Coin World*, published by Amos Press, Inc., 911 Vandermark Rd., Sidney, OH 45367. There are several monthly coin magazines, including *Coinage*, published by Behn-Miller Publications, Inc., Encino, Calif. Amos Press also publishes several stamp magazines, including *Linn's Stamp News* and *Scott Stamp Monthly*. These magazines provide current prices for coins and stamps.

[12]For an article that describes the alternative grading services, see Diana Henriques, "Don't Take Any Wooden Nickels," *Barron's*, 19 June 1989, 16, 18, 20, 32. For an analysis of commemorative coins, see R. W. Bradford, "How to Lose a Mint," *Barron's*, 6 March 1989, 54, 55.

[13]For a discussion of problems and opportunities, see "When to Put Your Money into Gems," *Business Week*, 16 March 1981, 158–161.

data and attempted to provide information on the return and risk characteristics of various investments.

Many theorists have studied the historical rates of return on common stocks, and a growing interest in bonds has caused investigators to assess their performance as well. Because inflation has been so pervasive, many studies include both nominal and real rates of return on investments. Still other investigators have examined the performance of such assets as real estate, foreign stocks, art, antiques, and commodities. This section reviews some of the major studies that provide background on the rates of return and risk for these investment alternatives. This should help you to make decisions on the alternatives you might want to examine when building your investment portfolio and the allocation to the various asset classes.

Stocks, Bonds, and T-Bills

A set of studies by Ibbotson and Sinquefield (I&S) examined historical nominal and real rates of return for seven major classes of assets in the United States: (1) large-company common stocks, (2) small-capitalization common stocks,[14] (3) long-term U.S. government bonds, (4) long-term corporate bonds, (5) intermediate-term U.S. government bonds, (6) U.S. Treasury bills, and (7) consumer goods (a measure of inflation).[15] For each asset, the authors calculated total rates of return before taxes or transaction costs.

These investigators computed geometric and arithmetic mean rates of return and computed nine series derived from the basic series. Four of these series were net returns reflecting different premiums: (1) a *risk premium*, which I&S defined as the difference in the rate of return that investors receive from investing in large-company common stocks (as represented by the stocks in the S&P 500 Index that is described in Chapter 5) rather than in risk-free U.S. Treasury bills; (2) a *small-stock premium*, which they defined as the return on small-capitalization stocks minus the return on large-company stocks; (3) a *horizon premium*, which they defined as the difference in the rate of return received from investing in long-term government bonds rather than short-term U.S. Treasury bills; and (4) a *default premium*, which they defined as the difference between the rates of return on long-term risky corporate bonds and long-term risk-free government bonds. I&S also computed the real inflation-adjusted rates of return for common stocks, small-capitalization stocks, Treasury bills, long-term government bonds, intermediate-term government bonds, and long-term corporate bonds.

A summary of the rates of return, risk premiums, and standard deviations for the basic and derived series appears in Table 3.6. As discussed in Chapter 1, the geometric means of the rates of return are always lower than the arithmetic means of the rates of return, and the difference between these two mean values increases with the standard deviation of returns.

During the period from 1926 to 1998, large-company common stocks returned 11.2 percent a year, compounded annually. To compare this to other investments, the results show that common stock experienced a risk premium of 7.2 percent and inflation-adjusted real returns of 7.9 percent per year. In contrast to all common stocks, the small-capitalization

---

[14]Small-capitalization stocks were broken out as a separate class of asset because several studies have shown that firms with relatively small capitalization (stock with low market value) have experienced rates of return and risk significantly different from those of stocks in general. Therefore, they were considered a unique asset class. We will discuss these studies in Chapter 7, which deals with the efficient markets hypothesis. The large-company stock returns are based upon the S&P Composite Index of 500 stocks—the S&P 500.

[15]The original study was Roger G. Ibbotson and Rex A. Sinquefield, "Stocks, Bonds, Bills, and Inflation: Year-by-Year Historical Returns (1926–1974)," *Journal of Business* 49, no. 1 (January 1976): 11–47. Although this study was updated in several monographs, the current update is contained in *Stocks, Bonds, Bills, and Inflation: 1999 Yearbook* (Chicago: Ibbotson Associates, 1999). A seventh asset class (intermediate-term U.S. government bonds) was not part of the original studies but was added during the past decade.

TABLE 3.6 **BASIC AND DERIVED SERIES: HISTORICAL HIGHLIGHTS (1926–1998)**

Series	Annual Geometric Mean Rate of Return	Arithmetic Mean of Annual Returns	Standard Deviation of Annual Returns
Large-company stocks	11.2%	13.2%	20.3%
Small-capitalization stocks	12.4	17.4	33.8
Long-term corporate bonds	5.8	6.1	8.6
Long-term government bonds	5.3	5.7	9.2
Intermediate-term government bonds	5.3	5.5	5.7
U.S. Treasury bills	3.8	3.8	3.2
Consumer price index	3.1	3.2	4.5
Equity risk premium	7.2	9.1	20.1
Small-stock premium	1.1	2.7	18.4
Default premium	0.5	0.5	3.0
Horizon premium	1.5	1.8	8.5
Large company stock—inflation adjusted	7.9	9.9	20.4
Small-capitalization stock—inflation adjusted	9.1	13.9	33.1
Long-term corporate bonds—inflation adjusted	2.6	3.1	9.9
Long-term government bonds—inflation adjusted	2.2	2.7	10.5
Intermediate-term government bonds—inflation adjusted	2.2	2.4	7.0
U.S. Treasury bills—inflation adjusted	0.7	0.8	4.1

Source: © *Stocks, Bonds, Bills, and Inflation: 1999 Yearbook*™, Ibbotson Associates, Chicago (annually updates work by Roger G. Ibbotson and Rex A. Sinquefield). Used with permission. All rights reserved.

stocks (which are represented by the smallest 20 percent of stocks listed on the NYSE measured by market value) experienced a geometric mean return of 12.4 percent, which was a premium compared to all common stocks of 1.1 percent.

Although large cap common stocks and small-capitalization stocks experienced higher rates of return than the other asset groups, their returns were also more volatile as measured by the standard deviations of annual returns.

Long-term U.S. government bonds experienced a 5.3 percent annual return, a real return of 2.2 percent, and a horizon premium (compared to Treasury bills) of 1.5 percent. Although the returns on these bonds were lower than those on stocks, they were also far less volatile.

The annual compound rate of return on long-term corporate bonds was 5.8 percent, the default premium compared to U.S. government bonds was 0.5 percent, and the inflation-adjusted return was 2.6 percent. Although corporate bonds provided a higher return, as one would expect, the volatility of corporate bonds was slightly lower than that experienced by long-term government bonds.

The nominal return on U.S. Treasury bills was 3.8 percent a year, whereas the inflation-adjusted return was 0.7 percent. The standard deviation of nominal returns for T-bills was the lowest of the series examined, which reflects the low risk of these securities and is consistent with the lowest rate of return.

This study reported the rates of return, return premiums, and risk measures on various asset groups in the United States. As noted, the rates of return were generally consistent with the uncertainty (risk) of annual returns as measured by the standard deviations of annual returns.

WORLD PORTFOLIO PERFORMANCE

Expanding this analysis from domestic to global securities, Reilly examined the performance of numerous assets, not only in the United States, but around the world.[16] Specifically, for the period from 1980 to 1997, he examined the performance of stocks, bonds, cash (the equivalent of U.S. T-bills), real estate, and commodities from the United States,

[16] Frank K. Reilly, "An Analysis of Global Capital Market Returns," Mimeo (January 1999).

TABLE 3.7 **SUMMARY RISK-RETURN RESULTS FOR ALTERNATIVE CAPITAL MARKET ASSETS: 1980–1997**

	Arithmetic Mean	Geometric Mean	Standard Deviation	Coefficient of Variation[b]	Beta 18 Years
S&P 500	17.89	17.13	13.22	0.74	1.32
Ibbotson Small-Cap Stock	17.52	16.12	17.47	1.00	1.33
Wilshire 5000	17.13	16.33	13.60	0.79	1.36
Russell 1000	17.57	16.77	13.55	0.77	1.34
Russell 1000 Value	16.89	16.13	13.12	0.78	1.21
Russell 1000 Growth	17.04	15.97	15.78	0.93	1.47
Russell 2000	13.65	12.35	16.63	1.22	1.49
Russell 2000 Value	18.51	17.25	16.44	0.89	1.28
Russell 2000 Growth	13.37	11.66	19.76	1.48	1.71
Russell 3000	17.37	16.56	13.56	0.78	1.36
Russell 3000 Value	18.11	17.39	12.73	0.70	1.22
Russell 3000 Growth	16.66	15.57	15.88	0.95	1.49
IFC Emerging Markets Stock	11.78	8.57	27.06	2.30	0.56
MSCI EAFE	16.22	14.29	21.66	1.34	1.24
Toronto Stock Exchange 300	8.46	7.53	14.02	1.66	1.21
Financial Times All-Shares	13.83	13.06	12.58	0.91	1.23
Frankfurt Allgemeine Index (FAZ)	14.79	11.89	25.82	1.75	1.10
Nikkei Index	6.98	4.79	20.63	2.95	1.01
Tokyo Stock Exchange Index	7.54	5.35	20.61	2.73	0.85
M-S World Stock	12.31	11.36	14.32	1.16	1.26
Brinson GSMI	14.40	13.99	9.70	0.67	1.00
LB Goverment Bond	10.70	10.47	7.15	0.67	0.28
LB Corporation Bond	11.80	11.38	9.96	0.84	0.40
LB Aggregate Bond	11.03	10.75	8.05	0.73	0.32
LB High-Yield Bond	14.32	13.69	12.25	0.85	0.44
ML World Government Bond	10.09	9.84	7.38	0.73	0.24
ML World Government Bond except U.S.	12.40	11.78	12.00	0.97	0.28
Wilshire Real Estate	13.37	12.12	15.42	1.15	0.00
Goldman Sachs Commodities	10.75	9.57	15.87	1.48	0.04
1-Year Government Bond[a]	8.57	8.51	3.77	0.44	0.06
Inflation	4.24	4.21	2.59	0.61	−0.02

Notes:

[a]The 1-year Government Bond is used as the risk-free of return in the portfolio performance measurement.

[b]Coefficient of Variation = Standard Deviation / Arithmetic Mean Rate of Return

[c]The Beta is calculated using monthly rates of return for 18 years (216 observations) and uses the Brinson GSMI series as the proxy for the market portfolio (i.e., benchmark).

[d]Betas of ML Government Bond and ML Non-U.S. Government Bond were calculated from 1986–1996.
Beta of Commodities was calculated from 1980–1996.

Source: Frank K. Reilly, "An Analysis of Global Capital Market Returns," Mimeo (January 1999).

Canada, Europe, Japan, and the emerging markets. He computed annual returns, risk measures, and correlations among the returns for alternative assets. Table 3.7 shows the geometric and arithmetic average annual rates of return, the standard deviations of returns, and the systematic risk (beta) for the 18-year period.

ASSET RETURN AND RISK The results in Table 3.7 generally confirm the expected relationship between annual rates of return and the risk of these securities. The riskier assets—those that had higher standard deviations—experienced the highest returns. For example, the MSCI EAFE and Frankfurt FAZ indexes had relatively high returns

TABLE 3.8 **CORRELATIONS AMONG GLOBAL CAPITAL MARKET ASSETS 1980–1997 (MONTHLY)**

	S&P 500	Wilshire 5000	IFC Emerging Market Stock	MSCI EAFE	M-S World Stock	Brinson GSMI
S&P 500	1.000	.989	.272	.470	.509	.902
Ibbotson Small Cap. Stk.	.780	.851	.261	.388	.422	.757
Wilshire 5000	.989	1.000	.280	.472	.513	.910
Russell 1000	.997	.996	.272	.467	.506	.908
Russell 1000 Value	.970	.965	.292	.465	.504	.883
Russell 1000 Growth	.976	.979	.245	.448	.487	.890
Russell 2000	.837	.902	.273	.420	.458	.812
Russell 2000 Value	.826	.883	.291	.423	.458	.804
Russell 2000 Growth	.819	.888	.252	.405	.443	.793
Russell 3000	.992	.999	.275	.468	.509	.910
Russell 3000 Value	.969	.970	.295	.468	.508	.888
Russell 3000 Growth	.972	.982	.247	.450	.489	.891
IFC Emerging Market Stock	.272	.280	1.000	.304	.295	.275
MSCI EAFE	.470	.472	.304	1.000	.992	.706
Toronto Stock Exchange 300	.754	.785	.293	.495	.551	.760
Financial Times All Shares	.618	.614	.404	.460	.466	.598
Frankfurt Allgem. Index (FAZ)	.467	.450	.361	.388	.393	.444
Nikkei Index	.378	.378	.328	.737	.729	.504
Tokyo Stock Exch. Index	.291	.289	.279	.699	.689	.419
M-S World Stock	.509	5.13	.295	.992	1.000	.736
Brinson GSMI	.902	.910	.275	.706	.736	1.000
LB Government Bond	.323	.297	−.093	.220	.222	.451
LB Corporation Bond	.362	.345	−.056	.226	.232	.483
LB Aggregate Bond	.333	.312	−.073	.222	.225	.463
LB High-Yield Bond	.461	.483	.104	.331	.340	.550
ML World Government Bond	.079	.040	−.246	.505	.495	.336
ML World Government Bond Ex U.S.	−.037	−.067	−.229	.539	.528	.239
Wilshire Real Estate	.661	.712	.245	.404	.435	.695
Goldman Sachs Commodities	.045	.042	−.042	.103	.118	.026
1-Year Government Bond	.141	.130	−.066	.135	.129	.280
Inflation	−.165	−.170	−.009	−.205	−.207	−.232

Source: Frank K. Reilly, "An Analysis of Global Capital Market Returns," Mimeo (January, 1999).

(16.22 and 14.79 percent) and very large standard deviations (21.66 and 25.82 percent). It is not a surprise that the highest risk asset class was Emerging Market stock at 27.06 percent, whereas risk-free U.S. cash equivalents (1-year government bonds) had low returns (8.57 percent) and the smallest standard deviation (3.77 percent). The data amassed by Reilly could be used to assess the relative risk of assets in a portfolio, as well as risk and return values for each asset.

RELATIVE ASSET RISK Calculating the coefficients of variation (CVs), which measure relative variability, Reilly found a wide range of values. The lowest CV was experienced by the low risk 1-year government bond. Japanese stocks had the highest CV value because of their large standard deviation and relatively low returns during this period. The CVs for stocks ranged from 0.70 to 1.75, with U.S. stocks toward the low end due to the strong rates of return during this period. Finally, the Brinson Global Security Market index had a rather low CV (0.67), demonstrating the benefits of global diversification.

CORRELATIONS BETWEEN ASSET RETURNS Table 3.8 is a correlation matrix of selected U.S. and world assets. The first column shows that U.S. equities have a rea-

FIGURE 3.6

GEOMETRIC MEAN RATES OF RETURN AND STANDARD DEVIATION FOR SOTHEBY'S INDEXES, S&P 500, BOND MARKET SERIES, 1-YEAR BONDS, AND INFLATION: 1976–1991

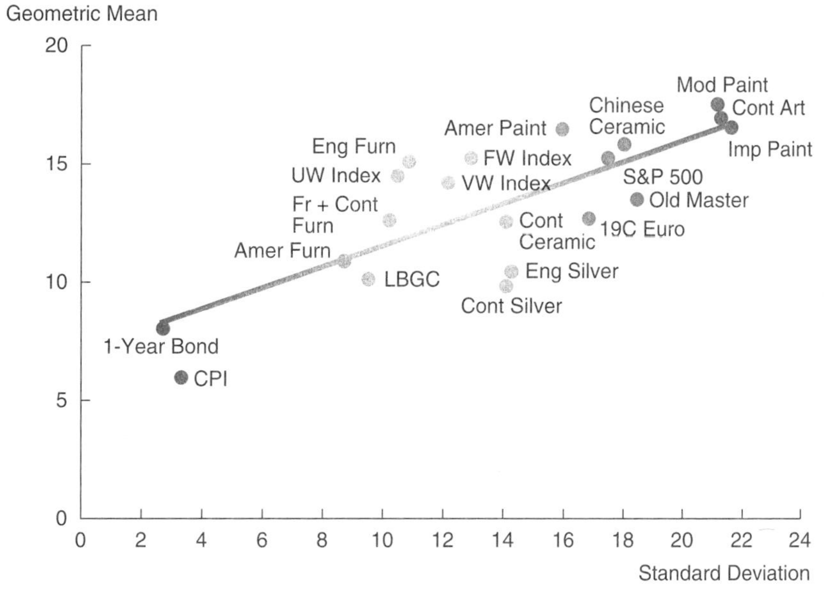
Geometric Mean
20
15
10
5
0
Mod Paint
Chinese Ceramic
Cont Art
Amer Paint
Imp Paint
Eng Furn
FW Index
UW Index
VW Index
S&P 500
Old Master
Fr + Cont Furn
Cont Ceramic
19C Euro
Amer Furn
LBGC
Eng Silver
Cont Silver
1-Year Bond
CPI
0 2 4 6 8 10 12 14 16 18 20 22 24
Standard Deviation

Source: Adapted from Frank K. Reilly, "Risk and Return on Art and Antiques: The Sotheby's Indexes," Eastern Finance Association Meeting, May 1987. (Updated through September 1991.)

sonably high correlation with Canadian and United Kingdom stocks (.754 and .618), but low correlation with emerging market stocks and Japanese stocks (.272 and .291). Also, U.S. equities show a negative correlation with world government bonds (−0.037). You will recall from our earlier discussion that you can use this information to build a diversified portfolio by combining those assets with low positive or negative correlations.

ART AND ANTIQUES

Unlike financial securities, where the results of transactions are reported daily, art and antique markets are fragmented and lack any formal transaction reporting system. This makes it difficult to gather data. The best-known series that attempt to provide information about the changing value of art and antiques were developed by Sotheby's, a major art auction firm. These value indexes cover 13 areas of art and antiques and a weighted aggregate series that is a combination of the 13.

Reilly examined these series for the period from 1976 to 1991 and computed rates of return, measures of risk, and the correlations among the various art and antique series.[17] Figure 3.6 shows these data and compares them with returns for one-year Treasury bonds, the Lehman Brothers Government/Corporate Bond Index, the Standard & Poor's 500 Stock Index, and the annual inflation rate.

These results vary to such a degree that it is impossible to generalize about the performance of art and antiques. As shown, the average annual compound rates of return (measured by the geometric means) ranged from a high of 16.8 percent (modern paintings) to a low of 9.99 percent (English silver). Similarly, the standard deviations varied from 21.67

[17]Frank K. Reilly, "Risk and Return on Art and Antiques: The Sotheby's Indexes," Eastern Finance Association Meeting, May 1987. The results reported are a summary of the study results and have been updated through September 1991.

percent (Impressionist–Postimpressionist paintings) to 8.74 percent (American furniture). The relative risk measures (the coefficients of variation) varied from a high of 1.33 (Continental silver) to a low value of 0.71 (English furniture). The annual rankings likewise changed over time.

Although there was a wide range of mean returns and risk, the risk–return plot in the figure indicates a fairly consistent relationship between risk and return during this 16-year period. Comparing the art and antique results to the bond and stock indexes indicates that the stocks and bonds experienced results in the middle of the art and antique series.

Analysis of the correlation matrix of these assets in Table 3.9 using annual rates of return reveals several important relationships. First, the correlations among alternative antique and art categories (for example, paintings and furniture) vary substantially from above 0.90 to negative correlations. Second, the correlations between rates of return on art/antiques and bonds are generally negative. Third, the correlations of art/antiques with stocks are typically small positive values. Finally, the correlation of art and antiques with percentage changes in the CPI (the rate of inflation) indicates that several of the categories have been fairly good inflation hedges since they were positively correlated with inflation (for example, Chinese ceramics), and they were clearly superior inflation hedges compared to long bonds and common stocks.[18] This would suggest that a properly diversified portfolio of art, antiques, stocks, and bonds might provide a fairly low-risk portfolio. It is important to reiterate the earlier observation that most art and antiques are considered to be quite illiquid and the transaction costs are fairly high compared to the financial assets we have discussed.

Real Estate

Somewhat similar to art and antiques, returns on real estate are difficult to derive because of the limited number of transactions and the lack of a national source of data for the transactions that allows one to accurately compute rates of return. In the study by Goetzmann and Ibbotson, the authors gathered data on commercial real estate through REITs and Commingled Real Estate Funds (CREFs) and estimated returns on residential real estate from a series created by Case and Shiller.[19] The summary of the real estate returns compared to various stock, bond, and an inflation series is contained in Table 3.10. As shown, the two commercial real estate series reflected strikingly different results. The CREFs had lower returns and low volatility, while the REIT index had higher returns and risk. Notably, the REIT returns were higher than those of common stocks, but the risk measure for real estate was lower (there was a small difference in the time period). The residential real estate series reflected lower returns and low risk. The longer-term results indicate that all the real estate series experienced lower returns than common stock, but they also had much lower risk.

Table 3.11 shows the correlations among annual returns for the various asset groups. The results indicate a relatively low positive correlation between commercial real estate and stocks. In contrast, there was negative correlation between stocks and residential real estate and farm real estate. This negative relationship with real estate was also true for 20-year government bonds. Several studies that considered international commercial real

[18]These results for stocks are consistent with Table 3.8 and several prior studies that likewise found a negative relationship between inflation and returns on stocks, which indicates that common stocks have been poor inflation hedges. See Eugene F. Fama, "Stock Returns, Real Activity, Inflation and Money," *American Economic Review* 71, no. 2 (June 1991): 545–565; and Jeffrey Jaffe and Gershon Mandelker, "The 'Fisher Effect' for Risky Assets: An Empirical Investigation," *Journal of Finance* 31, no. 2 (June 1976): 447–458.

[19]William N. Goetzmann and Roger G. Ibbotson, "The Performance of Real Estate as an Asset Class," *Journal of Applied Corporate Finance* 3, no 1 (spring 1990): 65–76; Carl Case and Robert Shiller, "Price of Single Family Homes Since 1970: New Indexes for Four Cities," National Bureau of Economic Research, Inc., Working Paper No. 2393 (1987).

TABLE 3.9

CORRELATION COEFFICIENTS AMONG ANNUAL RATES OF RETURN FOR ART, ANTIQUES, STOCKS, BONDS, AND INFLATION: 1976–1991 (SEPTEMBER YEAR END)

	Old Mast.	19C Euro.	Impr. Pt.-Im.	Mod. Paint.	Cont. Art	Amer. Paint.	Cont. Ceram.	Chin. Ceram.	Engl. Silver	Cont. Silver	Ameri. Furn.	Fr. & Cont. Furn.	Engl. Furn.	Fix Wt. Index	Unwtd. Index	Pr. W. Index	1-yr. T Bond	LBGC Bond	S&P 500	CPI
Old masters paintings	*																			
Nineteenth–century European paintings	0.948	*																		
Impressionist–post impressionist paintings	0.442	0.467	*																	
Modern paintings	0.403	0.473	0.969	*																
Continental art	0.780	0.652	0.566	0.476	*															
American paintings	0.599	0.515	0.464	0.386	0.674	*														
Continental ceramics	0.589	0.584	0.200	0.191	0.227	0.498	*													
Chinese ceramics	0.447	0.419	0.279	0.267	0.279	0.561	0.708	*												
English silver	0.394	0.497	0.117	0.186	0.057	−0.012	0.295	0.098	*											
Continental silver	0.628	0.709	0.354	0.404	0.301	0.054	0.600	0.270	0.729	*										
American furniture	−0.176	−0.204	0.185	0.165	−0.071	0.012	−0.251	−0.167	0.122	−0.168	*									
French and Continental furniture	0.648	0.755	0.116	0.192	0.310	0.143	0.622	0.459	0.541	0.764	−0.379	*								
English furniture	0.234	0.328	0.548	0.605	−0.016	0.433	0.471	0.449	0.105	0.222	0.043	0.178	*							
Fixed-weight index	0.817	0.835	0.851	0.838	0.727	0.637	0.536	0.525	0.359	0.622	0.001	0.525	0.550	*						
Unweighted index	0.859	0.872	0.740	0.731	0.700	0.677	0.666	0.611	0.450	0.686	−0.017	0.620	0.540	0.977	*					
Price-weighted index	0.828	0.826	0.791	0.776	0.733	0.723	0.610	0.593	0.397	0.611	0.000	0.536	0.555	0.984	0.990	*				
One-year Treasury bond	−0.331	−0.376	−0.089	−0.131	0.159	−0.109	−0.570	−0.269	−0.103	−0.302	0.130	−0.248	−0.612	−0.269	−0.309	−0.258	*			
LBGC bond index	−0.169	−0.182	−0.280	−0.308	−0.173	−0.308	−0.422	−0.318	0.052	−0.210	−0.159	−0.328	−0.351	−0.322	−0.366	−0.359	−0.080	*		
S&P 500	0.038	−0.026	−0.082	−0.134	−0.097	−0.127	−0.041	−0.015	−0.031	−0.058	0.144	−0.113	−0.030	−0.075	−0.080	−0.121	−0.224	0.127	*	
Consumer Price Index	0.008	0.010	0.064	0.056	0.161	0.283	0.290	0.462	0.127	0.085	0.118	0.338	−0.024	0.141	0.224	0.227	0.496	−0.647	−0.322	*

Source: Frank K. Reilly, "Risk and Return on Art and Antiques," July 1992.

TABLE 3.10

SUMMARY STATISTICS OF COMMERCIAL AND RESIDENTIAL REAL ESTATE SERIES COMPARED TO STOCKS, BONDS, T-BILLS, AND INFLATION

Series	Date	Geometric Mean	Arithm. Mean	Standard Deviation
ANNUAL RETURNS 1969–1987				
CREF (Comm.)	1969–87	10.8%	10.9%	2.6%
REIT (Comm.)	1972–87	14.2	15.7	15.4
C&S (Res.)	1970–86	8.5	8.6	3.0
S&P (Stocks)	1969–87	9,2	10.5	18.2
LTG (Bonds)	1969–87	7.7	8.4	13.2
TBILL (Bills)	1969–87	7.6	7.6	1.4
CPI (Infl.)	1969–87	6.4	6.4	1.8
ANNUAL RETURNS OVER THE LONG TERM				
I&S (Comm.)	1960–87	8.9%	9.1%	5.0%
CPIHOME (Res.)	1947–86	8.1	8.2	5.2
USDA (Farm)	1947–87	9.6	9.9	8.2
S&P (Stocks)	1947–87	11.4	12.6	16.3
LTG (Bonds)	1947–87	4.2	4.6	9.8
TBILL (Bills)	1947–87	4.9	4.7	3.3
CPI (Infl.)	1947–87	4.5	4.6	3.9

Source: William N. Goetzmann and Roger G. Ibbotson, "The Performance of Real Estate as an Asset Class," *Journal of Applied Corporate Finance* 3, no. 1 (spring 1990): 65–76. Reprinted with permission.

TABLE 3.11

CORRELATIONS OF ANNUAL REAL ESTATE RETURNS WITH THE RETURNS ON OTHER ASSET CLASSES

	I&S	CREF	CPI Home	C&S	Farm	S&P	20-Yr. Gvt.	1-Yr. Gvt.	Infl.
I&S	1								
CREF	0.79	1							
CPI Home	0.52	0.12	1						
C&S	0.26	0.16	0.82	1					
Farm	0.06	−0.06	0.51	0.49	1				
S&P	0.16	0.25	−0.13	−0.20	−0.10	1			
20-Yr. Gvt.	−0.04	0.01	−0.22	−0.54	−0.44	0.11	1		
1-Yr. Gvt.	0.53	0.42	0.13	−0.56	−0.32	−0.07	0.48	1	
Infl.	0.70	0.35	0.77	0.56	0.49	−0.02	−0.17	0.26	1

Note: Correlation coefficient for each pair of asset classes uses the maximum number of observations, that is, the minimum length of the two series in the pair.

Source: William N. Goetzmann and Roger G. Ibbotson, "The Performance of Real Estate as an Asset Class," *Journal of Applied Corporate Finance* 3, no. 1 (spring 1990): 65–76. Reprinted with permission.

estate and REITs indicated the returns were correlated with stock prices, but also provided significant diversification.[20]

These results imply that returns on real estate are equal to or slightly lower than returns on common stocks, but real estate possesses favorable risk results. Specifically, real estate had much lower standard deviations as unique assets, and either low positive or negative correlations with other asset classes in a portfolio context.

[20] P. A. Eichholtz, "Does International Diversification Work Better for Real Estate than for Stocks and Bonds?" *Financial Analysts Journal* 52, no. 1 (January–February 1996): 56–62; S. R. Mull and L. A. Socnen, "U.S. REITs as an Asset Class in International Investment Portfolios," *Financial Analysts Journal* 53, no. 2 (March–April 1997): 55–61; and D. C. Quan and S. Titman, "Commercial Real Estate Prices and Stock Market Returns: An International Analysis," *Financial Analysts Journal* 53, no. 3 (May–June 1997): 21–34.

THE INTERNET *Investments Online*

As this chapter describes, the variety of financial products is huge and potentially confusing to the novice (not to mention the experienced professional). Two good rules of investing are (1) stick to your risk tolerance; many people will try to sell instruments that may not be appropriate for the typical individual investor and (2) don't invest in something if you don't understand it. Web sites mentioned in Chapters 1 and 2 provide useful information on a variety of investments. Below we list a few others that may be of interest.

www.wiso.gwdg.de/ifbg/finance.html This site modestly labels itself as "Finance on the WWW." It contains an international selection of guides, sites, and general information. Among other features, it contains links to bond, stock, mutual fund, futures and options, exchange rates, financial services, and personal finance sites. For the more sophisticated user, links exist to sites that deal with investment research, law and finance, technical analysis, fundamental analysis, and portfolio analysis (topics that are discussed in future chapters!).

www.global-investor.com This site contains information on ADRs, offers global financial information, and allows users to follow the performance of the world's major markets. It provides a number of links to global, regional, and country markets.

www.nfsn.com The home page of the National Financial Services Network offers information on personal and commercial financial products and services, in addition to news, interest rate updates, and stock price quotes.

www.emgmkts.com The Emerging Markets Companion home page contains information on emerging markets in Asia, Latin America, Africa, and Eastern Europe. Available information and links include news, prices, market information, and research.

Other sites of interest include:

www.euro.net/innovation/Finance_Base/Fin_encyc.html This site contains an international financial encyclopedia of investing terms, instruments, and companies.

www.sothebys.com The home page of Sotheby's, Inc., the auction house, contains auction updates and information on collectibles, Internet resources, and featured upcoming sales.

www.christies.com This is the home page of another auction house, Christie's.

Summary

- Investors who want the broadest range of choices in investments must consider foreign stocks and bonds in addition to domestic financial assets. Many foreign securities offer investors higher risk-adjusted returns than do domestic securities. In addition, the low positive or negative correlations between foreign and U.S. securities make them ideal for building a diversified portfolio.
- Figure 3.7 summarizes the risk and return characteristics of the investment alternatives described in this chapter. Some of the differences are due to unique factors that we discussed. Foreign bonds are considered riskier than domestic bonds because of the unavoidable uncertainty due to exchange rate risk and country risk. The same is true for foreign and domestic common stocks. Such investments as art, antiques, coins, and stamps require heavy liquidity risk premiums. You should divide consideration of real estate investments between your personal home, on which you do not expect as high a return because of nonmonetary factors, and commercial real estate, which requires a much higher rate of return due to cash flow uncertainty and illiquidity.
- Studies on the historical rates of return for common stocks and other investment alternatives (including bonds, commodities, real estate, foreign securities, and art and antiques) point toward two generalizations.[21]

  1. A positive relationship typically holds between the rate of return earned on an asset and the variability of its historical rate of return. This is expected in a world of risk-averse investors who require higher rates of return to compensate for more uncertainty.

---

[21]An excellent discussion of global investing and extensive analysis of returns and risks for alternative asset classes is Roger G. Ibbotson and Gary P. Brinson, *Global Investing* (New York: McGraw-Hill, 1993).

FIGURE 3.7 **ALTERNATIVE INVESTMENTS RISK AND RETURN CHARACTERISTICS**

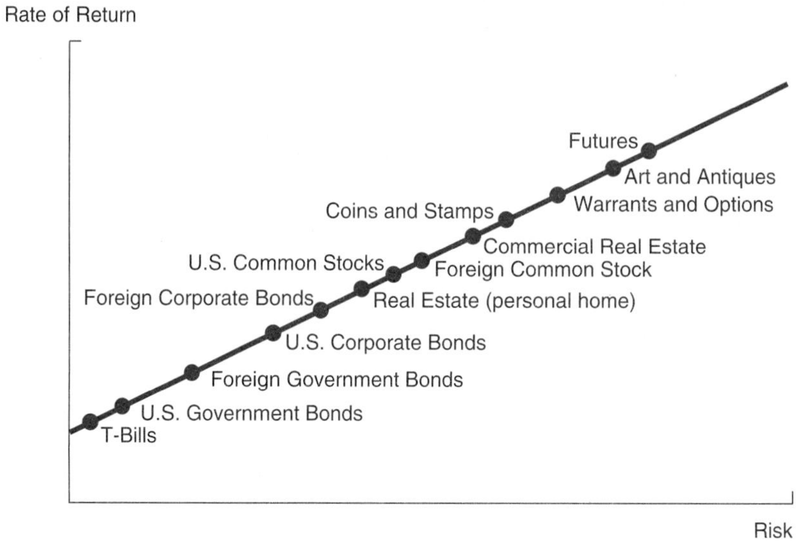
Rate of Return
Futures
Art and Antiques
Warrants and Options
Coins and Stamps
Commercial Real Estate
Foreign Common Stock
U.S. Common Stocks
Foreign Corporate Bonds
Real Estate (personal home)
U.S. Corporate Bonds
Foreign Government Bonds
U.S. Government Bonds
T-Bills
Risk

2. The correlation among rates of return for selected alternative investments is typically quite low, especially for U.S. and foreign stocks and bonds and between these financial assets and real assets, as represented by art, antiques, and real estate. This confirms the advantage of diversification among investments from around the world.

- In addition to describing many direct investments, such as stocks and bonds, we also discussed investment companies that allow investors to buy investments indirectly. These can be important to investors who want to take advantage of professional management but also want instant diversification with a limited amount of funds. With $10,000, you may not be able to buy many individual stocks or bonds, but you could acquire shares in a mutual fund, which would give you a share of a diversified portfolio that might contain 100 to 150 different U.S. and international stocks or bonds.
- Now that we know the range of domestic and foreign investment alternatives, our next task is to learn about the markets in which they are bought and sold. That is the objective of the next chapter. The discussion in Chapter 4 will help us understand how markets match buyers and sellers of investments. Later chapters will describe how investors evaluate the risk and return characteristics of alternative investments to build diversified portfolios that are consistent with their objectives.

Questions

1. What are the advantages of investing in the common stock rather than the corporate bonds of a company? Compare the certainty of returns for a bond with those for a common stock. Draw a line graph to demonstrate the pattern of returns you would envision for each of these assets over time.
2. Discuss three factors that cause U.S. investors to consider including global securities in their portfolios.
3. Discuss why international diversification reduces portfolio risk. Specifically, why would you expect low correlation in the rates of return for domestic and foreign securities?
4. Discuss why you would expect a *difference* in the correlation of returns between securities from the United States and from alternative countries (for example, Japan, Canada, South Africa).
5. Discuss whether you would expect any *change* in the correlations between U.S. stocks and the stocks for different countries. For example, discuss whether you would expect the correlation between U.S. and Japanese stock returns to change over time.
6. When you invest in Japanese or German bonds, what major additional risks must you consider besides yield changes within the country?
7. Some investors believe that international investing introduces additional risks. Discuss these risks and how they can affect your return. Give an example.

8. What alternatives to direct investment in foreign stocks are available to investors?
9. You are a wealthy individual in a high tax bracket. Why might you consider investing in a municipal bond rather than a straight corporate bond, even though the promised yield on the municipal bond is lower?
10. You can acquire convertible bonds from a rapidly growing company or from a utility. Speculate on which convertible bond would have the lower yield and discuss the reason for this difference.
11. Compare the liquidity of an investment in raw land with that of an investment in common stock. Be specific as to why and how they differ. (Hint: Begin by defining *liquidity*.)
12. What are stock warrants and call options? How do they differ?
13. Discuss why financial analysts consider antiques and art to be illiquid investments. Why do they consider coins and stamps to be more liquid than antiques and art? What must an investor typically do to sell a collection of art and antiques? Briefly contrast this procedure to the sale of a portfolio of stocks that are listed on the New York Stock Exchange.
14. You have a fairly large portfolio of U.S. stocks and bonds. You meet a financial planner at a social gathering who suggests that you diversify your portfolio by investing in emerging market stocks. Discuss whether the correlation results in Table 3.8 support this suggestion.
15. You are an avid collector/investor of American paintings. Based on the information in Figure 3.6, describe your risk–return results during the period from 1976 to 1991 compared to U.S. common stocks.
16. CFA *CFA Examination I (1993)*

    Chris Smith of XYZ Pension Plan has historically invested in the stocks of only U.S.-domiciled companies. Recently, he has decided to add international exposure to the plan portfolio.

    a. Identify and briefly discuss *three* potential problems that Smith may confront in selecting international stocks that he did not face in choosing U.S. stocks.
17. CFA *CFA Examination III (1993)*

    TMP has been experiencing increasing demand from its institutional clients for information and assistance related to international investment management. Recognizing that this is an area of growing importance, the firm has hired an experienced analyst/portfolio manager specializing in international equities and market strategy. His first assignment is to represent TMP before a client company's investment committee to discuss the possibility of changing their present "U.S. securities-only" investment approach to one including international investments. He is told that the committee wants a presentation that fully and objectively examines the basic, substantive considerations on which the committee should focus its attention, including both theory and evidence. The company's pension plan has no legal or other barriers to adoption of an international approach; no non-U.S. pension liabilities currently exist.

    a. Identify and briefly discuss *three* reasons for adding international securities to the pension portfolio and *three* problems associated with such an approach.
    b. Assume that the committee has adopted a policy to include international securities in its pension portfolio. Identify and briefly discuss *three* additional *policy-level* investment decisions the committee must make *before* management selection and actual implementation can begin.

Problems

1. Calculate the current horizon (maturity) premium on U.S. government securities based on data in the *Wall Street Journal*. The long-term security should have a maturity of at least 20 years.
2. Using a source of international statistics, compare the percentage change in the following economic data for Japan, Germany, Canada, and the United States for a recent year. What were the differences, and which country or countries differed most from the United States?
    a. Aggregate output (GDP)
    b. Inflation
    c. Money supply growth
3. Using a recent edition of *Barron's*, examine the weekly percentage change in the stock price indexes for Japan, Germany, Italy, and the United States. For each of three weeks, which foreign series moved most closely with the U.S. series? Which series diverged most from the U.S. series? Discuss these results as they relate to international diversification.

4. Using published sources (for example, *The Wall Street Journal, Barron's, Federal Reserve Bulletin*), look up the exchange rate for U.S. dollars with Japanese yen for each of the past 10 years (you can use an average for the year or a specific time period each year). Based on these exchange rates, compute and discuss the yearly exchange rate effect on an investment in Japanese stocks by a U.S. investor. Discuss the impact of this exchange rate effect on the risk of Japanese stocks for a U.S. investor.
5. *CFA Examination* (Adapted)
   The following information is available concerning the historical risk and return relationships in the U.S. capital markets:

U.S. CAPITAL MARKETS TOTAL ANNUAL RETURNS, 1960–1984

Investment Category	Arithmetic Mean	Geometric Mean	Standard Deviation of Return[a]
Common stocks	10.28%	8.81%	16.9%
Treasury bills	6.54	6.49	3.2
Long-term government bonds	6.10	5.91	6.4
Long-term corporate bonds	5.75	5.35	9.6
Real estate	9.49	9.44	3.5

[a]Based on arithmetic mean.

Source: Adapted from R. G. Ibbotson, Laurence B. Siegel, and Kathryn S. Love, "World Wealth: Market Values and Returns," *Journal of Portfolio Management* 12, no. 1 (fall 1985): 4–23.

   a. Explain why the geometric and arithmetic mean returns are not equal and whether one or the other may be more useful for investment decision making. [5 minutes]
   b. For the time period indicated, rank these investments on a risk-adjusted basis from most to least desirable. Explain your rationale. [6 minutes]
   c. Assume the returns in these series are normally distributed.
      1. Calculate the range of returns that an investor would have expected to achieve 95 percent of the time from holding common stocks. [4 minutes]
      2. Suppose an investor holds real estate for this time period. Determine the probability of at least breaking even on this investment. [5 minutes]
   d. Assume you are holding a portfolio composed entirely of real estate. Discuss the justification, if any, for adopting a mixed asset portfolio by adding long-term government bonds. [5 minutes]
6. You are given the following long-run annual rates of return for alternative investment instruments:

U.S. Government T-bills	4.50%
Large-cap common stock	12.50%
Long-term corporate bonds	5.80%
Long-term government bonds	5.10%
Small-capitalization common stock	14.60%

   a. On the basis of these returns, compute the following:
      1. The common-stock risk premium
      2. The small-firm stock risk premium
      3. The horizon (maturity) premium
      4. The default premium
   b. The annual rate of inflation during this period was 4 percent. Compute the real rate of return on these investment alternatives.

References

Elton, Edwin J., and Martin J. Gruber, eds. *Japanese Capital Markets*. New York: Harper & Row Publishers, 1990.

European Bond Commission. *The European Bond Markets*. Chicago: Probus Publishing, 1989.

Fabozzi, Frank J., ed. *The Japanese Bond Markets*. Chicago: Probus Publishing, 1990.

Fisher, Lawrence, and James H. Lorie. *A Half Century of Returns on Stocks and Bonds*. Chicago: University of Chicago Graduate School of Business, 1977.

Grabbe, J. Orlin. *International Financial Markets*. New York: Elsevier Science Publishing, 1986.

Hamao, Yasushi. "Japanese Stocks, Bonds, Inflation, 1973–1987." *Journal of Portfolio Management* 16, no. 2 (winter 1989).

lbbotson, Roger G., and Gary P. Brinson. *Global Investing*. New York: McGraw-Hill, 1993.

Lessard, Donald R. "International Diversification." In *The Financial Analyst's Handbook*, 2d ed., ed. Sumner N. Levine. Homewood, Ill.: Dow Jones–Irwin, 1988.

Malvey, Jack. "Global Corporate Bond Portfolio Management." In *The Handbook of Fixed-Income Securities*, 5th ed., ed. Frank J. Fabozzi. Chicago, Ill: Irwin Professional Publishing, 1997.

Murphy, Brian, David Won, and Deepak Gulrajani. "Valuation and Risk Analysis of International Bonds." In *The Handbook of Fixed-Income Securities,* 4th ed., ed. Frank J. Fabozzi and T. Dessa Fabozzi. Burr Ridge, Ill.: Irwin Professional Publishing, 1995.

Reilly, Frank K., and David J. Wright. "Global Bond Markets: An Analysis of Alternative Benchmarks and Risk–Return Performance." Midwest Finance Association Meeting (March 1995).

Rosenberg, Michael R. " International Fixed-Income Investing: Theory and Practice." In *The Handbook of Fixed-Income Securities,* 5th ed., ed. Frank J. Fabozzi. Chicago, Ill.: Irwin Professional Publishing, 1997.

Siegel, Laurence B., and Paul D. Kaplan. "Stocks, Bonds, Bills, and Inflation Around the World." In *Managing Institutional Assets*, ed. Frank J. Fabozzi. New York: Harper & Row, 1990.

Solnik, Bruno. *International Investments*, 4th ed., Reading, Mass.: Addison-Wesley Publishing, 2000.

Steward, Christopher, and Adam Greshin, "International Bond Markets and Instruments." In *The Handbook of Fixed-Income Securities,* 5th ed., ed. Frank J. Fabozzi. Chicago, Ill.: Irwin Professional Publishing, 1997.

Van der Does, Rein W. "Investing in Foreign Securities." In *The Financial Analyst's Handbook*, 2d ed., ed. Sumner N. Levine. Homewood, Ill.: Dow Jones–Irwin, 1988.

Wilson, Richard S., and Frank J. Fabozzi. *The New Corporate Bond Market.* Chicago: Probus Publishing, 1990.

Chapter 3 APPENDIX — COVARIANCE AND CORRELATION

COVARIANCE

Because most students have been exposed to the concepts of covariance and correlation, the following discussion is set forth in intuitive terms with examples to help the reader recall the concepts.[22]

Covariance is an absolute measure of the extent to which two sets of numbers move together over time, that is, how often they move up or down together. In this regard, *move*

[22]A more detailed, rigorous treatment of the subject can be found in any standard statistics text, including S. Christian Albright, *Statistics for Business and Economics* (New York: Macmillan, 1987), 63–67.

TABLE 3A.1 **CALCULATION OF COVARIANCE**

Observation	i	j	$i - \bar{i}$	$j - \bar{j}$	$i'j'$
1	3	8	−4	−4	16
2	6	10	−1	−2	2
3	8	14	+1	+2	2
4	5	12	−2	0	0
5	9	13	+2	+1	2
6	11	15	+4	+3	12
Σ	42	72			34
Mean	7	12			
Cov_{ij}	$= \frac{34}{6} = +5.67$				

together means they are generally above their means or below their means at the same time. Covariance between i and j is defined as:

$$\text{COV}_{ij} = \frac{\Sigma(i - \bar{i})(j - \bar{j})}{N}$$

If we define $(i - \bar{i})$ as i' and $(j - \bar{j})$ as j', then

$$\text{COV}_{ij} = \frac{\Sigma i'j'}{N}$$

Obviously, if both numbers are consistently above or below their individual means at the same time, their products will be positive, and the average will be a large positive value. In contrast, if the i value is below its mean when the j value is above its mean or vice versa, their products will be large negative values, giving negative covariance.

Table 3A.1 should make this clear. In this example, the two series generally moved together, so they showed positive covariance. As noted, this is an *absolute* measure of their relationship and, therefore, can range from $+\infty$ to $-\infty$. Note that the covariance of a variable with itself is its *variance*.

CORRELATION To obtain a relative measure of a given relationship, we use the correlation coefficient (r_{ij}), which is a measure of the relationship:

$$r_{ij} = \frac{\text{COV}_{ij}}{\sigma_i \sigma_j}$$

You will recall from your introductory statistics course that:

$$\sigma_i = \sqrt{\frac{\Sigma(i - \bar{i})^2}{N}}$$

If the two series move completely together, then the covariance would equal $\sigma_i\sigma_j$ and:

$$\frac{\text{COV}_{ij}}{\sigma_i \sigma_j} = 1.0$$

The correlation coefficient would equal unity in this case, and we would say the two series are perfectly correlated. Because we know that:

TABLE 3A.2 **CALCULATION OF CORRELATION COEFFICIENT**

Observation	$i - \bar{i}^a$	$(i - \bar{i})^2$	$j - \bar{j}^a$	$(j - \bar{j})^2$
1	−4	16	−4	16
2	−1	1	−2	4
3	+1	1	+2	4
4	−2	4	0	0
5	+2	4	+1	1
6	+4	16	+3	9
		42		34

$\sigma_j^2 = 42/6 = 7.00$ $\qquad\sigma_j^2 = 34/6 = 5.67$

$\sigma_j = \sqrt{7.00} = 2.65$ $\qquad\sigma_j = \sqrt{5.67} = 2.38$

$$r_{ij} = COV_{ij}/\sigma_i\sigma_j = \frac{5.67}{(2.65)(2.38)} = \frac{5.67}{6.31} = 0.898$$

$$r_{ij} = \frac{COV_{ij}}{\sigma_i\sigma_j}$$

we also know that $COV_{ij} = r_{ij}\sigma_i\sigma_j$. This relationship may be useful when computing the standard deviation of a portfolio, because in many instances the relationship between two securities is stated in terms of the correlation coefficient rather than the covariance.

Continuing the example given in Table 3A.1, the standard deviations are computed in Table 3A.2, as is the correlation between *i* and *j*. As shown, the two standard deviations are rather large and similar, but not exactly the same. Finally, when the positive covariance is normalized by the product of the two standard deviations, the results indicate a correlation coefficient of 0.898, which is obviously quite large and close to 1.00. Apparently, these two series are highly related.

PROBLEMS

1. As a new analyst, you have calculated the following annual rates of return for both Lauren Corporation and Kayleigh Industries.

Year	Lauren's Rate of Return	Kayleigh's Rate of Return
1996	5	5
1997	12	15
1998	−11	5
1999	10	7
2000	12	−10

Your manager suggests that because these companies produce similar products, you should continue your analysis by computing their covariance. Show all calculations.

2. You decide to go an extra step by calculating the coefficient of correlation using the data provided in Problem 1 above. Prepare a table showing your calculations and explain how to interpret the results. Would the combination of Lauren and Kayleigh be good for diversification?

Chapter

4 Organization and Functioning of Securities Markets*

After you read this chapter, you should be able to answer the following questions:

- What is the purpose and function of a market?
- What are the characteristics that determine the quality of a market?
- What is the difference between a primary and secondary capital market and how do these markets support each other?
- What are the national exchanges and how are the major securities markets around the world becoming linked (what is meant by "passing the book")?
- What are regional stock exchanges and over-the-counter (OTC) markets?
- What are the alternative market-making arrangements available on the exchanges and the OTC market?
- What are the major types of orders available to investors and market makers?
- What are the major functions of the specialist on the NYSE and how does the specialist differ from the central market maker on other exchanges?
- What are the major factors that have caused significant changes in markets around the world during the past 15 years?
- What are some of the major changes in world capital markets expected over the next decade?

The stock market, the Dow Jones Industrials, and the bond market are part of our everyday experience. Each evening on the television news broadcasts we find out how stocks and bonds fared; each morning we read in our daily newspapers about expectations for a market rally or decline. Yet most people have an imperfect understanding of how domestic and world capital markets actually function. To be a successful investor in a global environment, you must know what financial markets are available around the world and how they operate.

In Chapter 1, we considered why individuals invest and what determines their required rate of return on investments. In Chapter 2, we discussed the life cycle for investors and the alternative asset allocation decisions by investors during different phases. In Chapter 3, we learned about the numerous alternative investments available and why we should diversify with securities from around the world. This chapter takes a broad view of securities

*The authors acknowledge helpful comments on this chapter from Robert Battalio of Georgia State University and Paul Schultz of the University of Notre Dame.

markets and provides a detailed discussion of how major stock markets function. We conclude with a consideration of how global securities markets are changing.

We begin with a discussion of securities markets and the characteristics of a good market. Two components of the capital markets are described: primary and secondary. Our main emphasis in this chapter is on the secondary stock market. We consider the national stock exchanges around the world and how these markets, separated by geography and by time zones, are becoming linked into a 24-hour market. We also consider regional stock markets and the over-the-counter market and provide a detailed analysis of how alternative exchange markets operate. The final section considers numerous historical changes in financial markets since the mid-1970s, additional current changes, and significant changes expected into the next century. These numerous changes in our securities markets will have a profound effect on what investments are available to you from around the world and how you buy and sell them.

WHAT IS A MARKET?

This section provides the necessary background for understanding different securities markets around the world and the changes that are occurring. The first part considers the general concept of a market and its function. The second part describes the characteristics that determine how well a particular market will fulfill its function. The third part of the section describes primary and secondary capital markets and how they interact and depend on one another.

A **market** is the means through which buyers and sellers are brought together to aid in the transfer of goods and/or services. Several aspects of this general definition seem worthy of emphasis. First, a market need not have a physical location. It is only necessary that the buyers and sellers can communicate regarding the relevant aspects of the transaction.

Second, the market does not necessarily own the goods or services involved. When we discuss what is required for a good market, you will note that ownership is not involved; the important criterion is the smooth, cheap transfer of goods and services. In most financial markets, those who establish and administer the market do not own the assets. They simply provide a physical location or an electronic system that allows potential buyers and sellers to interact, and they help the market function by providing information and facilities to aid in the transfer of ownership.

Finally, a market can deal in any variety of goods and services. For any commodity or service with a diverse clientele, a market should evolve to aid in the transfer of that commodity or service. Both buyers and sellers will benefit from the existence of a market. Basically, we take markets for granted because they are vital to a smooth-operating economy. Still, it is important to recognize that the quality of alternative markets can differ.

CHARACTERISTICS OF A GOOD MARKET

Throughout this book, we will discuss markets for different investments, such as stocks, bonds, options, and futures, in the United States and throughout the world. We will refer to these markets using various terms of quality, such as *strong, active, liquid,* or *illiquid.* There are many financial markets, but they are not all equal—some are active and liquid, others are relatively illiquid, and inefficient in their operations. To appreciate these discussions, you should be aware of the characteristics that investors look for when evaluating the quality of a market. In this section, we describe those characteristics.

One enters a market to buy or sell a good or service quickly at a price justified by the prevailing supply and demand. To determine the appropriate price, participants must have timely and accurate information on the volume and prices of past transactions and on all currently outstanding bids and offers. Therefore, one attribute of a good market is *availability of* **information.**

Another prime requirement is **liquidity**, the ability to buy or sell an asset quickly and at a known price—that is, a price not substantially different from the prices for prior transactions, assuming no new information is available. An asset's likelihood of being sold quickly, sometimes referred to as its *marketability,* is a necessary, but not a sufficient, condition for liquidity. The expected price should also be fairly certain, based on the recent history of transaction prices and current bid-ask quotes.[1]

A component of liquidity is **price continuity**, which means that prices do not change much from one transaction to the next unless substantial new information becomes available. Suppose no new information is forthcoming, and the last transaction was at a price of $20; if the next trade were at 20 1/16, the market would be considered reasonably continuous.[2] A continuous market without large price changes between trades is a characteristic of a liquid market.

A market with price continuity requires *depth,* which means that numerous potential buyers and sellers must be willing to trade at prices above and below the current market price. These buyers and sellers enter the market in response to changes in supply and demand or both and thereby prevent drastic price changes. In summary, liquidity requires marketability and price continuity, which, in turn, require depth.

Another factor contributing to a good market is the **transaction cost**. Lower costs (as a percent of the value of the trade) make for a more efficient market. An individual comparing the cost of a transaction between markets would choose a market that charges 2 percent of the value of the trade compared with one that charges 5 percent. Most microeconomic textbooks define an efficient market as one in which the cost of the transaction is minimal. This attribute is referred to as *internal efficiency.*

Finally, a buyer or seller wants the prevailing market price to adequately reflect all the information available regarding supply and demand factors in the market. If such conditions change as a result of new information, the price should change accordingly. Therefore, participants want prices to adjust quickly to new information regarding supply or demand, which means that prices reflect all available information about the asset. This attribute is referred to as **external efficiency** or **informational efficiency**. This attribute is discussed extensively in Chapter 7.

In summary, a good market for goods and services has the following characteristics:

1. Timely and accurate information is available on the price and volume of past transactions and the prevailing bid and ask prices.
2. It is liquid, meaning an asset can be bought or sold quickly at a price close to the prices for previous transactions (has price continuity), assuming no new information has been received. In turn, price continuity requires depth.
3. Transactions entail low costs, including the cost of reaching the market, the actual brokerage costs, and the cost of transferring the asset.
4. Prices rapidly adjust to new information; thus the prevailing price is fair because it reflects all available information regarding the asset.

---

[1]For a more formal discussion of liquidity and the effects of different market systems, see Sanford J. Grossman and Merton H. Miller, "Liquidity and Market Structure," *Journal of Finance* 43, no. 3 (July 1988): 617–633; and Puneet Handa and Robert A. Schwartz, "How Best to Supply Liquidity to a Securities Market," *Journal of Portfolio Management* 22, no. 2 (winter 1996): 44–51.

[2]You should be aware that common stocks are sold in increments of sixteenths of a dollar, or $0.0625. Therefore, 20 1/16 means the stock sold at $20.0625 per share.

ORGANIZATION OF THE SECURITIES MARKET

Before discussing the specific operation of the securities market, you need to understand its overall organization. The principal distinction is between **primary markets**, where new securities are sold, and **secondary markets,** where outstanding securities are bought and sold. Each of these markets is further divided based on the economic unit that issued the security. The following discussion considers each of these major segments of the securities market with an emphasis on the individuals involved and the functions they perform.

PRIMARY CAPITAL MARKETS

The primary market is where new issues of bonds, preferred stock, or common stock are sold by government units, municipalities, or companies to acquire new capital.[3]

GOVERNMENT BOND ISSUES

All U.S. government bond issues are subdivided into three segments based on their original maturities. **Treasury bills** are negotiable, non-interest-bearing securities with original maturities of one year or less. They are currently issued for three months, six months, or one year. **Treasury notes** have original maturities of 2 to 10 years, and they have generally been issued with 2-, 3-, 4-, 5-, 7-, and 10-year terms. Finally, **Treasury bonds** have original maturities of more than 10 years.

To sell bills, notes, and bonds, the Treasury relies on Federal Reserve System auctions. In an auction held each week, institutions and some individuals submit bids for T-bills at prices below par that imply specific yields. (The bidding process and pricing are discussed in detail in Chapter 15.)

Treasury notes and bonds are likewise sold at auction by the Federal Reserve, but the bids state yields rather than prices. That is, the Treasury specifies how much it wants and when the notes or bonds will mature. After receiving the competitive bid yields and quantity, the Treasury determines the stop-out yield bid (the highest yield it will accept) based on the bids received and how much it wants to borrow. The Fed also receives many noncompetitive bids from investors who are willing to pay the average price of the accepted competitive tenders. All noncompetitive bids are accepted.

MUNICIPAL BOND ISSUES

New municipal bond issues are sold by one of three methods: competitive bid, negotiation, or private placement. Competitive bid sales typically involve sealed bids. The bond issue is sold to the bidding syndicate of underwriters that submits the bid with the lowest interest cost in accordance with the stipulations set forth by the issuer. Negotiated sales involve contractual arrangements between underwriters and issuers wherein the underwriter helps the issuer prepare the bond issue and set the price and has the exclusive right to sell the issue. Private placements involve the sale of a bond issue by the issuer directly to an investor or a small group of investors (usually institutions).

Note that two of the three methods require an *underwriting* function. Specifically, in a competitive bid or a negotiated transaction, the investment banker typically underwrites the issue, which means the firm purchases the entire issue at a specified price, relieving the issuer from the risk and responsibility of selling and distributing the bonds. Subsequently, the underwriter sells the issue to the investing public. For municipal bonds, this underwriting function is performed by both investment banking firms and commercial banks.

---

[3]For an excellent set of studies related to the primary market, see Michael C. Jensen and Clifford W. Smith, Jr., eds., "Symposium on Investment Banking and the Capital Acquisition Process," *Journal of Financial Economics* 15, no. 1/2 (January–February 1986).

The underwriting function can involve three services: origination, risk-bearing, and distribution. Origination involves the design of the bond issue and initial planning. To fulfill the risk-bearing function, the underwriter acquires the total issue at a price dictated by the competitive bid or through negotiation and accepts the responsibility and risk of reselling it for more than the purchase price. Distribution means selling it to investors, typically with the help of a selling syndicate that includes other investment banking firms or commercial banks.

In a negotiated bid, the underwriter will carry out all three services. In a competitive bid, the issuer specifies the amount, maturities, coupons, and call features of the issue and the competing syndicates submit a bid for the entire issue that reflects the yields they estimate for the bonds. The issuer may have received advice from an investment firm on the desirable characteristics for a forthcoming issue, but this advice would have been on a fee basis and would not necessarily involve the ultimate underwriter who is responsible for risk-bearing and distribution. Finally, a private placement involves no risk-bearing, but an investment banker could assist in locating potential buyers and negotiating the characteristics of the issue.

Municipal bonds are either general obligation (GO) bonds that are backed by the full taxing power of the municipality, or revenue bonds that are dependent on the revenues from a specific project that was funded by an issue, such as a toll road, a hospital, or a sewage system. Commercial banks dominate the management of GO bond sales, and investment banking firms dominate revenue bond sales.

The municipal bond market has experienced two major trends during the past decade. First, it has shifted toward negotiated bond issues versus competitive bids. Currently, about 75 percent of issues are negotiated deals. Second, the market has shifted toward revenue bonds, wherein almost 70 percent of the market is revenue issues. These two trends are related because revenue issues tend to be negotiated underwritings. Although many states require that GO bond issues be sold through competitive bidding, they seldom impose such a requirement on revenue issues.[4]

Corporate Bond and Stock Issues

Corporate securities include bond and stock issues. Corporate bond issues are almost always sold through a negotiated arrangement with an investment banking firm that maintains a relationship with the issuing firm. In a global capital market that involves an explosion of new instruments, the origination function is becoming more important because the corporate chief financial officer (CFO) will probably not be completely familiar with the availability and issuing requirements of many new instruments and the alternative capital markets around the world. Investment banking firms compete for underwriting business by creating new instruments that appeal to existing investors and by advising issuers regarding desirable countries and currencies. As a result, the expertise of the investment banker can help reduce the issuer's cost of new capital.

Once a stock or bond issue is specified, the underwriter will put together a syndicate of other major underwriters and a selling group for its distribution. For common stock, **new issues** are typically divided into two groups. The first and largest group is *seasoned* new issues that are offered by companies that have outstanding stock with existing public markets. For example, in 1995 General Motors sold a new issue of common stock. General Motors common stock already had a large and active market, and the company decided to

---

[4]For a further discussion, see David S. Kidwell and Eric H. Sorensen, "Investment Banking and the Underwriting of New Municipal Issues," in *The Municipal Bond Handbook,* ed. F. J. Fabozzi, S. G. Feldstein, I. M. Pollack, and F. G. Zarb (Homewood, Ill.: Dow Jones/Irwin, 1983).

issue new shares, which increased the number of outstanding shares, to acquire new equity capital.

The second major category of new stock issues is referred to as **initial public offerings (IPOs)**, wherein a company decides to sell common stock to the public for the first time. At the time of an IPO offering, there is no existing public market for the stock, that is, the company has been closely held. An example would be an IPO by Polo Ralph Lauren in 1997, at $26 per share. The company is a leading manufacturer and distributor of men's clothing. The purpose of the offering was to get additional capital to expand its operations.

New issues (seasoned or IPOs) are typically underwritten by investment bankers, who acquire the total issue from the company and sell the securities to interested investors. The underwriter gives advice to the corporation on the general characteristics of the issue, its pricing, and the timing of the offering. The underwriter also accepts the risk of selling the new issue after acquiring it from the corporation.[5]

RELATIONSHIPS WITH INVESTMENT BANKERS The underwriting of corporate issues typically takes one of three forms: negotiated, competitive bids, or best-efforts arrangements. As noted, negotiated underwritings are the most common, and the procedure is the same as for municipal issues.

A corporation may also specify the type of securities to be offered (common stock, preferred stock, or bonds) and then solicit competitive bids from investment banking firms. This is rare for industrial firms but is typical for utilities, which may be required to sell the issue via a competitive bid by state laws. Although competitive bids typically reduce the cost of an issue, they also bring fewer services from the investment banker. The banker gives less advice but still accepts the risk-bearing function by underwriting the issue and fulfills the distribution function.

Alternatively, an investment banker can agree to support an issue and sell it on a *best-efforts basis.* This is usually done with speculative new issues. In this arrangement, the investment banker does not underwrite the issue because it does not buy any securities. The stock is owned by the company, and the investment banker acts *as a broker* to sell whatever it can at a stipulated price. The investment banker earns a lower commission on such an issue than on an underwritten issue. With any of these arrangements, the lead investment banker will typically form an underwriting syndicate of other investment bankers to spread the risk and also help in the sales. In addition, if the issue is large, the lead underwriter and underwriting syndicate will form a selling group of smaller firms to help in the distribution.

INTRODUCTION OF RULE 415 The typical practice of negotiated arrangements involving numerous investment banking firms in syndicates and selling groups has changed with the introduction of Rule 415, which allows large firms to register security issues and sell them piecemeal during the following two years. These issues are referred to as *shelf registrations* because, after they are registered, the issues lie on the shelf and can be taken down and sold on short notice whenever it suits the issuing firm. As an example, General Electric could register an issue of 5 million shares of common stock during 1999 and sell a million shares in early 2000, another million shares late in 2000, 2 million shares in early 2001, and the rest in late 2001.

Each offering can be made with little notice or paperwork by one underwriter or several. In fact, because relatively few shares may be involved, the lead underwriter often handles

---

[5]For an extended discussion of the underwriting process, see Richard A. Brealey and Stewart C. Myers, *Principles of Corporate Finance,* 6th ed. (New York: McGraw-Hill, 1997), Chapter 15.

the whole deal without a syndicate or uses only one or two other firms. This arrangement has benefited large corporations because it provides great flexibility, reduces registration fees and expenses, and allows firms issuing securities to request competitive bids from several investment banking firms.

On the other hand, some observers fear that shelf registrations do not allow investors enough time to examine the current status of the firm issuing the securities. Also, the follow-up offerings reduce the participation of small underwriters because the underwriting syndicates are smaller and selling groups are almost nonexistent. Shelf registrations have typically been used for the sale of straight debentures rather than common stock or convertible issues.[6]

Private Placements and Rule 144A

Rather than a public sale using one of these arrangements, primary offerings can be sold privately. In such an arrangement, referred to as a **private placement**, the firm designs an issue with the assistance of an investment banker and sells it to a small group of institutions. The firm enjoys lower issuing costs because it does not need to prepare the extensive registration statement required for a public offering. The institution that buys the issue typically benefits because the issuing firm passes some of these cost savings on to the investor as a higher return. In fact, the institution should require a higher return because of the absence of any secondary market for these securities, which implies higher liquidity risk.

The private placement market has been changed dramatically by the introduction of Rule 144A by the SEC. This rule allows corporations—including non-U.S. firms—to place securities privately with large, sophisticated institutional investors without extensive registration documents. The SEC intends to provide more financing alternatives for U.S. and non-U.S. firms and possibly increase the number, size, and liquidity of private placements.[7]

SECONDARY FINANCIAL MARKETS

In this section, we consider the purpose and importance of secondary markets and provide an overview of the secondary markets for bonds, financial futures, and stocks. Next, we consider national stock markets around the world. Finally, we will discuss regional and over-the-counter stock markets and provide a detailed presentation on the functioning of stock exchanges.

Secondary markets permit trading in outstanding issues; that is, stocks or bonds already sold to the public are traded between current and potential owners. The proceeds from a sale in the secondary market do not go to the issuing unit (the government, municipality, or company), but rather to the current owner of the security.

Why Secondary Markets Are Important

Before discussing the various segments of the secondary market, we must consider its overall importance. Because the secondary market involves the trading of securities initially sold in the primary market, *it provides liquidity to the individuals who acquired these securities.* After acquiring securities in the primary market, investors want to sell them again to acquire other securities, buy a house, or go on a vacation. The primary market

---

[6]For further discussion of Rule 415, see Robert J. Rogowski and Eric H. Sorensen, "Deregulation in Investment Banking: Shelf Registration, Structure and Performance," *Financial Management* 14, no. 1 (spring 1985): 5–15.

[7]For a discussion of the rule and private placements, see Michael Siconolfi and Kevin Salwen, "SEC Ready to Ease Private-Placement Rules," *Wall Street Journal,* 13 April 1990, C1, C5. For a discussion of some reactions to Rule 144A, see John W. Milligan, "Two Cheers for 144A," *Institutional Investor* 24, no. 9 (July 1990): 117–119; and Sara Hanks, "SEC Ruling Creates a New Market," *Wall Street Journal,* 16 May 1990, A12.

benefits greatly from the liquidity provided by the secondary market because investors would hesitate to acquire securities in the primary market if they thought they could not subsequently sell them in the secondary market. That is, without an active secondary market, potential issuers of stocks or bonds would have to provide a much higher rate of return to compensate investors for the substantial liquidity risk.

Secondary markets are also important to issuers because the prevailing market price of the securities is determined by transactions in the secondary market. New issues of outstanding stocks or bonds to be sold in the primary market are based on prices and yields in the secondary market. As a result, capital costs for the government, municipalities, and corporations are determined by investor expectations and actions that are reflected in market prices prevailing in the secondary market.[8] Even nonpublic IPOs are priced based on the prices and values of comparable stocks or bonds in the public secondary market.

SECONDARY BOND MARKETS

The secondary market for bonds distinguishes among those issued by the federal government, municipalities, or corporations.

SECONDARY MARKETS FOR U.S. GOVERNMENT AND MUNICIPAL BONDS U.S. government bonds are traded by bond dealers that specialize in either Treasury bonds or agency bonds. Treasury issues are bought or sold through a set of 35 primary dealers, including large banks in New York City and Chicago and some of the large investment banking firms (for example, Merrill Lynch, First Boston, Morgan Stanley Dean Witter). These institutions and other firms also make markets for government agency issues, but there is no formal set of dealers for agency securities.[9]

The major market makers in the secondary municipal bond market are banks and investment firms. Banks are active in municipal bond trading because they are involved in the underwriting of general obligation issues and they commit large parts of their investment portfolios to these securities. Also, many large investment firms have municipal bond departments that are active in underwriting and trading these issues.

SECONDARY CORPORATE BOND MARKETS The secondary market for corporate bonds has two major segments: security exchanges and an over-the-counter (OTC) market. The major exchange for corporate bonds is the New York Stock Exchange Fixed Income Market. By the end of 1998, more than 1,200 corporate bond issues were listed on this exchange with a combined par value of about $265 billion and a combined market value of approximately $270 billion.[10] On a typical day, there are about 1,600 trades with a total volume of about $31 million. Notably, currently all the trading on the NYSE's bond market is done through its *Automated Bond System (ABS),* which is a fully automated

---

[8]In the literature on market microstructure, it is noted that secondary markets also have an effect on market efficiency, the volatility of security prices, and the serial correlation in security returns. In this regard, see F. D. Foster and S. Viswanathan, "The Effects of Public Information and Competition on Trading Volume and Price Volatility," *Review of Financial Studies* 6, no. 1 (spring 1993): 23–56; C. N. Jones, G. Kaul, and M. L. Lipson, "Information, Trading and Volatility," *Journal of Financial Economics* 36, no. 1 (August 1994): 127–154; H. Bessembinder, Kalok Chan, and P. J. Sequin, "An Empirical Examination of Information Differences of Opinion, and Trading Activity," *Journal of Financial Economics* 40, no. 1 (January 1996): 105–134.

[9]For a discussion of non-U.S. bond markets, see European Bond Commission, *The European Bond Markets* (Chicago: Probus Publishing, 1989); and Frank J. Fabozzi, ed., *The Japanese Bond Market* (Chicago: Probus Publishing, 1990).

[10]*NYSE Fact Book* (New York: NYSE, 1999), 82. If you include U.S. government issues and non-U.S. issues of companies, banks, and governments, there are almost 2,100 issues with a par value and market value of more than $2,700 billion.

trading and information system that allows subscribing firms to enter and execute bond orders through terminals in their offices.[11] Users receive immediate execution reports and locked-in compared trades. In addition, 92 issues are listed on the American Stock Exchange (AMEX) with par value of over $11 billion, a total market value of almost $10 billion, and typical daily trading volume in excess of $1.4 million.

All corporate bonds not listed on one of the exchanges are traded over-the-counter by dealers who buy and sell for their own accounts. In sharp contrast to what occurs for stocks where most of the trading takes place on the national exchanges, such as the NYSE, in the United States about 90 percent of *corporate bond trades occur on the OTC market.* Virtually all large trades are carried out on the OTC market, even for the bonds that are listed on an exchange. The fact is, the NYSE bond market is considered the "odd-lot" market for bonds. As such, the prices reported on the exchanges are generally considered to be inexact estimates of prices associated with large transactions.[12]

The major bond dealers are the large investment banking firms that underwrite the issues, such as Merrill Lynch, Goldman Sachs, Salomon Smith Barney, Lehman Brothers, and Morgan Stanley Dean Witter. Because of the limited trading in corporate bonds compared to the fairly active trading in government bonds, corporate bond dealers do not carry extensive inventories of specific issues. Instead, they hold a limited number of bonds desired by their clients, and when someone wants to do a trade, they work more like brokers than dealers.

Financial Futures

In addition to the market for the bonds, a market has developed for futures contracts related to these bonds. These contracts allow the holder to buy or sell a specified amount of a given bond issue at a stipulated price. The two major futures exchanges are the Chicago Board of Trade (CBOT) and the Chicago Mercantile Exchange (CME). These futures contracts and the futures market are discussed in Chapters 11 and 23.

Secondary Equity Markets

The secondary equity market has historically been broken down into three major segments: (1) the major national stock exchanges, including exchanges in New York, Tokyo, London, Frankfurt, and Paris; (2) regional stock exchanges in such cities as Chicago, San Francisco, Boston, Osaka and Nagoya in Japan, and Dublin in Ireland; and (3) the over-the-counter (OTC) market, which involves trading in stocks not listed on an organized exchange. While it is still appropriate to discuss the overall structure in these terms, there has been a major trend toward consolidation and affiliation in this segment of global capital markets beginning in 1998 that should be understood. Therefore, following a discussion of alternative trading systems and market operations, we consider the trend toward consolidation of exchanges.

The first two segments, referred to as *listed securities exchanges,* differ in size and geographic emphasis. Both are composed of formal organizations with specific members and specific securities (stocks or bonds) that have qualified for listing. Although the exchanges typically consider similar factors when evaluating firms that apply for listing, the level of requirement differs (the national exchanges have more stringent requirements). Also, the prices of securities listed on alternative stock exchanges are determined using several different trading (pricing) systems that will be discussed in the next section.

---

[11]Gregory Zuckerman, "Electronic Trading in Bond Market Is Slow to Catch On," *Wall Street Journal,* 3 June 1998, C1.

[12]For an empirical analysis of the differences, see Arthur D. Warga, "Corporate Bond Price Discrepancies in the Dealer and Exchange Markets," *Journal of Fixed Income* 1, no. 3 (December 1991): 7–16.

SECURITIES EXCHANGES As indicated, the secondary stock market is composed of three segments: national stock exchanges, regional stock exchanges, and the over-the-counter market. We will discuss each of these separately because they differ in importance within countries and they have different trading systems. As an investor interested in trading global securities, you should be aware of these differences. Following a brief discussion of alternative trading systems and a consideration of call versus continuous markets, we describe the three segments of the equity market.

Alternative Trading Systems Although stock exchanges are similar in that only qualified stocks can be traded by individuals who are members of the exchange, they can differ in their *trading systems.* There are two major trading systems, and an exchange can use one of these or a combination of them. One is a *pure auction market,* in which interested buyers and sellers submit bid and ask prices for a given stock to a central location where the orders are matched by a broker who does not own the stock, but who acts as a facilitating agent. Participants refer to this system as *price-driven* because shares of stock are sold to the investor with the highest bid price and bought from the seller with the lowest offering price.

The other major trading system is a *dealer market* where individual dealers provide liquidity by buying and selling the shares of stock for themselves. Therefore, in such a market, investors wanting to buy or sell shares of a stock must go to a dealer. Ideally, dealers will compete against each other to provide the highest bid prices when you are selling and the lowest asking price when you are buying stock. When we discuss the various exchanges, we will indicate the trading system used.

Call versus Continuous Markets Beyond the alternative trading systems for equities, the operations of exchanges can differ in terms of when and how the stocks are traded.

In **call markets**, trading for individual stocks takes place at specified times. The intent is to gather all the bids and asks for the stock and attempt to arrive at a single price where the quantity demanded is as close as possible to the quantity supplied. This trading arrangement is generally used during the early stages of development of an exchange when there are few stocks listed or a small number of active investors/traders. If you envision an exchange with only a few stocks listed and a few traders, you would call the roll of stocks and ask for interest in one stock at a time. After determining all the available buy and sell orders, exchange officials attempt to arrive at a single price that will satisfy *most* of the orders, and all orders are transacted at this one price.

Notably, call markets also are used at the opening for stocks on the NYSE if there is an overnight buildup of buy and sell orders, in which case the opening price can differ from the prior day's closing price. Also, this concept is used if trading is suspended during the day because of some significant new information. In either case, the specialist or market maker would attempt to derive a new equilibrium price using a call-market approach that would reflect the imbalance and take care of most of the orders. For example, assume a stock had been trading at about $42 per share and some significant, new, positive information was released overnight or during the day. If it was overnight it would affect the opening; if it happened during the day it would affect the price established after trading was suspended. If the buy orders were three or four times as numerous as the sell orders, the price based on the call market might be $44, which is the specialists' estimate of a new equilibrium price that reflects the supply–demand caused by the new information. It is contended that this temporary use of the call-market mechanism contributes to a more orderly market and less volatility in such instances because it attempts to avoid major up and down price swings.

In a **continuous market**, trades occur at any time the market is open. Stocks in this continuous market are priced either by auction or by dealers. If it is a dealer market, numerous dealers are willing to make a market in the stock, which means that they are willing to buy or sell for their own account at a specified bid and ask price. If it is an auction market, enough buyers and sellers are trading to allow the market to be continuous; that is, when you come to buy stock, there is another investor available and willing to sell stock. A compromise between a pure dealer market and a pure auction market is a combination wherein the market is basically an auction market, but there exists an intermediary who is willing to act as a dealer if the pure auction market does not have enough activity. These dealers provide temporary liquidity to ensure that the market will be liquid as well as continuous.

The Chapter 4 Appendix contains two tables that list the characteristics of stock exchanges around the world and indicate whether the exchange provides a continuous market, a call-market mechanism, or a mixture of the two. Notably, although many exchanges are considered continuous, they also employ a call-market mechanism on specific occasions, such as at the open and during trading suspensions. The NYSE is such a market.

NATIONAL STOCK EXCHANGES Two U.S. securities exchanges have historically been considered national in scope: the New York Stock Exchange (NYSE) and the American Stock Exchange (AMEX). Outside the United States, each country typically has had one national exchange, such as the Tokyo Stock Exchange (TSE), the London Exchange, the Frankfurt Stock Exchange, and the Paris Bourse. These exchanges are considered national because of the large number of listed securities from companies within the countries, the prestige of the firms listed, the wide geographic dispersion within the country of the listed firms, and the diverse clientele of buyers and sellers.

The point that will be made in the subsequent discussion of the consolidation of the secondary equity market is that, similar to the emphasis of investors on global portfolios, the exchanges, either alone or with partners, are also working toward being global or major regional exchanges in order to respond to the needs of global investors. This is part of the trend toward "one-stop shopping" applied to the secondary equity market. Because of this trend, the following presentation will discuss the NYSE and the Tokyo Stock Exchange (TSE) separately because they have not been included in any external mergers, but have attempted to grow by adding international stocks to the list. Subsequently, we discuss explicitly the several mergers and affiliations of exchanges that have been or are being implemented around the world.

New York Stock Exchange (NYSE) The New York Stock Exchange (NYSE), the largest organized securities market in the United States, was established in 1817 as the New York Stock and Exchange Board. The Exchange dates its founding to when the famous Buttonwood Agreement was signed in May 1792 by 24 brokers.[13] The name was changed to the New York Stock Exchange in 1863.

At the end of 1998, approximately 3,114 companies had stock issues listed on the NYSE, for a total of 3,382 stock issues (common and preferred) with a total market value of almost $11.0 trillion. The specific listing requirements for the NYSE as of 1998 appear in Table 4.1.

The average number of shares traded daily on the NYSE has increased steadily and substantially, as shown in Table 4.2. Prior to the 1960s, the daily volume averaged less than

[13]The NYSE considers the signing of this agreement the birth of the Exchange and celebrated its 200th birthday during 1992. For a pictorial history, see *Life,* collectors' edition, spring 1992.

TABLE 4.1 **LISTING REQUIREMENTS FOR STOCKS ON THE NYSE AND THE AMEX**

	NYSE	AMEX
Pretax income last year[a]	$ 2,500,000	$ 750,000 latest year or two of last three years
Pretax income last two years	$ 2,000,000	
Net tangible assets	$18,000,000	$4,000,000
Shares publicly held	1,100,000	500,000
Market value of publicly held shares[b]	$18,000,000	$3,000,000[c]
Minimum number of holders of round lots (100 shares or more)	2,000	800

[a]For AMEX, this is *net* income last year.
[b]This minimum required market value varies over time, depending on the value of the NYSE Common Stock Index. For specifics, see the *1998 NYSE Fact Book,* 31–34.
[c]The AMEX only has one minimum.

Sources: *NYSE Fact Book* (New York: NYSE, 1998); and *AMEX Fact Book* (New York: AMEX, 1998). Reprinted by permission.

TABLE 4.2 **AVERAGE DAILY REPORTED SHARE VOLUME TRADED ON SELECTED STOCK MARKETS (× 1,000)**

Year	NYSE	AMEX	NASDAQ	TSE
1955	2,578	912	N.A.	8,000
1960	3,042	1,113	N.A.	90,000
1965	6,176	2,120	N.A.	116,000
1970	11,564	3,319	N.A.	144,000
1975	18,551	2,138	5,500	183,000
1980	44,871	6,427	26,500	359,000
1985	109,169	8,337	82,100	428,000
1990	156,777	13,158	131,900	500,000
1991	178,917	13,309	163,300	380,000
1992	202,266	14,157	190,800	269,000
1993	264,519	18,111	263,000	353,000
1994	291,357	17,945	295,100	342,200
1995	346,101	20,128	401,400	369,600
1996	411,953	22,158	543,700	405,500
1997	526,925	24,389	585,000(e)	420,000E
1998	673,590	29,009	801,747	450,000E

N.A. = not available. E = estimate.

Sources: *NYSE Fact Book* (New York: NYSE, various issues); *AMEX Fact Book* (New York: AMEX, various issues); *Tokyo Stock Exchange Fact Book* (Tokyo: TSE, various issues). Reprinted with permission.

3 million shares, compared with current average daily volume in excess of 673 million shares and record volume of over 1.2 billion shares on October 28, 1997.

The NYSE has dominated the other exchanges in the United States in trading volume. During the past decade, the NYSE has consistently accounted for about 80 percent of all shares traded on U.S. listed exchanges.[14]

[14]For a breakdown of shares traded and their value, see Securities and Exchange Commission, *Annual Report* (Washington, D.C.: U.S. Government Printing Office, annual); and *NYSE Fact Book* (New York: NYSE, annual).

TABLE 4.3 **MEMBERSHIP PRICES ON THE NYSE AND THE AMEX ($000)**

	NYSE		AMEX			NYSE		AMEX	
	High	Low	High	Low		High	Low	High	Low
1925	$150	$ 99	$ 38	$ 9	1990	$ 430	$ 250	$170	$ 84
1935	140	65	33	12	1991	440	345	120	80
1945	95	49	32	12	1992	600	410	110	76
1955	90	49	22	12	1993	775	500	163	92
1960	162	135	60	51	1994	830	760	205	155
1965	250	190	80	55	1995	1,050	785	152	105
1970	320	130	185	70	1996	1,450	1,225	210	150
1975	138	55	72	34	1997	1,750	1,175	420	200
1980	275	175	252	95	1998	2,000	1,225	600E	250E
1985	480	310	160	115					

Sources: *NYSE Fact Book* (New York: NYSE, various issues); *AMEX Fact Book* (New York: AMEX, various issues). Reprinted by permission of the New York Stock Exchange and the American Stock Exchange.

The volume of trading and relative stature of the NYSE is reflected in the price of a membership on the exchange (referred to as a seat). As shown in Table 4.3, the price of membership has fluctuated in line with trading volume and other factors that influence the profitability of membership.[15]

American Stock Exchange (AMEX) The American Stock Exchange (AMEX) was begun by a group who traded unlisted shares at the corner of Wall and Hanover Streets in New York City. It was originally called the Outdoor Curb Market. In 1910, it established formal trading rules and changed its name to the New York Curb Market Association. The members moved inside a building in 1921. The current name was adopted in 1953.

The AMEX has been a national exchange, distinct from the NYSE. The AMEX has emphasized foreign securities, listing 64 foreign issues in 1997. Trading in these issues constituted about 13 percent of total volume.[16]

The AMEX has become a major options exchange including options on stocks, and options on interest rates and stock indexes.

At the end of 1997 prior to the merger, 829 stock issues were listed on the AMEX.[17] As shown in Table 4.2, average daily trading volume has fluctuated substantially over time, growing to more than 24 million shares per day in 1997.

Tokyo Stock Exchange (TSE) Of the eight stock exchanges in Japan, those in Tokyo, Osaka, and Nagoya are the largest. The TSE dominates its country's market much as the NYSE does in the United States. Specifically, about 87 percent of trades in volume and 83 percent of value occur on the TSE.

The Tokyo Stock Exchange Co., Ltd., established in 1878, was replaced in 1943 by the Japan Securities Exchange, which was dissolved in 1947. The Tokyo Stock Exchange in its present form was established in 1949. The trading mechanism is a price-driven system wherein an investor submits bid and ask prices for stocks. At the end of 1997, there were about 1,700 companies listed with a total market value of 300.2 trillion yen (this equals

[15]For a discussion of trading volume and membership prices, see Anita Rashavan, "Stock Boom Doesn't Spur Bull Market in Seats," *Wall Street Journal,* 24 March 1993, C1, C25; and Greg Ip, "Prices Soften for Exchange Seats," *Wall Street Journal,* 27 May 1998, C1, C17.

[16]*AMEX Fact Book* (New York: AMEX, 1998).

[17]The requirements for listing on the AMEX appear in Table 4.1.

about 2.4 trillion dollars at an exchange rate of 125 yen to the dollar). As shown in Table 4.2, average daily share volume has increased from 90 million shares per day in 1960 to a peak of over 1 billion shares in 1988 prior to a decline to about 450 million shares in 1998.

Both domestic and foreign stocks are listed on the Tokyo Exchange. The domestic stocks are further divided between the First and Second Sections. The First Section contains about 1,200 stocks and the Second Section about 450 stocks. The 150 most active stocks on the First Section are traded on the trading floor. Trading in all other domestic stocks and all foreign stocks is conducted by a computer that matches buy and sell orders for each stock on the electronic book-entry display screen and returns confirmations to the trading parties.

Besides domestic stocks, foreign company stocks are listed and traded on the TSE foreign stock market. As of by the end of 1997, the TSE listed 77 foreign companies.

London Stock Exchange (LSE) The largest established securities market in the United Kingdom is the London Stock Exchange. Since 1973, it has served as the stock exchange of Great Britain and Ireland, with operating units in London, Dublin, and six other cities. Both listed securities (bonds and equities) and unlisted securities are traded on the LSE. The listed equity segment involves more than 2,600 companies with a market value in excess of 374 billion pounds (approximately \$561 billion at an exchange rate of \$1.50/pound). Of the 2,600 companies listed on the LSE, about 600 are foreign firms—the largest number on any exchange.

The pricing system on the LSE is done by competing dealers who communicate via computers in offices away from the stock exchange. This system is similar to the NASDAQ system used in the OTC market in the United States, which is described in the next section.

Divergent Trends—New Exchanges and Consolidations The global secondary equity market has been experiencing two trends that appear divergent, yet are reasonable in a dynamic global equity market with a range of economies that vary from being very developed to newly emerging. The first trend is the creation of a number of *new* stock exchanges around the world in emerging economies, including China, Russia, Sri Lanka, Poland, Hungary, and Peru. The second trend is toward *consolidation* of existing exchanges in developed countries through mergers or strong affiliations.

The creation of numerous new exchanges in emerging economies is based upon the need in these countries for capital to help individual firms grow. The point was made early in the chapter that a strong secondary market for securities is necessary to provide the liquidity that investors require if they are going to buy securities in the primary market from which firms acquire new capital. Put another way, if companies need new capital, and want to get it by selling stock, it is necessary to have a liquid secondary equity market—that is, a stock exchange.

The trend toward the consolidation of existing exchanges in developed markets, such as London, Frankfurt, and Paris, can be explained by the economies of scale required by these exchanges, including the need for significant expenditures for technology to remain globally competitive. To acquire and maintain the necessary technology is extremely expensive and a smaller exchange may not be able to afford this outlay. Further, once an exchange is created, there are substantial economies of scale—a trading system can probably handle 4,000 stocks as easily and cheaply as 400 stocks. The cost of, and the economies of scale related to, technology are the major reasons for most of the mergers and affiliations being proposed.

Another reason is the added liquidity provided by adding members to the exchange. Assume two exchanges, each with 200 members and 1,000 different stocks listed. If you combine the exchanges into 400 members and 2,000 stocks, each stock should benefit in terms of potential liquidity because there are more members (dealers) who are available to buy and sell the stocks and bring clients to the exchange.

Therefore, the normal evolution in the global economy with global capital markets should be the creation of new stock exchanges in emerging economies followed by the subsequent consolidation of these exchanges (20 years later) into regional exchanges (e.g., Pan-European) to meet the need for expensive technology and enhanced liquidity.

The following section discusses some of the recent consolidations to document this trend.

Recent Consolidations Although the rate of consolidations has increased recently, they began in 1995 when Germany's three largest exchanges merged into the one in Frankfurt.[18]

The recent merger movement of exchanges began when the NASD announced an intention to merge with the AMEX in March 1998.[19] Subsequently (June 1998), the Philadelphia Stock Exchange indicated that it would merge with the NASD/AMEX. Another combination in the United States occurred in July 1998 when the Chicago Board Options Exchange (CBOE) agreed to merge with the Pacific Exchange.[20] These two exchanges account for about 60 percent of options trading in the United States.

The major move toward consolidation in Europe occurred in July 1998 when the London Stock Exchange and the Frankfurt Stock Exchange laid the foundation for a possible pan-European market by announcing a strategic alliance.[21] Initially, the Paris exchange reacted by suggesting that it would form an alliance with other European exchanges left out of the London–Frankfurt alliance.[22] Subsequently, it softened its response and indicated that it would work toward joining the alliance during 1999.

This major initiative prompted several smaller exchanges in Europe to form alliances. In November 1998, the Dutch, Belgian, and Luxembourg stock exchanges indicated an alliance. This was followed in December by an alliance of the Stockholm, Copenhagen, and Oslo exchanges.[23]

Figure 4.1 attempts to summarize the numerous changes that have occurred. Given these changes, more consolidations and alliances will likely take place in the next few years.

The Global 24-Hour Market Our discussion of the global securities market will tend to emphasize the three markets in New York, London, and Tokyo because of their relative size and importance, and because they represent the major segments of a worldwide 24-hour stock market. You will often hear about a continuous market where investment firms "pass the book" around the world. This means that an active market in securities moves around the globe as trading hours for these three markets begin and end. Consider the indi-

---

[18]Andrew Fisher, "Top Three German Exchanges to Merge," *Financial Times,* 9 May 1995.

[19]Anita Raghavan, "NASDAQ's Parent Is in Negotiations to Take Control of the AMEX," *Wall Street Journal,* 12 March 1998, A1.

[20]Greg Ip, Silvia Ascarelli, and Jeffrey Hiday, "Mergers of Markets May Mean Trading Will Be Cheaper, Speedier and Easier," *Wall Street Journal,* 14 July 1998, C1, C13.

[21]George Graham and Simon Davies, "London-Frankfurt Link Paves Way for Pan-European Exchange," *Financial Times,* 8 July 1998, 1; Andrew Fisher, "London Link Offers Way into Top Tier," *Financial Times,* 8 July 1998, 20. There were other articles in the same edition of the paper. For a discussion of some concern expressed in the United States, see Suzanne McGee and Silvia Ascarelli, "European Market Link-Up Faces Hurdles," *Wall Street Journal,* 8 July 1998, C1, C15.

[22]Vincent Boland and Edward Luce, "Paris Bourse Plans Rival Alliance," *Financial Times,* 19 July 1998, 20.

[23]Gordan Cramb, "Benelux Markets Form Trading Link," *Financial Times,* 25 November 1998, 10; Valeros Skold and Tim Burt, "Oslo Set to Join Nordic Bourse Tie-Up," *Financial Times,* 11 December 1998, 24.

FIGURE 4.1 **THE MOVE TOWARD CONSOLIDATION AND AFFILIATION IN THE SECONDARY EQUITY MARKET**

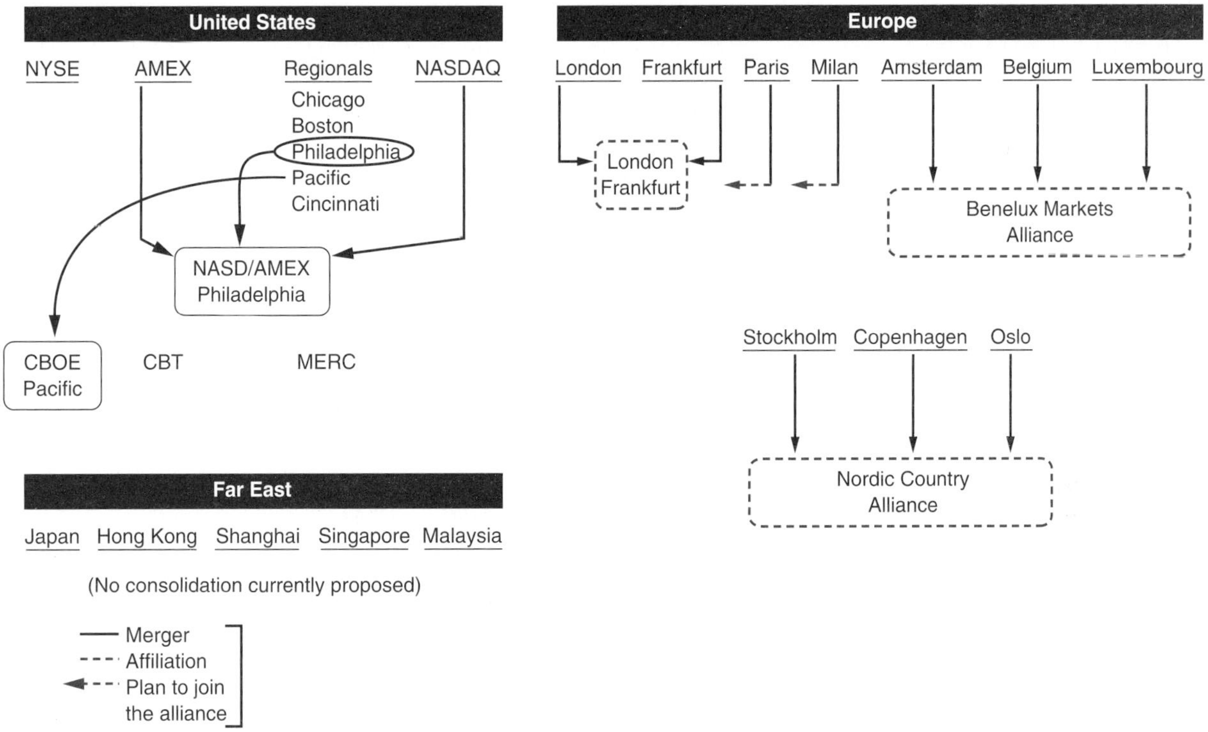
United States
NYSE
AMEX
Regionals
Chicago
Boston
Philadelphia
Pacific
Cincinnati
NASDAQ
NASD/AMEX Philadelphia
CBOE Pacific
CBT
MERC
Europe
London
Frankfurt
Paris
Milan
Amsterdam
Belgium
Luxembourg
London Frankfurt
Benelux Markets Alliance
Stockholm
Copenhagen
Oslo
Nordic Country Alliance
Far East
Japan
Hong Kong
Shanghai
Singapore
Malaysia
(No consolidation currently proposed)
Merger
Affiliation
Plan to join the alliance

vidual trading hours for each of the three exchanges, translated into a 24-hour eastern standard time (EST) clock:

	Local Time (24-hr. Notations)	24-Hour EST
New York Stock Exchange	0930–1600	0930–1600
Tokyo Stock Exchange	0900–1100	2300–0100
	1300–1500	0300–0500
London Stock Exchange	0815–1615	0215–1015

Imagine trading starting in New York at 0930 and going until 1600 in the afternoon, being picked up by Tokyo late in the evening and going until 0500 in the morning, and continuing in London (with some overlap) until it begins in New York again (with some overlap) at 0930. Alternatively, it is possible to envision trading as beginning in Tokyo at 2300 hours and continuing until 0500, when it moves to London, then ends the day in New York. This latter model seems the most relevant because the first question a London trader asks in the morning is "What happened in Tokyo?" and the U.S. trader asks "What happened in Tokyo and what *is* happening in London?" The point is, the markets operate almost continuously and are related in their response to economic events. Therefore, as an investor you are not dealing with three separate and distinct exchanges, but with one interrelated world market.[24] Clearly, this interrelationship is growing daily because of numerous multiple listings where stocks are listed on several exchanges around the world (such as the NYSE and TSE) and the availability of sophisticated telecommunications.

REGIONAL EXCHANGES AND THE OVER-THE-COUNTER MARKET

Within most countries, regional stock exchanges compete with and supplement the national exchanges by providing secondary markets for the stocks of smaller companies. Beyond these exchanges, trading off the exchange (the over-the-counter or OTC market) includes all stocks not listed on one of the formal exchanges. The size and significance of the regional exchanges versus the OTC market and the relative impact of these two sectors on the overall secondary stock markets vary among countries. In the first part of this section, we discuss the rationale for and operation of regional stock exchanges. The second part of the section describes the OTC market, including heavy emphasis on the OTC market in the United States where it is a significant component of the total secondary stock market.

REGIONAL SECURITIES EXCHANGES Regional exchanges typically have the same operating procedures as the national exchanges in the same countries, but they differ in their listing requirements and the geographic distributions of the listed firms. Regional stock exchanges exist for two main reasons: First, they provide trading facilities for local companies not large enough to qualify for listing on one of the national exchanges. Their listing requirements are typically less stringent than those of the national exchanges, as presented in Table 4.1.

Second, regional exchanges in some countries list firms that also list on one of the national exchanges to give local brokers who are not members of a national exchange access to these securities. As an example, American Telephone & Telegraph and General Motors are listed on both the NYSE and several regional exchanges. This dual listing or the use of unlisted trading privileges (UTP) allows a local brokerage firm that is not large enough to purchase a membership on the NYSE to buy and sell shares of a dual-listed stock (such as General Motors) without going through the NYSE and giving up part of the commission. The regional exchanges in the United States are:[25]

- Chicago Stock Exchange
- Boston Stock Exchange
- Cincinnati Stock Exchange

Following the recent consolidations, the remaining regional exchange volume is about 5 percent of total exchange volume in the United States.

In Japan, seven regional stock exchanges supplement the Tokyo Stock Exchange. The exchange in Osaka accounts for about 10 percent and that in Nagoya for about 2.3 percent

[24]For an example of global trading, see "How Merrill Lynch Moves Its Stock Deals All Around the World," *Wall Street Journal,* 9 November 1987, 1, 19; and *Opportunity and Risk in the 24-Hour Global Marketplace* (New York: Coopers & Lybrand, 1987). In response to this trend toward global trading, the International Organization of Securities Commissions (IOSCO) has been established. For a discussion of it, see David Lascelles, "Calls to Bring Watchdogs into Line," *Financial Times,* 14 August 1989, 10.

[25]The Philadelphia Exchange proposed a merger into the NASDAQ/AMEX in mid-1998 that was subsequently cancelled; the Pacific Stock Exchange, which emphasized stock options, merged with the CBOE as noted earlier.

of the total volume. The remaining exchanges together account for less than 1 percent of volume.

The United Kingdom has one stock exchange in London with operating units in seven cities, including Dublin, Belfast, and Glasgow. Germany has eight stock exchanges, including its national exchange in Frankfurt and regional exchanges in Düsseldorf, Munich, and Berlin.[26]

Without belaboring the point, each country typically has one national exchange that accounts for the majority of trading and several regional exchanges that have less stringent listing requirements to allow trading in smaller firms. Recently, several national exchanges have created second-tier markets that are divisions of the national exchanges to allow smaller firms to be traded as part of the national exchanges.[27]

OVER-THE-COUNTER (OTC) MARKET The over-the-counter (OTC) market includes trading in all stocks not listed on one of the exchanges. It can also include trading in listed stocks, which is referred to as the *third market,* and is discussed in the following section. The OTC market is not a formal organization with membership requirements or a specific list of stocks deemed eligible for trading.[28] In theory, any security can be traded on the OTC market as long as a registered dealer is willing to make a market in the security (willing to buy and sell shares of the stock).

Size of the OTC Market The U.S. OTC market is the largest segment of the U.S. secondary market in terms of the number of issues traded. It is also the most diverse in terms of quality. As noted earlier, about 3,500 issues are traded on the NYSE and about 900 issues on the AMEX. In contrast, almost 5,000 issues are actively traded on the OTC market's NASDAQ National Market System (NMS).[29] Another 1,000 stocks are traded on the NASDAQ system independent of the NMS. Finally, 1,000 OTC stocks are regularly quoted in *The Wall Street Journal* but not in the NASDAQ system. Therefore, a total of almost 7,000 issues are traded on the OTC market—substantially more than on the NYSE and AMEX combined.

Table 4.4 sets forth the growth in the number of companies and issues on NASDAQ. The growth in average daily trading is shown in Table 4.2 relative to some national exchanges. As of the end of 1998, 510 issues on NASDAQ were either foreign stocks or American Depository Receipts (ADRs). Trading in foreign stocks and ADRs represented over 5 percent of total NASDAQ share volume in 1998. About 300 of these issues trade on both NASDAQ and a foreign exchange, such as Toronto. In 1988, NASDAQ developed a link with the Singapore Stock Exchange that allows 24-hour trading from NASDAQ in New York to Singapore to a NASDAQ/London link and back to New York.

---

[26]As noted, the three largest exchanges have merged, which has created an exchange encompassing more than 80 percent of total volume. Recently, a similar idea has been proposed in the United States. Greg Ip, "Super-regional Exchange Is a Bold Idea," *Wall Street Journal,* 15 July 1998, C1, C18.

[27]An example of these second-tier markets is the Second Section on the TSE and the Unlisted Stock Market (USM) on the LSE. In both cases, the exchange is attempting to provide trading facilities for smaller firms without changing their listing requirements for the national exchange. An appendix at the end of this chapter contains information about exchanges around the world in both developed and emerging markets.

[28]The requirements of trading on different segments of the OTC trading system will be discussed later in this section.

[29]NASDAQ is an acronym for National Association of Securities Dealers Automated Quotations. The system is discussed in detail in a later section. To be traded on the NMS, a firm must have a certain size and trading activity and at least four market makers. A specification of requirements for various components of the NASDAQ system is contained in Table 4.5.

TABLE 4.4 **NUMBER OF COMPANIES AND ISSUES TRADING ON NASDAQ: 1980–1998**

Year	Number of Companies	Number of Issues
1980	2,894	3,050
1985	4,136	4,784
1990	4,132	4,706
1991	4,094	4,684
1992	4,113	4,764
1993	4,611	5,393
1994	4,902	5,761
1995	5,122	5,955
1996	5,556	6,384
1997	5,487	6,208
1998	5,068	5,583

Source: *NASDAQ Fact Book* (Washington, D.C.: National Association of Securities Dealers, 1999), 5.

Although the OTC market has the greatest number of issues, the NYSE has a larger total value of trading. In 1997 the approximate value of equity trading on the NYSE was about $5,700 billion, and NASDAQ was about $3,500 billion. Notably, the NASDAQ value exceeded what transpired on the LSE ($700 billion) and on the TSE ($873 billion).[30]

There is tremendous diversity in the OTC market because it imposes no minimum requirements. Stocks that trade on the OTC range from those of small, unprofitable companies to large, extremely profitable firms (such as Microsoft and Intel). On the upper end, all U.S. government bonds are traded on the OTC market as are the majority of bank and insurance stocks. Finally, about 100 exchange-listed stocks are traded on the OTC—the third market.

Operation of the OTC As noted, any stock can be traded on the OTC as long as someone indicates a willingness to make a market whereby the party buys or sells for his or her own account acting as a dealer.[31] This differs from most transactions on the listed exchanges, where some members keep the book and as brokers attempt to match buy and sell orders. Therefore, the OTC market is referred to as a *negotiated market,* in which investors directly negotiate with dealers.

The NASDAQ System *The National Association of Securities Dealers Automated Quotation (NASDAQ)* system is an automated, electronic quotation system for the vast OTC market. Any number of dealers can elect to make markets in an OTC stock. The actual number depends on the activity in the stock. The average number of market makers for all stocks on the NASDAQ system was 10.7 in 1997, according to the *NASDAQ Fact Book.*

NASDAQ makes all dealer quotes available immediately. The broker can check the quotation machine and call the dealer with the best market, verify that the quote has not changed, and make the sale or purchase. The NASDAQ system has three levels to serve firms with different needs and interests.

Level 1 provides a single median representative quote for the stocks on NASDAQ. This quote system is for firms that want current quotes on OTC stocks but do not consistently

[30]There will be a change in how some trades are counted on the NASD where riskless transfers are not counted as two trades. See Aaron Lucchetti, "NASDAQ to Change Way It Counts Some Trades," *Wall Street Journal,* 7 July 1998, C1.

[31]*Dealer* and *market maker* are synonymous.

buy or sell OTC stocks for their customers and are not market makers. This composite quote changes constantly to adjust for any changes by individual market makers.

Level 2 provides instantaneous current quotations on NASDAQ stocks by all market makers in a stock. This quotation system is for firms that consistently trade OTC stocks. Given an order to buy or sell, brokers check the quotation machine, call the market maker with the best market for their purposes (highest bid if they are selling, lowest offer if buying), and consummate the deal.

Level 3 is for OTC market makers. Such firms want Level 2, but they also need the capability to change their own quotations, which Level 3 provides.

Listing Requirements for NASDAQ Quotes and trading volume for the OTC market are reported in two lists: a National Market System (NMS) list and a regular NASDAQ list. As of 1999, there were four sets of listing requirements. The first, for initial listing on any NASDAQ system, is the least stringent. The second is for automatic (mandatory) inclusion on the NASDAQ/NMS system. For stocks on this system, reports include up-to-the-minute volume and last-sale information for the competing market makers as well as end-of-the-day information on total volume and high, low, and closing prices. In addition, two sets of criteria govern voluntary participation on the NMS by companies with different characteristics. Alternative 1 accommodates companies with limited assets or net worth but substantial earnings; Alternative 2 is for large companies that are not necessarily as profitable. The four sets of criteria are set forth in Table 4.5.

A Sample Trade Assume you are considering the purchase of 100 shares of Intel. Although Intel is large enough and profitable enough to be listed on a national exchange, the company has never applied for listing because it enjoys an active market on the OTC. (It is one of the volume leaders with daily volume typically above 1 million shares and often in excess of 5 million shares.) When you contact your broker, he or she will consult the NASDAQ electronic quotation machine to determine the current dealer quotations for INTC, the trading symbol for Intel.[32] The quote machine will show that about 35 dealers are making a market in INTC. An example of differing quotations might be as follows:

Dealer	Bid	Ask
1	$85\frac{1}{2}$	$85\frac{3}{4}$
2	$85\frac{3}{8}$	$85\frac{5}{8}$
3	$85\frac{1}{4}$	$85\frac{5}{8}$
4	$85\frac{3}{8}$	$85\frac{3}{4}$

Assuming these are the best markets available from the total group, your broker would call either Dealer 2 or Dealer 3 because they have the lowest offering prices. After verifying the quote, your broker would give one of these dealers an order to buy 100 shares of INTC at $85\frac{5}{8}$ ($85.625 a share). Because your firm was not a market maker in the stock, the firm would act as a broker and charge you $8,562.50 plus a commission for the trade. If your firm had been a market maker in INTC, with an asking price of $85\frac{5}{8}$, the firm would have sold the stock to you at $85\frac{5}{8}$ net (without commission). If you had been interested in selling

[32]Trading symbols are one- to four-letter codes used to designate stocks. Whenever a trade is reported on a stock ticker, the trading symbol appears with the figures. Many symbols are obvious, such as GM (General Motors), F (Ford Motors), GE (General Electric), and T (American Telephone & Telegraph).

TABLE 4.5A NASDAQ NATIONAL MARKET QUANTITATIVE STANDARDS

	Initial NASDAQ National Market Listing		Continued NASDAQ National Market
Standard	**Alternative 1**	**Alternative 2**	**Inclusion**
Registration under Section 12(g) of the Securities Exchange Act of 1934 or Equivalent	Yes	Yes	Yes
Net Tangible Assets[a]	\$4 million	\$12 million	\$1 million[b]
Net Income (In Last Fiscal Year or Two of Last Three Fiscal Years)	\$400,000	—	—
Pretax Income (In Last Fiscal Year or Two of Last Three Fiscal Years)	\$750,000	—	—
Public Float (Shares)[c]	500,000	1 million	200,000
Operating History	—	3 years	—
Market Value of Float	\$3 million	\$15 million	\$1 million
Minimum Bid Per Share	\$5	\$3	\$1[d]
Shareholders			
—if between 0.5 and 1 million shares publicly held	800	400	400[e] —
—if more than 1 million shares publicly held	400	400	—
—if more than 0.5 million shares publicly held and average daily volume in excess of 2,000 shares	400	400	—
Number of Market Makers	2	2	2

[a]"Net Tangible Assets" means total assets (excluding goodwill) minus total liabilities.
[b]Continued NASDAQ National Market inclusion requires net tangible assets of at least \$2 million if the issuer has sustained losses from continuing operations and/or net losses in two of its three most recent fiscal years or \$4 million if the issuer has sustained losses from the continuing operations and/or net losses in three of its four most recent fiscal years.
[c]Public float is defined as shares that are not "held directly or indirectly by any officer or director of the issuer and by any person who is the beneficial owner of more than 10 percent of the total shares outstanding. . . ."
[d]Or, in alternative, market value of public float of \$3 million and \$4 million of net tangible assets.
[e]Or 300 shareholders of round lots.

100 shares of Intel instead of buying, the broker would have contacted Dealer 1, who made the highest bid.

Changing Dealer Inventory Let us consider the price quotations by an OTC dealer who wants to change his or her inventory on a given stock. For example, assume Dealer 4, with a current quote of $85\frac{3}{8}$ bid–$85\frac{3}{4}$ ask, decides to increase his or her holdings of INTC. The NASDAQ quotes indicate that the highest bid is currently $85\frac{1}{2}$. Increasing the bid to $85\frac{1}{2}$ would bring some of the business currently going to Dealer 1. Taking a more aggressive action, the dealer might raise the bid to $85\frac{5}{8}$ and buy all the stock offered, including some from Dealers 2 and 3, who are offering it at $85\frac{5}{8}$. In this example, the dealer raises the bid price but does not change the asking price, which was above those of Dealers 2 and 3. This dealer will buy stock but probably will not sell any. A dealer who had excess stock would keep the bid below the market (lower than $85\frac{1}{2}$) and reduce the asking price to $85\frac{5}{8}$ or less.

TABLE 4.5B **QUANTITATIVE STANDARDS FOR DOMESTIC STOCKS IN THE NASDAQ SMALLCAP MARKET**

Initial Listing		Continued Listing	
Registration under Section 12(g) of the Securities Exchange Act of 1934 or Equivalent	Yes	Registration under Section 12(g) of The Securities Exchange Act of 1934 or Equivalent	Yes
Total Assets	$4 million	Total Assets	$2 million
Capital and Surplus	$2 million	Capital and Surplus	$1 million
Public Float (Shares)	100,000	Public Float (Shares)	100,000
Market Value of Public Float	$1 million	Market Value of Public Float	$200,000[a]
Market Makers	2[a]	Market Makers	2[a]
Bid Price per Share	$3	Bid Price per Share	$1[a,b]
Shareholders	300	Shareholders	300

Note: All amendments to entry and maintenance requirements also apply to non-Canadian foreign and American Depository Receipts, except for amended entry and maintenance requirements for price per share and market value of public float.

[a]A deficiency in the maintenance criteria for market value of public float, market makers, and bid price will be determined if the issuer fails any of these requirements for 10 consecutive days. If failure of any of the 10-day tests occur, the issuer will be notified promptly and will be given 30 calendar days to comply with the market-maker criteria and 90 calendar days to comply with the bid price or market value of public float requirements.

[b]The rule allows issuers that fail to meet the minimum bid price requirement to continue to qualify if they continue to meet the $1 million market value of public float and $2 million in capital and surplus requirements.

Source: *The NASDAQ Stock Market Fact Book* (Washington, D.C.: 1997), 51, 212.

Dealers constantly change their bid and ask prices or both, depending on their current inventories or changes in the outlook based on new information for the stock.[33]

THIRD MARKET As mentioned, the term **third market** describes over-the-counter trading of shares listed on an exchange. Although most transactions in listed stocks take place on an exchange, an investment firm that is not a member of an exchange can make a market in a listed stock. Most of the trading on the third market is in well-known stocks, such as AT&T, IBM, and Xerox, and in many of these stocks it accounts for over 10 percent of trading volume. The success or failure of the third market depends on whether the OTC market in these stocks is as good as the exchange market and whether the relative cost of the OTC transaction compares favorably with the cost on the exchange. This market is critical during the relatively few periods when trading is not available on the NYSE either because trading is suspended or the exchange is closed.[34]

FOURTH MARKET The term **fourth market** describes direct trading of securities between two parties with no broker intermediary. In almost all cases, both parties involved are institutions. When you think about it, a direct transaction is really not that unusual. If

[33]Some studies have examined the determinants of dealers' bid–ask spreads, including H. R. Stoll, "Inferring the Components of the Bid–Ask Spread: Theory and Empirical Tests," *Journal of Finance* 44, no. 1 (March 1989): 115–134.

[34]Craig Torres, "Third Market Trading Crowds Stock Exchanges," *Wall Street Journal,* 8 March 1990, C1, C9. For an analysis of the effect of this trading, see Robert H. Battalio, "Third-Market Broker-Dealers: Cost Competitors or Cream Skimmers," *Journal of Finance* 52, no. 1 (March 1997): 341–352.

you own 100 shares of AT&T Corp. and decide to sell it, there is nothing wrong with simply offering it to your friends or associates at a mutually agreeable price (for example, based on exchange transactions) and making the transaction directly.

Investors typically buy or sell stock through brokers because it is faster and easier. Also, you would expect to get a better price for your stock because the broker has a good chance of finding the best buyer. You are willing to pay a commission for these liquidity services. The fourth market evolved because of the substantial fees charged by brokers to institutions with large orders. At some point, it becomes worthwhile for institutions to attempt to deal directly with each other and bypass the brokerage fees. Assume an institution decides to sell 100,000 shares of AT&T, which is selling for about $65 per share, for a total value of $6.5 million. The average commission on such a transaction prior to the advent of negotiated rates in 1975 was about 1 percent of the value of the trade, or about $65,000. This cost made it attractive for a selling institution to spend some time and effort finding another institution interested in increasing its holdings of AT&T and negotiating a direct sale. Currently, such transactions cost about 5 cents per share, which implies a cost of $5,000 for the 100,000-share transaction. This is lower, but still not trivial. Because of the diverse nature of the fourth market and the lack of reporting requirements, no data are available regarding its specific size or growth.

DETAILED ANALYSIS OF EXCHANGE MARKETS

The importance of listed exchange markets requires that we discuss them at some length. In this section, we discuss several types of membership on the exchanges, the major types of orders, and the role and function of exchange market makers—a critical component of a good exchange market.

Exchange Membership

Listed U.S. securities exchanges typically offer four major categories of membership: (1) specialist, (2) commission broker, (3) floor broker, and (4) registered trader. Specialists (or exchange market makers), who constitute about 25 percent of the total membership on exchanges, will be discussed after a description of types of orders.

Commission brokers are employees of a member firm who buy or sell for the customers of the firm. When you place an order to buy or sell stock through a brokerage firm that is a member of the exchange, in many instances the firm contacts its commission broker on the floor of the exchange. That broker goes to the appropriate post on the floor and buys or sells the stock as instructed.

Floor brokers are independent members of an exchange who act as brokers for other members. As an example, when commission brokers for Merrill Lynch become too busy to handle all their orders, they will ask one of the floor brokers to help them. At one time, these people were referred to as *$2 brokers* because that is what they received for each order. Currently, they receive about $4 per 100-share order.[35]

Registered traders are allowed to use their memberships to buy and sell for their own accounts. They therefore save commissions on their own trading, and observers believe they have an advantage because they are on the trading floor. The exchanges and others are willing to allow these advantages because these traders provide the market with added liquidity, but regulations limit how they trade and how many registered traders can be in a

[35]These brokers received some unwanted notoriety in 1998: Dean Starkman and Patrick McGeehan, "Floor Brokers on Big Board Charged in Scheme," *Wall Street Journal,* 26 February 1998, C1, C21; and Suzanna McGee, " 'S2 Brokers' Worried about Notoriety from Charges of Illegal Trading Scheme," *Wall Street Journal,* 5 March 1998, C1, C22.

trading crowd around a specialist's booth at any time. In recent years, registered traders have become **registered competitive market makers (RCMMs)**, who have specific trading obligations set by the exchange. Their activity is reported as part of the specialist group.[36]

TYPES OF ORDERS

It is important to understand the different types of orders entered by investors and the specialist as a dealer.

MARKET ORDERS The most frequent type of order is a **market order**, an order to buy or sell a stock at the best current price. An investor who enters a market sell order indicates a willingness to sell immediately at the highest bid available at the time the order reaches the specialist on the exchange or an OTC dealer. A market buy order indicates that the investor is willing to pay the lowest offering price available at the time the order reaches the floor of the exchange or an OTC dealer. Market orders provide immediate liquidity for someone willing to accept the prevailing market price.

Assume you are interested in General Electric (GE) and you call your broker to find out the current "market" on the stock. The quotation machine indicates that the prevailing market is 75 bid–75¼ ask. This means that the highest current bid on the books of the specialist is 75; that is, $75 is the most that anyone has offered to pay for GE. The lowest offer is 75¼; that is, the lowest price anyone is willing to accept to sell the stock. If you placed a market buy order for 100 shares, you would buy 100 shares at $75.25 a share (the lowest ask price) for a total cost of $7,525 plus commission. If you submitted a market sell order for 100 shares, you would sell the shares at $75 each and receive $7,500 less commission.

LIMIT ORDERS The individual placing a **limit order** specifies the buy or sell price. You might submit a bid to purchase 100 shares of Coca-Cola stock at $65 a share when the current market is 70 bid–70¼ ask, with the expectation that the stock will decline to $65 in the near future.

You must also indicate how long the limit order will be outstanding. Alternative time specifications are basically boundless. A limit order can be instantaneous ("fill or kill," meaning fill the order instantly or cancel it). It can also be good for part of a day, a full day, several days, a week, or a month. It can also be open-ended, or good until canceled (GTC).

Rather than wait for a given price on a stock, your broker will give the limit order to the specialist, who will put it in a limit-order book and act as the broker's representative. When and if the market reaches the limit-order price, the specialist will execute the order and inform your broker. The specialist receives a small part of the commission for rendering this service.

SHORT SALES Most investors purchase stock ("go long") expecting to derive their return from an increase in value. If you believe that a stock is overpriced, however, and want to take advantage of an expected decline in the price, you can sell the stock short. A **short sale** is the sale of stock that you do not own with the intent of purchasing it back later at a lower price. Specifically, you would borrow the stock from another investor through your broker, sell it in the market, and subsequently replace it at (you hope) a price lower than the price at which you sold it. The investor who lent the stock has the proceeds of the sale as collateral. In turn, this investor can invest these funds in short-term, risk-free securities. Although a short sale has no time limit, the lender of the shares can decide to sell

---

[36]Prior to the late 1970s, there also were odd-lot dealers who bought and sold to individuals with orders for less than round lots (usually 100 shares). Currently, this function is handled by either the specialist or some large brokerage firm.

the shares, in which case your broker must find another investor willing to lend the shares.[37]

Three technical points affect short sales. First, a short sale can be made only on an *uptick trade,* meaning the price of the short sale must be higher than the last trade price. This is because the exchanges do not want traders to force a profit on a short sale by pushing the price down through continually selling short. Therefore, the transaction price for a short sale must be an uptick or, without any change in price, the previous price must have been higher than its previous price (a zero uptick). For an example of a zero uptick, consider the following set of transaction prices: 42, 42¼, 42¼. You could sell short at 42¼ even though it is no change from the previous trade at 42¼ because that trade was an uptick trade.

The second technical point concerns dividends. The short seller must pay any dividends due to the investor who lent the stock. The purchaser of the short-sale stock receives the dividend from the corporation, so the short seller must pay a similar dividend to the lender.

A final point is that short sellers must post the same margin as an investor who had acquired stock. This margin can be in any unrestricted securities owned by the short seller.

SPECIAL ORDERS In addition to these general orders, there are several special types of orders. A *stop loss order* is a conditional market order whereby the investor directs the sale of a stock if it drops to a given price. Assume you buy a stock at 50 and expect it to go up. If you are wrong, you want to limit your losses. To protect yourself, you could put in a stop loss order at 45. In this case, if the stock dropped to 45, your stop loss order would become a market sell order, and the stock would be sold at the prevailing market price. The stop loss order does not guarantee that you will get the $45; you can get a little bit more or a little bit less. Because of the possibility of market disruption caused by a large number of stop loss orders, exchanges have, on occasion, canceled all such orders on certain stocks and not allowed brokers to accept further stop loss orders on those issues.

A related type of stop loss tactic for short sales is a *stop buy order.* An investor who has sold stock short and wants to minimize any loss if the stock begins to increase in value would enter this conditional buy order at a price above that at which the investor sold the stock short. Assume you sold a stock short at 50, expecting it to decline to 40. To protect yourself from an increase, you could put in a stop buy order to purchase the stock using a market buy order if it reached a price of 55. This conditional buy order would hopefully limit any loss on the short sale to approximately $5 a share.

MARGIN TRANSACTIONS On any type of order, an investor can pay for the stock with cash or borrow part of the cost, leveraging the transaction. Leverage is accomplished by buying on **margin**, which means the investor pays for the stock with some cash and borrows the rest through the broker, putting up the stock for collateral.

As shown in Figure 4.2, the dollar amount of margin credit extended by members of the NYSE has increased consistently since 1991 and reached record levels in 1998. The interest rate charged on these loans by the investment firms is typically 1.50 percent above the rate charged by the bank making the loan. The bank rate, referred to as the *call money rate,* is generally about 1 percent below the prime rate. For example, in July 1999, the prime rate was 8.00 percent, and the call money rate was 6.75 percent.

---

[37]For a discussion of negative short-selling results, see William Power, "Short Sellers Take It on the Chin Again," *Wall Street Journal,* 29 June 1993, C1, C2; and William Power, "Short Sellers Set to Catch Tumbling Overvalued Stocks, *Wall Street Journal,* 28 December 1993, C1, C2. For a further discussion of short-selling events, see Carol J. Loomis, "Short Sellers and the Seamy Side of Wall Street," *Fortune,* 22 July 1996, 66–72; and Gary Weiss, "The Secret World of Short Sellers," *Business Week,* 5 August 1996, 62–68.

FIGURE 4.2 **BORROWING AGAINST STOCKS—AMOUNT OF MARGIN CREDIT EXTENDED BY BROKERS AND DEALERS AT END OF MONTH ($ BILLIONS)**

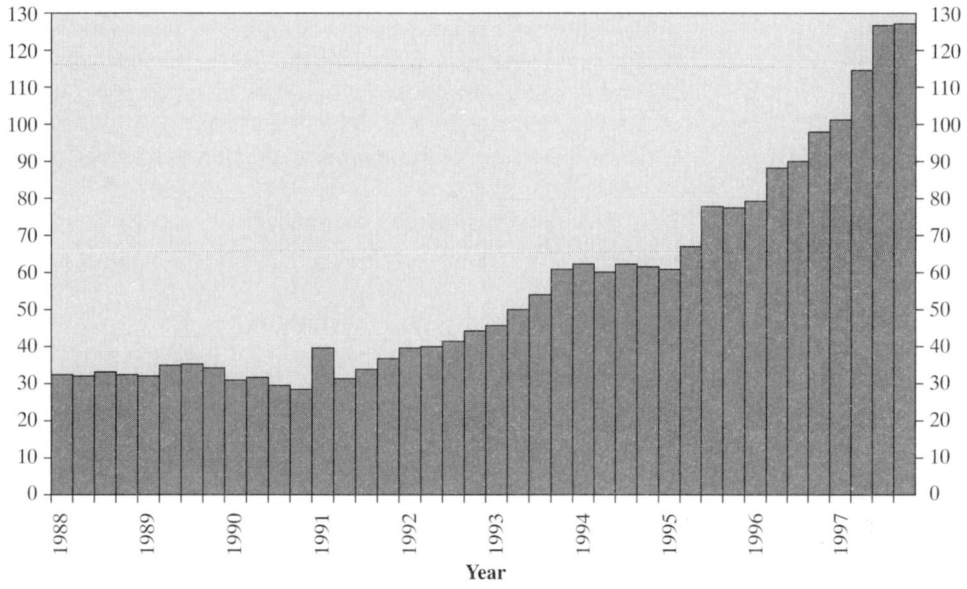
130
120
110
100
90
80
70
60
50
40
30
20
10
0
1988
1989
1990
1991
1992
1993
1994
1995
1996
1997
Year

Federal Reserve Board Regulations T and U determine the maximum proportion of any transaction that can be borrowed. These regulations were enacted during the 1930s because of the contention that the excessive credit extended for stock acquisition contributed to the stock market collapse of 1929. Since the enactment of the regulations, this *margin requirement* (the proportion of total transaction value that must be paid in cash) has varied from 40 percent (allowing loans of 60 percent of the value) to 100 percent (allowing no borrowing). As of July 1999, the initial margin requirement specified by the Federal Reserve was 50 percent, although individual investment firms can require higher rates.

After the initial purchase, changes in the market price of the stock will cause changes in the *investor's equity,* which is equal to the market value of the collateral stock minus the amount borrowed. Obviously, if the stock price increases, the investor's equity as a proportion of the total market value of the stock increases; that is, the investor's margin will exceed the initial margin requirement.

Assume you acquired 200 shares of a $50 stock for a total cost of $10,000. A 50 percent initial margin requirement allowed you to borrow $5,000, making your initial equity $5,000. If the stock price increases by 20 percent to $60 a share, the total market value of your position is $12,000, and your equity is now $7,000, or 58 percent ($7,000/$12,000). In contrast, if the stock price declines by 20 percent to $40 a share, the total market value would be $8,000, and your investor's equity would be $3,000, or 37.5 percent ($3,000/$8,000).

This example demonstrates that buying on margin provides all the advantages and the disadvantages of leverage. Lower margin requirements allow you to borrow more, increasing the percentage of gain or loss on your investment when the stock price increases or decreases. The leverage factor equals 1 percent margin. Thus, as in the example, if the margin is 50 percent, the leverage factor is 2, that is, 1/0.50. Therefore, when the rate of return on the stock is plus or minus 10 percent, the return on your equity is plus or minus

20 percent. If the margin declines to 33 percent, you can borrow more (67 percent), and the leverage factor is 3(1/0.33). When you acquire stock or other investments on margin, you are increasing the financial risk of the investment beyond the risk inherent in the security itself. You should increase your required rate of return accordingly.[38]

The following example shows how borrowing by using margin affects the distribution of your returns before commissions and interest on the loan. When the stock increased by 20 percent, your return on the investment was as follows:

1. The market value of the stock is $12,000, which leaves you with $7,000 after you pay off the loan.
2. The return on your $5,000 investment is:

$$\frac{7{,}000}{5{,}000} - 1 = 1.40 - 1$$
$$= 0.40 = 40\%$$

In contrast, if the stock declined by 20 percent to $40 a share, your return would be as follows:

1. The market value of the stock is $8,000, which leaves you with $3,000 after you pay off the loan.
2. The return on your $5,000 investment is:

$$\frac{3{,}000}{5{,}000} - 1 = 0.60 - 1$$
$$= -0.40 = -40\%$$

You should also recognize that this symmetrical increase in gains and losses is only true prior to commissions and interest. Obviously, if we assume a 6 percent interest on the borrowed funds (which would be $5,000 × 0.06 = $300) and a $100 commission on the transaction, the results would indicate a lower increase and a larger negative return as follows:

$$\text{20\% increase: } \frac{\$12{,}000 - \$5{,}000 - \$300 - \$100}{5{,}000} - 1$$
$$= \frac{6{,}600}{5{,}000} = -1$$
$$= 0.32 = 32\%$$
$$\text{20\% decline: } \frac{\$8{,}000 - \$5{,}000 - \$300 - \$100}{5{,}000} - 1$$
$$= \frac{2{,}600}{5{,}000} = -1$$
$$= -0.48 = -48\%$$

[38]For a discussion of margin calls following market declines in 1987 and 1990, see Karen Slater, "Margin Calls Create Dilemma for Investors," *Wall Street Journal,* 23 October 1987, 21; William Power, "Stocks' Drop Spurs Margin Calls Less Severe Than in Earlier Falls," *Wall Street Journal,* 15 August 1990, C1. For a discussion of margin debt as a market indicator, see Michael Siconolfi, "Does Margin-Loan Binge Signal Stock-Market Top?" *Wall Street Journal,* 23 April 1993, C1, C16.

In addition to the initial margin requirement, another important concept is the **maintenance margin**, which is the required proportion of your equity to the total value of the stock; the maintenance margin protects the broker if the stock price declines. At present, the minimum maintenance margin specified by the Federal Reserve is 25 percent, but, again, individual brokerage firms can dictate higher margins for their customers. If the stock price declines to the point where your equity drops below 25 percent of the total value of the position, the account is considered undermargined, and you will receive a **margin call** to provide more equity. If you do not respond with the required funds in time, the stock will be sold to pay off the loan. The time allowed to meet a margin call varies between investment firms and is affected by margin conditions. Under volatile conditions, the time allowed to respond to a margin call can be shortened drastically.

Given a maintenance margin of 25 percent, when you buy on margin you must consider how far the stock price can fall before you receive a margin call. The computation for our example is as follows: If the price of the stock is P and you own 200 shares, the value of the position is $200P$ and the equity in the account is $200P - \$5,000$. The percentage margin is $(200P - 5,000)/200P$. To determine the price, P, that is equal to 25 percent (0.25), we use the equation:

$$\frac{200P - \$5,000}{200P} = 0.25$$

$$200P - 5,000 = 50P$$

$$P = \$33.33$$

Therefore, when the stock is at \$33.33, the equity value is exactly 25 percent; so if the stock goes below \$33.33, the investor will receive a margin call.

To continue the previous example, if the stock declines to \$30 a share, its total market value would be \$6,000 and your equity would be \$1,000, which is only about 17 percent of the total value (\$1,000/\$6,000). You would receive a margin call for approximately \$667, which would give you equity of \$1,667, or 25 percent of the total value of the account (\$1,667/\$6,667).[39]

EXCHANGE MARKET MAKERS

Now that we have discussed the overall structure of the exchange markets and the orders that are used to buy and sell stocks, we can discuss the role and function of the market makers on the exchange. These people and the role they play differ among exchanges. For example, on U.S. exchanges these people are called **specialists**; on the TSE they are a combination of the *Saitori* and regular members. Most exchanges do not have a single market maker but have competing dealers. On exchanges that have central market makers, these individuals are critical to the smooth and efficient functioning of these markets.

As noted, a major requirement for a good market is liquidity, which depends on how the market makers do their job. Our initial discussion centers on the specialist's role in U.S. markets, followed by a consideration of comparable roles on exchanges in other countries.

U.S. MARKETS The specialist is a member of the exchange who applies to the exchange to be assigned stocks to handle.[40] The typical specialist will handle about 15 stocks.

[39]For a further discussion, see Georgette Jansen, "Cheap Margin Loans Are Tempting, but Beware," *Wall Street Journal, 23* April 1993, C1, C21.

[40]Each stock is assigned to one specialist. Most specialists are part of a unit that can be a formal organization of specialists (a specialist firm) or a set of independent specialists who join together to spread the workload and the risk of the stocks assigned to the unit. At the end of 1998, a total of 479 individual specialists made up 53 specialist units (about 9 specialists per unit).

The capital requirement for specialists changed in April 1998 in response to the October 1987 market crash. Specifically, the minimum capital required of each specialist unit was raised to $1 million or the value of 15,000 shares of each stock assigned, whichever is greater.

Functions of the Specialist Specialists have two major functions. First, they serve as *brokers* to match buy and sell orders and to handle special limit orders placed with member brokers. An individual broker who receives a limit order (or stop loss or stop buy order) leaves it with the specialist, who executes it when the specified price occurs. For this service, the specialist receives a portion of the broker's commission on the trade.

The second major function of a specialist is to act as a *dealer* to maintain a fair and orderly market by providing liquidity when the normal flow of orders is not adequate. In this capacity, the specialist must buy and sell for his or her own account (like an OTC dealer) when public supply or demand is insufficient to provide a continuous, liquid market.

Consider the following example. If a stock is currently selling for about $40 per share, the current bid and ask in an auction market (without the intervention of the specialist) might be a 40 bid–41 ask. Under such conditions, random market buy and sell orders might cause the stock price to fluctuate between 40 and 41 constantly—a movement of 2.5 percent between trades. Most investors would probably consider such a price pattern too volatile; the market would not be considered continuous. Under such conditions, the specialist is expected to provide "bridge liquidity" by entering alternative bids and asks or both to narrow the spread and improve the stock's price continuity. In this example, the specialist could enter a bid of 40½ or 40¾ or an ask of 40½ or 40¼ to narrow the spread to one-half or one-quarter point.

Specialists can enter either side of the market, depending on several factors, including the trend of the market. They are expected to buy or sell against the market when prices are clearly moving in one direction. Specifically, they are required to buy stock for their own inventories when there is an excess of sell orders and the market is definitely declining. Alternatively, they must sell stock from their inventories or sell it short to accommodate an excess of buy orders when the market is rising. Specialists are not expected to prevent prices from rising or declining, but only to ensure that the prices change in an orderly fashion (that is, to maintain price continuity). Evidence that they have fulfilled this requirement is that during recent years NYSE stocks traded unchanged from, or within one-eighth point of, the price of the previous trade about 95 percent of the time.

Another factor affecting specialists' decisions on how to narrow the spread is their current inventory position in the stock. For example, if they have large inventories of a given stock, all other factors being equal, they would probably enter on the ask (sell) side to reduce these heavy inventories. In contrast, specialists who have little or no inventory of shares because they had been selling from their inventories, or selling short, would tend toward the bid (buy) side of the market to rebuild their inventories or close out their short positions.

Finally, the position of the limit order book will influence how they act. Numerous limit buy orders (bids) close to the current market and few limit sell orders (asks) might indicate a tendency toward higher prices because demand is apparently heavy and supply is limited. Under such conditions, a specialist who is not bound by one of the other factors would probably opt to accumulate stock in anticipation of a price increase. The specialists on the NYSE have historically participated as dealers in 10 to 12 percent of all trades.

Specialist Income The specialist derives income from the broker and the dealer functions. The actual breakdown between the two sources depends on the specific stock. In an actively traded stock, such as IBM, a specialist has little need to act as a dealer because the substantial public interest in the stock creates a tight market (that is, a small bid–ask spread). In such a case, the main source of income would come from maintaining the limit orders for the stock. The income derived from acting as a broker for a stock such as IBM can be substantial and it is basically without risk.

In contrast, a stock with low trading volume and substantial price volatility would probably have a fairly wide bid–ask spread, and the specialist would have to be an active dealer. The specialist's income from such a stock would depend on his or her ability to trade it profitably. Specialists have a major advantage when trading because of their limit order books. Officially, only specialists are supposed to see the limit order book, which means that they would have a monopoly on very important information regarding the current supply and demand for a stock. The fact is that currently the specialists routinely share the limit order book with other brokers, so it is not a competitive advantage.[41]

Most specialists attempt to balance their portfolios between strong broker stocks that provide steady, riskless income and stocks that require active dealer roles. Notably, following the October 1987 market crash, specialists were required to increase their capital positions substantially, which would reduce their return on investment.[42]

TOKYO STOCK EXCHANGE (TSE) As of 1998, the TSE had a total of 124 "regular members" (100 Japanese members and 24 foreign members) and 1 *Saitori* member (4 *Saitori* firms merged during 1992). For each membership, the firm is allowed several people on the floor of the exchange, depending on its trading volume and capital position (the average number of employees on the floor is 20 per firm for a regular member and about 300 employees for the *Saitori* member).

Regular members buy and sell securities on the TSE either as agents or principals (brokers or dealers). *Saitori* members specialize in acting as intermediaries (brokers) for transactions among regular members, and they maintain the books for limit orders. (Stop loss and stop buy orders as well as short selling are not allowed.) Therefore, *Saitori* members match buy and sell orders for customers, handle limit orders, and are not allowed to deal with public customers; however, they do not act as dealers to maintain an orderly market. Only regular members are allowed to buy and sell for their own accounts. Therefore, the TSE is a two-way, continuous auction, order-driven market where buy and sell orders directly interact with one another with the *Saitori* acting as the auctioneer (intermediary) between firms submitting the orders.

Trading on the floor is enhanced by an electronic system called the Floor Order Routing and Execution System (FORES). This system is designed to: (1) automate order routing for small orders, (2) replace manual order books with electronic order books that can execute orders, and (3) computerize the reporting and confirmation process. All other stocks on the TSE are traded through a computer system called CORES, which stands for Computer-assisted Order Routing and Execution System. With CORES, orders become part of an electronic "book," which matches all buy and sell orders on the computer in accordance with trading rules. The system also automatically executes all orders for transactions at the last sale price and provides a narrow bid–ask spread within which orders are executed.

---

[41]Notably, if a major imbalance in trading arises due to new information, the specialist can request a temporary suspension of trading. For an analysis of what occurs during these trading suspensions, see Frank J. Fabozzi and Christopher K. Ma, "The Over-the-Counter Market and New York Stock Exchange Trading Halts," *Financial Review* 23, no. 4 (November 1988): 427–437. An example of a dramatic halt is discussed in Martha Brannigan, "Shares of Policy Management Nose-Dive 43%," *Wall Street Journal,* 7 April 1993, A4.

[42]For a rigorous analysis of specialist trading, see Ananth Madhaven and George Sofianos, "An Empirical Analysis of NYSE Specialist Trading," *Journal of Financial Economics* 48, no. 2 (May 1998): 189–210.

TSE membership is available to corporations licensed by the Minister of Finance. Member applicants may request any of four licenses: (1) to trade securities as a dealer, (2) to trade as a broker, (3) to underwrite new securities, or (4) to handle retail distribution of new or outstanding securities. A firm may have more than one license, but cannot act as a principal and agent in the same transaction. The minimum capital requirements for these licenses vary from 200 million to 3 billion yen ($2 million to $30 million), depending on the type of license.

Although Japan's securities laws allow foreign securities firms to obtain membership on the exchanges, the individual exchanges determine whether membership will be granted. Twenty-four foreign firms have become members of the TSE since 1986.[43]

LONDON STOCK EXCHANGE (LSE) Members on the LSE are either brokers who make markets in various equities and gilts (British government bonds) and jobbers who can deal with non-stock-exchange members, including the public and institutions.

Membership in the LSE is granted based on experience and competence, and there are no citizenship or residency requirements. Currently, more than 5,000 individual memberships are held by 214 broker firms and 22 jobbers. Although individuals gain membership, the operational unit is a firm that pays an annual charge equal to 1 percent of its gross revenues.

CHANGES IN THE SECURITIES MARKETS

During the past two decades, numerous changes have emerged because of the significant growth of trading by large financial institutions, such as banks, insurance companies, pension funds, and investment companies. Additional changes have transpired because of capital market globalization. In this section, we discuss these changes, consider their impact on the market, and speculate about future changes.

EVIDENCE AND EFFECT OF INSTITUTIONALIZATION

The growing influence of large financial institutions is shown by data on block trades (transactions involving at least 10,000 shares) in Table 4.6. Financial institutions are the main source of large block trades, and the number of block trades on the NYSE has grown steadily from a daily average of 9 in 1965 to almost 14,000 a day in 1998. On average, such trades constitute almost half of all the volume on the exchange.[44]

Several major effects of this institutionalization of the market have been identified:

1. Negotiated (competitive) commission rates
2. The influence of block trades
3. The impact on stock price volatility
4. The development of a National Market System (NMS)

[43]Some observers have questioned the pure economics of these memberships, but the firms have defended them as a means of becoming a part of the Japanese financial community. In this regard, see Marcus W. Brauchli, "U.S. Brokerage Firms Operating in Japan Have Mixed Results," *Wall Street Journal,* 16 August 1989, A1, A8.

[44]Although the influence of institutional trading is greatest on the NYSE, it is also a major factor on the AMEX, where block trades constituted about 43 percent of share volume in 1997, and on the NASDAQ-NMS, where block trades accounted for almost 50 percent of share volume in 1997. Evidence of continued institutional growth is that mutual fund sales in 1997 were a record $378 billion. See Robert McGough, "Stock Funds' Inflows Total $99 Billion in '96," *Wall Street Journal,* 29 May 1996, C1, C23.

TABLE 4.6 **BLOCK TRANSACTIONS[a] ON THE NYSE**

Year	Total Number of Block Transactions	Total Number of Shares in Block Trades (× 1,000)	Percentage of Reported Volume	Average Number of Block Transactions per Day
1965	2,171	48,262	3.1%	9
1970	17,217	450,908	15.4	68
1975	34,420	778,540	16.6	136
1980	133,597	3,311,132	29.2	528
1985	539,039	14,222,272	51.7	2,139
1986	665,587	17,811,335	49.9	2,631
1987	970,679	24,497,241	51.2	3,639
1988	768,419	22,270,680	54.5	3,037
1989	872,811	21,316,132	51.1	3,464
1990	843,365	19,681,849	49.6	3,333
1991	981,077	22,474,382	49.6	3,878
1992	1,134,832	26,069,383	50.7	4,468
1993	1,477,859	35,959,117	53.7	5,841
1994	1,654,505	40,757,770	55.5	6,565
1995	1,963,889	49,736,912	57.0	7,793
1996	2,348,457	58,510,323	55.9	9,246
1997	2,831,321	67,832,129	50.9	11,191
1998	3,518,200	82,656,678	48.7	13,961

[a]Trades of 10,000 shares or more.

Source: *NYSE Fact Book* (New York: NYSE, various issues). Reprinted by permission.

In the following sections, we discuss how each of these effects has affected the operation of the U.S. securities market.

Negotiated Commission Rates

BACKGROUND When the NYSE was formally established in 1792, it was agreed that members would carry out all trades in designated stocks on the exchange, and that they would charge nonmembers on the basis of a *minimum commission schedule* that outlawed price cutting. The minimum commission schedule was initially developed to compensate for handling small orders and made no allowance for the trading of large orders by institutions. As a result, institutional investors had to pay substantially more in commissions than the costs of the transactions justified.

The initial reaction to the excess commissions was "give-ups," whereby brokers agreed to pay part of their commissions (sometimes as much as 80 percent) to other investment firms designated by the institution making the trade that provided services to the institution. These commission transfers were referred to as *soft dollars*. Another response was the increased use of the third market, where commissions were not fixed as they were on the NYSE, and the use of the fourth market.

NEGOTIATED COMMISSIONS In 1970, the SEC began a program of negotiated commissions on large transactions and finally allowed negotiated commissions on all transactions on May 1, 1975 ("May Day").

The effect on commissions charged has been dramatic. Currently, commissions for institutions are in the range of 5 to 10 cents per share regardless of the price of the stock, which implies a large discount on high-priced shares. Individuals also receive discounts from numerous competing discount brokers who charge a straight transaction fee and provide no research advice or safekeeping services. These discounts vary depending on the size of the trade. Beyond using discount brokers for typical transactions initiated by a phone call to the broker, the emerging trend is transactions over the Internet, where there is a relatively low flat charge ($15–$20) irrespective of the size of the order. The overall effect of competitive commission rates has been that total commissions paid have shown a significant decline, and the size and structure of the industry have changed.[45]

THE IMPACT OF BLOCK TRADES

Because the increase in institutional trading has caused an increase in block trades, it is important to consider how block trades influence the market and understand how they trade.

BLOCK TRADES ON THE EXCHANGES The increase in block trading by institutions has strained the specialist system, which had three problems with block trading: capital, commitment, and contacts (the "three Cs"). First, specialists did not have the capital needed to acquire blocks of 10,000 or 20,000 shares. Second, even when specialists had the capital, they may have been unwilling to commit the capital because of the large risks involved. Finally, because of Rule 113, specialists were not allowed to directly contact institutions to offer a block brought by another institution. Therefore, they were cut off from the major source of demand for blocks and were reluctant to take large positions in thinly traded stocks.

BLOCK HOUSES This lack of capital, commitment, and contacts by specialists on the exchange resulted in the development of block houses. *Block houses* are investment firms (also referred to as *upstairs traders* because they are away from the exchange floor) that help institutions locate other institutions interested in buying or selling blocks of stock. A good block house has (1) the capital required to position a large block, (2) the willingness to commit this capital to a block transaction, and (3) contacts among institutions.

EXAMPLE OF A BLOCK TRADE Assume a mutual fund decides to sell 50,000 of its 250,000 shares of Ford Motors. The fund decides to do it through Goldman Sachs & Company (GS&Co.), a large block house and lead underwriter for Ford that knows institutions interested in the stock. After being contacted by the fund, the traders at Goldman Sachs contact several institutions that own Ford to see if any of them want to add to their position and to determine their bids. Assume that the previous sale of Ford on the NYSE was at $46\frac{3}{4}$ and GS& Co. receives commitments from four different institutions for a total of 40,000 shares at an average price of $46\frac{5}{8}$. Goldman Sachs returns to the mutual fund and bids $46\frac{1}{2}$ minus a negotiated commission for the total 50,000 shares. Assuming the fund accepts the bid, Goldman Sachs now owns the block and immediately sells 40,000 shares to the four institutions that made prior commitments. It also "positions" 10,000 shares; that is, it owns the 10,000 shares and must eventually sell them at the best price possible. Because GS&Co. is a member of the NYSE, the block will be processed ("crossed") on the exchange as one transaction of 50,000 shares at $46\frac{1}{2}$. The specialist on the NYSE might take some of the stock to fill limit orders on the book at prices between $46\frac{1}{2}$ and $46\frac{3}{4}$.

---

[45]Three papers examine the impact of regional exchanges and the practice of purchasing order flow that would normally go to the NYSE; see Robert H. Battalio, "Third Market Broker-Dealers: Cost Competitors or Cream Skimmers?" *Journal of Finance* 52, no. 1 (March 1997): 341–352; Robert Battalio, Jason Greene, and Robert Jennings, "Do Competing Specialists and Preferencing Dealers Affect Market Quality?" University of Notre Dame Working Paper (December 1995); and David Easley, Nicholas Kiefer, and Maureen O'Hara, "Cream/ Skimming or Profit Sharing? The Curious Role of Purchased Order Flow," *Journal of Finance* 51, no. 3 (July 1996): 811–833.

For working on this trade, GS&Co. receives a negotiated commission, but it has committed almost $470,000 to position the 10,000 shares. The major risk to GS&Co. is the possibility of a subsequent price change on the 10,000 shares. If it can sell the10,000 shares for 46½ or more, it will just about break even on the position and have the commission as income. If the price of the stock weakens, GS&Co. may have to sell the position at 46¼ and take a loss on it of about $2,500, offsetting the income from the commission.

This example indicates the importance of institutional contacts, capital to position a portion of the block, and willingness to commit that capital to the block trade. Without all three, the transaction would not take place.

Institutions and Stock Price Volatility

Some stock market observers speculate there should be a strong positive relationship between institutional trading and stock price volatility because institutions trade in large blocks, and it is contended that they tend to trade together. Empirical studies of the relationship between the proportion of trading by large financial institutions and stock price volatility have never supported the folklore.[46] In a capital market where trading is dominated by institutions, the best environment is one where all institutions are actively involved because they provide liquidity for one another and for noninstitutional investors.

National Market System (NMS)

The development of a National Market System (NMS) has been advocated by financial institutions because it is expected to provide greater efficiency, competition, and lower cost of transactions. Although there is no generally accepted definition of an NMS, four major characteristics are generally expected:

1. Centralized reporting of all transactions
2. Centralized quotation system
3. Centralized limit order book (CLOB)
4. Competition among all qualified market makers

CENTRALIZED REPORTING Centralized reporting requires a composite tape to report all transactions in a stock regardless of where the transactions took place. On the tape you might see a trade in GM on the NYSE, another trade on the Chicago Exchange, and a third on the OTC. The intent is to provide a tape that contains full information of all completed trades.

As of June 1975, the NYSE began operating a central tape that includes all NYSE stocks traded on other exchanges and on the OTC. The volume of shares reported on the consolidated tape is shown in Table 4.7. The recent breakdown among the seven exchanges and two OTC markets appears in Table 4.8. Therefore, this component of a National Market System (NMS) is available for stocks listed on the NYSE. As shown, although the volume of trading is dispersed among the exchanges and the NASD, the NYSE is clearly dominant and has increased its share since a low point in 1992.[47]

---

[46]In this regard, see Neil Berkman, "Institutional Investors and the Stock Market," *New England Economic Review* (November–December 1977): 60–77; and Frank K. Reilly and David J. Wright, "Block Trades and Aggregate Stock Price Volatility," *Financial Analysts Journal* 40, no. 2 (March–April 1984): 54–60.

[47]For a discussion of these changes, see Craig Torres and William Power, "Big Board Is Losing Some of Its Influence over Stock Trading," *Wall Street Journal,* 17 April 1990, A1, A6; William Power, "Big Board, at Age 200, Scrambles to Protect Grip on Stock Market," *Wall Street Journal,* 13 May 1992, A1, A8; and Pat Widder, "NASDAQ Has Its Eyes Set on the Next 100 Years," *Chicago Tribune,* 17 May 1992, Section 7, pp. 1, 4.

TABLE 4.7

CONSOLIDATED TAPE VOLUME (THOUSANDS OF SHARES)

1976	6,281,008	1993	81,926,892
1980	12,935,607	1994	88,870,770
1985	32,988,595	1995	106,554,583
1990	48,188,072	1996	126,340,065
1991	55,294,725	1997	159,451,717
1992	63,064,667	1998	203,727,877

Source: *NYSE Fact Book* (New York: NYSE, 1999).

TABLE 4.8

EXCHANGES AND MARKETS INVOLVED IN CONSOLIDATED TAPE WITH PERCENTAGE OF TRADES DURING 1998

	Percentage		Percentage
AMEX	0.00%	NASD	7.87%
Boston	1.41	NYSE	84.07
Chicago	4.01	Pacific	1.69
Cincinnati	0.88	Philadelphia	0.76
Instinet	0.00[a]		

[a]Instinet percent of trades included in NASD total after December 1, 1993.

Source: *NYSE Fact Book* (New York: NYSE, 1999): 25.

CENTRALIZED QUOTATION SYSTEM A centralized quotation system would list the quotes for a given stock (say, IBM) from all market makers on the national exchanges, the regional exchanges, and the OTC. With such a system, a broker who requested the current market quota for IBM would see all the prevailing quotes and should complete the trade on the market with the best quote.

Intermarket Trading System A centralized quotation system is currently available—the Intermarket Trading System (ITS), developed by the American, Boston, Chicago, New York, Pacific, and Philadelphia Stock Exchanges and the NASD. ITS consists of a central computer facility with interconnected terminals in the participating market centers. As shown in Table 4.9, the number of issues included, the volume of trading, and the size of trades have all grown substantially. Of the 4,535 issues included on the system in 1997, 3,711 were listed on the NYSE and 824 were listed on the AMEX.

With ITS, brokers and market makers in each market center indicate specific buying and selling commitments through a composite quotation display that shows the current quotes for each stock in every market center. A broker is expected to go to the best market to execute a customer's order by sending a message committing to a buy or sell at the price quoted. When this commitment is accepted, a message reports the transaction. The following example illustrates how ITS works.

A broker on the NYSE has a market order to sell 100 shares of IBM stock. Assuming the quotation display at the NYSE shows that the best current bid for IBM is on the Chicago Stock Exchange (CSE), the broker will enter an order to sell 100 shares at the bid on the CSE. Within seconds, the commitment flashes on the computer screen and is printed out at the CSE specialist's post where it is executed against the CSE bid. The transaction is reported back to New York and on the consolidated tape. Both brokers receive immediate confirmation and the results are transmitted to the appropriate market centers at the end of each day. Thereafter, each broker completes his or her own clearance and settlement procedure.

TABLE 4.9

INTERMARKET TRADING SYSTEM ACTIVITY

		Daily Average		
Year	Issues Eligible	Share Volume	Executed Trades	Average Size of Trade
1980	884	1,565,900	2,868	546
1985	1,288	5,669,400	5,867	966
1990	2,126	9,387,114	8,744	1,075
1995	3,542	12,185,064	10,911	1,117
1996	4,001	12,721,968	11,426	1,113
1997	4,535	15,429,377	14,057	1,098
1998	4,844	18,136,472	17,056	1,063

Source: *NYSE Fact Book* (New York: NYSE, 1999): 28.

The ITS system currently provides centralized quotations for stocks listed on the NYSE and specifies whether a bid or ask *away* from the NYSE market is superior to that *on* the NYSE. Note, however, that the system lacks several characteristics. It does not have the capability for automatic execution at the best market. Instead you must contact the market maker and indicate that you want to buy or sell, at which time the bid or ask may be withdrawn. Also, it is not mandatory that a broker go to the best market. Although the best price may be at another market center, a broker might consider it inconvenient to trade on that exchange if the price difference is not substantial. It is almost impossible to audit such actions. Still, even with these shortcomings, substantial technical and operational progress has occurred on a central quotation system.

CENTRAL LIMIT ORDER BOOK (CLOB) Substantial controversy has surrounded the idea of a central limit order book (CLOB) that would contain all limit orders from all exchanges. Ideally, the CLOB would be visible to everyone, and all market makers and traders could fill orders on it. Currently, most limit orders are placed with specialists on the NYSE and filled when a transaction on the NYSE reaches the stipulated price. The NYSE specialist receives some part of the commission for rendering this service. The NYSE has opposed a CLOB because its specialists do not want to share this lucrative business. Although the technology for a CLOB is available, it is difficult to estimate when it will become a reality.

COMPETITION AMONG MARKET MAKERS (RULE 390) Market makers have always competed on the OTC market, but competition has been opposed by the NYSE. The argument in favor of competition among market makers is that it forces dealers to offer better bids and asks, or they will not do any business. Several studies have indicated that competition among a large number of dealers (as in the OTC market) results in a smaller spread. In contrast, the NYSE argues that a central auction market forces all orders to one central location where the orders are exposed to all interested participants and this central auction results in the best market and execution, including many transactions at prices between the current bid and ask.

To help create a centralized market, the NYSE's Rule 390 requires members to obtain the permission of the exchange before carrying out a transaction in a listed stock off the exchange. This rule is intended to draw all volume to the NYSE so that the exchange can provide the most complete auction market. The exchange contends that Rule 390 is necessary to protect the auction market, arguing that its elimination would fragment the market, tempting members to trade off the exchange and to internalize many orders (that is, members would match orders from their own customers, which would keep these orders from exposure to the full auction market). Progress in achieving this final phase of the NMS has been slow because of strong opposition by members of the investment community and caution by the SEC.[48]

NEW TRADING SYSTEMS

As daily trading volume has gone from about 5 million shares to more than 600 million shares, it has become necessary to introduce new technology into the trading process. Currently, the NYSE routinely handles days with volume over 600 million and had a record daily high of more than 1.2 billion in 1998. The following discussion considers some technological innovations that assist in the trading process.

SUPER DOT Super Dot is an electronic order-routing system through which member firms transmit market and limit orders in NYSE-listed securities directly to the posts where securities are traded or to the member firm's booth. After the order has been executed, a report of execution is returned directly to the member firm office over the same electronic circuit, and the execution is submitted directly to the comparison systems. Member firms can enter market orders up to 2,099 shares and limit orders in round or odd lots up to 30,099 shares. An estimated 85 percent of all market orders enter the NYSE through the Super Dot system.

DISPLAY BOOK The Display Book is an electronic workstation that keeps track of all limit orders and incoming market orders. This includes incoming Super Dot limit orders.

OPENING AUTOMATED REPORT SERVICE (OARS) OARS, the opening feature of the Super Dot system, accepts member firms' preopening market orders up to 30,099 shares. OARS automatically and continuously pairs buy and sell orders and presents the imbalance to the specialist prior to the opening of a stock. This system helps the specialist determine the opening price and the potential need for a preopening call market.

MARKET ORDER PROCESSING Super Dot's postopening market order system is designed to accept member firms' postopening market orders up to 30,099 shares. The system provides rapid execution and reporting of market orders. During 1997, 92.4% of market orders were executed and reported in less than 60 seconds.

LIMIT ORDER PROCESSING The limit order processing system electronically files orders to be executed when and if a specific price is reached. The system accepts limit orders up to 99,999 shares and electronically updates the Specialists' Display Book. Good-until-canceled orders that are not executed on the day of submission are automatically stored until executed or canceled.

GLOBAL MARKET CHANGES

NYSE OFF-HOURS TRADING One of the major concerns of the NYSE is the continuing erosion of its market share for stocks listed on the NYSE due to global trading. Specifically, the share of trading of NYSE-listed stock has declined from about 80 to 85 percent during the early 1980s to about 75 percent in 1997. This reflects an increase in trading on regional exchanges and the third market, some increase in fourth-market trading, but mainly an increase in trading in foreign markets in London and Tokyo. The NYSE has attempted to respond to this by expanding its trading hours and listing more non-U.S. stocks.

[48]For a recent article, see Hans R. Stoll, "Organization of the Stock Market: Competition or Fragmentation," *Journal of Applied Corporate Finance* 5, no. 4 (winter 1993): 89–93.

The expansion of hours was initiated in May 1991, when the SEC approved a 2-year pilot program of two NYSE crossing sessions.

Crossing Session I (CSI) provides the opportunity to trade individual stocks at the NYSE closing prices after the regular session—from 4:15 P.M. to 5:00 P.M. In 1997, CSI averaged 358,000 shares per day and had a record of 14 million shares in September 1995. Crossing Session II (CSII) allows trading a collection of at least 15 NYSE stocks with a market value of at least $1 million. This session is from 4:00 P.M. to 5:15 P.M. During 1997, the average daily share volume during CSII was about 4.1 million shares.

Listing Foreign Stocks on the NYSE A major goal and concern for the NYSE is the ability to list foreign stocks on the exchange. The NYSE chairman, Richard A. Grasso, has stated on several occasions that the exchange recognizes that much of the growth in the coming decades will be in foreign countries and their stocks. As a result, the exchange wants to list a number of these stocks. The problem is that current SEC regulations will not allow the NYSE to list these firms because they follow less-stringent foreign accounting and disclosure standards. Specifically, many foreign companies issue financial statements less frequently and with less information than what is required by the SEC. As a result, about 360 foreign firms currently have shares traded on the NYSE (mainly through ADRs), but it is contended that 2,000 to 3,000 foreign companies would qualify for listing on the NYSE except for the accounting rules. The exchange contends that unless the rules are adjusted and the NYSE is allowed to compete with other world exchanges (the LSE lists more than 600 foreign stocks), it will eventually become a regional exchange in the global market. The view of the SEC is that they have an obligation to ensure that investors receive adequate disclosure. This difference hopefully will be resolved during 1999 in favor of allowing additional foreign listings.[49] Even with the stringent requirements, stocks from more than 60 companies were listed during 1997.

LONDON STOCK EXCHANGE The London Stock Exchange initiated several major changes on October 27, 1986, in an event referred to as the *Big Bang.* As a result of this event, brokers can act as market makers, jobbers can deal with the public and with institutions, and all commissions are fully negotiable.

The gilt market was restructured to resemble the U.S. government securities market. The Bank of England approved a system whereby 27 primary dealers make markets in U.K. government securities and transact with a limited number of interdealer brokers. This new arrangement has created a more competitive environment.

Trades are reported on a system called *Stock Exchange Automated Quotations (SEAQ) International,* which is an electronic market-price information system similar to NASDAQ. In addition, real-time prices are being shared with the NYSE while the NASD provides certain U.S. OTC prices to the London market. Also, as discussed earlier, 35 U.S. OTC stocks are available for 24-hour trading between New York, Tokyo, Singapore, and London.

Access to membership on the exchange has increased; foreign firms are admitted as members, and they can be wholly owned by non-U.K. firms. As a result, some U.S. banks have acquired British stockbrokers, and several major U.S. firms are now members of the exchange.

[49]The NYSE argument is supported in the following articles: William J. Baumol and Burton Malkiel, "Redundant Regulation of Foreign Security Trading and U.S. Competitiveness," *Journal of Applied Corporate Finance* 5, no. 4 (winter 1993): 19–27; and Franklin Edwards, "Listing of Foreign Securities on U.S. Exchanges," *Journal of Applied Corporate Finance* 5, no. 4 (winter 1993): 28–36.

Effects of the Big Bang Probably one of the most visually striking changes caused by the Big Bang occurred on the trading floor of the LSE. Prior to October 1986, the activity on the floor of the LSE was similar to that on the NYSE and the TSE—large numbers of people gathered around trading posts and moving between the phones and the posts. Currently, the exchange floor is completely deserted except for some traders in stock options. Once they introduced competitive market makers on the floor of the exchange, it was just as easy to buy and sell listed stocks away from the exchange using the quotes on SEAQ.

The rest of the Big Bang's effects can be summarized by the phrase "more business, less profit." Specifically, there is more activity throughout the system, but profit margins have declined or disappeared due to the intense competition. In the process, many firms have merged or been acquired by firms from the United States, Japan, or Germany that have been willing to accept lower returns to establish market presence.[50]

TOKYO STOCK EXCHANGE (TSE) The TSE experienced a "big bang" during 1998 that introduced more competition in trading commissions and also encouraged competition among market participants.

By late 1997, 25 foreign firms were members of the TSE. Four Japanese investment firms dominate the Japanese financial market: Nomura, Daiwa, Nikko, and Yamaichi. The foreign firms were less aggressive between 1992 and 1997 because of the dramatic slowdown in the Japanese economy and its securities market.[51]

Future Developments

In addition to the expected effects of the NMS and a global capital market, there are other changes that you should understand.

CONTINUING CONSOLIDATION OF SECURITY EXCHANGES Earlier in the chapter we discussed several mergers and affiliations among security exchanges in the United States and Europe. Because of the significant economic arguments in favor of these consolidations, we anticipate a continuation of this trend in the United States and Europe, as well as in the Far East and Latin America.

MORE SPECIALIZED INVESTMENT COMPANIES Although more individuals want to own stocks and bonds, they have increasingly acquired this ownership through investment companies because most individuals find it too difficult and time-consuming to do their own analysis. This increase in fund sales has caused an explosion of new funds (discussed in Chapters 3 and 26) that provide numerous opportunities to diversify in a wide range of asset classes.

This trend toward specialized funds will continue and could possibly include other investment alternatives, such as stamps, coins, and art. Because of the lower liquidity of foreign securities, stamps, coins, and art, many of these new mutual funds will be closed-end and will be traded on an exchange. These closed-end funds and their surge in popularity are discussed in Chapter 26.

CHANGES IN THE FINANCIAL SERVICES INDUSTRY The financial services industry is experiencing a major change in makeup and operation. Prior to 1960,

---

[50]Craig Forman, "Britain's Deregulation Leaves a Casualty Trail in Securities Industry," *Wall Street Journal,* 14 October 1987, 1, 18.

[51]For a discussion of the problems, see Robert Thomson, "New Plea to Japan to Reform Markets," *Financial Times,* 5 February 1993, 17; Gilliam Tett, "Tokyo Urged to Boost System of Regulation under Big Bang," *Financial Times,* 15 April 1998, 1; and James Kynge and John Ridding, "China Calls for Japan to Act as Asian Crisis Bites," *Financial Times,* 10 June 1998, 1.

the securities industry was composed of specialty firms that concentrated in specific investments, such as stocks, bonds, commodities, real estate, or insurance. A trend during the early 1980s focused on creating financial supermarkets that considered all these investment alternatives around the world. Prime examples would be Merrill Lynch, which acquired insurance and real estate subsidiaries, and Travelers Insurance, which acquired Salomon Brothers and Smith Barney. A subset includes firms that are global in coverage, but limit their product line to mainstream investment instruments, such as bonds, stocks, futures, and options. Firms in this category would include Merrill Lynch, Goldman Sachs, and recently merged Morgan Stanley Dean Witter, among others. At the other end of the spectrum, large banks, such as Citicorp, want to become involved in the investment banking business.

In contrast to financial supermarkets, some firms have decided not to be all things to all people. These firms are going the specialty, or "boutique," route, attempting to provide unique, superior financial products. Examples include discount brokers, investment firms that concentrate on institutional or individual investors, or firms that concentrate on an industry, such as banking.

It appears we are moving toward a world with two major groups. Specifically, one group would include a few global investment firms that deal in almost all the asset classes available, while the second group would include numerous firms that provide specialized services in unique products.

TRADING IN CYBERMARKETS Beyond these firm changes, the advances in technology continue to accelerate and promise to affect how the secondary market will be organized and operated.[52] Specifically, computerized trading has made tremendous inroads during the past five years and promises to introduce numerous additional changes into the 21st century in markets around the world. The 24-hour market will require extensive computerized trading. It is envisioned that the markets of the future will be floorless, global, and highly automated.

THE INTERNET *Investments Online*

Many Internet sites deal with different aspects of investing. Earlier site suggestions led you to information and prices of securities traded both in the United States and around the globe. Here are some additional sites of interest:

www.quote.com This site offers substantial market information, including price quotes on stocks, bonds, and options. Charts of price activity at 5-minute, 15-minute, daily, or weekly intervals are available. News headlines and stories from a number of sources are available on the site. Various research sources are offered, including Lipper, Disclosure, Zacks, First Call, and Options Analytics.

www.sec.gov The Web site of the SEC (Securities and Exchange Commission) offers news and information, investor assistance and complaint handling, SEC rules, enforcement, and data.

(continued)

[52]This includes the "Market 2000" report, prepared by the SEC, that is concerned with the organization and operation of securities markets in the United States. Notably, many emerging market exchanges are able to "leapfrog" to the latest technology. This also includes the technology innovations related to the merger of the NASD, the AMEX, and the Philadelphia Exchange discussed earlier. This is discussed in Paula Dwyer, A. Osterland, K. Capell, and S. Reier, "The 21st Century Stock Market," *Business Week,* 10 August 1998, 66–72; and Greg Ip, "Instinet Expands Its Presence," *Wall Street Journal,* 28 July 1999, C1, which discusses a new electronic market that will compete with the NYSE and the NASDAQ.

THE INTERNET *Investments Online (cont.)*

www.nyse.com and **www.nasdaq-amex.com** The Web sites of the New York Stock Exchange and the merged National Association of Securities Dealers Automated Quotation (NASDAQ) system and the American Stock Exchange offer information about the relevant market, price quotes, listings of firms, and investor services. The NASDAQ-AMEX site includes price quotes for SPDRs (S&P Depository Receipts, which represent ownership in the S&P 500 index or the S&P Midcap 400 index) and WEBS (World Equity Benchmark Shares, which track the Morgan Stanley Capital International [MSCI] indexes of 17 different countries).

www.etrade.com, www.schwab.com, and **www.ml.com** Many brokerage houses have Web pages. These are three examples of such sites. E*Trade Securities is an example of an online brokerage firm that allows investors to trade securities over the Internet. Schwab is a discount broker, whereas Merrill Lynch is a full-service broker with a reputation for good research.

Summary

- The securities market is divided into primary and secondary markets. Secondary markets provide the liquidity that is critical for primary markets. The major segments of the secondary markets include listed exchanges (the NYSE, AMEX, TSE, LSE, and regional exchanges), the over-the-counter market, the third market, and the fourth market. Because you will want to invest across these secondary markets within a country as well as among countries, you need to understand how the markets differ and how they are similar.
- Many of the dramatic changes in our securities markets during the past 30 years are due to an increase in institutional trading and to rapidly evolving global markets. It is important to understand what has happened and why it happened because numerous changes have occurred—and many more are yet to come. You need to understand how these changes will affect your investment alternatives and opportunities. You must look not only for the best investment, but also for the best securities market. This discussion should provide the background to help you make that trading decision.

Questions

1. Define *market* and briefly discuss the characteristics of a good market.
2. You own 100 shares of General Electric stock and you want to sell it because you need the money to make a down payment on a stereo. Assume there is absolutely no secondary market system in common stocks. How would you go about selling the stock? Discuss what you would have to do to find a buyer, how long it might take, and the price you might receive.
3. Define *liquidity* and discuss the factors that contribute to it. Give examples of a liquid asset and an illiquid asset, and discuss why they are considered liquid and illiquid.
4. Define a primary and secondary market for securities and discuss how they differ. Discuss why the primary market is dependent on the secondary market.
5. Give an example of an initial public offering (IPO) in the primary market. Give an example of a seasoned equity issue in the primary market. Discuss which would involve greater risk to the buyer.
6. Find an advertisement for a recent primary offering in *The Wall Street Journal.* Based on the information in the ad, indicate the characteristics of the security sold and the major underwriters. How much new capital did the firm derive from the offering before paying commissions?
7. Briefly explain the difference between a competitive bid underwriting and a negotiated underwriting.
8. The figures in Table 4.3 reveal a major difference in the price paid for a membership (seat) on the NYSE compared with one on the AMEX. How would you explain this difference?
9. What are the major reasons for the existence of regional stock exchanges? Discuss how they differ from the national exchanges.
10. Which segment of the secondary stock market (listed exchanges or the OTC) is larger in terms of the number of issues? Which is larger in terms of the value of the issues traded?

11. Discuss the three levels of NASDAQ in terms of what each provides and who would subscribe to each.
12. a. Define the third market. Give an example of a third-market stock.
    b. Define the fourth market. Discuss why a financial institution would use the fourth market.
13. Briefly define each of the following terms and give an example:
    a. Market order
    b. Limit order
    c. Short sale
    d. Stop loss order
14. Briefly discuss the two major functions and sources of income for the NYSE specialist.
15. Describe the duties of the *Saitori* member on the TSE. Discuss how these duties differ from those of the NYSE specialist.
16. Discuss why the U.S. equity market has experienced major changes since 1965.
17. What were give-ups? What are "soft dollars"? Discuss why soft dollars and give-ups existed when there were fixed commissions.
18. The discussion of block trades noted that the specialist is hampered by the three Cs. Discuss each of the three Cs as it relates to block trading.
19. Describe block houses and explain why they evolved. Describe what is meant by *positioning* part of a block.
20. a. Describe the major attributes of the National Market System (NMS).
    b. Briefly describe the ITS and what it contributes to the NMS. Discuss the growth of the ITS.
21. The chapter includes a discussion of expected changes in world capital markets. Discuss one of the suggested changes in terms of what has been happening or discuss an evolving change that was not mentioned.

Problems

1. The initial margin requirement is 60 percent. You have $40,000 to invest in a stock selling for $80 a share. Ignoring taxes and commissions, show in detail the impact on your rate of return if the stock rises to $100 a share and if it declines to $40 a share assuming: (a) you pay cash for the stock, and (b) you buy it using maximum leverage.
2. Lauren has a margin account and deposits $50,000. Assuming the prevailing margin requirement is 40 percent, commissions are ignored, and The Gentry Shoe Corporation is selling at $35 per share:
    a. How many shares can Lauren purchase using the maximum allowable margin?
    b. What is Lauren's profit (loss) if the price of Gentry's stock
        1. rises to $45?
        2. falls to $25?
    c. If the maintenance margin is 30 percent, to what price can Gentry Shoe fall before Lauren will receive a margin call?
3. Suppose you buy a round lot of Maginn Industries stock on 55 percent margin when the stock is selling at $20 a share. The broker charges a 10 percent annual interest rate, and commissions are 3 percent of the total stock value on both the purchase and sale. A year later you receive a $0.50 per share dividend and sell the stock for 27. What is your rate of return on the investment?
4. You decide to sell short 100 shares of Charlotte Horse Farms when it is selling at its yearly high of 56. Your broker tells you that your margin requirement is 45 percent and that the commission on the purchase is $155. While you are short the stock, Charlotte pays a $2.50 per share dividend. At the end of 1 year, you buy 100 shares of Charlotte at 45 to close out your position and are charged a commission of $145 and 8 percent interest on the money borrowed. What is your rate of return on the investment?
5. You own 200 shares of Shamrock Enterprises that you bought at $25 a share. The stock is now selling for $45 a share.
    a. If you put in a stop loss order at $40, discuss your reasoning for this action.
    b. If the stock eventually declines in price to $30 a share, what would be your rate of return with and without the stop loss order?
6. Two years ago, you bought 300 shares of Kayleigh Milk Co. for $30 a share with a margin of 60 percent. Currently, the Kayleigh stock is selling for $45 a share. Assuming no dividends and

ignoring commissions, (a) compute the annualized rate of return on this investment if you had paid cash and (b) your rate of return with the margin purchase.

7. The stock of the Michele Travel Co. is selling for $28 a share. You put in a limit buy order at $24 for one month. During the month, the stock price declines to $20, then jumps to $36. Ignoring commissions, what would have been your rate of return on this investment? What would be your rate of return if you had put in a market order? What if your limit order was at $18?

References

AMEX Fact Book. New York: AMEX, published annually.

Amihad, Y., T. Ho, and Robert Schwartz. *Market Making and the Changing Structure of the Securities Industry.* New York: Lexington-Heath, 1985.

Amihad, Y., and H. Mendelson. "Trading Mechanisms and Stock Returns: An Empirical Investigation." *Journal of Finance* 42, no. 3 (July 1987).

Barclay, Michael J., William G. Christie, Jeffrey H. Harris, Eugene Kandel, and Paul Schultz. "The Effects of Market Reform on the Trading Costs and Depth of NASDAQ Stocks." *Journal of Finance* 54, no. 1 (March, 1999).

Beidleman, Carl, ed. *The Handbook of International Investing.* Chicago: Probus Publishing, 1987.

Blume, Marshall E., and Jeremy J. Siegel. "The Theory of Security Pricing and Market Structure." *Financial Markets, Institutions and Instruments* 1, no. 3 (1992). New York University Salomon Center.

Blume, Marshall E., and Michael Goldstein. "Quotes, Order Flow, and Price Discovery." *Journal of Finance* 52, no. 1 (March 1997).

Christie, William, and Paul Schultz. "Why Do NASDAQ Market-Makers Avoid Odd-Eighth Quotes?" *Journal of Finance* 49, no. 5 (December 1994).

Cohen, Kalman, Steven Maier, Robert Schwartz, and David Whitcomb. *The Microstructure of Securities Markets.* Englewood Cliffs, N.J.: Prentice-Hall, 1986.

Dutts, Prajit, and Ananth Madhaven. "Competition and Collusion in Dealer Markets." *Journal of Finance* 52, no. 1 (March 1997).

Economides, Nicholas, and Robert A. Schwartz. "Electronic Call Market Trading." *Journal of Portfolio Management* 21, no. 3 (spring 1995).

Godek, P., "Why NASDAQ Market Makers Avoid Odd Eighth Quotes," *Journal of Financial Economics* 41, no. 3 (July, 1996).

Grabbe, J. Orlin. *International Financial Markets.* New York: Elsevier, 1986.

Grossman, S. J., and Merton H. Miller. "Liquidity and Market Structure." *Journal of Finance* 43, no. 2 (June 1988).

Harris, Jeffrey and Paul Schultz. "The Trading Profits of SOES Bandits." *Journal of Financial Economics* 50, no. 1 (October 1998).

Hasbrouck, Joel. "Assessing the Quality of a Security Market: A New Approach to Transaction-Cost Measurement." *Review of Financial Studies* 6, no. 1 (1993).

Ho, T., and Hans Stoll. "The Dynamics of Dealer Markets under Competition." *Journal of Finance* 38, no. 2 (June 1983).

Huang, Roger, and Hans Stoll. "Dealer versus Auction Markets: A Paired Comparison of Execution Costs on NASDAQ and the NYSE." *Journal of Financial Economics* 41, no. 3 (July 1996).

Ibbotson, Roger G., and Gary P. Brinson. *Global Investing.* New York: McGraw-Hill, 1993.

Kee, C. "Market Integration and Price Execution for NYSE-Listed Securities." *Journal of Finance* 48, no. 2 (June 1993).

Madhaven, Ananth. "Trading Mechanisms in Securities Markets." *Journal of Finance* 47, no. 2 (June 1992).

McInish, Thomas, and Robert A. Wood. "Hidden Limit Orders on the NYSE." *Journal of Portfolio Management* 21, no. 3 (spring 1995).

NASDAQ Fact Book. Washington, D.C.: National Association of Securities Dealers, published annually.

Neal, Robert. "A Comparison of Transaction Cost between Competitive Market Maker and Specialist Market Structures." *Journal of Business* 65, no. 3 (July 1992).

NYSE Fact Book. New York: NYSE, published annually.

Pagano, M. "Trading Volume and Asset Liquidity." *Quarterly Journal of Economics* 104, no. 2 (1989).

Petersen, M., and D. Fialkowski. "Posted versus Effective Spreads: Good Prices or Bad Quotes?" *Journal of Financial Economics* 35, no. 3 (June 1994).

Sherrerd, Katrina F., ed. *Execution Techniques, True Trading Costs, and the Microstructure of Markets.* Charlottesville, Va.: Association for Investment Management and Research, 1993.

Sobel, Robert. *N.Y.S.E.: A History of the New York Stock Exchange, 1935–1975.* New York: Weybright and Talley, 1975.

Sobel, Robert. *The Curbstone Brokers: The Origins of the American Stock Exchange.* New York: Macmillan, 1970.

Solnik, Bruno. *International Investments.* 3d ed. Reading, Mass.: Addison-Wesley, 1995.

Stoll, Hans. *The Stock Exchange Specialist System: An Economic Analysis.* Monograph Series in Financial Economics 1985, 2. New York University, 1985.

Stoll, Hans, and Robert Whaley. "Stock Market Structure and Volatility." *Review of Financial Studies* 3, no. 1 (1990).

Tokyo Stock Exchange Fact Book. Tokyo: TSE, published annually.

U.S. Congress, Office of Technology Assessment. *Trading Around the Clock: Global Securities Markets and Information Technology—Background Paper,* OTA-BP-CIT-66. Washington, D.C.: U.S. Government Printing Office, July 1990.

Viner, Aron. *Inside Japanese Financial Markets.* Homewood, Ill.: Dow Jones/Irwin, 1988.

Chapter 4

APPENDIX CHARACTERISTICS OF DEVELOPED AND DEVELOPING MARKETS AROUND THE WORLD

TABLE 4A DEVELOPED MARKETS AROUND THE WORLD

Country	Principal Exchange	Other Exchanges	Total Market Capitalization ($ Billions)	Available Market Capitalization ($ Billions)	Trading Volume ($ Billions)	Domestic Issues Listed	Total Issues Listed	Auction Mechanism	Official Specialists	Options/ Futures Trading	Price Limits	Principal Market Indexes
Australia	Sydney	5	82.3	53.5	39.3	N.A.	1,496	Continuous	No	Yes	None	All Ordinaries—324 issues
Austria	Vienna	—	18.7	8.3	37.2	125	176	Call	Yes	No	5%	GZ Aktienindex—25 issues
Belgium	Brussels	3	48.5	26.2	6.8	186	337	Mixed	No	Few	10%	Brussels Stock Exchange Index—186 issues
Canada	Toronto	4	186.8	124.5	71.3	N.A.	1,208	Continuous	Yes	Yes	None	TSE 300 Composite Index
Denmark	Copenhagen	—	29.7	22.2	11.1	N.A.	284	Mixed	No	No	None	Copenhagen Stock Exchange Index—38 issues
Finland	Helsinki	—	9.9	1.7	5.2	N.A.	125	Mixed	N.A.	N.A.	N.A.	KOP (Kansallis-Osake-Pannki) Price Index
France	Paris	6	256.5	137.2	129.0	463	663	Mixed	Yes	Yes	4%	CAC General Index—240 issues
Germany	Frankfurt	7	297.7	197.9	1,003.7	N.A.	355	Continuous	Yes	Options	None	DAX; FAZ (Frankfurter Allgemeine Zeitung)
Hong Kong	Hong Kong	—	67.7	37.1	34.6	N.A.	479	Continuous	No	Futures	None	Hang Seng Index—33 issues
Ireland	Dublin	—	8.4	6.4	5.5	N.A.	N.A.	Continuous	No	No	None	J&E Davy Total Market Index
Italy	Milan	9	137.0	73.2	42.6	N.A.	317	Mixed	No	No	10–20%	Banca Commerziale—209 issues
Japan	Tokyo	7	2,754.6	1,483.5	1,602.4	N.A.	1,576	Continuous	Yes	No	10% down	TOPIX—1,097 issues; TSE II—423 issues; Nikkei 225
Luxembourg	Luxembourg	—	1.5	0.9	0.1	61	247	Continuous	N.A.	N.A.	N.A.	Domestic Share Price Index—9 issues

continued

TABLE 4A *concluded*

Country	Principal Exchange	Other Exchanges	Total Market Capitalization ($ Billions)	Available Market Capitalization ($ Billions)	Trading Volume ($ Billions)	Domestic Issues Listed	Total Issues Listed	Auction Mechanism	Official Specialists	Options/ Futures Trading	Price Limits	Principal Market Indexes
Malaysia	Kuala Lumpur	—	199.3	95.0	126.4	430	478	Continuous	No	No	None	Kuala Lumpur Composite Index—83 issues
The Netherlands	Amsterdam	—	112.1	92.4	80.4	279	569	Continuous	Yes	Options	Variable	ANP—CBS General Index—51 issues
New Zealand	Wellington	—	6.7	5.3	2.0	295	451	Continuous	No	Futures	None	Barclay's International Price Index—40 issues
Norway	Oslo	9	18.4	7.9	14.1	N.A.	128	Call	No	No	None	Oslo Bors Stock Index—50 issues
Singapore	Singapore	—	28.6	15.6	8.2	N.A.	324	Continuous	No	No	None	Straits Times Index—30 issues; SES—32 issues
South Africa	Johannesburg	—	72.7	N.A.	8.2	N.A.	N.A.	Continuous	No	Options	None	JSE Actuaries Index—141 issues
Spain	Madrid	3	86.6	46.8	41.0	N.A.	368	Mixed	No	No	10%	Madrid Stock Exchange Index—72 issues
Sweden	Stockholm	—	59.0	24.6	15.8	N.A.	151	Mixed	No	Yes	None	Jacobson & Ponsbach—30 issues
Switzerland	Zurich	6	128.5	75.4	376.6	161	380	Mixed	No	Yes	5%	Société de Banque Suisse—90 issues
United Kingdom	London	5	756.2	671.1	280.7	1,911	2,577	Continuous	No	Yes	None	Financial Times—(FT) Ordinaries—750 issues; FTSE 100; FT 33
United States	New York	6	9,413.1	8,950.3	5,778.7	N.A.	3,358	Continuous	Yes	Yes	None	S&P 500; Dow Jones Industrial Average; Wilshire 5000; Russell 3000

Notes: Market capitalizations (both total and available) are as of December 31, 1990, except for South African market capitalization, which is from 1988. Available differs from total market capitalization by subtracting cross holdings, closely held and government-owned shares, and takes into account restrictions on foreign ownership. Number of issues listed are from 1988 except for Malaysia, which is from 1994. Trading volume data are 1990 except for Switzerland, which are from 1988. Trading institutions data are from 1987. Market capitalizations (both total and available) for all countries except the United States and South Africa are from the Salomon-Russell Global Equity Indices. U.S. market capitalization (both total and available) is from the Frank Russell Company. All trading volume information (except for Switzerland) and Malaysian total issues listed are from the *Emerging Stock Markets Factbook: 1991,* International Finance Corp., 1991. Trading institutions information is from Richard Roll, "The International Crash of 1987," *Financial Analysts Journal* (September/October 1988). South African market capitalization, number of issues listed for all countries (except Malaysia), and Swiss trading volume are reproduced courtesy of Euromoney Books, extracted from *The G.T. Guide to World Equity Markets: 1989, 1988.*

Source: Roger G. Ibbotson and Gary P. Brinson, *Global Investing* (New York: McGraw-Hill, 1993): 109–111. Reproduced with permission of The McGraw-Hill Companies.

TABLE 4B **EMERGING MARKETS AROUND THE WORLD**

Country	Principal Exchange	Other Exchanges	Market Capitalization ($ Billions)	Trading Volume ($ Billions)	Total Issues Listed	Auction Mechanism	Principal Market Indexes
Argentina	Buenos Aires	4	36.9	11.4	156	N.A.	Buenos Aires Stock Exchange Index
Brazil	São Paulo	9	189.2	109.5	544	Continuous	BOVESPA Share Price Index—83 issues
Chile	Santiago	—	68.2	5.3	279	Mixed	IGPA Index—180 issues
China	Shanghai	1	43.5	97.5	291	Continuous	Shanghai Composite Index
Colombia	Bogotá	1	14.0	2.2	90	N.A.	Bogotá General Composite Index
Greece	Athens	—	14.9	5.1	216	Continuous	Athens Stock Exchange Industrial Price Index
India	Bombay	14	127.5	27.3	4,413	Continuous	Economic Times Index—72 issues
Indonesia	Jakarta	—	47.2	11.8	216	Mixed	Jakarta Stock Exchange Index
Israel	Tel Aviv	—	10.6	5.5	267	Call	General Share Index—all listed issues
Jordan	Amman	—	4.6	0.6	95	N.A.	Amman Financial Market Index
Mexico	Mexico City	—	130.2	83.0	206	Continuous	Bolsa de Valores Index—49 issues
Nigeria	Lagos	—	2.7	N.A.	177	Call	Nigerian Stock Exchange General Index
Pakistan	Karachi	—	12.2	3.2	724	Continuous	State Bank of Pakistan Index
Philippines	Makati	1	55.5	13.9	189	N.A.	Manila Commercial & Industrial Index—25 issues
Portugal	Lisbon	1	16.2	5.2	195	Call	Banco Totta e Acores Share Index—50 issues
South Korea	Seoul	—	191.8	286.0	699	Continuous	Korea Composite Stock Price Index
Taiwan	Taipei	—	247.3	711.0	313	Continuous	Taiwan Stock Exchange Index
Thailand	Bangkok	—	131.4	80.2	389	Continuous	Securities Exchange of Thailand Price Index
Turkey	Istanbul	—	21.6	21.7	176	Continuous	Istanbul Stock Exchange Index—50 issues
Venezuela	Caracas	1	4.1	0.9	90	Continuous	Indice de Capitalization de la BVC
Zimbabwe	N.A.	—	1.8	0.2	64	N.A.	Zimbabwe S.E. Industrial Index

Notes: Market capitalizations, trading volume, and total issues listed are as of 1994. Market capitalization, trading volume, and total issues listed for Brazil and São Paulo only. Trading volume for the Philippines is for both Manila and Makati. Total issues listed for India is Bombay only. Trading institutions information is from 1987 and 1988. Market capitalizations, trading volume, and total issues listed are from the *Emerging Stock Markets Factbook: 1995,* International Finance Corp., 1995. Trading institutions information is from Richard Roll, "The International Crash of 1987." *Financial Analysts Journal* (September/October 1988).

Source: Roger G. Ibbotson and Gary P. Brinson, *Global Investing* (New York: McGraw-Hill, 1993): 125–126. Reproduced with permission of The McGraw-Hill Companies.

Chapter

5 Security-Market Indicator Series

After you read this chapter, you should be able to answer the following questions:

- What are some major uses of security-market indicator series (indexes)?
- What are the major characteristics that cause alternative indexes to differ?
- What are the major stock-market indexes in the United States and globally, and what are their characteristics?
- What are the major bond-market indexes for the United States and the world?
- What are some of the composite stock–bond market indexes?
- Where can you get historical and current data for all these indexes?
- What is the short-run relationship among many of these indexes (monthly)?

A fair statement regarding **security-market indicator series**—especially those outside the United States—is that everybody talks about them, but few people understand them. Even those investors familiar with widely publicized stock-market series, such as the Dow Jones Industrial Average (DJIA), usually know little about indexes for the U.S. bond market or for non-U.S. stock markets such as Tokyo or London.

Although portfolios are obviously composed of many different individual stocks, investors typically ask, "What happened to the market today?" The reason for this question is that if an investor owns more than a few stocks or bonds, it is cumbersome to follow each stock or bond individually to determine the composite performance of the portfolio. Also, there is an intuitive notion that most individual stocks or bonds move with the aggregate market. Therefore, if the overall market rose, an individual's portfolio probably also increased in value. To supply investors with a composite report on market performance, some financial publications or investment firms have developed stock-market and bond-market indexes.[1]

The initial section discusses several ways that investors use market indicator series. An awareness of these significant functions should provide an incentive for becoming familiar with these series and indicates why we present a full chapter on this topic. The second section considers what characteristics cause alternative indexes to differ. In this chapter, we discuss numerous stock-market and bond-market indexes. You should understand their differences and why one of them is preferable for a given task because of its characteristics. The third section presents the most well-known U.S. and global stock market series separated into groups based on the weighting scheme used. The fourth section considers bond-market indexes, which is a relatively new topic, not because the bond market is new, but because the creation and maintenance of total return bond indexes are new. Again, we

[1] Throughout this chapter and the book, we will use *indicator series* and *indexes* interchangeably, although *indicator series* is the more correct specification because it refers to a broad class of series; one popular type of series is an index, but there can be other types and many different indexes.

consider international bond indexes following the domestic indexes. In section five, we consider composite stock market–bond market series. Our final section examines how these indexes relate to each other over monthly intervals. This comparison demonstrates the important factors that cause high or low correlation among series. With this background, you should be able to make an intelligent choice of the indicator series that is best for you based upon how you want to use the index.

USES OF SECURITY-MARKET INDEXES

Security-market indexes have at least five specific uses. A primary application is to use the index values to compute total returns for an aggregate market or some component of a market over a specified time period and use the rates of return computed as a *benchmark* to judge the performance of individual portfolios. A basic assumption when evaluating portfolio performance is that any investor should be able to experience a rate of return comparable to the market return by randomly selecting a large number of stocks or bonds from the total market; hence, a superior portfolio manager should consistently do better than the market. Therefore, *an aggregate stock- or bond-market index can be used as a benchmark to judge the performance of professional money managers.* You should recall from our earlier discussion that you should also analyze the differential risk for the portfolios being judged as compared to the risk inherent in the benchmark.

Indicator series are also used to develop an index portfolio. As we will discuss later, it is difficult for most money managers to consistently outperform specified market indexes on a risk-adjusted basis over time. If this is true, an obvious alternative is to invest in a portfolio that will emulate this market portfolio. This notion led to the creation of *index funds,* whose purpose is to track the performance of the specified market series (index) over time, that is, derive similar rates of return.[2] The original index fund concept was related to common stocks. Subsequently, development of comprehensive, well-specified bond-market indexes and similar inferior performance relative to the bond market by most bond portfolio managers have led to a similar phenomenon in the fixed-income area (bond index funds).[3]

Securities analysts, portfolio managers, and others use security-market indexes to examine the factors that influence aggregate security price movements (that is, the indexes are used to measure aggregate market movements). A similar use is to analyze the relationship among stock and bond returns of different countries. An example is the analysis of the relationship among U.S., Japanese, and German stock or bond returns.

Another group interested in an aggregate market series is "technicians," who believe past price changes can be used to predict future price movements. For example, to project future stock price movements, technicians would plot and analyze price and volume changes for a stock market series like the Dow Jones Industrial Average.

Finally, work in portfolio and capital market theory has implied that the relevant risk for an individual risky asset is its *systematic risk,* which is the relationship between the rates of

---

[2]For a discussion of developments in indexing, see "New Ways to Play the Indexing Game," *Institutional Investor* 22, no. 13 (November 1988): 92–98; and Sharmin Mossavar-Rahmani, "Indexing Fixed-Income Assets," in *The Handbook of Fixed Income Securities,* 5th ed., ed. Frank J. Fabozzi (Chicago: Irwin Professional Publishing, 1997).

[3]See Fran Hawthorne, "The Battle of the Bond Indexes," *Institutional Investor* 20, no. 4 (April 1986); and Chris P. Dialynas, "The Active Decisions in the Selection of Passive Management and Performance Bogeys," in *The Handbook of Fixed Income Securities,* 5th ed., ed. Frank J. Fabozzi (Chicago: Irwin Professional Publishing, 1997).

return for a risky asset and the rates of return for a market portfolio of risky assets.[4] Therefore, it is necessary when computing the systematic risk for an individual risky asset (security) to relate its returns to the returns for an aggregate market index that is used as a proxy for the market portfolio of risky assets.

In summary, security market indexes are used:

- As benchmarks to evaluate the performance of professional money managers
- To create and monitor an index fund
- To measure market rates of return in economic studies
- For predicting future market movements by technicians
- As a proxy for the market portfolio of risky assets when calculating the systematic risk of an asset

DIFFERENTIATING FACTORS IN CONSTRUCTING MARKET INDEXES

Because the indicator series are intended to reflect the overall movements of a group of securities, it is necessary to consider which factors are important in computing an index that is intended to represent a total population.

The Sample

The size of the sample, the breadth of the sample, and the source of the sample used to construct a series are all important.

A small percentage of the total population will provide valid indications of the behavior of the total population *if* the sample is properly selected. In fact, at some point the costs of taking a larger sample will almost certainly outweigh any benefits of increased size. The sample should be *representative* of the total population; otherwise, its size will be meaningless. A large biased sample is no better than a small biased sample. The sample can be generated by completely random selection or by a nonrandom selection technique that is designed to incorporate the characteristics of the desired population. Finally, the *source* of the sample is important if there are any differences between segments of the population, in which case samples from each segment are required.

Weighting Sample Members

Our second concern is with the weight given to each member in the sample. Three principal weighting schemes are used: (1) a price-weighted series, (2) a value-weighted series, and (3) an unweighted series, or what would be described as an equally weighted series.

Computational Procedure

Our final consideration is selecting the computational procedure. One alternative is to take a simple arithmetic average of the various members in the series. Another is to compute an index and have all changes, whether in price or value, reported in terms of the basic index. Finally, some prefer using a geometric average of the components rather than an arithmetic average.

STOCK-MARKET INDICATOR SERIES

As mentioned in the introduction to this chapter, we hear a lot about what happens to the Dow Jones Industrial Average (DJIA) each day. In addition, you might also hear about

[4]This concept and its justification are discussed in Chapters 8 and 9. Subsequently, in Chapter 10 we consider the difficulty of finding an index that is an appropriate proxy for the market portfolio of risky assets.

other stock indexes, such as the NYSE Composite, the S&P 500 index, the NASDAQ index, or even the Nikkei Average. If you listen carefully, you will realize that these indexes change by differing amounts. Reasons for some differences are obvious, such as the DJIA versus the Nikkei Average, but others are not. This section will briefly review how the major series differ in terms of the characteristics discussed in the prior section. As a result, you should come to understand that the movements over time for alternative indexes *should* differ and you will understand why they differ.

The discussion of the indexes is organized by the weighting of the sample of stocks. We begin with the price-weighted series because some of the most popular indexes are in this category. The next group is the value-weighted series, which is the technique currently used for most indexes. Finally, we will examine the unweighted series.

Price-Weighted Series

A **price-weighted series** is an arithmetic average of current prices, which means that index movements are influenced by the differential prices of the components.

DOW JONES INDUSTRIAL AVERAGE The best-known price-weighted series is also the oldest and certainly the most popular stock-market indicator series, the Dow Jones Industrial Average (DJIA). The DJIA is a price-weighted average of 30 large, well-known industrial stocks that are generally the leaders in their industry (blue chips) and are listed on the NYSE. The DJIA is computed by totaling the current prices of the 30 stocks and dividing the sum by a divisor that has been adjusted to take account of stock splits and changes in the sample over time.[5] The divisor is adjusted so that the index value will be the same before and after the split. This is demonstrated in Table 5.1.

$$\text{DJIA}_t = \sum_{i=1}^{30} p_{it}/D_{adj}$$

where:

DJIA_t = the value of the DJIA on day t
p_{it} = the closing price of stock i on day t
D_{adj} = the adjusted divisor on day t

TABLE 5.1 **EXAMPLE OF CHANGE IN DJIA DIVISOR WHEN A SAMPLE STOCK SPLITS**

	Before Split	After Three-for-One Split by Stock A	
	Prices	Prices	
A	30	10	
B	20	20	
C	10	10	
	60 ÷ 3 = 20	40 ÷ X = 20	X = 2 (New Divisor)

[5]A complete list of all events that have caused a change in the divisor since the DJIA went to 30 stocks on October 1, 1928, is contained in Phyllis S. Pierce, ed., *The Business One Irwin Investor's Handbook* (Burr Ridge, Ill.: Dow Jones Books, annual). Prior to 1992, it was the *Dow Jones Investor's Handbook.* In May 1996 the DJIA celebrated its 100th birthday, which was acknowledged with two special sections entitled "A Century of Investing" and "100 Years of the DJIA," *Wall Street Journal,* 28 May 1996.

TABLE 5.2

DEMONSTRATION OF THE IMPACT OF DIFFERENTLY PRICED SHARES ON A PRICE-WEIGHTED INDICATOR SERIES

		PERIOD $T+1$	
	Period T	Case A	Case B
A	100	110	100.7
B	50	50	50
C	30	30	33
Sum	180	190	183
Divisor	3	3	3
Average	60	63.3	61
Percentage change		5.5	1.7

In Table 5.1, three stocks are employed to demonstrate the procedure used to derive a new divisor for the DJIA when a stock splits. When stocks split, the divisor becomes smaller as shown. The cumulative effect of splits can be derived from the fact that the divisor was originally 30.0, but as of July 1999 it was 0.197405.

The adjusted divisor ensures that the new value for the series is the same as it would have been without the split. In this case, the pre-split index value was 20. Therefore, after the split, given the new sum of prices, the divisor is adjusted downward to maintain this value of 20. The divisor is also changed in the rare instances of a change in the sample makeup of the series.

Because the series is price weighted, a high-priced stock carries more weight than a low-priced stock, so, as shown in Table 5.2, a 10 percent change in a \$100 stock (\$10) will cause a larger change in the series than a 10 percent change in a \$30 stock (\$3). In Case A, when the \$100 stock increases by 10 percent, the average rises by 5.5 percent; in Case B, when the \$30 stock increases by 10 percent, the average rises by only 1.7 percent.

The DJIA has been criticized on several counts. First, the sample used for the series is limited. It is difficult to conceive that 30 nonrandomly selected blue-chip stocks can be representative of the 3,000 stocks listed on the NYSE. Beyond the limited number, the stocks included are the largest and most prestigious companies in various industries. Therefore, it is contended that the DJIA probably reflects price movements for large, mature, blue-chip firms rather than for the typical company listed on the NYSE. Several studies have pointed out that the DJIA has not been as volatile as other market indexes and that the long-run returns on the DJIA are not comparable to the other NYSE stock indexes.

In addition, because the DJIA is price weighted, when companies have a stock split, their prices decline, and therefore their weight in the DJIA is reduced—even though they may be large and important. Therefore, the weighting scheme causes a downward bias in the DJIA, because the stocks that have higher growth rates will have higher prices, and because such stocks tend to split, they will consistently lose weight within the index.[6] Regardless of the several criticisms made of the DJIA, a fairly close relationship exists between the *daily* or monthly percentage changes for the DJIA and comparable price

[6]For discussions of these problems, see H. L. Butler, Jr., and J. D. Allen, "The Dow Jones Industrial Average Re-examined," *Financial Analysts Journal* 35, no. 6 (November–December 1979): 37–45. For several articles that consider the origin and performance of the DJIA during its 100 years, see "100 Years of the DJIA," section in the *Wall Street Journal,* 28 May 1996, R29–R56. For a recent discussion of differing results, see Greg Ip, "What's Behind the Trailing Performance of the Dow Industrials vs. the S & P 500?" *Wall Street Journal,* 20 August 1998, C1, C17.

changes for other NYSE indexes, as shown in a subsequent section of this chapter. Dow Jones also publishes an average of 20 stocks in the transportation industry and 15 utility stocks. Detailed reports of the averages are contained daily in the *Wall Street Journal* and weekly in *Barron's,* including hourly figures.

NIKKEI–DOW JONES AVERAGE Also referred to as the Nikkei Stock Average Index, the Nikkei–Dow Jones Average is an arithmetic average of prices for 225 stocks on the First Section of the Tokyo Stock Exchange (TSE). This is the best-known series in Japan, and it has been used to show stock price trends since the reopening of the TSE. Notably, it was formulated by Dow Jones and Company, and, similar to the DJIA, it is a price-weighted series, so a large price change for a small company will have the same impact as a similar price change of a large firm. It is also criticized because the 225 stocks that are included comprise only about 15 percent of all stocks on the First Section. The results for this index are reported daily in the *Wall Street Journal* and the *Financial Times* and weekly in *Barron's.*

Value-Weighted Series

A **value-weighted series** is generated by deriving the initial total market value of all stocks used in the series (Market Value = Number of Shares Outstanding × Current Market Price). This initial figure is typically established as the base and assigned an index value (the most popular beginning index value is 100, but it can vary—say, 10, 50). Subsequently, a new market value is computed for all securities in the index, and the current market value is compared to the initial "base" value to determine the percentage of change, which in turn is applied to the beginning index value.

$$\text{Index}_t = \frac{\Sigma P_t Q_t}{\Sigma P_b Q_b} \times \text{Beginning Index Value}$$

where:

Index_t = index value on day t
P_t = ending prices for stocks on day t
Q_t = number of outstanding shares on day t
P_b = ending price for stocks on base day
Q_b = number of outstanding shares on base day

A simple example for a three-stock index is shown in Table 5.3. As you can see, there is an *automatic adjustment* for stock splits and other capital changes with a value-weighted index because the decrease in the stock price is offset by an increase in the number of shares outstanding.

In a value-weighted index, the importance of individual stocks in the sample depends on the market value of the stocks. Therefore, a specified percentage change in the value of a large company has a greater impact than a comparable percentage change for a small company. As shown in Table 5.4, assuming the only change is a 20 percent increase in the value of Stock A, which has a beginning value of $10 million, the ending index value would be $202 million, or an index of 101. In contrast, if only Stock C increases by 20 percent from $100 million, the ending value will be $220 million or an index value of 110. The point is, price changes for the large market value stocks in a value-weighted index will dominate changes in the index value over time. This value-weighting effect was prevalent during 1998 when the market was being driven by large growth stocks—that is, almost all of the gain for the year was attributable to the largest 50 of the S&P 500 Index.

Table 5.5 is a summary of the characteristics of the major price-weighted, market-value-weighted, and equal-weighted stock price indexes for the United States and the major

TABLE 5.3

EXAMPLE OF A COMPUTATION OF A VALUE-WEIGHTED INDEX

Stock	Share Price	Number of Shares	Market Value
December 31, 1999			
A	$10.00	1,000,000	$ 10,000,000
B	15.00	6,000,000	90,000,000
C	20.00	5,000,000	100,000,000
Total			$200,000,000
			Base Value Equal to an Index of 100
December 31, 2000			
A	$12.00	1,000,000	$ 12,000,000
B	10.00	12,000,000[a]	120,000,000
C	20.00	5,500,000[b]	110,000,000
Total			$242,000,000

$$\text{New Index Value} = \frac{\text{Current Market Value}}{\text{Base Value}} \times \text{Beginning Index Value}$$

$$= \frac{\$242{,}000{,}000}{\$200{,}000{,}000} \times 100$$

$$= 1.21 \times 100$$

$$= 121$$

[a]Stock split two-for-one during the year.

[b]Company paid a 10 percent stock dividend during the year.

TABLE 5.4

DEMONSTRATION OF THE IMPACT OF DIFFERENT VALUES ON A MARKET-VALUE-WEIGHTED STOCK INDEX

		December 31, 1999		December 31, 2000			
				Case A		Case B	
Stock	Number of Shares	Price	Value	Price	Value	Price	Value
A	1,000,000	$10.00	$ 10,000,000	$12.00	$ 12,000,000	$10.00	$ 10,000,000
B	6,000,000	15.00	90,000,000	15.00	90,000,000	15.00	90,000,000
C	5,000,000	20.00	100,000,000	20.00	100,000,000	24.00	120,000,000
			$200,000,000		$202,000,000		$220,000,000
Index Value			100.00		101.00		110.00

foreign countries. As shown, the major differences are the number of stocks in the index, but more important, the *source* of the sample (stocks from the NYSE, the OTC, the AMEX, or from a foreign country, such as the United Kingdom or Japan).

Figure 5.1 shows the "Stock Market Data Bank" from the *Wall Street Journal* of May 27, 1999, which contains values for many of the U.S. stock indexes we have discussed. To gain an appreciation of the differences among indexes, you should examine the different 12-month percentage changes of alternative indexes in the third column from the left. Figure 5.2 shows a similar table for alternative indexes created and maintained by the *Financial Times*.

TABLE 5.5 **SUMMARY OF STOCK MARKET INDEXES**

Name of Index	Weighting	Number of Stocks	Source of Stocks
Dow Jones Industrial Average	Price	30	NYSE
Nikkei–Dow Jones Average	Price	225	TSE
S&P 400 Industrial	Market value	400	NYSE, OTC
S&P Transportation	Market value	20	NYSE, OTC
S&P Utilities	Market value	40	NYSE, OTC
S&P Financials	Market value	40	NYSE, OTC
S&P 500 Composite	Market value	500	NYSE, OTC
NYSE			
Industrial	Market value	1,420	NYSE
Utility	Market value	227	NYSE
Transportation	Market value	48	NYSE
Financial	Market value	864	NYSE
Composite	Market value	2,559	NYSE
NASDAQ			
Composite	Market value	4,879	OTC
Industrial	Market value	3,019	OTC
Banks	Market value	320	OTC
Insurance	Market value	107	OTC
Other finance	Market value	646	OTC
Transportation	Market value	91	OTC
Telecommunications	Market value	141	OTC
AMEX Market Value	Market value	900	AMEX
Dow Jones Equity Market Index	Market value	2,300	NYSE, AMEX, OTC
Wilshire 5000 Equity Value	Market value	5,000	NYSE, AMEX, OTC
Russell Indexes			
3,000	Market value	3,000	NYSE, AMEX, OTC
1,000	Market value	1,000 largest	NYSE, AMEX, OTC
2,000	Market value	2,000 smallest	NYSE, AMEX, OTC
Financial Times Actuaries Index			
All Share	Market value	700	LSE
FT100	Market value	100 largest	LSE
Small Cap	Market value	250	LSE
Mid Cap	Market value	250	LSE
Combined	Market value	350	LSE
Tokyo Stock Exchange Price Index (TOPIX)	Market value	1,800	TSE
Value Line Averages			
Industrials	Equal (geometric average)	1,499	NYSE, AMEX, OTC
Utilities	Equal	177	NYSE, AMEX, OTC
Rails	Equal	19	NYSE, AMEX, OTC
Composite	Equal	1,695	NYSE, AMEX, OTC
Financial Times Ordinary Share Index	Equal (geometric average)	30	LSE
FT-Actuaries World Indexes	Market value	2,275	24 countries, 3 regions (returns in \$, £, ¥, DM, and local currency)
Morgan Stanley Capital International (MSCI) Indexes	Market value	1,375	19 countries, 3 international, 38 international industries (returns in \$ and local currency)
Dow Jones World Stock Index	Market value	2,200	13 countries, 3 regions, 120 industry groups (returns in \$, £, ¥, DM, and local currency)
Euromoney—First Boston Global Stock Index	Market value	—	17 countries (returns in \$ and local currency)
Salomon-Russell World Equity Index	Market value	Russell 1000 and S-R PMI of 600 non-U.S. stocks	22 countries (returns in \$ and local currency)

FIGURE 5.1 STOCK MARKET DATA BANK

STOCK MARKET DATA BANK 5/26/99

MAJOR INDEXES

†12-MO HIGH	†12-MO LOW		DAILY HIGH	DAILY LOW	CLOSE	NET CHG	% CHG	†12-MO CHG	% CHG	FROM 12/31	% CHG
DOW JONES AVERAGES											
11107.19	7539.07	**30 Industrials**	10721.33	10518.70	x10702.16	+ 171.07	+ 1.62	+1765.59	+ 19.76	+1520.73	+ 16.56
3783.50	2345.00	**20 Transportation**	3477.01	3426.21	x3453.88	+ 0.55	+ 0.02	+ 121.38	+ 3.64	+ 304.57	+ 9.67
330.63	271.67	**15 Utilities**	331.20	327.64	x330.63	+ 2.15	+ 0.65	+ 53.21	+ 19.18	+ 18.33	+ 5.87
3366.13	2411.00	**65 Composite**	3255.20	3210.08	x3251.23	+ 35.55	+ 1.11	+ 434.66	+ 15.43	+ 380.40	+ 13.25
1296.00	900.71	**DJ Global-US**	1235.88	1210.32	1235.88	+ 19.27	+ 1.58	+ 204.17	+ 19.79	+ 66.54	+ 5.69
NEW YORK STOCK EXCHANGE											
651.35	477.20	**Composite**	624.94	615.41	624.84	+ 7.50	+ 1.21	+ 60.91	+ 10.80	+ 29.03	+ 4.87
808.78	593.49	**Industrials**	777.69	767.66	777.30	+ 7.36	+ 0.96	+ 77.48	+ 11.07	+ 33.65	+ 4.52
479.79	354.33	**Utilities**	472.98	465.05	472.15	+ 5.69	+ 1.22	+ 107.49	+ 29.48	+ 26.21	+ 5.88
560.33	351.13	**Transportation**	511.41	503.61	510.14	+ 1.76	+ 0.35	+ 17.53	+ 3.56	+ 27.76	+ 5.75
599.15	399.19	**Finance**	550.18	536.19	550.18	+ 12.16	+ 2.26	+ 9.11	+ 1.68	+ 28.76	+ 5.52
STANDARD & POOR'S INDEXES											
1367.56	957.28	**500 Index**	1304.85	1278.43	1304.76	+ 20.36	+ 1.59	+ 212.53	+ 19.46	+ 75.53	+ 6.14
1635.22	1134.73	**Industrials**	1566.10	1536.65	1565.37	+ 20.62	+ 1.33	+ 288.67	+ 22.61	+ 86.21	+ 5.83
269.21	229.71	**Utilities**	269.43	266.54	269.21	+ 2.07	+ 0.77	+ 37.17	+ 16.02	+ 9.59	+ 3.69
409.63	275.93	**400 MidCap**	393.88	387.48	393.88	+ 2.41	+ 0.62	+ 38.94	+ 10.97	+ 1.57	+ 0.40
194.44	128.70	**600 SmallCap**	176.38	174.48	175.38	– 0.30	– 0.17	– 13.03	– 6.92	– 1.99	– 1.12
287.08	200.77	**1500 Index**	274.24	268.93	274.24	+ 3.96	+ 1.47	+ 41.25	+ 17.70	+ 14.19	+ 5.46
NASDAQ STOCK MARKET											
2652.05	1419.12	**Composite**	2427.18	2339.12	2427.18	+ 46.28	+ 1.94	+ 646.08	+ 36.27	+ 234.49	+ 10.69
2260.66	1128.88	**Nasdaq 100**	2053.04	1960.55	2053.04	+ 54.00	+ 2.70	+ 843.58	+ 69.75	+ 217.03	+ 11.82
1534.20	882.40	**Industrials**	1451.02	1405.90	1449.93	+ 15.37	+ 1.07	+ 130.22	+ 9.87	+ 145.68	+ 11.17
2372.33	1346.58	**Insurance**	2364.71	2337.80	2361.15	+ 16.96	+ 0.72	+ 563.46	+ 31.34	+ 564.36	+ 31.41
2198.81	1486.32	**Banks**	1825.85	1810.36	1825.75	+ 6.74	+ 0.37	– 364.43	– 16.64	– 12.25	– 0.67
1381.92	690.19	**Computer**	1206.75	1151.37	1206.68	+ 30.81	+ 2.62	+ 451.58	+ 59.80	+ 72.49	+ 6.39
700.12	310.74	**Telecommunications**	643.65	619.21	643.42	+ 15.42	+ 2.46	+ 268.96	+ 71.83	+ 142.51	+ 28.45
OTHERS											
800.39	563.75	**Amex Composite**	783.13	775.97	782.66	+ 3.82	+ 0.49	+ 73.82	+ 10.41	+ 93.67	+ 13.60
713.04	494.35	**Russell 1000**	680.00	666.48	680.00	+ 10.16	+ 1.52	+ 107.78	+ 18.84	+ 37.13	+ 5.78
463.64	310.28	**Russell 2000**	436.94	429.71	435.41	+ 0.96	+ 0.22	– 14.85	– 3.30	+ 13.45	+ 3.19
734.62	509.10	**Russell 3000**	701.24	687.72	701.24	+ 9.81	+ 1.42	+ 100.90	+ 16.81	+ 36.97	+ 5.57
483.72	346.66	**Value-Line(geom.)**	450.14	446.14	449.71	+ 1.01	+ 0.23	– 28.11	– 5.88	+ 12.56	+ 2.87
12549.05	8620.80	**Wilshire 5000**	...	...	11969.09	+ 156.51	+ 1.32	+1665.02	+ 16.16	+ 651.50	+ 5.76

†-Based on comparable trading day in preceding year.

Source: *Wall Street Journal,* 27 May 1999, C2.

UNWEIGHTED PRICE INDICATOR SERIES

In an **unweighted index**, all stocks carry equal weight regardless of their price or market value. A $20 stock is as important as a $40 stock, and the total market value of the company is unimportant. Such an index can be used by individuals who randomly select stock for their portfolio and invest the same dollar amount in each stock. One way to visualize an unweighted series is to assume that equal dollar amounts are invested in each stock in the portfolio (for example, an equal $1,000 investment in each stock would work out to 50 shares of a $20 stock, 100 shares of a $10 stock, and 10 shares of a $100 stock). In fact, the actual movements in the index are typically based on *the arithmetic average of the percent changes in price or value for the stocks in the index.* The use of percentage price changes means that the price level or the market value of the stock does not make a difference—each percentage change has equal weight. This arithmetic average of percent changes procedure is used in academic studies when the authors specify equal weighting.

FIGURE 5.2 ***FINANCIAL TIMES* ACTUARIES SHARES INDICES**

FTSE Actuaries Share Indices — UK Series
Produced in conjunction with the Faculty and Institute of Actuaries

	£ Stlg May 27	Day's chge%	Euro Index	£ Stlg May 26	£ Stlg May 25	Year ago	Actual yield%	Cover	P/E ratio	Xd adj. ytd	Total Return
FTSE 100	6199.5	−0.6	7386.1	6236.8	6249.3	5862.3	2.26	1.62	27.31	71.85	2776.71
FTSE 250	5667.7	+0.3	6752.6	5652.4	5653.7	5898.5	2.81	1.85	19.20	70.11	2497.38
FTSE 250 ex Inv Co	5721.4	+0.3	6816.5	5703.1	5703.5	5965.0	2.93	1.90	17.94	73.66	2533.48
FTSE 350	2968.4	−0.5	3536.5	2982.2	2987.4	2860.9	2.34	1.66	25.63	34.77	2718.12
FTSE 350 ex Inv Co	2973.6	−0.5	3542.7	2987.7	2992.9	2863.6	2.35	1.67	25.40	35.12	1396.81
FTSE 350 Higher Yield	2970.7	−0.7	3539.3	2991.3	2985.1	2787.5	3.02	1.50	22.02	41.46	2342.38
FTSE 350 Lower Yield	2958.9	−0.2	3525.2	2965.5	2982.7	2941.5	1.61	1.99	31.09	27.24	2185.77
FTSE SmallCap	2551.68	+0.1	3040.10	2549.94	2557.36	2769.58	2.75	1.81	20.16	27.70	2280.07
FTSE SmallCap ex Inv Co	2524.96	+0.1	3008.27	2523.28	2531.40	2774.96	2.91	1.91	18.01	28.94	2283.30
FTSE All-Share	2882.07	−0.4	3433.73	2894.77	2899.95	2798.68	2.36	1.67	25.30	33.63	2678.59
FTSE All-Share ex Inv Co	2890.24	−0.5	3443.47	2903.31	2908.60	2803.28	2.38	1.68	24.98	34.09	1382.30
FTSE Fledgling	1403.99	......	1672.73	1404.47	1405.05	1501.28	2.77	1.23	29.43	15.21	1599.46
FTSE Fledgling ex Inv Co	1419.95	−0.1	1691.75	1421.21	1421.77	1533.94	3.13	1.26	25.33	17.27	1624.56
FTSE All-Small	1448.40	......	1725.64	1447.73	1451.16	1567.07	2.75	1.68	21.63	15.72	1652.18
FTSE All-Small ex Inv Co	1460.65	......	1740.24	1460.15	1463.99	1599.39	2.96	1.77	19.15	16.95	1679.23
FTSE AIM	978.0	−0.1	1165.2	979.0	980.9	1138.5	0.99	30.00†	0.14	3.41	899.83

Source: *Financial Times,* 28 May 1999, 36.

TABLE 5.6 **EXAMPLE OF AN ARITHMETIC AND GEOMETRIC MEAN OF PERCENTAGE CHANGES**

	Share Price			
Stock	***T***	***T* + 1**	**HPR**	**HPY**
X	10	12	1.20	0.20
Y	22	20	.91	−0.09
Z	44	47	1.07	0.07

$$\text{II} = 1.20 \times 0.91 \times 1.07 = 1.168 \qquad 1.168^{1/3} = 1.0531$$

$$\Sigma = 0.18 \qquad 0.18/3 = 0.06 = 6\%$$

Index Value (T) × 1.0531 = Index Value (T + 1)
Index Value (T) × 1.06 = Index Value (T + 1)

In contrast to computing an arithmetic average of percentage changes, both Value Line and the *Financial Times* Ordinary Share Index compute a *geometric* mean of the holding period returns *and* derive the holding period yield from this calculation. Table 5.6 contains an example of an arithmetic average and a geometric average. This demonstrates the downward bias of the geometric calculation. Specifically, the geometric mean of holding period yields (HPY) shows an average change of only 5.3 percent versus the actual change in wealth of 6 percent.

GLOBAL EQUITY INDEXES

As noted in this chapter's appendix, there are stock-market indexes available for most individual foreign markets similar to those we described for Japan (the Nikkei and TOPIX) and the United Kingdom (the several *Financial Times* indexes) described in Table 5.5. While these local indexes are closely followed within each country, a problem arises in comparing the results implied by these indexes across countries because of a lack of consistency among them in sample selection, weighting, or computational procedure. To solve these comparability problems, several groups have computed a set of country stock indexes with consistent sample selection, weighting, and computational procedure. As a result, these indexes can be directly compared and can be combined to create various regional indexes (for example, Pacific Basin). We will describe the three sets of global equity indexes.

FT/S&P-ACTUARIES WORLD INDEXES The FT/S&P-Actuaries World Indexes are jointly compiled by the Financial Times Limited, Goldman Sachs and Company, and Standard and Poor's (the "compilers") in conjunction with the Institute of Actuaries and the Faculty of Actuaries. Approximately 2,461 equity securities in 30 countries are measured, covering at least 70 percent of the total value of all listed companies in each country. Actively traded medium- and small-capitalization stocks are included along with major international equities. All securities included must allow direct holdings of shares by foreign nationals.

The indexes are market-value weighted and have a base date of December 31, 1986 = 100. The index results are reported in U.S. dollars, U.K. pound sterling, Japanese yen, German marks, and the local currency of the country. Performance results are calculated after the New York markets close and are published the following day in the *Financial Times* as shown in Table 5.7. In addition to the individual countries and the world index, there are several geographic subgroups, as shown in Table 5.7.

MORGAN STANLEY CAPITAL INTERNATIONAL (MSCI) INDEXES The Morgan Stanley Capital International Indexes consist of 3 international, 19 national, and 38 international industry indexes. The indexes consider some 1,375 companies listed on stock exchanges in 19 countries with a combined market capitalization that represents approximately 60 percent of the aggregate market value of the stock exchanges of these countries. All the indexes are market-value weighted. Table 5.8 contains the countries included, the number of stocks, and market values for stocks in the various countries and groups.

In addition to reporting the indexes in U.S. dollars and the country's local currency, the following valuation information is available: (1) price-to-book value (P/BV) ratio, (2) price-to-cash earnings (earnings plus depreciation) (P/CE) ratio, (3) price-to-earnings (P/E) ratio, and (4) dividend yield (YLD). These ratios help in analyzing different valuation levels among countries and over time for specific countries.

Notably, the Morgan Stanley group index for Europe, Australia, and the Far East (EAFE) is being used as the basis for futures and options contracts on the Chicago Mercantile Exchange and the Chicago Board Options Exchange. Several of the MSCI country indexes, the EAFE index, and a world index are reported daily in the *Wall Street Journal,* as shown in Figure 5.3.

DOW JONES WORLD STOCK INDEX In January 1993, Dow Jones introduced its World Stock Index with results beginning December 31, 1991. Composed of more than 2,200 companies worldwide and organized into 120 industry groups, the index includes 33 countries representing more than 80 percent of the combined capitalization of these countries. In addition to the 33 countries shown in Figure 5.4, the countries are grouped into three regions: Asia/Pacific, Europe/Africa, and the Americas. Finally, each country's index is calculated in its own currency as well as in the U.S. dollar. The index is reported daily in the *Wall Street Journal* (domestic), in the *Wall Street Journal Europe,* and in the *Asian Wall Street Journal.* It is published weekly in *Barron's.*[7]

COMPARISON OF WORLD STOCK INDEXES As shown in Table 5.9, the correlations between the three series since December 31, 1991, when the DJ series became available, indicate that the results with the alternative world stock indexes are quite comparable.

---

[7] "Journal Launches Index Tracking World Stocks," *Wall Street Journal,* 5 January 1993, C1.

TABLE 5.7 FT/S&P ACTUARIES WORLD INDEXES

FT/S&P ACTUARIES WORLD INDICES

The FT/S&P Actuaries World Indices are owned by FTSE International Limited, Goldman, Sachs & Co. and Standard & Poor's. The Indices are compiled by FTSE International and Standard & Poor's in conjunction with the Faculty of Actuaries and the Institute of Actuaries.

NATIONAL AND REGIONAL MARKETS	WEDNESDAY MAY 26 1999								TUESDAY MAY 25 1999					DOLLAR INDEX		
Figures in parentheses show number of lines of stock	US Dollar Index	Day's Change %	Pound Sterling Index	Yen Index	Euro Index	Local Currency Index	Local % chg on day	Gross Div. Yield	US Dollar Index	Pound Sterling Index	Yen Index	Euro Index	Local Currency Index	52 week High	52 week Low	Year ago (approx)
Australia (75)	216.51	−1.3	201.01	166.79	237.95	221.99	0.0	3.39	219.34	203.05	170.15	238.08	221.90	236.98	163.86	198.26
Austria (21)	174.75	−1.0	162.24	134.62	169.47	169.47	0.2	2.20	176.53	163.42	136.94	169.08	169.08	253.73	165.27	253.73
Belgium (22)	340.85	−2.1	316.45	262.58	323.63	323.63	−0.8	2.27	348.04	322.19	269.99	326.37	326.37	446.95	322.79	357.37
Brazil (29)	145.72	5.4	135.28	112.25	160.14	463.48	4.0	5.18	138.23	127.97	107.23	150.04	445.53	239.10	89.32	206.79
Canada (124)	219.22	−1.2	203.52	168.88	240.92	233.87	−0.2	1.58	221.83	205.35	172.08	240.78	234.36	242.37	159.94	242.37
Denmark (34)	420.54	−0.6	390.43	323.97	462.18	405.73	0.6	1.86	423.27	391.83	328.34	459.42	403.40	537.33	406.62	511.69
Finland (26)	637.68	−1.2	592.01	491.24	759.41	759.41	0.1	1.54	645.20	597.27	500.50	758.86	758.86	719.62	338.49	443.99
France (72)	328.55	−1.5	305.03	253.10	322.65	322.65	−0.3	2.09	333.59	308.81	258.77	323.54	323.54	354.45	253.86	328.64
Germany (53)	254.07	−0.9	235.88	195.73	246.56	246.56	0.3	1.61	256.38	237.34	198.88	245.73	245.73	325.61	226.35	303.12
Greece (35)	441.68	−3.8	410.05	340.25	485.41	982.51	−2.7	1.22	459.27	425.16	356.27	498.50	1009.66	467.85	211.47	300.61
Hong Kong, China (69)	371.64	0.4	345.03	286.29	408.43	370.01	0.4	3.00	370.05	342.56	287.06	401.66	368.43	407.18	196.64	285.43
Indonesia (21)	74.96	−4.5	69.59	57.74	82.38	372.47	−3.2	1.07	78.47	72.64	60.87	85.17	384.63	80.38	19.04	38.28
Ireland (14)	497.12	−1.5	461.52	382.96	526.51	526.51	−0.3	2.01	504.74	467.25	391.54	527.97	527.97	605.85	396.15	521.11
Italy (53)	161.32	−1.0	149.77	124.28	222.65	222.65	0.2	1.74	162.94	150.83	126.39	222.09	222.09	192.64	128.68	174.10
Japan (443)	110.93	0.4	102.98	85.45	121.91	85.45	−0.3	0.81	110.48	102.27	85.70	119.92	85.70	119.02	76.83	93.20
Mexico (29)	1668.64	1.8	1549.15	1285.45	1833.85	17669.39	3.5	1.60	1639.38	1517.61	1271.71	1779.41	17069.17	1870.23	787.15	1451.45
Netherlands (26)	498.21	−1.4	462.54	383.80	478.25	478.25	−0.2	2.03	505.27	467.74	391.95	479.03	479.03	562.73	394.92	529.83
New Zealand (19)	62.40	−1.6	57.93	48.07	68.58	62.19	0.4	3.73	63.38	58.67	49.17	68.80	61.94	72.33	45.68	69.59
Norway (37)	253.63	−0.8	235.46	195.38	278.74	270.27	0.1	1.72	255.69	236.70	198.35	277.54	270.00	323.73	181.86	323.73
Philippines (22)	107.79	−0.2	100.07	83.04	118.46	204.39	0.4	0.74	107.96	99.94	83.75	117.18	203.64	120.36	42.48	93.30
Portugal (18)	210.89	−0.7	195.79	162.46	276.19	276.19	0.6	2.32	212.32	196.54	164.70	274.62	274.62	296.74	194.13	291.55
Singapore (40)	269.20	−0.3	249.93	207.38	295.86	214.53	0.1	1.22	269.90	249.85	209.37	292.95	214.36	297.82	102.45	181.99
South Africa (31)	224.98	−1.4	208.87	173.32	247.26	308.24	−0.8	3.46	228.09	211.15	176.94	247.58	310.59	298.93	151.55	298.93
Spain (29)	368.85	−1.7	342.44	284.15	443.73	443.73	−0.4	1.63	375.16	347.29	291.02	445.74	445.74	435.19	290.81	396.60
Sweden (41)	560.12	−1.6	520.01	431.49	615.58	709.54	−0.7	1.92	568.98	526.72	441.38	617.58	714.37	628.19	379.18	611.47
Switzerland (29)	366.63	−1.0	340.38	282.44	402.93	345.51	0.1	1.35	370.21	342.72	287.19	401.84	345.04	441.65	307.73	414.95
Thailand (26)	35.03	0.2	32.52	26.98	38.49	50.52	0.4	1.64	34.95	32.35	27.11	37.93	50.30	42.39	8.15	21.73
United Kingdom (199)	389.65	−0.5	361.74	300.17	428.22	361.74	−0.2	2.34	391.62	362.54	303.79	425.08	362.54	417.04	307.96	385.50
USA (605)	538.04	1.6	499.52	414.48	591.31	538.04	1.6	1.25	529.81	490.46	410.99	575.07	529.81	564.34	390.12	446.35
Americas (787)	479.08	1.5	444.78	369.06	526.52	406.20	1.5	1.28	472.14	437.07	366.25	512.47	400.15	503.06	347.59	403.57
Europe (709)	349.84	−1.0	324.79	269.50	384.48	343.92	−0.1	1.98	353.40	327.15	274.14	383.58	344.36	386.24	282.63	367.09
Eurobloc (334)	99.15	−1.3	92.05	76.38	104.14	104.14	0.0	1.86	100.43	92.97	77.91	104.19	104.19	113.92	81.53	106.34
Nordic (138)	518.59	−1.2	481.46	399.50	569.94	565.25	−0.2	1.78	525.16	486.16	407.38	570.02	566.45	555.97	360.04	531.26
Pacific Basin (715)	120.55	0.2	111.92	92.87	132.49	95.04	−0.2	1.27	120.30	111.37	93.32	130.58	95.23	129.86	82.88	101.33
Euro–Pacific (1424)	215.56	−0.6	200.13	166.06	236.90	188.50	−0.2	1.76	216.92	200.81	163.27	235.45	188.78	227.88	166.00	212.11
North America (729)	516.50	1.4	479.52	397.89	567.64	517.04	1.5	1.26	509.13	471.31	394.94	552.62	509.47	541.76	374.92	433.41
Europe Ex. UK (510)	319.22	−1.3	296.36	245.91	350.83	325.12	−0.1	1.79	323.35	299.33	250.83	350.97	325.38	366.32	260.93	345.25
Europe Ex. Eurobloc (375)	97.52	−0.7	90.53	75.12	107.17	101.72	−0.2	2.10	98.23	90.94	76.20	106.62	101.94	103.93	77.40	100.08
Europe Ex. UK Ex. Eurobloc (176)	93.78	−1.3	87.07	72.25	103.07	98.16	−0.2	1.52	94.98	87.92	73.68	103.09	98.35	109.21	75.16	104.20
Pacific Ex. Japan (272)	211.13	−0.5	196.01	162.65	232.03	213.44	0.2	2.94	212.19	196.43	164.60	230.31	213.07	230.69	128.26	177.75
World Ex. Eurobloc (1908)	111.29	0.9	103.32	85.74	122.31	111.28	0.9	1.43	110.33	102.14	85.59	119.76	110.26	116.77	83.09	97.48
World Ex. US (1637)	216.25	−0.6	200.76	166.59	237.66	194.25	−0.1	1.78	217.55	201.39	168.76	236.14	194.45	228.52	165.95	215.04
World Ex. UK (2043)	313.21	0.7	290.79	241.29	344.22	286.73	0.9	1.40	311.13	288.02	241.35	337.70	284.18	327.39	236.11	280.46
World Ex. Japan (1799)	424.03	0.6	393.67	326.65	466.01	423.31	0.9	1.58	421.65	390.33	327.08	457.66	419.50	443.90	320.58	386.81
The World Index (2242)	319.83	0.6	296.93	246.38	351.50	293.70	0.8	1.49	318.09	294.46	246.75	345.26	291.42	335.13	242.36	289.35

 CONSTITUENT CHANGE 28/5/99: Addition: Delphi Automotive Systems (Medium-Small Cap) (USA).

Source: *Financial Times*, 28 May 1999, 37.

TABLE 5.8 MARKET COVERAGE OF MORGAN STANLEY CAPITAL INTERNATIONAL INDEXES AS OF AUGUST 26, 1998

	GDP EAFE	Weights[a] World	Companies in Index	U.S. $ Billion	Free EAFE[b]	World
Austria	1.5	0.9	20	24.1	0.4	0.2
Belgium	1.8	1.1	17	123.1	1.9	0.9
Denmark	1.3	0.8	22	64.1	1.0	0.5
Finland	1.0	0.6	20	70.0	1.1	0.5
Finland (free)	1.0	0.6	20	70.0	1.1	0.5
France	10.7	6.5	67	639.2	9.9	4.6
Germany	16.2	9.9	62	728.9	11.3	5.3
Ireland	0.5	0.3	17	31.6	0.5	0.2
Italy	9.4	5.7	52	331.0	5.1	2.4
The Netherlands	2.7	1.7	23	369.4	5.7	2.7
Norway	1.2	0.7	30	30.5	0.5	0.2
Norway (free)	1.2	0.7	30	30.5	0.5	0.2
Spain	4.2	2.6	31	207.6	3.2	1.5
Sweden	1.7	1.0	38	197.2	3.0	1.4
Sweden (free)	1.7	1.0	38	197.2	3.0	1.4
Switzerland	2.1	1.3	32	523.3	8.1	3.8
United Kingdom	9.7	5.9	136	1,466.4	22.7	10.6
Europe 14 (free)	64.6	39.4	587	4,849.8	74.9	35.2
Europe 14	64.6	39.4	587	4,849.8	74.9	35.2
Australia	2.6	1.6	54	147.6	2.3	1.1
Hong Kong	1.2	0.8	34	114.0	1.8	0.8
Japan	29.9	18.3	308	1,292.7	20.0	9.4
Malaysia	0.5	0.3	72	23.3	0.4	0.2
New Zealand	0.5	0.3	9	12.7	0.2	0.1
Singapore	0.7	0.4	35	32.1	—	0.2
Singapore (free)	—	—	35	32.8	0.5	—
Pacific	35.4	21.6	512	1,622.3	—	11.8
Pacific (free)	—	—	512	1,623.0	25.1	—
EAFE (free)	100.0	61.0	1,099	6,472.1	—	46.9
EAFE	—	—	1,099	6,472.8	100.0	—
Canada	—	24	78	264.1	—	1.9
United States	—	36.6	383	7,059.9	—	51.2
The World Index (free)	—	100.0	1,560	13,796.1	—	100.0
The World Index	—	—	1,560	13,796.8	—	—
Nordic countries	5.1	3.1	110	361.8	—	2.6
Europe 14 ex UK	54.9	33.5	451	3,383.3	—	24.5
Far East	32.3	19.7	449	1,462.0	—	10.6
Far East (free)	—	—	449	1,462.7	22.6	—
EASEA (EAFE ex. Japan)	70.1	42.7	791	5,179.4	—	37.5
North America	—	39.0	461	7,324.0	—	53.1
Kokusai (World ex. Japan)	—	81.8	1,252	12,503.4	—	90.6

[a]GDP weight figures represent the initial weights applicable for the first month. They are used exclusively in the MSCI "GDP weighted" indexes.

[b]*Free* indicates that only stocks that can be acquired by foreign investors are included in the index. If the number of companies is the same and the value is different, it indicates that the stocks available to foreigners are priced differently from domestic shares.

Source: Morgan Stanley Capital International (New York: Morgan Stanley & Co., 1998).

BOND-MARKET INDICATOR SERIES[8]

Investors know little about the several bond-market series because these bond series are relatively new and not widely published. Knowledge regarding these bond series is

[8]The discussion in this section draws heavily from Frank K. Reilly and David J. Wright, "Bond Market Indexes," *The Handbook of Fixed-Income Securities,* 5th ed., ed. Frank J. Fabozzi (Chicago: Irwin Professional Publishing, 1997).

FIGURE 5.3 **LISTING OF MORGAN STANLEY CAPITAL INTERNATIONAL STOCK INDEX VALUES FOR MAY 27, 1999**

Morgan Stanley Indexes

	MAY 25	MAY 24	% FROM 12/31/98
U.S.	1255.6	1277.5	+ 4.9
Britain	1837.6	1858.8	+ 5.4
Canada	807.3	827.0	+ 8.2
Japan	830.1	837.1	+ 19.3
France	1384.6	1394.8	+ 10.6
Germany	677.6	691.1	+ 2.73
Hong Kong	7206.8	7253.2	+ 21.3
Switzerland	866.4	886.10	− 2.8
Australia	584.8	593.5	+ 2.3
World Index	**1185.4**	**1200.1**	+ **3.1**
EAFE MSCI-p	**1414.7**	**1423.6**	+ **0.7**

As calculated by Morgan Stanley Capital International Perspective, Geneva. Each index, calculated in local currencies, is based on the close of 1969 equaling 100.

Source: *Wall Street Journal,* 27 May 1999, C12.

becoming more important because of the growth of fixed-income mutual funds and the consequent need to have a reliable set of benchmarks to use in evaluating performance.[9] Also, because the performance of many fixed-income money managers has been unable to match that of the aggregate bond market, interest has been growing in bond index funds, which requires the development of an index to emulate.[10]

Notably, the creation and computation of bond-market indexes is more difficult than a stock-market series for several reasons. First, the universe of bonds is much broader than that of stocks, ranging from U.S. Treasury securities to bonds in default. Second, the universe of bonds is changing constantly because of numerous new issues, bond maturities, calls, and bond sinking funds. Third, the volatility of prices for individual bonds and bond portfolios changes because bond price volatility is affected by duration, which is likewise changing constantly because of changes in maturity, coupon, and market yield (see Chapter 16). Finally, significant problems can arise in correctly pricing the individual bond issues in an index (especially corporate and mortgage bonds) compared to the current and continuous transactions prices available for most stocks used in stock indexes.

The subsequent discussion is divided into three subsections: (1) U.S. investment-grade bond indexes, including Treasuries; (2) U.S. high-yield bond indexes; and (3) global government bond indexes. Notably, all of these indexes indicate total rates of return for the portfolio of bonds, including price change, accrued interest, and coupon income reinvested. Also most of the indexes are market-value weighted using current prices and outstanding

[9]For a discussion of benchmark selection, see Chris P. Dialynas, "The Active Decisions in the Selection of Passive Management and Performance Bogeys," and Daralyn B. Peifer, "A Sponsor's View of Benchmark Portfolios," in *The Handbook of Fixed-Income Securities,* 5th ed., ed. Frank J. Fabozzi (Chicago, Ill.: Irwin Professional Publishing, 1997).

[10]For a discussion of this phenomenon, see Fran Hawthorne, "The Battle of the Bond Indexes," *Institutional Investor* 20, no. 4 (April 1986); and Sharmin Mossavar-Rahmani, "Indexing Fixed-Income Investments," in *The Handbook of Fixed-Income Securities,* 5th ed., ed. Frank J. Fabozzi (Chicago: Irwin Professional Publishing, 1997).

FIGURE 5.4 **DOW JONES WORLD STOCK INDEX LISTING**

DOW JONES GLOBAL INDEXES

5:30 p.m., Wednesday, May 26, 1999

REGION/ COUNTRY	DJ GLOBAL INDEXES, LOCAL CURRENCY	PCT. CHG.	IN U.S. DOLLARS: 5:30 P.M. INDEX	CHG.	PCT. CHG.	12-MO HIGH	12-MO LOW	12-MO CHG.	PCT. CHG.	FROM 12/31	PCT. CHG.
Americas			**301.23**	**+ 4.60**	**+ 1.55**	**316.29**	**219.47**	**+ 45.89**	**+ 17.97**	**+17.44**	**+ 6.15**
Brazil†	1139	+ 5.75	256.09	+18.11	+ 7.61	406.24	155.25	−113.82	− 30.77	+17.50	+ 7.33
Canada	206.64	− 0.29	162.40	− 0.80	− 0.49	174.70	117.73	− 11.53	− 6.63	+16.15	+11.05
Chile	211.02	+ 1.28	159.43	+ 1.86	+ 1.18	174.92	96.32	+ 0.40	+ 0.25	+28.49	+21.76
Mexico	414.17	+ 3.45	132.16	+ 2.78	+ 2.15	147.81	60.60	+ 19.88	+ 17.71	+43.13	+48.45
U.S.	1235.88	+ 1.58	1235.88	+19.27	+ 1.58	1296.00	900.71	+204.17	+ 19.79	+66.54	+ 5.69
Venezuela	391.49	+ 2.37	40.40	+ 0.89	+ 2.25	56.43	23.01	− 15.86	− 28.19	+ 0.47	+ 1.18
Latin America			**159.27**	**+ 6.11**	**+ 3.99**	**187.21**	**90.39**	**− 18.14**	**− 10.22**	**+30.95**	**+24.12**
Europe/Africa			**228.05**	**− 3.00**	**− 1.30**	**251.61**	**185.07**	**− 6.66**	**− 2.84**	**− 6.95**	**− 2.96**
Austria	123.58	+ 0.26	100.19	− 1.32	− 1.30	137.08	93.22	− 36.86	− 26.89	− 5.13	− 4.87
Belgium	289.21	− 0.82	234.68	− 5.66	− 2.36	307.75	225.59	− 8.89	− 3.65	−54.73	−18.91
Denmark	199.31	+ 0.18	167.78	− 0.54	− 0.32	210.95	156.84	− 31.26	− 15.70	−22.35	−11.75
Finland	918.75	− 0.27	668.40	−12.40	− 1.82	752.22	365.19	+194.64	+ 41.09	+63.88	+10.57
France	269.06	− 0.03	221.86	− 3.57	− 1.58	238.23	173.04	+ 10.15	+ 4.80	+ 0.85	+ 0.39
Germany	284.33	+ 0.26	229.97	− 3.03	− 1.30	280.68	195.52	− 20.64	− 8.23	−18.05	− 7.28
Greece	594.50	− 2.71	336.33	−12.69	− 3.64	358.78	181.78	+ 95.39	+ 39.59	+54.34	+19.27
Ireland	373.68	− 0.73	295.97	− 6.88	− 2.27	369.89	247.45	− 9.57	− 3.13	−39.67	−11.82
Italy	319.59	+ 0.30	212.59	− 2.72	− 1.26	252.46	169.16	− 4.74	− 2.18	−21.83	− 9.31
Netherlands	398.83	− 0.17	322.60	− 5.64	− 1.72	366.66	258.60	− 16.62	− 4.90	−23.43	− 6.77
Norway	174.59	+ 0.32	132.81	− 0.88	− 0.66	170.80	96.85	− 33.90	− 20.33	+16.69	+14.37
Portugal	354.23	+ 0.54	249.32	− 2.58	− 1.02	352.93	221.49	− 84.19	− 25.24	−48.57	−16.30
South Africa	188.45	− 0.71	82.58	− 0.97	− 1.16	116.10	57.78	− 30.31	− 26.85	+11.88	+16.80
Spain	405.01	− 0.48	247.94	− 5.13	− 2.03	293.48	194.86	− 6.99	− 2.74	−22.68	− 8.38
Sweden	431.36	− 0.76	279.43	− 4.63	− 1.63	317.82	190.08	− 21.45	− 7.13	+25.98	+10.25
Switzerland	392.41	+ 0.15	348.55	− 5.66	− 1.60	421.91	295.28	− 46.16	− 11.69	−47.38	−11.97
United Kingdom	237.51	− 0.34	202.85	− 1.43	− 0.70	217.02	162.40	+ 3.99	+ 2.01	+ 4.28	+ 2.15
Europe/Africa (ex. South Africa)			**236.36**	**− 3.11**	**− 1.30**	**260.76**	**191.94**	**− 5.26**	**− 2.18**	**− 8.03**	**− 3.29**
Europe/Africa (ex. U.K. & S. Africa)			**257.50**	**− 4.14**	**− 1.58**	**292.44**	**210.59**	**− 10.82**	**− 4.03**	**−15.39**	**− 5.64**
Asia/Pacific			**90.97**	**− 0.02**	**− 0.02**	**98.15**	**62.38**	**+ 15.92**	**+ 21.22**	**+ 9.94**	**+12.27**
Australia	181.14	+ 0.54	154.35	− 0.93	− 0.60	168.20	112.56	+ 24.60	+ 18.95	+13.34	+ 9.46
Hong Kong	248.81	+ 0.47	249.55	+ 1.16	+ 0.47	272.00	134.48	+ 65.61	+ 35.67	+45.49	+22.29
Indonesia	244.80	− 2.88	60.31	− 3.17	− 4.99	63.48	15.47	+ 28.26	+ 88.18	+19.87	+49.11
Japan	79.89	− 0.25	81.52	− 0.24	− 0.29	87.96	57.38	+ 12.55	+ 18.19	+ 7.33	+ 9.87
New Zealand	137.75	+ 0.42	135.66	− 1.47	− 1.07	157.99	99.94	− 13.46	− 9.02	+ 6.26	+ 4.84
Philippines	228.74	+ 0.62	156.04	+ 0.01	+ 0.01	175.79	60.68	+ 26.20	+ 20.17	+28.75	+22.59
Singapore	142.28	+ 0.42	133.30	+ 0.32	+ 0.24	145.54	59.89	+ 40.94	+ 44.32	+23.89	+21.84
South Korea	125.82	+ 3.13	80.12	+ 2.16	+ 2.77	89.81	25.38	+ 51.65	+181.43	+18.90	+30.86
Taiwan	181.11	+ 0.41	142.42	+ 0.48	+ 0.34	147.37	106.17	+ 0.17	+ 0.12	+19.13	+15.52
Thailand	77.82	+ 3.11	49.43	+ 1.42	+ 2.96	56.76	20.88	+ 15.49	+ 45.64	+ 9.67	+24.32
Asia/Pacific (ex. Japan)			**154.35**	**+ 0.85**	**+ 0.55**	**166.45**	**91.45**	**+ 34.64**	**+ 28.93**	**+23.65**	**+18.10**
World (ex. U.S.)			**150.49**	**− 1.14**	**− 0.75**	**159.31**	**115.37**	**+ 4.48**	**+ 3.07**	**+ 3.47**	**+ 2.36**
DJ WORLD STOCK INDEX			**210.25**	**+ 0.99**	**+ 0.47**	**220.75**	**160.36**	**+ 20.91**	**+ 11.04**	**+ 7.46**	**+ 3.68**

Indexes based on 6/30/82=100 for U.S., 12/31/91=100 for World.
†Local currency index shown in 000s.

Source: *Wall Street Journal,* 27 May 1999, C12.

TABLE 5.9

CORRELATIONS OF PERCENT PRICE CHANGES OF ALTERNATIVE WORLD STOCK INDEXES 12/31/91–12/31/98

	U.S. Dollars
FT–MS:	0.998
FT–DJ:	0.997
MS–DJ:	0.996

par values publicly held. Table 5.10 is a summary of the characteristics for the indexes available for these three segments of the bond market.

Investment-Grade Bond Indexes

As shown in Table 5.10, four investment firms have created and maintain indexes for Treasury bonds and other bonds considered investment grade; that is, the bonds are rated BBB or higher. As demonstrated in Reilly and Wright and shown in Chapter 4, the relationship among the returns for these bonds is strong (that is, the correlations among the returns average about 0.95), regardless of the segment of the market. This implies that the returns for these investment-grade bonds are being driven by aggregate interest rates—that is, shifts in the government yield curve.

High-Yield Bond Indexes

One of the fastest-growing segments of the U.S. bond market during the past 15 years has been the high-yield bond market, which includes bonds that are not investment grade—that is, they are rated BB, B, CCC, CC, and C. Because of this growth, four investment firms and two academicians created indexes related to this market. A summary of the characteristics for these indexes is included in Table 5.10. As shown in a study by Reilly and Wright, the relationship among the alternative high-yield bond indexes is weaker than among the investment-grade indexes, and this is especially true for the bonds rated CCC.[11]

MERRILL LYNCH CONVERTIBLE SECURITIES INDEXES In March 1988, Merrill Lynch introduced a convertible bond index with data beginning in January 1987. This index includes 600 issues in three major subgroups: U.S. domestic convertible bonds, Eurodollar convertible bonds issued by U.S. corporations, and U.S. domestic convertible preferred stocks. The issues included must be public U.S. corporate issues, have a minimum par value of $25 million, and have a minimum maturity of one year.

Global Government Bond Market Indexes

Similar to the high-yield bond market, the global bond market has experienced significant growth in size and importance during the recent five-year period. Unlike the high-yield bond market, this global segment is completely dominated by government bonds because few non-U.S. countries have a corporate bond market, much less a high-yield corporate bond market. Once again, several major investment firms have responded to the needs of investors and money managers by creating indexes that reflect the performance for the global bond market, certain individual countries, and several regions. As shown in Table 5.10, the various indexes have several similar characteristics, such as measuring total rates of return, using market-value weighting, and using trader pricing. At the same time, the total sample sizes differ as do numbers of countries included.

[11]Frank K. Reilly and David J. Wright, "An Analysis of High-Yield Bond Benchmarks," *Journal of Fixed Income* 3, no. 4 (March 1994): 6–24. The uniqueness of CCC bonds is demonstrated in Frank K. Reilly and David J. Wright, "High-Yield Bonds and Segmentation in the Bond Market," mimeo (January 1999).

TABLE 5.10 **SUMMARY OF BOND MARKET INDEXES**

Name of Index	Number of Issues	Maturity	Size of Issues	Weighting	Pricing	Reinvestment Assumption	Subindexes Available
U.S. Investment-Grade Bond Indexes							
Lehman Brothers	5,000+	Over 1 year	Over $100 million	Market value	Trader priced and model priced	No	Government, gov./corp., corporate, mortgage-backed, asset-backed
Merrill Lynch	5,000+	Over 1 year	Over $50 million	Market value	Trader priced and model priced	In specific bonds	Government, gov./corp., corporate, mortgage
Ryan Treasury	300+	Over 1 year	All Treasury	Market value and equal	Market priced	In specific bonds	Treasury
Salomon Brothers	5,000+	Over 1 year	Over $50 million	Market value	Trader priced	In one-month T-bill	Broad inv. grade, Treas.-agency, corporate, mortgage
U.S. High-Yield Bond Indexes							
Blume-Keim	233	Over 10 years	Over $25 million	Equal	Trader priced	Yes	Only composite
First Boston	423	All maturities	Over $75 million	Market value	Trader priced	Yes	Composite and by rating
Lehman Brothers	624	Over 1 year	Over $100 million	Market value	Trader priced	No	Composite and by rating
Merrill Lynch	735	Over 1 year	Over $25 million	Market value	Trader priced	Yes	Composite and by rating
Salomon Brothers	299	Over 7 years	Over $50 million	Market value	Trader priced	Yes	Composite and by rating
Global Government Bond Indexes (Initial Date of Index)							
Lehman Brothers (January 1987)	800	Over 1 year	Over $200 million	Market value	Trader priced	Yes	Composite and 13 countries, local and U.S. dollars
Merrill Lynch (December 1985)	9,736	Over 1 year	Over $50 million	Market value	Trader priced	Yes	Composite and 9 countries, local and U.S. dollars
J. P. Morgan (12/31/85)	445	Over 1 year	Over $100 million	Market value	Trader priced	Yes in index	Composite and 11 countries, local and U.S. dollars
Salomon Brothers (12/31/84)	400	Over 1 year	Over $250 million	Market value	Trader priced	Yes at local short-term rate	Composite and 14 countries, local and U.S. dollars

Source: Frank K. Reilly, Wenchi Kao, and David J. Wright, "Alternative Bond Market Indexes," *Financial Analysts Journal* 48, no. 3 (May–June, 1992): 14–58; Frank K. Reilly and David J. Wright, "An Analysis of High-Yield Bond Benchmarks," *Journal of Fixed Income* 3, no. 4 (March 1994): 6–24; and Frank K. Reilly and David J. Wright, "Global Bond Markets: Alternative Benchmarks and Risk–Return Performance," mimeo (May 1997).

An analysis of performance in this market indicates that the differences mentioned have caused some large differences in the long-term risk–return performance by the alternative indexes.[12] Also, the low correlation among the various countries is similar to stocks. Finally, there was a significant exchange rate effect on volatility and correlations.

COMPOSITE STOCK–BOND INDEXES

Beyond separate stock indexes and bond indexes for individual countries, a natural step is the development of a composite series that measures the performance of all securities in a given country. A composite series of stocks and bonds makes it possible to examine the benefits of diversifying with a combination of asset classes such as stocks and bonds in addition to diversifying within the asset classes of stocks or bonds.

Merrill Lynch–Wilshire U.S. Capital Markets Index (ML–WCMI)

A market-value-weighted index called Merrill Lynch–Wilshire Capital Markets Index (ML–WCMI) measures the total return performance of the combined U.S. taxable fixed-income and equity markets. It is basically a combination of the Merrill Lynch fixed-income indexes and the Wilshire 5000 common-stock index. As such, it tracks more than 10,000 stocks and bonds. The makeup of the index is as follows (as of December 1997):

Security	$ in Billions	Percent of Total
Treasury bonds	$1,085	20.89%
Agency bonds	166	3.20
Mortgage bonds	467	8.99
Corporate bonds	453	8.72
OTC stocks	331	6.37
AMEX stocks	105	2.02
NYSE stocks	2,586	49.92
	$5,193	100.00%

Brinson Partners Global Security Market Index (GSMI)

The Brinson Partners GSMI series contains both U.S. stocks and bonds, but also includes non-U.S. equities and nondollar bonds as well as an allocation to cash. The specific breakdown is as follows (as of January 1999):

	Percent
Equities	
U.S. large capitalization	35
U.S. small and mid-cap	15
Non-U.S.	17
Fixed Income	
U.S. domestic investment grade	18
International dollar bonds	2
Nondollar bonds	8
Cash	5
Total	100

[12]Frank K. Reilly and David J. Wright, "Global Bond Markets: Alternative Benchmarks and Risk–Return Performance," mimeo (May 1997).

Although related to the relative market values of these asset classes, the weights specified are not constantly adjusted. The construction of the GSMI used optimization techniques to identify the portfolio mix of available global asset classes that matches the risk level of a typical U.S. pension plan. The index is balanced to the policy weights monthly.

Because the GSMI contains both U.S. and international stocks and bonds, it is clearly the most diversified benchmark available with a weighting scheme that approaches market values. As such, it is closest to the theoretically specified "market portfolio of risky assets" referred to in the CAPM literature.[13]

COMPARISON OF INDEXES OVER TIME

This section discusses price movements in the different series for various monthly or annual intervals.

Correlations Among Monthly Equity Price Changes

Table 5.11 contains a matrix of the correlation coefficients of the monthly percentage of price changes for a set of U.S. and non-U.S. equity-market indexes during the 25-year period from 1972 to 1997.[14] Most of the correlation differences are attributable to sample differences, that is, differences in the firms listed on the alternative stock exchanges. Most of the major series—except the Nikkei Stock Average—are market-value-weighted indexes that include a large number of stocks. Therefore, the computational procedure is generally similar and the sample sizes are large or all-encompassing. Thus, the major difference between the indexes is that the stocks are from different segments of the U.S. stock market or from different countries.

There is a high positive correlation (0.92) between the alternative NYSE series (the S&P 500 and the NYSE composite). These indexes are also highly correlated with the Wilshire 5000 index that is value weighted, which means it is heavily influenced by the large NYSE stocks in the index.

In contrast, there are lower correlations between these NYSE series and the AMEX series (about 0.72) or the NASDAQ index (about 0.78). Further, the relationship between the Russell 2000 Index and the other U.S. series ranges from 0.73 to 0.91, which reflects the fact that the Russell 2000 series includes a sample of small-cap stocks from all exchanges.

The correlations among the U.S. series and those from Canada, the United Kingdom, Germany, and Japan support the case for global investing. The relationships among the two TSE series were correlated about 0.87 even though the sample sizes, weightings, and computations differ. These within-country results attest to the importance of the basic sample. In contrast, the U.S.–Canada and U.S.–U.K. correlations, which averaged about 0.73, and the U.S.–Japan correlations, which were about 0.30, confirm the benefits of global diversification because such low correlations reduce the variance of a portfolio.

[13]This GSMI series is used in a study that examines the effect of alternative benchmarks on the estimate of the security market and estimates of individual stock betas. See Frank K. Reilly and Rashid A. Akhtar, "The Benchmark Error Problem with Global Capital Markets," *Journal of Portfolio Management* 22, no. 1 (fall 1995). Brinson Partners has a Multiple Markets Index (MMI) that also contains venture capital and real estate. Because these assets are not actively traded, the value and rate of return estimates tend to be relatively stable, which reduces the standard deviation of the series.

[14]In earlier editions of the text, the correlations examined daily percentage price changes. The shift to monthly percentage price changes made it possible to consider a wider range of non-U.S. equity indexes. Notably, the monthly price change correlation results among U.S. indexes are similar to the daily results.

TABLE 5.11 **CORRELATION COEFFICIENTS AMONG MONTHLY PERCENTAGE PRICE CHANGES IN ALTERNATIVE EQUITY MARKET INDICATOR SERIES: JANUARY 1972 (WHEN AVAILABLE) TO DECEMBER 1997**

	S&P 500	NYSE	AMEX	NASDAQ Industr.	Wilshire 5000	Russell 2000[a]	Toronto SE 300	Tokyo SE	Nikkei	FAZ[b]	FT All-Share[b]	M-S World	FT/S&P World[c]
S&P 500	—												
NYSE	0.919	—											
AMEX	0.719	0.801	—										
NASDAQ Ind.	0.783	0.881	0.824	—									
Wilshire 5000	0.906	0.987	0.817	0.906	—								
Russell 2000	0.731	0.848	0.764	0.913	0.870	—							
Toronto 300	0.687	0.761	0.768	0.740	0.768	0.723	—						
Tokyo SE	0.302	0.299	0.245	0.251	0.284	0.249	0.269	—					
Nikkei	0.358	0.350	0.280	0.308	0.335	0.325	0.293	0.872	—				
FAZ	0.501	0.534	0.381	0.404	0.515	0.440	0.452	0.279	0.330	—			
FT All-Share	0.615	0.712	0.591	0.620	0.693	0.618	0.627	0.266	0.379	0.514	—		
M-S World	0.763	0.821	0.658	0.704	0.808	0.669	0.714	0.588	0.631	0.525	0.651	—	
FT/S&P World	0.590	0.695	0.508	0.589	0.666	0.572	0.616	0.664	0.731	0.505	0.617	0.960	—

[a]Russell 2000 series starts in 1979.

[b]FAZ and FT All-Share series start in 1983.

[c]FT/S&P World Index series starts in 1986.

Correlations among Monthly Bond Indexes

The correlations among the monthly bond return series in Table 5.12 consider a variety of bond series, including investment-grade bonds, U.S. high-yield bonds, and government bond indexes for several major non-U.S. countries (GE–Germany, JA–Japan, and UK–the United Kingdom). The correlations among the U.S. investment-grade bond series ranged from 0.90 to 0.99, confirming that although the *level* of interest rates differs due to the risk premium, the overriding factors that determine the rates of return for investment-grade bonds over time are *systematic* interest rate variables.

The correlations among investment-grade bonds and HY bonds are significantly lower (0.40 to 0.54), caused by definite equity characteristics of HY bonds.[15] Finally, the low and diverse relationships among U.S. investment-grade bonds and non-U.S. government bond series (0.14 to 0.33) reflect different interest-rate movements and exchange-rate effects (these non-U.S. government results are U.S. dollar returns). Again, these results support the concept of global diversification.

Mean Annual Stock Price Changes

The mean and standard deviation of annual percentage of price changes for the major stock indexes is contained in Table 5.13. One would expect differences among the price changes and measures of risk for the various series due to the different samples. For example, the NYSE series should have lower rates of return and risk measures than the AMEX and OTC series. The results generally confirm these expectations. For example, the Russell 2000 reflects the results for the small-capitalization segment of the U.S. stock market. This series, which began in 1979, shows higher returns and higher risk measures than the large-cap NYSE series during most individual years.

Regarding non-U.S. results, the Canadian results on the Toronto Exchange had higher average returns than the NYSE, and lower risk than the NASDAQ. The United Kingdom (that is, the FT All-Share) had higher returns than the NYSE indexes, but much larger variability, while Germany (the FAZ) had lower returns than the United States, but similar volatility. Finally, the Japanese markets experienced lower returns and slightly lower volatility than the U.S. markets. Remember, these non-U.S. stock results reflect the domestic price changes and do not consider the exchange-rate effect.

These results for the Japanese market were significantly affected by poor results during 1990 to 1997. Because the Japanese stock market had relatively low correlation with alternative U.S. stock-market indexes (Table 5.11), it indicates that Japan would have been a prime source of diversification benefits even with the higher volatility.

Annual Bond Rates of Return

Table 5.14 shows the mean and standard deviation of annual total rates of return for the Lehman Brothers bond-market indexes.[16] You cannot directly compare the bond and stock results because the bond results are *total* rates of return versus annual percentage price change results for stocks (most of the stock series do not report dividend data).

The major comparison for the bond series should be among the average rates of return and the risk measures, because although the monthly rates of return are correlated, we would expect a difference in the level of return due to the differential risk premiums. The results generally confirm our expectations (that is, there typically are lower returns and risk measures for the government series followed by higher returns and risk for corporate and mortgage bonds).

---

[15]For a detailed analysis of this point, see Frank K. Reilly and David J. Wright, "High Yield Bonds and Segmentation in the Bond Market," mimeo (June 1999).

[16]Because of the high correlations among the monthly rates of return as shown in Table 5.12, the results for various bond-market segments (government, corporate, mortgages) are similar regardless of the source (Lehman Brothers, Merrill Lynch, Salomon Brothers, Ryan). Therefore, only the Lehman Brothers risk–return results are presented in Table 5.14.

TABLE 5.12 CORRELATIONS AMONG MONTHLY BOND RETURNS FOR U.S. INVESTMENT-GRADE BONDS, U.S. HIGH-YIELD BONDS, AND NON-U.S. GOVERNMENT BONDS: 1985–1997

	LBGC	LBG	LBC	LBM	LBA	MLHYM	SBGE	SBJA	SBUK
LBGC	—								
LBG	0.997	—							
LBC	0.976	0.958	—						
LBM	0.919	0.905	0.927	—					
LBA	0.995	0.990	0.978	0.952	—				
MLHYM	0.457	0.419	0.548	0.454	0.465	—			
SBGE	0.308	0.321	0.259	0.298	0.308	−0.031	—		
SBJA	0.183	0.196	0.159	0.142	0.178	0.043	0.486	—	
SBUK	0.280	0.297	0.227	0.235	0.276	−0.013	0.656	0.455	—

TABLE 5.13 MEAN AND STANDARD DEVIATION OF ANNUAL PERCENTAGE PRICE CHANGE FOR STOCK PRICE SERIES 1972–1997

	Geometric Mean	Arithmetic Mean	Standard Deviation	Coefficient of Variation
DJIA	8.79	10.09	16.70	1.66
S&P 400	9.29	10.58	16.44	1.55
S&P 500	9.06	10.35	16.49	1.59
AMEX Value Index	10.04	12.26	22.07	1.80
NASDAQ Comp.	11.89	13.94	20.81	1.49
Russell 2000[a]	15.61	17.00	18.05	1.06
Wilshire 5000	9.29	10.69	17.07	1.60
Toronto S.E. Comp.	11.32	12.54	16.52	1.32
FT All-Share	10.37	14.36	31.94	2.22
FAZ	7.58	10.16	24.27	2.39
Nikkei	6.97	9.74	25.77	2.65
Tokyo S.E. Index	6.86	9.84	27.15	2.76
MS World	8.58	9.82	16.19	1.65

[a]The Russell 2000 index was initiated in 1979.

TABLE 5.14 MEAN AND STANDARD DEVIATION OF ANNUAL RATES OF RETURN FOR LEHMAN BROTHERS BOND INDEXES 1976–1997

	Geometric Mean	Arithmetic Mean	Standard Deviation	Coefficient of Variation
Government/Corporate	9.68	9.95	8.04	0.81
Government	9.65	9.77	7.15	0.73
Corporate	10.17	10.60	10.25	0.97
Mortgage-Backed	9.94	10.35	10.07	0.97
Yankee	10.34	10.73	9.63	0.90
Aggregate	9.75	10.02	8.17	0.82

THE INTERNET *Investments Online*

We've seen several previous Web sites which offer online users a look at current market conditions in the form of a time-delayed market index (some sites offer real-time stock and index prices, but only at a cost to their customers). Here are a few others:

www.bloomberg.com The site is somewhat of an Internet version of the "Bloomberg machine," which is prevalent in many brokerage house offices. It offers both news and current data on a wide variety of global market securities and indexes as well as information on interest rates, commodities, and currencies.

www.stockmaster.com The Stockmaster Web site offers information on a number of U.S. and overseas market indexes.

www.asx.com.au Australian Stock Exchange

www.bolsamadrid.es Madrid Stock Exchange; Web site is in Spanish

www.tse.com Toronto Stock Exchange

www.nikko.co.jp:80/SEC/index_e.html Nikko Stock Market index (Japan)

www.exchange.de/realtime/dax_d.html German Stock Exchange information

Here's a test of your Web information-seeking skills: see if you can find Web pages for some of the country stock exchanges listed in the Chapter 5 appendix.

Summary

- Given the several uses of security-market indicator series, you should know how they are constructed and the differences among them. If you want to use one of the many series to learn how the "market" is doing, you should be aware of what market you are dealing with so you can select the appropriate index. As an example, are you only interested in the NYSE or do you also want to consider the AMEX and the OTC? Beyond the U.S. market, are you interested in Japanese or U.K. stocks, or do you want to examine the total world market?[17]
- Indexes are also used as benchmarks to evaluate portfolio performance.[18] In this case, you must be sure the index (benchmark) is consistent with your investing universe. If you are investing worldwide, you should not judge your performance relative to the DJIA, which is limited to 30 U.S. blue-chip stocks. For a bond portfolio, the index should match your investment philosophy. Finally, if your portfolio contains both stocks and bonds, you must evaluate your performance against an appropriate combination of indexes.
- Whenever you invest, you examine numerous market indexes to tell you what has happened and how successful you have been. The selection of the appropriate indexes for information or evaluation will depend on how knowledgeable you are regarding the various series. The purpose of this chapter is to help you understand what to look for and how to make the right decision.

Questions

1. Discuss briefly several uses of security-market indicator series.
2. What major factors must be considered when constructing a market index? Put another way, what characteristics differentiate indexes?
3. Explain how a market indicator series is price weighted. In such a case, would you expect a $100 stock to be more important than a $25 stock? Why?
4. Explain how to compute a value-weighted series.
5. Explain how a price-weighted series and a value-weighted series adjust for stock splits.

[17]For a readable discussion on this topic, see Anne Merjos, "How's the Market Doing?" *Barron's,* 20 August, 1990, 18–20, 27, 28.

[18]Chapter 27 includes an extensive discussion of the purpose and construction of benchmarks and considers the evaluation of portfolio performance.

6. Describe an unweighted price-indicator series and describe how you would construct such a series. Assume a 20 percent price change in GM ($40/share; 50 million shares outstanding) and Coors Brewing ($25/share and 15 million shares outstanding). Explain which stock's change will have the greater impact on this index.
7. If you correlated percentage changes in the Wilshire 5000 equity index with percentage changes in the NYSE composite, the AMEX index, and the NASDAQ composite index, would you expect a difference in the correlations? Why or why not?
8. There are high correlations among the monthly percentage price changes for the alternative NYSE indexes. Discuss the reason for this similarity: is it size of sample, source of sample, or method of computation?
9. Compare stock price indicator series for the three U.S. equity-market segments (NYSE, AMEX, OTC) for the period 1972 to 1997. Discuss whether the results in terms of average annual price change and risk (variability of price changes) were consistent with economic theory.
10. Discuss the relationship (correlations) between the two stock price indexes for the Tokyo Stock Exchange (TSE). Examine the correlations among the TSE series and two NYSE series. Explain why these relationships differ.
11. You learn that the Wilshire 5000 market-value-weighted series increased by 16 percent during a specified period, whereas a Wilshire 5000 equal-weighted series increased by 23 percent during the same period. Discuss what this difference in results implies.
12. Why is it contended that bond-market indexes are more difficult to construct and maintain than stock-market indexes?
13. The Wilshire 5000 market-value-weighted index increased by 5 percent, whereas the Merrill Lynch–Wilshire Capital Markets Index increased by 15 percent during the same period. What does this difference in results imply?
14. The Russell 1000 increased by 8 percent during the past year, whereas the Russell 2000 increased by 15 percent. Discuss the implication of these results.
15. Based on what you know about the *Financial Times* (FT) World Index, the Morgan Stanley Capital International World Index, and the Dow Jones World Stock Index, what level of correlation would you expect among monthly rates of return? Discuss the reasons for your answer based on the factors that affect indexes.

Problems

1. You are given the following information regarding prices for a sample of stocks:

		PRICE	
Stock	**Number of Shares**	***T***	***T* + 1**
A	1,000,000	60	80
B	10,000,000	20	35
C	30,000,000	18	25

a. Construct a *price-weighted* series for these three stocks, and compute the percentage change in the series for the period from T to $T + 1$.

b. Construct a *value-weighted* series for these three stocks, and compute the percentage change in the series for the period from T to $T + 1$.

c. Briefly discuss the difference in the results for the two series.

2. a. Given the data in Problem 1, construct an equal-weighted series by assuming $1,000 is invested in each stock. What is the percentage change in wealth for this equal-weighted portfolio?

b. Compute the percentage of price change for each of the stocks in Problem 1. Compute the arithmetic average of these percentage changes. Discuss how this answer compares to the answer in 2a.

c. Compute the geometric average of the percentage changes in 2b. Discuss how this result compares to the answer in 2b.

3. For the past five trading days, on the basis of figures in the *Wall Street Journal,* compute the daily percentage price changes for the following stock indexes:
   a. DJIA
   b. S&P 400
   c. AMEX Market Value Series
   d. NASDAQ Industrial Index
   e. FT-100 Share Index
   f. Nikkei Stock Price Average

   Discuss the difference in results for a and b, a and c, a and d, a and e, a and f, e and f. What do these differences imply regarding diversifying within the United States versus diversifying between countries?

4.

	PRICE			**SHARES**		
Company	**A**	**B**	**C**	**A**	**B**	**C**
Day 1	12	23	52	500	350	250
Day 2	10	22	55	500	350	250
Day 3	14	46	52	500	175[a]	250
Day 4	13	47	25	500	175	500[b]
Day 5	12	45	26	500	175	500

[a]Split at close of Day 2
[b]Split at close of Day 3

   a. Calculate a Dow Jones Industrial Average for Days 1 through 5.
   b. What effects have the splits had in determining the next day's index? (Hint: Think of the relative weighting of each stock.)
   c. From a copy of the *Wall Street Journal,* find the divisor that is currently being used in calculating the DJIA. (Normally this value can be found on pages C2 and C3.)

5. Utilizing the price and volume data in Problem 4,
   a. Calculate a Standard & Poor's Index for Days 1 through 5 using a beginning index value of 10.
   b. Identify what effects the splits had in determining the next day's index. (Hint: Think of the relative weighting of each stock.)

6. Based on the following stock price and shares outstanding information, compute the beginning and ending values for a price-weighted index and a market-value-weighted index.

	DECEMBER 31, 1999		**DECEMBER 31, 2000**	
	Price	**Shares Outstanding**	**Price**	**Shares Outstanding**
Stock K	20	100,000,000	32	100,000,000
Stock M	80	2,000,000	45	4,000,000[a]
Stock R	40	25,000,000	42	25,000,000

[a]Stock split two-for-one during the year

   a. Compute the percentage change in the value of each index.
   b. Explain the difference in results between the two indexes.
   c. Compute the results for an unweighted index and discuss why these results differ from the others.

7. a. Assume a base index value of 100 at the beginning of 1972. Using the returns in Table 5.13, what would be your ending index value if you owned the stocks in the Nikkei Average through 1998?
   b. In addition to knowing this domestic rate of return, you are told that the exchange rate at the beginning of 1972 was ¥200 to the dollar and it was ¥120 to the dollar at the end of 1998. Compute the compound return in U.S. dollars.

References

Fisher, Lawrence, and James H. Lorie. *A Half Century of Returns on Stocks and Bonds.* Chicago: University of Chicago Graduate School of Business, 1997.

Ibbotson Associates. *Stocks, Bonds, Bills and Inflation.* Chicago: Ibbotson Associates, annual.

Lorie, James H., Peter Dodd, and Mary Hamilton Kimpton. *The Stock Market: Theories and Evidence.* 2d ed. Homewood, Ill.: Richard D. Irwin, 1985.

Reilly, Frank K., and David J. Wright, "Bond Market Indexes." In *The Handbook of Fixed-Income Securities,* 5th ed., ed. Frank J. Fabozzi. Chicago, Ill.: Irwin Professional Publishing, 1997.

Chapter 5 APPENDIX — FOREIGN STOCK-MARKET INDEXES

Index Name	Number of Stocks	Weights of Stocks	Calculation Method	History of Index
ATX-index (Vienna)	All stocks listed on the exchange	Market capitalization	Value weighted	Base year 1967, 1991 began including all stocks (Value = 100)
Swiss Market Index	18 stocks	Market capitalization	Value weighted	Base year 1988, stocks selected from the Basle, Geneva, and Zurich Exchanges (Value = 1500)
Stockholm General Index	All stocks (voting) listed on exchange	Market capitalization	Value weighted	Base year 1979, continuously updated (Value = 100)
Copenhagen Stock Exchange Share Price Index	All stocks traded	Market capitalization	Value weighted	Share price is based on average price of the day
Oslo SE Composite Index (Sweden)	25 companies			Base year 1972 (Value = 100)
Johannesburg Stock Exchange Actuaries Index	146 companies	Market capitalization	Value weighted	Base year 1959 (Value = 100)
Mexican Market Index	Variable number, based on capitalization and liquidity		Value weighted (adjustment for value of paid-out dividends)	Base year 1978, high dollar returns in recent years
Milan Stock Exchange MIB	Variable number, based on capitalization and liquidity		Weighted arithmetic average	Change base at beginning of each year (Value = 1000)
Belgium BEL-20 Stock Index	20 companies	Market capitalization	Value weighted	Base year 1991 (Value = 1000)
Madrid General Stock Index	92 stocks	Market capitalization	Value weighted	Change base at beginning of each year
Hang Seng Index (Hong Kong)	33 companies	Market capitalization	Value weighted	Started in 1969, accounts for 75 percent of total market
FT-Actuaries World Indexes	2,212 stocks	Market capitalization	Value weighted	Base year 1986
FT-SE 100 Index (London)	100 companies	Market capitalization	Value weighted	Base year 1983 (Value = 1000)
CAC General Share Index (French)	212 companies	Market capitalization	Value weighted	Base year 1981 (Value = 100)

Index Name	Number of Stocks	Weights of Stocks	Calculation Method	History of Index
Morgan Stanley World Index	1,482 stocks	Market capitalization	Value weighted	Base year 1970 (Value = 100)
Singapore Straits Times Industrial Index	30 stocks	Unweighted		
German Stock Market Index (DAX)	30 companies (Blue Chips)	Market capitalization	Value weighted	Base year 1987 (Value = 1000)
Frankfurter Allgemeine Zeitung Index (FAZ) (German)	100 companies (Blue Chips)	Market capitalization	Value weighted	Base year 1958 (Value = 100)
Australian Stock Exchange Share Price Indices	250 stocks (92 percent of all shares listed)	Market capitalization	Value weighted	Introduced in 1979
Dublin ISEQ Index	71 stocks (54 official, 17 unlisted). All stocks traded	Market capitalization	Value weighted	Base year 1988 (Value = 1000)
HEX Index (Helsinki)	Varies with different share price indexes	Market capitalization	Value weighted	Base changes every day
Jakarta Stock Exchange	All listed shares (148 currently)	Market capitalization	Value weighted	Base year 1982 (Value = 100)
Taiwan Stock Exchange Index	All ordinary stocks (listed for at least a month)	Market capitalization	Value weighted	Base year 1966 (Value = 100)
TSE 300 Composite Index (Toronto)	300 stocks (comprised of 14 subindexes)`	Market capitalization (adjusted for major shareholders)	Value weighted	Base year 1975 (Value = 1000)
KOSPI (Korean Composite Stock Price Index)	All common stocks listed on exchange	Market capitalization (adjusted for major shareholders)	Value weighted	Base year 1980 (Value = 100)

Chapter

6 Sources of Information on Global Investments

After you read this chapter, you should be able to answer the following questions:

- What are the major sources of information and data for aggregate economic analysis in the United States?
- What are the major sources for non-U.S. economic data, including the principal bibliographies?
- What are the major sources of information and data for aggregate security market analysis? Which sources are available annually, weekly, and daily?
- What investment firms provide analysis and recommendations for global markets?
- What are the major sources of information and data for industry analysis?
- What are the major sources of information and data for individual firm stock and bond analysis?
- What are the major investment magazines? Which magazines are available monthly, biweekly, and weekly?
- What are some major sources of information for mutual funds?
- What are the major academic journals that publish theoretical and empirical studies related to investments?
- What are the major computerized data sources?
- What are the major online databases?
- What are the names and addresses for the major sources of investment information?

In this chapter, we describe some of the major sources of information needed for global investment analysis. Relevant information is both important and difficult to obtain, especially in the current global capital market. The initial discussion considers sources of information related to aggregate economic analysis, including data from the government and various bank publications as well as sources of non-U.S. economic data. The second section considers sources of data for aggregate security market analysis. Again, we will review government publications, commercial publications, and brokerage firm reports. The third section considers sources of information for industry analysis, which generally receives significantly less attention than either the aggregate market or individual securities. As we will discuss, the major sources are industry publications, industry magazines, and information provided through industry trade associations. The fourth section on individual stock analysis considers company-generated information and numerous commercial publications provided to individual and institutional investors as well as brokerage firm reports. Finally, there are a growing number of investment magazines. The fifth section discusses sources of information for bond investors, including what is provided in government publications as well as numerous commercial publications. In many instances, bond information is included in publications with stock data.

Beyond the analysis of individual stocks and bonds, a point made throughout this textbook is that many investors implement their investment program using mutual funds. Therefore, there is a section dealing with sources of information on funds that considers basic descriptive information, but also sources of portfolio performance evaluation. Notably, this is an area of growing interest, and commercial publications are responding with new services and magazines.

Section six shifts from commercial publications and investment magazines for the typical investor to a discussion of academic journals that contain more theoretical and empirical studies expected to have a long-run impact on the investment process. We conclude the chapter with a discussion of a growing list of computerized data sources available to individuals and institutions. This includes large databases typically available on computer tapes as well as a growing number of online databases available through the Internet.

While it is not necessary to become completely familiar with each of the items mentioned in this chapter, it is important to become aware of what is available so that when you need specific data or information, you will know where to look for the material.

AGGREGATE ECONOMIC ANALYSIS

This section describes the data used to evaluate and estimate economic changes for the United States and other major countries, as contrasted to data regarding the aggregate securities markets (stocks, bonds, etc.).

U.S. Government Sources

It should come as no surprise that the main source of information on the U.S. economy is the federal government, which issues a variety of publications on the topic.

Federal Reserve Bulletin is a monthly publication issued by the Board of Governors of the Federal Reserve System. It is the primary source for almost all monetary data, including monetary aggregates, factors affecting member bank reserves, member bank reserve requirements, Federal Reserve open market transactions, and loans and investments of all commercial banks. In addition, the publication contains figures on financial markets, interest rates, and some stock-market statistics; data for corporate finance, including profits, assets, and liabilities of corporations; extensive nonfinancial statistics on output, the labor force, and the GDP; and a major section on international finance.

Survey of Current Business is a monthly publication issued by the U.S. Department of Commerce that gives details on national income and production figures. It is probably the best source for current, detailed information on all segments of the GDP and national income and contains industrial production data for numerous segments of the economy. The *Survey* is an excellent secondary source for labor statistics (employment and wages), interest rates, and statistics on foreign economic development. It also contains data regarding the leading, coincident, and lagging economic series previously published by the Department of Commerce.[1] These series are considered important by those who attempt to project peaks and troughs in the business cycle.

Economic Indicators—a monthly publication prepared for the Joint Economic Committee by the Council of Economic Advisers—contains monthly and annual data on output, income, spending, employment, production, prices, money and credit, federal finance, and international economies.

The *Quarterly Financial Report (QFR)* is prepared by the Federal Trade Commission and contains aggregate statistics on the financial position of U.S. corporations. Based on an

[1]These series are discussed more extensively in Chapter 14 where they are related to stock-market movements.

extensive quarterly sample survey, the *QFR* presents estimated statements of income and retained earnings, balance sheets, and related financial and operating ratios for all manufacturing corporations. The publication also includes data on mining and trade corporations. The statistical data are classified by industry and, within the manufacturing group, by size.

Business Statistics is a biennial supplement to the *Survey of Current Business* that contains extensive historical data for about 2,500 series contained in the survey. The historical section contains monthly data for the past 4 or 5 years, quarterly data for the previous 10 years, and annual data back to 1947 if available. A notable feature is a section of explanatory notes for each series that describes the series and indicates the original source for the data.

Historical Chart Book is an annual supplement to the *Federal Reserve Bulletin* that includes long-range financial and business series. There is an excellent section on the various series that indicates the source of the data.

Economic Report of the President is published each January wherein the president transmits to Congress what has transpired during the past year, what is the current environment, and what he considers to be the major economic problems that will face the country during the coming year. This publication also contains an extensive document, "The Annual Report of the Council of Economic Advisers," which includes a detailed discussion of developments in the domestic and international economies gathered by the council (the group that advises the president on economic policy). An appendix contains statistical tables relating to income, employment, and production. The tables typically provide annual data from the 1940s, and in some instances from 1929.

Statistical Abstract of the United States, published annually since 1878, is the standard summary of statistics on the social, political, and economic organization of the United States. Prepared by the Bureau of the Census, it is designed to serve as a convenient statistical reference and as a guide to other statistical publications and sources. This large volume includes data from many statistical publications, both government and private.

BANK PUBLICATIONS

In addition to government material, much data on the economy are published by various banks. These generally appear monthly, are free of charge, and can be categorized as publications of the Federal Reserve Banks or commercial banks.

PUBLICATIONS OF FEDERAL RESERVE BANKS The Federal Reserve System is divided into 12 Federal Reserve Districts with a major Federal Reserve Bank in each location as follows:[2]

1. Boston
2. New York
3. Philadelphia
4. Cleveland
5. Richmond
6. Atlanta
7. Chicago
8. St. Louis
9. Minneapolis
10. Denver
11. Dallas
12. San Francisco

Each of the Federal Reserve district banks has a research department that issues periodic reports. Although the various bank publications differ, monthly reviews—which are available to interested parties—are published by all district banks. These reviews typically

[2]Specific addresses for each of the district banks and names of major personnel are contained in the *Federal Reserve Bulletin,* published monthly by the Federal Reserve Board.

contain one or several articles as well as regional economic statistics. A major exception is the St. Louis Federal Reserve Bank, which publishes statistical releases weekly, monthly, and quarterly that contain extensive national and international data in addition to its monthly review.[3]

PUBLICATIONS OF COMMERCIAL BANKS A number of large banks prepare monthly letters available to interested individuals. These letters generally include commentary on the current and future outlook of the economy and specific industries or segments of the economy.

Non-U.S. Economic Data

In addition to data on the U.S. economy, data on other countries where you might consider investing are also important to acquire. Some of the available sources follow.[4]

The *Economic Intelligence Unit (EIU)* publishes 83 separate quarterly reviews and an annual supplement covering the economic and business conditions and outlook for 160 countries. For each country, the reviews consider the economy, trade and finance, and trends in investment and consumer spending, along with comments on its political environment. Tables contain data on economic activity and foreign trade.

The EIU also publishes *European Trends,* which discusses the aggregate economic environment for the overall European community and the world.

The *Organization for Economic Cooperation and Development (OECD)* publishes semiannual surveys showing recent trends and policies and assesses short-term prospects for each country. An annual volume, *Historical Statistics,* contains annual percentage change data for the most recent 20 years.

The *Economist* prepares country reports on more than 100 countries around the world that contain extensive economic and demographic statistics. Of greater importance is a detailed discussion that critically analyzes the current economic and political environment in the country and considers the future outlook. It is possible to subscribe to reports for a selected list of countries or for all of them. The reports are updated twice a year.

Worldwide Economic Indicators is an annual book published by the Business International Corporation that contains data for 131 countries on population, GDP by activity, wages and prices, foreign trade, and a number of specific items for the most recent 4 years.

Demographic Yearbook, published by the United Nations, consists of statistics on population, births, deaths, life expectancy, marriages, and divorces for approximately 240 countries.

International Marketing Data and Statistics, published by Euromonitor Publications Inc. of London, is an annual guide that contains data for 132 non-European countries covering population, employment, production, trade, the economy, and other economic data.

United Nations Statistical Yearbook is a reference book that contains extensive economic statistics on all UN countries (population, construction, industrial production, etc.).

Eurostatistics, a monthly publication by the *Statistical Office of European Communities (Luxembourg),* contains statistics for short-term economic analysis in 10 European community countries and the United States. There are generally data for 6 years covering industrial production, employment and unemployment, external trade, prices, wages, and finance.

---

[3]An individual can request to be put on the mailing list for these publications by writing to Federal Reserve Bank of St. Louis, P.O. Box 442, St. Louis, MO 63166. Most of them are free.

[4]This discussion draws heavily from P. M. Daniells, *Business of Information Sources,* 2d ed. (Berkeley, Calif.: University of California Press, 1986).

U.S. International Trade Administration, International Economic Indicators, is a quarterly publication of the U.S. Government Printing Office that includes comparative economic indicators and trends in the United States and its seven principal industrial competitors: France, Germany, Italy, The Netherlands, United Kingdom, Japan, and Canada. The data are organized in five parts: general indicators, trade indicators, price indicators, finance indicators, and labor indicators. The sources for the data are contained at the back of the booklet.

International Financial Statistics, a monthly publication (with a yearbook issue) of the International Monetary Fund, is an essential source of current financial statistics, such as exchange rates, fund position, international liquidity, money and banking statistics, interest rates (including LIBOR), prices, and production.[5]

International Monetary Fund, Balance of Payments Yearbook is a two-part publication. The first part contains detailed balance-of-payments figures for over 110 countries, and the second part contains world totals for balance-of-payments components and aggregates.

United Nations, Yearbook of International Trade Statistics is an annual report on import statistics over a 4-year period for each of 166 countries. The commodity figures for each country are given by commodity code.

United Nations Yearbook of National Accounts Statistics is a comprehensive source of national account data that contains detailed statistics for 155 countries on domestic product and consumption expenditures, national income, and disposable income for a 12-year period.

Some individual countries publish national income studies with detailed breakdowns as well as annual statistical reports that contain the more important statistics and include bibliographical sources for the tables. Brazil, Great Britain, Japan, and Switzerland are a few examples.

Similar to the United States, major banks in various countries publish bulletins or letters that contain statistical reviews for individual countries. Examples include:

- *Bank of Canada Review* (monthly)
- *Bank of England* (quarterly)
- *Bank of Japan* (monthly)
- *National Bank of Belgium* (monthly)
- *Deutsche Bundesbank* (monthly)

In addition to these specific sources of data, you should be aware of the following bibliographies:

- G. R. Dicks, ed., *Sources of World Financial and Banking Information* (Westport, CT: Greenwood Press, 1981). A descriptive list of nearly 5,000 financial and banking sources arranged by country.
- David Hoopes, ed., *Global Guide to International Business* (New York: File Publications, 1983). A descriptive list of source information about individual countries.
- *Index of International Statistics* (Washington, DC: Congressional Information Service). A monthly descriptive guide and index to statistical publications by the world's major international government organizations.

---

[5]LIBOR is an acronym for London Interbank Borrowing Rate. It is used as a base rate for many international financial transactions.

AGGREGATE SECURITY-MARKET ANALYSIS

Several government publications provide useful data on the stock and bond markets, but the bulk of detailed information is provided by private firms. Some of the government publications discussed earlier (e.g., *Federal Reserve Bulletin* and *Survey of Current Business*) contain financial market data, such as interest rates and stock prices.

GOVERNMENT PUBLICATIONS

The main source of data in this area is the Securities and Exchange Commission (SEC)—the federal agency that regulates the operation of the securities markets and collects data in this regard. The *Annual Report of the SEC* is published for the fiscal year ending in June. It contains a detailed discussion of important developments during the year and comments on the SEC's disclosure system and regulation of the securities markets. Finally, it includes a statistics section containing historical data on many security-market series.

COMMERCIAL PUBLICATIONS

Considering the numerous advisory services in existence, a section dealing with their publications could become voluminous. Therefore, our intent is to list and discuss only *major* services and allow you to develop your own list of other available sources. An excellent source of advertisements for these services is *Barron's.* A publication that lists and briefly describes these publications is the *Fortune Investment Information Directory.*[6] Sources are arranged by frequency of publication: annual, weekly, daily.

ANNUAL SECURITY-MARKET PUBLICATIONS *New York Stock Exchange Fact Book* is an annual publication of the New York Stock Exchange. The book is an outstanding source of current and historical data on stock and bond activity on the NYSE.

NASDAQ-AMEX Fact Book is an annual data book for the combined OTC-AMEX market. It contains extensive data on trading volume and information related to the stocks on the NASDAQ system and discusses past growth and future plans for the NASDAQ-AMEX market systems. Prior to 1998 the AMEX had a separate fact book.

Tokyo Stock Exchange Fact Book is an annual publication in English, containing information on the TSE. It is similar to the fact books prepared by U.S. institutions and contains extensive data related to stocks and bond and options trading on the exchange. Copies are available through the New York office of the TSE.

Emerging Stock Markets Factbook is an annual publication of the International Finance Corporation (IFC). The *Factbook* contains five sections:

1. A background on the IFC and its emerging markets database, which contains statistics on stock markets in developing countries.
2. Extensive statistical data related to both developed and developing countries.
3. Stock indexes for 52 developing countries. There is a description of the index methodology and an analysis of performance for many of the countries using the IFC index and a commonly used local stock index.
4. A statistical analysis of 33 emerging markets.
5. A directory of pertinent information for more than 50 stock exchanges in developing countries.

---

[6]This directory contains extensive listings of print material (newspapers, magazines), audiovisual material, electronic sources (software, databases), and interpersonal sources (seminars). It is published by the Dushkin Publishing Group, Inc., Sluice Dock, Guilford, CT 06437.

American Banker Yearbook is an annual publication by the publisher of *American Banker,* a daily newspaper serving the financial services industry (this newspaper is described later in this section). The *Yearbook* contains a review of annual events that affect the banking industry plus an extensive statistical section that includes operating and size data on commercial banks, finance companies, mortgage banking, thrifts, and also international banks (the top 100 banks in the world).

The Bond Buyer Yearbook is an annual publication by the publisher of the *Bond Buyer,* a daily newspaper related to the fixed-income market (this newspaper is described later in this section). In addition to a review of the major events of the year, there are extensive statistics related to the municipal bond market, such as the volume of long- and short-term issues in total by purpose and by states, the interest rates on alternative issues, the top underwriter, and the top counseling firms. This is the major source of data related to the tax-exempt bond market.

The Business One Irwin Investor's Handbook is an annual publication that covers the complete DJIA results for each year along with earnings and dividends for the series since 1939. It also contains data on other U.S. stock indexes. A recent important addition is data for a number of individual foreign stocks and historical data for a number of non-U.S. stock indexes (e.g., Japan, Hong Kong, Singapore, Australia, Philippines, Thailand). Individual reports on common and preferred stocks and bonds listed on the NYSE and AMEX, including high and low prices, volume, dividends, and the year's most active stocks, are also included.[7]

Business and Investment Almanac, published annually by Irwin Professional Publishing, contains a wide range of information on the economy, various industries, U.S. and foreign securities markets, and individual investments (stocks, bonds, options, futures, real estate, diamonds, and other collectibles). It concludes with a helpful business and information directory.

The Wall Street Waltz is a book that contains 90 charts dealing with financial cycles and trends of historical interest put together by Kenneth Fisher. Examples include "Price-to-Book Value Ratios" from 1921; "Stock Prices Abroad" (stock prices for seven foreign countries); and a chart of the South Seas Bubble from 1719 to 1720. It provides excellent historical and current perspectives.

S&P Trade and Security Statistics is a service of Standard and Poor's that includes historical data on various economic and security price series and a monthly supplement that updates the series for the recent period. There are two major sets of data: (1) business and financial and (2) security price index record. Within the business and finance section are long-term statistics on trade, banking, industry, prices, agriculture, and the financial sector.

The security price index record contains historical data for all of Standard and Poor's indexes. This includes the 500 stocks broken down into 88 individual groups. The four main groups are industrials, rails, utilities, and financial firms. There also are four supplementary group series: capital goods companies, consumer goods, high-grade common stocks, and low-priced common stocks. In addition, there is a quarterly series of earnings and dividends for each of the four main groups from 1946 to the present. The booklet also contains daily stock sales on the NYSE since 1918 and historical yields for a number of corporate and government bond series.

Stocks, Bonds, Bills, and Inflation is published annually by Ibbotson Associates and contains monthly rates of return for seven primary U.S. capital market series and a number of derived series. The primary series are (1) large-cap common stocks, (2) small-cap

[7]Prior to 1992, this was titled *The Dow Jones Investor's Handbook,* published by Irwin Professional Publishing.

common stocks, (3) long-term corporate bonds, (4) long-term government bonds, (5) intermediate-term government bonds, (6) U.S. Treasury bills, and (7) inflation. Besides the extensive data (which are also available on disk), there is a detailed discussion of the results over time and consideration of how the data can be used by portfolio managers, regulators, and corporate treasurers.

WEEKLY SECURITY-MARKET PUBLICATIONS *Barron's,* a weekly publication of Dow Jones and Company, typically contains about eight articles on topics of interest to investors. In the middle of the paper is an extensive statistical section, "Market Week," that contains the most complete weekly listing of prices and quotes for all U.S. financial markets. It provides weekly data on individual stocks and the latest information on earnings and dividends as well as quotes on commodities, stock options, and financial futures. Also included in the publication is an extensive statistical section with detailed information on the U.S. securities market for the past week.[8] There is also a fairly extensive set of world security-market indicator series and interest rates around the world as well as an "International Trader" section that discusses price movements in the major global stock markets.

Asian Wall Street Journal is a weekly publication of the *Wall Street Journal* that concentrates on the Asian region. It includes detailed economic news and stock and bond quotes related to this area of the global market.

Credit Markets is a weekly newspaper by the publishers of the *Bond Buyer.* It provides a longer-term overview of the major news items that affect the aggregate Treasury and corporate bond market and individual bonds. There is an extensive statistical section listing bond calls, redemptions, and the long-term future underwriting calendar, along with several security-market series.

Banking World is a weekly newspaper from the publishers of *American Banker.* It summarizes all the major news stories from Washington, the Federal Reserve, and financial services industry sectors. There is news on marketing, technology, federal and state regulations, and specific financial firms.

Financial Services Week is a weekly publication from Fairchild Publications that is billed as "The Financial Planner's Newspaper." It contains articles on the overall stock and bond market, insurance, and special features, such as "Planning for Dentists" and "Baby Boomers and Financial Services." There is also consideration of tax changes and other legislation of importance to those involved in personal financial planning.

International Financing Review is a weekly magazine that contains stories and data regarding international investment banking firms and the international securities markets. Emphasis is on fixed-income securities, global economies, and politics. It is published by IFR Publishing Ltd.

Equities International, a weekly magazine that is also produced by IFR Publishing, deals with global markets but concentrates on equity instruments, such as common stock, warrants, convertibles, options, and futures. The emphasis is on major trends and events in countries around the world. There is a complete listing of stock-market indexes for major global markets.

Euro Week, billed as "The Euromarket's First Newspaper," includes discussions related to notes, bonds, and stocks throughout Europe as well as longer articles on major news items in individual countries. A capital markets guide provides information on forthcoming

[8]For a discussion of the features in *Barron's* and how the series are used by technicians, see Martin E. Zweig, *Understanding Technical Forecasting.* Free copies are available from the *Wall Street Journal,* Educational Service Bureau, P.O. Box 300, Princeton, NJ 08540.

securities issues. Finally, there is a listing of market indexes for various countries and a quarterly listing of the top investment banking firms in various categories (Eurobonds, Euro-equities) based on the value of the issues underwritten.

DAILY SECURITY-MARKET PUBLICATIONS The *Wall Street Journal,* published by Dow Jones and Company, is a daily national business newspaper published five days a week. It contains complete listings for the NYSE, the AMEX, the NASDAQ-OTC market, U.S. bond markets, options markets, and commodities quotations. There also are a number of quotes for foreign stocks and an extensive list of non-U.S. stock market indicator series, including local indexes and the Dow Jones global country indexes. It is recognized worldwide as a prime source of financial and business information for the United States.[9]

Investor Daily, billed as "America's Business Newspaper," was initiated in 1984 as competition to the *Wall Street Journal.* It provides much of the same information but attempts to provide added information related to stock prices, earnings, and trading volume. An extensive set of U.S. general market indexes, including several unique to it, are included. It contains little information on non-U.S. markets.

The *Financial Times* is published five times a week in London with issues printed in New York and Los Angeles. Although it could be considered a British version of the *Wall Street Journal,* it is actually much more because it has a true *world* perspective on the financial news. In addition to reporting financial news related to England, it discusses the U.S. economy and security markets, including extensive stock and bond quotes and security-market indicator series. It also contains news and data for Japan and other countries. Most important, however, is its global perspective in discussing and interpreting the news, which is critical to those involved in global investing.

The *Bond Buyer* is a daily newspaper (five days a week) that concentrates on news and quotes related to the overall bond market, with special emphasis on the municipal bond market—its caption reads, "The Authority on Municipal Bonds Since 1891." Besides news stories on events that affect bonds, there are extensive listings of new and forthcoming bond sales, bond calls and redemptions, and information on bond ratings. There also are numerous market indicator series reported with the emphasis on fixed-income series.

The *American Banker* is referred to as "The Daily Financial Services Newspaper." It contains articles of interest to bankers and others involved in the financial services industry on such topics as legislation and general news of the industry and major banks. There also is a brief summary of the financial markets related to Treasuries, financial futures, and mortgage securities.

BROKERAGE FIRM REPORTS

As a means of competing for investor's business, brokerage firms provide, among other services, information and recommendations on the outlook for securities markets (bonds and stocks). These reports are typically prepared monthly and distributed to customers (or potential customers) of the firm free of charge. In the competition for institutional business, investment firms have generated reports that are quite extensive and sophisticated. Among the brokerage firms issuing these reports are Goldman, Sachs and Company; Merrill Lynch, Pierce, Fenner & Smith; Morgan Stanley Dean Witter and Company; and Smith Barney Salomon Brothers.

[9]For a discussion of many of the features of the *Wall Street Journal,* see "A Future Manager's Guide to the *Wall Street Journal.*" Copies are available from the *Wall Street Journal,* Educational Service Bureau, P.O. Box 300, Princeton, NJ 08540.

Beyond these reports on the U.S. securities markets, several investment banking firms publish extensive reviews of the world capital markets. The economic outlook for the major countries is discussed along with import/export and exchange rate considerations that culminate in evaluations of the outlook for particular industries specified as *global industries* and recommendations related to world bond and stock markets. Examples of such publications include:

- Goldman, Sachs International Corporation's monthly publication, *World Investment Strategy Highlights,* begins with world investment factors, such as economic activity, monetary conditions, and interest rates, and moves to individual country reports for about 12 individual countries and groups. The culmination is a recommended world portfolio strategy that considers individual country expectations and exchange rate forecasts.

  Goldman also publishes a "Quarterly Chart Book" that contains numerous charts dealing with fundamental economic and market data of use to analysts and portfolio managers.
- Morgan Stanley Capital International has a monthly publication that provides up-to-date pricing and valuation data on individual stocks and world industries. For example, it is assumed that an analyst or a portfolio manager would evaluate U.S. chemical firms as part of the global chemical industry, not just the U.S. chemical industry. This set of world data allows the analyst or portfolio manager to examine stocks across industries and countries.

  The firm also has a quarterly publication that provides over 20 years of share price information (adjusted for capital changes) for 1,700 of the largest companies in the world, representing over 75 percent of the world's market capitalization. The most recent balance sheet is provided, along with 5 years of operating data.
- The Merrill Lynch Capital Markets Group publishes "World Bond Market Monitor," a biweekly analysis of international bond yields, spreads, and yield curves that specifically considers the U.S. dollar bond market, the floating rate note market, U.K. sterling bond market, Japanese yen bond market, Deutschemark (DM) bond market, Dutch guilder bond market, and several other countries along with data on world inflation and yields in currency hedged instruments. It also has a monthly publication, "International Fixed Income Strategy," which considers the global perspective for the dollar; the world climate for bonds; and specific market perspectives for the Japanese yen, the sterling bond market, and Deutschemark (DM) bonds. It concludes with a recommended international fixed-income strategy for the coming six months.
- Salomon Brothers Inc. has three interlocking monthly reports: "Global Fixed-Income Investment Strategy," "Global Equity Investment Strategy," and "Global Economic Outlook and Asset Allocation." Based on the outlook for the U.S. and world economies and markets, it makes a recommendation for a total world portfolio, including a global fixed-income-equity allocation that considers the exchange rate outlook.
- Nomura Research Institute (NRI)[10] publishes *Nomura Investment Review,* a monthly publication that analyzes and projects the general investment climate in Japan and the rest of the world. Although the emphasis is on the Japanese economy and its securities markets, there also is an extensive discussion of the world stock markets as well as various sectors (industries). The result is a world portfolio structure recommendation and suggestions for specific stocks.

[10]The Nomura Research Institute is an independently managed research company affiliated with the Nomura Securities Company, Ltd.

- Daiwa Securities Company, Ltd., has a quarterly publication, *Tokyo Stock Market Quarterly Review,* that includes an in-depth analysis of the Japanese economy and securities market and discusses numerous markets around the world.

INDUSTRY ANALYSIS

There are only a few publications with extensive information on a wide range of industries. The major sources of data on various industries are industry publications and trade association magazines.

Industry Publications

Standard and Poor's Industry Survey is a two-volume reference work divided into 34 segments dealing with 69 major domestic industries. Coverage in each area is divided into a basic analysis and a current analysis. The *basic analysis* examines the long-term prospects for a particular industry based on an analysis of historical trends and problems. Major segments of the industry are spotlighted, and a comparative analysis of the principal companies in the industry is included. The *current analysis* discusses recent developments and provides statistics for an industry and specific companies along with appraisals of the industry's investment outlook.

Standard and Poor's Analysts Handbook contains selected income account and balance sheet items along with related financial ratios for the Standard and Poor's industry groups. (It is typically not available until about seven months after year-end.) With these fundamental income and balance sheet series, it is possible to compare the major factors bearing on group stock price movements (e.g., sales, profit margins, earnings, assets, debt). These data are used extensively in the industry analysis chapter. Figure 6.1 is a sample page from the *Handbook.*

Value Line Industry Survey is an integral part of the *Value Line Investment Survey.* The reports for the 1,700 companies included are divided into 91 industries and updated by industry. The industry report contains summary statistics for the industry on assets, earnings, and important ratios similar to what is included for companies. There also is an industry stock price index as well as a table that provides comparative data for all the individual companies in the industry on timeliness rank, safety rank, and financial strength. The discussion considers the major factors affecting the industry and concludes with an investment recommendation for the industry.

Industry Magazines

The magazines published for various industries are excellent sources of data and general information. Depending on the industry, there can be several publications (e.g., the computer industry has spawned at least five such magazines). Examples of industry publications include:

- *Computers*
- *Real Estate Today*
- *Chemical Week*
- *Modern Plastics*
- *Paper Trade Journal*
- *Automotive News*

TRADE ASSOCIATIONS Trade associations are organizations set up by those involved in an industry or a general area of business to provide information for such topics as education, advertising, lobbying for legislation, and problem solving. Trade associations

FIGURE 6.1 **SAMPLE PAGE FROM *STANDARD AND POOR'S ANALYSTS HANDBOOK***

CHEMICALS

Per Share Data — Adjusted to stock price index level. Average of stock price indexes, 1941-1943=10

	Sales	Oper. Profit	Profit Margin %	Depr.	Income Taxes	Cash Flow	Earnings Per Share	Earnings % of Sales	Dividends Per Share	Dividends % of Earn.	Prices 1941-1943=10 High	Prices 1941-1943=10 Low	Price/Earn. Ratio High	Price/Earn. Ratio Low	Div. Yields % High	Div. Yields % Low	Book Value Per Share	Book Value % Return	Working Capital	Capital Expenditures
1965	34.52	8.59	24.88	2.64	2.55		3.41	9.88	1.89	55.43	76.78	68.78	22.52	20.17	2.75	2.46	21.94	15.54	9.90	4.88
1966	38.18	8.97	23.49	2.88	2.58		3.50	9.17	1.94	55.43	75.38	49.82	21.54	14.23	3.89	2.57	23.51	14.89	9.93	5.41
1967	38.63	8.12	21.02	3.15	1.99		2.84	7.35	1.87	65.85	60.53	50.87	21.31	17.91	3.68	3.09	24.40	11.64	10.21	5.07
1968	43.96	9.37	21.31	3.51	2.56		3.16	7.19	2.00	63.29	61.43	50.20	19.44	15.89	3.98	3.26	26.25	12.04	11.21	4.59
1969	47.18	9.55	20.24	3.70	2.52		3.17	6.72	1.94	61.20	57.95	40.08	18.28	12.64	4.84	3.35	27.17	11.67	11.79	5.40
1970	47.51	8.89	18.71	3.90	1.95		2.70	5.68	1.90	70.37	47.11	36.93	17.45	13.68	5.14	4.03	27.77	9.72	11.75	5.95
1971	49.55	9.36	18.89	3.99	2.07		2.93	5.91	1.90	64.85	58.71	47.56	20.04	16.23	3.99	3.24	29.48	9.94	12.97	5.25
1972	54.18	10.77	19.88	4.15	2.66		3.61	6.66	1.97	54.57	67.13	56.40	18.60	15.62	3.49	2.93	30.64	11.78	14.51	5.00
1973	64.00	13.54	21.16	4.23	3.91		5.10	7.97	2.08	40.78	72.95	55.46	14.30	10.87	3.75	2.85	33.84	15.07	16.39	6.39
1974	85.47	17.01	19.90	4.76	5.10		6.79	7.94	2.21	32.55	68.80	47.20	10.13	6.95	4.68	3.21	38.34	17.71	18.71	10.26
1975	80.33	15.24	18.97	4.92	4.18		5.51	6.86	2.18	39.56	74.63	48.76	13.54	8.85	4.47	2.92	39.26	14.03	17.59	11.95
1976	91.16	17.47	19.17	5.49	4.52		6.59	7.23	2.48	37.63	89.70	67.27	13.61	10.21	3.69	2.76	43.27	15.23	18.93	12.97
1977	101.01	18.44	18.26	6.37	4.31	12.52	6.16	6.10	2.78	45.13	72.45	52.70	11.76	8.56	5.28	3.84	46.55	13.23	19.77	12.10
1978	112.76	20.82	18.46	7.21	5.07	14.36	7.16	6.35	3.10	43.30	59.62	46.05	8.33	6.43	6.73	5.20	50.65	14.14	22.27	12.13
1979	129.30	22.59	17.47	7.51	5.13	16.67	9.17	7.09	3.38	36.86	61.04	51.75	6.66	5.64	6.53	5.54	54.58	16.80	24.87	12.48
1980	140.37	20.86	14.86	7.73	4.03	15.79	8.07	5.75	3.56	44.11	64.88	49.70	8.04	6.16	7.16	5.49	60.53	13.33	25.83	15.11
1981	143.65	21.09	14.68	7.72	4.79	15.42	7.71	5.37	3.37	43.71	73.84	52.81	9.58	6.85	6.38	4.56	65.84	11.71	29.45	15.26
1982	159.01	21.85	13.74	9.56	5.52	14.76	5.21	3.28	3.57	68.52	63.30	45.44	12.15	8.72	7.86	5.64	65.63	7.94	26.03	15.89
1983	161.68	23.41	14.48	10.18	6.66	14.46	4.98	3.08	3.66	73.49	81.75	57.95	16.41	11.64	6.32	4.48	66.32	7.51	22.60	12.06
1984	168.26	26.85	15.96	9.84	7.97	17.39	7.39	4.39	4.00	54.13	75.82	61.58	10.26	8.33	6.50	5.28	68.72	10.75	21.35	13.35
1985	151.04	24.21	16.03	10.47	3.84	13.35	2.34	1.55	3.91	...	91.58	63.14	39.14	26.98	6.19	4.27	60.10	3.89	18.64	13.90
1986	142.01	27.14	19.11	11.64	5.92	19.59	7.95	5.60	6.04	75.97	132.68	87.43	16.69	11.00	6.91	4.55	58.74	13.53	20.02	13.63
1987	171.62	33.40	19.46	12.25	10.21	24.99	12.75	7.43	4.72	37.02	185.85	118.65	14.58	9.31	3.98	2.54	68.96	18.49	25.94	15.02
1988	200.84	44.65	22.23	13.38	11.09	31.10	17.73	8.83	5.19	29.27	151.64	128.15	8.55	7.23	4.05	3.42	84.36	21.02	21.86	21.12
1989	219.60	47.21	21.50	14.44	11.15	32.59	18.15	8.27	6.88	37.91	184.92	146.63	10.19	8.08	4.69	3.72	74.17	24.47	17.12	24.06
1990	245.58	45.20	18.41	16.35	10.16	30.63	14.28	5.81	6.84	47.90	186.89	124.41	13.09	8.71	5.50	3.66	82.40	17.33	23.51	30.16
1991	230.78	38.20	16.55	17.32	6.00	24.80	7.48	3.24	6.98	93.32	190.89	136.71	25.52	18.28	5.11	3.66	83.86	8.92	25.35	25.75
1992	232.50	35.39	15.22	17.90	3.69	22.54	4.64	2.00	7.09	...	213.51	184.11	46.02	39.68	3.85	3.32	61.90	7.50	19.87	23.33
1993	211.25	37.77	17.88	18.74	4.45	25.38	6.64	3.14	7.22	...	214.23	185.65	32.26	27.96	3.89	3.37	60.32	11.01	18.13	20.15
1994	225.07	44.58	19.81	17.48	9.24	33.15	15.67	6.96	7.49	47.80	258.78	212.03	16.51	13.53	3.53	2.89	68.40	22.91	23.65	17.96
1995	267.75	60.24	22.50	18.65	15.41	43.96	25.31	9.45	8.43	33.31	304.70	225.31	12.04	8.90	3.74	2.77	77.66	32.59	21.19	24.01

Source: *Analysts Handbook,* 1995 Edition (New York: Standard & Poor's, Inc.). Reprinted by permission of Standard & Poor's Corporation.

typically gather extensive statistics for the industry. Examples of such organizations include:[11]

- Iron and Steel Institute
- American Railroad Association
- National Consumer Finance Association
- Institute of Life Insurance
- American Bankers Association
- Machine Tool Association

INDIVIDUAL STOCK AND BOND ANALYSIS

The most extensive material is available on individual firms' stocks and bonds. The sources of these publications include individual companies; commercial publishing firms, which produce a vast array of material; reports provided by investment firms; and several investment magazines, which discuss the overall financial markets and provide opinions on individual companies and their stocks or bonds. We will discuss each of these sources and specific publications; however, you should keep in mind that many of the sources previously listed, such as the *Wall Street Journal* and *Barron's,* also include discussions of individual stocks or bonds.

Company-Generated Information

An obvious source of information about a company is the company itself. Indeed, for some small firms, it may be the only source of information because trading activity in the firm's stock is not sufficient to justify its inclusion in publications of commercial services or brokerage firms.

ANNUAL REPORTS Every firm with publicly traded stock must prepare and distribute to its stockholders an annual report of financial operations and current financial position. In addition to basic information, most reports discuss what happened during the year and outline future prospects. Most firms also publish quarterly financial reports that include brief income statements for the interim period and, sometimes, a balance sheet. These reports can be obtained directly from the company. To find an address for a company, you should consult Volume 1 of *Standard and Poor's Register of Corporations, Directors, and Executives,* which contains an alphabetical listing, by business name, of approximately 37,000 corporations.

SECURITY PROSPECTUS When a firm wants to sell securities (bonds, preferred stock, or common stock) in the primary market to raise new capital, the SEC requires that it file a registration statement describing the securities being offered. It must provide extensive financial information beyond what is required in an annual report as well as nonfinancial information on its operations and personnel. A condensed version of the registration statement, referred to as a *prospectus,* is published by the underwriting firm and contains most of the relevant information. Copies of a prospectus for a current offering can be obtained from the underwriter or from the company. Investment banking firms will often advertise offerings in such publications as the *Wall Street Journal, Barron's,* or the *Financial Times.*

[11]For a more extensive list, see *Encyclopedia of Associations* (Detroit: Gale Research Company, 1977); and *The World Guide to Trade Associations* (New York: R. R. Bowker, 1986).

REQUIRED SEC REPORTS In addition to registration statements, the SEC requires three *periodic* statements from publicly held firms. First, the 8-K form is filed each month. reporting any action that affects debt, equity, amount of capital assets, voting rights, or other changes that might have a significant impact on the stock.

Second, the 9-K form is an unaudited report filed every six months containing revenues, expenses, gross sales, and special items. It typically contains more extensive information than the quarterly statement.

Finally, the 10-K form is an annual version of the 9-K but is even more complete. The SEC requires that firms indicate in their annual reports that a copy of their 10-K is available from the company—on request and without charge.

COMMERICAL PUBLICATIONS

Numerous advisory services supply information on the aggregate market and individual stocks. A partial list follows.

STANDARD AND POOR'S PUBLICATIONS *Standard and Poor's Corporation Records* is a set of seven volumes. The first six contain basic information on all types of corporations (industrial, financial) and are arranged alphabetically. The volumes are in binders and are updated throughout the year. The seventh volume is a daily news volume that contains recent data on all companies listed in all the volumes.

Standard and Poor's Stock Reports are comprehensive two-page reports on numerous companies with stocks listed on the NYSE and AMEX and traded OTC. They include the near-term sales and earnings outlook, recent developments, key income statement and balance sheet items, and a chart of stock price movements. They are in bound volumes by exchange and are revised every three to four months. A sample page is shown in Figure 6.2.

Standard and Poor's Stock Guide is a monthly publication that contains compact, pertinent financial data on more than 5,000 common and preferred stocks. A separate section covers over 400 mutual fund issues. For each stock, the guide provides information on price ranges (historical and recent), dividends, earnings, financial position, institutional holdings, and a ranking for earning and dividend stability. It is a very useful quick reference for almost all actively traded stocks, as is shown by the example in Figure 6.3.

Standard and Poor's Bond Guide is a monthly publication containing the most pertinent comparative financial and statistical information on a broad list of bonds, including domestic and foreign bonds (about 3,900 issues), 200 foreign government bonds, and about 650 convertible bonds.

The *Outlook* is a weekly publication of Standard and Poor's Corporation that advises investors about the general market environment and specific groups of stocks or industries (e.g., high-dividend stocks, stocks with low price-to-earnings ratios, high-yield bonds, stocks likely to increase their dividends). Weekly stock index figures for 88 industry groups and other market statistics are included.

Daily Stock Price Records is published quarterly by Standard and Poor's, with individual volumes for the NYSE, the AMEX, and the OTC market. Each quarterly book is divided into two parts. Part 1, "Major Technical Indicators of the Stock Market," is devoted to market indicators widely followed as technical guides to the stock market and includes price indicator series, volume series, and data on odd lots and short sales. Part 2, "Daily and Weekly Stock Action," gives daily high, low, close, and volume information as well as monthly data on short interest for individual stocks, insider trading information, a 200-day moving average of prices, and a weekly relative strength series. The books for the NYSE and AMEX are available from 1962 to the present; the OTC books begin in 1968.

FIGURE 6.2 **SAMPLE PAGE FROM *STANDARD AND POOR'S STOCK REPORTS***

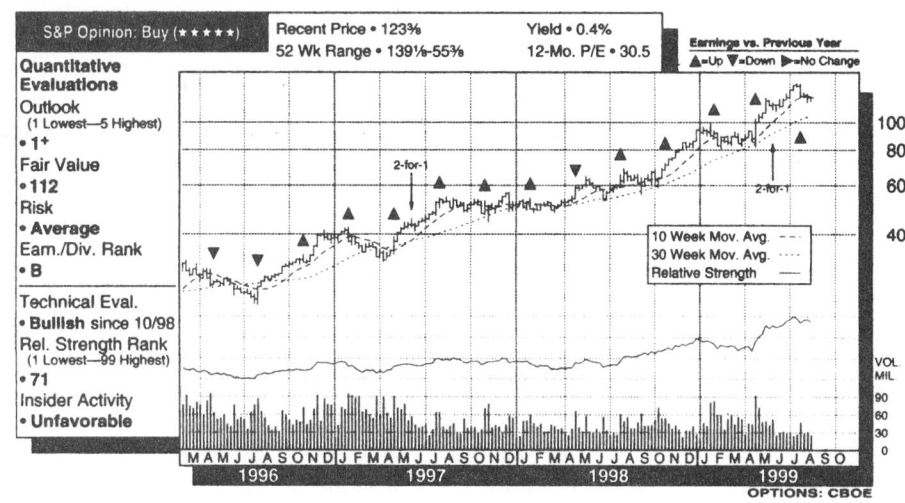

STANDARD
&POOR'S
STOCK REPORTS

Int'l Business Machines

NYSE Symbol **IBM**
In S&P 500

19-JUN-99 **Industry:** Computers (Hardware)

Summary: The world's largest technology company, IBM offers a diversified line of computer hardware equipment, application and system software, and related services.

S&P Opinion: Buy (★★★★★)

Recent Price • 123⅜
52 Wk Range • 139⅛-55⅜
Yield • 0.4%
12-Mo. P/E • 30.5

Quantitative Evaluations
Outlook
(1 Lowest—5 Highest)
• 1+
Fair Value
• 112
Risk
• **Average**
Earn./Div. Rank
• B

Technical Eval.
• **Bullish** since 10/98
Rel. Strength Rank
(1 Lowest—99 Highest)
• 71
Insider Activity
• **Unfavorable**

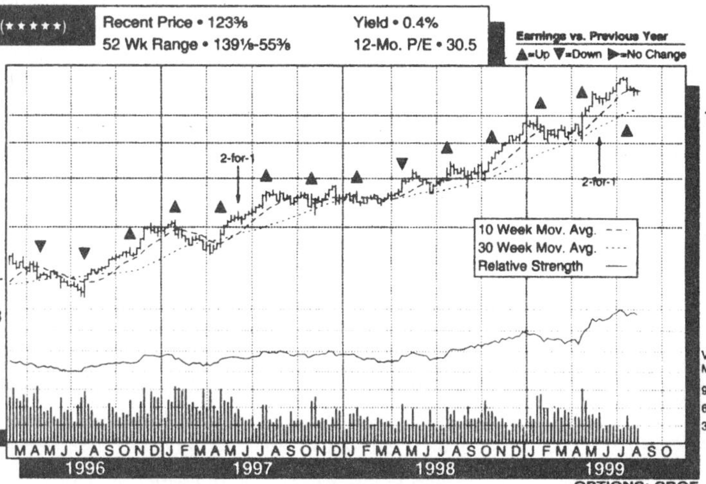

Earnings vs. Previous Year
▲=Up ▼=Down ▶=No Change
2-for-1
2-for-1
10 Week Mov. Avg.
30 Week Mov. Avg.
Relative Strength
100
80
60
40
VOL. MIL.
90
60
30
0
M A M J J A S O N D J F M A M J J A S O N D J F M A M J J A S O N D J F M A M J J A S O
1996
1997
1998
1999

OPTIONS: CBOE

Overview - 27-JUL-99

We project revenue growth of 11% for 1999. Hardware sales growth should be helped by improved personal computer (PC) sales and new server offerings. Indeed, hardware sales for the first half of the year surged 19%, buoyed by healthy PC and Netfinity server sales. Services growth should remain at its stellar 20% pace, and software revenues should continue to rise, aided by IBM's successful middleware offerings. In addition, both segments should benefit from increasing demand for IBM's e-business solutions offerings. While pricing pressures in hardware should continue to weigh on total gross margins, we see only a gradual decline as IBM's sales mix is increasingly weighted toward its services and software units, and it continues to focus on manufacturing efficiencies. Meanwhile, IBM continues to control operating expenses. We project 1999 EPS of $3.92, rising to $4.50 in 2000.

Valuation - 27-JUL-99

We continue to recommend buying the shares, based on IBM's improved earnings momentum and cash flow. The stock strengthened significantly in 1998, with IBM's outlook the most positive it has been in recent memory, reflecting impressive new product introductions, sounder businesses, and signs that investment in faster-growing segments is paying off. In addition, the "annuity-like" revenue streams of its services and software units are becoming a larger portion of IBM's sales mix, enhancing revenue and earnings predictability. We expect IBM's P/E (price-earnings) ratio to continue to expand as these improved earnings growth prospects, better cash flow and earnings predictability are reflected in the stock's valuation. As this P/E expansion occurs, we expect the shares to outperform the overall market.

Key Stock Statistics

S&P EPS Est. 1999	3.92	Tang. Bk. Value/Share	9.85
P/E on S&P Est. 1999	31.5	Beta	1.21
S&P EPS Est. 2000	4.50	Shareholders	622,092
Dividend Rate/Share	0.48	Market cap. (B)	$223.9
Shs. outstg. (M)	1814.8	Inst. holdings	49%
Avg. daily vol. (M)	6.473		

Value of $10,000 invested 5 years ago: $ 91,622

Fiscal Year Ending Dec. 31

	1999	1998	1997	1996	1995	1994
Revenues (Million $)						
1Q	20,317	17,618	17,308	16,559	15,735	13,373
2Q	21,905	18,823	18,872	18,183	17,531	15,351
3Q	—	20,095	18,605	18,062	16,754	15,431
4Q	—	25,131	23,723	23,143	21,920	19,897
Yr.	—	81,667	78,508	75,947	71,940	64,052
Earnings Per Share ($)						
1Q	**0.78**	**0.53**	0.59	0.35	0.53	0.16
2Q	**1.28**	**0.75**	0.73	0.63	0.74	0.28
3Q	—	**0.78**	0.69	0.61	-0.24	0.29
4Q	—	**1.24**	**1.06**	0.98	0.77	0.52
Yr.	—	**3.28**	**3.00**	**2.50**	**1.76**	**1.24**

Next earnings report expected: late October

Dividend Data (Dividends have been paid since 1916.)

Amount ($)	Date Decl.	Ex-Div. Date	Stock of Record	Payment Date
0.220	Jan. 26	Feb. 08	Feb. 10	Mar. 10 '99
0.120	Apr. 27	May. 06	May. 10	Jun. 10 '99
2-for-1	Jan. 26	May. 27	May. 10	May. 26 '99
0.120	Jul. 27	Aug. 06	Aug. 10	Sep. 10 '99

Source: *Standard & Poor's Stock Reports* (New York: Standard & Poor's Corp., 1999). Reprinted by permission of Standard & Poor's Corporation.

FIGURE 6.3 **EXAMPLE FROM *STANDARD AND POOR'S STOCK GUIDE***

120 **MAR-MBI** Standard & Poor's

¶ S&P 500 # MidCap 400 ✤ SmallCap 600 • Options

Index	Ticker	Name of Issue (Call Price of Pfd. Stocks)	Market	Com. Rank. & Pfd. Rating	Inst. Hold Cos	Inst. Hold Shs. (000)	Principal Business	Price Range 1971-97 High	1971-97 Low	1998 High	1998 Low	1999 High	1999 Low	July, 1999 Jul. Sales in 100s	Last Sale Or Bid High	Low	Last	%Div Yield	P-E Ratio	EPS 5 Yr Growth	% Annualized Total Return 12 Mo	36 Mo	60 Mo
✤1	MCS	✓Marcus Corp	NY,Ph	↓A–	98	11934	Hotels:restaurants:theatres	20 15/16	5/16	19 1/16	12 7/16	16 9/16	10 1/2	3484	13 1/2	11 7/16	11 15/16	1.8	16	1	–22.1	–4.9	1.1
2	MRBA	✓Marimba Inc	NNM	NR	5	250	Internet-based softwr solut'n	...	...	...	...	74 3/8	20	46526	51 15/16	25 1/8	26 3/16	...	d	...	...	...	...
3•[1]	MRL	✓Marine Drilling	NY,Ph	B–	172	30007	Contract drill'g o & g wells	246 7/8	3/4	26 11/16	7	17 3/4	5 15/16	144154	15 5/8	12 5/8	14 15/16	...	65	NM	34.3	21.3	23.0
4	MARPS	✓Marine Petrol Tr[51]	NSC	NR	6	109	Oil & gas royalties-Gulf Oil	45	5	19 1/2	12 1/8	19	12 3/8	131	15	13 13/16	14	9.6	9	3	3.1	12.4	11.5
5	HZO	✓MarineMax Inc	NY	NR	15	1016	Recreational boat dealer/svcs	...	...	14 3/16	7 9/16	13	7 1/8	1622	12 1/8	11 1/4	11 7/16	...	6	...	6.4	...	...
6	MPN	✓Mariner Post-Acute Network	NY,Ph,P	NR	127	32329	Oper long-term hlth centers	20 1/4	3 11/16	21 1/2	2 3/4	5 1/8	1/4	179997	1 3/16	1/4	5/8	...	d	Neg	–94.8	–57.1	–41.5
7	TUG	✓Maritrans Inc	NY	B–	32	6590	U.S.coast marine transporter	10 1/4	1 3/4	11 5/8	6 9/16	6 7/8	5	9352	5 9/16	5	5 1/8	7.8	14	...	–39.8	–1.1	4.9
#8•[1]	IV	✓Mark IV Industries	NY,Ch,P	B+	195	31199	Power transfer eqp/audio prod	28	1/32	24 1/8	12 1/8	21 7/8	12 13/16	37380	21 7/8	20 1/2	21 3/8	1.0	13	–6	12.6	4.9	9.0
9	MKL	✓Markel Corp	NY	B+	105	1666	Insurance broker/underwriter	161 1/8	7 1/2	187	132	193	160	1351	192	180	191 1/2	...	19	22	12.2	29.1	34.9
10	MSGI	✓Marketing Services Group	NNM	C	13	1301	Provide telemarketing svcs	28 3/4	5/8	5 9/16	2	60 1/8	3 1/8	62676	30 1/2	20 1/8	20 5/8	...	d	–25	535	56.9	37.4
11	MKTW	✓MarketWatch.com	NNM	NR	50	1287	Internet financial news svcs	...	...	...	...	130	38 1/8	17043	59 3/4	38 1/8	39 5/8	...	d	...	...	...	...
12	NRG	✓MarkWest Hydrocarbon	AS	NR	20	2766	Natural gas processing svcs	25	10	22 1/2	7	11 3/8	5 3/4	5210	8 7/8	7 7/8	8 1/4	...	d	...	–44.3	...	...
13	MTY	✓Marlton Technologies	AS	B–	8	1042	Mfr custom trade show exhibits	29	3/8	7 5/8	2 3/4	5 1/4	3	1231	4	3 1/2	3 5/8	...	10	16	–43.1	11.4	31.1
¶14	MAR	✓Marriott Intl 'A'	NY	NR	461	125367	Hotel mgmt/franchising	...	...	37 15/16	19 3/8	44 1/2	29	91278	38 3/8	33 15/16	35 1/16	0.6	21	23	8.5	...	...
¶15•[2]	MMC	✓Marsh & McLennan	NY,B,Ch,P	A	892	170936	Insur brokerage & agency serv	53 9/16	2 9/16	64 9/16	43 3/8	81 1/2	57 1/8	124062	81 1/2	75 5/8	78	2.4	21	12	27.6	40.0	25.6
16	MARSA	✓Marsh Supermkts'A'	NNM	A	17	1915	Food chain, Indiana & Ohio	23 1/2	1	18 1/4	13	18	11	823	16	14 1/8	15 1/2	2.8	12	–12	–7.4	14.8	10.3
#17•[3]	MRIS	✓Marshall & Ilsley	NNM	A–	255	30366	Commercial bkg,Wisconsin	62 1/4	1 3/8	62 1/4	39 3/8	72 3/4	54 3/8	39308	69 3/4	64 1/4	64 5/8	1.5	21	22	16.9	37.4	27.9
✤18•[2]	MI	✓Marshall Indus[56]	NY,Ch,P,Ph	B	142	12246	Dstr electronic comp:tools	43 1/8	1/4	34 13/16	21 1/2	38 9/16	12 3/8	24825	38 9/16	36	37 1/4	...	28	–7	59.4	11.5	11.1
#19	MLM	✓Martin Marietta Materials	NY,Ch,Ph,P	NR	334	42031	Aggregates/bldg materials	38 1/2	16 1/2	62 3/16	35 13/16	68 1/8	49 3/16	20158	60 3/8	54 7/16	54 7/16	1.0	19	17	11.0	35.8	21.9
20	MVL	✓Marvel Enterprises	NY,Ch,Ph	NR	46	12539	Design,mkt,dstr spcl toys	26 1/4	7 9/16	11 5/16	4 5/16	9 3/4	5 3/8	9051	7 1/2	5 9/16	6 3/8	...	d	Neg	–34.2	–27.9	...
¶21•[4]	MAS	✓Masco Corp	NY,B,Ch,P	B+	728	272772	Bldg & home improv't prod	26 7/8	1 3/16	33	20 3/4	32 7/16	25 1/4	205211	31 1/2	28 9/16	29 3/4	1.5	19	NM	5.7	31.3	20.4
✤22•[5]	MSX	✓MascoTech, Inc	NY,Ch,P	B	146	14690	Mfr powertrain,chassis,auto pd	28 1/8	1 1/2	26 7/16	15 1/4	17 3/4	14	15580	17 1/8	16	16 13/16	1.9	10	NM	–22.5	8.4	5.0
23•[6]	MYS	✓Masisa S.A.[57]ADS	NY,P	NR	26	4404	Mfr particle board, Chile	34 3/4	8 11/16	11 1/2	4 1/2	11 1/8	5 3/8	3168	11 1/16	10 3/8	11	2.5	12	...	58.8	–10.5	–11.4
24•[7]	MTZ	✓MasTec Inc	NY,Ch,Ph	B	89	6855	Telephone/elec sv	55 3/4	1 1/16	34 3/16	12 3/8	37 1/4	19 5/8	30616	37 1/4	26 11/16	35 5/8	...	..	–19	49.2	30.2	45.8
25	MAST	✓Mastech Corp	NNM	NR	168	14243	Info technology services	18 3/16	5 11/16	30 7/16	15 1/2	30 3/4	10 3/8	110524	21 3/4	16	16 7/8	...	20	38	–29.3	...	...
26	MATVY	✓Matav-Cable Sys ADS[60]	NNM	NR	15	9566	Cable TV services	20 3/4	12 7/8	27 13/16	14 3/4	47 3/8	19 7/8	2770	47 3/8	40 1/4	43	...	..	...	75.8	49.9	...
27	MXC	✓MATEC Corp	AS	B–	6	180	Steel cable:electr:instr	8 7/8	9/16	6	3 1/4	4 1/4	3 5/16	53	3 3/4	3 3/8	3 1/2B	...	29	NM	–6.7	2.5	7.7
✤28•[8]	MSC	✓Material Sciences	NY,Ch,Ph	B	81	7854	Steel coil protective coat'gs	22 3/8	3 7/8	13 3/16	6 1/2	16	6 3/8	7446	15 13/16	12 15/16	13 13/16	...	17	–5	32.3	–4.0	–2.9
29	MLK	✓Matlack Systems	NY,Ch,Ph	C	21	3475	Bulk commodities trucking	12 1/4	2 1/16	12 1/4	6 5/8	7 5/8	4 7/8	1307	5 15/16	5 3/16	5 7/16	...	d	Neg	–26.3	–8.6	–11.6
30	MC	✓Matsushita El Ind[63] ADR	NY,B,Ch,P,Ph	NR	77	4698	Japan mfr consumer elec eq	219 1/16	6 3/16	182 1/4	128	239	157 1/2	2042	239	198	233	0.4	75	57	46.5	11.6	7.9
¶31•[4]	MAT	✓Mattel, Inc	NY,B,Ch,P,Ph	A–	768	257462	Design,mfg,market toys	42 1/4	1 5/16	46 9/16	21 1/4	30 5/16	21 3/8	594448	26 3/4	23 1/4	23 5/8	1.5	16	–3	–37.7	–0.6	7.1
32	MLP	✓Maui Land & Pineapple	AS	NR	5	327	Land devel/pineapple business	...	...	21 3/8	8 13/16	30 3/4	9	3759	30 3/4	15	18 7/8	...	21	...	82.2	...	...
33	MAVK	✓Maverick Tube	NNM,Ch	B–	56	2953	Mfr welded tube for o&g ind	51 1/4	2 3/16	26 7/8	5	15 1/2	5 3/8	31471	14 1/4	11 5/16	13 15/16	...	d	–14	68.9	32.0	26.8
34	MAV	✓Mavesa, S.A. ADS[64]	NY,Ch	NR	31	14552	Mfr,dstr food/soap products	10 7/8	5 1/4	6 1/4	2 3/8	5	2 1/4	9008	3 1/2	2 7/8	3 1/16	2.6	..	...	–1.4	...	...
35	MAXC	✓Maxco Inc	NNM	B–	8	390	Distrib construction supplies	12 1/2	7/16	11 1/2	6	8 3/4	4 1/2	548	7 1/2	5 7/8	7	...	58	–18	–9.7	–9.7	–4.1
36•[9]	MAXI	✓Maxicare Health Plans	NNM	NR	46	11471	Multi-state HMO services	31 1/8	6 3/8	13 1/8	2 5/8	7	3 3/4	29201	6	4 1/4	4 3/4	...	d	Neg	–32.1	–31.6	–17.3
37	MXG	✓Maxim Group	NY	NR	65	9229	Franchisor floor cover'g ctrs	17 7/8	5 1/4	24 9/16	14 1/16	25 5/8	6	23138	9 3/16	6	6 5/16	...	d	–47	–71.8	–19.8	–11.1
#38•[10]	MXIM	✓Maxim Integrated Prod	NNM	B+	462	116513	Mfr,mkt integrated circuits	38 3/16	1/16	45 1/2	22 9/16	73 1/2	39 7/8	356641	73 1/2	60 1/16	64 1/16	...	50	48	100	65.1	64.0
39	MMP	✓Maxim Pharmaceuticals	AS	NR	9	483	Dvlp therapeutics & vaccines	19 1/4	6 3/4	23	11 5/8	15 5/8	8 3/4	11291	10 3/8	8 3/4	9 1/4	...	d	...	–51.0	1.6	...
40	WS	Wrrt(Pur 1 com at$10.50)	AS	....	1	.2		9 1/2	1 1/4	12	2 1/4	7 1/8	2 9/16	787	3 1/8	2 9/16	2 1/8	...	..	...	...	...	...
41	MMS	✓MAXIMUS Inc	NY	NR	123	11111	Consult'g svs to gvt agencies	32 1/8	16	37	20 7/16	41 1/8	21 13/16	8602	36	28 1/8	35 3/8	...	30	...	34.8	...	...
42•[11]	MXTR	✓Maxtor Corp	NNM	NR	116	46810	Hard disk storage prod	...	...	16 1/4	6 3/4	21 1/4	4 1/4	261885	6 3/4	4 5/8	5 3/8	...	..	...	–22.8	...	...
43	MXWL	✓Maxwell Technologies	NNM	C	60	3734	Defense/comm'l electr sys	39 3/8	2 9/16	42 1/4	16 3/8	40 5/8	15 7/16	20783	33 5/8	22 3/4	26	...	23	NM	3.5	58.7	44.5
44	MMX	✓Maxx Petroleum[67]	AS,To	NR	12	4803	Oil & gas acq,dvlp,prodn, Cdn	12 9/16	13/16	5 3/4	1 7/8	3 1/2	1 13/16	361	3 1/4	2 13/16	2 7/8	...	d	Neg	–11.5	–25.2	–15.9
#45	MXM	✓MAXXAM Inc	AS,B,Ch,P,Ph	B–	103	2361	Alum'n/forest prod:RE mgmt	67 5/8	2 1/8	65 1/4	41 1/2	64 3/4	43	1119	64 1/4	61 3/8	61 5/8	...	8	NM	5.1	15.5	11.1
✤46	MAM	✓Maxxim Medical[68]	NY,Ch,Ph	B+	147	9713	Mfr medical/therapy products	26 7/16	4	30 3/8	16 1/8	30 3/8	14 1/8	11954	24	23	23 3/8	...	16	19	–7.9	10.9	9.5
¶47•[5]	MAY	✓May Dept Stores	NY,B,C,Ch,P,Ph	A+	834	250669	Large department store chain	38 1/16	1 3/16	47 1/4	33 3/16	45 3/8	36	133043	43 5/8	38 1/8	38 11/16	2.3	15	4	–7.4	...	...
¶48•[4]	MYG	✓Maytag Corp	NY,B,Ch,P	B	620	56303	Mfrs major home appliances	37 9/16	4	64 1/2	35 3/8	74 15/16	52 1/8	124005	74 1/4	68	69 5/8	1.0	19	NM	60.2	54.4	32.3
49	MAZL	✓Mazel Stores	NNM	NR	18	2478	'Close-out'/mdse strs/whlsale	29 1/4	11	20 3/8	8 3/8	16 1/4	8	1147	10 1/4	8 1/8	9 3/4	...	20	...	–40.5	...	...
¶50•[8]	MBI	✓MBIA Inc	NY,Ch,Ph,P	A+	677	89943	Insurance for muni bonds	67 3/8	5 5/16	80 15/16	46 1/16	71 1/8	56 3/4	53306	66 15/16	56 15/16	57 5/8	1.4	12	4	–13.7	16.5	16.5

Uniform Footnote Explanations-See Page 1. Other: [1]CBOE:Cycle 2. [2]P:Cycle 1. [3]ASE,Ph:Cycle 3. [4]ASE:Cycle 1. [5]CBOE:Cycle 3. [6]CBOE:Cycle 1. [7]CBOE,Ph:Cycle 1. [8]Ph:Cycle 2. [9]ASE:Cycle 3. [10]P:Cycle 2. [11]Ph:Cycle 1. [51]Units of int. [52]9 Mo Sep'97. [53]®$0.84,'96. [54]Stk dstr of Jackpot Enterprises. [55]2 Mo Dec'97. [56]Avnet Inc plan acq,$39 in cash or 0.82 com. [57]Ea ADS rep 30 ord, no par. [58]Approx. [59]Stk dstr of National Beverage Corp,'91. [60]Ea ADS rep 2 ord NIS 1. [61]To be determined. [62]Restated fr $0.78,'96. [63]Each ADR equal 10 com yen 50 par. [64]Ea ADS rep 60 com,nominal val Bs.10. [65]10 Mo Jan'96. [66]Re-spec cond.. [67]Sep'97 & prior pricing in $Cdn. [68]Mgt group plan acq,$26. [69]Excl ESOP Shs.

MOODY'S PUBLICATIONS *Moody's Industrial Manual* resembles the Standard & Poor's Corporation records service except this service is organized by type of corporation (i.e., industrial, utility, etc.). The two-volume industrial service is published once a year and covers industrial companies listed on the NYSE, the AMEX, and regional exchanges. One section concentrates on international industrial firms. Like all Moody's manuals, there is a news report volume that covers events that occurred after publication of the basic manual.

Moody's OTC Industrial Manual is similar to the *Moody's Industrial Manual* of listed firms but is limited to stocks traded on the OTC market.

Moody's has manuals for various sectors as well. *Moody's Public Utility Manual* provides information on public utilities, including electric and gas, gas transmission, telephone, and water companies. *Moody's Transportation Manual* covers the transportation sector, including railroads, airlines, steamship companies, electric railway, bus and truck lines, oil pipelines, bridge companies, and automobile and truck leasing companies. *Moody's Bank and Finance Manual* covers the field of financial services represented by banks, savings and loan associations, credit agencies of the U.S. government, all phases of the insurance industry, investment companies, real estate firms, real estate investment trusts, and miscellaneous financial enterprises.

Moody's Municipal and Government Manual contains data on the U.S. government, all the states, state agencies, and over 13,500 municipalities. It also includes some excellent information and data on foreign governments and international organizations.

Moody's International Manual provides financial information on about 3,000 major foreign corporations.

VALUE LINE PUBLICATIONS *The Value Line Investment Survey* is published in two parts. Volume 1 contains basic historic information on about 1,700 companies, including a number of analytical measures of earnings stability, growth rates, a common stock safety factor, and a timing factor rating. A number of studies have examined the usefulness of the timing factor ratings for investment purposes. The results of these studies will be discussed in the efficient markets chapter.

The *Investment Survey* also includes extensive two-year *projections* for the given firms and three-year *estimates* of performance. As an example, in early 2000 it will include an earnings projection for 2000, 2001, and 2002–2004. The second volume contains a weekly service that provides general investment advice and recommends individual stocks for purchase or sale. An example of a Value Line company report is shown in Figure 6.4.

The *Value Line OTC Special Situations Service* is published 24 times a year. It serves the experienced investor who is willing to accept high risk in the hope of realizing exceptional capital gains. Each issue discusses past recommendations and presents 8 to 10 new stocks for consideration.

Brokerage Firm Reports

Besides the products of these information firms, many brokerage firms prepare reports on individual companies and their securities. Some of these reports are objective and contain only basic information, but others make specific recommendations (e.g., buy, hold, sell).

INVESTMENT MAGAZINES

Many periodicals cover the securities industry for the benefit of professionals and individual investors. As noted earlier, although many of these publications emphasize individual companies and their stocks, they also discuss the overall financial markets and industries. Again, the order of presentation will be based on frequency of publication: monthly, biweekly, weekly.

FIGURE 6.4

SAMPLE LISTING FROM *VALUE LINE*

HARCOURT GENERAL NYSE-H | RECENT PRICE 47 | P/E RATIO 20.3 (Trailing: 26.1 / Median: 24.0) | RELATIVE P/E RATIO 1.22 | DIV'D YLD 1.8% | VALUE LINE 1826

TIMELINESS 3 Raised 8/28/98
SAFETY 2 Raised 8/27/99
TECHNICAL 4 Lowered 7/30/99
BETA .95 (1.00 = Market)

2002-04 PROJECTIONS

	Price	Gain	Ann'l Total Return
High	95	(+100%)	20%
Low	70	(+50%)	12%

Insider Decisions

	O	N	D	J	F	M	A	M	J
to Buy	0	0	0	0	0	0	0	0	1
Options	0	0	1	6	0	0	1	0	0
to Sell	0	0	0	1	0	0	0	0	0

Institutional Decisions

	3Q1998	4Q1998	1Q1999
to Buy	91	103	93
to Sell	75	74	89
Hld's(000)	45000	45520	45005

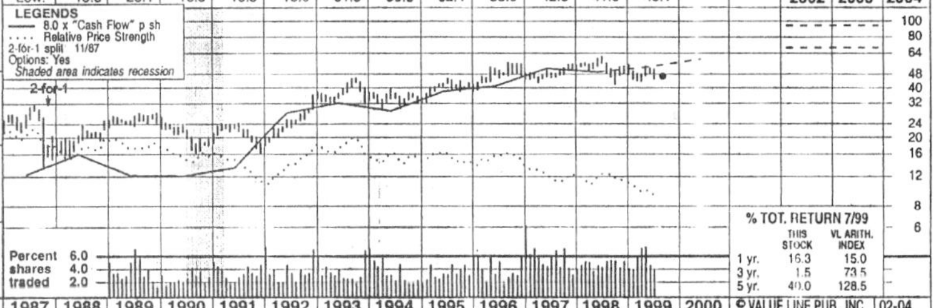
LEGENDS
8.0 x "Cash Flow" p sh
Relative Price Strength
2-for-1 split 11/87
Options: Yes
Shaded area indicates recession
2-for-1
Target Price Range
2002 2003 2004
100
80
64
48
40
32
24
20
16
12
8
6
Percent shares traded
6.0
4.0
2.0

% TOT. RETURN 7/99

	THIS STOCK	VL ARITH. INDEX
1 yr.	16.3	15.0
3 yr.	1.5	73.5
5 yr.	40.0	128.5

1983	1984	1985	1986	1987	1988	1989	1990	1991	1992	1993	1994	1995	1996	1997	1998	1999	2000	© VALUE LINE PUB., INC.	02-04
					25.8	28.5	27.0	24.8	36.6	46.1	39.5	45.8	57.0	55.7	61.9	55.5		High	
					15.8	23.1	16.5	16.5	18.0	31.3	30.3	32.4	38.0	42.6	41.9	43.1		Low	
12.39	12.18	13.29	13.68	14.22	31.69	26.02	29.18	45.41	46.94	46.10	39.76	41.06	45.52	51.38	58.87	*64.30*	*69.45*	Revenues per sh [A]	*88.50*
1.27	1.43	1.75	1.89	1.54	2.02	1.53	1.52	1.69	3.54	4.07	3.64	4.78	5.14	6.54	6.23	*6.70*	*7.45*	"Cash Flow" per sh	*10.15*
.76	.95	1.17	1.23	.93	.85	.73	.67	d.66	1.35	1.93	1.57	2.31	2.62	1.78	1.96	*2.25*	*2.70*	Earnings per sh [A B]	*4.15*
.14	.17	.22	.27	.32	.37	.41	.45	.49	.53	.57	.61	.65	.69	.73	.77	*.81*	*.85*	Div'd Decl'd per sh [C] ■	*1.20*
.73	.69	.95	1.19	1.17	1.68	1.87	2.25	2.17	2.55	2.02	2.47	2.98	3.36	2.71	3.83	*4.70*	*4.90*	Cap'l Spending per sh	*5.70*
3.46	4.73	5.31	6.78	7.41	8.25	21.06	22.11	5.98	11.67	13.26	13.20	12.73	14.30	11.76	12.87	*14.30*	*16.10*	Book Value per sh [D]	*26.50*
74.94	75.25	72.72	72.93	73.14	73.34	73.55	73.67	79.02	79.18	79.30	79.34	73.91	72.27	71.88	71.94	*72.30*	*72.70*	Capital Shs Outst'g [E]	*74.00*
11.6	11.6	13.7	18.6	27.1	22.4	34.2	33.5	--	16.7	19.0	22.7	17.0	17.6	27.1	27.4	*Bold figures are Value Line estimates*		Avg Ann'l P/E Ratio	*19.5*
.98	1.08	1.11	1.26	1.81	1.86	2.59	2.49	--	1.01	1.12	1.49	1.14	1.10	1.56	1.44			Relative P/E Ratio	*1.30*
1.6%	1.5%	1.4%	1.2%	1.3%	1.9%	1.6%	2.0%	2.3%	2.4%	1.6%	1.7%	1.7%	1.5%	1.5%	1.4%			Avg Ann'l Div'd Yield	*1.5%*

CAPITAL STRUCTURE as of 4/30/99
Total Debt $1995.2 mill. **Due in 5 Yrs** $460.0 mill.
LT Debt $1856.2 mill. **LT Interest** $140.0 mill.
(Total interest coverage: 3.5x) (68% of Cap'l)

Leases, Uncapitalized Annual rentals $78 mill.
Pension Liability None

Capital Stock 72,033,536 shares (32% of Cap'l)
Incl. .9 mill. Series A limited vote shs.
20.0 mill. Class B preferential vote shs.
51.1 mill. Common shs.
as of 6/7/99
MARKET CAP: $3.4 billion (Mid Cap)

1989	1990	1991	1992	1993	1994	1995	1996	1997	1998	1999	2000		02-04
1913.8	2149.5	3587.8	3716.9	3655.7	3154.2	3034.7	3289.9	3692.0	4235.0	*4665*	*5050*	Revenues ($mill) [A]	*6550*
7.9%	5.7%	8.8%	11.2%	13.2%	13.8%	16.3%	16.0%	16.7%	16.9%	*16.5%*	*16.5%*	Operating Margin	*16.0%*
58.6	62.5	185.4	173.6	169.3	163.1	175.7	180.4	343.2	306.2	*320*	*345*	Depreciation ($mill)	*440*
54.1	49.3	d39.1	106.6	153.6	125.5	177.6	190.9	126.9	141.6	*165*	*195*	Net Profit ($mill)	*310*
39.8%	34.7%	--	39.2%	36.4%	37.5%	34.0%	34.0%	36.0%	38.0%	*38.0%*	*38.0%*	Income Tax Rate	*38.0%*
2.8%	2.3%	NMF	2.9%	4.2%	4.0%	5.9%	5.8%	3.4%	3.3%	*3.5%*	*3.9%*	Net Profit Margin	*4.7%*
1126.4	1616.3	d.8	548.4	712.1	1146.0	824.8	984.9	491.6	524.4	*570*	*690*	Working Cap'l ($mill)	*925*
737.9	803.1	980.2	1086.1	1090.6	1123.3	959.9	939.1	1564.7	1988.1	*1950*	*2000*	Long-Term Debt ($mill)	*2200*
1548.9	1629.0	472.8	924.4	1051.6	1047.4	941.1	1033.5	845.5	925.7	*1035*	*1170*	Shr. Equity ($mill)	*1960*
4.2%	4.0%	.7%	7.4%	9.0%	7.6%	11.6%	11.5%	7.2%	6.7%	*7.5%*	*8.0%*	Return on Total Cap'l	*9.0%*
3.5%	3.0%	NMF	11.5%	14.6%	12.0%	18.9%	18.5%	15.0%	15.3%	*16.0%*	*16.5%*	Return on Shr. Equity	*16.0%*
1.6%	1.0%	NMF	7.1%	10.4%	7.5%	13.8%	13.8%	9.0%	9.5%	*10.0%*	*11.5%*	Retained to Com Eq	*11.0%*
54%	65%	NMF	38%	29%	38%	27%	26%	40%	38%	*36%*	*31%*	All Div'ds to Net Prof	*29%*

CURRENT POSITION ($MILL.)	1997	1998	4/30/99
Cash Assets	82.6	115.2	107.7
Receivables	526.0	618.4	295.4
Inventory (FIFO)	676.4	706.6	732.2
Other	199.9	208.8	411.6
Current Assets	1484.9	1649.0	1546.9
Accts Payable	346.4	392.4	347.6
Debt Due	14.4	10.0	139.0
Other	632.5	722.2	744.0
Current Liab.	993.3	1124.6	1230.6

ANNUAL RATES of change (per sh)	Past 10 Yrs.	Past 5 Yrs.	Est'd '96-'98 to '02-'04
Revenues	10.0%	2.5%	*9.5%*
"Cash Flow"	12.5%	14.0%	*9.5%*
Earnings	8.0%	19.5%	*12.0%*
Dividends	8.5%	6,5%	*8.5%*
Book Value	5.5%	4.5%	*12.5%*

Fiscal Year Ends	QUARTERLY REVENUES ($ mill.) [A] Jan.31	Apr.30	Jul.31	Oct.31	Full Fiscal Year
1996	698.4	844.3	879.2	868.0	3289.9
1997	769	880	1052	991	3692
1998	900	1037	1162	1136	4235
1999	975	1167	*1308*	*1215*	*4665*
2000	*1055*	*1260*	*1410*	*1325*	*5050*

Fiscal Year Ends	EARNINGS PER SHARE [A, B] Jan.31	Apr.30	Jul.31	Oct.31	Full Fiscal Year
1996	.23	.14	1.44	.81	2.62
1997	.21	.04	1.42	.11	1.78
1998	d.21	d.24	1.54	.87	1.96
1999	d.28	d.33	*1.87*	*.99*	*2.25*
2000	*d.21*	*d.29*	*2.08*	*1.12*	*2.70*

Cal-endar	QUARTERLY DIVIDENDS PAID [C] ■ Mar.31	Jun.30	Sep.30	Dec.31	Full Year
1995	16	.16	.16	.17	.65
1996	.17	.17	.17	.18	.69
1997	.18	.18	.18	.19	.73
1998	.19	.19	.19	.20	.77
1999	.20	.20	.20		

BUSINESS: Harcourt General, Inc. is a leading publisher (Harcourt Brace) in educational, scientific, technical, medical, legal, and trade fields. Provides career training and assessment products and services. 54%-owned Neiman Marcus Group includes Bergdorf Goodman and NM Direct. '98 acquisitions include Mosby, Inc. (medical publishing) and GartnerLearning (info. tech. training). '98 deprec. rate: 26%. Has 26,400 employees, 8,050 stockholders. Officers & Directors hold 1% of Common stock, 1% of Series A stk., 75% of Class B stk. 4 instit'ns hold 31% of Com. stk. (2/99 proxy). Chairman and C.E.O.: Richard A. Smith. Co-C.O.O.s & Presidents: Robert A. Smith and Brian J. Knez. Incorp.: Delaware. Address: 27 Boylston St., Chestnut Hill, MA 02467. Tel.: 617-232-8200.

The report of a rebound from seasonal losses is due from Harcourt General. This year's $0.33-a-share drain in the fiscal second quarter was deeper than the year before, despite a 13% revenue increase. Preparations in anticipation of a strong textbook market caused an Education Group loss of $48.9 million, $1.7 million heavier than last year. A greater impact on the year-to-year comparison came in the Worldwide Scientific, Technical, Medical (STM) Group. Although its acquisition of medical publisher Mosby, Inc. last November added substantial revenues, it burdened operating income with goodwill and integration costs. In addition, this year, the Neiman Marcus Group contribution in the three months was $1.3 million less.

The spinoff of most of Harcourt's NMG holding is due before November. As previously reported, the move is intended to lift the value of both companies in a market that appraises pure-play entities more highly than conglomerates. The proposal calls for a tax-free distribution of 21.4 million of Harcourt's 26.4 million NMG shares to Harcourt shareholders. These will be named Class B stock, with the right to elect 80% of Neiman's directors. Although members of Harcourt C.E.O. Richard Smith's family will continue in the top management of both companies, the separation could facilitate more specialization. Shareholders of both companies still must approve the deal.

Harcourt's focus is increasingly on technology-based training. The NETg subsidiary is a leader in the rapidly expanding field. It recently announced an agreement with IBM to cooperate in providing quality training for information technology professionals. The deal gives IBM customers access to all NETg services, and expands the offerings of NETg to include IBM instructor-led and computer-based training.

This mature business retains the flexibility to pursue new directions. This quality supports our projections for above-average earnings progress. Large stock ownership aligns management interests with those of other holders. The neutrally ranked shares offer better 3- to 5-year prospects than most stocks.

Edmund B. Swort, CFA August 27, 1999

(A) Fiscal year ends Oct. 31st. (B) Diluted earnings. Excludes nonrecur income (loss): '84, 53¢; '86, 49¢; '87, 1¢; '88, 28¢; '89, $12.43; '90, 84¢; '91, ($3.22) '92, $5.40; '93, 22¢; '94, 65¢; '95, (15¢); '97, ($3.42). Next earnings report due early Sept. (C) Next dividend meeting about Sept. 16. Goes ex about Oct. 13. Div'd paym't dates: end of Jan., April, July, October. ■ Div'd reinvestment plan available. (D) Incl. intangibles. In '98: $1.8 bill., $24.99/sh. (E) In mill., adjusted for stk. split.

Company's Financial Strength	B++
Stock's Price Stability	85
Price Growth Persistence	55
Earnings Predictability	40

Source: Copyright © 1999 by Value Line Publishing, Inc. Reprinted by permission; All Rights Reserved.

MONTHLY MAGAZINES *Money,* a monthly publication of Time Inc., deals specifically with topics of interest to individual investors, including articles on individual companies and general investment suggestions (e.g., "How to Determine Your Net Worth" and

"The Why and How of Investing in Foreign Securities"). Also, each issue presents a financial planning discussion with an individual or a couple.

Institutional Investor is a monthly publication of Institutional Investors Systems aimed at professional investors and portfolio managers. It emphasizes events in the investment industry as they relate to corporate finance, pensions, money management, portfolio strategy, and global stock markets. A popular annual feature is the selection of a group of sell-side equity analysts—an "All-American Analysts Team." This concept has been expanded to involve an "All-American Fixed-Income Team" and an international team.

Financial Planning, a monthly publication billed by its publisher, Financial Services Information Company, as "The Magazine for Financial Service Professionals," is intended for individuals involved in financial planning. It contains feature articles on alternative investment products and procedures, important regulatory information affecting financial planning (e.g., tax legislation), various industries, and specific classes of investments (e.g., mutual funds, real estate, equipment leasing).

Global Finance, a monthly magazine published by Global Information, Inc., contains a number of articles on trends around the world. It is an international version of *Institutional Investor* because it is written for the practicing money manager or investment professional. It also contains regular columns on venture capital, hedging, and investment strategies.

Global Investor is published monthly (but it produces combined issues for July/August and December/January) by Euromoney Publications PLC. Like *Global Finance,* it contains articles on various markets, international instruments, and specific money management firms. It features regular columns on the overall bond and stock markets and an extensive section on international bond and stock indexes.

BIWEEKLY MAGAZINES *Forbes* is published twice monthly and contains 12 to 14 articles on individual companies, industries, and the market. Several regular columnists discuss the economy, the aggregate money and stock markets, and the commodity markets, and they include specific stock recommendations.

Fortune, published biweekly by Time Inc., provides extensive articles on the economy, politics, individual companies, securities markets, and personal investing. The magazine is well known for its special annual reports on the *Fortune* 500 and the *Fortune* 1000 largest industrial firms in the country. The magazine also publishes a listing of large nonindustrial firms and major foreign companies. The importance of this information on non-U.S. firms is growing with the increase in globalization.

Financial World, published twice a month, generally contains about six articles on companies, industries, and the overall market along with several regular features on taxes and options. A separate section reports market data.

Pension and Investments, published by Crain Communications, Inc., is a biweekly newspaper of corporate and institutional investing with special editions in May and October. It is referred to as "The International Newspaper of Money Management" and is intended for those who invest in pension fund assets as either corporate managers or money managers. The stories and interviews are related to pension fund management, such as asset class decisions by pension funds. There is substantial consideration of personnel changes within firms. The special editions report on industrywide surveys on investment performance and the size of portfolios under management.

WEEKLY MAGAZINES *Business Week* is published weekly by McGraw-Hill. Although not strictly an investment magazine, it contains numerous articles on companies and industries as well as several features of importance to investors, including a weekly production index and a leading economic index. The magazine also has initiated several special issues compiling such lists as the Top 1,000 U.S. firms and the Top 500 global firms.

The *Economist* is a weekly magazine published in London and New York by the Economist Newspaper, Inc. It is directed to worldwide reporting similar to what the *Financial Times* does on a daily basis. Beyond a set of articles dealing with the major events around the world, the magazine contains two major sections. The first, "World Politics and Current Affairs," is divided into sections on American Survey, Asia, International, Europe, and Britain. The second section, "Business, Finance and Science," has sections on business, finance, and science and technology. There also is an excellent set of economic and financial indicators from around the world. Similar to the *Financial Times,* this magazine is required reading for a global investor.

The *Wall Street Transcript* is published weekly as a composite of sources of information other than market quotations. It contains texts of speeches made at analysts' meetings, copies of brokerage house reports on companies and industries, and interviews with corporate officials. It includes discussions of forthcoming new stock issues.

The *Media General Financial Weekly* features a series of articles and columns. Of primary interest is a comprehensive set of financial and statistical information on 3,400 common stocks, including every common stock listed on the NYSE and the AMEX and over 700 OTC issues. It also presents stock price charts on 60 major industry groups.

OBTAINING INFORMATION ON BONDS

As might be expected, the data needs of bond investors differ considerably from those of stockholders. For one thing, there is less emphasis on fundamental analysis because, except for speculative-grade bonds and revenue obligations, most bond investors rely on the rating agencies for credit analysis. An exception is large institutions that employ in-house analysts to confirm assigned agency ratings or to uncover incremental return opportunities. Because of the large investments by these institutions, the total dollar rewards from only a few basis points can be substantial. As you might expect, the institutions enjoy economies of scale in research. Finally, there are a few private research firms that concentrate on the independent appraisal of bonds.

Required Information

In addition to information on the risk of default, bond investors need information on (1) market and economic conditions and (2) intrinsic bond features. Market and economic information allows investors to stay abreast of the general tone of the bond market, overall interest rate developments, and yield-spread behavior in different market sectors. Bond investors also require information on bond indenture provisions, such as call features and sinking-fund provisions.

Some of this information is readily available in the *Wall Street Journal, Barron's, Business Week, Fortune,* and *Forbes.* In addition, two popular sources of bond data are the *Federal Reserve Bulletin* and the *Survey of Current Business.*

A number of other sources of specific information are important to bond investors. The following are specifically concerned with information on and analysis of bonds.

- *Treasury Bulletin* (monthly)
- *Standard and Poor's Bond Guide* (monthly)
- *Moody's Bond Record* (monthly)
- *Moody's Bond Survey* (weekly)
- *Fitch Rating Register* (monthly)

- *Fitch Corporate Credit Analysis* (monthly)
- *Fitch Municipal Credit Analysis* (monthly)
- *Investment Dealers Digest* (weekly)
- *Credit Markets* (weekly)
- *Duff and Phelps Credit Decisions* (weekly)
- *The Bond Buyer* (daily)

Sources of Bond Quotes

The listed information sources fill three needs of investors: evaluating the risk of default, staying abreast of bond market and interest rate conditions, and obtaining information on specific bonds. Another important data need is current bond quotes and prices.

Unfortunately, many of the prime sources of bond prices are not widely distributed. For example, *Bank and Quotation Record* is a valuable, though not widely circulated, source that provides monthly price information for government and agency bonds, listed and OTC corporate bonds, municipal bonds, and money market instruments. Current quotes on municipal bonds are available only through a fairly costly publication that is used by many financial institutions—*The Blue List of Current Municipal Offerings.* It contains over 100 pages of price quotes for municipal bonds, municipal notes, and industrial development and pollution-control revenue bonds.

Daily information on all publicly traded Treasury issues, most agency obligations, and numerous corporate issues is published in the *Wall Street Journal.* Similar data are available weekly in *Barron's.* Both publications include corporate bond quotes for bonds listed on the New York and American exchanges that represent a minor portion of the total corporate bond market. You will recall that the majority of corporate bond trading is on the OTC market. Finally, major bond dealers maintain firm quotes on a variety of issues for clients. We will discuss bond quotes in more detail in Chapter 15.

SOURCES OF INFORMATION ON MUTUAL FUNDS

Because there is a wide variety of types of funds available, you should examine the performance of various funds over time to derive some understanding of their goals and management philosophies. Daily quotations for numerous open-end funds appear in the *Wall Street Journal.* A description of what is provided is shown in Figure 6.5. The *Wall Street Journal* provides information on a fund's objective, NAV, offer price, load, expense ratio, and historical returns ranked on a 5-point scale.[12]

A comprehensive weekly list of quotations with data on dividend income and capital gain for the previous 12 months is carried in *Barron's.* In addition, *Barron's* publishes quarterly updates on the performance of a number of funds over the previous 10 years. *Barron's* lists closed-end stock and bond funds with their current net asset values, current market quotes, and the percentage of difference between the two figures.

A major source of comprehensive historical information is an annual publication issued by Arthur Wiesenberger Services—*Investment Companies.* This book contains statistics for

---

[12]NAV is net asset value per share for the fund, which is equal to the market value of all assets in the fund (stocks and/or bonds) minus any liabilities, divided by the number of shares outstanding.

FIGURE 6.5 **DESCRIPTION OF DAILY MUTUAL FUND QUOTATIONS IN THE *WALL STREET JOURNAL* FOR ALTERNATIVE DAYS**

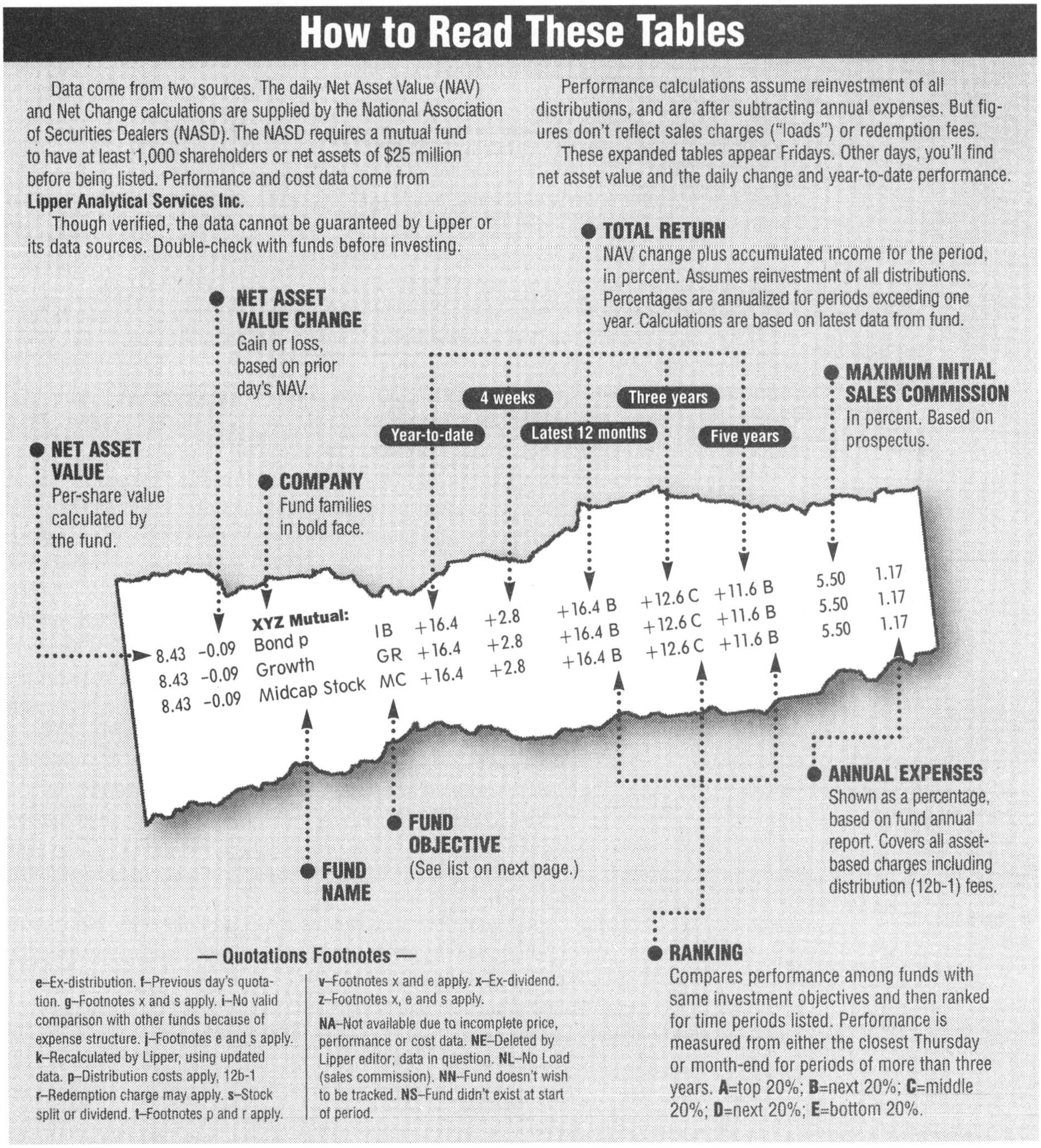

How to Read These Tables

Data come from two sources. The daily Net Asset Value (NAV) and Net Change calculations are supplied by the National Association of Securities Dealers (NASD). The NASD requires a mutual fund to have at least 1,000 shareholders or net assets of $25 million before being listed. Performance and cost data come from **Lipper Analytical Services Inc.**

Though verified, the data cannot be guaranteed by Lipper or its data sources. Double-check with funds before investing.

Performance calculations assume reinvestment of all distributions, and are after subtracting annual expenses. But figures don't reflect sales charges ("loads") or redemption fees.

These expanded tables appear Fridays. Other days, you'll find net asset value and the daily change and year-to-date performance.

TOTAL RETURN
NAV change plus accumulated income for the period, in percent. Assumes reinvestment of all distributions. Percentages are annualized for periods exceeding one year. Calculations are based on latest data from fund.
NET ASSET VALUE CHANGE
Gain or loss, based on prior day's NAV.
4 weeks
Three years
Year-to-date
Latest 12 months
Five years
MAXIMUM INITIAL SALES COMMISSION
In percent. Based on prospectus.
NET ASSET VALUE
Per-share value calculated by the fund.
COMPANY
Fund families in bold face.
XYZ Mutual:
8.43 -0.09 Bond p IB +16.4 +2.8 +16.4 B +12.6 C +11.6 B 5.50 1.17
8.43 -0.09 Growth GR +16.4 +2.8 +16.4 B +12.6 C +11.6 B 5.50 1.17
8.43 -0.09 Midcap Stock MC +16.4 +2.8 +16.4 B +12.6 C +11.6 B 5.50 1.17
ANNUAL EXPENSES
Shown as a percentage, based on fund annual report. Covers all asset-based charges including distribution (12b-1) fees.
FUND OBJECTIVE
(See list on next page.)
FUND NAME
RANKING
Compares performance among funds with same investment objectives and then ranked for time periods listed. Performance is measured from either the closest Thursday or month-end for periods of more than three years. A=top 20%; B=next 20%; C=middle 20%; D=next 20%; E=bottom 20%.

— Quotations Footnotes —

e–Ex-distribution. **f**–Previous day's quotation. **g**–Footnotes x and s apply. **i**–No valid comparison with other funds because of expense structure. **j**–Footnotes e and s apply. **k**–Recalculated by Lipper, using updated data. **p**–Distribution costs apply, 12b-1 **r**–Redemption charge may apply. **s**–Stock split or dividend. **t**–Footnotes p and r apply. **v**–Footnotes x and e apply. **x**–Ex-dividend. **z**–Footnotes x, e and s apply.

NA–Not available due to incomplete price, performance or cost data. **NE**–Deleted by Lipper editor; data in question. **NL**–No Load (sales commission). **NN**–Fund doesn't wish to be tracked. **NS**–Fund didn't exist at start of period.

over 600 mutual funds arranged alphabetically. It describes each major fund, including a brief history, investment objectives and portfolio analysis, statistical history, special services, personnel, advisors and distributors, sales charges, and a chart of the value of a hypothetical $10,000 investment over 10 years. The Wiesenberger book also contains a summary list with annual rates of return and price volatility measures for a number of additional funds.

Wiesenberger has two other services. Every three months, the firm publishes *Management Results,* which updates the long-term performance of more than 400 mutual funds, arranged alphabetically and grouped by investment objective. The firm's monthly publication, *Current Performance and Dividend Record,* reports the dividend and short-run performance of more than 400 funds.

Another source of analytical historical information on funds is *Forbes.* This biweekly financial publication typically discusses individual companies and their investment potential. In addition, the magazine's August issue contains an "Annual Survey of Mutual Funds." The survey includes information regarding each fund's yield, its sales charge, and its annual expense ratio.

Business Week publishes a "Mutual Fund Scoreboard" for open-end, equity, and fixed-income funds. The magazine publishes a comparable one for closed-end, fixed-income funds and equity funds. Besides information on performance (both risk-adjusted performance and total return), sales charges (including those for 12b-1 plans), expenses, and portfolio yield and maturity, an accompanying table contains telephone numbers for all the funds. The *Business Week* fund listings contain information on funds' after-tax returns, 10-year trend analysis, and investment style (e.g., growth versus value, small capitalization versus large capitalization-oriented).

Morningstar provides a number of services for mutual fund investors. Its basic service is *Morningstar Mutual Funds,* which evaluates the performance of over 1,300 open-end mutual funds and provides a very informative one-page sheet on each fund. This sheet provides up-to-date information on the fund's objective and its risk-adjusted performance relative to the risk-adjusted performance of all other funds in the same class (e.g., equity, hybrid, taxable bond, or tax-free bond). There also is an analysis of performance and a discussion of the fund's investment strategy based on an interview with the fund manager.

In addition, the firm publishes an annual source book that provides a year-end profile of 2,400 open-end funds, a source book for 370 closed-end funds, a monthly performance report (similar to the stock guide) on 2,500 mutual funds, and an annual reference publication of the elite 500 open- and closed-end funds.

The newest service for mutual funds is "The Value Line Mutual Fund Survey." The service, which is modeled after their well-regarded company analysis service, covers 2,000 funds—1,500 established funds and 500 newer, smaller funds. Each fund survey contains performance data, portfolio data, and tax data. Notably, the report considers what happened during the latest bull and bear markets.

THEORETICAL AND EMPIRICAL ANALYSIS

Academic Journals

The material in academic journals differs from that in investment magazines in timeliness and general orientation. Investment magazines are concerned with the current investment environment and with providing advice for current action. The material is generally non-quantitative. In contrast, academic journals contain more quantitative articles as well as theoretical or empirical studies related to investments that could have long-run implications.

Journal of Finance is a quarterly published by the American Finance Association. The articles are almost all by academicians and are rather theoretical and empirical. The typical issue includes 15 articles, notes and comments, and book reviews.

Journal of Financial Economics is published quarterly by North Holland Publishing Company in collaboration with the Simon Graduate School of Management of the University of Rochester. It publishes academic research in the areas of consumption and investment decisions under uncertainty, portfolio analysis, efficient markets, and the normative theory of financial management.

The *Review of Financial Studies* is published quarterly by Oxford University Press for the Society for Financial Studies. Its purpose is to publish new research in financial economics balanced between theoretical and empirical research. Although the subject matter appears similar to that of the *Journal of Financial Economics,* it places a stronger emphasis on the theoretical treatment of topics.

Journal of Financial and Quantitative Analysis is a quarterly published by the University of Washington School of Business Administration in cooperation with the New York University Leonard N. Stein School of Business. Almost all of its articles are by academicians and deal with topics in investments and corporate finance.

Financial Analysts Journal is published six times a year by the Association of Investment Management and Research (AIMR). Each issue contains six or seven articles of interest to financial analysts and portfolio managers, a regular feature on securities regulation, and book reviews. The articles are authored by either academicians or practitioners.

Journal of Portfolio Management is published quarterly by Institutional Investors Systems as a forum for academic research of interest to the practicing portfolio manager. Over half the articles are written by academicians, but they are written for the practitioner. Many articles are less technical and mathematical versions of studies previously published in heavily academic journals.

Journal of Fixed Income is published quarterly by Institutional Investor, Inc., as a forum for academic research related to fixed-income securities that can be understood and read by professional analysts and portfolio managers. The topics range from credit analysis and interest rates forecasting to various bond portfolio management strategies.

The *Journal of Investing* is a quarterly publication of Institutional Investor, Inc., that includes topics of asset allocation, global investing, risk management, real estate, mutual funds, and consulting. The emphasis is on readable and useful articles.

The *Journal of Derivatives* is a quarterly publication by Institutional Investor, Inc., as a forum to publish new developments in both derivative theory and practice. It provides a practical analysis of the latest derivative innovations and practical insights.

Real Estate Finance is a quarterly publication of Institutional Investor, Inc., that is intended to provide critical analysis on the latest financing techniques, securitization trends, IRS rulings, and environmental issues related to real estate.

Financial Management, published quarterly by the Financial Management Association, is intended for executives and academicians interested in the financial management of a firm. It contains investment-related articles on such topics as stock splits, dividend policy, mergers, initial public offerings, and stock listings when it is shown that such events are important to the investment and financing decisions of a firm.

The *Financial Review* is a quarterly journal sponsored by the Eastern Finance Association. About half of its articles are concerned with capital markets, investments, and portfolio management.

Journal of Financial Research is a joint quarterly publication of the Southern Finance Association and the Southwestern Finance Association. It contains articles on financial management, investments, financial institutions, capital market theory, and portfolio theory.

Financial Services Review is a quarterly journal sponsored by the Academy of Financial Services and published by JAI Press, Inc. It is a journal devoted to publishing academic research on individual financial management, which involves examining the application and effect of all facets of finance on the financial planning decisions made by individuals.

The *C.F.A. Digest* is published quarterly by the Institute of Chartered Financial Analysts (a subsidiary of the Association of Investment Management and Research). Its purpose is to provide, as a service to members of the investment community, about 20 abstracts of published articles from a wide variety of academic and nonacademic journals that are of interest to financial analysts and portfolio managers.

There are a number of general business and economics journals that include articles on finance and some specifically on investments. One of the foremost is the *Journal of Business,* published by the University of Chicago, which has outstanding articles in the area of investments. Other journals to consider include: *Quarterly Review of Economics and Finance* (University of Illinois), *International Review of Economics and Finance* (JAI Press, Inc.), *Review of Business and Economic Research* (University of New Orleans), *Journal of Business Research* (North Holland Publishing), *American Economic Review* (American Economic Association), *Journal of Political Economy* (University of Chicago), *Rand Journal of Economics* (American Telephone and Telegraph), and the *Journal of Applied Corporate Finance* (Bank of America).

COMPUTERIZED DATA SOURCES

In addition to the numerous published sources of data, some financial service firms have developed computerized data sources. The following discussion considers (1) major data banks and (2) the well-known online data systems. Space limitations restrict the discussion to major sources.

Data Banks

Compustat is a computerized bank of financial data developed by Standard & Poor's and is currently handled by a subsidiary, Investors Management Services. The Compustat tapes contain 20 years of data for approximately 2,220 listed industrial companies, 1,000 OTC companies, 175 utilities, 120 banks, and 500 Canadian firms. Quarterly tapes contain 20 years of quarterly financial data for over 2,000 industrial firms and 12 years of quarterly data for banks and utilities. The financial data on the annual tapes include almost every possible item from each firm's balance sheet and income statement as well as stock-market data (stock prices and trading volume).

Value Line Data Base contains historical annual and quarterly financial and market data for 1,600 industrial and finance companies beginning in 1954. It also provides quarterly data from 1963. In addition to historical data, it gives estimates of dividends and earnings for the coming year and the Value Line opinion regarding stock price stability and investment timing.

Compact Disclosure is a database on a compact disk with information on over 4,000 public companies filing with the SEC. It is available from Disclosure Information Group of Bethesda, Maryland.

University of Chicago Stock Price Tapes is a set of monthly and daily stock price tapes developed by the Center for Research in Security Prices (CRSP) at the University of Chicago Graduate School of Business. The monthly tapes contain month-end prices from January 1926 to the present (updated annually) for every stock listed on the NYSE. Stock prices are adjusted for all stock splits, dividends, and any other capital changes. Monthly AMEX data beginning from July 1962 were added to the NYSE monthly file to create the current NYSE/AMEX monthly file with information on approximately 6,100 securities.

The daily stock price tape contains the daily high, low, close, and volume figures since July 1962 for every stock listed on the NYSE and AMEX (approximately 5,600 securities). In 1988, the CRSP developed its NASDAQ historical data file with daily price quotes, volume, and information about capitalization and distributions to shareholders for over 9,600 common stocks traded on the NASDAQ system since December 14, 1972. These tapes are updated at the end of each calendar year and supplied to subscribers each spring.

The *Media General Data Bank,* compiled by Media General Financial Services, Inc., includes current price and volume data plus major corporate financial data on 2,000 major companies. In addition, it contains 10 years of daily price and volume information on over 8,000 issues of approximately 4,000 firms on the NYSE, the AMEX, and the OTC market. Finally, it includes price and volume data on several major market indexes.

ISL Daily Stock Price Tapes are prepared by Interactive Data Corporation. They contain the same information as the *Daily Stock Price Records.*

ONLINE DATABASES

Bi Data provides international statistical data, including national accounts, labor statistics, foreign trade, consumption, prices, and production. It is produced by Business International Corp. and sold by General Electric Information Service.

Commodities Market Data Bank provides statistical data on all traded commodities. Data Resources Inc. (DRI) is the producer and vendor.

Bloomberg is a data service that also includes very useful analytical programs for the analysis of bonds and stocks. Although the system initially emphasized bonds, it has been expanding its capability in domestic and international equities and derivatives. The firm publishes a monthly magazine that discusses new data and analytical program uses.

Bridge Information System is a comprehensive worldwide securities database. Global stocks, options, bonds, commodities, futures, indexes, currencies, and other derivatives are available on the Bridge system. Numerous, easy-to-read tables and graphs are available through a Microsoft Windows–based system. The firm publishes a monthly magazine that describes new additions to the database.

CompuServe, Inc. provides references, statistical data, and full-text retrieval of information on numerous topics, including financial and investment data from Compustat and the Value Line databases. CompuServe, Inc., is the producer and vendor.

Quick Quote provides current price quotations, trading volume information, and high–low data for the securities of U.S. public corporations. CompuServe, Inc., is the producer and vendor.

Dow Jones News/Retrieval Service supplies texts of articles appearing in major financial publications, including the *Wall Street Journal* and *Barron's.* The *StockQuote Reporter* service provides quotes on stocks, bonds, and mutual funds. Dow Jones & Company is the producer and vendor of both.

DRI Capsule/EEI Capsule services provide over 3,700 U.S. social and economic statistical time series on such topics as population, income, money supply, and interest rates. The producer is DRI and the vendor is Business Information Services.

THE INTERNET *Investments Online*

Many of the sources listed in the chapter and in the Reference section of the chapter have Internet Web sites which are not difficult to find; some of them have already been listed in the Internet boxes in prior chapters. For example:

www. bog.frb.fed.us The Web site of the Board of Governors of the Federal Reserve System has pages containing current analysis of the U.S. economy. Links to the 12 regional Federal Reserve Banks are found at **www.bog.frb.fed.usotherfrb.htm** and each has their own treasure trove of information and data.

www.doc.gov The Web site of the U.S. Department of Commerce has numerous links to economic and statistical information, including links to Department Bureaus such as the Census and Economic Analysis.

www.ita.doc.gov/ita_home/itakeyin.html The home page of the International Trade Administration is another source with a wealth of information and data on trade issues and various industries.

www.economist.com What periodicals such as *Fortune* or *Business Week* are to U.S. business analysis, *The Economist* is to surveyors of the global economy, especially UK and the EC. Its blend of news and economic analysis make it a good source of global information and commentary.

Here are a few others you may use to gather information about interest rates and financial markets in various economies:

www.jpmorgan.com This site has a number of pages related to performance in various markets. For example, its government bond index is found at **www.jpmorgan.com/MarketDataInd/GovernBondIndex/GovernBondIndex.html** and its emerging markets bond index is at **www.jpmorgan.com/MarketDataInd/EMBI/embi.html**. The site contains information on the composition of these indexes.

www.dir.co.jp/InfoManage/datarsc.html This site from Daiwa Capital Markets features information on performance of various components of the Japanese markets.

www.global-investor.com/dir/global/bonds.htm This site has links to yield curve and index data for several bond indexes.

www.psa.com The U.S. Public Securities Association home page contains information on a variety of bond market topics: newsletters, reports, and links to a number of other sites dealing with asset-backed securities, mortgage securities, corporate, treasury, money market securities, legislative issues, and other information of interest to both investors and brokers.

The *GTE Financial System One Quotation Service* provides current quotations and statistical data on U.S. and Canadian stocks, bonds, options, and commodities along with other market data. GTE Information Systems, Inc., is the producer and vendor.

The *Information Bank* provides extensive information on current affairs based on abstracts from numerous English-language publications. New York Times Information Service is the producer and vendor.

Quotron 800 provides up-to-the-minute quotations and statistics for a broad range of stocks, bonds, options, and commodities. Quotron Systems, Inc., is the producer and vendor.[13]

[13]An excellent source for additional computer databases and software as well as general information on business and economics is *The Irwin Business and Investment Almanac*, edited by Sumner W. Levine and Caroline Levine (Burr Ridge, Ill.: Irwin Professional Publishing, annual).

Summary

As an investor you must be aware of sources of information on the U.S. and world economies, the securities markets around the globe, alternative industries, and individual firms. You should use the information in this chapter as a starting point and spend time in a university library examining these and the many other sources available. Six books that will help are:

- Paul Wasserman, ed., *Encyclopedia of Business Information Sources,* 3d ed. (Detroit: Gale Research Co., 1976).
- P. M. Daniells, *Business Information Sources,* 2d ed. (Berkeley: University of California Press, 1986).
- Sylvia Michanie, *Course Syllabus for Information Sources of Business and Economics* (Brooklyn, NY. Pratt Institute School of Library and Information Science, 1977).
- *Fortune Investment Information Directory* (Guilford, Conn.: The Dushkin Publishing Group, Inc., 1986). This booklet contains a listing and brief description of numerous newspapers, magazines, investment letters, and books. There also is an excellent listing of software and databases of interest to investors in stocks, bonds, futures, and options.
- *Encyclopedia of Information Systems and Services* (Detroit: Gale Research Co., 1988).
- *Guide to American Directories* (Coral Springs, Fla.: B. Klein Publications, 1987).

Questions

1. Name at least three sources of information on the gross domestic product for the past 10 years.
2. Name two sources of information on rates of exchange with major foreign countries.
3. Assume you want to compare production in the steel and auto industries to industrial production for the economy. Discuss how you would do it, what data you would use, and where you would get the data.
4. You are told that a relationship exists between the growth rate of the money supply and stock price movements. Where would you obtain the data to test this relationship?
5. You are an analyst for Growth Stock Investment Company. The head of research tells you about a tip on an OTC firm, the Shamrock Corporation. He wants data on the company's sales, earnings, and recent stock price movements. Discuss several sources for this information. (One source is insufficient because the company may not be big enough to be included in some of them.)
6. The head of your research department indicates that the investment committee has decided to become involved in global investing. To get started, the committee wants you to recommend two sources of macroeconomic data for various countries, two sources of industry information, and two sources of company data. Discuss your recommendations.
7. As an individual investor, discuss four publications to which you believe you should subscribe (besides *The Wall Street Journal*). Indicate what each publication can give you and why it is appropriate for you as an individual investor. Be sure that at least two of these sources relate to global investing.
8. As the director of a newly established investment research department at a money management firm, discuss the first four investment services to which you will subscribe, and justify each selection.
9. Select one company each from the NYSE, the AMEX, and the OTC, and look up the name and address of the financial officers you would contact at each firm to obtain recent financial reports.

References

SOURCES OF INVESTMENT INFORMATION

American Banker-Bond Buyer, a division of International Thomson Publishing Corporation, One State Street Plaza, New York, NY 10004.

Bloomberg, P.O. Box 888, Princeton, NJ 08542-0888.

Bridge Information Systems, Inc., 717 Office Parkway, St. Louis, MO 63141.

Business One Irwin Investor's Handbook is available from Irwin Professional Publishing, Burr Ridge, IL 60521.

Business Statistics is obtained from Superintendent of Documents, U.S. Government Printing Office, Washington, DC 20402.

Center for Research in Security Prices, Graduate School of Business, University of Chicago, Chicago, IL 60637.

CompuServe, Inc., 5000 Arlington Centre Boulevard, Columbus, OH 43220.

Data Resources, Inc. (DRI), 29 Hartwell Avenue, Lexington, MA 02173.

Dow Jones & Co., 200 Burnett Road, Chicopee, MA 01021.

Economic Indicators is available from Superintendent of Documents, U.S. Government Printing Office, Washington, DC 20402.

Economic Report of the President may be obtained from Superintendent of Documents, U.S. Government Printing Office, Washington, DC 20402.

Euromoney Publications PLC, Nestor House, Playhouse Yard, London ECUV 5EX. The address for North American subscriptions: Reed Business Publishing, 205 East 42nd Street, New York, NY 10017.

Federal Reserve Bulletin is available from the Division of Administrative Services, Board of Governors of the Federal Reserve System, Washington, DC 20551.

Financial Times is available from Bracken House, Cannon Street, London EC4P 4BY England. U.S. office: 44 East 60th Street, New York, NY 10022.

Global Information, Inc., 55 John Street, New York, NY 10038.

GTE Information Systems, Inc., East Park Drive, Mount Laurel, NJ 08054.

Ibbotson Associates, 225 North Michigan Ave., Chicago, IL 60601-7676.

IFR Publishing Ltd., 97 Middlesex Street, London EL 7EZ.

Institutional Investor Systems, Inc., 488 Madison Avenue, New York, NY 10022.

Interactive Data Corporation, 122 E. 42nd Street, New York, NY 10017.

International Finance Corporation, 1818 H Street, N.W., Washington, DC 20433.

Investors Management Services, P.O. Box 239, Denver, CO 80201.

London Stock Exchange, Trogmorton Street, London EG2N 1HP, England.

Media General Financial Services, Inc., P. O. Box 26991, Richmond, VA 23261.

Moody's Investor's Services, Inc., 99 Church Street, New York, NY 10007.

National Association of Securities Dealers, Inc. (NASD), 1735 K Street, N.W., Washington, DC 20006.

New York Stock Exchange, 11 Wall Street, New York, NY 10005.

New York Times Information Services, Inc., 1719-A Route 10, Parsippany, NJ 07054.

Quarterly Financial Report is available from Superintendent of Documents, U.S. Government Printing Office, Washington, DC 20402.

Quotron Systems, Inc., 5454 Beethoven Street, Los Angeles, CA 90066.

Securities and Exchange Commission, 450 5th Street, N.W., Washington, DC 20549.

Standard & Poor's Corporation, 345 Hudson Street, New York, NY 10014.

Statistical Abstract of the United States is available from the Superintendent of Documents, U.S. Government Printing Office, Washington, DC 20402.

Statistical Bulletin is available from the Superintendent of Documents, U.S. Government Printing Office, Washington, DC 20402.

Survey of Current Business is available from Superintendent of Documents, U.S. Government Printing Office, Washington, DC 20402.

Tokyo Stock Exchange. The Exchange has an office in New York: TSE, New York Research Office, 45 Broadway, New York, NY 10006.

Value Line Services is available from Arnold Bernhard and Company, Inc., 5 East 44th Street, New York, NY 10017.

Part

2 DEVELOPMENTS IN INVESTMENT THEORY

N
E
W
S

The chapters in Part I provided background on why individuals invest their funds and what they expect to derive from this activity. We also argued very strongly for a global investment program, described the major instruments and capital markets in a global investment environment, and showed the relationship among these instruments and markets. Finally, we discussed where you can get relevant information on these instruments and markets.

We now are ready to discuss how to analyze and value the various investment instruments available. In turn, valuation requires the estimation of expected returns (cash flows) and a determination of the risk involved in the securities. Before we can begin the analysis, we need to understand several major developments in investment theory that have influenced how we specify and measure risk in the valuation process. The purpose of the five chapters in this part is to provide this background on risk and asset valuation.

Chapter 7 describes the concept of efficient capital markets, which hypothesizes that security prices reflect the effect of all information. This chapter considers why markets should be efficient, discusses how one goes about testing this hypothesis, describes the results of the tests, and discusses the implications of the results for those engaged in technical and fundamental analysis as well as portfolio management.

Chapter 8 provides an introduction to portfolio theory, which was developed by Harry Markowitz. This theory provided the first rigorous measure of risk for investors and showed how one selects alternative assets to diversify and reduce the risk of a portfolio. Markowitz also derived a risk measure for individual securities within the context of an efficient portfolio.

Following the development of the Markowitz portfolio model, William Sharpe and several other academicians extended the Markowitz model into a general equilibrium asset pricing model that included an alternative risk measure for all risky assets. Chapter 9 contains a detailed description of these developments and an explanation of the relevant risk measure implied by this valuation model, referred to as the *capital asset pricing model* (CAPM). We introduce the CAPM at this early point in the book because the risk measure implied has been used extensively in various valuation models.

Chapter 9 also contains a discussion of an alternative asset pricing model referred to as the *arbitrage pricing theory* (APT). This theory was developed by Steve Ross in response to criticisms of the CAPM because of its restrictive assumptions and the difficulty in testing it. The fundamental differences between the CAPM and the APT models is that APT requires fewer assumptions and is considered a multivariate risk model compared to the CAPM, which is referred to as a single risk variable model (beta).

In Chapter 10, we return to the asset pricing models and consider the effect of changing some of the assumptions of the models. More important, we review the numerous studies that have empirically tested the CAPM and generated divergent results, including one that casts serious doubt on the basic model. We also revisit the "benchmark problem," which contends that it is not possible to use this model to analyze portfolio performance because the proxy typically used for the required market portfolio is clearly incomplete.

This chapter also includes a review of the APT model and how it differs from the CAPM. This is followed by a discussion of numerous studies that have tested the usefulness of the APT model compared to the CAPM. Again, the results are mixed in terms of supporting the model. Some observers question whether it is possible to test this model because the factors cannot be identified.

In addition to the development of asset pricing models, another major development has been the creation and development of new markets and instruments beyond stocks and bonds. The greatest growth and development has been in the area referred to as *derivatives,* which includes options and futures. These instruments create a wider range of risk–return opportunities for investors. Chapter 11 provides an initial description of these instruments, including an understanding of the fundamental principles that determine their prices. Again, these derivative pricing principles can and should be applied to other assets, including stocks, and especially bonds.

Chapter

7 Efficient Capital Markets

After you read this chapter, you should be able to answer the following questions:

- What is meant by the concept that capital markets are efficient?
- Why *should* capital markets be efficient?
- What are the specific factors that contribute to an efficient market?
- Given the overall efficient market hypothesis, what are the three subhypotheses and what are the implications of each?
- How do you test the weak-form efficient market hypothesis (EMH) and what are the results of the tests?
- How do you test the semistrong-form EMH and what are the test results?
- How do you test the strong-form EMH and what are the test results?
- For each set of tests, which results support the hypothesis and which results indicate an anomaly related to the hypothesis?
- What are the implications of the empirical results for:
  - technical analysis?
  - fundamental analysis?
  - portfolio managers with superior analysts?
  - portfolio managers with inferior analysts?
- What is the evidence related to the EMH for markets in foreign countries?

An **efficient capital market** is one in which security prices adjust rapidly to the arrival of new information and, therefore, the current prices of securities reflect all information about the security. Some of the most interesting and important academic research over the past 25 years has analyzed whether our capital markets are efficient. This extensive research is important because its results have significant real-world implications for investors and portfolio managers. In addition, the efficiency of capital markets is one of the most controversial areas in investment research because opinions regarding the efficiency of capital markets differ widely.

Because of its importance and the controversy, you need to understand the meaning of the terms *efficient capital markets* and *efficient market hypothesis (EMH)*. You should understand the analysis performed to test the EMH and the results of studies that either support or contradict the hypothesis. Finally, you should be aware of the implications of these results when you analyze alternative investments and work to construct a portfolio.

We consider the topic of efficient capital markets at this point for two reasons. First, the discussions in previous chapters have given you an understanding of how the capital markets function, so now it seems natural to consider the efficiency of the market in terms of how prices react to new information. Second, the overall evidence on capital market efficiency is best described as mixed; some studies support the hypothesis and others do not. The implications of these diverse results are important for you as an investor involved in analyzing securities and working to build a portfolio.

There are four major sections in this chapter. The first discusses why we would expect capital markets to be efficient and the factors that contribute to an efficient market where the prices of securities reflect available information.

The single efficient market hypothesis has been divided into three subhypotheses to facilitate testing. The second section describes these three subhypotheses and the implications of each.

Section three is the largest section because it contains a discussion of the tests used to examine the three subhypotheses and reviews the results of numerous studies. This review of the research reveals that a large body of evidence supports the EMH, but a growing number of other studies do not support the hypothesis. These results that do not support the EMH indicate that there are a number of **anomalies.**

The final section discusses the implications of these results for an investor who uses either technical analysis or fundamental analysis or for a portfolio manager who has access to superior or inferior analysts. This includes a discussion of how an analyst can take advantage of the anomalies noted in our review of the evidence from the tests. We conclude with a brief discussion of the evidence for markets in foreign countries.

As noted, we will discuss numerous empirical studies of efficient markets in this chapter. Because space limitations preclude dealing with them in depth, we encourage you to consult the literature cited in the footnotes and the reference section at the end of this chapter.

WHY SHOULD CAPITAL MARKETS BE EFFICIENT?

As noted earlier, in an efficient capital market, security prices adjust rapidly to the infusion of new information, and, therefore, current security prices fully reflect all available information. To be absolutely correct, this is referred to as an **informationally efficient market**. Although the idea of an efficient capital market is relatively straightforward, we often fail to consider *why* capital markets *should* be efficient. What set of assumptions imply an efficient capital market?

An initial, and very important, premise of an efficient market requires that *a large number of competing profit-maximizing participants analyze and value securities,* each independently of the others.

A second assumption is that *new information regarding securities comes to the market in a random fashion,* and the timing of one announcement is generally independent of others.

The third assumption is especially crucial: *The competing investors attempt to adjust security prices rapidly to reflect the effect of new information.* Although the price adjustment may be imperfect, it is unbiased. This means that sometimes the market will overadjust, and other times it will underadjust, but you cannot predict which will occur at any given time. Security prices adjust rapidly to new information because of the many profit-maximizing investors competing against one another.

The combined effect of (1) information coming in a random, independent fashion and (2) numerous competing investors analyzing the new information and adjusting stock prices rapidly to reflect this new information means that one would expect price changes to be independent and random. The adjustment process requires a large number of investors following the movements of the security, analyzing the impact of new information on its value, and buying or selling the security until its price adjusts to reflect the new information. This scenario implies that (1) informationally efficient markets require some minimum number of competing investors who analyze new information and trade and (2) more trading by numerous competing investors should cause a faster price adjustment, making the market more efficient. We will return to this need for trading and investor attention when we discuss some anomalies of the EMH.

Finally, because security prices adjust to all new information, these security prices should reflect all information that is publicly available at any point in time. Therefore, the security prices that prevail at any time should be an unbiased reflection of all currently available information, including the risk involved in owning the security. Therefore, in an efficient market, *the expected returns implicit in the current price of the security should reflect its risk.*

ALTERNATIVE EFFICIENT MARKET HYPOTHESES

Most of the early work related to efficient capital markets was based on the *random walk hypothesis,* which contended that changes in stock prices occurred randomly. This early academic work contained extensive empirical analysis without much theory behind it. Fama attempted to formalize the theory and organize the growing empirical evidence.[1] Fama presented the efficient market theory in terms of a *fair game* model.

Expected Return or Fair Game Model[2]

Unlike work done under the random walk hypothesis, which dealt with price movement over time, the fair game model deals with price at a specified point in time. It assumes that the price of a security fully reflects all available information at that point in time. The model requires that the price-formation process be specified in enough detail so that it is possible to indicate what is meant by "fully reflect." Most of the available models of equilibrium prices formulate prices in terms of rates of return that are dependent on alternative definitions of risk. All such expected return theories of price formation can be described notationally as follows:

$$E(\bar{P}_{j,t+1} \mid \phi_t) = [1 + E(\bar{r}_{j,t+1} \mid \phi_t]P_{j,t}$$

where:

E = expected value operator
$P_{j,t}$ = price of security j at time t
$P_{j,t+1}$ = price of security j at time $t + 1$
$r_{j,t+1}$ = the one period percent rate of return for security j during period $t + 1$
ϕ_t = the set of information that is assumed to be "fully reflected" in the security price at time t

This equation indicates that the expected price of security *j,* given the full set of information available at time t (ϕ_t), is equal to the current price times 1 plus the expected return on security *j,* given the set of available information. This expected future return should reflect the set of information available at *t,* which includes the state of the world at time *t,* including all current and past values of any relevant variables, such as inflation, interest rates, earnings, GDP, and so forth. In addition, it is assumed that this information set includes knowledge of *all the relevant relationships among variables*—that is, it considers how alternative economic series relate to each other and how they relate to security prices.

If equilibrium market prices can be stated in terms of expected returns that "fully reflect" the information set ϕ_t, this implies that it is not possible to derive trading systems or

[1]Eugene F. Fama, "Efficient Capital Markets: A Review of Theory and Empirical Work," *Journal of Finance* 25, no. 2 (May 1970): 383–417.

[2]This section is drawn from Fama, *ibid.*

investment strategies based on this current very encompassing information set and experience returns beyond what should be expected on the basis of an asset's risk. Thus, let us define $x_{j,t+1}$ as the difference between the actual price in $t + 1$ and the expected price in $t + 1$:

$$x_{j,t+1} = P_{j,t+1} - E(P_{j,t-1}\,\phi_t)$$

The above equation can be described as a definition of *excess market value* for security j because it is the difference between the actual price and the expected price projected at t on the basis of the information set ϕ_t. In an efficient market:

$$E(\bar{x}_{j,i+1}\,\phi_t) = 0$$

This equation indicates that the market reflects a "fair game" with respect to the information set ϕ_t. This means that investors can be confident that *current prices fully reflect all available information and are consistent with the risk involved.*

Beyond articulating the efficient market (EM) theory in terms of a fair game model, in his original article, Fama divided the overall efficient market hypothesis (EMH) and the empirical tests of the hypothesis into three subhypotheses depending on the information set involved: (1) weak-form EMH, (2) semistrong-form EMH, and (3) strong-form EMH.

In a later article Fama again divided the empirical results into three groups, but shifted empiricals results among the prior categories.[3] Basically, the weak-form category was broadened to include numerous studies previously considered in the semistrong-form category. Therefore, the following discussion uses the original categories but organizes the presentation of test results using the new categories.

In the remainder of this section, we describe the three hypotheses and the implications of each. In the following section, we describe how researchers have tested each of these hypotheses and briefly discuss the results of numerous studies.

Weak-Form Efficient Market Hypothesis

The **weak-form EMH** assumes that current stock prices fully reflect all *security-market information,* including the historical sequence of price, rates of return, trading volume data, and other market-generated information, such as odd-lot transactions, block trades, and transactions by exchange specialists or other unique groups. Because the EMH assumes that current market prices already reflect all past returns and any other security-market information, this hypothesis implies that past rates of return and other market data should have no relationship with future rates of return (i.e., rates of return should be independent). Therefore, you should gain little from any trading rule that decides whether to buy or sell a security based on past rates of return or any other past market data.

Semistrong-Form Efficient Market Hypothesis

The **semistrong-form EMH** asserts that security prices adjust rapidly to the release of *all public information:* That is, current security prices fully reflect all public information. The semistrong hypothesis encompasses the weak-form hypothesis because all the market information considered by the weak-form hypothesis—such as stock prices, rates of return, and trading volume—is public. Public information also includes all nonmarket information, such as earnings and dividend announcements, price-to-earnings (P/E) ratios, dividend-yield (D/P) ratios, book value–market value (BV/MV) ratios, stock splits, news about the economy, and political news. This hypothesis implies that investors who base

[3]Eugene F. Fama, "Efficient Capital Markets: II," *Journal of Finance* 46, no. 5 (December 1991): 1575–1617.

their decisions on important new information *after it is public* should not derive above-average profits from their transactions because the security price already reflects all such new public information.

STRONG-FORM EFFICIENT MARKET HYPOTHESIS

The **strong-form EMH** contends that stock prices fully reflect *all information from public and private sources.* This means that no group of investors has monopolistic access to information relevant to the formation of prices. Therefore, no group of investors should be able to consistently derive above-average profits. The strong-form EMH encompasses both the weak-form and the semistrong-form EMH. Further, the strong-form EMH extends the assumption of efficient markets, in which prices adjust rapidly to the release of new public information, to assume perfect markets, in which all information is cost-free and available to everyone at the same time.

TESTS AND RESULTS OF ALTERNATIVE EFFICIENT MARKET HYPOTHESES

Now that you understand the three components of the EMH and what each of them implies regarding the effect on security prices of different sets of information, we can consider how a person doing research in this area tests to see whether the hypotheses are supported by the data. Therefore, in this section we discuss the specific tests used to gauge support for the hypotheses and we summarize the results of these tests.

Like most hypotheses in finance and economics, the evidence on the EMH is mixed. Results from some studies have supported the hypothesis and indicate that capital markets are efficient. Results from some other studies have not been consistent with the hypotheses and have revealed some anomalies related to these hypotheses, raising questions about support for the EMH.

WEAK-FORM HYPOTHESIS: TESTS AND RESULTS

Researchers have formulated two groups of tests of the weak-form EMH. The first category involves statistical tests of independence between rates of return. The second entails a comparison of risk–return results for trading rules that make investment decisions based on past market information versus results from a simple buy-and-hold policy, which assumes that you buy stock at the beginning of a test period and hold it to the end.

STATISTICAL TESTS OF INDEPENDENCE As discussed earlier, the EMH contends that security returns over time should be independent of one another because new information comes to the market in a random, independent fashion, and security prices adjust rapidly to this new information. Two major statistical tests have been used to verify this independence.

First, **autocorrelation tests** of independence measure the significance of positive or negative correlation in returns over time. Does the rate of return on day t correlate with the rate of return on day $t - 1$, $t - 2$, or $t - 3$?[4] Those who believe that capital markets are efficient would expect insignificant correlations for all such combinations.

Several researchers have examined the serial correlations among stock returns for several relatively short time horizons, including 1 day, 4 days, 9 days, and 16 days.[5] The

---

[4]For a discussion of tests of independence, see S. Christian Albright, *Statistics for Business and Economics* (New York: Macmillan Publishing, 1987), 515–517.

[5]Eugene F. Fama, "The Behavior of Stock Market Prices," *Journal of Business* 38, no. 1 (January 1965): 34–105; and Eugene Fama and James MacBeth, "Risk, Return and Equilibrium: Empirical Tests," *Journal of Political Economy* 81, no. 3 (May–June 1973): 607–636.

results typically indicated insignificant correlation in stock returns over time. The typical range of correlation coefficients was from + 0.10 to − 0.10, and these correlations were typically not statistically significant. Some recent studies that considered portfolios of stocks with different market values (size) have indicated that the autocorrelation is stronger for portfolios of small stocks.[6] Therefore, although the older results tend to support the hypothesis, the more recent studies cast doubt on it for portfolios of small firms, although these results could be affected by nonsynchronous trading for small-firm stocks.

The second statistical test of independence is the **runs test.**[7] Given a series of price changes, each price change is designated either a plus (+) if it is an increase in price or a minus (−) if it is a decrease in price. The result is a set of pluses and minuses as follows: + + + − + − − + + − − + +. A run occurs when two consecutive changes are the same; two or more consecutive positive or negative price changes constitute one run. When the price changes in a different direction, such as when a negative price change is followed by a positive price change, the run ends and a new run may begin. To test for independence, you would compare the number of runs for a given series to the number in a table of expected values for the number of runs that should occur in a random series.

Studies that have examined stock price runs have confirmed the independence of stock price changes over time. The actual number of runs for stock price series consistently fell into the range expected for a random series. Therefore, these statistical tests have confirmed the independence of stock price changes over time. These statistical tests of independence have been repeated for stocks traded on the OTC market, and the results supported the EMH.[8]

Although short horizon stock returns have generally supported the weak-form EMH, several studies that examined price changes for individual *transactions* on the NYSE found significant serial correlations. Notably, none of these studies attempted to show that the dependence of transaction price movements could be used to earn above-average, risk-adjusted returns. Apparently, the significant correlation among individual transactions returns is due to the market-making activities of the specialist, but investors probably cannot use this small imperfection to derive excess profits after considering the trading rule's substantial transactions costs.[9]

TESTS OF TRADING RULES The second group of tests of the weak-form EMH was developed in response to the assertion that the prior statistical tests of independence were too rigid to identify the intricate price patterns examined by technical analysts. Technical analysts do not accept a set number of positive or negative price changes as a signal of a move to a new equilibrium in the market—they typically look for a general consistency in the price and volume trends over time. Such a trend might include both positive and negative changes. For this reason, technical analysts felt that their **trading rules** were too sophisticated and complicated to be simulated by rigid statistical tests.

---

[6]Jennifer Conrad and Gantam Kaul, "Time Variation in Expected Returns," *Journal of Business* 61, no. 4 (October 1988): 409–425; and Andrew W. Lo and A. Craig MacKinley, "Stock Market Prices Do Not Follow Random Walks: Evidence from a Simple Specifications Test," *Review of Financial Studies* 1, no. 1 (spring 1988): 41–66.

[7]For the details of a runs test, see Albright, *Statistics for Business and Economics,* 695–699.

[8]Robert L. Hagerman and Richard D. Richmond, "Random Walks, Martingales and the OTC," *Journal of Finance* 28, no. 4 (September 1973): 897–909.

[9]J. Campbell, S. Grossman, and J. Wang, "Trading Volume and Serial Correlation in Stock Returns," *Quarterly Journal of Economics* 108, no. 3 (1993): 905–934; L. Glosten, "Insider Trading, Liquidity, and the Role of the Monopolist Specialist," *Journal of Business* 54, no. 2 (April 1989): 579–596; and L. Harris, "A Transactions Data Study of Weekly and Intradaily Patterns in Stock Returns," *Journal of Financial Economics* 16, no. 1 (May 1986): 99–117.

In response to this objection, investigators attempted to examine alternative technical trading rules through simulation. Advocates of an efficient market hypothesized that investors could not derive profits above a buy-and-hold policy, or abnormal profits, using any trading rule that depended solely on any past market information about such factors as price, volume, short sales, advance-decline ratios, or specialist activity.

The trading rule studies compared the risk–return results derived from such a simulation, including transactions costs, to the results from a simple buy-and-hold policy. Three major pitfalls can negate the results of a trading rule study:

1. The investigator should *use only publicly available data* in the decision rule. For example, the earnings for a firm as of December 31 may not be publicly available until April 1, so you should not factor in an earnings report until then.
2. When computing the returns from a trading rule, you should *include all transactions costs* involved in implementing the trading strategy because most trading rules involve many more transactions than a simple buy-and-hold policy.
3. You must *adjust the results for risk* because a trading rule might simply select a portfolio of high-risk securities that should experience higher returns.

Researchers have encountered two operational problems in carrying out these tests of specific trading rules. First, some technical trading rules require too much subjective interpretation of data to simulate mechanically. Second, the almost infinite number of potential trading rules makes it impossible to test all of them. As a result, only the better-known technical trading rules have been examined.

Another factor you should recognize is that some simulation studies have been somewhat biased. Specifically, the operational problems noted above have restricted the studies to relatively simple trading rules, which many technicians contend are rather naive.

In addition, these studies typically employ readily available data from the NYSE, which is biased toward well-known, heavily traded stocks that certainly should trade in efficient markets. Because markets should be more efficient with higher numbers of aggressive, profit-maximizing investors attempting to adjust stock prices to reflect new information, market efficiency depends on trading volume. Specifically, *more trading in a security should promote market efficiency.* Alternatively, for securities with relatively few stockholders and little trading activity, the market could be inefficient because fewer investors would be analyzing the effect of new information and this limited interest would result in insufficient trading activity to move the price of the security quickly to a new equilibrium value that would reflect the new information. Therefore, using only active, heavily traded stocks in the trading rule tests could bias the results toward finding efficiency.

RESULTS OF SIMULATIONS OF SPECIFIC TRADING RULES In the most popular trading technique, **filter rules,** an investor trades a stock when the price change exceeds a filter value set for it. As an example, an investor using a 5 percent filter would envision a positive breakout if the stock were to rise 5 percent from some base, suggesting that the stock price would continue to rise. A technician would acquire the stock to take advantage of the expected continued rise. In contrast, a 5 percent decline from some peak price would be considered a breakout on the downside, and the technician would expect a further price decline and would sell any holdings of the stock, and possibly even sell the stock short.

Studies of this trading rule have used a range of filters from 0.5 percent to 50 percent. The results indicated that small filters would yield above-average profits before taking account of trading commissions. However, small filters generate numerous trades and, therefore, substantial trading costs. When these trading commissions were considered, all the trading profits turned to losses. Alternatively, larger filters did not yield returns above those of a simple buy-and-hold policy.[10]

Researchers have simulated other trading rules that used past market data other than stock prices.[11] Trading rules have been devised that use odd-lot figures, advance-decline ratios, short sales, short positions, and specialist activities. These simulation tests have generated mixed results. Most of the early studies suggested that these trading rules generally would not outperform a buy-and-hold policy on a risk-adjusted basis after taking account of commissions, while a couple of recent studies have indicated support for specific trading rules.[12] Therefore, most evidence from simulations of specific trading rules indicates that these trading rules have not been able to beat a buy-and-hold policy. Therefore, these results generally support the weak-form EMH, but the results are not unanimous.

Semistrong-Form Hypothesis: Tests and Results

Recall that the semistrong-form EMH asserts that security prices adjust rapidly to the release of all public information; that is, security prices fully reflect all public information. Using the organization adopted by Fama, studies that have tested the semistrong-form EMH can be divided into the following sets:

1. Studies to predict future rates of return using available public information beyond the pure market information, such as prices and trading volume, considered in the weak-form tests. These studies of aggregate market returns or individual stock returns can involve either *time-series analysis* of returns or the *cross-section distribution* of returns or other characteristics (e.g., price/earnings ratios, size based upon market value, or price/book value ratios) for individual stocks. Those who believe in the EMH would contend that it would not be possible to predict *future* returns using past returns or to predict the distribution of future returns using any public information.
2. Event studies that examine how fast stock prices adjust to specific significant economic events. A corollary approach would be to test whether it is possible to invest in a security after the public announcement of a significant event and experience significant abnormal rates of return. Again, advocates of the EMH would expect security prices to adjust very rapidly, such that it would not be possible for investors to experience superior risk-adjusted returns by investing after the public announcement of any significant information and paying normal transactions costs.

ADJUSTMENT FOR MARKET EFFECTS For any of these tests, you need to adjust the security's rates of return for the rates of return of the overall market during the

[10]Eugene Fama and Marshall Blume, "Filter Rules and Stock Market Trading Profits," *Journal of Business* 39, no. 1 (January 1966 Supplement): 226–241.

[11]Many of these trading rules are discussed in Chapter 21 on technical analysis.

[12]George Pinches, "The Random Walk Hypothesis and Technical Analysis," *Financial Analysts Journal* 26, no. 2 (March–April 1970): 104–110. Two studies have indicated support for some technical trading rules that use a three-part filter or adjust relative strength for the January effect; see John S. Brush, "Eight Relative Strength Models Compared," *Journal of Portfolio Management* 13, no. 1 (fall 1986): 21–28; and Stephen W. Pruitt and Richard E. White, "Who Says Technical Analysis Can't Beat the Market?" *Journal of Portfolio Management* 14, no. 3 (spring 1988): 55–58. For a study that casts doubt on the ability to implement such trading rules in the real world, see Ray Ball, S. P. Kothari, and Charles Wasley, "Can We Implement Research on Stock Trading Rules?" *Journal of Portfolio Management* 21, no. 2 (winter 1995): 54–63. A recent study that tests a set of relatively simple trading rules finds that they have significant forecasting power, but concludes that the returns do not outweigh the trading costs involved. See Hendrik Bessembinder and Kalok Chan, "Market Efficiency and Returns to Technical Analysis," *Financial Management* 27, no. 2 (summer 1998): 5–17.

period considered. A 5 percent return in a stock during the period surrounding an announcement is not meaningful until you know what the aggregate stock market did during the same period and how this stock normally acts under such conditions. If the market had experienced a 10 percent return during this period, the 5 percent return for the stock may be lower than expected.

Authors of studies prior to 1970 generally recognized the need to make such adjustments for market movements. They typically assumed that the individual stocks should experience returns equal to the aggregate stock market. This assumption meant that the market adjustment process simply entailed subtracting the market return from the return for the individual security to derive its **abnormal rate of return,** as follows:

$$AR_{it} = R_{it} - R_{mt}$$

where:

AR_{it} = abnormal rate of return on security i during period t
R_{it} = rate of return on security i during period t
R_{mt} = rate of return on a market index during period t

In the example where the stock experienced a 5 percent increase while the market increased 10 percent, the stock's abnormal return would be minus 5 percent.

Some authors have adjusted the rates of return for securities by an amount different from the market rate of return because they recognize that based on work with the CAPM, all stocks do not change by the same amount as the market. That is, as will be discussed in Chapter 9, some stocks are more volatile than the market, and some are less volatile. These possibilities mean that you must determine an *expected* rate of return for the stock based on the market rate of return *and* the stock's relationship with the market. As an example, suppose a stock is generally 20 percent more volatile than the market. In such a case, if the market experiences a 10 percent rate of return, you would expect this stock to experience a 12 percent rate of return. Therefore, you would determine the abnormal return by computing the difference between the stock's actual rate of return and its **expected rate of return** as follows:

$$AR_{it} = R_{it} - E(R_{it})$$

where:

$E\,(R_{it})$ = the expected rate of return for stock i during period t based on the market rate of return and the stock's normal relationship with the market (its beta)

Continuing with the example, if the stock that was expected to have a 12 percent return (based on a market return of 10 percent and a stock beta of 1.20) had only a 5 percent return, its abnormal rate of return during the period would be minus 7 percent. Over the normal long-run period, you would expect the abnormal returns for a stock to be zero. Specifically, during one period the returns may exceed expectations, and in the next period they may fall short of expectations.

To summarize, there are two sets of tests of the semistrong-form EMH. In the first set, investigators attempt to predict the future rates of return for individual stocks or the aggregate market (i.e., predict the time series) using public information, such as the aggregate price-earnings ratio, dividend yield, or the risk premium spread for bonds. Alternatively, analysts look for public information regarding individual stocks that will allow them to predict the cross-sectional distribution of risk-adjusted rates of return (i.e., test whether it is possible to use such variables as the price/earnings ratio, market value size, price/book value ratio, the price-earnings to growth rate (PEG) ratio, or the dividend yield to predict which stocks will experience above-average or below-average risk-adjusted rates of return). In the second set of tests (event studies), they examine abnormal rates of return for the period immediately after an announcement of a significant economic event to determine whether it is possible for an investor to derive above-average risk-adjusted rates of return by investing after the release of public information.

In both sets of tests, the emphasis is on the analysis of abnormal rates of return that deviate from long-term expectations, or returns that are adjusted for a stock's specific risk characteristics and overall market rates of return during the period.

RESULTS OF RETURN PREDICTION STUDIES The *time-series tests* assume that in an efficient market the best estimate of *future* rates of return will be the long-run *historical* rates of return. The point of the tests is to determine whether there is any public information that will provide superior estimates of returns for a short-run horizon (1 to 6 months) or a long-run horizon (1 to 5 years).

The results of these studies have indicated that there is limited success in predicting short-horizon returns, but the analysis of long-horizon returns has been quite successful. Rozeff and Shiller postulated that the aggregate dividend yield (D/P) was a proxy for the risk premium on stocks.[13] Their results indicated a positive relationship between the D/P and future stock-market returns. An analysis and explanation of this relationship for long horizons of 2 to 4 years is contained in papers by Fama and French, which show that the predictive power increases with the horizon.[14] A subsequent study by Balvers, Cosimano, and McDonald showed that within an efficient market framework, stock prices do not have to follow a random walk and *long-run* returns on stocks can be predicted as long as you can predict aggregate output.[15]

Several studies have considered dividend yield and two variables related to the term structure of interest rates: (1) a default spread, which is the difference between the yields on lower-grade and Aaa-rated long-term corporate bonds (this spread has been used in earlier chapters of this book as a proxy for a market risk premium); and (2) the *term structure or horizon spread,* which is the difference between the long-term Aaa yield and the yield on 1-month Treasury bills.[16] These studies find that these variables can be used to predict stock returns and bond returns and have even been useful for predicting returns for foreign common stocks.[17]

The reasoning for these empirical results is that when the two most significant variables—the dividend yield (D/P) and the default spread—are high, it implies that investors

[13]Michael Rozeff, "Dividend Yields as Equity Risk Premiums," *Journal of Portfolio Management* 11, no. 1 (fall 1984): 68–75; and Robert Shiller, "Stock Prices and Social Dynamics," *Brookings Papers on Economic Activity* 2 (1984): 457–510.

[14]Eugene F. Fama and Kenneth R. French, "Dividend Yields and Expected Stock Returns," *Journal of Financial Economics* 22, no. 1 (October 1988): 3–25; and Eugene F. Fama and Kenneth R. French, "Business Conditions and Expected Returns on Stocks and Bonds," *Journal of Financial Economics* 25, no. 1 (November 1989): 23–49.

[15]Ronald J. Balvers, Thomas F. Cosimano, and Bill McDonald, "Predicting Stock Returns in an Efficient Market," *Journal of Finance* 45, no. 4 (September 1990): 1109–1128.

[16]Donald B. Keim and Robert F. Stambaugh, "Predicting Returns in Stock and Bond Markets," *Journal of Financial Economics* 17, no. 2 (December 1986): 357–390; John Y. Campbell, "Stock Returns and the Term Structure," *Journal of Financial Economics* 18, no. 2 (June 1987): 373–399; and Nai-fu Chen, "Financial Investment Opportunities and the Macroeconomy," *Journal of Finance* 46, no. 2 (June 1991): 529–594.

[17]Harvey Campbell, "The World Price of Covariance Risk," *Journal of Finance* 46, no. 1 (March 1991): 111–157.

are expecting or requiring a high return on stocks and bonds, and this occurs when the economic environment has been poor, as reflected in the growth rate of output. Such a poor economic environment indicates a low wealth environment wherein investors perceive higher risk for investments, which means that in order to invest and shift consumption from the present to the future, investors will require a high rate of return.

A study by Pesaran and Timmermann considered a number of business cycle variables and found that the predictive power of various economic factors related to stock returns changes through time and tends to vary with the volatility of returns.[18] Specifically, the predictability of returns was low during the calm markets of the 1960s, but predictions based upon economic factors could have been exploited even considering transactions costs during the volatile markets of the 1970s.

QUARTERLY EARNINGS STUDIES An important set of studies involves quarterly earnings reports, which can be considered part of the time-series analysis. The question is, is it possible to predict future returns for a stock based on publicly available quarterly earnings reports?

Numerous studies by Latané and associates on the usefulness of quarterly reports consistently have failed to support the semistrong EMH.[19] A study by Joy, Litzenberger, and McEnally (JLM) examined firms that experienced unanticipated changes in quarterly earnings using three categories based on how actual earnings deviated from expectations: (1) any deviation from expectations, (2) a deviation of plus or minus 20 percent, and (3) a deviation of at least 40 percent.[20] They examined abnormal price changes from 13 weeks prior to the announcement to 26 weeks following it. The abnormal price movements for the "any deviation" category for companies with "positive earnings surprises" (i.e., actual earnings above analysts expectations) was about 1 to 2 percent during the period compared to transaction costs of 2 to 3 percent, indicating a lack of profit opportunities. For the 20-percent-above-expectations category, the post-announcement gain was about 4 percent compared to 5 to 6 percent gains when actual earnings were 40 percent above expectations. These abnormal returns exceeded transaction costs. The price adjustment to "negative earning surprises" (i.e., actual earnings below expectations) was more rapid, and there were no abnormal returns for any category.

These results suggest that favorable information contained in quarterly earnings reports (i.e., positive earnings surprises) is not instantaneously reflected in stock prices and that a significant relationship exists between the size of the earnings surprise and the post-announcement stock price change.

In reviewing these studies, Joy and Jones noted problems in several of the earlier studies that they believed were remedied in subsequent studies.[21] Ball reviewed 20 studies of price reaction to earnings announcements and found that the post-announcement risk-adjusted abnormal returns are consistently positive, which is inconsistent with market

[18]M. Hashem Pesaran and Allann Timmermann, "Predictability of Stock Returns: Robustness and Economic Significance," *Journal of Finance* 50, no. 4 (September 1995): 1201–1228.

[19]Representative studies in the area are H. A. Latané, O. Maurice Joy, and Charles P. Jones, "Quarterly Data, Sort-Rank Routines, and Security Evaluation," *Journal of Business* 43, no. 4 (October 1970): 427–438; and C. Jones and R. Litzenberger, "Quarterly Earnings Reports and Intermediate Stock Price Trends," *Journal of Finance* 25, no. 1 (March 1970): 143–148.

[20]O. Maurice Joy, Robert H. Litzenberger, and Richard W. McEnally, "The Adjustment of Stock Prices to Announcements of Unanticipated Changes in Quarterly Earnings," *Journal of Accounting Research* 15, no. 2 (fall 1977): 207–225.

[21]O. Maurice Joy and Charles P. Jones, "Earnings Reports and Market Efficiencies: An Analysis of Contrary Evidence," *Journal of Financial Research* 2, no. 1 (spring 1979): 51–63.

efficiency.[22] He contended that the abnormal returns are due to problems with the capital asset pricing model (the CAPM is discussed in Chapter 9) used to derive expected returns, not market inefficiencies. Watts found significant abnormal returns even after making all the adjustments suggested by Ball.[23] He explicitly showed that the abnormal returns were due to market inefficiencies rather than the CAPM, but noted that the abnormal returns were small and not completely consistent over time.

The more recent earnings announcement studies have used the concept of *standardized unexpected earnings (SUE)*.[24] Rather than examine the percentage differences between actual and expected, this technique normalizes the difference between actual and expected earnings for the quarter by the standard error of estimate from the regression used to derive the expected earnings figure. Therefore, the SUE is:

$$\frac{\text{Reported EPS}_t - \text{Predicted EPS}_t}{\text{Standard Error of Estimate for the Estimating Regression Equation}}$$

The predicted earnings are estimated by a time-series model that considers the earnings during the prior 20 quarters and includes quarterly dummy variables that adjust for any seasonal factors. Therefore, the SUE indicates how many standard errors the reported EPS figure is above or below the predicted EPS figure. The typical categories are greater than 4.0, between 4.0 and 3.0, between 3.0 and 2.0, and so on, all the way to less than minus 4.0.

An extensive analysis by Rendleman, Jones, and Latané (RJL) using a very large sample and daily returns provided evidence that large SUEs were accompanied by significant abnormal stock price changes.[25] These results contrasted with the earlier findings by Reinganum that the abnormal returns between high and low SUE portfolios were not statistically different from zero.[26] The RJL results were confined for the time period examined by Reinganum (1975–1977), but also from 1971 to 1980. RJL also examined the impact of different risk adjustments and concluded that the results were not sensitive to the risk adjustments. The analysis of daily data from 20 days before a quarterly earnings announcement to 90 days after the announcement indicated that 31 percent of the total response in stock returns came before the announcement, 18 percent on the announcement day, and 51 percent afterwards.

Foster, Olsen, and Shevlin examined several reasons for the return drift following earnings announcements and confirmed the prior results using different earnings expectations models.[27] The unexpected earnings explained over 80 percent of the subsequent stock price

---

[22]Ray Ball, "Anomalies in Relationships between Securities' Yields and Yield-Surrogates," *Journal of Financial Economics* 6, no. 2/3 (June–September 1978): 103–126.

[23]Ross L. Watts, "Systematic 'Abnormal' Returns after Quarterly Earnings Announcements," *Journal of Financial Economics* 6, no. 2/3 (June–September 1978): 127–150.

[24]These include Henry A. Latané and Charles P. Jones, "Standardized Unexpected Earnings—A Progress Report," *Journal of Finance* 32, no. 5 (December 1977): 1457–1465; and Henry A. Latané and Charles Jones, "Standardized Unexpected Earnings: 1971–1977," *Journal of Finance* 34, no. 3 (June 1979): 717–724.

[25]Richard J. Rendleman, Jr., Charles P. Jones, and Henry A. Latané, "Empirical Anomalies Based on Unexpected Earnings and the Importance of Risk Adjustments," *Journal of Financial Economics* 10, no. 3 (November 1982): 269–287; and C. P. Jones, R. J. Rendleman, Jr., and H. A. Latané, "Earnings Announcements: Pre- and Post-Responses," *Journal of Portfolio Management* 11, no. 3 (spring 1985): 28–32.

[26]Marc R. Reinganum, "Misspecification of Capital Asset Pricing," *Journal of Financial Economics* 9, no. 1 (March 1981): 19–46.

[27]George Foster, Chris Olsen, and Terry Shevlin, "Earnings Releases, Anomalies, and the Behavior of Security Returns," *Accounting Review* 59, no. 4 (October 1984): 574–603.

drift for the total time period and during several subperiods. Bernard and Thomas review the prior studies and attempt to explain this pervasive drift.[28]

In summary, these results indicate that the market has not adjusted stock prices to reflect the release of quarterly **earnings surprises** as fast as expected by the semistrong EMH. As a result, it appears that earnings surprises can be used to predict returns for individual stocks.[29]

CALENDAR STUDIES Another set of studies that attempted to predict rates of return are the *calendar studies,* which questioned whether some regularities exist in the rates of return during the calendar year that would allow investors to predict returns on stocks. These include numerous studies on "the January anomaly" and those that consider a variety of other daily and weekly regularities.

The January Anomaly Several years ago, Branch proposed a unique trading rule for taking advantage of tax selling.[30] Investors tend to engage in tax selling at the end of the year to establish losses on stocks that have declined. After the new year, there is a tendency to reacquire these stocks or to buy other stocks that look attractive. This scenario would produce downward pressure on stock prices in late November and December and positive pressure in early January. Those who believe in efficient markets would not expect such a seasonal pattern to persist; it should be eliminated by arbitrageurs who would buy in December and sell in early January.

Dyl supported the tax-selling hypothesis when he found that December trading volume was abnormally high for stocks that had declined during the previous year and that volume was abnormally low for stocks that had experienced large gains.[31] He found significant abnormal returns during January for stocks that had experienced losses during the prior year.

Roll confirmed the price pattern on the last day of December and the first four days of January.[32] Stocks with negative returns during the prior year had higher returns around January 1 and 2. The results also indicated that smallness had an effect beyond volatility and tax selling. To examine the impact of transaction costs, Roll assumed a purchase on the second-to-last day of the year and a sale of the fourth day of the new year. This trading rule generated returns of 6.89 percent for the NYSE and 14.2 percent for the AMEX. Applying the 6.77 percent commissions estimated by Stoll and Whaley for small firms, they still had excess returns of 3.94 percent for the NYSE and 10.3 percent for the AMEX. Assuming a purchase at the high price for the second-to-last trading day and sales at the low price on the fourth day of the new year—and adding commissions—there was no profit on the NYSE, but there was an excess return on the AMEX. Roll concluded that because of transaction costs, arbitrageurs must not be eliminating the January tax-selling anomaly.

Keim analyzed the relation between abnormal returns and market value during each month of the year. Overall he found a negative relationship between size and abnormal returns, but the strongest relationship was always in January, where nearly 50 percent of the

---

[28]Victor L. Bernard and Jacob K. Thomas, "Post-Earnings-Announcement Drift: Delayed Price Response or Risk Premium?" *Journal of Accounting Research* 27, Supplement (1989).

[29]Academic studies such as these that have indicated the importance of earnings surprises have led *The Wall Street Journal* to publish a section on "earnings surprises" in connection with regular quarterly earnings reports.

[30]Ben Branch, "A Tax Loss Trading Rule," *Journal of Business* 50, no. 2 (April 1977): 198–207. These results were generally confirmed in Ben Branch and Kyun Chun Chang, "Tax-Loss Trading—Is the Game Over or Have the Rules Changed?" *The Financial Review* 20, no. 1 (February 1985): 55–69.

[31]Edward A. Dyl, "Capital Gains Taxation and Year-End Stock Market Behavior," *Journal of Finance* 32, no. 1 (March 1977): 165–175.

[32]Richard Roll, "Vas Ist Das?" *Journal of Portfolio Management* 9, no. 2 (winter 1983): 18–28.

overall size effect occurred.[33] In fact, more than 50 percent of the January effect was concentrated in the first week of trading, particularly on the first day of the year.

Following the earlier work by Rozeff and Kinney,[34] Reinganum found large abnormal returns at the beginning of January, consistent with tax-loss selling.[35] Still, small firms that did very well the prior year also experienced large abnormal returns in early January, which is not consistent with the tax-selling hypothesis.

Brown, Keim, Kleidon, and Marsh examined the January effect using Australian data because the year-end for tax purposes in Australia is June 30, making the seasonal tax effect occur in July.[36] The results indicated the largest seasonals in January and July. Although the results for July support the tax-selling hypothesis, the January impact cannot be explained. Berges, McConnell, and Schlarbaum document the January effect using Canadian data for the period 1951–1980, but Canada did not introduce the capital gains tax until 1973.[37] Therefore, the tax-loss hypothesis cannot explain the January effect they found. Also of interest, they did not find the small-firm effect in January.

Chang and Pinegar indicate support for the tax-loss selling hypothesis based on an analysis of long-term government and corporate bonds, with most of the support coming from lower-rated bonds (BB and B).[38] Because they also derived January gains that could not be explained by tax selling, they felt that tax-loss selling is probably not the only cause of January gains. Tinic and West highlighted the January effect by examining the seasonality of the relationship between expected return and risk.[39] They found that there was no significant risk–return relationship in any single month (except January), nor during the other 11 months combined.

Keim analyzed dividend yields and stock returns overall and found a nonlinear relationship in January.[40] Specifically, the zero dividend securities had the largest return, and for the rest of the groups there was a positive relationship between the dividend yield and the stock returns. He likewise found a strong seasonal pattern because the dividend yield–stock return relationship only existed during January. Lakonishok and Smidt found a year-end effect in trading volume for small firms—the most active day being the last day of the year with above-normal trading activity continuing in January.[41]

---

[33]Donald B. Keim, "Size-Related Anomalies and Stock Return Seasonality," *Journal of Financial Economics* 12, no. 1 (June 1983): 13–32.

[34]Michael S. Rozeff and William R. Kinney, Jr., "Capital Market Seasonality: The Case of Stock Returns," *Journal of Financial Economics* 3, no. 4 (December 1976): 379–402.

[35]Marc R. Reinganum, "The Anomalous Stock Market Behavior of Small Firms in January: Empirical Tests for Tax-Loss Selling Effects," *Journal of Financial Economics* 12, no. 1 (January 1983): 89–104.

[36]Philip Brown, Donald B. Keim, Allan W. Kleidon, and Terry A. Marsh, "Stock Return Seasonalities and the Tax-Loss Selling Hypothesis," *Journal of Financial Economics* 12, no. 1 (June 1983): 105–127.

[37]Angel Berges, John J. McConnell, and Gary G. Schlarbaum, "The Turn-of-the-Year in Canada," *Journal of Finance* 39, no. 1 (March 1984): 185–192.

[38]Eric C. Chang and J. Michael Pinegar, "Return Seasonality and Tax-Loss Selling in the Market for Long-Term Government and Corporate Bonds," *Journal of Financial Economics* 17, no. 2 (December 1986): 391–415.

[39]Seha M. Tinic and Richard R. West, "Risk and Return: January vs. the Rest of the Year," *Journal of Financial Economics* 13, no. 4 (December 1984): 561–574.

[40]Donald B. Keim, "Dividend Yields and Stock Returns: Implications of Abnormal January Returns," *Journal of Financial Economics* 14, no. 3 (September 1985): 473–489; Donald B. Keim, "Dividend Yields and the January Effect," *Journal of Portfolio Management* 12, no. 2 (winter 1986): 54–60.

[41]Josef Lakonishok and Seymour Smidt, "Volume and Turn-of-the-Year Behavior," *Journal of Financial Economics* 13, no. 3 (September 1984): 435–455; and Josef Lakonishok and Seymour Smidt, "Trading Bargains in Small Firms at Year-End," *Journal of Portfolio Management* 12, no. 3 (spring 1986): 24–29.

The January anomaly is intriguing because it is so pervasive. Its relationship with the small-firm effect is fascinating because of the apparent speed of impact. This seasonal impact also influences the dividend yield effect and trading volume, and a tax-loss explanation of this anomaly has received mixed support. Despite numerous studies, the January anomaly poses as many questions as it answers.[42]

Other Calendar Effects Although not as significant as the January anomaly, several other "calendar" effects have been examined, including a monthly effect, a weekend/day-of-the-week effect, and an intraday effect. Ariel found a significant monthly effect wherein all the market's cumulative advance occurred during the first half of trading months.[43]

The weekend effect has been documented by French and by Gibbons and Hess.[44] French found that the mean return for Monday was significantly negative during 5-year subperiods and during the full period. In contrast, the average return for the other 4 days was positive. Gibbons and Hess likewise found negative returns on Monday for individual stocks and Treasury bills, and this was confirmed by Keim and Stambaugh who found negative Monday results back to 1928 for individual exchange-listed stocks and for active OTC stocks.[45] The Monday effect was similar for different size firms that were exchange-traded or OTC.

Rogalski decomposed the Monday effect that is typically measured from Friday close to Monday close into a *weekend effect* from Friday close to Monday open and a *Monday trading effect* from Monday open to the Monday close.[46] He showed that the negative Monday effect found in prior studies occurs from the Friday close to the Monday open (i.e., the weekend effect). After adjusting for the weekend effect, the Monday trading effect was positive. When the day-of-the-week returns were segmented into January and the rest of the year, the Monday effect was on average positive in January and negative for all other months. Also, the size effect only existed in January.

Two studies have examined this question using intraday observations. Smirlok and Stacks examined hourly observations between 1963 and 1983 for the total period and for three subperiods.[47] They found a change in the pattern of returns before and after 1974. The results for the period 1974–1983 were consistent with Rogalski wherein the Monday effect is concentrated in the weekend effect. In contrast, before 1974 the Monday effect occurred during the Monday trading period. These results imply a shift in the timing of the weekend effect wherein recently the negative effect is during the weekend. Notably, the Monday

---

[42]An article that reviews these studies and others is Donald B. Keim, "The CAPM and Equity Return Regularities," *Financial Analysts Journal* 42, no. 3 (May–June 1986): 19–34. For a study that applies this hypothesis to bonds, see William E. Maxwell, "The January Effect in the Corporate Bond Market: A Systematic Examination," *Financial Management* 27, no. 2 (summer 1998): 18–30. For a study that evaluates the tax-loss-selling hypothesis against the window-dressing hypothesis, see Richard W. Sias and Laura T. Starks, "Institutions and Individuals at the Turn-of-the-Year," *Journal of Finance* 52, no. 4 (September 1997): 1543–1562.

[43]Robert A. Ariel, "A Monthly Effect in Stock Returns," *Journal of Financial Economics* 8, no. 1 (March 1987): 161–174.

[44]Kenneth R. French, "Stock Returns and the Weekend Effect," *Journal of Financial Economics* 18, no. 1 (March 1980): 55–70; and Michael R. Gibbons and Patrick Hess, "Day of the Week Effects and Asset Returns," *Journal of Business* 54, no. 4 (October 1981): 579–596. For a subsequent note, see Josef Lakonishok and Maurice Levi, "Weekend Effects on Stock Returns: A Note," *Journal of Finance* 37, no. 2 (June 1982): 883–889.

[45]Donald B. Keim and Robert F. Stambaugh, "A Further Investigation of the Weekend Effect in Stock Returns," *Journal of Finance* 39, no. 3 (July 1984): 819–835.

[46]Richard J. Rogalski, "New Findings Regarding Day-of-the-Week Returns over Trading and Non-Trading Periods: A Note," *Journal of Finance* 39, no. 5 (December 1984): 1603–1614.

[47]Michael Smirlok and Laura Stacks, "Day-of-the-Week and Intraday Effects in Stock Returns," *Journal of Financial Economics* 17, no. 1 (September 1986): 197–210.

trading effect has turned positive because the negative Monday morning effect is swamped by positive Monday afternoon returns.

Harris examined the NYSE transactions data, which allowed an analysis across firms and over time.[48] The analysis of trading and nontrading returns indicated that for *large firms,* the negative Monday effect occurred before the market opened (it was a weekend effect), whereas for smaller firms most of the negative Monday effect occurred during the day on Monday (it was a Monday trading effect). An analysis of 15-minute intervals during the day indicated that the only differences occurred during the first 45 minutes of the day—on Monday mornings prices tended to drop; on other weekday mornings, they increased. Price patterns during the day were otherwise similar. Finally, prices tended to rise on the last trade of the day. This effect is further refined by Wang, Li, and Erickson, who find that the Monday effect occurs primarily in the last two weeks of the month.[49]

PREDICTING CROSS-SECTIONAL RETURNS Assuming an efficient market, all securities should lie along a security market line that relates the expected rate of return to an appropriate risk measure. That is, *all securities should have equal risk-adjusted returns* because security prices should reflect all public information that would influence the security's risk. Therefore, studies in this category attempt to determine if it is possible to predict the future distribution of risk-adjusted rates of return (i.e., using public information, is it possible to determine what stocks will enjoy above-average, risk-adjusted returns, and which stocks will experience below-average, risk-adjusted returns?).

These studies typically examine the usefulness of alternative measures of size or quality as a tool to rank stocks in terms of risk-adjusted returns. The reader should be forewarned that all of these tests involve *a joint hypothesis* because not only do they consider the efficiency of the market, but also they are dependent on the asset pricing model that provides the measure of risk used in the test. Specifically, if the results of a test determine that it is possible to predict future risk-adjusted returns, these results could occur *either* because the market is not efficient, *or* because the measure of risk is faulty and, therefore, the measures of risk-adjusted returns are wrong.

Price-Earnings Ratios and Returns Basu tested the EMH by examining the relationship between the historical price-earnings (P/E) ratios for stocks and their returns.[50] Some have suggested that low P/E stocks will outperform high P/E stocks because growth companies enjoy high P/E ratios, but the market tends to overestimate the growth potential and thus overvalues these growth companies while undervaluing low-growth firms with low P/E ratios. A relationship between the historical P/E ratios and subsequent risk-adjusted market performance would constitute evidence against the semistrong EMH because it would imply that investors could use publicly available P/E ratios to predict future abnormal returns.

Basu divided the stocks into five P/E classes and determined the risk and return for portfolios of high and low P/E ratio stocks. Risk-adjusted performance measures indicated that low P/E ratio stocks experienced superior results relative to the market, whereas high P/E ratio stocks had significantly inferior results.[51] Although there was some impact of taxes

---

[48]Lawrence Harris, "A Transaction Data Study of Weekly and Intradaily Patterns in Stock Returns," *Journal of Financial Economics* 16, no. 1 (May 1986): 99–117.

[49]Ko Wang, Yuming Li, and John Erickson, "A New Look at the Monday Effect," *Journal of Finance* 52, no. 5 (December 1997): 2171–2186.

[50]S. Basu, "Investment Performance of Common Stocks in Relation to Their Price-Earnings Ratios: A Test of the Efficient Market Hypothesis," *Journal of Finance* 32, no. 3 (June 1977): 663–682; and S. Basu, "The Information Content of Price-Earnings Ratios," *Financial Management* 4, no. 2 (summer 1975): 53–64.

[51]Composite performance measures are discussed in Chapter 27.

and transaction costs, it was concluded that publicly available P/E ratios possess valuable information. Obviously, these results are not consistent with semistrong efficiency.

Peavy and Goodman examined P/E ratios with adjustments for firm size, industry effects, and infrequent trading.[52] After these adjustments, they found that the risk-adjusted returns for stocks in the lowest P/E ratio quintile were superior to those in the highest P/E ratio quintile.

Price-Earnings/Growth Rate Ratios During the past decade there has been a significant increase in the use of the ratio of a stock's price-earnings ratio divided by the firm's expected growth rate of earnings (referred to as the PEG ratio) as a relative valuation tool, especially for stocks of growth companies that have P/E ratios substantially above average. Advocates of the PEG ratio have generally hypothesized an inverse relationship between the PEG ratio and subsequent rates of return—that is, advocates of the PEG ratio expect that stocks with relatively low PEG ratios (i.e., less than one) will experience above-average rates of return while stocks with relatively high PEG ratios (i.e., in excess of three or four) will have below-average rates of return. The results from a published study by Peters using a sample of above-average growth companies and quarterly rebalancing supported the hypothesis of an inverse relationship during the period 1982–1989.[53] These results that would constitute an anomaly and would not support the EMH were generally confirmed by several subsequent unpublished studies done by analysts at several investment firms.[54] A more recent study by Reilly and Marshall examined a sample of stocks from the Value Line universe. The authors assumed annual rebalancing and divided the sample on the basis of a risk measure (beta), market value size, and by expected growth rate.[55] Except for stocks with low betas and those with very low expected growth rates, the results were not consistent with the hypothesis of an inverse relationship between the PEG ratio and subsequent rates of return. Notably, the study contained results that appeared to support both the small cap hypothesis and the P/E anomaly (i.e., an inverse relationship between P/E and returns).

In summary, the results related to using the PEG ratio to select stocks are mixed—several studies that assume either monthly or quarterly rebalancing have results that indicate an anomaly because the authors use public information and derive above-average rates of return, while the results of a recent study with annual rebalancing indicated that no consistent relationship exists between the PEG ratio and subsequent rates of return.

The Size Effect Two authors simultaneously examined the impact of size (measured by total market value) on risk-adjusted rates of return.[56] All stocks of the NYSE (Banz) or on

---

[52]John W. Peavy III and David A. Goodman, "The Significance of P/Es for Portfolio Returns," *Journal of Portfolio Management* 9, no. 2 (winter 1983): 43–47.

[53]Donald J. Peters, "Valuing a Growth Stock," *Journal of Portfolio Management* 17, no. 3 (spring 1991): 49–51.

[54]Claudia Mott, Daniel Cohen, and Kevin Condon, "Focus on Factor: P/E to Growth," Prudential Securities (October 22, 1993); David Lipshutz, "Low P/E Ratio to Growth Rate as a Stock Selection Strategy: When Analysts Love 'Em But Investors Don't Trust 'Em," Morgan Stanley Dean Witter (August 13, 1997); David Lipshutz, "If You Liked PEG, You'll Love PEGY," Morgan Stanley Dean Witter (October 20, 1997); David Lipshutz, "PEGY Update: Loving the Unloved," Morgan Stanley Dean Witter (December 16, 1997); and Steven De Sanatis and Claudia Mott, "Focus on a Factor: P/E to Growth Works Well in a Mid-Cap Universe," Prudential Securities (January 22, 1997).

[55]Frank K. Reilly and Dominic R. Marshall, "Using P/E/Growth Ratios to Select Stocks," University of Notre Dame (January 1999).

[56]R. W. Banz, "The Relationship between Return and Market Value of Common Stocks," *Journal of Financial Economics* 9, no. 1 (March 1981): 3–18; and Marc R. Reinganum, "Misspecification of Capital Asset Pricing: Empirical Anomalies Based on Earnings Yield and Market Values," *Journal of Financial Economics* 9, no. 1 (March 1981): 19–46.

the NYSE and the AMEX (Reinganum) were ranked by market value and divided into 10 equally weighted portfolios. The risk-adjusted returns for extended periods (10 to 15 years) indicated that the small firms consistently experienced significantly larger risk-adjusted returns than the larger firms. In addition, they contended that it was really the size—not the P/E ratio—that caused the Basu results. Subsequently, Basu reexamined Reinganum's results using a different sample period and different portfolio creation techniques and found that the highest risk-adjusted returns were in portfolios with small firms and low P/E ratios.[57]

As noted, these studies on market efficiency are dual tests of the EMH *and* the CAPM. Abnormal returns may occur because the markets are not efficient or because the market model does not provide correct estimates of expected returns. Reinganum contended that the abnormal returns were the result of the simple one-period CAPM—an inadequate description of the real-world capital markets.[58]

Roll suggested that the riskiness of the small firms was improperly measured.[59] Because small firms are traded less frequently, this causes an increase in serial correlation of prices over time and a decrease in the variance of returns, which also means that the covariance of returns for the stock with the market portfolio is reduced, so the stock's beta is lower. Earlier, Dimson suggested adding lagged and leading market returns to the market model and summing the coefficients to arrive at the beta for infrequently traded stocks.[60] Reinganum computed betas for the alternative market value portfolios using the standard *ordinary least squares (OLS) model* and using Dimson's *aggregated coefficients model* and found a substantial difference in the estimated betas (e.g., the smallest firm portfolio beta was 0.75 using OLS and 1.69 using the aggregated coefficients method).[61] The difference between betas narrowed with size until the largest firm portfolio beta was 0.98 with OLS and 0.97 with aggregated coefficients. Although the results demonstrated that the risk for small firms was underestimated, these larger betas still could not explain the very large differences in rates of return.

Chan, Chen, and Hsich applied a multifactor pricing model with several risk variables and found the difference in risk-adjusted returns between the top and bottom groups was only about 1 or 2 percent, compared with about 12 percent before the multifactor adjustment for risk.[62] The authors contend that these results imply that most of the difference in size-related returns can be explained by *complete measures of risk.*

Stoll and Whaley confirmed that total market value varies inversely with risk-adjusted returns but also found a strong positive correlation between average price per share and market value; firms with small market value have low stock prices.[63] Because transaction costs vary inversely with price per share, they must be considered when examining the

[57]S. Basu, "The Relationship between Earnings, Yield, Market Value, and Return for NYSE Common Stocks," *Journal of Financial Economics* 12, no. 1 (June 1983): 129–156.

[58]Marc R. Reinganum, "Abnormal Returns in Small Firm Portfolios," *Financial Analysts Journal* 37, no. 2 (March–April 1981): 52–57.

[59]Richard Roll, "A Possible Explanation of the Small Firm Effect," *Journal of Finance* 36, no. 4 (September 1981): 879–888.

[60]Elroy Dimson, "Risk Measurement When Shares Are Subject to Infrequent Trading," *Journal of Financial Economics* 7, no. 2 (June 1979): 197–226.

[61]Marc R. Reinganum, "A Direct Test of Roll's Conjecture on the Firm Size Effect," *Journal of Finance* 37, no. 1 (March 1982): 27–35.

[62]K. C. Chan, Nai-fu Chen, and David A. Hsich, "An Exploratory Investigation of the Firm Size Effect," *Journal of Financial Economics* 14, no. 3 (September 1985): 451–471.

[63]Hans R. Stoll and Robert E. Whaley, "Transactions Costs and the Small Firm Effect," *Journal of Financial Economics* 12, no. 1 (June 1983): 57–80.

small-firm effect. Transaction costs include both the dealer's bid–ask spread and the broker's commission, which both vary inversely with price. Specifically, the proportional bid–ask spread varied from 2.93 percent for small-value stocks to 0.69 percent for large-value stocks, and the broker's commission was 3.84 percent for small firms and 2.02 percent for large firms. This indicates a total difference in transaction cost of 4.06 percent between large and small firms—that is, a combined cost of 2.93 plus 3.84 (6.77 percent) for small firms, and 0.69 plus 2.02 (2.71 percent) for large firms. This differential in transaction cost—with frequent trading—can have a significant impact on the results. Assuming daily transactions, the original small-firm effects are reversed, whereas with less trading, the original abnormal returns recur. These results imply that subsequent size effect studies must consider realistic transaction costs and specify holding period assumptions.

Reinganum investigated a buy-and-hold strategy for longer periods of time and had results that were similar to an annual trading strategy.[64] Two holding period strategies were considered: a one-year holding period, with rebalancing every year; and a buy-and-hold strategy from 1963 through 1980. With annual rebalancing, the small-firm portfolio grew from $1 in 1963 to over $46 without commissions, whereas $1 in the largest-firm portfolio grew to about $4. With no rebalancing, a dollar in the small-firm portfolio grew to about $11, whereas $1 in the large-firm portfolio again grew to over $4. Transaction costs with annual rebalancing were not considered because the differential returns were so large that any reasonable transaction costs could not overcome this return superiority. In summary, the small firms outperformed the large firms after considering risk and transaction costs, assuming annual rebalancing.

Most studies on size effect used large databases and long time periods (30 to 50 years) to show that this phenomenon has existed for many years. In contrast, Brown, Kleidon, and Marsh examined the performance over various intervals of time and concluded that *the small firm effect is not stable.*[65] During some periods, they found the negative relationship derived by others, but during others (e.g., 1967 to 1975), large firms outperformed the small firms. Some recent analysis indicates that this positive relationship held during the periods of 1984–1987, 1989–1990, and 1995–1998. Reinganum acknowledges this instability, but contends that the small-firm effect is still a long-run phenomenon.[66]

Neglected Firms and Trading Activity Arbel and Strebel considered an additional influence beyond size—attention or neglect.[67] They measured attention in terms of the number of analysts who regularly follow a stock and divided the stocks into three groups: (1) highly followed, (2) moderately followed, and (3) neglected. They confirmed the small-firm effect but also found a neglected-firm effect caused by lack of information and limited institutional interest. The neglected-firm concept applied across size classes. A more recent study, by Beard and Sias, provided contrary results—they found no evidence of a neglected-firm premium after controlling for capitalization.[68]

---

[64]Marc R. Reinganum, "Portfolio Strategies Based on Market Capitalization," *Journal of Portfolio Management* 9, no. 2 (winter 1983): 29–36.

[65]Philip Brown, Allen W. Kleidon, and Terry A. Marsh, "New Evidence on the Nature of Size-Related Anomalies in Stock Prices," *Journal of Financial Economics* 12, no. 1 (June 1983): 33–56.

[66]Marc R. Reinganum, "A Revival of the Small Firm Effect," *Journal of Portfolio Management* 18, no. 3 (spring 1992): 55–62.

[67]Avner Arbel and Paul Strebel, "Pay Attention to Neglected Firms!" *Journa. of Portfolio Management* 9, no. 2 (winter 1983): 37–42.

[68]Craig Beard and Richard Sias, "Is There a Neglected Firm Effect?" *Financial Analysts Journal* 53, no. 5 (September–October 1997): 19–23.

James and Edmister examined the impact of trading volume by considering the relationship between returns, market volume, and trading activity.[69] They confirmed the relationship between size and rates of return and then considered the impact of trading volume as an alternative explanation because of a strong positive correlation between size and trading activity. A relationship between return and trading activity would justify the excess return for small stocks on the basis of a liquidity premium. The results indicated there was not the hypothesized inverse relationship between trading activity and mean daily returns. A test on firms with comparable trading activity confirmed the size effect. In summary, the size effect could not be explained by differential trading activity.

Barry and Brown hypothesized that firms with less information require higher returns.[70] Using the period of listing as a proxy for information, they found a negative relationship between returns and the period of listing after adjusting for firm size and the January effect.

Firm size has emerged as a major predictor of future returns and an anomaly in the efficient markets literature. There have been numerous attempts to explain the anomaly in terms of superior risk measurements, transaction costs, analysts' attention, trading activity, and differential information. In general, no single study has been able to explain these very unusual results. Apparently, the two strongest explanations are risk measurements and higher transaction costs. Depending on the frequency of trading, these two factors may account for much of the differential. Given these results, Dimson and Marsh warn that the size effect must be considered in any event study that uses long intervals and contains sample firms with significantly different market values.[71]

Book Value–Market Value Ratio The ratio that relates the book value (BV) of a firm's equity to the market value (MV) of its equity was initially suggested by Rosenberg, Reid, and Lanstein as a predictor of stock returns.[72] They found a significant positive relationship between a firm's historical BV/MV ratio and future stock returns and contended that this relationship was evidence against the EMH.

The strongest support for the importance of this ratio was provided by Fama and French, who evaluated the joint effects of market beta, size, E/P ratio, leverage, and the BV/MV ratio on the cross-section average returns on the NYSE, AMEX, and NASDAQ stocks.[73] They analyzed the hypothesized positive relationship between beta and expected returns, and concluded that the positive relationship found in empirical studies before 1969 disappeared between 1963 and 1990. In contrast, the negative relationship between size and average return was significant by itself and after inclusion of other variables.

In addition, Fama and French found a significant positive relationship between the BV/MV ratio and average return that persisted when other variables are included. Most importantly, *both* size and the BV/MV ratio are significant when included together, and they dominate other ratios. Specifically, although leverage and the E/P ratio were significant by themselves or when considered with size, they become insignificant when *both* size and the BV/MV ratio are considered.

---

[69]Christopher James and Robert Edmister, "The Relation between Common Stock Returns, Trading Activity, and Market Value," *Journal of Finance* 38, no. 4 (September 1993): 1075–1086.

[70]Christopher B. Barry and Stephen J. Brown, "Differential Information and the Small Firm Effect," *Journal of Financial Economics* 13, no. 2 (June 1984): 283–294.

[71]Elroy Dimson and Paul Marsh, "Event Study Methodologies and the Size Effect: The Case of UK Press Recommendations," *Journal of Financial Economics* 17, no. 1 (September 1986): 113–142.

[72]Barr Rosenberg, Kenneth Reid, and Ronald Lanstein, "Persuasive Evidence of Market Inefficiency," *Journal of Portfolio Management* 11, no. 3 (spring 1985): 9–17.

[73]Eugene F. Fama and Kenneth R. French, "The Cross-Section of Expected Stock Returns," *Journal of Finance* 47, no. 2 (June 1992): 427–465.

TABLE 7.1

AVERAGE MONTHLY RETURNS ON PORTFOLIOS FORMED ON SIZE AND BOOK-TO-MARKET EQUITY; STOCKS SORTED BY ME (DOWN) AND THEN BE/ME (ACROSS); JULY 1963 TO DECEMBER 1990

In June of each year *t*, the NYSE. AMEX, and NASDAQ stocks that meet the CRSP-COMPUSTAT data requirements are allocated to 10 size portfolios using the NYSE size (ME) breakpoints. The NYSE, AMEX, and NASDAQ stocks in each size decile are then sorted into 10 BE/ME portfolios using the book-to-market ratios for year $t - 1$. BE/ME is the book value of common equity plus balance-sheet deferred taxes for fiscal year $t - 1$, over market equity for December of year $t - 1$. The equal-weighted monthly portfolio returns are then calculated for July of year *t* to June of year $t + 1$.

Average monthly return is the time-series average of the monthly equal-weighted portfolio returns (in percent).

The All *column* shows average returns for equal-weighted size decile portfolios. The All *row* shows average returns for equal-weighted portfolios of the stocks in each BE/ME group.

		Book-to-Market Portfolios									
	All	Low	2	3	4	5	6	7	8	9	High
All	1.23	0.64	0.98	1.06	1.17	1.24	1.26	1.39	1.40	1.50	1.63
Small-ME	1.47	0.70	1.14	1.20	1.43	1.56	1.51	1.70	1.71	1.82	1.92
ME-2	1.22	0.43	1.05	0.96	1.19	1.33	1.19	1.58	1.28	1.43	1.79
ME-3	1.22	0.56	0.88	1.23	0.95	1.36	1.30	1.30	1.40	1.54	1.60
ME-4	1.19	0.39	0.72	1.06	1.36	1.13	1.21	1.34	1.59	1.51	1.47
ME-5	1.24	0.88	0.65	1.08	1.47	1.13	1.43	1.44	1.26	1.52	1.49
ME-6	1.15	0.70	0.98	1.14	1.23	0.94	1.27	1.19	1.19	1.24	1.50
ME-7	1.07	0.95	1.00	0.99	0.83	0.99	1.13	0.99	1.16	1.10	1.47
ME-8	1.08	0.66	1.13	0.91	0.95	0.99	1.01	1.15	1.05	1.29	1.55
ME-9	0.95	0.44	0.89	0.92	1.00	1.05	0.93	0.82	1.11	1.04	1.22
Large-ME	0.89	0.93	0.88	0.84	0.71	0.79	0.83	0.81	0.96	0.97	1.18

Source: Eugene F Fama and Kenneth French, "The Cross-Section of Expected Stock Returns," *Journal of Finance* 47, no. 2 (June 1992): 446. Reprinted with permission.

A demonstration of the significance of both size and the BV/MV ratio can be seen from the results in Table 7.1, which shows the separate and combined effect of the two variables. As shown, controlling for size, BV/MV captures strong variation in average returns (0.70 to 1.92 percent). Alternatively, controlling for the BV/MV ratio leaves a size effect in average returns (if you have the high BV/MV portfolio, you can increase your return from 1.18 to 1.92 by moving from large ME to small ME). These positive results for the BV/MV ratio were replicated by Chan, Hamao, and Lakonishok for returns on Japanese stocks.[74]

Given the results of the Fama-French study, which casts doubt on the CAPM and the use of beta as well as the significant support for the BV/MV ratio as an indicator of returns, several studies of these results followed. The studies focused on two questions: (1) Is beta really dead whereby no relationship exists between beta and rates of returns? and (2) Why and how does the BV/MV ratio help predict rates of return? In contrast to Fama-French (who measured beta with monthly returns), Kothari, Shanken, and Sloan (KSS) measured beta with annual returns to avoid some of the trading problems with monthly data.[75] Using annual betas, KSS found substantial compensation for beta risk and suggested that the relationship between returns and the BV/MV ratio may be periodic and was not significant over a longer period. Alternatively, Pettengill, Dundaram, and Matthur note that these

[74]Louis K. Chan, Yasushi Hamao, and Josef Lakonishok, "Fundamentals and Stock Returns in Japan," *Journal of Finance* 41, no. 5 (December 1991): 1739–1789.

[75]S. P. Kothari, Jay Shanken, and Richard G. Sloan, "Another Look at the Cross Section of Expected Stock Returns," *Journal of Finance* 50, no. 2 (March 1995): 185–224.

studies typically used *realized returns* to test the model when the theory specifies *expected returns.* When adjusting for expectations concerning negative market excess returns, they found a consistent and significant relationship between beta and returns.[76]

A study by Fairfield examined the characteristics and usefulness of the BV/MV ratio (referred to as the P/B ratio). Fairfield's valuation model illustrates (in accounting terms) that the P/B ratio depends on the expected *level* of future profitability, while the P/E ratio depends on the expected *changes* in future profitability.[77] The evidence indicated that the P/B ratio was related to future ROE, while the P/E was related to future growth in earnings. Finally, P/Bs were more stable than P/Es and high P/B–P/E firms generally maintained their classifications.

As a follow-up to their earlier study, Fama and French examined whether the behavior of stock price to size and the BV/MV ratio reflected earnings changes.[78] The analysis centered on the relationship of high and low BV/MV stocks and profitability, which was measured as earnings-to-book-equity (ROE). Notably, low BV/MV stocks (generally referred to as growth stocks) tended to have high ROE in the years prior to forming portfolios, but lower ROE in subsequent years. In contrast, high BV/MV stocks (generally referred to as value stocks) experienced low ROE prior to the portfolio formation, but increases in ROE after the formation. The BV/MV ratios were persistent, which is consistent with Fairfield. Size played a more important role in the small-stock portfolios, while the BV/MV ratio was more important for firms with high BV/MV ratios (i.e., value stocks).

The original Fama-French results were confirmed in a study by Dennis, Perfect, Snow, and Wiles.[79] They not only confirmed that the optimal combination was portfolios of small firms with high BV/MV ratios, but showed that this superiority prevailed after assuming a 1 percent transaction cost and annual rebalancing. It is shown that the best results are derived assuming rebalancing every four years.

In summary, the tests of publicly available ratios that can be used to predict the cross section of expected returns for stocks have provided substantial evidence in conflict with the semistrong-form EMH. Significant results were found for E/P ratios, market value size, neglected firms, leverage, and BV/MV ratios. While recent work has indicated that the optimal combination appears to be size and the BV/MV ratio, results of studies by Jensen, Johnson, and Mercer indicate that this combination of variables only works during periods of expansive monetary policy.[80]

---

[76]Glenn Pettengill, Sridhar Dundaram, and Ike Matthur, "The Conditional Relation between Beta and Returns," *Journal of Financial and Quantitative Analysis* 30, no. 1 (March 1995): 101–115. For another defense of beta, see K. Grundy and Burton Malkiel, "Reports of Beta's Death Are Greatly Exaggerated," *Journal of Portfolio Management* 22, no. 3 (spring 1996): 36–45.

[77]Patricia M. Fairfield, "P/E, P/B, and the Present Value of Future Dividends," *Financial Analysts Journal* 50, no. 4 (July–August 1994): 23–31.

[78]Eugene F. Fama and Kenneth French, "Size and Book-to-Market Factors in Earnings and Returns," *Journal of Finance* 50, no. 1 (March 1995): 131–155.

[79]Patrick Dennis, Steven Perfect, Karl Snow, and Kenneth Wiles, "The Effects of Rebalancing on Size and Book-to-Market Ratio Portfolio Returns," *Financial Analysts Journal* 51, no. 3 (May–June 1995): 47–57. For a study that shows CEOs do not acknowledge these results, see H. Shefrin and M. Statman, "Making Sense of Beta, Size, and Book-to-Market," *Journal of Portfolio Management* 21, no. 2 (winter 1995): 26–34. Also, see Peter J. Knez and Mark J. Ready, "On the Robustness of Size and Book-to-Market in Cross Sectional Regressions," *Journal of Finance* 52, no. 4 (September 1997).

[80]Gerald R. Jensen, Jeffrey Mercer, and Robert R. Johnson, "Business Conditions, Monetary Policy, and Expected Security Returns," *Journal of Financial Economics* 40, no. 2 (February 1996): 213–237; Gerald R. Jensen, Robert R. Johnson, and Jeffrey M. Mercer, "New Evidence on Size and Price-to-Book Effects in Stock Returns," *Financial Analysts Journal* 53, no. 1 (November–December 1997): 34–42; and Gerald R. Jensen, Robert R. Johnson, and Jeffrey M. Mercer, "The Inconsistency of Small-Firm and Value Stock Premiums," *Journal of Portfolio Management* 24, no. 2 (winter 1998): 27–36. These are discussed further in Chapter 14.

RESULTS OF EVENT STUDIES The use of event studies to test the EMH has been a major growth sector during the past 20 years. Recall that these studies examine how abnormal rates of return react to significant economic information. Those who advocate the EMH would expect returns to adjust very quickly to announcements of new information, which means that it is not possible for investors to experience positive abnormal rates of return by acting after the announcement. Because of space constraints, it is impossible to consider the many studies, but only to summarize the results for some of the more popular events considered.

Numerous studies have examined the price reaction to specific events, such as stock splits, exchange listings, and earnings announcements. Therefore, the discussion of results is organized by event or item of public information. Specifically, we will review the results of **event studies** that examined the price movements and profit potential surrounding stock splits, the sale of initial public offerings, exchange listings, unexpected world or economic events, and the announcement of significant accounting changes. We will see that the results for most of these studies have supported the semistrong-form EMH.

Stock Split Studies One of the more popular economic events to examine is stock splits. Some observers believe the prices of stocks that split will increase in value because the shares are priced lower, which increases demand for them. In contrast, advocates of efficient markets would not expect a change in value, reasoning that the firm has simply issued additional stock and nothing fundamentally affecting the value of the firm has occurred.

A well-known test of the semistrong hypothesis is the FFJR study, which asserts that stock splits alone should not cause higher rates of return because they add nothing to the value of a firm.[81] It is assumed that any relevant information (e.g., earnings growth) that caused the split would have already been discounted.[82]

One reason for expecting a price increase is that companies typically raise their dividends when they split their stock. The dividend change has an information effect because it indicates that management is confident that it will have a new, higher level of earnings in the future, which will justify a higher level of dividends. Therefore, it is contended that any price increase that accompanies a dividend increase is not caused by the dividend itself, but by the expected earnings information it transmits.

To adjust for the market effect, FFJR derived unique parameters for each stock relative to the market and computed abnormal returns for the period 20 months before and after the stock split. The analysis was intended to determine whether the positive stock price effects took place before or after the split. The total sample was divided into two groups: stocks that split and increased their dividend rate, and those that split but did not increase their dividend rate.

Both groups experienced positive abnormal price changes prior to the split. Stocks that split but did *not* increase their dividend experienced abnormal price declines following the split and within 12 months lost all their accumulated abnormal gains. In contrast, stocks that split and increased their dividend experienced no abnormal returns after the split.

These results, which indicated that stock splits do not result in higher rates of return for stockholders after the split, support the semistrong EMH because they indicate that investors cannot gain from the information on a split after the public announcement.

---

[81]E. F. Fama, L. Fisher, M. Jensen, and R. Roll, "The Adjustment of Stock Prices to New Information," *International Economic Review* 10, no. 1 (February 1969): 1–21.

[82]For a detailed analysis of why firms split their stock, see Josef Lakonishok and Baruch Lev, "Stock Splits and Stock Dividends: Why, Who and When," *Journal of Finance* 42, no. 4 (September 1987): 913–932.

Hausman, West, and Largay confirmed this conclusion when they examined monthly data.[83] Reilly and Drzycimski also found strong support for the EMH using daily price and volume data for the period surrounding the split announcement.[84] In contrast, Grinblatt, Masulis, and Titman reported positive results on the day of the announcement and subsequent days.[85]

In summary, most studies attribute no short-run or long-run positive impact on security returns because of a stock split, although the results are not unanimous.[86]

Initial Public Offerings During the past 25 years, a number of closely held companies have gone public by selling some of their common stock. Determining the appropriate price for an initial public offer (IPO) is a difficult task. Because of uncertainty about price and the risk involved in underwriting such issues, it has been hypothesized that underwriters would tend to underprice these new issues.[87]

Given this general expectation of underpricing, the studies in this area have generally considered the following questions: (1) How great is the underpricing on average? Does the underpricing vary over time, and, if so, why? (2) What factors cause different amounts of underpricing for alternative issues? (3) How fast does the market adjust the price for the underpricing?

The answer to the first set of questions seems to be an average underpricing of about 15 percent, but it varies over time as shown by the results in Table 7.2.[88] Numerous factors have been suggested for the differential underpricing of alternative issues, but the major variables seem to be various risk measures, the size of the firm, the prestige of the underwriter, and the status of the firm's accounting firm.[89] Finally, the question of direct interest to the EMH is how fast the price is adjusted to the underpricing. The more recent results

---

[83]W. H. Hausman, R. R. West, and J. A. Largay, "Stock Splits, Price Changes, and Trading Profits: A Synthesis," *Journal of Business* 44, no. 1 (January 1971): 69–77.

[84]Frank K. Reilly and Eugene F. Drzycimski, "Short-Run Profits from Stock Splits," *Financial Management* 10, no. 3 (summer 1981): 64–74.

[85]Mark S. Grinblatt, Ronald W. Masulis, and Sheridan Titman, "The Valuation Effects of Stock Splits and Stock Dividends," *Journal of Financial Economics* 13, no. 4 (December 1984): 461–490. For a recent study on long-run returns, see H. Desai and P. Jain, "Long-Run Common Stock Returns Following Splits and Reverse Splits," *Journal of Business* 70, no. 2 (April 1997): 409–433.

[86]Another question of interest related to stock splits is the impact on the liquidity and volatility of the stocks involved. For a study on this question, see Ohlson and Penman, "Volatility Increases Subsequent to Stock Splits," *Journal of Financial Economics* 14, no. 2 (June 1985): 251–266.

[87]For a discussion of the reasons for a bias toward underpricing of IPOs, see Frank K. Reilly and Kenneth Hatfield, "Investor Experience with New Stock Issues," *Financial Analysts Journal* 25, no. 5 (September–October 1969): 73–80.

[88]Example studies that measured these returns include Roger G. Ibbotson, "Price Performance of Common Stock New Issues," *Journal of Financial Economics* 2, no. 3 (September 1975): 235–272; Dennis E. Logue, "On the Pricing of Unseasoned New Issues, 1965–1969," *Journal of Financial and Quantitative Analysis* 8, no. 1 (January 1973): 91–103; Frank K. Reilly, "Further Evidence on Short-Run Results for New Issue Investors," *Journal of Financial and Quantitative Analysis* 8, no. 1 (January 1973): 83–90; Frank K. Reilly, "New Issues Revisited," *Financial Management* 6, no. 4 (winter 1977): 28–42; and B. M. Neuberger and C. A. Lachapelle, "Unseasoned New Issue Price Performance on Three Tiers: 1975–1980," *Financial Management* 12, no. 3 (fall1983): 23–28.

[89]See Randolph Beatty and Jay Ritter, "Investment Banking, Reputation, and the Underpricing of Initial Public Offerings," *Journal of Financial Economics* 15, no. 1 (March 1986): 213–232; J. R. Ritter, "The 'Hot' Issue Market of 1980," *Journal of Business* 57, no. 2 (April 1984): 215–240; K. Rock, "Why New Issues Are Underpriced," *Journal of Financial Economics* 15, no. 1 (March 1986): 187–212; and R. Michaely and W. H. Shaw, "Does the Choice of Auditor Convey Quality in an Initial Public Offering?" *Financial Management* 24, no. 4 (winter 1995): 15–30.

TABLE 7.2

NUMBER OF OFFERINGS, AVERAGE INITIAL RETURN, AND GROSS PROCEEDS OF INITIAL PUBLIC OFFERINGS IN 1960–1992

Year	Number of Offerings[a]	Average Initial Return, %[b]	Gross Proceeds $ Millions[c]
1960	269	17.83	553
1961	435	34.11	1,243
1962	298	−1.61	431
1963	83	3.93	246
1964	97	5.32	380
1965	146	12.75	409
1966	85	7.06	275
1967	100	37.67	641
1968	368	55.86	1,205
1969	780	12.53	2,605
1970	358	−0.67	780
1971	391	21.16	1,655
1972	562	7.51	2,724
1973	105	−17.82	330
1974	9	−6.98	51
1975	14	−1.86	264
1976	34	2.90	237
1977	40	21.02	151
1978	42	25.66	247
1979	103	24.61	429
1980	259	49.36	1,404
1981	438	16.76	3,200
1982	198	20.31	1,334
1983	848	20.79	13,168
1984	516	11.52	3,932
1985	507	12.36	10,450
1986	953	9.99	19,260
1987	630	10.39	16,380
1988	435	5.27	5,750
1989	371	6.47	6,068
1990	276	9.47	4,519
1991	367	11.83	16,420
1992	509	10.90	23,990
1960–69	2,661	21.25	7,988
1970–79	1,658	8.95	6,868
1980–89	5,155	15.18	80,946
1990–92	1,152	10.85	44,929
Total	10,626	15.26	140,731

[a]The number of offerings excludes Regulation A offerings (small issues, raising less than $1.5 million during the 1980s), real estate investment trusts (REITs), and closed-end funds. Data are from Roger G. Ibbotson and Jeffry F. Jaffe, "'Hot Issues' Markets," *Journal of Finance* (September 1975) for 1960–70; Jay R. Ritter, "The 'Hot Issues' Market of 1980," *Journal of Business* (April 1984) for 1971–82; *Going Public: The IPO Reporter* for 1983–84; and Investment Dealer's Digest Information Services and Security Data Company for 1985–92. Returns data for 1988–92 exclude best efforts offerings. If these are included, the average initial returns for these years would presumably be higher.

[b]Initial returns are computed as the percentage return from the offering price to the end-of-the-calendar-month bid price, less the market return, for offerings in 1960–76. For 1977–92, initial returns are computed as the percentage return from the offering price to the end-of-the-first-day bid price, without adjusting for initial market movements. Data are from Ibbotson and Jaffe (op. cit.) for 1960–70, Ritter (op. cit.) for 1971–82, and prepared by the authors for 1983–92. Initial returns for 1988–92 prepared with the assistance of Zhewei Ma.

[c]Gross proceeds data come from various issues of the *S.E.C. Monthly Statistical Bulletin* and *Going Public: The IPO Reporter* for 1960–87, and Securities Data Co. for 1988–92. Only the U.S. portion of international equity offerings is included in the gross proceeds figures.

Source: Roger G. Ibbotson, Jody L. Sindelar, and Jay R. Ritter, "The Market Problems with the Pricing of Initial Public Offerings," *Journal of Applied Corporate Finance* 7, no. 1 (spring 1994): 69.

indicate that the price adjustment takes place within one day after the offering.[90] Therefore, on average there is some underpricing of IPOs when they are offered, but only the few investors who receive allocations of the original issue will benefit. Further, Hanley and Wilhelm show that institutional investors capture the vast majority (70 percent) of the short-term profits.[91]

The evidence indicates that investors who acquire the stock after the initial adjustment do not experience abnormal returns. This is best documented by Ritter, who shows that a strategy of investing in IPOs at the end of the first day of public trading and holding them for three years would have resulted in a wealth relative to 0.83 compared to a portfolio of matched stocks from the NYSE or AMEX.[92]

Exchange Listing Another significant economic event for a firm and its stock is the decision to become listed on a national exchange, especially the NYSE. Such a listing is expected to increase the market liquidity of the stock and add to its prestige. Two questions are important. First, does an exchange listing increase a stock's liquidity and permanently increase the value of the firm? Second, can an investor derive abnormal returns from investing in the stock when a new listing is announced or around the time of the actual listing? On the first question, the results are inconclusive regarding the effect on liquidity, while the overall consensus is that listing on a national exchange does not cause a permanent change in the long-run value of a firm.[93] The results about abnormal returns surrounding the listing have been mixed. The studies generally agreed that the stocks' prices increased before any listing announcements and that stock prices consistently declined after the actual listing. The crucial question is, what happens between the listing announcement and the actual listing (a period of 4 to 6 weeks)? Most recent studies point toward profit opportunities immediately after the announcement that a firm is applying for listing, and some suggest the possibility of excess returns from price declines after the

---

[90] See Robert E. Miller and Frank K. Reilly, "An Examination of Mispricing, Returns, and Uncertainty for Initial Public Offerings," *Financial Management* 16, no. 2 (January 1987): 33–38; Andrew J. Chalk and John W. Peavy III, "Initial Public Offerings: Daily Returns, Offering Types, and the Price Effect," *Financial Analysts Journal* 43, no. 5 (September–October 1987): 65–69; and Kathleen Weiss Hanley, "Underpricing of Initial Public Offerings and the Partial Adjustment Phenomenon," *Journal of Financial Economics* 34. no. 2 (October 1993): 231–250. For an excellent review of the research on this topic, see Roger G. Ibbotson, Jody L. Sindelar, and Jay R. Ritter, "The Market Problems with the Pricing of Initial Public Offerings," *Journal of Applied Corporate Finance* 7, no. 1 (spring 1994): 66–74.

[91] Kathleen Weiss Hanley and William J. Wilhelm, Jr., "Evidence on the Allocation of Initial Public Offerings," *Journal of Financial Economics* 37, no. 2 (February 1995): 239–257.

[92] Jay R. Ritter, "The Long-Run Performance of Initial Public Offerings," *Journal of Finance* 46, no. 1 (March 1991): 3–27. Subsequent analysis of factors affecting long-run performance is contained in Alan Bravand and Paul A. Gompers, "Myth or Reality? The Long-Run Underperformance of Initial Public Offerings: Evidence from Venture and Non-Venture Capital-Backed Companies," *Journal of Finance* 52, no. 5 (December 1977): 1791–1821; and Richard B. Carter, Frederick Dark, and Asai K. Singh, "Underwriter Reputation, Initial Returns, and the Long-Run Performance of IPO Stocks," *Journal of Finance* 53, no. 1 (February 1998): 285–311.

[93] Regarding liquidity effects, see William G. Christie and Roger D. Huang, "Market Structures and Liquidity: A Transactions Data Study of Exchange Listings," *Journal of Financial Intermediation* 3 (1993): 300–326; and Gregord Kadlec and J. J. McConnell, "The Effect of Market Segmentation and Illiquidity on Asset Prices: Evidence from Exchange Listings," *Journal of Finance* 49, no. 2 (June 1994): 611–636. Regarding changes in long-term value, see James C. VanHorne, "New Listings and Their Price Behavior," *Journal of Finance* 25, no. 4 (September 1970): 783–794; and Waldemar M. Goulet, "Price Changes, Managerial Actions, and Insider Trading at the Time of Listing," *Financial Management* 3, no. 1 (spring 1974): 30–36.

actual listing.[94] A study by Dharan and Ikenberry confirms that on average, there is a relative price decline after listing, but they also show that the results differ by size of firm.[95] They find that the major impact is on small firms that tend to list prior to a decline in performance—in contrast to large firms that do not experience poor performance. Finally, studies that have examined the impact of listing on the risk of the securities found no significant change in systematic risk or the firm's cost of equity.[96]

In summary, these studies on exchange listings indicate no long-run effects on value or risk. They do, however, provide some evidence of short-run profit opportunities from public information, which does not support the semistrong-form EMH.

Unexpected World Events and Economic News The results of several studies of the response of security prices to world or economic news have supported the semistrong-form EMH. Reilly and Drzycimski examined the reaction of stock prices to unexpected world events and found that prices adjusted to the news before the market opened or before it reopened after the announcement.[97] Pierce and Roley examined the response to announcements about money supply, inflation, real economic activity, and the discount rate and found either no impact or an impact that did not persist beyond the announcement day.[98] When Jain analyzed hourly stock returns and trading volume response to surprise announcements about money supply, price changes, industrial production, and the unemployment rate, he found that money supply and price changes had an impact that was reflected in about one hour.[99]

Announcements of Accounting Changes Numerous studies have analyzed the impact of announcements of accounting changes on stock prices. In efficient markets, security prices should react quickly and predictably to announcements of accounting changes. An announcement of an accounting change that affects the economic value of the firm should cause a rapid change in stock prices. An accounting change that affects reported earnings, but has no economic significance, should not affect stock prices. An example would be the analysis of stock price movements surrounding an accounting change in depreciation method from accelerated to straight line, which increases reported earnings. The results of several studies generally supported the EMH because there was no indication of positive price changes following the change. In fact, there were some negative stock return effects because it was postulated that firms making such an accounting change are typically performing poorly.

---

[94]See Gary Sanger and John McConnell, "Stock Exchange Listings, Firm Value and Security Market Efficiency: The Impact of NASDAQ," *Journal of Financial and Quantitative Analysis* 2l, no. 1 (March 1986): 1–25; John J. McConnell and Gary Sanger, "The Puzzle in Post-Listing Common Stock Returns," *Journal of Finance* 42, no. 1 (March 1987): 119–140; and John J. McConnell and Gary Sanger, "A Trading Strategy for New Listings on the NYSE," *Financial Analysts Journal* 40, no. 1 (January–February 1989): 38–39.

[95]Bala G. Dharan and David L. Ikenberry, "The Long-Run Negative Drift of Post-Listing Stock Returns," *Journal of Finance* 50, no. 5 (December 1995): 1547–1574.

[96]Frank J. Fabozzi, "Does Listing on the AMEX Increase the Value of Equity?" *Financial Management* 10, no. 1 (spring 1981): 43–50; and Kent Baker and James Spitzfaden, "The Impact of Exchange Listing on the Cost of Equity Capital," *The Financial Review* 17, no. 3 (September 1982): 128–141.

[97]Frank K. Reilly and Eugene F. Drzycimski, "Tests of Stock Market Efficiency Following Major World Events," *Journal of Business Research* 1, no. 1 (summer 1973): 57–72.

[98]Douglas Pierce and Vance Roley, "Stock Prices and Economic News, " *Journal of Business* 59, no. 1 (January 1985): 49–67.

[99]Prom C. Jain, "Response of Hourly Stock Prices and Trading Volume to Economic News," *Journal of Business* 61, no. 2 (April 1988): 219–231.

Another example involves studies done during periods of high inflation when many firms will change their inventory method from first-in, first-out (FIFO) to last-in, first-out (LIFO). Such a change causes a decline in reported earnings but benefits the firm because it reduces its taxable earnings and, therefore, tax expenses. Advocates of efficient markets would expect positive price changes from the tax savings, and study results confirmed this expectation. Although reported earnings were lower than with FIFO, stock prices generally increased for these firms.

Therefore, these studies indicate that the securities markets react quite rapidly to accounting changes and adjust security prices as one would expect on the basis of the true value (i.e., analysts are able to pierce the accounting veil and value securities on the basis of the true economic impact of the events).[100]

Corporate Events An area that has received substantial analysis during the last few years is corporate finance events, such as mergers and acquisitions, reorganizations, and various security offerings (common stock, straight bonds, convertible bonds). Again there are two general questions of interest: (1) What is the market impact of these alternative events? and (2) How fast does the market react to these events and adjust the security prices?

On the question of the reaction to corporate events, the answer is almost unanimous that prices react as one would expect based on the underlying economic impact of the action. An example would be the reaction to mergers where the stock of the firm being acquired increases in line with the premium offered by the acquiring firm, whereas the stock of the acquiring firm typically declines or experiences no change because of the concern that they overpaid for the firm. On the question of speed of reaction, the evidence indicates fairly rapid adjustment, with the time period shortening as shorter interval data are analyzed (i.e., using daily data, most studies find that the price adjustment is completed in about 3 days). Numerous studies related to financing decisions are reviewed by Smith.[101] The rapidly growing number of studies on corporate control that consider mergers and reorganizations are reviewed by Jensen and Warner.[102] For a brief review of studies related to equity offerings and debt offerings, see the studies by Spiess and Affleck-Graves.[103]

SUMMARY ON THE SEMISTRONG-FORM EMH Clearly, the evidence from tests of the semistrong EMH is mixed. The hypothesis receives strong and almost unanimous support from the numerous event studies on a range of events, including stock splits, initial public offerings, world events and economic news, accounting changes, and a variety of corporate finance events. About the only mixed results come from exchange listing studies.

---

[100]For an extensive review of studies directed to this contention, see William H. Beaver, *Financial Reporting: An Accounting Revolution* (Englewood Cliffs, N.J.: Prentice-Hall, Inc., 1981), especially Chapter 6. For an article that reviews numerous studies of accounting and stock prices, see Michael J. Brennan, "A Perspective on Accounting and Stock Prices," *Journal of Applied Corporate Finance* 8, no. 1 (spring 1995): 43–52.

[101]Clifford W. Smith, Jr., "Investment Banking and the Capital Acquisition Process," *Journal of Financial Economics* 15, no. 1/2 (January/February 1986): 3–29.

[102]Michael C. Jensen and Jerald B. Warner, "The Distribution of Power among Corporate Managers, Shareholders, and Directors," *Journal of Financial Economics* 20, no. 1/2 (January/March 1988): 3–24.

[103]Katherine Spiess and John Affleck-Graves, "Underperformance in Long-Run Stock Returns Following Seasoned Equity Offerings," *Journal of Financial Economics* 38, no. 3 (July 1995): 243–267; and Katherine Spiess and John Affleck-Graves, "The Long-Run Performance of Common Stock Following Debt Offerings," *Journal of Financial Economics,* forthcoming.

In sharp contrast, the numerous studies on predicting rates of return over time or for a cross section of stocks presented evidence that indicated markets were not semistrong efficient. This included time-series studies on dividend yields, risk premiums, calendar patterns, and quarterly earnings surprises. Equally pervasive were the anomalous results for cross-sectional predictors, such as market value size, the BV/MV ratio (both of these when there is expansive monetary policy), E/P ratios, and neglected firms.

Strong-Form Hypothesis: Tests and Results

The strong-form EMH contends that stock prices fully reflect *all information*, public and private. This implies that no group of investors has access to *private information* that will allow them to consistently experience above-average profits. This extremely rigid hypothesis requires not only that stock prices must adjust rapidly to new public information, but also that no group has access to private information.

Tests of the strong-form EMH have analyzed returns over time for different identifiable investment groups to determine whether any group consistently received above-average risk-adjusted returns. To consistently earn positive abnormal returns, the group must have continuing access to important private information or an ability to consistently act on public information before other investors. Such results would indicate that security prices were not adjusting rapidly to *all* new information.

Investigators interested in testing this form of the EMH have analyzed the performance of four major groups of investors. First, several researchers have analyzed the returns experienced by *corporate insiders* from their stock trading. Another group of studies analyzed the returns available to *stock exchange specialists.* The third group of tests examined the ability of the group of *security analysts* at Value Line and elsewhere to select stocks that will outperform the market. Finally, a number of studies have examined the overall performance of *professional money managers.* The analysis of money managers' performance emphasized the risk-adjusted returns experienced by mutual funds because of the availability of data. Recently. these tests have been replicated for pension plans and endowment funds.

CORPORATE INSIDER TRADING Corporate insiders are required to report to the SEC each month their transactions (purchases or sales) in the stock of the firm for which they are insiders. Insiders include major corporate officers, members of the board of directors, and owners of 10 percent or more of any equity class of securities. About 6 weeks after the reporting period, this insider trading information is made public by the SEC. These insider trading data have been used to identify how corporate insiders have traded and determine whether they bought on balance before abnormally good price movements and sold on balance before poor market periods for their stock.[104] The results of these studies have generally indicated that corporate insiders consistently enjoyed above-average profits, especially on purchase transactions.

Jaffe found that public investors who consistently traded with the insiders based on announced insider transactions would have enjoyed excess risk-adjusted returns (after commissions).[105] Kerr tested this trading rule and concluded that the market had eliminated

[104]The early studies on this topic are James H. Lorie and Victor Niederhoffer, "Predictive and Statistical Properties of Insider Trading," *Journal of Law and Economics* 11 (April 1968): 35–53; Joseph E. Finnerty, "Insiders and Market Efficiency," *Journal of Finance* 31, no. 4 (September 1976): 1141–1148; and Joseph E. Finnerty, "Insiders Activity and Inside Information: A Multivariate Analysis," *Journal of Financial and Quantitative Analysis* 11, no. 2 (June 1976): 205–215.

[105]Jeffrey F. Jaffe, "Special Information and Inside Trading," *Journal of Business* 47, no. 2 (April 1974): 410–428.

this inefficiency.[106] Trivoli contended that you can substantially increase the returns from using insider trading information by combining it with key financial ratios.[107] Nunn, Madden, and Gombola contended that you should consider which group of insiders (board chair, officers, directors versus other insiders) is doing the buying and selling.[108] Seyhun also agreed that the realizable return to investors who attempt to act on insider reports was not positive after considering total transaction costs. Finally, a study by Pettit and Venkatesh has results that show a significant relationship between insider trading and longer-term security performance.[109]

Overall, these results provide mixed support for the EMH. Although several studies indicate the ability for insiders to experience abnormal profits, an almost equal number of studies indicate it is no longer possible for the noninsider to use this information to receive excess returns. Lee and Solt and subsequent authors found it is not possible to use *aggregate* insider trading activity as a guide to market timing.[110] Notably, because of investor interest in these data as a result of academic research, the *Wall Street Journal* currently publishes a monthly column entitled "Inside Track" that discusses the largest insider transactions.

STOCK EXCHANGE SPECIALISTS Several studies examining the function of stock exchange specialists have determined that specialists have monopolistic access to certain very important information about unfilled limit orders. One would expect specialists to derive above-average returns from this information. This expectation is generally supported by the data. Specialists seem generally to make money because they typically sell shares at higher prices than they purchase shares. Also, they apparently make money when they buy or sell after unexpected announcements and when they trade in large blocks of stock.

An SEC study in the early 1970s examined the rates of return earned on capital by the specialists.[111] The results indicated that these rates of return were substantially above normal, which would not support the strong-form EMH. In fairness to current specialists, the prevailing environment differs substantially from that in the early 1970s. More recent results indicate that specialists are experiencing much lower rates of return following the introduction of competitive rates and other trading practices that have reduced specialists' fees.

---

[106]Halbert Kerr, "The Battle of Insider Trading and Market Efficiency," *Journal of Portfolio Management* 6, no. 4 (summer 1980): 47–50. These results are supported by Michael S. Rozeff and Mir A. Zaman, "Market Efficiency and Insider Trading: New Evidence," *Journal of Business* 61, no. 1 (January 1988): 25–44.

[107]George W. Trivoli, "How to Profit from Insider Trading Information," *Journal of Portfolio Management* 6, no. 4 (summer 1980): 51–56.

[108]Kenneth P. Nunn, Jr., Gerald P. Madden, and Michael J. Gombola, "Are Some Insiders More 'Inside' Than Others?" *Journal of Portfolio Management* 9, no. 3 (spring 1982): 18–22. This was supported in H. Nejat Seyhun, "Insiders' Profits, Costs of Trading, and Market Efficiency," *Journal of Financial Economics* 16, no. 2 (June 1986): 189–212.

[109]R. Richardson Pettit and P. C. Venkatesh, "Insider Trading and Long-Run Return Performance," *Financial Management* 24, no. 2 (summer 1995): 88–103.

[110]Wayne Y. Lee and Michael E. Solt, "Insider Trading: A Poor Guide to Market Timing," *Journal of Portfolio Management* 12, no. 4 (summer 1986): 65–71. These results are generally confirmed in H. N. Seyhun, "The Information Content of Aggregate Insider Trading," *The Journal of Business* 61, no. 1 (January 1988): 1–24; and in M. Chowdhury, J. S. Howe, and J. C. Lin, "The Relation between Aggregate Insider Transactions and Stock Market Returns," *Journal of Financial and Quantitative Analysis* 28, no. 3 (September 1993): 431–437.

[111]*Report of the Special Study of the Security Markets* (Washington, D.C.: Securities and Exchange Commission, 1963): Part 2, 54.

SECURITY ANALYSTS Several tests have considered whether it is possible to identify a set of analysts who have the ability to select stocks that are undervalued. These tests involve determining whether there are significant abnormal returns available to those who invest after the recommendations by some set of analysts are public. These studies and those that follow regarding the performance of money managers are more realistic and relevant than the prior discussion that considered corporate insiders and stock exchange specialists because these analysts and money managers are full-time investment professionals with no obvious advantage except emphasis and training. If anyone should be able to select undervalued stocks, it should be these "pros." The first group of tests examine Value Line rankings, followed by an analysis of recommendations by individual analysts.

The Value Line Enigma Value Line (VL) is a large, well-known advisory service that publishes financial information on approximately 1,700 stocks. Included in its report is a timing rank, which indicates Value Line's expectation regarding a firm's common stock performance over the coming 12 months. A rank of 1 indicates VL expects the most favorable performance and 5 indicates VL expects the worst performance. This ranking system, initiated in April 1965, assigns numbers based on four factors:

1. An earnings and price rank of each security relative to all others
2. A price momentum factor
3. Year-to-year relative changes in quarterly earnings
4. A quarterly earnings "surprise" factor (i.e., actual quarterly earnings compared with VL estimated earnings.)

The firms are ranked based on a composite score for each firm. The top and bottom 100 are ranked 1 and 5 respectively, the next 300 from the top and bottom are ranked 2 and 4, and the rest (approximately 900) are ranked 3. Rankings are assigned every week based on the latest data. Notably, all the data used to derive the four factors are public information.

The preliminary ranking is made every Wednesday, and the final ranking is sent to the printer on Friday (there are typically five or six changes between Wednesday and Friday due to unusual new information). The new rankings are ready to be distributed on the following Wednesday, and Value Line attempts a staggered mailing so that everyone receives the weekly *Survey* on Friday.

Several years after the ranking was started, Value Line indicated that the performance of the stocks in the various ranks differed substantially. Specifically, it was contended that the stocks rated 1 substantially outperformed the market, and the stocks rated 5 seriously underperformed the market (the performance figures did not include dividend income but also did not charge commissions).

Black tested the Value Line system over the period 1965–1970 by constructing portfolios grouped by rank and revising the portfolios monthly.[112] He concluded that rank-1 firms outperformed rank-5 firms by 20 percent per year on a risk-adjusted basis and that even with round-trip transaction costs of 2 percent, the net rate of return for a long position in rank-1 stocks would have been positive. Holloway examined the top 100 stocks and concluded that if you adjusted your portfolio weekly, the returns would be superior before transaction costs—but not after.[113] Alternatively, assuming annual portfolio revisions, there were abnormal returns after transaction costs.

---

[112]Fischer Black, "Yes, Virginia, There Is Hope: Tests of the Value Line Ranking System," *Financial Analysts Journal* 29, no. 5 (September–October 1973): 10–14.

[113]Clark Holloway, "A Note on Testing an Aggressive Investment Strategy Using Value Line Ranks," *Journal of Finance* 36, no. 3 (June 1981): 711–719.

Copeland and Mayers found that the abnormal returns were consistent with the rankings, but only the returns for rank 5 were significantly negative, implying that VL has the ability to select underperformers.[114] An analysis of a strategy of buying upgraded stocks and selling short stocks that were downgraded indicated significant negative abnormal returns for down-ranked stocks, but only limited significance for stocks that were upgraded. Finally, although the negative abnormal returns for the rank-5 portfolios were *statistically* significant, the trading rules were not profitable after transaction costs.

Stickel found that although all rank changes affect stock prices, the most significant impact occurs when stocks go from rank 2 to 1.[115] Other changes in rank were followed by statistically significant changes that were much smaller than for a move from 2 to 1. Stickel contends that the price movements require three days, but he counts Thursday as Day 0 because some people might receive the *Value Line Survey* on Thursday. Clearly, after Monday, there is no significant impact. Also, smaller firms experienced a larger reaction to changes in rank, and the change requires several days. However, acting on the rank change from 2 to 1 for the smallest firms would not be profitable due to the large transaction costs of small firms. Therefore, although evidence shows that there is information content in VL rank changes and that the price adjustment is not instantaneous, some recent evidence indicates that the absolute price change is possibly *not* large enough to generate excess returns after transaction costs.

To see if the VL record is a result of the firm size phenomenon, Huberman and Kandel examined the relationship between the VL recommendation and firm size.[116] The overall results indicated no relationship between the VL rankings and size. Also, although the VL investment service favors large firms, the system appears to be better at predicting the relative returns on small-firm stocks.

Peterson examined the daily price changes around the release of initial reviews and consequent new rankings of stocks.[117] The analysis considers the day before official release, the release day, and the following day (typically Thursday, Friday, and Monday). The portfolio returns for stocks ranked 1 were significant on Days −1, 0, and +1, individually and combined. In general, there were no significant abnormal returns for stocks assigned any other ranking, which implies that these other rankings contain very little information. Notably, there were no significant price changes after Day +1. It is concluded that there is information in some of the rankings (mainly rank 1), but the market is fairly efficient in adjusting to them.

Finally, as noted previously, one of the four factors considered by VL when ranking firms is quarterly earnings "surprises." Affleck-Graves and Mendenhall contend that the longer-term abnormal returns from the VL ranking are really caused by the quarterly post-earnings announcement drift that follows the earnings' "surprise" as discussed earlier.[118] That is, the authors contend that this VL anomaly is caused by the quarterly earnings anomaly.

---

[114]Thomas E. Copeland and David Mayers, "The Value Line Enigma (1965–1978): A Case Study of Performance Evaluation Issues," *Journal of Financial Economics* 10, no. 3 (November 1982): 289–321.

[115]Scott E. Stickel, "The Effect of Value Line Investment Survey Changes on Common Stock Prices," *Journal of Financial Economics* 14, no. 1 (March 1985): 121–143.

[116]Gur Huberman and Shmuel Kandel, "Value Line Rank and Firm Size," *Journal of Business* 60, no. 4 (October 1987): 577–589; and Gur Huberman and Shmuel Kandel, "Market Efficiency and Value Line's Record," *Journal of Business* 63, no. 2 (April 1990): 187–216.

[117]David R. Peterson, "Security Price Reactions to Initial Reviews of Common Stock by the Value Line Investment Survey," *Journal of Financial and Quantitative Analysis* 22, no. 4 (December 1987): 483–494.

[118]John Affleck-Graves and Richard R. Mendenhall, "The Relation between the Value Line Enigma and Post-Earnings-Announcement Drift," *Journal of Financial Economics* 31, no. 1 (February 1992): 75–96.

The studies on the Value Line enigma indicate that there is information in the VL rankings (especially either rank 1 or 5) and in changes in the rankings (especially going from 2 to 1). Although these changes in rank have a larger effect on smaller firms, there is no direct relationship between the VL rankings and the size anomaly. Further, most of the recent evidence indicates that the market is fairly efficient because the abnormal adjustments appear to be complete by Day +2. An analysis of study results over time indicates a faster adjustment to the rankings during recent years. In fact, a study by Hulbert indicates weaker performance for rank-1 stocks after 1983.[119] Also, although there are statistically significant price changes, there is mounting evidence that it is not possible to derive abnormal returns from announcements after considering realistic transaction costs. Some of the strongest evidence in this regard is the fact that Value Line's Centurion Fund, which concentrates on rank-1 stocks, has consistently underperformed the market over the past decade.

Analysts' Recommendations Mixed evidence exists regarding whether analysts possess private information. Studies by Lloyd-Davies and Canes and by Lin, Smith, and Syed found that the prices of stocks mentioned in the *Wall Street Journal* column "Heard on the Street" experience a significant change on the day the column appears, in contrast to Desai and Jain, who examined the performance of stocks recommended by "superstar" money managers at *Barron's* roundtable and found abnormal returns of 1.91 percent from the meeting date to the publication date, but *zero* abnormal returns for all postpublication holding periods.[120] A recent comprehensive examination of analysts' recommendations by Womack finds that analysts appear to have both market timing and stock picking ability, especially in connection with sell recommendations that are relatively rare.[121]

PERFORMANCE OF PROFESSIONAL MONEY MANAGERS As discussed previously, the studies of professional money managers are more realistic and widely applicable than the analysis of insiders and specialists because money managers typically do not have monopolistic access to important new information. Still, they are highly trained professionals who work full time at investment management. Therefore, if any "normal" set of investors should derive above-average profits, it would be this group. Also, if any noninsider should derive inside information, professional money managers would because they conduct extensive management interviews.

Most studies on the performance of money managers have examined mutual funds because performance data are readily available. Only recently have data been available for bank trust departments, insurance companies, and investment advisors. The original mutual fund studies indicated that most funds could not match the performance of a buy-and-hold policy.[122] When risk-adjusted returns were examined *without* considering commission

---

[119]Mark Hulbert, "Proof of Pudding," *Forbes,* 10 December 1990, 316.

[120]Peter Lloyd-Davies and Michael Canes, "Stock Prices and the Publication of Second-Hand Information," *Journal of Business* 51, no. 1 (January 1987): 43–56; Pu Lin, Stanley D. Smith, and Axmat A. Syed, "Security Price Reaction to The *Wall Street Journal's* Securities Recommendations," *Journal of Financial and Quantitative Analysis* 25, no. 3 (September 1990): 399–410; and Hemang Desai and Prem Jain, "An Analysis of the Recommendations of the 'Superstars' Money Managers at *Barron's* Annual Roundtable," *Journal of Finance* 50, no. 4 (September 1995): 1257–1273.

[121]Kent L. Womack, "Do Brokerage Analysts' Recommendations Have Investment Value?" *Journal of Finance* 51, no. 1 (March 1996): 137–167.

[122]Notable studies include William F. Sharpe, "Mutual Fund Performance," *Journal of Business* 39, no. 1 (January 1966 Supplement): 119–139; Michael Jensen, "The Performance of Mutual Funds in the Period 1945–1964," *Journal of Finance* 23, no. 2 (May 1968): 389–416; and Jack L. Treynor, "How to Rate Management of Investment Funds," *Harvard Business Review* 43, no. 1 (January–February 1965): 63–75. These studies and others on this topic are reviewed in Chapter 27.

costs, slightly more than half of the money managers did better than the overall market. When commission costs, load fees, and management costs were considered, approximately two-thirds of the mutual funds did *not* match aggregate market performance. Also, Shukla and Trzcinka (ST) found that funds were generally inconsistent in their performance and the only persistence was in inferior performance, which led Stewart to contend that consistency should be a major factor in judging performance.[123]

Studies by Henriksson and by Chang and Lewellen provided similar results on performance.[124] In contrast, Ippolito found that funds during the period 1965–1984 beat the market after research and transaction costs.[125] Finally, Elton, Gruber, Davis, and Aklarka used a three-factor model to measure risk and found that during the Ippolito period, the abnormal returns using more extensive risk measurement were negative.[126] Therefore, the vast majority of money manager studies support the EMH with results that indicate mutual fund managers generally cannot beat a buy-and-hold policy.

As noted, recently it has been possible to get performance data for pension plans and endowment funds. Given these data, a study by Brinson. Hood, and Beebower as well as several other studies have documented that the performances of pension plans did not match that of the aggregate market.[127] Likewise, Berkowitz, Finney, and Logue documented that the performance of endowment funds was not able to beat a buy-and-hold policy.[128]

The figures in Table 7.3 provide a rough demonstration of these results. These data are collected by Frank Russell Analytical Services as part of its performance evaluation service. Table 7.3 contains the median rates of return for several investment groups compared to the Standard & Poor's 500 Index.[129]

Looking at the long-term, 10-year results, the first set of universes are banks that experienced returns above the Standard & Poor's 500 during the long-term periods (6, 8, 10 years), but not during the recent periods. The mutual funds never had superior results (apparently, during 1998, about 90 percent of the mutual funds underperformed the S&P 500). Finally, the four equity-style universes typically did better. In summary, 7 of the 10 universes beat the market for the 10-year period. Notably, these results are *not* adjusted for risk. Interestingly, these results are generally not consistent with the mutual fund results and would not support the strong-form EMH.

---

[123]Ravi Shukla and Charles Trzcinka, "Persistent Performance in the Mutual Fund Market: Tests with Funds and Investment Advisors," *Review of Quantitative Finance and Accounting* 4, no. 2 (June 1994): 115–135; and Scott D. Stewart, "Is Consistency of Performance a Good Measure of Manager Skill?" *Journal of Portfolio Management* 24, no. 3 (spring 1998): 22–32.

[124]Roy t. Henriksson, "Market Timing and Mutual Fund Performance: An Empirical Investigation," *Journal of Business* 57, no. 1, part 1 (January 1984): 73–96; and Eric C. Chang and Wilber G. Lewellen, "Market Timing and Mutual Fund Investment Performance," *Journal of Business* 57, no. 1, part 1 (January 1984): 57–72.

[125]Richard A. Ippolito, "Efficiency with Costly Information: A Study of Mutual Fund Performance, 1965–84," *Quarterly Journal of Economics* 104, no. 1 (March 1989): 1–23.

[126]Edwin Elton, Martin J. Gruber, Sanjiv Davis, and Matt Aklarka, "Efficiency with Costly Information: A Reinterpretation of Evidence from Managed Portfolios" (New York University Graduate School of Business, 1994).

[127]Gary P. Brinson, Randolph Hood, and Gilbert Beebower, "Determinants of Portfolio Performance," *Financial Analysts Journal* 43, no. 4 (July–August 1986): 39–44; Alicia Munnell, "Who Should Manage the Assets of Collectively Bargained Pension Plans?" *New England Economic Review* (July–August 1983): 18–30; and Richard A. Ippolito and John A. Turner, "Turnover Fees and Pension Plan Performance," *Financial Analysts Journal* 43, no. 6 (November–December 1987): 16–26.

[128]Stephen A. Berkowitz, Louis D. Finney, and Dennis E. Logue, *The Investment Performance of Corporate Pension Plans* (New York: Quorum Books, 1988).

[129]The results for these individual accounts have an upward bias because they consider only accounts retained (e.g., if a firm or bank does a poor job on an account and the client leaves, those results would not be included).

TABLE 7.3 **ANNUALIZED RATES OF RETURN DURING ALTERNATIVE PERIODS ENDING DECEMBER 31, 1997**

	1 Year	2 Years	4 Years	6 Years	8 Years	10 Years
U.S. Equity Broad Universe Medians						
Equity accounts	30.6	26.6	21.5	18.1	17.0	18.3
Equity pooled accounts	30.5	26.4	21.6	17.4	16.2	17.5
Equity-oriented separate accounts	30.7	26.8	21.4	18.3	17.3	18.5
Special equity pooled accounts	25.9	22.6	18.2	18.8	17.9	19.5
Mutual Fund Universe Medians						
Balanced mutual funds	20.2	16.8	13.5	12.0	12.4	13.0
Equity mutual funds	26.3	22.8	18.2	16.1	15.1	16.2
U.S. Equity-Style Universe Medians						
Growth equity accounts	31.3	26.3	20.8	16.4	18.0	19.2
Small capitalization accounts	25.5	24.4	19.4	19.6	18.0	19.7
Value equity accounts	30.4	26.7	21.6	19.4	16.7	18.2
Market-oriented accounts	31.0	27.0	21.9	18.3	17.3	18.6
S&P 500 Index	33.4	28.2	23.0	18.1	16.7	18.0
Number of Universes with Returns above the S&P 500	0	0	0	5	6	7

Source: Frank Russell Company, Tacoma, WA. Reprinted with permission.

CONCLUSIONS REGARDING THE STRONG-FORM EMH The tests of the strong-form EMH generated mixed results, but the bulk of relevant evidence supported the hypothesis. The results for two unique groups of investors (corporate insiders and stock exchange specialists) did not support the hypothesis because both groups apparently have monopolistic access to important information and use it to derive above-average returns.

Tests to determine whether there are analysts with private information concentrated on the Value Line rankings and publications of analysts' recommendations. The results for Value Line rankings have changed over time and currently lean toward support for the EMH. Specifically, although it appears that the VL rankings have information, it also appears that the adjustment to rankings and ranking changes is fairly rapid, and that trading is not profitable after transaction costs. Also, there is a question whether the Value Line anomaly is really due to the quarterly earnings surprise anomaly. Alternatively, the evidence regarding the value of analysts' recommendations is mixed, but apparently some analysts' recommendations (especially sell recommendations) seem to contain significant information.

Finally, the performance by professional money managers has generally provided support for the strong-form EMH. The vast majority of money manager performance studies, which have typically examined the performance of mutual fund managers, have indicated that the investments by these highly trained, full-time investors could not consistently outperform a simple buy-and-hold policy on a risk-adjusted basis. This has been consistently true for mutual funds, with mixed results for pension plans and endowment funds. Because these money managers are similar to most investors who do not have consistent access to inside information, these results are considered more relevant to the hypothesis. Therefore, there appears to be overall support for the strong-form EMH as applied to most investors.

IMPLICATIONS OF EFFICIENT CAPITAL MARKETS

Having reviewed numerous studies related to different facets of the EMH, the important question is: What does this mean to individual investors, financial analysts, portfolio managers, and institutional investors? Overall, the results of numerous studies indicate that the capital markets are efficient as related to numerous sets of information. At the same time, a growing number of studies have uncovered a substantial number of instances where the market apparently does not adjust rapidly to public information. Given these mixed results regarding the existence of efficient capital markets, it is very important to consider the implications of this contrasting evidence of market efficiency.

The following discussion considers the implications of both sets of evidence. Specifically, given results that support the EMH, we consider what techniques will not work and what you do if you can't beat the market. In contrast, because of the evidence that fails to support the EMH, we discuss what information should he considered when attempting to actively manage a portfolio and derive superior investment results.

Efficient Markets and Technical Analysis

The assumptions of technical analysis directly oppose the notion of efficient markets. A basic premise of technical analysis is that stock prices move in trends that persist.[130] Technicians believe that when new information comes to the market, it is not immediately available to everyone but typically is disseminated from the informed professional to the aggressive investing public and then to the great bulk of investors. Also, technicians contend that investors do not analyze information and act immediately. This process takes time. Therefore, they hypothesize that stock prices move to a new equilibrium after the release of new information in a gradual manner, which causes trends in stock price movements that persist for certain periods.

Technical analysts believe that nimble traders can develop systems to detect the beginning of a movement to a new equilibrium (called a "breakout"). Hence, they hope to buy or sell stock immediately after its breakout to take advantage of the subsequent price adjustment.

The belief in this pattern of price adjustment directly contradicts advocates of the EMH who believe that security prices adjust to new information very rapidly. These EMH advocates do not contend, however, that prices adjust perfectly, which means there can be an overadjustment or underadjustment. Still, because it is not certain whether the market will over- or underadjust at any time, you cannot derive abnormal profits from adjustment errors.

If the capital market is weak-form efficient as indicated by most of the results and prices fully reflect all relevant information, no technical trading system that depends only on past trading data should have any value. By the time the market information is public, the price adjustment has taken place. Therefore, a purchase or sale using a technical trading rule that only uses historical market information should not generate abnormal returns after considering risk and transaction costs.

Efficient Markets and Fundamental Analysis

As you know from our prior discussion, fundamental analysts believe that, at any time, there is a basic intrinsic value for the aggregate stock market, various industries, or individual securities and that these values depend on underlying economic factors. Therefore, a fundamental analyst would determine the intrinsic value of an investment asset at a point

[130]Chapter 21 contains an extensive discussion of technical analysis.

in time by examining the variables that determine value, such as future earnings' cash flows, interest rates, and risk variables. If the prevailing market price differs from the intrinsic value by enough to cover transaction costs, an investor should take appropriate action: Buy if the market price is substantially below intrinsic value and sell if it is above. Fundamental analysts believe that occasionally market price and intrinsic value differ, but eventually investors recognize the discrepancy and correct it.

If you can do a superior job of *estimating* intrinsic value, you can consistently make superior market timing (asset allocation) decisions or acquire undervalued securities and generate above-average returns. Fundamental analysis involves aggregate market analysis, industry analysis, company analysis, and portfolio management. The divergent results from the EMH research have important implications for all of these components of fundamental analysis and are discussed in the following subsections.

AGGREGATE MARKET ANALYSIS WITH EFFICIENT CAPITAL MARKETS Chapters 13 and 14 make a strong case that intrinsic value analysis should use a top-down approach and begin with aggregate market analysis. Still the EMH implies that if you examine only *past* economic events, it is unlikely that you will outperform a buy-and-hold policy because the market adjusts very rapidly to known economic events. Evidence suggests that the market experiences long-run price movements, but to take advantage of these movements in an efficient market, you must do a superior job of *estimating* the relevant economic variables that cause these long-run movements. Put another way, if you only use *historical* data to estimate future values and invest on the basis of these estimates from historical data, you will not experience superior risk-adjusted returns.

INDUSTRY AND COMPANY ANALYSIS WITH EFFICIENT CAPITAL MARKETS As discussed in Chapter 19, the wide range of returns from different industries and companies during a period of time and over time clearly justifies industry and company analysis. Again, the EMH does not contradict the potential value of such fundamental analyses, but it does imply that to be successful you need to (1) understand the relevant variables that affect rates of return, and (2) do a superior job of *estimating* movements in these relevant valuation variables. To demonstrate this, Malkiel and Cragg developed a model that did an excellent job of explaining *past* stock price movements using historical data. When this valuation model was used to project *future* stock price changes but continued using *past* company data, however, the results were consistently inferior to a buy-and-hold policy.[131] This implies that, even with a good valuation model, you *cannot* select stocks that will provide superior returns using only past data as inputs.

Another study showed that the crucial difference between stocks that enjoyed the best and worst price performance during a given year was the relationship between expected earnings of professional analysts and actual earnings (i.e., earnings surprises). Specifically, stock prices increased if actual earnings substantially exceeded expected earnings (i.e., there was a positive earnings surprise) and fell if earnings did not reach expected levels (i.e., there was a negative earnings surprise).[132] Thus, if you can do a superior job of projecting earnings and your expectations *differ from the consensus,* you will probably have a

---

[131]Burton G. Malkiel and John G. Cragg, "Expectations and the Structure of Share Prices," *American Economic Review* 60, no. 4 (September 1970): 601–617.

[132]Gary A. Benesh and Pamela P. Peterson, "On the Relation between Earnings Changes, Analysts' Forecasts and Stock Price Fluctuations," *Financial Analysts Journal* 41, no. 6 (November–December 1986).

superior stock selection record. Put another way, *you must be able to predict earnings surprises.*[133]

The quest to be a superior analyst holds some good news and some suggestions. The good news is related to the strong-form tests that indicated the likely existence of superior analysts. It was shown that the rankings by Value Line contained information value, even though it might not be possible to profit from it after transaction costs. Also, the short-run and long-term price adjustment to the publication of analysts' recommendations indicates that there are superior analysts. The point is, there clearly are some superior analysts, but there are only a limited number of them and it is not easy to be among this select group. Most notably, to be a superior analyst, your must do an superior job of *estimating* the relevant valuation variables and predicting earnings surprises.

The suggestions for those involved in fundamental analysis are based on the studies that considered the cross section of future returns. As noted, these studies indicated that E/P ratios, size, and the BV/MV ratios were able to differentiate future return patterns with size and the BV/MV ratio appearing to be the optimal combination. Therefore, these factors should be considered when selecting a universe of stocks for intensive analysis or analyzing individual stocks. In addition, the evidence suggests that the monetary environment is very important and neglected firms should be given extra consideration.

HOW TO EVALUATE ANALYSTS OR INVESTORS If you want to determine if an individual is a superior analyst or investor, you should examine the performance of numerous securities that this analyst or investor recommends over time in relation to the performance of a set of randomly selected stocks of equal risk. The stock selections of a superior analyst or investor should *consistently* outperform the randomly selected stocks. The consistency requirement is crucial because you would expect a portfolio developed by random selection to outperform the market about half the time.

CONCLUSIONS ABOUT FUNDAMENTAL ANALYSIS A text on investments can indicate the relevant variables that you should analyze and describe the important analysis techniques, but estimating the relevant variables is as much an art and a product of hard work as it is a science. If the estimates could be done on the basis of some mechanical formula, you could program a computer to do it, and there would be no need for analysts. Therefore, the superior analyst or successful investor must understand what variables are relevant to the valuation process and have the ability to do a superior job of *estimating* these variables. Alternatively, one can be superior if he or she has the ability to interpret the impact or estimate the effect of some public information better than others.

Efficient Markets and Portfolio Management

As noted, a number of studies have indicated that professional money managers generally do not beat a buy-and-hold policy on a risk-adjusted basis. One explanation for this generally inferior performance is that there are no superior analysts and the cost of research forces the results of merely adequate analysis into the inferior category. Another explanation, which is favored by the author and has some empirical support from the Value Line and the analyst recommendation results, is that money management firms employ both superior and inferior analysts, and the gains from the recommendations by the few superior

[133]This is a major point made in H. Russell Fogler, "A Modern Theory of Security Analysis," *Journal of Portfolio Management* 19, no. 3 (spring 1993): 6–14. Additional suggestions of what security analysts should do is contained in Peter L. Bernstein, "The Expected Return of the Security Analyst," *Financial Analysts Journal* 54, no. 2 (March–April 1998): 4, 6–8.

analysts are offset by the costs of the research department and the poor results due to the recommendations of the inferior analysts.

This raises the question: Should a portfolio be managed actively or passively? The point of the following discussion is that the decision of how one manages the portfolio (actively or passively) should depend on whether the manager has access to superior analysts. A portfolio manager with access to superior analysts or an investor who feels he or she has the time and expertise to be a superior investor can manage a portfolio actively, looking for undervalued securities based upon superior fundamental analysis, including predicting earnings surprises, and attempting to time the market wherein asset allocation is shifted between aggressive and defensive positions, depending on the investor's outlook for the market. In contrast, without superior analysts or the time and ability to be a superior investor, you should manage passively and assume that all securities are properly priced based on their levels of risk. The following subsections consider these two alternatives in more detail.[134]

PORTFOLIO MANAGEMENT WITH SUPERIOR ANALYSTS A portfolio manager with access to superior analysts who have unique insights and analytical ability should follow their recommendations. The superior analysts should make investment recommendations for a certain proportion of the portfolio, and the portfolio manager should ensure that the risk preferences of the client are maintained.

Also, the superior analysts should be encouraged to concentrate their efforts in mid-cap stocks that possess the liquidity required by institutional portfolio managers, but because they do not receive the substantial attention given to the large cap stocks, the markets for these neglected stocks may be less efficient than the market for large cap stocks.

Recall that capital markets are expected to be efficient because many investors receive new information and analyze its effect on security values. If the number of analysts following a stock differ, one could conceive of differences in the efficiency of the markets. New information on large cap stocks is well publicized and rigorously analyzed. As a result, the price of these securities should adjust rapidly to reflect the new information. In contrast, mid-cap firms receive less publicity, fewer analysts follow these firms because there is less institutional interest in them, and prices adjust less rapidly to new information. Therefore, the possibility of finding temporarily undervalued securities among these relatively neglected stocks is greater. Again, in line with the cross-section study results, these superior analysts should pay particular attention to neglected firms' BV/MV ratio, to the size of stocks being analyzed, and to the monetary policy environment.[135]

PORTFOLIO MANAGEMENT WITHOUT SUPERIOR ANALYSTS If you do not have access to superior analysts, your procedure should be as follows. First, you should *measure your risk preferences* or those of your clients. Then build a portfolio to

[134]For a discussion of this decision based upon active-manager skill, see Eric H. Sorenson, Keith Miller, and Vele Samak, "Allocating between Active and Passive Management," *Financial Analysts Journal* 54, no. 5 (September–October 1998): 18–31.

[135]The strongest evidence in this regard is contained in Eugene F. Fama and Kenneth French, "The Cross-Section of Expected Stock Returns," *Journal of Finance* 47, no. 2 (June 1992): 427–465. One should also read several of the follow-up studies on the BV/MV ratio (P/B) that were discussed earlier in this chapter, as well as the Jensen, Johnson, and Mercer studies that indicated the importance of the monetary environment. Further support for considering monetary policy is contained in Willem Thorbecke, "On Stock Market Returns and Monetary Policy," *Journal of Finance* 52, no. 2 (June 1997): 635–654; and Alex D. Patelis, "Stock Return Predictability and the Role of Monetary Policy," *Journal of Finance* 52, no. 5 (December 1997): 1951–1972.

match this risk level by investing a certain proportion of the portfolio in risky assets and the rest in a risk-free asset as will be discussed in Chapter 9.

You must *completely diversify* the risk-asset portfolio on a global basis so it moves consistently with the world market. In this context, proper diversification means eliminating all unsystematic (unique) variability. In Chapter 3, we discussed studies that estimated the number of securities needed to gain most of the benefits (over 90 percent) of a completely diversified portfolio was about 15 to 20. More than 100 stocks are required for complete diversification. To decide how many securities to actually include in your portfolio, you must balance the added benefits of complete worldwide diversification against the costs of research for the additional stocks. To diversify globally will require international securities that are probably best added via mutual funds.

Finally, you should *minimize transaction costs.* Assuming that the portfolio is completely diversified and is structured for the desired risk level, excessive transaction costs that do not generate added returns will detract from your expected rate of return. Three factors are involved in minimizing total transaction costs.

1. Minimize taxes. Methods of accomplishing this objective vary, but it should receive prime consideration.
2. Reduce trading turnover. You should trade only to liquidate part of the portfolio or to maintain a given risk level.
3. When you trade, minimize liquidity cost by trading relatively liquid stocks. To accomplish this, you should submit limit orders to buy or sell several stocks at prices that approximate the specialist's quote. That is, you would put in limit orders to buy stock at the bid price or sell at the ask price. The stock that is bought or sold first is the most liquid one; all other orders should be withdrawn.

In summary, if you do not have access to superior analysts, you should do the following:

1. Determine and quantify your risk preferences.
2. Construct the appropriate risk-level portfolio by dividing the total portfolio between lending or borrowing risk-free assets and a portfolio of risky assets.
3. Diversify completely on a global basis to eliminate all unsystematic risk.
4. Maintain the specified risk level by rebalancing when necessary.
5. Minimize taxes and total transaction costs.

THE RATIONALE AND USE OF INDEX FUNDS As the prior discussion indicates, efficient capital markets and a limited number of superior analysts imply that many portfolios should be managed so that their performance matches that of the aggregate market, minimizing the costs of research and trading. The idea is, if you don't have superior analysts who can beat the market, then simply attempt to *match* the market at the lowest cost. In response to this desire, several institutions have introduced *market funds,* also referred to as *index funds,* which are security portfolios designed to duplicate the composition and therefore the performance of a selected market index series.

Three major investment services started equity index funds in the early 1970s that were intended to match the performance of the S&P 500 index: American National Bank and Trust Company of Chicago; Batterymarch Financial Management Corporation of Boston; and Wells Fargo Investment Advisors, a division of Wells Fargo Bank in San Francisco. Analysis by the author has documented that the correlation of quarterly rates of return for these index funds and the S&P 500 has historically exceeded 0.98. This shows that the funds generally fulfill their stated goal of matching market performance.

Although these initial index funds were available only to institutional investors, subsequently a number of index mutual funds have become available to individuals. In addition, this concept has been extended beyond U.S. stocks to other areas of investments. Index bond funds attempt to emulate the bond-market indexes discussed in Chapter 5. Also, there are indexes that focus on specific segments of the market, such as international bond index funds, international stock index funds that target specific countries, and even index funds that target small capitalization stocks in the United States and Japan.[136]The point is, when portfolio managers decide they want a given asset class in their portfolio to aid diversification, they often look for index funds for the asset class. The use of index funds to get representation may be easier and less costly in terms of research and commissions, and it may provide the same or better performance than what is available from active portfolio management.[137] Such an approach is consistent with the discussion in Chapter 2 that indicated that the most significant factor explaining portfolio performance is asset allocation.

EFFICIENCY IN EUROPEAN EQUITY MARKETS

With rare exception, the discussion in this chapter has been concerned with the efficiency of U.S. markets. The growing importance of world markets raises a natural question about the efficiency of securities markets outside the United States. Numerous studies have dealt with this set of questions, and a discussion of them would substantially lengthen the chapter. Fortunately, a monograph by Hawawini contains a review of numerous studies that examined the behavior of European stock prices and evaluated the efficiency of European equity markets.[138] The monograph lists over 280 studies covering 14 Western European countries from Austria to the United Kingdom classified by country and within each country into the following five categories:

1. Market model, beta estimation, and diversification
2. Capital asset pricing model and arbitrage pricing model
3. Weak-form tests of market efficiency
4. Semistrong-form tests of market efficiency
5. Strong-form tests of market efficiency

Hawawini offers the following overall conclusion after acknowledging that European markets are smaller and less active than U.S. markets.

> Our review of the literature indicates that despite the peculiarities of European equity markets, the behavior of European stock prices is, with few exceptions, surprisingly similar to that of U.S. common stocks. That is true even for countries with extremely narrow equity markets such as Finland. The view that most European equity markets, particularly those of smaller countries, are informationally inefficient does not seem to be borne out by the data. We will see that most of the results of empirical tests performed on European common stock prices are generally in line with those reported by researchers who used U.S. data.

[136]For a discussion of some of these indexes, see James A. White, "The Index Boom: It's No Longer Just the S&P 500 Stock Index," *Wall Street Journal,* 19 May 1991, C1, C3.

[137]Two articles that indicate this trend are Terry Williams, "Sandoz Indexes All Large Cap Stocks," *Pensions and Investments*, 8 January 1996, 1; and Sabine Schramm, "Indexed Assets Top $1 Trillion," *Pensions and Investments*, 23 February 1998, 1.

[138]Gabriel Hawawini, *European Equity Markets: Price Behavior and Efficiency*, Monograph 1984–4/5, Monograph Series in Finance and Economics, Salomon Brothers Center for the Study of Financial Institutions, Graduate School of Business, New York University, 1984.

THE INTERNET *Investments Online*

Capital market prices reflect current news items fairly quickly. On the other hand, a portfolio manager should not ignore news just because prices adjust quickly. News provides information the manager can use to structure portfolios and allows him or her to update potential future scenarios.

A number of news sources are available on the Internet. Some of them, such as **www.bloomberg.com, www.ft.com,** and **www.wsj.com,** were listed in previous chapters. Other sites include:

www.pointcast.com This is the Web site of Pointcast, a system that allows you to have news sent directly to your PC, at no charge.

www.cnnfn.com This is the financial network site for the Cable News Network (CNN). The CNN Web site is **www.cnn.com**

www.cnbc.com This is the Web site of the CNBC cable TV station.

www.abcnews.com, www.cbs.com, and **www.nbcnews.com** These are the URLs for news from ABC, CBS, and NBC. The NBC site is the home page of the MSNBC station, which can be reached at **www.msnbc.com** as well.

This implies that when one considers securities markets outside the United States, it is appropriate to assume a level of informational efficiency similar to that for U.S. markets.

Summary

- The efficiency of capital markets has implications for your investment analysis and the management of your portfolio. Capital markets should be efficient because numerous rational, profit-maximizing investors react quickly to the release of new information. Assuming prices reflect new information, they are unbiased estimates of the securities' true, intrinsic value, and there should be a consistent relationship between the return on an investment and its risk.
- The voluminous research on the EMH has been divided into three segments, which have been tested separately. The weak-form EMH states that stock prices fully reflect all market information, so any trading rule that uses past market data to predict future returns should not provide superior risk-adjusted rates of return after transaction costs. The results of most studies consistently supported this hypothesis.
- The semistrong-form EMH asserts that security prices adjust rapidly to the release of all public information. The tests of this hypothesis either examined the opportunities to predict future rates of return (either a time series or a cross section), or they involved event studies in which investigators analyzed whether investors could derive above-average returns from trading on the basis of public information. The test results for this hypothesis were clearly mixed. On the one hand, the results for almost all the event studies related to such events as stock splits, initial public offerings, economic announcements, and accounting changes consistently supported the semistrong hypothesis. In contrast, several studies that examined the ability to predict differential rates of return on the basis of unexpected quarterly earnings, P/E ratios, size, neglected stocks, and the BV/MV ratio, as well as several calendar effects, generally did not support the hypothesis.
- The strong-form EMH states that security prices reflect all information. This implies that nobody has private information so no group should be able to derive above-average returns consistently. Studies that examined the results for corporate insiders and stock exchange specialists do not support the strong-form hypothesis. An analysis of individual analysts as represented by Value Line or by recommendations published in the *Wall Street Journal* gives mixed results. The results indicated that the Value Line rankings have significant information but it may not be possible to profit from it after transaction costs, whereas the recommendations by analysts indicated the existence of private information by some superior analysts. In contrast, the performance by professional money

managers generally supported the EMH because their risk-adjusted investment performance (whether mutual funds, pension funds, or endowment funds) was typically inferior to results achieved with buy-and-hold policies.

- We conclude the chapter with a very important discussion of the implications of all these empirical results. An understanding of these implications is crucial for investors, analysts (fundamental or technical), or portfolio managers because it impacts the subsequent presentations on valuation and portfolio management. The EMH indicates that technical analysis should be of limited value. All forms of fundamental analysis are useful, but they are difficult to implement because they require the ability to *estimate future values* for relevant economic variables. Superior analysis is possible but is *very difficult* because it requires superior projections of the relevant variables, i.e., you need to be accurate and different. Those who manage portfolios should constantly evaluate investment advice to determine whether it is superior.
- Without access to superior analytical advice, you should run your portfolio like an index fund. In contrast, those with superior analytical ability should be allowed to make decisions, but they should concentrate their efforts on mid-cap firms and neglected firms, where there is a higher probability of discovering misvalued stocks. In the analysis, there should be particular concern with alternative firms' BV/MV ratio, the firms' size, and the monetary policy environment.
- This chapter contains some good news and some bad news. The good news is that the practice of investment analysis and portfolio management is not an art that has been lost to the great computer in the sky. Viable careers still await those willing to extend the effort and able to accept the pressures. The bad news is that many bright, hardworking people with extensive resources make the game tough. In fact, those competitors have created a fairly efficient capital market in which it is extremely difficult for most analysts and portfolio managers to achieve superior results.[139]

Questions

1. Discuss the rationale for expecting an efficient capital market. What factor would you look for to differentiate the market for two alternative stocks? Specifically, why should the efficiency of the markets for the stocks differ?
2. Define and discuss the weak-form EMH. Describe the two sets of tests used to examine the weak-form EMH.
3. Define and discuss the semistrong-form EMH. Describe the two sets of tests used to examine the semistrong-form EMH.
4. What is meant by the term *abnormal rate of return?*
5. Describe how you would compute the abnormal rate of return for a stock for a period surrounding an economic event. Give a brief example for a stock with a beta of 1.40.
6. When testing the EMH by comparing alternative trading rules to a buy-and-hold policy, there are three common mistakes that can bias the results against the EMH. Discuss each individually and explain why it would cause a bias.
7. Describe the results of a study that supported the semistrong-form EMH. Discuss the nature of the test and why the results support the hypothesis.
8. Describe the results of a study that did *not* support the semistrong-form EMH. Discuss the nature of the test and specifically why the results reported did not support the hypothesis.
9. For many EMH tests, it is noted that it is really a test of a "joint hypothesis." Discuss what is meant by this concept and, in this instance, what are the joint hypotheses being tested.
10. Define and discuss the strong-form EMH. Why do some observers contend that the strong-form hypothesis requires a perfect market in addition to an efficient market? Be specific.
11. Discuss how you would test the strong-form EMH. Why are these tests relevant? Give a brief example.
12. Describe the results of a study that did *not* support the strong-form EMH. Discuss the test involved and why the test results did not support the hypothesis.

---

[139]For a fairly recent discussion that supports market efficiency despite the challenges from long-term return anomalies, see Eugene F. Fama, "Market Efficiency, Long-Term Returns and Behavioral Finance," *Journal of Financial Economics* 49, no. 3 (September 1998): 283–306.

13. Describe the results of a study that supported the strong-form EMH. Discuss the test involved and why these test results support the hypothesis.
14. What does the EMH imply for the use of technical analysis?
15. What does the EMH imply for fundamental analysis? Discuss specifically what it does *not* imply.
16. In a world of efficient capital markets, what do you have to do to be a superior analyst? Be specific. How would you test whether an analyst were truly superior?
17. What advice would you give to your superior analysts in terms of the set of firms to analyze and variables that should be considered in the analysis? Discuss your reasoning for this advice.
18. How should a portfolio manager without any superior analysts run his or her portfolio?
19. What are the goals of an index fund? Discuss the contention that index funds are the ultimate answer in a world with efficient capital markets.
20. At a social gathering, you meet the portfolio manager for the trust department of a local bank. He confides to you that he has been following the recommendations of the department's six analysts for an extended period and has found that two are superior, two are average. and two are clearly inferior. What would you recommend that he do to run his portfolio?
21. Discuss whether you were surprised by Hawawini's summary of findings related to the EMH for the European equity markets.
22. Describe a test of the weak-form EMH for the Japanese stock market and indicate where you would get the required data.
23. CFA *CFA Examination I (1992)*
    a. List and briefly define the *three* forms of the Efficient Market Hypothesis. [6 minutes]
    b. Discuss the role of a portfolio manager in a perfectly efficient market. [9 minutes]
24. CFA *CFA Examination II (1993)*

    Tom Max, TMP's quantitative analyst, has developed a portfolio construction model about which he is very excited. To create the model, Max made a list of the stocks currently in the S&P 500 Stock Index and obtained annual operating cash flow, price, and total return data for each issue for the past five years. As of each year-end, this universe was divided into five equal-weighted portfolios of 100 issues each, with selection based solely on the price/cash flow rankings of the individual stocks. Each portfolio's average annual return was then calculated.

    During this 5-year period, the linked returns from the portfolios with the lowest price/cash flow ratio generated an annualized total return of 19.0 percent, or 3.1 percentage points better than the 15.9 percent return on the S&P 500 Stock Index. Max also noted that the lowest price/cash flow portfolio had a below-market beta of 0.91 over this same time span.

    a. Briefly comment on Max's use of the beta measure as an indicator of portfolio risk in light of recent academic tests of its explanatory power with respect to stock returns. [5 minutes]
    b. You are familiar with the literature on market anomalies/inefficiencies. Against this background, discuss Max's use of a single-factor model (i.e., price/cash flow) in his research. [8 minutes]
    c. Identify and briefly describe *four* specific concerns about Max's test procedures and/or model design. (The issues already discussed in your answers to parts a and b above may *not* be used in answering part c.) [12 minutes]
25. CFA *CFA Examination III (1995)*
    a. Briefly explain the concept of the *efficient market hypothesis* (EMH) and each of its three forms—*weak, semistrong,* and *strong*—and briefly discuss the degree to which existing empirical evidence supports each of the three forms of the EMH. [8 minutes]
    b. Briefly discuss the implications of the efficient market hypothesis for investment policy as it applies to:
       (i) technical analysis in the form of charting, and
       (ii) fundamental analysis. [4 minutes]
    c. Briefly explain *two* major roles or responsibilities of portfolio managers in an efficient market environment. [4 minutes]
    d. Briefly discuss whether active asset allocation among countries could consistently outperform a world market index. Include a discussion of the implications of *integration versus segmentation* of international financial markets as it pertains to portfolio diversification, but ignore the issue of stock selection. [6 minutes]

Problems

1. Compute the abnormal rates of return for the following stocks during period t (ignore differential systematic risk):

Stock	R_{it}	R_{mt}
B	11.5%	14.0%
F	10.0	8.5
T	14.0	9.6
C	12.0	15.3
E	15.9	12.4

R_{it} = return for stock i during period t
R_{mt} = return for the aggregate market during period t

2. Compute the abnormal rates of return for the five stocks in Problem 1, assuming the following systematic risk measures (betas):

Stock	i
B	0.95
F	1.25
T	1.45
C	0.75
E	−0.30

3. Compare the abnormal returns in Problems 1 and 2, and discuss the reason for the difference in each case.
4. You are given the following data regarding the performance of a group of stocks recommended by an analyst and a set of stocks with matching betas.

Stock	Beginning Price	Ending Price	Dividend
C	43	47	1.50
C-match	22	24	1.00
R	75	73	2.00
R-match	42	38	1.00
L	28	34	1.25
L-match	18	16	1.00
H	52	57	2.00
H-match	38	44	1.50
S	63	68	1.75
S-match	32	34	1.00

Based on the individual and composite results for these stocks (assume equal weights), would you judge this individual to be a superior analyst? Discuss your reasoning.

5. Look up the daily trading volume for the following stocks during a recent 5-day period.
   - Merck
   - Anheuser Busch
   - Intel
   - McDonald's
   - General Electric

   Randomly select five stocks from the NYSE and examine their daily trading volume for the same 5 days.
   a. What are the average daily volumes for the two samples?
   b. Would you expect this difference to have an impact on the efficiency of the markets for the two samples? Why or why not?

References

Ball, Ray, "The Theory of Stock Market Efficiency: Accomplishments and Limitations," *Journal of Applied Corporate Finance* 8, no. 1 (spring 1995).

Berkowitz, Stephen A., Louis D. Finney, and Dennis Logue. *The Investment Performance of Corporate Pension Plans.* New York: Quorum Books, 1988.

Bernard, Victor, "Capital Markets Research in Accounting during the 1980s: A Critical Review." In *The State of Accounting Research as We Enter the 1990s,* ed. Thomas J. Frecka. Urbana: University of Illinois Press, 1989.

Fama, Eugene F. "Efficient Capital Market: II," *Journal of Finance* 46, no. 5 (December 1991).

Haugen, Robert A. *The New Finance.* Englewood Cliffs, N.J.: Prentice Hall, 1995.

Hawawini, Gabriel. *European Equity Markets: Price Behavior and Efficiency.* Monograph 1984–4/5. Monograph Series in Finance and Economics, Salomon Brothers Center for the Study of Financial Institutions, Graduate School of Business, New York University, 1984.

Keim, Donald B., "The CAPM and Equity Return Regularities," *Financial Analysts Journal* 41, no. 3 (May–June 1986).

Keim, Donald B., and Robert F. Stambaugh, "Predicting Returns in Stock and Bond Markets," *Journal of Financial Economics* 17, no. 2 (December 1986).

Lev, Baruch, "On the Usefulness of Earnings and Earning Research: Lessons and Directions from Two Decades of Empirical Research." *Journal of Accounting Research* (Supplement, 1989).

Lorie, James H., Peter Dodd, and Mary Hamilton Kimpton. *The Stock Market: Theories and Evidence.* 2d ed. Homewood, Ill.: Richard D. Irwin, 1985.

Malkiel, Burton G. *A Random Walk Down Wall Street.* New York: W. W. Norton, 1995.

Ou, J., and S. Penman, "Financial Statement Analysis and the Prediction of Stock Returns." *Journal of Accounting and Economics* (November 1989).

Chapter 8

An Introduction to Portfolio Management

After you read this chapter, you should be able to answer the following questions:

- What do we mean by *risk aversion* and what evidence indicates that investors are generally risk averse?
- What are the basic assumptions behind the Markowitz portfolio theory?
- What do we mean by *risk* and what are some of the alternative measures of risk used in investments?
- How do you compute the expected rate of return for an individual risky asset or a portfolio of assets?
- How do you compute the standard deviation of rates of return for an individual risky asset?
- What do we mean by the *covariance* between rates of return and how do you compute covariance?
- What is the relationship between covariance and correlation?
- What is the formula for the standard deviation for a portfolio of risky assets and how does it differ from the standard deviation of an individual risky asset?
- Given the formula for the standard deviation of a portfolio, why and how do you diversify a portfolio?
- What happens to the standard deviation of a portfolio when you change the correlation between the assets in the portfolio?
- What is the risk-return–efficient frontier of risky assets?
- Is it reasonable for alternative investors to select different portfolios from the portfolios on the efficient frontier?
- What determines which portfolio on the efficient frontier is selected by an individual investor?

One of the major advances in the investment field during the past few decades has been the recognition that the creation of an optimum investment portfolio is not simply a matter of combining a lot of unique individual securities that have desirable risk–return characteristics. Specifically, it has been shown that you must consider the relationship *among* the investments if you are going to build an optimum portfolio that will meet your investment objectives. The recognition of what is important in creating a portfolio was demonstrated in the derivation of portfolio theory.

This chapter explains portfolio theory step by step. It introduces you to the basic portfolio risk formula that you must understand when you are combining different assets. When you understand this formula and its implications, you will increase your understanding of not only why you should diversify your portfolio, but also *how* you should diversify. The subsequent chapter introduces asset pricing models and capital market theory with an emphasis on determining the appropriate risk measure for individual assets.

SOME BACKGROUND ASSUMPTIONS

Before presenting portfolio theory, we need to clarify some general assumptions of the theory. This includes not only what we mean by an *optimum portfolio,* but also what we mean by the terms *risk aversion* and *risk.*

One basic assumption of portfolio theory is that as an investor you want to maximize the returns from your investments for a given level of risk. To adequately deal with such an assumption, certain ground rules must be laid. First, your portfolio should *include all of your assets and liabilities,* not only your stocks or even your marketable securities, but also such items as your car, house, and less-marketable investments, such as coins, stamps, art, antiques, and furniture. The full spectrum of investments must be considered because the returns from all these investments interact, and *this relationship between the returns for assets in the portfolio is important.* Hence, a good portfolio is *not* simply a collection of individually good investments.

Risk Aversion

Portfolio theory also assumes that investors are basically **risk averse**, meaning that, given a choice between two assets with equal rates of return, they will select the asset with the lower level of risk. Evidence that most investors are risk averse is that they purchase various types of insurance, including life insurance, car insurance, and health insurance. Buying insurance basically involves an outlay of a given amount to guard against an uncertain, possibly larger outlay in the future. When you buy insurance, this implies that you are willing to pay the current known cost of the insurance policy to avoid the uncertainty of a potentially large future cost related to a car accident or a major illness. Further evidence of risk aversion is the difference in promised yield (the required rate of return) for different grades of bonds that supposedly have different degrees of credit risk. As you might know from reading about corporate bonds, the promised yield on bonds increases as you go from AAA (the lowest risk class) to AA to A, and so on. This increase in promised yields means that investors require a higher rate of return to accept higher risk.

This does not imply that everybody is risk averse, or that investors are completely risk averse regarding all financial commitments. The fact is, not everybody buys insurance for everything. Some people have no insurance against anything, either by choice or because they cannot afford it. In addition, some individuals buy insurance related to some risks such as auto accidents or illness, but they also buy lottery tickets and gamble at race tracks or in casinos, where it is known that the expected returns are negative, which means that participants are willing to pay for the excitement of the risk involved. This combination of risk preference and risk aversion can be explained by an attitude toward risk that is not completely risk averse or risk preferring, but is a combination of the two that depends on the amount of money involved. Friedman and Savage speculate that this is the case for people who like to gamble for small amounts (in lotteries or nickel slot machines), but buy insurance to protect themselves against large potential losses, such as fire or accidents.[1]

While recognizing this diversity of attitudes, our basic assumption is that most investors committing large sums of money to developing an investment portfolio are risk averse. Therefore, we expect a positive relationship between expected return and expected risk. Notably, this is also what we generally find in terms of long-run historical results—that is, there is generally a positive relationship between the rates of return on various assets and their measures of risk as shown in Chapter 3.

[1]Milton Friedman and Leonard J. Savage, "The Utility Analysis of Choices Involving Risk," *Journal of Political Economy* 56, no. 3 (August 1948): 279–304.

DEFINITION OF RISK Although there is a difference in the specific definitions of *risk* and *uncertainty,* for our purposes and in most financial literature the two terms are used interchangeably. In fact, one way to define risk is *the uncertainty of future outcomes.* An alternative definition might be *the probability of an adverse outcome.* Subsequently, in our discussion of portfolio theory, we will consider several measures of risk that are used when developing the theory.

MARKOWITZ PORTFOLIO THEORY

In the 1950s and early 1960s, the investment community talked about risk, but there was no specific measure for the term. To build a portfolio model, however, investors had to quantify their risk variable. The basic portfolio model was developed by Harry Markowitz, who derived the expected rate of return for a portfolio of assets and an expected risk measure.[2] Markowitz showed that the variance of the rate of return was a meaningful measure of portfolio risk under a reasonable set of assumptions, and he derived the formula for computing the variance of a portfolio. This formula for the variance of a portfolio not only indicated the importance of diversifying your investments to reduce the total risk of a portfolio, but also showed *how* to effectively diversify. The Markowitz model is based on several assumptions regarding investor behavior:

1. Investors consider each investment alternative as being represented by a probability distribution of expected returns over some holding period.
2. Investors maximize one-period expected utility, and their utility curves demonstrate diminishing marginal utility of wealth.
3. Investors estimate the risk of the portfolio on the basis of the variability of expected returns.
4. Investors base decisions solely on expected return and risk, so their utility curves are a function of expected return and the expected variance (or standard deviation) of returns only.
5. For a given risk level, investors prefer higher returns to lower returns. Similarly, for a given level of expected return, investors prefer less risk to more risk.

Under these assumptions, *a single asset or portfolio of assets is considered to be efficient if no other asset or portfolio of assets offers higher expected return with the same (or lower) risk, or lower risk with the same (or higher) expected return.*

ALTERNATIVE MEASURES OF RISK One of the best-known measures of risk is the *variance,* or *standard deviation of expected returns.*[3] It is a statistical measure of the dispersion of returns around the expected value whereby a larger variance or standard deviation indicates greater dispersion, all other factors being equal. The idea is that the more disperse the expected returns, the greater the uncertainty of those returns in any future period.

Another measure of risk is the *range of returns.* In this case, it is assumed that a larger range of expected returns, from the lowest to the highest return, means greater uncertainty and risk regarding future expected returns.

Instead of using measures that analyze all deviations from expectations, some observers believe that when you invest you should be concerned only with *returns below expectations,* which means that you only consider deviations below the mean value. A measure that

[2]Harry Markowitz, "Portfolio Selection," *Journal of Finance* 7, no. 1 (March 1952): 77–91; and Harry Markowitz, *Portfolio Selection—Efficient Diversification of Investments* (New York: John Wiley & Sons, 1959).

[3]We consider the variance and standard deviation as one measure of risk because the standard deviation is the square root of the variance.

only considers deviations below the mean is the *semivariance.* Extensions of the semivariance measure only computed expected returns *below zero* (that is, negative returns), or returns below some specific asset such as T-bills, the rate of inflation, or a benchmark. These measures of risk implicitly assume that investors want to *minimize the damage* from returns less than some target rate. Assuming that investors would welcome positive returns or returns above some target rate, the returns above expectations or a target return is not considered when measuring risk.

Although there are numerous potential measures of risk, we will use the variance or standard deviation of returns because (1) this measure is somewhat intuitive, (2) it is a correct and widely recognized risk measure, and (3) it has been used in most of the theoretical asset pricing models.

EXPECTED RATES OF RETURN

The expected rate of return for *an individual investment* is computed as shown in Table 8.1. The expected return for an individual risky asset with the set of potential returns and an assumption of equal probabilities used in the example would be 11 percent.

The expected rate of return for a *portfolio* of investments is simply the weighted average of the expected rates of return for the individual investments in the portfolio. The weights are the proportion of total value for the investment.

The expected rate of return for a hypothetical portfolio with four risky assets is shown in Table 8.2. The expected return for this portfolio of investments would be 11.5 percent. The effect of adding or dropping any investment from the portfolio would be easy to determine because you would use the new weights based on value and the expected returns for each of the investments. This computation of the expected return for the portfolio $[E(R_{port})]$ can be generalized as follows:

$$E(R_{port}) = \sum_{i=1}^{n} W_i E(R_i)$$

where:

$\boldsymbol{W_i}$ = **the percent of the portfolio in asset *i***
$\boldsymbol{E(R_i)}$ = **the expected rate of return for asset *i***

TABLE 8.1 **COMPUTATION OF EXPECTED RETURN FOR AN INDIVIDUAL RISKY ASSET**

Probability	Possible Rate of Return (Percent)	Expected Return (Percent)
.25	.08	.0200
.25	.10	.0250
.25	.12	.0300
.25	.14	.0350
		$E(R)$ = .1100

TABLE 8.2 **COMPUTATION OF THE EXPECTED RETURN FOR A PORTFOLIO OF RISKY ASSETS**

Weight (W_i) (Percent of Portfolio)	Expected Security Return $E(R_i)$	Expected Portfolio Return ($W_i \times E(R_i)$)
.20	.10	.0200
.30	.11	.0330
.30	.12	.0360
.20	.13	.0260
		$E(R_{port})$ = .1150

Variance (Standard Deviation) of Returns for an Individual Investment

As noted, we will be using the variance or the standard deviation of returns as the measure of risk (recall that the standard deviation is the square root of the variance). Therefore, at this point, we will demonstrate how you would compute the standard deviation of returns for an individual investment. Subsequently, after discussing some other statistical concepts, we will consider the determination of the standard deviation for a *portfolio* of investments.

The variance, or standard deviation, is a measure of the variation of possible rates of return, R_i, from the expected rate of return $[E(R_i)]$ as follows:

$$\text{Variance } (\sigma^2) = \sum_{i=1}^{n}[R_i - E(R_i)]^2 P_i$$

where P_i is the probability of the possible rate of return, R_i.

$$\text{Standard Deviation } (\sigma) = \sqrt{\sum_{i=1}^{n}[R_i - E(R_i)]^2 P_i}$$

The computation of the variance and standard deviation of the expected rate of return for the individual risky asset in Table 8.1 is set forth in Table 8.3.

Variance (Standard Deviation) of Returns for a Portfolio

Two basic concepts in statistics, covariance and correlation, must be understood before we discuss the formula for the variance of the rate of return for a portfolio.

COVARIANCE OF RETURNS In this section, we discuss what the covariance of returns is intended to measure, give the formula for computing it, and present an example of the computation. **Covariance** is a measure of the degree to which two variables "move together" relative to their individual mean values over time. In portfolio analysis, we usually are concerned with the covariance of *rates of return* rather than prices or some other variable.[4] A positive covariance means that the rates of return for two investments tend to

TABLE 8.3 **COMPUTATION OF THE VARIANCE OF THE EXPECTED RATE OF RETURN FOR AN INDIVIDUAL RISKY ASSET**

Possible Rate of Return (R_i)	Expected Return $E(R_i)$	$R_i - E(R_i)$	$[R_i - E(R_i)]^2$	P_i	$(R_i - E(R_i))^2 P_i$
.08	.11	.03	.0009	.25	.000225
.10	.11	.01	.0001	.25	.000025
.12	.11	.01	.0001	.25	.000025
.14	.11	.03	.0009	.25	.000225
					.000500

Variance (σ^2) = .00050

Standard Deviation (σ) = .02236

[4]Returns, of course, can be measured in a variety of ways, depending on the type of asset. You will recall that we defined returns (R_i) in Chapter 1 as:

$$R_i = \frac{\text{EV} - \text{BV} + \text{CF}}{\text{BV}}$$

where EV is ending value, BV is beginning value, and CF is the cash flow during the period.

TABLE 8.4 **COMPUTATION OF MONTHLY RATES OF RETURN: 1998**

	Coca-Cola			Exxon		
Date	Closing Price	Dividend	Rate of Return (%)	Closing Price	Dividend	Rate of Return (%)
12/97	66.688	0.14		61.188	0.41	
1/98	64.750		−3.11	59.313		−3.71
2/98	68.625		5.98	63.750	0.41	8.17
3/98	77.438	0.15	13.06	67.625		5.40
4/98	75.875		−2.21	73.063		8.04
5/98	78.375		3.29	70.500	0.41	−2.95
6/98	85.500	0.15	9.28	71.375		0.66
7/98	80.500		−6.01	70.250		−1.58
8.98	65.125		−19.10	65.438	0.41	−6.27
9/98	57.625	0.15	−11.29	70.625		7.26
10/98	67.563		16.94	71.625		1.42
11/98	70.063	0.15	3.92	75.000	0.41	5.28
12/98	67.000		−4.58	73.125		−3.03
		$E(R_{\text{Coca-Cola}})$ =	0.52		$E(R_{\text{Exxon}})$ =	1.56

FIGURE 8.1 **TIME SERIES OF MONTHLY RATES OF RETURN FOR COCA-COLA: 1998**

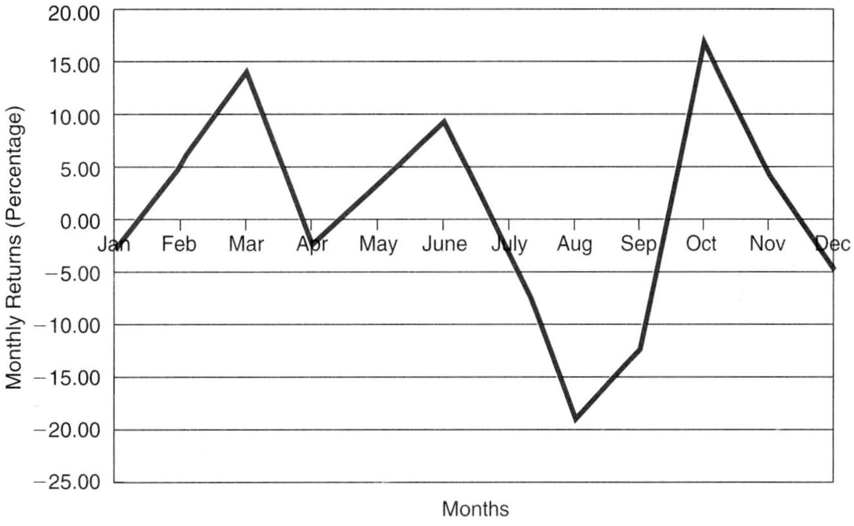
20.00
15.00
10.00
5.00
0.00
−5.00
−10.00
−15.00
−20.00
−25.00
Monthly Returns (Percentage)
Jan
Feb
Mar
Apr
May
June
July
Aug
Sep
Oct
Nov
Dec
Months

move in the same direction relative to their individual means during the same time period. In contrast, a negative covariance indicates that the rates of return for two investments tend to move in different directions relative to their means during specified time intervals over time. The *magnitude* of the covariance depends on the variances of the individual return series, as well as on the relationship between the series.

Table 8.4 contains the monthly closing prices and dividends for Coca-Cola and Exxon. You can use these data to compute monthly rates of return for these two stocks during 1998. Figures 8.1 and 8.2 contain a time-series plot of the monthly rates of return for the two stocks during 1998. Although the rates of return for the two stocks moved together

FIGURE 8.2

TIME SERIES OF MONTHLY RATES OF RETURN FOR EXXON: 1998

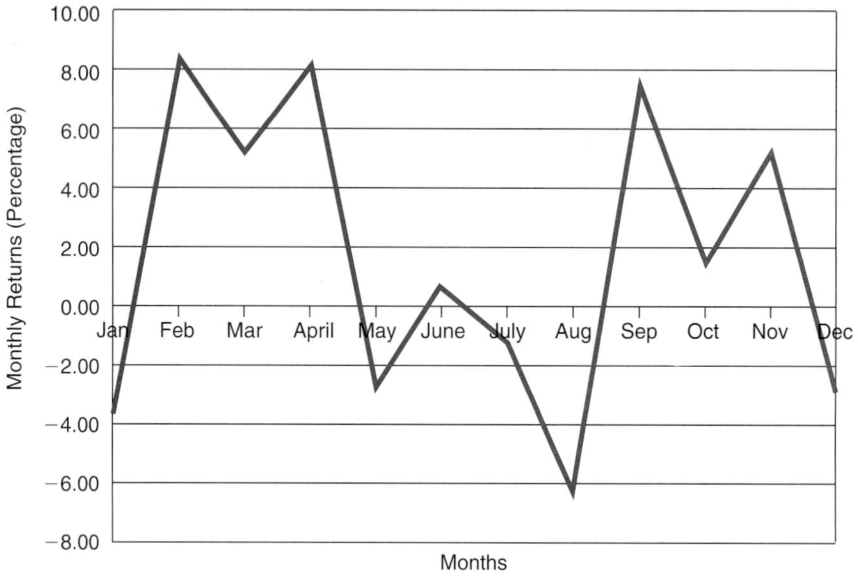
10.00
8.00
6.00
4.00
2.00
0.00
−2.00
−4.00
−6.00
−8.00
Monthly Returns (Percentage)
Jan
Feb
Mar
April
May
June
July
Aug
Sep
Oct
Nov
Dec
Months

during some months, in other months they moved in opposite directions. The covariance statistic provides an *absolute* measure of how they moved together over time.

For two assets, *i* and *j,* the covariance of rates of return is defined as:

$$\text{Cov}_{ij} = E\{[R_i - E(R_i)][R_j - E(R_j)]\}$$

When we apply this formula to the monthly rates of return for Coca-Cola and Exxon during 1998, it becomes:

$$\frac{1}{12}\sum_{i=1}^{n}[R_i - E(R_i)][R_j - E(R_j)]$$

As can be seen, if the rates of return for one stock are above (below) its mean rate of return during a given period, and the returns for the other stock are likewise above (below) its mean rate of return during this same period, then the *product* of these deviations from the mean is positive. If this happens consistently, the covariance of returns between these two stocks will be some large positive value. If, however, the rate of return for one of the securities is above its mean return while the return on the other security is below its mean return, the product will be negative. If this contrary movement happened consistently, the covariance between the rates of return for the two stocks would be a large negative value.

Table 8.5 contains the monthly rates of return during 1998 for Coca-Cola and Exxon as computed in Table 8.4. One might expect the returns for the two stocks to have reasonably low covariance because of the differences in the products of these firms. The expected returns $E(R)$ were the arithmetic mean of the monthly returns:

$$E(R_i) = \frac{1}{12}\sum_{i=1}^{12} R_{it}$$

TABLE 8.5 **COMPUTATION OF CONVARIANCE OR RETURNS FOR COCA-COLA AND EXXON: 1998**

	Monthly Return (%)				
Date	Coca-Cola (R_i)	Exxon (R_j)	Coca-Cola $R_i - E(R_i)$	Exxon $R_j - E(R_j)$	Coca-Cola $[R_j - E(R_i)]$ × Exxon $R_j - E(R_j)$
1/98	−3.11	−3.71	−3.63	−5.27	19.10
2/98	5.98	8.17	5.47	6.61	36.17
3/98	13.06	5.40	12.54	3.84	48.20
4/98	−2.21	8.04	−2.72	6.48	−17.66
5/98	3.29	−2.95	2.78	−4.50	−12.52
6/98	9.28	0.66	8.77	−0.90	−7.91
7/98	−6.01	−1.58	−6.53	−3.13	20.46
8/98	−19.10	−6.27	−19.62	−7.82	153.49
9/98	−11.29	7.26	−11.80	5.70	−67.24
10/98	16.94	1.42	16.42	−0.14	−2.33
11/98	3.92	5.28	3.41	3.73	12.69
12/98	−4.58	−3.03	−5.09	−4.59	23.36
	$E(R_i) =$ 0.52	$E(R_j) =$ 1.56			Sum = 205.82

$Cov_{ij} = 205.82/12 = 17.15$

and

$$E(R_j) = \frac{1}{12}\sum_{j=1}^{12} R_{jt}$$

All figures (except those in the last column) were rounded to the nearest hundredth of 1 percent. As shown in Table 8.4, the average monthly return was 0.52 percent for Coca-Cola and 1.56 percent for Exxon stock. The results in Table 8.5 show that the covariance between the rates of return for these two stocks was:

$$\begin{aligned} \text{Cov}_{ij} &= \frac{1}{12} \times 205.82 \\ &= 17.15 \end{aligned}$$

Interpretation of a number such as 17.15 is difficult; is it high or low for covariance? We know the relationship between the two stocks is generally positive, but it is not possible to be more specific. Figure 8.3 contains a scatter diagram with paired values of R_{it} and R_{jt} plotted against each other. This plot demonstrates the linear nature and strength of the relationship and shows several instances during 1998 when Coca-Cola experienced negative returns relative to its mean return when Exxon had positive rates of return relative to its mean.

COVARIANCE AND CORRELATION Covariance is affected by the variability of the two individual return series. Therefore, a number such as the 17.15 in our example might indicate a weak positive relationship if the two individual series were volatile, but would reflect a strong positive relationship if the two series were stable. Obviously, you want to "standardize" this covariance measure taking into consideration the variability of the two individual return series, as follows:

FIGURE 8.3 **SCATTER PLOT OF MONTHLY RATES OF RETURN FOR COCA-COLA AND EXXON: 1998**

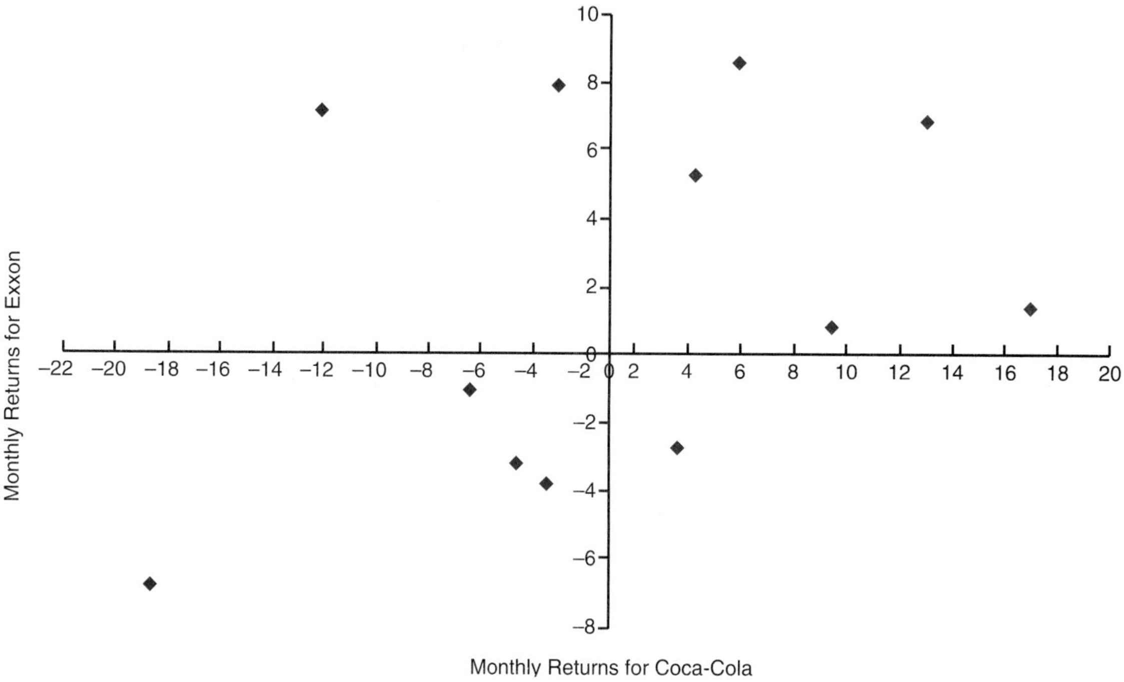
Monthly Returns for Exxon
Monthly Returns for Coca-Cola
10
8
6
4
2
0
−2
−4
−6
−8
−22 −20 −18 −16 −14 −12 −10 −8 −6 −4 −2 0 2 4 6 8 10 12 14 16 18 20

$$r_{ij} = \frac{\text{Cov}_{ij}}{\sigma_i \sigma_j}$$

where:

r_{ij} = the correlation coefficient of returns
σ_i = the standard deviation of R_{it}
σ_j = the standard deviation of R_{jt}

Standardizing the covariance by the individual standard deviations yields the **correlation coefficient** (r_{ij}), which can vary only in the range −1 to +1. A value of +1 would indicate a perfect positive linear relationship between R_i and R_j, meaning the returns for the two stocks move together in a completely linear manner. A value of −1 indicates a perfect negative relationship between the two return series such that when one stock's rate of return is above its mean, the other stock's rate of return will be below its mean by the comparable amount.

To calculate this standardized measure of the relationship, you need to compute the standard deviation for the two individual return series. We already have the values for $R_{it} - E(R_i)$ and $R_{jt} - E(R_j)$ in Table 8.5. We can square each of these values and sum them as shown in Table 8.6 to calculate the variance of each return series.

$$\sigma_i^2 = \frac{1}{12}(1166.38) = 97.20$$

TABLE 8.6

COMPUTATION OF STANDARD DEVIATION OF RETURN FOR COCA-COLA AND EXXON: 1998

	Coca-Cola		Exxon	
Date	$R_i - E(R_i)$	$[R_i - E(R_i)]^2$	$R_j - E(R_j)$	$[R_j - E(R_j)]^2$
1/98	−3.63	13.15	−5.27	27.76
2/98	5.47	29.90	6.61	43.76
3/98	12.54	157.37	3.84	14.77
4/98	−2.72	7.42	6.48	42.02
5/98	2.78	7.72	−4.50	20.29
6/98	8.77	76.84	−0.90	0.81
7/98	−6.53	42.63	−3.13	9.82
8/98	−19.62	384.77	−7.82	61.23
9/98	−11.80	139.29	5.70	32.46
10/98	16.42	269.76	−0.14	0.02
11/98	3.41	11.60	3.73	13.89
12/98	−5.09	25.92	−4.59	21.05
		Sum = 1,166.38		Sum = 287.87
	Variance$_i$ = 1166.38/12 =	97.20	Variance$_j$ = 287.87/12 =	23.99
	Standard Deviation$_i$ = $(97.20)^{1/2}$ =	9.86	Standard Deviation$_j$ = $(23.99)^{1/2}$ =	4.90

and

$$\sigma_j^2 = \frac{1}{12}(287.87) = 23.99$$

The standard deviation for each series is the square root of the variance for each, as follows:

$$\sigma_i = \sqrt{97.20} = 9.86$$
$$\sigma_j = \sqrt{23.99} = 4.90$$

Thus, based on the covariance between the two series and the individual standard deviations, we can calculate the correlation coefficient between returns for Coca-Cola and Exxon as

$$r_{ij} = \frac{\text{Cov}_{ij}}{\sigma_i \sigma_j} = \frac{17.15}{(9.86)(4.90)} = \frac{17.15}{48.31} = .355$$

Obviously, this formula also implies that

$$\text{Cov}_{ij} = r_{ij}\,\sigma_i\sigma_j = (.355)(9.86)(4.90) = 17.15$$

as computed in Table 8.5.

STANDARD DEVIATION OF A PORTFOLIO

As noted, a correlation of +1.0 would indicate perfect positive correlation, and a value of −1.0 would mean that the returns moved in a completely opposite direction. A value of zero would mean that the returns had no linear relationship, that is, they were uncorrelated statistically. That does *not* mean that they are independent. The value of

$r_{ij} = 0.355$ is significant but not high. This relatively low correlation is not unusual for stocks in diverse industries. Correlation between stocks of companies *within* some industries approach 0.85.

PORTFOLIO STANDARD DEVIATION FORMULA Now that we have discussed the concepts of covariance and correlation, we can consider the formula for computing the standard deviation of returns for a *portfolio* of assets, our measure of risk for a portfolio. As noted, Harry Markowitz derived the formula for computing the standard deviation of a portfolio of assets.[5]

In Table 8.2, we showed that the expected rate of return of the portfolio was the weighted average of the expected returns for the individual assets in the portfolio; the weights were the percentage of value of the portfolio. Under such conditions, we can easily see the impact adding or deleting an asset would have on the portfolio's expected return.

One might assume it is possible to derive the standard deviation of the portfolio in the same manner, that is, by computing the weighted average of the standard deviations for the individual assets. This would be a mistake. Markowitz derived the general formula for the standard deviation of a portfolio as follows:[6]

$$\sigma_{\text{port}} = \sqrt{\sum_{i=1}^{n} w_i^2 \sigma_i^2 + \sum_{\substack{i=1}}^{n} \sum_{\substack{i=1 \\ i \neq j}}^{n} w_i w_j \,\text{Cov}_{ij}}$$

where:

σ_{port} = the standard deviation of the portfolio
w_i = the weights of the individual assets in the portfolio, where weights are determined by the proportion of value in the portfolio
σ_i^2 = the variance of rates of return for asset i
Cov_{ij} = the covariance between the rates of return for assets i and j, where $\text{Cov}_{ij} = r_{ij}\sigma_i\sigma_j$

This formula indicates that the standard deviation for a portfolio of assets is a function of the weighted average of the individual variances (where the weights are squared), *plus* the weighted covariances between all the assets in the portfolio. The standard deviation for a portfolio of assets encompasses not only the variances of the individual assets, but *also* includes the covariances between pairs of individual assets in the portfolio. Further, it can be shown that, in a portfolio with a large number of securities, this formula reduces to the sum of the weighted covariances.

Although most of the subsequent demonstration will consider portfolios with only two assets because it is possible to show the effect in two dimensions, we will demonstrate the computations for a three-asset portfolio. Still, it is important at this point to consider what happens in a large portfolio with many assets. Specifically, what happens to the portfolio's standard deviation when you add a new security to such a portfolio? As shown by the formula, we see two effects. The first is the asset's own variance of returns, and the second is the covariance between the returns of this new asset and the returns of *every other asset that is already in the portfolio.* The relative weight of these numerous covariances is substantially greater than the asset's unique variance, and the more assets in the portfolio, the more this is true. This means that the important factor to consider when adding an investment to a portfolio that contains a number of other investments is

[5]Markowitz, *Portfolio Selection.*

[6]For the detailed derivation of this formula, see Markowitz, *Portfolio Selection.*

not the investment's own variance, but *its average covariance with all the other investments in the portfolio.*

In the following examples we will consider the simple case of a two-asset portfolio. We do these relatively simple calculations and provide graphs with two assets to demonstrate the impact of different covariances on the total risk (standard deviation) of the portfolio.

DEMONSTRATION OF THE PORTFOLIO STANDARD DEVIATION CALCULATION Because of the assumptions used in developing the Markowitz portfolio model, any asset or portfolio of assets can be described by two characteristics: the expected rate of return and the expected standard deviation of returns. Therefore, the following demonstrations can be applied to two *individual* assets with the indicated return–standard deviation characteristics and correlation coefficients, two *portfolios* of assets, or two *asset classes* with the indicated return–standard deviation characteristics and correlation coefficients.

Equal Risk and Return—Changing Correlations Consider first the case in which both assets have the same expected return and expected standard deviation of return. As an example, let us assume

$$E(R_1) = 0.20$$
$$E(\sigma_1) = 0.10$$
$$E(R_2) = 0.20$$
$$E(\sigma_2) = 0.10$$

To show the effect of different covariances, assume different levels of correlation between the two assets. Consider the following examples where the two assets have equal weights in the portfolio ($W_1 = 0.50$; $W_2 = 0.50$). Therefore, the only value that changes in each example is the correlation between the returns for the two assets.

Recall that

$$\text{Cov}_{ij} = r_{ij}\sigma_i\sigma_j$$

Consider the following alternative correlation coefficients and the covariances they yield. The covariance term in the equation will be equal to $r_{1,2}$ (0.10)(0.10) because both standard deviations are 0.10.

a. $r_{1,2} = 1.00$; $\text{Cov}_{1,2} = (1.00)(0.10)(0.10) = 0.01$
b. $r_{1,2} = 0.50$; $\text{Cov}_{1,2} = (0.50)(0.10)(0.10) = 0.005$
c. $r_{1,2} = 0.00$; $\text{Cov}_{1,2} = 0.000$
d. $r_{1,2} = -0.50$; $\text{Cov}_{1,2} = -0.005$
e. $r_{1,2} = -1.00$; $\text{Cov}_{1,2} = -0.01$

Now let us see what happens to the standard deviation of the portfolio under these five conditions. Recall that

$$\sigma_{\text{port}} \sqrt{\sum_{i=1}^{n} w_i^2\sigma_i^2 + \sum_{i=1}^{n}\sum_{\substack{i=1 \\ i \neq j}}^{n} w_i w_j \text{Cov}_{ij}}$$

When this general formula is applied to a two-asset portfolio, it is

$$\sigma_{\text{port}} = \sqrt{w_1^2\sigma_1^2 + w_2^2\sigma_2^2 + 2w_1w_2r_{1,2}\sigma_1\sigma_2}$$

or

$$\sigma_{\text{port}} = \sqrt{x_1^2\sigma_1^2 + w_2^2\sigma_2^2 + 2w_1w_2\text{Cov}_{1,2}}$$

Thus, in Case a,

$$\begin{aligned}\sigma_{\text{port (a)}} &= \sqrt{(0.5)^2(0.10)^2 + (0.5)^2(0.10)^2 + 2(0.5)(0.5)(0.01)}\\ &= \sqrt{(0.25)(0.01) + (0.25)(0.01) + 2(0.25)(0.01)}\\ &= \sqrt{0.01}\\ &= 0.10\end{aligned}$$

In this case, where the returns for the two assets are perfectly positively correlated ($r_{1,2} = 1.0$), the standard deviation for the portfolio is, in fact, the weighted average of the individual standard deviations. The important point is that we get no real benefit from combining two assets that are perfectly correlated; they are like one asset already because their returns move together.

Now consider Case b, where $r_{1,2}$ equals 0.50.

$$\begin{aligned}\sigma_{\text{port (b)}} &= \sqrt{(0.5)^2(0.10)^2 + (0.5)^2(0.10)^2 + 2(0.5)(0.5)(0.005)}\\ &= \sqrt{(0.0025) + (0.0025) + 2(0.25)(0.005)}\\ &= \sqrt{0.0075}\\ &= 0.0868\end{aligned}$$

The only term that changed from Case a is the last term, $\text{Cov}_{1,2}$, which changed from 0.01 to 0.005. As a result, the standard deviation of the portfolio declined by about 13 percent, from 0.10 to 0.0868. Note that *the expected return did not change* because it is simply the weighted average of the individual expected returns; it is equal to 0.20 in both cases.

You should be able to confirm through your own calculations that the standard deviations for Portfolios c and d are as follows:

c. 0.0707
d. 0.05

The final case where the correlation between the two assets is -1.00 indicates the ultimate benefits of diversification.

$$\begin{aligned}\sigma_{\text{port (e)}} &= \sqrt{(0.5)^2(0.10)^2 + (0.5)^2(0.10)^2 + 2(0.5)(0.5)(-0.01)}\\ &= \sqrt{(0.0050) + (-0.0050)}\\ &= \sqrt{0}\\ &= 0\end{aligned}$$

Here, the negative covariance term exactly offsets the individual variance terms, leaving an overall standard deviation of the portfolio of zero. *This would be a risk-free portfolio.*

Figure 8.4 illustrates a graph of such a pattern. Perfect negative correlation gives a mean combined return for the two securities over time equal to the mean for each of them, so the returns for the portfolio show no variability. Any returns above and below the mean for

FIGURE 8.4

TIME PATTERNS OF RETURNS FOR TWO ASSETS WITH PERFECT NEGATIVE CORRELATION

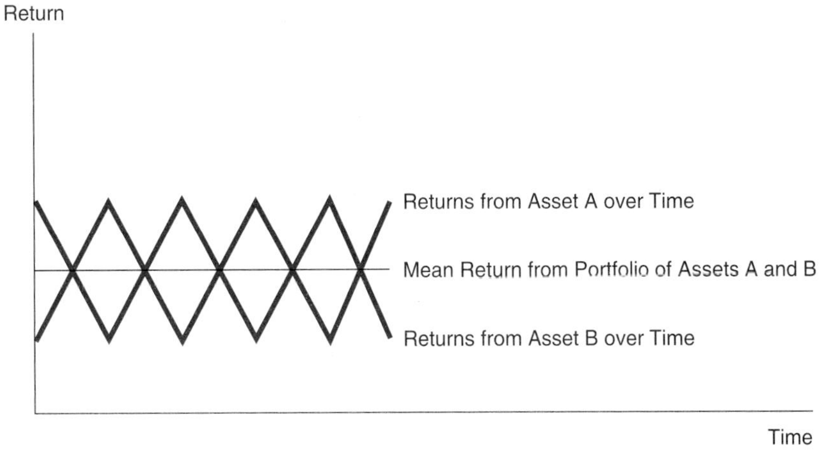
Return
Returns from Asset A over Time
Mean Return from Portfolio of Assets A and B
Returns from Asset B over Time
Time

each of the assets are *completely offset* by the return for the other asset, so there is *no variability* in total returns, that is, *no risk,* for the portfolio. This combination of two assets that are completely negatively correlated provides the maximum benefits of diversification—it completely eliminates risk.

The graph in Figure 8.5 shows the difference in the risk–return posture for these five cases. As noted, the only effect of the change in correlation is the change in the standard deviation of this two-asset portfolio. Combining assets that are not perfectly correlated does *not* affect the expected return of the portfolio, but it *does* reduce the risk of the portfolio (as measured by its standard deviation). When we eventually reach the ultimate combination of perfect negative correlation, risk is eliminated.

Combining Stocks with Different Returns and Risk The previous discussion indicated what happens when only the correlation coefficient (covariance) differs between the assets. We now consider two assets (or portfolios) with different expected rates of return and individual standard deviations.[7] We will show what happens when we vary the correlations between them. We will assume two assets with the following characteristics:

Asset	$E(R_i)$	W_i	σ_i^2	σ_i
1	.10	.50	.0049	.07
2	.20	.50	.0100	.10

The previous set of correlation coefficients gives a different set of covariances because the standard deviations are different. For example, the covariance in Case b where $r_{1,2} = 0.50$ would be $(0.50)(0.07)(0.10) = 0.0035$.

[7]As noted, these could be two asset classes. For example, asset 1 could be low risk–low return bonds and asset 2 could be higher return–higher risk stocks.

FIGURE 8.5

RISK–RETURN PLOT FOR PORTFOLIOS WITH EQUAL RETURNS AND STANDARD DEVIATIONS BUT DIFFERENT CORRELATIONS

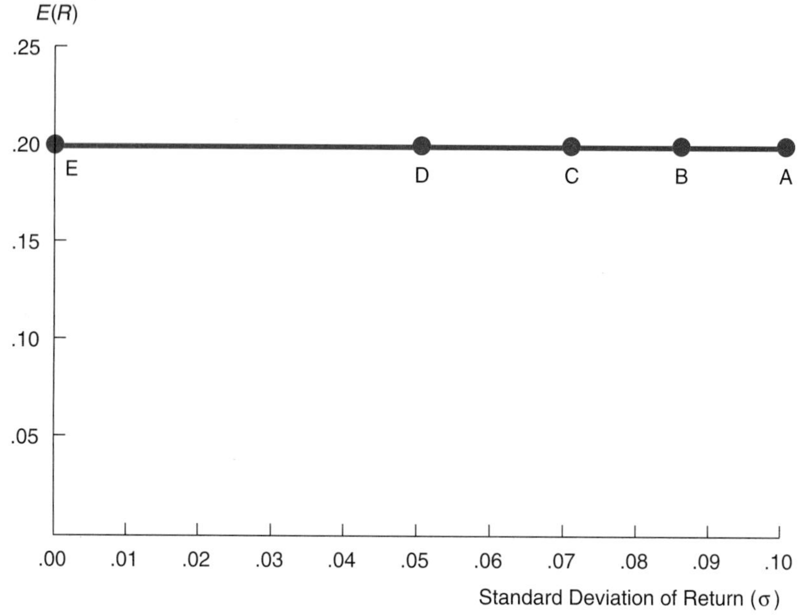
E(R)
.25
.20
.15
.10
.05
E
D
C
B
A
.00
.01
.02
.03
.04
.05
.06
.07
.08
.09
.10
Standard Deviation of Return (σ)

Case	Correlation Coefficient	Covariance ($r_{ij}\sigma_i\sigma_j$)
a	+1.00	.0070
b	+0.50	.0035
c	0.00	.0000
d	−0.50	−.0035
e	−1.00	−.0070

Because we are assuming the same weights in all cases (0.50 − 0.50), the expected return in every instance will be

$$E(R_{port}) = 0.50(0.10) + 0.50(0.20)$$
$$= 0.15$$

The standard deviation for Case a will be

$$\sigma_{port\ (a)} = \sqrt{(0.5)^2(0.07)^2 + (0.5)^2(0.10)^2 + 2(0.5)(0.5)(0.0070)}$$
$$= \sqrt{(0.001225) + (0.0025) + (0.5)(0.0070)}$$
$$= \sqrt{0.007225}$$
$$= 0.085$$

Again, with perfect positive correlation, the standard deviation of the portfolio is the weighted average of the standard deviations of the individual assets:

$$(0.5)(0.07) + (0.5)(0.10) = 0.085$$

As you might envision, changing the weights with perfect positive correlation causes the standard deviation for the portfolio to change in a linear fashion. This is an important point to remember when we discuss the capital asset pricing model (CAPM) in the next chapter.

For Cases b, c, d, and e, the standard deviation for the portfolio would be as follows:[8]

$$\sigma_{\text{port (b)}} = \sqrt{(0.001225) + (0.0025) + (0.5)(0.0035)}$$
$$= \sqrt{0.005475}$$
$$= 0.07399$$
$$\sigma_{\text{port (c)}} = \sqrt{(0.001225) + (0.0025) + (0.5)(0.00)}$$
$$= 0.0610$$
$$\sigma_{\text{port (d)}} = \sqrt{(0.001225) + (0.0025) + (0.5)(-0.0035)}$$
$$= 0.0444$$
$$\sigma_{\text{port (e)}} = \sqrt{(0.003725) + (0.5)(-0.0070)}$$
$$= 0.015$$

Note that, in this example, with perfect negative correlation the standard deviation of the portfolio is not zero. This is because the different examples have equal weights, but the individual standard deviations are not equal.[9]

Figure 8.6 shows the results for the two individual assets and the portfolio of the two assets assuming the correlation coefficients vary as set forth in Cases a through e. As before, the expected return does not change because the proportions are always set at 0.50 − 0.50, so all the portfolios lie along the horizontal line at the return, $E(R) = 0.15$.

Constant Correlation with Changing Weights If we changed the weights of the two assets while holding the correlation coefficient constant, we would derive a set of combinations that trace an ellipse starting at Asset 2, going through the 0.50 – 0.50 point, and ending at Asset 1. We can demonstrate this with Case c, in which the correlation coefficient of zero eases the computations. We begin with 100 percent in Asset 2 (Case f) and change the weights as follows, ending with 100 percent in Asset m (Case m):

Case	W_1	W_2	$E(R_i)$
f	.00	1.00	.20
g	.20	.80	.18
h	.40	.60	.16
i	.50	.50	.15
j	.60	.40	.14
k	.80	.20	.12
m	1.00	.00	.10

[8]In all the following examples we will skip some steps because you are now aware that only the last term changes. You are encouraged to work out the individual steps to ensure that you understand the computational procedure.

[9]The two appendixes to this chapter show proofs for equal weights with equal variances and solve for the appropriate weights to get zero standard deviation when standard deviations are not equal.

FIGURE 8.6 **RISK-RETURN PLOT FOR PORTFOLIOS WITH DIFFERENT RETURNS, STANDARD DEVIATIONS, AND CORRELATIONS**

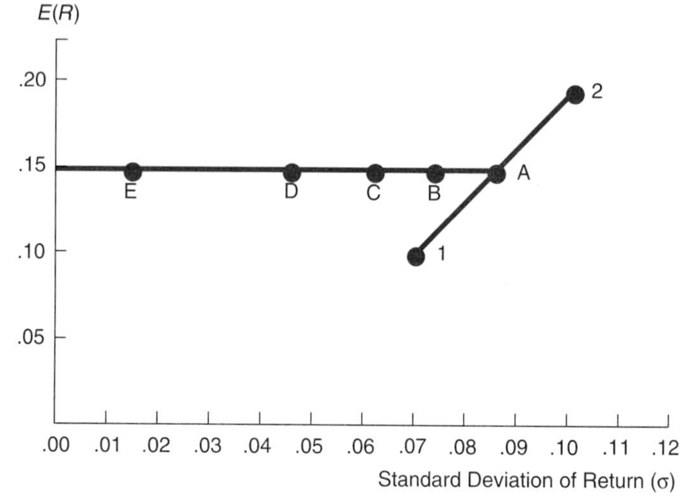
E(R)
.20
.15
.10
.05
2
A
E
D
C
B
1
.00
.01
.02
.03
.04
.05
.06
.07
.08
.09
.10
.11
.12
Standard Deviation of Return (σ)

We already know the standard deviation (σ) for Portfolio i. In Cases f, g, h, j, k, and m, the standard deviations would be[10]

$$\begin{aligned}\sigma_{\text{port (g)}} &= \sqrt{(0.20)^2(0.07)^2 + (0.80)^2(0.10)^2 + 2(0.20)(0.80)(0.00)}\\ &= \sqrt{(0.04)(0.0049) + (0.64)(0.01) + (0)}\\ &= \sqrt{0.006596}\\ &= 0.0812\end{aligned}$$

$$\begin{aligned}\sigma_{\text{port (h)}} &= \sqrt{(0.40)^2(0.07)^2 + (0.60)^2(0.10)^2 + 2(0.40)(0.60)(0.00)}\\ &= \sqrt{0.004384}\\ &= 0.0662\end{aligned}$$

$$\begin{aligned}\sigma_{\text{port (j)}} &= \sqrt{(0.60)^2(0.07)^2 + (0.40)^2(0.10)^2 + 2(0.60)(0.40)(0.00)}\\ &= \sqrt{0.003364}\\ &= 0.0580\end{aligned}$$

$$\begin{aligned}\sigma_{\text{port (k)}} &= \sqrt{(0.80)^2(0.07)^2 + (0.20)^2(0.10)^2 + 2(0.80)(0.20)(0.00)}\\ &= \sqrt{0.003536}\\ &= 0.0595\end{aligned}$$

These alternative weights with a constant correlation would yield the following risk–return combinations:

---

[10]Again, you are encouraged to fill in the steps we skipped in the computations.

Case	W_1	W_2	$E(R_i)$	$E(\sigma_{port})$
f	0.00	1.00	0.20	0.1000
g	0.20	0.80	0.18	0.0812
h	0.40	0.60	0.16	0.0662
i	0.50	0.50	0.15	0.0610
j	0.60	0.40	0.14	0.0580
k	0.80	0.20	0.12	0.0595
m	1.00	0.00	0.10	0.0700

A graph of these combinations appears in Figure 8.7 for the curve with $r_{1,2} = +0.00$. You could derive a complete curve by simply varying the weighting by smaller increments.

A notable result is that with low, zero, or negative correlations, it is possible to derive portfolios that have *lower risk than either single asset.* In our set of examples where $r_{ij} = 0.00$, this occurs in Cases h, i, j, and k. This ability to reduce risk is the essence of diversification. In turn, we see that the crucial factors that affect diversification are the correlations between assets and the weighting among them.

As shown in Figure 8.7, the curvature in the graph depends on the correlation between the two assets or portfolios. With $r_{ij} = +1.00$, the combinations lie along a straight line between the two assets. When $r_{ij} = 0.50$, the curve is to the right of our $r_{ij} = 0.00$ curve, while the $r_{ij} = -0.50$ is to the left. Finally, when $r_{ij} = -1.00$, the graph would be two straight lines that would touch at the vertical line (zero risk) with some combination. As discussed in Appendix B of this chapter, it is possible to solve for the specified set of weights that would give a portfolio with zero risk. In this case, it is $W_1 = 0.412$ and $W_2 = 0.588$.

A THREE-ASSET PORTFOLIO

A demonstration of what occurs with a three-asset class portfolio is useful because it shows the dynamics of the portfolio process when we add additional assets to a portfolio. It also

FIGURE 8.7 **PORTFOLIO RISK-RETURN PLOTS FOR DIFFERENT WEIGHTS WHEN $r_{i,j}$ = +1.00; +0.50; 0.00; −0.50; −1.00**

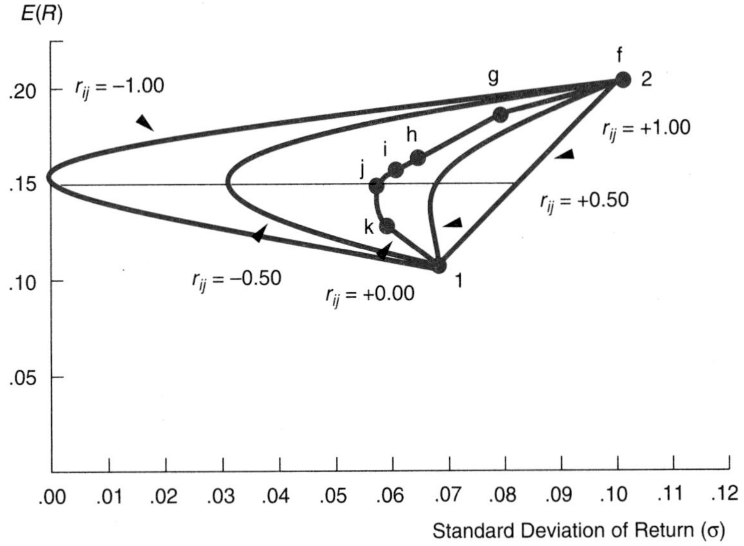
E(R)
.20
.15
.10
.05
r_{ij} = −1.00
r_{ij} = +1.00
r_{ij} = +0.50
r_{ij} = −0.50
r_{ij} = +0.00
f
g
h
i
j
k
1
2
.00 .01 .02 .03 .04 .05 .06 .07 .08 .09 .10 .11 .12
Standard Deviation of Return (σ)

shows the rapid growth in the computations required, which is why we will stop at three assets.

In this example, we will combine three asset classes we have been discussing: stocks, bonds, and cash equivalents.[11] We will assume the following characteristics for these assets:

Asset Classes	$E(R_i)$	$E(\sigma_i)$	W_i
Stocks (S)	.12	.20	.60
Bonds (B)	.08	.10	.30
Cash equivalent (C)	.04	.03	.10

The correlations are as follows:

$$r_{S,B} = 0.25; \; r_{S,C} = -0.08; \; r_{B,C} = 0.15$$

Given the weights specified, the $E(R_p)$ is:

$$\begin{aligned} E(R_p) &= (0.60)(0.12) + (0.30)(0.08) + (0.10)(0.04) \\ &= (0.072 + 0.024 + 0.004) = 0.100 = 10.00\% \end{aligned}$$

When we apply the generalized formula to the expected standard deviation of a three-asset class, it is as follows:

$$\sigma_p^2 = \left[W_S^2\sigma_S^2 + W_B^2\sigma_B^2 + W_C^2\sigma_C^2\right] + \left[2W_SW_B\sigma_S\sigma_B r_{S,B} + 2W_SW_C\sigma_S\sigma_C r_{S,C} + 2W_BW_C\sigma_B\sigma_C r_{B,C}\right]$$

Using the characteristics specified, the standard deviation of this three-asset class portfolio (σ_p) would be:

$$\begin{aligned} \sigma_p^2 &= \left[(0.6)^2(0.20)^2 + (0.3)^2(0.10)^2 + (0.1)^2(0.03)^2\right] \\ &\quad + \left\{\left[2(0.6)(0.3)(0.20)(0.10)(0.25)\right] + \left[2(0.6)(0.1)(0.20)(0.03)(-0.08)\right]\right. \\ &\quad \left. + \left[2(0.3)(0.1)(0.10)(0.03)(0.15)\right]\right\} \\ &= \left[0.015309\right] + \left\{\left[0.0018\right] + \left[-0.0000576\right] + \left[0.000027\right]\right\} \\ &= 0.0170784 \\ \sigma_p &= (0.0170784)^{1/2} = 0.1306 = 13.06\% \end{aligned}$$

ESTIMATION ISSUES It is important to keep in mind that the results of this portfolio asset allocation depend on the accuracy of the statistical inputs. In the current instance, this means that for every asset (or asset class) being considered for inclusion in the portfolio, you must estimate its expected returns and standard deviation. In addition, the correlation coefficient among the entire set of assets must also be estimated. The number of correlation estimates can be significant—for example, for a portfolio of 100 securities, the number is 4,950 (that is, 99 + 98 + 97 + . . .). The potential source of error that arises from these approximations is referred to as *estimation risk.*

[11]The asset allocation articles regularly contained in the *Wall Street Journal* generally refer to these three asset classes.

It is possible to reduce the number of correlation coefficients that must be estimated by assuming that stock returns can be described by a single index market model as follows:

$$R_i = a_i + b_i R_m + \epsilon_i$$

where:

b_i = the slope coefficient that relates the returns for security i to the returns for the aggregate stock market
R_m = the returns for the aggregate stock market

If all the securities are similarly related to the market and a b_i derived for each one, it can be shown that the correlation coefficient between two securities i and j is given as:

$$r_{ij} = b_i b_j \frac{\sigma_m^2}{\sigma_i \sigma_j}$$

where σ_m^2 = the variance of returns for the aggregate stock market.

This reduces the number of estimates from 4,950 to 100—that is, once you have derived a slope estimate (b_i) for each security, the correlation estimates can be computed. Keep in mind that this assumes that the single index market model provides a good estimate of security returns.

The Efficient Frontier

If we examined different two-asset combinations and derived the curves assuming all the possible weights, we would have a graph like that in Figure 8.8. The envelope curve that contains the best of all these possible combinations is referred to as the **efficient frontier**. Specifically, *the efficient frontier represents that set of portfolios that has the maximum rate of return for every given level of risk, or the minimum risk for every level of return.* An example of such a frontier is shown in Figure 8.9. Every portfolio that lies on the efficient frontier has either a higher rate of return for equal risk or lower risk for an equal rate of return than some portfolio beneath the frontier. Thus, we would say that Portfolio A *dominates* Portfolio C because it has an equal rate of return but substantially less risk. Similarly, Portfolio B dominates Portfolio C because it has equal risk but a higher expected rate of return. Because of the benefits of diversification among imperfectly correlated assets, we would expect the efficient frontier to be made up of *portfolios* of investments rather than

FIGURE 8.8 **NUMEROUS PORTFOLIO COMBINATIONS OF AVAILABLE ASSETS**

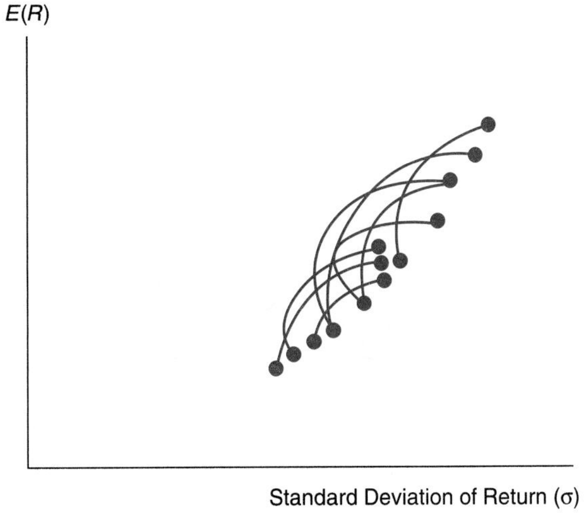
E(R)
Standard Deviation of Return (σ)

FIGURE 8.9 **EFFICIENT FRONTIER FOR ALTERNATIVE PORTFOLIOS**

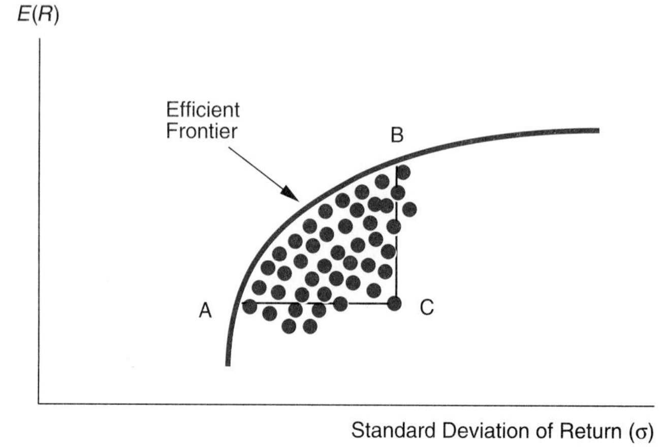
E(R)
Efficient
Frontier
B
A
C
Standard Deviation of Return (σ)

individual securities. Two possible exceptions arise at the end points, which represent the asset with the highest return and that asset with the lowest risk.

As an investor, you will target a point along the efficient frontier based on your utility function and your attitude toward risk. No portfolio on the efficient frontier can dominate any other portfolio on the efficient frontier. All of these portfolios have different return and risk measures, with expected rates of return that increase with higher risk.

The Efficient Frontier and Investor Utility

The curve in Figure 8.9 shows that the slope of the efficient frontier curve decreases steadily as you move upward. This implies that adding equal increments of risk as you move up the efficient frontier gives you diminishing increments of expected return. To evaluate this slope, we calculate the slope of the efficient frontier as follows:

$$\frac{\Delta E(R_{\text{port}})}{\Delta E(\sigma_{\text{port}})}$$

An individual investor's utility curves specify the trade-offs he or she is willing to make between expected return and risk. In conjunction with the efficient frontier, these utility curves determine which *particular* portfolio on the efficient frontier best suits an individual investor. Two investors will choose the same portfolio from the efficient set only if their utility curves are identical.

Figure 8.10 shows two sets of utility curves along with an efficient frontier of investments. The curves labeled U_1 are for a strongly risk-averse investor (with U_3 U_2 U_1). These utility curves are quite steep, indicating that the investor will not tolerate much additional risk to obtain additional returns. The investor is equally disposed toward any $E(R)$, $E(\sigma)$ combinations along a specific utility curve, such as U_1.

The curves labeled $U_{1'}$ ($U_{3'}$ $U_{2'}$ $U_{1'}$) characterize a less risk-averse investor. Such an investor is willing to tolerate a bit more risk to get a higher expected return.

The **optimal portfolio** is the portfolio on the efficient frontier that has the highest utility for a given investor. It lies at *the point of tangency between the efficient frontier and the curve with the highest possible utility.* A conservative investor's highest utility is at point *X* in Figure 8.10, where the curve U_2 just touches the efficient frontier. A less–risk-averse investor's highest utility occurs at point *Y*, which represents a portfolio with a higher expected return and higher risk than the portfolio at *X*.

FIGURE 8.10 SELECTING AN OPTIMAL RISKY PORTFOLIO ON THE EFFICIENT FRONTIER

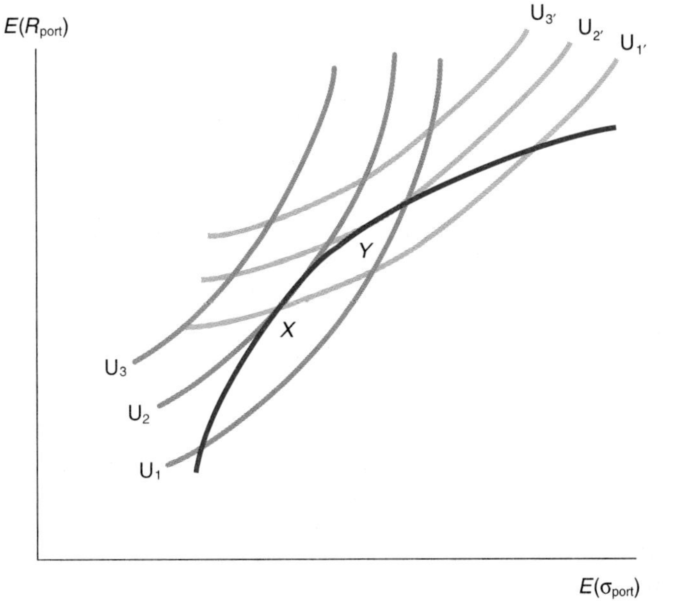
$E(R_{port})$
$U_{3'}$
$U_{2'}$
$U_{1'}$
Y
X
U_3
U_2
U_1
$E(\sigma_{port})$

THE INTERNET *Investments Online*

By seeking to operate on the efficient frontier, portfolio managers try to minimize risk for a certain level of return, or maximize return for a given level of risk. Software programs, called *optimizers,* are used by portfolio managers to determine the shape of the efficient frontier as well as to determine some of the portfolios that lie on it. Financial planners use information on past returns and manager performance, in addition to optimizers, to make recommendations to their clients. Some interesting Web sites for money managers includes:

www.pionlie.com This is the home page for *Pensions and Investments,* a newspaper for money managers. Items on the home page include links to news of interest to managers, PIPER performance data on over 3,000 equity, fixed-income, real estate, and global portfolios managed by over 1,100 management firms, research (with links to thousands of articles and listings), and other links to organizations, such as central banks, consultants, and sellers of investment-related products. The performance section shows, among other items, returns, risk and graphic analyses of over 60 PIPER-style universes and over 90 benchmark portfolios.

www.investmentnews.com *Investment News* is a sister publication to *Pensions and Investments,* with a focus toward the financial advisor. This site includes information on financial planning, the mutual fund industry, regulation, equity performance and industry trends.

www.micropal.com This site provides fund information for over 38,000 funds in 19 countries. Performance data are available over daily, weekly, and monthly intervals. Users can see performance by fund objective, read economic commentaries, and screen and sort the site's database.

www.riskview.com The creators of this home page want to help people identify risk in their portfolios. It includes access to risk and return for about 3,000 equities from 29 countries. The site features historical return and volatility measures, risk–return analysis, and forecasts of future volatilities and correlations.

(continued)

THE INTERNET *Investments Online (cont.)*

www.altivest.com The home page of Alternative Investment Corporation seeks to encourage investors to use convertible securities and "convertible arbitrage" in their portfolios (convertible arbitrage, as explained on this site, involves going long in a convertible security while shorting shares of the underlying equity). It presents an interesting application of this chapter since the firm attempts to identify investments with low correlations to the stock and bond markets in an effort to shift investors' efficient frontier outward. If a site visitor enters data from his or her current portfolio, an optimizer program will compute two portfolio solutions (maximum return for the portfolio's current risk, and minimum risk for the portfolio's current return).

Summary

- The basic Markowitz portfolio model derived the expected rate of return for a portfolio of assets and a measure of expected risk, which is the standard deviation of expected rate of return. Markowitz shows that the expected rate of return of a portfolio is the weighted average of the expected return for the individual investments in the portfolio. The standard deviation of a portfolio is a function not only of the standard deviations for the individual investments, but *also* of the covariance between the rates of return for all the pairs of assets in the portfolio. In a large portfolio, these covariances are the important factors.
- Different weights or amounts of a portfolio held in various assets yield a curve of potential combinations. Correlation coefficients among assets are the critical factor you must consider when selecting investments because you can maintain your rate of return while reducing the risk level of your portfolio by combining assets or portfolios that have low positive or negative correlation.
- Assuming numerous assets and a multitude of combination curves, the efficient frontier is the envelope curve that encompasses all of the best combinations. It defines the set of portfolios that has the highest expected return for each given level of risk, or the minimum risk for each given level of return. From this set of dominant portfolios, you select the one that lies at the point of tangency between the efficient frontier and your highest utility curve. Because risk–return utility functions differ among investors, your point of tangency and, therefore, your portfolio choice will probably differ from those of other investors.
- At this point, we understand that an optimum portfolio is a combination of investments, each having desirable individual risk–return characteristics that also fit together based on their correlations. This deeper understanding of portfolio theory should lead you to reflect back on our earlier discussion of global investing. Because many foreign stock and bond investments provide superior rates of return compared with U.S. securities *and* have low correlations with portfolios of U.S. stocks and bonds as shown in Chapter 3, including these foreign securities in your portfolio will help you to reduce the overall risk of your portfolio while possibly increasing your rate of return.

Questions

1. Why do most investors hold diversified portfolios?
2. What is covariance, and why is it important in portfolio theory?
3. Why do most assets of the same type show positive covariances of returns with each other? Would you expect positive covariances of returns between *different* types of assets such as returns on Treasury bills, General Electric common stock, and commercial real estate? Why or why not?
4. What is the relationship between covariance and the correlation coefficient?
5. Explain the shape of the efficient frontier.
6. Draw a properly labeled graph of the Markowitz efficient frontier. Describe the efficient frontier in exact terms. Discuss the concept of dominant portfolios and show an example of one on your graph.
7. Assume you want to run a computer program to derive the efficient frontier for your feasible set of stocks. What information must you input to the program?
8. Why are investors' utility curves important in portfolio theory?

9. Explain how a given investor chooses an optimal portfolio. Will this choice always be a diversified portfolio, or could it be a single asset? Explain your answer.
10. Assume that you and a business associate develop an efficient frontier for a set of investments. Why might the two of you select different portfolios on the frontier?
11. Draw a hypothetical graph of an efficient frontier of U.S. common stocks. On the same graph, draw an efficient frontier assuming the inclusion of U.S. bonds as well. Finally, on the same graph, draw an efficient frontier that includes U.S. common stocks, U.S. bonds, and stocks and bonds from around the world. Discuss the differences in these frontiers.
12. Stocks K, L, and M each have the same expected return and standard deviation. The correlation coefficients between each pair of these stocks are:

K and L	correlation coefficient = +0.8
K and M	correlation coefficient = +0.2
L and M	correlation coefficient = −0.4

Given these correlations, a portfolio constructed of which pair of stocks will have the lowest standard deviation? Explain.

Problems

1. Considering the world economic outlook for the coming year and estimates of sales and earnings for the pharmaceutical industry, you expect the rate of return for Lauren Labs common stock to range between −20 percent and +40 percent with the following probabilities:

Probability	Possible Returns
0.10	−0.20
0.15	−0.05
0.20	0.10
0.25	0.15
0.20	0.20
0.10	0.40

Compute the expected rate of return $[E(R_i)]$ for Lauren Labs.

2. Given the following market values of stocks in your portfolio and their expected rates of return, what is the expected rate of return for your common stock portfolio?

Stock	Market Value ($ Mil.)	$E(R_i)$
Phillips Petroleum	$15,000	0.14
Starbucks	17,000	−0.04
International Paper	32,000	0.18
Intel	23,000	0.16
Walgreens	7,000	0.12

3. The following are the monthly rates of return for Madison Software Corp. and for General Electric during a 6-month period.

Month	Madison Software	General Electric
1	−.04	.07
2	.06	−.02
3	−.07	−.10
4	.12	.15
5	−.02	−.06
6	.05	.02

Compute the following:

a. Expected monthly rate of return $[E(R_i)]$ for each stock.

b. Standard deviation of returns for each stock.

c. The covariance between the rates of return.

d. The correlation coefficient between the rates of return.

What level of correlation did you expect? How did your expectations compare with the computed correlation? Would these two stocks offer a good chance for diversification? Why or why not?

4. You are considering two assets with the following characteristics:

$$E(R_1) = .15 \qquad E(\sigma_1) = .10 \qquad W_1 = .5$$
$$E(R_2) = .20 \qquad E(\sigma_2) = .20 \qquad W_2 = .5$$

Compute the mean and standard deviation of two portfolios if $r_{1,2} = 0.40$ and -0.60, respectively. Plot the two portfolios on a risk–return graph and briefly explain the results.

5. Given: $E(R_1) = .10$
$E(R_2) = .15$
$E(\sigma_1) = .03$
$E(\sigma_2) = .05$

Calculate the expected returns and expected standard deviations of a two-stock portfolio in which Stock 1 has a weight of 60 percent under the following conditions:

a. $r_{1,2} = 1.00$
b. $r_{1,2} = 0.75$
c. $r_{1,2} = 0.25$
d. $r_{1,2} = 0.00$
e. $r_{1,2} = -0.25$
f. $r_{1,2} = -0.75$
g. $r_{1,2} = -1.00$

Calculate the expected returns and expected standard deviations of a two-stock portfolio having a correlation coefficient of 0.70 under the following conditions:

a. $w_1 = 1.00$
b. $w_1 = 0.75$
c. $w_1 = 0.50$
d. $w_1 = 0.25$
e. $w_1 = 0.05$

6. Given: $E(R_1) = 0.12$
$E(R_2) = 0.16$
$E(\sigma_1) = 0.04$
$E(\sigma_2) = 0.06$

Plot the results on a return–risk graph. Without calculations, draw in what a curve with varying weights would look like if the correlation coefficient had been 0.00; or if it had been −0.70.

7. The following are monthly percentage price changes for four market indexes:

Month	DJIA	S&P 400	AMEX	NIKKEI
1	.03	.02	.04	.04
2	.07	.06	.10	−.02
3	−.02	−.01	−.04	.07
4	.01	.03	.03	.02
5	.05	.04	.11	.02
6	−.06	−.04	−.08	.06

Compute the following:

a. Expected monthly rate of return for each series.

b. Standard deviation for each series.

c. Covariance between the rates of return for the following indexes:
DJIA—S&P 400
S&P 400—AMEX
S&P 400—NIKKEI
AMEX—NIKKEI

d. The correlation coefficients for the same four combinations.

e. Using the answers from parts a, b, and d, calculate the expected return and standard deviation of a portfolio consisting of equal parts of (1) the S&P and the AMEX and (2) the S&P and the NIKKEI. Discuss the two portfolios.

8. The standard deviation of Shamrock Corp. stock is 19 percent. The standard deviation of Cagney Co. stock is 14 percent. The covariance between these two stocks is 100. What is the correlation between Shamrock and Cagney stock?

References

Elton, Edwin J., and Martin J. Gruber. *Modern Portfolio Theory and Investment Analysis.* 5th ed. New York: John Wiley & Sons, Inc., 1995.

Farrell, James L., Jr. *Portfolio Management: Theory and Application.* 2d ed. New York: McGraw-Hill, 1997.

Harrington, Diana R. *Modern Portfolio Theory, the Capital Asset Pricing Model, and Arbitrage Pricing Theory: A User's Guide.* 2d ed. Englewood Cliffs, N.J.: Prentice-Hall, 1987.

Maginn, John L., and Donald L. Tuttle, eds. *Managing Investment Portfolios: A Dynamic Process.* 2d ed. Sponsored by The Institute of Chartered Financial Analysts. Boston: Warren, Gorham & Lamont, 1990.

Markowitz, Harry. "Portfolio Selection." *Journal of Finance* 7, no. 1 (March 1952).

Markowitz, Harry. *Portfolio Selection: Efficient Diversification of Investments.* New York: John Wiley & Sons, 1959.

Chapter 8 APPENDIX

A. Proof That Minimum Portfolio Variance Occurs with Equal Weights When Securities Have Equal Variance

When $E(\sigma_1) = E(\sigma_2)$, we have:

$$E(\sigma^2_{\text{port}}) = w_1^2E(\sigma_1)^2 + (1 - w_1)^2E(\sigma_1)^2 - 2w_1(1 - w_1)r_{1,2}E(\sigma_1)^2$$
$$= E(\sigma_1)^2\left[w_1^2 + 1 - 2w_1 + w_1^2 + 2w_1r_{1,2} - 2w_1^2r_{1,2}\right]$$
$$= E(\sigma_1)^2\left[2w_1^2 + 1 - 2w_1 + 2w_1r_{1,2} - 2w_1^2r_{1,2}\right]$$

For this to be a minimum,

$$\frac{\partial E(\sigma^2_{\text{port}})}{\partial w_1} = 0 = E(\sigma_1)^2\left[4w_1 \times 2 + 2r_{1,2} \times 4w_1r_{1,2}\right]$$

Assuming $E(\sigma_1)^2 > 0$,

$$4w_1 - 2 + 2r_{1,2} - 4w_1r_{1,2} = 0$$
$$4w_1(1 - r_{1,2}) - 2(1 - r_{1,2}) = 0$$

from which

$$w_1 = \frac{2(1 - r_{1,2})}{4(1 - r_{1,2})} = \frac{1}{2}$$

regardless of $r_{1,2}$. Thus, if $E(\sigma_1) = E(\sigma_2)$, $E(\sigma^2_{port})$ will *always* be minimized by choosing $w_1 = w_2 = ½$, regardless of the value of $r_{1,2}$, except when $r_{1,2} = +1$ (in which case $E(\sigma_{port}) = E(\sigma_1) = E(\sigma_2)$. This can be verified by checking the second-order condition

$$\frac{\partial E(\sigma^2_{port})}{\partial w_1^2} > 0$$

PROBLEMS

1. The following information applies to Questions 1a and 1b. The general equation for the weight of the first security to achieve minimum variance (in a two-stock portfolio) is given by

$$w_1 = \frac{E(\sigma_2)^2 - r_{1,2}\,E(\sigma_1)E(\sigma_2)}{E(\sigma_1)^2 + E(\sigma_2)^2 - 2r_{1,2}\,E(\sigma_1)E(\sigma_2)}$$

1a. Show that $w_1 = 0.5$ when $E(\sigma_1) = E(\sigma_2)$.
1b. What is the weight of Security 1 that gives minimum portfolio variance when $r_{1,2} = 0.5$, $E(\sigma_1) = 0.04$, and $E(\sigma_2) = 0.06$?

Chapter 8 APPENDIX

B. DERIVATION OF WEIGHTS THAT WILL GIVE ZERO VARIANCE WHEN CORRELATION EQUALS −1.00

$$\begin{aligned} E(\sigma^2_{port}) &= w_1^2E(\sigma_1)^2 + (1 - w_1)^2E(\sigma_2)^2 + 2w_1(1 - w_1)r_{1,2}E(\sigma_1)E(\sigma_2) \\ &= w_1^2E(\sigma_1)^2 + E(\sigma_2)^2 - 2w_1E(\sigma_2) - w_1^2E(\sigma_2)^2 + 2w_1r_{1,2}E(\sigma_1)E(\sigma_2) - 2w_1^2r_{1,2}E(\sigma_1)E(\sigma_2) \end{aligned}$$

If $r_{1,2} = 1$, this can be rearranged and expressed as

$$\begin{aligned} E(\sigma^2_{port}) &= w_1^2\left[E(\sigma_1)^2 + 2E(\sigma_1)E(\sigma_2) + E(\sigma_2)^2\right] - 2w\left[E(\sigma_2)^2 + E(\sigma_1)E(\sigma_2)\right] + E(\sigma_2)^2 \\ &= w_1^2\left[E(\sigma_1) + E(\sigma_2)\right]^2 - 2w_1E(\sigma_2)\left[E(\sigma_1) - E(\sigma_2)\right] + E(\sigma_2)^2 \\ &= \left\{w_1\left[E(\sigma_1) + E(\sigma_2)\right] - E(\sigma_2)\right\}^2 \end{aligned}$$

We want to find the weight, w_1, which will reduce $E(\sigma^2_{port})$ to *zero;* therefore,

$$w_1[E(\sigma_1) + E(\sigma_2)] - E(\sigma_2) = 0$$

which yields

$$w_1 = \frac{E(\sigma_2)}{E(\sigma_1) + E(\sigma_2)}, \text{ and } w_2 = 1 - w_1 = \frac{E(\sigma_1)}{E(\sigma_1) + E(\sigma_2)}$$

PROBLEM

1. Given two assets with the following characteristics:

$E(R_1) = .12$	$E(\sigma_1) = .04$
$E(R_2) = .16$	$E(\sigma_2) = .06$

Assume that $r_{1,2} = -1.00$. What is the weight that would yield a zero variance for the portfolio?

Chapter 9

An Introduction to Asset Pricing Models

After you read this chapter, you should be able to answer the following questions:

- What are the assumptions of the capital asset pricing model?
- What is a risk-free asset and what are its risk–return characteristics?
- What is the covariance and correlation between the risk-free asset and a risky asset or portfolio of risky assets?
- What is the expected return when you combine the risk-free asset and a portfolio of risky assets?
- What is the standard deviation when you combine the risk-free asset and a portfolio of risky assets?
- When you combine the risk-free asset and a portfolio of risky assets on the Markowitz efficient frontier, what does the set of possible portfolios look like?
- Given the initial set of portfolio possibilities with a risk-free asset, what happens when you add financial leverage (that is, borrow)?
- What is the market portfolio, what assets are included in this portfolio, and what are the relative weights for the alternative assets included?
- What is the capital market line (CML)?
- What do we mean by complete diversification?
- How do we measure diversification for an individual portfolio?
- What are systematic and unsystematic risk?
- Given the CML, what is the separation theorem?
- Given the CML, what is the relevant risk measure for an individual risky asset?
- What is the security market line (SML), and how does it differ from the CML?
- What is *beta,* and why is it referred to as a standardized measure of systematic risk?
- How can you use the SML to determine the expected (required) rate of return for a risky asset?
- Using the SML, what do we mean by an undervalued and overvalued security, and how do we determine whether an asset is undervalued or overvalued?
- What is an asset's characteristic line, and how do you compute the characteristic line for an asset?
- What is the impact on the characteristic line when you compute it using different return intervals (such as weekly versus monthly) and when you employ different proxies (that is, benchmarks) for the market portfolio (for example, the S&P 500 versus a global stock index)?
- What is the arbitrage pricing theory (APT) and how does it differ from the capital asset pricing model (CAPM) in terms of assumptions?
- How does the APT differ from the CAPM in terms of risk measures?

Following the development of portfolio theory by Markowitz, two major theories have been put forth that employ the theory to derive a model for the valuation of risky assets. In this chapter, we introduce these two models. The background on asset pricing models is important at this point in the book because the risk measures implied by these models are a necessary input for our subsequent discussion on the valuation of risky assets. The bulk of the presentation concerns capital market theory and the capital asset pricing model (CAPM) that was developed almost concurrently by three individuals. Subsequently, an alternative asset valuation model has been proposed, the arbitrage pricing theory (APT). This theory and the implied pricing model are likewise introduced and discussed.

CAPITAL MARKET THEORY: AN OVERVIEW

Because capital market theory builds on portfolio theory, this chapter begins where the discussion of the Markowitz efficient frontier ended. We assume that you have examined the set of risky assets and derived the aggregate efficient frontier. Further, we assume that you and all other investors want to maximize your utility in terms of risk and return, so you will choose portfolios of risky assets on the efficient frontier at points where your utility maps are tangent to the frontier as shown in Figure 8.10. When you make your investment decision in this manner, you are referred to as a *Markowitz efficient investor.*

Capital market theory extends portfolio theory and develops a model for pricing all risky assets. The final product, the *capital asset pricing model (CAPM),* will allow you to determine the required rate of return for any risky asset.

We begin with the background of capital market theory that includes the underlying assumptions of the theory and a discussion of the factors that led to its development following the Markowitz portfolio theory. Principal among these factors was the analysis of the effect of assuming the existence of a risk-free asset. This is the subject of the next section.

We will see that assuming the existence of a risk-free rate has significant implications for the potential return and risk and alternative risk–return combinations. This discussion implies a central portfolio of risky assets on the efficient frontier, which we call the *market portfolio.* We discuss the market portfolio in the third section and what it implies regarding different types of risk.

The fourth section considers which types of risk are relevant to an investor who believes in capital market theory. Having defined a measure of risk, we consider how you determine your required rate of return on an investment. You can then compare this required rate of return to your estimate of the asset's expected rate of return during your investment horizon to determine whether the asset is undervalued or overvalued. The section ends with a demonstration of how to calculate the risk measure implied by capital market theory.

The final section discusses an alternative asset pricing model, the arbitrage pricing theory (APT). This model requires fewer assumptions than the CAPM and contends that the required rate of return for a risky asset is a function of *multiple* factors. This is in contrast to the CAPM, which is a single-factor model, that is, the CAPM assumes that the risk of an asset is determined by a single variable, its beta. There is a brief demonstration of how to evaluate the risk of an asset and determine its required rate of return using the APT model.

Background for Capital Market Theory

When dealing with any theory in science, economics, or finance, it is necessary to articulate a set of assumptions that specify how the world is expected to act. This allows the theoretician to concentrate on developing a theory that explains how some facet of the world will respond to changes in the environment. In the first part of this section, we consider the main assumptions that underlie the development of capital market theory. The second part of the section considers the major assumptions that allowed theoreticians to extend the portfolio model's techniques for combining investments into an optimal portfolio to a model that explains how to determine the value of those investments (or other assets).

ASSUMPTIONS OF CAPITAL MARKET THEORY Because capital market theory builds on the Markowitz portfolio model, it requires the same assumptions, along with some additional ones:

1. All investors are Markowitz efficient investors who want to target points on the efficient frontier. The exact location on the efficient frontier and, therefore, the specific portfolio selected, will depend on the individual investor's risk–return utility function.
2. Investors can borrow or lend any amount of money at the risk-free rate of return (RFR). Clearly, it is always possible to lend money at the nominal risk-free rate by buying risk-free securities such as government T-bills. It is not always possible to borrow at this risk-free rate, but we will see that assuming a higher borrowing rate does not change the general results.
3. All investors have homogeneous expectations; that is, they estimate identical probability distributions for future rates of return. Again, this assumption can be relaxed. As long as the differences in expectations are not vast, their effects are minor.
4. All investors have the same one-period time horizon such as one month, six months, or one year. The model will be developed for a single hypothetical period, and its results could be affected by a different assumption. A difference in the time horizon would require investors to derive risk measures and risk-free assets that are consistent with their investment horizons.
5. All investments are infinitely divisible, which means that it is possible to buy or sell fractional shares of any asset or portfolio. This assumption allows us to discuss investment alternatives as continuous curves. Changing it would have little impact on the theory.
6. There are no taxes or transaction costs involved in buying or selling assets. This is a reasonable assumption in many instances. Neither pension funds nor religious groups have to pay taxes, and the transaction costs for most financial institutions are less than 1 percent on most financial instruments. Again, relaxing this assumption modifies the results, but it does not change the basic thrust.
7. There is no inflation or any change in interest rates, or inflation is fully anticipated. This is a reasonable initial assumption, and it can be modified.
8. Capital markets are in equilibrium. This means that we begin with all investments properly priced in line with their risk levels.

You may consider some of these assumptions unrealistic and wonder how useful a theory we can derive with these assumptions. In this regard, two points are important. First, as mentioned, relaxing many of these assumptions would have only minor influence on the model and would not change its main implications or conclusions. Second, a theory should never be judged on the basis of its assumptions, but rather on how well it explains and helps us predict behavior in the real world. If this theory and the model it implies help us explain the rates of return on a wide variety of risky assets, it is useful, even if some of its assumptions are unrealistic. Such success implies that the questionable assumptions must be unimportant to the ultimate objective of the model, which is to explain asset pricing and rates of return on assets.

DEVELOPMENT OF CAPITAL MARKET THEORY The major factor that allowed portfolio theory to develop into capital market theory is the concept of a risk-free asset. Following the development of the Markowitz portfolio model, several authors considered the implications of assuming the existence of a **risk-free asset**, that is, an asset with *zero variance.* As we will show, such an asset would have zero correlation with all other risky assets and would provide the *risk-free rate of return (RFR).* It would lie on the vertical axis of a portfolio graph.

This assumption allows us to derive a generalized theory of capital asset pricing under conditions of uncertainty from the Markowitz portfolio theory. This achievement is generally attributed to William Sharpe, for which he received the Nobel Prize, but Lintner and Mossin derived similar theories independently.[1] Consequently, you may see references to the Sharpe-Lintner-Mossin (SLM) capital asset pricing model.

Risk-Free Asset

As noted, the assumption of a risk-free asset in the economy is critical to asset pricing theory. Therefore, this section explains the meaning of a risk-free asset and shows the effect on the risk and return measures when this risk-free asset is combined with a portfolio on the Markowitz efficient frontier.

We have defined a **risky asset** as one from which future returns are uncertain and we have measured this uncertainty by the variance, or standard deviation of expected returns. Because the expected return on a risk-free asset is entirely certain, the standard deviation of its expected return is zero ($\sigma_{RF} = 0$). The rate of return earned on such an asset should be the risk-free rate of return (RFR), which, as we discussed in Chapter 1, should equal the expected long-run growth rate of the economy with an adjustment for short-run liquidity. The next sections show what happens when we introduce this risk-free asset into the risky world of the Markowitz portfolio model.

COVARIANCE WITH A RISK-FREE ASSET Recall that the covariance between two sets of returns is

$$\text{Cov}_{ij} = \sum_{i=1}^{n}[R_i - E(R_i)][R_j - E(R_j)]/n$$

Because the returns for the risk-free asset are certain, $\sigma_{RF} = 0$, which means that $R_i = E(R_i)$ during all periods. Thus, $R_i - E(R_i)$ will also equal zero, and the product of this expression with any other expression will equal zero. Consequently, the covariance of the risk-free asset with any risky asset or portfolio of assets will always equal zero. Similarly, the correlation between any risky asset *i,* and the risk-free asset, RF, would be zero because it is equal to

$$r_{RF,i} = \text{Cov}_{RF,i}/\sigma_{RF}\sigma_j$$

COMBINING A RISK-FREE ASSET WITH A RISKY PORTFOLIO What happens to the average rate of return and the standard deviation of returns when you combine a risk-free asset with a portfolio of risky assets such as those that exist on the Markowitz efficient frontier?

Expected Return Like the expected return for a portfolio of two risky assets, the expected rate of return for a portfolio that includes a risk-free asset is the weighted average of the two returns:

[1]William F. Sharpe, "Capital Asset Prices: A Theory of Market Equilibrium under Conditions of Risk," *Journal of Finance* 19, no. 3 (September 1964): 425–442; John Lintner, "Security Prices, Risk and Maximal Gains from Diversification," *Journal of Finance* 20, no. 4 (December 1965): 587–615; and J. Mossin, "Equilibrium in a Capital Asset Market," *Econometrica* 34, no. 4 (October 1966): 768–783.

$$E(R_{\text{port}}) = w_{\text{RF}}(\text{RFR}) + (1 - w_{\text{RF}})E(R_i)$$

where:

w_{RF} = the proportion of the portfolio invested in the risk-free asset
$E(R_i)$ = the expected rate of return on risky Portfolio i

Standard Deviation Recall from Chapter 8 that the expected variance for a two-asset portfolio is

$$E(\sigma^2_{\text{port}}) = w_1^2\sigma_1^2 + w_2^2\sigma_2^2 + 2w_1w_2r_{1,2}\sigma_1\sigma_2$$

Substituting the risk-free asset for Security 1, and the risky asset portfolio for Security 2, this formula would become

$$E(\sigma^2_{\text{port}}) = w^2_{\text{RF}}\sigma^2_{\text{RF}} + (1 - w_{\text{RF}})^2\sigma_i^2 + 2w_{\text{RF}}(1 - w_{\text{RF}})r_{\text{RF},i}\sigma_{\text{RF}}\sigma_i$$

We know that the variance of the risk-free asset is zero, that is, $\sigma^2_{\text{RF}} = 0$. Because the correlation between the risk-free asset and any risky asset, *i*, is also zero, the factor $r_{\text{RF},i}$ in the equation above also equals zero. Therefore, any component of the variance formula that has either of these terms will equal zero. When you make these adjustments, the formula becomes

$$E(\sigma^2_{\text{port}}) = (1 - w_{\text{RF}})^2\sigma_i^2$$

The standard deviation is

$$E(\sigma_{\text{port}}) = \sqrt{(1 - w_{\text{RF}})^2\sigma_i^2}$$
$$= (1 - w_{\text{RF}})\sigma_i$$

Therefore, the standard deviation of a portfolio that combines the risk-free asset with risky assets is *the linear proportion of the standard deviation of the risky asset portfolio.*

The Risk–Return Combination Because both the expected return *and* the standard deviation of return for such a portfolio are linear combinations, a graph of possible portfolio returns and risks looks like a straight line between the two assets. Figure 9.1 shows a graph depicting portfolio possibilities when a risk-free asset is combined with alternative risky portfolios on the Markowitz efficient frontier.

You can attain any point along the straight line RFR-A by investing some portion of your portfolio in the risk-free asset w_{RF} and the remainder $(1 - w_{\text{RF}})$ in the risky asset portfolio at Point A on the efficient frontier. This set of portfolio possibilities dominates all the risky asset portfolios on the efficient frontier below Point A because some portfolio along Line RFR-A has equal variance with a higher rate of return than the portfolio on the original efficient frontier. Likewise, you can attain any point along the Line RFR-B by investing in some combination of the risk-free asset and the risky asset portfolio at Point B. Again, these potential combinations dominate all portfolio possibilities on the original efficient frontier below Point B (including Line RFR-A).

You can draw further lines from the RFR to the efficient frontier at higher and higher points until you reach the point where the line is tangent to the frontier, which occurs in Figure 9.1 at Point M. The set of portfolio possibilities along Line RFR-M dominates *all* portfolios below Point M. For example, you could attain a risk and return combination between the RFR and Point M (Point C) by investing one-half of your portfolio in the risk-free asset (that is, lending money at the RFR) and the other half in the risky portfolio at Point M.

FIGURE 9.1

PORTFOLIO POSSIBILITIES COMBINING THE RISK-FREE ASSET AND RISKY PORTFOLIOS ON THE EFFICIENT FRONTIER

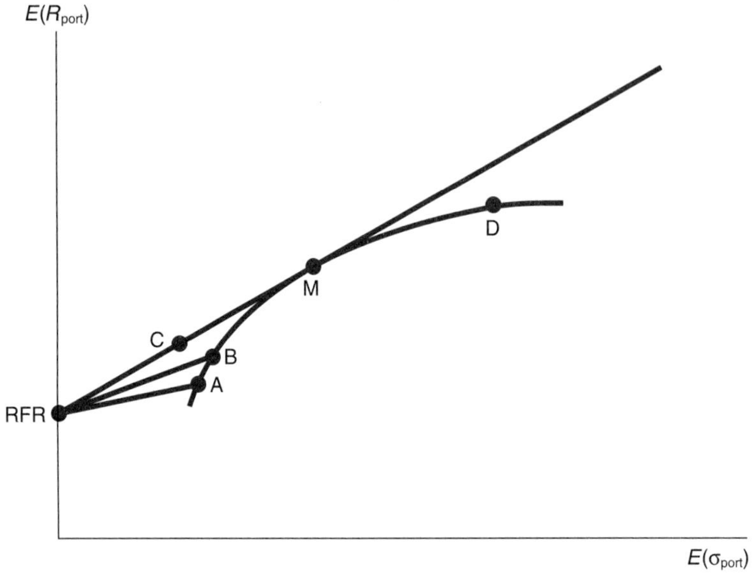
E(R_port)
D
M
C
B
A
RFR
E(σ_port)

Risk–Return Possibilities with Leverage An investor may want to attain a higher expected return than is available at Point M in exchange for accepting higher risk. One alternative would be to invest in one of the risky asset portfolios on the efficient frontier beyond Point M such as the portfolio at Point D. A second alternative is to add *leverage* to the portfolio by *borrowing* money at the risk-free rate and investing the proceeds in the risky asset portfolio at Point M. What effect would this have on the return and risk for your portfolio?

If you borrow an amount equal to 50 percent of your original wealth at the risk-free rate, w_{RF} will not be a positive fraction, but rather a negative 50 percent ($w_{RF} = -0.50$). The effect on the expected return for your portfolio is:

$$\begin{aligned} E(R_{port}) &= w_{RF}(\text{RFR}) + (1 - w_{RF})E(R_M) \\ &= -0.50(\text{RFR}) + [1 - (-0.50)]E(R_M) \\ &= -0.50(\text{RFR}) + 1.50E(R_M) \end{aligned}$$

The return will increase in a *linear* fashion along the Line RFR-M because the gross return increases by 50 percent, but you must pay interest at the RFR on the money borrowed. For example, assume that $E(\text{RFR}) = .06$ and $E(R_M) = .12$. The return on your leveraged portfolio would be:

$$\begin{aligned} E(R_{port}) &= -0.50(0.06) + 1.5(0.12) \\ &= -0.03 + 0.18 \\ &= 0.15 \end{aligned}$$

The effect on the standard deviation of the leveraged portfolio is similar.

$$\begin{aligned} E(\sigma_{port}) &= (1 - w_{RF})\sigma_M \\ &= [1 - (-0.50)]\sigma_M = 1.50\sigma_M \end{aligned}$$

FIGURE 9.2

DERIVATION OF CAPITAL MARKET LINE ASSUMING LENDING OR BORROWING AT THE RISK-FREE RATE

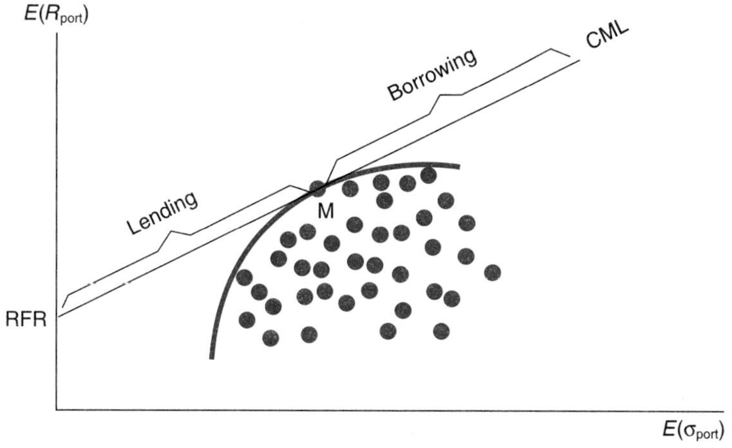
$E(R_{port})$
CML
Borrowing
Lending
M
RFR
$E(\sigma_{port})$

where:

σ_M = the standard deviation of the M portfolio

Therefore, *both return and risk increase in a linear fashion along the original Line RFR-M,* and this extension dominates everything below the line on the original efficient frontier. Thus, you have a new efficient frontier: the straight line from the *RFR* tangent to Point M. This line is referred to as the capital market line (CML) and is shown in Figure 9.2.

Our discussion of portfolio theory stated that, when two assets are perfectly correlated, the set of portfolio possibilities falls along a straight line. Therefore, because the CML is a straight line, it implies that all the portfolios on the CML are perfectly positively correlated. This positive correlation appeals to our intuition because all these portfolios on the CML combine the risky asset Portfolio M and the risk-free asset. You either invest part of your portfolio in the risk-free asset and the rest in the risky asset portfolio M, or you borrow at the risk-free rate and invest these funds in the risky asset portfolio. In either case, all the variability comes from the risky asset M portfolio. The only difference between the alternative portfolios on the CML is the magnitude of the variability, which is caused by the proportion of the risky asset portfolio in the total portfolio.

The Market Portfolio

Because Portfolio M lies at the point of tangency, it has the highest portfolio possibility line, and everybody will want to invest in Portfolio M and borrow or lend to be somewhere on the CML. This portfolio must, therefore, include *all risky assets.* If a risky asset were not in this portfolio in which everyone wants to invest, there would be no demand for it and therefore no value.

Because the market is in equilibrium, it is also necessary that all assets are included in this portfolio in *proportion to their market value.* If, for example, an asset accounts for a higher proportion of the M portfolio than its market value justifies, excess demand for this asset will increase its price until its relative market value becomes consistent with its proportion in the portfolio.

This portfolio that includes all risky assets is referred to as the **market portfolio**. It includes not only U.S. common stocks, but *all* risky assets, such as non-U.S. stocks, U.S. and non-U.S. bonds, options, real estate, coins, stamps, art, or antiques. Because the market portfolio contains all risky assets, it is a **completely diversified portfolio**, which means that all the risk unique to individual assets in the portfolio is diversified away. Specifically, the unique risk of any asset is offset by the unique variability of the other assets in the portfolio.

This unique (diversifiable) risk is also referred to as **unsystematic risk.** This implies that only **systematic risk**, which is defined as the variability in all risky assets caused by macroeconomic variables, remains in the market portfolio. This systematic risk, measured by the standard deviation of returns of the market portfolio, can change over time with changes in the macroeconomic variables that affect the valuation of all risky assets.[2] Examples of such macroeconomic variables would be variability of growth in the money supply, interest rate volatility, and variability in such factors as industrial production, corporate earnings, and cash flow.

HOW TO MEASURE DIVERSIFICATION As noted earlier, all portfolios on the CML are perfectly positively correlated, which means that all portfolios on the CML are perfectly correlated with the completely diversified market portfolio M. This implies a measure of complete diversification.[3] Specifically, a completely diversified portfolio would have a correlation with the market portfolio of +1.00. This is logical because complete diversification means the elimination of all the unsystematic or unique risk. Once you have eliminated all unsystematic risk, only systematic risk is left, which cannot be diversified away. Therefore, completely diversified portfolios would correlate perfectly with the market portfolio because it has only systematic risk.

DIVERSIFICATION AND THE ELIMINATION OF UNSYSTEMATIC RISK As discussed in Chapter 8, the purpose of diversification is to reduce the standard deviation of the total portfolio. This assumes imperfect correlations among securities.[4] Ideally, as you add securities, the average covariance for the portfolio declines. An important question is, about how many securities must be included to arrive at a completely diversified portfolio? To discover the answer, you must observe what happens as you increase the sample size of the portfolio by adding securities that have some positive correlation. The typical correlation among U.S. securities is about 0.5 to 0.6.

One set of studies examined the average standard deviation for numerous portfolios of randomly selected stocks of different sample sizes.[5] For example, Evans and Archer computed the standard deviation for portfolios of increasing numbers up to 20 stocks. The results indicated a large initial impact wherein the major benefits of diversification were achieved rather quickly. Specifically, about 90 percent of the maximum benefit of diversification was derived from portfolios of 12 to 18 stocks. Figure 9.3 shows a graph of the effect.

---

[2]For an analysis of changes in the standard deviation of returns for stocks in the United States, which is referred to as stock price volatility, see G. William Schwert, "Why Does Stock Market Volatility Change over Time?" *Journal of Finance* 44, no. 5 (December 1989): 1115–1153; Peter S. Spiro, "The Impact of Interest Rate Changes on Stock Price Volatility," *Journal of Portfolio Management* 16, no. 2 (winter 1990): 63–68; James M. Poterba and Lawrence H. Summers, "The Persistence of Volatility and Stock Market Fluctuations," *American Economic Review* 76, no. 4 (December 1981): 1142–1151; R. R. Officer, "The Variability of the Market Factor of the New York Stock Exchange," *Journal of Business* 46, no. 3 (July 1973): 434–453.

[3]James Lorie, "Diversification: Old and New," *Journal of Portfolio Management* 1, no. 2 (winter 1975): 25–28.

[4]The discussion in Chapter 8 leads one to conclude that securities with negative correlation would be ideal. Although this is true in theory, it is difficult to find such assets in the real world.

[5]John L. Evans and Stephen H. Archer, "Diversification and the Reduction of Dispersion: An Empirical Analysis," *Journal of Finance* 23, no. 5 (December 1968): 761–767; Thomas M. Tole, "You Can't Diversify without Diversifying," *Journal of Portfolio Management* 8, no. 2 (winter 1982): 5–11.

FIGURE 9.3

NUMBER OF STOCKS IN A PORTFOLIO AND THE STANDARD DEVIATION OF PORTFOLIO RETURN

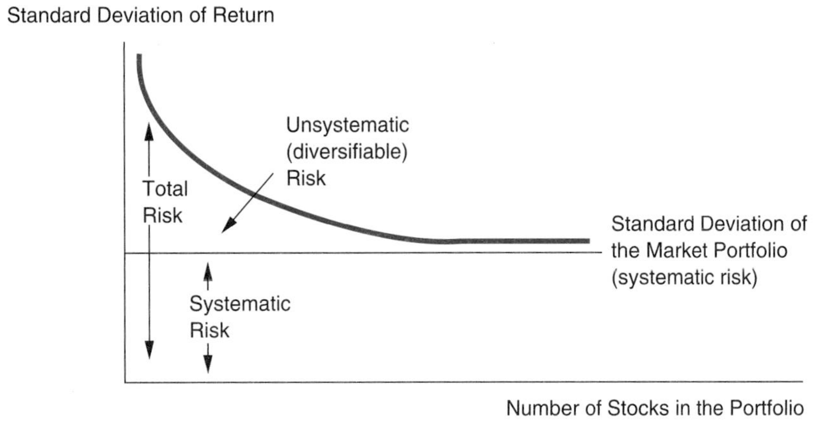
Standard Deviation of Return
Unsystematic
(diversifiable)
Risk
Total
Risk
Standard Deviation of
the Market Portfolio
(systematic risk)
Systematic
Risk
Number of Stocks in the Portfolio

A study by Statman compared the benefits of lower risk from diversification to the added transaction costs with more securities. It concluded that a well-diversified stock portfolio must include at least 30 stocks for a borrowing investor and 40 stocks for a lending investor.[6]

By adding stocks to the portfolio that are not perfectly correlated with stocks in the portfolio, you can reduce the overall standard deviation of the portfolio, but you *cannot eliminate variability.* The standard deviation of your portfolio will eventually reach the level of the market portfolio, where you will have diversified away all unsystematic risk, but you still have market or systematic risk. You cannot eliminate the variability and uncertainty of macroeconomic factors that affect all risky assets. At the same time, you will recall from the discussion in Chapter 3 that you can attain a lower level of systematic risk by diversifying globally versus only investing in the United States because some of the systematic risk factors in the U.S. market (such as U.S. monetary policy) are not correlated with systematic risk variables in other countries such as Germany and Japan. As a result, if you diversify globally you eventually get down to a world systematic-risk level.

THE CML AND THE SEPARATION THEOREM The CML leads all investors to invest in the same risky asset portfolio, the M portfolio. Individual investors should only differ regarding their position on the CML, which depends on their risk preferences.

In turn, how they get to a point on the CML is based on their *financing decisions.* If you are relatively risk averse, you will lend some part of your portfolio at the RFR by buying some risk-free securities and investing the remainder in the market portfolio of risky assets. For example, you might invest in the portfolio combination at Point A in Figure 9.4. In contrast, if you prefer more risk, you might borrow funds at the RFR and invest everything (all of your capital plus what you borrowed) in the market portfolio, building the portfolio at Point B. This financing decision provides more risk but greater returns than the market portfolio. As discussed earlier, because portfolios on the CML dominate other portfolio

[6]Meir Statman, "How Many Stocks Make a Diversified Portfolio?" *Journal of Financial and Quantitative Analysis* 22, no. 3 (September 1987): 353–363.

FIGURE 9.4 CHOICE OF OPTIMAL PORTFOLIO COMBINATIONS ON THE CML

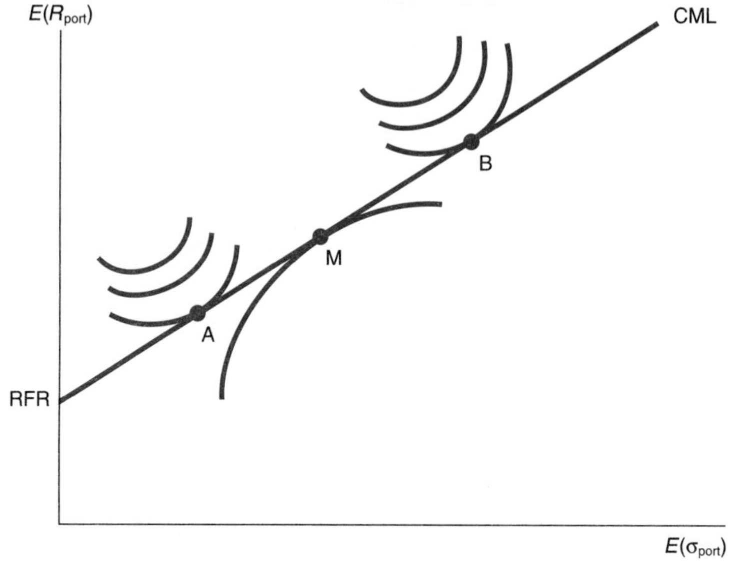
$E(R_{port})$
CML
B
M
A
RFR
$E(\sigma_{port})$

possibilities, the CML becomes the efficient frontier of portfolios, and investors decide where they want to be along this efficient frontier. Tobin called this division of the investment decision from the financing decision the **separation theorem.**[7] Specifically, to be somewhere on the CML efficient frontier, you initially decide to invest in the market portfolio M, which means that you will be on the CML. This is your *investment* decision. Subsequently, based on your risk preferences, you make a separate *financing* decision either to borrow or to lend to attain your preferred point on the CML.

A RISK MEASURE FOR THE CML In this section, we show that the relevant risk measure for risky assets is *their covariance with the M portfolio,* which is referred to as their systematic risk. The importance of this covariance is apparent from two points of view.

First, in discussing the Markowitz portfolio model, we noted that the relevant risk to consider when adding a security to a portfolio is *its average covariance with all other assets in the portfolio.* In this chapter, we have shown that *the only relevant portfolio is the M portfolio.* Together, these two findings mean that the only important consideration for any individual risky asset is its average covariance with all the risky assets in the M portfolio, or simply, *the asset's covariance with the market portfolio.* This covariance, then, is the relevant risk measure for an individual risky asset.

Second, because all individual risky assets are a part of the M portfolio, one can describe their rates of return in relation to the returns for the M portfolio using the following linear model:

$$R_{it} = a_i + b_i R_{Mt} + \epsilon$$

[7]James Tobin, "Liquidity Preference as Behavior Towards Risk," *Review of Economic Studies* 25, no. 2 (February 1958): 65–85.

where:

$R_{i,t}$ = return for asset i during period t
a_i = constant term for asset i
b_i = slope coefficient for asset i
R_{Mt} = return for the M portfolio during period t
ϵ = random error term

The variance of returns for a risky asset could be described as

$$\begin{aligned}\text{Var}(R_{it}) &= \text{Var}(a_i + b_i R_{Mt} + \epsilon)\\ &= \text{Var}(a_i) + \text{Var}(b_i R_{Mt}) + \text{Var}(\epsilon)\\ &= 0 + \text{Var}(b_i R_{Mt}) + \text{Var}(\epsilon)\end{aligned}$$

Note that $\text{Var}(b_i R_{Mt})$ is the variance of return for an asset related to the variance of the market return, or the *systematic variance or risk.* Also, $\text{Var}(\epsilon)$ is the residual variance of return for the individual asset that is not related to the market portfolio. This residual variance is the variability that we have referred to as the unsystematic or *unique risk or variance* because it arises from the unique features of the asset. Therefore:

$$\text{Var}(R_{i,t}) = \text{Systematic Variance} + \text{Unsystematic Variance}$$

We know that a completely diversified portfolio such as the market portfolio has had all the unsystematic variance eliminated. Therefore, the unsystematic variance of an asset is not relevant to investors, because they can and do eliminate it when making an asset part of the market portfolio. Therefore, investors should not expect to receive added returns for assuming this unique risk. Only the systematic variance is relevant because it *cannot* be diversified away, because it is caused by macroeconomic factors that affect all risky assets.

THE CAPITAL ASSET PRICING MODEL: EXPECTED RETURN AND RISK

Up to this point, we have considered how investors make their portfolio decisions, including the significant effects of a risk-free asset. The existence of this risk-free asset resulted in the derivation of a capital market line (CML) that became the relevant efficient frontier. Because all investors want to be on the CML, an asset's covariance with the market portfolio of risky assets emerged as the relevant risk measure.

Now that we understand this relevant measure of risk, we can proceed to use it to determine an appropriate expected rate of return on a risky asset. This step takes us into the **capital asset pricing model (CAPM)**, which is a model that indicates what should be the expected or required rates of return on risky assets. This transition is important because it helps you to value an asset by providing an appropriate discount rate to use in any valuation model. Alternatively, if you have already estimated the rate of return that you think you will earn on an investment, you can compare this *estimated* rate of return to the *required* rate of return implied by the CAPM and determine whether the asset is undervalued, overvalued, or properly valued.

To accomplish the foregoing, we demonstrate the creation of a security market line (SML) that visually represents the relationship between risk and the expected or the required rate of return on an asset. The equation of this SML, together with estimates for the return on a risk-free asset and on the market portfolio, can generate expected or

FIGURE 9.5 **GRAPH OF SECURITY MARKET LINE**

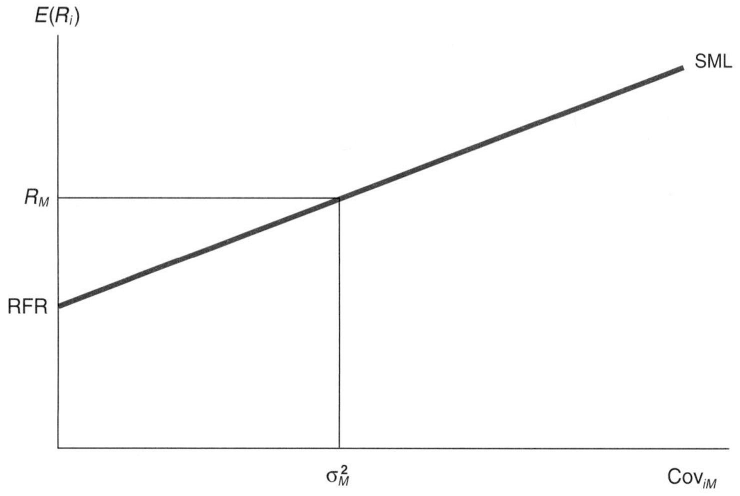
E(Ri)
SML
RM
RFR
σ²M
CoviM

required rates of return for any asset based on its systematic risk. You compare this required rate of return to the rate of return that you estimate that you will earn on the investment to determine if the investment is undervalued or overvalued. After demonstrating this procedure, we finish the section with a demonstration of how to calculate the systematic risk variable for a risky asset.

The Security Market Line (SML)

We know that the relevant risk measure for an individual risky asset is its covariance with the market portfolio ($\text{Cov}_{i,M}$). Therefore, we can draw the risk–return relationship as shown in Figure 9.5 with the systematic covariance variable ($\text{Cov}_{i,M}$) as the risk measure.

The return for the market portfolio (R_M) should be consistent with its own risk, which is the covariance of the market with itself. If you recall the formula for covariance, you will see that the covariance of any asset with itself is its variance, $\text{Cov}_{i,i} = \sigma_i^2$. In turn, the covariance of the market with itself is the variance of the market rate of return $\text{Cov}_{m,m} = \sigma_M^2$. Therefore, the equation for the risk–return line in Figure 9.5 is:

$$E(R_i) = \text{RFR} + \frac{R_M - \text{RFR}}{\sigma_M^2}(\text{Cov}_{i,M})$$

$$= \text{RFR} + \frac{\text{Cov}_{i,M}}{\sigma_M^2}(R_M - \text{RFR})$$

Defining $\text{Cov}_{i,M}/\sigma_M^2$ as beta, (β_i), this equation can be stated:

$$E(R_i) = \text{RFR} + \beta_i(R_M - \text{RFR})$$

Beta can be viewed as a *standardized* measure of systematic risk. Specifically, we already know that the covariance of any asset *i* with the market portfolio (Cov_{iM}) is the relevant risk measure. Beta is a standardized measure of risk because it relates this covariance to the

FIGURE 9.6

GRAPH OF SML WITH NORMALIZED SYSTEMATIC RISK

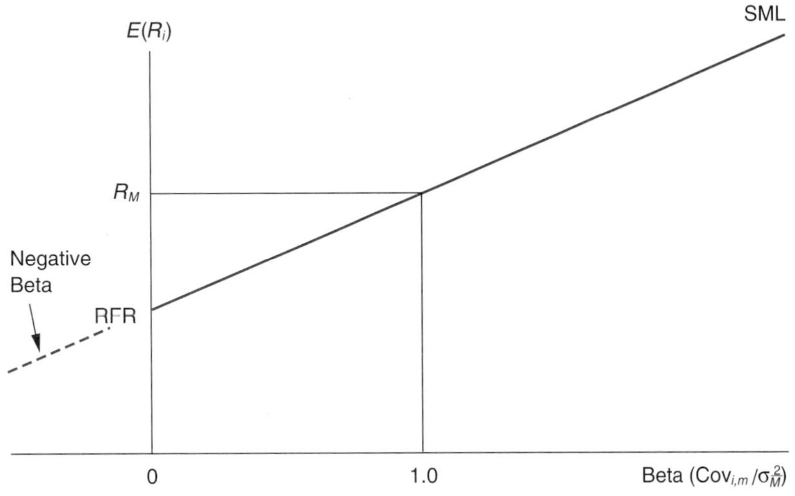
E(Ri)
SML
RM
Negative
Beta
RFR
0
1.0
Beta (Covi,m/σ²M)

variance of the market portfolio. As a result, the market portfolio has a beta of 1. Therefore, if the β_i for an asset is above 1.0, the asset has higher normalized systematic risk than the market, which means that it is more volatile than the overall market portfolio.

Given this standardized measure of systematic risk, the SML graph can be expressed as shown in Figure 9.6. This is the same graph as in Figure 9.5, except there is a different measure of risk. Specifically, the graph in Figure 9.6 replaces the covariance of an asset's returns with the market portfolio as the risk measure with the standardized measure of systematic risk (beta), which is the covariance of an asset with the market portfolio divided by the variance of the market portfolio.

DETERMINING THE EXPECTED RATE OF RETURN FOR A RISKY ASSET The equation above and the graph in Figure 9.6 tell us that the expected rate of return for a risky asset is determined by the RFR plus a risk premium for the individual asset. In turn, the risk premium is determined by the systematic risk of the asset (β_i), and the prevailing **market risk premium** (R_M − RFR). To demonstrate how you would compute the expected or required rates of return, consider the following example stocks assuming you have already computed betas:

Stock	Beta
A	0.70
B	1.00
C	1.15
D	1.40
E	−0.30

Assume that we expect the economy's RFR to be 6 percent (0.06) and the return on the market portfolio (R_M) to be 12 percent (0.12). This implies a market risk premium of

6 percent (0.06). With these inputs, the SML equation would yield the following expected (required) rates of return for these five stocks:

$$
\begin{aligned}
E(R_i) &= \text{RFR} + \beta_i(R_M - \text{RFR}) \\
E(R_A) &= 0.06 + 0.70\,(0.12 - 0.06) \\
&= 0.102 = 10.2\% \\
E(R_B) &= 0.06 + 1.00\,(0.12 - 0.06) \\
&= 0.12 = 12\% \\
E(R_C) &= 0.06 + 1.15\,(0.12 - 0.06) \\
&= 0.129 = 12.9\% \\
E(R_D) &= 0.06 + 1.40\,(0.12 - 0.06) \\
&= 0.144 = 14.4\% \\
E(R_E) &= 0.06 + (-0.30)\,(0.12 - 0.06) \\
&= 0.06 - 0.018 \\
&= 0.042 = 4.2\%
\end{aligned}
$$

As stated, these are the expected (required) rates of return that these stocks should provide based on their systematic risks and the prevailing SML.

Stock A has lower risk than the aggregate market, so you should not expect (require) its return to be as high as the return on the market portfolio of risky assets. You should expect (require) Stock A to return 10.2 percent. Stock B has systematic risk equal to the market's (beta = 1.00), so its required rate of return should likewise be equal to the expected market return (12 percent). Stocks C and D have systematic risk greater than the market's so they should provide returns consistent with their risk. Finally, Stock E has a *negative* beta (which is quite rare in practice), so its required rate of return, if such a stock could be found, would be below the RFR.

In equilibrium, *all* assets and *all* portfolios of assets should plot on the SML. That is, all assets should be priced so that their **estimated rates of return**, which are the actual holding period rates of return that you anticipate, are consistent with their levels of systematic risk. Any security with an estimated rate of return that plots above the SML would be considered underpriced because it implies that you *estimated* you would receive a rate of return on the security that is above its *required* rate of return based on its systematic risk. In contrast, assets with estimated rates of return that plot below the SML would be considered overpriced. This position relative to the SML implies that your estimated rate of return is below what you should require based on the asset's systematic risk.

In an efficient market in equilibrium, you would not expect any assets to plot off the SML because, in equilibrium, all stocks should provide holding period returns that are equal to their required rates of return. Alternatively, a market that is "fairly efficient" but not completely efficient may misprice certain assets because not everyone will be aware of all the relevant information for an asset.

As we discussed in Chapter 7 on the topic of efficient markets, a superior investor has the ability to derive value estimates for assets that are consistently superior to the consensus market evaluation. As a result, such an investor will earn better rates of return than the average investor on a risk-adjusted basis.

IDENTIFYING UNDERVALUED AND OVERVALUED ASSETS Now that we understand how to compute the rate of return one should expect or require for a specific risky asset using the SML, we can compare this *required* rate of return to the asset's

TABLE 9.1

PRICE, DIVIDEND, AND RATE OF RETURN ESTIMATES

Stock	Current Price (P_t)	Expected Price (P_{t+1})	Expected Dividend (D_{t+1})	Estimated Future Rate of Return (Percent)
A	25	27	0.50	10.0%
B	40	42	0.50	6.2
C	33	39	1.00	21.2
D	64	65	1.10	3.3
E	50	54	—	8.0

TABLE 9.2

COMPARISON OF REQUIRED RATE OF RETURN TO ESTIMATED RATE OF RETURN

Stock	Beta	Required Return $E(R_i)$	Estimated Return	Estimated Return Minus $E(R_i)$	Evaluation
A	0.70	10.2	10.0	−0.2	Properly valued
B	1.00	12.0	6.2	−5.8	Overvalued
C	1.15	12.9	21.2	8.3	Undervalued
D	1.40	14.4	3.3	−11.1	Overvalued
E	−0.30	4.2	8.0	3.8	Undervalued

estimated rate of return over a specific investment horizon to determine whether it would be an appropriate investment. To make this comparison, you need an independent estimate of the return outlook for the security based on either fundamental or technical analysis techniques that will be discussed in subsequent chapters. Let us continue the example for the five assets discussed in the previous section.

Analysts in a major trust department have been following these five stocks. Based on extensive fundamental analysis, the analysts provide the price and dividend outlooks contained in Table 9.1. Given these projections, you can compute the estimated rates of return the analysts would anticipate during this holding period.

Table 9.2 summarizes the relationship between the required rate of return for each stock based on its systematic risk as computed earlier and its estimated rate of return (from Table 9.1) based on the current and future prices, and its dividend outlook. This difference between estimated return and expected (required) return is sometimes referred to as a stock's *alpha* or its excess return. This alpha can be positive (the stock is undervalued) or negative (the stock is overvalued). If the alpha is zero, the stock is on the SML and is properly valued in line with its systematic risk.

Plotting these estimated rates of return and stock betas on the SML we specified earlier gives the graph shown in Figure 9.7. Stock A is almost exactly on the line, so it is considered properly valued because its estimated rate of return is almost equal to its required rate of return. Stocks B and D are considered overvalued because their estimated rates of return during the coming period are below what an investor should expect (require) for the risk involved. As a result, they plot below the SML. In contrast, Stocks C and E are expected to provide rates of return greater than we would require based on their systematic risk. Therefore, both stocks plot above the SML, indicating that they are undervalued stocks.

Assuming that you trusted your analyst to forecast estimated returns, you would take no action regarding Stock A, but you would buy Stocks C and E and sell Stocks B and D. You might even sell Stocks B and D short if you favored such aggressive tactics.

FIGURE 9.7 **PLOT OF ESTIMATED RETURNS ON SML GRAPH**

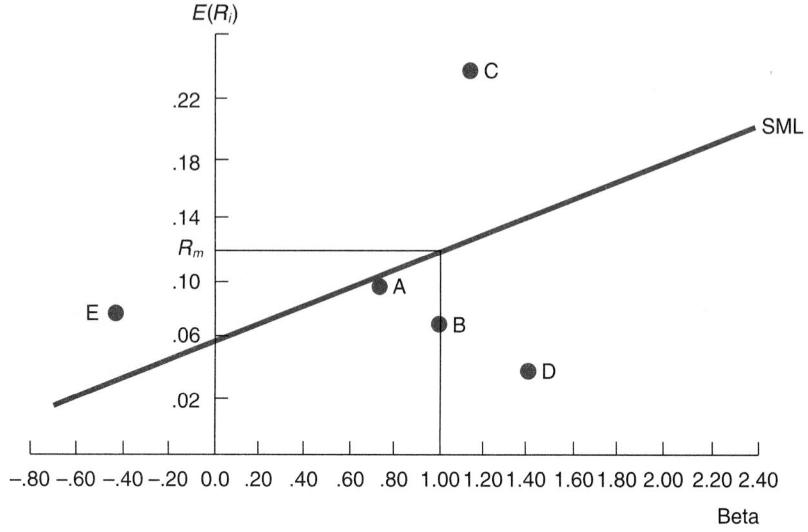
E(R_i)
.22
.18
.14
R_m
.10
.06
.02
A
B
C
D
E
SML
−.80 −.60 −.40 −.20 0.0 .20 .40 .60 .80 1.00 1.20 1.40 1.60 1.80 2.00 2.20 2.40
Beta

FIGURE 9.8 **SCATTER PLOT OF RATES OF RETURN**

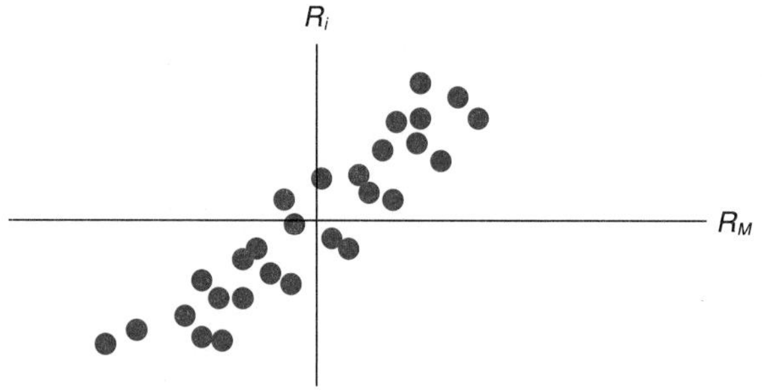
R_i
R_M

CALCULATING SYSTEMATIC RISK: THE CHARACTERISTIC LINE

The systematic risk input for an individual asset is derived from a regression model, referred to as the asset's **characteristic line** with the market portfolio:

$$R_{i,t} = \alpha_i + \beta_i R_{M,t} + \epsilon$$

where:

$R_{i,t}$ = the rate of return for asset i during period t
$R_{M,t}$ = the rate of return for the market portfolio M during period t
α_i = the constant term, or intercept, of the regression, which equals $\bar{R}_i - \beta_i \bar{R}_m$
β_i = the systematic risk (beta) of asset i equal to $\text{Cov}_{i,M}/\sigma_M^2$
ϵ = the random error term

The characteristic line is the regression line of best fit through a scatter plot of rates of return for the individual risky asset and for the market portfolio of risky assets over some designated past period, as shown in Figure 9.8.

The Impact of the Time Interval In practice the number of observations and the time interval used in the regression vary. Value Line Investment Services derives characteristic lines for common stocks using weekly rates of return for the most recent five years (260 weekly observations). Merrill Lynch, Pierce, Fenner & Smith uses monthly rates of return for the most recent five years (60 monthly observations). Because there is no theoretically correct time interval for analysis, we must make a trade-off between enough observations to eliminate the impact of random rates of return and an excessive length of time, such as 15 or 20 years, over which the subject company may have changed dramatically. Remember that what you really want is the *expected* systematic risk for the potential investment. In this analysis, you are analyzing historical data to help you derive a reasonable expectation of the asset's future systematic risk.

A couple of studies have considered the effect of the time interval used to compute betas (weekly versus monthly). Statman examined the relationship between Value Line (VL) betas and Merrill Lynch (ML) betas and found a relatively weak relationship.[8] Reilly and Wright examined a larger sample and analyzed the differential effects of return computation, market index, and the time interval and likewise found a weak relationship between VL and ML betas.[9] They showed that the major cause of the significant differences in beta was the use of monthly versus weekly return intervals.

They also found that the interval effect depended on the sizes of the firms. The shorter weekly interval caused a larger beta for large firms and a smaller beta for small firms. For example, from 1975 to 1979, the average beta for the smallest decile of firms using monthly data was 1.682, but the average beta for these small firms using weekly data was only 1.080. The authors concluded that the return time interval makes a difference, and the impact of the time interval increases as the size of the firm declines.

The Effect of the Market Proxy Another significant decision when computing an asset's characteristic line is which indicator series to use as a proxy for the market portfolio of all risky assets. Most investigators use the Standard & Poor's 500 Composite Index as a proxy for the market portfolio, because the stocks in this index encompass a large proportion of the total market value of U.S. stocks. Also, it is a value-weighted series, which is consistent with the theoretical market series. Still, this series contains only U.S. stocks, most of them listed on the NYSE. You will recall our earlier discussion where it was noted that the theoretically correct market portfolio of all risky assets should include U.S. stocks and bonds, non-U.S. stocks and bonds, real estate, coins, stamps, art, antiques, and any other marketable risky asset from around the world.[10]

EXAMPLE COMPUTATIONS OF A CHARACTERISTIC LINE The following examples show how you would compute characteristic lines for Coca-Cola based on the monthly rates of return during 1998.[11] Twelve is not enough observations for statistical purposes, but it should provide a good example. We demonstrate the computations using two different proxies for the market portfolio. The first is the typical analysis in which the

---

[8]Meir Statman, "Betas Compared: Merrill Lynch vs. Value Line," *Journal of Portfolio Management* 7, no. 2 (winter 1981): 41–44.

[9]Frank K. Reilly and David J. Wright, "A Comparison of Published Betas," *Journal of Portfolio Management* 14, no. 3 (spring 1988): 64–69.

[10]Substantial discussion surrounds the market index used and its impact on the empirical results and usefulness of the CAPM. This concern is discussed further and demonstrated in the subsequent section on computing an asset's characteristic line. The effect of the market proxy is also considered when we discuss the arbitrage pricing theory (APT) in this chapter and in Chapter 27 when we discuss the evaluation of portfolio performance.

[11]These betas are computed using only monthly price changes for Coca-Cola, the S&P 500, and the M-S World Index (dividends are not included). This is done for simplicity but is also based on a study indicating that betas derived with and without dividends are correlated 0.99: William Sharpe and Guy M. Cooper, "Risk–Return Classes of New York Stock Exchange Common Stocks," *Financial Analysts Journal* 28, no. 2 (March–April 1972): 35–43.

S&P 500 is used as the market proxy. The second example uses the Morgan Stanley (M-S) World Equity Index as the market proxy. This analysis allows us to demonstrate the effect of a more complete proxy of stocks.

The monthly price changes are computed using the closing prices for the last day of each month. These data for Coca-Cola, the S&P 500, and the M-S World Index are contained in Table 9.3. Figure 9.9 contains the scatter plot of the percentage price changes for Coca-Cola and the S&P 500. During this 12-month period, Coca-Cola had returns that varied when compared with the aggregate market returns as proxied by the S&P 500. As a result, the covariance between Coca-Cola and the S&P 500 series was a fairly large positive value (38.97). The covariance divided by the variance of the S&P 500 market portfolio (38.44) indicates that Coca-Cola's beta relative to the S&P 500 was equal to 1.01. This analysis indicates that during this limited time period Coca-Cola was slightly riskier than the aggregate market proxied by the S&P 500.

When we draw this characteristic line on Figure 9.9, the scatter plots are reasonably close to the characteristic line, which is consistent with the correlation coefficient of 0.61. The computation of the characteristic line for Coca-Cola using the M-S World Index as the proxy for the market is contained in Table 9.3, and the scatter plots are in Figure 9.10. At this point, it is important to consider what one might expect to be the relationship between the beta relative to the S&P 500 versus the betas with the M-S World Index. This requires a consideration of the two components in the computation of beta: (1) the covariance between the stock and the benchmark and (2) the variance of returns for the benchmark series. Notably, there is no obvious answer regarding what will happen for either series because one would typically expect both components to change. Specifically, the covariance of Coca-Cola with the S&P 500 will probably be higher than with the other series because you are matching a U.S. stock with a U.S. market index rather than a world index. Thus, the covariance with the other indexes will generally be smaller. At the same time, the variance of returns for the world stock index should typically also be smaller than the variance for the S&P 500 because it is a more diversified stock portfolio.

Therefore, the direction of change for the beta will depend on the relative change in the two components. An empirical observation is that generally the beta is smaller with the world stock index because the covariance is definitely lower, but the variance is only slightly smaller.[12] The results of this example were not consistent with expectations. The beta with the world stock index was larger (1.27 vs. 1.01) because the covariance was unexpectedly larger (40.63 vs. 38.97), whereas the variance of the market proxy was smaller as hypothesized (31.92 for the M-S series vs. 38.44 for the S&P 500).

The differences in beta were not consistent with expectations. The fact that they differed is significant and reflects the potential problem that can occur in a global environment where it becomes difficult to select the appropriate proxy for the market portfolio.

ARBITRAGE PRICING THEORY (APT)

At this point, we have discussed the basic theory of the CAPM, the effects of changing some of its major assumptions, and its dependence on a market portfolio of all risky assets. In addition, the model assumes that investors have quadratic utility functions and that the distribution of security prices is normal—that is, symmetrically distributed, with a variance term that can be estimated.

[12]For a demonstration of this effect for a large sample that confirms these expectations, see Frank K. Reilly and Rashid A. Akhtar, "The Benchmark Error Problem with Global Capital Markets," *Journal of Portfolio Management* 22, no. 1 (fall 1995): 33–52.

TABLE 9.3 COMPUTATION OF BETA FOR COCA-COLA WITH SELECTED INDEXES

Date	Index: S&P 500	Index: M-S World	Return: S&P 500	Return: M-S World	Return: Coca Cola	S&P 500 $R_{S\&P} - E(R_{S\&P})$ (1)	M-S World $R_{M\text{-}S} - E(R_{M\text{-}S})$ (2)	Coca-Cola $R_{KO} - E(R_{KO})$ (3)	(4)[a]	(5)[b]
12/97	970.43	933.60								
1/98	980.28	961.50	1.02	2.99	−3.11	−1.16	1.08	−3.63	4.21	−3.93
2/98	1,049.34	1,025.30	7.04	6.64	5.98	4.87	4.73	5.47	26.63	25.86
3/98	1,101.75	1,067.40	4.99	4.11	13.06	2.82	2.20	12.54	35.37	27.60
4/98	1,111.75	1,059.30	0.91	−0.76	−2.21	−1.27	−2.66	−2.72	3.45	7.26
5/98	1,090.82	1,061.80	−1.88	0.24	3.29	−4.06	−1.67	2.78	−11.28	−4.64
6/98	1,133.84	1,085.70	3.94	2.25	9.28	1.77	0.35	8.77	15.50	3.03
7/98	1,120.67	1,082.70	−1.16	−0.28	−6.01	−3.34	−2.18	−6.53	21.79	14.25
8/98	957.98	937.10	−14.58	−13.45	−19.10	−16.75	−15.35	−19.62	328.66	301.77
9/98	1,017.01	952.40	6.24	1.63	−11.29	4.06	−0.27	−11.80	−47.97	3.22
10/98	1,098.67	1,037.20	8.03	8.90	16.94	5.85	7.00	16.42	96.15	114.94
11/98	1,163.63	1,097.60	5.91	5.82	3.92	3.74	3.92	3.41	12.73	13.34
12/98	1,229.23	1,150.00	5.64	4.77	−4.58	3.46	2.87	−5.09	−17.63	−14.60
Average			2.18	1.91	0.52			Total =	467.61	487.50
Standard Deviation			6.20	5.65	10.30					

$Cov_{KO,S\&P} = 467.61/12 = 38.97$

$Cov_{KO,M\text{-}S} = 487.50/12 = 40.63$

$Var_{S\&P} = St.Dev._{S\&P}^2 = 6.2^2 = 38.44$

$Var_{M\text{-}S} = St.Dev._{M\text{-}S}^2 = 5.65^2 = 31.92$

$Beta_{KO,S\&P} = 38.97 / 38.44 = 1.01$

$Beta_{KO,M\text{-}S} = 40.63 / 31.92 = 1.27$

$Alpha_{KO,S\&P} = 0.52 - (1.01 * 2.18) = -1.68$

$Alpha_{KO,M\text{-}S} = 0.52 - (1.27 * 1.91) = -1.91$

$Correlation\ coef._{KO,S\&P} = 38.97 / (6.2 * 10.30) = 0.61$

$Correlation\ coef._{KO,M\text{-}S} = 40.625 / (5.65 * 10.30) = 0.70$

[a]Column (4) is equal to column (1) multiplied by column (3)

[b]Column (5) is equal to column (2) multiplied by column (3)

FIGURE 9.9

SCATTER PLOT OF COCA-COLA AND THE S&P 500 WITH CHARACTERISTIC LINE FOR COCA-COLA: 1998

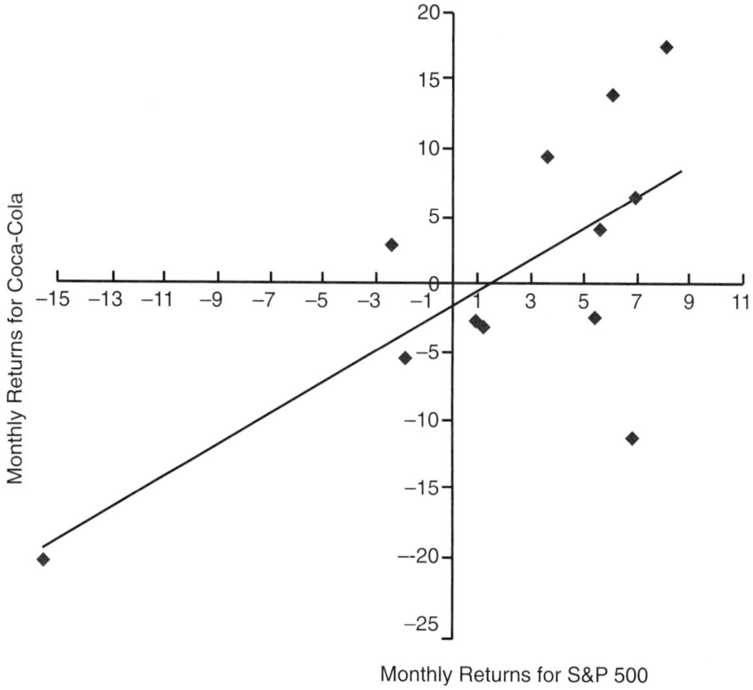
Monthly Returns for Coca-Cola
Monthly Returns for S&P 500
20
15
10
5
0
-5
-10
-15
-20
-25
-15 -13 -11 -9 -7 -5 -3 -1 1 3 5 7 9 11

FIGURE 9.10

SCATTER PLOT OF COCA-COLA AND THE M-S WORLD WITH CHARACTERISTIC LINE FOR COCA-COLA: 1998

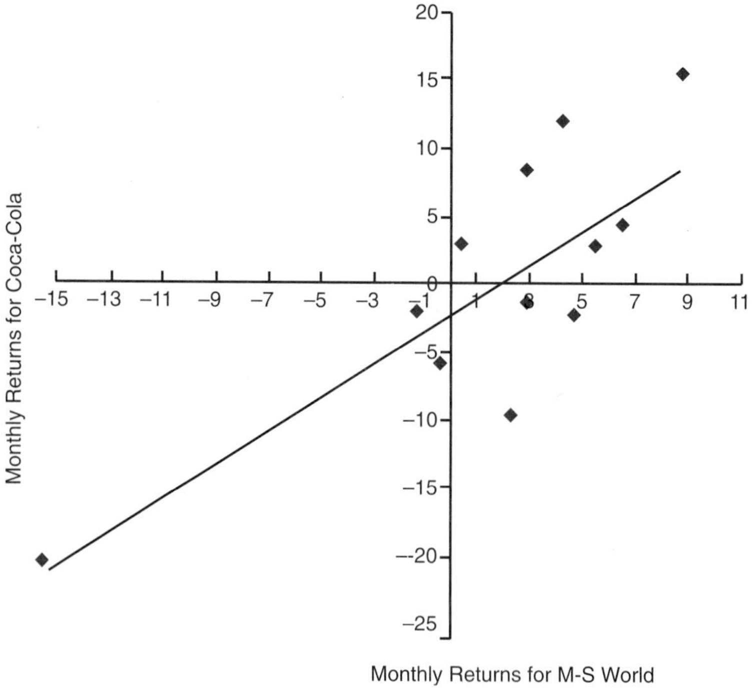
Monthly Returns for Coca-Cola
Monthly Returns for M-S World
20
15
10
5
0
-5
-10
-15
-20
-25
-15 -13 -11 -9 -7 -5 -3 -1 1 3 5 7 9 11

Some tests of the CAPM indicate that the beta coefficients for individual securities are not stable, but the beta of portfolios generally were stable assuming long enough sample periods and adequate trading volume. Some studies have also supported a positive linear relationship between rates of return and systematic risk for portfolios of stock. In contrast, a set of papers by Roll criticized the usefulness of the model because of its dependence on a market portfolio of risky assets, and Roll contends that such a portfolio is not currently available.[13] Roll points out that when the CAPM is used to evaluate portfolio performance, it is necessary to select a proxy for the market portfolio as a benchmark for performance. It has been shown in the Reilly-Akhtar paper that the performance results can be changed substantially depending upon the market proxy used.

Given these questions, the academic community has considered an alternative asset pricing theory that is reasonably intuitive and requires only limited assumptions. This **arbitrage pricing theory (APT)**, developed by Ross in the early 1970s and initially published in 1976, has three major assumptions:[14]

1. Capital markets are perfectly competitive.
2. Investors always prefer more wealth to less wealth with certainty.
3. The stochastic process generating asset returns can be represented as a K factor model (to be described).

Equally important, the following major assumptions are *not* required: (1) quadratic utility function, (2) normally distributed security returns, and (3) a market portfolio that contains all risky assets and is mean-variance efficient. Obviously, if a theory without these assumptions is able to explain differential security prices, it would be considered a superior theory because it is simpler (that is, it requires fewer assumptions).

As noted, the theory assumes that the stochastic process generating asset returns can be represented as a K factor model of the form

$$R_i = E_i + b_{i1}\delta_1 + b_{i2}\delta_2 + \ldots + b_{ik}\delta_k + \epsilon_i \qquad \text{for } i = 1 \text{ to } N$$

where:

R_i = **return on asset *i* during a specified time period**
E_i = **expected return for asset *i***
b_{ik} = **reaction in asset *i*'s returns to movements in a common factor**
δ_k = **a common factor with a zero mean that influences the returns on all assets**
ϵ_i = **a unique effect on asset *i*'s return that, by assumption, is completely diversifiable in large portfolios and has a mean of zero**
N = **number of assets**

Two terms require elaboration: δ_k and b. As indicated, the δ_k terms are the *multiple* factors expected to have an impact on the returns of *all* assets. Examples of such factors might include inflation, growth in GDP, major political upheavals, or changes in interest rates. The APT contends there are many such factors, in contrast to the CAPM, where it is contended that the only relevant variable is the covariance of the asset with the market portfolio, that is, its beta coefficient.

[13]Richard Roll, "A Critique of the Asset Pricing Theory's Tests," *Journal of Financial Economics* 4, no. 4 (March 1977): 129–176; Richard Roll, "Ambiguity When Performance Is Measured by the Securities Market Line," *Journal of Finance* 33, no. 4 (September 1978): 1051–1069; and Richard Roll, "Performance Evaluation and Benchmark Error II," *Journal of Portfolio Management* 7, no. 2 (winter 1981): 17–22.

[14]Stephen Ross, "The Arbitrage Theory of Capital Asset Pricing," *Journal of Economic Theory* 13, no. 2 (December 1976): 341–360; Stephen Ross, "Return, Risk, and Arbitrage," in *Risk and Return in Finance,* ed. I. Friend and J. Bicksler (Cambridge: Ballinger, 1977), 189–218.

Given these common factors, the β_{ik} terms determine how each asset reacts to this common factor. To extend the earlier example, although all assets may be affected by growth in GDP, the effects will differ across assets. For example, stocks of cyclical firms that produce autos, steel, or heavy machinery will have larger b_{ik} terms for this common factor than noncyclical firms, such as grocery chains. Likewise, you will hear discussions about interest-sensitive stocks: All stocks are affected by changes in interest rates, but some stocks experience larger effects. It is possible to envision other examples of common factors, such as inflation, exchange rates, interest rate spreads, and so on. Still, in the application of APT, *the factors are not identified.* That is, when we discuss the empirical studies, three, four, or five factors that affect security returns will be identified, but *there is no indication of what these factors represent.*

Similar to the CAPM model, it is assumed that the unique effects (ϵ_i) are independent and will be diversified away in a large portfolio. The APT assumes that, in equilibrium, the return on a zero-investment, zero-systematic-risk portfolio is zero when the unique effects are diversified away. This assumption and some theory from linear algebra imply that the expected return on any asset i [$E(R_i)$] can be expressed as

$$E(R_i) = \lambda_0 + \lambda_1 b_{i1}, + \lambda_2 b_{i2} + \ldots + \lambda_k \beta_{ik}$$

where:

λ_0 = the expected return on an asset with zero systematic risk where $\lambda_0 = E_0$
λ_1 = the risk premium related to each of the common factors—for example, the risk premium related to interest rate risk ($\lambda_i = E_i = E_0$)
b_i = the pricing relationship between the risk premium and asset i—that is, how responsive asset i is to this common factor K

Consider the following example of two stocks and a two-factor model:

λ_1 = changes in the rate of inflation. The risk premium related to this factor is 1 percent for every 1 percent change in the rate ($\lambda_1 = .01$)
λ_2 = percent growth in real GDP. The average risk premium related to this factor is 2 percent for every 1 percent change in the rate ($\lambda_2 = .02$)
λ_0 = the rate of return on a zero-systematic-risk asset (zero beta: $b_{0j} = 0$) is 3 percent ($\lambda_0 = .03$)

The two assets (X, Y) have the following response coefficients to these factors:

b_{x1} = the response of asset X to changes in the rate of inflation is 0.50 ($b_{x1} = .50$). This asset is not very responsive to changes in the rate of inflation
b_{y1} = the response of asset Y to changes in the rate of inflation is 2.00 ($b_{y1} = 2.00$)
b_{x2} = the response of asset X to changes in the growth rate of real GDP is 1.50 ($b_{x2} = 1.50$)
b_{y2} = the response of asset Y to changes in the growth rate of real GDP is 1.75 ($b_{y2} = 1.75$)

These response coefficients indicate that if these are the major factors influencing asset returns, asset Y is a higher-risk asset, and therefore its expected (required) return should be greater, as shown below:

$$\begin{aligned} E(R_i) &= \lambda_0 + \lambda_1 b_{i1} + \lambda_2 b_{i2} \\ &= .03 + (.01)b_{i1} + (.02)b_{i2} \end{aligned}$$

Therefore:

$$\begin{aligned} E(R_x) &= 0.03 + (0.01)(0.50) + (0.02)(1.50) \\ &= 0.065 = 6.5\% \\ E(R_y) &= 0.03 + (0.01)(2.00) + (0.02)(1.75) \\ &= 0.085 = 8.5\% \end{aligned}$$

THE INTERNET *Investments Online*

Asset pricing models show how risk measures or underlying return-generating factors will affect asset returns. Estimates from such models are usually proprietary and are available from providers only by buying their research. Of course, users can always purchase their raw data elsewhere (see some of our earlier Internet discussions) and develop their own estimates of beta and factor sensitivities.

www.valueline.com The Value Line Investment Survey has been a long-time favorite of investors and many local and college/university libraries subscribe to it. It is a popular source of finding a stock's beta. Value Line Publishing, Inc.'s Web site contains useful information for the online researcher and student of investments. Its site features investment-related articles, business forecasts, and a product directory, which lists the investment survey as well as Value Line's mutual fund and options services.

www.barra.com For subscribers, Barra's Web site offers extensive data and analytical analysis. Links offer information on portfolio management, investment data, market indices, and research. Barra offers its clients data, software, and consulting, as well as money management services for equity, fixed income, currency, and other global financial instruments. Barra estimates multiple factor models, and their global and single-country equity models provide risk analysis on over 25,000 globally traded securities, including predicted and historical beta values.

www.wsharpe.com or **www.stanford.edu/~wfsharpe** William F. Sharpe, the 1990 winner of the Nobel Prize in Economics because of his development of the Capital Asset Pricing Model, has a home page on the Internet. Among other items, Web surfers can read drafts of a sophisticated textbook in progress, as well as some of his published papers and case studies. Sharpe's site offers monthly returns data on a number of mutual funds, stock indices, and bond indices, as well as links to other finance sites.

If the prices of the assets do not reflect these returns, we would expect investors to enter into arbitrage arrangements whereby they would sell overpriced assets short and use the proceeds to purchase the underpriced assets until the relevant prices were corrected. Given these linear relationships, it should be possible to find an asset or a combination of assets with equal risk to the mispriced asset, yet a higher return.

EMPIRICAL TESTS OF THE APT

Studies by Roll and Ross and by Chen have provided results that support the APT because the model was able to explain different rates of return, in some cases with results that were superior to those of the CAPM.[15] In contrast, results of Reinganum's study do not support the model because it did not explain small-firm results.[16] Finally, Dhrymes and Shanken both questioned the usefulness of the model because it was not possible to identify the factors. Under these conditions, they question whether the theory is testable.[17]

At this time, the theory is relatively new and will be subject to continued testing. The important points to remember are that the model requires fewer assumptions and considers multiple factors to explain the risk of an asset.

---

[15]Richard Roll and Stephen A. Ross, "An Empirical Investigation of the Arbitrage Pricing Theory," *Journal of Finance* 35, no. 5 (December 1980): 1073–1103; and Nai-fu Chen, "Some Empirical Tests of Theory of Arbitrage Pricing," *Journal of Finance* 18, no. 5 (December 1983): 1393–1414.

[16]Marc R. Reinganum, "The Arbitrage Pricing Theory: Some Empirical Results," *Journal of Finance* 36, no. 2 (May 1981): 313–321.

[17]Phoebus J. Dhrymes, "The Empirical Relevance of Arbitrage Pricing Models," *Journal of Portfolio Management* 10, no. 4 (summer 1984): 35–44; Jay Shanken, "The Arbitrage Pricing Theory: Is It Testable?" *Journal of Finance* 37, no. 5 (December 1982): 1129–1140.

Summary

- The assumptions of capital market theory expand on those of the Markowitz portfolio model and include consideration of the risk-free rate of return. The correlation and covariance of any asset with a risk-free asset are zero, so that any combination of an asset or portfolio with the risk-free asset generates a linear return and risk function. Therefore, when you combine the risk-free asset with any risky asset on the Markowitz efficient frontier, you derive a set of straight-line portfolio possibilities.
- The dominant line is the one that is tangent to the efficient frontier. This dominant line is referred to as the *capital market line (CML),* and all investors should target points along this line depending on their risk preferences.
- Because all investors want to invest in the risky portfolio at the point of tangency, this portfolio—referred to as the market portfolio—must contain all risky assets in proportion to their relative market values. Moreover, the investment decision and the financing decision can be separated because, although everyone will want to invest in the market portfolio, investors will make different financing decisions about whether to lend or borrow based on their individual risk preferences.
- Given the CML and the dominance of the market portfolio, the relevant risk measure for an individual risky asset is its covariance with the market portfolio, that is, its *systematic risk.* When this covariance is standardized by the covariance for the market portfolio, we derive the well-known beta measure of systematic risk and a security market line (SML) that relates the expected or required rate of return for an asset to its beta. Because all individual securities and portfolios should plot on this SML, you can determine the expected (required) return on a security based on its systematic risk (its beta).
- Alternatively, assuming security markets are not always completely efficient, you can identify undervalued and overvalued securities by comparing your estimate of the rate of return to be earned on an investment to its expected (required) rate of return. The systematic risk variable (beta) for an individual risky asset is computed using a regression model that generates an equation referred to as the asset's *characteristic line.*
- We concluded the chapter with a discussion of an alternative asset pricing model—the arbitrage pricing theory (APT) model. This included a discussion of the necessary assumptions and the basics of the model as well as an example of its use. We also considered some of the tests of the model that have generated mixed results. Because of the mixed results and the importance of the topic, it is likely that testing of this model will continue.

Questions

1. Explain why the set of points between the risk-free asset and a portfolio on the Markowitz efficient frontier is a straight line.
2. Draw a graph that shows what happens to the Markowitz efficient frontier when you combine a risk-free asset with alternative risky asset portfolios on the Markowitz efficient frontier. Explain this graph.
3. Draw and explain why the line from the RFR that is tangent to the efficient frontier defines the dominant set of portfolio possibilities.
4. Discuss what risky assets are in Portfolio M and why they are in it.
5. Discuss leverage and its effect on the CML.
6. Discuss and justify a measure of diversification for a portfolio in terms of capital market theory.
7. What changes would you expect in the standard deviation for a portfolio of between 4 and 10 stocks, between 10 and 20 stocks, and between 50 and 100 stocks?
8. Discuss why the investment and financing decisions are separate when you have a CML.
9. Given the CML, discuss and justify the relevant measure of risk for an individual security.
10. Capital market theory divides the variance of returns for a security into systematic variance and unsystematic or unique variance. Describe each of these terms.
11. The capital asset pricing model (CAPM) contends that there is systematic and unsystematic risk for an individual security. Which is the relevant risk variable and why is it relevant? Why is the other risk variable not relevant?
12. How does the SML differ from the CML?

13. *CFA Examination I (1993)*
    Identify and briefly discuss *three* criticisms of beta as used in the Capital Asset Pricing Model (CAPM). [6 minutes]
14. *CFA Examination I (1993)*
    Briefly explain whether investors should expect a higher return from holding Portfolio A versus Portfolio B under Capital Asset Pricing Theory (CAPM). Assume that both portfolios are fully diversified. [6 minutes]

	Portfolio A	Portfolio B
Systematic risk (beta)	1.0	1.0
Specific risk for each individual security	High	Low

15. *CFA Examination II (1994)*
    You have recently been appointed chief investment officer of a major charitable foundation. Its large endowment fund is currently invested in a broadly diversified portfolio of stocks (60 percent) and bonds (40 percent). The foundation's board of trustees is a group of prominent individuals whose knowledge of modern investment theory and practice is superficial. You decide a discussion of basic investment principles would be helpful.
    a. Explain the concepts of *specific risk, systematic risk, variance, covariance, standard deviation,* and *beta* as they relate to investment management. [12 minutes]

    You believe that the addition of other asset classes to the endowment portfolio would improve the portfolio by reducing risk and enhancing return. You are aware that depressed conditions in U.S. real estate markets are providing opportunities for property acquisition at levels of expected return that are unusually high by historical standards. You believe that an investment in U.S. real estate would be both appropriate and timely, and have decided to recommend a 20 percent position be established with funds taken equally from stocks and bonds.

    Preliminary discussions revealed that several trustees believe real estate is too risky to include in the portfolio. The board chairman, however, has scheduled a special meeting for further discussion of the matter and has asked you to provide background information that will clarify the risk issue.

    To assist you, the following expectational data have been developed:

			CORRELATION MATRIX			
Asset Class	**Return**	**Standard Deviation**	**U.S. Stocks**	**U.S. Bonds**	**U.S. Real Estate**	**U.S. T-Bills**
U.S. Stocks	12.0%	21.0%	1.00			
U.S. Bonds	8.0	10.5	0.14	1.00		
U.S. Real Estate	12.0	9.0	−0.04	−0.03	1.00	
U.S. Treasury Bills	4.0	0.0	−0.05	−0.03	0.25	1.00

    b. Explain the effect on *both* portfolio risk *and* return that would result from the addition of U.S. real estate. Include in your answer *two* reasons for any change you expect in portfolio risk. (Note: It is *not* necessary to compute expected risk and return.) [8 minutes]
    c. Your understanding of capital market theory causes you to doubt the validity of the expected return and risk for U.S. real estate. Justify your skepticism. [5 minutes]
16. *CFA Examination II (1998)*
    The Arbitrage Pricing Theory (APT) and the Capital Asset Pricing Model (CAPM) have received much attention from practitioners and academicians for use in asset pricing and valuation.
    a. Explain the difference between APT and the CAPM with respect to:

i. investor utility functions.
ii. distribution of returns.
iii. the market portfolio.
[9 minutes]

b. Explain *one* conceptual difference between APT and the CAPM other than those listed in Part A. [6 minutes]

Problems

1. Assume that you expect the economy's rate of inflation to be 3 percent, giving a RFR of 6 percent and a market return (R_M) of 12 percent.
   a. Draw the SML under these assumptions.
   b. Subsequently, you expect the rate of inflation to increase from 3 percent to 6 percent. What effect would this have on the RFR and the R_M? Draw another SML on the graph from Part a.
   c. Draw an SML on the same graph to reflect an RFR of 9 percent and an R_M of 17 percent. How does this SML differ from that derived in Part b? Explain what has transpired.
2. You expect a RFR of 10 percent and the market return (R_M) of 14 percent. Compute the expected (required) return for the following stocks, and plot them on an SML graph.

Stock	Beta	$E(R_i)$
U	0.85	
N	1.25	
D	−0.20	

3. You ask a stockbroker what the firm's research department expects for the three stocks in Problem 2. The broker responds with the following information:

Stock	Current Price	Expected Price	Expected Dividend
U	22	24	0.75
N	48	51	2.00
D	37	40	1.25

   Plot your estimated returns on the graph from Problem 2 and indicate what actions you would take with regard to these stocks. Discuss your decisions.
4. Select a stock from the NYSE and collect its month-end prices for the latest 13 months to compute 12 monthly percentage of price changes ignoring dividends. Do the same for the S&P 500 series. Prepare a scatter plot of these series on a graph and draw a visual characteristic line of best fit (the line that minimizes the deviations from the line). Compute the slope of this line from the graph.
5. Given the returns derived in Problem 4, compute the beta coefficient using the formula and techniques employed in Table 9.3. How many negative products did you have for the covariance? How does this computed beta compare to the visual beta derived in Problem 4?
6. Look up the index values and compute the monthly rates of return for either the FT World Index or the Morgan Stanley World Index.
   a. Compute the beta for your NYSE stock from Problem 4 using one of these world stock indexes as the proxy for the market portfolio.
   b. How does this world stock index beta compare to your S&P beta? Discuss the difference.
7. Look up this stock in *Value Line* and record the beta derived by *VL*. How does this *VL* beta compare to the beta you computed using the S&P 500? Discuss reasons why the betas might differ.
8. Select a stock that is listed on NASDAQ and plot the returns during the past 12 months relative to the S&P 500. Compute the beta coefficient. Did you expect this stock to have a higher or lower beta than the NYSE stock? Explain your answer.
9. Given the returns for the NASDAQ stock in Problem 8, plot the stock returns relative to monthly rates of return for the NASDAQ composite Index and compute the beta coefficient. Does this

beta differ from that derived in Problem 8? If so, how can you explain this? (Hint: Analyze the specific components of the formula for the beta coefficient. How did the components differ between Problems 8 and 9?)

10. Using the data from the prior questions, compute the beta coefficient for the NASDAQ composite Index relative to the S&P 500 Index. A priori, would you expect a beta less than or greater than 1.00? Discuss your expectations and the actual results.
11. Based on five years of monthly data, you derive the following information for the companies listed.

Company	a_i (Intercept)	σ_i	r_{iM}
Intel	0.22	12.10%	0.72
Ford	0.10	14.60	0.33
Anheuser Busch	0.17	7.60	0.55
Merck	0.05	10.20	0.60
S&P 500	0.00	5.50	1.00

a. Compute the beta coefficient for each stock.
b. Assuming a risk-free rate of 8 percent and an expected return for the market portfolio of 15 percent, compute the expected (required) return for all the stocks and plot them on the SML.
c. Plot the following estimated returns for the next year on the SML and indicate which stocks are undervalued or overvalued.
   - Intel—20%
   - Ford—15%
   - Anheuser Busch—19%
   - Merck—10%

12. Calculate the expected (required) return for each of the following stocks when the risk-free rate is 0.08 and you expect the market return to be 0.14.

Stock	Beta
A	1.72
B	1.14
C	0.76
D	0.44
E	0.03
F	−0.79

13. The following are the historic returns for the Anita Computer Company:

Year	Anita Computer	General Index
1	37	15
2	9	13
3	−11	14
4	8	−9
5	11	12
6	4	9

Based on this information, compute the following:

a. The correlation coefficient between Anita Computer and the General Index.

b. The standard deviation for the company and the index.
c. The beta for the Anita Computer Company.

CFA

14. *CFA Examination II (1995)*

The following information describes the expected return and risk relationship for the stocks of two of WAH's competitors.

	Expected Return	Standard Deviation	Beta
Stock X	12.0%	20%	1.3
Stock Y	9.0	15	0.7
Market Index	10.0	12	1.0
Risk-free rate	5.0		

Using only the data shown above:

a. Draw and label a graph showing the Security Market Line and position stocks X and Y relative to it using the template provided in the answer book. [5 minutes]
b. Compute the alphas *both* for stock X *and* for stock Y. Show your work. [4 minutes]
c. Assume that the risk-free rate increases to 7 percent with the other data in the matrix above remaining unchanged. Select the stock providing the higher expected risk-adjusted return and justify your selection. Show your calculations. [6 minutes]

CFA

15. *CFA Examination II (1998)*

An analyst expects a risk-free return of 4.5 percent, a market return of 14.5 percent, and the returns for Stocks A and B that are shown in the following table.

STOCK INFORMATION

Stock	Beta	Analyst's Estimated Return
A	1.2	16%
B	0.8	14%

a. Show on the graph provided in the Answer Book:
   i. where Stock A and B would plot on the Security Market Line (SML) if they were fairly valued using the Capital Asset Pricing Model (CAPM).
   ii. where Stock A and B actually plot on the same graph according to the returns estimated by the analyst and shown in the table. [6 minutes]
b. State whether Stock A and B are undervalued or overvalued if the analyst uses the SML for strategic investment decisions. [4 minutes]

References

Brinson, Gary P., Jeffrey J. Diermeier, and Gary Schlarbaum. "A Composite Portfolio Benchmark for Pension Plans." *Financial Analysts Journal* 42, no. 2 (March–April 1986).

Chen, F. N., Richard Roll, and Steve Ross. "Economic Forces and the Stock Market." *Journal of Business* 59, no. 3 (July 1986).

Handa, Puneet, S. P. Kothari, and Charles Wasley. "The Relation between the Return Interval and Betas: Implications of the Size Effect." *Journal of Financial Economics* 23, no. 1 (June 1989).

Hawawini, Gabriel A. "Why Beta Shifts as the Return Interval Changes." *Financial Analysts Journal* 39, no. 3 (May–June 1983).

Reilly, Frank K., and Rashid A. Akhtar. "The Benchmark Error Problem with Global Capital Markets." *Journal of Portfolio Management* 22, no. 1 (fall 1995).

Chapter

10 EXTENSIONS AND TESTING OF ASSET PRICING THEORIES

After you read this chapter, you should be able to answer the following questions:

- What happens to the capital market line (CML) when you assume there are differences in the risk-free borrowing and lending rates?
- What is a zero-beta asset and how does its use impact the CML?
- What happens to the security market line (SML) when you assume transactions costs, heterogeneous expectations, different planning periods, and taxes?
- What are the major questions considered when empirically testing the CAPM?
- What are the empirical results from tests that examine the stability of beta?
- How do alternative published estimates of beta compare?
- What are the empirical test results of studies that examine the relationship between systematic risk and return?
- What other variables besides beta have had a significant impact on returns?
- What is the theory and practice regarding the "market portfolio"? How does this difference between theory and the market proxy relate to the benchmark problem?
- Assuming there is a benchmark problem, what variables are affected by it?
- What are the major assumptions *not* required by the APT model compared to the CAPM?
- How do you test the APT by examining anomalies found with the CAPM?
- What are the empirical test results related to the APT?
- Why do some authors contend that the APT model is untestable?
- What are the concerns related to the multiple factors of the APT model?

Chapters 8 and 9 introduced in detail the Markowitz portfolio theory and the capital asset pricing model (CAPM). This chapter considers several extensions of the CAPM, relaxes some of the assumptions, and examines the impact of these changes on the model. More important, we discuss the empirical tests of the theory. As we will discuss, some of the early results supported the predictive ability of the CAPM, but also raised some questions, including a contention by Roll that it is not possible to test the model. We also discuss in some detail the study by Fama and French that raises serious questions about the relationship between beta and rates of return. This is followed by a discussion of the results of several studies that have responded to the Fama-French contentions.

In Chapter 9, we discussed a well-regarded alternative asset pricing model—the arbitrage pricing theory (APT)—developed by Stephen Ross. Again, we will discuss the empirical tests of the APT. The empirical tests of this alternative theory yield mixed results, including a suggestion that the APT is likewise untestable.

RELAXING THE ASSUMPTIONS

In Chapter 9, several assumptions were set forth related to the CAPM. In this section, we discuss the impact on the capital market line (CML) and the security market line (SML) when we relax several of these assumptions.

Differential Borrowing and Lending Rates

One of the first assumptions of the CAPM was that investors could borrow and lend any amount of money at the risk-free rate. It is reasonable to assume that investors can *lend* unlimited amounts at the risk-free rate by buying government securities (e.g., T-bills). In contrast, one may question the ability of investors to borrow unlimited amounts at the T-bill rate because it is usually lower than the prime rate, and most investors must pay a premium relative to the prime rate when borrowing money. For example, when T-bills are yielding 5 percent, the prime rate will probably be about 7 percent, and most individuals would have to pay about 8 percent to borrow at the bank.

The effect of this differential is that there will be two different lines going to the Markowitz efficient frontier, as shown in Figure 10. 1. The segment *RFR–F* indicates the investment opportunities available when an investor combines risk-free assets (i.e., lending at the RFR) and Portfolio F on the Markowitz efficient frontier. It is not possible to extend this line any farther if it is assumed that you cannot borrow at this risk-free rate to acquire further units of Portfolio F. If it is assumed that you can borrow at R_b, the point of tangency from this rate would be on the curve at point *K*. This indicates that you could borrow at R_b and use the proceeds to invest in Portfolio K to extend the CML along the line segment *K–G*. Therefore, the CML is made up of *RFR–F–K–G;* that is, a line segment (*RFR–F*), a curve segment (*F–K*), and another line segment (*K–G*). This implies that you can either lend or borrow, but the borrowing portfolios are not as profitable as when it was assumed that you could borrow at the RFR. In this instance, because you must pay a borrowing rate that is higher than the RFR, your net return is less—that is, the slope of the borrowing line (*K–G*) is below that for *RFR–F*.[1]

FIGURE 10.1 **INVESTMENT ALTERNATIVES WHEN THE COST OF BORROWING IS HIGHER THAN THE COST OF LENDING**

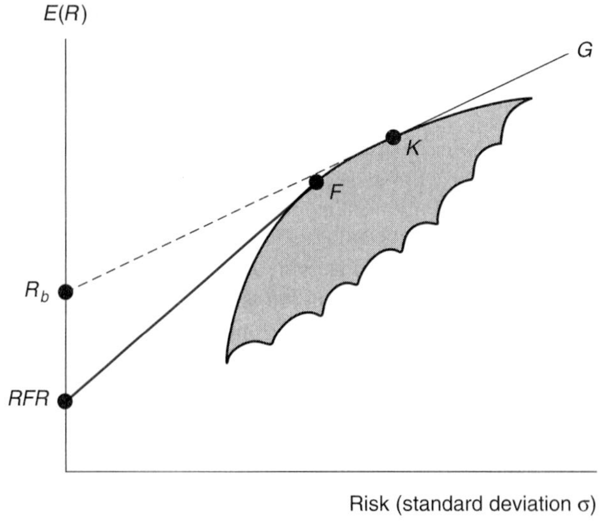
E(R)
G
K
F
R_b
RFR
Risk (standard deviation σ)

ZERO-BETA MODEL

If the market portfolio (M) is mean-variance efficient (i.e., it has the lowest risk for a given level of return among the attainable set of portfolios), an alternative model, derived by Black, does not require a risk-free asset.[2] Specifically, within the set of feasible alternative portfolios, several portfolios exist where the returns are completely uncorrelated with the market portfolio; the beta of these portfolios with the market portfolio is zero. From among the several zero-beta portfolios, you would select the one with minimum variance. Although this portfolio does not have any systematic risk, it does have some unsystematic risk. The availability of this zero-beta portfolio will not affect the CML, but it will allow construction of a linear SML, as shown in Figure 10.2. In the model, the intercept is the expected return for the zero-beta portfolio. Similar to the proof in Chapter 9, the combinations of this zero-beta portfolio and the market portfolio will be a linear relationship in return and risk because the covariance between the zero-beta portfolio (R_z) and the market portfolio likewise is similar to the risk-free asset. Assuming the return for the zero-beta portfolio is greater than that for a risk-free asset, the slope of the line through the market portfolio would not be as steep; that is, the market risk premium would be smaller. The equation for this zero-beta CAPM line would be

$$E(R_i) = E(R_z) + B_i[E(R_m) - E(R_z)]$$

Obviously, the risk premiums for individual assets would be a function of the beta for the individual security and the market risk premium:

$$[E(R_m) - E(R_z)]$$

Some of the empirical results discussed in the next section support this model with its higher intercept and flatter slope. Alternatively, several studies have specifically tested this model

FIGURE 10.2 **SECURITY MARKET LINE WITH A ZERO-BETA PORTFOLIO**

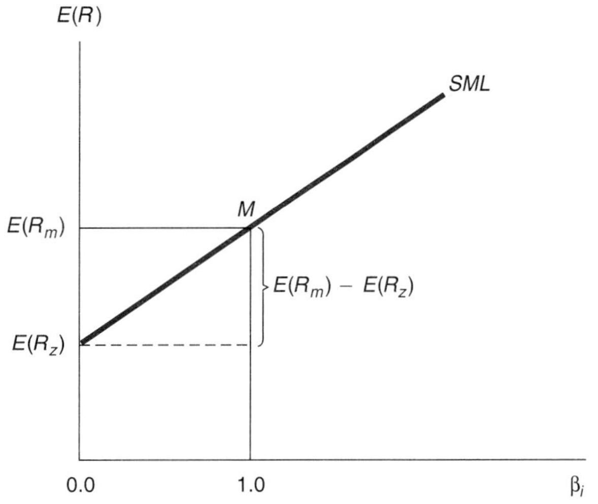
E(R)
SML
M
E(R_m)
E(R_m) − E(R_z)
E(R_z)
0.0
1.0
β_i

---

[1]For a detailed discussion, see Michael Brennan, "Capital Market Equilibrium with Divergent Borrowing and Lending Rates," *Journal of Financial and Quantitative Analysis* 4, no. 1 (March 1969): 4–14.

[2]Fischer Black, "Capital Market Equilibrium with Restricted Borrowing," *Journal of Business* 45, no. 3 (July 1972): 444–445.

and had conflicting results. Specifically, studies by Gibbons and Shanken rejected the model.[3] In contrast, the results of a study by Stambaugh supported the zero-beta CAPM.[4]

TRANSACTION COSTS

The basic assumption is that there are no transaction costs, so investors will buy or sell mispriced securities until they again plot on the SML. For example, if a stock plots above the SML, it is underpriced (its estimated return is greater than justified by its risk level). As a result, investors should buy it and bid up its price until its estimated return is in line with its risk—that is, until it plots on the SML. With transaction costs, investors will not correct all mispricing because in some instances the cost of buying and selling the mispriced security will offset any potential excess return. Therefore, securities will plot very close to the SML—but not exactly on it. Thus, the SML will be a band of securities, as shown in Figure 10.3, rather than a single line. Obviously, the width of the band is a function of the amount of the transaction costs. In a world with a large proportion of purchases and sales by institutions at pennies per share and with numerous discount brokers available for individual investors, the band should be quite narrow.

The existence of transaction costs also will affect the extent of diversification by investors. In Chapter 9, we discussed the relationship between the number of stocks in a portfolio and the variance of the portfolio (see Figure 9.3). Initially, the variance declined rapidly, approaching about 90 percent of complete diversification with about 15 to 18 securities. An

FIGURE 10.3 **SECURITY MARKET LINE WITH TRANSACTION COSTS**

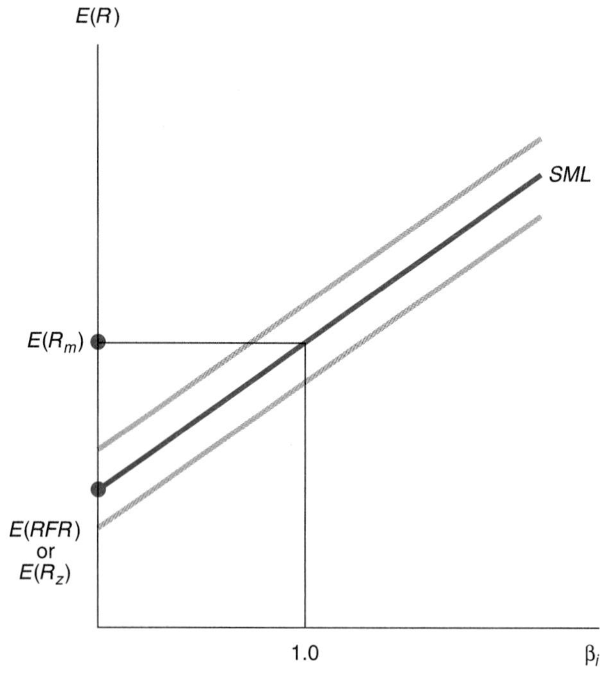
E(R)
SML
E(Rm)
E(RFR)
or
E(Rz)
1.0
βi

[3]Michael Gibbons, "Multivariate Tests of Financial Models: A New Approach," *Journal of Financial Economics* 10, no. 1 (March 1982): 3–28; and Jay Shanken, "Multivariate Tests of the Zero Beta CAPM," *Journal of Financial Economics* 14, no. 3 (September 1985): 327–348.

[4]Robert Stambaugh, "On the Exclusion of Assets from Tests of the Two-Parameter Model: A Sensitivity Analysis," *Journal of Financial Economics* 10, no. 4 (November 1982): 237–268.

important question is: How many securities must be added to derive the last 10 percent? Clearly, the existence of transaction costs indicates that at some point the additional cost of diversification relative to its benefit would be excessive for most investors, especially when considering the costs of monitoring and analyzing the added securities.[5]

HETEROGENOUS EXPECTATIONS AND PLANNING PERIODS

If all investors have different expectations about risk and return, each would have a unique CML and/or SML, and the composite graph would be a set (band) of lines with a breadth determined by the divergence of expectations. If all investors had similar information and background, the band would be reasonably narrow.

The impact of *planning periods* is similar. Recall that the CAPM is a one-period model, and the period employed should be the planning period for the individual investor. Thus, if you are using a one-year planning period, your CML and SML could differ from mine, which assumes a one-month planning period.

TAXES

The rates of return that we normally record and that were used throughout the model were pretax returns. In fact, the actual returns for most investors are affected as follows:

$$E(R_i)(AT) = \frac{(P_e - P_b) \times (1 - T_{cg}) + (Div) \times (1 - T_i)}{P_b}$$

where:

$R_i(AT)$ = **after-tax rate of return**
P_e = **ending price**
P_b = **beginning price**
T_{cg} = **tax on capital gain or loss**
Div = **dividend paid during period**
T_i = **tax on ordinary income**

Clearly, tax rates differ between individuals and institutions. Hence, for many institutions that do not pay taxes, the original pretax model is correctly specified—that is, T_{cg} and T_i take on values of zero. Alternatively, if investors have heavy tax burdens, this could cause major differences in the CML and SML among investors, depending on their marginal tax rates.[6] Several recent studies have examined the effect of the differential taxes on dividends versus capital gains. Although most of the studies have indicated that this tax difference has had an impact, the evidence is not unanimous.[7]

---

[5]The impact of transaction costs and illiquidity on risk and asset pricing is considered in E. Dimson, "Risk Management When Shares Are Subject to Infrequent Trading," *Journal of Financial Economics* 7, no. 2 (June 1979): 197–226; M. J. Brennan and A. Subramanyam, "Market Microstructure and Asset Pricing on the Compensation for Illiquidity in Stock Returns," *Journal of Financial Economics* 41, no. 3 (July 1996): 341–344.

[6]For a detailed consideration of this, see Fischer Black and Myron Scholes, "The Effects of Dividend Yield and Dividend Policy on Common Stock Prices and Returns," *Journal of Financial Economics* 1, no. 1 (March 1979): 1–22; and Robert Litzenberger and K. Ramaswamy, "The Effect of Personal Taxes and Dividends on Capital Asset Prices: Theory and Empirical Evidence," *Journal of Financial Economics* 7, no. 2 (June 1979): 163–196.

[7]Edwin Elton, Martin Gruber, and Joel Rentzler, "A Single Examination of the Empirical Relationship between Dividend Yields and Deviations from the CAPM," *Journal of Banking and Finance* 7, no. 1 (March 1983): 135–146; Roger Gordon and David Bradford, "Taxation and the Stock Market Valuation of Capital Gains and Dividends: Theory and Empirical Results," *Journal of Public Economics* 14, no. 4 (October 1980): 109–136; Merton Miller and Myron Scholes, "Dividends and Taxes: Some Empirical Evidence," *Journal of Political Economy* 90, no. 4 (December 1982): 1118–1141; and William Christie, "Dividend Yield and Expected Returns," *Journal of Financial Economics* 28, no. 1 (November–December 1990): 95–125.

EMPIRICAL TESTS OF THE CAPM

When we discussed the assumptions of capital market theory, we pointed out that a theory should not be judged on the basis of its assumptions, but on *how well it explains the relationships that exist in the real world.* When testing the CAPM, two major questions should concern us. The first is: *How stable is the measure of systematic risk (beta)?* Because beta is our principal risk measure, it is important to know whether past betas can be used as estimates of future betas. Also, what do we know about the alternative published estimates of beta? The second question is basic to the theory: *Is there a positive linear relationship as hypothesized between beta and the rate of return on risky assets?* More specifically, how well do returns conform to the following SML equation:

$$E(R_i) = RFR + \beta_i(R_m - RFR)$$

Some specific questions might include:

- Does the intercept approximate the RFR that prevailed during the period?
- Was the slope of the line positive? Was it consistent with the slope implied by the risk premium $(R_m - RFR)$ that prevailed during the test period?

We consider these two major questions in the following section.

Stability of Beta

Numerous studies have examined the stability of beta and generally reached similar conclusions. Levy examined weekly rates of return for 500 NYSE stocks and concluded that the risk measure was *not* stable for individual stocks over short periods (52 weeks) but the stability of the beta for *portfolios* of stocks increased dramatically.[8] Further, the larger the portfolio of stocks (e.g., 25 or 50 stocks) and the longer the period (over 26 weeks), the more stable the beta of the portfolio. Specifically, the correlation of the betas for 50-stock portfolios over 26-week periods averaged above 0.91. Also, the betas tended to regress toward the mean. Specifically, high-beta portfolios tended to decline over time toward unity (1.00), whereas low-beta portfolios tended to increase over time toward unity. A study by Blume provided very similar results.[9] Tole also found that there was substantially greater stability in beta as the portfolio size increased.[10] He also contended that the benefit of larger portfolios extends beyond 100 stocks in the portfolio.

Another factor that affects the stability of beta is how many months are used to estimate the original beta and the test beta. Baesel found that the stability of the individual betas increased as the length of the estimation period increased.[11] Altman, Jacquillat, and Leavaseur found similar results using French data.[12] Roenfeldt, Griepentrog, and Pflamm (RGP) compared betas derived from 48 months of data to subsequent betas for 12, 24, 36,

[8]Robert A. Levy, "On the Short-Term Stationarity of Beta Coefficients," *Financial Analysts Journal* 27, no. 6 (November–December 1971): 55–62.

[9]Marshall E. Blume, "On the Assessment of Risk," *Journal of Finance* 26, no. 1 (March 1971): 1–10.

[10]Thomas M. Tole, "How to Maximize Stationarity of Beta," *Journal of Portfolio Management* 7, no. 2 (winter 1980): 45–49.

[11]Jerome B. Baesel, "On the Assessment of Risk: Some Further Considerations," *Journal of Finance* 29, no. 5 (December 1974): 1491–1494.

[12]Edward Altman, B. Jacquillat, and M. Levasseur, "Comparative Analysis of Risk Measures: France and the United States," *Journal of Finance* 29, no. 5 (December 1974): 1495–1511.

and 48 months.[13] The 48-month betas were not good for estimating subsequent 12-month betas, but were quite good for estimating 24-, 36-, and 48-month betas.

Theobald derived a set of analytical expressions that explained the Baesel empirical results and partially explained the findings of RGP regarding the improved stability as the period was lengthened.[14] Theobald contended that the optimal length could be over 120 months, assuming the beta did not shift during the period. Chen concluded that portfolio betas would be biased if individual betas were unstable, so he suggested a Bayesian approach to estimating these time-varying betas.[15]

Carpenter and Upton considered the influence of the trading volume on beta stability and contended that the predictions of betas were slightly better using the volume-adjusted betas.[16] This impact of volume on beta estimates is related to the discussion in Chapter 7 on the small-firm effect where it was noted that the estimated beta for low-volume securities was biased downward. This is confirmed in a study by Ibbotson, Kaplan, and Peterson.[17]

To summarize, individual betas were generally volatile over time whereas portfolio betas were stable. Also, it is important to use at least 36 months of data to estimate beta. Finally, the analyst should be conscious of the stock's trading volume and size.

Comparability of Published Estimates of Beta

In contrast to deriving your own estimate of beta for a stock, you may want to use a published source for speed or convenience, such as Merrill Lynch's *Security Risk Evaluation Report* (published monthly) and the weekly *Value Line Investment Survey.* Although the methods of computation differ for these two estimates, both services use the following market model equation:

$$(R_{i,t}) = RFR + \beta_i R_{m,t} + E_t$$

Notably, they differ in the data used. Specifically, Merrill Lynch estimates the beta using *60 monthly observations* and the S&P 500 as the market proxy, whereas the *Value Line* estimates beta using *260 weekly observations* and uses the NYSE composite series as the market proxy. They both use an adjustment process because of the regression tendencies, and their adjustment equations differ slightly.

Given these relatively minor differences, one would probably expect the published betas to be quite comparable. Statman examined the betas for 195 firms for a comparable five-year period and found the following relationship between the adjusted betas:[18]

$$\text{Merrill Lynch Adjusted Beta} = 0.127 + 0.879 \text{ Value Line Adjusted Beta}$$

These results are not consistent with equality. Notably, the R^2 was only 0.55 and did not indicate any systematic bias in the differences. When he examined 19 portfolios of 10 stocks

---

[13]Rodney L. Roenfeldt, Gary L. Griepentrog, and Christopher C. Pflamm, "Further Evidence on the Stationarity of Beta Coefficients," *Journal of Financial and Quantitative Analysis* 13, no. 1 (March 1978): 117–121.

[14]Michael Theobald, "Beta Stationarity and Estimation Period: Some Analytical Results," *Journal of Financial and Quantitative Analysis* 16, no. 5 (December 1981): 747–757.

[15]Son-Nan Chen, "Beta Nonstationarity, Portfolio Residual Risk, and Diversification," *Journal of Financial and Quantitative Analysis* 16, no. 1 (March 1981): 95–111.

[16]Michael D. Carpenter and David E. Upton, "Trading Volume and Beta Stability," *Journal of Portfolio Management* 7, no. 2 (winter 1981): 60–64.

[17]Roger G. Ibbotson, Paul D. Kaplan, and James D. Peterson, "Estimates of Small-Stock Betas Are Much Too Low," *Journal of Portfolio Management* 23, no. 4 (summer 1997): 104–111.

[18]Meir Statman, "Betas Compared: Merrill Lynch vs. Value Line," *Journal of Portfolio Management* 7, no. 2 (winter 1981): 41–44.

each, the coefficient of determination was almost the same as for individual stocks (0.54 versus 0.55). These results imply a small but significant difference in beta estimates.

Reilly and Wright examined over 1,100 securities for three nonoverlapping periods and confirmed the difference in beta found by Statman.[19] They also indicated that the reason for the difference was the alternative time intervals (i.e., weekly versus monthly observations). Also, they found that the security's market value affected both the size and the direction of the interval effect. Therefore, when estimating beta or using a published source, you must consider the return interval used and the firm's relative size.

RELATIONSHIP BETWEEN SYSTEMATIC RISK AND RETURN

The ultimate question regarding the CAPM is whether it is useful in explaining the return on risky assets. Specifically, is there a positive linear relationship between the systematic risk and the rates of return on these risky assets? Sharpe and Cooper found a positive relationship between return and risk, although it was not completely linear (i.e., they found that the returns increased with risk class except for the highest risk classes, where the returns leveled off and declined slightly).[20]

Douglas examined the relationship by analyzing a systematic risk variable and a variance of return measure relative to return.[21] The results indicated intercepts that were larger than the prevailing risk-free rates. Further, although the coefficient for the total risk variable (variance) was generally significant, the coefficients for the systematic risk variables were typically not significant.

Miller and Scholes noted that the Douglas results could be caused by errors in measuring stock betas.[22] Unsystematic risk and betas are highly correlated, and the distribution of returns for the stocks was very skewed. These problems were not able to fully explain the Douglas results.

Because of the statistical problems with individual stocks, Black, Jensen, and Scholes examined the risk and return for portfolios of stocks and found a positive linear relationship between monthly excess return and portfolio beta, although the intercept was higher than the zero value expected.[23] Figure 10.4 contains charts from this study, which show that (1) most of the measured SMLs had a positive slope, (2) the slopes change between periods, (3) the intercepts are not zero, and (4) the intercepts likewise change between periods.

Fama and MacBeth examined the relationship between the rates of return during a given month and betas, a beta-squared variable (to test for linearity), and a measure of unsystematic risk during the prior month.[24] Although the monthly results varied over time, the overall

[19]Frank K. Reilly and David J. Wright, "A Comparison of Published Betas," *Journal of Portfolio Management* 14, no. 3 (spring 1988): 64–69.

[20]William F. Sharpe and Guy M. Cooper, "Risk–Return Classes of New York Stock Exchange Common Stocks: 1931–1967," *Financial Analysis Journal* 28, no. 2 (March–April 1972): 46–54. A subsequent study that considered yield tilting portfolios confirmed many of these results. See William F. Sharpe and Howard B. Sosin, "Risk, Return, and Yield: New York Stock Exchange Common Stocks: 1928–1969," *Financial Analysts Journal* 32, no. 2 (March–April 1976): 33–42.

[21]G. W. Douglas, "Risk in the Equity Markets: An Empirical Appraisal of Market Efficiency," *Yale Economic Essays* 9, no. 1 (1969): 3–48.

[22]Merton H. Miller and Myron Scholes, "Rates of Return in Relation to Risk: A Re-Examination of Some Recent Findings," in *Studies in the Theory of Capital Markets,* ed. Michael Jensen (New York: Praeger, 1972).

[23]Fischer Black, Michael Jensen, and Myron Scholes, "The Capital Asset Pricing Model: Some Empirical Tests," in *Studies in the Theory of Capital Markets,* ed. Michael Jensen (New York: Praeger, 1972).

[24]Eugene Fama and R. MacBeth, "Risk, Return and Equilibrium: Empirical Tests," *Journal of Political Economy* 81, no. 2 (May–June 1973): 453–474.

FIGURE 10.4 **AVERAGE EXCESS MONTHLY RATES OF RETURN COMPARED TO SYSTEMATIC RISK DURING ALTERNATIVE TIME PERIODS**

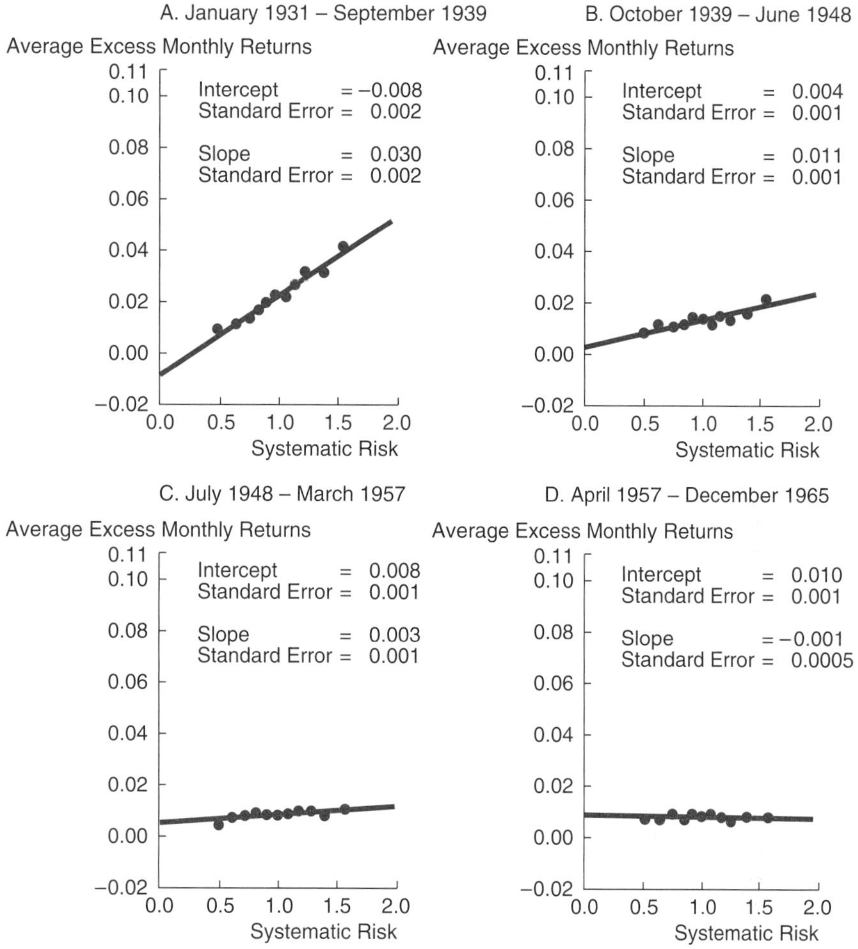
A. January 1931 – September 1939
Average Excess Monthly Returns
Intercept = −0.008
Standard Error = 0.002
Slope = 0.030
Standard Error = 0.002
Systematic Risk
B. October 1939 – June 1948
Average Excess Monthly Returns
Intercept = 0.004
Standard Error = 0.001
Slope = 0.011
Standard Error = 0.001
Systematic Risk
C. July 1948 – March 1957
Average Excess Monthly Returns
Intercept = 0.008
Standard Error = 0.001
Slope = 0.003
Standard Error = 0.001
Systematic Risk
D. April 1957 – December 1965
Average Excess Monthly Returns
Intercept = 0.010
Standard Error = 0.001
Slope = −0.001
Standard Error = 0.0005
Systematic Risk

Source: Michael C. Jensen, ed., *Studies in the Theory of Capital Markets* (New York: Praeger Publishers, 1972): 96–97. Reprinted with permission.

results supported the CAPM. The intercept was about equal to that implied by the RFR, the systematic risk coefficient was positive and significant, and neither of the coefficients for beta squared or for unsystematic risk were significant.

Effect of Skewness on the Relationship

Beyond the analysis of return and beta, several authors also have considered the impact of skewness on expected returns. You will recall from your statistics course that skewness reflects the presence of too many large positive or negative observations in a distribution. A normal distribution is referred to as symmetric, which means that balance exists between positive and negative observations. In contrast, if a return distribution has positive skewness, it means there is an abnormal number of large positive price changes.

Investigators considered skewness as a means to possibly explain the prior results wherein the model appeared to underprice low-beta stocks (so investors received returns above expectations) and overprice high-beta stocks (so investors received returns lower than expected). McEnally found results such as these, but also found that high-beta stocks had high positive skewness.[25] These results could be explained by investors who prefer stocks with high risk and high positive skewness that provide an opportunity for very large returns.

Kraus and Litzenberger examined this relationship more formally by testing a CAPM with a skewness term and found results that confirmed that investors are willing to pay for positive skewness.[26] They concluded that their three-moment CAPM corrects for the apparent mispricing of high- and low-risk stocks encountered with the standard CAPM. Subsequent testing of the model by Friend and Westerfield derived mixed results, but the importance of skewness was supported in studies by Sears and Wei and subsequently by Lim.[27]

Effect of Size, P/E, and Leverage

We know from our discussion in Chapter 7 dealing with the efficient markets hypothesis (EMH) that there has been extensive analysis of the size effect (the small-firm anomaly) and the P/E effect. Both of these variables were shown to have an inverse impact on returns after considering the CAPM. One could interpret these results as implying that these variables (size and P/E) are additional risk factors that need to be considered along with beta (similar to the skewness argument). Specifically, expected returns are a positive function of beta and a negative function of relative size, wherein investors require higher returns from relatively small firms even after allowing for beta. Investors would have a similar additional return requirement for stocks with relatively low P/E ratios.

An analysis by Bhandari finds that financial leverage (measured by the debt/equity ratio) also helps explain the cross section of average returns after both beta and size are considered.[28] This would imply a multivariate CAPM with three risk variables: beta, size, and financial leverage.

Effect of Book-to-Market Value: The Fama-French Study

A study that examined the viability and usefulness of the CAPM is quite damaging not only because of the depth of the analysis, but also because one of the authors, Eugene Fama has been a great supporter of the CAPM. The purpose of the study by Fama and French was to evaluate the joint roles of market beta, size, E/P, financial leverage, and the book-to-market equity ratio in the cross section of average returns on the NYSE, AMEX, and NASDAQ stocks.[29] Some of the earlier studies (including Fama-MacBeth) found a significant positive relationship between returns and beta. In contrast, this study finds that the relationship between beta and the average rate of return disappears during the more recent period 1963 to 1990, even when beta is used alone to explain average returns. In contrast, univariate tests between average returns and size, leverage, E/P, and book-to-market equity (BE/ME) indicate that all of these variables are significant and have the expected sign.

---

[25]Richard McEnally, "A Note on the Return Behavior of High Risk Common Stocks," *Journal of Finance* 29, no. 2 (May 1974): 199–202.

[26]Alan Kraus and Robert Litzenberger, "Skewness Preference and the Valuation of Risky Assets," *Journal of Finance* 31, no. 4 (September 1976): 1085–1094.

[27]Irwin Friend and Randolph Westerfield, "Co-Skewness and Capital Asset Pricing," *Journal of Finance* 35, no. 4 (September 1980): 897–914; R. Stephen Sears and John Wei, "The Structure of Skewness Preferences in Asset Pricing Models with Higher Moments," *Financial Review* 23, no. 1 (February 1988): 25–38; and Kian-Guan Lim, "A New Test of the Three-Moment Capital Asset Pricing Model," *Journal of Financial and Quantitative Analysis* 24, no. 2 (June 1989): 205–216.

[28]Laxims Chand Bhandari, "Debt/Equity Ratio and Expected Common Stock Returns: Empirical Evidence," *Journal of Finance* 43, no. 2 (June 1988): 507–528.

[29]Eugene F. Fama and Kenneth French, "The Cross Section of Expected Stock Returns," *Journal of Finance* 47, no. 2 (June 1992): 427–465.

In the multivariate tests, the results contained in Table 10.1 show that the negative relationship between size [In (ME)] and average returns is robust to the inclusion of other variables. Further, the positive relation between BE/ME and average returns also persists when the other variables are included. Interestingly, when both of these variables are included, the book-to-market value ratio (BE/ME) has the consistently stronger role in explaining average returns. The joint effect of size and BE/ME is shown in Table 10.1. The top row shows the univariate results and confirms the positive relationship between return versus the book-to-market ratio—i.e., as the book-to-market ratio increases, the returns go from 0.64 to 1.63. The left-hand column shows the negative relationship between return and size—i.e., as the size declines, the returns increase from 0.89 to 1.47. The body of the table shows that even within a size class, the returns increase with the BE/ME ratio. Similarly, within a BE/ME decile, there is generally a negative relationship for size. Hence, it is not surprising that the single highest average return is in the upper, right-hand corner (1.92), which is the portfolio with the smallest size and highest BE/ME stocks.

The authors conclude that between 1963 and 1990, size and book-to-market equity capture the cross-sectional variation in average stock returns associated with size, E/P, book-to-market equity, and leverage. Moreover, of the two variables, the book-to-market equity ratio seems to be more powerful and appears to subsume E/P and leverage.[30] Following these results, Fama-French suggested the use of a three-factor CAPM model and used this model in a subsequent study to explain a number of the anomalies from prior studies.[31]

Summary of CAPM Risk–Return Empirical Results

Most of the early evidence regarding the relationship between rates of return and systematic risk of portfolios indicated support for the CAPM. Still, the evidence was not without question because it was found that the intercepts were generally higher than implied by the RFR that prevailed, which is either consistent with a zero-beta model or the existence of higher borrowing rates. In a search for other variables that could explain the above-expected return for low-beta stocks and the below-expected returns for high-beta stocks, additional variables were considered. Several studies indicated support for including the third moment of the distribution (skewness) as a variable, assuming that investors preferred positive skewness and were willing to accept lower average rates of return for the opportunity for very large returns. The results indicated that positive skewness and high betas were correlated.

The efficient markets literature has provided extensive evidence that both size and the P/E ratio were variables that could help explain cross-sectional returns in addition to beta. Recent studies also have found that financial leverage and the book-to-market value of equity ratio (i.e., B/P ratio) have explanatory power regarding returns beyond beta.

The Fama-French study considered most of the other variables suggested and concluded that between 1963 and 1990, beta was not related to average returns on stocks when included with other variables, or when considered alone. Moreover, the two dominant variables were size and the book value to market value ratio, which was even stronger than size although both variables were significant.

[30]A prior study that documented the importance of the BE/ME ratio was Barr Rosenberg, Kenneth Reid, and Ronald Lanstein, "Persuasive Evidence of Market Inefficiency." *Journal of Portfolio Management* 11, no. 3 (spring 1985): 9–17. The relationship was confirmed in the Japanese market in Louis K. Chan, Yasusho Hamao, and Josef Lakonishok, "Fundamentals and Stock Returns in Japan," *Journal of Finance* 46, no. 5 (December 1991): 1739–1764.

[31]The three-factor model was suggested in Eugene F. Fama and Kenneth French, "Common Risk Factors in the Returns on Stocks and Bonds," *Journal of Financial Economics* 33, no. 1 (February 1993): 3–56. The model was used in Eugene F. Fama and Kenneth French, "Multifactor Explanations of Asset Pricing Anomalies," *Journal of Finance* 51, no. 1 (March 1996): 55–84.

TABLE 10.1

AVERAGE SLOPES (t-STATISTICS) FROM MONTH-BY-MONTH REGRESSIONS OF STOCK RETURNS ON β, SIZE, BOOK-TO-MARKET EQUITY, LEVERAGE, AND E/P: JULY 1963 TO DECEMBER 1990

Stocks are assigned the post-ranking β of the size-β portfolio they are in at the end of June of year t. BE is the book value of common equity plus balance-sheet deferred taxes, A is total book assets, and E is earnings (income before extraordinary items, plus income-statement deferred taxes, minus preferred dividends). BE, A, and E are for each firm's latest fiscal year ending in calendar year $t - 1$. The accounting ratios are measured using market equity ME in December of year $t - 1$. Firm size ln(ME) is measured in June of year t. In the regressions, these values of the explanatory variables for individual stocks are matched with returns for the CRSP tapes from the University of Chicago for the months from July of year t to June of year $t + 1$. The gap between the accounting data and the returns ensures that the accounting data are available prior to the returns. If earnings are positive, E(+)/P is the ratio of total earnings to market equity and E/P dummy is 0. If earnings are negative, E(+)/P is 0 and E/P dummy is 1.

The average slope is the time-series average of the monthly regression slopes for July 1963 to December 1990, and the t-statistic is the average slope divided by its time-series standard error.

On average, there are 2,267 stocks in the monthly regressions. To avoid giving extreme observations heavy weight in the regressions, the smallest and largest 0.5% of the observations of E(+)/P, BE/ME, A/ME, and A/BE are set equal to the next largest or smallest values of the ratios (the 0.005 and 0.995 fractiles). This has no effect on inferences.

β	ln(ME)	ln(BE/ME)	ln(A/ME)	ln(A/BE)	E/P Dummy	E(+)/P
0.15						
(0.46)						
	−0.15					
	(−2.58)					
−0.37	−0.17					
(−1.21)	(−3.41)					
		0.50				
		(5.71)				
			0.50	−0.57		
			(5.69)	(−5.34)		
					0.57	4.72
					(2.28)	(4.57)
	−0.11	0.35				
	(−1.99)	(4.44)				
	−0.11		0.35	−0.50		
	(−2.06)		(4.32)	(−4.56)		
	−0.16				0.06	2.99
	(−3.06)				(0.38)	(3.04)
	−0.13	0.33			−0.14	0.87
	(−2.47)	(4.46)			(−0.90)	(1.23)
	−0.13		0.32	−0.46	−0.08	1.15
	(−2.47)		(4.28)	(−4.45)	(−0.56)	(1.57)

Source: Eugene F. Fama and Kenneth French, "The Cross Section of Expected Stock Returns," *Journal of Finance* 47, no. 2 (June 1992): 439. Reprinted by permission.

Given the significance of the Fama-French study, several studies followed that considered these results. First, a study by Dennis, Perfect, Snow, and Wiles confirmed the Fama-French results.[32] They not only confirmed the optimal combination involved portfolios of small firms with high BV/MV ratios, but showed that this superiority prevailed after assuming 1 percent transaction costs and annual rebalancing. They subsequently showed that

[32]Patrick Dennis, Steven Perfect, Karl Snow, and Kenneth Wiles, "The Effects of Rebalancing on Size and Book-to-Market Ratio Portfolio Returns," *Financial Analysts Journal* 51, no. 3 (May–June 1995): 47–57.

the optimal results were derived if one assumes rebalancing every four years. Alternatively, two studies came out with contrary results related to the importance of beta. In contrast to Fama-French who measure beta with monthly returns, Kothari, Shanken, and Sloan (KSS) measure beta with annual returns to avoid trading problems involved with using monthly data.[33] Using annual betas, KSS found that there was substantial compensation for beta risk. They suggested that the relationship between rates of return and the BV/MV ratio may have been periodic to this time frame and might not be significant over a longer period. A study by Pettengill, Dundaram, and Matthur noted that empirical studies typically use realized returns to test the CAPM model when theory specifies expected returns.[34] When the authors adjust for expectations concerning negative market excess returns, they find a consistent and significant relationship between beta and rates of return. Jagannathan and Wang also employ a conditional CAPM that allows for changes in betas and the market risk premium.[35] It is shown that this specification of the model performs well in explaining the cross section of returns. Grundy and Malkiel also contend that beta is a very useful measure of risk during declining markets, which is when it is important.[36]

THE MARKET PORTFOLIO: THEORY VERSUS PRACTICE

Throughout our presentation of the CAPM, we noted that the market portfolio included *all* the risky assets in the economy. Further, in equilibrium, the various assets would be included in the portfolio in proportion to their market value. Therefore, this market portfolio should contain not only U.S. stocks and bonds, but also real estate, options, art, stamps, coins, foreign stocks and bonds, and so on, with weights equal to their relative market value.

Although this concept of a market portfolio is reasonable in theory, it is difficult—if not impossible—to implement when testing or using the CAPM. The easy part is getting a stock series for the NYSE, the AMEX, and major world stock exchanges, such as Tokyo, London, and Germany. There are stock series for the OTC market, too, but these series generally are incomplete. Also, as noted in Chapter 5, there is a growing number of world stock indexes. There also are some well-regarded U.S. bond series available (e.g., from Lehman Brothers, Merrill Lynch, Ryan Labs, and Salomon Brothers) and several world bond series (e.g., from J.P. Morgan, Salomon Brothers, and Merrill Lynch). Because of the difficulty in deriving series that are available monthly in a timely fashion for the numerous other assets mentioned, most studies have limited themselves to using a stock or bond series alone. In fact, the vast majority of studies have chosen the S&P 500 series or some other NYSE stock series that is obviously limited to only U.S. stocks, which constitutes *less than 20 percent* of a truly global risky asset portfolio (see Figure 3.1). At best, it was assumed that the particular series used as a proxy for the market portfolio was highly correlated with the true market portfolio.

Most academicians recognize this potential problem but assume that the deficiency is not serious. Several articles by Roll, however, concluded that, on the contrary, the use of

---

[33]S. P. Kothari. Jay Shanken, and Richard G. Sloan, "Another Look at the Cross Section of Expected Stock Returns," *Journal of Finance* 50, no. 2 (March 1995): 185–224.

[34]Glenn Pettengill, Sridhar Dundaram, and Ike Matthur, "The Conditional Relation between Beta and Returns," *Journal of Financial and Quantitative Analysis* 30, no. 1 (March 1995): 101–115.

[35]Ravi Jagannathan and Zhenyu Wang, "The Conditional CAPM and the Cross Section of Expected Returns," *Journal of Finance* 51, no. 1 (March 1996): 3–53.

[36]Kevin Grundy and Burton Malkiel, "Reports of Beta's Death Have Been Greatly Exaggerated," *Journal of Portfolio Management* 22, no. 3 (spring 1996): 36–44.

these indexes as a proxy for the market portfolio had very serious implications for tests of the model and especially for using the model when evaluating portfolio performance.[37] Roll referred to it as a **benchmark error** because the practice is to compare the performance of a portfolio manager to the return of an unmanaged portfolio of equal risk—that is, the market portfolio adjusted for risk would be the benchmark. Roll's point is that if the benchmark is mistakenly specified, you cannot measure the performance of a portfolio manager properly. A mistakenly specified market portfolio can have two effects. First, the beta computed for alternative portfolios would be wrong because the market portfolio used to compute the portfolio's systematic risk is inappropriate. Second, the SML derived would be wrong because it goes from the RFR through the improperly specified *M* portfolio. Figure 10.5 shows an example where the true portfolio risk (β_T) is underestimated (β_e) possibly because of the proxy market portfolio used in computing the estimated beta. As shown, the portfolio being evaluated may appear to be above the SML using β_e, which would imply superior management. If, in fact, the true risk (β_T) is greater, the portfolio will shift to the right and be below the SML, which would indicate inferior performance.

Figure 10.6 indicates that the intercept and slope will differ if (1) there is an error in selecting a proper risk-free asset and (2) if the market portfolio selected is not the correct mean-variance efficient portfolio. Obviously, it is very possible that under these conditions, a portfolio judged to be superior relative to the first SML (i.e., the portfolio plotted above the measured SML) could be inferior relative to the true SML (i.e., the portfolio would plot below the true SML).

FIGURE 10.5 **DIFFERENTIAL PERFORMANCE BASED ON AN ERROR IN ESTIMATING SYSTEMATIC RISK**

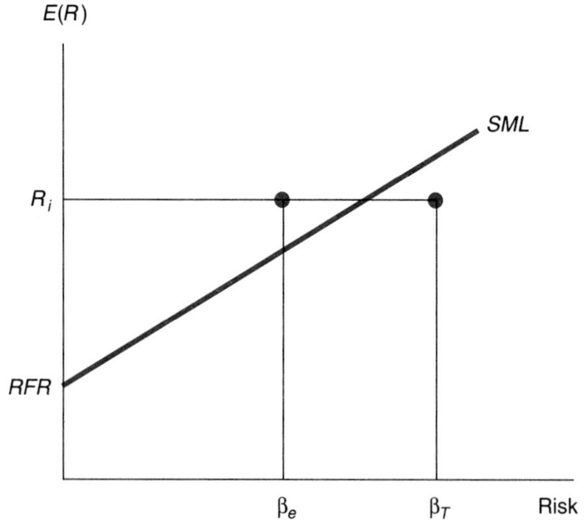
E(R)
SML
Ri
RFR
βe
βT
Risk

[37]Richard Roll, "A Critique of the Asset Pricing Theory's Tests," *Journal of Financial Economics* 4, no. 4 (March 1977): 129–176; Richard Roll, "Ambiguity When Performance Is Measured by the Securities Market Line," *Journal of Finance* 33. no. 4 (September 1978): 1051–1069; Richard Roll, "Performance Evaluation and Benchmark Error I," *Journal of Portfolio Management* 6, no. 4 (summer 1980): 5–12; and Richard Roll, "Performance Evaluation and Benchmark Error II," *Journal of Portfolio Management* 7, no. 2 (winter 1981): 17–22. This discussion draws heavily from these articles.

Roll contends that a test of the CAPM requires an analysis of whether the proxy used to represent the market portfolio is mean-variance efficient (on the Markowitz efficient frontier) and whether it is the true optimum market portfolio. Roll showed that if the proxy market portfolio (e.g., the S&P 500 index) is mean-variance efficient, it is mathematically possible to show a linear relationship between returns and betas derived with this portfolio. Unfortunately, this is not a true test of the CAPM because you are not working with the true SML (see Figure 10.7).

A demonstration of the impact of the benchmark problem is provided in a study by Reilly and Akhtar.[38] Table 10.2 shows the substantial difference in average beta for the 30 stocks in the DJIA during three alternative periods using three different proxies for the market portfolio: (1) the S&P 500 Index, (2) the Morgan Stanley World Stock Index, and (3) the Brinson Partners Global Security Market Index (GSMI). The GSMI includes not only U.S. and international stocks, but also U.S. and international bonds. The results in Table 10.2 are as one would expect because, as we know from Chapter 9, beta is equal to:

$$\text{Beta} = \frac{\text{Cov}_{i,m}}{\sigma_m^2}$$

where:

$\text{Cov}_{i,m}$ = the covariance between asset i and the m portfolio
σ_m^2 = the variance of the m portfolio

FIGURE 10.6

DIFFERENTIAL SML BASED ON MEASURED RISK-FREE ASSET AND PROXY MARKET PORTFOLIO

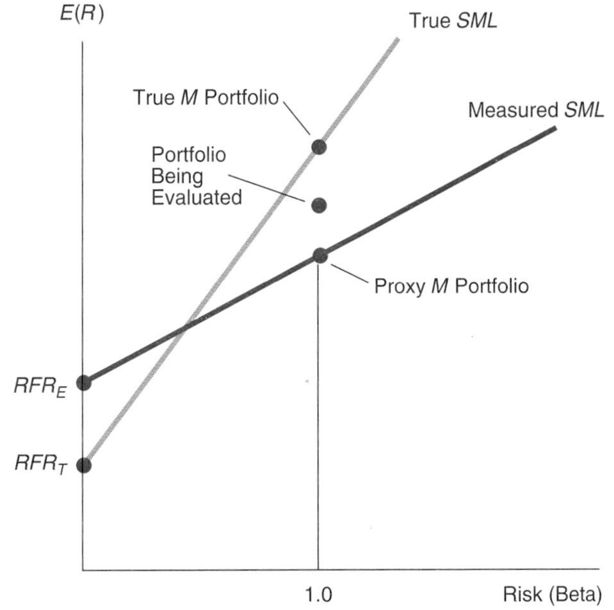
E(R)
True SML
True M Portfolio
Measured SML
Portfolio Being Evaluated
Proxy M Portfolio
RFR_E
RFR_T
1.0
Risk (Beta)

[38]Frank K. Reilly and Rashid A. Akhtar, "The Benchmark Error Problem with Global Capital Markets," *Journal of Portfolio Management* 22, no. 1 (fall 1995): 33–52.

FIGURE 10.7 **DIFFERENTIAL SML USING MARKET PROXY THAT IS MEAN-VARIANCE EFFICIENT**

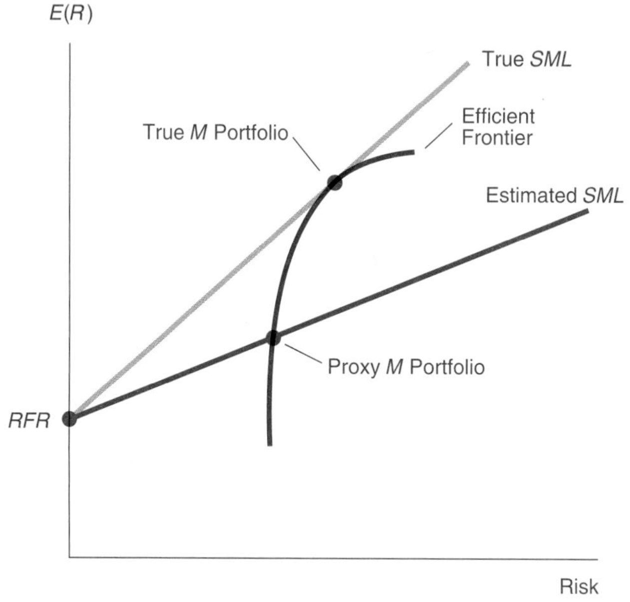
E(R)
True SML
True M Portfolio
Efficient Frontier
Estimated SML
Proxy M Portfolio
RFR
Risk

As we change from an all–U.S. stock index to a world stock index (M-S World) or a world stock and bond index (GSMI), we would expect the covariance with U.S. stocks to decline. The other component is the standard deviation for the market portfolio. As shown in the table, typically the M-S World Stock Index has a smaller variance than the S&P 500 because it is more diversified with international stocks. Therefore, while both covariance and market variance decline, the covariance effect dominates, so the beta is smaller with the M-S World Stock Index. In contrast, although the covariance between the U.S. stocks and the GSMI also is lower, the variance of the highly diversified GSMI market portfolio is substantially lower (about 25–33 percent). As a result, the beta is substantially larger (about 27 percent to 48 percent larger) when the Brinson Partners Index is used rather than the S&P 500 Index. Notably, the Brinson Index has a composition of assets that is substantially closer to the "true" *M* portfolio than either of the other proxies that contain only U.S. stocks or global stocks.

There also was a difference in the SMLs implied by each of the market proxies that only contain U.S. stocks or global stocks. Table 10.3 contains the average RFR, the market returns, and the slope of the SML during the three time periods for the three indexes and for market series from Japan (Nikkei), Germany (FAZ), and the United Kingdom (FT All-Share). Clearly, the slopes differ dramatically among the alternative indexes and over time. Needless to say, the benchmark used does make a difference.

Finally, it is necessary to combine the estimate of systematic risk (beta) with the estimated SML to determine the combined effect on the required rate of return for an asset. Table 10.4 shows that during specific time periods the difference between the highest and the lowest expected (required) return ranges from about 4 percent to 7.5 percent, with the highest expected returns when the market proxy was the Brinson GSMI because of the high betas. The differences in the expected (required) returns for individual stocks were similar (i.e., a range of about 4–5 percent), which can have a substantial impact on valuation.

TABLE 10.2 **AVERAGE BETA FOR THE 30 STOCKS IN THE DOW JONES INDUSTRIAL AVERAGE DURING ALTERNATIVE TIME PERIODS USING DIFFERENT PROXIES FOR THE MARKET PORTFOLIOS**

	Alternative Market Proxies		
Time Period	S&P 500	M-S World	Brinson GSMI
1983–1988			
Average beta	0.820	0.565	1.215
Mean index return	0.014	0.017	0.014
Standard deviation of index returns	0.049	0.043	0.031
1989–1994			
Average beta	0.991	0.581	1.264
Mean index return	0.010	0.004	0.008
Standard deviation of index returns	0.036	0.043	0.026
1983–1994			
Average beta	0.880	0.606	1.223
Mean index return	0.012	0.011	0.011
Standard deviation of index returns	0.043	0.043	0.029

Source: Frank K. Reilly and Rashid A. Akhtar, "The Benchmark Error Problem with Global Capital Markets," *Journal of Portfolio Management* 22, no. 1 (fall 1995): 33–52.

In summary, the concern is that an incorrect market proxy will affect the beta risk measures as well as the position and slope of the SML that is used to evaluate portfolio performance. In general, the errors will tend to overestimate the performance of portfolio managers because the proxy used for the market portfolio is probably not as efficient as the true market portfolio, so the slope of the SML will be underestimated. Also, the beta generally will be underestimated because the true market portfolio will have a lower variance than the typical proxy due to greater diversification.

Roll's benchmark problems, however, do not invalidate the value of the CAPM as *a normative model of asset pricing;* they only indicate a problem in *measurement* when attempting to test the theory and when using this model for evaluating portfolio performance. Therefore, it is necessary to develop a better market portfolio proxy similar to the Brinson GSMI and/or adjust the portfolio performance measures to reflect this measurement problem.

ARBITRAGE PRICING THEORY (APT)

At this point, we have discussed the basic theory of the CAPM, the impact of changing some of its major assumptions, the empirical evidence that does and does not support the theory, and its dependence on a market portfolio of all risky assets. In addition, the model assumes that investors have quadratic utility functions and that the distribution of security prices is normal (symmetrically distributed), with a variance term that can be estimated.

The tests of the CAPM indicated that the beta coefficients for individual securities were not stable, but the portfolio betas generally were stable assuming long enough sample periods and adequate trading volume. There was mixed support for a positive linear relationship between rates of return and systematic risk for portfolios of stock, with some recent evidence indicating the need to consider additional risk variables or a need for different risk

TABLE 10.3

COMPONENTS OF SECURITY MARKET LINES USING ALTERNATIVE MARKET PROXIES

	1983–1988			1989–1994			1983–1994		
	R_m	*RFR*	$(R_m - RFR)$	R_m	*RFR*	$(R_m - RFR)$	R_m	*RFR*	$(R_m - RFR)$
S&P 500	18.20	8.31	9.90	13.07	5.71	7.36	15.61	7.01	8.60
Nikkei	26.05	5.35	20.70	−3.62	4.70	−8.32	10.30	5.02	5.28
FAZ	16.36	5.01	11.35	7.97	7.83	0.14	12.09	6.42	5.67
FT AllShare	18.01	10.00	8.01	10.09	10.07	0.02	13.99	10.03	3.95
M-S World	22.64	8.31	14.33	5.18	5.71	−0.52	13.60	7.01	6.60
Brinson GSMI	18.53	8.31	10.22	10.18	5.71	4.48	14.28	7.01	7.28

RFR = risk-free return.

Source: Frank K. Reilly and Rashid Akhtar, "The Benchmark Error Problem with Global Capital Markets," *Journal of Portfolio Management* 22, no. 1 (fall 1995): 33–52.

TABLE 10.4

THE AVERAGE EXPECTED RETURNS FOR STOCKS IN THE DJIA BASED ON DIFFERENT BETAS AND SECURITY MARKET LINES DERIVED WITH ALTERNATIVE BENCHMARKS

	Mean Expected Rate of Return		
Time Period	S&P 500	M-S World	Brinson GSMI
1983–1988	16.41	17.72	20.75
1989–1994	13.00	5.40	11.36

Source: Frank K. Reilly and Rashid A. Akhtar, "The Benchmark Error Problem with Global Capital Markets," *Journal of Portfolio Management* 22, no. 1 (fall 1995): 33–52.

proxies. In addition, several papers by Roll criticized the tests of the model and the usefulness of the model in portfolio evaluation because of its dependence on a market portfolio of risky assets that is not currently available.

Consequently, the academic community has considered an alternative asset pricing theory that is reasonably intuitive and that requires only limited assumptions. This *arbitrage pricing theory (APT),* developed by Ross in the early 1970s and initially published in 1976, has three major assumptions:[39]

1. Capital markets are perfectly competitive.
2. Investors always prefer more wealth to less wealth with certainty.
3. The stochastic process generating asset returns can be expressed as a linear function of a set of K factors or indexes (to be described).

Equally important, the following major assumptions are *not* required: (1) quadratic utility function, (2) normally distributed security returns, and (3) a market portfolio that contains all risky assets and is mean-variance efficient. Obviously, if such a theory can explain differential security prices, it would be considered a superior theory to the CAPM because it

[39]Stephen Ross, "The Arbitrage Theory of Capital Asset Pricing," *Journal of Economic Theory* 13, no. 2 (December 1976): 341–360; and Stephen Ross, "Return, Risk, and Arbitrage," in *Risk and Return in Finance,* ed. I. Friend and J. Bicksler (Cambridge: Ballinger, 1977), 189–218.

is simpler (i.e., it requires fewer assumptions). Prior to discussing the empirical tests of the model, we provide a brief review of the basics of the model. The following review of the APT model is very similar to the discussion in Chapter 9. It is repeated here for the reader's convenience.

As noted, the theory assumes that the stochastic process generating asset returns can be represented as a K factor model of the form

$$R_i = E_i + b_{il}\delta_l + b_{i2}\delta_2 + \ldots + b_{ik}\delta_k + \epsilon_i \text{ for } i = 1 \text{ to } N$$

where:

R_i = return on asset *i* during a specified time period, $i = 1, 2, 3, \ldots m$
E_i = expected return for asset *i* if all the factors or indexes have zero changes
b_{ik} = reaction in asset *i*'s returns to movements in a common factor *K* or index *K*
δ_k = a set of common factors or indexes with a zero mean that influences the returns on all assets
ϵ_i = a unique effect on asset *i*'s return (i.e., a random error term that, by assumption, is completely diversifiable in large portfolios and has a mean of zero)
N = number of assets

Two terms require elaboration: δ_k and b_{ik}. As indicated, δ terms are the *multiple* factors expected to have an impact on the returns of *all* assets. Examples of these factors might include inflation, growth in GDP, major political upheavals, or changes in interest rates. The APT contends that there are many such factors that affect returns, in contrast to the CAPM, where the only relevant risk variable is the covariance of the asset with the market portfolio (i.e., the asset's beta).

Given these common factors, the b_{ik} terms determine how each asset reacts to a particular common factor. To extend the earlier example, although all assets may be affected by growth in GDP, the impact (i.e., reaction) to a factor will differ. For example, stocks of cyclical firms will have larger b_{ik} terms for the "growth in GDP" factor than will noncyclical firms, such as grocery chains. Likewise, you will hear discussions about interest-sensitive stocks. All stocks are affected by changes in interest rates; however, some experience larger impacts. For example, an interest-sensitive stock would have a b_k interest of 2.0 or more, whereas a stock that is relatively insensitive to interest rates would have a b_k of 0.5. Other examples of common factors include inflation, exchange rates, and interest rate spreads. Notably, when we apply the theory, *the factors are not identified.* That is, when we discuss the empirical studies, the investigators will note that they found three, four, or five factors that affect security returns, but *they will give no indication of what these factors represent.*

Similar to the CAPM model, it is assumed that the unique effects (ϵ_i) are independent and will be diversified away in a large portfolio. The APT assumes that in equilibrium the return on a zero-investment, zero-systematic-risk portfolio is zero when the unique effects are diversified away. This assumption and some theory from linear algebra imply that the expected return on any asset *i* (E_i), can be expressed as

$$E_0 = \lambda_0 + \lambda_1 b_{i1} + \lambda_2 b_{i2} + \ldots + \lambda_k b_{ik}$$

where:

λ_0 = the expected return on an asset with zero systematic risk where $\lambda_0 = E_0$
λ_i = the risk premium related to each of the common factors—for example, the risk premium related to the interest rate risk factor ($\lambda_i = E_i - E_0$)
b_i = the pricing relationship between the risk premium and asset *i*—that is, how responsive asset *i* is to this common factor *K*

For example, if we assume that the risk premium related to interest rate sensitivity is 0.02 and a stock that is sensitive to interest rates has a β_k (where K is interest rate sensitivity) of 2.0, this means that this factor would cause the stock's expected return to increase by 4 percent ($K = 2.0 \times 0.02$). Consider the following example of two stocks and a two-factor model.

K_1 = changes in the rate of inflation. The risk premium related to this factor is 1 percent for every 1 percent change in the rate ($\lambda_1 = 0.01$).
K_2 = percent growth in real GDP. The average risk premium related to this factor is 2 percent for every 1 percent change in the rate of growth ($\lambda_2 = 0.02$).
λ_0 = the rate of return on a zero-systematic risk asset (zero beta: $b_{0j} = 0$) is 3 percent ($\lambda_0 = 0.03$)

The two assets (X, Y) have the following response coefficients to these factors:

b_{x1} = the response of asset X to changes in the rate of inflation is 0.50 ($b_{x1} = 0.50$.). This asset is not very responsive to changes in the rate of inflation.
b_{y1} = the response of asset Y to changes in the rate of inflation is 2.00 ($b_{y1} = 2.00$)
b_{x2} = the response of asset X to changes in the growth rate of real GDP is 1.50 ($b_{x2} = 1.50$)
b_{y2} = the response of asset Y to changes in the growth rate of real GDP is 1.75 ($b_{y2} = 1.75$)

These response coefficients indicate that if these are the major factors influencing asset returns, asset Y is a higher risk asset, and, therefore, its expected return should be greater. The overall expected return equation will be

$$\begin{aligned} E_i &= \lambda_0 + \lambda_1 b_{i1} + \lambda_2 b_{i2} \\ &= 0.03 + (0.01)b_{i1} + (0.02)b_{i2} \end{aligned}$$

Therefore:

$$\begin{aligned} E_x &= 0.03 + (0.01)(0.50) + (0.02)(1.50) \\ &= 0.065 = 6.5\% \\ E_y &= 0.03 + (0.01)(2.00) + (0.02)(1.75) \\ &= 0.085 = 8.5\% \end{aligned}$$

If the prices of the assets do not reflect these expected returns, we would expect investors to enter into arbitrage arrangements whereby they would sell overpriced assets short and use the proceeds to purchase the underpriced assets until the relevant prices were corrected. Given these linear relationships, it should be possible to find an asset or a combination of assets with equal risk to the mispriced asset, yet providing a higher expected return.

Empirical Tests of the APT

Although the APT is relatively new, it has undergone numerous empirical studies. Before we begin discussing the empirical tests, remember the earlier caveat that when applying the theory, we do not know what the factors generated by the statistical model represent. This becomes a major point in some discussions of test results.

Roll-Ross Study

The Roll and Ross test followed a two-step procedure:[40]

1. Estimate the expected returns and the factor coefficients from time-series data on individual asset returns.

[40]Richard Roll and Stephen A. Ross, "An Empirical Investigation of the Arbitrage Pricing Theory," *Journal of Finance* 35, no. 5 (December 1980): 1073–1103.

2. Use these estimates to test the basic cross-sectional pricing conclusion implied by the APT. Specifically, are the expected returns for these assets consistent with the common factors derived in Step 1?

Roll and Ross tested the following pricing relationship:

$$H_0\text{: There exist nonzero constants } (E_0, \lambda_i, \ldots \lambda_k) \text{ such that}$$
$$E_1 - E_0 = \lambda_1 b_{i1} + \lambda_2 b_2 + \ldots \lambda_k b_{ik}$$

The specific b_i coefficients were estimated using factor analysis. The authors pointed out that the estimation procedure was generally appropriate for the model involved, but there is very little known about the small sample properties of the results. Therefore, they emphasized the tentative nature of the conclusions.

The data file was daily returns for the period July 1962 through December 1972. Stocks were put into 42 portfolios of 30 stocks each (1,260 stocks) by alphabetical order. The estimation of the factor model indicated that the maximum reasonable number of factors was five. The factors derived were applied to all 42 portfolios, with the understanding that the importance of the various factors might differ among portfolios (e.g., the first factor in Portfolio A might not be first in Portfolio B).

Assuming a risk-free rate of 6 percent ($\lambda_0 = 0.06$), the subsequent analysis indicated at least three important pricing factors, but probably not more than four. Further, the weight on the first two factors was quite heavy with changes in relative weights for the remaining three factors. When they allowed the model to estimate the risk-free rate (λ_0), only two factors were consistently significant, which indicates that the earlier estimate of three factors may have been an overestimate.

A subsequent test related returns to a security's own standard deviation, which should not affect expected return if the APT is valid because a security's diversifiable component would be eliminated by diversification, and the nondiversifiable components should be explained by the factor loadings. The test analyzed returns against the five factors plus the security's own standard deviation. The initial results indicated that the security's own standard deviation was statistically significant, which was evidence against the APT. Subsequently, they adjusted the results for skewness and found that the security's own standard deviation was insignificant, which supports the APT.

Finally, they tested whether the three or four factors that affect Group A were the same as the factors that affect Group B. The analysis involved testing for cross-sectional consistency by examining whether the λ_0 terms for the 42 groups are similar. The results yielded no evidence that the intercept terms were different, although the test was admittedly weak. The authors concluded that the evidence generally supported the APT, but acknowledged that these initial tests were weak.

Extensions of the Roll-Ross Tests

Cho, Elton, and Gruber tested the model by examining the number of factors in the return-generating process that were priced.[41] Because the APT model contends that more factors affect stock returns than are implied by the CAPM, they examined different sets of data to determine what happened to the number of factors priced in the model compared to prior studies that found between three and five significant factors. They simulated returns using the zero-beta CAPM with betas derived from Wilshire's fundamental betas and with betas derived from historical data. They found that five factors were required using the Roll-Ross

[41]D. Chinhyung Cho, Edwin J. Elton, and Martin J. Gruber, "On the Robustness of the Roll and Ross Arbitrage Pricing Theory," *Journal of Financial and Quantitative Analysis* 19, no. 1 (March 1984): 1–10.

procedures. The results using historical betas implied six factors were necessary, whereas the Wilshire fundamental betas indicated a need for three factors.

The authors concluded that even when returns are generated by a two-factor model, two or three factors are required to explain the returns. These results support the APT model because it allows for the consideration of these additional factors, which is not possible with the classical CAPM.

Dhrymes, Friend, and Gultekin (DFG) reexamined the techniques used in prior studies and contended that these techniques have several major limitations.[42] Although the division of the total sample of stocks into numerous portfolios of 30 stocks was necessary because of computer limitations, this practical constraint produced results that differed from large-sample results, especially for the total sample of over 1,000 stocks. Specifically, they found *no* relationship between the "factor loading" for groups of 30 stocks and for a group of 240 stocks.

Also, DFG could not identify the actual number of factors that characterize the return-generating process. When they applied the model to portfolios of different sizes, the number of factors changed. For example, for 15 securities, it is a two-factor model; for 30 securities, a three-factor model; for 45, a four-factor model; for 60, a six-factor model; and for 90, a nine-factor model. Also, with multiple factors it was difficult to know which of them were significant in explaining the returns.

Roll and Ross acknowledged that the factors differ with 30 stocks versus 240, but contended that the important consideration is whether the resulting estimates are *consistent* because it is not feasible to consider all of the stocks together.[43] When they tested for consistency, the model was generally supported. They point out that the number of factors is a secondary issue compared to how well the model explains the return-generating process compared to alternative models. Also, one would *expect* the number of factors to increase with the sample size because more potential relationships would arise (e.g., you would introduce industry effects). The relevant question is: How many of these factors are significant in a diversified portfolio?

Dhrymes, Friend, Gultekin, and Gultekin repeated the prior tests for larger groups of securities.[44] When they increased the number of securities in each group (30, 60, and 90 securities), both the number of factors that entered the model and the number of significant ("priced") factors increased, although most factors are not "priced." These results confirmed the DFG results. In addition, they found that the unique or total standard deviation for a period was as good at predicting subsequent returns as the factor loadings. Also, the number of time-series observations affected the number of factors discovered, and the group size of securities affected the model's intercept. These findings are not favorable to the empirical relevance of APT because they indicate extreme instability in the relationships and suggest that the risk-free rate implied by the model depends on group size and the number of observations. Also the fact that the total standard deviation is significant is discouraging.

The APT and Anomalies

An alternative set of tests of the APT considers how well it explains anomalies that are not explained by a competing model. Two anomalies considered are the small-firm effect and the January anomaly.

---

[42]Phoebus J. Dhrymes, Irwin Friend, and N. Bulent Gultekin, "A Critical Re-Examination of the Empirical Evidence on the Arbitrage Pricing Theory," *Journal of Finance* 39, no. 2 (June 1984): 323–346.

[43]Richard Roll and Stephen Ross, "A Critical Re-Examination of the Empirical Evidence on the Arbitrage Pricing Theory: A Reply," *Journal of Finance* 39, no. 2 (June 1984): 347–350.

[44]Phoebus J. Dhrymes, Irwin Friend, Mustofa N. Gultekin, and N. Bulent Gultekin, "New Tests of the APT and Their Implications," *Journal of Finance* 40, no. 3 (July 1985): 659–674.

Reinganum addressed the APT's ability to account for the differences in average returns between small firms and large firms.[45] Reinganum contended that this anomaly, which could not be explained by the CAPM, should be explained by the APT if the APT was to be considered a superior theory or an empirical replacement for the CAPM. Reinganum's test is conducted in two stages:

1. During Year Y − 1, factor loadings are estimated for all securities, and securities with similar factor loadings are put into common control portfolios that should have similar risk characteristics. (The author tests models with three, four, and five factors.) During Year Y, excess security returns are derived for each control portfolio from the daily returns of the individual stocks in the portfolio. Assuming that all stocks within a control portfolio have equal risk according to the APT, they should have similar average returns and the average excess returns should be zero.
2. Given the excess returns during Year Y, all the stocks were ranked on the basis of their market value at the end of Year Y − 1 and the excess returns of the firms in the bottom 10 percent of the size distribution were combined (equal weights) to form the average excess returns for Portfolio MV1. Similarly, nine other portfolios were formed, with MV10 containing excess returns for the largest firms.

Under the null hypothesis, the 10 portfolios should possess identical average excess returns, which should be insignificantly different from zero. If the 10 portfolios do not have identical average excess returns, this evidence would be inconsistent with the APT.

The ranking procedure described in Step 2 was done annually because the market values change, and firms are added and deleted. As stated, the APT would be supported if the average excess returns for the 10 portfolios equated zero.

The test results were *clearly inconsistent with the APT.* Specifically, the average excess returns of the 10 portfolios were not equal to zero for either a three-, four-, or five-factor model. The small-firm portfolio, MV1, experienced a positive and statistically significant average excess return, whereas Portfolio MV10 had a statistically significant negative average excess return. The mean difference in excess returns between the small and large firms was about 25 percent a year. Also, the mean excess returns of MV1 through MV10 were perfectly inversely ordered with firm size.

Reinganum also tested for significant differences between individual portfolio returns and the difference between the high and low portfolio each year. Both tests confirmed that the low-market-value portfolios outperformed the high-market-value portfolios regardless of whether excess returns were derived from the three-, four-, or five-factor model. The author concluded that these results did not support the APT, but he acknowledged that the analysis involved a joint test of several hypotheses implicit in the theory and that it was impossible to pinpoint the error.

A subsequent study by Chen supported the APT model compared to the CAPM and provided evidence related to the small-firm effect that was contrary to Reinganum.[46] Prior to discussing the tests, the author contended that problems caused by the need for a limited sample and the existence of multiple factors were related to the *testing* of the theory and should not reflect on the theory itself. The analysis employed 180 stocks and five factors.

---

[45]Mark R. Reinganum, "The Arbitrage Pricing Theory: Some Empirical Results," *Journal of Finance* 36, no. 2 (May 1981): 313–321.

[46]Nai-fu Chen, "Some Empirical Tests of the Theory of Arbitrage Pricing," *Journal of Finance* 38, no. 5 (December 1983): 1393–1414.

The cross-sectional results indicated that the first factor was highly correlated with beta. Chen's test of the two models for performance measurement was based on the contention that if the CAPM does not capture all the information related to returns, this remaining information will be in the residual series. In turn, if the APT can provide factors to explain these residual returns, it would be superior. He concluded that the CAPM was misspecified and that the missing price information was picked up by the APT.

The final tests examined whether some major variables have explanatory power after the factor loadings from the APT model. If so, it would cause one to reject the APT. The two variables considered based on prior CAPM studies were a stock's own variance and firm size. The results supported the APT because neither a stock's own variance nor a firm's size had explanatory power after adjusting for risk based on factor loadings. Again, these results are in contrast to the earlier results by Reinganum.

APT AND THE JANUARY EFFECT Given the January anomaly where returns in January are significantly larger than in any other month, Gultekin and Gultekin tested the ability of the APT model to adjust for this anomaly.[47] The APT model was estimated for each month and risk premia were *always* significant in January, but rarely priced in other months. It was concluded that the APT model, like the CAPM, can explain the risk–return relation only in January, which indicates that the APT model does not explain this anomaly any better than the CAPM.

Burmeister and McElroy estimated a linear factor model (LFM), the APT, and a CAPM.[48] They found a significant January effect that was not captured by any of the models. When they went beyond the January effect, however, they rejected the CAPM in favor of the APT.

THE APT AND INFLATION Elton, Gruber, and Rentzler extended the APT to consider the impact to inflation on asset returns.[49] After deriving an equilibrium model of real returns, they assumed the inflation factor was not priced, so they employed the APT model and compared the results to prior inflation-adjusted CAPM models. They contended that it was important to develop APT models with statistically identifiable factors that had economic meaning, such as inflation and growth in real GDP.

The Shanken Challenge to Testability of the APT

Similar to Roll's critique of the CAPM, a set of papers by Shanken challenged whether the APT can be empirically verified.[50] Rather than question specific tests or methods, Shanken questioned whether the APT is more susceptible to testing than the CAPM based on the usual empirical test that determines whether asset returns conform to a K factor model. One problem is that if returns are not explained by such a model, it is not considered a rejection of the model; however, if the factors do explain returns, it is considered support. Also, it is contended that APT has no advantage because the factors need not be observable, which means that equivalent sets of securities may conform to different factor structures. Therefore, the empirical formulation of the APT may yield different implications regarding the

[47]Mustofa N. Gultekin and N. Bulent Gultekin, "Stock Return Anomalies and the Tests of APT," *Journal of Finance* 42, no. 5 (December 1987): 1213–1224.

[48]Edwin Burmeister and Marjorie B. McElroy, "Joint Estimation of Factor Sensitivities and Risk Premia for the Arbitrage Pricing Theory," *Journal of Finance* 43, no. 3 (July 1988): 721–733.

[49]Edwin Elton, Martin Gruber, and Joel Rentzler, "The Arbitrage Pricing Model and Returns on Assets under Uncertain Inflation," *Journal of Finance* 38, no. 2 (May 1983): 525–537.

[50]Jay Shanken, "The Arbitrage Pricing Theory: Is It Testable?" *Journal of Finance* 37, no. 5 (December 1982): 1129–1140.

THE INTERNET *Investments Online*

The best way to stay on top of advances in theory is to stay in touch with those Web sites related to leading researchers, both academics and practitioners. As such, one Web site from Chapter 9 is particularly relevant to this chapter: **www.barra.com,** a leading provider of quantitative analysis and analytical tools. Periodically reviewing the Web site of a Nobel Prize winner such as William Sharpe's **www.wsharpe.com,** is a good way to stay close to the cutting edge, too. Several academic finance journals have Web sites that feature abstracts as well as selections and data sets from published articles. A particularly useful site along these lines is that of the *Journal of Finance,* **www.cob.ohio-state.edu/~fin/journal/jof.htm.** Another highly respected journal, *The Review of Financial Studies,* has a Web site at **www3.oup.co.uk/revfin/scope.**

expected returns for a given set of securities. Unfortunately, this implies that the theory cannot explain differential returns between securities because it cannot identify the relevant factor structure that explains the differential returns. This need to identify the relevant factor structure that affects asset returns is similar to the CAPM benchmark problem. In summary, each of the models has a problem with testing. Specifically, before you can test the CAPM, you must identify and use the true market portfolio, whereas before you can test the APT, you must identify the relevant factor structure that affects security returns.

Dybvig and Ross replied by suggesting that the APT is testable as an equality rather than the "empirical APT" proposed by Shanken.[51] Shanken responded that what has developed is a set of equilibrium APT pricing models that are testable, but the original arbitrage-based models ("APT") are not testable as originally specified.[52]

ALTERNATIVE TESTING TECHNIQUES Beyond those that were concerned with prior tests, several other articles have proposed alternative statistical techniques for testing the APT model. Jobson proposes that the APT be tested using a multivariate linear regression model.[53] Brown and Weinstein propose an approach to estimating and testing asset pricing models using a bilinear paradigm.[54] A number of subsequent papers have proposed new methodologies for testing the APT.[55]

---

[51]Philip H. Dybvig and Stephen A. Ross, "Yes, the APT Is Testable," *Journal of Finance* 40, no. 4 (September 1985): 1173–1188.

[52]Jay Shanken, "Multi-Beta CAPM or Equilibrium APT?: A Reply," *Journal of Finance* 40, no. 4 (September 1985):1189–1196.

[53]J. D. Jobson, "A Multivariate Linear Regression Test for the Arbitrage Pricing Theory," *Journal of Finance* 37, no. 4 (September 1982): 1037–1042.

[54]Stephen J. Brown and Mark I. Weinstein, "A New Approach to Testing Asset Pricing Models: The Bilinear Paradigm," *Journal of Finance* 38, no. 3 (June 1983): 711–743.

[55]Among the papers are Chinhyang Cho, "On Testing the Arbitrage Pricing Theory: Inter-Battery Factor Analysis," *Journal of Finance* 39, no. 5 (December 1984): 1485–1502; Gregory Connor and Robert Korajczyk, "Risk and Return in an Equilibrium APT: Applications of a New Test Methodology," *Journal of Financial Economics* 21, no. 2 (September 1988): 255–290; Robert McCulloch and Peter Rossi, "Posterior, Predictive, and Utility-Based Approaches to Testing the Arbitrage Pricing Theory," *Journal of Financial Economics* 28, no. 1 and 2 (November–December 1990): 7–38; Ravi Shakla and Charles Trzcinka, "Sequential Tests of the Arbitrage Pricing Theory: A Comparison of Principle Components and Maximum Likelihood Factors," *Journal of Finance* 45, no. 5 (December 1990): 1542–1564; and Punect Handa and Scott C. Linn, "Arbitrage Pricing with Estimation Risk," *Journal of Financial and Quantitative Analysis* 28, no. 1 (March 1993): 81–100.

Summary

- When we relax several of the major assumptions of the CAPM, the required modifications are reasonably minor and do not change the overall concept of the model. Empirical studies have indicated stable portfolio betas. especially when enough observations were used to derive the betas and there was adequate volume. Although the early tests confirmed the expected relationship between returns and systematic risk (with allowance for the zero-beta model), several subsequent studies indicated that the univariate beta model needed to be supplemented with additional variables that considered skewness, size, P/E, leverage, and the book value/market value ratio. A study by Fama and French contended that during the period 1963 to 1990, beta was not relevant. In their study, the most significant variables were book-to-market value (BE/ME) and size. Subsequent studies both supported their findings and differed with them because some more recent authors have found a significant relationship between beta and rates of return on stocks.
- Another problem has been raised by Roll, who contends that it is not possible to empirically derive a true market portfolio, so it is not possible to test the CAPM model properly or to use the model to evaluate portfolio performance. A study by Reilly and Akhtar provided empirical support for this contention by demonstrating significant differences in betas, SMLs, and expected returns with alternative benchmarks.
- Ross subsequently devised an alternative asset pricing model (the APT) with fewer assumptions that does not require a market portfolio. The results from the empirical tests of the APT have thus far been mixed. Also, Shanken contends that the nature of many of the tests are such that it is impossible to reject the theory.
- In conclusion, it is probably safe to assume that both the CAPM and APT will continue to be used to price capital assets. Coincident with their use will be further empirical tests of both theories, the ultimate goal being to determine which theory does the best job of explaining current and future returns. Notably, the APT model requires fewer assumptions and considers multiple factors to explain the risk of an asset.[56] At the same time, several authors (including Fama-French) have proposed either multifactor CAPMs or conditional CAPMs that allow for changing betas and market risk premiums over time.

Questions

1. In the empirical testing of the CAPM, what are two major concerns? Why are they important?
2. Briefly discuss why it is important for beta coefficients to be stationary over time.
3. Discuss the empirical results relative to beta stability for individual stocks and portfolios of stocks.
4. In the tests of the relationship between systematic risk (beta) and return, what are you looking for?
5. Draw an ideal SML. Based on the early empirical results, what did the actual risk–return relationship look like relative to the ideal relationship implied by the CAPM?
6. According to the CAPM, what assets are included in the market portfolio, and what are the relative weightings? In empirical studies of the CAPM, what are the typical proxies used for the market portfolio?
7. Assuming that the empirical proxy for the market portfolio is not a good proxy, what factors related to the CAPM will be affected?
8. Some studies related to the efficient market hypothesis generated results that implied additional factors beyond beta should be considered to estimate expected returns. What are these other variables and why should they be considered?
9. According to the Fama-French study, discuss what variables you should consider when selecting a cross section of stocks.
10. What are the major assumptions required by the APT? What critical assumptions of the CAPM are *not* required by the APT?
11. Briefly discuss one study that does not support the APT. Briefly discuss a study that supports the APT.

[56]For a discussion of how these models relate to each other, see William F. Sharpe, "Factor Models, CAPMs, and the APT," *Journal of Portfolio Management* 11, no. 1 (fall 1984): 21–25.

12. Briefly discuss why Shanken contends that the AFT is not testable.
13. *CFA Examination III (1986)*

CFA

Multifactor models of security returns have received increased attention. The arbitrage pricing theory (APT) probably has drawn the most attention and has been proposed as a replacement for the capital asset pricing model (CAPM).

a. Briefly explain the primary differences between APT and CAPM. [5 minutes]

b. Identify the *four* systematic factors suggested by Roll and Ross that determine an asset's riskiness. Explain how these factors affect an asset's expected rate of return. [10 minutes]

Problems

1. Given the following results, indicate what will happen to the beta for Stock E, relative to the market proxy, compared to the beta relative to the true market portfolio:

	Yearly Rates of Return		
Year	Stock E (percent)	Market Proxy (percent)	True Market (percent)
1	10	8	6
2	20	14	11
3	−14	−10	−7
4	−20	−18	−12
5	15	12	10

Discuss the reason for the differences in measured beta. Does the suggested relationship appear reasonable? Why or why not?

2. Draw the implied SMLs for the following two sets of conditions:

a. $RFR = 0.07$; $R_m\ (S + P\ 500) = 0.16$

b. $R_z = 0.09$; R_m (True) $= 0.18$

Under which set of conditions would it be more difficult for a portfolio manager to be superior?

3. Using the graph and equations from Problem 2, which of the following portfolios would be superior?

a. $R_a = 11\%$; $\beta = 0.09$

b. $R_b = 14\%$; $\beta = 1.00$

c. $R_c = 12\%$; $\beta = -0.40$

d. $R_d = 20\%$; $\beta = 1.10$

Does it matter which SML you use?

4. Draw the security market line for each of the following conditions:

a. (1) $RFR = 0.08 \quad R_m(\text{proxy}) = 0.12$

(2) $R_z = 0.06 \quad R_m(\text{true}) = 0.15$

b. Rader Tire has the following results for the last six periods. Calculate and compare the betas using each index.

Period	Return of Rader (percent)	Proxy Specific Index (percent)	True General Index (percent)
1	29	12	15
2	12	10	13
3	−12	−9	−8
4	17	14	18
5	20	25	28
6	−5	−10	0

c. If the current period return for the market is 12 percent and for Rader is 11 percent, are superior results being obtained for either index beta?

5. Under the following conditions, what are the expected returns for Stocks J and L?

$\lambda_0 = 0.05$	$b_{J1} = 0.80$
$K_1 = 0.02$	$b_{J2} = 1.40$
$K_2 = 0.04$	$b_{L1} = 1.60$
	$b_{L2} = 2.25$

References

Black, Fischer. "Capital Market Equilibrium with Restricted Borrowing." *Journal of Business* 45, no. 3 (July 1972).

Campbell, John Y., and John Ammer. "What Moves the Stock and Bond Markets? A Variance Decomposition for Long-Term Asset Returns." *Journal of Finance* 48, no. 1 (March 1993).

Chen, Nai-Fu. "Some Empirical Tests of the Theory of Arbitrage Pricing." *Journal of Finance* 38, no. 5 (December 1983).

Chen, Nai-fu, Richard Roll, and Stephen A. Ross. "Economic Forces and the Stock Market." *Journal of Business* 56, no. 3 (July 1986).

Elton, Edwin J., and Martin J. Gruber. *Modern Portfolio Theory and Investment Analysis.* 5th ed. New York: John Wiley & Sons, 1995.

Farrell, James L., Jr. *Portfolio Management Theory and Application.* 2d ed. New York: McGraw-Hill, 1997.

Handa, Punect, and Scott C. Linn. "Arbitrage Pricing with Estimation Risk." *Journal of Financial and Quantitative Analysis* 28, no. 1 (March 1993).

Lehmann, B. N., and D. M. Modest. "The Empirical Foundations of the Arbitrage Pricing Theory." *Journal of Financial Economics* 21, no. 3 (September 1988).

Roll, Richard, and Stephen A. Ross. "An Empirical Investigation of the Arbitrage Pricing Theory." *Journal of Finance* 35, no. 5 (December 1980).

Ross, Stephen A. "The Arbitrage Theory of Capital Asset Pricing." *Journal of Economic Theory* 13, no. 2 (December 1976).

Ross, Stephen A. "Risk, Return and Arbitrage." In *Risk and Return in Finance,* ed. I. Friend and J. Bicksler. Cambridge: Ballinger, 1977.

Shanken, Jay. "Multivariate Proxies and Asset Pricing Relations." *Journal of Financial Economics* 18, no. 1 (March 1987).

Chapter 11 An Introduction to Derivative Markets and Securities

After you read this chapter, you should be able to answer the following questions:

- What distinguishes a derivative security, such as a forward, futures, or option contract, from more fundamental securities, such as stocks and bonds?
- What are the important characteristics of forward, futures, and option contracts, and in what sense can they be interpreted as insurance policies?
- How are the markets for derivative securities organized and how do they differ from other security markets?
- What terminology is used to describe transactions that involve forward, futures, and option contracts?
- How are prices for derivative securities quoted and how should this information be interpreted?
- What are the similarities and differences between forward and futures contracts?
- What do the payoff diagrams look like for investments in forward and futures contracts?
- What do the payoff diagrams look like for investments in put and call option contracts?
- How are forward contracts, put options, and call options related to one another?
- How can derivatives be used in conjunction with stock and Treasury bills to replicate the payoffs to other securities and create arbitrage opportunities for an investor?
- How can derivative contracts be used to restructure cash flow patterns and modify the risks in existing investment portfolios?

So far, we have seen several ways in which individuals and institutions can design their investments to take advantage of future market conditions. We have also seen how investors can control the volatility associated with their positions—at least in part—by forming well-diversified portfolios of securities around a common investment theme, thereby reducing or eliminating the unsystematic component of a stock's risk.

In this chapter, we begin our formal investigation of the role played by **derivative securities** in modern investment portfolios. A derivative instrument is one for which the ultimate payoff to the investor depends directly on the value of another security or commodity. Earlier, we briefly described two basic types of derivatives: (1) forward and futures contracts and (2) option contracts. A call option, for example, gives its **owner** the right to purchase an underlying security, such as a stock or a bond, at a fixed price within a certain amount of time. Naturally, this right to purchase would most certainly be exercised only if the value of the underlying asset at the call's expiration date was greater than the contractual purchase price. In this manner, the option's ultimate value can be said to depend on—and thus derive from—that of the other (underlying) asset. Similarly, a forward contract to sell a specific bond for a fixed price at a future date will see its value to the investor rise or fall with decreases or increases in the market price of the underlying bond.

The growth of the markets in which derivative securities are created and exchanged has been nothing short of phenomenal. The last few decades have seen the emergence of forward. futures, and option contracts to trade such fundamental products as agricultural commodities. energy, precious metals, currencies, common stock, and bonds. There are even derivatives to trade hypothetical underlying assets (e.g., options and futures contracts on the Standard & Poor's stock indexes) as well as "combination" derivatives, such as option contracts that allow the investor to decide at a later date to enter into a futures contract involving another security or commodity. Interest rate swaps, which will be shown in Chapter 25 to be forward contracts on a short-term borrowing or lending rate, are a good example of the prodigious growth of these markets. Starting with the first swap in 1981, the volume of swap market activity had grown in size to the tens of trillions of dollars by the late 1990s. Although this sort of rapid expansion is not typical of all new derivative products, these instruments represent one of the true legacies of the financial markets in the latter part of the 20th century.

As we will see, derivative securities can be used by investors in the same way and for the same reasons as the underlying assets; an investor believing that a certain common stock will increase in value will likely benefit from either a purchase of the stock directly or through the acquisition of an option to purchase that stock at a predetermined price. The exact returns will not be equal for these two alternatives, but both will benefit from an upward movement in the stock's price. Ultimately, however, the real key to understanding how and why derivatives are used in practice lies in their ability to modify the risk and expected return characteristics of existing investment portfolios. That is, options and futures allow investors to **hedge** (or even increase) the risk of a collection of stocks in ways that go far beyond the diversification results presented in the preceding chapters. In addition, we will see that derivative securities also allow for the convenient duplication of cash flow patterns that already exist in other forms, thereby creating the possibility of **arbitrage** if two otherwise identical series of cash flows do not carry the same current price.

The balance of this chapter describes the fundamental nature and uses of forward, futures, and option contracts on common stock and bonds. (Subsequent chapters deal with more advanced forms of these products and valuation issues.) In the next section, we describe the basic terminology associated with the forward, futures, and option markets while the second section explains the similarities and differences in the payoff structures created by each of these instruments. Section three is devoted to developing the formal relationship between forwards and options, the result of which will be a series of conditions collectively known as **put-call parity.** In the final section, we briefly introduce two of the more popular ways in which derivatives have been used in managing stock and bond portfolios, with a particular emphasis on how derivatives can adjust risk to better suit the needs of the investor.

OVERVIEW OF DERIVATIVE MARKETS

As with any financial product, derivative transactions have a specific terminology that must be understood in order to use these instruments effectively. Unlike many other securities, however, the language used to describe forward, futures, and option contracts is often a confusing blend of jargon drawn from the equity, debt, and insurance markets with some unique expressions thrown in for good measure. Thus, we begin by summarizing the most important aspects of these products and the markets in which they trade.

The Language and Structure of Forward and Futures Markets

To most investors, the **forward contract** is the most basic derivative product available. Generally, a forward contract gives its holder both the *right and full obligation* to conduct a transaction involving another security or commodity—the underlying asset—at a predetermined future date and at a predetermined price. The future date on which the transaction is to be consummated is called the contract's *maturity* (or expiration) *date,* while the predetermined price at which the trade takes place is the forward **contract price.** Notice there must always be two parties (sometimes called **counterparties**) to a forward transaction: the eventual buyer (or **long position**), who pays the contract price and receives the underlying security, and the eventual seller (or **short position**), who delivers the security for the fixed price.

Forward contracts are not securities in the traditional sense; they are more appropriately viewed as *trade agreements* negotiated directly between two parties for a transaction that is scheduled to take place in the future. Suppose, for example, that two investors agree at date 0 (the present) to transfer a bond from one party to the other at the future date T. To specify the full terms of this agreement. the two parties must agree on which bond and how much of it is to be exchanged, the date and location at which this exchange will take place, and the price at which the bond will be bought and sold. Consequently, the terms that must be considered in forming a forward contract are the same as those that would be necessary for a bond transaction that settled immediately (i.e., a *spot market* transaction), but with two exceptions. First, the settlement date agreed to in the contract is purposefully set to be in the future. Second, the contract price—which we will represent as $F_{0,T}$, meaning a forward price set at date 0 for a contract that matures at date T—is usually different from the prevailing spot price (S_0) because of the different time frames involved. Typically, $F_{0,T}$ is chosen so that neither party needs to make an upfront payment to the other.

One important way in which spot and forward market transactions are similar is the conditions under which the long and short positions will profit. To illustrate this idea, suppose that at date T, the long position in a bond forward contract is obligated to pay \$ 1,000 ($= F_{0,T}$) for a bond that is worth S_T = \$1,050 (i.e., the spot price at date T). Since $F_{0,T} < S_T$, this will result in a profitable settlement for the long position in the contract since he will be able to acquire the bond for \$50 less than its current market value. On the other hand, the short position must deliver the bond at date T and will lose \$50 on her forward position; she would have profited if S_T had been below the contract price of \$1,000. Thus, just as if the bond had been purchased at date 0, the long position benefits when bond prices rise, at least relative to the contract price $F_{0,T}$. Conversely, the short position to the forward contract will gain from falling bond prices, just as if she had short sold the bond at date 0. Even though the timing of the trade's settlement has shifted, "buy low, sell high" is still the way to make a profit in the forward market.

Forward contracts are negotiated in the over-the-counter market. This means that forward contracts are agreements between two private parties—one of which is often a derivatives intermediary, such as a commercial or an investment bank—rather than traded through a formal security or commodity exchange. One advantage of this private arrangement is that the terms of the contract are completely flexible; they can be whatever any two mutually consenting counterparties agree to. Another desirable feature to many counterparties is that these arrangements may not require *collateral;* instead, the long and short positions sometimes trust each other to honor their respective commitments at date T. This lack of collateral means that forward contracts involve *credit* (or *default*) *risk,* which is one reason why commercial banks are often market makers in these instruments.

One disadvantage of a forward contract is that it is quite often *illiquid,* meaning that it might be difficult or costly for a counterparty to exit the contract before it matures. Illiquidity is really a by-product of the contract's flexibility because the more specifically tailored an agreement is to the needs of a particular individual, the less marketable it will be to someone else. **Futures contracts** solve this problem by standardizing the terms of the agreement (e.g., expiration date, identity and amount of the underlying asset) to the extent that it can be exchange traded. In contrast to the forward market, both parties in a futures contract trade through a centralized market, called a *futures exchange.* Although the standardization of contracts reduces the ability of the ultimate end-users to select the most desirable terms, it does create contract *homogeneity,* whereby the counterparties can always *unwind* a previous commitment prior to expiration by simply trading their existing position back to the exchange at the prevailing market price.

The *futures price* is analogous to the forward contract price and, at any time during the life of a contract, is set at a level such that a brand-new long or short position would not have to pay a premium to enter the agreement. However, the futures exchange will require both counterparties to post collateral, or *margin,* to protect itself against the possibility of default. (A futures exchange is not a credit-granting institution.) These margin accounts are held by the exchange's *clearinghouse* and are *marked-to-market* (i.e., adjusted for contract price movements) on a daily basis to ensure that both end-users always maintain sufficient collateral to guarantee their eventual participation. A list of some of the more popular futures contracts, along with the markets where they trade, is shown in Table 11. 1. Although generally quite diverse, all of these underlying assets have two things in common: *volatile price movements* and *strong interest* from both buyers and sellers.

Interpreting Futures Price Quotations: An Example

To illustrate how futures prices are typically quoted in financial markets, consider Table 11.2, which lists spot and futures prices for contracts on the Standard and Poor's 500 index as of February 5, 1999. Recall from Chapter 5 that the S&P 500 is a value-weighted index of the relative value of a broad collection of industrial, financial, utility, and transportation

TABLE 11.1 **POPULAR FUTURES CONTRACTS AND EXCHANGES**

Underlying Asset	Exchange
A. Physical Commodities	
Corn, soybeans, soybean meal, soybean oil, wheat	Chicago Board of Trade
Cattle—feeder, cattle—live, hogs, pork bellies Lumber Heating oil	Chicago Mercantile Exchange
Cocoa, coffee, sugar—world, sugar—domestic	Cocoa, Sugar, and Coffee Exchange
Copper, gold, silver	New York Commodity Exchange
Crude oil, heating oil, gasoline, natural gas Platinum	New York Mercantile Exchange
B. Financial Securities	
Yen, Deutschemark, Canadian dollar, Swiss franc, British pound, Mexican peso, Australian dollar, Treasury bills, Eurodollar (LIBOR), S&P 500 Index, Nikkei 225 Index, Russell 2000 Index	International Monetary Market (Chicago Mercantile Exchange)
Treasury bonds, Treasury notes, Municipal bond index, federal funds Dow Jones Industrials Average	Chicago Board of Trade
Eurodollar, British gilt, German bunds Euromarks, Eurofrancs, Eurolira FT-SE 100 Index	London International Financial Futures Exchange

companies representative of the entire United States stock market. At the close of trading on this particular day, the index level stood at 1239.40, which can be considered as the spot price of one "share" of the S&P index (i.e., S_0).[1] Table 11.2 also gives futures contract prices for eight different expiration dates falling in the months of March, June, September, and December for the years 1999 and 2000.

Focusing on a specific example, consider the futures contract that expires in March 1999. The closing (or last) contract price is listed as 1243.50 (i.e., $F_{0,T}$). This means that an investor taking a long position in this contract would be committing in February to buy a certain number of shares in the S&P 500 index—250 shares in the case of this contract—at a price of 1243.50 per share on the expiration date in March. Conversely, the short position in this contract would be committing to sell 250 S&P shares under the same conditions. It should once again be noted that, except for the margin posted with the futures exchange (i.e., the Chicago Mercantile Exchange for this contract), no money changes hands between the long and short positions at the origination of the contract in February.

Table 11.3 summarizes the net profit for this contract from the long position's point of view assuming a hypothetical set of S&P index levels on the March expiration date (i.e., S_T). The most important thing to note about the display is that the payoff to the long position is positive when the S&P index level rises (relative to the contract price of 1243.50), while a loss is incurred when the S&P index falls. For instance, if the expiration date level of the index is 1260.00, the long position will receive a profit of 16.50 per share (= 1260 − 1243.5). In that case, the profit owes to the fact that the contract allows the investor to buy stock that is worth 1260.00 for the predetermined price of only 1243.50. On the other hand, if the March index level turns out to be 1220, the futures contract still obligates the investor to purchase stock for the contract price, thus resulting in a loss of 23.50. This reinforces the fact that, as the buyer, the long position benefits when stock prices rise and suffers when

TABLE 11.2 **STANDARD AND POOR'S 500 INDEX FUTURES CONTRACT PRICE QUOTATIONS**

Session:D Contract Table
S & P 500 FUTURE
Exchange : Pricing Date: 2/ 5/99
Chicago Mercantile Exchange Delayed prices
Grey date = options trading

		Last	1Change	Time	High 2	Low	Tic	--AS REPORTED 2/5 -- 405201 OpenInt	105798 TotVol	2 Previous Close
Symbol										
1)SPX	spot	1239.40	-9.09	16:00	1251.8	1232.3	1799	0	0	1248.49
2)SPH9	Mar99	1243.50s	-15.80	Close	1259.0	1236.0	3782	390732	104852	1259.30
3)SPM9	Jun99	1255.20s	-15.90	Close	1271.0	1248.0	278	9133	757	1271.10
4)SPU9	Sep99	1267.00s	-15.90	Close		1261.4a	69	2519	102	1282.90
5)SPZ9	Dec99	1278.90s	-15.90	Close		1273.3a	70	1511	87	1294.80
6)SPH0	Mar00	1292.90s	-14.40	Close		1285.8a	77	129	0	1307.30
7)SPM0	Jun00	1306.90s	-12.90	Close		1298.3a	73	495	0	1319.80
8)SPU0	Sep00	1319.50s	-12.80	Close		1310.8a	69	0	0	1332.30
9)SPZ0	Dec00	1331.50s	-13.30	Close		1323.3a	69	682	0	1344.80

Source: Bloomberg L.P.

[1] In reality, actually purchasing the portfolio of 500 stocks comprising the S&P index would cost considerably more than $1,239.40. However, as the eventual profit or loss from a stock index futures contract is simply determined by the difference between the futures contract price and the spot price prevailing at contract expiration, this interpretation is nevertheless valid. The trading mechanics of these contracts will be described in greater detail in Chapter 23.

TABLE 11.3

NET PROFIT AT EXPIRATION FROM A LONG POSITION IN AN S&P 500 FUTURES CONTRACT

March S&P 500 Index Level	Futures Payoff at Expiration	Initial Futures Premium	Net Profit
1180.00	(1180 − 1243.5) = −63.50	0.00	−63.50
1200.00	(1200 − 1243.5) = −43.50	0.00	−43.50
1220.00	(1220 − 1243.5) = −23.50	0.00	−23.50
1240.00	(1240 − 1243.5) = −3.50	0.00	−3.50
1243.50	(1243.5 − 1243.5) = 0.00	0.00	0.00
1260.00	(1260 − 1243.5) = 16.50	0.00	16.50
1280.00	(1280 − 1243.5) = 36.50	0.00	36.50
1300.00	(1300 − 1243.5) = 56.50	0.00	56.50
1320.00	(1320 − 1243.5) = 76.50	0.00	76.50

prices fall, just as would be the case for an investor purchasing stock directly in the spot market. Of course, the short position to the contract, as the seller, would have the exact opposite payoffs as those shown in Table 11.3.

The data displayed in Table 11.2 contain other information useful to investors. First, recognize that the spot and all of the futures contract prices listed finished lower than they had been the day before; this can be seen from the negative entries in the "Change" column or by a direct comparison of the "Last" and "Previous Close" prices. This suggests that, although they depend on other factors as well, the futures contract prices are strongly linked to the prevailing level of the underlying spot index. Second, notice that the contract prices increase the farther into the future the expiration date occurs. That is, although all nine closing prices listed (i.e., the spot and the eight futures contracts) were set on the same day and correspond to the same S&P index share, the cost of that share gets increasingly more expensive the farther forward in time the delivery date is set. We will see later that this relationship is common for some securities but not for others. Finally, the display also lists the *open interest* and *trading volume* for each contract. Open interest is the number of outstanding contracts, while trading volume is the number of those contracts that changed hands that day. Thus, it appears in this case that the nearest-term contract (i.e., March 1999) is the most abundant and that about 26 percent (= 105,798 ÷ 405,201) of the total number of S&P contracts in existence were traded on February 5, 1999.

THE LANGUAGE AND STRUCTURE OF OPTION MARKETS

An **option contract** gives its holder the right—but not the obligation—to conduct a transaction involving an underlying security or commodity at a predetermined future date and at a predetermined price. Unlike the forward contract, the option gives the long position the right to decide whether or not the trade will eventually take place. On the other hand, the seller (or *writer*) of the option must perform on his side of the agreement if the buyer chooses to exercise the option. Thus, the obligation in the option market is inherently one-sided; buyers can do as they please, but sellers are obligated to the buyers under the terms of the agreement. As a consequence, two different types of options are needed to cover all potential transactions: a **call option**—the right to buy the underlying security—and a **put option**—the right to sell that same asset.

There are two prices that are important in evaluating an option position. The **exercise,** or striking, **price** is the price the call buyer will pay to—or the put buyer will receive from—the option seller if the option is exercised. The exercise price (represented here as X) is to an option what the contract price (i.e., $F_{0,T}$) is to a forward agreement. The second price of interest is the price that the option buyer must pay to the seller at date 0 to acquire the contract itself. To avoid confusion, this second price is typically referred to as the

option premium. A basic difference between options and forwards is that an option requires this up-front premium payment from buyer to seller while the forward ordinarily does not. This is because the forward contract allowed both the long and short positions to "win" at date T (depending on where S_T settled, relative to $F_{0,T}$), but the option agreement will only be exercised in the buyer's favor; hence the seller must be compensated at date 0, or she would never agree to the deal. Notice also that although a premium payment will be required for both puts and calls, it is quite likely that these two prices will differ. In the analysis that follows, we will define the date 0 premium to acquire an option expiring at date T as $C_{0,T}$ for a call and $P_{0,T}$ for a put. For example, in lieu of a long position in a bond forward contract, the investor in the previous example could have paid \$20 (= $C_{0,T}$) at date 0 for a call option that would have given him he right to buy the bond for \$1,000 (= X) at date T, but not required him to do so if $S_T < \$1,000$.

Options can be designed to provide a choice of when the contract can be exercised. **European** options can only be exercised at maturity (date T), while **American** contracts can be executed any time up to expiration. For a European-style call option, the buyer will only exercise when the expiration date market value of the underlying asset that could be purchased is greater than the exercise price. On the other hand, a European-style put option will only be rationally exercised when the date T price of the asset that could be sold is lower than X. (The decision to exercise an American-style contract is more complex and will be considered in a later chapter.)

Given these parameters, the date 0 premium for an option can be divided into two components: **intrinsic value** and **time premium**. Intrinsic value represents the value that the buyer could extract from the option if she exercised it immediately. For a call, this is the greater of either zero or the difference between the price of the underlying asset and the exercise price (i.e., max $[0, S_0 - X]$). For a put, intrinsic value would be max $[0, X - S_0]$ as X would now represent the proceeds generated from the asset's sale. An option with positive intrinsic value is said to be **in the money**, while one with zero intrinsic value is **out of the money**. For the special case where $S_0 = X$, the option is **at the money**. The time premium component is then simply the difference between the whole option premium and the intrinsic component: ($C_{0,T}$ − max $[0, S_0 - X]$) for a call and ($P_{0,T}$ − max $[0, X - S_0]$) for a put. The buyer is willing to pay this amount in excess of the option's immediate exercise value because of her ability to complete the transaction at a price of X that will remain in force until date T. Thus, the time premium is connected to the likelihood that the underlying asset's price will move in the anticipated direction by the contract's maturity.

Although a more complete discussion of valuing option premiums will be deferred until Chapter 24, several basic relationships can be seen now. First, because the buyer of a call option is never obligated to exercise, the contract should always at least be worth its intrinsic value. (The situation for put option prices or when the underlying asset pays a dividend can be more complicated and will be discussed later.) In any event, neither a call nor a put option can be worth less than zero. Second, for call options having the same maturity and based on the same underlying asset, the lower the exercise price, the higher will be the contract's intrinsic value and, hence, the greater its overall premium. Conversely, put options with higher exercise prices are more valuable than those with lower striking prices for the same reason. Third, increasing the amount of time until any option expires will increase the contract's time premium because it allows the price of the underlying security more opportunity to move in the direction anticipated by the investor (i.e., up for a call option, down for a put option). Finally, because they provide investors with more choices about exercising the agreement, American-style options are at least as valuable as otherwise comparable European-style contracts.

Like forwards and futures, options trade both in over-the-counter markets and on exchanges. When exchange-traded, just the seller of the contract is required to post a margin

TABLE 11.4 **POPULAR OPTION CONTRACTS AND EXCHANGES**

Underlying Asset	Exchange
A. Financial Securities	
Individual Equities S&P 100 Index	Chicago Board Options Exchange
Yen, Deutschemark, Canadian dollar, Swiss franc, British pound, Australian dollar, Mexican Peso S&P 500 Index	International Monetary Market (Chicago Mercantile Exchange)
B. Futures Options	
Cattle—feeder, cattle—live, hogs, pork bellies	Chicago Mercantile Exchange
Yen, Deutschemark, Canadian dollar, Swiss franc, British pound Eurodollar (LIBOR), 2 year Eurodollar S&P 500 Index	International Monetary Market (Chicago Mercantile Exchange)
Corn, soybeans, soybean meal, soybean oil, wheat Treasury bonds, Treasury notes Dow Jones Industrials Average	Chicago Board of Trade
British gilt, German bunds EuroLIBOR FT-SE 100 Index	London International Financial Futures Exchange
Crude oil, heating oil, gasoline, natural gas	New York Mercantile Exchange
Copper, gold, silver	New York Commodity Exchange

account because he is the only one obligated to perform on the contract at a later date. Also, options can be based on a wide variety of underlying securities, including futures contracts or other options. Table 11.4 lists the underlying assets and exchanges where a number of the most popular option contracts trade.

Interpreting Option Price Quotations: An Example

Table 11.5 shows data for a variety of call and put options on the S&P 500 index as of February 5, 1999. All the contracts listed expire in March 1999, making them comparable to the S&P 500 futures contract considered above. However, unlike the futures contracts, for which there was a single contract price for a given expiration month, Table 11.5 indicates that there are several March 1999 options having different exercise prices. In fact, the display lists bid and ask premium quotes for both puts and calls having striking prices ranging from 1210 to 1270.[2] Consistent with our earlier observation, notice that calls become more valuable (e.g., higher ask premiums) as the exercise price declines, with the opposite holding true for put options.

Consider the fortunes of two different investors, one of whom purchases a March S&P call struck at 1240 (i.e., X) and the other who buys a March 1240 put. At the origination of the transaction in February, these investors will pay their sellers the ask prices of \$48.50 (i.e., $C_{0,T}$) and \$44.50 (i.e., $P_{0,T}$, respectively. In return, the investor holding the call option has the right, but not the obligation, to buy one S&P share for 1240 at the expiration date in March. Since the current (i.e., spot) price of the index is 1239.40, this call option is out of the money and so the entire \$48.50 purchase price consists of time premium. Similarly, the investor holding the put option has the right, but not the obligation, to sell one S&P share for 1240 at the expiration date in March. The put is in the money, however, as this

[2]Recall that an investor buys a security from a dealer—in this case the options exchange—at the ask price and sells securities to the dealer at the bid price. The difference in these prices, which is the *bid-ask spread,* represents part of the compensation to the exchange for making a market in these contracts.

TABLE 11.5 STANDARD AND POOR'S 500 INDEX OPTION CONTRACT PRICE QUOTATIONS

OPTION BID ASK & GRAPH MONITOR

	Time	Current	Change	Open	High	Low	Prev Close
SPX	16:00	1239.40	-9.09	1248.49	1251.84	1232.33	1248.49

S&P 500 INDEX
Exchange :CBO
USD
Months Currently Trading
FEB99 MAR99 APR99 JUN99
SEP99 DEC99 JUN0 DEC0

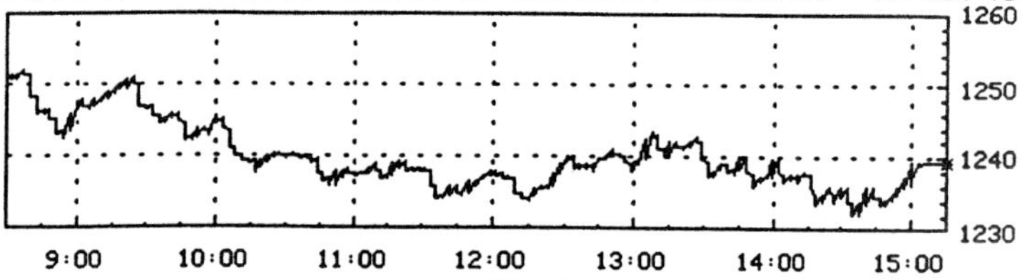
1260
1250
1240
1230
9:00
10:00
11:00
12:00
13:00
14:00
15:00

CALLS

SPX	MAR 99 Bid	Ask	Last	Volume
1) 1210	65 3/8	67 3/8	64y	24
2) 1225	54 7/8	56 7/8	58y	528
3) 1230	52 3/8	54 3/8	56y	76
4) 1240	46 1/2	48 1/2	47y	1304
5) 1245	43 3/8	45 3/8	44y	1774
6) 1250	41	42	40 1/4 y	1311
7) 1255	38	40	46y	270
8) 1260	35 5/8	37 5/8	35 1/2 y	74
9) 1265	32 3/4	34 3/4	34 1/2 y	10
10) 1270	29 7/8	31 7/8	37y	

PUTS

SPX	MAR 99 Bid	Ask	Last	Volume
11) 1210	31 1/2	33 1/2	35 1/2 y	11
12) 1225	36	38	40y	276
13) 1230	38 1/2	40 1/2	43y	56
14) 1240	42 1/2	44 1/2	45y	1799
15) 1245	44 3/8	46 3/8	45y	1420
16) 1250	46 3/8	48 3/8	48 3/8 y	1829
17) 1255	48 7/8	50 7/8	52y	269
18) 1260	51 1/2	53 1/2	54 1/2 y	55
19) 1265	53 5/8	55 5/8	51 1/2 y	
20) 1270	55 3/4	57 3/4	60 1/4 y	281

Source: Bloomberg L.P.

exercise price is higher than the current index level. Thus, the total put premium of \$44.50 can be divided into an intrinsic value component of \$0.60 (= 1240 − 1239.40) and a time premium of \$43.90 (= 44.50 − 0.60).

The expiration date net payoffs to these long option positions are listed in Table 11.6 for a variety of possible S&P index levels. Looking first at the call option payoffs in Panel A, notice that the investor will only exercise the contract to buy a share of the S&P index when the March S&P level is above 1240; at index levels at or below 1240, the investor will let the option expire worthless and simply lose his initial investment. Recognize, though, that while the call is in the money at index levels above 1240, the investor will not realize a net profit until the March index level rises above 1288.50, an amount equal to the exercise price plus the call premium (i.e., $X + C_{0,T}$). For the put option payoffs shown in Panel B, the holder will exercise the contract at March index levels below the exercise price, using the contract to sell for 1240 an S&P share that is worth less than that. However, the display also documents that the put investor will not realize a positive net profit until the index level falls below 1195.50 (i.e., $X - P_{0,T}$). For March S&P values above 1240, the put option expires out of the money.

INVESTING WITH DERIVATIVE SECURITIES

Although the preceding section highlighted many of the differences between forward and option agreements, the two types of derivatives are quite similar in terms of the benefits they produce for investors. The ultimate difference between forwards and options lies in the way the investor must pay to acquire those benefits. This concept, along with an examination of the basic payoff structures that exist in these markets, is described below.

TABLE 11.6 **NET PROFIT AT EXPIRATION FROM LONG POSITIONS IN S&P 500 CALL AND PUT OPTION CONTRACTS**

A. LONG CALL WITH EXERCISE PRICE OF 1240

March S&P 500 Index Level	Call Payoff at Expiration	Initial Call Premium	Net Profit
1180.00	0.00	−48.50	−48.50
1200.00	0.00	−48.50	−48.50
1220.00	0.00	−48.50	−48.50
1240.00	(1240 – 1240) = 0.00	−48.50	−48.50
1260.00	(1260 – 1240) = 20.00	−48.50	−28.50
1280.00	(1280 – 1240) = 40.00	−48.50	−8.50
1288.50	(1288.5 – 1240) = 48.50	−48.50	0.00
1300.00	(1300 – 1240) = 60.00	−48.50	11.50
1320.00	(1320 – 1240) = 80.00	−48.50	31.50

B. LONG PUT WITH EXERCISE PRICE OF 1240

March S&P 500 Index Level	Put Payoff at Expiration	Initial Put Premium	Net Profit
1180.00	(1240 – 1180) = 60.00	−44.50	15.50
1195.50	(1240 – 1195.5) = 44.50	−44.50	0.00
1200.00	(1240 – 1200) = 40.00	−44.50	−4.50
1220.00	(1240 – 1220) = 20.00	−44.50	−24.50
1240.00	(1240 –1240) = 0.00	−44.50	−44.50
1260.00	0.00	−44.50	−44.50
1280.00	0.00	−44.50	−44.50
1300.00	0.00	−44.50	−44.50
1320.00	0.00	−44.50	−44.50

The Basic Nature of Derivative Investing

Consider an investor—call him Investor 1—who has decided to purchase a share of stock in SAS Corporation six months from now, a time frame that coincides with an anticipated receipt of funds. We will assume that both SAS stock forward contracts and call options are available with the market prices of $F_{0,T}$ and $C_{0,T}$ (where $T = 0.50$ year) and that the exercise price of the call option, X, is equal to $F_{0,T}$. Thus, if the investor wants to secure the price now at which the stock purchase will eventually take place, he has two alternatives: a long position in the forward or the purchase of the call option. Figure 11. 1 compares the date 0 and date T cash flow exchanges for both possibilities.

The clear difference between these strategies at the time of origination is that the forward position requires no payment or receipt by either party to the transaction whereas the investor (i.e., the call buyer) must pay a cash premium to the seller of the option. As noted earlier, this front-end option payment releases the investor from the obligation to purchase SAS stock at date T if the terms of the contract turn out to be unfavorable (i.e., $S_T < X$). This is shown in the lower panel of Figure 11.1. When the expiration date price of SAS stock exceeds the exercise price, the investor will exercise the call and purchase the share of stock. Notice however, that this leads to exactly the same exchange as did the long forward contract. It is only when the stock price falls below X (and $F_{0,T}$) on date T that there is a difference between the two positions; under this condition, the right provided by the option *not* to purchase SAS stock is valuable since the investor will be required to execute his forward contract at a loss. In this sense, the call option can be viewed as the "good half"

FIGURE 11.1 **EXCHANGES FOR LONG FORWARD AND LONG CALL TRANSACTIONS**

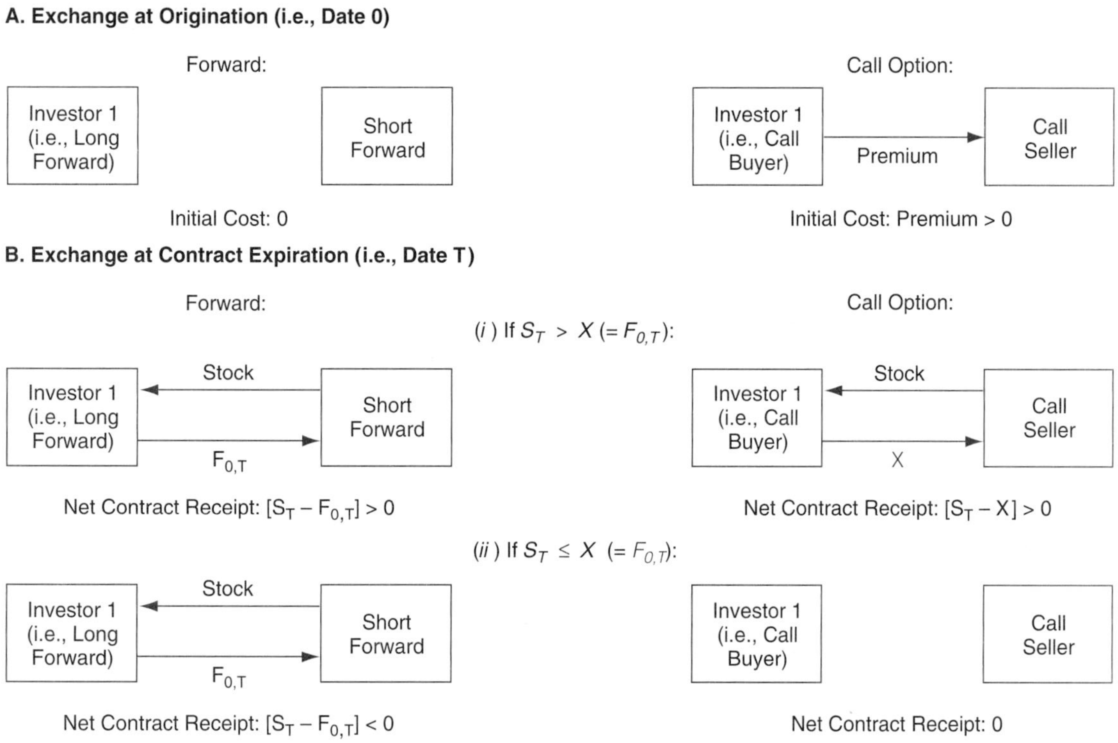
A. Exchange at Origination (i.e., Date 0)
Forward:
Investor 1 (i.e., Long Forward)
Short Forward
Initial Cost: 0
Call Option:
Investor 1 (i.e., Call Buyer)
Premium
Call Seller
Initial Cost: Premium > 0
B. Exchange at Contract Expiration (i.e., Date T)
Forward:
Call Option:
(i) If $S_T > X (= F_{0,T})$:
Stock
$F_{0,T}$
Net Contract Receipt: $[S_T - F_{0,T}] > 0$
X
Net Contract Receipt: $[S_T - X] > 0$
(ii) If $S_T \leq X (= F_{0,T})$:
Net Contract Receipt: $[S_T - F_{0,T}] < 0$
Net Contract Receipt: 0

of the long forward position because it allows for the future acquisition of SAS stock at a fixed price but doesn't require the transaction to take place.

This is the critical distinction between forward and option contracts. Both the long forward and the long call positions have been structured to provide the investor with exactly the same amount of "insurance" against the price of SAS stock rising over the next six months. That is, both contracts provide a payoff of $[S_T - X] = [S_T - F_{0,T}]$ whenever S_T exceeds X, which reduces the effective purchase price for the stock back down to X. The difference in contract design can then be viewed in terms of how the investor is required to pay for that price insurance. With a forward contract, no money is paid up front, but the investor will have to make a payment at the expiration date even if the stock price falls below $F_{0,T}$. Conversely, the call option will never require a future settlement payment, but the investor will have to pay the premium at origination. Thus, for the same date T benefit, the investor's decision between these two "insurance policies" comes down to choosing the certainty of a present premium payment (i.e., long call) versus the possibility of a future payment (i.e., long forward) that could potentially be much larger.

To see this distinction more clearly, suppose that Investor 1 plans to buy SAS stock in six months when some of the bonds in his portfolio mature. He is concerned that share values could rise substantially between now and the time he receives his investment funds and so to hedge that risk he considers two "insurance" strategies to lock in the eventual purchase price: (1) pay nothing now to take the long position in a six-month SAS stock forward contract with a contract price of $F_{0,T}$ = \$45, or (2) pay a premium of $C_{0,T}$ = \$3.24 for a six-month, European-style call option with an exercise price of X = \$45. Assuming that at the time of his decision the price of SAS stock is S_0 = \$40, the call option is out of the money, meaning that its intrinsic value is zero and the entire \$3.24 is time premium. As mentioned earlier, an obvious difference between these two strategies is that the option entails a front-end expense while the forward position does not. The other difference occurs at the expiration date, depending on whether the SAS stock price is above or below \$45. If, for instance, S_T = \$51, both the long forward position and the call option will be worth \$6 (i.e., 51 − 45) to the investor, reducing his net purchase price for SAS shares to \$45 (= 51 − 6). That is, when the stock settled above \$45 (i.e., the common value for $F_{0,T}$ and X), both the long forward and long call positions provided the same protection against rising prices. On the other hand, if S_T = \$41.75, the forward contract would have required that the investor pay \$4.25 (= 41.75 − 45) to his counterparty, which would have once again raised the net cost of his shares to \$45. With the call option, however, he could have let the contract expire without exercising it and purchased his SAS shares in the market for only \$41.75. Thus, in exchange for the option's front-end expense of \$3.24, the investor retains the possibility of paying less than \$45 for his eventual stock purchase.

The connection between forward contracts and put options can be made in a similar fashion. Suppose a different investor—call her Investor 2—has decided to liquidate a share of SAS stock from her portfolio in six months' time. Rather than risk a falling stock price over that period, she could arrange now to sell the share at that future date for a predetermined fixed price in one of two ways: a short forward position or the purchase of a put option. Figure 11.2 illustrates the exchanges for these alternatives. Once again, for the same insurance against SAS stock price declines, the choice comes down to the certainty of paying the put option premium versus the possibility of making a potentially larger payment with the forward contract by having to sell her stock for X (= $F_{0,T}$) when that value is considerably less than the stock's date T market price. Importantly, notice once again that the put option allows the investor to walk away from her obligation under the short forward position to sell her stock on the expiration date under disadvantageous conditions. Thus, in exchange for a front-end premium payment, the put option enables the investor to acquire the "good half" of the short position in a forward contract.

Basic Payoff Diagrams for Forward Contracts

Figures 11.1 and 11.2 show that the respective expiration date payoffs for long and short positions in a forward contract are $[S_T - F_{0,T}]$ and $[F_{0,T} - S_T]$ and that these values could be either positive or negative depending on the spot price prevailing at date T. These terminal payoffs are plotted against the possible expiration date values of the underlying security price in Figure 11.3. There are two interesting items in this display.

First, the payoffs to both long and short positions in the forward contract are *symmetric*, or two-sided, around the contract price. This, of course, is a direct result of the terms of the contract that fully obligate each party to complete the agreed-upon transaction—even at a financial loss. For instance, in the last example the investor holding a long position in a SAS stock forward contract with a contract price of \$45 lost \$4.25 when the date T price of SAS stock was \$41.75, but gained \$6 when S_T = \$51.

Second. the date T payoffs to the short and long positions are mirror images of each other; in market jargon, forward contracts are *zero-sum games* because the long position gains must be paid by the short position and vice versa. This illustration shows that when the date T spot price is lower than the contract price (i.e., S_1), the short position will receive the net payoff of $[F_{0,T} - S_1]$ from the long position while the settlement is reversed at S_2, where the security price is above $F_{0,T}$. Thus, forward markets reinforce the fundamental financial tenet that long positions benefit from rising prices while short positions benefit from falling prices. Finally, notice that these gains and losses can be quite large. In fact, the short forward position has the potential for unlimited loss while the long forward position has the potential for unlimited gain since there is no theoretical limit on how high the price

FIGURE 11.2 EXCHANGES FOR SHORT FORWARD AND LONG PUT TRANSACTIONS

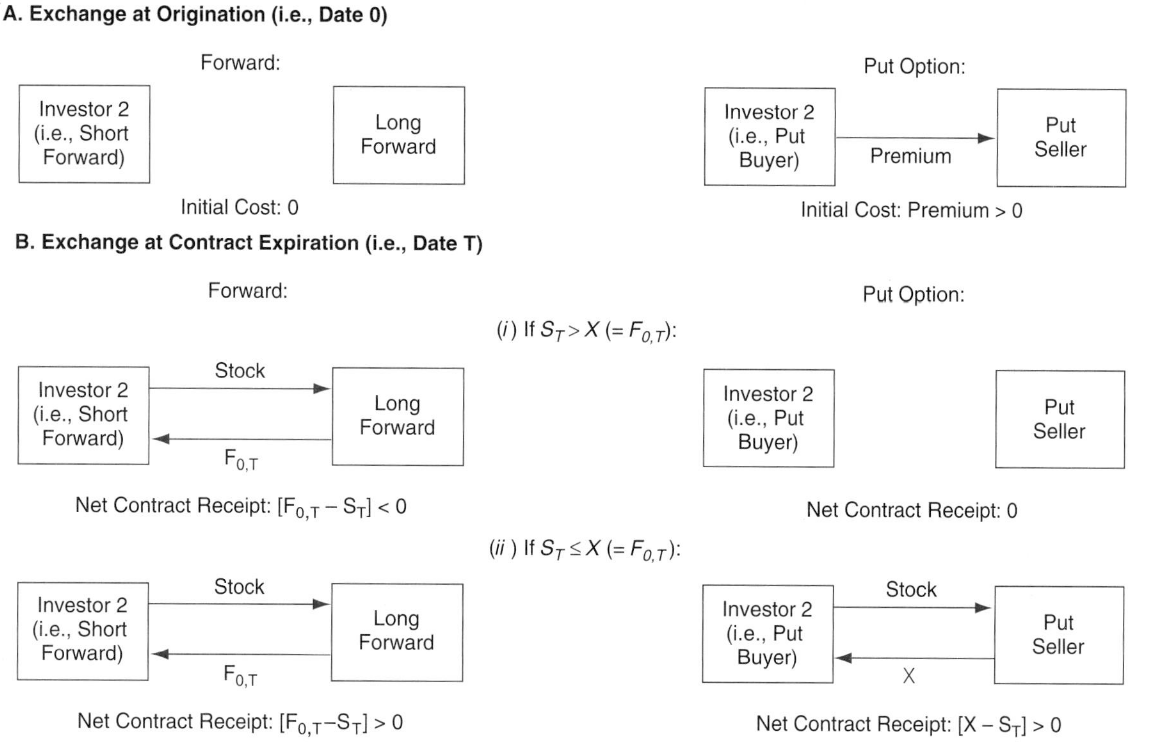
A. Exchange at Origination (i.e., Date 0)
Forward:
Investor 2 (i.e., Short Forward)
Long Forward
Initial Cost: 0
Put Option:
Investor 2 (i.e., Put Buyer)
Premium
Put Seller
Initial Cost: Premium > 0
B. Exchange at Contract Expiration (i.e., Date T)
Forward:
Put Option:
(i) If $S_T > X$ (= $F_{0,T}$):
Investor 2 (i.e., Short Forward)
Stock
$F_{0,T}$
Long Forward
Net Contract Receipt: [$F_{0,T} - S_T$] < 0
Investor 2 (i.e., Put Buyer)
Put Seller
Net Contract Receipt: 0
(ii) If $S_T \leq X$ (= $F_{0,T}$):
Investor 2 (i.e., Short Forward)
Stock
$F_{0,T}$
Long Forward
Net Contract Receipt: [$F_{0,T} - S_T$] > 0
Investor 2 (i.e., Put Buyer)
Stock
X
Put Seller
Net Contract Receipt: [$X - S_T$] > 0

for the underlying security can rise. Conversely, the loss potential for the long position (and the gain potential for the short position) is limited because the price of the underlying security cannot fall below zero.

Basic Payoff Diagrams for Call and Put Options

Figures 11.1 and 11.2 also show that options differ from forward contracts in two fundamental ways. Most directly, the expense of purchasing either a put or a call represents a sunk cost to the investor reducing her upside return relative to the comparable forward position. In exchange for this initial fee, the investor receives expiration date payoffs that are decidedly *asymmetric,* or one-sided. Figure 11.4 shows the net effect these differences have on the terminal payoffs to both long and short positions in call options, while Figure 11.5 provides a similar illustration for put option traders. This analysis assumes that both options are European-style, and so they actually reach expiration without having been exercised prematurely.

For call option positions, notice again that the buyer of the contract still benefits whenever the terminal security price (i.e., S_T) exceeds the contract purchase (i.e., exercise) price of X. However, given that the holder had to pay an initial premium of $C_{0,T}$, the position doesn't generate a positive payoff until S_T is greater than X by the amount of the premium paid. Put another way, although the call option is in the money (and hence will be exercised) when $S_T > X$, it will not produce a capital gain for the buyer until $S_T > (X + C_{0,T})$.[3] (Recall that this result was shown for the S&P 500 index option example in Table 11.6.)

[3]The expiration date payoffs shown in Figures 11.4 and 11.5 are somewhat inaccurate in that they show the net of the date T value of the option and its initial cost, which was paid at date 0. Thus, although this is an accurate way of portraying capital gains and losses from an accounting standpoint, it ignores the value differential in the timing of the two payments.

FIGURE 11.3 **EXPIRATION DATE PAYOFFS TO LONG AND SHORT FORWARD POSITIONS**

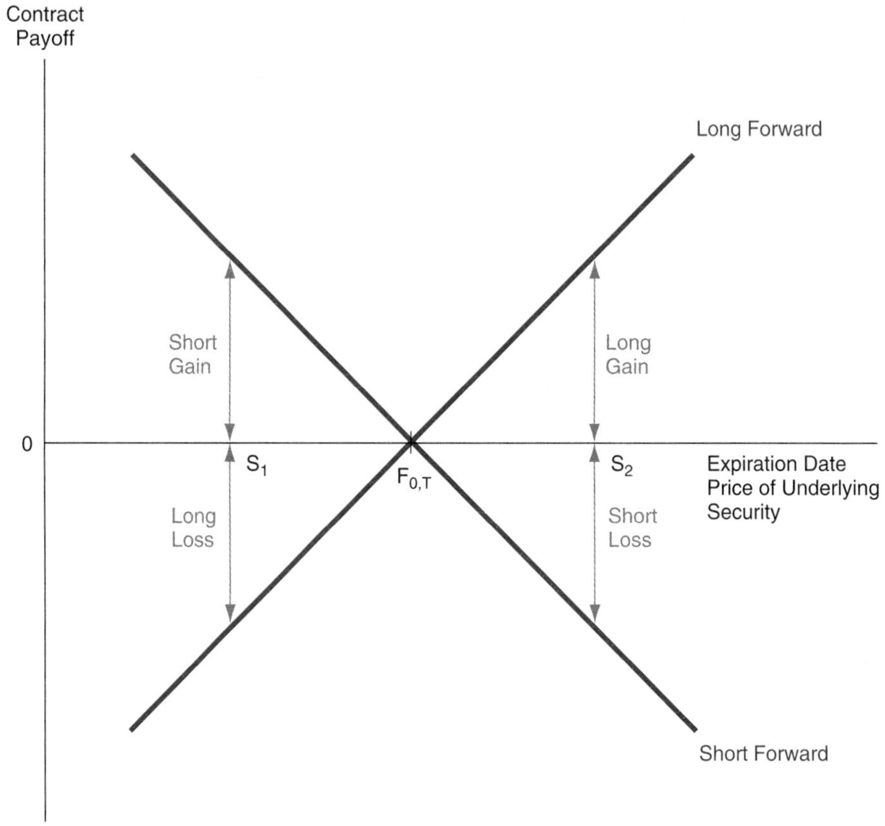
Contract Payoff
Long Forward
Short Gain
Long Gain
0
S1
F0,T
S2
Expiration Date Price of Underlying Security
Long Loss
Short Loss
Short Forward

When $X < S_T < (X + C_{0,T})$, the option is exercised at a loss, but this loss will be less than the full cost of the option, which is what the long position would incur if the call is not exercised. In fact, when $S_T < X$, the option is out of the money and the buyer who makes the rational decision to let the contract expire will lose $C_{0,T}$.

Notice, then, that the buyer of the call option has unlimited gain potential as the security price could rise indefinitely with losses limited to the option premium no matter how far prices fall. On the other hand, the short position benefits from a terminal price for the underlying asset beneath X, but only to the extent that he gets to keep the full amount of the option premium. When $S_T > X$, the seller of the call has unlimited liability. Like forward contracts, the call option is a zero-sum game between the long and short positions.

For the put option positions shown in Figure 11.5, the buyer benefits whenever $X > S_T$, and receives a positive payoff when the date T price of the underlying security falls below the contractual selling price, less the cost of the option. In this case, the put buyer's maximum capital gain is limited to $X - P_{0,T}$ as the underlying security itself is limited to a minimum price of zero; the best the put holder can hope for is to force the seller of the contract to buy worthless stock for X at the expiration date. On the other hand, as with the call option, the owner of an out-of-the-money put can only lose his initial investment of $P_{0,T}$, which will occur when $S_T > X$. Not surprisingly, the profit and loss opportunities for the put seller are exactly opposite of those for the put buyer. The contract seller will gain when $S_T > (X - P_{0,T})$, but this gain is limited to the amount of the option premium. A short position in a put also has limited loss potential, but at a maximum of $X - P_{0,T}$, this can still be a large amount.

FIGURE 11.4

EXPIRATION DATE PAYOFFS TO LONG AND SHORT CALL POSITIONS

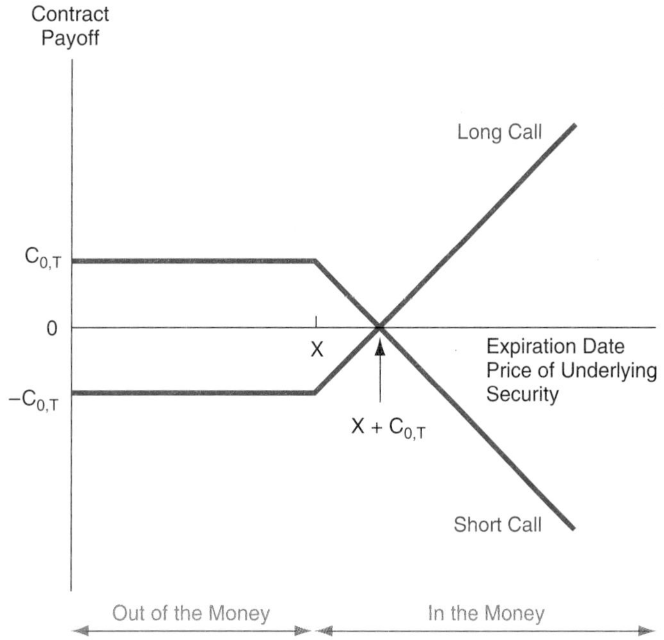
Contract
Payoff
Long Call
$C_{0,T}$
0
X
$-C_{0,T}$
Expiration Date
Price of Underlying
Security
$X + C_{0,T}$
Short Call
Out of the Money
In the Money

FIGURE 11.5

EXPIRATION DATE PAYOFFS TO LONG AND SHORT PUT POSITIONS

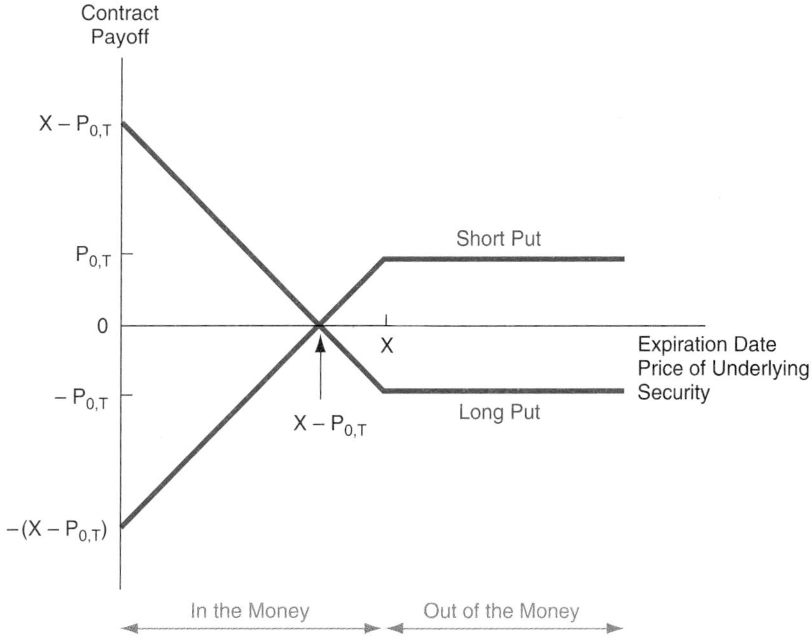
Contract
Payoff
$X - P_{0,T}$
Short Put
$P_{0,T}$
0
X
Expiration Date
Price of Underlying
Security
$- P_{0,T}$
$X - P_{0,T}$
Long Put
$-(X - P_{0,T})$
In the Money
Out of the Money

In summary, when they are held as investments, options are *directional views* on movements in the price of the underlying security. Call buyers and put sellers count on S_T to rise (or remain) above X, while put buyers and call sellers hope for S_T to fall (or remain) below the exercise price at the expiration date. However, the exact payoffs to each of these positions

TABLE 11.7 **HYPOTHETICAL STOCK AND OPTION PRICES**

Instrument	Exercise Price	Market Price	Intrinsic Value	Time Premium
SAS Stock	—	$40.00	—	—
Call: 1	$35.00	8.07	$5.00	$3.07
2	40.00	5.24	0.00	5.24
3	45.00	3.24	0.00	3.24
Put: 1	35.00	1.70	0.00	1.70
2	40.00	3.67	0.00	3.67
3	45.00	6.47	5.00	1.47

vary greatly for any given terminal security value. Importantly, option buyers—whether a put or a call—always have limited liability since they do not have to exercise an out-of-the-money position. This limited liability feature for option holders also means that the gain potential for the seller is limited as the two positions are mirror images of each other. For adverse price movements, though, option sellers face large potential losses, with the liability of the call writer being theoretically infinite just as if she had sold short the underlying security.

Option Payoff Diagrams: An Example

Although there will only be one value of $F_{0,T}$ that allows the present value of a forward contract to be zero (i.e., does not require an initial payment from either the long or the short position), we have seen that option contracts can be designed with several different values for the exercise price. It is interesting, therefore, to consider how the choice of the exercise price affects the instrument's expiration date payoff. Extending the last example, suppose that a share of SAS stock currently sells for $40, and six different SAS options—three calls and three puts—are available to investors. The options all expire on the same date in the future and have exercise prices of either $35, $40, or $45. Current market prices for these contracts, which are assumed to be European-style, are shown in Table 11.7 where they are broken down into their intrinsic value and time premium components.

Given that $S_0 = \$40$ call 1 (with X = 35) and put 3 (with X = 45) are both $5 in the money, which leaves $3.07 and $1.47, respectively, of their value in the form of time premium. Call 3 and put 1 are both currently $5 out of the money and so their market prices are purely time premium; someone buying either of these two contracts anticipates that stock prices will move in the desired direction by at least the option price *plus* $5. Notice that neither of the two at-the-money options, call 2 and put 2, have any intrinsic value, but they still sell in the market for different prices. Specifically, the call with X = $40 is more valuable than the comparable put option. As we will see shortly, this occurs because of **put-call parity**, which is the formal relationship that must exist between put and call options in efficient capital markets. (In fact, for options on a stock that does not pay a dividend, this situation should always hold. However, the value of an at-the-money put can exceed that of an at-the-money call if the underlying security is a stock, a bond, or currency that does pay a cash flow.) Finally, the last column of Table 11.7 shows that the time premium is largest for the at-the-money options because, at this point, the greatest amount of uncertainty exists as to whether the option will be in or out of the money (and hence valuable) at expiration.

It is instructive to compare the expiration date payoff diagrams for options on the same security with varying exercise prices but similar in every other respect. This is done for both call and put options in Figure 11.6. For simplicity, only the payoffs for the long positions in these contracts are shown. The call option payoffs portrayed in the first panel of the figure indicate that although it is the most expensive, the deepest in-the-money contract (call 1) becomes profitable the quickest, requiring only that S_T rise to $43.07 (= 35 + 8.07). Call 3,

FIGURE 11.6 **TERMINAL PAYOFFS TO OPTIONS WITH DIFFERENT EXERCISE PRICES**

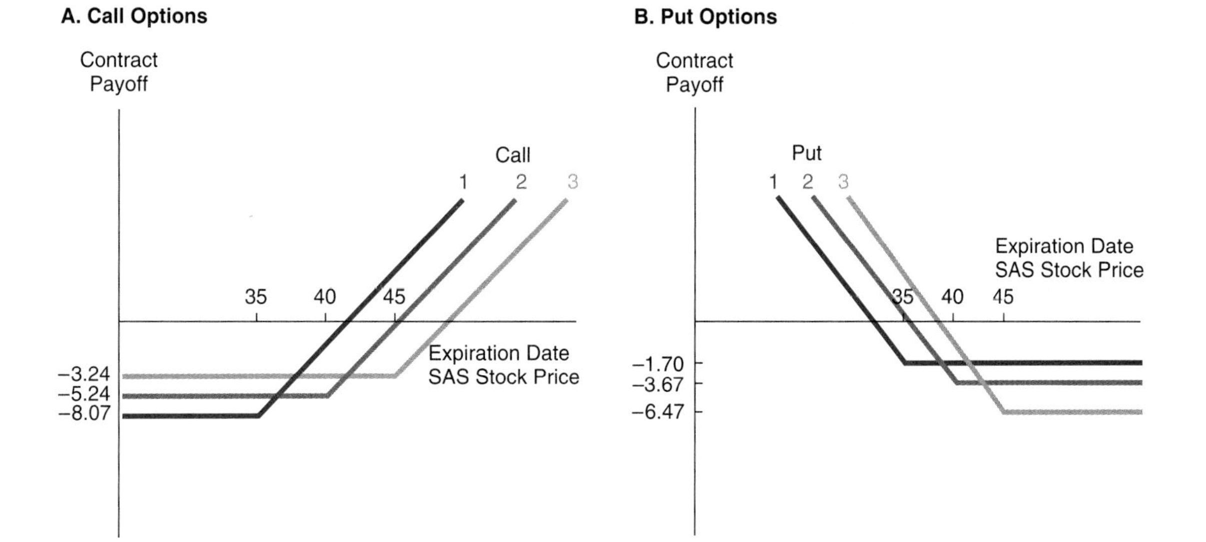
A. Call Options
Contract Payoff
Call
1 2 3
35 40 45
Expiration Date SAS Stock Price
−3.24
−5.24
−8.07
B. Put Options
Contract Payoff
Put
1 2 3
Expiration Date SAS Stock Price
35 40 45
−1.70
−3.67
−6.47

on the other hand, is the least expensive to purchase, but requires the greatest movement in the price of the underlying stock—to $48.24 in this example—before it provides a positive payoff to the investor. The put options illustrated in the second panel tell the same story, with put 1 (the out-of-the-money contract) costing the least but needing the largest price decline to be profitable at expiration. In general, by varying the exercise price on a series of options with otherwise identical contract terms, an investor can create just as many different risk–reward trade-offs for herself. This is one of several examples of how derivatives can be used to modify investment risk and to "customize" a desired payoff structure.

As a final extension of this example, let us compare the returns to an investment in either a put or a call option with an investment (or short sale) in a share of the underlying SAS stock. To focus on the important issues, we will limit the analysis to call 2 and put 2, the two at-the-money contracts. Table 11.8 summarizes the holding period returns for various positions assuming three different expiration date stock prices: $30, $40, and $50. Two different comparisons are made: (1) long stock versus long call and (2) short stock versus long put. In calculating the returns to the stock positions, we have measured the change in value of the SAS share as a percentage of the initial price of $40. For the option positions, the terminal payoffs of max $[0, S_T - 40]$ for the call and max $[0, 40 - S_T]$ for the put are listed relative to the contract's purchase price.

The most important thing to realize about these calculations is that both put and call options magnify the possible positive and negative returns of investing in the underlying security. In the case of the long call option position, for an initial cost of $5.24 the investor can retain the right to access the price appreciation of a share of SAS stock without spending $40 to own the share outright. This degree of financial *leverage* manifests itself in a 100 percent loss when the stock price falls by a quarter of that amount and a 91 percent gain when SAS shares increase in value from $40 to $50. Notably, if the stock price remains at $40, the owner of the share would not have lost anything while the call holder would have lost his entire investment, which was pure time premium at origination for the at-the-money contract. This suggests that in addition to anticipating the *direction* of the subsequent underlying stock price movement, the option investor also is taking a view on the *timing* of that movement. If the price of SAS stock had stayed at $40 through date T and

TABLE 11.11 REPLICATING A PUT OPTION

A. NET PORTFOLIO INVESTMENT AT INITIATION (DATE 0)

Portfolio	
Long 1 T-bill	$X(1 + RFR)^{-T}$
Short 1 WYZ stock	$-S_0$
Long 1 call option	$C_{0,T}$
Net investment:	$X(1 + RFR)^{-T} - S_0 + C_{0,T}$

B. PORTFOLIO VALUE AT OPTION EXPIRATION (DATE T)

Portfolio	(1) If $S_T \le X$:	(2) If $S_T > X$:
Long 1 T-bill	X	X
Short 1 WYZ stock	$-S_T$	$-S_T$
Long 1 call option	0	$(S_T - X)$
Net position:	$X - S_T$	0

assets represented in the first equation is always *redundant* because it can be defined in terms of the others. Three additional ways of manipulating this result are:

$$P_{0,T} = \frac{X}{(1 + RFR)^T} - S_0 + C_{0,T}$$

$$C_{0,T} = S_0 + P_{0,T} - \frac{X}{(1 + RFR)^T}$$

$$S_0 = \frac{X}{(1 + RFR)^T} - P_{0,T} + C_{0,T}$$

The first two of these equations indicate, respectively. that (1) the payoffs to a long position in a put option can be replicated by a portfolio consisting of a long position in a T-bill, a short stock position, and the purchase of a call option; and (2) a synthetic call option can be mimicked by a portfolio that is long in the stock and the put option and short in the T-bill. The final equation indicates that the payoff to the stock itself can be expressed by its derivative securities and the T-bill.

These results are useful in two ways. First, if there are not markets in either put or call options, the relationships summarized by these equations outline how investors can create the desired, but unavailable, pattern of cash flows through the appropriate "packaging" of the other three interrelated assets. Suppose, for example, that a put option on WYZ stock did not exist, but a call option does. Table 11.11 shows the date 0 and date T cash flows associated with the portfolio replicating the terminal payoff. Combining both panels of the display, an initial investment of $[X(1 + RFR)^{-T} - S_0 + C_{0,T}]$ leads to a final cash flow that is no less than zero and as large as $X - S_T$ whenever $X > S_T$. Expressed in a more traditional manner, the expiration date payoff to the synthetic put is max $[0, X - S_T]$.

Another way the alternative expressions for the put-call parity model (summarized by the three above equations) are used in practice is the identification of arbitrage opportunities. Even when a particular derivative instrument trades actively in the market, if its cash flows and risks can be duplicated, this leads to the possibility that the price of the actual instrument and the net cost of the replicating portfolio will differ. Using the numbers from the previous example, the date T distribution of max $[0, 50 - S_T]$ could be acquired through the synthetic strategy at a cost of \$2.25 (= 48.51 − 53 + 6.74) or through the purchase of the actual put for \$2.51.

FIGURE 11.6 **TERMINAL PAYOFFS TO OPTIONS WITH DIFFERENT EXERCISE PRICES**

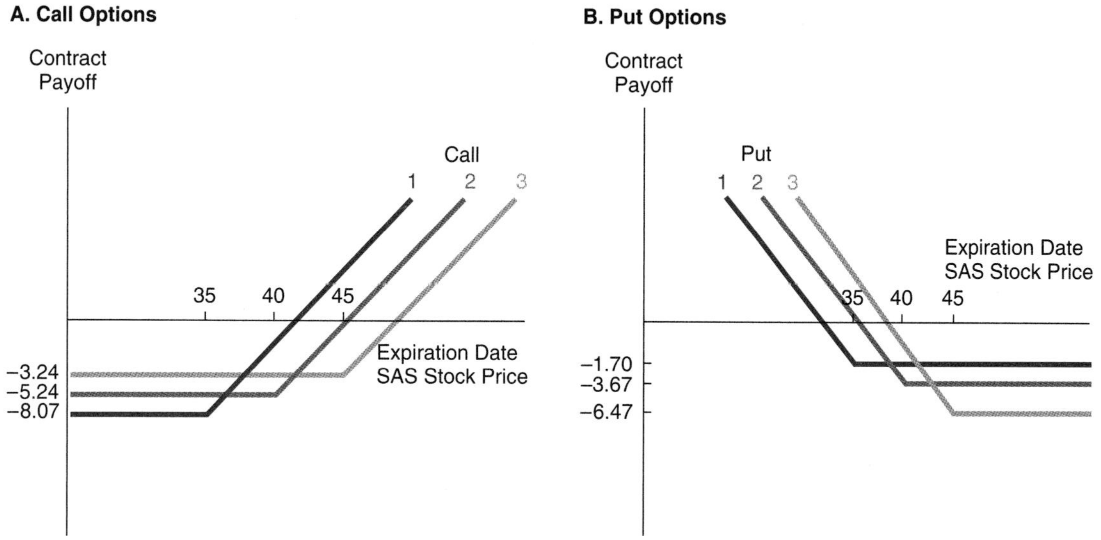
A. Call Options
Contract Payoff
Call
1
2
3
35
40
45
Expiration Date SAS Stock Price
-3.24
-5.24
-8.07
B. Put Options
Contract Payoff
Put
1
2
3
Expiration Date SAS Stock Price
35
40
45
-1.70
-3.67
-6.47

on the other hand, is the least expensive to purchase, but requires the greatest movement in the price of the underlying stock—to $48.24 in this example—before it provides a positive payoff to the investor. The put options illustrated in the second panel tell the same story, with put 1 (the out-of-the-money contract) costing the least but needing the largest price decline to be profitable at expiration. In general, by varying the exercise price on a series of options with otherwise identical contract terms, an investor can create just as many different risk–reward trade-offs for herself. This is one of several examples of how derivatives can be used to modify investment risk and to "customize" a desired payoff structure.

As a final extension of this example, let us compare the returns to an investment in either a put or a call option with an investment (or short sale) in a share of the underlying SAS stock. To focus on the important issues, we will limit the analysis to call 2 and put 2, the two at-the-money contracts. Table 11.8 summarizes the holding period returns for various positions assuming three different expiration date stock prices: $30, $40, and $50. Two different comparisons are made: (1) long stock versus long call and (2) short stock versus long put. In calculating the returns to the stock positions, we have measured the change in value of the SAS share as a percentage of the initial price of $40. For the option positions, the terminal payoffs of max $[0, S_T - 40]$ for the call and max $[0, 40 - S_T]$ for the put are listed relative to the contract's purchase price.

The most important thing to realize about these calculations is that both put and call options magnify the possible positive and negative returns of investing in the underlying security. In the case of the long call option position, for an initial cost of $5.24 the investor can retain the right to access the price appreciation of a share of SAS stock without spending $40 to own the share outright. This degree of financial *leverage* manifests itself in a 100 percent loss when the stock price falls by a quarter of that amount and a 91 percent gain when SAS shares increase in value from $40 to $50. Notably, if the stock price remains at $40, the owner of the share would not have lost anything while the call holder would have lost his entire investment, which was pure time premium at origination for the at-the-money contract. This suggests that in addition to anticipating the *direction* of the subsequent underlying stock price movement, the option investor also is taking a view on the *timing* of that movement. If the price of SAS stock had stayed at $40 through date T and

TABLE 11.8 **STOCK AND OPTION INVESTMENT RETURNS**

A. LONG STOCK VERSUS LONG CALL

Terminal Stock Price	Long Stock	Long Call
30	$\frac{30}{40} - 1 = -25.0\%$	$\frac{0}{5.24} - 1 = -100.0\%$
40	$\frac{40}{40} - 1 = 0.0\%$	$\frac{0}{5.24} - 1 = -100.0\%$
50	$\frac{50}{40} - 1 = 25.0\%$	$\frac{10}{5.24} - 1 = 90.8\%$

B. SHORT STOCK VERSUS LONG PUT

Terminal Stock Price	Short Stock	Long Put
30	$1 - \frac{30}{40} = 25.0\%$	$\frac{10}{3.67} - 1 = 172.5\%$
40	$1 - \frac{40}{40} = 0.0\%$	$\frac{0}{3.67} - 1 = -100.0\%$
50	$1 - \frac{50}{40} = -25.0\%$	$\frac{0}{3.67} - 1 = -100.0\%$

then rose to $50 on the following day, the stockholder would have experienced a 25 percent gain while the buyer of the call option would have seen the instrument expire worthless.

THE RELATIONSHIP BETWEEN FORWARD AND OPTION CONTRACTS

The preceding discussion highlighted the fact that positions in forward and option contracts can lead to similar investment payoffs if the price of the underlying security moves in the anticipated direction. As we saw, the difference in the payoffs to these derivatives came when the security's price changed adversely. This similarity in payoff structures suggests that there is a tractable set of relationships between these instruments. In fact, we will see that the values of five different securities can be linked: a risk-free bond, an underlying asset, a forward contract for the future purchase or sale of that asset, a call option, and a put option. These relationships, known as **put-call parity**, specify how the put and call premiums should be set relative to one another. Further, these conditions can be expressed in terms of the connection between these two option types and either the spot or forward market price for the underlying asset. They depend on the assumption that financial markets are free from arbitrage opportunities, meaning that securities (or portfolios of securities) offering identical payoffs with identical risks must sell for the same current price. As such, put-call parity represents an important first step in understanding how derivatives are valued in an efficient capital market.[4]

[4]The development of the relationships linking put and call option prices is commonly attributed to Hans R. Stoll, "The Relationship between Put and Call Option Prices," *Journal of Finance* 24, no. 5 (December 1969): 801–824. It has been embellished in many interesting ways, including Robert C. Merton, "The Relationship between Put and Call Option Prices: Comment," *Journal of Finance* 28, no. 1 (March 1973): 183–184; Joel S. Sternberg, "A Reexamination of Put-Call Parity on Index Futures," *Journal of Futures Markets* 14, no. 1 (spring 1994): 79–105; and Avraham Kamara and Thomas W. Miller, Jr., "Daily and Intradaily Tests for European Put-Call Parity," *Journal of Financial and Quantitative Analysis* 30, no. 4 (December 1995): 519–539.

TABLE 11.9 **PUT-CALL-SPOT PARITY**

A. NET PORTFOLIO INVESTMENT AT INITIATION (DATE 0)

Portfolio	
Long 1 WYZ Stock	S_0
Long 1 Put Option	$P_{0,T}$
Short 1 Call Option	$-C_{0,T}$
Net Investment:	$S_0 + P_{0,T} - C_{0,T}$

B. PORTFOLIO VALUE AT OPTION EXPIRATION (DATE T)

Portfolio	(1) If $S_T \le X$:	(2) If $S_T > X$:
Long 1 WYZ Stock	S_T	S_T
Long 1 Put Option	$(X - S_T)$	0
Short 1 Call Option	0	$-(S_T - X)$
Net Position:	X	X

PUT-CALL-SPOT PARITY

Suppose that at date 0 (the present) an investor forms the following portfolio involving three securities related to Company WYZ:

- Long in a share of WYZ common stock at a purchase price of S_0;
- Long in a put option to deliver one share of WYZ stock at an exercise price of X on the expiration date T. This put could be purchased for the price of $P_{0,T}$;
- Short in a call option allowing the purchase of one share of WYZ stock at an exercise price of X on the expiration date T. This call could be sold for the price $C_{0,T}$.

In this example, both of the WYZ options are European-style and have the same expiration date and exercise price. However, the specific values of the expiration date and exercise price do not affect the conclusion of the analysis that follows. Further, we will assume initially that WYZ stock does not pay a dividend during the life of the options.

With these definitions, notice in the top panel of Table 11.9 that the date 0 investment necessary to acquire this portfolio is $(S_0 + P_{0,T} - C_{0,T})$, which is the cost of the long positions in the stock and the put option less the proceeds generated by the sale of the call option.[5] A more interesting thing to consider is the value that this portfolio will have at the expiration date of the two options. Given that the stock's value at date T (i.e., S_T) is unknown when the investment is made at period 0, two general outcomes are possible: (1) $S_T \le X$ and (2) $S_T > X$. The bottom panel of Table 11.9 shows the value of each position as well as the net value of the whole portfolio at date T.

Notice that whenever the date T value of WYZ stock is less than the exercise price common to the put and call options, it is best for the investor to exercise the long position in the put and sell the WYZ share for X instead of its lower market value. Under the same condition, it will not be rational for the holder of the call to pay X for a share that is worth less. Therefore, the call will expire out of the money. On the other hand, when S_T exceeds X, the holder of the call will exercise the option to purchase WYZ stock for X from the investor

[5] In the "arithmetic" of engineering financial portfolios, a plus ("+") sign can be interpreted as a long position and a minus ("−") sign represents a short position. Thus the portfolio investment represented by $(S_0 + P_{0,T} - C_{0,T})$ can also be expressed as (long stock) + (long put) + (short call). Donald J. Smith, "The Arithmetic of Financial Engineering," *Journal of Applied Corporate Finance* 1, no. 4 (winter 1989): 49–58, explains this approach in more detail.

while the put would be out of the money. In either case, the net expiration date value of the position is X because the combination of options contained in the portfolio guarantees that the investor will sell the share of WYZ stock at date T for the fixed price X. That is, at stock prices lower than X, the investor will choose to sell the share at a profit, although he will be forced to sell at a loss when WYZ trades on the market at a price higher than X. The investor has, in effect, a guaranteed contract to sell the share of stock when the long put and short call positions are held jointly.

The consequence of this result is that when the investor commits ($S_0 + P_{0,T} - C_{0,T}$) to acquire the position at date 0, he knows that it will be worth X at date T. Thus, this particular portfolio has a comparable payoff structure to a U.S. Treasury bill, another risk-free, zero-coupon security that can be designed to have a face value of X and a maturity date T. In an arbitrage-free capital market, this means that the date 0 value of the portfolio must be equal to that of the T-bill, which is just the face value X discounted to the present using the risk-free rate. This "no arbitrage" condition can be formalized as follows:

$$S_0 + P_{0,T} - C_{0,T} = \frac{X}{(1 + RFR)^T}$$

where:

RFR = the annualized risk-free rate
T = the time to maturity (expressed in years)

Defining $[X\,(1 + RFR)^{-T}]$ as the present value of a T-bill, this equation can be expressed in "financial arithmetic" terms as:

$$\text{(long stock)} + \text{(long put)} + \text{(short call)} = \text{(long T-bill)}$$

In either form, this condition—known as the *put-call-spot* parity condition—indicates the efficient market linkages between prices for stock, T-bills, put options, and call options.

Put-Call Parity: An Example

As an example of how put-call parity might be used, suppose that WYZ stock is currently valued at \$53 and that call and put options on WYZ stock with an exercise price of \$50 sell for \$6.74 and \$2.51, respectively. Assuming that both options can only be exercised in exactly six months, the above equation suggests that we can "make" a synthetic T-bill by purchasing the stock, purchasing the put, and selling the call for a net price of \$48.77 (= 53.00 + 2.51 − 6.74). At the options' expiration date, this portfolio would have a terminal value of \$50. Thus, the risk-free rate implied by this investment can be established by solving the following equation for RFR:

$$48.77 = 50\,(1 + RFR)^{-0.5}$$

or

$$RFR = [(50 \div 48.77)^2 - 1] = 5.11\%$$

The practical application of this finding is that if the rate of return on an actual six-month T-bill with a face value of \$50 is not 5.11 percent, then an investor could exploit the difference. Suppose, for instance, that the actual T-bill rate is 6.25 percent and that there are no restrictions against using the proceeds from the short sale of any security. In such a situation, an investor wanting a risk-free investment would clearly choose the actual T-bill to lock in the higher return, while someone seeking a loan might attempt to secure a 5.11 percent borrowing rate by short-selling the synthetic T-bill. With an arithmetic rearrangement

TABLE 11.10 **A PUT-CALL PARITY ARBITRAGE EXAMPLE**

A. NET INITIAL INVESTMENT (DATE 0)

Transaction	
1. Long actual T-bill at 6.25%	−48.51
2. Short synthetic T-bill at 5.11%:	
Short WYZ stock	53.00
Short put option	2.51
Long call option	−6.74
Net receipt:	0.26

B. POSITION VALUE AT OPTION EXPIRATION (DATE T)

Transaction	(1) If $S_T \le 50$:	(2) If $S_T > 50$:
1. Long actual T-bill at 6.25%	50	50
2. Short synthetic T-bill at 5.11%:		
Short WYZ stock	$-S_T$	$-S_T$
Short put option	$-(50 - S_T)$	0
Long call option	0	$(S_T - 50)$
Net position:	0	0

of the parity condition in the previous equation, such an artificial short position can be obtained as (short stock) + (short put) + (long call) = (short T-bill).

With no transaction costs, a financial arbitrage could be constructed by combining a long position in the actual T-bill with a short sale of the synthetic portfolio. Given that the current value of the actual T-bill is \$48.51 = \$50 $(1.0625)^{-0.5}$], this set of transactions would generate the cash flows shown in Table 11.10 and produce a \$0.26 profit per each T-bill pair created. However, as the arbitrage trade did not require the investor to bear any risk (i.e., both the date 0 and date T values of the net position were known at inception) nor commit any capital, there is nothing in this example to prevent the investor from expanding the size of the trade to increasingly larger levels. Unfortunately, as additional transactions take place, the price discrepancy will disappear. In this case, the purchase of the actual T-bill and sale of the synthetic (short stock, short put, and long call) will continue until rates are equalized. This is how the markets remain efficient through arbitrage trading.

Another way of seeing this trade is

$$C_{0,T} - P_{0,T} = S_0 - X(1 + RFR)^{-T}$$

That is, the "no arbitrage" difference between the call and put prices should equal the difference between the stock price and the present value of the joint exercise price. The market-determined risk-free rate of 6.25 percent implies that the correct difference between the two derivatives should be \$4.49 (= 53 − 48.51), which is \$0.26 greater than the \$4.23 (= 6.74 − 2.51) actual difference. This discrepancy suggests that if you assume the actual T-bill is priced correctly, the call price is undervalued relative to the put option. Not surprisingly, then, notice that the arbitrage transaction requires the purchase of the call option while shorting the put option.

CREATING SYNTHETIC SECURITIES USING PUT-CALL PARITY

The preceding example demonstrates that a risk-free portfolio could be created by combining three risky securities: stock, a put option, and a call option. The parity condition developed above can be expressed in other useful ways as well. In particular, one of the four

TABLE 11.11 **REPLICATING A PUT OPTION**

A. NET PORTFOLIO INVESTMENT AT INITIATION (DATE 0)

Portfolio	
Long 1 T-bill	$X(1 + RFR)^{-T}$
Short 1 WYZ stock	$-S_0$
Long 1 call option	$C_{0,T}$
Net investment:	$X(1 + RFR)^{-T} - S_0 + C_{0,T}$

B. PORTFOLIO VALUE AT OPTION EXPIRATION (DATE T)

Portfolio	(1) If $S_T \leq X$:	(2) If $S_T > X$:
Long 1 T-bill	X	X
Short 1 WYZ stock	$-S_T$	$-S_T$
Long 1 call option	0	$(S_T - X)$
Net position:	$X - S_T$	0

assets represented in the first equation is always *redundant* because it can be defined in terms of the others. Three additional ways of manipulating this result are:

$$P_{0,T} = \frac{X}{(1 + RFR)^T} - S_0 + C_{0,.T}$$

$$C_{0,T} = S_0 + P_{0,T} - \frac{X}{(1 + RFR)^T}$$

$$S_0 = \frac{X}{(1 + RFR)^T} - P_{0,T} + C_{0,T}$$

The first two of these equations indicate, respectively. that (1) the payoffs to a long position in a put option can be replicated by a portfolio consisting of a long position in a T-bill, a short stock position, and the purchase of a call option; and (2) a synthetic call option can be mimicked by a portfolio that is long in the stock and the put option and short in the T-bill. The final equation indicates that the payoff to the stock itself can be expressed by its derivative securities and the T-bill.

These results are useful in two ways. First, if there are not markets in either put or call options, the relationships summarized by these equations outline how investors can create the desired, but unavailable, pattern of cash flows through the appropriate "packaging" of the other three interrelated assets. Suppose, for example, that a put option on WYZ stock did not exist, but a call option does. Table 11.11 shows the date 0 and date T cash flows associated with the portfolio replicating the terminal payoff. Combining both panels of the display, an initial investment of $[X(1 + RFR)^{-T} - S_0 + C_{0,T}]$ leads to a final cash flow that is no less than zero and as large as $X - S_T$ whenever $X > S_T$. Expressed in a more traditional manner, the expiration date payoff to the synthetic put is max $[0, X - S_T]$.

Another way the alternative expressions for the put-call parity model (summarized by the three above equations) are used in practice is the identification of arbitrage opportunities. Even when a particular derivative instrument trades actively in the market, if its cash flows and risks can be duplicated, this leads to the possibility that the price of the actual instrument and the net cost of the replicating portfolio will differ. Using the numbers from the previous example, the date T distribution of max $[0, 50 - S_T]$ could be acquired through the synthetic strategy at a cost of \$2.25 (= 48.51 − 53 + 6.74) or through the purchase of the actual put for \$2.51.

This is the same \$0.26 price differential we saw earlier when designing an arbitrage transaction involving the actual and synthetic T-bill. The put option arbitrage would be to short the actual put while buying the replicating portfolio (i.e., long T-bill, short stock, and long call), which is the same set of transactions we used in the T-bill arbitrage. This result underscores the important point that the put-call parity model only allows us to make *relative*—rather than absolute—statements about security values. Although we can change our perspective in identifying the misvalued instrument (e.g., T-bill versus put option), the real source of the market inefficiency came from examining the *difference* between the put and call prices in relation to the stock and T-bill prices. Consequently, all four securities need to be included in the arbitrage trade.

ADJUSTING PUT-CALL-SPOT PARITY FOR DIVIDENDS

A second extension of the put-call-spot parity model involves the payment of dividends to the shareholders of WYZ stock. Suppose for simplicity that in the basic portfolio listed in Table 11.9, WYZ stock pays a dividend of D_T immediately prior to the expiration of the options at date T. Assume further that the amount of this distribution is known when the investment is initiated, a condition that is almost certainly met for values of $T \leq 0.25$ year because U.S.-based companies typically pay quarterly dividends. The result of these modifications is that the terminal value of the long stock position will be $(S_T + D_T)$. On the other hand, the terminal payoffs to the put and call options remain max $[0, X - S_T]$ and max $[0, S_T - X]$, respectively, as the holders of the two derivative contracts will not participate directly in the payment of dividend to the stockholder.[6] Thus, the net date T value of the portfolio acquired originally for $(S_0 + P_{0,T} - C_{0,T})$ is $(X + D_T)$.

With the critical assumption that the dividend payment is known at date 0, the portfolio long in WYZ stock, long in the put, and short in the call once again can be viewed as equivalent to a T-bill. now having a face value of $(X + D_T)$. This allows the first equation to be adapted as follows:

$$S_0 + P_{0,T} - C_{0,T} = \frac{X + D_T}{(1 + RFR)^T} = \frac{X}{(1 + RFR)^T} + \frac{D_T}{(1 + RFR)^T}$$

which can be interpreted as:

(long stock) + (long put) + (short call) = (long T-bill) + (long present value of dividends).

Alternatively, it is often more useful to rearrange this equation as follows:

$$\left\{S_0 - \frac{D_T}{(1 + RFR)^T}\right\} + P_{0,T} - C_{0,T} = \frac{X}{(1 + RFR)^T}$$

In this form, the equation can be compared directly with the no-dividend put-call-spot parity result and shows that the current stock price must be *adjusted downward* by the present value of the dividend. With an initial stock price of \$53 and an annualized risk-free rate on a six-month T-bill of 6.25 percent, a \$1 dividend paid just before the expiration of a call and a put option with an exercise price of \$50 would result in a theoretical price differential of:

[6]The fact that the expiration date payoff to a call option on both a dividend- and nondividend-paying stock can be expressed as max $[0, S_T - X]$ does not mean that the two will generate the same dollar amount of cash flow. This is because the stock's value will be reduced by the payment of the dividend in the former case but not in the latter. Thus with the lower terminal payout, the call on the dividend-paying stock will be less valuable than an otherwise comparable contract on a nondividend-paying equity. We will explore this topic more fully in Chapter 24.

TABLE 11.12 **PUT-CALL-FORWARD PARITY**

A. Net Portfolio Investment at Initiation (Date 0)

Portfolio	
Long 1 forward contract	0
Long 1 put option	$P_{0,T}$
Short 1 call option	$-C_{0,T}$
Net investment:	$P_{0,T} - C_{0,T}$

Portfolio Value at Option Expiration (Date T)

Portfolio	(1) If $S_T \le X$:	(2) If $S_T > X$.
Long 1 forward contract	$(S_T - F_{0,T}$	$(S_T - F_{0,T})$
Long 1 put option	$(X - S_T)$	0
Short 1 call option	0	$-(S_T - X)$
Net position:	$(X - F_{0,T})$	$(X - F_{0,T})$

$$C_{0,0.5} - P_{0,0.5} = \left\{53 - \frac{1}{(1 + 0.0625)^{0.5}}\right\} - \frac{50}{(1 + 0.0625)^{0.5}} = \$3.52$$

This value differs from the parity differential for options on the nondividend-paying stock which was shown earlier to be \$4.49. Thus the payment of the dividend has reduced the price of the call relative to the put by \$0.97, which is the discounted amount of the \$1 cash distribution.

Put-Call-Forward Parity

At this point in our analysis of the structural relationships between derivative instruments and their underlying securities, we have not explicitly included forward or futures contracts. Suppose that instead of buying the stock in the spot market at date 0, we took a long position in a forward contract allowing us to purchase one share of WYZ stock at date T. The price of this acquisition, $F_{0,T}$, would be established by the forward agreement at date 0. As before, we will assume that this transaction is supplemented by the purchase of a put option and the sale of a call option, each having the same exercise price and expiration date. Table 11.12 summarizes both the initial and terminal cash flows to this position.

The bottom panel of the table reveals that this is once again a risk-free portfolio. There are, however, two important differences in its cash flow patterns. First, the net initial investment of $(P_{0,T} - C_{0,T})$ is substantially smaller than when the stock was purchased in the spot market. Second, the riskless terminal payoff of $(X - F_{0,T})$ also is smaller than before as the stock now must be purchased at date T rather than at date 0. This intuition leads directly to the *put-call-forward* parity condition:

$$P_{0,T} - C_{0,T} = \frac{X - F_{0,T}}{(1 + RFR)^T} = \frac{X}{(1 + RFR)^T} - \frac{F_{0,T}}{(1 + RFR)^T}$$

which says that for markets to be free from arbitrage, the difference between put and call prices must equal the discounted difference between the common exercise price and the contract price of the forward agreement. Just as $F_{0,T}$ did not appear in the spot market version of the parity condition, the current stock price does not appear in this equation.

This result implies that the only time that put and call prices should be equal to one another in an efficient market is when $X = F_{0,T}$. That is, although the put-call parity result holds for any common exercise price, there is only one value of X for which there would be no net cost to the option combination and that is the prevailing forward price. Recall, for example, that when WYZ stock did not pay a dividend, the theoretical difference between $C_{0,0.5}$ and $P_{0,0.5}$ was \$4.49 (= 53 − 48.51). This meant that an investor long in the call and short in the put with a joint \$50 exercise price would have what amounted to a forward contract to buy WYZ stock in six months at a price of \$50.[7] However, she would have to pay \$4.49 for this arrangement, suggesting that \$50 is a below-market forward price. How much below the prevailing forward contract price is \$50? By the future value of \$4.49, invested at the prevailing risk-free rate of 6.25 percent. Thus the no-arbitrage forward price under these circumstances should be \$54.63 [= 50 + 4.49 $(1 + 0.0625)^{0.5}$].

Another way to see this result comes from combining the put call-forward parity condition with the put-call-spot condition. Specifically, inserting the expression for $(P_{0,T} - C_{0,T})$ from the put-call-forward parity condition into the put-call-spot condition leaves:

$$S_0 + \left\{\frac{X}{(1 + RFR)^T} - \frac{F_{0,T}}{(1 + RFR)^T}\right\} = \frac{X}{(1 + RFR)^T}$$

which simplifies to:

$$S_0 = \frac{F_{0,T}}{(1 + RFR)^T}$$

This equation indicates that, in the absence of dividend payments, the spot price for the share of stock should simply be the discounted value of purchasing the same security in the forward market. Equivalently, this equation can be rewritten so that $F_{0,T} = S_0 (1 + RFR)^T$. In the above example, this means that the market-clearing (i.e., no net initial cost) contract price for a WYZ stock forward agreement should be $F_{0,0.5} = (53)(1 + 0.0625)^{0.5} = \$54.63$. Finally, in the case where dividends are paid, the equation for the put-call-forward parity condition can be inserted into the dividend-adjusted spot parity condition to produce the more general relationship between spot and forward prices:

$$\left\{S_0 - \frac{D_T}{(1 + RFR)^T}\right\} = \frac{F_{0,T}}{(1 + RFR)^T}$$

Thus, if a \$1 dollar dividend were paid on WYZ stock just prior to the maturity of the contract in six months, the forward price would be adjusted down to $F_{0,0.5} = (53)(1 + 0.0625)^{0.5} - 1 = \$53.63$ to account for the cash distribution that would benefit the actual shareholders but not the derivative holder.

AN INTRODUCTION TO THE USE OF DERIVATIVES IN PORTFOLIO MANAGEMENT

Beyond the unique risk–reward profiles they offer as stand-alone investments, derivatives also are used widely in investment management to restructure the fundamental nature of an existing portfolio of assets. Typically, the intent of this sort of restructuring is to modify the

[7] This interpretation follows by noting that the long call position will be exercised when $S_T \leq 50$ and the short put will be exercised against the investor when $S_T \leq 50$. Therefore, the investor's net option position produces an identical result to holding a long position in a forward contract with a contract price of \$50. Generalizing this result, any time we have a call and a put option on the same underlying stock with a common exercise price and expiration date, the following is true: (long call at X) + (short put at X) = (long forward at X). Similarly, shorting the call and buying the put produces a synthetic short forward position.

portfolio's risk. Although this topic will be covered more fully in Chapter 22, in this section, we review two prominent derivative applications in the management of equity positions: shorting forward contracts and purchasing **protective puts.**

Restructuring Asset Portfolios with Forward Contracts

Suppose the manager of a small corporate pension fund currently has all of her investable funds committed to a well-diversified portfolio of equity securities designed to reflect the movements of a broad indicator of the stock market's performance, such as Standard & Poor's 500 index. Implicit in this investment approach is the manager's belief that she cannot "add value" by trying to select superior individual securities. She does, however, feel that it is possible to take advantage of perceived trends at a macroeconomic level by switching her funds between her current equity holding and any of several other portfolios mimicking different asset classes (e.g.. fixed-income, cash equivalents), depending on her forecast of future events. Switching a portfolio's composition in an attempt to time general market movements instead of company-specific trends is known as *tactical asset allocation.*

The stock market has increased steadily over the past several months, and the pension fund has a present market value of $100 million. At this time, though, the manager has become concerned about the possibility that inflationary pressures will dampen corporate earnings and drive stock prices down. Although it is unclear now whether this concern will be realized, she feels confident that the uncertainty will be resolved in the coming quarter. Accordingly, she would like to shift her allocation from 100 percent equity to 100 percent T-bills for the next three months. There are two ways she can make this change. The most direct method would be to sell her stock portfolio and buy $100 million (less the transaction costs) of 90-day T-bills. When the T-bills mature in three months, she could then repurchase her original equity holdings.

The second approach would be to maintain her current stock holdings, but convert them into a synthetic risk-free position with a three-month forward contract specifying $100 million of the stock index as the underlying asset. As we will see later, the primary benefit of this approach is that it is often more cost-effective and quicker to implement. This is a classic example of a hedge position, wherein the price risk of the underlying asset is offset (rather than eliminated) by a supplementary derivative transaction. The following table captures the dynamics of this hedge at a basic level.

Economic Event	Actual Stock Exposure	Desired Forward Exposure
Stock prices fall	Loss	Gain
Stock prices rise	Gain	Loss

To neutralize the risk of falling stock prices, the fund manager will need to adopt a forward position that benefits from that potential movement. Said differently, the manager requires a hedge position with payoffs that are *negatively correlated* with those of the existing exposure. As we saw in Figure 11.3, this requires committing to the short side of the contract. This hedging argument is identical to the point we made in the portfolio formation analysis of Chapter 8 that it is always possible to combine two perfectly negatively correlated assets to create a risk-free position.

FIGURE 11.7 ALTERING THE SYSTEMATIC RISK OF A STOCK PORTFOLIO SYNTHETICALLY

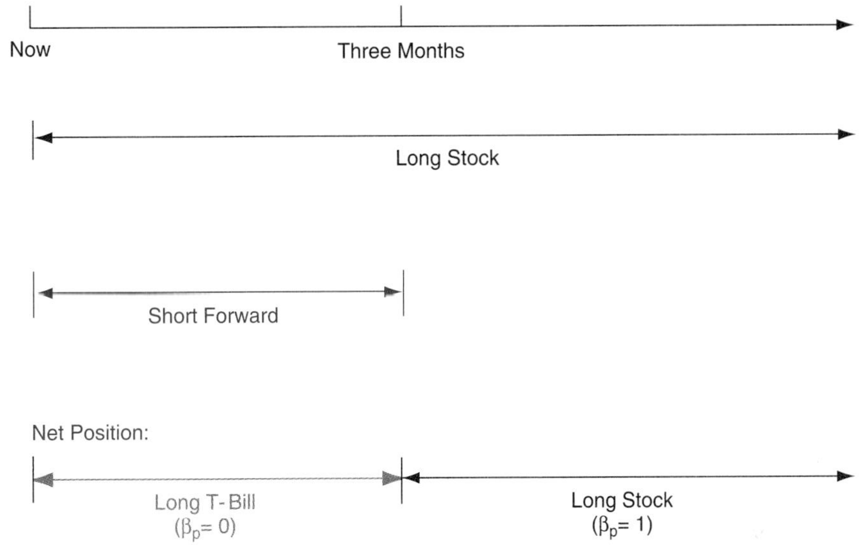
Now
Three Months
Long Stock
Short Forward
Net Position:
Long T-Bill
(β_p= 0)
Long Stock
(β_p= 1)

This synthetic restructuring is best understood through the effect that it has had on the systematic risk—or beta—of the portfolio. By its original construction, we will assume that the original stock holding had a beta of one, matching the volatility of a proxy for the market portfolio. The combination of being long \$100 million of stock and short a forward covering \$100 million of a stock index converts the systematic portion of the portfolio into a synthetic T-bill, which by definition has a beta of zero. Once the contract matures in three months, however, the position will revert to its original risk profile. This is illustrated in Figure 11.7. More generally, the short forward position can be designed to allow for intermediate combinations of stock and T-bills as well. To see this, let w_s be the stock allocation so that $(1 - w_s)$ is the allocation to the risk-free asset created synthetically. The net beta for the converted portfolio is simply a weighted average of the systematic risks of its equity and T-bill portions or:

$$\beta_P = (w_S)\,\beta_S + (1 - w_S)\,\beta_{RFR}$$

Thus, if the manager had wished to change the original allocation from 100 percent stock to a "60–40" mix of stock and T-bills, she would have shorted only \$40 million of the index forward to leave her with an unhedged equity position totaling \$60 million (i.e., w_s = 0.60 and $(1 - w_s) = 0.40$). By the above equation, this in turn would leave her with an adjusted portfolio beta of $[(0.6)(1) + (0.4)(0)] = 0.6$.

Protecting Portfolio Value with Put Options

Although the manager's concern in the previous example was to protect her stock portfolio against possible share price declines over the next three months, by shorting the stock index forward contract, she has effectively committed to "selling" her equity position—even if stock prices rise. That is, by using a derivative with a symmetric payoff structure to hedge her risk, the manager also has surrendered the upside potential of her original holding. Recognizing this, suppose instead that she attempted to design a hedge position correlated to her stock portfolio as shown in the following table.

Economic Event	Actual Stock Exposure	Desired Hedge Exposure
Stock prices fall	Loss	Gain
Stock prices rise	Gain	*No loss*

In seeking an asymmetric hedge, this manager wants a derivative contract that allows her to sell stock when prices fall but keep her shares when prices rise. As we have seen, she must purchase a put option to obtain this exposure.

The purchase of a put option to hedge the downside risk of an underlying security holding is called a *protective put* position and is the most straightforward example of a more general set of derivative-based strategies known as *portfolio insurance.*[8] To see this insurance interpretation, suppose that in lieu of the short forward position, the manager purchased a three-month, at-the-money put option on her $100 million stock portfolio. Under the prevailing market conditions, let us also assume that this put cost the manager an up-front premium of $1.324 million. The value of the protective put position (net of the initial cost of the hedge) is calculated in Table 11.13 for several different expiration date prices for the underlying stock portfolio. In particular, notice that with the exercise price set equal to the current portfolio value of $100 million, the put contract exactly offsets any expiration date share price decline while allowing the position to increase in value as stock prices increase. Thus the put provides the manager with insurance against falling prices with no *deductible.*[9]

An intriguing aspect of the terminal value of the combined stock and put option portfolio shown in the last column of Table 11.13 is that it resembles the payoff diagram of the long call option position illustrated earlier in Figure 11.4. A different way of seeing this is shown in Figure 11.8, which indicates that being long in the stock and long in the put generates the same net payoff as an at-the-money long call option holding "elevated" by $100 million. Given the put-call-spot parity results of the previous section, however. This should come as no surprise. Indeed, the no-arbitrage equation can be rewritten:

$$S_0 + P_{0,T} = C_{0,T} + \frac{X}{(1 + RFR)^T}$$

This expression says that the protective put method of providing portfolio insurance generates an equivalent expiration date payoff as a long position in a call option with the same characteristics as the put and a long position in a T-bill with a face value equal to the options' common exercise price. It is this final term that provides the "elevation" to the call payoff diagram in Figure 11.8. Thus the manager has two ways of providing

[8]The concept and use of portfolio insurance has received a great deal of scrutiny in research literature. See, for example, the studies by Mark Rubinstein, "Alternative Paths to Portfolio Insurance," *Financial Analysts Journal* 41, no. 4 (July–August 1985): 42–52; Mark Kritzman, "What's Wrong with Portfolio Insurance?" *Journal of Portfolio Management* 13, no. 1 (fall 1986): 13–17; and Harry M. Kat, "Portfolio Insurance: A Comparison of Alternative Strategies," *Journal of Financial Engineering* 1, no. 4 (1993): 415–442.

[9]In general, the deductible portion of the portfolio insurance contract can be defined as $[S_0 - X]$. For instance, with an exercise price of only 95, the manager would not receive compensation from the hedge until the portfolio value fell below $95 million; she would effectively be "self-insuring" the first $5 million of losses. Naturally, the larger this deductible amount, the lower the cost of the put option.

TABLE 11.13 **EXPIRATION DATE VALUE OF A PROTECTIVE PUT POSITION**

Potential Portfolio Value	Value of Put Option	Cost of Put Option	Net Protective Put Position
60	(100 − 60) = 40	−1.324	(60 + 40) − 1.324 = 98.676
70	(100 − 70) = 30	−1.324	(70 + 30) − 1.324 = 98.676
80	(100 − 80) = 20	−1.324	(80 + 20) − 1.324 = 98.676
90	(100 − 90) = 10	−1.324	(90 + 10) − 1.324 = 98.676
100	0	−1.324	(100 + 0) − 1.324 = 98.676
110	0	−1.324	(110 + 0) − 1.324 = 108.676
120	0	−1.324	(120 + 0) − 1.324 = 118.676
130	0	−1.324	(130 + 0) − 1.324 = 128.676
140	0	−1.324	(140 + 0) − 1.324 = 138.676

FIGURE 11.8 **TERMINAL PAYOFF TO AN "INSURED" STOCK POSITION**

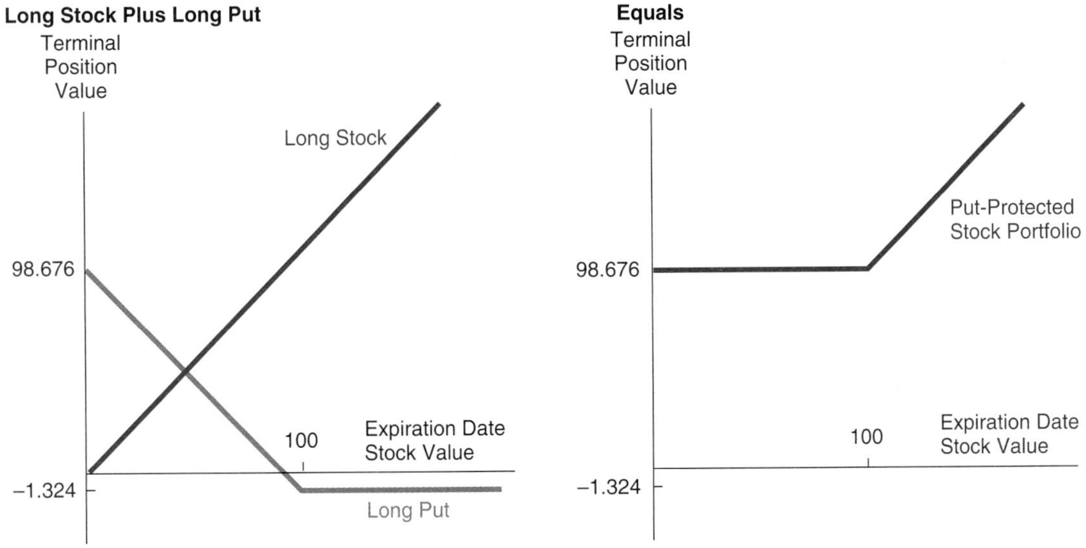
Long Stock Plus Long Put
Terminal Position Value
Long Stock
98.676
100
Expiration Date Stock Value
−1.324
Long Put
Equals
Terminal Position Value
Put-Protected Stock Portfolio
98.676
100
Expiration Date Stock Value
−1.324

price insurance for her current stock holding: (1) continue to hold her shares and purchase a put option, or (2) sell her shares and buy both a T-bill and a call option. Her choice between them will undoubtedly come down to specific logistic considerations, such as relative option prices and transaction costs.[10]

[10]Many authors have studied the effect that adding options to an underlying security position has on the risk of the combined portfolio. In particular, see Robert C. Merton, Myron S. Scholes, and Matthew L. Gladstein, "A Simulation of the Returns and Risk of Alternative Option Portfolio Investment Strategies," *Journal of Business* 51, no. 2 (April 1978): 183–242; and Richard M. Bookstaber and Roger G. Clarke, "Options Can Alter Portfolio Return Distributions," *Journal of Portfolio Management* 7, no. 3 (spring 1981): 63–70. For a good nontechnical discussion of this material, see Maarten L. Nederlof, "The Comparison of Strategies Using Derivatives," in *Derivative Strategies for Managing Portfolio Risk,* ed. K. Brown (Charlottesville, Va.: Association for Investment Management and Research, 1993).

THE INTERNET *Investments Online*

A good way to learn more about the basics of futures and options is to visit some derivative-related Web sites. Interesting futures and options exchange sites include:

www.cboe.com The Web site of the Chicago Board Options Exchange presents an overview of the exchange and options on equities, indexes, and LEAPS. Market data, including quotes, are available. The site offers educational materials for beginners and discussions of investment strategies. By inputting some data, users can compute the theoretical value of an option using the site's options calculator.

www.cbot.com The home page of the Chicago Board of Trade includes an overview of the Board, a dictionary of trading jargon, as well as price quotes and charts. The site offers government agriculture reports (since many commodities are traded on the CBOT) and weather reports (due to the effect of weather on commodity yields).

www.cme.com The Chicago Mercantile Exchange's Web site features similar information as the other exchanges: news, price quotes, product information, and educational resources. The Merc's site offers Web-based lessons on derivative strategies, and even offers an "Introduction to Hand Signals" (**www.cme.com/educational/hand1.htm**) used by floor traders.

www.liffe.com LIFFE stands for the London International Financial Futures and Options Exchange. It trades equity and short-term interest rate contracts. It is Europe's premier derivatives exchange, and it has a goal of being one of the most technologically advanced—so keep an eye on this Web site! Users can register online for free to gain access to the site's pages, which include information on money market, bond, equity, index, and commodity trading. It contains links to many countries' futures and options exchanges.

www.options-iri.com The Web site of the Investment Research Institute serves the investing public. It advertises option trading resources, but it also has several valuable (and free) educational resources. The site reviews option basics and option trading strategies (from the simple to the complex). It offers users a daily options market commentary, a market forecast, and free option quotes. This is a very useful site for those who want to get a flavor for how traders and investors use options.

Summary

- As their popularity in financial markets has increased over the past few decades, derivative securities have become an indispensable part of the investment manager's toolkit. Although forward, futures, and option contracts play important roles as stand-alone investments, the real advantage of derivatives is their ability to modify the risk–return characteristics of a collection of existing securities in a cost-effective manner. This use of forwards and options to restructure a portfolio synthetically has two dimensions. First, we saw that it is possible to combine derivatives with the underlying position in a way that replicates the cash flow patterns of another traded instrument. For instance, a well-diversified stock portfolio could be converted into the equivalent of a T-bill by shorting an appropriate amount of a stock index futures contract. Second, derivatives can also be used with the original portfolio to create a payoff structure that is otherwise unavailable. The use of a protective put to eliminate the downside risk of an equity holding while maintaining its upside profit potential is an example.
- At a fundamental level, forward and option contracts can be viewed as insurance policies that an investor can hold against adverse price movements in his underlying position. As forwards and options can be structured to provide exactly the same degree of "coverage," the basic difference between these contracts lies in how the investor must pay for the desired insurance. Forwards, with symmetrical terminal payoffs, typically do not require any initial payment but do obligate the investor to the possibility of an unfavorable transaction at a future date. Conversely, with options, which provide asymmetrical terminal payoffs, the investor must pay an up-front premium, but then has no further obligation to his counterparty.
- Given these similarities, it is not surprising that there are well-defined relationships that must exist in an efficient capital market between the prices of forward and option contracts. In particular, the put-call parity conditions delineated the linkages between five different securities: the under-

lying asset (e.g., stock), T-bills, forward contracts, call options, and put options. An important consequence of these relationships is that one of these securities is always redundant because its cash flow patterns can be replicated by the remaining instruments. This realization leads to another important use for derivatives: arbitrage investing. Through their ability to help create synthetic replicas of existing securities, derivatives provide investors with the possibility of riskless excess returns when the synthetic and actual instruments sell for different prices.

- Although this chapter provides a broad overview of the dynamics of these important financial contracts, there are several issues related to the use and management of derivative securities that remain to be addressed. Chief among these are ways in which individual positions in forwards, futures, and options are valued and the adjustments that investors need to make when designing derivatives on an underlying asset other than common stock. These topics will be considered in subsequent chapters after we have explored the valuation and investment applications of a more basic set of securities (i.e., stocks and bonds). For now, though, it is important to appreciate these instruments for their ability to assist investors in repackaging the risks and cash flows of their portfolios.

Questions

1. Explain why the difference between put and call prices depends on whether or not the underlying security pays a dividend during the life of the contracts.
2. When comparing futures and forward contracts, it has been said that futures are more liquid but forwards are more flexible. Explain what this statement means and comment on how differences in contract liquidity and design flexibility might influence an investor's preference in choosing one instrument over the other.
3. Compare and contrast the gain and loss potential for investors holding the following positions: long forward, short forward, long call, short call, long put, and short put. Indicate what the terms *symmetric* and *asymmetric* mean in this context.
4. CFA *CFA Examination III (June 1993)*
   The Franklin Medical Research Foundation is to be established with a gift from Mr. John Franklin in memory of his deceased wife. The foundation's grant-making and investment policy issues have been finalized. Receipt of the expected $45 million Franklin cash gift will not occur for 90 days, yet the committee believes current stock and bond prices are unusually attractive and wishes to take advantage of this perceived opportunity.
   a. Briefly describe two strategies which utilize derivative financial instruments and could be implemented to take advantage of the committee's market expectations.
   b. Evaluate whether or not it is appropriate for the foundation to undertake a derivatives-based hedge to bridge the expected 90-day time gap, considering both positive and negative factors.
5. CFA *CFA Examination II (June 1991)*
   Robert Chen, CFA, is reviewing the characteristics of derivative securities and their use in portfolios. Chen is considering the addition of either a short position in stock index futures or a long position in stock index options to an existing well-diversified portfolio of equity securities. Contrast the way in which each of these two alternatives would affect the risk and return of the resulting combined portfolios.
6. CFA *CFA Examination II (May 1997)*
   Current equity call prices for Furniture City are contained in the table below. In reviewing these prices, Jim Smith, CFA, notices discrepancies between several option prices and basic option pricing relationships.

CLOSING PRICES
FURNITURE CITY EQUITY CALL OPTIONS
MAY 31, 1997

		EXPIRATION MONTH			
Stock Close	Strike	June	July	August	September
119½	110	8⅞	12½	15	18
119½	120	1½	3¾	3	4¼
119½	130	1	2¼	2⅞	5

Identify three different apparent pricing discrepancies in the table. Identify which of the basic option-pricing relationships each discrepancy violates.(*Note:* The fact that option contracts do not always trade at the same time as the underlying stock should *not* be identified as a discrepancy.)

7. Explain how call and put options can represent a leveraged way of investing in the stock market and also enable investors to hedge their risk completely. Specifically, under what circumstances will the addition of an option increase the risk of an existing portfolio and under what circumstances will it decrease portfolio risk?
8. It has been said that from an investor's perspective a long position in a call option represents the "good half" of a long position in a forward contract. Explain what is meant by this statement. Also, describe what the "bad half" of the long forward position would have to be for this statement to be true.
9. Discuss the difficulties that having options in a security portfolio create for the measurement of portfolio risk. Specifically, explain why standard deviation is a deficient statistic for capturing the essence of risk in a put-protected portfolio. How could the standard deviation statistic be modified to account for this concern?
10. If the current price of a nondividend-paying stock is $32 and a one-year futures contract on that stock has a contract price of $35, explain how an investor could create an "off-market" long position in a forward contract at an exercise price of $25. Would this synthetic contract require a cash payment from either the long or short position? If so, explain which party would have to make the payment and how that payment should be calculated.

Problems

1. The common stock of Sophia Enterprises serves as the underlying asset for the following derivative securities: (1) forward contracts, (2) European-style call options, and (3) European-style put options.
   a. Assuming that all Sophia derivatives expire at the same date in the future, complete a table similar to that shown below for each of the following contract positions:
      (1) a long position in a forward with a contract price of $50;
      (2) a long position in a call option with an exercise price of $50 and a front-end premium expense of $5.20;
      (3) a short position in a call option with an exercise price of $50 and a front-end premium receipt of $5.20.

Expiration Date Sophia Stock Price	Expiration Date Derivative Payoff	Initial Derivative Premium	Net Profit
25	______	______	______
30	______	______	______
35	______	______	______
40	______	______	______
45	______	______	______
50	______	______	______
55	______	______	______
60	______	______	______
65	______	______	______
70	______	______	______
75	______	______	______

   In calculating net profit, ignore the time differential between the initial derivative expense or receipt and the terminal payoff.

   b. Graph the net profit for each of the three derivative positions, using net profit on the vertical axis and Sophia's expiration date stock price on the horizontal axis. Label the breakeven (i.e., zero profit) point(s) on each graph.
   c. Briefly describe the belief about the expiration date price of Sophia stock that an investor using each of these three positions implicitly holds.
2. Refer once again to the derivative securities using Sophia common stock as an underyling asset discussed in Problem 1.

a. Assuming that all Sophia derivatives expire at the same date in the future, complete a table similar to that shown below for each of the following contract positions:
(1) a short position in a forward with a contract price of $50,
(2) a long position in a put option with an exercise price of $50 and a front-end premium expense of $3.23;
(3) a short position in a put option with an exercise price of $50 and a front-end premium receipt of $3.23.

Expiration Date Sophia Stock Price	Expiration Date Derivative Payoff	Initial Derivative Premium	Net Profit
25	________	________	________
30	________	________	________
35	________	________	________
40	________	________	________
45	________	________	________
50	________	________	________
55	________	________	________
60	________	________	________
65	________	________	________
70	________	________	________
75	________	________	________

In calculating net profit, ignore the time differential between the initial derivative expense or receipt and the terminal payoff.

b. Graph the net profit for each of the three derivative positions, using net profit on the vertical axis and Sophia's expiration date stock price on the horizontal axis. Label the breakeven (i.e., zero profit) point(s) on each graph.

c. Briefly describe the belief about the expiration date price of Sophia stock that an investor using each of these three positions implicitly holds.

3. Suppose that an investor holds a share of Sophia common stock, currently valued at $50. She is concerned that over the next few months the value of her holding might decline and she would like to hedge that risk by supplementing her holding with one of three different derivative positions, all of which expire at the same point in the future:
(1) a short position in a forward with a contract price of $50;
(2) a long position in a put option with an exercise price of $50 and a front-end premium expense of $3.23;
(3) a short position in a call option with an exercise price of $50 and a front-end premium receipt of $5.20.

a. Using a table similar to the one shown below, calculate the expiration date value of the investor's combined (i.e., stock and derivative) position. In calculating net portfolio value, ignore the time differential between the initial derivative expense or receipt and the terminal payoff.

Expiration Date Sophia Stock Value	Expiration Date Derivative Payoff	Initial Derivative Premium	Combined Terminal Position Value
25	________	________	________
30	________	________	________
35	________	________	________
40	________	________	________
45	________	________	________
50	________	________	________
55	________	________	________
60	________	________	________
65	________	________	________
70	________	________	________
75	________	________	________

b. For each of the three hedge portfolios, graph the expiration date value of her combined position on the vertical axis, with potential expiration date share prices of Sophia stock on the horizontal axis.

c. Assuming that the options are priced fairly, use the concept of put-call parity to calculate the zero-value contract price (i.e., $F_{0,T}$ for a forward agreement on Sophia stock. Explain why this value differs from the $50 contract price used in parts a and b.

4. You strongly believe that the price of Breener Inc. stock will rise substantially from its current level of $137 and you are considering buying shares in the company. You currently have $13,700 to invest. As an alternative to purchasing the stock itself, you are also considering buying call options on Breener stock that expire in three months and have an exercise price of $140. These call options cost $10 each.
   a. Compare and contrast the size of the potential payoff and the risk involved in each of these alternatives.
   b. Calculate the three-month rate of return on both strategies assuming that at the option expiration date Breener's stock price has: (1) increased to $155, or (2) decreased to $135.
   c. At what stock price level will the person who sells you the Breener call option break even? Can you determine the maximum loss that the call option seller may suffer, assuming that he does not already own Breener stock?

5. The common stock of Company XYZ is currently trading at a price of $42. Both a put and a call option are available for XYZ stock, each having an exercise price of $40 and an expiration date in exactly six months. The current market prices for the put and call are $1.45 and $3.90, respectively. The risk-free holding period return for the next six months is 4 percent, which corresponds to an 8 percent annual rate.
   a. For each possible stock price in the following sequence, calculate the expiration date payoffs (net of the initial purchase price) for the following positions: (1) buy one XYZ call option, and (2) short one XYZ call option:

      20, 25, 30, 35, 40, 45, 50, 55, 60

      Draw a graph of these payoff relationships, using net profit on the vertical axis and potential expiration date stock price on the horizontal axis. Be sure to specify the prices at which these respective positions will break even (i.e.. produce a net profit of zero).
   b. Using the same potential stock prices as in part a, calculate the expiration date payoffs (net of the initial purchase price) for the following positions: (1) buy one XYZ put option, and (2) short one XYZ put option. Draw a graph of these payoff relationships, labeling the prices at which these investments will break even.
   c. Determine whether the $2.45 difference in the market prices between the call and put options is consistent with the put-call parity relationship for European-style contracts.

6. *CFA Examination III (June 1987)*

   On June 1, 1987, an institutional portfolio manager is managing a $1 million portfolio consisting of U.S. government bonds. Currently, the portfolio is fully invested in one bond issue—Government 8% Bonds due June 1, 2002, selling at a market price of 100.

   The manager is concerned about the outlook for interest rates over the next six months. The manager believes interest rates will move significantly with probabilities favoring a strong rise in rates, but a strong decline is also possible. For the next six-month holding period, the manager's goal is to structure a portfolio which will be substantially protected from a rate rise, but which will also participate in any market advances.

   Other available investment instruments are the following:

   (1) Futures Contract on Government 8 Percent Bonds, due 6/1/02

Futures Expiration	12/1/87
Futures Current Price	$101
Contract Size	$100,000

   (2) Option Contracts on Government 8 Percent Bonds, due 6/1/02 expiring 12/1/87

Option	Strike Price	Market Price	Contract Size
Calls	100	4.00	$100,000
Puts	100	2.00	$100,000

(3) Treasury Bills maturing 12/1/87, yielding 3 percent for six months.

a. Assume that the manager wishes to maintain the current bond holding. Design an option strategy that will achieve the manager's goal of protecting against an interest rate rise while also participating in any market advances.

b. Assume that the manager is willing to maintain or sell the current bond holding. With available instruments listed above, design two alternative portfolio structures which accomplish the same goal.

c. Based on the put-call parity relationship shown below, calculate which of the two strategies designed in part b should be implemented:

$$\text{Put Price} = \text{Call Price} - \text{Bond Price} + (\text{Present Value of Exercise Price})$$

7. Consider Commodity Z that has both exchange-traded futures and option contracts associated with it. As you look in today's paper, you find the following put and call prices for options that expire exactly six months from now:

Exercise Price	Put Price	Call Price
40	$0.59	$8.73
45	1.93	—
50	—	2.47

a. Assuming that the futures price of a six-month contract on Commodity Z is $48, what must be the price of a put with an exercise price of $50 in order to avoid arbitrage across markets? Similarly, calculate the "no arbitrage" price of a call with an exercise price of $45. In both calculations, assume that the yield curve is flat and the annual risk-free rate is 6 percent.

b. What is the "no arbitrage" price differential that should exist between the put and call options having an exercise price of $40? Is this differential satisfied by current market prices? If not, demonstrate an arbitrage trade to take advantage of the mispricing.

8. *CFA Examination III (June 1988)*

Frederick Selbst, a self-employed mechanical engineer, recently sold the patent rights for an industrial process that he developed. Selbst had been fairly successful in managing his personal savings and Keogh plans over the years. Because he is a "hands on," "do it myself" individual, he decided to retire from engineering and to manage his personal wealth since the money he received was more than enough to support him in early retirement. He also plans to take extended trips to remote areas, often leaving on very short notice.

Selbst often meets with you to seek advice on investment policy or to discuss new investment concepts. However, he has not given you discretionary authority over his portfolio and continues to select his own individual securities and execute his own trades.

Selbst has scheduled a meeting with you to discuss ways to control risk in his $10 million portfolio, now invested 90 percent in common stocks and 10 percent in cash equivalents. The portfolio of common stocks is broadly diversified but is not an index fund. He plans to use a risk-control strategy for the foreseeable future. In addition, Selbst has told you that he may need to withdraw $3 million from his $10 million portfolio to fund a commitment he has made to a limited partnership investment.

Selbst is at your office to discuss two possible ways to reduce risk: (1) buy stock index put options and (2) sell a fixed number of stock index futures. For the purpose of discussion, Selbst has given you two possible portfolios:

Portfolio 1:	Broadly diversified common stocks		$9,000,000
	Cash equivalents		950,000
	Hold stock index put options to sell $1,000,000 of stocks, at-the-money, expiring in three months		50,000
		Total	$10,000,000
Portfolio 2:	Broadly diversified common stocks		$9,000,000
	Cash equivalents (including futures margin)		1,000,000
	Sell $2,000,000 stock index futures, expiring in three months		0
		Total	$10,000,000

a. Compare and contrast Portfolio 1 and Portfolio 2 with respect to the distribution of returns and the systematic and specific risk.

b. Discuss for each portfolio the ease of constructing and revising the portfolio and the ability to withdraw $3 million, given the fact that Selbst has retained discretionary authority but is often unavailable. Based on your discussion, justify your choice of one of these portfolios for Selbst.

Portfolio 1 specifies the purchase of index puts. Alternatively, one of your staff recommends purchasing puts on each of the individual stocks in Selbst's portfolio. To compare the costs of these two approaches, you assume the portfolio to be protected has only 100 shares each of two stocks: X and Y. The index, called XY, is 50 percent invested in X and 50 percent invested in Y. Both individual stocks and the index have put options as indicated:

Stock/Index	Standard Deviation	Current Stock Price	Put Strike Price	Put Option Price (Per Share)
X (only)	35%	$60	$60	$6.3750
Y (only)	20	40	40	3.2500
XY	15	50	50	1.9375

All puts expire in three months and the T-bill rate for that period is 6 percent per annum.

Approach 1: Buy a put on X and a put on Y (covering 100 shares each). The cost of protecting the portfolio's current market value with puts (in-the-money) is (100 × $6.375) + (100 × $3.25) = $962.50. Note that the portfolio has 200 shares and puts covering 200 shares.

Approach 2: Buy puts on the XY index. The cost of two index puts is 200 × $1.9375 = $387.50.

c. Demonstrate numerically that, excluding the cost of the puts, the downside protection is the same for both Approach 1 and Approach 2.

d. Compare the costs and benefits of Approach 1 relative to Approach 2.

9. *CFA Examination III (June 1990)*

Industrial Products Corp. (IPC), a publicly held company, is considering going private. It is extremely important to IPC's management that the pension fund's present surplus level be preserved pending completion of buyout financing. For the next three months (until September 1, 1990), management's goal is to sustain no loss of value in the pension fund portfolio. Today (June 1, 1990), this value is $300 million. Of this total, $150 million is invested in equities in the form of an S&P 500 Index fund, producing an annual dividend yield of 4 percent; the balance is invested in a single U.S. government bond issue, having a coupon of 8 percent and a maturity of 6/01/2005. Since the "no-loss strategy" has only a three-month time horizon, management does not wish to sell any of the present security holdings.

Assume that sufficient cash is available to satisfy margin requirements, transaction costs, etc., and that the following market conditions exist as of June 1, 1990:

- the S&P 500 Index is at the 350 level, with a yield of 4.0 percent
- the U.S. government 8.0 percent bonds due 6/1/2005 are selling at 100; and
- U.S. Treasury Bills due on 9/1/90 are priced to yield 1.5 percent for the three-month period (i.e., 6 percent annually)

Available investment instruments are the following:

Contract	Expiration	Current Contract Price	Strike Price	Contract Size
S&P 500 Index future	9/1/90	$355.00	—	$175,000
Future on U.S. government 8% bonds due 6/1/2005	9/1/90	101.00	—	100,000
S&P 500 call option	9/1/90	8.00	350	35,000
S&P 500 put option	9/1/90	7.00	350	35,000
U.S. government 8% due 6/1/2005 call option	9/1/90	2.50	100	100,000
U.S. government 8% due 6/1/2005 put option	9/1/90	4.50	100	100,000

a. Assume that the management wishes to protect the portfolio against any losses (ignoring the costs of purchasing options or futures contracts), but wishes also to participate in any stock or bond market advances over the next three months. Using the above instruments, design two strategies to accomplish this goal, and calculate the number of contracts needed to implement each strategy.

b. Using the put-call parity relationship and the fair value formula for futures (both shown below), recommend which one of the two strategies designed in part a should be implemented. Justify your choice.

Put Price = Call price minus Security Price plus Present Value of (Exercise Price plus Income on the Underlying Security)

Futures Price = Underlying Security Price plus (Treasury Bill Income minus Income on the Underlying Security)

10. a. Use combinations of payoff diagrams similar to those shown in Figures 11.3–11.5 to demonstrate why the "synthetic put" version of the put-call-spot parity condition must hold in an arbitrage-free capital market.

b. Once again using the appropriate payoff diagrams, provide an explanation for the put-call-forward parity relationship of the following equation:

$$S_0 = \frac{F_{0,T}}{(1 + RFR)^T}$$

11. As an option trader, you are constantly looking for opportunities to make an arbitrage transaction (i.e., a trade in which you do not need to commit your own capital or take any risk, but still make a profit). Suppose you observe the following prices for options on DRKC Co. stock: $3.18 for a call with an exercise price of $60 and $3.38 for a put with an exercise price of $60. Both options expire in exactly six months and the price of a six-month T-bill is $97.00 (for face value of $100).

a. Using the put-call-spot parity condition, demonstrate graphically how you could synthetically recreate the payoff structure of a share of DRKC stock in six months using a combination of puts, calls, and T-bills transacted today.

b. Given the current market prices for the two options and the T-bill. calculate the no-arbitrage price of a share of DRKC stock.
c. If the actual market price of DRKC stock is $60, demonstrate the arbitrage transaction you could create to take advantage of the discrepancy. Be specific as to the positions you would need to take in each security and the dollar amount of your profit.

12. You are currently managing a stock portfolio worth $55 million and you are concerned that over the next four months equity values will be flat and may even fall. Consequently, you are considering two different strategies for hedging against possible stock declines: (1) buying a protective put, and (2) selling a *covered call* (i.e., selling a call option based on the same underlying stock position you hold). An over-the-counter derivatives dealer has expressed interest in your business and has quoted the following bid and offer prices (in millions) for at-the-money call and put options that expire in four months and match the characteristics of your portfolio:

	Bid	Ask
Call	$2.553	$2.573
Put	1.297	1.317

a. For each of the expiration date values for the unhedged equity position listed below, calculate the terminal values for a protective put strategy.

35, 40, 45, 50, 55, 60, 65, 70, 75

b. Draw a graph of the protective put payoff structure in part a and demonstrate how this position could have been constructed by using call options and T-bills, assuming a risk-free rate of 7 percent.
c. For each of these same expiration date stock values, calculate the terminal values for a covered call strategy.
d. Draw a graph of the covered call payoff structure in part c and demonstrate how this position could have been constructed by using put options and T-bills, again assuming a risk-free rate of 7 percent.

13. You are a market maker in derivative instruments linked to KemCo stock. In addition to acting as a dealer in KemCo call options, put options, and forward contracts, you also spend part of your time surveying other dealers in the industry looking for arbitrage profit opportunities. Currently. the market-clearing (i.e., zero-value) contract price for a KemCo forward contract with nine months to maturity is $45. Also, an average of the last few trades involving nine-month KemCo puts with a $45 exercise price revealed a contract price of $3.22.
a. If the nine-month T-bill is priced to yield an annual return of 6.5 percent, what bid–ask spread would you quote for a nine-month KemCo call option struck at a price of $45? In establishing this spread, first calculate the theoretical no-arbitrage price for the contract and then round this price up (or down) to the nearest one-eighth of a dollar for your ask (or bid) quote.
b. Given the prevailing market prices for the forward and put option contracts, what should be the fair market value of KemCo stock at the present time?
c. Assuming the actual market price of KemCo stock is $41, create an arbitrage portfolio that will allow you to profit from the discrepancy. Be specific as to the positions you would need to take in each security and the dollar amount of your profit.
d. Suppose that KemCo's management has just announced that it will pay a cash dividend in exactly nine months (i.e., just before the derivative contract expiration date). To make the existing stock and forward prices arbitrage-free, what would the amount of this dividend have to be?

References

Brown, Keith C., ed. *Derivative Strategies for Managing Portfolio Risk.* Charlottesville, Va.: Association for Investment Management and Research, 1993.

Burns, Terrence E., ed. *Derivatives in Portfolio Management.* Charlottesville, Va.: Association for Investment Management and Research, 1998.

Chance, Don M. *An Introduction to Options and Futures.* 4th ed. Fort Worth, Tex.: The Dryden Press, 1998.

Clarke, Roger G. *Options and Futures: A Tutorial.* Charlottesville, Va.: The Research Foundation of the Institute of Chartered Financial Analysts, 1992.

Dubofsky, David A. *Options and Financial Futures: Valuation and Uses.* New York: McGraw-Hill, 1992.

Garcia, C. B., and F. J. Gould. "An Empirical Study of Portfolio Insurance." *Financial Analysts Journal* 45, no. 4 (July–August 1987).

Gastineau, Gary L. *The Options Manual.* 3d ed. New York: McGraw-Hill, 1988.

Fabozzi, Frank J., and Gregory M. Kipnis, eds. *The Handbook of Stock Index Futures and Options.* Homewood, Ill.: Dow Jones Irwin, 1989.

Hull, John. *Options, Futures and Other Derivatives.* 3d ed. Englewood Cliffs, N.J.: Prentice-Hall, 1997.

Klemkosky, Robert C., and Bruce G. Resnick. "Put-Call Parity and Market Efficiency." *Journal of Finance* 34, no. 5 (December 1979).

Merton, Robert C., Myron S. Scholes, and Mathew L. Gladstein. "The Returns and Risks of Alternative Put–Option Portfolio Investment Strategies." *Journal of Business* 55, no. 1 (January 1982).

Moriarty, Eugene, Susan Phillips, and Paula Tosini. "A Comparison of Options and Futures in the Management of Portfolio Risk." *Financial Analysts Journal* 37, no. 1 (January–February 1981).

Rubinstein, Mark. "Portfolio Insurance and the Market Crash." *Financial Analysis Journal* 44. no. 1 (January–February 1988).

Tian, Yisong. "A Reexamination of Portfolio Insurance: The Use of Index Put Options." *Journal of Futures Markets* 16, no. 2 (April 1996).

Part 3 VALUATION PRINCIPLES AND PRACTICES

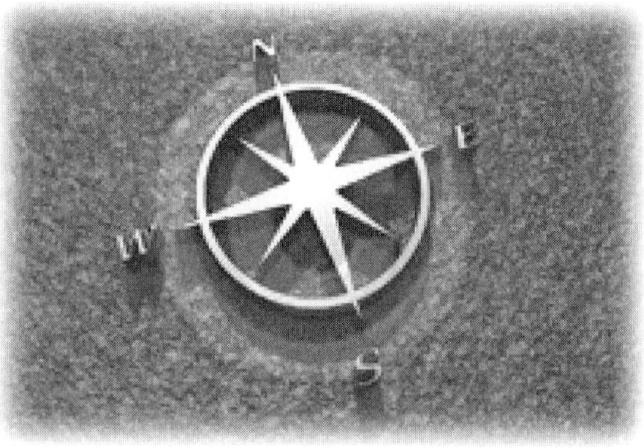
N
E
W
S

Based on the chapters in the first two parts, you know the purpose of investing and the importance of an appropriate asset allocation decision. You also know about the numerous investment instruments available on a global basis, and you have the background regarding the institutional characteristics of the capital markets. In addition, you are aware of the major developments in investment theory as they relate to efficient capital markets, portfolio theory, capital asset pricing, and derivative securities. Therefore, at this point you are in a position to consider the theory and practice of estimating the value of various securities, which is the heart of investing and leads to the construction of a portfolio that is consistent with your risk–return objectives. You will recall that the investment decision is based on a comparison of an asset's intrinsic value and its market price.

The major source of information regarding a stock or bond is the corporation's financial statements. Chapter 12 considers what financial statements are available and what information they provide, followed by a discussion of the financial ratios used to answer several important questions about a firm's liquidity, its operating performance, its risk profile, and its growth potential.

Chapter 13 considers the basic principles of valuation and applies those principles to the valuation of bonds, preferred stock, and common stock. Because it is recognized that the valuation of common stock is the most challenging task, we present two general approaches to equity valuation (discounted cash flow models and relative valuation ratios) and several techniques for each of these approaches. We conclude by reviewing the basic factors that determine the required rate of return for an investment and the growth rate of earnings and dividends for domestic and international firms.

Chapter 14 deals with a major question for the global investor that was introduced in Chapter 2—how to allocate assets across countries based on the state of their economies and the security markets. We examine some specific tools used in this macroeconomic analysis. Additionally, within each country it is necessary to make a further allocation among available asset classes including stocks, bonds, and cash.

Chapter

12 ANALYSIS OF FINANCIAL STATEMENTS

After you read this chapter, you should able to answer the following questions:

- What are the major financial statements provided by firms and what specific information does each of them contain?
- Why do we use financial ratios to examine the performance of a firm, and why is it important to examine performance relative to the economy and to a firm's industry?
- What are the major categories for financial ratios and what questions are answered by the ratios in these categories?
- What specific ratios help determine a firm's internal liquidity, operating performance, risk profile, growth potential, and external liquidity?
- How can the DuPont analysis help evaluate a firm's past and future return on equity?
- What are some of the major differences between U.S. and non-U.S. financial statements and how do these differences affect the financial ratios?
- What is a "quality" balance sheet or income statement?
- Why is financial statement analysis done if markets are efficient and forward-looking?
- What major financial ratios are used by analysts in the following areas: stock valuation, estimating and evaluating systematic risk, predicting the credit ratings on bonds, and predicting bankruptcy?

Financial statements are the main source of information for major investment decisions, including whether to lend money to a firm (invest in its bonds), to acquire an ownership stake in a firm (buy its preferred or common stock), or to buy warrants or options on a firm's stock. In this chapter, we first introduce a corporation's major financial statements and discuss why and how financial ratios are useful. In subsequent sections, we provide example computations of ratios that reflect internal liquidity, operating performance, risk analysis, growth analysis, and external liquidity. Because analysts deal with foreign stocks and bonds, we also discuss factors that affect the analysis of foreign financial statements. In the final section, we address four major areas in investments where financial ratios have been effectively employed.

Our example company in this chapter is Walgreen Company, the largest retail drugstore chain in the United States. It operates 2,549 drugstores in 35 states and Puerto Rico. General merchandise accounts for 25 percent and pharmacy generates almost 50 percent of total sales.

MAJOR FINANCIAL STATEMENTS

Financial statements are intended to provide information on the resources available to management, how these resources were financed, and what the firm accomplished with them. Corporate shareholder annual and quarterly reports include three required financial statements: the balance sheet, the income statement, and the statement of cash flows. In addition, reports that must be filed with the Securities and Exchange Commission (SEC) (for example, the 10-K and 10-Q reports), carry detailed information about the firm, such as information on loan agreements and data on product line and subsidiary performance. Information from the basic financial statements can be used to calculate financial ratios and to analyze the operations of the firm to determine what factors influence a firm's earnings, and cash flows and risk characteristics.

Generally Accepted Accounting Principles

Among the input used to construct the financial statements are **generally accepted accounting principles (GAAP)**, which are formulated by the Financial Accounting Standards Board (FASB). The FASB recognizes that it would be improper for all companies to use identical and restrictive accounting principles. Some flexibility and choice are needed because industries and firms within industries differ in their operating environments. Therefore, the FASB allows companies some flexibility to choose among appropriate GAAP for their use. This flexibility allows the firm's managers to choose accounting standards that best reflect company practice. On the negative side, this flexibility can allow firms to appear healthier than they really are. Given this possibility, the financial analyst must rigorously analyze the available financial information to separate those firms that *appear* attractive from those that actually are in good financial shape.

Fortunately, the FASB requires that financial statements include footnotes that inform analysts regarding which accounting principles were used by the firm. Because accounting principles frequently differ among firms, the footnote information assists the financial analyst in adjusting the financial statements of companies so the analyst can better compare "apples with apples."

Balance Sheet

The **balance sheet** shows what resources (assets) the firm controls and how it has financed these assets. Specifically, it indicates the current and fixed assets available to the firm *at a point in time* (the end of the fiscal year or the end of a quarter). In most cases, the firm owns these assets, but some firms lease assets on a long-term basis. How the firm has financed the acquisition of these assets is indicated by its mixture of current liabilities (accounts payable or short-term borrowing), long-term liabilities (fixed debt), and owners' equity (preferred stock, common stock, and retained earnings).

The balance sheet for Walgreen in Table 12.1 represents the *stock* of assets and its financing mix as of the end of Walgreen's fiscal year, August 31, 1996, 1997, and 1998.

Income Statement

The **income statement** contains information on the profitability of the firm during some *period of time* (a quarter or a year). In contrast to the balance sheet, which indicates the firm's financial position at a fixed point in time, the income statement indicates the *flow* of sales, expenses, and earnings during a period of time. The income statement for Walgreen for the years 1996, 1997, and 1998 appears in Table 12.2. We concentrate on earnings from operations after tax as the relevant net earnings figure. In the case of Walgreen, this is the same as net income; the firm has no nonrecurring or unusual income or expense items.

Statement of Cash Flows

Based upon our earlier discussion on valuation, you know that cash flows are a critical input. In response to a growing interest in this data, accountants now require firms to provide such information. The **statement of cash flows** integrates the information on the balance sheet and income statement. For a given period, it shows the effects on the firm's cash flow of income flows (based on the most recent year's income statement) and changes in various items on the balance sheet (based on the two most recent annual balance sheets). The

TABLE 12.1

WALGREEN COMPANY AND SUBSIDIARIES CONSOLIDATED BALANCE SHEET ($ MILLIONS): YEARS ENDED AUGUST 31, 1996, 1997, AND 1998

	1998	1997	1996
Assets			
Current Assets			
Cash and cash equivalents	$ 144	$ 73	$ 9
Trade accounts receivable—net of allowances	373	376	288
Inventories	2,027	1,733	1,632
Other current assets	79	144	90
Total Current Assets	2,623	2,326	2,019
Property, plant, and equipment	2,961	2,502	2,108
Less accumulated depreciation	817	748	659
Property—Net	2,144	1,754	1,448
Other noncurrent assets	135	127	166
Total assets	4,902	4,207	3,634
Liabilities and Shareholders' Equity			
Current Liabilities			
Short-term debt	$ 0	$ 0	$ 0
Current portion of long-term debt	0	0	0
Trade accounts payable	907	813	692
Accrued expenses and other liabilities	618	554	467
Income taxes payable	55	72	23
Total Current Liabilities	1,580	1,439	1,182
Long-Term Debt	0	0	0
Other Noncurrent Liabilities	384	282	263
Deferred Income Taxes	89	113	145
Preferred Stock, \$0.25 par value, authorized 8,000,000 shares; none issued	—	—	—
Common Shareholders' Equity			
Common stock, \$0.3125 par value, authorized 800 million shares; issued and outstanding 246,141,072 in 1998, 1997, and 1996	78	77	77
Paid-in Capital	118	30	0
Retained earnings	2,653	2,266	1,966
Total Common Shareholders' Equity	2,849	2,373	2,043
Total Liabilities and Common Shareholders' Equity	$4,902	$4,207	$3,634

Source: Walgreen annual reports.

result is a set of cash flow values that you can use to estimate the value of a firm and evaluate the risk and return of the firm's bonds and stock.

The statement of cash flows has three sections: cash flows from operating activities, cash flows from investing activities, and cash flows from financing activities. The sum total of the cash flows from the three sections is the net change in the cash position of the firm. This bottom-line number should equal the difference in the cash balance between the ending and beginning balance sheets. The statements of cash flow for Walgreen for 1996, 1997, and 1998 appear in Table 12.3.

CASH FLOW FROM OPERATING ACTIVITIES This section lists the sources and uses of cash that arise from the normal operations of a firm. In general, the net cash flow from operations is computed as the net income reported on the income statement in-

TABLE 12.2

WALGREEN COMPANY AND SUBSIDIARIES CONSOLIDATED STATEMENT OF INCOME ($ MILLIONS, EXCEPT PER-SHARE DATA): YEARS ENDED AUGUST 31, 1996, 1997, AND 1998

	1998	1997	1996
Net sales	$ 15,307	$ 13,363	$ 11,778
Cost of goods sold	11,140	9,682	8,515
Gross profit	4,167	3,681	3,264
Selling, general and administrative expenses	3,332	2,973	2,660
Operating profit (EBIT)	835	708	604
Interest Income	6	6	5
Interest Expense	1	2	2
Gain on sale of long term-care pharmacies	39	0	0
Operating income before income taxes	877	712	607
Provision for income taxes	340	276	235
Operating income after taxes	537	436	372
Cumulative effect of accounting change	(26)		
Reported net income	511	436	372
Reported net income available for Common	511	436	372
Per Common Share[a]			
Operating income after taxes[b]	$ 1.07	$ 0.88	$ 0.75
Reported net income	$ 1.02	$ 0.88	$ 0.75
Dividends declared	$ 0.25	$ 0.24	$ 0.22
Average Number of Common Shares Outstanding ('000)[a]	498,244	493,790	492,282

[a]Adjusted for stock splits.

[b]Does not include gain on sale of pharmacies and effect of accounting changes.

Source: Walgreen annual reports.

cluding changes in net working capital items (i.e., receivables, inventories, and so on) plus adjustments for noncash revenues and expenses (such as depreciation), or:

$$\text{Cash Flow from Operating Activities} = \text{Net Income} + \text{Noncash Revenue and Expenses} + \text{Changes in Net Working Capital Items}$$

Consistent with our discussion above, the cash account is not included in the calculations of cash flow from operations. Notably, Walgreen has been able to generate consistently large and growing cash flows from operations after accounting for consistent increases in receivables and inventory.

CASH FLOWS FROM INVESTING ACTIVITIES A firm makes investments in both its own noncurrent and fixed assets, and the equity of other firms (which may be subsidiaries or joint ventures of the parent firm. They are listed in the "investment" account of the balance sheet). Increases and decreases in these noncurrent accounts are considered investment activities. The cash flow from investing activities is the change in gross plant and equipment plus the change in the investment account. The changes are positive if they represent a source of funds; otherwise they are negative. The dollar changes in these accounts are computed using the firm's two most recent balance sheets. Most firms (including Walgreen) experience negative cash flows from investments due to significant capital expenditures.

TABLE 12.3

WALGREEN COMPANY AND SUBSIDIARIES CONSOLIDATED STATEMENT OF CASH FLOWS ($ MILLIONS): YEARS ENDED AUGUST 31, 1996, 1997, AND 1998

	1998	1997	1996
Cash Flow from Operating Activities:			
Net Income	$ 511	$ 436	$ 372
Adjustments to reconcile net income to net cash provided by operating activities:			
Cumulative effect of accounting changes	26	0	0
Depreciation and amortization	189	164	147
Gain on sale of long-term-care pharmacies	(37)	0	0
Deferred income taxes and other items	(1)	8	3
Other	29	8	5
Changes in operating assets and liabilities (used in) provided from continuing operations:			
(Increase) decrease in trade accounts receivable	(20)	(74)	(60)
(Increase) decrease in inventories	(299)	(101)	(178)
(Increase) decrease in other current assets	(3)	3	1
Increase (decrease) in trade accounts payable	94	121	85
Accrued expenses and other liabilities	99	73	42
Income taxes	(17)	12	(9)
Insurance reserve	0	0	3
Net Cash Provided by Operating Activities	$ 571	$ 650	$ 411
Cash Flow from Investing Activities:			
Additions to property, plant, and equipment	$(641)	$(485)	$(365)
Net borrowing against corporate-owned life insurance	9	(16)	47
Proceeds from the surrender of corporate-owned life insurance	58	0	0
Disposition of property and equipment	72	15	18
Net Cash Used in Investing Activities	$(502)	$(486)	$(299)
Cash Flow from Financing Activities:			
Cash dividends	$(123)	$(116)	$(105)
Cost of employee stock purchase and option plans	0	(18)	(13)
Proceeds from employee stock plans	105	35	(7)
Payments of long-term obligations	20	(1)	0
Net Cash Used in Financing Activities	2	$(100)	$(125)
Net increase (decrease) in cash and cash equivalents	71	64	(13)
Cash and cash equivalents—beginning of year	73	9	22
Cash and cash equivalents—end of year	$ 144	$ 73	$ 9

Source: Walgreen annual reports.

CASH FLOWS FROM FINANCING ACTIVITIES Cash flow from financing activities is computed as financing sources minus financing uses. Inflows are created by actions increasing notes payable and long-term liability and equity accounts, such as bond and stock issues. Financing uses (outflows) include decreases in such accounts (that is, the paydown of liability accounts or the repurchase of common shares). Dividend payments to equityholders are likewise a financing cash outflow.

The sum total of the cash flows from operating, investing, and financing activities is the net increase or decrease in the firm's cash. The statement of cash flows provides some of the cash flow detail that is lacking in the balance sheet and income statement.

ALTERNATIVE MEASURES OF CASH FLOW

There are several cash flow measures an analyst can use to determine the underlying health of the corporation.

CASH FLOW FROM OPERATIONS This includes the traditional measure of cash flow, which is equal to net income plus depreciation expense and deferred taxes. But as we have just seen, it is also necessary to adjust for changes in operating (current) assets and liabilities that either use or provide cash. For example, an increase in accounts receivable implies that either the firm is using cash to support this increase or the firm did not collect all the sales reported. In contrast, an increase in a current liability account, such as accounts payable, means that the firm acquired some assets but has not paid for them, which is a source (increase) of cash flow (that is, the firm's suppliers are implicitly providing financing to the firm). These changes in operating assets or liabilities can add to or subtract from the cash flow estimated from the traditional measure of cash flow: net income plus noncash expenses. The table below compares the cash flow from operations figures (Table 12.3) to the traditional cash flow figures for Walgreen from 1996 to 1998:

	Traditional Cash Flow Equals Net Income + Depreciation + Change in Def. Taxes	Cash Flow from Operations from Statement of Cash Flows
1998	699	571
1997	608	650
1996	522	411

In two of the three years the cash flow from operations was less than the traditional cash flow estimate because of the several adjustments needed to arrive at cash flow from operations. Therefore, using this more exact measure of cash flow, the Walgreen ratios would not have been as strong. For many firms this is fairly typical because the effect of working capital changes is often a large negative cash flow due to necessary increases in receivables or inventory (especially for high-growth companies).

FREE CASH FLOW **Free cash flow** modifies cash flow from operations to recognize that some investing and financing activities are critical to the firm. It is assumed that these expenditures must be made before a firm can use its cash flow for other purposes such as reducing debt outstanding or repurchasing common stock. The three additional items considered are: (1) capital expenditures (an investing expenditure), (2) the disposition of property and equipment (a divestment source of cash), and (3) dividends (a financing activity). These three items are subtracted from cash flow from operations as follows (some only subtract capital expenditures):

	Cash Flow from Operations	−	Capital Expenditures	+	Disposition of Property and Equipment	−	Dividends	=	Free Cash Flow
1998	571		641		72		193		(121)
1997	650		485		15		116		64
1996	411		364		18		105		(40)

For firms involved in leveraged buyouts, this free cash flow number is critical because the new owners typically want to use the free cash flow as funds available for retiring outstanding debt. It is not unusual for a firm's free cash flow to be a negative value. The free cash flow for Walgreen has been negative because of fairly heavy capital expenditures and larger dividends. Notably, this free cash flow value or a variation of it without dividends will be used in the subsequent cash flow valuation models.

PURPOSE OF FINANCIAL STATEMENT ANALYSIS

Financial statement analysis seeks to evaluate management performance in several important areas, including profitability, efficiency, and risk. Although we will necessarily analyze historical data, the ultimate goal is to provide insights that will help you to *project* future management performance, including pro forma balance sheets, income statements, cash flows, and risk. It is the firm's expected future performance that determines whether you should lend money to a firm or invest in it.

ANALYSIS OF FINANCIAL RATIOS

Analysts use financial ratios because numbers in isolation typically convey little meaning. Knowing that a firm earned a net income of $100,000 is less informative than also knowing the sales figure that generated this income ($1 million or $10 million) and the assets or capital committed to the enterprise. Thus, ratios are intended to provide meaningful *relationships* between individual values in the financial statements.

Because the major financial statements report numerous individual items, it is possible to produce numerous potential ratios, many of which will have little value. Therefore, you want to limit your examination to the most relevant ratios and categorize them into groups that provide information on important economic characteristics of the firm. It is also important to recognize the need for relative analysis.

IMPORTANCE OF RELATIVE FINANCIAL RATIOS

Just as a single number from a financial statement is of little use, an individual financial ratio has little value except in relation to comparable ratios for other entities. That is, *only relative financial ratios are relevant.* The important comparisons examine a firm's performance relative to

- The aggregate economy
- Its industry or industries
- Its major competitors within the industry
- Its past performance (time-series analysis)

The comparison to the aggregate economy is important because almost all firms are influenced by the economy's expansions and contractions (recessions) in the business cycle. It is unreasonable to expect an increase in the profit margin for a firm during a recession; a stable margin might be encouraging under such conditions. In contrast, a small increase in a firm's profit margin during a major business expansion may be a sign of weakness. Comparing a firm's financial ratios relative to a similar set of ratios for the economy will also help you to understand how a firm reacts to the business cycle and will help you *estimate* the future performance of the firm during subsequent business cycles.

Probably the most popular comparison relates a firm's performance to that of its industry. Different industries affect the firms within them differently, but this relationship is always significant. The industry effect is strongest for industries with homogeneous products, such as steel, rubber, glass, and wood products, because all firms within these industries experience coincidental shifts in demand. In addition, these firms employ fairly similar technology and production processes. For example, even the best-managed steel firm experiences a decline in sales and profit margins during a recession. In such a case, the relevant question might be, how did the firm perform relative to other steel firms? As part of this, you should examine an industry's performance relative to aggregate economic activity to understand how the industry responds to the business cycle.

Data for industry average and median financial ratios are published by a number of organizations, such as Dun & Bradstreet *(Industry Norms and Key Business Ratios);* Robert Morris Associates *(Annual Statement Studies);* Standard and Poor *(Analysts Handbook);* and the Federal Trade Commission *(Quarterly Financial Report for Manufacturing, Mining and Trade Corporations).* These sources are available at most libraries.

When comparing a firm's financial ratios to industry ratios, you may not feel comfortable using the average (mean) industry value when there is wide variation among individual firm ratios within the industry. This specific problem can be addressed by using industry median ratios (one-half of firms in the industry have ratios above the median value; one-half have ratios below it). An interquartile range for the ratio may also be helpful.

Alternatively, you may believe that the firm being analyzed is not typical—that is, it has a unique component. Under these conditions, a **cross-sectional analysis** may be appropriate, in which you compare the firm to a subset of firms within the industry that are comparable in size or characteristics. As an example, within the computer industry, you might want to compare IBM to such firms as Apple rather than to industry average data, which include numerous small firms that produce unique products or services.

Another practical problem with comparing a firm's ratios to an industry average is that many large firms are multiproduct and multi-industry in nature. Inappropriate comparisons can arise when a multi-industry firm is evaluated against the ratios from a single industry. Two approaches can help mitigate this problem. The first method is to use cross-sectional analysis by comparing the firm against a rival that operates in many of the same markets. The second method is to construct composite industry average ratios for the firm. To do this, the firm's annual report or 10-K filing is used to identify each industry in which the firm operates and the proportion of total firm sales derived from each industry. Composite industry average ratios are constructed by computing weighted average ratios based on the proportion of firm sales derived from each industry.

You also should examine a firm's relative performance over time to determine whether it is progressing or declining. This **time-series analysis** is helpful when estimating future performance. For example, some may want to calculate the average of a ratio for a 5- or 10-year period without considering the trend. This can result in misleading conclusions. For example, an average rate of return of 10 percent can be based on rates of return that have increased from 5 percent to 15 percent over time, or it can be based on a series that begins at 15 percent and declines to 5 percent. Obviously, the difference in the trend for these series would have a major impact on your estimate for the future. Ideally, you want to examine a firm's time series of *relative* financial ratios compared to its industry or the economy.

COMPUTATION OF FINANCIAL RATIOS

We divide the financial ratios into six major categories that will help us understand the important economic characteristics of a firm. In this section, we focus on describing the various ratios and computing them using Walgreen's data. Comparative analysis of Walgreen's ratios with the economy and industry will be discussed in a later section. The six categories are

1. Common size statements
2. Internal liquidity (solvency)
3. Operating performance
   a. Operating efficiency

TABLE 12.4 **WALGREEN COMPANY AND SUBSIDIARIES COMMON SIZE BALANCE SHEET[a]: YEARS ENDED AUGUST 31, 1994, 1995, 1996, 1997, AND 1998**

	1998	1997	1996	1995	1994
Assets					
Current Assets					
Cash and cash equivalents	2.94%	0.02%	0.24%	0.68%	2.68%
Trade accounts receivable—net of allowances	7.61	8.94	7.94	7.57	6.67
Inventories	41.35	41.19	44.91	44.70	43.43
Other current assets	1.61	3.42	2.47	2.79	3.68
Total Current Assets	53.51	55.29	55.57	55.74	57.51
Property, plant, and equipment	60.40	59.47	58.00	56.29	54.91
Less accumulated depreciation	16.67	17.78	18.14	17.89	17.59
Property—Net	43.74	41.69	39.86	38.40	37.32
Other noncurrent assets	2.75	3.02	4.58	5.86	5.17
Total assets	100.00%	100.00%	100.00%	100.00%	100.00%
Liabilities and Shareholders' Equity					
Current Liabilities					
Short-term debt	0.00%	0.00%	0.00%	0.00%	0.00%
Current portion of long-term debt	0.00	0.00	0.00	0.00	0.00
Trade accounts payable	18.50	19.32	19.04	18.64	18.32
Accrued expenses and other liabilities	12.61	13.17	12.86	13.78	17.03
Income taxes payable	1.12	1.71	0.63	0.72	0.77
Total Current Liabilities	32.23	34.20	32.53	33.14	36.12
Long-Term Debt	0.00	0.00	0.00	0.00	0.00
Other Noncurrent Liabilities	7.83	6.70	7.25	7.38	3.81
Deferred Income Taxes	1.82	2.69	4.00	4.37	5.97
Preferred Stock, $0.25 par value, authorized 8,000,000 shares; none issued	—	—	—	—	—
Common Shareholders' Equity					
Common stock, $0.15625 par value, authorized 1,600 million shares; issued and outstanding 498,243,522 in 1998, 493,789,966 in 1997, and 492,282,144 in 1996 and 1995	1.59	2.54	2.12	2.36	2.64
Paid-in capital	2.41	0.71			
Retained Earnings	54.12	53.86	54.11	52.75	51.46
Total Common Shareholders' Equity	58.12	56.40	56.23	55.11	54.10
Total Liabilities and Common Shareholders' Equity	100.00%	100.00%	100.00%	100.00%	100.00%

[a]Percentages may not add to 100.0% due to rounding.

   b. Operating profitability
4. Risk analysis
   a. Business risk
   b. Financial risk
5. Growth analysis
6. External liquidity (marketability)

COMMON SIZE STATEMENTS

Common size statements "normalize" balance sheet and income statement items to allow easier comparison of different-size firms. A common size balance sheet expresses all balance sheet accounts as a *percentage of total assets.* A common size income statement ex-

TABLE 12.5 **WALGREEN COMPANY AND SUBSIDIARIES COMMON SIZE INCOME STATEMENT[a]: YEARS ENDED AUGUST 31, 1994, 1995, 1996, 1997, AND 1998**

	1998	%	1997	%	1996	%	1995	%	1994	%
Net sales	15,307	100.00	13,363	100.00	11,778	100.00	10,395	100.00	9,235	100.00
Cost of goods sold	11,140	72.78	9,682	72.45	8,515	72.29	7,482	71.98	6,614	71.62
Gross profit	4,167	27.22	3,681	27.55	3,264	27.71	2,913	28.02	2,621	28.38
Selling, general, and administrative expenses	3,332	21.77	2,973	22.25	2,660	22.58	2,393	23.02	2,165	23.44
Operating profit	835	5.46	708	5.30	604	5.13	520	5.00	456	4.93
Interest Income	6	0.04	6	0.01	5	0.04	5	0.05	5	0.06
Interest Expense	1	0.01	2	0.00	2	0.02	1	0.01	3	0.03
Gain on sale of long-term-care pharmacies	37	0.24								
Operating income before income taxes	877	5.73	712	5.33	607	5.15	524	5.04	458	4.96
Provision for income taxes	340	2.22	276	2.07	235	2.00	203	1.95	176	1.91
Operating income after taxes	537	3.51	436	3.26	372	3.16	321	3.09	282	3.05
Cumulative effect on accounting change	(26)	(0.17)								
Reported net income	511	3.34	436	3.26	372	3.16	321	3.09	282	3.05
Operating income after taxes available for Common	537	3.51	436	3.26	372	3.16	321	3.09	282	3.05
Reported net income available for Common	511	3.34	436	3.26	372	3.16	321	3.09	282	3.05

[a]Percentages may not add to 100.0% due to rounding.

presses all income statement items as a *percentage of sales.* Table 12.4 is the common size balance sheet for Walgreen, and Table 12.5 contains the common size income statement. Common size ratios are useful to quickly compare two different-size firms and to examine trends over time within a single firm. Common size statements also give an analyst insight into the structure of a firm's financial statements—that is, the percentage of sales consumed by production costs or interest expense, the proportion of assets that are liquid, or the proportion of liabilities that are short-term obligations. For example, for Walgreen the common size balance sheet shows a small decline in the percent of current assets and an increase in the proportion of net property. Alternatively, the common size income statement in Table 12.5 shows Walgreen's cost of goods sold was quite stable from 1994 to 1998 in proportion to sales. As a result of this stability combined with a lower ratio for selling, general, and administrative expenses, the firm has experienced a consistent increase in its operating profit margin before and after taxes.

EVALUATING INTERNAL LIQUIDITY

Internal liquidity (solvency) ratios indicate the ability of the firm to meet future short-term financial obligations. They compare near-term financial obligations, such as accounts payable or notes payable, to current assets or cash flows that will be available to meet these obligations.

INTERNAL LIQUIDITY RATIOS

CURRENT RATIO Clearly the best-known liquidity measure is the current ratio, which examines the relationship between current assets and current liabilities as follows:

$$\text{Current Ratio} = \frac{\text{Current Assets}}{\text{Current Liabilities}}$$

For Walgreen, the current ratios were (all ratios are in thousands of dollars)

$$1998: \frac{2{,}623}{1{,}580} = 1.66$$

$$1997: \frac{2{,}326}{1{,}439} = 1.62$$

$$1996: \frac{2{,}019}{1{,}182} = 1.71$$

These current ratios experienced a small decline during the three years and are consistent with the "typical" current ratio. As always, it is important to compare these values with similar figures for the firm's industry and the aggregate market. If the ratios differ from the industry results, it is necessary to determine what causes the difference and what might explain it. This comparative analysis is considered in a subsequent section.

QUICK RATIO Some observers believe you should not consider total current assets when gauging the ability of the firm to meet current obligations because inventories and some other assets included in current assets might not be very liquid. As an alternative, they prefer the quick ratio, which relates current liabilities to only relatively liquid current assets (cash items and accounts receivable) as follows:

$$\text{Quick Ratio} = \frac{\text{Cash} + \text{Marketable Securities} + \text{Receivables}}{\text{Current Liabilities}}$$

This ratio is intended to indicate the amount of highly liquid assets available to pay near-term liabilities. Walgreen's quick ratios were

$$1998: \frac{517}{1{,}580} = 0.33$$

$$1997: \frac{499}{1{,}439} = 0.31$$

$$1996: \frac{297}{1{,}182} = 0.25$$

These quick ratios for Walgreen were below the norm and were fairly constant over the three years. As before, you should compare these values relative to other firms in the industry and to the aggregate economy. When possible, you should question management regarding the reason for these relatively low liquidity ratios.

CASH RATIO The most conservative liquidity ratio is the cash ratio, which relates the firm's cash and short-term marketable securities to its current liabilities as follows:

$$\text{Cash Ratio} = \frac{\text{Cash and Marketable Securities}}{\text{Current Liabilities}}$$

Walgreen's cash ratios were

$$1998: \frac{144}{1{,}580} = 0.09$$

$$1997: \frac{73}{1{,}439} = 0.05$$

$$1996: \frac{9}{1{,}182} = 0.01$$

The cash ratios during these three years have been quite low and they would be cause for concern except that the firm has strong lines of credit at various banks. Still, as an investor you would want to know the reason for these low levels and compare them to the ratio for other drugstore chains.

RECEIVABLES TURNOVER In addition to examining liquid assets relative to near-term liabilities, it is useful to analyze the quality (liquidity) of the accounts receivable. One way to do this is to calculate how often the firm's receivables turn over, which implies an average collection period. The faster these accounts are paid, the sooner the firm gets the funds that can be used to pay off its own current liabilities. Receivables turnover is computed as follows:

$$\text{Receivables Turnover} = \frac{\text{Net Annual Sales}}{\text{Average Receivables}}$$

Analysts typically derive the average receivables figure from the beginning receivables figure plus the ending value divided by two. Walgreen receivables turnover ratios were

$$1998: \frac{15{,}307}{(373 + 376)/2} = 40.9 \text{ times}$$

$$1997: \frac{13{,}363}{(376 + 288)/2} = 40.2 \text{ times}$$

It is not possible to compute a turnover value for 1996 because the tables used do not include a beginning receivables figure for 1996 (that is, we lack the ending receivables figure for 1995).

Given these annual receivables turnover figures, you can compute an average collection period as follows:

$$\text{Average Receivable Collection Period} = \frac{365}{\text{Annual Receivables Turnover}}$$

$$1998: \frac{365}{40.9} = 8.9 \text{ days}$$

$$1997: \frac{365}{40.2} = 9.1 \text{ days}$$

These results indicate that Walgreen currently collects its accounts receivable in about nine days on average, and this collection record is fairly stable. To determine whether these account collection numbers are good or bad, they should be related to the firm's credit policy and to comparable numbers for other firms in the industry. Such an analysis would indicate similar rapid collection periods for other drugstore chains since this is basically a cash business.

The receivables turnover is one of the ratios where *you do not want to deviate too much from the norm.* In an industry where the norm is 40 days, a collection period of 80 days would indicate slow-paying customers, which increases the capital tied up in receivables and the possibility of bad debts. You would want the firm to be somewhat below the norm (for example, 35 days versus 40 days), but a figure *substantially below* the norm, such as 20 days, might indicate overly stringent credit terms relative to your competition, which could be detrimental to sales.

INVENTORY TURNOVER Another current asset that should be examined in terms of its liquidity is inventory—the firm's inventory turnover and the implied processing time. Inventory turnover can be calculated relative to sales or cost of goods sold. The preferred turnover ratio is relative to cost of goods sold (CGS) because CGS does not include the profit implied in sales.

$$\text{Inventory Turnover} = \frac{\text{CGS}}{\text{Average Inventory}}$$

For Walgreen the turnover ratios are as follows:

$$1998: \frac{11{,}140}{(2{,}027 + 1{,}733)/2} = 5.9 \text{ times}$$

$$1997: \frac{9{,}682}{(1{,}733 + 1{,}632)/2} = 5.7 \text{ times}$$

Given the turnover values, you can compute the average inventory processing time as follows:

$$\text{Average Inventory Processing Period} = \frac{365}{\text{Annual Inventory Turnover}}$$

$$1998: \frac{365}{5.9} = 62 \text{ days}$$

$$1997: \frac{365}{5.7} = 64 \text{ days}$$

Although this seems like a low turnover figure, it is encouraging that the inventory processing period is declining. Still, it is always essential to examine this figure relative to an industry norm and/or the firm's prime competition. Notably, it will be affected by the products carried by the chain—for instance, if a drugstore chain adds high profit margin items, such as cosmetics and liquor, these products may have a lower turnover.

As with receivables, you don't want an extremely low inventory turnover value and long processing time because this implies that capital is being tied up in inventory and could signal obsolete inventory. Alternatively, an abnormally high inventory turnover and a short processing time could mean inadequate inventory that could lead to outages, backorders, and slow delivery to customers, which would adversely affect sales.

CASH CONVERSION CYCLE An alternative measure of overall internal liquidity is the cash conversion cycle, which combines information from the receivables turnover, the inventory turnover, and the accounts payable turnover. The point is, cash is tied up in assets for a certain number of days. Specifically, cash is committed to receivables for the collection period and is also tied up for a number of days in inventory—the inventory processing period. At the same time, the firm receives an offset to this capital commitment from its own suppliers, who provide interest-free loans to the firm by carrying the firm's payables. Specifically, the payables' payment period is equal to 365/the payables' turnover ratio. In turn, the payables turnover ratio is equal to:

$$\text{Payables Turnover Ratio} = \frac{\text{Cost of Goods Sold}}{\text{Average Trade Payables}}$$

For Walgreen the ratio is:

$$1998: \frac{11{,}140}{(907 + 813)/2} = 13.0 \text{ times}$$

$$1997: \frac{9{,}682}{(813 + 692)/2} = 12.9 \text{ times}$$

$$\text{Payables Payment Period} = \frac{365}{\text{Payables Turnover}}$$

$$1998: \frac{365}{13.0} = 28 \text{ days}$$

$$1997: \frac{365}{12.9} = 28 \text{ days}$$

Therefore the cash conversion cycle for Walgreen equals:

Year	Receivables Days	+	Inventory Processing Days	−	Payables Payment Period	=	Cash Conversion Cycle
1998	9		62		28		43 days
1997	9		64		28		45 days

Walgreen has improved (reduced) its inventory processing days, but is paying its bills at about the same speed, which has caused a small decline in its cash conversion cycle. Although the overall cash conversion cycle appears to be quite good (about 43 days), as always you should examine the firm's long-term trend and compare it to other drugstore chains.

EVALUATING OPERATING PERFORMANCE

The ratios that indicate how well the management is operating the business can be divided into two subcategories: (1) **operating efficiency ratios** and (2) **operating profitability ratios**. Efficiency ratios examine how the management uses its assets and capital, measured in terms of the dollars of sales generated by various asset or capital categories. Profitability ratios analyze the profits as a percentage of sales and as a percentage of the assets and capital employed.

Operating Efficiency Ratios

TOTAL ASSET TURNOVER The total asset turnover ratio indicates the effectiveness of the firm's use of its total asset base (net assets equals gross assets minus depreciation on fixed assets). It is computed as follows:

$$\text{Total Asset Turnover} = \frac{\text{Net Sales}}{\text{Average Total Net Assets}}$$

Walgreen's total asset turnover values were

$$1998: \frac{15{,}307}{(4{,}902 + 4{,}207)/2} = 3.4 \text{ times}$$

$$1997: \frac{13{,}363}{(4{,}207 + 3{,}634)/2} = 3.4 \text{ times}$$

You must compare this ratio to that of other firms in an industry because it varies substantially between industries. For example, total asset turnover ratios range from about 1 for large capital-intensive industries (steel, autos, and other heavy manufacturing companies) to over 10 for some retailing operations. It also can be affected by the use of leased facilities.

Again, you should consider a *range* of turnover values. It is poor management to have an exceedingly high asset turnover relative to your industry because this might imply too few assets for the potential business (sales) or the use of outdated, fully depreciated assets. It is equally poor management to have a low relative asset turnover because this implies tying up capital in an excess of assets relative to the needs of the firm.

Beyond the analysis of the total asset base, it is insightful to examine the utilization of some specific assets, such as inventories and fixed assets. Because we have already examined the receivables and inventory turnover as part of our liquidity analysis, we will examine the fixed asset ratio.

NET FIXED ASSET TURNOVER The net fixed asset turnover ratio reflects the firm's utilization of fixed assets. It is computed as follows:

$$\text{Fixed Asset Turnover} = \frac{\text{Net Sales}}{\text{Average Net Fixed Assets}}$$

Walgreen's fixed asset turnover ratios were

$$1998: \frac{15{,}307}{(2{,}144 + 1{,}754)/2} = 7.9 \text{ times}$$

$$1997: \frac{13{,}363}{(1{,}754 + 1{,}448)/2} = 8.3 \text{ times}$$

These turnover ratios must be compared with those of firms in the same industry and should consider the impact of leased assets, especially for retail firms. Also remember that an abnormally low turnover implies capital tied up in excessive fixed assets, while an abnormally high asset turnover ratio can indicate a lack of productive capacity to meet sales demand or the use of old, fully depreciated equipment that may be obsolete.

EQUITY TURNOVER In addition to specific asset turnover ratios, it is useful to examine the turnover for alternative capital components. An important one, equity turnover, is computed as follows:

$$\text{Equity Turnover} = \frac{\text{Net Sales}}{\text{Average Equity}}$$

Equity includes preferred and common stock, paid-in capital, and total retained earnings.[1] The difference between this ratio and total asset turnover is that it excludes current liabilities and long-term debt. Therefore, when examining this series, it is important to consider the firm's capital ratios because the firm can increase its equity turnover ratio by increasing its proportion of debt capital (that is, a higher debt/equity ratio).

Walgreen's equity turnover ratios were

out

$$1998: \frac{15{,}307}{(2{,}849 + 2{,}373)/2} = 5.9 \text{ times}$$

$$1997: \frac{13{,}363}{(2{,}373 + 2{,}043)/2} = 6.1 \text{ times}$$

Walgreen has experienced relative stability in this ratio during the past several years. In our later analysis of sustainable growth, we examine the variables that affect the equity turnover ratio to understand what caused any changes.

Given some understanding of the firm's record of operating efficiency, as shown by its ability to generate sales from its assets and capital, the next step is to examine its profitability in relation to its sales and capital.

Operating Profitability Ratios

The ratios in this category indicate two facets of profitability: (1) the rate of profit on sales (profit margin) and (2) the percentage return on capital employed.

GROSS PROFIT MARGIN Gross profit equals net sales minus the cost of goods sold. The gross profit margin is computed as

$$\text{Gross Profit Margin} = \frac{\text{Gross Profit}}{\text{Net Sales}}$$

The gross profit margins for Walgreen were

$$1998: \frac{4{,}167}{15{,}307} = 27.2\%$$

$$1997: \frac{3{,}681}{13{,}363} = 27.6\%$$

$$1996: \frac{3{,}264}{11{,}778} = 27.7\%$$

This ratio indicates the basic cost structure of the firm. An analysis over time relative to a comparable industry figure shows the firm's relative cost–price position. Walgreen has experienced a small decline in this margin during the last several years. As always, it is important to compare these margins and any changes with industry statistics.

OPERATING PROFIT MARGIN Operating profit is gross profit minus sales, general, and administrative (SG & A) expenses. The operating profit margin equals

$$\text{Operating Profit Margin} = \frac{\text{Operating Profit}}{\text{Net Sales}}$$

[1]Some investors prefer to consider only *owner's* equity, which would not include preferred stock.

For Walgreen the operating profit margins were

$$1998: \frac{835}{15{,}307} = 5.5\%$$

$$1997: \frac{708}{13{,}363} = 5.3\%$$

$$1996: \frac{604}{11{,}778} = 5.1\%$$

The variability of the operating profit margin over time is a prime indicator of the business risk for a firm. For Walgreen, this margin has experienced a small steady increase over time.

There are two additional deductions from operating profit—interest expense and net foreign exchange loss. This indicates operating income before income taxes.

In some instances, investors add back depreciation expense and compute a profit margin that consists of earnings before interest, taxes, depreciation and amortization (EBITDA). This alternative operating profit margin reflects all controllable expenses and is used as a proxy for pre-tax cash flow. It can provide great insights regarding the profit performance of heavy manufacturing firms with large depreciation charges. It also can indicate earnings available to pay fixed financing costs, as discussed in the section on financial risk.

NET PROFIT MARGIN This margin relates net income to sales. In the case of Walgreen, this is the same as operating income after taxes because the firm does not have any significant nonoperating adjustments, including the cumulative effect of accounting changes. The net income used is earnings after taxes but before dividends on preferred and common stock. For most firms this margin is equal to

$$\text{Net Profit Margin} = \frac{\text{Net Income}}{\text{Net Sales}}$$

As noted, Walgreen's net profit margin is based on income after taxes as follows:

$$1998: \frac{511}{15{,}307} = 3.3\%$$

$$1997: \frac{436}{13{,}363} = 3.3\%$$

$$1996: \frac{372}{11{,}778} = 3.2\%$$

This ratio should be computed based on sales and earnings from *continuing* operations because our analysis seeks to derive insights about *future* expectations. Therefore, results for continuing operations are relevant rather than the profit or loss that considers earnings from discontinued operations, the gain or loss from the sale of these operations, or any truly nonrecurring income or expenses.

COMMON SIZE INCOME STATEMENT Beyond these ratios, an additional technique for analyzing operating profitability is a common size income statement, which lists all expense and income items as a percentage of sales. Analyzing this statement for several years (five at least) will provide useful insights regarding the trends in cost figures and profit margins.

Table 12.5 shows a common size statement for Walgreen for five years. These statements were discussed earlier where the stability in the percentage of cost of goods was highlighted and the small decline in SG&A expenses caused an increase in the net margin.

Beyond the analysis of earnings on sales, the ultimate measure of the success of management is the profits earned on the assets or the capital committed to the enterprise. Several ratios help us evaluate this important relationship.

RETURN ON TOTAL CAPITAL The return on total capital ratio relates the firm's earnings to all the capital involved in the enterprise (debt, preferred stock, and common stock). Therefore, the earnings figure used is the net income from continuing operations (before any dividends) *plus* the interest paid on debt.

$$\text{Return on Total Capital} = \frac{\text{Net Income} + \text{Interest Expense}}{\text{Average Total Capital}}$$

Walgreen incurred interest expense for long- and short-term debt. The gross interest expense value used in this ratio differs from the "net" interest expense item in the income statement, which is measured as gross interest expense minus interest income.

Walgreen's rate of return on total capital was

$$1998: \frac{511 + 1}{(4{,}902 + 4{,}207)/2} = 11.2\%$$

$$1997: \frac{436 + 2}{(4{,}207 + 3{,}634)/2} = 11.2\%$$

This ratio indicates the firm's return on all the capital it employed. It should be compared with the ratio for other firms in the industry and the economy. If this rate of return does not match the perceived risk of the firm, one might question if the entity should continue to exist because the capital involved in the enterprise could be used more productively elsewhere in the economy. For Walgreen, the results are stable with an increase during the last several years.

RETURN ON OWNER'S EQUITY The return on owner's equity (ROE) ratio is extremely important to the owner of the enterprise (the common stockholder) because it indicates the rate of return that management has earned on the capital provided by the owner after accounting for payments to all other capital suppliers. If you consider all equity (including preferred stock), this return would equal

$$\text{Return on Total Equity} = \frac{\text{Net Income}}{\text{Average Total Equity}}$$

If an investor is concerned only with owner's equity (the common-shareholder's equity), the ratio would be calculated

$$\text{Return on Owner's Equity} = \frac{\text{Net Income} - \text{Preferred Dividend}}{\text{Average Common Equity}}$$

Walgreen generated return on owner's equity of

$$1998: \frac{511 - 0}{(2{,}849 + 2{,}373)/2} = 19.6\%$$

$$1997: \frac{436 - 0}{(2{,}373 + 2{,}043)/2} = 19.8\%$$

This ratio reflects the rate of return on the equity capital provided by the owners. It should correspond to the firm's overall business risk, but it also should reflect the financial risk assumed by the common stockholder because of the prior claims of the firm's bondholders.

THE DUPONT SYSTEM The importance of ROE as an indicator of performance makes it desirable to divide the ratio into several components that provide insights into the causes of a firm's ROE or any changes in it. This breakdown of ROE into component ratios is generally referred to as the **DuPont System**. To begin, the return on equity (ROE) ratio can be broken down into two ratios that we have discussed—net profit margin and equity turnover.

$$\text{ROE} = \frac{\text{Net Income}}{\text{Common Equity}} = \frac{\text{Net Income}}{\text{Net Sales}} \times \frac{\text{Net Sales}}{\text{Common Equity}}$$

This breakdown is an identity because we have both multiplied and divided by net sales. To maintain the identity, the common equity value used is the year-end figure rather than the average of the beginning and ending value. This identity reveals that ROE equals the net profit margin times the equity turnover, which implies that a firm can improve its return on equity by *either* using its equity more efficiently (increasing its equity turnover) or by becoming more profitable (increasing its net profit margin).

As noted previously, a firm's equity turnover is affected by its capital structure. Specifically, a firm can increase its equity turnover by employing a higher proportion of debt capital. We can see this effect by considering the following relationship:

$$\frac{\text{Net Sales}}{\text{Equity}} = \frac{\text{Net Sales}}{\text{Total Assets}} \times \frac{\text{Total Assets}}{\text{Equity}}$$

Similar to the prior breakdown, this is an identity because we have both multiplied and divided the equity turnover ratio by total assets. This equation indicates that the equity turnover ratio equals the firm's *total asset turnover* (a measure of efficiency) times the ratio of total assets to equity, which is a measure of financial leverage. Specifically, this latter ratio of total assets to equity indicates the proportion of total assets financed with debt. *All assets have to be financed by either equity or some form of debt* (either current liabilities or long-term debt). Therefore, the higher the ratio of assets to equity, the higher the proportion of debt to equity. A total asset/equity ratio of 2, for example, indicates that for every two dollars of assets there is a dollar of equity, which means the firm financed one-half of its assets with equity. This implies that it financed the other half with debt. A total asset/equity ratio of 3 indicates that only one-third of total assets was financed with equity, so two-thirds must have been financed with debt. This breakdown of the equity turnover ratio implies that a firm can increase its equity turnover either by increasing its total asset turnover (becoming more efficient) or by increasing its financial leverage ratio (financing assets with a higher proportion of debt capital). This financial leverage ratio is also referred to as the financial leverage multiplier whereby the first two ratios (profit margin and total asset turnover) equal return on total assets (ROTA) and ROTA times the financial leverage multiplier equals ROE.

Combining these two breakdowns, we see that a firm's ROE is composed of three ratios as follows:

$$\begin{aligned}\frac{\text{Net Income}}{\text{Common Equity}} &= \frac{\text{Net Income}}{\text{Net Sales}} \times \frac{\text{Net Sales}}{\text{Total Assets}} \times \frac{\text{Total Assets}}{\text{Common Equity}} \\ &= \begin{matrix}\text{Profit}\\\text{Margin}\end{matrix} \times \begin{matrix}\text{Total Asset}\\\text{Turnover}\end{matrix} \times \begin{matrix}\text{Financial}\\\text{Leverage}\end{matrix}\end{aligned}$$

As an example of this important set of relationships, the figures in Table 12.6 indicate what has happened to the ROE for Walgreen and the components of its ROE during the 17-year period from 1982 to 1998. As noted, these ratio values employ year-end balance sheet figures (assets and equity) rather than the average of beginning and ending data.

TABLE 12.6

COMPONENTS OF RETURN ON TOTAL EQUITY FOR WALGREEN COMPANY[a]

Year	(1) Sales/Total Assets	(2) Net Profit Margin (%)	(3)[b] Return on Total Assets	(4) Total Assets/ Equity	(5)[c] Return on Equity (%)
1982	3.31	2.75	9.09	2.06	18.73
1983	3.29	2.96	9.72	2.04	19.84
1984	3.26	3.11	10.16	2.03	20.60
1985	3.29	2.98	9.79	2.00	19.58
1986	3.06	2.82	8.62	2.16	18.64
1987	3.14	2.42	7.60	2.19	16.63
1988	3.23	2.64	8.54	2.12	18.12
1989	3.20	2.87	9.18	2.04	18.74
1990	3.16	2.89	9.12	2.02	18.42
1991	3.21	2.90	9.31	1.94	18.04
1992	3.15	2.95	9.30	1.92	17.90
1993	3.27	2.67	8.74	1.84	16.07
1994	3.17	3.05	9.69	1.85	17.91
1995	3.20	3.09	9.86	1.81	17.89
1996	3.24	3.16	10.23	1.78	18.19
1997	3.18	3.26	10.37	1.77	18.35
1998	3.12	3.34	10.42	1.72	17.92

[a]Ratios use year-end data for total assets and common equity rather than averages of the year.

[b]Column (3) is equal to column (1) times column (2).

[c]Column (5) is equal to column (3) times column (4); ROE is calculated using operating income after taxes.

The DuPont results in Table 12.6 indicate several significant trends:

1. The asset turnover ratio was stable with a total range of 3.06 to 3.31 and a small decline to 3.12 in 1998.
2. The profit margin series experienced a stable increase from 2.75 to 3.34.
3. The product of the total asset turnover and the net profit margin is equal to return on total assets (ROTA), which experienced an overall increase from 9.09 percent to 10.42 percent.
4. The financial leverage multiplier (total assets/equity) experienced a steady decline from 2.06 to 1.72. Notably, most of this debt is trade credit, which is noninterest bearing. The fact is, the firm has almost no interest-bearing debt, except for the long-term leases on drugstores, to be considered in the financial risk section.
5. Finally, as a result of the increasing ROTA and the declining financial leverage, the firm's ROE has been quite constant overall beginning at 18.73 and ending at 17.92.

AN EXTENDED DUPONT SYSTEM[2] Beyond the original DuPont System, some analysts have suggested using an extended DuPont System, which provides additional insights into the effect of financial leverage on the firm and also pinpoints the effect of

[2]The original DuPont System was the three-component breakdown discussed in the prior section. Because this analysis also involves the components of ROE, some still refer to it as the DuPont System. In our presentation, we refer to it as the extended DuPont System to differentiate it from the original three-component system.

income taxes on the firm's ROE. Because both financial leverage and tax rates have changed dramatically over the past decade, these additional insights are important.

In the prior presentation, we started with the ROE and divided it into components. In contrast, we now begin with the operating profit margin (EBIT divided by sales) and introduce additional ratios to derive an ROE value. Combining the operating profit margin and the total asset turnover ratio yields the following:

$$\frac{\text{EBIT}}{\text{Net Sales}} \times \frac{\text{Net Sales}}{\text{Total Assets}} = \frac{\text{EBIT}}{\text{Total Assets}}$$

This ratio is the operating profit return on total assets. To consider the negative effects of financial leverage, we examine the effect of interest expense as a percentage of total assets:

$$\frac{\text{EBIT}}{\text{Total Assets}} - \frac{\text{Interest Expense}}{\text{Total Assets}} = \frac{\text{Net Before Tax}}{\text{Total Assets}}$$

We consider the positive effect of financial leverage with the financial leverage multiplier as follows:

$$\frac{\text{Net Before Tax (NBT)}}{\text{Total Assets}} \times \frac{\text{Total Assets}}{\text{Common Equity}} = \frac{\text{Net Before Tax (NBT)}}{\text{Common Equity}}$$

This indicates the pretax return on equity. To arrive at ROE, we must consider the tax rate effect. We do this by multiplying the pretax ROE by a tax retention rate as follows:

$$\frac{\text{Net Before Tax}}{\text{Common Equity}} \times \left(100\% - \frac{\text{Income Taxes}}{\text{Net Before Tax}}\right) = \frac{\text{Net Income}}{\text{Common Equity}}$$

In summary, we have the following five components:

1. $\frac{\text{EBIT}}{\text{Sales}}$ = Operating Profit Margin
2. $\frac{\text{Sales}}{\text{Total Assets}}$ = Total Asset Turnover
3. $\frac{\text{Interest Expense}}{\text{Total Assets}}$ = Interest Expense Rate
4. $\frac{\text{Total Assets}}{\text{Common Equity}}$ = Financial Leverage Multiplier
5. $\left(100\% - \frac{\text{Income Taxes}}{\text{Net Before Tax}}\right)$ = Tax Retention Rate

To demonstrate the use of this extended DuPont System, Table 12.7 contains the calculations using the five components for the years 1982 through 1998. The first column indicates that the firm's operating profit margin peaked in 1985 and has subsequently generally declined. We know from the prior discussion that the firm's total asset turnover (column 2) has been fairly constant overall. As a result, operating return on assets has looked good. As discussed, because of almost no interest-bearing debt, column 4 shows a small negative impact of leverage.

Column 5 reflects the firm's operating performance before the positive impact of financing (the leverage multiplier) and any impact of taxes. These results show strong

TABLE 12.7 **EXTENDED DUPONT SYSTEM ANALYSIS FOR WALGREEN: 1982–1998[a]**

Year	(1) EBIT/Sales (Percent)	(2) Sales/Total Assets (Times)	(3) EBIT/Total Assets (Percent)[b]	(4) Interest Expense/Total Assets (Percent)	(5) Net before Tax/Total Assets (Percent)[c]	(6) Total Assets/ Common Equity (Times)	(7) Net before Tax/Common Equity (Percent)[d]	(8) Tax Retention Rate	(9) Return on Equity (Percent)[e]
1982	4.32	3.31	14.30	(0.85)	15.15	2.06	31.20	0.60	18.75
1983	5.16	3.29	17.00	0.25	16.75	2.04	34.20	0.56	19.30
1984	5.57	3.26	18.20	(0.24)	18.44	2.03	37.40	0.55	20.65
1985	5.63	3.29	18.50	0.43	18.07	2.00	36.10	0.54	19.57
1986	5.37	3.06	16.40	0.74	15.66	2.16	33.90	0.55	18.63
1987	4.92	3.14	15.50	1.22	14.28	2.19	31.30	0.53	16.69
1988	4.59	3.23	14.80	1.01	13.79	2.12	29.30	0.62	18.10
1989	4.71	3.20	15.10	0.57	14.53	2.04	29.70	0.63	18.79
1990	4.70	3.16	14.90	0.17	14.73	2.02	29.80	0.62	18.52
1991	4.77	3.21	15.30	0.44	14.86	1.94	28.80	0.63	18.00
1992	4.80	3.15	15.10	0.23	14.87	1.92	28.60	0.62	17.87
1993	4.90	3.31	16.20	0.26	15.94	1.82	29.00	0.61	17.80
1994	4.93	3.21	15.90	(0.10)	16.00	1.83	29.20	0.62	17.96
1995	5.00	3.20	15.99	0.04	15.95	1.81	28.90	0.61	17.70
1996	5.13	3.24	16.62	0.06	16.56	1.78	29.50	0.61	18.07
1997	5.30	3.18	16.85	0.05	16.80	1.77	29.74	0.61	18.14
1998	5.46	3.12	17.04	0.02	17.02	1.72	29.27	0.61	17.85

[a]The percents in this table may not be the same as in Table 12.5 due to rounding.

[b]Column (3) is equal to column (1) times column (2).

[c]Column (5) is equal to column (3) minus column (4).

[d]Column (7) is equal to column (5) times column (6).

[e]Column (9) is equal to column (7) times column (8); ROE is calculated using operating income after taxes.

performance by the firm overall. Column 6 reflects the steady decline in financial leverage. Column 8 shows the effect of lower tax rates and thus a higher overall tax retention rate that increased from the mid-50 percent range to the low 60 percent rate. In summary, this breakdown should likewise help you to understand *what* happened to a firm's ROE as well as *why* it happened. The intent is to determine what happened to the firm's internal operating results and its financial leverage, and what was the effect of external government tax policy. Although the two breakdowns should provide the same ending value, they may differ by small amounts because of rounding of components.

RISK ANALYSIS

Risk analysis examines the uncertainty of income flows for the total firm and for the individual sources of capital (that is, debt, preferred stock, and common stock). The typical approach examines the major factors that cause a firm's income flows to vary. More volatile income flows mean greater risk (uncertainty) facing the investor.

The total risk of the firm has two components: business risk and financial risk. The next section discusses the concept of business risk: how you measure it, what causes it, and how you measure its individual causes. The following section discusses financial risk and describes the ratios by which you measure it.

Business Risk[3]

Recall that **business risk** is the uncertainty of income caused by the firm's industry. In turn, this uncertainty is due to the firm's variability of sales caused by its products, customers, and the way it produces its products. Specifically, a firm's earnings vary over time because its sales and production costs vary. As an example, the earnings for a steel firm will probably vary more than those of a grocery chain because (1) over the business cycle, steel sales are more volatile than grocery sales, and (2) the steel firm's large fixed production costs make its earnings vary more than its sales.

Business risk is generally measured by the variability of the firm's operating income over time. In turn, the earnings variability is measured by the standard deviation of the historical operating earnings series. You will recall from Chapter 1 that the standard deviation is influenced by the size of the numbers, so investors standardize this measure of volatility by dividing it by the mean value for the series (i.e., the average operating earnings). The resulting ratio of the standard deviation of operating earnings divided by the average operating earnings is the familiar coefficient of variation (CV):

$$\begin{aligned}\text{Business Risk} &= f(\text{Coefficient of Variation of Operating Earnings})\\ &= \frac{\text{Standard Deviation of Operating Earnings } (OE)}{\text{Mean Operating Earnings}}\\ &= \frac{\sqrt{\sum_{i=1}^{n}(OE_i - \overline{OE})^2/N}}{\sum_{i=1}^{n} OE_i/N}\end{aligned}$$

The CV of operating earnings allows comparisons between standardized measures of business risk for firms of different sizes. To compute the CV of operating earnings, you need a

[3]For a further discussion on this general topic, see Eugene Brigham and Louis C. Gapenski, *Financial Management: Theory and Practice,* 8th ed. (Fort Worth, Tex.: Dryden, 1997), Chapters 6 and 10. For a detailed discussion of the computations, see Frank K. Reilly and Keith Brown, *Investment Analysis and Portfolio Management,* 5th ed. (Fort Worth, Tex.: Dryden, 1997).

minimum of 5 years up to about 10 years. Less than 5 years is not very meaningful, and data more than 10 years old are typically out of date. We cannot compute the CV of operating earnings of Walgreen because we have data for only 3 years.

Besides measuring overall business risk, we can examine the two factors that contribute to the variability of operating earnings: sales variability and operating leverage.

SALES VARIABILITY Sales variability is the prime determinant of earnings variability. Operating earnings must be as volatile as sales. Notably, the variability of sales is largely outside the control of management. Specifically, although the variability of sales is affected by a firm's advertising and pricing policy, the major cause is its industry. For example, sales for a firm in a cyclical industry, such as automobiles or steel, will be volatile over the business cycle compared to sales of a firm in a noncyclical industry, such as retail food or hospital supplies. Like operating earnings, the variability of a firm's sales is typically measured by the CV of sales during the most recent 5 to 10 years. The CV of sales equals the standard deviation of sales divided by the mean sales for the period.

$$\text{Sales volatility} = f(\text{Coefficient of Variation of Sales}) = \frac{\sqrt{\sum_{i=1}^{n}(S_i - \bar{S})^2/N}}{\sum_{i=1}^{n} S_i/N}$$

OPERATING LEVERAGE The variability of a firm's operating earnings also depends on its mixture of production costs. Total production costs of a firm with no *fixed* production costs would vary directly with sales, and operating profits would be a constant proportion of sales. The firm's operating profit margin would be constant and its operating profits would have the same relative volatility as its sales. Realistically, firms always have some fixed production costs (buildings, machinery, or relatively permanent personnel and such). Fixed production costs cause operating profits to vary more than sales over the business cycle. During slow periods, profits decline by a larger percentage than sales. In contrast, during an economic expansion, profits will increase by a larger percentage than sales.

The employment of fixed production costs is referred to as **operating leverage**. Clearly, greater operating leverage makes the operating earnings series more volatile relative to the sales series.[4] This basic relationship between operating profit and sales leads us to measure operating leverage as the percentage change in operating earnings relative to the percentage change in sales during a specified period as follows:

$$\text{Operating Leverage} = \frac{\sum_{i=1}^{n}\left|\frac{\%\Delta OE}{\%\Delta S}\right|}{N}$$

We take the absolute value of the percentage changes because the two series can move in opposite directions. The direction of the change is not important, but the relative size of the change is relevant. The more volatile the operating earnings as compared to the volatility of sales, the greater the firm's operating leverage.

[4]For a further treatment of this area, see James C. Van Horne, *Financial Management and Policy*, 9th ed. (Englewood Cliffs, N.J.: Prentice-Hall, 1993), Chapter 27; and C. F. Lee, Joseph E. Finnerty, and Edgar A. Norton, *Foundations of Financial Management* (St. Paul, Minn.: West Publishing Co., 1997), Chapter 5.

Financial Risk

Financial risk, you will recall, is the additional uncertainty of returns to equity holders due to a firm's use of fixed obligation debt securities. This financial uncertainty is in addition to the firm's business risk. When a firm sells bonds to raise capital, the interest payments on this capital precede the computation of common stock earnings, and these interest payments are fixed obligations. As with operating leverage, during good times the earnings available for common stock will experience a larger percentage increase than operating earnings, whereas during a business decline the earnings available to stockholders will decline by a larger percentage than operating earnings because of these fixed financial costs. Also, as a firm increases its debt financing with fixed contractual obligations, it increases its financial risk and the possibility of default and bankruptcy.

The acceptable level of financial risk for a firm depends on its business risk. If the firm has low business risk (i.e., stable operating earnings), investors are willing to accept higher financial risk. For example, retail food companies typically have rather stable operating earnings over time and therefore relatively *low* business risk, which means that investors and bond-rating firms will allow the firm to have *higher* financial risk.

Three sets of financial ratios help measure financial risk, and *all three* sets should be considered. First are balance sheet ratios that indicate the proportion of capital derived from debt securities compared to equity capital. Second are ratios that consider the earnings available to pay fixed financial charges. Third are ratios that consider the cash flows available.

Proportion of Debt (Balance Sheet) Ratios

The proportion of debt ratios indicate what proportion of the firm's capital is derived from debt compared to other sources of capital, such as preferred stock, common stock, and retained earnings. A higher proportion of debt capital compared to equity capital makes earnings more volatile and increases the probability that a firm will be unable to meet the required interest payments and will default on the debt. Therefore, higher proportion of debt ratios indicate greater financial risk. In the rest of this subsection, we describe the major proportion of debt ratios used to measure this risk.

DEBT–EQUITY RATIO The debt–equity ratio is equal to

$$\text{Debt–Equity Ratio} = \frac{\text{Total Long-Term Debt}}{\text{Total Equity}}$$

The debt figure includes all long-term fixed obligations, including subordinated convertible bonds. The equity typically is the book value of equity and includes preferred stock, common stock, and retained earnings. Some analysts prefer to exclude preferred stock and consider only common equity. Total equity is preferable if some of the firms being analyzed have preferred stock. Alternatively, if the preferred stock dividend is considered an interest payment, you might want to compute a ratio of debt plus preferred stock relative to common equity.

Two sets of debt ratios can be computed: *with and without deferred taxes.* Most balance sheets include an accumulated deferred tax figure, which comes just below long-term debt and other liabilities on the balance sheet. There is some controversy regarding whether you should treat these deferred taxes as a liability or as part of permanent capital. Some argue that if the deferred tax has accumulated because of the difference in accelerated and straight-line depreciation, this liability may never be paid. That is, as long as the firm continues to grow and add new assets, this total deferred tax account continues to grow and is never paid off. Alternatively, if the deferred tax account results from differences in the recognition of income on long-term contracts, such as government contracts, there will be a reversal, and this liability must eventually be paid. To resolve this question, you must determine the reason for the deferred tax account and examine its long-term trend.[5]

Walgreen's deferred tax account arose because of a depreciation difference, and it has typically grown over time. The following ratios are computed with the conservative assumption that includes deferred taxes as a long-term liability. The debt–equity ratios for Walgreen were

Including Deferred Taxes as Long-Term Debt

$$1998: \frac{473}{2,849} = 16.60\%$$

$$1997: \frac{395}{2,373} = 16.65\%$$

$$1996: \frac{408}{2,043} = 19.97\%$$

These ratios indicate a relatively small and declining debt burden for the firm over the three-year period.

LONG-TERM DEBT/TOTAL CAPITAL RATIO The debt–total capital ratio indicates the proportion of long-term capital derived from long-term debt capital. It is computed as

$$\text{L.T. Debt/Total L.T. Capital Ratio} = \frac{\text{Total Long-Term Debt}}{\text{Total Long-Term Capital}}$$

The long-term capital would include all long-term debt, any preferred stock, and total equity. The debt–total capital ratios for Walgreen were

Including Deferred Taxes as Long-Term Debt

$$1998: \frac{473}{3,322} = 14.24\%$$

$$1997: \frac{395}{2,768} = 14.27\%$$

$$1996: \frac{408}{2,452} = 16.64\%$$

Again, this ratio indicates a decrease in the firm's financial risk for the same reason as before (a large increase in equity capital).

TOTAL DEBT RATIOS In some cases, it is useful to compare total debt (current liabilities plus long-term liabilities) to total capital (total debt plus total equity). This ratio is especially revealing for a firm that derives substantial capital from short-term borrowing. The total debt–total capital ratios for Walgreen were

[5]For a further discussion of this, see Gerald I. White, Ashwinpaul C. Sondhi, and Dov Fried, *The Analysis and Use of Financial Statements*, 2d ed. (New York: Wiley, 1997), 1017–1018.

Including Deferred Taxes as Long-Term Debt

$$1998: \frac{2{,}053}{4{,}902} = 41.9\%$$

$$1997: \frac{1{,}834}{4{,}207} = 43.6\%$$

$$1996: \frac{1{,}591}{3{,}634} = 43.8\%$$

This ratio indicates that currently about 42 percent of Walgreen's assets are financed with debt. These ratios should be compared with those of other companies in the industry to evaluate their consistency with the business risk of this industry. Such a comparison with industry peers also would indicate how much higher this total debt ratio can go (i.e., the firm's unused debt capacity).

Although this ratio indicates a relatively low proportion of total debt, some observers would consider it too conservative because it includes accounts payable and accrued expenses, which are *noninterest-bearing debt.* In the case of Walgreen, if this noninterest-bearing debt along with deferred taxes is excluded from debt and from total capital, the ratio declines to a low proportion as follows:

$$\text{Total Interest-Bearing Debt/Total Capital} = \frac{\text{Total Interest-Bearing Debt}}{\text{Total Capital} - \text{Non-Int. Liab.}}$$

$$1998: \frac{384}{3{,}233} = 11.9\%$$

$$1997: \frac{282}{2{,}655} = 10.6\%$$

$$1996: \frac{263}{2{,}307} = 11.4\%$$

Earnings Flow Ratios

In addition to ratios that indicate the proportion of debt on the balance sheet, investors are giving greater attention to ratios that relate the *flow* of earnings that is available to meet the required interest and lease payments. A higher ratio of earnings relative to fixed financial charges indicates lower financial risk.

INTEREST COVERAGE The standard interest coverage ratio is computed as follows:

$$\text{Interest Coverage} = \frac{\text{Income before Interest and Taxes (EBIT)}}{\text{Debt Interest Charges}}$$

$$= \frac{\text{Net Income} + \text{Income Taxes} + \text{Interest Expense}}{\text{Interest Expense}}$$

This ratio indicates how many times the fixed interest charges are earned, based on the earnings available to pay these expenses.[6] Alternatively, one minus the reciprocal of the coverage

[6]The net income figure used in the analysis is the operating income after taxes because, once again, it is important to exclude earnings and cash flows that are considered nonrecurring. The idea is to consider only those earnings that should be available in the future (that is, those from ongoing operations).

ratio indicates how far earnings could decline before it would be impossible to pay the interest charges from current earnings. For example, a coverage ratio of 5 means that earnings could decline by 80 percent (1 minus ⅕), and the firm could still pay its fixed financial charges. Walgreen's interest coverage ratios (using the gross interest expense) were

$$1998: \frac{511 + 1 + 340}{1} = 852 \text{ times}$$

$$1997: \frac{436 + 2 + 276}{2} = 357 \text{ times}$$

$$1996: \frac{372 + 2 + 235}{2} = 305 \text{ times}$$

The ratios are extremely high and reflect almost no public interest-bearing debt.

CONSIDERATION OF LEASE PAYMENTS Although Walgreen has little public interest-bearing debt, similar to many retail firms the company stores generally operate in leased premises. Specifically, original noncancellable lease terms typically range from 10 to 20 years. In addition, they may contain escalation clauses and typically provide for contingent rentals based upon sales. For Walgreen, the minimum lease payment plus contingent rental for each year 1996–98 were as follows (in millions):

1998—437
1997—389
1996—351

The rule of thumb used by bond-rating agencies is to assume that one-third of the lease payment is the interest component. Therefore, if we add this implied interest cost to the interest expense figures used in prior ratios, the fixed financial charge coverage ratios become

$$\text{Fixed Financial Cost Coverage} = \frac{\text{EBIT}}{\text{Interest Expense} + \frac{1}{3}\text{ Lease Payments}}$$

$$1998: \frac{841}{1 + (437/3)} = \frac{841}{147} = 6 \text{ times}$$

$$1997: \frac{714}{2 + (389/3)} = \frac{714}{132} = 5 \text{ times}$$

$$1996: \frac{609}{2 + (351/3)} = \frac{609}{119} = 5 \text{ times}$$

These fixed financial cost coverage ratios show a substantially different picture than the prior coverage ratios, but the coverage ratios still show reasonable financial risk for a firm with very low business risk.

The trend of Walgreen's coverage ratios has been consistent with the overall trend in the proportion of debt ratios. The proportion of debt ratios and the earnings flow ratios do not always give consistent results because the proportion of debt ratios are not sensitive to changes in earnings or to changes in the interest rates on the debt. For example, if interest rates increase or if the firm replaces old debt with new debt that has a higher interest rate, no change would occur in the proportion of debt ratios, but the interest coverage ratio would decline. Also, the interest coverage ratio is sensitive to an increase or decrease in earnings. Therefore, the results using balance sheet ratios and coverage ratios can differ.

TOTAL FIXED CHARGE COVERAGES You might want to determine how well earnings cover *total* fixed financial charges, including any noncancellable lease payments and any preferred dividends paid out of earnings *after* taxes. If you want to consider preferred dividends, you must determine the pretax earnings needed to meet these preferred dividend payments, as follows:

$$\text{Fixed Charge Coverage} = \frac{\text{Income before Interest, Taxes, and Lease Payments}}{\text{Debt Interest} + \text{Lease Payments} + (\text{Preferred Dividend}/[1 - \text{Tax Rate}])}$$

CASH FLOW RATIOS

As an alternative to these earnings coverage ratios, analysts employ several cash flow ratios that relate the cash flow available from operations to either interest expense, total fixed charges, or the face value of outstanding debt. The first set of cash flow to interest expense or total fixed charges are an extension of the earnings coverage ratios. The second set of cash flow ratios are unique because they relate the *flow* of earnings plus noncash expenses to the *stock* of outstanding debt. These cash flow-to-outstanding-debt ratios have been significant variables in numerous studies concerned with predicting bankruptcies and bond ratings.[7]

CASH-FLOW COVERAGE RATIO These ratios are an alternative to the earnings coverage ratio. The motivation is that a firm's earnings and cash flow typically will differ substantially (these differences have been noted and will be considered in a subsequent section). To have ratios that can be compared to similar values for the industry and the aggregate market, the cash flow value used is the "traditional" measure of cash flow, which is equal to net income plus depreciation expense plus the change in deferred taxes (if there was an increase in deferred taxes) for the period (the depreciation expense and deferred tax values are typically given either in the cash flow statements or in the footnotes or in both). Therefore, the cash flow interest coverage ratios for Walgreen were:

$$1998: \frac{511 + 189 + (-24)}{1} = 676 \text{ times}$$

$$1997: \frac{436 + 164 + (-32)}{2} = 284 \text{ times}$$

$$1996: \frac{372 + 147 + 3}{2} = 261 \text{ times}$$

To compute a cash-flow coverage ratio comparable to the earnings coverage ratio, it is necessary to add back the interest charges to this cash flow value because interest expense was deducted to arrive at net income. In addition, we also consider one-third of lease payments as an interest component. Given these adjustments, the cash-flow coverage of fixed financial costs equals

[7] A list of studies in which ratios or cash flow variables are used to predict bankruptcies or bond ratings is included in the reference section.

$$\text{Cash-Flow Coverage of Fixed Financial Costs} = \frac{\text{Traditional Cash Flow} + \text{Int. Expense} + \frac{1}{3}\text{ Lease Payments}}{\text{Int. Expense} + \frac{1}{3}\text{ Lease Payments}}$$

$$1998: \frac{676 + 1 + 146}{147} = 5.6 \text{ times}$$

$$1997: \frac{568 + 2 + 130}{132} = 5.3 \text{ times}$$

$$1996: \frac{522 + 2 + 117}{119} = 5.4 \text{ times}$$

CASH FLOW–LONG-TERM DEBT RATIO Beyond relating cash flow to the required financing expense, several studies have used a ratio that relates cash flow to a firm's outstanding debt as a predictor of bankruptcy and found that this ratio was an excellent explanatory variable in these studies (as noted, these studies are listed in the references). The cash flow figure used in most studies is the traditional measure used in the prior cash-flow coverage ratios. Therefore, this ratio would be computed as

$$\text{Cash Flow/LT Debt} = \frac{\text{Net Income} + \text{Depreciation Expense} + \text{Change in Deferred Tax}}{\text{Book Value of Long-Term Debt}}$$

For Walgreen these ratios were computed based on operating earnings after taxes plus the depreciation expense and deferred taxes reported in the footnotes. Again, we computed these ratios assuming that deferred taxes are included as long-term debt as follows:

Including Deferred Taxes as Long-Term Debt

$$1998: \frac{511 + 1 + (-24)}{473} = 103\%$$

$$1997: \frac{436 + 164 + (-32)}{395} = 144\%$$

$$1996: \frac{372 + 147 + 3}{408} = 128\%$$

CASH FLOW–TOTAL DEBT RATIO Investors also should consider the relationship of cash flow to total debt to check that a firm has not had a significant increase in its short-term borrowing. For Walgreen, these ratios were

Including Deferred Taxes as Long-Term Debt

$$1998: \frac{488}{2{,}053} = 23.8\%$$

$$1997: \frac{568}{1{,}834} = 31.0\%$$

$$1996: \frac{522}{1{,}591} = 32.8\%$$

When you compare these ratios to those with only long-term debt, they reflect the firm's proportion of short-term debt due to short-term borrowing and trade accounts payable. As before, some analysts would exclude accounts payable and accrued expenses because they are noninterest-bearing. In the case of Walgreen, this would eliminate almost all current liabilities. As before, it is important to compare these flow ratios with similar ratios for other companies in the industry and with the overall economy to gauge the firm's relative performance. Alternatively, one might consider capitalizing the operating leases.

ALTERNATIVE MEASURES OF CASH FLOW As noted, these cash flow ratios used the traditional measure of cash flow. The requirement that companies must prepare and report the statement of cash flows to stockholders has raised interest in other, more exact measures of cash flow. The first is the *cash flow from operations,* which is taken directly from the statement of cash flows. A second measure is *free cash flow,* which is a modification of the cash flow from operations discussed earlier. The table below summarizes the values derived earlier in the chapter.

			Free Cash Flow	
Year	Traditional Cash Flow	Cash Flow from Operations	Before Div.	After Div.
1998	609	571	2	(121)
1997	608	650	180	64
1996	522	411	65	(40)

ANALYSIS OF GROWTH POTENTIAL

IMPORTANCE OF GROWTH ANALYSIS

The analysis of **sustainable growth potential** examines ratios that indicate how fast a firm should grow. Analysis of a firm's growth potential is important for both lenders and owners. Owners know that the value of the firm depends on its future growth in earnings and dividends. In the following chapter, we discuss various valuation models that determine the value of the firm based on alternative cash flows, your required rate of return for the stock, and the firm's expected growth rate of cash flows.

Creditors also are interested in a firm's growth potential because the firm's future success is the major determinant of its ability to pay obligations, and the firm's future success is influenced by its growth. Some financial ratios used in credit analysis measure the book value of a firm's assets relative to its financial obligations, assuming the firm can sell these assets to pay off the loan in case of default. Selling assets in a forced liquidation will typically yield only about 10 to 15 cents on the dollar. Currently, most analysts recognize that the more relevant analysis measures the ability of the firm to pay off its obligations as an ongoing enterprise, and its growth potential indicates its future status as an ongoing enterprise. This analysis is also more relevant if you are interested in rating changes.

DETERMINANTS OF GROWTH

The growth of business, like the growth of any economic entity, including the aggregate economy, depends on

1. the amount of resources retained and reinvested in the entity, and
2. the rate of return earned on the resources retained.

The more a firm reinvests, the greater its potential for growth. Alternatively, for a given level of reinvestment, a firm will grow faster if it earns a higher rate of return on the resources reinvested. Therefore, the growth of equity earnings is a function of two variables: (1) the percentage of net earnings retained (the firm's retention rate) and (2) the rate of return earned on the firm's equity capital (the firm's ROE).

$$\begin{aligned} g &= \text{Percentage of Earnings Retained} \times \text{Return on Equity} \\ &= \text{RR} \times \text{ROE} \end{aligned}$$

where:

g = potential (i.e., sustainable) growth rate
RR = the retention rate of earnings
ROE = the firm's return on equity

The retention rate is a decision by the board of directors based on the investment opportunities available to the firm. Theory suggests that the firm should retain earnings and reinvest them as long as the expected rate of return on the investment exceeds the firm's cost of capital.

As discussed earlier in the chapter, the firm's ROE is a function of three components:

- Net profit margin
- Total asset turnover
- Financial leverage (total assets/equity)

Therefore, a firm can increase its ROE by increasing its profit margin, by becoming more efficient (increasing its total asset turnover), or by increasing its financial leverage and financial risk. As discussed, you should examine and estimate each of the components when estimating the ROE for a firm.

The sustainable growth potential analysis for Walgreen begins with the retention rate (RR):

$$\text{Retention Rate} = 1 - \frac{\text{Dividends Declared}}{\text{Operating Income after Taxes}}$$

Walgreen RR figures were

$$1998\text{: } 1 - \frac{0.25}{1.02} = 0.75$$

$$1997\text{: } 1 - \frac{0.24}{0.88} = 0.73$$

$$1996\text{: } 1 - \frac{0.22}{0.75} = 0.71$$

These results, shown in Table 12.8, indicate that the retention rate for Walgreen has been extremely stable during the 17-year period at about 70 percent.

Table 12.6 contains the three components of ROE for the period 1982–1998. Table 12.8 contains the two factors that determine a firm's growth potential and the implied growth rate during the past 17 years. Overall, Walgreen has experienced a slight decline in its growth potential from about 14 percent in the early years to 12–13 percent recently.

TABLE 12.8 **WALGREEN COMPANY COMPONENTS OF GROWTH AND THE IMPLIED SUSTAINABLE GROWTH RATE**

Year	(1) Retention Rate[a]	(2) Return on Equity[b]	(3)[c] Sustainable Growth Rate
1982	0.72	18.73	13.49
1983	0.74	19.84	14.68
1984	0.74	20.60	15.24
1985	0.71	19.58	13.90
1986	0.70	18.64	13.05
1987	0.68	16.63	11.31
1988	0.71	18.12	12.87
1989	0.73	18.74	13.68
1990	0.72	18.42	13.26
1991	0.71	18.04	12.81
1992	0.71	17.90	12.71
1993	0.67	16.07	10.77
1994	0.70	17.91	12.54
1995	0.69	17.89	12.52
1996	0.71	18.19	12.91
1997	0.73	18.35	13.40
1998	0.75	17.92	13.44

[a]Operating income after taxes is used to calculate retention rate.

[b]From Table 12.6.

[c]Column (3) is equal to column (1) times column (2).

Table 12.8 reinforces our understanding of the importance of the firm's ROE. Walgreen's retention rate was quite stable throughout the period, implying that the firm's ROE determined its sustainable growth rate. This analysis indicates that the important consideration is the long-run outlook for the components of sustainable growth. As an investor, you need to *project* changes in each of the components of ROE and employ these projections to estimate an ROE to use in the growth model along with an estimate of the firm's long-run retention rate. We will come back to these concepts on numerous occasions when valuing the market, industries, and individual firms, especially growth companies where the ROEs are notably above average for the economy and vulnerable to competition.

EXTERNAL MARKET LIQUIDITY

Market Liquidity Defined

In Chapter 4 we discussed market liquidity as the ability to buy or sell an asset quickly with little price change from a prior transaction assuming no new information. AT&T and IBM are examples of liquid common stocks because you can sell them quickly with little price change from the prior trade. You might be able to sell an illiquid stock quickly, but the price would be significantly different from the prior price. Alternatively, the broker might be able to get a specified price, but could take several days doing so.

Determinants of Market Liquidity

Investors should know the liquidity characteristics of securities they currently own or may buy because liquidity can be important if they want to change the composition of their portfolios. Although the major determinants of market liquidity are reflected in market trading data, several internal corporate variables are good proxies for these market variables. The most important determinant of external market liquidity is the number of shares or the dollar value of shares traded (the dollar value adjusts for different price levels). More trading activity indicates a greater probability that you can find someone to take the other side of a desired transaction. Another measure of market liquidity is the bid–ask spread (a smaller spread indicates greater liquidity). Fortunately, certain internal corporate variables correlate highly with these market trading variables:

1. Total market value of outstanding securities (number of common shares outstanding times the market price per share)
2. Number of security owners

Numerous studies have shown that the main determinant of the bid–ask spread (besides price) is the dollar value of trading.[8] In turn, the value of trading correlates highly with the market value of the outstanding securities and the number of security holders. This relationship holds because with more shares outstanding, there will be more stockholders to buy or sell at any time for a variety of purposes. Numerous buyers and sellers provide liquidity.

You can estimate the market value of Walgreen's outstanding stock as the average number of shares outstanding during the year (adjusted for stock splits) times the average market price for the year (equal to the high price plus the low price divided by two) as follows:[9]

$$1998\text{: } 996 \text{ million} \times \left[(25 + 13)/2\right] = \$18.92 \text{ billion}$$
$$1997\text{: } 988 \text{ million} \times \left[(15 + 8)/2\right] = \$11.36 \text{ billion}$$
$$1996\text{: } 984 \text{ million} \times \left[(9 + 6)/2\right] = \$7.38 \text{ billion}$$

These market values would place Walgreen in the large-capitalization category, which usually begins at about $5 billion. Walgreen's stockholders number 43,000, including more than 600 institutions that own approximately 51 percent of the outstanding stock.

A final measure, **trading turnover** (the percentage of outstanding shares traded during a period of time), also indicates trading activity. During calendar year 1998, about 622 million shares of Walgreen were traded (adjusted for the 2-for-1 split in early 1999), which indicates turnover of approximately 62 percent (622 million/996 million). This compares with the average turnover for the NYSE of about 55 percent. These large values for market value, the number of stockholders and institutional holders, and the high trading turnover indicate a highly liquid market in the common stock of Walgreen. That is, Walgreen has extremely low external liquidity risk.

COMPARATIVE ANALYSIS OF RATIOS

We have discussed the importance of comparative analysis, but so far we have concentrated on the selection and computation of specific ratios. Table 12.9 contains most of the ratios discussed for Walgreen, the Retail Drug Store Industry (as derived from the S&P *Analysts Handbook*), and the S&P 400 Index. The three-year comparison should provide some insights, although you typically would want to examine data for a 5- to 10-year period. It is necessary to do the comparison for the period 1995–97 because industry and market data from Standard and Poor's were not available for 1998 until late in 1999.

---

[8]Studies on this topic were discussed in Chapter 4.

[9]These values are for the Walgreen fiscal year. Stock prices are rounded to the nearest whole dollar.

TABLE 12.9 SUMMARY OF FINANCIAL RATIOS FOR WALGREEN, S&P RETAIL DRUG STORES, S&P 400 INDEX: 1995–1997

	1997			1996			1995		
	Walgreen	Drug Stores	S&P 400	Walgreen	Drug Stores	S&P 400	Walgreen	Drug Stores	S&P 400
Internal Liquidity									
Current ratio	1.62	1.55	1.36	1.71	1.89	1.33	1.68	1.87	1.38
Quick ratio	0.31	0.23	0.93	0.25	0.37	0.92	0.25	0.31	0.94
Cash ratio	0.05	0.06	0.19	0.01	0.12	0.19	0.02	0.04	0.18
Receivables turnover	40.25	37.13	4.36	44.06	31.77	4.31	47.25	35.79	4.35
Average collection period	9.07	9.83	83.80	8.28	11.49	84.73	7.73	10.20	84.00
Working capital/sales	0.07	0.09	0.11	0.07	0.12	0.11	0.07	0.09	0.12
Operating Performance									
Total asset turnover	3.41	2.38	0.93	3.42	2.34	0.96	3.37	2.82	0.99
Inventory turnover (sales)[a]	7.94	5.74	10.26	7.63	5.81	10.01	8.49	6.65	9.81
Working capital turnover	15.07	11.46	9.13	14.07	8.19	9.03	14.14	10.70	8.59
Net fixed asset turnover	8.35	7.78	2.63	8.73	6.84	2.79	8.91	7.58	2.93
Equity turnover	6.05	5.18	3.00	6.14	4.95	3.11	6.18	5.67	3.27
Profitability									
Gross profit margin	27.55	—	—	27.71	—	—	28.02	—	—
Operating profit margin	5.30	7.06	17.04	5.13	6.80	16.07	5.00	6.51	15.47
Net profit margin[b]	3.26	1.96	6.13	3.16	3.26	5.93	3.09	2.84	5.32
Return on total capital[b]	11.17	7.33	10.65	10.96	11.75	10.66	10.45	12.59	10.04
Return on owners' equity[b]	19.75	10.36	18.76	19.38	16.14	18.80	19.06	16.14	17.76
Financial Risk									
Debt–equity ratio[c]	16.65	40.38	79.52	19.97	49.87	76.53	21.31	38.09	77.33
Long-term debt/long-term capital[c]	14.27	28.77	47.83	16.64	33.28	46.63	17.56	27.58	46.70
Total debt/total capital[c]	43.60	54.46	132.25	43.80	53.99	133.98	44.90	50.78	136.00
Interest coverage[b]	357.00	7.37	5.63	304.50	11.99	5.57	441.12	13.20	5.00
Cash flow/long-term debt[b,c]	144.00	42.19	44.82	128.00	41.13	45.21	119.00	61.55	42.96
Cash flow/total debt[b,c]	31.00	14.25	16.21	32.80	17.48	15.73	31.20	22.72	14.75
Growth Analysis[d]									
Retention rate[b]	0.73	0.59	0.62	0.71	0.71	0.62	0.70	0.66	0.61
Return on equity[b]	18.35	10.16	18.06	18.20	16.13	17.63	17.90	16.14	16.72
Total asset turnover	3.41	2.38	0.93	3.42	2.34	0.96	3.37	2.82	0.99
Total assets/equity	1.77	2.18	3.27	1.78	2.17	3.20	1.81	2.03	3.25
Net profit margin[b]	3.26	1.96	6.13	3.16	3.26	5.93	3.09	2.84	5.32
Sustainable growth rate[b]	13.40	5.99	11.17	12.86	11.45	10.95	12.53	10.65	10.14

[a]Computed using sales since cost of sales not available for industry and S&P 400.
[b]Calculated using operating income after taxes.
[c]Ratios include deferred taxes and long-term debt.
[d]Calculated using year-end data.

INTERNAL LIQUIDITY The three basic ratios (current ratio, quick ratio, and cash ratio) provided mixed results regarding liquidity for Walgreen relative to the industry and market. The current ratio is above the industry and market. The firm's receivables turnover has increased and its collection period is so fast that the collection period is substantially less than the S&P 400 and the retail drug store industry (9 days versus 10 and 84 in 1997). Because it has declined steadily, the difference is probably because of the firm's basic credit policy.

Overall, the comparisons indicate reasonably strong internal liquidity. An additional positive factor is the firm's ability to sell high-grade commercial paper and the existence of several major bank credit lines.

OPERATING PERFORMANCE This segment of the analysis considers efficiency ratios (turnovers) and profitability ratios. Given the nature of the analysis, the major comparison is relative to the industry. Walgreen's turnover ratios were substantially above those of the retail drug store industry. Specifically, during 1995–1997, all the turnover ratios for Walgreen exceeded comparable industry turnovers.

This was offset partially by profitability from sales, which was only adequate. Operating and net profit margins were consistently below the industry.

The profit performance related to invested capital was historically strong. The retail drug store industry return on total capital was consistently above the S&P 400, and Walgreen was above the retail drug store industry in all three years. The drug store industry experienced ROEs substantially above the market, and Walgreen attained higher ROEs than its industry in all three years.

FINANCIAL RISK Walgreen's financial risk ratios, measured in terms of proportion of debt, were consistently below those of the industry and the market, indicating a low financial risk posture. Similary the financial risk flow ratios for Walgreen were substantially above the market and its industry. These comparisons confirm that Walgreen has not increased its very low financial risk position during the past several years. Note that the financial risk ratios in Table 12.9 assume that deferred taxes are long-term debt, a conservative assumption for a firm with a strong growth pattern like Walgreen, but do not consider the firm's leases.

GROWTH ANALYSIS Walgreen has generally maintained a sustainable growth rate similar to its industry, and both Walgreen and the industry have outperformed the aggregate market. The reasons for a difference in growth for the firm and its industry is a higher ROE (except the industry in 1997), and the retention rate for Walgreen has been consistently higher.

In sum, Walgreen has adequate liquidity, a good operating record, and low financial risk even when you consider the leases on stores. Your success as an investor depends on how well you use these historical numbers to derive meaningful *estimates* of future performance and then use these estimates in a valuation model.

ANALYSIS OF NON-U.S. FINANCIAL STATEMENTS

As noted previously, your portfolio should encompass other economies and markets, numerous global industries, and many foreign firms in these global industries. You should recognize, however, that non-U.S. financial statements will differ widely from those in this chapter and a typical accounting course. Accounting conventions differ substantially among countries. Although it is impossible to discuss alternative accounting conventions in detail, we will consider some of the major differences in format and principle.

TABLE 12.10

COMPARATIVE BALANCE SHEET FORMATS

UNITED KINGDOM

Net assets employed
- Fixed assets
- Subsidiaries
- Associated companies
- Current assets
- Less: current liabilities
- Less: deferred liabilities

Assets represented by:
- Share capital
- Reserves

CANADA

Assets
- Current assets
- Investments
- Fixed assets
- Other assets

Liabilities and shareholders' equity
- Current liabilities
- Long-term debt
- Deferred income taxes
- Shareholders' equity

AUSTRALIA

Share capital and reserves and liabilities
- Share capital and reserves
- Long-term debt and deferred income taxes
- Current liabilities

Assets
- Fixed assets
- Investments
- Current assets

GERMANY

Assets
- Outstanding payments on subscribed share capital
- Fixed assets and investments
- Revolving assets
- Deferred charges and prepaid expenses
- Accumulated net loss (of period)

Liabilities and shareholders' equity
- Share capital
- Open reserves
- Adjustments to assets
- Reserves for estimated liabilities and accrued expenses
- Deferred income
- Accumulated net profit (of period)

Source: *Professional Accounting in 30 Countries,* pp. 51, 125–126, 169, 629, 746–749. Copyright © 1975 by the American Institute of Certified Public Accountants, Inc. Reprinted by permission of the AICPA.

ACCOUNTING STATEMENT FORMAT DIFFERENCES

Table 12.10 contains examples of balance sheet formats for several countries and indicates some major differences in accounts and the order of presentation. As an example, in the United Kingdom, fixed assets are presented above current assets, and current liabilities are automatically subtracted from current assets. In Australia, capital accounts are presented initially, and the current assets are placed below long-term assets. The balance sheet items are similar to those in the United States, but almost exactly opposite in presentation. Clearly, the accounts and presentation in Canada are similar to those in the United States. Germany's accounts also are similar except that they have numerous reserve accounts on the liability side. Besides finding similarities to the U.S. firms, you need to consider the techniques used to derive individual items.

The comparative income statement formats in Table 12.11 show that the U.K. statements have much less detail than U.S. statements. This limits your ability to analyze trends in expense items. Although Japanese statements are fairly similar to those of the United States, you should be aware of nonoperating income and expense items. These can be substantial because Japanese firms typically have heavy investments in the common stock of suppliers and customers as a sign of goodwill. The income and gains (or losses) from these equity holdings can be a substantial permanent component of a firm's net income.

The Australian statements, like the British, combine numerous expense items and include several items concerned with the distribution of the net income. Finally, income statements from Germany are highly detailed and contain many unusual income and expense items. These details provide numerous opportunities to control the profit or loss for the period.

TABLE 12.11 COMPARATIVE INCOME STATEMENT FORMATS

UNITED KINGDOM
Group turnover
Profit before taxation and extraordinary items
  Less: Taxation based on profit for the year
Profit after taxation and before extraordinary items
  Less: Extraordinary items
Profits attributable to shareholders of parent company

JAPAN
Sales
  Less: Cost of goods sold
Gross profit on sales
  Less: Selling and administrative expenses
Operating income
  Add: Nonoperating revenue
Gross profit for the period
  Less: Nonoperating expenses
Net income for the period

AUSTRALIA
Sales and revenue
  Less: Cost of sales
Operating profit
  Add: Income from investments
  Less: Interest to other persons
Pretax profit
  Less: Provision for income tax
Net profit before extraordinary items
  Less: Extraordinary items
Net profit after extraordinary items
Unappropriated profits, previous year
Prior year adjustments
Transfer from general reserve
Available for appropriation
Dividends
Transfer to general reserve
Transfer to capital profits reserve
Unappropriated profits, end of year

GERMANY
Net sales
Increase or decrease of finished and unfinished products
Other manufacturing costs for fixed assets
Total output
Raw materials and supplies, purchased goods consumed in sale
Gross profit
Income from profit transfer agreements
Income from trade investments
Income from other long-term investments
Other interest and similar income
Income from retirement and appraisal of fixed assets
Income from the cancellation of lump allowances
Income from the cancellation of overstated reserves
Other income, including extraordinary items
Income from loss transfer agreements
Total income
Wages and salaries
Social taxes
Expenses for pension plans and relief
Depreciation and amortization of fixed assets and investments
Depreciation and amortization of finance investments
Losses by deduction or on retirement of current assets
Losses on retirement of fixed assets and investments
Interest and similar expenses
Taxes on income and net assets
Other expenses
Profits transferable to parent company under profit transfer agreement
Profit or loss for the period
Profit or loss brought forward from preceding year
Release of reserves
Amounts appropriated to reserves out of profit of period
Accumulated net profit or loss

Source: *Professional Accounting in 30 Countries,* pp. 52, 350, 351, 630, 750, 753. Copyright © 1975 by the American Institute of Certified Public Accountants, Inc. Reprinted by permission of the AICPA.

DIFFERENCES IN ACCOUNTING PRINCIPLES

Beyond the differences in the presentation format, numerous differences appear in the accounting principles used to arrive at the income, expense, and balance sheet items. Choi and Bavishi compared accounting standards for 10 countries and highlighted the differences.[10] Table 12.12 synthesizes the differences in 32 specific items. Following a discussion of several major areas, the authors conclude

> Perhaps the major conclusion drawn from analyzing the annual reports of the world's leading industrial firms is that fundamental differences in accounting practices between each of ten

[10]Frederick D. S. Choi and Vinod B. Bavishi, "Diversity in Multinational Accounting," *Financial Executive* 50, no. 7 (August 1982): 36–39. This table also is presented and discussed in Frederick D. S. Choi and Gerhard G. Mueller, *International Accounting* (Englewood Cliffs, N.J.: Prentice-Hall, 1984), 72–76.

TABLE 12.12 **SYNTHESIS OF ACCOUNTING DIFFERENCES**

Accounting Principles	United States	Australia	Canada	France	Germany	Japan	The Netherlands	Sweden	Switzerland	United Kingdom
1. Marketable securities recorded at the lower of cost or market?	Yes	Yes	Yes	Yes	Yes	Yes	Yes	Yes	Yes	Yes
2. Provision for uncorrectable accounts made?	Yes	Yes	Yes	No	Yes	Yes	Yes	Yes	Yes	Yes
3. Inventory costed using FIFO?	Mixed	Yes	Mixed	Mixed	Yes	Mixed	Mixed	Yes	Yes	Yes
4. Manufacturing overhead allocated to year-end inventory?	Yes	Yes	Yes	Yes	Yes	Yes	Yes	Yes	No	Yes
5. Inventory valued at the lower of cost or market?	Yes	Yes	Yes	Yes	Yes	Yes	Yes	Yes	Yes	Yes
6. Accounting for long-term investments: less than 20 percent ownership: cost method?	Yes	Yes	Yes	Yes*	Yes	Yes	No (K)	Yes	Yes	Yes
7. Accounting for long-term investments: 21–50 percent ownership: equity method?	Yes	No (G)	Yes	Yes*	No (B)	No (B)	Yes	No (B)	No (B)	Yes
8. Accounting for long-term investments: more than 50 percent ownership: full consolidation?	Yes	Yes	Yes	Yes*	Yes	Yes	Yes	Yes	Yes	Yes
9. Both domestic and foreign subsidiaries consolidated?	Yes	Yes	Yes	Yes	No**	Yes	Yes	Yes	Yes	Yes
10. Acquisitions accounted for under the pooling-of-interest method?	Yes	No (C)	No (C)	No (C)	No (C)	No (C)	No (C)	No (C)	No (C)	No (C)
11. Intangible assets: goodwill amortized?	Yes	Yes	Yes	Yes	No	Yes	Mixed	Yes	No**	No**
12. Intangible assets: other than goodwill amortized?	Yes	Yes	Yes	Yes	Yes	Yes	Yes	Yes	No**	No**
13. Long-term debt includes maturities longer than one year?	Yes	Yes	Yes	Yes	No (D)	Yes	Yes	Yes	Yes	Yes
14. Discount/premium on long-term debt amortized?	Yes	Yes	Yes	No	No	Yes	Yes	No	No	No
15. Deferred taxes recorded when accounting income is not equal to taxable income?	Yes	Yes	Yes	Yes	Yes	Yes	Yes	No	No	Yes
16. Financial leases (long-term) capitalized?	Yes	No	Yes	No	No	No	No	No	No	No
17. Company pension fund contribution provided regularly?	Yes	Yes	Yes	Yes	Yes	Yes	Yes	Yes	Yes	Yes
18. Total pension fund assets and liabilities excluded from company's financial statement?	Yes	Yes	Yes	Yes	No	Yes	Yes	Yes	Yes	Yes
19. Research and development expensed?	Yes	Yes	Yes	Yes	Yes	Yes	Yes	Yes	Yes	Yes
20. Treasury stock deducted from owner's equity?	Yes	NF	Yes	Yes	No	Yes	Mixed	NF	NF	NF
21. Gains or losses on treasury stock taken to owner's equity?	Yes	NF	Yes	Yes	No	No**	Mixed	NF	NF	NF

TABLE 12.12 **(CONCLUDED)**

Accounting Principles	United States	Australia	Canada	France	Germany	Japan	The Netherlands	Sweden	Switzerland	United Kingdom
22. No general purpose (purely discretionary) reserves allowed?	Yes	Yes	Yes	No	No	No	No	No	No	Yes
23. Dismissal indemnities accounted for on a pay-as-you-go basis?	Yes	Yes	Yes	Yes	Yes	Yes	NF	Yes	NF	Yes
24. Minority interest excluded from consolidated income?	Yes	Yes	Yes	Yes	No	Yes	Yes	Yes	Yes	Yes
25. Minority interest excluded from consolidated owner's equity?	Yes	Yes	Yes	Yes	No	Yes	Yes	Yes	Yes	Yes
26. Are intercompany sales or profits eliminated on consolidation?	Yes	Yes	Yes	Yes	Yes	Yes	Yes	Yes	Yes	Yes
27. Basic financial statements reflect a historical cost valuation (no price level adjustment)?	Yes	No	Yes	No	Yes	Yes	No**	No	No	No
28. Supplementary inflation-adjusted financial statements provided?	Yes	No**	No**	No	No	No	No**	No	No**	Yes
29. Straight-line depreciation adhered to?	Yes	Yes	Yes	Mixed	Mixed	Mixed	Yes	Yes	Yes	Yes
30. No expense depreciation permitted?	Yes	No	Yes	No	Yes	Yes	No	No	No	No
31. Temporal method of foreign currency translation employed?	Yes	Mixed	Yes	No (E)	No (E)	Mixed	No (E)	No (L)	No (E)	No (E)
32. Currency translation gains or losses reflected in current income?	Yes	Mixed	Yes	Mixed	Mixed	Mixed	No (J)	Mixed	No (H)	No

Key
Yes—Predominant practice.
Yes*—Minor modifications, but still predominant practice.
No**—Minority practice.
No—Accounting principle in question is not adhered to.
NF—Not found.
Mixed—Alternative practices followed with no majority.
B—Cost method is used.
C—Purchase method is used.
D—Long-term debt includes maturities longer than four years.
E—Current rate method of foreign-currency translation.
F—Weighted average is used.
G—Cost or equity.
H—Translation gains and losses are deferred.
I—Market is used.
J—Owner's equity.
K—Equity.
L—Monetary/Nonmonetary.

Source: "Diversity in Multinational Accounting" by Frederick D. S. Choi and Vinod B. Bavishi. Reprinted with permission from *Financial Executive,* August 1982, copyright © 1982 by Financial Executives Institute, 10 Madison Avenue, P.O. Box 1938, Morristown, NJ 07962-1938.

TABLE 12.13 **MEAN DIFFERENCES IN AGGREGATE FINANCIAL RATIOS: UNITED STATES, JAPAN, KOREA (UNADJUSTED)**

Enterprise Category	Current Ratio	Quick Ratio	Debt Ratio	Times Interest Earned	Inventory Turnover
All Manufacturing					
Japan (976)	1.15	0.80	0.84	1.60	5.00
Korea (354)	1.13	0.46	0.78	1.80	6.60
United States (902)	1.94	1.10	0.47	6.50	6.80
Difference (U.S.–Japan)	40%	26%	(77%)	75%	26%
Difference (U.S.–Korea)	42%	58%	(66%)	73%	2%
Chemicals					
Japan (129)	1.30	0.99	0.79	1.80	7.10
Korea (54)	1.40	0.70	0.59	2.40	7.10
United States (n.a.)	2.20	1.30	0.45	6.50	6.50
Difference (U.S.–Japan)	42%	22%	(74%)	72%	(8%)
Difference (U.S.–Korea)	36%	45%	(31%)	62%	(9%)
Textiles					
Japan (81)	1.00	0.77	0.81	1.10	6.20
Korea (34)	1.00	0.37	0.83	1.30	4.90
United States (n.a.)	2.30	1.20	0.48	4.30	6.50
Difference (U.S.–Japan)	55%	38%	(70%)	74%	5%
Difference (U.S. Korea)	55%	70%	(74%)	70%	24%
Transportation					
Japan (85)	1.20	0.86	0.83	1.90	3.90
Korea (14)	0.95	0.40	0.91	1.90	18.60
United States (n.a.)	1.60	0.74	0.52	8.70	5.60
Difference (U.S.–Japan)	21%	(16%)	(61%)	78%	28%
Difference (U.S.–Korea)	40%	46%	(75%)	77%	(234%)

countries examined are not as extensive as was initially feared. Major differences observed relate to accounting for goodwill, deferred taxes, long-term leases, discretionary reserves, and foreign-currency translation. Having observed this comforting fact, the user must be cautioned against assuming that consistency and harmonization exist among the annual reports of all foreign companies.[11]

INTERNATIONAL RATIO ANALYSIS

The tendency is to analyze accounting statements using financial ratios similar to those discussed in this chapter. Although this is certainly legitimate, it is important to recognize that the representative ratio values and trends may differ among countries because of local accounting practices and business norms. Choi et al. compared a common set of ratios for a sample of companies in the United States, Japan, and Korea.[12] Table 12.13 com-

[11]Choi and Bavishi, "Diversity in Multinational Accounting," 39. Another comparison of accounting standards for the United States, the United Kingdom, the European Economic Community, and Canada is contained in Thomas G. Evans, Martin E. Taylor, and Oscar Holzmann, *International Accounting and Reporting* (New York: Macmillan, 1985), 106–113.

[12]Frederick D. S. Choi, Hisaaki Hino, Sang Kee Min, Sang Oh Nam, Junichi Ujiie, and Arthur J. Stonehill, "Analyzing Foreign Financial Statements: The Use and Misuse of International Ratio Analysis," *Journal of International Business Studies* (spring–summer 1983): 113–131, reprinted in Frederick D. S. Choi and Gerhard G. Mueller, *Frontiers of International Accounting: An Anthology* (Ann Arbor, Mich.: UMI Research Press, 1985).

TABLE 12.13 (CONCLUDED)

Enterprise Category	Average Collection Period	Fixed Asset Turnover	Total Asset Turnover	Profit Margin	Return on Total Assets	Return on Net Worth
All Manufacturing						
Japan (976)	86	3.10	0.93	.013	0.12	.071
Korea (354)	33	2.80	1.20	.023	.028	.131
United States (902)	43	3.90	1.40	.054	.074	.013
Difference (U.S.–Japan)	(102%)	22%	32%	26%	84%	49%
Difference (U.S.–Korea)	24%	29%	9%	57%	62%	6%
Chemicals						
Japan (129)	88	2.80	0.90	.015	.014	.065
Korea (54)	33	1.60	0.90	.044	.040	.100
United States (n.a.)	50	2.80	1.10	.073	.081	.148
Difference (U.S.–Japan)	(75%)	0%	19%	79%	83%	52%
Difference (U.S.–Korea)	34%	44%	19%	39%	50%	32%
Textiles						
Japan (81)	66	3.50	0.92	.003	.003	.017
Korea (34)	30	2.20	1.00	.010	.011	.064
United States (n.a.)	48	5.80	1.80	.027	.049	.094
Difference (U.S.–Japan)	(39%)	40%	50%	87%	93%	82%
Difference (U.S.–Korea)	36%	63%	44%	62%	78%	32%
Transportation						
Japan (85)	116	4.50	0.90	.017	.015	.092
Korea (14)	18	1.10	0.80	.026	.021	.221
United States (n.a.)	31	6.50	1.60	.049	.078	.161
Difference (U.S.–Japan)	278%	30%	44%	65%	80%	43%
Difference (U.S.–Korea)	40%	84%	50%	47%	73%	(37%)

Note: Parentheses indicate foreign ratios greater than U.S. ratios.

Source: Frederick D. S. Choi, Hisaaki Hino, Sang Kee Min, Sang Oh Nam, Junichi Ujiie, and Arthur J. Stonehill, "Analyzing Foreign Financial Statements: The Use and Misuse of International Ratio Analysis," *Journal of International Business Studies* (spring–summer 1983): 113–131.

pares the mean values for these ratios and the differences among them. These ratios differ substantially for all manufacturing as well as for specific important industries (chemical, textiles, and transportation). Following an extensive discussion of the ratios, the authors conclude

> On the basis of these findings, institutional, cultural, political and tax considerations in Japan and Korea do indeed cause their accounting ratios to differ from U.S. norms without necessarily reflecting better or worse financial risk and return characteristics being measured. . . .
>
> A major conclusion of our study is that accounting measurements reflected in corporate financial reports represent, in one sense, merely "numbers" that have limited meaning and significance in and of themselves. Meaning and significance come from and depend upon an understanding of the environmental context from which the numbers are drawn as well as the relationship between the numbers and the underlying economic phenomena that are the real items of interest.[13]

[13]Choi et al., "Analyzing Foreign Financial Statements," 131.

Financial Ratios
1. Average debt/equity
2. Average interest coverage
3. Average dividend payout
4. Average return on equity
5. Average retention rate
6. Average market price to book value
7. Average market price to cash flow
8. Average market price to sales
Variability Measures
1. Coefficient of variation of operating earnings
2. Coefficient of variation of sales
3. Coefficient of variation of net income
4. Systematic risk (beta)
Nonratio Variables
1. Average growth rate of earnings

Financial Ratios and Systematic Risk

As discussed in Chapter 7, the capital asset pricing model (CAPM) asserts that the relevant risk variable for an asset should be its systematic risk, which is its beta coefficient related to the market portfolio of all risky assets. In efficient markets, a relationship should exist between internal corporate risk variables and market-determined risk variables, such as beta. Numerous studies have tested this relationship by examining internal corporate variables intended to reflect business risk and financial risk.[18] Some of the significant variables (usually five-year averages) included were

Financial Ratios
1. Dividend payout
2. Total debt/total assets
3. Cash flow/total debt
4. Interest coverage
5. Working capital/total assets
6. Current ratio
Variability Measures
1. Variance of operating earnings
2. Coefficient of variation of operating earnings
3. Coefficient of variation of operating profit margins
4. Operating earnings beta (company earnings related to aggregate earnings)
Nonratio Variables
1. Asset size
2. Market value of stock outstanding

Financial Ratios and Bond Ratings

As will be discussed in Chapter 15, four financial services assign quality ratings to bonds on the basis of the issuing company's ability to meet all its obligations related to the bond.

[18]A list of studies in this area appears in the reference section at the end of the chapter.

An AAA or Aaa rating indicates high quality and almost no chance of default, whereas a C rating indicates the bond is already in default. Studies have used financial ratios to predict the rating to be assigned to a bond.[19] The major financial variables considered (again, typically five-year averages) were as follows:

Financial Ratios

1. Long-term debt/total assets
2. Total debt/total capital
3. Net income plus depreciation (cash flow)/long-term senior debt
4. Cash flow/total debt
5. Net income plus interest/interest expense (fixed charge coverage)
6. Cash flow/interest expense
7. Market value of stock/par value of bonds
8. Net operating profit/sales
9. Net income/owners' equity (ROE)
10. Net income/total assets
11. Working capital/sales
12. Sales/net worth (equity turnover)

Variability Measures

1. Coefficient of variation (CV) of net earnings
2. Coefficient of variation of return on assets

Nonratio Variables

1. Subordination of the issue
2. Size of the firm (total assets)
3. Issue size
4. Par value of all publicly traded bonds of the firm

Financial Ratios and Insolvency (Bankruptcy)

Analysts have always been interested in using financial ratios to identify which firms might default on a loan or declare bankruptcy. Several studies have attempted to identify a set of ratios for this purpose.[20] The typical study examines a sample of firms that have declared bankruptcy against a matched sample of firms in the same industry and of comparable size that have not failed. The analysis involves examining a number of financial ratios or cash flow variables expected to reflect declining liquidity for several years (usually five years) prior to the declaration of bankruptcy. The goal is to determine which ratios or set of ratios provide the best predictions of bankruptcy. Some of the models have been able to properly classify more than 80 percent of the firms one year prior to failure, and some achieve high classification results three to five years before failure. The financial ratios typically included in successful models were [21]

---

[19] A list of studies in this area appears in the reference section at the end of the chapter.

[20] A list of studies on this topic appears in the reference section at the end of the chapter.

[21] In addition to the several studies that have used financial ratios to predict bond ratings and failures, other studies have used cash flow variables or a combination of financial ratios and cash flow variables for these predictions, and the results have been quite successful. These studies are listed in the reference section at the end of the chapter. The five ratios designated by an asterisk (*) are the ratios used in the well-known Altman Z-score model following. Edward I. Altman, "Financial Ratios, Discriminant Analysis and the Prediction of Corporate Bankruptcy," *Journal of Finance* 23, no. 4 (September 1968): 589–609.

Financial Ratios

1. Cash flow/total debt
2. Cash flow/long-term debt
3. Sales/total assets*
4. Net income/total assets
5. EBIT/total assets*
6. Total debt/total assets
7. Market value of stock/book value of debt*
8. Working capital/total assets*
9. Retained earnings/total assets*
10. Current ratio
11. Cash/current liabilities
12. Working capital/sales

Limitations of Financial Ratios

We must reinforce the earlier point that you should always consider *relative* financial ratios. In addition, you should be aware of other questions and limitations of financial ratios:

1. Are alternative firms' accounting treatment comparable? As you know from prior accounting courses, there are several generally accepted methods for treating various accounting items, and the alternatives can cause a difference in results for the same event. Therefore, you should check on the accounting treatment of significant items and adjust the values for major differences. This becomes a critical consideration when dealing with non-U.S. firms.
2. How homogeneous is the firm? Many companies have several divisions that operate in different industries. This may make it difficult to derive comparable industry ratios.
3. Are the implied results consistent? It is important to develop a total profile of the firm and not depend on only one set of ratios (for example, internal liquidity ratios). As an example, a firm may be having short-term liquidity problems but be very profitable, and the profitability will eventually alleviate the short-run liquidity problems.
4. Is the ratio within a reasonable range for the industry? As noted on several occasions, you typically want to consider a *range* of appropriate values for the ratio because a value that is either too high or too low for the industry can be a cause for concern.

THE INTERNET *Investments Online*

Many publicly traded companies have Web sites that, among other information, contain financial data. Sometimes complete copies of the firm's annual report and SEC filings are on its home page. Since the focus of this chapter has been Walgreen's financial statements, here are some relevant sites:

www.walgreens.com/hm.html Walgreen's home page, with financial information available through links from this page.

At least three of Walgreen's competitors have Web sites featuring financial information.

www.cvs.com The home page for CVS Pharmacy

www.riteaid.com Rite Aid Corporation's home page

www.longs.com The Web site for Longs Drug Stores

Commerically oriented and government-sponsored databases are available through the Web, too:

www.sec.gov/edgarhp.htm This is the Web address for gaining entrance into the SEC's EDGAR (elec-

THE INTERNET *Investments Online (cont.)*

tronic data gathering, analysis, and retrieval database). Most firms' SEC filings are accessible through EDGAR, including filings for executive compensation, 10-K, and 10-Q forms for over 8,500 firms.

www.hoovers.com Hoover's Online is a commercial source of company-specific information, including financial statements and stock performance. Some data is available for free, including a company profile, news, stock price, and chart of recent stock price performance. It contains links to a number of sources, including the firm's annual report, SEC filings, and earnings per share estimates by Zacks.

www.dnb.com Dun & Bradstreet is a well-known source of financial information. Corporations make use of its business-credit reporting services. D&B publishes industry average financial ratios, which are useful in equity and fixed-income analysis.

Summary

- The overall purpose of financial statement analysis is to help you make decisions on investing in a firm's bonds or stocks. Financial ratios should be examined relative to the economy, the firm's industry, the firm's main competitors, and the firm's past relative ratios.
- The specific ratios can be divided into five categories, depending on the purpose of the analysis: internal liquidity, operating performance, risk analysis, growth analysis, and external market liquidity.
- When analyzing the financial statements for non-U.S. firms, you must consider differences in format and in accounting principles. These differences will cause different values for specific ratios in alternative countries.
- Four major uses of financial ratios are (1) stock valuation, (2) the identification of internal corporate variables affecting a stock's systematic risk (beta), (3) assigning credit quality ratings on bonds, and (4) predicting insolvency (bankruptcy).
- A final caveat: you can envision a large number of potential financial ratios through which to examine almost every possible relationship. The trick is not to come up with more ratios, but to attempt to limit the number of ratios so you can examine them in a meaningful way. This entails an analysis of the ratios over time relative to the economy, the industry, or the past. Any additional effort should be spent on deriving better comparisons for a limited number of ratios that provide insights into the questions of interest to you (for example, the firm's future operating performance or its business and financial risk).

Questions

1. Discuss briefly two decisions that require the analysis of financial statements.
2. Why do analysts use financial ratios rather than the absolute numbers? Give an example.
3. Besides comparing a company's performance to its total industry, discuss what other comparisons should be considered *within* the industry.
4. How might a jewelry store and a grocery store differ in terms of asset turnover and profit margin? Would you expect their return on total assets to differ assuming equal business risk? Discuss.
5. Describe the components of business risk, and discuss how the components affect the variability of operating earnings.
6. Would you expect a steel company or a retail food chain to have greater business risk? Discuss this expectation in terms of the components of business risk.
7. When examining a firm's financial structure, would you be concerned with the firm's business risk? Why or why not?
8. Give an example of how a cash flow ratio might differ from a proportion of debt ratio. Assuming these ratios differ for a firm (for example, the cash flow ratios indicate high financial risk,

while the proportion of debt ratio indicates low risk), which ratios would you follow? Justify your choice.

9. Why is the analysis of growth potential important to the common stockholder? Why is it important to the debt-investor?
10. Discuss the general factors that determine the rate of growth of *any* economic unit.
11. A firm is earning 24 percent on equity and has low business and financial risk. Discuss why you would expect it to have a high or low retention rate.
12. The Orange Company earned 18 percent on equity, whereas the Blue Company earned only 14 percent on equity. Does this mean that Orange will grow faster than Blue? Explain.
13. In terms of the factors that determine market liquidity, why do investors consider real estate to be a relatively illiquid asset?
14. Discuss some internal company factors that would indicate a firm's market liquidity.
15. Select one of the limitations of ratio analysis and indicate why you believe it is a major limitation.

Problems

1. The Shamrock Vegetable Company has the following results:

Net sales	$6,000,000
Net total assets	4,000,000
Depreciation	160,000
Net income	400,000
Long-term debt	2,000,000
Equity	1,160,000
Dividends	160,000

   a. Compute Shamrock's ROE directly. Confirm this using the three components.
   b. Using the ROE computed in part a, what is the expected sustainable growth rate for Shamrock?
   c. Assuming the firm's net profit margin went to 0.04, what would happen to Shamrock's ROE?
   d. Using the ROE in part c, what is the expected sustainable growth rate? What if dividends were only $40,000?

2. Three companies have the following results during the recent period.

	K	L	M
Net profit margin	.04	.06	.10
Total asset turnover	2.20	2.00	1.40
Total assets/equity	2.40	2.20	1.50

   a. Derive for each its return on equity based on the three DuPont components.
   b. Given the following earnings and dividends, compute the sustainable growth rate for each firm.

Earnings/share	2.75	3.00	4.50
Dividends/share	1.25	1.00	1.00

3. Given the following balance sheet, fill in the ratio values for 2000 and discuss how these results compare with both the industry average and Eddies' past performance.

EDDIES ENTERPRISES
CONSOLIDATED BALANCE SHEET:
YEARS ENDED DECEMBER 31, 1999 AND 2000

ASSETS (DOLLARS IN THOUSANDS)

	2000	1999
Cash	$ 100	$ 90
Receivables	220	170
Inventories	330	230
Total current assets	650	490
Property, plant, and equipment	1,850	1,650
Depreciation	350	225
Net properties	1,500	1,425
Intangibles	150	150
Total assets	2,300	2,065

LIABILITIES AND SHAREHOLDERS' EQUITY

	2000	1999
Accounts payable	$ 85	$ 105
Short-term bank notes	125	110
Current portion of long-term debt	75	—
Accruals	65	85
Total current liabilities	350	300
Long-term debt	625	540
Deferred taxes	100	80
Preferred stock (10%, $100 par)	150	150
Common stock ($2 par, 100,000 issued)	200	200
Additional paid-in capital	325	325
Retained earnings	550	470
Common shareholders' equity	1,075	995
Total liabilities and shareholders' equity	2,300	2,065

EDDIES ENTERPRISES
CONSOLIDATED STATEMENT OF INCOME:
YEARS ENDED DECEMBER 31, 1999 AND 2000
(DOLLARS IN THOUSANDS)

	2000	1999
Net sales	$3,500	$2,990
Cost of goods sold	2,135	1,823
Selling, general, and administrative expenses	1,107	974
Operating profit	258	193
Net interest expense	62	54
Income from operations	195	139
Income taxes	66	47
Net income	129	91
Preferred dividends	15	15
Net income available for common shares	114	76
Dividends declared	40	30

	Eddies (2000)	Eddies' Average	Industry Average
Current ratio	________	2.000	2.200
Quick ratio	________	1.000	1.100
Receivables turnover	________	18.000	18.000
Average collection period	________	20.000	21.000
Total asset turnover	________	1.500	1.400
Inventory turnover	________	11.000	12.500
Fixed-asset turnover	________	2.500	2.400
Equity turnover	________	3.200	3.000
Gross profit margin	________	.400	.350
Operating profit margin	________	8.000	7.500
Return on capital	________	.107	.120
Return on equity	________	.118	.126
Return on common equity	________	.128	.135
Debt/equity ratio	________	.600	.500
Debt/total capital ratio	________	.400	.370
Interest coverage	________	4.000	4.500
Fixed charge coverage	________	3.000	4.000
Cash flow/long-term debt	________	.400	.450
Cash flow/total debt	________	.250	.300
Retention rate	________	.350	.400

4. *CFA Examination I (1990)*
(Question 4 is composed of two parts, for a total of 20 minutes.)
The DuPont formula defines the net return on shareholders' equity as a function of the following components:

- operating margin
- asset turnover
- interest burden
- financial leverage
- income tax rate

Using *only* the data in the table shown below:

a. Calculate *each* of the *five* components listed above for 1985 *and* 1989, and calculate the return on equity (ROE) for 1985 *and* 1989, using all of the *five* components. Show calculations. [15 minutes]

b. Briefly discuss the impact of the changes in asset turnover *and* financial leverage on the change in ROE from 1985 to 1989. [5 minutes]

	1985	1989
INCOME STATEMENT DATA		
Revenues	$542	$979
Operating income	38	76
Depreciation and amortization	3	9
Interest expense	3	0
Pretax income	32	67
Income taxes	13	37
Net income after tax	19	30
BALANCE SHEET DATA		
Fixed assets	$ 41	$ 70
Total assets	245	291
Working capital	123	157
Total debt	16	0
Total shareholders' equity	159	220

References

GENERAL

Beaver, William H. *Financial Reporting: An Accounting Revolution.* Englewood Cliffs, N.J.: Prentice-Hall, 1989.

Bernstein, Leopold A., and John J. Wild. *Financial Statement Analysis: Theory, Application, and Interpretation.* 6th ed. Homewood, Ill.: Irwin/McGraw-Hill, 1998.

Chen, Kung H., and Thomas A. Shimerda. "An Empirical Analysis of Useful Financial Ratios." *Financial Management* 10, no. 1 (spring 1981).

Foster, George. *Financial Statement Analysis.* 2d ed. Englewood Cliffs, N.J.: Prentice-Hall, 1978.

Frecka, Thomas J., and Cheng F. Lee. "Generalized Financial Ratio Adjustment Processes and Their Implications." *Journal of Accounting Research* 27, no. 1 (spring 1983).

Gombola, Michael J., and Edward Ketz. "Financial Ratio Patterns in Retail and Manufacturing Organizations." *Financial Management* 12, no. 2 (summer 1983).

Heckel, Kenneth S., and Joshua Livnat. *Cash Flow and Security Analysis.* 2d ed. Burr Ridge, Ill.: Business One Irwin, 1996.

Helfert, Erich A. *Techniques of Financial Analysis.* 8th ed. New York: McGraw-Hill, 1993.

Higgins, Robert C. *Analysis for Financial Management.* 4th ed. Chicago: Irwin, 1995.

Johnson, W. Bruce. "The Cross-Sectional Stability of Financial Ratio Patterns." *Journal of Financial and Quantitative Analysis* 14, no. 5 (December 1979).

Lev, Baruch, and S. Ramu Thiagarajan. "Fundamental Information Analysis." *Journal of Accounting Research* 37, no. 2 (autumn 1993).

White, Gerald I., Ashwinpaul Sondhi, and Dov Fried. *The Analysis and Use of Financial Statements.* 2d ed. New York: Wiley, 1998.

ANALYSIS OF INTERNATIONAL FINANCIAL STATEMENTS

Arpan, Jeffrey S., and Lee H. Rodebaugh. *International Accounting and Multinational Enterprises.* New York: Wiley, 1981.

Choi, Frederick D. S., ed. *Multinational Accounting: A Research Framework for the Eighties.* Ann Arbor, Mich.: UMI Research Press, 1981.

Choi, Frederick D. S., and Vinod B. Bavishi. "Diversity in Multinational Accounting." *Financial Executive* 50, no. 7 (August 1982).

Choi, Frederick D. S., H. Hino, S. K. Min, S. O. Nam, J. Ujiie, and A. I. Stonehill. "Analyzing Foreign Financial Statements: The Use and Misuse of International Ratio Analysis." *Journal of International Business Studies* (spring–summer 1983).

Choi, Frederick D. S., and Gerhard G. Mueller. *International Accounting.* Englewood Cliffs, N.J.: Prentice-Hall, 1984.

Choi, Frederick D. S., and Gerhard G. Mueller. *Frontiers of International Accounting: An Anthology.* Ann Arbor, Mich.: UMI Research Press, 1985.

Evans, Thomas G., Martin E. Taylor, and Oscar Holzmann. *International Accounting and Reporting.* New York: Macmillan, 1985.

Fitzgerald, R., A. Stickler, and T. Watts. *International Survey of Accounting Principles and Practices.* Scarborough, Ontario: Price Waterhouse International, 1979.

Gray, S. J., J. C. Shaw, and L. B. McSweeney. "Accounting Standards and Multinational Corporations." *Journal of International Business Studies* 12, no. 1 (spring–summer 1981).

Nair, R. D., and Werner G. Frank. "The Impact of Disclosure and Measurement Practices in International Accounting Classifications." *Accounting Review* 55, no. 3 (July 1980).

FINANCIAL RATIOS AND STOCK VALUATION MODELS

Babcock, Guilford. "The Concept of Sustainable Growth." *Financial Analysts Journal* 26, no. 3 (May–June 1970).

Beaver, William, and Dale Morse. "What Determines Price–Earnings Ratios?" *Financial Analysts Journal* 34, no. 4 (July–August 1978).

Copeland, Tom, Tim Koller, and Jack Murrin. *Valuation: Measuring and Managing the Value of Companies,* 2d ed. New York: John Wiley & Co., 1996.

Damodaran, Aswath. *Damodaran on Valuation.* New York: John Wiley & Co., 1994.

Estep, Tony. "Security Analysis and Stock Selection: Turning Financial Information into Return Forecasts." *Financial Analysts Journal* 43, no. 4 (July–August 1987).

Fairfield, Patricia M. "P/E, P/B and the Present Value of Future Dividends." *Financial Analysts Journal* 50, no. 4 (July–August 1994).

Farrell, James L. "The Dividend Discount Model: A Primer." *Financial Analysts Journal* 41, no. 6 (November–December 1985).

Malkiel, Burton G., and John G. Cragg. "Expectations and the Structure of Share Prices." *American Economic Review* 60, no. 4 (September 1970).

Palepu, Krishna G., Victor L. Bernard, and Paul M. Healy. *Business Analysis and Valuation.* Cincinnati, Ohio: South-Western Publishing Co., 1996.

Wilcox, Jarrod W. "The P/B-ROE Valuation Model." *Financial Analysts Journal* 40, no. 1 (January–February 1984).

FINANCIAL RATIOS AND SYSTEMATIC RISK (BETA)

Beaver, William H., Paul Kettler, and Myron Scholes. "The Association between Market-Determined and Accounting-Determined Risk Measures." *Accounting Review* 45, no. 4 (October 1970).

Gahlon, James M., and James A. Gentry. "On the Relationship between Systematic Risk and the Degrees of Operating and Financial Leverage." *Financial Management* 11, no. 2 (summer 1982).

Mandelker, Gershon M., and S. Ghon Rhee. "The Impact of the Degrees of Operating and Financial Leverage on the Systematic Risk of Common Stock." *Journal of Financial and Quantitative Analysis* 19, no. 1 (March 1984).

Rosenberg, Barr. "Prediction of Common Stock Investment Risk." *Journal of Portfolio Management* 11, no. 1 (fall 1984).

Rosenberg, Barr. "Prediction of Common Stock Betas." *Journal of Portfolio Management* 11, no. 2 (winter 1985).

Thompson, Donald J., II. "Sources of Systematic Risk in Common Stocks." *Journal of Business* 49, no. 2 (April 1976).

FINANCIAL RATIOS AND BOND RATINGS

Ang, James S., and A. Kiritkumar. "Bond Rating Methods: Comparison and Validation." *Journal of Finance* 30, no. 2 (May 1975).

Fisher, Lawrence. "Determinants of Risk Premiums on Corporate Bonds." *Journal of Political Economy* 67, no. 3 (June 1959).

Gentry, James A., David T. Whitford, and Paul Newbold. "Predicting Industrial Bond Ratings with a Probit Model and Funds Flow Components." *Financial Review* 23, no. 3 (August 1988).

Kaplan, Robert S., and Gabriel Urwitz. "Statistical Models of Bond Ratings: A Methodological Inquiry." *Journal of Business* 52, no. 2 (April 1979).

Pinches, George E., and Kent A. Mingo. "The Role of Subordination and Industrial Bond Ratings." *Journal of Finance* 30, no. 1 (March 1975).

Standard and Poor's Corporation. "Corporation Bond Ratings: An Overview." 1978.

FINANCIAL RATIOS AND CORPORATE BANKRUPTCY

Altman, Edward I. "Financial Ratios, Discriminant Analysis, and the Prediction of Corporate Bankruptcy." *Journal of Finance* 23, no. 4 (September 1968).

Altman, Edward I. *Corporate Financial Distress and Bankruptcy.* 2d ed. New York: Wiley, 1993.

Altman, Edward I., Robert G. Haldeman, and P. Narayanan. "Zeta Analysis: A New Model to Identify Bankruptcy Risk of Corporations." *Journal of Banking and Finance* 1, no. 2 (June 1977).

Aziz, A., and G. H. Lawson. "Cash Flow Reporting and Financial Distress Models: Testing of Hypothesis." *Financial Management* 18, no. 1 (spring 1989).

Beaver, William H. "Alternative Accounting Measures as Predictors of Failure." *Accounting Review* 43, no. 1 (January 1968).

Beaver, William H. "Financial Ratios as Predictors of Failure." *Empirical Research in Accounting: Selected Studies,* 1966, supplement to vol. 4, *Journal of Accounting Research.*

Beaver, William H. "Market Prices, Financial Ratios, and the Prediction of Failure." *Journal of Accounting Research* 6, no. 2 (autumn 1968).

Casey, Cornelius, and Norman Bartczak. "Using Operating Cash Flow Data to Predict Financial Distress: Some Extensions." *Journal of Accounting Research* 23, no. 1 (spring 1985).

Collins, R. B. "An Empirical Comparison of Bankruptcy Prediction Models." *Financial Management* 9, no. 2 (summer 1980).

Dumbolena, I. G., and J. M. Shulman. "A Primary Rule for Detecting Bankruptcy: Watch the Cash." *Financial Analysts Journal* 44, no. 5 (September–October 1988).

Gentry, James A., Paul Newbold, and David T. Whitford. "Classifying Bankrupt Firms with Funds Flow Components." *Journal of Accounting Research* 23, no. 1 (spring 1985).

Gentry, James A., Paul Newbold, and David T. Whitford. "Predicting Bankruptcy: If Cash Flow's Not the Bottom Line, What Is?" *Financial Analysts Journal* 41, no. 5 (September–October 1985).

Gombola, M. F., M. E. Haskins, J. E. Katz, and D. D. Williams. "Cash Flow in Bankruptcy Prediction." *Financial Management* 16, no. 4 (winter 1987).

Largay, J. A., and C. P. Stickney. "Cash Flows Ratio Analysis and the W. T. Grant Company Bankruptcy." *Financial Analysts Journal* 36, no. 4 (July–August 1980).

Menash, Yaw M. "The Differential Bankruptcy Predictive Ability of Specific Price Level Adjustments: Some Empirical Evidence." *Accounting Review* 58, no. 2 (April 1983).

Ohlson, J. A. "Financial Ratios and the Probabalistic Prediction of Bankruptcy." *Journal of Accounting Research* 18, no. 2 (spring 1980).

Reilly, Frank K. "Using Cash Flows and Financial Ratios to Predict Bankruptcies." In *Analyzing Investment Opportunities in Distressed and Bankrupt Companies.* Charlottesville, Va.: The Institute of Chartered Financial Analysts, 1991.

Wilcox, Jarrod W. "A Prediction of Business Failure Using Accounting Data." *Empirical Research in Accounting: Selected Studies,* 1973, supplement to vol. 11, *Journal of Accounting Research.*

13 AN INTRODUCTION TO SECURITY VALUATION

After you read this chapter, you should be able to answer the following questions:

- What are the two major approaches to the investment process?
- What are the specifics and logic of the top-down (three-step) approach?
- What empirical evidence supports the usefulness of the top-down approach?
- When valuing an asset, what are the required inputs?
- After you have valued an asset, what is the investment decision process?
- How do you determine the value of bonds?
- How do you determine the value of preferred stock?
- What are the two primary approaches to the valuation of common stock?
- Under what conditions is it best to use the present value of cash flow approach for valuing a company's equity?
- Under what conditions is it best to use the relative valuation techniques for valuing a company's equity?
- How do you apply the discounted cash flow valuation approach and what are the major discounted cash flow valuation techniques?
- What is the dividend discount model (DDM) and what is its logic?
- What is the effect of the assumptions of the DDM when valuing a growth company?
- How do you apply the DDM to the valuation of a firm that is expected to experience temporary supernormal growth?
- How do you apply the present value of operating cash-flow technique?
- How do you apply the present value of free cash flow to equity technique?
- How do you apply the relative valuation approach?
- What are the major relative valuation ratios?
- How can you use the DDM to develop an earnings multiplier model?
- What does the DDM model imply are the factors that determine a stock's P/E ratio?
- What two general variables need to be estimated in any valuation approach?
- How do you estimate the major inputs to the stock valuation models: (1) the required rate of return and (2) the expected growth rate of earnings and dividends?
- What additional factors must be considered when estimating the required rate of return and growth rate for a foreign security?

At the start of this book, we defined an investment as a commitment of funds for a period of time to derive a rate of return that would compensate the investor for the time during which the funds are invested, for the expected rate of inflation during the investment horizon, and for the uncertainty involved. From this definition, we know that the first step in making an investment is determining your required rate of return.

Once you have determined this rate, some investment alternatives, such as savings accounts and T-bills, are fairly easy to evaluate because they provide stated cash flows. Most investments have expected cash flows and a stated market price (for example, common stock), and you must evaluate the investment to determine if its market price is consistent with your required return. To do this, you must estimate the value of the security based on its expected cash flows and your required rate of return. This is the process of estimating the value of an asset. After you have completed estimating a security's intrinsic value, you compare this estimated intrinsic value to the prevailing market price to decide whether you want to buy the security or not.

This **investment decision process** is similar to the process you follow when deciding on a corporate investment or when shopping for clothes, a stereo, or a car. In each case, you examine the item and decide how much it is worth to you (its value). If the price equals its estimated value or is less, you would buy it. The same technique applies to securities except that the determination of a security's value is more formal.

We start our investigation of security valuation by discussing the **valuation process**. There are two general approaches to the valuation process: (1) the top-down, three-step approach or (2) the bottom-up, stock valuation, stockpicking approach. Both of these approaches can be implemented by either fundamentalists or technicians. The difference between the two approaches is the perceived importance of economic and industry influence on individual firms and stocks.

Advocates of the top-down, three-step approach believe that both the economy/market and the industry effect have a significant impact on the total returns for individual stocks. In contrast, those who employ the bottom-up, stockpicking approach contend that it is possible to find stocks that are undervalued relative to their market price, and these stocks will provide superior returns *regardless* of the market and industry outlook.

Both of these approaches have numerous supporters, and advocates of both approaches have been quite successful.[1] In this book, we advocate and present the top-down, three-step approach because of its logic and empirical support. Although we believe that a portfolio manager or an investor can be successful using the bottom-up approach, we believe that it is more difficult to be successful because these stockpickers are ignoring substantial information from the market and the firm's industry.

Although we know that the value of a security is determined by its quality and profit potential, we also believe that the economic environment and the performance of a firm's industry influence the value of a security and its rate of return. Because of the importance of these economic and industry factors, we present an overview of the valuation process that describes these influences and explains how they can be incorporated into the analysis of security value. Subsequently, we describe the theory of value and emphasize the factors that affect the value of securities.

Next, we apply these valuation concepts to the valuation of different assets—bonds, preferred stock, and common stock. In this section, we show how the valuation models help investors calculate how much they should pay for these assets. In the final section, we emphasize the estimation of the variables that affect value (the required rate of return and the expected rate of growth). We conclude with a discussion of additional factors that must be considered when we extend our analysis to the valuation of international securities.

AN OVERVIEW OF THE VALUATION PROCESS

Psychologists suggest that the success or failure of an individual can be caused as much by his or her social, economic, and family environment as by genetic gifts. Extending this idea

[1]For the history and selection process of a legendary stockpicker, see Robert G. Hagstrom, Jr., *The Warren Buffett Way* (New York: Wiley, 1994), or Roger Lowenstein, *Buffett: The Making of an American Capitalist* (New York: Random House, 1995).

to the valuation of securities means we should consider a firm's economic and industry environment during the valuation process. Regardless of the qualities or capabilities of a firm and its management, the economic and industry environment will have a major influence on the success of a firm and the realized rate of return on its stock.

As an example, assume you own shares of the strongest and most successful firm producing home furnishings. If you own the shares during a strong economic expansion, the sales and earnings of the firm will increase and your rate of return on the stock should be quite high. In contrast, if you own the same stock during a major economic recession, the sales and earnings of this firm (and probably most or all of the firms in the industry) would likely experience a decline, and the price of its stock would be stable or decline. Therefore, when assessing the future value of a security, it is necessary to analyze the outlook for the aggregate economy, the security markets, and the firm's specific industry.

The valuation process is like the chicken-and-egg dilemma. Do you start by analyzing the macroeconomy and various industries before individual stocks, or do you begin with individual securities and gradually combine these firms into industries and the industries into the entire economy? For reasons discussed in the next section, we contend that the discussion should begin with an analysis of aggregate economies and overall securities markets and progress to different industries with a global perspective. Only after a thorough analysis of a global industry are you in a position to properly evaluate the securities issued by individual firms within the better industries. Thus, we recommend a three-step, top-down valuation process in which you first examine the influence of the general economy on all firms and the security markets, then analyze the prospects for various global industries with the best outlooks in this economic environment, and finally turn to the analysis of individual firms in the preferred industries and to the common stock of these firms. Figure 13.1 indicates the procedure recommended.

WHY A THREE-STEP VALUATION PROCESS?

General Economic Influences

Monetary and fiscal policy measures enacted by various agencies of national governments influence the aggregate economies of those countries. The resulting economic conditions influence all industries and companies within the economies.

Fiscal policy initiatives, such as tax credits or tax cuts, can encourage spending, whereas additional taxes on income, gasoline, cigarettes, and liquor can discourage spending. Increases or decreases in government spending on defense, on unemployment insurance or retraining programs, or on highways also influence the general economy. All such policies influence the business environment for firms that rely directly on such government expenditures. In addition, we know that government spending has a strong *multiplier effect.* For example, increases in road building increase the demand for earthmoving equipment and concrete materials. As a result, in addition to construction workers, the employees in those industries that supply the equipment and materials have more to spend on consumer goods, which raises the demand for consumer goods, which affects another set of suppliers.

Monetary policy produces similar economic changes. A restrictive monetary policy that reduces the growth rate of the money supply reduces the supply of funds for working capital and expansion for all businesses. Alternatively, a restrictive monetary policy that targets interest rates would raise market interest rates and therefore firms' costs, and make it more expensive for individuals to finance home mortgages and the purchase of other durable goods, such as autos and appliances. Monetary policy therefore affects all segments of an economy and that economy's relationship with other economies.

FIGURE 13.1 OVERVIEW OF THE INVESTMENT PROCESS

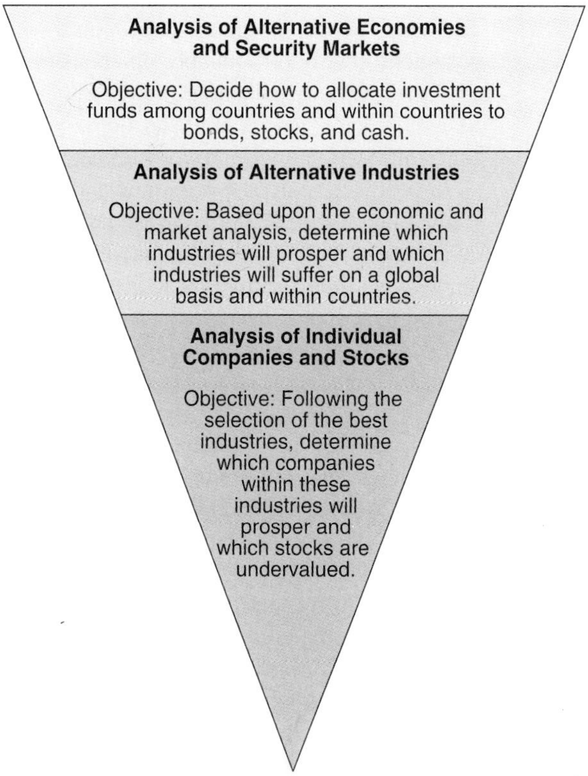
Analysis of Alternative Economies and Security Markets
Objective: Decide how to allocate investment funds among countries and within countries to bonds, stocks, and cash.
Analysis of Alternative Industries
Objective: Based upon the economic and market analysis, determine which industries will prosper and which industries will suffer on a global basis and within countries.
Analysis of Individual Companies and Stocks
Objective: Following the selection of the best industries, determine which companies within these industries will prosper and which stocks are undervalued.

Any economic analysis requires the consideration of inflation. As we have discussed, inflation causes differences between real and nominal interest rates and changes the spending and savings behavior of consumers and corporations. In addition, unexpected changes in the rate of inflation make it difficult for firms to plan, which inhibits growth and innovation. Beyond the impact on the domestic economy, differential inflation and interest rates influence the trade balance between countries and the exchange rate for currencies.

In addition to monetary and fiscal policy actions, such events as war, political upheavals in foreign countries, or international monetary devaluations produce changes in the business environment that add to the uncertainty of sales and earnings expectations and therefore the risk premium required by investors. For example, the political uncertainty in Russia during 1995–1999 caused a significant increase in the risk premium for investors in Russia and a subsequent reduction in investment and spending in Russia. In contrast, the end of apartheid in South Africa and its open election in 1994 were viewed as a positive event and led to a significant increase in economic activity in the country. Similarly, the peace accord in Northern Ireland in 1996 caused a major influx of investment and tourist dollars.

In short, it is difficult to conceive of any industry or company that can avoid the impact of macroeconomic developments that affect the total economy. Because aggregate economic events have a profound effect on all industries and companies within these industries, these macroeconomic factors should be considered before industries are analyzed.

Taking a global portfolio perspective, the asset allocation for a country within a global portfolio will be affected by its economic outlook. If a recession is imminent in a country, you would expect a negative impact on its security prices. Because of these economic expectations, investors would be apprehensive about investing in most industries in the country. Given these expectations, the country will be **underweighted** in portfolios relative to its weight based on its market value. Further, given these pessimistic expectations, any funds invested in the country would be directed to low-risk sectors of the economy.

In contrast, optimistic economic and stock market outlooks for a given country should lead an investor to increase the overall allocation to this country (**overweight** the country compared to its weights determined by its relative market value).[2] After allocating funds among countries, the investor looks for outstanding industries in each country. This search for the best industries is enhanced by the economic analysis because the future performance of an industry depends on the country's economic outlook *and* the industry's expected relationship to the economy during the particular phase of the business cycle.

INDUSTRY INFLUENCES

The second step in the valuation process is to identify those industries that will prosper or suffer in the long run or during the expected near-term economic environment. Examples of conditions that affect specific industries are strikes within a major producing country, import or export quotas or taxes, a worldwide shortage or an excess supply of a resource, or government-imposed regulations on an industry.

You should remember that alternative industries react to economic changes at different points in the business cycle. For example, firms typically increase capital expenditures when they are operating at full capacity at the peak of the economic cycle. Therefore, industries that provide plant and equipment will typically be affected toward the end of a cycle. In addition, alternative industries have different responses to the business cycle. As an example, cyclical industries, such as steel or autos, typically do much better than the aggregate economy during expansions, but they suffer more during contractions. In contrast, noncyclical industries, such as retail food, would not experience a significant decline during a recession, but also would not experience a strong increase during an economic expansion.

Another factor that will have a differential effect on industries is demographics. For example, it is widely recognized that the U.S. population is weighted toward "baby boomers" entering their late 50s and that there has been a large surge in the number of citizens over age 65. These two groups have heavy demand for second homes and medical care and the industries related to these segments (e.g., home furnishings and pharmaceuticals).

Firms that sell in international markets can benefit or suffer as foreign economies shift. An industry with a substantial worldwide market might experience low demand in its domestic market, but benefit from growing demand in its international market. As an example, much of the growth for Coca-Cola and Pepsi and the fast-food chains, such as McDonald's and Burger King, has come from international expansion in Europe and the Far East.

In general, an industry's prospects within the global business environment will determine how well or poorly an individual firm will fare, so industry analysis should precede company analysis. Few companies perform well in a poor industry, so even the best company in a poor industry is a bad prospect for investment. For example, poor sales and earnings in the farm equipment industry during the late 1980s had a negative impact on Deere and Co., a well-managed firm and probably the best firm in its industry. Though Deere per-

[2] We will show an example of a global asset allocation in Chapter 14.

formed better than other firms in the industry (some went bankrupt), its earnings and stock performance still fell far short of its past performance, and the company did poorly compared to firms in most other industries.

COMPANY ANALYSIS

After determining that an industry's outlook is good, an investor can analyze and compare individual firms' performance within the entire industry using financial ratios and cash flow values. As we discussed in Chapter 12, many financial ratios for firms are valid only when they are compared to the performance of their industries.

You undertake company analysis to identify the best company in a promising industry. This involves examining a firm's past performance, but more important, its future prospects. After you understand the firm and its outlook, you can determine its value. In the final step, you compare this estimated "intrinsic" value to the firm's market price and decide whether its stock or bonds are good investments.

Your final goal is to select the best stock or bonds within a desirable industry and include it in your portfolio based on its relationship (correlation) with all other assets in your portfolio. As we discuss in more detail in Chapter 20, the best stock for investment purposes may not necessarily be issued by the best company because the stock of the finest company in an industry may be overpriced, which would cause it to be a poor investment. You cannot know whether a security is undervalued or overvalued until you have analyzed the company, estimated its intrinsic value, and compared your estimated intrinsic value to the market price of the stock.

DOES THE THREE-STEP PROCESS WORK?

Although you might agree with the logic of the three-step investment process, you might wonder how well this process works in selecting investments. The results of several academic studies have supported this technique. First, studies indicated that most changes in an individual firm's *earnings* could be attributed to changes in aggregate corporate earnings and changes in the firm's industry, with the aggregate earnings changes being more important. Although the relative influence of the general economy and the industry on a firm's earnings varied among individual firms, the results consistently demonstrated that the economic environment had a significant effect on firm earnings.

Second, several studies have found a relationship between aggregate stock prices and various economic series, such as employment, income, or production. These results supported the view that a relationship exists between stock prices and economic expansions and contractions.[3]

Third, an analysis of the relationship between *rates of return* for the aggregate stock market, alternative industries, and individual stocks showed that most of the changes in rates of return for individual stocks could be explained by changes in the rates of return for the aggregate stock market and the stock's industry. Although the importance of the market effect tended to decline over time and the significance of the industry effect varied among industries, the combined market–industry effect on an individual stock's rate of return was still important.[4]

These results from academic studies support the use of the three-step investment process. This investment decision approach is consistent with the discussion in Chapter 2,

---

[3]For a further discussion of this and empirical support, see Geoffrey Moore and John P. Cullity, "Security Markets and Business Cycles" in *The Financial Analysts Handbook*, 2d ed., ed. Sumner N. Levine (Homewood, Ill.: Dow Jones–Irwin, 1988); and Jeremy Siegel, "Does It Pay Stock Investors to Forecast the Business Cycle?" *Journal of Portfolio Management* 18, no. 1 (fall 1991): 27–34.

[4]For an analysis, see Stephen L. Meyers, "A Re-Examination of Market and Industry Factors in Stock Price Behavior," *Journal of Finance* 28, no. 3 (June 1973): 695–705.

which contended that the most important decision is the asset allocation decision.[5] The asset allocation specifies: (1) what proportion of your portfolio will be invested in various nations' economies; (2) within each country, how you will divide your assets among stocks, bonds, or other assets; and (3) your industry selections, based on which industries are expected to prosper in the projected economic environment. We provide an example of global asset allocation in Chapter 14.

Now that we have described and justified the three-step process, we need to consider the theory of valuation. The application of this theory allows us to compute estimated values for the market, for alternative industries, and for individual firms and stocks. Finally, we compare these estimated values to current market prices and decide whether we want to make particular investments.

THEORY OF VALUATION

You may recall from your studies in accounting, economics, or corporate finance that the value of an asset is the present value of its expected returns. Specifically, you expect an asset to provide a stream of returns during the period of time you own it. To convert this estimated stream of returns to a value for the security, you must discount this stream at your required rate of return. This process of valuation requires estimates of (1) the stream of expected returns and (2) the required rate of return on the investment.

Stream of Expected Returns (Cash Flows)

An estimate of the expected returns from an investment encompasses not only the size but also the form, time pattern, and the uncertainty of returns, which affect the required rate of return.

FORM OF RETURNS The returns from an investment can take many forms, including earnings, cash flows, dividends, interest payments, or capital gains (increases in value) during a period. We will consider several alternative valuation techniques that use different forms of returns. As an example, one common stock valuation model applies a multiplier to a firm's earnings, whereas another valuation model computes the present value of a firm's operating cash flows, and a third model estimates the present value of dividend payments. Returns or cash flows can come in many forms, and you must consider all of them to evaluate an investment accurately.

TIME PATTERN AND GROWTH RATE OF RETURNS You cannot calculate an accurate value for a security unless you can estimate when you will receive the returns or cash flows. Because money has a time value, you must know the time pattern and growth rate of returns from an investment. This knowledge will make it possible to properly value the stream of returns relative to alternative investments with a different time pattern and growth rate of returns or cash flows.

---

[5]Authors who examine this question generally refer to it as market timing. Studies on this topic include Robert F. Vandell and Jerry L. Stevens, "Evidence of Superior Performance from Timing," *Journal of Portfolio Management* 15, no. 3 (spring 1989): 38–42; and Jerry Wagner, Steve Shellans, and Richard Paul, "Market Timing Works Where It Matters Most . . . in the Real World," *Journal of Portfolio Management* 18, no. 4 (summer 1992): 86–90. The classic study that established the importance of asset allocation is Gary P. Brinson, L. R. Hood, and G. L. Beebower, "Determinants of Portfolio Performance," *Financial Analysts Journal* 42, no. 4 (July–August 1986): 35–43; followed by Gary P. Brinson, Brian D. Singer, and G. L. Beebower, "Determinants of Portfolio Performance II: An Update," *Financial Analysts Journal* 47, no. 3 (May–June 1991): 40–48. A subsequent well-regarded application of these concepts by Abby J. Cohen is contained in Abby J. Cohen, "Economic Forecasts and the Asset Allocation Decision," in *Economic Analysis for Investment Professionals* (Charlottesville, Va.: AIMR, November 1996).

REQUIRED RATE OF RETURN

UNCERTAINTY OF RETURNS (CASH FLOWS) You will recall from Chapter 1 that the required rate of return on an investment is determined by (1) the economy's real risk-free rate of return, plus (2) the expected rate of inflation during the holding period, plus (3) a risk premium that is determined by the uncertainty of returns. All investments are affected by the risk-free rate and the expected rate of inflation because these two variables determine the nominal risk-free rate. Therefore, the factor that causes a difference in required rates of return is the risk premium for alternative investments. In turn, this risk premium depends on the uncertainty of returns or cash flows from an investment.

We can identify the sources of the uncertainty of returns by the internal characteristics of assets or by market-determined factors. Earlier, we subdivided the internal characteristics for a firm into business risk (BR), financial risk (FR), liquidity risk (LR), exchange rate risk (ERR), and country risk (CR). The market-determined risk measures are the systematic risk of the asset, its beta, or its multiple APT factors.

INVESTMENT DECISION PROCESS: A COMPARISON OF ESTIMATED VALUES AND MARKET PRICES

To ensure that you receive your required return on an investment, you must estimate the intrinsic value of the investment at your required rate of return, and then compare this estimated intrinsic value to the prevailing market price. You should not buy an investment if its market price exceeds your estimated value because the difference will prevent you from receiving your required rate of return on the investment. In contrast, if the estimated value of the investment exceeds the market price, you should buy the investment. In summary:

If Estimated Value > Market Price, Buy

If Estimated Value < Market Price, Don't Buy

For example, assume you read about a firm that produces athletic shoes and its stock is listed on the NYSE. Using one of the valuation models we will discuss, and making estimates of earnings, cash flow, and growth based on the company's annual report and other information, you estimate the company's stock value using your required rate of return as \$20 a share. After estimating this value, you look in the paper and see that the stock is currently being traded at \$15 a share. You would want to buy this stock because you think it is worth \$20 a share and you can buy it for \$15 a share. In contrast, if the current market price were \$25 a share, you would not want to buy the stock because based upon your valuation, it is overvalued.

The theory of value provides a common framework for the valuation of all investments. Different applications of this theory generate different estimated values for alternative investments because of the different payment streams and characteristics of the securities. The interest and principal payments on a bond differ substantially from the expected dividends and future selling price for a common stock. The initial discussion that follows applies the discounted cash flow method to bonds, preferred stock, and common stock. This presentation demonstrates that the same basic model is useful across a range of investments. Subsequently, because of the difficulty in estimating the value of common stock, we consider two general approaches and numerous techniques for the valuation of stock.

VALUATION OF ALTERNATIVE INVESTMENTS

VALUATION OF BONDS

Calculating the value of bonds is relatively easy because the size and time pattern of cash flows from the bond over its life are known. A bond typically promises

1. Interest payments every six months equal to one-half the coupon rate times the face value of the bond
2. The payment of the principal on the bond's maturity date

As an example, in 2000 a \$10,000 bond due in 2015 with a 10 percent coupon will pay \$500 every six months for its 15-year life. In addition, the bond issuer promises to pay the \$10,000 principal at maturity in 2015. Therefore, assuming the bond issuer does not default, the investor knows what payments (cash flows) will be made and when they will be made.

Applying the valuation theory, which states that the value of any asset is the present value of its cash flows, the value of the bond is the present value of the interest payments, which we can think of as an annuity of \$500 every six months for 15 years, and the present value of the principal payment, which in this case is the present value of \$10,000 in 15 years. The only unknown for this asset (assuming the borrower does not default) is the required rate of return that should be used to discount the expected stream of returns (cash flows). If the prevailing nominal risk-free rate is 9 percent, and the investor requires a 1 percent risk premium on this bond because there is some probability of default, the required rate of return would be 10 percent.

The present value of the interest payments is an annuity for 30 periods (15 years every six months) at one-half the required return (5 percent):[6]

$$\$500 \times 15.3725 = \$7,686$$

(present value of interest payments at 10 percent)

The present value of the principal is likewise discounted at 5 percent for 30 periods:[7]

$$\$10,000 \times 0.2314 = \$2,314$$

(present value of the principal payment at 10 percent)

This can be summarized as follows:

Present value of interest payments \$500 × 15.3725	= \$ 7,686
Present value of principal payment \$10,000 × 0.2314 =	2,314
Total value of bond at 10 percent	= \$10,000

This is the amount that an investor should be willing to pay for this bond, assuming that the required rate of return on a bond of this risk class is 10 percent. If the market price of the bond is above this value, the investor should not buy it because the promised yield to maturity at this higher price will be less than the investor's required rate of return.

Alternatively, assuming an investor requires a 12 percent return on this bond, its value would be:

\$500 × 13.7648 =	\$6,882
\$10,000 × 0.1741 =	1,741
Total value of bond at 12 percent =	\$8,623

This example shows that if you want a higher rate of return, you will not pay as much for an asset; that is, a given stream of cash flows has a lower value to you. As before, you would compare this computed value to the market price of the bond to determine whether you should invest in it.[8]

---

[6]The annuity factors and present value factors are contained in Appendix C at the end of the book.

[7]If we used annual compounding, this would be 0.239 rather than 0.2314. We use semiannual compounding because it is consistent with the interest payments and is used in practice.

[8]To test your mastery of bond valuation, check that if the required rate of return were 8 percent, the value of this bond would be \$11,729.

VALUATION OF PREFERRED STOCK

The owner of a preferred stock receives a promise to pay a stated dividend, usually each quarter, for an infinite period. Preferred stock is a **perpetuity** because it has no maturity. As was true with a bond, stated payments are made on specified dates although the issuer of this stock does not have the same legal obligation to pay investors as do issuers of bonds. Payments are made only after the firm meets its bond interest payments. Because this reduced legal obligation increases the uncertainty of returns, investors should require a higher rate of return on a firm's preferred stock than on its bonds. Although this differential in required return should exist in theory, it generally does not exist in practice because of the tax treatment accorded dividends paid to corporations. As described in Chapter 3, 80 percent of intercompany preferred dividends are tax-exempt, making the effective tax rate on them about 6.8 percent, assuming a corporate tax rate of 34 percent. This tax advantage stimulates the demand for preferred stocks by corporations and, because of this demand, the yield on them has generally been below that on the highest-grade corporate bonds.

Because preferred stock is a perpetuity, its value is simply the stated annual dividend divided by the required rate of return on preferred stock (k_p) as follows:

$$V = \frac{\text{Dividend}}{k_p}$$

Assume a preferred stock has a \$100 par value and a dividend of \$8 a year. Because of the expected rate of inflation, the uncertainty of the dividend payment, and the tax advantage to you as a corporate investor, your required rate of return on this stock is 9 percent. Therefore, the value of this preferred stock to you is

$$V = \frac{\$8}{0.09}$$
$$= \$88.89$$

Given this estimated value, you would inquire about the current market price to decide whether you would want to buy this preferred stock. If the current market price is \$95 you would decide against a purchase, whereas if it is \$80, you would buy the stock. Also, given the market price of preferred stock, you can derive its promised yield. Assuming a current market price of \$85, the promised yield would be

$$k_p = \frac{\text{Dividend}}{\text{Price}} = \frac{\$8}{\$85.00} = 0.0941$$

APPROACHES TO THE VALUATION OF COMMON STOCK

Because of the complexity and importance of valuing common stock, various techniques for accomplishing this task have been devised over time. These techniques fall into one of two general approaches: (1) the discounted cash-flow valuation techniques, where the value of the stock is estimated based upon the present value of some measure of cash flow, including dividends, operating cash flow, and free cash flow; and (2) the relative valuation techniques, where the value of a stock is estimated based upon its current price relative to variables considered to be significant to valuation, such as earnings, cash flow, book value, or sales. Figure 13.2 provides a visual presentation of the alternative approaches and specific techniques.

An important point is that *both of these approaches and all of these valuation techniques have several common factors.* First, all of them are significantly affected by the investor's *required rate of return* on the stock because this rate becomes the discount rate or is a major component of the discount rate. Second, all of them are affected by *the estimated growth rate of the variable* used in the valuation technique—for example, dividends, earnings, cash

FIGURE 13.2 COMMON STOCK VALUATION APPROACHES AND SPECIFIC TECHNIQUES

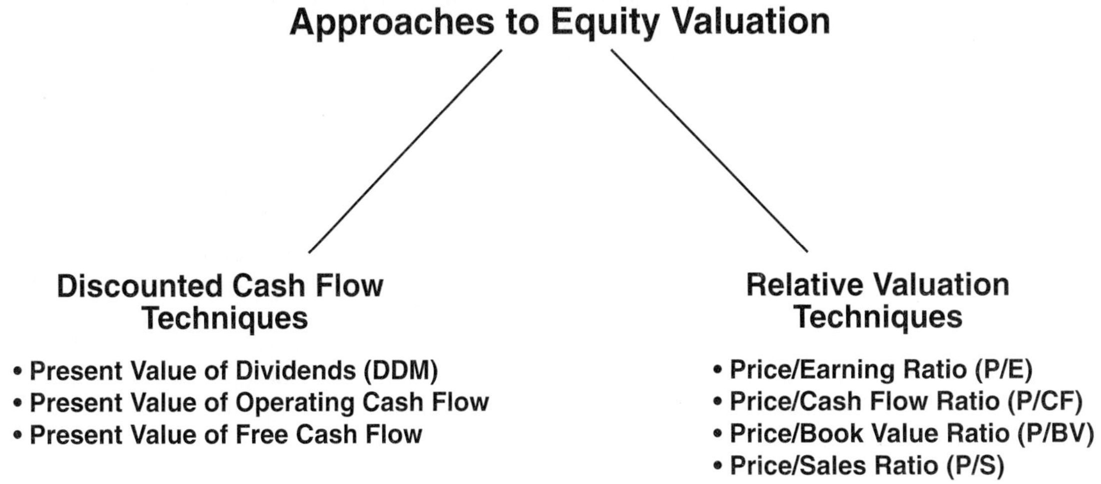
Approaches to Equity Valuation
Discounted Cash Flow Techniques
• Present Value of Dividends (DDM)
• Present Value of Operating Cash Flow
• Present Value of Free Cash Flow
Relative Valuation Techniques
• Price/Earning Ratio (P/E)
• Price/Cash Flow Ratio (P/CF)
• Price/Book Value Ratio (P/BV)
• Price/Sales Ratio (P/S)

flow, or sales. As noted in the efficient-market discussion, both of these critical variables must be *estimated.* As a result, different analysts using the same valuation techniques will derive different estimates of value for a stock because they have different estimates for these critical variable inputs.

The following discussion of equity valuation techniques considers the specific models and the theoretical and practical strengths and weaknesses of each of them. Notably, the authors' intent is to present these two approaches as complementary, *not* competitive, approaches—that is, you should learn and use both of them.

Why and When to Use the Discounted Cash-Flow Valuation Approach

These discounted cash-flow valuation techniques are obvious choices for valuation because they are the epitome of how we describe value—that is, the present value of expected cash flows. The major difference between the alternative techniques is how one specifies cash flow—that is, the measure of cash flow used.

The cleanest and most straightforward measure of cash flow is *dividends* because these are clearly cash flows that go directly to the investor, which implies that you should use *the cost of equity* as the discount rate. However, this dividend technique is difficult to apply to firms that do not pay dividends during periods of high growth, or that currently pay very limited dividends because they have high rate of return investment alternatives available. On the other hand, an advantage is that the reduced form of the dividend discount model (DDM) is very useful when discussing valuation for a stable, mature entity where the assumption of relatively constant growth for the long term is appropriate.

The second specification of cash flow is the *operating cash flow,* which is generally described as cash flows after direct costs (cost of goods and S, G & A expenses) and before any payments to capital suppliers. Because we are dealing with the cash flows available for all capital suppliers, the discount rate employed is the firm's *weighted average cost of capital* (WACC). This is a very useful model when comparing firms with diverse capital structures because you determine the value of the total firm and then subtract the value of the firm's debt obligations to arrive at a value for the firm's equity.

The third cash-flow measure is *free cash flow to equity,* which is a measure of cash flows available to the equity holder after payments to debt holders and after allowing for expenditures to maintain the firm's asset base. Because these are cash flows available to equity owners, the appropriate discount rate is the firm's *cost of equity.*

Beyond being theoretically correct, these models allow a substantial amount of flexibility in terms of changes in sales and expenses that implies changing growth rates over time. Once you understand how to compute each measure of cash flow, you can estimate cash flow for each year by constructing a pro-forma statement for each year or you can estimate overall growth rates for the alternative cash-flow values as we will demonstrate with the DDM.

A potential difficulty with these cash-flow techniques is that they are very dependent on the two significant inputs—(1) the growth rates of cash flows (both the *rate* of growth and the *duration* of growth), and (2) the estimate of the discount rate. As we will show in several instances, a small change in either of these values can have a significant impact on the estimated value. This is the problem when using any theoretical model: Everyone knows and uses the same model, but it is the *inputs* that are critical—GIGO: garbage in, garbage out!

Why and When to Use the Relative Valuation Techniques

As noted, a potential problem with the discounted cash-flow valuation models is that it is possible to derive intrinsic values that are substantially above or below prevailing prices depending on how you adjust your estimated inputs to the prevailing environment. An advantage of the relative valuation techniques is that they provide information about how the market is *currently* valuing stock at several levels—that is, the aggregate market, alternative industries, and individual stocks within industries. Following this chapter, which provides the background for these two approaches, we will demonstrate the alternative relative valuation ratios for the aggregate market, for an industry relative to the market, and for an individual company relative to its industry and relative to the aggregate market.

The good news is that this relative valuation approach provides information on how the market is currently valuing securities. The bad news is that it is providing information on current valuation. The point is, the relative valuation approach provides this information on current valuation, but it does not provide guidance on whether these current valuations are appropriate—that is, *all* valuations at a point in time could be too high or too low. For example, assume that the market becomes significantly overvalued. If you compare the value for an industry or stock to the very overvalued market, you might contend based on such a comparison that an industry is undervalued relative to the market. Unfortunately, your judgment may be wrong because of the benchmark you are using—that is, you might be comparing a fully valued industry to a *very* overvalued market.

Put another way, the relative valuation techniques are appropriate to consider under two conditions:

1. You have a good set of comparable entities—that is, either comparable industries or companies that are similar in terms of industry, size, and, it is hoped, risk.
2. The aggregate market is not at a valuation extreme—that is, it is not either seriously undervalued or overvalued.

Discounted Cash-Flow Valuation Techniques

All of these valuation techniques are based on the basic valuation model, which asserts that the value of an asset is the present value of its expected future cash flows as follows:

$$V_j = \sum_{t=1}^{n} \frac{CF_t}{(1+k)^t}$$

where:

V_j = value of stock j
n = life of the asset
CF_t = cash flow in period t
k = the discount rate that is equal to the investors' required rate of return for asset j, which is determined by the uncertainty (risk) of the stock's cash flows

As noted, the specific cash flows used will differ between techniques. They range from dividends (the best-known model) to operating cash flow and free cash flow. We begin with a fairly detailed presentation of the present-value-of-dividend model, referred to as the dividend discount model (DDM), because it is intuitively appealing and is the best-known model. Also, its general approach is similar to the approach used for implementing other discounted cash-flow models.

THE DIVIDEND DISCOUNT MODEL (DDM) The **dividend discount model** assumes that the value of a share of common stock is the present value of all future dividends as follows:[9]

$$\begin{aligned} V_j &= \frac{D_1}{(1+k)} + \frac{D_2}{(1+k)^2} + \frac{D_3}{(1+k)^3} \\ &\quad + \ldots + \frac{D_\infty}{(1+k)^\infty} \\ &= \sum_{t=1}^{n} \frac{D_t}{(1+k)^t} \end{aligned}$$

where:

V_j = value of common stock *j*
D_t = dividend during period *t*
k = required rate of return on stock *j*

An obvious question is: What happens when the stock is not held for an infinite period? A sale of the stock at the end of Year 2 would imply the following formula:

$$V_j = \frac{D_1}{(1+k)} + \frac{D_2}{(1+k)^2} + \frac{SP_{j2}}{(1+k)^2}$$

The value is equal to the two dividend payments during Years 1 and 2 plus the sale price (*SP*) for stock *j* at the end of Year 2. The expected selling price of stock *j* at the end of Year 2 (SP_{j2}) is simply the value of all remaining dividend payments.

$$SP_{j2} = \frac{D_3}{(1+k)} + \frac{D_4}{(1+k)^2} + \ldots + \frac{D_\infty}{(1+k)^\infty}$$

If SP_{j2} is discounted back to the present by $1/(1+k)^2$, this equation becomes

$$\begin{aligned} PV(SP_{j2}) &= \frac{\dfrac{D_3}{(1+k)} + \dfrac{D_4}{(1+k)^2} + \ldots + \dfrac{D_\infty}{(1+k)^\infty}}{(1+k)^2} \\ &= \frac{D_3}{(1+k)^3} + \frac{D_4}{(1+k)^4} + \ldots + \frac{D_\infty}{(1+k)^\infty} \end{aligned}$$

which is simply an extension of the original equation. Whenever the stock is sold, its value (that is, the sale price at that time) will be the present value of all future dividends. When

[9]This model was initially set forth in J. B. Williams, *The Theory of Investment Value* (Cambridge, MA: Harvard, 1938). It was subsequently reintroduced and expanded by Myron J. Gordon, *The Investment, Financing, and Valuation of the Corporation* (Homewood, Ill.: Irwin, 1962).

this ending value is discounted back to the present, you are back to the original dividend discount model.

What about stocks that pay no dividends? Again, the concept is the same, except that some of the early dividend payments are zero. Notably, there are expectations that *at some point* the firm will start paying dividends. If investors lacked such an expectation, nobody would be willing to buy the security. It would have zero value. A firm with a nondividend-paying stock is reinvesting its capital in very profitable projects rather than paying current dividends so that its earnings and dividend stream will be larger and grow faster in the future. In this case, we would apply the DDM as:

$$V_j = \frac{D_1}{(1+k)} + \frac{D_2}{(1+k)^2} + \frac{D_3}{(1+k)^3} + \ldots + \frac{D}{(1+k)^\infty}$$

where: $D_1 = 0$; $D_2 = 0$.

The investor expects that when the firm starts paying dividends in Period 3, it will be a large initial amount and dividends will grow faster than those of a comparable stock that had paid out dividends. The stock has value because of these *future* dividends. We will apply this model to several cases having different holding periods that will show you how it works.

One-Year Holding Period Assume an investor wants to buy the stock, hold it for one year, and then sell it. To determine the value of the stock—that is, how much the investor should be willing to pay for it—using the DDM, we must estimate the dividend to be received during the period, the expected sale price at the end of the holding period, and the investor's required rate of return.

To estimate the dividend for the coming year, adjust the current dividend for expectations regarding the change in the dividend during the year. Assume the company we are analyzing earned \$2.50 a share last year and paid a dividend of \$1 a share. Assume further the firm has been fairly consistent in maintaining this 40 percent payout over time. The consensus of financial analysts is that the firm will earn about \$2.75 during the coming year and will raise its dividend to \$1.10 per share.

A crucial estimate is the expected selling price for the stock a year from now. You can estimate this expected selling price by either of two alternative procedures. In the first, you can apply the dividend discount model where you estimate the specific dividend payments for a number of years into the future and calculate the value of the stock from these estimates. In the second procedure, the earnings multiplier model, you multiply the future expected earnings for the stock by an earnings multiple, which you likewise estimate, to find an expected sale price. We will discuss the earnings multiple model in a later section of the chapter. For now, assume you prefer the DDM. Applying this model, you project the sale price of this stock a year from now to be \$22.

Finally, you must determine the required rate of return. As discussed before, the nominal risk-free rate is determined by the real risk-free rate and the expected rate of inflation. A good proxy for this rate is the promised yield on one-year government bonds because your investment horizon (expected holding period) is one year. You estimate the stock's risk premium by comparing its risk level to the risk of other potential investments. In later chapters, we discuss how you can estimate this risk. For the moment, assume that one-year government bonds are yielding 10 percent, and you believe that a 4 percent risk premium over the yield of these bonds is appropriate for this stock. Thus, you specify a required rate of return of 14 percent.

In summary, you have estimated the dividend at \$1.10 (payable at year-end), an ending sale price of \$22, and a required rate of return of 14 percent. Given these inputs, you would estimate the value of this stock as follows:

$$
\begin{aligned}
V_1 &= \frac{\$1.10}{(1+0.14)} + \frac{\$22.00}{(1+0.14)} \\
&= \frac{1.10}{1.14} + \frac{22.00}{1.14} \\
&= 0.96 + 19.30 \\
&= \$20.26
\end{aligned}
$$

Note that we have not mentioned the current market price of the stock. This is because the market price is not relevant to you as an investor except as a comparison to the independently derived value based on your estimates of the relevant variables. Once we have calculated the stock's value as \$20.26, we can compare it to the market price and apply the investment decision rule: If the stock's market price is more than \$20.26, do not buy; if it is equal to or less than \$20.26, buy.

Multiple-Year Holding Period If you anticipate holding the stock for several years and then selling it, the valuation estimate is harder. You must forecast several future dividend payments and estimate the sale price of the stock several years in the future.

The difficulty with estimating future dividend payments is that the future stream can have numerous forms. The exact estimate of the future dividends depends on two projections. The first is your outlook for earnings growth because earnings are the source of dividends. The second projection is the firm's dividend policy, which can take several forms. A firm can have a constant percent payout of earnings each year, which implies a change in dividend each year, or the firm could follow a step pattern in which it increases the dividend rate by a constant dollar amount each year or every two or three years. The easiest dividend policy to analyze is one where the firm enjoys a constant growth rate in earnings and maintains a constant dividend payout. This set of assumptions implies that the dividend stream will experience a constant growth rate that is equal to the earnings growth rate.

Assume the expected holding period is three years, and you estimate the following dividend payments at the end of each year:

Year 1	\$1.10/share
Year 2	\$1.20/share
Year 3	\$1.35/share

The next estimate is the expected sale price (*SP*) for the stock three years in the future. Again, if we use the DDM for this estimate, you would need to project the dividend growth pattern for this stock beginning three years from now. Assume an estimated sale price using the DDM of \$34.

The final estimate is the required rate of return on this stock during this period. Assuming the 14 percent required rate is still appropriate, the value of this stock is

$$
\begin{aligned}
V &= \frac{1.10}{(1 + 0.14)^1} + \frac{1.20}{(1 + 0.14)^2} + \frac{1.35}{(1 + 0.14)^3} + \frac{34.00}{(1 + 0.14)^3} \\
&= \frac{1.10}{(1.14)} + \frac{1.20}{(1.30)} + \frac{1.35}{(1.4815)} + \frac{34.00}{(1.4815)} \\
&= 0.96 + 0.92 + 0.91 + 22.95 \\
&= \$25.74
\end{aligned}
$$

Again, to make an investment decision you would compare this estimated value for the stock to its current market price to determine whether you should buy.

At this point, you should recognize that the valuation procedure discussed here is similar to that used in corporate finance when making investment decisions, except that the cash flows are from dividends instead of returns to an investment project. Also, rather than estimating the scrap value or salvage value of a corporate asset, we are estimating the ending sale price for the stock. Finally, rather than discounting cash flows using the firm's cost of capital, we use the individual's required rate of return on the company's equity. In both cases, we are looking for excess present value, which means that the present value of expected cash inflows—that is, the estimated intrinsic value of the asset—exceeds the present value of cash outflows, which is the market price of the asset.

Infinite Period Model We can extend the multiperiod model by extending our estimates of dividends 5, 10, or 15 years into the future. The benefits derived from these extensions would be minimal, however, and you would quickly become bored with this exercise. Instead, we will move to the infinite period dividend discount model, which assumes investors estimate future dividend payments for an infinite number of periods.

Needless to say, this is a formidable task! We must make some simplifying assumptions about this future stream of dividends to make the task viable. The easiest assumption is that *the future dividend stream will grow at a constant rate for an infinite period.* This is a rather heroic assumption in many instances, but where it does hold, we can use the model to value individual stocks as well as the aggregate market and alternative industries. This model is generalized as follows:

$$V_j = \frac{D_0(1 + g)}{(1 + k)} + \frac{D_0(1 + g)^2}{(1 + k)^2} + \dots + \frac{D_0(1 + g)^n}{(1 + k)^n}$$

where:

V_j = the value of stock j
D_0 = the dividend payment in the current period
g = the constant growth rate of dividends
k = the required rate of return on stock j
n = the number of periods, which we assume to be infinite

In the appendix to this chapter, we show that with certain assumptions, this infinite period constant growth rate model can be simplified to the following expression:

$$V_j = \frac{D_1}{k - g}$$

You will probably recognize this formula as one that is widely used in corporate finance to estimate the cost of equity capital for the firm—that is, $k = D/V + g$.

To use this model for valuation, you must estimate (1) the required rate of return (k) and (2) the expected growth rate of dividends (g). After estimating g, it is a simple matter to estimate D_1, because it is the current dividend (D_0) times ($1 + g$).

Consider the example of a stock with a current dividend of $1 a share, which you expect to rise to $1.09 next year. You believe that, over the long run, this company's earnings and dividends will continue to grow at 9 percent; therefore, your estimate of *g* is 0.09. For the long run, you expect the rate of inflation to decline, so you set your long-run required rate of return on this stock at 13 percent; your estimate of *k* is 0.13. To summarize the relevant estimates:

$$g = 0.09$$
$$k = 0.13$$
$$D_1 = 1.09\ (\$1.00 \times 1.09)$$
$$V = \frac{1.09}{0.13 - 0.09} = \frac{1.09}{0.04} = \$27.25$$

A small change in any of the original estimates will have a large impact on *V* as shown by the following examples:

1. $g = 0.09$; $k = 0.14$; $D_1 = \$1.09$. (We assume an increase in *k*.)

$$V = \frac{\$1.09}{0.14 - 0.09} = \frac{\$1.09}{0.05} = \$21.80$$

2. $g = 0.10$; $k = 0.13$; $D_1 = \$1.10$. (We assume an increase in *g*.)

$$V = \frac{\$1.10}{0.13 - 0.10} = \frac{\$1.10}{0.03} = \$36.67$$

These examples show that as small a change as 1 percent in either *g* or *k* produces a large difference in the estimated value of the stock. The crucial relationship that determines the value of the stock is the *spread between the required rate of return (k) and the expected growth rate of dividends (g)*. Anything that causes a decline in the spread will cause an increase in the computed value, whereas any increase in the spread will decrease the computed value.

Infinite Period DDM and Growth Companies

As noted in the appendix, the infinite period DDM has the following assumptions:

1. Dividends grow at a constant rate.
2. The constant growth rate will continue for an infinite period.
3. The required rate of return *(k) is greater than the infinite growth rate (g)*. If it is not, the model gives meaningless results because the denominator becomes negative.

What is the effect of these assumptions if you want to use this model to value the stock of growth companies, such as Intel, Merck, Microsoft, McDonald's, and Wal-Mart? **Growth**

companies are firms that have the opportunities and abilities to earn rates of return on investments that are consistently above their required rates of return.[10] You will recall from corporate finance that the required rate of return for a corporation is its weighted average cost of capital (WACC). An example might be Intel, which has a WACC of about 12 percent, but is currently earning about 25 percent on its invested capital. Therefore, we would consider Intel a growth company. To exploit these outstanding investment opportunities, these firms generally retain a high percentage of earnings for reinvestment, and their earnings will grow faster than those of the typical firm. You will recall from the discussion in Chapter 12 that a firm's substainable growth is a function of its retention rate and its return on equity (ROE). Notably, as discussed below, the earnings growth pattern for these growth companies is inconsistent with the assumptions of the infinite period DDM.

First, the infinite period DDM assumes dividends will grow at a constant rate for an infinite period. This assumption seldom holds for companies currently growing at above average rates. As an example, Intel and Wal-Mart have both grown at rates in excess of 30 percent a year for several years. It is unlikely that they can maintain such extreme rates of growth because of the inability to continue earning the ROEs implied by this growth for an infinite period in an economy where other firms will compete with them for these high rates of return.

Second, during the periods when these firms experience abnormally high rates of growth, their rates of growth probably exceed their required rates of return. There is *no* automatic relationship between growth and risk; a high-growth company is not necessarily a high-risk company. In fact, a firm growing at a high *constant rate* would have lower risk (less uncertainty) than a low-growth firm with an unstable earnings pattern.

In summary, some firms experience periods of abnormally high rates of growth for some finite periods of time. The infinite period DDM cannot be used to value these true growth firms because these high-growth conditions are temporary and therefore inconsistent with the assumptions of the DDM. In the following section we discuss how to supplement the DDM to value a firm with temporary supernormal growth. In Chapter 20 we will discuss additional models used for estimating the stock value of growth companies.

Valuation with Temporary Supernormal Growth

Thus far, we have considered how to value a firm with different growth rates for short periods of time (one to three years) and how to value a stock using a model that assumes a constant growth rate for an infinite period. It was noted that the assumptions of the model make it impossible to use the infinite period constant growth model to value true growth companies. A company cannot permanently maintain a growth rate higher than its required rate of return because competition will eventually enter this apparently lucrative business, which will reduce the firm's profit margins and therefore its ROE and growth rate. Therefore, after a few years of exceptional growth—i.e., a period of temporary supernormal growth—a firm's growth rate is expected to decline. Eventually its growth rate is expected to stabilize at a constant level consistent with the assumptions of the infinite period DDM.

To determine the value of a temporary supernormal growth company, you must combine the previous models. In analyzing the initial years of exceptional growth, you examine each year individually. If the company is expected to have two or three stages of supernormal growth, you must examine each year during these stages of growth. When the firm's growth rate stabilizes at a rate below the required rate of return, you can compute the

[10]Growth companies are discussed in Ezra Salomon, *The Theory of Financial Management* (New York: Columbia University Press, 1963); and Merton Miller and Franco Modigliani, "Dividend Policy, Growth, and the Valuation of Shares," *Journal of Business* 34, no. 4 (October 1961): 411–433. Models to value growth companies are discussed in Chapter 20.

remaining value of the firm assuming constant growth using the DDM and discount this lump-sum constant growth value back to the present. The technique should become clear as you work through the following example.

The Bourke Company has a current dividend (D_0) of \$2 a share. The following are the expected annual growth rates for dividends.

Year	Dividend Growth Rate
1–3	25%
4–6	20
7–9	15
10 on	9

The required rate of return for the stock (the company's cost of equity) is 14 percent. Therefore, the value equation becomes

$$V_i = \frac{2.00(1.25)}{1.14} + \frac{2.00(1.25)^2}{(1.14)^2} + \frac{2.00(1.25)^3}{(1.14)^3}$$
$$+ \frac{2.00(1.25)^3(1.20)}{(1.14)^4} + \frac{2.00(1.25)^3(1.20)^2}{(1.14)^5}$$
$$+ \frac{2.00(1.25)^3(1.20)^3}{(1.14)^6} + \frac{2.00(1.25)^3(1.20)^3(1.15)}{(1.14)^7}$$
$$+ \frac{200.(1.25)^3(1.20)^3(1.15)^2}{(1.14)^8} + \frac{2.00(1.25)^3(1.20)^3(1.15)^3}{(1.14)^9}$$
$$+ \frac{\dfrac{2.00(1.25)^3(1.20)^3(1.15)^3(1.09)}{(0.14 - 0.09)}}{(1.14)^9}$$

The computations in Table 13.1 indicate that the total value of the stock is \$94.36. As before, you would compare this estimate of intrinsic value to the market price of the stock when deciding whether to purchase the stock. The difficult part of the valuation is estimating the supernormal growth rates and determining *how long* each of the growth rates will last.

To summarize this section, the initial present value of cash flow stock valuation model considered was the dividend discount model (DDM). Following an explanation of the basic model and the derivation of its reduced form, we noted that the infinite period DDM cannot be applied to the valuation of stock for growth companies because the abnormally high growth rate of earnings for the growth company is inconsistent with the assumptions of the infinite period constant growth DDM model. Subsequently we modified the DDM model to evaluate companies with temporary supernormal growth. In the following sections we discuss the other present value of cash flow techniques assuming a similar set of scenarios.

Present Value of Operating Cash Flows

In this model, you are deriving the value of the total firm because you are discounting the total operating cash flows prior to the payment of interest to the debt holders. Also, because you are discounting the total firm's operating cash flow, you would use the firm's weighted average cost of capital (WACC) as your discount rate. Therefore, once you estimate the

TABLE 13.1

COMPUTATION OF VALUE FOR THE STOCK OF A COMPANY WITH TEMPORARY SUPERNORMAL GROWTH

Year	Dividend	Discount Factor (14 percent)	Present Value
1	$ 2.50	0.8772	$ 2.193
2	3.12	0.7695	2.401
3	3.91	0.6750	2.639
4	4.69	0.5921	2.777
5	5.63	0.5194	2.924
6	6.76	0.4556	3.080
7	7.77	0.3996	3.105
8	8.94	0.3506	3.134
9	10.28	0.3075[b]	3.161
10	11.21		
	$224.20[a]	0.3075[b]	68.941
		Total value =	$94.355

[a]Value of dividend stream for Year 10 and all future dividends (that is, $11.21/(0.14 − 0.09) = $224.20).

[b]The discount factor is the ninth-year factor because the valuation of the remaining stream is made at the end of Year 9 to reflect the dividend in Year 10 and all future dividends.

value of the total firm, you subtract the value of debt, assuming your goal is to estimate the value of the firm's equity. The total value of the firm is equal to:

$$V_j = \sum_{t=1}^{n} \frac{OCF_t}{(1 + WACC_j)^t}$$

where:

V_j = value of firm j
n = number of periods assumed to be infinite
OCF_t = the firm's operating cash flow in period t. The specification of operating cash flow will be discussed in Chapter 20.
$WACC_j$ = firm j's weighted average cost of capital. The computation of the firm's WACC will be discussed in Chapter 20 800

Similar to the process with the DDM, it is possible to envision this as a model that requires estimates for an infinite period. Alternatively, if you are dealing with a mature firm whereby its operating cash flows have reached a stage of stable growth, you can adapt the infinite period constant growth DDM model as follows:

$$V_j = \frac{OCF_1}{WACC_j - g_{OCF}}$$

where:

OCF_1 = operating cash flow in period 1 equal to $OCF_0(1 + g_{OCF})$
g_{OCF} = long-term constant growth rate of operating cash flow

Alternatively, assuming that the firm is expected to experience several different rates of growth for OCF, these estimates can be divided into three or four stages, as demonstrated with the temporary supernormal dividend growth model. Similar to the dividend model, the analyst must estimate the *rate* of growth and the *duration* of growth for each of these periods of supernormal growth as follows:

Year	OCF Growth Rate
1–4	20%
5–7	16
8–10	12
11 on	7

Therefore, the calculations would estimate the specific OCFs for each year through Year 10 based on the expected growth rates, but you would use the infinite growth model estimate when the growth rate reached stability after Year 10. As noted, after determining the value of the total firm V_j, you must subtract the value of all nonequity items, including accounts payable, total interest-bearing debt, deferred taxes, and preferred stock, to arrive at the estimated value of the firm's equity. This calculation will be demonstrated in Chapter 20.

Present Value of Free Cash Flows to Equity

The third discounted cash-flow technique deals with "free" cash flows to equity, which would be derived *after* operating cash flows have been adjusted for debt payments (interest and principle) and after deducting capital expenditures necessary to maintain the firm's asset base. Also, these cash flows precede dividend payments to the common stockholder. Such cash flows are referred to as "free" because they are what is left after meeting all obligations to other capital suppliers (debt and preferred stock) and after providing the funds needed to maintain the firm's asset base.

Notably, because these are cash flows available to equity owners, the discount rate used is the firm's cost of equity (k) rather than the firm's WACC.

$$V_j = \sum_{t=1}^{n} \frac{FCF_t}{(1 + k_j)^t}$$

where:

V_j = value of the stock of firm j
n = number of periods assumed to be infinite
FCF_t = the firm's free cash flow in period t. The specification of free cash flow will be discussed in Chapter 20

Again, how an analyst would implement this general model depends upon the firm's position in its life cycle. That is, if the firm is expected to experience stable growth, analysts can use the infinite growth model. In contrast, if the firm is expected to experience a period of temporary supernormal growth, analysts should use the multistage growth model similar to the process used with dividends and for operating cash flow.

RELATIVE VALUATION TECHNIQUES

In contrast to the various discounted cash-flow techniques that attempt to estimate a specific value for a stock based on its estimated growth rates and its discount rate, the relative valuation techniques implicitly contend that it is possible to determine the value of an economic entity (i.e., the market, an industry, or a company) by comparing it to similar entities on the basis of several relative ratios that compare its stock price to relevant variables that affect a stock's value, such as earnings, cash flow, book value, and sales. Therefore, in this section, we discuss the following relative valuation ratios: (1) price/earnings (P/E), (2) price/cash flow (P/CF), (3) price/book value (P/BV), and price/sales (P/S). We begin with the P/E ratio, also referred to as the earnings multiplier model, because it is the most popular relative valuation ratio. In addition we will show that the P/E ratio can be directly related to the DDM in a manner that indicates the variables that affect the P/E ratio.

Earnings Multiplier Model

As noted, many investors prefer to estimate the value of common stock using an **earnings multiplier model**. The reasoning for this approach recalls the basic concept that the value of any investment is the present value of future returns. In the case of common stocks, the returns that investors are entitled to receive are the net earnings of the firm. Therefore, one way investors can estimate value is by determining how many dollars they are willing to pay for a dollar of expected earnings (typically represented by the estimated earnings during the following 12-month period). For example, if investors are willing to pay 10 times expected earnings, they would value a stock they expect to earn \$2 a share during the following year at \$20. You can compute the prevailing earnings multiplier, also referred to as the **price/earnings (P/E) ratio**, as follows:

$$\text{Earnings Multiplier} = \text{Price/Earnings Ratio}$$
$$= \frac{\text{Current Market Price}}{\text{Expected 12-Month Earnings}}$$

This computation of the current earnings multiplier (P/E ratio) indicates the prevailing attitude of investors toward a stock's value. Investors must decide if they agree with the prevailing P/E ratio (that is, is the earnings multiplier too high or too low?) based upon how it compares to the P/E ratio for the aggregate market, for the firm's industry, and for similar firms and stocks.

To answer this question, we must consider what influences the earnings multiplier (P/E ratio) over time. For example, over time the aggregate stock market P/E ratio, as represented by the S&P 400 Index, has varied from about 6 times earnings to about 25 times earnings.[11] The infinite period dividend discount model can be used to indicate the variables that should determine the value of the P/E ratio as follows:[12]

$$P_i = \frac{D_1}{k - g}$$

If we divide both sides of the equation by E_1 (expected earnings during the next 12 months), the result is

$$\frac{P_i}{E_1} = \frac{D_1/E_1}{k - g}$$

[11]When computing historical P/E ratios, the practice is to use earnings for the past 12 months rather than expected earnings. Although this will influence the level, it demonstrates the changes in the P/E ratio over time. Although it is appropriate to use historical P/E ratios for past comparison, we strongly believe that investment decisions should emphasize future P/E ratios that use *expected* earnings.

[12]In this formulation of the model we use P rather than V (that is, the value is stated as the estimated price of the stock). Although the factors that determine the P/E are the same for growth companies, this formula cannot be used to estimate a specific value because these firms do not have dividends and the $(k - g)$ assumptions don't apply.

Thus, the P/E ratio is determined by

1. The *expected* dividend payout ratio (dividends divided by earnings)
2. The *estimated* required rate of return on the stock (k)
3. The *expected* growth rate of dividends for the stock (g)

As an example, if we assume a stock has an expected dividend payout of 50 percent, a required rate of return of 12 percent, and an expected growth rate for dividends of 8 percent, this would imply the following:

$$D/E = 0.50; k = 0.12; g = 0.08$$

$$\begin{aligned} P/E &= \frac{0.50}{0.12 - 0.08} \\ &= 0.50/0.04 \\ &= 12.5 \end{aligned}$$

Again, a small change in either k or g or both will have a large impact on the earnings multiplier, as shown in the following three examples.

1. D/E = 0.50; $k = 0.13$; $g = 0.08$. (In this example, we assume an increase in k.)

$$\begin{aligned} P/E &= \frac{0.50}{0.13 - 0.08} \\ &= \frac{0.50}{0.05} \\ &= 10 \end{aligned}$$

2. D/E = 0.50; $k = 0.12$; $g = 0.09$. (In this example, we assume an increase in g and the original k.)

$$\begin{aligned} P/E &= \frac{0.50}{0.12 - 0.09} \\ &= \frac{0.50}{0.03} \\ &= 16.7 \end{aligned}$$

3. D/E = 0.50; $k = 0.11$; $g = 0.09$. (In this example, we assume a fairly optimistic scenario where k declines to 11 percent and there is an increase in the expected growth rate of dividends to 9 percent).

$$\begin{aligned} P/E &= \frac{0.50}{0.11 - 0.09} \\ &= \frac{0.50}{0.02} \\ &= 25 \end{aligned}$$

As before, *the spread between k and g is the main determinant of the size of the P/E ratio.* Although the dividend payout ratio has an impact, we are generally referring to a firm's long-run target payout, which is typically rather stable with little effect on year-to-year changes in the P/E ratio (earnings multiplier).

After estimating the earnings multiple, you would apply it to your estimate of earnings for the next year (E_1) to arrive at an estimated value. In turn, E_1 is based on the earnings for the current year (E_0) and your expected growth rate of earnings. Using these two estimates, you would compute an estimated value of the stock and compare this estimated value to its market price.

Consider the following estimates for an example firm:

$$\begin{aligned} D/E &= 0.50 \\ k &= 0.12 \\ g &= 0.09 \\ E_0 &= \$2.00 \end{aligned}$$

Using these estimates, you would compute an earnings multiple of:

$$P/E = \frac{0.50}{0.12 - 0.09} = \frac{0.50}{0.03} = 16.7$$

Given current earnings (E_0) of \$2.00 and a g of 9 percent, you would expect E_1 to be \$2.18. Therefore, you would estimate the value (price) of the stock as

$$\begin{aligned} V &= 16.7 \times \$2.18 \\ &= \$36.41 \end{aligned}$$

As before, you would compare this estimated value of the stock to its current market price to decide whether you should invest in it.

The Price/Cash Flow Ratio

The growth in popularity of this relative valuation technique can be traced to concern over the propensity of some firms to manipulate earnings per share, whereas cash flow values are generally less prone to manipulation. Also, as noted, cash flow values are important in fundamental valuation (when computing the present value of cash flow), and they are critical when doing credit analysis where "cash is king." The price to cash flow ratio is computed as follows:

$$P/CF_j = \frac{P_t}{CF_{t+1}}$$

where:

P/CF_j = the price/cash flow ratio for firm j
P_t = the price of the stock in period t
CF_{t+1} = the expected cash flow per share for firm j

Regarding what variables affect this ratio, the factors are similar to the P/E ratio. Specifically, the main variables should be the expected growth rate of the cash flow variable used and the risk of the stock as indicated by the uncertainty or variability of the cash flow series over time. The specific cash flow measure used is typically EBITDA, but it will vary depending upon the nature of the company and industry and which cash flow specification (for example, operating cash flow or free cash flow) is the best measure of performance for this industry. An appropriate ratio can also be affected by the firm's capital structure.

THE PRICE/BOOK VALUE RATIO

The price/book value (P/BV) ratio has been widely used for many years by analysts in the banking industry as a measure of relative value. The book value of a bank is typically considered a good indicator of intrinsic value because most bank assets, such as bonds and commercial loans, have a value equal to book value. This ratio gained in popularity and credibility as a relative valuation technique for all types of firms based upon a study by Fama and French that indicated a significant inverse relationship between P/BV ratios and excess rates of return for a cross section of stocks.[13] The P/BV ratio is specified as follows:

$$P/BV_j = \frac{P_t}{BV_{t+1}}$$

where:

P/BV_j = the price/book value ratio for firm j
P_t = the price of the stock in period t
BV_{t+1} = the estimated end-of-year book value per share for firm j

As with other relative valuation ratios, it is important to match the current price with the estimated book value that is expected to prevail at the end of the year. The difficulty is that this future book value is not generally available. One can derive an estimate based upon the historical growth rate for the series or use the growth rate implied by the sustainable growth formula: g = (ROE) (Retention Rate).

THE PRICE/SALES RATIO

The price/sales (P/S) ratio has a volatile history. It was a favorite of Phillip Fisher, a well-known money manager in the late 1950s, his son, and others.[14] Recently the P/S ratio has been suggested as useful by Martin Leibowitz, a widely admired stock and bond portfolio manager.[15] These advocates consider this ratio meaningful and useful for two reasons. First, they believe that strong and consistent sales growth is a requirement for a growth company. Although they note the importance of an above-average profit margin, they contend that *the growth process must begin with sales.* Second, given all the data in the balance sheet and income statement, sales information is subject to less manipulation than any other data item. The specific P/S ratio is:

$$P/S_j = \frac{P_t}{S_{t+1}}$$

where:

P/S_j = the price to sales ratio for firm j
P_t = the price of the stock in period t
S_{t+1} = the expected sales per share for firm j

---

[13] Eugene Fama and Kenneth French, "The Cross Section of Expected Returns," *Journal of Finance* 47, no. 2 (June 1992). This study was discussed in Chapter 7.

[14] Phillip A. Fisher, *Common Stock and Uncommon Profits,* rev. ed. (Woodside, Calif.: PSR Publications, 1984); Kenneth L. Fisher, *Super Stocks* (Homewood, Ill.: Dow Jones–Irwin, 1984); and A. J. Senchak, Jr., and John D. Martin, "The Relative Performance of the PSR and PER Investment Strategies," *Financial Analysts Journal* 43, no. 2 (March–April, 1987): 46–56.

[15] Martin L. Leibowitz, *Sales Driven Franchise Value* (Charlottesville, Va.: The Research Foundation of the Institute of Chartered Financial Analysts, 1997).

Again, it is important to match the current stock price with the firm's expected sales per share, which may be difficult to derive for a large cross section of stocks. Two caveats are relevant to the price to sales ratio. First, it is important to recognize that this particular relative valuation ratio varies dramatically by industry. For example, the sales per share for retail firms, such as Kroger or Wal-Mart, are typically much higher than sales per share for computer or microchip firms. The reason for this difference is related to the second consideration, the profit margin on sales. The point is, retail food stores have high sales per share, which will cause a low P/S ratio, which is considered good until one realizes that these firms have low net profit margins. Therefore, your relative valuation analysis using the P/S ratio should be between firms in the same or similar industries.

ESTIMATING THE INPUTS: THE REQUIRED RATE OF RETURN AND THE EXPECTED GROWTH RATE OF VALUATION VARIABLES

This section deals with estimating two inputs that are critical to the valuation process irrespective of which approach or technique is being used: the required rate of return (k) and the expected growth rate of earnings and other valuation variables—i.e., book value, cash flow, sales, and dividends.

We will review these factors and discuss how the estimation of these variables differs for domestic versus foreign securities. Although the valuation procedure is the same for securities around the world, k and g differ among countries. Therefore, we will review the components of the required rate of return for U.S. securities and then consider the components for foreign securities. Following this, we will turn to the estimation of the growth rate of earnings, cash flow, and dividends for domestic stocks and then discuss estimating growth for foreign stocks.

Required Rate of Return (k)

This discussion is a brief review of the determinants of the nominal required rate of return on an investment, including a consideration of factors for non-U.S. markets. As noted above, it is necessary to estimate the investor's required rate of return on an investment irrespective of which approach is used or which of the techniques is applied. This required rate of return will be the discount rate for most cash flow models and affects all the relative valuation techniques. The only instance of a difference in the discount rate is between the present value of dividends and the present value of free cash flow techniques, which use the required rate of return on equity (k), and the present value of operating cash flow technique, which uses the weighted average cost of capital (WACC). Even in this latter instance, the cost of equity is a critical input to estimating the firm's WACC.

Recall that three factors influence an investor's required rate of return:

1. The economy's real risk-free rate (RRFR)
2. The expected rate of inflation (I)
3. A risk premium (RP)

THE ECONOMY'S REAL RISK-FREE RATE This is the absolute minimum rate that an investor should require. It depends on the real growth rate of the investor's home economy because capital invested should grow at least as fast as the economy. As noted previously, this rate can be affected for short periods of time by temporary tightness or ease in the capital markets.

THE EXPECTED RATE OF INFLATION Investors are interested in real rates of return that will allow them to increase their rate of consumption. Therefore, if investors expect a given rate of inflation, they should increase their required nominal risk-free rate of return (NRFR) to reflect any expected inflation as follows:

$$\text{NRFR} = [1 + \text{RRFR}]\,[1 + E(\text{I})] - 1$$

where:

E(I) = expected rate of inflation

The two factors that determine the NRFR affect all investments, from U.S. government securities to highly speculative land deals. Investors who hope to calculate security values accurately must carefully estimate the expected rate of inflation. Not only does the NRFR affect all investments, but its extreme volatility makes its estimation difficult.

THE RISK PREMIUM The risk premium (RP) causes differences in the required rates of return among alternative investments that range from government bonds to corporate bonds to common stocks. The RP also explains the difference in the expected return among securities of the same type. For example, this is the reason corporate bonds with different ratings of Aaa, Aa, or A have different yields, and why different common stocks have widely varying earnings multipliers despite similar growth expectations.

In Chapter 1, we noted that investors demand a risk premium because of the uncertainty of returns expected from an investment. A measure of this uncertainty of returns was the dispersion of expected returns. We suggested several internal factors that influence a firm's variability of returns, such as its business risk, financial risk, and liquidity risk. We noted that securities of foreign firms or of domestic companies with significant foreign sales and earnings (e.g., Coca-Cola and McDonald's) bring additional risk factors, including exchange rate risk and country (political) risk.

Changes in the Risk Premium Because different securities have different patterns of returns and different guarantees to investors, we expect their risk premiums to differ. In addition, the risk premiums for the same securities can *change over time.* For example, Figure 13.3 shows the spread between the yields to maturity for Aaa-rated corporate bonds and Baa-rated corporate bonds from 1966 through 1998. This yield spread, or difference in yield, is a measure of the risk premium for investing in higher-risk bonds (Baa) compared to low- risk bonds (Aaa). As shown, the yield spread varied from about 0.40 percent to 2.69 percent (from less than one-half of 1 percent to almost 3 percent).

Figure 13.4 contains a plot of the *ratio* of the yields for the same period, which indicates the percentage risk premium of Baa bonds compared to Aaa bonds. You might expect a larger difference in yield between Baa and Aaa bonds if Aaa bonds are yielding 12 percent rather than 6 percent. The yield ratio in Figure 13.4 adjusts for this size difference. This shows that even adjusting for the yield level difference, the risk premium ratio varies from about 1.06 to 1.31—a 6 percent premium to a 31 percent premium over the base yield on Aaa bonds. This change in risk premium over time occurs because either investors perceive a change in the level of risk of Baa bonds compared to Aaa bonds, or there is a change in the amount of return that investors require to accept the same level of risk. In either case, this change in the risk premium for a set of assets implies a change in the slope of the security market line (SML). This change in the slope of the SML was demonstrated in Chapter 1.

In Chapter 18 we will discuss the controversy regarding an appropriate equity market risk premium and the question of possible changes in the long-run equity risk premium.

FIGURE 13.3 **TIME-SERIES PLOT OF MOODY'S CORPORATE BOND YIELD SPREADS (Baa–Aaa): MONTHLY 1966–1998**

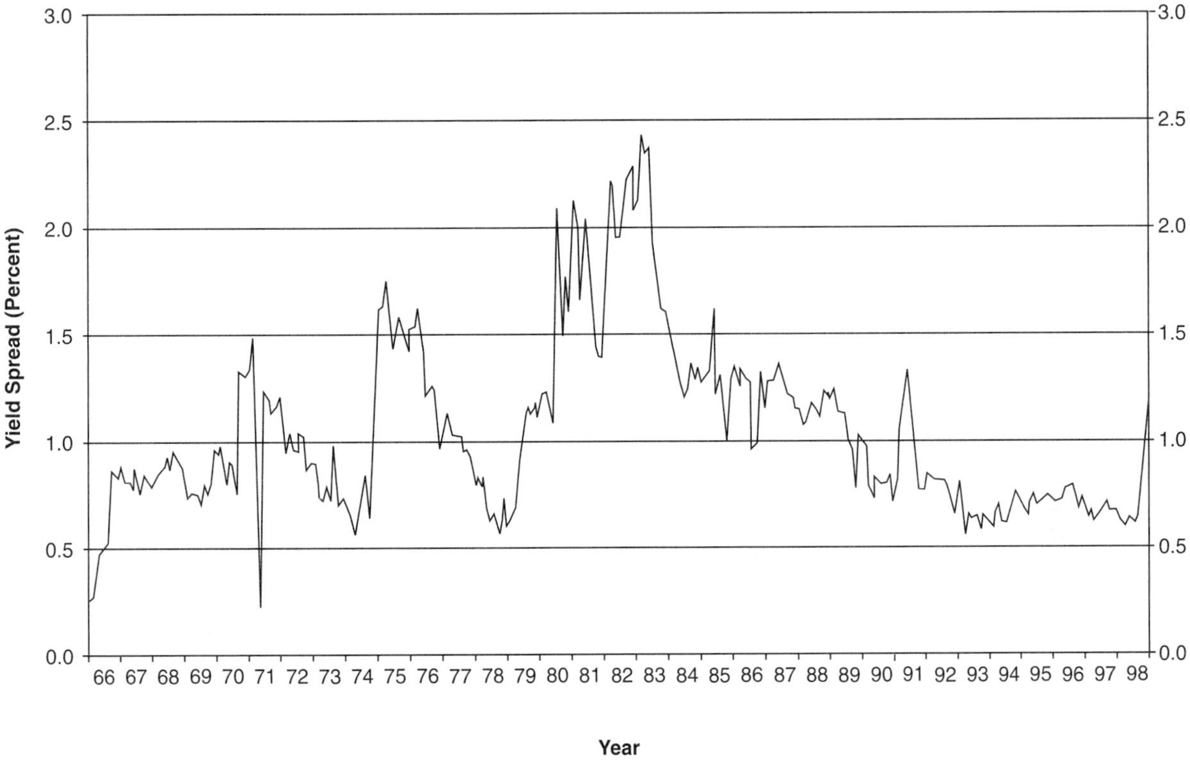

Yield Spread (Percent)
3.0
2.5
2.0
1.5
1.0
0.5
0.0
66 67 68 69 70 71 72 73 74 75 76 77 78 79 80 81 82 83 84 85 86 87 88 89 90 91 92 93 94 95 96 97 98
Year

Source: Lehman Brothers.

ESTIMATING THE REQUIRED RETURN FOR FOREIGN SECURITIES

Our discussion of the required rate of return for investments has been limited to the domestic market. Although the basic valuation model and its variables are the same around the world, there are significant differences in the specific variables. This section points out where these differences occur.

FOREIGN REAL RFR Because the RRFR in other countries should be determined by the real growth rate within the particular economy, the estimated rate can vary substantially among countries due to differences in an economy's real growth rate. An example of differences in the real growth rate of gross domestic product (GDP) can be seen in Table 13.2. There is a range of estimates for 2000 of 3.3 percent (that is, −0.8 percent for Japan compared to 2.5 percent for France). This difference in the growth rates of real GDP implies a substantial difference in the RRFR for these countries.

INFLATION RATE To estimate the NRFR for a country, you must also estimate its expected rate of inflation and adjust the NRFR for this expectation. Again, this rate of inflation typically varies substantially among countries. The price change data in Table 13.3 show that the expected rate of inflation during 2000 varied from −1.1 percent in Japan to 2.3 percent in the United States. Assuming equal growth, this implies a difference in the nominal required rate of return between these two countries of 3.4 percent. Such a difference in k can have a substantial impact on estimated values as demonstrated earlier. Again,

FIGURE 13.4 TIME-SERIES PLOT OF MOODY'S CORPORATE BOND YIELD (Baa YIELD/Aaa YIELD): MONTHLY 1966–1998

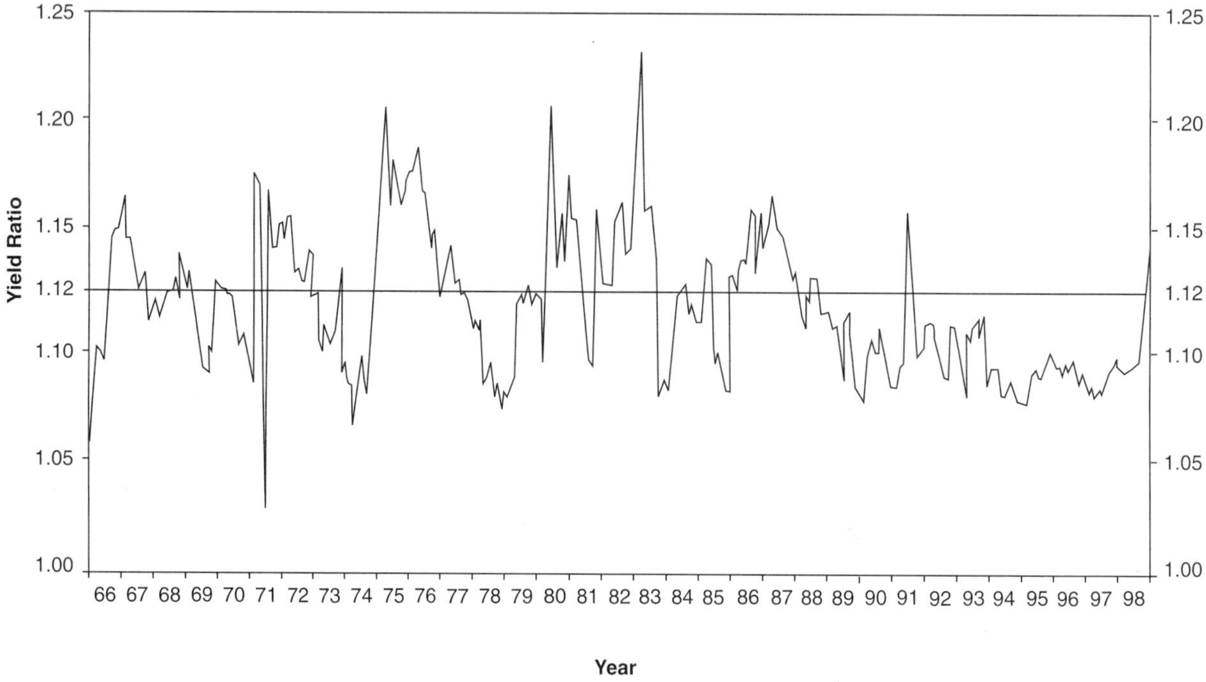
Yield Ratio
1.25
1.20
1.15
1.12
1.10
1.05
1.00
66 67 68 69 70 71 72 73 74 75 76 77 78 79 80 81 82 83 84 85 86 87 88 89 90 91 92 93 94 95 96 97 98
Year

Source: Lehman Brothers.

you must make a separate estimate for each individual country in which you are evaluating securities.

To demonstrate the combined impact of differences in real growth and expected inflation, Table 13.4 shows the results of the following computation for the six countries based on the year 2000 estimates:

$$\text{NRFR} = (1 + \text{Real Growth}) \times (1 + \text{Expected Inflation}) - 1$$

Given the differences between countries in the two components, the range in the NRFR of 6.0 percent is not surprising (4.1 percent for the United Kingdom and the United States versus −1.9 percent for Japan). As demonstrated earlier, such a difference in *k* for an investment will have a significant impact on its value.

RISK PREMIUM You must also derive a risk premium for the investments in each country. Again, the five risk components differ substantially between countries: business risk, financial risk, liquidity risk, exchange rate risk, and country risk. *Business risk* can vary because it is a function of the variability of economic activity within a country and of the operating leverage used by firms within the country. Firms in different countries assume significantly different *financial risk* as well. For example, Japanese firms use substantially more financial leverage than U.S. or U.K. firms. Regarding *liquidity risk,* the U.S. capital markets are acknowledged to be the most liquid in the world, with Japan and the U.K. being close behind. In contrast, some emerging markets are quite illiquid and investors need to add a significant liquidity risk premium.

TABLE 13.2

GROWTH OF REAL GDP (PERCENTAGE CHANGES FROM PREVIOUS YEAR)

Period	United States	Japan	Germany	France	United Kingdom	Italy
1987	3.7%	4.6%	1.7%	1.9%	4.5%	3.0%
1988	4.4	5.8	3.6	3.4	4.6	4.2
1989	2.5	4.8	4.0	3.6	1.9	3.2
1990	0.8	5.6	4.6	2.5	1.0	1.9
1991	0.1	3.6	3.3	1.2	−1.2	1.5
1992	2.1	1.5	1.5	1.2	−0.5	1.0
1993	3.0	0.1	−1.9	−0.7	1.9	−0.4
1994	3.5	0.5	2.9	2.8	4.0	2.1
1995	2.0	0.9	1.9	2.2	2.5	3.0
1996	2.8	3.9	1.4	1.6	2.5	0.7
1997	3.9	1.4	2.2	2.3	3.5	1.5
1998	3.8	−2.7	2.9	3.0	2.4	1.4
1999E	3.7	−1.3	1.4	2.2	0.6	1.2
2000E	1.8	−0.8	1.8	2.5	2.2	1.8

Source: "World Investment Strategy Highlights" (London: Goldman, Sachs International Ltd., May 1999). Reprinted by permission of Goldman, Sachs & Co.

TABLE 13.3

CHANGES IN CONSUMER OR RETAIL PRICES (PERCENTAGE CHANGES FROM PREVIOUS YEAR)

Period	United States	Japan	Germany	France	United Kingdom	Italy
1987	3.7%	0.1%	0.3%	3.3%	4.1%	4.6%
1988	4.1	0.7	1.3	2.7	4.9	5.0
1989	4.8	2.3	2.8	3.4	7.8	6.6
1990	5.4	3.0	2.7	3.4	9.5	6.1
1991	4.7	3.2	3.5	3.1	6.0	6.0
1992	3.0	1.7	4.0	2.8	3.7	5.2
1993	3.0	1.3	4.2	2.1	1.6	4.2
1994	2.6	0.7	2.7	2.1	2.4	3.9
1995	2.8	0.0	1.8	1.6	2.8	5.4
1996	2.9	0.1	1.5	2.0	3.0	3.9
1997	2.3	1.7	1.8	1.2	2.8	1.7
1998	1.6	0.7	0.9	0.7	2.7	1.7
1999E	1.9	−0.9	0.5	0.4	2.3	1.2
2000E	2.3	−1.1	0.5	0.6	1.9	1.3

Source: "World Investment Strategy Highlights" (London: Goldman, Sachs International Ltd., May 1999). Reprinted by permission of Goldman, Sachs & Co.

TABLE 13.4

ESTIMATES OF YEAR 2000 NOMINAL RFR FOR MAJOR COUNTRIES

Country	Real Growth in GDP[a]	Expected Inflation[b]	Nominal RFR
United States	1.8%	2.3%	4.1%
Japan	−0.8	−1.1	−1.9
Germany	1.8	0.5	2.3
France	2.5	0.6	3.1
United Kingdom	2.2	1.9	4.1
Italy	1.8	1.3	3.1

[a]Taken from Table 13.2
[b]Taken from Table 13.3

Source: Reprinted by permission of Goldman, Sachs & Co.

When investing globally, you also must estimate *exchange rate risk*, which is the additional uncertainty of returns caused by changes in the exchange rates for the currency of another country. This uncertainty can be small for a U.S. investor in a country such as Hong Kong because the currency is pegged to the U.S. dollar. In contrast, in some countries, substantial volatility in the exchange rate over time can mean significant differences in the domestic return for the country and return in U.S. dollars.[16] The level of volatility for the exchange rate differs between countries. The greater the uncertainty regarding future changes in the exchange rate, the larger the exchange rate risk for the country.[17]

Recall that country risk arises from unexpected events in a country, such as upheavals in its political or economic environment. Recent examples of political and economic disruptions have occurred in Russia when Boris Yeltsin engineered a significant change in his staff during 1998 and subsequently there was substantial uncertainty about the potential devaluation of the ruble. The result was a stock market decline of over 60 percent between January and August, 1998. Another example was the unrest in Indonesia during 1998 that led to riots and the eventual resignation of President Suharto. Such political unrest or a change in the economic environment creates uncertainties that increase the risk of investments in these countries. Before investing in such countries, investors must evaluate the additional returns they should require to accept this increased uncertainty.

Thus, when estimating required rates of return on foreign investments, you must evaluate these differences in fundamental risk factors and assign a unique risk premium for each country.

Expected Growth Rate of Dividends

After arriving at a required rate of return, the investor must estimate the growth rate of cash flows, earnings, and dividends because the alternative valuation models for common stock depend heavily on good estimates of growth (g) for these variables. The initial procedure we describe here is similar to the presentation in Chapter 12, where we used financial ratios to measure a firm's growth potential. Subsequently we will discuss the use of historical growth rates as an input to the estimate.

ESTIMATING GROWTH FROM FUNDAMENTALS The growth rate of dividends is determined by the growth rate of earnings and the proportion of earnings paid out in dividends (the payout ratio). Over the short run, dividends can grow faster or slower than earnings if the firm changes its payout ratio. Specifically, if a firm's earnings grow at 6 percent a year and it pays out exactly 50 percent of earnings in dividends, then the firm's dividends will likewise grow at 6 percent a year. Alternatively, if a firm's earnings grow at 6 percent a year and the firm increases its payout, then during the period when the payout ratio increases, dividends will grow faster than earnings. In contrast, if the firm reduces its payout ratio, dividends will grow slower than earnings for a period of time. Because there is a limit to how long this difference in growth rates can continue, most investors assume that the long-run dividend payout ratio is fairly stable. Therefore, analysis of the growth rate of dividends typically concentrates on an analysis of the growth rate of equity earnings. Also, as will be shown in Chapter 20, these earnings are the major factor driving the operating cash flows or the free cash flows for the firm.

When a firm retains earnings and acquires additional assets, if it earns some positive rate of return on these additional assets, the total earnings of the firm will increase because its

---

[16]Although we generally refer to these as domestic and U.S. dollar returns, you will also see references to *hedged* returns (for example, domestic) and *unhedged* returns (returns in U.S. dollars). In some cases, the hedged returns will adjust for the cost of hedging.

[17]For a thorough analysis of exchange rate determination and forecasting models, see Michael Rosenberg, *Currency Forecasting* (Burr Ridge, IL: Irwin Professional Publishing, 1996).

asset base is larger. How rapidly a firm's earnings increase depends on (1) the proportion of earnings it retains and reinvests in new assets and (2) the rate of return it earns on these new assets. Specifically, the growth rate (g) of equity earnings (that is, earnings per share) without any external financing is equal to the percentage of net earnings retained (the retention rate, which equals 1 − the payout ratio) times the rate of return on equity capital.

$$\begin{aligned} g &= (\text{Retention Rate}) \times (\text{Return on Equity}) \\ &= \text{RR} \times \text{ROE} \end{aligned}$$

Therefore, a firm can increase its growth rate by increasing its retention rate (reducing its payout ratio) and investing these added funds at its historic ROE. Alternatively, the firm can maintain its retention rate but increase its ROE. For example, if a firm retains 50 percent of net earnings and consistently has an ROE of 10 percent, its net earnings will grow at the rate of 5 percent a year, as follows:

$$\begin{aligned} g &= \text{RR} \times \text{ROE} \\ &= 0.50 \times 0.10 \\ &= 0.05 \end{aligned}$$

If, however, the firm increases its retention rate to 75 percent and invests these additional funds in internal projects that earn 10 percent, its growth rate will increase to 7.5 percent, as follows:

$$\begin{aligned} g &= 0.75 \times 0.10 \\ &= 0.075 \end{aligned}$$

If, instead, the firm continues to reinvest 50 percent of its earnings, but derives a higher rate of return on these investments, say 15 percent, it can likewise increase its growth rate, as follows:

$$\begin{aligned} g &= 0.50 \times 0.15 \\ &= 0.075 \end{aligned}$$

BREAKDOWN OF ROE Although the retention rate is a management decision, changes in the firm's ROE result from changes in its operating performance or its financial leverage. As discussed in Chapter 12, we can divide the ROE ratio into three components:

$$\begin{aligned} \text{ROE} &= \frac{\text{Net Income}}{\text{Sales}} \times \frac{\text{Sales}}{\text{Total Assets}} \times \frac{\text{Total Assets}}{\text{Equity}} \\ &= \begin{matrix}\text{Profit}\\ \text{Margin}\end{matrix} \times \begin{matrix}\text{Total Asset}\\ \text{Turnover}\end{matrix} \times \begin{matrix}\text{Financial}\\ \text{Leverage}\end{matrix} \end{aligned}$$

This breakdown allows us to consider the three factors that determine a firm's ROE.[18] Because it is a multiplicative relationship, an increase in any of the three ratios will cause an increase in ROE. The first two of the three ratios reflect operating performance and the third one indicates a firm's financing decision.

---

[18]You will recall from Chapter 12 (Table 12.8) that it is possible to employ an extended DuPont system that involves eight ratios. For purposes of this discussion, the three ratios indicate the significant differences among countries.

The first operating ratio, net profit margin, indicates the firm's profitability on sales. This ratio changes over time for some companies and is highly sensitive to the business cycle. For growth companies, this is one of the first ratios to decline because the increased competition forces price cutting, thus reducing profit margins. Also, during recessions profit margins decline because of price cutting or because of higher percentages of fixed costs due to lower sales.

The second component, total asset turnover, is the ultimate indicator of operating efficiency and reflects the asset and capital requirements of the business. Although this ratio varies dramatically by industry, within an industry it is an excellent indicator of management's operating efficiency.

The product of these first two components (profit margin and total asset turnover) equals the firm's return on assets (ROA), which reflects the firm's operating performance before the financing impact.[19]

The final component, total assets/equity, does not measure operating performance, but rather financial leverage. Specifically, it indicates how management has decided to finance the firm. This management decision regarding the financing of assets can contribute to a higher ROE, but it also has financial risk implications for the stockholder.

Knowing this breakdown of ROE, you must examine past results and expectations for a firm and develop *estimates* of the three components and therefore an estimate of a firm's ROE. This estimate of ROE combined with the firm's retention rate will indicate its future growth potential. This breakdown of ROE will be employed extensively in the market-industry-company analysis chapters.

ESTIMATING GROWTH BASED ON HISTORY Although the authors have a strong bias in favor of using the fundamentals to estimate future growth, which involves estimating the three or five components of ROE, we also believe in using all the information available to make this critical estimate. Therefore, we suggest that analysts also consider the historical growth rate of sales, earnings, cash flow, and dividends in this process.

Although we will demonstrate these computations for the market, for an industry, and for a company in subsequent chapters, the following discussion considers some suggestions on alternative calculations. In terms of the relevant period to consider, one is struck by the cliché "more is better" as long as you recognize that "recent is relevant." Specifically, about 20 years of annual observations would be ideal, but it is important to consider subperiods as well as the total period—that is, 20 years, two 10-year periods, and four 5-year periods would indicate the overall growth rate, but also would indicate if there were any *changes* in the growth rate in recent periods.

The specific measurement can be done using one or more of three techniques: (1) arithmetic or geometric average of annual percentage changes, (2) linear regression models, and (3) log-linear regression models. Irrespective of the measurement techniques used, we would strongly encourage a time-series plot of the data.

The arithmetic or geometric average technique involves computing the annual percentage change and then computing either the simple arithmetic average or the geometric average of these values for the alternative periods. As you will recall from the discussion in Chapter 3, the arithmetic average will always be a higher value than the geometric average (except when the annual values are constant) and the difference between the average values

[19]In Chapter 19, we will discuss a study that analyzes why and how alternative industries differ regarding the return on assets and the two components.

will increase with volatility. As noted in that discussion, we generally prefer the geometric mean because it provides the average annual compound growth rate.

The linear regression model goes well with the suggested time-series plot and is as follows:

$$\text{EPS}_t = a + bt$$

where:

EPS_t = earnings per period in period t
t = year t where t goes from 1 to n
b = the coefficient which indicates the average absolute change in the series during the period

It would be very informative to superimpose this regression line on the time-series plot because it would provide insights on changes in absolute growth.

The log-linear model considers that the series might be better described in terms of a constant *growth rate*. This model is as follows:

$$1n(\text{EPS}_t) = a + bt$$

where:

$1n(\text{EPS}_t)$ = the natural logarithm of earnings per share in period t
b = the coefficient which indicates *the average percentage change* in the series during the period

The analysis of these historical growth rates both visually with the time-series graph and the alternative calculations should provide you with significant insights into the trend of the growth rates as well as the *variability* of the growth rates over time. This could provide information on the unit's business risk.

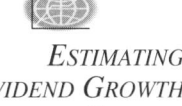

Estimating Dividend Growth for Foreign Stocks

The underlying factors that determine the growth rates for foreign stocks are similar to those for U.S. stocks, but the value of the equation's components may differ substantially from what is common in the United States. The differences in the retention rate or the components of ROE result from differences in accounting practices as well as alternative management performance or philosophy.

RETENTION RATES The retention rates for foreign corporations differ within countries, but differences also exist among countries due to differences in the countries' investment opportunities. As an example, firms in Japan have a higher retention rate than firms in the United States, whereas the rate of retention in France is much lower. Therefore, you need to examine the retention rates for a number of firms in a country as a background for estimating the standard rate within a country.

NET PROFIT MARGIN The net profit margin of foreign firms can differ because of different accounting conventions between countries. As noted in Chapter 12, foreign accounting rules allow firms to recognize revenue and allocate expenses differently from U.S. firms. For example, German firms are allowed to build up large reserves for various reasons. As a result, they report low earnings for tax purposes. Also, different foreign depreciation practices require adjustment of earnings and cash flows.

THE INTERNET *Investments Online*

Several sites that we discussed in earlier chapters contained financial calculators. By inputting the required data, users can determine if it is better to buy or lease a car, calculate returns, and determine how much money they will have if funds are invested at a certain rate of return over time. The sites listed below all contain financial calculators that may be of interest and use to investors and financial planners.

www.financenter.com

www.moneyadvisor.com

www.jamesko.com/financial_calculator.htm

http://fpc.net66.com

TOTAL ASSET TURNOVER Total asset turnover can likewise differ among countries because of different accounting conventions on the reporting of asset value at cost or market values. For example, in Japan a large part of the market values for some firms comes from their real estate holdings and their common stock investments in other firms. These assets are reported at cost, which typically has substantially understated their true value. This also means that the total asset turnover ratio for these firms is substantially overstated.

This ratio will also be impacted by leases that are not capitalized on the balance sheet—i.e., both assets and liabilities are understated.

TOTAL ASSET/EQUITY RATIO This ratio, a measure of financial leverage, differs among countries because of differences in economic environments, tax laws, management philosophies regarding corporate debt, and accounting conventions. In several countries, the attitude toward debt is much more liberal than in the United States. A prime example is Japan, where debt as a percentage of total assets is almost 50 percent higher than a similar ratio in the United States. Notably, most corporate debt in Japan entails borrowing from banks at fairly low rates of interest. Balance sheet debt ratios may be higher in Japan than in the United States or other countries, but because of the lower interest rates in Japan, the fixed-charge coverage ratios, such as the times interest earned ratio, might be similar to those in other countries. The point is, it is important to consider the several cash flow financial risk ratios along with the balance sheet debt ratios.

Consequently, when analyzing a foreign stock market or an individual foreign stock, when you estimate the growth rate for earnings and dividends you must consider the three components of the ROE just as you would for a U.S. stock. You must recognize that the financial ratios for foreign firms can differ from those of U.S. firms, as discussed in Chapter 12. Subsequent chapters on valuation applied to the aggregate market, to various industries, and to companies contain examples of these differences.

Summary

- As an investor, you want to select investments that will provide a rate of return that compensates you for your time, the expected rate of inflation, and the risk involved. To help you find these investments, this chapter considers the theory of valuation by which you derive the value of an investment using your required rate of return. We consider the two investment decision processes, which are the top-down, three-step approach and the bottom-up, stockpicking approach. Although it is recognized that either process can provide abnormal positive returns if the analyst is superior, we feel that a preferable approach is the top-down approach in which you initially consider the aggregate economy and market, then examine alternative global industries, and finally analyze individual firms and their stocks.

- We apply the valuation theory to a range of investments, including bonds, preferred stock, and common stock. Because the valuation of common stock is more complex and difficult, we suggest two alternative approaches (the present value of cash flows and the relative valuation approach) and several techniques for each of these approaches. Notably, we do *not* consider these competitive approaches, but suggest that *both* approaches should be used. Although we suggest using several different valuation models, the investment decision rule is always the same: If the estimated value of the investment is greater than the market price, you should buy the investment; if the estimated value of an investment is less than its market price, you should not invest in it.
- We conclude with a review of factors that you need to consider when estimating the value of stock with either approach—your required rate of return on an investment and the growth rate of earnings, cash flow, and dividends. Finally, we consider some unique factors that affect the application of these valuation models to foreign stocks.

Questions

1. Discuss the difference between the top-down and bottom-up approaches. What is the major assumption that causes the difference in these two approaches?
2. What is the benefit of analyzing the market and alternative industries before individual securities?
3. Discuss why you would not expect all industries to have a similar relationship to the economy. Give an example of two industries that have different relationships to the economy.
4. Discuss why estimating the value for a bond is easier than estimating the value for common stock.
5. Would you expect the required rate of return for a U.S. investor in U.S. common stocks to be the same as the required rate of return on Japanese common stocks? What factors would determine the required rate of return for stocks in these countries?
6. Would you expect the nominal RFR in the United States to be the same as in Germany? Discuss your reasoning.
7. Would you expect the risk premium for an investment in an Indonesian stock to be the same as that for a stock from the United Kingdom? Discuss your reasoning.
8. Would you expect the risk premium for an investment in a stock from Singapore to be the same as that for a stock from the United States? Discuss your reasoning.
9. Give an example of a stock where it would be appropriate to use the reduced form DDM for valuation and discuss why you feel that it is appropriate. Similarly, give an example and discuss a stock where it would not be appropriate to use the reduced form DDM.
10. Give an example of and discuss a stock that has temporary, supernormal growth where it would be appropriate (necessary) to use the modified DDM.
11. Under what conditions will it be ideal to use one or several of the relative valuation ratios to evaluate a stock?
12. Discuss a scenario where it would be appropriate to use one of the present value of cash flow techniques for the valuation.
13. Discuss why the two valuation approaches (present value of cash flows and the relative valuation ratios) are competitive or complementary.

Problems

1. What is the value to you of a 9 percent coupon bond with a par value of $10,000 that matures in 10 years if you want a 7 percent return? Use semiannual compounding.
2. What would be the value of the bond in Problem 1 if you wanted an 11 percent rate of return?
3. The preferred stock of the Clarence Radiology Company has a par value of $100 and a $9 dividend rate. You require an 11 percent rate of return on this stock. What is the maximum price you would pay for it? Would you buy it at a market price of $96?
4. The Baron Basketball Company (BBC) earned $10 a share last year and paid a dividend of $6 a share. Next year, you expect BBC to earn $11 and continue its payout ratio. Assume that you expect to sell the stock for $132 a year from now. If you require 12 percent on this stock, how much would you be willing to pay for it?
5. Given the expected earnings and dividend payments in Problem 4, if you expected a selling price of $110 and required an 8 percent return on this investment, how much would you pay for the BBC stock?

6. Over the long run, you expect dividends for BBC to grow at 8 percent and you require 11 percent on the stock. Using the infinite period DDM, how much would you pay for this stock?
7. Based on new information regarding the popularity of basketball, you revise your growth estimate for BBC to 9 percent. What is the maximum P/E ratio you will apply to BBC, and what is the maximum price you will pay for the stock?
8. The Shamrock Dogfood Company (SDC) has consistently paid out 40 percent of its earnings in dividends. The company's return on equity is 16 percent. What would you estimate as its dividend growth rate?
9. Given the low risk in dog food, your required rate of return on SDC is 13 percent. What P/E ratio would you apply to the firm's earnings?
10. What P/E ratio would you apply if you learned that SDC had decided to increase its payout to 50 percent? (Hint: This change in payout has multiple effects.)
11. Discuss three ways a firm can increase its ROE. Make up an example to illustrate your discussion.
12. It is widely known that grocery chains have low profit margins—on average they earn about 1 percent on sales. How would you explain the fact that their ROE is about 12 percent? Does this seem logical?
13. Compute a recent five-year average of the following ratios for three companies of your choice (attempt to select diverse firms):
    a. Retention rate
    b. Net profit margin
    c. Equity turnover
    d. Total asset turnover
    e. Total assets/equity

    Based on these ratios, explain which firm should have the highest growth rate of earnings.
14. You have been reading about the Maddy Computer Company (MCC), which currently retains 90 percent of its earnings ($5 a share this year). It earns an ROE of almost 30 percent. Assuming a required rate of return of 14 percent, how much would you pay for MCC on the basis of the earnings multiplier model? Discuss your answer. What would you pay for Maddy Computer if its retention rate was 60 percent and its ROE was 19 percent? Show your work.
15. Gentry Can Company's (GCC) latest annual dividend of $1.25 a share was paid yesterday and maintained its historic 7 percent annual rate of growth. You plan to purchase the stock today because you believe that the dividend growth rate will increase to 8 percent for the next three years and the selling price of the stock will be $40 per share at the end of that time.
    a. How much should you be willing to pay for the GCC stock if you require a 12 percent return?
    b. What is the maximum price you should be willing to pay for the GCC stock if you believe that the 8 percent growth rate can be maintained indefinitely and you require a 12 percent return?
    c. If the 8 percent rate of growth is achieved, what will the price be at the end of Year 3, assuming the conditions in part b?
16. In the *Federal Reserve Bulletin,* find the average yield of AAA and BBB bonds for a recent month. Compute the risk premium (in basis points) and the percentage risk premium on BBB bonds relative to AAA bonds. Discuss how these values compare to those shown in Figures 13.3 and 13.4.

References

Bhatia, Sanjiv, ed. *Global Equity Investing.* Proceedings of a seminar by the Association of Investment Management and Research. Charlottesville, Va.: AIMR, December 1, 1995.

Billingsley, Randall, ed. *Corporate Financial Decision Making and Equity Analysis.* Proceedings of a seminar by the Association of Investment Management and Research. Charlottesville, Va.: AIMR, January 18, 1995.

Copeland, T. E., Tim Koller, and Jack Murrin. *Valuation: Measuring and Managing the Value of Companies,* 2d ed. New York: Wiley, 1996.

Cornell, Bradford. *Corporate Valuation.* Burr Ridge, Ill.: Irwin Professional Publishing, 1993.

Damodaran, Aswath. *Damodaran on Valuation.* New York: Wiley, 1994.

Damodaran, Aswath. *Investment Valuation.* New York: Wiley, 1996.

Farrell, James L. "The Dividend Discount Model: A Primer." *Financial Analysts Journal* 41, no. 6 (November–December 1985).

Fogler, H. Russell, ed. *Blending Quantitative and Traditional Equity Analysis.* Proceedings of a seminar by the Association of Investment Management and Research. Charlottesville, Va.: AIMR, March 31, 1994.

Gastineau, Gary L., and Sanjiv Bhatia, eds. *Risk Management.* Proceedings of a seminar by the Association of Investment Management and Research. Charlottesville, Va.: AIMR, October 10, 1995.

Helfert, Erich A. *Techniques of Financial Analysis.* 10th ed. Burr Ridge, Ill.: Irwin McGraw-Hill, 2000.

Higgins, Robert C. *Analysis for Financial Management.* 4th ed. Chicago: Richard D. Irwin, Inc., 1995.

Levine, Sumner N., ed. *The Financial Analysts Handbook.* 2d ed. Homewood, Ill.: Dow Jones–Irwin, 1988.

Palepu, Krishna, Victor Bernard, and Paul Healy. *Business Analysis and Valuation.* Cincinnati, Ohio: SouthWestern Publishing, 1996.

Sharpe, William, and Katrina Sherrerd, eds. *Quantifying the Market Risk Premium Phenomenon for Investment Decision Making.* Proceedings of a seminar by the Association of Investment Management and Research. Charlottesville, Va.: AIMR, September 26, 1989.

Shaked, Israel. "International Equity Markets and the Investment Horizon." *Journal of Portfolio Management* 11, no. 2 (winter 1985).

Squires, Jan, ed. *Value and Growth Styles in Equity Investing.* Proceedings of a seminar by the Association of Investment Management and Research. Charlottesville, Va.: AIMR, February 15, 1995.

Squires, Jan, ed. *Equity Research and Valuation Techniques.* Proceedings of a seminar by the Association of Investment Management and Research. Charlottesville, Va.: AIMR, December 9, 1997.

Wagner, Jerry, Steven Shellans, and Richard Paul. "Market Timing Works Where It Matters Most . . . in the Real World." *Journal of Portfolio Management* 18, no. 4 (summer 1992).

Chapter 13 APPENDIX

DERIVATION OF CONSTANT GROWTH DIVIDEND DISCOUNT MODEL (DDM)

The basic model is

$$P_0 = \frac{D_1}{(1+k)^1} + \frac{D_2}{(1+k)^2} + \frac{D_3}{(1+k)^3} + \ldots + \frac{D_n}{(1+k)^n}$$

where:

P_0 = current price
D_i = expected dividend in period i
k = required rate of return on asset j

If growth rate (g) is constant,

$$P_0 = \frac{D_0(1+g)^1}{(1+k)^1} + \frac{D_0(1+g)^2}{(1+k)^2} + \ldots + \frac{D_0(1+g)^n}{(1+k)^n}$$

This can be written

$$P_0 = D_0\left[\frac{(1+g)}{(1+k)} + \frac{(1+g)^2}{(1+k)^2} + \frac{(1+g)^3}{(1+k)^3} + \ldots + \frac{(1+g)^n}{(1+k)^n}\right]$$

Multiply both sides of the equation by $\frac{1+k}{1+g}$.

$$\left[\frac{(1+g)}{(1+k)}\right]P_0 = D_0\left[1 + \frac{(1+g)}{(1+k)} + \frac{(1+g)^2}{(1+k)^2} + \ldots + \frac{(1+g)^{n-1}}{(1+k)^{n-1}}\right]$$

Subtract the previous equation from this equation:

$$\left[\frac{(1+k)}{(1+g)} - 1\right]P_0 = D_0\left[1 - \frac{(1+g)^n}{(1+k)^n}\right]$$

$$\left[\frac{(1+k)-(1+g)}{(1+g)}\right]P_0 = D_0\left[1 - \frac{(1+g)^n}{(1+k)^n}\right]$$

Assuming $k > g$, as $N \rightarrow \infty$, the term in brackets on the right side of the equation goes to 1, leaving:

$$\left[\frac{(1+k)-(1+g)}{(1+g)}\right]P_0 = D_0$$

This simplifies to

$$\left[\frac{(1+k-1-g)}{(1+g)}\right]P_0 = D_0$$

which equals

$$\left[\frac{k-g}{(1+g)}\right]P_0 = D_0$$

This equals

$$(k-g)P_0 = D_0(1+g)$$

$$D_0(1+g) = D_1$$

so:

$$(k-g)P_0 = D_1$$

$$P_0 = \frac{D_1}{k-g}$$

Gordon Model

Yield + growth = RRR

Remember, this model assumes

- A constant growth rate
- An infinite time period
- The required return on the investment (k) is greater than the expected growth rate (g)

Chapter 14 The Analysis of Alternative Economies and Security Markets: The Global Asset Allocation Decision

After you read this chapter, you should be able to answer the following questions:

- What are the expected and the empirical relationships between economic activity and security markets?
- What is the macroeconomic approach to estimating future market returns?
- What are the major macroeconomic techniques used to project the securities market?
- What is the leading economic indicator approach? What are its uses and shortcomings and can it be used to predict stock prices?
- What are the expected and the empirical relationships between the growth of the money supply and stock prices?
- What is meant by excess liquidity and how is it measured?
- What is the effect of monetary policy on stock prices in the United States and around the world?
- What are the expected and the empirical relationships between inflation, interest rates, and bond prices?
- What are the expected and the empirical relationships between inflation and stock prices?
- When analyzing world security markets, what is the relationship between inflation and interest rates in alternative countries? What is the effect of inflation and interest rates on exchange rates?
- How do the basic valuation variables differ among countries?
- How do stock price returns among countries correlate when considering domestic returns and returns in U.S. dollars?
- What factors should be considered when analyzing the outlook for a foreign economy and its stock and bond market?
- What is the asset allocation procedure for a global portfolio?
- For a world asset allocation, what is meant by normal weighting, underweighting, and overweighting?

In Chapter 13, we introduced the three-step investment process and found that, although we are ultimately interested in securities markets, we analyze economies because of the strong link between the overall economic environment in a country and the performance of its security markets. *Security markets reflect what is going on in an economy* because the value of an investment is determined by its expected cash flows and its required rate of return, and both of these factors are influenced by the aggregate economic environment. Therefore, if you want to estimate cash flows, interest rates, and risk premiums for securities, you need to consider aggregate economic analysis.

From this interrelated economy–security market perspective, we initiate discussion of the investment process in this chapter by examining various techniques that relate economic variables to security markets. The first section discusses in detail the expected relationship between economic activity and the security markets and provides empirical evidence of this relationship. Given this documented empirical relationship, we discuss several techniques that are part of this approach, including the use of leading economic indicators, the analysis of money supply growth, and other measures of monetary policy. Following from the analysis of monetary liquidity, we consider the effect of inflation on interest rates, bond prices, and stock returns.

Although most of the discussion focuses on the U.S. economy, we recognize the need to apply these techniques to other countries. To provide insights into this global investment process, we discuss an example of global investment analysis by an investment firm. The culmination of this analysis is a global asset allocation of investment funds among countries and further allocation within countries to specific asset classes: bonds, stocks, and cash equivalents.

In Chapter 13, we also discussed the importance of analyzing the general economy as part of arriving at an estimate of future aggregate market values that imply future returns from investing in common stocks and/or bonds. Three major techniques are available for analyzing securities markets. First is the *macroeconomic approach,* which attempts to project the outlook for securities markets based on an understanding of the underlying relationship between the aggregate economy and the securities markets. Second is the *microanalysis approach,* which involves using two approaches to valuation (the present value of cash flows and the relative valuation ratios) discussed in Chapter 13 to estimate a value for the aggregate stock market. Finally, the *technical analysis approach* assumes that the best way to determine future changes in security market values is to examine past movements in interest rates, security prices, and other market variables.

This chapter discusses the macroeconomic approach to security market analysis and considers the asset allocation decision that flows from this analysis. Chapter 18 presents the microanalysis of the security markets, and technical analysis techniques are discussed and demonstrated in Chapter 21.

ECONOMIC ACTIVITY AND SECURITY MARKETS

Fluctuations in security markets are related to changes in the aggregate economy. The price of most bonds is determined by the level of interest rates, which are influenced by overall economic activity and Federal Reserve policy. The price of a firm's stock reflects investor expectations about an issuing firm's performance in terms of earnings, cash flow, and the investor's required rate of return. This performance is likewise affected by the overall performance of the economy.

In its monitoring of business cycles, the National Bureau of Economic Research (NBER) has amassed substantial evidence that supports the relationship between security prices and economic behavior. Based on the relationship of alternative economic series to the behavior of the entire economy, the NBER has classified numerous economic series into three groups: leading, coincident, and lagging indicator series. Further, extensive

TABLE 14.1 **TIMING RELATIONSHIPS BETWEEN STOCK MARKET AND BUSINESS CYCLE PEAKS AND TROUGHS**

I. Stock Market Declines Associated with a Subsequent Recession

Stock Market Cycles*				Business Cycles				Lead of Stock Market over Business Cycle[a]	
Peak		Trough		Peak		Trough		Peak	Trough
Jan.	1953	Sep.	1953	Jul.	1953	May	1954	6.0	8.0
Aug.	1956	Oct.	1957	Aug.	1957	Apr.	1958	11.0	6.0
Aug.	1959	Oct.	1960	Apr.	1960	Feb.	1961	8.0	4.0
Nov.	1968	May	1970	Dec.	1969	Nov.	1970	12.0	6.0
Jan.	1973	Oct.	1974	Nov.	1973	Mar.	1975	10.0	5.0
Feb.	1980	Aug.	1982	Jan.	1980	Nov.	1982	(1.0)	3.0
							Average	7.7	5.3

II. False Signals

Dec.	1961	Jan.	1962
Apr.	1971	Nov.	1971
Sep.	1976	Mar.	1978

III. Stock Market Declines Associated with a Subsequent Growth Recession

Feb.	1966	Mar.	1968

[a]Defined as market declines of approximately 15 percent or more.

Source: Jason Benderly and Edward McKelvey, "The Pocket Chartbook," *Economic Research,* Goldman, Sachs & Co., December 1987.

Reprinted by permission of Goldman, Sachs & Co.

analysis of the relationship between the economy and the stock market has shown that the consistency of this relationship makes stock prices one of the better leading indicator series.

The evidence indicates a strong relationship between stock prices and the economy, and shows that stock prices consistently turn *before* the economy does.[1] The data in Table 14.1 document this relationship, beginning in the 1950s. Although this overall leading relationship appears to hold, the data also show several instances of false signals given by the stock market.

There are two possible reasons why stock prices lead the economy. One is that stock prices reflect *expectations* of earnings, dividends, and interest rates. As investors attempt to estimate these future variables, their stock price decisions reflect expectations for *future* economic activity, not current activity. A second possible reason is that the stock market reacts to various leading indicator series, the most important being corporate earnings, corporate profit margins, interest rates, and changes in the growth rate of the money supply. Because these series tend to lead the economy, when investors adjust stock prices to reflect expectations for these leading economic series, it makes stock prices a leading series as well.

Because stock prices lead the aggregate economy, our macroeconomic approach to market analysis concentrates on economic series that lead the economy by more than stock

[1]A detailed analysis of this relationship is contained in Geoffrey H. Moore and John P. Cullity, "Security Markets and Business Cycles," *The Financial Analysts Handbook,* 2d ed., ed. Sumner N. Levine (Homewood, Ill.: Dow Jones-Irwin, 1988). Also see Jeremy J. Siegel, "Does It Pay Stock Investors to Forecast the Business Cycle?" *Journal of Portfolio Management* 18. no. 1 (fall 1991).

prices do. First, we discuss cyclical indicator approaches developed by various research groups. These include the cyclical indicator approach of the NBER, along with several leading series developed by the Center for International Business Cycle Research (CIBCR) at Columbia University. Next, we consider an important leading series, the money supply, as well as other measures of monetary liquidity and policy. Finally, we discuss the research related to a number of economic series expected to affect security returns (e.g., production, inflation, and risk premiums).

CYCLICAL INDICATOR APPROACH TO FORECASTING THE ECONOMY

The *cyclical indicator approach* to forecasting the economy is based on the belief that the aggregate economy expands and contracts in discernible periods. This view of the economy has been investigated by the NBER, a nonprofit organization that attempts to interpret important economic facts scientifically and impartially. The NBER explains the business cycle as follows:

> The business cycle concept has been developed from the sequence of events discerned in the historical study of the movements of economic activity. Though there are many cross-currents and variations in the pace of business activity, periods of business expansion appear to cumulate to peaks. As they cumulate, contrary forces tend to gain strength, bringing about a reversal in business activity and the onset of a recession. As a recession continues, forces for an expansion gradually emerge until they become dominant and a recovery begins.[2]

The NBER examined the behavior of hundreds of economic time series in relation to past business cycles. (Recall that a time series reports the values for an economic variable over time, such as the monthly industrial production value for the period 1980–2000. Using this analysis, the NBER grouped various economic series into three major categories based on their relationship to the business cycle. The initial list of economic series that could predict turns in the economy was compiled in 1938, and it has undergone numerous revisions over the years. The most recent major revision occurred in 1983 with modifications in 1987, 1993, and 1997.[3]

Cyclical Indicator Categories

The first category, **leading indicators** of the business cycle, includes economic series that usually reach peaks or troughs before corresponding peaks or troughs in aggregate economic activity. The group currently includes the 10 series shown in Table 14.2, which indicates the median lead or lag for each series relative to business cycle peaks or troughs. One of the 10 leading economic series is common stock prices, which has a median lead of 4 months at peaks and troughs. Another leading series, the money supply in constant (1992) dollars, has a median lead of 5 months at peaks and 4 months at troughs.

The second category, **coincident indicators**, includes economic time series that have peaks and troughs that roughly coincide with the peaks and troughs in the business cycle.

[2]Julius Shiskin, "Business Cycle Indicators: The Known and the Unknown," *Review of the International Statistical Institute* 31, no. 3 (1963): 361–383.

[3]For a discussion of these changes, see Marie P. Hertzberg and Barry A. Beckman, "Business Cycle Indicators: Revised Composite Indexes," *Business Conditions Digest* (January 1989): 291–296; David Wassel, "Leading Index to Be Prepared by New Method," *Wall Street Journal,* 23 November 1993, A3; and *Business Cycle Indicators* (The Conference Board, February 1997).

TABLE 14.2 **ECONOMIC SERIES IN THE NBER LEADING INDICATOR GROUP**

	Median Lead (−) or Lag (+) (in Months)		
	Peaks	Troughs	All Turns
1. Average weekly hours of production workers (manufacturing)	−2	−3	−3
2. Average weekly initial claims for unemployment insurance (inverted)	−5	−1	−3
3. Manufacturers' new orders in 1992 dollars—consumer goods and materials	−2	−2	−2
4. Index of raw private housing units authorized by local building permits	−9	−6	−7
5. Index of stock prices, 500 common stocks	−4	−4	−4
6. M2 money supply in 1992 dollars	−5	−4	−5
7. Vendor performance (percentage of firms receiving slower deliveries)	−3	−4	−3
8. Changes in business and consumer credit outstanding	−4	−6	−5
9. Interest rate spread, 10-year Treasury yield less federal funds	−2	0	−1½
10. Index of consumer expectations	−4	−3	−3

Source: Geoffrey H. Moore, "The Leading Indicator Approach—Value, Limitations, and Future," presented at Annual Western Economic Association Meeting (June 1984), revised June 1986; Marie P. Hertzberg and Barry A. Beckman, "Business Cycle Indicators: Revised Composite Indexes," *Business Conditions Digest* 17, no. 1 (January 1989); and The Conference Board, "Business Cycle Indicators Project," in *Business Cycle Indicators* (February 1997).

As one might expect, the bureau uses many of these economic time series to help define the different phases of the cycle.

The third category, **lagging indicators**, includes series that experience their peaks and troughs after those of the aggregate economy. A listing and the average timing relationships for the coincident and lagging series appear in Table 14.3.

A final category, *selected series,* includes economic series that are expected to influence aggregate economic activity but do not fall neatly into one of the three main groups. This includes such series as U.S. balance of payments, federal surplus or deficit, and military contract awards.

COMPOSITE SERIES AND RATIO OF SERIES In addition to the individual economic series in each category, a composite time series combines these economic series—for example, the *composite leading indicator index.* This composite leading indicator series is widely reported in the press each month as an indicator of the current and future state of the economy. There also are composite coincident and lagging indicator series.

Some analysts have used a *ratio* of these composite series, contending that the ratio of the composite coincident series divided by the composite lagging series acts like a leading series, in some instances even leading the composite leading series. The rationale for expecting this leading relationship for the ratio is that the coincident series should turn before the lagging series, and the ratio of the two series will be quite sensitive to such changes. As a result, this ratio series is expected to lead both of the individual component series, especially at turning points.

Although movements for this ratio series are generally parallel to those of the leading series, its real value comes when it diverges from the pure leading indicator series because

TABLE 14.3 **ECONOMIC SERIES IN THE NBER COINCIDENT AND LAGGING INDICATOR SERIES**

	Median Lead (−) or Lag (+) (in Months)		
	Peaks	Troughs	All Turns
A. Coincident Indicator Series			
1. Employees on nonagricultural payrolls	−2	0	0
2. Personal income less transfer payments in 1992 dollars	0	−1	− ½
3. Index of industrial production	−3	0	− ½
4. Manufacturing and trade sales in 1992 dollars	−3	0	− ½
B. Lagging Indicator Series			
1. Average duration of unemployment in weeks (inverted)	+1	+8	+3½
2. Ratio of manufacturing and trade inventories to sales in 1992 dollars	+2	+3	+3
3. Average prime rate charged by banks	+4	+14	+5
4. Commercial and industrial loans outstanding in 1992 dollars	+2	+5	+4
5. Ratio of consumer installment credit outstanding to personal income	+6	+7	+7
6. Labor cost per unit of output in manufacturing, actual data as percentage of trend	+8½	+11	+10

Source: Moore, "The Leading Indicator Approach"; and Hertzberg and Beckman, "Business Cycle Indicators."

this signals a change in the normal relationship between the indicator series. For example, if the leading indicator series has been rising for a period of time, you would expect both the coincident and lagging series also to be rising, but the coincident series should be rising faster than the lagging series, so the ratio of the coincident to the lagging series should likewise be rising. In contrast, assume the leading indicator series is rising, but the ratio of coincident to lagging series is flattening out or declining. This change in trend in the ratio series could occur because the coincident series is not rising as fast as the lagging indicator series, or because the coincident series has turned down. Either scenario would indicate a possible end to an economic expansion or at least a less robust expansion.

An example of such a divergence appears in Figure 14.1. The pattern indicates that between 1991 and mid-1994, the ratio series increased at a faster rate than the leading series because the coincident series was rising while the lagging series declined dramatically from 1991 to 1993 and was flat from 1993 to mid-1994. It appears that both the ratio series and the leading series experienced softness during 1995 and have increased together from 1996 to the beginning of 1999.

Analytical Measures of Performance

When predicting the future based on an economic series, it is important to consider more than the behavior of the series alone. Certain analytical measures have been suggested for examining behavior within an alternative economic series.

DIFFUSION INDEXES As the name implies, *diffusion indexes* indicate how pervasive a given movement is in a series. Diffusion index values are measured by computing the percentage of reporting units in a series that indicate a given result. For example, if 100 companies constitute the sample reporting new orders for equipment, the diffusion index for this series would indicate what proportion of the 100 companies was reporting higher orders during an expansion. In addition to knowing that aggregate new

FIGURE 14.1 **INDICATOR SERIES PERFORMANCE**

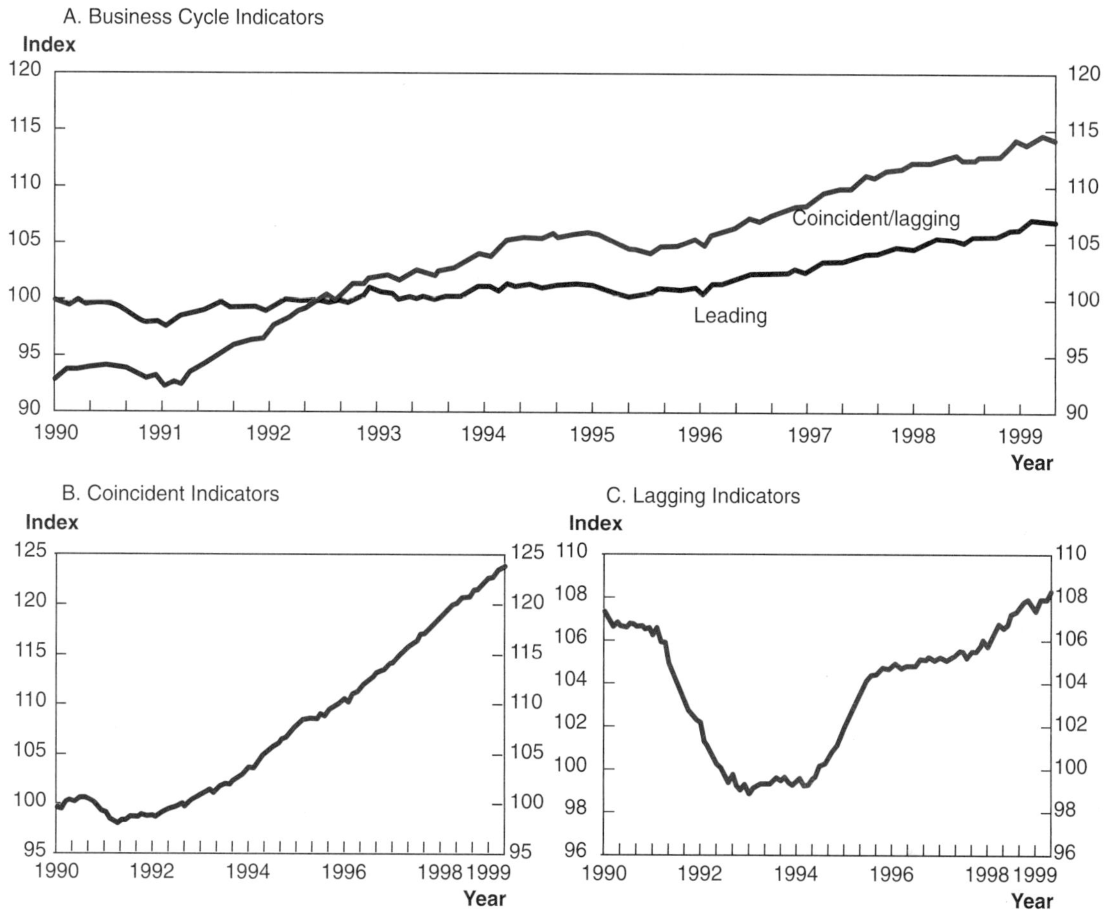
A. Business Cycle Indicators
Index
120
115
110
105
100
95
90
1990
1991
1992
1993
1994
1995
1996
1997
1998
1999
Year
Coincident/lagging
Leading
B. Coincident Indicators
Index
125
120
115
110
105
100
95
1990
1992
1994
1996
1998
1999
Year
C. Lagging Indicators
Index
110
108
106
104
102
100
98
96
1990
1992
1994
1996
1998
1999
Year

Source: Created by authors using data provided by the Conference Board from its *Business Cycle Indicators* database.

orders are increasing, it is helpful to know whether 55 percent or 95 percent of the companies in the sample are reporting higher orders. This information on the pervasiveness of the increase in new orders would help you project the future length and strength of an expansion.

You also would want to know the prevailing *trend* for a diffusion index. The diffusion index for a series almost always reaches its peak or trough before the peak or trough in the corresponding aggregate series. Therefore, you can use the diffusion index for a series to predict the behavior of the series itself. Assume that you are interested in the leading series, Manufacturers New Orders in 1992 dollars—Consumer Goods. If the diffusion index for this series drops from 85 percent to 75 percent and then to 70 percent, it indicates a widespread receipt of new orders, but it also indicates a *diminishing* breadth to the increase and possibly a forthcoming decline in the series itself.

Besides creating diffusion indexes for individual series, there is also a diffusion index that shows the percentage of the 10 leading indicators rising or falling during a given period. This particular diffusion index is widely reported each month as an indicator of the future state of the economy.

RATES OF CHANGE Knowing whether a series is increasing is useful, but more helpful is knowing that a 7 percent increase one month followed a 10 percent increase the previous month. The point is, the series is growing, but at a declining rate. Similar to the diffusion index, the rate of change values for a series reaches peaks or troughs prior to the peak or trough in the aggregate series.

DIRECTION OF CHANGE Direction of change tables show which series rose or fell (indicated by plus or minus signs) during the most recent period and how long the movement in this direction has persisted.

COMPARISON WITH PREVIOUS CYCLES A set of tables and charts shows the movements of individual series during the current business cycle and compares these movements to previous cycles for the same economic series. This comparison reveals whether a given series is moving slower or faster, or more strongly or weakly, than during prior cycles. This information can be useful because, typically, movements in the initial months of an expansion or contraction indicate their ultimate length and strength.[4]

Limitations of the Cyclical Indicator Approach

The NBER consistently has attempted to improve the usefulness of the cyclical indicators while acknowledging some limitations. The most obvious limitation is *false signals.* Past patterns might suggest that current indicator values signal a contraction, but then the indicator series turns up again and nullifies previous signals. A similar problem occurs when the indicators show hesitancy that is difficult to interpret. Some economic series may exhibit *high variability,* diminishing confidence in short-run signals as compared to projecting longer-term trends.

Another limitation is the *currency of the data* and *revisions.* The problem is that you might not get the original data very soon and then you have to be aware of subsequent revisions that may actually change the sign or direction of a series. Many of the series are seasonally adjusted, so you also must watch for changes in the seasonal adjustment factors.

Also, no series adequately reflects the service sector, which has grown to be a major factor in our economy. Further, no series represents the very important global economy or world securities markets. Similarly, the whole import–export sector is represented only in the "other series" group when, in fact, the export sector was the fastest-growing sector of our economy in the 1990s. Finally, there are numerous political or international developments that significantly influence the economy, but these factors cannot be incorporated into a statistical system.[5]

Leading Indicators and Stock Prices

Because stock prices are part of the composite set of leading indicators, an interesting question is whether we can use the composite leading series without stock prices to predict stock prices. A study that considered this question specified the decision rule in terms of percentage changes in the composite series.[6] Comparing the results of this decision rule to those of a buy-and-hold policy indicated that as long as the analysts had perfect

---

[4]Monthly presentations of all the series and analytical measures previously appeared in the U.S. Department of Commerce publication *Business Conditions Digest.* The government stopped publishing the *Digest* in 1990. The data now appear in the *Business Cycle Indicators* published by the Conference Board.

[5]These problems are discussed in Evan Koenig and Kenneth Emery, "Misleading Indicators? Using the Composite Leading Indicators to Predict Cyclical Turning Points," Federal Reserve Bank of Dallas, *Economic Review* (July 1991): 1–14.

[6]Bryan Heathcotte and Vincent P. Apilado, "The Predictive Content of Some Leading Economic Indicators for Future Stock Prices," *Journal of Financial and Quantitative Analysis* 9, no. 2 (March 1974): 247–258.

foresight regarding the correct percentage change to use, they beat a buy-and-hold policy. When they used the trading rule without foresight as to the best percentage change (merely using the percentage change that would have worked during the prior market cycle), they were not able to beat a buy-and-hold policy after subtracting commissions. Therefore, although these leading economic indicator series tend to lead the economy and can be used to predict aggregate economic activity, the composite leading indicator series does not consistently lead its own stock price component in a way that is useful for investment decisions.

Other Leading Indicator Series

The CIBCR at the Columbia Graduate School of Business has developed several additional leading indicator series. Monthly data for these series developed and maintained by the CIBCR are available in "The Leading Indicator Press Release." This release is published about the 10th day of each month with data as of 6 weeks prior to its release.

LONG-LEADING INDEX The CIBCR has developed its *Long-Leading Index* to provide earlier signals of major turning points in the economy than other leading indexes. It includes the following four series: (1) Dow Jones bond prices (20 bonds by percentage of face value); (2) the ratio of price to unit labor cost in manufacturing (1982 = 100); (3) M2 money supply, deflated (billion 1992 dollars); and (4) new housing building permits (1967 = 100). This index has anticipated recessions by 14 months, on average, and always by at least 7 months.

LEADING EMPLOYMENT INDEX The purpose of the CIBCR's *Leading Employment Index* (1967 = 100) is to forecast future changes in U.S. employment. It includes the following six component series:

1. Average workweek in manufacturing
2. Overtime hours in manufacturing
3. Percentage layoff rate (inverted)
4. Voluntary/involuntary part-time employment
5. Percentage short duration unemployment rate (inverted)
6. Initial claims for unemployment insurance (inverted)

LEADING INFLATION INDEX The CIBCR *Leading Inflation Index* is intended as a tool for forecasting inflation in the United States. It includes five variables:

1. The percentage employed of the working-age population
2. The growth rate of total debt (including business, consumer, and federal government debt
3. The growth rate of industrial material prices
4. The growth rate of an index of import prices
5. The percentage of businesspeople anticipating an increase in their selling prices, as determined by a Dun and Bradstreet survey

The leads for this series during the period 1950 to 1998 averaged 7 months at troughs, 4 months at peaks, and 5 months at all turns.

ANALYSIS OF ALTERNATIVE LEADING INDICATORS OF INFLATION A study by Garner examined the usefulness of the CIBCR series and four other series that have been suggested as leading indicators of inflation, including the price of gold and other composite series.[7] The results indicate that the composite indicators provide useful early indications of inflation turning points. Unfortunately, none of the series provides accurate estimates of the magnitude of inflation.

INTERNATIONAL LEADING INDICATOR SERIES In addition to developing leading indicators for the U.S. economy, the CIBCR also has developed a set of composite leading indicators for eight other major industrial countries: Canada, Germany, France, the United Kingdom, Italy, Japan, Australia, and Taiwan (Republic of China). These International Leading Indicator Series are part of an ongoing project to develop an international economic indicator (IEI) system. The series are comparable in data and analysis to the leading series for the United States.[8]

SURVEYS OF SENTIMENT AND EXPECTATIONS Consumer expectations seem to play a role as the economy approaches turning points in the business cycle. Two surveys of consumer expectations are reported monthly in the financial media. The University of Michigan Consumer Sentiment Index and the Conference Board Consumer Confidence Index both query a sample of households on their expectations over the next 6 months (Conference Board) or over the next year (Michigan). Although the two indexes sometimes deviate from each other month to month, over longer time periods they track each other fairly closely. Both indexes act as a leading indicator by rising and falling before the general level of economic activity does.

Other surveys of consumer and business expectations focus on the overall economy, and some focus on such areas as firms' capital spending or inventory investment plans. By subscribing to proprietary services or closely following the financial media, investment analysts can monitor how consumers and the business community feel about the economy and their spending plans. In general, the more optimistic they are, the better the prospects for increases in spending and economic growth. The more pessimistic they are, the worse the prospects for spending and growth. The problem with survey data is that individuals' and firms' reported plans may not come to fruition. Just because a survey reports that manufacturing firms expect to increase capital spending by a certain percentage does not mean they will actually do so.

Economic statistics released by the government are another source of helpful information about current economic trends, particularly concerning various economic sectors. Every Monday, *The Wall Street Journal* publishes a short commentary, "Tracking the Economy." The feature reports statistics that will be released during the coming week (for example, housing starts, agricultural production, GDP), their previous values, and their consensus forecasts. As you would expect from our discussion of efficient markets, investors react to economic "surprises" wherein the actual results deviate from the consensus forecasts (expectations).

MONETARY VARIABLES, THE ECONOMY, AND STOCK PRICES

Many academic and professional observers hypothesize a close relationship between stock prices and various monetary variables that are influenced by monetary policy. The best-

[7]C. Alan Garner, "How Useful Are Leading Indicators of Inflation?" Federal Reserve Bank of Kansas City *Economic Review* 80, no. 2 (Second Quarter 1995): 5–18.

[8]For an extended discussion, see Geoffrey H. Moore, "An Introduction to International Economic Indicators," *Business Cycles, Inflation, and Forecasting,* 2d ed. (New York: National Bureau of Economic Research, Studies in Business Cycles, No. 24, 1983).

known monetary variable in this regard is the *money supply.* You will recall from your economics course that the money supply can be measured in several ways, including currency plus demand deposits (referred to as the M1 money supply), and the M1 money supply plus time deposits (referred to as the M2 money supply). The government publishes other measures of the money supply, but M1 and M2 are the best known.[9] The Federal Reserve controls the money supply through various tools, the most useful of which is open market operations.

MONEY SUPPLY AND THE ECONOMY

In their classic work on the monetary history of the United States, Friedman and Schwartz thoroughly documented the relationship between changes in the growth rate of the money supply and subsequent changes in the economy.[10] Specifically, they demonstrated that declines in the rate of growth of the money supply have preceded business contractions by an average of 20 months, while increases in the growth rate of the money supply have preceded economic expansions by about 8 months.

Friedman suggests a transmission mechanism through which changes in the growth rate of the money supply affect the aggregate economy. He hypothesizes that, to implement planned changes in monetary policy, the Federal Reserve engages in open market operations, buying or selling Treasury bonds to adjust bank reserves and, eventually, the money supply. Because the Fed deals in government bonds, the initial liquidity impact affects the government bond market, creating excess liquidity for those who sold bonds to the Fed when the Federal Reserve was buying bonds, or there would be insufficient liquidity when the Federal Reserve sells bonds. Rising or falling government bond prices subsequently filter down to corporate bonds, and this change in liquidity eventually affects common stocks, and then the real goods market. The impact of money supply growth on stock prices is really part of the transmission process whereby money supply affects the aggregate economy. This liquidity transmission scenario implies that the initial effect of a change in monetary policy appears in financial markets (bonds and stocks) and only later in the aggregate economy.

MONEY SUPPLY AND STOCK PRICES

Numerous studies have tested the relationship suggested by this transmission mechanism. Specifically, do changes in the growth rate of the money supply precede changes in stock prices? The results of these studies have tended to change over time. The initial studies done in the 1960s and early 1970s generally indicated a strong *leading* relationship between money supply changes and stock prices.[11] Such results implied that changes in the growth rate of the money supply could serve as a leading indicator of stock price changes.

Subsequent studies questioned these findings.[12] Although these studies likewise found a relationship between the money supply and stock prices, the timing of the relationship

---

[9]For a discussion of alternative monetary series, see John R. Walter, "Monetary Aggregates: A User's Guide," Federal Reserve Bank of Richmond *Economic Review* (January/February 1989): 53–61.

[10]Milton Friedman and Anna J. Schwartz, "Money and Business Cycles," *Review of Economics and Statistics* 45, no. 1, part 2, supplement (February 1963): 32–78, reprinted in Milton Friedman, *The Optimum Quantity of Money and Other Essays* (Chicago: Aldine Publishing, 1969): 189–235.

[11]Studies that generally support this view include Beryl W. Sprinkel, *Money and Markets: A Monetarist View* (Homewood, Ill.: Richard D. Irwin, 1971); Michael W. Keran, "Expectations, Money, and the Stock Market," Federal Reserve Bank of St. Louis *Review* 53, no. 1 (January 1971): 16–31; and Kenneth Homa and Dwight Jaffee, "The Study of Money and Stock Prices," *Journal of Finance* 26, no. 5 (December 1971): 1015–1066.

[12]These studies include Richard V. L. Cooper, "Efficient Capital Markets and the Quantity Theory of Money," *Journal of Finance* 29, no. 3 (June 1974): 887–908; and M. S. Rozeff, "Money and Stock Prices: Market Efficiency and the Lag Effect of Monetary Policy," *Journal of Financial Economics* 1, no. 3 (September 1974): 245–302.

differed. These studies found that changes in the growth rate of the money supply did not lead stock prices but consistently *lagged* stock returns by about 1 to 3 months.

Studies in the 1980s examined the relationship of stock returns to anticipated and unanticipated money supply growth using weekly money supply data.[13] The results indicated that money changes affect stock prices, but the securities markets adjust stock prices very quickly to any unexpected changes in money supply growth. Therefore, to enjoy superior returns, it is necessary to *forecast unanticipated changes* in money supply growth.

Following more than a decade of very little research on this topic, several recent studies have found that monetary policy and the monetary environment do have an impact on stock returns. The initial research in this recent set of studies was done by Jensen, Johnson, and Mercer (JJM). The authors showed that the results of several earlier studies that examined the relationship between some economic variables and stock returns (e.g., default spreads, dividend yield, and term spreads) or some company variables and stock returns (e.g., size and price/book value ratios) can be significantly affected by the prevailing monetary environment.[14] Specifically, JJM showed that the business conditions proxies suggested by Fama and French[15] (i. e., the term spread, dividend yield, and default spread) have a different effect on stock returns depending on the prevailing monetary policy, where monetary policy is indicated by discount rate changes (i.e., declining discount rates imply an easy monetary policy, while rising discount rates imply a restrictive policy). The JJM studies also show that the relationship between stock price returns and both size and the price-to-book value ratio found in several studies[16] only holds during periods of easy monetary policy. A subsequent study by Thorbecke examined how stock returns respond to monetary policy shocks.[17] The results provided evidence that expansionary monetary policy increases ex-post stock returns. The most recent study by Patelis examines whether shifts in monetary policy can account for the predictability of excess stock returns.[18] The results of several statistical tests indicated that monetary policy variables were significant predictors of future stock returns, although they were not the only relevant factors (i.e., dividend yield was also relevant).

EXCESS LIQUIDITY AND STOCK PRICES Some analysts have looked beyond the growth rate of the money supply. Steven Einhorn of Goldman, Sachs & Co. contends that *excess liquidity* is the relevant monetary variable that influences stock prices. Excess

---

[13]These studies are found in Lawrence S. Davidson and Richard T. Froyen, "Monetary Policy and Stock Returns: Are Stock Markets Efficient?" Federal Reserve Bank of St. Louis *Review* 64, no. 3 (March 1982): 3–12; and R. W. Hafer, "The Response of Stock Prices to Changes in Weekly Money and the Discount Rate," Federal Reserve Bank of St. Louis *Review* 64, no. 3 (March 1985): 5–14.

[14]Gerald R. Jenson, Jeffrey Mercer, and Robert R. Johnson, "Business Conditions, Monetary Policy, and Expected Security Returns," *Journal of Financial Economics* 40, no. 2 (February 1996): 213–237; Gerald R. Jenson, Robert R. Johnson, and Jeffrey M. Mercer, "New Evidence on Size and Price-to-Book Effects in Stock Returns," *Financial Analysts Journal* 53, no. 6 (November–December 1997): 34–42; and Gerald R. Jenson, Robert R. Johnson, and Jeffrey M. Mercer, "The Inconsistency of Small Firm and Value Stock Premiums," *Journal of Portfolio Management* 24, no. 2 (winter 1998): 27–36.

[15]Eugene F. Fama and Kenneth French, "Business Conditions and Expected Returns on Stocks and Bonds," *Journal of Financial Economics* 25, no. 1 (January 1989): 23–49.

[16]These studies include Eugene F. Fama and Kenneth French, "Size and Book-to-Market Factors in Earnings and Returns," *Journal of Finance* 50, no. 1 (March 1995): 131–155; and Patricia M. Fairfield, "P/E, P/B, and Present Value of Future Dividends," *Financial Analysts Journal* 50, no. 4 (July–August 1994): 23–31.

[17]Willem Thorbecke, "On Stock Market Returns and Monetary Policy," *Journal of Finance* 52, no. 2 (June 1997): 635–654.

[18]Alex D. Patelis, "Stock Returns Predictability and the Role of Monetary Policy," *Journal of Finance* 52, no. 5 (December 1997):1951–1972.

FIGURE 14.2 **TIME SERIES PLOT OF "EXCESS LIQUIDITY" IN THE UNITED STATES: 1985–1998**

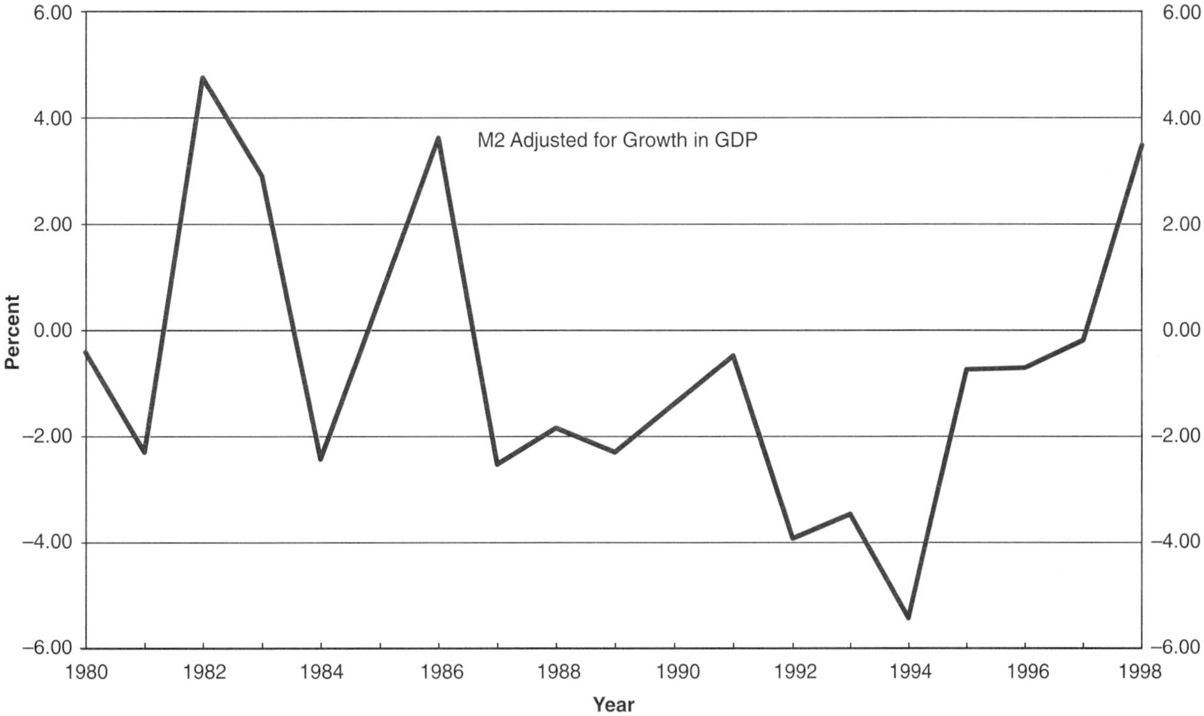
6.00
4.00
2.00
0.00
−2.00
−4.00
−6.00
Percent
M2 Adjusted for Growth in GDP
1980
1982
1984
1986
1988
1990
1992
1994
1996
1998
Year

Source: Chart contained in "Investment Strategy Chartbook," Abby Joseph Cohen and Gabrielle Napolitano (New York: Goldman, Sachs & Co., Quarterly).

liquidity is defined as the year-to-year percentage change in the M2 money supply adjusted for small time deposits less the year-to-year percentage change in nominal GDP. It is reasoned that the growth rate of nominal GDP indicates the need for liquidity in the economy. If the money supply growth rate exceeds the GDP growth rate, this indicates there is excess money (liquidity) in the economy that is available for buying securities. Therefore, it is reasoned that positive excess liquidity should lead to higher security prices.

Figure 14.2 contains a time series plot of excess liquidity in the United States since 1985. Our measure is somewhat different from that used by Goldman, Sachs—ours is equal to the annual growth rate of the M2 money supply minus the annual growth rate of GDP. As shown, it was negative during the period 1992 into 1997, yet U.S. stocks experienced outstanding returns during 1995–1998. This inconsistency could be caused by positive non-U.S. excess liquidity in some of our major trading partners, such as the United Kingdom, Germany, and Japan, who tend to invest in our stocks. These figures reveal positive excess liquidity for some periods in all these countries. This non-U.S. liquidity helped the U.S. stock market continue to rise in 1995–1998.

Other Economic Variables and Stock Prices

Chen, Roll, and Ross examined equity returns relative to a set of macroeconomic variables.[19] They found the following variables to be significant in explaining stock returns:

[19]Nai-Fu Chen, Richard Roll, and Stephen A. Ross, "Economic Forces and the Stock Market," *Journal of Business* 59, no. 3 (July 1986).

- Growth in industrial production
- Changes in the risk premium
- Twists in the yield curve
- Measures of unanticipated inflation
- Changes in expected inflation during periods of volatile inflation

The authors did not attempt to predict market returns, but suggested that these variables were important in explaining past returns.

INFLATION, INTEREST RATES, AND SECURITY PRICES

Because this chapter is concerned with the macroeconomic analysis of security markets, we should examine the macroeconomic impact of inflation and interest rates. We have noted throughout the book the critical role of expected inflation and nominal interest rates in determining the required rate of return used to derive the value of all investments. We would expect these variables that are very important in microeconomic valuation to also affect changes in the aggregate markets.

INFLATION AND INTEREST RATES Figure 14.3 contains a plot of long-term interest rates and the year-to-year percentage change in the consumer price index (CPI, a measure of inflation). This graph demonstrates the strong relationship between inflation and interest rates. We contended in our earlier discussion that when investors anticipated an increase in the rate of inflation, they would increase their required rates of return by a similar amount to derive constant real rates of return. The time series graph of the promised yield of Aaa corporate bonds and the annual rate of inflation in Figure 14.3 confirms the expected relationship overall, but also indicates an imperfect relationship between interest rates and inflation. If the relationship was perfect and investors were accurate in their *predictions* of future inflation, the difference between the interest rate and the inflation rate (the spread between them) would be fairly constant, reflecting the real return on corporate bonds. As shown, the spread between these two curves changes over time.

Figure 14.4 plots this spread and demonstrates the following results. Although the two curves generally move together, in some periods (1975–1979) the inflation rate exceeded the yield on the bonds, which implies that during these periods investors received *negative* real returns on corporate bonds. In contrast, during 1983–1985, the real rates of return on these bonds were in the 8 to 10 percent range, which clearly exceeds what most investors would expect on very low risk bonds.

This change in spread does not mean that there is not a relationship between inflation and interest rates; it only shows that *investors are not very good at predicting inflation.* Recall that the theoretical relationship is between *expected* inflation and interest rates, in contrast to these data that reflect actual inflation. Apparently, investors underestimated the rate of inflation during the periods of negative real returns, and overestimated the rate of inflation during periods when there were abnormally high real rates of return.

INTEREST RATES AND BOND PRICES The relationship between interest rates and bond prices is clearly negative because the only variable that changes in the valuation model is the discount factor. Specifically, the expected cash flows from a straight non-callable bond would not change, so an increase in interest rates will cause a decline in bond prices and a decline in interest rates will boost bond prices. For example, if you own a 10-year bond with a coupon of 10 percent, when interest rates go from 10 percent to 12 percent, the price of this bond will go from $1,000 (par) to $885. In contrast, if rates go from 10 percent to 8 percent, the price of the bond will go from $1,000 to $1,136.

FIGURE 14.3 TIME SERIES PLOT OF THE PROMISED YIELD OF MOODY'S AAA CORPORATE BONDS AND INFLATION: MONTHLY 1974–1998

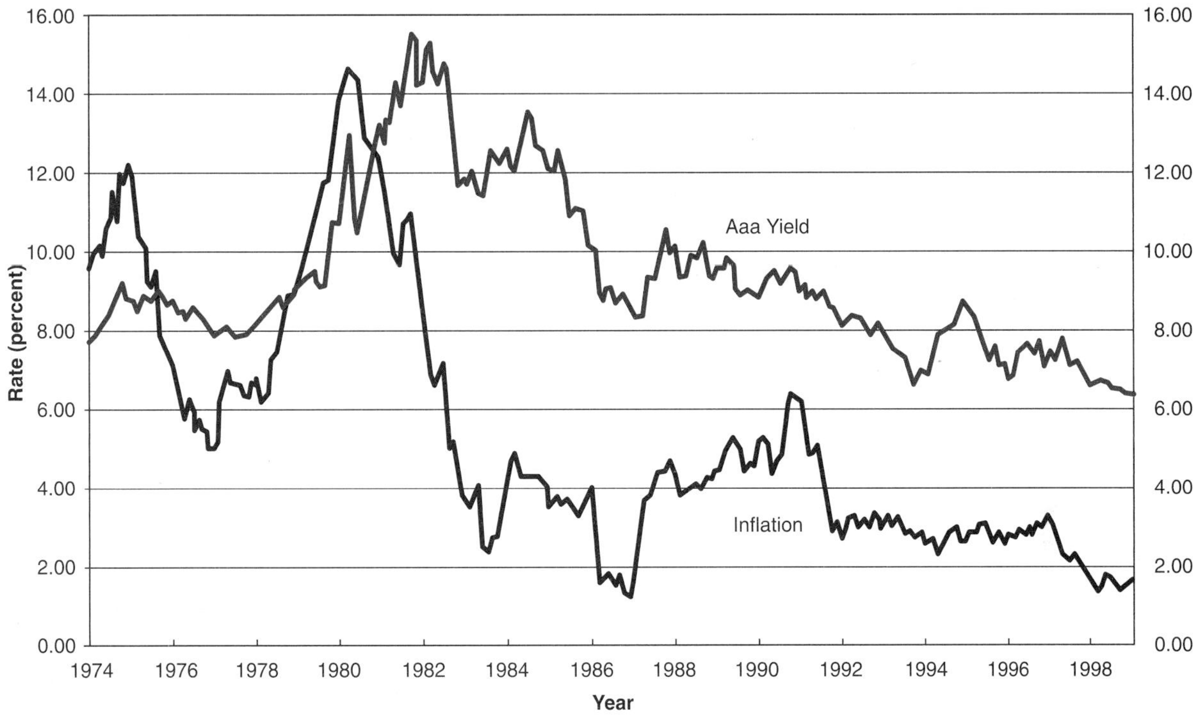
16.00
14.00
12.00
10.00
8.00
6.00
4.00
2.00
0.00
Rate (percent)
Aaa Yield
Inflation
1974
1976
1978
1980
1982
1984
1986
1988
1990
1992
1994
1996
1998
Year

Data Source: Moody's Investor's Service.

The size of the price change will depend on the characteristics of the bond. A longer-term bond will experience a larger price change for a change in interest rates.[20] Therefore, we can anticipate a negative relationship between inflation and the rates of return on bonds because inflation generally has a direct effect on interest rates, and in turn interest rates have an inverse effect on bond prices and rates of return. One example of empirical verification for this negative relationship is provided in Table 3.9, which shows a correlation of −0.647 between inflation and returns on long-term investment-grade bonds.

INTEREST RATES AND STOCK PRICES The relationship between interest rates and stock prices is not direct and consistent. The reason is that the cash flows from stocks can change along with interest rates, and we cannot be certain whether this change in cash flows will augment or offset the change in interest rates. To demonstrate this, consider the following potential scenarios following an increase in the rate of inflation and the effect on stock prices based on the DDM.

1. Interest rates rise due to an increase in the rate of inflation, and corporate earnings likewise experience an increase in growth because firms are able to increase prices in line with cost increases. In this case, stock prices might be fairly stable because the negative

[20]Chapter 16 contains a detailed discussion of the specific variables that influence bond price volatility.

FIGURE 14.4 **SPREAD BETWEEN PROMISED YIELD OF MOODY'S AAA CORPORATE BONDS AND INFLATION: MONTHLY 1974–1998**

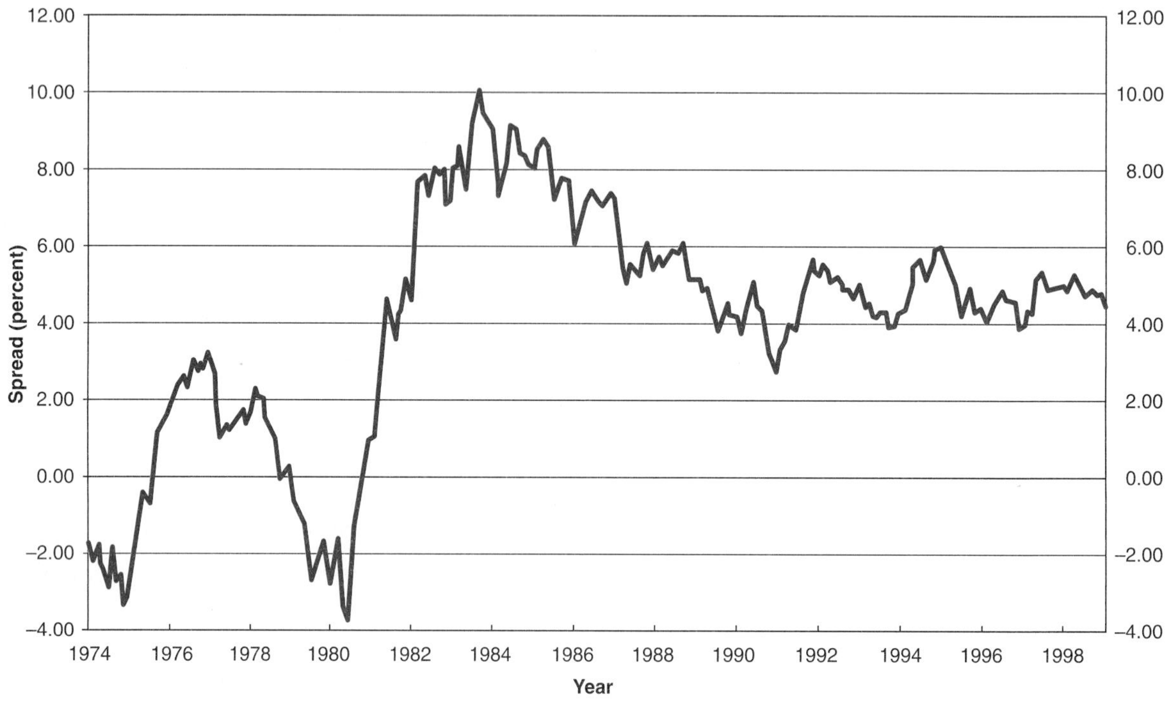
Spread (percent)
12.00
10.00
8.00
6.00
4.00
2.00
0.00
−2.00
−4.00
1974
1976
1978
1980
1982
1984
1986
1988
1990
1992
1994
1996
1998
Year

Data Source: Moody's Investor's Service.

effect of an increase in the required rate of return (k) is partially or wholly offset by the increase in the growth rate of earnings and dividends (g).

2. Interest rates increase, but expected cash flows change very little because firms are not able to increase prices in response to higher costs. This would cause a decline in stock prices similar to what happens with a bond. The required rate or return (k) would increase, but the growth rate of dividends (g) would be constant. As a result, the k–g spread discussed in Chapter 13 will widen and stock prices would decline.
3. Interest rates increase while cash flows decline because the factors that cause the rise in interest rates have a negative impact on earnings. For example, during 1981 to 1982, interest rates increased and remained high during a period of economic decline, which caused sales and earnings to decline. Alternatively, one can envision a period of inflation wherein the costs of production increase, but many firms are not able to increase prices, which causes a decline in profit margins. The impact of this set of events can be disastrous. Given this scenario, stock prices will experience significant decline because k will increase as g declines, causing a large increase in the k–g spread.

In contrast to these scenarios, you can envision a comparable set of scenarios when inflation and interest rates decline. The relationship between inflation, interest rates, and stock prices is not as direct or consistent as the relationship between interest rates and bonds. The effect of interest rate changes on stock prices will depend on what caused the change in interest rates and the effect of this event on the expected cash flows on common stock.

Notably, the actual relationship between inflation, interest rates, and stock prices is an empirical question and *the effect varies over time.* Therefore, although there has generally been a significant *negative* relationship between inflation, interest rates and the returns on stock, as shown in Chapter 3 (Table 3.9), this is not always true.[21] In addition, even when it is true for the overall market, certain industries or segments of the economy may have earnings and dividends that react positively to inflation and interest rate changes. In such an instance, their stock prices would be positively correlated with inflation and interest rates.[22]

Summary of Macroeconomic Analysis

There is ample evidence of a strong and consistent relationship between economic activity and the stock market, although stock prices consistently seem to turn from 4 to 9 months before the economy does. Therefore, to project the future direction of the stock market using the macroeconomic approach, you must either forecast economic activity about 12 months ahead or examine economic indicator series that lead the economy by more than stock prices do.

The results with the leading indicator series indicated that only with perfect foresight regarding the appropriate change to use with a diffusion index of the leading indicator series could an investor improve on a buy-and-hold policy. The results from studies of the relationship between the money supply and stock prices have indicated a significant relationship, but some research indicates that stock prices generally turn before the money supply does. The most recent research has indicated that monetary policy and the monetary environment do have a significant relationship to stock market returns. Therefore, it is a factor that should be considered when projecting market returns.

Alternative measures of the monetary environment were also considered, including U.S. and global excess liquidity. Although the historical results with U.S. excess liquidity were interesting, recent results have not been as consistent. Some contend that global liquidity has had an impact on the U.S. capital markets. Such a global monetary effect is not surprising and emphasizes the need to consider global macroeconomic variables. Alternatively, discount rate changes have been a very effective measure.

ANALYSIS OF WORLD SECURITY MARKETS

Although we have focused on the U.S. market to demonstrate the macroeconomic approach to forecasting movements in the securities markets, you must also consider a similar analysis for numerous foreign markets, including those in Japan, Canada, the United Kingdom, and Germany. Although it is not feasible to analyze each of these markets in detail, we can provide an example of such an analysis by reviewing the extensive analysis done by Goldman, Sachs & Co. This analysis is contained in a quarterly Goldman, Sachs publication, *World Investment Strategy Highlights,* as part of the firm's international research effort.

[21]A sample of studies on the topic of inflation and common stocks includes Frank K. Reilly, Glenn L. Johnson, and Ralph E. Smith, "Inflation, Inflation Hedges and Common Stocks," *Financial Analysts Journal* 26, no. 1 (January–February 1970): 104–110; Frank K. Reilly, "Companies and Common Stocks as Inflation Hedges," New York University, Center for the Study of Financial Institutions, *Bulletin* (April 1975); Jeffrey F. Jaffe and Gershon Mandelker, "The 'Fisher Effect' for Risky Assets: An Empirical Analysis," *Journal of Finance* 31, no. 2 (May 1976): 447–458; and Eugene F. Fama, "Stock Returns, Real Activity, Inflation and Money," *American Economic Review* 71, no. 4 (September 1981). For a more recent analysis of the factors that cause this relationship between inflation and stock returns, see Frank K. Reilly, "The Impact of Inflation on ROE, Growth and Stock Prices," *Financial Services Review* 6, no. 1 (1997): 1–17.

[22]Studies that examined alternative industries as inflation hedges include Stephen P. Ferris and Anil K. Makhija, "A Search for Common Stock Inflation Hedges," *Review of Business and Economic Research* 22, no. 2 (spring 1987): 27–36; and Frank K. Reilly, "Alternative Industries as Inflation Hedges," Financial Management Association Meeting (October 1987). Both studies found very few industries with positive correlations.

This publication draws on a number of other Goldman, Sachs publications to provide a world portfolio strategy as well as strategies for several individual countries.[23]

Goldman, Sachs uses a version of the three-step process (also referred to as the *top-down approach*), initially examining a country's aggregate economy and its components that relate to the valuation of securities—GDP, inflation, and interest rates. Table 14.4 contains the firm's forecast of GDP for several major countries. Note the fairly substantial differences in outlook for real GDP growth during 2000 (e.g., −0.8 percent for Japan versus 4.0 percent for Singapore).

Inflation and Exchange Rates

An analysis of historical and expected price changes in Table 14.5 also reveals differences in the outlook for inflation, ranging from −1.1 percent for Japan to 2.1 percent for the United States. These inflation estimates feed into an interest rate forecast for the end of 2000 in Table 14.6. This combination of forecasts indicates the expected trend in interest rates. The forecast for interest rates was clearly mixed. The overall range for expected long-term rates for mid-2000 was from 1.8 percent (Japan) to 5.0 percent (Canada).

Given these differences in inflation and interest rate levels and trends, you can expect major differences in the exchange rates. Table 14.7 presents the firm's forecast for several currencies. The forecasts for 6 months and 12 months imply trends during the year. These figures indicate that Goldman, Sachs expects the U.S. dollar to become weaker against most of the currencies during 1999–2000.

Based on this analysis of the underlying economies, Table 14.8 contains estimates of corporate earnings growth rates for various countries. It also gives estimates of other stock market variables, including dividend growth, price/earnings ratios, and dividend yields. Again, all series show major differences among countries. The estimated earnings growth rates for 1999 vary from zero expected growth for the United Kingdom to 14 percent for Italy. Likewise, the price/earnings ratio is expected to continue its historical variation, ranging in 1999 from about 18 times for Germany to 71 times for Japan.

Correlations among Returns

These substantial differences in economic performance and major changes in the underlying valuation variables indicate that there should be fairly low correlations among stock market returns for alternative countries. The correlation matrix of price changes in local currencies in Table 14.9 shows a fairly high correlation between the United States and the United Kingdom and Canada, and low correlations between the United States and Italy and Japan. Notably, the U.S.–Japan correlation increased during the early 1990s as our economies became more interdependent, but the correlations declined during the late 1990s when the Japanese economy and stock market experienced difficulty.

Table 14.10, a similar matrix in U.S. dollars, shows that all the correlations of returns with the United States decline when one considers the exchange rate effect. Comparisons such as these justify and encourage worldwide diversification of investments.

Individual Country Stock Price Changes

The stock market impact of exchange rates is shown in Table 14.11, which shows the percentage changes in stock prices in the local currency and adjusted for the U.S. dollar. The annual averages for local currency from 1994 to 1998 range from 0.4 percent for Japan to 13.9 percent for the United States. The percentage changes of stock prices in U.S. dollars ranged from 0.9 percent (Italy) to 13.9 percent (United States).

The significant impact of changes in exchange rates can be seen in two examples. Although the rate of change in Japan stock prices during 1994 was 8.0 percent, the change

[23]The other Goldman, Sachs publications used include *The International Economics Analyst, Financial Markets Perspectives, Investment Strategy Highlights, Japan Investment Strategy Highlights,* and *The U.K. Economics Analyst.*

TABLE 14.4 **FORECASTS FOR WORLD ECONOMIC ACTIVITY—REAL GDP GROWTH**

Country	1997	1998	1999E	2000E	10-Year Trend
		(percent per annum)			
United States	3.9	3.9	3.5	1.5	2.8
Japan	1.4	2.8	1.3	−0.8	3.1
Germany	2.2	2.8	1.4	1.8	2.6
United Kingdom	3.5	2.3	0.6	2.2	2.3
France	2.3	3.2	2.2	2.5	2.2
Italy	1.5	1.4	1.2	1.8	1.9
Mexico	6.8	4.8	1.5	3.0	3.0
Hong Kong	5.3	−5.1	−1.0	1.5	5.1
Singapore	8.0	1.5	2.0	4.0	5.8

E = estimate

Source: Adapted from *World Investment Strategy Highlights* (London: Goldman, Sachs International Corp., March 1999). Reprinted by permission of Goldman, Sachs & Co.

TABLE 14.5 **CONSUMER OR RETAIL PRICE CHANGES (PERCENTAGE CHANGES FROM PREVIOUS YEAR)**

Period	United States	Japan	Germany	France	United Kingdom	Italy	Hong Kong	Singapore
1988	4.1%	0.7%	1.3%	2.7%	4.9%	5.0%	NA	NA
1989	4.8	2.3	2.8	3.4	7.8	6.6	NA	NA
1990	4.4	3.0	2.7	3.5	9.5	6.1	NA	NA
1991	4.0	2.8	3.8	3.5	7.0	6.0	NA	NA
1992	3.0	1.7	4.0	2.8	3.7	5.2	NA	NA
1993	3.2	1.2	3.7	2.3	1.8	4.5	NA	NA
1994	2.6	0.7	2.7	2.1	2.4	3.9	8.1	3.1
1995	2.8	0.0	1.8	1.6	2.8	5.4	7.7	1.7
1996	2.6	0.0	1.8	1.8	2.9	3.8	6.8	2.0
1997	2.3	1.7	1.7	1.2	2.8	1.7	5.7	2.0
1998	1.6	0.7	1.0	0.7	2.7	1.7	4.1	−0.3
1999E	1.9	−0.9	0.5	0.4	2.3	1.2	−1.5	0.7
2000E	2.1	−1.1	0.5	0.6	1.9	1.3	1.0	1.2

E = estimate

Source: *World Investment Strategy Highlights* (London: Goldman, Sachs International Ltd., March 1999). Reprinted by permission of Goldman, Sachs & Co.

experienced by a U.S. citizen who invested in Japan during 1994 would have been 20.1 percent because of the significant strength of the yen. This increase in the rate of return (or decline in the negative price change) due to exchange rate changes relative to the U.S. dollar was fairly widespread during 1994. In contrast, during 1997 the U.S. dollar was quite strong, and all percentage stock price changes when converted to U.S. dollars were lower. For example, the change in Germany during 1997 was over 40 percent in local currency but only about 21 percent in U.S. dollars.

INDIVIDUAL COUNTRY ANALYSIS

Goldman, Sachs provides a detailed analysis of major countries that includes the country's economy and equity market, and culminates in a portfolio recommendation for investors in that country. Table 14.12 shows the major economic indicators for the United Kingdom reflecting a continuation of the economic expansion.

There is an analysis of the United Kingdom equity market in Table 14.13 following the economic projections. Goldman, Sachs feels that the overall economic outlook for the United Kingdom is moderate and declining, but the firm still expects U.K. equities to

TABLE 14.6

INTEREST RATE FORECASTS (PERCENT PER ANNUM)

Country	Current Rate[a]	Short Term (3 Months)	Long Term (12 Months)
United States			
3 month	4.9	5.2	4.7
10 year	5.2	5.1	4.7
Germany			
3 month	3.7	3.5	3.6
10 year	3.9	3.8	3.7
Japan			
3 month	0.2	0.2	0.4
10 year	1.8	1.3	1.8
France			
3 month	3.6	3.5	3.4
10 year	4.0	3.8	3.7
United Kingdom			
3 month	5.3	3.3	2.9
10 year	4.5	4.4	4.1
Canada			
3 month	4.9	5.0	4.5
10 year	5.2	5.1	5.0
Italy			
3 month	4.0	3.9	3.8
10 year	4.2	4.1	4.0

[a]1 March 1999

Source: *World Investment Strategy Highlights* (London: Goldman, Sachs International Ltd., March 1999). Reprinted by permission of Goldman, Sachs & Co.

TABLE 14.7

FORECAST OF EXCHANGE RATES AGAINST THE U.S. DOLLAR

	Canadian Dollar	Japanese Yen	British Pound	Euro	Swiss Franc
Current Rate	1.52	117	1.62	1.09	1.45
3 month	1.53	114	1.56	1.09	1.46
12 month	1.47	103	1.58	1.22	1.33

Source: Adapted from *World Investment Strategy Highlights* (London: Goldman, Sachs International Ltd., March 1999). Reprinted by permission of Goldman, Sachs & Co.

outperform bonds and short-term bonds (cash) during the next 12 months after inferior performance during the next 3 months.

World Asset Allocation

The final product of this analysis is a recommendation for an investor's world asset allocation. Table 14.14 begins with a division among bonds, equities, and cash. As of early 1999 Goldman, Sachs recommended that an investor should be at the middle of the range for both equity and cash, and slightly above midrange for bonds with a midrange exposure to commodities.

TABLE 14.8

COMPARATIVE STOCK MARKET STATISTICS

	United States	Japan	Hong Kong	United Kingdom	Germany	France	Italy
Earnings Growth							
1997	10	−31	11	3	14	31	11
1998	0	−32	−9	0	16	15	21
1999E	5	12	2	0	8	13	14
Dividend Growth							
1997	4	1	13	10	20	15	16
1998	5	−11	−13	6	15	11	25
1999E	6	8	−2	4	8	10	13
P/E							
1997	22.8	56.8	8.1	17.7	19.7	24.7	26.5
1998	30.2	79.5	—	19.1	19.5	25.4	27.4
1999E	30.7	71.1	—	19.1	18.1	22.5	23.9
D/Y							
1997	1.6	1.0	3.6	4.0	2.6	2.8	2.4
1998	1.2	0.8	3.3	3.6	2.3	2.3	1.9
1999E	1.3	0.8	3.2	3.4	2.6	2.4	1.9

Aggregates and multiples for earnings and dividend are based on a sample of all companies in each country. Note: Figures for the United States refer to the S&P Industrials Index and pertain to operating earnings.

Source: *World Investment Strategy Highlights* (London: Goldman, Sachs International Ltd., March 1999). Reprinted by permission of Goldman, Sachs & Co.

TABLE 14.9

CORRELATION OF PRICE RETURNS IN LOCAL CURRENCY: JANUARY 1986–JUNE 1999

	United States	Japan	Germany	United Kingdom	Canada	France
United States	—					
Japan	0.36	—				
Germany	0.53	0.31	—			
United Kingdom	0.72	0.36	0.57	—		
Canada	0.77	0.37	0.54	0.65	—	
France	0.58	0.43	0.75	0.61	0.56	—
Italy	0.35	0.38	0.54	0.44	0.39	0.60

Source: Prepared by the authors using data provided by Goldman, Sachs International Ltd. Reprinted by permission of Goldman, Sachs & Co.

TABLE 14.10

CORRELATION OF PRICE RETURNS IN U.S. DOLLARS: JANUARY 1986–JUNE 1999

	United States	Japan	Germany	United Kingdom	Canada	France
United States	—					
Japan	0.28	—				
Germany	0.44	0.30	—			
United Kingdom	0.62	0.45	0.56	—		
Canada	0.75	0.31	0.42	0.56	—	
France	0.50	0.45	0.75	0.59	0.45	—
Italy	0.29	0.37	0.48	0.36	0.33	0.52

Source: Prepared by the authors using data provided by Goldman, Sachs International Ltd. Reprinted by permission of Goldman, Sachs & Co.

TABLE 14.11 WORLD STOCK-MARKET PERFORMANCE: 1994–1998 (IN LOCAL CURRENCY AND U.S. DOLLARS)

	1994		1995		1996		1997		1998		Average 1994–1998	
	Local Currency	U.S. Dollars	Local Currency	U.S. Dollars	Local Currency	U.S. Dollars	Local Currency	U.S. Dollars	Local Currency	U.S. Dollars	Local Currency	U.S. Dollars
United States	−1.1	−1.1	33.8	33.8	20.1	20.1	31.3	31.3	27.9	27.9	22.4	22.4
Japan	7.8	20.6	2.1	−1.3	−6.3	−16.69	−17.3	−26.2	−8.5	5.5	−4.4	−3.6
Germany	−8.8	2.2	5.5	14.2	24.9	16	40.9	20.8	13.4	22.5	15.2	15.1
United Kingdom	−10.1	−4.9	19.2	18.3	11.4	22.8	21.8	17.2	12.7	13.9	11	13.5
France	−15.9	−7.1	0.5	9.7	26.8	19.3	29.4	11.8	26.9	36.7	13.5	14.1
Italy	4	9.8	−4.3	−2.1	8.6	13.3	6.4	4.1	4.2	5.2	22.7	22.8
World	−1	−1	33	33	21	21	31	30	27	26	21.9	21.8

Source: Computed by the authors using FT-stock indexes provided by Goldman, Sachs & Co.

TABLE 14.12

ECONOMIC OUTLOOK FOR THE UNITED KINGDOM

	Current Value	Historical Average
GDP Growth		
1998	2.3	2.2
1999E	0.6	
2000E	2.2	
Earnings Growth		
1998	3.0	6.2
1999E	0	
2000E	0	
Dividend Growth		
1998	10.0	4.8
1999E	6.0	
2000E	4.0	
Inflation (Consumer Price Index) (Percent)		
1998	2.7	4.6
1999E	2.3	
2000E	1.9	

INTEREST RATE OUTLOOK

	Current Rate	3 Months	12 Months
3-month CDs	5.3	3.3	2.9
10-year bond	4.5	4.1	4.0

E = estimate

Source: *World Investment Strategy Highlights* (London: Goldman, Sachs International Ltd., March 1999). Reprinted by permission of Goldman, Sachs & Co.

TABLE 14.13

RECENT STOCK MARKET PERFORMANCE FOR UNITED KINGDOM RELATIVE TO WORLD MARKET AND EXPECTED RATES OF RETURN OVER NEXT 3 AND 12 MONTHS

		Performance (Percent Change)		52-Week Range	
	Current Price	Last 3 Months	12 Months	High	Low
FT-SE 100	6484	7.3	12.4	6599	5770

EXPECTED RETURN (PERCENT)

	3 Months	12 Months
Equities	2.3	7.1
Bonds	4.1	4.0
Cash	3.3	2.9

Source: Adapted from *World Investment Strategy Highlights* (London: Goldman, Sachs International Ltd., March 1999). Reprinted by permission of Goldman, Sachs & Co.

TABLE 14.14 **ASSET ALLOCATION—WORLD PORTFOLIOS**

	Normal Range (Percent)	Weighting (Percent of Index)	Current Suggested Weighting[a] (Percent)
Bonds	**20–40**		**33.0**
Equities	**45–65**		**55.0**
United States		53.6	52.0
Canada		1.8	1.0
Japan		11.0	11.0
Hong Kong		1.1	1.1
Other Asia		1.0	0.9
United Kingdom		10.3	11.5
Germany		3.9	3.2
France		3.6	5.0
Italy		2.2	1.7
The Netherlands		2.4	3.0
Switzerland		2.8	3.2
Spain		1.2	2.2
Belgium		0.8	0.0
Sweden		1.1	2.2
Finland		0.6	0.7
Norway		0.1	0.0
Other Europe		1.3	1.0
Latin America		1.1	0.5
		100.0	**100.0**
Commodities	**0–10**		**3.0**
Cash	**0–20**		**9.0**

[a]It may not add up to 100 due to rounding.

Source: *World Investment Strategy Highlights* (London: Goldman, Sachs International Ltd., March 1999). Reprinted by permission of Goldman, Sachs & Co.

For the equity segment of the portfolio, the firm specified a neutral weighting for each country based on its relative market value. The relative market value of a country's equities is their value as a percentage of the total value of all world equities. For example, as shown in Table 14.14, the market value of U.S. equities is 53.6 percent of the total value of all equities in the world, whereas Japanese equities account for 11.0 percent of the total. A completely neutral portfolio regarding all equity markets would invest a proportion in each country equal to the relative market values of that country's equities. For example, if the value of stocks in a country constituted 10 percent of the value of all stocks in the world, a neutral outlook would lead you to invest 10 percent of your equity portfolio in this country. If you were bullish toward this country relative to other markets, you would *overweight* it, investing more than 10 percent of your equity portfolio there. As of the publication date of this report (March 1999), Goldman, Sachs was slightly bearish on the U.S. stock market because the market was close to fair value and expected returns were below those expected in some other countries, such as the United Kingdom, France, and Spain. Therefore, they recommended *underweighting* the United States (you should invest 52.0 percent of your equity portfolio in the United States versus a 53.6 percent market weighting). The firm was neutral regarding Japan and recommended that you marketweight Japanese stocks. Alternatively, the firm is recommending that you *overweight* the United Kingdom and France.

After completing the global market analysis, the next step is to analyze alternative industries worldwide within specified countries. Finally, you should consider alternative firms and their stocks in the preferred industries. This analysis is the subject of Chapters 19 and 20.

THE INTERNET *Investments Online*

The Internet contains a great many sources for economic and financial market information. Many banks, research firms, investment banks, stock brokerages, and government agencies feature data, analysis, or commentaries on their Web sites. Here are a few of the many Web resources you may wish to examine:

www.ms.com The home page of Morgan Stanley includes the Global Economic Forum. The Forum is a compilation of reports filed by 15 economists located around the world and is updated daily. Prior reports are available in an archive. This site features daily updates of the MSCI indexes of international markets and links to Morgan Stanley Dean Witter Equity Research pages.

www.dri.mcgraw-hill.com/index.htm Standard and Poor's DRI subsidiary home page features a number of links to S&P resources. Items of interest include a feature that gives a weekly analysis of international and U.S. economic news as well as current economic data.

www.yardeni.com Edward Yardeni is the chief economist of Deutsche Morgan Bank Securities. His home page contains links to market information, country information (including emerging markets), a weekly economic briefing, and studies of longer-term trends affecting the economy and financial markets. His site features a number of pull-down slides that provide links to Federal Reserve and U.S. Treasury information, as well as information about demographics, consumers, and marketing. The Stock Sector Derby section provides graphs of year-to-date performance of a variety of S&P 500 industry sectors.

www.whitehouse.gov/fsbr/esbr.html This is the Economics Statistics Briefing Room of the White House Web site. It includes links to data produced by a number of federal agencies.

www.bog.frb.fed.us This home page of the Board of Governors of the Federal Reserve System features data and information on a number of Fed-related activities, including research, money supply trends, Board actions, consumer information, and reports to Congress. The site includes links to each of the 12 regional Federal Reserve Banks and to a number of foreign central banks. The Philadelphia Fed's site includes access to the Livingston Surveys and Surveys of Professional Forecasters; both provide professional economists' judgments about future economic trends. The URL is **www.phil.frb.org/econ/index.html**.

Other sites of interest include:

www.worldbank.org Home page of the World Bank; features data and articles

www.bankamerica.com/econ_indicator/econ_indicator.html From the Web site of the Bank of America; features U.S. and global economic reviews, outlooks, and investment strategies

www.personalwealth.com Provides updates and analysis of movements in global equity markets

www.spglobal.com/index.html A Standard and Poor's site for index services; contains current headlines, weekly features, and information on the S&P stock indexes

Here's a variety of global links:

www.treasury.boi.ie Home page for the Bank of Ireland; offers economic updates

www.dkb.co.jp/english/index.html Home page for Dai-Ichi Kangyo Bank, Ltd.; has links to information about the Japanese economy

www.boj.or.jp/en/index.html Bank of Japan's Web site

www.indobiz.com Web site for Indonesia Business Center On-Line

www.bankofengland.co.uk The Bank of England's home page

www.bundesbank.de/index_e.html The Web site for Bundesbank, Germany's central bank

www.banque-france.fr/gb/home.htm The Bank of France's home page

www.ecb.int The Web site for the European Union central bank

Summary

In earlier chapters, we emphasized the importance of analyzing the aggregate markets before beginning any industry or company analysis. You must assess the economic and security-market outlooks and their implications regarding the bond, stock, and cash components of your portfolio. Then you proceed to consider the best industry or company.

- Three techniques are used to make the market decision: (1) the macroeconomic technique, which is based on the relationship between the aggregate economy and the stock market; (2) the microeconomic technique, which determines future market values by applying the two valuation approaches discussed in Chapter 13 to the aggregate stock market; and (3) technical analysis, which estimates future returns based on recent past returns. This chapter concentrates on the macroeconomic approach. The microeconomic analysis of equity markets will be considered in Chapter 18 as a prelude to industry analysis in Chapter 19 followed by company and stock analysis in Chapter 20. Technical analysis is covered in Chapter 21.
- The economy and the stock market have a strong, consistent relationship, but the stock market generally turns before the economy does. Therefore, the best macroeconomic projection techniques use economic series that likewise lead the economy, and possibly the stock market. The NBER leading indicator series (which includes stock prices) is one possibility, but the evidence does not support its use as a mechanical predictor of stock prices. Leading series for inflation and for other countries exist, but none of these series has been examined relative to stock prices.
- The money supply has been suggested as a predictor of aggregate market behavior based on its relationship to the economy. Some early studies indicated a strong relationship between the money supply and stock prices, and suggested that money supply changes turned before stock prices. Subsequent studies confirmed the link between money supply and stock prices, but they indicated that stock prices turn with or before money supply changes. The most recent results show that monetary policy has an important impact on stock price movements.
- The analysis of excess liquidity indicates an impact on stock prices, but also shows that global liquidity has become important.
- Although we emphasize the analysis of U.S. markets, we know it is also important to analyze numerous foreign markets. Such an analysis is demonstrated by a Goldman, Sachs' application of the three-step, or top-down, approach to major countries. This includes an economic analysis and a market analysis for each country. The analysis culminates with a recommendation for a world portfolio allocation among bonds, stocks, and cash. It also recommends an allocation of equity investments among countries in comparison to the country's normal weighting based on its relative market value.

This aggregate market analysis should lead you to a decision as to how much of your portfolio should be committed to bonds, stocks, and cash during the forthcoming investment period. The following three chapters deal with the fixed-income portion of your portfolio. Chapter 15 discusses bond fundamentals, Chapter 16 considers the analysis and valuation of individual bonds, and Chapter 17 presents alternative portfolio strategies for bond investors.

Questions

1. Why would you expect a relationship between economic activity and stock price movements?
2. At a lunch with some business associates, you discuss the reason for the relationship between the economy and the stock market. One of your associates contends that she has heard that stock prices typically turn before the economy does. How would you explain this phenomenon?

3. Could a diffusion index of a leading indicator series help you predict stock market movements? Why or why not?
4. Explain the following statements: (a) There is a strong, consistent relationship between money supply changes and stock prices; (b) Money supply changes cannot be used to predict stock price movements.
5. Discuss the rationale for the relationship of excess liquidity and security prices.
6. You are informed of the following estimates: nominal money supply is expected to grow at a rate of 7 percent, and GDP is estimated to grow at 4 percent. Explain what you think will happen to stock prices during this period and why.
7. The current rate of inflation is 3 percent and long-term Treasury bonds are yielding 7 percent. You estimate that the rate of inflation will increase to 6 percent. What do you expect to happen to long-term bond yields? Compute the effect of this change in inflation on the price of a 15-year, 10 percent coupon bond, with a current yield to maturity of 8 percent.
8. Some observers contend that it is harder to estimate the effect of a change in interest rates on common stocks than on bonds. Discuss this contention.
9. Based on the economic projections in Tables 14.5 through 14.8, would you expect the stock prices for the various countries to be highly correlated? Justify your answer with specific examples.
10. You are informed that a well-respected investment firm projects that the rate of return next year for the U.S. equity market will be 10 percent, and returns for German stocks will be 13 percent. Assume that all risks except exchange rate risk are equal and you expect the DM/U.S. dollar exchange rate to go from 1.50 to 1.30 during the year. Given this information, discuss where you would invest and why. Compute the effect if the exchange rate went from 1.50 to 1.90.

Problems

1. Prepare a table showing the percentage change for each of the last 10 years in (a) the Consumer Price Index (all items), (b) nominal GDP, (c) real GDP (in constant dollars), and (d) the GDP deflator. Discuss how much of nominal growth was due to *real* growth and how much was due to inflation.
2. CFA *CFA Examination I (June 1983)*
   There has been considerable growth in recent years in the use of economic analysis in investment management. Further significant expansion may lie ahead as financial analysts develop greater skills in economic analysis and these analyses are integrated more into the investment decision-making process. The following questions address the use of economic analysis in the investment decision-making process.
   a. 1. Differentiate among leading, lagging, and coincident indicators of economic activity, and give an example of each.
      2. Indicate whether the leading indicators are one of the best tools for achieving above-average investment results. Briefly justify your conclusion.
   b. Interest rate projections are used in investment management for a variety of purposes. Identify three significant reasons why interest rate forecasts may be important in reaching investment conclusions.
   c. Assume you are a fundamental research analyst following the automobile industry for a large brokerage firm. Identify and briefly explain the relevance of *three* major economic time series, economic indicators, or economic data items that would be significant to automotive industry and company research.
3. CFA *CFA Examination III (June 1985)*
   A U.S. pension plan hired two offshore firms to manage the non-U.S. equity portion of its total portfolio. Each firm was free to own stocks in any country market included in Capital International's Europe, Australia, and Far East Index (EAFE) and free to use any form of dollar and/or nondollar cash or bonds as an equity substitute or reserve. After 3 years had elapsed, the records of the managers and the EAFE Index were as shown on the next page:

SUMMARY: CONTRIBUTIONS TO RETURN

	Currency	Country Selection	Stock Selection	Cash/Bond Allocation	Total Return Recorded
Manager A	(9.0%)	19.7%	3.1%	0.6%	14.4%
Manager B	(7.4)	14.2	6.0	2.8	15.6
Composite of A&B	(8.2)	16.9	4.5	1.7	15.0
EAFE Index	(12.9)	19.9	—	—	7.0

You are a member of the plan sponsor's pension committee, which will soon meet with the plan's consultant to review manager performance. In preparation for this meeting, you go through the following analysis:

a. Briefly describe the strengths and weaknesses of each manager, relative to the EAFE Index data.
b. Briefly explain the meaning of the data in the Currency column.

4. Each week in *Barron's* in the data section entitled "Market Week" there is a table in the pages for the "International Trader" for Global Stock Markets. Consult the latest available issue of this publication and the issue one year earlier to find the following information.
   a. Show the closing value for five country indexes of your choice on each date relative to the yearly high for each year.
   b. Which countries have markets in downtrends? Which countries are in uptrends?
   c. Based on the percent range for the 52-week period [H − L/(H + L) 2], which is the most volatile market?
   d. For the five countries, calculate the percentage change over the one-year period in local currency and in U.S. dollars. Discuss how each country did relative to the World Index.
5. Using a source of financial data such as *Barron's* or *The Wall Street Journal:*
   a. Plot the weekly percentage changes in the S&P 400 index (y-axis) versus comparable weekly percentage changes in the M2 money supply figures (x-axis) for the past 10 weeks. Do you see a positive, negative, or zero correlation? (Monetary aggregates will lag the stock market aggregates.)
   b. Examine the trend in money rates (e.g., federal funds, 90-day T-bills, etc.) over the past 10 weeks. Is there a correlation between these money rates? Estimate the correlation between the individual money rates and percentage changes in M2.
6. For the past 10 weeks, examine the relationship between the weekly percentage changes in the S&P 400 Index and the DJIA. Plot the weekly percentage changes in each index using S&P as the x-axis and DJIA as the y-axis. Discuss your results as they relate to diversification. Do a similar comparison for the S&P 400 and the Nikkei Index and discuss these results as they relate to diversification.

References

Baker, H. Kent, ed. *Improving the Investment Decision Process—Better Use of Economic Inputs in Security Analysis and Portfolio Management.* Charlottesville, Va.: Association for Investment Management and Research, 1992.

Belfer, Nathan. "Economic Indicators and Their Significance." In *The Financial Analysts Handbook,* 2d ed., ed. Sumner N. Levine. Homewood, Ill.: Dow Jones-Irwin, 1988.

Diermeier, Jeffrey J. "Capital Market Expectations: The Macro Factors." In *Managing Investment Portfolios: A Dynamic Process,* 2d ed., ed. John L. Maginn and Donald L. Tuttle. Boston: Warren Gorham and Lamont, 1990.

Droms, William G., ed. *Initiating and Managing a Global Investment Program.* Charlottesville, Va.: Association for Investment Management and Research, 1991.

Fogler, H. Russell, and Darwin M. Bayston, eds. *Improving the Investment Decision Process: Quantitative Assistance for the Practitioner and for the Firm.* Charlottesville, Va.: The Institute of Chartered Financial Analysts, January 1984.

Investing Worldwide. An annual conference (started in 1990) sponsored by the Association of Investment Management and Research, Charlottesville, Va.

Solnik, Bruno. *Predictable Time-Varying Components of International Asset Returns.* Charlottesville, Va.: Association of Investment Management and Research, 1993.

Vertin, James R., ed. *Improving the Investment Decision Process: Applying Economic Analysis to Portfolio Management.* Charlottesville, Va.: The Institute of Chartered Financial Analysts, September 1984.

Part

4 Analysis and Management of Bonds

N
E
W
S

For most investors, bonds are like Rodney Dangerfield—"They get no respect!" This is surprising when one considers that the total market value of the bond market in the United States and in most other countries is substantially larger than the market value of the stock market. For example, by the end of 1998, the U.S. market value of all publicly issued bonds was more than $12 trillion, while the market value of all stocks was about $11 trillion. On a global basis, the values are about $26 trillion for bonds versus $23 trillion for stocks. Beyond the size factor, bonds have a reputation for low, unexciting rates of return. Although this may have been true 50 or 60 years ago, it certainly has not been true during the past 15 to 20 years. Specifically, the average annual compound rate of return on government/corporate bonds for the period 1978–1998 was slightly over 10 percent versus about 14 percent for common stocks. These rates of return along with corresponding standard deviations (8 percent for bonds versus 13 percent for stocks) and the relatively low correlations between stocks and bonds (about 0.35) indicate that there are substantial opportunities in bonds for individual and institutional investors to enhance their risk–return performance.

The chapters in this section are intended to provide: (a) a basic understanding of bonds and the bond markets around the world, (b) background on analyzing returns and risks in the bond market, and the valuation of bonds, including the numerous new fixed-income securities with very unusual cash flow characteristics, and (c) an understanding of what is involved in either active or passive bond portfolio management.

Chapter 15 describes the global bond market in terms of country participation and the makeup of the bond market in the largest countries. Also, the characteristics of bonds in alternative categories, such as government, corporate, and municipal, are discussed. We also discuss the many new corporate bond instruments developed in the United States, such as asset-backed securities, zero-coupon bonds, high-yield bonds and inflation protection securities. While the use of these securities has generally been limited to a few of the large developed markets, it is certain that they will eventually be used around the world. Finally, we consider the price information needed by bond investors and where to get it.

Chapter 16 is concerned with the analysis and valuation of bonds. This includes an initial detailed discussion of how one values a bond using a single discount rate or using spot rates from the theoretical spot rate curve, as well as the alternative rate of return measures for bonds. Subsequently we consider what factors affect yields on bonds, and what characteristics influence the volatility of bond returns. This latter discussion considers the very important concept of bond duration, which helps explain and measure bond price volatility and is important in active and passive bond portfolio management. We also consider a related concept of bond convexity and the impact of convexity on bond price volatility. Notably, these concepts are examined as they apply to option-free securities and securities with embedded options (which is becoming very common).

Chapter 17 considers how to use the background provided in Chapters 15 and 16 to create and manage a bond portfolio. There are three major categories of portfolio strategies that we consider in detail. The first is passive portfolio management strategies, which include either a simple buy-and-hold strategy or involve indexing to one of the major benchmarks. The second category includes active management strategies that can involve one of five alternatives: interest rate anticipation, valuation analysis, credit analysis, yield spread analysis, or bond swaps. The third category includes matched funding strategies, which include constructing dedicated portfolios, classical or contingent immunization portfolios, or horizon matching.

The fact that three chapters are devoted to the study of bonds and the length of the chapters attest to the importance of the topic and the extensive research done in this area. During the past 20 years, there have been more developments related to the valuation and portfolio management of bonds than of stocks. This growth of the fixed-income sector does not detract from the importance of equities, but certainly enhances the significance of fixed-income securities. Finally, readers of this book should keep in mind that this growth in the size, sophistication, and specialization of the bond market means that there are and will be numerous and varied career opportunities in the bond area ranging from trading these securities, valuation, credit analysis, and portfolio management—both domestically and globally.

Chapter

15 BOND FUNDAMENTALS

After you read this chapter, you should be able to answer the following questions:

- What are some of the basic features of bonds that affect their risk, return, and value?
- What is the current country structure of the world bond market and how has the makeup of the global bond market changed in recent years?
- What are the major components of the world bond market and the international bond market?
- What are bond ratings and what is their purpose? What is the difference between investment-grade bonds and high-yield (junk) bonds?
- What are the characteristics of bonds in the major bond categories, such as governments (including TIPS), agencies, municipalities, and corporates?
- How does the makeup of the bond market differ in major countries, such as the United States, Japan, the United Kingdom, and Germany?
- What are the important characteristics of corporate bond issues developed in the United States during the past decade, such as mortgage-backed securities, other asset-backed securities, zero-coupon and deep discount bonds, high-yield bonds, and structured notes?
- How do you read the quotes available for the alternative bond categories (e.g., governments, municipalities, corporates)?

The global bond market is large and diverse and represents an important investment opportunity. This chapter is concerned with publicly issued, long-term, nonconvertible debt obligations of public and private issuers in the United States and major global markets. In later chapters, we consider preferred stock and convertible bonds. An understanding of bonds is helpful in an efficient market because U.S. and foreign bonds increase the universe of investments available for the creation of a diversified portfolio.[1]

In this chapter, we review some basic features of bonds and examine the structure of the world bond market. The bulk of the chapter involves an in-depth discussion of the major fixed-income investments. The chapter ends with a brief review of the price information sources for bond investors. Chapter 16 discusses the valuation of bonds and considers several factors that influence bond value and bond price volatility.

BASIC FEATURES OF A BOND

Public bonds are long-term, fixed-obligation debt securities packaged in convenient, affordable denominations for sale to individuals and financial institutions. They differ from

---

Material on bonds and world bond markets in this chapter is based on information from "How Big Is the World Bond Market," 1998 update by Rosario Benavides of Salomon Brothers Inc., copyright © 1998 by Salomon Brothers, Inc., and "Size and Structure of the World Bond Market: 1998," ed. Dave Mozina, International Fixed Income Research, Merrill Lynch & Co., September 1998. Reprinted by permission.

[1]Meir Statman and Neal L. Ushman, "Bonds versus Stocks: Another Look," *Journal of Portfolio Management* 13, no. 3 (winter 1987): 33–38.

other debt, such as individual mortgages and privately placed debt obligations, because they are sold to the public rather than channeled directly to a single lender. Bond issues are considered fixed-income securities because they impose fixed financial obligations on the issuers. Specifically, the issuer agrees to

1. Pay a fixed amount of *interest periodically* to the holder of record
2. Repay a fixed amount of *principal* at the date of maturity

Normally, interest on bonds is paid every 6 months, although some bond issues pay in intervals as short as a month or as long as a year. The principal is due at maturity; this *par value* of the issue is rarely less than $1,000. A bond has a specified term to maturity, which defines the life of the issue. The public debt market typically is divided into three segments based on an issue's original maturity:

1. Short-term issues with maturities of 1 year or less. The market for these instruments is commonly known as the **money market**.
2. Intermediate-term issues with maturities in excess of 1 year, but less than 10 years. These instruments are known as **notes**.
3. Long-term obligations with maturities in excess of 10 years, called *bonds.*

The lives of debt obligations change constantly as the issues progress toward maturity. Thus, issues that have been outstanding in the secondary market for any period of time eventually move from long-term to intermediate to short-term. This change in maturity is important because a major determinant of the price volatility of bonds is the remaining life (maturity) of the issue.

BOND CHARACTERISTICS

A bond can be characterized based on (1) its intrinsic features, (2) its type, (3) its indenture provisions, or (4) the features that affect its cash flows and/or its maturity.

INTRINSIC FEATURES The coupon, maturity, principal value, and the type of ownership are important intrinsic features of a bond. The **coupon** of a bond indicates the income that the bond investor will receive over the life (or holding period) of the issue. This is known as *interest income, coupon income,* or *nominal yield.*

The **term to maturity** specifies the date or the number of years before a bond matures (or expires). There are two different types of maturity. The most common is a **term bond**, which has a single maturity date. Alternatively, a **serial obligation bond** issue has a series of maturity dates, perhaps 20 or 25. Each maturity, although a subset of the total issue, is really a small bond issue with generally a different coupon. Municipalities issue most serial bonds.

The **principal**, or **par value**, of an issue represents the original value of the obligation. This is generally stated in $1,000 increments from $1,000 to $25,000 or more. Principal value is *not* the same as the bond's market value. The market prices of many issues rise above or fall below their principal values because of differences between their coupons and the prevailing market rate of interest. If the market interest rate is above the coupon rate, the bond will sell at a discount to par. If the market rate is below the bond's coupon, it will sell at a premium above par. If the coupon is comparable to the prevailing market interest rate, the market value of the bond will be close to its original principal value.

Finally, bonds differ in terms of ownership. With a **bearer bond**, the holder, or bearer, is the owner, so the issuer keeps no record of ownership. Interest from a bearer bond is obtained by clipping coupons attached to the bonds and sending them to the issuer for payment. In contrast, the issuers of **registered bonds** maintain records of owners and pay the interest directly to them.

TYPES OF ISSUES In contrast to common stock, companies can have many different bond issues outstanding at the same time. Bonds can have different types of collateral and be either senior, unsecured, or subordinated (junior) securities. **Secured (senior) bonds** are backed by a legal claim on some specified property of the issuer in the case of default. For example, mortgage bonds are secured by real estate assets; equipment trust certificates, which are used by railroads and airlines, provide a senior claim on the firm's equipment.

Unsecured bonds (debentures) are backed only by the promise of the issuer to pay interest and principal on a timely basis. As such, they are secured by the general credit of the issuer. **Subordinate (junior) debentures** possess a claim on income and assets that is subordinated to other debentures. Income issues are the most junior type because interest on them is paid only if it is earned. Although income bonds are unusual in the corporate sector, they are very popular municipal issues, where they are referred to as **revenue bonds**. Finally, **refunding issues** provide funds to prematurely retire another issue.

The type of issue has only a marginal effect on comparative yield because it is the credibility of the issuer that determines bond quality. A study of corporate bond price behavior found that whether the issuer pledged collateral did not become important until the bond issue approached default.[2] The collateral and security characteristics of a bond influence yield differentials only when these factors affect the bond's quality ratings.

INDENTURE PROVISIONS The indenture is the contract between the issuer and the bondholder specifying the issuer's legal requirements. A trustee (usually a bank) acting on behalf of the bondholders ensures that all the indenture provisions are met, including the timely payment of interest and principal. All the factors that dictate a bond's features, its type, and its maturity are set forth in the indenture.

FEATURES AFFECTING BOND'S MATURITY Investors should be aware of the three alternative call option features that can affect the life (maturity) of a bond. One extreme is a *freely callable* provision that allows the issuer to retire the bond at any time with a typical notification period of 30 to 60 days. The other extreme is a *noncallable* provision wherein the issuer cannot retire the bond prior to its maturity.[3] Intermediate between these is a *deferred call* provision, which means the issue cannot be called for a certain period of time after the date of issue (e.g., 5 to 10 years). At the end of the deferred call period, the issue becomes freely callable. Callable bonds have a **call premium**, which is the amount above maturity value that the issuer must pay to the bondholder for prematurely retiring the bond.

A *nonrefunding provision* prohibits a call and premature retirement of an issue from the proceeds of a lower-coupon refunding bond. This is meant to protect the bondholder from a typical refunding, but it is not foolproof. An issue with a nonrefunding provision can be called and retired prior to maturity using other sources of funds, such as excess cash from operations, the sale of assets, or proceeds from a sale of common stock. This occurred on

[2]W. Braddock Hickman, *Corporate Bond Quality and Investor Experience* (Princeton, N.J.: Princeton University Press, 1958).

[3]The main issuer of noncallable bonds between 1985 and 1998 was the U.S. Treasury. Corporate long-term bonds typically have contained some form of call provision, except during periods of relatively low interest rates (e.g., 1994–1997) when the probability of exercising the option was very low. We discuss this notion in more detail in Chapter 16 in connection with the analysis of embedded options.

several occasions during the 1980s and 1990s when many issuers retired nonrefundable high-coupon issues early because they could get the cash from one of these other sources and felt that this was a good financing decision.

Another important indenture provision that can affect a bond's maturity is the **sinking fund**, which specifies that a bond must be paid off systematically over its life rather than only at maturity. There are numerous sinking-fund arrangements, and the bondholder should recognize this as a feature that can change the stated maturity of a bond. The size of the sinking fund can be a percentage of a given issue or a percentage of the total debt outstanding, or it can be a fixed or variable sum stated on a dollar or percentage basis. Similar to a call feature, sinking fund payments may commence at the end of the first year or may be deferred for 5 or 10 years from date of the issue. The amount of the issue that must be repaid before maturity from a sinking fund can range from a nominal sum to 100 percent. Like a call, the sinking-fund feature typically carries a nominal premium, but is generally smaller than the straight call premium (e.g., 1 percent). For example, a bond issue with a 20-year maturity might have a sinking fund that requires that 50 percent of the issue be retired every year beginning in year 10. By year 20, half of the issue has been retired and the rest is paid off at maturity. Sinking-fund provisions have a small effect on comparative yields at the time of issue, but have little subsequent impact on price behavior.

A sinking-fund provision is an obligation and must be carried out regardless of market conditions. Although a sinking fund allows the issuer to call bonds on a random basis, most bonds are retired for sinking-fund purposes through direct negotiations with institutional holders. Essentially, the trustee negotiates with an institution to buy back the necessary amount of bonds at a price slightly above the current market price.

Rates of Return on Bonds

The rate of return on a bond is computed in the same way as the rate of return on stock or any asset. Its is determined by the beginning and ending price and the cash flows during the holding period. The major difference between stocks and bonds is that the interim cash flow on bonds (i.e., the interest) is contractual and accrues over time as discussed below, whereas the dividends on stock may vary. Therefore, the holding period return (HPR) for a bond will be

$$\text{HPR}_{i,t} = \frac{P_{i,t+1} + Int_{i,t}}{P_{i,t}}$$

where:

$\text{HPR}_{i,t}$ = the holding period return for bond i during period t
$P_{i,t+1}$ = the market price of bond i at the end of period t
$P_{i,t}$ = the market price of bond i at the beginning of period t
$Int_{i,t}$ = the interest paid or accrued on bond i during period t. Because the interest payment is contractual, it accrues over time and if a bond owner sells the bond between interest payments, the sale price includes accrued interest[4]

The holding period yield (HPY) is:

$$\text{HPY} = \text{HPR} - 1$$

Note that the only contractual factor is the amount of interest payments. The beginning and ending bond prices are determined by market forces, as discussed in Chapter 13. Notably, the ending price is determined by market forces unless the bond is held to maturity, in which case the investor will receive the par value. These price variations in bonds mean that investors in bonds can experience capital gains or losses. Interest rate volatility has increased substantially since the 1960s, and this has caused large price fluctuations in

[4]The concept of accrued interest will be discussed further in Chapter 16 when we consider the valuation of bonds.

bonds.[5] As a result, capital gains or losses have become a major component of the rates of return on bonds.

THE GLOBAL BOND-MARKET STRUCTURE[6]

The market for fixed-income securities is substantially larger than the listed equity exchanges (NYSE, TSE, LSE) because corporations tend to issue bonds rather than common stock. Federal Reserve figures indicate that in the United States during 1998, 20 percent of all new security issues were equity, which included preferred as well as common stock. Corporations issue less common or preferred stock because firms derive most of their equity financing from internally generated funds (i.e., retained earnings). Also, although the equity market is strictly corporations, the bond market in most countries has four noncorporate sectors: the pure government sector (e.g., the Treasury in the United States), government agencies (e.g., FNMA), state and local government bonds (municipals), and international bonds (e.g., Yankees and Eurobonds in the United States).

The size of the global bond market and the distribution among countries can be gleaned from Table 15.1, which lists the dollar value of debt outstanding and the percentage distribution for the major bond markets for the years 1993, 1995, and 1997. There has been substantial overall growth, including a 32 percent increase in the total in 1997 compared with

TABLE 15.1 **TOTAL DEBT OUTSTANDING IN THE 13 MAJOR[a] BOND MARKETS: 1993–1997 (U.S. DOLLAR NOMINAL VALUE, IN BILLIONS)**

	1997		1995		1993	
	Total Value	Percentage of Total	Total Value	Percentage of Total	Total Value	Percentage of Total
United States	11,218	47.8	9,446	42.5	8,148	46.0
Japan	4,173	17.8	4,796	21.6	3,762	21.2
Germany	2,943	12.5	3,078	13.9	2,117	11.9
Italy	1,271	5.4	1,101	5.0	786	4.4
United Kingdom	856	3.6	571	2.6	452	2.6
France	961	4.1	1,035	4.7	730	4.1
Canada	524	2.2	507	2.3	464	2.6
Sweden	201	0.9	248	1.1	180	1.0
Denmark	266	1.1	292	1.3	227	1.3
Switzerland	241	1.0	218	1.0	189	1.1
Netherlands	342	1.5	393	1.8	295	1.7
Belgium	339	1.4	406	1.8	282	1.6
Australia	132	0.6	131	0.6	96	0.5
Total	**23,468**	**100.0%**	**22,222**	**100.0%**	**17,727**	**100.0%**

[a]Only includes bonds with maturities over 1 year. (Floating rates are excluded.)

Source: "Size and Structure of the World Bond Market: 1998," Merrill Lynch International Fixed Income Research, September 1998.

[5]The analysis of bond price volatility is discussed in detail in Chapter 16.

[6]For a further discussion of global bond markets and specific national bond markets, see *International Bond Handbook,* International Bond Research Unit, James Capel & Co., London, 1987; Christopher Steward and Adam M. Greshin, "International Bond Markets and Instruments," Christopher Steward and Adam Greshin, "International Bond Investing and Portfolio Management," and Michael R. Rosenberg, "International Fixed Income Investing: Theory and Practice," all in *The Handbook of Fixed-Income Securities,* 5th ed., ed. Frank J. Fabozzi (Chicago: Irwin Professional Publishing, 1997).

1993. Also, the country trends are significant. Specifically, the U.S. market went from about 46 percent of the total world market in 1993 to almost 48 percent in 1997. In contrast, Japan went from about 21 percent to less than 18 percent in 1997. The German, Italian, and U.K. markets increased as a percentage of the global bond market during the last several years, whereas the Canadian market experienced an overall decline.

PARTICIPATING ISSUERS

There are generally five different issuers in a country: (1) the federal government (e.g., the U.S. Treasury), (2) agencies of the federal government, (3) various state and local political subdivisions (known as municipalities), (4) corporations, and (5) international issues. The division of bonds among these five types for the three largest markets and the United Kingdom during 1993, 1995, and 1997 is contained in Table 15.2.

TABLE 15.2

MAKEUP OF BONDS OUTSTANDING IN THE UNITED STATES, JAPAN, GERMANY, AND THE UNITED KINGDOM: 1993–1997

	1997		1995		1993	
	Total Value	Percentage of Total	Total Value	Percentage of Total	Total Value	Percentage of Total
A. United States (U.S. dollars in billions)						
Government	2,741	24.4	2,547	27.0	2,275	27.9
Federal agency	2,848	25.4	2,405	25.5	1,907	23.4
Municipal	1,074	9.6	1,025	10.9	1,119	13.7
Corporate	2,956	26.3	2,498	26.4	2,041	25.0
International[a]	1,599	14.3	971	10.3	807	9.9
Total	11,218	100.0%	9,446	100.0%	8,148	100.0%
B. Japan (yen in trillions)						
Government	182	43.3	213	43.2	247	45.5
Government-associated organization	66	15.8	75	15.2	78	14.4
Municipal	25	5.9	36	7.3	42	7.7
Bank debentures	78	18.5	76	15.4	65	11.9
Corporate	40	9.5	46	9.3	53	9.8
International[a]	30	7.1	47	9.6	58	10.7
Total	421	100.0%	493	100.0%	542	100.0%
C. Germany (deutschemarks in billions)						
Government	1,224	23.2	1,092	24.7	969	26.5
Agency	157	3.0	181	4.1	148	4.1
State and local	774	14.7	697	15.8	595	16.3
Bank	1,990	37.7	1,607	36.4	1,316	36.0
Corporate	5	0.1	3	0.1	3	0.1
International[a]	1,125	21.3	833	18.9	624	17.1
Total	5,275	100.0%	4,413	100.0%	3,655	100.0%
D. United Kingdom (pounds in billions)						
Government	317	61.3	233	63.3	191	62.4
Agency	—	—	—	—	—	—
Municipal	—	—	—	—	—	—
Corporate	36	7.0	19	5.2	17	5.6
International[a]	164	31.7	116	31.5	98	32.0
Total	518	100.0%	369	100.0%	305	100.0%

[a]Includes foreign and Eurobonds.

Source: "Size and Structure of the World Bond Market: 1998," Merrill Lynch International Fixed Income Research, September 1998.

GOVERNMENT The market for government securities is the largest sector in Japan and the United Kingdom. It involves a variety of debt instruments issued to meet the growing needs of these governments. In Germany, the government sector is smaller, but is growing in size due to deficits related to reunification of the country.

GOVERNMENT AGENCIES Agency issues have become a major segment in the U.S. market (over 25 percent), but are a smaller proportion in other countries (e.g., about 16 percent in Japan, about 3 percent in Germany, and nonexistent in the United Kingdom). These agencies represent political subdivisions of the government, although the securities are *not* typically direct obligations of the government. The U.S. agency market has two types of issuers: government-sponsored enterprises and federal agencies. The proceeds of agency bond issues are used to finance many legislative programs. In the United States, many of these obligations carry government guarantees, although they are not direct obligations of the government. In other countries, the relationship of an agency issue to the government varies. In most countries, the market yields of agency obligations generally exceed those from pure government bonds. Thus, they represent a way for investors to increase returns with only marginally higher risk.

MUNICIPALITIES Municipal debt includes issues of states, school districts, cities, or other political subdivisions. Unlike government and agency issues, the interest income on municipal bonds in the United States is not subject to federal income tax, although capital gains are taxable. Moreover, these bonds are exempt from state and local taxes when they are issued by the investors' home state. That is, the interest income on a California issue would not be taxed to a California resident, but would be taxable to a New York resident. The interest income of Puerto Rican issues enjoys total immunity from federal, state, and local taxes.

As shown in Table 15.2, the municipal bond market has declined in the United States from almost 14 percent to less than 10 percent. In Japan and Germany, the bond market has declined slightly, to almost 6 percent in Japan, and almost 15 percent in Germany. It is nonexistent in the United Kingdom. Also, although each country has unique tax laws, the income from a non-U.S. municipal bond typically would not be exempt for a U.S. investor.

CORPORATIONS The major nongovernmental issuer of debt is the corporate sector. The importance of this sector differs dramatically among countries. It is a stable factor in the United States; a small sector in Japan where it is supplemented by bank debentures; and a small, declining proportion of the U.K. market. Finally, it is a declining part of the German market because most German firms get their financing through bank loans, which explains the large increasing percentage of bank debt in Germany.

The market for corporate bonds is commonly subdivided into several segments: industrials, public utilities, transportation, and financial issues. The specific makeup varies between countries. Most U.S. issues are industrials and utilities. Most foreign corporations do not issue public debt but borrow from the banks.

The corporate sector provides the most diverse issues in terms of type and quality. In effect, the issuer can range from the highest investment-grade firm, such as American Telephone and Telegraph or IBM, to a relatively new, high-risk firm that defaulted on previous debt securities.[7]

---

[7]It is possible to distinguish another sector that exists in the United States but not in other countries—institutional bonds. These are corporate bonds issued by a variety of *private, nonprofit institutions,* such as schools, hospitals, and churches. They are not broken out because they are only a minute part of the U.S. market and do not exist elsewhere.

INTERNATIONAL The international sector has two components: (1) foreign bonds, such as Yankee bonds and Samurai bonds; and (2) Eurobonds, including Eurodollar, Euroyen, Eurodeutschemark, and Eurosterling bonds.[8] Although the relative importance of the international bond sector varies by country (from a low of 7 percent in Japan to a high of almost 32 percent in the United Kingdom), it has grown in both absolute and relative terms in all these countries. Although Eurodollar bonds have historically made up over 50 percent of the Eurobond market, the proportion has declined as investors have attempted to diversify their Eurobond portfolios. Specifically, Eurodollar bonds constituted about 85 percent of the market in 1984, but only 45 percent in 1997. Clearly, the desire for diversification changes with the swings in the value of the U.S. dollar.

Participating Investors

Numerous individual and institutional investors with diverse investment objectives participate in the bond market. Individual investors are a minor portion because of the market's complexity and the high minimum denominations of most issues. Institutional investors typically account for 90 to 95 percent of the trading, although different segments of the market are more institutionalized than others. For example, institutions are involved heavily in the agency market, whereas they are much less active in the corporate sector.

A variety of institutions invest in the bond market. Life insurance companies invest in corporate bonds and, to a lesser extent, in Treasury and agency securities. Commercial banks invest in municipal bonds and government and agency issues. Property and liability insurance companies concentrate on municipal bonds and Treasuries. Private and government pension funds are heavily committed to corporates and invest in Treasuries and agencies. Finally, fixed-income mutual funds have grown substantially in size and their demand spans the full spectrum of the market as they develop bond funds that meet the needs of a variety of investors. As we will discuss in Chapter 26, municipal bond funds and corporate bond funds (including high-yield bonds) have experienced significant growth.

Alternative institutions tend to favor different sectors of the bond market based on two factors: (1) the tax code applicable to the institution and (2) the nature of the institution's liability structure. For example, because commercial banks are subject to normal taxation and have fairly short-term liability structures, they favor short- to intermediate-term municipals. Pension funds are virtually tax-free institutions with long-term commitments, so they prefer high-yielding, long-term government or corporate bonds. Such institutional investment preferences can affect the short-run supply and demand of loanable funds and impact interest rate changes.

Bond Ratings

Agency ratings are an integral part of the bond market because most corporate and municipal bonds are rated by one or more of the rating agencies. The exceptions are very small issues and bonds from certain industries, such as bank issues. These are known as *nonrated bonds.* There are four major rating agencies: (1) Duff and Phelps, (2) Fitch Investors Service, (3) Moody's, and (4) Standard and Poor's.

Bond ratings provide the fundamental analysis for thousands of issues. The rating agencies analyze the issuing organization and the specific issue to determine the probability of default and inform the market of their analyses through their ratings.[9]

---

[8]These bonds will be discussed in more detail later in this chapter.

[9]For a detailed listing of rating classes and a listing of factors considered in assigning ratings, see "Bond Ratings" and "Bond Rating Outlines," in *The Financial Analysts Handbook,* 2d ed., ed. Sumner N. Levine (Homewood, Ill.: Dow Jones-Irwin, 1988), 1102–1138. For a study that examines the value of two bond ratings, see L. Paul Hsueh and David S. Kidwell, "Bond Ratings: Are Two Better Than One?" *Financial Management* 17, no. 1 (spring 1988): 46–53. A very thorough discussion and analysis of the bond rating industry is contained in Richard Cantor and Frank Packer, "The Credit Rating Industry," *Journal of Fixed Income* 5, no 3 (December 1995): 10–34.

The primary question in bond credit analysis is whether the firm can service its debt in a timely manner over the life of a given issue. Consequently, the rating agencies consider expectations over the life of the issue, along with the historical and current financial position of the company. Although the agencies have done an admirable job, mistakes happen.[10] A study indicated that the rating services have tended to overestimate the risk of default, which has resulted in unnecessarily high risk premiums given the default probabilities.[11] We consider default estimation further when we discuss high-yield (junk) bonds.

Several studies have examined the relationship between bond ratings and issue quality as indicated by financial variables. The results clearly demonstrated that bond ratings were positively related to profitability, size, and cash flow coverage, and they were inversely related to financial leverage and earnings instability.[12]

The original ratings assigned to bonds have an impact on their marketability and effective interest rate. Generally, the four agencies' ratings agree. When they do not, the issue is said to have a *split rating.* Seasoned issues are regularly reviewed to ensure that the assigned rating is still valid. If not, revisions are made either upward or downward. Revisions are usually done in increments of one rating grade.[13] The ratings are based on both the company and the issue. After an evaluation of the creditworthiness of the total company is completed, a company rating is assigned to the firm's most senior unsecured issue. All junior bonds receive lower ratings based on indenture specifications. Also, an issue could receive a higher rating than justified because of credit-enhancement devices, such as the attachment of bank letters of credit, surety, or indemnification bonds from insurance companies.

The agencies assign letter ratings depicting what they view as the risk of default of an obligation. The letter ratings range from AAA (Aaa) to D. Table 15.3 describes the various ratings assigned by the major services. Except for slight variations in designations, the meaning and interpretation is basically the same. The agencies modify the ratings with + and − signs for Duff and Phelps, Fitch, and S&P, or with numbers (1-2-3) for Moody's. As an example, an A+ bond is at the top of the A-rated group.

The top four ratings—AAA (or Aaa), AA (or Aa), A, and BBB (or Baa)—are generally considered to be *investment-grade securities.* The next level of securities is known as *speculative bonds* and includes the BB- and B-rated obligations. The C categories are generally either income obligations or revenue bonds, many of which are trading flat. (Flat bonds are in arrears on their interest payments.) In the case of D-rated obligations, the issues are in outright default, and the ratings indicate the bonds' relative salvage values.[14]

---

[10]W. Braddock Hickman, *Corporate Bond Quality and Investor Experience* (Princeton, N.J.: Princeton University Press, 1958).

[11]Gordon Pye, "Gauging the Default Premium," *Financial Analysts Journal* 30, no. 1 (January–February 1974): 49–52.

[12]See, for example, Robert S. Kaplan and Gabrial Urwitz, "Statistical Models of Bond Ratings: A Methodological Inquiry," *Journal of Business* 52, no 2 (April 1979): 231–262; Ahmed Belkaoui, "Industrial Bond Ratings: A New Look," *Financial Management* 9, no. 3 (fall 1980): 44–52; and James A. Gentry, David T. Whitford, and Paul Newbold, "Predicting Industrial Bond Ratings with a Probit Model and Funds Flow Components," *The Financial Review* 23, no. 3 (August 1988): 269–286.

[13]Bond rating changes and bond-market efficiency are discussed in Chapter 16. Split ratings are discussed in R. Billingsley. R. Lamy, M. Marr, and T. Thompson, "Split Ratings and Bond Reoffering Yields," *Financial Management* 14, no. 2 (summer 1985): 59–65; L. H. Ederington, "Why Split Ratings Occur," *Financial Management* 14, no. 1 (spring 1985): 37–47; and P. Liu and W. T. Moore, "The Impact of Split Bond Rating on Risk Premia," *The Financial Review* 22, no. 1 (February 1987).

[14]Bonds rated below investment-grade are also referred to as "high-yield bonds" or "junk" bonds. These high-yield bonds will be discussed in more detail in the subsequent section on corporate bonds.

TABLE 15.3 **DESCRIPTION OF BOND RATINGS**

	Duff & Phelps	Fitch	Moody's	Standard & Poor's	Definition
High Grade	AAA	AAA	Aaa	AAA	The highest rating assigned to a debt instrument, indicating an extremely strong capacity to pay principal and interest. Bonds in this category are often referred to as *gilt edge securities.*
	AA	AA	Aa	AA	High-quality bonds by all standards with strong capacity to pay principal and interest. These bonds are rated lower primarily because the margins of protection are less strong than those for Aaa and AAA bonds.
Medium Grade	A	A	A	A	These bonds possess many favorable investment attributes, but elements may suggest a susceptibility to impairment given adverse economic changes.
	BBB	BBB	Baa	BBB	Bonds are regarded as having adequate capacity to pay principal and interest, but certain protective elements may be lacking in the event of adverse economic conditions that could lead to a weakened capacity for payment.
Speculative	BB	BB	Ba	BB	Bonds regarded as having only moderate protection of principal and interest payments during both good and bad times.
	B	B	B	B	Bonds that generally lack characteristics of other desirable investments. Assurance of interest and principal payments over any long period of time may be small.
Default	CCC	CCC	Caa	CCC	Poor-quality issues that may be in default or in danger of default.
	CC	CC	Ca	CC	Highly speculative issues that are often in default or possess other marked shortcomings.
	C	C			The lowest-rated class of bonds. These issues can be regarded as extremely poor in investment quality.
		C		C	Rating given to income bonds on which no interest is being paid.
		DDD, DD, D		D	Issues in default with principal or interest payments in arrears. Such bonds are extremely speculative and should be valued only on the basis of their value in liquidation or reorganization.

Sources: *Bond Guide* (New York: Standard & Poor's Corporation, monthly); *Bond Record* (New York: Moody's Investors Services, Inc., monthly); *Rating Register* (New York: Fitch Investors Service, Inc., monthly).

ALTERNATIVE BOND ISSUES

We have described the basic features available for all bonds and the overall structure of the global bond market in terms of the issuers of bonds and investors in bonds. In this section, we provide a detailed discussion of the bonds available from the major issuers of bonds. The presentation is longer than you would normally expect because when we discuss each issuing unit, such as governments, municipalities, or corporations, we consider the bonds available in several of the major world financial centers, such as Japan, Germany, and the United Kingdom.

Domestic Government Bonds

UNITED STATES As shown in Table 15.2, the U.S. fixed-income market is dominated by U.S. Treasury obligations. The U.S. government with the full faith and credit of the U.S. Treasury issues Treasury bills (T-bills), which mature in less than 1 year, and two forms of long-term obligations: government notes, which have maturities of 10 years or less, and Treasury bonds, with maturities of 10 to 30 years. Current Treasury obligations come in denominations of $1,000 and $10,000. The interest income from the U.S. government securities is subject to federal income tax but exempt from state and local levies. These bonds are popular because of their high credit quality, substantial liquidity, and noncall feature.

Short-term T-bills differ from notes and bonds because they are sold at a discount from par to provide the desired yield. The return is the difference between the purchase price and the par at maturity. In contrast, government notes and bonds carry semiannual coupons that specify the nominal yield of the obligations.

Government notes and bonds have some unusual features. First, the period specified for the deferred call feature on Treasury issues is very long and is generally measured relative to the maturity date rather than from date of issue. They generally cannot be called until 5 years prior to their maturity date. Notably, *all* issues since 1989 have been noncallable.

Treasury Inflation Protected Securities (TIPS)[15] The Treasury began issuing these inflation-indexed bonds in January 1997 to appeal to investors who wanted or needed a *real* default-free rate of return. To ensure the investors will receive the promised yield in real terms, the bond principal and interest payments are indexed to the *Consumer Price Index for All Urban Consumers (CPI-U)* published by the Bureau of Labor Statistics. Because inflation is generally not known until several months after the fact, the index value used has a 3-month lag built in—for example, for a bond issued on June 30, 1999, the beginning base index value used would be the CPI value as of March 30, 1999. Following the issuance of a TIPS bond, its principal value is adjusted every 6 months to reflect the inflation since the base period. In turn, the interest payment is computed based on this adjusted principal—that is, the interest payments equal the original coupon times the adjusted principal. The example in Table 15.4 demonstrates how the principal and interest payments are computed. As shown, both the interest payments and the principal payment are adjusted over time to reflect the prevailing inflation, thereby ensuring that the investor receives a *real* rate of return on these bonds of 3.50 percent. It is interesting that the promised yield on TIPS bonds was about 3.40 percent when originally issued in early 1997 but increased to about 3.80 percent in mid-1999.

Notably, these bonds can also be used to derive the prevailing market estimate of the expected rate of inflation during the remaining maturity of the TIPS bond. For example, if we assume that when the bond is issued on July 15,1999, it sells at par for a YTM of 3.50 percent, while a nominal Treasury note of equal maturity is sold at YTM of 5.75 percent. This differential implies that investors expect an average annual rate of inflation of 2.25 percent

---

[15]This section draws heavily from the following excellent article: Pu Shen, "Features and Risks of Treasury Inflation Protection Securities," Federal Reserve Bank of Kansas City *Economic Review* (First Quarter 1998): 23–38. Other brief articles on the topic are: William R. Emmons, "Indexed Bonds and Falling Inflation Expectations," *Monetary Trends* (Federal Reserve Bank of St. Louis, September 1997); and Frank A. Schmid, "Extracting Inflation Expectations from Bond Yields," *Monetary Trends* (Federal Reserve Bank of St. Louis, April 1999).

TABLE 15.4

PRINCIPAL AND INTEREST PAYMENT FOR A TREASURY INFLATION PROTECTED SECURITY (TIPS)

Par Value—$1,000
Issued on July 15, 1999
Maturity on July 15, 2004
Coupon—3.50%
Original CPI Value—170.00

Date	Index Value[a]	Rate of Inflation	Accrued Principal	Interest Payment[b]
7/15/99	170.00	—	$1,000.00	—
1/15/00	172.55	0.015	1,015.00	$17.76
7/15/00	175.14	0.015	1,030.22	18.03
1/15/01	178.12	0.017	1,047.74	18.34
7/15/01	181.50	0.019	1,067.65	18.68
1/15/02	185.13	0.020	1,089.00	19.06
7/15/02	188.83	0.020	1,110.78	19.44
1/15/03	192.23	0.018	1,130.77	19.79
7/15/03	195.69	0.018	1,151.13	20.14
1/15/04	199.62	0.020	1,174.15	20.55
7/15/04	204.60	0.025	1,203.50	21.06

[a]The CPI index value is for the period 3 months prior to the date.

[b]Semiannual interest payment equals 0.0175 (accrued principal).

during this 5-year period. If, a year later, the spread increased to 2.45 percent, it would indicate that investors expect a further increase in the inflation rate during the next 4 years.

JAPAN[16] The second-largest government bond market in the world is Japan's. It is controlled by the Japanese government and the Bank of Japan (Japanese Central Bank). Japanese government bonds are an attractive investment vehicle for those favoring the Japanese yen because their quality is equal to that of U.S. Treasury securities (they are guaranteed by the government of Japan) and they are very liquid. There are three maturity segments: medium-term (2, 3, or 4 years), long-term (10 years), and super-long (private placements for 15 and 20 years). Bonds are issued in both registered and bearer form, although registered bonds can be converted to bearer bonds through the registrar at the Bank of Japan.

Medium-term bonds are issued monthly through a competitive auction system similar to that of U.S. Treasury bonds. Long-term bonds are authorized by the Ministry of Finance and issued monthly by the Bank of Japan through an underwriting syndicate consisting of major financial institutions. Most super-long bonds are sold through private placement to a few financial institutions. Federal government bonds, which are the most liquid of all Japanese bonds, account for over 40 percent of the Japanese bonds outstanding and over 80 percent of total bond trading volume in Japan.

[16]For additional discussion, see *International Bond Handbook* (London: James Capel & Co., 1987); Nicholas Sargan, Kermit L. Schoenhotz, Steven Blitz, and Sahar Elhabashi, *Trading Patterns in the Japanese Government Bond Market* (New York: Salomon Brothers, 1986); Aron Viner, *Inside Japanese Financial Markets* (Homewood, Ill.: Dow Jones-Irwin, 1988); Edwin J. Elton and Martin J. Gruber, eds., *Japanese Capital Markets* (New York: Harper & Row, 1990); and Frank J. Fabozzi, ed., *The Japanese Bond Markets* (Chicago: Probus Publishing, 1990).

At least 50 percent of the trading in Japanese government bonds will be in the so-called *benchmark issue* of the time. The benchmark issue is selected from 10-year coupon bonds. (As of early 1999, the benchmark issue was a 1.40 percent coupon bond maturing in 2009.) The designation of a benchmark issue is intended to assist smaller financial institutions in their trading of government bonds by ensuring these institutions that they would have a liquid market in this particular security. Compared to the benchmark issue, which accounts for about 50 percent of total trading in all Japanese government bonds, the comparable most active U.S. bond within a class accounts for only about 10 percent of the volume.

The yield on this benchmark bond is typically about 30 basis points below other comparable Japanese government bonds, reflecting its superior marketability. In the U.S. market, the most liquid bond sells at a yield differential of only 10 basis points. The benchmark issue changes when a designated issue matures or because of a decision by the Bank of Japan. Because of the difference in yield and liquidity, institutions that are interested in buying and holding (versus trading) acquire the nonbenchmark issues because of their higher yields. Notably, by taking these nonbenchmark issues out of circulation, these institutions ensure that they will not be traded, which confirms assumptions about their lack of liquidity.

GERMANY[17] The third-largest bond market in the world is the German market, although the government segment of this market is relatively small. Table 15.2 showed that approximately 40 percent of domestic deutschemark bonds are issued by the major commercial banks, whereas the federal government issues about 25 percent through the German Central Bank.

The German capital market is dominated by commercial banks because Germany makes no formal distinction between investment, merchant, or commercial banks as the United States and the United Kingdom do. As a result, firms arrange their financing primarily through bank loans, and these banks in turn raise their capital through public bond issues. Therefore, corporate domestic bonds are substantially less than 1 percent of the total.

Bonds issued by the Federal Republic of Germany, referred to as *bund* bonds, are issued in amounts up to DM 4 billion (4 billion deutschemarks) with a minimum denomination of DM 100. Original maturities are normally 10 or 12 years, although 30-year bonds have been issued.

Although bonds are issued as bearer bonds, individual bonds do not exist. A global bond is issued and held in safekeeping within the Germany Securities Clearing System (the *Kassenverein*). Contract notes confirming the terms and ownership of each issue are then distributed to individual investors. Sales are based on these contract notes. Bonds are issued through a fixed quota system by the Federal Bond Syndicate, made up of the Bundesbank and 17 banks, including certain resident branches of foreign banks. These government bunds are very liquid because the Bundesbank makes a market at all times. They also are the highest credit quality because they are guaranteed by the German government.

Bunds are quoted and traded on the German stock exchanges. Daily prices are determined by the Bundesbank, and market makers use this benchmark level as the basis for trading. Although listed on the exchanges, government bonds are primarily traded over the counter and interest is paid annually.

---

[17]For additional information on the German bond market, see Graham Bishop, "Deutschemark," in *Salomon Brothers International Bond Manual,* 2d ed. (New York: Salomon Brothers, 1987); and *The European Bond Markets,* ed. The European Bond Commission (Chicago: Probus Publishing, 1989).

UNITED KINGDOM[18] The U.K. government bond market changed dramatically on October 17, 1986 (the day of the Big Bang when the trading rules and organizations in the securities business in the United Kingdom were changed). The roles of jobbers and brokers changed so that broker-dealers could act as principals or agents with negotiated commission structures. In addition, the number of primary dealers in the "gilt" market was expanded from 7 gilt jobbers to 27 primary dealers.

Maturities in this market range from short gilts (maturities of less than 5 years) to medium gilts (5 to 15 years) to long gilts (15 years and longer). Government bonds either have a fixed redemption date or a range of dates with redemption at the option of the government after giving appropriate notice. Alternatively, some bonds are redeemable on a given date or at any time afterwards at the option of the government. Government bonds are normally registered, although bearer delivery is available.

Gilts are issued through the Bank of England (the British central bank) using the tender method, whereby prospective purchasers tender offering prices at which they hope to be allotted bonds. The price cannot be less than the minimum tender price stated in the prospectus. If the issue is oversubscribed, allotments are made first to those submitting the highest tenders and continue until a price is reached where only a partial allotment is required to fully subscribe the issue. All successful allottees pay the lowest allotment prices.

These issues are extremely liquid and are highly rated because they are guaranteed by the British government. All gilts are quoted and traded on the London Stock Exchange and pay interest semiannually.

Government Agency Issues

In addition to pure government bonds, the federal government in each country can establish agencies that have the authority to issue their own bonds. The size and importance of these agencies differ among countries. They are a large and growing sector of the U.S. bond market, a much smaller component of the bond markets in Japan and Germany, and nonexistent in the United Kingdom.

UNITED STATES Agency securities are obligations issued by the U.S. government through various political subdivisions, such as a government agency or a government-sponsored corporation. Six government-sponsored enterprises and over two dozen federal agencies issue these bonds. Table 15.5 lists selected characteristics of the more popular government-sponsored and federal agency obligations, including market size, typical denominations, tax features, and the availability of bond quotes.[19] The issues in the table are representative of the wide variety of available obligations.

Agency issues usually pay interest semiannually, and the minimum denominations vary between $1,000 and $10,000. These obligations are not direct Treasury issues, yet they carry the full faith and credit of the U.S. government. Moreover, unlike government obligations, some of the issues are subject to state and local income tax, whereas others are exempt.[20]

One agency issue offers particularly attractive investment opportunities: GNMA (*Ginnie Mae*) pass-through certificates, which are obligations of the Government National

[18]For further discussion, see Ian C. Collier, *An Introduction to the Gilt-Edged Market* (London: James Capel & Co., 1987); and *The European Bond Markets.*

[19] We will no longer distinguish between federal agency and government-sponsored obligations; instead, the term *agency* shall apply to either type of issue.

[20]Federal National Mortgage Association (Fannie Mae) debentures, for example, are subject to state and local income tax, whereas the interest income from Federal Home Loan Bank bonds is exempt. In fact, a few issues are exempt from federal income tax as well (e.g., public housing bonds).

TABLE 15.5 AGENCY ISSUES: SELECTED CHARACTERISTICS

Type of Security	Minimum Denomination	Form	Life of Issue	Tax Status	How Interest Is Earned
Government-Sponsored					
Banks for cooperatives (co-ops)	$ 5,000	B, BE	No longer issued Longest issue due 1/02/86	Federal: Taxable State: Exempt Local: Exempt	Semiannual interest, 360-day year
Federal farm credit banks Consolidated systemwide notes	50,000	BE	5 to 365 days	Federal: Taxable State: Exempt Local: Exempt	Discount actual, 360-day year
Consolidated systemwide bonds	5,000	BE	6 and 9 months	Federal: Taxable State: Exempt Local: Exempt	Interest payable at maturity, 360-day year
	1,000	BE	13 months to 15 years	Federal: Taxable State: Exempt Local: Exempt	Semiannual interest
Federal Home Loan Bank					
Consolidated discount notes	100,000	BE	30 to 360 days	Federal: Taxable State: Exempt Local: Exempt	Discount actual, 360-day year
Consolidated bonds	10,000[a]	B, BE	1 to 20 years	Federal: Taxable State: Exempt Local: Exempt	Semiannual interest, 360-day year
Federal Home Loan Mortgage					
Corporation debentures	10,000[a]	BE	18 to 30 years	Federal: Taxable State: Taxable Local: Taxable	Semiannual interest, 360-day year
Participation certificates	100,000	R	30 years (12-year average life)	Federal: Taxable State: Taxable Local: Taxable	Monthly interest and principal payments
Federal interstate credit banks	5,000	B, BE	No longer issued Longest issue date 1/05/87	Federal: Taxable State: Exempt Local: Exempt	Semiannual interest, 360-day year
Federal National Mortgage Association discount notes	50,000[a]	B	30 to 360 days	Federal: Taxable State: Taxable Local: Taxable	Discount actual, 360-day year
Debentures	10,000[a]	B, BE	1 to 30 years	Federal: Taxable State: Taxable Local: Taxable	Semiannual interest, 360-day year

(continued)

Mortgage Association.[21] These bonds represent an undivided interest in a pool of federally insured mortgages. The bondholders receive monthly payments from Ginnie Mae that include both principal and interest because the agency "passes through" mortgage payments made by the original borrower (the mortgagee) to Ginnie Mae.

The coupons on these pass-through securities are related to the interest charged on the pool of mortgages. The portion of the cash flow that represents the repayment of the

[21]For a further discussion of mortgage-backed securities, see Frank J. Fabozzi and Chuck Ramsey, "Mortgages and Overview of Mortgage-Backed Securities"; Lakhbir S. Hayre, Cyrus Mohebbi, and Thomas A. Zimmerman, "Mortgage Pass-Through Securities"; and Chris Ames, "Collateralized Mortgage Obligations," all in *The Handbook of Fixed-Income Securities,* 5th ed., ed. Frank J. Fabozzi (Chicago, Ill.: Irwin Professional Publishing, 1997).

TABLE 15.5 (CONCLUDED)

Type of Security	Minimum Denomination	Form	Life of Issue	Tax Status	How Interest Is Earned
Government National Mortgage Association					
Mortgage-backed bonds	25,000	B, R	1 to 25 years	Federal: Taxable State: Taxable Local: Taxable	Semiannual interest, 360-day year
Modified pass-throughs	25,000[a]	R	12 to 40 years (12-year average)	Federal: Taxable State: Taxable Local: Taxable	Monthly interest and principal payments
Student Loan Marketing Association discount notes	100,000	B	Out to 1 year	Federal: Taxable State: Exempt Local: Exempt	Discount actual, 360-day year
Notes	10,000	R	3 to 10 years	Federal: Taxable State: Exempt Local: Exempt	Semiannual interest, 360-day year
Floating rate notes	10,000[a]	R	6 months to 10 years	Federal: Taxable State: Exempt Local: Exempt	Interest rate adjusted weekly to an increment over the average auction rate on 91-day Treasury bills and payable quarterly
Tennessee Valley Authority (TVA)	1,000	R, B	5 to 25 years	Federal: Taxable State: Exempt Local: Exempt	Semiannual interest, 360-day year
U.S. Postal Service	10,000	R, B	25 years	Federal: Taxable State: Exempt Local: Exempt	Semiannual interest, 360-day year

Notes: Form B = Bearer; R = Registered; BE = Book entry form. Debt issues sold subsequent to December 31, 1982, must be in registered form.

[a]Minimum purchase with increments in $5,000.

Source: *United States Government Securities* (New York: Merrill Lynch Government Securities, Inc., 1985); *Handbook of Securities of the United States Government and Federal Agencies,* 31st ed. (New York: First Boston Corporation, 1984).

principal is tax-free, but the interest income is subject to federal, state, and local taxes. The issues have minimum denominations of $25,000 with maturities of 25 to 30 years but an average life of only 12 years because as mortgages in the pool are paid off, payments and prepayments are passed through to the investor. Therefore, unlike most bond issues, the monthly payment is not fixed. In fact, the monthly payment is *very uncertain* because of the prepayment schedule that can vary dramatically over time when interest rates change.

The point that will be made in Chapter 16 in connection with the valuation of bonds with embedded options is that mortgages generally have a call option whereby the homeowner has the option to prepay the mortgage (i.e., call the mortgage loan) when it is advantageous because of interest rates or if it is necessary due to the sale of the house. Therefore, there are prepayments on these securities for two reasons: (1) because homeowners pay off their mortgages when they sell their homes and (2) because owners refinance their homes when mortgage interest rates decline as they did in 1995 and 1997. A major disadvantage of GNMA issues is that they can be seriously depleted by prepayments, which means that their *maturities are very uncertain.*

The rates of return on these pass-throughs are relatively attractive compared to corporates. Also, most of the return is tax-free in later years because the tax-free part of the payment (the return of principal) is large.

JAPAN The agencies in Japan, referred to as *government associate organizations,* account for about 15 percent of the total Japanese bond market. This agency market includes a substantial amount of public debt, but almost twice as much is privately placed with major financial institutions. Public agency debt is issued like government debt.

GERMANY The agency market in Germany finances about 5 percent of the public debt. The major agencies are the Federal Railway, which issues *Bahn* or *Bundesbahn* bonds, and the Federal Post Office, which issues *Post* or *Bundespost* bonds. These Bahns and Posts are issued up to DM 2 billion. The issue procedure is similar to that used for regular government bonds. Bahns and Posts are relatively liquid, although less liquid than government bunds. These agency issues are implicitly guaranteed by the government.

UNITED KINGDOM As shown in Table 15.2, there are no agency bond issues in the United Kingdom.

Municipal Bonds

Municipal bonds are issued by states, counties, cities, and other political subdivisions. Again, the size of the municipal bond market (referred to as *local authority* in the United Kingdom) varies substantially among countries. It is about 10 percent of the total U.S. market, compared to about 6 percent in Japan, 15 percent in Germany, and nonexistent in the United Kingdom. Because of the size and popularity of this market in the United States, we will discuss only the U.S. municipal bond market.

Municipalities in the United States issue two distinct types of bonds: general obligation bonds and revenue issues. **General obligation bonds** (GOs) are essentially backed by the full faith and credit of the issuer and its entire taxing power. Revenue bonds, in turn, are serviced by the income generated from specific revenue-producing projects of the municipality, for example, bridges, toll roads, hospitals, municipal coliseums, and waterworks. Revenue bonds generally provide higher returns than GOs because of their higher default risk. Should a municipality fail to generate sufficient income from a project designated to service a revenue bond, it has no legal debt service obligation until the income becomes sufficient.

GO municipal bonds tend to be issued on a serial basis so that the issuer's cash flow requirements will be steady over the life of the obligation. Therefore, the principal portion of the total debt service requirement generally begins at a fairly low level and builds up over the life of the obligation. In contrast, most municipal revenue bonds are term issues, so the principal value is not due until the final maturity date or the last few payment dates.[22]

The most important feature of municipal obligations is that the interest payments are exempt from federal income tax as well as from taxes in the locality and state in which the obligation was issued. This means that their attractiveness varies with the investor's tax brackets.

You can convert the tax-free yield of a municipal to an equivalent taxable yield (ETY) using the following equation:

---

[22]For a more detailed discussion of the overall municipal bond market, see Sylvan G. Feldstein and Frank J. Fabozzi, "Municipal Bonds." For an excellent discussion of the credit analysis of these bonds, see Sylvan G. Feldstein, "Guidelines in the Credit Analysis of General Obligation and Revenue Municipal Bonds." Both chapters are in *The Handbook of Fixed-Income Securities.*

$$ETY = \frac{i}{(1 - t)}$$

where:

ETY = equivalent taxable yield
i = coupon rate of the municipal obligations
t = marginal tax rate of the investor

An investor in the 35 percent marginal tax bracket would find that a 6 percent yield on a municipal bond selling close to its par value is equivalent to a 9.23 percent fully taxable yield according to the following calculation:

$$ETY = \frac{0.06}{(1 - 0.35)} = 0.0923$$

Because the tax-free yield is the major benefit of municipal bonds, an investor's marginal tax rate is a primary concern in evaluating them. As a rough rule of thumb, using the tax rates expected in 1999, an investor must be in the 28 to 30 percent tax bracket before the lower yields available in municipal bonds are competitive with those from fully taxable bonds. However, although the interest payment on municipals is tax-free, any capital gains are not (which is why the ETY formula is correct only for a bond selling close to its par value).

MUNICIPAL BOND INSURANCE A growing feature of the U.S. municipal bond market is *municipal bond insurance,* which provides that an insurance company will guarantee to make principal and interest payments in the event that the issuer of the bonds defaults. The insurance is placed on the bond at date of issue and is *irrevocable* over the life of the issue. The issuer purchases the insurance for the benefit of the investor, and the municipality benefits from lower interest costs due to lower default risk, which causes an increase in the rating on the bond and increased marketability. Others who would benefit from the insurance are small government units not widely known and bonds with a complex security structure.

As of 1999, approximately 40 percent of all new municipal bond issues were insured. There are six private bond insurance firms: a consortium of four large insurance companies entitled the Municipal Bond Investors Assurance (MBIA), American Municipal Bond Assurance Corporation (AMBAC), the Financial Security Assurance (FSA), the Financial Guaranty Insurance Company (FGIC), Capital Guaranty Insurance Company (CGIC), and Connie Lee Insurance Company. These firms will insure either general obligation or revenue bonds. To qualify for private bond insurance, the issue must initially carry an S&P rating of BBB or better. Currently, the rating agencies will give an AAA (Aaa) rating to bonds insured by these firms because all the insurance firms have AAA ratings. Issues with these private guarantees have enjoyed a more active secondary market and lower required yields.[23]

---

[23]For a discussion of municipal bond insurance, see Sylvan Feldstein and Frank J. Fabozzi, "Municipal Bonds," in *the Handbook of Fixed-Income Securities;* and D. S. Kidwell, E. H. Sorenson, and J. M. Wachowicz, "Estimating the Signaling Benefits of Debt Insurance: The Case of Municipal Bonds," *Journal of Financial and Quantitative Analysis* 22, no. 3 (September 1987): 299–313. For a discussion of a problem due to the popularity of insurance, see Constance Mitchell, "Bond Insurers Nearing Their Capacity for Backing Some Municipalities' Debt," *Wall Street Journal,* 1 June 1992, C1, C7.

Corporate Bonds

Again, the importance of corporate bonds varies across countries. The absolute dollar value of corporate bonds in the United States is substantial and has grown overall and as a percentage of U.S. long-term capital. At the same time, corporate debt as a percentage of total U.S. debt has declined from 18 percent to 13 percent because of the faster increase in government debt caused by large government deficits prior to 1998 and the growth of agency debt. The pure corporate sector in Japan is small and declining, whereas bank debentures comprise a significant segment (over 20 percent). The pure corporate sector in Germany is almost nonexistent, whereas bank debentures that are used to finance loans to nonbank corporations are the largest segment. The proportion of corporate debt in the United Kingdom is in the 5 to 6 percent range.

U.S. CORPORATE BOND MARKET Utilities dominate the U.S. corporate bond market. The other important segments include industrials (which rank second to utilities), rail and transportation issues, and financial issues. This market includes debentures, first-mortgage issues, convertible obligations, bonds with warrants, subordinated debentures, income bonds (similar to municipal revenue bonds), collateral trust bonds backed by financial assets, equipment trust certificates, and asset-backed securities (ABS) including mortgage-backed bonds.

If we ignore convertible bonds and bonds with warrants, the preceding list of obligations varies by the type of collateral behind the bond. Most bonds have semiannual interest payments, sinking funds, and a single maturity date. Maturities range from 25 to 40 years, with public utilities generally on the longer end and industrials preferring the 25- to 30-year range. Nearly all corporate bonds provide for deferred calls after 5 to 10 years. The deferment period varies directly with the level of the interest rates. Specifically, during periods of higher interest rates, bond issues typically will carry a 7- to 10-year deferment, while during periods of lower interest rates, the deferment periods will be much shorter.

On the other hand, corporate notes—with maturities of 5 to 7 years—are generally noncallable. Notes become popular when interest rates are high because issuing firms prefer to avoid long-term obligations during such periods. In contrast, during periods of low interest rates, such as 1995 and 1997, most corporate issues did not include a call provision because corporations did not believe that they would be able to exercise the call option and did not want to pay the higher yield required to include them.

Generally, the average yields for industrial bonds will be the lowest of the three major sectors, followed by utility returns, with yields on transportation bonds generally being the highest. The difference in yield between utilities and industrials occurs because utilities have the largest supply of bonds, so yields on their bonds must be higher to increase the demand for these bonds.

Some corporate bonds have unique features or security arrangements that will be discussed in the following subsections.[24]

Mortgage Bonds The issuer of a mortgage bond has granted to the bondholder a first-mortgage lien on some piece of property or possibly all the firm's property. Such a lien provides greater security to the bondholder and a lower interest rate for the issuing firm. Additional mortgage bonds can be issued, assuming certain protective covenants related to earnings or assets are met by the issuer.

Equipment Trust Certificates Equipment trust certificates are issued by railroads (the biggest issuers), airlines, and other transportation firms with the proceeds used to purchase

[24]For a further discussion, see Frank J. Fabozzi, Harry Sauvain, Richard Wilson, and John Ritchie, "Corporate Bonds," in *The Handbook of Fixed-Income Securities.*

equipment (freight cars, railroad engines, and airplanes), which serves as the collateral for the debt. Maturities range from 1 to about 15 years. The fairly short maturities reflect the nature of the collateral, which is subject to substantial wear and tear and tends to deteriorate rapidly.

Equipment trust certificates are appealing to investors because of their attractive yields and low default record. Although they lack the visibility of other corporate bonds, they typically are fairly liquid.

Collateral Trust Bonds As an alternative to pledging fixed assets or property, a borrower can pledge financial assets, such as stocks, bonds, or notes, as collateral. The bonds secured by these assets are termed *collateral trust bonds.* These pledged assets are held by a trustee for the benefit of the bondholder.

Collateralized Mortgage Obligations (CMOs)[25] Earlier we discussed mortgage bonds backed by pools of mortgages that pay bondholders proportionate shares of principal and interest paid on the mortgages in the pool. You will recall that the pass-through monthly payments are necessarily both interest and principal and that the bondholder is subject to early retirement if the mortgagees prepay because the house is sold or the mortgage refinanced. As a result, when you acquire the typical mortgage pass-through bonds, you receive monthly payments (which may not be ideal), and you would be uncertain about the size and timing of the payments.

Collateralized mortgage obligations (CMOs) were developed to offset some of the problems with the traditional mortgage pass-throughs. The first CMO was issued in June 1983, and the current total issuance exceeds $1 trillion. The main innovation of the CMO instrument is the segmentation of irregular mortgage cash flows to create securities that are high-quality, short-, medium-, and long-term collateralized bonds. Specifically, CMO investors own bonds that are collateralized by a pool of mortgages or by a portfolio of mortgage-backed securities. The bonds are serviced with the cash flows from these mortgages, but rather than the straight pass-through arrangement, the CMO substitutes a *sequential distribution process* that creates a series of bonds with varying maturities to appeal to a wider range of investors.

The prioritized distribution process is as follows:

- Several classes of bonds (these are referred to as *tranches*) are issued against a pool of mortgages, which are the collateral. As an example, let us assume a CMO issue with four classes (tranches) of bonds. In such a case, the first three (e.g., Classes A, B, C) would pay interest at their stated rates, beginning at their issue date, and the fourth class would be an accrual bond (referred to as a *Z bond*).[26]
- The cash flows received from the underlying mortgages are applied first to pay the interest on the bonds, and then to retire these bonds.

[25]For a detailed discussion, see Chris Ames, "Collateralized Mortgage Obligations," in *the Handbook of Fixed-Income Securities.*

[26]The four-class CMO was the typical configuration during the 1980s and is used here for demonstration purposes. By 1992, CMOs were issued with 18 to 20 classes. More advanced CMOs are referred to as REMICs, which are intended to provide greater certainty regarding the cash flow patterns for various components of the pool or some of those investing in the pool. Discussions of these REMICs include Robert A. Kulason and Michael Waldman, *Understanding TAC and PAC CMO Structures* (New York: Salomon Brothers, 1988); Mark J. Latimer, "Regarding REMICs," *Secondary Mortgage Markets* (McLean, Va.: Freddie Mac, 1991); Andrew S. Carron, "Understanding CMOs, REMICs, and Other Mortgage Derivatives," *Fixed Income Research* (New York: The First Boston Corp., 1992).

- The classes of bonds are retired sequentially. All principal payments are directed first to the shortest-maturity class A bonds until they are completely retired. Then all principal payments are directed to the next shortest-maturity bonds (i.e., the class B bonds). The process continues until all the classes have been paid off.
- During the early periods, the accrual bonds (the class Z bonds) pay no interest, but the interest accrues as additional principal, and the cash flow from the mortgages that collateralize these bonds is used to pay interest on and retire the bonds in the other classes. Subsequently, all remaining cash flows are used to pay off the accrued interest, pay any current interest, and then to retire the Z bonds.

This prioritized sequential pattern means that the A-class bonds are fairly short term and each subsequent class is a little longer term until the Z-class bond, which is a long-term bond. It also functions like a zero-coupon or PIK bond for the initial years.

Besides creating bonds that pay interest in a more normal pattern (quarterly or semiannually) and that have more predictable maturities, these bonds are considered very high quality securities (AAA) because of the structure and quality of the collateral. To obtain an AAA rating, CMOs are structured to ensure that the underlying mortgages will always generate enough cash to support the bonds issued, even under the most conservative prepayment and reinvestment rates. In fact, most CMOs are overcollateralized.

Further, the credit risk of the collateral is minimal because most are backed by mortgages guaranteed by a federal agency (GNMA, FNMA) or by the FHLMC. Those mortgages that are not backed by agencies carry private insurance for principal and interest and mortgage insurance. Notably, even with this AAA rating, the yield on these CMOs typically has been higher than the yields on AA industrials. This premium yield has, of course, contributed to their popularity and growth.

Asset-Backed Securities (ABSs) A rapidly expanding segment of the securities market is that of *asset-backed securities (ABSs),* which involve *securitizing debt.* This is an important concept because it substantially increases the liquidity of these individual debt instruments, whether they be individual mortgages, car loans, or credit card debt. This general class of securities was introduced in 1983. Since then, more than $700 billion in asset-backed securities have been issued. Beyond the mortgage securities, this market is dominated by securities backed by automobile loans and credit card receivables.

Certificates for automobile receivables (CARs) CARs are securities collateralized by loans made to individuals to finance the purchase of cars. Auto loans are self-amortizing, with monthly payments and relatively short maturities (i.e., 2 to 5 years). These auto loans can either be direct loans from a lending institution or indirect loans that are originated by an auto dealer and sold to the ultimate lender. CARs typically have monthly or quarterly fixed interest and principal payments, and expected weighted average lives of 1 to 3 years with specified maturities of 3 to 5 years. The expected actual life of the instrument typically is shorter than the specified maturity because of early payoffs when cars are sold or traded in. The cash flows of CARs are comparable to short-term corporate debt. They provide a significant yield premium over General Motors Acceptance Corporation (GMAC) commercial paper, which is the most liquid short-term corporate alternative. The popularity of these collateralized securities makes them important not only by themselves, but also as an indication of the potential for issuing additional collateralized securities backed by other assets and/or other debt instruments.[27]

---

[27]For further discussion, see Thomas Zimmerman, "Auto-Loan-Backed Securities," in *The Handbook of Fixed-Income Securities.*

Credit card receivables Since 1992, the fastest-growing segment of the ABS market has been securities supported by credit card loans. Credit card receivables are considered to be a revolving credit ABS, in contrast to auto loan receivables that are referred to as an installment contract ABS—because of the nature of the loan. Specifically, whereas the mortgaged-backed and auto loan securities amortize principal, the principal payments from credit card receivables are not paid to the investor but are retained by the trustee to reinvest in additional receivables. This allows the issuer to specify a maturity for the security that is consistent with the needs of the issuer and the demands of the investors.

When buying a credit card ABS, the indenture specifies (1) the intended maturity for the security; (2) the "lockout period" during which no principal will be paid; and (3) the structure for repaying the principal, which can be accomplished through a single-bullet payment, such as a bond, or distributed monthly with the interest payment over a specified amortization period. For example, a 5-year ABS could have a lockout period of 4 years followed by a 12-month amortization of the principal.

Beyond this standard arrangement, revolving credit securities are protected by early amortization events that can force early repayment if specific payout events occur that are detrimental to the investor (e.g., an increase in the loss rate or if the issuer goes into bankruptcy or receivership). Although this early amortization feature protects the investor from credit problems, it causes an early payment that may not be desirable.[28]

Variable-Rate Notes Introduced in the United States in the mid-1970s, variable-rate notes became popular during periods of high interest rates. The typical **variable-rate note** possesses two unique features:

1. After the first 6 to 18 months of the issue's life, during which a minimum rate is often guaranteed, the coupon rate floats, so that every 6 months it changes to follow some standard. Usually it is pegged 1 percent above a stipulated short-term rate. For example, the rate might be the preceding 3 weeks' average 90-day T-bill rate.
2. After the first year or two, the notes are redeemable at par, at the *holder's* option, usually at 6-month intervals.

Such notes represent a long-term commitment on the part of the borrower, yet provide the lender with all the characteristics of a short-term obligation. They typically are available to investors in minimum denominations of $1,000. However, although the 6-month redemption feature provides liquidity, the variable rates can cause the issues to experience wide swings in semiannual coupons.[29]

Zero-Coupon and Deep Discount Bonds The typical corporate bond has a coupon and maturity. In turn, the value of the bond is the present value of the stream of cash flows (interest and principal) discounted at the required yield to maturity (YTM). Alternatively, some bonds do not have any coupons or have coupons that are below the market rate at the time of issue. Such securities are referred to as *zero-coupon* or *minicoupon bonds* or *original-issue discount (OID) bonds.* A zero-coupon discount bond promises to pay a stipulated principal amount at a future maturity date, but it does not promise to make any interim interest payments. Therefore, the price of the bond is the present value of the principal payment at the maturity date using the required discount rate for this bond. The

[28]For further discussion, see David R. Howard, "Credit Card ABS," in *The Handbook of Fixed-Income Securities.*

[29]For an extended discussion, see Richard S. Wilson, "Domestic Floating-Rate and Adjustable-Rate Debt Securities," in *The Handbook of Fixed-Income Securities.* Adjustable-rate preferred stocks also are discussed in Richard S. Wilson, *Corporate Senior Securities* (Chicago: Probus Publishing, 1987), Chapter 6.

return on the bond is the difference between what the investor pays for the bond at the time of purchase and the principal payment at maturity.

Consider a zero-coupon, $10,000 par value bond with a 20-year maturity. If the required rate of return on bonds of equal maturity and quality is 8 percent and we assume semiannual discounting, the initial selling price would be $2,082.89 because the present-value factor at 8 percent compounded semiannually for 20 years is 0.208289. From the time of purchase to the point of maturity, the investor would not receive any cash flow from the firm. The investor must pay taxes, however, on the implied interest on the bond, although no cash is received. Because an investor subject to taxes would experience severe negative cash flows during the life of these bonds, they are primarily of interest to investment accounts not subject to taxes, such as pensions, IRAs, or Keogh accounts.[30]

A modified form of zero-coupon bond is the OID bond where the coupon is set substantially below the prevailing market rate, for example, a 5 percent coupon on a bond when market rates are 12 percent. As a result, the bond is issued at a deep discount from par value. Again, taxes must be paid on the implied 12 percent return rather than the nominal 5 percent, so the cash flow disadvantage of zero-coupon bonds, though lessened, remains.

High-Yield Bonds A segment of the corporate bond market that has grown in size, importance, and controversy is **high-yield bonds**, also referred too as *speculative-grade bonds* and *junk bonds.* These are corporate bonds that have been assigned a bond rating as noninvestment grade, that is, they have a rating below BBB or Baa. The title of speculative-grade bonds is probably the most objective because bonds that are not rated investment grade are speculative grade. The designation of *high-yield bonds* was by Drexel Burnham Lambert (DBL) as an indication of the returns available for these bonds relative to Treasury bonds and investment-grade corporate bonds. The *junk bond* designation is obviously somewhat derogatory and refers to the low credit quality of the issues.

Brief history of the high-yield bond market Based on a specification that bonds rated below BBB make up the high-yield market, this segment has existed as long as there have been rating agencies. Prior to 1980, most of the high-yield bonds were referred to as *fallen angels,* which means they were bonds that were originally issued as investment-grade securities but because of changes in the firm over time, the bonds were downgraded into the high-yield sector (BB and below).

The market changed in the early 1980s when DBL began aggressively underwriting high-yield bonds for two groups of clients: (1) small firms that did not have the financial strength to receive an investment-grade rating by the rating agencies, and (2) large and small firms that issued high-yield bonds in connection with leveraged buyouts (LBOs). The high-yield bond market went from a residual market that included fallen angels to a new-issue market where bonds were underwritten with below-investment-grade ratings.

The individual credited with leading the development of this new-issue, high-yield market is Michael Milken, a bond trader/salesman at DBL. Milken examined the returns and risks related to speculative-grade securities pre-1975 and became convinced that the promised and realized rates of return on these speculative-grade bonds were higher than justified by their default experience. He convinced a number of institutional investors of the superior risk-adjusted returns available on these bonds, which helped create a demand for them. At the same time, Milken and DBL became active in underwriting a large

[30]These bonds will be discussed further in Chapter 16 in the section on volatility and duration and in Chapter 17 when we consider immunization.

TABLE 15.6 **HIGH-YIELD BONDS—NEW ISSUE VOLUME 1977–1998**

	PUBLIC		144A		TOTAL		
Year	Number of Issues	Principal Amount ($ Millions)	Number of Issues	Principal Amount ($ Millions)	Number of Issues	Principal Amount ($ Millions)	Average Issue Size ($ Millions)
1977	61	$ 1,040.2			61	$ 1,040.2	17.05
1978	82	1578.5			82	1,578.5	19.25
1979	56	1,399.8			56	1,399.8	25.00
1980	45	1,429.3			45	1,429.3	31.76
1981	34	1,536.3			34	1,536.3	45.19
1982	52	2,691.5			52	2,691.5	51.76
1983	95	7,765.2			95	7,765.2	81.74
1984	131	15,238.9			131	15,238.9	116.33
1985	175	15,684.8			175	15,684.8	89.63
1986	226	33,261.8			226	33,261.8	147.18
1987	190	30,522.2			190	30,522.2	160.64
1988	160	31,095.2			160	31,095.2	194.34
1989	130	28,753.2			130	28,753.2	221.18
1990	10	1,397.0			10	1,397.0	139.70
1991	48	9,967.0			48	9,967.0	207.65
1992	245	39,755.2	29	$ 3,810.8	274	43,566.0	159.00
1993	341	57,163.7	95	15,096.8	436	72,260.5	165.74
1994	191	34,598.8	81	7,733.5	272	42,332.3	155.63
1995	152	30,139.1	94	14,242.0	246	44,381.1	180.41
1996	142	30,739.4	217	35,172.9	359	65,912.3	183.60
1997	103	19,822.0	576	98,885.0	679	118,707.0	174.83
1998	116	29,844.0	604	111,044.7	720	140,888.7	195.68

Note: Includes nonconvertible, corporate debt rated below investment grade by Moody's or Standard & Poor's. Excludes mortgage- and asset-backed issues, as well as non-144a private placements.

Source: Merrill Lynch & Co.; Securities Data Company.

number of these high-yield bond issues for small firms and LBOs.[31] As a result, the high-yield bond market exploded in size and activity beginning in 1983. As shown in Table 15.6, there were a limited number of new high-yield issues in the late 1970s, and they were not very large issues (the average size was less than $30 million). Therefore, they accounted for only about 4 to 7 percent of all public straight debt issues. Beginning in 1983, more large issues became common (the average size of an issue currently is almost $200 million), and high-yield issues became a significant percentage of the total new-issue bond market (typically between 15 and 20 percent). As of 1999, the total outstanding high-yield debt constituted about 20 percent of outstanding corporate debt in the United States.

---

[31]After the growth and development of the high-yield bond market, Michael Milken and DBL were indicted for securities law violations. DBL settled with the SEC and paid a fine without admitting guilt. In early 1990, Milken agreed to a plea bargain with the SEC that involved a fine and a prison term. It is the author's opinion that observers should separate the development of the high-yield bond market and the securities law violations. Although not condoning the securities law violations, almost everyone would acknowledge that the development of the high-yield debt market has had a positive impact on the capital-raising ability of the economy. For an analysis of this impact, see Glenn Yago, *Junk Bonds* (New York: Oxford University Press, 1991); and Kevin J. Perry and Robert A. Taggart Jr., "The Growing Role of Junk Bonds in Corporate Finance," *Journal of Applied Corporate Finance* 1, no. 1 (spring 1988): 37–45. An update on its characteristics is contained in Martin S. Fridson, "The State of the High-Yield Bond Market: Overshooting or Return to Normallcy," *Journal of Applied Corporate Finance* 7, no. 1 (spring 1994); 85–97; and Joseph V. Amato, "The High-Yield Bond Market," in *The Handbook of Fixed-Income Securities.*

TABLE 15.7 **DISTRIBUTION OF RATINGS FOR HIGH-YIELD BONDS: DECEMBER 31, 1993–DECEMBER 31, 1998**

	By Par Amount					
Average S&P Rating	**1998**	**1997**	**1996**	**1995**	**1994**	**1993**
BB	39.8	46.8	48.2	49.2	45.8	43.4
B	49.6	44.8	45.1	45.6	49.9	48.4
CCC/CC/C[a]	10.6	8.4	6.7	5.2	4.3	8.2

[a]Includes nonrated bonds.

Source: Martin S. Fridson, "This Year in High Yield," *Extra Credit* (New York: Merrill Lynch & Co., January/February 1994–1999.

An important point bears repeating: Although the high-yield debt market has existed for many years, its real emergence as a major component of the U.S. capital market did not occur until 1983. This is relevant when considering the liquidity and default experience for these securities.

Distribution of high-yield bond ratings Table 15.7 contains the distribution of ratings for all outstanding high-yield issues as of December 31, 1993–1998. As shown, the heavy concentration by both issues and par amount is in the B class, which contains almost half of all issues. There was an increase, then a decrease in the BB category that grew to over 49 percent then declined to less than 40 percent in 1998.

Ownership of high-yield bonds The major owners of high-yield bonds have been mutual funds, insurance companies, and pension funds. As of the end of 1998, over 100 mutual funds were either exclusively directed to invest in high-yield bonds or included such bonds in their portfolio. Notably, there has been a shift of ownership away from insurance companies and savings and loans toward mutual funds. This shift mainly occurred during the dark days of 1989–1990 when regulators "encouraged" the insurance companies and S&Ls to reduce or eliminate high-yield bonds from their portfolios.

The purpose of this discussion has been to introduce you to high-yield bonds because of the growth in size and importance of this segment of the market for individual and institutional investors. We revisit this topic in Chapter 17 on bond portfolio management, where we review the historical rates of return and alternative risk factors, including the default experience for these bonds. All of this must be considered by potential investors in these securities.[32]

JAPANESE CORPORATE BOND MARKET The corporate bond market in Japan is made up of two components: (1) bonds issued by industrial firms or utilities and (2) bonds issued by banks to finance loans to corporations. As noted in connection with Table 15.2, the pure corporate bond sector has declined in relative size over time to less

[32]For additional discussion of these bonds, see Robert Solof, *Historical Perspectives on the Use of High-Yield Securities in Corporate Creation: A Hundred Years of "Junk"* (New York: Drexel Burnham Lambert, February 1989); Edward I. Altman, ed., *The High-Yield Debt Market* (Homewood, Ill.: Dow Jones-Irwin, 1990); Frank J. Fabozzi, ed., *The New High-Yield Debt Market* (New York: Harper Business, 1990); Martin S. Fridson, *High-Yield Bonds* (Chicago: Probus Publishing, 1989); Frank K. Reilly, ed., *High-Yield Bonds: Analysis and Risk Assessment* (Charlottesville, Va.: Institute of Chartered Financial Analysts, 1990); and Jane Tripp Howe, *Junk Bonds: Analysis and Portfolio Strategies* (Chicago: Probus Publishing, 1988).

than 10 percent of the total. In contrast, the dollar amount of bank debentures is over 18 percent of the total.

Japanese corporate bonds are regulated by the *Kisaikai,* a council composed of 22 bond-related banks and seven major securities companies. It operates under the authority of the Ministry of Finance (MOF) and the Bank of Japan (BOJ) to determine bond-issuing procedures. Specifically, the Kisaikai fixes the coupons on corporate bonds in relation to coupons on long-term government bonds to prevent any competition with the government bond market.

Because of numerous bankruptcies during the 1930s depression, the government mandated that all corporate debt be secured. During the 1970s and 1980s, there was pressure to relax these requirements. Before this was allowed, domestic Japanese firms began issuing convertible bonds because they were not bound by the collateral rule. Also, foreign firms began issuing unrestricted Euroyen bonds, and domestic firms began selling straight debt in the Euroyen market. Finally, the requirement was abolished during 1988.

The issuance of unsecured debt has led to the birth of bond-rating agencies, which were not needed with completely secured debt. The Japan Bond Research Institute was established in 1979, followed by Mikuni's Credit Rating Company in 1981 and by the following firms in 1985 and 1986: Japan Credit Rating Agency, Ltd.; Nippon Investors Service, Inc.; and Moody's Japan K.K. (a subsidiary of Moody's Investor's Service, Inc.).

The Ministry of Finance specifies minimum corporate requirements and issuing requirements. Also, the ministry controls the issuance system that specifies who can issue bonds and when they can be issued. In addition, lead-underwriting managers are predetermined in accordance with a lead manager rotating system that ensures balance among the big-four securities firms in Japan (Nomura, Nikko, Daiwa, and Yamaichi Capital Management).

Bank Bonds The substantial issuance of bank bonds is because of the banking system in Japan, which is segmented into the following components:

- Commercial banks (13 big-city banks and 64 regional banks)
- Long-term credit banks (3)
- Mutual loan and savings banks (6)
- Specialized financial institutions

During the post–World War II reconstruction, several banks were permitted to obtain funding by issuing medium- and long-term debentures at rates above yields on government bonds. These funds were used to make mortgage loans to firms in the industrial sector to rebuild plant and equipment. Currently, these financial institutions sell 5-year coupon debentures and 1-year discount debentures directly to individual and institutional investors. The long-term credit banks are not allowed to take deposits and thus depend on the debentures to obtain funds. These bonds are traded in the OTC market.[33]

GERMAN CORPORATE BOND MARKET Germany likewise has a combination sector in corporates that includes pure corporate bonds and bank bonds. Here the contrast is even larger because nonbank corporate bonds are almost nonexistent, whereas bank bonds make up almost 38 percent of the total bond market.

[33]For further discussion of this market, see Aron Viner, *Inside Japanese Financial Markets* (Homewood, Ill.: Dow Jones-Irwin, 1988), Chapters 5 and 6; and Frank J. Fabozzi, ed., *The Japanese Bond Markets* (Chicago: Probus Publishing, 1990.

Bank bonds may be issued in collateralized or uncollateralized form. For the collateralized bonds, the largest categories are mortgage bonds and commercial bonds.

German mortgage bonds are collateralized bonds of the issuing bank backed by mortgage loans. Due to the supervision of these bonds and the mortgage collateral, these bonds are considered to be very high quality. They are issued in bearer or registered form. Most registered bonds are sold to domestic institutions and cannot be listed on a stock exchange because they are not considered securities. Alternatively, the bearer bonds, which are transferred by book-entry, are sold in small denominations, are traded on the exchanges, and enjoy an active secondary market.

German commercial bonds are subject to the same regulation and collateralization as mortgage bonds. The difference is that the collateral consists of loans to or guarantees by a German public-sector entity rather than a first mortgage. Possible borrowers include the federal government, its agencies (the federal railway or the post office), federal states, and agencies of the European Economic Community (EEC). The credit quality of these loans is excellent. Mortgage and commercial bonds have identical credit standing and trade at very narrow spreads.

Schuldscheindarlehen are private loan agreements between borrowers and large investors (usually a bank) who make the loans but who can (with the borrower's permission) sell them or divide the loans among several investors. These instruments are like a negotiable loan participation. All participants receive a copy of the loan agreement, and a letter of assignment gives the participant title to a share of principal and interest, although the bank acts as the agent. These loan agreements, which come in various sizes, account for a substantial proportion of all funds raised in Germany. A large volume of these private loan agreements exists, but because the market is not very liquid they typically are used for the investment of large sums to maturity.

U.K. CORPORATE BOND MARKET Corporate bonds in the United Kingdom are available in three forms: debentures, unsecured loans, and convertible bonds. The values of securities in each class are about equal. The maturity structure of the corporate bond market is fairly wide because during the 1980s, the preference of investors shifted toward long-maturity bonds. The coupon structure of corporate bonds also is broad with high-coupon bonds issued during the 1980s. The higher end of the coupon range, which goes from 10 to 14 percent, is due to the unsecured segment of this market. In contrast, convertible bonds have the low coupons. Almost all U.K. corporate bonds are callable term bonds.

Corporate bonds in the United Kingdom have been issued through both public offerings and private placements. Early in the 1980s, the market tended toward private placements. Since the Big Bang in October 1986, there have been more public offerings. Prior to the Big Bang, corporate bonds were traded on the stock exchange. Subsequently, primary dealers have begun trading corporate bonds directly with each other. All corporate bonds are issued in registered form.

INTERNATIONAL BONDS

Each country's international bond market has two components. The first, *foreign bonds,* are issues sold primarily in one country and currency by a borrower of a different nationality. An example would be U.S. dollar–denominated bonds sold in the United States by a Japanese firm. (These are referred to as *Yankee bonds.*) Second are *Eurobonds,* which are bonds underwritten by international bond syndicates and sold in several national markets. An example would be Eurodollar bonds that are securities denominated in U.S. dollars, underwritten by an international syndicate, and sold to non-U.S. investors outside the United States. The relative size of these two markets (foreign bonds versus Eurobonds) varies by country.

UNITED STATES The Eurodollar bond market has been much larger than the Yankee bond market (about $635 billion versus $220 billion). However, because the Eurodollar bond market is heavily affected by changes in the value of the U.S. dollar, it has experienced slower growth during periods when the dollar was weak. Such periods have created a desire for diversification by investors.

Yankee bonds are issued by foreign firms who register with the SEC and borrow U.S. dollars, using issues underwritten by a U.S. syndicate for delivery in the United States. These bonds are traded in the United States and pay interest semiannually. Over 60 percent of Yankee bonds are issued by Canadian corporations and typically have shorter maturities and longer call protection than U.S. domestic issues, which increase their appeal.

The Eurodollar bond market is dominated by foreign investors, and the center of trading is in London. Eurodollar bonds pay interest annually, so it is necessary to adjust the standard yield calculation that assumes semiannual compounding. The Eurodollar bond market currently comprises almost 40 percent of the total Eurobond market.

JAPAN Before 1985, the Japanese international bond market was dominated (over 90 percent) by foreign bonds (Samurai bonds) with the balance in Euroyen bonds. After the issuance requirements for Euroyen bonds were liberalized in 1985, the ratio of issuance swung heavily in favor of Euroyen bonds.

Samurai bonds are yen-denominated bonds sold by non-Japanese issuers and mainly sold in Japan. The market is fairly small and has limited liquidity. The market has experienced very little growth in terms of yen, but substantial growth in U.S. dollar terms because of changes in the exchange rate.

Euroyen bonds are yen-denominated bonds sold in markets outside Japan by international syndicates. As indicated, this market has grown substantially since 1985 because of the liberal issue requirements and favorable exchange-rate movements that make yen-denominated securities desirable.

GERMANY All deutschemark bonds of foreign issuers can be considered Eurobonds. This is because the stability of German currency reduces the importance of the distinction between foreign bonds (DM-denominated bonds sold in Germany by non-German firms) and Euro-DM bonds (DM bonds sold outside Germany). Both types of bonds share the same primary and secondary market procedures, are free of German taxes, and have similar yields, and the amount outstanding is almost equal.

UNITED KINGDOM U.K. foreign bonds, referred to as *bulldog bonds,* are sterling-denominated bonds issued by non-English firms and sold in London. Eurosterling bonds are sold in markets outside London by international syndicates.

Similar to other countries, the U.K. international bond market has become dominated by the Eurosterling bonds. As of 1998, the ratio of Eurobonds versus foreign bonds had grown to 25-to-1. The procedure for issuing and trading Eurosterling bonds is similar to that of other Eurobonds.

OBTAINING INFORMATION ON BOND PRICES

As might be expected, the price information needs of bond investors are considerably different from those of stockholders. We know that there is substantial up-to-the-minute information on numerous listed and OTC stocks based on recent transactions. In sharp contrast, almost all bond trading (in dollar volume) is done on the OTC market, and these transactions are not reported. As a result, almost all prices reported are based upon self-reporting of yield estimates by bond dealers who trade government, corporate, or municipal bonds. There was some discussion of this in Chapter 5 when we considered the creation and maintenance of bond indexes. Given this background, the following discussion considers how investors read and interpret bond price information reported in newspapers and quote sheets.

Interpreting Bond Quotes

Essentially, all bonds are quoted on the basis of either yield or price. Price quotes are always interpreted as a *percentage of par.* For example, a quote of 98½ is not interpreted as \$98.50, but 98½ percent of par. The dollar price is derived from the quote, given the par value. If the par value if \$5,000 on a municipal bond, then the price of an issue quoted at 98½ would be \$4,925. Actually, the market follows three systems of bond pricing: one system for corporates, another for governments (both Treasury and agency obligations), and a third for municipals.

CORPORATE BOND QUOTES Figure 15.1 is a listing of NYSE corporate bond quotes that appeared in *The Wall Street Journal* on June 9, 1999. The data pertain to trading activity on June 8. Several quotes have been designated for illustrative purposes. The first issue designated in column one is an American Telephone and Telegraph (ATT) issue and is representative of most corporate prices. In particular, the 8⅛22 indicates the coupon and maturity of the obligation; in this case, the ATT issue carries an 8.125 percent coupon and matures in 2022. The next column provides the *current* yield of the obligation and is found by comparing the coupon to the current market price. For example, a bond with an 8.125 percent coupon selling for 105.375 would have a 7.7 percent current yield. This is *not* the YTM or even necessarily a good approximation to it. Both of these yields will be discussed in Chapter 16.

The next column gives the volume of \$1,000 par value bonds traded that day (in this case, 52 bonds were traded). The next column indicates closing quotes, followed by the column for the net change in the closing price from the last day the issue was traded. In this case, ATT closed at 105.375, which was up ¼ from the prior day (\$25).

The second example in Column 1 is Alza, which refers to an Alza Corp. zero coupon bond ("zr") due in 2014. As discussed, zero coupon securities do not pay interest but are redeemed at par at maturity. Because there is no coupon, they sell at a deep discount, which implies a yield. Again, since there are no coupon payments, they do not report a current yield.

Finally, the third example in Column 1 is a convertible ("cv") bond from Argosy that has a 12 percent coupon and is due on 2001. The conversion feature means that the bond is convertible into the common stock of the company. The letters "dc" before the coupon mean "deep discount" and indicates that the original coupon was set below the going rate at the time of issue. An example of such a bond would be a 5 percent coupon bond issued when market rates were 9 or 10 percent. Alternatively, "vj" in front of a bond issue means that the firm is in receivership or bankruptcy. The small letter "f" that will usually follow the maturity date of such a bond means that the issue is trading *flat,* which means the issuer is not meeting its interest payments. Therefore, the coupon of the obligation is inconsequential and there is a dash in the current yield column because there are no coupon payments.

All fixed-income obligations, with the exception of preferred stock, are traded on an *accrued interest basis.* The prices pertain to the value of all *future* cash flows from the bond and exclude interest that has accrued to the holder since the last interest payment date. The actual price of the bond will exceed the quote listed because accrued interest must be added. Assume a bond with a 7⅛ percent coupon. If 2 months have elapsed since interest

FIGURE 15.1 **SAMPLE CORPORATE BOND QUOTATIONS**

NEW YORK EXCHANGE BONDS

Quotations as of 4 p.m. Eastern Time
Tuesday, June 8, 1999

Volume $13,574,000

	Domestic Tue.	Domestic Mon.	All Issues Tue.	All Issues Mon.
Issues Traded	239	209	249	215
Advances	91	87	95	87
Declines	107	83	111	87
Unchanged	41	39	43	41
New highs	2	3	3	3
New lows	26	20	26	20

SALES SINCE JANUARY 1
(000 omitted)

1999	1998	1997
$1,497,233	$1,699,099	$2,626,029

Dow Jones Bond Averages

–1998– High	–1998– Low	–1999– High	–1999– Low		––1999–– Close	––1999–– Chg.	––1999–– %Yld	––1998–– Close	––1998–– Chg.
107.17	104.42	106.88	102.22	20 Bonds	102.22	–0.37	7.13	104.93	+0.12
104.71	101.88	104.72	99.80	10 Utilities	99.80	–0.44	7.08	102.56	+0.02
109.81	106.48	109.44	104.63	10 Industrials	104.63	–0.31	7.17	107.30	+0.21

CORPORATION BONDS
Volume, $12,893,000

Bonds	Cur Yld.	Vol.	Close	Net Chg.
AES Cp 8s8	8.6	300	92⅞	– 1⅛
ATT 5⅛01	5.2	50	98½	+ ⅛
ATT 7⅛02	7.0	42	102⅛	– ¼
ATT 6¾04	6.7	51	101½	+ ⅛
ATT 5⅝04	5.8	11	96¾	– ⅜
ATT 8.2s05	8.0	180	102¼	...
ATT 7½06	7.2	60	104⅝	– ⅛
ATT 7¾07	7.3	25	106⅝	...
ATT 6s09	6.4	74	94	– ¼
① → ATT 8⅛22	7.7	52	105⅜	+ ¼
ATT 8⅛24	7.7	3	105½	+ ½
ATT 8.35s25	7.7	10	108	+ ⅛
ATT 6½29	7.1	75	91¼	– ⅜
ATT 8⅝31	8.0	34	107½	– ⅛
Aames 10½02	14.0	47	75	...
Aetna 6⅜03	6.4	50	99¾	+ ⅛
AlldC zr99	...	10	98 29/32	+ 1/32
AlldC zr2000	...	25	93¼	+ ⅛
AlldC zr03	...	15	75¼	– ¾
AlldC zr07	...	15	55¾	– ½
② → Alza zr14	...	8	53	...
AExC 6⅛00	6.2	10	99½	– 1
ARetire 5¾02	cv	60	84½	– ½
Amresco 10s03	13.0	75	77	– 2⅜
Amresco 10s04	12.5	131	80	...
AnnTaylr 8¾00	8.7	20	100⅝	– ⅜
③ → Argosy 12s01	cv	22	101¾	– ⅞
BkrHgh zr08	...	10	76	+ 3
BellPa 7⅛12	7.1	10	100¾	– ¼
BellsoT 6½00	6.4	35	100⅞	...
BellsoT 6¼03	6.2	10	100⅜	– ⅛
BellsoT 7s05	6.9	10	101¼	– ¾
BellsoT 5⅞09	6.2	150	95⅜	– 1
BellsoT 8¼32	7.6	31	108⅛	+ ⅛
BellsoT 7⅞32	7.7	195	102⅛	+ ⅛
BellsoT 7½33	7.4	21	100¾	...
BellsoT 6¾33	7.1	136	94½	...
BellsoT 7⅝35	7.5	229	101¼	– ¼
BethSt 8⅜01	8.3	10	100¾	+ ⅛
BethSt 8.45s05	8.4	108	100½	– ⅛
Bevrly 9s06	9.1	10	99¼	– 1
Bluegrn 8¼12	cv	25	94½	+ 2½
Bordn 8⅜16	8.4	118	100	– 1⅞
BosCelts 6s38	9.8	22	61½	...
BoydGm 9¼03	8.9	5	104½	+ 1⅝
BrnSh 9½06	9.1	5	104⅝	– ⅜
BurNo 3.20s45	6.3	35	50¾	+ ⅝
Caterplnc 6s07	6.2	53	97	...
Centrtrst 7½01	cv	77	95⅝	+ ⅜
ChaseM 7⅞04	7.8	33	100¾	+ ⅝
ChaseM 6¼06	6.3	25	98⅝	– ⅜
ChaseM 6¾08	6.8	25	99½	– ⅛
ChaseM 6½09	6.7	30	97⅜	– ⅝
CPoM 7¼12	7.2	9	101¼	...
CPoV 7¼12	7.2	5	100½	– ⅛
ChespkE 9⅝05	10.5	25	91¾	+ 2⅞
ChespkE 9⅛06	10.0	39	91	+ 1⅛
ChespkE 8½12	11.0	2	77	+ 2
ChckFul 7s12	cv	105	128	– 1
Clardge 11¾02f	...	69	58	– 2
ClrkOil 9½04	9.4	50	101⅜	...
CoeurDA 7¼05	cv	20	61½	+ ½
Coeur 6⅜04	cv	18	61½	...
CompUSA 9½00	9.5	23	100	+ ¼
Consec 8⅛03	7.9	10	103⅜	+ ⅝
ConPort 10½04	30.0	45	35	– ⅛
ConPort 10¾06	35.8	79	30	– 6½
Convrse 7s04	cv	21	49	– 2
DR Hrtn 10s06	9.6	141	104	– ½
DVI 9⅞04	9.9	25	100¼	+ 1⅞
DataGen 6s04	cv	36	88	– ½
DelcoR 8⅝07	8.5	10	102	+ ¼
DukeEn 7s00	6.9	25	100 25/32	...
DukeEn 6¼04	6.4	49	98	+ ¼
DukeEn 7⅞24	7.7	5	102⅝	...
DukeEn 6¾25	7.1	4	95⅝	...
DukeEn 7½25	7.4	20	101½	...
DukeEn 7s33	7.2	20	97	– ½
FedNM zr19s	...	10	26	– ½
FUnRE 8⅞03	8.8	15	100¾	+ ¾
FordCr 6⅜08	6.6	18	96	– ½
GBCB 8⅜07	8.5	10	98½	– ½
GMA 8.40s99	8.4	15	100 15/32	– ⅛
GMA 7s00	7.0	10	100 21/32	...
GMA 5½01	5.6	15	98¼	– ⅜
GMA 5⅝01	5.7	20	98⅞	– ¼
GMA 7s02	6.9	55	101⅜	– ⅛
GMA 6⅝02	6.6	19	100⅛	+ ¼
GMA 5⅞03	6.0	7	97¾	– ⅛
GMA 8¾05	7.7	3	113¾	+ 1¼
GMA dc6s11	6.5	44	92¼	– ½
GMA zr12	...	40	385	– 1
GMA zr15	...	8	320	...
GenesisH 9¾05	11.0	30	88½	+ 1
GaPw 6⅛99	6.1	25	99 13/16	– 1/32
GulfMo 5s56f	8.2	10	60⅝	– ⅞
Hallwd 10s05	12.2	82	82	– 2½
HlthcrR 6.55s02	cv	30	91	...
Hilton 5s06	cv	95	93	– ⅝
HuntPly 11¾04	11.0	10	106½	+ ½
IntgHlth 5¾01	cv	81	62	...

Source: *Wall Street Journal,* 9 June 1999.

was paid, the current holder of the bond is entitled to ⅔ or one-third of the bond's semiannual interest payment that will be paid in 4 months. More specifically, the 7⅛ percent coupon provides semiannual interest income of $35.625. the investor who held the obligation for 2 months beyond the last interest payment date is entitled to one-third (⅓) of that $35.625 in the form of accrued interest. Therefore, whatever the current price of the bond, an accrued interest value of $11.87 will be added. If a bond is trading "flat" as discussed above, accrued interest would not be added.

TREASURY AND AGENCY BOND QUOTES Figure 15.2 illustrates the quote system for Treasury and agency issues. These quotes resemble those used for OTC securities because they contain both bid and ask prices, rather than high, low, and close. For U.S. Treasury bond quotes, a small "n" behind the maturity date indicates that the obligation is a Treasury *note.* A small "p" indicates it is a Treasury note on which nonresident aliens are exempt from withholding taxes on the interest.

All other obligations in this section are Treasury bonds. The security identification is different because it is not necessary to list the issuer. Instead, the usual listing indicates the coupon, the month and year of maturity, and information on a call feature of the obligation. For example, if a quote carried a maturity of 2000–2005, this would mean that the issue has a deferred call feature until 2000 (and is thereafter freely callable) and a (final) maturity date of 2005. The bid–ask figures provided are stated as a percentage of par. The yield figure provided is yield to maturity, or *promised* yield based on the asking price. This system is used for Treasuries, agencies, and municipals.

Quote 1 is a 5⅝ percent obligation of 1999 that demonstrates the basic difference in the price system of government bonds (i.e., Treasuries and agencies). The bid quote is 100:08, and the ask is 100:10. Governments are traded in thirty-seconds of a point (rather than eighths), and the figures to the right of the colons indicate the number of thirty-seconds in the fractional bid or ask. In this case, the bid price is actually 100.25 percent of par. These quotes also are notable in terms of the bid–ask spread, which typically is 2 or 3 thirty-seconds, or about one-half the size of the smallest possible spread for most stocks, which is ⅛. This small spread reflects the outstanding liquidity and low transaction costs for Treasury securities.

The lower section of the first column contains quotes for U.S. Treasury securities that have been "stripped." Specifically, the typical bond that promises a series of coupon payments and its principal at maturity is divided into separate units whereby each coupon payment and the principal payment are treated like a zero-coupon bond that matures on that date. The security labeled ② was originally a coupon that was to be paid in February 2003. The asking yield (5.82) is referred to as the spot rate for this maturity (spot rate will be discussed in Chapter 16). The coupon interest payment with no principal is designated as "ci" (stripped coupon interest), while the other strip for February 2003 containing only the principal payment is designated "np" (Treasury note, stripped principal).

The securities listed in the Treasury bill section only report dates and days to maturity and no coupons. This is because these are pure discount securities, that is, the return is the difference between the price you pay and par at maturity.[34]

The final section contains the original Treasury Inflation Protection Securities (TIPS) discussed earlier. Notice the accrued principal in the last column that reflects the inflation since the bond was issued. The bond designated ③ was the original bond issued in January 1997, so it has the highest value of 1.043, and yield to maturity is computed using this as the principal amount to be paid at maturity.

MUNICIPAL BOND QUOTES Figure 15.3 contains municipal bond quotes from *The Blue List of Current Municipal Offerings.* These are ordered according to states and then alphabetically within states. Each issue gives the amount of bonds being offered (in

---

[34]For a discussion of calculating yields, see Bruce D. Fielitz, "Calculating the Bond Equivalent Yield for T-Bills," *Journal of Portfolio Management* 9, no. 3 (spring 1983): 58–60.

FIGURE 15.2 **SAMPLE QUOTES FOR TREASURY BONDS, NOTES, AND BILLS**

TREASURY BONDS, NOTES & BILLS

Tuesday, June 8, 1999

Representative and Indicative Over-the-Counter quotations based on $1 million or more.

Treasury bond, note and bill quotes are as of mid-afternoon. Colons in bond and note bid-and-asked quotes represent 32nds; 101:01 means 101 1/32. Net changes in 32nds. Treasury bill quotes in hundredths, quoted in terms of a rate discount. Days to maturity calculated from settlement date. All yields are to maturity and based on the asked quote. Most recently auctioned treasury bonds and notes, and current 13-week and 26-week bills are boldfaced. For bonds callable prior to maturity, yields are computed to the earliest call date for issues quoted above par and to the maturity date for issues quoted below par. n-Treasury note. i-Inflation-indexed. wi-When issued. iw-Inflation-indexed when issued; daily change is expressed in basis points.

Source: Dow Jones/Cantor Fitzgerald.

U.S. Treasury strips as of 3 p.m. Eastern time, also based on transactions of $1 million or more. Colons in bid-and-asked quotes represent 32nds; 99:01 means 99 1/32. Net changes in 32nds. Yields calculated on the asked quotation. ci-stripped coupon interest. bp-Treasury bond, stripped principal. np-Treasury note, stripped principal. For bonds callable prior to maturity, yields are computed to the earliest call date for issues quoted above par and to the maturity date for issues below par.

Source: Bear, Stearns & Co. via Street Software Technology Inc.

GOVT. BONDS & NOTES

Rate	Maturity Mo/Yr	Bid	Asked	Chg.	Ask Yld.
6	Jun 99n	100:01	100:03	-1	4.27
6 3/4	Jun 99n	100:03	100:05	....	3.93
6 3/8	Jul 99n	100:04	100:06	-1	4.37
5 7/8	Jul 99n	100:03	100:05	-1	4.68
6 7/8	Jul 99n	100:07	100:09	-1	4.79
6	Aug 99n	100:06	100:08	-1	4.55
8	Aug 99n	100:18	100:20	-1	4.48
5 7/8	Aug 99n	100:06	100:08	-1	4.68
6 7/8	Aug 99n	100:13	100:15	-1	4.69
5 3/4	Sep 99n	100:07	100:09	-1	4.77
7 1/8	Sep 99n	100:20	100:22	-1	4.80
6	Oct 99n	100:10	100:12	-1	4.87
5 5/8	Oct 99n	100:06	100:08	....	4.94
7 1/2	Oct 99n	100:29	100:31	....	4.94
5 7/8	Nov 99n	100:10	100:12	....	4.97
7 7/8	Nov 99n	101:05	101:07	-1	4.97
5 5/8	Nov 99n	100:08	100:10	....	4.95
7 3/4	Nov 99n	101:08	101:10	....	4.92
① → 5 5/8	Dec 99n	100:08	100:10	....	5.04
7 3/4	Dec 99n	101:13	101:15	....	5.04
6 3/8	Jan 00n	100:22	100:24	-1	5.08
5 3/8	Jan 00n	100:06	100:08	....	4.96
7 3/4	Jan 00n	101:21	101:23	....	4.99
5 7/8	Feb 00n	100:15	100:17	....	5.06
8 1/2	Feb 00n	102:07	102:09	-1	5.05
5 1/2	Feb 00n	100:08	100:10	....	5.04
7 1/8	Feb 00n	101:12	101:14	....	5.07
5 1/2	Mar 00n	100:07	100:09	....	5.13
6 7/8	Mar 00n	101:09	101:11	-1	5.14
5 1/2	Apr 00n	100:05	100:07	....	5.22
5 5/8	Apr 00n	100:09	100:11	....	5.22
6 3/4	Apr 00n	101:08	101:10	....	5.22
6 3/8	May 00n	100:30	101:00	....	5.26
8 7/8	May 00n	103:08	103:10	....	5.18
5 1/2	May 00n	100:06	100:08	....	5.23
6 1/4	May 00n	100:28	100:30	....	5.25
5 3/8	Jun 00n	100:01	100:03	....	5.28
5 7/8	Jun 00n	100:17	100:19	....	5.29

U.S. TREASURY STRIPS

Mat.	Type	Bid	Asked	Chg.	Ask Yld.
Aug 99	ci	99:06	99:06	+ 2	4.54
Aug 99	np	99:04	99:04	....	4.78
Nov 99	ci	97:29	97:30	+ 1	4.93
Nov 99	np	97:28	97:29	....	5.01
Feb 00	ci	96:20	96:21	....	5.07
Feb 00	np	96:20	96:21	....	5.06
May 00	ci	95:11	95:12	....	5.16
May 00	np	95:10	95:11	+ 1	5.21
Aug 00	ci	93:29	93:30	....	5.36
Aug 00	np	93:29	93:29	+ 1	5.38
Nov 00	ci	92:19	92:20	....	5.44
Nov 00	np	92:18	92:19	....	5.46
Feb 01	ci	91:06	91:07	....	5.53
Feb 01	np	91:06	91:07	....	5.53
May 01	ci	89:29	89:30	....	5.57
May 01	np	89:29	89:30	....	5.57
Aug 01	ci	88:19	88:21	....	5.60
Aug 01	np	88:19	88:20	....	5.61
Nov 01	ci	87:11	87:12	....	5.63
Nov 01	np	87:09	87:10	....	5.66
Feb 02	ci	85:30	86:00	− 1	5.70
May 02	ci	84:22	84:24	− 1	5.73
May 02	np	84:24	84:25	− 1	5.72
Aug 02	ci	83:15	83:17	− 1	5.74
Aug 02	np	83:14	83:16	− 1	5.75
Nov 02	ci	82:12	82:15	− 1	5.70
② → Feb 03	ci	80:27	80:30	− 1	5.82
Feb 03	np	80:31	81:01	− 1	5.79
May 03	ci	79:22	79:24	− 1	5.84
Aug 03	ci	78:17	78:20	− 4	5.83
Aug 03	np	78:17	78:20	− 1	5.84
Nov 03	ci	77:16	77:19	− 1	5.81
Feb 04	ci	76:05	76:08	− 2	5.88
Feb 04	np	76:09	76:12	− 3	5.84
May 04	ci	75:00	75:04	− 3	5.89
May 04	np	75:01	75:05	− 3	5.88
Aug 04	ci	74:02	74:05	− 3	5.85
Aug 04	np	73:28	73:31	− 3	5.90
Nov 04	ci	72:20	72:24	− 3	5.95
Nov 04	bp	72:14	72:18	− 2	5.99
Nov 04	np	72:22	72:26	− 3	5.93
Feb 05	ci	71:16	71:20	− 2	5.96
Feb 05	np	71:17	71:21	− 2	5.95
May 05	ci	70:13	70:17	− 2	5.98
May 05	bp	70:06	70:10	− 2	6.03
May 05	np	70:16	70:20	− 2	5.95

TREASURY BILLS

Maturity	Days to Mat.	Bid	Asked	Chg.	Ask Yld.
Jun 10 '99	1	4.55	4.47	+0.21	4.53
Jun 17 '99	8	4.42	4.34	+0.25	4.40
Jun 24 '99	15	4.33	4.25	+0.17	4.32
Jul 01 '99	22	4.15	4.07	+0.19	4.14
Jul 08 '99	29	4.28	4.20	+0.15	4.27
Jul 15 '99	36	4.28	4.24	+0.15	4.32
Jul 22 '99	43	4.41	4.37	+0.16	4.45
Jul 29 '99	50	4.44	4.40	+0.14	4.49
Aug 05 '99	57	4.46	4.42	+0.12	4.51
Aug 12 '99	64	4.49	4.47	+0.10	4.57
Aug 19 '99	71	4.53	4.51	+0.10	4.61
Aug 26 '99	78	4.50	4.48	+0.11	4.59
Sep 02 '99	85	4.46	4.44	+0.05	4.55
Sep 09 '99	92	4.49	4.48	....	4.59
Sep 16 '99	99	4.60	4.58	+0.09	4.70
Sep 23 '99	106	4.60	4.58	+0.07	4.71
Sep 30 '99	113	4.61	4.59	+0.07	4.72
Oct 07 '99	120	4.67	4.65	+0.04	4.79
Oct 14 '99	127	4.70	4.68	+0.05	4.82
Oct 21 '99	134	4.72	4.70	+0.07	4.85
Oct 28 '99	141	4.70	4.68	+0.05	4.83
Nov 04 '99	148	4.74	4.72	+0.03	4.88
Nov 12 '99	156	4.74	4.72	+0.03	4.89
Nov 18 '99	162	4.74	4.72	+0.01	4.89
Nov 26 '99	170	4.74	4.72	+0.01	4.89
Dec 02 '99	176	4.74	4.72	−0.02	4.90
Dec 09 '99	183	4.77	4.76	+0.01	4.95
Jan 06 '00	211	4.69	4.67	....	4.85
Feb 03 '00	239	4.64	4.62	+0.01	4.81
Mar 02 '00	267	4.74	4.72	+0.02	4.92
Mar 30 '00	295	4.78	4.76	+0.03	4.97
Apr 27 '00	323	4.76	4.74	+0.01	4.97
May 25 '00	351	4.81	4.80	+0.01	5.04

INFLATION-INDEXED TREASURY SECURITIES

Rate	Mat.	Bid/Asked	Chg.	*Yld.	Accr. Prin.
3.625	07/02	99-25/26	....	3.677	1032
3.375	01/07	96-22/23	− 01	3.867	1043 ← ③
3.625	01/08	97-27/28	− 02	3.909	1023
3.875	01/09	99-26/27	− 02	3.890	1008
3.625	04/28	95-06/07	− 01	3.900	1022
3.875	04/29	99-16/17	+ 01	3.899	1006

*-Yld. to maturity on accrued principal.

Source: *Wall Street Journal*, 9 June 1999.

FIGURE 15.3 **QUOTES FOR MUNICIPALS**

INDIANA

No. of Bonds Offered	Municipal Issuer	Special Characteristics	Coupon	Maturity	Price/YTM	Broker
100	INDIANA BD BK REV (HOOSIER) EQUIP)	*B/E*	4.300	01/01/96N/C	100	NORWESMN
550	INDIANA HEALTH FAC FING AUTH	METHODIST	5.625	09/01/02N/C	101	PRUBACG
45	INDIANA HEALTH FAC FING AUTH	P/R @ 102	7.750	08/15/20C00	5.25	EQUITSEC
200	INDIANA PORT COMMN PORT REV		6.750	07/01/10	993/4	NOYESDAV
3115	INDIANA ST OFFICE BLDG COMMN	P/R @ 102	8.200	07/01/01C97	4.60	MORGANNT
200	INDIANA ST OFFICE BLDG COMMN	MBIA	0.000	07/01/05	5.60	BEARSTER ←①
335	INDIANA ST RECREATIONAL DEV		6.050	07/01/14	6.45	SMITHBCH
115	INDIANA ST TOLL RD COMMN TOLL	M/S/F 11	9.000	01/01/15ETM	6.30	DRIZOS ←②
95	INDIANA ST TOLL RD COMMN TOLL		9.000	01/01/15ETM	6.30	EMMET
1000	INDIANA ST TOLL RD COMMN TOLL	N/C S/F 11	9.000	01/01/15ETM	6.00	WILLIAMA
100	ELKHART CNTY IND HOSP AUTH REV (ELKHART GEN HOSP)	*B/E* RFDG	6.200	07/01/01N/C	5.40	BLAIRWM
45	FORT WAYNE IND HOSP AUTH HOSP	S/F 97	6.875	01/01/02ETM	5.85	EMMET
100	FORT WAYNE IND HOSP AUTH HOSP	P/R @ 102	9.125	07/01/15C95	3.80	GABRIELE
55	GOSHEN IND CMNTY SCHS		6.600	07/01/97	4.75	NBDBKIND
10	INDIANAPOLIS IND ARPT AUTH REV (CA @ 102.01 @ 100)	US AIR	7.500	07/01/09C97	100	HSH ←③
15	INDIANAPOLIS IND ARPT AUTH REV	US AIR	7.500	07/01/19	8.25	STERLING
500	INDIANAPOLIS IND GAS UTIL REV		4.300	06/01/98	5.00	CITYSEC
60	INDIANAPOLIS IND LOC PUB IMPT		0.000	08/01/07N/C	8.10	SAPNY
25	INDIANAPOLIS IND LOC PUB IMPT		6.750	02/01/20	100	COUGHLIN
200	LAKE CENTRAL IND MULTI-		6.000	01/15/02ETM	5.25	CREWASSC
300	MICHIGAN CITY IND SEW WKS REV		5.200	08/01/07	5.70	NOYESDAV
	Thursday May 28, 1994				PAGE 15.A	

Source: *The Blue List of Current Municipal Offerings,* 28 May 1994, 15A. The Blue List Division of Standard & Poor's Corp., New York. Reprinted by permission of Standard & Poor's Corp.

thousands of dollars), the name of the security, the purpose or description of the issue, the coupon rate, the maturity (which includes month, day, and year), the yield or price, and the dealer offering the bonds. Bond quote 1 is for $200,000 of Indiana State Office Building bonds. The letters MBIA indicate that the bonds are guaranteed by the Municipal Bond Insurance Association (MBIA). These are zero (0.000) coupon bonds due July 1, 2005. In this instance, the yield to maturity is given (5.60 percent). To determine the price, compute the discount value or look up in a yield book the price of a zero coupon bond, due in about 8 years to yield 5.60 percent. The dealer offering the bonds is Bearster. A list in the back of the publication gives the name and phone number of the firm.

The second bond is for $115,000 of Indiana State Toll Road bonds with a 9 percent coupon. These bonds have an M/S/F (mandatory sinking fund) that becomes effective in 2011, although the bond matures in 2015. The letters ETM mean that the sinking fund is put into "escrow till maturity." The market yield on these bonds is 6.30 percent, which means the bond would be selling at a premium.

Bond quote 3 refers to $10,000 of Indianapolis, Indiana, Airport Authority revenue bonds that are backed by a contract with US Air. Although the bonds mature in 2009, they are callable beginning in 1997 (C97) at 102 of par. The coupon is 7.50 percent and, in this case, the price of the bond is listed (100), which means its market yield also is 7.50 percent. Such bonds are called *dollar bonds.*

THE INTERNET *Investments Online*

This chapter discusses some of the basics of bonds—terminology, ratings, and the differences between corporate and municipal bonds. Bonds are much simpler to evaluate than stocks because they are debt, not ownership claims, and because they (usually) have a fixed time to maturity and known cash flows to the investor (barring default). Bonds are an important part of many individual and institutional portfolios, and here are some helpful Web sites for bond information:

www.bonds-online.com This Web site covers the gamut of bonds. It offers information and price quotes on a wide variety of instruments, including Treasuries, savings bonds, corporates, municipals, inflation-indexed bonds, and zero coupon bonds. The site features a "bond professor" that answers queries about fixed-income securities, and site visitors can submit their own questions. Other information includes a capital markets commentary, a savings bond calculator, and a matrix of municipal yields by credit quality and years to maturity.

www.prusec.com/daily.htm Prudential Securities Market Commentaries is one of the brokerage house's sites that focuses on bonds. It features eight daily market commentaries on such topics as the financial markets, municipals, Treasuries, and corporates, as well as the stock market. Some commentaries span the trading day, beginning with pre-opening thoughts, offering a mid-day update, and ending with an after-the-close summary of what happened during the day.

The three bond ratings firms with interesting Web sites are Fitch's Investor's Service LP (**www.fitchinv.com**), Moody's Investor Services (**www.moodys.com**), and **www.standardandpoors.com/ratings**. These sites feature ratings, research, products, and services. Moody's includes an economic commentary, a discussion of its rating track record, and an overview of its rating process. In addition to featuring bond ratings, Moody's site offers country sovereign risk ratings. Standard & Poor's site offers selected research reports, ratings, and the agency's rating criteria.

www.bradynet.com This site is a good information source for emerging markets' fixed-income securities. It features bond prices, indexes, and yield curves for different countries, as well as analysis and research.

www.bondmarkets.com This is an issues-and-information-oriented site. It has information and updates on legislative and regulatory issues affecting the bond market, including such sectors as corporate, mortgage, and municipal bond markets.

The "+" in the far left column indicates a new item since the prior issue of *The Blue List.* A "#" in the column prior to the yield to maturity or the price indicates that the price or yield has changed since the last issue. It is always necessary to call the dealer to determine the current yield/price because these quotes are at least one day old when they are published.

Summary

- We considered the basic features of bonds: interest, principal, and maturity. Certain key relationships affect price behavior. Price is essentially a function of coupon, maturity, and prevailing market interest rates. Bond price volatility depends on coupon and maturity. As will be demonstrated in Chapter 16, bonds with longer maturities and/or lower coupons respond most vigorously to a given change in market rates.
- Each bond has unique intrinsic characteristics and can be differentiated by type of issue and indenture provisions. Major benefits to bond investors include high returns for nominal risk, the potential for capital gains, certain tax advantages, and possibly additional returns from active trading of bonds. Aggressive bond investors must consider market liquidity, investment risks, and interest rate behavior. We introduced high-yield (junk) bonds because of the growth in size and status of this segment of the bond market.

- The global bond market includes numerous countries. The non-U.S. markets have experienced strong relative growth, whereas the U.S. market has been stable, but constitutes less than half the world bond market. The four major bond markets (the United States, Japan, Germany, and the United Kingdom) have a different makeup in terms of the proportion of governments, agencies, municipals, corporates, and international issues. The various market sectors also are unique in terms of liquidity, yield spreads, tax implications, and operating features.
- To gauge default risk, most bond investors rely on agency ratings. For additional information on the bond market, prevailing economic conditions, and intrinsic bond features, individual and institutional investors rely on a host of readily available publications discussed in Chapter 6. Although extensive up-to-date quotes are available on Treasury bonds and notes, trading and price information for corporates and municipals is relatively difficult to find and is expensive.
- The world bond market is large and is continuing to grow at a strong rate due to government deficits around the world and the need for capital by corporations. It is also very diverse in terms of country alternatives and issuers within countries. This chapter provides the fundamentals that will allow us to consider the valuation of individual bonds in Chapter 16, and the alternative bond portfolio techniques in Chapter 17.

Questions

1. Explain the difference between calling a bond and a bond refunding.
2. Identify the three most important determinants of the price of a bond. Describe the effect of each.
3. Given a change in the level of interest rates, discuss how two major factors will influence the relative change in price for individual bonds.
4. Briefly describe two indenture provisions that can affect the maturity of a bond.
5. Explain the differences in taxation of income from municipal bonds and income from U.S. Treasury bonds and corporate bonds.
6. For several institutional participants in the bond market, explain what type of bond each is likely to purchase and why.
7. Why should investors be aware of the trading volume for bonds in their portfolio?
8. What is the purpose of bond ratings?
9. Based on the data in Table 15.1, which is the fastest-growing bond market in the world? Which markets are losing market share?
10. Based on the data in Table 15.2, discuss the makeup of the German bond market and how and why it differs from the U.S. market.
11. Discuss the positives and negatives of investing in a government agency issue rather than a straight Treasury bond.
12. Discuss the difference between a foreign bond (e.g., a Samurai) and a Eurobond (e.g., a Euroyen issue).
13. CFA *CFA Examination I (1993)*
    List *three* differences between Eurodollar and Yankee bonds.

Problems

1. An investor in the 28 percent tax bracket is trying to decide which of two bonds to purchase. One is a corporate bond carrying an 8 percent coupon and selling at par. The other is a municipal bond with a 5½ percent coupon, and it, too, sells at par. Assuming all other relevant factors are equal, which bond should the investor select?
2. What would be the initial offering price for the following bonds (assume semiannual compounding):
   a. A 15-year zero-coupon bond with a yield to maturity (YTM) of 12 percent.
   b. A 20-year zero-coupon bond with a YTM of 10 percent.
3. An 8.4 percent coupon bond issued by the state of Indiana sells for $1,000. What coupon rate on a corporate bond selling at its $1,000 par value would produce the same after-tax return to the investor as the municipal bond if the investor is in
   a. the 15 percent marginal tax bracket?
   b. the 25 percent marginal tax bracket?
   c. the 35 percent marginal tax bracket?

4. The Shamrock Corporation has just issued a $1,000 par value zero-coupon bond with an 8 percent yield to maturity, due to mature 15 years from today (assume semiannual compounding).
   a. What is the market price of the bond?
   b. If interest rates remain constant, what will be the price of the bond in 3 years?
   c. If interest rates rise to 10 percent, what will be the price of the bond in 3 years?
5. Complete the information requested for each of the following $1,000 face value, zero-coupon bonds, assuming semiannual compounding.

Bond	Maturity (Years)	Yield (Percent)	Price ($)
A	20	12	?
B	?	8	601
C	9	?	350

References

Altman, Edward I., ed. *The High Yield Debt Market.* Homewood, Ill.: Dow Jones-Irwin, 1990.

Altman, Edward I., and Scott A. Nammacher. *Investing in Junk Bonds.* New York: John Wiley & Sons, 1987.

Barnhill, Theodore M., William F. Maxwell, and Mark R. Shenkman, eds. *High-Yield Bonds.* New York: McGraw-Hill, 1999.

Beidleman, Carl, ed. *The Handbook of International Investing.* Chicago: Probus Publishing, 1987.

Douglas, Livingston G. *The Fixed Income Almanac.* Chicago: Probus Publishing, 1993.

Elton, Edwin J., and Martin J. Gruber, eds. *Japanese Capital Markets.* New York: Harper & Row, 1990.

European Bond Commission. *European Bond Markets.* Chicago: Probus Publishing, 1989.

Fabozzi, Frank J., ed. *Advances and Innovations in the Bond and Mortgage Markets.* Chicago: Probus Publishing, 1989.

Fabozzi, Frank J., ed. *The Japanese Bond Market.* Chicago: Probus Publishing, 1990.

Fabozzi, Frank J., ed. *The New High-Yield Debt Market.* New York: Harper Business, 1990.

Fridson, Martin S. *High-Yield Bonds.* Chicago: Probus Publishing, 1989.

Grabbe, J. Orlin. *International Financial Markets.* New York: Elsevier, 1986.

Howe, Jane Tripp. *Junk Bonds: Analysis and Portfolio Strategies.* Chicago: Probus Publishing, 1988.

Norton, Joseph, and Paul Spellman, eds. *Asset Securitization.* Cambridge, Mass.: Basil Blackwell, Inc., 1991.

Van Horne, James C. *Financial Market Rates and Flows.* 5th ed. Englewood Cliffs, N.J.: Prentice Hall, 1998.

Viner, Aron. *Inside Japanese Financial Markets.* Homewood, Ill.: Dow Jones-Irwin, 1988.

Wilson, Richard S. *Corporate Senior Securities.* Chicago: Probus Publishing, 1987.

Wilson, Richard S., and Frank J. Fabozzi. *The New Corporate Bond Market.* Chicago: Probus Publishing, 1990.

Yago, Glenn. *Junk Bonds.* New York: Oxford University Press, 1991.

Chapter

16 The Analysis and Valuation of Bonds

After you read this chapter, you should be able to answer the following questions:

- How do you determine the value of a bond based on the present value formula?
- What are the alternative bond yields that are important to investors?
- How do you compute the following major yields on bonds: current yield, yield to maturity, yield to call, and compound realized (horizon) yield?
- What are spot rates and forward rates and how do you calculate these rates from a yield to maturity curve?
- What is the spot rate yield curve and forward rate curve?
- How and why do you use the spot rate curve to determine the value of a bond?
- What are the alternative theories that attempt to explain the shape of the term structure of interest rates?
- What factors affect the level of bond yields at a point in time?
- What economic forces cause changes in bond yields over time?
- When yields change, what characteristics of a bond cause differential price changes for individual bonds?
- What is meant by the duration of a bond, how do you compute it, and what factors affect it?
- What is modified duration and what is the relationship between a bond's modified duration and its volatility?
- What is the convexity for a bond, how do you compute it, and what factors affect it?
- Under what conditions is it necessary to consider both modified duration and convexity when estimating a bond's price volatility?
- What happens to the duration and convexity of bonds that have embedded call options?
- What is effective duration and effective convexity and when are they useful?
- What is empirical duration and how is it used with common stocks and other assets?
- What is the static yield spread and option-adjusted spread?

In this chapter, we apply the valuation principles that were introduced in Chapter 13 to the valuation of bonds. This chapter is concerned with how one goes about finding the value of bonds using the traditional single yield to maturity rate and using multiple spot rates. We will also come to understand the several measures of yields for bonds. It also is important to understand why these bond values and yields change over time. To do this, we begin with a review of value estimation for bonds using the present value model introduced in Chapter 13. This background on valuation allows us to understand and compute the expected rates of return on bonds, which are their yields. We need to understand how to measure alternative yields on bonds because they are very important to bond investors.

After mastering the measurement of bond yields, we consider what factors influence the level of bond yields and what economic forces cause changes in yields over time. This is followed by a consideration of the alternative shapes of the yield curve and the alternative theories that explain changes in its shape. We discuss the effects of various characteristics and indenture provisions that affect the required returns and, therefore, the value of specific bond issues. This includes such factors as time to maturity, coupon, callability, and sinking funds.

We return to the consideration of bond value and acknowledge that when yields change, all bond prices do not change in the same way. An understanding of the factors that affect the price changes for bonds has become more important during the past several decades because the price volatility of bonds has increased substantially. Before 1950, the yields on bonds were fairly low and both yields and prices were stable. In this environment, bonds were considered a very safe investment and most investors in bonds intended to hold them to maturity. During the last several decades, however, the level of interest rates has increased substantially because of inflation, and interest rates have also become more volatile because of changes in the rate of inflation and monetary policy. As a result, bond prices and rates of return on bonds have been much more volatile and the rates of return on bond investments have increased. Although this increase in interest rate volatility has affected all bonds, the impact is more significant on bonds with embedded options, such as call features.

THE FUNDAMENTALS OF BOND VALUATION

The value of bonds can be described in terms of dollar values or the rates of return they promise under some set of assumptions. In this section, we describe both the present value model, which computes a specific value for the bond using a single discount value, and the yield model, which computes the promised rate of return based on the bond's current price.

The Present Value Model

In our introduction to valuation theory in Chapter 13, we saw that the value of a bond (or any asset) equals the present value of its expected cash flows. The cash flows from a bond are the periodic interest payments to the bondholder and the repayment of principal at the maturity of the bond. Therefore, the value of a bond is the present value of the semiannual interest payments plus the present value of the principal payment. Notably, the standard technique is to use a single interest rate discount factor, which is the required rate of return on the bond. We can express this in the following present value formula that assumes semiannual compounding.[1]

$$P_m = \sum_{t=1}^{2n} \frac{C_i/2}{(1 + i/2)^t} + \frac{P_p}{(1 + i/2)^{2n}}$$

where:

P_m = the current market price of the bond
n = the number of years to maturity
C_i = the annual coupon payment for bond i
i = the prevailing yield to maturity for this bond issue
P_p = the par value of the bond

The value computed indicates what an investor would be willing to pay for this bond to realize a rate of return that takes into account expectations regarding the RFR, the expected

[1]Almost all U.S. bonds pay interest semiannually so it is appropriate to use semiannual compounding wherein you cut the annual coupon rate in half and double the number of periods. To be consistent, you should also use semiannual compounding when discounting the principal payment of a coupon bond or even a zero-coupon bond. All our present value calculations assume semiannual compounding.

rate of inflation, and the risk of the bond. The standard valuation technique assumes holding the bond to the maturity of the obligation. In this case, the number or periods would be the number of years to the maturity of the bond (referred to as its *term to maturity*). In such a case, the cash flows would include all the periodic interest payments and the payment of the bond's par value at the maturity of the bond.

We can demonstrate this formula using an 8 percent coupon bond that matures in 20 years with a par value of $1,000. This calculation implies that an investor who holds this bond to maturity will receive $40 every 6 months (one half of the $80 coupon) for 20 years (40 periods) and $1,000 at the maturity of the bond in 20 years. If we assume a prevailing yield to maturity for this bond of 10 percent (the market's required rate-of-return on the bond), the value for the bond using the above equation would be:

$$P_m = \sum_{t=1}^{40} \frac{80/2}{(1 + .10/2)^t} + \frac{\$1,000}{(1 + .10/2)^{40}}$$

We know that the first term is the present value of an annuity of $40 every 6 months for 40 periods at 5 percent, while the second term is the present value of $1,000 to be received in 40 periods at 5 percent. This can be summarized as follows:

Present value of interest payments:		
$40 × 17.1591	=	$686.36
Present value of principal payment		
$1,000 × 0.1420	=	142.00
Total value of bond at 10%		$828.36

As expected, the bond will be priced at a discount to its par value because the market's required rate of return of 10 percent is greater than the bond's coupon rate, i.e., $828.36 or 82.836 percent of par.

Alternatively, if the market's required rate was 6 percent, the value would be computed the same way except we would compute the present value of the annuity at 3 percent for 40 periods and the present value of the principal at 3 percent for 40 periods as follows:

Present value of interest payments:		
$40 × 23.1148	=	$ 924.59
Present value of principal payment		
$1,000 × 0.3066	=	306.60
Total value of bond at 6%		$1,231.19

Because the bond's discount rate is lower than its coupon, the bond would sell at a premium above par value—that is, $1,231.19 or 123.119 of par.

THE PRICE–YIELD CURVE When you know the basic characteristics of a bond in terms of its coupon, maturity, and par value, the only factor that determines its value (price) is the market discount rate—its required rate of return. As shown above, as we increase the required rate, the price declines. It is possible to demonstrate the specific relationship between the price of a bond and its yield by computing the bond's price at a range of yields as shown in Table 16.1.

TABLE 16.1 **PRICE–YIELD RELATIONSHIP FOR A 20-YEAR, 8 PERCENT COUPON BOND ($1,000 PAR VALUE)**

Required Yield	Price of Bond
2	$1,985.09
4	1,547.12
6	1,231.19
8	1,000.00
10	828.36
12	699.05
14	600.07
16	522.98

FIGURE 16.1 **THE PRICE–YIELD CURVE FOR A 20-YEAR, 8 PERCENT COUPON BOND**

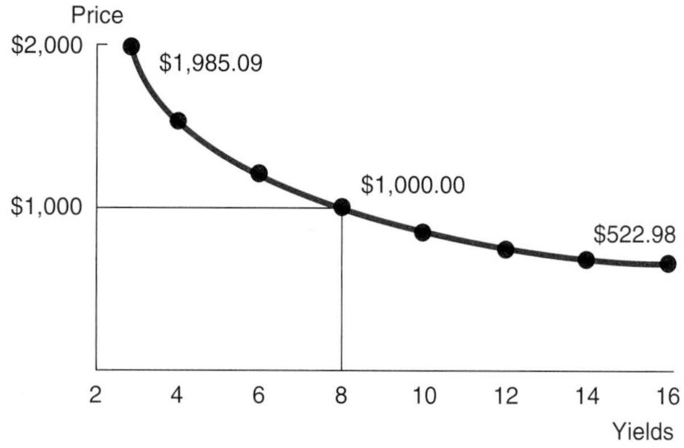
Price
$2,000
$1,985.09
$1,000
$1,000.00
$522.98
2
4
6
8
10
12
14
16
Yields

A graph of this relationship between the required return (yield) on the bond and its price is referred to as the price–yield curve, as shown in Figure 16.1. Besides demonstrating that price moves inverse to yield, it shows three other important points:

1. When the yield is below the coupon rate, the bond will be priced at a **premium** to its par value.
2. When the yield is above the coupon rate, the bond will be priced at a **discount** to its par value.
3. The price–yield relationship is not a straight line; rather, it is *convex.* As yields decline, the price increases at an increasing rate, and as the yield increases, the price declines at a declining rate. This concept of a convex price–yield curve is referred to as *convexity* and will be discussed further in a later section.

The Yield Model

Instead of determining the value of a bond in dollar terms, investors often price bonds in terms of **yields**—the promised rates of return on bonds under certain assumptions. Thus far, we have used cash flows and our required rate of return to compute an estimated value for the bond. To compute an expected yield, we use the current market price (P_m) and the expected cash flows to *compute the expected yield on the bond.* We can express this approach using the same present value model. The difference is that in the equation on page 543, it was assumed that we knew the appropriate discount rate (the required rate of return), and we computed the estimated value (price) of the bond. In this case, it is assumed that we know the price of the bond and we compute the discount rate (yield) that will give us the current market price (P_m).

$$P_m = \sum_{t=1}^{2n} \frac{C_i/2}{(1 + i/2)^t} + \frac{P_p}{(1 + i/2)^{2n}}$$

where the variables are the same as previously, except

i = the discount rate that will discount the expected cash flows to equal the current market price of the bond.

This i value gives the expected ("promised") yield of the bond under various assumptions to be noted, assuming you pay the price P_m. In the next section, we will discuss several types of bond yields that arise from the assumptions of the valuation model.

Approaching the investment decision stating the bond's value as a yield figure rather than a dollar amount, you consider the relationship of the computed bond yield to your required rate of return on this bond. If the computed bond yield is equal to or greater than your required rate of return, you should buy the bond; if the computed yield is less than your required rate of return, you should not buy the bond.

These approaches to pricing bonds and making investment decisions are similar to the two alternative approaches by which firms make investment decisions. We referred to one approach, the net present value (NPV) method, in Chapter 13. With the NPV approach, you compute the present value of the net cash flows from the proposed investment at your cost of capital and subtract the present value cost of the investment to get the net present value (NPV) of the project. If this NPV is positive, you consider accepting the investment; if it is negative, you reject it. This is basically the way we compared the value of an investment to its market price.

The second approach is to compute the **internal rate of return (IRR)** on a proposed investment project. The IRR is the discount rate that equates the present value of cash outflows for an investment with the present value of its cash inflows. You compare this discount rate, or IRR (which is also the expected rate of return on the project), to your cost of capital, and accept any investment proposal with an IRR equal to or greater than your cost of capital. We do the same thing when we price bonds on the basis of yield. If the expected yield on the bond (yield to maturity, yield to call, or horizon yield) is equal to or exceeds your required rate of return on the bond, you should invest in it; if the expected yield is less than your required rate of return on the bond, you should not invest in it.

COMPUTING BOND YIELDS

Bond investors traditionally have used five yield measures for the following purposes:

Yield Measure	Purpose
Nominal yield	Measures the coupon rate.
Current yield	Measures the current income rate.
Promised yield to maturity	Measures the expected rate of return for bond held to maturity.
Promised yield to call	Measures the expected rate of return for bond held to first call date.
Realized (horizon) yield	Measures the expected rate of return for a bond likely to be sold prior to maturity. It considers specific reinvestment assumptions and an estimated sales price. It also can measure the actual rate of return on a bond during some past period of time.

Nominal and current yields are mainly descriptive and contribute little to investment decision making. The last three yields are all derived from the present value model as described in the equation on page 543.

When we present the last three yields based on the present value model, we consider two calculation techniques. First, we consider a fairly simple calculation for the approximate values for each of these yields to provide reasonable estimates. Second, we use the present value model to get accurate values. We provide both techniques because an exact answer with the present value model requires several calculations. In some cases, the approximate yield value is adequate.

To measure an expected realized yield (also referred to as the horizon yield or total return), a bond investor must estimate a bond's future selling price. Following our presentation of bond yields, we present the procedure for finding these prices. After a brief presentation on yields for tax-free bonds, we conclude the valuation segment with a demonstration of valuing bonds using spot rates, which is becoming more prevalent.

NOMINAL YIELD

Nominal yield is the coupon rate of a particular issue. A bond with an 8 percent coupon has an 8 percent nominal yield. This provides a convenient way of describing the coupon characteristics of an issue.

CURRENT YIELD

Current yield is to bonds what dividend yield is to stocks. It is computed as

$$CY = C_i / P_m$$

where:

CY = the current yield on a bond
C_i = the annual coupon payment of bond i
P_m = the current market price of the bond

Because this yield measures the current income from the bond as a percentage of its price, it is important to income-oriented investors who want current cash flow from their investment portfolios. An example of such an investor would be a retired person who lives on this investment income. Current yield has little use for most other investors who are interested in total return because it excludes the important capital gain or loss component.

PROMISED YIELD TO MATURITY

Promised yield to maturity is the most widely used bond yield figure because it indicates the fully compounded rate of return promised to an investor who buys the bond at prevailing prices, *if two assumptions hold true.* Specifically, the *promised* yield to maturity will be equal to the investor's *realized* yield *if* these assumptions are met. The first assumption is that the investor holds the bond to maturity. This assumption gives this value its shortened name, *yield to maturity* (YTM). The second assumption is implicit in the present value method of computation. Referring to the equation on page 543, recall that it related the current market price of the bond to the present value of all cash flows as follows:

$$P_m = \sum_{t=1}^{2n} \frac{C_i/2}{(1 + i/2)^t} + \frac{P_p}{(1 + i/2)^{2n}}$$

To compute the YTM for a bond, we solve for the rate i that will equate the current price (P_m) to all cash flows from the bond to maturity. As noted, this resembles the computation of the internal rate of return (IRR) on an investment project. Because it is a present value–based computation, it implies a reinvestment rate assumption because it discounts the cash flows. That is, the equation assumes that *all interim cash flows (interest payments) are reinvested at the computed YTM*. That is why this is referred to as a *promised* YTM because the bond will provide this computed YTM *only if* you meet its conditions:

1. You hold the bond to maturity.
2. You reinvest all the interim cash flows at the computed YTM rate.

If a bond promises an 8 percent YTM, you must reinvest coupon income at 8 percent to realize that promised return. If you spend (do not reinvest) the coupon payments or if you cannot find opportunities to reinvest these coupon payments at rates as high as its promised YTM, then the actual realized yield you earn will be less than the promised yield to maturity. As will be demonstrated in the section on realized return, if you can reinvest at rates above the YTM, your realized (horizon) return will be greater than the promised YTM. The income earned on this reinvestment of the interim interest payments is referred to as **interest-on-interest**.[2]

The impact of the reinvestment assumption (i.e., the interest-on-interest earnings) on the actual return from a bond varies directly with the bond's coupon and maturity. A higher coupon and/or a longer term to maturity will increase the loss in value from failure to reinvest the coupon cash flow at the YTM. Therefore, a higher coupon or a longer maturity makes the reinvestment assumption more important.

Figure 16.2 illustrates the impact of interest-on-interest for an 8 percent, 25-year bond bought at par to yield 8 percent. If you invested $1,000 today at 8 percent for 25 years and reinvested all the coupon payments at 8 percent, you would have approximately $7,100 at the end of 25 years. We will refer to this money that you have at the end of your investment horizon as your **ending-wealth value**. To prove that you would have an ending-wealth value of $7,100, look up the compound interest factor for 8 percent for 25 years (6.8493) or 4 percent for 50 periods (which assumes semiannual compounding and is 7.1073). In the case of U.S. bonds, the semiannual compounding is the appropriate procedure because almost all U.S. bonds pay interest every 6 months.

Figure 16.2 shows that this $7,100 is made up of $1,000 principal return, $2,000 of coupon payments over the 25 years ($80 a year for 25 years), and $4,100 in interest earned on the semiannual coupon payments reinvested at 4 percent semiannually. If you never reinvested any of the coupon payments, you would have an ending-wealth value of only $3,000. This ending-wealth value of $3,000 derived from the beginning investment of $1,000 gives you an actual (realized) yield to maturity of only 4.5 percent. That is, the rate that will discount $3,000 back to $1,000 in 25 years is 4.5 percent. Reinvesting the coupon payments at some rate between 0 and 8 percent would cause your ending-wealth position to be above $3,000 and below $7,100; therefore, your actual rate of return would be somewhere between 4.5 percent and 8 percent. Alternatively, if you managed to reinvest the coupon payments at rates consistently above 8 percent, your ending-wealth position would be above $7,100, and your realized (horizon) rate of return would be above 8 percent.

Interestingly, during periods of very high interest rates, you often hear investors talk about "locking in" high yields. Many of these people are subject to **yield illusion** because they do not realize that attaining the high promised yield requires that they reinvest all the coupon payments at the very high promised yields. For example, if you buy a 20-year bond with a promised yield to maturity of 15 percent, you will actually realize the promised 15 percent yield *only* if you are able to reinvest all the coupon payments at 15 percent over the next 20 years.

---

[2]This concept is developed in Sidney Homer and Martin L. Leibowitz, *Inside the Yield Book* (Englewood Cliffs, N.J.: Prentice-Hall, 1972), Chapter 1.

FIGURE 16.2 **THE EFFECT OF INTEREST-ON-INTEREST ON TOTAL REALIZED RETURN**

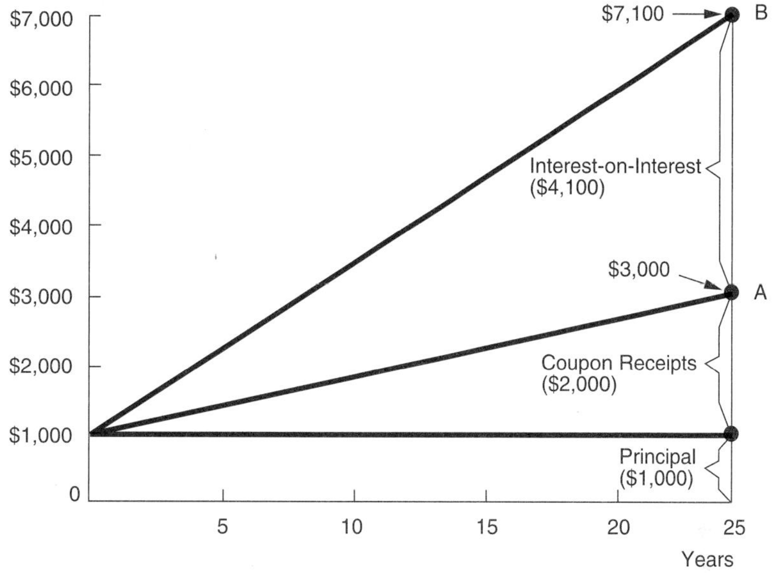
$7,000
$6,000
$5,000
$4,000
$3,000
$2,000
$1,000
0
$7,100
B
Interest-on-Interest ($4,100)
$3,000
A
Coupon Receipts ($2,000)
Principal ($1,000)
5
10
15
20
25
Years

Promised yield at time of purchase: 8.00%

Realized yield over the 25-year investment horizon with no coupon reinvestment (A): 4.50%

Realized yield over the 25-year horizon with coupons reinvested at 8% (B): 8.00%

COMPUTING THE PROMISED YIELD TO MATURITY The promised yield to maturity can be computed in two ways: finding an approximate annual yield, or using the present value model with semiannual compounding. The present value model gives an investor a more accurate result and is the technique used by investment professionals.

The approximate promised yield (APY) measure is easy to calculate:

$$\text{APY} = \frac{C_i + \dfrac{P_p - P_m}{n}}{\dfrac{P_p + P_m}{2}}$$

$$= \frac{\text{Coupon} + \text{Annual Straight-Line Amortization of Capital Gain or Loss}}{\text{Average Investment}}$$

where variables are as defined earlier. This approximate value for the promised yield to maturity assumes interest is compounded annually, and it does not require the multiple computations of the present value model. An 8 percent bond with 20 years remaining to maturity and a current price of $900 has an approximate yield of 8.95 percent as follows:

$$\text{APY} = \frac{80 + \dfrac{1000 - 900}{20}}{\dfrac{1000 + 900}{2}} = \frac{80 + 5}{950}$$

$$= 8.95\%$$

The present value model provides a more accurate yield to maturity value. Again, the equation on page 543 shows the promised yield valuation model:

$$P_m = \sum_{t=1}^{2n} \frac{C_i/2}{(1 + i/2)^t} + \frac{P_p}{(1 + i/2)^{2n}}$$

All variables are as described previously. This model is more accurate than the approximate promised yield model, but also is more complex because the solution requires iteration. The present value equation is a variation of the internal rate of return (IRR) calculation where we want to find the discount rate, *i*, that will equate the present value of the cash flows to the market price of the bond (P_m). Using the prior example of an 8 percent, 20-year bond, priced at \$900, the equation gives us a semiannual promised yield to maturity of 4.545 percent, which implies an annual promised YTM of 9.09 percent.[3]

$$\begin{aligned} 900 &= 40 \sum_{t=1}^{40} \left(\frac{1}{(1.04545)^t}\right) + 1000 \left(\frac{1}{(1.04545)^{40}}\right) \\ &= 40(18.2574) + 1{,}000\,(0.1702) \\ &= 900 \end{aligned}$$

The values for $1/(1 + i)$ were taken from the present value interest factor tables in the appendix at the back of the book using interpolation.

Comparing the results of this equation with those of the approximate promised yield computation, you find a variation of 14 basis points (8.95 percent versus 9.09 percent). As a rule, the approximate promised yield tends to understate the present value promised yield for issues selling below par value (that is, trading at a discount) and to overstate the promised yield for a bond selling at a premium. The size of the differential varies directly with the length of the holding period. Although the estimated yield values differ, the rankings of yields estimated using the APY formula will generally be identical to those determined by the present value method.

YTM FOR A ZERO-COUPON BOND In several instances we have discussed the existence of zero-coupon bonds that only have the one cash inflow at maturity. This single cash flow means that the calculation of YTM is substantially easier as shown by the following example:

Assume a zero-coupon bond, maturing in 10 years with a maturity value of \$1,000 selling for \$311.80. Because you are dealing with a zero-coupon bond, there is only the one cash flow from the principal payment at maturity. Therefore, you simply need to determine what is the discount rate that will discount \$1,000 to equal the current market price of \$311.80 in 20 periods (10 years of semiannual payments). The equation is as follows:

$$\$311.80 = \frac{\$1000}{(1 + i)^{20}}$$

[3]You will recall from your corporate finance course that you start with one rate (e.g., 9 percent or 4.5 percent semiannual) and compute the value of the stream. In this example, the value would exceed \$900, so you would select a higher rate until you had a present value for the stream of cash flows of less than \$900. Given the discount rates above and below the true rate, you would do further calculations or interpolate between the two rates to arrive at the correct discount rate that would give you a value of \$900.

You will see that i = 6 percent, which implies an annual rate of 12 percent. For future reference, this yield also is referred to as the 10-year spot rate, which is the discount rate for a single cash flow to be received in 10 years.

Promised Yield to Call

Although investors use promised YTM to value most bonds, they must estimate the return on certain callable bonds with a different measure—the **promised yield to call (YTC)**. Whenever a bond with a call feature is selling for a price above par (that is, at a premium) equal to or greater than its call price, a bond investor should consider valuing the bond in terms of YTC rather than YTM. This is because the marketplace uses the lowest, most conservative yield measure in pricing a bond. When bonds are trading at or above a specified **crossover price**, which is approximately the bond's call price plus a small premium that increases with time to call, the yield to call will provide the lowest yield measure.[4] The crossover price is important because at this price the YTM and the YTC are equal—this is the *crossover yield.* When the bond rises to this price above par, the computed YTM becomes low enough that it would be profitable for the issuer to call the bond and finance the call by selling a new bond at this prevailing market interest rate.[5] Therefore, the YTC measures the promised rate of return the investor will receive from holding this bond until it is retired at the first available call date, that is, at the end of the deferred call period. Note that if an issue has multiple call dates at different prices (the call price will decline for later call dates), it will be necessary to compute which of these scenarios provides the lowest yield—this is referred to as computing *yield to worst.* Investors must consider computing the YTC for their bonds after a period when numerous high-yielding, high-coupon bonds have been issued. Following such a period, interest rates will decline, bond prices will rise, and the high-coupon bonds will subsequently have a high probability of being called.

COMPUTING PROMISED YIELD TO CALL Again, there are two methods for computing the promised yield to call: the approximate method and the present value method. Both methods assume that you hold the bond until the first call date. The present value method also assumes that you reinvest all coupon payments at the YTC rate.

Yield to call is calculated using variations of the equations on pages 543 and 549. The approximate yield to call (AYC) is computed as follows:

$$\text{AYC} = \frac{C_i + \dfrac{P_c - P_m}{nc}}{\dfrac{P_c + P_m}{2}}$$

where:

AYC = the approximate yield to call (YTC)
P_c = the call price of the bond (generally equal to par value plus 1 year's interest)
P_m = the market price of the bond
C_i = the annual coupon payment of bond i
nc = the number of years to first call date

---

[4] For a discussion of the crossover price and yield, see Homer and Leibowitz, *Inside the Yield Book,* Chapter 4.

[5] Extensive literature exists on the refunding of bond issues, including W. M. Boyce and A. J. Kalotay, "Optimum Bond Calling and Refunding," *Interfaces* (November 1979): 36–49; R. S. Harris, "The Refunding of Discounted Debt: An Adjusted Present Value Analysis," *Financial Management* 9, no. 4 (winter 1980): 7–12; A. J. Kalotay, "On the Structure and Valuation of Debt Refundings," *Financial Management* 11, no. 1 (spring 1982): 41–42; and John D. Finnerty, "Evaluating the Economics of Refunding High-Coupon Sinking-Fund Debt," *Financial Management* 12, no. 1 (spring 1983): 5–10.

This equation is comparable to APY, except that P_c has replaced P_p in the equation and nc has replaced n.

To find the AYC of a 12 percent, 20-year bond that is trading at 115 ($1,150) with 5 years remaining to first call and a call price of 112 ($1,120), we substitute these values into the above equation.

$$\text{AYC} = \frac{120 + \dfrac{1120 - 1150}{5}}{\dfrac{1120 + 1150}{2}} = 10.04\%$$

This bond's approximate YTC is 10.04 percent, assuming that the issue will be called after 5 years at the call price of 112. To confirm that yield to call is the more conservative and more accurate value for a bond callable in 5 years, you can compute the approximate promised YTM. Using the equation on page 543 indicates a promised YTM of 10.47 percent.

To compute the YTC by the present value method, we would adjust the semiannual present value equation to give

$$P_m = \sum_{t=1}^{2nc} \frac{C_i/2}{(1 + i/2)^t} + \frac{P_c}{(1 + i/2)^{2nc}}$$

where:

P_m = the current market price of the bond
C_i = the annual coupon payment of bond i
nc = the number of years to first call date
P_c = the call price of the bond

Following the present value method, we solve for i, which typically requires several computations or extrapolation to get the exact yield.

Realized (Horizon) Yield

The final measure of bond yield, **realized yield** or **horizon yield**, measures the expected rate of return of a bond that you expect to sell prior to its maturity. In terms of the equation, the investor has a holding period (*hp*) or investment horizon that is less than n. Realized (horizon) yield can be used to estimate rates of return attainable from various trading strategies. Although it is a very useful measure, it requires several additional estimates not required by the other yield measures. Specifically, the investor must estimate the expected future selling price of the bond at the end of the holding period. Also, this measure requires a specific estimate of the reinvestment rate for the coupon flows prior to the liquidation of the bond. This technique also can be used by investors to measure their actual yields after selling bonds.

COMPUTING REALIZED (HORIZON) YIELD The realized yields are variations on the promised yield equations. The approximate realized yield (ARY) is calculated as follows:

$$\text{ARY} = \frac{C_i + \dfrac{P_f - P_m}{hp}}{\dfrac{P_f + P_m}{2}}$$

where:

ARY = the approximate realized (horizon) yield
C_i = the annual coupon payment of the bond i
P_f = the future selling price of the bond
P_m = the current market price of the bond
hp = the holding period of the bond (in years)

Again, the same two variables change: the holding period (hp) replaces n, and P_f replaces P_p. Keep in mind that P_f is not a contractual value but is *calculated* by defining the years remaining to maturity as $n - hp$ and by estimating a future market interest rate, i. We describe the computation of the future selling price (P_f) in the next section.

Once we determine hp and P_f, we can calculate the approximate realized yield. Assume you acquired an 8 percent, 20-year bond for \$750. Over the next two years, you expect interest rates to decline. As you know, when interest rates decline, bond prices increase. Suppose you anticipate that, when interest rates decline, the bond price will rise to \$900. The approximate realized yield in this case for the two years would be:

$$\text{ARY} = \frac{80 + \dfrac{900 - 750}{2}}{\dfrac{900 + 750}{2}} = 18.79\%$$

The estimated high realized (horizon) yield reflects your expectation of substantial capital gains in a fairly short period of time. Similarly, the substitution of P_f and hp into the present value model provides the following realized yield model:

$$P_m = \sum_{t=1}^{2hp} \frac{C_t/2}{(1 + i/2)^t} + \frac{P_f}{(1 + i/2)^{2hp}}$$

Again, this present value model requires you to solve for the i that equates the expected cash flows from coupon payments and the estimated selling price to the current market price. Because of the small number of periods in hp, the added accuracy of this measure is somewhat marginal. It has been suggested that because realized yield measures are based on an uncertain future selling price, the approximate realized (horizon) yield method is appropriate under many circumstances. In contrast, if you are going to use this technique to measure historical performance, you should use the more accurate present value model.

You will note from the present value realized yield formula in the above equation that the coupon flows are implicitly discounted at the computed realized (horizon) yield. In many cases, this is an inappropriate assumption because available market rates might be very different from the computed realized (horizon) yield. Therefore, to derive a realistic estimate of the expected realized yield, you also need to estimate your expected reinvestment rate during the investment horizon. We will demonstrate this in a subsequent subsection.

Therefore, to complete your understanding of computing expected realized yield for alternative investment strategies, the next section considers the calculation of future bond prices. This is followed by a section on calculating a realized (horizon) return with different reinvestment rates.

CALCULATING FUTURE BOND PRICES

Dollar bond prices need to be calculated in two instances: (1) when computing realized (horizon) yield, you must determine the future selling price (P_f) of a bond if it is to be sold before maturity or first call, and (2) when issues are quoted on a promised yield basis, as with municipals. You can easily convert a yield-based quote to a dollar price by using the equation on page 543, which does not require iteration. (You need only solve for P_m.) The coupon (C_i) is given, as is par value (P_p), and the promised YTM, which is used as the discount rate.

Consider a 10 percent, 25-year bond with a promised YTM of 12 percent. You would compute the price of this issue as

$$\begin{aligned} P_m &= 100/2 \sum_{t=1}^{50} \frac{1}{\left(1+\dfrac{0.120}{2}\right)^t} + 1000 \frac{1}{\left(1+\dfrac{0.120}{2}\right)^{50}} \\ &= 50(15.7619) + 1000(0.0543) \\ &= \$842.40 \end{aligned}$$

In this instance, we are determining the prevailing market price of the bond based on the current market YTM. These market figures indicate the consensus of all investors regarding the value of this bond. An investor with a required rate of return on this bond that differs from the market YTM would estimate a different value for the bond.

In contrast to the current market price, you will need to compute a future price (P_f) when estimating the expected realized (horizon) yield performance of alternative bonds. Investors or portfolio managers who consistently trade bonds for capital gains need to compute expected realized (horizon) yield rather than promised yield. They would compute P_f through the following variation of the realized yield equation:

$$P_f = \sum_{t=1}^{2n-2hp} \frac{C_i/2}{(1+i/2)^t} + \frac{P_p}{(1+i/2)^{2n-2hp}}$$

where:

P_f = the future selling price of the bond
P_p = the par value of the bond
n = the number of years to maturity
hp = the holding period of the bond (in years)
C_i = the annual coupon payment of bond i
i = the expected market YTM at the end of the holding period

This equation is a version of the present value model that is used to calculate the expected price of the bond at the end of the holding period (hp). The term $2n - 2hp$ equals the bond's remaining term to maturity at the end of the investor's holding period, that is, the number of 6-month periods remaining after the bond is sold. Therefore, the determination of P_f is based on four variables: two that are known and two that must be estimated by the investor.

Specifically, the coupon (C_i) and the par value (P_p) are given. The investor must forecast the length of the holding period, and therefore the number of years remaining to maturity at the time the bond is sold ($n - hp$). The investor also must forecast the expected market YTM at the time of sale (i). With this information, you can calculate the future price of the bond. The real difficulty (and the potential source of error) in estimating P_f lies in predicting hp and i.

Assume you bought the 10 percent, 25-year bond just discussed at \$842, giving it a promised YTM of 12 percent. Based on an analysis of the economy and the capital market, you expect this bond's market YTM to decline to 8 percent in 5 years. Therefore, you want to compute its future price (P_f) at the end of year 5 to estimate your expected rate of return, assuming you are correct in your assessment of the decline in overall market interest rates. As noted, you estimate the holding period (5 years), which implies a remaining life of 20 years, and the market YTM of 8 percent. A semiannual model gives a future price:

$$\begin{aligned} P_f &= 50 \sum_{t=1}^{40} \frac{1}{(1.04)^t} + 1000 \frac{1}{(1.04)^{40}} \\ &= 50(19.7928) + 1000\,(0.2083) \\ &= 989.64 + 208.30 \\ &= \$1{,}197.94 \end{aligned}$$

Based on this estimate of the selling price, you would estimate the approximate realized (horizon) yield on this investment on an annual basis as

$$\begin{aligned} \text{APY} &= \frac{100 + \dfrac{1198 - 842}{5}}{\dfrac{1198 + 842}{2}} \\ &= \frac{100 + 71.20}{1020} \\ &= 0.1678 \\ &= 16.78\% \end{aligned}$$

REALIZED (HORIZON) YIELD WITH DIFFERENTIAL REINVESTMENT RATES

The realized yield equation on page 553 is the standard present value formula with the changes in holding period and ending price. As such, it includes the implicit reinvestment rate assumption that all cash flows are reinvested at the computed i rate. There may be instances where such an implicit assumption is not appropriate, given your expectations for future interest rates. Assume that current market interest rates are very high and you invest in a long-term bond (e.g., a 20-year, 14 percent coupon) to take advantage of an expected decline in rates from 14 percent to 10 percent over a 2-year period. Computing the future price (equal to $1,330.95) and using the realized yield equation to estimate the realized (horizon) yield, we will get the following fairly high realized rate of return:

$$\begin{aligned} P_m &= \$1{,}000 \\ hp &= 2 \text{ years} \\ P_f &= \sum_{t=1}^{36} 70/(1 + 0.05)^t + \$1{,}000/(1.05)^{36} \\ &= \$1{,}158.30 + \$172.65 \\ &= \$1{,}330.95 \\ \$1{,}000 &= \sum_{t=1}^{4} \frac{70}{(1 + i/2)^t} + \frac{1330.95}{(1 + i/2)^4} \\ i &= 27.5\% \end{aligned}$$

As noted, this calculation assumes that all cash flows are reinvested at the computed i (27.5 percent). However, it is unlikely that during a period when market rates are going from 14 percent to 10 percent, you could reinvest the coupon at 27.5 percent. It is more appropriate and realistic to explicitly estimate the reinvestment rates and calculate the realized yields based on your *ending-wealth position.* This procedure is more precise and realistic, and it is easier because it does not require iteration.

The basic technique calculates the value of all cash flows at the end of the holding period, which is the investor's ending-wealth value. We compare this ending-wealth value to our *beginning-wealth value* to determine the *compound rate of return that equalizes these two values.* Adding to our prior example, assume we have the following cash flows:

$$P_m = \$1{,}000$$
$$i = \text{interest payments of } \$70 \text{ in 6, 12, 18, and 24 months}$$
$$P_f = \$1{,}330.95 \text{ (the ending market value of the bond)}$$

The ending value of the four interest payments is determined by our assumptions regarding specific reinvestment rates. Assume each payment is reinvested at a different declining rate that holds for its time period (that is, the first three interest payments are reinvested at progressively lower rates and the fourth interest payment is received at the end of the holding period).

$$\begin{aligned}
i_1 \text{ at } 13\% \text{ for 18 months} &= \$70 \times (1 + 0.065)^3 = \$\ 84.55 \\
i_2 \text{ at } 12\% \text{ for 12 months} &= \$70 \times (1 + 0.06)^2 = \quad 78.65 \\
i_3 \text{ at } 11\% \text{ for 6 months} &= \$70 \times (1 + 0.055) = \quad 73.85 \\
i_4 \text{ not reinvested} &= \$70 \times (1.0) = \quad \underline{70.00} \\
\text{Future Value of Interest Payments} &= \$307.05
\end{aligned}$$

Therefore, our total ending-wealth value is

$$\$1{,}330.95 + \$307.05 = \$1{,}638.00$$

The compound realized (horizon) rate of return is calculated by comparing our ending-wealth value (\$1,638) to our beginning-wealth value (\$1,000) and determining what interest rate would equalize these two values over a 2-year holding period. To find this, compute the ratio of ending wealth to beginning wealth (1.638). Find this ratio in a compound value table for four periods (assuming semiannual compounding). Table C.3 at the end of the book indicates that the realized rate is somewhere between 12 percent (1.5735) and 14 percent (1.6890). Interpolation gives an estimated semiannual rate of 13.16 percent, which indicates an annual rate of 26.32 percent. Using a calculator or computer, it is equal to $(1.638)^{1/4} - 1$. This compares to an estimate of 27.5 percent when we assume an implicit reinvestment rate of 27.5 percent.

This realized (horizon) yield computation specifically states the expected reinvestment rates as contrasted to assuming the reinvestment rate is equal to the computed realized yield. The actual assumption regarding the reinvestment rate can be very important.

The steps to calculate an expected realized (horizon) yield can be summarized as follows:

1. Calculate the future value at the horizon date of all coupon payments reinvested at estimated rates.
2. Calculate the expected sales price of the bond at your expected horizon date based on your estimate of the required yield to maturity at that time.
3. Sum the values in (1) and (2) to arrive at the total ending-wealth value.
4. Calculate the ratio of the ending-wealth value to the beginning value (the purchase price of the bond). Given this ratio and the time horizon, compute the compound rate of interest that will grow to this ratio over this time horizon.

$$\left(\frac{\text{Ending-wealth value}}{\text{Beginning value}}\right)^{1/2n} - 1$$

5. If all calculations assume semiannual compounding, double the interest rate derived from (4).

PRICE AND YIELD DETERMINATION ON NONINTEREST DATES

So far, we have assumed that the investor buys (or sells) a bond precisely on the date that interest is due, so the measures are accurate only when the issues are traded on coupon payment dates. If the approximate yield method is used, sufficient accuracy normally is obtained by extrapolating for transactions on noninterest payment dates. You already are dealing with an approximation, and a bit more is probably acceptable.

However, when the semiannual model is used, and when more accuracy is necessary, another version of the price and yield model must be used for transactions on noninterest payment dates. Fortunately, the basic models need be extended only one more step because the value of an issue that trades X years, Y months, and so many days from maturity is found by extrapolating the bond value (price or yield) for the month before and the month after the day of transaction. Thus, the valuation process involves full months to maturity rather than years or semiannual periods.[6]

ACCRUED INTEREST Having computed a value for the bond at a noninterest payment date, it is also necessary to consider the notion of *accrued interest.* Because the interest payment on a bond, which is paid every 6 months, is a contractual promise by the issuer, the bond investor has the right to receive a portion of the semiannual interest payment if he/she held the bond for some part of the 6-month period. For example, assume an 8 percent, $1,000 par value bond that pays $40 every 6 months. If you sold the bond 2 months after the prior interest payment, you have held it for one-third of the 6-month period and would have the right to one-third of the $40 ($13.33). This is referred to as the accrued interest on the bond. Therefore, when you sell the bond, there is a calculation of the bond's remaining value until maturity, that is, its price. What you receive is this price *plus* the accrued interest ($13.33).

YIELD ADJUSTMENTS FOR TAX-EXEMPT BONDS

Municipal bonds, Treasury issues, and many agency obligations possess one common characteristic: Their interest income is partially or fully tax-exempt. This tax-exempt status affects the valuation of taxable versus nontaxable bonds. Although you could adjust each present value equation for the tax effects, it is not necessary for our purposes. We can envision the approximate impact of such an adjustment, however, by computing the fully taxable equivalent yield, which is one of the most often cited measures of performance for municipal bonds.

The **fully taxable equivalent yield (FTEY)** adjusts the promised yield computation for the bond's tax-exempt status. To compute the FTEY, we determine the promised yield on a tax-exempt bond using one of the yield formulas and then adjust the computed yield to reflect the rate of return that must be earned on a fully taxable issue. It is measured as

$$\text{FTEY} = \frac{i}{1 - T}$$

where:

i = the promised yield on the tax-exempt bond
T = the amount and type of tax exemption. (i.e., the investor's marginal tax rate)

For example, if the promised yield on the tax-exempt bond is 6 percent and the investor's marginal tax rate is 30 percent, the taxable equivalent yield would be:

$$\text{FTEY} = \frac{0.06}{1 - 0.30} = \frac{0.06}{0.70} = 0.0857$$
$$= 8.57\%$$

[6] For a detailed discussion of these calculations, see Chapter 4 in Frank J. Fabozzi, ed., *The Handbook of Fixed-Income Securities,* 5th ed. (Chicago, Ill.: Irwin Professional Publishing, 1997).

The FTEY equation has some limitations. It is applicable only to par bonds or current coupon obligations, such as new issues, because the measure considers only interest income, ignoring capital gains, which are not tax-exempt. Therefore, we cannot use it for issues trading at a significant variation from par value (premium or discount).

BOND YIELD BOOKS Bond value tables, commonly known as *bond books* or *yield books,* can eliminate most of the calculations for bond valuation. A bond yield table is like a present value interest factor table in that it provides a matrix of bond prices for a stated coupon rate, various terms to maturity (on the horizontal axis), and promised yields (on the vertical axis). Such a table allows you to determine either the promised yield or the price of a bond.

As might be expected, access to sophisticated calculators or computers has substantially reduced the need for and use of yield books. In addition, to truly understand the meaning of alternative yield measures, you must master the present value model and its variations that generate values for promised YTM, promised YTC, realized (horizon) yield, and bond prices.

BOND VALUATION USING SPOT RATES

Thus far, we have used the valuation model, which assumes that we discount all cash flows by one common yield, reflecting the overall required rate of return for the bond. Similarly, we compute the yield on the bond (YTM, YTC, horizon yield) as the single interest rate that would discount all the flows from the bond to equal the current market price of the bond. It was noted in the YTM calculations that this was a "promised" yield that depended on two assumptions: holding the bond to maturity and reinvesting all cash flows at the computed YTM (the IRR assumption). Notably, this second assumption often is very unrealistic because it requires a flat, constant yield curve. We know that it is extremely rare for the yield curve to be flat, much less remain constant for any period of time. The yield curve typically is upward sloping for several reasons, which we discuss in a later section. Investors at any point in time require *a different rate of return for flows at different times.* For example, if investors are buying alternative zero-coupon bonds (promising a single cash flow at maturity), they will almost always require different rates of return if they are offered a bond that matures in 2 years, 5 years, or 10 years.

As mentioned earlier, the rates used to discount a flow at a point in time are called spot rates. It is possible to demonstrate the desire for different rates by examining the rates on government discount notes with different maturities (i.e., spot rates) as of mid-1999 as shown in Table 16.2. These rates indicate that investors require 5.22 percent for a 2-year flow, 5.48 percent for the cash flow in 5 years, and 5.86 percent for the cash flow in 10 years. Although these differences in required rates for alternative maturities are noticeable, they are not nearly as large as they were during the years 1993–1994. The difference in yield between the 1-year bond (4.99 percent) and the 30-year bond (5.95 percent) (referred to as the *maturity spread*) was 96 basis points in mid-1999; however, it was over 250 basis points in mid-1993.

Because of these differences in spot rates across maturities, bond analysts and bond portfolio managers recognize that it is inappropriate to discount all the flows for a bond at one single rate where the rate used is often based on the yield to maturity for a government bond with that maturity. For example, when asked about the value of a particular 20-year bond rated AA, a bond trader typically will respond that the bond should trade a certain number of basis points higher than comparable maturity Treasury bonds (e.g., "plus 70

TABLE 16.2 **YIELDS ON U.S. TREASURY STRIPS WITH ALTERNATIVE MATURITIES**

Maturity	Yield
1 Year	4.99
2 Years	5.22
3 Years	5.33
4 Years	5.42
5 Years	5.48
6 Years	5.58
7 Years	5.64
8 Years	5.68
9 Years	5.79
10 Years	5.86
12 Years	6.01
14 Years	6.14
16 Years	6.23
18 Years	6.26
20 Years	6.28
25 Years	6.16
30 Years	5.95

Source: *Wall Street Journal,* 18 May 1999.

basis points"). This means that if 20-year Treasury bonds are currently yielding 6.06 percent, this AA-rated bond should trade at about a 6.76 percent yield. Notably, this rate would determine the price for the bond with no consideration given to the specific cash flows of this security (i.e., high or low coupon). Therefore, there is a growing awareness that the valuation formula should be specified such that all cash flows should be discounted at spot rates consistent with the timing of the flows as follows:

$$P_m = \sum_{t=1}^{2n} \frac{C_t}{(1 + i_t/2)^t}$$

where:

P_m = the market price for the bond
C_t = the cash flow at time t
n = the number of years
i_t = the spot rate for Treasury securities at time t

Note that this valuation model requires a different discount rate for each flow so it is not possible to use the annuity concept. Also, the principal payment at the end of the year n is no different from the interest coupon flow.

To demonstrate the effect of this procedure, consider the following hypothetical spot rate curve for the next 5 years (in Table 16.3) and three example bonds with equal maturities of 5 years, but with very different cash flows.

Beyond the differences in value because of the differences in cash flows and the rising spot rate curve, a significant comparison is the value that would be derived using a single discount rate based on the 5-year maturity of all three bonds. If we assume two alternative yields to maturity of 6 percent and 6.5 percent for 5-year bonds, the values for the three bonds are:

	6%	6.5%
Bond A	$ 60 × 8.5302 = $ 511.81	$ 60 × 8.4254 = $ 505.52
	$1,000 × 0.7441 = 744.10	$1,000 × 0.7270 = 727.00
	Total Value = $1,255.91	= $1,232.52
Bond B	$ 30 × 8.5302 = $ 255.90	$ 30 × 8.4254 = $ 252.76
	$1,000 × 0.7441 = 744.10	$1,000 × 0.7270 = 727.00
	Total Value = $1,000.00	= $ 979.76
Bond C	$1,000 × 0.7441 = $ 744.10	$1,000 × 0.7270 = $ 727.00
	Total Value = $ 744.10	= $ 727.00

Because there is a rising spot-yield curve, we know the YTM would be somewhere between these two values. The point is, valuing the bonds with these single rates tends to generate a value that is greater than that derived from the spot rate curve. This implies that the single-rate valuation technique would overvalue these bonds relative to the more appropriate technique that considers each flow as a single bond discounted by its own spot rate.

WHAT DETERMINES INTEREST RATES?

Now that we have learned to calculate various yields on bonds and to determine the value of bonds using yields and spot rates, the question arises as to what causes differences and changes in yields over time. Market interest rates cause these effects because the interest rates reported in the media are simply the prevailing YTMs for the bonds being discussed. For example, when you hear that the interest rate on long-term government bonds declined from 6.80 percent to 6.70 percent, this means that the price of this particular bond increased such that the computed YTM at the former price was 6.80 percent, but the computed YTM

TABLE 16.3 **DEMONSTRATION OF DIFFERENT VALUATION OF ALTERNATIVE 5-YEAR MATURITY BONDS WITH UNIQUE CASH FLOWS, DISCOUNTED USING THE SPOT RATE CURVE**

			Cash Flows					
			Bond A		Bond B		Bond C	
Maturity (Years)	Spot Rate	Discount Factor	$	PV	$	PV	$	PV
0.5	5.00	0.9756	60	$ 58.536	30	$ 29.268	—	—
1.0	5.20	0.9499	60	56.994	30	28.497	—	—
1.5	5.50	0.9218	60	55.308	30	27.654	—	—
2.0	5.70	0.8937	60	53.622	30	26.811	—	—
2.5	5.80	0.8668	60	52.008	30	26.004	—	—
3.0	5.90	0.8399	60	50.394	30	25.197	—	—
3.5	6.10	0.8103	60	48.618	30	24.309	—	—
4.0	6.30	0.7803	60	46.818	30	23.409	—	—
4.5	6.40	0.7532	60	45.192	30	22.596	—	—
5.0	6.50	0.7270	1,060	770.620	1,030	748.810	1,000	727.00
Total Present Value				$1,238.110		$982.555		$727.00

at the new, higher price is 6.70 percent. Yields and interest rates are the same. They are different terms for the same concept.

We have discussed the inverse relationship between bond prices and interest rates. When interest rates decline, the prices of bonds increase; when interest rates rise, there is a decline in bond prices. It is natural to ask which of these is the driving force—bond prices or bond interest rates? It is a simultaneous change, and you can envision either factor causing it. Most practitioners probably envision the changes in interest rates as causes because they constantly use interest rates to describe changes. They use interest rates because they are comparable across bonds, whereas the price of a bond depends not only on the interest rate, but also on its specific characteristics, including its coupon and maturity. The point is, as demonstrated in Table 16.1 and Figure 16.1, when you change the interest rate (yield) on a bond, you simultaneously change its price in the opposite direction. Later in the chapter we will have a further discussion of the specific price–yield relationship for individual bonds and demonstrate that this price–yield relationship differs among bonds based on their particular coupon and maturity.

Understanding interest rates and what makes them change is necessary for an investor who hopes to maximize returns from investing in bonds. Therefore, in this section we review our prior discussion of the following topics: what causes overall market interest rates to rise and fall, why alternative bonds have different interest rates, and why the difference in rates (i.e., the yield spread) between alternative bonds changes over time. To accomplish this, we begin with a general discussion of what influences interest rates and then consider the **term structure of interest rates** (shown by yield curves), which relates the interest rates on a set of comparable bonds to their terms to maturity. The term structure is important because it implies a set of spot rates that can be used in the valuation of bonds. In addition, it reflects what investors expect to happen to interest rates in the future and it dictates their current risk attitude. In this section, we specifically consider the calculation of spot rates and forward rates from the reported yield curve. Finally, we turn to the concept of *yield spreads,* which measure the differences in yields between alternative bonds. We describe various yield spreads and explore changes in them over time.

FORECASTING INTEREST RATES

As discussed, the ability to forecast interest rates and changes in these rates is critical to successful bond investing. Later, we consider the major determinants of interest rates, but for now you should keep in mind that interest rates *are the price for loanable funds.* Like any price, they are determined by the supply and demand for these funds. On the one side, investors are willing to provide funds (the supply) at prices based on their required rates of return for a particular borrower. On the other side, borrowers need funds (the demand) to support budget deficits (government), to invest in capital projects (corporations), or to acquire durable goods (cars, appliances) or homes (individuals).

Although lenders and borrowers have some fundamental factors that determine supply and demand curves, the prices for these funds (interest rates) also are affected for short periods by events that shift the curves. Examples include major government bond issues that affect demand, or significant changes in Federal Reserve monetary policy that affect the supply of money.

Our treatment of interest rate forecasting recognizes that you must be aware of the basic determinants of interest rates and monitor these factors. We also recognize that detailed forecasting of interest rates is a very complex task that is best left to professional economists. Therefore, our goal as bond investors and bond portfolio managers is to monitor current and expected interest rate behavior. We should attempt to continuously assess the major factors that affect interest rate behavior but also rely on others—such as economic

FIGURE 16.3

YIELDS OF INTERNATIONAL LONG-TERM GOVERNMENT BONDS: QUARTERLY 1990–1998

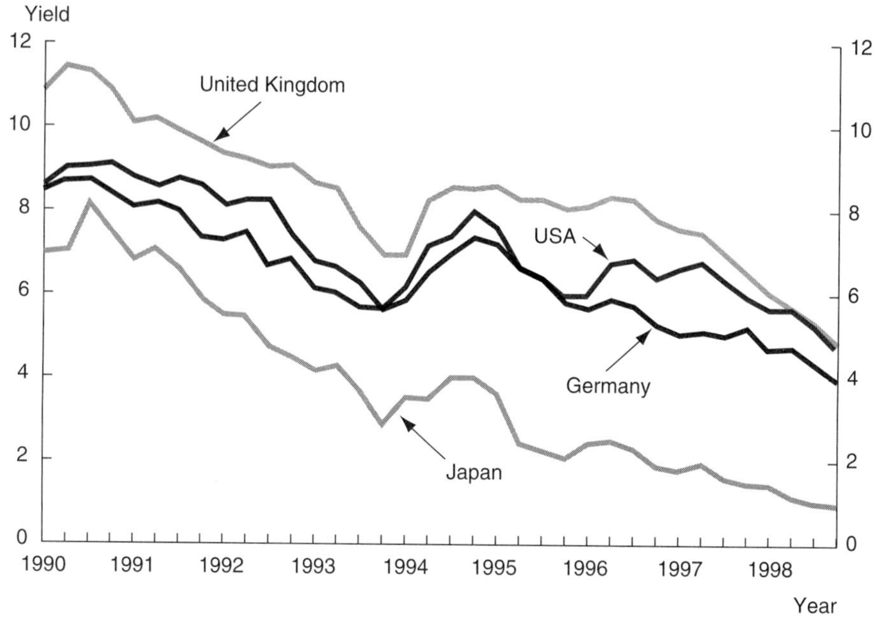
Yield
12
10
8
6
4
2
0
United Kingdom
USA
Germany
Japan
1990
1991
1992
1993
1994
1995
1996
1997
1998
Year

Sources: Federal Reserve Bank; *International Financial Statistics* (various issues).

consulting firms, banks, or investment banking firms—for detailed insights on such topics as the real RFR and the expected rate of inflation.[7] This is precisely the way most bond portfolio managers operate.

Fundamental Determinants of Interest Rates

As shown in Figure 16.3, average interest rates (yields) for long-term (10-year) U.S. government bonds during the period from 1990 through 1998 went from about 8.20 percent to less than 5 percent. These results were midway between those of the United Kingdom and Japan. U.K. bonds went from about 11 percent to 7 percent, while the rate on Japanese government bonds declined from 7 percent to less than 1 percent. As a bond investor, you should understand *why* these differences exist and *why* interest rates changed.

As you know from your knowledge of bond pricing, bond prices increased dramatically during periods when market interest rates dropped, and some bond investors experienced very attractive returns. In contrast, some investors experienced substantial losses during periods when interest rates increased. A casual analysis of this chart, which covers about 9 years, indicates the need for monitoring interest rates. Essentially, the factors causing interest rates (i) to rise or fall are described by the following model:

$$i = \text{RFR} + I + \text{RP}$$

[7] Sources of information on the bond market and interest rate forecasts would include Merrill Lynch's *Fixed Income Weekly* and *World Bond Market Monitor;* Goldman Sach's *Financial Market Perspectives* and *The Pocket Chartroom;* and the Federal Reserve Bank of St. Louis, *Monetary Trends.*

where:

RFR = the real risk-free rate of interest
***I* = the expected rate of inflation**
RP = the risk premium

The relationship shown in this equation should be familiar from our presentations in Chapters 1 and 13. It is a simple but complete statement of interest rate behavior. The more difficult task is estimating the *future* behavior of such variables as real growth, expected inflation, and economic uncertainty. In this regard, interest rates, like stock prices, are extremely difficult to forecast with any degree of accuracy.[8] Alternatively, we can visualize the source of changes in interest rates in terms of the economic conditions and issue characteristics that determine the rate of return on a bond:

$$\begin{aligned} i &= f(\text{Economic Forces} + \text{Issue Characteristics}) \\ &= (\text{RFR} + I) + \text{RP} \end{aligned}$$

This rearranged version of the previous equation helps isolate the determinants of interest rates.[9]

EFFECT OF ECONOMIC FACTORS The real risk-free rate of interest (RFR) is the economic cost of money, that is, the opportunity cost necessary to compensate individuals for forgoing consumption. As discussed previously, it is determined by the real growth rate of the economy with short-run effects due to ease or tightness in the capital market.

The expected rate of inflation is the other economic influence on interest rates. We add the expected level of inflation (*I*) to the real risk-free rate (RFR) to specify the nominal RFR, which is a market rate like the current rate on government T-bills. Given the stability of the real RFR, it is clear that the wide swings in nominal risk-free interest rates during the years covered by Figure 16.3 occurred because of expected inflation.[10] Besides the unique country and exchange rate risk that we discuss in the section on risk premiums, differences in the rates of inflation between countries have a major impact on their level of interest rates.

To sum up, one way to estimate the nominal RFR is to begin with the real growth rate of the economy, adjust for short-run ease or tightness in the capital market, and then adjust this real rate of interest for the expected rate of inflation.

Another approach to estimating the nominal rate or changes in the rate is the macroeconomic view, where the supply and demand for loanable funds are the fundamental economic determinants of *i*. As the supply of loanable funds increases, the level of interest rates declines, other things being equal. Several factors influence the supply of funds. Government monetary policies imposed by the Federal Reserve have a significant impact on

---

[8] For an overview of interest rate forecasting, see Frank J. Jones and Benjamin Wolkowitz, "The Determinants of Interest Rates," and W. David Woolford, "Forecasting Interest Rates," in *The Handbook of Fixed-Income Securities,* 4th ed., ed. Frank J. Fabozzi and T. Dessa Fabozzi (Burr Ridge, Ill.: Irwin Professional Publishing, 1995).

[9] For an extensive exploration of interest rates and interest rate behavior, see James C. Van Horne, *Financial Market Rates and Flows,* 5th ed. (Englewood Cliffs, N.J.: Prentice-Hall, 1998).

[10] In this regard, see R. W. Hafer, "Inflation: Assessing Its Recent Behavior and Future Prospects," Federal Reserve Bank of St. Louis *Review* 65, no. 7 (August–September 1983): 36–41; and C. Alan Garner, "How Useful Are Leading Indicators of Inflation?" Federal Reserve Bank of Kansas City *Economic Review* 80, no. 2 (Second Quarter 1995): 5–18.

the supply of money. The savings patterns of U.S. and non-U.S. investors also affect the supply of funds. Non-U.S. investors have become a stronger influence on the U.S. supply of loanable funds during recent years, as shown by the significant purchases of U.S. securities by non-U.S. investors, most notably the Japanese during the early 1990s. It is widely acknowledged that this foreign supply of funds has been very beneficial to the United States because it has helped reduce interest rates and the cost of capital.

Interest rates increase when the demand for loanable funds increases. The demand for loanable funds is affected by the capital and operating needs of the U.S. government, federal agencies, state and local governments, corporations, institutions, and individuals. Federal budget deficits increase the Treasury's demand for loanable funds. Likewise, the level of consumer demand for funds to buy houses, autos, and appliances affects rates, as does corporate demand for funds to pursue investment opportunities. The total of all groups determines the aggregate demand and supply of loanable funds and the level of the nominal RFR.[11]

THE IMPACT OF BOND CHARACTERISTICS The interest rate of a specific bond issue is influenced not only by all the factors that affect the nominal RFR, but also by its unique issue characteristics. These issue characteristics influence the bond's risk premium (RP). The economic forces that determine the nominal RFR affect all securities, whereas issue characteristics are unique to individual securities, market sectors, or countries. Thus, the differences in the yields of corporate and Treasury bonds are not caused by economic forces, but rather by different issue characteristics that cause differences in the risk premiums.

Bond investors separate the risk premium into four components:

1. The quality of the issue as determined by its risk of default relative to other bonds
2. The term to maturity of the issue, which can affect yield and price volatility
3. Indenture provisions, including collateral, call features, and sinking-fund provisions
4. Foreign bond risk, including exchange rate risk and country risk

Of the four factors, quality and maturity have the greatest impact on the risk premium for domestic bonds, while exchange rate risk and country risk are important components of risk for non-U.S. bonds.

The credit quality of a bond reflects the ability of the issuer to service outstanding debt obligations. This information is largely captured in the ratings issued by the bond rating firms. As a result, bonds with different ratings have different yields. For example, AAA-rated obligations possess lower risk of default than BBB obligations, so they can provide lower yield.

Notably, the risk premium differences between bonds of different quality levels have changed dramatically over time, depending on prevailing economic conditions. When the economy experiences a recession or a period of economic uncertainty, the desire for quality increases, and investors bid up prices of higher-rated bonds, which reduces their yields. This difference in yield is referred to as the quality spread. It also has been suggested by Dialynas and Edington that this yield spread is influenced by the volatility of interest rates.[12] This variability in the risk premium over time was demonstrated and discussed in Chapters 1 and 13. The U.S. market experienced a dramatic demonstration of a short-run risk premium

---

[11] For an example of an estimate of the supply and demand for funds in the economy, see *Prospects for Financial Markets in 1999* (New York: Salomon Bros, Smith Barney, 1998). This is an annual publication of Salomon Brothers Smith Barney that gives an estimate of the flow of funds in the economy and discusses its effect on various currencies and interest rates. It concludes with recommendations for portfolio strategy on the basis of these expectations.

[12] Chris P. Dialynas and David H. Edington, "Bond Yield Spreads: A Postmodern View," *Journal of Portfolio Management* 19, no. 1 (fall 1992): 68–75.

explosion during the period August to October 1998 in response to several global events, including Russia defaulting on its debt.

Term to maturity also influences the risk premium because it affects an investor's level of uncertainty as well as the price volatility of the bond. In the section on the term structure of interest rates, we will discuss the typical positive relationship between the term to maturity of a bond issue and its interest rate.

As discussed in Chapter 15, indenture provisions indicate the collateral pledged for a bond, its callability, and its sinking-fund provisions. Collateral gives protection to the investor if the issuer defaults on the bond because the investor has a specific claim on some assets in case of liquidation.

Call features indicate when an issuer can buy back the bond prior to its maturity. A bond is called by an issuer when interest rates have declined, so typically it is not to the advantage of the investor who must reinvest the proceeds at a lower interest rate. Obviously, an investor will charge the issuer for including the call option, and the cost of the option (which is a higher yield) will increase with the level of interest rates. Therefore, more protection against having the bond called reduces the risk premium. The significance of call protection increases during periods of high interest rates. When you buy a bond with a high coupon, you want protection from having it called away when rates decline.[13]

A sinking fund reduces the investor's risk and causes a lower yield for several reasons. First, a sinking fund reduces default risk because it requires the issuer to reduce the outstanding issue systematically. Second, purchases of the bond by the issuer to satisfy sinking-fund requirements provide price support for the bond because of the added demand. These purchases by the issuer also contribute to a more liquid secondary market for the bond because of the increased trading. Finally, sinking-fund provisions require that the issuer retire a bond before its stated maturity, which causes a reduction in the issue's average maturity. The decline in average maturity tends to reduce the risk premium of the bond much as a shorter maturity would reduce yield.[14]

We know that foreign currency exchange rates change over time and that this increases the risk of global investing. Differences in the variability of exchange rates among countries arise because the trade balances and rates of inflation differ among countries. More volatile trade balances and inflation rates in a country make its exchange rates more volatile, which will add to the uncertainty of future exchange rates. These factors increase the exchange rate risk premium.

In addition to the ongoing changes in exchange rates, investors always are concerned with the political and economic stability of a country. If investors are unsure about the political environment or the economic system in a country, they will increase the risk premium they require to reflect this country risk.[15]

Term Structure of Interest Rates

The term structure of interest rates (or the *yield curve,* as it is more popularly known) is a static function that relates the term to maturity to the yield to maturity for a sample of

---

[13] William Marshall and Jess B. Yawitz, "Optimal Terms of the Call Provision on a Corporate Bond," *Journal of Financial Research* 3, no. 3 (fall 1980): 203–211; Michael G. Ferri, "Systematic Return Risk and the Call Risk of Corporate Debt Instruments," *Journal of Financial Research* 1, no. 1 (winter 1978): 1–13; and Bryan Stanhouse and Duane Stock, "How Changes in Bond Call Features Affect Coupon Rates," *Journal of Applied Corporate Finance* 12, no. 1 (spring 1999): 92–99.

[14] For a further discussion of sinking funds, see A. J. Kalotay, "On the Management of Sinking Funds," *Financial Management* 10, no. 2 (summer 1981): 34–40; and A. J. Kalotay, "Sinking Funds and the Realized Cost of Debt," *Financial Management* 11, no. 1 (spring 1982): 43–54.

[15] In this regard, see David T. Beers, "Standard & Poor's Sovereign Ratings Criteria," and Allen A. Vine, "High-Yield Analysis of Emerging Markets Debt," both in *The Handbook of Fixed-Income Securities.*

FIGURE 16.4

TREASURY YIELD CURVES

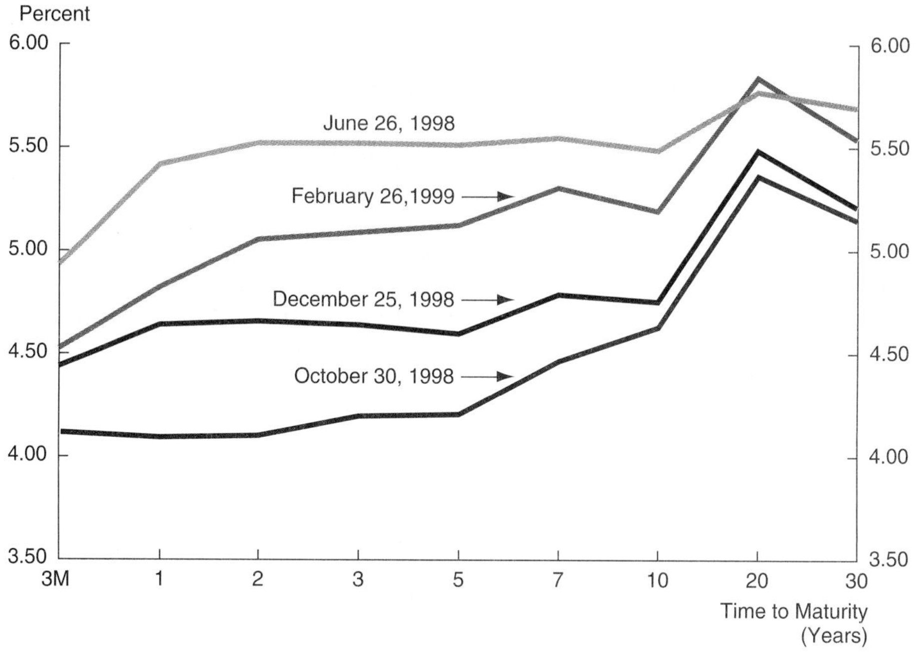
Percent
6.00
5.50
5.00
4.50
4.00
3.50
June 26, 1998
February 26,1999
December 25, 1998
October 30, 1998
3M
1
2
3
5
7
10
20
30
Time to Maturity (Years)

Source: Curves made by authors using data from *Federal Reserve Bulletin* (Washington, D.C., various issues.)

bonds at *a given point in time.*[16] Thus, it represents a cross section of yields for a category of bonds that are comparable in all respects but maturity. Specifically, the quality of the issues should be constant, and ideally you should have issues with similar coupons and call features within a single industry category. You can construct different yield curves for Treasuries, government agencies, prime-grade municipals, AAA utilities, and so on. The accuracy of the yield curve will depend on the comparability of the bonds in the sample.

As an example, Figure 16.4 shows yield curves for a sample of U.S. Treasury obligations. It is based on the yield to maturity information for a set of comparable Treasury issues from a publication such as the *Federal Reserve Bulletin* or the *Wall Street Journal.* These promised yields were plotted on the graph, and a yield curve was drawn that represents the general configuration of rates. These data represent yield curves at four different points in time to demonstrate the changes in yield levels and in the shape of the yield curve over time.

All yield curves, of course, do not have the same shape as those in Figure 16.4. Although individual yield curves are static, their behavior over time is quite fluid. As shown, the level of the curve decreased from June 1998 to October 1998 and then increased in December 1998 and increased further in February 1999. Also, the shape of the yield curve can undergo dramatic alterations, following one of the four patterns shown in Figure 16.5. The rising yield curve is the most common and tends to prevail when interest rates are at low or

[16] For a discussion of the theory and empirical evidence, see Richard W. McEnally and James V. Jordan, "The Term Structure of Interest Rates," in *The Handbook of Fixed-Income Securities.*

FIGURE 16.5 **TYPES OF YIELD CURVES**

A Rising Yield Curve is formed when the yields on short-term issues are low and rise consistently with longer maturities and flatten out at the extremes.

A Declining Yield Curve is formed when the yields on short-term issues are high and yields on subsequently longer maturities decline consistently.

A Flat Yield Curve has approximately equal yields on short-term and long-term issues.

A Humped Yield Curve is formed when yields on intermediate-term issues are above those on short-term issues and the rates on long-term issues decline to levels below those for the short-term and then level out.

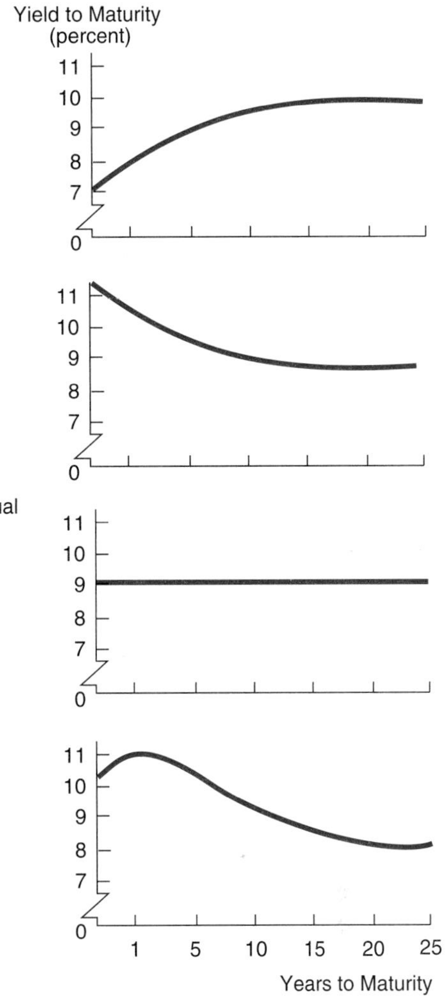
Yield to Maturity (percent)
11
10
9
8
7
0
1
5
10
15
20
25
Years to Maturity

modest levels. The declining yield curve tends to occur when rates are relatively high. The flat yield curve rarely exists for any period of time. The humped yield curve prevails when extremely high rates are expected to decline to more normal levels. Note that the slope of the curve tends to level off after 15 years.

Why does the term structure assume different shapes? Three major theories attempt to explain this: the expectations hypothesis, the liquidity preference hypothesis, and the segmented market hypothesis.

Before we discuss these three alternative hypotheses, we must first discuss two previously noted rates that not only are an integral part of the term structure, but also are important in the valuation of bonds. The next two subsections will deal with the specification and computation of *spot rates* and *forward rates.* Earlier, we discussed and used spot rates to value bonds with the idea that any coupon bond can be viewed as a collection of zero-coupon securities.

TABLE 16.4 **MATURITY AND YIELD TO MATURITY FOR HYPOTHETICAL TREASURY SECURITIES**

Maturity (Years)	Coupon Rate	Price	Yield-to-Maturity
0.50	0.0000	96.15	0.0800
1.00	0.0000	92.19	0.0830
1.50	0.0850	99.45	0.0890
2.00	0.0900	99.64	0.0920
2.50	0.1100	103.49	0.0940
3.00	0.0950	99.49	0.0970

Sources: *Federal Reserve Bulletin;* Moody's *Bond Guide.*

CREATING THE THEORETICAL SPOT-RATE CURVE[17] Earlier in the chapter, we discussed the notion that the yield on a zero-coupon bond for a given maturity is the spot rate for the maturity. Specifically, the spot rate is defined as the discount rate for a cash flow at a specific maturity. At that time, we used the rates on a series of zero-coupon government bonds created by stripping coupon government bonds.

In this case, we will construct a theoretical spot rate curve from the observable yield curve that is based on the existing yields of Treasury bills and the most recent Treasury coupon securities (referred to as *on-the-run* Treasury issues). One might expect the theoretical spot rate curve and the spot rate curve derived from the stripped zero-coupon bonds used earlier to be the same. The fact is, while they are close, they will not be exactly the same because the stripped zero-coupon bonds will not be as liquid as the on-the-run issues. In addition, there are instances where institutions will have a strong desire for a particular spot maturity and this preference will distort the term structure relationship. Therefore, while it is possible to use the stripped zero-coupon curve for a general indication, if you are going to use the spot rates for significant valuation, you would want to use the theoretical spot rate curve.

The process of creating a theoretical spot rate curve from coupon securities is called *bootstrapping* wherein it is assumed that the value of the Treasury coupon security should be equal to the value of the package of zero-coupon securities that duplicates the coupon bond's cash flow. Table 16.4 lists the maturity and YTM for six hypothetical Treasury bonds that will be used to calculate the initial spot rates.

Consider the 6-month Treasury bill in Table 16.4. As discussed earlier, a Treasury bill is a zero-coupon instrument so its annualized yield of 8 percent is equal to the spot rate. Similarly, for the 1-year Treasury bill, the cited yield of 8.3 percent is equal to the 1-year spot rate. Given these two spot rates, we can compute the spot rate for a theoretical 1.5-year zero-coupon Treasury. The price should equal the present value of three cash flows from an actual 1.5-year coupon Treasury, where the yield used for discounting a specific coupon payment is the spot rate corresponding to the cash flow.

Using $100 as par, the *cash flow* for the 1.5-year, 8.50 percent coupon Treasury is as follows:

0.5 years	$0.085 \times \$100 \times 0.5$	=	$ 4.25
1.0 years	$0.085 \times \$100 \times 0.5$	=	$ 4.25
1.5 years	$0.085 \times \$100 \times 0.5 + \$100$	=	$104.25

[17] This discussion of the theoretical spot rate curve and the subsequent presentation on calculating forward rates draws heavily from Frank J. Fabozzi, "The Structure of Interest Rates," in *The Handbook of Fixed-Income Securities.*

The present value of the cash flows discounted at the appropriate spot rates is then

$$\frac{4.25}{(1+z_1)^1}+\frac{4.25}{(1+z_2)^2}+\frac{104.25}{(1+z_3)^3}$$

where:

z_1 = one-half the annualized 6-month theoretical spot rate
z_2 = one-half the 1-year theoretical spot rate
z_3 = one-half the 1.5-year theoretical spot rate

Because the 6-month spot rate and 1-year spot rate are 8.0 percent and 8.3 percent, respectively, we know that

$$z_1 = 0.04 \quad \textit{and} \quad z_2 = 0.0415$$

We can compute the present value of the 1.5-year coupon Treasury security as

$$\frac{4.25}{(1.0400)^1}+\frac{4.25}{(1.0415)^2}+\frac{104.25}{(1+z_3)^3}$$

Because the price of the 1.5-year coupon Treasury security (from Table 16.4) is \$99.45, the following relationship must hold:

$$99.45=\frac{4.25}{(1.0400)^1}+\frac{4.25}{(1.0415)^2}+\frac{104.25}{(1+z_3)^3}$$

We can solve for the theoretical 1.5-year spot rate as follows:

$$99.45 = 4.08654 + 3.91805 + \frac{104.25}{(1+z_3)^3}$$

$$91.44541 = \frac{104.25}{(1+z_3)^3}$$

$$\frac{104.25}{91.44541} = (1+z_3)^3$$

$$(1+z_3)^3 = 1.140024$$

$$z_3 = 0.04465$$

Doubling this yield, we obtain the bond-equivalent yield of 0.0893 or 8.93 percent, which is the theoretical 1.5-year spot rate. That rate is the rate that the market would apply to a 1.5-year zero-coupon Treasury, if such a security existed.

Given the theoretical 1.5-year spot rate, we can obtain the theoretical 2-year spot rate. The cash flow for the 2-year, 9.0 percent coupon Treasury in Table 16.4 is

0.5 years	0.090 × \$100 × 0.5	=	\$ 4.50
1.0 years	0.090 × \$100 × 0.5	=	\$ 4.50
1.5 years	0.090 × \$100 × 0.5	=	\$ 4.50
2.0 years	0.090 × \$100 × 0.5 + 100	=	\$104.50

The present value of the cash flow is then

$$\frac{4.50}{(1+z_1)^1}+\frac{4.50}{(1+z_2)^2}+\frac{4.50}{(1+z_3)^3}+\frac{104.50}{(1+z_4)^4}$$

where:

z_4 = one-half the 2-year theoretical spot rate

Because the 6-month spot rate, 1-year spot rate, and 1.5-year spot rate are 8 percent, 8.3 percent, and 8.93 percent, respectively, then

$$z_1 = 0.04 \quad z_2 = 0.0415 \qquad \textit{and} \qquad z_3 = 0.04465$$

Therefore, the present value of the 2-year coupon Treasury security is

$$\frac{4.50}{(1.0400)^1}+\frac{4.50}{(1.0415)^2}+\frac{4.50}{(1.04465)^3}+\frac{104.50}{(1+z_4)^4}$$

Because the price of the 2-year, 9.0 percent coupon Treasury security is \$99.64, the following relationship must hold:

$$99.64 = \frac{4.50}{(1.0400)^1}+\frac{4.50}{(1.0415)^2}+\frac{4.50}{(1.04465)^3}+\frac{104.50}{(1+z_4)^4}$$

We can solve for the theoretical 2-year spot rate as follows:

$$99.64 = 4.32692 + 4.14853 + 3.94730 + \frac{104.50}{(1+z_4)^4}$$

$$87.21725 = \frac{104.50}{(1+z_4)^4}$$

$$(1+z_4)^4 = 1.198158$$

$$z_4 = 0.046235$$

Doubling this yield, we obtain the theoretical 2-year spot rate bond-equivalent yield of 9.247 percent.

One can follow this approach sequentially to derive the theoretical 2.5-year spot rate from the calculated values of z_1, z_2, z_3, z_4 (the 6-month, 1-year, 1.5-year, and 2-year spot rates), and the price and the coupon of the bond with a maturity of 2.5 years. Subsequently, one could derive the theoretical spot rate for 3 years. The spot rates thus obtained are shown in Table 16.5. They represent the term structure of spot interest rates for maturities up to 3 years, based on the prevailing bond price quotations.

As shown, with a rising YTM curve, the theoretical spot rate will increase at a faster rate such that the difference increases with maturity (i.e., the theoretical spot rate curve will be above a positively sloped YTM curve).

CALCULATING FORWARD RATES FROM THE SPOT RATE CURVE

Now that we have derived the theoretical spot rate curve, it is possible to determine what this curve implies regarding the market's expectation of *future* short-term rates, which are

TABLE 16.5 **THEORETICAL SPOT RATES**

Maturity (Years)	Yield-to-Maturity	Theoretical Spot Rate
0.50	0.0800	0.08000
1.00	0.0830	0.08300
1.50	0.0890	0.08930
2.00	0.0920	0.09247
2.50	0.0940	0.09468
3.00	0.0970	0.09787

referred to as *forward rates.* The following illustrates the process of extrapolating this information about expected future interest rates.

Consider an investor who has a 1-year investment horizon and is faced with the following two alternatives:

Alternative 1: Buy a 1-year Treasury bill.

Alternative 2: Buy a 6-month Treasury bill and, when it matures in 6 months, buy another 6-month Treasury bill.

The investor will be indifferent between the two alternatives if they produce the same return on the 1-year investment horizon. The investor knows the spot rate on the 6-month Treasury bill and the 1-year Treasury bill. However, she does not know what yield will be available on a 6-month Treasury bill 6 months from now. The yield on a 6-month Treasury bill 6 months from now is called a **forward rate**. Given the spot rate for the 6-month Treasury bill and the 1-year bill, we can determine the forward rate on a 6-month Treasury bill *that will make the investor indifferent between the two alternatives.*

At this point, however, we need to digress briefly and recall several present value and investment relationships. First, if you invested in a 1-year Treasury bill, you would receive \$100 at the end of one year. The price of the 1-year Treasury bill would be

$$\frac{100}{(1 + z_2)^2}$$

where:

z_2 = one-half the bond-equivalent yield of the theoretical 1-year spot rate

Second, suppose you purchased a 6-month Treasury bill for \$X. At the end of 6-months, the value of this investment would be

$$X(1 + z_1)$$

where:

z_1 = one-half the bond-equivalent yield of the theoretical 6-month spot rate

Let ${}_{t+0.5}r_{0.5}$ represent one-half the forward rate (expressed as a bond-equivalent yield) on a 6-month Treasury bill (0.5) available 6 months from now ($t + 0.5$). If the investor were to renew her investment by purchasing that bill at that time, then the future dollars available at the end of the year from the \$X investment would be

$$X(1 + z_1)(1 + {}_{t+0.5}r_{0.5}) = 100$$

Third, it is easy to use that formula to find out how many dollars the investor must invest in order to get \$100 one year from now. This can be found as follows:

$$(1 + z_1)(1 + {}_{t+0.5}r_{0.5}) = 100$$

which gives us

$$X = \frac{100}{(1 + z_1)(1 + {}_{t+0.5}r_{0.5})}$$

We are now prepared to return to the investor's choices and analyze what that situation says about forward rates. The investor will be indifferent between the two alternatives confronting her if she makes the same dollar investment and receives \$100 from both alternatives at the end of 1 year. That is, the investor will be indifferent if

$$\frac{100}{(1 + z_2)^2} = \frac{100}{(1 + z_1)(1 + {}_{t+0.5}r_{0.5})}$$

Solving for ${}_{t+0.5}r_{0.5}$ we get

$${}_{t+0.5}r_{0.5} = \frac{(1 + z_2)^2}{(1 + z_1)} - 1$$

Doubling r gives the bond-equivalent yield for the 6-month forward rate 6 months from now.

We can illustrate the use of this formula with the theoretical spot rates shown in Table 16.5. From that table, we know that

Six-month bill spot rate = 0.080 so $z_1 = 0.0400$
One-year bill spot rate = 0.083 so $z_2 = 0.0415$

Substituting into the formula, we have

$$\begin{aligned}{}_{t+0.5}r_{0.5} &= \frac{(1.0415)^2}{(1.0400)} - 1 \\ &= 0.043\end{aligned}$$

Therefore, the forward rate 6 months from now ($t + 0.5$) on a 6-month Treasury security, quoted annually, is 8.6 percent (0.043×2). Let us confirm our results. The price of a 1-year Treasury bill with \$100 maturity is

$$\frac{100}{(1.0415)^2} = 92.19$$

If \$92.19 is invested for 6 months at the 6-month spot rate of 8 percent, the amount at the end of 6 months would be

$$92.19(1.0400) = 95.8776$$

If \$95.8776 is reinvested for another 6 months in a 6-month Treasury bill offering 4.3 percent for 6 months (8.6 percent annually), the amount at the end of 1 year would be

$$95.8776(1.043) = 100$$

Both alternatives will have the same \$100 payoff if the 6-month Treasury bill yield 6 months from now is 4.3 percent (8.6 percent on a bond-equivalent basis). This means that, if an investor is guaranteed a 4.3 percent yield on a 6-month Treasury bill 6 months from now, she will be indifferent between the two alternatives.

We used the theoretical spot rates to compute the forward rate. The resulting forward rate is called the *implied forward rate.*

It is possible to use the yield curve to calculate the implied forward rate for any time in the future for any investment horizon. This would include 6-month or 1-year forward rates for each year in the future. The 1-year forward rates would be designated as follows:

$_{t+1}r_1$ = **the 1-year forward rate, 1 year from now ($t + 1$)**
$_{t+2}r_1$ = **the 1-year forward rate, 2 years from now ($t + 2$)**
$_{t+3}r_1$ = **the 1-year forward rate, 3 years from now ($t + 3$)**

Given the calculations, it is clear that with a rising spot rate curve, the forward rate curve would be above the spot rate curve. From Table 16.5, we have the following 1-year spot rates, which imply the following 1-year forward rates:

Maturity (Years)	Spot Rates	1-Year Forward Rates
1.0	0.08300	
2.0	0.09247	0.1020
3.0	0.09787	0.1087

Therefore:

$$_{t+1}r_1 = \frac{(1.09247)^2}{(1.08300)} - 1 = \frac{1.19349}{1.08300} - 1 = 0.1020$$

$$_{t+2}r_1 = \frac{(1.09787)^3}{(1.09247)^2} - 1 = \frac{1.32328}{1.19349} - 1 = 0.1087$$

Specifically, the 1-year forward rate that is expected 1 year from now ($_{t+1}r_1$) is 10.20 percent, while the 1-year forward rate that is expected 2 years from now ($_{t+2}r_1$) is 10.87 percent.

TERM-STRUCTURE THEORIES

EXPECTATIONS HYPOTHESIS According to the expectations hypothesis, the shape of the yield curve results from the interest rate expectations of market participants. More specifically, it holds that *any long-term interest rate simply represents the geometric* *mean of current and future 1-year interest rates expected to prevail over the maturity of the issue.* In essence, the term structure involves a series of intermediate and long-term interest rates, each of which is a reflection of the geometric average of current and expected 1-year interest rates. Under such conditions, the equilibrium long-term rate is the rate the long-term bond investor would expect to earn through successive investments in short-term bonds over the term to maturity of the long-term bond.

Generally, this relationship can be formalized as follows:

$$(1 + {}_tR_n) = [(1 + {}_tR_1)(1 + {}_{t+1}r_1) \ldots (1 + {}_{t+n-1}r_1)]^{1/N}$$

where:

R_n = the actual long-term rate
N = the term to maturity (in years) of long issue
R = the current 1-year rate
${}_{t+i}r_1$ = the expected 1-year yield during some future period, $t + i$ (these future 1-year rates are referred to as *forward rates*)

Given the relationship set forth in this equation, the formula for computing the one-period forward rate beginning at time $t + n$ and implied in the term structure at time t is:

$$1 + {}_{t+n}r_{1t} = \frac{(1 + {}_tR_{1t})(1 + {}_{t+1}r_{1t})(1 + {}_{t+2}r_{1t}) \ldots (1 + {}_{t+n-1}r_{1t})(1 + {}_{t+n}r_{1t})}{(1 + {}_tR_{1t})(1 + {}_{t+1}r_{1t}) \ldots (1 + {}_{t+n-1}r_{1t})}$$

$$= \frac{(1 + {}_tR_{n+1})^{n+1}}{(1 + {}_tR_n)^n}$$

$${}_{t+n}r_{1t} = \frac{(1 + {}_tR_{n+1})^{n+1}}{(1 + {}_tR_n)^n} - 1$$

where ${}_{t+n}r_{1t}$ is the 1-year forward rate prevailing at $t + n$, using the term structure at time t.

Assume that the 5-year spot rate is 10 percent (${}_tR_5 = 0.10$) and the 4-year spot rate is 9 percent (${}_tR_4 = 0.09$). The forward 1-year rate 4 years from now implied by these spot rates can be calculated as follows:

$${}_{t+4}r_{1t} = \frac{(1 + {}_tR_5)^5}{(1 + {}_tR_4)^4} - 1$$

$$= \frac{(1 + 0.10)^5}{(1 + 0.09)^4} - 1$$

$$= \frac{1.6105}{1.4116} - 1$$

$$= 1.1409 - 1 = 0.1409 = 14.09\%$$

The term structure at time t implies that the 1-year spot rate 4 years from now (during Year 5) will be 14.09 percent. This concept and formula can be used to derive future rates for multiple years. Thus, the 2-year spot rate that will prevail 3 years from now could be calculated using the 3-year spot rate and the 5-year spot rate. The general formula for computing the j-period forward rate beginning at time $t + n$ as of time t is

$${}_{t+n}r_{jt} = \sqrt[j]{\frac{(1 + {}_tR_{n+j})^{n+j}}{(1 + {}_tR_n)^n}} - 1$$

As a practical approximation of the equation at the top of this page, it is possible to use the *arithmetic* average of 1-year rates to generate long-term yields.

The expectations theory can explain any shape of yield curve. Expectations for rising short-term rates in the future cause a rising yield curve; expectations for falling short-term rates in the future will cause long-term rates to lie below current short-term rates, and the yield curve will decline. Similar explanations account for flat and humped yield curves.

Consider the following explanation by the expectations hypothesis of the shape of the term structure of interest rates using arithmetic averages:

$_{t}R_1 = 5\frac{1}{2}\%$ **the 1-year rate of interest prevailing now (period t)**
$_{t+1}r_1 = 6\%$ **the 1-year rate of interest expected to prevail next year (period $t + 1$)**
$_{t+2}r_1 = 7\frac{1}{2}\%$ **the 1-year rate of interest expected to prevail 2 years from now (period $t + 2$)**
$_{t+3}r_1 = 8\frac{1}{2}\%$ **the 1-year rate of interest expected to prevail 3 years from now (period $t + 3$)**

Using these values, and the known rate on a 1-year bond, we compute rates on 2-, 3-, or 4-year bonds (designated R_2, R_3, and R_4) as follows:

$_{t}R_1 = 5\frac{1}{2}$ **percent**
$_{t}R_2 = (0.055 + 0.06)/2 = 5.75$ **percent**
$_{t}R_3 = (0.055 + 0.06 + 0.075)/3 = 6.33$ **percent**
$_{t}R_4 = (0.055 + 0.06 + 0.075 + 0.085)/4 = 6.88$ **percent**

In this illustration (which uses the arithmetic average as an approximation of the geometric mean), the yield curve is upward-sloping because, at present, investors expect future short-term rates to be above current short-term rates. This is not the formal method for constructing the yield curve. Rather, the yield curve is constructed on the basis of the prevailing promised yields for bonds with different maturities.

The expectations hypothesis attempts to explain *why* the yield curve is upward-sloping, downward-sloping, humped, or flat by explaining the expectations implicit in yield curves with different shapes. The evidence is fairly substantial and convincing that the expectations hypothesis is a workable explanation of the term structure. Because of the supporting evidence, its relative simplicity, and the intuitive appeal of the theory, the expectations hypothesis of the term structure of interest rates is rather widely accepted.

Consistent Investor Actions Besides the theory and empirical support, it is also possible to present a scenario wherein investor actions will cause the yield curve postulated by the theory. The expectations hypothesis predicts a declining yield curve when interest rates are expected to fall in the future rather than rise. In such a case, long-term bonds would be considered attractive investments because investors would want to lock in prevailing higher yields (which are not expected to be as high in the future) or they would want to capture the increase in bond prices (as capital gains) that will accompany a decline in rates. By the same reasoning, investors will avoid short-term bonds or sell them and reinvest the funds in long-term bonds that will experience larger price increases if rates decline. The point is, investor expectations will reinforce the declining shape of the yield curve as they bid up the prices of long-maturity bonds (forcing yields to decline) and short-term bond issues are avoided or sold (so prices decline and yields rise). At the same time, there is confirming action by suppliers of bonds. Specifically, government or corporate issuers will avoid selling long bonds at the current high rates, waiting until the rates decline. In the meantime, they will issue short-term bonds, if needed, while waiting for lower rates. Therefore, in the long-term market, you will have an increase in demand and a decline in the supply and vice versa in the short-term market. These shifts between long- and short-term maturities will continue until equilibrium occurs or expectations change.

LIQUIDITY PREFERENCE HYPOTHESIS The theory of liquidity preference holds that long-term securities should provide higher returns than short-term obligations because investors are willing to sacrifice some yields to invest in short-maturity obligations to avoid the higher price volatility of long-maturity bonds. Another way to interpret the liquidity preference hypothesis is to say that lenders prefer short-term loans, and, to induce them to lend long term, it is necessary to offer higher yields.

The liquidity preference theory contends that uncertainty causes investors to favor short-term issues over bonds with longer maturities because short-term bonds can easily be converted into predictable amounts of cash should unforeseen events occur. This theory argues that the yield curve should slope upward and that any other shape should be viewed as a temporary aberration.

This theory can be considered an extension of the expectations hypothesis because the formal liquidity preference position contends that the liquidity premium inherent in the yields for longer maturity bonds should be added to the expected future rate in arriving at long-term yields. Specifically, the liquidity premium (L) compensates the investor in long-term bonds for the added uncertainty because of less-stable prices. Because the liquidity premium (L) is provided to compensate the long-term investor, it is simply a variation of the equation on page 574 as follows:

$$(1 + {}_tR_N) = [(1 + {}_tR_1)(1 + {}_{t+1}r_1 + L_2)\ldots(1 + {}_{t+N-1}r_1 + L_n)]^{1/N}$$

In this specification, the Ls are not the same, but would be expected to increase with time. The liquidity preference theory has been found to possess some strong empirical support.[18]

To see how the liquidity preference theory predicts future yields and how it compares with the pure expectations hypothesis, let us predict future long-term rates from a single set of 1-year rates: 6 percent, 7.5 percent, and 8.5 percent. The liquidity preference theory suggests that investors add increasing liquidity premiums to successive rates to derive actual market rates. As an example, they might arrive at rates of 6.3 percent, 7.9 percent, and 9.0 percent.

As a matter of historical fact, the yield curve shows an upward bias, which implies that some combination of the expectations theory and the liquidity preference theory will more accurately explain the shape of the yield curve than either of them alone. Specifically, actual long-term rates consistently tend to be above what is envisioned from the price expectations hypothesis. This tendency implies the existence of a liquidity premium.

SEGMENTED MARKET HYPOTHESIS Despite meager empirical support, a third theory for the shape of the yield curve is the segmented market hypothesis, which enjoys wide acceptance among market practitioners. Also known as the *preferred habitat,* the *institutional theory,* or the *hedging pressure theory,* it asserts that different institutional investors have different maturity needs that lead them to confine their security selections to specific maturity segments. That is, investors supposedly focus on short-, intermediate-, or long-term securities. This theory contends that the shape of the yield curve ultimately is a function of these investment policies of major financial institutions.

Financial institutions tend to structure their investment policies in line with such factors as their tax liabilities, the types and maturity structure of their liabilities, and the level of earnings demanded by depositors. For example, because commercial banks are subject to normal corporate tax rates, and their liabilities are generally short- to intermediate-term time and demand deposits, they consistently invest in short- to intermediate-term municipal bonds.

---

[18] See Reuben A. Kessel, "The Cyclical Behavior of the Term Structure of Interest Rates," Occasional Paper 91, National Bureau of Economic Research, 1965; Phillip Cagan, *Essays on Interest Rates* (New York: Columbia University Press for the National Bureau of Economic Research, 1969); and J. Huston McCulloch, "An Estimate of the Liquidity Premium," *Journal of Political Economy* 83, no. 1 (January–February 1975): 95–119.

The segmented market theory contends that the business environment, along with legal and regulatory limitations, tends to direct each type of financial institution to allocate its resources to particular types of bonds with specific maturity characteristics. In its strongest form, the segmented market theory holds that the maturity preferences of investors and borrowers are so strong that investors never purchase securities outside their preferred maturity range to take advantage of yield differentials. As a result, the short- and long-maturity portions of the bond market are effectively segmented, and yields for a segment depend on the supply and demand *within* that maturity segment.

TRADING IMPLICATIONS OF THE TERM STRUCTURE Information on maturities can help you formulate yield expectations by simply observing the shape of the yield curve. If the yield curve is declining sharply, historical evidence suggests that interest rates will probably decline. Expectations theorists would suggest that you need to examine only the prevailing yield cure to predict the direction of interest rates in the future.

Based on these theories, bond investors use the prevailing yield curve to predict the shapes of future yield curves. Using this prediction and knowledge of current interest rates, investors can determine expected yield volatility by maturity sector. In turn, the maturity segments that experience the greatest yield changes give the investor the largest potential price change opportunities.[19]

Yield Spreads

Another technique that helps make good bond investments or profitable trades is the analysis of *yield spreads*—the differences in promised yields between bond issues or segments of the market at any point in time. Such differences are specific to the particular issues or segments of the bond market. Thus they add to the rates determined by the basic economic forces (RFR + I).

There are four major yield spreads:

1. Different *segments* of the bond market may have different yields. For example, pure government bonds will have lower yields than government agency bonds, and government bonds have much lower yields than corporate bonds.
2. Bonds in different *sectors* of the same market segment may have different yields. For example, prime-grade municipal bonds will have lower yields than good-grade municipal bonds; you will find spreads between AA utilities and BBB utilities, or between AAA industrial bonds and AAA public utility bonds.
3. Different *coupons* or *seasoning* within a given market segment or sector may cause yield spreads. Examples include current coupon government bonds versus deep-discount governments or recently issued AA industrials versus seasoned AA industrials.
4. Different *maturities* within a given market segment or sector also cause differences in yields. You will see yield spreads between short-term agency issues and long-term agency issues, or between 3-year prime municipals and 25-year prime municipals.

The differences among these bonds cause yield spreads that may be either positive or negative. More important, *the magnitude or the direction of a spread can change over time.* These changes in size or direction of yield spreads offer profit opportunities. We say that the spread narrows whenever the differences in yield become smaller; it widens as the differences increase. Table 16.6 contains data on a variety of past yield spreads.

---

[19] Gikas A. Hourdouvelis, "The Predictive Power of the Term Structure during Recent Monetary Regimes," *Journal of Finance* 43, no. 2 (June 1988): 339–356.

TABLE 16.6 SELECTED MEAN YIELD SPREADS (REPORTED IN BASIS POINTS)

Comparisons	1990	1991	1992	1993	1994	1995	1996	1997	1998
1. Long Governments[a]—Short Governments	109	267	295	227	37	80	89	37	68
2. Long Aaa Corporates[b]—Long Governments	68	91	60	49	44	79	45	72	85
3. Long Aaa Corporates[c]—Long Municipals	217	183	189	153	173	132	169	167	124
4. Long Baa Municipals[d]—Long Aaa Municipals	47	33	36	51	55	26	30	14	35
5. Baa Utilities[e]—Aa Utilities	54	36	37	55	47	60	54	34	46
6. Aa Industrials[f]—Aa Utilities	−6	−20	−16	−11	−15	−8	−6	−17	−27

Note: Yield spreads are equal to the yield on the first bond minus the yield on the second bond—for example, the yield on long governments minus the yield on short governments.

[a]Median yield to maturity of a varying number of bonds with 2 to 5 years' maturity and more than 10 years, respectively.

[b]Long Aaa corporates based on yields to maturity on selected long-term bonds.

[c]Long-term municipal issues based on Bond Buyer Series, a representative list of high-quality municipal bonds with a 20-year period to maturity being maintained.

[d]General obligation municipal bonds only.

[e]Based on a changing list of representative issues.

Sources: *Federal Reserve Bulletin;* Moody's *Bond Guide.*

As a bond investor, you should evaluate yield spread changes because these changes influence bond price behavior and comparative return performance. You should attempt to identify (1) any normal yield spread that is expected to become abnormally wide or narrow in response to an anticipated swing in market interest rates, or (2) an abnormally wide or narrow yield spread that is expected to become normal.

Economic and market analysis help develop these expectations of potential for yield spreads to change. Taking advantage of these changes requires a knowledge of historical spreads and an ability to *predict* not only future total market changes, but also why and when specific spreads will change.[20]

WHAT DETERMINES THE PRICE VOLATILITY FOR BONDS?

In this chapter, we have learned about alternative bond yields, how to calculate them, what determines bond yields (interest rates), and what causes them to change. Now that we understand why yields change, we can logically ask, what is the effect of these yield changes on the prices and rates of return for different bonds? We have discussed the inverse relationship between changes in yields and the price of bonds, so we can now discuss *the specific factors that affect the amount of price change for a yield change* in different bonds. This can also be referred to as the *interest rate sensitivity* of a bond. This section lists the specific factors that affect bond price changes for a given change in interest rates (i.e., the interest rate sensitivity of a bond) and demonstrates the effect for different bonds.

A given change in interest rates can cause vastly different percentage price changes for alternative bonds, which implies different interest rate sensitivity. This section will help

[20]An article that identifies four determinants of relative market spreads and suggests scenarios when they will change is Chris P. Dialynas and David H. Edington, "Bond Yield Spreads: A Postmodern View," *Journal of Portfolio Management* 19, no. 1 (fall 1992): 68–75.

you understand what causes these differences in interest rate sensitivity. To maximize your rate of return from an expected decline in interest rates, for example, you need to know which bonds will benefit the most from the yield change. This section helps you make this bond selection decision.

Throughout this section, we talk about bond price changes or bond price volatility interchangeably. A bond price change is measured as the percentage change in the price of the bond, computed as follows:

$$\frac{\text{EPB}}{\text{BPB}} - 1$$

where:

EPB = the ending price of the bond
BPB = the beginning price of the bond

Bond price volatility also is measured in terms of percentage changes in bond prices. A bond with high price volatility or high interest rate sensitivity is one that experiences large percentage price changes for a give change in yields.

Bond price volatility is influenced by more than yield behavior alone. Malkiel used the bond valuation model to demonstrate that the market price of a bond is a function of four factors: (1) its par value, (2) its coupon, (3) the number of years to its maturity, and (4) the prevailing market interest rate.[21] Malkiel's mathematical proofs showed the following relationships between yield (interest rate) changes and bond price behavior:

1. Bond prices move inversely to bond yields (interest rates).
2. For a given change in yields (interest rates), longer-maturity bonds post larger price changes; thus, bond price volatility is *directly* related to term to maturity.
3. Price volatility (percentage of price change) increases at a diminishing rate as term to maturity increases.
4. Price movements resulting from equal absolute increases or decreases in yield are *not* symmetrical. A decrease in yield raises bond prices by more than an increase in yield of the same amount lowers prices.
5. Higher coupon issues show smaller percentage price fluctuation for a given change in yield; thus, bond price volatility is *inversely* related to coupon.

Homer and Leibowitz showed that the absolute level of market yields also affects bond price volatility.[22] As the level of prevailing yields rises, the price volatility of bonds increases, *assuming a constant percentage change in market yields.* It is important to note that if you assume a constant percentage change in yield, the basis-point change will be greater when rates are high. For example, a 25 percent change in interest rates when rates are at 4 percent will be 100 basis points; the same 25 percent change when rates are at 8 percent will be a 200 basis-point change. In the discussion of bond duration, we will see that this difference in basis point change is important.

Tables 16.7, 16.8, and 16.9 demonstrate these relationships assuming semiannual compounding. Table 16.7 demonstrates the effect of maturity on price volatility. In all four

---

[21]Burton G. Malkiel, "Expectations, Bond Prices, and the Term Structure of Interest Rates," *Quarterly Journal of Economics* 76, no. 2 (May 1962): 197—218.

[22]Sidney Homer and Martin L. Leibowitz, *Inside the Yield Book* (Englewood Cliffs, N.J.: Prentice-Hall, 1972).

TABLE 16.7 **EFFECT OF MATURITY ON BOND PRICE VOLATILITY**

	PRESENT VALUE OF AN 8 PERCENT BOND ($1,000 PAR VALUE)							
Term to Maturity	1 Year		10 Years		20 Years		30 Years	
Discount rate (YTM)	7%	10%	7%	10%	7%	10%	7%	10%
Present value of interest	$ 75	$ 73	$ 569	$498	$ 858	$686	$1,005	$757
Present value of principal	934	907	505	377	257	142	132	54
Total value of bond	$1,009	$980	$1,074	$875	$1,115	$828	$1,137	$811
Percentage change in total value	−2.9		−18.5		−25.7		−28.7	

TABLE 16.8 **EFFECT OF COUPON ON BOND PRICE VOLATILITY**

	PRESENT VALUE OF 20-YEAR BOND ($1,000 PAR VALUE)							
	0 Percent Coupon		3 Percent Coupon		8 Percent Coupon		12 Percent Coupon	
Discount rate (YTM)	7%	10%	7%	10%	7%	10%	7%	10%
Present value of interest	$ 0	$ 0	$322	$257	$ 858	$686	$1,287	$1,030
Present value of principal	257	142	257	142	257	142	257	142
Total value of bond	$257	$142	$579	$399	$1,115	$828	$1,544	$1,172
Percentage change in total value	−44.7		−31.1		−25.7		−24.1	

TABLE 16.9 **EFFECT OF YIELD LEVEL ON BOND PRICE VOLATILITY**

	PRESENT VALUE OF A 20-YEAR, 4 PERCENT BOND ($1,000 PAR VALUE)							
	(1) Low Yields		(2) Intermediate Yields		(3) High Yields		(4) 100 Basis-Point Change at High Yields	
Discount rate (YTM)	3%	4%	6%	8%	9%	12%	9%	10%
Present value of interest	$ 602	$ 547	$462	$396	$370	$301	$370	$343
Present value of principal	562	453	307	208	175	97	175	142
Total value of bond	$1,164	$1,000	$769	$604	$545	$398	$545	$485
Percentage change in total value	−14.1		−21.5		−27.0		−11.0	

maturity classes, we assume a bond with an 8 percent coupon and assume that the discount rate (YTM) changes from 7 percent to 10 percent. The only difference among the four cases is the maturities of the bonds. The demonstration involves computing the value of each bond at a 7 percent yield and at a 10 percent yield and noting the percentage change in price. As shown, this change in yield caused the price of the 1-year bond to decline by only 2.9 percent; the 30-year bond declined by almost 29 percent. Clearly, the longer-maturity bond experienced the greater price volatility.

Also, price volatility increased at a decreasing rate with maturity. When maturity doubled from 10 years to 20 years, the percent change in price increased by less than 50 percent (from 18.5 percent to 25.7 percent). A similar change occurred when going from 20 years to 30 years. Therefore, this table demonstrates the first three of our price–yield relationships: Bond price is inversely related to yields, bond price volatility is positively related to term to maturity, and bond price volatility increases at a decreasing rate with maturity.

It also is possible to demonstrate the fourth relationship with this table. Using the 20-year bond, if you computed the percentage change in price related to an *increase* in rates (e.g., from 7 percent to 10 percent), you would get the answer reported—a 25.7 percent decrease. In contrast, if you computed the effect on price of a *decrease* in yields from 10 percent to 7 percent, you would get a 34.7 percent increase in price (from \$828 to \$1,115). This demonstrates that prices change more in response to a decrease in rates (from 10 percent to 7 percent) than to a comparable increase in rates (from 7 percent to 10 percent).

Table 16.8 demonstrates the coupon effect. In this set of examples, all the bonds have equal maturity (20 years) and experience the same change in YTM (from 7 percent to 10 percent). The table shows the *inverse* relationship between coupon rate and price volatility: The smallest coupon bond (the zero) experienced the largest percentage price change (almost 45 percent), versus a 24 percent change for the 12 percent coupon bond.

Table 16.9 demonstrates the yield level effect. In these examples, all the bonds have the same 20-year maturity and the same 4 percent coupon. In the first three cases, the YTM changed by a constant 33.3 percent (i.e., from 3 percent to 4 percent, from 6 percent to 8 percent, and from 9 percent to 12 percent). Note that the first change is 100 basis points, the second is 200 basis points, and the third is 300 basis points. The results in the first three columns confirm the statement that when rates change by a *constant percentage,* the change in the bond price is larger when the rates are at a higher level.

The fourth column shows that if you assume a *constant basis-point change in yields,* you get the opposite results. Specifically, a 100 basis-point change in yields from 3 percent to 4 percent provides a price change of 14.1 percent, while the same 100 basis-point change from 9 percent to 10 percent results in a price change of only 11 percent. Therefore, the yield level effect can differ, depending on whether the yield change is specified as a constant percentage change or a constant basis-point change.

Thus, the price volatility of a bond for a given change in yield (i.e., its interest rate sensitivity) is affected by the bond's coupon, its term to maturity, the level of yields (depending on what kind of change in yield), and the direction of the yield change. However, although both the level and direction of change in yields affect price volatility, they cannot be used for trading strategies. When yields change, the two variables that have a dramatic effect on a bond's interest rate sensitivity are coupon and maturity.

Trading Strategies

Knowing that coupon and maturity are the major variables that influence a bond's interest rate sensitivity, we can develop some strategies for maximizing rates of return when interest rates change. Specifically, if you expect a major *decline* in interest rates, you know that bond prices will increase, so you want a portfolio of bonds with the *maximum interest rate sensitivity* so that you will enjoy maximum price changes (capital gains) from the change in interest rates. In this situation, the previous discussion regarding the effect of maturity and coupon indicates that you should attempt to build a portfolio of long-maturity bonds with low coupons (ideally a long-term zero-coupon bond). A portfolio of such bonds should experience the maximum price appreciation for a given decline in market interest rates.

In contrast, if you expect an *increase* in market interest rates, you know that bond prices will decline, and you want a portfolio with *minimum interest rate sensitivity* to minimize the capital losses caused by the increase in rates. Therefore, you would want to change your portfolio to short-maturity bonds with high coupons. This combination should provide minimal price volatility for a change in market interest rates.

Duration Measures

Because the price volatility (interest rate sensitivity) of a bond varies inversely with its coupon and directly with its term to maturity, it is necessary to determine the best combination of these two variables to achieve your objective. This effort would benefit from a composite measure that considered both coupon and maturity.

A measure of the interest rate sensitivity of a bond is referred to as **duration**. This concept and its development as a tool in bond analysis and portfolio management has existed for over 50 years. Notably, several specifications of duration have been derived over the past 20 years. First, **Macaulay duration**, developed over 60 years ago by Frederick Macaulay, is a measure of the time flow of cash from a bond.[23] A modified version of Macaulay duration can be used under certain conditions to indicate the price volatility of a bond in response to interest rate changes. Second, **modified duration** is derived by making a small adjustment (modification) to the Macaulay duration value. As noted above, under certain restrictive conditions (most important, there are no embedded options), modified duration can provide an approximation to the interest rate sensitivity of a bond (or any financial asset). Third, **effective duration** is a direct measure of the interest rate sensitivity of a bond (or any financial instrument) where it is possible to estimate price changes for an asset using a valuation model. Finally, **empirical duration** measures directly the percentage price change of an asset for an actual change in interest rates. This can be used as an estimate for an asset when there is no exact valuation model available. Because of the development of many new financial instruments, which have very unique cash flows *that change with interest rates,* effective duration and empirical duration have become widely used because of their flexibility and ability to provide a useful measure of interest rate sensitivity—the primary goal of duration. Therefore, in this section we discuss and demonstrate these four duration measures, including their limitations.

MACAULAY DURATION Macaulay showed that the duration of a bond was a more appropriate measure of time characteristics than the term to maturity of the bond because duration considers both the repayment of capital at maturity and the size and timing of coupon payments prior to final maturity. Using annual compounding, duration (D) is

$$D = \frac{\sum_{t=1}^{n} \frac{C_t(t)}{(1+i)^t}}{\sum_{t=1}^{n} \frac{C_t}{(1+i)^t}}$$

where:

t = the time period in which the coupon or principal payment occurs
C_t = the interest or principal payment that occurs in period t
i = the yield to maturity on the bond

The denominator in this equation is the price of a bond as determined by the present value model. The numerator is the present value of all cash flows *weighted according to the time to cash receipt.* The following example, which demonstrates the specific computations for two bonds, shows the procedure and highlights some of the properties of duration. Consider the following two sample bonds:

	Bond A	Bond B
Face value	$1,000	$1,000
Maturity	10 years	10 years
Coupon	4%	8%

[23]Frederick R. Macaulay, *Some Theoretical Problems Suggested by the Movements of Interest Rates, Bond Yields, and Stock Prices in the United States since 1856* (New York: National Bureau of Economic Research, 1938).

TABLE 16.10

COMPUTATION OF MACAULAY DURATION (ASSUMING 8 PERCENT MARKET YIELD)

BOND A

(1) Year	(2) Cash Flow	(3) PV at 8%	(4) PV of Flow	(5) PV as % of Price	(6) (1) × (5)
1	$ 40	0.9259	$ 37.04	0.0506	0.0506
2	40	0.8573	34.29	0.0469	0.0938
3	40	0.7938	31.75	0.0434	0.1302
4	40	0.7350	29.40	0.0402	0.1608
5	40	0.6806	27.22	0.0372	0.1860
6	40	0.6302	25.21	0.0345	0.2070
7	40	0.5835	23.34	0.0319	0.2233
8	40	0.5403	21.61	0.0295	0.2360
9	40	0.5002	20.01	0.0274	0.2466
10	1,040	0.4632	481.73	0.6585	6.5850
Sum			$ 731.58	1.0000	8.1193

Duration = 8.12 Years

BOND B

(1) Year	(2) Cash Flow	(3) PV at 8%	(4) PV of Flow	(5) PV as % of Price	(6) (1) × (5)
1	$ 80	0.9259	$ 74.07	0.0741	0.0741
2	80	0.8573	68.59	0.0686	0.1372
3	80	0.7938	63.50	0.0635	0.1906
4	80	0.7350	58.80	0.0588	0.1906
5	80	0.6806	54.44	0.0544	0.2720
6	80	0.6302	50.42	0.0504	0.3024
7	80	0.5835	46.68	0.0467	0.3269
8	80	0.5403	43.22	0.0432	0.3456
9	80	0.5002	40.02	0.0400	0.3600
10	1,080	0.4632	500.26	0.5003	5.0030
Sum			$1,000.00	1.0000	7.2470

Duration = 7.25 Years

Assuming annual interest payments and an 8 percent yield to maturity on the bonds, duration is computed as shown in Table 16.10.[24] If duration is computed by discounting flows using the yield to maturity of the bond, it is called *Macaulay duration.*

Characteristics of Macaulay Duration This example illustrates several characteristics of Macaulay duration. First, the Macaulay duration of a bond with coupon payments always will be less than its term to maturity because duration gives weight to these interim interest payments.

Second, there is *an inverse relationship between coupon and duration.* A bond with a larger coupon will have a shorter duration because more of the total cash flows come earlier in the form of interest payments. As shown in Table 16.10, the 8 percent coupon bond has a shorter duration than the 4 percent coupon bond.

A zero-coupon bond or a pure discount bond, such as a Treasury bill, will have *duration equal to its term to maturity.* In Table 16.10, if you assume a single payment at maturity, duration will equal term to maturity because the only cash flow comes in the final (maturity) year—that is, you receive 100 percent of cash flows in year *n.*

[24]We assume annual interest payments to reduce the space requirements and computations. In practice you would assume semiannual payments that would cause a slightly shorter duration since you receive half the payments earlier.

FIGURE 16.6 **DURATION VERSUS MATURITY**

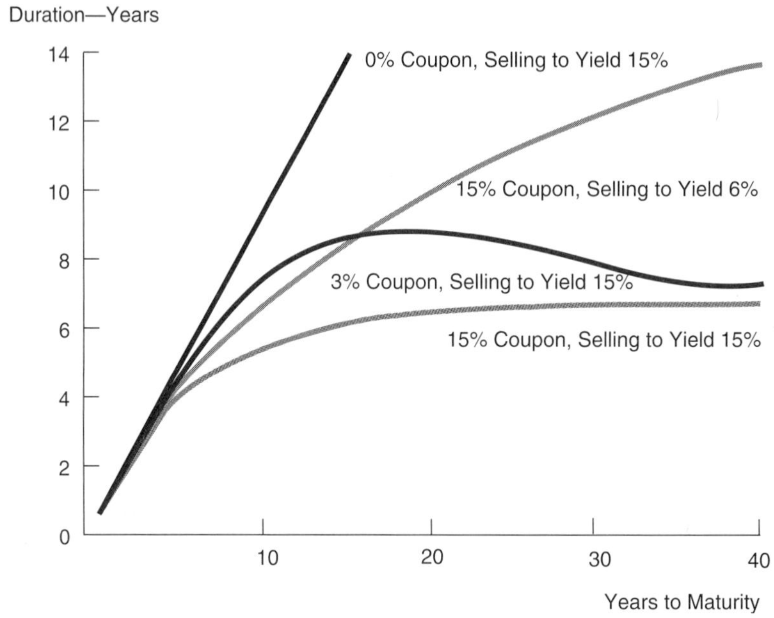
Duration—Years
14
12
10
8
6
4
2
0
0% Coupon, Selling to Yield 15%
15% Coupon, Selling to Yield 6%
3% Coupon, Selling to Yield 15%
15% Coupon, Selling to Yield 15%
10
20
30
40
Years to Maturity

Third, there is *generally a positive relationship between term to maturity and Macaulay duration,* but duration increases at a decreasing rate with maturity. Therefore, a bond with longer term to maturity almost always will have a higher duration. The relationship is not direct because as maturity increases the present value of the principal declines in value.

As shown in Figure 16.6, the shape of the duration–maturity curve depends on the coupon and the yield to maturity. The curve for a zero-coupon bond is a straight line, indicating that duration equals term to maturity. In contrast, the curve for a low-coupon bond selling at a deep discount (due to a high YTM) will turn down at long maturities, which means that under these conditions, the longer-maturity bond will have lower duration because the discounted value of the principal payment becomes insignificant, which shifts the weight to the early interest payments, causing a decline in Macaulay duration.

Fourth, all else the same, there is an *inverse relationship between YTM and duration.* A higher yield to maturity of a bond reduces its duration. As an example, in Table 16.10, if the yield to maturity had been 12 percent rather than 8 percent, the duration for the 4 percent bond would have gone from 8.12 to 7.75, and the duration of the 8 percent bond would have gone from 7.25 to 6.80.[25] The combined effect of the inverse relationships between duration and both coupon and yield can be seen with the curve for the 15 percent coupon and yield bond where the duration tops out at about 6 years. The real-world example of such a bond would be a high-yield bond.

Finally, sinking funds and call provisions can have a dramatic effect on a bond's duration. They can change the total cash flows for a bond and, therefore, significantly change its duration. Between these two factors, the characteristic that causes the greatest uncertainty is the call feature—it is difficult to estimate when it will be exercised since it is a

[25]These properties are discussed and demonstrated in Frank K. Reilly and Rupinder Sidhu, "The Many Uses of Bond Duration," *Financial Analysts Journal* 36, no. 4 (July–August 1980): 58–72; and Frank J. Fabozzi, Mark Pitts, and Ravi E. Dattatreya, "Price Volatility Characteristics of Fixed-Income Securities," in *The Handbook of Fixed-Income Securities.*

function of changes in interest rates. We consider this further when we discuss the effect of embedded options on the duration and convexity of a bond.

A summary of Macaulay duration characteristics is as follows:

- The duration of a zero-coupon bond will *equal* its term to maturity.
- The duration of a coupon bond always will be less than its term to maturity.
- There is an *inverse* relationship between coupon and duration.
- There is generally a *positive* relationship between term to maturity and duration. Note that the duration of a coupon bond increases at a decreasing rate with maturity and the shape of the duration/maturity curve will depend on the coupon and YTM of the bond. Also, the duration of a deep discount bond will decline at very long maturities (over 20 years).
- There is an *inverse* relationship between yield to maturity and duration.
- Sinking funds and call provisions can cause a dramatic change in the duration of a bond. The effect of embedded options is discussed in a subsequent section.

Modified Duration and Bond Price Volatility

An adjusted measure of duration called *modified duration* can be used to approximate the interest rate sensitivity of an option-free (straight) bond. Modified duration equals Macaulay duration (computed in Table 16.10) divided by 1 plus the current yield to maturity divided by the number of payments in a year. As an example, a bond with a Macaulay duration of 10 years, a yield to maturity (i) of 8 percent, and semiannual payments would have a modified duration of

$$D_{mod} = 10/\left(1 + \frac{0.08}{2}\right)$$
$$= 10/(1.04) = 9.62$$

It has been shown, both theoretically and empirically, that price movements of option-free bonds *will vary proportionally* with modified duration for *small changes in yields.*[26] Specifically, as shown in the following equation, an estimate of the percentage change in bond price equals the change in yield times modified duration:

$$\frac{\Delta P}{P} \times 100 = -D_{mod} \times \Delta i$$

where:

ΔP = the change in price for the bond
P = the beginning price for the bond
$-D_{mod}$ = the modified duration of the bond
Δi = the yield change in basis points divided by 100. For example, if interest rates go from 8.00 to 8.50 percent, $\Delta i = 50/100 = 0.50$.

Consider a bond with Macaulay $D = 8$ years and $i = 0.10$. Assume that you expect the bond's YTM to decline by 75 basis points (e.g., from 10 percent to 9.25 percent). The first step is to compute the bond's modified duration as follows:

[26]A generalized proof of this is contained in Michael H. Hopewell and George Kaufman, "Bond Price Volatility and Term to Maturity: A Generalized Respecification," *American Economic Review* 63, no. 4 (September 1973): 749–753. The importance of the specification "for small changes in yields" will become clear when we discuss convexity in the next section. Because modified duration is an approximate measure of interest rate sensitivity, the "years" label is not appropriate.

$$D_{mod} = 8/\left(1 + \frac{0.10}{2}\right)$$
$$= 8/(1.05) = 7.62$$

The estimated percentage change in the price of the bond is as follows:

$$\%\Delta P = -(7.62) \times \frac{-75}{100}$$
$$= (-7.62) \times (-0.75)$$
$$= 5.72$$

This indicates that the bond price should increase by approximately 5.72 percent in response to the 75 basis-point decline in YTM. If the price of the bond before the decline in interest rates was \$900, the price after the decline in interest rates should be approximately \$900 × 1.0572 = \$951.48.

The modified duration is always a negative value for a noncallable bond because of the inverse relationship between yield changes and bond price changes. Also, remember that this formulation provides an *estimate* or *approximation* of the percent change in the price of the bond. The following section on convexity shows that this formula that uses only modified duration provides an exact estimate of the percentage price change only for very small changes in yields of option-free securities.

TRADING STRATEGIES USING MODIFIED DURATION We know that the longest duration security provides the maximum price variation. Table 16.11 demonstrates that numerous ways exist to achieve a given level of duration. The following discussion indicates that an active bond investor who wants to adjust his/her portfolio for anticipated interest rate changes can use this measure of interest rate sensitivity to structure a portfolio to take advantage of changes in market yields.

If you expect a *decline* in interest rates, you should *increase* the average modified duration of your bond portfolio to experience maximum price volatility. If you expect an *increase* in interest rates, you should *reduce* the average modified duration of your portfolio to minimize your price decline. Note that the modified duration of your portfolio is the market-value-weighted average of the modified durations of the individual bonds in the portfolio.

Bond Convexity

Modified duration allows us to estimate bond price changes for a change in interest rates. However, the equation we used to make this calculation (on page 585) is accurate only for *very small changes* in market yields. We will see that the accuracy of the estimate of the price change deteriorates with larger changes in yields because the modified duration calculation is a *linear* approximation of a bond price change that follows a *curvilinear* (convex) function. To understand the effect of this **convexity**, we must consider the price–yield relationship for alternative bonds.[27]

THE PRICE–YIELD RELATIONSHIP FOR BONDS Because the price of a bond is the present value of its cash flows at a particular discount rate, if you are given the

[27]For a further discussion of this topic, see Mark L.Dunetz and James M. Mahoney, "Using Duration and Convexity in the Analysis of Callable Bonds," *Financial Analysts Journal* 44, no. 3 (May–June 1988): 53–73; and Fabozzi, Pitts, and Dattatreya, "Price Volatility Characteristics of Fixed-Income Securities," in *The Handbook of Fixed Income Securities.*

TABLE 16.11

BOND DURATION IN YEARS FOR BOND YIELDING 6 PERCENT UNDER DIFFERENT TERMS

	COUPON RATES			
Years to Maturity	0.02	0.04	0.06	0.08
1	0.995	0.990	0.985	0.981
2	4.756	4.558	4.393	4.254
10	8.891	8.169	7.662	7.286
20	14.981	12.980	11.904	11.232
50	19.452	17.129	16.273	15.829
100	17.567	17.232	17.120	17.064
∞	17.167	17.167	17.167	17.167

Source: L. Fisher and R. L. Weil, "Coping with the Risk of Interest Rate Fluctuations: Returns to Bondholders from Naive and Optimal Strategies," *Journal of Business* 44, no. 4 (October 1971): 418. Copyright © 1971 by The University of Chicago Press. Reprinted by permission of The University of Chicago Press.

TABLE 16.12

PRICE–YIELD RELATIONSHIPS FOR ALTERNATIVE BONDS

A. 12 PERCENT, 20-YEAR		B. 12 PERCENT, 3-YEAR		C. ZERO-COUPON, 30-YEAR	
Yield	Price	Yield	Price	Yield	Price
1.0%	$2,989.47	1.0%	$1,324.30	1.0%	$741.37
2.0	2,641.73	2.0	1,289.77	2.0	550.45
3.0	2,346.21	3.0	1,256.37	3.0	409.30
4.0	2,094.22	4.0	1,224.06	4.0	304.78
5.0	1,878.60	5.0	1,192.78	5.0	227.28
6.0	1,693.44	6.0	1,162.52	6.0	169.73
7.0	1,533.88	7.0	1,133.21	7.0	126.93
8.0	1,395.86	8.0	1,104.84	8.0	95.06
9.0	1,276.02	9.0	1,077.37	9.0	71.29
10.0	1,171.59	10.0	1,050.76	10.0	53.54
11.0	1,080.23	11.0	1,024.98	11.0	40.26
12.0	1,000.00	12.0	1,000.00	12.0	30.31

coupon, maturity, and a yield for a bond, you can calculate its price at a point in time. The price–yield curve provides a set of prices for a specific maturity-coupon bond at a point in time using a range of yields to maturity (discount rates). As an example, Table 16.12 lists the computed prices for a 12 percent, 20-year bond assuming yields from 1 percent to 12 percent. The table shows that if you discount the flows from this bond at a yield of 1 percent, you would get a price of $2,989.47; discounting these same flows at 10 percent gives a price of $1,171.59. The graph of these prices relative to the yields that produced them (Figure 16.7) indicates that the price–yield relationship for this bond is not a straight line but a curvilinear relationship. That is, it is convex.

Two points are important about the price–yield relationship:

1. This relationship can be applied to a single bond, a portfolio of bonds, or any stream of future cash flows.
2. The convex price–yield relationship will differ among bonds or other streams, depending on the nature of the cash flow stream, that is, its coupon and maturity. For example,

FIGURE 16.7 PRICE–YIELD RELATIONSHIP AND MODIFIED DURATION AT 4 PERCENT YIELD

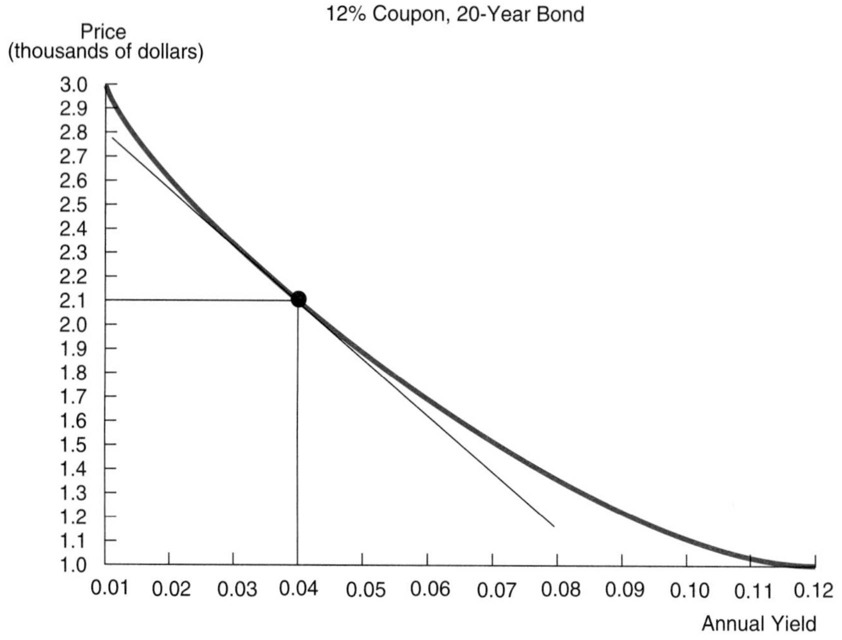
12% Coupon, 20-Year Bond
Price
(thousands of dollars)
3.0
2.9
2.8
2.7
2.6
2.5
2.4
2.3
2.2
2.1
2.0
1.9
1.8
1.7
1.6
1.5
1.4
1.3
1.2
1.1
1.0
0.01 0.02 0.03 0.04 0.05 0.06 0.07 0.08 0.09 0.10 0.11 0.12
Annual Yield

the price–yield relationship for a high-coupon, short-term security will be almost a straight line because the price does not change as much for a change in yields (e.g., the 12 percent, 3-year bond in Table 16.12). In contrast, the price–yield relationship for a low-coupon, long-term bond will curve radically (i.e., be very convex), as shown by the zero-coupon, 30-year bond in Table 16.12. These differences in convexity are shown graphically in Figure 16.8. The curved nature of the price–yield relationship is referred to as the bond's *convexity.*

The Desirability of Convexity As shown by the graph in Figure 16.8, because of the convexity of the price–yield relationship, as yield increases, the rate at which the price of the bond declines becomes slower. Similarly, when yields decline, the rate at which the price of the bond increases becomes faster. Therefore, convexity is considered a desirable trait. Specifically, if you have two bonds with equal duration but one has greater convexity, you would want the bond with greater convexity because it would have better price performance whether yields rise (price declines less) or yields fall (the bond price increases more).

Given this price–yield curve, modified duration is the percentage change in price for a nominal change in yield as follows:[28]

$$D_{mod} = \frac{\frac{dP}{di}}{P}$$

Notice that the *dP/di* line is tangent to the price–yield curve *at a given yield* as shown in Figure 16.9. For *small* changes in yields (i.e., from y^* to either y_1 or y_2), this tangent

[28]In mathematical terms, modified duration is the first differential of this price–yield relationship with respect to yield.

FIGURE 16.8 **PRICE–YIELD CURVES FOR ALTERNATIVE BONDS**

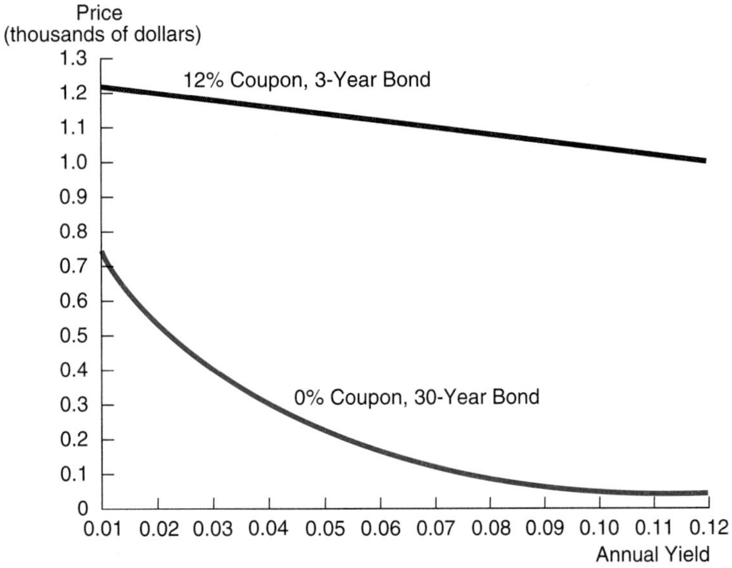
Price
(thousands of dollars)
1.3
1.2
1.1
1.0
0.9
0.8
0.7
0.6
0.5
0.4
0.3
0.2
0.1
0
12% Coupon, 3-Year Bond
0% Coupon, 30-Year Bond
0.01 0.02 0.03 0.04 0.05 0.06 0.07 0.08 0.09 0.10 0.11 0.12
Annual Yield

straight line gives a good estimate of the actual price changes. In contrast, for larger changes in yields (i.e., from y^* to either y_3 or y_4), the straight line will estimate the new price of the bond at less than the actual price shown by the price–yield curve. This misestimate arises because the modified-duration line is a linear estimate of a curvilinear relationship. Specifically, the estimate using only modified duration will *underestimate* the actual price *increase* caused by a yield decline and *overestimate* the actual price *decline* caused by an increase in yields. This graph, which demonstrates the convexity effect, also shows that price changes are *not* symmetric when yields increase or decrease. As shown, when rates decline, there is a larger price error than when rates increase because, due to convexity, when yields decline prices rise at an *increasing* rate, while prices decline at a *decreasing* rate when yields rise.

DETERMINANTS OF CONVEXITY Convexity is a measure of the curvature of the price–yield relationship. In turn, because modified duration is the slope of the curve at a given yield, convexity indicates changes in duration. Mathematically, convexity is the second derivative of price with respect to yield (d^2P/di^2) divided by price. Specifically, convexity is the percentage change in dP/di for a given change in yield:

$$\text{Convexity} = \frac{\dfrac{d^2P}{di^2}}{P}$$

Convexity is a measure of how much a bond's price–yield curve deviates from the linear approximation of that curve. As indicated by Figures 16.7 and 16.9 for *noncallable* bonds, convexity always is a positive number, implying that the price–yield curve lies above the modified-duration (tangent) line. Figure 16.8 illustrates the price–yield relationship for two bonds with very different coupons and maturities. (The yields and prices are contained in Table 16.12.)

These graphs demonstrate the following relationship between these factors and the convexity of a bond.

FIGURE 16.9 **PRICE APPROXIMATION USING MODIFIED DURATION**

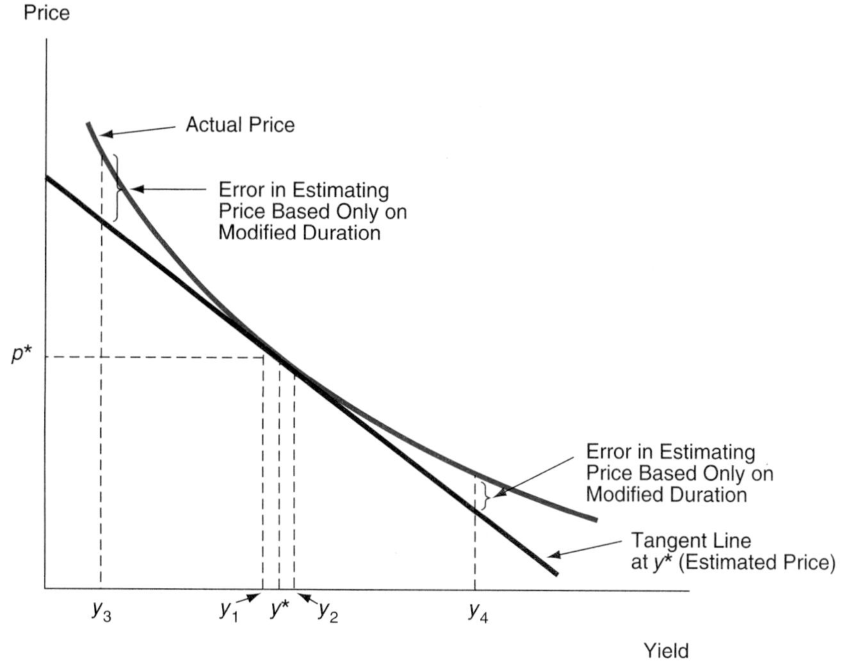
Price
Actual Price
Error in Estimating Price Based Only on Modified Duration
p*
Error in Estimating Price Based Only on Modified Duration
Tangent Line at y* (Estimated Price)
y3
y1
y*
y2
y4
Yield

Source: Frank J. Fabozzi, Mark Pitts, and Ravi E. Dattatreya, "Price Volatility Characteristics of Fixed-Income Securities," in *The Handbook of Fixed-Income Securities,* 5th ed. (Irwin Professional Publishing, © 1997), p. 92.

- There is an *inverse* relationship between coupon and convexity (yield and maturity constant)—that is, lower coupon, higher convexity.
- There is a *direct* relationship between maturity and convexity (yield and coupon constant)—that is, longer maturity, higher convexity.
- There is an *inverse* relationship between yield and convexity (coupon and maturity constant). This means that the price–yield curve is more convex at its lower-yield (upper left) segment.

Therefore, a short-term, high-coupon bond, such as the 12 percent coupon, 3-year bond in Figure 16.8, has very low convexity—it is almost a straight line. In contrast, the zero-coupon, 30-year bond has high convexity.

Notably, the determinants of duration and convexity for option-free bonds are very similar. Specifically, the three factors are the same—maturity, coupon, and yield—and the direction of impact is the same—that is, maturity is direct and both coupon and yield are inverse. Therefore, high duration bonds have high convexity.

THE MODIFIED-DURATION–CONVEXITY EFFECTS In summary, the change in a bond's price resulting from a change in yield can be attributed to two sources: the bond's modified duration and its convexity. The relative effect of these two factors on the price change will depend on the characteristics of the bond (i.e., its convexity) and the size of the yield change. For example, if you are estimating the price change for a 300 basis-point change in yield for a zero-coupon, 30-year bond, the convexity effect would be fairly large because this bond would have high convexity, and a 300 basis-point change in yield is relatively large. In contrast, if you are dealing with only a 10 basis-point change in yields, the convexity effect would be minimal because it is a small change in yield. Similarly, the convexity effect would be small for a larger yield change if you are concerned with a bond with small convexity (i.e., a high-coupon, short-maturity bond) because its price–yield curve is almost a straight line.

In conclusion, modified duration can help you derive an *approximate* percentage bond price change for a given change in interest rates, but you must remember that it is only a good estimate when you are considering small yield changes. The point is, you must also consider the convexity effect on price change when you are dealing with large yield changes and/or when the securities or cash flows have high convexity.

COMPUTATION OF CONVEXITY Again, the formula for computing the convexity of a stream of cash flows looks fairly complex, but it can be broken down into manageable steps. You will recall from our convexity equation above that

$$\text{Convexity} = \frac{\frac{d^2P}{di^2}}{P}$$

In turn,

$$\frac{d^2P}{di^2} = \frac{1}{(1+i)^2}\left[\sum_{t=1}^{n} \frac{CF_t}{(1+i)^t}(t^2+t)\right]$$

Table 16.13 contains the computations related to this calculation for a 3-year bond with a 12 percent coupon and 9 percent YTM assuming annual flows.

The convexity for this bond is very low because it has a short maturity, high coupon, and high yield. Note that *the convexity of a security will vary along the price–yield curve.* You will get a different convexity at a 3 percent yield that at a 12 percent yield. In terms of the computation, the maturity and coupon will be the same, but you will use a different discount rate that reflects where you are on the curve. This is similar to the earlier observation that *you will get a different modified duration at different points on the price–yield curve* because the slope varies along the curve. You also can see this mathematically because, depending on where you are on the curve, you will be using a different market yield, and the Macaulay and modified durations are inverse to the discount rate.[29]

To compute the price change attributable to the convexity effect after you know the bond's convexity, use this equation:

$$\text{Price Change Due to Convexity} = \tfrac{1}{2} \times \text{Price} \times \text{Convexity} \times (\Delta \text{ in yield})^2$$

Table 16.14 shows the change in bond price considering the duration effect and the convexity effect for an 18-year bond with a 12 percent coupon and 9 percent YTM. For demonstration purposes, we assumed a decline of 100 and 300 basis points (BP) in rates (i.e., 9 percent to 8 percent and 9 percent to 6 percent).

With the 300 BP change, if you considered only the modified-duration effect, you would have *estimated* that the bond went from 126.50 to 158.30 (a 25.14 percent increase), when, in fact, the actual price is closer to 164.41, which is about a *30 percent increase.*

Duration and Convexity for Callable Bonds

The discussion and presentation thus far regarding Macaulay and modified durations and convexity have been concerned with option-free bonds. A callable bond is different because it provides the issuer with an option to call the bond under certain conditions and pay it off with funds from a new issue sold at a lower yield. Observers refer to this as a bond with an

[29]In the appendix there is a table that combines the computation of Macaulay and modified duration and convexity using semiannual cash flows.

TABLE 16.13 **COMPUTATION OF CONVEXITY**

$$\text{Convexity} = \frac{d^2P/di^2}{PV \text{ of Cash Flows}} = \frac{d^2P/di^2}{\text{Price}}$$

$$\frac{d^2P}{di^2} = \frac{1}{(1+i)^2}\left[\sum_{t=1}^{n}(t^2+t)\frac{CF_t}{(1+i)^t}\right]$$

$$\text{Convexity} = \frac{d^2P/di^2}{\text{Price}}$$

Example: 3-Year Bond, 12% Coupon, 9% YTM

(1) Year	(2) CF_t	(3) PV @ 9%	(4) PV CF	(5) $t^2 + t$	(4) × (5)
1	120	0.9174	$ 110.09	2	$ 220.18
2	120	0.8417	101.00	6	606.00
3	120	0.7722	92.66	12	1,111.92
3	1,000	0.7722	772.20	12	9,266.40
			Price = $1,075.95		$11,204.50

$$\frac{1}{(1+i)^2} = \frac{1}{(1.09)^2} = \frac{1}{1.19} = 0.84$$

$$\$11{,}204.50 \times 0.84 = \$9{,}411.78$$

$$\text{Convexity} = \frac{9411.78}{1075.95} = 8.75$$

embedded option. We noted earlier that the duration of a bond can be seriously affected by an embedded call option if interest rates decline substantially below a bond's coupon rate. In such a case, the issuer will likely call the bond, which will dramatically change the maturity and the duration of the bond. For example, assume a firm issues a 30-year bond with a 9 percent coupon with a deferred call provision whereby the bond can be called in 6 years at 109 percent of par. If the bond is issued at par, its original *duration to maturity* will be about 11 years. A year later, if rates decline to about 7 percent, its duration to maturity will still be over *10 years* because duration is inversely related to yield and yields have declined. Notably, at a yield of 7 percent, this bond will probably trade at *yield to call* because at a 7 percent yield the firm will likely exercise its option and call the bond in 5 years. Notably, the bond's *duration to first call* would be about *4 years.* Clearly, there is a significant difference between duration to maturity (over 10 years) and duration to first call (about 4 years).

To understand the impact of the call feature on the duration and convexity of a bond, it is important to consider what determines the price of a callable bond. A callable bond is a combination of a noncallable bond plus a *call option* that was *sold to the issuer,* which allows the issuer to call the bond under the conditions discussed earlier. Because the call option is owned by the issuer, it has negative value for the investor in the bond. Thus the bondholder's position is:

Long a Callable Bond = Long a Noncallable Bond + A Short Position in a Call Option

Therefore, the value (price) of a callable bond is equal to:

Callable Bond Price = Noncallable Bond Price − Call Option Price

TABLE 16.14 **ANALYSIS OF BOND PRICE CHANGE CONSIDERING DURATION AND CONVEXITY**

Example: 18-Year Bond, 12% Coupon, 9% YTM
Price: 126.50
Modified Duration: 8.38 (D^*)
Convexity: 107.70
Estimate of Price Change Using Duration:
Percent Δ Price = D^* (Δ in YLD/100)
Estimate of Price Change from Convexity:
Price Change = ½ × Price × Convexity × (Δ in YLD)^2

A. Change in Yield: −100 BP

Duration Change: $-8.38 + \left(\frac{-100}{100}\right) = +8.38\%$

$+8.38\% \times 126.50 = +10.60$

Convexity Change: $\frac{1}{2} \times (126.50) \times 107.70 \times (0.01)^2$
$= 63.25 \times 107.70 \times 0.0001$
$= 6{,}812.03 \times 0.0001 = 0.68$

Combined Effect:
126.50
+ 10.60 (Duration)
137.10
+0.68 (Convexity)
137.78

B. Change in Yield: −300 BP

Duration Change: $-8.38 \times \left(\frac{-300}{100}\right) = +25.14\%$

$126.50 \times 1.2514 = 158.30\ (+31.80)$

Convexity Effect: $\frac{1}{2} \times (126.50) \times 107.70 \times (0.03)^2$

$6{,}812.03 \times 0.0009 = 6.11$

Combined Effect:
126.50
+ 31.80 (Duration)
158.30
+6.11 (Convexity)
164.41

Given this valuation, anything that increases the value of the call option will reduce the value of the callable bond.[30] The point is, when interest rates decline, the right-hand side of this equation experiences a conflict between the value of the noncallable bond that

[30]For a further discussion of the effect of these embedded options, see Frank J. Fabozzi, Mark Pitts, and Ravi E. Dattatreya, "Price Volatility Characteristics of Fixed-Income Securities," and Frank J. Fabozzi, Andrew J. Kalotay, and George O. Williams, "Valuation of Bonds with Embedded Options." Both are in *The Handbook of Fixed-Income Securities.* Also see Kurt Winkelmann, "Uses and Abuses of Duration and Convexity," *Financial Analysts Journal* 45, no. 5 (September–October 1989): 72–75; and Chapter 14 in Frank J. Fabozzi, *Bond Markets, Analysis and Strategies,* 3d ed. (Upper Saddle River, N.J.: Prentice Hall, 1996).

increases in value, and the negative effect of the call option that also increases. Notably, if the value of the call option increases faster than the value of the noncallable bond, the overall value of the callable bond will *decline* when interest rates decline and this is referred to as *negative duration.*

OPTION-ADJUSTED DURATION[31] Given these two extreme values of: (1) duration to maturity, and (2) duration to first call, the investment community derives a duration estimate that is referred to as an option-adjusted or call-adjusted duration based on *the probability that the issuing firm will exercise its call option* for the bond when the bond becomes freely callable. This option-adjusted duration will be somewhere between these two extreme values. Specifically, when interest rates are substantially above the coupon rate, the probability of the bond being called is very small (i.e., the call option has very little value) and the option-adjusted duration will approach the duration to maturity. In contrast, if interest rates decline to levels substantially below the coupon rate, the probability of the bond being called at the first opportunity is very high (i.e., the call option is very valuable and will probably be exercised) and the option-adjusted duration will approach the duration to first call. In summary, the bond's option-adjusted duration will be somewhere between these two extremes with the exact option-adjusted duration depending on the level of interest rates relative to the bond's coupon rate.

The option-adjusted duration can also be envisioned or computed based on the duration of the two components, as follows:

$$\text{Option-Adjusted Duration} = \text{Duration of the Noncallable Bond} - \text{Duration of the Call Option}$$

If one conceives of duration as interest rate sensitivity, we know that at high interest rates a change in yield will have little if any impact on the value of the option. Thus the duration (i.e., interest rate sensitivity) of the option would be close to zero and the option-adjusted duration would equal that of a noncallable bond. In contrast, when yields decline below the coupon yield, the call option will be very interest rate sensitive since the option will experience a large increase in value at low yields. Thus the duration (i.e., the interest rate sensitivity) of the option will be fairly high and have a large impact on the callable bond's option-adjusted duration—it will drive the duration of the callable bond toward the duration to first call. In fact, it is possible to conceive of an option that is very leveraged such that it is extremely interest rate sensitive (i.e., has a very large duration that exceeds the duration of the noncallable bond) resulting in a *negative option-adjusted duration.* An example is a mortgage-backed security that might *decline* in price when there is a *decline* in interest rates.

CONVEXITY OF CALLABLE BONDS Figure 16.10 shows what happens to the price of a callable bond versus the value of a noncallable bond when interest rates increase or decline. Starting from yield y^* (which is close to the par value yield), if interest rates *increase,* the value of the call option declines because at market interest rates that are substantially above the coupon rate, it is unlikely the issuer will want to call the issue. Therefore, the call option has very little value and the price of the callable bond will be similar to the price of a noncallable bond. In contrast, when interest rates *decline* below y^*, there is an increase in the probability that the issuer will want to use the call option—that

[31]The discussion in this subsection will consider the option-adjusted duration on a conceptual and intuitive basis. For a detailed mathematical treatment, see Dunetz and Mahoney, "Using Duration and Convexity in the Analysis of Callable Bonds."

FIGURE 16.10 **NONCALLABLE AND CALLABLE BOND PRICE–YIELD RELATIONSHIP**

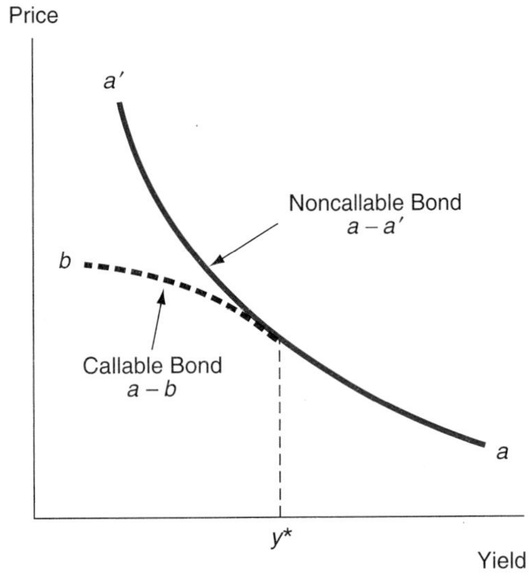
Price
a′
Noncallable Bond
a – a′
b
Callable Bond
a – b
a
y*
Yield

Source: Frank J. Fabozzi, Mark Pitts, and Ravi E. Dattatreya, "Price Volatility Characteristics of Fixed-Income Securities," in *The Handbook of Fixed-Income Securities,* 5th ed., Frank J Fabozzi (Chicago, Ill.: Irwin Professional Publishing, 1997). Reprinted by permission of the publisher.

is, the value of the call option increases. As a result, the value of the callable bond will deviate from the value of the noncallable bond—that is, the price of the callable bond will initially not increase as fast as the noncallable bond price and eventually will not increase at all. This is what is shown in curves *a–b.*

In the case of the noncallable bond, we indicated that it had *positive convexity* because as yields declined, the price of the bond increased at a *faster* rate. With the callable bond, when rates decline, the price increases at a *slower* rate and eventually does not change at all. This pattern of price–yield change for a callable bond is referred to as *negative convexity.*

Needless to say, this price pattern (negative convexity) is one of the risks of a callable bond versus a noncallable bond, especially if there is a chance of declining interest rates.

LIMITATIONS OF MACAULAY AND MODIFIED DURATION

It is important to understand Macaulay and modified duration because of the perspective they provide regarding factors that affect the volatility and interest rate sensitivity of bonds. However, it also is important for bond analysts and portfolio managers to recognize the serious limitations of these measures in the real world. The major limitations are as follows:

First, as noted in the discussion of convexity, the percent change estimates using modified duration are good only for small-yield changes. This was demonstrated in Figure 16.9. As a result, two bonds with equal duration may experience different price changes for large-yield changes—depending on *differences in the convexity* of the bonds.

Second, it is difficult to determine the interest rate sensitivity of a portfolio of bonds when there is a change in interest rates and the yield curve experiences *a nonparallel shift.* It was noted earlier that the duration of a portfolio is the weighted average of the durations of the bonds in the portfolio. Everything works well as long as all yields change by the same amount—that is, there is a parallel shift of the yield curve. However, when yields change, the yield curve *seldom* experiences a parallel shift. Assuming a nonparallel shift, which yield do you use to describe the change—the short-, intermediate-, or long-maturity yield? Two portfolios that begin the period with the same duration can have different ending durations and perform very differently, depending on how the yield curve changed (i.e., did it steepen or flatten?) and the composition of the portfolio (i.e., relative to its duration, was it a bullet or a barbell?). Consider the following simple example for two portfolios that have a duration of 4.50 years:

Bond	Coupon	Maturity (Years)	Yield	Modified Duration	Weights
Portfolio A					
A	7.00	4	7.00	2.70	0.555
B	9.00	20	9.00	6.75	0.445
Portfolio B					
C	8.00	10	8.00	4.50	1.000

As shown, the modified durations are equal at the initiation of the portfolio. Assume a non-parallel change in yields where the *yield curve steepens.* Specifically, 4-year yields decline to 6 percent, 10-year yields do not change, and 20-year yields rise to 10 percent. Portfolio B would experience a very small change in value because of stability in yield for 10-year bonds. In contrast, the price for 4-year bonds will experience a small increase (because of small duration) and the value of 20-year bonds will experience a large decline. Overall, the value of portfolio A will decline because of the weight of bond B in the portfolio and its large decline in value due to its large modified duration. Obviously, if the yield curve had flattened or inverted, the barbell portfolio would have benefited from the change. This differential performance because of the change in the shape of the yield curve (i.e., it did not experience a parallel shift) is referred to as *yield curve risk,* which cannot be captured by the traditional duration–convexity presentation.

The third limitation of Macaulay and modified durations involves our initial calculation. We assumed that cash flows from the bond *were not affected by yield changes*—that is, we assumed option-free bonds. Later, we saw the effect on the computed duration and convexity when we considered the effect of an embedded call option in Figure 16.10. Specifically, we saw that the option-adjusted duration would be some value between the duration to maturity and duration to first call and the specific value would depend on the current market yield relative to the bond's coupon. Further, we saw that when interest rates declined with an embedded option, the convexity of the bond went from some positive value to *negative* convexity because the price of the callable bond increased at a slower rate or it did not change when the yields declined (i.e., there is *price compression*).

Because of these limitations, practitioners have developed a way to approximate the duration of a bond or any security that will be impacted by a change in interest rates. This is referred to as *effective duration,* which is discussed in the following section.

EFFECTIVE DURATION[32] As noted previously, the purpose of duration is to indicate the price change of an asset to a change in yield—that is, it is *a measure of the interest rate sensitivity of an asset.* Because modified duration is based on Macaulay duration, it can provide a reasonable approximation of the interest rate sensitivity of a bond that experiences a small-yield change and one that is option free—if yield changes do not change the cash

[32]This section benefited substantially from the very thorough presentation in Gerald W. Buetow, Jr. and Robert Johnson, "Effective Duration and Convexity for Bonds with Embedded Options," *Handbook of Fixed Income Securities,* 6th ed., forthcoming.

flows for the bond. Unfortunately, the Macaulay and modified-duration measures cannot be used: (1) for large-yield changes, (2) for assets with embedded options, or (3) for assets that are affected by variables other than interest rates, such as common stocks or real estate.

To overcome these limitations, practitioners use *effective duration,* a direct measure of the interest rate sensitivity of a bond or any asset where it is possible to use a pricing model to estimate the market prices surrounding a change in interest rates. As we will demonstrate, using this measure it is possible to derive negative durations (which is not mathematically possible with Macaulay) or durations that are longer than the maturity of the asset (likewise not possible with Macaulay). Specifically, effective duration measures the interest rate sensitivity of a bond taking into consideration that the cash flows of the bond can change when yields change due to the existence of embedded options (e.g., call or put options). It is also possible to calculate the effective duration for an option-free bond, in which case the computed value will be equal to what would be derived for small-yield changes using modified duration.

Notably, to implement the effective duration formula, it is necessary to use an interest rate model and corresponding pricing model that will provide price estimates for the asset when interest rates and cash flows change. The formulas for calculating effective duration and effective convexity are:

$$\text{Effective Duration } (D_{Eff}) = \frac{(P_-) - (P_+)}{2PS}$$

$$\text{Effective Convexity } (C_{Eff}) = \frac{(P_-) + (P_+) - 2P}{PS^2}$$

where:

P_- = the estimated price of the asset after a downward shift in interest rates
P_+ = the estimated price of the asset after an upward shift in interest rates
P = the current price of the asset (before any interest rate shifts)
S = the assumed shift in the term structure

The formulas are implemented by assuming small changes in yield (10 basis points) both down and up and using a pricing model to estimate the expected market prices (both P_- and P_+) at the new yields. Everything else in the formulas is given. Consider the following bond that we will initially assume is option free:

Par Value	\$1,000
Coupon	6%
Maturity	8 years
Initial YTM	6%
Initial Price (P)	100

Given this initial scenario, we assume a change in yields of 10 basis points. The prices for the yields to maturity of 5.90 percent (P_-) and 6.10 percent (P_+) are:

$$0.0590\ (P_-) = 100.42760054$$
$$0.0610\ (P_+) = \underline{\ 99.57457612}$$
$$(P_-) - (P_+) = 0.85302442$$
$$2PS = (2)(100)(0.001) = 0.20$$

$$D_{Eff} = \frac{0.85302442}{0.20} = 4.265122$$

Because this is a noncallable bond (option-free), we know that this effective duration equals the modified duration we would derive based upon the Macaulay duration of 4.39.

$$D_{mod} = \frac{4.39}{\left(1 + \frac{0.06}{2}\right)} = \frac{4.39}{1.03} = 4.262$$

The difference is due to the rounding of the Macaulay duration.

The bond's effective convexity would equal:

$$\begin{aligned} C_{Eff} &= \frac{(P_{-}) + (P_{+}) - 2P}{PS^2} \\ &= \frac{100.42760054 + 99.57457612 - 200}{(100)(0.001)^2} \\ &= \frac{200.00217666 - 200}{0.0001} \\ &= \frac{0.00217666}{0.0001} = 21.766 \end{aligned}$$

We know from our earlier discussion that at a lower yield the duration would be higher. Specifically, if we assumed a YTM of 4 percent, the effective and modified durations would be about 4.34 compared to about 4.27 at 6 percent.

Let us now assume that the bond is callable at 106 of par after 3 years. Using the Black, Derman and Toy no-arbitrage binomial model to estimate prices for this bond beginning at a yield of 4 percent, we derive the following prices:[33]

$$\begin{aligned} 0.0390\ (P_{-}) &= 108.55626094 \\ 0.0410\ (P_{+}) &= 107.92318176 \\ 0.04\ (P) &= 108.24082177 \end{aligned}$$

$$\begin{aligned} D_{Eff} &= \frac{108.55626094 - 107.92318176}{(2)(108.24082177)(0.001)} \\ &= 2.92 \end{aligned}$$

As expected, because of the embedded call option that would have increased in value with a decline in yields, this duration value (2.92) would be lower than the duration for the option-free bond discussed above (4.34). In contrast, the effective durations for callable bonds at higher yields would be equal to the durations for option-free bonds because the value of the option approaches zero.

The effective convexity of this callable bond at 4 percent would be:

$$\begin{aligned} C_{Eff} &= \frac{108.55626094 + 107.92318176 - [2(108.24082177)]}{(108.24082177)(0.001)^2} \\ &= -20.33 \end{aligned}$$

As discussed, this is an example of negative convexity because the price increase is limited because of the increasing value of the call option. For comparison purposes, the convexity

---

[33] F. Black, E. Derman, and Wo Toy, "A One-Factor Model of Interest Rates and Its Application to Treasury Bond Options," *Financial Analysts Journal* 46, no. 1 (January–February 1990): 33–39.

of the option-free bond at 4 percent is 23.76, which is, as expected, slightly higher than its convexity of 21.77 at 6 percent (recall that both duration and convexity is inversely related to yield).

Putable Bonds Although it is not feasible to discuss in detail the properties of bonds with put options (putable bonds), it is possible to envision the effects if one considers the basic value of a putable bond as follows:

$$\text{Value of Putable Bond} = \text{Value of Nonputable Bond} + \text{Value of the Put Option}$$

In this instance, the investor owns the option, which means it has a positive impact on the value of the bond and this option *increases* in value when interest rates *increase*. Therefore, when rates increase, the price of the bond does not decline as much as an option-free bond, but when rates decline, its price pattern is similar to that of an option-free bond because the value of the put option approaches zero.

A visual presentation of the effect of the call option on the price–yield curve was contained in Figure 16.10. Alternatively, Figures 16.11 and 16.12 contain the effective duration–yield curves and the effective convexity–yield curves, which show the significant impact of embedded options on the effective duration and convexity of fixed income securities.

EFFECTIVE DURATION GREATER THAN MATURITY Because effective duration is simply interest rate sensitivity, it is possible to have an asset that is highly levered such that its interest rate sensitivity exceeds its maturity. For example, there are 5-year, collateralized mortgage obligations (CMOs) that are highly levered and their prices will change by 15 percent to 20 percent when interest rates change by 100 basis points. Using the formula discussed, you would compute an effective duration of 15 or 20 for a 5-year maturity security.

NEGATIVE EFFECTIVE DURATION We know from the formula for Macaulay duration that it is not possible to compute a negative duration. Further, in the calculation for price volatility where we use modified duration, we use $-D^*$ to reflect the negative relationship between price changes and interest rate changes for *option-free bonds*. At the same time, we know that when we leave the world of option-free bonds and consider bonds with embedded options, it is possible to envision cases where bond prices move in the same direction as yields, which implies negative duration. A prime example would be mortgage-backed securities where a significant decline in interest rates will cause a substantial increase in refinancing prepayments by homeowners, which will reduce the value of these bonds to holders. Therefore, you would see a decline in interest rates *and* a decline in the price of these mortgage-backed bonds, which implies *negative duration.* Another way to explain a price decline with lower interest rates is the value formula—that is, with lower interest rates, the value of the call option increases in value by more than the value of the noncallable bond, which implies a decline in the value of the callable bond.

EMPIRICAL DURATION[34] In the preceding discussion of effective duration, the point was made that these computations required the use of an interest rate model and a pricing model that considered cash flow changes when yields changed and generated market price estimates that were inputs into the effective duration and effective convexity

[34]The discussion in this section considered the analysis in Lakhbir Hayre and Hubert Chang, "Effective and Empirical Durations of Mortgage Securities," *Journal of Fixed Income* 6, no. 4 (March 1997): 17–33.

FIGURE 16.11 **EFFECTIVE DURATION–YIELD CURVES**

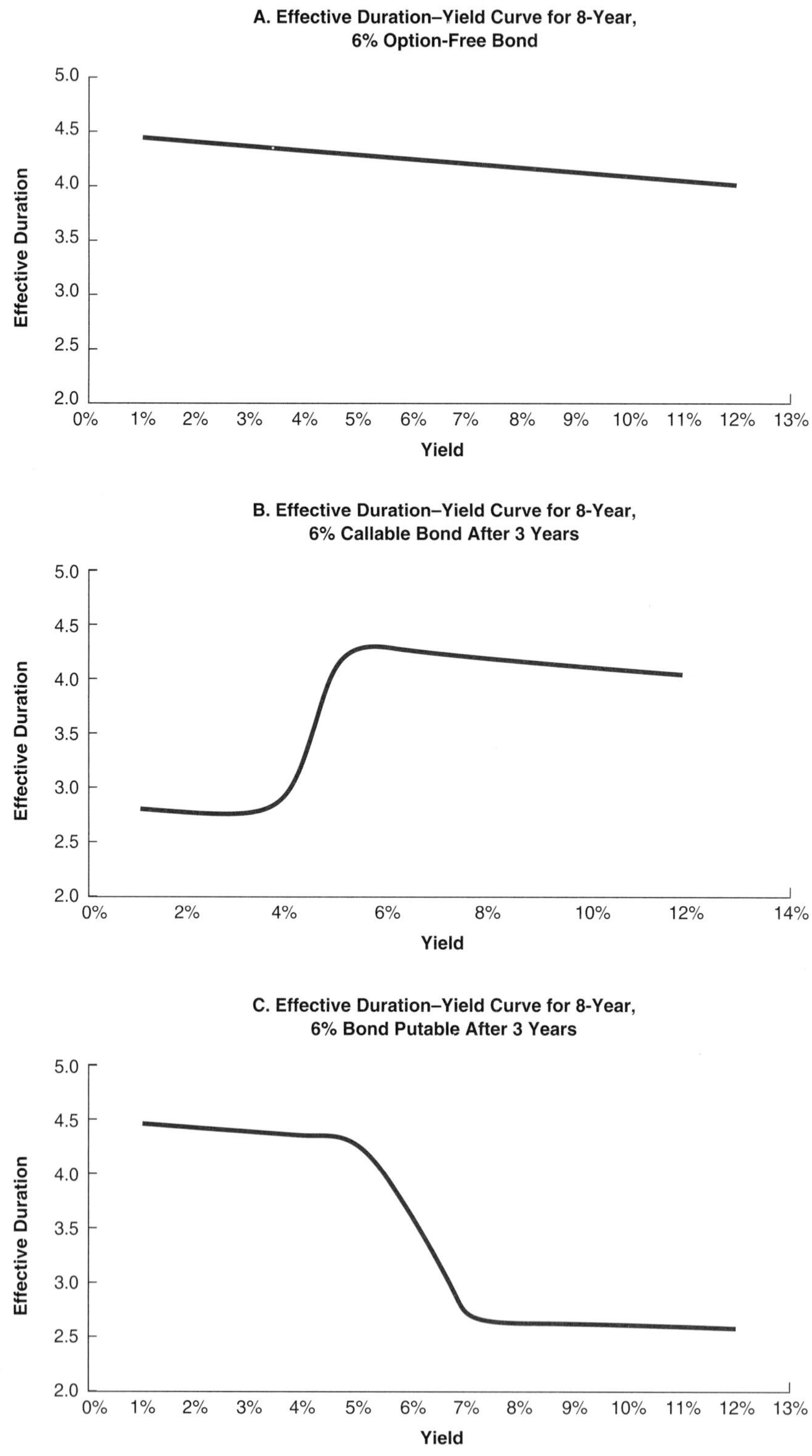
A. Effective Duration–Yield Curve for 8-Year, 6% Option-Free Bond
Effective Duration
5.0
4.5
4.0
3.5
3.0
2.5
2.0
0% 1% 2% 3% 4% 5% 6% 7% 8% 9% 10% 11% 12% 13%
Yield
B. Effective Duration–Yield Curve for 8-Year, 6% Callable Bond After 3 Years
Effective Duration
5.0
4.5
4.0
3.5
3.0
2.5
2.0
0% 2% 4% 6% 8% 10% 12% 14%
Yield
C. Effective Duration–Yield Curve for 8-Year, 6% Bond Putable After 3 Years
Effective Duration
5.0
4.5
4.0
3.5
3.0
2.5
2.0
0% 1% 2% 3% 4% 5% 6% 7% 8% 9% 10% 11% 12% 13%
Yield

FIGURE 16.12 **EFFECTIVE CONVEXITY–YIELD CURVES**

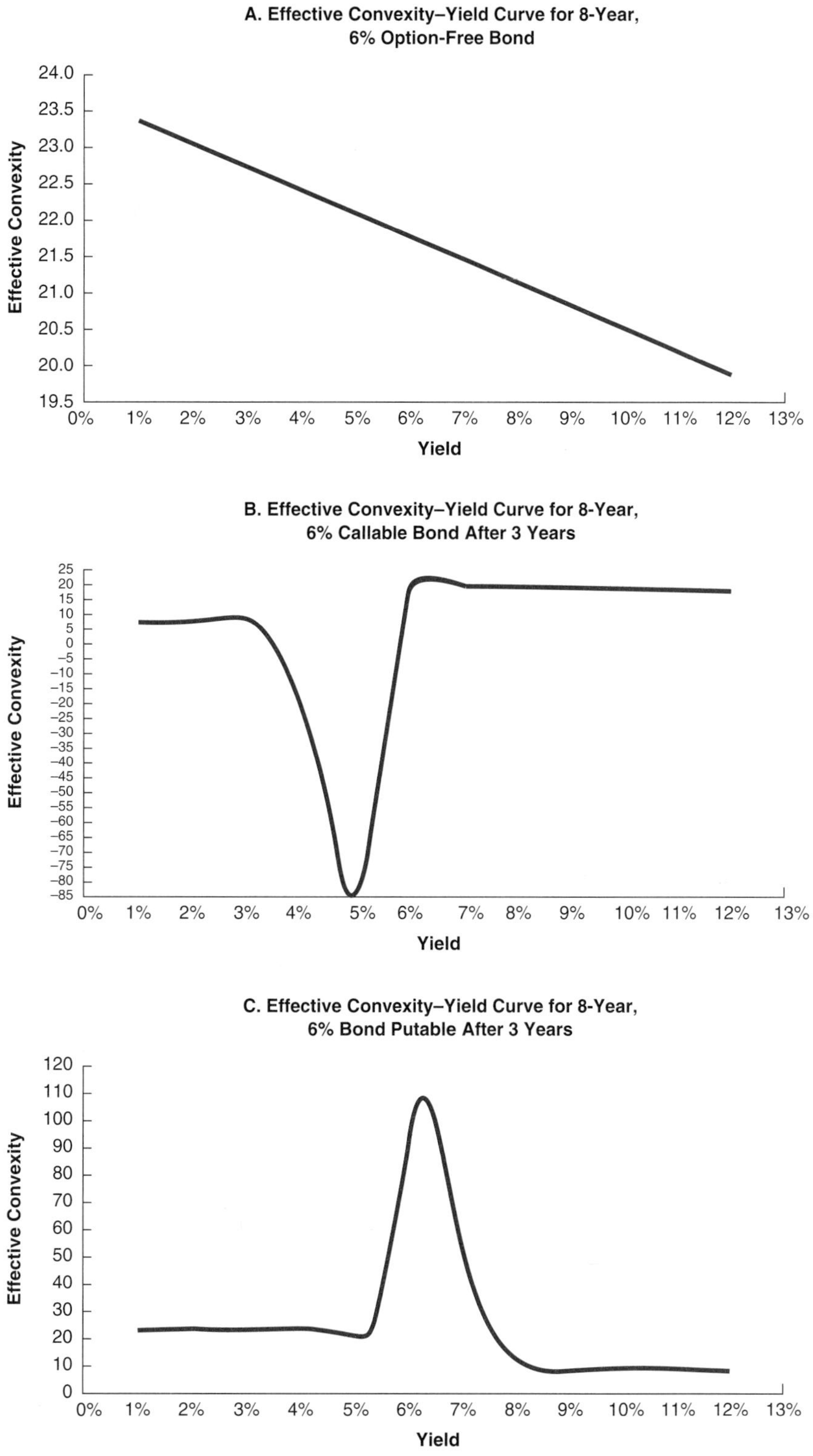
A. Effective Convexity–Yield Curve for 8-Year,
6% Option-Free Bond
Effective Convexity
24.0
23.5
23.0
22.5
22.0
21.5
21.0
20.5
20.0
19.5
0% 1% 2% 3% 4% 5% 6% 7% 8% 9% 10% 11% 12% 13%
Yield
B. Effective Convexity–Yield Curve for 8-Year,
6% Callable Bond After 3 Years
Effective Convexity
25 20 15 10 5 0 −5 −10 −15 −20 −25 −30 −35 −40 −45 −50 −55 −60 −65 −70 −75 −80 −85
0% 1% 2% 3% 4% 5% 6% 7% 8% 9% 10% 11% 12% 13%
Yield
C. Effective Convexity–Yield Curve for 8-Year,
6% Bond Putable After 3 Years
Effective Convexity
120 110 100 90 80 70 60 50 40 30 20 10 0
0% 1% 2% 3% 4% 5% 6% 7% 8% 9% 10% 11% 12% 13%
Yield

formulas. The question arises regarding what happens when you want to estimate interest rate sensitivity for an asset class where it is not possible to generate well-specified market price estimates in response to yield changes. The classic example would be common stocks where there is an impact on price when interest rates change, but the interest rate effect can be overpowered by the growth rate effect that is likewise unknown. The other obvious example would be bonds with exotic embedded options (including mortgage-backed bonds) where prices can change based upon the value of the exotic option that is difficult to price. In order to derive some estimate of interest rate sensitivity under such circumstances, analysts and portfolio managers employ **empirical duration**, which is the actual percentage price change for an asset in response to a change in yield during a specified time period. The concept is best described by recalling the formula to determine the percentage price change for a bond using modified duration as follows:

$$\%\Delta Price = -D_{mod} \times (\Delta i)$$

where:

D_{mod} = **the modified Macaulay duration**
Δi = **the change in interest rates in basis points divided by 100**

The typical assumption is that we know D_{mod} and Δi and can solve for approximate percentage price change. Given this relationship, we can solve for D_{mod} as follows:

$$-D_{mod} = \frac{\%\Delta Price}{\Delta R}$$

When we solve for it this way, it is no longer D_{mod} (modified duration), but D_{emp}—empirical duration. Given this formulation, if you observe a change in interest rates (Δi) and the change in the price of an asset during the same time period, you can solve for the empirical duration of the asset. Consider the following simple example.

- Interest rates decline by 200 BP.
- The price of a bond increases by 10 percent.

$$D_{emp} = -\frac{10}{-200/100} = -\frac{10}{-2}$$
$$= 5$$

Therefore, the change in price coincident with a change in interest rates indicates that this bond has an empirical duration (D_{emp}) of 5. This is a direct measure of the bond's interest rate sensitivity. Notably, thinking of duration in this way, it is not appropriate to describe it as a measure of time (i.e., in years). As noted, it is a measure of interest rate sensitivity and you should think of it as *the approximate percentage change in price for a 100-basis-point change in interest rates.*

While this simple example indicates the concept of empirical duration, the technique that is generally suggested for estimating empirical duration is to employ the following regression model:

$$\frac{\Delta P}{P} = \alpha + D^{**}\Delta Y + u$$

where:

$$\frac{\Delta P}{P} = \textbf{percentage change in price}$$
$$\alpha = \textbf{constant term}$$
$$D^{**} = \textbf{an estimate of } D_{emp} \textbf{ (empirical duration)}$$
$$\Delta Y = \textbf{change in yield in basis points}$$
$$u = \textbf{random error term}$$

The time interval for the data and the time period considered can vary based upon the asset and purpose of the analysis. When working with bonds some analysts employ daily data for short time periods (months), while investigators using the concept for stocks or real estate (to be discussed) have employed weekly and monthly data for longer time periods (quarters or years).

EMPIRICAL DURATION FOR COMMON STOCK If one considers the Macaulay duration of common stock, it is possible to envision a fairly high number because you are dealing with a perpetuity, and some growth stocks pay low dividends for many years. The values derived by Reilly and Sidhu, using various assumptions of price and growth, ranged from 10 years to 20 years.[35] In contrast, using empirical duration one gets very different results.

Because we are dealing with the interest rate sensitivity of an asset, it is possible to compute an empirical duration for common stock that is much lower than what is implied by Macaulay duration and it is more variable. Observing a change in interest rates and the accompanying percentage change in stock prices would indicate the interest rate sensitivity of stocks. Leibowitz conducted such an analysis and derived a rolling, 1-year effective duration for the S&P 500 that ranged *from about zero to almost seven.*[36] When measuring the interest rate sensitivity of common stocks over time, you would expect changes because the correlation between stock and bond returns varies substantially over time.[37] In addition you might anticipate significant differences in the effective duration for alternative stocks. For example, you would expect a large difference in the interest rate sensitivity (empirical duration) of a banking or utility stock (which is very interest rate sensitive) compared to the empirical duration of a small cap or technology stock where its value is based more on changes in its specific growth expectations than interest rates.

YIELD SPREADS WITH EMBEDDED OPTIONS

Earlier in the chapter we discussed the analysis of yield spread as a technique to enhance bond investments or bond trades. At this point, it is necessary to revisit the concept of yield spreads, keeping in mind the term structure of interest rates, but more important, with an awareness of the significant impact that interest rate volatility has on the value of embedded options in bonds. In this revisitation, we will consider two spreads: (1) **static yield**

[35]Frank K. Reilly and Rupinder Sidhu, "The Many Uses of Bond Duration," *Financial Analysts Journal* 36, no. 4 (July–August 1980): 58–72.

[36]Martin L. Leibowitz, *New Perspectives on Asset Allocation* (Charlottesville, Va.: The Research Foundation of the Institute of Chartered Financial Analysts, 1987).

[37]For a specific analysis of the intertemporal correlation between stock returns and Treasury bond returns (which implies the relationship with interest rates), see Frank K. Reilly, David J. Wright, and Kam C. Chan, "An Analysis of Changes in Bond Market Volatility" (University of Notre Dame Working Paper, February, 1999).

spreads that consider the total term structure, and (2) **option-adjusted spreads** that consider changes in the term structure and alternative estimates of the volatility of interest rates.

STATIC YIELD SPREADS

You will recall that the traditional yield spread compares the yields between two bonds with similar coupons and equal maturities as follows:

8%—20-Year AA Corporate Bond	8.20%
8%—20-Year Treasury Bond	7.10%
Yield Spread	1.10%
	110 b.p.

There are three problems with this "traditional" yield spread:

- The two yields do not consider the prevailing term structures of interest rates, but only consider the yield spread at the one-point on the curve (at 20 years).
- The analysis does not consider the fact that the corporate bond could have an embedded option (put or call), whereby expected interest rate volatility may alter the cash flow for this bond.
- While not true in this example, it is possible that investors would compare two bonds with equal maturities but different coupon cash flow (e.g., a zero-coupon bond versus a coupon bond).

The first concern (neglect of the term structure) suggests the consideration of the *static spread.* It is contended that the proper way to compare non-Treasury bonds of the same maturity but with different coupon rates is to compare them to a portfolio of Treasury securities that have the same cash flow. The way to do this, if there is not an existing Treasury bond with the specified flows, is to discount the corporate bond's cash flow as if the flows were risk free. Specifically, discount them using the prevailing Treasury spot rates for the life of the corporate bond. Consider the following example:

Corporate Bond—8%, five-year bond

If we discount this bond's flows using the hypothetical Treasury spot rate curve contained in Table 16.15, the price would be \$1040.56, which is what this bond would sell at if it were a Treasury bond. In fact, the bond is priced at \$1006.70. The *static spread* is the spread that will make the present value of the cash flows from the corporate bond when discounted at the Treasury spot rate plus the spread, equal to the corporate bond's market price. To put it another way, how much of a static spread across all points on the Treasury spot rate curve is required to generate the current market price for this bond? Adding 70 basis points to every spot rate generates a price above \$1006.70 which indicates that we need to consider a larger spread. As shown in Table 16.16, using a spread of 80 basis points generates a price of \$1006.70, which equals the current price of the corporate bond, which indicates that there is a static spread for the bond of 80 basis points or 0.80 percent.

OPTION-ADJUSTED SPREAD

As noted, the traditional spread was a problem because it did not consider the full-term structure or the impact of interest rate volatility. The term structure problem was addressed by estimating the static spread.

The interest rate volatility factor is considered by the option-adjusted spread (OAS) analysis. Why is interest rate volatility a problem? The point is, as discussed earlier in the chapter, if a bond has an embedded call option, this option can affect the bond's expected cash flow. The likelihood of the call being exercised will depend on future interest rates, the remaining maturity of the bond, the call price, and other costs of a call and new issue.

TABLE 16.15

CALCULATION OF THE PRICE OF A 5-YEAR, 8 PERCENT COUPON BOND USING TREASURY SPOT RATES

Period	Cash Flow	Treasury Spot Rate	Present Value
1	$ 40	6.20	$ 38.80
2	40	6.30	37.60
3	40	6.40	36.40
4	40	6.50	35.20
5	40	6.60	34.00
6	40	6.70	32.84
7	40	6.80	31.64
8	40	6.90	30.48
9	40	7.00	29.36
10	1040	7.10	734.24
		Theoretical Price	$1040.56

TABLE 16.16

CALCULATION OF THE STATIC SPREAD FOR A 5-YEAR, 8 PERCENT COUPON CORPORATE BOND

Period	Cash Flow	Treasury Spot Rate	80 b.p. Spread Spot Rate	Present Value
1	$ 40	6.20	7.00	$ 38.64
2	40	6.30	7.10	37.30
3	40	6.40	7.20	35.98
4	40	6.50	7.30	34.66
5	40	6.60	7.40	33.36
6	40	6.70	7.50	32.07
7	40	6.80	7.60	30.81
8	40	6.90	7.70	29.57
9	40	7.00	7.80	28.35
10	1040	7.10	7.90	705.95
			Present Value	$1006.70

The goal of the OAS is similar to the static spread except that the technique allows for a *change in the term structure* over time based on some estimates of interest rate volatility.

The concept of OAS is best understood by a presentation of the steps involved in estimating the OAS for a specific bond as follows:

1. Based upon the prevailing Treasury yield curve, estimate the term structure of interest rates (i.e., the prevailing Treasury spot rate curve) and the implied short-term forward rates derived from the spot rates.
2. Select a probability distribution for short-term Treasury spot rates. This should be based on the current term structure and the historical behavior of interest rates. The significant estimate is the volatility of interest rates—that is, how much will the forward rates change each period?
3. Using the probability distribution and Monte Carlo simulation, it is possible to randomly generate a large number of interest rate paths (e.g., 1,000).
4. For bonds with embedded options (such as callable bonds), develop rules for determining when the option will be exercised. For example, given the coupon, maturity, and call option, at what interest rate will the issue be called?
5. For each path generated in step 3, determine the cash flows from the bond, given (a) the information about the bond (i.e., its call provision) and (b) the rules established in step 4 for calling the bond.

6. For an assumed spread relative to the Treasury term structure of spot rates along a path, calculate a present value for all paths created in step 3.
7. Calculate the *average* present value for all paths.
8. Compare the average present value calculated in step 7 to the market price of the bond. If they are equal, the assumed spread used in step 6 is the option-adjusted spread. If they are not, try another spread and repeat steps 6, 7, and 8.

The computed option-adjusted spread is the average spread over the Treasury spot rate curve based on the potential paths that can be realized in the future for interest rates. The reason it is referred to as "option adjusted" is because the potential paths of cash flow are adjusted to reflect the effect of the options embedded in the bonds.

The following are some technical issues that an analyst should be aware of when attempting to estimate the OAS and also factors that can cause differences in an estimate of the OAS for a bond by alternative dealers.

- It is necessary to have a large number of paths for the simulation.
- The estimate of the probability distribution which includes the volatility is crucial. Notably, if alternative firms differ in this estimate of expected interest rate volatility, it can cause differences in the OAS estimate.
- It is necessary to determine the relationship between short-term rates and refinancing rates. Specifically, how much more does the firm have to pay above the short-term forward rate (i.e., the refinancing rate is a long-term rate)? Empirically, what is this relationship?
- A call rule must be specified. This depends upon the coupon rate for the bond and other costs. It has been assumed to be almost 300 bp below the coupon rate (e.g., 5.8 percent with at least 3 years to maturity).

As noted, different assumptions regarding these technical issues can cause different estimates of the OAS by alternative dealers. The critical estimate is the expected interest rate volatility and this can vary between dealers, and also individual dealers can change their estimates over time.

THE INTERNET *Investments Online*

Bond valuation focuses on bond mathematics, the term structure, and bond features that add to the yield (such as callability) or lead to lower yields (such as putability). Bonds are normally easier to evaluate than stocks, given their stated life, cash flows, and discount rates that can be read from the term structure. Nonetheless, bond pricing can become quite complicated if the bond has complex options or attributes. It is not surprising that bond-market commentary typically focuses on interest rate trends and factors that can affect credit quality.

www.bondcalc.com This site discusses a software pricing system for fixed-income securities. It includes a description of basic and sophisticated bond analyses.

www.bondtrac.com This site offers much bond data to subscribers. It has links to various bond market pages, including municipal, corporate, and agency sites.

www.moneyline.com The Moneyline Web site features bond prices, analysis, and market commentaries for the investor. It covers a number of bond sectors, including Treasury bonds, notes, and bills; agencies; money markets; corporate bonds; emerging market debt; and mortgage-backed securities.

www.bondsonline.com This site provides current yield-curve information on Treasuries and yield spread for corporate bonds. It also covers pricing quotation of individual bonds.

Summary

- The value of a bond equals the present value of all future cash flows accruing to the investor. Cash flows for the conservative bond investor include periodic interest payments and principal return; cash flows for the aggressive investor include periodic interest payments and the capital gain or loss when the bond is sold prior to its maturity. Bond investors can maximize their yields by accurately estimating the level of interest rates, and more importantly, by estimating changes in interest rates, yield spreads, and credit quality. Similarly, they must compare coupon rates, maturities, and call features of alternative bonds.
- There are five bond yield measures: nominal yield, current yield, promised yield to maturity, promised yield to call, and realized (horizon) yield. The promised YTM and promised YTC equations include the interest-on-interest (or coupon reinvestment) assumption. For the realized (horizon) yield computation, the investor estimates the reinvestment rate and the future selling price for the bond. The fundamental determinants of interest rates are a real risk-free rate, the expected rate of inflation, and a risk premium.
- The yield curve (or the term structure of interest rates) shows the relationship between the yields on a set of comparable bonds and the term to maturity. Based upon this yield curve it is possible to derive a theoretical spot rate curve. In turn, these spot rates can be used to value bonds using an individual spot rate for each cash flow. This valuation approach is becoming more useful in a world where bonds have very different cash flows. In addition, these spot rates imply investor expectations about future rates referred to as forward rates. Yield curves exhibit four basic patterns. Three theories attempt to explain the shape of the yield curve: the expectations hypothesis, the liquidity preference hypothesis, and the segmented market hypothesis.
- It is important to understand what causes changes in interest rates and how these changes in rates affect the prices of bonds. Differences in bond price volatility are mainly a function of differences in yield, coupon, and term to maturity. There are four duration measures that have been used as measures of bond price volatility or interest rate sensitivity. The Macaulay duration measure incorporates coupon, maturity, and yield in one measure. In turn, modified duration (which is directly related to Macaulay duration) provides an estimate of the response of bond prices to changes in interest rates under certain assumptions. Because modified duration provides a straight-line estimate of the curvilinear price–yield function, you must consider modified duration together with the convexity of a bond for large changes in yields and/or when dealing with securities that have high convexity. Notably, an embedded call option feature on a bond can have a significant impact on its duration (the call feature can shorten it dramatically) and on its convexity (the call feature can change the convexity from a positive value to a negative value). Following a discussion of some of the limitations of Macaulay and modified durations as measures of interest rate sensitivity, effective duration is introduced as a direct measure of interest rate sensitivity—i.e., it is the estimated percentage change in price for a 100-basis-point change in interest rates and allows for changes in cash flow due to changes in interest rates. Notably, with effective duration, it is possible to have durations longer than maturity as well as negative duration.
- Finally, there are instances when it is very difficult to estimate the price effect of a change in interest rates as required for effective duration—such as with some mortgage-backed securities, common stock, and real estate. In these instances analysts consider estimating empirical duration, which is based on the analysis of historical data on price changes that accompany interest rate changes. While it is possible to derive such estimates for a range of assets, it is important to remember that the values derived can vary dramatically and are notoriously unstable.
- We concluded the chapter with a revisitation to yield spreads for bonds with embedded options. To take account of the spread across the total term structure of interest rates we described and demonstrated the static spread. In order to consider the impact of interest rate volatility on the embedded options, we discussed and described the steps to estimate the option-adjusted spread (OAS) for these bonds.

Given the background in bond valuation and the factors that influence bond value and bond return volatility, we are ready to consider how to build a bond portfolio that is consistent with our goals and objectives. Bond portfolio analysis is the topic for Chapter 17.

Questions

1. Why does the present value equation appear to be more useful for the bond investor than for the common stock investor?
2. What are the important assumptions made when you calculate the promised yield to maturity? What are the assumptions when calculating promised YTC?
3. a. Define the variables included in the following model:

$$i = (\text{RFR}, I, \text{RP})$$

   b. Assume that the firm whose bonds you are considering is not expected to break even this year. Discuss which factor will be affected by this information.
4. We discussed three alternative hypotheses to explain the term structure of interest rates. Briefly discuss the three hypotheses and indicate which one you think best explains the alternative shapes of a yield curve.

CFA ©

5. *CFA Examination I (June 1982)*
   a. Explain what is meant by *structure of interest rates.* Explain the theoretical basis of an upward-sloping yield curve [8 minutes]
   b. Explain the economic circumstances under which you would expect to see the inverted yield curve prevail. [7 minutes]
   c. Define "real" rate of interest. [2 minutes]
   d. Discuss the characteristics of the market for U.S. Treasury securities. Compare it to the market for AAA corporate bonds. Discuss the opportunities that may exist in bond markets that are less than efficient. [8 minutes]
   e. Over the past several years, fairly wide yield spreads between AAA corporates and Treasuries have occasionally prevailed. Discuss the possible reasons for this. [5 minutes]

CFA ©

6. *CFA Examination III (June 1982)*
   As the portfolio manager for a large pension fund, you are offered the following bonds:

	Coupon	Maturity	Price	Call Price	Yield to Maturity
Edgar Corp. (new issue)	14.00%	2002	$101.3/4	$114	13.75%
Edgar Corp. (new issue)	6.00	2002	48.1/8	103	13.60
Edgar Corp. (1972 issue)	6.00	2002	48.7/8	103	13.40

   Assuming that you expect a decline in interest rates over the next 3 years, identify and justify which of these bonds you would select. [10 minutes]
7. You expect interest rates to decline over the next six months.
   a. Given your interest rate outlook, state what kinds of bonds you want in your portfolio in terms of duration and explain your reasoning for this choice.
   b. You must make a choice between the following three sets of noncallable bonds. In each case, select the bond that would be best for your portfolio given your interest rate outlook and the consequent strategy set forth in part a. In each case briefly discuss why you selected the bond.

		Maturity	Coupon	Yield to Maturity
Case 1:	Bond A	15 years	10%	10%
	Bond B	15 years	6%	8%
Case 2:	Bond C	15 years	6%	10%
	Bond D	10 years	8%	10%
Case 3:	Bond E	12 years	12%	12%
	Bond F	15 years	12%	8%

8. At the present time, you expect a decline in interest rates and must choose between two portfolios of bonds with the following characteristics:

	Portfolio A	Portfolio B
Average maturity	10.5 years	10.0 years
Average YTM	7%	10%
Modified duration	5.7 years	4.9 years
Modified convexity	125.18	40.30
Call features	Noncallable	Deferred call features that range from 1 to 3 years

Select one of the portfolios and discuss three factors that would justify your selection.

9. The Chartered Finance Corporation has issued a bond with the following characteristics:

Maturity—25 years
Coupon—9%
Yield to maturity—9%
Callable—after 3 years @ 109
Duration to maturity—8.2 years
Duration to first call—2.1 years

a. Discuss the concept of call-adjusted duration and indicate the approximate value (range) for it at the present time.
b. Assuming interest rates increase substantially (i.e., to 13 percent), discuss what will happen to the call-adjusted duration and the reason for the change.
c. Assuming interest rates decline substantially (i.e., they decline to 4 percent), discuss what will happen to the bond's call-adjusted duration and the reason for the change.
d. Discuss the concept of negative convexity as it relates to this bond.

10. *CFA Examination I (1990)*
Duration may be calculated by *two* widely used methods. Identify these *two* methods, and briefly discuss the primary differences between them. [5 minutes]

11. *CFA Examination II (1995)*
Option-adjusted duration and *effective duration* are alternative measures used by analysts to evaluate fixed-income securities with embedded options.
Briefly describe *each* measure and how to apply *each* to the evaluation of fixed-income securities with embedded options. [8 minutes]

12. *CFA Examination II (1995)*
As a portfolio manager, during a discussion with a client, you explain that historical return and risk premia of the type presented in the following table are frequently used in forming estimates of future returns for various types of financial assets. Although such historical data are helpful in forecasting returns, most users know that history is an imperfect guide to the future. Thus, they recognize that there are reasons why these data should be adjusted if they are to be employed in the forecasting process.

U.S. HISTORICAL RETURN AND RISK PREMIA (1926–1994)

	Per Year
Inflation rate	3.0%
Real interest rate on Treasury bills	0.5%
Maturity premium of long Treasury bonds over Treasury bills	0.8%
Default premium of long corporate bonds over long Treasury bonds	0.6%
Risk premium on stock over long Treasury bonds	5.6%
Return on Treasury bills	3.5%
Return on long corporate bonds	4.9%
Return on large-capitalization stocks	9.9%

a. As shown in the table, the historical real interest rate for Treasury bills was 0.5 percent per year and the maturity premium on Treasury bonds over Treasury bills was 0.8 percent. Briefly describe and justify *one* adjustment to *each* of these two data items that should be made before they can be used to form expectations about future real interest rates and Treasury bond maturity premia. [6 minutes]

b. You recognize that even adjusted historical economic and capital markets data may be of limited use when estimating future returns. Independent of your part a response, briefly describe *three* key circumstances that should be considered when forming expectations about future returns. [8 minutes]

CFA

13. *CFA Examination I (1992)*

A portfolio manager at Superior Trust Company is structuring a fixed-income portfolio to meet the objectives of a client. This client plans on retiring in 15 years and wants a substantial lump sum at that time. The client has specified the use of AAA-rated securities.

The portfolio manager compares coupon U.S. Treasuries with zero-coupon stripped U.S. Treasuries and observes a significant yield advantage for the stripped bonds.

Maturity	Coupon U.S. Treasuries	Zero-Coupon Stripped U.S. Treasuries
3 year	5.50%	5.80%
5 year	6.00%	6.60%
7 year	6.75%	7.25%
10 year	7.25%	7.60%
15 year	7.40%	8.80%
30 year	7.75%	7.75%

Briefly discuss *two* reasons why zero-coupon stripped U.S. Treasuries could yield more than coupon U.S. Treasuries with the same final maturity. [5 minutes]

CFA

14. *CFA Examination II (1993)*

a. In terms of option theory, explain the impact on the offering yield of adding a call feature to a proposed bond issue. [5 minutes]

b. Explain the impact on *both* bond duration and convexity of adding a call feature to a proposed bond issue. [10 minutes]

Assume that a portfolio of corporate bonds is managed to maintain targets for modified duration and convexity.

c. Explain how the portfolio could include *both* callable and noncallable bonds while maintaining the targets. [5 minutes]

d. Describe *one* advantage and *one* disadvantage of including callable bonds in this portfolio. [5 minutes]

CFA

15. *CFA Examination II (1996)*

The shape of the U.S. Treasury yield curve appears to reflect two expected Federal Reserve reductions in the Federal Funds rate. The first reduction of approximately 50 basis points (BP) is expected 6 months from now, and the second reduction of approximately 50 BP is expected 1 year from now. The current U.S. Treasury term premiums are 10 BP per year for each of the next 3 years (out through the 3-year benchmark.)

You agree that the two Federal Reserve reductions described above will occur. However, you believe that they will be reversed in a single 100 BP increase in the Federal Funds rate 2½ years from now. You expect term premiums to remain 10 BP per year for each of the next 3 years (out through the 3-year benchmark.)

a. Describe *or* Draw the shape of the Treasury yield curve out through the 3-year benchmark. (*Note to Candidates:* Be sure to label your axes and relevant data points carefully.) [4 minutes]

b. State which term structure theory supports the shape of the U.S. Treasury yield curve described in part a. Justify your choice. [6 minutes]

Kent Lewis, an economist, also expects two Federal Reserve reductions in the Federal Funds rate, but believes that the market is too optimistic about how soon they will occur. Lewis believes that the first 50 BP reduction will be made 1 year from now and that the second 50 BP reduction will be made 1½ years from now. He expects these reductions to be reversed by a single 100 BP increase 2½ years from now. He believes that the market will adjust to reflect his beliefs when new economic data are released over the next 2 weeks.

Assume you are convinced by Lewis's argument and are authorized to purchase either the 2-year benchmark U.S. Treasury or a Cash/3-year benchmark U.S. Treasury barbell weighted to have the same duration as the 2-year U.S. Treasury.

c. Select an investment in *either* the 2-year benchmark U.S. Treasury (bullet) *or* the Cash/3-year benchmark U.S. Treasury barbell. Justify your choice. [5 minutes]

16. *CFA Examination II (1997)*

Beth Goetz, CFA, has decided to add some asset-backed securities (ABS) to her fixed-income portfolio. She has narrowed the choice to automobile ABS and fixed-rate home equity loan (second mortgage) ABS.

Automobile ABS are available at a pricing spread of 75 basis points over comparable-maturity Treasuries, with a zero-volatility spread of 67 basis points. Home equity loan ABS are available at a pricing spread of 85 basis points over comparable-maturity Treasuries, with an option-adjusted spread of 60 basis points.

a. Explain why pricing spread is not an appropriate measure of yield advantage for ABS. [3 minutes]
b. Describe the concepts of:
   (i) zero-volatility spread.
   (ii) option-adjusted spread. [8 minutes]
c. Explain why option-adjusted spread is the appropriate measure of yield for a second mortgage ABS. [4 minutes]

17. *CFA Examination II (1998)*

The asset-backed securities (ABS) market has grown in the past few years partly as a result of credit enhancements to ABS.

a. Describe a "letter of credit" and the risk to the investor associated with relying exclusively on this type of credit enhancement. [6 minutes]
b. Describe "early amortization" and the risk to the investor associated with relying exclusively on this type of credit enhancement. [6 minutes]

18. *CFA Examination II (1998)*

Rachel Morgan owns a newly issued U.S. government agency fixed-rate pass-through mortgage-backed security (MBS) and wants to evaluate the sensitivity of its principal cash flow to the following interest rate scenario:

- Interest rates instantaneously decline by 250 basis points for all maturities, remain there for 1 year, and then,
- interest rates instantaneously increase 350 basis points for all maturities and remain there for the next year.

Currently, the MBS is priced close to par and the yield curve is "flat." Morgan does not expect the shape of the yield curve to change during her interest rate scenario.

a. (i) State whether, in the interest rate scenario described above, the MBS principal cash flows:
   - increase or decrease in the first year.
   - increase or decrease in the second year.

   (ii) Discuss the reason why principal cash flows change. [6 minutes]

Morgan also wants to evaluate the price sensitivity of her MBS to changes in interest rates. She knows that modified duration and effective duration are two possible measures she could use to evaluate price sensitivity.

b. Select *and* justify with *one* reason which duration measure Morgan should use to evaluate the price sensitivity of her MBS. [6 minutes]

Morgan also owns a newly issued U.S. government agency collateralized mortgage obligation interest-only (IO) security.

c. State whether the IO security price increases or decreases in the first year of the interest rate scenario described above. Justify your response. [6 minutes]

CFA

19. *CFA Examination III (1996)*

One common goal among fixed-income portfolio managers is to earn high incremental returns on corporate bonds versus government bonds of comparable durations. The approach of some corporate-bond portfolio managers is to find and purchase those corporate bonds having the largest initial spreads over comparable-duration government bonds. John Ames, HFS's fixed-income manager, believes that a more rigorous approach is required if incremental returns are to be maximized.

The table below presents data relating to one set of corporate/government spread relationships present in the market at a given date:

CURRENT AND EXPECTED SPREADS AND DURATIONS OF HIGH-GRADE CORPORATE BONDS (1-YEAR HORIZON)

Bond Rating	Initial Spread over Governments	Expected Horizon Spread	Initial Duration	Expected Duration 1 Year from Now
Aaa	31 BP	31 BP	4 years	3.1 years
Aa	40 BP	50 BP	4 years	3.1 years

a. Recommend purchase of *either* Aaa *or* Aa bonds for a 1-year investment horizon given a goal of maximizing incremental returns. Show your calculations. (Base your decision *only* on the information presented in the table above.) [6 minutes]

Ames chooses not to rely *solely* on initial spread relationships. His analytical framework considers a full range of other key variables likely to impact realized incremental returns, including:

- call provisions, and
- potential changes in interest rates.

b. Describe *two* variables, *in addition to those identified above,* that Ames should include in his analysis *and* explain how *each* of these *two* variables could cause realized incremental returns to differ from those indicated by initial spread relationships. [10 minutes]

CFA

20. *CFA Examination III (1998)*

Charles Investment Management, Inc., a fixed-income manager of U.S.-only portfolios, has provided significant excess returns for its clients through duration and sector management. The firm defines sectors as either government bonds or corporate bonds. Several of the manager's clients have asked the firm about the possibility of investing in international fixed-income markets. These clients mention the favorable performance of these markets, as exemplified by the "international fixed-income aggregate index" in the accompanying table. The clients are asking Charles to transfer the same management techniques that it has successfully applied in the U.S. market to international fixed-income markets.

ANNUALIZED RATES OF RETURN

Bond Index	1 Year	5 Year
International fixed-income aggregate index, unhedged	1.0%	15.9%
International fixed-income aggregate index, hedged	6.5	7.2

a. Infer from the table the effect of changes in the U.S. dollar on international fixed-income returns for U.S. investors in the past 1-year *and* 5-year periods. [6 minutes]

b. Explain why the firm's techniques to generate excess returns through duration *and* sector management in U.S. fixed-income markets may not be transferrable to international fixed-income markets. [6 minutes]

CFA

21. *CFA Examination II (1999)*

On May 30, 1999, Janice Kerr is considering purchasing one of the following newly issued 10-year AAA corporate bonds shown in the following exhibit. Kerr notes that the yield curve is currently flat and assumes that the yield curve shifts in an instantaneous and parallel manner.

BOND CHARACTERISTICS

Description	Coupon	Price	Callable	Call Price
Sentinel due May 30, 2009	6.00%	100.00	Noncallable	Not applicable
Colina due May 30, 2009	6.20%	100.00	Currently callable	102.00

a. Contrast the effect on the price of *both* bonds if yields decline more than 100 basis points. (No calculation is required). [6 minutes]

b. State and explain under which *two* interest rate forecasts Kerr would prefer the Colina bond over the Sentinel bond. [6 minutes]

c. State the directional price change, if any, assuming interest rate volatility increases, of *each* of the following: [6 minutes]

(i) the Sentinel bond

(ii) the Colina bond

Problems

1. Four years ago, your firm issued $1,000 par, 25-year bonds, with a 7 percent coupon rate and a 10 percent call premium.

   a. If these bonds are now called, what is the *approximate* yield to call for the investors who originally purchased them?

   b. If these bonds are now called, what is the *actual* yield to call for the investors who originally purchased them at par?

   c. If the current interest rate is 5 percent and the bonds were not callable, at what price would each bond sell?

2. Assume that you purchased an 8 percent, 20-year, $1,000 par, semiannual payment bond priced at $1,012.50 when it has 12 years remaining until maturity. Compute:

   a. Its approximate yield to maturity

   b. Its actual yield to maturity

   c. Its yield to call if the bond is callable in 3 years with an 8 percent premium.

3. Calculate the duration of an 8 percent, $1,000 par bond that matures in 3 years if the bond's YTM is 10 percent and interest is paid semiannually.

   a. Calculate this bond's modified duration.

   b. Assuming the bond's YTM goes from 10 percent to 9.5 percent, calculate an estimate of the price change.

4. Two years ago, you acquired a 10-year zero-coupon, $1,000 par value bond at a 12 percent YTM. Recently you sold this bond at an 8 percent YTM. Using semiannual compounding, compute the annualized horizon return for this investment.

5. A bond for the Webster Corporation has the following characteristics:

Maturity—12 years
Coupon—10%
Yield to maturity—9.50%
Macaulay duration—5.7 years
Convexity—48
Noncallable

a. Calculate the approximate price change for this bond using only its duration assuming its yield to maturity increased by 150 basis points. Discuss the impact of the calculation, including the convexity effect.

b. Calculate the approximate price change for this bond (using only its duration) if its yield to maturity declined by 300 basis points. Discuss (without calculations) what would happen to your estimate of the price change if this was a callable bond.

6. *CFA Examination I (1992)*

The table below shows selected data on a German government bond (payable in Deutschemarks) and a U.S. government bond. Identify the components of return and calculate the total return in U.S. dollars for both of these bonds for the year 1991. Show the calculations for *each* component. (Ignore interest on interest in view of the short time period.) [8 minutes]

		Market Yield			**Exchange Rate (DM/$U.S.)**	
	Coupon	**1/1/91**	**1/1/92**	**Modified duration**	**1/1/91**	**1/1/92**
German Government Bond	8.50%	8.50%	8.00%	7.0	1.55	1.50
U.S. Government Bond	8.00%	8.00%	6.75%	6.5	—	—

7. *CFA Examination I (1993)*

Philip Morris has issued bonds that pay semiannually with the following characteristics:

Coupon	Yield-to-Maturity	Maturity	Macaulay Duration
8%	8%	15 years	10 years

a. Calculate modified duration using the information above. [5 minutes]

b. Explain why modified duration is a better measure than maturity when calculating the bond's sensitivity to changes in interest rates. [5 minutes]

c. Identify the direction of change in modified duration if:

(i) the coupon of the bond were 4 percent, not 8 percent

(ii) the maturity of the bond were 7 years, not 15 years [5 minutes]

d. Define convexity and explain how modified duration *and* convexity are used to approximate the bond's percentage change in price, given a change in interest rates. [5 minutes]

8. *CFA Examination I (1993)*

You are a U.S. investor considering purchase of one of the following securities. Assume that the currency risk of the German government bond will be hedged, and the 6-month discount on Deutschemark forward contracts is −0.75 percent versus the U.S. dollar.

Bond	Maturity	Coupon	Price
U.S. government	June 1, 2003	6.50%	100.00
German government	June 1, 2003	7.50%	100.00

Calculate the expected price change required in the German government bond that would result in the two bonds having equal total returns in U.S. dollars over a 6-month horizon. [8 minutes]

CFA 9. *CFA Examination II (1990)*
The following are the average yields on U.S. Treasury bonds at two different points in time:

	Yield-to-Maturity	
Term to Maturity	**January 15, 19XX**	**May 15, 19XX**
1 year	7.25%	8.05%
2 years	7.50%	7.90%
5 years	7.90%	7.70%
10 years	8.30%	7.45%
15 years	8.45%	7.30%
20 years	8.55%	7.20%
25 years	8.60%	7.10%

a. Assuming a pure expectations hypothesis, define a forward rate. Describe how you would calculate the forward rate for a 3-year U.S. Treasury bond 2 years from May 15, 19XX, using the actual term structure above. [3 minutes]
b. Discuss how *each* of the *three* major term structure hypotheses could explain the January 15, 19XX, term structures shown above. [6 minutes]
c. Discuss what happened to the term structure over the time period and the effect of this change on U.S. Treasury bonds of 2 years *and* 10 years. [5 minutes]
d. Assume that you invest solely on the basis of yield spreads, and in January 19XX acted upon the expectation that the yield spread between 1-year and 25-year U.S. Treasuries would return to a more typical spread of 170 basis points. Explain what you would have done on January 15, 19XX, and describe the result of this action based upon what happened between January 15, 19XX, and May 15, 19XX. [7 minutes]

CFA 10. *CFA Examination II (1992)*
a. Using the information in the table below, calculate the projected price change for Bond B if the yield-to-maturity for this bond falls by 75 basis points. [7 minutes]
b. Describe the shortcoming of analyzing Bond A strictly to call or to maturity. Explain an approach to remedy this shortcoming. [6 minutes]

MONTICELLO CORPORATION BOND INFORMATION

	Bond A (Callable)	Bond B (Noncallable)
Maturity	2002	2002
Coupon	11.50%	7.25%
Current price	125.75	100.00
Yield-to-maturity	7.70%	7.25%
Modified duration to maturity	6.20	6.80
Convexity to maturity	0.50	0.60
Call date	1996	—
Call price	105	—
Yield to call	5.10%	—
Modified duration to call	3.10	—
Convexity to call	0.10	—

CFA 11. *CFA Examination II (1992)*
U.S. Treasuries represent a significant holding in Monticello's pension portfolio. You decide to analyze the yield curve for U.S. Treasury Notes.

a. Using the data in the table below, calculate the 5-year spot and forward rates assuming annual compounding. Show calculations. [8 minutes]

U.S. TREASURY NOTE YIELD CURVE DATA

Years to Maturity	Par Coupon Yield-to-Maturity	Calculated Spot Rates	Calculated Forward Rates
1	5.00	5.00	5.00
2	5.20	5.21	5.42
3	6.00	6.05	7.75
4	7.00	7.16	10.56
5	7.00	□	□

b. Define and describe *each* of the following *three* concepts:
- Yield-to-maturity
- Spot rate
- Forward rate

Explain how these *three* concepts are related. [9 minutes]

You are considering the purchase of a zero-coupon U.S. Treasury Note with 4 years to maturity.

c. Based on the above yield curve analysis, calculate *both* the expected yield-to-maturity and the price for the security. Show calculations. [8 minutes]

12. *CFA Examination III (1992)*

Emily Maguire, manager of the actively managed non-government bond portion of PTC's pension portfolio, has received a fact sheet containing data on a new security offering. It will be a bond issued by a U.S. corporation but denominated in Australian dollars (A$), with both principal and interest payable in that currency.

The terms of the offering made in June 1992 are as follows:
- Issuer—Student Loan Marketing Association (SLMA—a U.S. government sponsored corporation)
- Rating—AAA
- Coupon Rate—8.5 percent payable quarterly
- Price—Par
- Maturity—June 30, 1997 (noncallable)
- Principal and interest payable in Australian dollars (A$)

As an alternative, Maguire finds that 5-year U.S. dollar-pay notes issued by SLMA yield 6.75 percent.

She prepares an analysis directed at several specific questions, beginning with the following table of economic data for Australia and the United States.

	UNITED STATES			AUSTRALIA		
Major Economic Indicators	**1990**	**1991**	**1992E**	**1990**	**1991**	**1992E**
Real GNP (annual change)	1.1%	−0.5%	2.2%	1.6%	−0.5%	3.0%
Consumer expenditures (annual change)	0.9%	0.0%	1.0%	1.1%	−0.2%	2.0%
Inflation (annual change)	5.4%	4.2%	3.4%	7.3%	3.2%	3.9%
Long-bond yield (end-of-year)	8.1%	7.2%	7.0%	9.8%	10.0%	10.2%
Trade balance (U.S. $ billions)	−100	−83	−80	−30	−20	−25

Assuming that interest rates fall 100 basis points in both the U.S. and Australian markets over the next year, identify which of these two bonds will increase the most in value, and justify your answer. [7 minutes]

CFA

13. *CFA Examination II (1993)*
The following table shows yields to maturity on U.S Treasury securities as of January 1, 1993:

Term to Maturity	Yield to Maturity
1 year	3.50%
2 years	4.50%
3 years	5.00%
4 years	5.50%
5 years	6.00%
10 years	6.60%

a. Based on the data in the table, calculate the implied forward 1-year rate of interest at January 1, 1996. [5 minutes]
b. Describe the conditions under which the calculated forward rate would be an unbiased estimate of the 1-year spot rate of interest at January 1, 1996. [5 minutes]

Assume that 1 year earlier, at January 1, 1992, the prevailing term structure for U.S. Treasury securities was such that the implied forward 1-year rate of interest at January 1, 1996, was significantly higher than the corresponding rate implied by the term structure at January 1, 1993.

c. On the basis of the pure expectations theory of the term structure, briefly discuss two factors that could account for such a decline in the implied forward rate. [8 minutes]

Multiple scenario forecasting frequently makes use of information from the term structure of interest rates.

d. Briefly describe how the information conveyed by this observed decrease in the implied forward rate for 1996 could be used in making a multiple scenario forecast. [5 minutes]

CFA

14. *CFA Examination III (1993)*
TMP is working with the officer responsible for the defined-benefit pension plan of a U.S. company. She has come to the firm for advice on what she calls "the key elements of non-U.S. dollar fixed-income investing."

The following information, based on TMP's assessment of the Italian market, has been developed to illustrate the process by which market and currency expectations are integrated.

ITALIAN GOVERNMENT SECURITIES DATA

Security	Modified Duration	Current Price	Current Yield to Maturity	Expected Yield to Maturity in 3 Months
Bill	0.25	100.00	12.50%	12.50%
Note	6.00	100.00	10.00%	9.00%

LIRA/$(US) EXCHANGE RATE

Current Rate	Expected Rate in 3 Months
L1500/$1.00 (US)	L1526/$1.00 (US)

Based on the information provided above, calculate the expected return (in U.S. dollars) on *each* security over the 3-month period. [9 minutes]

CFA

15. *CFA Examination I (1994)*
Bonds of Zello Corporation with a par value of $1,000 sell for $960, mature in 5 years, and have a 7 percent annual coupon rate paid semiannually.
   a. Calculate the:
      (i) current yield;
      (ii) yield-to-maturity (to the nearest whole percent, i.e. 3 percent, 4 percent, 5 percent, etc.); *and*
      (iii) horizon yield (also called total return) for an investor with a 3-year holding period and a reinvestment rate of 6 percent over the period. At the end of 3 years, the 7 percent coupon bonds with 2 years remaining will sell to yield 7 percent.
   Show your work. [9 minutes]
   b. Cite *one* major shortcoming for *each* of the following fixed-income yield measures:
      (i) current yield;
      (ii) yield to maturity; *and*
      (iii) horizon yield (also called total return). [6 minutes]

CFA

16. *CFA Examination I (1994)*
During 1990, Disney issued $2.3 billion face value of zero-coupon subordinated notes that resulted in gross proceeds of $965 million. The notes:
   - mature in 2005;
   - can be exchanged for cash by the note holder at any time for the U.S. dollar equivalent of the current market value of 19.651 common shares of Euro Disney per $1,000 face value of notes; and
   - are callable at any time at their issuance price plus accrued interest.

On March 11, 1993, Disney called the notes at a price of $483.50, which is equivalent to a yield to maturity of 6%. On the call date, Euro Disney common stock traded at a price of 86.80 French francs per share and the currency exchange rate for U.S. dollars ($US) to French francs (Ffr) was:

	$US/Ffr	Ffr/$US
Exchange rate:	.1761	5.6786

   a. Calculate, as of the call date:
      (i) the price of a share of Euro Disney expressed in U.S. dollars; *and*
      (ii) the exchange value (conversion value) of a $1,000 face value note in U.S. dollars. [6 minutes]
   b. On July 21, 1993, Disney issued, at par, $300 million of 100-year bonds with a coupon rate of 7.55 percent. The bonds are callable in 30 years at 103.02. From Disney's point of view, state *three* disadvantages of calling the zero-coupon notes and effectively replacing part of that debt capital with the issue of 100-year bonds. [8 minutes]

CFA

17. *CFA Examination II (1994)*
Table 1 below shows the characteristics of two annual pay bonds from the same issuer with the same priority in the event of default, and Table 2 below displays spot interest rates. Neither bond's price is consistent with the spot rates.

Using the information in Tables 1 and 2, recommend *either* Bond A *or* Bond B for purchase. Justify your choice. [10 minutes]

TABLE 1 BOND CHARACTERISTICS

	Bond A	Bond B
Coupons	Annual	Annual
Maturity	3 years	3 years
Coupon Rate	10%	6%
Yield-to-maturity	10.65%	10.75%
Price	98.40	88.34

TABLE 2 SPOT INTEREST RATES

Term	Spot Rates (Zero Coupon)
1 year	5%
2 year	8%
3 year	11%

18. *CFA Examination II (1996)*
You ran a regression of the yield of KC Company's 10-year bond on the 10-year U.S. Treasury benchmark's yield using month-end data for the past year. You found the following result:

$$\text{Yield}_{KC} = 0.54 + 1.22\ \text{Yield}_{\text{Treasury}}$$

where Yield_{KC} is the yield on the KC bond and $\text{Yield}_{\text{Treasury}}$ is the yield on the U.S. Treasury bond.
The modified duration on the 10-year U.S. Treasury is 7.0 years, and modified duration on the KC bond is 6.93 years.
a. Calculate the percentage change in the price of the 10-year U.S. Treasury, assuming a 50 basis-point change in the yield on the 10-year U.S. Treasury. [3 minutes]
b. Calculate the percentage change in the price of the KC bond, using the regression equation above, assuming a 50 basis-point change in the yield on the 10-year U.S. Treasury. [6 minutes]

19. *CFA Examination II (1997)*
Table 1 shows prices as a function of yields for four tranches of a collateralized mortgage obligation (CMO).

TABLE 1 PRICES FOR FOUR CMO TRANCHES AT SELECTED YIELDS

	YIELD (%)				
CMO Tranche	6.0	6.5	7.0	7.5	8.0
T-1	111.5	105.5	100.0	95.0	90.5
T-2	107.5	104.0	100.0	95.5	90.5
T-3	112.0	105.5	100.0	95.5	92.0
T-4	104.5	102.0	100.0	98.5	97.5

a. Calculate the effective duration of Tranche T-3. Assume that the relevant current yield is 7.0 percent. Show your work. [5 minutes]
b. Identify the tranche with the negative convexity. Calculate the effective convexity of this tranche. Show your work. [5 minutes]

Table 2 shows the option-adjusted spread for four different mortgage pass-through securities.

TABLE 2 MORTGAGE PASS-THROUGH OPTION-ADJUSTED SPREADS (ASSUMING INTEREST RATE VOLATILITY OF 8 PERCENT)

Security	Option-Adjusted Spread (In Basis Points)
A	43
B	70
C	89
D	99

c. Identify which of the patterns of option-adjusted spreads shown in Table 3 is plausible if the assumed interest rate volatility is 12 percent rather than the 8 percent assumed in Table 2. Justify your choice. [5 minutes]

TABLE 3 MORTGAGE PASS-THROUGH OPTION-ADJUSTED SPREADS (ASSUMING INTEREST RATE VOLATILITY OF 12 PERCENT)

	Option-Adjusted Spread (In Basis Points)	
Security	Pattern A	Pattern B
A	−13	103
B	20	120
C	49	129
D	69	129

CFA

20. *CFA Examination II (1998)*
Patrick Wall is considering the purchase of one of the two bonds described in the following table. Wall realizes his decision will depend primarily on effective duration, and he believes that interest rates will decline by 50 basis points at all maturities over the next 6 months.

BOND DESCRIPTIONS

Characteristic	CIC	PTR
Market price	101.75	101.75
Maturity date	June 1, 2008	June 1, 2008
Call date	Noncallable	June 1, 2003
Annual coupon	6.25%	7.35%
Interest payment	Semiannual	Semiannual
Effective duration	7.35	5.40
Yield to maturity	6.02%	7.10%
Credit rating	A	A

a. Calculate the percentage price change forecasted by effective duration for *both* the CIC and PTR bonds if interest rates decline by 50 basis points over the next 6 months. Show your work. [6 minutes]

b. Calculate the 6-month horizon return (in percent) for *each* bond, if the actual CIC bond price equals 105.55 and the actual PTR bond price equals 104.15 at the end of 6 months. Assume you purchased the bonds to settle on June 1, 1998. Show your work. [6 minutes]

Wall is surprised by the fact that although interest rates fell by 50 basis points, the actual price change for the CIC bond was greater than the price change forecasted by effective duration, whereas the actual price change for the PTR bond was less than the price change forecasted by effective duration.

c. Explain why the actual price change would be greater for the CIC bond and the actual price change would be less for the PTR bond. [6 minutes]

CFA

21. *CFA Examination II (1999)*

a. Discuss how *each* of the following theories for the term structure of interest rates could explain an upward slope of the yield curve:
   (i) Pure Expectations (Unbiased)
   (ii) Uncertainty and Term Premiums (Liquidity Preference)
   (iii) Market Segmentation [9 minutes]

The following are the current coupon yields to maturity and spot rates of interest for six U.S. Treasury securities. Assume all securities pay interest annually.

YIELDS TO MATURITY AND SPOT RATES OF INTEREST

Term to Maturity	Current Coupon Yield to Maturity	Spot Rate of Interest
1-Year Treasury	5.25%	5.25%
2-Year Treasury	5.75	5.79
3-Year Treasury	6.15	6.19
5-Year Treasury	6.45	6.51
10-Year Treasury	6.95	7.10
30-Year Treasury	7.25	7.67

b. Compute, under the Pure Expectations theory, the 2-year implied forward rate 3 years from now, given the information provided in preceding table. State the assumption underlying the calculation of the implied forward rate. [6 minutes]

References

Fabozzi, Frank J. *Fixed Income Mathematics.* Chicago: Probus Publishing, 1988.

Fabozzi, Frank J. *Bond Markets, Analysis and Strategies.* 3d ed. Upper Saddle River, N.J.: Prentice-Hall, 1996.

Fama, Eugene F. "Forward Rates as Predictors of Future Spot Rates." *Journal of Financial Economics* 3, no. 4 (October 1976).

Sundaresan, Suresh. *Fixed Income Markets and Their Derivatives.* Cincinnati, Ohio: South-Western College Publishing, 1997.

Tuckman, Bruce. *Fixed Income Securities.* New York: John Wiley & Sons, 1995.

Van Horne, James C. *Financial Market Rates and Flows.* 5th ed. Englewood Cliffs, N.J.: Prentice-Hall, 1998.

Chapter 16 APPENDIX

TABLE 16A.1 **CALCULATION OF DURATION AND CONVEXITY FOR AN 8 PERCENT 5-YEAR BOND SELLING TO YIELD 6 PERCENT**

Period	Cash Flow	Discount Factor	PV	PV × t	PV × t × (t + 1)
1	40.00	0.9709	38.83	38.83	77.67
2	40.00	0.9426	37.70	75.41	226.22
3	40.00	0.9151	36.61	109.82	439.27
4	40.00	0.8885	35.54	142.16	710.79
5	40.00	0.8626	34.50	172.52	1,035.13
6	40.00	0.8375	33.50	201.00	1,406.97
7	40.00	0.8131	32.52	227.67	1,821.32
8	40.00	0.7894	31.58	252.61	2,273.50
9	40.00	0.7664	30.66	275.91	2,759.10
10	1,040.00	0.7441	773.86	7,738.58	85,124.34
		Total	1,085.30	9,234.50	95,874.32

$$\text{Macaulay Duration} = \frac{9{,}234.50}{2 \times 1{,}085.30} = 4.25$$

$$\text{Modified Duration} = \frac{4.25}{1.03} = 4.13$$

$$\text{Convexity} = \frac{95{,}874.32}{(1.03)^2 \times 2^2 \times 1{,}085.30} = 20.82$$

Chapter

17 BOND PORTFOLIO MANAGEMENT STRATEGIES

After you read this chapter, you should be able to answer the following questions:

- What are the four major alternative bond portfolio management strategies available?
- What are the two specific passive portfolio management strategies available?
- What are the five alternative strategies available within the active bond portfolio management category?
- What is meant by matched-funding techniques and what are the four specific strategies available in this category?
- What are the major contingent procedure strategies that are also referred to as structured active management strategies?
- What are the implications of capital market theory for those involved in bond portfolio management?
- What is the evidence on the efficient market hypothesis as it relates to bond markets?
- What are the implications of efficient market studies for those involved in bond portfolio management?

In this chapter, we shift attention from bond valuation and analysis to the equally important bond portfolio management strategies. In the first section, we discuss the alternative portfolio management strategies. This includes a detailed consideration of the four major strategies: passive management, active management, matched-funding techniques, and structured active management. Next, we consider the implications of capital market theory and bond market efficiency on bond portfolio management.

ALTERNATIVE BOND PORTFOLIO STRATEGIES

Bond portfolio management strategies can be divided into four groups:[1]

1. Passive portfolio strategies
   a. Buy and hold
   b. Indexing
2. Active management strategies
   a. Interest rate anticipation
   b. Valuation analysis
   c. Credit analysis
   d. Yield spread analysis
   e. Bond swaps

[1]This breakdown benefited from the discussion in Martin L. Leibowitz, "The Dedicated Bond Portfolio in Pension Funds—Part I: Motivations and Basics," *Financial Analysts Journal* 42, no 1 (January–February 1986): 61–75.

3. Matched-funding techniques
   a. Dedicated portfolio, exact cash match
   b. Dedicated portfolio, optimal cash match and reinvestment
   c. Classical ("pure") immunization
   d. Horizon matching
4. Contingent procedures (structured active management)
   a. Contingent immunization
   b. Other contingent procedures

We discuss each of these alternatives because they are all viable for certain portfolios with different needs and risk profiles. Prior to the 1960s, only the first two groups were available, and most bond portfolios were managed on the basis of buy and hold. The 1960s and early 1970s saw growing interest in alternative active bond portfolio management strategies. The investment environment during the late 1970s and early 1980s was characterized by record-breaking inflation and interest rates, extremely volatile rates of return in bond markets, and the introduction of many new financial instruments in response to the increase in return volatility. Since the mid-1980s, we have seen matched funding techniques or contingent portfolio management techniques to meet the emerging needs of institutional clients.

Passive Management Strategies

Two specific passive portfolio strategies exist. First is a **buy-and-hold strategy** in which a manager selects a portfolio of bonds based on the objectives and constraints of the client with the intent of holding these bonds to maturity. In the second passive strategy—**indexing**—the objective is to construct a portfolio of bonds that will equal the performance of a specified bond index, such as the Lehman Brothers Corporate/Government Bond Index.

BUY-AND-HOLD STRATEGY The simplest portfolio management strategy is to buy and hold. Obviously not unique to bond investors, it involves finding issues with desired quality, coupon levels, term to maturity, and important indenture provisions, such as call features. Buy-and-hold investors do not consider active trading to achieve attractive returns, but rather look for vehicles whose maturities (or duration) approximate their stipulated investment horizon to reduce price and reinvestment risk. Many successful bond investors and institutional portfolio managers follow a modified buy-and-hold strategy wherein an investment is made in an issue with the intention of holding it until the end of the investment horizon. However, they still actively look for opportunities to trade into more desirable positions.[2]

Whether the investor follows a strict or modified buy-and-hold approach, the key ingredient is finding investment vehicles that possess attractive maturity and yield features. The strategy does not restrict the investor to accept whatever the market has to offer, nor does it imply that selectivity is unimportant. Attractive high-yielding issues with desirable features and quality standards are actively sought. For example, these investors recognize that agency issues generally provide incremental returns relative to Treasuries with a little sacrifice in quality, that utilities provide higher returns than comparable rated industrials, and that various call features affect the risk and realized yield of an issue. Thus, successful buy-and-hold investors use their knowledge of markets and issue characteristics to seek out attractive realized yields. Aggressive buy-and-hold investors also incorporate timing considerations into their investment decisions by using their knowledge of market rates and expectations.

---

[2]Obviously, if the strategy becomes too modified, it would become one of the active strategies.

INDEXING STRATEGY As discussed in the chapter on efficient capital markets, numerous empirical studies have demonstrated that the majority of money managers have not been able to match the risk–return performance of common stock or bond indexes. As a result, many clients have opted to index some part of their bond portfolios, which means that the portfolio manager builds a portfolio that will match the performance of a selected bond-market index, such as the Lehman Brothers Index, Merrill Lynch Index, or Salomon Brothers Index. In such a case, the portfolio manager is not judged on the basis of risk and return compared to an index, but by how closely the portfolio *tracks* the index. Specifically, the analysis of performance involves examining the **tracking error**, which equals the difference between the rate of return for the portfolio and the rate of return for the bond-market index. For example, if the portfolio experienced an annual rate of return of 8.2 percent during a period when the index had a rate of return of 8.3 percent, the tracking error would be 10 basis points.

When initiating an indexing strategy, the selection of the appropriate market index is very important because it directly determines the client's risk–return results. As such, it is necessary to be very familiar with all the characteristics of the index.[3] For bond indexes, it also is important to be aware of how the aggregate market and the indexes change over time.[4] Reilly and Wright demonstrated that the market has experienced significant changes in composition, maturity, and duration since 1975. After the appropriate bond index is selected, several techniques are available to accomplish the actual tracking.[5]

Active Management Strategies[6]

Five active management strategies are available, including interest rate anticipation, which involves economic forecasting, as well as valuation analysis and credit analysis, which require detailed bond and company analysis. Alternatively, yield spread analysis and bond swaps, which require economic and market analysis, are also available.

[3]An article that briefly discusses the indexes is F. Hawthorne, "The Battle of the Bond Indexes," *Institutional Investor* (April 1986). Two articles that discuss how the characteristics of indexes affect their performance in different interest rate environments are Chris P. Dialynas, "The Active Decisions in the Selection of Passive Management and Performance Bogeys," and Daralyn B. Peifer, "A Sponsor's View of Benchmark Portfolios." Both are in *The Handbook of Fixed-Income Securities,* 5th ed., ed. Frank J. Fabozzi (Chicago, Ill.: Irwin Professional Publishing, 1997). For an analysis of a relatively new comprehensive Treasury bond index, see Frank K. Reilly and David J. Wright, "Introducing a Comprehensive U.S. Treasury Bond Market Benchmark," in *Yield Curve Dynamics,* ed. Ronald J. Ryan (Chicago: Glenlake Publishing, 1997).

[4]An article that describes the major bond-market indexes, analyzes the relationship among them, and examines how the aggregate bond market has changed is Frank K. Reilly and David J. Wright, "Bond Market Indexes," in the *Handbook of Fixed-Income Securities,* 5th ed., ed. Frank J. Fabozzi (Chicago, Ill.: Irwin Professional Publishing, 1997). A similar study for high-yield indexes is Frank K. Reilly and David J. Wright, "An Analysis of High Yield Bond Benchmarks," *Journal of Fixed Income* 3, no. 4 (March 1994): 6–25.

[5]For a detailed discussion of the alternative tracking techniques available, see Sharmin Mossavar-Rahmoni, "Indexing Fixed-Income Assets," in *The Handbook of Fixed-Income Securities;* Sharmin Mossavar-Rahmoni, *Bond Index Funds* (Chicago: Probus Publishing, 1991); and Frank J. Fabozzi, *Bond Markets, Analysis and Strategies,* 3d ed. (Upper Saddle River, N.J.: Prentice-Hall, 1996), Chapter 18.

[6]For further discussion on this topic, see H. Gifford Fong, "Active Strategies for Managing Bond Portfolios," in *The Revolution in Techniques for Managing Bond Portfolios,* ed. Donald Tuttle (Charlottesville, Va.: The Institute of Chartered Financial Analysts, 1983), 21–38; and Thomas Vock, "Managing Global Fixed-Income Portfolios," in *Global Portfolio Management,* ed. Jan R. Squires (Charlottesville, Va.: Association for Investment Management and Research, 1996). For a set of readings, see *Global Bond Management*, ed. Jan R. Squires (Charlottesville, Va.: Association for Investment Management and Research, 1997); and Dwight Churchill, ed., *Fixed Income Management: Techniques and Practices,* (Charlottesville, Va.: Association for Investment Management and Research, 1994).

INTEREST RATE ANTICIPATION **Interest rate anticipation** is perhaps the riskiest active management strategy because it involves relying on uncertain forecasts of future interest rates. The idea is to preserve capital when an increase in interest rates is anticipated and achieve attractive capital gains when interest rates are expected to decline. Such objective usually are attained by altering the maturity (duration) structure of the portfolio (i.e., reducing portfolio duration when interest rates are expected to increase and increasing the portfolio duration when a decline in yields is anticipated). Thus, the risk in such portfolio restructuring is largely a function of these duration (maturity) alterations. When maturities are shortened to preserve capital, substantial income could be sacrificed and the opportunity for capital gains could be lost if interest rates decline rather than rise. Similarly, the portfolio shifts prompted by anticipation of a decline in rates are very risky. Specifically, if we assume that we are at a peak in interest rates, it is likely that the yield curve is downward-sloping, which means that bond coupons will decline with maturity. Therefore, the investor is sacrificing current income by shifting from high-coupon short bonds to longer-duration bonds. At the same time, the portfolio is purposely exposed to greater price volatility that could work against the portfolio if an unexpected increase in yields occurs. Note that the portfolio adjustments prompted by anticipation of an increase in rates involves less risk of an absolute capital loss. When you reduce the maturity, the worst that can happen is that interest income is reduced and/or capital gains are forgone (opportunity cost).

Once future (expected) interest rates have been determined, the procedure relies largely on technical matters. Assume that you expect an increase in interest rates and want to preserve your capital by reducing the duration of your portfolio. A popular choice would be high-yielding, short-term obligations, such as Treasury bills. Although your primary concern is to preserve capital, you would nevertheless look for the best return possible given the maturity constraint. Liquidity also is important because, after interest rates increase, yields may experience a period of stability before they decline, and you would want to shift positions quickly to benefit from the higher income and/or capital gains.

One way to shorten maturities is to use a *cushion bond*—a high-yielding, long-term obligation that carries a coupon substantially above the current market rate and that, due to its current call feature and call price, has a market price lower than what it should be given current market yields. As a result, its yield is higher than normal. An example would be a 10-year bond with a 12 percent coupon, currently callable at 110. If current market rates are 8 percent, this bond (if it were noncallable) would have a price of about 127; because of its call price, however, it will stay close to 110, and its yield will be about 10 percent rather than 8 percent. Bond portfolio managers look for cushion bonds when they expect a modest increase in rates because such issues provide attractive current income *and* protection against capital loss. Because these bonds are trading at an abnormally high yield, market rates would have to rise to that abnormal level before their price would react.

The portfolio manager who anticipates higher interest rates, therefore, has two simple strategies available: shorten the duration of the portfolio and/or look for an attractive cushion bond.[7] In either case, you would want very liquid issues.

A totally different posture is assumed by investors who anticipate a decline in interest rates. The significant risk involved in restructuring a portfolio to take advantage of a decline in interest rates are balanced by the potential for substantial capital gains and holding period returns. When you expect lower interest rates, you will recall that you should

[7]For an extended discussion of cushion bonds, see Sidney Homer and Martin L. Leibowitz, *Inside the Yield Book* (Englewood Cliffs, N.J.: Prentice Hall, 1972), Chapter 5.

increase the duration of the portfolio because the longer the duration, the greater the price volatility. Also, liquidity is important because you want to be able to close out the position quickly when the drop in rates has been completed.

Notably, because interest rate sensitivity is critical, it is important to recall that the higher the quality of an obligation, the more sensitive it is to interest rate changes. Therefore, high-grade securities should be used, such as Treasuries, agencies, or corporates rated AAA through BAA. Finally, you want to concentrate on noncallable issues or those with strong call protection because of the substantial call risk discussed in Chapter 16 in connection with the analysis of duration and convexity.

VALUATION ANALYSIS With **valuation analysis**, the portfolio manager attempts to select bonds based on their intrinsic value. In turn, the bond's value is determined based on its characteristics and the average value of these characteristics in the marketplace. As an example, a bond's rating will dictate a certain spread relative to comparable Treasury bonds: long maturity might be worth an added 60 basis points relative to short maturity (i.e., the maturity spread); a given deferred call feature might require a higher or lower yield; a specified sinking fund would likewise mean higher or lower required yields. Given all the characteristics of the bond and the normal cost of the characteristics in terms of yield, you would determine the required yield and, therefore, the bond's implied intrinsic value. After you have done this for a number of bonds, you would compare these derived bond values to the prevailing market prices to determine which bonds are undervalued or overvalued. Based on your confidence in the characteristic costs, you would buy the undervalued issues and ignore or sell the overvalued issues.

Success in valuation analysis is based on understanding the characteristics that are important in valuation and being able to accurately *estimate* the yield cost of these characteristics over time.

CREDIT ANALYSIS A **credit analysis** strategy involves detailed analysis of the bond issuer to determine expected changes in its default risk. This involves attempting to project changes in the quality ratings assigned to bonds by the four rating agencies discussed in Chapter 15.[8] These rating changes are affected by internal changes in the entity (e.g., changes in important financial ratios) and by changes in the external environment (i.e., changes in the firm's industry and the economy). During periods of strong economic expansion, even financially weak firms may survive and prosper. In contrast, during severe economic contractions, normally strong firms may find it very difficult to meet financial obligations. Therefore, historically there has been a strong cyclical pattern to rating changes: typically, downgradings increase during economic contractions and decline during economic expansions.

To use credit analysis as a portfolio management strategy, it is necessary to project rating changes prior to the announcement by the rating agencies. As the subsequent discussion on bond-market efficiency notes, the market adjusts rather quickly to bond rating changes—especially downgradings. Therefore, you want to acquire bond issues expected to experience upgradings and sell or avoid those expected to be downgraded.

---

[8]For a discussion of changes in the aggregate financial risk of U.S. corporations and the opportunities this has created, see Frank K. Reilly, "The Growing Importance of Credit Analysis," Working paper, University of Notre Dame (April 1999). For a presentation on credit analysis that emphasizes changes in credit ratings, see Jane Tripp Howe, "Credit Analysis for Corporate Bonds," in *The Handbook of Fixed-Income Securities*. For a set of readings on global credit analysis, see ed. Jan R. Squires, *Credit Analysis Around the World* (Charlottesville, Va.: Association for Investment Management and Research, 1998).

FIGURE 17.1 **YIELD SPREAD BETWEEN THE AVERAGE YIELD ON THE MERRILL LYNCH HIGH-YIELD MASTER INDEX AND THE 10-YEAR TREASURY INDEX: DECEMBER 1984–DECEMBER 1998**

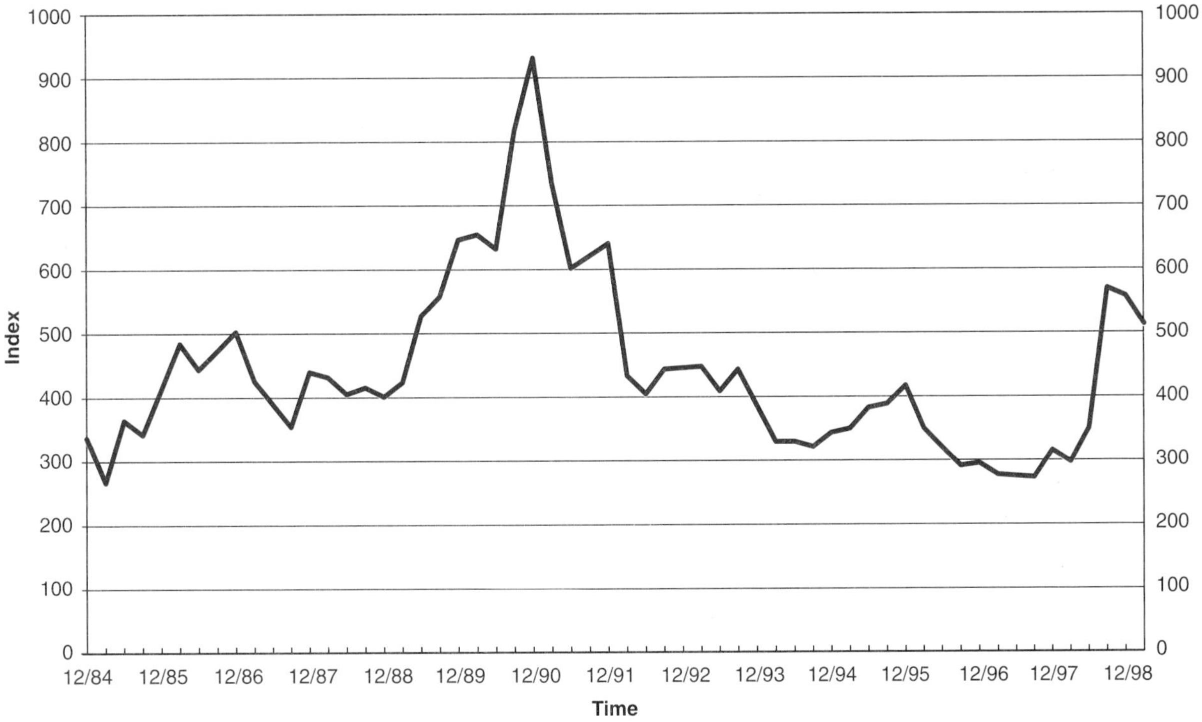
1000
900
800
700
600
500
400
300
200
100
0
Index
12/84
12/85
12/86
12/87
12/88
12/89
12/90
12/91
12/92
12/93
12/94
12/95
12/96
12/97
12/98
Time

Source: Martin S. Fridson, Chief High Yield Strategist, Merrill Lynch, and M. Christopher Garman, Analyst, High Yield Strategy, Merrill Lynch, "This Year in High Yield—1998." Reprinted by permission. Copyright © 1999 Merrill Lynch, Pierce, Fenner & Smith Incorporated.

Credit Analysis of High-Yield (Junk) Bonds One of the most obvious opportunities for credit analysis is the analysis of high-yield (junk) bonds. As demonstrated by several studies, the yield differential between junk bonds that are rated below BBB and Treasury securities ranges from about 200 basis points to over 1,000 basis points. Notably, these yield differentials vary substantially over time as shown by a time-series plot in Figure 17.1. Specifically, the average yield spread ranged from a low of less than 300 basis points in late 1984 and 1997 to a high of over 900 basis points during early 1991.

Although the spreads have changed, a study indicated that the average credit quality of high-yield bonds also changed over time.[9] As an example, interest coverage tends to fluctuate with the business cycle. In addition, the credit quality of bonds *within* rating categories tends to change over the business cycle.[10]

These changes in credit quality will make credit analysis of high-yield bonds not only more important, but also more difficult. This means that bond analysts–portfolio managers

[9]Barrie A. Wigmore, "The Decline in Credit Quality of New Issue Junk Bonds," *Financial Analysts Journal* 46, no. 5 (September–October 1990): 53–62.

[10]These changes are demonstrated in Reilly, "The Growing Importance of Credit Analysis."

TABLE 17.1 **AVERAGE CUMULATIVE DEFAULT RATES FOR CORPORATE BONDS: 1971–1994**

Ratings	Years since Issue: 5	10
AAA	0.08%	0.08%
AA	1.20	1.30
A	0.53	0.98
BBB	2.39	3.66
BB	10.79	15.21
B	23.71	35.91
CCC	45.63	57.39

Source: K. Scott Douglass and Douglas J. Lucas, "Historical Default Rates of Corporate Bond Issuers, 1971–1994" (New York: Moody's Investors Service, July 1995). © Moody's Investors Service.

need to engage in detailed credit analysis to select bonds that will survive. Given the spread in promised yields, if a portfolio manager can—through rigorous credit analysis—avoid bonds with a high probability of default, high-yield bonds will provide substantial rates of return for the investor.[11]

In summary, substantial rates of return can be derived by investing in high-yield bonds if you do the credit analysis required to avoid defaults, which occur with these bonds at substantially higher rates than the overall market. Several recent studies have shown that the average cumulative default rate for high-yield bonds after 10 years is between 30 percent and 35 percent. Of the high-yield bonds sold in 1988, about 33 percent had defaulted by 1998.[12]

Table 17.1 lists the results for a study that considers the full spectrum of bonds. It shows substantial differences in cumulative default rates for bonds with different ratings for the periods 5 and 10 years after issue. Over 10 years—the holding period that is widely discussed—the default rate for BBB investment-grade bonds is only 3.66 percent, but the default rate increases to over 15 percent for BB-rated, to almost 36 percent for B-rated bonds, and to over 57 percent for CCC-rated bonds.

These default rates do not mean that investors should avoid high-yield bonds, but they do indicate that extensive credit analysis is a critical component for success within this sector. Given the substantial yield spreads over Treasuries, you may experience high returns *if* you can avoid owning bonds that default or are downgraded. The route to avoiding such bond issues is through rigorous, enlightened credit analysis.

[11]For a presentation of the unique factors that must be considered when analyzing high-yield bonds, see Jane Tripp Howe, "Credit Considerations in Evaluating High-Yield Debt," and Allen A. Vine, "High-Yield Analysis of Emerging Markets Debt." Both of these are in *The Handbook of Fixed-Income Securities.*

[12]Although the details of the analysis differ, the overall results for cumulative defaults are quite consistent. See Edward I. Altman, "Measuring Corporate Bond Mortality and Performance," *Journal of Finance* 44, no. 4 (September 1989): 909–922; Paul Asquith, David W. Mullins, Jr., and Eric D. Wolff, "Original Issue High Yield Bonds: Aging Analysis of Defaults, Exchanges, and Calls," *Journal of Finance* 44, no. 4 (September 1989): 929–952; K. Scott Douglass and Douglas J. Lucas, "Historical Default Rates of Corporate Bond Issuers, 1970–1988" (New York: Moody's Investors Services, July 1989). The Altman and Douglass-Lucas studies are updated and discussed in Frank K. Reilly, ed., *High Yield Bonds: Analysis and Risk Assessment* (Charlottesville, Va.: Institute of Chartered Financial Analysts, 1990). Another review of these studies is Edward I. Altman, "Setting the Record Straight on Junk Bonds: A Review of the Research on Default Rates and Returns," *Journal of Applied Corporate Finance* 3, no. 2 (summer 1990): 82–95; and Edward I. Altman, "Revisiting the High-Yield Bond Market," *Financial Management* 21, no 2 (summer 1992): 78–92. For a recent update, see Martin S. Fridson and M. Christopher Garman, "This Year in High Yield—1998," *Extra Credit* (New York: Merrill Lynch, January–February 1999).

Investing in Defaulted Debt Beyond high-yield bonds that have high credit risk and high default rates, a new set of investment opportunities has evolved—investing in defaulted debt. While this sector requires an understanding of legal procedures surrounding bankruptcy as well as economic analysis, the returns have generally been consistent with the risk—i.e., between high-yield debt and common stock.[13]

Credit Analysis Models The credit analysis of high-yield bonds can use a statistical model or basic fundamental analysis that recognizes some of the unique characteristics of these bonds. The Altman–Nammacher book suggests that a modified *Z-score model* used to predict bankruptcy can also be used to predict default for these high-yield bonds or as a gauge of changes in credit quality. The Z-score model combines traditional financial measures with a multivariate techniques known as *multiple discriminant analysis* to derive a set of weights for the specified variables. The result is an overall credit score (zeta score) for each firm.[14] The model is of the form

$$\text{Zeta} = a_0 + a_1X_1 + a_2X_2 + a_3X_3 + \ldots + a_nX_n$$

where:

Zeta = the overall credit score
$X_1 \ldots X_n$ = the explanatory variables (ratios and market measures)
$a_0 \ldots a_n$ = the weightings or coefficients

The final model used in this analysis included the following seven financial measures:

X_1 = profitability: earnings before interest and taxes (EBIT)/total assets (TA)
X_2 = stability of profitability measure: the standard error of estimate of EBIT/TA (normalized for 10 years)
X_3 = debt service capabilities: EBIT/interest charges
X_4 = cumulative profitability: retained earnings/total assets
X_5 = liquidity: current assets/current liabilities
X_6 = capitalization levels: market value of equity/total capital (5-year average)
X_7 = size: total tangible assets (normalized)

The weightings, or coefficients, for the variables were not reported.[15]

In contrast to using a model that provides a composite credit score, most analysts simply adapt their basic corporate bond analysis techniques *to the unique needs of high-yield*

---

[13]For a discussion of the legal and economic analysis, see Edward I. Altman, *Corporate Financial Distress and Bankruptcy,* 2d ed. (New York: John Wiley & Sons, 1993); and Jane Tripp Howe, "Investing in Chapter 11 and Other Distressed Companies," in *The Handbook of Fixed-Income Securities.* For an analysis of the investment performance, see Edward I. Altman, "Defaulted Bonds: Demand, Supply, and Performance, 1987–1992," *Financial Analysts Journal* 49, no 3 (May–June 1993): 55–60; Edward I. Altman and Babe E. Simon, "The Investment Performance of Defaulted Bonds for 1994 and 1987–1994," New York University, Salomon Center (February 1995); G. Hradsky and Robert Long, "High Yield Losses and the Return Performance of Bankrupt Debt Issues, 1978–1988," *Financial Analysts Journal* 45, no. 4 (July–August 1989): 38–49; David J. Ward and Gary L. Griepentrog, "Risk and Return in Defaulted Bonds," *Financial Analysts Journal* 49, no. 3 (May–June 1993): 61–65; and Frank K. Reilly, David J. Wright, and Edward I. Altman, "Including Defaulted Bonds in the Capital Markets Asset Spectrum," *Journal of Fixed Income* 8, no. 3 (December 1998): 33–48.

[14]Edward I. Altman and Scott A. Nammacher, *Investing in Junk Bonds* (New York: John Wiley & Sons, 1987).

[15]Beyond this analysis of predicting default for individual issues, several studies have examined the aggregate default rate for high-yield bonds as follows: Jon G. Jonsson and Martin S. Fridson, "Forecasting Default Rates on High-Yield Bonds," *Journal of Fixed Income* 6, no. 1 (June 1996): 69–77; Jean Helwege and Paul Kleiman, "Understanding Aggregate Default Rates of High-Yield Bonds," *Journal of Fixed Income* 7, no. 1 (June 1997): 55–61; and Martin S. Fridson, M. Christopher Garman, and Sheg Wu, "Real Interest Rates and the Default Rate on High-Yield Bonds," *Journal of Fixed Income* 7, no. 2 (September 1997): 29–34.

bonds, which have characteristics of common stock.[16] Howe claims that the analysis of high-yield bonds is the same as with any bond except that five areas of analysis should be expanded.[17]

1. What is the firm's *competitive position* in terms of cost and pricing? This can be critical to a small firm.
2. What is the firm's *cash flow* relative to cash requirements for interest, research, growth, and periods of economic decline? Also, what is the firm's *borrowing capacity* that can serve as a safety net and provide flexibility?
3. What is the *liquidity value of the firm's assets*? Are these assets available for liquidation (are there any claims against them)? In many cases, asset sales are a critical part of the strategy for a leveraged buyout.
4. How good is the *total management team*? Is the team committed to and capable of operating in the high-risk environment of this firm?
5. What is the firm's *financial leverage* on an absolute basis and on a market-adjusted basis (using market value of equity and debt)?

Hynes suggests that the following areas require additional analysis as part of the process of evaluating cash flows when analyzing a leveraged buyout (which typically involves the issuance of high-yield debt).[18]

- Inherent business risk
- Earnings growth potential
- Asset redevelopment potential
- Refinancing capability

In addition to the potentially higher financial risk, an increase in business risk may exist if the firm sells off some operations that have favorable risk characteristics with the remaining operations—that is, business risk would increase if the firm sells a division or a company that has low correlation of earnings with other units of the firm. Further, a change in management operating philosophy could have a negative impact on operating earnings. The managements of leveraged buyout (LBO) firms are known for making optimistic growth estimates related to sales and earnings, so the analyst should evaluate these estimates very critically. Asset divestiture plans often are a major element of an LBO because they provide necessary capital that is used to reduce the substantial debt taken on as part of the buyout. Therefore, it is important to examine the liquidity of the assets, their estimated selling values, and the timing of these programs. You must ascertain whether the estimated sales prices for the assets are reasonable and whether the timing is realistic. In contrast, if the divestiture program is successful wherein the prices received are above normal expectations and the assets are sold ahead of schedule, this can be grounds for upgrading the

---

[16]For an analysis that shows the relationship of high-yield bonds to investment-grade bonds and common stock, see Frank K. Reilly and David J. Wright, "An Analysis of High-Yield Bond Benchmarks," *Journal of Fixed Income* 3, no. 4 (March 1994): 6–25. An updated version is in Theodore M. Barnhill, Jr., William F. Maxwell, and Mark R. Shenkman, eds., *High-Yield Bonds* (New York: McGraw-Hill, 1999).

[17]Jane Tripp Howe, "Credit Considerations in Evaluating High-Yield Bonds," in *The Handbook of Fixed-Income Securities*; and Jane Tripp Howe, *Junk Bonds: Analysis and Portfolio Strategies* (Chicago: Probus Publishing, 1988).

[18]Joseph Hynes, "Key Risk Factors for LBOs," *Speculative Grade Debt Credit Review* (New York: Standard & Poor's Corporation, June 15, 1987).

debt. Finally, it is necessary to constantly monitor the firm's refinancing flexibility. Specifically, what refinancing will be necessary, what does the schedule look like, and will the capital suppliers be receptive to the refinancing.[19]

The substantial increase in junk bonds issued and outstanding has been matched by an increase in research and credit analysis. The credit analysis of these bonds is similar to that of investment-grade bonds with an emphasis on the following factors: (1) *the use of cash flows* compared to debt obligations under very conservative assumptions, (2) the detailed analysis of *potential asset sales,* including a conservative estimate of sales prices, the asset's true liquidity, the availability of the assets, and a consideration of the timing of the sales, and (3) the recognition that high-yield bonds have many characteristics of common stock, which means that many equity analysis techniques are appropriate. An in-depth analysis of junk bonds is critical because of the number of issues, the wide diversity of quality within the junk bond universe, and the growing complexity of these issues.

High-Yield Bond Research Because of the growth of high-yield bonds, several investment houses have developed specialized high-yield groups that examine high-yield bond issues and monitor yield spreads in the aggregate junk bond market.

Merrill Lynch's monthly publication, *High-Yield,* provides an overview of the market and reviews several individual industries and firms within these main industries (e.g., retail, steel, building products, and textile). It also contains reports of research done by the firm on general questions about the high-yield market. The firm initiated a high-yield master bond return index in October 1984, and it tracks the yield spreads for high-yield bonds relative to Treasury issues. As noted earlier, the January/February issue of *High-Yield* always contains a detailed annual review of the market with extensive historical tables.

Merrill Lynch's weekly publication, *This Week in High Yield,* discusses current events in the high-yield market. This includes weekly yields and yield spreads for the various sectors of the market and news highlights for specific companies and issues.

High Yield Market Update, a Salomon Brothers Smith Barney monthly publication, presents monthly and cumulative long-term returns for its high-yield indexes (long-term and intermediate-term corporates, long-term utilities), as well as spreads between rating categories relative to appropriate Treasuries. The publication also features commentary on timely topics within the high-yield market.

The high-yield research group at First Boston publishes *Monthly Market Review,* which contains an extensive performance review of the HY (high-yield) bond market that examines returns by sectors and industries as well as considering yield spreads and changing volatility for these bonds. First Boston also publishes an annual *High Yield Handbook,* which reviews annual events and considers every aspect of risk, return, and correlation of high-yield bonds with other asset classes. There also is a very helpful listing of new issues, retirements, and defaults.

Lehman Brothers publishes a weekly review, *High Yield Portfolio Advisor,* which analyzes the performance of the firm's high-yield bond indexes and has detailed comments on news events that affect prominent industries in the high-yield market. The firm also publishes a monthly *High Yield Bond Market Report* that briefly discusses the returns and new issues for the month, contains extensive data on returns for all components of the HY market (BB, B, CCC, CC-D, nonrated, default), and contains descriptive statistics regarding

[19]For a set of presentations on credit analysis including distressed securities, see Ashwinpaul C. Sondhi, ed., *Credit Analysis of Nontraditional Debt Securities* (Charlottesville, Va.: Association for Investment Management and Research, 1995), and Jan R. Squires, ed., *Credit Analysis Around the World* (Charlottesville, Va.: Association of Investment Management and Research, 1998).

bonds in the composite index and various subindexes, such as average coupon, maturity, duration to worst, modified adjusted duration, price, and yield.

In addition, several bond-rating firms conduct research on these industries and firms. Standard & Poor's publication, *Speculative Grade Debt Credit Review,* discusses the credit analysis of high-yield bonds. The publication also includes a review of several major industries and specific comments on outstanding issues.

Duff & Phelps has three regular publications related to the high-yield bond market. *Credit Comments* is a weekly publication that discusses developments and changes in default rankings or buy/sell/hold suggestions. *Recommendations* is a monthly summary of current recommendations for over 400 bond issues, including month-end prices, default risk rankings, and yield spreads. Finally, *Profiles* is a quarterly bulletin that contains an updated financial profile for the companies in the high-yield service, including financial ratios, income statement items, and a cash flow summary.

YIELD SPREAD ANALYSIS As discussed in Chapter 16, spread analysis assumes normal relationships exist between the yields for bonds in alternative sectors (e.g., the spread between high-grade versus low-grade industrial or between industrial versus utility bonds). Therefore, a bond portfolio manager would monitor these relationships, and, when an abnormal relationship occurs, execute various sector swaps. The crucial factor is developing the background to know the normal yield relationship and to evaluate the liquidity necessary to buy or sell the required issues quickly enough to take advantage of the temporary abnormality.

The analysis of yield spreads has been enhanced by a paper by Dialynas and Edington that considers several specific factors that affect the aggregate spread.[20] It is acknowledged that the generally accepted explanation of changes in the yield spread is that it is related to the economic environment. Specifically, the spread widens during periods of economic uncertainty and recession because investors require larger risk premiums (i.e., larger spreads). In contrast, the spread will decline during periods of economic confidence and expansion. Although not denying the existence of such a relationship, the authors contend that a more encompassing factor is the impact of interest rate (yield) volatility. They contend that yield volatility will affect the spread via three effects: (1) yield volatility and the behavior of embedded options, (2) yield volatility and transactional liquidity, and (3) the effect of yield volatility on the business cycle.

Recall that the value of callable bonds is equal to the value of a noncallable bond minus the value of the call option. Obviously, if the value of the option goes up, the value of the callable bond will decline and its yield will increase. When yield volatility increases, the value of the call option increases, which causes a decline in the price of the callable bond, and a rise in the bond's yield and its yield spread relative to Treasury bonds. Similarly, an increase in yield volatility will raise the uncertainty facing bond dealers and cause them to increase their bid–ask spreads that reflect the transactional liquidity for these bonds. This liquidity will have a bigger effect on nongovernment bonds, so their yield spread relative to Treasury bonds will increase. Finally, interest rate volatility causes uncertainty for business executives and consumers regarding their cost of funds. This typically will precede an economic decline that will, in turn, lead to an increase in the yield spread. It is demonstrated that it is possible to have a change in yield spread for reasons other than economic uncertainty. If there is a period of greater yield volatility that is not a

[20]Chris P. Dialynas and David H. Edington, "Bond Yield Spreads—A Postmodern View," *Journal of Portfolio Management* 19, no. 1 (fall 1992): 60–75.

period of economic uncertainty, the yield spread will increase due to the embedded option effect and the transactional liquidity effect. Therefore, when examining yield spreads, you should pay particular attention to interest rate (yield) volatility.

BOND SWAPS **Bond swaps** involve liquidating a current position and simultaneously buying a different issue in its place with similar attributes but having a chance for improved return. Swaps can be executed to increase current yield, to increase yield to maturity, to take advantage of shifts in interest rates or the realignment of yield spreads, to improve the quality of a portfolio, or for tax purposes. Some swaps are highly sophisticated and require a computer for calculation. However, most are fairly simple transactions with obvious goals and risk. They go by such names as *profit takeouts, substitution swaps, intermarket spread swaps,* or *tax swaps.* Although many of these swaps involve low risk (such as the pure yield pickup swap), others entail substantial risk (the rate anticipation swap). Regardless of the risk involved, all swaps have one basic purpose: portfolio improvement.

Most swaps involve several different types of risk. One obvious risk is that the market will move against you while the swap is outstanding. Interest rates may move up over the holding period and cause you to incur a loss. Alternatively, yield spreads may fail to respond as anticipated. Possibly the new bond may not be a true substitute and so, even if your expectations and interest rate formulations are correct, the swap may be unsatisfactory because the wrong issue was selected. Finally, if the work-out time is longer than anticipated, the realized yield might be less than expected. You must be willing to accept such risks to improve your portfolio. The following subsections consider three of the more popular bond swaps.[21]

Pure Yield Pickup Swap The pure yield pickup involves swapping out of a low-coupon bond into a comparable higher-coupon bond to realize an automatic and instantaneous increase in current yield and yield to maturity. Your risks are (1) that the market will move against you and (2) that the new issue may not be a viable swap candidate. Also, because you are moving to a higher coupon obligation, there could be greater call risk.

An example of a pure yield pickup swap would be an investor who currently holds a 30-year, Aa-rated 10 percent issue that is trading at an 11.50 percent yield. Assume that a comparable 30-year, Aa-rated obligation bearing a 12 percent coupon priced to yield 12 percent becomes available. The investor would report (and realize) some book loss if the original issue was bought at par but is able to improve current yield and yield to maturity simultaneously if the new obligation is held to maturity as shown in Table 17.2.

The investor need not predict rate changes, and the swap is not based on any imbalance in yield spread. The object simply is to seek higher yields. Quality and maturity stay the same as do all other factors *except coupon.* The major risk is that future reinvestment rates may not be as high as expected, and, therefore, the total terminal value of the investment (capital recovery, coupon receipts, and interest-on-interest) may not be as high as expected or comparable to the original obligation. This reinvestment risk can be evaluated by analyzing the results with a number of reinvestment rates to determine the minimum reinvestment rate that would make the swap viable.

Substitution Swap The substitution swap generally is short term and relies heavily on interest rate expectations. Therefore, it is subject to considerably more risk than the pure yield pickup swaps. The procedure assumes a short-term imbalance in yield spreads between issues that are perfect substitutes. The imbalance in yield spread is expected to be

[21]For additional information on these and other types of bond swaps, see Sidney Homer and Martin L. Leibowitz, *Inside the Yield Book* (Englewood Cliffs, N.J.: Prentice Hall, 1972); Anand K. Bhattasharya and Frank J. Fabozzi, "Interest Rate Swaps," in *The Handbook of Fixed-Income Securities.*

TABLE 17.2 **A PURE YIELD PICKUP SWAP**

Pure Yield Pickup Swap: A bond swap involving a switch—from a low-coupon bond to a higher-coupon bond of similar quality and maturity—in order to pick up higher current yield and a better yield to maturity.

Example: Currently hold: 30-yr., 10.0% coupon priced at 874.12 to yield 11.5%.
Swap candidate: 30-yr., Aa 12% coupon priced at \$1,000 to yield 12.0%.

	Current Bond	Candidate Bond
Dollar investment	\$874.12	\$1,000.00[a]
Coupon	100.00	120.00
i on one coupon (12.0% for 6 months)	3.000	3.600
Principal value at year end	874.66	1,000.00
Total accrued	977.66	1,123.60
Realized compound yield	11.514%	12.0%

Value of swap: 48.6 basis points in one year (assuming a 12.0% reinvestment rate).

The rewards for a pure yield pickup swap are automatic and instantaneous in that both a higher-coupon yield and a higher yield to maturity are realized from the swap.
Other advantages include:

1. No specific work-out period needed because the investor is assumed to hold the new bond to maturity
2. No need for interest rate speculation
3. No need to analyze prices for overvaluation or undervaluation

A major disadvantage of the pure yield pickup swap is the book loss involved in the swap. In this example, if the current bond were bought at par, the book loss would be \$125.88 (\$1,000 − 874.12).
Other risks involved in the pure yield pickup swap include:

1. Increased risk of call in the event interest rates decline
2. Reinvestment risk is greater with higher-coupon bonds.

[a]Obviously, the investor can invest \$874.12—the amount obtained from the sale of the bond currently held—and still obtain a realized compound yield of 12.0%.

Swap evaluation procedure is patterned after a technique suggested by Sidney Homer and Martin L. Leibowitz.

Source: Adapted from the book *Inside the Yield Book* by Sidney Homer and Martin L. Leibowitz, Ph.D., © 1972, used by permission of the publisher, Prentice-Hall Inc., Englewood Cliffs, N.J., and New York Institute of Finance, New York, N.Y.

corrected in the near future. For example, the investor might hold a 30-year, 12 percent issue that is yielding 12 percent and be offered a comparable 30-year, 12 percent bond that is yielding 12.20 percent. Because the issue offered will trade at a price less than \$1,000 for every issue sold, the investor can buy more than one of the offered obligations.

You would expect the yield spread imbalance to be corrected by having the yield on the offering bond decline to the level of your current issue. Thus, you would realize capital gains by switching out of your current position into the higher-yielding obligation. This swap is described in Table 17.3.

Although a modest increase in current income occurs as the yield imbalance is corrected, attractive capital gains are possible, causing a differential in *realized yield.* The work-out time will have an important effect on the differential realized return. Even if the yield is not corrected until maturity, 30 years later, you will still experience a small increase in realized yield (about 10 basis points). In contrast, if the correction takes place in 1 year, the differential realized return is much greater, as shown in Table 17.3.

After the correction has occurred, you would have additional capital for a subsequent swap or other investment. Several risks are involved in this swap. In addition to the pressure

TABLE 17.3

A SUBSTITUTION SWAP

Substitution Swap: A swap executed to take advantage of temporary market anomalies in yield spreads between issues that are equivalent with respect to coupon, quality, and maturity.

Example: Currently hold: 30-yr., Aa 12.0% coupon priced at $1,000 to yield 12.0%.
Swap candidate: 30-yr., Aa 12% coupon priced at $984.08 to yield 12.2%.
Assumed work-out period: 1 year
Reinvested at 12.0%

	Current Bond	Candidate Bond
Dollar investment	$1,000.00	$ 984.08
Coupon	120.00	120.00
i on one coupon (12.0% for 6 months)	3.60	3.60
Principal value at year end (12.0% YTM)	1,000.00	1,000.00
Total accrued	1,123.60	1,123.60
Total gain	123.60	139.52
Gain per invested dollar	0.1236	0.1418
Realized compound yield	12.00%	13.71%
Value of swap: 171 basis points in one year		

The rewards for the substitution swap are additional basis-point pickups for YTM, additional realized compound yield, and capital gains that accrue when the anomaly in yield corrects itself.

In the substitution swap, any basis-point pickup (171 points in this example) will be realized only during the work-out period. Thus, in our example, to obtain the 171 basis-point increase in realized compound yield, you must swap an average of once a year and pick up an average of 20 basis points in yield to maturity on each swap.

Potential risks associated with the substitution swap include:

1. A yield spread thought to be temporary may, in fact, be permanent, thus reducing capital gains advantages.
2. The market rate may change adversely.

Swap evaluation procedure is patterned after a technique suggested by Sidney Home and Martin L. Leibowitz.

Source: Adapted from the book *Inside the Yield Book* by Sidney Homer and Martin L. Leibowitz, Ph.D., © 1972, used by permission of the publisher, Prentice-Hall Inc., Englewood Cliffs, N.J., and New York Institute of Finance, New York, N.Y.

of the work-out time, market interest rates could move against you, the yield spread may not be temporary, and the issue may not be a viable swap candidate (i.e., the spread may be due to the issue's lower quality).

Tax Swap The tax swap is popular with individual investors because it is a relatively simple procedure that involves no interest rate projections and few risks. Investors enter into tax swaps due to tax laws and realized capital gains in their portfolios. Assume you acquired $100,000 worth of corporate bonds and after 2 years sold the securities for $150,000, implying a capital gain of $50,000. One way to eliminate the tax liability of that capital gain is to sell an issue that has a comparable long-term capital loss.[22] If you had a long-term investment of $100,000 with a current market value of $50,000, you could execute a tax swap to establish the $50,000 capital loss. By offsetting this capital loss and the comparable capital gain, you would reduce your income taxes.

[22]Although this discussion with bond tax swaps, comparable strategies could be used with other types of investments.

TABLE 17.4

A TAX SWAP

Tax Swap: A swap undertaken when you wish to offset capital gains in other securities through the sale of a bond currently held and selling at a discount from the price paid at purchase. By swapping into a bond with as nearly identical features as possible, you can use the capital loss on the sale of the bond for tax purposes and still maintain your current position in the market.

Example: Currently hold: $100,000 worth of corporate bonds with current market value of $150,000 *and* $100,000 in N.Y., 20-year, 7% bonds with current market value of $50,000.
Swap candidate: $50,000 in N.Y., 20-year, 7.1% bonds

A. Corporate bonds sold and long-term capital gains profit established	$50,000	
Capital gains tax liability (assume you have 20% capital gains tax Rate) ($50,000 × 0.20)		$10,000
B. N.Y. 7s sold and long-term capital *loss* established	$50,000	
Reduction in capital gains tax liability ($50,000 × 0.20)		($10,000)
Net capital gains tax liability		0
Tax *savings* realized		$10,000
C. Complete tax swap by buying N.Y. 7.1s from proceeds of N.Y. 7s Sale (therefore, amount invested remains largely the *same*)[a]		
Annual tax-free interest income—N.Y. 7s	$ 7,000	
Annual tax-free interest income—N.Y.7.1s	$ 7,100	
Net *increase* in *annual* tax-free interest income	$ 100	

[a]N.Y. 7.1s will result in substantial capital gains when liquidated at maturity (because they were bought at deep discounts) and, therefore, will be subject to future capital gains tax liability. The swap is designed to use the capital loss resulting from the swap to offset capital gains from other investments. At the same time, your funds remain in a security almost identical to your previous holding while you receive a slight increase in both current income and YTM.

Because the tax swap involved no projections in terms of work-out period, interest rate changes, etc., the risks involved are minimal. Your major concern should be to avoid potential wash sales.

Municipal bonds are considered particularly attractive tax swap candidates because you can increase your tax-free income and use the capital loss (subject to normal federal and state taxation) to reduce capital gains tax liability. To continue our illustration, assume you own $100,000 worth of New York City, 20-year, 7 percent bonds that you bought at par, but they have a current market value of $50,000. Given this tax loss, you need a comparable bond swap candidate. Suppose you find a 20-year New York City bond with a 7.1 percent coupon and a market value of 50. By selling your New York 7s and instantaneously reinvesting in the New York 7.1s, you would eliminate the capital gains tax from the corporate bond transaction. In effect, you have $50,000 of tax-free capital gains, and you have increased your current tax-free yield. The money saved by avoiding the tax liability can then be used to increase the portfolio's yield, as shown in Table 17.4.

An important caveat is that *you cannot swap identical issues* (such as selling the New York 7s to establish a loss and then buying back the same New York 7s). If it is not a different issue, the IRS considers the transaction a *wash sale* and does not allow the loss. It is easier to avoid wash sales in the bond market than it is in the stock market because every bond issue, even with identical coupons and maturities, is considered distinct. Likewise, it is easier to find comparable bond issues with only modest differences in coupon, maturity, and quality. Tax swaps are common at year end as investors establish capital losses because the capital loss must occur in the same taxable year as the capital gain. This procedure differs from other bond swap transactions because it exists due to tax statutes rather than temporary market anomalies.

A GLOBAL FIXED-INCOME INVESTMENT STRATEGY

An active management strategy that considers one or several of the techniques discussed thus far should apply these techniques to a global portfolio. The optimum global fixed-income asset allocation must consider three interrelated factors: (1) the local economy in each country that includes the effect of domestic and international demand, (2) the impact of this total demand and domestic monetary policy on inflation and interest rates, and (3) the effect of the economy, inflation, and interest rates on the exchange rates among countries.[23] Based on the evaluation of these factors, a portfolio manager must decide the relative weight for each country. In addition, one might consider an allocation within each country among government, municipal, and corporate bonds. In the examples that follow, most portfolio recommendations concentrate on the country allocation and do not become more specific except in the case of the United States.

Table 17.5 is from the March 31, 1999, *Quarterly Investment Strategy* by UBS Brinson, a global institutional asset manager. The table's "Benchmark" column indicates what the asset allocation would be if Brinson had no opinion regarding the expected bond-market performance in the alternative countries. In most cases, this normal allocation is based on the country's relative market value. Here, the normal allocation is 29.6 percent for the United States, 20.5 percent for Japan, and the remaining 49.9 percent for the other countries, including 36.6 percent for the combined EMU countries. Clearly, Brinson *does* have an opinion regarding these countries (as shown in its market strategy) because it has overweighted the U.S. bond market with an allocation of 39.6 percent (versus 29.6 percent) and underweighted the Japan bond market with an allocation of only 4.8 percent (versus 20.5 percent). In turn, several other countries are heavily overweighted—Canada, Spain, Greece, and Sweden—while several are clearly underweighted, including Belgium, Italy, and the Netherlands. In addition, Brinson does a specific currency allocation among countries that would likewise be based on the normal policy weight unless the firm had an opinion on currencies. Again, Brinson has a definite opinion: it heavily underweighted the U.S. dollar, the Japanese yen, and the U.K. pound, and was overweighted in the EMU, Sweden, and Australia.

In making your own allocations based on these specific expectations, you would look for U.S. securities in which yields were expected to decline relative to Treasury securities and for bond markets in foreign countries that likewise had bullish interest rate expectations. Finally, you would look for countries in which the currency was expected to be strong relative to the United States.

In summary, assuming you want to actively manage a bond portfolio, this example shows an approach to the asset allocation decision on a global scale. Similar to our discussion on equity securities, global asset allocation requires substantially more research because you must evaluate each country—individually and relative to every other country. Finally, your global recommendation also must consider exchange rate changes—i.e., you must make a currency decision for each country.

---

[23]For a detailed discussion of the benefits of international bond investing as well as what is involved in the analysis, see Christopher B. Steward and Adam M. Greshin, "International Bond Investing and Portfolio Management"; Michael R. Rosenberg, "International Fixed Income Investing: Theory and Practice"; and Jack Malvey, "Global Corporate Bond Portfolio Management." All three are included in *The Handbook of Fixed-Income Securities.* For a discussion of global portfolio management including bonds, see William G. Droms, ed., *Initiating and Managing a Global Investment Program* (Charlottesville, Va.: Association of Investment Management and Research, 1991); Dwight D. Churchhill, ed., *Fixed-Income Management: Techniques and Practices* (Charlottesville, Va.: Association of Investment Management and Research, 1994); Jan R. Squires, ed., *Global Portfolio Management* (Charlottesville, Va.: Association of Investment Management and Research, 1996); Jan R. Squires, ed., *Global Bond Management* (Charlottesville Va.: Association of Investment Management and Research, 1997); and *Managing Currency Risk* (Charlottesville, Va.: Association of Investment Management and Research, 1997).

TABLE 17.5 **UBS BRINSON GLOBAL BOND PORTFOLIO STRATEGY: MARCH 31, 1999**

MARKET ALLOCATION AS OF MARCH 31, 1999

	Benchmark	Market Strategy	Over / Under Weight	Strategy Range (95% Freq.)
North America	**32.5%**	**45.3%**	**+12.8**	**+/−25%**
Canada	2.9	5.7	+2.8	0 to +10
United States	29.6	39.6	+10.0	+/−25
EMU	**36.6**	**29.0**	**−7.6**	**+/−25**
Austria	0.8	0.0	−0.8	0 to +10
Belgium	2.7	0.0	−2.7	0 to +10
Finland	0.8	0.0	−0.8	0 to +10
France	8.5	9.1	+0.6	0 to +10
Germany	8.6	8.1	−0.5	0 to +10
Ireland	0.3	0.0	−0.3	0 to +10
Italy	8.2	4.7	−3.5	0 to +10
Netherlands	2.9	0.0	−2.9	0 to +10
Portugal	0.4	0.0	−0.4	0 to +10
Spain	3.4	7.2	+3.8	0 to +10
Other Europe	**3.4**	**8.9**	**+5.5**	**0 to +20**
Denmark	1.4	2.4	+1.0	0 to +10
Greece[a]	0.0	2.0	+2.0	0 to +10
Sweden	1.5	4.5	+3.0	0 to +10
Switzerland	0.5	0.0	−0.5	0 to +10
United Kingdom	**6.3**	**6.3**	**0.0**	**0 to +25**
Japan	**20.5**	**4.8**	**−15.7**	**0 to +25**
Australia	**0.7**	**5.7**	**+5.0**	**0 to +10**
	100.0%	**100.0%**		

CURRENCY ALLOCATION

	Benchmark	Market Strategy[b]	Over / Under Weight	Strategy Range (95% Freq.)
North America	**32.5%**	**32.5%**		**+/−25%**
Canada	2.9	6.9	+4.0	0 to +10
United States	29.6	25.6	−4.0	+/−25
EMU	**36.6**	**40.9**	**+4.3**	**+/−25**
Other Europe	**3.4**	**7.4**		**0 to +20**
Denmark	1.4	1.4		0 to +10
Sweden	1.5	5.5	+4.0	0 to +10
Switzerland	0.5	0.5		0 to +10
United Kingdom	**6.3**	**0.0**	**−6.3**	**0 to +25**
Japan	**20.5**	**12.5**	**−8.0**	**0 to +25**
Australia	**0.7**	**6.7**	**+6.0**	**0 to +10**
	100.0%	**100.0%**		

[a]Not a component of the benchmark.

[b]The current strategy is not dependent on the client's base currency.

Totals may not add due to rounding.

Source: UBS Brinson, *Quarterly Investment Strategy,* 31 March 1999 (Chicago, Ill.: Brinson Partners).

FIGURE 17.2 **A PRESCRIBED SCHEDULE OF LIABILITIES**

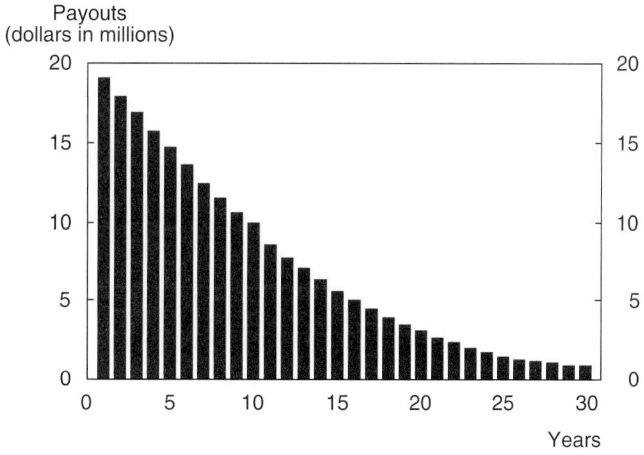
Payouts
(dollars in millions)
20
15
10
5
0
0
5
10
15
20
25
30
Years

Source: Martin L. Leibowitz, "The Dedicated Bond Portfolio in Pension Funds—Part I: Motivations and Basics," *Financial Analysts Journal* 42, no. 1 (January–February 1986). Reprinted by permission of *Financial Analysts Journal.*

MATCHED-FUNDING TECHNIQUES[24]

As discussed previously, because of an increase in interest rate volatility and the needs of many institutional investors, there has been a growth in the use of matched-funding techniques ranging from pure cash-matched dedicated portfolios to portfolios involved in contingent immunization.

DEDICATED PORTFOLIOS **Dedication** refers to bond portfolio management techniques that are used to service a prescribed set of liabilities. The idea is that a pension fund has a set of future liabilities, and those responsible for administering these liabilities want a money manager to construct a portfolio of assets with cash flows that will match this liability stream. Such a "dedicated" portfolio can be created in several ways. We will discuss two alternatives.

A **pure cash-matched dedicated portfolio** is the most conservative strategy. Specifically, the objective of pure cash-matching is to develop a portfolio of bonds that will provide a stream of payments from coupons, sinking funds, and maturing principal payments that will exactly match the specified liability schedules. As example of a typical liability stream for a retired-lives component of a pension system is shown in Figure 17.2.

The goal is to build a portfolio that will generate sufficient funds in advance of each scheduled payment to ensure that the payment will be met. One alternative is to find a number of zero-coupon Treasury securities that will exactly cash-match each liability. Such an exact cash-match is referred to as a *total passive* portfolio because it is designed so that any prior receipts would not be reinvested (i.e., it assumes a zero reinvestment rate).

Dedication with reinvestment is the same as the pure cash-matched technique except it is assumed that the bonds and other cash flows do not have to exactly match the liability

[24]An overview of these alternative strategies is contained in Martin L. Leibowitz, "The Dedicated Bond Portfolio in Pension Funds—Part I: Motivations and Basics," *Financial Analysts Journal* 42, no. 1 (January–February 1986): 68–75; and Martin L. Leibowitz, "The Dedicated Bond Portfolio in Pension Funds—Part II: Immunization, Horizon Matching, and Contingent Procedures," *Financial Analysts Journal* 42, no. 2 (March–April 1986): 47–57.

stream. Specifically, any inflows that precede liability claims can be reinvested at some reasonably conservative rate. This assumption allows the portfolio manager to consider a substantially wider set of bonds that may have higher return characteristics. In addition, the assumption of reinvestment within each period and between periods also will generate a higher return for the asset portfolio. As a result, the net cost of the portfolio will be lower, with almost equal safety, assuming the reinvestment rate assumption is conservative. An example would be to assume a reinvestment rate of 6 percent in an environment where market interest rates are currently ranging from 7 percent to 10 percent.

Potential problems exist with both of these approaches to a dedicated portfolio. For example, when selecting potential bonds for these portfolios, it is critical to be aware of call/prepayment possibilities (refundings, calls, sinking funds) with specific bonds or mortgage-backed securities. These prepayment possibilities become very important following periods of historically high rates. A prime example was the period 1982 to 1986, when interest rates went from over 18 percent to under 8 percent. Because of this substantial change in rates, many dedicated portfolios constructed without adequate concern for complete call protection were negatively affected when numerous bonds were called that were not expected to be called "under normal conditions." For example, bonds selling at deep discounts (which typically provide implicit call protection), when rates were 16 percent to 18 percent, went to par and above when rates declined to under 10 percent—and they were called. Obviously, the reinvestment of these proceeds at the lower rates caused many dedicated portfolios to be underfunded. Therefore, it is necessary to find bonds with complete call protection or to consider deep discount bonds under conservative interest rate conditions.

Although quality also is a legitimate concern, it is probably not necessary to invest only in Treasury bonds if the portfolio manager diversifies across industries and sectors. A diversified portfolio of AA or A industrial bonds can provide a current and total annual return of 40 to 60 basis points above Treasuries. This differential over a 30-year period can have a significant impact on the net cost of funding a liability stream.[25]

IMMUNIZATION STRATEGIES Instead of using a passive strategy, an active strategy, or a dedicated portfolio technique, a portfolio manager (after client consultation) may decide that the optimal strategy is to immunize the portfolio from interest rate changes. The *immunization techniques* attempt to derive a specified rate of return (generally quite close to the current market rate) during a given investment horizon regardless of what happens to market interest rates.

Components of Interest Rate Risk A major problem encountered in bond portfolio management is deriving a given rate of return to satisfy an ending-wealth requirement at a future specific date—that is, the **investment horizon**. If the term structure of interest rates were flat and market rates never changed between the time of purchase and the horizon date when funds were required, you could acquire a bond with a term to maturity equal to the desired investment horizon, and the ending wealth from the bond would equal the promised wealth position implied by the promised yield to maturity. Specifically, the ending-wealth position would be the beginning wealth times the compound value of a dollar at the promised yield to maturity. For example, assume you acquire a 10-year, $1 million bond with an 8 percent coupon at its par value (8 percent YTM). If conditions were as specified (there was a flat yield curve and there were no changes in the curve), your wealth position at the end of your 10-year investment horizon (assuming semiannual compounding) would be

$$\$1{,}000{,}000 \times (1.40)^{20} = \$1{,}000{,}000 \times 2.1911 = \$2{,}191{,}100$$

[25]For additional discussion of this strategy, see Peter E. Christensen and Frank J. Fabozzi, "Dedicated Bond Portfolios," in *The Handbook of Fixed-Income Securities*.

You can get the same answer by taking the $40,000 interest payment every 6 months and compounding it semiannually to the end of the period at 4 percent and adding the $1,000,000 principal at maturity. Unfortunately, in the real world, the term structure of interest rates typically is not flat and the level of interest rates is constantly changing. Consequently, the bond portfolio manager faces **interest rate risk** between the time of investment and the future target date. Interest rate risk is the uncertainty regarding the ending-wealth value of the portfolio due to changes in market interest rates between the time of purchase and the investor's horizon date. It involves two component risks: **price risk** and **coupon reinvestment risk**.

The price risk occurs because if interest rates change before the horizon date and the bond is sold before maturity, the realized market price for the bond will differ from the *expected* price, assuming there had been no change in rates. If rates increased after the time of purchase, the realized price for the bond in the secondary market would be below expectations, whereas if rates declined, the realized price would be above expectations. Because you do not know whether interest rates will increase or decrease, you are uncertain about the bond's future price.

The coupon reinvestment risk arises because the yield to maturity computation implicitly assumes that all coupon cash flows will be reinvested at the promised yield to maturity.[26] If, after the purchase of the bond, interest rates decline, the coupon cash flows will be reinvested at rates below the promised YTM, and the ending wealth will be below expectations. In contrast, if interest rates increase, the coupon cash flows will be reinvested at rates above expectations, and the ending wealth will be above expectations. Again, because you are uncertain about future rates, you are uncertain about these reinvestment rates.

Classical Immunization and Interest Rate Risk The price risk and the reinvestment risk caused by a change in interest rates have opposite effects on the ending-wealth position. An increase in interest rates will cause an ending price below expectations, but the reinvestment rate for interim cash flows will be above expectations. A decline in market interest rates will cause the reverse situation. Clearly, a bond portfolio manager with a specific target date (investment horizon) will attempt to eliminate these two interest rate risks. The process intended to eliminate interest rate risk is referred to as **immunization** and was discussed by Redington in the early 1950s.[27] It has been specified by Fisher and Weil as follows:

> A portfolio of investments in bonds is *immunized* for a holding period if its value at the end of the holding period, regardless of the course of interest rates during the holding period, must be at least as large as it would have been had the interest-rate function been constant throughout the holding period.
>
> If the realized return on an investment in bonds is sure to be at least as large as the appropriately computed yield to the horizon, then that investment is immunized.[28]

Fisher and Weil found a significant difference between the *promised* yields and the *realized* returns on bonds for the period 1925 to 1968, indicating the importance of immunizing a bond portfolio. They showed that it is possible to immunize a bond portfolio if you can assume that any change in interest rates will be the same for all—that is, if forward interest

---

[26]This point was discussed in detail in Chapter 16 and in Homer and Leibowitz, *Inside the Yield Book,* Chapter 1.

[27]F. M. Redington, "Review of the Principles of Life—Office Valuations," *Journal of the Institute of Actuaries* 78 (1952): 286–340.

[28]Lawrence Fisher and Roman L. Weil, "Coping with the Risk of Interest-Rate Fluctuations: Returns to Bondholders from Naive and Optimal Strategies," *Journal of Business* 44, no. 4 (October 1971): 408–431.

rates change, all rates will change by the same amount (there is a parallel shift of the yield curve). Given this assumption, Fisher and Weil proved that *a portfolio of bonds is immunized from interest rate risk if the duration of the portfolio is always equal to the desired investment horizon.* For example, if the investment horizon of a bond portfolio is 8 years, the *duration* of the bond portfolio should equal 8 years to immunize the portfolio. To attain a given duration, the weighted average duration (with weights equal to the proportion of value) is set at the desired length following an interest payment, and all subsequent cash flows are invested in securities *to keep the portfolio duration equal to the remaining investment horizon.*

Fisher and Weil showed that price risk and reinvestment rate risk are affected in opposite directions by a change in market rates and that duration is the time period when these two risks are of equal magnitude but opposite in direction.[29]

Application of the Immunization Principle Fisher and Weil simulated the effects of applying the immunization concept (a duration-matched strategy) compared to a naive portfolio strategy where the portfolio's maturity was equal to the investment horizon. They compared the ending-wealth ratio for the duration matched and for the naive strategy portfolios to a wealth ratio that assumed no change in the interest rate structure. In a perfectly immunized portfolio, the actual ending wealth should equal the expected ending wealth implied by the promised yield, so these comparisons should indicate which portfolio strategy does a superior job of immunization. The duration-matched strategy results were consistently closer to the promised yield results; however, the results were not perfect. The duration portfolio was not perfectly immunized because the basic assumption did not always hold; that is, when interest rates changed, all interest rates did not change by the same amount.

Bierwag and Kaufman pointed out several specifications of the duration measure.[30] The Macaulay duration measure, one of the duration measures discussed in Chapter 16, discounts all flows by the prevailing yield to maturity on the bond being measured.[31] Alternatively, Fisher and Weil defined duration using future one-period interest rates (forward rates) to discount the future flows.[32] Depending on the shape of the yield curve, the two definitions could give different answers. If the yield curve is flat, the two definitions will compute equal durations. Bierwag and Kaufman computed alternative measures of duration and found that, except at high coupons and long maturities, the duration values of the alternative definitions were similar, and the Macaulay definition is preferable because it is a function of the yield to maturity of the bond. This means you do not need a forecast of one-period forward rates over the maturity of the bond.[33]

Example of Classical Immunization Table 17.6 shows the effect of attempting to immunize a portfolio by matching the investment horizon and the duration of a bond portfolio using a single bond. The portfolio manager's investment horizon is 8 years, and the current yield to maturity for 8-year bonds is 8 percent. Therefore, if we assumed no change in yields, the ending-wealth ratio for an investor should be 1.8509 (1.08^8) with annual

[29]This also is noted and discussed in G. O. Bierwag and George G. Kaufman, "Coping with the Risk of Interest Rate Fluctuations: A Note," *Journal of Business* 50, no. 3 (July 1977): 364–370; and G. O. Bierwag, "Immunization, Duration, and the Term Structure of Interest Rates," *Journal of Financial and Quantitative Analysis* 12, no. 5 (December 1977): 725–742.

[30]Bierwag and Kaufman, "Coping with the Risk of Interest Rate Fluctuations," 364–370.

[31]Frederick R. Macaulay, *Some Theoretical Problems Suggested by the Movements of Interest Rates, Bond Yields, and Stock Prices in the United States since 1856* (New York: National Bureau of Economic Research, 1938).

[32]Fisher and Weil, "Coping with the Risk of Interest Rate Fluctuations," 408–431.

[33]Bierwag and Kaufman, "Coping with the Risk of Interest Rate Fluctuations," 367.

TABLE 17.6 **AN EXAMPLE OF THE EFFECT OF A CHANGE IN MARKET RATES ON A BOND (PORTFOLIO) THAT USES THE MATURITY STRATEGY VERSUS THE DURATION STRATEGY**

	Results with Maturity Strategy			Results with Duration Strategy		
Year	Cash Flow	Reinvestment Rate	End Value	Cash Flow	Reinvestment Rate	End Value
1	$ 80	.08	$ 80.00	$ 80	.08	$ 80.00
2	80	.08	166.40	80	.08	166.40
3	80	.08	259.71	80	.08	259.71
4	80	.08	360.49	80	.08	360.49
5	80	.06	462.12	80	.06	462.12
6	80	.06	596.85	80	.06	596.85
7	80	.06	684.04	80	.06	684.04
8	$1,080	.06	$1,805.08	$1,120.64[a]	.06	$1,845.72
Expected Wealth Ratio = 1.8509 or $1,850.90						

[a]The bond could be sold at its market value of $1,040.64, which is the value for an 8 percent bond with 2 years to maturity priced to yield 6 percent.

compounding.[34] As noted, this also should be the ending-wealth ratio for a completely immunized portfolio.

The example considers two portfolio strategies: (1) the maturity strategy, where the portfolio manager would acquire a bond with a term to maturity of 8 years, and (2) the duration strategy, where the portfolio manager sets the duration of the portfolio at 8 years. For the **maturity strategy**, the portfolio manager acquires an 8-year, 8 percent bond; for the **duration strategy**, the manager acquires a 10-year, 8 percent bond that has approximately an 8-year duration (8.12 years), assuming an 8 percent YTM (see Table 16.2). We assume a single shock to the interest rate structure at the end of Year 4, when rates go from 8 percent to 6 percent and stay there through Year 8.

As shown, due to the interest rate change, the ending-wealth ratio for the maturity strategy bond is *below* the desired wealth ratio because of the shortfall in the reinvestment cash flow after Year 4 when the interim coupon cash flow was reinvested at 6 percent rather than 8 percent. Note that *the maturity strategy eliminated the price risk* because the bond matured at the end of Year 8. Alternatively, the duration strategy portfolio likewise suffered a shortfall in reinvestment cash flow because of the change in market rates. In contrast to the maturity strategy, this reinvestment shortfall was partially offset by an *increase* in the ending value for the bond because of the decline in market rates. This second bond is sold at the end of Year 8 at 104.06 of par because it is an 8 percent coupon bond with 2 years to maturity selling to yield 6 percent. Because of this partial offset due to the price increase, the duration strategy had an ending-wealth value (1845.72) that was much closer to the expected wealth ratio (1850.90) than the maturity strategy (1805.08). The point is, the reinvestment rate shortfall was almost completely offset by the positive price effect.

If market interest rates had increased during this period, the maturity strategy portfolio would have experienced an *excess* of reinvestment income compared to the expected cash flow, and the ending-wealth ratio for this strategy would have been above expectations. In contrast, in the duration portfolio, the excess cash flow from reinvestment under this assumption would have been partially offset by a *decline* in the ending price for the bond (i.e., it would have sold at a small discount to par value). Although the ending-wealth ratio for the duration strategy would have been lower than the maturity strategy, it would have

[34]We use annual compounding to compute the ending-wealth ratio because the example uses annual observations.

been closer to the expected-wealth ratio. Although the maturity strategy would have provided a higher than expected ending value for this scenario, the whole purpose of immunization is to *eliminate uncertainty* due to interest rate changes by having the realized-wealth position equal the expected-wealth position. As shown, this is what is accomplished with the duration-matched strategy.

Another View of Immunization The prior example assumed that both bonds were acquired and held to the end of the investment horizon. An alternative way to envision what is expected to happen with an immunized portfolio is to concentrate on the specific growth path from the beginning-wealth position to the ending-wealth position and examine what happens when interest rates change.

Assume that the initial-wealth position is $1 million, your investment horizon is 10 years, and the coupon and current YTM are 8 percent. We know from an earlier computation that this implies that the expected ending-wealth value is $2,191,100 (with semiannual compounding). Figure 17.3A shows the compound growth rate path from $1 million to the expected ending value at $2,191,100. In Figure 17.3B, it is assumed that at the end of Year 2, interest rates increase 200 basis points from 8 percent to 10 percent. We know that with no prior rate changes, at the end of Year 2 the value of the portfolio would have grown at an 8 percent compound rate to $1,169,900 [$1.04^4 = 1.1699$]. Given the rate change, we know there will be two changes for this portfolio: (1) the price (value of the portfolio) will decline to reflect the higher interest rate, and (2) the reinvestment rate, which is the growth rate, will increase to 10 percent. An important question is: How much will the portfolio value decline? The answer depends on the modified duration of the portfolio when rates change. Fisher and Weil showed that *if the modified duration is equal to the remaining horizon, the price change will be such that at the new growth rate (10 percent), the new portfolio value will grow to the expected-wealth position.* You can approximate the change in portfolio value using the modified duration and the change in market rates. (Recall that this will not give an exact estimate because of the convexity of the portfolio.) The approximate change in price is 16 percent based on a modified duration of 8 years and a 200-basis-point change. This would imply an approximate portfolio value of $982,716 ($1,169,900 × 0.84). In fact, the actual value would be $1,003,743. (Recall that the estimated value based on using modified duration always is below the value implied by the price–yield curve.) If this new wealth grows at 10 percent a year for 8 years, the ending-wealth value will be

$$\$1{,}003{,}743 \times 2.1829 \text{ (5\% for 16 periods)} = \$2{,}191{,}070$$

The difference between the expected value and projected value is due to rounding. This example shows that the price decline is almost exactly offset by the higher reinvestment rate—assuming that the modified duration of the portfolio at the time of the rate change was equal to the remaining investment horizon.

What happens if the portfolio is not properly matched? If the modified duration is greater than the remaining horizon, the price change will be greater. Thus, if interest rates increase, the value of the portfolio after the rate change will be less than $1,003,743. In this case, even if the new value of the portfolio grew at 10 percent a year, it would not reach the expected ending-wealth value. This scenario is shown in Figure 17.3C where it is assumed that the portfolio value declined to $950,000. If this new value grew at 10 percent a year for the remaining 8 years, its ending value would be

$$\$950{,}000 \times 2.1829 \text{ (5\% for 16 periods)} = \$2{,}073{,}755$$

Therefore, the shortfall of $118,000 between the expected-wealth value and the realized-wealth value is because the portfolio was not properly duration matched (immunized) when interest rates changed.

FIGURE 17.3 **THE GROWTH PATH TO THE EXPECTED ENDING-WEALTH VALUE AND THE EFFECT OF IMMUNIZATION**

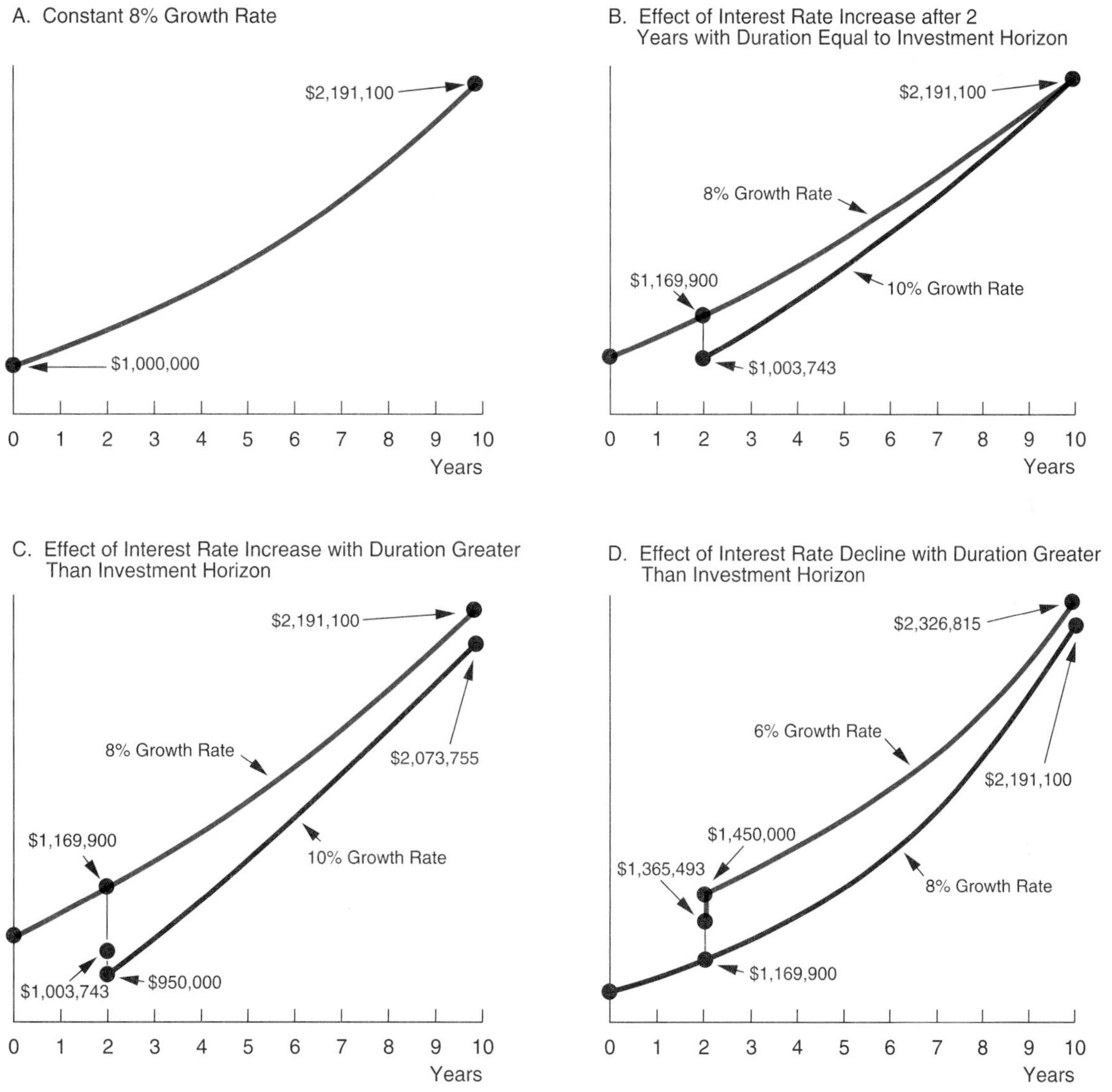
A. Constant 8% Growth Rate
$2,191,100
$1,000,000
0 1 2 3 4 5 6 7 8 9 10
Years
B. Effect of Interest Rate Increase after 2 Years with Duration Equal to Investment Horizon
$2,191,100
8% Growth Rate
$1,169,900
10% Growth Rate
$1,003,743
0 1 2 3 4 5 6 7 8 9 10
Years
C. Effect of Interest Rate Increase with Duration Greater Than Investment Horizon
$2,191,100
8% Growth Rate
$2,073,755
$1,169,900
10% Growth Rate
$1,003,743
$950,000
0 1 2 3 4 5 6 7 8 9 10
Years
D. Effect of Interest Rate Decline with Duration Greater Than Investment Horizon
$2,326,815
6% Growth Rate
$2,191,100
$1,450,000
$1,365,493
8% Growth Rate
$1,169,900
0 1 2 3 4 5 6 7 8 9 10
Years

Alternatively, if interest rates had declined, and the modified duration had been longer than 8 years, the portfolio value would have increased such that the new portfolio value would have been greater than the required value. Figure 17.3D shows what can happen if the portfolio is not properly matched and interest rates decline by 200 basis points to 6 percent. First, if the portfolio *is* properly matched, the value will increase to $1,365,493. If this new portfolio value grows at 6 percent for 8 years, its ending value will be

$$\$1{,}365{,}493 \times 1.6047 \text{ (3\% for 16 periods)} = \$2{,}191{,}207$$

Again, this deviates slightly from the expected ending-wealth value ($2,191,100) due to rounding. Alternatively, if the modified duration had been above 8 years, the new portfolio value would have been greater than the required current value of $1,365,493. Assume that because the duration of the portfolio exceeded the remaining horizon, the portfolio value increased to $1,450,000. If so, the ending value would be

$$\$1{,}450{,}000 \times 1.6047 \text{ (3\% for 16 periods)} = \$2{,}326{,}815$$

In this example, the ending-wealth value would have been greater than the expected-wealth value because you were mismatched and interest rates went in the right direction. When you are not duration matched, you are speculating on interest rate changes, and the result can be very good or very bad. The purpose of immunization is to avoid these uncertainties and to ensure the expected ending-wealth value ($2,191,100), regardless of interest rate changes.

Application of Classical Immunization Once you understand the reasoning behind immunization (i.e., it is meant to offset the components of interest rate risk) and the general principle (you need to match modified duration and the investment horizon), you might conclude that this strategy is fairly simply to apply. You might even consider it a passive strategy; simply match modified duration and the investment horizon, and you can ignore the portfolio until the end of the horizon period. The following discussion will show that *immunization is neither a simple nor a passive strategy.*

Except for the case of a zero-coupon bond, *an immunized portfolio requires frequent rebalancing* because the modified duration of the portfolio always should be equal to the remaining time horizon. The zero-coupon bond is unique because it is a pure discount bond. As such, because there is no cash flow, there is *no reinvestment risk* because the discounting assumes that the value of the bond will grow at the discount rate. For example, if you discount a future value at 10 percent, the present value factor assumes that the value will grow at a compound rate of 10 percent to maturity. Also, there is *no price risk* if you set the duration at your time horizon because you will receive the face value of the bond at maturity. Also, recall that the duration of a zero-coupon bond always is equal to its term to maturity. In summary, if you immunize by matching your horizon with a zero-coupon bond of equal duration, you do not have to rebalance.

In contrast, if you immunize a portfolio using coupon bonds, several characteristics of duration make it impossible to set a duration equal to the remaining horizon at the initiation of the portfolio and ignore it thereafter. First, *duration declines more slowly than term to maturity, assuming no change in market interest rates.* For example, assume you have a security with a computed duration of 5 years at a 10 percent market yield. A year later, if you compute the duration of the security at 10 percent, you will find that it has a duration of approximately 4.2 years; that is, although the term to maturity has declined by a year, the duration has declined by only 0.8 year. This means that, assuming no change in market rates, the portfolio manager must rebalance the portfolio to reduce its duration to 4 years. Typically, this is not difficult because cash flows from the portfolio can be invested in short-term T-bills if necessary.

Second, *duration changes with a change in market interest rates.* In Chapter 16, we discussed the inverse relationship between market rates and duration—with higher market rates, there will be lower duration and vice versa. Therefore, a portfolio that has the appropriate modified duration at a point in time can have its duration changed immediately if market rates change. If this occurs, a portfolio manager would have to rebalance the portfolio if the deviation from the required duration becomes too large.

Third, you will recall from our initial discussion of immunization that one of the assumptions is that when market rates change, they will change by the same amount and in the same direction (i.e., there will be a parallel shift of the yield curve). Clearly, if this does

FIGURE 17.4 **THE CONCEPT OF HORIZON MATCHING**

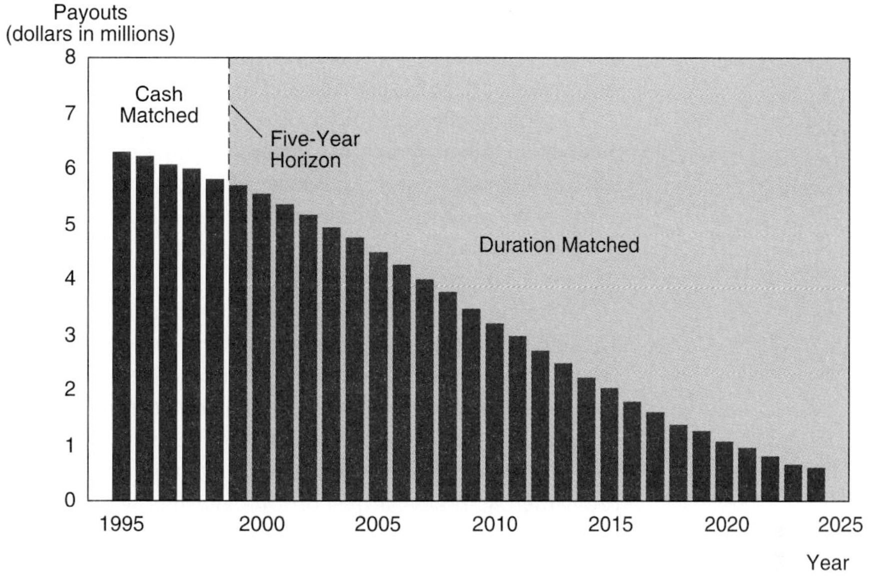

Payouts
(dollars in millions)
8
7
6
5
4
3
2
1
0
Cash
Matched
Five-Year
Horizon
Duration Matched
1995
2000
2005
2010
2015
2020
2025
Year

Source: Copyright © 1983 Salomon Brothers Inc. This chart was prepared for Salomon Brothers Inc. by Martin Leibowitz, a former Managing Director, Thomas E. Klaffky, Managing Director, Steven Mandel, Managing Director, and Alfred Weinberger, a former Director. Although the information in this chart has been obtained from sources that Salomon Brothers Inc. believes to be reliable, Salomon does not guarantee its accuracy, and such information may be incomplete or condensed. All figures included in this chart constitute our judgment as of the original publication date.

not happen, it will affect the performance of a portfolio of diffuse bonds. For example, assume you own a portfolio of long- and short-term bonds with a weighted average 6-year duration (e.g., 2-year duration bonds and 10-year duration bonds). Assume the term-structure curve changes such that short-term rates decline and long-term rates *rise* (there is an increase in the slope of the yield curve). In such a case, you would experience a major price decline in the long-term bonds, but would be penalized on reinvestment, assuming you generally reinvest the cash flow in short-term securities. This potential problem (caused by a change in the shape of the yield curve) suggests that you should attempt to bunch your portfolio selections close to the desired duration (i.e., use a bullet approach). For example, an 8-year duration portfolio should be made up of 7- to 9-year duration securities to avoid this yield curve reshaping problem.

Finally, there always can be a problem acquiring the bonds you select as optimum for your portfolio. For instance, you can buy long-duration bonds at the price you consider acceptable? In summary, it is important to recognize that classical immunization is *not a passive strategy* because it is subject to all of these potential problems.[35]

HORIZON MATCHING Horizon matching is a combination of two of the techniques discussed: cash-matching dedication and immunization. As shown in Figure 17.4, the liability stream is divided into two segments. In the first segment, the portfolio is constructed to provide a cash match for the liabilities during this horizon period (e.g., the first

[35]Several of these problems are discussed in Peter Christensen, Frank J. Fabozzi, and Anthony Lofaso, "Bond Immunization: An Asset/Liability Optimization Strategy," in *The Handbook of Fixed-Income Securities.*

5 years). The second segment is the remaining liability stream following the end of the horizon period—in the example, it is the 25 years after the horizon period. During this second time period, the liabilities are covered by a duration-matched strategy based on immunization principles. As a result, the client receives the certainty of cash matching during the early years and the cost saving and flexibility of duration-matched flows thereafter.

The combination technique also helps alleviate one of the problems with classical immunization: the potential for nonparallel shifts in the yield curve. Most of the problems related to nonparallel shifts are concentrated in the short end of the yield curve because this is where the most severe curve reshaping occurs. Because the short end is taken care of by the cash matching, these are not of concern and we know that the long end of the yield curve tends toward parallel shifts.

An important decision when using horizon matching is the length of the horizon period. The trade-off when making this decision is between the safety and certainty of cash matching and the cost and flexibility of duration-based immunization. The portfolio manager should provide to the client a set of horizon alternatives and the costs and benefits of each of them and allow the client to make the decision.

It also is possible to consider *rolling out* the cash-matched segment over time. Specifically, after the first year the portfolio manager would restructure the portfolio to provide a cash match during the original Year 6, which means that you would still have a 5-year horizon. The ability and cost of rolling out depends on movements in interest rates (ideally, you would want parallel shifts in the yield curve).[36]

Contingent Procedures

Contingent procedures are a form of structured active management. The procedure we discuss here is contingent immunization, which entails allowing the portfolio manager some opportunity to actively manage the portfolio with a structure that constrains the portfolio manager if he or she is unsuccessful.

CONTINGENT IMMUNIZATION Subsequent to the development and application of classical immunization, Leibowitz and Weinberger developed a portfolio strategy called *contingent immunization.*[37] Basically, it allows a bond portfolio manager to pursue the highest returns available through active strategies, while relying on classical bond immunization techniques to ensure a given minimal return over the investment horizon—that is, it allows active portfolio management with a safety net provided by classical immunization.

To understand contingent immunization, it is necessary to recall our discussion of classical immunization. Remember that when the portfolio duration is equal to the investment horizon, a change in interest rates will cause a change in the dollar value of the portfolio such that when the new asset value is compounded at the new market interest rate, it will equal the desired ending value. This required change in value occurs *only* when the modified duration of the portfolio is equal to the remaining time horizon, which is why the modified duration of the portfolio must be maintained at the horizon value.

Consider the following example of this process. Assume that our desired ending-wealth value is \$206.3 million. Given a specific ending value and the number of years to your horizon value, it is possible to determine how much you must invest today to attain that

---

[36]For a further discussion on this topic, see Martin L. Leibowitz, Thomas E. Klaffky, Steven Mandel, and Alfred Weinberger, *Horizon Matching: A New Generalized Approach for Developing Minimum-Cost Dedicated Portfolios* (New York: Salomon Brothers, 1983).

[37]Martin L. Leibowitz and Alfred Weinberger, "Contingent Immunization—Part I: Risk Control Procedures," *Financial Analysts Journal* 38, no. 6 (November–December 1982): 17–32; and Martin L. Leibowitz and Alfred Weinberger, "Contingent Immunization—Part II: Problem Areas," *Financial Analysts Journal* 39, no. 1 (January–February 1983): 35–50. This section draws heavily from these articles.

ending value if you assume a rate of return on the portfolio. Obviously, this is just the reverse of the price compounding exercise—i.e., you compute the present value of the ending value at the expected yield for the horizon period. In this case, we assume a 5-year horizon and a 15 percent return, which means we compute the present value of $206.3 million at 15 percent for 5 years or 7.5 percent for 10 periods assuming semiannual compounding. The present value factor of 0.48473 times the $206.3 million ending value equals $100 million—i.e., this is the required initial investment under these assumptions to attain the desired ending value. We can do it for other interest rates as follows:

Percent	Present Value Factor[a]	Required Investment ($ Mil.)	Percent	Present Value Factor[a]	Required Investment ($ Mil.)
10	0.6139	$126.65	16	0.4632	$95.56
12	0.5584	115.20	18	0.4224	87.14
14	0.5083	104.86	20	0.3855	79.53
15	0.48473	100.00			

[a]Present value for 10 periods (5 years) at one-half the annual percent.

Figure 17.5 reflects these calculations—i.e., the dark line indicates the required initial amount that must be invested at every yield level to attain $206.3 million in 5 years. Clearly at lower yields you need a larger initial investment (e.g., $126 million at 10 percent), and it declines with higher yields (e.g., less than $80 million at 20 percent). The dotted line in Figure 17.5 indicates that the price sensitivity of a portfolio with a modified duration of 5 years will have almost exactly the price sensitivity required.

FIGURE 17.5 **CLASSICAL IMMUNIZATION**

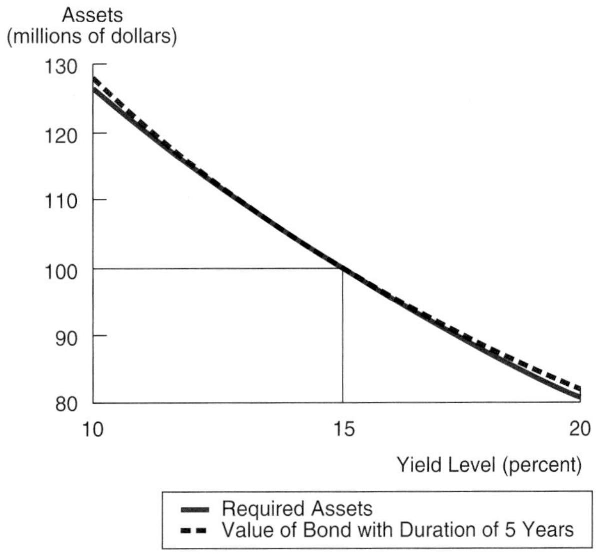
Assets
(millions of dollars)
130
120
110
100
90
80
10
15
20
Yield Level (percent)
Required Assets
Value of Bond with Duration of 5 Years

Source: Martin L. Leibowitz and Alfred Weinberger, "Contingent Immunization—Part I: Risk Control Procedures," *Financial Analysts Journal* 38, no. 6 (November–December 1982): 17–32. Reprinted by permission of *Financial Analysts Journal.*

Contingent immunization requires that the client be willing to accept a potential return below the current market return, referred to as a *cushion spread*—the difference between the current market return and some floor rate. This cushion spread in required yield provides flexibility for the portfolio manager to engage in active portfolio strategies. For example, if current markets are 15 percent, the client might be willing to accept a floor rate of 14 percent. If we assume the client initiated the fund with $100 million, the acceptance of this lower rate will mean that the portfolio manager does not have the same ending-asset requirements. Specifically, at 14 percent the required ending-wealth value would be $196.72 million (7 percent for 10 periods) compared to the $206.3 million at 15 percent. Because of this lower floor rate (and lower ending-wealth value), it is possible to experience some declines in the value of the portfolio while attempting to do better than the market through active management strategies.

Figure 17.6 shows the value of assets that are required at the beginning assuming a 14 percent required return and the implied ending-wealth value of $196.72 million. Notably, assuming current market rates of 15 percent, the required value of assets at the beginning would be $95.56 million, which is the present value of $196.72 million at 15 percent for 15 years. The difference between the client's initial fund of $100 million and the required assets of $95.56 million is the dollar cushion available to the portfolio manager. As noted, this dollar cushion arises because the client has agreed to a lower investment rate, and therefore a lower ending-wealth value.

At this point, the portfolio manager can engage in various active portfolio management strategies to increase the ending-wealth value of the portfolio above that required at 14 percent. As an example, assume that the portfolio manager believes that market rates will

FIGURE 17.6 **PRICE BEHAVIOR REQUIRED FOR FLOOR RETURN**

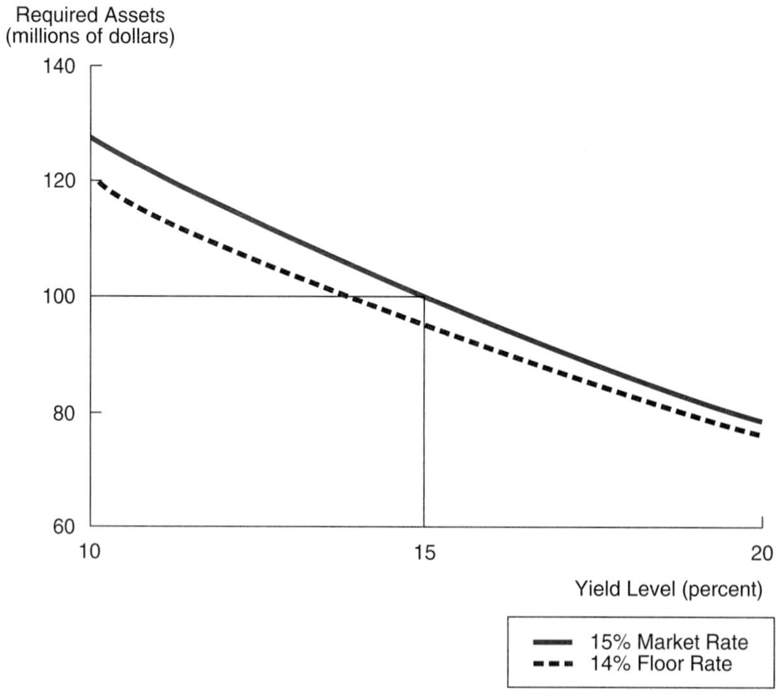
Required Assets
(millions of dollars)
140
120
100
80
60
10
15
20
Yield Level (percent)
15% Market Rate
14% Floor Rate

Source: Martin L. Leibowitz and Alfred Weinberger, "Contingent Immunization—Part I: Risk Control Procedures," *Financial Analysts Journal* 38, no. 6 (November–December 1982): 17–32. Reprinted by permission of *Financial Analysts Journal.*

decline. Under such conditions, the portfolio manager might consider acquiring a 30-year bond that has a duration greater than the investment horizon of 5 years and, therefore, has greater price sensitivity to changes in market rates. Hence, if rates decline as expected, the value of the long-duration portfolio will rise above the initial value. In contrast, if rates increase, the value of the portfolio will decline rapidly. In this case, depending on how high rates go, the value of the portfolio could decline to a value below that needed to reach the desired ending-wealth value of \$196.72 million.

Figure 17.7 shows what happens to the value of this portfolio if we assume an instantaneous change in interest rates when the fund is established. Specifically, if rates decline from 15 percent, the portfolio of long-duration, 30-year bonds would experience a large increase in value and develop a *safety margin*—a portfolio value above the required value. In contrast, if rates increase, the value of the portfolio will decline until you reach the asset value required at 14 percent. When the value of the portfolio reaches this point of minimum return (referred to as a *trigger point*), it is necessary to stop active portfolio management and use classical immunization with the remaining assets to ensure that you attain the desired ending-wealth value (i.e., \$196.72 million).

Potential Return The concept of *potential return* is helpful in understanding the objective of contingent immunization. This is the return the portfolio would achieve over the entire investment horizon if, at any point, the assets in hand were immunized at the prevailing market rate. Figure 17.8 contains the various potential rates of return based on dollar asset values shown in Figure 17.7. If the portfolio were immediately immunized when market

FIGURE 17.7 **SAFETY MARGIN FOR A PORTFOLIO OF 30-YEAR BONDS**

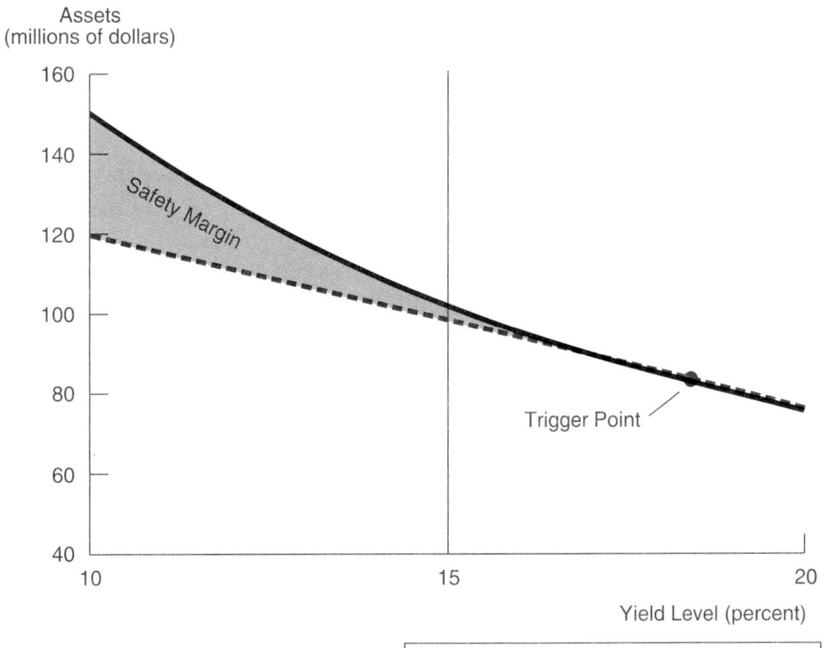
Assets
(millions of dollars)
160
140
120
100
80
60
40
10
15
20
Yield Level (percent)
Safety Margin
Trigger Point
Portfolio of 30-Year Bonds
Required Assets for 14% Floor Rate

Source: Martin L. Leibowitz and Alfred Weinberger, "Contingent Immunization—Part I: Risk Control Procedures," *Financial Analysts Journal* 38, no. 6 (November–December 1982): 17–32. Reprinted by permission of *Financial Analysts Journal.*

FIGURE 17.8

THE POTENTIAL RETURN CONCEPT

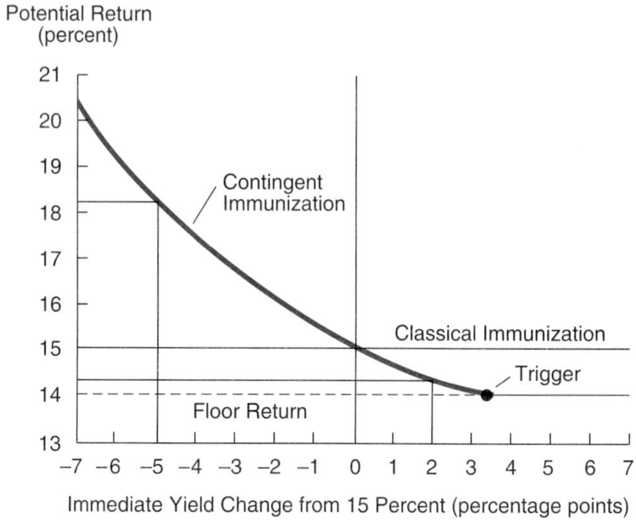
Potential Return (percent)
21
20
19
18
17
16
15
14
13
Contingent Immunization
Classical Immunization
Trigger
Floor Return
−7 −6 −5 −4 −3 −2 −1 0 1 2 3 4 5 6 7
Immediate Yield Change from 15 Percent (percentage points)

Source: Martin L. Leibowitz and Alfred Weinberger, "Contingent Immunization—Part I: Risk Control Procedures," *Financial Analysts Journal* 38, no. 6 (November–December 1982): pp. 17–32. Reprinted by permission of *Financial Analysts Journal.*

rates were 15 percent, it would naturally earn the 15 percent market rate; that is, its potential return would be 15 percent. Alternatively, if yields declined instantaneously to 10 percent, the portfolio's asset value would increase to $147 million (see Figure 17.7). If this $147 million portfolio were immunized at the market rate of 10 percent over the remaining 5-year period, the portfolio would compound at 10 percent to a total value of $239.45 million ($147 million × 1.6289, which is the compound growth factor for 5 percent and 10 periods). This ending value of $239.45 million represents an 18.25 percent realized (horizon) rate of return on the original $100 million portfolio. Consequently, as shown in Figure 17.8, if rates decline by 5 percent, the potential return for this portfolio at this point in time is 18.25 percent.

In contrast, if interest rates increased, the value of the portfolio will decline substantially and the potential return will decline. For example, if market rates rise to 17 percent (i.e., a yield change of 2 percent), the asset value of the 30-year bond portfolio will decline to $88 million (see Figure 17.7). If this portfolio of $88 million were immunized for the remaining 5 years at the prevailing market rate of 17 percent, the ending value would be $199 million. This ending value implies a potential return of 14.32 percent for the total period.

As Figure 17.7 shows, if interest rates rose to 18.50 percent, the 30-year bonds would decline to a value of $81.16 million (the trigger point) and the portfolio would have to be immunized. At this point, if the remaining assets of $81.16 million were immunized at this current market rate of 18.50 percent, the value of the portfolio would grow to $196.73 million ($81.16 × 2.424, which is the compound value factor for 9.25 percent for 10 periods). This ending value implies that the potential return for the portfolio would be exactly 14 percent as shown in Figure 17.8. Regardless of what happens to subsequent market rates, the portfolio has been immunized at the floor rate of 14 percent. That is a major characteristic of the contingent immunized portfolio; if there is proper monitoring, you will always know your trigger point where you must immunize and can be assured of receiving a return no less than the minimum rate of return specified.

FIGURE 17.9 **CONTINGENT IMMUNIZATION FLOOR PORTFOLIO OVER TIME**

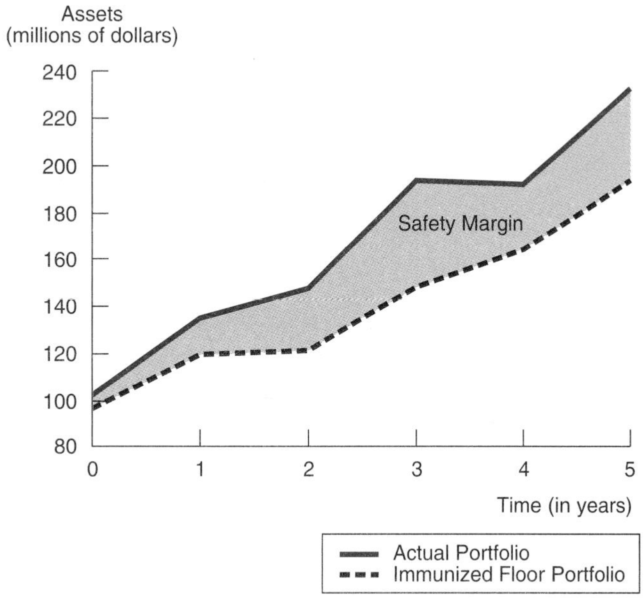
Assets
(millions of dollars)
240
220
200
180
160
140
120
100
80
0
1
2
3
4
5
Time (in years)
Safety Margin
Actual Portfolio
Immunized Floor Portfolio

Source: Martin L. Leibowitz and Alfred Weinberger, "Contingent Immunization—Part I: Risk Control Procedures," *Financial Analysts Journal* 38, no. 6 (November–December 1982): 17–32. Reprinted by permission of *Financial Analysts Journal.*

Monitoring the Immunized Portfolio Clearly, a crucial factor in managing a contingent immunized portfolio is monitoring it to ensure that if the asset value falls to the trigger point, it will be detected and the appropriate action taken to ensure that the portfolio is immunized at the floor-level rate. This can be done using a chart as in Figure 17.9. The top line is the current market value of the portfolio over time. The bottom line is the required value of the immunized floor portfolio. Specifically, the bottom line is *the required value of the portfolio* if we were to immunize at *today's rates* to attain the necessary ending-wealth value. This required minimum value for the portfolio is calculated by *computing the present value of the promised ending-wealth value at the prevailing market rate.*

To demonstrate how this floor portfolio would be constructed, consider our example where we derived a promised ending-wealth value in 5 years of $196.72 million based on an initial investment of $100 million and an acceptable floor rate of 14 percent. If 1 year after the initiation of the portfolio, market rates were 10 percent, you would need a minimum portfolio value of approximately $133.14 million to get to $196.72 million in 4 years. To compute this minimum required value, you multiply the $196.72 million (promised ending-wealth value) times the present value factor for 10 percent for 4 years, assuming semiannual compounding (.6761). The logic is that $133.14 million invested (immunized) at 10 percent for 4 years will equal $196.72 million.

If the active manager had predicted correctly that market rates would decline and had a long-duration portfolio under these conditions, the *actual* value of the portfolio would be much higher than this *minimum required* value, and there would be a safety margin. A year later (after year 2), you would determine the assets needed at the rate prevailing at that point in time. Assuming interest rates had increased to 12 percent, you could determine that you would need a floor portfolio of about $138.69 million. Specifically, this is the present

FIGURE 17.10 **COMPARISON OF RETURN DISTRIBUTIONS**

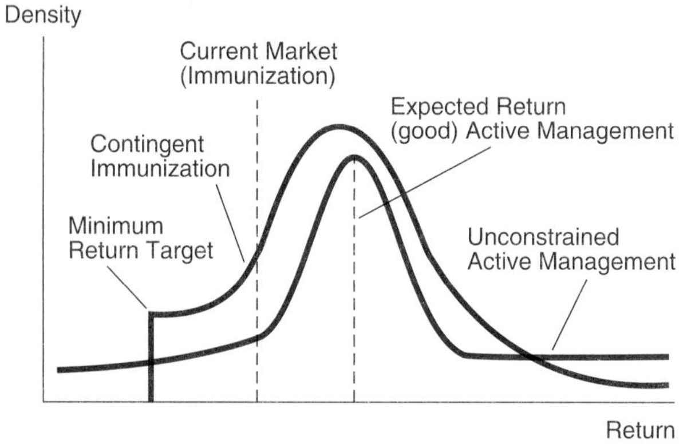
Density
Current Market
(Immunization)
Expected Return
(good) Active Management
Contingent
Immunization
Minimum
Return Target
Unconstrained
Active Management
Return

Source: Martin L. Leibowitz and Alfred Weinberger, "Contingent Immunization—Part II: Problem Areas," *Financial Analyst Journal* 39, no. 1 (January–February 1983): 35–50. Reprinted by permission of *Financial Analysts Journal.*

value of the $196.72 million for 3 years at 12 percent, assuming semiannual compounding (0.7050). Again, you would expect the actual value of the portfolio to be greater than this required floor portfolio, so you still have a safety margin. If you ever reached the point where the actual value of the portfolio was equal to the required floor value, you would stop the active management and immunize what was left *at the current market rate* to ensure that the ending value of the portfolio would be $196.72 million.

In summary, the contingent immunization strategy encompasses the opportunity for a bond portfolio manager to engage in various active portfolio strategies if the client is willing to accept a floor return (and ending-wealth value) that is below what is currently available. The graph in Figure 17.10 describes the trade-offs involved in contingent immunization. Specifically, by allowing for a slightly lower minimum target rate, the client is making it possible to experience a much higher potential return from active management by the portfolio manager.

IMPLICATIONS OF CAPITAL MARKET THEORY AND THE EMH ON BOND PORTFOLIO MANAGEMENT

The high level of interest rates that has prevailed since the latter part of the 1960s has provided increasingly attractive returns to bond investors, and the wide swings in interest rates that have accompanied these high market yields have provided numerous capital gains opportunities for bond portfolio managers. As a result, the average compound rates of return on bonds during the 1980s was the highest of any 10-year period in this century, and this performance has continued into the 1990s. Specifically, the results contained in Table 17.7 indicate that the annual returns on the aggregate of high-grade bonds during the period 1980–1998 ranged from −2.92 percent (the only negative annual return) to 32.62 percent, and the geometric mean returns of 10.64 percent were clearly impressive even compared to the average returns on common stocks of 17.37 percent. When these are compared to the long-term results since 1926 (see Figure 17.12), it appears that it will be

TABLE 17.7 **ANNUAL RATES OF RETURN, RISK MEASURES, AND RANGES OF RETURN FOR LEHMAN BROTHERS BONDS INDEXES AND THE S&P 500 TOTAL RETURN INDEX: 1980–1998**

	Arithmetic Mean	Geometric Mean	Standard Deviation	Coefficient of Variation[a]	High Year	Low Year
Lehman Brothers Government/Corporate	10.86	10.60	7.90	0.72	31.10	−3.51
Lehman Brothers Government	10.66	10.44	7.15	0.67	27.75	−3.38
Lehman Brothers Corporate	11.63	11.23	9.98	0.86	39.20	−3.92
Lehman Brothers Mortgage	11.26	10.85	10.14	0.90	43.04	−1.61
Lehman Brothers Yankee	11.65	11.26	9.72	0.83	35.82	−4.65
Lehman Brothers Aggregate	10.91	10.64	8.06	0.74	32.62	−2.92
S&P 500	18.09	17.37	13.20	0.73	37.57	−4.91

[a]Coefficient of Variation = Standard Deviation/Arithmetic Mean Return.

Source: *Global Family of Indices*—Historical Database 1973–1998, Lehman Brothers, Fixed Income Research. Reprinted with permission.

difficult to continue such performance. Still, these results indicate that there are some wonderful opportunities available in bonds. An important consideration for portfolio managers, therefore, is the proper role of fixed-income securities when considering the implications of portfolio theory, capital market theory, and research related to efficient capital markets.

Bonds and Total Portfolio Theory

The performance of bonds has improved even more than indicated by returns alone because bonds offer substantial diversification benefits. In an efficient market, neither stocks nor bonds should dominate a portfolio, but some combination of them should provide a superior risk-adjusted return compared to either one taken alone (assuming low correlation between stocks and bonds). In the study by Reilly, Kao, and Wright, which showed that stock returns were superior to bond yields, they also showed that, due to the low correlation between bonds and equities (about 0.30), the combination of the stocks and bonds in a portfolio vastly improved the return per unit of risk.[38]

Bonds and Capital Market Theory

Capital market theory contends that there should be an upward-sloping market line, meaning that greater return should be accompanied by greater risk. Compared to other market vehicles fixed-income securities were traditionally viewed as low risk, and their rates of return were typically modest until the late 1970s. At that time, the inflation rate and bond yields increased. Also, during periods of high economic uncertainty, such as the recessions of 1981–1982 and 1990–1991, the risk premiums on bonds increased substantially because the risk of default for low-rated obligations increased.[39] As demonstrated earlier in the chapter (Figure 17.1), the risk premium on junk bonds has fluctuated dramatically over time.

Capital market theory also relates the risk–return behavior of fixed-income securities to other financial assets. Because fixed-income securities are considered to be relatively

[38]Frank K. Reilly, Wenchi Kao, and David J. Wright, "Alternative Bond Market Indexes," *Financial Analysts Journal* 48, no. 3 (May–June 1992): 44–58.

[39]For a detailed discussion on this topic that considers several studies on the subject, see James C. Van Horne, *Financial Market Rates and Flows,* 5th ed. (Englewood Cliffs, N.J.: Prentice-Hall, 1998), Chapter 6.

FIGURE 17.11 **TOTAL RISK–RETURN COMPARISON FOR ALTERNATIVE CAPITAL MARKET ASSETS: 1980–1997**

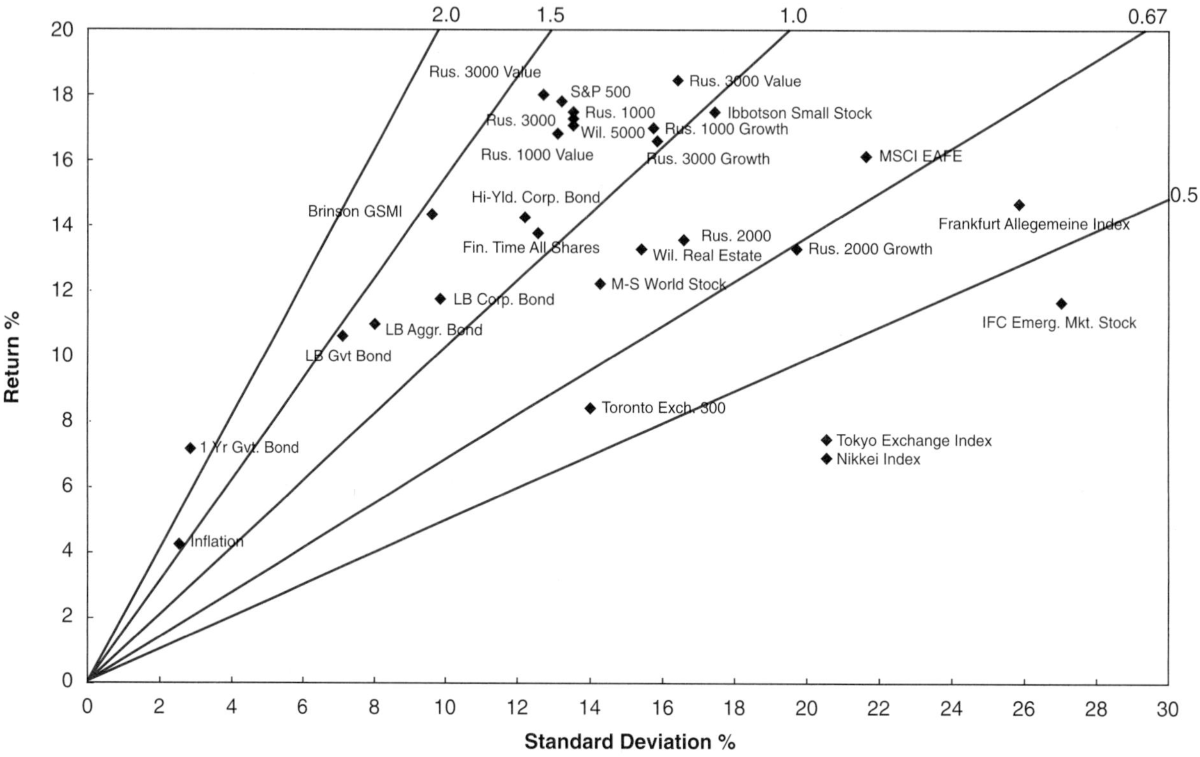
2.0
1.5
1.0
0.67
0.5
Rus. 3000 Value
S&P 500
Rus. 1000
Wil. 5000
Rus. 3000
Rus. 1000 Value
Rus. 3000 Value
Ibbotson Small Stock
Rus. 1000 Growth
Rus. 3000 Growth
MSCI EAFE
Brinson GSMI
Hi-Yld. Corp. Bond
Fin. Time All Shares
Rus. 2000
Wil. Real Estate
Rus. 2000 Growth
Frankfurt Allegemeine Index
M-S World Stock
LB Corp. Bond
LB Aggr. Bond
LB Gvt Bond
IFC Emerg. Mkt. Stock
Toronto Exch. 300
Tokyo Exchange Index
Nikkei Index
1 Yr Gvt. Bond
Inflation
Return %
Standard Deviation %
0
2
4
6
8
10
12
14
16
18
20
22
24
26
28
30

Source: Frank K. Reilly, "An Analysis of Capital Market Returns," University of Notre Dame Working Paper (May 1999).

conservative investments, we would expect them to be on the lower end of the capital market line. A study by Reilly examined the comparative risk–return characteristics of 30 classes of long-term securities.[40] Figure 17.11 shows the basic findings of the study and confirms the a priori expectations. Specifically, government and high-grade corporate bonds were at the low end of the risk spectrum, and it progressed to high-quality common stocks, small cap stocks, foreign stocks, and, finally, emerging market stocks. An annual analysis of capital market returns by Ibbotson Associates comparing corporate and government bonds (long- and intermediate-term) to common stocks (total NYSE and small-firm) and Treasury bill obligations indicated similar results. As Figure 17.12 shows, Treasury bills have the least risk and return, followed by government bonds, corporate bonds, large company common stocks, and finally small company common stocks.

Bond Price Behavior in a CAPM Framework

The capital asset pricing model (CAPM) is expected to provide a framework for explaining realized security returns as a function of nondiversifiable market risk. Bond returns should be linked directly to risk of default and interest rate risk. Although interest rate risk

[40]Frank K. Reilly, "An Analysis of Capital Market Returns," University of Notre Dame Working Paper (May 1999).

FIGURE 17.12 **MEAN RATE OF RETURN AND STANDARD DEVIATION OF RETURNS FOR COMMON STOCKS, GOVERNMENT AND CORPORATE BONDS, T-BILLS, AND INFLATION: 1926–1998**

	Geometric Mean	Arithmetic Mean	Standard Deviation
Large company stocks	11.2%	13.2%	20.3%
Small company stocks	12.4	17.4	33.8
Long-term corporate bonds	5.8	6.1	8.6
Long-term government bonds	5.3	5.7	9.2
Intermediate-term government bonds	5.3	5.5	5.7
U.S. Treasury bills	3.8	3.8	3.2
Inflation	3.1	3.2	4.5

Distribution

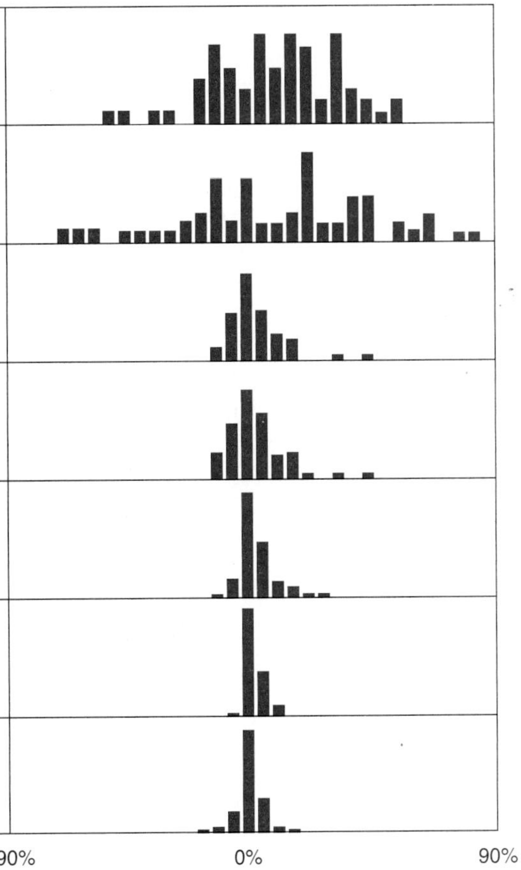
–90%
0%
90%

Note: The 1933 Small Company Stock Total Return was 142.9 percent.

Source: From *Stocks, Bonds, Bills, and Inflation 1999 Yearbook*™, Ibbotson Associates, Chicago (this book annually updates work by Roger G. Ibbotson and Rex A. Sinquefield). Used with permission. All Rights Reserved.

for investment-quality bonds should be nondiversifiable, some evidence exists that default risk also is largely nondiversifiable because default experience is closely related to the business cycle.[41] Therefore, because the major bond risks are largely nondiversifiable, this

[41]W. Braddock Hickman, *Corporate Bond Quality and Investor Experience* (New York: National Bureau of Economic Research, 1958); Thomas R. Atkinson, *Trends in Corporate Bond Quality* (New York: National Bureau of Economic Research, 1967); Dwight M. Jaffee, "Cyclical Variations in the Risk Structure of Interest Rates," *Journal of Monetary Economics* 1, no. 2 (July 1975): 309–325; Douglas J. Lucas and John G. Lonski, "Changes in Corporate Credit Quality 1970–1990," *Journal of Fixed Income* 1, no. 4 (March 1992): 7–14; Jean Helwege and Paul Kleiman, "Understanding Aggregate Default Rates of High-Yield Bonds," *Journal of Fixed Income* 7, no. 1 (June 1997): 55–61; and Martin S. Fridson, M. Christopher Garman, and Sheng Wu, "Real Interest Rates and the Default Rate on High-Yield Bonds," *Journal of Fixed Income* 7, no. 2 (September 1997): 29–34.

implies that we should be able to define bond returns in the context of the CAPM. Still, few studies have attempted it because of data-collection problems. Percival found only a modest effect of a computed beta on bond returns.[42] An analysis of beta and its relationship to the bond and issuer characteristics indicated that bond betas were more responsive to the intrinsic characteristics of the bond *issue* (i.e., coupon, maturity, duration, and call features) than of the issuer.

Reilly and Joehnk found that average bond betas had no significant or consistent relationships with agency ratings.[43] It was contended that, because the study involved only investment-grade securities, the major factor affecting bond prices was market interest rate movements. Evidence that high-grade bond risk is almost all systematic risk is found in the Reilly, Wright study, which shows that the returns among these investment-grade bonds, regardless of sector (government, corporate, mortgages) or ratings, were correlated 0.90 to 0.99.[44] This interest rate risk, which is a market-related, systematic risk factor, has an overpowering effect on price performance and largely negated the effects of differential default risk (a company-specific unique risk factor). It is this unique default risk that is reflected in comparative agency ratings. Notably, the overpowering effect of systematic interest rate risk does *not* prevail when one considers high-yield (junk) bonds. As shown by Reilly and Wright, the correlation between high-yield bonds and investment-grade bonds is *lower* than the correlation between high-yield bonds and common stock.[45] This strong correlation with stocks occurs because both high-yield bonds and common stocks have substantial unsystematic risk.

Alexander examined some of the assumptions of the market model as related to bonds and found two major problems.[46] First, the bond beta results were sensitive to the market index used.[47] Specifically, there were major differences with a pure stock index, a pure bond index, or a composite stock-bond index, and the pure bond index had the biggest problems. Second, the results were sensitive to the time period used; the bond betas increased during periods of high bond yields.

Weinstein computed betas for bonds using several market series and related the betas to term to maturity, coupon, and bond ratings.[48] The results for beta using alternative market indexes (pure stock, pure bond, combined) revealed a very strong correlation between the betas from the stock and the combined indexes, a fairly strong relationship between the betas from the bond and the combined indexes, and a weak relationship between the betas from pure stock and bond indexes. No significant relationship existed between the betas and bond ratings for the top four classes of ratings (similar to the findings of Reilly and Joehnk), but there was a weak relationship using the top six ratings. The author postulated a nonlinear relationship where the risk of default becomes significant only for low ratings.

---

[42]John Percival, "Corporate Bonds in a Market Model Context," *Journal of Business Research* 2, no. 4 (October 1974): 461–467.

[43]Frank K. Reilly and Michael D. Joehnk, "The Association between Market-Determined Risk Measures for Bonds and Bond Ratings," *Journal of Finance* 31, no. 5 (December 1976): 1387–1403.

[44]Frank K. Reilly and David J. Wright, "Bond Market Indexes," in *The Handbook of Fixed-Income Securities.*

[45]Frank K. Reilly and David J. Wright, "An Analysis of High Yield Bond Indices" in *High Yield Bonds,* ed. Theodore M. Barnhill, Jr., William F. Maxwell, and Mark R. Shenkman (New York: McGraw-Hill, 1999).

[46]Gordon J. Alexander, "Applying the Market Model to Long-Term Corporate Bonds," *Journal of Financial and Quantitative Analysis* 15, no. 5 (December 1980): 1063–1080.

[47]This is similar to the well-known work by Roll on market series.

[48]Mark I. Weinstein, "The Systematic Risk of Corporate Bonds," *Journal of Financial and Quantitative Analysis* 16, no. 3 (September 1981): 156–278.

In a subsequent study, Weinstein computed bond betas and examined their stability over time.[49] He used a model that allowed the systematic risk to vary consistently with the Black-Scholes-Merton options pricing model. The results indicated that a model that assumes bond betas change over time has more explanatory power than a constant risk model. Also, he found that a bond's beta was related to firm characteristics (e.g., debt–equity ratios, and the variance of rate of return on assets) and to bond characteristics (coupon, term to maturity).

Thus, evidence on the usefulness of the CAPM as related to the bond market is mixed. Specifically, there are obvious problems regarding the appropriate market index to use, the systematic risk measure is unstable, and the risk–return relationship did not hold for the higher-quality bonds. Finally, there appears to be a relationship between the systematic risk measure and some characteristics of the firm. However, systematic risk also is heavily impacted by the characteristics of the bond, such as its coupon and maturity, that affect the bond's duration and convexity. This is not surprising because we know from Chapter 16 that modified effective and empirical durations are measures of relative bond price volatility for a given change in market interest rates.

Bond-Market Efficiency

Two versions of the efficient market hypothesis (EMH) are examined in the context of fixed-income securities: the weak and the semistrong theories. The weak-form hypothesis contends that security price movements are independent events so historical price information is useless in predicting future price behavior. Studies of weak-form efficiency have examined the ability of investors to forecast interest rates because if you can forecast interest rates you can forecast bond price behavior. Also, interest rate expectations are important for bond portfolio management.

Several studies[50] reached the same conclusion: interest rate behavior cannot be consistently and accurately forecast! In fact, one study suggests that the best forecast is no forecast at all. The models developed ranged from a naive approach to fairly sophisticated techniques. Some models used historical information, some ignored it, and one study used the expectations of acknowledged experts. In all cases, the most naive model, or no forecast at all, provided the best measure of future interest rate behavior. Clearly, if it is not possible to forecast interest rates, then neither can bond prices be forecast using historical prices, all of which supports the weak-form EMH.

The semistrong EMH asserts that current prices fully reflect all public knowledge and that efforts to act on public information are largely unproductive. Several studies have examined the informational value of bond rating changes. Katz examined monthly changes in bond yields surrounding ratings changes and found a significant impact of the change.[51] Weinstein examined monthly bond returns surrounding the announcement of rating changes and found an effect during the 18 months to 7 months before the announcement, but no effect from 6 months before the announcement to 6 months after the announcement.[52]

---

[49]Mark I. Weinstein, "Bond Systematic Risk and the Option Pricing Model," *Journal of Finance* 38, no. 5 (December 1983): 1415–1429.

[50]See, for example, William A. Bomberger and W. J. Frazer, "Interest Rates, Uncertainty, and the Livingston Data," *Journal of Finance* 36, no. 3 (June 1981): 661–675; Stephen K. McNees," The Recent Record of Thirteen Forecasters," *New England Economic Review,* Federal Reserve Bank of Boston (September–October 1981): 3–10; and Adrian W. Throop, "Interest Rate Forecasts and Market Efficiency," Federal Reserve Bank of San Francisco *Economic Review* (spring 1981): 29–43.

[51]Steven Katz, "The Price Adjustment Process of Bonds to Rating Reclassifications: A Test of Bond Market Efficiency," *Journal of Finance* 29, no. 2 (May 1974): 551–559.

[52]Mark I. Weinstein, "The Effect of a Rating Change Announcement on Bond Price," *Journal of Financial Economics* 5, no 3 (December 1977): 329–350.

The Internet *Investments Online*

Fixed-income management analytics and software are typically proprietary. The sites listed here offer some additional information about the techniques discussed in the text and will give you insight into the use of various analytical and portfolio management techniques.

www.ryanlabs.com Ryan Labs is a leader in the construction and analysis of fixed-income indexes. Their site offers information on their research, data, indexing, consulting, and asset/liability management skills (this latter feature is of particular importance to portfolios that must be structured to meet a stream of cash outflows, such as a pension fund). The site discusses the quantitative nature of bond portfolio management, fixed-income index construction, and the variety of risk and reward measures that are used for bond investment analysis.

www.bondbasics.com BondBasics' home page offers daily analysis for institutional fixed-income investors. Their information and analysis is for subscribers only, but a sample site gives visitors a flavor of some of BondBasics' analytical products, including an analysis of the U.S. Treasury market, yield curve projections, and computing present values from the current term structure.

www.cms-info.com The home page of Capital Management Sciences allows users to move to sites featuring CMS's various products. CMS sells fixed-income analytical software to institutional investment managers. Research papers on fixed-income security analysis are offered free of charge to users who fill out an online form. BondEdge is a product offering "what-if" simulations, volatility appraisals, and other analytics to fixed-income portfolio managers. BondVu does single-security analysis, including valuation, horizon return analysis, swap analysis, and price-yield calculations, among others.

www.cboe.com/education/strategy/interestrate.htm This site offers visitors an overview of various ways to hedge against or gain additional exposure to interest rate moves with options contracts.

www.finpipe.com The Financial Pipeline contains information about securities, including bonds, derivatives and mutual funds, in an easily accessible form. Pages have links to a variety of topics, and include types of bonds, how bonds trade, characteristics of bonds, and bond management strategies.

Several brokerage houses offer fixed-income portfolio information and strategies with an orientation to the individual investor. Two such sites are:

www.prusec.com/ladder.htm Prudential Securities' site presents an overview of the bond laddering strategy.

www.deanwitter.com/tfi/milp.html Dean Witter's site discusses laddering strategies as well. It presents several hypothetical examples for retirement, college funding, and monthly income laddering strategies.

In contrast, several studies have examined the impact of bond rating changes on stock prices and returns. Pinches and Singleton found very little impact on stock prices due to the ratings change.[53] Griffin and Sanvicente found a significant stock price impact following bond downgradings.[54] Alternatively, they found no impact on stock prices during the months when an upgrading was announced, but there was an impact during the prior 11 months. Holthausen and Leftwich examined daily stock return data surrounding the announcement of bond rating changes and likewise found negative abnormal returns when bonds were downgraded, but little evidence of abnormal price changes surrounding the announcement of an upgrading.[55]

---

[53]George E. Pinches and Clay Singleton, "The Adjustment of Stock Prices to Bond Rating Changes," *Journal of Finance* 33, no. 1 (March 1978): 29–44.

[54]Paul A. Griffin and Antonio Z. Sanvicente, "Common Stock Returns and Rating Changes: A Methodological Comparison," *Journal of Finance* 37, no. 1 (March 1982): 103–119.

[55]Robert W. Holthausen and Richard W. Leftwich, "The Effect of Bond Rating Changes on Common Stock Prices," *Journal of Financial Economics* 17, no. 1 (September 1986): 57–89.

Summary

- During the past decade, there has been a significant increase in the number and range of bond portfolio management strategies available. Bond portfolio management strategies include the relatively straightforward buy-and-hold and bond indexing strategies, several alternative active portfolio strategies, dedicated cash matching, classical immunization, horizon matching, and contingent immunization. Although you should understand the alternatives available and how to implement them, you also should recognize that the choice of a specific strategy is based on the needs and desires of the client. In turn, the success of any strategy will depend on the background and talents of the portfolio manager.
- The risk–return performance of bonds as a unique asset class has been consistent with expectations. In addition, their inclusion has generally enhanced overall portfolio performance because of their low covariance with other financial assets. The application of CAPM concepts to bonds has been mixed because it has been difficult to derive acceptable measures of systematic risk, and the risk measures derived have been unstable.
- Studies in the bond market have supported the theory of weak-form efficiency. The evidence for semistrong efficiency has been mixed. The results that indicate a lack of efficiency could be due to the relatively inactive secondary markets for most corporate bonds, which causes pricing and adjustment problems compared to the active markets for equities.

Questions

1. What is meant by an indexing portfolio strategy and why is it used?
2. Briefly define the following bond swaps: pure yield pickup swap, substitution swap, and tax swap.
3. Briefly describe three active bond portfolio management strategies.
4. Discuss two variables you would examine very carefully if you were analyzing a junk bond, and indicate why they are important.
5. How would you explain to a casual observer the reason why high-yield bond returns are more correlated to common stock returns than to investment-grade bond returns?
6. What are the advantages and difficulties of a cash-matched dedicated portfolio?
7. Describe the two components of interest rate risk.
8. What is meant by bond portfolio immunization?
9. If the yield curve were flat and did not change, how would you immunize your portfolio?
10. You begin with an investment horizon of 4 years and a portfolio with a duration of 4 years with a market interest rate of 10 percent. A year later, what is your investment horizon? Assuming no change in interest rates, what is the duration of your portfolio relative to your investment horizon? What does this imply about your ability to immunize your portfolio?
11. It has been contended that a zero-coupon bond is the ideal financial instrument to use for immunizing a portfolio. Discuss the reasoning for this statement.
12. During a conference with a client, the subject of classical immunization is introduced. The client questions the fee charged for developing and managing an immunized portfolio. The client believes it is basically a passive investment strategy, so the management fee should be substantially lower. What would you tell the client to show that it is not a passive policy?
13. With contingent immunization, what do you give up and what do you gain?
14. CFA *CFA Examination III (1983)*

    The ability to *immunize* a bond portfolio is very desirable for bond portfolio managers in some instances.

    a. Discuss the components of interest rate risk. Assuming a change in interest rates over time, explain the two risks faced by the holder of a bond.

    b. Define immunization and discuss why a bond manager would immunize a portfolio.

    c. Explain why a duration-matching strategy is a superior technique to a maturity-matching strategy for the minimization of interest rate risk.

    d. Explain in specific terms how you would use a zero-coupon bond to immunize a bond portfolio. Discuss why a zero-coupon bond is an ideal instrument in this regard.

    e. Explain how *contingent immunization,* another bond portfolio management technique, differs from *classical immunization.* Discuss why a bond portfolio manager would engage in contingent immunization. [35 minutes]

15. *CFA Examination III (1986)*
During the past several years, there has been substantial growth in the dollar amount of portfolios managed using *immunization* and *dedication* techniques. Assume a client wants to know the basic differences between (1) classical immunization, (2) contingent immunization, (3) cash-matched dedication, and (4) duration-matched dedication.
 a. Briefly describe each of these four techniques.
 b. Briefly discuss the ongoing investment action you would have to carry out if managing an *immunized portfolio.*
 c. Briefly discuss three of the major considerations involved with creating a *cash-matched dedicated* portfolio.
 d. Describe two parameters that should be specified when using *contingent immunization.*
 e. Select one of the four alternative techniques that you believe requires the last degree of active management and justify your selection. [20 minutes]

16. *CFA Examination III (1988)*
After you have constructed a structured fixed-income portfolio (i.e., one that is dedicated, indexed, or immunized), it may be possible over time to improve on the initial optimal portfolio while continuing to meet the primary goal. Discuss three conditions that would be considered favorable for a restructuring—assuming no change in objectives for the investor—and cite an example of each condition. [10 minutes]

17. *CFA Examination III (1988)*
The use of bond index funds has grown dramatically in recent years.
 a. Discuss the reasons you would expect it to be easier or more difficult to construct a bond-market index than a stock-market index.
 b. It is contended that the *operational process* of managing a corporate bond index fund is more difficult than managing an equity index fund. Discuss three examples that support this contention. [15 minutes]

18. *CFA Examination III (1988)*
Hans Kaufmann is a global fixed-income portfolio manager based in Switzerland. His clients are primarily U.S.-based pension funds. He allocates investments in the United States, Japan, Germany, and the United Kingdom. His approach is to make investment allocation decisions among these four countries based on his global economic outlook. To develop this economic outlook, Kaufmann analyzes the following five factors for each country: real economic growth, inflation, monetary policy, interest rates, and exchange rates.

When Kaufmann believes that the four economies are equally attractive for investment purposes, he equally weights investments in the four countries. When the economies are not equally attractive, he overweights the country or countries where he sees the largest potential returns.

Tables 1 through 5 present relevant economic data and forecasts.
 a. Indicate, before taking into account currency hedging, whether Kaufmann should overweight or underweight investments in each country. Justify your position. [15 minutes]
 b. Briefly describe how your answer to part a might change with the use of currency hedging techniques. [5 minutes]

TABLE 1 REAL GNP/GDP (ANNUAL CHANGES)

	1985	1986	1987	1988E
United States	3.0%	2.9%	2.4%	2.7%
Japan	4.7	2.4	3.2	3.4
West Germany	2.0	2.5	1.5	2.1
United Kingdom	3.4	3.0	3.4	2.3

TABLE 2 GNP/GDP DEFLATOR (ANNUAL CHANGES)

	1985	1986	1987	1988E
United States	3.2%	2.6%	3.3%	3.8%
Japan	1.5	2.8	3.0	3.0
West Germany	2.2	3.1	2.5	2.2
United Kingdom	6.0	3.5	4.5	4.8

TABLE 3 NARROW MONEY (MI) (ANNUAL CHANGES)

	1985	1986	1987	1988E
United States	9.2%	13.4%	5.5%	7.0%
Japan	5.0	6.9	9.9	10.0
West Germany	4.3	8.5	7.5	8.5
United Kingdom	17.8	25.6	16.5	12.0

TABLE 4 LONG-TERM INTEREST RATES (ANNUAL RATES)

	1985	1986	1987	1988E
United States	10.6%	7.7%	8.8%	9.0%
Japan	6.5	5.2	6.1	6.1
West Germany	9.9	5.9	6.1	7.0
United Kingdom	10.6	9.9	9.8	9.5

TABLE 5 EXCHANGE RATES (CURRENCY PER U.S. DOLLARS)

	1985	1986	1987	1988E
United States (dollars)	1.00	1.00	1.00	1.00
Japan (yen)	228.08	163.87	141.22	140.09
West Germany (marks)	2.80	2.08	1.74	1.67
United Kingdom (pounds)	0.74	0.67	0.58	0.59

Sources: *World Economic Outlook,* October 1987; and Kaufmann's estimates.

CFA

19. *CFA Examination I (1990)*
Robert Devlin and Neil Parish are portfolio managers at the Broward Investment Group. At their regular Monday strategy meeting, the topic of adding international bonds to one of their portfolios came up. The portfolio, an ERISA-qualified pension account for a U.S. client, was currently 90 percent invested in U.S. Treasury bonds, and 10 percent invested in 10-year Canadian government bonds.

Devlin suggested buying a position in 10-year German government bonds, while Parish argued for a position in 10-year Australian government bonds.

a. Briefly discuss the *three* major issues that Devlin and Parish should address in their analysis of the return prospects for German and Australian bonds relative to those of U.S. bonds. [6 minutes]

Having made no changes to the original portfolio, Devlin and Parish hold a subsequent strategy meeting and decide to add positions in the government bonds of Japan, the United Kingdom, France, Germany, and Australia.

b. Identify and discuss *two* reasons for adding a broader mix of international bonds to the pension portfolio. [9 minutes]

CFA

20. *CFA Examination III (1990)*

The investment committee of the money management firm of Gentry, Inc. has typically been very conservative and has avoided investing in high-yield (junk) bonds, although they have had major positions in investment-grade corporate bonds. Recently, Pete Squire, a member of the committee, suggested that they should review their policy regarding junk bonds because they currently constitute over 25 percent of the total corporate bond market.

As part of this policy review, you are asked to respond to the following questions.

a. Briefly discuss the liquidity *and* pricing characteristics of junk bonds relative to *each* of the following types of fixed-income securities:
   - Treasuries;
   - high-grade corporate bonds;
   - corporate loans; and
   - private placements.

Briefly discuss the implications of these differences for Gentry's bond portfolio managers. The committee has learned that the correlation of rates of return between Treasuries and high-grade corporate bonds is approximately 0.98, while the correlation between Treasury/high-grade corporate bonds and junk bonds is approximately 0.45.

b. Briefly explain the reason for this difference in correlations, and briefly discuss its implications for bond portfolios.

The committee has also heard that durations at the times of issue for junk bonds are typically much shorter than for newly issued high-grade corporate bonds.

c. Briefly explain the reason for this difference in duration, and briefly discuss its implication for the volatility of high-yield bond portfolios. [15 minutes]

CFA

21. *CFA Examination II (1990)*

Greg Kemp, CFA, Chief Investment Officer of Anchor Advisors, has received the following recommendation from his bond management group.

> "We believe the current environment has focused excessive pessimism on high-grade corporate bonds. Fears of 'event risk' and weakness in the junk bond market have widened yield spreads to attractive levels.
>
> "It is recommended that our employee benefit bond accounts reduce their current U.S. Treasury weightings from 75 percent to 25 percent, with this money to be invested in callable Single-A and AA utility bonds with coupon rates between 9 percent and 11 percent. The durations of the bonds purchased will be equal to those sold."

Kemp accepts the idea that yield spreads are wider than normal between U.S. Treasury bonds and corporate issues. Interest rates on long-term U.S. Treasury issues are currently 9 percent. He expects a significant (more than 100 basis points) drop in interest rates.

a. Kemp has some concerns about the volatility implications of the proposed trade in light of his understanding of the concepts of duration, convexity, and option-adjusted spreads. Given his interest rate expectations, identify and explain *two* key questions that Kemp should raise about the proposed trade. [10 minutes]

b. Recommend *two* modifications to the proposed trade that would address Kemp's concerns mentioned in part a. [5 minutes]

CFA

22. *CFA Examination II (1994)*

Bond analysis often requires more than traditional credit ratio analysis. Discuss *each* of the following *three* considerations as they relate to evaluating a specific fixed-income security:

(i) Competition within the Industry
(ii) Liquidation Value of Net Assets
(iii) Management [6 minutes]

CFA

23. *CFA Examinaton III (1999)*
A consultant suggests that the weighted-average portfolio duration calculation for a global bond portfolio is the same as for a domestic bond portfolio.
a. **State** whether the use of portfolio duration in international bond portfolio management is more limiting than in domestic bond portfolio management. **Support** your conclusion with *two* reasons. [8 minutes]
The consultant recognizes that currency, duration, and investing outside the benchmark are possible sources of excess return in global bond management. He is also curious about additional methods of adding value through global bond management.
b. **List** and **discuss** *two* additional potential sources of excess return. [6 minutes]

Problems

1. You have a portfolio with a market value of $50 million and a Macaulay duration of 7 years (assuming a market interest rate of 10 percent). If interest rates jump to 12 percent, what would be the estimated value of your portfolio using modified duration? Show all your computations.
2. Answer the following questions assuming that at the initiation of an investment account, the market value of your portfolio is $200 million, and you immunize the portfolio at 12 percent for 6 years. During the first year, interest rates are constant at 12 percent.
   a. What is the market value of the portfolio at the end of Year 1?
   b. Immediately after the end of the year, interest rates *decline* to 10 percent. Estimate the new value of the portfolio, assuming you did the required rebalancing (use only modified duration).
3. Compute the Macaulay duration under the following conditions:
   a. A bond with a 5-year term to maturity, a 12 percent coupon (annual payments), and a market yield of 10 percent.
   b. A bond with a 4-year term to maturity, a 12 percent coupon (annual payments), and a market yield of 10 percent.
   c. Compare your answers to parts a and b, and discuss the implications of this for classical immunization.
4. Compute the Macaulay duration under the following conditions:
   a. A bond with a 4-year term to maturity, a 10 percent coupon (annual payments), and a market yield of 8 percent
   b. A bond with a 4-year term to maturity, a 10 percent coupon (annual payments), and a market yield of 12 percent
   c. Compare your answers to parts a and b. Assuming it was an immediate shift in yields, discuss the implications of this for classical immunization.
5. A major requirement in running a contingent immunization portfolio policy is monitoring the relationship between the current market value of the portfolio and the required value of the floor portfolio. In this regard, assume a $300 million portfolio with a horizon of 5 years. The available market rate at the initiation of the portfolio is 14 percent, but the client is willing to accept 12 percent as a floor rate to allow you to use active management strategies. The current market values and current market rates at the end of Years 1, 2, and 3 are as follows:

End of Year	Market Value ($ Mil)	Market Yield	Required Floor Portfolio	Safety Margin (deficiency)
1	340.00	0.12		
2	375.00	0.10		
3	360.20	0.14		

   a. What is the required ending-wealth value for this portfolio?
   b. What is the value of the required floor portfolio at the end of Years 1, 2, and 3?
   c. Compute the safety margin or deficiency at the end of Years 1, 2, and 3.
6. Evaluate the following pure yield pickup swap: You currently hold a 20-year, Aa-rated, 9.0 percent coupon bond priced to yield 11.0 percent. As a swap candidate, you are considering a

20-year, Aa-rated, 11 percent coupon bond priced to yield 11.5 percent. (Assume reinvestment at 11.5 percent.)

	Current Bond	Candidate Bond
Dollar investment		
Coupon		
i on one coupon		
Principal value at year end		
Total accrued		
Realized compound yield		
Value of swap: ______ basis points in one year		

7. Evaluate the following substitution swap: You currently hold a 25-year, 9.0 percent coupon bond priced to yield 10.5 percent. As a swap candidate, you are considering a 25-year, Aa-rated, 9.0 percent coupon bond priced to yield 10.75 percent. (Assume a 1-year work-out period and reinvestment at 10.5 percent.)

	Current Bond	Candidate Bond
Dollar investment		
Coupon		
i on one coupon		
Principal value at year end		
Total accrued		
Realized compound yield		
Value of swap: ______ basis points in one year		

8. *CFA Examination III (1984)*
Reinvestment risk is a major factor for bond managers to consider when determining the most appropriate or optimal strategy for a fixed-income portfolio. Briefly describe each of the following bond portfolio management strategies, and explain how each deals with reinvestment risk:
   a. Active management
   b. Classical immunization
   c. Dedicated portfolio
   d. Contingent immunization [20 minutes]
9. *CFA Examination III (1985)*
A major requirement in managing a fixed-income portfolio using a contingent immunization policy is monitoring the relationship between the current market value of the portfolio and the required value of the floor portfolio. This difference is defined as the *margin of error.* In this regard, assume a $300 million portfolio with a time horizon of 5 years. The available market rate at the initiation of the portfolio is 12 percent, but the client is willing to accept 10 percent as a floor rate to allow use of active management strategies. The current market values and current market rates at the end of Years 1, 2, and 3 are as follows:

End of Year	Market Value ($Mil)	Market Yield	Required Floor Portfolio ($Mil)	Margin of Error ($Mil)
1	$340.9	10%		
2	405.5	8		
3	395.2	12		

Table 1
Present Value (use tables in back of book)

Table 2
Compound Value (use tables in back of book)
Assuming semiannual compounding:
a. Calculate the required ending-wealth value for this portfolio.
b. Calculate the value of the required floor portfolios at the end of Years 1, 2, and 3.
c. Compute the margin of error at the end of Years 1, 2, and 3.
d. Indicate the action that a portfolio manager utilizing a *contingent immunization* policy would take if the margin of error at the end of any year had been zero or negative.

CFA

10. *CFA Examination (1990)*
PTC's Investment Committee has decided to allocate 50 percent of the pension plan portfolio's fixed-income investment to non-U.S. government bonds (i.e., bonds representing non-U.S. sovereign credits). For a number of reasons, BAG—the Committee's consultant—has recommended against using a pure dedication approach to management of the bonds. Instead, it has presented the Committee with three alternative strategies for consideration, accompanied by the 15-year historical performance data for each strategy shown in Table 1.

TABLE 1

	15-Year Historical Universe Performance			
	Average Returns Annualized	Average Top Decile Returns (a) Annualized	Average Bottom Decile Returns (b) Annualized	Standard Deviation of Returns
Strategy Characteristics				
Active management	12.9%	15.6%	6.8%	18.6%
Duration shifts + or −40% of Salomon WGB Index (c)				
Deviations from country allocation benchmarks in Index are unrestricted				
Transactions permitted for any management purpose				
Fee: 35 basis points/year				
Passive management	11.8%	12.8%	10.7%	16.0%
Duration shifts + or − 5% of Salomon WGB Index (c)				
Country allocation deviations limited relative to index proportions				
Transactions permitted only for replacement of deteriorating credits				
Fee: 15 basis points/year				
Indexed management	11.3%	12.0%	11.0%	14.9%
Match return of Salomon WGB Index (c)				
No duration shifts permitted				
Transactions allowed only for portfolio rebalancing				
Fee: 6 basis points/year				

(a) Top decile returns are simple average of the 10 best manager records in BAG's 100-manager universe.
(b) Bottom decile returns are a simple average of the 10 worst manager records in BAG's 100-manager universe.
(c) Salomon Brothers World Government Bond Index (WGB)

a. Based on the management strategy characteristics set for the in Table 1, as well as your general knowledge, identify and explain *three* advantages of *each* strategy as an alternative for the Investment Committee to consider. In developing your response, regard yourself as a strong advocate as you explain the advantages of *each* of the three alternatives. [15 minutes]
b. Identify and explain *one* key *disadvantage* of *each* of the three strategies. [5 minutes]

PTC has now decided to index the segment of the fixed-income portfolio to be invested in non-U.S. government bonds, using the Salomon Brothers World Government Bond Index as the benchmark portfolio. Assume this index includes the sovereign credits of nine major countries in the proportions shown below:

Country	Weighting
Australia	2%
Canada	8%
Denmark	2%
France	11%
Germany	19%
Japan	37%
Netherlands	8%
Switzerland	2%
United Kingdom	11%

Several members of the Investment Committee favor use of the full replication approach to indexing the non-U.S. government bonds, while the chairman favors use of the stratified sampling approach. As the BAG representative assigned to the PTC account, you have been asked to assist the Committee in choosing between the two indexing methods.

c. Describe and evaluate *each* of these two indexing alternatives for the purpose of creating and managing a bond portfolio intended to represent the Salomon Brothers World Government Bond Index benchmark. [10 minutes]
d. Evaluate the appropriateness of using the Salomon Brothers World Government Bond Index as a benchmark for purposes of monitoring PTC's non-U.S. portfolio exposures in relation to its pension benefit liability exposures. [5 minutes]

CFA

11. *CFA Examination II (1996)*

PowerTool is the largest U.S. manufacturer of industrial hand tools. Its sales force is strong but clients have complained that marketing is weak. The industrial tool business is mature, with little or no future expected growth.

PowerTool has acquire Fenton Manufacturing, a small, innovative company whose sales are entirely in the retail tool market. The retail tool market is expected to grow at a 5 percent annual rate.

Fenton recently developed a patented line or rechargeable home power tools that displayed strong potential in test markets. Fenton expects this line to generate 50 percent of its sales within 5 years, but lacks a sales force to market this product line. Jerry Fenton, the company's founder, recently retired.

PowerTool management is highly respected and the company has experienced little management turnover. However, the Chief Executive Officer has announced her retirement after 18 years of service, and will be replaced by the current Chief Operating Officer.

You are a private investor with a large investment in PowerTool bonds, and wish to determine the effect of the acquisition of Fenton on PowerTool's bonds.

Table 1 presents financial ratios and debt ratings of PowerTool and Fenton prior to the merger, and pro forma ratios of the combined company following the acquisition.

TABLE 1 FINANCIAL RATIOS AND DEBT RATINGS: JUNE 1, 1996

Company	Total Debt to Total Capital	Pretax Interest Coverage	Operating Cash Flow to Total Debt	Debt Rating
PowerTool	30%	6.2x	50%	A+
Fenton	72%	2.1x	8%	Not rated
Combined	42%	5.4x	40%	To be determined

a. Explain how *each* of the following *three* ratios should be used to evaluate a firm's financial risk:
   (i) Total Debt to Total Capital,
   (ii) Pretax Interest Coverage, *and*
   (iii) Operating Cash Flow to Total Debt [9 minutes]

PowerTool has issued debt with the following covenants, which continue in force after its acquisition of Fenton.

Dividend Test Covenant
PowerTool may not pay any cash dividend or repurchase shares if such payment would result in total debt-to-capital in excess of 50 percent.

Put Option Covenant
If PowerTool's debt rating falls below A, bondholders have the right to redeem the bonds at a price of 105 plus accrued interest within 60 days following the change in rating.

b. Discuss the impact of *each* of the *two* debt covenants as described above on PowerTool's financial flexibility following its acquisition of Fenton:
   (i) Dividend Test covenant, *and*
   (ii) Put Option Covenant. [8 minutes]

Use only the information provided in the introduction in answering the following question.

c. Discuss, *from the PowerTool bondholders' point of view, two* advantages and *two* disadvantages to PowerTool of the acquisition of Fenton, with regard to the following product lines:
   - industrial tool business, and
   - retail tool business [12 minutes]

PowerTool debt has not yet been re-rated following the acquisition of Fenton. PowerTool bonds are currently trading at a price comparable to A-rated bonds.

Table 2 displays financial ratios used to determine bond ratings.

TABLE 2 BOND RATING CRITERIA: JUNE 1, 1996

Debt Rating	Total Debt to Total Capital	Pretax Interest Coverage	Operating Cash Flow to Total Debt
AA	26%	8.8x	75%
A	37%	4.6x	44%
BBB	48%	2.5x	29%

d. Recommend whether you should *hold* or *sell* the PowerTool bonds. Support your recommendations with *four* reasons drawn from the Introduction, Tables 1 and 2, and your answers to parts a through c. [13 minutes]

12. *CFA Examination II (1997)*

CFA

As a new employee at Clayton Asset Management, Emma Bennett has been assigned to evaluate the credit quality of BRT Corporation bonds. Clayton holds the bonds in its high-yield bond portfolio. The following information is provided to assist in the analysis.

BRT Corporation is a rapidly growing company in the broadcast industry. It has grown primarily through a series of aggressive acquisitions.

Early in 1996, BRT announced it was acquiring a competitor in a hostile takeover that would double its assets but also increase debt burdens. The credit rating of BRT debt fell from BBB to BB. The acquisition reduced the financial flexibility of BRT but increased its presence in the broadcasting industry.

Now, mid-1997, BRT has announced its merging with another large entertainment company. The merger will alter BRT's capital structure and place it as a leader in the broadcast industry. The early 1996 acquisition combined with this merger will increase the total assets of BRT by a factor of four. A large portion of the total assets are intangible, representing franchise and distribution rights.

Although the outlook for the broadcasting industry remains healthy, large telecommunication companies attempting to enter the broadcasting industry are keeping competitive pressures high. Laws and regulations also promote the competitiveness of the environment, but initial start-up costs make it difficult for new companies to enter the industry. Large capital expenditures are required to maintain and improve existing systems as well as to expand current business.

For Bennett's analysis, she has been provided with the financial data shown in Tables 1 through 4.

a. Calculate the following ratios using the *projected 1997* financial information:
   (i) Operating income to sales.
   (ii) Earnings before interest and taxes to total assets.
   (iii) Times interest earned.
   (iv) Long-term debt to total assets. [4 minutes]

b. Discuss the effect of the 1997 merger on the creditworthiness of BRT through an analysis of *each* of the ratios in part a. [8 minutes]

BRT Corporation 10-year bonds are currently rated BB and are trading at a yield to maturity of 7.70 percent. The current 10-year Treasury note is yielding 6.15 percent.

c. State and justify, based on your work in parts a and b, the information in Tables 3 and 4, and the introduction, whether Clayton should hold or sell the BRT Corporation bonds in its portfolio. Include a discussion of *two* qualitative factors. [10 minutes]

TABLE 1 BRT CORPORATION BALANCE SHEET DATA AT YEAR END—DECEMBER 31 (IN MILLIONS)

	1993	1994	1995	1996	Projected 1997
Current assets	$ 654	$ 718	$2,686	$ 2,241	$ 5,255
Net fixed assets	391	379	554	1,567	2,583
Other assets (Intangibles)	2,982	3,090	3,176	8,946	20,435
Total assets	$4,027	$4,187	$6,416	$12,754	$28,273
Current liabilities	$ 799	$ 876	$ 966	$ 1,476	$ 3,731
Long-term debt	2,537	2,321	2,378	7,142	15,701
Other liabilities	326	292	354	976	349
Total equity	365	698	2,718	3,160	8,492
Total liabilities and equity	$4,027	$4,187	$6,416	$12,754	$28,273

TABLE 2 BRT CORPORATION INCOME STATEMENT DATA YEARS ENDING DECEMBER 31 (IN MILLIONS EXCEPT PER-SHARE DATA)

	1993	1994	1995	1996	Projected 1997
Net Sales	$1,600	$1,712	$2,005	$4,103	$9,436
Operating Expenses	1,376	1,400	1,620	3,683	8,603
Operating Income	$ 224	$ 312	$ 385	$ 420	$ 833
Interest Expense	296	299	155	270	825
Income taxes	20	42	130	131	4
Net income	$ (92)	$ (29)	$ 100	$ 19	$ 4
Earnings per share	($ 0.86)	($ 0.24)	$ 0.83	$ 0.09	$ 0.01
Average price per share	$26.30	$34.10	$ 4.90	$40.10	$40.80
Average shares outstanding	107	120	121	198	359

TABLE 3 BRT CORPORATION SELECTED FINANCIAL RATIOS

	1993	1994	1995	1996	Projected 1997
Operating income to sales (%)	14.0%	18.2%	19.2%	10.2%	*
Sales to total assets	0.39x	0.41x	0.31x	0.32x	0.33x
Earnings before interest and taxes to total assets	5.5%	7.4%	6.0%	3.3%	*
Times interest earned	0.76x	1.04x	2.48x	1.55x	*
Long-term debt to total assets	63.0%	55.4%	37.0%	55.9%	*

TABLE 4 CLAYTON ASSET MANAGEMENT CREDIT RATING STANDARDS

	AVERAGE RATIOS BY RATING CATEGORY						
	AA	A	BBB	BB	B	CCC	CC
Financial Ratios							
Operating income to sales (%)	16.2	13.4	12.1	10.3	8.5	6.4	5.2
Sales to total assets	2.50x	2.00x	1.50x	1.00x	0.75x	0.50x	0.25x
Earnings before interest and taxes to total assets	15.0%	10.0%	8.0%	6.0%	4.0%	3.0%	2.0%
Times interest earned	5.54x	3.62x	2.29x	1.56x	1.04x	0.79x	0.75x
Long-term debt to total assets	19.5%	30.4%	40.2%	51.8%	71.8%	81.0%	85.4%
Bond Credit Spread Information							
Current yield spread in basis points over 10-year Treasuries	45	55	85	155	225	275	350

13. *CFA Examination II (1998)*
Jane Berry is a fixed-income analyst at an investment management firm. She has been following the developments at two companies, Sturdy Machines and Patriot Manufacturing, which are both U.S.-based industrial companies that sell their products worldwide. Both companies operate in cyclical industries.

Sturdy Machine's profits have suffered from a rising dollar and a slump in its business. The company has said that major cuts in its operating expenses are likely to be necessary if it is to make a profit next year. On the other hand, Patriot Manufacturing has been able to maintain its profitability and enhance its balance sheet, as shown in Table 1.

TABLE 1 FINANCIAL INFORMATION

Ratio	1995	1996	1997
Sturdy Machines			
Cash flow/total debt (%)	37.3	31.0	33.0
Total debt/capital (%)	38.2	40.1	41.3
Pretax interest coverage (×)	4.2	2.3	1.1
Patriot Manufacturing			
Cash flow/total debt (%)	34.6	38.0	43.1
Total debt/capital (%)	40.0	347.3	34.9
Pretax interest coverage (×)	2.7	4.5	6.1

Berry has been monitoring the bonds of these companies for possible purchase. She notices that a rating agency recently downgraded the senior debt of Sturdy Machines from A1 to A2 and upgraded the senior debt of Patriot Manufacturing from A3 to A2. Berry has received the following yield quotes from a broker:

- Sturdy Machines 7.50 percent due June 1, 2008, was quoted at 7.10 percent.
- Patriot Manufacturing 7.50 percent due June 1, 2008, was quoted at 7.10 percent.

Recommend which bond Berry should buy. Justify your choice with *two* factors from Table 1 and *two* qualitative factors from the discussion above. [16 minutes]

CFA

14. *CFA Examination II (1999)*

Mike Smith, CFA, an analyst with Blue River Investments, is considering buying a Montrose Cable Company Corporate bond. He has collected the following balance sheet and income statement information for Montrose as shown in Exhibit 1. He has also calculated the three ratios shown in Exhibit 2 which indicate that the bond is currently rated "A" according to the firm's internal bond-rating criteria shown in Exhibit 4.

Smith has decided to consider some off-balance-sheet items in his credit analysis, as shown in Exhibit 3. Specifically, Smith wishes to evaluate the impact of each of the off-balance-sheet items on each of the ratios found in Exhibit 2.

a. Calculate the combined effect of the *three* off-balance-sheet items in Exhibit 3 on *each* of the following *three* financial ratios shown in Exhibit 2. [9 minutes]
   (i) EBITDA/interest expense.
   (ii) Long-term debt/equity.
   (iii) Current assets/current liabilities.

The bond is currently trading at a credit premium of 55 basis points. Using the internal bond-rating criteria in Exhibit 4, Smith wants to evaluate whether or not the credit yield premium incorporates the effect on the off-balance-sheet items.

b. State and justify whether or not the current credit yield premium compensates Smith for the credit risk of the bond based on the internal bond-rating criteria found in Exhibit 4. [6 minutes]

EXHIBIT 1 MONTROSE CABLE COMPANY: YEAR ENDED MARCH 31, 1999 (US$ THOUSAND)

Balance Sheet	
Current assets	$ 4,735
Fixed assets	43,225
Total assets	$47,960
Current liabilities	$ 4,500
Long-term debt	10,000
Total liabilities	$14,500
Shareholder's equity	33,460
Total liabilities and shareholder's equity	$47,960
Income Statement	
Revenue	$18,500
Operating and adminiastrative expenses	14,050
Operating income	$ 4,450
Depreciation and amortization	1,675
Interest expense	942
Income before income taxes	$ 1,833
Taxes	641
Net income	$ 1,192

EXHIBIT 2 SELECTED RATIOS AND CREDIT YIELD PREMIUM DATA FOR MONTROSE

EBITDA/interest expense	4.72
Long-term debt/equity	0.30
Current assets/current liabilities	1.05
Credit yield premium over U.S. Treasuries	55 basis points

EXHIBIT 3 MONTROSE OFF-BALANCE-SHEET ITEMS

- Montrose has guaranteed the long-term debt (principal only) of an unconsolidated affiliate. This obligation has a present value of $995,000.
- Montrose has sold $500,000 of accounts receivable with recourse at a yield of 8 percent.
- Montrose is a lessee in a new noncancelable operating leasing agreement to finance transmission equipment. The discounted present value of the lease payments is $6,144,000 using an interest rate of 10 percent. The annual payment will be $1,000,000.

EXHIBIT 4 BLUE RIVER INVESTMENTS: INTERNAL BOND-RATING CRITERIA AND CREDIT YIELD PREMIUM DATA

Bond Rating	Interest Coverage (EBITDA/ Interest Expense	Leverage (Long-term Debt/Equity)	Current Ratio (Current Assets/ Current Liabilities)	Credit Yield Premium over U.S. Treasuries (in Basis Points)
AA	5.00 to 6.00	0.25 to 0.30	1.15 to 1.25	30 bps
A	4.00 to 5.00	0.30 to 0.40	1.00 to 1.15	50 bps
BBB	3.00 to 4.00	0.40 to 0.50	0.90 to 1.00	100 bps
BB	2.00 to 3.00	0.50 to 0.60	0.75 to 0.90	125 bps

References

Altman, Edward I., ed. *The High Yield Debt Market.* Homewood, Ill.: Dow Jones-Irwin, 1990.

Barnhill, Theodore M., William F. Maxwell, and Mark R. Shenkman, eds. *High Yield Bonds.* New York: McGraw-Hill, 1999.

Bierwag, G. O., George G. Kaufman, and Alden Toevs, eds. *Innovations in Bond Portfolio Management: Duration Analysis and Immunization.* Greenwich, Conn.: JAI Press, 1983.

Cheung, Rayner, Joseph C. Bencivenga, and Frank J. Fabozzi. "Original Issue High-Yield Bonds: Historical Return and Default Experiences, 1977–1989." *The Journal of Fixed Income* 2, no. 2 (September 1992).

Choie, Kenneth S. "A Simplified Approach to Bond Portfolio Management: DDS." *Journal of Portfolio Management* 16, no. 3 (spring 1990).

Churchill, Dwight D., ed. *Fixed Income Management: Techniques and Practices.* Charlottesville, Va.: Association for Investment Management and Research, 1994.

Dattatreya, Ravi E., and Frank J. Fabozzi. *Active Total Return Management of Fixed Income Portfolios.* Rev. ed. Burr Ridge, Ill.: Irwin Professional Publishing, 1995.

Fabozzi, Frank J. *Bond Markets, Analysis and Strategies,* 3d ed. Upper Saddle River, N.J.: Prentice-Hall, 1996.

Fabozzi, Frank J., ed. *The New High-Yield Debt Market.* New York: Harper Business, 1990.

Fridson, Martin. *High Yield Bonds: Assessing Risk and Identifying Value in Speculative Grade Securities.* Chicago: Probus Publishing, 1989.

Howe, Jane Tripp. *Junk Bonds: Analysis and Portfolio Strategies.* Chicago: Probus Publishing, 1988.

Leibowitz, Martin L., William S. Krasker, and Ardavan Nozari. "Spread Duration: A New Tool for Bond Portfolio Management." *Journal of Portfolio Management* 16, no. 3 (spring 1990).

Reilly, Frank K., ed. *High Yield Bonds: Analysis and Risk Assessment.* Charlottesville, Va.: Institute of Chartered Financial Analysts, 1990.

Rosenberg, Michael R. *Currency Forecasting.* Burr Ridge, Ill.: Irwin Professional Publishing, 1996.

Ryan, Ronald J., ed. *Yield Curve Dynamics.* Chicago: Glen Lake Publishing Co. Ltd., 1997.

Squires, Jan R., ed. *Global Portfolio Management.* Charlottesville, Va.: Association for Investment Management and Research, 1996.

Squires, Jan R., ed. *Global Bond Management.* Charlottesville, Va.: Association for Investment Management and Research, 1997.

Squires, Jan R., ed. *Credit Analysis around the World.* Charlottesville, Va.: Association for Investment Management and Research, 1998.

Tuttle, Donald, ed. *The Revolution in Techniques for Managing Bond Portfolios.* Charlottesville, Va.: The Institute of Chartered Financial Analysts, 1983.

Wilson, Richard S., and Frank J. Fabozzi. *The New Corporate Bond Market.* Chicago: Probus Publishing, 1990.

Part 5 Analysis of Common Stock

Part 3 considered the basic valuation principles and practices applied to all securities and how this was applied to the global asset allocation decision and, in Part 4, we applied these principles to the analysis and management of bonds. In Part 5, we apply these same valuation principles and practices to the analysis of common stocks. The objective is to be in a position to make the critical risk–return decision at the market-industry-company stock level.

You will recall from Chapter 11 that successful investing requires several steps beginning with a valuation of the aggregate economy and market, the examination of various industries, and the analysis of individual companies and their securities. Globalization of the capital markets has definitely complicated this process wherein it is now necessary to consider markets on a worldwide basis followed by the analysis of *world* industries in numerous, complex foreign companies.

In Chapter 18 we begin the three-step, top-down approach and discuss how to analyze the aggregate stock market using the two general valuation approaches introduced in Chapter 13—the present value of cash flow models and the relative valuation ratios. In Chapter 19 we again demonstrate these two approaches to the valuation of an industry.

Chapter 20 on company analysis begins with a discussion of the difference between a company and its stock. In many instances, the common stock of a very fine company may not be a good investment, which is why we emphasize that company analysis and stock selection are two separate but dependent activities. Once again, the analysis procedure is built on the two valuation approaches employed for the market and industry. We also consider other techniques such as economic value added (EVA) that provide insights regarding the economic success of a firm and its management. The overall goal of this procedure is to select one of the best companies in a superior industry during a favorable market environment.

It was noted in Chapter 13 that it is not feasible to use the standard dividend discount model to value true growth companies. Therefore, there is a separate discussion in Chapter 20 in which we discuss several valuation models that have been specifically developed for the analysis of growth companies.

Throughout this section, we refer to the semistrong efficient market hypothesis. You will recall that, although many studies support this hypothesis, there is growing literature dealing with anomalies related to this hypothesis. The presentation in this section provides a consistent and justifiable valuation technique that can be used to find undervalued securities. You should never forget that the output of alternative valuation models is only as good as the estimated inputs and *the superior analyst is the one who provides the best estimates of risk growth.*

Chapter 21 deals with technical analysis, an alternative or supplement to the fundamental approach discussed in the prior chapters. Rather than estimating value based on external variables, the technical analyst believes that it is possible to project future stock price movements based on past stock price changes or other stock market data. Various techniques used by technical analysts for U.S. and world markets are discussed and demonstrated.

Chapter 22 deals with equity portfolio management strategies. We begin with a general discussion of passive versus active management styles. This is followed by a specific discussion of indexing, including the selection of an appropriate benchmark index, and a consideration of how one selects stocks to include in an indexed portfolio.

The overview of active equity portfolio management strategies includes a discussion of how one constructs an appropriate normalized benchmark portfolio that reflects the client's risk–return objectives and constraints. We consider how a manager implements one of the three major active management approaches: market-timing, sector or style rotation (e.g., growth versus value), or stockpicking. Notably, all of these approaches can and should consider global opportunities.

We conclude this chapter with a discussion of how equity portfolio managers can use derivatives for the following purposes: change the risk–return characteristics of a portfolio; make specific asset allocation decisions (including international allocations); and hedge portfolio inflows and outflows.

Chapter 18 STOCK-MARKET ANALYSIS

After you read this chapter, you should be able to answer the following questions:

- How do we apply the basic reduced form dividend discount model (DDM) to the valuation of the aggregate stock market?
- What would be the prevailing value of the market as represented by the S&P 400 based upon the reduced form DDM?
- What would be the prevailing value of the market (S&P 400) based upon the present value of free cash flow to equity (FCFE) model?
- What two components are involved in the two-part valuation procedure?
- Given the two components in the valuation procedure, which is more volatile?
- What steps are involved in estimating the earnings per share for an aggregate market series?
- What variables affect the aggregate operating profit margin and how do they affect it?
- What variables determine the level and changes in the market earnings multiplier?
- How do you arrive at an expected market value and an expected rate of return for the stock market?
- What has happened to the values for the other relative valuation ratios—i.e., the P/BV, P/CF, and P/S ratios?
- What additional factors must be considered when you apply this microanalysis approach to the valuation of stock markets around the world?
- What are some differences between stock-market statistics for the United States and those of other countries?

Interest in stock-market movements has grown during the past decade. More individuals own stock than ever before, and significant mergers are increasingly frequent. In earlier chapters, we emphasized the importance of analyzing the aggregate economy and alternative security markets before an industry or a company analysis. As discussed in Chapter 14, it is very important to use the economic and market outlook to make the asset allocation decision between stocks, bonds, or cash before you consider which is the best industry or company.

There are three techniques for making the security-market decision. The first is a macroanalysis approach, which is based on the strong relationship between the aggregate economy and alternative security markets. Chapter 14 was concerned with the macro techniques and discussed world asset allocation. The second technique involves microanalysis, which applies basic valuation models to the bond or equity markets. Chapter 16 discussed the micro valuation of bonds. The third technique is technical analysis, which assumes that past market series can be used to predict future market returns. This technique will be discussed in Chapter 21.

This chapter explains the microanalysis of a country's stock market. Your estimate of the future value for the stock market in a country implies an estimate of the rate of return you expect as an equity investor in the country during the holding period.

This chapter begins the three-step valuation process introduced in Chapter 13. We initiate the fundamental analysis of stocks, which determines the future value of the aggregate stock market on the basis of sales, earnings, cash flows, and risk factors. In this chapter, we estimate the aggregate market outlook based on the outlook for the economy. This will be followed in Chapter 19 by a discussion of how one analyzes alternative industries. Finally, in Chapter 20, we consider how to estimate the value of an individual firm and its stock.

The presentation of the fundamental valuation approaches to the aggregate stock market considers the two equity valuation approaches introduced in Chapter 13. Initially, we employ the present value of cash flow models. As before, we begin with a valuation using the present value of dividends—that is, the basic reduced form DDM. This is followed by a valuation using the present value of the free cash flow to equity (FCFE) model assuming the constant growth model. Subsequently, we demonstrate a valuation using the FCFE model assuming a three-stage growth scenario for a few years prior to constant growth. Notably, we do not employ the present value of operating free cash flow model in this chapter due to space constraints, but also because of the difficulty in estimating the debt for this index.

After the present value of cash flow valuation, we move to the relative valuation ratio techniques, beginning with a detailed analysis and valuation using the earnings multiple (P/E ratio) approach. Subsequently, we compute and analyze the trends for the other relative valuation ratios, P/BV, P/CF, and P/S. We do not attempt to use these ratios to derive a specific value of the market; rather, we discuss the trends for these ratios during the past 20 years to help you become familiar with them so that these relative ratios can be used subsequently in industry analysis and the company-stock analysis. In addition, it will be useful to compare industry and company valuation ratios to the relative valuation ratios for the market. We finish the chapter with a discussion of some unique factors that must be considered when applying these valuation techniques to foreign markets.

APPLYING THE DDM VALUATION MODEL TO THE MARKET

In Chapter 13, we worked with a valuation model that equated the value of an investment to

1. The stream of expected returns
2. The time pattern of expected returns
3. The required rate of return on the investment

Using this information, we employed the dividend discount model (DDM), which estimated the value of the stock (V_j) assuming a constant growth rate of dividends for an infinite period.

$$V_j = \frac{D_0(1+g)}{(1+k)} + \frac{D_0(1+g)^2}{(1+k)^2} + \ldots + \frac{D_0(1+g)^n}{(1+k)^n}$$

where:

V_j = **the value of stock** j
D_0 = **the dividend payment in the current period**
g = **the constant growth rate of dividends**
k = **the required rate of return on stock** j
n = **the number of periods, which is assumed to be infinite**

We used this model as the basis for the fundamental analysis of common stock. We also can use it to value a stock-market series. In the appendix to Chapter 13, it was shown that this model can be simplified to the following expression:

$$V_j = P_j = \frac{D_1}{k - g}$$

where:

P_j = the price of stock j
D_1 = dividend in period 1, which is equal to: $D_0(1 + g)$
k = the required rate of return for stock j
g = the constant growth rate of dividends

This model suggests that the parameters to be estimated are (1) the required rate of return (k) and (2) the expected growth rate of dividends (g). After estimating g, it is simple to estimate D_1 because it is the known current dividend (D_0) times $(1 + g)$.

Recall too that we can transform the dividend discount model into an earnings multiplier model by dividing both sides of the equation by E:

$$\frac{P_i}{E_1} = \frac{\frac{D_1}{E_1}}{k - g}$$

We call this P/E ratio the **earnings multiplier** or the *price/earnings ratio.* It is determined by

1. The expected dividend payout ratio (D_1/E_1)
2. The required rate of return on the stock (k)
3. The expected growth rate of dividends for the stock (g)

We will see that the estimation of this earnings multiplier is important because it varies between stocks and industries. Also the multiplier for the aggregate stock market varies widely over time and has a big impact on changes in the value of the market.

We showed previously that the difficult parameters to estimate are k and g, or, more specifically, the *spread* between k and g. Recall that very small changes in either k or g without an offset by the other variable can affect the spread and change the value of the aggregate market substantially.

MARKET VALUATION USING THE REDUCED FORM DDM

Because we have discussed the basic model several times, the emphasis in this section will be an application of the model to the valuation of the S&P 400 Index as of mid-1999. As noted, the critical estimates are the prevailing k and g for the U.S. equity market. The estimate of D_1 is the current D_0 for the latest 52-week period times $(1 + g)$. As of mid-1999, the recent trailing 52-week dividend estimate in *Barron's* was $20.00.

As discussed previously, the estimate of k is a function of the nominal risk-free rate (NRFR) plus a market risk premium (RP). Because both of these components are subject to interpretation, we will consider a range of values.

THE NOMINAL RISK-FREE RATE The alternatives for the NRFR are based upon the theoretical specifications that it should be a zero-coupon, default-free asset with a time to maturity that approximates the investor's holding period. The point is, such an asset would provide the asset's promised return (i.e., its yield to maturity) because there is no default risk, no reinvestment risk because it is a zero-coupon security, and no price risk because the asset matures at the end of the holding period. The range of suggested maturities goes from a three-month T-bill to an intermediate government bond (e.g. a 10-year Treasury), to the long-term government bond (e.g., a 30-year Treasury). As of mid-1999, these yields were:

3-Month Treasury Bill:	4.40%
10-Year Treasury:	5.50%
30-Year Treasury:	5.70%

THE EQUITY RISK PREMIUM The attitude toward the estimation of the equity risk premium has undergone significant changes during the 1990s. The initial empirical estimate of an equity risk premium was provided by the pioneering work of Ibbotson and Sinquefield, in their monograph for the *Financial Analysts Research Foundation.* They estimated the risk premium on common stock as the arithmetic mean of the difference in the annual rate of return from stocks minus the return on Treasury bills.[1] Although the original estimate was for 1926–1981, this estimated risk premium has been updated annually in a yearbook provided by Ibbotson Associates.[2] For example, the equity risk premium as of 1999 for 1926–1998 was 9.2 percent using the arithmetic mean of the annual values and 7.6 percent using the geometric mean of the annual values. The geometric mean is appropriate for long-run asset class comparisons, whereas the arithmetic mean is what you would use to estimate the premium for a given year (e.g., the *expected* performance next year). Because our application is to the long-term DDM model, the geometric mean value would probably be more appropriate, which implies using the 7.6 percent risk premium value.

An additional adjustment is suggested to reflect the belief that the typical investment horizon is longer than that implied by the T-bill rate. Assuming that most investors consider the intermediate time frame (5 years) a more appropriate investment horizon, the risk premium should be computed as the stock return less the return on intermediate government bonds. Given the typical upward-sloping yield curve, it is not surprising that this measure of the risk premium is about 1 percent less than the T-bill premium—i.e., the arithmetic mean of the annual risk premiums relative to intermediate government bonds was 8.2 percent during 1926–1998, and the geometric mean of the annual risk premiums was 6.7 percent. Therefore, the risk premium to use should be about *6.5 percent,* if you are interested in the long-term historical estimate.

Several authors have contended that there are problems with this estimate in a dynamic real-world environment. The major criticism is that it is *too long term* and assumes that the *market-risk premium is almost a constant value.*[3] Given that we are dealing with an average value that encompasses almost 75 years, this technique will not reflect any changes over time. There are ways to adjust for this constant value problem and there are other estimation approaches that have been suggested.

[1]Roger G. Ibbotson and Rex A. Sinquefield, *Stocks, Bonds, Bills and Inflation: The Past and Future* (Charlottesville, Va.: Financial Analysts Research Foundation, 1982).

[2]*Stocks, Bonds, Bills and Inflation* (Chicago, Ill.: Ibbotson Associates, annual).

[3]This is the contention contained in Michael Rozeff, "Dividend Yields Are Equity Risk Premiums," *Journal of Portfolio Management* 11, no. 1 (fall 1984): 68–75.

The first suggestion to adjust for the constant value is to use a constant period moving average for the Ibbotson–Sinquefield technique—e.g., instead of using a single mean value for the total period since 1926, employ a 20-year moving average of the series. This would reflect any trends in the series over time. Figure 18.1 shows the impact of employing a moving average and using the intermediate bond return as the risk-free asset. These time series plots also suggest that the risk premium series is not very stable since the 20-year moving average values vary from about 1 percent to 16 percent.

The paper by Rozeff referred to above discusses the equity risk premium (RP) concept similar to the presentation in this book.[4] This is followed by a review of alternative measures of the RP, including the Ibbotson–Sinquefield series, an estimate using the CAPM, and a brief consideration of the default risk premium (referred to as the credit risk series). Rozeff shows that, given some economic assumptions, the risk premium on equity is equal to the dividend yield. He further suggests that when the dividend yield exceeds 6 percent, it is an excellent time to buy stocks; when the yield is below 3 percent, it is generally a poor time to buy stocks. Some relatively casual empirical results were provided to support these contentions. The fact is, this decision rule has not worked during the period 1991–1998 and especially since 1995 because during the period 1995–1998, the dividend yield was consistently below 2.5 percent and yet, stocks experienced a rate of return that averaged about 24 percent (the highest 4-year average since 1926).

The credit risk premium concept has been referred to on several occasions in this book when discussing changes in the capital market risk premium. The notion is that changes in the absolute or percentage spread between the yield on BAA and AAA bonds indicates a change in the required rate of return by investors for accepting credit risk. Further, this

FIGURE 18.1

INTERMEDIATE-TERM EQUITY RISK PREMIUM: 20-YEAR MOVING ARITHMETIC AND GEOMETRIC AVERAGES

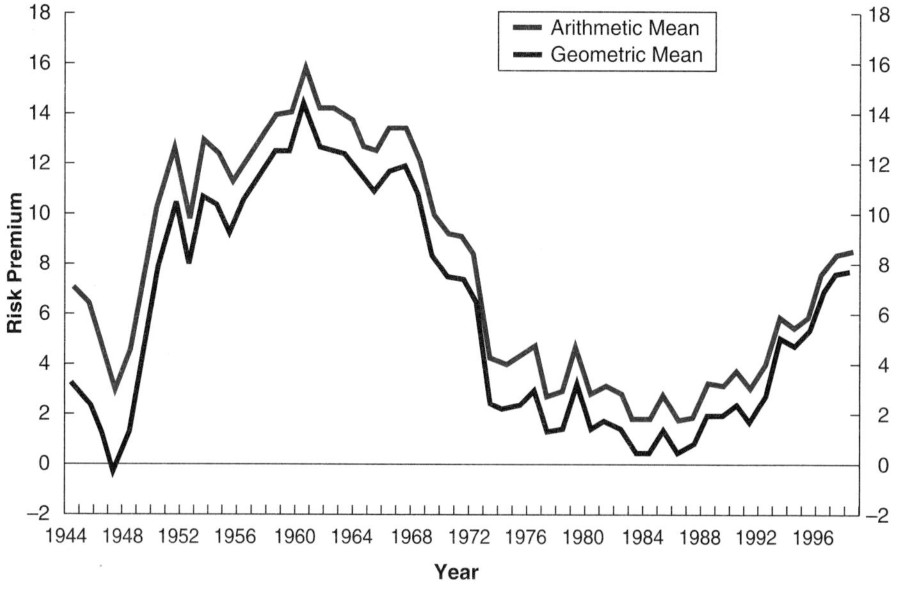
Arithmetic Mean
Geometric Mean
Risk Premium
18
16
14
12
10
8
6
4
2
0
−2
1944 1948 1952 1956 1960 1964 1968 1972 1976 1980 1984 1988 1992 1996
Year

[4] Ibid.

change in the credit risk premium implies a change in the slope of the security market line (SML). The percent yield spread is considered a preferable measure because it adjusts for the level of yields. An advantage of the credit risk measure is that it is based on current market results and reflects prevailing investor attitudes. For a recent plot of this credit yield spread, see Figure 1.7, which indicates a declining trend since 1985.

An alternative estimate of the equity risk premium is suggested by Reichenstein and Rich—namely the Value Line forecast of dividends and capital gain.[5] This estimated total market return less short-term government bond yield is shown to provide better and more consistent results than an earnings price value or dividend yield.

A comparison used by Woolridge to justify a change in the equity risk premium is the relative volatility of stocks versus bonds.[6] Woolridge argues that the risk premium for equity has declined from the 6 percent estimate based on the Ibbotson–Sinquefield data to about 2.5 percent because of the *increase* in bond market volatility relative to stock volatility.[7] Specifically, the equity risk premium spread has declined, not because stocks have become less volatile, but because bonds have become more volatile. Thus, the difference in risk between the two asset classes is less than before, so the risk premium spread has declined.

In summary, if you use the current intermediate government bond rate as your estimate of the minimal NRFR, these studies indicate that the equity risk premium should be somewhere between 2.5 percent and 6.0 percent, depending on the current environment. In turn, you can derive an indicator of the current environment by examining the dividend yield, the prevailing credit risk spread, or the relative volatility of bonds versus stocks.

Once you have estimated the required rate of return for the current period, you must determine whether the expected rate of inflation or the risk premium on common stock will change during your investment horizon.

THE CURRENT ESTIMATE OF RP AND k Based upon the prior discussion, the total range for the equity RP is from about 1.5 percent (the prevailing dividend yield on the major market indexes) to about 6.0 percent (the long-run geometric average of the historical returns according to the Ibbotson data). For purposes of applying these results, we will employ three alternative risk premiums: 2, 4, and 6 percent. If we combine these RPs with the prior nominal risk-free rates for government bonds, we derive the following matrix of required rates of return (k) for the S&P 400:

	RISK PREMIUMS		
Nominal RFR	**0.02**	**0.04**	**0.06**
0.044	0.064	0.084	0.104
0.055	0.075	0.095	0.115
0.057	0.077	0.097	0.117

[5]William Reichenstein and Steven P. Rich, "The Market Risk Premium and Long-Term Stock Returns," *Journal of Portfolio Management* 19, no. 4 (summer 1993): 63–72.

[6]Randall Woolridge, "Do Stock Prices Reflect Fundamental Values?" *Journal of Applied Corporate Finance* 8, no. 1 (spring 1995): 64–69.

[7]For an analysis of relative volatility of bonds versus stocks that is consistent with the Woolridge contention, see Frank K. Reilly and David J. Wright, "An Analysis of Changes in Bond Market Volatility," Working Paper, University of Notre Dame College of Business Administration (February 1999).

The matrix indicates a range of k from 0.064 (6.4 percent) to 0.117 (11.7 percent). The low required rate of return assumes investors have a very short-run horizon and a very small risk premium, while the high required return implies a long-run horizon and the use of the long-run historical risk premium.

For purposes of our subsequent estimate, we will use the diagonal values from this matrix: 0.064, 0.095, and 0.117.

ESTIMATING THE GROWTH RATE OF DIVIDENDS (g)

The earnings multiple that is applied to next year's earnings must take into account the expected growth rate (g) for common dividends.[8] There is a positive relationship between the earnings multiplier and the growth rate of earnings and dividends—the higher the expected growth rate, the higher the multiple.[9] When estimating g, you should consider the current expected rate of growth and estimate any *changes* in the growth rate. Such changes in expectations indicate a change in the relationship between k and g and will have a profound effect on the earnings multiplier.

As discussed in Chapters 12 and 13, a firm's growth rate is equal to (1) the proportion of earnings retained and reinvested by the firm—that is, its retention rate (b)—times (2) the rate of return earned on investments (ROE). An increase in either or both of these variables causes an increase in the expected growth rate (g) and an increase in the earnings multiplier. Therefore, the growth rate can be stated as:

$$g = f(b, \text{ROE})$$

where:

g = expected growth rate
b = the expected retention rate equal to 1 − D/E
ROE = the expected return on equity investments

Therefore, to estimate the growth rate, you need to estimate changes in the retention rate (b) and the return on equity (ROE). The plot in Figure 18.2 shows that the retention rate was relatively high (56 to 63 percent) during the 1970s, ranged between 45 and 62 percent during the 1980s, declined in 1991 when earnings declined but many firms did not cut their dividends, and returned to over 55 percent during 1994–98. Because the valuation model is a long-run model, you should estimate only relatively permanent changes, although short-run changes can affect expectations. Specifically, you should recognize that the annual retention rate which has been quite volatile (between 45 and 60 percent) is heavily impacted by annual earnings changes (as will be discussed in the dividend payout section).

The second variable that affects g is changes in the return on equity (ROE) defined as

$$\text{ROE} = \frac{\text{Net Income}}{\text{Equity}}$$

You will recall from the discussion in Chapter 12 that ROE can be broken down using the three-component Du Pont analysis as follows:

[8]You know that the g in the valuation model is the expected growth rate for dividends. In our discussion, we assume a relatively constant dividend-payout ratio (dividend/earnings), so the growth of dividends is dependent on the growth in earnings, and in the long run the growth rates are approximately equal.

[9]A paper that specifically examines this relationship is Patricia M. Fairfield, "P/E, P/B, and the Present Value of Future Dividends," *Financial Analysts Journal* 50, no. 4 (July/August 1994): 22–31.

FIGURE 18.2

TIME-SERIES PLOT OF THE S&P 400 RETENTION RATE: 1977–1998

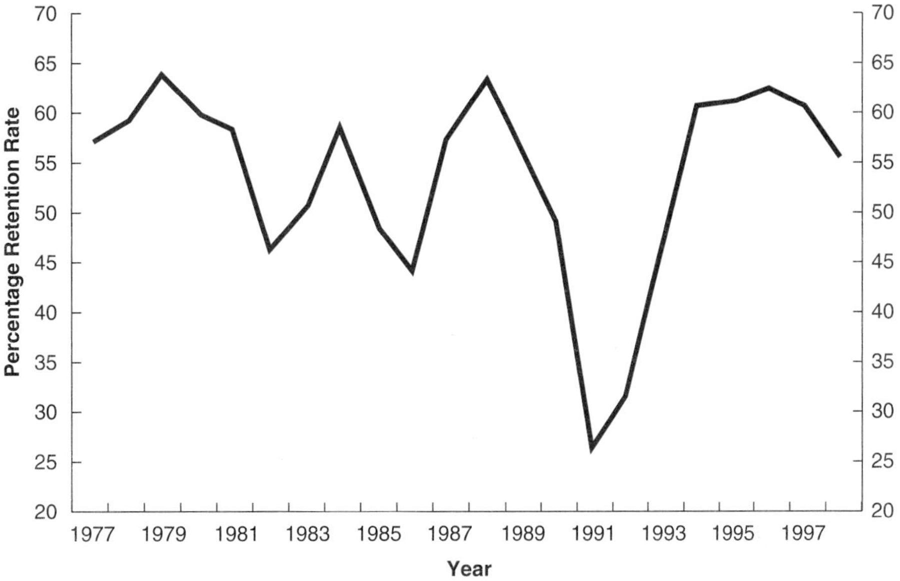
Percentage Retention Rate
70
65
60
55
50
45
40
35
30
25
20
1977
1979
1981
1983
1985
1987
1989
1991
1993
1995
1997
Year

$$\frac{\text{Net Income}}{\text{Equity}} = \frac{\text{Net Income}}{\text{Sales}} \times \frac{\text{Sales}}{\text{Total Assets}} \times \frac{\text{Total Assets}}{\text{Equity}}$$

$$= \begin{matrix}\text{Net Profit}\\\text{Margin}\end{matrix} \times \begin{matrix}\text{Total Asset}\\\text{Turnover}\end{matrix} \times \begin{matrix}\text{Financial}\\\text{Leverage}\end{matrix}$$

This equation shows that the ROE increases if either the total asset turnover or the profit margin increases. In addition, you can increase ROE by increasing financial leverage. Because the S&P 400 series includes historical information on total assets only since 1977, we examine this three-component breakdown of ROE for this 21-year period.

As shown in Figure 18.3, the ROE for the S&P 400 series experienced very little change over the 15-year period prior to the decline in 1991 and strong recovery in 1993–1998 to record levels. An analysis of the three components of ROE indicates what contributed to the overall change (or lack of change) over time. First, the profit margin (Figure 18.4) experienced steady increase after 1993. The second component, total asset turnover (Figure 18.5) increased in 1980 and 1981, but declined subsequently and overall was lower in 1997. Combining these two variables (PM and TATO) equals return on total assets that has been increasing since 1992 but has declined slightly during the total period from 1977 to 1998. Therefore, it appears that the major variable that contributed to the increase in ROE was the financial leverage ratio (Figure 18.6) that increased from about 2.00 to 3.40 in 1998.

All of this shows a need for an investor to estimate the long-term outlook for ROE, which in turn requires a long-term estimate for each of the three component ratios. Once established, multiply this long-term estimate of ROE by your estimate of b, the retention rate, to calculate an estimate of g. As an example, if you estimate, the *long-run* retention rate of firms will be 55 percent and their ROE will be about 14 percent; this means you would expect the long-run growth rate of

$$\begin{aligned} g &= b \times \text{ROE} \\ &= 0.55 \times 0.14 \\ &= 0.077 = 7.7\% \end{aligned}$$

FIGURE 18.3

S&P 400: RETURN ON EQUITY AND RETURN ON ASSETS: 1977–1998(P)

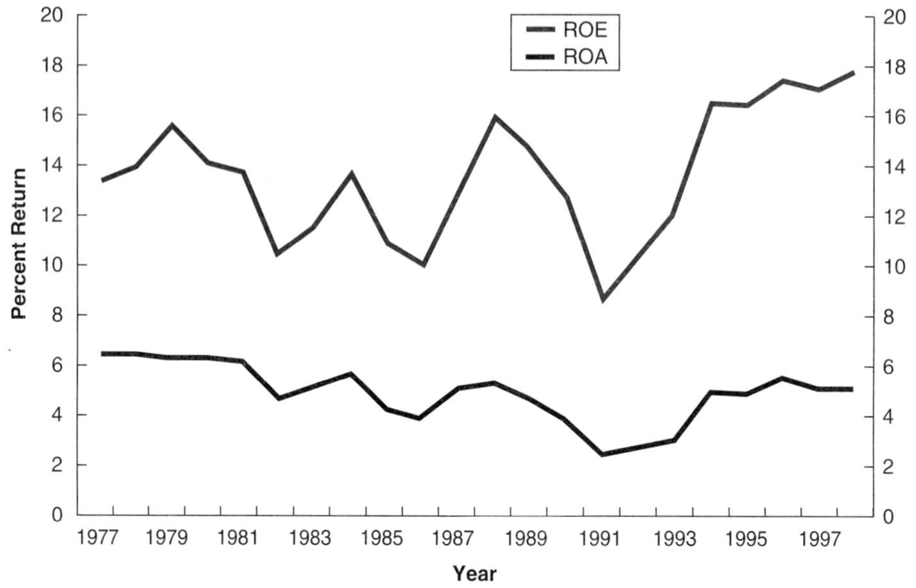
ROE
ROA
Percent Return
Year
20
18
16
14
12
10
8
6
4
2
0
1977
1979
1981
1983
1985
1987
1989
1991
1993
1995
1997

FIGURE 18.4

S&P 400: NET PROFIT MARGIN: 1977–1998E

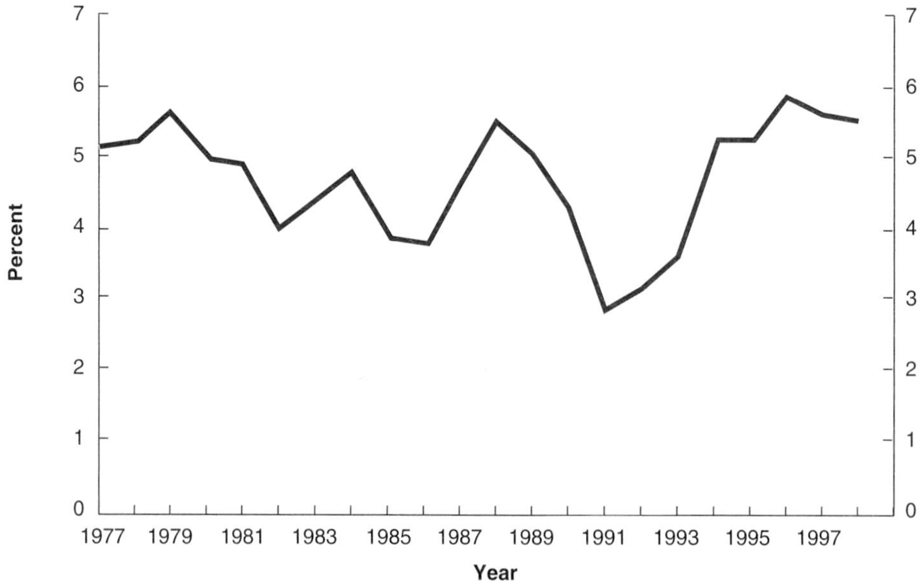
Percent
Year
7
6
5
4
3
2
1
0
1977
1979
1981
1983
1985
1987
1989
1991
1993
1995
1997

COMBINING THE ESTIMATES If we combine the several estimates, they are as follows:

$$D_0 = \$20.00$$
$$k = 0.064 - 0.095 - 0.117$$
$$g = 0.077$$
$$D_1 = 20.00(1 + g) = 20.00(1.077) = \$21.54$$

FIGURE 18.5

S&P 400: TOTAL ASSET TURNOVER: 1977–1998(P)

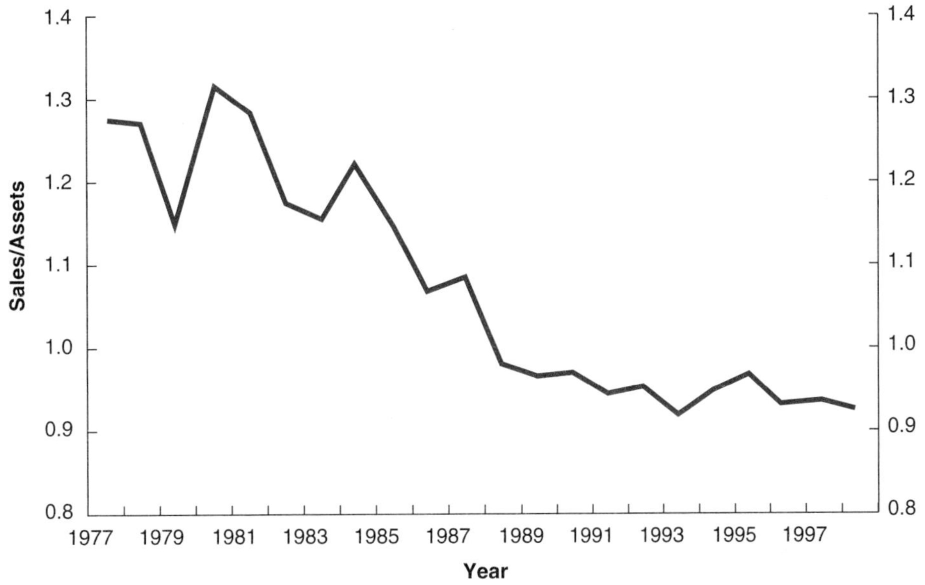
1.4
1.3
1.2
1.1
1.0
0.9
0.8
Sales/Assets
1977 1979 1981 1983 1985 1987 1989 1991 1993 1995 1997
Year

FIGURE 18.6

S&P 400: ASSETS/EQUITY: 1977–1998(P)

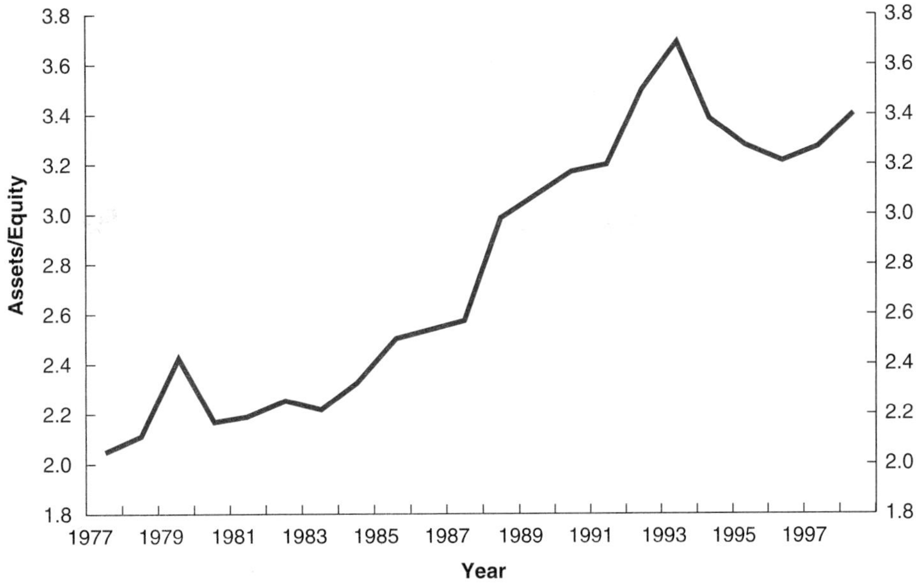
3.8
3.6
3.4
3.2
3.0
2.8
2.6
2.4
2.2
2.0
1.8
Assets/Equity
1977 1979 1981 1983 1985 1987 1989 1991 1993 1995 1997
Year

Using these values in the reduced form DDM indicates the following estimates:

1. $\frac{\$21.54}{0.064 - 0.077} = \frac{\$21.54}{-0.013} = \text{meaningless}$

2. $\frac{\$21.54}{0.095 - 0.077} = \frac{\$21.54}{0.018} = 1{,}196.67$

3. $\frac{\$21.54}{0.117 - 0.077} = \frac{\$21.54}{0.04} = 538.50$

These latter two estimated values, not including the one where the expected growth rate exceeds the very low k estimate, are below the prevailing index value of about 1,580. Assuming the dividend value of \$21.54 is reasonable, one needs to consider what k–g spread is necessary to justify the prevailing market value. Consider the following values:

$$\frac{\$21.54}{0.015} = 1{,}436.00$$

$$\frac{\$21.54}{0.014} = 1{,}538.57$$

$$\frac{\$21.54}{0.013} = 1{,}656.92$$

$$\frac{\$21.54}{0.012} = 1{,}795.00$$

$$\frac{\$21.54}{0.011} = 1{,}958.18$$

$$\frac{\$21.54}{0.010} = 2{,}154.00$$

It appears that the current market value implies (requires) a k–g spread approaching 1.3 percent, which means either a k below 0.095 or an expected growth rate above 0.077. The most likely would be a lower k approaching 0.090, which implies about a 3 percent RP with a long-term NRFR or a 4 percent RP with a short-term NRFR.

Market Valuation Using the Free Cash Flow to Equity (FCFE) Model

As indicated earlier, we will derive an estimate using this FCFE model under two scenarios: (1) a constant growth rate from the present, and then, (2) a two-stage growth rate assumption. Recall from Chapter 13 that this model requires an estimate of the expected growth rate of FCFE. We initially consider a constant growth version and then a two-stage growth model.

THE CONSTANT GROWTH FCFE MODEL To begin, the FCFE is defined (measured) as follows:[10]

Net Income
\+ *Depreciation Expense*
− *Capital Expenditures*
− *Δ in Working Capital*
− *Principal Debt Repayments*
\+ *New Debt Issues*

This technique attempts to determine the free cash flow that is available to the stockholders after payments to all other capital suppliers and after providing for the continued growth of the firm. The FCFE data for the S&P 400 Industrial Index for the period 1987–1998 is contained in Table 18.1

Although there was overall growth in the series for the period 1987–1997 (13 percent a year) and for 1987–1998 (11 percent a year), there was also substantial variation, including the peak value in 1988 and the low value in 1993. Therefore, for the constant growth version of the model, we will use the growth values used in the DDM as follows:

[10]For further discussion and detail, see Aswath Damodaran, *Damodaran on Valuation* (New York: John Wiley & Sons, 1994), Chapter 7.

TABLE 18.1 COMPONENTS OF FREE CASH FLOW TO EQUITY FOR THE S&P 400 INDEX 1987–1998

Year	Net Income	Depreciation Expense	Capital Expenditure	Δ in Working Capital	Principal Repayment	New Debt Issues	Total FCFE
1987	20.28	20.21	27.59	5.09	—	3.00	10.81
1988	26.59	23.59	35.43	−21.14	—	44.04	79.93
1989	26.83	24.21	40.98	−6.25	—	3.63	19.94
1990	24.77	26.31	43.93	−5.25	—	10.48	22.88
1991	16.91	27.50	40.33	−1.42	—	2.26	7.76
1992	19.05	29.48	39.36	−2.88	1.70	—	10.35
1993	21.93	28.72	39.28	6.63E	2.42	—	2.32
1994	32.83	29.58	39.97	6.63E	—	4.06	19.87
1995	35.44	33.06	46.16	6.63E	—	10.90	26.61
1996	41.15	36.11	53.49	−3.85	—	10.17	41.64
1997	43.80	39.79	60.54	−0.94	—	11.04	35.03
1998E	38.50	43.10	56.00	3.00	—	11.50	34.10

Source: *Financial Analysts Handbook* (New York: Standard & Poor's, 1998).

$$g = 0.077$$
$$k = 0.095; 0.117$$
$$\text{FCFE} = 34.10 \text{ in 1998 } (\text{FCFE}_0)$$
$$= (34.10)(1.077) = 36.73 \text{ in 1999 } (\text{FCFE}_1)$$
$$\text{Equity Values} = \frac{36.73}{0.095 - 0.077} = \frac{36.73}{0.018} = 2{,}040$$
$$= \frac{36.73}{0.117 - 0.077} = \frac{36.73}{0.04} = 918.25$$

In contrast to the DDM results, this model indicates that the market at its current price of about 1,600 is undervalued if one assumes a cost of equity of 9.5 percent. In contrast, the market is overvalued assuming a cost of equity of 11.7 percent. Recall that the 9.5 percent cost of equity is based upon using the 10-year Treasury bond as the NRFR and assumes a 4 percent market risk premium.

Alternatively, if we assume a lower perpetual growth rate of 7.2 percent, the value declines to 1,597 (36.73/0.023), and if our growth estimate is only 7 percent, the value declines to 1,469. Needless to say, the estimated value is very sensitive to the estimates of k and g and the resulting spread.

THE TWO-STAGE GROWTH FCFE MODEL If one considers only the period 1994–1998, the average annual percentage growth is about 15 percent with declines in the last 2 years. To demonstrate this model, we assumed the following above-average growth rates during the next 5 years (the first stage) followed by a second stage of constant growth at 7 percent.

1999—12%

2000—10%

2001—10%

2002—8%

2003—8%

2004 onward—7%

Assuming a k of 9.5 percent and an FCFE of 34.10 in 1998, the computations are as follows:

Year	FCFE	Discount Factor at 0.095		Present Value
1999	38.19	0.9132		34.88
2000	42.01	0.8340		35.04
2001	46.21	0.7616		35.19
2002	49.91	0.6954		34.71
2003	53.90	0.6353		34.24
Continuing Value[a]	2,307	0.6353		1,465.64
			Total P.V.	$1,639.70

[a] $\frac{57.67}{0.095 - 0.07} = 2,307$

As can be seen, this set of assumptions indicates an intrinsic market value very close to the current price of the market, which implies the following: (1) the market is properly valued at this time, and (2) investors who acquire a diversified portfolio of U.S. stocks at these prices should derive a long-run annual rate of return of about 9.5 percent. It is also possible to arrive at this market return estimate using the k estimate from the DDM as follows: $k = \frac{D}{P} + g$. Combining the current dividend yield of about 1.4 percent and the expected g of 7.7 percent implies a return of 9.1 percent. Notably, this is higher than what is expected by Emmons from the St. Louis Federal Reserve who derives expected growth based on the growth of nominal GDP of about 6 percent plus a dividend yield of 1.3 percent to arrive at a return estimate of about 7 percent (he stipulates a range of 5 to 7 percent).[11]

The next section will discuss and demonstrate the four alternative relative valuation ratios as follows: (1) the price/earnings ratio (P/E), (2) the price/book-value ratio (P/BV), (3) the price/cash flow ratio (P/CF), and (4) the price/sales ratio (P/S). We begin with the P/E ratio because it is the most well known and because it can be derived from the DDM. Finally, this model can be used to derive a specific expected market value, which implies an expected rate of return for the equity market.

VALUATION USING THE RELATIVE VALUATION APPROACH

Two-Part Valuation Procedure

We use the earnings multiplier version of the dividend discount model to value the stock market because it is a theoretically correct model of value assuming a constant growth of dividends for an infinite time period, which is a reasonable assumption for the aggregate stock market.[12] Also this valuation technique is consistently used in practice.

Recall that k and g are independent variables because k depends heavily on risk, whereas g is a function of the retention rate and the ROE. Therefore, this spread between k and g can

[11] William R. Emmons, "What Can 'Buy-and-Hold' Stock Investors Expect?" *Monetary Trends* (St. Louis: Federal Reserve Bank of St. Louis, June 1999).

[12] Recall that these assumptions may be unrealistic for many stocks, especially for stocks of growth companies. We will consider these problems and discuss alternative valuation models that consider such conditions in Chapter 20.

and does change over time. The following equations show that you can derive an estimate of this spread at a point in time by examining the prevailing dividend yield:

$$P_j = \frac{D_1}{k - g}$$

$$P_j/D_1 = 1/k - g$$

$$D_1/P_j = k - g$$

Although the dividend yield gives an estimate of the size of the prevailing spread, it does not indicate the values for the two individual components (k and g) or what caused the *change* in the spread. More important, it says nothing about the future spread, which is the critical value that must be determined based upon estimating values for k and g.

Importance of Both Components of Value

The ultimate objective of this microanalysis is to estimate the future market value for a major stock-market series, such as the S&P 400. This estimation process has two equally important steps:

1. Estimating the future earnings per share for the stock-market series
2. Estimating a future earnings multiplier for the stock-market series[13]

Some analysts have concentrated on estimating the earnings for a market series with little consideration of changes in the earnings multiplier for the series. An investor who considers only the earnings for the series and ignores the earnings multiplier (i.e., the P/E ratio), assumes that the earnings multiplier will be relatively constant over time. If this were correct, stock prices would generally move in line with earnings. The fallacy of this assumption is obvious when one examines data for the two components during the period from 1975 to 1998, as shown in Table 18.2.

The year-end stock price is the closing value for the S&P 400 series on the last trading day of the year. The next column is the percentage change in price for the year. The earnings figure is the earnings per share during the year for the S&P 400 series, and the next column shows the percentage change from the prior year. The fifth column is the historical earnings multiplier at the end of the year, which is equal to the year-end value for the S&P 400 series divided by the *historical* earnings for that year. As an example, at the end of 1975, the S&P 400 price series was equal to 100.88 and the earnings per share for the firms that made up the series were 8.58 for the 12 months ending 12/31/75. This implies an earnings multiplier of 11.76 (100.88/8.58). Although this may not be the ideal measure of the multiplier, it is consistent in its measurement and shows the changes in the relationship between stock prices and earnings over time. An alternative measure is to compute the multiplier using *next* year's earnings (i.e., stock price as of 12/31/75 versus earnings for the 12 months ending 12/31/76). This series likewise reflects substantial annual changes that are not quite as large as with historical earnings and a smaller multiple because it considers future earnings that are typically higher.

There were numerous striking examples where annual stock price movements for the S&P 400 series were opposite to earnings changes during the same year.

[13]Our emphasis will be on *estimating future values.* We will show the relevant variables and provide a procedural framework, but the final estimate depends on the ability of the analyst.

TABLE 18.2

ANNUAL CHANGES IN STOCK PRICES, CORPORATE EARNINGS, AND THE EARNINGS MULTIPLIER FOR S&P 400: 1975–1998

Year	Year-End Stock Prices	Percentage Change	Earnings per Share	Percentage Change	Year-End Earnings Multiple	Percentage Change	Earnings Multiple $t+1$	Percentage Change
1975	100.88	31.9	8.58	−10.7	11.76	47.8	9.44	5.9
1976	119.46	18.4	10.69	24.6	11.17	−5.0	10.43	10.6
1977	104.71	−12.3	11.45	7.1	9.14	−18.2	8.03	−23.0
1978	107.21	2.4	13.04	13.9	8.22	−10.1	6.58	−18.0
1979	121.02	12.9	16.29	24.9	7.43	−9.6	7.51	14.1
1980	154.45	27.6	16.12	−1.0	9.58	29.0	9.23	22.9
1981	137.12	−11.2	16.74	3.8	8.19	−14.5	10.39	12.6
1982	157.62	15.0	13.20	−21.1	11.94	45.8	10.67	2.7
1983	186.17	18.1	14.77	11.9	12.60	5.6	10.28	−3.7
1984	186.36	0.1	18.11	22.6	10.29	−18.4	12.20	18.6
1985	234.56	25.9	15.28	−15.6	15.35	49.2	16.14	32.4
1986	269.93	15.1	14.53	−4.9	18.58	21.0	13.31	−17.5
1987	285.85	5.9	20.28	39.6	14.10	−24.1	10.75	−19.2
1988	321.26	12.4	26.59	31.1	12.08	−14.3	11.97	11.4
1989	403.49	25.6	26.83	0.9	15.04	24.5	16.29	36.0
1990	387.42	−4.0	24.77	−7.7	15.64	4.0	22.91	40.6
1991	492.72	27.2	16.91	−31.7	29.14	86.3	25.86	12.9
1992	507.46	3.0	19.05	12.7	26.64	−8.6	23.14	−10.5
1993	540.19	6.4	21.93	15.1	24.63	−7.5	16.45	−28.9
1994	547.51	1.4	32.83	49.7	16.68	−32.3	15.45	−6.1
1995	721.19	31.7	35.44	8.0	20.35	22.0	17.53	13.4
1996	869.97	20.6	41.15	16.1	21.14	3.9	20.65	17.8
1997	1,121.38	28.9	42.13	2.4	26.62	25.9	28.75	39.2
1998	1,479.16	31.9	39.00	−7.4	37.93	42.5	NA	NA
With Signs								
Mean		14.6		8.1	16.27	9.6	14.39	6.5
Standard deviation		13.4		18.9		28.7		19.5
Coefficient of variation		0.9		2.3		3.0		3.0
Without Signs								
Mean		16.2		15.8		23.1		17.6
Standard deviation		10.7		12.8		19.0		10.1
Coefficient of variation		0.7		0.8		0.8		0.6

NA—not available

Source: *Standard & Poor's Analysts Handbook* (New York: Standard & Poor's Corporation, 1998). Reprinted by permission of Standard & Poor's Corp.

- 1975 profit *declined* by 10 percent; stock prices *increased* by 32 percent.
- 1977 profits *increased* by 7 percent; stock prices *declined* by 12 percent.
- 1980 profits *decreased* by 1 percent; stock prices *increased* by over 27 percent.
- 1982 profits *decreased* by 21 percent; stock prices *increased* by 15 percent.
- 1984 profits *increased* by almost 23 percent; stock prices were basically *unchanged.*
- 1985 profits *decreased* by 15 percent; stock prices *increased* by about 26 percent.
- 1989 profits were almost *unchanged;* stock prices *increased* by over 25 percent.
- 1991 profits *decreased* by almost 32 percent; stock prices *increased* by over 27 percent.
- 1994 profits *increased* by almost 50 percent; stock prices were basically *unchanged.*
- 1997 profits *increased* about 2 percent; stock prices *increased* almost 29 percent.
- 1998 profits *decreased* by 7 percent; stock prices *increased* almost 32 percent.

FIGURE 18.7

YEAR-END EARNINGS MULTIPLE FOR THE S&P 400 BASED ON HISTORICAL EARNINGS: 1975–1998(P)

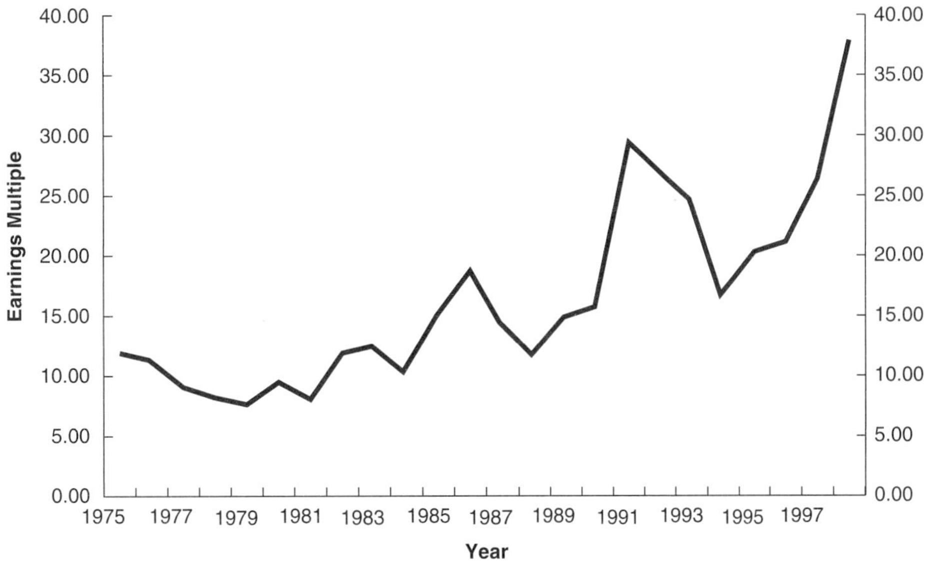
Earnings Multiple
40.00
35.00
30.00
25.00
20.00
15.00
10.00
5.00
0.00
1975
1977
1979
1981
1983
1985
1987
1989
1991
1993
1995
1997
Year

During each of these years, the major influences on stock price movements came from changes in the earnings multiplier. The greater volatility of the multiplier series compared to the earnings per share series can be seen from the summary figures at the bottom of Table 18.2 and from the graph of the earnings multiplier in Figure 18.7. The standard deviation of annual changes for the earnings multiplier series is much larger than the standard deviation of earnings changes (28.7 versus 18.9). The same is true for the relative volatility measures of the coefficient of variability (3.0 versus 2.3). Also, if you consider the mean annual percentage change of the two series without sign, the earnings multiplier series has a larger mean annual percent change value (23.1 versus 15.8) and a larger standard deviation of annual percentage change (19.0 versus 12.8). Therefore, these figures show that, of the two estimates required for market valuation, *the earnings multiplier is the more volatile component.*

The point of this discussion is not to reduce the importance of the earnings estimate, but to note that this calculation of future market value requires two separate estimates and *both* are important and necessary. Therefore, we will begin by considering a procedure for estimating aggregate earnings. Later, we discuss the factors that should be analyzed and the procedure for estimating the aggregate market earnings multiplier.

ESTIMATING EXPECTED EARNINGS PER SHARE

The estimate of expected earnings per share for the market series will consider the outlook for the aggregate economy and for the corporate sector. This requires the following steps:

1. Estimate sales per share for a stock-market series, such as the S&P 400. This estimate of sales involves a prior estimate of gross domestic product (GDP) because of the relationship between the sales of major industrial firms and this measure of aggregate economic

activity. Therefore, prior to estimating sales per share, we will consider sources for an estimate of GDP.

2. Estimate the operating profit margin for the series, which equals operating profit divided by sales. Given the data available from Standard and Poor's, we will define operating profit as earnings before interest, taxes, and depreciation (EBITDA).
3. Estimate depreciation per share for the next year.
4. Estimate interest expense per share for the next year.
5. Estimate the corporate tax rate for the next year.

These steps will lead to an estimate of net earnings per share that will be combined with an estimate of the earnings multiplier to arrive at an estimate of the ending price for the stock-market series.

ESTIMATING GROSS DOMESTIC PRODUCT

GDP is a measure of aggregate economic output or activity. Therefore, one would expect aggregate corporate sales to be related to GDP. We begin our estimate of sales for a stock-market series with a prediction of nominal GDP from one of several banks or financial service firms that regularly publish such estimates.[14] Using this estimate of nominal GDP, we can estimate corporate sales based on the historical relationship between S&P 400 sales per share and aggregate economic activity (GDP).[15]

ESTIMATING SALES PER SHARE FOR A MARKET SERIES

As noted, we will use a sales figure for an existing stock-market series—the S&P 400 Industrial Index.[16] The plot in Figure 18.8 shows the relationship between the annual percentage changes in GDP and S&P 400 sales per share contained in Table 18.3. Generally, there is a strong relationship between the two series whereby a large proportion of the percentage changes in S&P 400 sales per share can be explained by percentage changes in nominal GDP. The relationship is not stronger because (1) the S&P 400 sales series is more volatile than the GDP series and (2) the GDP series never experienced a decline. The equation for the least-squares regression line relating annual percentage changes (% Δ) in the two series for the period 1975–1997 is

$$\$\ \Delta \text{ S\&P 400 Sales}_t = \underset{(-0.85)}{-2.40} + \underset{(4.06)}{1.16}\ (\%\ \Delta \text{ in Nominal GDP}_t)$$

$$\text{Adj. } R^2 = 0.36$$

These results indicate that about 36 percent of the variance in percentage changes in S&P 400 sales can be explained by percentage changes in the nominal GDP. Thus, given an estimate of the expected percentage change in nominal GDP for next year, we can estimate the percentage change in sales for the S&P 400 series and therefore the amount of sales per share. For example, assume the consensus estimate by economists is that nominal GDP

[14]This would include projections by Standard & Poor's appearing late in the year in *The Outlook;* and projections by several of the large investment firms, such as Goldman, Sachs, & Company ("The Pocket Chartbook"), Merrill Lynch, as well as by banks. *The Wall Street Journal* publishes a survey of over 50 economists every 6 months that includes estimates of various interest rates, GDP, inflation, and the value of the dollar versus the Japanese yen. For a sample survey, see Fred R. Bleakley, "Economy's Strength Is Seen Cooling in Second Half," *Wall Street Journal,* 1 July 1996, A2.

[15]Because GDP includes imports and exports, we also considered a pure domestic series entitled "Final Sales of Domestic Product." A consideration of both series indicated that the GDP series provided superior regression results; therefore, it is used.

[16]Sales per share figures are available from 1945 in Standard & Poor's *Analysts Handbook* (New York: Standard & Poor's Corporation). Because the composite series include numerous companies of different sizes, all data are on a per-share basis. The book is updated annually, and some series are updated quarterly in a monthly supplement.

FIGURE 18.8

SCATTER PLOT OF ANNUAL PERCENTAGE CHANGES IN S&P 400 SALES AND GDP

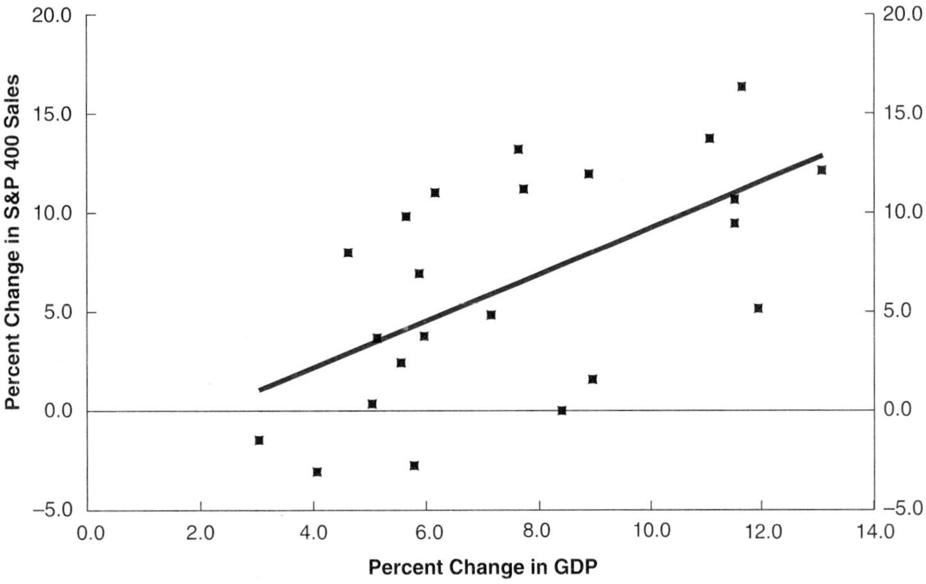
20.0
15.0
10.0
5.0
0.0
-5.0
Percent Change in S&P 400 Sales
0.0
2.0
4.0
6.0
8.0
10.0
12.0
14.0
Percent Change in GDP

next year will increase by approximately 6 percent (a 3 percent increase in real GDP plus 3 percent inflation). This estimate combined with the regression results implies the following estimated increase in S&P 400 sales:

$$\begin{aligned}\% \Delta \text{ S\&P 400 Sales} &= -0.024 + 1.16\,(0.06)\\ &= 0.046\\ &= 4.6\%\end{aligned}$$

Notably, this is referred to as a *point estimate of sales* because it is based on a point estimate of GDP. Although we know there is actually a *distribution* of estimates for GDP, we have used the mean value, or expected value, as our point estimate. In actual practice, you would probably consider several estimates and assign probabilities to each of them.

Alternative Estimates of Corporate Net Profits

Once sales per share for the market series have been estimated, the difficult estimate is the profit margin. Three alternative procedures are possible depending on the desired level of aggregation.

The first is a direct estimate of the *net* profit margin based on recent trends. As shown in Table 18.4, the net profit margin series is quite volatile because of changes in depreciation, interest, and the tax rate over time. As such, it is the most difficult series to estimate.

The second procedure would attempt to estimate the *net before tax* (NBT) profit margin. Once the NBT margin is derived, a separate estimate of the tax rate is obtained based on recent tax rates and current government tax pronouncements. Examples of critical tax rate estimates were those following the 1986 Tax Reform Act and those in 1993–1994 following the Clinton deficit reduction program.

The third method estimates an *operating* profit margin, defined as earnings before interest, taxes, and depreciation (EBITDA), as a percentage of sales. Because this measure of operating earnings as a percentage of sales is not influenced by changes in depreciation allowances, interest expense, or tax rates, it should be a stable series compared to either the

TABLE 18.3

NOMINAL GDP; FINAL SALES OF DOMESTIC PRODUCT, AND STANDARD AND POOR'S 400 INDUSTRIAL SALES PER SHARE: 1975–1997

Year	Nominal GDP (Billions of Dollars)	Percentage Change	Final Sales of Domestic Product (Billions of Dollars)	Percentage Change	S&P 400 (Dollar Value of Sales per Share)	Percentage Change
1975	1,630.6	8.9	1,636.9	10.4	185.2	1.7
1976	1,818.0	11.5	1,802.0	10.1	202.7	9.5
1977	2,026.9	11.5	2,003.8	11.2	224.2	10.6
1978	2,291.4	13.0	2,264.2	13.0	251.3	12.1
1979	2,557.5	11.6	2,540.6	12.2	292.4	16.3
1980	2,784.2	8.9	2,791.9	9.9	327.4	12.0
1981	3,115.9	11.9	3,087.8	10.6	344.3	5.2
1982	3,242.1	4.1	3,256.6	5.5	333.9	−3.0
1983	3,514.2	8.4	3,519.4	8.1	334.1	0.1
1984	3,902.4	11.0	3,835.0	9.0	379.7	13.7
1985	4,180.7	7.1	4,154.5	8.3	398.4	4.9
1986	4,422.2	5.8	4,412.6	6.2	387.8	−2.7
1987	4,692.3	6.1	4,668.1	5.8	430.4	11.0
1988	5,049.6	7.6	5,038.7	7.9	486.9	13.1
1989	5,438.7	7.7	5,407.0	7.3	541.4	11.2
1990	5,743.8	5.6	5,735.8	6.1	594.6	9.8
1991	5,916.7	3.0	5,919.0	3.2	586.9	−1.3
1992	6,244.4	5.5	6,237.4	5.4	601.4	2.5
1993	6,558.1	5.0	6,537.6	4.8	603.6	0.4
1994	6,947.0	5.9	6,885.7	5.3	626.3	3.8
1995	7,265.4	4.6	7,235.3	5.1	676.6	8.0
1996	7,636.0	5.1	7,610.2	5.2	701.9	3.7
1997	8,083.4	5.9	8,018.8	5.4	750.7	7.0
Average		7.6		7.6		6.5

Source: *Economic Report of the President,* 1998 (Washington, DC: U.S. Government Printing Office, 1998); and *Standard & Poor's Analysts Handbook* (New York: Standard & Poor's Corporation, 1998). Reprinted by permission of Standard & Poor's Corp.

net profit margin or net before tax margin series. Our analysis will begin with estimating this operating profit margin series.

After we estimate this operating profit margin, we will multiply it by the sales estimate to derive a dollar estimate of operating EBITDA. Subsequently, we will derive separate estimates of depreciation and interest expenses, which are subtracted from the EBITDA to arrive at earnings before taxes (EBT). Finally, we estimate the expected tax rate (T) and multiply EBT times $(1 - T)$ to get our estimate of net income. The following sections discuss the details of estimating earnings per share beginning with the operating profit margin.

ESTIMATING AGGREGATE OPERATING PROFIT MARGIN

Finkel and Tuttle hypothesized that the following four variables affected the aggregate profit margin.[17]

1. Capacity utilization rate
2. Unit labor costs
3. Rate of inflation
4. Foreign competition

[17]Sidney R. Finkel and Donald L. Tuttle, "Determinants of the Aggregate Profit Margin," *Journal of Finance* 26, no. 5 (December 1971): 1067–1075.

TABLE 18.4 **S&P 400 SALES PER SHARE AND COMPONENTS OF OPERATING PROFIT MARGIN: 1977–1997**

		EBITDA[a]		DEPRECIATION		INTEREST		INCOME TAX		NET INCOME	
Year	Sales per Share	Per Share	Percent of Sales	Per Share	Percent of Sales	Per Share	Percent of Sales	Per Share	Tax Rate	Per Share	Percent of Sales
1977	224.24	34.34	15.31	8.53	3.80	3.22	1.44	11.14	49.31	11.45	5.11
1978	251.32	38.63	15.37	9.64	3.84	3.81	1.52	12.14	48.21	13.04	5.19
1979	292.38	45.71	15.63	10.82	3.70	4.58	1.57	14.02	46.26	16.29	5.57
1980	327.36	48.11	14.70	12.37	3.78	5.95	1.82	13.67	45.89	16.12	4.92
1981	344.31	51.00	14.81	13.82	4.01	7.49	2.18	12.95	43.62	16.74	4.86
1982	333.86	47.68	14.28	15.30	4.58	8.23	2.47	10.95	45.34	13.20	3.95
1983	334.07	50.18	15.02	15.67	4.69	7.62	2.28	12.12	45.07	14.77	4.42
1984	379.70	57.11	15.04	16.31	4.30	8.54	2.25	14.15	43.86	18.11	4.77
1985	398.42	56.39	14.15	18.19	4.57	9.24	2.32	13.68	47.24	15.28	3.84
1986	387.76	54.70	14.11	19.41	5.01	9.75	2.51	11.01	43.11	14.53	3.75
1987	430.35	64.59	15.01	20.21	4.70	10.14	2.36	13.96	40.77	20.28	4.71
1988	486.92	80.02	16.43	23.59	4.84	14.84	3.05	15.00	36.07	26.59	5.46
1989	541.38	85.56	15.80	24.21	4.47	18.79	3.47	15.73	36.96	26.83	4.96
1990	594.55	87.52	14.72	26.31	4.43	20.17	3.39	16.27	39.64	24.77	4.17
1991	586.86	75.35	12.84	27.50	4.69	18.74	3.19	12.20	41.91	16.91	2.88
1992	601.39	76.74	12.76	29.48	4.90	16.20	2.69	12.01	38.67	19.05	3.17
1993	603.62	78.67	13.03	28.72	4.76	14.66	2.43	13.36	37.86	21.93	3.63
1994	626.26	94.06	15.02	29.58	4.72	12.77	2.04	18.88	36.51	32.83	5.24
1995	676.62	103.50	15.30	33.06	4.89	14.21	2.10	20.79	36.97	35.44	5.24
1996	701.91	115.45	16.45	36.11	5.14	14.32	2.04	23.87	36.71	41.15	5.86
1997	750.71	123.76	16.49	39.77	5.30	14.84	1.98	27.02	39.07	42.13	5.61

[a]This is used as an estimate of operating earnings.

Source: *Standard & Poor's Analysts Handbook* (New York: Standard & Poor's Corporation, 1998). Reprinted by permission of Standard & Poor's Corp.

CAPACITY UTILIZATION RATE One would expect a positive relationship between the capacity utilization rate and the profit margin because if production increases as a proportion of total capacity, there is a decrease in per-unit fixed production costs and fixed financial costs. The relationship may not be completely linear at very high rates of capacity utilization because operating diseconomies are introduced as firms are forced to use marginal labor and/or older plant and equipment to reach the higher capacity. The figures in Table 18.5 indicate that capacity utilization ranged from a peak of over 86 percent in 1979 to a trough of less than 73 percent during the recession of 1975.

UNIT LABOR COST The change in unit labor cost is a compound effect of two individual factors: (1) changes in wages per hour and (2) changes in worker productivity. Wage costs per hour typically increase every year by varying amounts depending on the economic environment. As shown in Table 18.5, the annual percentage increase in compensation per hour varied from 1.7 percent to 10.8 percent. If workers did not become more productive, this increase in per-hour wage costs would be the increase in per-unit labor cost. Fortunately, because of advances in technology and greater mechanization, the worker units of output per hour (labor productivity) have increased over time—our labor force has become *more productive.* If wages per hour increase by 5 percent and labor productivity increases by 5 percent, there would be no increase in unit labor costs because the workers would offset wage increases by producing more. Therefore, the increase in *per-unit labor cost* is a function of the percentage change in hourly wages minus the increase in productivity during the period.

TABLE 18.5

VARIABLES THAT AFFECT THE AGGREGATE PROFIT MARGIN: CAPACITY UTILIZATION RATE, PERCENTAGE CHANGE IN COMPENSATION, PRODUCTIVITY, UNIT LABOR COST, AND CONSUMER PRICE INDEX: 1975–1998(P)

		Compensation/ Work Hours	Output/Work Hours	Unit Labor Costs	
Year	Utilization Rate (Mfg.)	Percentage Change	Percentage Change	Percentage Change	Rate of Inflation
1975	72.9	10.1	2.7	7.2	7.00
1976	78.2	8.6	3.6	4.9	4.80
1977	82.6	8.0	1.6	6.3	6.80
1978	85.2	9.1	1.3	7.6	9.00
1979	85.3	9.5	−0.8	10.3	13.30
1980	79.5	10.8	−0.4	11.2	12.40
1981	78.3	9.7	1.1	8.5	8.90
1982	71.8	7.4	−0.8	8.2	3.90
1983	74.4	4.2	4.2	0.1	3.80
1984	79.8	4.2	1.7	2.5	4.00
1985	78.8	4.6	1.0	3.6	3.80
1986	78.7	5.2	2.6	2.5	1.10
1987	81.3	3.8	−0.2	4.0	4.40
1988	83.8	4.4	0.7	3.6	4.40
1989	83.6	2.7	0.6	2.1	4.60
1990	81.4	5.5	0.5	5.0	6.10
1991	77.9	4.9	0.7	4.2	3.10
1992	79.4	5.2	3.2	1.9	3.00
1993	80.5	2.3	0.1	2.2	2.70
1994	82.5	1.7	0.4	1.4	2.70
1995	82.8	2.5	0.2	2.4	2.54
1996	81.4	3.5	2.4	1.0	3.32
1997	81.7	3.7	1.4	2.3	1.70
1998(p)	81.0	4.2	2.0	2.1	1.40

Source: *Economic Report of the President,* 1999 (Washington, D.C.: U.S. Government Printing Office, 1999).

The actual relationship typically is not this exact due to measurement problems, but it is quite close as indicated by the figures in Table 18.5. For example, during 1983 productivity increased by as much as the hourly compensation did, so there was basically no change in unit labor cost. In contrast, during 1980, wage rates increased by 10.8 percent, productivity *declined* by 0.4 percent because of the recession, and, therefore, unit labor costs increased by 11.2 percent. Because unit labor is the major variable cost of a firm, one would expect a *negative* relationship between the operating profit margin and percentage changes in unit labor cost—that is, a small (below-average) change in unit labor cost, similar to what we have experienced since the early 1990s, should correspond to an above-average operating profit margin.

RATE OF INFLATION The precise effect of inflation on the aggregate profit margin is unresolved. Finkel and Tuttle hypothesized a positive relationship between inflation and the profit margin for several reasons. First, it was contended that a higher level of inflation increases the ability of firms to pass higher costs on to the consumer and thereby raise their profit margin. Second, assuming the classical demand-pull inflation, the increase in prices would indicate an increase in general economic activity, which typically is accompanied by higher margins. Finally, an increase in the rate of inflation might stimulate consumption as individuals attempt to shift their holdings from financial assets to real assets, which would contribute to an expansion.

In contrast, many observers doubt that most businesses can consistently increase prices in line with rising costs. Assume a 5 percent rate of inflation that impacts labor and material costs. The question is whether all firms can *completely* pass these cost increases along to their customers. If a firm increases prices at the same rate as cost increases, the result will be a *constant* profit margin, *not* an increase. Only if a firm can raise prices by *more than* cost increases can it increase its margin. Many firms are not able to raise prices in line with increased costs because of the elasticity of demand for their products.[18] Such an environment will cause the profit margin to decline. Given the alternative scenarios, it is contended that most firms will not be able to increase their profit margins or even hold them constant. Because many firms will experience lower profit margins during periods of inflation, it is expected that the aggregate profit margin will probably decline when there is an increase in the rate of inflation.

Given the contrasting expectations, one would need to consider the empirical evidence to determine how inflation has affected the operating profit margin.

FOREIGN COMPETITION Finkel and Tuttle contend that export markets are more competitive than domestic markets so export sales are made at a lower margin. This implies that lower exports by U.S. firms would increase profit margins. In contrast, Gray believed that only exports between independent firms should be considered, and they should be examined relative to total output exported.[19] Further, he felt that imports could have an important negative impact on the operating profit margin because they influence the selling price of all competing domestic products. Therefore, there is a divergence of expectations regarding the ultimate effect of foreign trade on the operating profit margin, so it is likewise an empirical question.

Analysis of the annual data for the period 1977 to 1997 by the authors confirmed that the relationship between the operating profit margin and the capacity utilization rate was always significant and positive, whereas the relationship between the unit labor cost and the operating profit margin was always negative and significant. Alternatively, the rate of inflation and foreign trade variables were never significant in the multiple regression. Finally, the simple correlation between the profit margin and inflation was consistently *negative.*

Therefore, when estimating the operating profit margin, you should concentrate on the capacity utilization rate for the economy and the rate of change in unit labor cost. As an example, consider what will happen at two extremes of the business cycle. At the end of an economic recession, the capacity utilization rate will be very low. Therefore, during the early stages of an economic recovery, there should be a large increase in capacity utilization as firms increase production and sales. At the same time, workers will not be asking for large wage increases, and as production increases, there will be large increases in labor productivity. As a result, unit labor costs will increase very slowly (or could decline). Therefore, as a result of an increase in capacity utilization and a very small increase (or a decline) in unit labor cost, there should be a large increase in the operating profit margin.

In contrast, at the peak of the business cycle, firms will be operating at full capacity, so there will be very small increases or possibly declines in capacity utilization. Also, one would expect a higher rate of inflation, which will prompt demands for large wage

[18]An extreme example of this inability is regulated industries that may not be able to raise prices at all until after lengthy hearings before regulatory agencies. Even then, the increase in rates may not match the cost increase.

[19]H. Peter Gray, "Determinants of the Aggregate Profit Margin: A Comment," *Journal of Finance* 31, no. 1 (March 1976): 163–165.

FIGURE 18.9 TIME-SERIES PLOT OF DEPRECIATION EXPENSE FOR THE S&P 400 INDEX

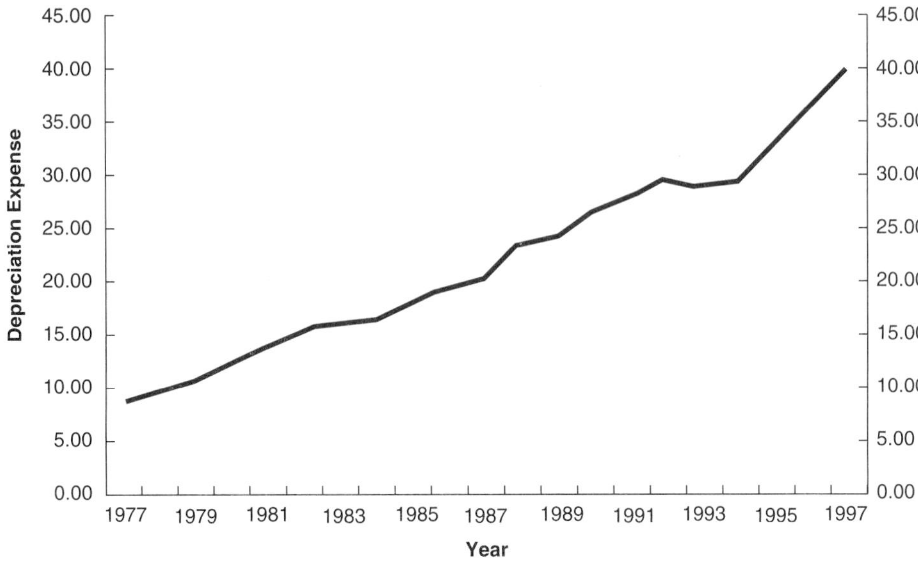
Depreciation Expense
45.00
40.00
35.00
30.00
25.00
20.00
15.00
10.00
5.00
0.00
1977
1979
1981
1983
1985
1987
1989
1991
1993
1995
1997
Year

increases during a time when you would expect small increases in labor productivity because firms are using marginal labor and production facilities. The effect will be large increases in unit labor cost. Therefore, as a result of very small increases or possibly decreases in capacity utilization and large increases in unit labor cost, there should be a major decline in the operating profit margin at the peak of a business cycle.

How do you use this information to estimate an operating profit margin? The most important estimate is *the direction of the change from current levels.* Assuming that you know the recent operating profit margin, your primary analysis should be concerned with deciding whether the profit margin will increase, decrease, or stay about the same based on your expectation regarding capacity utilization and changes in unit labor cost. The size of the estimated change in the operating profit margin will depend on where the economy is in the business cycle and the direction and size of the expected changes in capacity utilization and unit labor cost.

After estimating the operating profit margin, you can calculate the dollar value of EBITDA by applying this operating profit margin estimate to the previously estimated sales-per-share figure. The next step is to estimate depreciation per share, which we subtract from operating profits to get EBIT. Table 18.4 contains data on the operating earnings components for the period since 1977.

Estimating Depreciation Expense

As shown in Figure 18.9, the depreciation expense per share series has declined only once since 1977 (in 1993). This is not surprising because depreciation expense is an estimate of the fixed-cost expense related to the total fixed assets held by the S&P 400 industrial firms. Naturally, this fixed-asset base increases over time. Therefore, the relevant question when estimating depreciation expense is generally *not* whether it will increase or decrease, but by *how much will it increase.*

There are two suggestions for estimating depreciation expense. First, you can use time series analysis, which involves using the recent trend as a guide to the future increase. Probably the biggest external factor that could influence the rate of growth of the depreciation

TABLE 18.6 FOR THE S&P 400: RATIO OF DEPRECIATION EXPENSE TO NET PPE AND RATIO OF INTEREST EXPENSE TO LONG-TERM DEBT: 1977–1997

Year	Depre. Expense	Net PPE	Sales Net PPE	Dep. Exp. Net PPE	Interest Expense	Total Asset Turnover	L-T. Debt	L-T. Debt T. Assets	Int. Exp. L-T. Debt	L-T. Govt. Bond Yield
1977	8.53	83.64	2.68	10.20	3.25	1.27	32.09		10.13	8.03
1978	9.64	94.15	2.67	10.24	3.84	1.27	36.23		10.60	8.98
1979	10.82	106.89	2.74	10.12	4.58	1.30	39.22		11.68	10.12
1980	12.37	120.03	2.73	10.31	5.95	1.31	43.27		13.75	11.99
1981	13.82	134.37	2.56	10.29	7.49	1.28	49.06		15.27	13.34
1982	15.30	144.06	2.49	10.62	8.23	1.17	52.72		15.61	10.95
1983	15.67	142.26	2.35	11.02	7.62	1.15	50.08		15.60	9.56
1984	16.31	138.79	2.74	11.75	8.54	1.22	53.25		16.04	11.70
1985	18.19	150.20	2.65	12.11	9.24	1.15	50.08		15.60	9.56
1986	19.41	154.64	2.51	12.55	9.75	1.07	66.89		14.58	7.89
1987	20.21	160.39	2.68	12.60	10.14	1.08	69.89		14.51	9.20
1988	23.59	175.31	2.78	13.46	15.01	0.98	113.93		13.17	9.18
1989	24.21	193.23	2.80	12.53	18.79	0.97	117.56		15.98	8.16
1990	26.31	212.30	2.80	12.39	20.17	0.97	128.04		15.75	8.44
1991	27.50	216.63	2.71	12.69	18.74	0.94	130.03		14.38	7.30
1992	29.48	219.19	2.74	13.45	16.20	0.95	128.60	0.20	12.60	7.26
1993	28.72	217.14	2.78	13.23	14.66	0.92	126.18	0.19	11.62	6.54
1994	29.58	223.46	2.80	13.24	12.77	0.95	130.24	0.20	9.80	7.99
1995	33.06	237.84	2.84	13.90	14.21	0.97	141.14	0.20	10.07	6.03
1996	36.11	264.21	2.66	13.67	14.32	0.93	151.31	0.20	9.46	6.73
1997	39.77	286.11	2.62	13.90	14.84	0.94	162.35	0.20	9.14	6.02
Mean										
1977–1997				12.11					13.09	
1988–1997				13.25					12.20	
1993–1997				13.59					10.02	

Source: *Standard & Poor's Analysts Handbook* (New York: Standard & Poor's Corporation, 1998). Reprinted by permission of Standard & Poor's Corp.

expense series is recent capital expenditures. If capital expenditures have been above normal, you would expect subsequent depreciation expense to grow at an above-average rate. Recently, the average annual percentage increase in depreciation expense has been in the range of 5 to 8 percent. Because a column in the table indicates that depreciation is a percent of sales, you might consider this as an estimating approach—this would be a *mistake.* Depreciation is clearly a *fixed* expense, which means generally it is independent of sales and so should not be expected to vary with sales. As shown, depreciation as a percentage of sales has varied from 3.70 percent to over 5 percent, which is consistent with its fixed nature.

Second, you can derive an estimate based upon an estimate of property, plant, and equipment (PPE) and then apply the historical depreciation rate relative to the PPE account. This technique requires two steps. First, you must make an estimate of the PPE account based on the relationship between sales (that have been estimated) and PPE—that is, the expected PPE turnover based upon historical trends. Table 18.6 contains the historical PPE turnover series, which appears quite stable between 2.60 and 2.80 (see Figure 18.10). Therefore, given your estimate for sales, it is possible to derive an estimate of PPE. The second estimate is the ratio of depreciation to PPE, which is likewise contained in Table 18.6 and plotted in Figure 18.11. As shown, this ratio has experienced a fairly steady increase over time from about 10 percent in the late 1970s to almost 14 percent in 1997. One can speculate that this trend is the result of the increase in technology that has tended to

FIGURE 18.10

TIME-SERIES PLOT OF THE RATIO OF SALES TO PPE (PPE TURNOVER) FOR THE S&P 400 INDEX

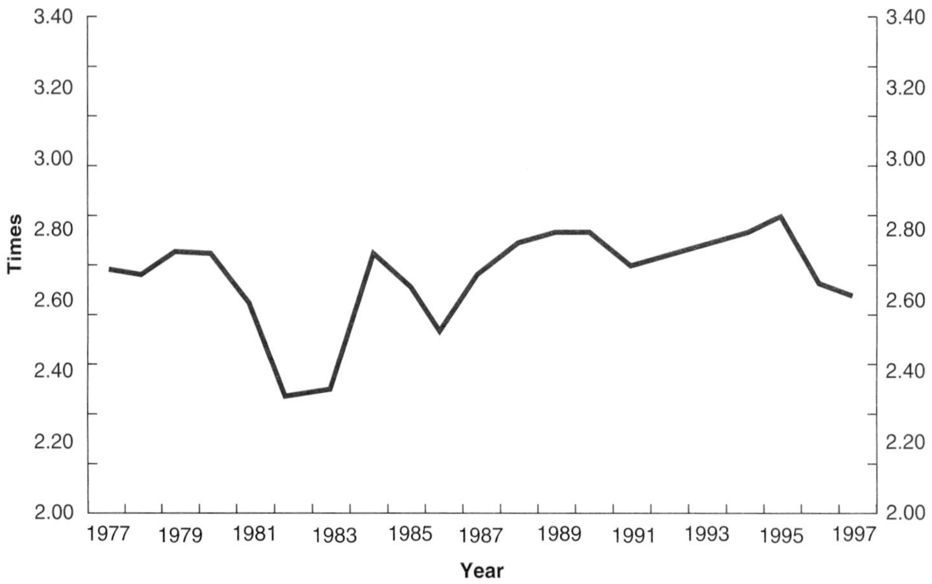
3.40
3.20
3.00
2.80
2.60
2.40
2.20
2.00
Times
1977
1979
1981
1983
1985
1987
1989
1991
1993
1995
1997
Year

FIGURE 18.11

TIME-SERIES PLOT OF THE RATIO OF DEPRECIATION EXPENSES TO PPE ACCOUNT FOR THE S&P 400 INDEX

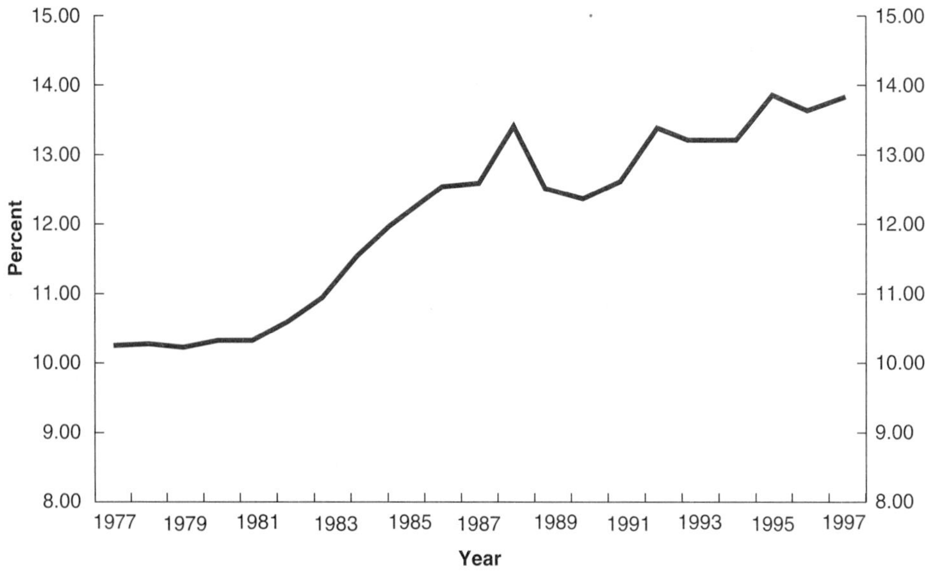
15.00
14.00
13.00
12.00
11.00
10.00
9.00
8.00
Percent
1977
1979
1981
1983
1985
1987
1989
1991
1993
1995
1997
Year

reduce the useful life for productive machinery, which implies a higher annual depreciation rate. Therefore, one would derive an estimate of depreciation expense based upon an estimate of PPE and the estimated ratio of depreciation to PPE.

Based on these factors, you would estimate what you expect for this year. After you have estimated the depreciation expense, you subtract it from the operating profit estimate to get an EBIT estimate.

FIGURE 18.12

TIME-SERIES PLOT OF DEBT OUTSTANDING FOR THE S&P 400 INDEX

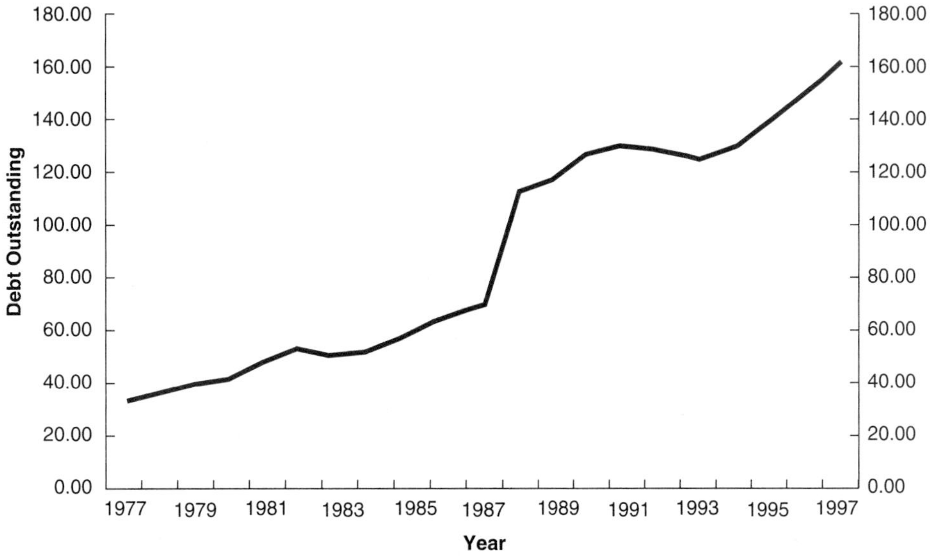

180.00
160.00
140.00
120.00
100.00
80.00
60.00
40.00
20.00
0.00
Debt Outstanding
1977
1979
1981
1983
1985
1987
1989
1991
1993
1995
1997
Year

Estimating Interest Expense

As shown in Table 18.4, interest expense of the companies in the S&P 400 series generally increased in absolute value until 1990 and increased as a percentage of sales from 1.44 percent in 1977 to a peak of 3.47 percent in 1989. This growth is consistent with our prior discussions, which alluded to the overall increase in debt financing and financial risk assumed by U.S. firms—especially during the 1980s. This strong growth of interest expense was reversed after the 1989–1990 recession because, as shown in Table 18.5 and Figure 18.12, (1) corporations reduced their debt levels in 1992 and 1993 before a small reversal in 1994, and (2) interest rates declined. The estimate of interest expense should be based on an estimate of debt outstanding (will it grow and by how much?) and the level of interest rates (do you expect interest rates to increase or decline in the future?)

A couple of examples should illustrate the point. In 1988, interest expense increased substantially to 15.01 from 10.14 in 1987. An analysis of the components indicates that this increase was completely due to a substantial increase in debt outstanding, as shown in Figure 18.12, that went from about 70 to almost 114 (a 63 percent increase), while the average interest rate, as shown in Figure 18.13, actually declined (from 14.51 percent to 13.17 percent). In contrast, as shown in Figure 18.14, from 1990 to 1994 interest expense declined steadily from 20.17 to 12.77. In this case, the decline was wholly attributable to a decline in interest rates shown in Figure 18.3. Specifically, during this period, long-term debt outstanding increased slightly from about 128 to 130, while interest rates declined steadily from 15.75 percent to 9.80 percent. The point is, to estimate interest expense you need to estimate each of these components (the amount of debt outstanding and the average interest rate on this debt) and determine the joint effect.

An estimate of debt outstanding requires two estimates: (1) the amount of total assets for the firm based upon the firm's expected total asset turnover, and (2) the expected capital structure based upon the average total debt to total asset ratio. Both of these ratios are included in Table 18.6.

Similar to depreciation, interest expense generally is a fixed expense that is impacted by corporate financing decisions and the cost of debt (i.e., interest rates). Therefore, interest

FIGURE 18.13

TIME-SERIES PLOT OF THE INTEREST RATE ON DEBT OUTSTANDING FOR THE S&P 400 INDEX

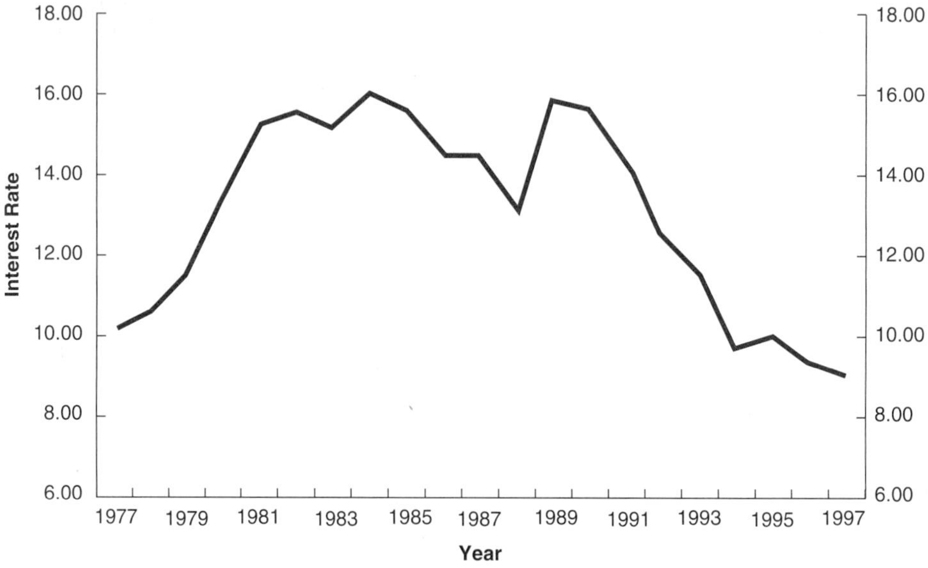
18.00
16.00
14.00
12.00
10.00
8.00
6.00
Interest Rate
1977 1979 1981 1983 1985 1987 1989 1991 1993 1995 1997
Year

FIGURE 18.14

TIME-SERIES PLOT OF INTEREST EXPENSES FOR THE S&P 400 INDEX

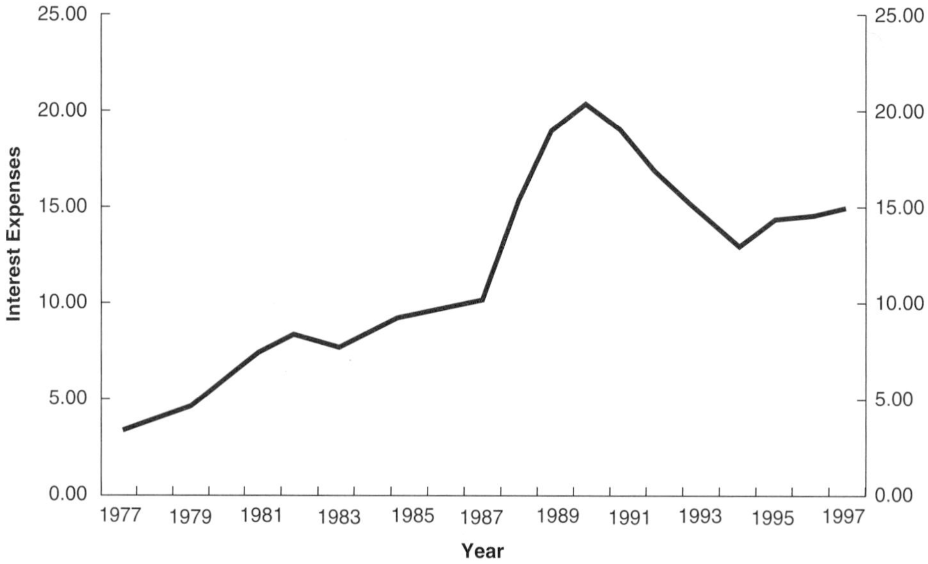
25.00
20.00
15.00
10.00
5.00
0.00
Interest Expenses
1977 1979 1981 1983 1985 1987 1989 1991 1993 1995 1997
Year

expense as a percent of sales is a very unstable value and this percent value should *not* be used when estimating interest expense.

After you have estimated the interest expense figure, this value is subtracted from the EBIT per share value to estimate EBT.

ESTIMATING THE TAX RATE

This is the final step in estimating the earnings per share for the S&P 400 series. As shown in Table 18.4, the average tax rate for the firms in the S&P 400 series during the late 1970s was in the 45 to 50 percent range. During the 1980s, it declined to almost 35 percent (in

1988) following the 1986 Tax Reform Act, then reversed and increased during the period 1989–1991, followed by declines in 1992–1996. Subsequently, it increased in 1997.

Estimating the future tax rate is difficult because it depends on political action. You must evaluate the current tax rate and recent tax legislation that affects business firms (e.g., tax credits). Once you have estimated the tax rate (T), you multiply one minus this tax rate $(1 - T)$ times the EBT per-share figure to derive an estimate of the net income per share for the S&P 400 series.

At this point, we have derived an estimate of sales per share for an aggregate stock-market series and discussed how to estimate an operating profit margin and several specific expense items to estimate earnings per share. In the next section, we demonstrate this procedure by estimating earnings per share for 1999.

Calculating Earnings per Share: An Example

The following demonstration for estimating earnings per share emphasizes the procedure rather than the actual numbers. An analyst engaged in this exercise would provide a very long, detailed analysis. In this example, we estimate earnings per share for the S&P 400 during 1999 using 1998 data (most of which is estimated).

STEP 1 Nominal GDP for 1999 is based on an estimate for 1998 of approximately $8,485 billion. In 1998, the economy was in the eighth year of expansion following a recession in 1989–1990. Therefore, 1999 is the ninth year of expansion, and real GDP is expected to increase by 2.0 percent and inflation will be approximately 2 percent. Therefore, nominal GDP in 1999 is estimated to increase by about 4.0 percent to $8,824 billion.

STEP 2 Corporate sales have had a strong relationship with nominal GDP as shown in Figure 18.2. During 1998, when nominal GDP increased by about 5 percent, S&P sales were relatively flat, due to weak exports, at an estimated $760 per share. In 1999 with GDP rising only 4 percent, there is an expectation of strong foreign sales because of economic recoveries in many foreign countries. Therefore, the consensus is that S&P industrial sales should increase by almost 6 percent to $805 per share.

STEP 3 The operating profit margin reached a peak of 16.49 percent in 1997, followed by a decline to 16.00 percent in 1998. This decline was a function of a lower utilization rate (81.5 percent in 1998 compared to 82 percent during 1997). For 1999, the outlook is for a small rebound in the operating profit margin because there should be almost no change in the capacity utilization rate. We also expect a very modest increase in unit labor cost. Specifically, we expect compensation per hour to experience a relatively small increase, along with limited gains in productivity since we are in the ninth year of expansion. Therefore, the outlook is for a 2 to 3 percent increase in unit labor cost. In summary, the outlook is for a small increase in the operating profit margin from 16.00 percent in 1998 to 16.20 percent in 1999. Applying this operating profit margin to the sales per share figure ($805) indicates an operating profit (EBITDA) of $130.40 ($0.162 \times \$805$).

STEP 4 The depreciation expense during 1998 was approximately $42.00 per share. Because the utilization rate is not very high and we are expecting a modest increase in sales, we expect an increase in capital expenditures of about 5 percent during 1999 and, therefore, an increase in depreciation expense of about 3.0 percent to $43.26 per share. Thus the estimated EBIT is $87.14 ($\$130.40 - \$43.26$).

STEP 5 Interest expense declined in 1998 because of a small increase in the debt level and a continued decline in interest rates during the year. Interest expense is estimated to be slightly lower in 1999 because initial interest rates were at a low level and did not begin to increase until June. Based on this interest rate scenario and no major change in leverage, interest expense is estimated at \$14.80 (\$170 × 0.087). When we subtract this interest expense from the EBIT estimate of \$87.14, we have an EBT of \$72.34.

STEP 6 Given the interest in reducing the tax burden, the 1997 tax rate is considered a temporary anomaly. The corporate tax rate during 1998 was expected to be slightly lower than the pre-1997 results—around 36 percent. The tax rate is expected to decline further to 35 percent during 1999. Applying a 65 percent after-tax rate to the NBT figure of \$72.34 indicates a net income estimate of \$47 a share.

This per-share estimate can be summarized as follows:

Sales	\$805.00	
EBITDA	130.40	(0.162)
Depreciation Expense	43.26	
EBIT	87.14	
Interest Expense	14.80	
EBT	72.34	
Taxes	25.32	(0.35)
Net Income (EPS)	\$47.02	

ESTIMATING THE EARNINGS MULTIPLIER FOR A STOCK-MARKET SERIES

Given our estimate of earnings per share, the next step is to estimate an earnings multiplier. A combination of the earnings per share estimate times the estimated earnings multiplier provides an estimate of the future value for the stock-market series. This estimated value for the stock-market series and an estimate of the dividend during the year are used to compute the expected rate of return for investors who own a portfolio of stocks during this holding period.

Our prior discussion related to Table 18.2 indicated that the earnings multiplier (i.e., P/E ratio) over time has been more volatile than the earnings per share series because the multiplier is very sensitive to changes in the spread between k and g. Earlier we discussed several instances where the changes in the earnings multiplier (P/E ratio) was the dominant factor in stock price changes. Because of the significance of the earnings multiplier, we will examine each of the variables in the P/E ratio equation to determine what determines the value for them and why they change. Given this understanding, we can consider the whole P/E ratio equation and demonstrate how an investor would estimate a value for the earnings multiplier.

Determinants of the Earnings Multiplier

Recall the variables that influence the earnings multiplier or the P/E ratio by using the equation generated from the dividend discount model:

$$\text{P/E} = \frac{D_1/E_1}{k - g}$$

where:

D_1 = dividends expected in period 1, which is equal to $D_0(1 + g)$
E_1 = earnings expected in period 1
D_1/E_1 = the dividend-payout ratio expected in period 1
k = the required rate of return on the stock
g = the expected growth rate of dividends for the stock

Therefore, the major variables that affect the earnings multiplier for common stocks in a country are

- The dividend-payout ratio
- The required rate of return on common stock in the country being analyzed
- The expected growth rate of dividends for the stocks in the country being analyzed

Because this equation is derived from the dividend discount model, it assumes constant growth for an infinite period. Also, the required rate of return is the long-term estimate. Therefore, the k and g projections are *long-term estimates*. Thus, although these variables can be impacted by near-term events, they should not experience major changes on a year-to-year basis.

It is easier to discuss the dividend-payout ratio after we have considered both k and g. Therefore, the order of discussion will be

- Estimating k, the required rate of return
- Estimating g, the growth rate of dividends
- Estimating D_1/E_1, the dividend-payout ratio

Estimating the Required Rate of Return (k)

The multiplier equation indicates that the earnings multiplier is inversely related to the required rate of return; the higher an investor's required rate of return, the less he or she will pay for a future earnings stream. Our prior discussions indicated that the required rate of return (k) is determined by (1) the economy's risk-free rate (RFR); (2) the expected rate of inflation during the period of investment (I); and (3) the risk premium (RP) for the specific investment.

Earlier in the chapter in connection with our discussion of cash flow models we derived a range of three estimates of k as follows:

NRFR	Risk Premium	Estimated k	Description
0.044	0.02	0.064	Short-term RFR and small RP
0.055	0.04	0.095	Intermediate RFR and midrange RP
0.057	0.06	0.117	Long-term RFR and historical RP

Estimating the Growth Rate of Dividends (g)

Again, earlier in the chapter we discussed the estimated growth rate of earnings and dividends in connection with the present value of cash flow models. You will recall that:

$$g = b \times \text{ROE}$$

After a discussion of the pattern of dividend payouts over the business cycle, it was suggested that an appropriate long-run retention rate (b) was 55 percent.

We estimated a long-run ROE based upon an analysis of the three components of the Du Pont analysis, which showed an overall increase in the ROE for the S&P 400 over the past 20 years as a result of recent strong profit margins combined with a decline in the total asset turnover that was offset by an increase in financial leverage. Long-run, we estimated an ROE of 14 percent. The combined result was:

$$\begin{aligned} g &= 0.55 \times 0.14 \\ &= 0.077 = 7.7\% \end{aligned}$$

Given these estimates of *k*, *g*, and dividend payout (1 minus the retention rate of 0.55), the following section discusses the estimation of the earnings multiples.

Estimating the Dividend-Payout Ratio (D_1/E_1)

Based on the P/E equation, there is a positive relationship between payout ratio and the P/E ratio. Therefore, if the *k–g* spread is constant and this dividend-payout ratio increases, there will be an increase in the earnings multiplier. At the same time, you should recognize that the dividend-payout ratio is equal to one minus the earnings retention rate (*b*). Therefore, if the dividend payout *increases,* there will be a *decline* in the earnings retention rate (*b*), which will cause a *decline* in the growth rate (*g*). Thus, there is a partial offset between changes in the dividend-payout rate and the expected growth rate (*g*).

In the discussion of the growth rate, we indicated that the retention rate was high in the 1970s, declined in the early 1980s, and has increased again since 1993. This implies that the payout ratio has declined recently.

DIVIDEND PAYOUT—ACTIVE OR RESIDUAL DECISION? When examining or attempting to estimate the dividend payout for the aggregate market or an individual firm, it is important to consider whether the dividend payout is (1) an active decision of management (and the board of directors) or (2) a residual outcome because the active decision is the dividend payment. Obviously, if the dividend payout rate is the active decision, the dividend payment would vary over time in line with earnings. In contrast, if the dividend payment is the active decision, this implies that the dividend payout is a residual decision. The dividend payments then would be reasonably stable and show fairly steady increases while the dividend payout ratio would be very volatile because it would be dictated by the earnings. That is, the dividend payout would increase dramatically during periods of low earnings and decline significantly during periods of abnormally high earnings.

The time series plots in Figures 18.15 and 18.16 support the residual payout theory because they show fairly constant changes in dividend payments (Figure 18.15) but high volatility for the dividend payout ratio in Figure 18.16 (the dividend payout was high during the recession in 1991 and quite low during the expansion in 1993–1997). This discus-

FIGURE 18.15 **EARNINGS PER SHARE AND DIVIDENDS PER SHARE FOR S&P 400: 1977–1997**

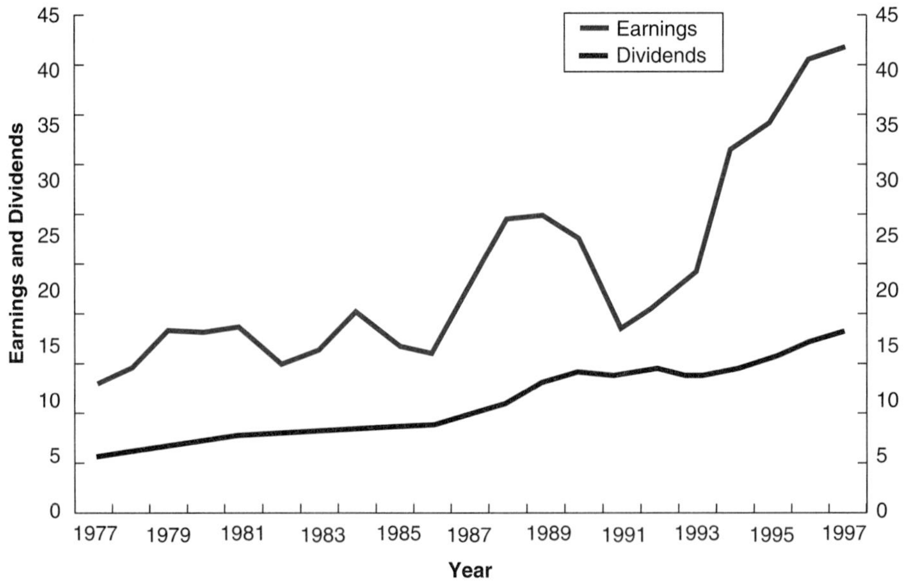

Earnings
Dividends
Earnings and Dividends
Year
45
40
35
30
25
20
15
10
5
0
1977
1979
1981
1983
1985
1987
1989
1991
1993
1995
1997

sion can be summarized as follows: the annual dividend payout is inversely related to earnings changes. Put another way, there is a positive relationship between the earnings retention rate and earnings changes. Therefore, when estimating the dividend payout ratio, it is necessary to estimate the dividend payment using time series analysis and then relate this estimated dividend to the earnings estimate. Because of its volatility, it is important *not* to emphasize annual dividend payout changes, but use a *long-run perspective* regarding the dividend payout ratio over the business cycle.

ESTIMATING AN EARNINGS MULTIPLIER: AN EXAMPLE

There are two ways to estimate the earnings multiplier based on our discussion of the multiplier variables. The first approach begins with the current earnings multiplier and attempts to estimate the direction and amount of any change based on your expectations for changes in the three major components. We will call this approach the *direction of change approach.*

In the second approach, you estimate a specific value for the earnings multiplier by deriving specific estimates for each of the three components in the P/E ratio equation. When using this approach, most analysts derive several estimates based on alternative optimistic or pessimistic scenarios. We will call this the *specific estimate approach.*

THE DIRECTION OF CHANGE APPROACH Begin with the current earnings multiplier and estimate the direction and extent of change for the dividend payout and the variables that influence k and g. The direction of the change is more important than its size.

The variables that must be estimated are

1. Changes in the dividend-payout ratio
2. Changes in the real RFR (Changes in k)
3. Changes in the rate of inflation (Changes in k)
4. Changes in the risk premium for common stock (Changes in k)
5. Changes in the earnings retention rate (Changes in g)
6. Changes in the return on equity (ROE) (Changes in g)

FIGURE 18.16 **TIME-SERIES PLOT OF S&P 400 PAYOUT RATIO: 1977–1997**

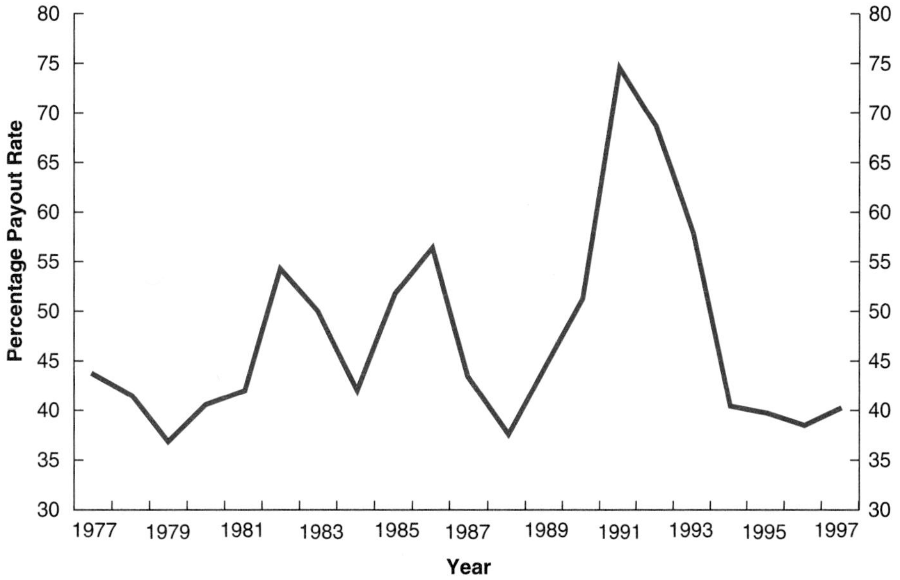

Percentage Payout Rate
80
75
70
65
60
55
50
45
40
35
30
1977
1979
1981
1983
1985
1987
1989
1991
1993
1995
1997
Year

The dividend-payout ratio is expected to increase slightly in the near term because recent payout values have been lower than the historical average because of the strong earnings growth, which has resulted in a substantial increase in the retention rate.

Given the three variables that affect the required rate of return on common stocks (k), there will probably be very little change in the real RFR in 1999 because there will be almost no change in the rate of real growth caused by higher productivity. The rate of inflation was quite low during 1998 and is expected to experience very little change in 1999. Finally, the risk premium is expected to experience a small increase for two reasons. First, we are in the ninth year of a business expansion wherein there could be more uncertainty. Second, although there was a decrease in stock price volatility during the early 1990s, at the current point in the market cycle, it could increase. Therefore, given the trends in the three components, overall one would expect a small increase in k during 1999.

The last two factors in the earnings multiplier estimate relate to the growth rate. We expect a small increase in the payout rate, which implies a small decline in the long-run retention rate. The outlook is for a small decrease in the aggregate ROE during 1999, although the profit margin in 1999 is expected to increase slightly relative to the lower margin in 1998. In contrast, there should be a small decline in the total asset turnover at this time in the economic expansion. Finally, we envision a small decline in the financial leverage ratio during 1999 as firms continue to reduce their financial leverage. The result of a slightly higher profit margin, a small decline in asset turnover, and a decline in financial leverage should be a decrease in the ROE during 1999. Therefore, with a small decrease in the retention rate and in ROE, you would estimate a small decline in the expected growth rate.[20] In summary, we expect

- An increase in the payout ratio
- A small increase in the required rate of return
- A small decline in the growth rate

Overall, this would imply a *small decline* in the earnings multiple. The earnings multiplier early in 1999 is about 30 times. This discussion would indicate that the multiplier could decline to about 27 times during 1999.

SPECIFIC ESTIMATE APPROACH This approach derives specific estimates for the earnings multiplier based on a range of estimates for the three variables: dividend payout (D/E), required rate of return (k), and growth (g). As indicated earlier, the retention rate has fluctuated between 45 and 65 percent during the past 10 years. Therefore, a reasonable dividend-payout ratio (D/E) would be 45 percent.

The required return (k) can be estimated using the interest rate on government bonds plus an estimate of the risk premium for common stocks. An appropriate risk premium could range from 2 percent to 6 percent, depending on the government security used to estimate a nominal risk-free rate. The 6 percent is based on the long-term geometric average risk premium as indicated by the Ibbotson–Sinquefield studies for the period 1926 to 1998 using T-bills as the risk-free investment. Notably, during the recent period (1977 to 1998), the risk premium has been in the range of 2.5 to 5.5 percent. As noted earlier, in early 1999, the rate on T-bills was about 4.40 percent, the rate on 5-year government bonds was about 5.50 percent, and the rate on long-term bonds was 5.70 percent. Notably, these interest rates

[20]This is the most reasonable scenario given the economic environment. At the same time, there have been changes in the value of common equity caused by asset write-offs and share repurchases. Both of these events can cause a significant decline in the equity account but have little impact on operating earnings. As a result, there has been a higher ROE simply because of a lower equity value.

are at the low end of the range for the past 20 years, and most observers expect a small increase during the year. If there is an adjustment to reflect this, you could conceive of the following possibilities:

	Expected at Year-End
A. 5-year government bonds	5.7%
Historical risk premium	6.0
Estimated k	11.7%
B. 5-year government bonds	5.7%
Low risk premium	2.0
Estimated k	7.7%
C. 5-year government bonds	5.7%
Medium risk premium	4.0
Estimated k	9.7%

Therefore, the required return (k) could be in the range of 7 to almost 12 percent.

The estimate of growth should be based on the current and expected return on equity (ROE) and the rate of retention. The graph in Figure 18.3 shows that the ROE for the S&P 400 was in the 10 to 18 percent range during the period 1977 to 1998. Assuming that 1999 is toward the end of an economic expansion that officially started in October 1991, a range of 12 to 16 percent for the ROE seems appropriate. As indicated earlier, the retention rate has been between 45 and 65 percent. Therefore, a conservative estimate of the growth rate would combine the 45 percent retention rate and an ROE of 12 percent: $0.45 \times 0.12 = 0.054$. An optimistic growth rate estimate would combine the 65 percent retention rate and a 16 percent ROE: $0.65 \times 0.16 = 0.104$. To summarize,

Dividend/earnings	0.35–0.55
Government securities	0.045–0.057
Equity risk premium	0.020–0.060
Required return (k)	0.07–0.12
ROE	0.120–0.160
Sustainable growth	0.06–0.08

By combining the most optimistic figures (with a positive k–g spread), we can derive a reasonably generous estimate. Using the pessimistic estimates, we can derive a very conservative estimate. The dividend-payout (D/E) figure should be consistent with the retention rate.

$$\text{High estimate: } D/E = 0.45$$
$$k = 0.09$$
$$g = 0.077\ (0.55 \times 0.14)$$
$$P/E = \frac{0.45}{0.090 - 0.077} = \frac{0.45}{0.013} = 34.6 \times$$

$$\text{Low estimate: } D/E = 0.60$$
$$k = 0.11$$
$$g = 0.06$$
$$P/E = \frac{0.60}{0.110 - 0.06} = \frac{0.60}{0.05} = 12 \times$$

Therefore, these data imply a range of earnings multipliers from about 12 times to 35 times with a midrange of about 24×. The midrange is consistent with the expectation of a P/E ratio of 27 derived from the direction of change approach.

CALCULATING AN ESTIMATE OF THE VALUE FOR THE MARKET SERIES

Previously, we estimated the earnings per share for Standard and Poor's 400 of \$47.00. Clearly, it would have been possible to derive additional earnings estimates.

In our work with the P/E, we developed several estimates for the price/earnings multiple that varied from about 12 to 35. At this point, we can combine these estimates of an earnings per share of \$47 and the several earnings multipliers and calculate the following estimates of value for Standard & Poor's 400 market series:

12.0 × \$47.00 =	564.00
18.0 × \$47.00 =	846.00
24.0 × \$47.00 =	1128.00
30.0 × \$47.00 =	1410.00
36.0 × \$47.00 =	1692.00

This example is intended to help you understand the estimation procedure. The estimation of values for D/E, k, and g was not as extensive as the process used by professional analysts. In addition, we used a point estimate for earnings per share rather than a range of estimates (pessimistic, optimistic, most likely), which would have been preferable. Our discussion has provided the skeleton of the process that includes the theoretical background that forms the foundation for the fundamental analysis of stocks. It is important to understand *the relevant variables and how they relate to the critical estimates of earnings per share and the earnings multiplier.* Notably, the two critical estimates that are necessary for both the present value of cash flow models and the earnings multiplier approach are k and g—that is, the required rate of return discount rate and the expected growth of earnings, cash flow, and dividends.

CALCULATING THE EXPECTED RATE OF RETURN ON COMMON STOCKS

Having estimated the expected value for the stock-market series, we can estimate the expected rate of return that this ending implies by using the following equation.

$$E(R_t) = \frac{\text{EV} - \text{BV} + \text{Div}}{\text{BV}}$$

where:

$E(R_t)$ = the expected rate of return during period t (We will assume a 1-year period.)
EV = the ending value for the stock-market series (We will use the several estimates of the ending value of the S&P 400 series derived in this section.)
BV = the beginning value for the stock-market series (You would typically use the current value for the stock-market series assuming you would be investing at this time.)
Div = the expected dividend payment on the stock-market series during the investment horizon

We will compute six rate-of-return estimates based on the six value estimates for the S&P 400 series. We will always assume the same beginning value for the S&P 400 that was the approximate closing value for 1998 (1479) and an estimate of the dividend per share during the next 12 months (23.00).[21] Therefore, the six estimates of expected rate of return are

$$\frac{564 - 1479 + 23.00}{1479} = -60.31\%$$

$$\frac{846 - 1479 + 23.00}{1479} = -41.24\%$$

$$\frac{1128 - 1479 + 23.00}{1479} = -22.18\%$$

$$\frac{1410 - 1479 + 23.00}{1479} = -3.11\%$$

$$\frac{1692 - 1479 + 23.00}{1479} = 15.96\%$$

As you would expect, there is a wide range of expected rates of return because of the range of ending values for the S&P 400. At this point, you either select the most reasonable estimate and use this value and the implied rate of return to make the investment decision, or you can assign probabilities to each of the estimates and derive an expected value estimate. In either case, you would compare this *expected* rate of return on common stocks to your *required* rate of return on common stocks. If we use the required k used in calculating the earnings multiplier, we know it is somewhere between 8 and 12 percent. Assuming that it is 9.5 percent, our investment decision would depend on whether the expected return calculated was equal to or greater than 9.5 percent as follows:

Estimate	Estimated Rate of Return	Required Rate of Return	Investment Decision
1	−60.30%	9.5%	Significant underweight
2	−41.24	9.5	Significant underweight
3	−22.18	9.5	Significant underweight
4	−3.11	9.5	Underweight
5	15.96	9.5	Overweight

Based on the discussion in Chapter 14, we know that this would cause us to underweight or overweight the U.S. equity market relative to either U.S. bonds or to stocks in other markets depending on the positive or negative excess returns.

One might want to compute the market value that would provide the desired return as follows:

$$\frac{x + 23.00}{1479} = 1.095$$

$$x = 1596.51$$

Other Relative Valuation Ratios

In addition to the P/E ratio, several other ratios are used by investors as indicators of relative value. Specifically, when doing an industry and company-stock analysis, analysts compare these valuation ratios to similar ratios for the aggregate market, other industries, and other

[21]This is an approximate estimate based on the expected earnings of $47.00 and a payout ratio of almost 50 percent, which is above the long-run payout.

stocks in an industry. Therefore, it is important to become familiar with the computation and historical movements for these ratios. The specific ratios considered are:

- the price-to-book-value ratio (P/BV)
- the price-to-cash-flow ratio (P/CF)
- the price-to-sales ratio (P/S)

CALCULATION OF RELATIVE VALUATION RATIOS The calculation of each of these ratios is generally straightforward with some differences in the measurement of the valuation variable (i.e., BV, CF, or S). In addition, it is necessary to decide whether one uses historical data or future values—i.e., do you compare current price to the *historical* valuation variable (e.g., cash flow for the prior year) or the *future expected* variable (e.g., the expected cash flow for the industry or company).

When computing this ratio for current valuation purposes, the *price-to-book-value (P/BV) ratio* is equal to the current stock price divided by the equity book value per share of the entity. When computing the ratio for historical exposition purposes, we use the average price each year, which is equal to the average of the high and low prices for the year. As noted, it is necessary to determine whether you want to use historical book value (i.e., compare the average stock price for year t to the book value at the end of year t) or use future book value (i.e., average stock price for year t to *estimated* book value for year $t + 1$). Similar to the P/E ratio, when you compute a ratio with a future value, the ratio will generally be lower and less volatile. Both sets of P/BV ratios are contained in Table 18.7 and plotted in Figure 18.17. The future ratios are computed using *actual* values for period $t + 1$ except for the last year (1997) where we computed the value for the $t + 1$ valuation variable assuming the average growth rate for the prior 20 years.

TABLE 18.7

RELATIVE VALUATION RATIOS FOR THE S&P 400 INDEX

	Price/Book-Value		Price/Cash-Flow (EBITDA)		Price/Sales		Price/Earnings	
Year	t	$t+1$	t	$t+1$	t	$t+1$	t	$t+1$
1977	1.33	1.22	5.49	4.83	0.49	0.44	9.55	8.39
1978	1.20	1.09	4.73	3.96	0.43	0.37	8.21	6.58
1979	1.17	1.07	4.28	4.07	0.40	0.35	7.11	7.18
1980	1.26	1.17	4.78	4.46	0.42	0.40	8.44	8.13
1981	1.22	1.19	4.64	4.97	0.41	0.42	8.45	10.72
1982	1.15	1.12	4.81	4.50	0.41	0.41	10.37	9.27
1983	1.43	1.41	5.75	5.08	0.52	0.46	11.84	9.66
1984	1.45	1.43	5.22	5.37	0.47	0.45	9.92	11.76
1985	1.66	1.67	6.25	6.16	0.52	0.54	13.68	14.38
1986	2.03	1.89	7.49	6.27	0.65	0.59	17.47	12.52
1987	2.42	2.32	8.02	6.47	0.75	0.67	15.99	12.20
1988	2.17	2.08	6.04	6.05	0.62	0.56	11.38	11.28
1989	2.51	2.39	7.29	7.14	0.67	0.61	13.59	14.72
1990	2.57	2.50	7.68	8.83	0.66	0.67	15.83	23.19
1991	2.73	3.01	9.66	8.84	0.73	0.71	25.36	22.51
1992	3.46	3.60	10.17	9.75	0.82	0.82	25.90	22.50
1993	3.80	3.45	10.28	8.33	0.86	0.83	23.72	15.85
1994	3.56	3.27	8.59	7.83	0.86	0.79	16.34	15.14
1995	3.90	3.80	9.33	8.24	0.94	0.91	18.03	15.53
1996	4.73	4.56	10.25	9.71	1.13	1.06	19.32	18.15
1997	5.78	5.57	12.28	12.93	1.34	1.31	22.97	26.22
1998(p)	7.11	NA	16.53	NA	1.67	NA	33.51	NA

The *price-to-cash-flow (P/CF) ratio* is equal to the average stock price for year *t* divided by either the historical or the estimated cash flow per share for the entity. Similar to most analysts, we use EBITDA as our measure of cash flow. Again, we use actual EBITDA in period $t + 1$ for the future ratio except for the final year where we estimate the components of EBITDA. The data are in Table 18.7 and the two series are plotted in Figure 18.18.

FIGURE 18.17

TIME-SERIES PLOT OF THE PRICE-TO-BOOK-VALUE RATIO FOR THE S&P 400 INDEX: 1977–1997

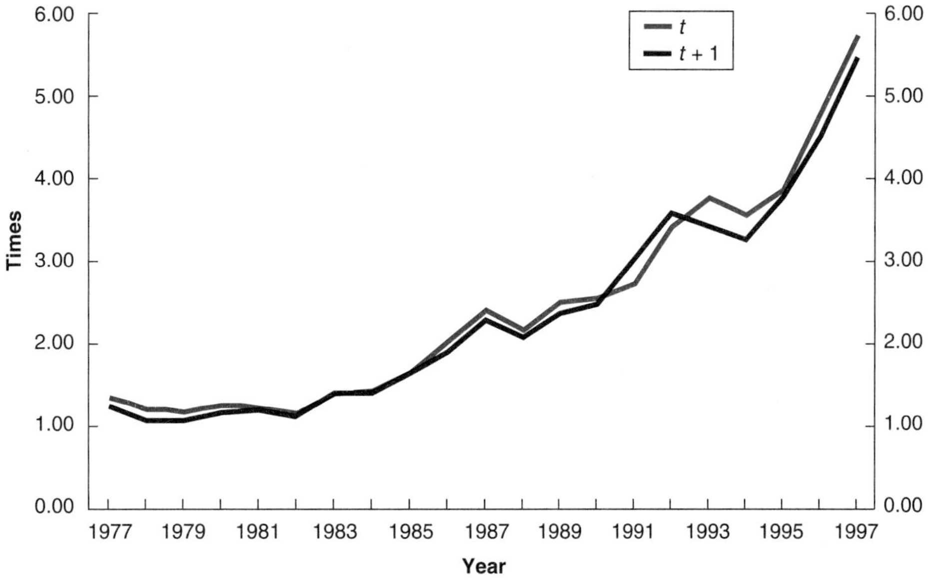

6.00
5.00
4.00
3.00
2.00
1.00
0.00
Times
t
t + 1
1977 1979 1981 1983 1985 1987 1989 1991 1993 1995 1997
Year

FIGURE 18.18

TIME-SERIES PLOT OF THE PRICE-TO-CASH-FLOW (EBITDA) RATIO FOR THE S&P 400 INDEX: 1977–1997

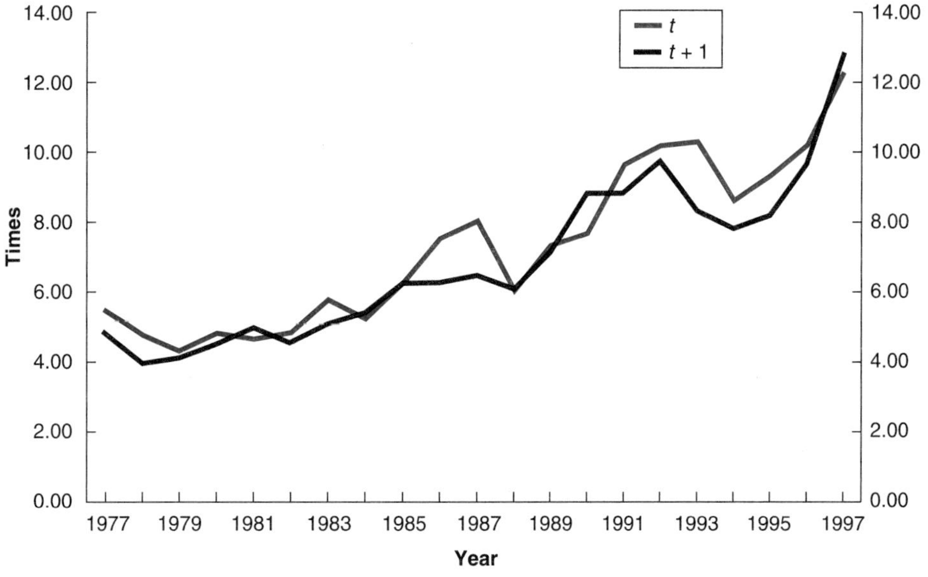

14.00
12.00
10.00
8.00
6.00
4.00
2.00
0.00
Times
t
t + 1
1977 1979 1981 1983 1985 1987 1989 1991 1993 1995 1997
Year

FIGURE 18.19

TIME-SERIES PLOT OF THE PRICE-TO-SALES RATIO FOR THE S&P 400 INDEX: 1977–1997

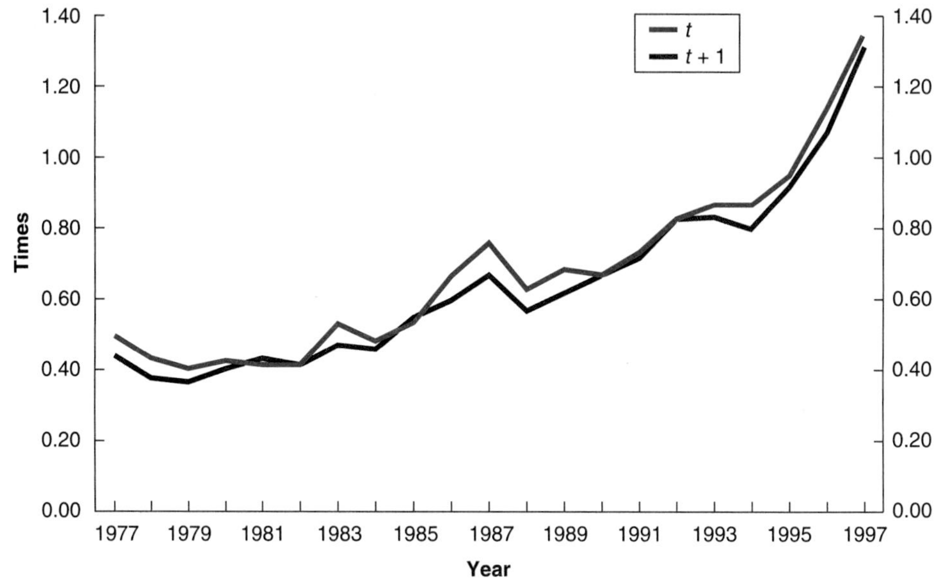
t
t + 1
Times
1.40
1.20
1.00
0.80
0.60
0.40
0.20
0.00
1977 1979 1981 1983 1985 1987 1989 1991 1993 1995 1997
Year

The *price-to-sales (P/S) ratio* is equal to the average stock price for year *t* divided by net sales per share during year *t* or an estimate of sales per share for year $t + 1$. Again, for the future P/S ratio we use actual sales per share during period $t + 1$ except for the final year where we estimate sales based upon the average sales growth during the prior 20 years. The results are in Table 18.7 and the two series are plotted in Figure 18.19.

As shown in the alternative time series plots, all the ratios (using the $t + 1$ values) have experienced overall increases during the 20-year period as follows:

Relative Valuation Ratio	Approximate Beginning Value (1977)	Approximate Ending Value (1997)
Price/Earnings	8.40	26.20
Price/Book Value	1.20	5.60
Price/Cash Flow	4.80	12.90
Price/Sales	0.40	1.30

To understand these higher valuation ratios, it is necessary to consider what factors drive the particular valuation ratio and whether these factors have changed over time. In the case of the P/E ratio, we know from DDM that the relevant variables are *k* and *g* for the economic unit. Therefore, when attempting to explain why the P/E has gone from about 8 times to 26 times, you would consider what has happened to these two variables. Without going into detail, we know that *k* has declined over time due to lower inflation and some evidence that the market risk premium has declined. In addition, the aggregate ROE has been increasing so that the expected growth rate should have increased. In summary, the *k–g* spread has declined substantially so a higher P/E is justified. How much higher it should be is subject to estimation and debate. Subsequently, we will discuss the relevant factors for the other ratios.

The plots also show considerable consistency between the time series using historical data for time *t* and future expected data for time *t* + 1. Given the similarity, the authors have a definite preference for using the *future* valuation variables. The point is, we know that when investors buy a stock, they are actually buying future earnings, cash flows, book values, or sales. Therefore, we will always refer to *future* P/E ratios that relate price to *expected* earnings. Although it is not always easy to obtain estimates for these alternative valuation variables beyond earnings, it is important to think in these terms if you want to use these ratios for valuation. The point is, similar to valuation using the P/E ratio, you will estimate the valuation variable (i.e., BV, CF, or Sales) and then apply an appropriate future multiple to the valuation variable to derive a price estimate.

ANALYSIS OF WORLD MARKETS

Although we have worked with the U.S. market to demonstrate the procedure for analyzing a country's stock market, investors should perform a similar analysis for non-U.S. markets, especially the major world markets—Japan, Canada, the United Kingdom, and Germany. We do not have the space to carry out a detailed analysis of each of these markets, but we can provide an example of the extensive analysis by a major investment firm. Specifically, Goldman, Sachs & Company provides a monthly publication entitled *World Investment Strategy Highlights* that contains a world portfolio strategy as well as a strategy for investors in several individual countries.

Overall, it is a top-down approach in which Goldman, Sachs initially examines the components of a country's economy that relate to the valuation of securities (i.e., GDP, capital investments, industrial production, inflation, and interest rates). In Chapter 14, we discussed the substantial difference in outlook for GDP growth during 1999 and 2000. Likewise, there are major differences in the outlook for inflation, which leads to major differences in expectations for exchange rates during 2000.

Given this approach, Table 18.8 contains forecasts for real GDP growth and inflation for six major countries. These data provide insights regarding individual countries in two areas. First is the status of their expansion, which began for most of the countries (except Japan) in 1993. Goldman, Sachs expected most countries, except Japan, to experience a continuation of their economic expansion in 1999 and 2000.

Going from the economy to results from corporations, Table 18.9 contains comparative results for firms in numerous countries regarding earnings growth and dividend growth. The range in results is substantial. For example, expected earnings growth in 2000 varies from 9 percent (United Kingdom) to 5 percent (Germany).

Because of the importance of interest rates in the valuation process, Table 18.10 contains long-term bond interest rate forecasts for seven countries for the short term (3 months) and the long term (12 months). As one might expect, the range of expected yields on long-term bonds is quite large—from 1.8 percent (Japan) to 5.0 percent (United States and Canada).

Putting the earnings growth estimate and interest rates together brings us to market valuation variables, including P/E ratios and dividend yields. The prevailing values for various countries contained in Table 18.11 indicate a wide range between countries (e.g., an estimated P/E during 2000 of about 18 for Germany versus 30 in the United States). The expected 2000 dividend yields range from less than 1.4 percent (United States) to 3.4 percent for the United Kingdom.

Individual Country Analysis

Following the summary of market statistics for the major equity markets, Goldman, Sachs provides a detailed analysis of each of the major countries. This begins with a discussion

TABLE 18.8

FORECASTS FOR COUNTRY REAL GDP GROWTH AND INFLATION (PERCENT PER ANNUM)

Country	1997	1998	1999E	2000E
United States				
GDP	3.9	3.9	3.7	1.8
Inflation	2.3	1.6	1.9	2.3
Japan				
GDP	1.4	−2.8	−1.3	−0.8
Inflation	1.7	0.7	−0.9	−1.1
Germany				
GDP	2.2	2.8	1.4	1.8
Inflation	1.7	1.0	0.5	0.5
United Kingdom				
GDP	3.5	2.3	0.6	2.2
Inflation	2.8	2.7	2.3	1.9
France				
GDP	2.3	3.2	2.2	2.5
Inflation	1.2	0.7	0.4	0.6
Italy				
GDP	1.5	1.4	1.2	1.8
Inflation	1.7	1.7	1.2	1.3

Source: Adapted from *World Investment Strategy Highlights* (London: Goldman, Sachs International Ltd.), May 1999. Reprinted by permission of Goldman, Sachs & Co.

TABLE 18.9

COMPARATIVE CORPORATE GROWTH STATISTICS

	United States	Japan	United Kingdom	Germany	France	Italy
Earnings Growth						
1998	−6	−68	−5	21	14	29
1999F	8	140	4	5	8	8
2000F	8	NA	9	5	6	7
Dividend Growth						
1998	5	−15	6	15	11	25
1999F	6	8	4	8	10	13
2000F	6	NA	5	5	8	9

Aggregates for earnings and dividend are based on an industrial sample of all the companies in each country.

F = forecast. NA = not available.

Note: Figures for the United States refer to the S&P Industrials Index and pertain to operating earnings.

Source: Adapted from *World Investment Strategy Highlights* (London: Goldman, Sachs International Ltd.), May 1999. Reprinted by permission of Goldman, Sachs & Co.

of the country's economy as part of an analysis of the country's equity market. Table 18.12 contains estimates of the major economic indicators for Germany. These projections reflect an economy struggling to prolong an economic expansion. Currently, government authorities are concerned about the future competitiveness of German firms in the European economic community.

TABLE 18.10 **INTEREST RATE FORECASTS (PERCENT PER ANNUM)**

Country	Current Rate[a]	Short Term (3 months)	Long Term (12 months)
United States			
10 year	5.3	5.3	5.0
Germany			
10 year	3.9	3.8	3.9
Japan			
10 year	1.5	1.3	1.8
France			
10 year	4.0	3.8	3.9
United Kingdom			
10 year	4.6	4.4	4.3
Canada			
10 year	5.2	5.1	5.0
Italy			
10 year	4.1	4.1	4.1

[a]May 1999.

Source: Adapted from *World Investment Strategy Highlights* (London: Goldman, Sachs International Ltd.), May 1999. Reprinted by permission of Goldman, Sachs & Co.

TABLE 18.11 **WORLD MARKET EVALUATION MATRIX**

	United States	Japan	United Kingdom	Germany	France	Italy
Industrial P/E						
1998	31.9	108.8	23.6	19.7	30.5	22.5
1999E	32.3	58.7	23.4	19.1	29.4	22.6
2000E	29.9	NA	21.5	18.3	27.7	21.0
Div. Yield						
1998	1.3	0.8	3.6	2.3	2.3	1.9
1999E	1.3	0.9	3.3	2.4	2.3	1.9
2000E	1.4	NA	3.4	2.7	2.5	2.1

Based on Datastream market indices.

E = estimate. NA = not available.

U.S. figures refer to S&P Composite Index and pertain to operating earnings. U.K. figures refer to FT-500 Index.

Source: Adapted from *World Investment Strategy Highlights* (London: Goldman, Sachs International Ltd.), May 1999. Reprinted by permission of Goldman, Sachs & Co.

Following the discussion of the economy and the projections, Goldman, Sachs analyzes the country's equity market. A summary for Germany is set forth in Table 18.13. Goldman, Sachs feels that the overall investment outlook for Germany is relatively weak because of the low earnings growth outlook. Therefore, they recommend a slight underweighting of German equities in a global portfolio.

TABLE 18.12 **MAJOR GERMAN ECONOMIC VARIABLES**

	Current Value	Historical Average
GDP Growth		
1998	2.8	2.2
1999F	1.4	
2000F	1.8	
Earnings Growth (Industrials)		
1998	21	7.4
1999F	5	
2000F	5	
Dividend Growth (Industrials)		
1998	15	4.0
1999F	8	
2000F	5	
Inflation (Consumer Price Index) (%)		
1998	1.0	2.0
1999F	0.5	
2000F	0.5	

INTEREST RATE OUTLOOK

	Current Rate	3 Months	12 Months
3 month	3.0	2.8	2.9
10 year	3.9	3.8	3.9

Source: Adapted from *World Investment Strategy Highlights* (London: Goldman, Sachs International Ltd.), May 1999. Reprinted by permission of Goldman, Sachs & Co.

TABLE 18.13 **STOCK INDEXES FOR THE GERMAN EQUITY MARKET AND EXPECTED RATES OF RETURN**

		Performance (% Change)		
		Last Month	YTD	12 Months
DAX	5349	1.8	−4.0	−2.5

	Expected Returns (%)	
	3 Months	12 Months
Equities	−0.2	1.8
Bonds	1.5	3.6
Cash	0.8	2.7

Source: Adapted from *World Investment Strategy Highlights* (London: Goldman, Sachs International Ltd.), May 1999. Reprinted by permission of Goldman, Sachs & Co.

THE INTERNET *Investments Online*

As the economy goes, so goes the stock market. As we've seen in an earlier chapter, the stock market is a leading economic indicator. Good economic insight will help with analyzing the current state and likely future path of the stock market. A number of good Internet sites offer analysis on the market, too.

www.ms.com Morgan Stanley Dean Witter's Web site has a link to their Global Strategy Bulletin, which contains an analysis of the U.S. economy and those of several other countries.

www.yardeni.com We've discussed Edward Yardeni's site in an earlier chapter. Of special relevance to this chapter are the forecasts for the economy, earnings, and stock market that appear on his site's pages. Information is available concerning the markets in a number of countries.

www.nabe.com The National Association of Business Economists' home page includes links to a number of economic information-related sites and data sources. Links include the Bureau of Economic Analysis (**www.bea.doc.gov**), which contains information about GDP and its components; and the U.S. government's publication, *Survey of Current Business.* Links to the Bureau of Labor Statistics (**stats.bls.gov**) provide data on various measures of inflation, unemployment, and productivity. Other links include the Census Bureau (**www.census.gov**); Congressional Budget Office (**www.cbo.gov**); Council of Economic Advisors (**www.whitehouse.gov/WH/EOP/CEA/html/CEA.html**); The Conference Board, publishers of the Index of Leading Economic Indicators (**www.conference-board.org**); and links to a number of sources of international data, from both U.S. and overseas statistical agencies. The site contains helpful industry information, too, with links to the *U.S. Industrial Outlook,* Federal Trade Commission, and a number of industry trade association sites.

www.agedwards.com The home page of A. G. Edwards & Son, Inc., allows visitors to obtain specific research reports on different topics, companies, and stocks. The site contains pages with the firm's analysis of economic trends, both in the United States and abroad. A separate site focuses on international perspectives.

Summary

- We consistently emphasize the importance of analyzing the economies and security markets before analyzing alternative industries or companies. You should determine whether the economic and market outlooks indicate an underweighting or overweighting related to investing in stocks, bonds, or cash before you consider which is the best industry or company.
- There are three techniques available to help you make the market decision. The first are macro techniques, which are based on the strong relationship between the economy and security markets. These models base their market projections on their outlook for the aggregate economy and certain components. The second are micro techniques, which estimate future market values by applying one of several basic valuation models to equity markets. The third is technical analysis wherein you analyze past and recent market movements for indications of future performance. In Chapter 14, we examined the macro techniques and discussed a world asset allocation. This chapter has been devoted to the microanalysis of equity markets in the United States and other countries. In Chapter 21 we will discuss numerous technical analysis tools.
- Our microanalysis of the United States equity market considered both approaches to equity analysis—the present value of cash flow techniques and the relative valuation ratio techniques. The cash flow techniques provided a range of estimates, most of which indicated that the market was fully valued, which implies that the rates of return on common stock in the near term will be lower than the long-run historical returns and certainly lower than during 1995–1998.
- We considered four relative valuation ratios, including the earnings multiple (P/E) approach where we discussed a two-step approach that included estimating EPS and the expected P/E ratio based upon the DDM. As a result, we generated a specific future market value and the expected

rate of return implied by the future market value. The other three ratios (P/BV; P/CF; and P/S) were defined and explained in anticipation of using them during industry and company analysis where the relative valuation technique compares an industry to the market and relates a company to both its industry and the aggregate market. The goal is to evaluate the relative value position of an industry or a stock. This initial analysis of the valuation ratios was intended to demonstrate the computations involved and show the consistent, substantial increase in all the ratios during the past 20 years. Subsequent analysis will need to consider what variables drive these relative valuation ratios and evaluate whether these variables have changed in a way that justifies these lofty ratio values.

- Finally, although we applied both sets of valuation techniques to the stock market in the United States, we know it is necessary to do a similar analysis for non-U.S. markets. An example of such an analysis by Goldman, Sachs shows how the firm applied the top-down approach to several major countries.

Following this aggregate market analysis, the next step is industry analysis, which is considered in the following chapter.

Questions

1. An investor believes the stock market will experience a substantial increase next year because corporate earnings are expected to rise by at least 12 percent. Do you agree or disagree? Why or why not?
2. In the library, find at least three sources of historical information on nominal and real GDP. Find two sources that generally provide an estimate of nominal GDP each year.
3. To arrive at an estimate of the *net profit margin,* why would you spend time estimating the operating profit margin and work down?
4. You are convinced that capacity utilization next year will decline from 82 percent to about 79 percent. Explain what effect this change will have on the operating profit margin.
5. You see an estimate that hourly wage rates will increase by 6 percent next year. How does this affect your estimate of the operating profit margin? What other information do you need to determine the effect of this wage rate increase and why do you need it?
6. You see an estimate that next year hourly wage rates will increase by 7 percent and productivity will increase by 5 percent. What would you expect to happen to unit labor cost? Discuss how this unit labor cost estimate would influence your estimate of the operating profit margin.
7. Assume that each of the following changes is independent (i.e., except for this change, all other factors remain unchanged). In each case, indicate what will happen to the earnings multiplier and why.
   a. The return on equity increases.
   b. The aggregate debt–equity ratio declines.
   c. Overall productivity of capital increases.
   d. The dividend-payout ratio declines.
8. Briefly discuss the two factors that must be considered (estimated) whether you are employing the present value of cash flow approaches or the relative valuation ratio approaches.
9. Discuss the difference between the constant growth DDM and the two-stage growth model. In your discussion, explain when you would use each of these models.

Problems

1. You are told that nominal GDP will increase by about 10 percent next year. Using Figure 18.8 and the regression equation, what increase would you expect in corporate sales? How would this estimate change if you gave more weight to the recent observations?
2. Currently, the dividend-payout ratio (D/E) for the aggregate market is 60 percent, the required return (k) is 13 percent, and the expected growth rate for dividends (g) is 7 percent.
   a. Compute the current earnings multiplier.
   b. You expect the D/E ratio to decline to 50 percent, but you assume there will be no other changes. What will be the P/E?

c. Starting with the initial conditions, you expect the dividend-payout ratio to be constant, the rate of inflation to increase by 3 percent, and the growth rate to increase by 2 percent. Compute the expected P/E.

d. Starting with the initial conditions, you expect the dividend-payout ratio to be constant, the rate of inflation to decline by 3 percent, and the growth rate to decline by 1 percent. Compute the expected P/E.

CFA

3. *CFA Examination III (1985)*

A U.S. pension plan hired two off-shore firms to manage the non-U.S. equity portion of its total portfolio. Each firm was free to own stocks in any country market included in Capital International's Europe, Australia, and Far East Index (EAFE), and to use any form of dollar and/or non-dollar cash or bonds as an equity substitute or reserve. After three years had elapsed, the records of the managers and the EAFE Index were as shown below:

SUMMARY: CONTRIBUTIONS TO RETURN

	Currency	Country Selection	Stock Selection	Cash/Bond Allocation	Total Return Recorded
Manager A	(9.0%)	19.7%	3.1%	0.6%	14.4%
Manager B	(7.4)	14.2	6.0	2.8	15.6
Composite of A&B	(8.2)	16.9	4.5	1.7	15.0
EAFE Index	(12.9)	19.9	—	—	7.0

You are a member of the plan sponsor's pension committee, which will soon meet with the plan's consultant to review manager performance. In preparation for this meeting, you go through the following analysis:

a. Briefly describe the strengths and weaknesses of each manager, relative to the EAFE Index data. (5 minutes)

b. Briefly explain the meaning of the data in the "Currency" column. (5 minutes)

4. As an analyst for Middle, Diddle, and O'Leary, you are forecasting the market P/E ratio using the dividend discount model. Because the economy has been expanding for 9 years, you expect the dividend-payout ratio will be at its low of 40 percent and that long-term government bond rates will rise to 7 percent. Because investors are becoming less risk-averse, the equity risk premium will decline to 3 percent. As a result, investors will require a 10 percent return, and the return on equity will be 12 percent.

a. What is the expected growth rate?

b. What is your expectation of the market P/E ratio?

c. What will be the value for the market index if the expectation is for earnings per share of $39.00?

d. What will be your rate of return if you acquired the index at a value of 700, you sold the index at the value computed in part c, and dividends during the year were $22.00?

5. You are given the following estimated per share data related to the S&P 400 for the year 2001:

Sales	$1,020.00
Depreciation	45.00
Interest expense	18.00

You are also informed that the estimated operating profit margin is 0.152 and the tax rate is 32 percent.

a. Compute the estimated EPS for 2001.

b. Assume that a member of the research committee for your firm feels that it is important to consider a range of operating profit margin (OPM) estimates. Therefore, you are asked to derive both optimistic and pessimistic EPS estimates using 0.149 and 0.155 for the OPM and holding everything else constant.

6. Given the three EPS estimates in Problem 5, you are also given the following estimates related to the market earnings multiple.

	Pessimistic	Consensus	Optimistic
D/E	0.65	0.55	0.45
Nominal RFR	0.10	0.09	0.08
Risk premium	0.05	0.04	0.03
ROE	0.10	0.13	0.16

a. Based on the three EPS and P/E estimates, compute the high, low, and consensus market value for the S&P 400 in 2001.

b. Assuming that the S&P 400 at the beginning of the year was priced at 1,600, compute your expected rate of return under the three scenarios from part a. Assuming your required rate of return is equal to the consensus, how would you weight the S&P 400 in your global portfolio?

7. You are analyzing the U.S. equity market based upon the Standard and Poor's 400 Industrial Index (S&P 400) and using the present value of free cash flow to equity technique. Your inputs are as follows:

Beginning FCFE: $40.00
$k = 0.09$

growth rates:

Year 1–3:	9%
4–6:	8%
7 and beyond	7%

a. Assuming that the current value for the S&P 400 is 1,600, would you underweight, overweight, or market weight the U.S. equity market?

b. Assume that there is a 1 percent increase in the rate of inflation—what would be the market's value and how would you weight the U.S. market?

References

Copeland, Basil L., Jr. "Inflation, Interest Rates and Equity Risk Premia." *Financial Analysts Journal* 38, no. 3 (May–June 1982).

Copeland, Tom, Tim Koller, and Jack Murrin. *Valuation.* 2d ed. New York: John Wiley & Sons, 1996.

Damodaran, Aswath. *Investment Valuation.* New York: John Wiley & Sons, 1996.

Fama, Eugene F., and Kenneth French. "Business Conditions and Expected Returns on Stocks and Bonds." *Journal of Financial Economics* 25, no. 1 (November 1989).

Fama, Eugene F., and Kenneth R. French. "Common Risk Factors in the Returns on Stocks and Bonds." *Journal of Financial Economics* 33, no. 1 (February 1993).

Finnerty, John D., and Dean Leistikow. "The Behavior of Equity and Debt Risk Premiums." *Journal of Portfolio Management* 19, no. 4 (summer 1993).

Gray, William S., III. "The Anatomy of a Stock Market Forecast." *Journal of Portfolio Management* 16, no. 1 (fall 1989).

Haugen, Robert A., and Nardin L. Baker. "Commonality in the Determinants of Expected Stock Returns." *Journal of Financial Economics* 41, no. 3 (July 1996).

Palepu, Krishna, Victor Bernard, and Paul M. Healy. *Business Analysis and Valuation*. Cincinnati, Ohio: South-Western College Publishing, 1996.

Reichenstein, William, and Steven P. Rich. "The Market Risk Premium and Long-Term Stock Returns." *The Journal of Portfolio Management* 19, no. 4 (summer 1993).

Reilly, Frank K., Frank T. Griggs, and Wenchi Wong. "Determinants of the Aggregate Stock Market Earnings Multiple." *Journal of Portfolio Management* 10, no. 1 (fall 1983).

Shiller, Robert J., and John Campbell. "Stock Prices, Earnings, and Expected Dividends." *Journal of Finance* 43, no. 3 (July 1988).

Vandell, Robert F., and George W. Keuter. *A History of Risk-Premia Estimates for Equities: 1944–1978*. Charlottesville, Va.: The Financial Analysts Research Foundation, 1989.

Chapter

19 Industry Analysis*

After you read this chapter, you should be able to answer the following questions:

- Is there a difference between the returns for alternative industries during specific time periods? What is the implication of these results?
- Is there consistency in the returns for individual industries over time? What do these results imply regarding industry analysis?
- Is the performance for firms within an industry consistent? What is the implication of these results for industry and company analysis?
- Is there a difference in risk among industries? What are the implications of these results for industry analysis?
- What happens to risk for individual industries over time? What does this imply for industry analysis?
- What are the two variables that need to be estimated whether you use cash flow models or relative valuation ratios?
- Given the present value of cash flow valuation techniques, how does an analyst determine the value of an industry using the DDM and assuming constant growth or two-stage growth?
- How does an analyst determine the value of an industry using the free cash flow to equity (FCFE) model assuming constant growth or two-stage growth?
- What are the steps involved in estimating earnings per share for an industry?
- What are the stages in the industrial life cycle and how does the stage in an industry's life cycle affect the sales estimate for an industry?
- What are the five basic competitive forces that determine the intensity of competition in an industry and, thus, its rate of return on capital?
- How does the procedure for estimating the operating profit margin differ for the aggregate market versus an industry?
- What are the two alternative procedures for estimating an industry earnings multiplier?
- What is involved in a macroanalysis of the industry earnings multiplier?
- What are the steps in the microanalysis of an industry earnings multiplier?
- After you estimate an industry earnings multiplier, how do you determine if the industry's multiplier is relatively high or low?
- How do analysts compare relative valuation ratios such as P/BV, P/CF, and P/S to comparable market ratios?
- How do industries differ in terms of what dictates their return on assets?
- What are some of the unique factors that must be considered in global industry analysis?

When asked about his or her job, a securities analyst typically will reply that he or she is an oil analyst, a retail analyst, or a computer analyst. A widely read trade publication, *The Institutional Investor,* selects an All-American analyst team each year based on industry

*The authors acknowledge the discussions on "The Business Cycle and Industry Sectors" and "Structural Economic Changes" provided by Professor Edgar Norton of Illinois State University.

groups. Investment managers talk about being in or out of the metals, the autos, or the utilities. This constant reference to industry groups is because most professional investors are extremely conscious of differences among alternative industries and organize their analyses and portfolio decisions according to industry groups. Recently, the Association for Investment Management and Research (AIMR) has responded to this interest by sponsoring a number of conferences that are specifically concerned with the techniques and topics relevant for specific industries.[1]

We share this appreciation of the importance of industry analysis as a component of the three-step fundamental analysis procedure initiated in Chapter 13. Industry analysis is the second step as we progress toward selecting specific firms and stocks for our investment portfolio. As the first step, in Chapter 14 we discussed the macroanalysis of the stock market to decide whether the expected rate of return from investing in common stocks was equal to or greater than our required rate of return. Based on this comparison, we would decide to be overweighted, market-weighted, or underweighted in stocks. We also discussed the microanalysis of the market in Chapter 18 to support the macroanalysis. Following this economic/market decision, we take the second step in this chapter when we analyze different industries to make a similar industry decision. The decision criteria are the same: Is the expected rate of return for an industry equal to or greater than our required rate of return for the industry? Based on this relationship, we decide how to weight the industry in our stock portfolio. We will take the final step in Chapter 20 when we analyze the individual companies and stocks within the alternative industries.

In the first section, we discuss the results of several studies that will help us identify the benefits and uses of industry analysis. Following that, we present two approaches for valuing industries that resemble the presentation in Chapter 18 for analyzing the aggregate stock market. We begin with the present value of cash flow models and then consider the several relative valuation ratios. Another section raises questions that are unique to industry analysis: What is the impact of the competitive environment within an industry and the effect of the intensity of competition on potential industry returns? We conclude the chapter with a demonstration of global industry analysis, which recognizes that many industries transcend U.S. borders and compete on a worldwide basis.

WHY DO INDUSTRY ANALYSIS?

Investment practitioners perform industry analysis because they believe it helps them isolate investment opportunities that have favorable return–risk characteristics. We likewise have recommended it as part of our three-step, top-down plan for valuing individual companies and selecting stocks for inclusion in our portfolio. What exactly do we learn from an industry analysis? Can we spot trends in industries that make them good investments? Studies of these questions indicate unique patterns in the rates of return and risk measures over time in different industries. In this section, we survey the results of studies that addressed these questions.

In the research we describe, investigators asked a set of questions designed to pinpoint the benefits and limitations of industry analysis. In particular, they wanted answers to the following questions:

[1]Examples of industries included in the AIMR series are health care, oil and gas, automotive, telecommunications, and the retail industry. Detailed references are contained at the end of the chapter.

- Is there a difference between the returns for alternative industries during specific time periods?
- Will an industry that performs well in one period continue to perform well in the future? That is, can we use past relationships between the market and an individual industry to predict future trends for the industry?
- Is the performance of firms within an industry consistent over time?

Several studies also considered questions related to risk:

- Is there a difference in the risk for alternative industries?
- Does the risk for individual industries vary, or does it remain relatively constant over time?

We consider the results of these studies and come to some general conclusions about the value of industry analysis. In addition, this assessment helps us interpret the results of our subsequent industry valuation.

CROSS-SECTIONAL INDUSTRY PERFORMANCE

To find out if the rates of return among different industries varied during a given time period (e.g., during the year 2000), researchers compared the performance of alternative industries during a specific time period. Similar performance during specific time periods for different industries would indicate that industry analysis is not necessary. For example, assume that during 2000, the aggregate stock market experienced a rate of return of 10 percent and the returns for *all* industries were bunched between 9 percent and 11 percent. If this was the result and this similarity in performance persisted for future periods, you might question whether it was worthwhile to conduct an industry analysis to find an industry that would return 11 percent when random selection would provide a return of about 10 percent (the average return).

Studies of the annual industry performance have found that different industries have consistently shown *wide dispersion in their rates of return* (e.g., a typical range of rates of return during a year will be from minus 30 percent to plus 50 percent). A specific example is the year 1998. As shown in Figure 19.1, although the aggregate stock market experienced a total return of about 24 percent (the S&P 500), the industry performance ranged from −58.88 percent (oil drillers) to 102.32 percent (communications technology). The long-term results that consider the average annual results over a 16½-year period confirm these results with a range from 1.87 percent (steel) to 36 percent (software). These results imply that *industry analysis is important and necessary* to uncover these substantial performance differences that will help identify both unprofitable and profitable opportunities.

INDUSTRY PERFORMANCE OVER TIME

In another group of investigations, researchers tried to determine whether individual industries that perform well in one time period would continue to perform well in subsequent time periods or at least outperform the aggregate market in the later time period. In this case, investigators found *almost no association* in individual industry performance year to year or over sequential rising or falling markets.

These studies imply that past performance alone does not help project future industry performance. The results do *not,* however, negate the usefulness of industry analysis. They simply confirm that variables that affect industry performance change over time and investors must project the future performance for individual industries on the basis of future estimates of these relevant variables.

PERFORMANCE OF THE COMPANIES WITHIN AN INDUSTRY

Other studies were designed to determine whether there is consistency in the performance of companies *within* an industry. If all the firms within an industry performed consistently during a specified time period, investors would not need company analysis. In such a case,

FIGURE 19.1 HOW THE DOW JONES U.S. INDUSTRY GROUPS FARED DURING 1998

Best Performers	% Change 12/31/97 to 12/31/98	Compound Ann. Chg. 6/30/82 to 12/31/98	Worst Performers	% Change 12/31/97 to 12/31/98	Compound Ann. Chg. 6/30/82 to 12/31/98
Communications tech.	+102.32%	+18.82%	Oil drillers	−58.88%	+3.27%
Entertainment	+90.34	+14.88	Oilfield equipment	−42.47	+4.57
Computers (excl. IBM)	+82.56	+18.39	Marine transportation	−39.75	+9.28
Computers (incl. IBM)	+80.42	+14.46	Casinos	−31.59	+14.48
Software	+79.04	+36.41	Heavy machinery	−31.30	+8.26
Drug retailers	+68.30	+24.40	Secondary oil cos.	−28.44	+3.90
Consumer services	+67.95	+18.77	Non-ferrous (excl. aluminum)	−27.16	+4.33
Specialty retailers	+67.68	+19.15	Real estate	−26.15	+9.20
Apparel retailers	+65.96	+23.04	Precious metals	−24.33	+2.01
Semiconductors	+63.20	+24.82	Lodging	−24.26	+13.62
Broadline retailers	+60.93	+19.17	Clothing and fabric	−19.08	+12.67
Broadcasting	+59.02	+20.88	Coal	−18.85	+4.72
Office equipment	+54.92	+17.01	Aerospace and defense	−18.53	+15.50
Food retailers	+52.58	+19.79	Transportation equipment	−17.93	+9.91
Automakers	+50.70	+14.87	Health care	−16.11	+12.25
Mining	+50.66	+10.35	Toys	−14.53	+13.16
Restaurants	+50.43	+18.54	Containers	−13.90	+14.27
Beverages	+48.13	+16.81	Steel	−13.03	+1.87

Source: *Wall Street Journal,* 2 January 1999, R3.

industry analysis alone would be enough because once you selected a profitable industry, you would know that all the stocks in that industry would do well.

These studies typically have found *wide dispersion* in the performance among companies in most industries. An alternative way to measure this same impact is to examine the industry influence on the returns for individual stocks. Studies that have done such an analysis have shown evidence of an industry effect in specific industries, such as oil or autos, but most stocks showed small industry effects. In addition, the results indicated that the industry impact on individual stocks has been declining over time.[2]

IMPLICATION OF DISPERSION WITHIN INDUSTRIES Citing such studies as these, some theorists have contended that industry analysis is useless because all firms in an industry do not move together. Obviously, consistent firm performance in an industry would be ideal because you would not need to do company analysis. For industries that have a strong, consistent industry influence, such as oil, gold, steel, autos, and railroads, you can reduce the extent of your company analysis after your industry analysis.

Most analysts do not expect such a strong industry influence, which means that a thorough *company* analysis is still necessary. Even for industries that do not have a strong industry influence, industry analysis is valuable because it is much easier to select a superior company from a good industry than to find a good company in an unhealthy industry. By selecting the best stocks within an industry with good expectations, you avoid the risk that your analysis and selection of a good company will be offset by poor industry performance.

[2]For example, see Stephen L. Meyers, "A Re-examination of Market and Industry Factors in Stock Price Behavior," *Journal of Finance* 28. no. 3 (June 1973): 695–705; and Miles Livingston, "Industry Movements of Common Stocks," *Journal of Finance* 32, no. 2 (June 1977): 861–874.

Differences in Industry Risk

Although a number of studies have focused on industry rates of return, few studies have examined industry risk measures. A study by Reilly and Drzycimski investigated two questions: (1) Did risk differ among industries during a given time period? (2) Were industry risk measures stable over time?[3] The study found *a wide range of risk* among different industries at a point in time, and the differences in the measures of industry risk typically widened during rising and falling markets. On a positive note, an analysis of the risk measures for individual industries over time indicated that they were *reasonably stable over time.*

We can interpret these findings as follows: although risk measures for different industries showed substantial dispersion during a period of time, individual industries' risk measures are stable over time. This means that the analysis of past industry risk is necessary, but this historical anaysis of risk is useful when you attempt to estimate the future risk for an industry.

Summary of Research on Industry Analysis

Earlier we noted that a number of academic studies have sought answers to questions dealing with industry analysis. The conclusions of the studies are:

- During any time period, the returns for different industries vary within a wide range, which means that industry analysis can be useful in the process of targeting investments.
- The rates of return for individual industries vary over time, so we cannot simply extrapolate past industry performance into the future.
- The rates of return of firms within industries also vary, so company analysis is a necessary follow-up to industry analysis.
- During any time period, different industries' risk levels vary within wide ranges, so we must examine and estimate the risk factors for alternative industries as well as returns.
- Risk measures for different industries remain fairly constant over time, so the historical risk analysis is useful when estimating future risk.

The results imply that industry analysis is necessary, both to avoid losses and to find better industries. Industry analysis is also important when you examine individual stocks to identify superior risk–return opportunities for investors.

THE BUSINESS CYCLE AND INDUSTRY SECTORS

Economic trends can and do affect industry performance. By identifying and monitoring key assumptions and variables, we can monitor the economy and gauge the implications of new information on our original economic outlook and industry analysis. Recall that in order to do better than the market averages on a risk-adjusted basis, we must have forecasts that differ from the market consensus *and* we must be correct more often than not.

Economic trends can take two basic forms: **cyclical changes** in the economy arise from the ups and downs of the business cycle, and **structural changes** occur when the economy is undergoing a major change in organization or in how it functions. For example, excess labor or capital may exist in some sectors whereas shortages of labor and capital exist elsewhere. The "downsizing" of corporate America during the 1990s, transitions from socialist to market economies in Eastern Europe, and the transition in the United States from a manufacturing to a service economy are all examples of structural change.[4] Industry analysts must examine structural changes for the implications they hold for the industry under review.

---

[3]Frank K. Reilly and Eugene Drzycimski, "Alternative Industry Performance and Risk," *Journal of Financial and Quantitative Analysis* 9, no. 3 (June 1974): 423–446.

[4]An excellent discussion of structural changes in the U.S. economy and the implications of these changes for the business cycle and the stock market is contained in William C. Dudley and Edward F. McKelvey, "The Brave New Business Cycle: No Recession in Sight" (New York: Goldman, Sachs & Co., January 1997).

FIGURE 19.2

THE STOCK MARKET AND THE BUSINESS CYCLE

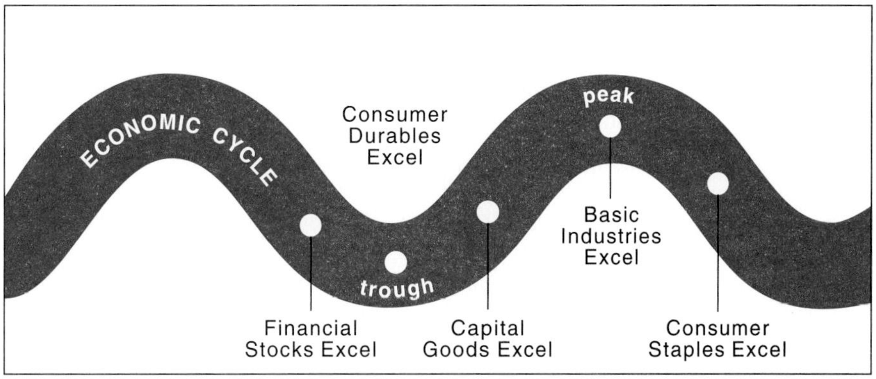
ECONOMIC CYCLE
Consumer Durables Excel
peak
Basic Industries Excel
trough
Financial Stocks Excel
Capital Goods Excel
Consumer Staples Excel

Source: Adapted from Susan E. Kuhn, "Stocks Are Still Your Best Buy," *Fortune,* 21 March 1994, 140. © 1994 Time Inc. All Rights Reserved.

Concerning the effects of business cycles on industry analysis, most observers believe that industry performance is related to the stage of the business cycle. What makes industry analysis challenging is that although this belief may be true on average, every business cycle is different and those who look only at history are in danger of missing the current and evolving trends that will determine future market performance.

Switching from one industry group to another over the course of a business cycle is known as a *rotation strategy.* When trying to determine which industry groups will benefit from the next stage of the cycle, investors need to identify and monitor key assumptions and variables related to economic trends and industry characteristics.

Figure 19.2 presents a stylized graphic of which industry groups typically perform well in the different stages of the business cycle. Toward the end of a recession, financial stocks begin to rise in value as investors begin to anticipate the end of the recession. They anticipate that banks' earnings will rise as both the economy and loan demand recover. Brokerage houses may also be attractive investments because their sales and earnings are expected to rise as investors trade securities and as businesses sell debt and equity during the economic recovery. These industry selections assume that the recession will end shortly, followed by positive economic news, including increases in loan demand, housing construction, and security offerings.

Once the economy hits bottom and begins its recovery, consumer durable stocks typically make attractive investments. Such stocks include industries that produce expensive consumer items, such as cars, personal computers, refrigerators, lawn tractors, and snow blowers. These industries are attractive investments because a reviving economy will increase consumer confidence and personal income. Pent-up demand for expensive consumer purchases that were likely delayed during the recession may be fulfilled during the coming recovery.

Once businesses finally recognize the economy is recovering and current levels of consumer spending are sustainable, they begin to think about modernizing, renovating, or purchasing new equipment to satisfy rising demand, lower costs, expand markets, or provide better service to customers. Thus, capital goods industries become attractive investments. Examples of capital goods industries include heavy equipment manufacturers, machine and tool die makers, and airplane manufacturers.

Cyclical industries include capital goods and consumer durables whose sales rise and. fall along with general economic activity. Cyclical industries are attractive investments during the early stages of an economic recovery because of their high degree of operating leverage, which means that they benefit greatly from the sales increases during an economic expansion.[5] Industries with high financial leverage (that is, higher industry debt ratios), such as banks, likewise benefit from rising sales or loan volume.[6]

Traditionally, toward the business cycle peak, the rate of inflation increases as demand starts to outstrip supply. Basic materials industries, which transform raw materials into finished products, become investor favorites. These industries include the oil, gold, aluminum, and timber industries. Because inflation has little influence on the cost of extracting or finishing these products, the higher prices allow these industries to experience higher profit margins.

During a recession, some industry sectors typically do better than others. Consumer staples, such as pharmaceuticals, food, and beverages, tend to perform better than other sectors during a recession because, although spending may drop in other areas, people still spend money on these necessities. As a result, these "defensive" industries generally maintain their values during market declines.

If a weak domestic economy means a weak currency, industries with large export components may benefit because their goods become more cost competitive in overseas markets. The most attractive industries will be those with large markets in growing economies.

We have identified certain industries that typically make attractive investments over the course of the business cycle. Generally, investors should not invest based upon the current economic environment because the efficient market has already incorporated current economic news into security prices. Rather, it is necessary to forecast important economic variables at least 3 to 6 months in the future and invest accordingly. The following subsection considers several important economic variables and discusses how changes in these variables may affect different industries.

Inflation

Higher inflation is generally perceived as being negative for the stock market, because it causes higher market interest rates, it increases uncertainty about future prices and costs (leading to higher risk perceptions), and it harms firms that cannot pass their cost increases on to consumers. Although these adverse effects are true for most industries, some industries benefit from inflation. Firms in natural resource industries benefit *if* their production costs do not rise with inflation, because their oil, mineral, or metal output will likely sell at higher prices. Industries that have high operating and financial leverage may benefit because many of their costs are fixed in nominal (current dollar) terms whereas revenues increase in line with inflation. Industries with high financial leverage may also gain because their debts are repaid in cheaper dollars.

Interest Rates

Banks generally benefit from volatile interest rates, because stable interest rates lead to heavy competitive pressures that squeeze their interest margins. Because high interest rates harm the construction industry, they generally help industries that supply the do-it-yourselfer. High interest rates also benefit those whose income is dependent on interest income—for example, retirees.

---

[5]Operating leverage arises from the existence of fixed costs in a firm's operating structure. Industries with large fixed expenses, such as rent or lease payments, depreciation, or take-or-pay contracts, will have high degrees of operating leverage. This means a small percentage change in sales can result in a large percentage change in operating income.

[6]As noted in Chapter 12, financial leverage arises from fixed financial costs (that is, interest expense) in a firm's capital structure. Industries that have extensive debt financing (such as banks or utilities) will have net income that is sensitive to small changes in operating income.

INTERNATIONAL ECONOMICS Both domestic and overseas events may cause the value of the U.S. dollar to fluctuate. A weaker U.S. dollar helps U.S. industries because their exports become comparatively cheaper in overseas markets while the goods of foreign competitors become more expensive in the United States. A stronger dollar has an opposite effect. Economic growth in world regions or specific countries benefits industries that have a large presence in those areas. The creation of free trade zones, such as the European Community and the North American Free Trade Zone, assist industries that produce goods and services that previously faced quotas or tariffs in partner countries.

CONSUMER SENTIMENT Because it comprises about two-thirds of GDP, consumption spending has a large impact on the economy. Optimistic consumers are more willing to spend and borrow money for expensive goods, such as houses, cars, new clothes, and furniture. Therefore, the performance of consumer cyclical industries will be affected by changes in consumer sentiment and by consumers' willingness and ability to borrow and spend money.

STRUCTURAL ECONOMIC CHANGES AND ALTERNATIVE INDUSTRIES

Influences other than the economy are part of the business environment. Demographics and changes in technology as well as political and regulatory environments all play a role in affecting the cash flow and risk prospects of different industries.

DEMOGRAPHICS In the past 50 years the United States has had a baby boom, a baby bust, and is now enjoying a baby boomlet as members of the baby-boom generation (those born between the end of World War II and the early 1960s) have children. The influx of the baby boom and "the graying of the baby boom" have had a large impact on U.S. consumption, from advertising strategies to house construction to concerns over social security and health care. The study of demographics includes much more than population growth and age distributions. Demographics also includes the geographical distribution of people, the changing ethnic mix in a society, and changes in income distribution. Corporate marketing strategists and Wall Street industry analysts observe demographic trends and determine their effect on different industries and firms.

In the 1990s, the fastest-growing age groups in the United States were those in their forties and fifties, teens, and those over 70; among the declining groups were those between ages 18 and 24. As of the year 2000, more than one in eight Americans are 65 years of age or older. The changing age profile of Americans has implications for resource availability, namely, a possible shortage of entry-level workers leading to an increase in labor costs. It also is going to be difficult to find qualified persons to replace the retiring baby boomers. The "graying"' of the U.S. population also affects U.S. savings patterns, as people in the 40 to 60 age bracket usually save more than younger people. These trends may bode well for the financial services industry, which offers assistance to those who want to invest their savings. Alternatively, a declining population of entry-level workers and a greater propensity for older Americans to save may have a negative impact on some industries, such as the retailing industry.

LIFESTYLES Lifestyles deal with how people live, work, form households, consume, enjoy leisure, and educate themselves. Consumer behavior is affected by trends and fads. The rise and fall of jeans, "designer" jeans, chinos, and other styles in clothes illustrates the sensitivity of some markets to changes in consumer tastes. The increase in divorce rates, dual-career families, population shifts away from cities, and computer-based education and entertainment have influenced numerous industries, including housing, automobiles, convenience and catalog shopping, services, and home entertainment. From an international perspective, some U.S.-brand goods—from blue jeans to movies—have a high demand overseas. They are perceived to be more "in style" and perhaps higher quality than items produced domestically. Sales in several industries have benefited from this exercise of consumer choice overseas.

TECHNOLOGY

Trends in technology can affect both the industry product and the manufacturing and delivery processes. For example, demand has fallen for carburetors on cars because of electronic fuel-injection technology. The engineering process has changed because of the advent of computer-aided design and computer-aided manufacturing. Perpetual improvement of designs in the semiconductor and microprocessor industry has made that industry a difficult one to evaluate. Innovations in process technology allowed steel minimills to grow at the expense of large steel producers. Advances in technology allow some plant sites and buildings to generate their own electricity, bypassing their need for power from the local electric utility. Trucks have reduced railroads' market share in the long-distance carrier industry, and planes, not trains, now mainly carry people long distances. The "information superhighway" is becoming a reality and may lead to linkages between telecommunications and cable TV systems. Changes in technology have spurred capital spending in technological equipment as firms try to use microprocessors and software as a means to gain competitive advantages. The future effect of the Internet is astronomical.

The retailing industry is a user of new technology. Some forecasters envision "relationship merchandising," in which customer databases will allow closer links between retail stores and customer needs.[7] Rather than doing market research to focus on aggregate consumer trends, specialized retailers can offer products that particular consumer segments desire in the locations that consumers prefer. Technology may allow retailers to become more organizationally decentralized and geographically diversified.

Major retailers already use a great deal of technology. Bar-code scanning speeds the checkout process and allows the firm to track inventory. Use of customer credit cards allows firms to track customer purchases and send custom-made sales announcements. Electronic data interchange (EDI) allows the retailer to electronically communicate with suppliers to order new inventory and pay accounts payable. Electronic funds transfer allows retailers to move funds quickly and easily between local banks and headquarters.

POLITICS AND REGULATIONS

Because political change reflects social values, today's social trend may be tomorrow's law, regulation, or tax. The industry analyst needs to project and assess political changes relevant to the industry under study.

Some regulations and laws are based on economic reasoning. Due to utilities' positions as natural monopolies, their rates must be reviewed and approved by a regulatory body.[8] Some regulation involves social ends. For example, the Food and Drug Administration protects consumers by reviewing new drugs. Public and worker safety concerns spurred creation of the Consumer Product Safety Commission, Environmental Protection Agency, and

---

[7]Carl E. Steidtmann, "General Trends in Retailing," in *The Retail Industry—General Merchandisers and Discounters,* ed. Charles Ingene (Charlottesville, Va.: Association for Investment Management and Research, 1993): 6–9.

[8]Technology can change natural monopolies. We mentioned earlier how some firms are generating their own electrical power. Advancing technology resulted in AT&T losing its monopoly in the early 1980s. As another example of technology change leading to regulatory change, by the mid- and late 1990s, numerous states were allowing electric utilities to compete for customers.

OSHA. Well-meaning, overzealous regulators or politicians may try to "micromanage" an industry, resulting in increasing firms' costs and restricting entry into the industry.

Some regulations arise because of concerns about fairness. Tax increases on higher incomes affect profitable firms and individuals. The oil windfall-profits tax that was instituted during the 1973 oil crisis taxed oil companies to reduce the benefit they would receive from selling oil at OPEC's higher prices.

Regulatory changes have affected numerous industries. The Depository Institution Deregulation and Monetary Control Act (DIDMCA) of 1980 transformed the savings and loan industry; the Financial Institutions Reform, Recovery and Enforcement Act of 1989 (FIRREA) was intended to reverse some of the excesses caused by the DIDMCA. Changing regulations and technology are bringing the various aspects of the financial services industry—banking, insurance, investment banking, and investment services—together.

Regulations and laws affect international commerce. International tax laws, tariffs, quotas, embargoes, and other trade barriers may affect different industries in various ways.

The retail industry is affected by several political and regulatory factors. First is the minimum-wage law, which specifies the minimum wage that can be paid to workers. A second factor is the uncertain result of health-care reform debate. Employer-paid health insurance would dramatically affect the labor costs of labor-intensive service industries, such as retailing. Third, because goods must first be delivered to the stores, regulations that affect the cost of shipping by airplane, ship, or truck will affect retailers' costs. Finally, trends toward open international markets lead to the elimination or reduction of tariffs and quotas, which allows retailers to offer imported goods at lower prices, which will assist them in expanding their international marketing.

ESTIMATING INDUSTRY RATES OF RETURN

Having determined that industry analysis helps an investor select profitable investment opportunities, how do we go about valuing an industry and estimating the expected rate of return that an investment will provide? Again, we consider the two equity valuation approaches introduced in Chapter 13—the present value of cash flows and the relative valuation ratios. Beginning with the present value of cash flow models, we demonstrate the DDM with the two-stage growth assumption and then assume constant growth for the retail drugstore industry. Following this we consider the present value of free cash flow (FCF) model. This will be followed by an analysis of the alternative relative valuation techniques with the price/earnings ratio and analysis of the P/BV, P/CF, and P/S ratios relative to the comparable market valuation ratios presented in Chapter 18.

Although our investment decision is always the same, the form of the comparison depends on which valuation approach is being used. In the case of the present value of cash flow techniques, we derive a present value for the industry using our required rate of return for the equity of the industry. Therefore, the critical comparison is the present value of the specified cash flow versus the prevailing value of the index. If our estimated present value exceeds the prevailing index value, it indicates we should overweight the industry. Alternatively, if the PV is less than the industry index, it implies that the industry is overvalued (i.e., the industry will not provide our required rate of return if acquired at this price) and we should underweight this industry in our portfolio.

In contrast, if we use the two-step P/E ratio approach, we compute an expected value at the end of our investment horizon and compute an expected rate of return for the period based on this ending value and the expected dividend return during the period. If this expected rate of return exceeds the required rate of return (k), you should overweight the industry; if the return is below k, you should underweight the industry.

To demonstrate industry analysis, we use Standard and Poor's Retail Store—Drug index to represent industrywide data for this industry. This retail store—drug index (hereinafter referred to as the retail drugstore [RDS] industry) contains three companies: (1) Longs Drug Stores, (2) Rite-Aid, and (3) Walgreen Company. The industry was selected because it should be reasonably familiar to most observers and because it is consistent with the subsequent company analysis of Walgreen.

Valuation Using the Reduced Form DDM

Recall that the reduced form DDM is:

$$P_i = \frac{D_1}{k - g}$$

where:

P_i = the price of industry i at time t
D_1 = expected dividend for industry i in period 1 equal to $D_0 (1 + g)$
k = the required rate of return on the equity for industry i
g = the expected long-run growth rate of earnings and dividend for industry i

As always, *the two major estimates for any valuation model are* k *and* g. We will discuss each of these at this point in the chapter with the understanding that we will use these estimates subsequently when applying the two-step, price/earnings ratio technique for valuation.

ESTIMATING THE REQUIRED RATE OF RETURN (k) Because the required rate of return (k) on all investments is influenced by the risk-free rate and the expected inflation rate, the differentiating factor in this case is the risk premium for the RDS industry versus the market. In turn, we discussed the risk premium in terms of fundamental factors, including business risk (BR), financial risk (FR), liquidity risk (LR), exchange rate risk (ERR), and country (political) risk (CR). Alternatively, you can estimate the risk premium based on the CAPM, which implies that the risk premium is a function of the systematic risk (beta) of the asset. Therefore, to derive an estimate of the industry's risk premium, you should examine the BR, FR, LR, ERR, and CR for the industry and compare these industry risk factors to those of the aggregate market. Alternatively, you can compute the systematic risk (beta) for the industry and compare this to the market beta of 1.0. Prior to calculating a beta for the industry, we briefly discuss the fundamental risk factors for the industry.

Business risk is a function of relative sales volatility and operating leverage. We know that the annual percentage changes in retail drugstore sales was less volatile than aggregate sales as represented by PCE. Also, the OPM (operating profit margin) for retail drugstores was less volatile than the S&P 400 OPM. Therefore, because both sales and the OPM for the RDS industry were less volatile than the market, operating profits are substantially less volatile. This implies that the business risk for the RDS industry is *below average.*

The *financial risk* for this industry is difficult to judge because of widespread use of building leases in the industry. Still, on the basis of the reported data on debt to total capital or interest coverage ratios, the FR for this industry is substantially below the market. Assuming substantial use of long-term lease contracts, this industry probably has financial risk *about equal* to the market.

To evaluate the liquidity risk for an industry, it is necessary to estimate the liquidity risk for all the firms in the industry and derive a composite view. The fact is, there is substantial variation in market liquidity among the firms in this industry. Walgreen is very liquid, whereas Longs Drug Stores and Rite-Aid are relatively illiquid. A conservative view is that the RDS industry probably has *above-average* liquidity risk.

Exchange rate risk (ERR) is the uncertainty of earnings due to changes in exchange rates faced by firms in this industry that sell outside the United States. The amount of ERR is determined by what proportion of sales is non-U.S., how these sales are distributed among countries, and the exchange rate volatility for these countries. This risk could range from an industry with very limited international sales (e.g., a service industry that is not involved overseas) to an industry that is clearly worldwide (e.g., the chemical or pharmaceutical industry). For a truly global industry, you need to examine the distribution of sales among specific countries because we know that the exchange rate risk varies among countries based on the volatility of exchange rates with the U.S. dollar. The ERR for the RDS industry would be *quite low* because sales and earnings for these drugstore firms are almost wholly attributable to activity within the United States.

The existence of *country risk* (*CR*) is likewise a function of the proportion of foreign sales, the specific foreign countries involved, and the stability of the political/economic system in these countries. As noted, there is very little CR in the United Kingdom and Japan, but there can be substantial CR in China, Russia, or South Africa. For the RDS industry, country risk would be very low because of limited foreign sales.

In summary, for the RDS industry, business risk is definitely below average, financial risk is about equal to the market, liquidity risk is above average, and exchange rate risk and country risk are almost nonexistent. The consensus is that the overall risk for the RDS industry is clearly lower than for the aggregate market on the basis of fundamental characteristics.

The *systematic risk* for the retail drugstore industry is computed using the market model as follows:

$$\%\Delta\, RDS_t = \alpha_i + \beta_i\,(\%\Delta \text{ S\&P } 500_t)$$

where:

$\%\,\Delta$ RDS$_t$ = the percentage price change in the retail drugstore (RDS) index during month t
α_i = the regression intercept for the RDS industry
β_i = the systematic risk measure for the RDS industry equal to $\text{Cov}_{i,m}/\sigma^2_m$

To derive an estimate for the RDS industry, the model specified was run with monthly data for the 5-year period 1994 to 1998. The results for this regression are as follows:

$\alpha_t = 0.004$	$R^2 = 0.66$
$\beta_t = 0.75$	$DW = 1.78$
t-value $= 8.70$	$F = 70.52$

The systematic risk ($\beta = 0.75$) for the RDS industry is clearly below unity, indicating a low-risk industry (i.e., risk less than the market). These results are quite consistent with the prior analysis of fundamental risk factors (BR, FR, LR, ERR, CR).

Translating this systematic risk into a required rate of return estimate (k) calls for using the security market line model as follows:

$$k_i = \text{RFR} + \beta_i (R_m - \text{RFR})$$

Recall that in Chapter 18 we derived three estimates for the required market rate of return based upon alternative risk premiums (0.064 − 0.095 − 0.117). For our purposes here, it seems like the midpoint is reasonable—i.e., a nominal RFR of 0.055 and an R_m of 0.095. This, combined with a beta for the industry at 0.75, indicates the following:

$$\begin{aligned} k &= 0.055 + 0.75\,(0.095 - 0.055) \\ &= 0.055 + 0.03 \\ &= 0.085 = 8.50\% \end{aligned}$$

A microestimate of fundamental risk below average and a risk estimate using the CAPM likewise below average implies an industry earnings multiple *above* the market multiple, all other factors being equal.

ESTIMATING THE EXPECTED GROWTH RATE (g) You will recall that earnings and dividend growth are determined by the retention rate and the return on equity.

$$g = f\,(\text{Retention Rate and Return on Equity})$$

We have consistently broken down return on equity into the following three components:

$$\begin{aligned} \frac{\text{Net Profit}}{\text{Equity}} &= \frac{\text{Net Income}}{\text{Sales}} \times \frac{\text{Sales}}{\text{Total Assets}} \times \frac{\text{Total Assets}}{\text{Equity}} \\ &= \begin{matrix}\text{Profit}\\ \text{Margin}\end{matrix} \times \begin{matrix}\text{Total Asset}\\ \text{Turnover}\end{matrix} \times \begin{matrix}\text{Financial}\\ \text{Leverage}\end{matrix} \end{aligned}$$

Therefore, we need to examine each of these variables in Table 19.1 to determine if they imply a difference in the expected growth rate for RDS as compared to the aggregate market (S&P 400).

Earnings Retention Rate The retention rate data in Table 19.1 indicate that the RDS industry has a higher retention rate (68 percent versus 53 percent). This means that the RDS industry would have a potentially *higher* growth rate, all else being the same (i.e., equal ROE).

Return on Equity Because the return on equity is a function of the net profit margin, total asset turnover, and a measure of financial leverage, these three variables are examined individually.

Historically, the net profit margin for the S&P 400 series has been consistently higher than the margin for the RDS industry. This is not surprising because retail firms typically have lower profit margins but higher turnover. This difference in profit margin increased in 1997 because the S&P 400 margin experienced a small change and the RDS industry margin declined substantially to less than 2 percent.

As noted, one would normally expect the total asset turnover (TAT) for a retail firm to be higher than the average company. This expectation has typically been confirmed because the average TAT for the S&P 400 was 1.09 versus 2.76 for the RDS industry. Beyond the overall difference, the spread between the two series changed over the period.

TABLE 19.1 EARNINGS MULTIPLIER FOR THE S&P 400 AND THE RDS INDUSTRY, AND INFLUENTIAL VARIABLES: 1977–1997

	Earnings Multiplier (t + 1)		Retention Rate		Net Profit Margin		Total Asset Turnover		Return on Total Assets		Total Assets/ Equity		Return on Equity	
Year	S&P 400	RDS	S&P 400	RDS	S&P 400	RDS	S&P 400	RDS	S&P 400	RDS	S&P 400	RDS	S&P 400	RDS
1977	9.42	8.39	56.80	79.90	5.15	4.07	1.27	2.84	6.54	11.56	2.08	1.53	13.60	17.68
1978	8.71	6.58	58.80	76.10	5.19	4.03	1.27	2.81	6.59	11.32	2.15	1.52	14.17	17.21
1979	7.61	7.18	63.70	72.60	5.57	3.47	1.30	3.00	7.24	10.41	2.20	1.65	15.93	17.18
1980	7.47	8.13	59.70	70.80	4.92	3.47	1.31	3.04	6.45	10.55	2.23	1.66	14.37	17.51
1981	9.21	10.72	58.10	69.00	4.86	3.45	1.28	3.03	6.22	10.45	2.25	1.65	14.00	17.25
1982	9.24	9.27	46.00	68.90	3.95	3.44	1.17	2.97	4.62	10.22	2.31	1.66	10.68	16.96
1983	13.83	9.66	50.40	70.70	4.42	3.79	1.15	2.86	5.08	10.84	2.28	1.88	11.59	20.38
1984	13.82	11.76	58.50	62.40	4.77	3.04	1.22	2.65	5.82	8.06	2.39	1.93	13.91	15.55
1985	13.93	14.38	48.50	59.20	3.84	2.96	1.15	2.68	4.42	7.93	2.54	1.88	11.22	14.91
1986	15.15	12.52	44.00	67.10	3.75	3.11	1.07	2.71	4.01	8.43	2.58	1.94	10.35	16.35
1987	15.70	12.20	57.00	68.40	4.77	2.88	1.08	2.80	5.15	8.06	2.62	2.04	13.50	16.45
1988	13.91	11.28	63.10	69.40	5.51	2.90	0.98	2.82	5.40	8.18	3.03	2.07	16.36	16.93
1989	14.01	14.72	55.97	67.71	5.01	2.79	0.97	2.82	4.86	7.87	3.16	2.03	15.36	15.97
1990	13.87	23.19	49.80	68.32	4.26	2.89	0.97	2.82	4.13	8.13	3.27	2.00	13.50	16.26
1991	15.59	22.51	28.19	67.19	2.97	2.91	0.94	2.85	2.80	8.31	3.24	1.83	9.09	15.25
1992	22.51	22.50	33.86	66.41	3.27	2.89	0.96	2.83	3.13	8.19	3.50	1.82	10.95	14.89
1993	15.43	15.85	41.96	53.17	3.73	2.15	0.92	2.79	3.42	6.00	3.76	1.88	12.86	11.27
1994	13.83	15.14	61.06	66.22	5.24	2.89	0.95	2.63	4.89	7.60	3.51	2.00	17.14	15.17
1995	15.46	15.53	60.61	66.33	5.24	2.84	0.97	2.66	5.08	7.55	3.32	2.03	16.87	15.33
1996	26.28	18.15	69.14	71.19	5.86	3.21	0.93	2.02	5.45	6.48	3.26	2.17	17.77	14.06
1997	26.36	26.22	60.31	59.05	5.61	1.96	0.94	2.23	5.27	4.37	3.33	2.18	17.55	9.53
Mean	14.35	14.09	53.26	67.62	4.66	3.10	1.09	2.76	5.07	8.60	2.81	1.87	13.85	15.82

Source: *Standard & Poor's Analysts Handbook* (New York: Standard & Poor's Corp., 1998). Reprinted by permission of Standard & Poor's Corp.

FIGURE 19.3

TIME-SERIES PLOT OF TOTAL ASSET TURNOVER FOR THE S&P 400 AND THE RDS INDUSTRY: 1977–1997

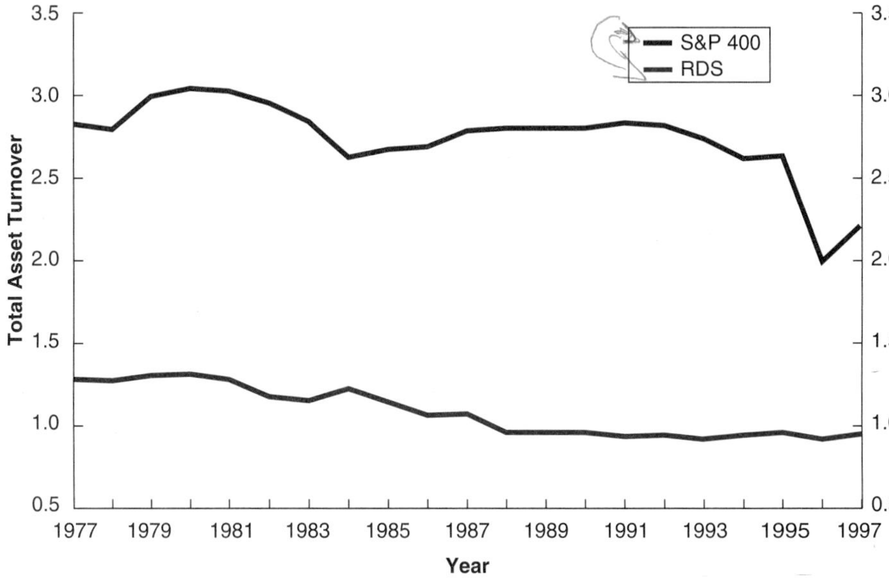

S&P 400
RDS
Total Asset Turnover
3.5
3.0
2.5
2.0
1.5
1.0
0.5
1977
1979
1981
1983
1985
1987
1989
1991
1993
1995
1997
Year

This change occurred because the TAT for the S&P 400 series declined steadily over the period while the TAT for the RDS industry declined sharply during the last two years from about 2.6 to about 2.2 as shown in Figure 19.3. Multiplying these two ratios indicates the industry's return on total assets (ROTA).[9]

$$\frac{\text{Net Income}}{\text{Sales}} \times \frac{\text{Sales}}{\text{Total Assets}} = \frac{\text{Net Income}}{\text{Total Assets}}$$

When we do this for the two series, the results in Table 19.1 indicate that the return on total assets (ROTA) for the S&P 400 series went from 6.54 percent in 1977 to 5.27 percent in 1997 and averaged 5.07 percent, whereas the ROTA for the RDS industry went from 11.56 percent to 4.37 percent and averaged 8.60 percent. Clearly the industry ROTA results were superior on average, although the industry experienced a serious decline in 1997 while the market's performance was quite strong. As a result, in 1997, the ROTA for the market series (S&P 400) was larger than that for the RDS industry.

The final component is the financial leverage multiplier (total assets/equity). As shown in Table 19.1 and Figure 19.4, the leverage multiplier for the S&P 400 increased overall from 2.08 to 3.33, whereas the leverage multiplier for the RDS industry went from 1.53 to 2.18. Although this higher financial leverage multiplier implies greater financial risk for both the S&P 400 series and the RDS industry, it also will contribute to a higher ROE, all else being the same.

[9]The reader is encouraged to read Appendix 19C to this chapter, which contains a discussion of an article by Selling and Stickney wherein they analyze the components of ROA and relate this to an industry's economics and its strategy: Thomas Selling and Clyde Stickney, "The Effects of Business Environment and Strategy on a Firm's Rate of Return on Assets," *Financial Analysts Journal* 39, no. 1 (January–February 1983).

FIGURE 19.4

TIME-SERIES PLOT OF FINANCIAL LEVERAGE FOR THE S&P 400 AND THE RDS INDUSTRY: 1977–1997

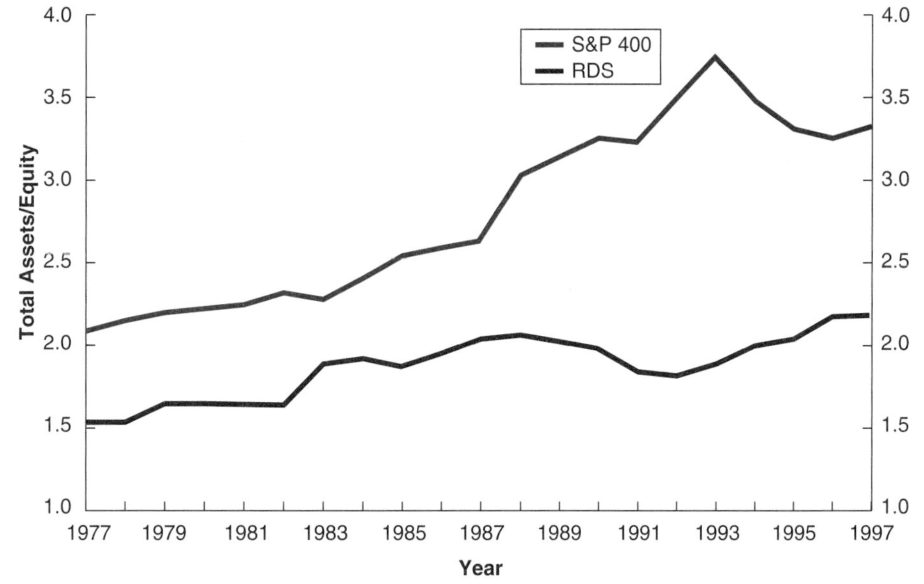
S&P 400
RDS
Total Assets/Equity
4.0
3.5
3.0
2.5
2.0
1.5
1.0
1977
1979
1981
1983
1985
1987
1989
1991
1993
1995
1997
Year

FIGURE 19.5

TIME-SERIES PLOT OF THE RETURN ON EQUITY FOR THE S&P 400 AND THE RDS INDUSTRY: 1977–1997

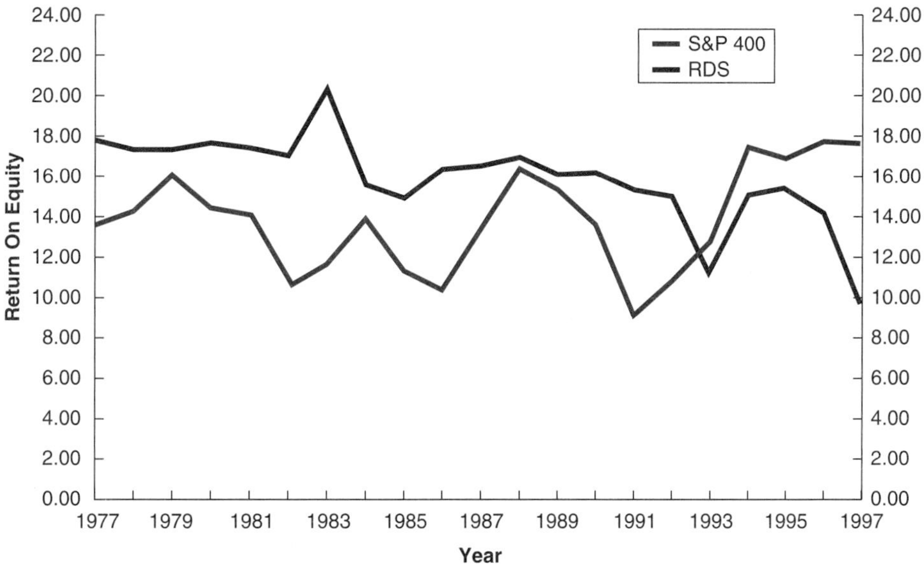
S&P 400
RDS
Return On Equity
24.00
22.00
20.00
18.00
16.00
14.00
12.00
10.00
8.00
6.00
4.00
2.00
0.00
1977
1979
1981
1983
1985
1987
1989
1991
1993
1995
1997
Year

This brings us to the final value of ROE, which is the product of the three ratios (profit margin, total asset turnover, and financial leverage), or the product of return on total asset and the financial leverage multiplier. The figures in Table 19.1 and the plot in Figure 19.5 indicate that the ROE for the RDS industry was higher than the market throughout the period until 1993. The average annual ROE was 15.82 percent for the RDS industry versus

13.85 percent for the S&P 400 series. These average percentages are quite consistent with what would be derived from multiplying the averages of the components from Table 19.1 as follows:

ROE ESTIMATE BASED ON TOTAL PERIOD AVERAGES (1977–1997)

	Profit Margin		Total Asset Turnover		Total Assets/ Equity		ROE
S&P 400	4.66	×	1.09	×	2.81	=	14.27
RDS Industry	3.10	×	2.76	×	1.87	=	16.00

Although examining the historical trends and the averages for each of the components is important, you should never lose sight of the fact that expectations of *future* performance will determine the equity value for the industry. In the current case, this analysis of expectations is very important because of the change in relative ROE beginning in 1993. As an analyst, it is necessary to determine whether the change that began in 1993 is a permanent change in the relative performance of this industry versus the market. In this case, you should be very concerned because of the consistently inferior performance of the RDS industry since 1993 and the very poor results for 1997. Specifically, if you use the results for the recent 5-year period (1993–1997), the ROE results are:

ROE ESTIMATE BASED ON RECENT 5-YEAR AVERAGES (1993–1997)

	Profit Margin		Total Asset Turnover		Total Assets/ Equity		ROE
S&P 400	5.14	×	0.94	×	3.44	=	16.62
RDS Industry	2.61	×	2.47	×	2.05	=	13.22

Notably, using the recent results, the ROE results are reversed. Combining these recent ROE results with alternative retention rates provides interesting growth estimates.

GROWTH ESTIMATES BASED ON RECENT ROE WITH HISTORICAL AND RECENT RETENTION RATES

	Recent ROE	Historical RR	Estimated *g*	Recent ROE	Recent RR	Estimated *g*
S&P 400	16.62	.53	8.81	16.62	.57	9.47
RDS Industry	13.22	.68	8.99	13.22	.63	8.33

The point is, using full-period retention results indicates almost equal expected *g*. Alternatively, using the retention rates for the recent 5-year period indicates a higher *g* for the market. Given the consistent decline in *g* for the industry when we consider the recent results (lower ROE, lower retention rate), it is probably appropriate to use a growth estimate for the RDS industry that is close to the recent conservative estimate—that is, 8.5 percent.

TABLE 19.2 **DIVIDEND DISCOUNT CALCULATIONS**

Year	Estimated Dividend	Discount Factor @ 8.5%	Present Value of Dividend
1999	5.37	—	—
2000	5.83	0.9217	5.37
2001	6.33	0.8495	5.38
2002	6.86	0.7829	5.37
2003	7.41	0.7216	5.35
2004	8.00	0.6650	5.32
2005	8.60	0.6129	5.27
2006	9.25	0.5649	5.23
Cont. Value[a]	660.00	0.5649	372.83
		Total Value	**$410.12**

[a]Constant Growth Rate = 7%

Continuing Value: $\dfrac{D_1}{k - g} = \dfrac{\$9.25\ (1.07)}{0.085 - 0.070} = \dfrac{\$9.90}{0.015} = \$660$

COMBINING THE ESTIMATES At this point we have the following estimates:

$$k = 0.085$$
$$g = 0.085$$
$$D_0 = \$4.95 \text{ (recent 12-month dividends)}$$
$$D_1 = \$4.95 \times 1.085 = \$5.37 \text{ (estimated dividend for 1999)}$$

Because of the equality between k and g (this g is above the long-run market norm of about 7 percent and probably cannot be sustained) we need to evaluate this industry using the temporary growth company model discussed in Chapter 13. We will assume the following growth pattern:

2000–2002	0.085
2003–2004	0.080
2005–2006	0.075
2007–onward	0.070

Using these estimates of k and this growth pattern, the computation of value for the industry using the DDM is contained in Table 19.2.

These computations imply a value of $410.12 compared to a price for the industry index of about $640.00 in mid-1999. Therefore, according to this valuation model and these k and g estimates, this industry is about 50 percent overvalued at this time. As will be shown below, a fairly small change in the $k - g$ spread can have a large effect on the estimated value.

If we assumed a constant growth rate of 7 percent from the beginning and a D_1 of $5.83, the value would be even lower as follows:

$$P = \frac{5.83}{(0.085 - 0.070)} = \frac{5.83}{0.015} = 388.67$$

This is clearly a low estimate of value since it assumes the base growth rate of 7 percent from the beginning. To demonstrate the effect of a change in the $k - g$ spread, if we assume a decline in this spread from 0.015 to 0.01 because of either a lower k or a higher g or some combination of the two, the value of the industry would be:

$$P = \frac{5.83}{0.010} = \$583$$

This is still below the current price of \$640, but if we reduce the spread to 0.009, the value becomes \$648 (5.83/0.009), which exceeds the prevailing price. The question becomes: how do you justify such a $k-g$ spread in terms of the two components? The point is, using this model, if you cannot justify a lower k than 8.50 percent or a higher long-run growth rate (g) than 7.00 percent, you would conclude that this industry is overvalued and should be underweighted in your portfolio.

Industry Valuation Using the Free Cash Flow to Equity (FCFE) Model

Similar to the presentation in Chapter 18, we initially define the FCFE series and present the series for the recent 12-year period, including an estimate for 1998 in Table 19.3. Given these data, we will consider the historical growth rates for the components and for the final FCFE series as inputs to estimating future growth for the valuation models. You will recall that FCFE is defined (measured) as follows:

Net Income
+ Depreciation expense
− Capital expenditures
− Δ in working capital
− Principal debt repayments
+ New debt issues

As noted, the FCFE data inputs and final annual value of FCFE for the RDS industry for the period 1987–1998 is contained in Table 19.3, along with 5-year and 10-year growth rates of the components. Using this data, we derive an estimate using the FCFE model under two scenarios: (1) a constant growth rate from the present, and (2) a two-stage growth rate assumption.

THE CONSTANT GROWTH RATE FCFE MODEL We know that the constant growth rate model requires that the growth rate (g) be lower than the required rate of return (k), which we have specified as 8.50 percent. In the current case, this is difficult because both the 10-year and the 5-year growth rates exceed this. Still, in order to use the model, we assume a 10 percent growth in 1999, and 7 percent long-run growth in subsequent years. The result is as follows:

$g = 0.07$ (long-run growth beginning in 2000)

$k = 0.085$

FCFE (1998) = \$8.41

FCFE (1999) = \$8.41 (1.10) = \$9.25 = $FCFE_0$

$$V = \frac{FCFE_1}{k - g}$$

$$= \frac{9.25\ (1.07)}{0.085 - 0.070} = \frac{9.90}{0.015}$$

$$= 660$$

TABLE 19.3 **COMPONENTS OF FREE CASH FLOW ANALYSIS FOR THE RETAIL DRUGSTORE INDUSTRY**

Year	Net Income	Depreciation Expense	Capital Expenditure	Δ in Work. Capital	Principal Repayment	New Debt Issues	Total FCFE
1987	5.53	2.63	5.80	2.37	—	2.00	1.99
1988	6.30	3.09	6.72	2.50	—	0.65	0.82
1989	6.69	3.39	6.02	9.36	—	7.00	1.70
1990	7.67	4.15	7.62	2.37	—	0.83	2.66
1991	8.26	4.03	7.73	0.16	4.40	—	—
1992	8.96	4.39	7.19	1.96	1.03	—	3.17
1993	7.09	4.75	9.24	0.14	—	2.71	5.17
1994	10.51	5.32	11.40	2.20	—	3.93	6.16
1995	11.76	6.02	13.97	3.30	—	4.16	4.67
1996	13.92	6.07	15.00	14.33	—	20.14	10.80
1997	10.77	8.45	17.40	(5.04)	3.74	—	3.12
1998E	15.62	9.46	20.76	3.71	—	7.80	8.41
5-Year Growth Rate	17.11	14.78	17.58	92.64	NMF	23.55	10.22
10-Year Growth Rate	9.51	11.84	11.94	4.04	NMF	28.21	26.21

E = Estimates.

This $660 value exceeds the industry price of about $640 that prevailed in mid-1999. This implies that the industry is undervalued and should be overweighted in the portfolio.

THE TWO-STAGE GROWTH FCFE MODEL As before, we assume a period of above-average growth for several years followed by a second period of constant growth at 7 percent. The period of above-average growth will be as follows based upon the 10 percent growth rate of FCFE experienced during the recent 5-year period.

1999	10%
2000	10%
2001	9%
2002	9%
2003	8%
2004	8%
2005–onward	7%

Assuming a k of 8.5 percent and an FCFE of $8.41 in 1998 and $9.25 in 1999, the value for the industry is as shown in Table 19.4. These results are very encouraging for the industry because the computed value of $716 is substantially above the recent market price of about $640. This apparent undervaluation would indicate that the industry should be overweighted in the portfolio.

Notably, the alternative present value of cash flow models have generated a fairly wide range of values as follows:

Model	Computed Value
Constant growth DDM	$389
Two-stage growth DDM	$410
Constant growth FCFE	$660
Two-stage growth FCFE	$716

TABLE 19.4 **COMPUTATION OF RDS INDUSTRY VALUE USING THE FCFE MODEL AND TWO-STAGE GROWTH**

Year	FCFE	Discount Factor @ 0.085	Present Value
2000	10.18	0.9217	9.38
2001	11.09	0.8495	9.42
2002	12.09	0.7829	9.47
2003	13.06	0.7216	9.42
2004	14.10	0.6650	9.38
Cont. Value[a]	1006.00	0.6650	668.99
		Total Present Value	**$716.06**

[a] $\frac{15.09}{0.085 - 0.070} = 1006$

Because of this wide range of estimated values whereby two indicate overvaluation and two indicate undervaluation, it is clear that a critical variable is the *k–g* spread. Specifically, the spread needs to be smaller for the DDM and could be larger for the FCFE models.

INDUSTRY ANALYSIS USING THE RELATIVE VALUATION APPROACH

This section contains a discussion and demonstration of the relative valuation ratio techniques: (1) price/earnings ratios (P/E), (2) the price to book value ratios (P/BV), (3) the price to cash flow ratios (P/CF), and (4) the price to sales ratios (P/S). Again, we will begin with the detailed demonstration of the P/E ratio approach, which provides a specific valuation and an expected rate of return for the industry based upon an estimate of future earnings per share and an industry multiple.

The analysis of the other relative valuation ratios is also more meaningful because we can compare the industry valuation ratios to the market valuation ratios while considering what factors affect the specific valuation ratios.

THE EARNINGS MULTIPLE TECHNIQUE

You will recall that the earnings multiple technique is a two-step process that involves (1) a detailed estimation of future earnings per share, and (2) an estimate of an appropriate earnings multiplier (P/E ratio) based upon a consideration of P/E determinants derived from the DDM.

ESTIMATING EARNINGS PER SHARE To estimate earnings per share, you must start by estimating sales per share. The first part of this section describes three techniques that provide help and insights for the sales estimate. Next, we derive an estimate of earnings per share, which implies a net profit margin for the industry. As in Chapter 18 where we estimated earnings per share for a stock-market series, we begin with the operating profit margin because it is less volatile and easier to estimate than the net profit margin. Then we subtract estimates of depreciation and interest expenses and apply a tax rate to find the earnings per share.

Forecasting Sales per Share Three techniques can be useful when deriving a sales forecast for an industry:

FIGURE 19.6 **LIFE CYCLE FOR AN INDUSTRY**

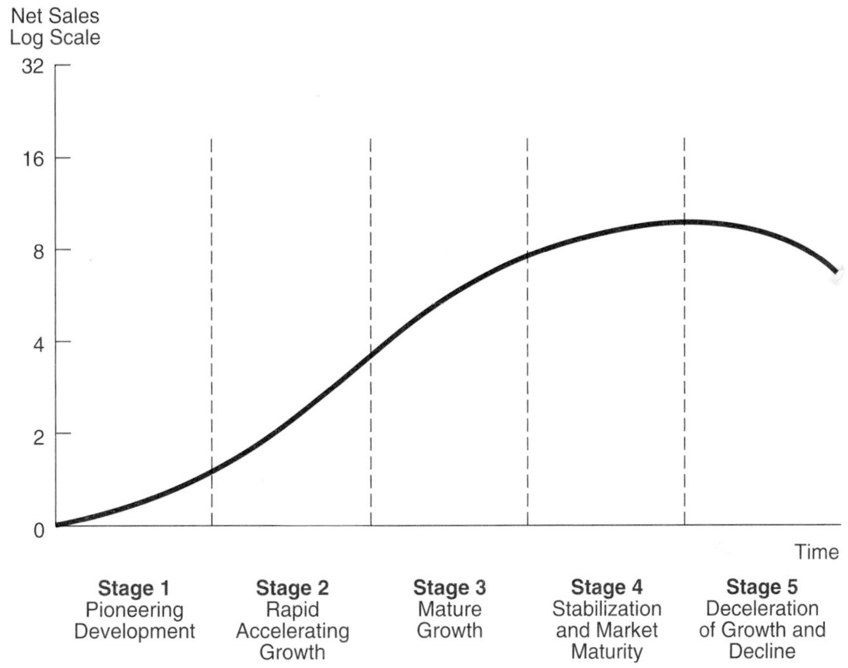
Net Sales
Log Scale
32
16
8
4
2
0
Time
Stage 1
Pioneering Development
Stage 2
Rapid Accelerating Growth
Stage 3
Mature Growth
Stage 4
Stabilization and Market Maturity
Stage 5
Deceleration of Growth and Decline

1. Industry life cycle
2. Input–output analysis
3. Industry–aggregate economy relationship

Notably, these techniques are *not* competing alternatives, but are complementary and supplementary. Together they will help you develop a complete picture of the current position and outlook of the industry under a variety of scenarios.

Sales forecasting and the industry life cycle An insightful analysis when predicting industry sales is to view the industry over time and divide its development into stages, similar to those that humans progress through as they move from birth to adolescence to adulthood to middle age to old age. The number of stages in this **industry life cycle analysis** can vary based on how much detail you want. A five-stage model would include:

1. Pioneering development
2. Rapid accelerating growth
3. Mature growth
4. Stabilization and market maturity
5. Deceleration of growth and decline

Figure 19.6 shows the growth path of sales during each stage. The vertical scale in logs reflects *rates* of growth, whereas the arithmetic horizontal scale has different widths representing different, unequal time periods. To estimate industry sales, you must predict the length of time for each stage. This requires answers to such questions as: How long will an industry grow at an accelerating rate (Stage 2)? How long will it be in a mature growth phase (Stage 3) before its sales growth stabilizes (Stage 4) and then declines (Stage 5)?

Besides being useful when estimating sales, this analysis of an industry's life cycle also can provide some insights into profit margins and earnings growth, although these profit measures do not necessarily parallel the sales growth. The profit margin series typically peaks very early in the total cycle and then levels off and declines as competition is attracted by the early success of the industry.

To illustrate the contribution of life cycle stages to sales estimates, we briefly describe these stages and their effects on sales growth and profits:

1. *Pioneering development.* During this start-up stage, the industry experiences modest sales growth and very small or negative profit margins and profits. The market for the industry's product or service during this time period is small, and the firms involved incur major development costs.
2. *Rapid accelerating growth.* During this rapid growth stage, a market develops for the product or service and demand becomes substantial. The limited number of firms in the industry face little competition and individual firms can experience substantial backlogs. The profit margins are very high. The industry builds its productive capacity as sales grow at an increasing rate as the industry attempts to meet excess demand. High sales growth and high profit margins that increase as firms become more efficient cause industry and firm profits to explode. During this phase, profits can grow at over 100 percent a year as a result of the low earnings base and because of the rapid growth of sales and net profit margins.
3. *Mature growth.* The success in Stage 2 has satisfied most of the demand for the industry goods or service. Thus future sales growth may be above normal, but it no longer accelerates. For example, if the overall economy is growing at 8 percent, sales for this industry might grow at a stabilizing rate of 15 percent to 20 percent a year. Also, the rapid growth of sales and the high profit margins attract competitors to the industry, which causes an increase in supply and lower prices such that the profit margins begin to decline to normal levels.
4. *Stabilization and market maturity.* During this stage, which is probably the longest phase, the industry growth rate declines to the point where it matches the growth rate of the aggregate economy or the segment of the economy of which the industry is a part. During this stage, investors can estimate growth easily because sales correlate highly with an economic series. Although sales grow in line with the economy, profit growth varies by industry because the competitive structure varies by industry, and by individual firms within the industry because management ability to control costs differs among companies. Competition produces tight profit margins, and the rates of return on capital (e.g., return on assets, return on equity) eventually become equal to or slightly below the competitive level.
5. *Deceleration of growth and decline.* At this stage of maturity, the industry's sales growth declines because of shifts in demand or growth of substitutes. Profit margins continue to be squeezed, and some firms experience low profits or even losses. Firms that remain profitable may show very low rates of return on capital. Finally, investors begin thinking about alternative uses for the capital tied up in this industry.

Although these are general descriptions of the alternative life cycle stages, they should help you identify the stage your industry is in, which should help you estimate its potential sales growth. Obviously, everyone is looking for an industry in the early phases of Stage 2 and hopes to avoid industries in Stages 4 or 5. Comparing the sales and earnings growth of an industry to similar growth in the economy should help you identify the industry's stage within the industrial life cycle.

Sales forecasting and input–output analysis Input–output analysis is another way to gain insights regarding the outlook for an industry by separating industries that supply the input for a specific industry from those that get its output. In other words, we want to identify an industry's suppliers and customers. This will help us identify (1) the future demand from customers and (2) the ability of suppliers to provide the goods and services required by the industry. The goal is to determine the long-run sales outlook for both the industry's suppliers and its major customers.[10] To extend this analysis to global industries, we must include worldwide suppliers and customers.

Sales forecasting and the industry–economy relationship A third technique used to forecast industry sales is to compare sales for the industry with one or several aggregate economic series that are related to the goods and services produced by the industry. That is, an analyst tries to find a relationship between the product or services of the industry and the economy. In the following example, we will demonstrate this industry–economy technique for the retail drugstore industry.

Demonstrating a sales forecast The retail drugstore (RDS) industry includes retailers of basic necessities, including pharmaceuticals and medical supplies and many nonmedical products, such as cosmetics, snacks, pop, and liquor. Therefore, we want a series that (1) reflects broad consumption expenditures and (2) gives weight to the impact of medical expenditures. The economic series we consider are personal consumption expenditures (PCE) and PCE-medical care. Table 19.5 contains the aggregate and per-capita values for the two series.

A casual analysis of these time series indicates that although personal consumption expenditures (PCE) have experienced reasonably steady growth of almost 8 percent a year during this period, PCE-medical care has grown at a faster rate of over 10 percent. As a result, as shown in the table's last column, medical care expenditures as a percentage of all PCE have grown from 9.6 percent in 1977 to over 15 percent in 1997. Obviously, as an analyst, you would be pleased because it appears that retail drugstore sales had benefited from this growth in medical expenditures, as shown by the annual growth of drugstore sales of 14 percent.

The scatter plot in Figure 19.7 indicates a strong linear relationship between retail drugstore sales per share and PCE-medical care. Although not shown, there also is a good relationship with PCE. Therefore, if you can accurately estimate changes in these economic series, you should derive a good estimate of expected sales for the RDS industry.

As the industry being analyzed becomes more specialized, you need a more individualized economic series that reflects the demand for the industry's product. The selection of an appropriate economic series is one place where an analyst can demonstrate knowledge and innovation. There also can be instances where industry sales are dependent on several components of the economy, in which case you should probably consider a multivariate model that would include two or more economic series. For example, if you were dealing with the tire industry, you might want to consider new-car production, new-truck production, and a series that would reflect the replacement tire demand.

You also should consider *per-capita* personal consumption expenditures–medical care. Although aggregate PCE-medical care increases each year, there also is an increase in the aggregate population, so the increase in the PCE-medical care per capita (the average PCE-medical care for each adult and child) will be less than the increase in the aggregate series. As an example, during 1998 aggregate PCE-medical care increased about 5.2 percent, but per-capita PCE-medical care increased only 4.8 percent. Finally, an analysis of the relationship between changes in the economic variable and changes in industry sales

[10]For an explanation of input–output analysis, see Howard B. Bonham, Jr., "The Use of Input–Output Economics in Common Stock Analysis," *Financial Analysts Journal* 23, no. 1 (January–February 1967): 27–31.

TABLE 19.5 **S&P RETAIL DRUGSTORE SALES AND VARIOUS ECONOMIC SERIES: 1977–1998**

				PER CAPITA		
Year	Retail Drug-store Sales ($/Share)	Personal Consumption Expenditures ($ Billions)	PCE-Medical Care ($ Billions)	Personal Consumption Expenditures (Dollars)	PCE-Medical Care (Dollars)	Medical Care as a Percentage of PCE
1977	43.99	1,271.5	122,4	5,773.3	555.8	9.6
1978	49.87	1,421.2	139.7	6,400.2	629.1	9.8
1979	73.39	1,583.7	157.8	7,036.9	701.2	10.0
1980	84.82	1,748.1	181.3	7,676.3	796.1	10.4
1981	95.50	1,926.2	213.6	8,376.0	928.8	11.1
1982	109.22	2,059.2	240.5	8,868.7	1,035.8	11.7
1983	118.85	2,257.5	265.7	9,634.8	1,134.0	11.8
1984	135.15	2,460.3	290.6	10,409.7	1,229.5	11.8
1985	153.30	2,667.4	319.3	11,185.7	1,339.0	12.0
1986	157.74	2,850.6	346.4	11,854.5	1,440.5	12.2
1987	191.72	3,052.2	384.7	12,570.6	1,584.4	12.6
1988	217.80	3,296.1	427.7	13,452.3	1,745.6	13.0
1989	239.68	3,523.1	471.9	14,243.8	1,907.9	13.4
1990	265.77	3,761.2	526.2	15,050.2	2,105.5	14.0
1991	283.50	3,902.4	571.9	15,446.3	2,263.7	14.7
1992	309.78	4,136.9	628.3	16,197.3	2,460.0	15.2
1993	329.20	4,378.2	680.5	16,961.9	2,636.4	15.5
1994	363.71	4,627.0	727.1	17,751.7	2,789.6	15.7
1995	413.52	4,953.9	776.2	18822	2,950.3	15.7
1996	434.15	5,215.7	806.8	19639	3,037.9	15.5
1997	549.51	5,493.7	843.4	20508	3,102.4	15.4
1998 (e)	612.86	5,800.7	887.5	21466	3,250.0	15.3
Mean Annual Growth	14.04%	7.68%	10.19%	6.64%	9.12%	

Source: *Standard & Poor's Analysts Handbook* (New York: Standard & Poor's Corporation, 1998). Reprinted by permission of Standard & Poor's Corp. *Economic Report of the President* (Washington, DC: U.S. Government Printing Office, 1999).

will indicate how the two series move together and highlight any changes in the relationship. Using annual percentage changes provides the following regression model:

$$\% \Delta \text{ Industry Sales} = \alpha_i + \beta_i (\% \Delta \text{ in Economic Series})$$

The size of the β_i coefficient should indicate how closely the two series move together. Assuming the intercept (α_i) is close to zero, a slope (β_i) value of 1.00 would indicate relatively equal percentages of change (e.g., this would indicate that a 10 percent increase in PCE typically is associated with a 10 percent increase in industry sales). A β_i of less than unity would imply that industry sales are not as volatile annually as the economy is. This analysis and the levels of relationship reflected in Figure 19.7 would help you find an economic series that closely reflects the demand for the industry's products; it also would indicate the form of the relationship.

As indicated in this analysis, the best relationship was between retail drugstore sales and PCE-medical care. The specific regression result was

$$\% \Delta \text{ Retail Drugstore Sales} = 5.38 + 0.58 (\% \Delta \text{ PCE-Medical Care})$$

$$(t\text{-values}) \qquad (1.75) \quad (1.96)$$

$$R^2 = 0.19$$

FIGURE 19.7 **SCATTER PLOT OF RDS SALES PER SHARE AND PCE-MEDICAL CARE: 1977–1998E**

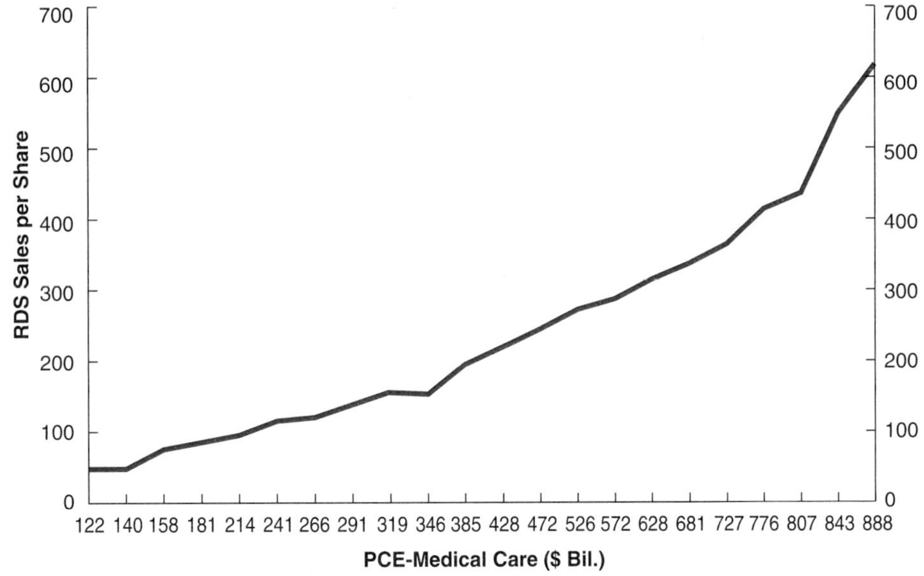
700
600
500
400
300
200
100
0
RDS Sales per Share
122 140 158 181 214 241 266 291 319 346 385 428 472 526 572 628 681 727 776 807 843 888
PCE-Medical Care ($ Bil.)

The specific sales estimate procedure would begin with an estimate of aggregate PCE for the coming year. Given the importance of the PCE series, it should be relatively easy to find one or several estimates. The next step would be to estimate any change (probably an increase) in the proportion of PCE spent on medical care. As noted, this proportion has grown steadily from 9.6 percent to 15.3 percent. Once you estimate this percentage, you apply it to the PCE estimate to arrive at an estimate of the percentage change in PCE-medical care. Finally, you would use this PCE-medical care estimate in a regression equation to derive a sales estimate for the industry. This procedure will be demonstrated in a subsequent section.

FORECASTING EARNINGS PER SHARE

Earnings Forecasting and the Analysis of Industry Competition Similar to the sales forecast that can be enhanced by the analysis of the industrial life cycle, an industry earnings forecast should be preceded by the analyses of the competitive structure for the industry. Specifically, a critical factor affecting the profit potential of an industry is the intensity of competition in the industry, as Porter has discussed in a series of books and articles.[11]

COMPETITION AND EXPECTED INDUSTRY RETURNS

Porter's concept of **competitive strategy** is described as the search by a firm for a favorable competitive position in an industry. To create a profitable competitive strategy, a firm must first examine the basic competitive structure of its industry because the potential profitability of a firm is heavily influenced by the profitability of its industry. After determining the competitive structure of the industry, you examine the factors that determine the

[11]Michael E. Porter, *Competitive Strategy: Techniques for Analyzing Industries and Competitors* (New York: Free Press, 1980): Michael Porter, "Industry Structure and Competitive Strategy: Keys to Profitability," *Financial Analysts Journal* 36, no. 4 (July–August 1980); and Michael Porter, *Competitive Advantage: Creating and Sustaining Superior Performance* (New York: Free Press, 1985), Chapter 1.

relative competitive position of a firm within its industry. In this section, we consider the competitive forces that determine the competitive structure of the industry. In the next chapter, our discussion of company analysis will cover the factors that determine the relative competitive position of a firm within its industry.

BASIC COMPETITIVE FORCES Porter believes that the **competitive environment** of an industry (the intensity of competition among the firms in that industry) determines the ability of the firms to sustain above-average rates of return on invested capital. As shown in Figure 19.8, he suggests that five competitive forces determine the intensity of competition, and that the relative effect of each of these five factors can vary dramatically among industries.

1. *Rivalry among the existing competitors.* For each industry analyzed, you must judge if the rivalry among firms is currently intense and growing, or if it is polite and stable. Rivalry increases when many firms of relatively equal size compete in an industry. When estimating the number and size of firms, be sure to include foreign competitors. Further, *slow growth* causes competitors to fight for market share and increases competition. *High fixed costs* stimulate the desire to sell at the full capacity, which can lead to price cutting and greater competition. Finally, look for *exit barriers,* such as specialized facilities or labor agreements. These can keep firms in the industry despite below-average or negative rates of return.
2. *Threat of new entrants.* Although an industry may have few competitors, you must determine the likelihood of firms entering the industry and increasing competition. *High barriers to entry,* such as low current prices relative to costs, keep the threat of new

FIGURE 19.8 **FORCES DRIVING INDUSTRY COMPETITION**

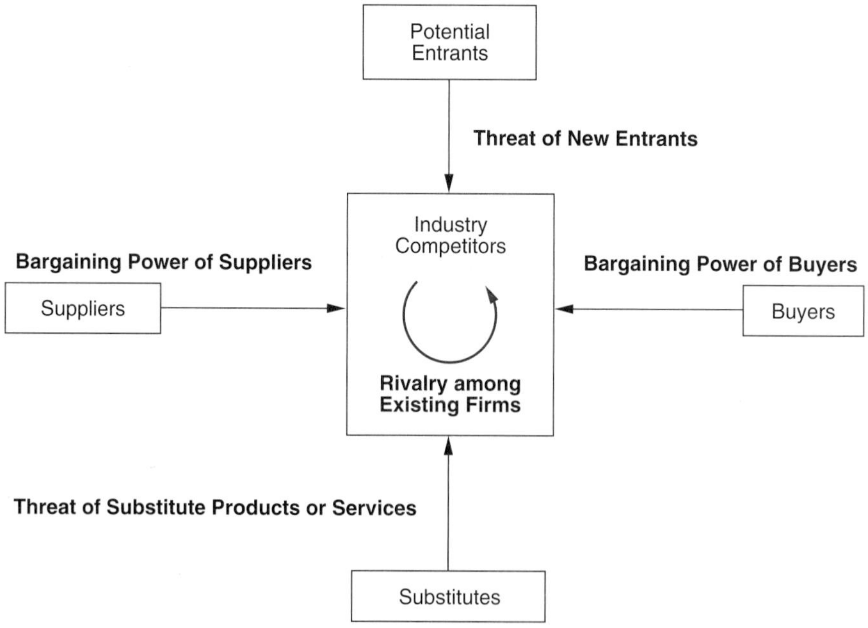
Potential Entrants
Threat of New Entrants
Industry Competitors
Bargaining Power of Suppliers
Bargaining Power of Buyers
Suppliers
Buyers
Rivalry among Existing Firms
Threat of Substitute Products or Services
Substitutes

Source: Adapted/reprinted with the permission of The Free Press, a division of Simon and Schuster, from *Competitive Strategy: Techniques for Analyzing Industries and Competitors,* by Michael E. Porter. Copyright © 1980 by The Free Press.

entrants low. Other barriers to entry include the need to invest large financial resources to compete and the availability of capital. Also, substantial economies of scale give a current industry member an advantage over a new firm. Further entrants might be discouraged if success in the industry requires extensive distribution channels that are hard to build because of exclusive distribution contracts. Similarly, high costs of switching products or brands, such as those required to change a computer or telephone system, keep competition low. Finally, government policy can restrict entry by imposing licensing requirements or limiting access to materials (lumber, coal). Without some of these barriers, it might be very easy for competitors to enter an industry, increasing the competition and driving down potential rates of return.

3. *Threat of substitute products.* Substitute products limit the profit potential of an industry because they limit the prices firms in an industry can charge. Although almost everything has a substitute, you must determine how close the substitute is in price and function to the product in your industry. As an example, the threat of substitute glass containers hurt the metal container industry. Glass containers kept declining in price, forcing metal container prices and profits down. In the food industry, consumers constantly substitute between beef, pork. chicken, and fish. The more commoditylike the product, the greater the competition and the lower the profit margins.
4. *Bargaining power of buyers.* Buyers can influence the profitability of an industry because they can bid down prices or demand higher quality or more services by bargaining among competitors. Buyers become powerful when they purchase a large volume relative to the sales of a supplier. The most vulnerable firm is a one-customer firm that supplies a single large manufacturer, as is common for auto parts manufacturers or software developers. Buyers will be more conscious of the costs of items that represent a significant percentage of the firm's total costs. This consciousness increases if the buying firm is feeling cost pressure from its customers. Also, buyers who know a lot about the costs of supplying an industry will bargain more intensely—for example, when the buying firm supplies some of its own needs and buys from the outside.
5. *Bargaining power of suppliers.* Suppliers can alter future industry returns if they increase prices or reduce the quality of the product or the services they provide. The suppliers are more powerful if they are few and if they are more concentrated than the industry to which they sell, and if they supply critical inputs to several industries, for which few, if any, substitutes exist. In this instance, the suppliers are free to change prices and services they supply to the firms in an industry. When analyzing supplier bargaining power, be sure to consider labor's power within each industry.

An investor needs to analyze these competitive forces to determine the intensity of the competition in an industry and assess the effect of this competition on the industry's long-run profit potential. You should examine each of these factors for every industry and develop a relative competitive profile. You need to update this analysis of an industry's competitive environment over time because an industry's competitive structure can and will change over time.

INDUSTRY PROFIT MARGIN FORECAST Similar to the aggregate market, the net profit margin is the most volatile and the hardest margin to estimate directly. Alternatively, it is suggested that you begin with the operating profit margin (EBITDA/Sales) and then estimate depreciation expense, interest expense, and the tax rate.

The Industry's Operating Profit Margin Recall that in the market analysis, we analyzed the factors that should influence the economy's operating profit margin, including

TABLE 19.6

PROFIT MARGINS AND COMPONENT EXPENSES FOR THE S&P 400 AND THE RDS INDUSTRY INDEX: 1977–1997

	EBITDA ($)		EBITDA Margin (%)		Depreciation Expense ($)		Interest Expense ($)		Tax Rate (%)		Net Profit Margin (%)	
Year	S&P 400	RDS	S&P 400	RDS	S&P 400	RDS	S&P 400	RDS	S&P 400	RDS	S&P 400	RDS
1977	32.20	3.94	14.36	8.96	8.53	0.41	3.22	0.13	48.90	48.60	5.15	4.07
1978	36.19	4.38	14.40	8.78	9.64	0.49	3.81	0.13	49.00	47.90	5.19	4.03
1979	42.01	5.31	14.37	7.24	10.82	0.71	4.58	0.23	46.00	45.70	5.57	3.47
1980	43.08	6.00	13.16	7.07	12.37	0.83	5.95	0.28	45.60	44.70	4.92	3.47
1981	44.50	6.85	12.92	7.17	13.82	1.02	7.49	0.39	43.30	44.20	4.86	3.45
1982	42.67	7.97	12.78	7.30	15.30	1.21	8.23	0.41	45.00	44.60	3.95	3.44
1983	45.57	9.48	13.64	7.98	15.67	1.40	7.62	0.43	44.60	45.00	4.42	3.79
1984	51.50	9.72	13.56	7.19	16.31	1.71	8.54	0.78	42.70	45.10	4.77	3.04
1985	53.23	10.73	13.36	7.00	18.19	2.02	9.24	0.73	46.70	45.90	3.84	2.96
1986	51.02	11.62	13.16	7.37	19.41	2.08	9.75	0.77	42.70	45.10	3.75	3.11
1987	58.89	13.57	13.68	7.08	20.21	2.63	10.14	1.17	40.50	43.90	4.77	2.88
1988	74.31	14.60	15.26	6.70	23.59	3.09	14.84	1.42	35.30	38.60	5.51	2.90
1989	79.52	16.08	14.69	6.71	24.21	3.39	18.79	1.65	37.00	37.80	5.01	2.79
1990	82.47	17.84	13.87	6.71	26.31	4.15	20.17	1.63	39.60	38.30	4.26	2.89
1991	75.10	18.49	12.80	6.52	27.50	4.03	18.74	1.32	41.19	36.70	2.97	2.91
1992	78.17	19.68	13.00	6.35	29.48	4.39	16.20	1.08	37.91	36.95	3.27	2.89
1993	82.16	20.56	13.61	6.25	28.72	4.75	14.66	0.80	37.27	39.29	3.73	2.15
1994	91.28	23.36	14.58	6.42	29.58	5.32	12.79	1.01	36.12	38.29	5.24	2.89
1995	104.67	26.93	15.47	6.51	33.06	6.02	14.21	1.57	36.62	38.62	5.24	2.84
1996	112.69	28.34	16.05	6.53	36.71	6.07	14.32	2.05	36.47	37.19	5.86	3.21
1997	123.15	38.81	16.40	7.06	39.77	8.45	14.84	3.08	35.62	45.11	5.61	1.96

Source: *Standard & Poor's Analysts Handbook* (New York: Standard & Poor's Corporation, 1998). Reprinted by permission of Standard & Poor's Corp.

capacity utilization, unit labor cost, inflation, and net exports. The most important variables were capacity utilization and unit labor cost. We cannot do such an analysis for most industries because the relevant variables typically are not available for individual industries. As an alternative, we can assume that movements in these industry profit margin variables are related to movements in similar economic variables. For example, when an increase in capacity utilization for the aggregate economy exists, there is probably a comparable increase in utilization for the auto industry or the chemical industry, The same could be true for unit labor cost and exports. If there is a stable relationship between these variables for the industry and the economy, you would expect a relationship to exist between the profit margins for the industry and the economy. Although it is not necessary that the relationship be completely linear, it is important for the relationship (whatever it is) to be generally stable.

The operating profit margin (OPM) for the S&P 400 Industrial Index and the retail drugstore (RDS) index is presented in Table 19.6. The time-series plot in Figure 19.9 indicates that the S&P 400 OPM experienced a decline during the 1980s and early 1990s, but increased steadily during the rest of the 1990s and ended the period with a record margin of over 16 percent. In contrast, the RDS OPM experienced a fairly steady decline with the exception of a small increase in 1997. The analysis of the relationship between the OPM for the market and industry using regression analysis was not useful, so it is not discussed. It appears that the best estimate for the RDS industry can be derived from the OPM time-series plot using what we know about the changing competitive environment and profit trends in the retail drugstore business. It is a matter of judgment for each specific industry

FIGURE 19.9 **TIME-SERIES PLOT OF OPERATING PROFIT MARGINS FOR THE S&P 400 AND THE RDS INDUSTRY: 1977–1997**

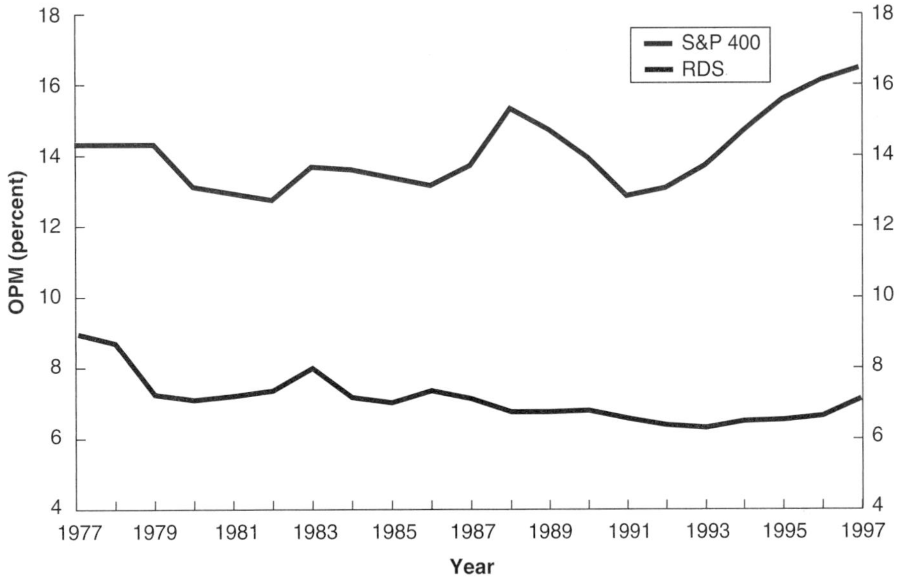
S&P 400
RDS
OPM (percent)
18
16
14
12
10
8
6
4
1977
1979
1981
1983
1985
1987
1989
1991
1993
1995
1997
Year

whether you use regression analysis and/or the time-series analysis. The point is, any such mathematical analysis should be considered a supplement to the economic analysis of the competitive environment for the industry.

Either regression analysis or time-series techniques can be useful tools, but *neither technique should be applied mechanically.* You should be aware of any unique factors affecting the specific industry, such as price wars, contract negotiations, building plans, or foreign competition. An analysis of these unique events is critical when estimating the final gross profit margin or when estimating a range of industry profit margins (optimistic, pessimistic, most likely).

Beyond this discussion, which is primarily concerned with an estimate of the near-term OPM, it also is important to consider the long-term profitability of the industry based on the competitive structure of the industry as discussed in an earlier section.

Industry Depreciation The next step is estimating industry depreciation, which typically is easier because the series generally is increasing; the only question is by how much. As shown in Table 19.6, except for 1991, the depreciation series for RDS increased every year since 1977. The results in Table 19.6 the time-series plots in Figure 19.10 relate depreciation for the S&P 400 and the RDS industry. To estimate depreciation expense, one can consider the two techniques used in the market analysis chapter (i.e., the time-series analysis and the specific estimate technique using the depreciation expense/PPE ratio) or an industry–market relationship. Figure 19.10 contains the time-series plot of depreciation expense for both the aggregate industrial market (the S&P 400) and the RDS industry.

An analysis of the graph as well as regression analysis of levels and annual percentage changes indicates that the relationship between this industry and the market is not good enough to use for an estimate. Alternatively, the depreciation expense series has been increasing at a fairly steady rate between 8 and 10 percent a year, so a time-series estimate could provide a viable estimate.

FIGURE 19.10 **TIME-SERIES PLOT OF DEPRECIATION FOR THE S&P 400 AND THE RDS INDUSTRY: 1977–1997**

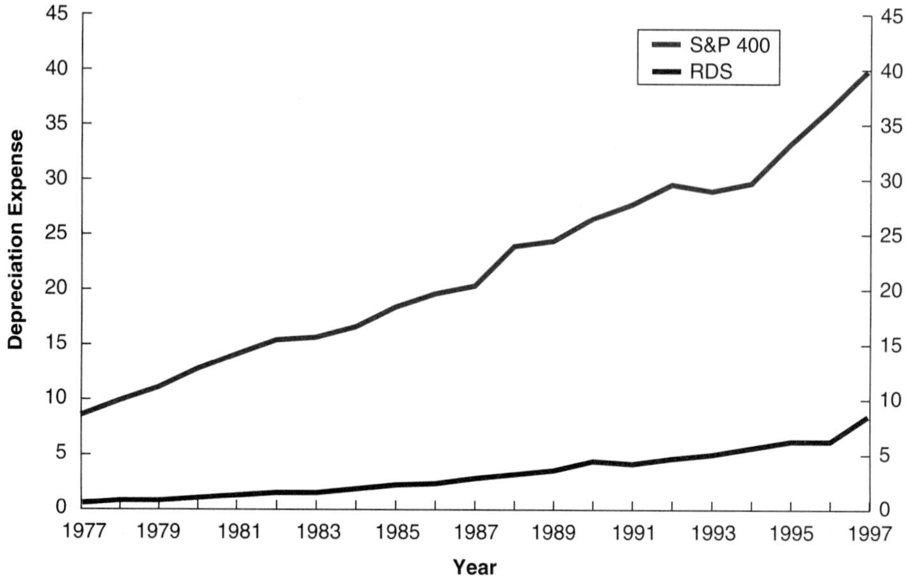
S&P 400
RDS
Depreciation Expense
Year
45
40
35
30
25
20
15
10
5
0
1977
1979
1981
1983
1985
1987
1989
1991
1993
1995
1997

Table 19.7 contains the components needed to derive a specific depreciation expense estimate similar to what we did for the S&P 400 using the following four steps:

1. Calculate the annual PPE turnover for the RDS industry.
2. Based upon your sales estimate and your expected PPE turnover ratio, estimate the expected PPE for next year.
3. Calculate the annual depreciation expense as a percent of PPE for the RDS industry.
4. Estimate depreciation expense as follows:

$$(\text{Estimated PPE}) \times \text{Estimated}\left(\frac{\text{Depreciation Expense}}{PPE}\right)\text{Ratio}$$

For example, the PPE turnover had tended to decline during the recent period with a recovery in 1997. A conservative estimate would be a PPE turnover of 7.40. This turnover value combined with a sales estimate for 1999 of $650 implies a PPE estimate of $87.84. In turn, the depreciation expense/PPE ratio was in the 10 percent range before 1996. Subsequently, 1996 was below the norm and 1997 was above historical levels. Using the recent 5-year average indicates an estimate of depreciation expense/PPE of 10.43 percent. Applying this estimated percent to the PPE estimate of $87.84 implies a depreciation expense estimate of $9.16 ($87.84 × 0.1043).

Subtracting an estimate of depreciation expense from the operating profit figure indicates the industry's net income before interest and taxes (EBIT).

Industry Interest Expense An industry's interest expense will be a function of its financial leverage and interest rates. As shown in Figure 19.11, interest expense for the RDS industry always has been relatively low when compared to the S&P 400 and did not increase at the same rate during the 1980s. Therefore, looking for a relationship between the two interest expense series would not be fruitful. Your estimate for the future should be based on

TABLE 19.7 **COMPONENTS FOR DERIVING SPECIFIC ESTIMATES FOR DEPRECIATION EXPENSE AND INTEREST EXPENSE FOR THE RDS INDUSTRY**

Year	Net Sales	Net PPE	PPE Turnover	Deprec. Exp.	Deprec. Exp. / PPE	Total Assets	T. Asset Turnover	L-T Debt	L-T Debt / T. Assets	Int. Exp.	Int. Exp. / L-T Debt
1977	43.99	3.32	13.25	0.41	0.12	15.51	2.84	1.25	0.08	0.13	0.10
1978	49.87	4.00	12.47	0.49	0.12	17.73	2.81	1.29	0.07	0.13	0.10
1979	73.39	6.18	11.88	0.71	0.11	24.49	3.00	2.69	0.11	0.23	0.09
1980	84.82	7.84	10.82	0.83	0.11	27.89	3.04	2.84	0.10	0.28	0.10
1981	95.50	9.68	9.87	1.02	0.11	31.53	3.03	2.48	0.08	0.39	0.16
1982	109.22	11.27	9.69	1.21	0.11	36.76	2.97	2.04	0.06	0.41	0.20
1983	118.85	12.90	9.21	1.40	0.11	41.61	2.86	1.82	0.04	0.43	0.24
1984	135.15	15.66	8.63	0.71	0.05	50.92	2.65	4.05	0.08	0.78	0.19
1985	153.30	18.56	8.26	2.02	0.11	56.74	2.70	8.25	0.15	1.14	0.14
1986	157.74	22.81	6.92	2.08	0.09	58.12	2.71	7.02	0.12	0.77	0.11
1987	191.72	26.45	7.25	2.63	0.10	68.54	2.80	8.76	0.13	1.17	0.13
1988	217.80	28.31	7.69	3.09	0.11	77.30	2.82	9.41	0.12	1.42	0.15
1989	239.68	30.80	7.78	3.39	0.11	85.05	2.82	16.41	0.19	1.65	0.10
1990	265.77	34.66	7.67	4.15	0.12	94.39	2.82	17.24	0.18	1.63	0.09
1991	283.50	37.55	7.55	4.03	0.11	99.34	2.85	12.84	0.13	1.32	0.10
1992	309.78	40.23	7.70	4.39	0.11	109.39	2.83	11.81	0.11	1.08	0.09
1993	329.20	43.63	7.55	4.75	0.11	118.19	2.79	14.52	0.12	0.80	0.06
1994	363.71	50.39	7.22	5.32	0.11	138.33	2.63	18.45	0.13	1.01	0.05
1995	413.52	58.69	7.05	6.02	0.10	155.38	2.66	22.61	0.15	1.57	0.07
1996	434.15	68.31	6.36	6.07	0.09	215.05	2.02	42.75	0.20	2.05	0.05
1997	549.51	73.01	7.53	8.45	0.12	246.75	2.23	39.01	0.16	3.08	0.08

Source: *Standard & Poor's Analysts Handbook* (New York: Standard and Poor's Corp., 1998). Reprinted by permission of Standard & Poor's Corp.

two separate estimates: (1) changes in the amount of debt outstanding for this industry during the year, and (2) an estimate of the level of interest rates (will they increase or decline?).

Estimating Interest Expense The historical data needed to derive a specific estimate of interest expense is also in Table 19.7. Recall the following steps used in Chapter 18:

1. Calculate the annual total asset turnover (TAT) for the RDS industry.
2. Use your 1999 sales estimate and an estimate of TAT to estimate total assets next year.
3. Calculate the annual long-term (interest-bearing) debt as a percentage of total assets for the RDS industry.
4. Using your estimate of total assets and long-term debt as a percentage of total assets, estimate long-term debt for the next year.
5. Calculate the annual interest cost as a percentage of long-term debt and analyze the trend of this series.
6. Estimate next year's interest cost of debt for this industry based upon your prior estimate of market yields.
7. Estimate interest expense based on the following estimates:

$$(\text{Interest Cost of Debt}) \times (\text{Outstanding Long-Term Debt})$$

For example, our sales estimate of \$650 and a TAT that has averaged 2.47 over the most recent years imply total assets of \$263 next year. Long-term, interest-bearing debt has averaged 15.17 percent of total assets for the RDS industry, which implies long-term debt next year of about \$40 (\$263 × 0.1517). In turn, interest expense as a percentage of long-term debt,

FIGURE 19.11

TIME-SERIES PLOT OF INTEREST EXPENSE FOR THE S&P 400 AND THE RDS INDUSTRY: 1977–1997

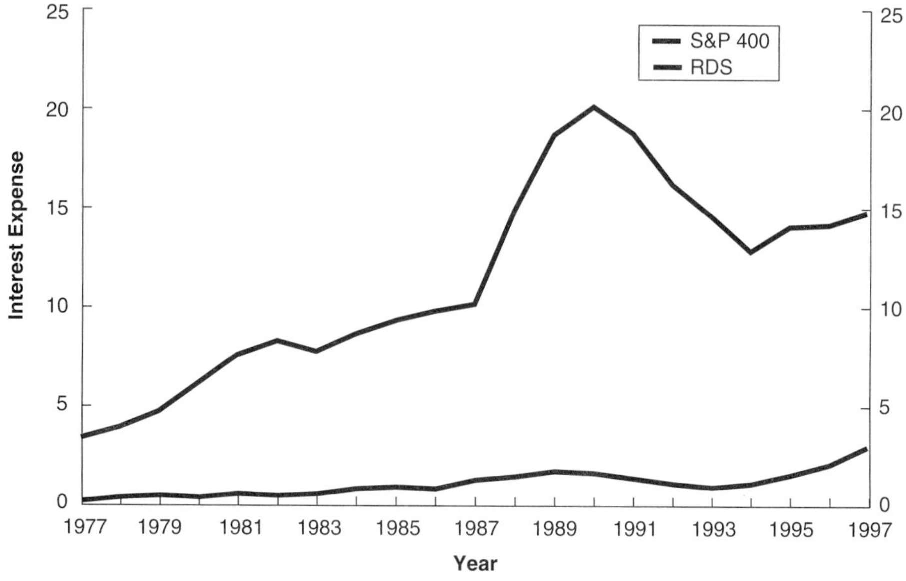

S&P 400
RDS
Interest Expense
25
20
15
10
5
0
1977
1979
1981
1983
1985
1987
1989
1991
1993
1995
1997
Year

ignoring an unusual rate for 1996, has averaged about 6.50 percent for this industry. Based upon the expectation of a small increase in market interest rates during 1999, we would estimate this interest rate to be 7.00 percent in 1999. This interest rate estimate combined with our long-term debt estimate of \$40 implies interest expense of \$2.80 (0.07 × \$40).

Industry Tax Rate As you might expect, tax rates differ between industries. An extreme example would be the oil industry where heavy depletion allowances cause lower taxes. In some instances, however, you can assume that tax law changes have similar impacts on all industries. To see if this is valid, you need to examine the relationship of tax rates over time for your industry and the aggregate market to determine if you can use regression analysis in your estimation process. Alternatively, a time-series plot could provide a useful estimate.

As shown in Figure 19.12, except for 1997, the RDS tax rate historically has moved with the economy's tax rate. Therefore, the time-series plot in this figure is fairly informative, although you still need to consider impending national legislation and unique industry tax factors. Once you have estimated the tax rate, you multiply the EBT per share value by (1 − tax rate) to get your estimate of earnings per share.

In addition to an estimate of earnings per share, you also should derive an estimate of the industry's net profit margin as a check on your EPS estimate. A time-series plot of the profit margin series for the industry and the S&P 400 is contained in Figure 19.13. Two important characteristics are notable. First, the S&P 400 net profit margin series is much more volatile than that for retail drugstores. Second, although both profit margin series showed an overall decline through 1993, the S&P 400 has experienced a strong recovery since 1993 to a margin of almost 6 percent. In contrast, the RDS margin started at about 4 percent and generally declined prior to a major drop in 1997 to 1.96 percent.

AN INDUSTRY EARNINGS ESTIMATE EXAMPLE Now that we have described how to estimate each variable in the equation to help you understand the procedure,

FIGURE 19.12

TIME-SERIES PLOT OF THE TAX RATES FOR THE S&P 400 AND THE RDS INDUSTRY: 1977–1997

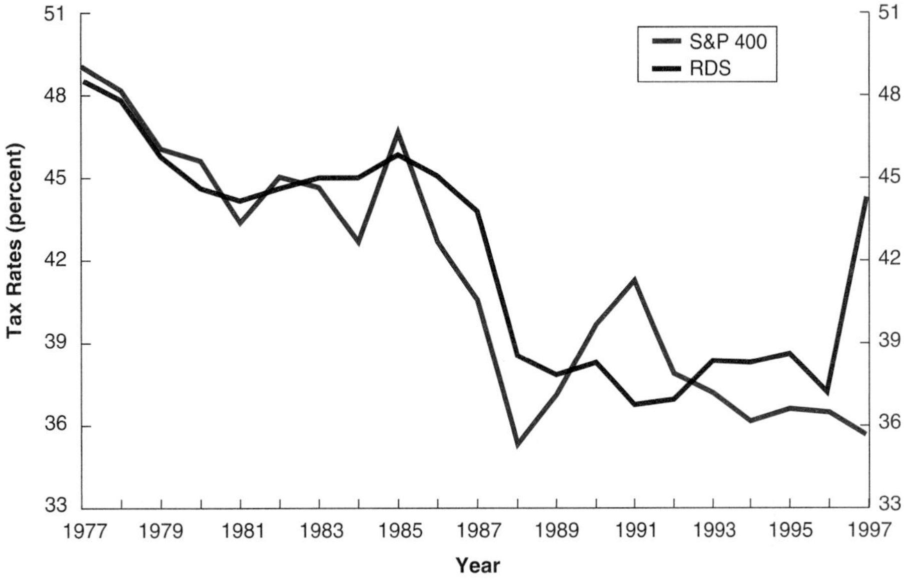
S&P 400
RDS
Tax Rates (percent)
51
48
45
42
39
36
33
1977
1979
1981
1983
1985
1987
1989
1991
1993
1995
1997
Year

FIGURE 19.13

TIME-SERIES PLOT OF NET PROFIT MARGINS FOR THE S&P 400 AND THE RDS INDUSTRY: 1977–1997

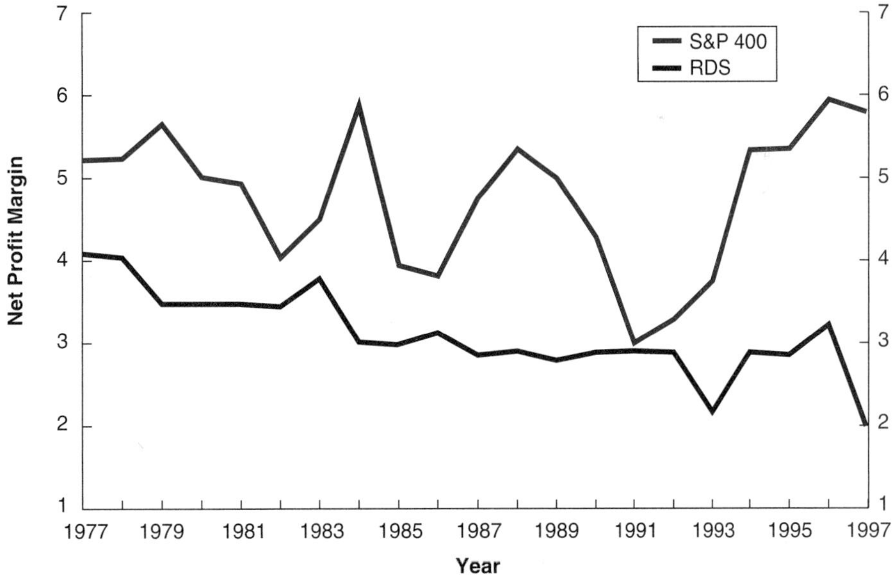
S&P 400
RDS
Net Profit Margin
7
6
5
4
3
2
1
1977
1979
1981
1983
1985
1987
1989
1991
1993
1995
1997
Year

the following is an estimate of earnings per share for the retail drugstore industry using the economic forecasts from Chapter 18 and the relationship between the RDS industry and the market. Our results are not as exact as those of a practicing analyst who would use this example as an *initial* estimate that would be modified based on his or her industry knowledge, current events, and expectations of future unique factors.

The regressions and the plots in Figure 19.7 indicated that the best relationship was between retail drugstore sales and PCE-medical care. The outlook for PCE is for an increase of 5.5 percent in 1998 (to about $5,800 billion) and a 5 percent increase in 1999 to $6,090 billion. It is further assumed that medical care expenditures will be 15.3 percent of PCE in 1998 and in 1999. This implies that PCE-medical care will be about $887 billion in 1998 and $932 billion in 1999 (a 5 percent increase). Using these results in the earlier equation indicates that retail drugstore sales in 1999 should be about $677, which implies a 23 percent increase over the 2 years from 1997.

The OPM for retail drugstores was 7.06 percent in 1997. Although the OPM for the S&P 400 declined slightly during 1998, retail drugstore margins were expected to experience stability at 7.05. The aggregate OPM was expected to experience a small rebound during 1999. Based on the time-series plot in Figure 19.9, this would indicate that retail drugstore margins should also increase to about 7.10 percent, which implies an operating profit per share for the retail drugstore industry of $48.07 (.071 × $677).

Aggregate depreciation for the S&P 400 series during 1998 was estimated to grow to 43.26 in 1999. Based upon the earlier specific estimate which implies growth similar to the market, the industry depreciation expense is estimated at $9.16 in 1999. Therefore, earnings before interest and taxes would be $38.91 ($48.07 − $9.16).

Given the decline in yields during 1998 and the small increase in rates envisioned during 1999 along with minor debt financing, our prior specific estimate of interest expense was $2.80 for 1999. Thus, EBT would be $36.11 ($38.91 − $2.80).

The tax rate for the retail drugstore industry has been higher than the aggregate during the last 2 years when the aggregate tax rate declined. The aggregate tax rate was expected to be relatively stable in 1998 and in 1999. Therefore, a rate of about 38 percent seems appropriate for the retail drugstore industry. This implies taxes of $13.72 ($36.11 × 0.38) and net income (earnings per share) of $22.39 ($36.11 − $13.72). This indicates a net profit margin for the RDS industry of 3.31 percent (22.39/677.00), which is slightly above the recent experience.

Given an estimate of the industry's net income per share, your next step is to estimate the earnings multiplier for this industry. Together, the earnings per share and the earnings multiplier provide an estimate of the expected value for the industry index. Given this expected value and an estimate of dividends per share during the holding period, you can compute an expected rate of return from investing in this industry.

ESTIMATING AN INDUSTRY EARNINGS MULTIPLIER This section discusses how to estimate an industry earnings multiplier using two alternative techniques: macroanalysis and microanalysis. In macroanalysis, you examine the relationship between the multiplier for the industry and the market. In microanalysis, you estimate the industry earnings multiplier by examining the specific variables that influence it: (1) the dividend-payout ratio, (2) the required rate of return for the industry(k), and (3) the expected growth rate of earnings and dividends for the industry (g).

Macroanalysis of an Industry Multiplier

Why a relationship? Given that this subsection considers the relationship between the earnings multiplier (P/E ratio) for an industry to the P/E for the aggregate market, a natural question is: Why do we *expect* a relationship? The reasons are based on the variables that influence the multiplier—the required rate of return, the expected growth rate of earnings and dividends, and the dividend-payout ratio. Specifically, as you know, the required rate of return (k) is a function of the nominal risk-free rate plus a risk premium. The fact is, the nominal risk-free rate is the same for all investment assets and is the major reason for

FIGURE 19.14

TIME-SERIES PLOT OF ANNUAL AVERAGE FUTURE EARNINGS MULTIPLIERS FOR THE S&P 400 AND THE RDS INDUSTRY: 1977–1997

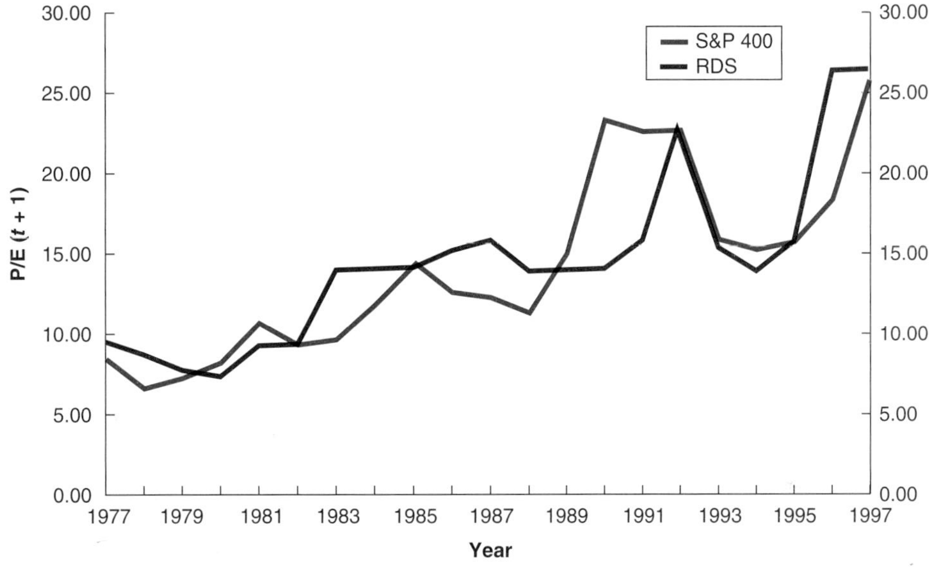
S&P 400
RDS
30.00
25.00
20.00
15.00
10.00
5.00
0.00
P/E (t + 1)
1977
1979
1981
1983
1985
1987
1989
1991
1993
1995
1997
Year

changes in k. Also, though the level of the risk premium may differ between the market and an industry, any *changes* in the RP are probably related.

Although the rate of growth (g) for an industry may differ from that of the market, and this difference in g is a major reason for the difference in the level of the P/E ratio, *changes* in the growth expectations for many industries will be related to changes in g for the market and for other industries because they are driven by macroeconomic growth factors that affect the overall market and most industries. Therefore, since the major factor causing a change in the P/E ratio for the aggregate market and alternative industries is a change in the k–g spread, and these two variables have several components that move together, it is not unreasonable to look for an overall (macro) relationship between changes in an industry's P/E and the market P/E ratio.

An examination of the relationship between the P/E ratios for 71 S&P industries and the S&P 400 index during four partially overlapping 21-year periods indicated a significant positive relationship between percentage changes in P/E ratios for most industries examined.[12] Notably, because there was a difference in the significance of the relationship between industries, it is necessary to evaluate the quality of the relationship between the P/E ratios for a specific industry and the market before using this technique.

The results in Table 19.1 and Figure 19.14 for the retail drugstore industry during the period 1977 to 1997 indicate a relatively close relationship between the market and the RDS industry. The P/E ratio for drugstores was generally above the market P/E ratio until 1989 when the market P/E increased while the P/E for drugstores was relatively stable. Notably, the industry P/E ratios are less volatile than the market P/E ratios. These results imply that the macroanalysis could be a useful input for this industry.

[12]Frank K. Reilly and Thomas Zeller, "An Analysis of Relative Industry Price–Earnings Ratios," *The Financial Review* (1974): 17–33.

Microanalysis of an Industry Multiplier In Chapter 18, we estimated the future earnings multiplier for the stock-market series in two ways. In the first, *the direction of change approach*, we estimated the changes for the three variables that determine the earnings multiplier—the dividend-payout ratio, the required rate of return, and the expected growth rate of earnings and dividends. Based on the consensus of changes, we estimated a direction of change for the multiplier from its current value. In the second approach, *the specific multiplier estimate,* we estimated a range of values for the three variables that determine the multiplier and derived a range of P/E ratio estimates. These two approaches provided several multiplier estimates that were used with our EPS estimate to compute a range of expected values for the market index that, in turn, provided expected rates of return on common stocks.

Our microanalysis of the industry multiplier could use the same two approaches. Although this would certainly be reasonable, it would not take advantage of the prior work on the stock-market multiplier. Because the variables that affect the stock-market multiplier also determine the industry multiplier, it should be possible to compare the two sets of variables.

Therefore, in our microanalysis, we estimate the three variables that determine the industry earnings multiplier and compare them to the comparable values for the market P/E. This allows us to determine whether the industry earnings multiplier *should* be above, below, or equal to the market multiplier. Once we feel confident about this relationship, it is easier to derive a specific estimate for the industry P/E ratio. As a first step, we need to recall the long-run relationship between the industry and market P/E ratios.

Industry multiplier versus the market multiplier Recall from Table 19.1 that the P/E ratios for the RDS industry typically were larger than the P/E ratios for the stock market prior to 1989. Obvious questions include: Why do the P/E ratios for this industry and the stock market differ over time? Beginning in 1989, why were investors willing to pay more for a dollar of earnings from the aggregate market than from retail drugstores? Why were the P/Es very similar from 1992 to 1997? In summary, why has the historical relationship that has prevailed between the P/E ratios for this industry and the stock market changed? A comparative analysis of the factors that determine the earnings multiplier should help us answer these questions.

Comparing dividend-payout ratios We can discuss the dividend-payout ratio directly or in terms of the retention rate because the retention rate is one minus the dividend-payout ratio. Analyzing the data in Table 19.1 indicates that the retention rates of retail drugstores have consistently been higher than the retention rates for the market (68 percent versus 53 percent). This indicates a higher dividend payout (lower retention rate) for the S&P 400, which implies a higher multiplier for the S&P 400, holding all other variables constant.

Estimating the required rate of return Recall that we estimated the required rate of return (k) earlier in the chapter in connection with the present value of cash flow valuation models. The final estimate indicated a beta of 0.75 for the industry, which was generally consistent with the fundamental risk characteristics of the industry. In turn, this beta in the prevailing SML implied a k of 8.50 percent. This 8.50 percent compares to the k for the aggregate stock market derived in Chapter 18 of 9.50 percent, which implies that all else the same, the industry P/E should be higher than the market P/E.

Estimating the expected growth rate (g) You will recall that we likewise estimated a growth rate for the industry early in this chapter in connection with the present value of cash flow models. Using the relationship

$$\begin{aligned} g &= \text{Retention Rate } (b) \times \text{Return on Equity (ROE)} \\ &= (b) \times (\text{ROE}) \end{aligned}$$

we estimated a g of about 9 percent based on long-run historical results, and a g of 8.33 percent using the results for the recent 5-year period 1993–1997. Because of the steady deterioration of both b and ROE for the RDS industry, we decided upon an estimate of industry growth close to the lower bound–8.50 percent.

This 8.50 percent growth rate estimate compares to the growth rates for the S&P 400 of between 8.81 percent (using the long-run retention rate) and 9.47 percent (using the recent 5-year retention rate). The mean of these two growth rates is 9.14 percent. If we opted to be near the high value because of the steady improvement of the components that determine growth, we would be around 9.25 percent. All these growth estimates exceed the industry g of about 8.50 percent, which implies that based on the growth factor, the industry multiple would be lower than the market multiple.

In summary, a comparison of the dividend-payout ratios indicates that the market P/E ratio should be higher; the required rate of return comparison indicates that the industry multiple should be higher; while the growth rate favors the market multiple. The consensus tends to favor a higher market multiple. Earlier it was discussed that the market multiple would need to be about 30 times to justify the prevailing market price. This implies an industry multiplier in the mid-20s—i.e., we will use an expected industry P/E of 25 times.

Industry expected value and rate of return At this point, we have an estimate of the industry earnings per share ($22.39) and an estimate for an industry earnings multiple in the mid-20s based on a comparison of the industry and market components. It is not possible to derive a specific estimate using the DDM formula because the k and g for the industry are roughly equal—i.e., both k and g are about 8.50 percent. Because the multiple estimate is necessarily not specific, it seems appropriate to consider an optimistic and a pessimistic estimate, with the initial estimate as follows:

Optimistic Multiple:	$30 \times \$22.39 = \$671.70$
Expected Multiple:	$25 \times \$22.39 = \$559.75$
Pessimistic Multiple:	$20 \times \$22.39 = \$447.80$

Given a current market price for the industry index of about $640.00, these results indicate that the industry is overpriced based upon general expectations and the pessimistic estimate, but is slightly underpriced if one favors the optimistic multiple. The specific calculation of rates of return during 1999 for the industry using these ending values, an estimate of dividends, and an index value during early 1999 is as follows:[13]

$$\text{Optimistic Rate of Return: } \frac{671.70 + 4.70}{640.00} = 1.057 - 1.0 = 5.7\%$$

$$\text{Expected Rate of Return: } \frac{559.75 + 4.70}{640.00} = 0.882 - 1.0 = -11.8\%$$

$$\text{Pessimistic Rate of Return: } \frac{447.80 + 4.70}{640.00} = 0.707 - 1.0 = -29.3\%$$

Comparing these estimated rates of return to the required rate of return for this industry of 8.50 percent indicates that, using this earnings multiple model, the industry is overpriced, even using an optimistic earnings multiple.

[13]We use this index value for early 1999 because it is more reasonable than the very inflated value that prevailed at the end of 1998.

OTHER RELATIVE VALUATION RATIOS

Similar to the market analysis, we need to consider the other three relative valuation ratios (P/BV; P/CF; and P/S) and compare their performance over time relative to similar ratios for the aggregate stock market as represented by the S&P 400.

Again, the calculations will employ the average annual price and *future* book value, cash flow, and sales. The input data derived for the industry and the S&P 400 (from Chapter 18) with 20-year and 10-year growth rates for each of these variables are contained in Table 19.8. Table 19.9 contains the four relative valuation ratios for the RDS industry and for the S&P 400 Index along with the ratio of the annual industry valuation ratio divided by the market valuation ratio. The idea is to determine for each valuation ratio the long-run relationship between the industry and the market, including any changes in this relationship. Subsequently, the goal is to explain the overall relationship and consider any changes that have occurred and whether these changes can be explained based upon the factors that should affect the particular relative valuation ratio.

The Price/Book Value Ratio

The time-series plot in Figure 19.15 shows the overall increase experienced by both the aggregate stock market and the RDS industry from less than two times to over five times. In addition, there has been a change in the relationship between the industry and the market—i.e., the industry P/BV ratio was larger from 1977 through 1989, after which the market P/BV ratio has been larger. The reason for this change in the relationship appears to be the change in ROE for the market and industry because the P/BV ratio should reflect the ability of the market, an industry, or a company to earn a return on capital that exceeds its cost of funds. In turn, this return on capital for the equity holder is the ROE, and we know from our earlier analysis that during the last decade, the ROE for the market has been increasing while the ROE for the RDS industry has steadily declined because of the decline in profit margin. Therefore, not only can we explain the difference, but also one might expect the difference in the P/BV ratios to increase unless the RDS industry can improve its profitability and ROE relative to the market.

The Price/Cash Flow Ratio

As shown in Table 19.9 and Figure 19.16, the P/CF ratio has increased for both the market and the RDS industry from about 6 times to about 15 times, and the industry ratio has consistently been larger by almost 50 percent—i.e., the industry–market ratio has ranged from 1.92 to 1.17. The reason for the difference in the P/CF ratios is akin to the P/E ratio—i.e., a difference in the growth rate of CF per share and the risk (volatility) of the CF series over time. As shown in Table 19.8, the growth rate of the industry CF has been almost twice as high as the growth of the market CF, and the industry CF series has also been more consistent in its growth. The only question that remains is whether the industry P/CF ratio should be 50 percent higher than the P/CF ratio for the market—i.e., does the difference in consistent growth of CF justify the fairly large difference in the P/CF ratios?

The Price/Sales Ratio

As shown in Table 19.9 and Figure 19.17, the P/S ratio for the market has more than tripled from about 0.40 to 1.31, while the industry P/S ratio has not quite doubled from 0.38 to 0.67. Because of this differential in the increase in the ratios, the industry–market ratio of P/S ratios has declined from 0.87 to 0.51. In terms of what should affect the P/S ratio, one can think of three factors: (1) sales growth rate; (2) the uncertainty (risk) of sales growth; and (3) the profitability of sales (i.e., the net profit margin). Because the industry and the market experienced a decline in the rate of growth for sales for the 10-year versus the 20-year period, it is not the rate of growth. Both have likewise experienced less volatility in sales growth. In contrast, the profit margin (PM) change is consistent with the difference

TABLE 19.8 **INPUTS FOR RELATIVE VALUATION RATIOS: THE RETAIL DRUGSTORE INDUSTRY AND THE S&P 400 INDEX: 1977–1998**

	Retail Drugstore Industry						S&P 400 Index					
Year	Mean Price	EPS	Cash Flow P/S	Book Value P/S	Net Sales P/S	Dividend P/S	Mean Price	EPS	Cash Flow P/S	Book Value P/S	Net Sales P/S	Dividend P/S
1977	18.93	1.79	2.20	9.35	43.99	0.36	109.40	11.45	19.94	82.21	224.24	4.95
1978	22.20	2.01	2.50	10.93	49.87	0.48	107.12	13.04	22.65	89.34	251.32	5.37
1979	22.38	2.55	3.26	13.95	73.39	0.70	115.79	16.29	27.06	98.71	292.38	5.92
1980	24.57	2.94	3.78	16.11	84.82	0.86	136.03	16.12	28.45	108.33	327.36	6.49
1981	34.62	3.29	4.31	18.45	95.50	1.02	141.48	16.74	30.52	116.06	344.31	7.01
1982	41.58	3.76	4.79	20.74	109.22	1.17	136.87	13.20	28.46	118.60	333.86	7.13
1983	56.70	4.50	5.90	23.34	118.85	1.32	174.90	14.77	30.41	122.32	334.07	7.32
1984	58.30	4.10	5.81	24.21	135.15	1.54	179.62	18.11	34.40	123.99	379.70	7.51
1985	68.28	4.22	6.24	26.82	153.30	1.72	208.99	15.28	33.44	125.89	398.42	7.87
1986	83.78	4.90	6.99	27.73	157.74	1.61	253.83	14.53	33.91	124.87	387.76	8.14
1987	98.93	5.53	8.16	30.79	191.72	1.75	324.30	20.28	40.46	134.19	430.35	8.72
1988	93.05	6.30	9.40	34.25	217.80	1.93	302.63	26.59	50.13	139.50	486.92	9.80
1989	107.46	6.69	10.07	38.31	239.68	2.16	364.58	26.83	50.02	145.34	541.38	11.95
1990	114.53	7.67	11.82	43.65	265.77	2.43	392.12	24.77	51.04	152.71	594.55	12.70
1991	139.70	8.26	12.29	50.94	283.50	2.71	428.81	16.91	44.41	157.05	586.86	12.51
1992	159.62	8.96	13.34	56.97	309.78	3.01	493.33	19.05	48.50	142.46	601.39	13.01
1993	162.19	7.09	11.84	60.04	329.20	3.32	520.21	21.93	50.61	136.91	603.62	12.51
1994	162.67	10.51	15.83	63.62	363.71	3.55	536.52	32.83	62.43	150.70	626.26	13.01
1995	215.26	11.76	17.77	68.93	413.52	3.96	638.97	35.44	68.51	163.94	676.62	13.96
1996	283.01	13.92	18.82	71.26	434.15	4.01	795.01	41.15	77.56	168.04	701.91	15.58
1997	411.75	10.77	19.22	70.88	549.51	4.41	1006.12	43.80	81.90	174.21	750.71	16.72
1998[a]	657.05	15.62	20.76	77.90	612.86	4.52	1285.70	38.37	77.80	180.76	767.83	17.28
20-yr. G	**18.46**	**10.80**	**11.16**	**10.32**	**13.36**	**11.87**	**13.23**	**5.54**	**6.36**	**3.59**	**5.74**	**6.02**
10-yr. G	**21.59**	**9.51**	**8.24**	**8.56**	**10.90**	**8.88**	**15.56**	**3.74**	**4.49**	**2.62**	**4.66**	**5.84**

[a]The 1998 earnings, cash flow, and book value and sales per share are estimated by the authors.

TABLE 19.9 RELATIVE VALUATION RATIOS FOR THE RDS INDUSTRY COMPARED TO SIMILAR VALUATION RATIOS FOR THE S&P 400 INDUSTRIAL INDEX: 1977–1997

	PRICE/EARNINGS$_{t+1}$			PRICE/CASH FLOW$_{t+1}$			PRICE/BOOK VALUE$_{t+1}$			PRICE/SALES$_{t+1}$		
Year	Retail Drug	S&P 400	Ratio Ind/Mkt	Retail Drug	S&P 400	Ratio Ind/Mkt	Retail Drug	S&P 400	Ratio Ind/Mkt	Retail Drug	S&P 400	Ratio Co/Mkt
1977	9.42	8.39	1.12	7.57	4.83	1.57	1.73	1.22	1.41	0.38	0.44	0.87
1978	8.71	6.58	1.32	6.81	3.96	1.72	1.59	1.09	1.47	0.30	0.37	0.83
1979	7.61	7.18	1.06	5.92	4.07	1.45	1.39	1.07	1.30	0.26	0.35	0.75
1980	7.47	8.13	0.92	5.70	4.46	1.28	1.33	1.17	1.14	0.26	0.40	0.65
1981	9.21	10.72	0.86	7.23	4.97	1.45	1.67	1.19	1.40	0.32	0.42	0.75
1982	9.24	9.27	1.00	7.05	4.50	1.57	1.78	1.12	1.59	0.35	0.41	0.85
1983	13.83	9.66	1.43	9.76	5.08	1.92	2.34	1.41	1.66	0.42	0.46	0.91
1984	13.82	11.76	1.18	9.34	5.37	1.74	2.17	1.43	1.52	0.38	0.45	0.84
1985	13.93	14.38	0.97	9.77	6.16	1.58	2.46	1.67	1.47	0.43	0.54	0.80
1986	15.15	12.52	1.21	10.27	6.27	1.64	2.72	1.89	1.44	0.44	0.59	0.74
1987	15.70	12.20	1.29	10.52	6.47	1.63	2.89	2.32	1.24	0.45	0.67	0.68
1988	13.91	11.28	1.23	9.24	6.05	1.53	2.43	2.08	1.17	0.39	0.56	0.69
1989	14.01	14.72	0.95	9.09	7.14	1.27	2.46	2.39	1.03	0.40	0.61	0.66
1990	13.87	23.19	0.60	9.32	8.83	1.06	2.25	2.50	0.90	0.40	0.67	0.60
1991	15.59	22.51	0.69	10.47	8.84	1.18	2.45	3.01	0.81	0.45	0.71	0.63
1992	22.51	22.50	1.00	13.48	9.75	1.38	2.66	3.60	0.74	0.48	0.82	0.59
1993	15.43	15.85	0.97	10.25	8.33	1.23	2.55	3.45	0.74	0.45	0.83	0.54
1994	13.83	15.14	0.91	9.15	7.83	1.17	2.36	3.27	0.72	0.39	0.79	0.50
1995	15.46	15.53	1.00	11.44	8.24	1.39	3.02	3.80	0.79	0.50	0.91	0.54
1996	26.28	18.15	1.45	14.72	9.71	1.52	3.99	4.56	0.87	0.52	1.06	0.49
1997	26.36	26.22	1.01	19.84	12.93	1.53	5.29	5.57	0.95	0.67	1.31	0.51
20-yr. G	**5.28**	**5.86**	—	**4.93**	**5.05**	—	**5.74**	**7.86**	—	**2.90**	**5.66**	—
10-yr. G	**5.32**	**7.96**	—	**6.54**	**7.17**	—	**6.23**	**9.12**	—	**3.99**	**7.00**	—
Mean	14.35	14.09	1.06	9.85	6.85	1.47	2.45	2.37	1.16	0.41	0.64	0.69

in the P/S ratios—the PM for the market has increased recently while the PM for the industry has declined. A major question that arises from these results is: Why has the industry P/S ratio experienced any increase when the only positive change for the industry is the greater consistency in sales growth?

Figure 19.18 is a summary of the four industry–market ratios for each of the valuation ratios. In general, the results indicate that investors' assessment of this industry relative to the market has deteriorated during this time period. Notably, the largest decline occurred in the P/BV ratios, which is caused by the decline in the industry's ROE which, in turn was caused by the lower industry profit margin in recent years.

GLOBAL INDUSTRY ANALYSIS

Because so many firms are active in foreign markets and because the proportion of foreign sales is growing for so many firms, we must expand industry analysis to include the effects of foreign firms on global trade and industry returns. To see why this is so, consider the auto industry. Besides Ford and General Motors, the auto industry for a global investor includes numerous firms from Japan, Germany, Italy, and Korea, among others. Thus we must extend the analysis described earlier to include global factors. This section presents an example of such an analysis for the European chemical industry performed by industry

FIGURE 19.15

TIME-SERIES PLOT OF THE PRICE/BOOK VALUE RATIOS FOR THE S&P 400 AND THE RDS INDUSTRY: 1977–1997

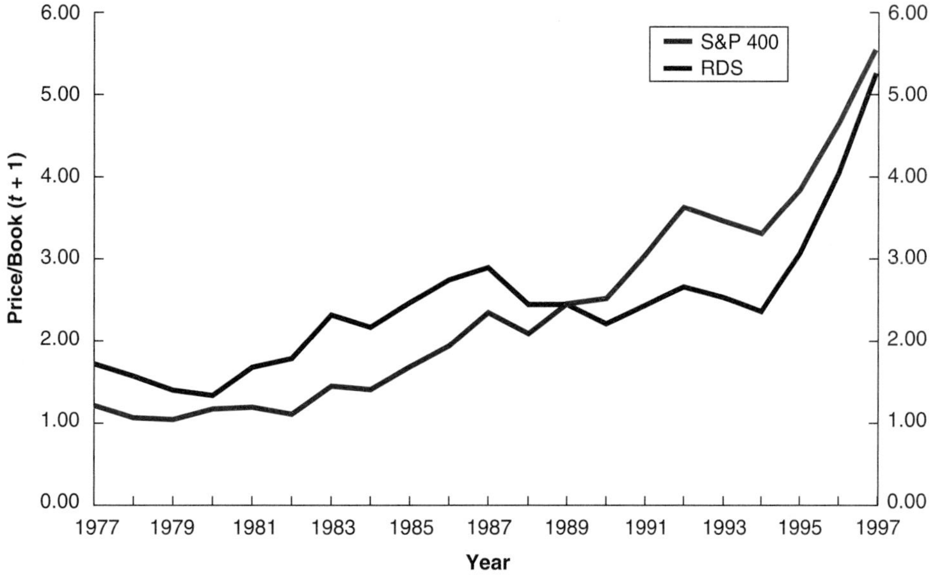
S&P 400
RDS
Price/Book (t + 1)
6.00
5.00
4.00
3.00
2.00
1.00
0.00
1977 1979 1981 1983 1985 1987 1989 1991 1993 1995 1997
Year

FIGURE 19.16

TIME-SERIES PLOT OF THE PRICE/CASH FLOW RATIOS FOR THE S&P 400 AND THE RDS INDUSTRY: 1977–1997

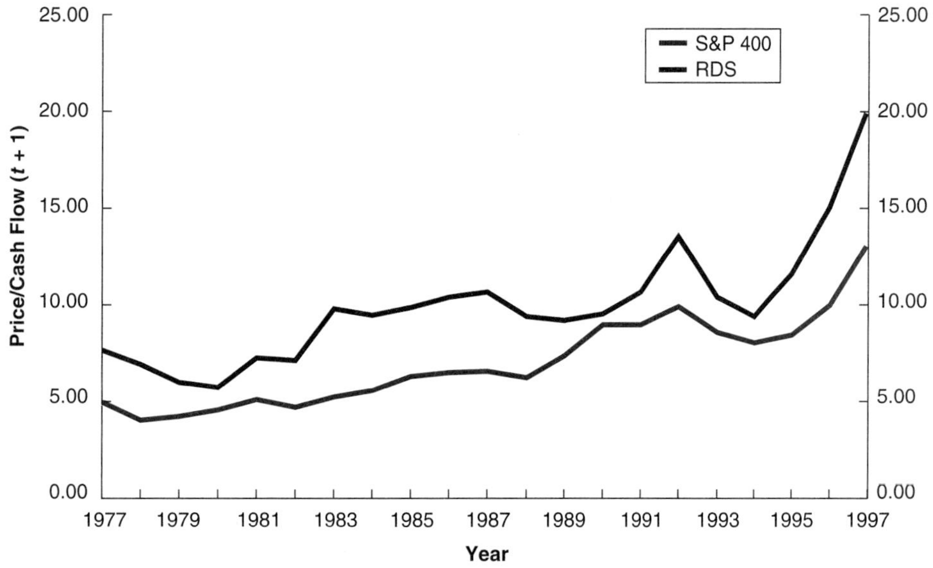
S&P 400
RDS
Price/Cash Flow (t + 1)
25.00
20.00
15.00
10.00
5.00
0.00
1977 1979 1981 1983 1985 1987 1989 1991 1993 1995 1997
Year

FIGURE 19.17

TIME-SERIES PLOT OF THE PRICE/SALES RATIOS FOR THE S&P 400 AND THE RDS INDUSTRY: 1977–1997

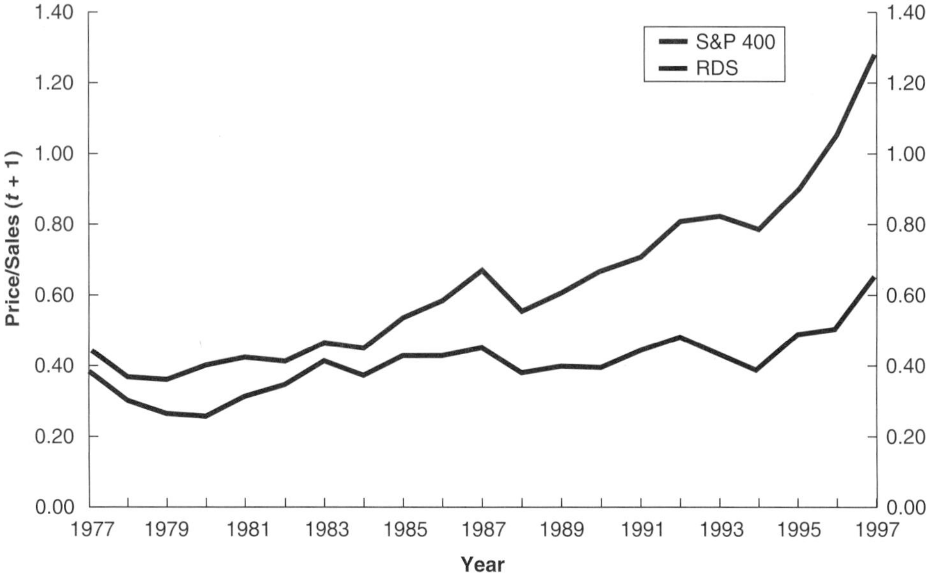

S&P 400
RDS
Price/Sales (t + 1)
1.40
1.20
1.00
0.80
0.60
0.40
0.20
0.00
1977
1979
1981
1983
1985
1987
1989
1991
1993
1995
1997
Year

FIGURE 19.18

TIME-SERIES PLOTS OF THE INDUSTRY–MARKET RELATIVE RATIO OF VALUATION RATIOS OF THE RDS INDUSTRY VERSUS THE S&P 400

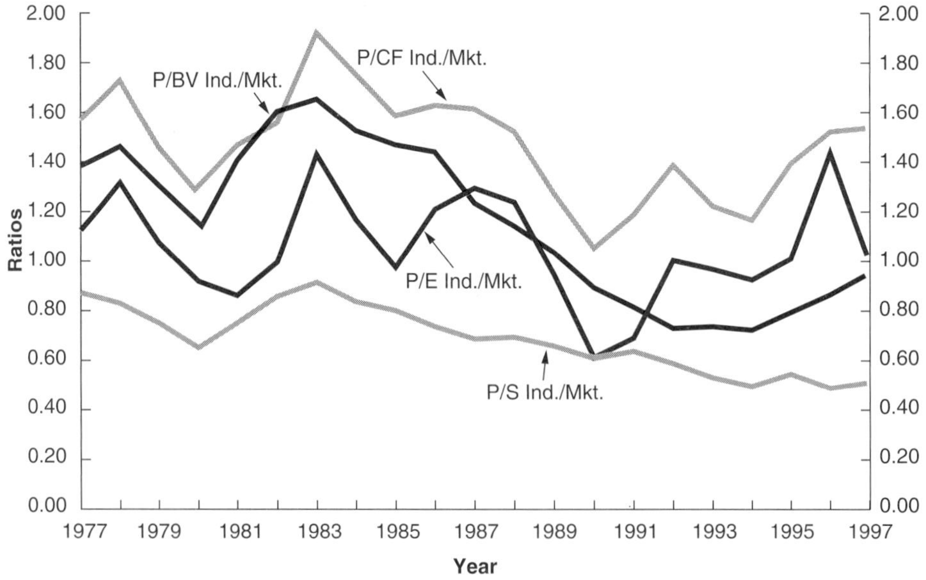

P/BV Ind./Mkt.
P/CF Ind./Mkt.
P/E Ind./Mkt.
P/S Ind./Mkt.
Ratios
2.00
1.80
1.60
1.40
1.20
1.00
0.80
0.60
0.40
0.20
0.00
1977
1979
1981
1983
1985
1987
1989
1991
1993
1995
1997
Year

TABLE 19.10 **ECONOMIC SCENARIO 1997–1999E (ANNUAL PERCENTAGE CHANGES)[a]**

	GDP			
	1997	1998E	1999E	10-Year Trend
Germany	2.3	2.7	2.8	2.7
France	3.2	2.8	2.4	2.1
United Kingdom	2.9	1.7	2.1	2.1
Italy	2.8	2.0	2.6	1.8
United States	3.7	3.0	2.5	2.4
Japan	−0.2	0.8	1.1	3.1

[a]Goldman, Sachs & Co. estimates.

Source: Jackie Ashurst, Charles K. Brown, Geoff Haire, Mark Tracey, John A. Murphy, and Jane Henderson, "The Major European Chemical/Pharma Groups—Industries in Flux" (London: Goldman, Sachs International Ltd., May 1998). Reprinted by permission of Goldman, Sachs & Co.

analysts at Goldman, Sachs & Company.[14] Although the report discusses individual firms in the industry, we emphasize the overall chemical industry.

THE EUROPEAN CHEMICAL INDUSTRY

Table 19.10 contains the expected economic outlook for the major European countries during the period 1997 to 1999. The economic outlook clearly varied depending upon the country. Specifically, Germany and Japan reflected increasing growth over the three years, in contrast to France and the United States where the outlook was for slower growth each year (the United Kingdom and Italy were a mixture).

PROFIT PERFORMANCE Table 19.11 shows EPS, ROE, the debt/equity ratio, and several measures of relative value (P/E, P/CF, P/B) for seven major companies, which reflects what happened to most other firms in this industry. These data indicate that about half the firms in the industry were expected to experience an increase in profit results during 1999 versus 1998. Also, the expected ROEs for 1999 were quite respectable. Similar to the past, the expected P/E ratios were wide ranging, as were the P/CF ratios. As noted in the financial statement analysis chapter, because of the differences among countries in accounting treatments, it is typically not possible to directly compare such ratios across countries, but only to examine them over time within a country.

Another segment of the analysis examined the currency factors involved in forecasting production for each country, and the export–import possibilities based on the exchange rate outlook. Table 19.12 lists exchange rate trends for each of the major countries relative to the U.S. dollar and on a trade-weighted basis to all currencies. The main point derived from these results for the period 1996–1998E is the cyclical changes—periods of strength followed by periods of weakness, then strength again. It emphasizes the importance of these exchange rate changes and the need to forecast them.

Overall, the prospects for the latter part of 1998 and into 1999 were considered relatively optimistic. The analysts were optimistic about earnings developments through the remainder of 1998 and 1999. Further, although valuations were above those that prevailed during the 1980s, the current levels could be justified based upon the improved earnings

[14]Jackie Ashurst, Charles K. Brown, Geoff Haire, Mark Tracey, John A. Murphy, and Jane Henderson, "The Major European Chemicals/Pharma Groups—Industries in Flux" (London: Goldman, Sachs International Ltd., May 1998).

TABLE 19.11 **KEY EARNINGS AND FINANCIAL STATISTICS FOR MAJOR CHEMICAL FIRMS[a]**

		EPS		1999E (%)		P/E	P/CF	P/B
Firm	Currency	1998	1999E	ROE	ND/Eq	1999E	1999E	1999
BASF	DM	5.0	4.9	11.8	−3	16.4	7.0	1.5
Bayer	DM	4.4	4.7	14	16	16.6	8.1	2.0
Hoechst	DM	34.0	47.5	14	93	15.5	6.3	2.5
AKZO	DFL	27.8	29.5	19.2	19	14.3	8.4	2.0
DSM	DFL	26.5	22.0	15.9	72	9.3	4.0	1.1
L'Air Liquide	FFr	52.2	55.6	12.4	37	21.0	9.8	2.6
Rhone-Poulenc	FFr	8.6	12.4	5	153	15.6	4.8	1.2

[a]Goldman, Sachs & Co. estimates.

Source: Jackie Ashurst, Charles K. Brown, Geoff Haire, Mark Tracey, John A. Murphy, and Jane Henderson, "The Major European Chemicals/Pharma Groups—Industries in Flux" (London: Goldman, Sachs International Ltd., May 1998). Reprinted by permission of Goldman, Sachs & Co.

TABLE 19.12 **EXCHANGE RATE TRENDS 1996–1998E[a]**

	DM Strength		SFr Strength		FFr Strength		DFL Strength		Sterling Strength		
	vs US$ %	Trade-Weighted %	vs US$ %	Trade-Weighted %	vs US$ %	Trade-Weighted %	vs US$ %	Trade-Weighted %	vs US$ %	vs DM %	Trade-Weighted %
1996											
Q1	+1	—	+15	+5	+6	−1	+1	—	−3	−4	−4
Q2	−9	−4	+18	+9	−5	—	−8	−3	−5	+4	+1
Q3	−5	−2	+10	+5	−3	−1	−5	−2	−1	+3	+2
Q4	−8	−4	+11	+8	−5	−2	−8	−4	+5	+13	+9
1997											
Q1	−13	−5	−21	−10	−11	−3	−13	−5	+7	+20	+16
Q2	−13	−4	−16	−6	−12	−3	−13	−4	+7	+21	+18
Q3	−21	−6	−22	−9	−20	−5	−21	−6	+5	+26	+20
Q4	−15	−4	−11	0	−14	−3	−16	−4	+2	+16	+13
1998											
Q1E[b]	−10	−3	−3	+5	−9	−2	−10	−3	+1	+11	+9
Q2E[b]	−3	−2	−3	+3	−1	+1	−3	−1	—	+3	+3
Q3E[b]	+3	—	+1	+1	—	—	+2	+1	—	−2	−1
Q4E[b]	—	+1	−3	−2	+1	−1	—	—	−1	−1	−1

[a]Year-on-year percentage changes.

[b]Projections at May 11, 1998 rates of DM1.77/\$, Sfr1.48/\$, FFr5.91/\$, DFL2.00/\$, \$1.63/£ and DM2.89/£.

Source: Jackie Ashurst, Charles K. Brown, Geoff Haire, Mark Tracey, John A. Murphy, and Jane Henderson, "The Major European Chemicals/Pharma Groups—Industries in Flux" (London: Goldman, Sachs International Ltd., May 1998). Reprinted by permission of Goldman, Sachs & Co.

quality. Finally, the analysts also felt the dollar outlook would probably not be helpful to earnings and valuation.

The rest of the report discussed the major chemical firms and made specific recommendations regarding each of them. This segment of the report on individual companies will be considered in our next chapter on company analysis.

THE INTERNET *Investments Online*

The Web is a source that can help researchers find information about an industry. Unfortunately, many industry analysis reports are available online but only to registered and paying clients of research firms, investment banks, and brokerage houses. Up-to-date Porter-type analyses are also not available free on the Internet for a variety of industries. Web searches for industry information can focus on exploring Web sites of competitors in the industry. Trade group Web sites may be found through keyword searches using terms and phrases relevant to the target industry.

Since this chapter focuses on the retail drugstore industry, a little investigation brought forth the sites described here; many more exist for your perusal.

www.lf.com This is the home page for Lebhar-Friedman, Inc., a publisher and provider of information about retailers. Their site for *Drug Store News* (**www.drugstorenews.com**) has a number of industry links, including suppliers, retailers, wholesalers, trade associations, information for pharmacists, and pharmacy-related links.

www.studentcenter.com Though not directly related to the chapter's topic, this site contains helpful information. The main purpose of the site is to help students with their job search. Because it links to industries and companies, it also provides information on a variety of firms in different industries. Over 35,000 firms in 1,000 industries are included in its database.

www.nacds.org This page is sponsored by the National Association of Chain Drug Stores. It contains links to data relevant to chain drugstores, from sales in different product categories to projected numbers of prescriptions. It offers news and links to related sites.

www.nwda.org This is a site of the National Wholesale Druggists Association. This page features links to managed care issues; public policy issues; and information for pharmacies, consumers, the press, manufacturers, analysts, and investors; as well as links to other health-related Web sites.

Summary

- Several studies have examined industry performance and risk. They have found wide dispersion in the performance of alternative industries during specified time periods, implying that industry analysis can help identify superior investments. They also showed inconsistent industry performance over time, implying that looking at only past performance of an industry has little value in projecting future performance. Also, the performance by firms within industries typically is not very consistent, so you must analyze individual companies in an industry following the industry analysis.
- The analysis of industry risk indicated wide dispersion in the measures of risk for different industries, but a fair amount of consistency in the risk measure over time for individual industries. These results imply that risk analysis and measurement are useful in selecting industries. The good news is that past risk measures may be of some value when estimating future risk.
- We discussed and demonstrated both approaches to the valuation of the RDS industry. The present value of cash flow models indicated a fairly wide range of value wherein the DDM models indicated overvaluation of the industry, while the FCFE models indicated that the industry was undervalued.
- The four relative valuation ratio techniques also provided a range of results, including the two-step earnings multiple technique where the results generally pointed toward overvaluation. The other three relative valuation ratios showed a tendency to decline over time relative to the market with a major decline in the P/BV ratio caused by a deterioration in the industry profit margin and its ROE.
- Global industry analysis must evaluate the effects not only of world supply, demand, and cost components for an industry, but also different valuation levels due to accounting conventions, and finally the impact of exchange rates on the total industry and the firms within it.

Questions

1. Briefly describe the results of studies that examined the performance of alternative industries during specific time periods and discuss their implications for industry analysis.
2. Briefly describe the results of the studies that examined industry performance over time. Do these results complicate or simplify industry analysis?
3. Assume all the firms in a particular industry have consistently experienced similar rates of return. Discuss what this implies regarding the importance of industry and company analysis for this industry.
4. Discuss the contention that differences in the performance of various firms within an industry limit the usefulness of industry analysis.
5. Several studies have examined the difference in risk for alternative industries during a specified time period. Describe the results of these studies and discuss their implications for industry analysis.
6. What were the results when industry risk was examined during successive time periods? Discuss the implication of these results for industry analysis.
7. Assume the industry you are analyzing is in the fourth stage of the industrial life cycle. How would you react if your industry–economic analysis predicted that sales per share for this industry would increase by 20 percent? Discuss your reasoning.
8. Discuss at what stage in the industrial life cycle you would like to discover an industry. Justify your decision.
9. Give an example of an industry in stage two of the industrial life cycle. Discuss your reasoning for putting the industry in stage two and any evidence that caused you to select this industry.
10. Discuss an example of input–output analysis to predict the sales for the auto industry. Discuss how you would use input–output analysis to predict the costs of production for the computer industry.
11. Discuss the impact of the threat of substitute products on the steel industry's profitability.
12. Discuss the two variables that must be considered whether you are using the present value of cash flow approach or the relative valuation ratio approach to valuation. Why are these variables relevant for either valuation approach?
13. List the three variables that are relevant when attempting to determine whether the earnings multiple (P/E ratio) for an industry should be higher, equal to, or lower than the market multiple. Assuming you are analyzing the retail food industry, discuss which of these variables would be most important in explaining the difference in earnings multiple. Why is it relevant?
14. Discuss when you would use the two-stage growth FCFE model rather than the constant growth model.
15. You are examining the P/CF ratio for an industry compared to the market and find that the industry ratio has always been at a discount to the market—e.g., the industry–market ratio of ratios is about 0.80. What variable(s) would you examine to explain this difference or to justify an increase in the industry–market ratio?
16. *CFA Examination II (1999).*

CFA

Elizabeth Coronado, CFA, is analyzing Nelson Motors, Inc., one of the largest and most profitable automobile manufacturers in North America. Since the early 1990s, the fastest growing and most profitable product segment for Nelson has been its sport utility vehicles (SUV) line shown in the following exhibit.

Coronado believes that applying the product life cycle model to Nelson's SUV product line will yield additional analytical insights into the company's recent rapid earnings growth.

a. Identify the current product life cycle stage for the Raven, Hawk, and Eagle. Justify your choice of product life cycle stage by citing evidence from the following exhibit. [6 minutes]

NELSON MOTORS ANNUAL SUV PRODUCTION AND FINANCIAL DATA

	1990	1991	1992	1993	1994	1995	1996	1997	1998	1999E	2000E
SUV Units Sold in Thousands											
Raven	5	10	35	70	90	100	110	112	110	105	90
Hawk	—	—	—	—	3	10	20	45	63	68	69
Eagle	—	—	—	—	—	—	—	5	32	70	110
Profit per Vehicle in $ Thousands											
Raven	9	10	9	8	8	7	7	6	5	4	3
Hawk	—	—	—	—	6	7	8	7	7	8	7
Eagle	—	—	—	—	—	—	—	10	10	11	12
Profit per SUV Model in $ Millions											
Raven	45	100	315	560	720	700	770	672	550	420	270
Hawk	—	—	—	—	18	70	160	315	441	544	483
Eagle	—	—	—	—	—	—	—	50	320	770	1320
Total SUV Division Profit in $ Millions	45	100	315	560	738	770	930	1,037	1,311	1,734	2,073
Total Nelson Motors Profit in $ Millions	1,125	1,250	1,575	1,600	1,994	1,974	2,214	2,357	2,960	3,470	3,989
SUV Division Profit % of Nelson Motors Profit	4%	8%	20%	35%	37%	39%	42%	44%	44%	50%	52%
Year over Year % Change in Total SUV Profit	—	122%	215%	78%	32%	4%	21%	12%	26%	32%	20%
Model Percent of SUV Division Profit											
Raven	100%	100%	100%	100%	98%	91%	83%	65%	42%	24%	13%
Hawk	—	—	—	—	2%	9%	17%	30%	34%	31%	23%
Eagle	—	—	—	—	—	—	—	5%	24%	44%	64%

Because of the high expectations associated with the Eagle, Nelson Motors' current P/E is above its five-year historic range and above the auto industry P/E. An auto analyst states that "Nelson Motors has the best of both worlds:

- increasing SUV profitability and
- declining expected future earnings volatility."

b. Evaluate *each* statement, using the data presented in the Exhibit (6 minutes).

17. *CFA Examination II (1999).*

Scott Kelly, a U.S.-based equity analyst, is analyzing the toy industry to determine which companies will be most competitive. He has determined that the U.S. toy industry is relatively mature and that revenue and earnings growth are slowing. His report contains the following statements:

- I recommend that we invest in toy companies with a substantial percentage of revenues derived from non-U.S. sales.
- Companies selected for the portfolio should derive a large portion of revenues from the largest discount toy retailer.
- I am particularly interested in a start-up company that has an exciting new toy coming out based on a very popular television show.
- Although MasterToy has the dominant market share, I feel that smaller companies will have better opportunities for growth in a mature market.

State whether *each* of Kelly's statements is valid or not valid. Cite *two* industry characteristics by *number* from the following Exhibit to support your decision. [16 minutes]

TOY INDUSTRY CHARACTERISTICS

Industry Life Cycle:

1. U.S. toy sales grew by 5% compounded annually over the past 10 years. However, toy sales in the U.S. were down 4% last year. Growth of toy sales is expected to be 1.5–3.0% annually for the next 5 years.
2. Non-U.S. toy sales grew by 7% compounded annually over the past 10 years. Sales growth is expected to be 7–8% for the next 5 years.
3. The toy industry is in a period of rapid consolidation. Companies faced with slower internal growth are considering acquisitions to enhance growth.

Demographics:

4. The birth rate in the U.S. is expected to decline by 3% annually for the next 3 years.
5. The birth rate in Europe and Asia is expected to increase by 2% annually for the next 3 years.
6. Age demographics are important drivers of demand both in the U.S. and in target non-U.S. markets (only 3% of the world's children live in the U.S.). Per capita consumption of toys in non-U.S. markets is lower than in the U.S.

Consumer Preference:

7. Brand names are one of the keys to success in both U.S. and non-U.S. markets. Consumers show a preference for products manufactured by well-regarded companies.
8. Marketing studies indicate that even technologically superior products will be hard to sell when manufactured by a company without a brand name or without a substantial advertising budget to support the product.
9. The top companies dedicate a large amount of money to focus groups and marketing studies in order to accurately gauge consumer preference.

Market Share:

10. The world's two largest toy manufacturers (MasterToy and FunToyz) control more than 75% of the U.S. market. No other manufacturer represents more than 5% in market share. Economies of scale are important for production, advertisement, and promotion.
11. The larger companies in the industry have the ability to develop lucrative and cost effective advertising in all media sectors. They have better bargaining power versus the competition and are more able to negotiate prime-time advertisements.
12. Marketing studies show that sales of products associated with hit movies and TV shows are much higher than for competing products without the entertainment tie-in.

Retail Environment/Distribution:

13. A major discount toy retailer's inventory-reduction program has negatively affected earnings for the group. This distribution channel has been critical to success in the past, accounting for a large percentage of sales. The company has adopted a new inventory control system in order to operate more efficiently.
14. To reduce dependence on traditional retail channels, companies are diversifying into direct mail and Internet commerce.
15. Global distribution of product is an essential component of long-term growth for industry leaders.

Diversification:

16. Diversification is a key to success. A niche product can quickly lose its appeal. Typically, companies that rely on one or two key products fail when popularity fades.
17. The top two toy manufacturers have a highly diversified product mix.

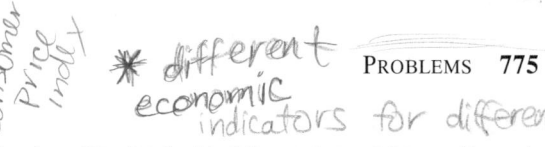

Problems

1. Select three industries from the S&P *Analysts Handbook* with different demand factors. For each industry, indicate what economic series you would use to predict the growth for the industry. Discuss why the economic series selected is relevant for this industry.
2. Prepare a scatter plot for one of the industries in Problem 1 of industry sales per share and observations from the economic series you suggested for this industry. Do this for the most recent 10 years using information available in the *Analysts Handbook*. Based on the results of the scatter plot, discuss whether the economic series was closely related to this industry's sales.
3. Based on an analysis of the results in Problem 2, discuss the stage of your industry in its life cycle.
4. Evaluate your industry in terms of the five factors that determine an industry's intensity of competition. Based on this analysis, what are your expectations about the industry's profitability in the short run (1 or 2 years) and the long run (5–10 years)?
5. Using the S&P *Analysts Handbook*, plot the latest 10-year history of the operating profit margin for the S&P 400 versus the S&P industry of your choice. Is there a positive, negative, or zero correlation?
6. Using the S&P *Analysts Handbook*, calculate the means for the following variables of the S&P 400 and the industry of your choice during the last 10 years:
   a. Price/earnings multiplier
   b. Retention rate
   c. Return on equity
   d. Equity turnover
   e. Net profit margin

   Briefly comment on how your industry and the S&P 400 differ for each of the variables.
7. Prepare a table listing the variables that influence the earnings multiplier for your chosen industry and the S&P 400 series for the most recent 10 years.
   a. Do the average dividend-payout ratios for your industry and the S&P 400 differ? How should the dividend payout influence the difference between the multipliers?
   b. Based on the fundamental factors, would you expect the risk for this industry to differ from that for the market? In what direction, and why? Calculate the industry beta using monthly data for 5 years. Based on the fundamental factors and the computed systematic risk, how does this industry's risk compare to the market? What effect will this difference in risk have on the industry multiplier relative to the market multiplier?
   c. Analyze and discuss the different components of growth (retention rate, total asset turnover, total assets/equity, and profit margin) for your chosen industry and the S&P 400 during the most recent 10 years. Based on this analysis, how would you expect the growth rate for your industry to compare with the growth rate for the S&P 400? How would this difference in expected growth affect the multiplier?
8. *CFA Examination II (1995)*

   As a securities analyst you have been asked to review a valuation of a closely held business, Wigwam Autoparts Heaven, Inc. (WAH) prepared by the Red Rocks Group (RRG). You are to give an opinion on the valuation and to support your opinion by analyzing each part of the valuation. WAH's sole business is automotive parts retailing.

   The RRG valuation includes a section called "Analysis of the Retail Autoparts Industry," based completely on the data in Table 1 and the following additional information.

   - WAH and its principal competitors each operated over 150 stores at year end 1994.
   - The average number of stores operated per company engaged in the retail autoparts industry is 5.3.
   - The major customer base for auto parts sold in retail stores consists of young owners of old vehicles. These owners do their own automotive maintenance out of economic necessity.

TABLE 1 SELECTED RETAIL AUTOPARTS INDUSTRY DATA

	1994	1993	1992	1991	1990	1989	1988	1987	1986	1985
Population 18–29 Years Old (Percentage Change)	−1.8%	−2.0%	−2.1%	−1.4%	−0.8%	−0.9%	−1.1%	−0.9%	−0.7%	−0.3%
Number of Households with Income More Than $35,000 (Percentage Change)	6.0%	4.0%	8.0%	4.5%	2.7%	3.1%	1.6%	3.6%	4.2%	2.2%
Number of Households with Income Less Than $35,000 (Percentage (Change)	3.0%	−1.0%	4.9%	2.3%	−1.4%	2.5%	1.4%	−1.3%	0.6%	0.1%
Number of Cars 5–15 Years Old (Percentage Change)	0.9%	−1.3%	−6.0%	1.9%	3.3%	2.4%	−2.3%	−2.2%	−8.0%	1.6%
Automotive Aftermarket Industry Retail Sales (Percentage Change)	5.7%	1.9%	3.1%	3.7%	4.3%	2.6%	1.3%	0.2%	3.7%	2.4%
Consumer Expenditures on Automotive Parts and Accessories (Percentage Change)	2.4%	1.8%	2.1%	6.5%	3.6%	9.2%	1.3%	6.2%	6.7%	6.5%
Sales Growth of Retail Autoparts Companies with 100 or More Stores	17.0%	16.0%	16.5%	14.0%	15.5%	16.8%	12.0%	15.7%	19.0%	16.0%
Market Share of Retail Autoparts Companies with 100 or More Stores	19.0%	18.5%	18.3%	18.1%	17.0%	17.2%	17.0%	16.9%	15.0%	14.0%
Average Operating Margin of Retail Autoparts Companies with 100 or More Stores	12.0%	11.8%	11.2%	11.5%	10.6%	10.6%	10.0%	10.4%	9.8%	9.0%
Average Operating Margin of All Retail Autoparts Companies	5.5%	5.7%	5.6%	5.8%	6.0%	6.5%	7.0%	7.2%	7.1%	7.2%

a. One of RRG's conclusions is that the retail autoparts industry as a whole is in the stabilization stage of the industry life cycle. Discuss *three* relevant items of data from Table 1 that support this conclusion. [9 minutes]

b. Another RRG conclusion is that WAH and its principal competitors are in the growth stage of their life cycle.

Cite *three* relevant items of data from Table 1 that support this conclusion.

Explain how WAH and its principal competitors can be in a growth stage while their industry as a whole is in the stabilization stage. [11 minutes]

9. You know the following about your industry (*I*) and the market (*M*):

ROE_I:	12%	ROE_M:	16%
RR_I:	60	RR_M:	0.55
$Beta_I$:	1.05	$Beta_M$:	1.00

Discuss what difference you would expect in the P/Es, and explain why you expect this difference.

References

Aber, John. "Industry Effects and Multivariate Stock Price Behavior." *Journal of Financial and Quantitative Analysis* 11, no. 5 (November 1976).

Fruhan, William E., Jr. *Financial Strategy.* Homewood, Ill.: Richard D. Irwin, 1979.

Goodman, D. A., and John W. Peavy III. "Industry Relative Price-Earnings Ratios as Indicators of Investment Returns." *Financial Analysts Journal* 39, no. 2 (March–April 1983): 60–66.

Porter, Michael E. *Competitive Advantage: Creating and Sustaining Superior Performance.* New York: Free Press, 1985.

Porter, Michael E. *Competitive Strategy: Techniques for Analyzing Industries and Competitors.* New York: Free Press, 1980.

Porter, Michael E. "How to Conduct an Industry Analysis." In *The Financial Analysts Handbook,* 2d ed., ed. Sumner N. Levine. Homewood, Ill.: Dow Jones-Irwin, 1988.

Stewart, Samuel S. "Forecasting Corporate Earnings." In *The Financial Analysts Handbook,* 2d ed., ed. Sumner N. Levine. Homewood, Ill.: Dow Jones-Irwin, 1988.

The following are proceedings from industry analysis seminars sponsored by the Association for Investment Management and Research:

Balog, James (ed.). *The Health Care Industry.* Charlottesville, Va.: Association for Investment Management and Research, 1993.

Bhatia, Sanjiv (ed.). *The Consumer Staples Industry.* Charlottesville, Va.: Association for Investment Management and Research, 1995.

Bhatia, Sanjiv (ed.). *The Media Industry.* Charlottesville, Va.: Association for Investment Management and Research, 1996.

Billingsley, Randall S. (ed.). *The Telecommunications Industry.* Charlottesville, Va.: Association for Investment Management and Research, 1994.

Petrie, Thomas A. (ed.). *The Oil and Gas Industries.* Charlottesville, Va.: Association for Investment Management and Research, 1993.

Shasta, Theodore (ed.). *The Automotive Industry.* Charlottesville, Va.: Association for Investment Management and Research, 1994.

Chapter 19

APPENDIX A. PREPARING AN INDUSTRY ANALYSIS

WHAT IS AN INDUSTRY?[15]

Identifying a company's industry can be difficult in today's business world. Although airlines, railroads, and utilities may be easy to categorize, what about manufacturing companies with three different divisions, none of which is dominant? Perhaps the best way to test whether a company fits into an industry grouping is to compare the operating results for the company and an industry. For our purposes, an industry is a group of companies with similar demand, supply, and operating characteristics.

The following is a set of guidelines for preparing an industry appraisal, including the topics to consider and some specific items to include.

CHARACTERISTICS TO STUDY

1. Price history reveals valuable long-term relationships
   a. Price/earnings ratios
   b. Common stock yields
   c. Price/book value ratios
   d. Price/cash flow ratios

[15]Reprinted and adapted with permission of Stanley D. Ryals, CFA; Investment Council, Inc.; La Crescenta, CA 91214.

2. Operating data show comparisons of
   a. Return on total investment (ROI)
   b. Return on equity (ROE)
   c. Sales growth
   d. Trends in operating profit margin
   e. Evaluation of stage in industrial life cycle
   f. Book value growth
   g. Earnings-per-share growth
   h. Profit margin trends (gross, operating, and net)
   i. Evaluation of exchange rate risk from foreign sales
3. Comparative results of alternative industries show
   a. Effects of business cycles on each industry group
   b. Secular trends affecting results
   c. Industry growth compared to other industries
   d. Regulatory changes
   e. Importance of overseas operations

FACTORS IN INDUSTRY ANALYSIS

MARKETS FOR PRODUCTS

1. Trends in the markets for the industry's major products: historical and projected
2. Industry growth relative to GDP or other relevant economic series; possible changes from past trends
3. Shares of market for major products among domestic and global producers; changes in market shares in recent years; outlook
4. Effect of imports on industry markets; share of market taken by imports; price and margin changes caused by imports; outlook for imports
5. Effect of exports on their markets; trends in export prices and units exported; outlook for exports
6. Expectations for the exchange rates in major non-U.S. countries; historical volatility of exchange rates; outlook for the level and volatility of exchange rates

FINANCIAL PERFORMANCE

1. Capitalization ratios; ability to raise new capital; earnings retention rate; financial leverage
2. Ratio of fixed assets to capital invested; depreciation policies; capital turnover
3. Return on total capital; return on equity capital; components of ROE
4. Return on foreign investments; need for foreign capital

OPERATIONS

1. Degrees of integration; cost advantages of integration; major supply contracts
2. Operating rates as a percentage of capacity; backlogs; new-order trends
3. Trends of industry consolidation
4. Trends in industry competition
5. New-product development; research and development expenditures in dollars and as a percentage of sales
6. Diversification; comparability of product lines

MANAGEMENT

1. Management depth and ability to develop from within; organizational structure
2. Board of directors: internal versus external members; compensation package

3. Flexibility to deal with product demand changes; ability to identify and eliminate losing operations
4. Record and outlook regarding labor relations
5. Dividend policy and historical progression

SOURCES OF INDUSTRY INFORMATION

1. Independent industry journals
2. Industry and trade associations
3. Government reports and statistics
4. Independent research organizations
5. Brokerage house research
6. Financial publishers (S&P; Moody's; Value Line)

Chapter 19 APPENDIX

B. DATA NEEDS FOR AN INDUSTRY ANALYSIS

DATA NEEDS FOR AN INDUSTRY ANALYSIS

Data Categories	Compilation
Product lines	By company
Buyers and their behavior	By year
Complementary products	By functional area
Substitute products	
Growth	
Rate	
Pattern (seasonal, cyclical)	
Determinants	
Technology of production and distribution	
Cost structure	
Economies of scale	
Value added	
Logistics	
Labor	
Marketing and selling	
Market segmentation	
Marketing practices	
Suppliers	
Distribution channels (if indirect)	
Innovation	
Types	
Sources	
Rate	
Economies of scale	
Competitors—strategy, goals, strengths and weaknesses, assumptions	
Social, political, legal environment	
Macroeconomic environment	

Source: Adapted and reprinted with the permission of The Free Press, a division of Simon & Schuster, from *Competitive Strategy: Techniques for Analyzing Industries and Competitors* by Michael E. Porter, p. 370. Copyright © 1980 by The Free Press.

Chapter 19
APPENDIX C. INSIGHTS ON ANALYZING INDUSTRY ROAs

INSIGHTS ON INDUSTRY ROAS

Beyond the normal analysis of ROA as a component of ROE (ROA times Total Assets/Equity equals ROE), an article by Selling and Stickney provides some interesting insights for industry analysis based upon an analysis of the two components of the ROA ratio (profit margin and total asset turnover) and what these two components signal regarding the industry strategy.[16] Given the two components of the ROA, it is possible to graph each of these values as shown in Figure 19C.1 and determine what each component contributed to the ROA at the point of intersection. As shown, it is possible to draw a constant ROA curve, which demonstrates that it is possible to achieve an 8 percent (or 4 percent) ROA with numerous combinations of profit margin and asset turnover. The particular combination of profit margin and asset turnover is generally dictated by the nature of the industry and the strategy employed by management. For example, many industries necessarily require large capital inputs for equipment (e.g., steel, auto, heavy machinery manufacturers). Therefore, the asset turnover is necessarily low, which means the profit margin must be higher. The firms in such an industry are typically in the upper left segment of the graph (segment *a*), and improvements of ROA in these industries are derived by increasing profit margins because it is difficult to increase asset turnover. In contrast, industries that have commodity-type products (e.g., retail food, paper, industrial chemicals) generally have low profit margins and succeed based upon high asset turnover. These industries are generally in the

FIGURE 19C.1 **ROA—THE TRADE-OFF OF PROFIT MARGIN AND ASSET TURNOVER**

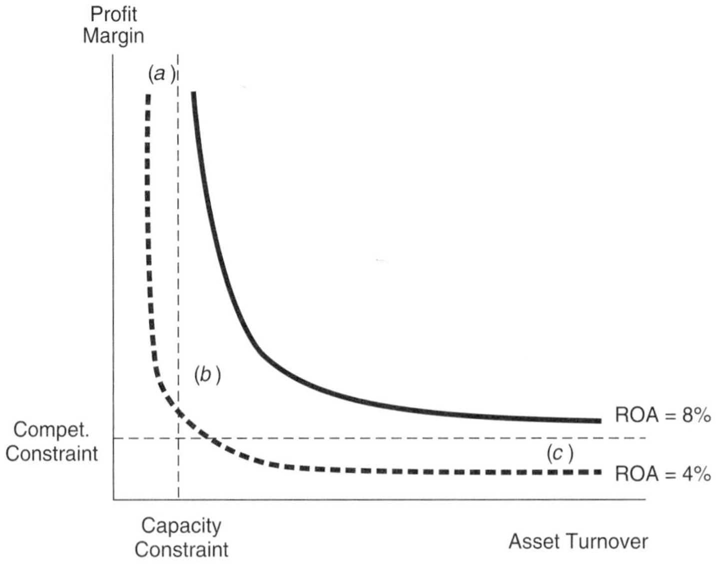
Profit Margin
(a)
(b)
(c)
ROA = 8%
ROA = 4%
Compet. Constraint
Capacity Constraint
Asset Turnover

Source: Thomas Selling and Clyde P. Stickney, "The Effects of Business Environment and Strategy on a Firm's Rate of Return on Assets," *Financial Analysts Journal* 45, no. 1 (January–February 1989): 43–52.

[16]Thomas Selling and Clyde P. Stickney, "The Effects of Business Environment and Strategy on a Firm's Rate of Return on Assets," *Financial Analysts Journal* 45, no. 1 (January–February 1989): 43–52.

lower right segment of the graph (segment *c*) and attempt to improve their ROA by increasing their asset turnover rather than the profit margin (i.e., they are constrained by price competition). Industries in the middle segment (*b*) are in a more balanced position and can attempt to improve the ROA by increasing *either* the profit margin or the asset turnover.

It is very important for an analyst to understand the nature of the industry and what contributes to the industry's ROA as well as what this implies about the constraints and opportunities facing the firms in the industry.

Chapter

20 Company Analysis and Stock Selection*

After you read this chapter, you should be able to answer the following questions:

- Why is it important to differentiate between company analysis and stock analysis?
- What is the difference between a growth company and a growth stock?
- How do we apply the two valuation approaches and the several valuation techniques to Walgreen?
- What techniques are useful when estimating the inputs to alternative valuation models?
- What techniques aid estimating company sales?
- How do we estimate the profit margins and earnings per share for a company?
- What procedures and factors do we consider when estimating the earnings multiplier for a firm?
- What two specific competitive strategies can a firm use to cope with the competitive environment in its industry?
- In addition to the earnings multiplier, what are some other relative valuation ratios?
- How do you apply the several present value of cash flow models to the valuation of a company?
- What are some value-added measures that can be used to evaluate the performance of a firm?
- What are the specific calculations required to compute economic value-added (EVA), market value-added (MVA), and the franchise value for a firm?
- What is the relationship between these value-added measures and changes in the market value of firms?
- When should we consider selling a stock?
- What is meant by a true growth company?
- What is the relationship between positive EVA and a growth company?
- Why is it inappropriate to use the standard dividend discount model to value a true growth company?
- What is the difference between no growth, simple growth, and dynamic growth?
- What is the growth duration model and what information does it provide when analyzing a true growth company and evaluating its stock?
- How can you use the growth duration model to derive an estimate of the P/E for a growth company?
- What is the flexible three-stage growth model and how would you describe the three stages?
- What are some additional factors that should be considered when analyzing a company on a global basis?

*The authors acknowledge comments and suggestions on this chapter by Professor Edgar Norton of Illinois State University.

At this point you have made two decisions about your investment in equity markets. First, after analyzing the economy and stock markets for several countries, you have decided that you should invest some portion of your portfolio in common stocks. Second, after analyzing various industries, you have identified those that appear to offer above-average risk-adjusted performance over your investment horizon. You must now answer the final questions in the fundamental analysis procedure: (1) Which are the best companies within these desirable industries? and (2) Are their stocks underpriced? Specifically, is the intrinsic value of the stock above its market value, or is the expected rate of return on the stock equal to or greater than its required rate of return?

We begin this chapter with a discussion of the difference between company analysis and stock selection. Company analysis should occur in the context of the prevailing economic and industry conditions. We discuss some competitive strategies that can help firms maximize returns in an industry's competitive environment. We demonstrate cash flow models and relative valuation ratios that can be used to identify undervalued stocks. Cash flow and earnings-oriented models are suggested as ways to determine a stock's intrinsic value. We also review factors that will help you determine when to sell a stock that you currently own and discuss the pressures and influences that affect professional stock analysts. We conclude with an example of the analysis of foreign stocks.

This chapter discusses a number of methods used by practicing analysts to estimate intrinsic values.

COMPANY ANALYSIS VERSUS THE SELECTION OF STOCK

This chapter is titled "Company Analysis and Stock Selection" to convey the idea that the common stocks of good companies are not necessarily good investments. As a final step of the analysis, you must compare the intrinsic value of a stock to its market value to determine if it should be purchased. The point is, the stock of a wonderful firm with superior management and strong performance measured by sales and earnings growth can be priced so high that the intrinsic value of the stock is below its current market price. In contrast, the stock of a company with less success based on its sales and earnings growth may have a stock market price that is below its intrinsic value. In this case, although the company is not as good, its stock could be the better investment.

The classic confusion in this regard concerns growth companies versus growth stocks. The stock of a growth company is not necessarily a growth stock. Recognition of this difference is absolutely essential for successful investing.

Growth Companies and Growth Stocks

Growth companies have historically been defined as companies that consistently experience above-average increases in sales and earnings. This definition has some limitations because many firms could qualify due to certain accounting procedures, mergers, or other external events.

In contrast, financial theorists define a growth company as a firm with the management ability and the opportunities to make investments that yield rates of return greater than the firm's required rate of return.[1] You will recall from financial management courses that this required rate of return is the firm's weighted average cost of capital (WACC). As an example, a growth company might be able to acquire capital at an average cost of 10 percent

[1] Ezra Solomon, *The Theory of Financial Management* (New York: Columbia University Press, 1963), 55–68; and Merton Miller and Franco Modigliani, "Dividend Policy, Growth and the Valuation of Shares," *Journal of Business* 34, no. 4 (October 1961): 411–433.

and yet have the management ability and the opportunity to invest those funds at rates of return of 15 to 20 percent. As a result of these investment opportunities, the firm's sales and earnings grow faster than those of similar risk firms and the overall economy. In addition, a growth company that has above-average investment opportunities should, and typically does, retain a large portion of its earnings to fund these superior investment projects.

Growth stocks are not necessarily shares in growth companies. A **growth stock** is a stock with a higher rate of return than other stocks in the market with similar risk characteristics. The stock achieves this superior risk-adjusted rate of return because at some point in time the market undervalued it compared to other stocks. Although the stock market adjusts stock prices relatively quickly and accurately to reflect new information, available information is not always perfect or complete. Therefore, imperfect or incomplete information may cause a given stock to be undervalued or overvalued at a point in time.[2]

If the stock is undervalued, its price should eventually increase to reflect its true fundamental value when the correct information becomes available. During this period of price adjustment, the stock's realized return will exceed the required return for a stock with its risk, and, during this period of adjustment, it will be considered a growth stock. Growth stocks are not necessarily limited to growth companies. A future growth stock can be issued by any type of company; the stock need only be undervalued by the market.

The fact is, if investors recognize a growth company and discount its future earnings stream properly, the current market price of the growth company's stock will reflect its future earnings stream. Those who acquire the stock of a growth company at this correct market price will receive a rate of return consistent with the risk of the stock, even when the superior earnings growth is attained. In many instances, overeager investors tend to inflate the price of a growth company's stock. Investors who pay the inflated price will earn a rate of return below the risk-adjusted required rate of return, despite the fact that the growth company fulfills its bright prospects. Several studies that have examined the stock price performance for samples of growth companies have found that their stocks performed poorly—that is, the stocks of growth companies have generally *not* been growth stocks.[3]

Defensive Companies and Stocks

Defensive companies are those whose future earnings are likely to withstand an economic downturn. One would expect them to have relatively low business risk and not excessive financial risk. Typical examples are public utilities or grocery chains—firms that supply basic consumer necessities.

There are two closely related concepts of a **defensive stock**. First, a defensive stock's rate of return is not expected to decline during an overall market decline, or decline less than the overall market. Second, our CAPM discussion indicated that an asset's relevant risk is its covariance with the market portfolio of risky assets—that is, an asset's systematic risk. A stock with low or negative systematic risk (a small positive or negative beta) may be considered a defensive stock according to this theory because its returns are unlikely to be harmed significantly in a bear market.

---

[2]An analyst is more likely to find such stocks outside the top tier of companies, because these top-tier stocks are scrutinized by numerous analysts; in other words, look for "neglected" stocks.

[3]Michael Solt and Meir Statman, "Good Companies, Bad Stocks," *Journal of Portfolio Management* 15, no. 4 (summer 1989): 39–44; and Hersh Shafrin and Meir Statman, "Making Sense of Beta, Size, and Book-to-Market," *Journal of Portfolio Management* 21, no. 2 (winter 1995): 26–34. Similar results for "excellent" companies are discussed in Michelle Clayman, "In Search of Excellence: The Investor's Viewpoint," *Financial Analysts Journal* 43, no. 3 (May–June 1987): 54–63; and in Michelle Clayman, "Excellence Revisited," *Financial Analysts Journal* 50, no. 3 (May–June 1994): 61–65.

CYCLICAL COMPANIES AND STOCKS

A **cyclical company's** sales and earnings will be heavily influenced by aggregate business activity. Examples would be firms in the steel, auto, or heavy machinery industries. Such companies will do well during economic expansions and poorly during economic contractions. This volatile earnings pattern is typically a function of the firm's business risk and can be compounded by financial risk.

A **cyclical stock** will experience changes in its rates of return greater than changes in overall market rates of return. In terms of the CAPM, these would be stocks that have high betas. The stock of a cyclical company, however, is not necessarily cyclical. A cyclical stock is the stock of any company that has returns that are more volatile than the overall market—that is, high-beta stocks.

SPECULATIVE COMPANIES AND STOCKS

A **speculative company** is one whose assets involve great risk, but that also has a possibility of great gain. A good example of a speculative firm is one involved in oil exploration.

A **speculative stock** possesses a high probability of low or negative rates of return and a low probability of normal or high rates of return. Specifically, a speculative stock is one that is overpriced, leading to a high probability that during the future period when the market adjusts the stock price to its true value, it will experience either low or possibly negative rates of return. Such an expectation might be the case for an excellent growth company whose stock is selling at an extremely high price/earnings ratio.

VALUE VERSUS GROWTH INVESTING

Some analysts also divide stocks into "growth" stocks and "value" stocks. As we discussed above, growth stocks are companies that will have positive earnings surprises and above-average risk-adjusted rates of return because the stocks are undervalued. If the analyst does a good job in identifying such companies, investors in these stocks will reap the benefits of seeing their stock prices rise after other investors identify their earnings growth potential. **Value stocks** are those that appear to be undervalued for reasons other than earnings growth potential. Value stocks are usually identified by analysts as having low P/E ratios or low ratios of price to book value. Notably, in these comparisons between growth and value stocks, the specification of a growth stock is not consistent with our discussion above. In this case a **growth stock** is generally the stock of a company that is experiencing rapid growth of sales and earnings (e.g., Intel and Microsoft). As a result, the stock has a high P/E and price-book-value ratio. Cycles appear over time during which value stocks sometimes outperform growth stocks; at other times growth stocks outperform value stocks. Figure 20.1 shows the recent performance of a growth and value stock index for the period 1993-1998. During this period it appears that growth stocks were the better investment choice based upon a surge in performance during 1998.

The major point of this section is that you must examine a company to determine its characteristics and derive an estimate of the value of its stock. Subsequently, you compare this intrinsic value of the stock to its current market price to determine whether you should acquire it—that is, will the stock provide a rate of return equal to or greater than what is consistent with its risk?

ECONOMIC, INDUSTRY, AND STRUCTURAL LINKS TO COMPANY ANALYSIS

The analysis of companies and their stocks is the final step in the top-down approach to investing. Rather than selecting stocks on the basis of company-specific factors (as with bottom-up analysis), top-down analysts review the current state and future outlook for domestic and international sectors of the economy. On the basis of this macroeconomic

FIGURE 20.1 **COMPARISON OF THE PERFORMANCE OF THE RUSSELL 3000 VALUE AND GROWTH STOCK INDEXES: 1994–1998**

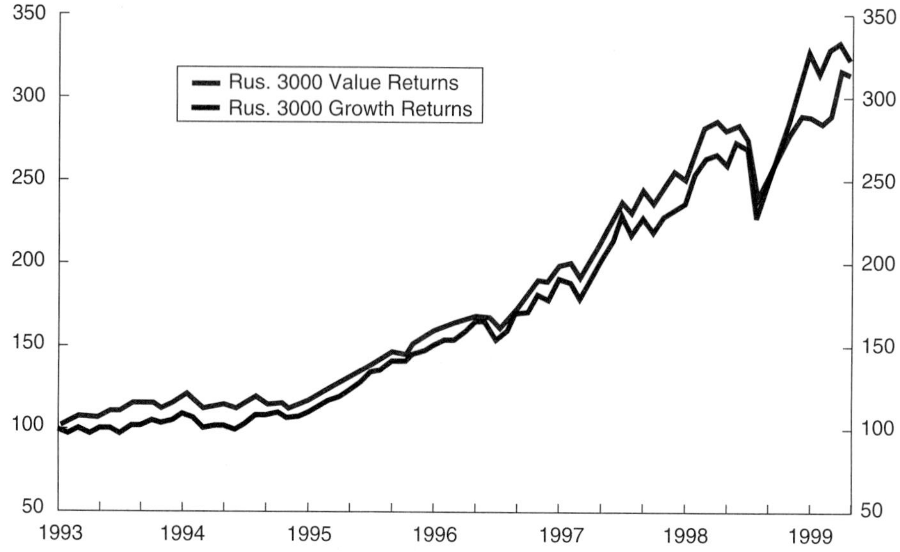
350
300
250
200
150
100
50
Rus. 3000 Value Returns
Rus. 3000 Growth Returns
1993
1994
1995
1996
1997
1998
1999

Source: Frank Russell & Co.

analysis, they identify industries that are expected to offer attractive returns in the expected future environment. Following these earlier macroanalyses, we turn our attention to the process of analyzing firms in the selected industries. Our analysis concentrates on the two significant determinants of a stock's intrinsic value: growth of the firm's expected cash flows and its risk.

ECONOMIC AND INDUSTRY INFLUENCES

If economic trends are favorable for an industry, the company analysis should focus on firms in that industry that are well positioned to benefit from the economic trends. Firms with sales or earnings particularly sensitive to macroeconomic variables should also be considered. As part of the analysis, research analysts will have to be familiar with the cash flow and risk attributes of the firms they are studying. In times of economic or industry growth, the most attractive candidates for purchase may not be the financially strong market leaders. Rather, the marginal firms in the industry or firms with high levels of operating leverage and financial leverage may benefit substantially. A modest percentage increase in revenue can be magnified into a much larger percentage rise in earnings and cash flow for the highly leveraged firm. The point is, all firms in an industry are not identical. They will have varying sensitivities to economic variables, such as economic growth, interest rates, input costs, and exchange rates, and will have different competitive strategies. Because each firm is different, an investor must examine each firm to determine the best candidates for purchase under current and expected economic conditions.

STRUCTURAL INFLUENCES

In addition to economic variables, other factors, such as social trends, technology. and political and regulatory influences, can have a major effect on some firms in an industry. Some firms in the industry can try to take advantage of demographic changes or shifts in consumer tastes and lifestyles, or invest in technology to lower costs and better serve their customers. Such firms may be able to grow and succeed despite unfavorable industry or economic conditions. For example, Wal-Mart became the nation's leading retailer in the

1990s because it benefited from smart management. The geographic location of many of its stores allowed it to benefit from rising regional population and lower labor costs. Its strategy, which emphasized everyday low prices, was appealing to consumers who had become concerned about the price and value of purchases. Wal-Mart's technologically advanced inventory and ordering systems, and the logistics of its distribution system, gave the retailer an advantage over less technologically progressive rivals.

During the initial stage of an industry's life cycle, the original firms in the industry can refine their technologies and move down the learning curve. Subsequent followers may also benefit from these initial actions and can learn from the leaders' mistakes and take the market lead away from them. Investors need to be aware of such strategies so they can evaluate companies and their stocks accordingly.

Political and regulatory events can create opportunities in an industry even when economic influences appear weak. Deregulation in trucking, airlines, and the financial services industries in the 1980s led to the creation of new companies and innovative strategies that returned continuing value to shareholders. If the saying "it's always darkest before dawn" has any truth to it, sharp price declines following bad industry news may be a good buying opportunity for investors with good analytical skills. Some stocks may deserve lower prices following some political or regulatory events; but if the market also punishes the stock prices of good companies or companies with smaller exposures to the bad news, then an astute analyst will identify buying opportunities of underpriced stocks within an industry.

The bottom line is that, although the economy plays a major role in determining overall market trends and industry groups display sensitivity to economic variables, other structural changes may counterbalance the economic effects, or company management may be able to minimize the impact of economic events on a company. Analysts who are familiar with industry trends and company strategies can issue well-reasoned buy-and-sell recommendations irrespective of the economic forecast.

COMPANY ANALYSIS

This section, "Company Analysis," groups various analysis components for discussion. "Firm Competitive Strategies" contains a continuation of the Porter discussion of an industry's competitive environment, and a later subsection discusses the basic SWOT analysis, where the objective is to articulate a firm's strengths, weaknesses, opportunities, and threats. These two analyses should provide a complete understanding of a firm's overall *strategic* approach. Given this background, you can tackle the fundamental valuation models using the analytical tools provided in Chapter 12, "Analysis of Financial Statement," and Chapter 13, "Introduction to Security Valuation." In the rest of this chapter, we discuss estimating intrinsic value by implementing the two valuation approaches: (1) the present value of cash flows, and (2) relative valuation ratio techniques. After applying the several valuation techniques to Walgreen, we discuss the significance of site visits to companies, how to prepare for an interview with management, and suggestions on when an investor should consider selling an asset. This is followed by a discussion of unique considerations regarding evaluation of international companies and their stocks. The final section of the chapter discusses the unique features of true growth companies and presents and demonstrates several models that can be used to derive a relative value or a specific value for growth companies.

Firm Competitive Strategies

In describing competition within industries, we identified five competitive forces that could affect the competitive structure and profit potential of an industry. They are: (1) current rivalry, (2) threat of new entrants, (3) potential substitutes, (4) bargaining power of suppliers, and (5) bargaining power of buyers. After you have determined the competitive structure of an industry, you should attempt to identify the specific competitive strategy employed by each firm and evaluate these strategies in terms of the overall competitive structure of the industry. As before, the analyst should identify and monitor the key assumptions and variables that affect the firm's attractiveness as a purchase candidate.

A company's competitive strategy can either be *defensive* or *offensive.* A **defensive competitive strategy** involves positioning the firm so that its capabilities provide the best means to deflect the effect of the competitive forces in the industry. Examples may include investing in fixed assets and technology to lower production costs or creating a strong brand image with increased advertising expenditures.

An **offensive competitive strategy** is one in which the firm attempts to use its strengths to affect the competitive forces in the industry and, in so doing, improves the firm's relative position in the industry. For example, Microsoft's domination in personal computer software is due to its ability to preempt rivals and its early affiliation with IBM by becoming the writer of operating system software for a large portion of the PC market. Similarly, Wal-Mart used its buying power to obtain price concessions from its suppliers. This cost advantage, coupled with a superior delivery system to its stores, allowed Wal-Mart to grow against larger competitors until it became the leading U.S. retailer. Another example would be a firm that expands its scale of production to deter potential entrants.

As an investor, you must understand the alternative competitive strategies available, determine each firm's strategy, judge whether the firm's strategy is reasonable for its industry, and, finally, evaluate how successful the firm is in implementing its strategy.

In the following sections, we discuss analyzing a firm's competitive position and strategy. The analyst must decide whether the firm's management is correctly positioning the firm to take advantage of industry and economic conditions. The analyst's opinion about management's decisions should ultimately be reflected in the analyst's estimates of the firm's growth of cash flow, dividends, earnings, and stock price.

Porter suggests two major competitive strategies: low-cost leadership and differentiation.[4] These two competitive strategies dictate how a firm has decided to cope with the five competitive conditions that define an industry's environment. The strategies available and the ways of implementing them differ within each industry.

LOW-COST STRATEGY The firm that pursues the low-cost strategy is determined to become *the* low-cost producer and, hence, the cost leader in its industry. Cost advantages vary by industry and might include economies of scale, proprietary technology, or preferential access to raw materials. In order to benefit from cost leadership, the firm must command prices near the industry average, which means that it must differentiate itself about as well as other firms. If the firm discounts price too much, it could erode the superior rates of return available because of its low cost. During the early 1990s, Wal-Mart was considered a low-cost source. The firm achieved this by volume purchasing of merchandise and lower-cost operations. As a result, the firm charged less, but still enjoyed higher profit margins and returns on capital than many of its competitors.

DIFFERENTIATION STRATEGY With the differentiation strategy, a firm seeks to identify itself as unique in its industry in an area that is important to buyers. Again, the possibilities for differentiation vary widely by industry. A company can attempt to differ-

---

[4]Michael E. Porter, *Competitive Strategy: Techniques for Analyzing Industries and Companies* (New York: The Free Press, 1980); Michael E. Porter, *Competitive Advantage: Creating and Sustaining Superior Performance* (New York: The Free Press, 1985).

TABLE 20.1 SKILLS, RESOURCES, AND ORGANIZATIONAL REQUIREMENTS NEEDED TO SUCCESSFULLY APPLY COST LEADERSHIP AND DIFFERENTIATION STRATEGIES

Generic Strategy	Commonly Required Skills and Resources	Common Organizational Requirements
Overall cost leadership	Sustained capital investment and access to capital Process engineering skills Intense supervision of labor Products designed for ease in manufacture Low-cost distribution system	Tight cost control Frequent, detailed control reports Structured organization and responsibilities Incentives based on meeting strict quantitative targets
Differentiation	Strong marketing abilities Product engineering Creative flair Strong capability in basic research Corporate reputation for quality or technological leadership Long tradition in the industry or unique combination of skills drawn from other businesses Strong cooperation from channels	Strong coordination among functions in R&D, product development, and marketing Subjective measurement and incentives instead of quantitative measures Amenities to attract highly skilled labor, scientists, or creative people

Source: Adapted/reprinted with the permission of The Free Press, a division of Simon & Schuster from *Competitive Strategy: Techniques for Analyzing Industries and Competitors* by Michael E. Porter, pp. 40–41. Copyright © 1980 by The Free Press.

entiate itself based on its distribution system (selling in stores, by mail order, or door-to-door), or some unique marketing approach. A firm employing the differentiation strategy will enjoy above-average rates of return only if the price premium attributable to its differentiation exceeds the extra cost of being unique. Therefore, when you analyze a firm using this strategy, you must determine whether the differentiating factor is truly unique, whether it is sustainable, its cost, and if the price premium derived from the uniqueness is greater than its cost (is the firm experiencing above-average rates of return?).

FOCUSING A STRATEGY Whichever strategy it selects, a firm must determine where it will focus this strategy. Specifically, a firm must select segments in the industry and tailor its strategy to serve these specific groups. For example, a low-cost strategy would typically exploit cost advantages for certain segments of the industry, such as being the low-cost producer for the expensive segment of the market. Similarly, a differentiation focus would target the special needs of buyers in specific segments. For example, in the athletic shoe market, companies have attempted to develop shoes for unique sport segments, such as tennis, basketball, aerobics, or walkers and hikers, rather than offering only shoes for runners. Firms thought that participants in these activities needed shoes with characteristics different from those desired by joggers. Equally important, they believed that these athletes would be willing to pay a premium for these special shoes. Again, you must ascertain if special possibilities exist, if they are being served by another firm, and if they can be priced to generate abnormal returns to the firm. Table 20.1 details some of Porter's ideas for the skills, resources, and company organizational requirements needed to successfully develop a cost leadership or differentiation strategy.

Next, you must determine which strategy the firm is pursuing and its success. Also, can the strategy be sustained? Further, you should evaluate a firm's competitive strategy over time, because strategies need to change as an industry evolves; different strategies work during different phases of an industry's life cycle. For example, differentiation strategies may work for an industry's firms during the growth stages. When the industry is in the mature stage, firms may try to lower their costs.

Through the analysis process, the analyst identifies what the company does well, what it doesn't do well, and where the firm is vulnerable to the five competitive forces. Some call this process developing a company's "story." This evaluation enables the analyst to determine the outlook and risks facing the firm. In summary, the industry's competitive forces and the firm's strategy for dealing with them is the key to determining the firm's long-run cash flows and risks of doing business.

Another framework for examining a firm's competitive position and its strategy is the SWOT analysis, the subject of the following section.

SWOT Analysis

SWOT analysis involves an examination of a firm's *S*trengths, *W*eaknesses, *O*pportunities, and *T*hreats. It should help you evaluate a firm's strategies to exploit its competitive advantages or defend against its weaknesses. Strengths and weaknesses involve identifying the firm's own (internal) abilities, or lack thereof. Opportunities and threats include external situations, such as: competitive forces, discovery and development of new technologies, government regulations, and domestic and international economic trends.

The *strengths* of a company give the firm a comparative advantage in the marketplace. Perceived strengths can include good customer service, high-quality products, strong brand image, customer loyalty, innovative R&D, market leadership, or strong financial resources. To remain strengths, they must continue to be developed, maintained, and defended through prudent capital investment policies.

Weaknesses result when competitors have potentially exploitable advantages over the firm. Once weaknesses are identified, the firm can select strategies to mitigate or correct the weaknesses. For example, a firm that is only a domestic producer in a global market can make investments that will allow it to export or produce its product overseas. Another example would be a firm with poor financial resources that would form joint ventures with financially stronger firms.

Opportunities, or environmental factors that favor the firm, can include a growing market for the firm's products, shrinking competition, favorable exchange rate shifts, a financial community that has confidence in the firm's future, or identification of a new market or product segment.

Threats are environmental factors that can hinder the firm in achieving its goals. Examples would include a slowing domestic economy (or sluggish overseas economies for exporters), an increase in industry competition, threats of entry, buyers or suppliers seeking to increase their bargaining power, or new technology that can hurt the industry's position. By recognizing and understanding opportunities and threats, an investor can make informed decisions about how the firm can exploit opportunities and mitigate threats.

Some Lessons from Lynch

Peter Lynch, the former portfolio manager of Fidelity Investments' highly successful Magellan Fund, looks for the following attributes when he analyzes firms.[5]

FAVORABLE ATTRIBUTES OF FIRMS The following attributes of firms may result in favorable stock market performance:

1. The firm's product is not faddish; it is one that consumers will continue to purchase over time. Investors should seek long-term investments by trying to recognize value in companies and stocks before others do.

[5]See his two books: Peter Lynch, *One Up on Wall Street* (New York: Simon & Schuster, 1989); and Peter Lynch, *Beating the Street* (New York: Simon & Schuster, 1993).

2. The company should have long-run some comparative competitive advantage over its rivals, otherwise its superior sales growth and profits will disappear over time.
3. The firm's industry or product has the potential for market stability, because it has little or no need to innovate, create product improvements, or fear that it may lose a technological advantage. Market stability means less potential for entry, which implies little need for costly investments or R&D.
4. The firm can benefit from cost reductions. An example would be a computer manufacturer that uses technology provided by suppliers competing to deliver a faster and less-expensive machine or computer chip.
5. Firms that buy back their shares or companies where management (insiders) are buying shares show that the firm and its insiders are putting their money into the firm.

CATEGORIZING COMPANIES Lynch recommends placing firms into one of six categories. Firms in each category possess different characteristics, so investors need to focus on different firm attributes to determine if the firm is an attractive investment. The six categories are:

1. *Slow growers.* These firms are at or near the top of the industry or product life cycle. They typically pay a regular dividend due to few attractive internal investments. The investor should focus on potentially profitable new products or acquisitions that will allow the firm to experience rising earnings and dividends.
2. *Stalwarts.* Stalwarts are expected to have faster earnings growth, but their consistent growth, priced into the stock price, makes large stock price changes unlikely. Investors should focus on the firm's current P/E ratio versus its historical relationships with the industry and market. Investors also should look for anything that might increase the stalwart's earnings growth rate.
3. *Fast growers.* These are smaller, aggressive firms with high earnings growth potential (say, 20 percent to 25 percent per year). Fast growers don't have to be in a fast-growing industry but may achieve growth by building on their competitive advantage and taking market share away from established rivals. These firms are risky because their stock prices tumble at the first sign of negative earnings surprises. Investors need to concentrate on *how the firm will sustain its growth rate.* How does current expansion compare to past growth? How is growth being financed? Is the firm maintaining its cash flow growth?
4. *Cyclicals.* These are firms whose sales and profits rise and fall with the business cycle. Investors need to focus on economic forecasts and the firm's internal conditions.
5. *Turnarounds.* These are firms with current internal weaknesses but external opportunities that may allow them to recover from difficult times. Because of typically high leverage and investor pessimism, these firms are risky investments but they can be rewarding. Investors need to study the firm's plans to correct its problems and/or the hiring of a top-level executive with experience in turnaround situations. Discussions with the firm's suppliers and customers can provide information about the success and timing of the turnaround plan and the rate of recovery.
6. *Asset plays.* These are firms with valuable assets that are hidden on the balance sheet. Such assets may include valuable land holdings, film libraries, trademarks, cable TV subscribers, or patents. Investors attempt to value the firm's major divisions on a "stand-alone" basis and then compare this intrinsic total value to the firm's per-share value in the market.

Investors should make use of research on the competitive forces in an industry, a firm's responses to those forces, SWOT analysis, and Lynch's suggestions.

ESTIMATING INTRINSIC VALUE

Now that the analysis of the economy, structural forces, the industry, a company, and its competitors is completed, it is time to estimate the intrinsic value of the firm's common stock. If the intrinsic value estimate exceeds the stock's current market price, the stock should be purchased. In contrast, if the current market price exceeds our intrinsic value estimate, we should avoid the stock.

As noted in Chapter 13, analysts use two general approaches to valuation. The techniques that serve each of these approaches are listed below:

A. Present value of cash flows (PVCF)
   1. Present value of dividends (DDM)
   2. Present value of free cash flow to equity (FCFE)
   3. Present value of free cash flow to the firm (FCFF)

B. Relative valuation techniques
   1. Price/earnings ratio (P/E)
   2. Price/cash flow ratio (P/CF)
   3. Price/book value ratio (P/BV)
   4. Price/sales ratio (P/S)

This section contains a brief presentation for each of these techniques as applied to the Walgreen Company, the largest retail drugstore chain in the United States. It operates 2,549 drugstores in 29 states and Puerto Rico. General merchandise accounts for 25 percent of total sales and its pharmacy operation generates almost 50 percent.

Although we limit our demonstration to Walgreen, your complete company analysis would cover all the firms in the retail drugstore industry to determine which stocks should perform the best. The objective is to estimate the expected return and risk for all the individual firms in the industry over your investment horizon. The initial presentation considers the present value of cash flow (PVCF) models. Table 20.2 contains historical data for Walgreen related to variables required for the PVCF models.

Present Value of Dividends

We learned in Chapter 13 that determining the present value of future dividends is a difficult task. Therefore, analysts apply one or more simplifying assumptions when employing the dividend discount models (DDMs). The typical assumption is that the stock's dividends will grow at a constant rate over time. Although unrealistic for fast-growing or cyclical firms, DDMs may be appropriate for some mature, slower-growing firms. More complex DDMs exist for more complicated growth forecasts. These include two-stage growth models (a period of fast growth followed by a period of constant growth) and three-stage growth models (a period of fast growth followed by a period of diminishing growth rates followed by a period of constant growth).[6]

For simplicity, we will initially discuss the constant growth DDM. We saw in Chapter 12 that when dividends grow at a constant rate, a stock's price should equal next year's dividend, D_1, divided by the difference between investors' required rate of return on the stock (k) and the dividend growth rate (g):

[6]These were discussed in Chapter 13. There is a detailed discussion of growth duration models later in this chapter.

TABLE 20.2

COMPONENTS OF FREE CASH FLOW VALUATION ANALYSIS FOR THE WALGREEN COMPANY: 1983–1998 (DOLLARS IN MILLIONS EXCEPT PER-SHARE DATA)[a]

Year	Dividend per Share	Net Income	Depreciation Expense	Capital Spending	Change in Working Capital	Principal Repayment	New Debt Issues	FCFE	EBIT	Tax Rate	FCFF	1-Tax Rate	Time
1983	0.020	70.00	25.00	−71.00	−15.00	−3.00	0.00	6.00	146.76	0.45	20.26	0.55	1
1984	0.025	85.00	29.00	−68.00	−56.00	−3.00	0.00	−13.00	181.04	0.45	5.45	0.55	2
1985	0.030	94.00	34.00	−97.00	−61.00	−3.00	20.00	−13.00	209.33	0.46	−10.91	0.54	3
1986	0.030	103.00	44.00	−156.00	−72.00	−5.00	92.00	6.00	229.27	0.45	−57.17	0.55	4
1987	0.035	104.00	54.00	−122.00	−118.00	−4.00	5.00	−81.00	242.53	0.46	−55.98	0.54	5
1988	0.040	129.00	59.00	−114.00	49.00	−4.00	31.00	150.00	262.81	0.38	156.21	0.62	6
1989	0.045	154.00	64.00	−121.00	−97.00	−4.00	0.00	−4.00	300.78	0.37	35.84	0.63	7
1990	0.050	175.00	70.00	−192.00	−69.00	−4.00	0.00	−20.00	284.00	0.38	−14.13	0.62	8
1991	0.060	195.00	84.00	−202.00	−129.00	−24.00	0.00	−76.00	321.00	0.38	−46.38	0.63	9
1992	0.065	221.00	92.00	−145.00	−32.00	−6.00	0.00	130.00	358.00	0.37	139.13	0.63	10
1993	0.075	245.00	105.00	−185.00	−28.00	−112.00	0.00	25.00	406.00	0.39	141.30	0.61	11
1994	0.085	282.00	118.00	−290.00	−58.00	−6.00	0.00	46.00	458.00	0.38	52.00	0.62	12
1995	0.100	321.00	132.00	−310.00	−104.00	−7.00	0.00	32.00	524.00	0.39	39.00	0.61	13
1996	0.110	372.00	147.00	−364.00	−116.00	0.00	2.00	41.00	607.00	0.39	39.00	0.61	14
1997	0.120	436.00	164.00	−485.00	34.00	−1.00	0.00	148.00	712.00	0.39	149.00	0.61	15
1998	0.125	500.00	189.00	−398.00	−126.00	0.00	11.00	176.00	835.00	0.39	176.32	0.61	16
Dividend Growth 1983–1998		12.14%						23.51%			14.48%		
Dividend Growth 1988–1998		12.07%						1.61%	12.25%		1.22%		
Dividend Growth 1993–1998		12.10%											
BV/PS Growth 1988–1998		14.34%											
ROE		19.60%											
Cost of Equity		10.50%											

[a]All per-share data are adjusted for prior stock splits, including the split that occurred in 1999.

Source: Walgreen's Annual Reports.

$$\text{Intrinsic Value} = D_1 / (k - g)$$

With constant dividend growth, next year's dividend should equal the current dividend, D_0, increased by the constant dividend growth rate: $D_1 = D_0 (1 + g)$. Because the current dividend is known, to estimate intrinsic value we need only estimate two parameters: the dividend growth rate and investors' required rate of return.

GROWTH RATE ESTIMATES If the stock has had fairly constant dividend growth over the past 5 to 10 years, one estimate of the constant growth rate is to use the actual growth of dividends over this period. The average compound rate of growth is found by computing

$$\text{Average Dividend Growth Rate} = \sqrt[n]{\frac{D_n}{D_0}} - 1$$

In the case of Walgreen, the 1988 dividend (D_0) was \$0.04 a share and the 1998 dividend (D_{10}) was \$0.125 a share. The average dividend growth rate was

$$\sqrt[10]{\frac{\$0.125}{\$0.04}} - 1 = \sqrt[10]{3.125} - 1 = 0.12068$$

or 12.07 percent. Clearly, it is inappropriate to blindly plug historical growth rates into our formulas because if we do, we've wasted our time analyzing economic, structural, industry, and company influences. Our analysis may have indicated that growth is expected to increase or decrease due to such factors as changes in government programs, demographic shifts, or changes in product mix. The historical growth rate may need to be raised or lowered to incorporate our findings.

In Chapter 12, we learned other ways to estimate future growth. The sustainable growth rate

$$g = \text{RR} \times \text{ROE}$$

assumes the firm will maintain a constant debt–equity ratio as it finances asset growth. We know from Chapters 12 and 19 that ROA can be expressed as the product of the firm's net profit margin and total asset turnover; ROE is the product of the net profit margin, total asset turnover, and the financial leverage multiplier. Thus, a firm's future growth rate and its components of ROE can be compared to those of its competitors, its industry, and the market. Although there is not necessarily a close relationship between the year-to-year growth in a firm's assets and its dividend cash flows, these calculations provide insight that, along with the rest of the top-down analysis, can assist the analyst in determining whether dividend growth may rise or fall in the future. For Walgreen, the sustainable growth rate calculation using 1998 data is[7]

$$\begin{aligned} g &= \text{RR} \times \text{ROE} = 0.75 \times 0.19 \\ &= 0.1425 = 14.25\% \end{aligned}$$

The dividend growth rate will be influenced by the age of the industry life cycle, structural changes, and economic trends. Economic–industry–firm analysis provides valuable

[7]This sustainable growth rate value differs from the one in Chapter 12 because this calculation uses year-end values for ROE, while in Chapter 12, the equity value is an average of the beginning and ending values.

information regarding future trends in dividend growth. Analysts who ask questions during interviews about management's plans to expand the firm, diversify into new areas, or change dividend policy can gather useful information about the firm's dividend policy. Averaging the historical growth rate of dividends (12.07 percent) and the implied sustainable growth estimate above of 14.25 percent indicates a value of 13.16 percent. Because we feel that a firm's ROE is the critical growth factor, we give this estimate more weight and we will use 14 percent for Walgreen's estimated *g*.

REQUIRED RATE OF RETURN ESTIMATE We know an investor's required rate of return has two basic components: the nominal risk-free interest rate and a risk premium. If the market is efficient, over time the return earned by investors should compensate them for the risk of the investment.

Notably, we must estimate *future* risk premiums to determine the stock's current intrinsic value. Estimates of the nominal risk-free interest rate are available from the initial analysis of the economy during the top-down approach. The risk premium of the firm must rely on other information derived from the top-down company analysis, including evaluation of the financial statements and capital market relationships.

In Chapter 12, we examined ratios that measure several aspects of the risk of a firm and its stock. Business risk, financial risk, liquidity risk, exchange rate risk, and country risk are fundamental risk factors to be reviewed in the context of our economy–industry–firm analysis. These measures can be compared against the firm's major competitors, its industry, and the overall market. This fundamental comparison will tell the analyst if the firm should have a higher or lower risk premium than other firms in the industry, the overall market, or the firm's historical risk premium. Accounting-based risk measures use historical data, whereas investment analysis requires an estimate of the future. Investors need to incorporate into the risk analysis any information uncovered during the top-down process that would lead to higher or lower risk estimates.

For a market-based risk estimate, the firm's characteristic line is estimated by regressing market returns on the stock's returns. We know the slope of this regression line is the stock's beta, or measure of systematic risk. Estimates of the economy's risk-free rate, the future long-run market return, and an estimate of the stock's beta help estimate next year's required rate of return:

$$R_{\text{stock}} = E(RFR) + \beta_{\text{stock}}\,[E(R_{\text{market}}) - E(RFR)]$$

Again, this estimate of beta begins with historical market information. Because beta is affected by changes in a firm's business and financial risks, as well as other influences, an investor should increase or lower the historical beta estimate based upon his or her analysis of the firm's future risk characteristics.

To demonstrate the estimate of the required rate of return equation for Walgreen, we make several assumptions regarding components of the security market line (SML) discussed in Chapter 8. First is the prevailing nominal risk-free rate (RFR), which is estimated at about 6.0 percent—the current yield to maturity for the intermediate-term government bond. The expected equity market rate of return (R_M) depends on the expected market risk premium on stocks. As noted earlier, there is substantial controversy on the appropriate estimate for the equity market risk premium—that is, the estimates range from a high of about 8 percent (the arithmetic mean of the actual risk premium since 1926) to a low of about 3 percent, which is the risk premium suggested in several recent academic studies. The authors reject both of these extreme values and suggest using a 5 percent risk premium (0.05) The final estimate is the firm's systematic risk value (beta), which is typically derived based upon the following regression model (the characteristic line) noted in Chapter 8.

$$R_{WAG} = \alpha + \beta_{WAG} R_M$$

where:

R_{WAG} = monthly rate of return for Walgreen
α = constant term
β_{WAG} = beta coefficient for Walgreen equal to $\frac{Cov_{W,M}}{\sigma_m^2}$
R_M = monthly rates of return for a market proxy—typically the S&P 500 Index

When this regression was run using monthly rates of return during the 5-year period 1994-1998 (60 observations), the beta coefficient was estimated at 0.90.

Putting together the RFR of 0.060 and the market risk premium of 0.05 implies an expected market return (R_M) of 0.110. This combined with the Walgreen beta of 0.90 indicates the following expected rate of return for Walgreen:

$$\begin{aligned} E(R) &= RFR + \beta_i(R_M - RFR) \\ &= 0.060 + 0.90(0.110 - 0.060) \\ &= 0.060 + 0.90(0.05) \\ &= 0.060 + 0.045 \\ &= .105 = 10.5\% \end{aligned}$$

The Present Value of Dividends Model (DDM)

At this point, the analyst would face a problem: the intent was to use the basic DDM, which assumed a constant growth rate for an infinite period. You will recall that the model also required that $k > g$ (the required rate of return is larger than the expected growth rate), which is not true in this case because $k = 10.5$ percent and $g = 14$ percent (see Table 20.2). Therefore, the analyst must employ a two- or three-stage growth model. Because of the fairly large difference between the current growth rate of 14 percent and the long-run constant growth rate of 8 percent, it seems reasonable to use a three-stage model, which includes a gradual transition period. We assume that the growth periods are as follows:

g_1 = 5 years (growing at 14 percent a year)
g_2 = 6 years (during this period it is assumed that the growth rate declines 1 percent per year for 6 years)
g_3 = constant perpetual growth of 8 percent

Therefore, beginning with 1999, when dividends were at an annual rate of $0.14, the future dividend payments will be as follows (the growth rate is in parentheses):[8]

High-Growth Period		PV @ 10.5%	Declining Growth Period		PV @ 10.5%
2000 (14%)	0.16	0.14	2005(13%)	0.30	0.17
2001 (14%)	0.18	0.15	2006 (12%)	0.34	0.17
2002 (14%)	0.21	0.16	2007 (11%)	0.38	0.17
2003 (14%)	0.24	0.16	2008 (10%)	0.42	0.17
2004 (14%)	0.27	0.16	2009 (9%)	0.45	0.17
		0.77	2010 (8%)	0.49	0.85

[8]Since the analysis is being done in July 1999 when the current stock price is $30.00 after a split, we will treat 1999 as year 0, and use split adjusted dividends.

Constant Growth Period:

$$P_{2009} = \frac{0.45(1 + 0.08)}{0.105 - 0.08} = \frac{0.49}{0.025} = \$19.60$$

The total value of the stock is the sum of the three present value streams discounted at 10.5 percent:

1. Present value of high-growth period	\$0.77
2. Present value of declining growth period	0.85
3. Present value of constant growth period	7.24
Total Present Value of Dividends	**\$8.86**

The estimated value based on the DDM is substantially lower than the market price in mid-1999 of about \$30.00. This estimated value also implies a low P/E ratio based upon expected earnings in 2000 of about \$0.72 per share (that is, about 12.3 times earnings) compared to the prevailing market P/E of more than 22 times 2000 earnings. In a subsequent section on relative valuation techniques, we compare Walgreen's P/E ratio to that of its industry and the market.

PRESENT VALUE OF FREE CASH FLOW TO EQUITY

As noted in Chapter 13, this technique resembles a present value of earnings concept except that it considers the capital expenditures required to maintain and grow the firm and the change in working capital required for a growing firm (that is, an increase in accounts receivable and inventory). The specific definition of free cash flow to equity (FCFE) is:

Net Income + Depreciation Expense − Capital
Expenditures − Δ in Working Capital − Principal
Debt Repayments + New Debt Issues

This technique attempts to determine the free cash flow that is available to the stockholders after payments to all other capital suppliers and after providing for the continued growth of the firm. As noted in Chapter 13, given the current FCFE values, the alternative forms of the model are similar to those available for the DDM, which in turn depends on the firm's growth prospects. Specifically, if the firm is in its mature constant growth phase, it is possible to use a model similar to the reduced form DDM:

$$\text{Value} = \frac{\text{FCFE}_1}{k - g_{\text{FCFE}}}$$

where:

FCFE = the expected free cash flow to equity in period 1
k = the required rate of return on equity for the firm
g_{FCFE} = the expected constant growth rate of free cash flow to equity for the firm

We already know from the prior dividend model that the firm's earnings are growing at a rate (about 14 percent) that exceeds the required rate of return. In the case of FCFE, it is necessary to consider the effect of capital expenditures relative to depreciation and changes in working capital as well as debt repayments and new debt issues. The historical data in

Table 20.2 shows that the FCFE series has had a volatile history with a growth rate exceeding 20 percent during the 15-year period. Such volatility makes it appropriate to use a more conservative 16 percent growth rate that is modestly higher than the growth of Walgreen's sales and book value. Therefore, the following example again uses a three-stage growth model with the following growth estimates:

g_1 = 16 percent for 5 years
g_2 = a constantly declining growth rate to 8 percent over 8 years
k = 10.5 percent cost of equity

The specific estimate of annual FCFE in $million beginning with the actual 1998 value of $176 million and an estimate of $204 million in 1999 are as follows:

High-Growth		PV @ 10.5%	Declining Growth		PV @ 10.5%
2000 (16%)	$237	$214	2005 (15%)	$493	271
2001 (16%)	275	225	2006 (14%)	562	280
2002 (16%)	319	237	2007 (13%)	636	287
2003 (16%)	370	248	2008 (12%)	712	291
2004 (16%)	429	261	2009 (11%)	790	292
		$1,185	2010 (10%)	869	291
			2011 (9%)	947	287
					$1,999

$$\text{Constant Growth Period Value} = \frac{1{,}023}{0.105 - 0.08} = \$40{,}920$$

The total value of the stock is the sum of the three present value streams discounted at 10.5 percent:

	($Mil)
1. Present value of high-growth cash flows	$ 1,185
2. Present value of declining growth cash flows	1,999
3. Present value of constant growth cash flows	12,402
Total present value of FCFE	**$15,586**

The outstanding shares in 1999 were approximately 1,003 million. Therefore, the per share value based upon the present value of FCFE is $15.54. Again, this estimated value is substantially lower than the prevailing market price of about $30. This value implies a P/E ratio of about 21.6 times estimated 2000 earnings of $0.72 per share.

PRESENT VALUE OF OPERATING FREE CASH FLOW

This is also referred to as *free cash flow to the firm* (FCFF) by Damodaran and *the entity DCF model* by Copeland, Koller, and Murrin.[9] The object is to determine a value for the total firm and subtract the value of the firm's debt obligations to arrive at a value for the

[9] Aswath Damodaran, *Damodaran on Valuation* (New York: Wiley, 1994), Chapter 8, and Tom Copeland, Tim Koller, and Jack Murrin, *Valuation: Measuring and Managing the Value of Companies,* 2d ed. (New York: Wiley, 1996), Chapter 5.

firm's equity. Notably, in this valuation technique, we discount the firm's operating free cash flow to the firm (FCFF) at the firm's weighted average cost of capital (WACC) rather than its cost of equity.

Operating free cash flow or *free cash flow to the firm* is equal to

$$\begin{aligned}&\text{EBIT}(1 - \text{Tax Rate}) + \text{Depreciation Expense}\\&\quad - \text{Capital Spending} - \Delta \text{ in Working Capital}\\&\quad - \Delta \text{ in other assets}\end{aligned}$$

This is the cash flow generated by a company's operations and available to all who have provided capital to the firm—both equity and debt. As noted, because it is the cash flow from *all capital suppliers,* it is discounted at the firm's WACC.

Again, the alternative specifications of this operating FCF model are similar to the DDM—that is, the specification depends upon the firm's growth prospects. Assuming an expectation of constant growth, you can use the reduced form model

$$\text{Firm Value} = \frac{\text{FCFF}_1}{\text{WACC} - g_{FCFF}} \text{ or } \frac{\text{Oper. FCF}_1}{\text{WACC} - g_{OFCF}}$$

where:

$FCFF_1$ = the free cash flow for the firm in period 1
Oper. FCF_1 = the firm's operating free cash flow in period 1
WACC = the firm's weighted average cost of capital
g_{FCFF} = the constant infinite growth rate of free cash flow for the firm
g_{OFCF} = the constant infinite growth rate of operating free cash flow

As noted in Table 20.2, the compound annual growth rate for operating free cash flow (free cash flow to the firm) during the 15-year period was 14.5 percent. An alternative measure of growth is the growth implied by the equation:

$$g = (\text{RR})(\text{ROIC})$$

where:

RR = the average retention rate
ROIC = EBIT (1− Tax Rate) /Total Capital

For Walgreen, the recent retention rate is about 75 percent and the ROIC is equal to

$$\text{ROIC} = \frac{\text{EBIT}(1 - \text{Tax Rate})}{\text{Total Capital}} = \frac{510}{2{,}650} = 0.1925$$
$$= 19.25\%$$

Therefore,

$$\begin{aligned}g &= (0.75)(0.1925)\\&= 0.1444 = 14.44\%\end{aligned}$$

The average of the two growth estimates (14.50 percent and 14.44 percent) is 14.47 percent. In the subsequent valuation calculation we will begin with a growth estimate for FCFF of 14 percent.

CALCULATION OF WACC We calculate the discount rate (i.e., the firm's WACC) using the following formula:

$$\text{WACC} = W_E k + W_D i$$

where:

W_E = the proportion of equity in total capital
k = the after-tax cost of equity (from the SML)
W_D = the proportion of debt in total capital[10]
i = the after-tax cost of debt[11]

The reader will recall from corporate finance courses that there are differences of opinion regarding how one should estimate the debt and equity weights—i.e., using proportions—based upon relative book values or based on relative market value weights. Without getting into the reasons for each choice, it is important to recognize that the use of market value weights will almost always result in a higher WACC because it will imply more equity financing since most firms have a P/BV ratio greater than one (for Walgreen the P/BV ratio is currently in excess of 5.0). To demonstrate this, we compute a WACC using both weightings. The cost of debt and cost of equity will be the same for both sets.

WACC USING BOOK VALUE WEIGHTS

$k_e = 0.105$ (from prior SML calculation)
$k_d = 0.043$ (current interest rate of 7% and recent tax of 39% of WAG)
$0.07 \times (1 - 0.39) = 0.043$
$W_d = 0.30$ (including leases)
$W_e = 0.70$

$$\begin{aligned}\text{WACC} &= (W_d \times k_d) + (W_e \times k_e)\\ &= (0.30 \times 0.043) + (0.70 \times 0.105)\\ &= 0.0129 + 0.0735 = 0.0863 = 8.63\%\end{aligned}$$

WACC USING MARKET VALUE WEIGHTS

$k_e = 0.105$ $\qquad W_e = 0.90$
$k_d = 0.043$ $\qquad W_d = 0.10$

$$\begin{aligned}\text{WACC} &= (W_d \times k_d) + (W_e \times k_e)\\ &= (0.10 \times 0.043) + (0.90 \times 0.105)\\ &= 0.0043 + 0.0945 = 0.0988 = 9.88\%\end{aligned}$$

Therefore, we have a range of 8.63 percent to 9.88 percent and an average of 9.25 percent. We will use 9 percent in the demonstration.

Again, because the expected growth rate of operating free cash flow is greater than the firm's WACC, we cannot use the reduced form model that assumes constant growth at this relatively high rate for an infinite period. Therefore, the following demonstration will em-

[10]The proportions of debt and equity capital used in the WACC estimate will be computed using both book value weights that consider the value of capitalized lease payments as debt, and market value weights.

[11]For this estimate we use the prevailing interest rate on corporate AA-rated bonds (7 percent), and Walgreen's recent tax rate of 39 percent.

ploy the three-stage growth model with growth duration assumptions similar to the prior examples.

Given these inputs for recent growth and the firm's WACC, the growth estimates for a three-stage growth model are

g_1 = 14 percent for 5 years
g_2 = a constantly declining rate to 7 percent over 6 years.[12]

The specific estimates for future operating FCF (or FCFF) are as follows, beginning from the 1998 value of $176 million, and an estimate for 1999 (year 0) of $202.

High-Growth Periods		PV at 9%	Declining Growth Periods		PV at 9%
2000	$230	$ 211	2005 (13%)	$440	$ 262
2001	263	221	2006 (12%)	492	269
2002	299	231	2007 (17%)	546	274
2003	341	242	2008 (10%)	601	277
2004	389	253	2009 (9%)	655	277
		$1,158	2010 (8%)	708	274
					$1,633

$$\text{Constant Growth} = \frac{\text{Oper. FCF}_{2011}}{0.09 - 0.07} = \frac{757}{0.02} = \$37{,}850$$

Thus, the total value of the firm is:

	($Mil)
1. Present value of high-growth cash flows	$ 1,158
2. Present value of declining growth cash flows	1,633
3. Present value of constant growth cash flows	14,668
Total present value of operating FCF	**$17,459**

Recall that the value of equity is the total value of the firm (PV of operating FCF) minus the current market value of debt, which is the present value of debt payments at the firm's cost of debt (0.07). The values are as follows:

Total present value of operating FCF	$17,459
Minus: value of debt[13]	4,250
value of equity	$13,209
Number of common shares	1,003 million
Value of equity per share	$13.17

[12]This 7 percent long-run growth rate assumption implies that we do not believe that FCFF can grow as fast as FCFE. Given a beginning growth rate of 14 percent and a long-run rate of 7 percent means that the growth rate will decline by 0.01 per year as shown in the following example.

[13]This includes the present value of minimum lease payments discounted at the firm's cost of debt (7 percent).

Again, this estimated value compares to the recent market value of about $30. The $13.17 value implies a P/E of about 18 times estimated 2000 earnings of $0.72 per share.

To summarize, the valuations derived from the present value of cash flow techniques are as follows:

Present value of dividends	$ 8.86
Present value of FCFE	$15.54
Present value of operating FCF (Also, the PV of FCFF)	$13.17

All of these prices must be compared to the prevailing market price of $30 to determine the investment decision.

RELATIVE VALUATION RATIO TECHNIQUES

In this section, we present the data required to compute the several relative valuation ratios and demonstrate the use of these relative valuation ratio techniques for Walgreen compared to the retail drugstore industry and the S&P 400 Industrial Index.

Table 20.3 contains the basic data required to compute the relative valuation ratios, and Table 20.4 contains the four sets of relative valuation ratios for Walgreen, its industry, and the aggregate market. This table also contains a comparison of the company ratios to similar ratios for the company's industry and the market. Such a comparison helps the analyst determine change in the relative valuation ratio over time and consider if the current valuation ratio for the company (Walgreen) is reasonable based on the financial characteristics of the firm versus its industry and the market. To aid in the analysis, four graphs contain the time series of the relative valuation ratios for the company, its industry, and the market. Four additional graphs show the relationship between the relative valuation ratios: for the company compared to its industry, and for the company compared to the stock market. Similar to the chapters on market analysis and industry analysis, we begin with the P/E ratio approach where we derive a specific value for the stock and a rate of return based upon an estimate of future EPS and an earnings multiple for the stock.

PRICE/EARNINGS RATIO As before, we derive a detailed estimate of Walgreen's earnings per share for 2000. Subsequently, we estimate the stock's earnings multiple based on macro and micro analysis of its components.

ESTIMATING COMPANY EARNINGS PER SHARE

Expected earnings per share is a function of the sales forecast and the estimated profit margin.

The sales forecast includes an analysis of the relationship of company sales to various relevant economic series and to the retail drugstore industry series. These comparisons tell us how the company is performing relative to the economy and to its closest competition.

COMPANY SALES FORECAST

Besides providing background on the company, these relationships can help us develop specific sales forecasts for Walgreen.

Table 20.5 contains data on sales for Walgreen from its annual report, sales per share for the retail drugstore industry, and several personal consumption expenditure (PCE) series for the period 1977 to 1998.

To examine the relationship of Walgreen sales to the economy, we considered several alternative series. The series that had the strongest relationship was personal consumption

TABLE 20.3 INPUTS FOR RELATIVE VALUATION TECHNIQUES: WALGREEN, RETAIL DRUGSTORE, S&P 400 INDEX: 1977–1998

	Walgreen					Retail Drugstore Industry					S&P 400 Index				
Year	Mean Price	EPS	Cash Flow P/S	Book Value P/S	Sales P/S	Mean Price	EPS	Cash Flow P/S	Book Value P/S	Sales P/S	Mean Price	EPS	Cash Flow P/S	Book Value P/S	Sales Price
1977	0.26	0.04	0.03	0.17	1.92	18.93	1.79	2.20	9.35	43.99	109.40	11.45	19.94	82.21	224.24
1978	0.37	0.05	0.04	0.18	2.17	22.20	20.1	2.50	10.93	49.87	107.12	13.04	22.65	89.34	251.32
1979	0.46	0.07	0.05	0.21	2.47	22.38	2.55	3.26	13.95	73.39	115.79	16.29	27.06	98.71	292.38
1980	0.53	0.08	0.06	0.23	3.09	24.57	2.94	3.78	16.11	84.82	136.03	16.12	28.45	108.33	327.36
1981	0.73	0.09	0.07	0.27	3.52	34.62	3.29	4.31	18.45	95.50	141.48	16.74	30.52	116.06	344.31
1982	1.26	0.12	0.16	0.62	3.88	41.58	3.76	4.79	20.74	109.22	136.87	13.20	28.46	118.60	333.86
1983	2.08	0.15	0.29	1.08	4.77	56.70	4.50	5.90	23.34	118.85	174.90	14.77	30.41	122.32	334.07
1984	2.31	0.17	0.23	0.85	5.54	58.30	4.10	5.81	24.21	135.15	179.62	18.11	34.40	123.99	379.70
1985	3.24	0.19	0.26	0.98	6.38	68.28	4.22	6.24	26.82	153.30	208.99	15.28	33.44	125.89	398.42
1986	4.35	0.21	0.33	1.23	7.40	83.78	4.90	6.99	27.73	157.74	253.83	14.53	33.91	124.87	387.76
1987	4.37	0.21	0.32	1.27	8.64	98.93	5.53	8.16	30.79	191.72	324.30	20.28	40.46	134.19	430.35
1988	4.07	0.26	0.39	1.46	9.85	93.05	6.30	9.40	34.25	217.80	302.63	26.59	50.13	139.50	486.92
1989	5.00	0.32	0.45	1.67	10.86	107.46	6.69	10.07	38.31	239.68	364.58	26.83	50.02	145.34	541.38
1990	5.82	0.36	0.52	1.99	12.20	114.53	7.67	11.82	43.65	265.77	392.12	24.77	51.04	152.71	594.55
1991	7.94	0.40	0.57	2.20	13.59	139.70	8.26	12.29	50.94	283.50	428.81	16.91	44.41	157.05	586.86
1992	9.38	0.45	0.78	2.51	15.08	159.62	8.96	13.34	56.97	309.78	493.33	19.05	48.50	142.46	601.39
1993	9.91	0.45	0.88	2.80	16.74	162.19	7.09	11.84	60.04	329.20	520.21	21.93	50.61	136.91	603.62
1994	10.12	0.57	1.00	3.20	18.63	162.67	10.51	15.83	63.62	363.71	536.52	32.83	62.43	150.70	626.26
1995	13.28	0.65	1.13	3.64	20.97	215.26	11.76	17.77	68.93	413.52	638.97	35.44	68.51	163.94	676.62
1996	18.19	0.75	1.30	4.15	23.70	283.01	13.92	18.82	71.26	434.15	795.01	41.15	77.56	168.04	701.91
1997	26.44	0.88	1.22	4.81	27.06	411.75	10.77	19.22	70.88	549.51	1006.12	43.80	81.90	174.21	750.71
1998	44.60	1.02	1.40	5.72	30.72	657.05	15.62	20.76	77.90	612.86	1285.70	38.37	77.80	180.76	767.83

Note: Walgreen had a 2-for-1 stock split on August 11, 1997.

TABLE 20.4 RELATIVE VALUATION VARIABLES: WALGREEN, RETAIL DRUGSTORE, S&P 400 INDEX: 1977–1997

	Price/Earnings Ratio$_{t+1}$					Price/Cash Flow Ratio$_{t+1}$					Price/Book Value$_{t+1}$					Price/Sales Ratio$_{t+1}$				
Year	Walgreen	Retail Drug	Ratio Co/Ind	S&P 400	Ratio Co/Mkt	Walgreen	Retail Drug	Ratio Co/Ind	S&P 400	Ratio Co/Mkt	Walgreen	Retail Drug	Ratio Co/Ind	S&P 400	Ratio Co/Mkt	Walgreen	Retail Drug	Raito Co/Ind	S&P 400	Ratio Co/Mkt
1977	5.20	9.42	0.55	8.39	0.62	6.50	7.57	0.86	4.83	1.35	1.44	1.73	0.83	1.22	1.18	0.12	0.38	0.32	0.44	0.28
1978	5.21	8.71	0.60	6.58	0.79	7.30	6.81	1.07	3.96	1.84	1.78	1.59	1.12	1.09	1.63	0.15	0.30	0.49	0.37	0.40
1979	5.75	7.61	0.76	7.18	0.80	8.36	5.92	1.41	4.07	2.05	2.00	1.39	1.44	1.07	1.87	0.15	0.26	0.56	0.35	0.42
1980	5.89	7.47	0.79	8.13	0.72	8.15	5.70	1.43	4.46	1.83	2.00	1.33	1.50	1.17	1.71	0.15	0.26	0.59	0.40	0.38
1981	6.35	9.21	0.69	10.72	0.59	4.56	7.23	0.36	4.97	0.92	1.19	1.67	0.71	1.19	1.00	0.19	0.32	0.59	0.42	0.44
1982	8.69	9.24	0.94	9.27	0.94	4.34	7.05	0.62	4.50	0.97	1.17	1.78	0.66	1.12	1.04	0.26	0.35	0.76	0.41	0.65
1983	12.58	13.83	0.91	9.66	1.30	9.22	9.76	0.94	5.08	1.81	2.46	2.34	1.05	1.41	1.74	0.37	0.42	0.89	0.46	0.81
1984	12.13	13.82	0.88	11.76	1.03	8.87	9.34	0.95	5.37	1.65	2.35	2.17	1.08	1.43	1.64	0.36	0.38	0.95	0.45	0.80
1985	15.40	13.93	1.11	14.38	1.07	9.95	9.77	1.02	6.16	1.62	2.64	2.46	1.07	1.67	1.58	0.44	0.43	1.01	0.54	0.81
1986	20.69	15.15	1.37	12.52	1.25	13.58	10.27	1.32	6.27	2.16	3.42	2.72	1.26	1.89	1.81	0.50	0.44	1.15	0.59	0.85
1987	16.81	15.70	1.07	12.20	1.38	11.35	10.52	1.08	6.47	1.75	2.99	2.89	1.04	2.32	1.29	0.44	0.45	0.98	0.67	0.67
1988	12.90	13.91	0.93	11.28	1.14	9.03	9.24	0.98	6.05	1.49	2.44	2.43	1.01	2.08	1.17	0.37	0.39	0.96	0.56	0.67
1989	14.08	14.01	1.01	14.72	0.96	9.71	9.09	1.07	7.14	1.36	2.51	2.46	1.02	2.39	1.05	0.41	0.40	1.01	0.61	0.67
1990	14.72	13.87	1.06	23.19	0.63	10.20	9.32	1.09	8.83	1.16	2.65	2.25	1.18	2.50	1.06	0.43	0.40	1.06	0.67	0.64
1991	17.84	15.59	1.14	22.51	0.79	10.18	10.47	0.97	8.84	1.15	3.17	2.45	1.29	3.01	1.05	0.53	0.45	1.17	0.71	0.74
1992	20.83	22.51	0.93	22.50	0.93	10.71	13.48	0.79	9.75	1.10	3.35	2.66	1.26	3.60	0.93	0.56	0.48	1.16	0.82	0.69
1993	17.39	15.43	1.13	15.85	1.10	9.91	10.25	0.97	8.33	1.19	3.10	2.55	1.22	3.45	0.90	0.53	0.45	1.19	0.83	0.64
1994	15.57	13.83	1.13	15.14	1.03	8.96	9.15	0.98	7.83	1.14	2.78	2.36	1.18	3.27	0.85	0.48	0.39	1.23	0.79	0.61
1995	17.70	15.46	1.14	15.53	1.14	10.25	11.44	0.90	8.24	1.24	3.20	3.02	1.06	3.80	0.84	0.56	0.50	1.13	0.91	0.62
1996	20.67	26.28	0.79	18.15	1.14	14.97	14.72	1.02	9.71	1.54	3.78	3.99	0.95	4.56	0.83	0.67	0.52	1.31	1.06	0.63
1997	25.92	26.36	0.98	26.22	0.99	18.82	19.83	0.95	12.93	1.46	4.62	5.29	0.87	5.57	0.83	0.86	0.67	1.28	1.31	0.66
Mean	13.92	14.35	0.95	14.09	0.99	9.76	9.85	1.00	6.85	1.47	2.62	2.45	1.09	2.37	1.24	0.41	0.41	0.94	0.64	0.62

Note: Walgreen had a 2-for-1 stock split on August 11, 1997.

TABLE 20.5 **WALGREEN, S&P RETAIL DRUGSTORE SALES, AND VARIOUS ECONOMIC SERIES: 1977–1998**

Year	Sales Walgreen Company ($ Millions)	Retail Drugstores ($/Share)	Personal Consumption Expenditures (PCE) ($ Billions)	PCE-Medical Care ($ Billions)	Medical Care as a Percentage of PCE
1977	1,223.2	43.99	1,271.5	122.4	9.6
1978	1,192.9	49.87	1,421.2	139.7	9.8
1979	1,334.5	73.39	1,583.7	157.8	10.0
1980	1,530.7	84.82	1,748.1	181.3	10.4
1981	1,743.5	95.50	1,926.2	213.6	11.1
1982	2,039.5	109.22	2,059.2	240.5	11.7
1983	2,360.6	118.85	2,257.5	265.7	11.8
1984	2,744.6	135.15	2,460.3	290.6	11.8
1985	3,161.9	153.30	2,667.4	319.3	12.0
1986	3,660.6	157.74	2,850.6	346.4	12.2
1987	4,281.8	191.72	3,052.2	384.7	12.6
1988	4,883.5	217.80	3,296.1	427.7	13.0
1989	5,380.1	239.68	3,523.1	471.9	13.4
1990	6,047.5	265.77	3,761.2	526.2	14.0
1991	6,733.0	283.50	3,902.4	571.9	14.7
1992	7,475.0	309.78	4,136.9	628.3	15.2
1993	8,294.8	329.20	4,378.2	680.5	15.5
1994	9,235.0	363.71	4,627.0	727.1	15.7
1995	10,395.1	413.52	4,953.9	776.2	15.7
1996	11,778.0	434.15	5,215.7	806.8	15.5
1997	13,363.0	549.51	5,493.7	843.4	15.4
1998	15,307.0	612.86	5,800.7	887.5	15.3
CGR	12.86%	13.69%	7.52%	6.47%	9.94%

CGR = Compound annual growth rate.

Source: Standard & Poor's *Analyst's Handbook* (New York: Standard & Poor's Corporation, 1999). Reprinted by permission of Standard & Poor's Corp. *Economic Report of the President* (Washington, D.C.: U.S. Government Printing Office, 1999).

expenditure for medicine (PCE-medical care).[14] The scatter plot of Walgreen sales and the PCE-medical care expenditures contained in Figure 20.2 indicates a strong linear relationship, including the fact that Walgreen sales grew faster than PCE-medical care (i.e., 12.86 percent versus 6.47 percent). As a result, Walgreen sales have gone from about 1.00 percent of PCE-medical care to 1.72 percent.

We also compared Walgreen sales and sales per share for the retail drugstore industry. Unfortunately, it did not reflect as strong a relationship and is not used subsequently.

The figures in the last column of Table 20.5 indicate that during this period, the proportion of PCE allocated to medical care went from about 9 percent in 1977 to over 15 percent in 1998. The increasing proportion of PCE spent on medical care is a function of the growing proportion of the population over 65 and the rising cost of medical care. Because Walgreen sales are growing faster than medical expenditures, these increases should continue to be beneficial for Walgreen because almost 50 percent of its sales is prescriptions. Notably, these increases in medical care expenditures continued during the economic recessions in 1981–1982 and in 1990–1991.

[14]The relationship between Walgreen sales and total PCE or per capital PCE was significant but not as strong as PCE-medical care.

FIGURE 20.2 SCATTER PLOT OF WALGREEN SALES AND PCE-MEDICAL CARE: 1977–1998

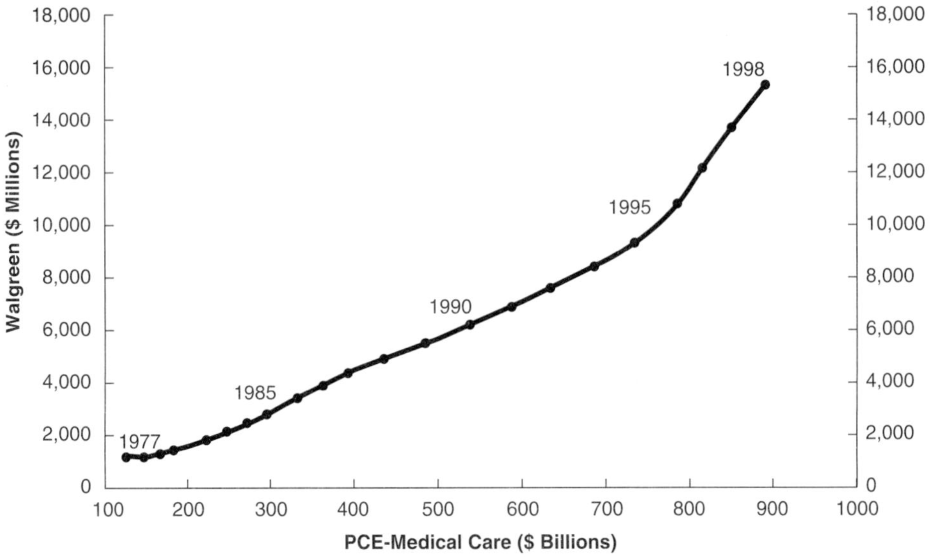
18,000
16,000
14,000
12,000
10,000
8,000
6,000
4,000
2,000
0
Walgreen ($ Millions)
1977
1985
1990
1995
1998
100
200
300
400
500
600
700
800
900
1000
PCE-Medical Care ($ Billions)

As shown in Table 20.6, the internal sales growth for Walgreen resulted from an increase in the number of stores (from 633 in 1975 to 2,549 in 1998) and an increase in the annual sales per store because of the upgrading of stores. The net increase in stores includes numerous new, large stores and the closing of many smaller stores. As a result, the average size of stores has increased. More important, the firm has increased its sales per thousand square feet, which is a critical value in the retailing industry.

SAMPLE ESTIMATE OF WALGREEN SALES The foregoing analysis indicates that you should use the Walgreen–PCE-medical care graph. To estimate PCE-medical care, you should initially project total PCE and then determine how much would be included in the medical care component. As noted in Chapter 19 in connection with the industry analysis, economists were forecasting an increase in PCE of 6.3 percent during 1999, which implied a 1999 estimate of $6,177 billion. In addition, it was estimated that the percentage of PCE spent on medical care in 1999 would be about 15.3 percent. This implies an estimate for PCE-medical care of $945 billion, which is about a 6.5 percent increase from 1998. Based on the graph in Figure 20.2, which shows the historical relationship between these two variables, this would imply an 11 percent increase in Walgreen sales to about $17.0 billion ($15.207 billion × 1.11) Notably, this estimate is below the firm's recent growth in sales.

Firms in this industry provide data on square footage and the number of stores. This allows us to compute an alternative sales estimate using these company data in Table 20.6 to support the prior estimate that was based on macroeconomic data. If we assume an increase in store area during 1999 of about 1.5 million square feet (which is less than in most years), the firm's total sales area would be about 27.50 million square feet. As noted, sales per square foot have likewise increased. Assuming a conservative increase to $600 of sales per thousand square feet implies a sales forecast of about $16.50 billion for 1999, a 10.8 percent increase over 1998 sales of $15.31 billion.

TABLE 20.6 **SALES, NUMBER OF STORES, AND SALES AREA FOR WALGREEN: 1977–1998**

Year	Sales ($ Millions)	Number of Stores	Annual Sales per Store ($ Millions)	Store Area (000 Square Feet)	Average Area per Store (000 Square Feet)	Sales per Thousand Square Feet
1977	1,223.2	626	1.95	5,188	8.29	235.77
1978	1,192.9	641	1.66	5,390	8.10	221.32
1979	1,334.5	688	1.94	5,851	8.50	228.08
1980	1,530.7	739	2.07	6,305	8.53	242.78
1981	1,743.5	821	2.12	7,209	8.78	241.85
1982	2,039.5	883	2.31	7,815	8.85	260.97
1903	2,360.6	941	2.51	8,402	8.93	280.96
1984	2.744.6	1,002	2.74	9,002	8.98	304.89
1985	3,161.9	1,095	2.89	10,010	9.14	315.87
1986	3,660.6	1,273	2.88	11,895	9.34	307.74
1987	4,281.8	1,356	3.16	12,844	9.47	333.37
1988	4.883.5	1,416	3.45	13,549	9.57	360.43
1989	5,380.1	1,484	3.63	14,272	9.62	376.97
1990	6,047.5	1.564	3.87	15,105	9.66	400.36
1991	6,733.0	1,646	4.09	15,877	9.65	424.07
1992	7,474.0	1.736	4.31	16,811	9.68	444.59
1993	8,294.8	1,836	4.52	17,950	9.78	462.11
1994	9,235.0	1,968	4.69	19,342	9.83	477.46
1995	10,395.1	2,085	4.99	20,731	9.94	501.43
1996	11,778.0	2.193	5.37	22,124	10.09	532.36
1997	13.363.0	2.358	5.67	23,935	10.15	558.30
1998	15,307.0	2,549	6.01	26,024	10.21	588.19
Average Annual Rate of Growth (%)	12.8	6.9	5.5	8.0	1.0	4.4

Source: Walgreen Company annual reports.

Another internal estimate is possible by using the number of stores and sales per store. Walgreen is expected to open at least 200 stores during 1999. Assuming it closes 40, this would be a net addition of 160 to 2,700 at the end of 1999. Assuming sales per store likewise continue to increase from $6.01 million to $6.25 million implies an estimate of $16.88 billion (2,700 × $6.25 million), which is an increase of 10 percent over 1998.

Given the three estimates, the preference is for an estimate close to the high value because of the positive economic environment and the company's ability to increase sales between 13 and 14 percent during 1998 and 1997. Therefore, we will assume an 11 percent increase, which implies a final sales forecast for 1999 of $17 billion.

Estimating the Company Profit Margin

The next step in projecting earnings per share is to estimate the firm's net profit margin, which should include three considerations: (1) identification and evaluation of the firm's specific competitive strategy—i.e., either low-cost or differentiation; (2) the firm's internal performance, including general company trends and consideration of any problems that might affect its future performance; and (3) the firm's relationship with its industry, which should indicate whether the company's past performance is attributable to its industry or if it is unique to the firm. These examinations should help us understand the firm's past performance, but should also provide the background to make a meaningful estimate for the future. In this analysis, we do not consider the company–economy relationship because the significant economywide profit factors are reflected in the industry results. Since we have already discussed these strategies in general, we concentrate on how they affect Walgreen.

WALGREEN COMPETITIVE STRATEGIES

Over the years, has Walgreen pursued a low-cost strategy or has the firm attempted to differentiate itself from its competitors in some unique way? Based on its annual reports, Walgreen has pursued both strategies with different segments of its business. The firm's size and buying power allow it to be a cost leader for some of its nonprescription products, such as liquor, ice cream, candy, and soft drinks. These items are advertised heavily to attract customer traffic and to build consumer loyalty. At the same time, Walgreen has attempted to build a very strong franchise in the medical prescription business based on differentiation in service. Computer technology in the prescription area makes it possible for the firm to distinguish itself by providing outstanding service to its prescription customers. Specifically, the firm refers to itself as the nation's prescription druggist based on the number of prescriptions it fills and a nationwide computer system that allows customers to have their prescriptions filled at any of the 2,549 Walgreen drugstores in the country. This leadership in the growing medical field is a major goal.

The Internal Performance

Profit margin figures for Walgreen and the retail drugstore industry are in Table 20.7. The profit margins for Walgreen increased from 1977 to the mid-1980s followed by a decline through 1988 and a recovery beginning in 1991. In contrast, the margins for the retail drugstore industry experienced a relatively steady decline after a peak in 1983. Overall, Walgreen experienced a positive trend in its operating and net profit margins over the past 21 years, which has caused its net profit margin to be similar to the industry prior to 1997 when the industry margin declined sharply. To predict future values, you need to determine the reason for the overall decline in the industry profit margin and, more important, what factors have caused Walgreen's strong positive performance.

INDUSTRY FACTORS Industry profit margins have declined over the past two decades due to price discounting by aggressive regional drug chains.[15] The discussion in Chapter 19 suggested this as one of the competitive structure conditions that affect long-run profitability. Industry analysts have observed, however, that price cutting has subsided, and they currently foresee relative price stability. In addition, drugstores have tended toward a more profitable product mix featuring high-profit-margin items, such as cosmetics, and this has had a positive influence on profit margins.

COMPANY PERFORMANCE Walgreen's profit margin has showed consistent improvement, and a major reason has been the change in corporate structure. The outlook for profit margins is good because the firm has developed a strong position in the pharmacy business and has invested in service (including mail-order prescriptions) and inventory control technology that will help the firm experience strong margins on this business. The firm also has emphasized other big-profit-margin items, such as greeting cards, photofinishing, and cosmetics.

Specific estimates for Walgreen's future margins typically would begin with an analysis of their relationship with drugstore industry margins using time-series plots, such as those in Figure 20.3.[16] This time-series plot for the period 1977–1997 showed good results for

---

[15]For a more complete discussion, see "Retailing—Drug Stores," *Standard & Poor's Industry Surveys* (New York: Standard & Poor's, 1998).

[16]Both the operating margin and the net before tax margin were analyzed; the results indicated that the net profit margins yielded the best relationships. The long-run relationship cannot be very good because over the total period the industry margin was declining while Walgreen experienced fairly steady increases as shown in Figure 20.3.

TABLE 20.7 **PROFIT MARGINS AND COMPONENT EXPENSES FOR THE S&P 400 INDEX AND THE RETAIL DRUGSTORE INDUSTRY: 1977–1997**

	Walgreen Company			Retail Drugstores		
Year	Operating Margin (%)	NBT Margin	Net Profit Margin (%)	Operating Margin (%)	NBT Margin	Net Profit Margin (%)
1977	3.11	2.66	1.46	8.96	7.92	4.07
1978	3.86	3.73	2.16	8.78	7.74	4.03
1979	3.86	3.79	2.25	7.24	6.39	3.47
1980	3.56	3.52	2.27	7.07	6.27	3.47
1981	3.40	3.54	2.42	7.17	6.18	3.45
1982	4.32	4.20	2.75	7.30	6.21	3.44
1983	5.16	5.11	2.96	7.98	6.89	3.79
1984	5.57	5.46	3.11	7.19	5.54	3.03
1985	5.63	5.49	2.98	7.00	5.47	2.96
1986	5.37	5.13	2.82	7.37	5.66	3.11
1987	4.92	4.54	2.42	7.08	5.13	2.88
1988	4.59	4.28	2.64	6.70	4.72	2.90
1989	4.71	4.53	2.87	6.71	4.49	2.79
1990	4.70	4.65	2.89	6.71	4.68	2.89
1991	4.77	4.63	2.90	6.52	4.60	2.91
1992	4.80	4.72	2.95	6.35	4.59	2.89
1993	4.90	4.82	2.96	6.25	4.67	2.80
1994	4.93	4.96	3.05	6.42	4.68	2.89
1995	5.00	5.04	3.09	6.51	4.63	2.84
1996	5.13	5.15	3.16	6.53	5.11	3.21
1997	5.30	5.33	3.84	7.06	3.57	1.96

Source: Standard & Poor's *Analysts Handbook* (New York: Standard & Poor's Corporation, 1998). Reprinted by permission of Standard & Poor's Corp. Walgreen Company annual reports.

Walgreen versus its industry prior to 1997. Specifically, the net profit margins for the company and industry have come together over time due to steady improvements by Walgreen. You also should consider any unique factors that would influence this long-run relationship, such as price wars that would be reported in business publications or an abnormal number of store openings or closings as reported by the firm in quarterly or annual earnings reports.

Following a consideration of the long-run company–industry profit margin relationship, you should analyze the firm's common size income statement for several years. As discussed in Chapter 12, the breakdown of the income statement depends on the consistent detail provided by the firm. Table 20.8 shows a common size income statement for Walgreen during the period 1995–1998. An analysis of the main items of interest—cost of goods sold and operating expense—was encouraging. The cost-of-sales percentage increased slightly (less than 1 percent) from 1995 to 1998. In contrast, there was a larger decline in the percentage of SG&A expense through 1998. As a result, the operating profit margin increased from 5.00 percent to 5.46 percent. Interest expense was not a factor. Finally, the tax rate remained between 38 and 40 percent during the last several years. Overall, the net operating income margin experienced a small but steady increase over the 4 years.

NET PROFIT MARGIN ESTIMATE The overall industry outlook is encouraging because of stable prices, an increase in mechanization within the industry, and the inclusion of more high-profit-margin items. Therefore, the industry profit margin is expected to

FIGURE 20.3 **TIME-SERIES PLOT OF NET PROFIT MARGIN FOR WALGREEN AND THE RETAIL DRUGSORE INDUSTRY: 1977–1997**

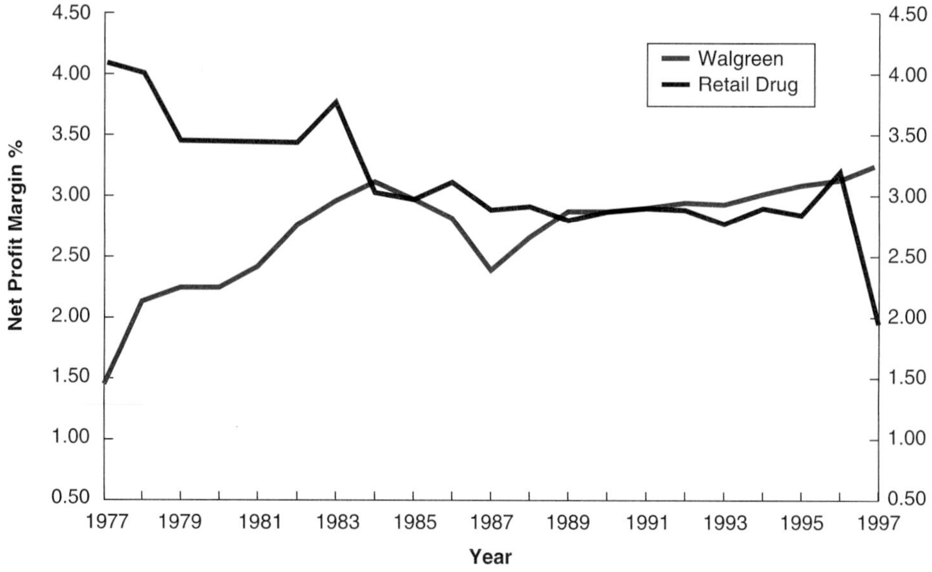
Net Profit Margin %
4.50
4.00
3.50
3.00
2.50
2.00
1.50
1.00
0.50
Walgreen
Retail Drug
1977
1979
1981
1983
1985
1987
1989
1991
1993
1995
1997
Year

increase slightly during 1999. Because of Walgreen's strong relationship to the industry profit margin and the increase in its margin since 1995 as shown in Table 20.8, it is estimated that the firm will show a further increase during 1999 to 3.50 percent.

COMPUTING EARNINGS PER SHARE This margin estimate, combined with the prior sales estimate of $17 billion, indicates net income of $596 million. Assuming about 1,003 million common shares outstanding, earnings should be about $0.60 per share for 1999, which is an increase of about 16 percent over the earnings of $0.51 per share in 1998. To find the value of Walgreen Company stock, our next step is to estimate its earnings multiplier.

ESTIMATING COMPANY EARNINGS MULTIPLIERS

As in our analysis of industry multipliers in Chapter 19, we use two approaches to estimate a company multiplier. First, we estimate the P/E ratio from the relationships among Walgreen, its industry, and the market. This is the macroanalysis. Second, we estimate a multiplier based on its three components: the dividend-payout ratio, the required rate of return, and the rate of growth. We then resolve the estimates derived from each approach and settle on one estimate.

Macroanalysis of the Earnings Multiplier

Table 20.4 and Figure 20.4 show the mean earnings multiple for the company, the retail drugstore industry, and the aggregate market for the period 1977–1997. Notably, all these earnings multipliers are computed using future earnings. Walgreen's relationship to its industry has changed dramatically over time. During the late 1970s and early 1980s, Walgreen's multiplier was consistently below the industry's. After 1987, the Walgreen

TABLE 20.8 **WALGREEN COMPANY AND SUBSIDIARIES COMMON SIZE INCOME STATEMENT:[a] YEARS ENDED AUGUST 31, 1995, 1996, 1997, AND 1998**

	1998	%	1997	%	1996	%	1995	%
Net Sales	15,307	100.00	13,363	100.00	11,778	100.00	10,395	100.00
Cost of goods sold	11,140	72.78	9,682	72.45	8,515	72.30	7,482	71.98
Gross Profit	4,167	27.22	3,681	27.55	3,263	27.70	2,913	28.02
Selling, general and administrative expenses	3,332	21.77	2,973	22.25	2,659	22.58	2,393	23.02
Operating Profit	835	5.46	708	5.30	604	5.13	520	5.00
Interest income	(6)	(0.04)	(6)	(0.04)	(5)	(0.04)	(5)	(0.05)
Interest expense	1	0.01	2	0.01	2	0.02	1	0.01
Operating Income before Income Taxes	840	5.49	712	5.33	607	5.15	524	5.04
Provision for income taxes	340	2.22	276	2.07	235	2.00	203	1.95
Operating Income After Taxes	500	3.27	436	3.26	372	3.16	321	3.09
Extraordinary loss (income)	(37)	(0.24)	—	—	—	—	—	—
Cumulative effect of accounting change	26	0.17	—	—	—	—	—	—
Reported Net Income	511	3.34	436	3.26	372	3.16	321	3.09
Operating Income After Taxes Available for Common	500	3.27	436	3.26	372	3.16	321	3.09
Reported Net Income Available for Common	511	3.34	436	3.26	372	3.16	321	3.09

[a]Percentages may not add to 100.0% due to rounding.

multiplier has followed the industry multiplier fairly closely. Similarly, the Walgreen earnings multiplier was lower than the market multiplier until 1982 and during 1990 and 1991, but they have been similar since 1992.

This pattern raises the question: Is the similarity of the Walgreen P/E relative to both its industry and the market that generally has prevailed since 1992 justified? The microanalyses should provide some insights regarding this question.

MICROANALYSIS OF THE EARNINGS MULTIPLIER

This historical data for the relevant series are contained in Table 20.9.[17] The relevant question is: Why has the earnings multiplier for Walgreen been similar to the market and industry earnings multiplier during the period 1992 to 1997? As before, we are looking for estimates of D/E, k, and g to find an earnings multiplier. We will use the historical data in Table 20.9 to determine patterns for the data and to develop future projections.

COMPARING DIVIDEND-PAYOUT RATIOS The dividend-payout ratio for Walgreen typically has been lower than its industry in recent years. The Walgreen–market comparison shows that Walgreen almost always had a lower payout, which by itself would imply a P/E ratio for Walgreen that is below the industry and the market P/E ratio.

[17]Although some prior tables included data through 1998 using estimates for specific ratios, it is not possible to do this for all the variables in Table 20.9 as of mid-1999. These data generally are not available until September.

FIGURE 20.4

TIME-SERIES PLOT OF MEAN PRICE/EARNINGS RATIOS FOR WALGREEN, THE RETAIL DRUGSTORE INDUSTRY, AND THE S&P 400

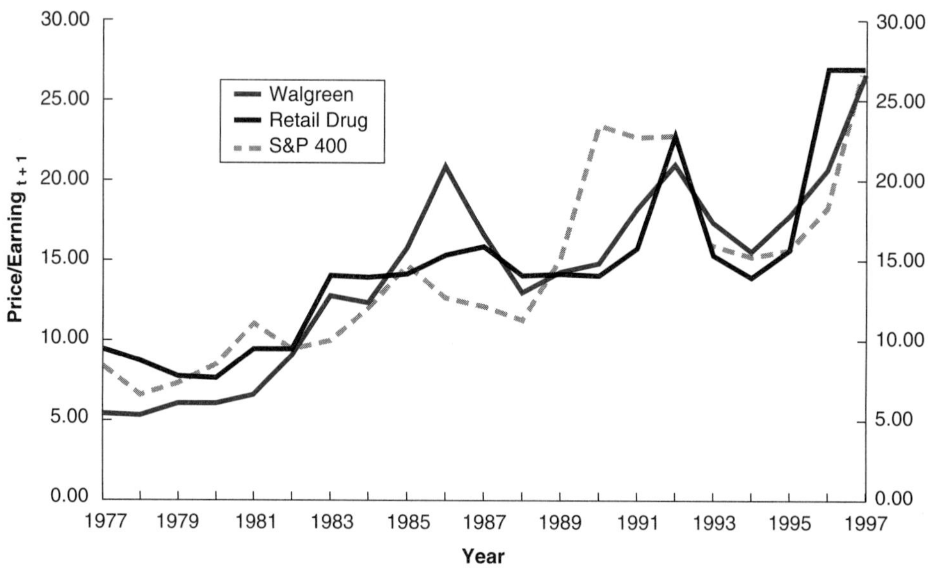
Walgreen
Retail Drug
S&P 400
Price/Earning t+1
30.00
25.00
20.00
15.00
10.00
5.00
0.00
1977
1979
1981
1983
1985
1987
1989
1991
1993
1995
1997
Year

ESTIMATING THE REQUIRED RATE OF RETURN To find Walgreen's required rate of return (k), we need to analyze the firm's fundamental risk characteristics (BR, FR, LR, ERR, and CR). Following this fundamental analysis of intrinsic factors, we also should derive an estimate based on the SML and a measure of Walgreen's systematic risk (i.e., its beta).

Walgreen should have relatively low business risk due to its stable sales growth compared to its industry and the aggregate economy. Notably, several measures of sales volatility did not support this expectation due to measurement problems. The coefficient of variation of sales that adjusts for absolute size indicated that Walgreen sales were less volatile than its industry, but more volatile than the market. It also is necessary to adjust for trend because a high-growth trend will cause a larger standard deviation due to the growth. To adjust for growth, we computed the standard deviation of annual percentage changes, which indicated that sales for Walgreen were less volatile. Therefore, after adjusting for size and trend, the results indicated that Walgreen sales were less volatile, which indicates lower business risk.

Several financial risk variables for Walgreen, its industry, and the aggregate market are shown in Table 20.10. Notably, these do not consider fairly large leases of stores. The firm's financial leverage ratio (notably, total assets/equity) has recently been less than 2.00, which is comparable to the industry and definitely lower than the aggregate market. Walgreen has an interest coverage ratio in excess of 10, a cash flow/long-term debt ratio of over 300 percent, and a cash flow/total debt ratio of about 30 percent. These financial risk ratios indicate that Walgreen has comparable financial risk to its industry and substantially lower financial risk than the aggregate stock market. As shown in Chapter 12, when the leases are considered, the firm's FR is fairly close to that of the market.

The firm's liquidity risk is quite low compared to its industry and the average firm in the market. Indicators of market liquidity are (1) the number of stockholders, (2) the number

TABLE 20.9

VARIABLES THAT INFLUENCE THE EARNINGS MULTIPLIER FOR WALGREEN, RETAIL DRUGSTORES, AND THE S&P 400: 1977–1998

	Walgreen						Retail Drugstores						S&P 400					
Year	D/E	NPM	TAT	ROA	TAE	ROE	D/E	NPM	TAT	ROA	TAE	ROE	D/E	NPM	TAT	ROA	TAE	ROE
1977	45.80	1.27	3.81	4.84	2.39	11.56	20.11	4.07	2.84	11.56	1.53	17.68	43.20	5.11	1.27	6.49	2.15	13.95
1978	30.31	2.16	3.45	7.45	2.34	17.44	23.90	4.03	2.81	11.32	1.52	17.21	41.20	5.19	1.27	6.59	2.22	14.63
1979	30.33	2.25	3.53	7.94	2.30	18.27	27.40	3.47	3.00	10.41	1.65	17.18	36.30	5.57	1.30	7.24	2,28	16.51
1980	30.47	2.27	3.60	8.17	2.16	17.65	29.20	3.47	3.04	10.55	1.66	17.51	40.30	4.92	1.31	6.45	2.30	14.82
1981	30.42	2.42	3.60	8.71	2.08	18.12	31.00	3.45	3.03	10.45	1.65	17.25	41.90	4.86	1.28	6.22	2,32	14.43
1982	26.93	2.75	3.59	9.87	2.06	20.34	31.10	3.44	2.97	10.22	1.66	16.96	54.00	3.95	1.17	4.62	2.40	11.09
1983	26.33	2.96	3.54	10.48	2.04	21.38	29.30	3.79	2.86	10.84	1.88	20.38	49.60	4.42	1.15	5.08	2.37	12.05
1984	25.84	3.11	3.52	10.95	2.03	22.22	37.60	3.04	2.65	8.06	1.93	15.55	41.50	4.77	1.22	5.82	2.51	14.61
1985	28.58	2.98	3.39	10.10	2.16	21.82	40.80	2.96	2.68	7.93	1.88	14.91	51.50	3.84	1.15	4.42	2.75	12.14
1986	29.81	2.82	3.39	9.56	2.16	20.65	31.90	3.11	2.71	8.43	1.94	16.35	56.00	3.75	1.07	4.01	2.90	11.64
1987	32.08	2.42	3.35	8.11	2.19	17.75	31.60	2.88	2.80	8.06	2.04	16.45	43.00	4.71	1.08	5.09	2.97	15.11
1988	28.59	2.64	3.40	8.98	2.12	19.03	30.60	2.90	2.82	8.18	2.07	16.93	36.90	5.46	0.98	5.35	3.56	19.06
1989	27.12	2.87	3.37	9.67	2.04	19.73	32.29	2.79	2.82	7.87	2.03	15.97	44.03	4.96	0.97	4.81	3.84	18.46
1990	28.19	2.89	3.16	9.13	2.02	18.45	31.68	2.89	2.82	8.13	2.00	16.26	50.20	4.17	0.97	4.04	4.01	16.22
1991	29.04	2.90	3.21	9.31	1.94	18.06	32.81	2.91	2.85	8.31	1.83	15.25	71.81	2.88	0.94	2.72	3.96	10.77
1992	29.21	195	3.15	9.29	1.92	17.89	33.59	2.89	2.83	8.19	1.82	14.89	66.14	3.17	0.96	3.03	4.41	13.37
1993	33.52	2.67	3.27	8.73	1.84	16.08	46.83	2.15	2.79	6.00	1.88	11.27	58.04	3.63	0.92	3.33	4.81	16.02
1994	29.82	3.05	3.17	9.67	1.85	17.92	33.78	2.89	2.63	7.60	2.00	15.17	38.94	5.24	0.95	4.98	4.38	21.79
1995	30.77	3.09	3.20	9.87	1.81	19.10	33.67	2.84	2.66	7.56	2.03	15.36	39.39	5.24	0.97	5.08	4.25	21.62
1996	28.95	3.16	3.24	10.24	1.78	19.40	28.81	3.21	2.02	6.48	2.17	14.06	37.86	5.86	0.93	5.45	4.49	24.49
1997	26.97	3.26	3.18	10.36	1.77	19.80	40.95	1.96	2.23	4.37	2.18	9.53	39.69	5.61	0.94	5.27	4.77	25.14
1998	24.27	3.51	3.12	10.95	1.72	19.60	NA	NA	NA	NA	NA	NA	NA	NA	NA	NA	NA	NA
Mean	29.70	2.75	3.37	9.20	2.03	18.74	32.38	3.10	2.76	8.60	1.87	15.82	46.74	4.63	1.09	5.05	3.32	16.09

D/E = Dividend payout, equal to dividends/earnings.

NPM = Net profit margin, equal to net income/sales.

TAT = Total asset turnover, equal to sales/total assets.

ROA = Return on assets.

TAE = Leverage ratio, equal to total assets/equity.

ROE = Return on equity, equal to net income/equity.

NA = Data not available.

Source: Standard & Poor's *Analysts Handbook* (New York: Standard & Poor's Corp., 1998). Reprinted by permission of Standard & Poor's Corp. Walgreen Annual Reports, various issues.

TABLE 20.10 **FINANCIAL RISK RATIOS FOR WALGREEN COMPANY, THE RETAIL DRUGSTORE INDUSTRY, AND THE S&P 400: 1977–1997**

	Walgreen Company				Retail Drugstores				S&P 400			
Year	Total Assets/ Equity	Interest Coverage	Cash Flow/ Long-Term Debt[a]	Cash Flow/ Total Debt[b]	Total Assets/ Equity	Interest Coverage	Cash Flow/ Long-Term Debt[a]	Cash Flow/ Total Debt[b]	Total Assets/ Equity	Interest Coverage	Cash Flow/ Long-Term Debt[a]	Cash Flow/ Total Debt[b]
1977	2.39	6.91	0.36	0.13	1.53	28.90	1.76	0.41	2.15	8.00	0.63	0.22
1978	2.34	7.93	0.43	0.18	1.52	30.90	1.94	0.42	2.22	7.60	0.63	0.22
1979	2.30	8.83	0.50	0.19	1.65	21.20	1.21	0.34	2.28	7.70	0.70	0.22
1980	2.16	9.01	0.60	0.20	1.66	20.10	1.33	0.35	2.30	6.00	0.66	0.21
1981	2.08	10.44	0.91	0.22	1.65	16.20	1.74	0.36	2.32	5.00	0.63	0.21
1982	2.06	13.38	1.40	0.24	1.66	17.40	2.43	0.36	2.40	4.00	0.54	0.18
1983	2.04	19.61	1.76	0.26	1.88	20.20	3.24	0.35	2.37	4.60	0.61	0.19
1984	2.03	25.23	2.14	0.27	1.93	10.60	1.43	0.24	2.51	4.10	0.65	0.19
1985	2.16	28.65	1.79	0.27	1.88	708.00	0.75	0.22	2.75	4.20	0.51	0.16
1986	2.16	17.11	0.90	0.23	1.94	12.70	0.99	0.24	2.90	3.60	0.51	0.15
1987	2.19	11.76	0.94	0.21	2.04	9.40	0.93	0.23	2.97	4.40	0.58	0.17
1988	2.12	11.46	0.92	0.20	2.07	8.20	1.00	0.24	3.56	3.80	0.44	0.15
1989	2.04	13.94	1.23	0.22	2.03	7.10	0.61	0.23	3.84	3.70	0.43	0.13
1990	2.02	11.22	1.67	0.26	2.00	8.20	0.69	0.25	4.01	3.60	0.40	0.12
1991	1.94	18.18	2.27	0.28	1.83	10.30	0.96	0.27	3.96	3.40	0.34	0.10
1992	1.93	23.53	1.65	0.28	1.82	13.40	1.13	0.27	4.41	4.00	0.38	0.11
1993	1.84	15.59	2.50	0.29	1.88	15.80	0.82	0.21	4.81	4.50	0.40	0.10
1994	1.85	10.51	2.80	0.23	2.00	16.70	0.86	0.23	4.38	5.60	0.50	0.13
1995	1.94	12.14	3.15	0.31	2.03	13.20	0.79	0.23	4.25	3.40	0.49	0.14
1996	1.90	11.40	3.30	0.33	2.17	11.99	0.47	0.17	4.49	4.70	0.51	0.15
1997	1.91	11.75	3.35	0.33	2.18	7.37	0.49	0.14	4.77	5.63	0.52	0.15

[a]Long-term debt does not include deferred taxes.

[b]Total debt is equal to total assets minus total equity, including preferred stock.

Source: Walgreen Annual Reports; Standard & Poor's *Analysts Handbook.*

of shares outstanding, (3) the number of shares traded, and (4) institutional interest in the stock. As of January 1, 1999, Walgreen had 27,600 holders of common stock—a relatively large number. At mid-1999, there were over one billion common shares outstanding (after the 1999 stock split) with a market value of over $30 billion. Clearly, Walgreen would qualify as an investment for institutions that require firms with large market value. Walgreen stock has an annual trading turnover of 48 percent, which is slightly below average. Financial institutions own about 450 million shares of Walgreen, which is about 45 percent of the outstanding shares. Therefore, Walgreen's large number of stockholders, fairly active trading of its stock, and strong institutional interest indicate that Walgreen has very little liquidity risk.

As discussed in Chapter 18, the exchange rate risk for companies depends on what proportion of sales and earnings are generated outside the United States and the volatility of the exchange rates in the specific countries. Walgreen has very little exchange rate risk or country risk because the firm has virtually no non-U.S. sales.

In summary, Walgreen has below-average business risk, financial risk equal to the market when we consider leases, low liquidity risk, and virtually no exchange rate and country risk. This implies that—based on fundamental factors—the overall risk for Walgreen should be lower than the market.

In addition to the consideration of fundamental factors, one should also consider market-determined risk (beta) based on the CAPM. As noted earlier in connection with the cash flow models, the stock's beta derived from 5 years of monthly data relative to the S&P 500 for the period 1994 to 1998 indicated a beta of 0.90.

These results are consistent with those derived from an analysis of the fundamental factors—both indicate that Walgreen's risk is below the aggregate market. This means that the risk premium and the required rate of return for Walgreen stock should be lower than the market. By itself, this lower required rate of return would suggest an earnings multiplier above the market multiplier.

ESTIMATING THE EXPECTED GROWTH RATE Recall that the expected growth rate (g) is determined by the firm's retention rate and its expected return on equity (ROE). We have already noted Walgreen's low dividend payout compared to the industry and the aggregate market, which implies a higher retention rate.

As we know from our earlier analysis using the DuPont model, a firm's ROE can be evaluated and estimated in terms of the three ratios: (1) net profit margin (NPM), (2) total asset turnover (TAT), and (3) the financial leverage multiplier. We also know from the discussion in Chapter 19 that NPM $\times$ TAT $=$ Return on Assets (ROA). Not only is it important to examine the relative impact of these two ratios, but it is also important to compare the ROA of alternative firms because it is a measure of operating performance—i.e., profitability and asset efficiency. In the case of Walgreen, the firm has experienced a small decline in TAT, but this has been more than offset by an increase in NPM. As a result, the firm's ROA has increased substantially from about 7 percent to over 10 percent. Notably, it has an ROA substantially above both its industry and the market.

Finally, the firm's ROE equals the ROA times the financial leverage multiplier (total assets/equity). It is notable that since 1977 Walgreen has reduced its leverage multiplier from 2.39 to 1.72 while both the industry and the market have experienced increases, (in particular, the market has increased from 2.08 to 3.33). As a result, the ROEs are similar but the financial risk is different—i.e., not only does Walgreen have a higher ROE, but it has lower financial risk (as noted earlier, with leases the FR is about equal to the market).

Using the results for the last three years (1995–1997), the ROEs would be approximately as follows:

	NPM	TAT	ROA	Total Assets/ Equity	ROE
Walgreen	3.17	3.21	10.18	1.79	18.22
Retail drugstores	2.67	2.30	6.14	2.13	13.08
S&P 400	5.57	0.95	5.29	3.30	17.46

The foregoing is meant to highlight the difference among the three units based on history. An analyst would need to *estimate* future components and derive an expected ROE that reflects the firm's *future* performance.

The demonstration can be extended by combining the average annual ROEs derived above and the average of recent retention rates from Table 20.11 to derive expected growth rates:

	Retention Rate	ROE	Expected Growth Rate
Walgreen	0.75	0.1822	0.1366
Retail drugstores	0.68	0.1308	0.0889
S&P 400	0.53	0.1746	0.0925

Taken alone, these higher expected growth rates for Walgreen would indicate that it should definitely have a higher multiple than its industry and the market.

COMPUTING THE EARNINGS MULTIPLIER Comparing our estimates of *D/E, k,* and *g* to comparable values for the industry and the market, we find that Walgreen's earnings multiplier based on the microanalysis should be greater than the multiplier for its industry and the market. Specifically, the dividend-payout ratio points toward a lower multiplier for Walgreen, whereas both the risk analysis and the expected growth rate would indicate a multiplier for Walgreen above that of its industry and the market.

The macroanalysis indicated that Walgreen's multiplier typically has been above that of its industry and the market. As noted, the microanalysis supported this relationship. Assuming a market multiple of about 20 and a retail drugstore multiplier of about 22, the multiplier for Walgreen should be between 24 and 26, with a tendency toward the upper end of the range and beyond (24-26-28 times). Alternatively, if we inserted some earlier estimated values for *D/E, k,* and *g* into the P/E ratio formula, we would not be able to derive an estimated multiplier for Walgreen because *g* is greater than *k.* As noted earlier in Chapter 13, because Walgreen is a true growth company, we cannot use the standard DDM formula to estimate a specific multiple. We would need to employ the direction of change and the macroanalysis estimates of 24-26-28 times.

ESTIMATE OF THE FUTURE VALUE FOR WALGREEN Earlier, we estimated 1999 earnings per share for Walgreen of about \$0.60 per share. Assuming multipliers of 24-26-28 implies the following estimated future values:

$$24 \times \$0.60 = \$14.40$$

$$26 \times \$0.60 = \$15.60$$

$$28 \times \$0.60 = \$16.80$$

TABLE 20.11 **EXPECTED GROWTH RATE COMPONENTS FOR WALGREEN COMPANY, THE RETAIL DRUGSTORE INDUSTRY, AND THE S&P 400: 1977–1997**

	WALGREEN			RETAIL DRUGSTORES			S&P 400		
Year	Retention Rate	ROE	Expected Growth Rate	Retention Rate	ROE	Expected Growth Rate	Retention Rate	ROE	Expected Growth Rate
1977	0.54	11.56	6.24	0.80	17.68	14.14	0.57	13.95	7.95
1978	0.70	17.44	12.21	0.76	17.21	13.08	0.59	14.63	8.63
1979	0.70	18.27	12.79	0.73	17.49	12.77	0.64	16.51	10.57
1980	0.70	17.65	12.36	0.71	17.51	12.43	0.60	14.82	8.89
1981	0.70	18.12	12.68	0.69	17.25	11.90	0.58	14.43	8.37
1982	0.73	20.34	14.85	0.69	16.96	11.70	0.45	11.09	4.99
1983	0.74	21.38	15.75	0.71	18.15	12.89	0.50	12.05	6.03
1984	0.74	22.22	16.51	0.62	15.15	9.39	0.59	14.61	8.62
1985	0.71	21.82	15.59	0.59	15.15	8.94	0.46	12.14	5.83
1986	0.70	20.65	14.50	0,68	16.52	11.23	0.44	11.64	5.12
1987	0.68	17.75	12.04	0.68	16.45	11.19	0.57	15.11	8.61
1988	0.71	19.30	13.79	0.63	16.87	10.63	0.61	19.06	11.63
1989	0.73	20.10	14.63	0.68	15.99	10.87	0.55	18.46	10.15
1990	0.72	19.70	14.11	0.68	16.28	11.07	0.49	16.22	7.95
1991	0.71	19.20	13.59	0.64	15.25	9.76	0.26	10.77	2.80
1992	0.71	19.10	13.56	0.66	14.89	9.83	0.32	13.37	4.28
1993	0.67	18.80	12.60	0.53	11.27	5.97	0.40	16.02	6.41
1994	0.70	19.10	13.37	0.66	15.17	10.01	0.60	21.79	13.07
1995	0.69	19.10	13.24	0.68	16.18	11.00	0.51	21.62	11.03
1996	0.71	19.40	13.75	0.71	19.53	13.90	0.62	24.49	15.22
1997	0.73	19.80	14.42	0.59	15.19	8.97	0.62	25.14	15.55
Mean:	0.70	19.09	13.46	0.67	16.29	11.03	0.52	16.09	8.65

MAKING THE INVESTMENT DECISION

In our prior discussions of valuation, we set forth the investment decision in two forms:

1. Compute the estimated value for an investment using your required rate of return as the discount rate. If this estimated value is equal to or greater than the current market price of the investment, buy it.
2. Compute the estimated future value for an investment using your required rate of return as one of the components. Given this future value, compute the expected rate of return you would receive if you bought the asset at the current market price and held the investment during the future period, typically assumed to be a year. If this expected rate of return is equal to or greater than your required rate of return, buy the investment; if the expected return is below your required rate of return, do not buy it.

The most obvious comparison is the estimated values derived using the present value of cash flow models and the values estimated using the earnings multiple model to the current market price of Walgreen of about $30 a share. The following is a summary of these estimated values. Recall that we could not calculate constant growth models because Walgreen has consistently experienced growth rates above its required rates of return (it is a true growth company).

Present Value of Cash Flow Models	
Three-Stage DDM	$8.86
Three-Stage FCFE	$15.54
Three-Stage FCFF (Operating FCF)	$13.17

Earnings Multiple Models	
24 times estimated earnings	\$14.40
26 times estimated earnings	\$15.60
28 times estimated earnings	\$16.80

Because none of the computed values is equal to or larger than the current market price of \$30.00, you would not recommend a purchase of the stock although Walgreen is clearly an outstanding firm; it is obviously a true growth company, but apparently is not expected to be a growth stock.

COMPARING EXPECTED RATE OF RETURN TO REQUIRED RATE OF RETURN In past demonstrations of this decision rule, we have computed an expected rate of return using the expected value and dividend. Although we will again use this technique, we also will introduce another technique for computing an expected rate of return based on the dividend discount model (DDM).

We can compute the expected rate of return, $E(R_i)$, based on our expected future value using the formula

$$E(R_i) = \frac{EV - BV + Div}{BV}$$

where:

EV = the estimated ending value of the stock
BV = the beginning value of the stock (typically its current market price)
Div = the expected dividend per share during the holding period

In our case, these values would be

$$EV = \$17.00 \text{ (at best)}$$
$$BV = \text{(assume \$30 a share)}$$
$$Div = \$0.14$$

Thus, we know that all the expected returns would be negative. Based on the k of 10.5 percent used in the valuation section, we would not buy this stock because its negative expected rates of return are below our required rate of return (10.5 percent).

The second technique used for deriving an expected rate of return is based on the dividend discount model. You will recall that the DDM states:

$$P_0 = \frac{D_1}{k - g}$$

Solving to estimate k:

$$k_i = \frac{D_1}{P_0} + g$$

In this equation, k serves as an estimate of the required rate of return when you assume that you know the firm's future growth rate. Alternatively, an investor can use this equation to estimate his or her *long-run* expected rate of return if you are estimating the future dividend and growth rate. For Walgreen, the P_0 would be the current price of the stock, D_1 would be the expected dividend during the investment horizon, and g would be the expected longer-run growth rate, as discussed in connection with Table 20.10.

As an example, assume a current price of \$30, an expected dividend of \$0.14 per share, and a growth rate of 14 percent, which is the growth rate we used in the earlier microestimate of the multiplier. Notably, it is slightly above the g implied by the average values in Table 20.10. This would imply the following estimate of your long-run expected rate of return on Walgreen common stock:

$$\begin{aligned} k &= \frac{0.14}{30.00} + 0.140 \\ &= 0.005 + 0.140 \\ &= 0.145 = 14.5\% \end{aligned}$$

This computation shows that you would expect a *long-run* rate of return from investing in Walgreen stock of 14.5 percent. If your required rate of return was 10.5 percent, you would buy this stock recognizing it is a *long-run* expectation.

ADDITIONAL MEASURES OF RELATIVE VALUE

The best-known measure of relative value for common stock is the price/earnings ratio or the earnings multiplier because it is derived from the dividend growth model and has stood the test of time as a useful measure of relative value. Although not rejecting the P/E ratio, analysts have begun to calculate three additional measures of relative value for common stocks—the price/book value ratio, the price/cash flow ratio, and the price/sales ratio. In this section, each of these valuation ratios is discussed and demonstrated.

Price/Book (P/BV) Value Ratio

The price-to-book-value ratio (P/BV) has gained prominence because of the studies by Fama and French and several subsequent authors.[18] The rationale is that book value can be a reasonable measure of value for firms. Also, individual firms that have consistent accounting practice (for example, firms in the same industry) can be meaningfully compared. Notably, this measure can apply to firms with negative earnings or even negative cash flows. You should not attempt to compare this ratio for firms with different levels of hard assets—that is, don't compare a heavy industrial firm to a service firm.

The annual P/BV ratios for Walgreen, its industry, and the market are in Table 20.4, along with the ratio of the company P/BV ratio relative to its industry and relative to the market ratio. In this instance, the major variable that should cause a difference in the P/BV ratio is the firm's return on investment (ROI) relative to its cost of capital (its WACC). Assuming that most firms in an industry have comparable WACCs, the major differential should be the firm's ROI because the larger the ROI–WACC difference, the greater the justified P/BV ratio. We will consider this in the subsequent section on EVA.

As shown in Figure 20.5, the P/BV ratios for the three components have increased from about 1.5–2.00 to 4.0–4.5. As shown in Figure 20.6, which contains a plot of relative

[18]Eugene F. Fama and Kenneth R. French, "The Cross Section of Expected Stock Returns," *Journal of Finance* 47, no. 2 (June 1992): 427–450; Barr Rosenberg, Kenneth Raid, and Ronald Lanstein, "Persuasive Evidence of Market Inefficiency," *Journal of Portfolio Management* 11, no. 3 (spring 1985): 9–17; and Patricia Fairfield, "P/E, P/B and the Present Value of Future Dividends," *Financial Analysts Journal* 50, no. 4 (July–August 19): 23–31.

FIGURE 20.5

TIME-SERIES PLOT OF PRICE/BOOK VALUE RATIOS FOR WALGREEN, THE RDS INDUSTRY, AND THE S&P 400

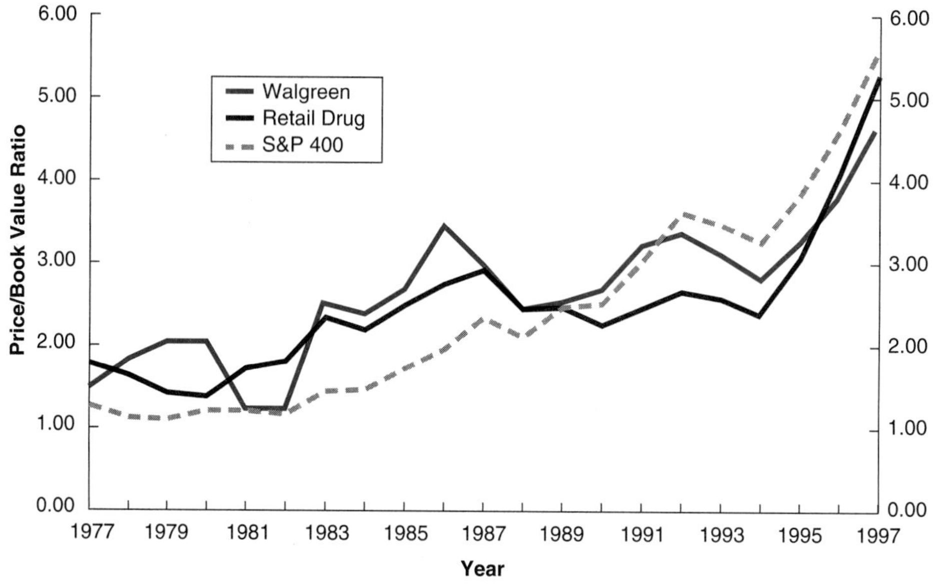
Price/Book Value Ratio
Walgreen
Retail Drug
S&P 400
6.00
5.00
4.00
3.00
2.00
1.00
0.00
1977
1979
1981
1983
1985
1987
1989
1991
1993
1995
1997
Year

FIGURE 20.6

TIME-SERIES PLOT OF RELATIVE PRICE/BOOK VALUE RATIOS FOR WALGREEN/INDUSTRY AND WALGREEN/MARKET

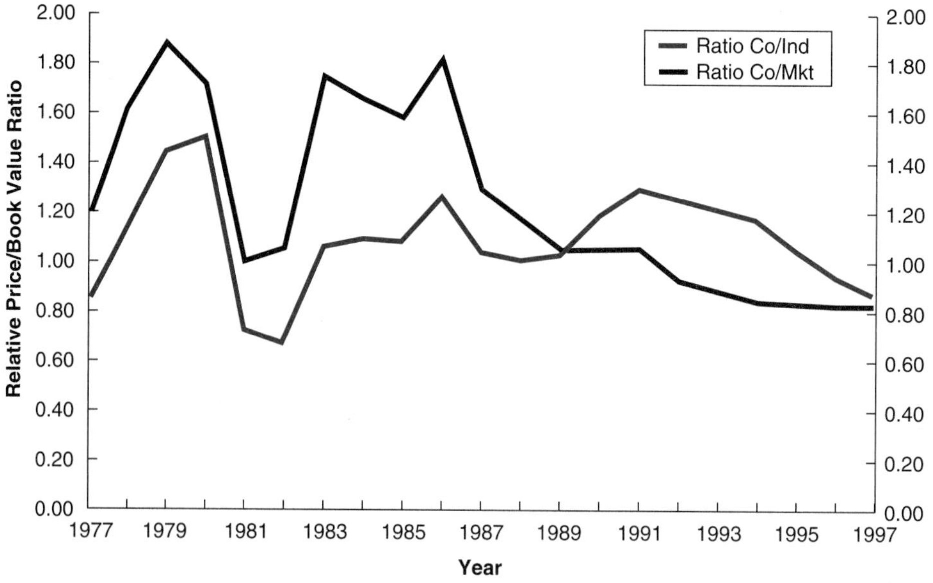
Relative Price/Book Value Ratio
Ratio Co/Ind
Ratio Co/Mkt
2.00
1.80
1.60
1.40
1.20
1.00
0.80
0.60
0.40
0.20
0.00
1977
1979
1981
1983
1985
1987
1989
1991
1993
1995
1997
Year

valuation ratios, Walgreen has experienced a larger increase in its P/BV ratio than its industry as indicated by its Co/Ind ratio that has gone from about 0.80 to about 0.90. This seems reasonable based upon the difference in ROE for the Co versus the industry. In contrast, the Co/Mkt ratio for Walgreen has *declined* from about 1.18 to about 0.83 at the end

FIGURE 20.7

TIME-SERIES PLOT OF PRICE/CASH FLOW RATIOS FOR WALGREEN, THE RDS INDUSTRY, AND THE S&P 400

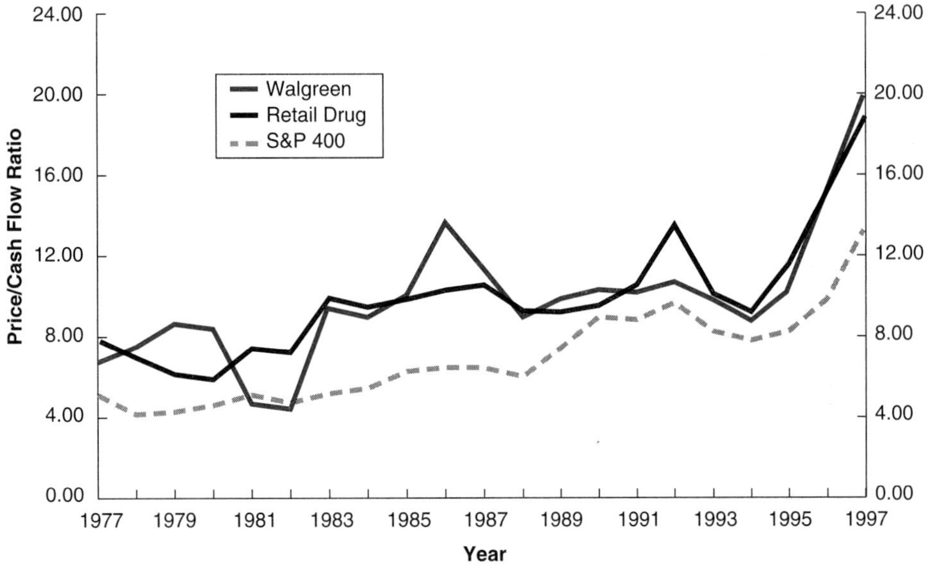
24.00
20.00
16.00
12.00
8.00
4.00
0.00
Price/Cash Flow Ratio
Walgreen
Retail Drug
S&P 400
1977
1979
1981
1983
1985
1987
1989
1991
1993
1995
1997
Year

of the period. This latter trend is interesting because the ROE for Walgreen has consistently been greater than for the S&P 400 until 1995 when the ROE for the S&P 400 rose substantially. One must question whether this declining trend in the Co/Mkt ratio is because the beginning relationship was too high.

PRICE/CASH FLOW (P/CF) RATIO

As noted in Chapter 12, the price/cash flow ratio has grown in prominence and use because many observers contend that a firm's cash flow is less subject to manipulation than its earnings per share and because cash flows are widely used in the present value of cash flow models discussed earlier. An important question is: Which of the several cash flow specifications should an analyst employ? In this analysis, we use the EBITDA cash flow measure equal to net income plus interest, depreciation, and taxes because this cash flow measure can be derived for both the retail drugstore industry and the market. Although it is certainly possible to employ any of the other cash flow measures discussed, a demonstration using this measure should provide a valid comparison for learning purposes.

The time-series graph of the P/CF ratios in Figure 20.7 shows a general increase for Walgreen and its industry from about 7 times in 1977 to almost 20 times in 1997, while the market P/CF ratio went from 5 times to 12 times. Notably, although the absolute value of the ratios increased, the graphs in Figure 20.8 show that Walgreen P/CF ratios relative to its industry experienced an overall decline from 0.84 and a high of 1.40 to an ending relative ratio of 0.93. Similarly, the Co/Mkt comparison started at 1.38, reached a high of 2.20, and ended at 1.42. This indicates an overall increase in the P/CF ratio, but no overall change in the P/CF ratio relative to the firm's industry and the overall market. In this case, the question becomes: What has happened to the firm's growth rate of cash flow and the risk of these cash flows that would justify this lack of change in the relative P/CF ratio?

PRICE/SALES (P/S) RATIO

The price-to-sales ratio (P/S) has had a long but generally neglected existence followed by a recent reawakening. In the late 1950s, Phillip Fisher in his classic book suggested this

FIGURE 20.8

TIME-SERIES PLOT OF RELATIVE PRICE/CASH FLOW RATIOS OF WALGREEN/INDUSTRY AND WALGREEN/MARKET

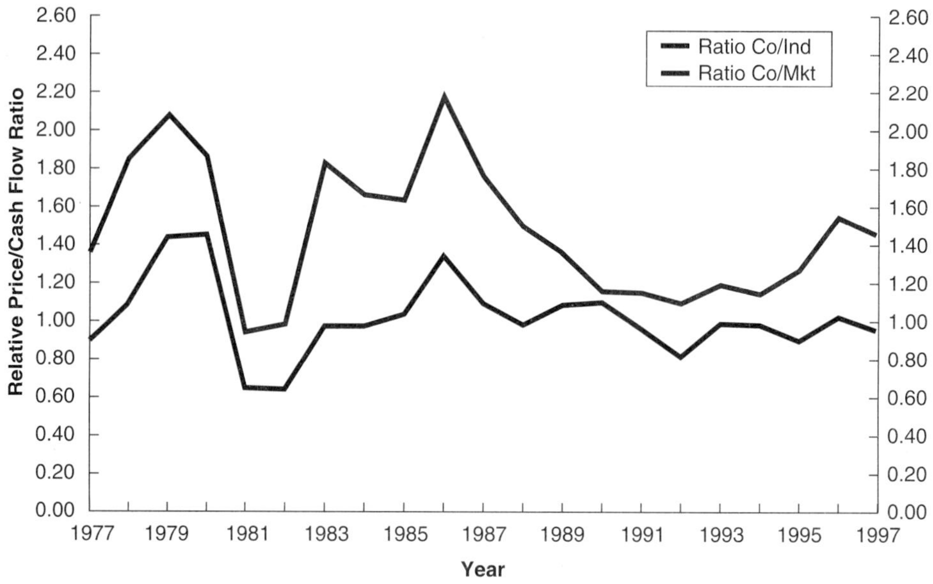
Ratio Co/Ind
Ratio Co/Mkt
Relative Price/Cash Flow Ratio
2.60
2.40
2.20
2.00
1.80
1.60
1.40
1.20
1.00
0.80
0.60
0.40
0.20
0.00
1977
1979
1981
1983
1985
1987
1989
1991
1993
1995
1997
Year

ratio as a valuable tool when considering investments, including growth stocks.[19] Subsequently, his son, Kenneth Fisher, used the ratio as a major stock selection variable in his widely read book.[20] Recently, P/S has been suggested as a valuable tool in a monograph by award-winning author Martin Leibowitz, and the ratio was espoused by O'Shaughnessy in his book that compared several stock selection techniques.[21] Leibowitz makes the point that sales growth drives all subsequent earnings and cash flow, while those who are concerned with accounting manipulation point out that sales is one of the purest numbers available. As noted in Chapter 12, this ratio is equal to the P/E ratio times the net profit margin (Earnings/Sales), which implies that it is heavily influenced by the profit margin of the entity being analyzed.

As shown in Table 20.4 and Figure 20.9, the P/S ratio for Walgreen has experienced a significant increase from 0.10 to 0.83, compared to a moderate increase by its industry (0.38 to 0.65) and a healthy increase by the market (from 0.42 to 1.30). This substantial relative performance by Walgreen is reflected in Figure 20.10, which shows the plot of relative ratios wherein the Co/Ind ratio increased notably from 0.31 to almost 1.30, while the Co/Mkt ratio went from 0.30 to 0.67. Similar to prior comparisons, the question the analyst must ask is whether the growth of sales, the risk related to the sales growth, and the profit margin of Walgreen can justify a much higher P/S ratio than its industry. The positive news is that Walgreen sales have experienced strong consistent growth relative to its industry. Also, Walgreen has shown a larger increase in its profit margin.

---

[19]Phillip A. Fisher, *Common Stocks and Uncommon Profits* (Woodside, Calif.: PSR Publications, 1958, 1960 rev. ed., 1984).

[20]Kenneth L. Fisher, *SuperStocks* (Woodside, Calif.: Business Classics, 1984).

[21]Martin L. Leibowitz, *Sales-Driven Franchise Value* (Charlottesville, Va.: The Research Foundation of the Institute of Chartered Financial Analysis, 1997); and James P. O'Shaughnessy, *What Works on Wall Street* (New York: McGraw-Hill, 1997).

FIGURE 20.9

TIME-SERIES PLOT OF PRICE/SALES RATIOS FOR WALGREEN, THE RDS INDUSTRY, AND THE S&P 400

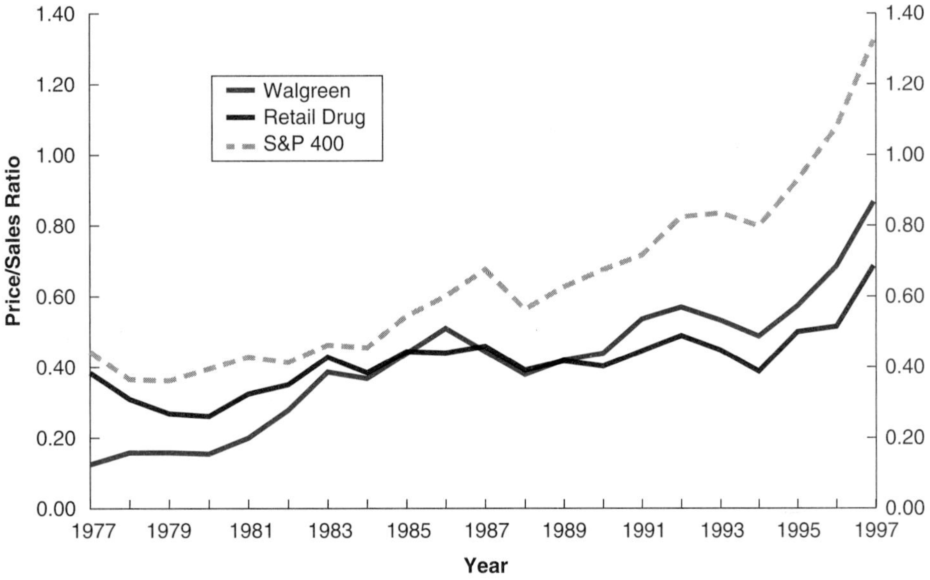
Walgreen
Retail Drug
S&P 400
Price/Sales Ratio
Year
1.40
1.20
1.00
0.80
0.60
0.40
0.20
0.00
1977
1979
1981
1983
1985
1987
1989
1991
1993
1995
1997

FIGURE 20.10

TIME-SERIES PLOT OF RELATIVE PRICE/SALES RATIOS FOR WALGREEN, THE RDS INDUSTRY, AND WALGREEN/MARKET

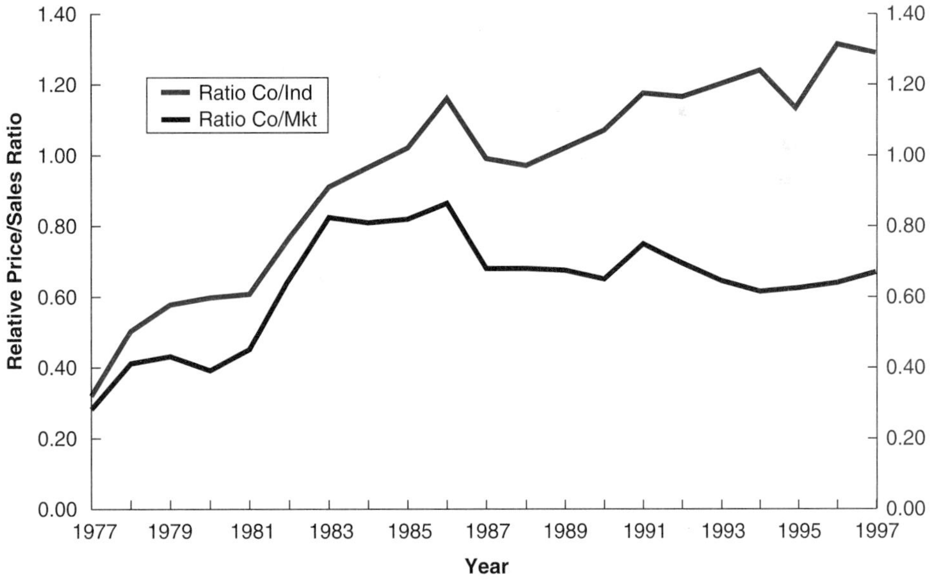
Ratio Co/Ind
Ratio Co/Mkt
Relative Price/Sales Ratio
Year
1.40
1.20
1.00
0.80
0.60
0.40
0.20
0.00
1977
1979
1981
1983
1985
1987
1989
1991
1993
1995
1997

SUMMARY OF RELATIVE VALUATION RATIOS

Notably, the four individual, relative valuation variables increased across the board—all four relative valuation ratios increased during the 20-year period for the firm, its industry, and the aggregate stock market. The widespread increases suggest that the relative valuation ratio changes are caused by changes in some aggregate economic variables, such as economic growth and economic risk factors. Interestingly, Dudley and McKelvey from

Goldman Sachs & Co. argued that the U.S. economy has experienced several significant changes during the past two decades that have caused an important change in the nature and length of our economic expansions and contractions.[22]

In addition to these overall increases for all three segments (firm, industry, and market), Walgreen has generally experienced a larger increase than its industry in terms of its P/E ratio, P/BV ratio, and P/S ratio, while lagging in terms of its P/CF ratio. Compared to the market, the firm's P/E ratio and P/S ratio increased more than the market, while its P/CF ratio and its P/BV ratios increased less than the market. Assuming that an investor wants to use these ratios to determine relative value or to make an investment decision, he or she must examine the basic valuation factors that affect the ratios to explain the differentials.

Now that we have considered the two major approaches to basic equity valuation, it is important to also consider some techniques used to analyze and derive values for growth companies. This is the purpose of the next section.

ANALYSIS OF GROWTH COMPANIES

Investment literature contains numerous accounts of the rapid growth of such companies as Wal-Mart, Cisco Systems, Intel, Merck, and Microsoft, along with stories about investors who became wealthy because of the timely acquisition of these stocks. These very high rates of return indicate that the proper valuation of true growth companies can be extremely rewarding. At the same time, for every successful Wal-Mart or Microsoft, there are numerous firms that did not survive. In addition, there are many instances where the stock price of a true growth company overcompensated for the firm's expected growth, and the subsequent returns to the stockholder were below expectations. As noted earlier, the common stock of a growth company is *not* always a growth stock.[23]

You are familiar with the dividend discount model and its basic assumptions—that is, that dividends are expected to grow at a *constant rate* for an *infinite time period.* As explained in Chapter 13. although these assumptions are reasonable when evaluating the aggregate market and some large industries, they can be very tenuous when analyzing individual securities. *These assumptions are extremely questionable for a growth company.*

Growth Company Defined

A growth company has the opportunities and ability to invest capital in projects that generate rates of return greater than the firm's cost of capital. Such a condition is considered to be *temporary* because, in a competitive economy, all firms should produce at the point where marginal revenue equals marginal cost, which means that the returns to the producer will exactly compensate for the risks involved. If the returns earned in an industry are below what is expected for the risk involved, some participants will leave the industry. In contrast, if the rates of return for a given industry exceed the rates of return expected based on the risk involved, other companies will enter the industry, increase the supply, and eventually drive prices down until the rates of return earned are consistent with the risk involved, resulting in a state of equilibrium.

Actual Returns above Expected Returns

The notion of a firm consistently earning rates of return above its required rate of return requires elaboration. Firms are engaged in business ventures that offer opportunities for investment of corporate capital, and these investments entail some risk. Investors determine

[22]William C. Dudley and Edward F. McKelvey, *The Brave New Business Cycle* (New York: Goldman, Sachs & Co., October 1997).

[23]See Michael Solt and Meir Statman, "Good Companies, Bad Stocks," *Journal of Portfolio Management* 15, no. 4 (summer 1989): 39–44.

their required return for owning a firm based on the risk of its investments compared to the risk of other firms. Based on the CAPM, one would expect the difference in the required rate of return to be a function of the difference in the stock's systematic risk. This required rate of return is referred to as the firm's *cost of equity.* If the market is in a state of equilibrium, the rates of return earned on risky investments by the firm should equal the rates of return required by investors. If a firm earns returns above those required for the systematic risk involved, these excess returns are referred to as *pure profits.*

One of the costs of production is the cost of the capital used. Therefore, in a competitive environment, marginal revenue should equal marginal costs (including capital costs), and there would be no excess returns or pure profits. Excess profits are possible only in a noncompetitive environment. Assume that a medical equipment firm is able to earn 20 percent on its capital, while investors require only 15 percent from the firm because of its systematic risk. The extra 5 percent is defined as pure profit, and numerous companies would enter the medical equipment field to enjoy the excess profits. These competitors would increase the supply of equipment and reduce the price that producers could charge for the equipment until the marginal returns equaled the marginal costs.

Because many firms have derived excess profits for a number of years, these excess returns are probably not due to a temporary disequilibrium, but rather because of some noncompetitive factors that exist, such as patents or copyrights that provide a firm or person with monopoly rights to a process or a manuscript for a specified period. During this period of protection from competition, the firm can derive above-normal returns without fear of competition. Also, a firm could possess other strategies, such as those discussed by Porter, that provide added profits (e.g., a unique marketing technique or other organizational characteristics). Finally, there may be significant barriers to entry, such as capital requirements.

In a purely competitive economy with no frictions, true growth companies would not exist because competition would not allow continuing excess return investments. The fact is, our economy is not perfectly competitive (although this typically is the best model to use) because there are a number of frictions that restrict competition. Therefore, it is possible for *temporary* true growth companies to exist in our economy. The question is: How long can they earn these excess profits?

Growth Companies and Growth Stocks

Recall that a growth stock is expected to experience above-average risk-adjusted rates of return during some future period. This means that any undervalued stock can be a growth stock, regardless of the type of company. Alternatively, the stock of a growth company that is overvalued could be a speculative stock because the probability of below-normal returns would be very high.

In this section, we discuss models that are meant to help you evaluate the unique earnings stream of a growth company. As a result, you should derive a better estimate of the firm's value and be able to judge whether the stock of a growth company is: (1) a growth stock, (2) a properly valued stock, or (3) a speculative overvalued stock.

Growth Companies and the Dividend Discount Model

We know it is impossible for a true growth firm to exist for an infinite time period in a relatively competitive economy. Further, even in an economy with some noncompetitive factors, a true growth firm should not be able to exist for very long because patents and copyrights run out, unusual management practices can be copied, and competitors can enter the industry. Therefore, the constant growth dividend discount growth model is *not* appropriate for the valuation of growth companies, and we must consider special valuation models that allow for the finite periods of abnormal growth and for the possibility of different rates of growth. The rest of the chapter deals with models for valuing growth companies.

ALTERNATIVE GROWTH MODELS[24]

In this section, we consider the full range of growth models, from those of no growth and negative growth to dynamic true growth. Knowledge of the full range will help you understand why the dividend growth model is not always applicable. We assume the company is an all-equity firm to simplify the computations.

NO-GROWTH FIRM

The no-growth firm is a mythical company that is established with a specified portfolio of investments that generate a constant stream of earnings (E) equal to r times the value of assets. Earnings are calculated after allowing for depreciation to maintain the assets at their original value. Therefore,

$$E = r \times \text{Assets}$$

It also is assumed that all earnings of the firm are paid out in dividends; if b is the rate of retention, $b = 0$. Hence,

$$E = r \times \text{Assets} = \text{Dividends}$$

Under these assumptions, the value of the firm is the discounted value of the perpetual stream of earnings (E). The discount rate (the required rate of return) is specified as k. In this case, it is assumed that $r = k$. The firm's rate of return on assets equals its required rate of return. The value of the firm is

$$V = \frac{E}{k} = \frac{(1 - b)E}{k}$$

In the no-growth case, the earnings stream never changes because the asset base never changes, and the rate of return on the assets never changes. Therefore, the value of the firm never changes, and investors continue to receive k on their investment.

$$k = E/V$$

LONG-RUN GROWTH MODELS

Long-run models differ from the no-growth models because *they assume some of the earnings are reinvested.* The initial case assumes a firm retains a constant dollar amount of earnings and reinvests these retained earnings in assets that obtain a rate of return above the required rate.

In all cases, it is postulated that the market value (V) of an all-equity firm is the capitalized value of three component forms of returns discounted at the rate k.

- E = the level of (constant) net earnings expected from existing assets, without further net investments.
- G = the growth component that equals the present value of capital gains expected from reinvested funds. The return on reinvested funds is equal to r, which equals mk (m is the relative rate of return operator). If m is equal to 1, then $r = k$. If m is greater than 1, the projects that generate these returns are considered true growth investments ($r > k$). If m is less than 1, the investments are generating returns (r) below the cost of capital ($r < k$).
- R = the reinvestment of net earnings (E) and is equal to bE, where b is a percent of retention between zero (no reinvestment) and unity (total reinvestment; no dividends).

[24]The discussion in this section draws heavily from Ezra Solomon, *The Theory of Financial Management* (New York: Columbia University Press, 1963), 55–63; and M. Miller and F. Modigliani, "Dividend Policy, Growth, and the Valuation of Shares," *The Journal of Business* 34, no. 4 (October 1961): 411–433.

SIMPLE GROWTH MODEL This model assumes the firm has growth investment opportunities that provide rates of return equal to r, where r is greater than k (m is above 1), Further, it is assumed that the firm can invest R dollars a year at these rates and that $R = bE$; R is a *constant dollar amount* because E is the constant earnings at the beginning of the period.

The value of G, the capital gain component, is computed as follows: the first investment of bE dollars yields a stream of earnings equal to bEr dollars, and this is repeated every year. Each of these earnings streams has a present value, as of the year it begins, of bEr/k, which is the present value of a constant perpetual stream discounted at a rate consistent with the risk involved. Assuming the firm does this every year, it has a series of investments, each of which has a present value of bEr/k. The present value of all these series is $(bEr/k)/k$, which equals bEr/k^2. But because $r = mk$, this becomes

20.1
$$\frac{bEmk}{k^2} = \frac{bEm}{k} \quad \text{(Gross Present Value of Growth Investments)}$$

To derive these flows, the firm must invest bE dollars each year. The present value of these annual investments is equal to bE/k. Therefore, the *net* present value of growth investments is equal to

20.2
$$\frac{bEm}{k} - \frac{bE}{k} \quad \text{(Net Present Value of Growth Investments)}$$

The important variable is the value of m, which indicates the relationship of r to k. Combining this growth component with the capitalized value of the constant earnings stream indicates that the value of the firm is

20.3
$$V = \frac{E}{k} + \frac{bEm}{k} - \frac{bE}{k}$$

This equation indicates that the value of the firm is equal to the constant earnings stream plus a growth component equal to the *net* present value of reinvestment in growth projects. By combining the first and third terms in Equation 20.3, it becomes

20.4
$$V = \frac{E(1 - b)}{k} + \frac{bEm}{k}$$

Because $E(1 - b)$ is the dividend (D), this model becomes

20.5
$$V = \frac{D}{k} + \frac{bEm}{k} \quad \text{(Present Value of Constant Dividend plus the Present Value of Growth Investment)}$$

It can be stated as earnings only by rearranging Equation 20.3.

20.6
$$V = \frac{E}{k} + \frac{bE(m - 1)}{k} \quad \text{(Present Value of Constant Earnings plus Present Value of Excess Earnings from Growth Investments)}$$

EXPANSION MODEL The expansion model assumes a firm retains earnings to reinvest but receives a rate of return on its investments that is equal to its cost of capital

($m = 1$, so $r = k$). The effect of such a change can be seen in Equation 20.2, where the net present value of growth investments would be zero. Therefore, Equation 20.3 would become

20.7
$$V = \frac{E}{k}$$

Equation 20.4 would become

20.8
$$V = \frac{E(1 - b)}{k} + \frac{bE}{k} = \frac{E}{k}$$

Equation 20.5 is still valid, but the present value of the growth investment component would be smaller because m would be equal to 1. Finally, the last term in Equation 20.6 would disappear.

This discussion indicates that simply because a firm retains earnings and reinvests them, it is not necessarily beneficial to the stockholder *unless the reinvestment rate is above the required rate* ($r > k$). Otherwise, the investor in a tax-free world would be as well off with all earnings paid out in dividends.

NEGATIVE GROWTH MODEL The negative growth model applies to a firm that retains earnings ($b > 0$) and reinvests these funds in projects that generate rates of return *below* the firm's cost of capital ($r < k$ or $m < 1$). The impact of this on the value of the firm can be seen from Equation 20.2, which indicates that with $m < 1$, the net present value of the growth investments would be *negative*. Therefore, the value of the firm in Equation 20.3 would be *less* than the value of a no-growth firm or an expansion firm. This also can be seen by examining the effect of $m < 1$ in Equation 20.6. The firm is withholding funds from the investor and investing them in projects that generate returns less than those available from comparable risk investments.

Such poor performance may be difficult to uncover because the firm's asset base will grow since it is retaining earnings and acquiring assets. Notably, the earnings of the firm will increase if it earns *any* positive rate of return on the new assets. *The earnings will not grow by as much as they should,* so the value of the firm will decline when investors discount this reinvestment stream at the firm's cost of capital.

WHAT DETERMINES THE CAPITAL GAIN COMPONENT? These equations highlight the factors that influence the capital gain component. All the equations beginning with 20.1 suggest that the gross present value of the growth investments is equal to

$$bEm/k$$

Therefore, three factors influence the size of this capital gain term. The first is b, the percentage of earnings retained for reinvestment. The greater the proportion of earnings retained, the larger the capital gain component. The second factor is m, which is critical because it indicates the relationship between the firm's rate of return on investments and the firm's required rate of return (i.e., its cost of capital). A value of 1 indicates the firm is earning only its required return. A firm with an m greater than 1 is a true growth company. The important question is: How much greater than 1 is the return? The final factor is the time period for the superior investments. How long can the firm make these superior return investments? This time factor often is overlooked because we have assumed an infinite horizon to simplify the computations. However, when analyzing growth companies, this time estimate is clearly a major consideration. In summary, the three factors that influence the capital gain component are

1. The amount of capital invested in growth investments (b)
2. The relative rate of return earned on the funds retained (m)
3. The time horizon for these growth investments

DYNAMIC TRUE GROWTH MODEL A dynamic true growth model applies to a firm that invests a constant *percentage* of *current* earnings in projects that generate rates of return above the firm's required rate ($r > k$, $m < 1$). In contrast to the simple growth model where the firm invests a *constant* dollar amount each year, in this model the amount invested is *growing* each year as earnings increase. As a result, the firm's earnings and dividends will grow at a *constant rate* that is equal to br (the percentage of earnings retained times the return on investments). In the current model, this would equal bmk, where m is greater than 1. Given these assumptions, the dynamic growth model for an infinite time period is the dividend discount model derived in the Appendix to Chapter 13:

$$V = \frac{D_1}{k - g}$$

Applying this model to a true growth company means that earnings and dividends are growing at a constant rate and *the firm is investing larger and larger dollar amounts in projects that generate returns greater than k.* Moreover, the DDM model implicitly assumes that the firm can continue to do this for *an infinite time period.* If the growth rate (g) is greater than k, the model blows up and indicates that the firm should have an infinite value. Durand[25] considered this possibility and concluded that, although many firms had current growth rates above the normal required rates of return, very few of their stocks were selling for infinite values. He explained this by contending that investors expected the reinvestment rate to decline or they felt that the investment opportunities would not be available for an infinite time period. Table 20.12 contains a summary of the alternative company characteristics.

TABLE 20.12 **SUMMARY OF COMPANY DESCRIPTIONS**

	Retention	Return on Investments
No-Growth Company	$b = 0$	$r = k$
Long-Run Growth (assumes reinvestment)		
Negative growth	$b > 0$	$r < k$
Expansion	$b > 0$	$r = k$
Simple long-run growth	$b > 0$ (constant $)	$r > k$
Dynamic long-run growth	$b > 0$ (constant $)	$r > k$

[25]David Durand, "Growth Stocks and the Petersburg Paradox," *Journal of Finance* 12, no. 3 (September 1957): 348–363.

THE REAL WORLD

Because these models are simplified to allow us to develop a range of alternatives, several of them are extremely unrealistic. In the real world, companies may combine these models. Unfortunately, most firms have made some investments where $r < k$, and many firms invest in projects that generate returns about equal to their cost of capital. Finally, most firms invest in *some* projects that provide rates of return above the firm's cost of capital ($r > k$). The crucial questions are: How much is invested in these growth projects? How long do these true growth opportunities last?

Given this understanding of growth companies and what creates their value, the rest of the chapter considers various models that help you understand how to identify a true growth company and estimate specific values for these growth companies. We begin with models that are intended to identify growth companies in terms of providing excess economic value, which some contend is due to franchise value. Subsequently, we consider several models that are intended to provide a valuation of these companies by concentrating on how long the superior growth can continue and, alternatively, the extent and length of the superior growth. This final model has some similarities to the three-stage cash flow models.

MEASURES OF VALUE ADDED[26]

In addition to the DDM, which feeds into the P/E ratio valuation technique and the supplementary P/BV, P/CF, ratios, there has been growing interest in a set of performance measures referred to as "value-added." An appealing characteristic of these value-added measures of performance is that they are directly related to the capital budgeting techniques used in corporation finance. Specifically, they consider *economic profit,* which is analogous to the net present value (NPV) technique used in corporate capital budgeting. These value-added measures are mainly used to measure management performance based on the ability of managers to add value to the firm. Notably, these measures are also being used by security analysts as possible indicators of future equity returns, based on the logic that superior management performance should be reflected in a company's stock returns. In the subsequent discussion, we concentrate on three measures of value-added: **economic value-added (EVA)** and **market value-added (MVA)** pioneered by Stern and Stewart,[27] and the **franchise factor** developed by Leibowitz and Kogelman.[28]

ECONOMIC VALUE ADDED (EVA)[29]

As noted, this measure of value-added is closely related to the net present value (NPV) technique. Specifically, with the NPV technique you evaluate the expected performance of an investment by discounting the future cash flows from a potential investment at the firm's weighted average cost of capital (WACC) and compare this sum of discounted future cash flows to the cost of the project. If the discounted cash flows are greater than its cost, the project is expected to generate a positive NPV, which implies that it will add to the value of the firm and therefore it should be undertaken. In the case of EVA, you evaluate the annual performance of management by comparing the firm's net operating profit less ad-

[26]This section benefited from Pamela P. Peterson and David Peterson, "Company Performance Measures of Value-Added" (Charlottesville Va.: The Research Foundation of the Institute of Chartered Financial Analysts, 1996).

[27]These concepts are described in detail in G. Bennett Stewart III, *The Quest for Value* (New York: Harper Business, 1991).

[28]Martin L. Leibowitz and Staley Kogelman, *Franchise Value and the Price-Earnings Ratio* (Charlottesville, Va.: Research Foundation of the Institute of Chartered Financial Analysts, 1994).

[29]This is a registered trademark of Stern, Stewart, & Co.

justed taxes (NOPLAT) to the firm's total cost of capital in dollar terms, including the cost of equity. In this analysis, if the firm's NOPLAT during a specific year exceeds its dollar cost of capital, it has a positive EVA for the year and has added value for its stockholders. In contrast, if the EVA is negative, the firm has not earned enough during the year to cover its cost of capital and the value of the firm has declined. Notably, NOPLAT indicates what the firm has earned for all capital suppliers and the dollar cost of capital is what all the capital suppliers required—including the firm's equity holders. The following summarizes the major calculations:[30]

EVA =

(A) Adjusted Operating Profits before Taxes
minus (B) Cash Operating Taxes
equals (C) Net Operating Profits Less Adjusted Taxes (NOPLAT)
minus (D) The Dollar Cost of Capital
equals (E) Economic Value-Added (EVA)

In turn, these items are calculated as follows:

OPERATING PROFIT (AFTER DEPRECIATION AND AMORTIZATION)

Add:	Implied Interest on Operating Leases
Add:	An Increase in the LIFO Reserve
Add:	Goodwill Amortization
Equals:	*(A) Adjusted Operating Profits before Taxes*

INCOME TAX EXPENSE

Add:	Decrease in Deferred Taxes
Add:	Tax Benefit from Interest Expenses
Add:	Tax Benefit from Interest on Leases
Less:	Taxes on Nonoperating Income
Equals:	*(B) Cash Operating Taxes*

(A) minus (B) equals: (C) Net Operating Profits Less Adjusted Taxes (NOPLAT)

Capital =

	Net Working Capital (current assets less noninterest-bearing liabilities)
Add:	LIFO Reserve
Add:	Net Plant, Property, and Equipment
Add:	Other Assets
Add:	Goodwill
Add:	Accumulated Goodwill Amortized
Add:	Present Value of Operating Leases
Equals:	*Capital*

[30]For a detailed discussion, see Stewart, *The Quest for Value,* or Peterson and Peterson, *Company Performance Measures of Value-Added.* For summary discussions, see Thomas P. Jones, "The Economic Value-Added Approach to Corporate Investments," in *Corporate Financial Decision Making and Equity Analysis* (Charlottesville, Va.: Association for Investment Management and Research, 1995); T. J. Sheehan, "To EVA or Not to EVA: Is That the Question?" *Journal of Applied Corporate Finance* 7, no. 2 (summer 1994): 84–87; G. B. Stewart, "EVA: Fact and Fantasy," *Journal of Applied Corporate Finance* 7, no. 2 (summer 1994): 71–84; and S. Tully, "The Real Key to Creating Wealth," *Fortune* September 1993, 38–40, 44, 45, 48, 50.

Weighted Average Cost of Capital (WACC) =
(Book Value of Debt/Total Book Value) × (the Market Cost of Debt)
(1 − Tax Rate)
(Book Value of Equity/Total Book Value) × (Cost of Equity)
(Cost of equity is based on the CAPM using the prevailing 10-year Treasury bond as the RFR, a calculated beta, and a market risk premium between 3 and 6 percent.)

(D) Dollar Cost of Capital = Capital × WACC
(E) Economic Value-Added (EVA) =
(C) Net Operating Profits Less Adjusted Taxes (NOPLAT) minus (D) Dollar Cost of Capital

---

EVA RETURN ON CAPITAL The preceding calculations provide a positive or negative dollar value, which indicates whether the firm earned an excess above its cost of capital during the year analyzed. There are two problems with this annual dollar value for EVA. First, how does one judge over time if the firm is prospering relative to its past performance? Although you would want the absolute EVA to grow over time, the question is whether the rate of growth of EVA is adequate for the additional capital provided. Second, how does one compare alternative firms of different sizes? Both of these concerns can be met by calculating an EVA return on capital equal to:

EVA/Capital

You would want this EVA rate of return on capital for a firm to remain constant over time, or, ideally, to grow, Also, using this ratio you can compare firms of different sizes and determine which firm has the largest *economic profit per dollar of capital.*

AN ALTERNATIVE MEASURE OF EVA An alternative but equal way to measure and think about EVA is to compare directly the firm's return on capital employed with the firm's average cost of capital (i.e., its WACC). As noted previously, it is this difference in the rates of return that identifies a company as a true growth company. Another way to measure EVA is to multiply this EVA spread (return on capital minus WACC) by the amount of capital employed. The appeal of this EVA spread approach is that it concentrates on the factors that create a growth company. Also, it helps the management and analysts recognize that true growth can be created either by increasing the firm's return on capital *or* by reducing its cost of capital.

An excellent example of this approach to the measurement and analysis of EVA is the work by Cohen and Napolitano of Goldman Sachs regarding EVA performance of the S&P 400 industrials.[31] As shown in Table 20.13 and Figure 20.11, the EVA spread for the S&P 400 has gone from a zero spread in 1986 to a negative spread during the 1990–1991 recession to a very healthy estimated 3.8 percent spread in 1999 because of both an increase in the return on capital *and* a decline in the WACC for these firms.

Market Value-Added (MVA)

In contrast to EVA, which generally is an evaluation of internal performance, MVA is a measure of external performance—how the market has evaluated the firm's performance in terms of the market value of debt and market value of equity compared to the capital invested in the firm.

---

[31]Abby Joseph Cohen and Gabrielle Napolitano, eds., *Investment Strategy Chartbook* (New York: Goldman, Sachs & Co., April 1999).

TABLE 20.13 **S&P INDUSTRIALS EVA AND SPREAD ANALYSIS**

	1986	1987	1988	1989	1990	1991	1992	1993	1994	1995	1996	1997	1998E	1999E
Return on Capital Employed (r):														
Nominal (a)	9.4%	11.2%	13.8%	11.5%	10.2%	7.1%	7.5%	8.4%	9.8%	11.8%	12.4%	12.6%	11.2%	11.6%
Real	7.5	7.6	9.7	6.7	4.8	2.9	4.4	5.5	7.1	9.0	9.5	10.3	9.6	9.6
Cost of Capital (c):*														
Nominal (b)	9.4%	9.9%	10.0%	9.8%	9.6%	9.2%	8.7%	7.7%	8.8%	8.5%	8.5%	8.1%	7.6%	7.8%
Real	7.5	6.3	6.0	5.0	4.1	5.0	5.6	4.7	6.2	5.7	5.6	5.7	6.0	5.8
Spread (r − c*)	0.0%	1.3%	3.7%	1.7%	0.6%	(2.1%)	(1.1%)	0.7%	0.9%	3.3%	3.9%	4.5%	3.6%	3.8%
EVA ($ per Share)	$0.04	$3.42	$10.63	$6.43	$2.54	($9.52)	($5.04)	$3.16	$4.36	$15.16	$18.54	$22.64	$18.86	$20.08
Consumer Price Index	1.9%	3.7%	4.1%	4.8%	5.4%	4.2%	3.1%	3.0%	2.6%	2.8%	2.9%	2.3%	1.6%	2.0%

(a) NOPLAT/Beginning-period adjusted capital.

(b) Weighted-average after-tax cost of debt and equity capital.

Source of Data: Standard & Poor's; Federal Reserve Board; Bureau of Labor Statistics; Goldman Sachs estimates; Abby Joseph Cohen and Gabrielle Napolitano, eds., *Investment Strategy Chartbook* (New York: Goldman, Sachs & Co., April 1999).

FIGURE 20.11 **TIME-SERIES PLOT OF RETURN ON CAPITAL, COST OF CAPITAL, AND EVA SPREAD FOR S&P 400 INDUSTRIALS: 1986–1999E**

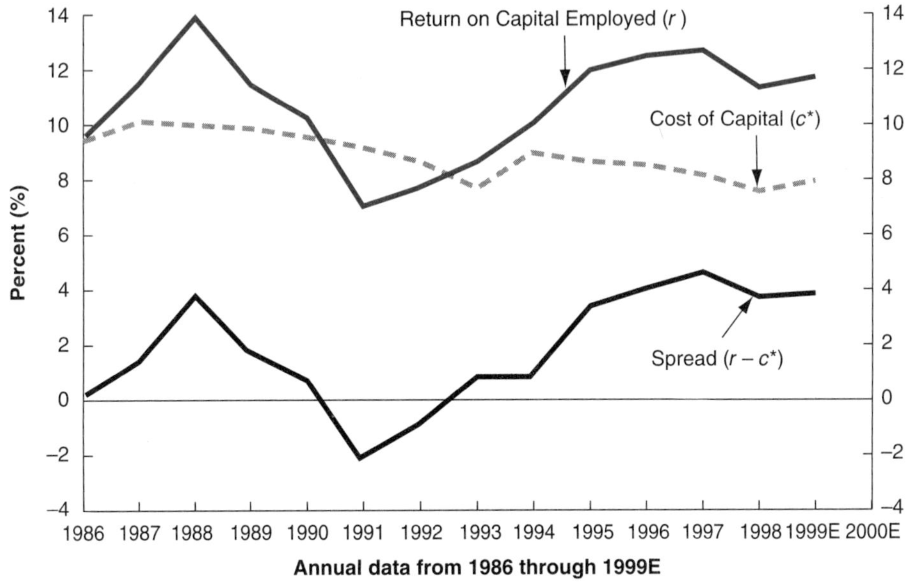
Return on Capital Employed (r)
Cost of Capital (c*)
Spread (r – c*)
Percent (%)
14
12
10
8
6
4
2
0
–2
–4
1986 1987 1988 1989 1990 1991 1992 1993 1994 1995 1996 1997 1998 1999E 2000E
Annual data from 1986 through 1999E

Source: Standard & Poor's; Federal Reserve Board; Goldman Sachs estimates; Abby Joseph Cohen and Gabrielle Napolitano, eds., *Investment Strategy Chartbook* (New York: Goldman, Sachs & Co., April 1999).

$$
\begin{aligned}
\text{Market Value-Added (MVA)} &= (\text{Market Value of Firm}) - \text{Capital} \\
&\quad - \text{Market Value of Debt} \\
&\quad - \text{Market Value of Equity}
\end{aligned}
$$

Again, to properly analyze this performance, it is necessary to look for positive changes over time—i.e., the percent change each year. It is important to compare these changes in MVA each year to those for the aggregate stock and bond markets because these market values can be impacted by interest rates and general economic conditions.

Relationships between EVA and MVA

Although EVA is used primarily for evaluating management performance, it also is being used by external analysts to evaluate management with the belief that superior internal performance should be reflected in a company's stock performance. Several studies have attempted to determine the relationship between the two variables (EVA and MVA), and the results have been mixed. Although the stock of firms with positive EVAs has tended to outperform the stocks of negative EVA firms, the differences are typically insignificant and the relationship does not occur every year. This poor relationship may be due to the timing of the analysis (how fast EVA is reflected in stocks) or because the market values (MVAs) are affected by factors other than EVA—e.g., MVA can be impacted by market interest rates and by changes in *future* expectations for a firm not considered by EVA—i.e., it appears that EVA does an outstanding job of evaluating management's *past* performance in terms of adding value. While one would certainly hope that superior past performance will continue, there is nothing certain about this relationship.

The Franchise Factor

The franchise factor concept is similar to EVA since it recognizes that, to add to the value of a firm, it is necessary to invest in projects that provide excess NPV—i.e., the firm must generate rates of return above its WACC. This technique is directly related to the valuation approach we have been using since the franchise value approach breaks a firm's observed P/E down into two components: (1) the P/E, based on the company's ongoing business (its base P/E); plus (2) a franchise P/E the market assigns to *the expected value of new and profitable business opportunities.* This can he visualized as:

$$\text{Franchise P/E} = \text{Observed P/E} - \text{Base P/E}$$

The base P/E is the reciprocal of the market discount rate k (it is $1/k$). For example, if the stock's market discount rate is 12 percent, the base P/E would be about 8.5X.

What determines the franchise P/E? Not surprising, it is a function of the relative rate of return on new business opportunities (the franchise factor) and the size of the superior return opportunities (the growth factor).

$$\text{Incremental Franchise P/E} = \text{Franchise Factor} \times \text{Growth Factor}$$
$$= \frac{R - k}{rk} \times G$$

where:

R = the expected return on the new opportunities
k = the current cost of equity
r = the current ROE on investment
G = the present value of the new growth projects relative to the current value of the firm

The critical factors determining the franchise P/E are the difference between R and k and the size of these growth opportunities relative to the firm's current size.[32]

As will be shown in the subsequent discussion, this analysis of franchise value or the franchise P/E are very similar to the growth company valuation models.

Growth Duration

The purpose of the growth duration model is to help you *evaluate* the high P/E ratio for the stock of a growth company by relating the P/E ratio to the firm's rate and duration of growth. A stock's P/E ratio is a function of (1) the firm's expected rate of growth of earnings per share, (2) the stock's required rate of return, and (3) the firm's dividend-payout ratio. Assuming equal risk and no significant difference in the payout ratio for different firms, the principal variable affecting differences in the earnings multiple for two firms *is the difference in expected growth.* Further, the growth estimate must consider the *rate* of growth and how long it will last—that is, the *duration* of expected growth. As noted earlier, no company can grow indefinitely at a rate substantially above normal. For example, Wal-Mart cannot continue to grow at 20 percent a year for an extended period, or it will eventually become the entire economy. In fact, Wal-Mart or any similar growth firm will eventually run out of high-profit investment projects. Recall that continued growth at a constant rate requires that larger amounts of money be invested in high-return projects. Eventually competition will encroach on these high-return investments, and the firm's growth rate will decline to a rate consistent with the rate for the overall economy. Ascertaining the duration of a firm's high-growth period therefore becomes significant.

---

[32]For further detail and examples of the application, see Leibowitz and Kogelman, *Franchise Value and the Price/Earnings Ratio.*

COMPUTATION OF GROWTH DURATION The growth duration concept was suggested by Holt, who showed that if you assume equal risk between a given security and a market security, such as the S&P 400, you can concentrate on the differential past growth rates for the market and the growth firm as a factor causing the alternative P/E ratios.[33] This allows you to compute the market's *implied growth duration* for the growth firm.

If $E'(0)$ is the firm's current earnings, then $E'(t)$ is earnings in period t according to the expression

20.9 $$E'(t) = E(0)(1 + G)^t$$

where G is the annual percentage growth rate for earnings. To adjust for dividend payments, it was assumed that all such payments are used to purchase further shares of the stock. This means the number of shares (N) will grow at the dividend rate (D). Therefore

20.10 $$N(t) = N(0)(1 + D)^t$$

To derive the total earnings for a firm, $E(t)$, the growth rate in per-share earnings and the growth in shares are combined as follows:

20.11 $$E(t) = E'(t)N(t) = E'(0)[(1 + G)(1 + D)]^t$$

Because G and D are small, this expression can be approximated by

20.12 $$E(t) \simeq E'(0)(1 + G + D)^t$$

Assuming the growth stock (g) and the nongrowth stock (a) have similar risk and payout, the market should value the two stocks in direct proportion to their earnings in year T, where T is the time when the growth company will begin to grow at the same rate as the market (i.e., the nongrowth stock). In other words, *current prices should be in direct proportion to the expected future earnings ratio that will prevail in year T.* This relationship can be stated

20.13 $$\left(\frac{P_g(0)}{P_a(0)}\right) \simeq \left(\frac{E_g(0)(1 + G_g + D_g)^T}{E_a(0)(1 + G_a + D_a)^T}\right)$$

or

20.14 $$\left(\frac{P_g(0)/E_g(0)}{P_a(0)/E_a(0)}\right) \simeq \left(\frac{1 + G_g + D_g}{1 + G_a + D_a}\right)^T$$

As a result, the *P/E ratios of the two stocks are in direct proportion to the ratio of composite growth rates raised to the Tth power.* You can solve for T by taking the log of both sides as follows:

20.15 $$\ln\left(\frac{P_g(0)/E_g(0)}{P_a(0)/E_a(0)}\right) \simeq T \ln\left(\frac{1 + G_g + D_g}{(1 + G_a + D_a}\right)$$

---

[33]Charles C. Holt, "The Influence of Growth Duration on Share Prices," *Journal of Finance* 7, no. 3 (September 1962): 465–475.

The growth duration model answers the question: How long must the earnings of the growth stock grow at the past rate, relative to the nongrowth stock, to justify its prevailing above-average P/E ratio? You must then determine whether the *implied* growth duration estimate is reasonable in terms of the company's potential.

Consider the following example. The stock of a well-known growth company is selling for \$60 a share with expected per-share earnings of \$2.00 (its earnings multiple is 30). The growth firm's EPS growth rate during the past 5- and 10-year periods has been 17 percent a year, and its dividend yield has been 1 percent. In contrast, the S&P 400 Industrial Index has a current P/E ratio of 20, an average dividend yield of 2 percent, and an average growth rate of 7 percent. Therefore, the comparison looks as follows:

	S&P 400	Growth Company
P/E ratio	20.00	30.00
Average growth rate	0.07	0.17
Dividend yield	0.02	0.01

Inserting these values into Equation 20.15 yields the following:

$$1\text{n}\left(\frac{30.00}{20.00}\right) = T1\text{n}\left(\frac{1 + 0.17 + 0.01}{1 + 0.07 + 0.02}\right)$$

$$1\text{n}(1.50) = T1\text{n}\left(\frac{1.18}{1.09}\right)$$

$$1\text{n}(1.50) = T1\text{n}\,(1.083)$$

$$T = 1\text{n}(1.50)/1\text{n}(1.083)(\text{log base }10)$$

$$= 0.1761/0.0345$$

$$= 5.10 \text{ years}$$

These results indicate the market is implicitly assuming that the growth company can continue to grow at this composite rate (18 percent) for about 5 more years, after which it is assumed the growth company will grow at the same rate (9 percent) as the aggregate market (i.e., the S&P 400). You must now ask: Can this superior growth rate be sustained by this growth company for at least this period? If the implied growth duration is greater than you believe is reasonable, you would advise against buying the stock. If the implied duration is below your expectations, you would recommend buying the stock.

INTRA-INDUSTRY ANALYSIS Besides comparing a company to a market series, you can directly compare two firms. For an intercompany analysis, you should compare firms in the same industry because the equal risk assumptions of this model are probably more reasonable.

Consider the following example from the computer software industry:

	Company A	Company B
P/E ratios	31.00	25.00
Average annual growth rate	0.1700	0.1200
Dividend yield	0.0100	0.0150
Growth rate plus dividend yield	0.1800	0.1350
Estimate of T[a]		5.53 years

[a]Readers should check to see that they get the same answer.

These results imply that the market expects Company A to grow at an annual total rate of 18 percent for about 5.5 years, after which it will grow at Company B's rate of 13.5 percent. If you believe the implied duration is too long, you will prefer Company B; if you believe it is reasonable or low, you will recommend Company A.

AN ALTERNATIVE USE OF *T* Instead of solving for *T* and then deciding whether the figure derived is reasonable, you can use this formulation to compute a reasonable P/E ratio for a security relative to the aggregate market (or another stock) if the implicit assumptions are reasonable for the stock involved. Assume that you estimate the composite growth of a company to be about 18 percent a year compared to the market growth of 8 percent. Further, you believe that this firm can continue to grow at this above-normal rate for about 7 years. Using Equation 20.15, this becomes

$$
\begin{aligned}
\ln(X) &= 7 \times \ln \frac{1.18}{1.08} \\
&= 7 \times \ln (1.0926) \\
&= 7 \times (0.03846) \\
&= 0.26922
\end{aligned}
$$

To determine what the P/E ratio should be given these assumptions, you must derive the antilog of 0.26922, which is approximately 1.859. Therefore, assuming the market multiples is 20, the earnings multiple for this growth company should be about 1.859 times the market P/E ratio, or 37.18.

Alternatively, if you expect that the firm can maintain this differential growth for only 5 years, you would derive the antilog for 0.1923 (5 × 0.03846). The answer is 1.557, which implies a P/E ratio of 31.14 for the stock.

FACTORS TO CONSIDER When using the growth duration technique, remember the following factors: First, the technique assumes equal risk, which may be acceptable when comparing two large, well-established firms or relating them to a market proxy (e.g., IBM and Apple Computer to each other or to the S&P 400). It is probably *not* a valid assumption when comparing a small firm to the aggregate market.

Second, which growth estimate should be used? In the typical case, 5- and 10-year historical growth rates are used. Which time interval is most relevant if historical rates are used? It may be more appropriate to use the *expected* rate of growth based on the factors that affect *g* (i.e., the retention rate and the components of ROE).

Third, the growth duration technique assumes that stocks with higher P/E ratios have the higher growth rates. However, in many cases the stock with the higher P/E ratio does not have a higher historical growth rate, which generates a useless negative growth duration value. Inconsistency between growth and the P/E ratio could be attributed to one of four factors:

1. A major difference in the risk involved.
2. Inaccurate growth rate estimates. Possibly the firm with the higher P/E ratio is *expected* to grow faster in the future. Consider the historical growth rate used and whether you expect any changes in the firm's growth rate.
3. The stock with a low P/E ratio relative to its growth rate is undervalued. (Before you accept this possibility, consider the first two factors.)
4. The stock with a high P/E and a low growth rate is overvalued. (Before this is accepted, consider the second factor.)

The growth duration concept is valid, *given the assumptions made,* and can help you evaluate growth investments. It is not universally valid, though, because its answers are only as good as the data inputs (relative growth rates) and the applicability of the assumptions. The answer must be evaluated based on the analyst's knowledge.

The technique probably is most useful for helping spot overvalued growth companies with very high multiples. In such a case, the technique will highlight that the company must continue to grow at some very high rate for an extended period of time to justify its high P/E ratio (e.g., 15 to 20 years). Also, it can help you decide between two growth companies in the same industry by comparing each to the market, the industry, or directly to each other. Such a comparison has provided interesting insights wherein the new firms in an industry were growing faster than the large competitor, but their P/E ratios were *substantially* higher and implied that these new firms had to maintain this large growth rate superiority for *over 10 years* to justify the much higher P/E ratio.

A Flexible Growth Stock Valuation Model

Mao developed an investment opportunities growth model that incorporated some previous work on growth stock valuation by Solomon and by Miller and Modigliani.[34] These authors had recognized the true nature of a growth firm, but they assumed unrealistic infinite growth horizons to simplify the exposition, which meant the models were not applicable to practical problems.

Mao developed a three-stage valuation model that considered (1) *a dynamic growth period* during which the firm invests a constant percentage of current earnings in growth projects, (2) *a simple growth period* during which the firm invests a constant dollar amount in growth opportunities, and, finally, (3) *a declining growth period* during which the amount invested in growth investments declines to zero. The model was theoretically correct and realistic but required difficult computations and was somewhat rigid in its assumptions about the parameters b (the retention rate), r (the return on growth investments), and k (the required rate of return on the stock). As a result, the model has not been applied as widely as expected. In this section, we discuss the flexible growth model, apply it to a growth company, and discuss the effects of varying the parameters.

THE VALUATION MODEL Mao assumed that the price of the stock is equal to (1) the present value of current earnings, E, discounted to infinity at the required rate of return, k ($P = E/k$), plus (2) the net present value of growth opportunities, assuming three stages of growth.

The dynamic growth stage lasts for n_1 years during which the firm has opportunities to invest a given percentage of current earnings in growth projects where r is greater than k. Because b is a constant percentage of a growing earnings stream, the dollar amount invested in these growth projects grows at an exponential rate. The value of the dynamic investments is given by

20.16
$$\left(\frac{r-k}{k}\right)(bE)\sum_{t=1}^{n_1}\frac{(1+br)^{t-1}}{(1+k)^t} \quad \text{(Value of Dynamic Growth Opportunities)}$$

The simple growth stage lasts for n_2 years during which the firm invests a constant dollar amount in growth projects ($r > k$). The value of these projects is given by

[34]James C. Mao, "The Valuation of Growth Stocks: The Investment Opportunities Approach," *Journal of Finance* 21, no. 1 (March 1966): 95–102.

20.17
$$\left(\frac{r-k}{k}\right)(bE)\sum_{t=1}^{n_2}\frac{1}{(1+k)^t} \quad \text{(Value of Simple Growth Opportunities)}$$

During the final declining growth stage, which lasts n_3 years, the firm has opportunities to invest in growth projects, but the dollar amount declines steadily from bE to zero. The amount of the decline is steady at $1/n_3$ each year. As an example, if bE equals $100,000 and n_3 is 20, then the amount invested in growth projects would decline by $5,000 a year. The value of this component is

20.18
$$\left(\frac{r-k}{k}\right)(bE)\sum_{t=1}^{n_3}\frac{(n_3-t+1)}{n_3(1+k)^t} \quad \text{(Value of Declining Growth Opportunities)}$$

The complete model combines the no-growth component (E/k) plus the three growth components. If the final summation term in Equation 20.16 is designated A, the final term in Equation 20.17 is designated B, and the final term in Equation 20.18 is designated C, this formulation can be written as follows:

20.19
$$P=\frac{E}{k}+\left(\frac{r-k}{k}\right)(bE)\left[A+\frac{(1+br)^{n_1-1}}{(1+k)^{n_1}}B+\frac{(1+br)^{n_1-1}}{(1+k)^{n_1+n_2}}C\right]$$

Mao provided tables that contained values for A and C, given several combinations of the parameters. B is simply the present value of an annuity. Even with the tables and no change in the parameters, the computations are rather tedious.

FLEXIBLE PARAMETERS The Mao model assumes (1) no change in the required rate of return (k), (2) the same rate of return on all growth projects (r), and (3) the same retention rate (b) during the three growth periods. Mao probably assumed constant parameters to avoid complicating a technique that already involved extensive computations. Still, there are indications that investors probably change their required return (k) during different phases of the firm's life cycle. Malkiel contends it is logical to require a higher return on high-growth stocks because the stream of returns is such that these stocks are inherently longer-duration securities.[35] At the other extreme, a firm may become more subject to cyclical variations during its declining years, which would indicate higher business risk and a higher required rate of return (k).

Regarding the return on investments (r), it could be too optimistic to assume that during the period of simple growth, the firm can continue to earn very high rates, even on a stable dollar amount. Many analysts might prefer a longer n^2 period and a somewhat smaller r.

Finally, is it realistic to assume a constant retention rate (b) over the life of a firm? Most observers would expect a high retention rate during the early years when growth opportunities are abundant and capital is scarce, and a lower retention rate during the later years when growth investment opportunities are limited, the levels of earnings and cash flow are high, and outside capital is available. The model would be more useful and realistic if the parameters could be changed.

APPLICATION OF THE MODEL Using a computer program that requires three statements for each case allows you to consider several alternative sets of parameters,

---

[35]Burton G. Malkiel, "Equity Yields, Growth, and the Structure of Share Prices," *American Economic Review* 53, no. 5 (December 1963): 1004–1031.

including most pessimistic, most optimistic, and most likely. For a high P/E stock, you should determine the required sets of estimates that justify the prevailing market price. When applying this technique to evaluate growth companies, you should consider the following suggestions:

1. The earnings figure (E) is assumed to be the figure for the coming year. A crude estimate is the actual earnings for the most recent year times the growth rate for the past 5 or 10 years. Practicing analysts would use their estimate of future growth.
2. The estimated retention rate (b) can be the average retention rate during the last several years.
3. The estimate of the return on investment (r) is obviously crucial.[36] You can compute the average ROE during the recent period or estimate the three components (total asset turnover, financial leverage, and the profit margin) and use the product of these three estimates. Alternatively, Mao suggested computing the increase in earnings per share during some period divided by the amount of earnings retained over a comparable period with a 1-year lag (e.g., the increase in earnings per share for the period 1997 to 2001 divided by the retained earnings for the period 1996 to 2000). This computation attempts to estimate the firm's current return on retained earnings rather than the traditional average ROE, which is current net earnings divided by current equity. This average ROE is heavily influenced by past performance and uses historical equity, which can become seriously distorted over time. The Mao estimate is akin to a marginal ROE.
4. The required return estimate (k) could be the actual return derived from all common stocks or the return experienced by the specific stock during some recent period. Alternatively, you could use a required rate of return based on the CAPM and the stock's beta. Because this model is *extremely sensitive to changes in k*, you definitely should consider a *range* of ks.

AN EXAMPLE Assume the following for a firm that you consider to be a true growth company:

- Earnings: 2000 \$2.50
  2001 (estimated) \$2.88 (\$2.50 × 1.15)
- Annual growth rate in EPS (1996–2000) 0.15
- Retention rate (1996–2000) 0.65
- Average return on equity (1996–2000) 0.24
- Marginal return on equity (1996–2000) 0.26
- Estimated r for analysis 0.25

Given these estimates of the major parameters, you can derive a number of stock price values by simply changing the values for the three ns (n_1, n_2, n_3) and consider alternative required returns. You can change the values for each of these parameters for each growth period. In this example, they will be constant at these historical values to simplify the presentation. Subsequent estimates should consider alternative parameters. For the example, the initial estimates of the ns are relatively conservative (5, 5, 10) and are changed to more liberal estimates as follows:

[36]An article that discusses the components of growth is Guilford C. Babcock, "The Concept of Sustainable Growth," *Financial Analysts Journal* 26, no. 3 (May–June 1970): 236–242.

TABLE 20.14 **ESTIMATED VALUES FOR STOCK ASSUMING ALTERNATIVE TIME PERIODS AND REQUIRED RATES OF RETURN (E = \$2.88; B = 0.65; R = 0.25)**

n_1	n_2	n_3	0.08	0.10	0.12	0.14	0.16
5	5	10	91.03	62.79	45.67	34.55	26.96
5	10	15	102.92	68.72	48.72	36.15	27.80
10	10	15	154.15	95.72	63.55	44.46	32.46
15	15	20	242.31	136.49	83.39	54.40	37.48

A. $n_1 = 5$
$n_2 = 5$
$n_3 = 10$

B. $n_1 = 5$
$n_2 = 10$
$n_3 = 15$

C. $n_1 = 10$
$n_2 = 10$
$n_3 = 15$

D. $n_1 = 15$
$n_2 = 15$
$n_3 = 20$

The k_s considered ranged from 8 percent to 16 percent in increments of 2 percent. The results in Table 20.14 indicate a wide range of estimated values for this stock. You must select the best estimate of the three time periods and, most important, an estimate of k for this stock based on its systematic risk and the expected security market line (SML). Because almost all growth companies have above-average systematic risk (i.e., betas above 1.00), the required return typically will exceed the expected market return.

Assume the following estimates regarding the SML: RFR = 0.06; Rm = 0.10. If the stock has a beta of 1.5, the estimated required return would be

$$k = \text{RFR} + \beta_i(Rm - \text{RFR})$$
$$k = 0.06 + 1.5(0.10 - 0.06)$$
$$k = 0.12$$

This would indicate further consideration of the 0.12 percent column and the adjoining columns. Comparing these prices to the current market price will indicate whether the stock should be included in the portfolio.

You can graph the stock values for a given set of n values and different ks. Using several sets of ns will produce a set of curves sloping downward to the right as shown in Figure 20.12. There are two ways to use this graph to examine the model results. First, compare the current market price to the range of computed values. The prevailing price should be within the total range, and you should get an indication of relative valuation depending on whether the current market price is at the upper or lower end of the valuation range. Second, determine the implied rate of return by drawing the current market price horizontally across the valuation curves. Because the valuation curves generally represent the full range of feasible parameters, the intersection of the current market price line with

FIGURE 20.12

ESTIMATED STOCK PRICES FOR A GROWTH COMPANY USING THE FLEXIBLE GROWTH MODEL

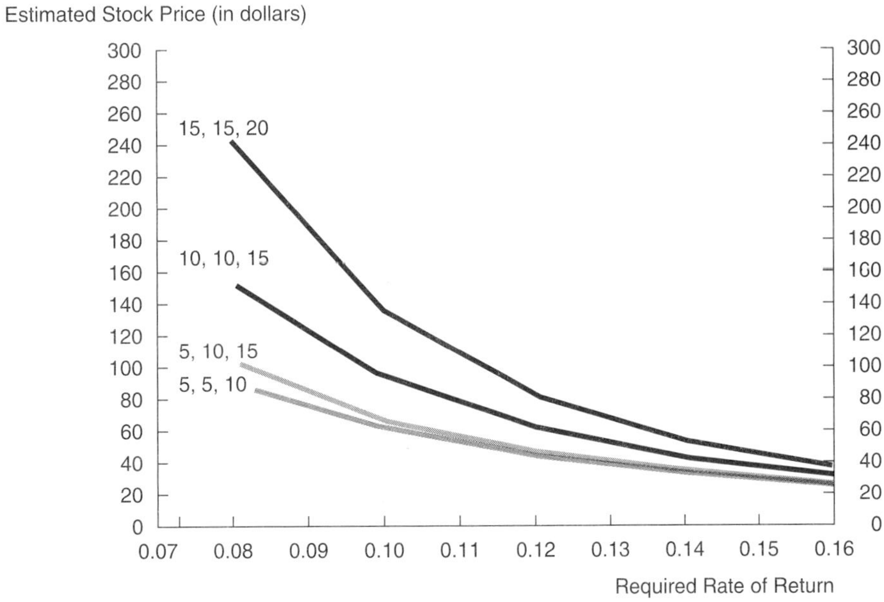
Estimated Stock Price (in dollars)
300
280
260
240
220
200
180
160
140
120
100
80
60
40
20
0
15, 15, 20
10, 10, 15
5, 10, 15
5, 5, 10
0.07
0.08
0.09
0.10
0.11
0.12
0.13
0.14
0.15
0.16
Required Rate of Return

the curve to the right indicates the highest k that can be expected—with the most liberal parameters—if you buy the stock at the current market price. The curve to the left indicates the lowest k possible if you buy the stock at today's price.

SITE VISITS AND THE ART OF THE INTERVIEW

Brokerage house analysts and portfolio managers have access to persons that the typical small investor does not. Analysts frequently have contact with corporate personnel by telephone (conference calls), at formal presentations, or during plant site visits. Though insider trading laws restrict the analyst's ability to obtain material nonpublic information, these visits facilitate dialog between the corporation and the investor community. The analyst can gather information about the firm's plans and strategies, which helps the analyst understand the firm's prospects as an investment.

Interviewing is an art. The analyst wants information about the firm, and top management wants to put the firm in the best light possible. Thus, the analyst must be prepared to focus the interview on management's plans, strategies, and concerns. Management will typically indicate that earnings estimates may be "too high," "too low," or "about right." Discussions of new products under development are also valuable. Analysts try to gauge the sensitivity of the firm's revenues, costs, and earnings to different scenarios by asking "what if" questions.

Analysts have frequent telephone contact with the firm's investor relations (IR) department, which wants analysts to know about company pronouncements. Notably, they will try to put as good a "spin" as possible on negative news events.

The chief financial officer and chief executive officer of the firm also meet with security analysts and discuss the firm's planning process and major issues confronting the industry. Subsequently, management is interested in the analyst's report because it should represent a fair, informed, and independent appraisal of the firm.

The analyst should talk to people other than top managers. Talking to middle managers or factory workers during a plant tour, visiting stores, and talking with customers provides insights beyond those of management. The firm's major customers can provide information regarding product quality and customer satisfaction. The firm's suppliers can furnish information about rising or falling supply orders and the timeliness of payments.

WHEN TO SELL

Our analysis has focused on determining if a stock should be purchased. In fact, when we make a purchase, a subsequent question gains prominence: When should the stock be sold? Many times holding on to a stock too long leads to a return below expectations or less than what was available earlier. When stocks decline in value immediately following a portfolio manager's purchase, is this a further buying opportunity, or does the decline indicate that the stock analysis was incorrect?

The answer to when to sell a stock is contained in the same collection of research that convinced the analyst to purchase the stock in the first place. The analyst should have identified the key assumptions and variables driving the expectations for the stock. Analysis of the stock doesn't end when intrinsic value is computed and the research report is written. Once the key value drivers are identified, the analyst must continually monitor and update his or her knowledge base about the firm. Notably, if the key assumptions and variables appear to have weakened, it is time to reevaluate, and possibly sell, the stockholding.

The stock should also be closely evaluated when the current price approaches the intrinsic value estimate. When the stock becomes fairly priced, it may be time to sell it and reinvest the funds in other underpriced stocks. In short, if the "story" for buying the stock still appears to be true, continue to hold it. If the "story" changes, it may be time to sell the stock. If you know why you bought the stock, you'll be able to recognize when to sell it.

INFLUENCES ON ANALYSTS

Stock analysts and portfolio managers are, for the most part, highly trained individuals who possess expertise in financial analysis and background in their industry. A computer hardware analyst knows as much about industry trends and new product offerings as any industry insider. A pharmaceutical analyst is able to independently determine the market potential of drugs undergoing testing and the FDA approval process. So why don't more brokerage house customers and portfolio managers who receive the analysts' expert advice achieve investment success? The following subsections discuss several factors that make it difficult to "beat the market."

Efficient Markets

As noted in Chapter 7, the efficient market is difficult to outsmart, especially if you are considering actively traded and frequently analyzed companies. Information about the economy, a firm's industry, and the firm itself is reviewed by numerous bright analysts, investors, and portfolio managers. Because of the market's ability to review and absorb information, stock prices generally approximate fair market value. Investors look for situations where stocks may not be fairly valued. Notably, because there are numerous bright, hardworking analysts, it is difficult to successfully, frequently, and consistently find undervalued shares. The analyst's best place to seek attractive stocks is not among well-known companies and actively traded stocks, because they are analyzed by dozens of Wall Street researchers. Stocks with smaller market capitalizations, those not covered by many analysts, or those whose shares are mainly held by individual investors may be the best places to search for inefficiencies. Smaller capitalization stocks sometimes are too small for time-constrained analysts or too small for purchase by institutional investors.[37] The price of stocks not researched by many analysts ("neglected stocks") may not reflect all relevant information.[38]

PARALYSIS OF ANALYSIS Analysts spend most of their time in a relentless search for one more contact or one more piece of information. Such a search can keep the analyst's mind off their stock recommendation. Analysts need to develop a systematic approach for gathering, monitoring, and reviewing relevant information about economic trends, industry competitive forces, and company strategy. Otherwise they become too busy collecting data, searching for all the answers. The analyst must evaluate the information as a whole to discern patterns that indicate the intrinsic value of the stock. Rather than searching for one more piece of information, analysts should evaluate what they already know about the stock's prospects.

Because markets are generally efficient, the consensus view about the firm is already reflected in its stock price. To earn above-average returns, the analyst must have expectations that differ from the consensus *and* the analyst must be correct. Thus, the analyst may want to concentrate on identifying what is wrong with the market consensus, or what surprises may upset the market consensus—that is, *estimate earning surprises.*

FORCES PULLING ON THE ANALYST Although such linkages should not exist, at times communication occurs between a firm's investment banking and stock analysis division. If the investment bankers assist a firm in a stock or bond offering, it will be difficult for an analyst to issue a negative evaluation of the company. Advisory fees have been lost because of a negative stock recommendation. Despite attempts to ensure the independence of stock analysts, at times firm politics may get in the way.

The analyst is in frequent contact with the top officers of the company he or she analyzes. Although there are guidelines about receiving gifts and favors, it is sometimes difficult to separate personal friendship and impersonal corporate relationships. Corporate officials may try to convince the analyst that his pessimistic report is in error or suggest that it glosses over recent positive developments. To mitigate these problems, an analyst should call the company's investor relations department immediately *after* changing a recommendation to explain his or her perspective. The analyst needs to maintain independence and have confidence in his or her analysis.

GLOBAL COMPANY ANALYSIS

One of our goals in this book is to demonstrate investment techniques that can be applied to foreign markets, industries, and companies. A major problem of global analysis is getting the data required for the analysis.

In this section, we continue the analysis of the European chemical industry that we started in Chapter 19. The objective is to see how to evaluate individual companies and

[37]According to SEC regulations, mutual funds cannot own more than 10 percent of a firm's shares. For some large funds, this constraint will make the resulting investment too small to have any significant impact on fund returns, so they do not bother to consider such stocks for purchase.

[38]Information on the number of analysts covering a stock is available from research firms, such as IBES and Zacks.

TABLE 20.15 **EARNINGS AND DIVIDEND PER SHARE FOR MAJOR EUROPEAN CHEMICAL FIRMS**

		Earnings per Share			
Company	Currency	1998E	1999E	Dividends per Share (1999E)	Dividend Payout (1999)
BASF	DM	5.0	4.9	2.0	0.408
Bayer	DM	4.4	4.7	2.1	0.447
Ciba	Sfr	8.9	10.4	2.5	0.240
AKZO	DFL	26.0	27.8	9.5	0.342
DSM	DFL	26.5	22.0	10.0	0.455
Air Liquide	FFr	47.4	52.2	18.9	0.362
BOC	BP	53.5	61.7	33.0	0.535
AGA	SKr	5.1	6.0	3.4	0.567

E = Estimate.

Source: Jackie Ashurst, Charles K Brown, G. Haire, Mark Tracey, J. A. Murphy, and J. Henderson, "The Major European Chemicals/Pharma Groups" (London: Goldman Sachs International Ltd., May 1998). Copyright 1998 by Goldman Sachs.

select specific stocks for your investment portfolio. Again, we will work with tables assembled by Goldman Sachs.

Earnings per Share Analysis

Table 20.15 contains estimated earnings per share for the major chemical firms for 1998 and 1999. This two-period comparison shows the outlook for these firms. Most estimates indicate a mixed pattern of growth among the firms for 1999. The dividend data indicate a range of payouts from about 24 to 56 percent.

Common Stock Statistics

Given the prior analysis, Table 20.16 contains measures of stock performance and relative value for the firms in the industry. The absolute P/E ratios show the differences in the earnings multipliers among countries. The table contains interesting information on the individual stock P/E ratios relative to the average P/E ratio in the local market. As an example, Bayer's P/E ratio for 1999 is 16.6, which is only 89 percent of the average of all stocks in Germany. In contrast, Air Liquide has a P/E ratio of 22.4, which is 102 percent of the average for stocks in France. This shows that two stocks in the same industry could have different relative valuations in different countries due to variations in accounting conventions or social attitudes. Such differences in measures of relative valuation among countries should decline in the future as international accounting standards become more prevalent and global capital markets become more integrated.

The price/cash flow ratios likewise reflect major differences in relative valuation among countries. Again, these differences could be due to differences in real value or differences in accounting practices.

Share Price Performance

Table 20.17 compares the stock price changes for the major chemical firms. The results indicate large differences in absolute and relative stock performances. This comparison is very interesting because it demonstrates the effect of diversification when making foreign investments. The results deteriorate when they are compared to both the S&P 500 and the FT-Europe Index and to each stock's local market index. In summary, during this particular period, both the FT-Europe and most local markets were strong, which hurt these relative comparisons.

TABLE 20.16 COMMON STOCK STATISTICS FOR MAJOR EUROPEAN CHEMICAL FIRMS

Company	P/E			P/CF			P/E Relative[d]			EV/EBITDA[e]			EV/EBIT			Gross Dividend Yield (%)		
	1997	1998E	1999E	1997	1998E	1999E	1997	1998E	1999E	1997	1998E	1999E	1997	1998E	1999E	1997	1998E	1999E
Commodity																		
BASF	16.3	16.0	16.4	6.8	7.0	7.0	0.75	0.66	0.78	6.5	6.6	6.5	10.6	11.2	11.3	3.6	3.6	3.6
DSM	7.1	7.8	9.3	3.5	3.7	4.0	0.38	0.34	0.46	3.3	2.9	3.0	5.8	5.1	5.8	4.9	4.9	4.9
EVC	17.2	nm	15.8	3.5	2.9	2.7	0.91	nm	0.78	4.5	3.2	3.2	26.5	9.5	11.1	7.7	7.7	7.7
Kemira	12.6	12.4	11.1	5.0	5.0	4.5	0.84	0.64	0.67	5.7	5.6	5.3	10.5	10.2	9.4	3.7	4.0	4.2
Solvay	18.1	18.4	17.9	6.2	7.0	6.7	1.20	0.91	0.95	6.5	6.3	6.1	12.5	12.2	11.9	2.9	2.9	2.9
Hybrid																		
Akzo Nobel	18.7	16.3	15.2	10.7	9.2	8.8	0.99	0.72	0.75	8.8	8.1	7.8	13.6	12.1	11.5	2.0	2.1	2.2
Albright & Wilson*	13.4	12.5	11.2	9.6	7.8	7.2	0.78	0.63	0.61	7.8			10.4			3.9	4.1	4.3
Bayer	19.5	17.9	16.6	8.8	8.7	8.1	0.89	0.74	0.79	8.2	7.8	7.2	12.9	11.9	10.9	3.4	3.6	3.8
Degussa[b]*	23.9	21.6	19.0	9.1	8.3	7.6	1.09	0.89	0.90	10.4			20.3			2.0	2.2	2.4
Hoechst	23.7	23.7	17.9	8.3	10.7	9.2	1.08	0.98	0.85	8.7	10.0	8.9	16.6	19.4	15.3	2.9	3.1	3.3
ICI	36.7	26.1	19.1	18.0	13.0	10.9	2.14	1.30	1.04	12.0	12.0	11.0	20.4	16.9	14.7	2.6	2.8	2.9
Rhône-Poulenc	31.1	27.2	23.0	10.7	11.9	11.4	1.44	1.07	1.05	9.9	9.0	8.6	17.0	15.0	13.3	1.8	1.9	2.2
Specialty																		
AGA	27.7	24.3	20.8	10.7	9.8	8.7	1.76	1.47	1.49	10.0	8.7	7.7	19.3	16.3	13.8	2.4	2.6	2.7
Air Liquide	27.6	24.6	22.4	13.1	11.5	10.5	1.28	0.97	1.02	10.9	9.3	8.4	17.4	15.0	13.5	2.0	2.2	2.4
BOC[b]	16.4	18.2	15.8	9.0	9.6	8.2	0.99	0.94	0.84	7.7	8.2	7.5	11.6	13.1	11.9	3.0	3.2	3.4
BTP[a]*	25.7	23.2	20.7	18.4	16.7	14.7	1.49	1.16	1.13	14.0			17.4			2.3	2.4	2.5
Ciba Specialty Chem.	22.7	21.4	18.3	13.5	12.0	10.7	0.94	0.70	0.69	11.7	8.9	7.9	16.9	12.6	10.8	1.1	1.1	1.3
Clariant	29.0	22.0	18.4	12.8	11.4	10.4	1.20	0.72	0.70	10.5	9.7	9.1	16.1	14.2	12.8	0.8	1.1	1.4
Croda*	22.4	21.6	20.2	15.4	13.1	11.7	0.81	0.80	0.80	11.4			15.8			2.2	2.3	2.5
Elementis*	17.9	14.0	10.8	14.4	24.9	30.3	1.00	0.81	0.82	7.5			11.4			2.3		
Henkel	27.8	24.1	21.0	11.3	10.7	9.8	1.27	0.99	0.99	9.4	8.9	8.5	18.3	16.5	15.1	1.4	1.6	1.9
Inspec*	13.9	16.0	14.7	5.2	9.7	8.9	0.81	0.80	0.80	9.6			12.4			2.2	2.3	2.5
Laporte*	17.2	16.3	15.1	7.5	12.1	11.1	1.11	0.91	0.77	9.9			12.6			3.0	3.2	3.4
SKW Trostberg[c]*	17.8	17.1	13.7	6.2	5.7	5.3	0.81	0.70	0.65	8.2			15.6			2.8	3.1	3.2
Yule Catto*	16.9	15.1	13.1	18.8	12.0	11.0	0.99	0.88	0.76	21.7			26.2			2.4	2.7	2.9

*Company not covered, consensus estimates provided by I/B/E/S.

[a]March year end.

[b]September year end.

[c]1997 figures are estimates.

[d]Relative to local market.

[e]EV = market cap + net debt + minorities (+ pension liabilities for German companies).

Source: Jackie Ashurst, Charles K. Brown, G. Haire, M. Tracey, J. A. Murphy, and J. Henderson, "The Major European Chemicals/Pharma Groups" (London: Goldman Sachs International Ltd., May 1998). Copyright 1998 by Goldman Sachs.

TABLE 20.17 **SHARE PRICE PERFORMANCE FOR MAJOR EUROPEAN CHEMICAL FIRMS**

	Absolute			Relative to FT-A Europe			Relative to Local Market		
%	1 Month	3 Month	12 Month	1 Month	3 Month	12 Month	1 Month	3 Month	12 Month
BASF	−2.6	25.0	17.4	−2.7	9.0	−18.3	−3.0	7.3	−21.7
DSM	−1.6	7.1	5.2	−1.8	−6.6	−26.8	−2.8	−11.3	−30.6
EVC	−6.7	8.3	−30.0	−6.9	−5.5	−51.3	−7.8	−10.2	−53.8
Kemira	−0.5	12.6	21.4	−0.7	−1.8	−15.5	−10.1	−16.3	−27.4
Solvay	0.7	19.1	30.1	0.5	3.9	−9.4	−0.8	1.7	−6.5
Commodity Average	*−2.1*	*14.4*	*8.8*	*−2.3*	*−0.2*	*−24.2*	*−4.9*	*−5.8*	*−28.0*
Akzo Nobel	2.9	13.1	62.8	2.7	−1.4	13.4	1.7	−6.3	7.5
Albright & Wilson	1.4	27.9	18.5	1.2	11.6	−17.5	1.4	17.2	−8.0
Bayer	−5.1	2.7	17.4	−5.3	−10.5	−18.3	−5.6	−11.8	−21.7
Degussa	−5.8	8.8	36.4	−6.0	−5.1	−5.1	−6.3	−6.5	−9.1
Hoechst	−0.2	3.0	10.2	−0.4	−10.2	−23.3	−0.7	−11.5	−26.5
ICI	7.9	15.7	57.2	7.7	0.9	9.5	7.9	6.0	22.1
Rhône-Poulenc	7.5	15.5	65.9	7.3	0.7	15.5	4.3	−6.9	8.8
Hybrid Average	*1.1*	*19.6*	*39.1*	*0.9*	*4.3*	*−3.1*	*0.4*	*4.5*	*−1.8*
AGA	13.1	24.4	19.1	12.9	8.5	−17.1	11.9	8.3	−10.1
Air Liquide	3.5	25.2	33.5	3.2	9.2	−7.1	0.3	1.0	−12.5
BOC	3.5	4.4	0.3	3.3	−9.0	−30.2	3.5	−4.4	−22.1
BTP	32.0	47.6	94.9	31.8	28.7	35.7	32.0	35.2	51.3
Ciba Specialty Chemicals	−2.1	12.4	44.5	−2.3	−2.0	0.6	−2.7	1.5	−5.8
Clariant	2.7	18.6	104.4	2.5	3.4	42.3	2.0	7.1	33.2
Croda	13.2	28.7	55.5	13.0	12.2	8.3	13.2	17.9	20.7
Elementis	14.6	30.0	49.1	14.3	13.3	3.8	14.5	19.0	15.8
Henkel	2.2	24.7	56.8	2.0	8.8	9.2	1.7	7.1	4.6
Inspec	27.0	49.5	58.0	26.8	30.4	10.0	27.0	36.9	22.6
Laporte	9.3	28.9	35.9	9.1	12.4	−5.4	9.3	18.0	5.5
SKW Trostberg	−6.2	3.2	9.6	−6.4	−10.0	−23.7	−6.6	−11.3	−26.9
Yule Catto	15.3	19.0	18.7	15.1	3.8	−17.4	15.3	9.0	−7.9
Specialty Average	*9.9*	*24.3*	*44.6*	*9.6*	*8.4*	*0.7*	*9.3*	*11.2*	*5.3*

Source: Jackie Ashurst, Charles K. Brown, G. Haire, M. Tracey, J. A. Murphy, and J. Henderson, "The Major European Chemicals/Pharma Groups" (London: Goldman Sachs International Ltd., May 1998). Copyright 1998 by Goldman Sachs.

INDIVIDUAL COMPANY ANALYSIS

The report concludes with a summary of the strengths and potential problems of each individual company. Table 20.18 summarizes the operating and stock results for Bayer, a German firm considered to be one of the world's leading chemical companies. The analysts' discussion that accompanies the business sector analysis in Table 20.19 breaks down sales by product sector and indicates the percent of profit and profit margin for each sector. In addition, there is a geographic breakdown that highlights the firm's global expansion.

Based upon the sales, earnings, and valuation outlook for the firm, the analyst refers to the stock as a "market performer," which implies that it is expected to experience a return consistent with the aggregate European markets. Also, a stock price chart for Bayer (Figure 20.13) shows the absolute and relative movements for the firm's stock. As shown, although the stock price increased, it clearly underperformed the aggregate German market represented by the DAX 30 index.

TABLE 20.18 **COMPANY AND STOCK PRICE DATA FOR BAYER**

Bayer **Market Performer**

Price:	DM	78.75	Net Debt:	DMm	2,818	Price Target:	DM85
Market Value:	DMbn	57.3	Minorities[a]:	DMm	9581	Rel. to Germany 1 Month:	−5.6%
12-Month Range:	DM	85.5–57.1	Ent. Value:	DMbn	69.7	3 Months:	−11.8%
FT/S&P Germany:		266.9	No. Shares:	m	727	12 Months:	−21.7%

Year to December:	Sales DMm	Pre-Tax Profit DMm	DVFA EPS DM	Net Div DM	CFPS DM	P/E	P/E Rel	P/CF	Gross Yield %
1996	48,608	4,464	3.8	1.70	8.0	20.5	0.75	9.9	3.1
1997	55,005	5,108	4.0	1.90	8.9	19.5	0.89	8.8	3.4
1998E	56,780	5,525	4.4	2.00	9.1	17.9	0.74	8.7	3.6
1999E	60,000	6,020	4.7	2.10	9.7	16.6	0.79	8.1	3.8

Options/Convertibles/Warrants: O/C/W
Listed ADRs: No. Non listed BAYRY, 1:1

Ticker. BAYG.F
[a]Includes pension liabilities

Source: Jackie Ashurst, Charles K. Brown, G. Haire, M. Tracey, J. A. Murphy, and J. Henderson, "The Major European Chemicals/Pharma Groups" (London: Goldman Sachs International Ltd., May 1998). Copyright 1998 by Goldman Sachs.

TABLE 20.19 **ANALYSIS OF SALES, PROFITS, AND PROFIT MARGIN BY BUSINESS SECTOR AND GEOGRAPHY FOR BAYER**

BAYER BUSINESS SECTOR ANALYSIS 1997

	Sales		Trading Profit		Margin
	DMm	%	DMm	%	%
Health Care	13,635	25	1,871	34	13.7
Agriculture	5,697	10	945	17	16.6
Polymers	16,798	31	1,540	28	9.2
Chemicals	10,762	20	591	11	5.5
Agfa Group	8,113	15	481	9	5.9
Total	**55,005**	**100**	**5,428**	**100**	**9.9**

BAYER GEOGRAPHICAL ANALYSIS 1997

	Sales		Operating Profit		Margin
	DMm	%	DMm	%	%
Europe	25,961	47	3,542	65	13.6
North America	14,943	27	1,394	26	9.3
Latin America	4,425	8	155	3	3.5
Others	9,676	18	337	6	3.5
Total	**55,005**	**100**	**5,428**	**100**	**9.9**

Source: Jackie Ashurst, Charles K. Brown, G. Haire, M. Tracey, J. A. Murphy, and J. Henderson, "The Major European Chemicals/Pharma Groups" (London: Goldman Sachs International Ltd., May 1998). Copyright 1998 by Goldman Sachs.

FIGURE 20.13 **BAYER PRICE PERFORMANCE 1996–1998**

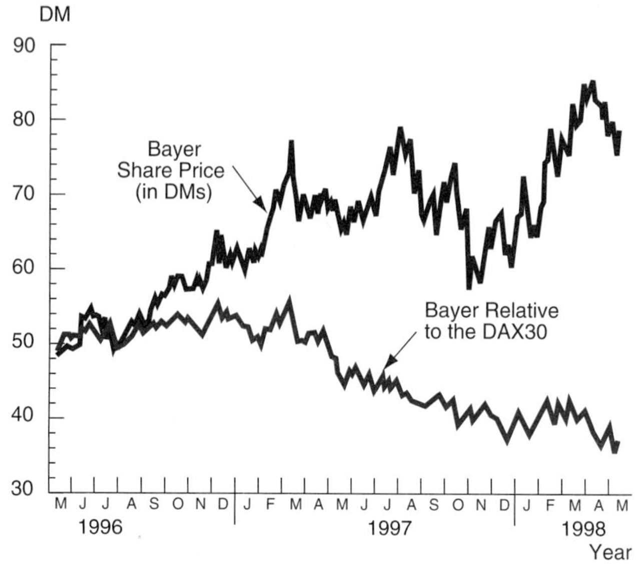
DM
90
80
70
60
50
40
30
Bayer Share Price (in DMs)
Bayer Relative to the DAX30
M J J A S O N D J F M A M J J A S O N D J F M A M
1996
1997
1998
Year

Source: Jackie Ashurst, Charles K. Brown, G. Haire, M. Tracey, J. A. Murphy, and J. Henderson, "The Major European Chemicals/Pharma Groups" (London: Goldman Sachs International Ltd., May 1998). Copyright 1998 by Goldman Sachs.

THE INTERNET *Investments Online*

Many helpful sites have been reviewed in prior chapters, for example, individual firm sites and the SEC's EDGAR database for firm-specific information. Investment bank and brokerage house sites may also prove valuable, though they may expect payment for access to their published research on different firms. Still, many sites exist that allow users to examine free information and investing tips:

www.better-investing.com The home page for the National Association of Investment Clubs offers company information and investing ideas in addition to resources for those interested in setting up their own investment club.

www.fool.com This is the home page for the Motley Fool; despite its name, it is a well-known and popular site for investors to visit. It is chock-full of data, articles, educational resources, news, and investing ideas.

www.cfonews.com Corporate Financials Online provides links to news about selected publicly traded firms.

www.ibes.com The home page for the Institutional Brokers Estimate System. IBES maintains a database of analysts' earnings expectations on a variety of stocks. The database contains earnings per share estimates from 800 brokers on 18,000 stocks in 52 countries. The site offers free reports on a selected number of firms.

www.zacks.com This is the Web site for Zacks Investment Research. When the user types in a ticker symbol for one of the 8,700 stocks covered, Zacks provides links to a company profile, financials, analysts' consensus earnings estimates, and the number of analysts recommending strong buy, moderate buy, hold, moderate sell, and strong sell. Links allow the user to order brokerage reports.

www.valueline.com This site was mentioned in an earlier chapter. The Value Line Investment Survey is a favorite source of information for many investors.

www.financialweb.com This site provides links to investment newsletters, stock screening features, educational features, company links, and news.

THE INTERNET *Investments Online (cont.)*

investor.msn.com The home page of Microsoft Investor allows users to track investments, follow the market, read daily editorial and market summaries, and obtain company profiles.

www.marketedge.com MarketEdge, part of the Thomson Investors Network, has company stock reports for over 7,000 firms that are updated twice a month. Visitors can find possible investments by screening stocks on seven different variables.

www.nyssa.org The home page of the New York Society of Security Analysts includes many financial Web links and sources of market and company information.

Summary

- This chapter demonstrates how to complete the fundamental analysis process by analyzing a company and deciding whether you should buy its stock. This requires a separate analysis of a company and its stock. A wonderful firm can have an overpriced stock, or a mediocre firm can have an underpriced stock.
- Although the chapter is mainly concerned with discussing and demonstrating several alternative valuation techniques, the initial section contained a discussion of the strategic alternatives available to firms in response to different competitive pressures in their industries. The alternative corporate strategies include low-cost leadership or differentiation. Either of these strategies should be focused toward alternative segments of the market and, if properly implemented, should help the company attain above-average rates of return. In addition, we discussed SWOT analysis, which helps an analyst assess a firm's strengths and weaknesses as well as its external opportunities and threats. Following your economic and industry analysis, this strategic analysis of the firm ensures that you fully understand the firm's goals, objectives, and strategy. You should now be in a position to properly estimate the intrinsic value of the stock based upon your knowledge of the company.
- When estimating a stock's intrinsic value you can follow one or both of two approaches (the present value of cash flow, or the analysis of relative valuation ratios). Each of these approaches includes several techniques. We reviewed how to estimate the major inputs to the techniques and demonstrated what the results would be when these techniques are applied to Walgreen.
- After we derived several estimated values for Walgreen based upon the present value of cash flow techniques, we applied the relative valuation ratios beginning with P/E ratios and a detailed valuation of the firm using this technique.
- In addition, we considered the other relative valuation ratios variables that affect investor decisions. Specifically, we computed and analyzed the price/book value ratio, the price/cash flow ratio, and the price/sales ratio, and compared these company relative valuation ratios to comparable ratios for both the retail drugstore industry and the aggregate market.
- The investment decision is based upon three comparisons. First, we compute the expected value of the stock discounted to the present and compare this intrinsic value to the prevailing market price. If the stock's intrinsic value exceeds the market price, we would buy the stock. Second, we compute the estimated rate of the return on the stock during our holding period on the basis of the expected value of the stock and the expected dividend. If this estimated rate of return exceeds our required rate of return, we would buy the stock. Finally, we compute the expected long-run rate of return based upon the stock's expected dividend yield plus the expected growth rate for the firm. Again, if this expected long-run rate of return exceeds our required rate of return, we would consider buying the stock for the long run.
- Because of the profit potential of investing in growth companies as well as the difficulty in estimating the intrinsic value of these firms, we considered the concept of growth companies, the alternative specifications for growth companies, and then several techniques that provide insights on the valuation of these firms. These techniques include economic value-added (EVA), the franchise

factor model, a growth duration model that emphasizes the importance of estimating how long superior growth is expected to last, and, finally, a three-step valuation model that considers periods of differential growth progressing from dynamic growth to simple growth and then declining growth. These models not only help the analyst arrive at a specific value for the stock, but also concentrate attention on the relevant factors that determine "true" growth which determines the intrinsic value of these growth companies. As noted at the beginning of the chapter, the critical question is—is the stock of the growth company going to be a growth stock?

- We concluded the chapter with a continuation of our example of global analysis by reviewing the company analysis related to the European chemical industry. This demonstration showed the importance of differential demand and cost factors among countries as well as between companies. The significance of different accounting conventions and the impact of exchange rate differences were likewise highlighted.

Questions

1. Give an example of a growth company and discuss why you identify it as such. Based on its P/E, do you think it is a growth stock? Explain.
2. Give an example of a cyclical stock and discuss why you have designated it as such. Is it issued by a cyclical company?
3. A biotechnology firm is growing at a compound rate of over 21 percent a year. (Its ROE is over 30 percent, and it retains about 70 percent of its earnings.) The stock of this company is priced at about 65 times next year's earnings. Discuss whether you consider this a growth company or a growth stock.
4. Select a company outside the retail drugstore industry and indicate what economic series you would use for a sales projection. Discuss why this is a relevant series.
5. Select a company outside the retail drugstore industry and indicate what industry series you would use in an industry analysis. (Use one of the industry groups designated by Standard & Poor's.) Discuss why this industry series is appropriate. Were there other possible alternatives?
6. Select a company outside the retail drugstore industry and, based on reading its annual report and other public information, discuss what you perceive to be its competitive strategy (i.e., low-cost producer or differentiation).
7. Discuss a company that is known to be a low-cost producer in its industry and consider what makes it possible for the firm to be a cost leader. Do the same for a firm known for differentiating.
8. Under what conditions would you use a two- or three-stage cash flow model rather than the constant growth model?
9. What is the rationale for using the price/book value (P/BV) ratio as a measure of relative value?
10. What would you look for to justify a price/book value ratio of 3.0? What would you expect to be the characteristics of a firm with a P/BV ratio of 0.6?
11. Why has the price/cash flow (P/CF) ratio become a popular measure of relative value during the recent past? What factors would help explain a difference in this ratio for two firms?
12. Assume that you uncover two stocks with substantially different price/sales ratios (e.g., 0.5 versus 2.5). Discuss the factors that might explain the difference.
13. Specify the major components for the calculation of economic value-added (EVA) and describe what a positive EVA signifies.
14. Discuss why you would want to use EVA return on capital rather than absolute EVA to compare two companies or to evaluate a firm's performance over time.
15. Differentiate between EVA and MVA and discuss the relatively weak relationship between these two measures of performance. Is this relationship surprising to you? Explain.
16. Discuss the two factors that determine the franchise value of a firm. Assuming a firm has a base cost of equity of 11 percent and does not have a franchise value, what will be its P/E?
17. You are told that a company retains 80 percent of its earnings, and its earnings are growing at a rate of about 8 percent a year versus an average growth rate of 6 percent for all firms. Discuss whether you would consider this a growth company.
18. It is contended by some that in a completely competitive economy, there would never be a true growth company. Discuss the reasoning behind this contention.

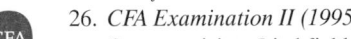

19. Why is it not feasible to use the dividend discount model in the valuation of true growth companies?
20. Discuss the major assumptions of the growth duration model. Why could these assumptions present a problem?
21. You are told that a growth company has a P/E ratio of 10 times and a growth rate of 15 percent compared to the aggregate market, which has a growth rate of 8 percent and a P/E ratio of 11 times. What does this comparison imply regarding the growth company? What else do you need to know to properly compare the growth company to the aggregate market?
22. Given the alternative companies described in the chapter (negative growth, simple growth, dynamic growth), indicate what your label would be for the Walgreen Company. Justify your label.
23. Indicate and justify a label for General Motors.
24. What are the variables you must estimate if you want to use the Mao three-stage growth valuation model?
25. *CFA Examination I (1993)*
    Using book value to measure profitability and to value a company's stock has limitations. Discuss *five* such limitations from an accounting perspective. Be specific. [10 minutes]
26. *CFA Examination II (1995)*
    On your visit to Litchfield Chemical Corp. (LCC), you learned that the board of directors has periodically debated the company's dividend payout policy.
    a. Briefly discuss *two* arguments *for* and *two* arguments *against* a high dividend payout policy. [8 minutes]

    A director of LCC said that the use of dividend discount models by investors is "proof" that "the higher the dividend, the higher the stock price."

    b. Using a constant growth dividend discount model as a basis of reference, evaluate the above director's statement. [8 minutes]
    c. Explain how an increase in dividend payout would affect *each* of the following (holding all other factors constant):
    (i) Internal (implied, normalized, or sustainable) growth rate; and
    (ii) Growth in book value. [8 minutes]
27. *CFA Examination II (1997)*
    The Soft Corporation (SC) is planning to acquire a slower growth competitor, which will materially increase SC's sales volume. The company to be acquired has pretax margins that are approximately the same as those of SC. SC plans to issue $300 million in long-term debt to finance the entire cost of the acquisition.
    a. Discuss how SC's potential acquisition might *decrease* its valuation based on a constant growth dividend discount model. Be sure to comment on *each* of the three factors in such a model. [9 minutes]
    b. Discuss *two* reasons why SC's potential acquisition might *increase* the P/E multiple investors are willing to pay for SC. [4 minutes]
28. *CFA Examination II (1999)*
    A generalized model for the value of any asset is the present value of the expected cash flows:

$$\text{Value} = \sum_{t=1}^{N} \frac{CF_t}{(1+k)^t}$$

where:

N = life of the asset
CF_t = cash flow in period t
k = appropriate discount rate

Both stock and bond valuation models use a discounted cash flow approach, which includes the estimation of three factors (N, CF_t, k).

Explain why *each* of these *three* factors is generally more difficult to estimate for common stocks than for traditional corporate bonds. [12 minutes]

Problems

1. Select two stocks in an industry of your choice, and perform a common size income statement analysis over a two-year period.
   a. Discuss which firm is more cost effective.
   b. Discuss the relative year-to-year changes in gross profit margin, operating profit margin, and net profit margin for each company.
2. Select a company outside the retail store industry, and examine its operating profit margin relative to the operating margin for its industry during the most recent 10-year period. Discuss the annual results in terms of levels and percentage changes.
3. Select any industry except chemicals and provide general background information on two *non*-U.S. companies from public sources (see Chapter 6). This background information should include their products, overall size (sales and assets), growth during the past 5 years (sales and earnings), ROE during the last 2 years, current stock price, and P/E ratio.
4. Given Hitech's beta of 1.75 and a risk-free rate of 7 percent, what is the expected rate of return assuming
   a. a 15 percent market return?
   b. a 10 percent market return?
5. Select three companies from any industry except retail drugstores.
   a. Compute their P/E ratios using last year's average price [(high plus low)/2] and earnings.
   b. Compute their growth rate of earnings over the last 5 years.
   c. Look up the most recent beta reported in Value Line.
   d. Discuss the relationships between P/E, growth, and risk.
6. What is the implied growth duration of Kayleigh Industries given the following:

	S&P 400	Kayleigh Industries
P/E ratios	16	24
Average growth	0.06	0.14
Dividend yield	0.04	0.02

7. Lauren Industries has an 18 percent annual growth rate compared to the market rate of 8 percent. If the market multiple is 14, determine P/E ratios for Lauren Industries, assuming its beta is 1.0 and you feel it can maintain its superior growth rate for
   a. the next 10 years.
   b. the next 5 years.
8. You are given the following information about two computer software firms and the S&P 400:

	Company A	Company B	S&P 400
P/E ratio	30.0	27.0	18.0
Average annual growth rate	0.18	0.15	0.07
Dividend yield	0.00	0.01	0.02

   a. Compute the growth duration of each company stock relative to the S&P 400.
   b. Compute the growth duration of Company A relative to Company B.
   c. Given these growth durations, what determines your investment decision?

CFA

9. *CFA Examination II (June 1981)*
   The value of an asset is the present value of the expected returns from the asset during the holding period. An investment will provide a stream of returns during this period, and it is necessary to discount this stream of returns at an appropriate rate to determine the asset's present value. A dividend valuation model such as the following is frequently used,

$$P_i = \frac{D_1}{(k_i - g_i)}$$

where:

P_i = the current price of common stock i
D_1 = the expected dividend in period 1
k_i = the required rate of return on stock i
g_i = the expected constant growth rate of dividends for stock i

a. *Identify* the three factors that must be estimated for any valuation model, and *explain* why these estimates are more difficult to derive for common stocks than for bonds. [9 minutes]

b. *Explain* the principal problem involved in using a dividend valuation model to value
   (1) companies whose operations are closely correlated with economic cycles.
   (2) companies that are of giant size and are maturing.
   (3) companies that are of small size and are growing rapidly.
   Assume all companies pay dividends. [6 minutes]

CFA

10. *CFA Examination I (June 1985)*
Your client is considering the purchase of $100,000 in common stock which pays no dividends and will appreciate in market value by 10 percent per year. At the same time, the client is considering an opportunity to invest $100,000 in a lease obligation that will provide the annual year-end cash flows listed in Table 1. Assume that each investment will be sold at the end of 3 years and that you are given no additional information.

Calculate the present value of each of the two investments assuming a 10 percent discount rate, and state which one will provide the higher return over the 3-year period. Use the data in Table 1, and show your calculations. [10 minutes]

TABLE 1 ANNUAL CASH FLOW FROM LEASE

End of Year	
1	$ -0-
2 Lease receipts	15,000
3 Lease receipts	25,000
3 Sale proceeds	$100,000

PRESENT VALUE OF $1

Period	6%	8%	10%	12%
1	0.943	0.926	0.909	0.893
2	0.890	0.857	0.826	0.797
3	0.840	0.794	0.751	0.712
4	0.792	0.735	0.683	0.636
5	0.747	0.681	0.621	0.567

CFA

11. *CFA Examination I (1990)*
The constant growth dividend discount model can be used both for the valuation of companies and for the estimation of the long-term total return of a stock.

Assume:	$20 =	the price of a stock today
	8% =	the expected growth rate of dividends
	$0.60 =	the annual dividend one year forward

a. Using *only* the above data, compute the expected long-term total return on the stock using the constant growth dividend discount model. Show calculations.
b. Briefly discuss *three* disadvantages of the constant growth dividend discount model in its application to investment analysis.
c. Identify *three* alternative methods to the dividend discount model for the valuation of companies. [10 minutes]

12. *CFA Examination I (1992)*

Mulroney recalled from her CFA studies that the constant growth discounted dividend model (DDM) was one way to arrive at a valuation for a company's common stock. She collected current dividend and stock price data for Eastover and Southampton, shown in Table 2.

a. Using 11 percent as the required rate of return (i.e., discount rate) and a projected growth rate of 8 percent, compute a constant growth DDM value for Eastover's stock and compare the computed value for Eastover to its stock price indicated in Table 2. Show calculations. [10 minutes]

Mulroney's supervisor commented that a two-stage DDM may be more appropriate for companies such as Eastover and Southampton. Mulroney believes that Eastover and Southampton could grow more rapidly over the next 3 years and then settle in at a lower but sustainable rate of growth beyond 1994. Her estimates are indicated in Table 3.

b. Using 11 percent as the required rate of return, compute the two-stage DDM value of Eastover's stock and compare that value to its stock price indicated in Table 2. Show calculations. [15 minutes]
c. Discuss *two* advantages and *three* disadvantages of using a constant growth DDM. Briefly discuss how the two-stage DDM improves upon the constant growth DDM. [10 minutes]

TABLE 2 CURRENT INFORMATION

	Current Share Price	Current Dividends per Share	1992 EPS Estimate	Current Book Value per Share
Eastover (EO)	$ 28	$ 1.20	$ 1.60	$ 17.32
Southampton (SHC)	48	1.08	3.00	32.21
S&P 500	415	12.00	20.54	159.83

TABLE 3 PROJECTED GROWTH RATES

	Next 3 Years (1992, 1993, 1994)	Growth Beyond 1994
Eastover (EO)	12%	8%
Southampton (SHC)	13%	7%

13. *CFA Examination I (1992)*

In addition to the discounted dividend model (DDM) approach, Mulroney decided to look at the price/earnings ratio and price/book ratio, relative to the S&P 500, for both Eastover and Southampton. Mulroney elected to perform this analysis using 1987–1991 and current data.

a. Using the data in Tables 4 and 5, compute *both* the current and the 5-year (1987–1991) average relative price/earnings ratios and relative price/book ratios for Eastover and Southampton. Discuss *each* company's current relative price/earnings ratio as compared to its 5-year average relative price/earnings ratio and *each* company's current relative price/book ratio as compared to its 5-year average relative price/book ratio. [10 minutes]
b. Briefly discuss *one* disadvantage for *each* of the relative price/earnings and relative price/book approach to valuation. [5 minutes]

TABLE 4 EASTOVER COMPANY (EO)

	1986	1987	1988	1989	1990	1991
Earnings per share	$ 1.27	$ 2.12	$ 2.68	$ 1.56	$ 1.87	$ 0.90
Dividends per share	0.87	0.90	1.15	1.20	1.20	1.20
Book value per share	14.82	16.54	18.14	18.55	19.21	17.21
Stock price						
High	28	40	30	33	28	30
Low	20	20	23	25	18	20
Close	25	26	25	28	22	27
Average P/E	18.9x	14.2x	9.9x	18.6x	12.3x	27.8x
Average price/book	1.6x	1.8x	1.5x	1.6x	1.2x	1.5x

SOUTHAMPTON COMPANY (SHC)

	1986	1987	1988	1989	1990	1991
Earnings per share	$1.66	$3.13	$3.55	$5.08	$2.46	$1.75
Dividends per share	0.77	0.79	0.89	0.98	1.04	1.08
Book value per share	24.84	27.47	29.92	30.95	31.54	32.21
Stock price						
High	34	40	38	43	45	46
Low	21	22	26	28	20	26
Close	31	27	28	39	27	44
Average P/E	16.6x	9.9x	9.0x	7.0x	13.2x	20.6x
Average price/book	1.1x	1.1x	1.1x	1.2x	1.0x	1.1x

S&P 500

	1986	1987	1988	1989	1990	1991	5-Year Average (1987–1991)
Average P/E	15.8x	16.0x	11.1x	13.9x	15.6x	19.2x	15.2x
Average price/book	1.8x	2.1x	1.9x	2.2x	2.1x	2.3x	2.1x

TABLE 5 CURRENT INFORMATION

	Current Share Price	Current Dividends per Share	1992 EPS Estimate	Current Book Value per Share
Eastover (EO)	$28	$1.20	$1.60	$17.32
Southampton (SHC)	48	1.08	3.00	32.21
S&P 500	415	12.00	20.54	159.83

CFA

14. *CFA Examination I (1993)*
At year-end 1991, the Wall Street consensus was that Philip Morris' earnings and dividends would grow at 20 percent for 5 years after which growth would fall to a market-like 7 percent. Analysts also projected a required rate of return of 10 percent for the U.S. equity market.
    a. Using the data in Table 6 and the multistage dividend discount model, calculate the intrinsic value of Philip Morris stock at year-end 1991. Assume a similar level of risk for Philip Morris stock as for the typical U.S. stock. Show all work. [7 minutes]
    b. Using the data in Table 6, calculate Philip Morris' price/earnings ratio and the price/earnings ratio relative to the S&P 500 Stock Index as of December 31, 1991. [3 minutes]
    c. Using the data in Table 6, calculate Philip Morris' price/book ratio and the price/book ratio relative to the S&P 500 Stock Index as of December 31, 1991. [3 minutes]

TABLE 6 PHILIP MORRIS CORPORATION: SELECTED FINANCIAL STATEMENT AND OTHER DATA—YEARS ENDING DECEMBER 31 ($ MILLIONS EXCEPT PER-SHARE DATA)

	1991	1981
Income Statement		
Operating revenue	$56,458	$10,886
Cost of sales	25,612	5,253
Excise taxes on products	8,394	2,580
Gross profit	$22,452	$ 3,053
Selling, general, and administrative expenses	13,830	1,741
Operating income	$ 8,622	$ 1,312
Interest expense	1,651	232
Pretax earnings	$ 6,971	$ 1,080
Provision for income taxes	3,044	420
Net earnings	$ 3,927	$ 660
Earnings per share	$4.24	$0.66
Dividends per share	$1.91	$0.25
Balance Sheet		
Current assets	$12,594	$ 3,733
Property, plant, and equipment, net	9,946	3,583
Goodwill	18,624	634
Other assets	6,220	1,230
Total assets	$47,384	$ 9,180
Current liabilities	$11,824	$ 1,936
Long-term debt	14,213	3,499
Deferred taxes	1,803	455
Other liabilities	7,032	56
Stockholders' equity	12,512	3,234
Total liabilities and stockholders' equity	$47,384	$ 9,180
Other Data		
Philip Morris:		
Common shares outstanding (millions)	920	1,003
Closing price common stock	$80.250	$6.125
S&P 500 Stock Index:		
Closing price	417.09	122.55
Earnings per share	16.29	15.36
Book value per share	161.08	109.43

CFA

15. *CFA Examination I (1993)*
    a. State *one* major advantage and *one* major disadvantage of *each* of the *three* valuation methodologies you used to value Philip Morris stock in Question 14. [6 minutes]
    b. State whether Philip Morris stock is undervalued or overvalued as of December 31, 1991. Support your conclusion using your answers to previous questions and any data provided. (The past 10-year average S&P 500 Stock Index relative price/earnings and price/book ratios for Philip Morris were 0.80 and 1.61, respectively.) [9 minutes]

CFA

16. *CFA Examination II (1995)*
    Your supervisor has asked you to evaluate the relative attractiveness of the stocks of two very similar chemical companies: Litchfield Chemical Corp. (LCC) and Aminochem Company

(AOC). AOC also has a June 30 fiscal year end. You have compiled the data in Table 7 for this purpose. Use a one-year time horizon and assume the following:

- Real gross domestic product is expected to rise 5 percent;
- S&P 500 expected total return of 20 percent;
- U.S. Treasury bills yield 5 percent; and
- 30-year U.S. Treasury bonds yield 8 percent.

a. Calculate the value of the common stock of LCC and AOC using the constant growth dividend discount model. Show your work. [5 minutes]
b. Calculate the expected return over the next year of the common stock of LCC and AOC using the Capital Asset Pricing Model. Show your work. [5 minutes]
c. Calculate the internal (implied, normalized, or sustainable) growth rate of LCC and AOC. Show your work. [5 minutes]
d. Recommend LCC *or* AOC for investment, Justify your choice by using your answers to A, B, and C and the information in Table 7. [10 minutes]

TABLE 7

	Litchfield Chemical (LCC)	**Aminochem (AOC)**
Current stock price	$50	$30
Shares outstanding (millions)	10	20
Projected earnings per share (fiscal 1996)	$4.00	$3.20
Projected dividend per share (fiscal 1996)	$0.90	$1.60
Projected dividend growth rate	8%	7%
Stock beta	1.2	1.4
Investors' required rate of return	10%	11%
Balance sheet data (millions)		
Long-term debt	$100	$130
Stockholders' equity	$300	$320

17. *CFA Examination II (1997)*
Westfield Capital Management Company's equity investment strategy is to invest in companies with low price-to-book ratios, while taking into account differences in solvency and asset utilization. Westfield is considering investing in the shares of either Jerry's Department Stores (JDS) or Miller Stores (MLS).
a. Calculate *each* of the following ratios for *both* JDS and MLS. Use *only* the financial data in Table 8. Show your work. [6 minutes]
(i) Price-to-book ratio
(ii) Total-debt-to-equity ratio
(iii) Fixed-asset utilization (turnover)
b. Select, based on part a, the company that best meets Westfield's investment criteria. Justify your choice. [4 minutes]
c. Describe, based on Tables 9 and 10, the balance sheet adjustments in *each* of the following areas required to enhance the comparability of JDS and MLS. (A total of *four* adjustments is required.) [8 minutes]
(i) Leases
(ii) Sale of receivables with recourse
(iii) Inventory valuation method
(iv) Pensions
d. Calculate each of the following ratios for *both* JDS and MLS using the adjusted financial data from part c. Ignore any income tax effects. Show your work. [12 minutes]
(i) Book value per common share
(ii) Total-debt-to-equity ratio

(iii) Fixed-asset utilization (turnover)

e. Select, based on part d, the company that best meets Westfield's investment criteria. Justify your choice. [4 minutes]

TABLE 8 JERRY'S DEPARTMENT STORES AND MILLER STORES: SELECTED FINANCIAL DATA AT MARCH 31, 1997 (IN MILLIONS EXCEPT PER-SHARE DATA)

	JDS	MLS
Sales	$21,250	$18,500
PP&E	$ 5,700	$ 5,500
Short-term debt	$ 0	$ 1,000
Long-term debt	$ 2,700	$ 2,500
Common equity	$ 6,000	$ 7,500
Issued and outstanding shares as of 3/31/97	250	400
Per share market price on 5/30/97	$ 51.50	$ 49.50

TABLE 9 JERRY'S DEPARTMENT STORES: DATA EXTRACTED FROM MARCH 31, 1997, FINANCIAL STATEMENT FOOTNOTES

1. The Company conducts the majority of its operations from leased premises, which include distribution centers, warehouses, offices, and retail stores. Future minimum lease payments for noncancelable real and personal property operating leases are as follows:

	Operating Leases ($ in millions)
1997	$ 259
1998	213
1999	183
2000	160
2001	144
Thereafter	706
Total minimum lease payments	$1,665
Present value of lease payments	$1,000
Weighted-average interest rate	10%

2. During the fiscal year ended March 31, 1997, the Company sold $800 million of its accounts receivable with recourse, all of which were outstanding at year end.
3. Merchandise inventory. Substantially all merchandise inventory is valued at the lower of cost (first-in, first-out) or market.
4. Substantially all of the Company's employees are enrolled in Company-sponsored defined-contribution profit sharing and retirement savings plans.

TABLE 10 MILLER STORES: DATA EXTRACTED FROM MARCH 31, 1997, FINANCIAL STATEMENT FOOTNOTES

1. The Company's real estate policy is to own its stores; thus, the Company has no operating leases.
2. The Company does not sell or securitize its accounts receivable.
3. All inventories are valued on the last-in, first-out (LIFO) cost basis. As of March 31, 1997, inventories were $700 million lower than they would have been had the first-in, first-out (FIFO) cost basis been used.
4. Actuarial present value of accumulated (ABO) and projected (PBO) benefit obligation for its pension plan at March 31, 1997, was as follows ($ in millions):

	ABO	PBO
Vested	$1,550	$1,590
Nonvested	40	210
Total	$1,590	$1,800

Plan assets at fair value = $3,400.
Accrued pension per 3/31/97 balance sheet = $0.

Note: Questions 18–22 are all related.

18. *CFA Examination II (1998)*
Janet Ludlow is preparing a report on U.S.-based manufacturers in the electric toothbrush industry and has gathered the information shown in Table 11 and Exhibit 1.

TABLE 11 RATIOS FOR ELECTRIC TOOTHBRUSH INDUSTRY INDEX AND BROAD STOCK MARKET INDEX

Year	1992	1993	1994	1995	1996	1997
Return on equity						
Electric toothbrush industry index	12.5%	12.0%	15.4%	19.6%	21.6%	21.6%
Market index	10.2	12.4	14.6	19.9	20.4	21.2
Average P/E						
Electric toothbrush industry index	28.5x	23.2x	19.6x	18.7x	18.5x	16.2x
Market index	10.2	12.4	14.6	19.9	18.1	19.1
Dividend payout ratio						
Electric toothbrush industry index	8.8%	8.0%	12.1%	12.1%	14.3%	17.1%
Market index	39.2	40.1	38.6	43.7	41.8	39.1
Average dividend yield						
Electric toothbrush industry index	0.3%	0.3%	0.6%	0.7%	0.8%	1.0%
Market index	3.8	3.2	2.6	2.2	2.3	2.1

Ludlow's report concludes that the electric toothbrush industry is in the maturity (i.e., late) phase of its industry life cycle.

a. Select and justify *three* factors from Table 11 that *support* Ludlow's conclusion. [6 minutes]

EXHIBIT 1 CHARACTERISTICS OF THE ELECTRIC TOOTHBRUSH MANUFACTURING INDUSTRY

- *Industry Sales Growth*—Industry sales have grown at 15–20 percent per year in recent years and are expected to grow at 10–15 percent per year over the next 3 years.
- *Non-U.S. Markets*—Some U.S. manufacturers are attempting to enter fast-growing non-U.S. markets, which remain largely unexploited.
- *Mail Order Sales*—Some manufacturers have created a new niche in the industry by selling electric toothbrushes directly to customers through mail order. Sales for this industry segment are growing at 40 percent per year.
- *U.S. Market Penetration*—The current penetration rate in the United States is 60 percent of households and will be difficult to increase.
- *Price Competition*—Manufacturers compete fiercely on the basis of price, and price wars within the industry are common.
- *Niche Markets*—Some manufacturers are able to develop new, unexploited niche markets in the United States based on company reputation, quality, and service.
- *Industry Consolidation*—Several manufacturers have recently merged, and it is expected that consolidation in the industry will increase.
- *New Entrants*—New manufacturers continue to enter the market.

b. Select and justify *three* factors from Exhibit 1 that *refute* Ludlow's conclusion. [6 minutes]

Questions 19 through 22 relate to QuickBrush Company and SmileWhite Corporation. A total of 73 minutes is allocated to these questions. Use the first few minutes to review Tables 12, 13, and 14, Exhibits 2 and 3, and the questions themselves.

CFA

19. *CFA Examination II (1998)*
After describing the electric toothbrush industry, Janet Ludlow's report focuses on two companies, QuickBrush Company and SmileWhite Corporation. Her report concludes:

> QuickBrush is a more profitable company than SmileWhite, as indicated by the 40 percent sales growth and substantially higher margins it has produced over the last few years. SmileWhite's sales and earnings are growing at a 10 percent rate and produce much lower margins. We do not think SmileWhite is capable of growing faster than its recent growth rate of 10 percent whereas QuickBrush can sustain a 30 percent long-term growth rate.

a. Criticize Ludlow's analysis and conclusion that QuickBrush is more profitable, as defined by return on equity (ROE), than SmileWhite and that it has a higher sustainable growth rate. Use only the information provided in Tables 12 and 13. Support your criticism by calculating and analyzing:
   - the five components that determine ROE.
   - the two ratios that determine sustainable growth. [20 minutes]

b. Explain how QuickBrush has produced an average annual earnings per share (EPS) growth rate of 40 percent over the last 2 years with an ROE that has been declining. Use only the information provided in Table 12. [8 minutes]

TABLE 12 QUICKBRUSH COMPANY: FINANCIAL STATEMENTS—YEARLY DATA ($000 EXCEPT PER-SHARE DATA)

	December 1995	December 1996	December 1997
Income Statement			
Revenue	$3,480	$5,400	$7,760
Cost of goods sold	2,700	4,270	6,050
Selling, general, and admin. expense	500	690	1,000
Depreciation and amortization	30	40	50
Operating income (EBIT)	$ 250	$ 400	$ 660
Interest expense	0	0	0
Income before taxes	$ 250	$ 400	$ 660
Income taxes	60	110	215
Income after taxes	$ 190	$ 290	$ 445
Diluted EPS	$0.60	$0.84	$1.18
Average shares outstanding (000)	317	346	376

	December 1995	December 1996	December 1997	3-Year Average
Financial Statistics				
COGS as % of sales	77.59%	79.07%	77.96%	78.24%
SG&A as % of sales	14.37	12.78	12.89	13.16
Operating margin	7.18	7.41	8.51	
Pretax income/EBIT	100.00	100.00	100.00	
Tax rate	24.00	27.50	32.58	

	December 1995	December 1996	December 1997
Balance Sheet			
Cash and cash equivalents	$ 460	$ 50	$ 480
Accounts receivable	540	720	950
Inventories	300	430	590
Net property, plant, and equipment	760	1,830	3,450
Total assets	$2,060	$3,030	$5,470
Current liabilities	$ 860	$1,110	$1,750
Total liabilities	$ 860	$1,110	$1,750
Stockholders' equity	1,200	1,920	3,720
Total liabilities and equity	$2,060	$3,030	$5,470
Market price per share	$21.00	$30.00	$45.00
Book value per share	$3.79	$5.55	$9.89
Annual dividend per share	$0.00	$0.00	$0.00

TABLE 13 SMILEWHITE CORPORATION: FINANCIAL STATEMENTS—YEARLY DATA ($000 EXCEPT PER-SHARE DATA)

	December 1995	December 1996	December 1997
Income Statement			
Revenue	$104,000	$110,400	$119,200
Cost of goods sold	72,800	75,100	79,300
Selling, general, and admin. expense	20,300	22,800	23,900
Depreciation and amortization	4,200	5,600	8,300
Operating income	$6,700	$6,900	$7,700
Interest expense	600	350	350
Income before taxes	$6,100	$6,550.	$7,350
Income taxes	2,100	2,200	2,500
Income after taxes	$4,000	$4,350	$4,850
Diluted EPS	$2.16	$2.35	$2.62
Average shares outstanding (000)	1,850	1,850	1,850

	December 1995	December 1996	December 1997	3-Year Average
Financial Statistics				
COGS as % of sales	70.00%	68.00%	66.53%	68.10%
SG&A as % of sales	19.52	20.64	20.05	20.08
Operating margin	6.44	6.25	6.46	
Pretax income/EBIT	91.04	94.93	95.45	
Tax rate	34.43	33.59	34.01	

	December 1995	December 1996	December 1997
Balance Sheet			
Cash and cash equivalents	$ 7,900	$ 3,300	$ 1,700
Accounts receivable	7,500	8,000	9,000
Inventories	6,300	6,300	5,900
Net property, plant, and equipment	12,000	14,500	17,000
Total assets	$33,700	$32,100	$33,600
Current liabilities	$ 6,200	$ 7,800	$ 6,600
Long-term debt	9,000	4,300	4,300
Total liabilities	$15,200	$12,100	$10,900
Stockholders' equity	18,500	20,000	22,700
Total liabilities and equity	$33,700	$32,100	$33,600
Market price per share	$23.00	$26.00	$30.00
Book value per share	$10.00	$10.81	$12.27
Annual dividend per share	$1.42	$1.53	$1.72

20. *CFA Examination II (1998)*
In her forecast of 1998 earnings per share for QuickBrush Company, Janet Ludlow has made the assumptions shown in Exhibit 2:

EXHIBIT 2 FORECAST ASSUMPTIONS: QUICKBRUSH 1998 EPS

Revenue	will rise 30% from 1997
Cost of goods sold (as % of sales)	3-year historical average
Selling, general, and administrative expense (as % of sales)	3-year historical average
Depreciation and amortization	2% of 1997 property, plant, and equipment
Interest expense	zero
Tax rate	34%
Shares outstanding	no change

Construct a 1998 projected income statement for OuickBrush using the percent-of-sales forecasting method based on 1997 data in Table 12 and the assumptions in Exhibit 2 above. [6 minutes]

21. *CFA Examination II (1998)*
Janet Ludlow's firm requires all its analysts to use a two-stage dividend discount model (DDM) and the Capital Asset Pricing Model (CAPM) to value stocks. Using the CAPM and DDM, Ludlow has valued QuickBrush Company at $63 per share. She now must value SmileWhite Corporation.

TABLE 14 VALUATION INFORMATION: DECEMBER 1997

	QuickBrush	SmileWhite
Beta	1.35	1.15
Market price	$45.00	$30.00
Intrinsic value	$63.00	?

Notes:

Risk-free rate	4.50%
Expected market return	14.50%

a. Calculate the required rate of return for SmileWhite using the information in Table 14 and the CAPM. Show your work. [6 minutes]
Ludlow estimates the following EPS and dividend growth rates for SmileWhite:

First 3 years:	12 percent per year
Years thereafter:	9 percent per year

b. Estimate the intrinsic value of SmileWhite using the data from Table 13 and Table 14 above, and the two-stage DDM. Show your work. [12 minutes]
c. Recommend QuickBrush or SmileWhite stock for purchase by comparing each company's intrinsic value with its current market price. Show your work. [6 minutes]
d. Describe *one* strength of the two-stage DDM in comparison with the constant growth DDM. Describe *one* weakness inherent in all DDMs. [6 minutes]

CFA

22. *CFA Examination II (1998)*
The information in Exhibit 3 comes from the 1997 financial statements of QuickBrush Company and SmileWhite Corporation:

EXHIBIT 3 NOTES TO THE 1997 FINANCIAL STATEMENTS

	QuickBrush	SmileWhite
Goodwill	The company amortizes goodwill over 20 years.	The company amortizes goodwill over 5 years.
Property, plant, and equipment	The company uses a straight-line depreciation method over the economic lives of the assets, which range from 5 to 20 years for buildings.	The company uses an accelerated depreciation method over the economic lives of the assets, which range from 5 to 20 years for buildings.
Accounts receivable	The company uses a bad debt allowance of 2 percent of accounts receivable.	The company uses a bad debt allowance of 5 percent of accounts receivable.

Determine which company has the higher quality of earnings by discussing *each* of the *three* notes. [9 minutes]

CFA

23. *CFA Examination II (1998)*
An analyst expects a risk-free return of 4.5 percent, a market return of 14.5 percent, and the returns for Stocks A and B that are shown in Table 15.

TABLE 15 STOCK INFORMATION

Stock	Beta	Analyst's Estimated Return
A	1.2	16%
B	0.8	14%

a. Show on a graph:
   (i) where Stocks A and B would plot on the Security Market Line (SML) if they were fairly valued using the Capital Asset Pricing Model (CAPM).
   (ii) where Stocks A and B actually plot on the same graph according to the returns estimated by the analyst and shown in Table 15. [6 minutes]
b. State whether Stock A and Stock B are undervalued or overvalued if the analyst uses the SML for strategic investment decisions. [4 minutes]

CFA

24. *CFA Examination II (1999)*
Scott Kelly is reviewing MasterToy's financial statements in order to estimate its sustainable growth rate. Using the information presented in the following exhibit
a. (i) Identify and calculate the *three* components of the DuPont formula.
   (ii) Calculate the ROE for 1999 using the three components of the DuPont formula.
   (iii) Calculate the sustainable growth rate for 1999. [13 minutes]

Kelly has calculated actual and sustainable growth for each of the past four years and finds in each year that its calculated sustainable growth rate substantially exceeds its actual growth rate.
b. Cite *two* courses of action (other than ignoring the problem) Kelly should encourage MasterToy to take, assuming the calculated sustainable growth rate continues to exceed the actual growth rate. [6 minutes]

MASTERTOY, INC.: ACTUAL 1998 AND ESTIMATED 1999 FINANCIAL STATEMENTS FOR FISCAL YEAR ENDING DECEMBER 31 ($ MILLIONS, EXCEPT PER-SHARE DATA)

	1998	1999e	Change (%)
Income Statement			
Revenue	$4,750	$5,140	7.6
Cost of goods sold	$2,400	$2,540	
Selling, general, and administrative	1,400	1,550	
Depreciation	180	210	
Goodwill amortization	10	10	
Operating income	$ 760	$ 830	8.4
Interest expense	20	25	
Income before taxes	$ 740	$ 805	
Income taxes	265	295	
Net income	$ 475	$ 510	
Earnings per share	$1.79	$1.96	8.6
Average shares outstanding (millions)	265	260	
Balance Sheet			
Cash	$ 400	$ 400	
Accounts receivable	$ 680	$ 700	
Inventories	$ 570	$ 600	
Net property, plant, and equipment	$ 800	$ 870	
Intangibles	$ 500	$ 530	
Total assets	$2,950	$3,100	
Current liabilities	$ 550	$ 600	
Long-term debt	$ 300	$ 300	
Total liabilities	$ 850	$ 900	
Stockholders' equity	$2,100	$2,200	
Total liabilities and equity	$2,950	$3,100	
Book value per share	$7.92	$8.46	
Annual dividend per share	$0.55	$0.60	

References

Bhatia, Sanjiv, ed. *Global Equity Investing.* Charlottesville, Va.: Association of Investment Management and Research, 1995.

Born, Jeffery, James Moses, and Dennis Officer. "Changes in Dividend Policy and Subsequent Earnings." *Journal of Portfolio Management* 14, no. 4 (summer 1988).

Copeland, Tom, Tim Koller, and Jack Murrin. *Valuation: Measuring and Managing the Value of Companies.* New York: Wiley, 1996.

Cottle, Sidney, Roger F. Murray, and Frank E. Block. *Graham and Dodd's Security Analysis.* 5th ed. New York: McGraw-Hill, 1988.

Damodaran, Aswath. *Damodaran on Valuation.* New York: Wiley, 1994.

Hackel, Kenneth S., and Joshua Livnat. *Cash Flow and Security Analysis.* 2d ed. Burr Ridge, Ill.: Irwin Professional Publishing, 1996.

Hassel, J., and Robert Jennings. "Relative Forecast Accuracy and the Timing of Earnings Forecast Announcements." *The Accounting Review* 61, no. 1 (January 1986).

Imhoff, Eugene, and G. Lobo. "Information Content of Analysts' Composite Forecast Revisions." *Journal of Accounting Research* 22, no. 3 (autumn 1984).

Jaffe, Jeffery, Donald Keim, and Randolph Westerfield. "Earnings Yields, Market Values, Stock Returns." *Journal of Finance* 44, no. 1 (March 1989).

Jennings, Robert. *Reaction of Financial Analysts to Corporate Management Earnings per Share Forecasts.* New York: Financial Analysts Research Foundation, Monograph No. 20, 1984.

Johnson, R. S., Lyle Fiore, and Richard Zuber. "The Investment Performance of Common Stocks in Relation to Their Price-Earnings Ratios: An Update of the Basu Study." *Financial Review* 24, no. 3 (August 1989).

Levine, Sumner N., ed. *The Financial Analysts Handbook.* 2d ed. Homewood, Ill.: Dow Jones-Irwin, 1988.

Palepu, Krishna, Victor Bernard, and Paul Healy. *Business Analysis and Valuation.* Cincinnati, Ohio: Southwestern Publishing, 1996.

Porter, Michael E. *Competitive Advantage: Creating and Sustaining Superior Performance.* New York: The Free Press, 1985.

Squires, Jan R., ed. *Equity Research and Valuation Techniques.* Charlottesville, Va.: Association for Investment Management and Research, 1997.

Squires, Jan R., ed. *Value and Growth Styles in Equity Investing.* Charlottesville, Va.: Association for Investment Management and Research, 1995.

Waymire, G. "Additional Evidence on the Information Content of Management Earnings Forecasts." *Journal of Accounting Research* 22, no. 3 (autumn 1984).

Chapter

21 TECHNICAL ANALYSIS*

After you read this chapter, you should be able to answer the following questions:

- How does technical analysis differ from fundamental analysis?
- What are the underlying assumptions of technical analysis?
- What major assumption causes a difference between technical analysis and the efficient market hypothesis?
- What are the major advantages of technical analysis compared to fundamental analysis?
- What are the major challenges to the assumptions of technical analysis and its rules?
- What is the logic for the major contrary opinion rules used by technicians?
- What are some of the significant rules used by technicians who want to follow the smart money and what is the logic of those rules?
- What is the breadth of market measures and what are they intended to indicate?
- What are the three types of price movements postulated in the Dow Theory and how are they used by a technician?
- Why do technicians consider the volume of trading important and how do they use it in their analysis?
- What are support and resistance levels, how are they identified, and how are they used by technicians?
- What is the purpose of moving average lines and how does the technician use one or several of them to detect major changes in trends?
- What is the rationale behind the relative strength line for an industry or a stock and how is it interpreted?
- How are bar charts different from point-and-figure charts?
- What are some uses of technical analysis in foreign security markets?
- How is technical analysis used when analyzing bond markets?

> The market reacted yesterday to the report of a large increase in the short interest on the NYSE.
>
> Although the market declined today, it was not considered bearish because of the light volume.
>
> The market declined today after three days of increases due to profit taking by investors.

These and similar statements appear daily in the financial news. All of them have as their rationale one of numerous technical trading rules. Technical analysts develop technical trading rules from observations of past price movements of the stock market and individual stocks. The philosophy behind technical analysis is in sharp contrast to the efficient market hypothesis that we studied, which contends that past performance has no influence on future performance or market values. It also differs from what we learned about fundamental analysis, which involves making investment decisions based on the

*Richard T. McCabe, Chief Market Analyst at Merrill Lynch Capital Markets, provided very helpful comments and material for this chapter.

examination of the economy, an industry, and company variables that lead to an estimate of value for an investment, which is then compared to the prevailing market price of the investment. In contrast to the efficient market hypothesis or fundamental analysis, **technical analysis** involves the examination of past market data, such as prices and the volume of trading, which leads to an estimate of future price trends and, therefore, an investment decision. Whereas fundamental analysts use economic data that are usually separate from the stock or bond market, the technical analyst believes that using data *from the market itself* is a good idea because "the market is its own best predictor." Therefore, technical analysis is an alternative method of making the investment decision and answering the questions: What securities should an investor buy or sell? And when should these investments be made?

Technical analysts see no need to study the multitude of economic, industry, and company variables to arrive at an estimate of future value because they believe that past price movements will signal future price movements. Technicians also believe that a change in the price trend may predict a forthcoming change in the fundamental variables, such as earnings and risk, earlier than the change is perceived or anticipated by most fundamental analysts. Are technicians correct? Many investors using these techniques claim to have experienced superior rates of return on many investments. In addition, many newsletter writers base their recommendations on technical analysis. Finally, even the major investment firms that employ many fundamental analysts also employ technical analysts to provide investment advice. Numerous investment professionals as well as individual investors believe in and use technical trading rules to make their investment decisions. Therefore, whether you are a fan of technical analysis or an advocate of the efficient market hypothesis, you should still have an understanding of the basic philosophy and reasoning behind these technical approaches. To help you understand technical analysis, we begin this chapter with an examination of the basic philosophy underlying all technical approaches to market analysis and company analysis. Subsequently, we consider the advantages and potential problems with the technical approach. The majority of the chapter involves the presentation and discussion of alternative technical trading rules applicable to both the U.S. market and foreign securities markets. We conclude the chapter with a discussion of examples where technical analysis is applied to foreign security markets and bond markets to demonstrate the diversity of this approach.

UNDERLYING ASSUMPTIONS OF TECHNICAL ANALYSIS

Technical analysts base trading decisions on examinations of prior price and volume data to determine past market trends from which they predict future behavior for the market as a whole and for individual securities. Several assumptions lead to this view of price movements.

1. The market value of any good or service is determined solely by the interaction of supply and demand.
2. Supply and demand are governed by numerous factors, both rational and irrational. Included in these factors are those economic variables relied on by the fundamental analyst as well as opinions, moods, and guesses. The market weighs all these factors continually and automatically.
3. Disregarding minor fluctuations, *the prices for individual securities and the overall value of the market tend to move in trends, which persist for appreciable lengths of time.*

4. Prevailing trends change in reaction to shifts in supply and demand relationships. These shifts, no matter why they occur, can be detected sooner or later in the action of the market itself.[1]

Certain aspects of these assumptions are controversial, leading fundamental analysts and advocates of efficient markets to question their validity. Those aspects are emphasized above.

The first two assumptions are almost universally accepted by technicians and nontechnicians alike. Almost anyone who has had a basic course in economics would agree that, at any point in time, the price of a security (or any good or service) is determined by the interaction of supply and demand. In addition, most observers would acknowledge that supply and demand are governed by many variables. The only difference in opinion might concern the influence of the irrational factors. A technical analyst might expect the irrational influence to persist for some time, whereas other market analysts would expect only a short-run effect with rational beliefs prevailing over the long run. Certainly, everyone would agree that the market continually weighs all these factors.

A stronger difference of opinion arises over the technical analysts' third assumption about the *speed of adjustment* of stock prices to changes in supply and demand. Technical analysts expect stock prices to move in trends that persist for long periods because they believe that new information that affects supply and demand does not come to the market at one point in time, but rather enters the market *over a period of time.* This pattern of information access occurs because of different sources of information or because certain investors receive the information or perceive fundamental changes earlier than others. As various groups ranging from insiders to well-informed professionals to the average investor receive the information and buy or sell a security accordingly, its price moves gradually toward the new equilibrium. Therefore, technicians do not expect the price adjustment to be as abrupt as fundamental analysts and efficient market supporters do, but they expect a *gradual price adjustment* to reflect the gradual flow of information.

Figure 21.1 shows this process. The figure shows that new information causes a decrease in the equilibrium price for a security, but the price adjustment is not rapid. It occurs as a trend that persists until the stock reaches its new equilibrium. Technical analysts look for the beginning of a movement from one equilibrium value to a new equilibrium value. Technical analysts do not attempt to predict the new equilibrium value. They look for the start of a change so that they can get on the bandwagon early and benefit from the move to the new equilibrium by buying if the trend is up or selling if the trend is down. Obviously, rapid adjustment of prices as expected by those who espouse an efficient market would keep the ride on the bandwagon so short that investors could not get onboard and benefit from the ride.

ADVANTAGES OF TECHNICAL ANALYSIS

Although technicians understand the logic of fundamental analysis, technical analysts see benefits in their approach compared to fundamental analysis. Most technical analysts admit that a fundamental analyst with good information, good analytical ability, and a keen sense of the impact of information on the market should achieve above-average returns.

[1]These assumptions are summarized in Robert A. Levy, "Conceptual Foundations of Technical Analysis," *Financial Analysts Journal* 22, no. 4 (July–August 1966): 83.

FIGURE 21.1

TECHNICIANS' VIEW OF PRICE ADJUSTMENT TO NEW INFORMATION

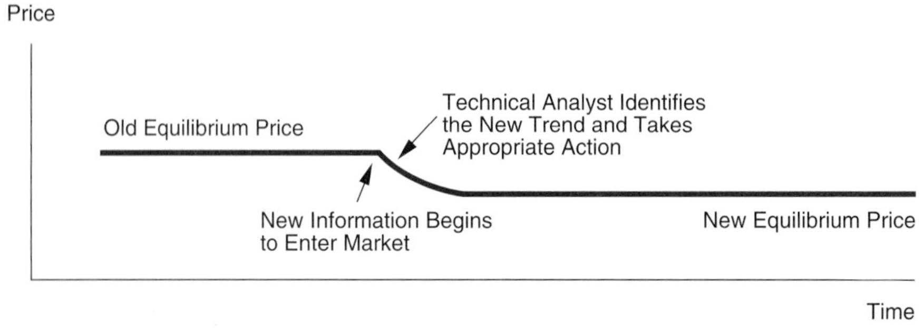
Price
Technical Analyst Identifies the New Trend and Takes Appropriate Action
Old Equilibrium Price
New Information Begins to Enter Market
New Equilibrium Price
Time

However, this statement requires qualification. According to technical analysts, it is important to recognize that the fundamental analysts can experience superior returns *only* if they obtain new information before other investors and process it *correctly* and *quickly.* Technical analysts do not believe that the vast majority of investors can consistently get new information before other investors and consistently process it correctly and quickly.

In addition, technical analysts claim that a major advantage of their method is that *it is not heavily dependent on financial accounting statements*—the major source of information about the past performance of a firm or industry. As you know from Chapters 18–20, the fundamental analyst evaluates such statements to help project future return and risk characteristics for industries and individual securities. The technician points out several major problems with accounting statements:

1. They lack a great deal of information that security analysts need, such as details on sales and general expenses or information related to sales, earnings, and capital used by product line.
2. According to GAAP (Generally Accepted Accounting Principles), corporations may choose among several procedures for reporting expenses, assets, or liabilities, and these alternative procedures can produce vastly different values for expenses, income, return on assets, and return on equity. As a result, an investor can have trouble comparing the statements of two firms in the same industry, much less firms in different industries.
3. Many psychological factors and other nonquantifiable variables do not appear in financial statements. Examples include employee training and loyalty, customer goodwill, and general investor attitude toward an industry. Investor attitudes could become important when investors become concerned about the risk from restrictions or taxes on such products as tobacco or alcohol or when firms do business in countries that have significant political risk.

Therefore, because technicians are suspicious of financial statements, they consider it advantageous not to depend on them. As we will show, most of the data used by technicians, such as security prices, volume of trading, and other trading information, are derived from the stock market itself.

Also, a fundamental analyst must process new information correctly and *quickly* to derive a new intrinsic value for the stock or bond before the other investors can. Technicians, on the other hand, need only quickly recognize a movement to a new equilibrium value *for whatever reason*—that is, they need not know about an event and determine the effect of the event on the value of the firm and its stock.

Finally, assume a fundamental analyst determines that a given security is under- or overvalued a long time before other investors. He or she still must determine when to make the purchase or sale. Ideally, the highest rate of return would come from making the transaction just before the change in market value occurs. For example, assume that based on your analysis in February, you expect a firm to report substantially higher earnings in June. Although you could buy the stock in February, you would be better off waiting until about May to buy the stock so your funds would not be tied up for an extra 3 months, but you may be reluctant to wait that long. Because most technicians do not invest until the move to the new equilibrium is under way, they contend that they are more likely to experience ideal timing compared to the fundamental analyst.

CHALLENGES TO TECHNICAL ANALYSIS

Those who question the value of technical analysis for investment decisions question the usefulness of this technique in two areas. First, they challenge some of its basic assumptions. Second, they challenge some of its specific trading rules and their long-run usefulness. In this section, we consider both of these challenges.

Challenges to Technical Analysis Assumptions

The major challenge to technical analysis is based on the results of empirical tests of the efficient market hypothesis (EMH). As discussed in Chapter 7, for technical trading rules to generate superior risk-adjusted returns after taking account of transactions costs, the market would have to be slow to adjust prices to the arrival of new information—that is, it would have to be inefficient. (This is referred to as the weak-form efficient market hypothesis.) The two sets of tests of the weak-form EMH are: (1) the statistical analysis of prices to determine if prices moved in trends or were a random walk, and (2) the analysis of specific trading rules to determine if their use could beat a buy-and-hold policy after considering transactions costs and risk. Almost all the studies testing the weak-form efficient market hypothesis using statistical analysis have found that prices do not move in trends based on statistical tests of autocorrelation and runs. These results support the efficient market hypothesis.

Regarding the analysis of specific trading rules, as discussed in Chapter 7, numerous technical trading rules exist that have not been or cannot be tested. Still, the vast majority of the results for the trading rules tested support the hypothesis.

Challenges to Technical Trading Rules

An obvious challenge to technical analysis is that the past price patterns or relationships between specific market variables and stock prices may not be repeated. As a result, a technique that previously worked might miss subsequent market turns. This possibility leads most technicians to follow several trading rules and to seek a consensus of all of them to predict the future market pattern.

Other critics contend that many price patterns become self-fulfilling prophecies. For example, assume that many analysts expect a stock selling at $40 a share to go to $50 or more if it should rise above its current pattern and "break through" its channel at $45. As soon as it reaches $45, enough technicians will buy to cause the price to rise to $50, exactly as predicted. In fact, some technicians may place a limit order to buy the stock at such a breakout point. Under such conditions, the increase, if it is not supported by strong fundamentals, will probably be only temporary and the price will return to its true equilibrium.

Another problem with technical analysis is that the success of a particular trading rule will encourage many investors to adopt it. It is contended that this popularity and the resulting competition will eventually neutralize the value of the technique. If numerous investors focus on a specific technical trading rule, some of them will attempt to anticipate what will happen prior to the completed price pattern and either ruin the expected historical price pattern or eliminate profits for most users of the trading rule by causing the price to change faster than expected. For example, suppose it becomes known that technicians who invest on the basis of the amount of short selling have been enjoying high rates of return. Based on this knowledge, other technicians will likely start using these data and thus accelerate the stock price pattern following changes in the amount of short selling. As a result, the trading rule that provided high rates of return previously may no longer be profitable after the first few investors react.

Further, as we will see when we examine specific trading rules, *they all require a great deal of subjective judgment.* Two technical analysts looking at the same price pattern may arrive at widely different interpretations of what has happened and, therefore, will come to different investment decisions. This implies that the use of various techniques is neither completely mechanical nor obvious. Finally, as we will discuss in connection with several trading rules, *the standard values that signal investment decisions can change over time.* Therefore, technical analysts must adjust the specified values that trigger investment decisions over time to conform to the new environment. In other cases, trading rules are abandoned because it appears they no longer work.

TECHNICAL TRADING RULES AND INDICATORS

To help you understand the specific technical trading rules, Figure 21.2 shows a typical stock price cycle that could be an example for the overall stock market or for an individual stock. The graph shows a peak and trough, along with a rising trend channel, a flat trend channel, a declining trend channel, and indications of when a technical analyst would ideally want to trade.

The graph begins with the end of a declining (bear) market that finishes in a **trough** followed by an upward trend that breaks through the **declining trend channel**. Confirmation that the trend has reversed would be a buy signal. The technical analyst would buy stocks in general or an individual stock that showed this pattern.

The analyst would then look for the development of a **rising trend channel**. As long as the stock price stayed in this rising channel, the technician would hold the stock(s) for the upward ride. Ideally, you want to sell at the **peak** of the cycle, but you cannot identify a peak until after the trend changes.

If the stock (or the market) begins trading in a flat pattern, it will necessarily break out of its rising trend channel. At this point, some technical analysts would sell, but most would hold to see if the stock experiences a period of consolidation and then breaks out of the **flat trend channel** on the upside and begins rising again. Alternatively, if the stock were to break out of the channel on the downside, the technician would take this as a sell signal and would expect a declining trend channel. The next buy signal would come after the trough when the price breaks out of the declining channel and establishes a rising trend. Subsequently, we will consider strategies to detect these changes in trend and the importance of volume in this analysis.

There are numerous technical trading rules and a range of interpretations for each of them. Almost all technical analysts watch many alternative rules and decide on a buy or sell decision based on a *consensus* of the signals because complete agreement of all the rules is rare. This section discusses most of the well-known techniques. The presentation on domestic indicators is divided into four sections based on the attitudes of technical analysts. The first group includes trading rules used by analysts who like to trade against the crowd

FIGURE 21.2 **TYPICAL STOCK MARKET CYCLE**

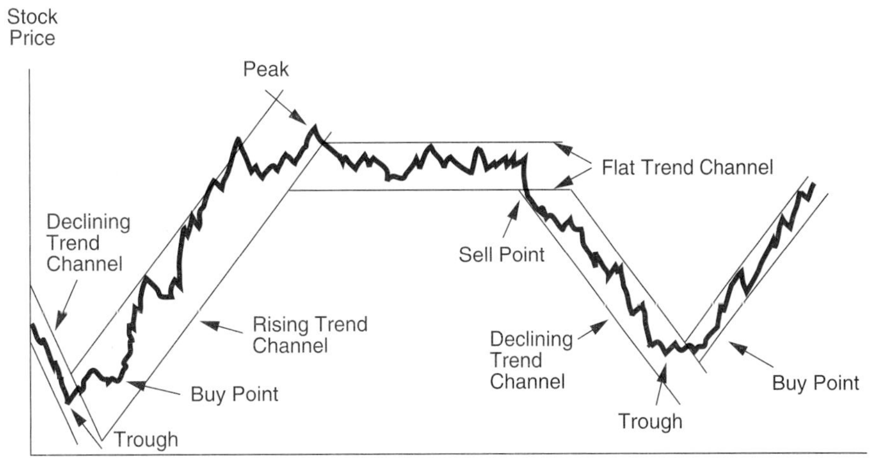
Stock
Price
Peak
Flat Trend Channel
Declining
Trend
Channel
Sell Point
Rising Trend
Channel
Declining
Trend
Channel
Buy Point
Buy Point
Trough
Trough

using contrary-opinion signals. The second group of rules attempts to emulate astute investors, that is, the smart money. The next section includes technical indicators that are very popular but not easily classified. The fourth section covers pure price and volume techniques, including the famous Dow Theory. The final sections describe how these technical trading rules have been applied to foreign securities markets and bond markets.

CONTRARY-OPINION RULES

Many technical analysts rely on technical trading rules developed from the premise that the majority of investors are wrong as the market approaches peaks and troughs. Therefore, these technicians try to determine when the majority of investors is either strongly bullish or bearish and then trade in the opposite direction.[2]

MUTUAL FUND CASH POSITIONS Mutual funds hold some part of their portfolio in cash for one of several reasons. The most obvious reason is that they need cash to liquidate shares that fundholders sell back to the fund. Another reason is that the money from new investments in the mutual fund may not have been invested. A third reason might be the portfolio manager's bearish outlook for the market, inspiring an asset allocation decision to increase the fund's defensive cash position.

Mutual funds' ratios of cash as a percentage of the total assets in their portfolios (the *cash ratio* or *liquid asset ratio*) are reported in the press, including monthly figures in *Barron's*.[3] This percentage of cash has varied in recent years from a low point of about 5 percent to a high point near 13 percent, although the range has increased during the past several years and there appears to be a declining trend to the series.

Contrary-opinion technicians consider the mutual funds a good proxy for the institutional investor. They also believe that mutual funds usually are wrong at peaks and troughs.

[2]Prior editions of this book included the percentage of odd-lot purchases and sales or odd-lot short sales as a percentage of total odd-lot sales as contrary-opinion rules. These are no longer included because odd-lot volume now accounts for a small proportion of total trading volume and is no longer considered a valid indication of small-investor sentiment.

[3]*Barron's* is a prime source for numerous technical indicators. For a readable discussion of relevant data and their use, see Martin E. Zweig, *Understanding Technical Forecasting* (New York: Dow Jones & Co., 1987).

FIGURE 21.3 TIME-SERIES PLOT OF DOW JONES INDUSTRIAL AVERAGE AND MUTUAL FUND CASH-TO-ASSET RATIO (CASH/TOTAL ASSETS)

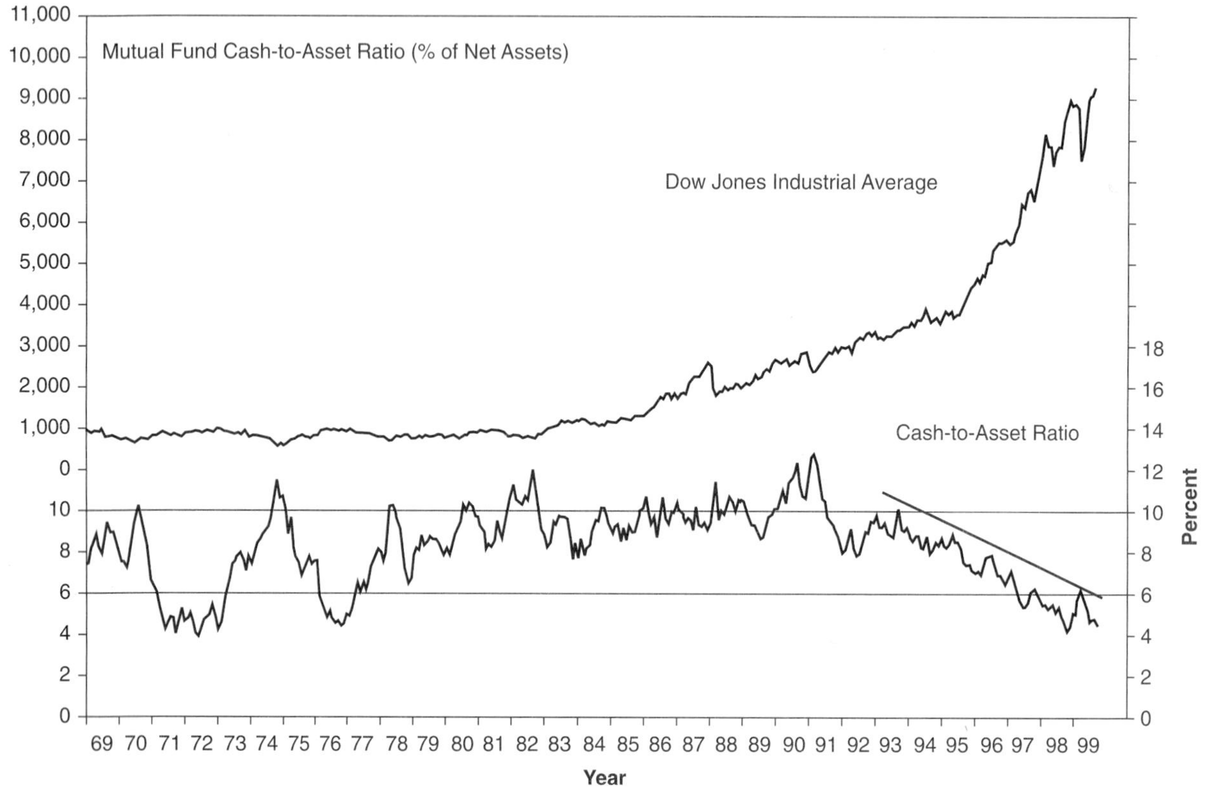
11,000
10,000
9,000
8,000
7,000
6,000
5,000
4,000
3,000
2,000
1,000
0
10
8
6
4
2
0
Mutual Fund Cash-to-Asset Ratio (% of Net Assets)
Dow Jones Industrial Average
Cash-to-Asset Ratio
18
16
14
12
10
8
6
4
2
0
Percent
69 70 71 72 73 74 75 76 77 78 79 80 81 82 83 84 85 86 87 88 89 90 91 92 93 94 95 96 97 98 99
Year

Source: *Where the Indicators Stand* (New York: Merrill Lynch, May 1999) Reprinted by permission of Merrill Lynch. Source of Data: Investment Company Institute.

Thus, they expect mutual funds to have a high percentage of cash near the trough of a market cycle, implying that they are bearish exactly at the time that they should be fully invested to take advantage of the impending market rise. At the market peak, technicians expect mutual funds to be almost fully invested with a low percentage of cash. This would indicate a bullish outlook by the mutual funds when they should be selling stocks and realizing gains for some part of their portfolios. Therefore, contrary-opinion technicians would watch for the mutual fund cash position to approach one of the extremes and would act contrary to the mutual funds. Specifically, they would tend to buy when the cash ratio approaches 13 percent and to sell when the cash ratio approaches 5 percent.

Figure 21.3 contains a time-series plot of the Dow Jones Industrial Average (DJIA) and the mutual fund cash ratio. It shows apparent bullish signals in 1970, in late 1974, in 1982, and in late 1990 near market troughs. Bearish signals appeared in 1971, 1972 to 1973, and 1976 prior to market peaks. The cash ratio has been falling since the summer of 1993 and as of May 1999 was the lowest it had been since 1976.

A high mutual fund cash position also can be considered as a bullish indicator because of potential buying power. Whether the cash balances have built up because of stock sales completed as part of a selling program or because investors have been buying mutual funds (as during the period 1996–1998), technicians believe these cash funds will eventually be invested and will cause stock prices to increase. This "liquidity" concept was widely discussed as a major cause of the market rise in 1997 and 1998. Alternatively, a low cash ratio would mean that the institutions have bought heavily and are left with little potential buying power. Obviously, the low cash position in May 1999 would not be a positive market factor.

A couple of studies have examined this mutual fund cash ratio and its components as a predictor of market cycles. They concluded that the mutual fund liquid asset ratio was not as strong a predictor of market cycles as suggested by technical analysts.[4]

CREDIT BALANCES IN BROKERAGE ACCOUNTS Credit balances result when investors sell stocks and leave the proceeds with their brokers, expecting to reinvest them shortly. The amounts are reported by the SEC and the NYSE in *Barron's*. Because technical analysts view these credit balances as pools of potential purchasing power, they interpret a decline in these balances as bearish because it indicates lower purchasing power as the market approaches a peak. Alternatively, technicians view a buildup of credit balances as an increase in buying power and a bullish signal.

Note that the data used to interpret the market environment are stated in terms of an increase or decline in the credit balance series rather than comparing these balances to some other series. This assumption of an absolute trend could make interpretation difficult as market levels change.

INVESTMENT ADVISORY OPINIONS Many technicians believe that if a large proportion of investment advisory services have a bearish attitude, this signals the approach of a market trough and the onset of a bull market. It is reasoned that because most advisory services tend to be trend followers, the number of bears usually is greatest when market bottoms are approaching. They develop this trading rule from the ratio of the number of advisory services that are bearish as a percentage of the number of services expressing an opinion.[5] A "bearish sentiment index" of 60 percent indicates a pervasive bearish attitude by advisory services, and contrarians would consider this a bullish indicator. In contrast, a decline of this bearish sentiment index to below 20 percent indicates a pervasive bullish attitude by advisory services, which technicians would interpret as a bearish sign. Figure 21.4 shows a time-series plot of the DJIA and both the bearish sentiment index and the bullish sentiment index. As of January 1999, the percentage of bullish services moved up to 60 percent, which is a sell signal, but has backed off recently. As of May 1999, both indexes still carry a negative rating.

OTC VERSUS NYSE VOLUME The ratio of OTC volume on the NASDAQ system to NYSE volume is considered by technicians as a measure of speculative trading. Speculative trading typically peaks at market peaks. Figure 21.5 contains a time-series plot of the NASDAQ Composite Average and the OTC/NYSE volume ratio.

Notably, the interpretation of the ratio has changed—that is, the decision rules have changed. Specifically, in 1990, the decision rules were 90 percent (this indicated heavy speculative trading) and 70 percent (this indicated low speculative trading and an oversold market). The decision rules were changed to 100 percent and 80 percent in 1994 and to 112

---

[4]Paul H. Massey, "The Mutual Fund Liquidity Ratio: A Trap for the Unwary," *Journal of Portfolio Management* 5, no. 2 (winter 1979): 18–21; and R. David Ranson and William G. Shipman, "Institutional Buying Power and the Stock Market," *Financial Analysts Journal* 37, no. 5 (September–October 1981): 62–68.

[5]This ratio is compiled by Investors Intelligence, Larchmont, NY 10538. Richard McCabe at Merrill Lynch uses this series as one of his "Investor Sentiment Indicators."

FIGURE 21.4 **TIME-SERIES PLOT OF DOW JONES INDUSTRIAL AVERAGE AND THE BULLISH AND BEARISH SENTIMENT INDEXES**

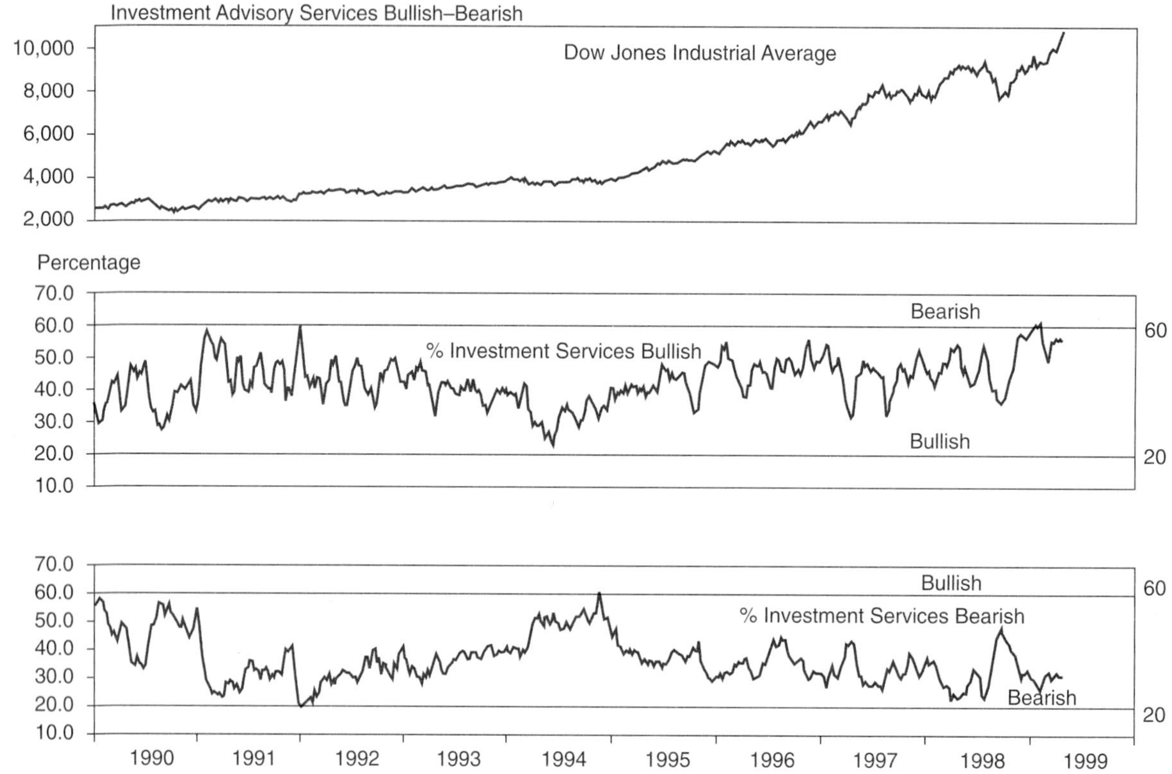
Investment Advisory Services Bullish–Bearish
10,000
8,000
6,000
4,000
2,000
Dow Jones Industrial Average
Percentage
70.0
60.0
50.0
40.0
30.0
20.0
10.0
Bearish
% Investment Services Bullish
Bullish
60
20
70.0
60.0
50.0
40.0
30.0
20.0
10.0
Bullish
% Investment Services Bearish
Bearish
60
20
1990
1991
1992
1993
1994
1995
1996
1997
1998
1999

Source: *Where the Indicators Stand* (New York: Merrill Lynch, May 1999). Source of data: Investor Intelligence, Larchmont NY 10538.

percent and 87 percent in 1996. The source of this rising drift in the decision rules was faster growth in the number of stocks listed on the OTC, rapid growth in OTC trading volume over the year, and dominance of the OTC market by a few large-cap stocks. In 1998, it was decided to stop using the percent values and detect excess speculative activity by using the *direction* of the volume ratio as a guide. As shown in Figure 21.5, as of mid-1999, the ratio was in the middle of the rising channel, which implies no excesses.

THE CHICAGO BOARD OPTIONS EXCHANGE (CBOE) PUT/CALL RATIO The CBOE equity (only) put/call ratio is a relatively new tool of contrary-opinion technicians. They use put options, which give the holder the right to sell stock at a specified price for a given time period, as signals of a bearish attitude. The technicians reason that a higher put/call ratio indicates a more pervasive bearish attitude, which they consider a bullish indicator.

As shown in Figure 21.6, this ratio fluctuates between 0.50 and 0.30. It typically has been substantially less than 1 because investors tend to be bullish and avoid selling short or buying puts. The current decision rule states that a put/call ratio above 0.50—fifty puts are traded for every one hundred calls—is considered bullish, while a relatively low put/call ratio of 0.35 or less is considered a bearish sign. The value of the ratio in mid-1999 was rated negative because it was approaching 0.35.

FIGURE 21.5 **TIME-SERIES PLOT OF NASDAQ COMPOSITE AVERAGE AND THE RATIO OF OTC VOLUME TO NYSE VOLUME (3-WEEK AVERAGE)**

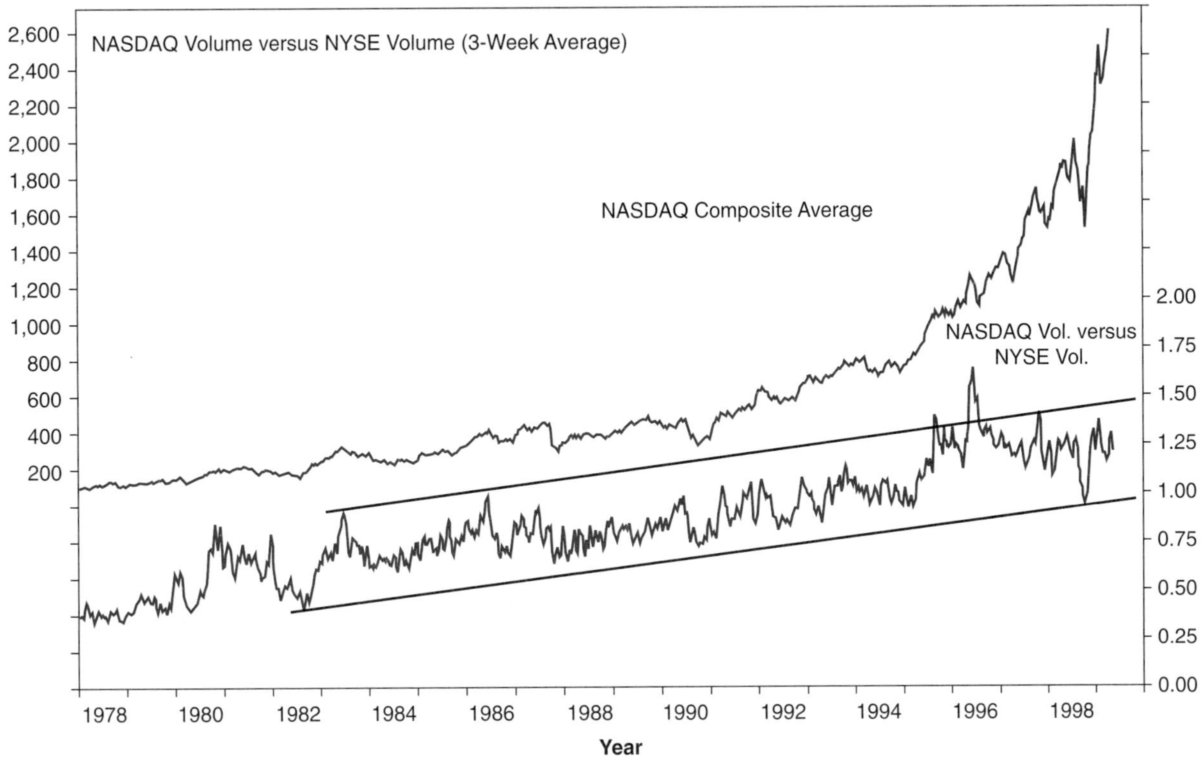
NASDAQ Volume versus NYSE Volume (3-Week Average)
NASDAQ Composite Average
NASDAQ Vol. versus NYSE Vol.
2,600
2,400
2,200
2,000
1,800
1,600
1,400
1,200
1,000
800
600
400
200
2.00
1.75
1.50
1.25
1.00
0.75
0.50
0.25
0.00
1978
1980
1982
1984
1986
1988
1990
1992
1994
1996
1998
Year

Source: *Where the Indicators Stand* (New York: Merrill Lynch, May 1999). Reprinted by permission of Merrill Lynch.

FUTURES TRADERS BULLISH ON STOCK INDEX FUTURES Another relatively new measure used by contrary-opinion technicians is the percentage of speculators in stock index futures who are bullish. Specifically, an advisory service (Market Vane) surveys other firms that provide advisory services for the futures market along with individual traders involved in the futures market to determine whether these futures traders are bearish or bullish regarding stocks. A plot of the series in Figure 21.7 indicates that these technicians would consider it a bearish sign when more than 75 percent of the speculators are bullish, and it is bullish if the portion of bullish speculators declines to 25 percent or lower. As of mid-1999, the series was within the specified boundaries indicating a neutral environment.

As you can see, technicians who seek to be contrary to the market have several series that provide measures of how the majority of investors are investing. They then take the opposite action. They generally would follow several of these series to provide a consensus regarding investors' attitudes.

Follow the Smart Money

Some technical analysts have created a set of indicators that they expect to indicate the behavior of smart, sophisticated investors and create rules to follow them. In this section, we discuss some of the more popular indicators of what smart investors are doing.

THE CONFIDENCE INDEX Published by *Barron's,* the Confidence Index is the ratio of *Barron's* average yield on 10 top-grade corporate bonds to the yield on the Dow

FIGURE 21.6 **TIME-SERIES PLOT OF DOW JONES INDUSTRIAL AVERAGE AND THE CBOE EQUITY (ONLY) PUT/CALL RATIO (5-DAY AVERAGE)**

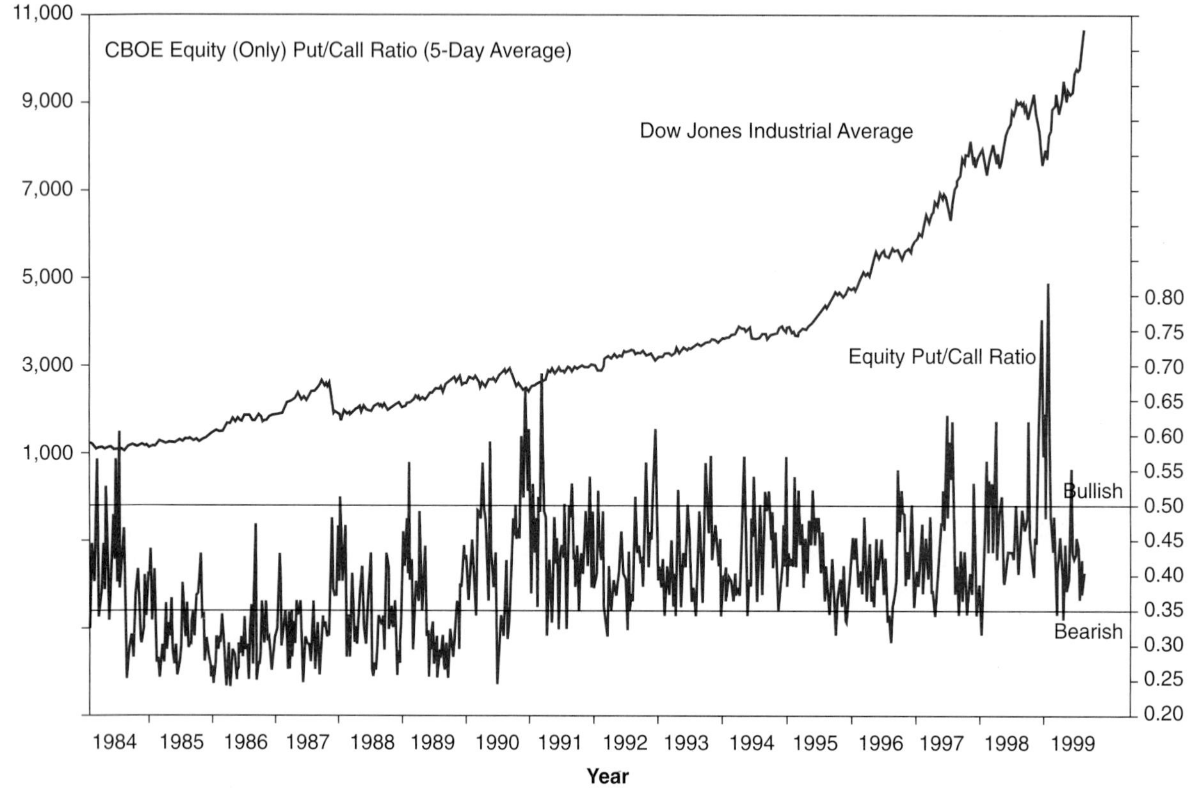
11,000
9,000
7,000
5,000
3,000
1,000
CBOE Equity (Only) Put/Call Ratio (5-Day Average)
Dow Jones Industrial Average
Equity Put/Call Ratio
Bullish
Bearish
0.80
0.75
0.70
0.65
0.60
0.55
0.50
0.45
0.40
0.35
0.30
0.25
0.20
1984 1985 1986 1987 1988 1989 1990 1991 1992 1993 1994 1995 1996 1997 1998 1999
Year

Source: *Where the Indicators Stand* (New York: Merrill Lynch, May 1999). Reprinted with permission from Merrill Lynch.

Jones average of 40 bonds. This index measures the difference in yield spread between high-grade bonds and a large cross section of bonds.[6] Because the yields on high-grade bonds always should be lower than those on a large cross section of bonds, this ratio should never exceed 100. It approaches 100 as the spread between the two sets of bonds gets smaller.

Technicians believe the ratio is a bullish indicator because, during periods of high confidence, investors are willing to invest more in lower-quality bonds for the added yield. This investment attitude should cause a decrease in the average yield for the large cross section of bonds relative to the yield on high-grade bonds. Therefore, this ratio of yields, which is the Confidence Index, will increase. In contrast, when investors are pessimistic, they avoid investing in low-quality bonds and increase their investments in high-grade bonds. This shift in investment preference increases the yield spread between high-grade and average bonds, which causes the Confidence Index to decline.

[6]Historical data for this series are contained in the *Dow Jones Investor's Handbook* (Princeton, N.J.: Dow Jones Books, annual). Current figures appear in *Barron's*.

FIGURE 21.7 **TIME-SERIES PLOT OF DOW JONES INDUSTRIAL AVERAGE AND PERCENTAGE OF FUTURES TRADERS BULLISH ON STOCK INDEX FUTURES**

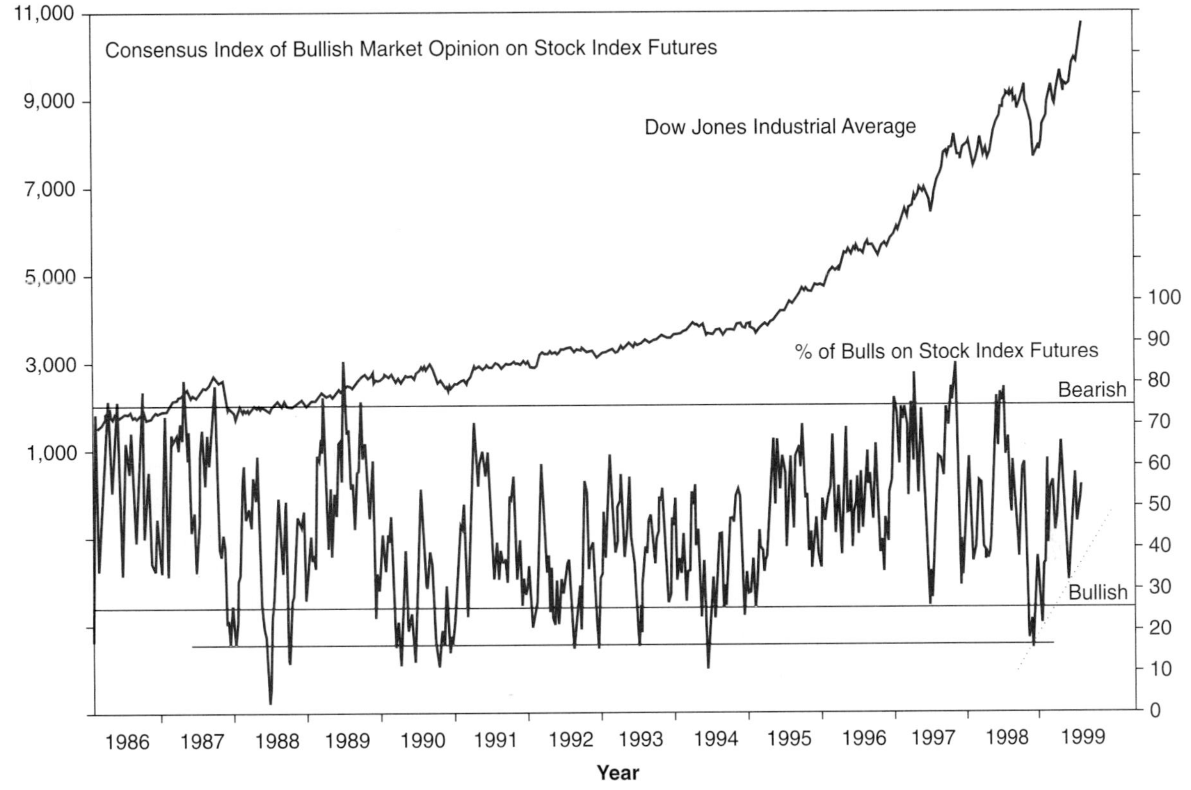
11,000
9,000
7,000
5,000
3,000
1,000
Consensus Index of Bullish Market Opinion on Stock Index Futures
Dow Jones Industrial Average
% of Bulls on Stock Index Futures
Bearish
Bullish
100
90
80
70
60
50
40
30
20
10
0
1986
1987
1988
1989
1990
1991
1992
1993
1994
1995
1996
1997
1998
1999
Year

Source: *Where the Indicators Stand* (New York: Merrill Lynch, May 1999). Reprinted by permission of Merrill Lynch. Data Courtesy of Market Vane.

Unfortunately, this interpretation of bond investor behavior is almost solely demand-oriented. Specifically, it assumes that changes in the yield spread are caused almost exclusively by changes in investor demand for different quality bonds. In fact, the yield differences have frequently changed because the supply of bonds in one of the groups increased. For example, a large issue of high-grade AT&T bonds could cause a temporary increase in yields on all high-grade bonds, which would reduce the yield spread and cause an increase in the Confidence Index without any change in investors' attitudes. Such a change in the supply of bonds can cause the series to generate a false signal of a change in confidence.

Advocates of the index believe that it reflects investor attitudes toward financial assets. Several studies have found that this index has been of little use in predicting stock price movements.

T-BILL–EURODOLLAR YIELD SPREAD An alternative measure of investor attitude or confidence on a global basis is the spread between T-bill yields and Eurodollar rates. It is reasoned that, at times of international crisis, this spread widens as money flows to safe-haven U.S. T-bills, which causes a decline in this ratio. The stock market has tended to reach a trough shortly thereafter.

SHORT SALES BY SPECIALISTS Data for total short sales on the NYSE, along with those for the specialists on the exchange, appear weekly in *Barron's.* It should be no surprise after our discussion in Chapter 4 that technicians who want to follow smart money watch the specialists. Specialists regularly engage in short selling as a part of their market-making function, but they can exercise discretion in this area when they feel strongly about expected market changes.

The normal ratio of specialists' short sales to total short sales has been approximately 40 percent.[7] Technicians view a decline in this ratio below 30 percent as a bullish sign because it means that specialists are attempting to minimize their participation in short sales. A ratio above 50 percent is a bearish sign.

Note two points about this ratio. First, do not expect it to be a long-run indicator; the nature of the specialists' portfolio probably will limit it to short-run movements. Second, there is a 2-week lag in reporting these data.

Although a graph of the specialist short-sales ratio indicated some support for the ratio as a buying signal, when used as a trading rule it provided insignificant excess returns.[8]

DEBIT BALANCES IN BROKERAGE ACCOUNTS (MARGIN DEBT) Debit balances in brokerage accounts represent borrowing (margin debt) by knowledgeable investors from their brokers. These balances indicate the attitude of a sophisticated group of investors who engage in margin transactions. Therefore, an increase in debit balances by this astute group would be a bullish sign. In contrast, a decline in debit balances would indicate selling as these sophisticated investors liquidate their positions and could indicate less capital available for investing. In either case, this would be a bearish indicator.

Monthly data on margin debt is reported in *Barron's.* Unfortunately, this series does not include borrowing by investors from other sources, such as banks. Also, because it is an absolute value, technicians would need to look for changes in the trend of borrowing.

Other Market Environment Indicators

In this section, we discuss several indicators that show overall market sentiment and that are used to make investment decisions related to the aggregate market.

BREADTH OF MARKET Breadth of market measures the number of issues that have increased each day and the number of issues that have declined. It helps explain the cause of a change of direction in a composite market series, such as the DJIA or the S&P 400 Index. As discussed in Chapter 5, the major stock-market series are heavily influenced by the stocks of large firms because most indexes are value-weighted. As a result, it is possible for a stock-market series to increase, but the majority of the individual issues will not. This divergence between the value for the aggregate index and its components is a problem because it means that most stocks are not participating in the rising market. Such a situation can be detected by examining the advance–decline figures for all stocks on the exchange, along with the overall market index.

A useful way to specify the advance–decline series for analysis is to create a cumulative series of net advances or net declines. Each day major newspapers publish figures on the number of issues on the NYSE that advanced, declined, or were unchanged. The figures for a 5-day sample, as would be reported in *Barron's,* are shown in Table 21.1. These

[7]Notably, during the early 1970s, the norm for this short-sales ratio was about 55 percent, and it became about 45 percent post-1981. Therefore, this is an example of another technique for which the decision ratio has changed over time.

[8]Frank K. Reilly and David Whitford, "A Test of the Specialists' Short Sale Ratio," *Journal of Portfolio Management* 8, no. 2 (winter 1982): 12–18.

TABLE 21.1 **DAILY ADVANCES AND DECLINES ON THE NEW YORK STOCK EXCHANGE**

Day	1	2	3	4	5
Issues traded	3,608	3,641	3,659	3,651	3,612
Advances	2,310	2,350	1,558	2,261	2,325
Declines	909	912	1,649	933	894
Unchanged	389	379	452	457	393
Net advances (advances minus declines)	+1,401	+1,438	−91	+1,328	+1,431
Cumulative net advances	+1,401	+2,839	+2,548	+3,876	+5,307
Changes in DJIA	+40.47	+43.99	−15.25	+60.50	+71.40

Sources: New York Stock Exchange and *Barron's*.

figures, along with changes in the DJIA at the bottom of the table, indicate to a technician a strong market advance because the DJIA was increasing and the net advance figure was strong, indicating that the market increase was broadly based and extended to most individual stocks. Even the results on Day 3, when the market declined 15 points, were somewhat encouraging. Although the market was down, it was a relatively small net decline and the individual stocks were split just about 50–50, which points toward a fairly even environment.

An alternative specification of the advance–decline series, a **diffusion index**, shows the daily total of stocks advancing plus one-half the number unchanged, divided by the total number of issues traded. To smooth the series, Merrill Lynch computes a 5-week moving average of these daily figures as shown in Figure 21.8.

Crossings from below to above 50 indicate the market's intermediate-term trend if the moving average series has turned from down to up. This advance–decline series also is used to measure intermediate trends and to signal overbought levels if it reaches very high levels of 56 to 60. Alternatively, the market is considered oversold when the diffusion index gets down to 40–44.

As of mid-1999, the diffusion indicator had turned up from the intermediate oversold level of 45 in early 1999 and was neutral and improving at about 53. The usefulness of the advance–decline series is supposedly greatest at market peaks and troughs when the composite value-weighted market series might be moving either up or down, but the majority of individual stocks might be moving in the opposite direction. As an example, near a peak, the DJIA would be increasing, but the net advance–decline ratio would become negative, the cumulative advance–decline series would level off and decline, and the advance–decline diffusion index would go below 50 percent. The *divergence* between the trend for the market index and the various advance–decline series would signal a market peak.

In contrast, as the market approached a trough, the composite market index would be declining, but the daily advance–decline ratio would become positive, the cumulative advance–decline index would turn up, and the diffusion index would rise above 50 percent before the aggregate market index increased.[9] In summary, a technician would look for the advance–decline series to indicate a change in trend before the composite stock-market series.[10]

[9]Ideally, the performance of the series should work at both peaks and troughs. In fact, it appears to work best at peaks. Apparently at troughs, the secondary stocks, which make up most of the issues, may remain weak until the low point and keep the advance–decline figures negative.

[10]This series also has been used to evaluate non-U.S. indexes. See Linda Sandler, "Advance–Decline Line, a Popular Indicator, Warns of Correction in Tokyo Stock Market," *Wall Street Journal,* 26 August 1988, C1.

FIGURE 21.8 TIME-SERIES PLOT OF DOW JONES INDUSTRIAL AVERAGE AND 5-WEEK MOVING AVERAGE OF THE ADVANCE-DECLINE DIFFUSION INDEX

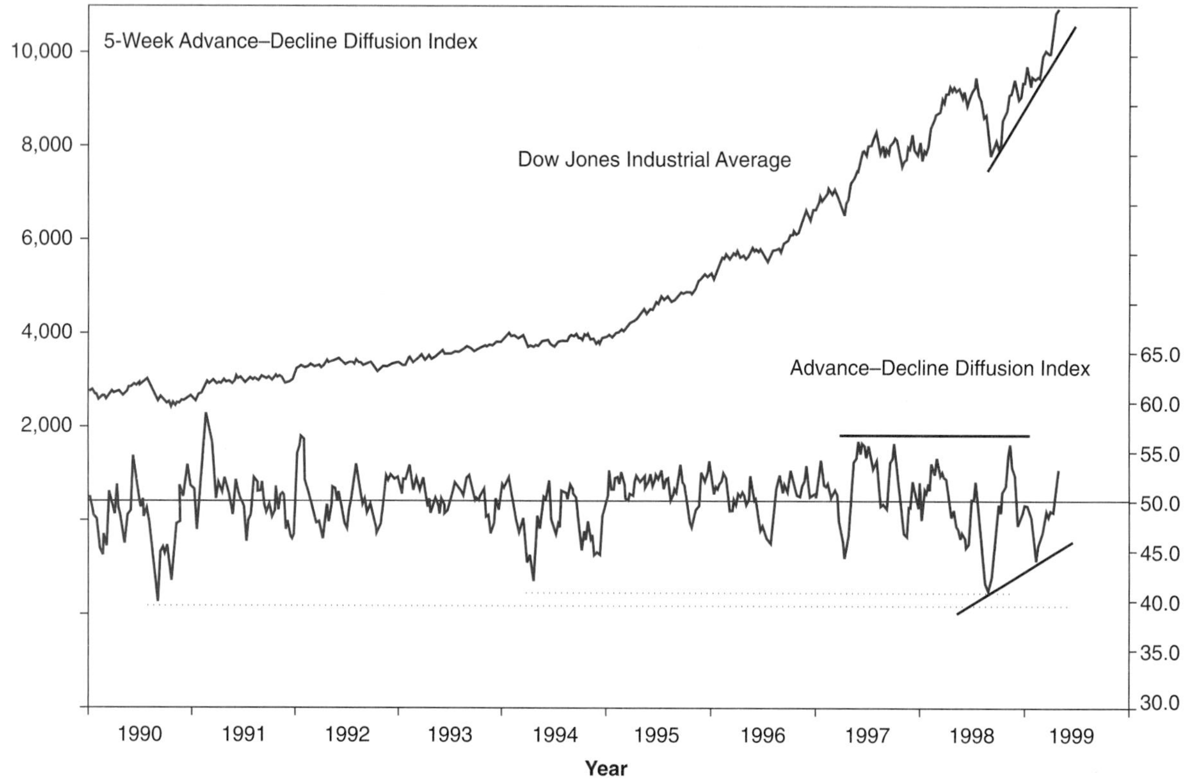
5-Week Advance–Decline Diffusion Index
Dow Jones Industrial Average
Advance–Decline Diffusion Index
10,000
8,000
6,000
4,000
2,000
65.0
60.0
55.0
50.0
45.0
40.0
35.0
30.0
1990
1991
1992
1993
1994
1995
1996
1997
1998
1999
Year

Source: *Where the Indicators Stand* (New York: Merrill Lynch, May 1999). Reprinted by permission of Merrill Lynch.

SHORT INTEREST The short interest is the cumulative number of shares that have been sold short by investors and not covered. This means the investor has not purchased the shares sold short and returned them to the investor from whom they were borrowed. Technicians compute a short-interest ratio as the outstanding short interest divided by the average daily volume of trading on the exchange. For example, if the outstanding short interest on the NYSE was 4,000 million shares and the average daily volume of trading on the exchange was 900 million shares, the short-interest ratio would be 4.44 (4,000/900). This means the outstanding short interest equals about 4 days' trading volume.

Technicians probably interpret this ratio contrary to your initial intuition. Because short sales reflect investors' expectations that stock prices will decline, one would typically expect an increase in the short-interest ratio to be bearish. On the contrary, technicians consider a high short-interest ratio bullish because it indicates *potential demand* for the stock by those who previously sold short and have not covered the short sale.

This is another example of a change in the decision value over time. Before 1994, the range for the short-interest ratio was between 2.0 and 3.0. Based on recent experience where the short-interest ratio has gotten as high as 6.0 or 7.0, a technician would be bullish when the short-interest ratio approached 6.0 and bearish if it declined toward 4.0. The short-interest position is calculated by the stock exchanges and the NASD as of the twentieth of each month and is reported about 2 days later in the *Wall Street Journal.*

FIGURE 21.9 **PERCENTAGE OF NYSE COMMON STOCKS ABOVE THEIR 200-DAY MOVING AVERAGE**

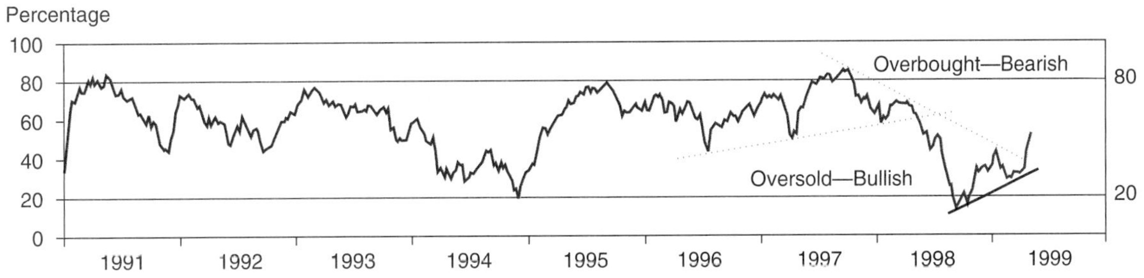
Percentage
100
80
60
40
20
0
Overbought—Bearish
Oversold—Bullish
80
20
1991
1992
1993
1994
1995
1996
1997
1998
1999

Source: *Where the Indicators Stand* (New York: Merrill Lynch, May 1999). Reprinted by permission of Merrill Lynch.

Various studies have examined the short-interest series as a predictor of stock price movements, with mixed results. For every study that supports the technique, another indicates that it should be rejected.[11] Technical analysts have pointed out that this ratio—and any ratio that involves short selling—has been affected by new techniques for short selling, such as options and futures.

STOCKS ABOVE THEIR 200-DAY MOVING AVERAGE Technicians often compute moving averages of a series to determine its general trend. To examine individual stocks, the 200-day **moving average** of prices has been fairly popular. From these moving-average series for numerous stocks, Media General Financial Services calculates how many stocks currently are trading above their 200-day moving-average series, and this is used as an indicator of general investor sentiment. As shown in Figure 21.9, the market is considered to be *overbought* and it is bearish when more than 80 percent of the stocks are trading above their 200-day moving average. In contrast, if less than 20 percent of the stocks are selling above their 200-day moving average, the market is considered to be *oversold,* which is bullish and means investors should expect a positive correction. As shown in Figure 21.9, as of mid-1999, the percent of stocks selling above their 200-day moving average is neutral because it is about 50 percent, which is midway between the bullish and bearish trigger points.

BLOCK UPTICK–DOWNTICK RATIO As discussed in Chapter 4, about 50 percent of NYSE volume comes from block trading by institutions. The exchange can determine whether the price change that accompanied a particular block trade was higher or lower than the price of the prior transactions. If the block trade price is above the prior transaction price, it is referred to as an **uptick**; if the block trade price is below the prior transaction price, it is referred to as a **downtick**.

It is assumed that if the block trade was initiated by a buyer, you would expect an uptick; if it was initiated by a seller, you would expect a downtick. This led to the development of the **uptick (buyers)–downtick (sellers) ratio**, which indicates institutional investor sentiment. This ratio generally has fluctuated in the range of 0.70, which indicates an oversold condition that is bullish, to about 1.10, which indicates an overbought environment and a bearish sentiment.

[11]See Joseph Vu and Paul Caster, "Why All the Interest in Short Interest?" *Financial Analysts Journal* 43, no. 4 (July–August 1987): 77–79.

STOCK PRICE AND VOLUME TECHNIQUES

In the introduction to this chapter, we examined a hypothetical stock price chart that demonstrated the market cycle and its peaks and troughs. Also, we considered rising and declining trend channels and breakouts from channels that signal new price trends or reversals of the price trends. Although these price patterns are important, most technical trading rules for the overall market and individual stocks consider both stock price movements and corresponding volume movements. Because technicians believe that prices move in trends that persist, they seek to predict future price trends from an astute analysis of past price trends along with an analysis of changes in the volume of trading.

THE DOW THEORY Any discussion of technical analysis using price and volume data should begin with a consideration of the Dow Theory because it was among the earliest work on this topic and remains the basis for many technical indicators. In this section, we show how Charles Dow combined price and volume information to analyze both individual stocks and the overall stock market.

Charles Dow published the *Wall Street Journal* during the late 1800s.[12] Dow described stock prices as moving in trends analogous to the movement of water. He postulated three types of price movements over time: (1) major trends that are like tides in the ocean, (2) intermediate trends that resemble waves, and (3) short-run movements that are like ripples. Followers of the Dow Theory hope to detect the direction of the major price trend (tide), recognizing that intermediate movements (waves) may occasionally move in the opposite direction. They recognize that a major market advance does not go straight up, but rather includes small price declines as some investors decide to take profits.

Figure 21.10 shows the typical bullish pattern. The technician would look for every recovery to reach a new peak above the prior peak, and this price rise should be accompanied by heavy trading volume. Alternatively, each profit-taking reversal that follows an increase to a new peak should have a trough above the prior trough, with relatively light trading volume during the reversals, indicating that there is limited interest in profit taking at these levels. When this pattern of price and volume movements changes, the major trend may be entering a period of consolidation or a major reversal. When using the Dow Theory to analyze the overall stock market, technicians also look for confirmation of peaks and troughs in the industrial stock price series by subsequent peaks and troughs in the transportation series. Such an "echo" indicates that the change in direction and the major trend is being confirmed across the total market.

IMPORTANCE OF VOLUME As noted in the description of the Dow Theory, technicians watch volume changes along with price movements as an indicator of changes in supply and demand for individual stocks or stocks in general. A price movement in one direction means that the net effect on price is in that direction, but the price change alone does not tell us how widespread the excess demand or supply is at that time. Therefore, the technician looks for a price increase on heavy volume relative to the stock's normal trading volume as an indication of bullish activity. Conversely, a price decline with relatively heavy volume is bearish. A generally bullish pattern would be when price increases are accompanied by heavy volume and the small price reversals occur with light trading volume, indicating limited interest in selling and taking profits.

---

[12]A study that discusses and provides support for the Dow Theory is David A. Glickstein and Rolf E. Wubbels, "Dow Theory Is Alive and Well," *Journal of Portfolio Management* 9, no. 3 (spring 1983): 28–32. The Dow Jones Industrial Average celebrated its 100th anniversary in 1996. The *Wall Street Journal* published a special supplement on May 28, 1996, to commemorate the event.

FIGURE 21.10 **SAMPLE BULLISH PRICE PATTERN**

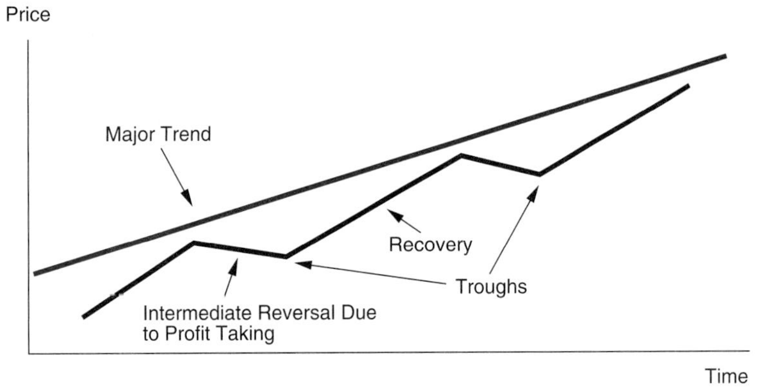
Price
Major Trend
Recovery
Troughs
Intermediate Reversal Due
to Profit Taking
Time

Technicians also use a ratio of upside–downside volume as an indicator of short-term momentum for the aggregate stock market. Each day the stock exchanges announce the volume of trading that occurred in stocks that experienced an increase divided by the volume of trading in stocks that declined. These data are reported daily in the *Wall Street Journal* and weekly in *Barron's*. Technicians consider this ratio to be an indicator of investor sentiment and use it to pinpoint excesses. Specifically, the ratio typically ranges between a value of 0.50 and 2.00 and is upside-biased. Technicians believe that a value of 1.50 or more indicates an overbought position that is bearish. Alternatively, a value of 0.75 and lower would reflect an oversold position and is considered bullish. As of May 1999, the ratio stands at about 1.25, which is considered neutral.

SUPPORT AND RESISTANCE LEVELS A **support level** is the price range at which the technician would expect a substantial increase in the demand for a stock. Generally, a support level will develop after a stock has enjoyed a meaningful price increase and the stock has begun to experience profit taking. Technicians reason that, at some price below the recent peak, other investors will buy who did not buy prior to the first price increase and have been waiting for a small reversal to get into the stock. When the price reaches this support price, demand surges and price and volume begin to increase again.

A **resistance level** is the price range at which the technician would expect an increase in the supply of stock and any price increase to reverse abruptly. A resistance level tends to develop after a stock has experienced a steady decline from a higher price level. It is reasoned that the decline in price leads some investors who acquired the stock at a higher price to look for an opportunity to sell it near their break-even points. Therefore, the supply of stock owned by these investors is *overhanging* the market. When the price rebounds to the target price set by these investors, this overhanging supply of stock comes to the market and dramatically reverses the price increase on heavy volume.

It is also possible to envision a set of support and resistance levels for a stock in a rising or declining trend wherein the resistance level is a price where a number of holders feel it is appropriate to take a profit. In this latter case, there might be a succession of resistance levels over time.

Figure 21.11 shows a daily price chart for Lucent Technology with an increasing pattern of support and resistance levels that reflect that the stock is in a bullish trend. This rising channel of support and resistance helps the technician to identify if there is a slowdown in

FIGURE 21.11 TIME-SERIES PLOT OF DAILY PRICES FOR LUCENT TECHNOLOGY WITH INDICATIONS OF SUPPORT AND RESISTANCE LEVELS

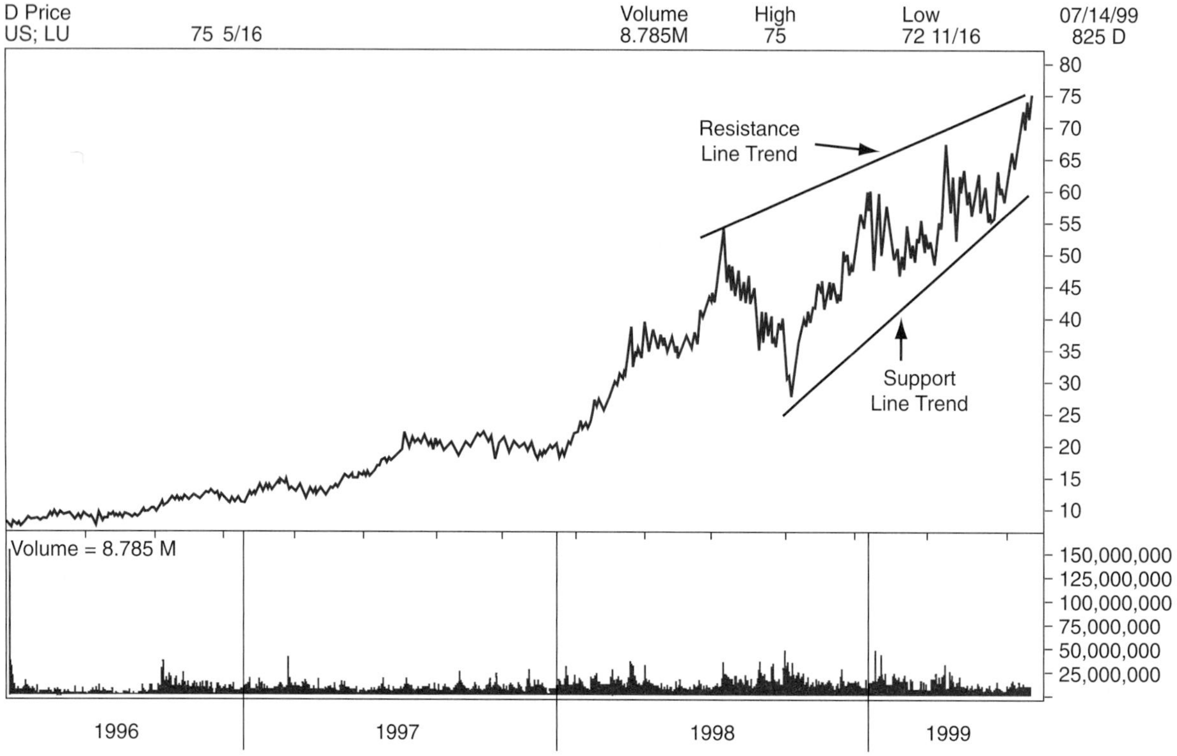
D Price
US; LU
75 5/16
Volume
8.785M
High
75
Low
72 11/16
07/14/99
825 D
Resistance
Line Trend
Support
Line Trend
80
75
70
65
60
55
50
45
40
35
30
25
20
15
10
Volume = 8.785 M
150,000,000
125,000,000
100,000,000
75,000,000
50,000,000
25,000,000
1996
1997
1998
1999

Source: Bridge Information Systems, Inc.

the price increases or if there is a bearish change in trend whereby the prices go below the support line that reflects the bullish trend. Thus far, the price pattern has been very well behaved with prices contained in the bullish band.

MOVING-AVERAGE LINES Earlier, we discussed how technicians use a moving average of past stock prices as an indicator of the long-run trend and how they examine current prices relative to this trend for signals of a change. We also noted that a 200-day moving average is a relatively popular measure for individual stocks and the aggregate market. In this discussion, we want to add a 50-day moving-average price line and consider large volume.

Figure 21.12 is a weekly price and volume chart for Motorola, Inc. (MOT) from the Bridge System for a 5-year period ending in July 1999. It also contains a 50-day and 200-day moving-average (MA) line. As noted, MA lines are meant to reflect the overall trend for the price series, with the shorter MA series (50-day versus 200-day) reflecting shorter trends. Two comparisons involving the MA series are considered important. The first comparison is the specific prices relative to the shorter-run MA series, which in this case is the 50-day MA series. If the overall price trend of a stock or the market has been down, the moving-average price line generally would lie above current prices. If prices reverse and break through the moving-average line *from below* accompanied by heavy trading volume, most technicians would consider this a strongly *positive* change and speculate that this

FIGURE 21.12 **DAILY STOCK PRICES FOR MOTOROLA—FEBRUARY 1995 TO JULY 1999, WITH 50-DAY AND 200-DAY MOVING-AVERAGE LINES**

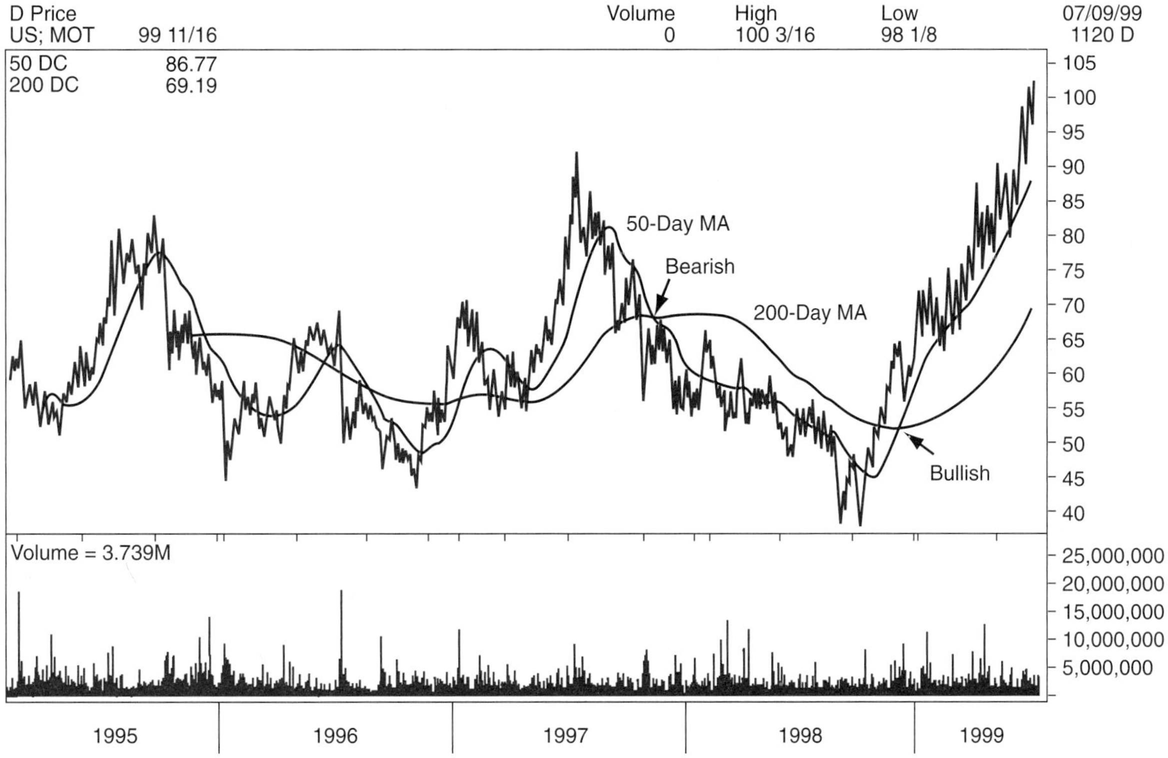
D Price
US; MOT 99 11/16
Volume 0
High 100 3/16
Low 98 1/8
07/09/99
1120 D
50 DC 86.77
200 DC 69.19
50-Day MA
Bearish
200-Day MA
Bullish
105
100
95
90
85
80
75
70
65
60
55
50
45
40
Volume = 3.739M
25,000,000
20,000,000
15,000,000
10,000,000
5,000,000
1995
1996
1997
1998
1999

Source: Bridge Information Systems, Inc.

breakthrough signals a reversal of the declining trend. In contrast, if the price of a stock had been rising, the moving-average line would also be rising, but it would be below current prices. If current prices broke through the moving-average line *from above* accompanied by heavy trading volume, this would be considered a bearish pattern that would signal a reversal of the long-run rising trend.

The second comparison is between the 50- and 200-day MA lines. Specifically, when these two lines cross, it signals a change in the overall trend. Specifically, if the 50-day MA line crosses the 200-day MA line from below on good volume, this would be a bullish indicator (buy signal) because it signals a reversal in trend from negative to positive. In contrast, when the 50-day line crosses the 200-day line from above, it signals a change to a negative trend and would be a sell signal. The price-volume chart in Figure 21.12 contains two recent strong signals for Motorola based on the moving-average lines. Specifically, in mid-1997, the stock price for Motorola peaked and in September broke through the 50-day MA line from above, which is an initial bearish signal. Then in late 1997, the 50-day MA line broke through the 200-day MA line from above, confirming the sell signal at a price of about $67. The price continued to decline to a low of less than $40 prior to a strong upward move whereby the price series broke through the 50-day moving-average line from below in late 1998, which is a bullish signal. Near year-end 1998, the bullish buy signal was confirmed when the 50-day MA line broke through the 200-day MA line at a price of about $53. Since this strong buy signal, the price for Motorola has risen fairly consistently into July to a price of $99.

Overall, for a *bullish* trend, the 50-day MA line should be above the 200-day MA line as it has been for Motorola since early 1999. Notably, if this positive gap between the 50-day and the 200-day MA lines gets too large (which happens with a fast run up in price), a technician might consider this an indication that the stock is temporarily overbought, which is bearish for the short run. A *bearish* trend is when the 50-day MA line is always below the 200-day MA line. If the gap was large on the downside, it might be considered a signal of an oversold stock, which is bullish for the short-run. A gap is generally considered too large when the average prices differ by 15 percent or more.

In the case of Motorola, one would need to be concerned regarding this trading rule because the current "gap" between the 50-day moving average and the 200-day moving average is getting quite large—i.e., it is the difference between about 86 and 69, a gap of almost 25 percent, indicating an overbought condition, which is bearish for Motorola stock in the short run.

RELATIVE STRENGTH Technicians believe that once a trend begins, it will continue until some major event causes a change in direction. They believe this is also true of *relative* performance. If an individual stock or an industry group is outperforming the market, technicians believe it will continue to do so.

Therefore, technicians compute weekly or monthly **relative-strength (RS) ratios** for individual stocks and industry groups as the ratio of the price of a stock or an industry index relative to the value for some stock-market series, such as the S&P 500. If this ratio increases over time, it shows that the stock or industry is outperforming the market, and a technician would expect this superior performance to continue. Relative-strength ratios work during declining as well as rising markets. In a declining market, if a stock's price declines less than the market does, the stock's relative-strength ratio will continue to rise. Technicians believe that if this ratio is stable or increases during a bear market, the stock should do well during the subsequent bull market.[13] The relative-strength line in Figure 21.13 indicates that Motorola's stock price performance relative to the S&P 500 generally declined with some brief recoveries since mid-1995 until a trough in about July 1998. Since that point, the relative strength line has experienced a steady upward trend, which supports the bullish pattern discussed in connection with the MA lines. The fact that this relative-strength line was positive at year-end 1998 when the MA lines crossed would have supported the buy signal for Motorola at that time.

Merrill Lynch publishes relative-strength charts for industry groups as well as a moving-average of the RS values to help identify the general direction of RS. Figure 21.14 describes how to read the charts.

BAR CHARTING Technicians use charts that show daily, weekly, or monthly time series of stock prices. For a given interval, the technical analyst plots the high and low prices and connects the two points vertically to form a bar. Typically, he or she will also draw a small horizontal line across this vertical bar to indicate the closing price. Finally, almost all bar charts include the volume of trading at the bottom of the chart so that the technical analyst can relate the price and volume movements. A typical bar chart in Figure 21.15 shows data for the DJIA from the *Wall Street Journal* along with volume figures for the NYSE.

---

[13]A study that supports the technique is James Bohan, "Relative Strength: Further Positive Evidence," *Journal of Portfolio Management* 7, no. 1 (fall 1981): 39–46. A study that rejects the technique is Robert D. Arnott, "Relative Strength Revisited," *Journal of Portfolio Management* 6, no. 3 (spring 1979): 19–23. Finally, a study that combines it with modern portfolio theory is John S. Brush and Keith Boles, "The Predictive Power in Relative Strength and CAPM, " *Journal of Portfolio Management* 9, no. 4 (summer 1983): 20–23.

FIGURE 21.13

WEEKLY RELATIVE-STRENGTH LINE FOR MOTOROLA RELATIVE TO THE S&P 500 INDEX: 1995–JULY 1999

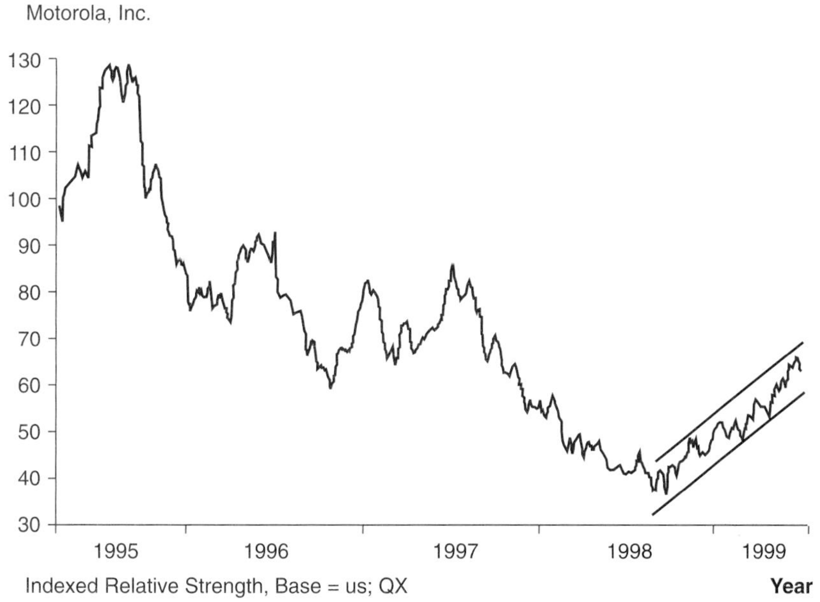
Motorola, Inc.
130
120
110
100
90
80
70
60
50
40
30
1995
1996
1997
1998
1999
Indexed Relative Strength, Base = us; QX
Year

Source: Bridge Information Systems, Inc.

MULTIPLE INDICATOR CHARTS We have been presenting charts that demonstrate one technical analysis technique for teaching purposes. In practice, technicians include as many price and volume series as are reasonable on one chart., such as two MA lines (50-day and 200-day) along with a relative-strength line and an MA line running through the relative-strength line. Notably, based on the performance of *several* technical indicators, they try to arrive at a consensus about the future movement for the stock.

POINT-AND-FIGURE CHARTS Another graph that is popular with technicians is the point-and-figure chart.[14] Unlike the bar chart, which typically includes all ending prices and volumes to show a trend, the point-and-figure chart includes only significant price changes, regardless of their timing. The technician determines what price interval to record as significant (one point, two points, and so on) and when to note price reversals.

To demonstrate how a technical analyst would use such a chart, assume you want to chart a volatile stock that is currently selling for $40 a share. Because of its volatility, you believe that anything less than a two-point price change is not significant. Also, you consider anything less than a four-point reversal, meaning a movement in the opposite direction, quite minor. Therefore, you would set up a chart similar to the one in Figure 21.16, which starts at 40 and progresses in two-point increments. If the stock moves to 42, you would place an X in the box above 40 and do nothing else until the stock rose to 44 or dropped to 38 (a four-point reversal from its high of 42). If it dropped to 38, you would move a column to the right, which indicates a reversal in direction, and begin again with an O to designate a decline at 38 (fill in boxes at 42 and 40). If the stock price dropped to 34, you would enter an O at 36 and another at 34. If the stock then rose to 38 (another four-

[14]Daniel Seligman, "The Mystique of Point-and-Figure," *Fortune*, March 1962, 113–115.

FIGURE 21.14 **HOW TO READ INDUSTRY GROUP CHARTS**

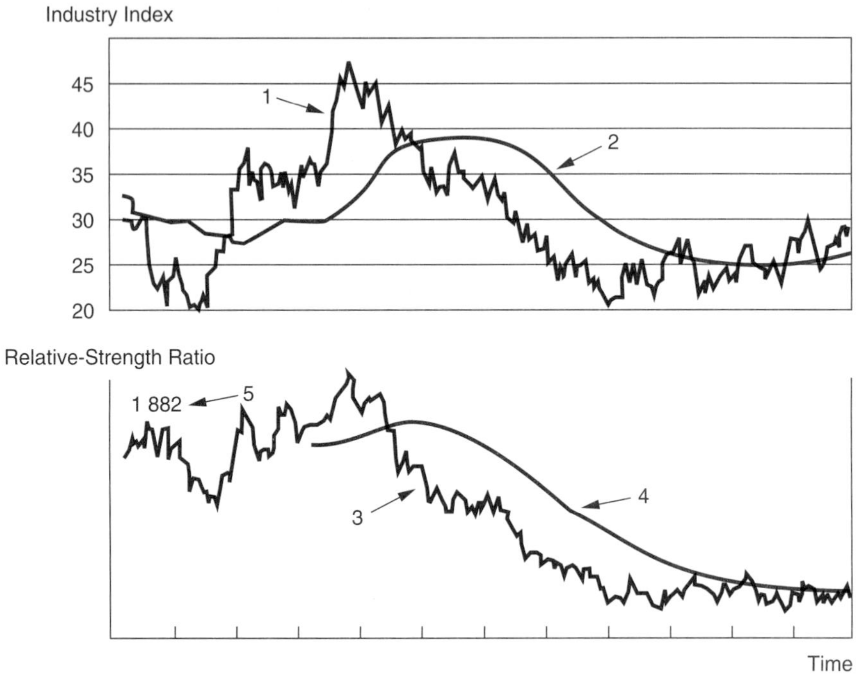
Industry Index
45
40
35
30
25
20
1
2
Relative-Strength Ratio
1 882
5
3
4
Time

The industry group charts in this report display the following elements:

1. A line chart of the weekly close of the Standard & Poor's Industry Group Index for the past 9½ years, with the index range indicated to the left.
2. A line of the seventy-five-week moving average of the Standard & Poor's Industry Group Index.
3. A relative-strength line of the Standard & Poor's Industry Group Index compared with the New York Stock Exchange Composite Index.
4. A seventy-five-week moving average of relative strength.
5. A volatility reading that measures the maximum amount by which the index has outperformed (or underperformed) the NYSE Composite Index during the time period displayed.

Source: *Technical Analysis of Industry Groups* (New York: Merrill Lynch, monthly). Reprinted by permission of Merrill Lynch. All Rights Reserved.

point reversal), you would move to the next column and begin with an X at 38, going up (fill in 34 and 36). If the stock then went to 46, you would fill in more Xs as shown and wait for further increases or a reversal.

Depending on how fast the prices rise and fall, this process might take anywhere from two to six months. Given these figures, the technical analyst would attempt to determine trends just as with the bar chart.

As always, you look for breakouts to either higher or lower price levels. A long horizontal movement with many reversals but no major trends up or down would be considered *a period of consolidation.* The technician would speculate that during this period, the stock is moving from buyers to sellers and back again with no strong support from either group that would indicate a consensus about its direction. Once the stock breaks out and moves up or down after a period of consolidation, analysts anticipate a major move because previous trading set the stage for it. In other words, the longer the period of consolidation, the larger the subsequent move.

Point-and-figure charts differ from bar charts by providing a compact record of movements because they only consider significant price changes for the stock being analyzed.

FIGURE 21.15 **A TYPICAL BAR CHART**

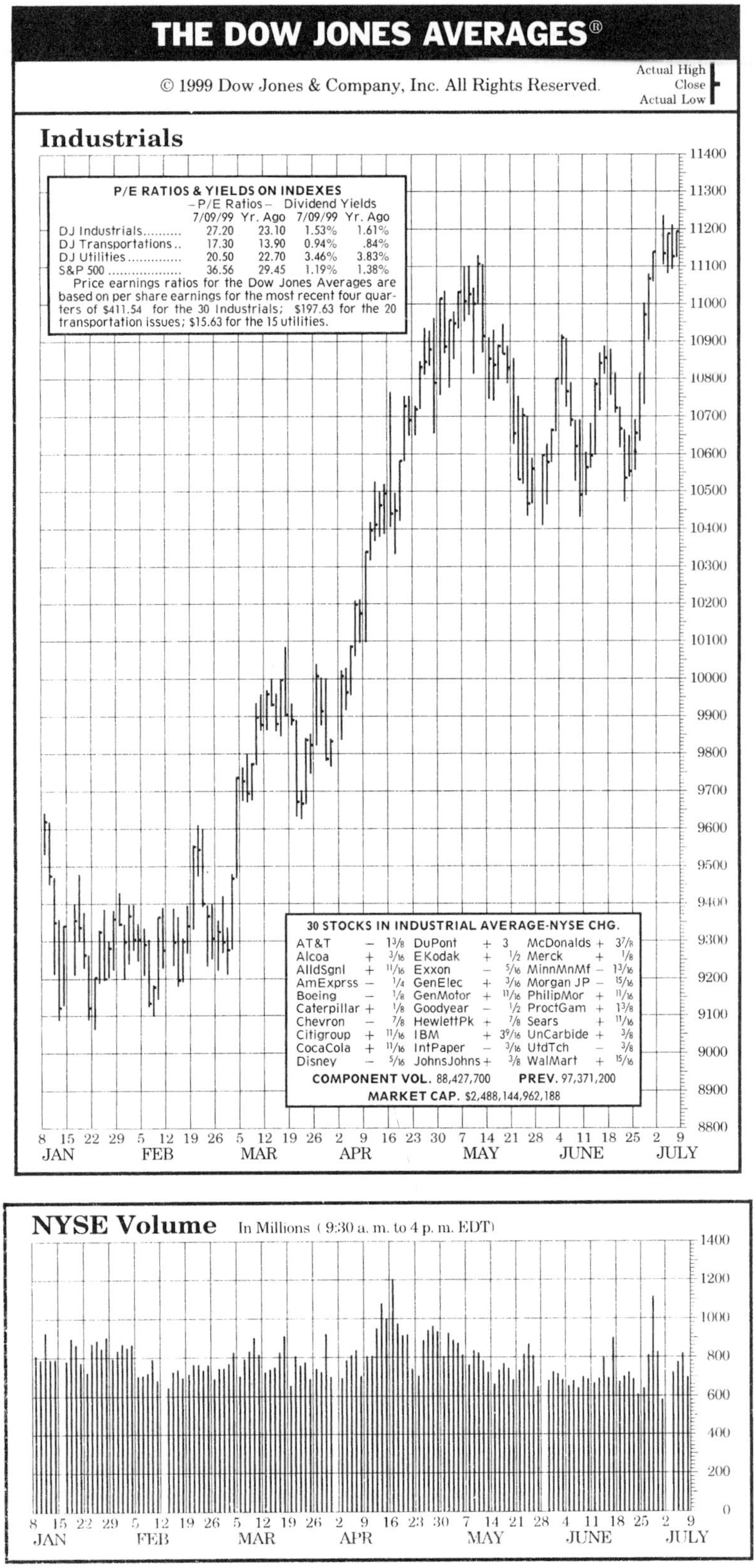
THE DOW JONES AVERAGES®
© 1999 Dow Jones & Company, Inc. All Rights Reserved.
Actual High
Close
Actual Low
Industrials
P/E RATIOS & YIELDS ON INDEXES
–P/E Ratios– Dividend Yields
7/09/99 Yr. Ago 7/09/99 Yr. Ago
DJ Industrials.......... 27.20 23.10 1.53% 1.61%
DJ Transportations.. 17.30 13.90 0.94% .84%
DJ Utilities............. 20.50 22.70 3.46% 3.83%
S&P 500 .... 36.56 29.45 1.19% 1.38%
Price earnings ratios for the Dow Jones Averages are based on per share earnings for the most recent four quarters of $411.54 for the 30 Industrials; $197.63 for the 20 transportation issues; $15.63 for the 15 utilities.
30 STOCKS IN INDUSTRIAL AVERAGE-NYSE CHG.
AT&T – 1 3/8 DuPont + 3 McDonalds + 3 7/8
Alcoa + 3/16 EKodak + 1/2 Merck + 1/8
AlldSgnl + 11/16 Exxon – 5/16 MinnMnMf – 1 3/16
AmExprss – 1/4 GenElec + 3/16 Morgan JP – 15/16
Boeing – 1/8 GenMotor + 11/16 PhilipMor + 11/16
Caterpillar + 1/8 Goodyear – 1/2 ProctGam + 1 3/8
Chevron – 7/8 HewlettPk + 7/8 Sears + 11/16
Citigroup + 11/16 IBM + 3 9/16 UnCarbide + 3/8
CocaCola + 11/16 IntPaper – 3/16 UtdTch – 3/8
Disney – 5/16 JohnsJohns + 3/8 WalMart + 15/16
COMPONENT VOL. 88,427,700 PREV. 97,371,200
MARKET CAP. $2,488,144,962,188
11400
11300
11200
11100
11000
10900
10800
10700
10600
10500
10400
10300
10200
10100
10000
9900
9800
9700
9600
9500
9400
9300
9200
9100
9000
8900
8800
8 15 22 29 5 12 19 26 5 12 19 26 2 9 16 23 30 7 14 21 28 4 11 18 25 2 9
JAN FEB MAR APR MAY JUNE JULY
NYSE Volume In Millions (9:30 a. m. to 4 p. m. EDT)
1400
1200
1000
800
600
400
200
0
8 15 22 29 5 12 19 26 5 12 19 26 2 9 16 23 30 7 14 21 28 4 11 18 25 2 9
JAN FEB MAR APR MAY JUNE JULY

Source: "The Dow Jones Averages" *Wall Street Journal,* 12 July 1999.

FIGURE 21.16 **SAMPLE POINT-AND-FIGURE CHART**

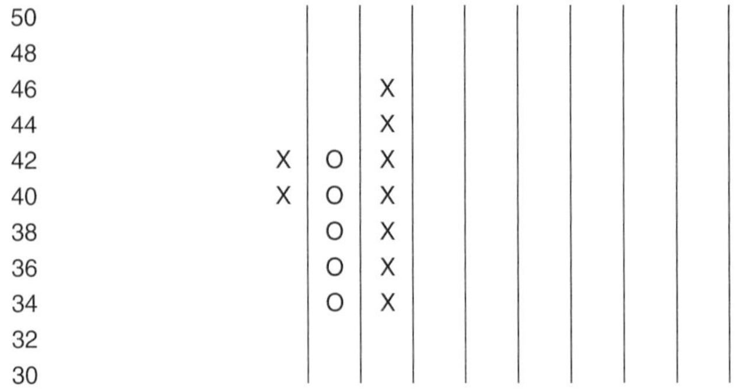
50
48
46
44
42
40
38
36
34
32
30

Therefore, some technicians prefer point-and-figure charts because they are easier to work with and give more vivid pictures of price movements.

This section discussed widely used technical indicators. As noted on several occasions, technical analysts generally do not concentrate on only a few indicators or even general categories, but seek to derive an overall feel for the market or a stock based on a *consensus of numerous technical indicators.*

Technical Analysis of Foreign Markets

Our discussion thus far has concentrated on U.S. markets, but as numerous analysts and firms have discovered, these techniques apply to foreign markets as well. Merrill Lynch, for instance, prepares separate technical analysis publications for individual countries such as Japan, Germany, and the United Kingdom, as well as a summary of all world markets. The examples that follow show that when analyzing non-U.S. markets, many techniques are limited to using price and volume data rather than the more detailed market information described for the U.S. market. This emphasis on price and volume data is necessary because the more detailed information that is available on the U.S. market through the SEC, the stock exchanges, the NASDAQ system, and various investment services is not always available in other countries.

FOREIGN STOCK MARKET SERIES Figure 21.17 contains the weekly time-series plot and 10-week and 40-week moving-average series for the United Kingdom FTSE 100 Index. This chart shows the strong rising trend by the United Kingdom stock market during the period 1994 to June 1999.

In the written analysis, the market analyst at Merrill Lynch estimated support and resistance levels for the United Kingdom Stock Exchange series and commented on the medium-term outlook for the German stock market. A small note of caution was expressed because of the 10 percent gap between the 10-week and 40-week moving-average lines that could be a signal for an overbought market in the short run.

Merrill Lynch publishes similar charts and discussions for 10 other countries and a summary release that compares the countries and ranks them by stock and currency performance. The next section discusses the technical analysis of currency markets.

TECHNICAL ANALYSIS OF FOREIGN EXCHANGE RATES On numerous occasions, we have discussed the importance of changes in foreign exchange rates and their impact on the rates of return on foreign securities. Because of the importance of these relationships, technicians who trade bonds and stocks in world markets examine the time-series data of various individual currencies, such as the British pound. They also analyze the

FIGURE 21.17

MERRILL LYNCH GRAPH AND SUMMARY COMMENTS ON THE UNITED KINGDOM STOCK MARKET

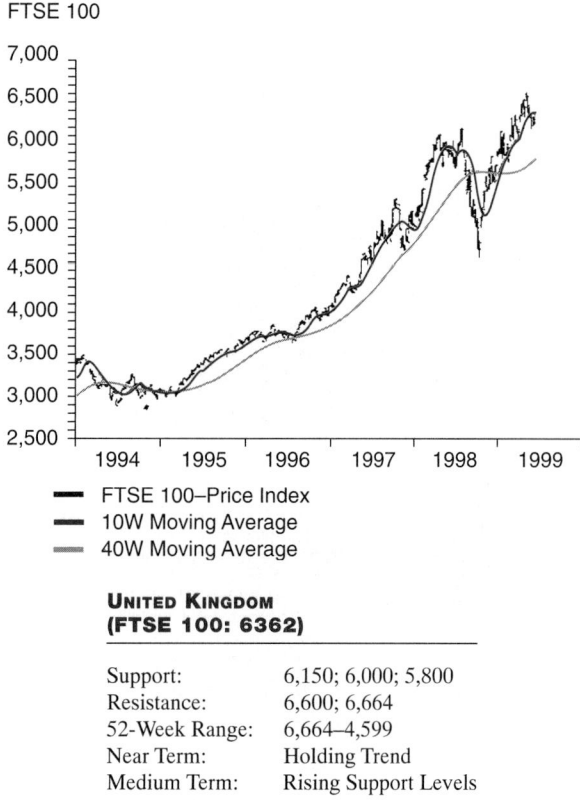

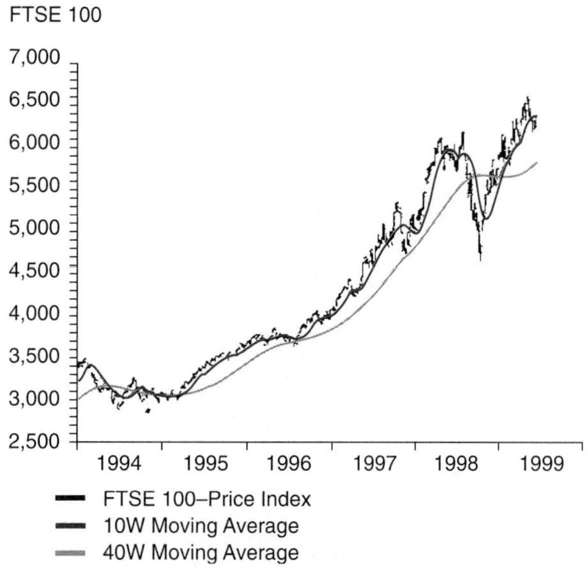
FTSE 100
7,000
6,500
6,000
5,500
5,000
4,500
4,000
3,500
3,000
2,500
1994
1995
1996
1997
1998
1999
FTSE 100–Price Index
10W Moving Average
40W Moving Average

UNITED KINGDOM
(FTSE 100: 6362)

Support:	6,150; 6,000; 5,800
Resistance:	6,600; 6,664
52-Week Range:	6,664–4,599
Near Term:	Holding Trend
Medium Term:	Rising Support Levels

Source: *The Global Technician* (New York: Merrill Lynch, 8 June 1999).

spread between currencies, such as the difference between the Japanese yen (¥) and the German deutsche mark (DM). Finally, an analysis of the composite dollar performance over time, as shown in Figure 21.18 is used to identify short-term momentum as well as resistance and support levels, and long-term trend lines. As of June 1999, the analyst was concerned about near-term resistance despite the strong momentum thus far in 1999.

TECHNICAL ANALYSIS OF BOND MARKETS

Thus far, we have described technical tools for the analysis of the stock market in the United States and the world. Although we have emphasized the use of technical analysis in stock markets, you should be aware that technicians also apply these techniques to the bond market. The theory and rationale for technical analysis of bonds are the same as for stocks and many of the same trading rules are used. As with stocks, the techniques apply to an individual bond, several bonds, or a bond index. A major difference is that it is generally not possible to consider the volume of trading of bonds since these data generally are not available because most bonds are traded OTC, where volume is not reported.

Figure 21.19 demonstrates the use of technical analysis techniques applied to a world bond-yield series. The top panel contains a time-series graph of daily global bond yields that shows a steady decline during the latter half of 1998 with a trough in December followed by a rising trend into June 1999. The 55-day moving-average line confirms this overall movement and shows a confirmation of the change in direction in late January 1999 when the

FIGURE 21.18

TIME-SERIES PLOT OF U.S. DOLLAR TRADE-WEIGHTED EXCHANGE RATES

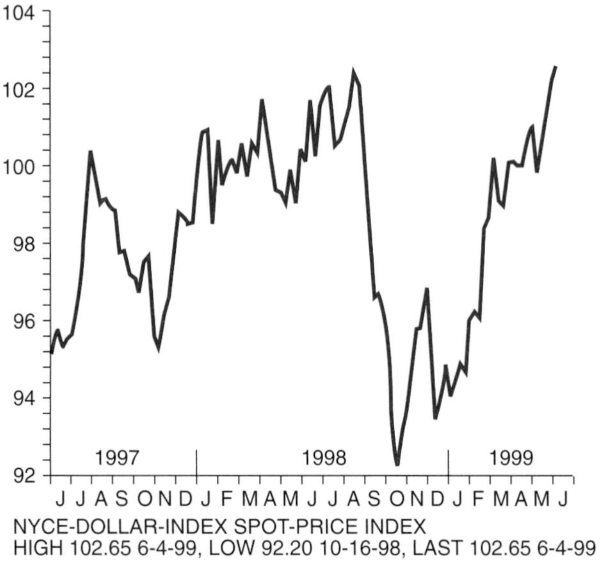
104
102
100
98
96
94
92
1997
1998
1999
J J A S O N D J F M A M J J A S O N D J F M A M J
NYCE-DOLLAR-INDEX SPOT-PRICE INDEX
HIGH 102.65 6-4-99, LOW 92.20 10-16-98, LAST 102.65 6-4-99

Source: *The Global Technician* (New York: Merrill Lynch, 8 June 1999). Source of data: Datastream.

FIGURE 21.19

TECHNICAL ANALYSIS OF A DAILY VALUE-WEIGHTED WORLD BOND-YIELD SERIES, INCLUDING A MOVING AVERAGE OF YIELDS AND A RELATIVE-STRENGTH INDEX

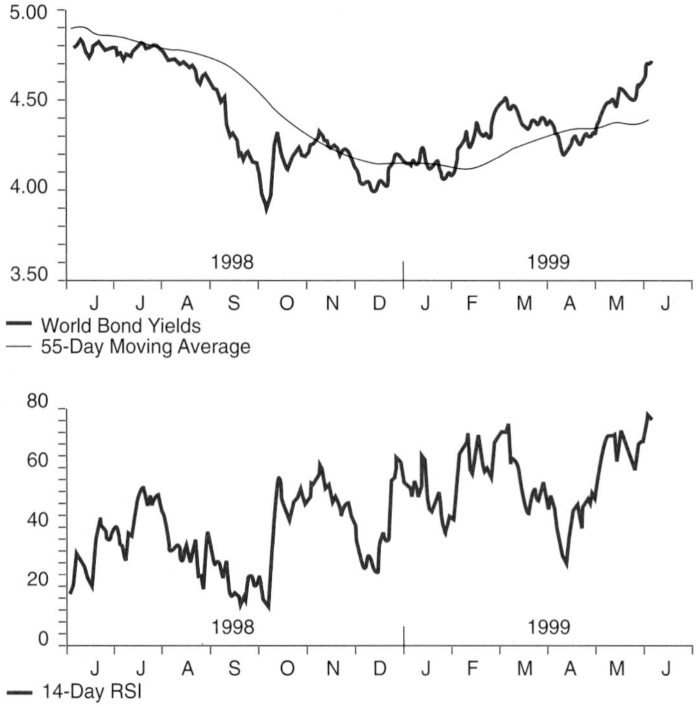
5.00
4.50
4.00
3.50
1998
1999
J J A S O N D J F M A M J
World Bond Yields
55-Day Moving Average
80
60
40
20
0
1998
1999
J J A S O N D J F M A M J
14-Day RSI

Source: *The Global Technician* (New York: Merrill Lynch, 8 June 1999).

THE INTERNET *Investments Online*

By its nature, technical analysis uses charts and graphs, and many Web sites offer them for use by investors and analysts; some are free, but some of the sites for more sophisticated users require payment for access. Here are several interesting sites:

www.mta-usa.org This is the home page of the Market Technicians Association, a professional group of chartists whose goal is to enhance technical analysis and educate investors about its role. The group sponsors the Chartered Market Technician (CMT) designation. This site features news groups, investment links, training and education sources, access to the organization's newsletter, and a list of technical analysis indicators.

www.bigcharts.com This site offers free intraday and historical charts and price quotes. Its database includes over 24,000 stocks, mutual funds, and indexes. Users can learn which stocks have the largest percentage gain (loss) in price and volume, and which stocks are hitting new 52-week highs (lows). Other features include momentum charts, stocks with the largest short interest, and a variety of other charts of interest to technicians.

www.dailystocks.com This site contains information of interest to both technicians and fundamentalists. It has several stock screening features, market commentary sources, and information on earnings, insider trading, and many more links.

www.investools.com The INVESTools home page offers news, reports, data, links to a variety of customized charts, investment newsletter links, and insights from featured advisors.

www.stockmaster.com This site offers basic stock charts, including price and volume charts.

www.dbc.com The home page of the Data Broadcasting Corporation has information about fixed-income and equity securities; news; research resources; and market updates on indexes, currencies, futures, new high/lows, and international indexes.

yield series rose above the moving-average line where it stayed except for a brief period in April. The lower panel is a 14-day relative-strength index (RSI) that confirms the strong momentum in yields based on a rising relative strength, but also an overall positive trend in the RSI. This set of technical graphs provides important insights to a global bond portfolio manager interested in the future outlook for global bond yields. These examples show how technical analysis can be and is applied to the bond market as well as to the stock market.

Summary

- Whether you want to base your investment decisions on fundamental analysis, technical analysis, or a belief in efficient markets, you should be aware of the principles and practice of technical analysis. Numerous investors believe in and use technical analysis, the large investment houses provide extensive support for technical analysis, and a large proportion of the discussion related to securities markets in the media is based on a technical view of the market. Now that you are aware of technical analysis principles, techniques, and indicators, you will recognize this tendency of security market commentators.
- Two main differences separate technical analysts and those who believe in efficient markets. The first, related to the information dissemination process, is concerned with whether one assumes that everybody gets the information at about the same time. The second difference is concerned with how quickly investors adjust security prices to reflect new information. Technical analysts believe that the information dissemination process differs for different people. They believe that news takes time to travel from the insider and expert to the individual investor. They also believe that price adjustments are not instantaneous. As a result, they contend that security prices move in trends that persist and, therefore, past price trends and volume information along with other market indicators can help you determine future price trends.

- We discussed technical trading rules under four general categories: contrary-opinion rules, follow-the-smart-money tactics, other market indicators, and stock price and volume techniques. These techniques and trading rules also can be applied to foreign markets and to the analysis of currency exchange rates. In addition, technical analysis has been used to determine the prevailing sentiment (trends) in the bond market.
- Most technicians follow several indicators and decision rules at any point in time and attempt to derive a consensus decision to buy, sell, or do nothing.[15] Many technicians often conclude to do nothing.

Questions

1. Technical analysts believe that one can use past price changes to predict future price changes. How do they justify this belief?
2. Technicians contend that stock prices move in trends that persist for long periods of time. What do technicians believe happens in the real world to cause these trends?
3. Briefly discuss the problems related to fundamental analysis that are considered advantages for technical analysis.
4. Discuss some disadvantages of technical analysis.
5. If the mutual fund cash position were to increase close to 12 percent, would a technician consider this cash position bullish or bearish? Give two reasons why the technical analyst would think this way.
6. Assume a significant decline in credit balances at brokerage firms. Discuss why a technician would consider this bearish.
7. If the bearish sentiment index of advisory service opinions were to increase to 61 percent, discuss why a technician would consider this bullish or bearish.
8. Suppose the ratio of specialists' short sales to total short sales increases to 70 percent. Discuss why a technician would consider this bullish or bearish.
9. Why is an increase in debit balances considered bullish?
10. Describe the Dow Theory and its three components. Which component is most important? What is the reason for an intermediate reversal?
11. Describe a bearish price and volume pattern, and discuss why it is considered bearish.
12. Discuss the logic behind the breadth of market index. How is it used to identify a peak in stock prices?
13. During a 10-day trading period, the cumulative net advance series goes from 1,572 to 1,053. During this same period, the DJIA goes from 11,200 to 12,050. As a technician, discuss what this set of events would mean to you.
14. Explain the reasoning behind a support level and a resistance level.
15. What is the purpose of computing a moving-average line for a stock? Describe a bullish pattern using a 50-day moving-average line and the stock volume of trading. Discuss why this pattern is considered bullish.
16. Assuming a stock price and volume chart that also contains a 50-day and a 200-day MA line, describe a bearish pattern with the two MA lines and discuss why it is bearish.
17. Explain how you would construct a relative-strength series for an individual stock or an industry group. What would it mean to say a stock experienced good relative strength during a bear market?
18. Discuss why most technicians follow several technical rules and attempt to derive a consensus.

Problems

1. Select a stock on the NYSE and construct a daily high, low, and close bar chart for it that includes its volume of trading for 10 trading days.
2. Compute the relative-strength ratio for the stock in Problem 1 relative to the S&P 500 Index. Prepare a table that includes all the data and indicates the computations as follows:

---

[15]An analysis using numerous indicators is Jerome Baesel, George Shows, and Edward Thorp, "Can Joe Granville Time the Market?" *Journal of Portfolio Management* 8, no. 3 (spring 1982): 5–9.

Closing Price		Relative-Strength Ratio	
Day	Stock	S&P 500	Stock Price/S&P 500

3. Plot the relative-strength ratio computed in Problem 2 on your bar chart. Discuss whether the stock's relative strength is bullish or bearish.
4. Currently Charlotte Art Importers is selling at $32 per share. Although you are somewhat dubious about technical analysis, you want to know how technicians who use point-and-figure charts would view this stock. You decide to note one-point movements and three-point reversals. You gather the following price information:

Date	Price	Date	Price	Date	Price
4/1	23½	4/18	33	5/3	27
4/4	28½	4/19	35⅜	5/4	26½
4/5	28	4/20	37	5/5	28
4/6	28	4/21	38½	5/6	28¼
4/7	29¾	4/22	36	5/9	28⅛
4/8	30½	4/25	35	5/10	28¼
4/11	30½	4/26	34¼	5/11	29⅛
4/12	32⅛	4/27	33⅛	5/12	30¼
4/13	32	4/28	32⅞	5/13	29⅞

Plot the point-and-figure chart using Xs for uptrends and Os for downtrends. How would a technician evaluate these movements? Discuss why you would expect a technician to buy, sell, or hold the stock based on this chart.

5. Assume the following daily closings for the Dow Jones Industrial Average:

Day	DJIA	Day	DJIA
1	11,010	7	11,220
2	11,100	8	11,130
3	11,165	9	11,250
4	11,080	10	11,315
5	11,070	11	11,240
6	11,150	12	11,310

a. Calculate a 4-day moving average for Days 4 through 12.
b. Assume that the index on Day 13 closes at 11,300. Would this signal a buy or sell decision?

6. The cumulative advance–decline line reported in *Barron's* at the end of the month is 21,240. During the first week of the following month, the daily report for the *Exchange* is as follows:

Day	1	2	3	4	5
Issues Traded	3,544	3,533	3,540	3,531	3,521
Advances	1,737	1,579	1,759	1,217	1,326
Declines	1,289	1,484	1,240	1,716	1,519
Unchanged	518	470	541	598	596

a. Compute the daily net advance–decline line for each of the 5 days.
b. Compute the cumulative advance–decline line for each day and the final value at the end of the week.

References

Brown, David P., and Robert H. Jennings. "On Technical Analysis." *The Review of Financial Studies* 2, no. 4 (October 1989).

Colby, Robert W., and Thomas A. Mayers. *The Encyclopedia of Technical Market Indicators.* Homewood, Ill.: Dow Jones-Irwin, 1988.

Dines, James. *How the Average Investor Can Use Technical Analysis for Stock Profits.* New York: Dines Chart Corporation, 1974.

Edwards, R. D., and John Magee, Jr. *Technical Analysis of Stock Trends.* 6th ed. Boston, Mass.: New York Institute of Finance, 1992.

Fosback, Norman G. *Stock Market Logic.* Fort Lauderdale, Fla.: The Institute for Economic Research, 1976.

Grant, Dwight. "Market Timing: Strategies to Consider." *Journal of Portfolio Management* 5, no. 4 (summer 1979).

Jagadeesh, Narasimhan. "Evidence of Predictable Behavior of Security Returns." *Journal of Finance* 45, no. 3 (July 1990).

Levy, Robert A. *The Relative Strength Concept of Common Stock Price Forecasting.* Larchmont, N.Y.: Investors Intelligence, 1968.

Meyers, Thomas A. *The Technical Analysis Course.* Chicago: Probus, 1989.

Murphy, John J. *Technical Analysis of the Futures Markets.* 2d ed. New York: McGraw-Hill, 1985.

Pring, Martin J. *Technical Analysis Explained.* 3d ed. New York: McGraw-Hill, 1991.

Shaw, Alan R. "Market Timing and Technical Analysis." In *The Financial Analysts Handbook.* 2d ed., ed. Sumner N. Levine. Homewood, Ill.: Dow Jones-Irwin, 1988.

Sweeney, Richard J. "Some New Filter Rule Tests: Methods and Results." *Journal of Financial and Quantitative Analysis* 23, no. 3 (September 1988).

Zweig, Martin E. *Winning on Wall Street.* New York: Warner Books, 1986.

Chapter

22 Equity Portfolio Management Strategies

After you read this chapter, you should be able to answer the following questions:

- What are the two generic equity portfolio management styles?
- What are three techniques for constructing a passive index portfolio?
- How does the goal of a passive equity portfolio manager differ from the goal of an active manager?
- What are the three themes that active equity portfolio managers can use?
- What stock characteristics differentiate value-oriented and growth-oriented investment styles?
- What is style analysis and what does it indicate about a manager's investment performance?
- What techniques are used by active managers in an attempt to outperform their benchmark?
- What are the differences between the integrated, strategic, tactical, and insured approaches to asset allocation?
- How can futures and options be used to help manage an equity portfolio?

Recent chapters have reviewed how to analyze industries and companies, how to estimate a stock's intrinsic value, and how technical analysis can assist in stock-picking. Some equity portfolios are constructed one stock at a time. Research staffs analyze the economy, industries, and companies; evaluate firms' strategies and competitive advantages; and recommend individual stocks for purchase or for sale.

Other equity portfolios are constructed using computer-intensive, rather than analyst-intensive, methods. Computers analyze relationships between stocks and market sectors to identify undervalued stocks. Quantitative "screens" and factor models are used to construct portfolios of stocks with such attributes as low P/E ratios, low price/book ratios, small capitalization, or high dividend yield; those neglected by analysts; or stocks whose returns are strongly correlated with economic variables, such as interest rates. Computer programs detect trading patterns and place buy-and-sell orders depending on past price movements. Computers also examine pricing relationships between the stock, options, and futures markets and place orders across these markets to arbitrage small price differences.

Managers of equity portfolios do not need to focus on the security selection process to produce superior investment returns. They can also increase an investor's wealth through their asset allocation decisions. For example, a manager acting as a market timer might split his funds into two index portfolios—one containing stocks and the other containing bonds—and then shift the allocation between these portfolios depending on which asset class he believes will perform the best during the coming period. The benefit of this strategy, which is formally known as *tactical* asset allocation, comes from correctly predicting broad market movements rather than trends for individual companies. Similarly, *insured* asset allocation is an attempt to limit investment losses by shifting funds between an existing equity portfolio and a risk-free security depending on changing market conditions.

As we saw in chapter 11, equity portfolio return profiles can be modified by the use of futures and options. It is possible to trade futures contracts on major indexes, as well as acquire options on stock market indexes, on selected industry groups, and on individual stocks. These derivative securities can assist the portfolio manager in shifting a portfolio's exposure to systematic and unsystematic risk.

PASSIVE VERSUS ACTIVE MANAGEMENT

Equity portfolio management styles fall into either a passive or an active category. Unlike the immunization of bond portfolios, no middle ground exists between active and passive equity management strategies. Some argue that "hybrid" active/passive equity portfolio management styles exist, but such styles really are variations of active management philosophies. Similar to traditional active management, hybrid-style managers invest to find undervalued sectors or securities. The following discussion reviews the traditional meaning of the terms *passive* and *active* portfolio management.

Passive equity portfolio management is a long-term buy-and-hold strategy. Usually stocks are purchased so the portfolio's returns will track those of an index over time. Because of the goal of tracking an index, this approach to investing is generally referred to as "indexing." Occasional rebalancing is needed as dividends must be reinvested and because stocks merge or drop out of the target index and other stocks are added. Notably, the purpose of an indexed portfolio is not to "beat" the target index, but to match its performance. A manager of an equity index portfolio is judged on how well he or she tracks the target index—that is, minimizes the deviation between portfolio and index returns (i.e., tracking error) similar to the bond index portfolio manager.

Active equity portfolio management is an attempt by the manager to outperform, on a risk-adjusted basis, a passive benchmark portfolio. A *benchmark portfolio* is a passive portfolio whose average characteristics (including such factors as beta, dividend yield, industry weighting, and firm size) match the risk–return objectives of the client.

When deciding whether to follow an active or a passive strategy (or some combination of the two), an investor must assess the trade-off between the low-cost but less-exciting alternative of indexing versus the higher-cost but potentially more lucrative alternative of active management. Not surprisingly, Sorensen, Miller, and Samak have noted that the critical factor in this evaluation is the stock-picking skill of the portfolio manager. Using pension fund performance data from the 1985–1997 period, they showed that the optimal allocation to indexing declines as managerial skill increases. However, they also conclude that some indexing is appropriate for funds in most risk objective classes.[1]

Table 22.1 reports the amount of money invested in the U.S. equity and fixed-income markets using active and indexed strategies for two recent years. The data are compiled from a survey of the strategies employed by more than 2,500 professional money management firms on behalf of their clients. Three conclusions are notable. First, active management strategies dominate indexed portfolios in terms of the total amount of money controlled by the investment management industry. Second, the indexed sector of the industry is growing quite rapidly, a trend driven in part by the lower management fees

[1]Eric H. Sorensen, Keith L. Miller, and Vele Samak, "Allocating between Active and Passive Management," *Financial Analysts Journal* 54, no. 4 (September/October 1998): 18–31.

TABLE 22.1 **ACTIVE AND PASSIVE INVESTMENT IN THE U.S. EQUITY AND FIXED-INCOME MARKETS**

Strategy	1995 (Billions)	1994 (Billions)	% Change
Active Equity	$1,945.10	$1,338.01	45.4
Indexed Equity	275.22	135.54	103.1
Active Fixed Income	1,677.45	1,370.63	22.4
Indexed Fixed Income	82.73	32.69	153.3

Source: Nelson Investment Management Network.

charged for passive portfolios. Third, although the amount of money managed in active equity and fixed-income strategies is roughly comparable, equity indexing is far more popular than fixed-income indexing.

In the following sections, we examine more closely the mechanics of passive and active equity portfolio management.

AN OVERVIEW OF PASSIVE EQUITY PORTFOLIO MANAGEMENT STRATEGIES

Passive equity portfolio management attempts to design a portfolio to replicate the performance of a specific index. The key word here is *replicate.* As discussed in Chapter 2, the portfolio manager who earns higher returns by violating the client's policy statement should be fired; a passive manager who isn't really passive should likewise be dismissed. A passive manager earns his or her fee by constructing a portfolio that closely tracks the performance of a specified equity index (referred to as the *benchmark index*) that meets the client's needs and objectives. If the manager attempts to outperform the index selected, he or she violates the passive premise of the portfolio.

In Chapter 7, we presented several reasons for investing in a passive equity portfolio. Strong evidence indicates that the stock market is fairly efficient. For most active managers, the costs of actively managing a portfolio (1 to 2 percent of the portfolio's assets) are difficult to overcome. As we saw earlier, the S&P 500 index typically outperforms most equity mutual funds on an annual basis. Note that, although the S&P 500 is the most popular index to track, a client can choose from among about 30 different indexes.[2]

Chapter 5 contained a summary description of many different market indexes. Domestic U.S. equity indexes include the S&P 500, 400, and 100; the Major Market index; the NASDAQ composite index; and the Wilshire 5000. The *Wall Street Journal* publishes the daily values of indexes for the organized exchanges, the OTC market, and various industry groups. Indexes exist for small capitalization stocks (Russell 2000), for value- or growth-oriented stocks (Russell Growth index and the Russell Value index), for numerous world regions (such as the EAFE index), as well as for smaller regions, individual countries, and types of countries (emerging markets). As passive investing has grown in popularity, money managers have created an index fund for virtually every broad market category.[3]

[2]The growing popularity of index funds is discussed in Jeffrey M. Laderman, "The Stampede to Index Funds," *Business Week,* 1 April 1996, 78–79.

[3]See, for example, Robert Fernholz, Robert Garvy, and John Hannon, "Diversity-Weighted Indexing," *Journal of Portfolio Management* 24, no. 2 (winter 1998): 74–82; and Ajay Khorana, Edward Nelling, and Jeffrey J. Trester, "The Emergence of Country Index Funds," *Journal of Portfolio Management* 24, no. 4 (summer 1998): 78–84.

The goal of a passive portfolio is to match the returns to the index as closely as possible. But because of cash inflows and outflows and company mergers and bankruptcies, securities must be bought and sold, which means that there inevitably will be differences between portfolio and benchmark returns over time. In addition, even though index funds generally attempt to minimize turnover and the resultant transactions fees, they necessarily have to do some rebalancing, which means that the long-run return performance of index funds will lag the benchmark index. Certainly, substantial or prolonged deviations of the portfolio's returns from the index's returns would be a cause for concern.

Index Fund Construction Techniques

There are three basic techniques for constructing a passive index portfolio: full replication, sampling, and quadratic optimization or programming. The most obvious technique is **full replication** wherein all the securities in the index are purchased in proportion to their weights in the index. This technique helps ensure close tracking, but it may be suboptimal for two reasons. First, the need to buy many securities will increase transaction costs that will detract from performance. Second, the reinvestment of dividends will also result in high commissions when many firms pay small dividends at different times in the year.

The second technique, **sampling**, addresses the problem of numerous stock issues. Statistical theory teaches us that we don't need to ask everyone in the United States for his or her opinion to determine who may win an election. Thus, opinion pollsters query only a small sample of the population to gauge public sentiment. Sampling techniques also can be applied to passive portfolio management. With sampling, a portfolio manager would only need to buy a representative sample of stocks that comprise the benchmark index. Stocks with larger index weights are purchased according to their weight in the index; smaller issues are purchased so their aggregate characteristics (e.g., beta, industry distribution, and dividend yield) approximate the underlying benchmark. With fewer stocks to purchase, larger positions can be taken in the issues acquired, which should lead to proportionately lower commissions. Further, the reinvestment of dividend cash flows will be less problematic because fewer securities need to be purchased to rebalance the portfolio. The disadvantage of sampling is that portfolio returns will almost certainly not track the returns for the benchmark index as closely as with full replication.

Figure 22.1 estimates the **tracking error** that occurs from sampling.[4] For example, full replication of the S&P 500 would (in theory) have almost no tracking error. As smaller samples are used to replicate the S&P's performance, the potential tracking error increases. There must be an analysis of the costs (larger tracking errors) and the benefits (easier management, lower trading commissions) of using smaller samples.

Rather than obtaining a sample based on industry or security characteristics, **quadratic optimization** or programming techniques can be used to construct a passive portfolio. With quadratic programming, historical information on price changes and correlations between securities are input to a computer program that determines the composition of a portfolio that will minimize tracking error with the benchmark. A problem with this technique is that it relies on *historical* price changes and correlations, and, if these factors change over time, the portfolio may experience very large tracking errors.

Some passive portfolios are not based on a published index. Sometimes customized passive portfolios, called **completeness funds**, are constructed to complement active portfolios that do not cover the entire market. For example, a large pension fund may allocate some of its holdings to active managers expected to outperform the market. Many times

---

[4]As noted earlier, the quality of an index portfolio is not measured by the magnitude of its returns; rather, it is measured by its tracking error, or the degree to which the portfolio's returns deviate from those of the benchmark index. See Roger Clarke, S. Krase, and Meir Statman, "Tracking Errors, Regret, and Tactical Asset Allocation," *Journal of Portfolio Management* 20, no. 3 (spring 1994): 16–24.

FIGURE 22.1 **EXPECTED TRACKING ERROR BETWEEN THE S&P 500 INDEX AND PORTFOLIOS COMPRISED OF SAMPLES OF FEWER THAN 500 STOCKS**

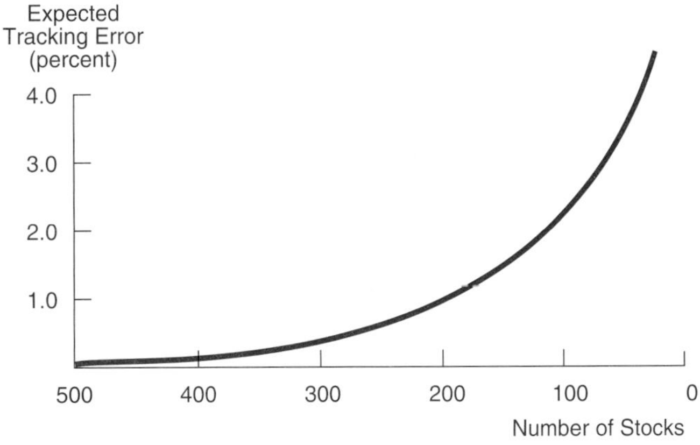
Expected
Tracking Error
(percent)
4.0
3.0
2.0
1.0
500
400
300
200
100
0
Number of Stocks

these active portfolios are overweighted in certain market sectors or stock types. In this case, the pension fund sponsor may want the remaining funds to be invested passively to "fill the holes" left vacant by the active managers. The performance of the completeness fund will be compared to a customized benchmark that incorporates the characteristics of the stocks not covered by the active managers.

For example, suppose a pension fund hires three active managers to invest part of the fund's money. One manager emphasizes small capitalization U.S. stocks, the second invests only in Pacific Rim countries, and the third invests in U.S. stocks with low P/E ratios. To ensure adequate diversification, the pension fund may want to passively invest the remaining assets in a completeness fund that will have a customized benchmark that includes large- and mid-capitalization U.S. stocks, U.S. stocks with normal to high P/E ratios, and international stocks outside the Pacific Rim.

Still other passive portfolios and benchmarks exist for investors with certain unique needs and preferences.[5] Some investors may want their funds to be invested only in stocks that pay dividends or in a company that produces a product or service that the investor deems socially responsible. Benchmarks can be produced that reflect these desired attributes, and passive portfolios can be constructed to track the performance of the customized benchmark over time so investors' special needs can be satisfied.[6]

AN OVERVIEW OF ACTIVE EQUITY PORTFOLIO MANAGEMENT STRATEGIES

The goal of active portfolio management is to earn a portfolio return that exceeds the return of a passive benchmark portfolio, net of transaction costs, on a risk-adjusted basis. An important issue for active managers and their clients to resolve is the selection of an

[5]Recall our discussion in Chapter 2 on investors' objectives and constraints; two of the constraints were legal and regulatory requirements and unique needs and preferences.

[6]See Sharmin Mossavar-Rahmani, "Customized Benchmarks in Structured Management," *Journal of Portfolio Management* 13, no. 4 (summer 1988): 65–68; and Chris P. Dialynas, "The Active Decisions in the Selection of Passive Management and Performance Bogeys," in *The Handbook of Fixed Income Securities,* 5th ed., ed. Frank Fabozzi (Chicago, Ill.: Irwin Professional Publishing, 1997).

appropriate benchmark (sometimes called a "normal" portfolio). The benchmark should incorporate the average qualities of the portfolio strategy of the client. Thus, an active portfolio manager who invests mainly in small capitalization stocks with low P/E ratios because the client specified this strategy should not have her performance compared to a broad market index, such as the S&P 500.

A first step in constructing the normal benchmark portfolio for the manger above may be to include, on an equally weighted basis, all stocks with market capitalizations under $1 billion and P/E ratios less than 80 percent of the S&P 500 P/E ratio. Computerized databases allow the construction of such passive benchmarks so you can monitor the returns over time. This benchmark portfolio will be the standard by which the small stock, low P/E manager is evaluated.

The job of an active equity manager is not easy. If transaction costs and fees total 1.5 percent of the portfolio's assets annually, the portfolio has to earn a return 1.5 percentage points above the passive benchmark just to keep pace with it. If the manager's strategy involves overweighting specific market sectors in anticipation of price increases, the risk of the active portfolio may well exceed that of the passive benchmark, so the active portfolio's return will have to exceed the benchmark by an even wider margin to compensate for its higher risk.

Thus, active managers must overcome two difficulties relative to the benchmark. First, an actively managed portfolio will have higher transaction costs. Second, active portfolios can often have higher risk than the passive benchmark.

One key to success is for active managers to *be consistent* in their area of expertise. Market gyrations occur and investment styles go in and out of favor. Successful long-term investing requires that you maintain your investment philosophy and composure while other are deviating from theirs. Another key to success is to *minimize the trading activity* of the portfolio. Attempts to time price movements over short horizons will result in lower profits because of growing commissions.

Active managers use three generic themes to time the market and add value to their portfolios in comparison to the benchmark. First, they can try to time the equity market by shifting funds into and out of stocks, bonds, and T-bills depending on broad market forecasts and estimated risk premiums. Second, they can shift funds among different equity sectors and industries (financial stocks, consumer cyclicals, durable goods, and so on) or among investment styles (large capitalization, small capitalization, value, growth, and so on) to catch the next "hot" concept before the rest of the market does. Third, equity managers can do stock-picking, looking at individual issues in an attempt to find undervalued stocks—i.e., buy low and sell high. The following discussion describes some of the strategies used to implement these investment themes.

Global portfolios can apply the economic analysis discussed in Chapter 14 to identify different countries whose equity markets are potentially undervalued or overvalued. The global portfolio can then overweight or underweight those countries relative to a global benchmark portfolio as shown in Chapter 14. Solnik has argued that if the investor sets the benchmark for a very long-term horizon, such a portfolio should not be unduly affected by the attendant currency risks.[7]

Some global portfolio managers emphasize industry analysis rather than a country allocation.[8] As competition is becoming more global, some analysts examine industries and firms while disregarding country boundaries. For example, Caterpillar and Komatsu

[7]Bruno Solnik, "Global Asset Management," *Journal of Portfolio Management* 24, no. 4 (summer 19998): 43–51.

[8]For example, see Richard A. Weiss, "Global Sector Rotation: A New Look at an Old Idea," *Financial Analysts Journal* 54, no. 3 (May/June 1998): 6–8.

FIGURE 22.2 **THE STOCK MARKET AND THE BUSINESS CYCLE**

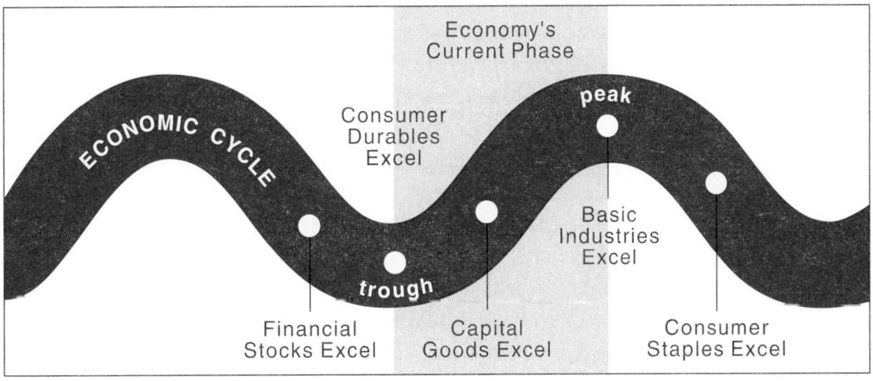
Economy's
Current Phase
ECONOMIC CYCLE
peak
Consumer
Durables
Excel
Basic
Industries
Excel
trough
Financial
Stocks Excel
Capital
Goods Excel
Consumer
Staples Excel

Source: Susan E. Kuhn, "Stocks Are Still Your Best Buy," *Fortune,* 21 March 1994, 140. © 1994 Time Inc. All Rights Reserved.

compete globally in the heavy equipment industry while Boeing and Airbus compete globally in the airline manufacturing industry. These global portfolio managers analyze economic trends, industry competitive forces, and company strengths and strategies with a global perspective. The analyses of financial statements (Chapter 12), industries (Chapter 19), and companies (Chapter 20) are applied in a global, rather than a national, setting in order to identify undervalued industrial sectors and firms.

A **sector rotation strategy** involves positioning the portfolio to take advantage of the market's next move. Often this means emphasizing or overweighting (relative to the benchmark portfolio) certain economic sectors or industries in response to the next expected phase of the business cycle. Figure 22.2 contains suggestions on how sector rotators may position their portfolios to take advantage of stock market trends during the economic cycle.

"Sector" also can include different stock attributes. Because the market seems to favor some attributes more than others over time, sector rotation may involve overweighting stocks with certain characteristics, such as small or large capitalization stocks, high or low P/E stocks, or stocks classified as "value" or "growth" stocks. A standard measure of a value stock is one with a below-average P/E ratio or price/book ratio. The low market ratios indicate that the stocks are potentially undervalued. Growth stocks are those whose earnings are expected to grow at a high rate. As a result, they typically have above-average P/Es, P/BV and P/CF ratios, and high ROEs.

Earnings momentum and **price momentum** strategies are used because the market at times seems to reward the stocks of companies whose earnings have steady, above-average growth, or whose prices are rising because of market optimism.

The existence of computer databases has encouraged the use of computer screening and other quantitatively based methods of evaluating stocks. These screening methods search for portfolios of stocks with certain characteristics rather than examining individual stocks to determine whether they are underpriced.

The simplest computer screens identify groups of stocks based on a set of attributes. Screens also are used to narrow the list of thousands of stocks to a manageable few that can then be evaluated using more traditional analytical means. Stocks can be screened on many company and stock price characteristics. For example, it is possible to generate a list of "value" stocks with at least a 20 percent return on equity, stable or growing dividends over the past 10 years, and below-market P/E ratios.

More complicated quantitative strategies are available that are similar in some ways to sector rotation. Factor models, similar to those used in the APT, can identify stocks whose earnings or prices are sensitive to economic variables, such as exchange rates, inflation, interest rates, or consumer sentiment. With this information, portfolios can be "tilted" by trading those stocks most sensitive to the analyst's economic forecast. The manager can try to improve the portfolio's relative performance in a recession by purchasing stocks that are *least* sensitive to the analyst's pessimistic forecast.[9]

Some quantitatively oriented portfolio managers use what is called a long–short approach to investing. In the long–short approach, stocks are passed through a number of screens and assigned a rank. Stocks at the top of the ranking are purchased; stocks at the bottom are sold short. Such a strategy can be neutral on the overall market, since the value of the long position can approximate that of the short position. The performance of the top-ranked stocks is expected to exceed that of the lower-ranked stocks, regardless of whether the overall stock market rises, falls, or trades in a narrow range.

How do managers know that these quantitative models have the potential to offer above-average risk-adjusted returns? The answer is that they hope the future will be similar to the past because these quantitative strategies have been **backtested**. This involves using computers to examine the composition and returns of portfolios based on historical data to determine if the strategy would have worked successfully in the past. The risk of testing an investment strategy in this way is that relationships that existed in the past are not guaranteed to hold in the future.

Some managers let the computers do all the work. Neural networks are computer programs that attempt to imitate the thinking patterns of the human brain. They use vast databases and artificial intelligence capabilities to find cause-and-effect patterns in stock returns.[10] The computer attempts to discover undervalued securities by identifying abnormal risk-adjusted return patterns and "learning" what stock attributes drive the market.

Active managers also use quadratic programming to solve the efficient frontier optimization problem of Markowitz (see Chapter 8). The manager's expectations about returns, risk, and correlations are used by the optimizer to select portfolios that offer the optimal risk–return trade-off.

Linear programming techniques can be used to construct portfolios that maximize an objective (such as expected return) while satisfying linear constraints dealing with such items as the portfolio's beta, dividend yield, and diversification. As with almost all models, the output is only as good as the inputs, which in this case are expectations (estimates) of return, standard deviations, and correlations among alternative assets and the aggregate market.

VALUE VERSUS GROWTH INVESTING: A CLOSER LOOK

One of the most important developments in active equity management during the last several years has been the creation of portfolio strategies based on value- and growth-oriented investment styles. Indeed, it is now common for money management firms to define themselves as "value stock managers" or "growth stock managers" when selling their services to clients. Table 22.2 indicates how pervasive these styles have become. Based on the sur-

[9]See Richard Roll and Stephen A. Ross, "The Arbitrage Pricing Theory Approach to Strategic Portfolio Planning," *Financial Analysts Journal* 51, no. 1 (January/February 1995): 122–131.

[10]See Delvin D. Hawley, John D. Johnson, and Dijjotam Raina, "Artificial Neural Systems: A New Tool for Financial Decision-Making," *Financial Analysts Journal* 46, no. 6 (November/December 1990): 63–72; George S. Swales, Jr., and Young Yoon, "Applying Artificial Neural Networks to Investment Analysis," *Financial Analysts Journal* 48, no. 4 (September/October 1992): 78–80; and Richard C. Grinold and Ronald N. Kahn, *Active Portfolio Management* (Chicago, Ill.: Probus Publishing, 1995).

TABLE 22.2 **GROWTH AND VALUE INVESTMENT PORTFOLIOS**

	1995	1994
Growth Portfolios		
Number of Domestic Equity Products	1,015	936
Total Assets under Management (billions)	\$799.55	\$552.52
Value Portfolios		
Number of Domestic Equity Products	748	702
Total Assets under Management (billions)	\$696.71	\$504.03

Source: Nelson Investment Management Network.

vey of 2,500 money managers described earlier, the data show that by 1995, more than 1,000 different growth-oriented investment products were in existence managing almost \$800 billion. Although the value style does not appear to be quite as popular with investors, it is still well represented with almost \$700 billion invested in about 750 different products.

The distinction between value and growth investing can be best appreciated by considering the thought process of a representative manager for each style.[11] In Chapter 13 we saw that the price-earnings ratio for any company can be expressed as:

$$\text{P/E Ratio} = \frac{(\text{Current Price Per Share})}{(\text{Earnings Per Share})}$$

where the earnings per share (EPS) measure can be based on either current or future (i.e., forecasted) firm performance. In broad terms, value and growth managers will focus on different aspects of this equation when deciding whether a stock should be added to an existing portfolio. Specifically, a growth-oriented investor will:

- focus on the EPS component (i.e., the denominator) of the P/E ratio and its economic determinants;
- look for companies that he or she expects to exhibit rapid EPS growth in the future; and
- often implicitly assume that the P/E ratio will remain constant over the near term, meaning that the stock price will rise as forecasted earnings growth is realized.

On the other hand, a value-oriented investor will:

- focus on the price component (i.e., the numerator) of the P/E ratio; he or she must be convinced that the price of the stock is "cheap" by some means of comparison;
- not care a great deal about current earnings or the fundamental drivers of earnings growth; and
- often implicitly assume that the P/E ratio is below its natural level and that the market will soon "correct" this situation by increasing the stock price with little or no change in earnings.

[11]This motivation is based on an excellent overview of value- and growth-oriented investment styles that can be found in Jon A. Christopherson and C. Nola Williams, "Equity Style: What It Is and Why It Matters," in *The Handbook of Equity Style Management,* ed. T. Daniel Coggin and Frank J. Fabozzi (New Hope, Pa.: Frank J. Fabozzi Associates, 1995).

FIGURE 22.3 CHARACTERISTICS OF GROWTH AND VALUE STOCKS

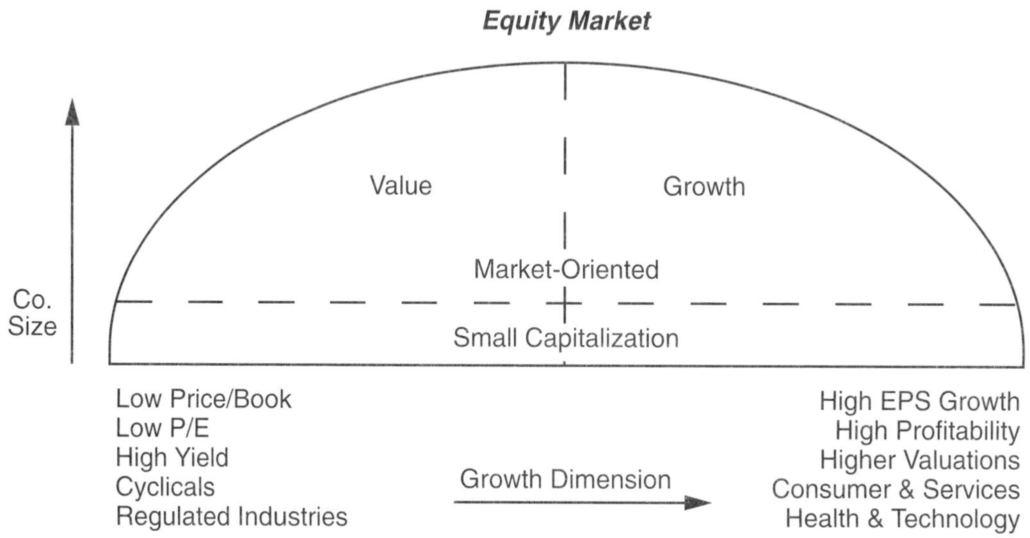
Equity Market
Value
Growth
Market-Oriented
Small Capitalization
Co.
Size
Low Price/Book
Low P/E
High Yield
Cyclicals
Regulated Industries
Growth Dimension
High EPS Growth
High Profitability
Higher Valuations
Consumer & Services
Health & Technology

Source: Frank Russell Company.

In summary, a growth investor focuses on the current and future economic "story" of a company, with less regard to share valuation. The value investor, on the other hand, focuses on share price in anticipation of a market correction and, possibly, improving company fundamentals.

The conceptual difference between value and growth investing may be reasonably straightforward, but classifying individual stocks into the appropriate style is not always simple in practice. Since detailed company valuations are time-consuming to produce, most analysts rely on more easily obtained financial indicators—such as P/E and P/B ratios, dividend yields, and EPS growth rates—to define both an individual equity holding as well as the style benchmark portfolio. Figure 22.3 shows one approach along these lines for classifying firms according to style and market capitalization. Notice that value stocks are defined as those that are relatively cheap (e.g., low P/B, high yield) and with modest growth opportunities (e.g., regulated firms) while growth stocks tend to be more expensive, reflecting their superior earnings potential (e.g., technology firms).

As noted earlier, one advantage of defining value and growth investment styles in this manner is that it makes computerized screening of an equity database quite easy. For instance, Table 22.3 shows a representative set of growth stocks (Panel A) and value stocks (Panel B) contained in the Bridge Information Systems U.S. equity database. For this example, growth stocks were defined as follows: Current P/E (PE) $>$ 25, Current P/B (PBK) $>$ 6, Dividend Yield (AYLD) $<$ 1.0%, and historical five-year EPS growth (GRWEPS) $>$ 27% per year. The value stocks were established by the following criteria: PE $<$ 8, PBK $<$ 1, AYLD $>$ 7%, and GRWEPS $<$ 4%. Not surprisingly, the growth screen uncovered several technology stocks (e.g., America Online, Intel) and other well-known firms with rapid earnings growth (e.g., Gap, Times Mirror). Conversely, 15 of the 20 value firms listed had negative current earnings (and, hence, negative P/E ratios) and all but two had negative earnings growth. Of course, this sort of screening does not insure investment success, particularly since it relied on historical data. The challenge for growth managers is to figure out which stocks in Panel A will continue to exhibit exceptional earnings momentum while value managers must determine which firms in Panel B have fundamentally sound businesses that can be acquired cheaply.

TABLE 22.3 **REPRESENTATIVE VALUE AND GROWTH PORTFOLIOS**

Panel A. Growth-Oriented Stocks

SYM	SYM	NA	PE	PBK	AYLD	GRWEPS	BETA
US;ADBE	US;ADBE	ADOBE SYSTEMS INC	32.8	7.01	0.34	54.9	1.44
US;AOL	US;AOL	AMERICA ONLINE INC	593.0	89.46	0.00	80.1	2.61
US;CAH	US;CAH	CARDINAL HEALTH INC	44.7	8.22	0.14	27.6	0.69
US;CL	US;CL	COLGATE PALMOLIVE CO	35.8	11.99	0.59	27.9	1.45
US;COF	US;COF	CAPITAL ONE FINANCIA	39.3	8.48	0.05	29.6	1.55
US;DL	US;DL	DIAL CORP	32.6	8.79	0.24	585.7	0.77
US;EXPD	US;EXPD	EXPEDITORS INTERNATI	31.8	6.46	0.12	36.1	2.05
US;FDS	US;FDS	FACTSET RESEARCH SYS	69.7	13.35	0.20	33.5	1.55
US;GDT	US;GDT	GUIDANT CORP	53.2	28.61	0.00	35.8	1.65
US;GLW	US;GLW	CORNING INC	41.2	9.37	0.30	192.0	1.50
US;GPS	US;GPS	GAP INC	49.1	24.81	0.19	56.3	2.01
US;HH	US;HH	HOOPER HOLMES INC	31.1	6.92	0.22	59.1	1.36
US;INTC	US;INTC	INTEL CORP	29.4	8.12	0.12	27.3	0.96
US;NDN	US;NDN	99 CENTS ONLY STORES	42.4	6.90	0.00	28.6	1.13
US;PAYX	US;PAYX	PAYCHEX INC	65.3	20.34	0.65	32.1	0.82
US;TJX	US;TJX	TJX COMPANIES INC	25.3	9.50	0.32	64.1	1.40
US;TMC	US;TMC	TIMES MIRROR CO	74.6	6.82	0.35	182.6	0.68
US;TRC	US;TRC	TEJON RANCH CO	87.5	7.10	0.22	38.1	0.91
US;TYC	US;TYC	TYCO INTERNATIONAL	35.6	6.99	0.13	32.6	1.34
US;USTC	US;USTC	US TRUST CORP	27.6	6.53	0.89	204.9	1.01

Found: 20
[BIR]RF <--- Main Menu 22-APR-99 Page: 1 of 1
[BIR]RF (c)BRIDGE

Panel B. Value-Oriented Stocks

SYM	SYM	NA	PE	PBK	AYLD	GRWEPS	BETA
US;AHPI	US;AHPI	ALLIED HEALTHCARE PR	−1.7	0.28	8.00	−97.5	2.31
US;BRU	US;BRU	BURLINGTON RESOURCES	7.1	0.90	9.43	−19.9	0.32
US;CMO	US;CMO	CAPSTEAD MORTGAGE CO	−1.3	0.68	41.40	−80.9	1.85
US;ECGOF	US;ECGOF	AMERICAN ECO CORP	−1.1	0.38	26.35	−41.9	0.73
US;FARL	US;FARL	FARREL CORP	7.2	0.62	7.27	−10.6	0.96
US;FFP	US;FFP	FFP PARTNERS LP	3.5	0.16	86.55	−74.6	0.37
US;FNL	US;FNL	FANSTEEL INC	7.9	0.85	10.20	−78.2	0.99
US;FUR	US;FUR	FIRST UNION REAL EST	−5.2	0.64	7.76	−85.8	1.02
US;GLR	US;GLR	G AND L REALTY CORP	−16.7	0.55	13.57	−38.9	−0.07
US;HBW	US;HBW	HOWARD B WOLF INC	−11.1	0.57	8.26	−45.5	0.00
US;HFD	US;HFD	HOST FUNDING INC	−4.7	0.93	28.80	−64.6	0.68
US;ICOC	US;ICOC	ICO INC	−11.8	0.19	55.74	−43.6	0.70
US;JII	US;JII	JOHNSTON INDUSTRIES	−29.2	0.39	17.14	−88.1	0.69
US;MTLM	US;MTLM	METAL MANAGEMENT INC	−2.6	0.46	7.30	0.0	2.79
US;NU	US;NU	NORTHEAST UTILITIES	−13.4	0.91	8.39	−98.9	0.03
US;OWOS	US;OWOS	OWOSSO CORP	−53.1	0.73	8.47	−80.3	0.00
US;PAH	US;PAH	PATRIOT AMERICAN HOS	−2.6	0.41	15.39	−95.6	2.47
US;PFG	US;PFG	PENNCORP FINANCIAL G	0.0	0.05	30.00	−88.6	1.44
US;PRT	US;PRT	PRIME RETAIL INC	−26.8	0.62	12.59	0.0	0.91
US;SGD	US;SGD	SCOTTS LIQUID GOLD I	−5.0	0.69	8.00	−41.4	−0.14

Found: 23
[BIR]RF <--- Main Menu 22-APR-99 Page: 1 of 2
[BIR]RF/PC/PG2 (c)BRIDGE

Source: Bridge Information Systems, 22 April 1999.

FIGURE 22.4

CUMULATIVE PERFORMANCE OF DOMESTIC VALUE AND GROWTH STOCK INDEXES

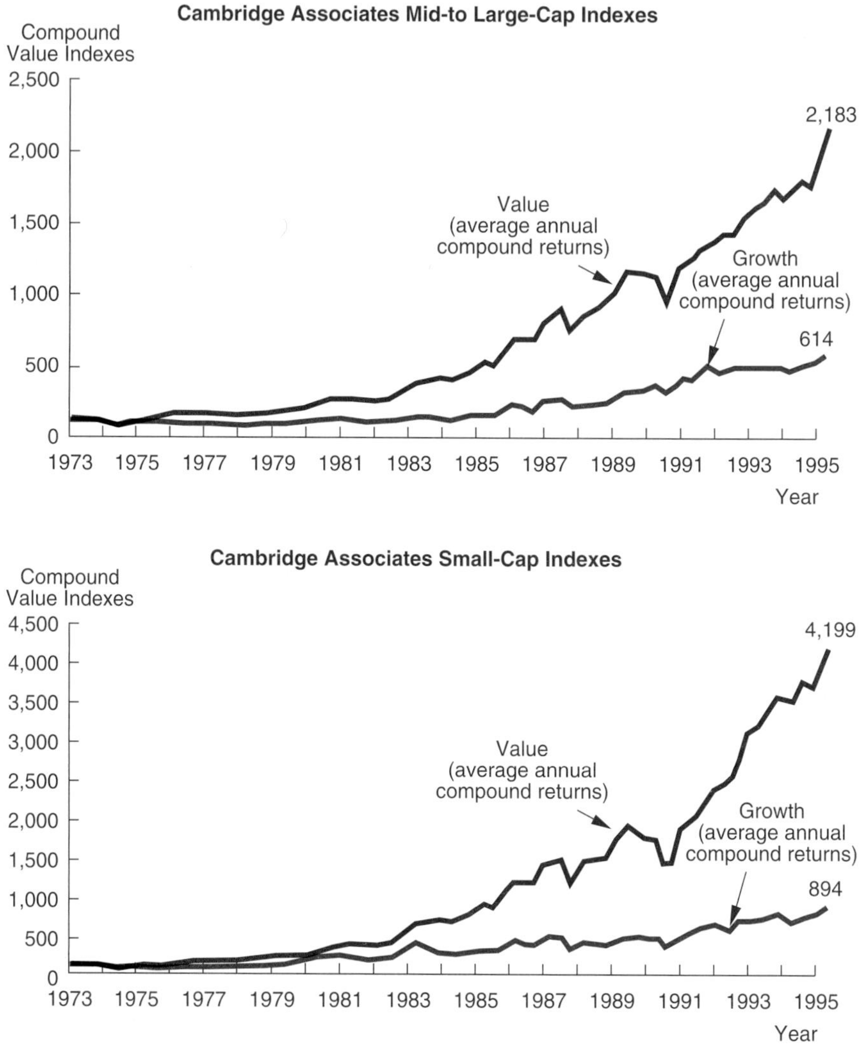
Cambridge Associates Mid-to Large-Cap Indexes
Compound Value Indexes
2,500
2,000
1,500
1,000
500
0
2,183
Value (average annual compound returns)
Growth (average annual compound returns)
614
1973 1975 1977 1979 1981 1983 1985 1987 1989 1991 1993 1995
Year
Cambridge Associates Small-Cap Indexes
Compound Value Indexes
4,500
4,000
3,500
3,000
2,500
2,000
1,500
1,000
500
0
4,199
Value (average annual compound returns)
Growth (average annual compound returns)
894
1973 1975 1977 1979 1981 1983 1985 1987 1989 1991 1993 1995
Year

Note: March 31, 1973 = 100.

Source: Calculated from data provided by Standard & Poor's Compustat.

Although investors appear to pay somewhat more attention to growth-oriented strategies, research has shown that a value approach to portfolio management tends to provide superior returns. In particular, Capaul, Rowley, and Sharpe studied the performance of value and growth portfolios (defined by relative P/B ratios) in six countries: the United States, the United Kingdom, Japan, France, Germany, and Switzerland.[12] Over a 10-year period ending in June 1992, they demonstrated that global value stocks outperformed global growth stocks by an average of 3.3 percent per year. Further, value stocks outperformed growth stocks in each of the six countries considered separately. Figure 22.4, which

[12]Carlo Capaul, Ian Rowley, and William F. Sharpe, "International Value and Growth Stock Returns," *Financial Analysts Journal* 49, no.1 (January/February 1993): 27–36.

FIGURE 22.5 **VALUE–GROWTH RETURN SPREAD**

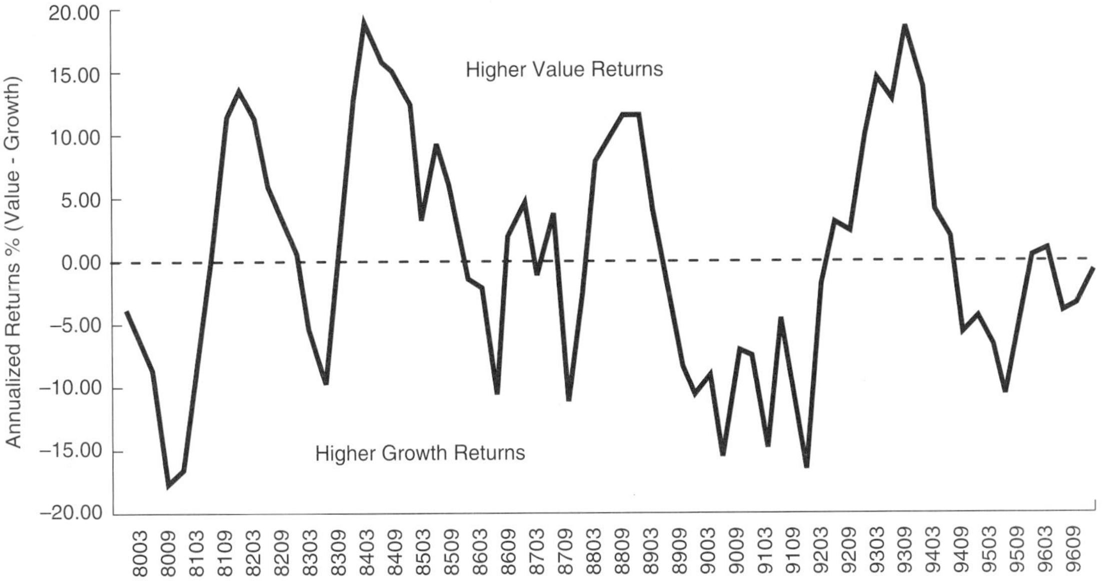
Annualized Returns % (Value - Growth)
20.00
15.00
10.00
5.00
0.00
−5.00
−10.00
−15.00
−20.00
Higher Value Returns
Higher Growth Returns
8003
8009
8103
8109
8203
8209
8303
8309
8403
8409
8503
8509
8603
8609
8703
8709
8803
8809
8903
8909
9003
9009
9103
9109
9203
9209
9303
9309
9403
9409
9503
9509
9603
9609

Relative rolling 12-month performance based on the Russell 1000 Value and Growth indices.

Source: Fidelity Management and Research Company.

looks at the value–growth return spread for firms with different market capitalizations, documents the substantial cumulative effect that this outperformance can have on an investor's wealth over time.

It is tempting to conclude that value is unambiguously superior to growth as an investment style. However, it is important to note that although value investing produces higher average returns than growth investing, this does not occur with much consistency from one investment period to another. In fact, Figure 22.5 shows that there are significant differences in the value–growth return spread (based on the rolling annual performance of the Russell 1000 Value and Growth indices) over time. During this analysis, the spread ranged from almost 20 percent in favor of value investing to almost 20 percent to the advantage of the growth style. Conversely, Figure 22.6 illustrates that the spread between value and growth return standard deviations, while itself volatile, is consistently negative, meaning that the growth strategy is consistently riskier than the value approach. This finding is also supported by the fact that the growth stocks in Table 22.3 tend to have larger beta coefficients than the value stocks.

AN OVERVIEW OF STYLE ANALYSIS

As we have seen, there are many approaches to managing a portfolio of equity securities. The different styles that have evolved over the years include forming portfolios around stock characteristics, such as market capitalization, leverage, industry sector, relative valuation, and growth potential. Returns-based **style analysis** is an attempt to explain the variability in the observed returns to a security portfolio in terms of the movements in the returns to a series of benchmark portfolios designed to capture the essence of a particular security characteristic. Effectively, style analysis determines the combination of long positions in a collection of passive indexes that best mimics the past performance of a security portfolio.

FIGURE 22.6 **VALUE–GROWTH VOLATILITY SPREAD**

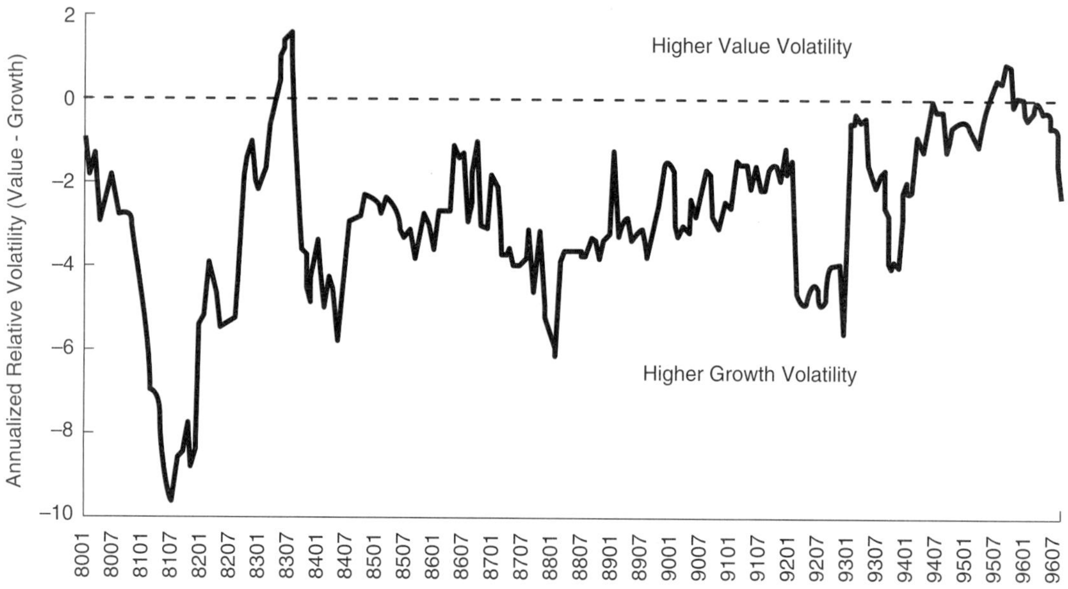
Higher Value Volatility
Higher Growth Volatility
Annualized Relative Volatility (Value - Growth)
2
0
–2
–4
–6
–8
–10
8001
8007
8101
8107
8201
8207
8301
8307
8401
8407
8501
8507
8601
8607
8701
8707
8801
8807
8901
8907
9001
9007
9101
9107
9201
9207
9301
9307
9401
9407
9501
9507
9601
9607

Relative rolling 12-month volatility based on the Russell 1000 Value and Growth indices.

Source: Fidelity Management and Research Company.

The process of returns-based style analysis involves using the past returns to a manager's portfolio along with those to a series of indexes representing different investment styles in an effort to determine the relationship between the fund and those specific styles. Generally speaking, the more highly correlated a fund's returns are with a given style index, the greater the weighting that style is given in the statistical assessment. The goals of the analysis are to better understand the underlying influences responsible for the portfolio's performance and to properly classify the manager's strategy when comparing his or her investment prowess with that of other managers. Thus, regardless of whatever investment objective a manger might profess to follow, style analysis allows the portfolio to "speak for itself."

Figure 22.7 shows a simple **style grid** that could be used to classify a manager's performance along two dimensions: firm size (large cap, small cap) and value–growth characteristics. An investor whose portfolio produced returns best mimicked by the returns to indexes representing a small-cap value style (such as Manager A) would be plotted in the lower left quadrant of the grid. These grids are also useful in establishing the implicit investment style for any of the popular stock market indicators described in Chapter 5. For example, Figure 22.8 shows the style plot points for the S&P 500, S&P Midcap, Wilshire 5000, NASDAQ Composite, Russell 3000 (R3), Russell 2000 (R2), and Russell 1000 (R1), among others.[13] One interesting result in this display is that the S&P 500 can be characterized as a large-cap, "blended" (i.e., between value and growth) fund. As such, it may not be the appropriate performance benchmark for someone managing a mid-cap, growth-oriented portfolio.

Formally, style analysis relies on the *constrained least squares* procedure, with the returns to the manager's portfolio designated as the dependent variable and the returns to the

[13]Figure 22.8 also plots the investment style for various subsets of the Russell indexes. For example, R1V and R1G are, respectively, the value and growth "halves" of the Russell 1000. They are created by ranking the 1,000 companies in the index by their price-to-book ratios and assigning those with the lowest (highest) ratios to the value (growth) subindex.

FIGURE 22.7 A STYLE ANALYSIS GRID

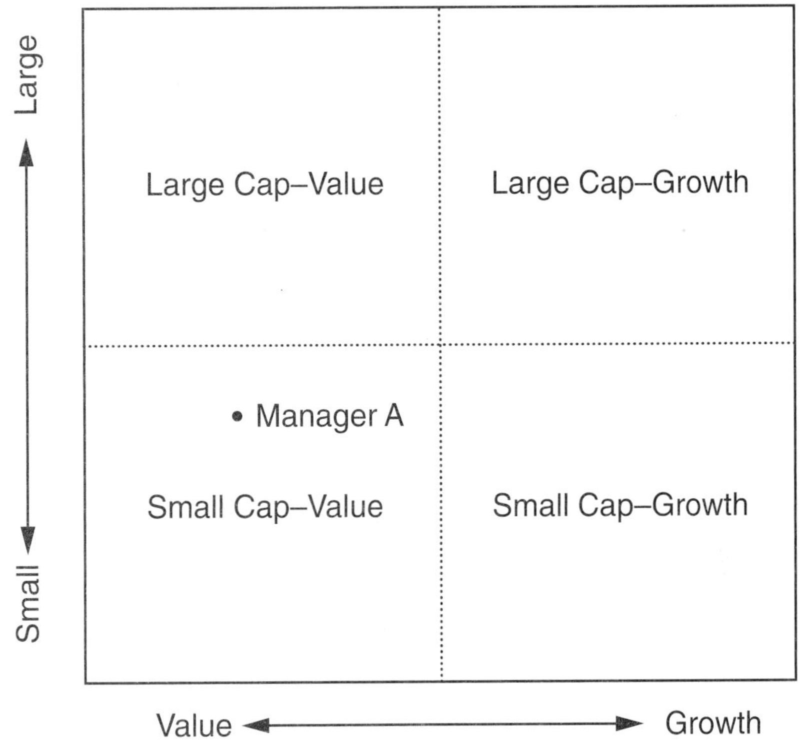
Large
Small
Large Cap–Value
Large Cap–Growth
• Manager A
Small Cap–Value
Small Cap–Growth
Value
Growth

Source: Fidelity Management and Research Company.

style index portfolios as the independent variables. In practice, there are often three constraints employed: (1) no intercept term is specified, (2) the coefficients must sum to one, and (3) all the coefficients must be non-negative. As developed by William Sharpe, returns-based style analysis is simply an application of an asset class factor model:[14]

$$R_{pt} = [b_{p1}F_{1t} + b_{p2}F_{2t} + \ldots + b_{pn}F_{nt}] + e_{pt}$$

where:

R_{pt} = the t-th period return to the portfolio of manager p
F_{jt} = the t-th period return to the j-th style factor
b_{pj} = the sensitivity of portfolio p to style factor j
e_{pt} = the portion of the return variability in portfolio p not explained by variability in the set of factors

As with any regression equation, the coefficient of determination can be defined as $R^2 = 1 - [\sigma^2(e_p)/\sigma^2(R_p)]$. Because of the way the factor model is designed, R^2 can be interpreted as the percentage of manager p's return variability due to the portfolio's *style,* with $(1 - R^2)$ due to his or her *selection* skills.

The benchmark portfolios that are selected as style analysis factors should be consistent with the manager's pronounced style. This suggests that a different set of indexes might be

[14]William F. Sharpe, "Asset Allocation: Management Style and Performance Measurement," *Journal of Portfolio Management* 18, no. 2 (winter 1992): 7–19.

FIGURE 22.8 **INVESTMENT STYLE OF POPULAR STOCK MARKET INDICATORS**

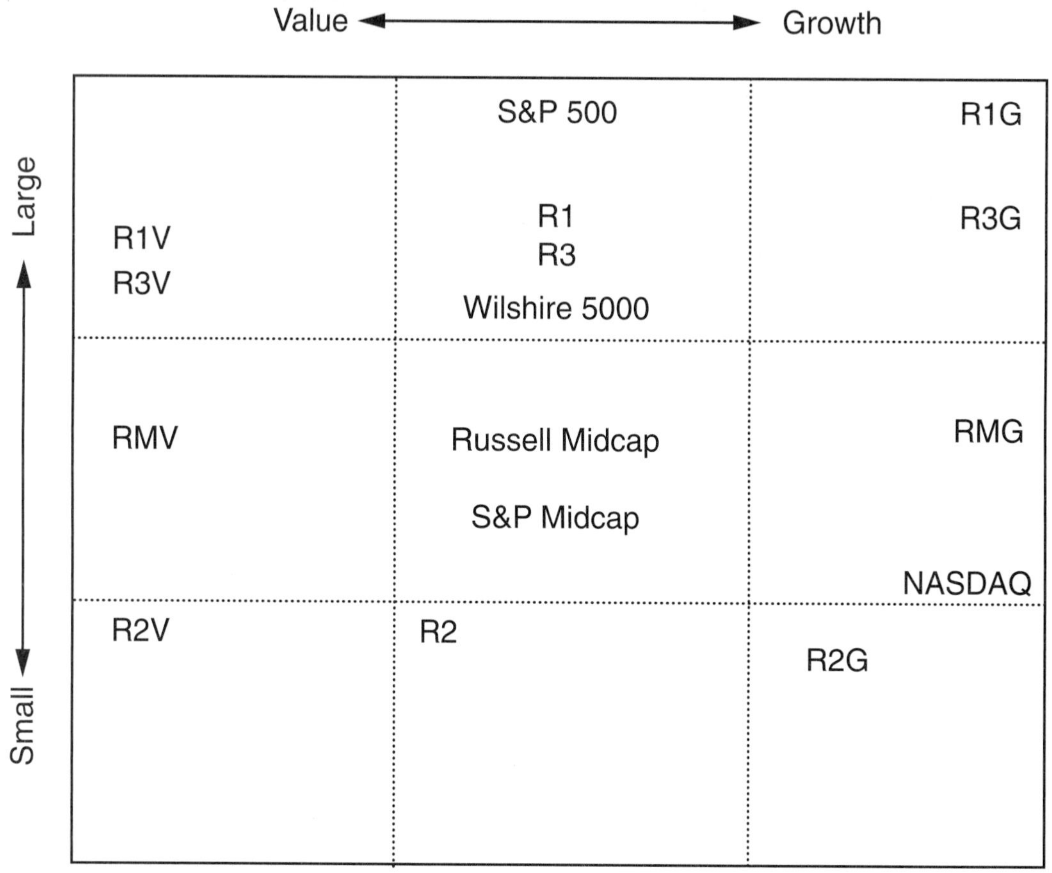
Value
Growth
Large
Small
S&P 500
R1G
R1V
R3V
R1
R3
Wilshire 5000
R3G
RMV
Russell Midcap
S&P Midcap
RMG
NASDAQ
R2V
R2
R2G

Source: Fidelity Management and Research Company.

specified for a domestic equity fund than for an international bond fund. Also, an effective benchmark portfolio should be easy to measure, available as a realistic investment alternative to an actively managed portfolio, and as uncorrelated as possible with the other style indexes. Within these broad guidelines, there are a virtually unlimited number of different benchmarks that could be used in practice. Three popular approaches are:

- *Sharpe:* Uses portfolios of T-bills, intermediate-term government bonds, long-term government bonds, corporate bonds, mortgage-related securities, large-capitalization value stocks, large-capitalization growth stocks, medium capitalization stocks, small-capitalization stocks, non-U.S. bonds, European stocks, and Japanese stocks.
- *BARRA:* Uses portfolios formed around 13 different security characteristics, including variability in markets, past firm success, firm size, trading activity, growth orientation, earnings-to-price ratio, book-to-price ratio, earnings variability, financial leverage, foreign income, labor intensity, yield, and low capitalization.[15]

[15]For more on the conceptual development of the BARRA style factors, see Richard Grinold and Ronald N. Kahn, "Multiple-Factor Models for Portfolio Risk," in *A Practitioner's Guide to Factor Models,* ed. John Peavy (Charlottesville, Va.: Research Foundation of the Institute of Chartered Financial Analysts, 1994).

- *Ibbotson Associates:* In its simplest style model, uses portfolios formed around five different characteristics: cash (i.e., T-bills), large-capitalization growth, small-capitalization growth, large-capitalization value, and small-capitalization value.[16]

To illustrate how this process can be implemented, Sharpe measured the investment styles of two large institutional equity portfolios—Vanguard Trustee's U.S. Fund and Fidelity Magellan Fund—over a recent five-year interval. Both portfolios performed well during the period, generating respective average annual returns of 15.5 percent and 20.6 percent. However, Figure 22.9 shows that the managers of these portfolios followed very different styles. The bar charts indicate the extent to which each portfolio's returns were correlated with the underlying style factors. Accordingly, the Trustees' Fund is best thought of as being a small-cap value fund over this period while the Magellan Fund was a small-to-mid-cap growth portfolio with some global exposure. Also, security selection accounted for a relatively small amount of Magellan's return variability (2.7 percent), but was more of a consideration (7.8 percent) in the Trustees' portfolio.

Finally, style analysis can also be used to determine whether a manager is able to maintain a consistent investment style over time. This can be accomplished by reestimating the optimal combination of mimicking style indexes as additional performance data become available and then overlaying the plot points on the same grid. Figure 22.10 shows the connected sequence of plot points—or "snail trails" as they are sometimes called—for four different mutual funds managed by Fidelity Investments. Two of these funds (Equity Income and Growth Company) have well-defined style mandates and have been able to achieve relatively stable investment policies. The other two—Desinty I and Contrafund—have exhibited considerable *style drift,* which in both cases is consistent with their flexible investment missions. Of course, an investor needs to be cautious about a manager whose portfolio exhibits unintentional style drift.

ASSET ALLOCATION STRATEGIES

An equity portfolio does not stand in isolation: rather it is part of an investor's overall investment portfolio. Many times the equity portfolio is part of a balanced portfolio that contains holdings in various long- and short-term debt securities (such as bonds and Treasury bills) in addition to equities.

In such situations, the portfolio manager must consider more than just the composition of the equity or the bond component of the portfolio. The manger also must determine the appropriate mix of asset categories in the entire portfolio. There are four general strategies for determining the asset mix of a portfolio as follows: the integrated, strategic, tactical, and insured asset allocation methods.

Integrated Asset Allocation

The integrated asset allocation strategy separately examines (1) capital market conditions and (2) the investor's objectives and constraints. These factors are then combined to establish the portfolio asset mix that offers the best opportunity for meeting the investor's needs given the capital market forecast. The actual returns from the portfolio are the used as inputs to an iterative process in which changes over time in the investor's objectives and constraints are noted along with changes in capital market expectations. The optimal portfolio is then revised based on this update of investor needs and capital market expectations.

[16]See R. Cummisford and Scott Lummer, "Controlling the Limitations of Style Analysis," *Journal of Financial Planning* 9, no. 5 (October 1996): 70–76.

FIGURE 22.9 **STYLE ANALYSIS FOR TWO MUTUAL FUNDS**

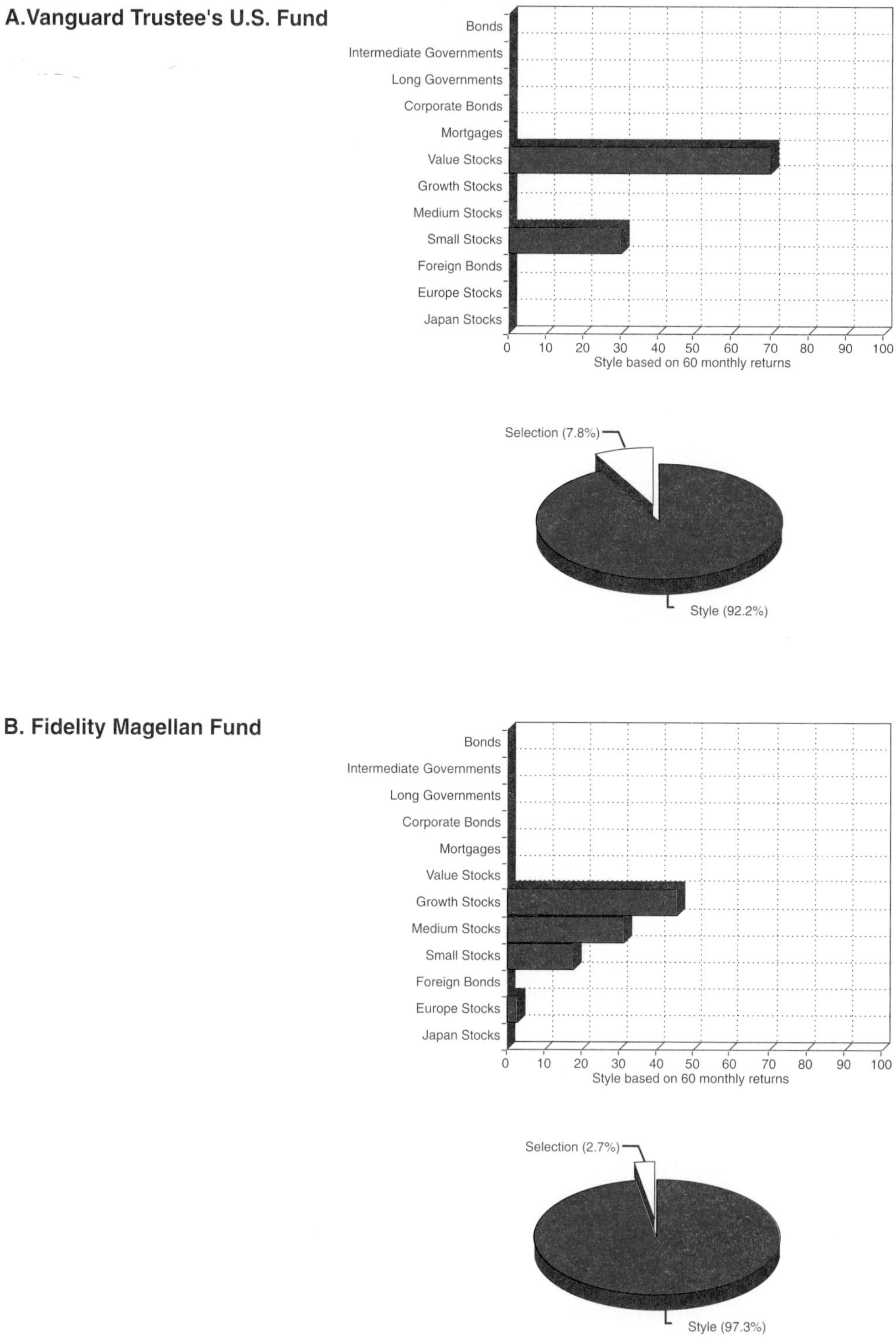
A. Vanguard Trustee's U.S. Fund
Bonds
Intermediate Governments
Long Governments
Corporate Bonds
Mortgages
Value Stocks
Growth Stocks
Medium Stocks
Small Stocks
Foreign Bonds
Europe Stocks
Japan Stocks
0 10 20 30 40 50 60 70 80 90 100
Style based on 60 monthly returns
Selection (7.8%)
Style (92.2%)
B. Fidelity Magellan Fund
Bonds
Intermediate Governments
Long Governments
Corporate Bonds
Mortgages
Value Stocks
Growth Stocks
Medium Stocks
Small Stocks
Foreign Bonds
Europe Stocks
Japan Stocks
0 10 20 30 40 50 60 70 80 90 100
Style based on 60 monthly returns
Selection (2.7%)
Style (97.3%)

Source: William F. Sharpe, "Asset Allocation: Management Style and Performance Measurement," *Journal of Portfolio Management* 18, no. 2 (winter 1992): 7–19.

FIGURE 22.10 **MUTUAL FUND STYLES OVER TIME**

A. Style Consistency

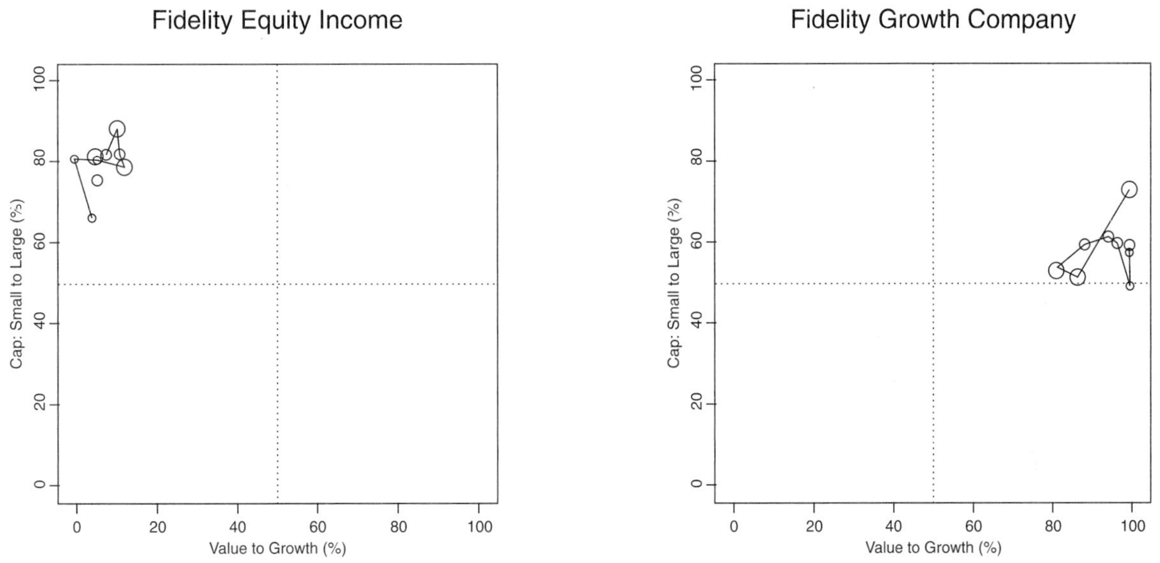
Fidelity Equity Income
Fidelity Growth Company
Cap: Small to Large (%)
Value to Growth (%)
0
20
40
60
80
100

B. Style Flexibility

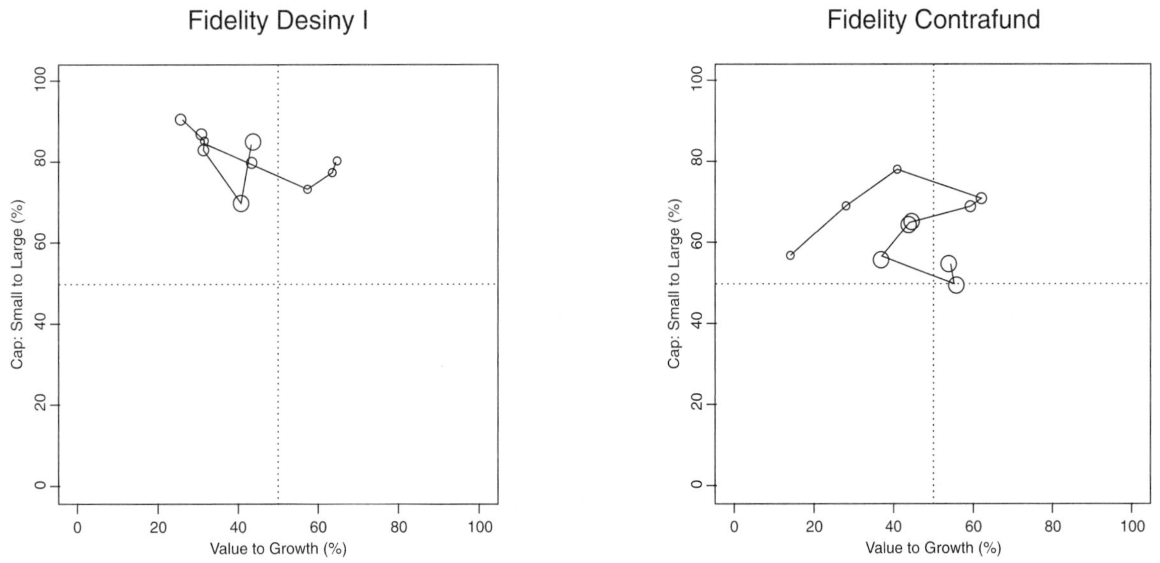
Fidelity Desiny I
Fidelity Contrafund
Cap: Small to Large (%)
Value to Growth (%)
0
20
40
60
80
100

Source: Fidelity Management and Research Company.

FIGURE 22.11 **INTEGRATED ASSET ALLOCATION**

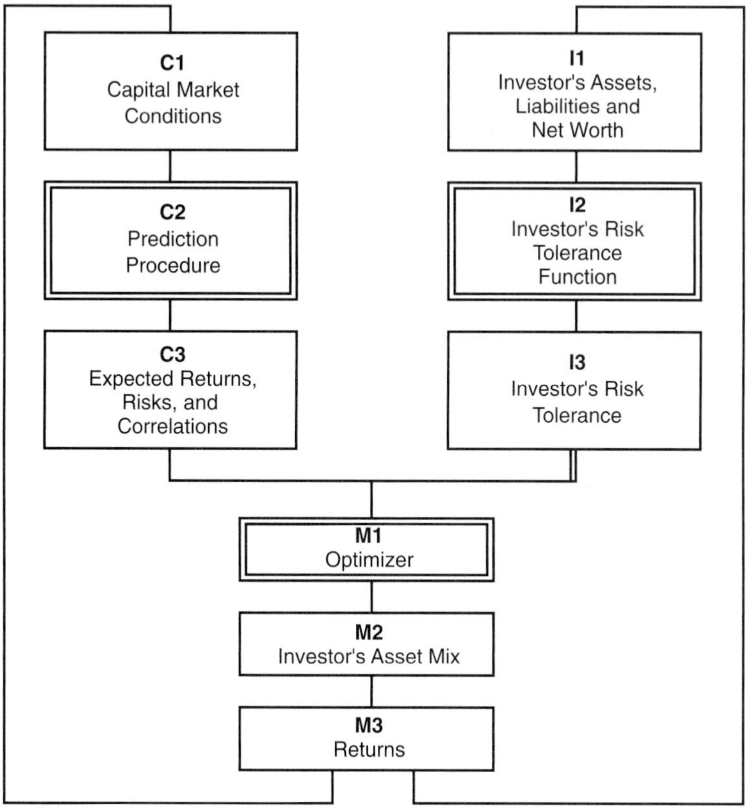
C1
Capital Market Conditions
I1
Investor's Assets, Liabilities and Net Worth
C2
Prediction Procedure
I2
Investor's Risk Tolerance Function
C3
Expected Returns, Risks, and Correlations
I3
Investor's Risk Tolerance
M1
Optimizer
M2
Investor's Asset Mix
M3
Returns

Source: William F. Sharpe, "Integrated Asset Allocation," *Financial Analysts Journal* 43, no. 5 (September/October 1987): 25–32.

This integrated approach to portfolio formation is illustrated in Figure 22.11. As described by Sharpe, there are three key steps to integrated asset allocation.[17] First, both capital market conditions and investor-specific objectives and constraints (e.g., risk tolerance, investment horizon, tax status) are summarized before the asset mix is determined. The processes by which the capital market and investor-specific data are summarized are shown in boxes C2 and I2, respectively, with the outcomes of those processes being boxes C3 and I3. An example of C3 might be the Markowitz efficient frontier containing portfolios of optimal risk–expected return combinations; the end-product of I3 might be captured in an investment policy statement.

The second step in the integrated asset allocation process is to combine the information from the first step in order to select the single best portfolio for the investor in question. This is captured by the optimizer box in M1, with the resulting asset mix being shown in M2. One simple way of seeing how M1 might work would be to calculate the *expected utility (EU)* of each prospective asset mix using the following formula:

[17]William F. Sharpe, "Integrated Asset Allocation," *Financial Analysts Journal* 43, no. 5 (September/October 1987): 25–32. An expanded discussion on this topic by the same author can be found in "Asset Allocation," in *Managing Investment Portfolios,* 2d ed., ed. John L. Maginn and Donald L. Tuttle (Boston, Mass.: Warren, Gorham & Lamont, 1990).

TABLE 22.4 **OPTIMAL PORTFOLIO SELECTION: AN EXAMPLE**

Panel A. Prospective Efficient Portfolios (C3)

Portfolio	Asset Mix: Stock	Bond	ER	σ^2
A	20%	80%	7%	7%
B	50	50	8	13
C	80	20	9	20

Panel B. Risk Tolerance Factors (I3)

Investor	RT	
1	5	(i.e., *less* tolerant)
2	40	(i.e., *more* tolerant)

Panel C. Expected Utility Results (M2)

	A	B	C
Investor #1 *EU*:	**5.6**	5.4	5.0
Investor #2 *EU*:	6.8	7.8	**8.5**

$$EU_{pk} = ER_p - \left(\frac{\sigma_p^2}{RT_k}\right) = ER_p - (\text{Risk Penalty})$$

where ER_p and σ_p^2 are the expected return and variance for portfolio p (which come from C3) and RT_k is the risk tolerance factor for investor k (which comes from I3). The risk tolerance factor is an estimate intended to capture the essence of an investor's attitude toward risk-bearing. Notice that the higher this number, the more risk tolerant the investor is and, hence, the less portfolio p has its expected return "penalized" by its risk level. The optimal asset mix for any particular investor is then the one that generates the highest level of expected utility.

As an example of the first two stages of the integrated asset allocation process, Panel A of Table 22.4 shows the expected returns and variances for three different potential asset mixes (C3) while Panel B lists risk tolerance factors for two investors (I3). Panel C shows the result of the expected utility calculations that combine this information (M2). For instance, the expected utility generated by Portfolio A for Investor 1 is 5.6 (= 7 − 7/5), which is the largest value of the three potential allocations and therefore his optimal asset mix. Conversely, Investor 2 is more tolerant of risk and finds that Portfolio 3, which generates an expected utility level of 8.5 (= 9 − 20/40), is her optimal allocation. Notice that the risk tolerance factor effectively deflates the risk penalty, allowing more risk tolerant investors to pursue more volatile portfolios with higher expected returns.

The third stage of the integrated portfolio process occurs after enough time has passed that the optimal portfolio's actual performance can be compared with the manager's original expectations. This evaluation process is represented by box M3 in Figure 22.11. Following this assessment, the manager can then make adjustments to the portfolio by including any new information into the optimization process. Adjustments to the initial asset mix can result from either a fundamental change in capital market conditions (e.g., increased inflation) or a change in the investor's circumstances (e.g., increased risk tolerance). It is this "feedback loop" that makes portfolio management a *dynamic* process.

STRATEGIC ASSET ALLOCATION

Strategic asset allocation is used to determine the long-term policy asset weights in a portfolio. Typically, long-term average asset returns, risk, and covariances are used as estimates of future capital market results. Efficient frontiers are generated using this historical return information and the investor decides which asset mix is appropriate for his or her needs during the planning horizon. This results in a *constant-mix* asset allocation with periodic rebalancing to adjust the portfolio to the specified asset weights.

One way to think of the strategic allocation process is as being equivalent to the integrated asset allocation process shown in Figure 22.11 but without the feedback loops. That is, as just described, the manager will determine the long-term asset allocation that is best suited for a particular investor by optimizing information from both the capital market and that investor. However, once this asset mix is established, the manager does not constantly attempt to adjust the allocation according to temporary changes in market and investor circumstances. Thus, the strategic allocation should define the basic nature of the trade-off between opportunity and safety that confronts the investor.[18]

As an example of strategic asset allocation, Table 22.5 shows the asset mixes for both large (Panel A) and small-to-midsize (Panel B) defined-benefit pension plans. The display lists average allocations for corporate, union, and public sector plans as of both 1997 and 1998. There are several interesting things to note. First, regardless of type, large plans appear to invest more heavily in equities than do smaller plans. Second, regardless of size, corporate and public funds invest more heavily in equities than do union funds, which allocate around half their capital to fixed-income and cash equivalent securities. (Generally speaking, portfolios tilted more toward stocks than bonds and cash are considered to be riskier.) Third, no fund takes a particularly big position in foreign securities, although union plans make by far the smallest global allocations. Finally, consistent with the idea of a strategic allocation as a long-term view, these asset mixes remained relatively stable over the two years in question.

TACTICAL ASSET ALLOCATION

Unlike an investor's strategic allocation, which is set with a long-term focus and modified infrequently, a tactical approach to asset allocation constantly adjusts the asset class mix in the portfolio in an attempt to take advantage of changing market conditions. With tactical asset allocation, these adjustments are driven solely by perceived changes in the relative values of the various asset classes; the investor's risk tolerance and investment constraints are assumed to be constant over time. In Figure 22.11, it is equivalent to an integrated approach to asset allocation that removes the feedback loop involving investor-specific information (i.e., I2).

Tactical asset allocation is frequently based on the premise of *mean reversion,* which holds that whatever a security's return has been in the recent past, it will eventually revert to its long-term average (mean) value. This assessment is usually done on a comparative basis. For instance, suppose that the ratio of stock and bond returns is normally 1.2, reflecting the greater degree of risk in the equity market. Then, if in the most recent investment period, stock returns were double those of bond returns, the tactical investor might determine that bonds were now undervalued relative to stock and most likely to be the best-performing asset class in the coming period. Accordingly, he should then overweight the fixed-income component of his portfolio, shifting, say, from a 60–40 percent initial mix of stocks and bonds to a 50–50 percent split.

For the preceding description, notice that tactical asset allocation is an inherently *contrarian* method of investing. That is, the investor adopting this approach will always be

[18]See D. Don Ezra, "Strategic Asset Allocation and Total Portfolio Returns," in *Asset Allocation in a Changing World,* ed. T. Burns (Charlottesville, Va.: Association for Investment Management and Research, 1998).

TABLE 22.5

STRATEGIC ASSET ALLOCATIONS FOR DEFINED-BENEFIT PENSION PLANS

Panel A. Sponsors of over $100 million

	CORPORATE		UNION		PUBLIC	
Asset Class	**1998**	**1997**	**1998**	**1997**	**1998**	**1997**
Cash/Equivalents	4.2%	4.7%	5.4%	5.9%	2.4%	2.7%
U.S. Equity	49.1	46.9	37.4	35.1	45.7	43.8
International Equity	6.6	6.8	8	1.0	7.5	7.6
U.S. Fixed Income	30.4	30.0	42.7	42.0	35.1	35.4
Int'l Fixed Income	.8	.8	.1	.3	1.6	1.7
U.S. Balanced Accounts	2.1	2.3	2.4	2.5	2.8	3.4
Int'l Balanced Accounts	.2	.2	n/a	n/a	.1	n/a
Equity Real Estate	1.3	1.5	2.1	2.0	2.2	2.3
Mortgages	.2	.2	1.7	2.4	.5	.6
Company's Own Stock	.9	.9	.2	.2	n/a	n/a
Convertibles	.1	.1	n/a	n/a	n/a	n/a
GIC's	1.0	1.2	.6	1.3	.5	.6
Venture Capital	.3	.3	n/a	.1	.4	.5
Gen'l Insurance Account	1.3	2.0	3.5	3.6	.3	.1
Other	1.8	1.9	3.3	3.6	.7	1.1

Panel B. Sponsors of $10 million to $100 million

	CORPORATE		UNION		PUBLIC	
Asset Class	**1998**	**1997**	**1998**	**1997**	**1998**	**1997**
Cash/Equivalents	8.4%	9.1%	7.2%	7.5%	6.2%	6.1%
U.S. Equity	37.9	36.2	32.1	29.1	39.3	38.3
International Equity	1.8	2.4	.4	.3	2.4	2.5
U.S. Fixed Income	32.6	30.6	46.4	44.5	44.6	45.5
Int'l Fixed Income	.4	.5	n/a	.1	.6	.2
U.S. Balanced Accounts	3.0	2.9	.4	.6	3.9	3.5
Int'l Balanced Accounts	.1	.1	n/a	n/a	n/a	n/a
Equity Real Estate	.4	.3	.7	.8	.8	.9
Mortgages	.4	.3	.5	.6	n/a	.1
Company's Own Stock	.6	.6	.1	.1	n/a	n/a
Convertibles	.2	.2	.1	.1	n/a	n/a
GIC's	1.6	2.1	1.2	1.7	1.0	1.1
Venture Capital	.1	.2	n/a	n/a	.3	.3
Gen'l Insurance Account	9.5	10.1	7.4	9.4	.3	.3
Other	4.0	4.3	4.3	5.0	.6	1.2

Source: Nelson Investment Management Network.

buying the asset class that is currently out of favor—on a relative basis, at least—and selling the asset class with the highest market value. In the above example, this was the case when the investor underweighted his stock allocation after stock prices rose substantially compared to bond prices. How frequently the investor chooses to adjust the asset class mix in the portfolio will depend on several factors, such as the general level of volatility in the capital markets, the relative size of the equity and fixed-income risk premiums, and changes in the fundamental macroeconomic environment.[19]

[19]A good overview of these strategies can be found in Charles H. DuBois, "Tactical Asset Allocation: A Review of Current Techniques," in *Active Asset Allocation,* ed. R. Arnott and F. Fabozzi (Chicago, Ill.: Probus Publishing, 1992).

INSURED ASSET ALLOCATION

Insured asset allocation likewise results in continual adjustments in the portfolio allocation. Insured asset allocation assumes that expected market returns and risks are constant over time, while the investor's objectives and constraints change as his or her wealth position changes. For example, rising portfolio values increase the investor's wealth and consequently his or her ability to handle risk, which means the investor can increase his or her exposure to risky assets. Declines in the portfolio's value lower the investor's wealth, consequently decreasing his or her ability to handle risk, which means the portfolio's exposure to risky assets must decline. Often, insured asset allocation involves only two assets, such as common stocks and T-bills. As stock prices rise, the asset allocation increases the stock component. As stock prices fall, the stock component of the mix falls while the T-bill component increases. This is opposite of what would happen under tactical asset allocation. Insured asset allocation is like the integrated approach without the feedback loop on the capital market side (i.e., C2 in Figure 22.11). It is sometimes called a *constant proportion* strategy because of the shifts that occur as wealth changes.

SELECTING AN ACTIVE ALLOCATION METHOD

Which asset allocation strategy is used depends on the perceptions of the variability in the client's objectives and constraints and the perceived relationship between past and future capital market conditions. If you believe that capital market conditions are relatively constant over time, you might use insured asset allocation. If you believe that the client's goals, risk preferences, and constraints are constant, you likewise might use tactical asset allocation. Integrated asset allocation assumes that both the investor's needs and capital market conditions are variable and therefore must be constantly monitored. Under these conditions, the portfolio mix must be updated constantly to reflect current changes in these parameters.

USING FUTURES AND OPTIONS IN EQUITY PORTFOLIO MANAGEMENT

There has been growing recognition that derivative instruments are ideal tools for accomplishing myriad changes in a portfolio irrespective of the specific strategy of the manager. For example, the systematic and unsystematic risk of equity portfolios can be modified by using futures and options derivatives, as can the portfolio mix between equities and other assets. Cash inflows and outflows can be hedged through appropriate derivative strategies. Due to the cost, risk, and restrictions of short selling, shorting futures contracts and purchasing puts are attractive alternatives to short selling for long–short managers.

MODIFYING PORTFOLIO RISK AND RETURN: A REVIEW

As discussed in Chapter 11, futures and options can affect the risk and return distribution for a portfolio. Generally, a dollar-for-dollar relationship exists between the changes in the price of the underlying security and the price of the corresponding futures contract. In effect, being long (short) in futures is identical to subtracting (adding) cash from (to) the portfolio. Long futures positions have the effect of increasing the exposure of the portfolio to the asset; shorting futures decreases the portfolio's exposure. Suppose Panel A of Figure 22.12 represents a portfolio's probability distribution of returns. Long positions in futures on the portfolio's underlying asset *increase* the portfolio's exposure (or sensitivity) to price changes of the asset. As shown in Panel B of Figure 22.12, as a result, the return distribution widens, indicating a larger return variance. Shorting futures has the effect of decreasing the portfolio's sensitivity to the underlying asset. Panel C of Figure 22.12 shows the effect on the portfolio if futures are sold. In this case, the variance of returns declines, causing a "narrower" return distribution.

Figure 22.12 illustrates that futures have a symmetrical impact on portfolio returns, since their impact on the portfolio's upside and downside return potential is the same. This

FIGURE 22.12 **HOW RETURN DISTRIBUTIONS ARE MODIFIED WHEN FUTURES CONTRACTS ARE PURCHASED OR SOLD**

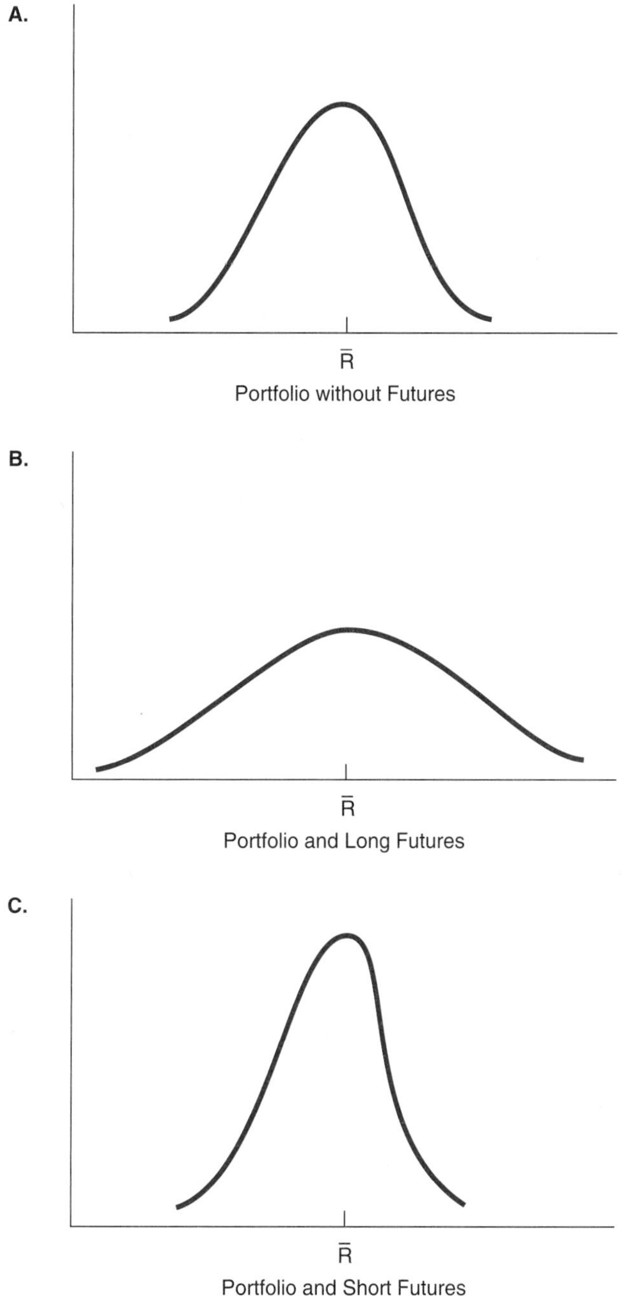
A.
R̄
Portfolio without Futures
B.
R̄
Portfolio and Long Futures
C.
R̄
Portfolio and Short Futures

is because of the close relationship between changes in the price of the futures contract and changes in the price of the underlying asset.

In contrast, options give their owner the right (but not the obligation) to buy or sell the underlying asset. Because options provide this choice of whether or not to exercise the option, it means that options do not have a symmetrical impact on returns. For example, as

FIGURE 22.13

EXAMPLES OF TRUNCATED RETURN DISTRIBUTIONS WHEN OPTIONS ARE USED TO MODIFY PORTFOLIO RISK

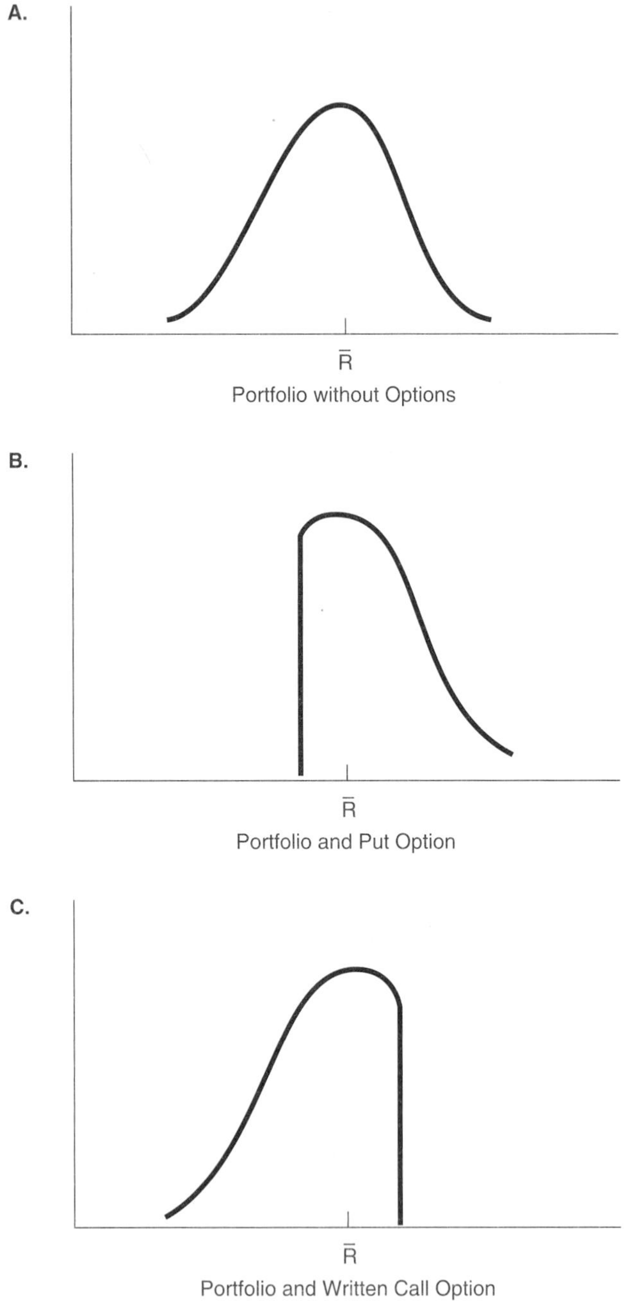
A.
R̄
Portfolio without Options
B.
R̄
Portfolio and Put Option
C.
R̄
Portfolio and Written Call Option

will be shown in Chapter 24, buying a call option limits losses; buying a put when the investor owns the underlying security has the effect of controlling downside risk, as shown in Figure 22.13, Panel B. Writing a covered call, on the other hand, limits upside returns while not appreciably affecting loss potential, as seen in Figure 22.13, Panel C; writing a put option has the same effect.

TABLE 22.6 **COMPARATIVE STOCK AND STOCK FUTURES TRADING COSTS (AS OF DECEMBER 1997)**

Cost Factor	United States (S&P 500)	Japan (Nikkei 225)	United Kingdom (FT-SE 100)	France (CAC 40)	Germany (DAX)	Hong Kong (Hang Seng)
A. Stocks						
Commissions	0.12%	0.20%	0.20%	0.25%	0.25%	0.50%
Market Impact	0.30	0.70	0.70	0.50	0.50	0.50
Taxes	0.00	0.21	0.50	0.00	0.00	0.34
Total	0.42%	1.11%	1.40%	0.75%	0.75%	1.34%
B. Futures						
Commissions	0.01%	0.05%	0.02%	0.03%	0.02%	0.05%
Market Impact	0.05	0.10	0.10	0.10	0.10	0.10
Taxes	0.00	0.00	0.00	0.00	0.00	0.00
Total	0.06%	0.15%	0.12%	0.13%	0.12%	0.15%

Source: Joanne M. Hill, "Derivatives in Equity Portfolios," in *Derivatives in Portfolio Management,* ed. T. Burns (Charlottesville, Va.: Association for Investment Management and Research, 1998).

THE USE OF FUTURES IN ASSET ALLOCATION

In times of changing market conditions, shifting a portfolio's asset allocation must be done quickly to take advantage of the manager's forecast. Such changes are costly since securities must be identified and then sold and bought to facilitate the reallocation. Commissions and the market impact of large trades can harm the portfolio's return potential.

Rather than identifying specific securities for sale and purchase, and then issuing large buy-and-sell orders, the portfolio manager can use futures to accomplish the change in asset allocation. Long or short positions in the appropriate futures contracts can quickly and easily change the portfolio's asset mix at lower transaction costs than trading large quantities of securities. For instance, Table 22.6 shows that when all the costs of trading are considered, the average expense of physically rebalancing a U.S. equity portfolio is about 42 basis points of the position's value, while the same trade with an index futures contract would cost just 6 basis points. Trading costs in Japan, the United Kingdom, France, Germany, and Hong Kong, though different in absolute level, reflect this same general trend. Other countries with traded stock index futures not shown in Table 22.6 include Switzerland, Canada, Italy, the Netherlands, Australia, Sweden, Spain, and Malaysia.

Futures also can be used to achieve a proper stock/bond mix in a multiple-manager environment. Many medium and large pension funds divide the portfolio among different individual managers to exploit their specialized expertise in managing different asset classes (e.g., small-cap growth, emerging stock markets, high-yield debt). In such an environment, the overall pension fund manager can use futures to maintain the desired asset allocation; otherwise he or she would have to disrupt the specialized managers by adding or removing funds to or from them because of reallocation.

THE USE OF DERIVATIVES IN EQUITY PORTFOLIOS

Regardless of whether the equity portfolio is passively or actively managed, futures and options can be used to help control cash inflows and outflows from the portfolio. In reality, most options used to modify portfolio risk are options whose underlying "security" is another derivative security—a futures contract. These options are called futures options or options on futures; they are discussed in Chapter 24.

Hedging Portfolio Inflows and Outflows

When a large sum of money is deposited with a manager, the fund's asset composition changes; the lump-sum cash inflow has the effect of reducing the portfolio's exposure to equities since a larger proportion of the portfolio's assets are currently in cash. A potential problem is that, if the portfolio manager wants to quickly invest the funds in the market, he or she may purchase inappropriate securities. Also, large purchases can lead to sizable commissions and a price-pressure impact on the stocks purchased.

A better strategy would be to use long positions in stock index futures contracts so the total contract value approximates the size of the inflow. Alternatively, you could purchase index call options. As a result, the money is immediately invested in stocks with lower commissions and a smaller price impact than if the stocks had been purchased outright. Once the futures positions are acquired, the manager has time to decide what assets to buy, and the specific stocks can be acquired in an orderly manner. The smaller purchases over time will reduce the price pressure. As these purchases are made, the futures contracts can be liquidated.

Similarly, a large planned withdrawal from a portfolio usually is done by selling securities over time so that when the withdrawal date occurs, the needed funds are available for transfer. The sale of securities causes an increase in cash holdings, which reduces the portfolio's equity exposure. A possible strategy to counterbalance the effect of a larger cash position is to take long positions in futures contracts as securities are sold. The net effect is to maintain the portfolio's overall exposure to stocks while accumulating cash. When the cash is withdrawn, the futures contracts can be unwound such that the portfolio's operations have not been disrupted.

Using Futures in Passive Equity Portfolio Management

A passive investment strategy generally seeks to buy and hold a portfolio of equity securities. With a passive investment strategy, the manager is expected to manage cash inflows and outflows without harming the ability of the portfolio to track its target index. The prior example on hedging a cash inflow or outflow is directly applicable to passive portfolio management. Instead of investing all cash inflows in the index or a subsample of the index, the manager can purchase an appropriate number of futures contracts to maintain the portfolio's structure and reduce the portfolio's tracking error relative to the index during the time period when the manager invests the funds in the index stocks. Similarly, anticipated cash outflows can be hedged when the portfolio manager is liquidating part of the portfolio over time. The hedge maintains the portfolio's exposure to the market through the use of futures contracts.

Options can be used to a limited extent in passive management. When cash rebalancing is imperfect and an index fund becomes overweighted in a sector or in individual stocks relative to its index, it is possible to sell call options on the individual stocks or on industry groups to correct the portfolio's weights.

Using Futures in Active Equity Portfolio Management

Active management often attempts to adjust the portfolio's systematic risk, unsystematic risk, or both. Systematic risk is a portfolio's exposure to price fluctuations caused by changes in the overall stock market. Unsystematic risk includes the portfolio's exposure to industries, sectors, or firms that is different from the benchmark.

MODIFYING SYSTEMATIC RISK An equity portfolio's systematic risk is the sensitivity of the portfolio's value to changes in the benchmark index measured by the portfolio's beta. If a rising market is expected, active portfolio managers will want to increase their portfolio's beta while expectations of a falling market will invite managers to reduce their portfolio's betas.

Traditionally, when the market was expected to rise, active mangers would sell low-beta stocks and buy high-beta stocks to raise the portfolio's weighted average beta.

Alternatively, the use of futures provides quicker and cheaper way to change the portfolio's beta with less disruption to the traits of the portfolio. As discussed in Chapter 11, long or short positions in futures contracts allow the manager to increase or decrease a portfolio's beta.

MODIFYING UNSYSTEMATIC RISK Opportunities exist for controlling the unsystematic risk in an equity portfolio. Futures and options on futures exist for a limited number of sectors, while there are options for numerous components of the equity market. There are option contracts on market indexes, such as the S&P 100 and S&P 500; for stock groups, such as consumer goods and cyclicals; and for selected industries, such as banks, utilities, pharmaceuticals, and mining. There are also options on over 1,400 individual stocks. Thus, even when industry option contracts don't exist, portfolio managers can buy or sell individual stock options for the industry to modify their exposure.

Options trading can be used to take advantage of the portfolio manager's forecasts for certain sectors and industries, by trading either sector options or options of firms in the industry. Options on index futures also can be used to exploit anticipated market changes. Because of their truncation effect on return distributions, options on index futures can affect both a portfolio's systematic and unsystematic risk.

For example, a manger can buy call options when anticipating a rise in the market, in a sector or industry, or in a group of individual stocks. The lower call premiums can provide more leverage than using futures, and options contracts can allow greater precision in targeting sectors of the market rather than an entire index. The maximum loss for such strategies is limited to the call premium.

Similarly, investors can buy put options on an index future, a sector, or group of stocks in anticipation of a decline in value. Calls can be written on the market and subsets of the market when declining or stable values are forecast. Writing put options on the market and its subsectors can generate income when the portfolio managers expect the value of the market or subsectors to be stable or to rise.

MODIFYING THE CHARACTERISTICS OF AN INTERNATIONAL EQUITY PORTFOLIO

Futures and options can be used to modify or hedge positions in international equity portfolios. International portfolios represent positions in both the securities and the currencies of the countries involved. Futures and options contracts on major currencies allow the portfolio manager to manage the risks of each of these components separately. Currency futures and options on currency futures can be used to modify the currency exposure of an international stock portfolio without affecting the actual holdings of the portfolios. For example, a portfolio manager may be bullish on German stocks but also may believe that the deutschemark is currently overvalued relative to the U.S. dollar. He or she can purchase the German securities and then adjust the overall currency exposure of the portfolio through the use of currency options and futures.

Consider the following example. Assume a stock portfolio has the equivalent of $30 million invested: $9 million in the United States; $12 million in Germany; the remainder in the United Kingdom. Thus, the current allocation across countries and currencies is: 30 percent United States, 40 percent Germany, and 30 percent United Kingdom. Assume the manager believes that the deutschemark is overvalued and expects a strengthening pound. Given this currency outlook, the manager wishes to reduce her exposure to the deutschemark by $4.5 million (or −15 percent of the portfolio) while increasing her exposure to the pound by $4.5 million (or +15 percentage points). In other words, the desired *currency* allocation is: 30 percent U.S. dollar, 25 percent German deutschemark, and 45 percent U.K. pound.

Traditional currency rebalancing would require rebalancing the country allocation whereby the manger would lose the chance to participate in security markets thought to be

THE INTERNET *Investments Online*

Equity portfolio management is the "how-to"—it applies what we know of stock selection and portfolio theory to the practice of constructing, monitoring, and updating equity portfolios to meet the needs of individual or institutional clients. Several professional money managers describe their services on the Internet, and here's a sampling of some of them:

www.russell.com The home page of Frank Russell and Company contains descriptions of Russell's many services. Of special interest to us are the links to Russell's indexes, including its various style indexes, for the United States and several other countries. Reading through this site and the array of services that Russell offers will show the importance and practical nature of topics discussed in this and the other portfolio management chapters.

www.firstquadrant.com First Quadrant is a leader in the application of quantitative investment techniques to equity portfolio management. The product section of this site features a description of its quantitative perspective of style management. Other sections allow users to order copies of research monographs and published articles by First Quadrant personnel.

www.wilshire.com Wilshire Associates, Inc., offers indexes, consulting, and other services to investors. This home page offers links to a market environment commentary and to information about its indexes (the Wilshire 5000 is a widely used benchmark to represent to total equity market in the United States). The site offers a description of each Wilshire index, including such helpful information as the fundamental characteristics of each index and their exposure to different stock-market sectors.

www.cboe.com The Chicago Board Options Exchange has some pages of interest on its Web site. Testimonials and descriptions of how institutional investors use options are available at **www.cboe.com/institutional/testimon.htm.** Descriptions of option strategies, such as the protective put, long call, and protective collar, are at **www.cboe.com/institutional/portfolio.htm.** Discussions of issues and strategies relevant to the use of options in portfolio management can be found at **www.cboe.com/institutional/whitepap.htm.**

undervalued. Also, such security rebalancing would be costly and time consuming, and cause the portfolio manager to ignore what she does best, namely identify undervalued markets and securities. The point is, she would be forced to make stock allocation decisions based on currency forecasts.

To reduce her exposure to the German currency by \$4.5 million, the manager could short an appropriate number of deutschemark futures contracts, which would obligate her at the contract expiration date to pay deutschemarks in exchange for receiving \$4.5 million. Simultaneously, she would also take long positions in \$4.5 million worth of pound sterling futures contracts expiring at the same time. When these contracts mature, the manager will pay \$4.5 million and receive an equivalent amount of pounds in return. The net effect of these positions taken together is that the manager has exchanged a portion of the deutschemark-denominated cash flows generated by her security portfolio for pound-denominated cash flows.

Following these transactions, the security allocation across these countries remains as before: 30 percent United States, 40 percent Germany, 30 percent United Kingdom. However, through the use of currency hedging, the portfolio's exposure to the (presumably overvalued) deutschemark is only 25 percent, while exposure to the (presumably undervalued) pound is 45 percent. The use of derivatives allows the portfolio manager to shift currency exposures in a quicker, less costly manner than reallocating stocks across countries, while allowing the manager to maintain the desired exposure to undervalued securities.

Summary

- Passive equity portfolios attempt to track the returns of an established benchmark, such as the S&P 500, or some other benchmark that meets the investor's needs. Active portfolios attempt to add value relative to their benchmark by market timing and/or by seeking to buy undervalued stocks.
- There are several methods for constructing and managing a passive portfolio, including full replication of a benchmark or sampling. Also, several active management strategies exist, including sector rotation, the use of factor models, quantitative screens, and linear programming methods. Value- and growth-oriented strategies have become particularly popular in recent years, and style analysis helps the investor determine the exact investment style the manager is using.
- Since equity portfolios typically are used with other assets in an investor's overall portfolio, we reviewed several common asset allocation strategies, including integrated asset allocation, strategic asset allocation, tactical asset allocation, and insured asset allocation. The basic difference between these strategies is whether they rely on current market expectations or long-run projections, and whether the investor's objectives and constraints remain constant over the planning horizon or change with market conditions.
- We also examine the use of derivative securities in equity portfolio management. Futures can be used to hedge against portfolio cash inflows and outflows; to keep a passive portfolio fully invested and help minimize tracking error; and to change an actively managed portfolio's beta. Alternatively, options can be used to modify a portfolio's unsystematic risk. Finally, derivatives can be used in managing currency exposures in international equity portfolios.

Questions

1. Why have passive portfolio management strategies increased in use over time?
2. What is meant by an indexing portfolio strategy and what is the justification for this strategy? How might it differ from another passive portfolio?
3. Briefly describe four techniques considered active equity portfolio management strategies.
4. Describe several techniques for constructing a passive portfolio.
5. Discuss three strategies active managers can use to add value to their portfolios.
6. How do trading costs and market efficiencies affect the active manager? How may an active manager try to overcome these obstacles to success?
7. Discuss how the four asset allocation strategies differ from one another.
8. *CFA Examination III (June 1994)*
   Recent empirical research has suggested that holding portfolios of stocks classified as "value" (low price/book ratio) as opposed to "growth" (high price/book ratio) in both U.S. and international markets has resulted in enhanced risk-adjusted returns. Critique the efficient market hypothesis in light of these findings.
9. Why might it be easier to construct a bond-market index than a stock-market index portfolio?
10. What are the trade-offs involved when constructing a portfolio using a full replication versus a sampling method?
11. Because of inflationary expectations, you expect natural resource stocks, such as mining companies and oil firms, to perform well over the next 3 to 6 months. As an active portfolio manager, describe the various methods available to take advantage of this forecast.

Problems

1. You have a portfolio with a market value of $50 million and a beta (measured against the S&P 500) of 1.2. if the market rises 10 percent, what value would you expect your portfolio to have?
2. Given the monthly returns below, how well did the passive portfolio track the S&P 500 benchmark? Find the R^2, alpha, and beta of the portfolio. Compute the average tracking error with and without sign.

Month	Portfolio Return	S&P 500 Return
January	5.0%	5.2%
February	−2.3	−3.0
March	−1.8	−1.6
April	2.2	1.9
May	0.4	0.1
June	−0.8	−0.5
July	0.0	0.2
August	1.5	1.6
September	−0.3	−0.1
October	−3.7	−4.0
November	2.4	2.0
December	0.3	0.2

3. Using the Ibbotson data on asset returns from Chapter 3 (Table 3.6), what percentage of the equity risk premium is consumed by trading costs of 1.5 percent? Assuming a normal distribution of returns, what is the probability that an active manager can earn a return that will overcome these trading costs?

CFA

4. *CFA Examination III (June 1992)*
   Global Advisers Company (GAC) is an SEC-registered investment counseling firm solely involved in managing international securities portfolios. After much research on the developing economy and capital markets of the country of Otunia, GAC has decided to include an investment in the Otunia stock market in its Emerging Market Commingled Fund. However, GAC has not yet decided whether to invest actively or by indexing. Your opinion on the active versus indexing decision has been solicited. A summary of the research findings follows.

   Otunia's economy is fairly well diversified across agricultural and natural resources, manufacturing (both consumer and durable goods), and a growing finance sector. Transaction costs in securities markets are relatively large in Otunia because of high commissions and government "stamp taxes" on securities trades. Accounting standards and disclosure regulations are quite detailed, resulting in wide public availability of reliable information about companies' financial performance.

   Capital flows into and out of Otunia and foreign ownership of Otunia securities are strictly regulated by an agency of the national government. The settlement procedures under these ownership rules often cause long delays in settling trades made by nonresidents. Senior finance officials in the government are working to deregulate capital flows and foreign ownership, but GAC's political consultant believes that isolationist sentiment may prevent much real progress in the short run.

   a. Briefly discuss four aspects of the Otunia environment that favor investing actively and four aspects that favor indexing.
   b. Recommend whether GAC should invest in Otunia actively or by indexing and justify your recommendation based on the factors identified in part a.

CFA

5. *CFA Examination III (June 1995)*
   Betty Black's investment club wants to buy the stock of either NewSoft Inc. or Capital Corp. In this connection, Black has prepared the table shown below. You have been asked to help her interpret the data, based on your forecast for a healthy economy and a strong market over the next 12 months.

	NewSoft Inc.	Capital Corp.	S&P 500 Index
Current Price	$30	$32	n/a
Industry	Computer Software	Capital Goods	n/a
P/E Ratio (current)	25×	14×	16×
P/E Ratio (5-yr avg.)	27×	16×	16×
P/B Ratio (current)	10×	3×	3×
P/B Ratio (5-yr avg.)	12×	4×	2×
Beta	1.5	1.1	1.0
Dividend Yield	0.3%	2.7%	2.8%

NewSoft's shares have higher price/earnings (P/E) and price/book (P/B) ratios than those of Capital Corp. Identify and briefly discuss three reasons why the disparity in ratios may not indicate that NewSoft's shares are overvalued relative to the shares of Capital Corp. Answer the question in terms of the two ratios, and assume that there have been no extraordinary events affecting either company.

6. As the chief investment officer for a money management firm specializing in taxable individual investors, you are trying to establish a strategic asset allocation for two different clients. You have established that Ms. A has a risk tolerance factor of 8 while Mr. B's risk tolerance factor is 27. The characteristics for four model portfolios are listed below:

	Asset Mix			
Portfolio	Stock	Bond	ER	σ^2
1	5%	95%	8%	5%
2	25	75	9	10
3	70	30	10	16
4	90	10	11	25

a. Calculate the expected utility of each prospective portfolio for each of the two clients.
b. Which portfolio represents the optimal strategic allocation for Ms. A? Which portfolio is optimal for Mr. B? Explain why there is a difference in these two outcomes.
c. For Ms. B, what level of risk tolerance would leave her indifferent between having Portfolio 1 or Portfolio 2 as her strategic allocation? Demonstrate.

7. *CFA Examination II (June 1995)*
Briefly discuss whether active asset allocation among countries could consistently outperform a world market index. Include a discussion of the implications of *integration versus segmentation* of international financial markets as it pertains to portfolio diversification, but ignore the issue of stock selection.

8. *CFA Examination III (June 1995)*
Giselle Donovan is the newly appointed Chief Financial Officer of Bontemps International (BI), an import/export firm conducting a worldwide trading business from its principal office in New York. BI is a financially healthy, rapidly growing firm with a young workforce. All liabilities are denominated in U.S. dollars. Its ERISA-qualified defined-benefit pension plan is structured as shown below:

		Percent Allocation	Prior Year Total Return
Higher-Risk Asset Classes			
U.S. equities (large capitalization)		35%	10.0%
U.S. equities (small capitalization)		10	12.0
International equities		5	7.0
Total equities		50%	
Lower-Risk Asset Classes			
U.S. Treasury bills (1-year duration)		10%	4.5
U.S. intermediates and mortgage-backed securities (4-year duration)		39	1.0
U.S. long-term bonds (10-year duration)		1	19.0*
Total fixed income		50%	
Total		100%	10.0%
Present value of plan liabilities	$298 million		
Market value of plan assets	$300 million		
Surplus	$ 2 million		
Duration of liabilities	10 years		
Actuarial return assumption	7.0%		
BI Board's long-term total return objective	9.0%		

*Income element 7.0%, gain element 12.0%.

The Board is concerned about the pension portfolio's downside risk and wants to adopt a formal policy for rebalancing the plan's assets in response to fluctuations in market values. Donovan asks you to review the major strategies that the Board should consider. You are aware of three strategies used to reallocate between higher-risk and lower-risk assets: "Constant Mix," "Constant Proportion," and "Buy and Hold."

a. Describe the primary characteristics of each of these three strategies as they relate to changes in market values. Identify the market environment in which each strategy should provide the best relative performance.
b. Recommend one strategy for the Board's consideration, taking their concerns into account. Justify your choice.

CFA

9. *CFA Examination III (June 1986)*

Futures contracts and options on futures contracts can be used to modify risk.

a. Identify the fundamental distinction between a futures contract and an option on a futures contract, and briefly explain the difference in the manner that futures and options modify portfolio risk.
b. The risk or volatility of an individual asset can be reduced either by writing a covered call option against the asset or by purchasing a put option on the asset. Explain the difference in the extent to which each of these two option strategies modifies an individual asset's risk. In your answer, describe the effect of each strategy on the potential upside and downside performance of the asset.

References

Bernstein, Richard. *Style Investing: Unique Insight into Equity Management.* New York, N.Y.: John Wiley & Sons, 1995.

Bhatia, Sanjiv, ed. *Global Equity Investing.* Charlottesville, Va.: Association for Investment Management and Research, 1996.

Erb, Claude B., Campbell R. Harvey, and Tadas E. Viskanta. *Country Risk in Global Financial Management.* Charlottesville, Va.: Research Foundation of the Institute of Chartered Financial Analysts, 1997.

Grossman, Sanford J. "Dynamic Asset Allocation and the Informational Efficiency of Markets," *Journal of Finance* 50, no. 3 (July 1995): 773–787.

Klein, Robert A., and Jess Lederman, eds. *Equity Style Management.* Chicago, Ill.: Irwin Professional Publishing, 1995.

Levine, Sumner N., ed. *The Financial Analysts Handbook.* 2d ed. Homewood, Ill.: Dow Jones-Irwin, 1988.

Maginn, John L., and Donald L. Tuttle, eds. *Managing Investment Portfolios.* 2d ed. Boston, Mass.: Warren, Gorham, and Lamont, 1990.

Michaud, Richard O. *Investment Styles, Market Anomalies, and Global Stock Selection.* Charlottesville, Va.: Research Foundation of the Institute of Chartered Financial Analysts, 1999.

Squires, Jan R., ed. *Value and Growth Styles in Equity Investing.* Charlottesville, Va.: Association for Investment Management and Research, 1995.

Part

6 DERIVATIVE SECURITY ANALYSIS

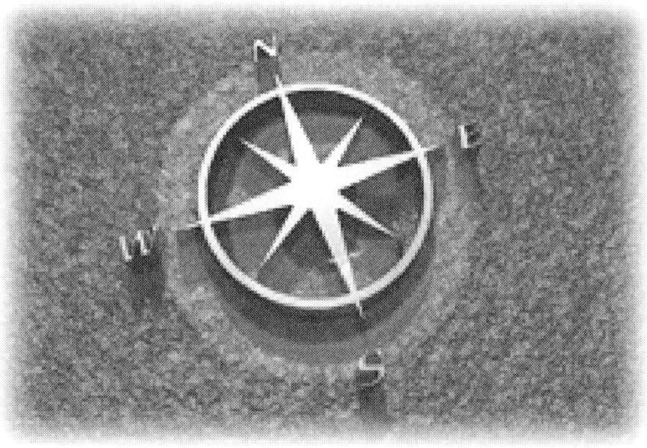

In recent years, it has been difficult to read the financial press without encountering at least a passing reference to an economic scandal attributed to trading in derivative securities. Procter and Gamble's ill-fated swap transactions with Banker's Trust and the equity index futures trades that brought down Barings Bank give the casual reader the impression that derivatives are highly volatile instruments used only by those investors interested in placing speculative "bets." Of course, nothing could be further from the truth. Although it is true that the companies in these examples either miscalculated or misunderstood the nature of their investment positions, the vast majority of derivative transactions are used by individuals and institutions seeking to reduce the risk exposures generated by their other business ventures.

Derivatives, in their many forms, have become a vital part of modern security markets, trailing only stocks and bonds in terms of importance. Unlike stocks and bonds, however, their widespread use is a relatively recent phenomenon, and misconceptions still exist about how derivatives work and the proper way for investors to trade them. The chapters in this section address this concern by providing the investor with a framework for understanding how derivatives are valued and used in practice. Building on the introduction to the topic in Chapter 11, this material considers the mechanics of the two basic contract forms—forwards and options—as well as several of the more sophisticated ways in which derivatives are used in combination with other securities.

Chapter 23 analyzes forward and futures contracts—the most prevalent form of derivative instrument. The similarities and differences between forward and futures contracts are described, with particular emphasis on the creation of (and subsequent adjustments to) margin accounts and the concept of basis risk. In addition, the calculation of the optimal hedge ratio and the arbitrage-free approach to determining the contract delivery price are discussed. The chapter concludes with an examination of the features of forward and futures contracts that are designed to offset financial (as opposed to commodity) risk exposures, including interest rate, equity, and currency price movements. Applications and investment strategies involving each of these contract types illustrate this discussion.

In Chapter 24, the focus turns to option contracting. The discussion begins with a consideration of how option markets are organized and how both puts and calls are quoted and traded. Several different option-based investment and hedging strategies are described as well as how these contracts can be used in conjunction with other securities to create customized payoff distributions. The chapter concludes with a formal treatment of how option contracts are valued in an efficient market. Starting with the simple two-state option pricing model, which contains the essence of the basic valuation argument, the discussion progresses to include state-of-the-art approaches such as the binomial and the Black-Scholes models. In this development, special attention is paid to the role that price volatility plays in the valuation process.

Chapter 25, the last chapter of this section, considers three additional classes of derivative products. First, the rapidly developing market for swap, cap, and floor agreements is examined. After describing how these instruments are related to typical forward and option contracts, the discussion concentrates on the many ways in which investors and corporate risk managers use these products in practice. In particular, applications involving four different exposures—interest rates, exchange rates, commodity prices, and equity prices—are developed. Second, the fundamentals of warrants and convertible securities are described. The emphasis of this discussion is on the option-like features of these instruments and how they alter the risk-return dynamics of traditional debt and equity products. Finally, the chapter concludes with an examination of the market for structured notes—instruments that can be viewed as "straight" bond issues into which derivatives have been embedded.

Chapter

23 FORWARD AND FUTURES CONTRACTS

After you read this chapter, you should be able to answer the following questions:

- What are the differences in the way forward and futures contracts are structured and traded?
- How are the margin accounts on a futures contract adjusted for daily changes in market conditions?
- How can an investor use forward and futures contracts to hedge an existing risk exposure?
- What is a hedge ratio and how should it be calculated?
- What economic functions do the forward and futures markets serve?
- How are forward and futures contracts valued after origination?
- What is the relationship between futures contract prices and the current and expected spot price for the underlying commodity or security?
- How can an investor use forward and futures contracts to speculate on a particular view about changing market conditions?
- How do agricultural futures contracts differ from those based on financial instruments, such as stock indexes, bonds, and currencies?
- How can forward and futures contracts be designed to hedge interest rate risk?
- How are implied forward rates and actual forward rates related?
- What is stock index arbitrage and how is it related to program trading?
- How can forward and futures contracts be designed to hedge foreign exchange rate risk?
- What is interest rate parity and how would you construct a covered interest arbitrage transaction?

As we saw in Chapter 11, forward and futures contracts are the most straightforward form of *derivative instrument* because they allow an investor to lock in the purchase or sales price of a transaction that will not be completed until a later date. Having laid the foundation for why these contracts exist and how they are used, in this chapter we continue our discussion along several lines. First, we take a closer look at the contract terms and trading mechanics of forwards and futures. In particular, we examine the important differences that exist between the two markets and describe the process by which futures contracts are **marked to market** on a daily basis. Further, we discuss how these contracts are used to hedge the price risk inherent in an existing or anticipated position and how **hedge ratios** are computed.

Second, we consider how forward and futures contracts are priced in an efficient capital market. Given that these instruments are not really securities in the same sense that stocks and bonds are, the notion of traditional security valuation is not quite appropriate in this market. Instead, valuation involves specifying the proper relationship between the forward contract price and the spot price for the underlying position. In general, we develop the "no arbitrage" result that the forward contract price should be equal to the spot price plus the cumulative costs of transporting the underlying security or commodity from the present to the future delivery date. These carrying costs can be either positive or negative; therefore, the correct forward contract price can be either higher or lower than the spot price.

Finally, we demonstrate several applications and strategies in which an investor can use forward and futures contracts. This demonstration concentrates on a class of contracts—*financial forward and futures*—that are particularly useful to investors. The underlying securities in financial futures include stock indexes, Treasury bonds, bank deposits, and foreign currencies. The use of these financial futures will be illustrated in a series of applications designed to demonstrate the connections between cash and futures markets.

AN OVERVIEW OF FORWARD AND FUTURES TRADING

Forward contracts are agreements negotiated directly between two parties in the OTC (i.e., nonexchange-traded) markets. A typical participant in a forward contract is a commercial or investment bank that, serving the role of the market maker, is contacted directly by the customer (although customers can form an agreement directly with one another). Forward contracts are individually designed agreements and can be tailored to the specific needs of the ultimate end-user. Futures contracting, on the other hand, is more complicated. An investor wishing either to buy or to sell in the futures market gives his order to a broker (a *futures commission merchant*), who then passes it to a trader on the floor of an exchange (*the trading pit*). After a trade has been agreed on, details of the deal are passed to the **exchange clearinghouse**, which catalogs the transaction. The ultimate end-users in a futures contract never deal with each other directly. Rather, they always transact with the clearinghouse, which is also responsible for overseeing the delivery process, settling daily gains and losses, and guaranteeing the overall transaction. Figure 23.1 highlights the differences in how these contracts are created.[1]

As an example, let us consider the traditional agricultural commodity futures that have been traded for more than 130 years beginning with the creation of the Chicago Board of Trade (CBT), the world's oldest and largest derivatives exchange. Futures contracts based on a wide array of commodities and securities have been created and now trade on almost 100 exchanges worldwide. Table 23.1 lists the leading derivatives markets in the United States and the world, ranked by relative trading volume. Notice that 2 of the top 3 and 6 of the top 10 exchanges in the world are located in the United States. Additionally, Figure 23.2 shows price and trade activity data for a representative sample of commodity futures contracts; financial futures will be described in detail later in the chapter. Each of these commodity contracts is standardized in terms of the amount and type of the commodity involved and the available dates on which it can be delivered. As we will see, this standardization can lead to an important source of risk that may not exist in forward contracts.

To interpret the display in Figure 23.2, consider the gold futures contract traded on the Commodity Exchange (COMEX), a division of the New York Mercantile Exchange (NYM). Each contract calls for the long position to buy, and the short position to sell, 100 troy ounces of gold in the appointed months. With commodity futures, it usually is the case that delivery can take place any time during the month at the discretion of the short position. Contracts are available with settlement dates every other month for the next 18 months and then twice a year for another three years. An investor committing on this particular date to a long position in the June 2000 contract is obligated to buy 100 ounces of gold 14 months

[1]For a more detailed discussion of the futures trading process, see Roger G. Clarke, *Options and Futures: A Tutorial* (Charlottesville, Va.: Research Foundation of the Institute of Chartered Financial Analysts, 1992). Some of this discussion is based on this book.

FIGURE 23.1 **FORWARD AND FUTURES TRADING MECHANICS**

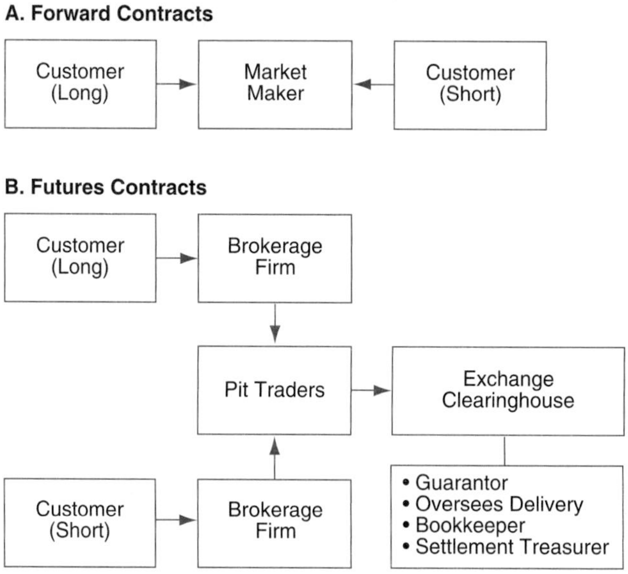
A. Forward Contracts
Customer (Long)
Market Maker
Customer (Short)
B. Futures Contracts
Customer (Long)
Brokerage Firm
Pit Traders
Exchange Clearinghouse
Customer (Short)
Brokerage Firm
• Guarantor
• Oversees Delivery
• Bookkeeper
• Settlement Treasurer

TABLE 23.1 **LEADING DERIVATIVES EXCHANGES RANKED BY RELATIVE TRADING VOLUME**

A. U.S. Futures Exchanges (1995 Data)

Exchange Name and Abbreviation	% of Trading Volume
Chicago Board of Trade (CBT)	41.9
Chicago Mercantile Exchange (CME)	37.3
New York Mercantile Exchange (NYMEX)	16.1
Coffee, Sugar and Cocoa Exchange (CSCE)	2.3
New York Cotton Exchange (CTN)	1.8
Mid-America Commodity Exchange (MCE)	0.8
Kansas City Board of Trade (KC)	0.4
Minneapolis Grain Exchange (MPLS)	0.2

B. International Futures and Options Exchanges (1998 Data)

Exchange and Country	% of Trading Volume
CBT, United States	18.2
EUREX, Germany and Switzerland	16.0
CME, United States	14.4
Chicago Board Options Exchange, United States	13.0
London International Financial Futures Exchange, United Kingdom	12.9
AMEX, United States	6.0
NYMEX, United States	6.0
BM&F, Brazil	5.7
Amsterdam Exchange, Netherlands	4.2
Pacific Stock Exchange, United States	3.6

Source: Chicago Mercantile Exchange and Futures Industry Association.

FIGURE 23.2 **COMMODITY FUTURES QUOTATIONS**

	Open	High	Low	Settle	Change	Lifetime High	Lifetime Low	Open Interest
CORN (CBT) 5,000 bu.; cents per bu.								
Mar	215¼	217½	215	217¼	+ 1½	305	209½	150,939
May	220¾	223½	220¾	223	+ 1¼	299	217	71,837
July	226	228½	226	228	+ 1¼	312	223	73,370
Sept	233	234¼	232¼	233¾	+ ¾	280	229¾	18,122
Dec	238¾	240½	238¼	239¾	+ ¼	291½	235	42,398
Mr00	247½	248	246½	247¾	+ ¼	270	242½	4,813
July	255	256	254½	256	+ ¼	278½	250½	1,682
Dec	255	256	255	255½	+ ¼	279½	250	1,438
Est vol 38,000; vol Wd 91,491; open Int 364,934, −1,202.								
OATS (CBT) 5,000 bu.; cents per bu.								
Mar	106½	106¾	105¾	106½	+ ¼	166½	104¼	7,767
May	100¼	109¾	100¼	109¾	+ ½	161	100¼	4,537
July	112¾	113¼	112½	113	+ ¼	150	112½	2,362
Sept	116¾	116¾	116½	116½	....	140	113	966
Dec	122½	122½	121¾	122	− ¼	147	121½	1,847
Est vol 1,000; vol Wd 543; open Int 17,494, −90.								
SOYBEANS (CBT) 5,000 bu.; cents per bu.								
Mar	507½	509½	503¾	508¾	+ 1¼	694	503¾	66,890
May	511	513	508	512¾	+ 1¼	671	508	31,557
July	516	518	512½	517½	+ 1¼	728	512½	32,807
Aug	517	519	514	518½	+ ½	618¼	514	10,276
Sept	518	520	516	519	+ ½	616½	514½	2,794
Nov	525	528	522½	527½	+ 1¼	680	520½	20,798
Est vol 40,000; vol Wd 67,176; open Int 166,296, −77.								
COTTON (CTN)-50,000 lbs.; cents per lb.								
Mar	60.45	60.55	58.50	59.13	− 1.26	77.25	57.35	27,572
May	61.10	61.20	59.60	59.98	− 1.03	76.80	58.51	18,424
July	61.75	61.80	60.20	60.65	− .95	77.31	59.51	12,640
Oct	62.00	62.10	61.10	61.18	− 1.22	77.05	60.70	1,655
Dec	62.69	62.75	61.70	61.84	− .86	74.10	61.70	13,579
Mr00	63.65	63.30	63.30	62.85	− .83	71.80	63.10	1,601
May		....	....	63.35	− .90	75.40	65.00	583
July		....	....	63.90	− .85	73.25	65.75	260
Est vol 14,500; vol Wd 6,271; open Int 76,334, +279.								
ORANGE JUICE (CTN)-15,000 lbs.; cents per lb.								
Mar	103.80	104.50	102.55	104.45	+ 1.05	127.75	86.05	15,856
May	103.40	103.80	101.75	102.25	− .70	130.00	90.80	6,397
July	103.05	103.05	101.50	101.50	− 1.40	132.00	95.50	3,061
Sept	101.50	101.50	101.50	101.50	− 1.65	132.00	96.20	803
Nov	102.70	102.70	102.70	101.50	− 1.15	132.75	97.20	621
Ja00		....	....	101.50	− .95	133.00	98.20	340
Mar		....	....	101.50	− .95	131.00	99.20	107
Est vol 2,600; vol Wd 2,652; open Int 27,185, +144.								
WHEAT (CBT) 5,000 bu.; cents per bu.								
Mar	265½	268	265¼	267¾	+ 2	384½	263	67,560
May	276½	279	275½	278½	+ 2¼	355	274	20,627
July	286½	288¾	286	288¼	+ 2	389	284	38,142
Sept	298	299	297½	298½	+ 1¼	344	294½	3,288
Dec	310½	311½	310¼	311	+ ¾	365	306	4,163
Est vol 14,000; vol Wd 32,244; open Int 133,825, +3,619.								
COPPER-HIGH (Cmx.Div.NYM)-25,000 lbs.; cents per lb.								
Feb	65.85	65.85	65.30	65.45	+ 1.00	94.60	63.50	891
Mar	65.55	66.30	65.55	65.80	+ 1.00	98.20	63.70	40,676
Apr	66.25	66.25	65.75	66.25	+ 1.00	96.00	64.65	2,093
May	66.40	67.10	66.40	66.60	+ 1.00	98.50	64.55	7,367
June		....	....	66.90	+ 1.00	91.00	65.65	1,495
July	67.50	67.70	67.10	67.30	+ 1.00	95.75	65.40	6,321
Aug	67.70	67.70	67.70	67.70	+ 1.00	90.50	65.50	1,408
Sept	68.25	68.25	67.90	68.10	+ 1.00	94.60	66.60	3,663
Oct		....	....	68.40	+ .95	90.00	66.90	987
Nov		....	....	68.75	+ .95	86.90	67.50	871
Dec	69.30	69.45	68.90	69.10	+ .95	86.00	67.50	5,089
Ja00	69.60	69.60	69.60	69.45	+ .95	83.80	68.00	229
Feb		....	....	69.80	+ 1.15	79.50	68.30	343
Mar	70.50	70.50	70.50	70.10	+ 1.15	83.00	68.40	537
May	71.10	71.10	71.10	70.55	+ 1.15	77.70	69.40	189
July	71.30	71.30	71.30	71.05	+ 1.15	78.10	71.25	560
Sept	71.90	71.90	71.90	71.55	+ 1.15	78.60	70.20	432
Est vol 11,000; vol Wd 10,924; open Int 73,790, −1,751.								
GOLD (Cmx.Div.NYM)-100 troy oz.; $ per troy oz.								
Feb	288.00	291.00	287.80	290.20	+ 2.20	349.50	277.50	1,905
Apr	289.50	292.00	289.20	291.20	+ 1.90	351.20	280.00	96,060
June	291.20	294.00	291.00	293.10	+ 1.90	520.00	282.00	25,131
Aug	294.00	294.00	294.00	295.00	+ 1.90	327.00	288.40	6,737
Oct	296.00	296.00	296.00	296.80	+ 1.90	327.00	287.00	2,797
Dec	297.00	299.50	297.00	298.60	+ 1.90	358.70	286.50	12,597
Fb00		....	....	299.70	+ 1.90	312.00	294.00	6,962
Apr		....	....	301.40	+ 2.00	311.00	298.00	1,120
June	302.00	303.50	302.00	303.10	+ 2.10	473.50	290.50	10,491
Dec		....	....	308.10	+ 2.30	474.50	299.00	6,525
Ju01		....	....	313.00	+ 2.50	447.00	319.00	2,401
Dec		....	....	317.90	+ 2.60	429.50	308.10	4,656
Ju02		....	....	322.90	+ 2.80	385.00	325.00	1,614
Dec		....	....	327.90	+ 2.90	....	....	1,301
Ju03		....	....	332.90	+ 3.00	....	....	643
Est vol 36,000; vol Wd 31,986; open Int 180,942, −350.								
PLATINUM (NYM)-50 troy oz.; $ per troy oz.								
Apr	353.50	364.00	352.00	362.00	+ 7.10	410.00	333.50	10,945
July	357.50	365.00	357.50	364.90	+ 7.10	413.50	340.00	1,479
Oct		....	....	367.70	+ 7.10	367.00	340.00	1,081
Est vol 1,185; vol Wd 1,185; open Int 13,508, +79.								
SILVER (Cmx.Div.NYM)-5,000 troy oz.; cnts per troy oz.								
Feb		....	....	576.0	+ 21.7	538.0	515.0	225
Mar	554.0	580.0	554.0	576.0	+ 21.7	690.0	458.5	54,687
May	562.0	581.0	555.5	576.8	+ 21.4	656.0	469.0	14,094
July	555.5	580.0	555.5	576.7	+ 21.0	680.0	472.0	10,336
Sept	567.0	580.0	557.0	577.4	+ 20.8	698.0	480.0	3,952
Dec	559.0	580.0	556.0	577.4	+ 21.1	720.0	477.0	6,395
Mr00	562.5	562.5	562.0	578.0	+ 21.5	562.5	496.0	1,487
July	563.0	563.0	563.0	579.8	+ 21.1	590.0	502.0	1,097
Dec	577.0	577.0	570.0	581.0	+ 20.5	685.0	497.0	1,981
Dc01	578.0	578.0	578.0	583.0	+ 20.5	680.0	500.0	415
Dc02		....	....	584.0	+ 21.5	613.0	511.0	370
Est vol 40,000; vol Wd 39,822; open Int 95,084, +5,350.								
CRUDE OIL, Light Sweet (NYM) 1,000 bbls.; $ per bbl.								
Mar	12.38	12.43	11.99	12.02	− 0.36	20.20	11.10	102,484
Apr	12.49	12.53	12.15	12.18	− 0.31	20.27	11.35	57,694
May	12.58	12.66	12.25	12.30	− 0.31	20.29	11.63	46,211
June	12.74	12.80	12.42	12.43	− 0.31	20.47	11.48	37,953
July	12.76	12.89	12.61	12.58	− 0.31	20.14	12.20	23,555
Aug	12.95	13.02	12.76	12.72	− 0.27	19.47	12.51	16,573
Sept	13.09	13.17	13.09	12.86	− 0.31	20.10	12.72	12,528
Oct	13.31	13.31	13.31	13.00	− 0.31	20.14	12.92	10,997
Nov	13.42	13.45	13.42	13.14	− 0.31	19.90	13.07	17,097
Dec	13.50	13.59	13.32	13.28	− 0.31	20.75	13.14	52,063
Ja00	13.74	13.74	13.64	13.42	− 0.32	19.15	13.35	15,991
Feb	13.85	13.85	13.80	13.55	− 0.33	20.16	13.55	8,564
Mar	13.95	13.95	13.95	13.66	− 0.34	20.10	13.70	12,775
Apr	....	....	....	13.77	− 0.34	19.16	13.85	5,447
May	....	....	....	13.88	− 0.34	19.16	14.39	1,256
June	....	....	....	13.99	− 0.34	20.10	14.05	10,716
July	....	....	....	14.10	− 0.34	17.88	14.80	1,436
Aug	....	....	....	14.21	− 0.34	17.47	14.80	3,252
Sept	....	....	....	14.32	− 0.34	17.70	14.40	2,405
Oct	....	....	....	14.43	− 0.34	17.55	15.53	1,080
Nov	....	....	....	14.53	− 0.34	17.68	15.63	3,571
Dec	14.99	14.99	14.97	14.63	− 0.34	20.75	14.65	26,308
Ja01	....	....	....	14.72	− 0.35	17.18	15.15	484
Feb	....	....	....	14.81	− 0.35	17.15	15.02	328
June	....	....	....	15.15	− 0.35	18.13	15.34	3,454
Dec	....	....	....	15.66	− 0.36	20.98	15.65	16,464
Dc02	....	....	....	16.39	− 0.36	21.38	16.83	6,296
Dc03	....	....	....	17.27	− 0.09	22.00	16.95	5,049
Dc04	....	....	....	17.72	− 0.09	19.27	17.20	4,076
Est vol 108,516; vol Wd 119,184; open Int 507,377, +5,614.								
NATURAL GAS, (NYM) 10,000 MMBtu.; $ per MMBtu's								
Mar	1.760	1.855	1.747	1.829	+ .016	2.600	1.730	53,395
Apr	1.800	1.890	1.786	1.855	+ .050	2.440	1.765	23,634
May	1.830	1.910	1.820	1.882	+ .047	2.380	1.810	15,658
June	1.865	1.925	1.850	1.902	+ .034	2.384	1.840	16,433
Aug	1.915	1.965	1.910	1.905	+ .025	2.390	1.890	10,719
Sept	1.950	1.985	1.940	1.975	+ .020	2.380	1.920	12,097
Oct	2.025	2.040	2.000	2.033	+ .015	2.415	1.970	9,457
Nov	2.190	2.205	2.170	2.188	+ .011	2.535	2.115	9,321
Dec	2.330	2.365	2.330	2.350	+ .010	2.680	2.213	13,060
Ja00	2.410	2.430	2.390	2.410	+ .010	2.680	2.295	14,192
Feb	2.335	2.345	2.310	2.330	+ .008	2.565	2.240	5,913
Mar	2.255	2.260	2.235	2.248	+ .008	2.475	2.119	4,749
Apr	2.180	2.180	2.160	2.730	+ .008	2.360	2.015	4,447
May	2.160	2.160	2.140	2.148	+ .006	2.339	1.960	4,398
June	2.175	2.175	2.155	2.166	+ .006	2.320	2.001	7,133
July	2.190	2.190	2.175	2.181	+ .006	2.325	2.005	2,502
Aug	2.200	2.200	2.180	2.188	+ .006	2.320	2.005	2,202
Sept	2.205	2.205	2.180	2.193	+ .006	2.370	2.100	1,853
Oct	2.235	2.235	2.210	2.223	+ .006	2.346	2.100	1,916
Nov	2.365	2.365	2.365	2.352	+ .006	2.469	2.240	2,341
Dec	2.515	2.515	2.515	2.502	+ .006	2.620	2.380	2,623
Ja01	2.565	2.565	2.560	2.552	+ .006	2.675	2.400	4,092
Feb	2.470	2.470	2.470	2.457	+ .006	2.522	2.305	2,087
Apr	2.275	2.275	2.255	2.261	+ .006	2.315	2.120	1,972
May	2.260	2.260	2.236	2.242	+ .006	2.305	2.119	1,447
June	2.270	2.270	2.246	2.252	+ .006	2.301	2.095	802
July	2.260	2.260	2.256	2.262	+ .006	2.310	2.095	1,553
Aug	2.280	2.280	2.280	2.267	+ .006	2.280	2.102	766
Sept	2.290	2.290	2.290	2.276	+ .006	2.290	2.137	690
Oct	2.320	2.320	2.320	2.302	+ .006	2.320	2.133	924
Est vol 66,154; vol Wd 55,107; open Int 254,691, +6,567.								

Source: *Wall Street Journal*, 5 February 1999.

later for the contract price of $303.10 per ounce. The volume statistics show that almost 32,000 gold contracts changed hands on the last reported trading day. Open interest—the total number of outstanding contracts of any maturity—was 180,942, down 350 contracts from the previous day.[2]

Another important difference between forward and futures contracts is how the two types of agreements account for the possibility that a counterparty will fail to honor its obligation. Forward contracts may not require either counterparty to post collateral, in which case each is exposed to the potential default of the other during the entire life of the contract. In contrast, the futures exchange requires each customer to post an *initial* **margin account** in the form of cash or government securities when the contract is originated. (The futures exchange, as a well-capitalized corporation, does not post collateral to protect customers from its potential default.) This margin account is then adjusted, or marked to market, at the end of each trading day according to that day's price movements. All outstanding contract positions are adjusted to the **settlement price**, which is set by the exchange after trading ends to reflect the midpoint of the closing price range.

The marked-to-market process effectively credits or debits each customer's margin account for daily trading gains or losses as if the customer had closed out her position, even though the contract remains open. For example, Figure 23.2 indicates that the settlement price of the June 2000 gold contract increased by $2.10 per ounce from the previous trading day. This price increase benefits the holder of a long position by $210 (= $2.10 per ounce × 100 ounces). Specifically, if she had entered into the contract yesterday, she would have a commitment to buy gold for $301.00, which she could now sell for $303.10. Accordingly, her margin account will be increased by $210. Conversely, any party who is short June gold futures will have his margin account reduced by $210 per contract. To ensure that the exchange always has enough protection, collateral accounts are not allowed to fall below a predetermined *maintenance level,* typically about 75 percent of the initial level. If this $210 adjustment reduced the short position's account beneath the maintenance margin, he would receive a **margin call** and be required to restore the account to its full initial level or face involuntary liquidation.

To summarize, the main trade-off between forward and futures contracts is *design flexibility* versus *credit and liquidity risks,* as highlighted by the following comparison.

	Futures	Forwards
Design flexibility:	Standardized	Can be customized
Credit risk:	Clearinghouse risk	Counterparty risk
Liquidity risk:	Depends on trading	Negotiated exit

These differences represent extremes; some forward contracts, particularly in foreign exchange, are quite standard and liquid while some futures contracts now allow for greater flexibility in the terms of the agreement. Also, forwards require less managerial oversight and intervention—especially on a daily basis—because of the lump-sum settlement at delivery (i.e., no margin accounts or marked-to-market settlement), a feature that is often important to unsophisticated or infrequent users of these products.

[2]New contracts are created when a new customer comes to the exchange at a time when no existing contract holder wishes to liquidate his position. On the other hand, if an existing customer wants to close out her short position and there is not a new customer to take her place, the contract price will be raised until an existing long position is enticed to sell back his agreement, thereby canceling the contract and reducing open interest by one.

HEDGING WITH FORWARDS AND FUTURES

HEDGING AND THE BASIS

The goal of a *hedge* transaction is to create a position that, once added to an investor's portfolio, will offset the price risk of another, more fundamental holding. The word "offset" is used here rather than "eliminate" because the hedge transaction attempts to neutralize an exposure that remains on the balance sheet. In Chapter 11, we expressed this concept with the following chart, which assumes that the underlying exposure results from a long commodity position:

Economic Event	Actual Commodity Exposure	Desired Hedge Exposure
Commodity prices fall	Loss	Gain
Commodity prices rise	Gain	Loss

In this case, a short position in a forward contract based on the same commodity would provide the desired negative price correlation. By virtue of holding a short forward position against the long position in the commodity, the investor has entered into a **short hedge**. A **long hedge**, on the other hand, is created by supplementing a short commodity holding with a long forward position.

The basic premise behind either a short or a long hedge is that as the price of the underlying commodity changes, so too will the price of a forward contract based on that commodity. Further, the implicit hope of the hedger is that the spot and forward prices change in a predictable way relative to one another. For instance, the short hedger in the above example is hoping that if commodity prices fall and reduce the value of her underlying asset, the forward contract price also will fall by the same amount to create an offsetting gain on the derivative. Thus, a critical feature that affects the quality of a hedge transaction is the way in which the spot and forward prices change over time.

To understand better the relationship between spot and forward price movements, it is useful to develop the concept of the **basis**. At any date *t*, the basis is the spot price minus the forward price for a contract maturing at date *T*:

$$\mathrm{B}_{t,T} = \mathrm{S}_t - F_{t,T}$$

where:

S_t = the date t spot price
$F_{t,T}$ = the date t forward price for a contract maturing at date T

Potentially, a different level of the basis may exist on each trading date *t*. Two facts always are true, however. First, the *initial basis* at date 0 ($\mathrm{B}_{0,T}$) always will be known since both the current spot and forward contract prices can be observed. Second, the *maturity basis* at date *T* ($\mathrm{B}_{T,T}$) always is zero whenever the commodity underlying the forward contract matches the asset held exactly. For this to occur, the forward price must *converge* to the spot price as the contract expires ($F_{T,T} = S_T$).

Consider again the investor who hedged her long position in a commodity by agreeing to sell it at date *T* through a short position in a forward contract. The value of the combined position is ($F_{0,T} - S_0$). If the investor decides to liquidate her entire position (including the hedge) prior to maturity, she will not be able to deliver the commodity to satisfy her forward obligation as originally intended. Instead, the investor will have to (1) sell her commodity position on the open market for S_t, and (2) "buy back" her short forward position for the new contract price of $F_{t,T}$.[3] The profit from the short hedge liquidated at date t is:

$$B_{t,T} - B_{0,T} = (S_t - F_{t,T}) - (S_0 - F_{0,T})$$

The term $B_{t,T}$ often is called the *cover basis* because that is when the forward contract is closed out, or covered.

This equation highlights an important fact about hedging. Once the hedge position is formed, the investor no longer is exposed to the absolute price movement of the underlying asset alone. Instead, she is exposed to **basis risk** because the terminal value of her combined position is defined as the cover basis minus the initial basis. Notice, however, that only the cover basis is unknown at date 0, and so her real exposure is to the *correlation* between future changes in the spot and forward contract prices. If these movements are highly correlated, the basis risk will be quite small. In fact, it is usually possible to design a forward contract based on a specific underlying asset and deliverable on exactly the desired future date. This sort of customized design reduces basis risk to zero, since $F_{T,T} = S_T$. Conversely, basis risk is a possibility when contract terms are standardized, and is most likely to occur in the futures market where standardization is the norm.

To illustrate the concept of basis risk, suppose the investor wishes to hedge a long position of 100,000 pounds of cotton that she is planning to sell in April. Figure 23.2 shows that cotton futures contracts do exist, but with delivery months in either March or May. With each contract requiring the delivery of 50,000 pounds of cotton, she decides to short two of the May contracts, specifically intending to liquidate her position a month early. Suppose that on the date she initiates her short hedge, the spot cotton price was \$0.5763 per pound and the May futures contract price was \$0.5998 per pound. This means that her initial basis was −2.35 cents, which she hopes will move toward zero in a smooth and predictable manner. Suppose, in fact, that when she closes out her combined position in April, cotton prices have declined so that S_t = \$0.5660 and $F_{t,T}$ = \$0.5753, leaving a cover basis of −0.93 cent. This means the basis has increased in value, or *strengthened,* which is to the short hedger's advantage. The net April selling price for her cotton is \$0.5905 per pound, which is equal to the spot price of \$0.5660 plus the net futures profit of \$0.0245 (= 0.5998 − 0.5753). Notice that this is lower than the original futures price but considerably higher than the April spot price. Thus, the short hedger has benefited by exchanging pure price risk for basis risk.

Although it is difficult to generalize, substantial indirect evidence exists that minimizing basis risk is the primary goal of most hedgers. For example, Brown and Smith noted that the phenomenal growth of OTC products to manage interest rate risk—despite the existence of exchange-traded contracts—is a response to the desire to create customized solutions.[4] Further, a survey by Jesswein, Kwok, and Folks showed that corporate risk managers preferred to hedge their firms' foreign exchange exposure with forward contracts rather than with futures by a ratio of about five to one.[5] Finally, Edwards and Canter as well as Pirrong chronicled the severe difficulties the German firm Metallgesellschaft A. G. had

---

[3]The mechanics of liquidating a forward or futures contract prior to maturity will be described in the next section.

[4]Keith C. Brown and Donald J. Smith, *Interest Rate and Currency Swaps: A Tutorial* (Charlottesville, Va.: Research Foundation of the Institute of Chartered Financial Analysts, 1995).

[5]Kurt Jesswein, Chuck C. Y. Kwok, and William R. Folks, "What New Currency Risk Products Are Companies Using and Why?" *Journal of Applied Corporate Finance* 8, no. 3 (fall 1995): 103–114.

in trying to hedge the energy-related positions on its balance sheet with exchange-traded futures positions.[6]

Calculating the Optimal Hedge Ratio

In the preceding example, the decision to short two cotton futures contracts was a simple one because the investor held exactly twice as much of the same commodity as was covered by a single contract. In most cases, calculating the appropriate hedge ratio, or the number of futures contracts per unit of the spot asset, is not that straightforward. The approach suggested by both Johnson and Stein is to choose the number of contracts that minimizes the variance of net profit from a hedged commodity position. The determination of the required number of contracts can be established as follows.[7]

Consider the position of a short hedger who is long one unit of a particular commodity and short N forward contracts on that commodity. Rewriting the previous equation for the profit from a short hedge and allowing for a variable number of contracts, the net profit (Π_t) of this position at date t can be written:

$$\Pi_t = (S_t - S_0) - (F_{t,T} - F_{0,T})(N) = (\Delta S) - (\Delta F)(N)$$

The variance of this value is then given as:

$$\sigma_{\Pi}^2 = \sigma_{\Delta S}^2 + (N^2)\sigma_{\Delta F}^2 - 2(N)\text{COV}_{\Delta S,\,\Delta F}$$

where:

COV = the covariance of changes in the spot and forward prices

Minimizing this expression and solving for N leaves:

$$N^* = \frac{\text{COV}_{\Delta S,\,\Delta F}}{\sigma_{\Delta F}^2} = \left(\frac{\sigma_{\Delta S}}{\sigma_{\Delta F}}\right)\rho$$

where:

ρ = the correlation coefficient between the spot and forward price changes[8]

The optimal hedge ratio (N^*) can be interpreted as the ratio of the spot and forward price standard deviations multiplied by the correlation coefficient between the two series. Recalling from Chapter 1 that standard deviation is a measure of a position's *total* risk, this means that the optimal number of contracts is determined by the ratio of total volatilities deflated by ρ to account for the *systematic* relationship between the spot and forward prices. (It is, in fact, directly comparable to the beta coefficient of a common stock.) An

[6]Franklin R. Edwards and Michael S. Canter, "The Collapse of Metallgesellschaft: Unhedgeable Risks, Poor Hedging Strategy, or Just Bad Luck?" *Journal of Applied Corporate Finance* 8, no. 1 (spring 1995): 86–105; and Stephen C. Pirrong, "Metallgesellschaft: A Prudent Hedger Ruined or a Wildcatter on NYMEX?" *Journal of Futures Markets* 17, no. 5 (August 1997): 543–578.

[7]Leland L. Johnson, "The Theory of Hedging and Speculation in Commodity Futures," *Review of Economic Studies* 27 (1959–60): 139–160; and Jerome L. Stein, "The Simultaneous Determination of Spot and Futures Prices," *American Economic Review* 51, no. 5 (December 1961): 1012–1025.

[8]Given data for spot and forward prices, σ_{Π}^2 in the variance equation is a function of just one variable, N. Thus, differentiating this equation with respect to N leaves $[d\sigma_{\Pi}^2/dN] = 2(N)\sigma_{\Delta F}^2 - 2\ \text{COV}_{\Delta S,\,\Delta F}$, which can be set equal to zero and solved for N^*. It is easily confirmed that the second derivative of this function is positive and so N^* is a minimizing value.

important implication of this is that the best contract to use in hedging an underlying spot position is the one that has the highest value of ρ. What if, for instance, a clothing manufacturer wanted to hedge the eventual purchase of a large quantity of wool, a commodity for which no exchange-traded futures contract exists? The expression for N^* suggests that it may be possible to form an effective **cross hedge** if prices for a contract based on a related commodity (e.g., cotton) are highly correlated with wool prices. In fact, the expected basis risk of such a cross hedge can be measured as $(1 - \rho^2)$. Finally, note that the value for N^* also can be calculated as the slope coefficient of a regression using ΔS and ΔF as the dependent and independent variables, respectively.[9] In the regression context, ρ^2 is called the coefficient of determination or, more commonly, R^2. Some examples of these calculations are presented in subsequent sections.

FORWARD AND FUTURES CONTRACTS: BASIC VALUATION CONCEPTS

Forward and futures contracts are not securities but rather *trade agreements* that enable both buyers and sellers of an underlying commodity or security to lock in the eventual price of their transaction. As such, they typically require no front-end payment from either the long or short position to motivate the other's participation and, consequently, the contract's initial market value usually is zero. Once the terms of the agreement are set, however, any change in market conditions will likely increase the value of the contract to one of the participants. For example, an obligation made in November to purchase soybeans in March for \$220 per ton is surely quite valuable in January if soybean prices in the spot market are already \$250 and no additional harvest is anticipated in the next 2 months. The valuation of these agreements, which is different for futures and forward contracts, is described below.

Valuing Forwards and Futures

Suppose that at date 0 you had contracted in the forward market to buy Q ounces of gold at date T for $F_{0,T}$. At date t, prior to the maturity date T, you decide that this long position is no longer necessary for your portfolio and you want to get rid of the future price risk it entails. Accordingly, you want to **unwind** your original obligation. One way to do this is to take a short position in a date t forward contract designed to offset the terms of the first. That is, at date t you would agree to sell Q ounces of gold at date T for the price of $F_{t,T}$. This is shown in the upper panel of Figure 23.3. Notice that because you now have contracts to buy and sell Q ounces of gold, you have no exposure to gold price movements between dates t and T. The profit or loss on this pair of forward contracts is $(Q)\ [F_{t,T} - F_{0,T}]$, or the difference between the selling and purchase prices multiplied by the quantity involved. However, this amount would not be received (if $F_{t,T} > F_{0,T}$) or paid until date T, meaning that the value of the original long forward position when it is sold on date t (i.e., its unwind value) would be the *present value* of $(Q)\ [F_{t,T} - F_{0,T}]$, or:

$$V_{t,T} = (Q)\left[F_{t,T} - F_{0,T}\right] \div (1 + i)^{(T-t)}$$

where:

i = the appropriate annualized discount rate

[9]Some have questioned whether regression-based hedge ratios are stable enough to be useful in practice. Recent work, however, has concluded that they are stationary. See Robert Ferguson and Dean Leistikow, "Are Regression Approach Futures Hedge Ratios Stationary?" *Journal of Futures Markets* 18, no. 7 (October 1998): 851–866.

FIGURE 23.3 **UNWIND VALUES FOR FORWARD AND FUTURES CONTRACTS**

Date 0 (Origination)	Date *t* (Unwind)	Date *T* (Maturity)

A. Forward Contract

- Long Forward ($F_{0,T}$)
- Short Forward ($F_{t,T}$)
- Contract Unwind Value: $V_{t,T} = (Q)[F_{t,T} - F_{0,T}] \div (1 + i)^{(T-t)}$

B. Futures Contract

- Long Futures ($F^*_{0,T}$)
- Short Futures ($F^*_{t,T}$)
- Contract Unwind Value: $V^*_{t,T} = (Q)[F^*_{t,T} - F^*_{0,T}]$

This equation expresses the date *t* value of a long forward contract maturing at date *T*. Notice two things about this amount. First, $V_{t,T}$ can be either positive or negative depending on whether $F_{t,T}$ is greater or less than the original contract price, $F_{0,T}$. This means that any forward contract carries the potential for symmetric payoffs to both participants. Second, the value of the short side of the same contract is just $(Q)\,[F_{0,T} - F_{t,T}] \div (1 + i)^{(T-t)}$, reinforcing the fact that forward contracts are *zero-sum games* since whatever the long position gains, the short position loses, and vice versa. For example, if you had originally agreed to a long position in a six-month gold forward at $F_{0.05}$ = \$400, and after three months the new forward contract price is $F_{0.25,\,0.5}$ = \$415, the value of your position would be \$1,464.68 (= (100) (415 − 400) ÷ $(1.1)^{0.25}$), assuming a 10 percent discount rate. Conversely, the value of the original short position would then have to be − \$1,464.68. Finally, notice that as date *t* approaches date *T*, the value of the contract simply becomes $(Q)(F_{T,T} - F_{0,T})$.

Valuing a futures contract is conceptually similar to valuing a forward contract with one important difference. As we saw earlier, futures contracts are marked to market on a daily basis, and this settlement amount was not discounted to account for the temporal difference between dates *t* and *T*. That is, the date *t* value of the futures contract is simply the undiscounted difference between the futures prices at the origination and unwind (or cover) dates, multiplied by the contract quantity, as shown in the bottom panel of Figure 23.3. Thus, the forward contract valuation equation can be adapted for futures as:

$$V^*_{t,T} = (Q)(F^*_{t,T} - F^*_{0,T})$$

where:

*** = the possibility that forward and futures prices for the same commodity at the same point in time might be different**

Cox, Ingersoll, and Ross showed that $F^*_{0,T}$ and $F_{0,T}$ would be equal if short-term interest rates (*i* in the forward valuation equation) are known, but need not be the same under other circumstances.[10]

[10]John Cox, Jonathan Ingersoll, and Stephen Ross, "The Relation between Forward Prices and Futures Prices," *Journal of Financial Economics* 9, no, 4 (December 1981): 321–346.

Typically, for commodities and securities that support both forward and futures markets, differences between $F^*_{0,T}$ and $F_{0,T}$ exist but are relatively small. For instance, Cornell and Reinganum established few economically meaningful differences between forward and futures prices in the foreign exchange market, while Park and Chen found that certain agricultural and precious metal futures prices were significantly higher than the analogous forward prices. More recently, Grinblatt and Jegadeesh documented that the historical differences in prices for Eurodollar forward and futures contracts are due to a mispricing of the latter, although this mispricing has been eliminated over time.[11] Finally, note once again that $V^*_{t,T}$ can be either positive or negative depending on how contract prices have changed since inception.

The Relationship Between Spot and Forward Prices

In many respects, the relationship between the spot and forward prices at any moment in time is a more challenging question than how the contract is valued. We can understand the intuition for this relationship with an example: You have agreed at date 0 to deliver 5,000 bushels of corn to your counterparty at date T. What is a "fair" price ($F_{0,T}$) to charge? Recognizing that the contract price can be anything that two parties agree to, one way to look at this question is to consider how much it will cost you to fulfill your obligation. If you wait until date T to purchase the corn on the spot market, you have a *speculative* position since your purchase price (S_T) will be unknown when you commit to a selling price.

Alternatively, suppose you buy the corn now for the current cash price of S_0 per bushel and store it until you have to deliver it at date T. Under this scheme, the forward contract price you would be willing to commit to would have to be high enough to cover: (1) the present cost of the corn, and (2) the cost of storing the corn until contract maturity. In general, these storage costs, denoted here as $SC_{0,T}$, can involve several things, including commissions paid for the physical warehousing of the commodity ($PC_{0,T}$) and the cost of financing the initial purchase of the underlying asset ($i_{0,T}$) but less any cash flows received ($D_{0,T}$) by owning the asset between dates 0 and T. Thus, in the absence of arbitrage opportunities, the forward contract price should be equal to the current spot price plus the **cost of carry** necessary to transport the asset to the future delivery date:

$$F_{0,T} = S_0 + SC_{0,T} = S_0 + (PC_{0,T} + i_{0,T} - D_{0,T})$$

Notice that even if the funds needed to purchase the commodity at date 0 are not borrowed, $i_{0,T}$ accounts for the opportunity cost of committing one's own financial capital to the transaction.

This cost of carry model is useful in practice because it applies in a wide variety of cases. For some commodities, such as corn or cattle, physical storage is possible but the costs are enormous. Also, neither of these assets pays periodic cash flows in the traditional sense of the term. In such situations, it is quite likely that $F_{0,T} > S_0$ and the market is said to be in **contango**. On the other hand, common stock is costless to store but often pays a dividend. The presence of this cash flow sometimes makes it possible for the basis to be positive (i.e., $F_{0,T} < S_0$), meaning that $SC_{0,T}$ can be negative. There is another reason why $SC_{0,T}$ might be less than zero. For certain storable commodities that do not pay a dividend, $F_{0,T} < S_0$ can occur when there is effectively a "premium" placed on currently owning the

[11]Bradford Cornell and Marc R. Reinganum, "Forward and Futures Prices: Evidence from Foreign Exchange Markets," *Journal of Finance* 36, no. 5 (December 1981): 1035–1045; H Y. Park and Andrew H. Chen, "Differences between Forward and Futures Prices: A Further Investigation of Marking to Market Effects," *Journal of Futures Markets* 5, no. 7 (February 1985): 77–88; and Mark Grinblatt and Narasimhan Jegadeesh, "Relative Pricing of Eurodollar Futures and Forward Contracts," *Journal of Finance* 51, no. 4 (September 1996): 1499–1522.

commodity. This premium, called a **convenience yield**, results from a small supply of the commodity at date 0 relative to what is expected at date T after, say, a crop harvest. (Crude oil is another commodity that sometimes satisfies this condition, although not as indicated in Figure 23.2.) Although it is extremely difficult to quantify, the convenience yield can be viewed as a potential negative storage cost component that works in a manner similar to $D_{0,T}$. A futures market in which $F_{0,T} < S_0$ is said to be **backwardated**.

An immediate implication of the cost of carry model is that there should be a direct relationship between contemporaneous forward and spot prices; indeed, this positive correlation is the objective of any well-designed hedging strategy. A related question involves the relationship between $F_{0,T}$ and the spot price expected to prevail at the time the contract matures (i.e., $E(S_T)$). There are three possibilities. First, the *pure expectations* hypothesis holds that, on average, $F_{0,T} = E(S_T)$, so that futures prices serve as unbiased forecasts of future spot prices. When this is true, futures prices serve an important *price discovery* function for participants in the applicable market. Conversely, $F_{0,T}$ could be less than $E(S_T)$, a situation that Keynes and Hicks argued would arise whenever short hedgers outnumber long hedgers.[12] In that case, a risk premium in the form of a lower contract price would be necessary to attract a sufficient number of long speculators. For reasons that are not entirely clear, this situation is termed *normal backwardation.* Finally, a *normal contango* market occurs when the opposite is true, specifically, when $F_{0,T} > E(S_T)$.

The existence of a risk premium in the futures market is hotly debated. Kamara surveyed the early literature on the subject and found the evidence from the commodity markets to be mixed. He concluded that although the normal backwardation hypothesis was supported, futures markets are mainly driven by risk-averse hedgers who have been able to acquire "cheap" insurance. Krehbiel and Collier examined the price behavior in the Eurodollar and Treasury bill futures markets and found evidence consistent with the existence of risk premia that were necessary to balance net hedging and net speculative positions. Finally, Brooks documented that the risk premia priced into Eurodollar futures contracts have a substantial impact on other financial securities as well. Specifically, he showed that prices for interest rate swaps—which can be viewed as portfolios of Eurodollar contracts—are biased upward, causing borrowers who use swaps to convert their variable-rate loans into synthetic fixed-rate debt to make higher payments, on average, than if they had not hedged.[13]

FINANCIAL FORWARDS AND FUTURES: APPLICATIONS AND STRATEGIES

Originally, forward and futures markets were organized largely around trading agricultural commodities, such as corn and wheat. Although markets for these products remain strong, the most significant recent developments in this area have involved the use of financial securities as the asset underlying the contract. In fact, Table 23.2 shows that the 10 most heavily traded derivative contracts in the world are based on financial securities. In this

[12]John Maynard Keynes, *A Treatise on Money* (London: Macmillan, 1930); and John Hicks, *Value and Capital* (Oxford: Clarendon Press, 1939).

[13]See Avraham Kamara, "The Behavior of Futures Prices: A Review of Theory and Evidence," *Financial Analysts Journal* 40, no. 4 (July–August 1984): 68–75; Tim Krehbiel and Roger Collier, "Normal Backwardation in Short-Term Interest Rate Markets," *Journal of Futures Markets* 16, no. 8 (December 1996): 899–913; and Robert Brooks, *Interest Rate Modeling and the Risk Premiums in Interest Rate Swaps* (Charlottesville, Va.: Research Foundation of the Institute of Chartered Financial Analysts, 1997).

TABLE 23.2 **LEADING INTERNATIONAL DERIVATIVE CONTRACTS RANKED BY TRADING VOLUME**

Contract, Exchange, and Country	1997 Volume	1998 Volume
U.S. Treasury Bonds, CBT, United States	85,111,733	98,459,876
3-mo. Eurodollar, CME, United States	86,397,906	93,266,197
Bund, EUREX, Germany and Switzerland	26,483,369	78,440,580
3-mo. Euromark, LIFFE, United Kingdom	37,043,571	46,891,965
U.S. Treasury Bonds Option, CBT, United States	26,651,471	35,027,073
Interest Rate, BM&F, Brazil	33,081,617	30,967,199
3-mo. Sterling, LIFFE, United Kingdom	17,233,678	29,355,767
S&P 100 Index Option, CBOE, United States	31,514,131	29,199,084
3-mo. Eurodollar Option, CME, United States	25,935,928	28,195,549
BOBL, EUREX, Germany and Switzerland	20,682,716	27,753,352

Source: Futures Industry Association.

section, we take a detailed look at three different types of financial forwards and futures: interest rate, equity index, and foreign exchange.

INTEREST RATE FORWARDS AND FUTURES

Interest rate forwards and futures were among the first derivatives to specify a financial security as the underlying asset. The earliest versions of these contracts were designed to lock in the forward price of a particular fixed-coupon bond, which in turn locks in its yield. As we will see in Chapter 25, this market has progressed to where such contracts as *forward rate agreements* and *interest rate swaps* now fix the desired interest rate directly without reference to any specific underlying security. To understand the nuances of the most popular exchange-traded instruments, it is useful to separate them according to whether they involve long- or short-term rates.

LONG-TERM INTEREST RATE FUTURES

TREASURY BOND AND NOTE CONTRACT MECHANICS The U.S. Treasury bond and note contracts at the Chicago Board of Trade (CBT) are among the most popular of all the financial futures contracts; in fact, Table 23.2 shows that the T-bond contract has historically been the most frequently traded futures contract of any kind. A similar T-bond contract is available at the London International Financial Futures Exchange (LIFFE) and a smaller version—one-half the delivery amount—at the MidAmerica Commodity Exchange (MCE). Delivery dates for both note and bond futures fall in March, June, September, and December. Figure 23.4 shows a representative set of quotes for these contracts.

Both the T-bond and the longer-term T-note contracts traded at the CBT call for the delivery of $100,000 face value of the respective instruments. For the T-bond contract, any Treasury bond that has at least 15 years to the nearest call date or to maturity (if non-callable) can be used for delivery. Bonds with maturities ranging from 6.5 to 10 years and 4.25 to 5.25 years can be used to satisfy the 10-year and 5-year T-note contracts, respectively. Delivery can take place on any day during the month of maturity, with the last trading day of the contract falling 7 business days prior to the end of the month.

Mechanically, the quotation processes for T-bond and T-note contracts work the same way. For example, the settlement price of 124-19, for the March 1999 T-bond contract on the CBT represents $124\frac{19}{32}$ percent of the face amount, or $124,593.75. The contract price went down by 31 **ticks** (−31) from the previous day's settlement, meaning that the short side had its margin account increased by $\frac{31}{32}$ percent of $100,000—or $968.75—where each $\frac{1}{32}$ movement in the bond's price equals $31.25 (i.e., 1,000 ÷ 32).

Although T-bond and T-note futures contracts are called interest rate futures, what the long and short positions actually agree to is the price of the underlying bond. Once that

FIGURE 23.4 **TREASURY BOND AND NOTE FUTURES QUOTATIONS**

	Open	High	Low	Settle	Change	Lifetime High	Lifetime Low	Open Interest
TREASURY BONDS (CBT)-$100,000; pts. 32nds of 100%								
Mar	125-17	125-29	124-05	124-19	– 31	134-26	103-04	612,631
June	125-00	125-05	123-24	124-05	– 31	134-02	110-07	158,464
Sept	123-28	124-01	123-09	123-23	– 30	131-06	115-11	7,797
Dec	....	....	....	123-03	– 30	128-28	118-07	3,267
Est vol 660,000; vol Wd 454,386; open Int 782,159, +29,083.								
TREASURY BONDS (MCE)-$50,000; pts. 32nds of 100%								
Mar	125-12	125-13	124-05	124-24	– 25	134-28	124-00	13,077
Est vol 8,000; vol Wd 4,618; open Int 13,106, +436.								
TREASURY NOTES (CBT)-$100,000; pts. 32nds of 100%								
Mar	117-26	118-00	116-28	117-06	– 20	123-22	112-04	506,367
June	117-27	117-27	117-01	117-09	– 21	120-21	113-18	19,598
Est vol 225,000; vol Wd 123,597; open Int 526,440, +911.								
5 YR TREAS NOTES (CBT)-$100,000; pts. 32nds of 100%								
Mar	12-165	12-195	112-00	12-055	– 11.0	116-15	112-00	263,315
June	113-04	113-04	112-29	113-01	– 12.0	116-08	112-29	4,944
Est vol 100,000; vol Wd 69,198; open Int 268,264, –2,462.								
2 YR TREAS NOTES (CBT)-$200,000, pts. 32nds of 100%								
Mar	105-13	05-145	05-085	05-102	– 3.0	106-30	105-08	40,954
Est vol 2,000; vol Wd 1,962; open Int 40,966, –23.								

Source: *Wall Street Journal,* 5 February 1999.

price is set, however, the yield will be locked in. When a yield is quoted, it is for reference only and typically assumes a coupon rate of 8 percent and 20 years to maturity. For the March 1999 bond contract, the settlement yield would be 5.8908 percent, which can be established by solving for the internal rate of return in the following "bond math" problem:

$$\$1,245.9375 = \sum_{t=1}^{40} \frac{\$40}{(1 + i/2)^t} + \frac{\$1,000}{(1 + i/2)^{40}}$$

This pricing formula takes into account the fact that Treasury bonds pay semiannual interest. So, a 20-year, 8 percent bond makes 40 coupon payments of 4 percent each. Thus, the long position in this contract has effectively agreed in February to buy a 20-year T-bond in March priced to yield 5.89 percent. If, in March, the actual yield on the 20-year bond is below 5.89 percent (i.e., the bond's price is greater than $124,593.75), the long position will have made a wise decision. Thus, the long position in this contract gains as prices rise and rates decrease and loses as increasing rates lead to lower bond prices.

Because the bond and note futures contracts allow so many different instruments to qualify for delivery, the seller would naturally choose to deliver the least expensive bond if there were no adjustments made for varying coupon rates and maturity dates. To account for this, the CBT uses **conversion factors** to correct for the differences in the deliverable bonds. The conversion factor is based on the price of a given bond if its yield is 8 percent at the time of delivery and the face value is $1. For example, the March 1999 conversion factor for the 9 percent T-bond maturing in November 2018 would be 1.0979, calculated as:

$$1.0979 = \sum_{t=1}^{39} \frac{0.045}{(1 + 0.04)^t} + \frac{1}{(1 + 0.04)^{39}}$$

The actual delivery price, or invoice price, for that Treasury bond would be the quoted futures price, $124,593.75, times the conversion factor, 1.0979, for a total of $136,791.48 (plus accrued interest). The buyer must pay more than $124,593.75 because the seller is delivering "more valuable" bonds since their coupon rate exceeds 8 percent.

The conversion factors used by the CBT are technically correct only when the Treasury yield curve is flat at 8 percent. Therefore, there usually will be a *cheapest to deliver* bond that maximizes the difference between the invoice price (the amount received by the short) and the cash market price (the amount paid by the short to acquire the delivery bond). Market participants always know which bond is the cheapest to deliver. Therefore, the T-bond futures contract trades as if this particular security were the actual underlying delivery bond. In fact, the cheapest to deliver security usually is the T-bond with the longest duration when yields are above 8 percent, and the one with the shortest duration for yields less than 8 percent.

A DURATION-BASED APPROACH TO HEDGING In Chapter 16, we stressed that the main benefit of calculating the duration statistic was its ability to link interest rate changes to bond price changes by the formula:

$$\left(\frac{\Delta P}{P}\right) \approx -D\left(\frac{\Delta(1 + i/n)}{(1 + i/n)}\right)$$

We also saw that a more convenient way to write this expression is:

$$\left(\frac{\Delta P}{P}\right) \approx -\left(\frac{D}{(1 + i/n)}\right)\Delta\,(1 + i/n) = -D_{\text{mod}}\,\Delta(i/n)$$

where:

D_{mod} = **the bond's modified duration, combining the Macaulay duration and its periodic yield into a single measure**

Earlier in this chapter, we noted that the objective of hedging was to select a hedge ratio (N) such that $\Delta S - \Delta F\,(N) = 0$, where S is the current spot price of the underlying asset and F is the current futures contract price. Rewriting this leaves:

$$N^* = \frac{\Delta S}{\Delta F}$$

Using the modified duration relationship, this optimal hedge ratio can now be expanded as follows:

$$N^* = \frac{\Delta S}{\Delta F} = \frac{\left(\frac{\Delta S}{S}\right)}{\left(\frac{\Delta F}{F}\right)} \times \frac{S}{F} = \frac{-D_{\text{mod}S} \times \Delta(i_S/n)}{-D_{\text{mod}F} \times \Delta(i_F/n)} \times \frac{S}{F}$$

or

$$N^* = \frac{D_{\text{mod}S}}{D_{\text{mod}F}} \times \beta_i \times \frac{S}{F}$$

where:

β_i = **the "yield beta"**

The yield beta is also called the ratio of changes in the yields applicable to the two instruments where n is the number of payment periods per year (e.g., $n = 2$ for semiannual coupon bonds).[14]

[14]In an early study on the topic, Gerald Gay, Robert Kolb, and Raymond Chiang, "Interest Rate Hedging: An Empirical Test of Alternative Strategies," *Journal of Financial Research* 6, no. 3 (fall 1983): 187–197, tested the duration-based hedge ratio against several other more naive approaches and found that it reduced the risk of the underlying bond position by the greatest amount.

As a general example of the duration-based approach to setting hedge ratios, consider the following fixed-income securities, each making annual payments (i.e., $n = 1$):

Instrument	Coupon	Maturity	Yield
A	8%	10 years	10%
B	10%	15 years	8%

How much of instrument B is necessary to hedge A? This question can be answered in three steps. First, using the method shown in Chapter 16 (and summarized in Appendix 23A), the duration statistics for each position are:

$$D_A = 7.0439 \text{ so } D_{\text{modA}} = (7.0439) \div (1.10) = 6.4036 \text{ years}$$
$$D_B = 8.8569 \text{ so } D_{\text{modB}} = (8.8569) \div (1.08) = 8.2009 \text{ years}$$

Second, we will assume that yield beta is unity (i.e., $\beta_i = 1$). In general, this is calculated by observing historical yield curve movements across the 10- and 15-year maturities. Finally, current prices are easily confirmed to be 87.71 for security A and 117.12 for security B assuming par value of 100. Thus, the duration-based hedge ratio is:

$$N^* = \left(\frac{6.4036}{8.2009}\right)(1)\left(\frac{87.71}{117.12}\right) = 0.5847$$

or 0.5847 unit of B short for every one unit of A held long.

TREASURY FUTURES APPLICATIONS

Hedging a Future Funding Commitment In late July, the treasurer of a U.S.-based company begins to arrange the details of an anticipated 15-year, $100 million funding. He feels that the company will be ready to launch its new debt issue in mid- to late September, but is concerned that between July and September, interest rates may rise, thereby increasing the company's funding cost. Consequently, he decides to hedge this exposure in the T-bond futures market. In this case, he will need to take a *short* position in the futures market, which will appreciate in value if interest rates increase, thereby offsetting the higher payments that will be required on the underlying debt.

The treasurer feels that if the bond issue was placed today, the credit standing of the firm would lead to a funding cost of 8.25 percent for the 15-year period. He knows that a September T-bond futures contract is trading at a price of 103–02 to yield 7.70 percent. He is also aware that bond yields beyond 10 years to maturity tend to move in a parallel fashion to one another so he is comfortable that a yield beta of one is appropriate. Further, the treasurer is aware that T-bond futures can't hedge for changes in the firm's risk premium over the risk-free rate; he will have to live with this source of basis risk.

If he plans to launch his new issue at par value, how many T-bond futures contracts would he need to short today? Assuming semiannual coupons for both the Treasury and corporate issues, their durations can be calculated using the closed-form equation shown in Appendix 23A:

$$D_{\text{corp}} = \frac{1.04125}{0.04125} - \frac{1.04125 + [30(0.04125 - 0.04125)]}{0.04125[(1.04125)^{30} - 1] + 0.04125} = 17.74 \text{ periods}$$

and

$$D_{\text{trsy}} = \frac{1.0385}{0.0385} - \frac{1.0385 + [40(0.04 - 0.0385)]}{0.04[(1.0385)^{40} - 1] + 0.0385} = 20.86 \text{ periods}$$

These statistics are denominated in "half years" so that the hedge ratio will be expressed in the same terms used to price the bonds. With these statistics we can calculate the modified durations as follows: $D_{\text{modC}} = 17.04$ (= 17.74 ÷ 1.04125) and $D_{\text{modT}} = 20.09$ (= 20.86 ÷ 1.0385). Finally, since each T-bond futures contract is standardized to a denomination of \$100,000, the treasurer can calculate the optimal number of contracts to short as:

$$(\text{Number of Contracts}) = \frac{(17.04)}{(20.09)} \times (1.0) \times \frac{(\$100{,}000{,}000)}{(\$103{,}062.50)} = 822.97, \text{ or } 823 \text{ contracts}$$

A T-Bond/T-Note (NOB) Futures Spread Frequently, speculators in the bond market will have a clear view on a change in the overall shape of the yield curve but be less certain as to the actual direction in future rate movements. Suppose, for instance, you think the yield curve—which is currently upward sloping across all maturities—will flatten, but you're not sure in which of several ways this might occur:

- Short-term rates rise and long-term rates fall.
- Short- and long-term rates both rise, but short-term rates rise by more.
- Short- and long-term rates both fall, but short-term rates fall by less.

Clearly, taking a long or short position in a single futures contract linked to a single point on the yield curve is too speculative, given your view; you could be right about the shape shift but guess wrong about direction. One way to mitigate this unwanted risk while investing (based on your view) is to go both long and short in contracts representing different points on the yield curve. This is known as the Treasury "Notes over Bond" **spread** (or "NOB" spread) strategy.

Suppose in mid-February you observe the following price quotes (along with their implied yields to maturity) for T-bond and T-note futures contracts maturing in June:

Contract	Settle Price	Implied Yield
20-yr, 8% T-bond	103–02	7.70%
10-yr, 8% T-note	104–02	7.42%

Notice that your expectation of a flattening yield curve is identical to the view that the 28 basis point yield gap (= 0.0770 − 0.0742) between the longer- and shorter-term contracts will shrink. If you also feel this will occur by mid-June, the appropriate strategy would be:

- Go long in one Treasury bond futures.
- Go short in one Treasury note futures.

The net profit from this joint position when you close out the two contracts is calculated as the sum of the profits on the short T-note position and the long T-bond contract, or:

$$\left[\frac{104.0625 - \text{June T-note Price}}{100} + \frac{\text{June T-bond Price} - 103.0625}{100}\right](\$100{,}000)$$

To see how this combined position would pay off if your view is correct, consider two scenarios in which the yield curve flattens to where there is no difference between 10- and 20-year rates by the time you close your positions in June:

1. *Rates increase to 8.00 percent by June.*
   In this case, both futures contracts will sell at par and so your net profit will be:

$$\text{Net Profit} = [0.040625 - 0.030625](\$100{,}000) = \$1{,}000$$

   Notice that this same calculation can be done on a "price tick" basis:

$$\begin{aligned}\text{Net Profit} &= \{[(104\text{–}02) - (103\text{–}02)] - [(100\text{–}00) - (100\text{–}00)]\}(\$31.25)\\ &= (32\text{ ticks})(\$31.25) = \$1{,}000\end{aligned}$$

   which is equivalent to the change in the number of ticks in the NOB spread multiplied by the dollar value of a tick (i.e., $31.25).
2. *Rates decrease to 7.00 percent by June.*
   Except when both bonds trade at par, it is generally not the case that two bonds with different maturities—but the same coupon and same yield—will trade at the same price. In this scenario, the settlement prices on the two futures contracts will be:

$$P_{\text{T-note}} = \sum_{t=1}^{20} \frac{\$4}{(1 + 0.035)^t} + \frac{\$100}{(1 + 0.035)^{20}} = \$107.11 \approx 107\text{–}04$$

   and

$$P_{\text{T-bond}} = \sum_{t=1}^{40} \frac{\$4}{(1 + 0.035)^t} + \frac{\$100}{(1 + 0.035)^{40}} = \$110.68 \approx 110\text{–}22$$

   so that the net profit from the NOB spread will be:

$$\begin{aligned}\text{Net Profit} &= \{[(104\text{–}02) - (103\text{–}02)] - [(107\text{–}04) - (110\text{–}22)]\}(\$31.25)\\ &= (32 + 114)(\$31.25) = \$4{,}562.50\end{aligned}$$

   Interpreting this outcome differently, you made $7,625.00 on your long position in the T-bond contract (= [(110–22) − (103–02)](31.25)), but you lost $3,062.50 on your short T-note position (= [(104–02) − (107–04)](31.25)) for a net gain of $4,562.50.

These results show that the futures spread allows speculators to separate their views on yield curve shape from an explicit forecast of a change in the curve's position. When using this strategy, however, the investor must be careful to recognize that, because the duration of the T-bond is greater than that of the T-note, the former will be more sensitive to a given rate change.

SHORT-TERM INTEREST RATE FUTURES

Short-term interest rate futures have become the most rapidly expanding segment of the exchange-traded market. Currently, investors can hedge their exposures to several different money market rates (e.g., T-bill, LIBOR, Banker's Acceptance, Federal Funds) denominated in a multitude of currencies (e.g., U.S. dollar, Swiss franc, British sterling). In the following analysis, we concentrate on two of these contracts: Eurodollar and Treasury bill.

EURODOLLAR AND TREASURY BILL CONTRACT MECHANICS The Eurodollar contract traded at the International Monetary Market (IMM) on the Chicago

FIGURE 23.5 **EURODOLLAR AND TREASURY BILL FUTURES QUOTATIONS**

EURODOLLAR (CME)-$1 million; pts of 100%

	Open	High	Low	Settle	Chg	Yield Settle	Yield Chg	Open Interest
Feb	95.01	95.01	94.99	95.00	....	5.00	....	18,870
Mar	95.00	95.00	94.97	94.99	– .01	5.01	+ .01	448,858
Apr	94.98	94.99	94.98	94.99	– .02	5.01	+ .02	1,969
May	94.98	94.98	94.98	94.98	– .03	5.02	+ .03	1,262
June	95.01	95.04	94.95	94.98	– .03	5.02	+ .03	437,737
Sept	95.00	95.01	94.93	94.95	– .05	5.05	+ .05	394,906
Dec	94.70	94.71	94.63	94.65	– .04	5.35	+ .04	262,751
Mr00	94.87	94.88	94.79	94.82	– .05	5.18	+ .05	244,401
June	94.81	94.83	94.74	94.76	– .06	5.24	+ .06	157,200
Sept	94.76	94.77	94.69	94.70	– .07	5.30	+ .07	127,029
Dec	94.64	94.64	94.56	94.57	– .06	5.43	+ .06	118,217
Mr01	94.70	94.70	94.63	94.64	– .06	5.36	+ .06	96,147
June	94.67	94.67	94.60	94.61	– .06	5.39	+ .06	82,197
Sept	94.65	94.65	94.58	94.59	– .06	5.41	+ .06	67,722
Dec	94.50	94.51	94.46	94.47	– .06	5.53	+ .06	55,364
Mr02	94.56	94.56	94.51	94.53	– .06	5.47	+ .06	50,615
June	94.54	94.54	94.48	94.50	– .06	5.50	+ .06	48,773
Sept	94.49	94.50	94.45	94.47	– .06	5.53	+ .06	40,554
Dec	94.38	94.38	94.33	94.35	– .06	5.65	+ .06	37,551
Mr03	94.43	94.43	94.37	94.39	– .06	5.61	+ .06	28,988
June	94.40	94.40	94.34	94.35	– .06	5.65	+ .06	27,429
Sept	94.36	94.36	94.30	94.32	– .06	5.68	+ .06	31,501
Dec	94.23	94.23	94.18	94.19	– .06	5.81	+ .06	18,431
Mr04	94.20	94.23	94.20	94.22	– .07	5.78	+ .07	17,729
June	94.20	94.20	94.16	94.18	– .07	5.82	+ .07	14,175
Sept	94.13	94.15	94.13	94.15	– .07	5.85	+ .07	13,419
Dec	93.98	94.00	93.97	94.00	– .07	6.00	+ .07	11,270
Mr05	94.06	94.06	94.01	94.04	– .07	5.96	+ .07	11,026
June	94.00	94.00	93.97	94.00	– .07	6.00	+ .07	9,583
Sept	93.96	93.96	93.94	93.96	– .07	6.04	+ .07	9,210
Dec	93.79	93.81	93.79	93.81	– .07	6.19	+ .07	6,451
Mr06	93.88	93.88	93.83	93.85	– .07	6.15	+ .07	6,220
June	93.80	93.81	93.79	93.81	– .07	6.19	+ .07	5,021
Sept	93.77	93.78	93.76	93.78	– .07	6.22	+ .07	5,727
Dec	....	....	....	93.63	– .07	6.37	+ .07	5,727
Mr07	93.70	93.70	93.65	93.67	– .07	6.33	+ .07	5,166
June	93.63	93.63	93.61	93.63	– .07	6.37	+ .07	4,708
Sept	93.59	93.59	93.57	93.59	– .07	6.41	+ .07	4,238
Dec	93.44	93.44	93.42	93.44	– .07	6.56	+ .07	5,137
Mr08	93.48	93.48	93.46	93.48	– .07	6.52	+ .07	3,908
June	93.44	93.44	93.41	93.44	– .07	6.56	+ .07	4,034
Sept	93.39	93.40	93.38	93.40	– .07	6.60	+ .07	3,483

Est vol 517,777; vol Wd 310,343; open int 2,946,257, +1,471.

TREASURY BILLS (CME)-$1 mil.; pts. of 100%

	Open	High	Low	Settle	Chg	Discount Settle	Discount Chg	Open Interest
Mar	95.68	95.69	95.66	95.69	– .01	4.31	+ .01	2,150
June	....	....	....	95.72	– .03	4.28	+ .03	124

Est vol 389; vol Wd 105; open int 2,274, +52.

LIBOR-1 MO. (CME)-$3,000,000; points of 100%

	Open	High	Low	Settle	Chg	Discount Settle	Discount Chg	Open Interest
Feb	95.04	95.05	95.04	95.05	....	4.95	....	11,767
Mar	95.00	95.01	94.99	95.00	– .01	5.00	+ .01	4,411
Apr	95.05	95.05	95.04	95.06	– .01	4.95	+ .01	3,274
May	95.05	95.05	95.05	95.05	– .02	4.95	+ .02	638
June	95.04	95.04	95.04	95.04	– .03	4.96	+ .03	414
July	....	....	....	95.04	– .03	4.96	+ .03	186

Est vol 2,413; vol Wd 1,927; open int 20,862, +97.

Source: *Wall Street Journal*, 5 February 1999.

Mercantile Exchange (CME, or "Merc"), as well as a comparable contract traded on the LIFFE, has become enormously successful since it was launched in the early 1980s. Delivery dates occur monthly for a brief period before following the March, June, September, December cycle (the so-called IMM dates) and now extend 10 years into the future. The final trading and settlement date is the second London business day before the third Wednesday of the delivery month. A representative set of quotes is shown in Figure 23.5. Also traded on the LIFFE (although not shown here) are similar contracts for hedging Euro-IBOR (i.e., the "Euro" currency), Eurosterling, Euromark, Eurolira, and Euroswiss rates.

Hypothetically, the Eurodollar contract requires the long position to make a $1,000,000, 90-day bank deposit with the short position at the maturity date. Unlike the Treasury bond and note futures just described, however, this contract requires all outstanding obligations to be settled in cash. This provision is necessary because the contract nominally requires the long position to make, and the short position to receive, a 90-day Euro-time deposit. However, that is something that the short position can't legally do unless it is a financial institution chartered for such business. The underlying interest rate is the 3-month (i.e., 90-day) LIBOR that is quoted on a 360-day bank add-on basis. As we will see, arbitrage trading should drive the sequence of Eurodollar (or LIBOR) futures rates to equal the forward rates implied by the yield curve for interbank lending in the cash market. That is, in an efficient market, the futures rates should be close to the comparable implied forward rates.

In Figure 23.5, the quoted contract price for the March 2000 contract is 94.82, which is not an actual purchase price but merely an index calculated as 100 minus the settlement yield of 5.18 (percent). Eurodollar futures use this settlement price index because it conveniently preserves the inverse relation between price and yield. Thus, a long position in this contract can still be thought to "win" when prices rise—and the short position wins with falling prices—even though it is the opposite movement in the underlying interest rate that matters.

The minimum price change, or "tick," for this contract is one basis point and equals a \$25 change in the value of the contract. Therefore, the *basis point value* of the contract is \$25 (= \$1,000,000 × 0.0001 × 90/360). Thus, the five tick (−0.05) decline in the price of the March contract means that LIBOR increased by five basis points from the prior day's settlement. This would benefit a person who acquired a short position at the close of the prior day inasmuch as he would have a locked-in borrowing cost for the 90-day period from March to June 2000 that is now five basis points lower than the market level. In fact, all sellers of this contract gained \$125 per contract (i.e., \$25 per tick times five ticks) in their margin accounts.

Finally, notice that the trading volume on the Eurodollar contract is less than that of the T-bond contract (shown in Figure 23.4), but the total open interest for all delivery months is about four times as great. Also, the Eurodollar open interest is spread over the various delivery dates to a greater extent than for the T-bond contract. In fact, the Eurodollar contract is the "deepest" financial futures contract available with, as noted, maturities going out 10 years. This makes it possible to hedge a LIBOR-based exposure a decade into the future. Brown and Smith interpreted these trading patterns as suggesting that T-bond futures are used in the market more as a speculative trading contract and that Eurodollar futures are used more frequently as a buy-and-hold hedging instrument.[15]

Figure 23.5 also lists quotes for the available Treasury bill futures traded at the IMM. This contract requires the long position to buy, and the short position to sell, a 90-day Treasury bill at maturity and can be settled in cash or with a physical exchange. Similar to the Eurodollar derivative, the T-bill contract is standardized to an amount of \$1,000,000 so that each basis point change in the price (or rate) is worth \$25 per contract. Again, the quoted price is a price index, 100 minus the settlement discount rate. In the absence of arbitrage, the T-bill futures rates should be close to the implied forward discount rates calculated from the cash market T-bill rates.

The T-bill contract at the IMM has lost much of its market share in recent years because it is dominated by competing contracts in two important applications. First, because many more corporate and banking transactions are tied to LIBOR—which can be viewed as a risk-free rate plus a credit spread—than to the T-bill rate, more end-users prefer the Eurodollar contract for hedging their interest rate exposures. Indeed, T-bill open interest is less than 1 percent that of the Eurodollar contract. Second, the T-bill contract is seldom used for speculative purposes in lieu of T-bond futures because the duration of the underlying instrument (a 3-month T-bill) in the T-bill contract is so much shorter than that of the latter (a 20-year bond), meaning that its price will increase by less if the anticipated rate change is

[15]Keith C. Brown and Donald J. Smith, "Recent Innovations in Interest Rate Risk Management and the Reintermediation of Commercial Banking," *Financial Management* 17, no. 4 (winter 1988): 45–58.

FIGURE 23.6 **USING INTEREST RATE FUTURES TO ADJUST DURATION**

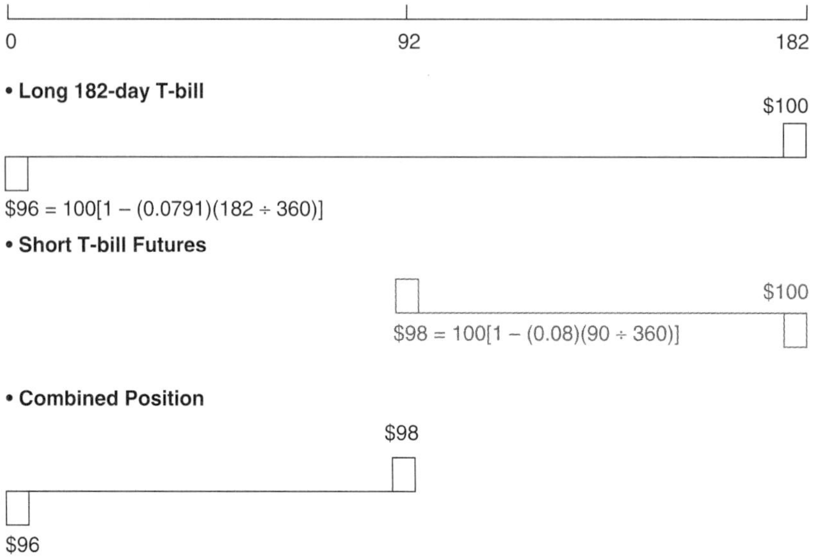
0
92
182
• Long 182-day T-bill
$100
$96 = 100[1 – (0.0791)(182 ÷ 360)]
• Short T-bill Futures
$100
$98 = 100[1 – (0.08)(90 ÷ 360)]
• Combined Position
$98
$96

realized. Nevertheless, the following examples will show that T-bill futures play an important (if limited) economic role in financial markets.

SHORT-TERM INTEREST RATE FUTURES APPLICATIONS

Altering Bond Duration with Futures Contracts An investor currently holds a 6-month (i.e., 182-day) Treasury bill. Because of a fear that inflationary pressures will increase interest rates toward the end of the coming quarter, she would like to reduce her exposure by converting this position into a 3-month T-bill. There are two ways to do this. First, she could sell her current holding and buy the shorter-term instrument she desires, a strategy that might entail nontrivial transaction costs. Second, she could accomplish the same change synthetically by supplementing her 6-month bill with a short position in a T-bill futures contract maturing in 92 days. This is what she decides to do.

Figure 23.6 shows the net effect of combining the long position in the 182-day T-bill with a short position in the T-bill futures (ignoring for simplicity the margin account on the derivative). In this illustration, the discount yield for the cash market instrument is 7.91 percent, leading to a price of $96 (per par value of 100). Also, the futures discount yield is 8 percent; that is, the investor is committed to deliver a 90-day T-bill at a price of $98 when the contract matures. The display assumes that she settles her futures obligation by giving up the remaining 90 days of her original T-bill in exchange for $98. This indicates that the combined position is equivalent to a 92-day Treasury bill with a current price of $96 and a "face" value of $98. Thus, shorting the futures contract has effectively converted a 6-month holding into a 3-month instrument with an implied discount yield of 7.99 percent (= [(98 − 96) ÷ 98][360 ÷ 92]).

Because Treasury bills, as zero-coupon securities, have durations equal to their maturities, a different way of interpreting this example is that the short position in a T-bill futures contract has allowed the investor to *reduce* the duration of her holding from 6 to 3 months. Conversely, although not shown in Figure 23.6, a long futures position can lengthen duration. For example, had the investor held a 92-day T-bill and supplemented it with a long T-bill futures contract maturing at the same date, she would have locked in her reinvestment rate for another 90-day T-bill position. Consequently, being long in the 92-day bill and long in the bill futures is equivalent to being long in a 182-day T-bill, which *increases* her investment duration from 3 to 6 months.[16]

Creating a Synthetic Fixed-Rate Funding with a Eurodollar Strip Suppose that on March 15 a senior loan officer for a large regional bank is considering an investment scheme for lending $2,000,000 in temporary cash balances to a "large cap" manufacturing firm. The plan would last for one year and have the payment rate reset on a quarterly basis at LIBOR. At the planning stage, the LIBOR yield curve appears as follows:

90-day LIBOR	5.00%
180-day LIBOR	5.10
270-day LIBOR	5.20
360-day LIBOR	5.30

Given the debt market convention that the funding rates on floating-rate deal structures always are determined in advance and paid in arrears, she knows that her loan receipt for the first 3 months would be based on the prevailing 5.00 percent rate and be receivable in 90 days. Her concern is what her receipts might be in the subsequent three quarters and, specifically, she is worried that they may fall to an unacceptable level. Accordingly, she considers using the Eurodollar futures market to hedge her exposure.

As a prelude to checking futures contract price quotes, she calculates the forward rates implied by the current yield curve. Using money-market implied forward rate formulas shown in Appendix 23B, these computations generate:

$$_{180}IFR_{90} = \left[\frac{(0.051)(180) - (0.050)(90)}{(180 - 90)}\right]\left[\frac{1}{1 + \left(\frac{(90)(0.050)}{360}\right)}\right] = 5.14\%$$

$$_{270}IFR_{180} = \left[\frac{(0.052)(270) - (0.051)(180)}{(270 - 180)}\right]\left[\frac{1}{1 + \left(\frac{(180)(0.051)}{360}\right)}\right] = 5.27\%$$

$$_{360}IFR_{270} = \left[\frac{(0.053)(360) - (0.052)(270)}{(360 - 270)}\right]\left[\frac{1}{1 + \left(\frac{(270)(0.052)}{360}\right)}\right] = 5.39\%$$

She checks with her trading desk for quotes on the relevant Eurodollar futures contracts and receives the following information:

Contract Expiration	**Settlement Price**
June	94.86
September	94.73
December	94.61

[16]For a related discussion, see Jess B. Yawitz and William J. Marshall, "The Use of Futures in Immunized Portfolios," *Journal of Portfolio Management* 11, no. 2 (winter 1985): 51–58.

The futures settlement prices indicate LIBOR contract rates that are identical to the implied forward rates, suggesting there is no arbitrage potential between the cash and futures markets on this date.

To lock in her receipts for the $2,000,000 loan, the banker would go long a *strip* of Eurodollar futures contracts. That is, she takes long positions in two June contracts, two September contracts, and two December contracts. (Recall that the long position in a Eurodollar contract gains when the price index rises with a falling LIBOR; this is the protection she is seeking.) With these positions, her quarterly interest receipts will be fixed at the following levels:

$$\text{June Receipt} = (\$2{,}000{,}000)\left[\frac{(0.0500)(90)}{360}\right] = \$25{,}000$$

$$\text{September Receipt} = (\$2{,}000{,}000)\left[\frac{(0.0514)(90)}{360}\right] = \$25{,}700$$

$$\text{December Receipt} = (\$2{,}000{,}000)\left[\frac{(0.0527)(90)}{360}\right] = \$26{,}350$$

$$\text{March (Next Year) Receipt} = (\$2{,}000{,}000)\left[\frac{(0.0539)(90)}{360}\right] = \$26{,}950$$

Although these cash inflows are fixed in advance, they clearly differ in amount from quarter to quarter. To get a better indication of her overall return, the banker asks herself the following question: What quarterly annuity payment does this sequence of receipts imply? This amount can be calculated as the solution to:

$$\frac{\$25{,}000}{\left[1+\frac{(0.050)(90)}{360}\right]} + \frac{\$25{,}700}{\left[1+\frac{(0.051)(180)}{360}\right]} + \frac{\$26{,}350}{\left[1+\frac{(0.052)(270)}{360}\right]} + \frac{\$26{,}950}{\left[1+\frac{(0.053)(360)}{360}\right]}$$

$$= \frac{\text{Annuity}}{\left[1+\frac{(0.050)(90)}{360}\right]} + \frac{\text{Annuity}}{\left[1+\frac{(0.051)(180)}{360}\right]} + \frac{\text{Annuity}}{\left[1+\frac{(0.052)(270)}{360}\right]} + \frac{\text{Annuity}}{\left[1+\frac{(0.053)(360)}{360}\right]}$$

Solving this formula for "Annuity" gives a value of $25,989.38, where the discount rates are from the prevailing cash market LIBOR curve. Finally, notice that this annuity payment, when expressed on a full 360-day percentage basis, is:

$$\left[\frac{\$25{,}989.38}{\$2{,}000{,}000}\right]\left[\frac{360}{90}\right] = 5.198\%$$

which is a time-weighted average of the 90-day spot LIBOR and the series of three implied forward rates.

Creating a TED Spread As noted earlier, one of the features that makes the Eurodollar futures contract such a popular hedging vehicle is the rate it is based on—3-month LIBOR. This rate can be thought of as equivalent to the 3-month T-bill yield *plus* a risk premium (i.e., credit spread). Sometimes, bond traders will have a view on future movements in this credit spread; for example, a trader might believe the current difference between the LIBOR and T-bill yield is too narrow and that it will soon widen. The problem with trying to play this view with a short position in the Eurodollar contract alone, however, is even if the trader is right about the spread, the general level of interest rates could still decline by more than enough to offset any spread gains.

FIGURE 23.7 **TED SPREAD FOR 3-MONTH CONTRACTS**

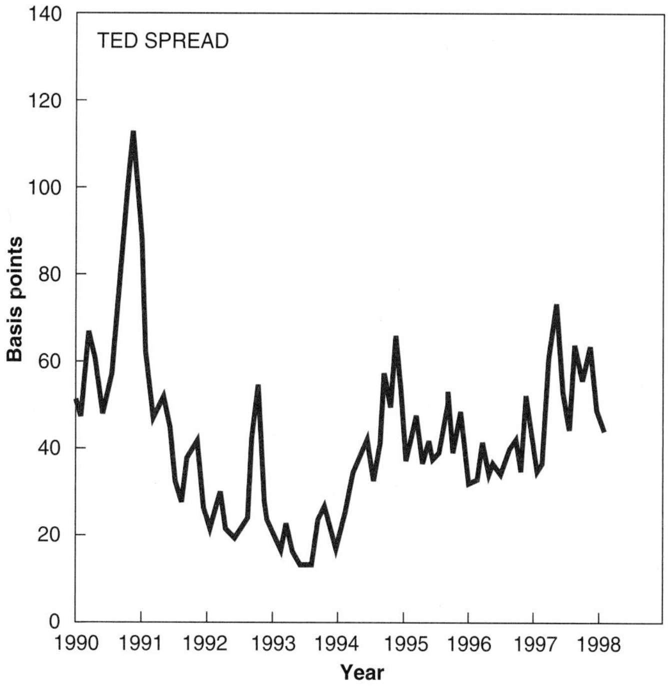
TED SPREAD
Basis points
140
120
100
80
60
40
20
0
1990 1991 1992 1993 1994 1995 1996 1997 1998
Year

Source: Federal Reserve Bank of Cleveland.

The solution to this dilemma is to isolate the credit spread component in LIBOR through a strategy known as the *TED* (Treasury/EuroDollar) *spread.* The TED spread is created by taking simultaneous, but opposite, positions in both a Eurodollar and T-bill futures contract having the same maturity. In the parlance of the market, we have the following definitions.

Long a TED Spread = (Long T-Bill Futures) + (Short Eurodollar Futures)
Short a TED Spread = (Short T-Bill Futures) + (Long Eurodollar Futures)

Notice that a long position in a TED spread will gain when the credit spread increases; the short TED spread benefits from a narrowing of the credit spread. Figure 23.7 shows how volatile the 3-month TED spread has been over time.

To see how an investor can profit from this volatility, consider the following example. Suppose that in early August you observe the following prices in the Eurodollar and T-bill futures markets:

	T-Bill	Eurodollar	Spread
September contracts	95.24	94.80	44 bp
December contracts	94.68	94.11	57 bp
March contracts	94.42	93.86	56 bp

Recall that the difference between the T-bill and Eurodollar price indexes is the spread built into the Eurodollar contract for a particular maturity.

If you believe the economy will remain sluggish for an extended period of time and that credit spreads currently are too narrow in the short-term contract, you would want to take a long TED spread position (i.e., short the Eurodollar futures and buy the T-bill contract). After you establish this position using the September contracts, the Federal Reserve Board tightens rates again so that by mid-September the following prices prevail when you unwind the strategy:

New September T-bill contract	94.55
New September Eurodollar contract	93.95
New spread	0.60

This new spread is more closely aligned with the December and March contracts. The profit on your transaction is calculated as (New TED spread) − (Original TED spread), or (94.55 − 93.95) − (95.24 − 94.80) = 16 basis points.

With each contract standardized so that a basis point is worth $25, the profit per contract-pair from this trade would be (16 × $25) = $400. Another way to see this profit is that you made an 85-basis-point profit on the short position in the Eurodollar contract (= 94.80 − 93.95) but lost 69 basis points on the long T-bill contract (= 94.55 − 95.24). However, if both rates had declined, you still would have made money if the T-bill yield had fallen by more than LIBOR.

Stock Index Futures

Another important form of financial futures contracting specifies an equity index as the underlying asset. In this section, we consider the basics of stock index futures trading and discuss two applications for these instruments, including a popular form of computer-assisted trading known as stock index arbitrage.

STOCK INDEX FUTURES CONTRACT FUNDAMENTALS Like interest rate futures, stock index futures were originally intended to provide a hedge against movements in an underlying financial asset. We have just seen that some interest rate futures can be settled with either a cash or physical transfer. As detailed in Chapter 5 and the introductory example in Chapter 11, however, the underlying financial asset for a stock index futures contract is a hypothetical creation that does not exist in practice and therefore cannot be delivered to settle a contract. Thus, stock index futures can only be settled in cash, similar to the Eurodollar (i.e., LIBOR) contract.

Stock index futures are intended to provide general hedges against stock market movements and can be applied to either whole (i.e., diversified) portfolios or individual stocks. Hedging an individual stock with an index futures contract is done in an attempt to isolate the unsystematic portion of that security's risk. Additionally, stock index futures often are used to convert entire stock portfolios into synthetic riskless positions to exploit an apparent mispricing between stock in the cash and futures markets. This strategy, commonly called **stock index arbitrage**, is the most prominent example of a wider class of computer-assisted trading schemes known as *program trading.*

Figure 23.8 lists quotes for futures contracts on several U.S. and foreign stock indexes, including the Dow Jones Industrial Average, the Standard and Poor's 500, the Standard and Poor's Midcap 400, the Nikkei 225 (Japan), the CAC 40 (France), the DAX 30 (Germany), and the FT-SE 100 (England). For instance, an investor planning in February to buy stock in June can hedge against his eventual purchase price increasing with rising market prices by entering the long position of the June 1999 S&P 500 contract. With a settlement price of

FIGURE 23.8 **STOCK INDEX FUTURES QUOTATIONS**

DJ INDUSTRIAL AVERAGE (CBOT)-$10 times average

	Open	High	Low	Settle	Chg	High	Low	Open Interest
Mar	9412	9445	9295	9350	– 67	9760	7220	15,329
June	9507	9510	9380	9426	– 68	9810	7670	1,366
Sept		....	....	9506	– 66	9891	7875	969
Dec	9560	9640	9540	9586	– 65	9974	7987	260
Dc00	10000	10000	9950	9950	– 63	10300	8100	45

Est vol 16,000; vol Wed 14,457; open int 17,969, +324.
Idx prl: High 9397.96; Low 9274.89; Close 9304.50 −62.31

S&P 500 INDEX (CME)-$250 times index

	Open	High	Low	Settle	Chg	High	Low	Open Interest
Mar	127910	128530	125200	125930	– 19.20	129420	902.85	391,408
June	128900	128900	126520	127110	– 19.40	130250	914.85	8,414
Sept	128000	130090	127590	128290	– 19.50	131370	927.35	2,400
Dec		....	....	129480	– 19.80	132520	960.70	1,479
Mr00		....	....	130730	– 21.30	133850	970.00	129
June		....	....	131980	– 22.80	135200	980.00	496

Est vol 118,403; vol Wed 103,617; open int 405,008, −681.
Idx prl: High 1272.16; Low 1248.37; Close 1248.49 −235.80

S&P MIDCAP 400 (CME)-$500 times index

	Open	High	Low	Settle	Chg	High	Low	Open Interest
Mar	381.00	381.50	373.05	374.00	– 7.45	398.90	274.30	16,432

Est vol 772; vol Wed 1,087; open int 16,432, +272.
Idx prl: High 379.04; Low 372.16; Close 372.25 −6.60

NIKKEI 225 STOCK AVERAGE (CME)-$5 times index

	Open	High	Low	Settle	Chg	High	Low	Open Interest
Mar	14200.	14230.	14105.	14150.	– 75	17150.	12690.	20,719
June	14100.	14100.	14050.	14050.	– 25	16755.	12640.	188

Est vol 794; vol Wed 510; open int 20,913, −44.
Idx prl: High 14255.67; Low 13925.14; Close 14086.85 −74.46

NASDAQ 100 (CME)-$100 times index

	Open	High	Low	Settle	Chg	High	Low	Open Interest
Mar	212800	214300	203400	204450	– 81.25	216500	109000	14,215
June	209800	211000	206325	206950	– 51.25	218600	110800	172

Est vol 7,879; vol Wed 6,809; open int 14,417, +824.
Idx prl: High 2121.62; Low 2027.56; Close 2027.66 −92.28

CAC-40 STOCK INDEX (MATIF)-FFr 50 per index pt.

	Open	High	Low	Settle	Chg	High	Low	Open Interest
Feb	4237.0	4281.0	4168.5	4174.0	– 17.0	4519.5	2997.0	110,945
Mar	4248.0	4284.0	4176.5	4181.0	– 17.0	4569.4	3541.5	61,801
Sept		....	....	4166.5	– 17.0	4296.5	3716.0	19,433
Mr00		....	....	4224.0	– 17.0	4343.5	3705.0	2,590
Sept		....	....	4211.0	– 17.0	....	....	315

Est vol 56,558; vol Wd 68,807; open int 195,087, −2,564.

DAX-30 GERMAN STOCK INDEX (EUREX)
DM 100 times index

	Open	High	Low	Settle	Chg	High	Low	Open Interest
Mar	5175.0	5226.0	5070.0	5074.5	– 30.5	5510.0	3928.0	186,222
June	5198.5	5241.5	5135.0	5137.0	+ 17.0	5522.0	4514.0	58,290

Est vol 39,671; vol Wd 60,518; open int 245,006, +5,267.
The index: High na; Low na; Close na,na

FT-SE 100 INDEX (LIFFE)-£10 per index point

	Open	High	Low	Settle	Chg	High	Low	Open Interest
Mar	5980.0	6050.0	5918.0	5950.0	+ 15.0	6244.0	4773.0	165,545
June	6020.0	6070.0	5965.0	5989.0	+ 12.0	6167.0	5255.0	17,163
Sept	....	....	....	6033.0	+ 14.0	6210.5	6005.0	1,700

Est vol 30,467; vol Wd 26,686; open int 184,408, −223.

Source: *Wall Street Journal,* 5 February 1999.

1271.10 for this contract (shown in the display as "127110"), he has obligated himself to the theoretical purchase of 250 "shares" of the S&P 500 on the third Friday of June for \$317,775 (= 1271.10 × 250). The minimum contract price movement is 0.10 points, which equals \$25. Thus, if the actual level of the S&P index on the contract settlement date turned out to be 1273.30, the long position would gain \$550, or \$25 times 22 "ticks" (i.e., (1273.30 − 1271.10) ÷ 0.10), thereby reducing the net purchase price for his desired equity investment.

STOCK INDEX FUTURES VALUATION AND INDEX ARBITRAGE Earlier we established that the key to understanding the pricing of futures contracts is the concept of arbitrage. To see how this works for index contracts, suppose that at date 0 an investor takes the following positions: (1) purchases a portfolio of stock representing the underlying stock index for S_0, and (2) goes short a stock index future (with an expiration date of T) for $F_{0,T}$. Assume further that in order to avoid making any investment at date 0, the funds for the long position are borrowed at the risk-free rate of RFR. Upon unwinding this position at date t, the net profit (Π) is given by:

$$\Pi = (F_{0,T} - F_{t,T}) + (S_t - S_0 - S_0RFR_t + S_0d_t) = (F_{0,T} - F_{t,T}) + [S_t - S_0(1 + RFR_t - d_t)]$$

where:

d_t = the dividend yield accruing to the stocks comprising the index between dates 0 and t

In other words, the profit you make on this short hedge in stock index futures will consist of two components: the net difference in the futures position and the net difference in the underlying index position (after adding borrowing costs and subtracting dividends received from the initial purchase).

Now assume the long position in the stock portfolio is held until the expiration of the futures contract (i.e., date $t = T$). The advantage of doing this is that the cash settlement feature of the stock index futures contract ensures that the futures price and index level will converge. That is, at date T we will have $F_{T,T} = S_T$, which means that the short hedge profit (Π) equation can be written:

$$\Pi = [F_{0,T} - S_0 - S_0(RFR_t - d_T)]$$

As before, $RFR_t - d_T$ is called the net cost of carry and represents the difference between the borrowing cost paid and the dividend received.

If the dividend yield is known at date 0, this position is riskless and requires no initial investment. Thus, buying and selling among arbitrageurs trading in both the stock and futures markets should ensure that $\Pi = 0$. Thus, the futures price set at date 0 will be:

$$F_{0,T} = S_0 + S_0(RFR_t - d_T)$$

As in the cost of carry model discussed earlier, the futures price could be set below the spot level of the index (i.e., a backwardated market) if $(\text{RFR}_t - d_T) < 0$. That is, the index futures contract will be priced lower than the current level of the stock price whenever the dividends received by holding stock exceed the borrowing cost.

To see how this parity relationship helps establish the appropriate level of the stock index futures price, assume that one "share" of the S&P 500 index can be purchased for 1250.00 and that the dividend yield and risk-free rate over the holding period are 1.5 percent and 2.5 percent, respectively. Under these conditions, the contract price on a 6-month S&P 500 futures should be $F_{0,0.5} = 1250 + 1250(0.025 - 0.015) = 1262.50$. Now suppose that you construct a short hedge position by (1) purchasing the index at 1250.00 and (2) shorting the futures at 1262.50. If the position is held to expiration, your profit at various expiration date levels of the S&P will be as shown in Table 23.3. Notice that your net profit remains constant no matter the level of the index at the expiration date. More importantly, this net profit can be expressed as $(31.25) \div (1250) = 2.5$ percent, which is the assumed cost of borrowing.

IMPLEMENTING AN INDEX ARBITRAGE STRATEGY What if the parity condition between the stock index and the stock index futures price does not hold? Could you design a portfolio to take advantage of the situation? Specifically, suppose that in the preceding example the actual contract price on a 6-month S&P 500 futures was 1265.50 (i.e., $F_{0,T} > S_0 + S_0(RFR_t - d_T)$). You could then implement the following arbitrage transaction:

TABLE 23.3 **STOCK INDEX FUTURES VALUATION EXAMPLE**

	S&P AT EXPIRATION IS:				
	1220	1240	1260	1280	1300
Net Futures Profit	42.50	22.50	2.50	(17.50)	(37.50)
Net Index Profit	(30.00)	(10.00)	10.00	30.00	50.00
Dividend	18.75	18.75	18.75	18.75	18.75
Net Profit	31.25	31.25	31.25	31.25	31.25

(1) short the stock index future at a price of 1265.50; (2) borrow money at 2.5 percent to purchase the stock index at 1250.00; and (3) hold the position until maturity, collecting 18.75 in dividends and then selling the stock to repay your loan. Your net profit at maturity would be 1265.50 − 1250 − 1250 (0.025 − 0.015) = 3.00. However, since this strategy was riskless (i.e., the sales price of the stock and the dividends were known in advance) and none of your own capital was used, it is an arbitrage profit.

This is *stock index arbitrage,* which is possible whenever the index futures price is set at a level sufficiently different from the theoretical value for $F_{0,T}$ to account for trading costs. For example, if the actual level of $F_{0,T} < S_0 + S_0(RFR_t - d_T)$, the previous strategy could be reversed: (1) buy the stock index future at a price of $F_{0,T}$, (2) lend money at RFR_t and short the stock index at S_0, and (3) cover the position at the expiration date of the futures contract. Indeed, index arbitrage is a very popular form of trading. Figure 23.9 reports that about 10 percent of all computer-assisted program trading used this strategy. Further, program trading accounted for about one-fifth of trading volume on the New York Stock Exchange. Both of these totals can get much higher around contract expiration dates (i.e., the so-called triple witching days).

One important side effect of this sort of trading activity is that stock index futures prices tend to stay close to the theoretical levels expressed by the preceding valuation equation. To see why this occurs, notice that the arbitrage "prescription" for a futures settlement price that is too low (too high) is to go long (short) in the contract which, when done in sufficient volume, adjusts the price in the proper direction. The empirical evidence tends to support this view, particularly after transaction costs and other trading realities are considered. Cornell, for instance, found that stock index futures prices tracked their model values more closely as the market matured, although Keim and Smirlock detected some temporal (i.e., day-of-the-week, January) pricing patterns.[17] In response to the allegation that index arbitrage caused the worldwide stock market crash of October 1987, Roll documented that countries with the greatest level of program trading activity experienced less-pronounced price declines.[18] This finding is consistent with the notion that index arbitrage reduces volatility by stabilizing cash and futures prices.

A STOCK INDEX FUTURES APPLICATION

Isolating the Unsystematic Risk of an Individual Stock In Chapter 11, we demonstrated how stock index futures could alter the systematic risk of an otherwise well-diversified

[17]Bradford Cornell, "Taxes and the Pricing of Stock Index Futures: Empirical Results," *Journal of Futures Markets* 5, no. 1 (1985): 89–101; and Donald B. Keim and Michael Smirlock, "Pricing Patterns in Stock Index Futures," in *The Handbook of Stock Index Futures and Options,* ed. F. Fabozzi and G. Kipnis (Homewood, Ill.: Dow Jones-Irwin, 1989).

[18]Richard Roll, "The International Crash of October 1987," *Financial Analysts Journal* 44, no. 5 (September–October 1988): 19–35.

FIGURE 23.9 **PROGRAM TRADING AND STOCK INDEX ARBITRAGE**

PROGRAM TRADING

NEW YORK—Program trading in the week ended Jan. 29 accounted for 18.8%, or an average 161 million daily shares, of New York Stock Exchange volume.

Brokerage firms executed an additional 57.1 million daily shares of program trading away from the Big Board, mostly on foreign markets. Program trading is the simultaneous purchase or sale of at least 15 different stocks with a total value of $1 million or more.

Of the program total on the Big Board, 10.3% involved stock index arbitrage, down from 10.4% in the prior week. In this strategy, traders dart between stocks and stock-index options and futures to capture fleeting price differences.

Some 68% of program trading was executed by firms for their customers, while 28.4% was done for their own accounts, or principal trading. An additional 3.6% was designated as customer facilitation, in which firms use principal positions to facilitate customer trades.

Of the five most-active firms, Deutsche Bank Securities, BNP Securities, Bear Stearns and Salomon Smith Barney executed all or most of their program activity for customers as agent, while Credit Suisse First Boston executed most of its program activity as principal for its own accounts.

NYSE PROGRAM TRADING

Volume (in millions of shares) for the week ended Jan. 29, 1999

Top 15 Firms	Index Arbitrage	Derivative-Related*	Other Strategies	Total
CS First Boston	4.0	....	100.6	104.6
Deutsche Bank Securities	20.2	0.1	81.5	101.8
BNP Securities	....	....	88.1	88.1
Bear Stearns	....	....	71.5	71.5
Salomon Smith Barney	0.6	....	69.0	69.6
Morgan StanleyDn Wttr	1.0	....	45.4	46.4
W&D Securities	....	....	40.9	40.9
TLW Securities LLC	1.1	1.5	36.6	39.2
Lehman Brothers	....	3.1	33.8	36.9
Intercative Brokers	....	....	22.4	22.4
CIBC Wood Gundy	7.5	....	14.1	21.6
RBC Dominion	15.8	....	5.4	21.2
Donaldson Lufkin	....	....	20.1	20.1
Merrill Lynch	1.6	....	16.9	18.5
Goldman Sachs	....	....	18.4	18.4
OVERALL TOTAL	83.3	4.8	716.8	804.9

*Other derivative-related strategies besides index arbitrage
Source: New York Stock Exchange

Source: *Wall Street Journal*, 5 February 1999.

portfolio. When the holding is an individual stock, this process can isolate the unique attributes of the company. Recall from Chapter 1 that:

$$\text{Total Stock Risk} = \text{Systematic Risk} + \text{Unsystematic Risk}$$

with the systematic component representing about 25–30 percent of the total risk for the typical firm. Thus, using stock index futures to adjust the stock's beta to zero effectively isolates the unsystematic portion of risk.

To see how this might work, suppose that in mid-February you own 75,000 shares of Merck, a multinational pharmaceutical firm. The current price of Merck stock is $46.75, and you calculate the company's beta at 0.99. You like the stock as an investment because of the quality of its management and some other unique attributes of the firm, but you are concerned that over the next few months the aggregate stock market might undergo a sizable correction that could more than offset any firm-specific gains.

To protect yourself, you decide to sell June S&P 500 futures contracts, which are currently trading at a settlement price of 1271.10. At this price, we have seen that the implied dollar value of a single contract is $317,775. The current value of your Merck stock is $3,506,250. Since the stock's beta can be defined as $\rho\,[\sigma_{\Delta S} \div \sigma_{\Delta F}]$, the optimal hedge ratio formula developed earlier can be adapted to provide the appropriate hedge ratio:

$$N^* = \left[\frac{\text{Market Value of Spot Position}}{\text{Value Implied by Futures Contract}}\right]\beta$$
$$= \left[(\$3{,}506{,}250) \div (\$317{,}775)\right](0.99) = 10.92$$

so you decide to short 11 contracts.

Now suppose that by mid-June when your futures position expires, the S&P 500 index settles at a level of 1251.10 while the price of Merck stock has increased to 47.50. Although you have made a modest profit on your common stock holding (i.e., \$56,250, or 1.60 percent), you will also benefit from a trading profit on the futures position of \$55,000 (= (11) [1271.10 − 1251.10](250)). As a result, your total return is \$111,250, which, expressed as a percentage of your original investment of \$3,506,250, is equivalent to an unsystematic appreciation in Merck's stock of 3.17 percent. Notice in this case that the difference between this amount and the gross increase of 1.60 percent in Merck stock is equal to the 1.57 percent (= [1251.1 ÷ 1271.1] − 1) that the stock index future position fell.

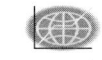

CURRENCY FORWARDS AND FUTURES

Whether in the spot or forward markets, foreign exchange (FX) transactions often involve a confusing blend of unique terminology and market conventions. Although these conventions are easily assimilated, they represent an initial barrier to understanding how FX deals work. Thus, we begin our analysis of currency derivatives with a brief overview of some of the fundamental features of these products.

THE MECHANICS OF CURRENCY TRANSACTIONS The market for foreign currency is no different than any other market in that buyer and seller negotiate for the exchange of a certain amount of a predetermined commodity at a fixed cash price. The challenge in FX transactions is that the "commodity" involved is someone else's currency. This means that the transaction can be viewed in two ways. For example, suppose that Company A agrees to pay 100 U.S. dollars to Company B in exchange for 67 British pounds. In this case, is Company A buying sterling (GBP) or selling dollars (USD)?[19] Similarly, is Company B selling pounds or buying dollars? The answer is that both are correct, depending on one's point of view.

Because of this dual interpretation, the price for all FX transactions also can be quoted in two ways. Assuming that Company A is a U.S.-based firm, it would probably think of the transaction as the purchase of 67 pounds at a cost of 100 dollars, which would yield the price of USD 1.4925/GBP (= 100/67). This method of quoting FX prices is called the *direct,* or *American,* convention. Notice that under this convention, the pound (i.e., the foreign currency from the U.S. firm's perspective) is treated as the commodity, and its price per unit is expressed in terms of dollars. On the other hand, if Company B is a British corporation, its managers would likely think of prices in terms of the amount of sterling they have to pay to acquire dollars. Here that amount translates into a price of GBP 0.67/USD. Treating the dollar as the commodity yields the *indirect,* or *European,* quotation method. Of course, the direct and indirect quotes are just *reciprocals* of one another, as they describe the same transaction from two different perspectives.

Figure 23.10 shows a representative set of FX quotes. Four prices are listed beside each currency. The first two columns report the current and previous days' dollar price,

[19]Currency traders often use three-letter abbreviations to denote a particular currency. Some of the more common abbreviations include USD (U.S. dollars), CAD (Canadian dollars), GBP (British pounds), JPY (Japanese yen), CHF (Swiss franc), DEM (German mark), FRF (French franc), and EUR (the "Euro" currency). For a more complete listing, see Gary L. Gastineau, *Dictionary of Financial Risk Management* (Chicago, Ill.: Probus Publishing, 1992).

FIGURE 23.10 **SPOT AND FORWARD CURRENCY QUOTATIONS**

EXCHANGE RATES

The New York foreign exchange mid-range rates below apply to trading among banks in amounts of $1 million and more, as quoted at 4 p.m. Eastern time by Telerate and other sources. Retail transactions provide fewer units of foreign currency per dollar. Rates for the 11 Euro currency countries are derived from the latest dollar-euro rate using the exchange ratios set 1/1/99.

	U.S. $ equiv.		Currency per U.S. $	
Country	Thu	Wed	Thu	Wed
Argentina (Peso)	1.0002	1.0005	.9998	.9995
Australia (Dollar)	.6485	.6412	1.5420	1.5596
Austria (Schilling)	.08238	.08215	12.139	12.173
Bahrain (Dinar)	2.6525	2.6525	.3770	.3770
Belgium (Franc)	.02810	.02802	35.586	35.686
Brazil (Real)	.5540	.5587	1.8050	1.7900
Britain (Pound)	1.6451	1.6353	.6079	.6115
1-month forward	1.6441	1.6342	.6082	.6119
3-months forward	1.6423	1.6325	.6089	.6126
6-months forward	1.6413	1.6311	.6093	.6131
Canada (Dollar)	.6708	.6616	1.4907	1.5115
1-month forward	.6708	.6615	1.4909	1.5117
3-months forward	.6707	.6615	1.4909	1.5117
6-months forward	.6710	.6617	1.4904	1.5113
Chile (Peso)	.002048	.002038	488.25	490.75
China (Renminbi)	.1208	.1208	8.2775	8.2777
Colombia (Peso)	.0006353	.0006344	1574.07	1576.22
Czech. Rep. (Koruna)				
Commercial rate	.03034	.03040	32.956	32.892
Denmark (Krone)	.1524	.1521	6.5615	6.5725
Ecuador (Sucre)				
Floating rate	.0001385	.0001385	7220.00	7220.00
Finland (Markka)	.1907	.1901	5.2450	5.2598
France (Franc)	.1728	.1723	5.7865	5.8029
1-month forward	.1730	.1726	5.7787	5.7951
3-months forward	.1736	.1731	5.7601	5.7766
6-months forward	.1745	.1740	5.7311	5.7473
Germany (Mark)	.5796	.5780	1.7253	1.7302
1-month forward	.5804	.5787	1.7230	1.7279
3-months forward	.5823	.5806	1.7174	1.7224
6-months forward	.5852	.5836	1.7088	1.7136
Greece (Drachma)	.003528	.003527	283.47	283.52
Hong Kong (Dollar)	.1291	.1291	7.7485	7.7488
Hungary (Forint)	.004534	.004555	220.57	219.55
India (Rupee)	.02355	.02355	42.465	42.462
Indonesia (Rupiah)	.0001152	.0001183	8680.00	8450.00
Ireland (Punt)	1.4394	1.4353	.6947	.6967
Israel (Shekel)	.2456	.2447	4.0715	4.0869
Italy (Lira)	.0005855	.0005838	1708.07	1712.91
Japan (Yen)	.008918	.008862	112.13	112.64
1-month forward	.008919	.008862	112.13	112.84
3-months forward	.008919	.008863	112.12	112.83
6-months forward	.008920	.008864	112.10	112.81
Jordan (Dinar)	1.4104	1.4104	.7090	.7090
Kuwait (Dinar)	3.3025	3.3135	.3028	.3018
Lebanon (Pound)	.0006631	.0006631	1508.00	1508.00
Malaysia (Ringgit-b)	.2632	.2632	3.8000	3.8000
Malta (Lira)	2.6247	2.6247	.3810	.3810
Mexico (Peso)				
Floating rate	.09920	.09899	10.081	10.102
Netherland (Guilder)	.5144	.5130	1.9440	1.9495
New Zealand (Dollar)	.5519	.5496	1.8119	1.8195
Norway (Krone)	.1311	.1308	7.6283	7.6458
Pakistan (Rupee)	.01943	.01949	51.480	51.300
Peru (new Sol)	.2951	.2942	3.3885	3.3985
Philippines (Peso)	.02595	.02601	38.530	38.450
Poland (Zloty)	.2710	.2705	3.6900	3.6975
Portugal (Escudo)	.005654	.005638	176.85	177.35
Russia (Ruble) (a)	.04322	.04325	23.140	23.120
Saudi Arabia (Riyal)	.2666	.2666	3.7507	3.7508
Singapore (Dollar)	.5926	.5923	1.6875	1.6882
Slovak Rep. (Koruna)	.02668	.02665	37.480	37.530
South Africa (Rand)	.1658	.1663	6.0305	6.0150
South Korea (Won)	.0008544	.0008545	1170.40	1170.30
Spain (Peseta)	.006813	.006794	146.78	147.19
Sweden (Krona)	.1277	.1267	7.8303	7.8903
Switzerland (Franc)	.7072	.7055	1.4140	1.4175
1-month forward	.7070	.7075	1.4144	1.4135
3-months forward	.7138	.7119	1.4010	1.4047
6-months forward	.7203	.7183	1.3883	1.3921
Taiwan (Dollar)	.03100	.03101	32.261	32.251
Thailand (Baht)	.02720	.02717	36.770	36.800
Turkey (Lira)	.00000297	.00000299	336273.00	334643.00
United Arab (Dirham)	.2723	.2723	3.6725	3.6725
Uruguay (New Peso)				
Financial	.09149	.09149	10.930	10.930
Venezuela (Bolivar)	.001735	.001734	576.38	576.57

SDR	1.3901	1.3950	.7194	.7169
Euro	1.1336	1.1304	.8821	.8846

Special Drawing Rights (SDR) are based on exchange rates for the U.S., German, British, French, and Japanese currencies. Source: International Monetary Fund.

a-Russian Central Bank rate. Trading band lowered on 8/17/98. b-Government rate.

The Wall Street Journal daily foreign exchange data from 1996 forward may be purchased through the Readers' Reference Service (413) 592-3600.

Source: *Wall Street Journal,* 5 February 1999.

respectively, for trading one unit of that currency (i.e., direct quotes). For instance, the prevailing price of a Norwegian krone on that date was USD 0.1311, which was 0.03 cent higher than the day before. The last two columns express these same prices in indirect terms (e.g., NKR 7.6283/USD = 1 ÷ USD 0.1311/NKR). Thus, the terms of a spot FX transaction can be structured to meet the particular needs of the counterparties involved.

Another important aspect of the FX markets highlighted by this display is that although many currencies trade in the spot market, relatively few also quote prices for forward transactions. In this list, only the British, Canadian, French, German, Japanese, and Swiss currencies have forward contracts. These contracts, which are negotiated in the over-the-counter market with a currency dealer (such as a multinational bank), carry maturities 1, 3, and 6 months into the future. For example, an investor wishing to buy French francs would pay USD 0.1728 per franc if the transaction were completed immediately, USD 0.1730 if the transaction were negotiated now but consummated in 30 days, and USD 0.1736 or USD 0.1745 for exchanges completed in 90 or 180 days, respectively.

FIGURE 23.11 **CURRENCY FUTURES QUOTATIONS**

	Open	High	Low	Settle	Change	Lifetime High	Lifetime Low	Open Interest
JAPAN YEN (CME)-12.5 million yen; $ per yen (.00)								
Mar	.8906	.9007	.8812	.8943	+ .0036	.9319	.6997	70,969
June	.8975	.9100	.8964	.9046	+ .0037	.9430	.7086	4,940
Sept	.9165	.9165	.9165	.9153	+ .0040	.9500	.7680	1,494
Dec	.9175	.9175	.9175	.9260	+ .0045	.9600	.8630	289
Est vol 26,262; vol Wed 18,067; open int 77,692, −625.								
DEUTSCHEMARK (CME)-125,000 marks; $ per mark								
Mar	.5798	.5813	.5761	.5806	+ .0008	.6347	.5540	56,116
June	.5798	.5836	.5798	.5834	+ .0006	.6285	.5565	1,601
Sept	.5840	.5850	.5840	.5864	+ .0005	.6300	.5840	168
Est vol 10,947; vol Wed 6,623; open int 57,945, +78.								
CANADIAN DOLLAR (CME)-100,000 dlrs.; $ per Can $								
Mar	.6618	.6710	.6618	.6698	+ .0089	.7247	.6290	51,004
June	.6635	.6718	.6635	.6700	+ .0089	.7172	.6300	3,834
Sept	.6664	.6720	.6664	.6704	+ .0089	.7080	.6310	1,047
Dec	.6660	.6725	.6660	.6708	+ .0089	.6785	.6320	990
Est vol 16,308; vol Wed 4,409; open int 56,991, −141.								
BRITISH POUND (CME)-62,500 pds.; $ per pound								
Mar	1.6340	1.6446	1.6292	1.6440	+ .0092	1.7150	1.5950	54,254
June	1.6310	1.6430	1.6280	1.6424	+ .0092	1.7060	1.5880	1,791
Sept		....	....	1.6420	+ .0100	1.6980	1.6254	230
Est vol 8,556; vol Wed 6,822; open int 56,305, −398.								
SWISS FRANC (CME)-125,000 francs; $ per franc								
Mar	.7092	.7105	.7039	.7097	....	.7890	.6635	56,463
June	.7120	.7166	.7112	.7162	....	.7930	.6695	481
Sept	....	....	....	.7224	....	.7831	.7175	320
Est vol 15,392; vol Wed 12,918; open int 57,277, +1,854.								
AUSTRALIAN DOLLAR (CME)-100,000 dlrs.; $ per A.$								
Mar	.6415	.6510	.6374	.6491	+ .0074	.6510	.5710	21,467
Est vol 4,693; vol Wed 1,371; open int 21,500, +455.								
MEXICAN PESO (CME)-500,000 new Mex. peso, $ per MP								
Mar	.09600	.09660	.09585	.09648	+ 00325	.10565	.07500	10,635
June	.09055	.09120	.09055	.09113	+ 00325	.10230	.06900	5,461
Sept	....	....	....	.08640	+ 00400	.09510	.06350	547
Dec	....	....	....	.08240	+ 00400	.09440	.06700	199
Est vol 1,148; vol Wed 3,543; open int 16,842, −741.								

Source: *Wall Street Journal*, 5 February 1999.

In the situation where it costs increasingly more dollars to buy the same franc the farther out in the future it is delivered, the dollar is said to be trading at a **forward discount** to the franc. Conversely, the franc is at a **forward premium** to the dollar. Notice that this relationship depends on the currencies being compared. In this set of quotes, the U.S. dollar is trading at a forward discount to the French franc, German mark, and Japanese yen, while it is at a forward premium to the British pound. (The U.S. dollar's relationships with the Swiss franc and Canadian dollar are mixed.) It should come as no surprise by now that the relationship between the spot and forward FX rates is not a random one. In fact, we will see shortly that whether a particular currency trades at a discount or a premium to another depends on the relative level of the investment rates in the two countries.

Figure 23.11 lists quotes for a sample of exchange-traded currency futures contracts. These specific instruments are traded at the International Monetary Market at the CME. Each contract follows the convention that the U.S. dollar is the native monetary unit and the foreign currency is the commodity, meaning that all prices are quoted using the direct method. Also, notice that these contracts are standardized to deliver a set number of units of the foreign currency on a specific date in the future. For instance, the March Mexican peso contract negotiated on that date required the long position to purchase—and the short position to deliver—500,000 pesos at the price of USD 0.09648 per peso. By convention, all currency futures on the IMM mature on the third Wednesday of the stated delivery month and can be settled with a wire transfer of the foreign currency. Notice that the dollar traded at a substantial forward premium to the peso at this point in time.

FIGURE 23.12 **INTEREST RATE PARITY**

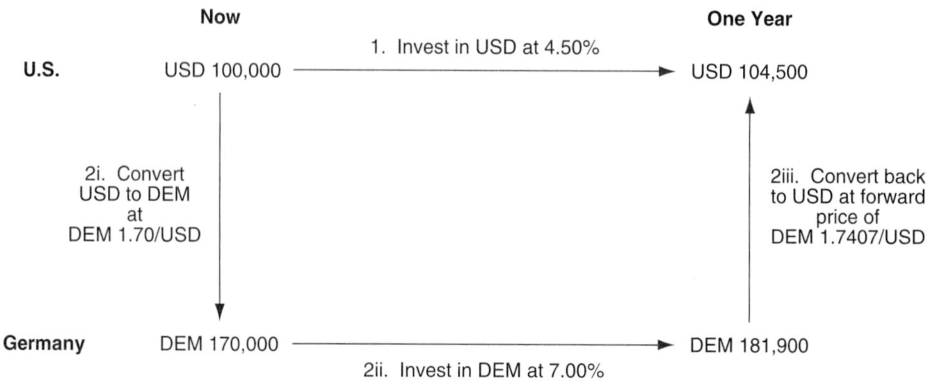
Now
One Year
U.S.
USD 100,000
1. Invest in USD at 4.50%
USD 104,500
2i. Convert USD to DEM at DEM 1.70/USD
2iii. Convert back to USD at forward price of DEM 1.7407/USD
Germany
DEM 170,000
DEM 181,900
2ii. Invest in DEM at 7.00%

INTEREST RATE PARITY AND COVERED INTEREST ARBITRAGE A key concept in FX risk management is **interest rate parity**, a condition that specifies the "no arbitrage" relationship between spot and forward FX rates (as priced into the futures contracts) and the level of interest rates in each currency. This connection is best seen through an example. Suppose that an institutional investor has USD 100,000 to invest for one year and is considering two different riskless alternatives. The first strategy entails the purchase of a U.S. Treasury bill. Assume that under current market conditions, the effective U.S. dollar risk-free interest rate is 4.50 percent per annum for a one-year maturity, so that a direct T-bill investment would return USD 104,500 at the end of the 12 months.

For the second strategy, suppose that the investor also can sell the USD 100,000 in the spot market at the current exchange rate of DEM 1.70/USD (or, equivalently, USD 0.5882/DEM) to obtain a total of 170,000 German marks. We assume that that amount can then be invested in a German risk-free security (i.e., bund) at an annualized rate of 7.00 percent, returning DEM 181,900 at the end of the year. Of course, to make this return comparable to the dollar-denominated proceeds from the first strategy, the marks will have to be converted back into U.S. currency. If this translation is negotiated at the end of the investment, however, the investor will be subjected to foreign exchange risk in that he will not know at date 0 what the DEM/USD exchange rate will be at date T. Thus, to make the second strategy riskless, the investor must enter into a forward contract to exchange marks back into dollars at the end of the year. The question then is what would the exchange rate priced into a one-year forward contract have to be at date 0 to leave the investor indifferent between these two strategies?

These investments are depicted in Figure 23.12. The essence of the arbitrage argument is that the one-year forward FX rate must be such that USD 104,500 equals DEM 181,900. Otherwise, an arbitrage opportunity would exist, or at least a dominating investment choice. Therefore, the forward contract rate consistent with interest rate parity is DEM 1.7407/USD (= 181,900 ÷ 104,500) on an indirect basis, or USD 0.5745/DEM quoted directly. Notice that this is a breakeven value in the sense that it allows the 4.50 percent investment return in the United States to be equal to the 7.00 percent available in Germany when the two are converted to the same currency. That is, the German return must be "deflated" by 250 basis points to leave the investor indifferent between the two strategies. This reduction occurs because, to invest in the mark-denominated security, the investor buys marks at a price of USD 0.5882/DEM but must sell them back in the forward market at the lower price of USD 0.5745/DEM. Thus, the loss on the round-trip currency translation required in the second strategy adjusts its net return down to the 4.50 percent available on the direct dollar investment.[20]

If the actual one-year forward contract FX rate were higher than this breakeven level—say, for instance, DEM 1.77/USD—the currency translation loss would be greater than 250 basis points, leaving the dollar-based strategy the more profitable choice. Given that there is now a difference between the returns to two otherwise comparable riskless investments, arbitrage is possible. In this case, an arbitrageur could enter the following transactions:

1. Borrow DEM 170,000 at 7.00 percent, agree to repay DEM 181,900 in one year;
2. Sell the marks on the spot market at DEM 1.70/USD, receive USD 100,000;
3. Invest the USD 100,000 at 4.50 percent, receive USD 104,500 in one year;
4. Sell USD 104,500 forward at DEM 1.77/USD, agree to receive DEM 184,965;
5. Repay the DEM loan, collect net profit of DEM 3,065.

If, on the other hand, the actual one-year forward rate were lower than breakeven—for instance, DEM 1.71/USD—the arbitrageur would implement the opposite trade:

1. Borrow USD 100,000 at 4.50 percent, agree to repay USD 104,500 in one year;
2. Sell the dollars on the spot market at DEM 1.70/USD, receive DEM 170,000;
3. Invest the DEM 170,000 at 7.00 percent, receive DEM 181,900 in one year;
4. Buy USD 104,500 forward at DEM 1.71/USD, agree to pay DEM 178,695;
5. Repay the dollar loan, collect net profit of DEM 3,205.

These strategies are known as **covered interest arbitrage** because the arbitrageur will always hold the security denominated in the currency that is the least expensive to deliver in the forward market. In this sense, the arbitrage position is hedged, or covered, against adverse foreign exchange movements while receiving the largest amount of net interest income. In practice, traders involved in covered interest arbitrage strategies utilize bank rates (e.g., LIBOR) for borrowing and lending, which injects a slight amount of credit risk into the scheme. After surveying the empirical evidence, Solnik has concluded that the ability to take these arbitrage positions keeps interest rate parity a viable description of the way spot and forward prices are set for the world's major currencies.[21]

With exchange rates quoted on an *indirect basis* (i.e., foreign currency [FC] per U.S. dollar), the general formula for the forward rate implied by interest rate parity is:

$$\text{Forward} = \text{Spot} \times \left(\frac{1 + (\text{Foreign Interest Rate}) \left(\dfrac{T}{365}\right)}{1 + (\text{U.S. Interest Rate}) \left(\dfrac{T}{365}\right)} \right)$$

where:

T = the number of days from the joint settlement of the futures and cash positions until they mature

[20]Under these conditions, the actual currency loss is calculated as 0.5745/0.5882 − 1 = −2.33 percent. This, in turn, means the dollar-denominated return to the second strategy is (1 + 0.07) × (1 − 0.0233) − 1 = 4.50 percent.

[21]Bruno Solnik, *International Investments,* 3d ed. (Reading, Mass.: Addison-Wesley Publishing, 1996).

In the last example, $T = 365$ so that DEM 1.7407/USD = DEM 1.70/USD × (1.07/1.045). This formula also assumes that the rates in question are quoted on a 365-day basis. If U.S. money market rates such as LIBOR are used, then the equation should be adjusted to a 360-day year.

Letting S_0 and $F_{0,T}$ once again denote the current spot and forward prices for an instrument that matures at date T, the above expression can be rewritten as:

$$\frac{F_{0,T}}{S_0} = \left(\frac{1 + (RFR_{FC}) \left(\frac{T}{365} \right)}{1 + (RFR_{USD}) \left(\frac{T}{365} \right)} \right)$$

where:

RFR_{USD} = the annualized risk-free rate in the United States
RFR_{FC} = the annualized risk-free rate in the foreign market

This equation defines the relationship between four different prices, all of which are determined at date 0: spot foreign exchange rate, forward foreign exchange rate, U.S. investment rate, and foreign investment rate. Importantly, notice that, if the markets are aligned properly, $F_{0,T}$ will be greater than S_0 whenever RFR_{FC} is greater than RFR_{USD}, with the opposite holding when $RFR_{FC} < RFR_{USD}$. With indirect currency quotes, $F_{0,T} > S_0$ implies that the foreign currency is at a forward discount to the dollar. In other words, the country with the *lowest* investment rate should see its currency trade at a forward premium. The intuition behind this is that to keep investment capital from flowing to the country with the highest returns, the currency translation must adjust accordingly. Thus, the high-interest country will suffer from a weaker forward value for its currency.[22]

A CURRENCY FUTURES APPLICATION

Calculating Implied World Investment Rates Suppose that you are the cash manager for a multinational company and you have \$1,000,000 in short-term balances that you can invest in sovereign-issued paper for the next 4 months. On Thursday, February 4, 1999, you obtain the following quotes for both spot and futures exchange rates for several currencies:

Currency	Spot (USD/FC)	June 1999 Futures (USD/FC)
German Mark	0.5796	0.5834
Japanese Yen	0.008918	0.009046
Swiss Franc	0.7072	0.7162
Canadian Dollar	0.6708	0.6700
British Pound	1.6451	1.6424
Mexican Peso	0.09920	0.09113

[22]When using direct quotes (i.e., USD/FC), the interest rate parity condition must be adjusted by taking the reciprocal of the ratio on the left-hand side: $[S_0 \div F_{0,T}] = [(1 + RFR_{FC}(T \div 365)) \div (1 + RFR_{USD}(T \div 365)]$. In the above example, with the direct quotes for the spot and forward being USD 0.5882/DEM (= 1/1.70) and USD 0.5745/DEM, respectively, we have S_0 = USD 0.5882/DEM = USD 0.5745/DEM × (1.07/1.045).

If you enter into any of these transactions, they will settle on Monday, February 8 (i.e., two business days later). The futures contracts mature on Wednesday, June 16, 1999, which leaves a 128-day investment window from settlement to maturity.

You also observe that a U.S. Treasury bill maturing at virtually the same time (i.e., June 17) pays a bond equivalent (i.e., 365-day) yield of 4.49 percent. Before checking the actual quotes for foreign-currency-denominated government paper from these other countries, you first calculate the investment rates implied by the interest rate parity relationship. Specifically, for the six countries listed above, you compute:

$$\text{Implied Rate} = \left[\left(\frac{\text{Spot}}{\text{Futures}}\right)\left(1 + (\text{U.S. Interest Rate})\left(\frac{128}{365}\right)\right) - 1\right]\left(\frac{365}{128}\right)$$

which is just the parity relationship rearranged to use direct currency quotes and to isolate the foreign interest rate. Notice that the direct parity formulation is the correct one to use because of the convention prevailing in the U.S. currency futures market. For British sterling, this calculation yields an implied 128-day annualized investment rate of:

$$\left[\left(\frac{1.6451}{1.6424}\right)\left(1 + (0.0449)\left(\frac{128}{365}\right)\right) - 1\right]\left(\frac{365}{128}\right) = 0.04966 = 4.97\%$$

This means that with the current spot and futures prices for exchanging dollars and pounds, you would be indifferent between receiving a 4-month investment rate of 4.49 percent in the United States or 4.97 percent in England.

Summarizing this calculation for all of the countries leaves:

Country	Implied 128-Day Rate
Germany	2.60%
Japan	0.39
Switzerland	0.85
Canada	4.84
Great Britain	4.97
Mexico	30.14

You can now compare these figures to the actual investment rates in each of the countries to determine if a futures-based synthetic foreign bond strategy is warranted. If, for example, the actual British 4-month gilt rate were 5.50 percent, you could exceed the 4.49 percent dollar-denominated T-bill return by (1) exchanging your dollars for pounds in the spot market at USD 1.6451/GBP, (2) investing for 128 days in the sterling-based security at 5.50 percent, and (3) translating your proceeds back into dollars at maturity using the futures rate of USD 1.6424/GBP.

Finally, notice that the countries with implied rates higher than 4.49 percent (i.e., Canada, Great Britain, and Mexico) are those whose currencies sold at a forward discount to the U.S. dollar over this 128-day window. Conversely, Germany, Japan, and Switzerland had currencies at a forward premium to the dollar and thus had implied investment rates less than 4.49 percent. One caution necessary in interpreting these yields properly is that it is imperative that the futures and spot FX quotes were obtained simultaneously and pertain to the same investment denomination. In this example, these conditions were more than likely violated to some extent.

THE INTERNET *Investments Online*

Some sites that focus on the use of these derivative products include:

www.fiafii.org This is the Web site of the Futures Industry Association. It features information and tutorials on futures. It is a good source of news about the futures markets, regulations, and the different exchanges.

www.e-analytics.com/fudir.htm The Web site of Equity Analytics is a collection of papers and information on topics such as future contracts, exchanges, cost of carry arbitrage, backward options, forward rates, and a number of other sophisticated investment instruments and strategies.

www.futuresmag.com *Futures Magazine*'s Web site features "hot market" analysis, technical analysis, and links to data and information about derivatives markets. A keyword search feature allows users to find *Futures Magazine* articles dealing with topics of interest.

Summary

- There is no question that forward and futures contracts have become an important feature of the modern investment landscape. As the most fundamental type of derivative instruments available, they greatly increase the alternatives that investors have to create and manage their portfolios and establish new trading opportunities. In this chapter, we discuss how these contracts work and the ways they are used in practice. As different mechanisms for accomplishing the same goals, forwards and futures differ primarily in the areas of design flexibility and collateralization. Specifically, forward agreements generally are more flexible but carry more credit risk, while the process of marking margin accounts to market on a daily basis makes futures contracts more secure (to the exchange, at least) even as the standardization of contract terms makes them less adaptable.
- We also show that hedging is key to understanding forward-based contracting and that the basis is the most important concept in understanding hedging. In particular, the basis, which is defined as the difference between spot and forward prices at any point in time, contains the essence of a short hedge position so that the hedger effectively trades the price risk of the underlying asset for the basis risk inherent in the spot-forward combination. This notion also leads to the calculation of an optimal hedge ratio, which specifies the appropriate number of contracts by minimizing the amount of basis (i.e., correlation) risk in the combined position.
- Although forward and futures contracts are not securities, their contract settlement prices still must follow certain regularities for these markets to remain efficient. For example, the cost of carry model suggests that in order to avoid arbitrage, the forward price should be equal to the spot price plus the cost of transporting the underlying asset to the future delivery date. These carrying costs can include commissions for physical storage, an opportunity cost for the net amount of invested capital, and a premium for the convenience of consuming the asset now. When forward prices are set in this manner, the market value of a new contract should be zero, although this value can become either positive or negative as the contract matures under changing market conditions.
- Finally, we illustrate these concepts with detailed examinations of three types of financial futures contracts: interest rate, equity index, and foreign exchange. In addition to describing the dynamics of each of these markets, we discuss different applications, including those involving hedging, speculation, and arbitrage. These applications produce some useful adaptations of the basic concepts, such as duration- and beta-based hedge ratios for interest rate and stock index futures as well as the currency futures version of the cost of carry model known as interest rate parity. Although no such list of applications could ever be complete, they should provide an understanding of why these instruments have become so important in financial markets.

Questions

1. We have futures contracts on Treasury bonds, but we do not have futures contracts on individual corporate bonds. We have cattle and pork belly futures but no chicken futures. Explain why the market has developed in this manner. What do you think are the most important characteristics for the success of a new futures contract concept?

2. "Hedgers trade price risk for basis risk." What is meant by this statement? In particular, explain the concept of the basis in a hedge transaction and how forward and futures contracts can be selected to minimize risk.
3. Suppose you are a derivatives trader specializing in creating customized commodity forward contracts for clients and then hedging your position with exchange-traded futures contracts. Your latest position is an agreement to deliver 100,000 gallons of unleaded gasoline to a client in 3 months.
   a. Explain how you can hedge your position using gasoline futures contracts.
   b. In calculating your hedge ratio, how must you account for the different valuation procedures used for forward and futures contracts? That is, what difference does it make that forward contracts are valued on a discounted basis while futures contracts are marked to market without discounting?
   c. If the only available gasoline futures contracts call for the delivery of 42,000 gallons and mature in either 2 or 4 months, describe the nature of the basis risk involved in your hedge.
4. A multinational corporation is about to embark on a major financial restructuring program. One critical stage will be the issuance of 7-year Eurobonds sometime within the next month. The CFO is concerned with recent instability in capital markets and with the particular event that market yields rise prior to issuance, forcing the corporation to pay a higher coupon rate on the bonds. It is decided to hedge that risk by selling 10-year Treasury note futures contracts. Notice that this is a classic cross hedge wherein 10-year Treasury notes are used to manage the risk of 7-year Eurobonds.

   Describe the nature of the basis risk in the hedge. In particular, what specific events with respect to the shape of the Treasury yield curve and the Eurobond spread over Treasuries could render the hedge ineffective? In other words, under what circumstances would the hedge fail and make the corporation worse off.?
5. *CFA Examination II (May 1997)*

   Mike Lane will have $5 million to invest in 5-year U.S. Treasury bonds 3 months from now. Lane believes interest rates will fall during the next three months and wants to take advantage of prevailing interest rates by hedging against a decline in interest rates. Lane has sufficient funds to pay the costs of entering into and maintaining a futures position.
   a. Describe what action Lane should take using 5-year U.S. Treasury note futures contracts to protect against declining interest rates.

   Assume 3 months have gone by and despite Lane's expectations, 5-year cash and forward market interest rates have increased by 100 basis points compared with the 5-year forward market interest rates of 3 months ago.
   b. Discuss the effect of higher interest rates on the value of the futures position that Lane entered into in part a.
   c. Discuss how the return from Lane's hedged position differs from the return he could now earn if he had not hedged in part a.
6. Eurodollar futures contracts are based on LIBOR, an add-on yield, while Treasury bill futures contracts are based on the T-bill rate, a discount yield. Despite different quotation conventions, these contracts use the same "discount" price index (100 − Yield). Explain the function of this price index and why the same design can be used for both contracts.
7. You own an equally weighted portfolio of 50 different stocks worth about $5,000,000. The stocks are from several different industries, and the portfolio is reasonably well diversified. Which do you think would provide you with the best overall hedge: a single position in an index futures or 50 different positions in futures contracts on the individual stocks? What are the most important factors to consider in making this decision?
8. *CFA Examination II (June 1991)*

   Four factors affect the value of a futures contract on a stock index. Three of these factors are: the current price of the stock index, the time remaining until the contract maturity (delivery) date, and the dividends on the stock index. Identify the fourth factor and explain how and why changes in this factor affect the value of the futures contract.
9. It is often stated that a stock index arbitrage trade is easier to implement when the stock index futures contract price is above its theoretical level than when it is below that value. What

institutional realities might make this statement true? Describe the steps involved in forming the arbitrage transaction in both circumstances. To the extent that the statement is valid, what does it suggest about the ability of the stock index futures market to remain efficient?

CFA

10. *CFA Examination III (June 1989)*
The World Ecosystem Consortium (WEC) pension trust holds $100 million in long-term U.S. Treasury bonds. To reduce interest rate risk you, as an independent advisor to the WEC, suggest that the trust diversify by investing $30 million in German government bonds (bunds) for 6 months. You point out that a fixed currency futures hedge (shorting a fixed number of contracts) could be used by WEC's pension trust to protect the $30 million in bunds against exchange rate losses over the 6 months.
Explain how a fixed currency futures hedge could be constructed for the WEC trust by shorting currency futures contracts to protect against exchange rate losses. Describe one characteristic of this hedge that WEC's investment committee might deem undesirable.
11. There are currency futures contracts that allow for the exchange of Mexican pesos and U.S. dollars, while other contracts allow for the exchange of Swiss francs and U.S. dollars. If I am an investor based in Zurich, explain how I could use these contracts to convert the payoff to a peso-denominated asset back into francs in 2 months.
12. Explain why the currency of Country A, whose interest rates are twice as great as those in Country B, must trade at a forward discount. If there were no difference between the spot and forward exchange rates in this interest rate environment, what arbitrage trade could be constructed to take advantage of the situation?

Problems

1. It is March 9 and you have just entered into a short position in a soybean meal futures contract. The contract expires on July 9 and calls for the delivery of 100 tons of soybean meal. Further, because this is a futures position, it requires the posting of a $3,000 initial margin and a $1,500 maintenance margin; for simplicity, however, assume that the account is marked to market on a monthly basis. Assume the following represent the contract delivery prices (in dollars per ton) that prevail on each settlement date:

March 9 (initiation)	$173.00
April 9	179.75
May 9	189.00
June 9	182.50
July 9 (delivery)	174.25

a. Calculate the equity value of your margin account on each settlement date, including any additional equity required to meet a margin call. Also compute the amount of cash that will be returned to you on July 9, and the gain or loss on your position, expressed as a percentage of your initial margin commitment.
b. Assuming that the underlying soybean meal investment pays no dividend and requires a storage cost of 1.5 percent (of current value), calculate the current (i.e., March 9) spot price for a ton of soybean meal, and the implied May 9 price for the same ton. In your calculations, assume that an annual risk-free rate of 8 percent prevails over the entire contract life.
c. Now suppose that on March 9 you also entered into a long forward contract for the purchase of 100 tons of soybean meal on July 9. Assume further that the July forward and futures contract prices always are identical to one another at any point in time. Calculate the cash amount of your gain or loss if you unwind both positions in their respective markets on May 9 and June 9, taking into account the prevailing settlement conditions in the two markets.

2. It is March 1 and you are a new derivatives trader making a market in forward contracts in Commodity W. One month ago (February 1), you began your operations with the following transactions, which are described from your perspective:

- With Client A: (1) Short a June 1 forward for 10,000 units at a contract price of $25.50/unit.
  (2) Long a September 1 forward for 15,000 units at a contract price of $26.20/unit.

- With Client B: (3) Short a September 1 forward for 25,000 units at a contract price of $26.40/unit.

Your current (i.e., March 1) contract price quotes are as follows:

Contract	Bid	Ask
June	$24.95	$25.15
September	25.65	25.85

The appropriate discount rate is 9 percent per annum.

a. If Client A just called you wanting to unwind both of its contracts, calculate a fair cash amount that can be used in settlement today. Would you pay or receive this amount?

b. If these contracts had been exchange-traded futures contracts instead of OTC forward contracts, how would this settlement amount need to be adjusted (assuming the same March 1 contract prices)?

c. Calculate the dollar amount you would lose if Client B called you to default its contractual obligation. (Hint: Compute this amount in the same manner you calculated the net settlement in part a.)

d. At the time you negotiated the three original agreements (i.e., February 1), did you have any price exposure on the September contracts? If so, what type of future price movements would be harmful to your net profit on the expiration date?

3. You are a coffee dealer anticipating the purchase of 82,000 pounds of coffee in 3 months. You are concerned that the price of coffee will rise, so you take a long position in coffee futures. Each contract covers 37,500 pounds and so, rounding to the nearest contract, you decide to go long in two contracts. The futures price at the time you initiate your hedge is 55.95 cents per pound. Three months later, the actual spot price of coffee turns out to be 58.56 cents per pound and the futures price is 59.20 cents per pound.

   a. Determine the effective price at which you purchased your coffee. How do you account for the difference in amounts for the spot and hedge positions?

   b. Describe the nature of the basis risk in this long hedge.

CFA

4. *CFA Examination III. (June 1983)*

   In February 1983, the United American Company is considering the sale of $100 million in 10-year debentures that will probably be rated AAA like the firm's other bond issues. The firm is anxious to proceed at today's rate of 10.5 percent.

   As Treasurer, you know that it will take about 12 weeks (May) to get the issue registered and sold. Therefore, you suggest that the firm hedge the pending issue using Treasury bond futures contracts. (Each Treasury bond contract is for $1,000,000.)

   Explain how you would go about hedging the bond issue, and describe the results, assuming that the following two sets of future conditions actually occur. (Ignore commissions and margin costs, and assume a 1-to-1 hedge ratio.) Show all calculations.

	Case 1	Case 2
Current Values—February 1983		
Bond Rate	10.5%	10.5%
June 1983 Treasury bonds	78.875	78.875
Estimated Values—May 1983		
Bond Rate	11.0%	10.0%
June 1983 Treasury bonds	75.93	81.84
Present Value of a $1 Annuity		
10 years at 10.5 percent	6.021	6.021

5. The corporate treasurer of XYZ Corp. manages the firm's pension fund. On February 15, 1993, the treasurer is informed that the pension fund will be required to sell its $100 million (face

value) Treasury bond portfolio on August 15, 1993, because of a pending change in the structure of the plan.

The portfolio consists entirely of a single bond issue with a maturity date of August 2019. The bond pays coupons of 7¼ percent and is currently priced at 97–12. This corresponds to a yield of 7.479 percent. These T-bonds were originally purchased at par, so the current price reflects a modest capital loss. The treasurer is concerned that further weakness in the dollar could raise market rates and exacerbate this loss before the August sale date.

Your task is to construct a hedge using T-bond futures to offset, or at least reduce, the risk exposure. Assume an August 1993 futures contract exists with the quoted price of 101–04 and a reference yield to maturity of 7.887 percent (based on an 8 percent coupon and 20 years to maturity). To complete the task, construct a numerical example to show the optimal number of contracts necessary to provide the desired price protection.

a. Assuming that interest rates do not change between February and August 1993, what will be the value of the T-bond portfolio? Briefly explain why this differs from the current value of $97.375 million.
b. As of August 1993, calculate the respective durations of the bond issue in the portfolio and the bond underlying the futures contract. Using the current yields to maturity, translate these into modified duration form. (Note: In your computation, recall that T-bonds pay semiannual interest.)
c. Assuming that the yield beta (β_i) between the instruments is equal to one, calculate the number of futures contracts required to form the optimal hedge. In this calculation, keep in mind that the face value of the bond underlying the futures contract is $100,000.

6. A bond speculator currently has positions in two separate corporate bond portfolios: a long holding in Portfolio 1 and a short holding in Portfolio 2. All the bonds have the same credit quality. Other relevant information on these positions includes:

Portfolio	Bond	Market Value (mil.)	Coupon Rate	Compounding Frequency	Maturity	Yield to Maturity
1	A	$ 6.0	0%	Annual	3 yrs.	7.31%
	B	4.0	0	Annual	14 yrs.	7.31
2	C	11.5	4.6	Annual	9 yrs.	7.31

Treasury bond futures (based on $100,000 face value of 20-year T-bonds having an 8 percent semiannual coupon) with a maturity exactly 6 months from now are currently priced at 109–24 with a corresponding yield to maturity of 7.081 percent. The "yield betas" between the futures contract and bonds A, B, and C are 1.13, 1.03. and 1.01, respectively. Finally, the modified duration for the T-bond underlying the futures contract is 10.355 years.

a. Calculate the modified duration (expressed in years) for each of the two bond portfolios. What will be the *approximate* percentage change in the value of each if all yields increase by 60 basis points on an annual basis?
b. Without performing the calculations, explain which of the portfolios will *actually* have its value impacted to the greatest extent (in absolute terms) by the shift in yields. (Hint: This explanation requires knowledge of the concept of *bond convexity.*)
c. Assuming the bond speculator wants to hedge her *net* bond position, what is the optimal number of futures contracts that must be bought or sold? Start by calculating the optimal hedge ratio between the futures contract and the two bond portfolios separately and then combine them.

CFA

7. *CFA Examination II (May 1998)*
Susan Baker is an investor who seeks to find arbitrage pricing discrepancies in the marketplace over the next 6 months. She has noted the following data:

Instrument	Spot Price	Futures Price for Contract Expiring in 6 Months	Income from Treasury Note for 6 Months	Finance Charge for 6 Months
U.S. Treasury note deliverable on the futures contract	$101	$100 (invoice price)	$4.50	$2.50

List the components of the arbitrage transaction and calculate the arbitrage profits, if any, that are available to exploit a possible pricing discrepancy. Show your calculations.

8. Consider a hypothetical Euromarket security simply called "paper." "Paper" trades and is quoted on a discount yield basis, the same as U.S. Treasury bills and commercial paper. Listed below are the current rate quotes for "paper" issues of two different maturities, each having a face value of $100,000:

90-day	7.50%
180-day	7.50%

Suppose further that a futures market also exists in 90-day "paper" and that you have just obtained a quote on a contract that matures in exactly 90 days from now at 7.50 percent. Assuming you can either buy or sell any of these securities (including the futures contract) at the quoted rates, show that a financial arbitrage opportunity exists. Calculating the implied forward discount rate will be useful. Demonstrate the sequence of transactions necessary to generate this arbitrage profit and indicate how much profit you would make. In these calculations, you may ignore the marked to market effects on the futures contract, assuming the exchange will hold any long position as collateral instead of cash.

9. As a relationship officer for a money-center commercial bank, one of your corporate accounts has just approached you about a 1-year loan for $1,000,000. The customer would pay a quarterly interest expense based on the prevailing level of LIBOR at the beginning of each 3-month period. As is the bank's convention on all such loans, the amount of the interest payment would then be paid at the end of the quarterly cycle when the new rate for the next cycle is determined. You observe the following LIBOR yield curve in the cash market:

90-day LIBOR	4.60%
180-day LIBOR	4.75
270-day LIBOR	5.00
360-day LIBOR	5.30

a. If 90-day LIBOR rises to the levels "predicted" by the implied forward rates, what will the dollar level of the bank's interest receipt be at the end of each quarter during the 1-year loan period?

b. If the bank wanted to hedge its exposure to failing LIBOR on this loan commitment, describe the sequence of transactions in the futures markets it could undertake.

c. Assuming the yields inferred from the Eurodollar futures contract prices for the next three settlement periods are equal to the implied forward rates, calculate the annuity value that would leave the bank indifferent between making the floating-rate loan and hedging it in the futures market, and making a 1-year fixed-rate loan. Express this annuity value in both dollar and annual (360-day) percentage terms.

10. Suppose that one day in early April, you observe the following prices on futures contracts maturing in June: 93.35 for Eurodollar and 94.07 for T-bill. These prices imply 3-month LIBOR and T-bill settlement yields of 6.65 percent and 5.93 percent, respectively. You think that over the next quarter the general level of interest rates will rise while the credit spread built into LIBOR will narrow. Demonstrate how you can use a TED (Treasury/Eurodollar) spread, which is a simultaneous long (short) position in a Eurodollar contract and short (long) position in the T-bill contract, to create a position that will benefit from these views.
11. An investment bank engages in stock index arbitrage for its own and customer accounts. On a particular day, the S&P index at the New York Stock Exchange is 602.25 when the futures contract for delivery in 90 days is 614.75. If the annualized 90-day interest rate is 8.00 percent and the (annualized) dividend yield is 3 percent, would program trading involving stock index arbitrage possibly take place? If so, describe the transactions that should be undertaken and calculate the profit that would be made per each "share" of the S&P 500 index used in the trade.
12. The treasurer of a middle market, import-export company has approached you for advice on how to best invest some of the firm's short-term cash balances. The company, which has been a client of the bank that employs you for a few years, has $250,000 that it is able to commit for a 1-year holding period. The treasurer is currently considering two alternatives: (1) invest all the funds in a 1-year U.S. Treasury bill offering a bond equivalent yield of 4.25 percent, and (2) invest all the funds in a Swiss government security over the same horizon, locking in the spot and forward currency exchanges in the FX market. A quick call to the bank's FX desk gives you the following two-way currency exchange quotes:

	Swiss Francs per U.S. Dollar	U.S. Dollar per Swiss Franc
Spot	1.5035	0.6651
1-year CHF futures	—	0.6586

a. Calculate the 1-year bond equivalent yield for the Swiss government security that would support the interest rate parity condition.
b. Assuming the actual yield on a 1-year Swiss government bond is 5.50 percent, which strategy would leave the treasurer with the greatest return after 1 year?
c. Describe the transactions that an arbitrageur could use to take advantage of this apparent mispricing and calculate what the profit would be for a $250,000 transaction.

References

Bautista, Carl, and Kris Mahabir. "Managing Risk and Capturing Opportunities with Derivative Securities." In *Fixed Income Management: Techniques and Practices,* ed. D. Churchill. Charlottesville, Va.: Association for Investment Management and Research, 1994.

Chance, Don M. *An Introduction to Derivatives.* 4th ed. Fort Worth, Tex.: Dryden Press, 1998.

Duffie, Darrell. *Futures Markets.* Englewood Cliffs, N.J.: Prentice-Hall, 1989.

Hull, John C. *Introduction to Futures and Options Markets.* 3d ed. Englewood Cliffs, N.J.: Prentice-Hall, 1998.

Kolb, Robert W. *Financial Derivatives.* Miami, Fla.: Kolb Publishing, 1993.

Siegel, Daniel, and Diane F. Siegel. *Futures Markets.* Hinsdale, Ill.: Dryden Press, 1990.

Smithson, Charles W., Clifford W. Smith, Jr., and D. Sykes Wilford. *Managing Financial Risk.* Burr Ridge, Ill.: Richard D. Irwin, 1995.

Telser, Lester G. "Futures Trading and the Storage of Cotton and Wheat." *Journal of Political Economy* 66 (June 1958).

Working, Holbrook. "Economic Functions of Futures Markets." In *Selected Writings of Holbrook Working.* Chicago, Ill.: Chicago Board of Trade, 1977.

Chapter 23

APPENDIX

A. A CLOSED-FORM EQUATION FOR CALCULATING DURATION

To calculate the duration statistic, it helps to think of a bond that pays a fixed coupon for a finite maturity as being just a portfolio of zero-coupon cash flows. Duration is then the weighted average of the payment (i.e., maturity) dates of those zero-coupon cash flows. What the duration statistic essentially does is convert a bond with any given coupon and maturity into what it would look like if it had been a zero-coupon bond. Thus, a bond's duration is its *zero-coupon equivalent maturity.*

To see how this calculation works, consider a nonamortizing, 5-year bond with a face value of \$1,000 making annual coupon payments of \$120 (i.e., 12 percent). Assuming a current yield-to-maturity of 10 percent, this bond will trade at a premium and its weighted average payment date (i.e., duration) is 4.074 years, as shown in Table 23A.1. Interpreting the coupon bond as a portfolio of zero-coupon cash flows, the duration of 4.0740 years is the weighted average maturity of that portfolio, where the weights are the respective shares of market value (e.g., the 1-year zero-coupon cash flow is 10. 14 percent of the value of the portfolio, the 5-year zero 64.64 percent).

This 5-year coupon bond with a duration of 4.0740 years is "equivalent" in terms of price risk to a zero-coupon bond having a maturity of 4.0740 years. As we saw in Chapter 16, this suggests that when the interest rate increases by 1 percent above its original level (i.e., $[\Delta(1 + i) \div (1 + i)] = 0.01$), then the price of this bond will decline by about 4.074 percent.

The Macaulay duration can be calculated with the following formula:

$$D = \frac{\dfrac{1 \times C}{\left(1 + \dfrac{Y}{n}\right)^1} + \dfrac{2 \times C}{\left(1 + \dfrac{Y}{n}\right)^2} + \dfrac{3 \times C}{\left(1 + \dfrac{Y}{n}\right)^3} + \ldots + \dfrac{(n \times T) \times (C + F)}{\left(1 + \dfrac{Y}{n}\right)^{n \times T}}}{\dfrac{C}{\left(1 + \dfrac{Y}{n}\right)^1} + \dfrac{C}{\left(1 + \dfrac{Y}{n}\right)^2} + \dfrac{C}{\left(1 + \dfrac{Y}{n}\right)^3} + \ldots + \dfrac{(C + F)}{\left(1 + \dfrac{Y}{n}\right)^{n \times T}}}$$

where:

C = the periodic coupon payment
F = the face value at maturity
T = the number of years until maturity
n = the payments per year
Y = the yield to maturity

Note that the denominator of this equation is just P, the price of the security. The numerator is the present value of the cash flows weighted by the time the payment is made; the

TABLE 23A.1 **A DURATION CALCULATION**

Year	Cash Flow	PV at 10%	PV ÷ Price	Year × (PV ÷ Price)
1	\$120	\$ 109.09	0.1014	0.1014
2	120	99.17	0.0922	0.1844
3	120	90.16	0.0838	0.2514
4	120	81.96	0.0762	0.3047
5	\$1,120	695.43	0.6464	3.2321
		Price = \$1,075.82		Duration = 4.0740 years

first by 1, the second by 2, and so forth. With some algebraic manipulation, this formula reduces to the following closed-form equation:

$$D = \frac{1 + \frac{Y}{n}}{\frac{Y}{n}} - \frac{1 + \frac{Y}{n} + \left[(n \times T)\left(\frac{C}{F} - \frac{Y}{n}\right)\right]}{\frac{C}{F}\left[\left(1 + \frac{Y}{n}\right)^{n \times T} - 1\right] + \frac{Y}{n}}$$

where:

C/F = the coupon rate per period

Note that the duration statistic in this equation is calculated on the basis of the underlying periodic cash flows even though it is often annualized when reporting the statistic by dividing it by n.

In the numerical example above, $Y = 0.10$, $n = 1$, $T = 5$, $C/F = 0.12$, and $Y/n = 0.10$. The bond's duration can therefore be solved as:

$$D = \frac{1 + 0.10}{0.10} - \frac{1 + 0.10 + 5\,(0.12 - 0.10)}{0.12\left[(1 + 0.10)^5 - 1\right] + 0.10} = 4.0740$$

As a second example of this formula, what is the duration of a 30-year Treasury bond with a $7\frac{5}{8}$ percent coupon and a stated yield to maturity of 7.72 percent? Here you need to recall that T-bonds pay semiannual interest and so the appropriate definitions of the variables are: $C/F = 0.038125$, $T = 30$, $n = 2$, and $Y/n = 0.0386$. Therefore:

$$D = \frac{1 + 0.0386}{0.0386} - \frac{1 + 0.0386 + 60(0.038125 + 0.0386)}{(0.038125)\left[(1 + 0.0386)^{60} - 1\right] + 0.0386} = 24.18 \text{ periods}$$

or 12.09 years. Although the method summarized by Table 23A.1 always will work for any nonamortizing bond, the closed-form expression is considerably quicker when a large number of coupon payments are involved.

Chapter 23 APPENDIX B. CALCULATING MONEY MARKET IMPLIED FORWARD RATES

Implied forward rates are an essential factor in understanding how short-term interest rate futures contracts are priced. In our discussion of the expectations hypothesis of the yield curve in Chapter 16, we saw that implied forward rates represented the sequence of future short-term rates that were built into the yield to maturity of a longer-term security. However, implied forward rates can have another interpretation. Consider an investor who is deciding between the following strategies for making a two-year investment: (1) buy a single 2-year, zero-coupon bond yielding 6 percent per annum; or (2) buy a 1-year, zero-coupon bond with a 5 percent yield and replace it at maturity with another 1-year instrument. An implied forward rate is the answer to the following question: At what rate must the investor be able to reinvest the interim proceeds from the second strategy to exactly equal the total return from the first investment? In other words, the implied forward rate is a *breakeven* reinvestment rate. In the notation of Chapter 16, we want to solve for ${}_2r_1$ in the following equation:

$$(1 + 0.06)^2 = (1 + 0.05)\,(1 + {}_2r_1)$$

or ${}_2r_1 = [(1 + 0.06)^2 \div (1 + 0.05)] - 1 = 7\%$. An alternative interpretation is that investing for 2 years with a return of 6 percent per year is exactly the same as investing for 1 year at 5 percent, with the principal and interest then reinvested for a second year at 7 percent.

Implied forward money market rates can be interpreted in the same way as bond yields, but they must be calculated differently because of differences in the quotation methods for the various rates. For example, T-bill rates are quoted on a *discount yield* (DY) basis using the following pricing formula:

$$P = F - \left[F \times DY \times \frac{T}{360}\right] = F\left[1 - DY \times \frac{T}{360}\right]$$

where:

F = the face value of the underlying instrument
P = the current price of the underlying instrument
T = the number of days to maturity

For example, a Treasury bill with 91 days to maturity, a $10,000 face value, and a discount yield of 4.67 percent would sell for a current price of:

$$\text{P} = \$10{,}000\left[1 - (0.0467) \times \frac{91}{360}\right] = \$9{,}881.95$$

On the other hand, we have seen that LIBOR is a bank *add-on yield* (AY) that is used to figure out how much money an investor will have at maturity given an initial investment of P (i.e., interest is "added on"):

$$F = P + \left[P \times AY \times \frac{T}{360}\right] = P\left[1 + AY \times \frac{T}{360}\right]$$

With this expression, a 60-day investment of $50,000 in a bank deposit paying LIBOR equal to 5.30 percent would be worth $50,441.67 at maturity. Notice that both the T-bill discount rate and LIBOR are based on a presumed 360-day year, the standard U.S. money market practice.

With these quotation conventions, Smith has shown that the implied forward rate between two money market instruments quoted on an add-on basis (e.g., LIBOR) can be calculated as:

$${}_BAY_A = \left[\frac{(B \times AY_B) - (A \times AY_A)}{B - A}\right]\left[\frac{1}{1 + \left(\dfrac{A \times DY_A}{360}\right)}\right]$$

where AY_A and AY_B are add-on yields for A and B days from settlement to maturity, with $B > A$.[23] The implied forward rate (${}_BAY_A$) also is on an add-on basis and has a maturity of $(B - A)$ days. That is, ${}_BAY_A$ corresponds to the time period between date A and date B. For

[23]Donald J. Smith, "The Calculation and Use of Money Market Implied Forward Rates," *Journal of Cash Management* 98. no. 5 (September/October 1989): 46–49.

money market instruments quoted on a discount yield basis (e.g., T-bill). a slightly different formula applies:

$$_BDY_A = \left[\frac{(B \times DY_B) - (A \times DY_A)}{B - A}\right]\left[\frac{1}{1 - \left(\frac{A \times DY_A}{360}\right)}\right]$$

where DY_A and DY_B are discount yields for A and B days from settlement to maturity, and $B > A$. The implied forward rate ($_ADY_B$) also is on a discount yield basis and has a maturity of $(B - A)$ days, assuming a 360-day year. Notice that these formulas have a common structure, differing only in that the add-on formula has a "plus" sign in the denominator of the second term while the discount yield has a "minus."

As an example of these calculations, consider the following short-term yield curves for T-bills and LIBOR:

Maturity	T-bill	LIBOR
30 days	4.00%	4.15%
60 days	4.10	4.25
90 days	4.20	4.35

What is the implied forward T-bill rate between days 30 and 60? Using $DY_A = 0.0400$, $DY_B = 0.0410, A = 30$ days, and $B = 60$ days for T-bills, we have:

$$_{60}DY_{30} = \left[\frac{(60 \times 0.0410) - (30 \times 0.0400)}{60 - 30}\right]\left[\frac{1}{1 - \left(\frac{30 \times 0.0400}{360}\right)}\right] = 4.21\%$$

This means that buying a 30-day T-bill at 4.00 percent and then again at 4.21 percent in another 30 days would have the same total return as the 60-day T-bill at 4.10 percent.

As a second example, what is the implied forward LIBOR between days 60 and 90? Using $AY_A = 0.0425, AY_B = 0.0435, A = 60$ days, and $B = 90$ days for LIBOR, we have:

$$_{90}AY_{60} = \left[\frac{(90 \times 0.0435) - (60 \times 0.0425)}{90 - 60}\right]\left[\frac{1}{1 + \left(\frac{60 \times 0.0425}{360}\right)}\right] = 4.52\%$$

That is, investing in a 60-day bank deposit at 4.25 percent and then a 30-day deposit at 4.52 percent would have the same total return (or cost of funds) as the 90-day deposit at 4.35 percent. This can be confirmed by examining the cash flows on the transactions. For example, the total return on a \$100,000, 60-day deposit at 4.25 percent would be \$100,708. This amount reinvested in a 30-day deposit at 4.52 percent would provide a total of \$101,087, equaling the payoff on a \$100,000, 90-day deposit at 4.35 percent.

Chapter 24 Option Contracts

After you read this chapter, you should be able to answer the following questions:

- How are options traded on exchanges and in OTC markets?
- How are options for stock, stock indexes, foreign currency, and futures contracts quoted in the financial press?
- How can investors use option contracts to hedge an existing risk exposure?
- What are the three steps in establishing the fundamental "no arbitrage" value of an option contract?
- What is the binomial (or two-state) option pricing model and in what way is it an extension of the basic valuation approach?
- What is the Black-Scholes option pricing model and how does it extend the binomial valuation approach?
- What is the relationship between the Black-Scholes and the put-call parity valuation models?
- How does the payment of a dividend by the underlying asset impact the value of an option?
- How can models for valuing stock options be adapted to other underlying assets, such as stock indexes, foreign currency, or futures contracts?
- How do American- and European-style options differ from one another?
- What is implied volatility and what is its role in the contract valuation process?
- What are exotic options and how are they valued?
- How do investors use options with the underlying security or in combination with one another to create payoff structures tailored to a particular need or view of future market conditions?
- What differentiates a spread from a straddle, a strangle, or a range forward?

Broken down to the most basic level, only two kinds of derivative contracts exist: forwards, which fix the price or rate of an underlying asset; and options, which allow holders to decide at a later date whether such a fixing is in their best interest. With our initial examination of forward and futures contracts now complete, this chapter turns our attention to issues concerning the trading and valuation of option contracts. We will develop the discussion in four parts. First, we will consider more closely the contract terms and trading mechanics for both call and put options. Options trade on exchanges as well as in the OTC dealer markets and can be based on a wide array of securities and commodities. To focus this discussion, we concentrate on options that have financial instruments as underlying securities, including options on individual stocks, stock indexes, foreign currency, and futures contracts. A formal discussion of options on interest rates is highlighted in the next chapter.

The second topic we explore is how option contracts are valued in an efficient capital market. We show that, at least intuitively, this can be viewed as a simple, three-step process: (1) creating a riskless hedge portfolio combining options with the underlying security, (2) invoking a no-arbitrage assumption about the rate of return that such a portfolio should earn, and (3) solving for the option value consistent with the first two steps. We show that several of the most widely used valuation models, including the **binomial** and the **Black-Scholes**, are consistent with this approach. In this analysis, it is important to keep in mind that we will be *valuing* options and not *pricing* them. Indeed, prices are established through the actions of buyers and sellers; investors and analysts use valuation models to estimate what those prices should be.

Third, we consider several extensions and advanced topics in option valuation. In particular, we show how the Black-Scholes model for call options on stock can be adapted to value put options, as well as the other financial assets commonly used as underlying assets. We describe how the payment of dividends affects an option's value and how the model can be adjusted accordingly. We discuss the practical differences between the European and American styles of contracting, and we also examine price or return volatility—the role it plays in the valuation process and the ways an investor can estimate it in practice. We conclude the section with an examination of **exotic options**, which are designed to have payoffs that differ from those of standard contracts.

Finally, several option-based investment and hedging strategies are examined. After describing protective put and covered call strategies, we demonstrate how options can be used in combination with one another to create risk–reward trade-offs that do not otherwise exist in financial markets. In this sense, options can be used as building blocks to help investors design customized payoff schemes. We consider three broad classes of option combination strategies: **straddles**, which involve the purchase and sale of both puts and calls; **spreads**, in which the investor simultaneously buys one call (or put) while selling another; and **range forwards**, which require the purchase of a call and the concurrent sale of a put, or vice versa.

AN OVERVIEW OF OPTION MARKETS AND CONTRACTS

In Chapter 23, we discussed the primary difference between forward and futures contracts: Futures are standardized and trade on exchanges while forward contracts have negotiable terms and therefore must be arranged in the OTC market. With the development of organized option exchanges during the past three decades, option contracts offer investors similar trading alternatives. The most important features of how these contracts are traded and quoted in the financial press are highlighted below.

Option Market Conventions

Option contracts have been traded for centuries in the form of separate agreements or embedded in other securities. Malkiel, for example, tells the story of how call options were used to speculate on flower prices during the tulip bulb frenzy in seventeenth-century Holland.[1] Then, and for most of the time until now, options were arranged and executed in private transactions. Collectively, these private transactions represent the OTC market for options. Like forward contracts, OTC option agreements can be structured around any terms or underlying asset to which two parties can agree. This has been a particularly useful mechanism when the underlying asset is too illiquid to support a widely traded contract. Also, credit risk is a paramount concern in this market because OTC agreements typically are not collateralized. This credit risk is one-sided with an option agreement because the buyer worries about the seller's ability to honor his obligations, but the seller has received everything he will get up front and is not concerned about the buyer's creditworthiness.

As in all security markets, OTC options ultimately are created in response to the needs and desires of the corporations and individual investors who use these products. Financial

[1]See Burton G. Malkiel, *A Random Walk Down Wall Street,* 6th ed. (New York: Norton, 1996).

institutions, such as money-center banks and investment banks, serve as market makers by facilitating the arrangement and execution of these deals. Over the years, various trade associations of broker-dealers in OTC options have emerged (and, in some cases, faded), including the Put and Call Brokers and Dealers Association, which helped arrange private stock option transactions, and the International Swap and Derivatives Association, which monitors the activities of market makers for interest rate and foreign exchange derivatives. These trade groups create a common set of standards and language to govern industry transactions.

In April 1973, the Chicago Board of Trade changed the dynamics of option trading when it opened the Chicago Board Options Exchange (CBOE). Specializing in stock and stock index options, the CBOE has introduced two important aspects of market uniformity. Foremost, contracts offered by the CBOE are standardized in terms of the underlying common stock, the number of shares covered, the delivery dates, and the range of available exercise prices. This standardization, which increases the possibility of basis risk, was meant to help develop a secondary market for the contracts. The rapid increase in trading volume on the CBOE and other options exchanges suggests that this feature is desirable compared to OTC contracts that must often be held to maturity due to a lack of liquidity.

The centralization of the trading function also necessitated the creation of the **Options Clearing Corporation (OCC)**, which acts as the guarantor of each CBOE-traded contract. Therefore, end-users in option transactions ultimately bear the credit risk of the OCC. For this reason, even though the OCC is independent of the exchange, it demands the option seller to post margin to guarantee future performance. Again, the option buyer will not have a margin account because a future obligation to the seller is nonexistent. Finally, this central market structure makes monitoring, regulation, and price reporting much easier than in the decentralized OTC markets.

Price Quotations for Exchange-Traded Options

EQUITY OPTIONS Options on the common stock of individual companies have traded on the CBOE since 1973. Several other markets, including the American (AMEX), Philadelphia (PHLX), and Pacific (PSE) Stock Exchanges, began trading their own contracts shortly afterward. The CBOE remains the largest exchange in terms of the number of companies for which options are listed with a market share of about 40 percent, but the AMEX is now a close second with just under 35 percent of the total listings. Options on each of these exchanges are traded similarly, with a typical contract for 100 shares of stock. Because exchange-traded contracts are not issued by the company whose common stock is the underlying asset, they require secondary transactions in the equity if exercised.[2]

Panel A of Figure 24.1 displays price quotations for a sample of equity options as well as a list of the most actively traded contracts on February 11, 1999. To interpret this exhibit, suppose that an investor wanted to buy an option on Dell Computer common stock, a quote for which is highlighted on the chart. The first column indicates that Dell shares closed that day at a price of \$101.875, while the next two columns list the exercise prices and expiration months for the available contracts. By convention, stock options expire on the Saturday following the third Friday of the designated month. The next two columns show the volume (number of contracts traded) and closing price, respectively, for Dell calls; the final two columns provide similar information for Dell puts.

Assume this investor wanted to buy a May 1999 Dell call with an exercise price of \$100. This contract would cost a total of \$1,725.00, calculated as the stated "per share" price of \$17.25 multiplied by 100 shares. In exchange for that payment, the holder of this American-style call would then be able to exercise the option in mid-May—or any time

[2]Call options issued directly by the firm whose common stock is the underlying asset are called *warrants*. We discuss the use and valuation of these contracts in Chapter 25.

FIGURE 24.1 STOCK OPTION QUOTATIONS

A. Regular Expiration Dates

Thursday, February 11, 1999

Composite volume and close for actively traded equity and LEAPS, or long-term options, with results for the corresponding put or call contract. Volume figures are unofficial. Open interest is total outstanding for all exchanges and reflects previous trading day. Close when possible is shown for the underlying stock on primary market. CB-Chicago Board Options Exchange. AM-American Stock Exchange. PB-Philadelphia Stock Exchange. PC-Pacific Stock Exchange. NY-New York Stock Exchange. XC-Composite. p-Put.

MOST ACTIVE CONTRACTS

Option/Strike				Vol	Exch	Last	Net Chg	a-Close	Open Int
Ph Mor	Jun	40		12,315	AM	3⅞	− ¾	40⅝	31,223
Cendant01	Jan 01	20	p	9,854	XC	5¾	+ ⅜	18¼	3,087
Netscpe	Feb	70	p	8,575	XC	2 11/16	− 4 9/16	70 7/16	38,612
MCI Wrld	Mar	85		8,386	XC	2½	+ 1	80 7/16	10,350
Intel	Feb	140		7,142	AM	1 1/16	+ 7/16	133¼	25,282
Ph Mor	Mar	45		6,698	AM	⅝	− ⅛	40⅝	13,470
Ph Mor	Mar	40		6,575	AM	2 3/16	− 7/16	40⅝	1,494
Ph Mor	Mar	47½		6,575	AM	5/16	− 1/16	40⅝	5,351
AmOnline	Feb	160		6,527	XC	5¾	+ 3⅜	164 11/16	40,476
Ph Mor	Jun	40	p	6,368	AM	3⅜	+ ⅛	40⅝	5,183
DellCptr	Feb	105		6,360	AM	4⅛	+ 1½	101⅞	19,511
DellCptr	Feb	100		6,267	AM	6½	+ 2	101⅞	26,332
Compaq	Feb	45		6,238	XC	1 3/16	+ ⅜	44 13/16	21,076
ClenaCp	Feb	22½		5,618	XC	1⅛	+ ⅜	22¼	21,999
Intel	Feb	130		5,541	AM	5¼	+ 1⅜	133¼	11,806
Oracle	Mar	60		5,513	CB	4⅜	+ 1⅞	59 9/16	7,961
GTelev	Mar	22½	p	5,000	XC	½	− ¼	26 5/16	342
Intel	Feb	135		4,845	AM	2 7/16	+ ⅝	133¼	14,777
Ph Mor	Sep	50		4,725	AM	1 9/16	− 3/16	40⅝	515
Cisco	Feb	100		4,545	XC	6¼	+ 3⅛	104⅞	26,076
TycoLb	Mar	75		4,462	PB	4⅛	+ 1⅞	75 7/16	4,786
Hewlet	Feb	80		4,358	CB	1⅜	+ 11/16	75¼	6,760
HarrahE	Mar	15		4,218	CB	1	− 1/16	15 9/16	803
AmOnline	Feb	165		4,128	XC	4⅞	+ 3¾	164 11/16	25,338
Cisco	Feb	105		4,094	XC	3⅛	+ 1¾	104⅞	31,540
TycoLb	Mar	70		3,800	PB	7⅛	+ 1¾	75 7/16	5,020
Ph Mor	Mar	40	p	3,656	AM	1 13/16	+ ⅛	40⅝	4,873
Cendant	Feb	20		3,564	XC	¼	− 1	18¼	81,051
MCI Wrld	Feb	80		3,458	XC	2	+ 1 3/16	80 7/16	34,692
MerrLyn	Feb	75		3,436	XC	¾	+ 9/16	71 11/16	15,994
I B M	Feb	170		3,432	XC	9½	+ 6⅛	178 13/16	6,428
TelMex	Mar	50	p	3,415	XC	1⅜	− ⅞	53¼	3,024
I B M	Feb	180		3,390	XC	2⅞	+ 2¼	178 13/16	7,752
AmOnline	Feb	170		3,368	XC	2⅞	+ 2 9/16	164 11/16	31,722
AmOnline	Feb	150		3,347	XC	14	+ 6⅞	164 11/16	29,874
MicrTc	Apr	70		3,225	XC	7⅝	+ ⅝	68 11/16	7,594
Micsft	Feb	170		3,053	PC	1¼	+ 3/16	162¾	16,667
I B M	Feb	175		3,028	XC	5⅜	+ 4	178 13/16	4,465
DellCptr	Jan 00	22½		3,000	AM	80¼	− 4	101⅞	2,771
DellCptr	Feb	95	p	2,984	AM	2½	− 2	101⅞	9,658

WSJ Complete equity option listings and data are available in The Wall Street Journal Interactive Edition at http://wsj.com on the Internet's World Wide Web.

Option/Strike		Exp.	–Call– Vol.	Last	–Put– Vol.	Last
A M R	60	Mar	818	2 3/16	47	6⅝
AT&T	80	Mar	537	9⅛	133	1 13/16
88 3/16	80	Apr	315	11⅛	45	3
88 3/16	85	Feb	947	3⅞	428	1
88 3/16	85	Mar	255	6¼	49	3
88 3/16	85	Apr	276	8⅛	132	4⅞
88 3/16	90	Feb	2720	1 7/16	57	3½
88 3/16	90	Mar	304	4¼	4	6⅛
88 3/16	90	Apr	343	5	50	9¼
88 3/16	95	Feb	383	⅝	5	9⅞
88 3/16	95	Mar	376	2¼	4	11¼
88 3/16	95	Apr	235	3⅜	...	...
88 3/16	100	Mar	862	1⅛	...	...
88 3/16	100	Apr	678	2⅜	...	...
AbleTel	7½	Mar	150	2¾	310	¾
9 9/16	10	Mar	808	1⅜	30	2⅛
9 9/16	12½	Jun	235	1 9/16	...	...
A M D	17½	Feb	345	½	183	¾
17 3/16	20	Feb	90	⅛	2448	3
17 3/16	20	Mar	181	⅜	2100	3⅜
17 3/16	22½	Mar	1000	7/16	1	5½
Airtch	70	Feb	2092	20	...	...
90 7/16	70	Jul	1635	23⅛	...	...
90 7/16	85	Feb	315	5¾	22	½
90 7/16	90	Feb	1088	1⅞	77	2 1/16
90 7/16	90	Mar	510	4¼	...	...
Alcatl	20	Mar	180	2⅞	556	1
Alcoa	85	Mar	1000	5⅜	...	...
AldSgnl	45	Feb	331	⅜	1	2⅜
Allste	35	Feb	286	3	10	¼
37 11/16	40	Apr	311	1⅜	...	...
Altera	50	Mar	4	9⅞	266	1 13/16
58 15/16	55	Feb	289	5	35	1⅛
58 15/16	60	Feb	262	1 7/16	10	3¼
Amazon	70	Feb	...	...	331	⅜
109⅞	80	Feb	3	24⅜	286	¼
109⅞	90	Feb	32	19⅜	776	1
109⅞	90	Mar	212	22¾	392	6½
109⅞	100	Feb	636	12⅞	1046	2½
109⅞	103⅜	Feb	251	10	167	3¾
109⅞	110	Feb	1880	5⅛	377	7⅛
109⅞	110	Mar	335	15	83	15
109⅞	120	Feb	542	2 9/16	82	12½
109⅞	120	Mar	465	10¼	61	23¼
109⅞	126⅜	Feb	612	1 7/16	10	24⅛
109⅞	130	Feb	715	1¼	80	21¾
109⅞	130	Mar	277	8	6	29½
109⅞	140	Feb	232	7/16	124	30¾
109⅞	140	Mar	248	6⅜	1	38⅛
AmeriTrde	90	Feb	254	14½	243	5⅜
98½	95	Feb	274	12	48	8⅝
98½	100	Feb	628	10⅜	117	8⅞
98½	110	Feb	331	5⅛	...	...
98½	120	Feb	371	3½	...	...
AmOnline	120	Feb	18	42¾	1747	3/16
164 11/16	125	Mar	210	41⅜	325	2 9/16
164 11/16	125	Apr	30	40⅝	373	6
164 11/16	130	Feb	65	33	274	⅜
164 11/16	135	Mar	58	30⅜	254	3
164 11/16	140	Feb	483	24¼	944	⅜
164 11/16	140	Mar	122	28	257	4⅞
164 11/16	145	Feb	423	19¾	967	13/16
164 11/16	145	Mar	210	26	622	6
164 11/16	150	Feb	3347	14	2453	1¼
164 11/16	150	Mar	885	22⅛	901	7⅜
164 11/16	150	Apr	393	27⅜	126	12¾
164 11/16	150	Jul	239	37¾	119	22¾
164 11/16	155	Feb	2948	11½	1445	1 11/16
164 11/16	155	Mar	822	19	167	9
164 11/16	155	Apr	232	24½	6	16⅝
164 11/16	160	Feb	6527	5¾	1620	3¼
164 11/16	160	Mar	1443	16⅞	87	11¾
164 11/16	160	Apr	501	22	40	18⅞
164 11/16	160	Jul	342	32⅜	5	27⅛
164 11/16	165	Feb	4128	4⅞	290	6
164 11/16	165	Mar	731	13½	32	16
164 11/16	170	Feb	3368	2⅞	437	8⅜
164 11/16	170	Mar	2098	11⅞	47	17¼
164 11/16	175	Feb	1929	1⅝	150	13⅜
164 11/16	180	Feb	447	⅞	5	25
164 11/16	180	Mar	489	8⅛	30	27⅜
164 11/16	180	Apr	1820	13¾	10	31⅜
164 11/16	185	Feb	839	5/16	4	29
164 11/16	185	Mar	337	6¾	100	35
164 11/16	200	Mar	419	4⅛	9	43⅜
AmWest	22½	Feb	506	¼	...	...
AmExpr	100	Feb	452	3¼	201	2⅛
101 1/16	110	Feb	458	3/16	...	...
Am Hom	50	Feb	375	6	...	...
56⅜	50	Apr	375	7⅜	...	...
56⅜	55	Feb	250	1 13/16	119	⅜
56⅜	55	Mar	251	3½	...	...
56⅜	60	Feb	1020	7/16	3	3¾
AmIntG	100	Feb	345	7	17	⅜
106 15/16	105	Feb	467	2⅞	84	1⅜
Amgen	120	Mar	273	9⅛	17	5⅜
124¾	125	Feb	619	2½	143	3¼
A M P	50	May	155	6⅛	300	3¼
52 13/16	55	May	558	2⅞	250	5
Amresco	10	Sep	...	...	325	2 3/16
10¼	15	Jun	560	1½	...	...
Analog	25	Feb	505	5⅞	...	...
Anheusr	70	Mar	302	4⅜	40	1¼
Aon Cp	55	Apr	875	3¼	...	...
AppleC	37½	Feb	315	2½	63	½
39⅝	40	Feb	1149	13/16	124	1 7/16
39⅝	40	Mar	241	2¾	15	3⅛
Aplbee	22½	Feb	678	3	...	...
25 13/16	25	Aug	800	3	...	...
ApplMg	5	Apr	...	...	530	1 3/16
4 15/16	7½	Apr	...	...	307	3
AplMat	60	Feb	638	7½	237	⅞
67 1/16	60	Mar	299	10	301	2⅜
67 1/16	65	Feb	1059	4	325	2¼
67 1/16	65	Mar	549	6½	91	4⅞
67 1/16	70	Feb	1199	1¾	71	5
67 1/16	70	Mar	889	4⅛	25	7¾
67 1/16	75	Feb	352	9/16	15	8¾
67 1/16	75	Mar	817	2⅜	5	10⅞
AscendC	70	Feb	1186	5½	91	⅞
74⅞	75	Feb	713	2¼	50	2⅜
AsiaPlp	5	Mar	...	...	1000	3/16
AtHome	100	Feb	281	11	167	3
109⅞	100	Jul	277	25⅞	251	21¼
109⅞	105	Feb	283	8¼	43	4½
109⅞	110	Feb	364	5½	6	6¼
109⅞	115	Feb	311	3½	10	11½
109⅞	120	Feb	361	2¼	2	17
Avon	30	Apr	...	...	924	⅜
Aware	35	Feb	605	1 7/16	15	2½
Aztar	5	May	...	...	700	11/16
BEA Sys	12½	Mar	342	5⅛	10	½
17 3/16	15	Jun	340	4⅛	...	...
BMC Sft	50	Feb	466	½	20	5¼
BP Amoco	80	Mar	...	...	385	2
BakrHu	20	Apr	467	¾	...	...
BancOne	50	Feb	200	1 11/16	322	⅞
BankNY	40	Mar	415	7/16	...	...
BkTokyoM	12½	May	343	⅞	...	...
BankAm	55	Mar	...	...	2003	1
64 15/16	55	May	50	12⅛	1530	2 5/16
64 15/16	60	Mar	179	6¼	1260	2 3/16
64 15/16	60	May	39	8½	1771	4
64 15/16	60	Aug	100	10	610	5¾
64 15/16	65	Feb	830	1⅝	169	1 15/16
64 15/16	65	Mar	319	3½	146	4⅜
64 15/16	70	Feb	472	⅛	...	...
64 15/16	70	Mar	1188	1⅜	...	...
64 15/16	75	Mar	395	⅜	4	12
BkBost	35	Feb	65	2⅛	300	7/16
37 1/16	40	Feb	390	¼	1	3⅜
37 1/16	40	Mar	1170	1 5/16	...	...
BarickG	20	Apr	244	1 3/16	30	2 7/16
BedBth	32½	Mar	777	1⅞	...	...
BellAtl	60	Mar	321	1⅜	1	3⅞
BellSo	45	Feb	753	1¾	615	½
46⅜	45	Apr	306	3⅜	...	...
BestBuy	80	Feb	127	8⅞	341	½
90 1/16	85	Feb	192	6	518	1⅛
Beth S	5	Apr	775	3⅜	...	...
bynd.com	25	Feb	8	3⅜	630	1¼
Biogen	80	Jul	...	...	2500	5
94 13/16	85	Feb	329	10	10	¼
94 13/16	95	Mar	483	6⅜	7	7⅛
94 13/16	95	Apr	329	8¼	...	...
CBS Cp	35	Feb	663	2	77	13/16
36¾	35	Mar	767	2⅞	4	1¼
CHS Elec	15	Mar	404	1⅛	...	...
CMGI Inc	100	Feb	283	16⅜	172	3¾
112	105	Feb	274	13	1	7
112	110	Feb	349	11	36	8¼
112	115	Feb	326	8	16	9⅞
112	120	Feb	485	5⅞	...	...
CNET	100	Feb	165	28	306	1⅜
129½	105	Feb	371	24¾	124	2¾
Capstd	5	Mar	235	½	...	...
Caribnr	7½	Mar	833	1⅛	...	...
Casella	25	Jun	338	2¾	...	...
Celgene	20	Jul	260	2⅛	...	...
Cellstar	10	Mar	160	2⅞	255	15/16
Cendant	17½	Feb	360	1⅛	123	⅜
18¼	17½	Mar	621	2	350	1
18¼	17½	Aug	192	3⅞	286	2⅜
18¼	20	Feb	3564	¼	222	2
18¼	20	Mar	1060	13/16	682	2⅛
18¼	20	May	465	1 13/16	41	3¼
18¼	22½	Feb	416	1/16	110	3¾
18¼	22½	Mar	856	⅜	...	...
18¼	22½	May	266	1 1/16	...	...
18¼	22½	Aug	234	1 13/16	...	...
18¼	25	May	329	⅜	53	6½
CntyCm	30	Mar	1000	3¾	130	1⅛
ChancellMda	45	Feb	337	3⅞	15	¾
50¾	50	Feb	345	2 3/16	6	3⅜
50¾	50	Mar	362	4¼	13	5⅛
50¾	55	Feb	929	9/16	51	7¼
50¾	65	Mar	...	...	250	16
Chase n	70	Feb	40	6⅜	250	⅜
76⅛	75	Feb	525	2⅜	103	1 9/16
76⅛	85	Mar	243	1⅛	...	...
76⅛	90	Sep	265	5¼	...	...
Chevrn	85	Mar	423	1	45	7⅛
ChlRex	22½	Mar	505	2⅛	...	...
23	25	Mar	514	1½	...	...
Chubb	45	Feb	315	13¾	...	...
ClenaCp	20	Feb	363	2¾	20	½
22¼	22½	Feb	5618	1⅛	25	1¼
22¼	25	Feb	454	½	5	3¼
22¼	25	Mar	809	1¾	1	4⅜
CirCty	45	Jul	...	...	505	3
Circus	12½	Mar	1113	2 9/16	...	...
15 1/16	15	Feb	273	7/16	13	½
15 1/16	15	Mar	1905	1	...	...
Cisco	90	Feb	214	15½	304	3/16
104⅞	95	Feb	661	10¼	1599	7/16
104⅞	95	Mar	252	13¾	261	3¾
104⅞	100	Feb	4545	6¼	2922	1¼
104⅞	100	Mar	811	10⅛	187	5½
104⅞	100	Apr	1153	12⅝	78	7⅜
104⅞	105	Feb	4094	3⅛	987	3⅛
104⅞	105	Mar	867	7½	377	7¾
104⅞	105	Apr	752	10⅛	52	9¾
104⅞	110	Feb	2821	1⅛	246	6½
104⅞	110	Mar	857	5¼	425	11¼
104⅞	110	Apr	535	7¾	20	13¼
104⅞	115	Feb	1102	⅜	51	13⅛
104⅞	115	Mar	605	3½	341	15¼
104⅞	120	Feb	736	⅛	37	17½
104⅞	120	Mar	865	2 7/16	46	17¾
Citigroup	47½	Mar	158	7¾	306	⅞
53⅜	50	Feb	352	3⅞	175	5/16
53⅜	50	Mar	413	5⅛	170	1 7/16
53⅜	55	Feb	2443	11/16	99	2 5/16
53⅜	55	Mar	1787	2⅜	57	3⅜
53⅜	60	Feb	625	1/16	39	6¼
53⅜	60	Mar	370	13/16	43	7⅛
CitrixSys	80	Feb	38	5¾	260	1 9/16
ClearCh	55	Mar	25	6⅜	300	2⅜
Coke	60	Mar	77	5¾	725	1 3/16
64⅜	65	Feb	1082	⅞	227	1½
64⅜	70	Feb	261	1/16	47	5½
64⅜	80	May	423	7/16	...	...
CellTel	60	Jul	50	18	320	7
72⅞	80	Feb	...	...	250	9⅜
Compaq	35	Apr	34	10¾	608	13/16
44 13/16	40	Feb	407	5	733	3/16
44 13/16	40	Mar	204	6¼	454	1⅛
44 13/16	40	Apr	680	7	741	2
44 13/16	42½	Feb	746	2¾	217	½
44 13/16	45	Feb	6238	1 3/16	972	1½
44 13/16	45	Mar	1959	3⅛	140	3¼
44 13/16	45	Apr	1250	4	98	4
44 13/16	47½	Feb	1383	½	10	3
44 13/16	47½	Mar	458	1⅜	...	...
44 13/16	50	Feb	1464	3/16	24	5¼
44 13/16	50	Mar	851	1⅛	12	6⅜
44 13/16	50	Apr	880	2 1/16	18	7¼
44 13/16	65	Jul	545	1 5/16	...	...
CmptHrz	17½	Feb	252	1¼	40	1 9/16
Comsat	30	Mar	20	⅞	500	1 9/16
29⅜	30	Apr	...	...	500	2⅛
Conoco	22½	Apr	275	9/16	...	...
Cnseco	25	Mar	20	4⅜	400	1
CtlAir B s	40	Mar	290	¾	...	...
CntwCrd	40	Feb	...	...	250	1⅛
DelmlChr	85	Jul	425	15⅛	...	...
DaouSys	7½	Jul	300	1 1/16	...	...
DlBdcst	17½	Feb	318	⅞	108	1⅜
17 1/16	17½	Mar	348	2¾	5	2⅞
17 1/16	20	Feb	682	¼	15	3⅛
17 1/16	20	Mar	234	1⅝	8	4¼
DataGn	17½	Mar	372	1¾	...	...
DayHud	65	Mar	266	2⅛	...	...
DellCptr	57½	Feb	275	26½	248	¼
101⅞	65	Feb	239	37	65	⅛
101⅞	80	Feb	500	21¾	197	⅜
101⅞	80	Mar	66	24	729	2 3/16
101⅞	85	Feb	508	17¾	1501	¾
101⅞	85	Mar	113	20	768	3⅜
101⅞	90	Feb	1289	13⅛	2804	1⅜
101⅞	90	Mar	550	17½	518	4⅞
101⅞	95	Feb	2349	9½	2984	2½
101⅞	95	Mar	955	14½	517	7
101⅞	100	Feb	6267	6⅛	2275	4⅝
101⅞	100	Mar	2745	11⅛	190	9
101⅞	100	May	758	17¼	109	15
101⅞	105	Feb	6360	4⅛	400	7
101⅞	105	Mar	1881	9	214	11⅝
101⅞	105	May	337	15	4	17¼
101⅞	110	Mar	1522	7⅛	98	15
101⅞	115	Feb	1472	1¼	1	15
101⅞	115	Mar	723	5½	282	18¾
101⅞	120	Feb	1369	⅝	148	20⅛
101⅞	120	Mar	1118	4¼	591	22¼
101⅞	125	Feb	295	¼	...	...
101⅞	125	Mar	549	2⅞	2	26⅝
101⅞	140	Mar	364	1⅛	...	...
DellPneLd	25	May	500	10	2	2 3/16
32½	30	Feb	1306	2½	519	⅞
DiaOff	22½	Mar	...	...	410	1 9/16
22¾	40	Mar	300	1/16	...	...
Disney	35	Feb	1082	⅞	92	¾
35 5/16	35	Mar	633	2	11	1⅞
35 5/16	35	Apr	251	2 11/16	37	2 1/16
Dow Ch	100	Jun	402	3½	...	...
DuPont	65	Jul	13	1 7/16	500	12
ETradeGr	40	Feb	370	8⅝	299	⅞
48¼	40	Mar	236	11¾	160	3½
48¼	45	Feb	611	4⅜	455	2¼
48¼	47½	Feb	365	3¾	43	3¼
48¼	50	Feb	870	2⅜	161	4⅞
48¼	50	Mar	540	6½	11	9
48¼	55	Feb	418	1¼	20	8¾
48¼	55	Mar	367	5⅛	4	14⅜
48¼	55	Jul	429	12	...	...
48¼	60	Feb	241	⅜	1	13½
48¼	60	Mar	342	3⅞	...	...
EMC	95	Apr	1518	15⅜	...	...
104⅛	100	Feb	1273	6⅛	253	1¾
104⅛	100	Mar	242	10½	67	6¼
104⅛	105	Feb	1603	3⅛	164	3¾
104⅛	110	Feb	383	1¼	...	...
104⅛	110	Mar	328	5⅜	...	...
ESCMed	5	Feb	...	...	300	¼
5¼	7½	Feb	...	...	250	2
Erthlink	65	Feb	330	4¾	36	3¾
66 13/16	70	Feb	424	2 15/16	51	7¾
EclpSurg	10	Feb	510	3	...	...
13⅜	12½	Feb	232	¾	10	⅜
Elan	55	Jul	...	...	500	1¼
78 1/16	75	Apr	301	6¼	40	2¾
78 1/16	85	Jul	500	4⅛	...	...
EDS	50	Mar	1042	1 11/16	10	4⅛
EnrnOG	15	Apr	1010	3	...	...
EntreMd	15	Feb	739	9	59	⅜
25 11/16	20	Feb	402	6¼	961	1
25 11/16	20	Mar	172	7⅜	383	2⅜
25 11/16	22½	Feb	284	4⅜	272	1⅞
25 11/16	25	Feb	595	3⅜	750	2⅞
25 11/16	25	Mar	205	5⅛	486	4⅜
25 11/16	30	Feb	1312	1 9/16	160	5⅞
25 11/16	30	Mar	356	3⅜	45	7¼
25 11/16	30	May	241	5⅛	...	...
25 11/16	35	Feb	675	7/16	12	10
25 11/16	35	Aug	23	4⅞	300	15⅜
EricTel	30	Apr	348	1	2	5
Excite	35	Feb	...	...	345	1/16
105¼	80	Feb	1225	22¾	146	½
105¼	85	Feb	318	17½	204	13/16
105¼	95	Feb	278	10⅜	201	2
105¼	100	Feb	265	7½	234	3⅜
105¼	110	Feb	259	3½	...	...
105¼	115	Feb	380	2¼	10	13
ExodsCm	80	Feb	361	11½	138	2
ExprScpt	70	Mar	250	4¼	...	...
Exxon	60	Apr	...	...	510	½
70⅜	65	Apr	...	...	326	1 3/16
70⅜	70	Feb	283	1½	456	1
70⅜	70	Mar	33	3⅛	620	2¼
70⅜	70	Apr	18	3⅜	495	3
70⅜	75	Mar	273	⅝	...	...
70⅜	75	Jul	310	3⅜	10	6
FDX Cp	70	Feb	1	15½	280	1/16
86 1/16	70	Apr	6	16¼	1945	1½
86 1/16	80	Apr	6	10½	1014	4
86 1/16	85	Feb	570	3¼	206	1½
F N M	65	Mar	750	8	160	1⅛
71 15/16	75	Mar	129	1⅞	750	4⅞
Fingerhl	12½	Apr	351	11¾	10	3/16
24½	15	Feb	1256	9½	...	...
24½	15	Mar	1294	9¼	...	...
24½	15	Apr	171	9¼	1002	3/16
24½	17½	Feb	647	6⅞	60	1/16
24½	17½	Mar	247	7⅛	10	⅛
24½	17½	Apr	901	6¾	...	...
24½	20	Feb	1543	4⅜	208	1/16
24½	20	Mar	709	4⅜	...	...
24½	20	Apr	927	4¾	...	...
24½	22½	Feb	1501	2	110	1/16
24½	22½	Jul	2	2¼	315	½
FtAmFin	25	Jul	270	5	3	3⅛
Firstar	85	Feb	126	1 13/16	1000	1 5/16
86 7/16	90	Mar	300	2	...	...
FdLionB	10	Jul	500	1	...	...
FordMot	55	Jun	510	7⅞	501	2⅞
60⅛	60	Feb	809	1⅜	81	1¼
ForeSys	17½	Mar	319	1 3/16	12	2⅜
16¼	20	Mar	943	½	10	4
FerstL	40	Feb	1610	7⅞	...	...
48¼	40	Mar	2100	8⅝	...	...
FHLB	47½	Apr	...	...	320	5/16
58 1/16	50	Apr	...	...	320	11/16
FruitL	15	Feb	233	7/16	20	1
14 7/16	20	Aug	302	1⅜	...	...
Gadzks	7½	Mar	247	15/16	...	...
Gtwy2000	75	Feb	312	3⅛	63	2 15/16
76⅛	75	Mar	534	6⅜	15	5½
76⅛	80	Mar	815	4½	18	9
Gemstr	60	Mar	375	7¼	20	5⅛
Gen El	90	Mar	48	11⅛	395	1½
100	90	Jun	...	...	278	3¾
100	95	Feb	168	5	614	½
100	100	Feb	996	1⅞	554	2
100	100	Mar	587	4¼	127	5
100	105	Feb	284	¼	21	5½

FIGURE 24.1 **STOCK OPTION QUOTATIONS (CONCLUDED)**

B. Long-Term Equity Anticipation Securities (LEAPS)

			-Call-		-Put-	
Option/Strike		Exp.	Vol.	Last	Vol.	Last
Allstate	30	Jan 00	200	9 7/8	...	...
37 11/16	45	Jan 00	215	2 3/4	...	...
Amazon	100	Jan 00	1604	44 1/8	3	32 1/8
109 7/8	200	Jan 01	253	34 3/4	...	...
AmerOn o	65	Jan 00	228	100 5/8	12	4 1/2
AmOnline o	70	Jan 01	32	105 1/4	250	10 3/4
AmerOn	70	Jan 00	216	43 3/4	2	49 1/2
AmerOn o	90	Jan 00	236	85 7/8	...	...
AmOnline	200	Jan 01	259	55 3/4	...	...
ApldMatl	40	Jan 00	528	30 1/2	707	3
67 1/16	60	Jan 00	286	18 3/4	1	9 5/8
ApldMat	70	Jan 01	1	21 1/2	200	18 7/8
NatnsBk	75	Jan 00	525	6 3/4	...	...
64 15/16	80	Jan 00	665	5 1/4	...	...
BkBost	37 1/2	Jan 00	...	...	504	6 3/8
Cendant01	10	Jan 01	353	10 3/4	...	...
CUC Int	20	Jan 00	203	3 7/8	2	4 5/8
Cendant01	20	Jan 01	52	6 1/8	9854	5 3/4
CUC Int	30	Jan 00	1539	1 5/8	80	11 7/8
18 1/4	40	Jan 00	1272	5/8	20	21
ChaseM	45	Jan 00	200	32 7/8	...	...
76 1/8	60	Jan 00	225	22	...	...
76 1/8	80	Jan 00	420	11	...	...
Cisco01	100	Jan 01	219	35	13	22 5/8
Travelers	30	Jan 00	217	25 7/8	16	1 1/8
Travelrs01	30	Jan 01	246	28 1/8	7	2 1/2
53 5/8	60	Jan 01	207	12 7/8	1	14 3/8
Travelers	60	Jan 00	212	7 1/2	50	11 3/8
Compaq	40	Jan 00	257	12 1/4	45	5 1/2
44 13/16	50	Jan 00	801	7 3/4	10	11
44 13/16	60	Jan 00	663	4 3/4	...	...
DellCptr	22 1/2	Jan 00	3000	80 1/4	...	...
101 7/8	35	Jan 00	500	69 1/4	30	2 3/16
101 7/8	100	Jan 01	315	41	22	30 7/8
101 7/8	100	Jan 00	369	29 1/2	5	24 1/4
101 7/8	120	Jan 00	372	21 1/2	...	...
101 7/8	120	Jan 01	206	34 1/2	...	...
DuPont	65	Jan 00	3	3 7/8	370	13 5/8
Exxon	65	Jan 00	...	...	236	4 1/2
70 3/8	80	Jan 00	323	4	20	11 1/8
FDX	70	Jan 00	...	...	300	6
GTE	60	Jan 00	432	10 1/4	400	5
Hmstke	7 1/2	Jan 00	...	...	230	1
9 1/4	10	Jan 00	1515	2 1/8	50	2 1/4
Inprise	10	Jan 01	200	15/16	...	...
MCI Wrld	50	Jan 00	1243	34 1/4	...	...
80 7/16	70	Jan 00	214	20	...	...
McDnlds	90	Jan 00	782	8 3/4	...	...
Microsft	160	Jan 00	208	29	...	...
162 3/4	220	Jan 01	293	20 1/4	5	63
Monsanto	60	Jan 01	201	11 3/4	...	...
NetwkAsc	65	Jan 01	200	11	...	...
NewmMin	20	Jan 01	405	6 5/8	5	6
PhilMor	30	Jan 01	1394	13 5/8	43	3
40 3/8	30	Jan 00	152	12 3/8	567	2
40 3/8	35	Jan 01	883	10 5/8	35	5 1/8
40 3/8	35	Jan 00	170	8 1/2	919	3 3/8
40 3/8	40	Jan 00	819	6	311	5 3/8
40 3/8	40	Jan 01	965	8 1/4	53	6 7/8
40 3/8	45	Jan 00	2501	4 1/4	52	8 1/2
40 3/8	50	Jan 01	446	4 3/4	22	13
40 3/8	50	Jan 00	1799	2 3/4	56	12 1/8
40 3/8	55	Jan 00	425	1 1/2	20	16 5/8
40 3/8	60	Jan 00	382	15/16	72	19 5/8
RJRNab	20	Jan 00	870	7 5/8	13	1 11/16
ReadRt	12 1/2	Jan 01	200	5 1/4	...	...
SchergPl	40	Jan 01	1210	20 3/8	...	...
54 5/16	50	Jan 01	1210	14 5/8	...	...
SeagateT	30	Jan 00	10	12 1/4	2014	3 1/2
Seagate	30	Jan 01	1	15 7/8	2000	5 5/8
SwstAirl	25	Jan 00	205	7 3/4	...	...
TelMex01	55	Jan 01	500	12 1/8	...	...
TelMex	55	Jan 00	503	8 1/2	...	...
WellsFrgo	34	Jan 00	850	5 3/8	...	...
Yahoo	140	Jan 00	...	...	300	40 1/4

VOLUME & OPEN INTEREST SUMMARIES

AMERICAN			
Call Vol:	31,822	Open Int:	2,108,734
Put Vol:	20,512	Open Int:	1,177,413
CHICAGO BOARD			
Call Vol:	19,897	Open Int:	3,029,215
Put Vol:	11,811	Open Int:	2,087,692
PACIFIC			
Call Vol:	13,187	Open Int:	1,230,650
Put Vol:	2,204	Open Int:	966,557
PHILADELPHIA			
Call Vol:	6,978	Open Int:	824,964
Put Vol:	1,745	Open Int:	363,404
TOTAL			
Call Vol:	71,884	Open Int:	7,193,563
Put Vol:	36,272	Open Int:	4,595,066

Source: *Wall Street Journal,* 12 February 1999.

before then—by paying \$10,000 (= \$100 × 100) and receive 100 Dell shares from the option seller, who is obligated to make that exchange at the buyer's request. That request will only be rational if the mid-May price of Dell is greater than \$100. If that price closes below \$100, the investor will simply let the call expire without acting on the option; that is her right as the derivative buyer. Finally, notice that with the February share price being \$101.875, the investor could immediately recover \$1.875 of the \$17.25 she paid for the contract. Thus, her time premium of \$15.375 (= \$17.25 − \$1.875) preserves her right to buy Dell stock at a price of \$100 for the next 3 months even if the market value of those shares moves higher.[3]

Consider another investor who sells the "May 100" Dell put. In return for an up-front receipt of \$1,500 (= \$15 × 100), he now must stand ready to buy 100 shares of stock in mid-May for \$10,000 if the option holder chooses to exercise his option to sell. The stock price will, of course, have to fall from its current level before this would occur. The investor in this case has sold an out-of-the-money contract and hopes that it will stay out of the money through expiration, letting the passing of time "decay" the time premium to zero. As we saw earlier, the front-end premium is all that sellers of put or call options ever

[3]Recall from Chapter 11 that a call option's value can be divided into two components: the *intrinsic value,* which is the greater of either zero or the stock price minus the exercise price, and the *time premium.* In this example, the Dell call is said to be *in the money* because it has positive intrinsic value, whereas an option with no intrinsic value is *out of the money.*

receive, and they hope to retain as much of it as possible. Like the long position in the call, the short put position benefits from an increase in Dell share prices.

Finally, notice that all the options listed in panel A of Figure 24.1 expire within a few months of the quotation date. In fact, the expiration dates available for these exchange-traded contracts are the two nearest-term months (February and March for Dell) and up to two additional months from a quarterly cycle beginning in either January, February, or March. In the case of Dell options, May 1999 (which is part of the quarterly cycle beginning in February) is the additional month listed. Panel B of the figure lists quotations for long-term equity anticipation securities (LEAPS), which are simply call and put options with longer expiration dates. Like the contracts just described, LEAPS are also traded on the CBOE and have comparable terms. For instance, a Dell call with the same \$100 striking price expiring in January 2000 would cost the investor \$2,950 (= \$29.50 × 100). Thus, by extending the expiration date by 7 months (i.e., from May 1999 to January 2000), the option's price increases from \$17.25 to \$29.50. Of course, since these two contracts had the same exercise price, this difference is purely because of additional time premium. The effect that time to expiration has on the value of an option will be examined in greater detail shortly.

STOCK INDEX OPTIONS As we saw in Chapter 11, options on stock indexes, such as Standard and Poor's 100 or 500, are patterned closely after equity options; however, they differ in one important way: Index options can only be settled in cash. This is because of the underlying index, which is a hypothetical portfolio that would be quite costly to duplicate in practice. First traded on the CBOE in 1983, index options are popular with investors for the same reason as stock index futures: They provide a relatively inexpensive and convenient way to take an investment or hedging position in a broad-based indicator of market performance. Index puts are particularly useful in portfolio insurance applications, such as the protective put strategy described earlier and again at the end of this chapter.

Prices for four of the more widely traded contracts are listed in Figure 24.2. They are interpreted in the same way as equity option prices, with each contract demanding the transfer of 100 "shares" of the underlying index. For example, the March S&P 500 index call and put contracts with an exercise price of 1270 could be purchased for \$3,200 (= \$32 × 100) and \$4,500 (= \$45 × 100), respectively. On the expiration date, which will be the third Friday of the month, the holder of the call would exercise the contract to "buy" \$127,000 worth of the index if the prevailing S&P 500 level is greater than 1270, with the put being exercised at index levels less than 1270.

FOREIGN CURRENCY OPTIONS Foreign currency options are structurally parallel to the currency futures contracts discussed in Chapter 23. That is, each contract allows for the sale or purchase of a set amount of foreign (i.e., non-U.S. dollar) currency at a fixed exchange (FX) rate. A currency call option is like the long position in the currency futures since it permits the contract holder to buy the currency at a later date. (Of course, unlike futures, options do not require that this exchange be made.) A currency put is therefore the option analog to being short in the futures market. These contracts exist for several major currencies, including the Euro, Australian dollars, French francs, Japanese yen, German deutschemarks, British pounds, and Swiss francs. The majority of currency options trading, which began in 1982, occurs on the PHLX. Figure 24.3 shows quotes from a sample of the available contracts, along with the spot foreign exchange rates for the same trading day.

Like the FX futures market, all the prices are quoted from the perspective of U.S.-based investors. Consider, for example, an investor who lives in New York and holds Canadian dollar–denominated provincial government bonds in her portfolio. It is February, and when the bonds come due in one month, she will need to convert the proceeds back into U.S. dollars, which exposes her to a possible weakening in the Canadian currency. Accordingly, she

FIGURE 24.2 STOCK INDEX OPTION QUOTATIONS

S & P 100 INDEX(OEX)

Mar	410 p	243	1/4	...	3,268
Mar	460 p	5	1/2	- 1/8	2,472
Mar	490 c	1	132 5/8	+ 6 3/8	566
Mar	490 p	54	1 1/16	- 3/8	2,075
Feb	500 p	141	1/16	...	5,611
Feb	510 p	316	1/16	- 1/16	2,952
Mar	510 c	10	120 3/4	+ 16 7/8	4,259
Mar	510 p	195	1 1/4	- 1 5/8	7,314
Feb	520 p	193	1/16	- 1/16	4,809
Mar	520 p	566	2 1/16	- 1 9/16	4,646
Apr	520 p	12	5 1/8	- 2 1/8	1,076
Feb	525 p	7	1/8	- 1/16	984
Feb	530 p	506	1/16	- 3/16	3,527
Mar	530 p	385	2 3/8	- 1 5/8	4,738
Apr	530 p	100	5 3/4	- 1 7/8	670
Feb	540 c	6	84 1/8	- 11 5/8	72
Feb	540 p	396	1/8	- 1/4	6,711
Mar	540 p	305	3 3/8	- 1 1/2	3,013
Apr	540 p	1	7 7/8	- 4	1,598
Feb	545 p	528	1/8	- 5/16	2,057
Feb	550 p	1,001	3/16	- 3/8	8,481
Mar	550 c	12	79	- 1	1,496
Mar	550 p	514	3 1/4	- 2 3/4	5,471
Apr	550 p	27	9	- 3 3/8	3,253
May	550 p	200	14 1/4	- 3 7/8	610
Feb	555 p	487	1/4	- 7/16	2,569
Feb	560 p	633	5/16	- 7/16	6,708
Mar	560 p	285	4 3/8	- 3 5/8	3,282
Apr	560 p	26	10 1/2	- 4 1/2	579
May.	560 p	102	16	- 4 1/8	84
Feb	565 p	639	1/4	- 3/4	3,432
Feb	570 p	1,015	5/16	- 1	6,123
Mar	570 p	432	6	- 3 1/2	3,752
Apr	570 p	25	12 1/2	- 3 1/4	3,401
May	570 p	8	21	+ 2	299
Feb	575 c	121	49 1/2	+ 7 3/4	368
Feb	575 p	1,324	7/16	- 1 3/16	3,216
Mar	575 p	2	9	- 2 1/2	435
Feb	580 c	231	44 3/4	+ 11 1/8	1,426
Feb	580 p	2,909	5/8	- 1 5/8	6,965
Mar	580 p	462	6 3/4	- 5 1/4	3,207
Apr	580 p	2	13 1/2	- 5 3/4	532
Feb	585 c	176	40	+ 6 7/8	457
Feb	585 p	754	11/16	- 2 1/16	4,472
Mar	585 p	300	9 1/8	- 4 7/8	362
Feb	590 c	620	35 3/4	+ 9 3/8	1,942
Feb	590 p	2,813	7/8	- 2 5/8	5,904
Mar	590 c	615	47	+ 11 7/8	1,703
Mar	590 p	1,237	8 5/8	- 5 1/8	1,638
Apr	590 c	1	54 1/2	+ 6	162
Apr	590 p	8	17 1/4	- 6 1/4	329
Feb	595 c	17	33 3/4	+ 13 3/8	196
Feb	595 p	1,220	1	- 3 1/2	5,539
Mar	595 c	210	41 3/4	+ 7 3/4	1,477
Mar	595 p	39	11 5/8	- 4 7/8	1,077
Feb	600 c	974	25	+ 7	5,536
Feb	600 p	6,791	1 3/8	- 4 3/8	12,559
Mar	600 c	3	38 1/8	+ 9 5/8	2,534
Mar	600 p	286	10 1/2	- 6 1/8	3,208
Apr	600 c	7	46	+ 6 1/2	1,072
Apr	600 p	37	18 1/4	- 7	1,149
May	600 p	53	24 1/2	- 8 1/4	316
Feb	605 c	349	27	+ 12 5/8	3,380
Feb	605 p	3,980	1 13/16	- 5 9/16	8,195
Mar	605 c	11	35 5/8	+ 8 1/2	695
Mar	605 p	478	12	- 9	890
Feb	610 c	2,032	22	+ 11	10,431
Feb	610 p	9,576	2 3/8	- 7	16,211
Mar	610 c	50	33	+ 9	4,067
Mar	610 p	306	13 3/4	- 7 3/4	3,640
Apr	610 p	613	22 1/4	- 5 3/4	2,942
Feb	615 c	3,190	18	+ 9 5/8	5,788
Feb	615 p	5,842	3 1/4	- 8	6,795
Mar	615 c	83	26 1/4	+ 5 1/8	2,266
Mar	615 p	140	16	- 7 1/2	533
Feb	620 c	9,624	14 3/4	+ 8 3/4	7,745
Feb	620 p	9,608	4 1/4	- 10	7,280
Mar	620 c	409	26 1/2	+ 7 1/2	3,187
Feb	680 c	930	1/16	...	7,452
Feb	680 p	3	66	+ 13	10
Mar	680 c	617	2 7/16	+ 1 1/16	3,755
Apr	680 c	200	6 5/8	+ 7/8	415
Feb	690 c	240	1/16	...	3,589
Mar	690 c	326	1 1/8	+ 3/8	2,598
Mar	700 c	292	3/4	+ 3/8	2,911
Apr	700 c	13	3 1/8	+ 1 1/4	1,484

Call Vol. ......61,509 Open Int. ...225,896
Put Vol. ......64,881 Open Int. ...367,412

S & P 500 INDEX-AM(SPX)

Mar	725 p	100	1/8	- 3/4	4,733
Mar	750 p	115	1/8	- 1/16	14,434
Mar	850 p	20	1/2	...	1,187
Mar	900 p	5	1/2	- 15/16	10,796
Apr	900 p	12	2 1/2	- 1	182
Mar	950 p	175	1	- 7/8	12,247
Apr	950 p	59	3 7/8	- 2 1/8	412
Feb	975 p	20	1/16	- 3/16	2,040
Mar	975 p	7	1 7/8	- 1	15,029
Mar	995 p	39	1 3/4	- 2	8,543
Feb	1005 p	100	1/16	- 1/4	2,387
Mar	1005 c	2	232	- 5	470
Mar	1005 p	3	3 1/8	- 1 3/8	5,554
Mar	1025 p	46	2 1/2	- 3	23,725
Apr	1025 p	495	7 7/8	- 4 7/8	1,543
Feb	1050 p	21	3/16	- 3/16	6,239
Mar	1050 p	815	4 1/8	- 2 3/8	27,085
Feb	1075 p	695	1/8	- 5/8	4,152
Mar	1075 p	81	4 7/8	- 4 3/8	11,809
Apr	1075 p	100	13 3/4	- 4 3/4	34
Feb	1100 c	10	147	+ 24	110
Feb	1100 p	2,918	1/4	- 3/4	13,372
Mar	1100 p	1,302	6	- 6	22,300
Apr	1100 p	2	22 1/8	- 1 3/8	1,589
Feb	1125 p	117	9/16	- 15/16	5,904
Mar	1125 c	27	139 1/2	+ 19 1/2	12,790
Mar	1125 p	18	10 7/8	- 4 7/8	14,535
Apr	1125 p	98	19	- 10	779
Feb	1150 p	556	1/2	- 2 1/2	10,189
Mar	1150 c	2	111	- 9	49,994
Mar	1150 p	2,925	11 1/2	- 9 7/8	15,149
Apr	1150 p	1,161	24	- 9 5/8	5,923
Feb	1175 c	1	70	+ 20	1,559
Feb	1175 p	735	1 15/16	- 4 1/16	6,391
Mar	1175 c	4	92	+ 14	13,804
Mar	1175 p	431	16	- 10	16,021
Feb	1180 p	161	1 1/2	- 4 5/8	5,568
Feb	1185 p	104	1 1/2	- 5 3/8	2,456
Feb	1190 p	361	2	- 8	1,539
Mar	1190 p	100	19	- 14 1/2	1,326
Feb	1200 c	74	52	+ 17 1/2	3,241
Feb	1200 p	1,236	2 1/8	- 8 3/8	11,403
Mar	1200 c	49	77 1/2	+ 18	14,882
Feb	1265 c	224	8 3/4	+ 4 5/8	2,760
Mar	1265 c	10	23 1/8	- 11 7/8	2,582
Mar	1265 p	4	45	- 18	2,555
Feb	1270 c	115	7 1/2	+ 5 7/16	2,211
Feb	1270 p	100	28	- 27	543
Mar	1270 c	9	32	+ 8 3/4	1,723
Mar	1270 p	211	45	- 26	2,316
Feb	1275 c	4,988	5 1/8	+ 3 5/8	10,845
Feb	1275 p	185	25 3/4	- 29 1/4	5,565
Mar	1275 c	478	29 1/2	+ 12	15,957
Mar	1275 p	1	53	- 16	11,775
Apr	1275 p	7	62	- 17	540
Feb	1280 c	30	2 1/8	+ 1 1/16	174
Feb	1280 p	3	57 1/2	- 5 1/2	38
Mar	1280 c	201	24 1/2	+ 6 1/2	533
Feb	1290 c	92	1 1/4	+ 3/4	224
Mar	1290 c	3	21	- 1/8	11
Feb	1295 c	243	1 1/2	+ 1 1/16	2,461
Feb	1295 p	1	53	- 25	1,296
Feb	1300 c	1,379	1 1/8	+ 7/8	10,890
Feb	1300 p	53	48	- 29	1,541
Mar	1300 c	908	20	+ 9	11,556
Mar	1300 p	15	58 1/2	- 29 1/2	8,800
Apr	1300 c	2	34	+ 8 3/4	1,128
Feb	1310 c	272	1/2	...	922
Feb	1325 c	170	1/4	+ 3/16	3,902
Mar	1325 c	1,258	9 1/2	+ 3 1/2	9,070
Mar	1325 p	6	77	- 6	39
Apr	1325 c	225	17 3/4	- 1/4	1,455
Feb	1350 c	1,433	1/16	- 1/16	9,979
Feb	1350 p	1	105 1/2	- 23 1/2	2,071
Mar	1350 c	1,541	6	+ 3	23,915
Mar	1350 p	26	99	- 36	5,545
Mar	1375 c	1,489	2 3/4	+ 1 1/4	7,382
Mar	1375 p	25	123	- 21	49
Apr	1375 c	2	9	+ 1 1/2	554
Mar	1400 c	10	1 1/4	+ 3/4	7,028
Apr	1425 c	200	2 3/4	- 1/8	2,212
Mar	1450 c	20	5/16	- 1/16	6,457
Mar	1500 p	250	254	- 20	5,847

Call Vol. ......33,083 Open Int. ...883,273
Put Vol. ......42,280 Open Int..1,125,719

DJ INDUS AVG(DJX)

Jun	72 p	500	1 1/16	- 1/2	799
Mar	80 p	14	3/8	- 1/2	10,847
Mar	84 c	2	10 1/2	+ 1 3/4	446
Mar	84 p	20	13/16	- 7/16	6,763
Feb	85 p	5	1/8	- 1/16	432
Feb	86 p	20	1/16	- 3/16	455
Mar	86 p	10	1	- 5/8	557
Feb	88 c	80	4 7/8	+ 7/8	191
Mar	88 p	39	1 1/4	- 7/8	8,719
Jun	88 p	21	4	- 7/8	2,739
Feb	89 c	9	4 5/8	+ 1 13/16	131
Feb	89 p	147	1/4	- 7/16	813
Mar	89 p	235	1 5/8	- 5/8	462
Feb	90 c	11	4	+ 1 3/16	1,320
Feb	90 p	500	3/16	- 9/16	3,117
Mar	90 c	1	5 1/2	- 1	4,833
Mar	90 p	45	1 11/16	- 15/16	5,195
Feb	91 c	178	3 1/4	+ 1 1/2	831
Feb	91 p	23	1/2	- 11/16	2,656
Mar	91 p	22	2 9/16	- 9/16	623
Feb	92 c	158	2 5/16	+ 1 3/8	1,079
Feb	92 p	249	1/2	- 1 1/16	1,475
Mar	92 c	79	4	+ 3/8	2,768
Mar	92 p	99	2 1/4	- 1 1/8	4,942
Jun	92 p	519	4 3/4	- 1 3/8	3,767
Feb	93 c	125	1 1/2	+ 3/4	1,766
Feb	93 p	251	3/4	- 1 3/8	1,864
Mar	93 c	15	3 1/2	+ 7/8	3,246
Mar	93 p	63	2 1/2	- 1 1/4	3,750
Feb	94 c	92	15/16	+ 9/16	877
Feb	94 p	147	1 1/8	- 1 7/8	1,316
Mar	94 c	17	2 7/16	+ 5/16	6,196
Mar	94 p	24	3 1/8	- 1 1/8	6,574
Feb	95 c	487	1/4	+ 1/16	2,477
Feb	95 p	132	2	- 1 3/4	2,352
Mar	95 c	10	2 1/4	+ 1/2	7,183
Mar	95 p	5	4	- 1	7,262
Feb	96 c	25	1/4	+ 1/8	4,077
Feb	96 p	67	2 5/8	- 1 7/8	1,879
Mar	96 c	17	1 7/8	+ 11/16	8,334
Mar	96 p	21	4	- 1 7/8	1,040
Jun	96 c	25	4 7/8	+ 3/8	87
Jun	96 p	24	6 1/2	- 1 1/4	826
Sep	96 p	1	6	- 1/8	84
Feb	97 c	125	1/16	...	1,470
Feb	97 p	20	4 1/2	...	810
Mar	97 p	4	4 3/8	- 2 3/8	37
Feb	98 p	21	4 1/4	- 2 1/2	177
Mar	98 c	5	1 1/8	- 1/8	72
Mar	99 p	14	6	- 1 3/8	271
Feb	100 c	100	1/16	...	2,105
Mar	100 p	15	7 1/2	- 1 1/4	6,772
Feb	104 p	10	11	- 1/4	211
Sep	104 c	22	3 1/2	- 1/4	305
Sep	104 p	5	12 5/8	...	...

Call Vol. ....1,656 Open Int. ...101,179
Put Vol. ....3,342 Open Int. ...160,746

NASDAQ-100(NDX)

Mar	1060 c	4	1/4	- 1 7/16	26
Mar	1100 p	40	3/8	- 1/8	324
Mar	1380 p	1	2 1/8	- 71 7/8	3
Mar	1500 p	9	7	- 2 1/4	41
Mar	1580 p	4	9 1/2	- 6 3/4	60
Feb	1660 p	70	11/16	- 1 5/16	585
Mar	1700 p	19	14 7/8	- 15 1/8	608
Mar	1720 p	3	18 1/4	- 9 1/4	81
Feb	1740 c	5	273	- 62 1/2	7
Feb	1740 p	102	1 1/2	- 4 1/4	469
Mar	1760 p	1	24	- 21	591
Feb	1800 p	47	1 13/16	- 7 1/16	559
Mar	1800 p	27	34	- 19	245
Feb	1820 c	20	194	+ 48	1
Feb	1820 p	15	4 7/8	- 7 1/8	227
Mar	1820 p	3	37	- 15 1/4	85
Feb	1840 p	201	5 1/8	- 9 1/8	195
Mar	1840 p	1	41 1/2	- 23 1/2	209
Feb	1860 c	12	170	+ 17	110
Feb	1860 p	25	8	- 10 1/2	526
Feb	1880 c	25	100 1/4	+ 19 3/8	106
Feb	1880 p	56	6 7/8	- 21 1/8	456
Mar	1880 p	104	47 3/4	- 22 1/8	55
Feb	1900 c	1	144	+ 74	689
Feb	1900 p	167	7	- 23 1/2	165
Mar	1900 p	2	57	- 20	171
Feb	1920 c	11	108	+ 43	106
Feb	1920 p	90	8 3/4	- 28 1/4	389
Mar	1920 p	560	75	- 16 5/8	282
Feb	1940 c	19	108 1/2	+ 59 1/2	266
Feb	1940 p	68	11 7/8	- 35 1/8	495
Mar	1940 c	2	150 7/8	- 8 1/2	41
Mar	1940 p	3	74	- 26	163
Feb	1960 c	18	89 1/8	+ 51 1/8	831
Feb	1960 p	245	17 1/4	- 35 3/4	2,869
Mar	1960 p	260	71 1/4	- 41 3/4	87
Feb	1980 c	26	70	+ 37	961
Feb	1980 p	680	20	- 44 1/4	960
Mar	1980 c	184	145	- 24 1/2	251
Mar	1980 p	151	70	- 45 1/4	176
Feb	2020 c	357	56 1/4	+ 39 1/8	1,230
Feb	2020 p	447	31	- 66 5/8	248
Mar	2020 c	6	114	- 11	104
Mar	2020 p	109		...	250
Feb	2040 c	2,037	38 3/4	+ 25 3/8	1,375
Feb	2040 p	4	39	- 75 1/2	43
Mar	2040 c	20	108	+ 41	18
Mar	2040 p	10	94 1/2	- 62 1/2	29
Feb	2060 c	194	30	+ 21 3/8	542
Mar	2060 c	93	90 1/2	+ 35 1/2	121
Feb	2080 c	67	23	+ 16	399
Mar	2080 c	4	60	- 19 5/8	11
Feb	2100 c	96	18 1/4	+ 14 3/8	876
Feb	2100 p	20	112 7/8	- 52 1/8	455
Mar	2100 c	21	64 3/4	+ 17 5/8	300
Mar	2100 p	10	135 1/2	- 59 1/2	230
Feb	2120 c	802	11 1/8	+ 8 1/4	940
Feb	2140 c	472	7 1/2	+ 4 11/16	163
Feb	2160 c	157	5 5/8	+ 4 1/8	448
Mar	2160 c	204	42	+ 7	256
Feb	2180 c	18	2	+ 1	418
Mar	2180 p	1	190	...	...
Feb	2200 c	397	2 1/8	+ 1 5/8	493
Mar	2200 c	8	34 3/8	+ 11 1/8	119
Feb	2220 c	106	1 3/16	+ 11/16	242
Feb	2240 c	55	5/16	- 2 3/16	184
Feb	2280 c	15	1/8	- 1/4	245
Mar	2280 c	105	18 1/4	+ 3	506

Call Vol. ......5,586 Open Int......14,700
Put Vol. ....3,774 Open Int......19,969

Source: *Wall Street Journal,* 12 February 1999.

buys the March put on the Canadian dollar with an exercise price of USD 0.675/CAD for a total price of USD 360.00 (= 50,000 × 0.0072). This option would allow the holder to sell CAD 50,000 in March for a total price of USD 33,750 (= 50,000 × 0.675). Obviously, our investor will only exercise the contract if the spot USD/CAD price prevailing in March is less than 0.675 (i.e., if the Canadian dollar weakened relative to the U.S. currency).

FIGURE 24.3 FOREIGN CURRENCY OPTION QUOTATIONS

OPTIONS
PHILADELPHIA EXCHANGE

		Calls Vol.	Calls Last	Puts Vol.	Puts Last
Euro					113.45
62,500 Euro-cents per unit.					
112	Feb	...	0.01	1000	0.10
112	Mar	...	0.01	4	0.50
114	Feb	...	0.01	3	1.17
116	Feb	...	...	1	2.94
116	Mar	4	0.20	...	...
Australian Dollar					64.62
50,000 Australian Dollars-cents per unit.					
62½	Mar	...	0.01	60	0.21
50,000 Australian Dollars-cents per unit.					
62	Feb	20	3.00	...	...
British Pound					162.94
31,250 Brit. Pounds-cents per unit.					
160	Jun	...	0.01	2	1.80
162	Jun	20	3.00	105	2.70
164	Mar	...	...	15	2.31
Canadian Dollar					67.07
50,000 Canadian Dollars-cents per unit.					
67½	Feb	...	0.01	60	0.40
67½	Mar	...	...	60	0.72
68	Mar	10	0.25	...	...
68	Jun	4	0.80	...	...
German Mark					57.99
62,500 German Marks-cents per unit.					
56	Mar	...	0.01	85	0.07
Japanese Yen					87.50
6,250,000J.Yen-100ths of a cent per unit.					
72	Feb	5	15.53	...	0.01
77	Mar	5	10.70	...	...
80	Jun	...	0.01	23	0.93
84½	Mar	...	0.01	4	0.40
86½	Feb	5	1.33	10	0.21
86½	Mar	5	2.40	...	...
89	Jun	...	0.01	1	3.60
6,250,000J.Yen-European Style.					
87	Feb	...	0.01	60	0.30
89	Feb	...	0.01	30	1.76
Swiss Franc					71.16
62,500 Swiss Francs-European Style.					
67	Feb	32	4.00	...	0.01
69	Feb	32	1.96	...	...
69	Mar	32	2.25	...	...
69½	Mar	...	0.01	30	0.31
70	Mar	16	1.48	48	0.44
70½	Feb	30	0.34	60	0.15
71	Feb	25	0.14	37	0.30
72	Feb	...	...	30	1.10
72	Mar	48	0.52	16	1.45
62,500 Swiss Francs-cents per unit.					
72	Jun	...	0.01	16	2.08
73	Jun	9	0.92	4	2.57
75	Jun	2	0.53	...	...

Call Vol ...... 1,399 Open Int ... 30,373
Put Vol .... 3,909 Open Int ... 42,461

Key Currency Cross Rates
Late New York Trading Feb 11, 1999

	Dollar	Euro	Pound	SFranc	Guilder	Peso	Yen	Lira	D-Mark	FFranc	CdnDlr
Canada	1.4926	1.6763	2.4222	1.0463	.76069	.14936	.01303	.00087	.85710	.25556	....
France	5.8406	6.5596	9.4781	4.0944	2.9766	.58447	.05099	.00339	3.3539	....	3.9130
Germany	1.7415	1.9558	2.8260	1.2208	.88752	.17427	.01520	.00101	....	.29816	1.1667
Italy	1724.0	1936.3	2797.8	1208.6	878.64	172.52	15.051	....	990.0	295.18	1155.1
Japan	114.55	128.65	185.89	80.301	58.379	11.463	....	.06644	65.778	19.613	76.745
Mexico	9.9930	11.223	16.217	7.0053	5.0928	....	.08724	.00580	5.7383	1.7110	6.6950
Netherlands ..	1.9622	2.2037	3.1842	1.3755	....	.19635	.01713	.00114	1.1267	.33595	1.3146
Switzerland ...	1.4265	1.6021	2.3149	....	.72700	.14275	.01245	.00083	.81914	.24424	.95571
U.K.	.61622	.69208	...	.43198	.31405	.06167	.00538	.00036	.35385	.10551	.41285
Euro	.89039	....	1.4449	.62418	.45378	.08910	.00777	.00052	.51129	.15245	.59654
U.S.	....	1.1231	1.6228	.70102	.50964	.10007	.00873	.00058	.57423	.17122	.66997

Source: Telerate

Source: *Wall Street Journal,* 12 February 1999.

Finally, because the spot rate is USD 0.66997/CAD, this option is in the money—that is, the contract price of 0.0072 consists of 0.00503 (= 0.675 − 0.66997) of intrinsic value and 0.00217 of time premium.

OPTIONS ON FUTURES CONTRACTS Although they have existed for decades in the OTC markets, options on futures contracts have only been exchange-traded since 1982. Also known as futures options, they give the holder the right, but not the obligation, to enter into a futures contract on an underlying security or commodity at a later date and at a predetermined price. Purchasing a call on a futures allows for the acquisition of a long position in the futures market, while exercising a put would create a short futures position. On the other hand, the seller of the call would be obligated to enter into the short side of the futures contract if the option holder decided to exercise the contract, while the seller of the put might be forced into a long futures position. Figure 24.4 lists quotations for options based on a wide variety of underlying assets, including agricultural, metal, and energy commodities; Treasury bonds and notes; foreign currencies; and stock indexes. Consistent with the trading patterns for the futures contracts we examined earlier, futures options on financial assets represent the largest part of the market.

FIGURE 24.4 FUTURES OPTION QUOTATIONS

AGRICULTURAL

CORN (CBT)
5,000 bu.; cents per bu.

Strike	Calls-Settle			Puts-Settle		
Price	Mar	May	Jly	Mar	May	Jly
200	16	23	....	⅛	⅛	2
210	6¼	14¾	22⅛	⅜	2½	4⅞
220	1¼	8½	16⅛	5⅜	6	8¼
230	¼	5	11⅝	14¼	12¼	13⅝
240	⅛	2¾	8½	24	19¾	20¼
250	⅛	1½	6½	34	28½	28

Est vol 10,000 Wd 5,556 calls 6,211 puts
Op int Wed 152,897 calls 119,332 puts

SOYBEANS (CBT)
5,000 bu.; cents per bu.

Strike	Calls-Settle			Puts-Settle		
Price	Mar	May	Jly	Mar	May	Jly
450	45¼	51½	59½	⅛	1¾	3½
475	20⅝	31	....	⅜	6¼	8½
500	2¾	15¾	25½	7½	15½	18⅞
525	¼	7½	15½	30	32	34
550	....	3⅜	9⅝	54¾	52½	52¼
575	⅛	1⅜	5¾	79¾	76¼	73

Est vol 15,000 Wd 9,154 calls 6,595 puts
Op int Wed 154,215 calls 85,593 puts

SOYBEAN MEAL (CBT)
100 tons; $ per ton

Strike	Calls-Settle			Puts-Settle		
Price	Mar	May	Jly	Mar	May	Jly
120	....	....	....	.05	1.55	2.00
125	6.10	7.60	....	.30	2.60	3.50
130	1.85	4.75	8.00	1.25	4.60	5.15
135	.40	2.85	5.75	4.50	7.80	7.75
140	.10	1.75	4.00	9.30	11.60	11.10
145	.05	1.25	3.00	14.20	16.10	15.00

Est vol 2,000 Wd 1,166 calls 477 puts
Op int Wed 52,354 calls 34,963 puts

SOYBEAN OIL (CBT)
60,000 lbs.; cents per lb.

Strike	Calls-Settle			Puts-Settle		
Price	Mar	May	Jly	Mar	May	Jly
2000	....	1.200	1.500	....	.320	.400
2050	.300	....	....	....	.500	....
2100	.100	.630	.930	.500	.740	.820
2150	.050	.460	....	.900	1.070	1.120
2200	.040	.330	.580	1.400	1.430	1.440
2250	.020	.230	.450	1.900	1.840	1.810

Est vol 8,000 Wd 3,117 calls 1,070 puts
Op int Wed 48,644 calls 25,537 puts

WHEAT (CBT)
5,000 bu.; cents per bu.

Strike	Calls-Settle			Puts-Settle		
Price	Mar	May	Jly	Mar	May	Jly
250	13	....	37½	⅜	3¼	3¼
260	5	19¼	30	2½	6	7½
270	1½	13½	24	9¼	10¼	11
280	⅝	9¼	19	17¾	15	16
290	¼	6	14¾	27½	22¼	21¼
300	⅛	4¼	11	37¼	31	27½

Est vol 4,000 Wd 2,893 calls 4,523 puts
Op int Wed 96,613 calls 68,058 puts

INDEX

DJ INDUSTRIAL AVG (CBOT)
$100 times premium

Strike	Calls-Settle			Puts-Settle		
Price	Feb	Mar	Apr	Feb	Mar	Apr
92	26.20	43.70	61.95	3.60	21.05	31.70
93	18.50	37.10	55.30	5.80	24.45	35.00
94	12.00	30.70	48.90	14.20	28.25	38.60
95	6.95	25.35	43.10	20.70	32.60	42.70
96	3.45	19.95	37.60	28.65	37.50	47.15
97	1.40	15.80	32.50	37.70	43.00	52.00

Est vol 500 Wd 179 calls 300 puts
Op int Wed 7,019 calls 11,035 puts

S&P 500 STOCK INDEX (CME)
$250 times premium

Strike	Calls-Settle			Puts-Settle		
Price	Feb	Mar	Apr	Feb	Mar	Apr
1255	19.70	42.80	....	12.20	35.30	....
1260	16.60	39.90	64.60	14.10	39.50	50.20
1265	13.80	37.00	....	16.30	41.80	....
1270	11.30	34.30	58.30	18.80	44.00	54.00
1275	9.10	31.60	55.00	21.60	46.50	56.00
1280	7.20	29.10	52.20	24.70	49.00	57.80

Est vol 14,941 Wd 6,224 calls 6,493 puts
Op int Wed 89,441 calls 161,934 puts

OIL

CRUDE OIL (NYM)
1,000 bbls.; $ per bbl.

Strike	Calls-Settle			Puts-Settle		
Price	Mar	Apr	May	Mar	Apr	May
1100	.88	1.18	1.44	.03	.25	.39
1150	.45	.84	1.13	.10	.41	.57
1200	.19	.57	.86	.34	.64	.80
1250	.06	.39	.66	.71	.96	1.10
1300	.03	.24	.49	1.18	1.31	1.42
1350	.02	.15	.36	1.67	1.71	1.79

Est vol 14,654 Wd 15,453 calls 11,-
947 puts
Op int Wed 284,777 calls 216,915 puts

HEATING OIL No.2 (NYM)
42,000 gal.; $ per gal.

Strike	Calls-Settle			Puts-Settle		
Price	Mar	Apr	May	Mar	Apr	May
28	....	....	....	.0015	.0047	....
29	....	....	....	....	.0070	.0094
30	.0088	....	....	.0049	.0107	.0130
31	.0052	.0151	....	.0113	.0146	.0175
32	.0022	.0111	.0195	.0183	.0206	.0225
33	.0015	.0060	.0150	.0276	.0354	.0279

Est vol 2,996 Wd 604 calls 139 puts
Op int Wed 42,034 calls 19,212 puts

GASOLINE-Unlead (NYM)
42,000 gal.; $ per gal.

Strike	Calls-Settle			Puts-Settle		
Price	Mar	Apr	May	Mar	Apr	May
31	....	....	....	....	....	....
32	.0170	....	....	.0026	.0018	....
33	.0099	....	....	.0055	....	....
34	.0050	....	....	.0106	.0065	....
35	.0027	....	....	.0183	....	....
36	.0013	....	....	.0269	.0135	.0130

Est vol 1,646 Wd 1,038 calls 134 puts
Op int Wed 22,616 calls 14,485 puts

NATURAL GAS (NYM)
10,000 MMBtu.; $ per MMBtu.

Strike	Calls-Settle			Puts-Settle		
Price	Mar	Apr	May	Mar	Apr	May
175	.118	....	....	.031	.058	.075
180	.086	.144	.187	.049	.078	.097
185	.057	.114	.160	.073	.101	.119
190	.038	.092	.135	.101	.126	.145
195	.025	.074	.114	.138	.158	.173
200	.017	.059	.096	.180	.192	.204

Est vol 21,752 Wd 4,523 calls 5,795 puts
Op int Wed 166,610 calls 139,795 puts

CURRENCY

DEUTSCHEMARK (CME)
125,000 marks; cents per mark

Strike	Calls-Settle			Puts-Settle		
Price	Mar	Apr	May	Mar	Apr	May
5650	....	....	....	0.15	....	....
5700	0.77	....	....	0.28	0.46	....
5750	0.48	....	....	0.49	....	....
5800	0.28	0.66	....	0.79	0.89	....
5850	....	....	....	....	1.21	....
5900	....	0.34	....	....	....	....

Est vol 402 Wed 313 calls 223 puts
Op int Wed 9,620 calls 7,136 puts

CANADIAN DOLLAR (CME)
100,000 Can.$, cents per Can.$

Strike	Calls-Settle			Puts-Settle		
Price	Mar	Apr	May	Mar	Apr	May
6600	1.15	....	....	0.19	0.43	....
6650	0.79	....	....	0.33	0.60	....
6700	0.50	....	....	0.54	....	....
6750	0.30	....	....	0.84	....	....
6800	0.17	0.42	....	1.21	....	....
6850	0.09	....	....	1.63	....	....

Est vol 635 Wed 497 calls 43 puts
Op int Wed 11,189 calls 7,747 puts

BRITISH POUND (CME)
62,500 pounds; cents per pound

Strike	Calls-Settle			Puts-Settle		
Price	Mar	Apr	May	Mar	Apr	May
1600	2.56	....	....	0.46	1.10	....
1610	1.82	....	....	0.72	1.50	....
1620	1.20	1.98	....	1.10	1.96	....
1630	0.76	....	....	1.66	....	....
1640	0.48	1.10	....	2.38	....	....
1650	0.28	....	....	3.18	....	....

Est vol 475 Wed 128 calls 89 puts
Op int Wed 11,306 calls 7,747 puts

METALS

COPPER (CMX)
25,000 lbs.; cents per lb.

Strike	Calls-Settle			Puts-Settle		
Price	Mar	Apr	May	Mar	Apr	May
62	4.35	5.25	6.05	.10	.65	1.10
64	2.65	3.80	4.70	.40	1.20	1.75
66	1.35	2.65	3.55	1.10	2.00	2.50
68	.55	1.75	2.60	2.30	3.05	3.60
70	.20	1.05	1.85	3.90	4.40	4.85
72	.05	.65	1.30	5.80	5.95	6.25

Est vol 600 Wd 354 calls 90 puts
Op int Wed 21,966 calls 5,183 puts

GOLD (CMX)
100 troy ounces; $ per troy ounce

Strike	Calls-Settle			Puts-Settle		
Price	Mar	Apr	Jun	Mar	Apr	Jun
280	9.40	10.00	13.70	.10	1.00	2.10
285	4.40	5.90	9.50	.10	1.60	3.60
290	.50	2.90	7.00	1.30	3.60	5.80
295	.10	1.30	4.40	5.80	7.40	8.20
300	.10	.70	3.30	10.80	12.10	12.10
305	.10	.50	2.10	15.70	16.20	15.80

Est vol 6,200 Wd 2,495 calls 4,046 puts
Op int Wed 323,419 calls 125,295 puts

SILVER (CMX)
5,000 troy ounces; cts per troy ounce

Strike	Calls-Settle			Puts-Settle		
Price	Mar	Apr	May	Mar	Apr	May
500	56.5	60.0	63.0	.1	2.0	4.8
525	31.7	38.0	43.5	.2	5.4	9.4
550	8.0	20.7	27.0	1.5	12.7	19.0
575	.7	11.0	18.5	19.0	27.5	34.5
600	.1	6.2	12.5	43.5	47.5	53.0
625	.1	4.0	8.5	68.5	70.0	74.5

Est vol 1,800 Wd 1,476 calls 1,074 puts
Op int Wed 63,657 calls 22,939 puts

INTEREST RATE

T-BONDS (CBT)
$100,000; points and 64ths of 100%

Strike	Calls-Settle			Puts-Settle		
Price	Mar	Jun	Sep	Mar	Jun	Sep
123	1-54	....	....	0-08	....	....
124	1-03	2-30	3-08	0-22	2-11	3-18
125	0-32	....	....	0-50	....	....
126	0-13	1-37	2-19	1-30	3-18	4-27
127	0-04	....	....	2-22	....	....
128	0-01	0-62	1-41	3-19	4-41	5-44

Est. vol. 95,000;
Wd vol. 55,415 calls; 47,150 puts
Op. int. Wed 622,414 calls; 594,256 puts

T-NOTES (CBT)
$100,000; points and 64ths of 100%

Strike	Calls-Settle			Puts-Settle		
Price	Mar	Jun	Sep	Mar	Jun	Sep
115	2-13	....	....	0-01	0-37	....
116	1-15	2-11	....	0-03	0-56	....
117	0-28	1-36	1-53	0-16	1-16	2-03
118	0-05	1-06	....	0-57	1-50	....
119	0-01	0-47	1-05	1-53	2-26	....
120	0-01	0-31	....	2-52	3-09	....

Est vol 44,000 Wd 24,977 calls 17,-
165 puts
Op int Wed 306,723 calls 270,638 puts

5 YR TREAS NOTES (CBT)
$100,000; points and 64ths of 100%

Strike	Calls-Settle			Puts-Settle		
Price	Mar	Jun	Sep	Mar	Jun	Sep
11100	....	....	....	0-02	0-19	....
11150	0-38	....	....	0-04	0-26	....
11200	0-15	....	....	0-13	0-36	....
11250	0-05	....	....	0-35	0-48	....
11300	0-01	0-53	....	0-63	0-63	....
11350	0-01	0-39	....	1-31	1-17	....

Est vol 4,400 Wd 4,965 calls 8,342 puts
Op int Wed 119,208 calls 89,346 puts

EURODOLLAR (CME)
$ million; pts. of 100%

Strike	Calls-Settle			Puts-Settle		
Price	Feb	Mar	Apr	Feb	Mar	Apr
9450	....	7.35	....	....	.00	.10
9475	2.35	4.85	....	.00	.05	.25
9500	.05	2.40	.70	.20	.40	.95
9525	.00	.25	.25	2.65	2.70	3.00
9550	.00	.05	.10	....	5.15	....
9575	....	.00	....	....	7.65	....

Est. vol. 62,762;
Wd vol. 32,238 calls; 32,983 puts
Op. int. Wed 1,537,526 calls; 1,081,-
297 puts

Source: *Wall Street Journal,* 12 February 1999.

To understand how these contracts work, consider a commodity futures option. The April call option on copper with a striking price of \$0.68 per pound would cost the buyer \$0.0175 per pound of copper covered by the futures position. As each copper futures contract on the Commodity Exchange (COMEX) requires the transfer of 25,000 pounds of the metal, the total purchase price for this futures call is \$437.50 (= 25,000 × 0.0175). Also, because the April copper futures price on this day was \$0.6665, this contract was out of the money so that its per-ounce price of 1.75 cents was purely a time premium.

As with any call position, the holder will only exercise at the expiration date if the prevailing price of the underlying asset exceeds the exercise price; she will let it expire worthless otherwise. This payoff structure might fit the need of an electronic appliance manufacturer exposed to higher copper prices as a factor of production or a speculator bullish on copper prices. In this example, suppose that on the expiration date of the option, the contract price of the April copper futures has risen to \$0.71. At this point, the holder will exercise her option and assume a long position in an April futures with a contract price of \$0.68 per pound, which will require posting a margin account. Her new position will immediately be marked to market, however, and \$750 (= [0.71 − 0.68] × 25,000) will be added to her margin account. Alternatively, she may decide to unwind her "below market" futures contract immediately and take the \$750 in cash.

The primary attraction of this derivative is the leverage that it provides to an investor. In this example, the call buyer has been able to control 25,000 pounds of copper for two months for an investment of \$437.50. Had she purchased the copper, it would have cost her \$16,662.50 (= 25,000 × 0.6665), assuming that the spot and futures prices were the same on this date. Further, even if it only required a 5 percent margin, a long position in the copper futures contract would necessitate a cash outlay of \$833.13. Since leverage is the driving force behind this market, in most cases the option is set up to expire at virtually the same time as the underlying futures contract. This indicates that actually acquiring a futures position is not a primary concern of the option users.

THE FUNDAMENTALS OF OPTION VALUATION

Although we know that options can be used by investors to anticipate future levels of security prices, the key to understanding how they are valued comes from recognizing that they also are risk reduction tools. Specifically, in this section we show that an option's theoretical value depends on combining it with its underlying security to create a *synthetic risk-free portfolio.* That is, it always is theoretically possible to use the option as a perfect *hedge* against fluctuations in the value of the asset on which it is based.

Recall that this was essentially the same approach we used in Chapter 11 to establish the put-call parity relationships. The primary differences between put-call parity and what follows are twofold. First, the portfolio implied by the put-call parity transaction did not require special calibration; it simply consisted of one stock long, one put long, and one call short— a mixture that required no adjustment prior to the expiration date. However, hedging an underlying asset position's risk with a single option position—whether it is a put or a call—often involves using multiple contracts and frequent changes in the requisite number to maintain the riskless portfolio. Second, the put-call parity paradigm did not demand a forecast of the underlying asset's future price level whereas the following analysis will. Indeed, we will see that *forecasting the volatility of future asset prices* is the most important input the investor must provide in determining option values.

THE BASIC APPROACH

While the mathematics associated with option valuation can be complex, the fundamental intuition behind the process is straightforward and can be illustrated quite simply. Suppose you have just purchased a share of stock in WYZ Corp. for \$50. The stock is not expected to pay a dividend during the time you plan to hold it, and you have forecast that in one year the stock price will either rise to \$65 or fall to \$40. This can be summarized as follows:

Today	One Year
	65
50	
	40

Suppose further that you can either buy or sell a call option on WYZ stock with an exercise price of \$52.50. If this is a European-style contract that expires in exactly one year, it will have the following possible expiration date values:

Today	One Year
	max[0,65 − 52.5] = 12.50
C_0	
	max[0,40 − 52.5] = 0

Although you do not know what the call option is worth today, you know what it is worth at expiration, given your forecast of future WYZ stock prices. The dilemma is establishing what the option should sell for today (i.e., C_0).

This question can be answered in three steps. First, design a hedge portfolio consisting of one share of WYZ stock held long and some number of call options (i.e., h), so that the combined position will be riskless. The number of call options needed can be established by ensuring that the portfolio has the same value at expiration no matter which of the two forecasted stock values occurs, or:

$$65 + (h)(12.50) = 40 + (h)(0)$$

leaving:

$$h = \frac{(65 - 40)}{(0 - 12.5)} = -2.00$$

There are both *direction* and *magnitude* dimensions to this number. That is, the negative sign indicates that, in order to create the necessary negative correlation between two assets that are naturally positively correlated, call options must be *sold* to hedge a long stock position. Further, given that the range of possible expiration date option outcomes (i.e., 12.5 − 0) is only half as large as the range for WYZ stock (i.e., 65 − 40), twice as many options must be sold as there is stock in the hedge portfolio. The value h is known as the *hedge ratio.*[4] Thus, the risk-free hedge portfolio can be created by purchasing one share of stock and selling two call options.

The second step in the option valuation process assumes capital markets that are free from arbitrage. Specifically, suppose no arbitrage possibilities exist in these markets so that

[4]In some valuation models (e.g.. Black-Scholes), the hedge ratio is expressed as the option's potential volatility divided by that for the stock. In this example, that would be $(0 - 12.5) \div (65 - 40) = -0.5$, meaning that the option is half as volatile in dollar terms as the share of stock. Of course, this alternative calculation is just the reciprocal of the value of $h = -2.00$.

all riskless investments are priced to earn the risk-free rate over the time until expiration. That is, the hedge portfolio costing $[50 − (2)($C_0$)] today would "grow" to the certain value of $40 by the following formula:

$$[50 - (2.00)(C_0)](1 + RFR)^T = 40$$

where:

RFR = the annualized risk-free rate
T = the time to expiration (i.e., one year)

Two unknown values exist in this formula: C_0 and RFR. Finding a suitable estimate for RFR seldom is a problem because the investor can use as a proxy the yield-to-maturity on a U.S. Treasury security of appropriate length. For example, if the one-year T-bill yield is 8 percent, the formula for C_0 can be solved as follows:

$$C_0 = \frac{50 - 40/1.08}{2.00} = \$6.48$$

This bit of algebraic manipulation is the third and final step in establishing the call's fair market value. That is, $6.48 represents the fundamental value of a one-year call option on WYZ stock, given both the prevailing market prices for two other securities (i.e., stock and T-bills) and the investor's forecast of future share values. Of course, since the security prices are observable, the investor's share value forecast becomes the critical element in determining if this value is a reasonable estimate. Finally, since the call option is currently out of the money, this amount is purely a time premium.

Improving Forecast Accuracy

Because it is unrealistic to assume only two possible outcomes for future WYZ share prices, the quality of the preceding valuation is highly suspect. To improve the accuracy of this process, the expiration date forecast of stock prices can be expanded to allow for numerous possibilities. To see the consequences of this expansion in the simplest terms possible, consider a revised forecast that includes only one additional potential price falling between the previous extreme values:

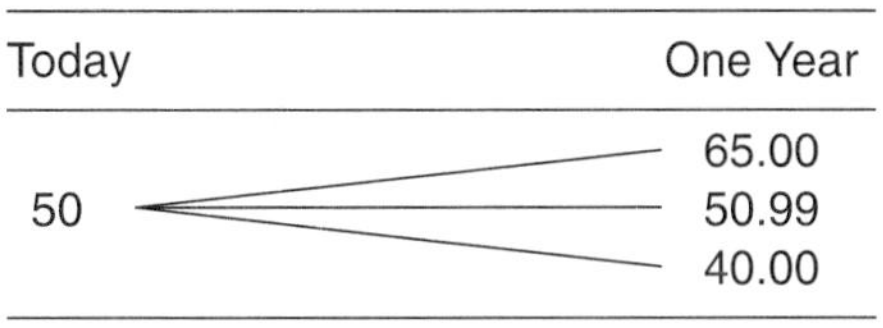
Today
One Year
50
65.00
50.99
40.00

Although the three-step riskless hedge approach to calculating C_0 is still conceptually valid, the exact methodology must be modified because it is now impossible to calculate a hedge ratio that simultaneously accounts for all three date T possibilities. That is, there will be several different hedge ratios defined by each distinct pair of future share prices, which, in turn, means that it is impossible for the preceding valuation process to consider all three possible stock outcomes at once.

The solution to this problem involves dividing the time to expiration into as many *subintervals* as necessary so that at any point in time the subsequent price can only move up or down. In this example, only one additional subinterval is needed. Figure 24.5 shows how the WYZ stock price forecast might be embellished in this manner. This illustration, which is sometimes called a *stock price tree,* indicates that before the current stock price can

FIGURE 24.5 **FORECASTED STOCK PRICE TREE (THREE TERMINAL OUTCOMES)**

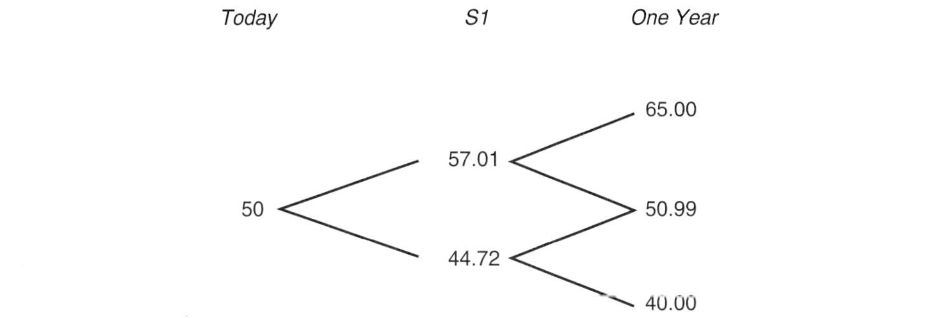
Today
S1
One Year
65.00
57.01
50
50.99
44.72
40.00

reach, say, \$65 in one year, it must first move up to \$57.01 in subperiod S1 before moving up a second time to its final value of \$65. Similarly, the lower extreme of \$40 can only be reached by two consecutive "down" price changes. On the other hand, there are two different paths to the terminal outcome in the middle: one "up" followed by one "down" or a down movement followed by an up movement both reach \$50.99.

Once the investor fills in all the details in this price tree, the call option's value can be solved by working backward on each pair of possible outcomes from the future. If, for instance, one up movement left the price of WYZ stock at \$57.01, a price change over the remaining subperiod could be characterized as:

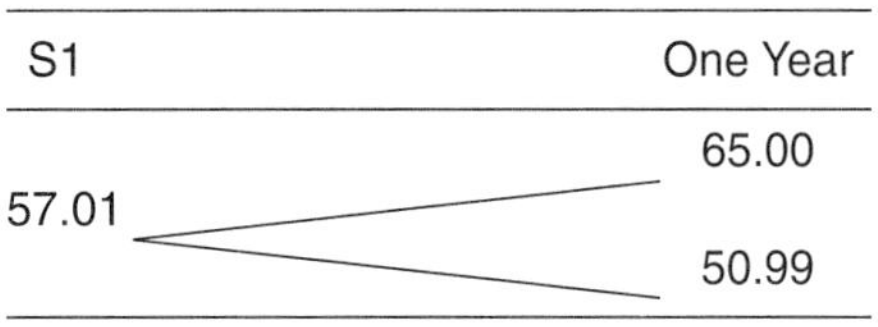
S1
One Year
65.00
57.01
50.99

The change in the value of the call option from this uppermost state of subinterval S1 (i.e., C_{11}) can then be shown as:

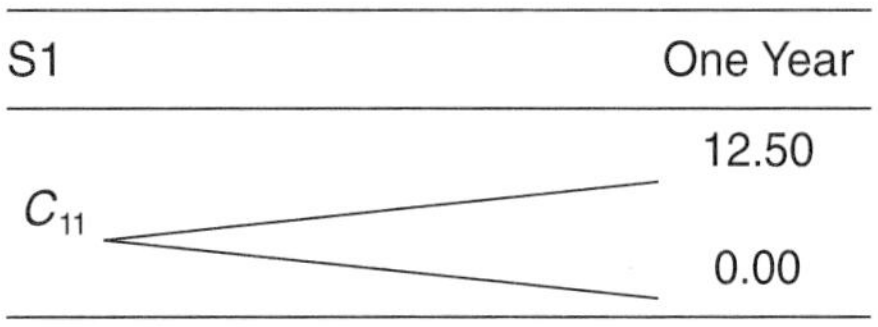
S1
One Year
12.50
C11
0.00

With $X = 52.50$, the call option would be in the money at expiration only if WYZ stock moves up in price again. This suggests a hedge ratio of:

$$h = \frac{(65.00 - 50.99)}{(0.00 - 12.50)} = -1.12$$

meaning that the riskless hedge portfolio at this point would contain one share of stock long and 1.12 calls short. The intermediate option value is then found by solving:

$$[57.01 - (1.12)(C_{11})](1.08)^{0.5} = [65 - (1.12)(12.50)] = 50.99$$

or:

$$C_{11} = \frac{57.01 - 50.99/1.0392}{1.12} = \$7.09$$

Here the factor 1.0392 [$= (1.08)^{0.5}$] is roughly one-half the annual risk-free rate (plus one) since the original holding period was divided into two subintervals of equal length (i.e., six months each).

Having established the value for C_{11}, the value for the option corresponding to an S1 share price of \$44.72 (i.e., C_{12}) can be established by the same three-step procedure with the stock and option price trees truncated as follows:

S1	One Year
	50.99
44.72	
	40.00

and:

S1	One Year
	0.00
C_{12}	
	0.00

Notice that in this case the call option is certain to be out of the money at the expiration date one subinterval hence. That is, given this forecast of potential stock prices, if the WYZ stock falls in value to \$44.72 after one subperiod, even a subsequent recovery to \$50.99 (i.e., an up move in the second subperiod) would leave the share price below the \$52.50 exercise price of the call option. Thus, it is clear that C_{12} must be \$0.00; any security that is certain to be worthless in the future must also be worthless today. Further, it should also be noted that the concept of forming a riskless hedge portfolio under such circumstances is meaningless.

These intermediate calculations have little meaning to the investor who only cares about the current value of the option. They are, however, a necessary evil as C_0 cannot be established before determining C_{11} and C_{12}. With these values in hand, the relevant part of the stock price tree is:

Today	S1
	57.01
50.00	
	44.72

with the corresponding call option tree being given by:

Today	S1
	7.09
C_0	
	0.00

FIGURE 24.6

TREE OF CALCULATED OPTION VALUES (THREE TERMINAL OUTCOMES)

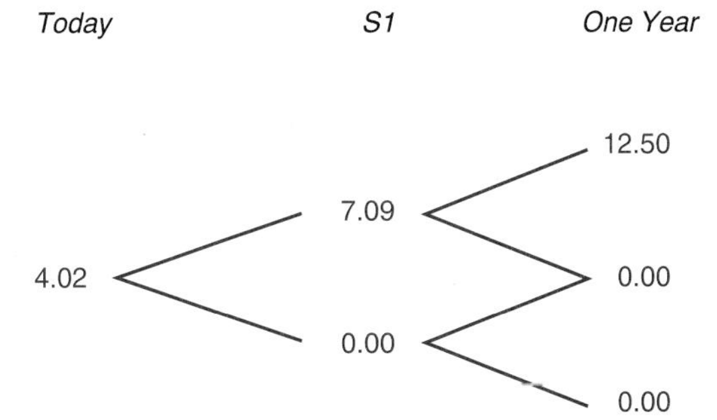

Today
S1
One Year
12.50
7.09
4.02
0.00
0.00
0.00

Once again applying the three-step valuation process, the initial (i.e., date 0) hedge ratio is:

$$h = \frac{(57.01 - 44.72)}{(0.00 - 7.09)} = -1.73$$

so that the riskless hedge portfolio at inception would short 1.73 calls for every share held long. The current option value is then found by solving:

$$[50.00 - (1.73)(C_0)](1.08)^{0.5} = [44.72 - (1.73)(0.00)] = 44.72$$

or:

$$C_{11} = \frac{50.00 - 44.72/1.0392}{1.73} = \$4.02$$

These initial, intermediate, and terminal option values are summarized in Figure 24.6.

Two interesting things resulted from this expansion from two to three possible stock price outcomes. First, notice that the addition of a third potential terminal stock price had the effect of reducing the date 0 option value from \$6.48 to \$4.02. Although this reduction was a consequence of choosing a third stock price (i.e., \$50.99) that caused the option to be out of the money—selecting a value closer to \$65.00 would have increased C_0—it does underscore once again that the option valuation process critically depends on the investor's stock price forecast. Second, notice also that the hedge ratio changes with stock price changes prior to the expiration date. That is, the composition of the riskless hedge portfolio must be rebalanced after each share price movement. For example, from the initial position of being short 1.73 calls against one share held long, an upward movement in WYZ stock from \$50.00 to \$57.01 would require buying back 0.61 (= 1.73 − 1.12) options. Thus, replicating a risk-free position with stock and call options is a *dynamic* process, a point to which we will return shortly.

This valuation process can become even more precise as more terminal share price outcomes are included in the forecast. Of course, as this happens, the number of pairwise calculations and the number of necessary subperiods will also increase. Consequently, although the three-step valuation method is quite flexible, there is a trade-off between realism and the volume of required calculations. To see how even seemingly minor expansions of the stock price forecast can dramatically increase the computational burden, consider the implications of including four potential expiration date stock prices:

FIGURE 24.7 **FORECASTED STOCK PRICE TREE (FOUR TERMINAL OUTCOMES)**

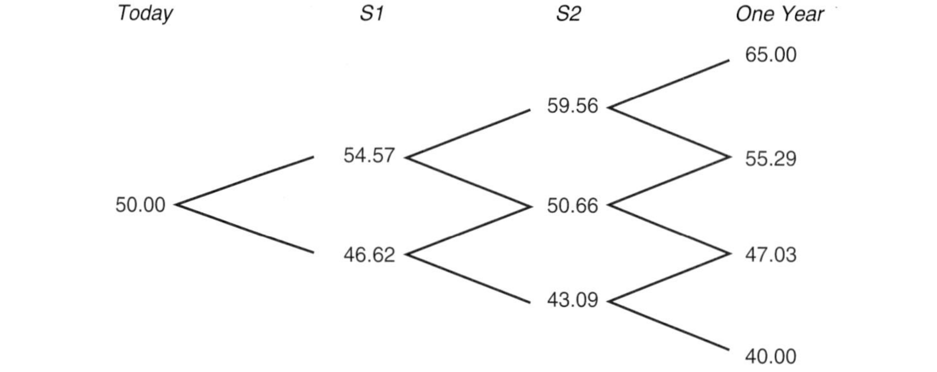
Today
S1
S2
One Year
65.00
59.56
54.57
55.29
50.00
50.66
46.62
47.03
43.09
40.00

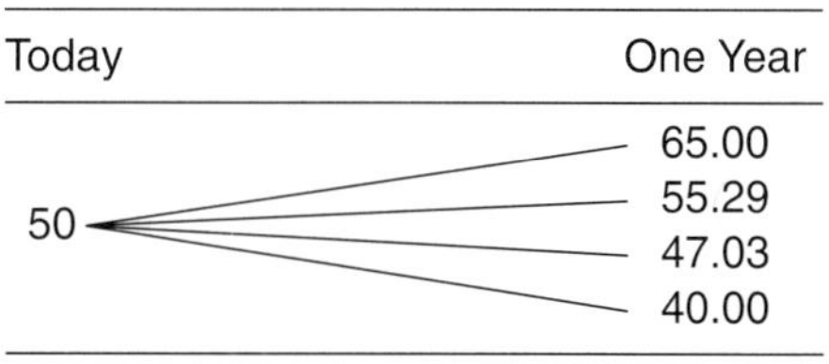
Today
One Year
50
65.00
55.29
47.03
40.00

Valuing the option in this case will require the creation of two subintervals (S1 and S2) and five intermediate stock price forecasts. These are illustrated in Figure 24.7.

In order to compute C_0, the investor must now work recursively backward through calculations for the five intermediate option values: C_{21}, C_{22}, and C_{23} subperiod S2 and C_{11} and C_{12} in subperiod 1. Of course, each of these calculations applies the same three-step riskless hedge process outlined earlier, appropriately modified for the new length of a subperiod (i.e., one-third of a year instead of six months). If, for instance, two consecutive up movements took the price of WYZ stock from \$50.00 to \$54.57 to \$59.56, a price change over the remaining subperiod could be characterized as:

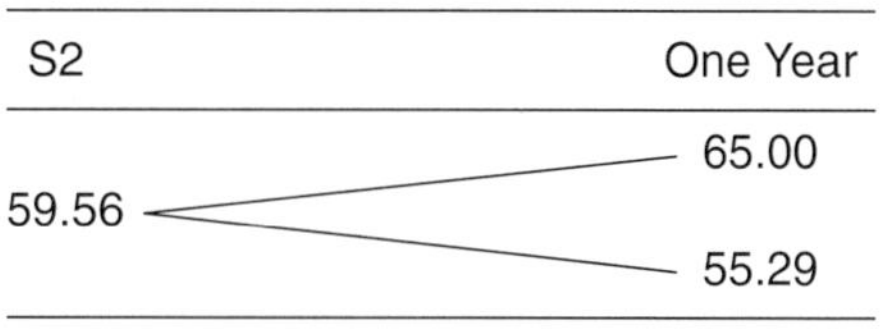
S2
One Year
59.56
65.00
55.29

The change in the value of the call option from this uppermost state of subinterval S2 (i.e., C_{21}) can then be shown as:

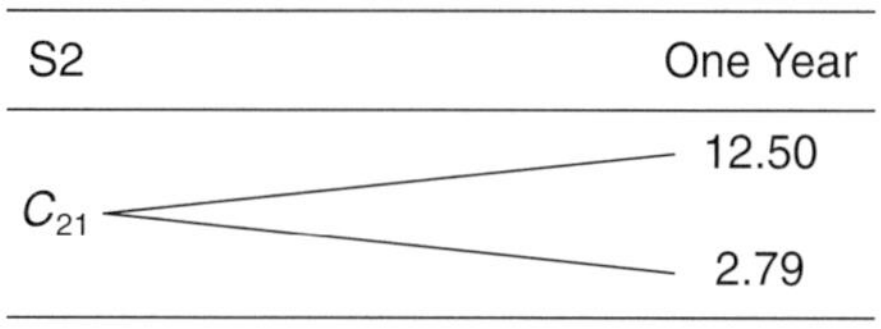
S2
One Year
C21
12.50
2.79

Given its exercise price of \$52.50, the call option would be certain to be in the money for both expiration date stock values. This suggests a hedge ratio of:

$$h = \frac{(65.00 - 55.29)}{(2.79 - 12.50)} = -1.00$$

FIGURE 24.8 **TREE OF CALCULATED OPTION VALUES (FOUR TERMINAL OUTCOMES)**

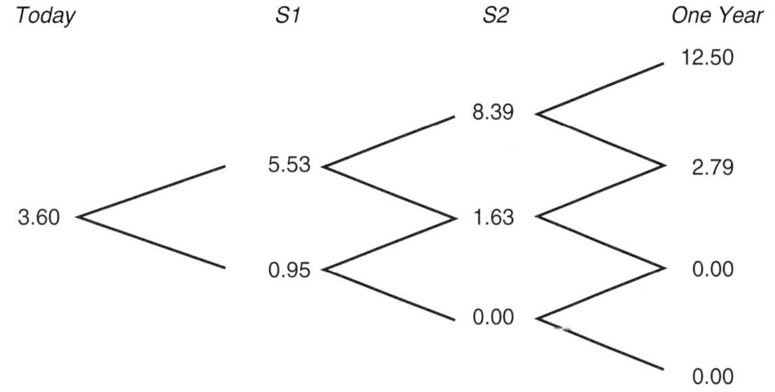
Today
S1
S2
One Year
12.50
8.39
5.53
2.79
3.60
1.63
0.95
0.00
0.00
0.00

meaning that the riskless hedge portfolio at this point would contain one share of stock long and one call short. As we have seen, C_{21} can then be found by solving:

$$[59.56 - (1.00)(C_{21})](1.08)^{0.33} = [65 - (1.00)(12.50)] = 52.50$$

or:

$$C_{21} = \frac{59.56 - 52.50/1.026}{1.00} = \$8.39$$

Notice that the discount factor of 1.026 $[=(1.08)^{0.33}]$ is now based on roughly one-third of the annual risk-free rate since the one-year option expiration period was adjusted to accommodate three subintervals of equal length. Solving for the remaining values in turn leaves the option value tree shown in Figure 24.8. Notice once again that the net effect of these particular forecast improvements has been to reduce the current value of the derivative even farther to \$3.60.

THE BINOMIAL OPTION PRICING MODEL

A crucial element of this basic approach to option valuation is that future changes in the underlying asset's price always can be simplified to one of two possibilities: an up movement or a down movement. For that reason, this analytical development is part of a more general valuation methodology known as the *two-state option pricing model.*[5] One difficulty with the preceding examples, however, is that they required the investor to specify cash amounts for each of the future potential stock prices in all the subperiods demanded by the forecast. This can be a rather daunting task as the number of terminal outcomes is allowed to grow larger with the time to expiration of the contract.

To simplify this forecasting process, suppose an investor focuses her estimates on how stock prices change from one subperiod to the next, rather than on the dollar levels. That is, beginning with today's known price for a stock, for the next subperiod she forecasts: (1) one plus the percentage change associated with an up (u) movement, and (2) one plus the percentage change associated with a down (d) movement. Further, to limit the number

---

[5]See Richard J. Rendleman Jr. and Brit J. Bartter, "Two-State Option Pricing," *Journal of Finance* 34, no. 5 (December 1979): 1093–1110; and John C. Cox, Stephen A. Ross, and Mark Rubinstein, "Option Pricing: A Simplified Approach," *Journal of Financial Economics* 7, no. 3 (September 1979): 229–264.

FIGURE 24.9

BINOMIAL MODEL FORECAST TREES

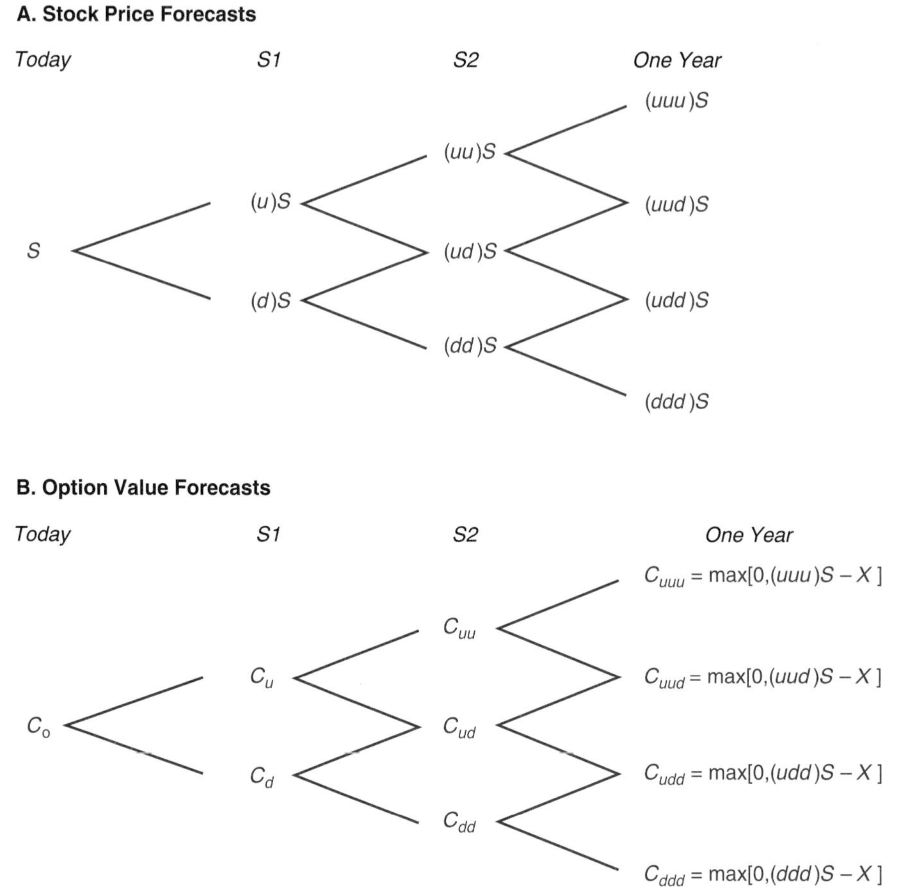
A. Stock Price Forecasts
Today
S1
S2
One Year
(uuu)S
(uu)S
(u)S
(uud)S
S
(ud)S
(d)S
(udd)S
(dd)S
(ddd)S
B. Option Value Forecasts
Today
S1
S2
One Year
Cuuu = max[0,(uuu)S – X]
Cuu
Cu
Cuud = max[0,(uud)S – X]
Co
Cud
Cd
Cudd = max[0,(udd)S – X]
Cdd
Cddd = max[0,(ddd)S – X]

of required forecasts, suppose she also assumes that the same values for *u* and *d* apply to every up and down price change in all subsequent subperiods. With these assumptions, the investor need only forecast three things: *u, d,* and *N*—the total number of subperiods.

Figure 24.9 shows the effect that these modifications—which represent the essence of the **binomial option pricing model**—have on the forecasted stock price and option value trees. Consistent with the four-outcome version of the preceding example, this illustration allows for three subperiods (i.e., $N = 3$). The upper panel of the display shows that after an up and a down movement during the first two subperiods, the initial stock price of S will have changed to $(ud)S$. Of course, the values $(ud)S$ and $(du)S$ are equal, meaning that the forecast does not depend on whether the stock price begins its journey by rising or falling. As before, once *u, d,* and *N* are determined, the expiration date payoffs to the option (i.e., C_{uuu}, C_{uud}, C_{udd} and C_{ddd}) are established.

As before, the initial value for the call, C_0, can be solved by working backward through the tree and solving for each of the remaining intermediate option values. However, another distinct advantage of the binomial model relative to the basic three-step approach is that these intermediate values are much easier to compute. In fact, in the *j*th state in any subperiod, the value of the option can be calculated by:

$$C_j = \frac{(p)C_{ju} + (1 - p)C_{jd}}{r}$$

where:

$$p = \frac{r - d}{u - d}$$

and:

r = one plus the risk-free rate over the subperiod

If p is interpreted as the probability of an up movement in the security's price, which would then mean that $(1 - p)$ is the probability of a down move, then the formula for C_j has an intuitively appealing interpretation. That is, the option's value at any point in time can be viewed as its expected value one subperiod hence discounted back to the current time. Further, although p was not an explicit part of the investor's forecast, it is nevertheless generated by the model. In this sense, p is referred to as the *implied probability* of an upward price movement. To ensure that this interpretation holds, the binomial model requires that $d < r < u$, a condition that is quite reasonable in practice.

This equation can be extended to a more useful format by recognizing that the value for C_j it generates is one of the inputs for valuing the option in the preceding subperiod. Thus, the formula for an option in subperiod t can be inserted into the right-hand side of the formula for subperiod $t - 1$. Carrying this logic all the way back to date 0, the binomial option valuation model becomes:

$$C_0 = \left\{ \sum_{j=0}^{N} \frac{N!}{(N - j)!j!} p^j (1 - p)^{N-j} \max\left[0, (u^j d^{N-j})S - X\right] \right\} \div r^N$$

where:

$N! = [(N)(N - 1)(N - 2) \ldots (2)(1)]$

To interpret this formula, the ratio $[N! \div (N - j)!j!]$ is the "combinatorial" way of stating how many distinct paths lead to a particular terminal outcome, $p^j(1 - p)^{N-j}$ is the probability of getting to that outcome, and $\max[0, (u^j d^{N-j})S - X]$ is the payoff associated with that outcome. Letting m be the smallest integer number of up moves guaranteeing that the option will be in the money at expiration (i.e., $u^m d^{N-m})S > X$), this formula can be reduced further to:

$$C_0 = \left\{ \sum_{j=m}^{N} \frac{N!}{(N - j)!j!} p^j (1 - p)^{N-j} \left[(u^j d^{N-j})S - X\right] \right\} \div r^N$$

As an example of how this model works, assume the investor has gathered contract terms and price data and has made her forecasts as follows: $S = 50.00$, $X = 52.50$, T = one year, RFR = 8 percent (through expiration), $u = 1.09139$, $d = 0.92832$, and $N = 3$. By these forecasts, the investor has divided the one-year life of the option into three subperiods and estimated up and down moves during any subperiod as slightly greater than 9 and 7 percent, respectively. Also, the values for r and p implied by these forecasts are 1.026 ($= (1.08)^{0.33}$) and 0.599 ($= [1.026 - 0.92832] \div [1.09139 - 0.92832]$). By the second binomial equation, which ignores the two terminal option outcomes in the first formula that are equal to zero, the value of a one-year European-style call option with an exercise price of \$52.50 is:

$$C_0 = \frac{(3)(0.599)^2(0.401)(2.79) + (1)(0.599)^3(12.50)}{(1.026)^3} = \$3.60$$

It is not surprising that this is the same value the three-step approach produced in the previous example because the forecasted stock price tree in Figure 24.7 was generated with these same values of u and d (e.g., $(uu)S = (1.09139)^2(50) = \$59.56$). We also can confirm that the tree of forecasted option values illustrated in Figure 24.8 may be replicated through repeatedly calculating the "state j" equation.[6] Finally, with this notation, the hedge ratio for any state j becomes:

$$h_j = \frac{(u - d)S_j}{(C_{jd} - C_{ju})}$$

Thus, a share of stock held long could be hedged initially by shorting 1.78 call options [= (1.09139 − 0.92832)(50) ÷ (0.95 − 5.53)], a position that would be rebalanced to 1.32 calls after one subperiod if the first price change was positive.

The Black-Scholes Valuation Model

The binomial model is a *discrete* method for valuing options because it allows security price changes to occur in distinct upward or downward movements. It also can be assumed that prices change *continuously* throughout time. This was the approach taken by Black and Scholes in developing their celebrated equation for valuing European-style options.[7] This is not a more realistic assumption because it presumes that security prices change when markets are closed (e.g., at night, on weekends). The advantage of the Black-Scholes approach—identical in spirit to the basic three-step, riskless hedge method outlined earlier—is that it leads to a relatively simple, closed-form equation that is capable of valuing options accurately under a wide array of circumstances.

Specifically, the Black-Scholes model assumes that stock price movements can be described by a statistical process known as *geometric Brownian motion.* Ultimately, this process is summarized by a volatility factor, σ, which is analogous to the investor's stock price forecasts in the previous models. Formally, the stock price process assumed by Black and Scholes is:

$$\frac{\Delta S}{S} = \mu[\Delta T] + \sigma\varepsilon[\Delta T]^{1/2}$$

That is, a stock's return ($\Delta S/S$) from the present through any future period T has both an expected component ($\mu[\Delta T]$) and a "noise" component ($\sigma\varepsilon[\Delta T]^{1/2}$), where μ is the mean return and ε is the standard normally distributed random error term.[8]

Assuming the continuously compounded risk-free rate and the stock's variance (i.e., σ^2) remain constant until the expiration date T, Black and Scholes used the riskless hedge intuition to derive the following formula for valuing a call option on a nondividend-paying stock:

---

[6]For example, C_{uu} = [(0.599)(12.50) + (0.401)(2.79)] ÷ (1.026) = \$8.39.

[7]See Fischer Black and Myron Scholes, "The Pricing of Options and Corporate Liabilities." *Journal of Political Economy* 81, no. 2 (May–June 1973): 637–654. For an interesting related discussion of this model, see Fischer Black, "How We Came Up with the Option Formula," *Journal of Portfolio Management* 15, no. 2 (winter 1989): 4–8.

[8]For a detailed analysis of the mathematics underlying the Black-Scholes model, see John Hull, *Options, Futures, and Other Derivatives,* 3d ed. (Englewood Cliffs, N.J.: Prentice-Hall, 1997).

$$C_0 = SN(d_1) - X(e^{-(RFR)T})N(d_2)$$

where $e^{-(RFR)T}$ is the discount function for continuously compounded variables,

$$d_1 = [(\ln(S/X) + (RFR + 0.5\sigma^2)[T])] \div (\sigma[T]^{1/2})$$

and

$$d_2 = d_1 - \sigma[T]^{1/2}$$

with $\ln(\cdot)$ being the natural logarithm function. The variable $N(d)$ represents the cumulative probability of observing a value drawn from the standard normal distribution (i.e., one with a mean of zero and a standard deviation of one) equal to or less than d. As the standard normal distribution is symmetric around zero, a value of $d = 0$ would lead to $N(d) = 0.5000$; positive values of d would then have cumulative probabilities greater than 50 percent, with negative values of d leading to cumulative probabilities of less than one-half.

Values for $N(d)$ can be established in two ways. First, an investor can use a table of calculated values for the standard normal distribution, such as the one shown in Appendix D at the end of the book. For example, if the value of d_1 is 0.65, $N(d_1)$ could be established by finding the entry corresponding to the 0.6 row and the 0.05 column, or 0.7422. This means that 74.22 percent of the observations in the standard normal distribution have a value of 0.65 or less. Notice also that if d_1 had been -0.65. the value of $N(-d_1) = 1 - N(d_1) = 1 - 0.7422 = 0.2578$, which must be the case since the distribution is symmetric.

A second approach to calculating cumulative normal probabilities is approximating them with the following formula:

$$N(d) \approx \begin{cases} 0.5e^{-(d^2)/2-281/(83-351/d)} & \text{if } d < 0 \\ 1 - 0.5e^{-(d^2)/2-281/(83+351/d)} & \text{if } d \geq 0 \end{cases}$$

For example, with $d = 0.65$, we have an approximate probability of:

$$N(0.65) \approx 1 - 0.5e^{-(0.65^2)/2-281(83+351/0.65)} = 0.7422$$

This matches the actual value to the fourth decimal place, and will likely lead to reasonable valuations.[9]

The **Black-Scholes valuation model** has several attractive features. A joint examination of the expressions for C, d_1, and d_2 reveals that the option's value is a function of five variables:

1. current security price
2. exercise price
3. time to expiration
4. risk-free rate
5. security price volatility

[9]For more on this approximation method, as well as how it can be written into a program usable on a hand-held financial calculator, see Peter Carr, "A Calculator Program for Option Values and Implied Standard Deviations," *Journal of Financial Education* 17, no. 1 (fall 1988): 89–93.

FIGURE 24.10

FACTORS AFFECTING BLACK-SCHOLES OPTION VALUES

	WILL CAUSE AN INCREASE/DECREASE IN THE:	
An Increase in the:	**Call Value**	**Put Value**
Security price (S)	Increase	Decrease
Exercise price (X)	Decrease	Increase
Time to expiration (T)	Increase	Increase or decrease
Risk-free rate (RFR)	Increase	Decrease
Security volatility (σ)	Increase	Increase

Functionally, the Black-Scholes model holds that $C = f(S, X, T, RFR, \sigma)$. The first and fourth factors are observable market prices, and the second and third variables are defined by the contract itself. Thus, the only variable an investor must provide in the Black-Scholes framework is the volatility factor. As noted earlier, the estimate of σ embeds the investor's forecast of future stock prices.

The value of the call option will rise with increases in each of the five factors *except* the exercise price. Figure 24.10 summarizes these relationships. Specifically, the middle column of the figure shows what will happen to the value of the call when one of the five factors increases. The intuition behind the first three of these relationships is straightforward. In particular, an increase in the underlying asset's price (i.e., S) will increase the call's intrinsic value; a larger exercise price (i.e., X) will reduce the intrinsic value. Also, the longer the option has until it expires, the more valuable the time premium component. This is because a greater opportunity exists for the contract to finish in the money. On the other hand, the relationships between C, RFR, and σ are less obvious. An increase in RFR will increase the call's value because this reduces the present value of X, an expense that the call holder must pay at expiration to exercise the contract. Similarly, when the volatility of the underlying asset's price increases, the call becomes more valuable since this increases the probability that the option will be deeper in the money at expiration.[10]

Another useful facet of the Black-Scholes model is that the hedge ratio at any moment in time is simply $N(d_1)$, the partial derivative of the call's value with respect to the stock price (i.e., $\delta C/\delta S$). Under this interpretation, $N(d_1)$ is the change in the option's value given a one dollar change in the underlying security's price. For this reason, $N(d_1)$ often is called the option's **delta**, and it indicates the number of stock shares that can be hedged by a single call—the exact reciprocal of the previous interpretation of the hedge ratio, h. Finally, although the Black-Scholes model was developed several years before the binomial framework, the former can be viewed as an extension of the latter. Specifically, as the number of subperiods (i.e., N) is allowed to approach infinity, the up or down price movements begin to occur on a continuous basis. If the values of u and d are then set equal to $e^{\sigma[\Delta T]^{1/2}}$ and $e^{-\sigma[\Delta T]^{1/2}}$, respectively, the binomial model collapses to become the Black-Scholes formula.

As an example of Black-Scholes valuation, consider the following values for the five input variables: $S = 40$, $X = 40$, $T =$ one year, $RFR = 9$ percent, and $\sigma = 0.30$. To calculate the fundamental value of a European-style call option under these conditions, which again will be purely time premium, first calculate:

$$d_1 = (\ln(40/40) + (0.09 + 0.5(0.3)^2)[1]) \div (0.3[1]^{1/2}) = 0.45$$

[10]In more technical terms, these relationships can be summarized as $\delta C/\delta S > 0$, $\delta C/\delta RFR > 0$, $\delta C/\delta T > 0$, $\delta C/\delta\sigma > 0$, and $\delta C/\delta X < 0$.

TABLE 24.1 **EXAMPLE OF BLACK-SCHOLES VALUATION**

Stock Price	Call Value	Hedge Ratio
$25	$0.44	0.1321
30	1.51	0.3054
35	3.53	0.5020
40	6.49	0.6736
45	10.19	0.8003
50	14.42	0.8837
55	18.98	0.9347

Note: Assumes $X = 40$, $T = 1$ year, $RFR = 9\%$, and $\sigma = 0.30$.

and

$$d_2 = 0.45 - 0.3[1]^{1/2} = 0.15$$

so that

$$N(d_1) = 1 - 0.5e^{-(0.45^2)/2 - 281/(83+351/0.45)} = 0.6736$$

and

$$N(d_2) = 1 - 0.5e^{-(0.15^2)/2 - 281/(83+351/0.15)} = 0.5596.$$

Thus,

$$C_0 = (40)(0.6736) - 40(e^{-.09})(0.5596) = \$6.49.$$

$N(d_1)$ says that the call option will change in value by about 67 cents for every dollar of a change in the underlying asset which, in turn, suggests a hedge ratio of one-and-a-half calls short for every stock share held long. Table 24.1 shows how both the option's value and $N(d_1)$ change as the security's value changes—with the other factors held constant. Notably, the hedge ratios range in value from 0 to 1, and increase as stock prices increase. Therefore, the deeper in the money the option is, the closer its price movements will come to duplicating those of the stock itself. The relationship between stock prices and call option prices for this example is shown in Figure 24.11. The delta, or hedge ratio, associated with a given stock price is simply the slope of a line tangent to the call option price curve.

ESTIMATING VOLATILITY Just as the growth rate of dividends (i.e., g) was a crucial element in establishing the fundamental value of common stock using the dividend discount model, option valuation depends critically on an accurate forecast of the underlying asset's future price level. Of course, in the Black-Scholes framework, this means selecting the proper σ. From the description of the geometric Brownian motion process, it should be clear that σ is equivalent to the standard deviation of returns to the underlying asset. This value can be estimated in two ways. First, it can be calculated in the traditional manner using historical returns. Specifically, calculate the day *t price relative* as $R_t = \ln(P_t \div P_{t-1})$. If a series of price relatives are then calculated for a sequence of N days in the recent past, the mean and standard deviation of this series can be calculated as:

FIGURE 24.11 **BLACK-SCHOLES VALUES**

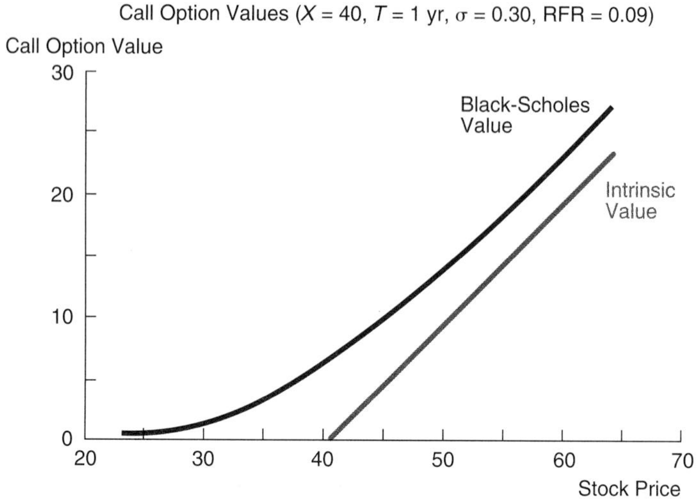
Call Option Values (X = 40, T = 1 yr, σ = 0.30, RFR = 0.09)
Call Option Value
30
20
10
0
20
30
40
50
60
70
Stock Price
Black-Scholes Value
Intrinsic Value

$$\bar{R} = \left(\frac{1}{N}\right)\sum_{t=1}^{N} R_t \text{ and } \sigma^2 = \left(\frac{1}{N-1}\right)\sum_{t=1}^{N}(R_t - \bar{R})^2$$

The factor σ is expressed in terms of daily price movements. To annualize this value, σ can be multiplied by the square root of the number of trading days in thc ycar (usually assumed to be 250), which then becomes the estimate of volatility employed in the Black-Scholes formula. The advantage of historical volatility is that it is easy to compute and requires no prior assumption about stock market efficiency; its disadvantage is its presumption that stock price behavior in the future will continue as it has in the past, a sometimes dubious assumption in a rapidly changing world.[11] Table 24.2 lists 30-day historical volatilities for a representative sample of optionable stocks during January 1999.

An alternative to relying on historical price movements is a second volatility estimation approach that involves the Black-Scholes equation. Recall that if we know all five input factors—*S, X, T, RFR,* and σ—we can solve for the value of the call option. However, because σ is the only unobservable input, and if we know the current price of the option (call it C^*) and the four other variables, we can calculate the level of σ that forces the Black-Scholes value to equal C^*. That is, the volatility implied by current market prices is established by finding σ^* such that $C^* = f(S, X, T, RFR, \sigma^*)$. Accordingly, the value σ^* is known as the **implied volatility**. No simple closed-form solution exists for performing this calculation; it must be done by trial and error.

Implied volatility is advantageous because it calculates the same volatility forecast investors use to set option prices. The disadvantage of implied volatility is its presumption that markets are efficient in that the option price set in the market corresponds directly to that generated by the Black-Scholes equation. Beckers has shown that implied volatilities do a better job than historical volatilities of predicting future stock price movements;

[11]For a good discussion of how stock price volatility has changed over time, see Charles P. Jones and Jack W. Wilson, "Is Stock Price Volatility Increasing?" *Financial Analysts Journal* 45, no. 6 (November–December 1989): 20–26.

TABLE 24.2 **HISTORICAL VOLATILITY ESTIMATES**

Company	Ticker	30-Day Volatility Estimate
American Express	AXP	45.10%
Applied Materials	AMAT	70.58
Ashland Inc.	ASH	20.50
Burlington Northern Sante Fe	BNI	29.69
British Telecom	BTY	39.77
Citigroup	C	48.71
Coca Cola	KO	30.43
Data General	DGN	73.00
Dell Computer	DELL	49.31
Enron	ENE	42.27
Halliburton	HAL	66.55
Intel	INTC	52.37
Litton Industries	LIT	22.92
Lucent Technologies	LU	57.14
Nike	NKE	50.19
Philip Morris	MO	36.96
Qualcomm Inc.	QCOM	56.85
Sunglass Hut	RAYS	97.14
Texas Utilities	TXU	19.83
Yahoo! Inc.	YHOO	131.38

Source: Chicago Board Options Exchange, 14 February 1999.

however, Figlewski cautions that σ^* can be "noisy" because it picks up not only the true level of volatility but any misestimate inherent in the valuation process.[12]

As an example of this calculation, Brown, Harlow, and Tinic estimated the volatilities implied by the S&P 500 index call option contract for the 121-day period surrounding the stock market crash in October 1987.[13] These calculations are reproduced in Figure 24.12. In this display, the time variable is denominated relative to "Black Monday" [i.e., Day 0], which occurred on October 19, 1987. To see how much market risk changed with the crash, the *average* implied volatility measure for the period Day −60 to Day −5 (i.e., the period beginning approximately two and a half months before the crash) was 18.9 percent. The comparable statistic for the period Day +5 to Day +60 was 43.3 percent. Moreover, on Black Monday itself, the implied volatility rose to 145 percent, more than seven and a half times its pre-crash level!

PROBLEMS WITH BLACK-SCHOLES VALUATION

The Black-Scholes option valuation model is popular with investors for at least two reasons: It is computationally convenient and it produces reasonable values under a wide variety of conditions. There are, however, circumstances in which the model is less than

[12]See Stan Beckers, "Standard Deviations Implied in Option Prices as Predictors of Future Stock Price Variability," *Journal of Banking and Finance* 5, no. 3 (September 1981): 363–381; Stephen Figlewski, "What Does an Option Pricing Model Tell Us about Option Prices?" *Financial Analysts Journal* 45, no. 5 (September–October 1989): 12–15; and Charles J. Corrado and Thomas W. Miller Jr., "Efficient Option-Implied Volatility Estimators," *Journal of Futures Markets* 16, no. 3 (June 1996): 247–272. For an exhaustive review of the literature on this topic, see Stewart Mayhew, "Implied Volatility," *Financial Analysts Journal* 51, no. 4 (July–August 1995), pp. 8–20.

[13]See Keith C. Brown, W. V. Harlow, and Seha M. Tinic, "How Rational Investors Deal with Uncertainty (Or, Reports of the Death of Efficient Market Theory Are Greatly Exaggerated)," *Journal of Applied Corporate Finance* 2, no. 3 (fall 1989): 45–58.

FIGURE 24.12 **IMPLIED VOLATILITIES AND THE STOCK MARKET CRASH OF 1987**

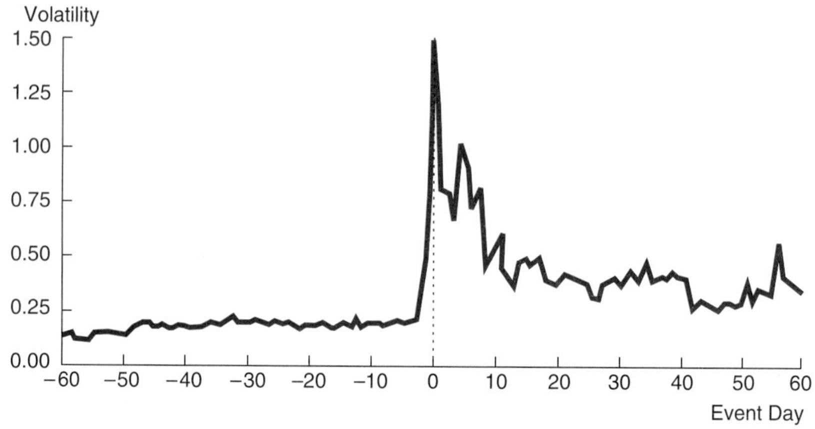
Volatility
1.50
1.25
1.00
0.75
0.50
0.25
0.00
−60 −50 −40 −30 −20 −10 0 10 20 30 40 50 60
Event Day

desirable. The implied volatilities just described have also been useful in determining whether the fundamental values produced by the Black-Scholes model match the traded prices for option contracts. In one of the earliest empirical tests of the Black-Scholes equation, MacBeth and Merville showed for a sample of six stocks that implied volatilities tended to be overly large when the associated call options were in the money and too small for out-of-the-money contracts.[14] Assuming that at-the-money options are priced fairly by the market, this suggested that in-the-money options were priced higher by investors than their Black-Scholes values, with the opposite being true for the out-of-the-money contracts. Thus, for the authors' sample of stocks, the Black-Scholes model overvalued out-of-the-money call options and undervalued in-the-money contracts. Interestingly, in two different studies, Rubinstein found evidence that both supported and contradicted these results.[15]

In general, any violation of the assumptions upon which the Black-Scholes model is based could lead to a misvaluation of the option contract. For instance, it was already noted that stock prices do not change continuously, meaning that stocks that are less actively traded might have options that are priced differently in the market than those stocks that trade frequently. Indeed, Figlewski has noted how such market imperfections as brokerage fees, bid–ask spreads, and inflexible position sizes can create arbitrageable differences between option values and prices.[16] He cautioned that Black-Scholes values are best viewed as approximations, best suited for comparing prices of different contracts. Further, Black has noted that other conditions of the model are almost certain to be violated in practice, such as the assumption that the risk-free rate and volatility level remain constant until the expiration date. He discusses how some of these problems can be exploited by investors.[17]

[14]See James D. MacBeth and Larry J. Merville, "An Empirical Examination of the Black-Scholes Call Option Pricing Model," *Journal of Finance* 34, no. 5 (December 1979): 1173–1186.

[15]See Mark Rubinstein, "Nonparametric Tests of Alternative Options Pricing Models Using All Reported Trades and Quotes on the 30 Most Active CBOE Options Classes from August 23, 1976, through August 31, 1978," *Journal of Finance* 40, no. 2 (June 1985): 455–480, and "Implied Binomial Trees," *Journal of Finance* 49, no. 3 (July 1994): 771–818.

[16]See Stephen Figlewski, "Options Arbitrage in Imperfect Markets," *Journal of Finance* 44, no. 5 (December 1989): 1289–1311.

[17]See Fischer Black, "How to Use the Holes in Black-Scholes," *Journal of Applied Corporate Finance* 1, no. 4 (winter 1989): 67–73.

OPTION VALUATION: EXTENSIONS AND ADVANCED TOPICS

The preceding discussion has concentrated on the valuation of European-style call options having a nondividend-paying stock as the underlying asset. Many other conditions and underlying assets exist for which options need to be valued. This section explores several extensions of the basic approach as well as other important topics relevant to the valuation process.

VALUING EUROPEAN-STYLE PUT OPTIONS

The put-call-spot parity model of Chapter 11 held that, in an efficient market, the value of a European-style put on a nondividend-paying security should be equivalent to a portfolio short in the security while long in both a call option and a Treasury bill having a face value equal to the common exercise price X. Converting the discounting process for the T-bill to be a continuous function, this relationship can be expressed:

$$P_0 = C_0 + X(e^{-(RFR)T}) - S$$

This formula implies that if we know the prices of the security, the call option, and the T-bill, we can solve for the value of the put option. Alternatively, if the Black-Scholes value for C is inserted into this expression, we have:

$$P_0 = [SN(d_1) - X(e^{-(RFR)T})N(d_2)] + X(e^{-(RFR)T}) - S$$

which can be manipulated to equal:

$$P_0 = X(e^{-(RFR)T})N(-d_2) - SN(-d_1)$$

where all the notation is the same as before. This is the Black-Scholes put option valuation model.

The comparative statics of put option valuation were shown in the final column of Figure 24.10. In particular, the value of the put will increase with higher levels of X but decline with an increase in S because of the effect these movements have on the contract's intrinsic value. Like the call option, the put's value benefits from an increase in σ since this increases the likelihood that the contract will finish deep in the money. Also, an increase in the risk-free rate reduces the present value of X, which hurts the holder of the put who receives the striking price if the contract is exercised. Finally, the sign of $\delta P/\delta T$ could be either positive or negative depending on the trade-off between the longer time over which the security price could move in the desired direction and the reduced present value of the exercise price received by the seller at expiration.

In the preceding example of a Black-Scholes call option valuation, we had the following inputs: $S = 40$, $X = 40$, $T =$ one year, $RFR = 9$ percent, and $\sigma = 0.30$. With these assumptions, d_1 and d_2 still are 0.45 and 0.15, respectively, but now we need to compute $N(-0.45) = 1 - 0.6736 = 0.3264$ and $N(-0.15) = 1 - 0.5596 = 0.4404$. Thus:

$$P_0 = 40(e^{-.09})(0.4404) - 40(0.3264) = \$3.04$$

Finally, the hedge ratio for the put option in this model is $[N(d_1) - 1]$, which in this case is -0.3264 and indicates that the put option's value will *decrease* by approximately 33 cents for every dollar *increase* in S.

Valuing Options on Dividend-Bearing Securities

We learned earlier that the put-call parity relationship required an adjustment when the underlying asset common to both the put and call options paid a dividend. This adjustment is needed because the payment of the dividend reduces the asset's market value, converting the investor's return from capital appreciation to cash flow. Thus, other than the tax implications of this conversion, the underlying asset's owner should not lose any overall net worth over the payment of the dividend. On the other hand, the problem for the prospective call option owner is that he will not receive the dividend; therefore, the reduction in the present value of the stock will reduce the value of his derivative contract. Being rational, he will reduce the price he is willing to pay for the call option on the dividend-bearing security. Consequently, dividends become a sixth factor in the option valuation process.

The original Black-Scholes valuation model can be modified to incorporate dividend payments in two ways. The most straightforward and most accurate approach is reducing the current share price by the present value of the dividends paid during the option's life and then using this amount in place of the actual stock price. That is, replace S in the model with $S' = S - PV$ (dividends). For example, for the case of the one-year, at-the-money call option with an exercise price of \$40 that we saw earlier, assume that a dividend payment of \$1 is made in six months, with another \$1 paid just prior to expiration. Recalling that the continuously compounded risk-free rate and volatility factors were 9 percent and 30 percent, respectively, we would then have:

$$S' = 40 - (1)e^{-(0.09)(0.5)} - (1)e^{-(0.09)(1.0)} = 38.13$$

When inserted into the formulas for d_1 and d_2, this S' would generate values of 0.29 and -0.01, respectively.

With these inputs, the Black-Scholes valuation then becomes:

$$C_0 = (38.13)N(0.29) + (40)e^{-0.09}N(0.01) = (38.13)(0.6141) - (36.56)(0.4960) = \$5.28$$

This amount can be compared to the \$6.49 contract value for an otherwise identical call on a nondividend-paying share that we estimated earlier. In particular, the reduction in option value (i.e., \$1.21) is not as great as the present value of the dividends (i.e., \$1.87). This is due to the possibility that the option would have expired out of the money even without the dividend payment, meaning that the dividend-induced stock price reduction will not always affect the contract's terminal payoff. Also, the hedge ratio in the above formula is reduced from its original level of 0.6736 to 0.6141.

The second approach to adjusting the option valuation process for dividend payments involves modifying the model itself rather than the stock price input. This requires expressing the dividend in *yield* form, defined as the annual payment divided by the current stock price, and assuming that this yield is paid continuously. Merton first showed that the Black-Scholes model can be rewritten as:

$$C_0 = (e^{-(D)T})SN(d_1) - X(e^{-(RFR)T})N(d_2)$$

with:

$$d_1 = [\ln((e^{-(D)T})S/X) + (RFR + 0.5\sigma^2)[T]] \div (\sigma[T]^{1/2})$$

and:

$$d_2 = d_1 - \sigma[T]^{1/2}$$

where:

D = the annualized dividend yield[18]

The yield appears as a "discount" factor to the current stock value in two places in these equations. If we set $S' = (e^{-(D)T})S$, this second dividend adjustment is seen as just a continuous version of the first.

Extending the original example, we now have six factors to include: $S = 40$, $X = 40$, T = one year, RFR = 9 percent, σ = 30 percent, and $D = (2/40) = 5$ percent. Plugging these into the model, we get values of 0.28 for d_1 and -0.02 for d_2 so that:

$$C_0 = (e^{-0.05})(40)N(0.28) - (e^{-0.09})(40)N(-0.02)$$
$$= (38.05)(0.6103) - (36.56)(0.4920) = \$5.23$$

This amount differs from the first adjustment process amount because the assumption of a continuous dividend stream does not match the reality of how these payments are made. However, by modifying the model's structure instead of the input level, this approach is often much more convenient.

Valuing American-Style Options

The preceding valuation discussion assumed European-style options. If the contract had been American-style—that is, its exercise is not limited to the expiration date—how would the valuation process change? The uncertainty over the possibility of early exercise makes the derivation of an exact closed-form analog to the Black-Scholes equation an elusive goal. Instead Roll, Geske, and Whaley have designed elaborate approximation procedures for estimating the value of American-style calls, which have proven quite useful in practice.[19] Further, Johnson and Barone-Adesi and Whaley, among others, have taken different approaches to address the issue of American put valuation.[20]

A formal summary of these models is beyond the scope of this discussion; however, we can consider several fundamental properties. Most important is that an American put or call has to be at least as valuable as its European-style counterpart because, by definition, the American option gives the holder more choices than the simpler contract. In other words, the American contract holder can exercise at the same time as the European option owner (i.e., at expiration) as well as any point prior to that terminal date. Since we have seen that an option's value ultimately derives from the choice to exercise the agreement or not, a better set of terms for that decision means a more valuable contract. Letting C_a and C_e represent the values of American and European calls, this relationship can be expressed as:

---

[18]See Robert C. Merton, "Theory of Rational Option Pricing," *Bell Journal of Economics and Management* 4, no. 1 (spring 1973): 141–183.

[19]The development of what is commonly called the Roll-Geske-Whaley model can be found in three separate articles: Richard Roll, "An Analytic Valuation Formula for Unprotected American Call Options on Stocks with Known Dividends," *Journal of Financial Economics* 5, no. 2 (November 1977): 251–258; Robert Geske, "A Note on an Analytical Valuation Formula for Unprotected American Call Options on Stocks with Known Dividends," *Journal of Financial Economics* 7, no. 4 (June 1979): 375–380; and Robert E. Whaley, "On the Valuation of American Call Options on Stocks with Known Dividends," *Journal of Financial Economics* 9, no. 2 (June 1981): 207–212.

[20]See H. E. Johnson, "An Analytic Approximation for the American Put Price," *Journal of Financial and Quantitative Analysis* 18, no. 1 (March 1983): 143–151; and Giovanni Barone-Adesi and Robert E. Whaley, "The Valuation of American Call Options and the Expected Ex-Dividend Stock Price Declines," *Journal of Financial Economics* 17, no. 1 (September 1986): 91–112.

$$S \geq C_a(S,T,X) \geq C_e(S,T,X) \geq \max[0, S - Xe^{-(RFR)T}] \geq \max[0, S - X] \geq 0$$

This expression says that (1) the American call is at least as valuable as the European contract, (2) neither call can be more valuable than the underlying stock, and (3) both contracts are at least as valuable as their intrinsic values, expressed on both a nominal and discounted basis. For puts, a similar boundary condition would be:

$$X \geq P_a(S,T,X) \geq P_e(S,T,X) \geq \max[0, Xe^{-(RFR)T} - S] \geq 0$$[21]

For a stock that does not pay dividends, C_a and C_c will be equal to one another. At any point prior to expiration, the above relationship shows that $C_a(S,T,X) - \max[0, S - X] > 0$, and $\max[0, S - X]$ is the value the investor would extract from the option's exercise. Therefore, without the depression in the stock's price caused by the dividend payment, an investor wishing to liquidate his American call position would sell it rather than exercise it so as not to surrender the contract's time premium. Thus, in the absence of dividends to consider during the life of the option, the American call offers choices that the investor neither wants nor will be willing to pay for. This result implies that the Black-Scholes model for C_e can be used to value C_a as well.

When the stock pays dividends, however, this situation changes. Suppose an investor holds an American call option on a stock just prior to its ex-dividend date. On the ex-date—call it date t—the value of the stock will decline by about the dividend amount, leaving $S_t = S_{t-1} - (\text{dividend})_t$ assuming no other new information impacted the share's value from the previous day. The value of the option will decline accordingly, from $C(S_{t-1})$ to $C(S_t)$ Of course, selling the contract on the day prior to the ex-date will not be possible since rational buyers will know what will happen the following day. Therefore, the investor must decide on date $t - 1$ whether he should exercise his contract and receive only the intrinsic value of $\max[0, S_{t-1} - X]$. This will be the proper choice if the loss of the option's time premium is less than $C(S_{t-1}) - C(S_t)$, which will likely occur when the option is close to maturity (and, hence, the time premium is low) and the stock's dividend is large. Because the American option allows the investor the possibility of preserving value when the European contract cannot, we must have $C_a > C_e$ for almost all cases.

Deciding to exercise a put prior to maturity does not depend on the presence of dividends. Indeed, dividend payments increase a put's value because they reduce the underlying common stock's value without an offset in the exercise price. Instead, the relevant issue is the limited liability of the stock itself. For example, suppose an investor holds an American put on a nearly bankrupt company. The contract, which is struck at \$50, has three more months before it expires, and the stock is currently selling for \$1. In this case, the option holder would evaluate the trade-off between exercising the contract today to capture the \$49 intrinsic value or waiting three months and hoping the stock becomes worthless. That is, she must decide whether she would rather have \$49 now or the present value of the possibility of receiving \$50. Depending on the discount rate and the estimated recovery probability, it is quite likely that she will exercise now.

On the other hand, the European put does not offer the investor this choice. Further, since the stock's expected return is positive, an efficient capital market would predict that the price of the nondividend-paying stock will be higher in three months, thereby reducing the expiration date value of the contract below \$49. Consequently, without the ability to ex-

[21] For a complete development of these boundary conditions, see Don M. Chance, *Introduction to Derivatives,* 4th ed. (Fort Worth, Tex.: Dryden Press, 1997).

FIGURE 24.13 **COMPARING AMERICAN AND EUROPEAN PUT VALUES**

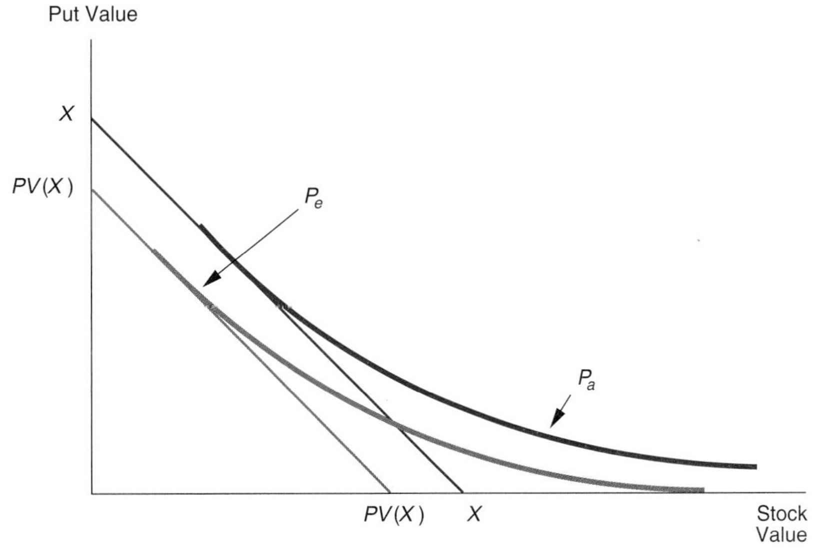
Put Value
X
PV(X)
Pe
Pa
PV(X)
X
Stock Value

ercise the put prior to expiration, the European put sometimes can be worth less than its intrinsic value—unadjusted for the time value of money—which always is a lower bound for the American contract. Thus, P_e can be either greater or less than max[0, $X - S$], with the latter situation most likely to occur at extremely low values of S and large values of T. The above boundary condition shows that P_e must only be greater than the discounted version of the intrinsic value formula, or max[0, $Xe^{-(RFR)T} - S$]. These relationships are illustrated in Figure 24.13.

Other Extensions of the Black-Scholes Model

The dividend-adjusted Black-Scholes model is also quite useful in valuing options for underlying assets other than common stock. Three of the more important applications along these lines follow.

STOCK INDEX OPTIONS As we have discussed, stock index options are fundamentally no different than regular stock options. That is, it is reasonable to assume that the index levels follow geometric Brownian motion just as the stock itself does. The primary difference is that, as a hypothetical creation, the stock index cannot be delivered to settle the contract and so it must be settled in cash. Beyond that, because it is a well-diversified portfolio, the volatility of the stock index's price usually is quite a bit lower than the typical stock. Finally, the applicable dividend yield can be assumed to be the average annualized yield on the index during the option's life, which is likely to be known to investors at least one calendar quarter into the future.

Suppose the Standard and Poor's 100 currently is at a level of 601.40 and a call option on the index with an exercise price of 600 is being offered at a price of \$17.75. An investor wants to determine whether the fair value of this contract is above or below the market price. The option is set to expire in exactly 61 days, which translates to 0.1671 (= 61/365) year. The dividend yield on the S&P 100 is 2.00 percent, and the annualized yield on a 61-day Treasury bill is 5.70 percent. The investor forecasts the index's volatility to be 18 percent, and establishes that:

$$d_1 = [\ln(601.40e^{-(0.02)0.1671}/600) + (0.057 + 0.5(0.18)^2)[0.1671]] \div (0.18[0.1671]^{1/2}) = 0.1525$$

and:

$$d_2 = 0.1525 - 0.18[0.1671]^{1/2} = 0.0789$$

Using the cumulative normal probability approximation function, this leads to $N(d_1) = 0.5607$ and $N(d_2) = 0.5315$. Thus, she estimates the call's value to be:

$$C_0 = (599.39)(0.5607) - (600)(e^{-(0.057)0.1671})(0.5315) = \$20.20$$

Since this is higher than the market price of the option (i.e., \$17.75), the contract appears undervalued. This is not necessarily an arbitrage opportunity, however, as the investor's valuation was based on two assumptions that may not match the consensus view of other market participants: (1) the Black-Scholes framework is appropriate, and (2) the index's volatility is 18 percent and not something lower. This, of course, is always the challenge confronting investors in an uncertain world.

FOREIGN CURRENCY OPTIONS Recall that prices for exchange-traded currency options are quoted in U.S. cents per unit of foreign currency, reflecting that a call option is the right to buy a fixed amount of foreign currency with U.S. dollars. Let RFR_f and RFR_d be the risk-free rates in the foreign and U.S. domestic markets, respectively. Further, let σ be the volatility of the exchange rate between the United States and the foreign country, denominated in USD per unit of FC. Garman and Kohlhagen showed that the Black-Scholes model for European-style calls and puts under these conditions can be written as:[22]

$$C_0 = (e^{-(RFR_f)T})SN(d_1) - X(e^{-(RFR_d)T})N(-d_2)$$
$$P_0 = X(e^{-(RFR_d)T})N(d_2) - (e^{-(RFR_f)T})SN(-d_1)$$

where:

$$\mathbf{d_1 = [\ln(e^{-(RFR_f)T}S/X) + (RFR_d + 0.5\sigma^2)[T]] \div (\sigma[T]^{1/2})}$$
$$\mathbf{d_2 = d_1 - \sigma[T]^{1/2}}$$
S = the spot exchange rate quoted on a direct (i.e., USD/FC) basis

Again, this formula is equivalent to the dividend-adjusted Black-Scholes model for stock options when RFR_f is interpreted as the "dividend yield" on the foreign currency. As an example of valuing FX options, suppose the spot exchange rate between the U.S. dollar and the British pound is USD 1.50/GBP, and the risk-free rates in the United States and England are 4.5 percent and 9 percent, respectively. With these market conditions, interest rate parity holds that the dollar should trade at a forward premium relative to the pound. To the extent that forward FX rates "predict" future spot rates, this suggests that the dollar price of sterling will fall. Thus, an at-the-money put option should be more valuable to an investor than an at-the-money sterling call. To see if this is the case, consider the valuation of six-month contracts where $S = 1.50$, $X = 1.50$, $RFR_d = 4.5$ percent, $RFR_f = 9$ percent, $\sigma = 13$ percent, and $T = 0.5$. With these inputs, $S' = S(e^{-(.09)0.5}) = 1.434$ so that:

[22]See Mark B. Garman and Steven W. Kohlhagen, "Foreign Currency Option Values," *Journal of International Money and Finance* 2, no. 3 (December 1983): 231–237, as well as Nahum Biger and John Hull, "The Valuation of Currency Options," *Financial Management* 12, no. 1 (spring 1983): 24–28.

$$d_1 = [\ln(1.434/1.50) + (0.045 + 0.5(0.13)^2)[0.5]] \div (0.13[0.5]^{1/2}) = -0.20$$

and:

$$d_2 = -0.20 - 0.13[0.5]^{1/2} = -0.29$$

Therefore, the option values are:

$$C_0 = (1.434)(0.4207) - (1.50)(e^{-(0.045)0.5})(0.3859) = \$0.037$$

and:

$$P_0 = (1.50)(e^{-(0.045)0.5})(0.6141) - (1.434)(0.5793) = \$0.070$$

as expected.

FUTURES OPTIONS In the preceding chapter, we showed that in the absence of physical storage costs or dividends, the futures contract price (F) should simply be the spot price (S) of the underlying asset carried forward to date T at the risk-free rate. With continuous yields, this can be written as $F = Se^{(RFR)T}$. Black showed that substituting F for S in the Black-Scholes formula for call options leaves:[23]

$$\begin{aligned} C_0 &= [e^{-(RFR)T})F]N(d_1) - (e^{-(RFR)T})XN(d_2) \\ &= (e^{-(RFR)T})[FN(d_1) - XN(d_2)] \end{aligned}$$

where:

$$\mathbf{d_1 = (\ln(F/X) + 0.5\sigma^2[T]) \div (\sigma[T]^{1/2})}$$
$$\mathbf{d_2 = d_1 - \sigma[T]^{1/2}}$$

In the expressions for d_1 and d_2, the risk-free rate factor drops out because a risk-free hedge portfolio with futures and call options requires no initial investment since futures contracts require no front-end payment. Also, here σ represents the futures price volatility, which normally is assumed to be equal to the underlying asset volatility. Put options on futures contracts can then be valued like the call options described above.

EXOTIC OPTIONS

Throughout the chapter, we have seen that the terminal payoff to a standard call option that has an exercise price of X and expires at date T can be written $\max[0, S_T - X]$. As investors have become comfortable with how these contracts work, a growing market has developed for options offering variations on this basic payoff scheme. Three such nonstandard, or *exotic,* contracts that are particularly popular in practice are *Asian, lookback,* and *digital* options. The payoff formulas for these exotic contracts can be summarized as follows:

Asian call:	$\max[0, \text{Average}(S) - X]$
Lookback call:	$\max[0, \text{Max}(S) - X]$
Digital call	$\$Q$ if $S_T > X$ or $\$0$ if $S_T \leq X$.

[23] See Fischer Black, "The Pricing of Commodity Contracts," *Journal of Financial Economics* 3, no. 1/2 (January–March 1976): 167–179.

FIGURE 24.14

FORECASTED STOCK PRICE AND REGULAR CALL VALUE TREES

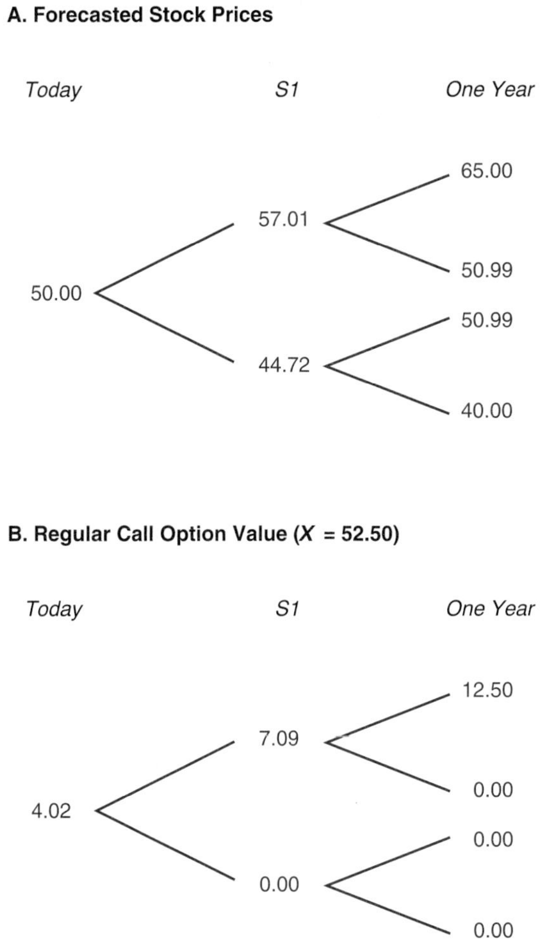
A. Forecasted Stock Prices
Today
S1
One Year
65.00
57.01
50.99
50.00
50.99
44.72
40.00
B. Regular Call Option Value (X = 52.50)
Today
S1
One Year
12.50
7.09
0.00
4.02
0.00
0.00
0.00

To see the impact of these nonstandard payoffs on option valuation, let us return to the simple binomial model described by Figures 24.5 and 24.6. In that example, the European-style call option expiring in two subperiods had an exercise price of \$52.50, and the risk-free rate was 3.92 percent per subperiod. For convenience, the stock price and option value trees have been reproduced in a slightly modified form in Figure 24.14. From the stock price forecasts in panel A, the values for up and down movements can be calculated as u = 1.1402 (= 57.01/50 = 65/57.01) and d = 0.8944 (= 44.72/50 = 40/44.72), so that the implied probability of an upward price move is 0.5891 (= [1.0392 − 0.8944]/[1.1402 − 0.8944]). With these conditions, we saw that the value of the regular call option is \$4.02.

ASIAN OPTIONS As indicated above, Asian options are contracts whose terminal payoffs are determined by the *average price* of the underlying security during the life of the contract. The effect of this averaging process is shown in panel A of Figure 24.15. Notice that for a terminal stock price of \$50.99, the payoff for the Asian call will be different depending on whether the subperiod S1 share price was \$57.01 or \$44.72. That is, the payoff to the Asian call is *path dependent* in that how the price of the underlying security arrived

FIGURE 24.15 **EXOTIC CALL OPTION VALUES**

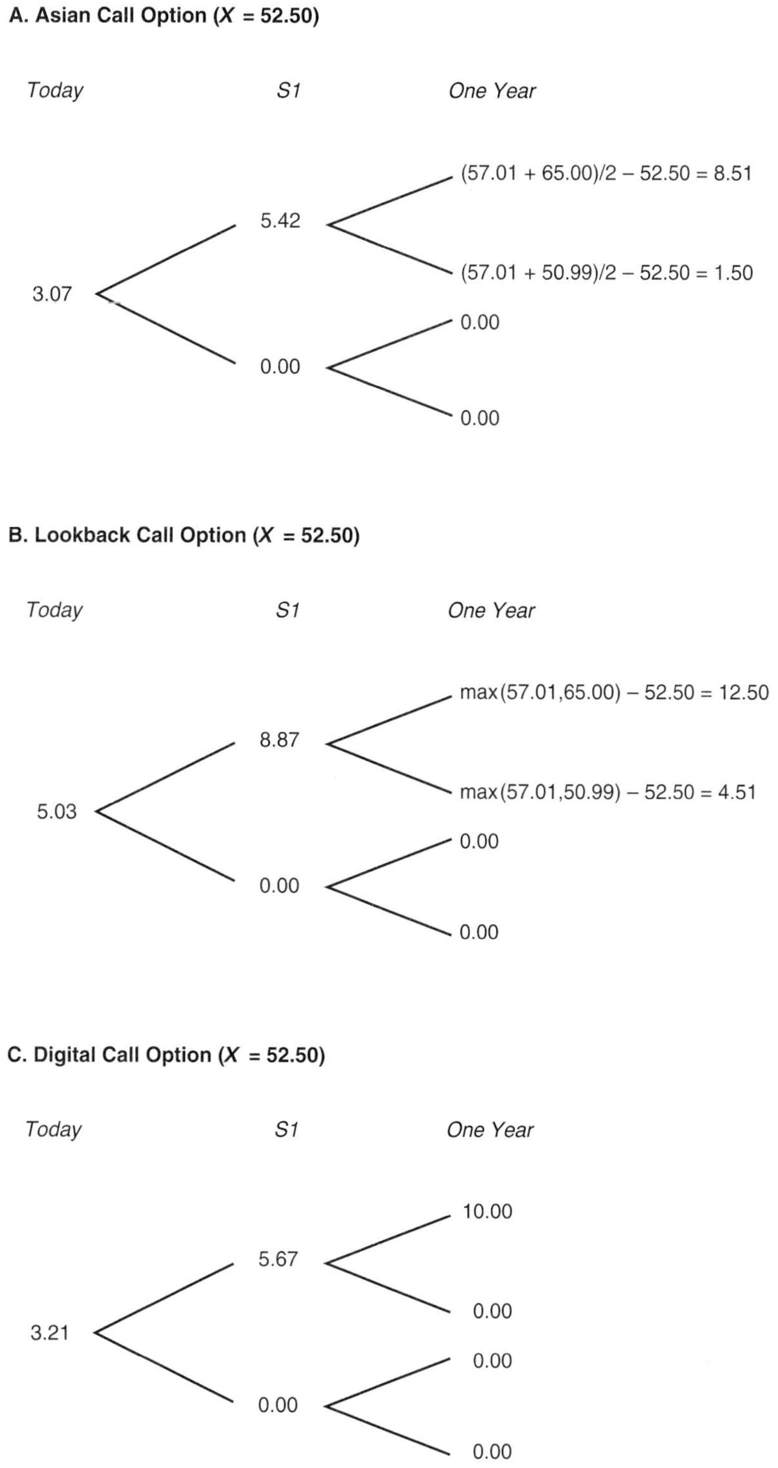
A. Asian Call Option (X = 52.50)
Today
S1
One Year
(57.01 + 65.00)/2 – 52.50 = 8.51
5.42
(57.01 + 50.99)/2 – 52.50 = 1.50
3.07
0.00
0.00
0.00
B. Lookback Call Option (X = 52.50)
Today
S1
One Year
max(57.01,65.00) – 52.50 = 12.50
8.87
max(57.01,50.99) – 52.50 = 4.51
5.03
0.00
0.00
0.00
C. Digital Call Option (X = 52.50)
Today
S1
One Year
10.00
5.67
0.00
3.21
0.00
0.00
0.00

at its terminal level (i.e., "up" then "down" versus "down" then "up") will affect the payoff. On the other hand, notice that standard call options are *path independent;* all that matters is the terminal share price and not how it got there.[24]

Once the expiration date payoffs are established, valuing the Asian contract proceeds in the same manner as for the standard option. That is, using the probabilities implied by u, d, and r, we can establish C_{11} as:

$$C_{11} = \frac{(0.5891)(8.51) + (0.4109)(1.50)}{1.0392} = \$5.42$$

so that:

$$C_0 = \frac{(0.5891)(5.42) + (0.4109)(0.00)}{1.0392} = \$3.07$$

Notice that the value for the Asian call is lower than that for the regular contract, a consequence of the fact that the averaging process *reduces* the volatility of the stock price movement.

Asian options are especially useful when an investor is trying to hedge an inventory of commodities or securities, rather than a single position. For instance, an oil importer who makes frequent purchases may want to hedge against price increases on all of his acquisition dates over the next three months. However, because there is no single purchase date, he may prefer that the contract be based on his average purchase price during the quarter. Thus, an Asian call option would be appropriate.

LOOKBACK OPTIONS As another example of a path dependent payoff, lookback options guarantee the holder a distribution based on the maximum price the underlying security achieves during the life of the contract. Panel B of Figure 24.15 shows that even if the terminal price of the stock is \$50.99, the lookback call would still pay \$4.51 (= 57.01 − 52.50) if the S1 price had been \$57.01. However, if the share price had initially fallen to \$44.72 before rising to \$50.99, the lookback option would be out of the money since neither of these values is greater than the exercise price of \$52.50. Like the Asian option, once these terminal payoffs are established, the current value of the lookback contract can be established as:

$$C_{11} = \frac{(0.5891)(12.50) + (0.4109)(4.51)}{1.0392} = \$8.87$$

and:

$$C_0 = \frac{(0.5891)(8.87) + (0.4109)(0.00)}{1.0392} = \$5.03$$

Notice that the value of the lookback option (\$5.03) is greater than that of the regular call option. This increased value is a direct result of the lookback contract *preserving* volatility by basing the payoff on the highest stock price regardless of when that value occurred during the option's life. For this reason, lookback options are always designed to be

[24]For more analysis of path dependent option contracts, see S. Eckl, J. N. Robinson, and D. C. Thomas, *Financial Engineering* (Cambridge, Mass.: Blackwell Publishing, 1991).

European-style; there is no need to have the exercise flexibility that an American-style contract provides if you are guaranteed the highest price no matter what happens by the expiration date. Of course, the buyer pays for this desirable feature in the form of a higher front-end premium. As such, lookback options represent a way of making speculative a bet against the stock price forecast assumed by the market as a whole.

DIGITAL OPTIONS The payoff to a digital, or binary, option is a fixed amount regardless of how deep in the money the contract is at expiration. It is not path dependent because, as with the standard format, the payoff depends only on the terminal stock price. Panel C of Figure 24.15 assumes a digital payoff of \$10 for an in-the-money option. In this case, the current value of the digital call is:

$$C_0 = \frac{(0.5891)(5.67)}{1.0392} = \frac{(0.5891)^2(10.00)}{(1.0392)^2} = \$3.21$$

Although this amount is lower than the regular call value of \$4.02, there is no way to generalize this result because the \$10 payoff was selected by the buyer rather than determined by market forces. For instance, if the digital payoff had been \$15, the value of the contract would be \$4.82 ($= \$15 \times (0.5891)^2 \div (0.0392)^2$). In fact, the value of this exotic option is simply the present value of the fixed payoff ($\$9.26 = \$10 \div (1.0392)^2$ in this example) multiplied by the probability that the contract finishes in the money (34.70 percent $= (0.5891)^2$). Digital options are often used by investors who have a very specific view about the expiration date trading range of the underlying security.

OPTION TRADING STRATEGIES

The introductory analysis in Chapter 11 highlighted two ways in which investors use options. First, we saw that the asymmetrical payoff structures they possess as stand-alone positions allowed investors to isolate the benefits of an anticipated change in the value of an underlying security while limiting the downside risk of an adverse price movement. Options are a leveraged alternative to making a direct investment in the asset on which the contract is based. Second, we also saw that put options could be used in conjunction with an existing portfolio to limit the portfolio's loss potential. After revisiting this protective put application in the context of individual stock holdings, in this section we will consider a **covered call** option strategy as another method for modifying the risk or enhancing the return of an existing equity position. Specifically, we will see that selling a call option while holding the underlying security can generate income for the investor in an otherwise static market environment.

This section also introduces a third way in which options are used: in *combination* with one another to create customized payoff distributions that do not exist in more fundamental securities, like stocks or bonds. In designing such combinations, the investor usually attempts to exploit a very specific view about future economic conditions. For example, he may feel that a particular company's stock returns will be extraordinarily volatile but have no clear impression about the price movement direction. On the other hand, he may feel that another company's shares will trade within a very narrow range around their current price during the next few months. In developing all these strategies, we will return to the hypothetical example of SAS Corporation, which has exchange-traded common stock as well as call and put options. Current prices for SAS stock and six different derivatives, all of which expire at the same time, are reproduced in Table 24.3.

TABLE 24.3 **HYPOTHETICAL SAS CORPORATION STOCK AND OPTION PRICES**

Instrument	Exercise Price	Market Price	Intrinsic Value	Time Premium
Stock:	—	$40.00	—	—
Call: #1	$35.00	8.07	$5.00	$3.07
#2	40.00	5.24	0.00	5.24
#3	45.00	3.24	0.00	3.24
Put: #1	35.00	1.70	0.00	1.70
#2	40.00	3.67	0.00	3.67
#3	45.00	6.47	5.00	1.47

TABLE 24.4 **EXPIRATION DATE VALUE OF A PROTECTIVE PUT POSITION**

Potential SAS Stock Value	Value of Put Option	Cost of Put Option	Net Protective Put Position
20	(40 − 20) = 20	−3.67	(20 + 20) − 3.67 = 36.33
25	(40 − 25) = 15	−3.67	(25 + 15) − 3.67 = 36.33
30	(40 − 30) = 10	−3.67	(30 + 10) − 3.67 = 36.33
35	(40 − 35) = 5	−3.67	(35 + 5) − 3.67 = 36.33
40	0	−3.67	(40 + 0) − 3.67 = 36.33
45	0	−3.67	(45 + 0) − 3.67 = 41.33
50	0	−3.67	(50 + 0) − 3.67 = 46.33
55	0	−3.67	(55 + 0) − 3.67 = 51.33
60	0	−3.67	(60 + 0) − 3.67 = 56.33

Protective Put Options

Although we have seen that the protective put strategy is most often used to provide insurance for price declines in entire portfolios, Brown and Statman have noted that the technique can also be employed with individual equity positions.[25] To see how this "insured stock" concept works, consider an investor who holds SAS stock in her portfolio but is concerned that an unexpected downturn in the company's product sales may lead to a decline in the value of her position in the coming months. To hedge against this firm-specific exposure, she decides to purchase an at-the-money put option on SAS shares. From Table 24.3, this would mean that she would spend $3.67 to buy put #2 with an exercise price of $40. If at expiration the price of SAS had declined below $40, the put option would pay her the difference.

The effect of this acquisition is shown in Table 24.4, which lists the expiration date value of the combined protective put position for a range of possible SAS prices. As noted earlier, the primary benefit of the insured stock strategy is that it creates a combined payoff equivalent to holding a call option on SAS stock. That is, the protective put holding preserves the investor's upside potential from rising share prices but limits her losses when share prices fall. In this case, the at-the-money put insures her against any losses beyond the $3.67 initial put premium. This is the same outcome the investor would have if instead of the put-protected SAS shares, she had held an at-the-money SAS call option and a T-bill; the risk-free security provides the safety and the call option provides the potential for price appreciation. Recall from the put-call parity model of Chapter 11 that this result was shown as:

---

[25]See Keith C. Brown and Meir Statman, "The Benefits of Insured Stocks for Corporate Cash Management," *Advances in Futures and Options Research* 2 (1987): 243–261.

FIGURE 24.16 **TERMINAL NET PAYOFFS TO THREE PROTECTIVE PUT POSITIONS**

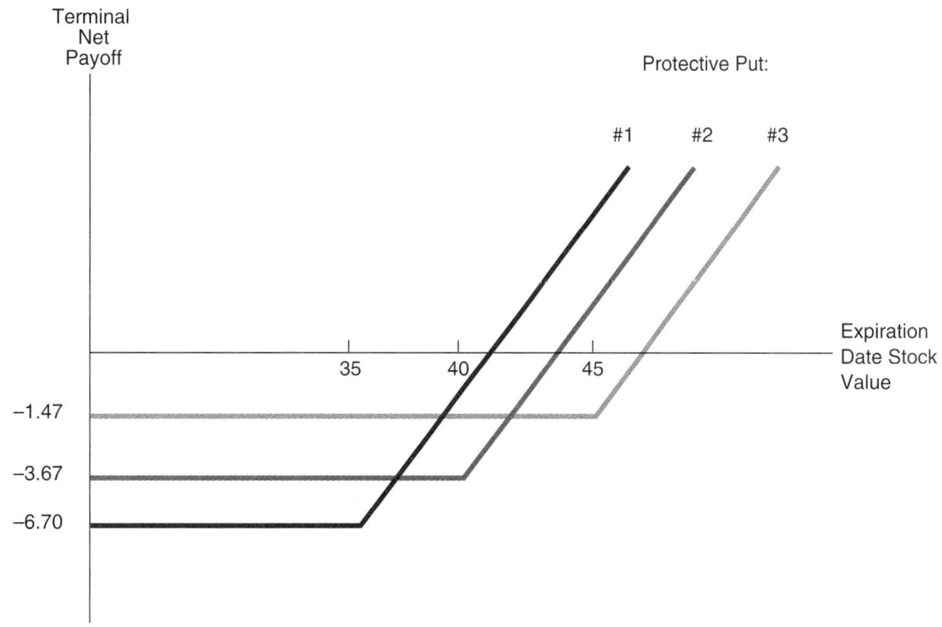
Terminal
Net
Payoff
Protective Put:
#1
#2
#3
35
40
45
Expiration
Date Stock
Value
–1.47
–3.67
–6.70

$$S_0 + P_{0,T} = C_{0,T} + PV(X)$$

which can be rewritten as follows:

$$(\text{Long Stock}) + (\text{Long Put}) = (\text{Long Call}) + (\text{Long T-bill})$$

To extend the insurance interpretation of the protective put, Figure 24.16 shows the expiration date payoffs (net of the initial \$40 purchase price for the investor's SAS shares) for using each of three put options available to her. To interpret this display, if SAS shares are priced at \$40 on the expiration date, for protective put #2 (i.e., the at-the-money contract), the investor's combined position will be worth \$36.33, giving her a net loss of \$3.67. The main thing about this illustration is the trade-off it shows between the risk and reward potential of the various positions. Put #1 has the smallest front-end expense but its \$35 exercise price forces the investor to bear the first \$5 of SAS stock price declines; this \$5 "deductible" leads to the largest potential loss of three positions at \$6.70 (= 1.70 + 5.00). However, for this degree of self-insuring on the part of the investor, protective put #1 has, at \$41.70 (= 35.00 + 6.70), the smallest breakeven price. Conversely, put #3, with an exercise price above the current share value, does not break even until SAS prices reach \$46.47, but has a maximum possible loss of only \$1.47 and therefore provides the best downside protection.

Covered Call Options

Another popular way in which derivatives are used to alter the payoff structure of an equity position involves the sale of call options. When investors sell call options based on an underlying position they own, they are said to be *writing* covered calls. Usually, the purpose of this strategy is to generate additional income for a stock holding that is not expected to

TABLE 24.5

EXPIRATION DATE VALUE OF A COVERED CALL POSITION

Potential SAS Stock Value	Value of Call Option	Proceeds from Call Option	Net Covered Call Position
20	0	5.24	(20 − 0) + 5.24 = 25.24
25	0	5.24	(25 − 0) + 5.24 = 30.24
30	0	5.24	(30 − 0) + 5.24 = 35.24
35	0	5.24	(35 − 0) + 5.24 = 40.24
40	0	5.24	(40 − 0) + 5.24 = 45.24
45	−(45 − 40) = −5	5.24	(45 − 0) + 5.24 = 45.24
50	−(50 − 40) = −10	5.24	(50 − 0) + 5.24 = 45.24
55	−(55 − 40) = −15	5.24	(55 − 0) + 5.24 = 45.24
60	−(60 − 40) = −20	5.24	(60 − 0) + 5.24 = 45.24

change in value much over the near term. By selling a call in such a situation, an investor receives the premium from the option contract to bolster an otherwise small (or negative) return. The danger, of course, is that the value of the stock position rises above the exercise price by the end of the contract's life causing the shares to be called away at the lower price.[26]

For example, suppose now that our investor believes that over the next few months the value of her SAS stock will neither rise nor fall by an appreciable amount. Accordingly, she decides not to insure her position against losses, but instead to increase the cash flow of the investment by selling an at-the-money call option (call #2). In exchange for granting the contract buyer the right to purchase her stock for $40 at the expiration date, she receives an immediate payment of $5.24. Using the same potential stock prices as before, the expiration date values for the covered call position are listed in Table 24.5. The construction of the terminal payoff diagram—once again net of the current SAS share price—is depicted in Figure 24.17.

Both the numbers and the pictures from these displays indicate that the expiration date payoff to the covered call position is comparable in form to that of a short position in a put option. Once again, this can be seen directly by adjusting the put-call parity condition as follows:

$$\text{(Long Stock)} + \text{(Short Call)} = \text{(Long T-bill)} + \text{(Short Put)}$$

Notice from Figure 24.17 that there are two dimensions to the price risk inherent in this strategy. First, if by the option expiration date, SAS stock has risen above $40, the investor will be forced to sell her shares for less than they are actually worth. However, this will represent a lost opportunity only at prices above $45.24, an amount equal to the exercise price plus the initial call premium. Second, if SAS stock experiences a decline in value, her potential loss is not hedged beyond the $5.24 in premium income that she received for selling the call; after prices fall beyond $31.09 (= $40 − $5.24 − $3.67), she would have been better off purchasing the at-the-money protective put option. Thus, to be profitable, the covered call strategy requires that the investor guess correctly that share values will remain in a reasonably narrow band around their present levels.

Straddles, Strips, and Straps

A straddle is the simultaneous purchase (or sale) of a call and a put option with the same underlying asset, exercise price, and expiration date. More precisely, a long straddle

[26]See James W. Yates Jr., and Robert W. Kopprasch Jr., "Writing Covered Call Options: Profits and Risks," *Journal of Portfolio Management* 7 (fall 1980), for more analysis of the covered call strategy.

FIGURE 24.17 **TERMINAL NET PAYOFF TO A COVERED CALL POSITION**

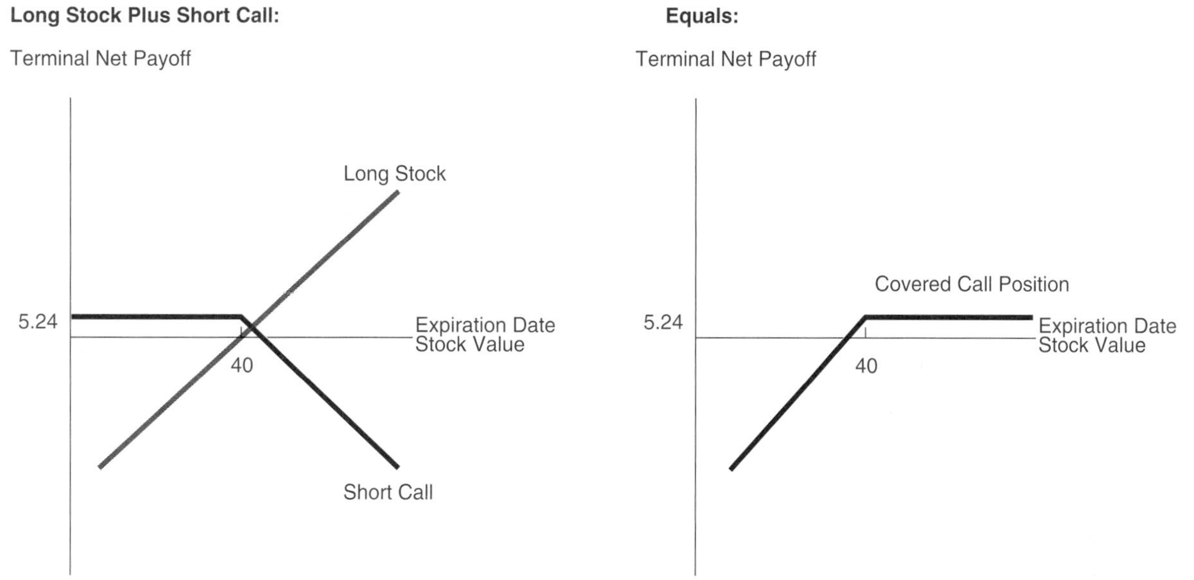
Long Stock Plus Short Call:
Terminal Net Payoff
Long Stock
5.24
40
Expiration Date
Stock Value
Short Call
Equals:
Terminal Net Payoff
Covered Call Position
5.24
40
Expiration Date
Stock Value

TABLE 24.6 **EXPIRATION DATE PAYOFFS TO A LONG STRADDLE POSITION**

SAS Stock Price at Expiration	Value of Calls	Value of Puts	Cost of Options	Net Profit
$20.00	$0.00	$20.00	$−8.91	$11.09
25.00	0.00	15.00	−8.91	6.09
30.00	0.00	10.00	−8.91	1.09
35.00	0.00	5.00	−8.91	−3.91
40.00	0.00	0.00	−8.91	−8.91
45.00	5.00	0.00	−8.91	−3.09
50.00	10.00	0.00	−8.91	1.09
55.00	15.00	0.00	−8.91	6.09
60.00	20.00	0.00	−8.91	11.09

requires the purchase of the put and the call, while a short straddle sells both contracts. The long straddle takes positions in both a call and a put, giving the investor a combination that will appreciate in value whether stock prices rise or fall in the future. Buying two options increases the initial cost; that is, to profit from this investment, stock price movements must be more pronounced than if the investor had predicted changes in a single direction. In this sense, a straddle is a *volatility* play; the buyer expects stock prices to move strongly one way or the other, while the seller hopes for lower-than-normal volatility.

To illustrate this combination, suppose an investor (who does not hold SAS stock) purchases a put and a call, each with an exercise price of $40. The cost of this purchase will be the combined prices of call #2 and put #2, or $8.91 (= $5.24 + $3.67). Recalling that the terminal values of the options are max[0, S_T − 40] and max[0, 40 − S_T], respectively, the expiration date payoffs to the straddle position (net of the initial cost, unadjusted for the time value differential) are shown in Table 24.6. These are illustrated in Figure 24.18, which also depicts the payoff to the seller of the straddle. The breakeven points on this graph occur at $31.09 (= $40 − $8.91) and $48.91 (= $40 + $8.91).

FIGURE 24.18 **THE STRADDLE ILLUSTRATED**

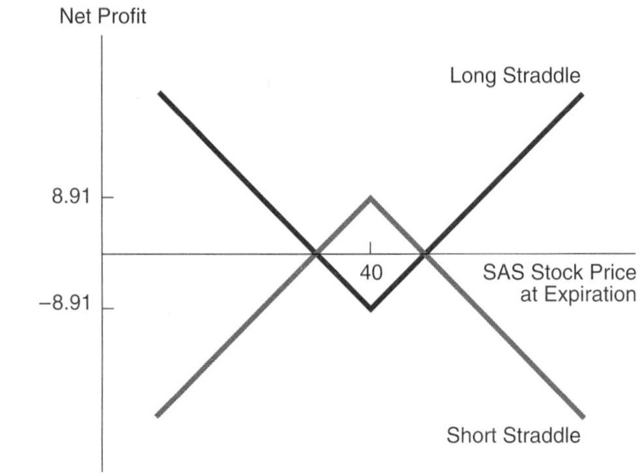
Net Profit
Long Straddle
8.91
40
SAS Stock Price at Expiration
−8.91
Short Straddle

Not surprisingly, the expiration date values to the long and short positions are mirror images of each other; if the individual options themselves are zero-sum games, so too must be any combination of contracts. In particular, the buyer of the straddle is hoping for a dramatic event—such as a company-specific technological breakthrough or the impending judgment in a major lawsuit—that will either increase or decrease the stock price from its present \$40 by at least \$8.91. Conversely, the best result for the straddle seller is for SAS stock to continue to trade at its current price through the expiration date (i.e., no volatility at all) so that both options expire worthless. The seller's position is particularly interesting because it demonstrates that it is possible to make money in the stock market even when prices do not change.

The long straddle position assumes implicitly that the investor has no intuition about the likely direction of future stock price movements. A slight modification of this format is overweighting either the put or call position to emphasize a directional belief while maintaining a contract that would profit from a price movement the other way. A long *strap* position is the purchase of two calls and one put with the same exercise price, suggesting an investor who thinks stock prices are more likely to increase. An investor with a more "bearish" view could create a long *strip* position by purchasing two puts and only one call. The terminal payoffs to both of these combinations are listed in Table 24.7, which again assumes the use of the two at-the-money SAS contracts.

Panel A of the table shows that for the higher up-front payment of \$14.15 (= (2 × \$5.24) + \$3.67), the strap will accelerate the payoff in a rising market relative to the straddle. The settlement payment when SAS stock finishes above \$40 on the expiration date is twice as great because the strap has doubled the investor's number of calls. The gross payoff when the price falls below \$40 remains the same; however, the net amount received is considerably lower because the extra contract the investor purchased would then be out of the money. The net terminal value of the strip position tells a similar story, only with the acceleration of the profit generated by failing stock prices. The strap is more expensive than the strip under these conditions because SAS is a nondividend-paying common stock that is expected to increase in price to provide the investor with a positive expected return.

Strangles One final variation on the straddle theme is an option combination known as a *strangle*. Like the straddle, a strangle is the simultaneous purchase or sale of a call and a put on the

TABLE 24.7

EXPIRATION DATE PAYOFFS TO LONG STRAP AND LONG STRIP POSITIONS

A. Strap Position (Two Calls and One Put)

SAS Stock Price at Expiration	Value of Calls	Value of Puts	Cost of Options	Net Profit
$20.00	$0.00	$20.00	$−14.15	$5.85
25.00	0.00	15.00	−14.15	0.85
30.00	0.00	10.00	−14.15	−4.15
35.00	0.00	5.00	−14.15	−9.15
40.00	0.00	0.00	−14.15	−14.15
45.00	10.00	0.00	−14.15	−4.15
50.00	20.00	0.00	−14.15	5.85
55.00	30.00	0.00	−14.15	15.85
60.00	40.00	0.00	−14.15	25.85

B. Strip Position (Two Puts and One Call)

SAS Stock Price at Expiration	Value of Calls	Value of Puts	Cost of Options	Net Profit
$20.00	$0.00	$40.00	$−12.58	$27.42
25.00	0.00	30.00	−12.58	17.42
30.00	0.00	20.00	−12.58	7.42
35.00	0.00	10.00	−12.58	−2.58
40.00	0.00	0.00	−12.58	−12.58
45.00	5.00	0.00	−12.58	−7.58
50.00	10.00	0.00	−12.58	−2.58
55.00	15.00	0.00	−12.58	2.42
60.00	20.00	0.00	−12.58	7.42

same underlying security with the same expiration date. Unlike the straddle, however, the options used in the strangle do not have the same exercise price; instead, they are chosen so that both are out of the money. By buying two out-of-the-money contracts, the investor reduces the original straddle position's initial cost. Offsetting this reduced cost, though, is that stock prices will have to change in either direction by a greater amount before the strangle becomes profitable. Thus, the strangle can be viewed as having a more modest risk–reward structure than the straddle.

As an example, suppose the investor purchased call #3 and put #1 for a combined price of $4.94 (= $3.24 + $1.70). If the price of SAS stock remained between the put exercise price of $35 and the call exercise price of $45, both contracts would expire worthless and the investor would lose his entire initial investment. Accordingly, prices would have to decline to $30.06 (= $35 − $4.94) or increase to $49.94 (= $45 + $4.94) before the investor would break even on the position. Figure 24.19 shows that these breakeven points for the strangle are outside those for the straddle described earlier. Thus, among the set of "volatility bets," the strangle costs less to implement than the straddle but requires greater movement in the underlying security's price before it generates a positive return. Finally, by varying the exercise prices on the two options—which is possible in the OTC market—the investor can create a strangle position that offers the exact trade-off between initial cost and future expected profit that he desires.

Chooser Options

The straddle is a special case of a wider class of option contracts sometimes called *chooser* options. With a chooser option, the investor selects an exercise price and expiration date but doesn't have to decide if the option should be a put or a call until after the contract is

FIGURE 24.19 **COMPARING THE LONG STRANGLE AND LONG STRADDLE POSITIONS**

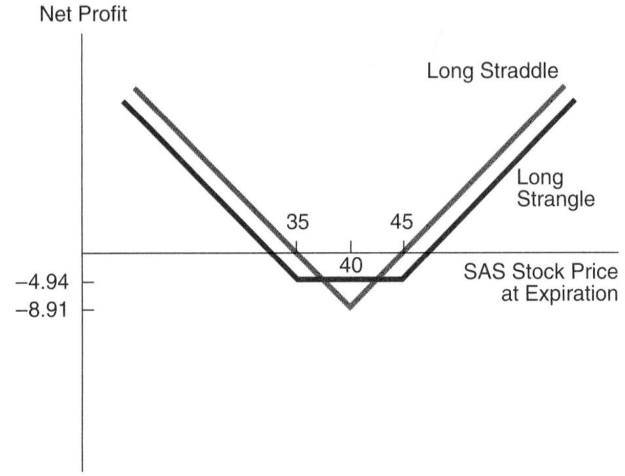
Net Profit
Long Straddle
Long
Strangle
35
45
40
SAS Stock Price
at Expiration
−4.94
−8.91

purchased. That is, the straddle is just a chooser option for which the decision can be deferred until the expiration date. Rubinstein has shown that the value of a chooser option will depend on when the investor has to make the put or call choice.[27]

At one extreme, if the decision has to be made immediately, the buyer will select the option most likely to be in the money at expiration. In the previous example, with $X = 40$, we have seen that this will be the call. Thus, a chooser option in this case is worth \$5.24. At the other extreme, a chooser option that allows the holder to defer the decision until expiration is, as noted above, equivalent to holding both a put and a call for the entire time to expiration. Consequently, the straddle price of \$8.91 is the upper bound of the chooser option value struck at \$40. The usual design for the chooser contract requires the holder to make a choice after the initial purchase but before expiration, which would create a position worth somewhere between \$5.24 and \$8.91.

SPREADS As described by Black, option spreads are the purchase of one contract and the sale of another, where the options are alike in all respects except for one distinguishing characteristic.[28] For example, in a *money* spread, the investor would sell an out-of-the-money call and purchase an in-the-money call on the same stock and expiration date. Alternatively, a *calendar* (or time) spread requires the purchase and sale of two calls—or two puts—with the same exercise price but different expiration dates. Option spreads are often used when one contract is perceived to be misvalued relative to the other. For instance, if an investor determines that a call option with an exercise price of X_1 and an expiration date T is selling at too high a price in the market, he can short it, thereby speculating on an eventual correction. However, if a broad-based increase in the stock market occurs before this contract-specific correction, he stands to lose a great deal because the short call position has unlimited liability. Thus, when he sells the first option, he can hedge some or all of the risk by buying a call with an exercise price of X_2 expiring at T.

[27]See Mark Rubinstein, "Options for the Undecided," in *From Black-Scholes to Black Holes* (London, England: Risk Magazine, 1992).

[28]See Fischer Black, "Fact and Fantasy in the Use of Options," *Financial Analysis Journal* 31, no. 4 (July–August 1975): 36–41, 61–72.

TABLE 24.8

EXPIRATION DATE PAYOFFS TO A BULL MONEY SPREAD POSITION

SAS Stock Price at Expiration	Value of Calls	Value of Puts	Cost of Options	Net Profit
$20.00	0.00	$0.00	$−4.83	$−4.83
25.00	0.00	0.00	−4.83	−4.83
30.00	0.00	0.00	−4.83	−4.83
35.00	0.00	0.00	−4.83	−4.83
40.00	5.00	0.00	−4.83	0.17
45.00	10.00	0.00	−4.83	5.17
50.00	15.00	−5.00	−4.83	5.17
55.00	20.00	−10.00	−4.83	5.17
60.00	25.00	−15.00	−4.83	5.17

FIGURE 24.20

COMPARING THE BULL MONEY SPREAD AND LONG CALL POSITIONS

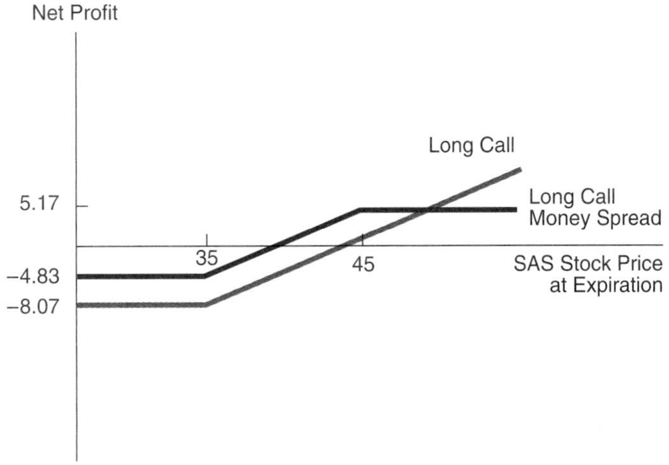

Net Profit
Long Call
5.17
Long Call
Money Spread
35
45
SAS Stock Price
at Expiration
−4.83
−8.07

Returning to the data for SAS options, suppose the investor purchases the in-the-money call (call #1) and sells the contract that is out of the money (call #3). In this case, the option he buys is more valuable than the one he sells, leading to a net cash outlay of $4.83 (= $8.07 − $3.24). At the common expiration date, three price ranges should be considered. If SAS stock settles below $35, both options will expire worthless, and the investor will lose all of his initial investment. With an SAS price above $45, both contracts will be exercised, meaning that the investor must sell at $45 the share he bought for $35, leaving a $10 gross profit. Finally, if SAS prices fall between the two exercise prices, the investor's option will be in the money while the contract he sold will not. This situation is summarized by the net payoff calculations shown in Table 24.8.

This combination is sometimes called a *bull* money spread because it will be profitable when stock prices rise. Specifically, with the initial cost of $4.83, the investor's breakeven point occurs when the stock price rises to $39.83 (= $35 + $4.83). His benefit stops increasing if SAS shares reach $45 since this is where the short position in call #3 becomes a liability. Figure 24.20 contrasts this situation with the outright purchase of the in-the money call. This contract would cost $8.07 initially, leading to the higher breakeven price of $43.07. It would not have a constraint on the upside profit potential, however, so once a share price of $48.24 is reached (= 45 + (8.07 − 4.83)), it would become the preferable

FIGURE 24.21

A BEAR MONEY SPREAD WITH PUT OPTIONS

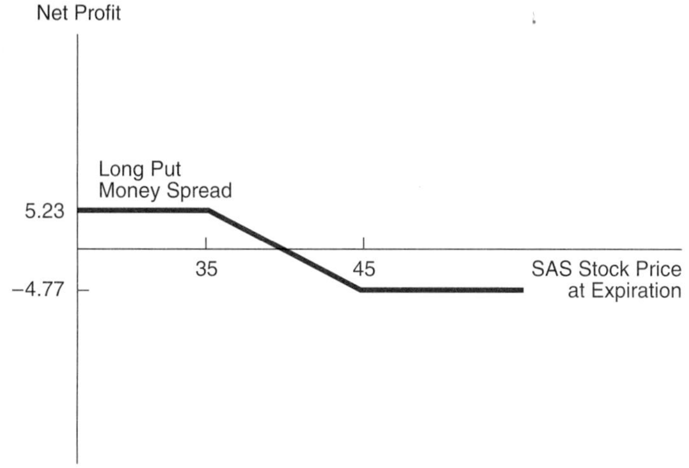
Net Profit
Long Put
Money Spread
5.23
35
45
−4.77
SAS Stock Price
at Expiration

alternative. Thus, in exchange for a lower initial purchase price, the bull spread investor is giving up the benefits of rising SAS prices after some point—a strategy that makes sense only if he expects the share price to settle within a fairly narrow range.

The profit for a *bear* money spread (the purchase of call #3 and the sale of call #1) is the opposite of that for the bull money spread. That is, buying a bear spread is equivalent to selling a bull spread. Consequently, a long bear spread position might be used by an investor who believed stock prices might decline, but did not want to be short in the stock. Notice that a spread transaction also can be created using put options. For instance, suppose a new investor undertakes the simultaneous purchase of put #3 and sale of put #1. Her net cost to acquire the position would be $4.77 (= $6.47 − $1.70), which would then generate the terminal payoffs displayed in Figure 24.21. If SAS stock settled at $45 or higher, both puts would be worthless and the investor would lose all of her initial investment. If the expiration date share price was $35 or less, both options would be in the money, leaving the investor with a net position of $5.23 (= $45 − $35 − $4.77). Thus, this is the put option version of a bear money spread.

A final extension of this concept is the *butterfly* spread. Suppose an investor designed the following portfolio of SAS options: long one call #1, short two calls #2, and long one call #3. This position is equivalent to holding:

- a bull money spread (i.e., buy call #1 and sell call #2), and
- a bear money spread (i.e., buy call #3 and sell call #2).

The net purchase price for these transactions is $0.83 (= ($8.07 − $5.24) + ($3.24 − $5.24)). The expiration date payoffs are listed in Table 24.9 and show that the value of the position peaks at a stock price of $40 and that the investor can lose, at most, her initial investment. The breakeven stock prices are $35.83 and $44.17. This form of the butterfly spread is equivalent to a hedged version of a short straddle position. That is, in exchange for receiving a smaller potential payoff (i.e., $4.17 versus $8.91) from a view on low volatility, the investor has limited her losses if SAS's stock price is more explosive than she expected. This trade-off is shown in Figure 24.22.

TABLE 24.9 **EXPIRATION DATE PAYOFFS TO A BUTTERFLY SPREAD**

SAS Stock Price at Expiration	Value Bull Spread	Value Bear Spread	Cost of Options	Net Profit
$20.00	$0.00	$0.00	$−0.83	$−0.83
25.00	0.00	0.00	−0.83	−0.83
30.00	0.00	0.00	−0.83	−0.83
35.00	0.00	0.00	−0.83	−0.83
40.00	5.00	0.00	−0.83	4.17
45.00	5.00	−5.00	−0.83	−0.83
50.00	5.00	−5.00	−0.83	−0.83
55.00	5.00	−5.00	−0.83	−0.93
60.00	5.00	−5.00	−0.83	−0.83

FIGURE 24.22 **COMPARING THE BUTTERFLY SPREAD AND SHORT STRADDLE POSITIONS**

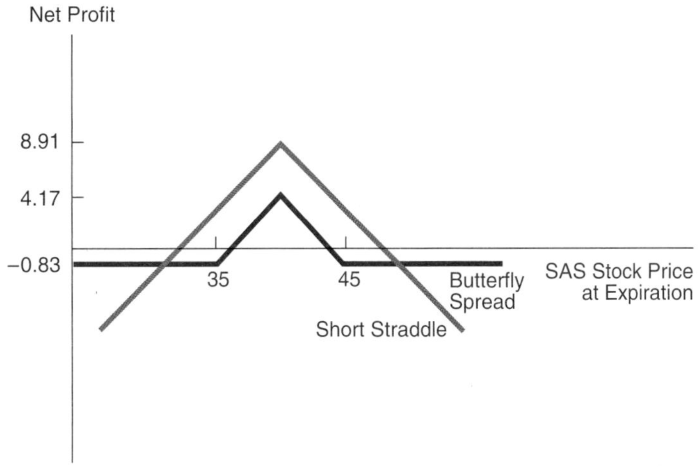
Net Profit
8.91
4.17
−0.83
35
45
Butterfly Spread
Short Straddle
SAS Stock Price at Expiration

RANGE FORWARDS

Despite a name that suggests otherwise, range (or "flexible") forwards are combinations of two option positions. They most often are used in hedging (as opposed to direct investment) applications, particularly in the management of foreign currency risk.[29] To see what they are and how they might be used in this context, suppose that the treasurer of a U.S. multinational corporation knows today that he will have a bill for imported goods that must be paid in three months. This bill, denominated in German marks and requiring a payment of DEM 1,000,000, presents a challenge for a dollar-based company because it must buy the marks it needs rather than generate them in the natural flow of business. As shown in Chapter 23, this is a classic opportunity to use derivatives to hedge the firm's FX exposure.

After contacting a number of dealers in the OTC market, the treasurer establishes prices and terms for several DEM forward and option contracts. These are listed in Table 24.10,

[29]For a more complete discussion of range forward applications, see Roger G. Clarke and Mark P. Kritzman, *Currency Management: Concepts and Practices* (Charlottesville, Va.: Research Foundation of the Institute of Chartered Financial Analysts, 1996): and Charles Smithson, Clifford W. Smith Jr., and D. Sykes Wilford, *Managing Financial Risk* (Burr Ridge, Ill.: Richard D. Irwin, 1995).

TABLE 24.10 **HYPOTHETICAL DEM DERIVATIVE PRICES AND TERMS**

Derivative	Contract/Striking Price (USD/DEM)	Expiration	DEM Amount	Price (USD/DEM)
Forward:	$0.67	3 months	1,000,000	—
Calls:	0.64	3 months	1,000,000	0.034
	0.67	3 months	1,000,000	0.015
	0.70	3 months	1,000,000	0.004
Puts:	0.64	3 months	1,000,000	0.004
	0.67	3 months	1,000,000	0.015
	0.70	3 months	1,000,000	0.034

FIGURE 24.23 **COMPARING LONG POSITIONS IN REGULAR AND RANGE FORWARDS**

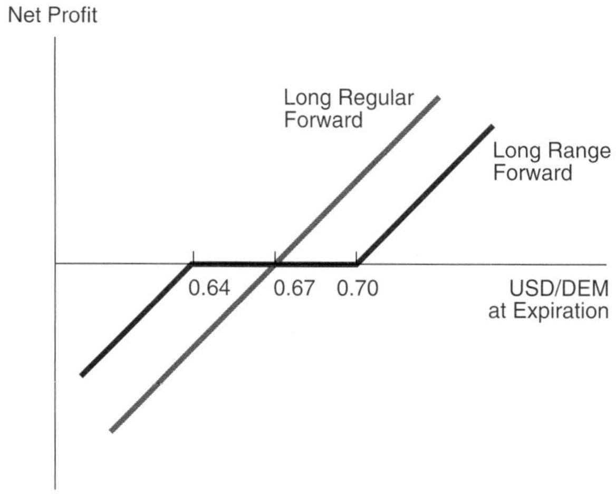
Net Profit
Long Regular Forward
Long Range Forward
0.64
0.67
0.70
USD/DEM at Expiration

which states prices on a direct (i.e., USD/DEM) basis. The treasurer could lock in a three-month forward rate of USD 0.67/DEM without cost in two ways. First, he could commit to a long position in the DEM forward with a contract amount of DEM 1,000,000. Second, he could buy the DEM call option struck at USD 0.67/DEM and pay for it by selling the DEM put at the same exercise rate. As shown in Chapter 11, the put-call parity model indicates that buying a call and selling a put with the same exercise rate is equivalent to a long forward position. Further, this second strategy would generate a zero-cost forward (i.e., $C_0 = P_0$) only when the common exercise rate is set equal to the prevailing forward rate.

As a third alternative, what if the treasurer: (1) bought the 0.70 call for USD $0.004 per mark, and (2) sold the 0.64 put for the same price? Once again, this would be a costless combination of options; however, since the two options do not have a common exercise price, this combination is not equivalent to the actual forward—it is a range forward. At the expiration date, one of three things will happen: (1) if the spot FX rate is greater than USD 0.70/DEM, the treasurer will exercise his call and buy marks at that level; (2) if the spot FX rate is less than USD 0.64/DEM, the dealer to whom the treasurer sold the put will force him to buy marks for USD 0.64 per mark, and (3) if the spot FX rate is in between these extremes, both options will finish out of the money and the treasurer will buy the required currency at the regular market price. This payoff scheme is contrasted with the regular contract in Figure 24.23.

If the treasurer takes a long position in the regular forward contract, he will buy his marks at USD 0.67/DEM, whether or not the prevailing exchange rate in three months is

THE INTERNET *Investments Online*

Additional information on options contracts and strategies can be found at:

www.cboe.com/products Among the products featured on this CBOE page are interest rate options, flex options, and international-index options. Flex options are featured at **www.cboe.com/institutional/flex.html.**

www.finance.wat.ch/cbt/options This page on the Finance Watch site presents an overview of options, option prices, and the use of hedges and different trading strategies.

www.optionmax.com This is the site of a software seller, but the pages here include descriptions of options strategies, from the simple to the complex, and charts of the resulting payoff patterns.

above or below this level. Thus, although he is protected against a weakening dollar, he cannot benefit if the domestic currency strengthens. With a long position in the range forward, though, in exchange for worse FX "insurance"—namely, a maximum purchase USD 0.70/DEM—he could pay as little as USD 0.64/DEM if the dollar gets stronger. Finally, many zero-cost range forwards could be created; for any desired out-of-the money call option, there will be an out-of-the-money put at some exercise price that has the same premium. In fact, the actual forward contract can be viewed as a zero-cost range forward for which the put and the call options are both struck at USD 0.67/DEM.[30]

Summary

- Along with forwards and futures, options represent another basic form of derivative contracting. Like the forward positions to which they are linked, puts and calls are used as either stand-alone investments or as supplements to an existing collection of assets. In the latter application, they provide investors with a convenient and inexpensive way to restructure the risk–reward trade-off in a portfolio. The flexibility of this form of contracting permits investors to create unique payoff structures by combining different options in various ways. Option straddles, for instance, allow the holder to take advantage of a view on the underlying asset's volatility while remaining neutral about the direction of future price movements. Forward contracts can be viewed as a specifically chosen pair of options; and these contracts are special cases of option combinations known as range forwards.
- We consider how option contracts are valued in an efficient market. Although the mathematics of some valuation models can be formidable, the intuition behind the process is not. Each of three models we discuss—the two-state, the binomial, and the Black-Scholes—is based on the same three-step evolution. The first step is combining options with the underlying asset in order to create a riskless position. Invariably, this synthetic risk-free portfolio requires the sale (purchase) of multiple calls (puts) to offset to the full cash exposure of a single share of stock held long. This hedge ratio changes with movements in the underlying asset's price and the passage of time; therefore, the riskless hedge portfolio needs to be rebalanced frequently. Once it is formed, however, the option's value can be established by assuming that the hedge portfolio should earn the risk-free rate (i.e., the "no arbitrage" condition) and solving for the option value that makes this assumption true.
- The Black-Scholes model is extremely flexible. Although originally created for European-style call options on nondividend-bearing stock, this model extends easily to valuing put options and options on dividend-paying stocks. The payment of dividends decreases the value of an otherwise identical call option, but not by the amount of the dividend itself. We also discuss how volatility, the only user-provided variable in the valuation model, is either estimated directly from a historical series of asset prices or implied from option prices themselves.

[30]In the market for derivatives used to hedge interest rate exposures, the range forward is called an interest rate *collar*. We will see this concept in Chapter 25.

- We discuss the process for valuing American-style puts and calls and how this differs from the valuation of their European counterparts. Further, we explain how the Black-Scholes model could be adapted to value options on other underlying assets, such as stock indexes, foreign currency, or commodity futures contracts. An introduction to the use and valuation of several exotic options having nonstandard payoffs is also offered.

Questions

1. Straddles have been described as "volatility plays." Explain what this means for both long and short straddle positions. Given the fact that volatility is a primary factor in how options are priced, under what conditions might an investor who believes that markets are efficient ever want to create a straddle?
2. Put-call-forward parity and range forward positions both involve the purchase of a call option and the sale of a put option (or vice versa) on the same underlying asset. Describe the relationship between these two trading strategies. Is one a special case of the other?
3. *CFA Examination II (June 1993)*
   Michelle Industries issued a Swiss-franc denominated five-year discount note for CHF 200 million. The proceeds were converted to U.S. dollars to purchase capital equipment in the U.S. The company wants to hedge this currency exposure and is considering the following alternatives:
   (i) At-the-money Swiss Franc call options
   (ii) Swiss franc forwards
   (iii) Swiss franc futures
   Contrast the essential characteristics of each of these three derivative instruments. Evaluate the suitability of each in relation to Michelle's hedging objective, including both advantages and disadvantages.
4. *CFA Examination III (June 1991)*
   Six factors affect the value of call options on stocks. Three of these factors are: the current price of the stock, the time remaining until the option expires, and the dividend on the stock. Identify the other three factors and explain how and why changes in each of these three factors affect the value of call options.
5. "Although options are risky investments, they are valued by virtue of their ability to convert the underlying asset into a synthetic risk-free security." Explain what this statement means, being sure to describe the basic three-step process for valuing option contracts.
6. In valuing currency options with the Black-Scholes model, we saw that the risk-free rate on the foreign currency was equivalent to the dividend yield when an individual stock or stock index was the underlying asset. Discuss the appropriateness of this analogy. What sort of transaction involving foreign currency would be required to make this parallel exact?
7. Describe the condition under which it would be rational to exercise both an American-style put and call stock option before the expiration date. In both cases, comment specifically on the role that dividends play.
8. Explain why a change in the time to expiration (i.e., T) can have either a positive or negative impact on the value of a European-style put option. In this explanation, it will be useful to contrast the put's reaction with that of a European-style call, for which an increase in T has an unambiguously positive effect.
9. Currency option traders often speak of "buying low volatility (or 'vol') and selling high vol" rather than buying or selling the option itself. What does this mean exactly? From this perspective, what is the real underlying asset: volatility or foreign currency?
10. It has been shown empirically that stock volatility decreases as a stock's price increases. Comment on how this phenomenon would tend to bias the call and put option values generated by the Black-Scholes model, which assumes that volatility remains constant.
11. On October 19, 1987, the stock market (as measured by the Dow Jones Industrial Average) lost almost one-quarter of its value in a single day. Nevertheless, some traders made a profit buying call options on the stock index and then liquidating their positions before the market closed. Explain how this is possible, assuming that it was not a case of the traders taking advantage of spurious upward "ticks" in stock prices.

Problems

CFA

1. *CFA Examination III (June 1987)*

   You are considering the sale of a call option with an exercise price of $100 and one year to expiration. The underlying stock pays no dividends, its current price is $100, and you believe it will either increase to $120 or decrease to $80. The risk-free rate of interest is 10 percent.

   a. Describe the specific steps involved in applying the binomial option pricing model to calculate the option's value.

   b. Compare the binomial option pricing model to the Black-Scholes option pricing model.

CFA

2. *CFA Examination III (June 1992)*

   You have decided to buy protective put options to protect the U.S. stock holdings of one of Global Advisers Company's (GAC) portfolios from a potential price decline over the next three months. You have researched the stock index options available in the U.S. and have assembled the following information:

Stock Index Option	Current Index Value	Underlying Value of One Put	Strike Price of Put	Put Premium	Average Daily Trading Volume of Puts
S&P 100	$365.00	$100 times index	365	$10.25	10,000
S&P 500	390.00	$100 times index	390	11.00	4,000
NYSE	215.00	$100 times index	215	6.25	1,000

(For each stock index option, the total cost of one put is the put premium times 100.)

	Beta vs. S&P 500	Correlation with Portfolio
Portfolio	1.05	1.00
S&P 100	0.95	0.86
S&P 500	1.00	0.95
NYSE	1.03	0.91

   a. Using all relevant data from the above tables, calculate for each stock index option both the number and cost of puts required to protect a $7,761,700 diversified equity portfolio from loss. Show all calculations.

   b. Recommend and justify which stock index option to use to hedge the portfolio, including reference to two relevant factors other than cost.

   You know that it is very unlikely that the current stock index values will be exactly the same as the put strike prices at the time you make your investment decision.

   c. Explain the importance of the relationship between the strike price of the puts and the current index values as it affects your investment decision.

   d. Explain how an option pricing model may help you make an investment decision in this situation.

CFA

3. *CFA Examination II (May 1998)*

   Joel Franklin is a portfolio manager responsible for derivatives. Franklin observes an American-style option and a European-style option with the same strike price, expiration, and underlying stock. Franklin believes that the European-style option will have a higher premium than the American-style option.

   a. Critique Franklin's belief that the European-style option will have a higher premium.

   Franklin is asked to value a one-year European-style call option for Abaco Ltd. Common stock, which last traded at $43.00. He has collected the following information:

Closing stock price	\$43.00
Call and put option exercise price	45.00
One-year put option price	4.00
One-year Treasury bill rate	5.50%
Time to expiration	One year

b. Calculate, using put-call parity and information provided above, the European-style call option value.
c. State the effect, if any, of each of the following three variables on the value of a call option: (i) an increase in short-term interest rate, (ii) an increase in stock price volatility, and (iii) a decrease in time to option expiration.

4. Assuming that a one-year call option with an exercise price of \$38 is available for the stock of the DEW Corp., consider the following price tree for DEW stock over the next year:

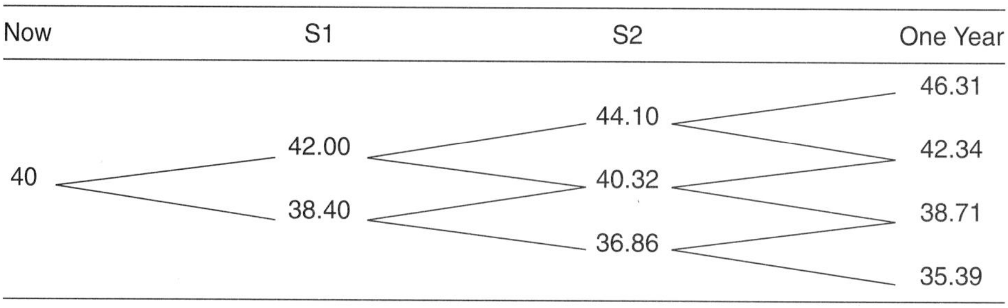
Now
S1
S2
One Year
46.31
44.10
42.00
42.34
40
40.32
38.40
38.71
36.86
35.39

a. If the sequence of stock prices that DEW stock follows over the year is 40.00, 42.00, 40.32, and 38.71, describe the composition of the initial riskless portfolio of stock and options you would form and all the subsequent adjustments you would have to make to keep this portfolio riskless. Assume the one-year risk-free rate is 6 percent.
b. Given the initial DEW price of \$40, what are the probabilities of observing each of the four terminal stock prices in one year? (Hint: In arriving at your answer, it will be useful to consider (i) the number of different ways that a particular terminal price could be achieved and (ii) the probability of an up or down movement.)
c. Use the binomial option model to calculate the present value of this call option.
d. Calculate the value of a one-year put option on DEW stock having an exercise price of \$38; be sure your answer is consistent with the correct response to part c.

5. Listed below is a two-period price tree for a share of stock in SAB Corp.:

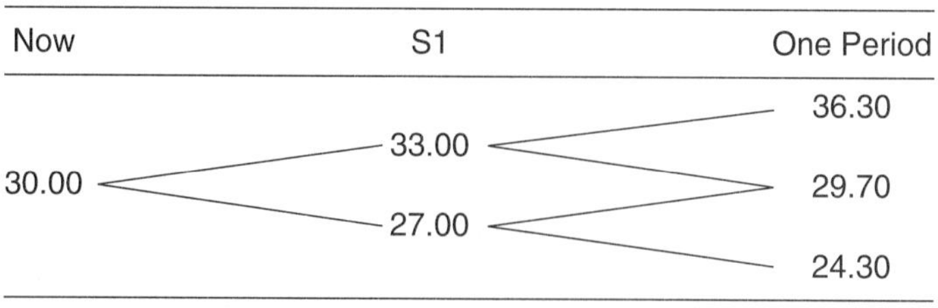
Now
S1
One Period
36.30
33.00
30.00
29.70
27.00
24.30

a. Using the binomial model, calculate the current fair value of a regular call option on SAB stock with the following characteristics: $X = 28$, $RFR = 5$ percent (per subperiod). You should also indicate the composition of the implied riskless hedge portfolio at the valuation date.
b. Using the same stock price tree, and assuming that the values of X and RF remain the same, calculate: (i) the value of an Asian-style (i.e., average price) call option, (ii) the value of a lookback call option, and (iii) the value of a digital call option with a fixed payout of $Q = 5$.

6. Consider the following questions on the pricing of options on the stock of ARB Inc.:

a. A share of ARB stock sells for $75 and has a standard deviation of returns equal to 20 percent per year. The current risk-free rate is 9 percent and the stock pays two dividends: (i) a $2 dividend just prior to the option's expiration day, which is 91 days from now (i.e., exactly one quarter of a year); and (ii) a $2 dividend 182 days from now (i.e., exactly one-half year). Calculate the Black-Scholes value for a European-style call option with an exercise price of $70.
b. What would be the price of a 91-day European-style put option on ARB stock having the same exercise price?
c. Calculate the change in the call option's value that would occur if ARB's management suddenly decided to suspend dividend payments and this action had no effect on the price of the company's stock.
d. Briefly describe (without calculations) how your answer in part a would differ under the following separate circumstances: (i) the volatility of ARB stock increases to 30 percent, and (ii) the risk-free rate decreases to 8 percent.

7. Consider the following data relevant to valuing a European-style call option on a non-dividend-paying stock: $X = 40$, $RFR = 9$ percent, $T =$ six months (i.e., 0.5), and $\sigma = 0.25$.
a. Compute the Black-Scholes option and hedge ratio values for the series of hypothetical current stock price levels shown in Table 24.1.
b. Explain why the values in part a differ from those shown in Table 24.1.
c. For $S = 40$, calculate the Black-Scholes value for a European-style put option. How much of this value represents time premium?

8. Suppose the current contract price of a futures contract on Commodity Z is $46.50 and the expiration date is in exactly six months (i.e., $T = 0.5$). The annualized risk-free rate over this period is 5.45 percent and the volatility of futures price movement is 23 percent, which is equal to that of the underlying commodity.
a. Calculate the values for both a call option and a put option or this futures contract, assuming both have an exercise price of $46.50 and a six-month expiration date.
b. Suppose the market prices for these contracts agree with the values you computed in part a. You decide to buy the call option and sell the put option. What sort of position have you just created? Under what circumstances (i.e., for what view of subsequent market conditions) would it make sense for an investor to create such a position?

9. Suppose the current value of the Standard and Poor's 500 index is 653.50 and the dividend yield on the index is 2.8 percent. Also, the yield curve is flat at a continuously compounded rate of 5.5 percent.
a. If you estimate the volatility factor for the index to be 16 percent, calculate the value of an index call option with an exercise price of 670 and an expiration date in exactly three months.
b. If the actual market price of this option is $17.40, calculate its implied volatility coefficient.
c. Besides volatility estimation error, explain why your valuation and the option's traded price might differ from one another.

10. Consider the following price data for TanCo stock in two different subperiods:
Subperiod A: 168.375; 162.875; 162.5; 161.625; 160.75; 157.75; 157.25; 157.75; 161.125; 162.5; 157.5; 156.625; 157.875; 155.375; 150.5; 155.75; 154.25; 155.875; 156; 152.75; 150.5; 150.75
Subperiod B: 122.5; 124.5; 121.875; 120.625; 119.5; 118.125; 117.75; 119.25; 122.25; 121.625; 120; 117.75; 118.375; 115.625; 117.75; 117.5; 118.5; 117.625; 114.625; 110.75
a. For each subperiod, calculate the annualized historical measure of stock volatility that could be used in pricing an option for TanCo. In your calculations, you may assume that there are 250 trading days in a year.
b. Suppose now that you decide to gather additional data for each subperiod. Specifically, you obtain information for a call option with a current price of $12.25 and the following characteristics: $X = 115$; $S = 120.625$; time to expiration $= 62$ days; $RFR = 7.42$ percent; and dividend yield $= 3.65$ percent. Here the risk-free rate and dividend yields are stated on an annual basis. Use the volatility measure from subperiod B and the Black-Scholes model to obtain the "fair value" for this call option. Based on your calculations, is the option currently priced as it should be? Explain.

11. In March, a derivatives dealer offers you the following quotes for June British pound option contracts (expressed in U.S. dollars per GBP):

Contract	Strike Price	Market Price of Contract: Bid	Offer
Call	USD 1.40	0.0642	0.0647
Put		0.0255	0.0260
Call	1.44	0.0417	0.0422
Put		0.0422	0.0427
Call	1.48	0.0255	0.0260
Put		0.0642	0.0647

a. Assuming each of these contracts specifies the delivery of GBP 31,250 and expires in exactly three months, complete a table similar to the following (expressed in dollars) for a portfolio consisting of the following positions:
   (i) Long a 1.44 call
   (ii) Short a 1.48 call
   (iii) Long a 1.40 put
   (iv) Short a 1.44 put

June USD/GBP	Net Initial Cost	Call 1.44 Profit	Call 1.48 Profit	Put 1.40 Profit	Put 1.44 Profit	Net Profit
1.36	—	—	—	—	—	—
1.40	—	—	—	—	—	—
1.44	—	—	—	—	—	—
1.48	—	—	—	—	—	—
1.52	—	—	—	—	—	—

b. Graph the total net profit (i.e., cumulative profit less net initial cost, ignoring time value considerations) relationship using the June USD/GBP rate on the horizontal axis (be sure to label the breakeven point(s)). Also, comment briefly on the nature of the currency speculation represented by this portfolio.

c. If in exactly one month (i.e., in April) the spot USD/GBP rate falls to 1.385 and the effective annual risk-free rates in the United States and England are 5 percent and 7 percent, respectively, calculate the equilibrium price differential that should exist between a long 1.44 call and a short 1.44 put position. (Hint: Consider what sort of forward contract this option combination is equivalent to and treat the British interest rate as a dividend yield.)

CFA

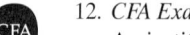

12. *CFA Examination III (June 1986)*

An institutional bond portfolio manager wants to increase the return on his existing holding of $1.0 million par value Government 11 percent bonds due June 1, 2006. The current market price of the bonds is 111. The manager has decided on June 1, 1986 to implement a covered option writing program on the portfolio. Available option information is listed below:

Options on Government 11% Bonds Due 2006 Expiring in 1986		Current Market Price of Option	Par Value of Bonds on Underlying Option	Option Commission $100 Par Value
December 112	CALLS	$1.65	$25,000	.05
December 109½	PUTS	$2.25	$25,000	.05

Standard deviation of the price of Government 11 percent bonds due in 2006 over 6-month holding periods has been 10 percent.

a. Design a "straddle-like" option-writing strategy for the manager.
b. Calculate the breakeven market prices for the underlying Government bond as a result of the "straddle-like" option-writing strategy.
c. Comment on the potential for a "straddle" option-writing strategy to add return to the portfolio.

13. In mid-May, there are two outstanding call option contracts available on the stock of ARB Co.:

Call #	Exercise Price	Expiration Date	Market Price
1	$50	August 19	$8.40
2	60	August 19	3.34

a. Assuming that you form a portfolio consisting of *one* call #1 held long and *two* calls #2 held short, complete the following table showing your intermediate steps. In calculating net profit, be sure to include the net initial cost of the options.

Price of ARB Stock at Expiration	Profit on Call #1 Position	Profit on Call #2 Position	Net Profit on Total Position
$40	—	—	—
45	—	—	—
50	—	—	—
55	—	—	—
60	—	—	—
65	—	—	—
70	—	—	—
75	—	—	—

b. Graph the net profit relationship in part a, using stock price on the horizontal axis. What is (are) the breakeven stock price(s)? What is the point of maximum profit?
c. Under what market conditions will this strategy (which is known as a *call ratio spread*) generally make sense? Does the holder of this position have limited or unlimited liability?

14. In developing the butterfly spread position, we showed that it could be broken down into two call option money spreads. Using the price data for SAS stock options from Table 24.3, demonstrate how a butterfly payoff structure similar to that shown in Figure 24.22 could be created using put options. Be specific as to the contract positions involved in the trade and show the expiration date net payoffs for the combined transaction.

CFA ©

15 *CFA Examination III (May 1997)*
Ken Webster manages a $100 million equity portfolio benchmarked to the S&P 500 index. Over the past two years, the S&P 500 index has appreciated 60 percent. Webster believes the market is overvalued when measured by several traditional fundamental/economic indicators. He is concerned about maintaining the excellent gains the portfolio has experienced in the past two years but recognizes that the S&P index could still move above its current 668 level. Webster is considering the following *option collar* strategy:

- Protection for the portfolio can be attained by purchasing an S&P 500 index put with a strike price of 665 (just out of the money).
- The put can be financed by selling two 675 calls (farther out of the money, for every put purchased.
- Because the combined delta of the two calls is less than 1 (that is, $2 \times 0.36 = 0.72$), the options will not lose more than the underlying portfolio advances.

The information in the following table describes the two options used to create the collar.

OPTIONS TO CREATE THE COLLAR

Characteristics	675 Call	665 Put
Option price	$4.30	$8.05
Option implied volatility	11.00%	14.00%
Option's delta	0.36	0.44
Contracts needed for collar	602	301

Notes:
- Ignore transaction costs.
- S&P 500 historical 30-day volatility = 12.00%.
- Time to option expiration = 30 days.

a. Describe the potential returns of the combined portfolio (the underlying portfolio plus the option collar) if after 30 days the S&P 500 index has: (i) risen approximately 5 percent to 701.00, (ii) remained at 668 (no change), and (iii) declined by approximately 5 percent to 635.
b. Discuss the effect on the hedge ratio (delta) of each option as the S&P 500 approaches the level for each of the potential outcomes listed in part a.
c. Evaluate the pricing of each of the following in relation to the volatility data provided: (i) the put, (ii) the call, and (iii) the collar.
d. Explain the term *wasting asset* in the context of the suggested collar strategy and discuss its effect on Webster's management of the portfolio.

References

Bookstaber, Richard M. *Option Pricing and Investment Strategies.* 3d ed. Chicago, Ill.: Probus Publishing, 1991.

Brenner, Menachem, Georges Courtadon, and Marti Subrahmanyam. "Options on the Spot and Options on Futures." *Journal of Finance* 40, no. 5 (December 1985).

Briys, Eric, Mondher Bellalah, Huu Minh Mai, and Francois De Varenne. *Options, Futures, and Exotic Derivatives.* New York: John Wiley and Sons, 1998.

Cox, John C., and Mark, Rubinstein. *Option Markets.* Englewood Cliffs, N.J.: Prentice-Hall, 1985.

Dubofsky. David A. *Options and Financial Futures: Valuation and Uses.* New York: McGraw-Hill, 1992.

Gastineau, Gary. *The Options Manual.* 3d ed. New York: McGraw-Hill, 1988.

Kolb, Robert W. *Options.* 3d ed. Cambridge, Mass.: Blackwell Publishers, 1997.

McMillan, Lawrence G. *Options as a Strategic Investment.* 3d ed. Upper Saddle River, N.J.: Prentice Hall, 1992.

Shastri, Kuldeep, and Kishore Tandon. "Options on Futures Contracts: A Comparison of European and American Pricing Models." *Journal of Futures Markets* 6, no. 4 (winter 1986).

Smith, Clifford W., Jr. "Option Pricing: A Review." *Journal of Financial Economics* 3, no. 1/2 (January–March 1976).

Stoll, Hans R., and Robert E. Whaley. *Futures and Options: Theory and Applications.* Cincinnati, Ohio: South-Western Publishing, 1993.

Chapter 25

Swap Contracts, Convertible Securities, and Other Embedded Derivatives

After you read this chapter, you should be able to answer the following questions:

- What are forward rate agreements and how can they be used to reduce the interest rate exposure of a borrower or an investor?
- What are interest rate swaps and how can they transform the cash flows of a fixed or floating rate security?
- How does the swap market operate and how are swap contracts quoted and priced?
- How can swaps be interpreted as a pair of capital market transactions and how does this aid in the swap valuation process?
- How is credit risk measured in the interest rate swap market?
- What are interest rate caps and floors and how are they related to interest rate swaps?
- What is an interest rate swaption and how can it be used to "monetize" an otherwise non-marketable asset?
- How does a currency swap differ from a "plain vanilla" interest rate swap and what is it used for?
- How can the swap contracting concept be adapted to manage equity and commodity price risk?
- How do the derivatives in convertible securities and warrant issues differ from traditional exchange-traded products?
- What are the similarities and differences between convertible preferred stock and convertible bonds?
- What are structured notes and what factors make their existence possible?
- How can securities with embedded derivatives reduce the funding cost of a corporate borrower?

Although derivatives only come in two basic "flavors"—forwards and options—the preceding chapters have shown that they can be used in a virtually unlimited number of situations by simply changing the contract terms or the nature of the underlying asset. In this chapter, we discuss several more ways in which these instruments can be modified to the specific needs of a particular end-user. Invariably, these modifications involve combining derivatives with other assets or liabilities to create the most highly valued cash flow pattern. We look at two general approaches to forming these combinations: "packages" of derivatives, such as **interest rate swaps**, caps, and floors; and derivatives that have been "embedded" in more fundamental assets, such as equity or debt issues.

To begin, we consider the market for OTC interest rate agreements—one of the fastest-growing segments of the derivatives industry in the past 20 years. In this examination, we once again focus on the differences between forward-based and option-based agreements while exploring the connection between the two. We then extend our discussion of swap contracting to include agreements based on foreign exchange, equity, and commodity price movements. Finally, we conclude the chapter with an overview of the myriad ways in which forwards and options are incorporated into other financial instruments. This includes an analysis of convertible securities, **warrants**, and **structured notes**. These innovations allow investors to acquire any of four different exposures—interest rate, currency, equity, or commodity price risk—in a creative and cost-effective manner.

OTC INTEREST RATE AGREEMENTS

In addition to futures and options contracts, an extremely active OTC market exists for products designed to manage an investor's or an issuer's interest rate risk. In describing strategies involving these instruments, it is useful to classify them as either forward-based or option-based contracts.[1]

Forward-Based Interest Rate Contracts

FORWARD RATE AGREEMENTS The **forward rate agreement** (FRA) is the most basic of the OTC interest rate contracts. In an FRA, two parties agree today to a future exchange of cash flows based on two different interest rates. One of the cash flows is tied to a yield that is fixed at the deal's origination (the fixed rate); the other is determined at some later date (the floating rate). On the contract's settlement date, the difference between the two interest rates is multiplied by the FRA's **notional principal** (the "scale" of the transaction) and prorated to the length of the holding period. As the London Interbank Offer Rate (LIBOR) is frequently used as the floating rate index, FRAs and the OTC equivalent of the Eurodollar futures contracts traded at the Chicago Mercantile Exchange, with two important exceptions: (1) FRAs typically require no collateral account, and (2) they are not marked to market on a daily basis.

An FRA's settlement date and maturity are defined by its name: a 3 × 6 FRA allows the investor to lock in three-month LIBOR, three months forward; a 12 × 18 FRA locks in six-month LIBOR, one year forward, and so forth. FRA market makers quote a bid–offer spread on a rate basis. For example, suppose the FRA rates for three-month LIBOR shown in Table 25.1 prevail in the market at date zero, with current three-month LIBOR assumed to be 4.50 percent. This means that on a 3 × 6 FRA, the market maker is prepared to pay a fixed rate of 4.81 percent for receipt of three-month LIBOR and to receive a fixed rate of 4.85 percent for payment of LIBOR. In either case, there will be no payment until LIBOR is revealed in month 3. Settlement can then be made in arrears at month 6 or in advance at month 3. If in arrears, the settlement flow will be adjusted to the actual number of days in the holding period and calculated by the following formula:

$$[\text{LIBOR} - \text{Fixed Rate}] \times [\text{Notional Principal}] \times \left[\frac{\text{Number of Days}}{360}\right]$$

[1]Some of the discussion in this section is based on Keith C. Brown and Donald J. Smith, *Interest Rate and Currency Swaps: A Tutorial* (Charlottesville, Va.: Research Foundation of the Institute of Chartered Financial Analysts, 1995).

TABLE 25.1 **INDICATIVE BID–OFFER QUOTES ON 3-MONTH FORWARD RATE AGREEMENTS**

Period	Bid	Offer
3 × 6	4.81%	4.85%
6 × 9	5.20	5.24
9 × 12	5.64	5.68
12 × 15	6.37	6.41
15 × 18	6.78	6.82
18 × 21	7.10	7.14
21 × 24	7.36	7.40

FIGURE 25.1 **A MATCHED PAIR OF 3 × 6 FRA TRANSACTIONS**

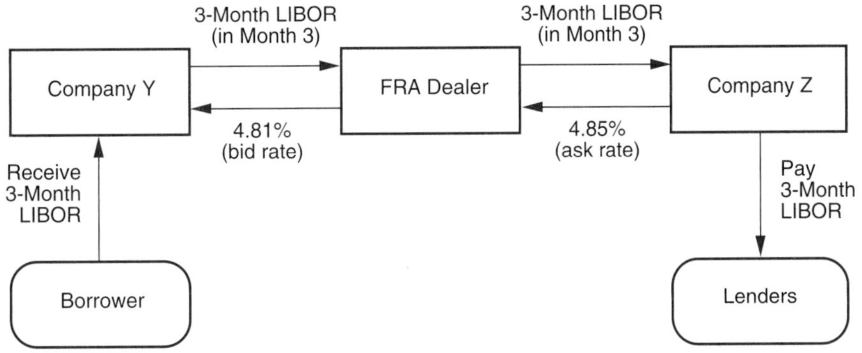
3-Month LIBOR
(in Month 3)
3-Month LIBOR
(in Month 3)
Company Y
FRA Dealer
Company Z
4.81%
(bid rate)
4.85%
(ask rate)
Receive
3-Month
LIBOR
Pay
3-Month
LIBOR
Borrower
Lenders

recalling that in the U.S. market, LIBOR is based on a 360-day year. The advance settlement amount is calculated as the present value of the in-arrears amount, using the prorated level of the realized LIBOR as the discount rate. Notice that this settlement occurs on a net basis—that is, only a single check for the rate differential will be written.

To see how an FRA might be used, suppose that Company Z decides to borrow financial capital for a six-month period, in two three-month installments. Because of the "set in advance, pay in arrears" convention for interest rate determination used in most debt markets, the firm finds itself exposed to rising interest rates over the next three months because the level of its second interest payment will not be established until the end of that period. (The amount of company Z's first three-month payment would be known at origination.) To solve this problem, the firm can acquire a 3 × 6 FRA whereby it pays the dealer's quoted fixed rate of 4.85 percent in exchange for receiving three-month LIBOR at the settlement date. This is illustrated on the right-hand side of Figure 25.1, which depicts both the borrowing and derivative transactions.

Once the dealer has committed to the FRA with Company Z, two things occur. First, Company Z no longer is exposed to a rising funding cost because it now has a forward contract that obligates the dealer to "sell" it the LIBOR it needs in month 3 at a "price" of 4.85 percent. Second, the dealer now is exposed to rising LIBOR because it will be obligated to make the net settlement payment if LIBOR exceeds 4.85 percent three months from now. That is, Company Z has effectively used the FRA to transfer its interest rate exposure to the dealer. Unless the dealer wishes to hold this position as a speculation that rates will subsequently fall, the exposure can be hedged by "buying" LIBOR from another counterparty for its bid rate of 4.81 percent. This alternative is shown on the left-hand-side of Figure

25.1 as a second FRA with Company Y, which is assumed to be an investor in a variable-rate asset who is naturally concerned about falling rates.

Now suppose that three-month LIBOR is 5.00 percent on the rate determination date in month 3 and that the agreements with Companies Y and Z were negotiated to have a notional principal of $10 million. If its contract specified settlement in arrears at month 6, Company Y would be obligated to pay the market maker $4,750, calculated as:

$$[0.0500 - 0.0481] \times [10{,}000{,}000] \times \left[\frac{90}{360}\right]$$

assuming there are 90 days between months 3 and 6. If settled in advance, the month 3 payment would be:

$$4{,}750 \div \left[1 + \frac{90 \times 0.0500}{360}\right] = \$4{,}691.36$$

Similarly, the payment from the dealer to Company Z would be $3,750 (= [0.0500 − 0.0485] × [10,000,000] × [90/360]) in month 6, or $3,703.70 if accelerated to month 3. By matching the FRAs, the market maker is fully hedged from interest rate risk. Its spread of four basis points, which translates into $1,000, compensates for the costs (e.g., transaction costs, credit risk) of making a market in these contracts.

Finally, although the terms "buy" and "sell" are awkward, they are commonly used when describing FRA transactions. Since the FRA has an initial value of zero and therefore is neither an asset nor a liability, a counterparty doesn't really buy or sell anything. Instead, the parties to the transaction enter into a contract that may obtain a positive or a negative value—depending on the direction of future interest rate level changes. Nevertheless, this language is consistent with interpreting LIBOR as the "commodity" involved in the deal. In that case, the fixed rate is then the price paid or received in exchange for LIBOR, so that the payer of the fixed rate (Company Z) is said to be buying LIBOR, with the fixed-rate receiver (Company Y) selling LIBOR.

INTEREST RATE SWAPS Although FRAs are quite useful, they represent a "one time only" solution to an interest rate risk management problem since they have a single settlement date. In fact, both investors and borrowers are routinely exposed to interest rate movements at regular intervals over an extended period of time, such as for the buyer and seller of a **floating rate note** that resets its coupon rate twice annually for several years according to movements in six-month LIBOR.[2] In that case, several "exposure dates" would need to be hedged, which could be accomplished with a series of FRAs. For example, suppose that an investor holding a one-year FRN paying quarterly coupons of three-month LIBOR becomes concerned that rates may fall in the future, thereby depressing the level of her last three coupons. (Recall that by convention her first coupon, payable in three months, is based on current LIBOR, which was assumed to be 4.50 percent.) Accordingly, she offsets this exposure by agreeing to receive the fixed rate on three separate FRA contracts: the

[2]As we discussed briefly in Chapter 15, a floating (or variable) rate note is a debt instrument that is similar to a fixed-income bond in that it pays coupons at regular (e.g., semiannual) dates during its life. The difference is that the floating-rate note, or FRN, pays a coupon that is adjusted in a predetermined way with changes in some reference rate. For instance, a typical payment formula might be to reset the coupon every six months at LIBOR + 0.25 percent, meaning that the coupon amount would vary directly with LIBOR. Do not confuse the two acronyms FRA and FRN: The former is an over-the-counter forward contract; the latter is a bond.

FIGURE 25.2 **CONVERTING A FLOATING RATE NOTE WITH A SERIES OF FRAs**

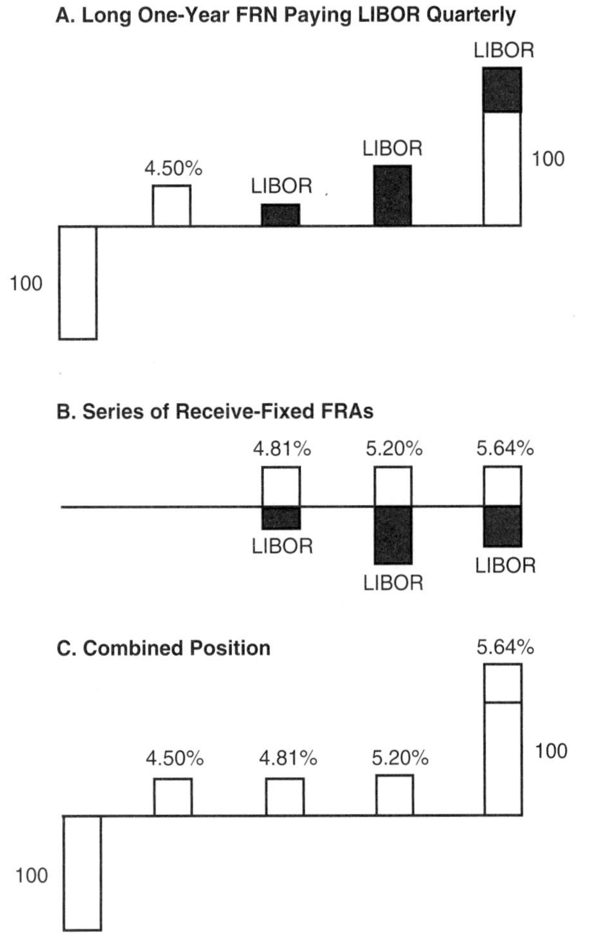
A. Long One-Year FRN Paying LIBOR Quarterly
LIBOR
4.50%
LIBOR
LIBOR
100
100
B. Series of Receive-Fixed FRAs
4.81%
5.20%
5.64%
LIBOR
LIBOR
LIBOR
C. Combined Position
5.64%
4.50%
4.81%
5.20%
100
100

3 × 6, the 6 × 9, and the 9 × 12. Given the bid rates quoted in Table 25.1, these positions transform the cash flows on the floating-rate asset as shown in Figure 25.2.

This series of FRAs locks in the coupon levels, but they are at different fixed rates and require three separate contracts. This may be inconvenient to the investor, who might prefer a single contract that covers all the future coupon dates using the same fixed rate. This is exactly what an interest rate swap does. Specifically, the swap contract can be viewed as a prepackaged series of forward contracts to buy or sell LIBOR (i.e., FRAs) at the same fixed rate. Alternatively, an FRA can be viewed as a one-date interest rate swap. Of course, for the swap and FRA markets to remain efficient, the single fixed rate on the swap would have to be the appropriate average of 4.50 percent, 4.81 percent, 5.20 percent, and 5.64 percent. For simplicity, assume that each quarterly settlement period is exactly 0.25 year. This average can be approximated by solving for the internal rate of return on the hedged FRN:

$$100 = \frac{4.50 \times (0.25)}{(1 + \text{IRR})^1} + \frac{4.81 \times (0.25)}{(1 + \text{IRR})^2} + \frac{5.20 \times (0.25)}{(1 + \text{IRR})^3} + \frac{100 + [5.64 \times (0.25)]}{(1 \times \text{IRR})^4}$$

or IRR = 1.258 percent. Thus, 5.03 percent (1.258 × 4) would be the fixed rate on a one-year, receive-fixed swap consistent with the forward rate agreements listed in Table 25.1. Notice that this IRR calculation is a very accurate approximation for the forward rate "annuitization" process we saw in Chapter 23. Specifically, a more general way to determine the swap fixed rate (SFR) that represents the appropriate average of this sequence of spot and forward LIBOR would be to solve the following equation:

$$\frac{(4.50)(0.25)(\text{NP})}{\left[1+\frac{i_{0,3}}{4}\right]}+\frac{(4.81)(0.25(\text{NP})}{\left[1+\frac{i_{0,6}}{4}\right]}+\frac{(5.20)(0.25)(\text{NP})}{\left[1+\frac{i_{0,9}}{4}\right]}+\frac{(5.64)(0.25)(\text{NP})}{\left[1+\frac{i_{0,12}}{4}\right]}$$

$$=$$

$$\frac{(\text{SFR})(0.25)(\text{NP})}{\left[1+\frac{i_{0,3}}{4}\right]}+\frac{(\text{SFR})(0.25)(\text{NP})}{\left[1+\frac{i_{0,6}}{4}\right]}+\frac{(\text{SFR})(0.25)(\text{NP})}{\left[1+\frac{i_{0,9}}{4}\right]}+\frac{(\text{SFR})(0.25)(\text{NP})}{\left[1+\frac{i_{0,12}}{4}\right]}$$

where NP is the swap's notional principal and $i_{0,t}$ is the spot discount rate for a cash flow received or paid at a date t months in the future. For a given interest rate term structure and contract notional principal, SFR is the only unknown element in this equation and can be solved for accordingly.[3]

Although interest rate swaps are priced off the LIBOR forward yield curve, they are quoted off the Treasury bond yield curve. That is, the fixed rate side of a U.S. dollar–based swap generally is broken down to two components for trading purposes: (1) the yield of a Treasury bond with a maturity comparable to that of the swap; and (2) a risk premium term known as the **swap spread**. Because the floating rate side of the agreement typically is based on LIBOR "flat" (i.e., without any adjustment), the swap dealer can incorporate his bid–ask profit margin directly into this swap spread. Table 25.2 lists a representative set of fixed-rate quotes for U.S. dollar swaps, both in absolute and swap spread terms. Each of the swaps represented in this table assumes semiannual settlement dates with six-month LIBOR as the floating rate. For example, the swap dealer would be willing to pay the fixed rate of 5.47 percent on a five-year contract, a rate that is 65 basis points greater than the five-year T-bond yield. Notice that swaps with maturities as long as 30 years are quoted, although most contracts are transacted with maturities of 10 years or less.

With the fixed rate on the swap linked to a bond (i.e., 365-day) yield and the floating rate as a money market (360-day in the U.S. market) yield, the swap settlement cash flows are calculated in a slightly different manner than for FRAs. Specifically, while the swap is still a net settlement contract, the date t fixed- and floating-rate payments are determined separately as:

$$(\text{Fixed} - \text{Rate Payment})_t = (\text{Swap Fixed Rate}) \times \left(\frac{\text{Number of Days}}{365}\right) \times (\text{Notional Principal})$$

and

$$(\text{Floating-Rate Payment})_t = (\text{Reference Rate})_{t-1} \times \left(\frac{\text{Number of Days}}{360}\right) \times (\text{Notional Principal})$$

[3]See Vipul S. Bansal, M. E. Ellis, and John F. Marshall, "The Pricing of Short-Dated and Forward Interest Rate Swaps," *Financial Analysts Journal* 49, no. 2 (March–April 1993): 82–87; and Robert Brooks, *Interest Rate Modeling and the Risk Premiums in Interest Rate Swaps* (Charlottesville, Va.: Research Foundation of the Institute of Chartered Financial Analysts, 1997).

TABLE 25.2 INTEREST RATE SWAP AND SWAP SPREAD QUOTES

A. Absolute (i.e., T-Bond + Swap Spread) Basis

	Security	Time	Bid	Ask	Change	Open	High	Low	PRV CLS
US SWAPS									
1) USSWAP2	Curncy	15:40	5.2800	5.3200	+0.0400	5.2600	5.3000	5.2360	5.2600
2) USSWAP3	Curncy	15:40	5.3600	5.4000	+0.0100		5.4900		5.3700
3) USSWAP4	Curncy	15:40	5.4100	5.4500	+0.0200	5.3800	5.7000	5.3238	5.4100
4) USSWAP5	Curncy	15:40	5.4700	5.5100	+0.0400	5.4000	5.4900	5.3538	5.4500
5) USSW6	Curncy	15:40	5.5100	5.5500	+0.0500	5.4280	5.5300	5.4113	5.4800
6) USSWAP7	Curncy	15:40	5.5500	5.5900	+0.0400	5.5300	5.8200	5.4690	5.5300
7) USSW8	Curncy	15:40	5.5900	5.6300	+0.0500	5.5330	5.6100	5.5162	5.5600
8) USSW9	Curncy	15:40	5.6200	5.6600	+0.0500	5.5800	5.6400	5.5612	5.5900
9) USSWAP10	Curncy	15.:40	5.6700	5.7100	+0.0400	5.6400	5.6900	5.6075	5.6500
10) USSWAP15	Curncy	15:40	5.8500	5.8900	+0.0500	5.8150	5.8700	5.8050	5.8200
11) USSWAP20	Curncy	15:40	5.9500	5.9900	+0.0500	5.9200	5.9700	5.9050	5.9200
12) USSWAP30	Curncy	15:40	5.9600	6.000	+0.0700	5.9100	5.9800	5.8700	5.9100

B. Swap Spread Basis

	Security	Time	Bid	Ask	Change	Open	High	Low	PRV CLS
DLR-DLR SWAP SPREAD									
1) $$SWAP2	Index	15:40	48	52	−1	53	53	48	53
2) $$SWAP3	Index	15:40	55	59	—	59	60	55	55
3) $$SWAP4	Index	15:40	60	64	+2	62	65	60	58
4) $$SWAP5	Index	15:40	65	69	+3	65	70	65	66
5) $$SWAP7	Index	15:40	70	74	+3	70	74	69	71
6) $$SWAP10	Index	15:40	74	78	+1	77	78	74	73
7) $$SWAP15	Index	15:40	92	96	—	95	96	92	92
8) $$SWAP20	Index	15:40	103	107	+1	106	108	102	106
9) $$SWAP30	Index	15:40	59	63	—	63	63	59	59

SPREAD OFF U.S. TREASURY
NOTE: 20 YR SPREAD OFF 10YR NOTE

Source: Bloomberg, 10 February 1999.

In these equations, the fixed rate never changes and the floating rate reference rate (i.e., LIBOR) always is determined at the beginning of a given settlement period.

As an example of these calculations, assume that Counterparty A is an institutional investor who currently holds a three-year bond paying a semiannual coupon of 7.00 percent. He feels that interest rates are likely to rise in the near term and, although he does not want to sell this position, he is concerned about a reduction in the bond's value. Consequently, the investor decides to convert his investment into a synthetic floating-rate note whose coupons will rise with future LIBOR increases. Specifically, he accomplishes this by agreeing to pay the fixed rate on a three-year interest rate swap contract with Counterparty B (i.e., the swap dealer). The terms of this agreement would be summarized as follows:

- Origination Date: February 10, 1999
- Maturity Date: February 10, 2002
- Notional Principal: $30 million
- Fixed-Rate Payer: Counterparty A (i.e., the investor)
- Swap Fixed Rate: 5.40 percent (semiannual, actual/actual bond basis)

FIGURE 25.3

CONVERTING CASH FLOWS FROM A FIXED-RATE BOND ISSUE WITH A SWAP AGREEMENT

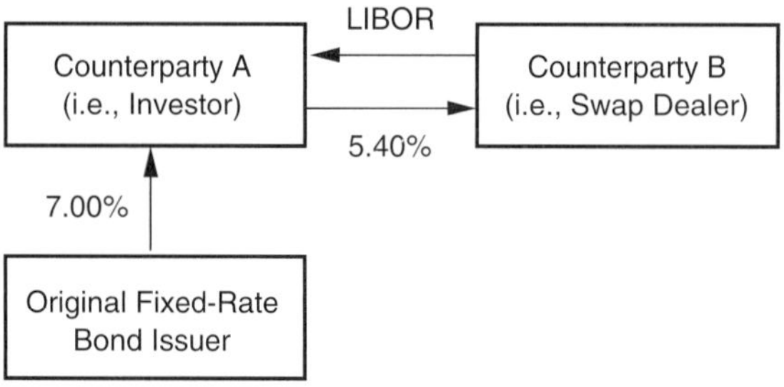
LIBOR
Counterparty A
(i.e., Investor)
Counterparty B
(i.e., Swap Dealer)
5.40%
7.00%
Original Fixed-Rate
Bond Issuer

$$\text{Net Interest Income} = (7.00\%)(360/365) + [\text{LIBOR} - (5.40\%)(360/365)]$$
$$= \text{LIBOR} + 1.57\%$$

TABLE 25.3

SETTLEMENT CASH FLOWS FOR A 3-YEAR "PLAIN VANILLA" INTEREST RATE SWAP (FIXED-PAYER'S PERSPECTIVE)

Settlement Date	Number of Days	Current LIBOR	Fixed-Rate Payment	Floating-Rate Receipt	Net Payment (Receipt)
2/10/99	—	5.00%	—	—	
8/10/99	181	5.30%	803,342	754,167	49,175
2/10/00	184	5.85%	816,658	812,667	3,991
8/10/00	182	6.00%	807,781	887,250	(79,469)
2/10/01	184	5.60%	816,658	920,000	(103,342)
8/10/01	181	5.20%	803,342	844,667	(41,325)
2/10/02	184	5.35%	816,658	797,333	19,325

- Fixed-Rate Receiver: Counterparty B (i.e., the swap dealer)
- Floating Rate: Six-month LIBOR (money market basis)
- Settlement Dates: February 10 and August 10 of each year
- LIBOR Determination: Set in advance, paid in arrears

This "fixed-for-floating" transaction—the most basic form of a swap—is often called a *plain vanilla* agreement. Figure 25.3 illustrates the effect of combining the swap with the underlying bond position while Table 25.3 lists the settlement cash flows from the investor's perspective for a hypothetical time-series of six-month LIBOR. In this display, the fixed-rate payer makes the net settlement payment when the day count-adjusted level of LIBOR is less than 5.40 percent; the fixed-rate receiver makes the settlement payment when LIBOR exceeds 5.40 percent.

Plain vanilla swaps are generally used for the same reason as FRAs: namely, to restructure the cash flows of an interest-sensitive asset or liability. In this example, the investor has reduced the price sensitivity (i.e., duration) of his asset by converting the fixed-rate coupon into one that adjusts to shifting market conditions. We saw in Chapter 22 that making this change synthetically with derivatives—rather than through a physical rebalancing of the portfolio–is the more cost-effective method. Given A's original coupon rate of 7 percent, the net annualized cash flow he will receive after accounting for the swap position will be:

Fixed-Rate Bond Coupon Receipt		= (7.00%) × (360/365)	= 6.90%
Swap:	(i) LIBOR Receipt		= LIBOR
	(ii) Fixed Payment	= [(5.40%) × (360/365)]	= (5.33%)
Net Interest Income:			= LIBOR + 1.57%

where this amount has been adjusted to a 360-day year. Thus, the net impact of combining the swap with the fixed-rate bond is to convert that security into a variable-rate asset paying a coupon of LIBOR plus 157 basis points.

There is another important way of viewing this swap transaction. With the swap agreement, Counterparty A is effectively paying the fixed-rate coupons he receives from his bond in exchange for receiving floating-rate coupons. That is, the pay-fixed swap position can be viewed as equivalent to holding a portfolio consisting of: (1) a long position in a par-value FRN paying semiannual coupons of LIBOR, and (2) a short position in a part-value fixed-rate note paying semiannual coupons of 5.40 percent. This capital market interpretation is illustrated in Figure 25.4. Notice that by essentially buying and selling two different par-value instruments, no net principal amount exists at origination or maturity; this is what allows the swap's principal to be notional (i.e., not actually exchanged). Thus, all the swap agreement really does is transform the nature of the coupon payments.

The immediate consequence of this interpretation is that at any point in time the value of the pay-fixed swap position can be calculated as the present value of the floating-rate cash flows held as an asset minus the present value of the fixed-rate bond cash flows that is a liability, or:

(PV of Pay-Fixed Swap) = (PV of FRN Paying LIBOR) − (PV of Fixed-Rate Bond Paying 5.40%)

FIGURE 25.4 **A CAPITAL MARKET INTERPRETATION OF AN INTEREST RATE SWAP**

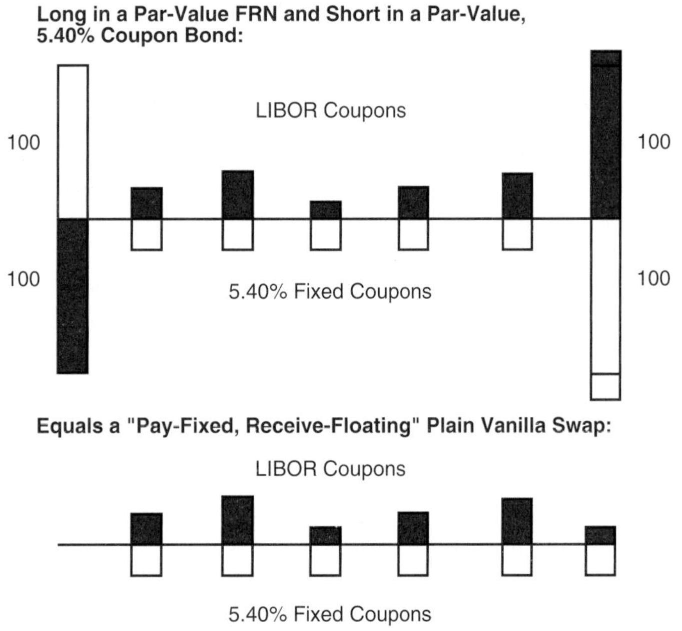
Long in a Par-Value FRN and Short in a Par-Value, 5.40% Coupon Bond:
LIBOR Coupons
100
100
100
100
5.40% Fixed Coupons
Equals a "Pay-Fixed, Receive-Floating" Plain Vanilla Swap:
LIBOR Coupons
5.40% Fixed Coupons

For example, suppose that one year after this swap was originated, yields have generally risen so that the fixed rate on a new two-year swap (i.e., the remaining time until the original maturity) is 6.40 percent. The value of this swap under these conditions can be established in two steps. First, on any settlement date, the FRN will be valued at par since its coupon always is reset according to current market conditions. Second, the market value of a bond paying a coupon of only 5.40 percent will fall, which benefits Counterparty A to whom this is a liability. Thus, using the new swap rate as a discount factor, A's position in the agreement (which as a forward contract had no value at origination) is now worth:

$$100 - \left[\sum_{t=1}^{4} \frac{(5.40/2)}{(1 + 0.064/2)^t} + \frac{100}{(1 + 0.064/2)^4}\right] = 1.8497$$

or 1.8497 percent of notional principal. Therefore, if Counterparty A chose to unwind his contract at this time, the dealer would be willing to pay as much as \$554,908 (= 0.018497 × \$30 million) and then find a new swap counterparty who would pay the now current fixed rate of 6.40 percent. The \$554,908 is considered to be the marked-to-market value of the swap. Given that interest rates have risen since inception, the original contract is now an asset to the fixed-rate payer (i.e., Counterparty A) and a liability to the fixed-rate receiver (i.e., the dealer).

An important characteristic of the swap agreement is that it becomes an *asset* to one participant and a *liability* to the other as soon as market conditions change after the terms of the contract are set. This means that swaps entail credit risk. To see why, consider what would happen to Counterparty A if, on a particular settlement date when LIBOR was 10 percent, the swap dealer was unable to make the net settlement payment. In that case, the investor would receive only the 7 percent coupon from his bond rather than the 11.57 percent (= LIBOR + 1.57 percent) coupon he expected from his synthetic FRN. The possibility that the swap counterparty either cannot or will not honor its obligation means that the synthetic floating-rate note carries *more* credit risk than the original fixed-rate bond. Further, notice that the swap dealer also will be concerned about the ability of Counterparty A to perform on the agreement when LIBOR is less than 5.40 percent. Thus, like any forward arrangement, the credit risk on a swap runs two ways.

What would it cost Counterparty A if, with exactly two years remaining on the contract described above, the swap dealer suffered bankruptcy and defaulted on the remainder of the agreement? To retain his synthetic FRN, the investor would have to find a new swap dealer to replace the old contract. Unfortunately, with the change in market conditions, Counterparty A will now have to pay 6.40 percent to receive LIBOR over the next two years, implying an additional cost of 50 basis points (times 30 million) each settlement period. Thus, the economic consequence to A of the dealer's default can be measured as:

$$\sum_{t=1}^{4} \frac{[(0.064/2) - (0.054/2)] \times (30{,}000{,}000)}{(1 + 0.064/2)^t} = \$554{,}908$$

which, of course, is the same amount as the marked-to-market value of the swap. Thus, this figure represents the current potential default loss for the counterparty to whom the swap is an asset.[4]

Finally, although interest rate swaps have been in existence since 1981, relatively little empirical evidence exists on how they are priced in the marketplace because of the

[4]For an interesting discussion of credit risk in the swap market, see Eric H. Sorensen and Thierry F. Bollier, "Pricing Interest Rate Swap Default Risk," *Financial Analysts Journal* 50, no. 3 (May–June 1994): 23–33.

nonpublic nature of the information about these contracts. The available evidence includes Kim and Koppenhaver's investigation of commercial bank activity in the swap market; Sun, Sundaresan, and Wang, who examined the consistency of bid–ask quotes issued by two swap dealers with different credit grades; and Brown, Harlow, and Smith, as well as Minton, who tested several theoretical relationships designed to explain the historical pattern of variation in the swap spread component.[5] Although each of the studies examined a different aspect of the swap contracting process, the collective evidence they present is consistent with the notion that this market works in an orderly and efficient manner. Further, the mechanics of swap pricing, which have matured over time, seem to be integrated with other affiliated securities, such as Treasury notes and bills and Eurodollar futures contracts.

OPTION-BASED INTEREST RATE CONTRACTS

In this section, we discuss three types of OTC interest rate option arrangements as well as their relationship with interest rate swaps: (1) caps and floors, the two most basic option-based products; (2) collars, special combinations of caps and floors; and (3) options that allow the holder to enter into a swap contract at a later date.

CAPS AND FLOORS Interest rate cap and floor agreements are equivalent to portfolios of interest rate option contracts, with each contract corresponding to a different settlement period. A **cap agreement** is a series of cash settlement interest rate options, typically based on LIBOR. The seller of the cap, in return for the option premium that is usually paid at origination, is obliged to pay the difference between LIBOR and the exercise, or cap, rate (times the fraction of the year, times the notional principal) whenever that difference is positive. The seller of a **floor agreement** makes settlement payments only when LIBOR is below the floor rate. No payment is made if LIBOR is above the floor or below the cap rate. As with swaps and FRAs, settlement can be either in advance or in arrears. Payment in arrears is more common because these contracts usually are used to hedge exposure to floating-rate bank loans and notes, which typically settle in arrears.

From these descriptions, the date t settlement payments on cap and floor agreements can be written as follows:

$$\textit{Cap Settlement}\text{: (Notional Principal)} \times \left(\frac{\text{Number of Days}}{360}\right) \times \max\left[\text{LIBOR}_{t-1} - X_c, 0\right]$$

and

$$\textit{Floor Settlement}\text{: (Notional Principal)} \times \left(\frac{\text{Number of Days}}{360}\right) \times \max\left[X_f - \text{LIBOR}_{t-1}, 0\right]$$

where:

X_c = **the cap exercise rate**
X_f = **the floor exercise rate**

[5]See Sung-Hwa Kim and Gary D. Koppenhaver, "An Empirical Analysis of Bank Interest Rate Swaps," *Journal of Financial Services Research* 7, no. 1 (January 1993): 57–72; Tong-sheng Sun, Suresh Sundaresan, and Ching Wang, "Interest Rate Swaps: An Empirical Investigation," *Journal of Financial Economics* 34, no. 1 (August 1993): 77–99; Keith C. Brown, W. V. Harlow, and Donald J. Smith, "An Empirical Analysis of Interest Rate Swap Spreads," *Journal of Fixed Income* 3, no. 3 (March 1994): 61–78; and Bernadette A. Minton, "An Empirical Examination of Basic Valuation Models for Plain Vanilla U.S. Interest Rate Swaps," *Journal of Financial Economics* 44, no. 2 (May 1997): 251–277.

(Recall once again that a 360-day year is used because of the quotation convention for U.S. dollar LIBOR.) For example, consider a three-year, semiannual settlement, 8 percent cap on six-month LIBOR. The buyer of the cap pays the writer an up-front premium, quoted as a percentage of the notional principal. Assuming the cost is 120 basis points and the notional principal is $100 million, the cost of the cap is $1,200,000.[6] Suppose that settlement dates are on the 15th of May and November of each year and that LIBOR on one particular May 15th is 9⅛ percent. The holder of the cap will receive settlement in arrears the following November in the amount of $575,000, calculated as (9.125 percent − 8 percent) × $100 million × (184/360).

The payoff relationships for caps and floors can be illustrated using traditional, option-style diagrams. Figure 25.5 portrays an 8 percent cap and a 4 percent floor on LIBOR. Notice that the payoff diagram for the cap looks like a typical call option on a commodity and the floor takes the form of a put option. Indeed, following the convention where LIBOR is the commodity, caps are referred to as "calls on LIBOR" and floors as "puts on LIBOR." Alternatively, a cap agreement on LIBOR is a series of put options on an underlying Eurodollar time deposit. In effect, the owner of the option has the right, but not the obligation, to sell to the cap writer a time deposit having a coupon rate equal to the cap rate in the amount of the notional principal of the contract. The owner exercises that option if current LIBOR exceeds the cap rate, thus selling a relatively low coupon deposit at par value. The proceeds of that sale can then be used to buy a time deposit that earns the higher market rate. The gain on those hypothetical transactions is equivalent to the payoff on the cap agreement. Whether one interprets a cap as a call on LIBOR or a put on a time deposit (and, similarly, a floor as a put on LIBOR or a all on a time deposit) is purely a matter of semantic preference.[7]

COLLARS An **interest rate collar** is a combination of a cap and a floor, a long position in one and a short position in the other. To buy a 4 percent–8 percent collar on LIBOR is to buy an 8 percent cap and to write a 4 percent floor. The buyer will receive cash payments when LIBOR exceeds 8 percent, make payments when LIBOR is below 4 percent, and neither receive nor pay if LIBOR is between 4 percent and 8 percent. Often the motive for a firm to buy a collar is to reduce the initial cost of acquiring the protection from higher levels of LIBOR, as the up-front receipt from selling the floor can be used to offset the cost of buying the cap.

A special interest rate collar occurs when the initial premiums on the cap and the floor are equal and therefore offset each other. For instance, suppose that the premium on a three-year, 4 percent floor is 120 basis points, which matches the premium on the 8 percent cap. The combination is known as zero-cost, or zero-premium, collar. This is a useful concept because it is easy to show that an interest rate swap is just a special case of a zero-cost interest rate collar. To see this, consider again the 4 percent–8 percent zero-cost collar on LIBOR that was constructed from buying the 8 percent cap and selling the 4 percent floor. Now tighten the collar by lowering the cap rate to 7 percent. The up-front premium paid by

[6]In practice, interest rate caps and floors are quoted by market makers on a volatility basis, for instance, 18.5 percent bid and 19.5 percent offered. That measure of volatility (stated as a standard deviation), plus the exercise rate, the current term structure of interest rates, and the time-frame for the contract, are then entered into an option pricing model to obtain the actual amount of the premium. Hull has shown that this amount can be established by adapting Black's model for valuing futures options to price each separate option in the contract (i.e., "caplets" and "floorlets"), and then summing them across all settlement dates. See John C. Hull, *Options, Futures, and Other Derivatives,* 3d ed. (Englewood Cliffs, N.J.: Prentice-Hall, 1997).

[7]A good review of these instruments can be found in Peter A. Abken, "Interest Rate Caps, Collars, and Floors," Federal Reserve Bank of Atlanta *Economic Review* 74 (November–December 1989): 2–24.

FIGURE 25.5

PAYOFF DIAGRAMS FOR BUYING AND WRITING AN INTEREST RATE CAP AND FLOOR

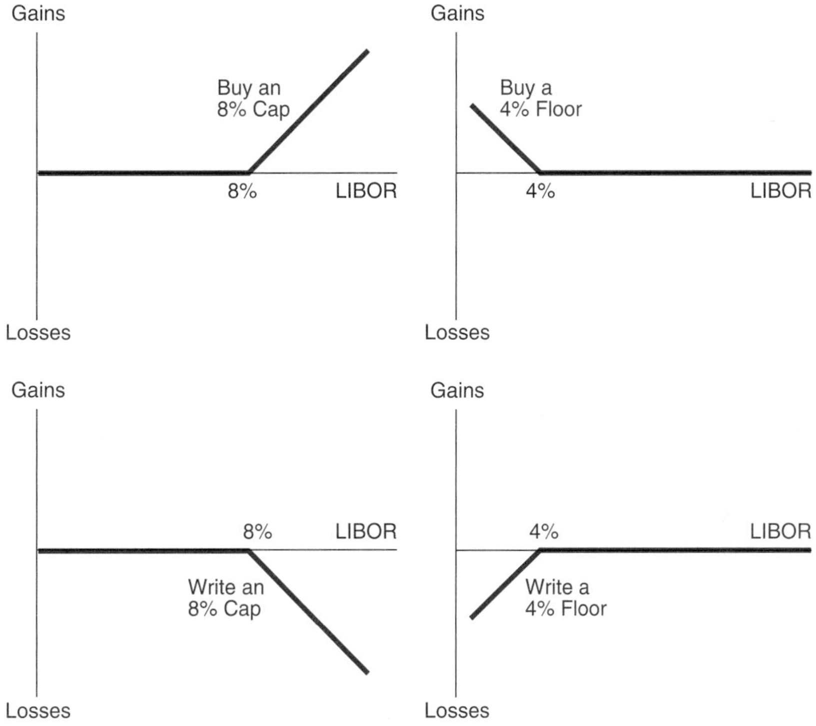
Gains
Buy an
8% Cap
8%
LIBOR
Losses
Gains
Buy a
4% Floor
4%
LIBOR
Losses
Gains
8%
LIBOR
Write an
8% Cap
Losses
Gains
4%
LIBOR
Write a
4% Floor
Losses

the buyer must go up; an insurance policy providing protection whenever LIBOR exceeds 7 percent has to cost more than a policy that pays off only when LIBOR moves above 8 percent. Suppose that premium is 200 basis points (times the notional principal). To keep the collar at a zero initial cost, the written floor must then generate additional premium for the seller as well. This will require a higher floor rate because a contract in which the seller makes settlement payments whenever LIBOR is less than 5 percent certainly will be worth more than one with a floor rate of 4 percent. If we keep tightening the collar at some exercise rate common to both the cap and the floor, say 6 percent, the combination will be zero-cost. That will be the pay-fixed swap fixed rate that prevails in the market. This is illustrated in Figure 25.6.

To summarize, buying a 6 percent cap and writing a 6 percent floor on LIBOR is equivalent in terms of settlement cash flows to an interest rate swap paying a fixed rate of 6 percent and receiving LIBOR. When LIBOR is above 6 percent, the net settlement receipt on the swap is the same as the receipt on the in-the-money cap that is owned. When LIBOR is below 6 percent, the net settlement payment on the swap is the same as the payment on the in-the-money floor that has been sold. Similarly, writing a cap and buying a floor at the same exercise rate is identical to a receive-fixed interest rate swap. Notice that a cap-floor combination at the same exercise rate always has the same payoffs as a swap contract. However, only when the combination also nets to a zero initial cost does that common rate match the prevailing swap fixed rate. This relationship is known as *cap-floor-swap parity,* and is the swap market analog to the put-call-forward parity formula first discussed in Chapter 11 and extended to the range forward strategy in Chapter 24.

FIGURE 25.6

AN ILLUSTRATION OF CAP-FLOOR-SWAP PARITY

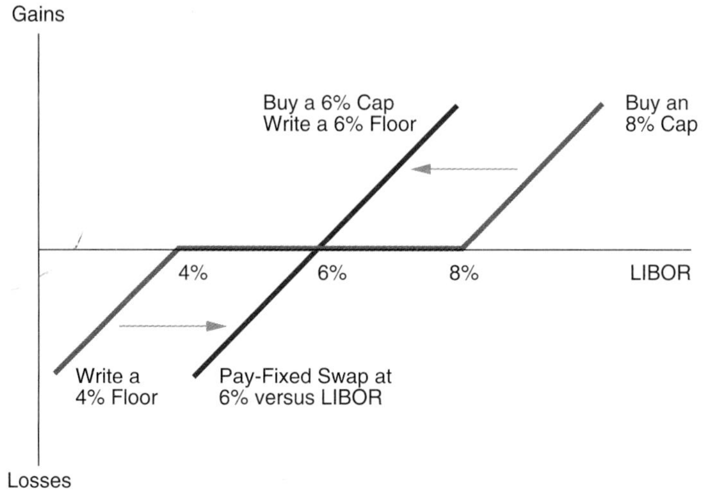
Gains
Buy a 6% Cap
Write a 6% Floor
Buy an
8% Cap
4%
6%
8%
LIBOR
Write a
4% Floor
Pay-Fixed Swap at
6% versus LIBOR
Losses

Along with the "portfolio of FRAs" and "pair of bonds" ways of viewing a swap contract, cap-floor-swap parity shows that a third interpretation exists: The swap can be viewed as a pair of option positions. This can be used to test the internal consistency of credit risk and valuation models for swaps. For example, because selling a cap and buying a floor at the same exercise rate can offer the same cash flows as a receive-fixed swap, the projected credit risk on the swap must be comparable to the credit risk on the floor agreement. (Note that a firm bears the counterparty's credit risk on purchased options, and not on written options, because only with purchased options is the firm relying on the other party's future performance.) This parity relationship also implies that variations of the option valuation models discussed in Chapter 24 can be used in the valuation of swap contracts.[8]

SWAP OPTIONS ("SWAPTIONS") A **swaption** gives the holder of the option the right, but not the obligation, to enter into an interest rate swap having a predetermined fixed rate at some later date. As with all options, there are two types of these agreements: *receiver* and *payer* swaptions. A receiver swaption gives the buyer the right, but not the obligation, to enter into a swap on prearranged terms (fixed rate, maturity, notional principal, floating rate index, settlement periods, documentation, etc.) as the fixed-rate receiver. The seller of the option, in return for the up-front premium, must enter the swap as the fixed-rate payer on demand of the buyer. Naturally, the buyer will only exercise the receiver swaption if the market swap rate is less than the strike rate at the maturity of the option; that is, if she can receive an above-market fixed rate while paying LIBOR.

On the other hand, a payer swaption gives the buyer the right, but not the obligation, to enter into a swap on prearranged terms as the fixed-rate payer, with the seller of the option obligated to receive the fixed rate at the buyer's request. Holders of a payer swaption will only exercise the contract if the market pay-fixed swap rate prevailing at the option exercise date is higher than the strike rate, thereby entitling them to pay a below-market fixed rate while receiving LIBOR.

Swaptions are most useful to those firms that presently are not sure if they will be exposed to future interest rate movements. An example would be a bond portfolio manager

[8]The relationship between swap, cap, and floor agreements is described in Rudy Yaksick, "Swaps, Caps, and Floors: Some Parity and Price Identities," *Journal of Financial Engineering* 1, no. 1 (1992): 105–115.

FIGURE 25.7

CALL MONETIZATION WITH SWAPTIONS: ORIGINATION

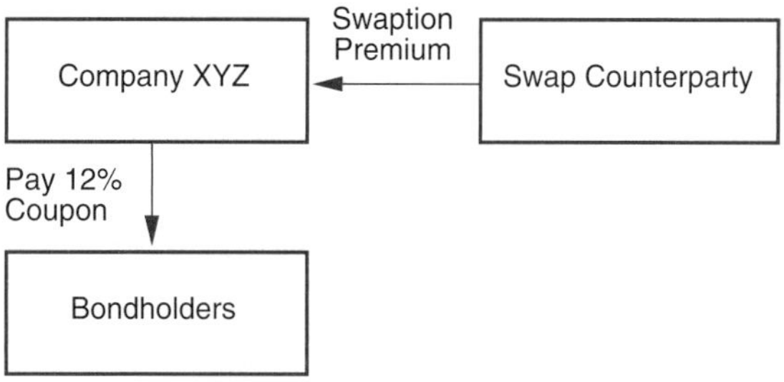
Company XYZ
Swaption Premium
Swap Counterparty
Pay 12% Coupon
Bondholders

who may be forced to liquidate part of his holdings in a year's time. In such a situation, the bond manager might like to have the option of fixing the future interest rate at the levels priced into today's yield curve.

Brown and Smith have shown how swaptions also can be used in the management of callable debt.[9] Suppose that three years ago, Company XYZ issued 15-year, fixed-rate callable debt with a coupon rate of 12 percent. Now, interest rates for XYZ's credit grade have fallen to 8 percent, but the outstanding debt issue still has two years before its call deferment period is over. Clearly, the issuing company would call the debt today if it could (i.e., it would rather make 8 percent coupon payments than 12 percent); the call option it implicitly holds on the bond it issued is currently in the money. However, it must wait for two years to exercise the call, during which time interest rates may rise back above 12 percent. Further, because the option cannot be detached from the original bond, it cannot be sold separately in today's market.

One solution to this dilemma involves the use of swaptions. Consider what would happen if the issuing firm entered into the following transaction today: Sell a two-year receiver option on a 10-year swap, giving the buyer the choice to receive the fixed rate of 12 percent. The benefit of doing this is that the company will receive a premium for selling the swaption at origination. This receipt of cash, which is illustrated in Figure 25.7, is analogous to what the company would have received if it had been able to sell the call feature embedded in the underlying bond directly in the marketplace.

To see what this will cost the company, consider what happens in two years when the swaption expires and the bond can be called. If interest rates are 12 percent or greater, neither the bond option nor the swap option will be exercised and they both expire out of the money. The issuing company continues to pay a 12 percent coupon for the next 10 years. This is shown in panel A of Figure 25.8. Conversely, if interest rates are less than 12 percent, both the bond option and swap option will be exercised by their respective holders. To Company XYZ, this means: (1) it can refinance its original debt with a 10-year FRN (assumed to pay LIBOR), and (2) it will be forced to pay a fixed rate of 12 percent as per the terms of the swaption. Thus, the net effect is that the issuing company will continue to pay a 12 percent coupon for the next 10 years. (Panel B of Figure 25.8 illustrates this set of transactions.)

The key point here is that, by selling the swaption today, the company has committed itself to paying a 12 percent coupon for the remaining life of the original bond. This was done in exchange for an up-front swaption premium received at origination. Thus, even though the bond's call option could not be sold directly, it has been effectively "monetized" in the swaption market. Not surprisingly, this strategy is often referred to as *call monetization.*

[9]See Keith C. Brown and Donald J. Smith, "Forward Swaps, Swap Options, and the Management of Callable Debt," *Journal of Applied Corporate Finance* 2, no. 4 (spring 1990): 59–71.

FIGURE 25.8 CALL MONETIZATION WITH SWAPTIONS: EXPIRATION DATE

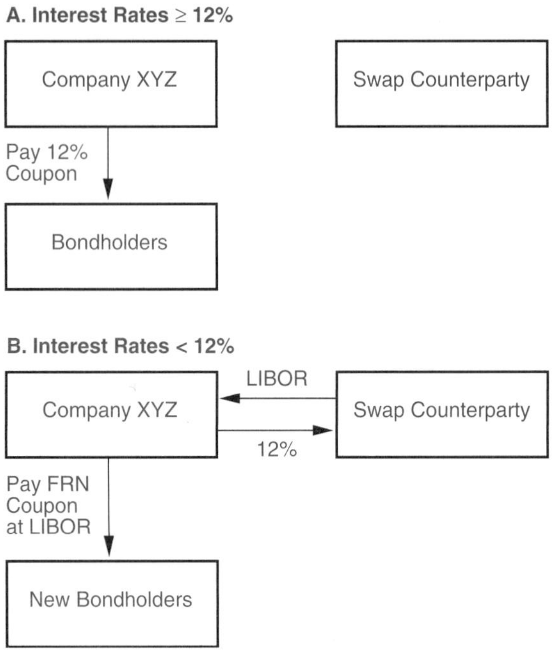
A. Interest Rates ≥ 12%
Company XYZ
Swap Counterparty
Pay 12% Coupon
Bondholders
B. Interest Rates < 12%
Company XYZ
LIBOR
12%
Swap Counterparty
Pay FRN Coupon at LIBOR
New Bondholders

One important caution is that the swap rates and bond rates do not necessarily move in the same fashion. This will create basis risk in that a swap market instrument is being used as a substitute for a capital market instrument (i.e., the bond's call feature). In this example, the worst-case result for the company would have been if the fixed-rate on a 10-year swap was below 12 percent in two years, but its debt refunding rate in the capital market was above 12 percent. This result, which could occur if Company XYZ's credit quality deteriorates over the next two years, would mean that the company would be forced to enter into a swap it doesn't want (or unwind the position at a disadvantage) and not be able to refinance its borrowing profitably.

SWAP CONTRACTING EXTENSIONS

Although interest rate swaps are by far the most prevalent OTC rate contract, three other important extensions of this concept have developed recently. All these agreements, which preserve the essential feature of a swap contract by exchanging cash flows based on two different rates or prices, include (1) currency (i.e., foreign exchange) swaps, (2) equity index-linked swaps, and (3) commodity swaps.

CURRENCY SWAPS

Like the plain vanilla swap agreements, a **currency swap** is an agreement where in two counterparties make periodic cash flow exchanges based on two different interest rates.[10] These contracts, also known as cross-currency swaps, differ from the single-currency

[10]A good collection of readings on both the currency swap market and applications of these instruments can be found in Carl R. Beidleman, ed., *Cross Currency Swaps* (Homewood, Ill.: Business One-Irwin, 1992). Also, Christopher Géczy, Bernadette A. Minton, and Catherine Schrond, "Why Firms Use Currency Derivatives," *Journal of Finance* 52, no. 4 (September 1997): 1323–1354, provide a good overview of corporate uses of these contracts.

FIGURE 25.9 **A BASIC CURRENCY SWAP TRANSACTION**

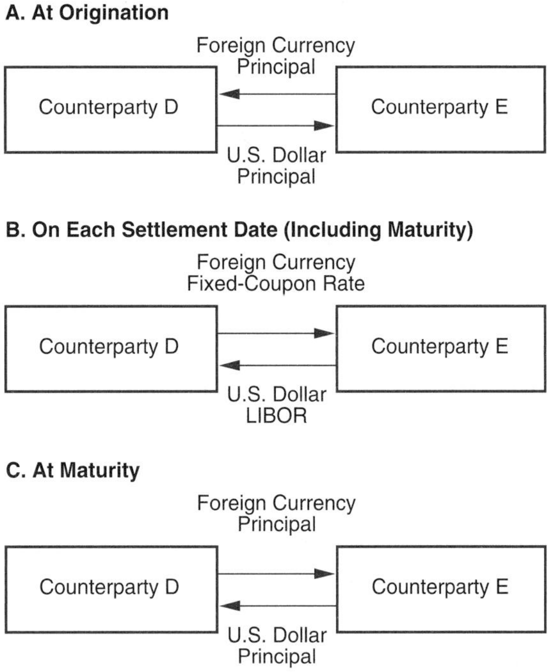
A. At Origination
Foreign Currency Principal
Counterparty D
Counterparty E
U.S. Dollar Principal
B. On Each Settlement Date (Including Maturity)
Foreign Currency Fixed-Coupon Rate
Counterparty D
Counterparty E
U.S. Dollar LIBOR
C. At Maturity
Foreign Currency Principal
Counterparty D
Counterparty E
U.S. Dollar Principal

version in two ways. First, because the associated cash flows are denominated in different monetary units, the principal amounts usually are exchanged at the origination and maturity dates of the contract. Second, because there are two currencies involved, the interest rates defining the transaction can be expressed on either a fixed- or floating-rate basis in either or both currencies. Assuming that the U.S. dollar is one of the currencies involved in the deal, this leaves the following four possibilities: (1) a fixed rate in the foreign currency versus a fixed rate in U.S. dollars, (2) a fixed rate in the foreign currency versus a floating rate in U.S. dollars, (3) a floating rate in the foreign currency versus a fixed rate in U.S. dollars, and (4) a floating rate in the foreign currency versus a floating rate in U.S. dollars. Although all of these formats are available, the predominant currency swap exchanges a fixed rate in the foreign currency for U.S. dollar LIBOR. This structure is shown in Figure 25.9.

This diagram shows that two distinct types of exchanges exist: principal at both origination and maturity and coupon interest on all the settlement dates. It is customary that both principal exchanges be executed at the spot foreign exchange (FX) rate prevailing at the initiation date, regardless of subsequent market FX rates. Further, similar to interest rate swap, the floating-rate side of the coupon exchanges in the standard currency swap usually is quoted flat. Thus, the dollar cash flow paid by Counterparty E on each settlement date is determined by multiplying the relevant LIBOR (which would have been determined at the previous settlement date) by the U.S. dollar principal amount, adjusted by the day count factor. The periodic cash flow that Counterparty D is obligated to pay is the product of the quoted fixed rate and the foreign currency–based principal amount. Because the cash flows differ in denomination, currency swaps do not settle on a net basis.

To see how these conventions translate into cash flows, suppose Counterparty D has agreed to pay Counterparty E 8.65 percent on a four-year, British pound swap. Assume further that the transaction can be summarized as follows:

TABLE 25.4

SETTLEMENT CASH FLOWS FOR A U.S. DOLLAR/BRITISH POUND CURRENCY SWAP

Settlement Date	Number of Days	Assumed Current LIBOR	Fixed-Rate Payment	Floating-Rate Receipt
A. Initial Exchange of Principal				
11/15/00	–	5.75%	USD 34.400	GBP 20.000
B. Coupon Exchanges				
5/15/01	181	6.00%	GBP 0.858	USD 0.994
11/15/01	184	6.25%	0.872	1.055
5/15/02	181	6.70%	0.858	1.087
11/15/02	184	7.25%	0.872	1.178
5/15/03	181	7.00%	0.858	1.254
11/15/03	184	6.75%	0.872	1.187
5/15/04	182	5.50%	0.863	1.167
C. Final Coupon and Principal Exchange				
11/15/04	184	5.75%	GBP 0.872 and GBP 20.000	USD 0.967 and USD 34.400

- Origination Date: November 15, 2000
- Maturity Date: November 15, 2004
- Notional Principal: GBP 20 million and USD 34.4 million
- Fixed-Rate Payer: Counterparty D
- Swap Fixed Rate: 8.65 percent in pounds sterling (semiannual bond basis)
- Fixed-Rate Receiver: Counterparty E
- Floating Rate: Six-month LIBOR in U.S. dollars (money market basis)
- Settlement Dates: November 15 and May 15 of each year
- LIBOR Determination: Set in advance, paid in arrears

The initial and ultimate principal exchanges are based on the spot exchange rate of USD 1.72/GBP that is assumed to have prevailed at the swap origination date. Given the rate conventions in each country, the pound-denominated coupon settlement payments are computed as [0.0865 × (Number of days ÷ 365) × GBP 20 million] while the dollar-based cash flows are determined by [LIBOR × (Number of days ÷ 360) × USD 34.4 million]. These amounts are shown in Table 25.4 from the perspective of Counterparty D (i.e., the fixed-rate payer).[11]

[11]Although the most typical form of a currency swap is this fixed foreign currency/floating dollar structure, that is not always the most useful way to package cash flows. If, for instance, Counterparty D had wanted to pay a fixed rate in U.S. dollars (USD), instead of LIBOR, in exchange for fixed sterling (GBP) receipts, the standard fixed/floating currency swap can be easily repackaged by combining it with a floating/fixed U.S. dollar interest rate swap. As a practical matter, if both of these transactions were executed simultaneously with the same market maker, the corporate end-user (i.e., Counterparty D) would not undertake two separate transactions. Rather, to minimize the requisite documentation and bookkeeping, the swap intermediary in this case would undoubtedly offer the counterparty a direct, blended quote of "receive fixed USD, pay fixed GBP," leaving LIBOR out altogether. These fixed/fixed swaps were once known as CIRCUS swaps, standing for "combined interest rate and currency swaps."

As an example of why such a transaction might be used, suppose that Counterparty E is a British pension fund that would like to invest GBP 20 million in a fixed-rate note making semiannual coupon payments for the next four years. Given the current pricing in the market, however, the coupon on sterling-denominated, par-value fixed-rate bonds issued by companies with an acceptable Aa credit rating is 8.40 percent. Suppose, on the other hand, that the pension fund buys a four-year floating rate note from an Aa-rated American corporation paying LIBOR flat for USD 34.4 million. In this case, the pension manager could purchase the dollar-denominated FRN and enter into the "pay USD floating/receive GBP fixed" swap outlined above. The combination of these two transactions, shown in Figure 25.10 would leave the investor with the equivalent of owning a pound-denominated bond paying a fixed rate of 8.65 percent in sterling, a yield "pickup" of 25 points relative to the direct issue market. Thus, by using the swap to transform both the rate sensitivity and currency denomination of the dollar FRN, the pension fund has created a more desirable package of cash flows than was otherwise available. In this sense, we can view any financial security as a substitute for any other financial security, once the appropriate repackaging has been accomplished.[12]

As with plain vanilla interest rate swaps, currency swaps can be viewed as a pair of bond transactions. Specifically, panel B of Figure 25.10 shows that, from Counterparty E's perspective, the swap can be interpreted as a portfolio containing: (1) a long position in a fixed-rate, pound-denominated bond and (2) a short position in a USD FRN. This intuition is useful in calculating the value of the agreement after origination, which is:

$$\text{Value of Currency Swap (in GBP)} = (\text{PV of GBP fixed cash flows}) - [(\text{PV of USD FRN}) \div (\text{Spot USD/GBP})]$$

There are two important features of this equation. First, the swap's value depends on changes in three fundamental factors: British interest rates, U.S. interest rates, and the USD/GBP exchange rate. Second, on any given settlement date, the floating rate note should once again be valued at par, which assumes no change in counterparty creditworthiness. This simplifies the swap valuation calculation tremendously.

Suppose, for example, that exactly two years (i.e., four settlement dates) after this agreement was originated, the fixed rate on a new two-year "receive GBP fixed, pay USD LIBOR" swap has fallen to 7.65 percent while the prevailing exchange rate has moved to USD 1.82/GBP. Assuming, for the ease of computation, that all the remaining GBP cash flows on the existing contract are 0.865 million (= (0.0865) × (1/2) × (20.0 million)), Counterparty E's position in the swap is worth:

$$\left[\sum_{t=1}^{4} \frac{\text{GBP } 0.865}{(1 + 0.0765/2)^t} + \frac{\text{GBP } 20.0}{(1 + 0.0765/2)^4}\right] - \frac{\text{USD } 34.4}{(\text{USD } 1.82/\text{GBP})}$$
$$= (20.364) - (18.901) = \text{GBP } 1.463 \text{ million}$$

Of course, this amount also represents a liability to Counterparty D; like any derivative a currency swap is a zero-sum game. Finally, notice that both the GBP rate decline and the

[12]An important mitigating factor that must once again be considered with any swap-based investment scheme is the credit risk of the swap counterparty. Whether the presence of this additional exposure in this case explains the 25 bp investment advantage would, of course, depend on an assessment of the likelihood that Counterparty D would default on the swap agreement under adverse market conditions. For a theoretical discussion on this topic see Ian A. Cooper and Antonio S. Mello, "The Default Risk of Swaps," *Journal of Finance* 46, no. 2 (June 1991): 597–620.

FIGURE 25.10 TRANSFORMING A BOND INVESTMENT WITH A CURRENCY SWAP

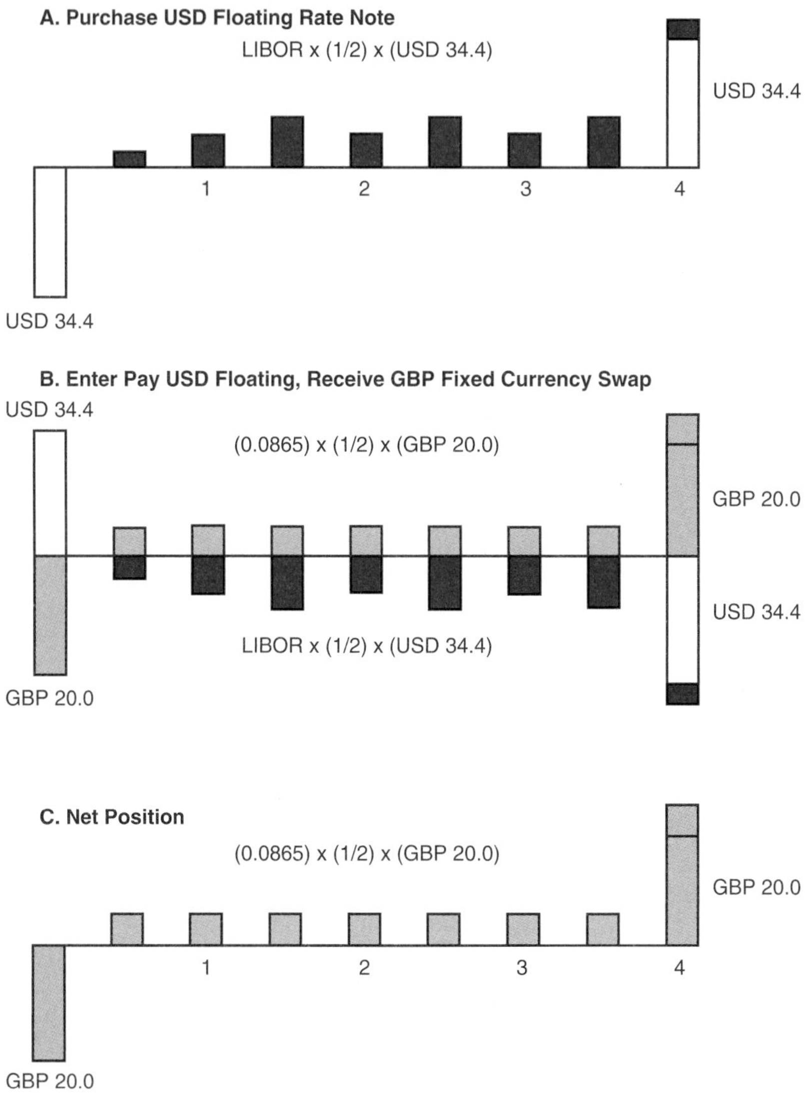
A. Purchase USD Floating Rate Note
LIBOR x (1/2) x (USD 34.4)
USD 34.4
1
2
3
4
USD 34.4
B. Enter Pay USD Floating, Receive GBP Fixed Currency Swap
USD 34.4
(0.0865) x (1/2) x (GBP 20.0)
GBP 20.0
USD 34.4
LIBOR x (1/2) x (USD 34.4)
GBP 20.0
C. Net Position
(0.0865) x (1/2) x (GBP 20.0)
GBP 20.0
1
2
3
4
GBP 20.0

exchange rate increase have changed the swap's value in the same direction by increasing the value of the pound-denominated asset and reducing the translated value of the dollar liability, respectively. Thus, even though the swap was originally negotiated to have no net value to either counterparty, it will become an asset to one and a liability to the other as soon as market conditions change.

Equity Index–Linked Swaps

Similar in form to interest rate swaps, **equity** index–linked **swaps** are equivalent to portfolios of forward contracts calling for the exchange of cash flows based on two different investment rates: (1) a variable debt rate (e.g., three-month LIBOR) and (2) the return to an equity index (e.g., Standard and Poor's 500). The index-linked payment is based on either the total return (i.e., dividends plus capital gain or loss) or just the percentage index change for the settlement period plus a fixed spread adjustment, which is expressed in basis points and can be negative. The floating-rate payments typically are based on LIBOR flat. Like interest rate and currency swaps, equity swaps are traded in the OTC markets and can have maturities out to 10 years or beyond.

In addition to the S&P 500, equity swaps can be structured around foreign indexes, such as TOPIX (Japan), FT-SE 100 (Great Britain), DAX (Germany), CAC 40 (France), TSE 35 (Canada), EOE (Netherlands), and Hang Seng (Hong Kong). These agreements also can be designed so that the cash flows are denominated in the same currency or in two different currencies. The equity index–based cash flow typically is denominated in the currency of the index's country of origination, but the swap can be designed so that this payment is automatically hedged into a different currency. Further, these agreements specify a notional principal that is not exchanged at origination but serves the purpose of converting percentage returns into cash flows. This notional principal can either be variable or fixed during the life of the agreement, but the same notional principal applies to both sides of the transaction.

The equity swap market has developed for several reasons. First, these agreements allow investors to take advantage of overall price movements in a specific country's stock market without having to purchase the equity securities directly.[13] This has the advantage of reducing both the transaction costs and tracking errors associated with assembling a portfolio that mimics the index as well as allowing the investor to avoid dividend withholding taxes normally associated with cross-border investing. Second, creating a direct equity investment in a foreign country may be difficult for some companies where prohibited by law or operating policy. Finally, an investment fund wanting to accumulate foreign index returns denominated in their domestic currency may not be able or legally permitted to obtain sufficient exchange-traded futures or option contracts to hedge a direct equity investment. The equity swap can be structured so that there is no need for separate hedging transactions.

The most common application for an equity swap involves a counterparty that receives the index-based payment in exchange for making the floating-rate payment. For example, consider a pension fund that currently has a substantial portion of its asset portfolio invested in floating-rate notes paying quarterly coupons based on LIBOR. If the manager of this fund wants to alter her existing asset allocation by converting some of these debt-based cash flows into equity-based receipts, she has two ways to do so. First, she can sell the existing floating-rate notes and purchase a portfolio of equities directly in the market. Alternatively, the manager can enter into an equity swap with an initial notional principal equal to the amount of the existing debt holdings she wants to convert. As we have seen, from the standpoint of reducing transaction costs, the second alternative is clearly preferable. The mechanics of this arrangement are illustrated in Figure 25.11.

The net return to the fund in this example is simply the return on the equity index plus the spread adjustment. Further, if the floating-rate notes held as an asset yield more than LIBOR, this incremental amount would increase the overall net return. Assuming that both cash flows are denominated in the same currency, the net settlement payment on the equity swap from the company's standpoint can be calculated as the difference between the variable-rate outflow and the equity-linked inflow, where:

$$\text{Payment} = [\text{LIBOR} - \text{Spread}] \times [\text{Notional Principal}] \times \left[\frac{(\text{Number of Days})}{360}\right]$$

and

$$\text{Receipt} = \left[\frac{\text{Index}_{\text{new}} - \text{Index}_{\text{old}}}{\text{Index}_{\text{old}}}\right] \times [\text{Notional Principal}]$$

[13]For a more detailed analysis of the uses and development of this product, see Julie A. Allen and Janet L. Showers, "Equity-Index-Linked Derivatives: A User's Guide" (New York: Salomon Brothers, 1991).

FIGURE 25.11 **ALTERING AN ASSET ALLOCATION POSITION WITH AN EQUITY SWAP**

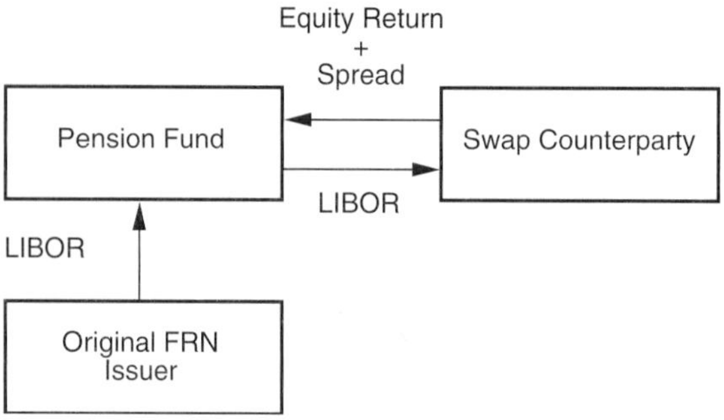
Equity Return
+
Spread
Pension Fund
Swap Counterparty
LIBOR
LIBOR
Original FRN Issuer

where Index_{new} and Index_{old} represent the index levels occurring on the current and immediate past settlement dates, assuming all dividends are reinvested. Notice here that to minimize calculations, the settlement payment is computed using (LIBOR − Spread) rather than adding a separate inflow for the equity spread itself. Gastineau investigated indicative spread quotes for various indexes throughout the world and found that, while some were positive (e.g., 90 bp for DAX, 25 bp for FT-SE), other were negative (e.g., −10 bp for S&P 500, −60 bp for Hang Seng).[14] However, he noted that the equity swap quotations methods are not standardized across all dealers; therefore, the quoted values may not be directly comparable.

Another way to view the effect of this swap-based cash flow transformation is shown in Figure 25.12. Here, it should be clear that equity swaps differ from interest rate and currency swaps in one important way. Specifically, because there is no guarantee that the equity index will appreciate in value from one settlement period to the next, it is possible that the company receiving the equity index will have to make a double payment. First, the usual debt-related cash flow, based on LIBOR, will have to be paid. Second, whenever Index_{new} is less than Index_{old}, the company will make an equity index–based payment to (i.e., "receive" a negative payment from) its counterparty. Thus, rather than netting one cash flow against the other, the company will pay both when the value of the equity index declines. (Examples of this situation are represented by the third and fifth payments in the figure.)

COMMODITY SWAPS

The preceding equity example demonstrates that the swap contracting mechanism can be applied to economic variables other than interest and exchange rates. In particular, a fast-growing market exists for OTC derivative agreements designed to hedge exposures to commodity prices. To date, these **commodity swaps** have been used mostly by corporate liability managers to fix the level of one or more of the firm's production costs, with the most active markets in energy, precious metals, and base metals. As in the rate swap markets, the growth of commodity swaps primarily has been attributable to the constraints imposed on hedgers and speculators by the rigid standardization of exchange-traded futures contracts.

A commodity swap effectively fixes the price of a commodity over a certain period in the same way that an interest rate swap fixes the value of LIBOR. That is, on each settlement date, the two counterparties exchange cash flows based on: (1) a fixed commodity price that does not change over the life of the agreement and (2) a variable commodity

[14]See Gary L. Gastineau, "Using Swaps in Equity Portfolios," in *Derivative Strategies for Managing Portfolio Risk*, edited by K. Brown (Charlottesville, Va.: Association for Investment Research and Management, 1993). See also Don Chance and Don Rich, "The Pricing of Equity Swaps and Swaptions," *Journal of Derivatives* 5, no. 2 (summer 1998): 19–31.

FIGURE 25.12 **CONVERTING A BOND WITH AN EQUITY SWAP**

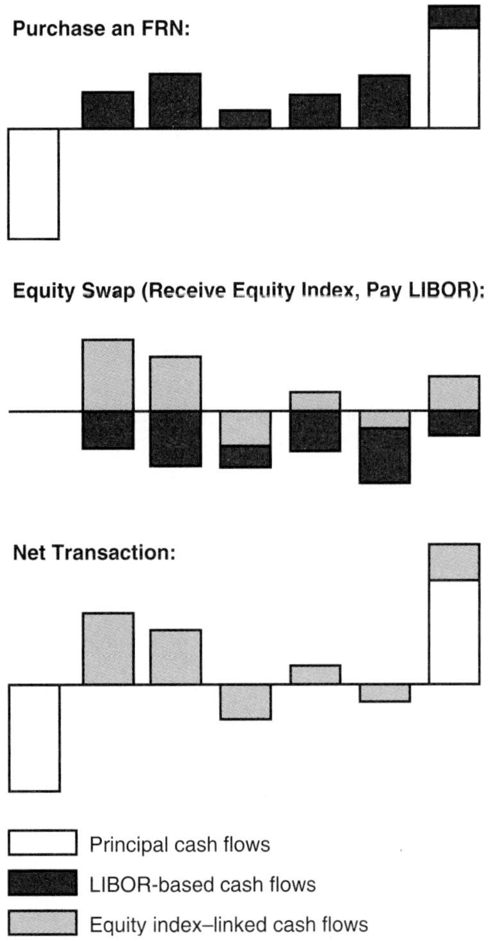
Purchase an FRN:
Equity Swap (Receive Equity Index, Pay LIBOR):
Net Transaction:
Principal cash flows
LIBOR-based cash flows
Equity index–linked cash flows

price that does. The equivalent of the floating-rate index in a commodity swap is the price of a commodity index (e.g., West Texas Intermediate Oil index, COMEX gold index), which is periodically reset over the contract's life. The agreement also sets a notional amount of the commodity on which the periodic cash exchanges are based, but no physical delivery ever takes place.

To illustrate how a commodity swap works and who might benefit, consider the following situations for two different corporations. Company OIL is an independent oil producer with production limited to 250,000 barrels a month. Because of high production costs, OIL needs to guarantee that it receives an average price of at least \$14.50 per barrel. On the other hand, Company CHM uses a monthly average of 250,000 barrels of West Texas Intermediate (WTI) crude oil in the production of its petrochemicals. Because of the competitive nature of its business and the highly elastic demand for its products, CHM's operations will lose financial viability if oil prices rise above \$15.50 per barrel over the next three years.

Clearly, OIL and CHM are concerned about falling and rising oil prices, respectively. As such, they are good candidates for a three-year oil swap with monthly settlement and a "notional principal" of 250,000 barrels. Suppose, therefore, that working through a swap

FIGURE 25.13

ILLUSTRATION OF AN OIL-ORIENTED COMMODITY SWAP

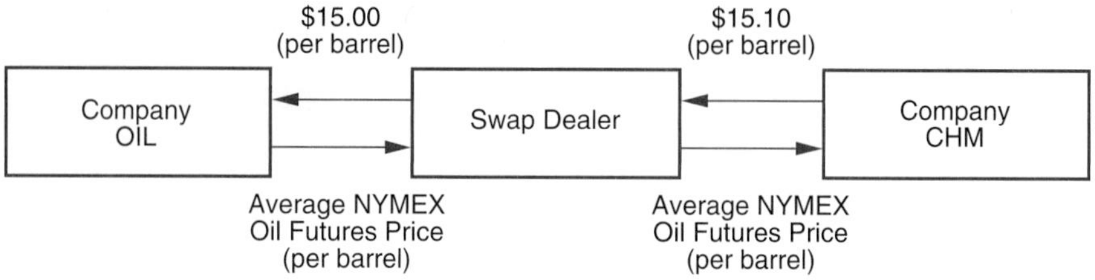
$15.00
(per barrel)
$15.10
(per barrel)
Company
OIL
Swap Dealer
Company
CHM
Average NYMEX
Oil Futures Price
(per barrel)
Average NYMEX
Oil Futures Price
(per barrel)

dealer, they arrange the transactions illustrated in Figure 25.13, where the monthly WTI index value is determined as the average of the daily settlement prices for the crude oil futures contract traded on the New York Mercantile Exchange (NYMEX). By their agreements with the swap dealer, OIL is effectively fixing the price of its oil sales at $15.00 per barrel and CHM is fixing the price of its purchase at $15.10. Examples of the actual settlement transactions are as follows:

- If average oil futures settlement price is $16.15:
  OIL pays to Dealer: ($16.15 − $15.00) × (250,000 barrels) = $287,500
  CHM receives from Dealer: ($16.15 − $15.10) × (250,000 barrels) = $262,500.
- If average oil futures settlement price is $14.40:
  OIL receives from Dealer: ($15.00 − $14.40) × (250,000 barrels) = $150,000
  CHM pays to Dealer: ($15.10 − $14.40) × (250,000 barrels) = $175,000.

Thus, barring default of one of the counterparties, the swap dealer in this matched transaction has no exposure to crude oil prices and simply collects the spread of $25,000 each month.

Using commodity swaps to maintain the economic viability of a high-cost project, such as oil drilling or gold mining, is not merely a matter of convenience. Because reopening an oil field or a mine can be quite costly, there typically will be a limited period of time during which it pays to keep them running at a loss. Thus, it often is prudent for producers (e.g., Company OIL) to enter into receive-fixed commodity swaps to remove price volatility at time when the operation is particularly vulnerable. Commodity swaps also can be used to reverse forward positions previously transacted if the counterparty to those agreements changed its view of future prices. For example, airlines often use forward contracts to lock in the price of jet fuel two or three years out. If a carrier felt that prices would decrease to a level below the contracted price, a swap could neutralize the long forward positions allowing the user effectively to pay the market price.[15]

WARRANTS AND CONVERTIBLE SECURITIES

A popular investment strategy in recent years has involved the creation of security "packages" in which derivatives are combined with, or embedded into, more basic instruments,

[15]For more on how commodity swaps and other derivative products can be used to hedge oil price movements, see Keith C. Brown and Robert F. Semmens, "Perspectives on Integration in the Oil Industry: Innovations from the Financial Market," in *Oil in the New World Order,* ed. K. Gillespie and C. Henry (Gainesville, Fla.: University of Florida Press, 1994).

such as stock shares or bonds. In this section, we take a detailed look at two important variations on this theme: (1) bonds with warrants that give the investor the right to buy additional shares of the company's common stock; and (2) securities, such as debt or preferred stock, that the investor can convert into other securities.

WARRANTS

By its most commonly used definition, a **warrant** is an equity call option issued directly by the company whose stock serves as the underlying asset. The key feature that distinguishes it from an ordinary call option is that, if exercised, the company will create new shares of stock to give to the warrantholder. Thus, the exercise of a warrant will increase the total number of outstanding shares, which reduces the value of each individual share. Because of this dilutive effect, the warrant will not be as valuable as an otherwise comparable option contract. Indeed, the valuation of warrants is complicated by many factors, such as how and when the number of outstanding warrants will be exercised, what the company's current capital structure looks like, and what the company plans to do with the new capital it will receive if and when the warrant is exercised.

Galai and Schneller proposed a simple warrant valuation model in which a firm is presently financed with all equity and the warrants it issues are European-style.[16] On its expiration date T, the warrant will be worth:

$$W_T = \max\left[\frac{V_T + N_W X}{N + N_W} - X, 0\right]$$

where:

N = the current number of outstanding shares
N_W = the number of new shares created if the warrants are exercised
V_T = the value of the firm before the warrants are exercised
X = the exercise price

They show that this terminal value can be rewritten as:

$$W_T = \left[\frac{1}{1 + (N_W/N)}\right] C_T$$

where:

C_T = the expiration date value of a regular call option with otherwise identical terms as the warrant

Consequently, at any point prior to expiration, the value of the warrant should be equal to the value of the call deflated (i.e., diluted) by the factor $[1 + (N_w/N)]^{-1}$.

Although warrants can be issued as stand-alone instruments, more frequently a company will attach them to a bond issue to lower its initial funding cost. Warrants created in this manner usually can be detached from the debt instrument by the buyer and traded separately. Suppose, for example, a firm with 1,000,000 shares of common stock outstanding at a current share price of \$100 attempts to raise an additional \$10 million by issuing a 10-year bond paying annual coupons. Given its current credit rating, assume further that the yield it would have to pay for a straight debt issue is 8.50 percent. The firm could lower this borrowing cost by attaching to the bond European-style equity warrants that mature in

[16]See Dan Galai and Meir I. Schneller, "Pricing Warrants and the Value of the Firm," *Journal of Finance* 33, no. 5 (December 1978): 1333–1342.

exactly one year and have an exercise price of \$115 per share. Assuming the firm eventually hopes to raise an additional \$5.75 million with these warrants, it will have to create new derivative contracts to cover 50,000 shares (\$5.75 million ÷ \$115).

Assuming that the one-year risk-free rate is 7 percent and the volatility of the firm's common stock is 25 percent, the Black-Scholes value for a one-year call option to buy one share at X = \$115 can be calculated as \$7.09. In turn, this means that the warrants are worth \$6.75 (= 7.09 ÷ [1 + (50,000/1,000,000)] per share. If each warrant allows for the purchase of one share and the face value of a single bond is \$1,000, the firm will issue 10,000 bonds with five warrants attached to each. Assuming it pays an 8.50 percent coupon, the total proceeds it would generate from the sale of each bond with the warrants attached would be \$1,033.75, or \$1,000 for the bond and \$33.75 (= 5 × \$6.75) for the warrants. Thus, the firm can reduce its funding cost to 8.00 percent—the solution to the yield-to-maturity in the following bond calculation:

$$1033.75 = \sum_{t=1}^{10} \frac{85}{(1+y)^t} + \frac{1000}{(1+y)^{10}}$$

Packaging warrants with bonds to reduce debt expenses for the issuer and enhance return potential for the investor can be done in a variety of ways. In particular, a recent trend in financial markets is for a firm to attach to its bonds an option that is based on an underlying asset other than the company's own stock. To date, alternative structures have included foreign exchange and stock index transactions. For instance, Rogalski and Seward detail the development of the market for *foreign currency exchange warrants,* which give the holder the right, but not the obligation, to purchase a predetermined number of U.S. dollars for a price denominated in a foreign currency.[17] Although called warrants, these contracts are closer in form to traditional call options on the dollar (or, equivalently, put options on the foreign currency) because they do not result in any direct change to the issuing firm's capital structure. That is, no dilutive valuation effect exists for these derivatives since there are no new shares of stock issued. Beyond that, these instruments generally can be settled only in cash but can be detached and traded separately from the original bond.[18]

Convertible Securities

A convertible security gives its owner the right, but not the obligation, to convert the existing investment into another form. Typically, the original security is either a bond or a share of preferred stock, which can be exchanged into common stock according to a predetermined formula. From this description, it should be clear that a convertible security is a hybrid issue consisting of a regular bond or preferred stock holding and a call option that allows for the conversion. Similar to warrants, they have been popular with issuers because they generally lead to a lower initial borrowing cost and represent a future supply of equity capital. In fact, Pinches noted that these securities often are used in connection with mergers because they generate capital without immediately diluting the equity base of the acquiring firm.[19] On the other hand, investors in convertibles gain the upside potential of common stock while actually holding a less risky asset.

[17]See Richard J. Rogalski and James K. Seward, "Corporate Issues of Foreign Currency Warrants," *Journal of Financial Economics* 30, no. 2 (December 1991): 347–366.

[18]For several additional discussions about how warrants are used in capital markets, see Jack Clark Francis, William W. Toy, and J. Gregg Whittaker, *The Handbook of Equity Derivatives* (Chicago, Ill.: Irwin Professional Publishing, 1995).

[19]See George E. Pinches, "Financing with Convertible Preferred Stock, 1960–1967," *Journal of Finance* 25, no. 1 (March 1970): 56–63. See also S. R. McGuire, *The Handbook of Convertibles* (New York, N.Y.: Simon & Schuster, 1991).

CONVERTIBLE PREFERRED STOCK

To see how convertible securities work, let us consider the dynamics of convertible preferred stock. As suggested above, owning a share of convertible preferred is equivalent to holding a portfolio long in a normal share of preferred stock and long in a call option on the firm's common stock that can be exercised by surrendering the preferred stock. There generally is no waiting period before the conversion can be made, and the conversion privilege usually never expires. This means that the *minimum value of the convertible* issue must be:

max[Preferred Stock Value, Conversion Value]

where the **conversion value** is the value of the common stock into which the preferred issue can be exchanged.

Suppose that for a $1,000,000 investment, an institutional investor could purchase 25,000 shares of a convertible preferred issue with the following terms (per share):

- Current Convertible Share Price: $40.00
- Annual Convertible Dividend: $ 3.00
- Convertible Yield: 7.50% (= $3 ÷ $40)
- Regular Preferred Yield: 10.00%
- Current Common Stock Price: $20.00
- Conversion Ratio: 1.75

With these conditions, the share value of a regular preferred stock issue paying a $3 dividend would be $30.00 (= $3 ÷ 0.10 percent), or the perpetual dividend amount divided by the prevailing regular yield. This means that the convertible issue sells at a 33 percent premium to the regular preferred. Also, given the **conversion ratio** of 1.75 shares of common to each share of preferred, the conversion value of the convertible issue is $35 (= 1.75 × $20). Thus, the minimum price of the convertible security would be $35, the greater of the regular preferred price and the conversion value. Since the market price of the convertible still is above this level, this implies a **conversion premium** of 14.29 percent (= [$40 − $35] ÷ $35), meaning that the convertible currently is selling based on its option value.

The future value of the convertible issue will depend on two events: (1) interest rate movements, which directly affect the yield on the regular preferred stock component, and (2) changes in common stock prices, given the 1.75 conversion ratio. Consider the matrix of minimum values for various levels of these two variables, shown in Table 25.5. In this situation, the value of the convertible preferred stock will likely be driven by its conversion value when interest rates and common stock prices are high and by its preferred stock value when rates and share prices are low.

CONVERTIBLE BONDS

Like convertible preferred stock, a convertible bond can be viewed as a prepackaged portfolio containing two distinct securities: a regular bond and an option to exchange the bond

TABLE 25.5 **MINIMUM CONVERTIBLE PREFERRED STOCK VALUES AS A FUNCTION OF REGULAR PREFERRED YIELDS AND COMMON STOCK PRICES**

		Common Stock Prices		
		15	20	25
Yield	*8%:*	37.50	37.50	43.75
	10%:	30.00	35.00	43.75
	12%:	26.25	35.00	43.75

FIGURE 25.14 **CONVERTIBLE BOND INFORMATION SUMMARY**

CUSIP	ISSUE	MOODY'S RATING	INT. DATES	ANN.? S.F. THOUS	CURR. CALL PRICE	AMT. OUTS MILL.	CONV. PRICE	SHS. PER $1,000 DEB.	CURRENT PRICE COM	CURRENT PRICE DEB.	DEB. YIELDS CURR.	DEB. YIELDS MAT.	DEB. CONV VALUE	ANTIC. COM. PRICE	1998 PRICE RANGE COM.		1998 PRICE RANGE DEB		LAT ANN. PER EARNS	COM ANN DIV
841338AG	•Southeast Banking Corp. (FL) cv sub cap nt 6.50 1999	C r	[1]09/15/1991	None	100.00	50.0	34.38	29.09	—	—	—	—	0	0	—	—	—	—	—	N
849176AA	Sports Authority, Inc. (The) cv sub nt 5.25 2001[2]	B1	J&J 31	None		149.5	—	—	—	—	—	5.3	—	—	—	—	—	—	0.7	N
784642AA	SRI Corp. cv sub deb 8.75 2008[3] ...	Ba3 r	J&J 1	1250-'94	100.00	25.0	14.17	70.57	19¾	280¾b	3.3	5.2	268¼	39¾	29¼	-18¼	400¾	-280¾	—	0.5
853258AA	•Standard Commercial Corp cv sub deb 7.25 2007	B2 r	M31&S 30	None	101.45	60.0	32.45	31.75	•10	82¾	7.9	10.3	82¾	26¾	17¼	-10	93	-82¾	2.18	N
857473AB	State Street Boston Corp. cv sub deb 7.75 2008	A2 r	M&N 1	None		50.0	5.75	173.91	• —	—	0.8	7.8	1123¼	0	—	—	—	—	—	N
861589AE	•Stone Container Corp. cv sub deb 6.75 2007	B3	F&A 15	None	101.35	115	33.94	29.46	•19¼	89¼	7.9	8.6	60	30¾	22¼	-15	95	-80½	d4.29	N
863238AA	StreamLogic Corp. cv sub deb 6.00 2012[4]	C r	M&S 15	5%-'0	100.00	75.0	48.50	20.62	—	48¼b	12	11.1	100	23¾	—		48¼	-48¼	d2.32	N
866762AG	•Sun Co., Inc. cv sub deb 6.75 2012	Baa3r	J&D 15	5%-'97	100.00	150	40.81	24.50	•37¼	108	6.8	5.9	59¾	44¼	44¾	-34¾	109	—	3.03	1.0
866933AA	Sun Healthcare Group, Inc. cv sub deb 6.00 2004	B3	M&S 1	None	100.00	83.3	21.84	—	•14¾	88¼b	—	8.5	100	19¼	20¾	-14¼	104¾	-88¼	0.75	N
866933AE	cv jr sub deb 7.00 2028[2]	B3	FMA&N 1	None		300	—	—	—	—	—	7.0	—	—	—		—	—	0.75	N
86736FAC	Sunglass Hut Intl Inc cv sub nt 5.25 2003	B3	J&D 15	None		100	—	—	—	78¼b	—	10.3	—	—	—		83¼	-71¼	d1.27	0.
86768KAA	Sunrise Assisted Living, Inc. cv sub nt 5.50 2002[2]	B2	J&D 15	None		130	37.19	26.89	30¼	104¼b	—	4.4	100	38¾	46¼	-27¾	135¾	-100	0.21	N
870738AB	•Swift Energy Co. cv sub nt 6.25 2006	B1	M&N 15	None		100	—	—	—	89	5.9	—	—	—	—		100¼	-88¼	1.35	1.
871609AA	SynOptics Communications, Inc cv sub deb 5.25 2003	Ba3	M&N 15	Yes		100	42.61	42.61	—	102¾b	5.8	—	0	43¾	—		109	-94¾	—	N
878742AB	•Teck Corp. (Canada) cv sub deb 3.75 2006	Baa3r	J&J 15	None	887.92	170	21.48	46.55	—	—	3.8	3.8	0	0	—		—	—	—	0.2
87924HAA	Tele-Communications Intl Inc. cv sub deb 4.50 2006	B3	F&A 15	None		345	—	—	—	100¾b	6	4.4	—	—	—		105¼	-84¼	d1.04	N
879700AA	Telxon Corp. cv sub deb 7.50 2012	B2 r	J&D 1	5%-'97	100.00	40.0	26.75	37.38	24¾	100b	8.4	7.5	45¾	26¾	38¾	-21¾	140	-96	0.96	0.0
88033GAD	•Tenet Healthcare Corp. sub ex deb 6.00 2005[5]	B1	J&D 1	None	103.00	320	38.55	25.94	• —	86½	5.6	8.5	0	33¾	—		96	-85	d0.64	N
883559AE	•Thermo Instrument Systems, Inc. cv sub deb ser rg 4.00 2005	Baa3r	J&J 15	None		250	35.65	28.05	•20	90½	—	4.0	100	32¼	35½	-19¾	114	-89	1.21	N
883655AA	ThermoQuest Corp. sub bd 5.00 2000[2]	Baa3	F&A 15	None		96.25	—	—	—	94½b	—	8.0	—	—	—		120¼	-94½	0.83	N
883666AA	•ThermoTrex Corp. gtd cv sub deb 3.25 2007	Baa3r	M&N 1	None	100.00	124.5	27.00	37.04	—	88	—	4.8	100	23¼	—		100	-86	0.44	N
640376AA	Thomas Nelson, Inc. cv sub nt 5.75 1999[2]	B1	M31&N 30	None	100.82	50.0	58.82	17.00	•13¾	99¼b	5.7	6.3	25¼	58¾	15¾	-10½	102¾	-95¼	0.74	0.
	Time Warner, Inc. LYONS 0.00 2012[6]	Ba1	N.P.	None	397.27		—	—	—	1	—	flat	—	—	—		—	—	—	N
	LYONS 0.00 2013[7]	Ba1 r	N.P.	None	476.74		—	—	—	—	—	—	—	—	—		—	—	—	N
887315AQ	•Time Warner, Inc. (New) cv sub deb 8.75 2015[8]	Ba2	JAJ&O 15	None			—	—	—	—	—	8.8	—	—	—		—	—	d0.13	N
887364AC	Times Mirror Co. (The) LYONS 0.00 2017[2]	A3	N.P.	None	494.52	500	50.38	5.83	•60¾	43¾b	—	—	100	22	65¼	-57	44¾	-41¾	2.35	0.7
872623AA	TPI Enterprises, Inc. gtd cv sub deb 8.25 2002	B3	J&J 15	None	101.65	45.0	6.50	154.00	—	—	9.4	8.3	1½	0	—		—	—	—	N
912325AA	U.S. Office Products Co. cv sub nt 5.50 2001	B3	F&A 1	None		143.75	28.50	35.08	—	74¾b	4.3	10.6	119¾	21¼	—		113¾	-74¼	2.25	N
907818AA	•Union Pacific Corp. cv deb 4.75 1999	Baa3	A&O 1	None			—	—	—	—	—	4.8	—	—	—		—	—	1.76	N
911684AA	•United States Cellular Corp. LYONS 0.00 2015	Baa3	N.P.	None		650	—	—	—	37½f	—	flat	—	—	—		39	-36¾	1.29	1.
911843AF	United States Filter Corp. cv sub nt 4.50 2001	Ba3	J&D 15	None	101.80	414	39.50	25.32	•27	102	—	3.9	100	40¼	36½	-26¾	114½	-101¼	d3.13	N
911843AC	cv sub nt 6.00 2005[2]	Ba3	M&S 15	None		140	27.50	36.36	•27	—	—	6.0	0	0	36½	-26¾	—	—	d3.13	N
913174AB	United Waste Systems, Inc. cv sub nt 4.50 2003[2]	Ba2	J&D 1	None		152	32.50	—	• —	—	—	4.5	100	0	—		—	—	0.88	N
902917AB	•USA Waste Services, Inc. (DE) cv sub nt 4.00 2002[9]	Ba1 r	F&A 1	None	101.60	500	43.56	22.96	• —	—	—	4.0	0	0	—		—	—	—	N
903290AD	USF&G Corp. cv zero cpn 0.00 2009	A3 r	N.P.	None	640.82	245	33.89	29.49	• —	65¾b	—	—	61¾	22½	—		77¼	-65¾	2.55	N
902905AT	USX Corp. bd 6.75 2000[10]	Baa2	FMA&N 1	None		106.88	—	—	• —	—	—	6.8	—	—	—		—	—	1.59	N
902905AU	nt 6.85 2008[10]	Baa2r	M&S 1	None			—	—	—	101b	—	6.7	—	—	—		102	-100	1.59	N
918005AA	•UtiliCorp United Inc. cv sub deb 6.625 2011	Ba1 r	J&J 1	None	100.63	50.0	23.68	42.22	•35¼	—	5.6	6.6	114	0	39¾	-34¼	970	—	2.27	1.8
918905AC	•Vaihi, Inc. (New) LYONS 0.00 2007	B1	N.P.	None	485.09	329.6	—	—	—	53	—	—	—	—	—		73	-52¼	0.49	N
925524AC	•Viacom Inc. ex sub deb 8.00 2006[11]	B1	J&J 15	None	103.00		50.00	20.00	•67¼	103¾	8.3	7.4	69	52	69¾	-39¼	104¼	-101	2.08	N
92855MAB	Vivra, Inc. cv sub nt 5.00 2001[2]	Ba3	J&J 1	None		150	—	—	—	—	5.1	5.0	—	—	—		—	—	1.27	N
961137AA	Weston (Roy F.), Inc. (New) cv sub deb 7.00 2002	B3 r	A&O 15	None	100.00	30.0	21.13	47.33	3¾	91¼b	8.6	9.5	16¾	19¾	4¾	-2¾	93¾	-89¼	d1.18	0.
961896AE	Wetterau Inc. cv sub deb 7.00 2000	Baa2r	J&D 15	None	101.40	107.5	33.00	30.30	—	—	7	7.0	0	0	—		—	—	—	N
966837AA	Whole Foods Market, Inc. sub deb 0.00 2016[2]	B2		None		268.51	—	—	—	38¼b	—	—	—	—	—		42¼	-37¾	1.05	N
92929QAF	•WMX Technologies Inc. cv sub nt 2.00 2005[12]	Ba1	J&J 24	None	843.03	550	26.07	38.34	• —	—	2.2	2.0	124¾	0	—		—	—	—	0.6
981443AA	•World Color Press, Inc. cv sub nt 6.00 2007	B1 r	A&O 1	None	104.20	132	41.47	24.11	•34¼	108½	—	4.9	100	45	36¼	-25¾	110¾	-96	1.65	N
981904AB	•WorldCorp, Inc. cv sub deb 7.00 2004	Caa1	M&N 15	None	103.00	65.0	11.06	90.41	•0¾	15	10	12.1	41¼	1¾	1¾	-0¼	50	-15	d1.29	N
98155FAA	•WorldWay Corp. cv sub deb 6.25 2011[13]	B1 r	A&O 15	2500-'97	100.00	50.0	47.50	21.05	• —	—	8.6	6.3	0	0	—		—	—	1.02	N
983919AA	Xilinx, Inc. cv sub nt 5.25 2002[2]	B2	M&N 1	None		250	—	—	—	97¾b	5.3	5.9	—	—	—		108¼	-92¾	1.72	N
	Yasuda Trust & Banking Co. cv eurobd 2.375 2001	Ba1	A&O 23	None		100	—	—	—	—	—	2.4	—	—	—		—	—	—	0.2
	cv eurobd 1.75 2002	Ba1	F&A 20	None		100	—	—	—	—	—	1.8	—	—	—		—	—	—	0.
989349AB	•Zenith Electronics Corp. cv sub deb 6.25 2011	Ca r	A&O 1	5%-'97	100.00	115	31.25	32.00	0¾	—	8.4	6.3	34¾	0	7¾	-0¼	—	—	d4.49	N

[1]Due 03-15-99..Co. filed for Chap. 11 [2]Private placement. [3]Now Selective Ins. Group [4]Form. Micropolis Corp. [5]Form. National Medical Enterprises, Inc. [6]Amt. outstg. 1.65149 billion. [7]Amt. outstg. 2.415 billion. [8]Amt. outstg. 3.05 billion. [9]Merged with United Waste Systems 8-26-97. [10]Form. U.S. Steel [11]Amt. outstg. 1.06987 billion. [12]Form. WMX Technologies [13]Form. Carolina Freight Corp.

Notes: Moody's ratings are subject to change. Because of the possible time lapse between Moody's assignment or change of a rating and your use of this monthly publication, we suggest you verify the current rating of any security or issuer in which you are interested. For standard abbreviations and symbols, see page 2.

Source: *Moody's Bond Record,* August 1998.

for a prespecified number of shares of the issuing firm's common stock. Thus, a convertible bond represents a hybrid investment involving elements of both the debt and equity markets. From the investor's standpoint, there are both advantages and disadvantages to this packaging. Specifically, although the buyer receives equity-like returns with a "guaranteed" terminal payoff equal to the bond's face value, he or she must also pay the option premium, which, as we will see shortly, is embedded in the price of the security.[20] Conversely, the issuer of a convertible bond increases the company's leverage while providing a potential source of equity financing in the future. Figure 25.14 shows a portion of a page from *Moody's Bond Record* summarizing the pertinent details of a sample of outstanding convertible bonds issued by U.S.-based companies.

[20]In fact, some authors have argued that the risk–return dynamics that convertible bonds offer to investors are sufficiently unique as to merit their own asset class. See Scott L. Lummer and Mark W. Riepe, "Convertible Bonds as an Asset Class: 1957–1992," *Journal of Fixed Income* 3, no. 2 (September 1993): 47–56.

FIGURE 25.15 **DETAILS OF STONE CONTAINER CORPORATION'S CONVERTIBLE BOND ISSUE**

```
STONE CONTAINER      STO6 3/4 02/15/07
CONV TO            29.4640 SHRS(PER      1000.0)STO    (NY  ) $11 3/8    (  0.30)DP 100%
CONVERTIBLE UNTIL  2/15/ 7                            ISSUER INFORMATION
 SECURITY INFORMATION                                 NAME     STONE CONTAINER
 CPN FREQ          SEMI-AN                            TYPE     INDUSTRIAL
 CPN TYPE          FIXED                IDENTIFICATION #'s      REDEMPTION INFO
 MTY/REFUND TYP CV/CALL/SINK            CUSIP     861589AE9     MATURITY DT     2/15/07
 CALC TYP ( 49)CONVERTIBLE              MLNUM E5845             REFUNDING DT    2/16/96
 DAY COUNT( 5) 30/360                                           NEXT CALL DT 11/20/98
 MARKET ISS        US DOMESTIC                                  WORKOUT DT      2/15/07
 COUNTRY/CURR      USA /USD                                     RISK FACTOR     6.2815
 COLLATERAL TYP SUB DEBENTURES              ISSUANCE INFO
 AMT ISSUED             115,000(M)      ANNOUNCE DT    2/11/92          RATINGS
 AMT OUTSTAND            45,200(M)      1ST SETTLE DT  2/20/92  MOODY     B3   /*+
 MIN PC/INC        1,000/      1,000    1ST CPN DT     8/15/92  S & P     B-   /*+
 PAR AMT                 1,000.00       INT ACCRUE DT  2/20/92  COMP      B3
 LEADMGR/UWRTR                          PRICE @ ISSUE  100      DCR       NR
 EXCHANGE         NEW YORK                                      FI        NR

NOTES HAVE PROSPECTUS, DTC, REGISTERED
NOT CALLABLE BEFORE 2/16/96. POISON PUT. OMMITTED DIV 7/28/92. O/S AMT PER 97
AR.
```

Source: Bloomberg, 21 October 1998.

As an example of how one such issue is structured and priced, consider the 6.75 percent coupon convertible subordinated debentures ("cv. Sub deb") issued by Stone Container Corporation, a NYSE-traded company. Stone Container is the industry leader in manufacturing containerboard, corrugated containers, bags, and sacks. The listing for this issue, which is scheduled to mature in February 2007, is shown on the sixth line from the top. After showing the issue's CUSIP identifier, contract terms, and default rating, (i.e., B3), the entry in the fourth column indicates that this bond pays interest semiannually on February 15 and August 15. The bond issue has \$115 million outstanding and is callable at 101.35 percent of par. At the time of this report (i.e., August 1998), the listed price of the debenture was 89.25 percent of par and the share price of Stone Container common stock was 19.875. Additional details of this security are shown in Figure 25.15, which was generated by Bloomberg.

As spelled out at the top of Figure 25.15—and approximated in the ninth column of Figure 25.14—each \$1,000 face value of this bond can be converted into 29.464 shares of Stone Container common stock. As in the convertible preferred example, this statistic is called the instrument's **conversion ratio**. At the listed share price of \$19.875, an investor exercising her conversion option would have received only \$585.60 (= \$19.875 × 29.464) worth of stock, an amount considerably below the current market value of the bond. In fact, the **conversion parity price** (i.e., the common stock price at which immediate conversion would make sense) is equal to \$30.29, which is the bond price of \$892.50 divided by the conversion ratio of 29.464. The prevailing market price of 19.875 is far below this parity level, meaning that the conversion option is currently out of the money. Of course, if the conversion parity price ever fell below the market price for the common stock, an astute investor could buy the bond and immediately exchange it into stock with a greater market value.

As indicated in the sixth column of Figure 25.14, most convertible bonds are also callable by the issuer. Of course, a firm will never call a bond selling for less than its call price (which is the case with the Stone Container debenture). In fact, firms often wait until the bond is selling for significantly more than its call price before calling it.[21] If the company calls the bond under these conditions, investors will have an incentive to convert the bond into the stock that is worth more than they would receive from the call price; this situation is referred to as *forcing conversion.* Two other factors also increase the investor's incentive to convert their bonds. First, some instruments have conversion prices that step up over time according to a predetermined schedule. Since a stepped-up conversion price leads to a lower number of shares received, it becomes more likely that investors will exercise their option just before the conversion price increases. Second, a firm can help to encourage conversion by increasing the dividends on the stock, thereby making the income generated by the shares more attractive relative to the income from the bond.

Another important characteristic when evaluating convertible bonds is the **payback** or *break-even time,* which measures how long the higher interest income from the convertible bond (compared to the dividend income from the common stock) must persist to make up for the difference between the price of the bond and its conversion value (i.e., the conversion premium). The calculation is as follows:

$$\text{Payback} = \frac{\text{Bond Price} - \text{Conversion Value}}{\text{Bond Income} - \text{Income from Equal Investment in Common Stock}}$$

For instance, the annual coupon yield payment on the Stone Container convertible bond is \$67.50, while the firm's dividend yield, which suspended payment of cash dividends in January 1997, is zero. Thus, assuming you sold the bond for \$892.50 and used the proceeds to purchase 44.906 shares (= \$892.50/\$19.875) of Stone Container stock, the payback period would be:

$$\frac{\$892.50 - \$585.60}{\$67.50 - \$0.00} = 4.55 \text{ years}$$

It is also possible to calculate the combined value of the investor's conversion option and issuer's call feature that are embedded in the debenture. In the Stone Container example, with a market price of \$892.50, the convertible's yield-to-maturity can be calculated as the solution to:

$$\$892.50 = \sum_{t=1}^{17} \frac{33.75}{(1 + y/2)^t} + \frac{1000}{(1 + y/2)^{17}}$$

or $y = 8.56$ percent (reported as 8.6 percent in the thirteenth column of Figure 25.14). This computation assumes 17 semiannual coupon payments of \$33.75 (= 67.5 ÷ 2). Since the yield on a Stone Container debt issue with no embedded options and the same (B3) credit rating and maturity was 9.51 percent, the present value of a "straight" fixed-income security with the same cash flows would be:

$$\$841.53 = \sum_{t=1}^{17} \frac{33.75}{(1 + 0.04755)^t} + \frac{1000}{(1 + 0.04755)^{17}}$$

This means that the net value of the combined options is \$50.97, or \$892.50 minus \$841.53. Using the Black-Scholes valuation model, it is easily confirmed that an eight-and-a-half-

[21]An empirical study of this issue revealed that almost all the convertible securities studied were called later than the theoretically optimal time. See Jonathan E. Ingersoll Jr., "An Examination of Corporate Call Policies on Convertible Securities," *Journal of Finance* 32, no. 2 (May 1977): 463–478. Also see Frank J. Fabozzi, *Bond Markets, Analysis and Strategies,* 3d ed. (Saddle River, N.J.: Prentice Hall, 1996).

FIGURE 25.16 **ILLUSTRATING THE VALUE OF A CONVERTIBLE BOND**

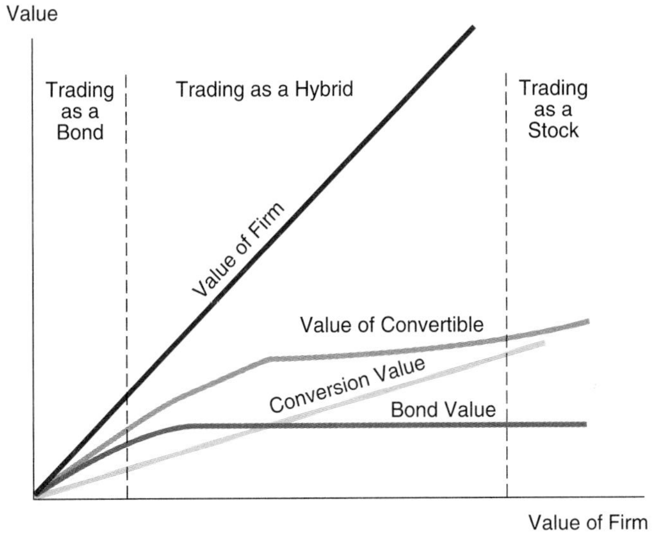
Value
Trading as a Bond
Trading as a Hybrid
Trading as a Stock
Value of Firm
Value of Convertible
Conversion Value
Bond Value
Value of Firm

year call option to buy *one* share of Stone Container stock—which does not pay a dividend—at an exercise price of \$30.29 (i.e., the conversion parity value) is equal to \$6.74.[22] Thus the value of the investor's conversion option—which allows for the acquisition of 29.464 shares—must be \$198.59 (= 29.464 × \$6.74). This means that the value of the issuer's call feature under these conditions must be \$147.62 (= \$198.59 − \$50.97).

Figure 25.16 illustrates the value of a convertible bond in a more general way. The horizontal axis plots the value of the firm, which establishes an upper bound for the value of a convertible since it cannot sell for more than the firm's assets. Thus, there is a firm value line that bisects the plane and the value of the convertible must be below that line. Note that the line for the bond value is relatively flat for a wide range of firm values because higher firm values do not increase the value of the bond since bondholders receive only their promised payments. In contrast, at fairly low firm values, the value of the bond drops off as bankruptcy becomes more likely. Conversion value rises directly with the value of the firm. The figure shows that for low firm values, the bond value will be the minimum value of the convertible, whereas the convertible's price will be driven by its conversion potential for high firm values. Finally, the line for the value of the convertible shows that when the firm value is low, the convertible will act more like a bond, trading for only a slight premium over the bond value (as is the case with the Stone Container debenture discussed earlier). Alternatively, when firm values are high, the convertible will act more like a stock, selling for only a slight premium over the conversion value. In the fairly wide middle range, the convertible will trade as the hybrid security that acts somewhat like a bond and somewhat like a stock.

OTHER EMBEDDED DERIVATIVES

For many years, the nature of borrowing and lending in securitized capital markets remained quite stable, with companies typically issuing bonds at par value and paying either

[22]This calculation assumes the following input values: $S = 19.875$, $X = 30.29$, $T = 8.5$, $RFR = 0.05$, $\sigma = 0.30$, and $D = 0.00$.

a fixed or floating rate of interest in the same currency in which the money was borrowed. With few exceptions, the choice of maturity or coupon structure was driven by the economic situation faced by the borrower, rather than the investor. Over the past decade, however, this scenario has greatly changed with the development of the *structured note* market. Generally speaking, structured notes are debt issues that have their principal or coupon payments linked to some other underlying variable. Examples include bonds whose coupons are tied to the appreciation of an equity index, such as the S&P 500, or a zero-coupon bond with a principal amount tied to the appreciation of an oil price index.

Crabbe and Argilagos have pointed out several common features that distinguish structured notes from regular fixed-income securities, two of which are important for our discussion.[23] First, structured notes are designed for and targeted to a specific investor with a very particular need. That is, these are not "generic" instruments, but products tailored to address an investor's special constraints, which often are themselves created by tax, regulatory, or institutional policy restrictions. Second, after structuring the financing to meet the investor's needs, the issuer typically will hedge that unique exposure with swaps or exchange-traded derivatives. Inasmuch as the structured note most likely required an embedded derivative to create the desired payoff structure for the investor, this unwinding of the derivative position by the issuer generates an additional source of profit opportunity for the bond underwriter.

The growth of this market has been quite rapid. From its ostensible origin in the mid-1980s, Crabbe and Argilagos report that just under $100 billion of these notes were issued annually by the middle of the next decade. Equally impressive is the wide variety of economic risks that have been embedded and the maze of new acronyms that has accompanied these innovations (e.g., FLAG, LYON, SPEL, STEER, PERCS, and ICON). We will take a detailed look at four such structures representative of the major exposures an investor might desire: currency, equity, commodity, and interest rates.

Dual Currency Bonds

A dual currency bond is a debt instrument that has coupons denominated in a different currency than its principal amount. They have been popular funding instruments, particularly in the Euromarkets, for more than a decade and have been designed to include virtually all the world's major currencies. These bonds can be viewed as a combination of two simpler financial instruments: (1) a single-currency fixed-coupon bond, and (2) a forward contract to exchange the bond's principal into a predetermined amount of a foreign currency. They often are sold to investors who are willing to "take a view" over the longer term in the foreign exchange markets. By having the currency forward attached to the bond, fixed-income portfolio managers who might otherwise be restricted from trading in FX have the potential to enhance their performance if their beliefs about future market conditions prove correct.

To demonstrate a structure typical of these products, consider a five-year bond paying an annual coupon of 9 percent in U.S. dollars and redemption amount of JPY 110,000. The initial price of the bond is USD 1,020, relative to a par value of USD 1,000. Assuming further that a regular five-year, dollar-denominated bond of comparable risk yielding 9 percent could have been issued at par, this means that the forward contract portion of the dual currency instrument is "off market" because it carries a present value of USD 20. Table 25.6 shows the cash flows for this structure from the investor's point of view. It also demonstrates how it can be assembled from its more basic component parts.

[23]See Leland E. Crabbe and Joseph D. Argilagos, "Anatomy of the Structured Note Market," *Journal of Applied Corporate Finance* 7, no. 3 (fall 1994): 85–98. Also see Ira G. Kawaller, "Understanding Structured Notes," *Derivatives Quarterly* 1, no. 3 (spring 1995).

TABLE 25.6 CASH FLOWS FOR A DUAL CURRENCY BOND FROM INVESTORS' PERSPECTIVE

	YEAR					
	0	1	2	3	4	5
Transaction						
1. Long 9% USD bond	−USD 1,000	+USD 90	+ USD 90	+USD 90	+USD 90	+USD 1,090
2. Long yen forward (pay USD, receive JPY)	−USD 20	—	—	—	—	+JPY 110,000 and − USD 1,000
3. Long dual currency bond (Transaction 1 + Transaction 2)	−USD 1,020	+USD 90	+USD 90	+USD 90	+USD 90	+JPY 110,000 and +USD 90

Notice that the embedded forward contract allows the bondholder to exchange the USD 1,000 for JPY 110,000, generating an implied *nominal* exchange rate of JPY 110/USD (or, equivalently, USD 0.0091/JPY). However, given that the investor has to pay an additional USD 20 today for this future transaction, this is not the *effective* exchange rate that the investor faces. Indeed, the fact that the investor is willing to pay the additional USD 20 suggests that JPY 110/USD is a favorable price to purchase yen forward. The effective exchange rate built into this transaction can be established by dividing JPY 110,000 by the sum of USD 1,000 and the future value (in year 5) of USD 20. Calculating this latter amount as 30.77 ($= 20 \times (1.09)^5$), the effective exchange rate becomes JPY 106.72/USD ($= 110{,}000 \div (1{,}000 + 30.77)$).

There are at least two reasons why this dual currency bond might trade at a premium over a single-currency 9 percent coupon bond of comparable creditworthiness. First, it is possible that the five-year forward exchange rate between yen and dollars in JPY 106.72/USD, meaning that at USD 1,020, the bond is priced properly. The more likely possibility, though, is that the five-year forward rate actually is JPY 110/USD, and that investors are "paying up" for a desirable FX exposure that they cannot acquire in any other way. If this is true, the issuer—who is effectively short the regular dollar bond and short in the yen forward—can unwind its derivative position at a profit, thereby reducing its funding cost below 9 percent. That is, the issuer's commitment to "sell" JPY 110,000 to the investor in year 5 can be offset by a long position in a separate yen forward (which, once again, is usually done with the bond's underwriter as the counterparty) at the market forward exchange rate of JPY 110/JSD. Thus, the issuer's net borrowing cost can be calculated by solving for the yield as follows:

$$1{,}020 = \sum_{t=1}^{5} \frac{90}{(1+y)^t} + \frac{1000}{(1+y)^5}$$

or $y = 8.49$ percent. This 51 basis-point differential from the "plain vanilla" borrowing rate of 9 percent represents the issuer's compensation for creating an investment vehicle that is tailored to the needs of the investor.

EQUITY INDEX–LINKED NOTES

In May 1996, Merrill Lynch & Co. raised $110,000,000 by issuing 11,000,000 units of an S&P 500 Market Index Target-Term Security (MITTS) at a price of $10 per unit.[24] These MITTS units had a maturity date of May 10, 2001, making them comparable in form to a

[24]We would like to thank Jim Spilman and Scott Soules of Merrill Lynch for their insights into the creation and trading of this security.

five-year bond even though they traded on the New York Stock Exchange. Indeed, Merrill Lynch issued them as a series of Senior Debt Securities making no coupon payments prior to maturity. At maturity, a unitholder received the original issue price plus a "supplemental redemption amount," the value of which depended on where the Standard and Poor's 500 index settled relative to a predetermined initial level. Given that this supplemental amount could not be less than zero, the total payout to the investor at maturity can be written:

$$10 + \max\left[0. \left\{10 \times \left(\frac{\text{Final S\&P Value} - \text{Initial S\&P Value}}{\text{Initial S\&P Value}}\right) \times 1.10\right\}\right]$$

where the initial S&P value was specified as 638.26. The cover page from the prospectus for this deal is shown in Figure 25.17.

From the preceding description, recognize that the MITTS structure combines a five-year, zero-coupon bond with an S&P index call option, both of which were issued by Merrill Lynch. Thus, the MITTS investor essentially owns a "portfolio" that is (1) long in a bond and (2) long in an index call option position. This particular security was designed primarily for those investors who wanted to participate in the equity market but, for regulatory or taxation reasons, were not permitted to do so directly. For example, the manager of a fixed-income mutual fund might be able to enhance her return performance by purchasing this "bond" and then hoping for an appreciating stock market. Notice that the use of the call option in this design makes it fairly easy for Merrill Lynch to market to its institutional customers because it is a "no lose" proposition; the worst-case scenario for the investor is that she simply gets her money back without interest in five years. (Of course, the customer carries the company's credit risk for this period.) Thus, unlike the dual currency bond where the investor could either gain or lose from changing exchange rates, at origination the MITTS issue had no downside exposure to stock price declines.

The call option embedded in this structure is actually a partial position. To see this, we can rewrite the option portion of the note's redemption value as:

$$\max\left[0, \left\{10 \times \left(\frac{\text{Final S\&P} - 638.26}{638.26}\right) \times 1.10\right\}\right] = \max\left[0, \left\{\left(\frac{11}{638.26}\right)(\text{Final S\&P} - 638.26)\right\}\right]$$

or

$$(0.0172)\{\max[0, (\text{Final S\&P} - 638.26)]\}$$

Thus, given that a regular index option would have a terminal payoff of max[0, (Final S&P $- X$)], where X is the exercise price, the derivative in the MITTS represents 1.72 percent of this amount. The terminal payoffs to the MITTS embedded option are shown in Table 25.7, along with those to a regular index call option for several potential May 2001 levels of the S&P 500 index. Notice that although the MITTS and regular options become in the money at the same point (i.e., 638.26), only the latter produces a "dollar-for-dollar" payoff with increasing values of the index beyond this point. The payoff to the call feature in the structured note still rises for any S&P level above 638.26, but gains only $0.0172 for every one point gained by the index.

Rewriting the redemption value in this fashion also makes valuing the MITTS issue a more transparent process. This can be accomplished by recognizing that the value of the entire structure simply should be the value of the bond portion plus the value of the option component; any price "synergy" for the packaging will be a market-driven phenomenon. Specifically, on October 9, 1998, the closing price for the MITTS issue with the ticker

FIGURE 25.17 **PROSPECTUS FOR MERRILL LYNCH'S MITTS ISSUE**

PROSPECTUS SUPPLEMENT
(To Prospectus dated April 4, 1996)

11,000,000 Units
Merrill Lynch & Co., Inc.
S&P 500 Market Index Target-Term Securities[SM] due May 10, 2001
"MITTS®"

An aggregate principal amount of $110,000,000 of S&P Market Index Target-Term Securities[SM] due May 10, 2001 (the "Securities" or "MITTS®") of Merrill Lynch & Co., Inc. (the "Company") are being offered hereby. Each $10 principal amount of Securities will be deemed a "Unit" for purposes of trading and transfer. Units will be transferable by the Depository (as hereinafter defined), as more fully described below.

The Securities are debt securities of the Company, which are being issued in denominations of $10 and integral multiples thereof, will bear no periodic payments of interest and will mature on May 10, 2001. At maturity, a beneficial owner of a Security will be entitled to receive, with respect to each Security, the principal amount thereof plus an interest payment, if any (the "Supplemental Redemption Amount"), based on the percentage increase, if any, in the S&P 500 Composite Stock Price Index (the "Index") over the Starting Index Value. The Supplemental Redemption Amount will in no event be less than zero. The Securities are not redeemable or callable by the Company prior to maturity. At maturity, a beneficial owner of a Security will receive the principal amount of such Security plus the Supplemental Redemption Amount, if any, however, there will be no other payment of interest, periodic or otherwise.

The Supplemental Redemption Amount payable with respect to a Security at maturity will equal the product of (A) the principal amount of the applicable Security, (B) the percentage increase from the Starting Index Value to the Ending Index Value, and (C) the Participation Rate. The Starting Index Value equals 638.26 which was the closing value of the Index on the date the Securities were priced by the Company for initial sale to the public (the "Pricing Date"). The Ending Index Value, as more particularly described herein, will be the average (arithmetic mean) of the closing values of the Index on certain days, or, if certain events occur, the closing value of the Index on a single day prior to the maturity of the Securities. The Participation Rate equals 110%.

For information as to the calculation of the Supplemental Redemption Amount which will be paid at maturity, the calculation and the composition of the Index, and certain tax consequences to beneficial owners of the Securities, see "Description of Securities", "The Index", and "Certain United States Federal Income Tax Considerations", respectively, in this Prospectus Supplement. For other information that should be considered by prospective investors, see "Risk Factors" beginning on page S-5 of this Prospectus Supplement.

Ownership of the Securities will be maintained in book-entry form by or through the Depository. Beneficial owners of the Securities will not have the right to receive physical certificates evidencing their ownership except under the limited circumstances described herein.

The Securities have been approved for listing on the New York Stock Exchange under the symbol "MIX", subject to official notice of issuance.

THESE SECURITIES HAVE NOT BEEN APPROVED OR DISAPPROVED BY THE SECURITIES AND EXCHANGE COMMISSION OR ANY STATE SECURITIES COMMISSION NOR HAS THE SECURITIES AND EXCHANGE COMMISSION OR ANY STATE SECURITIES COMMISSION PASSED UPON THE ACCURACY OR ADEQUACY OF THIS PROSPECTUS SUPPLEMENT OR THE PROSPECTUS. ANY REPRESENTATION TO THE CONTRARY IS A CRIMINAL OFFENSE.

	Price to Public(1)	Underwriting Discount(1)	Proceeds to the Company(2)
Per Unit	$10	$.25	$9.75
Total	$110,000,000	$2,750,000	$107,250,000

(1) The "Price to Public" and "Underwriting Discount" for any single transaction to purchase 100,000 to (but not including) 500,000 Units will be $9.95 per Unit and $.20 per Unit, respectively, and the "Price to Public" and "Underwriting Discount" for any single transaction to purchase 500,000 Units or more will be $9.80 per Unit and $.05 per Unit, respectively.

(2) Before deduction of expenses payable by the Company.

The Securities are offered by the Underwriter, subject to prior sale, when, as, and if issued by the Company and accepted by the Underwriter and subject to certain other conditions. The Underwriter reserves the right to reject orders in whole or in part. It is expected that delivery of the Securities will be made in New York, New York on or about May 13, 1996.

This Prospectus Supplement and the accompanying Prospectus may be used by the Underwriter in connection with offers and sales related to market-making transactions in the Securities. The Underwriter may act as principal or agent in such transactions. Such sales will be made at prices related to prevailing market prices at the time of sale.

Merrill Lynch & Co.

The date of this Prospectus Supplement is May 7, 1996.

"MITTS" is a registered service mark and "Market Index Target-Term Securities" is a service mark owned by Merrill Lynch & Co., Inc.

TABLE 25.7

TERMINAL PAYOFFS TO MITTS EMBEDDED CALL OPTION AND REGULAR INDEX CALL OPTION (X = 638.26)

Terminal S&P Value	Regular Index Call	MITTS Call
575	0.00	0.00
600	0.00	0.00
625	0.00	0.00
650	11.74	0.20
675	36.74	0.63
700	61.74	1.06
725	86.74	1.49
750	111.74	1.92
775	136.74	2.35
800	161.74	2.78
825	186.74	3.21
850	211.74	3.64
875	236.74	4.07
900	261.74	4.50
925	286.74	4.93
950	311.74	5.36
975	336.74	5.79
1000	361.74	6.22
1025	386.74	6.65
1050	411.74	7.08
1075	436.74	7.51
1100	461.74	7.94

symbol MIX was \$15.75, while the S&P 500 closed at 984.39. Further, the semiannually compounded yield of a zero-coupon (i.e., "stripped") Treasury bond on this date was 4.42 percent. Assuming that a credit spread of 95 basis points is appropriate for Merrill Lynch's credit rating (i.e., Aa3 and AA− by Standard and Poor's and Moody's, respectively) and the remaining time to maturity (i.e., two years and seven months, or 5.167 half-years), the bond portion of the MITTS issue should be worth:

$$\text{MITTS Bond Value} = \frac{10}{\left(1 + \frac{.0537}{2}\right)^{5.167}} = \$8.72$$

This means that the investor is paying \$7.03 (= \$15.75 − \$8.72) for the embedded index call.

Whether \$7.03 represents a fair price for the MITTS call depends on the value of the regular index option, which, as we saw in Chapter 24, can be calculated with the dividend yield-adjusted version of the Black-Scholes model. To perform this computation, some additional inputs are needed. First, the S&P dividend yield on October 9, 1998, was 1.11 percent. Second, the number of days between October 9, 1998, and May 10, 2001, is 944. Third, the continuously compounded equivalent of the quoted risk-free rate is 4.37 percent.[25] Finally, the volatility of the S&P 500 index returns over the time to the MITTS issue's maturity is assumed to be 36.74 percent, a level approximated from the prevailing

[25]This value can be established by solving for r in the following equation:

$$e^r = (1 + (0.0442)/2))^2$$

or

$$r = \ln[(1 + (0.0442/2))^2] = 0.0437$$

implied volatilities for exchange-traded index options on that date. (Note that October 1998 was an unusually volatile period for global and U.S. securities markets, as characterized by high implied volatilities and increased credit spreads.)

The value of an index call option with an exercise price of 638.26 can now be generated by the Black-Scholes formula using the following inputs: $S = 984.39$, $X = 638.26$, $T = 2.586$ ($=944/365$), $RFR = 0.0437$, $D = 0.0111$, and $\sigma = 0.3674$. Under these conditions we have:

$$d_1 = [\ln(984.39e^{-(0.0111)2.586}/638.26) + (0.0437 + 0.5(0.3674)^2)(2.586)] \div (0.3674[2.586]^{1/2}) = 1.17$$

and

$$d_2 = 1.17 - 0.3674[2.586]^{1/2} = 0.58$$

so that $N(d_1) = 0.8793$ and $N(d_2) = 0.7192$. Thus the index call's Black-Scholes value is:

$$C_0 = (984.39)(e^{-(0.0111)2.586})(0.8793) - (638.26)(e^{-(0.0437)2.586})(0.7192) = 431.06$$

The value of the embedded MITTS call is then established by multiplying 431.06 by 0.0172, which leaves a value of 7.41. Thus, on this particular date, the MITTS issue was priced in the market below its theoretical value, presenting investors with a potential buying opportunity depending on their transaction costs. Note, however, that the embedded call is still priced above the index option's adjusted intrinsic value of 5.95 ($= [984.39 - 638.26] \times 0.0172$).

Commodity-Linked Bull and Bear Bonds

Besides linking their payoffs to currency or equity indexes, fixed-income securities can be designed to give an investor exposure to commodity price movements as well. As with the commodity swaps we saw earlier, the commodities involved in these structures are seldom exchanged but instead represented in the form of "cash settlement only" derivatives. Thus, virtually no theoretical limit exists to the number of different underlying assets that can be embedded into a bond issue. However, recall that innovation in the structured note market is dictated by investor demands, which to date have tended to concentrate on either oil or precious metals. As in the previous examples, the primary attractions to the investor of gaining the desired exposure through the purchase of structured notes are their convenience and their ability to avoid restrictions on taking commodity positions directly.

A particularly interesting form of the commodity-linked bond is the so-called bull and bear note. This structure gets its name from a bond that is issued in two portions: a bull tranche, whose principal redemption amount increases directly with the price of the designated commodity; and a bear tranche, whose principal refunding declines with increasing commodity prices. One of the first issues of this kind occurred in October 1986 when the Kingdom of Denmark raised \$120 million in two separate \$60 million tranches, each having a different payoff structure depending on the movement of an index of gold prices.[26] Both of these gold-linked note tranches had a seven-year maturity, paid an annual coupon of 3 percent, and were issued at a price of 100.125 percent of par value. The principal redemptions for each \$1,000 of face value for the two tranches were:

[26] Additional details of this bull-and-bear structure are explained in Julian Walmsley, *The New Financial Instruments* 2d ed. (New York: John Wiley & Sons, 1998), which also contains descriptions of an exhaustive set of such deals. It is recommended reading for anyone wishing to learn more about the development of these innovative products.

Bull Redemption: (\$1,000) × [1.158 × (Index at Redemption ÷ Initial Index)]

and

Bear Redemption: (\$1,000) × {2.78 − [1.158 × (Index at Redemption ÷ Initial Index)]}

Finally, for both tranches, maximum and minimum redemption levels of \$2,280 and \$500, respectively, were set.

Table 25.8 shows the redemption amount that the Kingdom of Denmark is obligated to pay on each tranche for a series of gold index levels relative to the initial level, which was set at 426.50. The final column of this display shows what the average redemption value was when the two tranches are considered together. Notice that this average amount does not vary—that is, *the issuer has no net exposure to gold price movements.* Unlike the dual currency bond example considered earlier, which required the issuer to adopt an additional derivative position to offset the instrument's inherent FX exposure, the virtue of this two-tranche approach is that the commodity exposure is neutralized internally. That is, the Kingdom of Denmark is effectively both long and short gold in equal amounts across the bear and bull segments, respectively. An immediate consequence of this is that they have a fixed funding cost for the full \$120 million issue, calculated by solving:

$$1001.25 = \sum_{t=1}^{7} \frac{30}{(1+y)^t} + \frac{1390}{(1+y)^7}$$

or $y = 7.42$ percent. At the time this deal was launched, a regular seven-year, par-value debt issue would have required a yield of about 8 percent, a fact that underscores the Kingdom of Denmark's incentive to create this structure in the first place.

The attraction for the investors, of course, is the ability to purchase a fixed-income security that also allows for participation in gold price movements. In exchange for accepting a lower-than-market coupon, buyers of the bull (bear) tranche will receive a redemption value that exceeds their purchase price if the gold index increases (declines). Figure 25.18,

TABLE 25.8 **REDEMPTION VALUES FOR THE "BULL AND BEAR" GOLD-LINKED NOTE (IN U.S. DOLLARS)**

Terminal Gold Index	Bull Tranche	Bear Tranche	Average
100	500	2,280	1,390
150	500	2,280	1,390
200	543	2,237	1,390
250	679	2,101	1,390
300	815	1,965	1,390
350	950	1,830	1,390
400	1,086	1,694	1,390
450	1,222	1,558	1,390
500	1,358	1,422	1,390
550	1,493	1,287	1,390
600	1,629	1,151	1,390
650	1,765	1,015	1,390
700	1,901	879	1,390
750	2,036	744	1,390
800	2,172	608	1,390
850	2,280	500	1,390
900	2,280	500	1,390

which shows the redemption values for the two tranches in a graphical form, suggests that the commodity derivatives embedded in this transaction are not simple forward or option positions. Rather, the minimum and maximum principal payoffs effectively convert the gold exposure into a call option money spread—a bull spread for the bull tranche, a bear for the bear—as described in Chapter 24. The investors, who undoubtedly will be different people for the two positions, pay for this spread position through a reduction in their average yield-to-maturity relative to the regular bond.

SWAP-LINKED NOTES

As we have seen, interest rate swaps are efficient mechanisms for transforming the cash flows of existing debt issues. They also are quite useful in the new-issue market when the desired rate exposures of the borrower and lender do not coincide naturally. Imagine, for example, that Company LMN wishes to raise $50 million by issuing a fixed-rate note with semiannual coupon payments over a three-year period. Having floated a similar issue in the capital markets recently, however, LMN finds that little "appetite" exists for another one of its fixed-rate notes. On the other hand, a large institutional investor is willing to accept LMN's credit risk on a privately placed loan, providing that the deal can be structured to its satisfaction. In particular, the fund manager for this investment company thinks that interest rates are going to decline substantially over the next few years and wants to design the loan contract to take advantage of that possibility. Accordingly, she wants the semiannual coupon on the note to move inversely with the level of some variable interest rate index, such as LIBOR. This sort of arrangement is known as a *reverse floating rate* contract; the coupon rate changes as the general level of interest rates moves, but in the opposite direction.

Suppose the specific structure that LMN and the investor agree on resets the coupon on a semiannual basis at a level equal to 12 percent minus LIBOR. Thus, if six-month LIBOR on a particular settlement date is 7.5 percent, the coupon payment will be 4.5 percent (times one-half times $50 million). Conversely, a LIBOR of only 3.75 percent would generate a coupon of 8.25 percent. In this way, the investor gains the desired benefit from falling rates and does so in a convenient form that entails less credit risk than if it had transformed a regular bond issue with a derivative on its own. In addition, the reverse floater will actually benefit more from a rate decline than would a fixed-rate note of identical maturity. Specifically,

FIGURE 25.18 **REDEMPTION VALUES FOR THE "BULL AND BEAR" GOLD-LINKED NOTE**

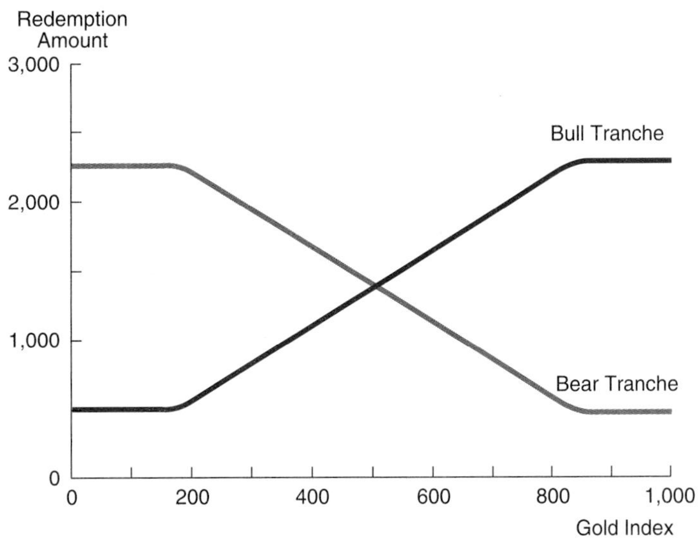
Redemption Amount
3,000
2,000
1,000
0
Bull Tranche
Bear Tranche
0
200
400
600
800
1,000
Gold Index

FIGURE 25.19

CONVERTING A RESERVE FLOATING-RATE NOTE WITH A SWAP

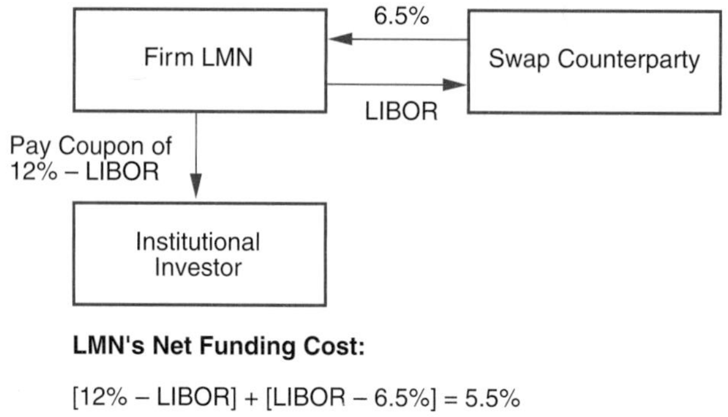
6.5%
Firm LMN
Swap Counterparty
LIBOR
Pay Coupon of
12% – LIBOR
Institutional
Investor
LMN's Net Funding Cost:
[12% – LIBOR] + [LIBOR – 6.5%] = 5.5%

while the price of a fixed-rate bond paying constant coupons will appreciate when yields fall, the reverse floater will increase the investor's periodic cash flow as well.

Unfortunately, although this design satisfies the investor's requirements, it does not do the same for the issuer. This discrepancy can be easily remedied, though, by combining Company LMN's debt position with a swap in which it receives the fixed rate and pays LIBOR. This is illustrated in Figure 25.19, assuming a three-year fixed swap rate of 6.5 percent against six-month LIBOR. One helpful way to see how a swap must be written to fix the coupon on this reverse rate structure is to notice that paying a coupon of 12 percent minus LIBOR is equivalent to paying a coupon of 12 percent and receiving one of LIBOR. Thus, to neutralize LMN's floating-rate exposure, it must pay out LIBOR on the swap.

Figure 25.19 also shows that the net synthetic fixed-rate funding cost to Company LMN is 5.5 percent (assuming the swap fixed rate has been converted to a 360-day year basis). This will only be true, however, whenever LIBOR does not exceed 12 percent. If LIBOR is greater than 12 percent, the benefit from paying lower coupons to the investor will stop—the coupon rate can never go negative—but LMN will continue having to make the higher net settlement payment on the swap, which raises the effective borrowing cost above 5.5 percent. Consequently, because there is an implicit cap on LIBOR built into the reverse floating-rate contract, Company LMN will need to offset this by purchasing an actual cap agreement with an exercise rate of 12 percent and a notional principal of $50 million. This option will not be expensive because it is quite far out of the money but it will not be free, which means the net funding cost will be somewhat greater than 5.5 percent.

Earlier in the chapter, we saw that an interest rate swap can be interpreted as a pair of capital market transactions. In this particular case, a "receive 6.5 percent fixed, pay LIBOR" swap can be viewed as a portfolio long in a fixed-rate note paying 6.5 percent and short in a LIBOR-based floating-rate note. Recalling that "+" represents a long position and "−" represents a short position, the synthetic fixed-rate issue from Company LMN's perspective can be written as follows:

$$
\begin{aligned}
-\text{(Synthetic Fixed Rate Bond at 5.5\%)} &= -\text{(Reverse Floater at 12\%} - \text{LIBOR)} \\
&\quad + \text{(Receive 6.5\%, Pay LIBOR Swap)} \\
&\quad + \text{(Cap at 12\% Exercise Rate)} \\
&= -\text{(Reverse Floater at 12\%} - \text{LIBOR)} \\
&\quad - \text{(FRN at LIBOR)} + \text{(Fixed Rate Bond at 6.5\%)} \\
&\quad + \text{(Cap at 12\% Exercise Rate).}
\end{aligned}
$$

FIGURE 25.20

CONVERTING A LEVERAGED RESERVE FLOATER WITH TWO SWAPS

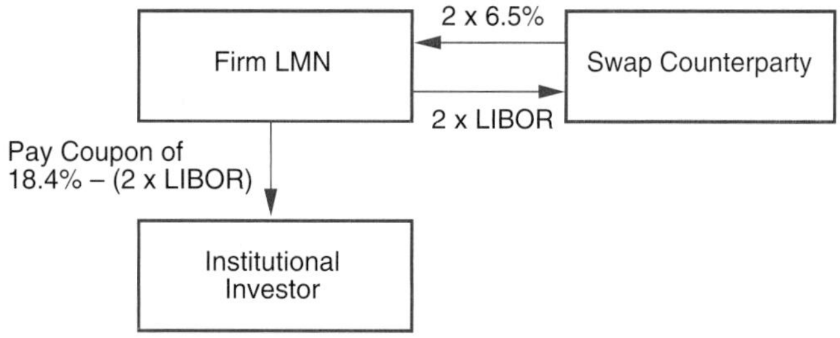
2 x 6.5%
Firm LMN
Swap Counterparty
2 x LIBOR
Pay Coupon of
18.4% – (2 x LIBOR)
Institutional
Investor

LMN's Net Funding Cost:

[18.4% – (2 x LIBOR)] + ([2 x LIBOR) – (2 x 6.5%)] = 5.4%

As in the previous examples, this sort of structured solution would only make sense to the issuer if it could ultimately obtain funding cost that was lower than a direct fixed-rate loan. The biggest reason for this is that while a direct fixed-rate loan would carry no credit risk for Company LMN, the structured loan would because of the swap and cap positions. Thus, the swap-based borrowing is never as good as a direct approach, and therefore requires a lower cost to entice the issuer.

As a final extension of this concept, consider what would have happened if the institutional investor decided to take an even more aggressive view of falling interest rates and requested that the coupon reset the formula to 18.4 percent minus (2 × LIBOR). Such a design is called a *leveraged* reverse floating-rate note, with the leverage coming from the fact that the coupon increases twice as fast as the decline in yields. Figure 25.20 indicates that to convert this to a fixed-rate issue, Company LMN would have to enter into two $50 million receive-fixed swaps (or, more practically, one contract with a notional principal of $100 million). As before, to fix its funding cost completely, it also would have to purchase two $50 million cap agreements with a cap rate of 9.2 percent (= 18.4 percent ÷ 2). This converted position, which would have a net funding cost of 5.4 percent before factoring in the cost of the caps, can be represented as:

$$
\begin{aligned}
-\text{(Synthetic Fixed-Rate Bond at 5.4\%)} &= -\text{(Reverse Floater at 18.4\%} - 2 \times \text{LIBOR)} \\
&\quad + \text{(2 Receive 6.5\%, Pay LIBOR Swaps)} \\
&\quad + \text{(2 Caps at 9.2 \% Exercise Rate)} \\
&= -\text{(Reverse Floater at 18.4\%} - 2 \times \text{LIBOR)} \\
&\quad - \text{(2 FRNs at LIBOR)} + \text{(2 Fixed-Rate Bonds at 6.5\%)} \\
&\quad + \text{(2 Caps at 9.2\% Exercise Rate).}
\end{aligned}
$$

Although the net coupon on this swapped leveraged structure is lower than on the swapped unleveraged reverse floater, the cost of the required options will be more than twice as expensive since two contracts must be purchased at a lower cap rate.[27]

[27]For a more complete examination of how swaps can be used to create structured investment payoffs, see Keith C. Brown and Donald J. Smith, "Structured Swaps," in *Yearbook of Fixed Income Investing,* ed. J. Finnerty and M. Fridson (Burr Ridge, Ill.: Irwin Professional Publishing, 1995).

THE INTERNET *Investments Online*

Bonds, a relatively simple finance and investment instrument, can become as complex as an equity to value when they contain embedded options such as convertibility, warrants, or callability. Several Web sites can help students and investors learn more about these advanced applications of derivatives:

www.altinvest.com We first saw this home page in Chapter 8. The Alternative Investment Corporation seeks to encourage investors to use convertible securities and "convertible arbitrage" in their portfolios (convertible arbitrage, as explained on this site, involves going long in a convertible security while shorting shares of the underlying equity). The site contains examples of how the use of convertible securities can enhance a portfolio's return without affecting its risk.

www.calamos.com Calamos Asset Management, Inc. specializes in research, investment, and management of convertible securities. This site features descriptions of convertibles, including their uses and characteristics, and their benefits to issuers and investors. A chart shows the relative performance of convertibles compared to a variety of other bonds. In addition, news, analysis, and market updates are available here, as are several good FAQs (frequently asked questions) about convertibles and their place in a portfolio.

www.goldmansachs.com/qs/ A page on the Goldman Sachs Web site features research papers on quantitative strategies by Goldman analysts, many of which involve derivative securities.

www.dir.co.jp/InfoManage/datarsc.html The site of the Daiwa Warrant Index includes data and information on how the index is constructed.

www.optionscentral.com The Options Clearing Corporation is the issuer and guarantor of all exchange-traded options contracts in the United States. Their home page allows users to download free software and videos. It features a "Strategy of the Month" for options trading and has a number of resource links to exchanges that trade options.

www.optionsanalysis.com The home page of Options Analysis offers free and purchased information to visitors, including price and volume analysis for many different stock options. It features an options primer and calculated value of options' implied volatilities over different time frames.

www.netservers.com/~waldemar/wl.html Waldemar's List, as it is known, contains links to a number of futures-related Web sites on the Internet. It includes links to publishers, newsletters, software, and information from the basic to the complex about trading. It offers links to traders' home pages, where traders discuss their triumphs and near-misses on the trading floor.

Summary

- The genius of modern financial markets is that they continuously provide new products and strategies to meet the constantly changing needs of anyone willing to pay the required price. In this chapter, we explore several ways in which derivatives can aid in that development process. In particular, we see that innovation sometimes takes the form of creating a new set of instruments, such as interest rate and currency swaps, while at other times it involves packaging existing securities in a creative way. Structured notes, which combine bonds with a derivative position based on a different sort of underlying asset, are a good example of this latter approach. It is important to keep in mind that the ultimate purpose of this financial engineering is to help borrowers and lenders manage one of four types of potential exposures: interest rate, currency, equity, or commodity price risk.
- We began our discussion with an examination of the market for OTC interest rate agreements. Although forward rate agreements are the most basic product in this category, interest rate swaps are the most popular. Swap contracts can be interpreted in three unique ways: as a series of FRAs, as a portfolio of bond positions, or as a zero-cost collar, which consists of a pair of cap and floor agreements. We then extended the "plain vanilla" swap concept to include contracts designed to handle other exposures, such as currency, equity, and commodity swaps, as well as the growing

market for swap options. Since all of these agreements are traded off of the organized exchanges, they are extremely flexible in the terms available—the primary appeal to investors and issuers.

- We conclude with an analysis of several ways in which derivatives can be embedded into other securities to create customized payoff distributions. Because these hybrid structures often are designed to the specific needs of a particular investor, the investor must "pay up" for the customization. Warrants, which are call options on common stock issued directly by the company itself, can be attached to a debt issue to offer investors the upside potential of equity with the safety of a bond. Further, bonds and preferred stock issues can be set up to allow for conversion into common stock at the investor's option. In both cases, the issuing firm will likely end up with a lower front-end funding cost because of the options it has implicitly sold. Finally, a class of instruments known as structured notes carries this concept even farther by embedding into bonds derivatives that often are based on exposures that may not appear on the issuer's balance sheet. These instruments epitomize how much value derivatives can add when they are used properly, and are indicative of the ways in which investors are likely to see them appear in the market for years to come.

Questions

CFA

1. *CFA Examination III (June 1994)*
   Several Investment Committee members for the pension fund you work for have asked about Interest Rate Swap agreements and how they are used in the management of domestic fixed-income portfolios.
   a. Define an interest rate swap and briefly describe the obligation of each party involved.
   b. Cite and explain two examples of how interest rate swaps could be used by a fixed-income portfolio manager to control risk or improve return.
2. Explain how an interest rate swap can be viewed as either a series of forward rate agreements, a pair of bond transactions, or a pair of option agreements. To make your description more precise, take the point of view of the fixed-rate receiver in the swap.
3. "When the yield curve is upward sloping, the fixed rate on a multiyear swap must be higher than the current level of LIBOR. With a downward-sloping yield curve, the opposite will occur." Explain what is meant by this statement and why it must be true.
4. Three years ago, you entered into a five-year interest rate swap agreement by agreeing to pay a fixed rate of 7 percent in exchange for six-month LIBOR. If your counterparty were to default today when the fixed rate on a new two-year swap is 6.5 percent, would you experience an economic loss? Explain.
5. If the fixed rate on a five-year, plain vanilla swap is currently 8 percent, what would happen if you: (1) bought a five-year cap agreement with an exercise rate of 7 percent, and (2) sold a five-year, 7 percent floor agreement? Use the concept of cap-floor-swap parity to describe the kind of position you have created and discuss whether or not a front-end cash payment would be necessary and whether you or your counterparty would receive it.

CFA

6. *CFA Examination III (June 1995)*
   A colleague has asked you about the effects of using interest rate swaptions in a fixed-income portfolio.
   a. Explain how the purchase of an interest rate receiver's swaption would modify:
      (i) the risk characteristics of a fixed-income portfolio; and
      (ii) the return characteristics of a fixed-income portfolio.
   b. Explain two potential disadvantages of using swaptions to help manage risk in a fixed-income portfolio.

CFA

7. *CFA Examination III (June 1995)*
   The manager of Bontemps International (BI) defined-benefit pension plan's fixed-income portfolio has shown exceptional security selection skills, and has produced returns consistently above those on BI's fixed-income benchmark portfolio. The Board wants to allocate more money to this manager to enhance further the fund's alpha. This action would increase the proportion allocated to fixed income and decrease the proportion in equities. However, the Board wants to keep the present fixed income/equity proportions unchanged.

a. Identify two distinct strategies using derivative financial instruments that the Board could use to increase the fund's allocation to the fixed-income manager without changing the present fixed-income/equity proportions. Briefly explain how each of these two strategies would work. (Note: Make sure that equity swaps are one of the two strategies that you choose.)
b. Briefly discuss one advantage and one disadvantage of each of the strategies you identified in part a above. Present your discussion in terms of the effect(s) of these advantages and disadvantages on the portfolio's:
(i) risk characteristics; and
(ii) return characteristics.

CFA

8. *CFA Examination III (June 1995)*
The Board of Bontemps International (BI) will substantially increase the company's defined-benefit pension fund's allocation to international equities in the future. However, the Board wants to retain the ability to reduce temporarily this exposure without making the necessary transactions in the cash markets. You develop a way to meet the Board's condition:

"BI enters into a swap arrangement with Bank A for a given notional amount and agrees to pay the EAFE (Europe, Australia, and Far East) Index return (in U.S. dollars) in exchange for receiving the LIBOR interest rate plus 0.2 percent (20 basis points).

On the same notional amount, BI arranges another swap with Bank B under which BI receives the return on the S&P 500 Index (in U.S. dollars) in exchange for paying the interest rate on the U.S. Treasury bill plus 0.1 percent (10 basis points).

Both swaps would be for a one-year term."

From BI's perspective, identify and briefly describe:
(i) the major risk that this transaction would eliminate;
(ii) the major risk that this transaction would not eliminate (i.e., retain), and
(iii) three risks that this transaction would create.

CFA

9. *CFA Examination III (May 1997)*
A pension plan is currently underfunded by about $400 million. This situation will be resolved soon when the plan sponsor issues a $400 million private placement two-year floater bond that will be placed into the plan under a stipulation that it will be held to maturity. This bond will carry an interest rate of 50 basis points (or 0.5 percent) above the rate of U.S. Treasury bills.

The actual as well as desired asset allocation is 50 percent bonds and 50 percent domestic equities. When the bond is added, the portfolio will become significantly overweighted in fixed-income instruments. In addition, the overall duration will be decreased for the next two years. When the bond matures, the proceeds can be used to buy equities and liquid bonds with longer maturities. One Board member has suggested that futures or swaps could be used to keep the portfolio allocation in line with the desired asset allocation during the two-year period before the floater's maturity.
a. Describe the transactions needed to restore the desired 50 percent/50 percent portfolio allocation using each of the following two derivative instruments: (i) futures, and (ii) swaps.
b. Discuss one advantage and one disadvantage of using futures instead of swaps to implement this strategy.

10. We have seen that equity warrants are not as valuable as an otherwise identical call option on the stock of the same company. Explain why this must be the case. Also, what is the incentive for a firm to issue a warrant rather than issuing stock directly?
11. Bonds and preferred stock that are convertible into common stock are said to provide investors with both upside potential and downside protection. Explain how one security can possess both attributes. What implications do these features have for the way a convertible security is priced?
12. Describe the conditions necessary for structured note issue to be successful. How can an issuer come to know what the particular economic needs of a potential investor happen to be?

Problems

1. With the interest rate swap quotations shown in Table 25.2, calculate the swap cash flows from the point of view of the fixed-rate receiver on a two-year swap with a notional principal of $22.5 million. You may assume the relevant part of the settlement date pattern and the realized LIBOR path shown in Table 25.3 for the three-year agreement. Also, calculate the fixed-rate payment on a 365-day basis and the floating-rate payments on a 360-day basis.
2. Suppose that on February 10, 1999, the treasurer for Company W wishes to restructure the coupon payments of one of her outstanding debt issues. The bond in question is scheduled to pay semiannual interest on March 1 and September 1 each year until February 10, 2004, and has a coupon rate of 6.50 percent with a face value of $35 million. On the same day, the treasurer for Company X wants to restructure the interest payments on his $50 million, four-year floating-rate note having its coupon reset each February 1 and August 1 to a reference rate of LIBOR flat. The maturity of this floating-rate bond is February 1, 2001.
   a. Using the plain vanilla interest rate swap quotes in Table 25.2, describe how both treasurers, working with a dealer, can use a swap agreement to alter synthetically their current cash flow obligations. Specifically, assume that Company W wishes to wind up with floating-rate exposure while Company X desires fixed-rate debt.
   b. Assuming that the dealer negotiates these swap transactions simultaneously, will they represent a matched book? If not, describe two remaining sources of market exposure that the dealer still faces.
3. The treasurer of a British brewery is planning to enter a plain vanilla, three-year, quarterly settlement interest rate swap to pay a fixed rate of 8 percent and to receive three-month sterling LIBOR. But first he decides to check various cap-floor combinations to see if any might be preferable. A market maker in British pound sterling OTC options presents the treasurer with the following price list for three-year, quarterly settlement caps and floors:

	Interest Rate Caps		**Interest Rate Floors**	
Strike Rate	**Buy**	**Sell**	**Buy**	**Sell**
7%	582 bp	597 bp	320 bp	335 bp
8	398	413	401	416
9	205	220	502	517

   The prices are in basis points, which when multiplied by the notional principal give the actual purchase or sale price in pounds sterling. These quotes are from the perspective of the market maker, not the firm. That is, the treasurer could buy a 9 percent cap from the market maker for 220 bp, or sell one for 205 bp. The strike rates are quoted on a 365-day basis, as is sterling LIBOR.

   In financial analysis of this sort, the treasurer assumes that the three-year cost of funds on fully amortizing debt would be about 8.20 percent (for quarterly payments). Should another structure be considered in lieu of the plain vanilla swap?
4. Corporation XYZ seeks $50 million, five-year fixed-rate funding. The firm is confident that it can issue a 9½ percent coupon bond (semiannual payments) at par value. Since the five-year Treasury issue yields 8.25 percent, this funding could be attained at 125 basis points over Treasuries—a reasonable spread given XYZ's credit rating. The corporate treasurer would like to explore the possibility of issuing an FRN, possibly an innovative type, and using the interest rate swap market to create synthetic fixed-rate funding. According to XYZ's capital markets group, the following FRNs could be launched:

Type	Reset Formula
"Traditional" floater	LIBOR + 0.25%
"Bull" (i.e., reverse) floater	18.40% − LIBOR
"Bear" floater	(2 × LIBOR) − 9.10%

Assume that each FRN could be placed at par value and that the flotation costs for the fixed-rate bond and various variable-rate issues are the same (and can therefore be ignored in the comparison). Note that the FRNs are quoted on a money market (360-day) basis and reset the coupon rate semiannually based on the prevailing six-month LIBOR. A quick canvassing of the swap market generates the following representative quotes on a five-year swap with semiannual settlements:

Dealer's Bid	Dealer's Ask
$T + 85$	$T + 95$

a. What specific swap transactions are needed to transform each FRN into a synthetic fixed rate? What synthetic fixed rate can be attained by each of the structures? Is the rate fixed for all possible levels of LIBOR? (Note: Calculate all synthetic funding rates on a 365-day basis.)
b. What would be the funding cost if XYZ raised the desired $50 million by issuing $25 million of a traditional FRN and $25 million of a bull floater?
c. Which structure would you recommend for XYZ?
d. What types of investors might be interested in acquiring a bull floater? If the motive was speculative, what would be the investor's view on the future path for LIBOR?
e. What types of investors might be interested in acquiring a bear floater? If an investor's motive was to hedge exposure to LIBOR, what might its balance sheet look like?

5. An Australian pension fund compares two investment alternatives. The first is a five-year Eurobond bearing an 11½ percent coupon rate (paid annually). The bond would have a face value of AUD 100 million and could be acquired at a price of 99.625 (percent of par value). The second is a five-year, AUD 100 million floating-rate note (FRN) that can be purchased at par. The FRN would have a semiannual coupon reset formula of the six-month bank bills' rate (BBR) plus 1.00 percent, and make coupon payments "in arrears" calculated on an actual/365 basis. The corporation can enter five-year, semiannual settlement interest rate swaps to pay a fixed rate (quoted on an actual/actual basis) of 10.25 percent, against BBR flat.
   a. Calculate and compare the fixed-rate yields to maturity for the two alternatives. Which delivers the higher return? Demonstrate.
   b. The interest rate swap involves credit risk for the pension fund. If the counterparty happened to default when the replacement swap fixed rate was 10.75 percent (SABB), what would be the financial impact on the pension fund? Assume a notional principal of AUD 100 million, exactly three remaining years to maturity, and use of the swap fixed rate as the discount factor in calculating the present value.
6. As a swap dealer, you have just been contacted by a prospective corporate counterparty who wishes to do a three-year "fixed/fixed" yen/sterling currency swap. In particular, the corporation needs to pay a fixed interest rate in Japanese yen and to receive a fixed rate in British pound sterling. Your current spot FX and three-year currency swap quotes (versus six-month U.S. dollar LIBOR) are as follows:

		Japanese Yen	British Pound Sterling
Spot Exchange Rate		JPY 127.47/USD	USD 1.82/GBP
Currency Swap:	Bid	4.85%	9.83%
	Offer	4.92	9.93

These quotes imply that you would be willing to pay 4.85 percent in yen to receive U.S. dollar LIBOR, but you would need to receive 4.92 percent in yen when paying LIBOR. Your bid–offer spread is seven basis points in yen. Note that the bid–offer spread is higher in sterling because each basis point is not worth as much (since sterling would be at a forward discount to yen).

a. Describe the sequence of transactions necessary to construct this swap from the counterparty's perspective, including your quotes for both of the fixed rates.
b. Construct a chart similar to Table 25.4 summarizing the cash flow exchanges on each exchange date, again adopting the end user's viewpoint. In this analysis, assume that the deal is to be scaled to a transaction size of USD 25 million and that the number of days in the settlement payments alternates between 182 and 183, starting with 183 days between the origination date and the first settlement date.

7. Suppose that on April 15, 1987, a French corporation entered into an annual-settlement, three-year currency swap to receive 12.72 percent in U.S. dollars (USD) and to pay 14.88 percent in French francs (FRF). Suppose that the spot market exchange rate was FRF 8.4435/USD at the time, or USD 0.118433/FRF. The principal on the swap was USD 100 million, which equals FRF 844.35 million. The scheduled cash flows on the swap from the perspective of the French corporation were the following:

	Receive	Pay
April 15, 1988	USD 12,720,000	FRF 125,639,280
April 15, 1989	USD 12,720,000	FRF 125,639,280
April 15, 1990	USD 112,720,000	FRF 969,989,280

On April 15, 1988, just after the initial coupon exchange, the corporation decides to cancel the remainder of its swap position and negotiate a lump-sum settlement with its counterparty. On that date, plain vanilla two-year fixed/fixed currency swaps were quoted by a number of dealers at 10.20 percent in USD versus 12.78 percent in FRF. The spot market exchange rate was FRF 9.4829/USD, or USD 0.105453/FRF.

a. Calculate the amount of the swap unwind payment (in FRF) suggested by these new market conditions.
b. Would the French corporation pay or receive this amount? Explain.

8. On December 2, the manager of a tactical asset allocation fund that is currently invested entirely in floating-rate debt securities decides to shift a portion of her portfolio to equities. To effect this change, she has chosen to enter into the "receive equity index" side of a one-year equity swap based on movements in the S&P 500 index plus a spread of 10 basis points. The swap is to have quarterly settlement payments with the floating-rate side of the agreement pegged to three-month LIBOR denominated in U.S. dollars. At the origination of the swap, the value of the S&P 500 index was 463.11 and three-month LIBOR was 3.50 percent. The notional principal of the swap is set for the life of the agreement at $50 million, which matches the amount of debt holdings in the fund that she would like to convert to equity.

a. Calculate the net cash receipt or payment—from the fund manager's perspective—on each future settlement date, assuming the value for the S&P 500 index (with all dividends reinvested) and LIBOR are as follows:

Settlement Date	Number of Days	S&P Level	LIBOR Level
December 2 (initial year)	—	463.11	3.50%
March 2 (following year)	90	477.51	3.25%
June 2	92	464.74	3.75%
September 2	92	480.86	4.00%
December 2	91	482.59	—

b. Explain why the fund manager might want the notional principal on this swap to vary over time and what the most logical pattern for this variation would be.

9. *CFA Examination III (June 1996)*

CFA

On June 30, 1996, Help for Students (HFS) Foundation owns $10 million (face amount) of 6% coupon SteelCo. bonds, currently priced at par, which it must hold to maturity on June 30, 1998, two years from now. John Ames, HFS's fixed-income manager, expects that the yield curve, now normal in shape (i.e., positively sloped), will undergo an upward shift and invert sometime prior to maturity. He wishes to enter into a swap on the $10 million notional amount of the holding to take advantage of this yield curve forecast. Assume that HFS's policy permits such action.

SELECTED JUNE 30, 1996, MARKET DATA

	Price	Yield
September 1996 Eurodollar Future	94.9	5.1%
2-year swap fixed rate	n/a	5.5%

a. Identify and explain an interest rate swap arrangement that could achieve Ames's goal in this particular instance. Base your response on the data above and assume quarterly cash flows.

b. Describe the direction and calculate the amount of the first quarterly cash flow (on September 30, 1996) under this arrangement. (*Note: Assume that 90-day spot LIBOR on June 30, 1996, equals the September 1996 Eurodollar futures contract settlement yield.*)

c. Explain the effect of the interest rate swap created in part a above on the sensitivity of HFS's portfolio value to interest rate changes.

d. Describe the role of the Eurodollar forward rate curve in pricing the fixed-rate payment side of the interest rate swap created in part a above.

e. Identify a strategy that would use options to replicate the position of a fixed-rate payer in a swap and explain how this strategy would accomplish its purposes. (Assume no transaction costs.)

10. A Spanish pension fund is considering buying a five-year floating-rate note named "El Oso Grande." El Oso Grande would have a coupon reset formula of three times six-month (Spanish peseta) LIBOR minus 24 percent, subject to a minimum coupon rate of 0 percent if peseta LIBOR were to fall below 8 percent. Currently, six-month peseta LIBOR is 11.20 percent, so the initial coupon would be based on a rate of 9.60 percent. The five-year, semiannual payment, 100 million peseta floating-rate note can be bought at par value. The pension fund intends to use derivative instruments to convert El Oso Grande into a synthetic fixed-rate asset. Quotes for five-years, semiannual settlement interest rate swaps, caps, and floors on six-month Spanish peseta LIBOR are obtained form a Madrid commercial bank specializing in derivative products.

Interest Rate Swaps: The pension fund can pay a fixed rate of 13.50 percent and receive six-month peseta LIBOR, or the fund can receive a fixed rate of 13.35 percent and pay six-month peseta LIBOR.

Interest Rate Caps:

Strike Rate	The Fund Buys the Cap	The Fund Writes the Cap
24%	125bp	90 bp

Interest Rate Floors:

Strike Rate	The Fund Buys the Floor	The Fund Writes the Floor
8%	175 bp	140 bp

(Recall that the premiums on the caps and floors are quoted as a percentage of the notional principal.)

a. Indicate the specific combination of transactions that provides a synthetic fixed-rate asset to the pension fund.
b. Calculate the "all-in," fixed rate of return. Assume that Spanish peseta LIBOR, the coupon rate on El Oso Grande, the swap fixed rate, and the strike rate on the caps and floors are all stated on a semiannual bond basis.

11. You are considering the purchase of a convertible bond issued by Bildon Enterprises, a non-investment-grade medical service firm. The issue has seven years to maturity and pays a semiannual coupon rate of 7.625 percent (i.e., 3.8125 percent per period). The issue is callable by the company at par and can be converted into 48.852 shares of Bildon common stock. The bond currently sells for $965 (relative to par value of $1,000), and Bildon stock trades at $12.125 a share.
    a. Calculate the current conversion value for the bond. Is the conversion option embedded in this bond in the money or out of the money? Explain.
    b. Calculate the conversion parity price for Bildon stock that would make conversion of the bond profitable.
    c. Bildon does not currently pay its shareholders a dividend, having suspended these distributions six months ago. What is the payback (i.e., break-even time) for this convertible security and how should it be interpreted?
    d. Calculate the convertible's current yield to maturity. If a "straight" Bildon fixed-income issue with the same cash flows would yield 9.25 percent, calculate the net value of the combined options (i.e., the issuer's call and the investor's conversion) embedded in the bond.
12. On May 26, 1991, Svensk Exportkredit (SEK), the Swedish export credit corporation, issued a Bull Indexed Silver Opportunity Note (BISON). Consider an extended version of this BISON issue that has the following terms:

Maturity:	May 26, 1993
Coupon:	6.50%, paid annually in arrears
Face Value:	USD 30 million
Purchase Price:	100.125% of par value

Additionally, this BISON includes a redemption feature that, for each USD 1,000 of face value held at maturity, repays the investor's principal according to the following formula:

$$\text{USD } 1{,}000 + [(\text{spot silver price per ounce} - \text{USD } 4.46) \times (\text{USD } 224.21525)]$$

a. Demonstrate that, from SEK's perspective, the BISON represents a combination of a straight debt issue priced at a small premium and a derivative contract. Be explicit as to the type of derivative contract and the underlying asset on which it is based. What implicit speculative position are the investors who buy these bonds taking?
b. Calculate the yield to maturity for an investor holding USD 10,000 in face value of these BISON if the May 1993 spot price for silver is (i) USD 4.96 per ounce, or (ii) USD 3.96 per ounce.
c. In May 1991 (i.e., when the BISON were used), the prevailing delivery price on a two-year silver futures contract was USD 4.35 per ounce. If SEK wanted to hedge its BISON-related exposure to silver prices with an offsetting futures position at this price, what type of position would need to be entered? Ignoring margin accounts and underwriting fees, calculate SEK's average annualized borrowing cost of funds for the resulting synthetic straight bond.

13. In July 1986, Guinness Finance B.V. placed a three-year, $100 million Eurobond issue known as *Stock Performance Exchange Linked* (SPEL) bonds. The concept of the SPEL is that the bond has its principal redemption amount tied to the level of the NYSE composite index at maturity (i.e., NY_3) by the following formula:

$$\text{Variable Redemption Amount} = \max\{100{,}100 \times (1 + [(NY_3 - 166) \div 166])\}$$

Notice that the investor is guaranteed redemption at par as a minimum. The bond also pays an annual coupon of 3 percent, which is 0.5 percent below the average annual dividend yield of shares on the NYSE. At the time the SPEL was launched, the NYSE composite index stood at 134.

a. Demonstrate that the SPEL is a combination of a regular debt issue and an equity option by analyzing the pattern of annual cash flows generated by the issue. In your work, assume a par value of 100.
b. The SPEL bonds were issued at a price of 100.625. Assuming that Guinness would ordinarily have to pay a borrowing cost of 7.65 percent on a three-year "straight" bond (i.e., one with no attached options), calculate the implicit dollar price of the equity index option embedded in this issue. How much of this amount represents intrinsic value and how much is time premium?

14. A firm has 100,000 shares of stock outstanding priced at $35 per share. The firm has no debt and does not pay a dividend. To raise more capital, it plans to issue 10,000 warrants, each allowing for the purchase of one share of stock at a price of $50. The warrants are European-style and expire in five years. The standard deviation of the firm's common stock is 34 percent and the continuously compounded, five-year risk-free rate is 5.2 percent.

a. Estimate the fair value of the warrants, first using the relevant information to calculate the Black-Scholes value of an analogous call option.
b. Determine the stock price at expiration, assuming the warrants are exercised if the value of the firm is at least $5,200,000.
c. Using the information in parts a and b about initial and terminal warrant and stock prices, discuss the relative merits of these two ways of making an equity investment in the firm.

References

Beidleman, Carl R., ed. *Interest Rate Swaps.* Homewood, Ill.: Business One-Irwin, 1991.

Bicksler, James, and Andrew H. Chen. "An Economic Analysis of Interest Rate Swaps." *Journal of Finance* 41, no. 3 (July 1986).

Campbell, Tim S., and William A. Kracaw. *Financial Risk Management.* New York: HarperCollins, 1993.

Constantinides, George M. "Warrant Exercise and Bond Conversion in Competitive Markets." *Journal of Financial Economics* 13, no. 3 (September 1984).

Dattareya, Ravi E., Raj E. S. Venkatesh, and Vijaya Venkatesh. *Interest Rate and Currency Swaps.* Chicago, Ill.: Probus Publishing, 1994.

Duffie, Darrell, and Kenneth J. Singleton. "An Econometric Model of the Term Structure of Interest-Rate Swap Yields." *Journal of Finance* 52, no. 4 (September 1997): 1287–1321.

Eckl, S., J. N. Robinson, and D. C. Thomas. *Financial Engineering: A Handbook of Derivative Products.* Cambridge, Mass.: Basil Blackwell, 1991.

Finnerty, John D. "An Overview of Corporate Securities Innovation." *Journal of Applied Corporate Finance* 4, no. 4 (winter 1992).

Galitz, Lawrence C. *Financial Engineering.* Burr Ridge, Ill.: Irwin Professional Publishing, 1995.

Intersoll, Jonathan E., Jr. "A Contingent Claims Valuation of Convertible Securities." *Journal of Financial Economics* 4, no. 3 (May 1977).

Litzenberger, Robert H. "Swaps: Plain and Fanciful." *Journal of Finance* 47, no. 3 (July 1992).

Smithson, Charles, Clifford W. Smith Jr., and D. Sykes Wilford. *Managing Financial Risk,* 3d ed. Burr Ridge, Ill.: Richard D. Irwin, 1998.

Wall, Larry D., and John J. Pringle. "Alternative Explanations of Interest Rate Swaps: A Theoretical and Empirical Analysis." *Financial Management* 18, no. 2 (summer 1989).

Part 7 Investment Companies and Evaluating Portfolio Performance

This final section of the book contains two chapters: the first deals with professional asset management, and the second is concerned with the evaluation of portfolio performance. The asset management chapter is mainly of concern to individual investors, while both individual and institutional investors need to be aware of how one evaluates the performance of a portfolio.

Because many investors employ professional asset managers to manage their assets, Chapter 26 is an important wrap-up to their asset allocation and portfolio construction process. After a broad overview of the different ways that professional asset management firms can be organized, the chapter describes how the asset management industry has changed over time and how professional managers are compensated for their expertise. Particular emphasis is paid to the role of the investment company (also more commonly called mutual funds), which manage the majority of assets held by individual investors. The discussion includes a description of the major forms of investment companies and the general types of funds available, such as money market, growth, aggressive growth, income, balanced, and bond funds. It is argued that almost any investment objective can be met by investing in one or several investment companies.

There is also a discussion of ethical and regulatory issues that arise when hiring a professional asset manager. Two issues that are of special concern are designing compensation contracts to provide managers with the proper incentives to act in the investor's best interest and the proper use of trading commission fees. The chapter concludes with an extensive analysis of the data sources available to investors about investment companies and the performance of these professional managers over time. The results of the research into fund performance indicate that, on average, investment companies have not been able to consistently outperform the aggregate market, although there is some recent evidence of performance persistence. However, it is noted that even with the average performance shortfall, investment companies are capable of fulfilling a number of functions that are important to investors.

We conclude the book with a chapter dealing with the evaluation of portfolio performance. After a discussion of what is required of a portfolio manager, we review in detail the major risk-adjusted portfolio performance models including a recent performance attribution model that, in turn, is capable of evaluating a global portfolio that necessarily includes the effect of currency allocation. We also consider how the alternative models relate to each other. This is followed by a demonstration of their use with a sample of mutual funds.

As always, it is important to understand potential problems with a technique or models. Therefore, we consider potential problems with the performance measures including a review of Roll's benchmark problem and its effect on these performance models. It is demonstrated that this benchmark problem has become more significant with the growth of global investing. Finally, because the factors that determine success in bonds differ from what is important in equities, we review and evaluate several alternative models used to evaluate the performance of bond portfolio managers.

Chapter 26 Professional Asset Management

After you read this chapter, you should be able to answer the following questions:

- What are the different ways that professional asset management firms can be organized?
- How has the structure of the asset management industry changed over time?
- How are managers at investment advisory firms compensated?
- Who manages the investment company portfolio and how are its managers compensated?
- How do you compute the net asset value (NAV) for investment companies?
- What is the difference between closed-end and open-end investment companies?
- What is the difference between the NAV and the market price for a closed-end fund?
- What are load fees, 12b-1 fees, and management fees and how do they influence investment company performance?
- What are the two major means of fund distribution and what has been the trend for each approach?
- Given the breakdown of all funds by investment objectives, which groups have experienced relative growth or decline?
- Given a desire to have a personal portfolio manager perform certain functions for you, how do investment companies help fulfill this need?
- What are the ethical dilemmas involved in the professional asset management industry?
- What has been the risk-adjusted performance of mutual funds relative to alternative market indexes?

So far, we have discussed how to analyze the aggregate market, alternative industries, and individual companies as well as their stocks and bonds in order to build a portfolio that is consistent with your investment objectives. Part 6 centered on alternative investment vehicles, such as options, warrants, convertibles, and futures, that provide additional risk–return possibilities beyond those available from a straight stock–bond portfolio. This chapter introduces another possibility: entrusting your money to a professional portfolio manager. As we will see, using a professional money manager can entail establishing a private account with an investment advisor or purchasing shares of an established security portfolio managed by an investment company. In either form, professionally managed investments often represent a substantial portion of an individual's total holdings.

The efficient market studies we have seen indicated that few individual investors outperform the aggregate market averages. This makes using professional asset managers a potentially appealing alternative for several reasons, including the additional services they provide. For example, it is often the case that an investment company offers an investor a cost-effective way to choose among a wide variety of diversified portfolios spanning the risk–return spectrum. However, this relationship also creates potential conflicts between the goals of the investor and the goals of the manager; we will consider some ethical implications of the investor–manager contract as well.

The initial sections of this chapter explain the two ways in which asset management firms are typically organized and charge for their services. In this discussion, we will pay particular attention to investment companies, which are the most prevalent way in which individual investors employ professional investment counsel. Subsequently, we describe how investment company shares are traded in the secondary market and how these companies can be divided into classes based on investment objectives and the types of securities in their portfolios. One important classification that we will see focuses on investment companies that invest in stocks and bonds from around the world.

To choose among the approximately 7,000 investment companies available, you need to understand how to access and interpret publicly available data and then to evaluate performance. We continue our discussion with a presentation of some sources of information on investment companies that can help you make decisions of an increasingly global nature. We then conclude with a consideration of the results from some major studies of investment company performance and the implications of these findings for investors.

THE ASSET MANAGEMENT INDUSTRY: STRUCTURE AND EVOLUTION

At the most basic level, there are two ways in which professional asset management firms are organized. In arguably the most straightforward structure, individuals as well as institutional investors, such as the sponsors of pension and endowment funds, make contracts directly with a **management and advisory firm** for its services. These services can range from providing standard banking transactions (savings accounts, personal loans) to advising clients on structuring their own portfolios to actually managing the investment funds themselves. Although banking and financial advice were once the main services these firms offered, the last several decades have seen a dramatic shift toward the *assets under management* (AUM) approach. In that arrangement, the management firm becomes the custodian of the investor's capital, usually with full discretion as to how those funds are invested. An important feature of this structure is that each client of the management firm has a *separate account.* That is, even if investors select the firm because of its expertise in a particular niche—say, selecting small capitalization growth stocks—the assets of each client will be accounted for separately regardless of whether the firm employs a single "model" portfolio. This situation is illustrated in Panel A of Figure 26.1.

A second general approach to asset management involves the *commingling* of investment capital from several clients. An **investment company** invests a pool of funds belonging to many individuals in a single portfolio of securities. In exchange for this commitment of capital, the investment company issues to each investor new shares representing his or her proportional ownership of the mutually held securities portfolio, which is commonly known as a *fund.* For example, suppose an investment company sells 10 million shares to the public at $10 a share, thereby raising $100 million. If the fund's purpose is to emphasize blue-chip common stocks, the manager would invest the proceeds of the fund share sale ($100 million less any brokerage fees) in the stock of such companies as AT&T, IBM, Xerox, and General Electric. Each investor who bought shares of the investment company would then own the appropriate percentage of the overall fund, rather than any portion of the shares in the portfolio themselves. Panel B of Figure 26.1 shows how this structure might work.

There are important differences between these two organizational forms. Private management and advisory firms typically develop a personal relationship with their clients, getting to know the specific investment objectives and constraints of each. The collection of

FIGURE 26.1 **OPERATING STRUCTURES OF ASSET MANAGEMENT COMPANIES**

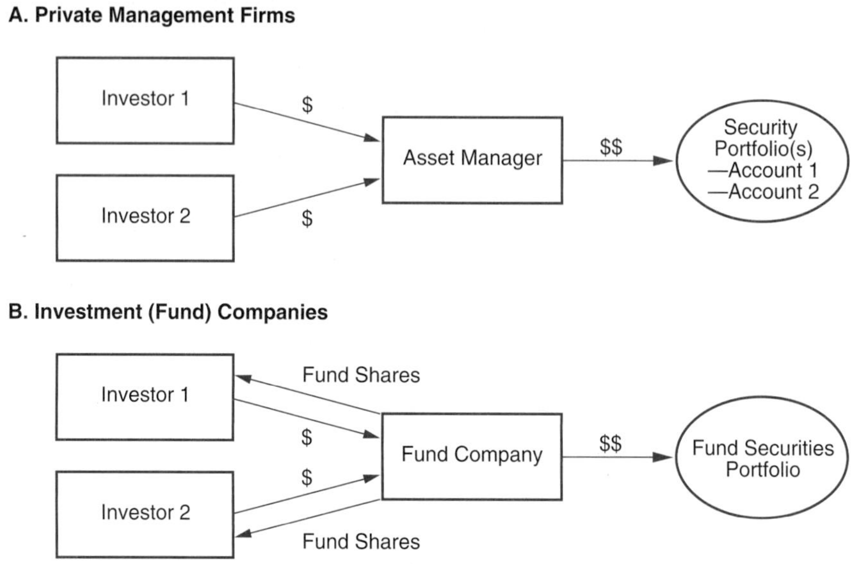
A. Private Management Firms
Investor 1
Investor 2
$
$
Asset Manager
$$
Security Portfolio(s)
—Account 1
—Account 2
B. Investment (Fund) Companies
Investor 1
Investor 2
Fund Shares
$
$
Fund Company
$$
Fund Securities Portfolio
Fund Shares

assets held in the various separate accounts can then be tailored to these special needs, even if a general "blueprint" portfolio is used for all clients. Of course, special attention comes at a cost, and for this reason private management firms are used mainly by investors with substantial levels of capital, such as pension fund sponsors and high net worth individuals. Conversely, a mutual fund offered by an investment company is formed as a general solution to an investment problem and then marketed to investors who might fit that profile. Not surprisingly, the primary clients who seek professional asset management through investment companies are individual investors with relatively small pools of capital. In fact, the Investment Company Institute (a nonprofit industry trade association) reported that in 1997 about 78 percent of mutual fund shares were held by households with only 10 percent being held by business organizations.[1]

It is not unusual for professional asset management firms to combine these two structures by offering private advisory services as well as publicly traded funds. For instance, consider T. Rowe Price Associates, a multi-asset, independent advisory firm located in Baltimore, Maryland. Founded in 1937, T. Rowe Price has seen its business grow to the point where it managed almost $150 billion by the end of 1998, compared with less than $54 billion AUM just four years earlier. The majority of this capital is invested in the firm's various public mutual fund portfolios, but T. Rowe Price also has several hundred private clients, including corporate retirement funds, public funds and unions, foundations and endowments, and individual investors.[2]

The AUM growth that T. Rowe Price has experienced during the past few years has been typical for the entire industry. Table 26.1 charts the top 50 asset management companies as of the end of 1994 and 1998. A striking feature of these lists is the rapid increase in the

[1]See Chapter 4 of *1998 Mutual Fund Fact Book* (Washington, D.C.: Investment Company Institute).

[2]This, and much more, information is available from T. Rowe Price's public home page maintained on Nelson's Investment Manager Network (**www.nelnet.com**) on the World Wide Web.

TABLE 26.1 **ASSETS UNDER MANAGEMENT (AUM) FOR LEADING FIRMS**

	December 31, 1998		December 31, 1994	
Rank	Firm	AUM ($MM)	Firm	AUM ($MM)
1	Fidelity Management & Research	$694,688	Fidelity Management & Research	$314,543
2	Merrill Lynch Asset Management Group	501,229	Bankers Trust Company	186,797
3	State Street Global Advisors	490,000	Merrill Lynch Asset Management Group	163,822
4	Barclays Global Investors	469,435	Capital Group	162,634
5	The Vanguard Group	463,083	Wells Fargo/BMZ	158,392
6	Bankers Trust Company	337,834	State Street Global Advisors	140,413
7	Prudential Investments	337,504	Alliance Capital Management	121,290
8	Metropolitan Life Insurance Co.	330,000	Franklin/Templeton Group	114,100
9	J. P. Morgan Investment Management	316,193	J. P. Morgan Investment Management	111,983
10	Putnam Investments	300,000	American Express Financial/IDS	102,128
11	Capital Research & Management Company	296,485	Putnam Investments	95,182
12	Alliance Capital Management	286,659	INVESCO	94,066
13	Scudder Kemper Investments	281,188	Scudder Stevens & Clark	91,253
14	ML Asset Management	278,750	The Northern Trust Company	82,353
15	The Northern Trust Company	236,020	Wellington Management Company	81,970
16	American Express Retirement Services	212,400	The Vanguard Group	81,743
17	Wellington Management Company	209,430	Citibank Global Asset Management	73,999
18	AXA Investment Managers	208,000	Pacific Investment Management Company (PIMCO)	72,175
19	Chase Asset Management	189,603	Smith Barney Capital	69,114
20	General Accident Investment Management	188,009	Kemper Financial Services	62,748
21	Goldman Sachs Asset Management	182,279	Dreyfus Corp.	62,055
22	SEI Investments	177,000	New England Investment Cos.	56,609
23	Mercury Fund Managers Limited	171,711	PNC Asset Management Group	56,422
24	Brinson Partners/UBS	162,794	T. Rowe Price Associates	53,705
25	Pacific Investment Management Company (PIMCO)	157,963	Dean Witter InterCapital	51,197
26	T. Rowe Price Associates	147,970	Federated Investors	50,743
27	Morgan Stanley Dean Witter Investment Management	141,879	Van Kampen American Capital	46,699
28	BlackRock	132,000	John Nuveen Co.	46,497
29	Franklin Resources	126,730	Chase Manhattan Corp.	44,839
30	John Hancock Mutual Life Insurance Company	126,063	Bank of New York	42,599
31	Janus Capital Corporation	108,299	TCW Group	41,981
32	Federated Investors	107,121	SunTrust Banks	41,811
33	INVESCO	102,692	Chemical Bank Portfolio Group	41,725
34	Oppenheimer Funds	99,133	Bank of America Investment Mgmt Services	41,328
35	Citibank Global Asset Management	98,894	NationsBank	40,771
36	MFS Institutional Advisors	97,527	Union Bank of Switzerland	38,685
37	SG Asset Management	94,107	GE Investments	38,230
38	Standard Life Assurance Company	92,000	Goldman Sachs Asset Management	37,400
39	Templeton Investment Counsel	90,111	Brinson Partners	36,540
40	AIG Global Investment Corp.	83,694	Boatmen's Trust Co.	36,420
41	AIM Advisors	83,200	Morgan Stanley Asset Management	35,678
42	CIGNA Investments	82,300	National Bank of Detroit	35,590
43	Capital Guardian Trust Company	81,298	Mitchell Hutchins Asset Management	34,394
44	American Century Investments	80,069	Harris Bankcorp.	33,827
45	Sanford C. Bernstein & Co.	78,984	Massachusetts Financial Services	33,432
46	New York Life Insurance Company	78,809	U.S. Trust Company of New York	33,032
47	First American Asset Management	78,000	Mellon Capital Management	31,910
48	Henderson Investors	76,994	Banc One Investment Corp.	31,537
49	U.S. Trust Company of New York	75,036	HSBC Asset Management	30,488
50	Mellon Capital Management	73,225	Fiduciary Trust Co. Int'l	29,903

Source: *Nelson's Directory of Investment Managers* and Goldman, Sachs.

number of large asset management firms, defined as those organizations with AUM of more than $100 billion. In 1994, there were only 10 such firms; by 1998, there were 33. Much of this asset growth can be explained by the strong performance of the U.S. equity market during this period, but another important contributing factor was the consolidation trend that marked the industry. Typical of this phenomenon was the merger of the asset management groups Union Bank of Switzerland and Brinson Partners (ranked 36 and 39 on the 1994 list, respectively) to become Brinson Partners/UBS (ranked 24 on the 1998 list). This consolidation trend is likely to continue as the competition among existing asset management firms for the flow of new investment capital is expected to increase significantly.[3]

PRIVATE MANAGEMENT AND ADVISORY FIRMS

Despite the notable movement toward larger management companies that offer a broader range of services and products, the majority of private management and advisory firms are still much smaller and more narrowly focused on a particular niche of the market. To examine one fairly typical organization in greater detail, we will consider Provident Investment Counsel, a growth-oriented equity and fixed-income manager located in Pasadena, California. Provident utilizes a "bottom up" security selection process with their portfolio managers looking for companies that have exceptional profitability, market share, return on equity, and earnings growth. Provident's clients include both institutional investors and high net worth individuals (with between $2 million and $5 million in assets) in both separate and commingled accounts. The firm offers management of both taxed and nontaxed products. Table 26.2 shows the myriad investment products that Provident offers, along with the minimum investment accepted in each.

Like the industry as a whole, Provident saw the assets under its management increase steadily over the past several years. Panel A of Table 26.3 reports that between December 1994 and December 1998, the firm's AUM grew by almost 60 percent, from $11.8 billion to $18.4 billion. During the same period, the median separate account size jumped from $24.8 million to almost $35 million. This account size suggests that Provident's clients tend to be institutional investors, and the client profile summarized in panel B of Table 26.3 shows this to be true. Indeed, the company offers services to more than 350 clients, but the majority of these are—and the vast majority of the assets comes from—institutional investors. Perhaps because of the minimum investment restrictions, relatively few of the clients are individual investors and the assets they represent are slightly more than 2 percent (399 ÷ 18,441) of Provident's business.

Panel C of Table 26.3 shows fee schedules representative of both the equity and fixed-income management services that Provident offers. Typical of the entire industry, these fees are not flat amounts but are expressed as percentages of invested capital on an annual basis. Further, they are also graduated on a declining scale so that the more capital an investor commits to the firm, the lower his or her average cost would be. For example, an individual with $15 million would pay annual fees of $137,500 ($10{,}000{,}000 \times 0.01 + 5{,}000{,}000 \times 0.0075$), or 0.92 percent of total invested capital. On the other hand, the fee paid by a pension fund with $115 million under management would be $650,000

[3]A good economic analysis of the professional asset management business can be found in M. Hurley, S. Meers, B. Bornstein, and N. Struminghers, *The Coming Evolution of the Investment Management Industry: Opportunities and Strategies* (New York: Goldman, Sachs & Co., October 1995). See also G. Brinson, "Investment Management in the 21st Century," and B. Putnam, "Thoughts about the Asset Management Industry of the Future," both in *The Future of Investment Management* (Charlottesville, Va.: Association for Investment Management and Research, 1998).

TABLE 26.2 REPRESENTATIVE PRIVATE MANAGEMENT FIRM INVESTMENT PRODUCTS

	Large Cap	Mid Cap	Small Cap
Equity:	$5 Million	$5 Million	
	$2 Million Commingled Fund (Delaware Business Trust)	$5 Million Commingled Fund (Delaware Business Trust)	$10 Million Commingled Fund (closed)
	$2 Million for Sponsored Program Affiliates	$2 Million for Sponsored Program Affiliates	
Balanced:	$5 Million		
	$2 Million for Sponsored Program Affiliates		
Concentrated:	$5 Million		
	$2 Million for Sponsored Program Affiliates		
Tax-Sensitive Management:	$5 Million Equity, Balanced, Fixed		
	$2 Million for Sponsored Program Affiliates Equity, Balanced, Fixed		
Concentrated Tax-Sensitive Management:	$5 Million		
	$2 Million for Sponsored Program Affiliates		
Active Fixed Income:	$5 Million Separately Managed		
	$2 Million for Sponsored Program Affiliates		

Source: Provident Investment Counsel

(10,000,000 × 0.01 + 10,000,000 × 0.0075 + 95,000,000 × 0.005), or 0.57 percent. Of course, one advantage to the investor of having the fee schedule tied directly to AUM is that as the management firm performs better for the client, its fees will increase. This reward system helps to align the incentives of the investor and the manager.

MANAGEMENT OF INVESTMENT COMPANIES

As noted earlier, an investment company typically is a corporation that has as its major assets the portfolio of marketable securities referred to as a fund. The management of the portfolio of securities and most of the other administrative duties are handled by a separate

TABLE 26.3 **REPRESENTATIVE PRIVATE MANAGEMENT FIRM: AUM, CLIENTS, AND FEES**

A. Assets under Management

			Account Size	
Date	Assets Managed ($mil.)	No. of Institutional Clients	Average ($mil.)	Median ($mil.)
12/98	18,441.0	206	85.1	34.9
12/97	17,608.0	226	74.2	30.6
12/96	17,808.0	233	72.3	30.4
12/95	14,578.0	237	61.5	27.8
12/94	11,833.0	230	51.4	24.8

B. Clients

	No. of Clients	Assets ($mil.)
Corp. retirement funds	132	7,175.0
Public funds	37	4,092.0
Unions (Taft-Hartley)	18	1,283.0
Found., endow., assns.	66	1,293.0
Co-mingled funds	3	972.0
General Insurance Accounts	NA	NA
Limited Partnerships	NA	NA
Mutual funds	18	2,741.0
Individuals: IRAs & other	55	399.0
Other	5	100.0
Taxable Corporate	20	386.0

C. Fee Schedule

Large Cap Growth Equity Accounts:
- 1.00% on the first $10,000,000
- 0.75% on the next $10,000,000
- 0.50% above $20,000,000

Fixed-Income Accounts:
- 0.375% on the first $25,000,000
- 0.30% over $25,000,000

Source: *Nelson's Directory of Investment Managers,* Provident Investment Counsel.

investment management company hired by the board of directors of the investment company. This legal description oversimplifies the typical arrangement. The actual management usually begins with an investment advisory firm that starts an investment company and selects a board of directors for the fund. Subsequently, this board of directors hires the investment advisory firm as the fund's portfolio manager.

The contract between the investment company (the portfolio of securities) and the investment management company indicates the duties and compensation of the management company. The major duties of the investment management company include investment research, the management of the portfolio, and administrative duties, such as issuing securities and handling redemptions and dividends. The management fee is generally stated as a percentage of the total value of the fund and typically ranges from one-quarter to one-half of 1 percent, with a sliding scale as the size of the fund increases.

To achieve economies of scale, many management companies start numerous funds with different characteristics. The variety of funds allows the management group to appeal to many investors with different risk–return preferences. In addition, it allows investors to switch among funds as economic or personal conditions change. This "family of funds" promotes flexibility and increases the total capital managed by the investment firm.

VALUING INVESTMENT COMPANY SHARES

When clients have their invested capital held in separate accounts, as is typical in a private management and advisory firm, the value of any given account can be calculated by simply totaling the market value of the securities held in the portfolio less fees. When the securities are held jointly, as they are in an investment company, the appropriate way to value a client's investment is to multiply the number of shares in the fund he or she owns by the per-share value of the entire security fund. This per-share value is known as the **net asset value (NAV)** of the investment company. It equals the total market value of all the firm's assets divided by the total number of fund shares outstanding, or:

$$\text{Fund NAV} = \frac{(\text{Total Market Value of Fund Portfolio}) - (\text{Fund Expenses})}{(\text{Total Fund Shares Outstanding})}$$

Notice that the NAV for an investment company is analogous to the share price of a corporation's common stock; like common stock, the NAV of the fund shares will increase as the value of the underlying assets (the fund security portfolio) increases.

In an earlier example we saw that an investment company with a \$100 million blue-chip stock portfolio and 10 million outstanding shares would have an NAV of \$10. What would happen, however, if during a holding period the value of the stock portfolio increased to \$112.5 million while the fund incurred \$0.1 million in trading expenses and management fees? If no new shares were sold during the period, the net value of the total investment company is \$112.4 million, which leaves a net asset value for each existing fund share of \$11.24 ([112,500,000 − 100,000] ÷ 10,000,000). Thus, the NAV provides an immediate reflection of the investment company's market value net of operating expenses. Also, had the investment company made any capital gain or dividend distributions to its investors, these too would be reflected in the NAV calculation because they would reduce the value of the fund portfolio. For publicly traded funds, NAVs are calculated and reported on a daily basis.

CLOSED-END VERSUS OPEN-END INVESTMENT COMPANIES

Investment companies begin like any other company—someone sells an issue of common stock to a group of investors. An investment company, however, uses the proceeds to purchase the securities of other publicly held companies rather than buildings and equipment. An open-end investment company (often referred to as a **mutual fund**) differs from a closed-end investment company (typically referred to as a *closed-end fund*) in the way each operates *after* the initial public offering.

Closed-End Investment Companies

A **closed-end investment company** operates like any other public firm. Its stock trades on the regular secondary market, and the market price of its shares is determined by supply and demand. The typical closed-end investment company offers no further shares and does not repurchase the shares on demand. Thus, if you want to buy or sell shares in a closed-end fund, you must make transactions in the public secondary market. The shares of many of these funds are listed on the NYSE. No new investment dollars are available for the investment company unless it makes another public sale of securities. Similarly, no funds can be withdrawn unless the investment company decides to repurchase its stock, which is quite unusual.

The closed-end investment company's NAV is computed twice daily based on prevailing market prices for the portfolio securities. The *market price* of the investment company shares is determined by the relative supply and demand for the investment company stock in the public secondary market. When buying or selling shares of a closed-end fund, you pay or receive this market price plus or minus a regular trading commission. You should recognize that *the NAV and the market price of a closed-end fund are almost never the same!* Over the long run, the market price of these shares has historically been from 5 to 20 percent below the NAV (i.e., closed-end funds typically sell at a discount to NAV). Figure 26.2 is a list of closed-end stock funds, including general equity funds; specialized equity funds; convertible securities, dual-purpose funds; and world equity funds as quoted in *Barron's.* The figure also contains a listing of closed-end bond funds, including loan participation funds, high-yield bond funds, world income funds, national municipal bond funds, and single state municipal bond funds.

Table 26.4 shows the dramatic growth in the number and value of closed-end stock funds based on recent new fund issues sales. Another growth indicator is that as of 1986, there were eight diversified common stock funds and 18 specialized and convertible funds listed in *Barron's.* By 1995, the number had grown to 57 general and specialized equity funds, 93 world equity funds, and 16 convertible securities and dual-purpose funds. The growth of closed-end bond funds has been even more dramatic. After many years of relative stability, the number of bond funds listed in *Barron's* increased from about 20 in 1986 to several hundred in 1999. We discuss several international bond funds later in the chapter.

At the time of the quotes in Figure 26.2, most of the funds were selling at discounts to their NAV. This typical relationship has prompted questions from investors: Why do these funds sell at a discount? Why do the discounts differ between funds? What are the returns available to investors from funds that sell at large discounts? This final question arises because an investor who acquires a portfolio at a price below market value (i.e., below NAV) expects an above-average dividend yield. Still, the total rate of return on the fund depends on what happens to the discount during the holding period. If the discount relative to the NAV declines, the investment should generate positive excess returns. If the discount increases, the investor will likely experience negative excess returns. The analysis of these discounts remains a major question of modern finance.[4]

The interest in closed-end funds has led Thomas J. Herzfeld Advisors, a firm that specializes in closed-end funds, to create an index that tracks the market price performance of a sample of U.S. closed-end funds that invest principally in U.S. equities. The price-weighted series is based on fund market values rather than on NAVs. In addition to its market price index, Herzfeld also computes the average discount from NAV. The graph in Figure 26.2 indicates that the average discount from NAV changes over time and has a major impact on the market performance of the index. For example, during the first quarter of 1999, the average discount increased to about 11 percent. Despite this, the performance of the Herzfeld closed-end average during this quarter was ahead of the DJIA.

---

[4]Studies over the years include Charles Lee, Andrei Shleifer, and Richard Thaler, "Investor Sentiment and the Closed-End Fund Puzzle," *Journal of Finance* 46, no. 1 (March 1991): 76–110: Michael Barclay, Clifford Holderness, and Jeffrey Pontiff, "Private Benefits from Block Ownership and Discounts on Closed-End Funds," *Journal of Financial Economics* 33, no. 3 (June 1993): 263–292; Burton Malkiel, "The Structure of Closed-End Fund Discounts Revisited," *Journal of Portfolio Management* 21, no. 4 (summer 1995): 32–38; and Peter Klibanoff, Owen Lamont, and Thierry A. Wizman, "Investor Reaction to Salient News in Closed-End Country Funds," *Journal of Finance* 53, no. 2 (April 1998): 673–699. For a discussion of bond funds, see Malcolm Richards, Donald Fraser, and John Groth, "The Attractions of Closed-End Bond Funds," *Journal of Portfolio Management* 8, no. 2 (winter 1982): 56–61.

FIGURE 26.2 **CLOSED-END FUNDS**

CLOSED-END FUNDS

Closed-end funds sell a limited number of shares and invest in securities. Unlike open-end funds, closed-ends generally do not buy their shares back from investors who wish to sell. Instead, shares trade on a stock exchange. The following list, provided by Lipper, shows the ticker symbol and exchange where each fund trades (A: American; C: Chicago; N: NYSE; O: Nasdaq; T: Toronto; z: does not trade on an exchange). The data also include the fund's most recent net asset value (NAV), share price and the percentage difference between the market price and NAV (the premium or discount), unless indicated by a footnote otherwise. For equity funds, the final column provides 52-week returns based on market prices plus dividends; for bond funds, the past 12 months' income distributions as a percentage of the market price at last month's end. Footnotes: a: the Net Asset Value and the market price are ex dividend. b: the NAV is fully diluted. c: NAV is as of Thursday's close. d: NAV as of Wednesday's close. e: NAV assumes rights offering is fully subscribed. v: NAV is converted at the commercial Rand rate. y: NAV and market price are in Canadian dollars. N/A: Information is not available or is not applicable. ♣Free annual or semiannual reports are available by phoning 1-800-965-2929 or faxing 1-800-747-9384. Daily closed-end listings are available in The Wall Street Journal Interactive Edition at http://wsj.com on the Internet's World Wide Web.

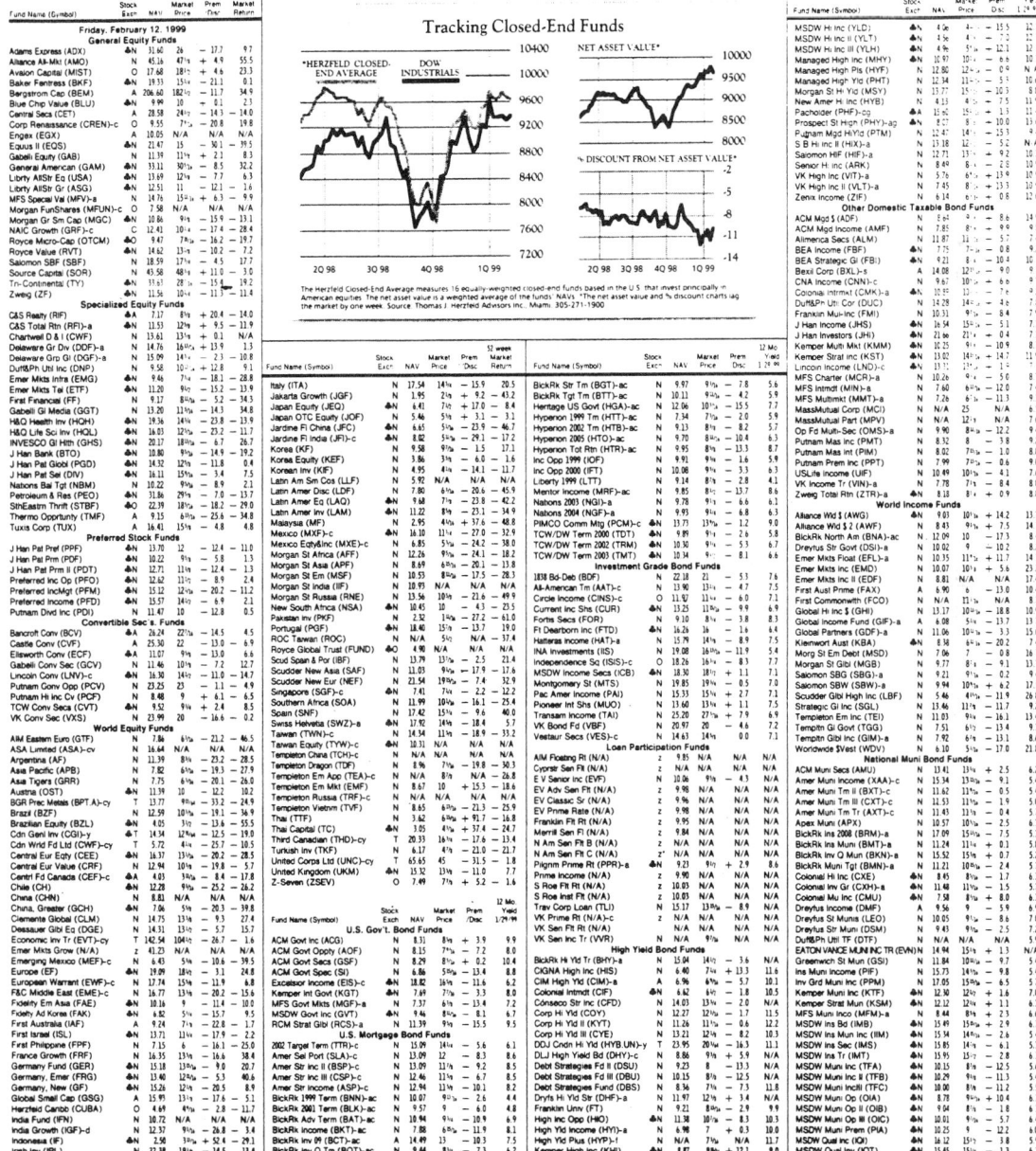

Tracking Closed-End Funds

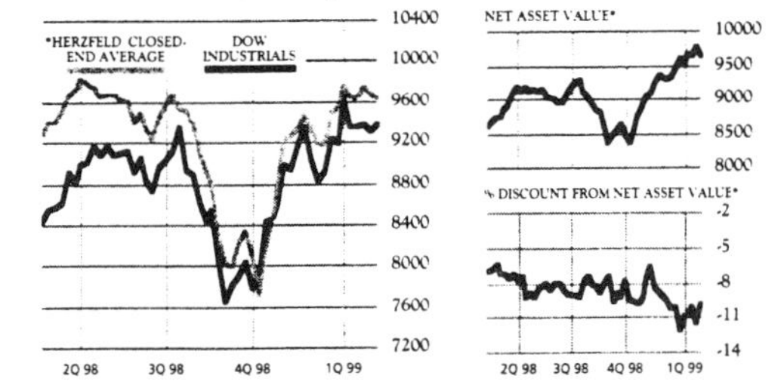

*HERZFELD CLOSED-END AVERAGE
DOW INDUSTRIALS
10400
10000
9600
9200
8800
8400
8000
7600
7200
2Q 98 3Q 98 4Q 98 1Q 99
NET ASSET VALUE*
10000
9500
9000
8500
8000
% DISCOUNT FROM NET ASSET VALUE*
-2
-5
-8
-11
-14
2Q 98 3Q 98 4Q 98 1Q 99

The Herzfeld Closed-End Average measures 16 equally-weighted closed-end funds based in the U.S. that invest principally in American equities. The net asset value is a weighted average of the funds' NAVs. *The net asset value and % discount charts lag the market by one week. Source: Thomas J. Herzfeld Advisors Inc., Miami. 305-271-1900

Friday, February 12, 1999

Fund Name (Symbol)	Stock Exch	NAV	Market Price	Prem /Disc	52 week Market Return
General Equity Funds					
Adams Express (ADX)	♣N	31.60	26	− 17.7	9.7
Alliance All-Mkt (AMO)	N	45.16	47 3/8	+ 4.9	55.5
Avalon Capital (MIST)	O	17.68	18 1/2	+ 4.6	23.3
Baker Fentress (BKF)	♣N	19.33	15 1/4	− 21.1	0.1
Bergstrom Cap (BEM)	A	206.60	182 1/2	− 11.7	34.9
Blue Chip Value (BLU)	♣N	9.99	10	+ 0.1	2.3
Central Secs (CET)	A	28.58	24 1/2	− 14.3	− 14.0
Corp Renaissance (CREN)-c	O	9.55	7 9/16	− 20.8	19.8
Engex (EGX)	A	10.05	N/A	N/A	N/A
Equus II (EQS)	♣N	21.47	15	− 30.1	− 39.5
Gabelli Equity (GAB)	N	11.39	11 5/8	+ 2.1	8.3
General American (GAM)	♣N	33.11	30 5/16	− 8.5	32.2
Librty AllStr Eq (USA)	♣N	13.69	12 5/8	− 7.7	6.3
Librty AllStr Gr (ASG)	♣N	12.51	11	− 12.1	− 1.6
MFS Special Val (MFV)-a	N	14.76	15 11/16	+ 6.3	− 9.9
Morgan FunShares (MFUN)-c	O	7.58	N/A	N/A	N/A
Morgan Gr Sm Cap (MGC)	♣N	10.86	9 1/8	− 15.9	− 13.1
NAIC Growth (GRF)-c	C	12.41	10 1/4	− 17.4	− 28.4
Royce Micro-Cap (OTCM)	♣O	9.47	7 15/16	− 16.2	− 19.7
Royce Value (RVT)	♣N	14.62	13 1/8	− 10.2	− 7.2
Salomon SBF (SBF)	N	18.59	17 3/4	− 4.5	17.7
Source Capital (SOR)	N	43.58	48 3/8	+ 11.0	− 3.0
Tri-Continental (TY)	♣N	33.63	28 7/16	− 15.4	19.2
Zweig (ZF)	♣N	11.56	10 1/4	− 11.3	− 11.4
Specialized Equity Funds					
C&S Realty (RIF)	♣A	7.17	8 5/8	+ 20.4	− 14.0
C&S Total Rtn (RFI)-a	♣N	11.53	12 5/8	+ 9.5	− 11.9
Chartwell D & I (CWF)	N	13.61	13 5/8	+ 0.1	N/A
Delaware Gr Div (DDF)-a	N	14.76	16 13/16	+ 13.9	1.3
Delaware Grp Gl (DGF)-a	N	15.09	14 3/4	− 2.3	− 10.8
Duff&Ph Util Inc (DNP)	N	9.58	10 13/16	+ 12.8	9.1
Emer Mkts Infra (EMG)	♣N	9.46	7 3/4	− 18.1	− 28.8
Emer Mkts Tel (ETF)	♣N	11.20	9 1/2	− 15.2	− 13.9
First Financial (FF)	N	9.17	8 11/16	− 5.2	− 34.3
Gabelli Gl Media (GGT)	N	13.20	11 5/16	− 14.3	34.8
H&Q Health Inv (HQH)	♣N	19.36	14 3/4	− 23.8	− 13.9
H&Q Life Sci Inv (HQL)	♣N	16.03	12 5/16	− 23.2	− 11.7
INVESCO Gl Hlth (GHS)	♣N	20.17	18 13/16	− 6.7	26.7
J Han Bank (BTO)	♣N	10.80	9 3/16	− 14.9	− 19.2
J Han Pat Globl (PGD)	♣N	14.32	12 5/8	− 11.8	0.4
J Han Pat Sel (DIV)	♣N	16.11	15 9/16	− 3.4	7.5
Nations Bal Tgt (NBM)	N	10.22	9 5/16	− 8.9	2.1
Petroleum & Res (PEO)	♣N	31.86	29 5/8	− 7.0	− 13.7
SthEastrn Thrift (STBF)	♣O	22.39	18 5/16	− 18.2	− 29.0
Thermo Opprtunty (TMF)	A	9.15	6 13/16	− 25.6	− 34.8
Tuxis Corp (TUX)	A	16.41	15 5/8	− 4.8	4.8
Preferred Stock Funds					
J Han Pat Pref (PPF)	♣N	13.70	12	− 12.4	− 11.0
J Han Pat Prm (PDF)	♣N	10.22	9 5/8	− 5.8	1.3
J Han Pat Prm II (PDT)	♣N	12.71	11 1/8	− 12.4	− 1.3
Preferred Inc Op (PFO)	♣N	12.62	11 1/2	− 8.9	2.4
Preferred IncMgt (PFM)	♣N	15.12	12 1/16	− 20.2	− 11.2
Preferred Income (PFD)	♣N	15.57	14 1/2	− 6.9	2.1
Putnam Divd Inc (PDI)	N	11.47	10	− 12.8	0.5
Convertible Sec's. Funds					
Bancroft Conv (BCV)	♣A	26.24	22 7/16	− 14.5	4.5
Castle Conv (CVF)	A	25.30	22	− 13.0	− 6.9
Ellsworth Conv (ECF)	♣A	11.07	9 5/8	− 13.0	6.6
Gabelli Conv Sec (GCV)	N	11.46	10 5/8	− 7.2	12.7
Lincoln Conv (LNV)-c	♣N	16.30	14 1/2	− 11.0	− 14.7
Putnam Conv Opp (PCV)	N	23.25	23	− 1.1	− 4.9
Putnam Hi Inc Cv (PCF)	N	8.48	9	+ 6.1	− 6.5
TCW Conv Secs (CVT)	♣N	9.52	9 3/4	+ 2.4	8.5
VK Conv Sec (VXS)	N	23.99	20	− 16.6	− 0.2
World Equity Funds					
AIM Eastern Euro (GTF)	N	7.86	6 3/16	− 21.2	− 46.5
ASA Limited (ASA)-cv	N	16.64	N/A	N/A	N/A
Argentina (AF)	N	11.39	8 3/4	− 23.2	− 28.5
Asia Pacific (APB)	N	7.82	6 5/16	− 19.3	− 27.9
Asia Tigers (GRR)	N	7.75	6 3/16	− 20.1	− 26.0
Austria (OST)	♣N	11.39	10	− 12.2	10.2
BGR Prec Metals (BPT.A)-cy	T	13.77	9 13/64	− 33.2	− 24.9
Brazil (BZF)	N	12.59	10 3/16	− 19.1	− 36.9
Brazilian Equity (BZL)	♣N	4.05	3 1/2	− 13.6	− 55.5
Cdn Genl Inv (CGI)-y	♣T	14.34	12 35/64	− 12.5	− 19.0
Cdn Wrld Fd Ltd (CWF)-cy	T	5.72	4 1/4	− 25.7	− 10.5
Central Eur Eqty (CEE)	♣N	16.37	13 1/16	− 20.2	− 28.5
Central Eur Value (CRF)	N	12.94	10 3/8	− 19.8	− 5.7
Centrl Fd Canada (CEF)-c	♣A	4.03	3 11/16	− 8.4	− 17.8
Chile (CH)	♣N	12.28	9 3/16	− 25.2	− 26.2
China (CHN)	N	8.81	N/A	N/A	N/A
China, Greater (GCH)	♣N	7.06	5 5/8	− 20.3	− 39.8
Clemente Global (CLM)	N	14.75	13 3/8	− 9.3	27.4
Dessauer Glbl Eq (DGE)	N	14.31	13 1/2	− 5.7	15.7
Economic Inv Tr (EVT)-cy	T	142.54	104 1/2	− 26.7	− 1.6
Emer Mkts Grow (N/A)	z	41.23	N/A	N/A	N/A
Emerging Mexico (MEF)-c	N	6.43	5 3/4	− 10.6	− 39.5
Europe (EF)	♣N	19.09	18 1/2	− 3.1	24.8
European Warrant (EWF)-c	N	17.74	15 5/8	− 11.9	6.8
F&C Middle East (EME)-c	N	16.77	13 3/8	− 20.2	− 15.6
Fidelity Em Asia (FAE)	♣N	10.16	9	− 11.4	− 10.0
Fidelty Ad Korea (FAK)	♣N	6.82	5 3/4	− 15.7	9.5
First Australia (IAF)	A	9.24	7 1/8	− 22.8	− 1.7
First Israel (ISL)	♣N	13.71	11 1/4	− 17.9	− 2.2
First Philippine (FPF)	N	7.15	6	− 16.1	− 25.0
France Growth (FRF)	N	16.35	13 5/8	− 16.6	38.4
Germany Fund (GER)	♣N	15.18	13 13/16	− 9.0	20.7
Germany, Emer (FRG)	♣N	13.40	12 11/16	− 5.3	40.6
Germany, New (GF)	♣N	15.26	12 1/8	− 20.5	8.9
Global Small Cap (GSG)	A	15.93	13 1/8	− 17.6	− 5.1
Herzfeld Caribb (CUBA)	O	4.69	4 9/16	− 2.8	− 11.7
India Fund (IFN)	N	10.72	N/A	N/A	N/A
India Growth (IGF)-d	N	12.37	9 1/16	− 26.8	− 3.4
Indonesia (IF)	♣N	2.50	3 13/16	+ 52.4	− 29.1
Irish Inv (IRL)	N	22.38	19 1/8	− 14.5	13.4
Italy (ITA)	N	17.54	14 3/4	− 15.9	20.5
Jakarta Growth (JGF)	N	1.95	2 1/8	+ 9.2	− 43.2
Japan Equity (JEQ)	♣N	6.41	7 1/2	+ 17.0	− 8.4
Japan OTC Equity (JOF)	N	5.46	5 5/8	+ 3.1	− 3.1
Jardine Fl China (JFC)	♣N	6.65	5 1/16	− 23.9	− 46.7
Jardine Fl India (JFI)-c	♣N	8.02	5 11/16	− 29.1	− 17.2
Korea (KF)	N	9.58	9 7/16	− 1.5	17.1
Korea Equity (KEF)	N	3.86	3 5/8	− 6.0	− 1.6
Korean Inv (KIF)	N	4.95	4 1/4	− 14.1	− 11.7
Latin Am Sm Cos (LLF)	N	5.92	N/A	N/A	N/A
Latin Amer Disc (LDF)	N	7.80	6 3/16	− 20.6	− 45.9
Latin Amer Eq (LAQ)	♣N	9.68	7 3/8	− 23.8	− 42.2
Latin Amer Inv (LAM)	♣N	11.22	8 5/8	− 23.1	− 34.9
Malaysia (MF)	N	2.95	4 1/16	+ 37.6	− 48.8
Mexico (MXF)-c	♣N	16.10	11 3/4	− 27.0	− 32.9
Mexico Eqty&Inc (MXE)-c	N	6.85	5 3/16	− 24.2	− 38.0
Morgan St Africa (AFF)	N	12.26	9 5/16	− 24.1	− 18.2
Morgan St Asia (APF)	N	8.69	6 15/16	− 20.1	− 13.8
Morgan St Em (MSF)	N	10.53	8 11/16	− 17.5	− 28.3
Morgan St India (IIF)	N	10.93	N/A	N/A	N/A
Morgan St Russia (RNE)	N	13.56	10 5/8	− 21.6	− 49.9
New South Africa (NSA)	♣N	10.45	10	− 4.3	− 23.5
Pakistan Inv (PKF)	N	2.32	1 11/16	− 27.2	− 61.0
Portugal (PGF)	♣N	18.40	15 7/8	− 13.7	19.0
ROC Taiwan (ROC)	N	N/A	5 1/2	N/A	− 37.4
Royce Global Trust (FUND)	♣O	4.90	N/A	N/A	N/A
Scud Spain & Por (IBF)	N	13.79	13 7/16	− 2.5	21.4
Scudder New Asia (SAF)	N	11.03	9 1/16	− 17.9	− 17.6
Scudder New Eur (NEF)	N	21.54	19 15/16	− 7.4	32.9
Singapore (SGF)-c	♣N	7.41	7 1/4	− 2.2	− 12.2
Southern Africa (SOA)	N	11.99	10 1/16	− 16.1	− 25.4
Spain (SNF)	N	17.42	15 3/4	− 9.6	40.0
Swiss Helvetia (SWZ)-a	♣N	17.92	14 5/8	− 18.4	5.7
Taiwan (TWN)-c	N	14.34	11 5/8	− 18.9	− 33.2
Taiwan Equity (TYW)-c	♣N	10.31	N/A	N/A	N/A
Templeton China (TCH)-c	N	N/A	N/A	N/A	N/A
Templeton Dragon (TDF)	N	8.96	7 3/16	− 19.8	− 30.3
Templeton Em App (TEA)-c	N	N/A	8 7/8	N/A	− 26.8
Templeton Em Mkt (EMF)	N	8.67	10	+ 15.3	− 18.6
Templeton Russia (TRF)-c	N	N/A	N/A	N/A	N/A
Templeton Vietnm (TVF)	N	8.65	6 13/16	− 21.3	− 25.9
Thai (TTF)	N	3.62	6 15/16	+ 91.7	− 16.8
Thai Capital (TC)	♣N	3.05	4 3/16	+ 37.4	− 24.7
Third Canadian (THD)-cy	T	20.33	16 3/4	− 17.6	− 13.4
Turkish Inv (TKF)	N	6.17	4 7/8	− 21.0	− 21.7
United Corps Ltd (UNC)-cy	T	65.65	45	− 31.5	− 1.8
United Kingdom (UKM)	♣N	15.32	13 5/8	− 11.0	7.7
Z-Seven (ZSEV)	O	7.49	7 7/8	+ 5.2	− 1.6

Fund Name (Symbol)	Stock Exch	NAV	Market Price	Prem /Disc	12 Mo. Yield 1/29/99
U.S. Gov't. Bond Funds					
ACM Govt Inc (ACG)	N	8.31	8 5/8	+ 3.9	9.9
ACM Govt Oppty (AOF)	N	8.15	7 9/16	− 7.2	8.0
ACM Govt Secs (GSF)	N	8.29	8 5/16	+ 0.2	10.4
ACM Govt Spec (SI)	N	6.86	5 15/16	− 13.4	8.8
Excelsior Income (EIS)-c	♣N	18.82	16 5/8	− 11.6	6.2
Kemper Int Govt (KGT)	♣N	7.69	7 7/16	− 3.3	8.0
MFS Govt Mkts (MGF)-a	N	7.37	6 3/8	− 13.4	7.2
MSDW Govt Inc (GVT)	♣N	9.46	8 11/16	− 8.1	6.7
RCM Strat Glbl (RCS)-a	N	11.39	9 5/8	− 15.5	9.5
U.S. Mortgage Bond Funds					
2002 Target Term (TTR)-c	N	15.09	14 1/4	− 5.6	6.1
Amer Sel Port (SLA)-c	N	13.09	12	− 8.3	8.6
Amer Str Inc II (BSP)-c	N	13.09	11 7/8	− 9.2	8.5
Amer Str Inc III (CSP)-c	N	12.46	11 5/8	− 6.7	8.5
Amer Str Income (ASP)-c	N	12.94	11 5/8	− 10.1	8.2
BlckRk 1999 Term (BNN)-ac	N	10.07	9 13/16	− 2.6	4.4
BlckRk 2001 Term (BLK)-ac	N	9.57	9	− 6.0	4.8
BlckRk Adv Term (BAT)-ac	N	10.94	9 3/4	− 10.9	6.9
BlckRk Income (BKT)-ac	N	7.88	6 15/16	− 11.9	8.1
BlckRk Inv 09 (BCT)-ac	A	14.49	13	− 10.3	7.5
BlckRk Inv Q Tm (BQT)-ac	N	9.44	8 3/4	− 7.3	6.2
BlckRk Str Tm (BGT)-ac	N	9.97	9 3/16	− 7.8	5.6
BlckRk Tgt Tm (BTT)-ac	N	10.11	9 11/16	− 4.2	5.9
Heritage US Govt (HGA)-ac	N	12.06	10 3/16	− 15.5	7.7
Hyperion 1999 Tm (HTT)-ac	N	7.34	7 3/16	− 2.0	5.9
Hyperion 2002 Tm (HTB)-ac	N	9.13	8 3/8	− 8.2	5.7
Hyperion 2005 (HTO)-ac	N	9.70	8 11/16	− 10.4	6.3
Hyperion Tot Rtn (HTR)-ac	N	9.95	8 5/8	− 13.3	8.7
Inc Opp 1999 (IOF)	N	9.91	9 3/4	− 1.6	5.9
Inc Opp 2000 (IFT)	N	10.08	9 3/4	− 3.3	6.3
Liberty 1999 (LTT)	N	9.14	8 7/8	− 2.8	4.1
Mentor Income (MRF)-ac	N	9.85	8 1/2	− 13.7	8.6
Nations 2003 (NGI)-a	N	9.78	9 1/8	− 6.6	6.1
Nations 2004 (NGF)-a	N	9.93	9 1/4	− 6.8	6.3
PIMCO Comm Mtg (PCM)-c	♣N	13.73	13 9/16	− 1.2	9.0
TCW/DW Term 2000 (TDT)	♣N	9.89	9 5/8	− 2.6	5.8
TCW/DW Term 2002 (TRM)	♣N	10.30	9 3/4	− 5.3	6.7
TCW/DW Term 2003 (TMT)	♣N	10.34	9 1/2	− 8.1	6.6
Investment Grade Bond Funds					
1838 Bd-Deb (BDF)	N	22.18	21	− 5.3	7.6
All-American Tm (AAT)-c	N	13.90	13 1/4	− 4.7	7.5
Circle Income (CINS)-c	O	11.97	11 1/4	− 6.0	7.1
Current Inc Shs (CUR)	♣N	13.25	11 15/16	− 9.9	6.9
Fortis Secs (FOR)	N	9.10	8 3/4	− 3.8	8.3
Ft Dearborn Inc (FTD)	♣N	16.26	16	− 1.6	6.4
Hatteras Income (HAT)-a	N	15.79	14 3/8	− 8.9	7.5
INA Investments (IIS)	N	19.08	16 13/16	− 11.9	5.4
Independence Sq (ISIS)-c	O	18.26	16 3/4	− 8.3	7.7
MSDW Income Secs (ICB)	♣N	18.30	18 1/2	+ 1.1	7.1
Montgomery St (MTS)	N	19.85	19 3/4	− 0.5	7.0
Pac Amer Income (PAI)	N	15.33	15 3/4	+ 2.7	7.1
Pioneer Int Shs (MUO)	N	13.60	13 3/4	+ 1.1	7.5
Transam Income (TAI)	N	25.20	27 3/16	+ 7.9	6.9
VK Bond Fd (VBF)	N	20.97	20	− 4.6	7.2
Vestaur Secs (VES)-c	N	14.63	14 5/8	0.0	7.1
Loan Participation Funds					
AIM Floating Rt (N/A)	z	9.85	N/A	N/A	N/A
Cyprstr Sen Flt (N/A)	z	N/A	N/A	N/A	N/A
E V Senior Inc (EVF)	N	10.06	9 5/8	− 4.3	N/A
EV Adv Sen Flt (N/A)	z	9.98	N/A	N/A	N/A
EV Classic Sr (N/A)	z	9.96	N/A	N/A	N/A
EV Prime Rate (N/A)	z	9.98	N/A	N/A	N/A
Franklin Flt Rt (N/A)	z	9.95	N/A	N/A	N/A
Merrill Sen Fl (N/A)	z	9.84	N/A	N/A	N/A
N Am Sen Flt B (N/A)	z	N/A	N/A	N/A	N/A
N Am Sen Flt C (N/A)	z*	N/A	N/A	N/A	N/A
Pilgrim Prime Rt (PPR)-a	♣N	9.23	9 1/2	+ 2.9	8.6
Prime Income (N/A)	z	9.90	N/A	N/A	N/A
S Roe Flt Rt (N/A)	z	10.03	N/A	N/A	N/A
S Roe Inst Flt (N/A)	z	10.03	N/A	N/A	N/A
Trav Corp Loan (TLI)	N	15.17	13 13/16	− 8.9	N/A
VK Prime Rt (N/A)-c	z	N/A	N/A	N/A	N/A
VK Sen Flt Rt (N/A)		N/A	N/A	N/A	N/A
VK Sen Inc Tr (VVR)	N	N/A	9 7/16	N/A	N/A
High Yield Bond Funds					
BlckRk Hi Yld Tr (BHY)-a	N	15.04	14 1/2	− 3.6	N/A
CIGNA High Inc (HIS)	N	6.40	7 1/4	+ 13.3	11.6
CIM High Yld (CIM)-a	A	6.96	6 9/16	− 5.7	10.1
Colonial Intmdt (CIF)	♣N	6.62	6 1/2	− 1.8	10.5
Cónseco Str Inc (CFD)	N	14.03	13 3/4	− 2.0	N/A
Corp Hi Yld (COY)	N	12.27	12 1/16	− 1.7	11.5
Corp Hi Yld II (KYT)	N	11.26	11 3/16	− 0.6	12.2
Corp Hi Yld III (CYE)	N	13.21	12 1/8	− 8.2	10.3
DDJ Cndn Hi Yld (HYB.UN)-y	T	23.95	20 3/64	− 16.3	11.1
DLJ High Yield Bd (DHY)-c	N	8.86	9 3/8	+ 5.9	N/A
Debt Strategies Fd II (DSU)	N	9.23	8	− 13.3	N/A
Debt Strategies Fd III (DBU)	N	10.15	8 7/8	− 12.5	N/A
Debt Strategies Fund (DBS)	N	8.36	7 3/4	− 7.3	11.8
Dryfs Hi Yld Str (DHF)-a	N	11.97	12 3/8	+ 3.4	N/A
Franklin Univ (FT)	N	9.21	8 15/16	− 2.9	9.9
High Inc Opp (HIO)	♣N	11.38	10 7/16	− 8.3	10.3
High Yld Income (HYI)-a	N	6.98	7	+ 0.3	10.0
High Yld Plus (HYP)-f	N	N/A	7 3/16	N/A	11.7
Kemper High Inc (KHI)	♣N	8.87	9 15/16	+ 12.1	9.0
MSDW Hi Inc (YLD)	♣N	4.96	[illegible]	− 15.5	12.3
MSDW Hi Inc II (YLT)	♣N	4.56	[illegible]	− 7.0	12.7
MSDW Hi Inc III (YLH)	♣N	4.96	5 9/16	+ 12.1	12.1
Managed High Inc (MHY)	♣N	10.97	10 1/4	− 6.6	10.1
Managed High Pls (HYF)	N	12.80	12 11/16	− 0.9	N/A
Managed High Yld (PHT)	N	12.34	11 11/16	− 5.3	10.6
Morgan St Hi Yld (MSY)	N	13.77	15 3/16	+ 10.3	8.8
New Amer Hi Inc (HYB)	N	4.13	4 7/16	+ 7.5	11.9
Pacholder (PHF)-cg	♣A	15.60	15 13/16	+ 1.3	11.4
Prospect St High (PHY)-ag	♣N	8.07	8 7/8	+ 10.0	13.6
Putnam Mgd HiYld (PTM)	N	12.47	14 5/16	+ 15.3	9.4
S B Hi Inc II (HIX)-a	N	13.18	12 1/2	− 5.2	N/A
Salomon HIF (HIF)-a	N	12.71	13 7/8	+ 9.2	10.2
Senior Hi Inc (ARK)	N	8.49	8 1/4	− 2.8	10.9
VK High Inc (VIT)-a	N	5.76	6 9/16	+ 13.9	10.9
VK High Inc II (VLT)-a	N	7.45	8 7/16	+ 13.3	10.9
Zenix Income (ZIF)	N	6.14	6 3/16	+ 0.8	12.0
Other Domestic Taxable Bond Funds					
ACM Mgd $ (ADF)	N	8.64	[illegible]	+ 8.6	14.0
ACM Mgd Income (AMF)	N	7.85	8 5/8	+ 9.9	9.9
Allmerica Secs (ALM)	N	11.87	11 3/16	− 5.7	7.4
BEA Income (FBF)	♣N	7.75	7 11/16	− 0.8	9.2
BEA Strategic Gl (FBI)	♣N	9.21	8 1/4	− 10.4	10.7
Bexil Corp (BXL)-s	A	14.08	12 13/16	− 9.0	9.3
CNA Income (CNN)-c	N	9.67	10 5/16	+ 6.6	9.3
Colonial Intrmkt (CMK)-a	♣N	10.97	[illegible]	− 7.6	9.2
Duff&Ph Util Cor (DUC)	N	14.28	14 15/16	+ 4.6	7.8
Franklin Mul-Inc (FMI)	N	10.31	9 7/16	− 8.4	7.9
J Han Income (JHS)	♣N	16.54	15 11/16	− 5.1	7.1
J Han Investors (JHI)	♣N	21.66	21 3/4	+ 0.4	7.1
Kemper Multi Mkt (KMM)	♣N	10.25	9 1/8	− 10.9	8.7
Kemper Strat Inc (KST)	♣N	13.02	14 15/16	+ 14.7	11.9
Lincoln Income (LND)-c	♣N	13.31	13 9/16	+ 1.9	7.5
MFS Charter (MCR)-a	N	10.26	9 3/4	− 5.0	8.3
MFS Intmdt (MIN)-a	N	7.60	6 11/16	− 12.0	7.4
MFS Multimkt (MMT)-a	N	7.26	6 7/16	− 11.3	9.1
MassMutual Corp (MCI)	N	N/A	25	N/A	6.5
MassMutual Part (MPV)	N	N/A	12 3/8	N/A	7.6
Op Fd Multi-Sec (OMS)-a	N	9.90	8 11/16	− 12.2	9.4
Putnam Mas Inc (PMT)	N	8.32	8	− 3.8	9.2
Putnam Mas Int (PIM)	N	8.02	7 15/16	− 1.0	8.8
Putnam Prem Inc (PPT)	N	7.99	7 15/16	− 0.6	9.0
USLife Income (UIF)	N	10.49	10 1/16	− 4.1	7.6
VK Income Tr (VIN)-a	N	7.78	7 1/8	− 8.4	8.8
Zweig Total Rtn (ZTR)-a	♣N	8.18	8 1/4	+ 0.9	8.8
World Income Funds					
Alliance Wld $ (AWG)	♣N	9.03	10 5/16	+ 14.2	13.3
Alliance Wld $ 2 (AWF)	N	8.43	9 1/16	+ 7.5	14.7
BlckRk North Am (BNA)-ac	N	12.09	10	− 17.3	8.4
Dreyfus Str Govt (DSI)-a	N	10.02	9	− 10.2	8.2
Emer Mkts Float (EFL)-a	N	10.35	11 9/16	+ 11.7	14.3
Emer Mkts Inc (EMD)	N	10.07	10 5/8	+ 5.6	23.2
Emer Mkts Inc II (EDF)	N	8.81	N/A	N/A	17.4
First Aust Prime (FAX)	A	6.90	6	− 13.0	10.4
First Commonwlth (FCO)	N	N/A	11 1/16	N/A	8.7
Global Hi Inc $ (GHI)	N	13.17	10 11/16	− 18.8	10.9
Global Income Fund (GIF)-a	A	6.08	5 1/4	− 13.7	13.7
Global Partners (GDF)-a	N	11.06	10 11/16	− 3.3	15.6
Kleinwort Aust (KBA)	♣N	8.38	6 11/16	− 20.2	7.4
Morg St Em Debt (MSD)	N	7.06	7	− 0.8	16.7
Morgan St Glbl (MGB)	N	9.77	8 7/8	− 9.1	13.3
Salomon SBG (SBG)-a	N	9.21	9 3/16	− 0.2	9.4
Salomon SBW (SBW)-a	N	9.94	10 9/16	+ 6.2	17.5
Scudder Glbl High Inc (LBF)	N	5.46	4 13/16	− 11.9	26.8
Strategic Gl Inc (SGL)	N	13.46	11 7/8	− 11.7	9.2
Templeton Em Inc (TEI)	N	11.03	9 1/4	− 16.1	13.4
Templtn Gl Govt (TGG)	N	7.51	6 1/2	− 13.4	9.1
Templtn Glbl Inc (GIM)-a	N	7.92	6 7/8	− 13.1	8.6
Worldwide $Vest (WDV)	N	6.10	5 1/16	− 17.0	21.8
National Muni Bond Funds					
ACM Muni Secs (AMU)	N	13.41	13 3/4	+ 2.5	6.2
Amer Muni Income (XAA)-c	N	15.34	13 15/16	− 9.1	5.4
Amer Muni Tm II (BXT)-c	N	11.62	11 9/16	− 0.5	5.4
Amer Muni Tm III (CXT)-c	N	11.53	11 5/16	− 1.9	5.0
Amer Muni Tm Tr (AXT)-c	N	11.43	11 3/8	− 0.4	5.7
Apex Muni (APX)	N	10.57	10 5/16	− 2.5	6.3
BlckRk Ins 2008 (BRM)-a	N	17.09	15 13/16	− 7.5	5.1
BlckRk Ins Muni (BMT)-a	N	11.24	11 1/4	+ 0.1	5.8
BlckRk Inv Q Mun (BKN)-a	N	15.52	15 5/8	+ 0.7	5.2
BlckRk Muni Tgt (BMN)-a	N	11.21	10 15/16	− 2.4	5.7
Colonial Hi Inc (CXE)	♣N	8.45	8 5/16	− 1.7	6.1
Colonial Inv Gr (CXH)-a	♣N	11.48	11 5/16	− 1.5	5.7
Colonial Mu Inc (CMU)	♣N	7.58	8 3/16	+ 8.0	6.1
Dreyfus Income (DMF)	A	9.56	9	− 5.9	6.9
Dreyfus St Munis (LEO)	N	10.05	9 3/16	− 8.6	7.0
Dreyfus Str Muni (DSM)	N	9.43	9 3/16	− 2.5	7.2
Duff&Ph Util TF (DTF)	N	N/A	N/A	N/A	5.9
EATON VANCE MUNI INC TR (EVN)	N	14.94	15 1/8	+ 1.3	N/A
Greenwich St Mun (GSI)	N	11.84	10 11/16	− 9.7	5.4
Ins Muni Income (PIF)	N	15.73	14 3/16	− 9.8	5.4
Inv Grd Muni Inc (PPM)	N	17.05	15 15/16	− 6.5	5.7
Kemper Muni Inc (KTF)	♣N	12.30	12 1/2	+ 1.6	7.0
Kemper Strat Mun (KSM)	♣N	12.12	12 1/4	+ 1.1	6.1
MFS Muni Inco (MFM)-a	N	8.44	8 5/8	+ 2.3	6.6
MSDW Ins Bd (IMB)	♣N	15.49	15 15/16	+ 2.9	6.1
MSDW Ins Mun Inc (IIM)	♣N	15.34	14 15/16	− 2.6	5.4
MSDW Ins Sec (IMS)	♣N	15.85	14 7/8	− 6.1	5.3
MSDW Ins Tr (IMT)	♣N	15.95	15 1/2	− 2.8	6.1
MSDW Muni Inc (TFA)	♣N	10.15	8 7/8	− 12.5	5.6
MSDW Muni Inc II (TFB)	♣N	10.29	9 1/8	− 11.3	5.4
MSDW Muni IncIII (TFC)	♣N	10.00	8 7/8	− 11.2	5.5
MSDW Muni Op (OIA)	♣N	8.78	9 11/16	+ 10.4	6.1
MSDW Muni Op II (OIB)	♣N	9.04	8 7/8	− 1.8	6.1
MSDW Muni Op III (OIC)	♣N	10.01	9 7/16	− 5.7	6.4
MSDW Muni Prem (PIA)	♣N	10.25	9	− 12.2	6.0
MSDW Qual Inc (IQI)	♣N	16.12	15 1/2	− 3.8	5.9
MSDW Qual Inv (IQT)	♣N	15.45	15 1/4	− 1.3	6.1

Source: *Barron's*, 15 February 1999.

TABLE 26.4

NUMBER OF CLOSED-END FUND INITIAL PUBLIC OFFERINGS AND NEW FUNDS RAISED

Year	Number of Funds	Amount Raised
1981	1	$ 62 million
1982	0	—
1983	4	58 million
1984	4	106 million
1985	3	614 million
1986	28	5 billion
1987	34	9 billion
1988	66	20 billion
1989	39	9 billion
1990	38	6 billion
1991	43	11 billion
1992	98	18 billion
1993	126	19 billion
1994	41	7 billion
1995	3	480 million

Source: Thomas J. Herzfeld Advisors, Inc., P.O. Box 161465, Miami, Florida 33116. Reprinted by permission of Thomas J. Herzfeld Advisors, Inc.

TABLE 26.5

OPEN-END INVESTMENT COMPANIES: NUMBER AND VALUE OF ASSETS: 1945–1997

	Number of Reporting Funds	Assets ($ Billions)		Number of Reporting Funds	Assets ($ Billions)
1945	73	$ 1.3	1986	1,356	424.2
1950	98	2.5	1987	1,781	453.8
1955	125	7.8	1988	2,109	472.3
1960	161	17.0	1989	2,253	553.9
1965	170	35.2	1990	2,362	568.5
1970	361	47.6	1991	2,603	853.1
1975	390	42.2	1992	2,984	1,100.1
1980	458	58.4	1993	3,638	1,510.1
1981	486	55.2	1994	4,394	1,550.5
1982	539	76.8	1995	4,764	2,067.3
1983	653	113.6	1996	5,305	2,637.4
1984	820	137.8	1997	5,765	3,430.8
1985	1,071	251.7			

Note: Does not include money market and short-term bond funds.

Sources: *1975 Mutual Fund Fact Book, 1981 Mutual Fund Fact Book, 1996 Mutual Fund Fact Book,* and *1998 Mutual Fund Fact Book* (Washington, D.C.: Investment Company Institute). Reprinted by permission of Investment Company Institute.

Open-End Investment Companies

Open-end investment companies, or mutual funds, continue to sell and repurchase shares after their initial public offerings. They stand ready to sell additional shares of the fund at the NAV, with or without sales charge, or to buy back (redeem) shares of the fund at the NAV, with or without redemption fees.

Open-end investment companies have enjoyed substantial growth since World War II, as shown by the figures in Table 26.5. Clearly, open-end funds account for a substantial portion of invested assets, and they provide a very important service for over 100 million accounts.

LOAD VERSUS NO-LOAD OPEN-END FUNDS One distinction of open-end funds is that some charge a sales fee for share sales. The offering price for a share of a *load fund* equals the NAV of the share plus a sales charge, which can be as large as 7.5 to 8.0 percent of the NAV. A fund with an 8 percent sales charge (load) would give an individual who invested $1,000 shares in the fund that are worth $920. Such funds generally charge no redemption fee, which means the shares can be redeemed at their NAV. These funds typically are quoted with an NAV and an offering price. The NAV price is the redemption (bid) price, and the offering (ask) price equals the NAV divided by 1.0 minus the percent load. For example, if the NAV of a fund with an 8 percent load is $8.50 a share, the offering price would be $9.24 ($8.50/0.92). The 74-cent differential is really 8.7 percent of the NAV. The load percentage typically declines with the size of the order.

A **no-load fund** imposes no initial sales charge so it sells shares at their NAV. Some of these funds charge a small redemption fee of about one-half of 1 percent. In the *Wall Street Journal,* quotes for these no-load funds list bid prices as the NAV with the designation "NL" (no-load) for the offering price—that is, the bid and offer are the same. The number of no-load funds has increased substantially in recent years. The *Wall Street Journal* lists more than 350 no-load funds, and *Barron's* lists more than 800.

Between the full-load fund and the pure no-load fund, several important variations exist. The first is the **low-load fund**, which imposes a front-end sales charge when the fund is bought, but it is typically in the 3 percent range rather than 7 to 8 percent. Generally, low-load funds are used for bond funds or equity funds offered by management companies that also offer no-load funds. For example, most Fidelity Management funds were no-load prior to 1985, but several of their newer funds have carried a low load of 3 percent. Alternatively, some funds—previously charging full loads—have reduced their loads.

The second major innovation is the **12b-1 plan**, named after a 1980 SEC ruling. This plan permits funds to deduct as much as 0.75 percent of average net assets *per year* to cover distribution costs, such as advertising, brokers' commissions, and general marketing expenses. A large and growing number of no-load funds are adopting these plans, as are a few low-load funds. You can determine if a fund has a 12b-1 plan only by reading the prospectus or using an investment service that reports charges in substantial detail.

Finally, some funds have instituted **contingent, deferred sales loads** in which a sales fee is charged when the fund is sold if it is held for less than some time period, perhaps three or four years.

Fund Management Fees

In addition to selling charges (loads or 12b-1 charges), all investment firms charge annual **management fees** to compensate professional managers of the fund. Similar to the compensation structure for private management firms, such a fee typically is a percentage of the average net assets of the fund varying from about 0.25 to 1.00 percent. Most of these management fees are on sliding scales that decline with the size of the fund. For example, a fund with assets under $1 billion might charge 1 percent, funds with assets between $1 billion and $5 billion might charge 0.50 percent, and those over $5 billion would charge 0.25 percent.

These management fees are a major factor driving the creation of new funds. More assets under management generate more fees, but the costs of management do not increase at the same rate as the managed assets because substantial economies of scale exist in managing financial assets. Once the research staff and management structure have been established, the incremental costs do not rise in line with the assets under management. For example, the cost of managing $1 billion of assets is *not* twice the cost of managing $500 million.

TYPES OF INVESTMENT COMPANIES BASED ON PORTFOLIO MAKEUP

Common Stock Funds

Some funds invest almost solely in common stocks; others invest in preferred stocks, bonds, and so forth. Within common stock funds, wide differences are found in emphasis, including funds that focus on growth companies, small cap stocks, companies in specific industries (e.g., Chemical Fund, Oceanography Fund), certain classes of industry (e.g., Technology Fund), or even geographic areas (such as the Northeast Fund or international funds). Different common stock funds can suit almost any taste or investment objective. Therefore, you must decide whether you want a fund that invests only in common stock; then you must consider the type of common stock you desire. Table 26.6 provides a list of mutual fund objectives and definitions for those objectives.

Balanced Funds

Balanced funds diversify outside the stock market by combining common stock with fixed-income securities, including government bonds, corporate bonds, convertible bonds, or preferred stock. The ratio of stocks to fixed-income securities will vary by fund, as stated in each fund's prospectus.

Bond Funds

Bond funds concentrate on various types of bonds to generate high current income with minimal risk. They are similar to common stock funds; however, their investment policies differ. Some funds concentrate on U.S. government or high-grade corporate bonds, others hold a mixture of investment-grade bonds, and some concentrate on high-yield (junk) bonds. Management strategies also can differ, ranging from buy-and-hold to extensive trading of the portfolio bonds.

In addition to government, mortgage, and corporate bond funds, a change in the tax law in 1976 caused the creation of numerous municipal bond funds. These funds provide investors with monthly interest payments that are exempt from federal income taxes, although some of the interest may be subject to state and local taxes. To avoid the state tax, some municipal bond funds concentrate on bonds from specific states, such as the New York Municipal Bond Fund, which allows New York residents to avoid most state taxes on the interest income.

Money Market Funds

Money market funds were initiated during 1973 when short-term interest rates were at record levels. These funds attempt to provide current income, safety of principal, and liquidity by investing in diversified portfolios of short-term securities, such as Treasury bills, banker certificates of deposit, bank acceptances, and commercial paper. They typically are no-load funds and impose no penalty for early withdrawal. Also, they generally allow holders to write checks against their account.[5] Table 26.7 documents the significant growth of these funds. Changes in their growth rate usually are associated with investor attitudes toward the stock market. When investors are bullish toward stocks, they withdraw funds from their money market accounts to invest; when they are uncertain, they shift from stocks to the money funds. Because of the interest in money market funds, Monday editions of the *Wall Street Journal* provide a special section within the mutual fund section titled "Money Market Funds."

---

[5]For a list of names and addresses of money market funds, write to Investment Company Institute, 1775 K Street N.W., Washington, DC 20006. A service that concentrates on money market funds is *Donoghue's Money Letter,* 770 Washington Street, Holliston, MA 01746. An analysis of performance is contained in Michael G. Ferri and H. Dennis Oberhelman, "How Well Do Money Market Funds Perform?" *Journal of Portfolio Management* 7, no. 3 (spring 1981): 18–26.

TABLE 26.6 MUTUAL FUND OBJECTIVES

Stock Funds

Aggressive growth funds seek maximum capital growth; current income is not a significant factor. These funds invest in stocks out of the mainstream, such as new companies, companies fallen on hard times, or industries temporarily out of favor. They may use investment techniques involving greater than average risk.

Growth funds seek capital growth; dividend income is not a significant factor. The invest in the common stock of well-established companies.

Growth and income funds seek to combine long-term capital growth and current income. These funds invest in the common stock of companies whose share value has increased and that have displayed a solid record of paying dividends.

Precious metals/gold funds seek capital growth. Their portfolios are invested primarily in securities associated with gold and other precious metals.

International funds seek growth in the value of their investments. Their portfolios are invested primarily in stocks of companies located outside the U.S.

Global equity funds seek growth in the value of their investments. They invest in stocks traded worldwide, including the U.S.

Income-equity funds seed a high level of income by investing primarily in stocks of companies with good dividend-paying records.

Bond and Income Funds

Flexible portfolio funds allow their money managers to anticipate or respond to changing market conditions by investing in stocks or bonds or money market instruments, depending on economic changes.

Balanced funds generally seek to conserve investors' principal, pay current income, and achieve long-term growth of principal and income. Their portfolios are a mix of bonds, preferred stocks, and common stocks.

Income-mixed funds seek a high level of income. These funds invest in income-producing securities, including both stocks and bonds.

Income-bond funds seek a high level of current income. These funds invest in a mix of corporate and government bonds.

U.S. government income funds seek current income. They invest in a variety of government securities, including Treasury bonds, federally guaranteed mortgage-backed securities, and other government notes.

GNMA (Ginnie Mae) funds seek a high level of income. The majority of their portfolios is invested in mortgage securities backed by the Government National Mortgage Association (GNMA).

Global bond funds seek a high level of income. These funds invest in debt securities of companies and countries worldwide, including the U.S.

Corporate bond funds seek a high level of income. The majority of their portfolios is invested in corporate bonds, with the balance in U.S. Treasury bonds or bonds issued by a federal agency.

High-yield bond funds seek a very high yield, but carry a greater degree of risk than corporate bond funds. The majority of their portfolios is invested in lower-rated corporate bonds.

National municipal bond funds—long-term seek income that is not taxed by the federal government. They invest in bonds issued by states and municipalities to finance schools, highways, hospitals, bridges, and other municipal works.

State municipal bond funds—long-term seek income that is exempt from both federal tax and state tax for residents of that state. They invest in bonds issued by a single state.

Money Market Funds

Taxable money market funds seek to maintain a stable net asset value. These funds invest in the short-term, high-grade securities sold in the money market, such as Treasury bills, certificates of deposit of large banks, and commercial paper. The average maturity of their portfolios is limited to 90 days or less.

Tax-exempt money market funds—national seek income that is not taxed by the federal government with minimum risk. They invest in muncipal securities with relatively short maturities.

Tax-exempt money market funds—state seek income that is exempt from both federal tax and state tax for residents of that state. They invest in municipal securities with relatively short maturities issued by a single state.

Source: *A Guide to Mutual Funds* (Washington, D.C.: Investment Company Institute), 1999.

BREAKDOWN BY FUND CHARACTERISTICS

Table 26.8 groups funds by their method of sale and by investment objectives. The two major means of distribution are (1) by a sales force and (2) by direct purchase from the fund or direct marketing. Sales forces would include brokers, such as Merrill Lynch; commission-based financial planners; or dedicated sales forces, such as those of American Express Retirement Services. Almost all mutual funds acquired from these individuals charge sales fees (loads) from which salespeople are compensated.

Investors typically purchase shares of directly marketed funds through the mail, telephone, bankwire, or an office of the fund. These direct sales funds usually impose a low

TABLE 26.7 **TAXABLE MONEY MARKET FUNDS (MILLIONS OF DOLLARS)**

Year	Number of Funds	Total Accounts Outstanding	Average Maturity (Days)	Total Net Assets
1975	36	208,777	93	$ 3,695.7
1976	48	180,676	110	3,585.8
1977	50	177,522	76	3,887.7
1978	61	467,803	42	10.858.0
1979	76	2,307,852	34	45,214.2
1980	96	4,745,572	24	74,447.7
1981	159	10,282.095	34	181,910.4
1982	281	13,101,347	37	206,607.5
1983	307	12,276,639	37	162,549.5
1984	329	13,556,180	43	209,731.9
1985	345	14,435,386	42	207,535.3
1986	359	15,653,595	40	228,345.8
1987	388	16,832,666	31	$254,676.4
1988	431	17,630,528	28	272,293.3
1989	463	20,173,265	38	358,719.2
1990	508	21,577,559	41	414,733.3
1991	554	21,863,352	50	452,559.2
1992	586	21,770,693	51	451,353.4
1993	628	21,586,862	49	461,903.9
1994	644	23,338,196	34	500,427.8
1995	672	27,852,374	52	629,729.2
1996	665	29,901,153	49	761,754.8
1997	682	32,960,623	46	898,083.1

Source: *1998 Mutual Fund Fact Book* (Washington, D.C.: Investment Company Institute). Reprinted by permission of Investment Company Institute.

sales charge or none at all. In the past, because they had no sales fee, they had to be sold directly because a broker had no incentive to sell a no-load fund. This has changed recently because some brokerage firms, most notably Charles Schwab & Co., have developed agreements with specific no-load funds whereby they will sell these funds to their clients and collect a fee from the fund. As of April 1999, Schwab had a list of 1,000 no-load funds that they would sell through their OneSource service. As seen in the most recent figures available in Table 26.8, the division between these two major distribution channels is currently about 54 to 34 percent in favor of the sales force method, although there has been a steady shift toward direct marketing. Given the investor preference for no-load funds and the increasing availability through firms like Charles Schwab, this trend toward direct marketed funds should continue.

The breakdown by investment objective indicates the investment companies' response to a shift in investor emphasis. The growth of an alternative investment objective category reflects not only the overall growth of the industry, but also the creation of new funds in response to the evolving demands of investors. For example, aggressive growth, growth, and growth and income funds have continued to grow and generally increased their percentages. Finally, the growing desire for international diversification is reflected in strong relative growth in international and global equity funds. This trend is discussed more thoroughly in the next section.

GLOBAL INVESTMENT COMPANIES

As discussed throughout this text, serious thought should be given to global diversification of your investment portfolio. Funds that invest in non-U.S. securities are generally called *foreign funds.* More specific designations include either *international funds* or *global funds.* International funds include only non-U.S. stocks from such countries as Germany, Japan, Singapore, and Korea. Global funds contain both U.S. and non-U-S. securities. Ideally, a global fund should invest in a large number of countries. Both international and global funds fall into familiar categories: money funds, long-term government and corporate bond funds, and equity funds. In turn, an international equity fund might limit its focus to a segment of the non-U.S. market, such as the European Fund or Pacific Basin Fund, or to a single country, such as Germany, Italy, Japan, or Korea. In the chapter on global investing,

TABLE 26.8 **TOTAL NET ASSETS BY FUND CHARACTERISTICS ($ MILLIONS)**

	1997		1995		1993	
	Dollars	Percent	Dollars	Percent	Dollars	Percent
Total net assets	$3,430,794.9	100.0	$2,067,337.3	100.0	$1,510,047.3	100.0
Method of Sale						
Sales force	N/A	N/A	1,117,451.5	54.1	876,474.4	58.0
Direct marketing	N/A	N/A	700,727.3	33.9	487,811.4	32.3
Variable annuity	N/A	N/A	247,753.0	12.0	144,566.6	9.6
Not offering shares	N/A	N/A	1,405.5	0.0	1,194,9	0.1
Investment Objective						
Aggressive growth	370,208.7	10.8	190,822.3	9.2	123,734.5	8.2
Growth	675,507.6	19.7	354,235.0	17.1	167,145.2	11.1
Growth and income	843,284.3	24.6	429,202.7	20.8	276,952.0	18.3
Precious metals	3,090.3	0.1	4,727.5	0.2	5,564.6	0.4
International	209,966.7	6.1	120,736.3	5.8	71,024.8	4.7
Global equity	137,207.3	4.0	76,001.6	3.8	43,269.7	2.9
Flexible portfolio	80,416.5	2.3	52,435.9	2.5	34,973.6	2.3
Balanced	131,133.9	3.7	81,288.0	3.9	58,031.2	3.8
Income equity	160,057.2	4.7	93,314.1	4.5	61,262.5	4.1
Income—mixed	105,272.6	3.1	77,404.4	3.7	53,934.3	3.6
Income—bond	128,986.1	3.8	66,111.2	3.2	55,467.1	3.7
U.S. government income	74,683.2	2.2	87,926.7	4.3	116,448.7	7.7
Ginnie Mae	53,833.2	1.6	55,257.0	2.7	73,200.5	4.9
Global bond	41,338.3	1.2	33,412.3	1.6	38,235.2	2.5
Corporate bond	40,430.2	1.2	31,731.9	1.5	27,517.1	1.8
High-yield bond	104,420.8	3.0	59,715.9	2.9	48,708.5	3.2
Long-term municipal bond	144,423.2	4.2	135,789.0	6.6	140,999.4	9.3
Long-term state municipal bond	126,534.8	3.7	117,225.5	5.7	113,578.4	7.5

Sources: *1995 Mutual Fund Fact Book, 1996 Mutual Fund Fact Book,* and *1998 Mutual Fund Fact Book* (Washington, DC: Investment Company Institute). Reprinted by permission of Investment Company Institute.

there was an extensive discussion about investing in emerging markets. Given the need to invest in a diversified portfolio of emerging markets, an emerging market mutual fund that contains a number of them is an ideal vehicle for this asset allocation.

Although most global or international funds are open-end funds (either load or no-load), a significant number are closed-end funds, including most of the single country and the emerging market funds. These funds have opted to be closed-end because being closed-end, they are not subject to major investor liquidations that require the sale of stocks in the portfolio on an illiquid foreign stock exchange. Because of the growth and popularity of foreign funds, most sources of information include separate sections on foreign stock or bond funds.

A final alternative that all investors—particularly those in the United States—should appreciate is the large number of non-U.S. investment companies that offer both domestic and global products in their local markets. In fact, the Investment Company Institute reported that of $7,159,064 million invested worldwide in open-end investment companies at the end of 1997, almost 40 percent of these assets were controlled by firms located outside the United States. In order, the largest concentrations of these AUM occurred in France, Luxembourg, Japan, Italy, Canada, Spain, and Germany. Further, of the 34,591 investment companies in operation during 1997, fewer than 7,000 were domiciled in the United States. From these statistics it is reasonable to assume that no single region of the world has a monopoly on investment management skill.

FIGURE 26.3 DESCRIPTION OF MUTUAL FUND QUOTATIONS IN THE *WALL STREET JOURNAL*

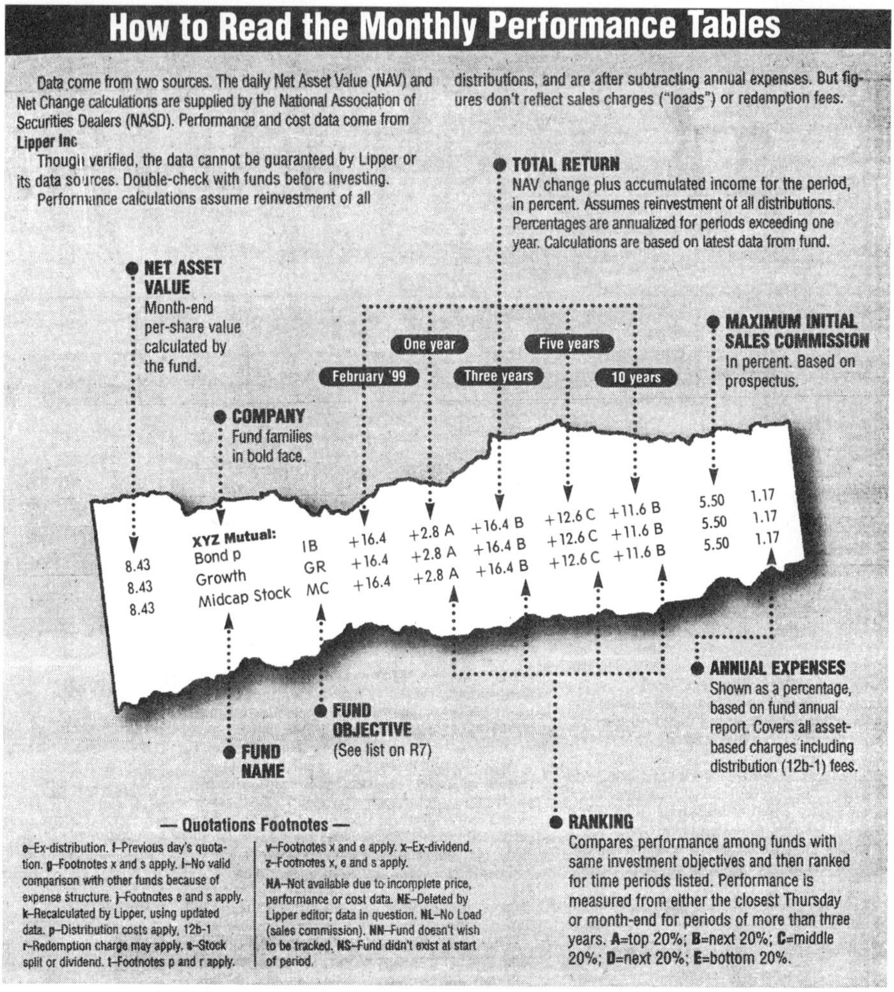
How to Read the Monthly Performance Tables
Data come from two sources. The daily Net Asset Value (NAV) and Net Change calculations are supplied by the National Association of Securities Dealers (NASD). Performance and cost data come from Lipper Inc.
Though verified, the data cannot be guaranteed by Lipper or its data sources. Double-check with funds before investing.
Performance calculations assume reinvestment of all distributions, and are after subtracting annual expenses. But figures don't reflect sales charges ("loads") or redemption fees.
TOTAL RETURN
NAV change plus accumulated income for the period, in percent. Assumes reinvestment of all distributions. Percentages are annualized for periods exceeding one year. Calculations are based on latest data from fund.
NET ASSET VALUE
Month-end per-share value calculated by the fund.
One year
Five years
February '99
Three years
10 years
MAXIMUM INITIAL SALES COMMISSION
In percent. Based on prospectus.
COMPANY
Fund families in bold face.
XYZ Mutual:
8.43 Bond p IB +16.4 +2.8 A +16.4 B +12.6 C +11.6 B 5.50 1.17
8.43 Growth GR +16.4 +2.8 A +16.4 B +12.6 C +11.6 B 5.50 1.17
8.43 Midcap Stock MC +16.4 +2.8 A +16.4 B +12.6 C +11.6 B 5.50 1.17
ANNUAL EXPENSES
Shown as a percentage, based on fund annual report. Covers all asset-based charges including distribution (12b-1) fees.
FUND OBJECTIVE
(See list on R7)
FUND NAME
— Quotations Footnotes —
e-Ex-distribution. f-Previous day's quotation. g-Footnotes x and s apply. l-No valid comparison with other funds because of expense structure. j-Footnotes e and s apply. k-Recalculated by Lipper, using updated data. p-Distribution costs apply, 12b-1 r-Redemption charge may apply. s-Stock split or dividend. t-Footnotes p and r apply.
v-Footnotes x and e apply. x-Ex-dividend. z-Footnotes x, e and s apply.
NA-Not available due to incomplete price, performance or cost data. NE-Deleted by Lipper editor; data in question. NL-No Load (sales commission). NN-Fund doesn't wish to be tracked. NS-Fund didn't exist at start of period.
RANKING
Compares performance among funds with same investment objectives and then ranked for time periods listed. Performance is measured from either the closest Thursday or month-end for periods of more than three years. A=top 20%; B=next 20%; C=middle 20%; D=next 20%; E=bottom 20%.

Source: *Wall Street Journal,* 1 March 1999.

SOURCES OF INFORMATION

Because a wide variety of funds are available, you should examine the performance of various funds over time to understand their goals and management philosophies. Daily quotations for numerous open-end funds appear in the *Wall Street Journal.* These quotations and the information provided have been enhanced dramatically since 1992, and the *Journal* now provides a comprehensive listing of historical returns and rankings on a monthly basis. (A description of the performance data provided is shown in Figure 26.3.)

A comprehensive weekly list of quotations with data on dividend income and capital gain for the previous 12 months is carried in *Barron's.* In addition, *Barron's* publishes quarterly updates on the performance of several funds over the previous 10 years. As shown earlier in Figure 26.1, *Barron's* lists closed-end stock and bond funds with their current net asset values, current market quotes, and the percentage of difference between the two figures.

A major source of comprehensive historical information is *Investment Companies,* an annual publication is issued by CDA/Wiesenberger. This book contains statistics for over 600

FIGURE 26.4

SAMPLE PAGE FROM 1998 CDA/WIESENBERGER *INVESTMENT COMPANIES YEARBOOK*

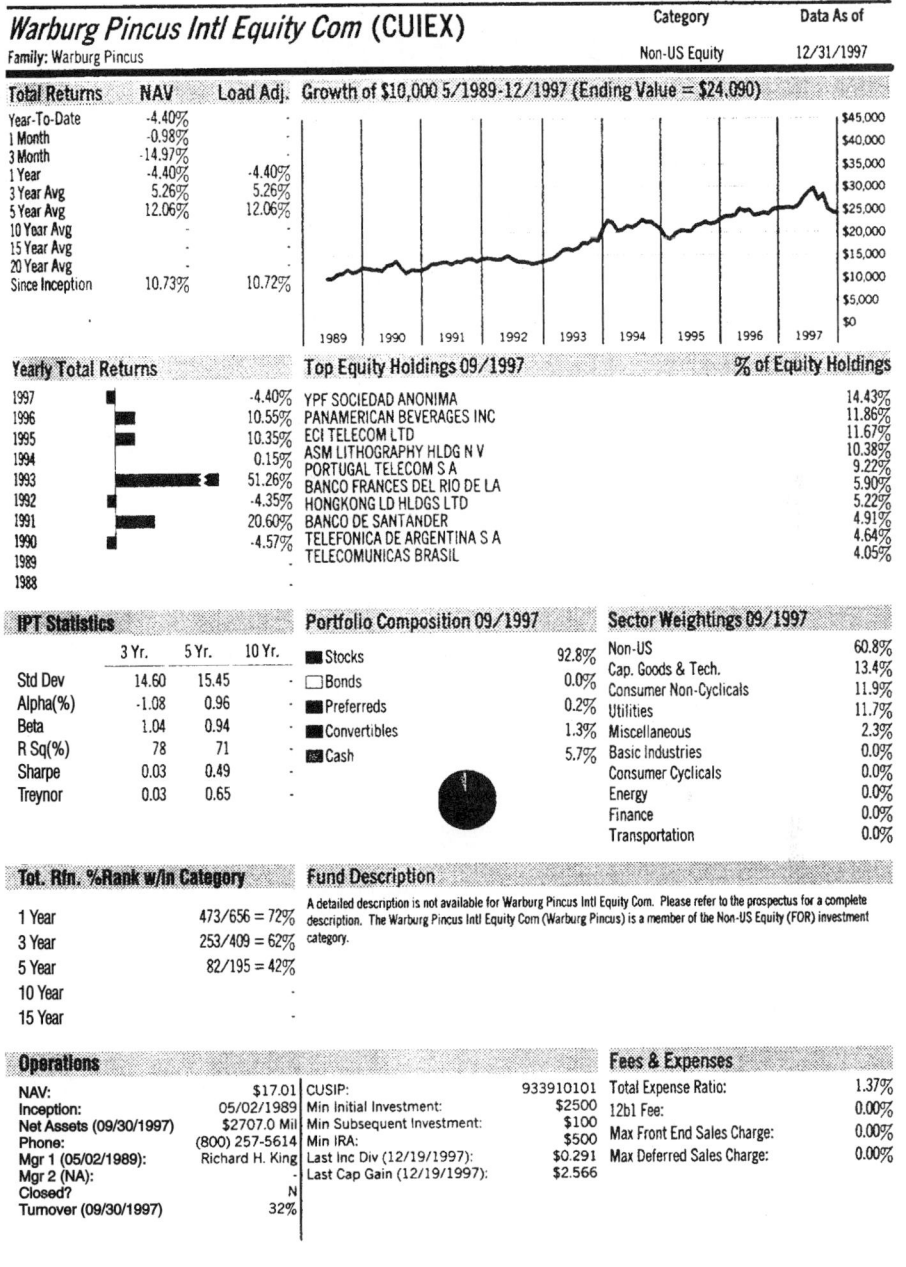

Warburg Pincus Intl Equity Com (CUIEX)

Family: Warburg Pincus

Category	Data As of
Non-US Equity	12/31/1997

Total Returns	NAV	Load Adj.
Year-To-Date	-4.40%	-
1 Month	-0.98%	-
3 Month	-14.97%	-
1 Year	-4.40%	-4.40%
3 Year Avg	5.26%	5.26%
5 Year Avg	12.06%	12.06%
10 Year Avg	-	-
15 Year Avg	-	-
20 Year Avg	-	-
Since Inception	10.73%	10.72%

Growth of $10,000 5/1989-12/1997 (Ending Value = $24,090)

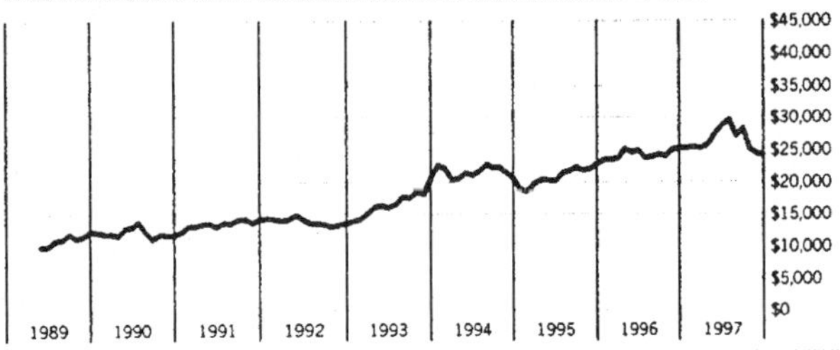
$45,000
$40,000
$35,000
$30,000
$25,000
$20,000
$15,000
$10,000
$5,000
$0
1989
1990
1991
1992
1993
1994
1995
1996
1997

Yearly Total Returns	
1997	-4.40%
1996	10.55%
1995	10.35%
1994	0.15%
1993	51.26%
1992	-4.35%
1991	20.60%
1990	-4.57%
1989	-
1988	-

Top Equity Holdings 09/1997	% of Equity Holdings
YPF SOCIEDAD ANONIMA	14.43%
PANAMERICAN BEVERAGES INC	11.86%
ECI TELECOM LTD	11.67%
ASM LITHOGRAPHY HLDG N V	10.38%
PORTUGAL TELECOM S A	9.22%
BANCO FRANCES DEL RIO DE LA	5.90%
HONGKONG LD HLDGS LTD	5.22%
BANCO DE SANTANDER	4.91%
TELEFONICA DE ARGENTINA S A	4.64%
TELECOMUNICAS BRASIL	4.05%

IPT Statistics	3 Yr.	5 Yr.	10 Yr.
Std Dev	14.60	15.45	-
Alpha(%)	-1.08	0.96	-
Beta	1.04	0.94	-
R Sq(%)	78	71	-
Sharpe	0.03	0.49	-
Treynor	0.03	0.65	-

Portfolio Composition 09/1997	
Stocks	92.8%
Bonds	0.0%
Preferreds	0.2%
Convertibles	1.3%
Cash	5.7%

Sector Weightings 09/1997	
Non-US	60.8%
Cap. Goods & Tech.	13.4%
Consumer Non-Cyclicals	11.9%
Utilities	11.7%
Miscellaneous	2.3%
Basic Industries	0.0%
Consumer Cyclicals	0.0%
Energy	0.0%
Finance	0.0%
Transportation	0.0%

Tot. Rtn. %Rank w/in Category	
1 Year	473/656 = 72%
3 Year	253/409 = 62%
5 Year	82/195 = 42%
10 Year	-
15 Year	-

Fund Description

A detailed description is not available for Warburg Pincus Intl Equity Com. Please refer to the prospectus for a complete description. The Warburg Pincus Intl Equity Com (Warburg Pincus) is a member of the Non-US Equity (FOR) investment category.

Operations

NAV:	$17.01
Inception:	05/02/1989
Net Assets (09/30/1997)	$2707.0 Mil
Phone:	(800) 257-5614
Mgr 1 (05/02/1989):	Richard H. King
Mgr 2 (NA):	-
Closed?	N
Turnover (09/30/1997)	32%

CUSIP:	933910101
Min Initial Investment:	$2500
Min Subsequent Investment:	$100
Min IRA:	$500
Last Inc Div (12/19/1997):	$0.291
Last Cap Gain (12/19/1997):	$2.566

Fees & Expenses	
Total Expense Ratio:	1.37%
12b1 Fee:	0.00%
Max Front End Sales Charge:	0.00%
Max Deferred Sales Charge:	0.00%

mutual funds. Arranged alphabetically, it describes each major fund, including a brief history, investment objectives and portfolio analysis, statistical history, special services available, personnel, advisors and distributors, sales charges, and a chart of the value of a hypothetical $10,000 investment over 10 years. Figure 26.4 shows a sample page for the Warburg Pincus International Equity Fund. The CDA/Wiesenberger book also contains a summary list with annual rates of return and price volatility measures for a number of additional funds.

FIGURE 26.5 **SAMPLE FUND RATING PAGE FROM *FORBES***

▲▼ FUND SURVEY

Stock funds

This chart is a picture of how wonderful investing in stocks can be. A consequence of that rise has been that many funds either have paid out big distributions or are sitting on a powder keg of unrealized appreciation. In response, we've added a tax efficiency measure to this table. It penalizes funds for past distributions and for accumulated gains that would have to be distributed if winning positions were liquidated. Unless you retain a fund in a tax-free account, pay attention to the tax grade.

To be sure, a loser like Comstock Partners Capital Value is a model of tax efficiency because there have been no gains. Where the grade can be helpful is in choosing between funds that are otherwise closely matched. As always, the things that matter are performance in both good and bad markets, and the cost of ownership.

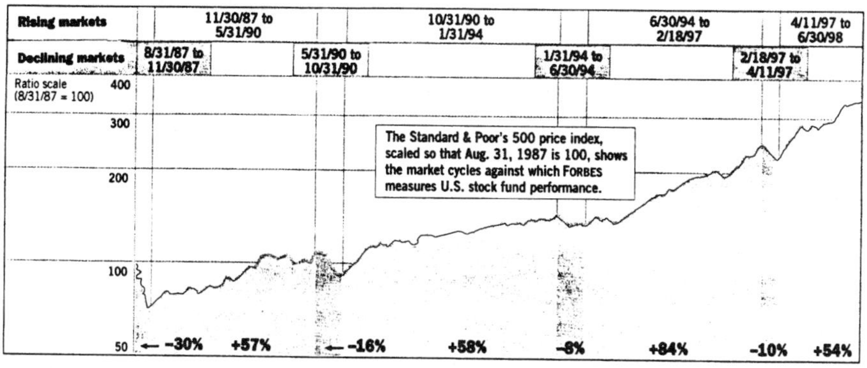

Rising markets
11/30/87 to 5/31/90
10/31/90 to 1/31/94
6/30/94 to 2/18/97
4/11/97 to 6/30/98
Declining markets
8/31/87 to 11/30/87
5/31/90 to 10/31/90
1/31/94 to 6/30/94
2/18/97 to 4/11/97
Ratio scale (8/31/87 = 100)
400
300
200
100
50
The Standard & Poor's 500 price index, scaled so that Aug. 31, 1987 is 100, shows the market cycles against which FORBES measures U.S. stock fund performance.
−30%
+57%
−16%
+58%
−8%
+84%
−10%
+54%

MARKET PERFORMANCE UP ▲	DOWN ▼	Fund/800 phone	Annualized total return 8/31/87 to 6/30/98	3-year	Tax efficiency	Assets 6/30/98 ($mil)	Weighted average P/E	Median market cap ($bil)	Maximum sales charge	Annual expenses per $100
		STANDARD & POOR'S 500 STOCK AVERAGE	15.2%	30.1%						
		FORBES STOCK FUND COMPOSITE	13.4%	23.4%			28.2	$14.0		$1.14
C	■ B	AAL Capital Growth Fund-A/553-6319	—*	29.2%	B	$2,936	31.4	$26.7	4.00%	$0.98
		AAL Equity Income-A[1]/553-6319	—*	17.7	–	212	26.8	11.4	4.00	1.11
		AAL Mid Cap Stock-A/553-6319	—*	18.6	A	662	28.5	2.4	4.00	1.30
B	D	AARP Growth–Capital Growth/225-2470	13.9%	28.1	B	1,462	26.2	25.1	none	0.88
D	A	AARP Growth–Growth & Income/225-2470	14.3	26.2	B	7,726	23.4	14.3	none	0.68
		Accessor Growth Fund-Advisor/759-3504	—*	29.8	C	120	33.6	94.2	none	0.93
		Accessor Small to Mid Cap-Advisor/759-3504	—*	31.1	C	199	17.7	2.0	none	1.25
		Accessor Value & Income-Advisor/759-3504	—*	27.7	C	122	14.7	16.3	none	1.08
A	C	Acorn Fund/922-6769	15.2	22.9	D	3,967	29.3	0.7	none	0.86
C	C	Addison Capital Shares/526-6397	12.5	25.7	F	82	21.3	6.3	none	1.75
		Advantus Cornerstone Fund-A/665-6005	—*	22.8	–	143	24.4	7.1	5.00	1.09a
		Advantus Enterprise Fund-A/665-6005	—*	12.8	–	54	33.8	0.9	5.00	1.26a
C	C	Advantus Horizon Fund-A/665-6005	13.0	25.9	D	71	37.4	22.3	5.00	1.39a
D	B	AIM Advisor–Large Cap Value-A/347-1919	13.2	23.9	D	202	23.5	19.6	5.50	1.46a
C	A	AIM Blue Chip-A/347-1919	14.3	29.0	A	1,577	32.4	18.3	5.50	1.27a

Three-year return 6/30/95 through 6/30/98. ■ Fund rated for three periods only; maximum allowable grade A. *Fund not in operation or did not meet asset minimum for full period. †Closed to new investors. §Distributor may impose redemption fee whose proceeds revert to the fund. a: Net of absorption of expenses by fund sponsor. b: Includes back-end load that reverts to distributor. NA: Not applicable or not available. [1]Formerly AAL Utilities Fund.
Sources: Forbes; Lipper Analytical Services; Morningstar, Inc.

Rules, page 188. For more funds: www.forbes.com/funds

Source: *Forbes,* August 1998.

CDA/Wiesenberger also offers several other services, in both print and software formats. *Mutual Funds Update* and *Mutual Funds Report* are monthly publications with information on more than 9,500 funds, as well as commentary on the industry. *Closed-End Weekly Review* provides information about the weekly performance of closed- end funds, and *FundEdge* is analytical software for investors in the closed-end fund industry.

Another source of analytical historical information funds is *Forbes.* This biweekly financial publication typically discusses individual companies and their investment potential.

FIGURE 26.5 **SAMPLE FUND RATING PAGE FROM *FORBES* (CONCLUDED)**

▲▼ **FUND SURVEY**

Foreign stock funds

Unlike global funds, these have no U.S. exposure at all. That offers two advantages: You, rather than a fund sponsor, select precisely how much of your portfolio is overseas, and secondly, come tax time, if only one area of your investments has had a rough stretch, you can harvest the loss to offset other capital gains. With the Asian crisis, Asian and emerging markets funds have fared miserably, while European funds have done well. It will not always be thus. Our advice: If you want to go abroad, consider the whole world rather than just a specific region. And don't be overly swayed by recent results.

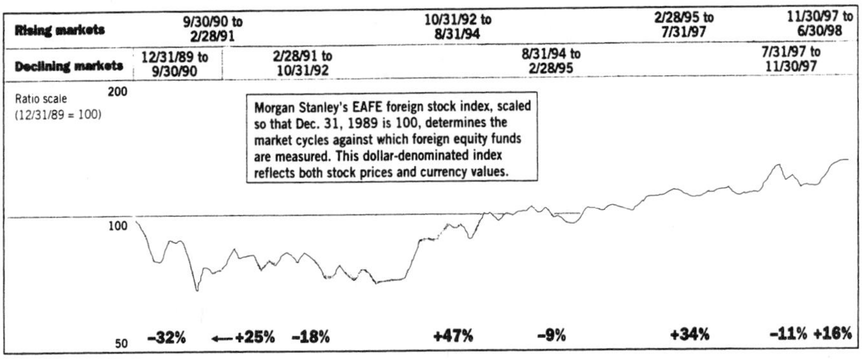
Rising markets
9/30/90 to 2/28/91
10/31/92 to 8/31/94
2/28/95 to 7/31/97
11/30/97 to 6/30/98
Declining markets
12/31/89 to 9/30/90
2/28/91 to 10/31/92
8/31/94 to 2/28/95
7/31/97 to 11/30/97
Ratio scale (12/31/89 = 100)
200
100
50
Morgan Stanley's EAFE foreign stock index, scaled so that Dec. 31, 1989 is 100, determines the market cycles against which foreign equity funds are measured. This dollar-denominated index reflects both stock prices and currency values.
-32%
←+25%
-18%
+47%
-9%
+34%
-11% +16%

Market performance UP ▲	Market performance DOWN ▼	Fund/800 phone	Annualized total return 12/31/89 to 6/30/98	Annualized total return 3-year	Tax efficiency	Assets 6/30/98 ($mil)	Weighted average P/E	Median market cap ($bil)	Maximum sales charge	Annual expenses per $100
		MORGAN STANLEY CAPITAL INTL EAFE INDEX	4.9%	10.7%						
		FORBES FOREIGN STOCK FUND COMPOSITE	6.8%	9.1%			25.4	$9.5		$1.51
		Accessor Intl Equity-Advisor/759-3504	—*	18.0%	-	$179	25.4	$9.5	none	$1.60
		Acorn International Fund/922-6769	—*	15.7	B	1,861	28.5	0.6	none	1.19
		Advantus Intl Balanced-A/665-6005	—*	11.3	-	63	NA	5.5	5.00%	1.99a
		AIM Advisor–Intl Value-C/347-1919	—*	19.4	-	135	24.7	16.5	5.50	2.46
		AIM Developing Markets-A[1]/347-1919	—*	-0.6	-	135	18.6	3.5	4.75	2.00a
■C	■C	AIM Emerging Markets-A[1]/347-1919	—*	-12.3	B	142	18.5	2.4	4.75	2.00a
C	D	AIM Europe Growth-A[1]/347-1919	7.0%	21.5	A	690	30.8	18.4	5.50	1.89
		AIM International–Equity-A/347-1919	—*	17.3	A	2,736	30.3	9.2	5.50	1.46a
D	C	AIM International Growth-A[1]/347-1919	5.3	13.5	F	198	27.0	11.0	5.50	1.82

Three-year return 6/30/95 through 6/30/98. ■Fund rated for three periods only; maximum allowable grade A. *Fund not in operation or did not meet asset minimum for full period. †Closed to new investors. §Distributor may impose redemption fee whose proceeds revert to the fund. a: Net of absorption of expenses by fund sponsor. b: Includes back-end load that reverts to distributor. NA: Not applicable or not available. [1]Formerly GT funds.
Sources: Forbes; Lipper Analytical Services; Morningstar, Inc.

Rules, page 180. For more funds: www.forbes.com/funds

Source: *Forbes*, August 1998.

In addition, the magazine's August issue contains an annual survey of mutual funds. A sample page in Figure 26.5 demonstrates the survey reports on annual average 10-year returns and last-12-month returns. The survey also provides information regarding each fund's yield, its sales charge, and its annual expense ratio. Notably, the survey includes a separate section on foreign stock funds as shown.

Business Week publishes a "Mutual Fund Scoreboard." Figure 26.6 contains a sample of this scoreboard for open-end equity funds. The magazine publishes a comparable one for

FIGURE 26.6 **MUTUAL FUND SCOREBOARD**

MUTUAL FUND SCOREBOARD

FUND	OVERALL RATING (COMPARES RISK-ADJUSTED PERFORMANCE OF EACH FUND AGAINST ALL FUNDS)	CATEGORY	RATING (COMPARES RISK-ADJUSTED PERFORMANCE OF FUND WITHIN CATEGORY)	SIZE ASSETS $MIL.	SIZE % CHG. 1997-98	FEES SALES CHARGE (%)	FEES EXPENSE RATIO (%)	1998 RETURNS (%) PRE-TAX	1998 RETURNS (%) AFTER-TAX	1998 RETURNS (%) YIELD
COLUMBIA BALANCED	A	Domestic Hybrid	A	925.8	17	No load	0.68	20.1	17.1	2.9
COLUMBIA COMMON STOCK	A	Large-cap Blend	B+	754.5	–4	No load	0.77	26.3	23.0	0.5
COLUMBIA GROWTH	B	Large-cap Growth	B	1588.2	20	No load	0.71	30.3	29.0	0.2
COLUMBIA SPECIAL	C–	Mid-cap Growth	B	869.0	–30	No load	0.98	16.6	16.6	0.0
CONCERT INVMT. GROWTH & INCOME B (n)		Large-cap Blend		1191.4	–1	5.00**	1.88†	18.1	17.1	0.0
CONCERT INVESTMENT GROWTH B (o)		Large-cap Blend		4105.5	2	5.00**	1.88†	27.3	25.3	0.0
CRABBE HUSON EQUITY A (p)	C–	Mid-cap Value	F	205.7	–46	No load	1.42†	–8.8	–9.6	0.6
DAVIS FINANCIAL A	B+	Financial	B	460.7	60	4.75	1.07†	14.2	14.2	0.0
DAVIS N.Y. VENTURE A	B	Large-cap Value	C–	6820.3	47	4.75	0.91†	14.7	14.1	0.4
DELAWARE A	B+	Domestic Hybrid	B	640.6	12	5.75	0.97†	17.4	15.3	2.0
DELAWARE DECATUR INCOME A	B	Large-cap Value	C	1947.0	0	5.75	0.88†	9.9	5.4	2.5
DELAWARE DECATUR T/R A	B	Large-cap Value	C	1014.4	13	5.75	1.13†	10.6	7.4	1.4
DELAWARE DELCAP A	D	Mid-cap Growth	C	674.4	–10	5.75	1.36†	17.7	14.1	0.0
DELAWARE SMALL CAP VALUE A	C	Small-cap Value	C	282.2	0	5.75	1.39†	–5.1	–5.3	0.6
DELAWARE TREND A	D	Small-cap Growth	B	446.8	–11	5.75	1.34†	13.6	10.1	0.0
DFA INTERNATIONAL SMALL COMPANY		Foreign		272.7	34	No load	0.75	8.2	7.5	1.9
DODGE & COX BALANCED	B+	Domestic Hybrid	B	5770.0	14	No load	0.55	6.7	4.4	3.2
DODGE & COX STOCK	B	Large-cap Value	C	4458.4	9	No load	0.57	5.4	3.2	1.6
DOMINI SOCIAL EQUITY	A	Large-cap Blend	A	635.8	111	No load	1.17†	33.0	32.6	0.0
DREYFUS	C–	Large-cap Value	F	2591.1	–1	No load	0.71	17.2	16.8	0.9
DREYFUS APPRECIATION	A	Large-cap Growth	A	4168.9	111	No load	0.87	30.9	30.6	0.5
DREYFUS BALANCED	B+	Domestic Hybrid	B	322.1	–13	No load	0.96	9.7	7.3	2.8
DREYFUS DISCIPLINE STOCK	B+	Large-cap Blend	B	2817.6	71	No load	0.90†	26.6	25.3	0.6
DREYFUS GROWTH & INCOME	C	Large-cap Value	D	1777.5	–9	No load	1.01	12.8	11.2	0.9
DREYFUS GROWTH OPPORTUNITY	C	Large-cap Value	D	469.4	–6	No load	1.06	16.1	14.9	0.7
DREYFUS MIDCAP INDEX	C	Mid-cap Blend	C	273.0	6	1.00*	0.50	18.4	12.9	1.1
DREYFUS NEW LEADERS	C–	Mid-cap Blend	C–	691.5	–20	1.00*	1.12	–4.0	–4.5	0.0
DREYFUS PREMIER CORE VALUE A (q)	C	Large-cap Value	D	556.2	–5	5.75	1.14†	7.1	5.0	0.5
DREYFUS PREMIER WORLDWIDE GROWTH B	B+	World	A	658.5	121	4.00**	2.00†	27.7	27.6	0.0
DREYFUS S&P 500 INDEX	A	Large-cap Blend	B+	2153.1	50	1.00*	0.50	28.1	27.7	1.0
DREYFUS SMALL COMPANY VALUE	C	Small-cap Value	C	327.4	–19	1.00*	1.21	–6.3	–6.3	0.0
DREYFUS THIRD CENTURY	C	Large-cap Growth	C	1049.0	30	No load	0.97	30.2	27.3	0.0
DRIEHAUS INTERNATIONAL GROWTH		Foreign		222.3	22	No load	2.11	15.2	14.0	0.0
EATON VANCE BALANCED A (r)	B+	Domestic Hybrid	C	271.2	3	5.75	0.97	13.4	9.1	2.3
EATON VANCE TAX-MGD. GROWTH B		Large-cap Blend		2194.1	205	5.00**	1.50†	24.5	24.5	0.0
EATON VANCE UTILITIES A (s)	C	Utilities	D	409.3	12	5.75	1.13	23.6	22.6	2.3
ENTERPRISE GROWTH A	B+	Large-cap Growth	B	827.6	95	4.75	1.43†	30.9	29.7	0.0
EUROPACIFIC GROWTH	C	Foreign	A	20797.9	10	5.75	0.86†	15.5	14.1	1.2
EVERGREEN B		Mid-cap Blend		727.7	32	5.00**	2.19†	6.2	6.1	0.0
EVERGREEN BALANCED B (t)	B+	Domestic Hybrid	C	557.9	360	5.00**	1.35†	12.7	7.7	2.6
EVERGREEN FOUNDATION B		Domestic Hybrid		1372.2	47	5.00**	2.04†	11.1	10.5	1.4
EVERGREEN GROWTH & INCOME B		Mid-cap Blend		1014.0	41	5.00**	2.21†	4.4	3.7	0.2
EVERGREEN SMALL CO. GROWTH B (u)	D	Small-cap Growth	D	218.7	–84	5.00**	1.36†	–17.0	–20.2	0.0
EVERGREEN TAX STRATEGIC B		Domestic Hybrid		248.0	88	5.00**	2.18†	5.0	4.6	1.4
EVERGREEN VALUE A	C	Large-cap Value	C–	467.7	18	4.75	1.01†	9.5	6.0	0.8
EXCELSIOR BLENDED EQUITY A	B	Large-cap Blend	C	665.0	23	No load	0.99	28.7	28.2	0.3
EXCELSIOR INTERNATIONAL	D	Foreign	C–	230.1	29	No load	1.43	7.9	7.7	0.6
EXCELSIOR VALUE & RESTRUCT. A	B	Mid-cap Blend	B+	597.1	160	No load	0.89	10.3	10.0	0.5
EXECUTIVE INVESTORS BLUE CHIP	B+	Large-cap Blend	B	419.5	0	4.75	0.75†	17.8	17.1	0.5
EXPEDITION EQUITY INSTITUTIONAL		Large-cap Blend		319.0	28	No load	1.09	28.5	26.6	0.3
FAM VALUE	B	Small-cap Value	A	357.7	8	No load	1.24	6.2	4.1	0.5
FASCIANO	B	Small-cap Growth	A	233.2	318	No load	1.30	7.2	6.3	0.1
FEDERATED AMERICAN LEADERS B		Large-cap Value		1620.7	72	5.50**	1.89†	16.6	13.2	0.1
FEDERATED EQUITY-INCOME B		Large-cap Blend		1224.1	47	5.50**	1.84†	14.9	12.9	0.9
FEDERATED GROWTH STRAT. A	C–	Mid-cap Growth	B	601.5	23	5.50	1.14	16.3	16.3	0.0
FEDERATED SMALL CAP STRAT. B		Small-cap Blend		234.2	22	5.50**	2.19†	0.9	0.9	0.0
FEDERATED STOCK & BOND A	B+	Domestic Hybrid	B	206.2	23	5.50	1.21†	11.2	8.7	3.3
FEDERATED STOCK	B+	Large-cap Value	B+	1534.2	26	No load	0.99	17.3	14.4	0.9
FEDERATED UTILITY A	C	Utilities	C	809.8	4	5.50	1.14	13.7	8.8	2.4
FIDELITY ADVISOR BALANCED T	C	Domestic Hybrid	D	2997.2	0	3.50	1.17†	15.5	12.5	2.5
FIDELITY ADVISOR EQUITY GROWTH T	B	Large-cap Growth	B	5194.8	25	3.50	1.29†	38.7	35.2	0.0
FIDELITY ADVISOR EQUITY INCOME T	B	Large-cap Value	B	2637.0	17	3.50	1.21†	16.1	14.8	0.6
FIDELITY ADVISOR GROWTH & INCOME T		Large-cap Blend		399.6	176	3.50	1.59†	30.3	30.2	0.2
FIDELITY ADVISOR GROWTH OPP. T	B+	Large-cap Value	B+	24823.6	18	3.50	1.27†	24.0	22.8	0.7
FIDELITY ADVISOR MIDCAP T		Mid-cap Blend		367.2	8	3.50	1.44†	14.4	13.7	0.0
FIDELITY ADVISOR NATURAL RES. T	D	Natural Resources	C	279.5	–45	3.50	1.39†	–16.3	–17.0	0.1
FIDELITY ADVISOR OVERSEAS T.	C–	Foreign	B	1138.1	3	3.50	1.65†	11.3	11.0	0.2
FIDELITY ADVISOR STRAT. OPP. T	C–	Small-cap Blend	C	444.8	–15	3.50	1.23†	0.8	0.3	0.0
FIDELITY ASSET MANAGER	B	Domestic Hybrid	C–	12879.2	6	No load	0.74	16.1	11.4	2.9
FIDELITY ASSET MANAGER: GROWTH	C	Domestic Hybrid	D	5119.9	10	No load	0.80	18.1	14.5	1.6

*Includes redemption fee. **Includes deferred sales charge. †12(b)-1 plan in effect. ‡Not currently accepting new accounts. §Less than 0.5% of assets. NA=Not available. NM=Not meaningful. (n) Formerly Common Sense Growth & Income B. (o) Formerly Common Sense Growth B. (p) Formerly Crabbe Huson Equity Prim. (q) Formerly Dreyfus Core Value Inv. (r) Formerly EV Traditional Investors. (s) Formerly EV Traditional Total Return. (t) Formerly Keystone Balanced K-1. (u) Formerly Keystone Small Company Growth S-4.

closed-end, fixed-income funds and equity funds. Besides information on performance (both before-tax and after-tax returns for 1–3–5–10 years), sales charges (including those for 12b-1 plans), expenses, portfolio yield and rank within objective, the table also contains portfolio information and telephone numbers for all the funds.

Morningstar is a well-regarded information service for mutual funds. Its basic service is the monthly "Morningstar Mutual Funds," which provides an informative one-page sheet

FIGURE 26.6

MUTUAL FUND SCOREBOARD (CONCLUDED)

Equity Funds

AVERAGE ANNUAL TOTAL RETURNS (%) 3 YEARS PRETAX	3 YEARS AFTERTAX	5 YEARS PRETAX	5 YEARS AFTERTAX	10 YEARS PRETAX	10 YEARS AFTERTAX	HISTORY RESULTS VS. ALL FUNDS	PORTFOLIO DATA TURNOVER	CASH %	FOREIGN %	P-E RATIO	UNTAXED GAINS (%)	LARGEST HOLDING COMPANY (% ASSETS)	RISK LEVEL	BEST QTR	BEST %RET	WORST QTR	WORST %RET	TELEPHONE
16.8	13.6	14.8	12.2	NA	NA	32	High	1	2	37	17	Microsoft (3)	Very low	IV 98	12.9	III 98	-4.8	800-547-1707
24.1	20.3	20.6	17.7	NA	NA	11	Average	2	1	37	29	Microsoft (4)	Low	IV 98	23.3	III 98	-11.5	800-547-1707
25.8	22.3	21.3	18.2	18.8	15.4	2211	High	1	NA	42	39	Microsoft (4)	Average	IV 98	25.6	III 98	-14.6	800-547-1707
14.1	11.1	14.5	11.4	16.8	14.1	2113	High	16	2	41	30	American Stores (5)	High	IV 98	23.2	III 98	-12.8	800-547-1707
19.2	15.5	NA	NA	NA	NA	2	Average	1	7	29	7	Dell Computer (3)			NA		NA	800-544-5445
23.4	19.9	NA	NA	NA	NA	1	High	5	4	36	6	MCI WorldCom (3)			NA		NA	800-544-5445
8.6	5.5	10.0	7.6	NA	NA	134	High	5	1	24	0	Amgen (4)	High	II 97	18.8	III 98	-19.9	800-541-9732
29.5	28.6	25.5	23.9	NA	NA	111	Very low	1	4	23	74	American Express (7)	Average	IV 98	20.1	III 98	-15.9	800-279-0279
24.7	23.5	21.8	20.1	20.4	18.0	1111	Very low	4	5	25	26	American Express (6)	Average	IV 98	21.4	III 98	-14.4	800-279-0279
18.5	15.2	15.6	12.7	14.4	11.6	2332	Average	3	4	28	24	Rite Aid (4)	Very low	IV 98	15.1	III 98	-5.5	800-523-4640
19.7	14.7	17.7	13.5	13.9	10.2	4322	Average	2	10	27	5	Bestfoods (3)	Low	II 97	13.7	III 98	-9.8	800-523-4640
20.3	16.5	18.8	15.3	15.2	12.0	3322	Average	4	10	27	12	Bestfoods (3)	Low	II 97	15.3	III 98	-10.9	800-523-4640
15.2	11.1	13.4	9.6	14.7	12.4	1323	High	9	NA	43	24	Staples (5)	High	IV 98	24.7	III 98	-16.3	800-523-4640
15.5	13.0	12.1	10.2	15.4	13.6	2143	Average	4	NA	20	21	Trigon Healthcare (2)	Average	II 97	15.3	III 98	-16.0	800-523-4640
14.5	11.4	14.0	11.3	19.0	15.7	1113	High	6	3	45	24	EMC/Mass. (4)	High	IV 98	22.9	III 98	-15.8	800-523-4640
NA	NA	NA	NA	NA	NA			4	NA	NA	21	NA			NA		NA	310-395-8005
14.1	12.0	14.2	12.2	14.1	12.1	2323	Low	4	9	24	13	ALCOA (2)	Very low	II 97	11.0	III 98	-7.9	800-621-3879
18.3	16.3	18.3	16.5	16.1	14.3	2312	Low	5	9	24	18	Pharmacia & Upjohn (3)	Average	II 97	15.4	III 98	-14.3	800-621-3879
30.1	29.8	24.3	23.8	NA	NA	311	Very low	1	0	34	32	Microsoft (6)	Low	IV 98	24.6	III 98	-9.8	800-762-6814
14.6	11.4	12.2	7.9	11.8	8.5	3435	Very high	3	4	25	22	General Electric (3)	Average	IV 98	20.3	III 98	-12.9	800-373-9387
28.1	27.8	24.6	24.1	18.5	17.5	2411	Very low	4	6	31	32	Pfizer (6)	Low	IV 98	20.5	III 98	-10.2	800-373-9387
12.9	9.8	13.3	10.6	NA	NA	33	Very high	12	3	27	7	Biogen (2)	Very low	IV 98	10.8	III 98	-7.1	800-373-9387
27.8	25.2	23.1	21.0	19.9	17.9	1311	Average	1	4	32	25	Microsoft (3)	Average	IV 98	22.6	III 98	-12.2	800-373-9387
14.4	10.4	12.2	9.2	NA	NA	33	High	14	3	26	14	Biogen (3)	Average	IV 98	18.5	III 98	-11.7	800-373-9387
17.8	14.1	14.5	10.0	12.0	8.6	4432	High	4	5	26	24	Coastal (3)	Average	IV 98	20.5	III 98	-11.4	800-373-9387
22.7	19.2	18.2	15.4	NA	NA	121	Low	8	0	31	15	America Online (3)	Average	IV 98	27.8	III 98	-14.6	800-373-9387
10.4	8.7	11.8	9.6	14.2	11.7	2124	Average	11	4	29	26	Metromedia Fiber Net Cl. A (2)	High	II 97	17.8	III 98	-20.4	800-373-9387
17.7	12.5	17.2	12.6	13.6	9.6	4312	Average	2	8	23	13	Waste Management (2)	Average	II 97	15.3	III 98	-14.6	888-338-8084
24.3	24.2	19.8	19.6	NA	NA	21	Very low	8	38	30	25	Pfizer (5)	Low	IV 98	19.9	III 98	-13.0	800-554-4611
27.6	26.6	23.4	21.8	NA	NA	311	Very low	3	2	33	38	Microsoft (3)	Low	IV 98	21.3	III 98	-10.1	800-373-9387
16.6	15.0	16.4	14.3	NA	NA	13	High	1	2	23	-7	Emmis Broadcasting Cl. A (2)	Average	IV 98	24.6	III 98	-27.2	800-373-9387
27.9	24.3	21.4	17.6	16.8	14.2	2421	Average	4	NA	36	35	Merck (4)	Average	IV 98	24.3	III 98	-11.4	800-373-9387
NA	NA	NA	NA	NA	NA			6	100	36	7	Nokia Cl. A ADR (3)			NA		NA	800-560-6111
16.2	12.0	14.8	11.4	13.3	9.9	3332	Low	3	13	33	21	Sofamor/Danek Group (3)	Very low	II 97	11.2	III 98	-5.2	800-225-6265
NA	NA	NA	NA	NA	NA	1	Very low	6	6	36	16	Automatic Data Processing (2)			NA		NA	800-225-6265
15.5	12.1	11.5	8.8	12.8	9.6	2243	High	3	30	26	33	Energis (17)	Low	IV 98	14.4	I 94	-7.7	800-225-6265
31.8	30.4	26.0	24.5	20.3	18.1	2211	Low	4	NA	40	31	Bristol-Myers Squibb (4)	Average	IV 98	26.8	III 98	-14.0	800-432-4320
14.4	12.5	11.3	9.6	13.3	11.9	3133	Low	14	100	27	24	Mannesmann (3)	Average	IV 98	17.9	III 98	-13.6	800-421-4120
16.8	16.3	NA	NA	NA	NA	2	Very low	18	1	27	44	Clear Channel Communs. (4)			NA		NA	800-343-2898
15.8	12.1	13.5	10.7	12.1	9.5	3432	Average	4	1	33	24	Johnson & Johnson (2)	Very low	II 97	10.4	I 94	-4.4	800-343-2898
15.1	14.1	NA	NA	NA	NA	2	Very low	11	3	29	24	Intel (3)			NA		NA	800-343-2898
18.5	17.7	NA	NA	NA	NA	2	Low	15	3	28	21	Webster Financial (1)			NA		NA	800-343-2898
-1.7	-5.2	5.3	1.9	13.6	10.3	1124	High	8	1	30	-13	DeVry (2)	Very high	II 97	17.9	III 98	-29.4	800-343-2898
12.9	12.1	NA	NA	NA	NA	3	Average	1	4	25	8	Perkin-Elmer (1)			NA		NA	800-343-2898
17.9	14.0	17.1	13.7	14.8	11.9	2422	Average	9	3	30	28	General Electric (3)	Average	II 97	11.7	III 98	-9.2	800-343-2898
26.1	24.6	20.9	19.2	18.1	16.6	3221	Low	0	4	33	55	Pfizer (5)	Average	IV 98	22.4	III 98	-12.1	800-446-1012
8.2	7.5	5.9	5.1	6.9	6.1	4444	High	6	99	27	13	Brambles Industries (3)	High	IV 98	16.3	III 98	-14.9	800-446-1012
22.6	21.8	21.3	20.5	NA	NA	11	Low	-2	12	28	15	Philip Morris (3)	Average	IV 98	22.9	III 98	-20.5	800-446-1012
21.5	19.7	19.3	17.2	NA	NA	412	High	12	3	33	9	General Electric (3)	Low	IV 98	19.7	III 98	-13.1	800-423-4026
NA	NA	NA	NA	NA	NA			1	NA	36	25	McKesson (4)			NA		NA	800-922-2085
18.0	16.6	16.0	14.8	16.0	15.0	1322	Very low	12	NA	18	38	Conmed (6)	Low	III 97	17.0	III 98	-15.2	800-932-3271
18.1	17.1	17.5	16.0	15.6	14.1	1413	Average	20	NA	27	5	Pulitzer Publishing (4)	Average	II 97	14.3	III 98	-13.4	800-848-6050
21.8	18.6	NA	NA	NA	NA	1	Average	1	5	26	13	PECO Energy (3)			NA		NA	800-341-7400
20.1	17.8	NA	NA	NA	NA	2	Average	4	5	27	16	Bristol-Myers Squibb (2)			NA		NA	800-341-7400
22.2	19.0	17.6	14.0	15.8	12.8	1422	High	3	3	42	25	America Online (2)	High	IV 98	27.3	III 98	-20.3	800-341-7400
15.3	15.2	NA	NA	NA	NA	3	High	3	2	30	12	S&P 500 Index (Fut.) (6)			NA		NA	800-341-7400
16.1	12.4	13.9	10.8	11.8	9.0	3432	Average	4	6	26	13	Federated High-Yield (4)	Very low	II 97	10.5	III 98	-5.2	800-341-7400
24.1	19.9	20.9	17.4	16.2	13.0	3211	Average	1	6	26	24	Lexmark International Cl. A (2)	Low	IV 98	16.5	III 98	-11.3	800-341-7400
17.2	13.2	13.2	10.2	14.0	11.2	2232	High	11	3	22	19	PECO Energy (3)	Low	IV 97	12.9	I 94	-7.2	800-341-7400
15.3	12.8	10.8	8.8	13.4	11.1	2242	Average	5	9	29	21	American Home Products (2)	Low	II 97	12.6	III 98	-5.9	800-522-7297
26.0	23.2	22.5	20.4	NA	NA	11	High	6	2	38	36	Johnson & Johnson (3)	Average	IV 98	24.1	III 98	-6.0	800-522-7297
18.8	17.1	18.8	17.3	NA	NA	12	Average	3	8	24	29	Citicorp (3)	Low	IV 98	17.8	III 98	-12.3	800-522-7297
NA	NA	NA	NA	NA	NA		Average	10	6	33	15	Time Warner (3)			NA		NA	800-843-3001
23.3	21.5	20.8	19.1	20.2	18.3	1121	Low	7	12	29	2	Fannie Mae (5)	Low	IV 98	20.5	III 98	-7.7	800-522-7297
NA	NA	NA	NA	NA	NA	2	Very high	8	1	30	16	McKesson (3)			NA		NA	800-522-7297
2.7	0.4	6.4	4.6	11.9	9.8	1114	High	5	29	23	-24	Total Cl. B ADR (6)	High	III 97	14.2	IV 97	-13.2	800-522-7297
11.7	10.3	9.1	8.2	NA	NA	243	Average	8	98	24	-2	Alcatel Alsthom (2)	Average	IV 98	17.3	III 98	-17.8	800-522-7297
8.9	6.3	10.6	8.6	13.0	10.6	2233	High	1	6	20	17	Whole Foods Market (8)	High	III 97	18.1	III 98	-18.0	800-522-7297
17.0	13.4	12.1	9.5	13.9	11.6	2242	High	13	2	34	14	Philip Morris (2)	Low	IV 98	14.1	III 98	-5.8	800-544-8888
20.6	17.2	14.3	12.0	NA	NA	42	High	6	NA	31	16	BellSouth (5)	Low	IV 98	16.1	III 98	-8.2	800-544-8888

DATA: MORNINGSTAR, INC., CHICAGO, IL.

Source: *Business Week*, 1 February 1999.

that evaluates the performance of open-end mutual funds. An example sheet for a fund is included as Figure 26.7. This sheet provides up-to-date information on the fund's objective and its risk-adjusted performance relative to an appropriate benchmark. There is also an analysis of performance and investment strategy based on an interview with the fund manager. The one-page sheet is best described as a *Value Line* sheet for a mutual fund. A similar service evaluates several hundred closed-end funds.

FIGURE 26.7 **SAMPLE PAGE FROM "MORNINGSTAR MUTUAL FUNDS"**

Fidelity Magellan

Ticker	Load	NAV	Yield	SEC Yield	Total Assets	Mstar Category
FMAGX	Closed	$113.18	0.6%	—	$76,290.4 mil	Large Blend

Prospectus Objective: Growth

Fidelity Magellan Fund seeks capital appreciation.

The fund invests primarily in common stocks and convertible securities, with up to 20% of assets invested in debt securities of all types and qualities. It features domestic corporations operating primarily in the United States, domestic corporations that have significant activities and interests outside the U.S., and foreign companies. No limitations are placed on total foreign investment, but no more than 40% of assets may be invested in companies operating exclusively in one foreign country.

The fund closed to new investment in 1965 and reopened in 1981. It closed again in 1997.

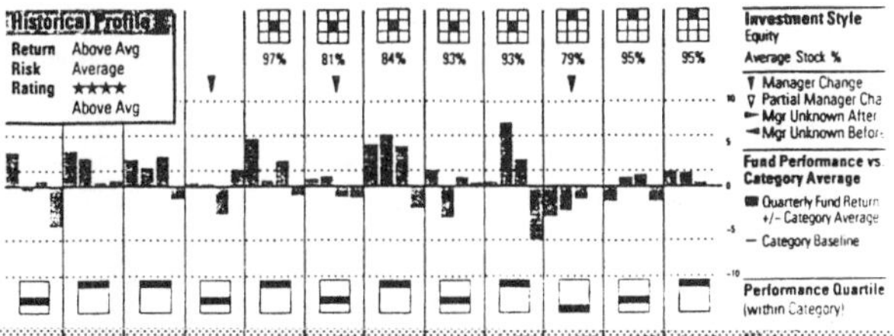
Historical Profile
Return Above Avg
Risk Average
Rating ★★★★ Above Avg
97%
81%
84%
93%
93%
79%
95%
95%
Investment Style
Equity
Average Stock %
Manager Change
Partial Manager Cha
Mgr Unknown After
Mgr Unknown Befor
Fund Performance vs. Category Average
Quarterly Fund Return +/- Category Average
— Category Baseline
Performance Quartile (within Category)

Portfolio Manager(s)

Robert E. Stansky, CFA. Since 6-96. '78 Nichols C.; MBA'83 New York U. Stansky joined Fidelity Management & Research in 1983 as a portfolio manager. Funds previously managed: Fidelity Growth Company (04-87 - 06-96), Fidelity Emerging Growth (12-90 - 04-91)

1987	1988	1989	1990	1991	1992	1993	1994	1995	1996	1997	11-98	History
40.10	48.32	59.85	53.93	68.61	63.01	70.85	66.80	85.98	80.65	95.27	113.18	NAV
1.00	22.77	34.58	-4.51	41.03	7.02	24.66	-1.81	36.82	11.69	26.59	21.90	Total Return %
-4.26	6.16	2.90	-1.39	10.54	-0.60	14.60	-3.13	-0.71	-11.26	-6.76	0.33	+/- S&P 500
-3.11	5.57	3.16	-0.43	8.56	-1.18	14.92	0.54	-0.83	-9.87	-6.71	0.82	+/- Wilshire Top 750
1.56	2.24	2.60	1.42	2.46	1.93	1.22	0.18	0.88	1.41	1.57	0.21	Income Return %
-0.56	20.52	31.98	-5.93	38.57	5.09	23.43	-1.99	35.94	10.28	25.03	21.69	Capital Return %
67	6	10	68	11	53	3	60	17	98	64	10	Total Rtn % Rank Cat
0.72	0.90	1.24	0.83	1.30	1.25	0.75	0.13	0.59	1.10	1.25	0.20	Income $
9.02	0.00	3.82	2.42	5.43	8.82	6.50	2.64	4.69	12.85	5.21	2.62	Capital Gains $
1.08	1.14	1.08	1.03	1.06	1.05	1.00	0.99	0.96	0.92	0.64	0.61	Expense Ratio %
1.18	1.33	2.13	2.54	2.47	1.57	2.11	1.07	0.39	0.95	1.75	0.77	Income Ratio %
96	101	87	82	135	172	155	132	120	155	67	34	Turnover Rate %
7,800.1	8,971.1	12,699.6	12,325.7	19,257.1	22,268.9	31,705.1	36,441.5	53,702.3	53,988.7	63,766.2	76,290.4	Net Assets $mil

Performance 11-30-98

	1st Qtr	2nd Qtr	3rd Qtr	4th Qtr	Total
1994	-1.59	-4.49	5.43	-0.90	-1.81
1995	8.44	15.77	10.60	-1.46	36.82
1996	1.79	1.00	1.67	6.85	11.69
1997	-0.56	16.55	9.67	-0.40	26.59
1998	14.22	3.37	-11.05	—	—

Trailing	Total Return%	+/- S&P 500	+/- Wil Top 750	% Rank All	% Rank Cat	Growth of $10,000
3 Mo	23.08	1.05	0.72	9	10	12,308
6 Mo	7.64	0.15	0.48	7	13	10,764
1 Yr	23.29	-0.37	-0.16	5	15	12,329
3 Yr Avg	19.46	-7.19	-6.30	15	76	17,050
5 Yr Avg	18.98	-3.98	-2.80	11	51	23,846
10 Yr Avg	19.03	0.29	0.81	5	7	57,084
15 Yr Avg	18.24	0.83	1.43	2	1	123,471

Tax Analysis	Tax-Adj Ret%	%Rank Cat	%Pretax Ret	%Rank Cat
3 Yr Avg	15.70	78	80.7	77
5 Yr Avg	15.90	56	83.8	64
10 Yr Avg	15.87	18	83.4	53

Potential Capital Gain Exposure: 44% of assets

Risk Analysis

Time Period	Load-Adj Return %	Risk %Rank[1] All	Risk %Rank[1] Cat	Morningstar Return	Morningstar Risk	Morningstar Risk-Adj Rating
1 Yr	19.59					
3 Yr	18.26	71	71	1.26	0.87	★★★
5 Yr	18.25	77	88	1.36	0.97	★★★★
10 Yr	18.67	70	68	1.62	0.93	★★★★★

Average Historical Rating (156 months): 4.7★s

[1]1=low, 100=high

Category Rating (3 Yr)

1
2
3
4
5
Worst
Best

Return Below Avg
Risk Above Avg

Other Measures	Standard Index S&P 500	Best Fit Index S&P 500
Alpha	-5.5	-5.5
Beta	0.99	0.99
R-Squared	95	95
Standard Deviation	19.25	
Mean	19.46	
Sharpe Ratio	0.84	

Portfolio Analysis 09-30-98

Share change since 03-98 Total Stocks: 343	Sector	PE	YTD Ret%	% Assets
⊕ General Electric	Industrials	33.5	24.50	[illegible]
⊕ Microsoft	Technology	59.8	88.78	[illegible]
⊕ Intel	Technology	33.1	53.44	[illegible]
⊕ Cisco Systems	Technology	80.2	102.80	[illegible]
⊖ Merck	Health	37.3	48.12	[illegible]
⊕ Wal-Mart Stores	Retail	40.7	91.75	[illegible]
⊕ Home Depot	Retail	50.4	69.38	[illegible]
⊕ MCI WorldCom	Services	—	95.04	[illegible]
⊕ Lucent Technologies	Technology	NMF	116.00	[illegible]
⊕ America Online	Services	NMF	287.00	[illegible]
⊕ Philip Morris	Staples	21.4	27.40	[illegible]
⊖ Bristol-Myers Squibb	Health	35.3	30.33	[illegible]
⊕ IBM	Technology	26.6	58.95	[illegible]
⊕ Schering-Plough	Health	47.2	73.52	[illegible]
⊕ Time Warner	Services	NMF	71.31	[illegible]
⊕ Fannie Mae	Financials	23.2	29.40	[illegible]
⊕ American Home Products	Health	26.4	42.13	[illegible]
⊕ AT & T	Services	18.0	3.11	[illegible]
⊕ Tyco Intl	Industrials	—	46.24	[illegible]
⊕ Warner-Lambert	Health	55.6	84.22	[illegible]
⊕ Dell Computer	Technology	73.3	189.50	[illegible]
⊕ Johnson & Johnson	Health	31.0	24.95	[illegible]
⊕ American Intl Group	Financials	27.1	29.90	[illegible]
⊕ Gap	Retail	41.4	108.70	[illegible]
⊕ Wells Fargo	Financials	25.2	10.66	[illegible]

Current Investment Style

Style: Value Blnd Growth; Size: Large Med Small

	Stock Port Avg	Relative S&P 500 Current	Relative S&P 500 Hist
Price/Earnings Ratio	35.2	1.13	1.03
Price/Book Ratio	8.5	1.15	0.88
Price/Cash Flow	24.6	1.13	1.02
3 Yr Earnings Growth	20.6	1.10	1.30
1 Yr Earnings Est%	15.3	1.50	—
Debt % Total Cap	30.8	0.70	0.95
Med Mkt Cap $mil	54,599	1.0	0.5

Analysis by Russel Kinnel 12-07-98

Fidelity Magellan Fund manager Bob Stansky inspires confidence.

The fund is running 33 basis points ahead of the S&P 500, so it has a chance to beat the index for the first calendar year since 1993. Strong stock picks in the retail and technology sectors account for the strong showing.

Just as important as the pickup in returns are the signs that Stansky has gotten the handle of steering this $76 billion supertanker. He has concentrated his efforts on the largest stocks in order to ensure adequate liquidity, and he waits patiently for the right time to buy.

Stansky stands pat when the market is rallying but dives in when corrections hit, thus minimizing the costs of buying popular stocks. Stansky made the biggest sector changes of his tenure this summer when the market sold off sharply. (The turnover rate has picked up a bit since the March 1998 number on the page.) Many of Stansky's favorite tech stocks were on sale, so he loaded up his cart, boosting tech from 14% to 20% of the portfolio. He trimmed energy, financials, and industrials to make room. In addition, Stansky boosted the fund's concentration in its top stocks while selling smaller positions. The portfolio slimmed down from 470 holdings to 350, and the top 10 stocks represent 22% of assets, up from 17%.

The moves also had a dramatic impact on the portfolio's median market cap, which went from half that of the S&P to on par with the index. That's certainly a logical development for a fund of this size, though it probably won't help Fidelity's contention that this isn't a quasi-index fund. On the other hand, Stansky's tech splurge has boosted the fund's projected growth rate and valuations from index level to well above those of the index.

Slowly but surely, Stansky is taking the fund into the growth territory that brought him success at Growth Company. It's a respectable investment despite its asset handicap.

Special Securities % of assets 09-30-98

○ Restricted/Illiquid Secs	0
● Emerging-Markets Secs	Trace
● Options/Futures/Warrants	Yes

Composition % of assets 09-30-98		Market Cap	
Cash	6.4	Giant	53.5
Stocks*	93.5	Large	32.9
Bonds	0.0	Medium	12.7
Other	0.0	Small	0.8
		Micro	0.0

*Foreign (% of stocks) 4.9

Sector Weightings	% of Stocks	Rel S&P	5-Year High
Utilities	0.4	0.1	9
Energy	6.8	0.9	25
Financials	12.6	0.8	17
Industrials	12.3	1.0	31
Durables	3.3	1.2	16
Staples	4.5	0.5	10
Services	16.1	1.2	17
Retail	10.8	1.7	11
Health	12.8	1.0	15
Technology	20.3	1.3	42

Address:	82 Devonshire Street Boston, MA 02109 800-544-8888
Inception:	05-02-63
Advisor:	Fidelity Management & Research
Subadvisor:	FMR (U.K.)/FMR (Far East)
Distributor:	Fidelity Distributors
NTF Plans:	Muriel Siebert

Minimum Purchase:	Closed	Add: $250 IRA: —
Min Auto Inv Plan:	Closed	Systematic Inv: $100
Sales Fees:	3.00%L	
Management Fee:	0.30%+0.52% max./0.27% min.(G)+(-)0.20%P	
Actual Fees:	Mgt: 0.43%	Dist: —
Expense Projections:	3Yr: $49	5Yr: $64 10Yr: $105
Avg Brok Commission:	$0.0328	Income Distrib: Semi-Ann.
Total Cost (relative to category):	Below Avg	

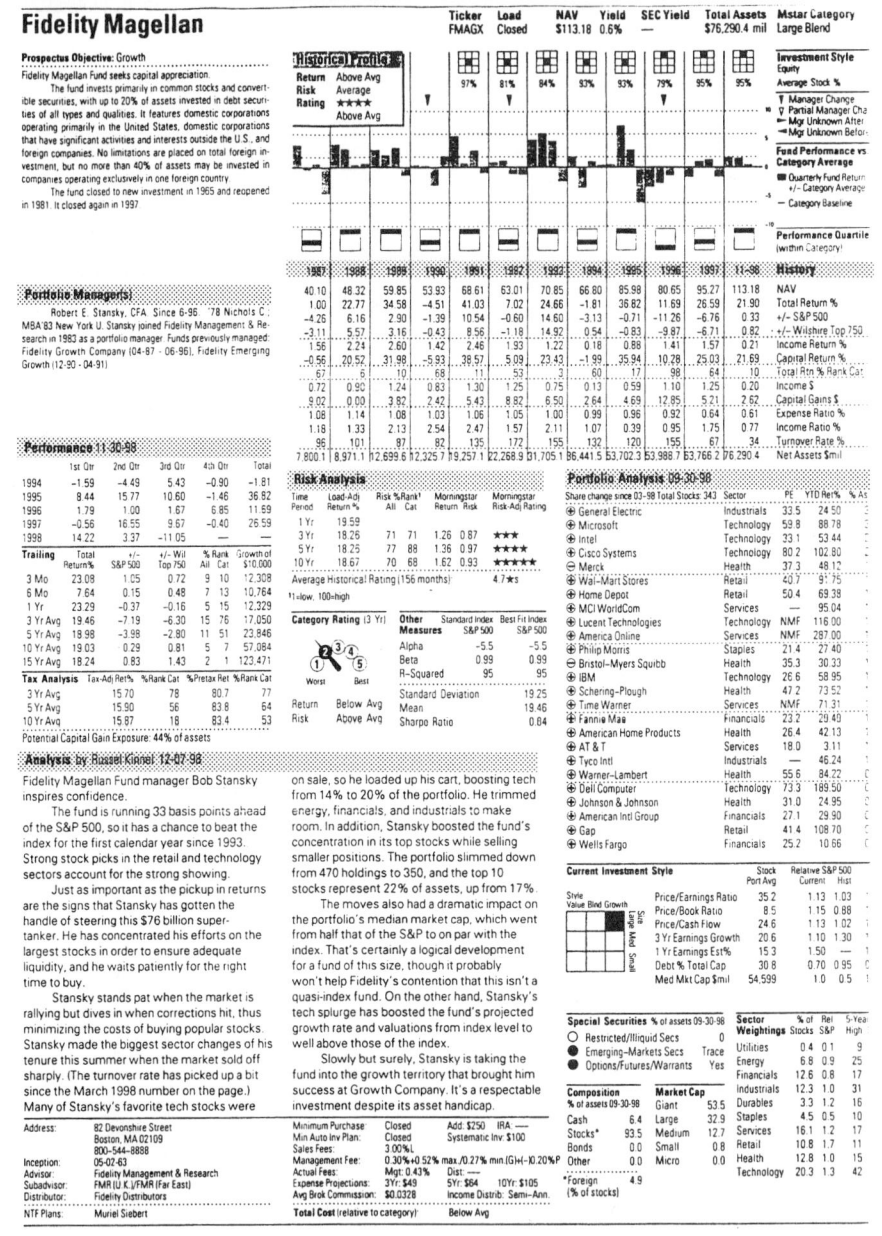

Source: "Morningstar Mutual Funds," February 1999.

One of the most useful features of the information provided by *Morningstar* is a performance and risk rating system. *Morningstar* gives each fund between one and five stars based on the fund's weighted risk-adjusted return performance over several time periods. The star ratings are interpreted as follows: Lowest Rating (1), Below Average (2), Neutral (3), Above Average (4), and Highest Rating (5). The Fidelity Magellan fund summarized in Figure 26.7 received an overall four-star rating in this assessment, although its 10-year per-

FIGURE 26.8 **MUTUAL FUND INFORMATION FROM BLOOMBERG AND BRIDGE INFORMATION SERVICES**

A. Bloomberg

	OBJECTIVE	ASSETS (MIL)
FMAGX US FIDELITY MAGELLAN	Growth	$72042.39

Fidelity Magellan is an open-end fund which seeks to provide capital appreciation. The Fund seeks to meet its objective by investing its assets primarily in equity securities of domestic, foreign and multinational issuers of all sizes that offer potential for growth.

Current Data		
1) GP NAV	$	128.88
52Wk Hi 3/18	$	131.14
52Wk Lo 10/ 8	$	88.75
3) BETA vs SPX		.99
Current Returns		
4) TRA 3 Mo Return		6.28
YTD Return		6.67
1 Yr Return		25.24
3 Yr Return		25.57
5 Yr Return		22.17
Sharpe Ratio		1.34

Hist Returns	
1998	33.63
1997	26.59
1996	11.69
1995	36.82
1994	-1.81
1993	24.66
1992	7.01
1991	41.03
1990	-4.51
1989	34.58
1988	22.76

Distributions - Semi-Annual	Income	Cap Gain
YTD	$ .00	$ .00
1998	$ .67	$ 5.15
1997	$ 1.25	$ 5.21
1996	$ 1.10	$ 12.85
1995	$ .59	$ 4.69
1994	$ .13	$ 2.64

7) DVD Dividends / Splits
8) MHD Fund Holdings
9) EDGR SEC Filings

B. Bridge Information Services

us;FMAGX Name: Fidelity Magellan Fund ADJ Cusip: 316184-10-0
Objective: GRD Growth - Domestic NAV: 128.88
Load: 3.00% Offer Pr: 132.87

Perf. as of 28-Feb-99	Total Return	SEC 482 Return	Percentile Rank in Obj
1 month	-3.19%		33
3 month	11.69%		22
YTD	1.89%		22
1 year	25.20%	29.62%	17
2 year - ann	29.36%		17
3 year - ann	24.07%		27
5 year - ann	20.17%	19.75%	36
10 year - ann	19.38%	19.53%	16

Net Assets: 83,552 M (as of 31-Dec-98)	
Equities	96.7%
Convertibles	0.0%
Preferred	0.0%
Bonds	0.0%
Cash	3.3%

Last 12 Mos.	
Yield:	0.51%
Income Divs:	0.67
Cap Gain Divs:	5.15
Expense Ratio:	0.60%
Port Turnover:	37.00%

Beta	
1 Year	1.091
3 Year	1.011
5 Year	1.032
10 Year	1.028

fmagx/fnd 29-Mar-99 13:28 NYC (c)BRIDGE

formance merited five stars. *Morningstar* also gave Magellan an "above average risk" rating when comparing it to other funds in the same objective class.

Finally, investors should be aware of the tremendous amount of investment data that is now available over the Internet and from other online sources. In fact, virtually all private and public asset management companies now have their own Web sites that are easily reached through standard search engines. (We saw earlier that Nelson's Investment Manager Network (**www.nelnet.com**) is a particularly good site for information about private advisory and management firms.) Further, Bloomberg and Bridge Information Services, two of the more popular online information services, provide investors with a combination of both unique information and data gathered from other sources. Figure 26.8 shows representative pages from both Bloomberg and Bridge for the Fidelity Magellan fund.

ETHICS AND REGULATION IN THE PROFESSIONAL ASSET MANAGEMENT INDUSTRY

The issue of ethical behavior arises any time one person is hired to perform a service for or look after the interests of another. This topic is particularly important for the asset management business because the entire industry is based on handling someone else's money. Not surprisingly, then, the investment industry is highly regulated to ensure a minimum level of acceptable practice. Table 26.9 describes the four principal securities laws that govern investment companies, including the Investment Company Act of 1940, the Securities Act of 1933, the Securities Exchange Act of 1934, and the Investment Advisers Act of 1940. Notice that a primary intention of these regulations is to guarantee that investment companies keep accurate and detailed transaction records and that account information is reported to investors in a fair and timely manner. The primary federal regulation governing the management of private pension funds is the Employee Retirement Income Security Act (ERISA), which was enacted in 1974.[6]

Investors are well aware of the securities scandals of the 1980s that made such individuals as Ivan Boesky and Michael Milken household names. Unfortunately, transgressions of this nature attest to the fact that although regulations can punish those found in violation of the law, they cannot prevent all such abuses from occurring. Absolute prevention requires self-regulation on the part of the asset manager in the form of a strict set of personal ethical standards. Avera has outlined four general principles that should form the cornerstone of the standards of conduct in the profession.[7] First, managers must conduct themselves with integrity and dignity and act in an ethical manner in all dealings. Second, they should perform financial analysis in a professional and ethical manner that reflects credit on the profession. Third, managers should act with competence and strive to maintain and improve competence in themselves. Finally, they should always use proper care and exercise independent professional judgment.

The Association for Investment Management and Research (AIMR) has developed for its worldwide membership of security analysts and money managers a rigorous Code of Ethics and Standards of Professional Conduct based on these principals. A summary list of the code and standards is presented in Appendix B. These standards provide asset managers with precisely defined conduct and actions that are acceptable (or, more to the point, unacceptable) in daily practice. For example, the general principle that managers should use proper care becomes a specific requirement that they must be able to justify the suitability of any investment decision made on behalf of a particular client. AIMR expects all of its members, which includes everyone holding the Chartered Financial Analyst (CFA) designation, to uphold these standards on a voluntary basis. Violations deemed severe enough can result in the loss of a manager's charter.

Many ethical lapses, such as plagiarizing research reports or falsifying performance statements, are unambiguously wrong. Others, however, are not as clear-cut. We will conclude this section with a discussion of two examples of how possible conflicts between

---

[6]The main feature of ERISA is the *prudent man* statute, which outlines the level of fiduciary care that the manager is required to provide to the investor. For a good discussion of this topic, see Diane Del Guerico, "The Distorting Effect of the Prudent-Man Laws on Institutional Equity Investments," *Journal of Financial Economics* 40, no. 1 (January 1996): 31–62.

[7]William F. Avera, "Definition of Industry Ethics and Development of a Code," in, *Good Ethics: The Essential Element of a Firm's Success,* ed. K. Baker (Charlottesville, Va.: Association for Investment Management and Research, 1994). For an interesting discussion of the investing public's perception of ethics in the asset management industry, see also Scott L. Lummer, "Public Perception of the Investment Industry: Trends and Counteractions," in the same volume.

TABLE 26.9 **PRINCIPAL SECURITIES LAWS FOR THE ASSET MANAGEMENT INDUSTRY**

- **The Investment Company Act of 1940** regulates the structure and operations of mutual funds. Among other things, the 1940 Act requires mutual funds to maintain detailed books and records, safeguard their portfolio securities, and file semiannual reports with the U.S. Securities and Exchange Commission (SEC).
- **The Securities Act of 1933** requires the federal registration of all public offerings of securities, including mutual fund shares. The 1933 Act also requires that all prospective investors receive a current prospectus describing the fund.
- **The Securities Exchange Act of 1934** regulates broker-dealers, including mutual fund principal underwriters and others who sell mutual fund shares, and requires them to register with the SEC. Among other things, the 1934 Act requires registered broker-dealers to maintain extensive books and records, segregate customer securities in adequate custodial accounts, and file detailed, annual financial reports with the SEC.
- **The Investment Advisers Act of 1940** requires federal registration of all investment advisers to mutual funds. The Advisers Act contains various antifraud provisions and requires fund advisers to meet recordkeeping, reporting, and other requirements.

Source: *1998 Mutual Fund Fact Book* (Washington, D.C.: Investment Company Institute).

the manager and the investor can arise from accepted business practices. The first example is related to the way in which managers are compensated for their service. We saw earlier in the chapter that asset management companies—both public and private—typically receive fees based on AUM. The managers at these companies, in turn, are often compensated with a base salary and a bonus that depends on the performance of their portfolios relative to those of their peers. Brown, Harlow, and Starks argued that this arrangement is analogous to a golf or tennis tournament where the players with the best relative performance at the end of the competition receive the largest payoffs.[8] They documented that managers with the worst relative performance midway through a compensation period were more likely to increase the risk of the portfolio in an effort to increase their final standing. Of course, altering fund risk to enhance their own compensation suggests that some managers may not always act in their clients' best interest.

A second potential ethical dilemma for professional asset managers involves the use of **soft dollars**. Soft dollars are generated when a manager commits the investor to paying a brokerage commission that is higher than the simple cost of executing a stock trade in exchange for the manager receiving additional bundled services from the broker. A typical example of this practice would be for a manager to route her trades through a non-discount broker in order to receive security research reports that the brokerage firm produces. It may not be hard for the manager to justify how this additional research benefits the investor—who, of course, is ultimately paying for the service—but the story is quite different if instead of research the manager receives from the broker "perks," such as office equipment, secretarial services, or even personal travel. Several authors have argued that this practice can result in an expropriation of investor wealth by the manager, although Horan and Johnsen document that the use of soft dollars is actually a cost-effective way for investors to monitor a manager's behavior.[9] In May 1998, AIMR adopted a comprehensive set of

[8]Keith C. Brown, W. V. Harlow, and Laura T. Starks, "Of Tournaments and Temptations: An Analysis of Managerial Incentives in the Mutual Fund Industry," *Journal of Finance* 51, no. 1 (March 1996).

[9]Stephen M. Horan and D. Bruce Johnsen, *The Welfare Effects of Soft Dollar Brokerage: Law and Economics* (Charlottesville, Va.: The Research Foundation of the Institute of Chartered Financial Analysts, forthcoming). See also Marshall E. Blume, "Soft Dollars and the Brokerage Industry," *Financial Analysts Journal* 49, no. 2 (March–April 1993): 36–44.

voluntary standards designed to give its members guidance on the permissible uses of soft dollar arrangements.

In summary, it is important for investors to recognize that potential ethical conflicts will exist any time they hire a professional investment manager. Investors are protected by the series of regulations that govern the security industry as well as the strict standards imposed by trade associations, such as AIMR. Of course, perhaps the best protection that investors have is that the vast majority of the thousands of investment advisors and managers throughout the world are unwilling to do anything that would jeopardize their personal and professional reputations.

PERFORMANCE OF INVESTMENT COMPANIES

Investment company performance has been one of the most widely studied topics in all of finance. There are two primary reasons for this: (1) These funds reflect the performance of professional money managers, and (2) fund data have been available for a long time. Although a more complete discussion of performance measurement techniques will be presented in Chapter 27, it is useful to conclude this chapter with a summary of what has been written on mutual fund investing.

Analysis of Overall Performance

When Sharpe evaluated the overall performance of mutual funds, only 32 percent of the funds outperformed the DJIA.[10] Further, comparing the ranks of the funds between the first and second halves of the sample period led Sharpe to conclude that past performance was not the best predictor of future performance.

An examination of the relationship between performance and the expense ratio indicated that good performance was associated with low expense ratios. Finally, analysis of *gross* performance, with expenses added back to the returns, indicated that 56 percent of the funds did better than the DJIA. Therefore, Sharpe concluded that the average mutual fund manager selected a portfolio at least as good as the DJIA, but after deducting the operating costs of the fund, most achieved *net* returns below those of the DJIA.

The results of a study by Jensen indicated that on average the funds earned 1.1 percent less per year than they should have earned for their level of risk.[11] Analysis of gross returns with expenses added back indicated that 42 percent did better than the overall market on a risk-adjusted basis, whereas the analysis of net returns indicated that only 34 percent of the funds outperformed the market. The gross returns indicate the forecasting ability of the funds because these results do not penalize the funds for operating expenses (only brokerage commissions). Jensen concluded that on average these funds could not beat a buy-and-hold policy.

Carlson examined the overall performance of mutual funds with emphasis on the effects of the market series used for comparison and the time period.[12] The results depended heavily on which market series were used: the S&P 500, the NYSE composite, or the DJIA. For the total period, most fund groups outperformed the DJIA, but only a few had gross returns better than the S&P 500 or the NYSE composite. Using net returns, *none* of

---

[10] William F. Sharpe, "Mutual Fund Performance," *Journal of Business* 39, no. 1, part 2 (January 1966): 119–138.

[11] Michael C. Jensen, "The Performance of Mutual Funds in the Period 1945–1964," *Journal of Finance* 23, no. 2 (May 1968): 389–416.

[12] Robert S. Carlson, "Aggregate Performance of Mutual Funds, 1948–1967," *Journal of Financial and Quantitative Analysis* 5, no. 1 (March 1970): 1–32.

the groups outperformed the S&P 500 or the NYSE composite. Analysis of the performance factors indicated consistency over time for return or risk alone, but no consistency in the risk-adjusted performance. Less than one-third of the funds that performed above average during the first half did so in the second half. Lehmann and Modest likewise found substantial differences between benchmarks, but also concluded that average performance was consistently inferior to the overall market performance.[13] A study by Grinblatt and Titman examined performance using portfolio holdings, which does not require a market benchmark.[14] Notably, using this technique they find that portfolio managers who manage aggressive growth stocks earned significantly positive risk-adjusted returns during 1976–1985.

All the early studies were concerned with evaluating the performance of U.S. equity funds. Given the growing tendency toward global stock and bond investing, several authors have examined the performance of international equity and fixed-income funds.

Cumby and Glen examined the performance of international funds compared to the Morgan Stanley world equity index and a U.S. index.[15] Using two risk-adjusted performance measures, they found no evidence that the performance of the funds surpassed that of a broad international index during the sample period. Bailey and Lim examined the performance of country funds (e.g., France, Germany, Korea, Spain) to see if these funds helped investors attain international diversification.[16] They found that country fund returns often resembled domestic U.S. stock returns more than returns from foreign stock portfolios—that is, these funds would not provide the expected benefits of diversification. Cai, Chan, and Yamada showed that Japanese mutual funds tend to underperform their benchmarks.[17]

Blake, Elton, and Gruber examined the performance of bond mutual funds and found that the bond funds generally underperformed relevant bond indexes.[18] Because the underperformance was about equal to the management fees, it is suggested that these funds performed about equal to the indexes—before expenses. They also found no evidence that past performance could predict future performance.

Cornell and Green examined the performance of low-grade (high-yield) bond funds and found that the returns on low-grade bond funds for the total period were about equal to the return on high-grade bonds.[19] They used a two-factor risk model that allowed for the impact of interest rates and stock returns. After adjusting for risk using this two-factor model, they concluded that the return on low-grade bonds were not statistically different from the returns on high-grade bonds.

---

[13]Bruce N. Lehmann and David M. Modest, "Mutual Fund Performance Evaluations: A Comparison of Benchmarks and Benchmark Comparisons," *Journal of Finance* 42, no. 2 (June 1987): 233–265.

[14]Mark Grinblatt and Sheridan Titman, "Performance Measurement without Benchmarks: An Examination of Mutual Fund Returns," *Journal of Business* 66, no. 1 (January 1993): 47–68.

[15]Robert E. Cumby and Jack D. Glen, "Evaluating the Performance of International Mutual Funds," *Journal of Finance* 45, no. 2 (June 1990): 497–522.

[16]Warren Bailey and Joseph Lim, "Evaluating the Diversification Benefits of the New Country Funds," *Journal of Portfolio Management* 18, no. 3 (spring 1992): 74–80.

[17]J. Cai, K. C. Chan, and T. Yamada, "The Performance of Japanese Mutual Funds," *Review of Financial Studies* 10, no. 2 (summer 1997): 237–274.

[18]Christopher R. Blake, Edwin J. Elton, and Martin J. Gruber, "The Performance of Bond Mutual Funds," *Journal of Business* 66, no. 3 (July 1993): 371–403.

[19]Bradford Cornell and Kevin Green, "The Investment Performance of Low-Grade Bond Funds," *Journal of Finance* 46, no. 1 (March 1991): 29–48.

IMPACT OF FUND OBJECTIVES

A fund investor needs to know whether the fund's performance is consistent with its stated objective. For example, does the performance of a balanced fund reflect less risk and lower return than an aggressive growth fund? To answer this, several studies have examined the relationship between funds' stated objectives and their measures of risk and return.

McDonald examined the overall performance of a sample of mutual funds relative to their stated objectives and found a positive relationship between stated objectives and measures of risk, with risk measures increasing as objectives become more aggressive.[20] Beyond finding a positive relationship between return and risk. the risk-adjusted performance indicated that the more aggressive funds outperformed the more conservative funds during this period. Brown and Goetzmann have developed an alternative fund classification system based on investment style that does a superior job of predicting future fund performance.[21] Bogle examined the relationship between fund performance and investment style, as defined by the nine categories of the *Morningstar* equity style box. He found that low-cost, passively managed index funds have generally delivered the highest risk-adjusted returns in each category.[22]

CONSISTENCY OF PERFORMANCE

Although several studies have considered consistency along with overall performances, some studies have concentrated on it. When Klemkosky examined rankings of risk-adjusted performance for adjacent time periods, he found some consistency between the four-year periods, but relatively low consistency between the adjacent two-year periods.[23] Klemkosky concluded that investors should not use past performance to predict short-run future performance. Dunn and Theisen examined institutional portfolios over a 10-year period looking for consistent success.[24] After finding that historical results give little help in explaining future results, they concluded that historical performance should be given very little weight when selecting a managcr.

In contrast to these past studies, several more recent studies have found persistence in fund performance. Grinblatt and Titman used a multiple portfolio benchmark and found that differences between funds persisted over time and, therefore, past performance is useful information.[25] Similarly, Hendricks, Patel, and Zeckhauser found persistence in the short run in terms of relative performance with the strongest evidence for a one-year evaluation horizon.[26] Rather than examine calendar periods, Bauman and Miller attempted to predict performance rankings when the measurement period encompassed full stock market cycles.[27] They found the correlations of portfolio performance rankings from one

---

[20]John G. McDonald. "Objectives and Performance of Mutual Funds. 1960–1969," *Journal of Financial and Quantitative Analysis* 9, no. 3 (June 1974): 311–333.

[21]Stephen J. Brown and William N. Goetzmann, "Mutual Fund Styles," *Journal of Financial Economics* 43, no. 1 (March 1997): 373–399.

[22]John C. Bogle, "The Implications of Style Analysis for Mutual Fund Performance Evaluation," *Journal of Portfolio Management* 24, no. 4 (summer 1998): 34–42.

[23]Robert C. Klemkosky, "How Consistently Do Managers Manage?" *Journal of Portfolio Management* 3, no. 2 (winter 1977): 11–15.

[24]Patricia C. Dunn and Rolf D. Theisen, "How Consistently Do Active Managers Win?" *Journal of Portfolio Management* 9, no. 4 (summer 1983): 47–50.

[25]Mark Grinblatt and Sheridan Titman, "The Persistence of Mutual Fund Performance," *Journal of Finance* 47, no. 5 (December 1992): 1977–1984.

[26]Darryl Hendricks, Jayendu Patel, and Richard Zeckhauser, "Hot Hands in Mutual Funds: Short-Run Persistence of Relative Performance, 1974–1988," *Journal of Finance* 48, no. 1 (March 1993): 93–130.

[27]W. Scott Bauman and Robert E. Miller, "Can Managed Portfolio Performance Be Predicted?" *Journal of Portfolio Management* 20, no. 4 (summer 1994): 31–40.

full market cycle to the next was positive and meaningful. Brown and Goetzmann examined performance persistence with specific concern for survivorship bias.[28] They found evidence of performance persistence, but acknowledged that it was strongly dependent on the time period of study and also correlation across winning funds due to common themes. Elton, Gruber, and Blake also found evidence of persistent performance, and this is repeated in Gruber.[29] Finally, Malkiel provides very insightful mixed results.[30] Specifically, he found evidence of performance persistence in the 1970s, but the persistence rules did *not* work during the 1980s.

What Performance Studies Mean to You

What functions would you want your own personal portfolio manager to perform for you? The list would probably include:

1. Determine your risk–return preferences and develop a portfolio that is consistent with them.
2. Diversify your portfolio to eliminate unsystematic risk.
3. Maintain your portfolio diversification and your desired risk class while allowing flexibility so you could shift between alternative investment instruments as desired.
4. Attempt to achieve a risk-adjusted performance that is superior to aggregate market performance. Some investors may be willing to sacrifice diversification for superior returns in limited segments of their portfolios.
5. Administer the account, keep records of costs, provide timely information for tax purposes, and reinvest dividends if desired.

Although the performance studies typically reviewed only risk-adjusted performance, all of these functions should be considered to put performance into perspective. Therefore, let us consider each of these functions and discuss how mutual funds fulfill them.

Mutual funds do not determine your risk preference. However, once you determine your risk–return preferences, you can choose a mutual fund from a large and growing variety of alternative funds designed to meet almost any investment goal. Recall that the empirical studies indicated that the funds generally were consistent in meeting their stated goals for investment strategies, risk, and returns.

Diversifying your portfolio to eliminate unsystematic risk is one of the major benefits of mutual funds. Many funds provide *instant diversification.* This is especially beneficial to small investors who do not have the resources to acquire 100 shares of 10 or 12 different issues required to reduce unsystematic risk. By initiating an investment in a fund with about $1,000 you can participate in a portfolio of securities that is correlated about 0.90 with the market portfolio, which means that it is about 90 percent diversified. Although diversification varies among funds, typically about three-quarters of the funds have a correlation with the market above 0.90. Therefore, most funds provide excellent diversification, especially if they state this as an objective.

---

[28]Stephen J. Brown and William N. Goetzmann, "Performance Persistence," *Journal of Finance* 50, no. 2 (June 1995):679–698.

[29]Edwin Elton, Martin J. Gruber, and Christopher Blake, "The Persistence of Risk-Adjusted Mutual Fund Performance," *Journal of Business* 69, no. 2 (April 1996): 133–157; and Martin J. Gruber, "Another Puzzle: The Growth in Actively Managed Mutual Funds," *Journal of Finance* 51, no. 3 (July 1996): 783–809.

[30]Barton G. Malkiel, "Returns from Investing in Equity Mutual Funds: 1971 to 1991," *Journal of Finance* 50, no. 2 (June 1995): 549–572.

The third function of your portfolio manager is to maintain the diversification and your desired risk class. It is not too surprising that mutual funds have generally maintained the stability of their correlation with the market because few change the makeup of reasonably well diversified portfolios substantially. Strong evidence exists regarding the consistency of the risk class for individual funds even when there was inconsistency in risk-adjusted performance.

Mutual funds have met the desire for flexibility to change investment instruments by the initiation of numerous funds within a given management company. Typically, investment groups, such as T. Rowe Price or Fidelity Investments, will allow you to shift among their funds without a charge simply by calling the fund. Therefore, you can shift among an aggressive stock fund, a money market fund, and a bond fund for much less than it would cost you in time and money to buy and sell numerous individual issues.

The fourth function of your portfolio manager is to provide risk-adjusted performance that is superior to the aggregate market, which implies that it is superior to a naive buy-and-hold policy. As indicated in the prior discussion, the majority of empirical evidence indicates that on average fund managers' results in selecting undervalued securities are about as good as, or only slightly better than, the results of a naive buy-and-hold policy. This conclusion is based on *gross* returns. Unfortunately, the evidence from *net* returns, after research and trading costs, indicates that most funds do not do as well as a naive buy-and-hold policy. Notably, some recent studies indicate that there *is* some persistence in performance. The shortfall in performance of about 1 percent a year roughly matches the average cost of research and trading commissions.

In response to these findings, several investment management firms have started index funds based on the philosophy, "if you can't beat 'em, join 'em." These *market index funds* do not attempt to beat the market, but merely try to match the composition, and, therefore, the performance of some specified market index, such as the S&P 500 index. Because these index funds have no research costs and minimal trading expenses, their returns typically have correlated with the chosen indexes at rates in excess of 0.99 with very low expenses. Also, their management fees are substantially below those charged by active managers.

Although institutions have used index funds for many years, such funds were not generally available for individual investors until 1989 when several major investment company sponsors initiated such funds. Currently, several equity index funds are available.

The final function of a portfolio manager is account administration. This is another significant benefit of most mutual funds because they allow automatic reinvestment of dividends with no charge and consistently provide records of total cost. Further, each year they supply statements of dividend income and capital gain distribution that can be used to prepare tax returns.

In summary, as an investor, you probably want your portfolio manager to perform a set of functions. Typically, mutual funds can help you accomplish four of the five functions at a lower cost in terms of time and money than doing the work on your own. This convenience and service have, on average, cost about 1 percent a year in terms of performance.

Finally, assuming that you decide to build your portfolio with mutual funds, it is important to minimize your trading. A study by Nesbitt showed that individual investors who attempt to select undervalued securities generally buy into asset categories near their peaks and sell after they level off or fall.[31] This results in an underperformance of about 1 percent a year.

---

[31]Stephen L. Nesbitt, "Buy High, Sell Low: Timing Errors in Mutual Fund Allocations," *Journal of Portfolio Management* 22, no. 1 (fall 1995): 57–60.

THE INTERNET *Investments Online*

As mutual funds have grown in popularity as a means to gain instant diversification and professional management, so have the number of Web sites devoted to some aspect of mutual fund investing. Any of the major fund companies (Fidelity, T. Rowe Price, Vanguard, Scudder, and so on) will have interesting Web sites to visit. Here are some others:

investools.com This is a site with links to several publications. The Closed End Fund Digest site (**investools.com/cgi-bin/server.pl/Newsletters/CEFD**) is a newsletter on closed-end funds. This site offers descriptions of the newsletter's features. A sample copy can be viewed online.

www.wiesenberger.com The home page of Wiesenberger offers an overview of the firm's various investment products. Both closed-end and open-end investment company data, analysis, and software can be purchased, hard copy or online, from this firm. This site has a page with links to many mutual fund sites, including mutual fund families and variable annuity firms.

www.fundsinteractive.com/index.shtml The Mutual Funds Interactive Web site offers basic information about mutual fund investing, via charts, market commentary, and fund price quotes. It has a number of educational features, including a Q&A section, a manager profile, and discussions of various investment topics and of the different types of mutual funds.

www.mfea.com A good place to start if you want to learn more about mutual funds is this home page for the Mutual Fund Education Alliance. This site, called the Mutual Fund Investor's Center, offers a great deal of information. The Fund Center allows users to research, track, and customize their own fund portfolio from a list of over 1,000 funds. Investors can search by a specific fund's name or search for funds by their characteristics, including investment category, level of 12b-1 fee, expense ratio, and sales charge. Investors can also discover the three top-performing funds year-to-date in different investment categories and find the lowest cost fund by investment category. The Education Center page deals with the basics of mutual fund investing, while the Planning and Retirement Center page covers information and investment strategies for retirement, future education, and children. The site has links to a number of fund families.

www.investorguide.com/MutualFunds.htm The InvestorGuide Web site was reviewed in Chapter 1. This page from that Web site focuses on mutual fund investing and has links to a variety of mutual fund-related sites. Topics include learning about mutual funds, getting performance data and ratings, screening mutual funds, and obtaining a mutual fund prospectus.

www.stocksmart.com/tr/tmf.html This site ranks the current performance of over 7,400 mutual funds and compares their relative performance to that of the S&P 500 and to a peer comparison group. It includes, as well, some data of interest to stock and bond investors.

www.mfcafe.com The Mutual Fund Cafe site is designed for mutual fund business and marketing professionals. It includes information and updates on legal issues, the SEC, accounting issues, industry news, and interviews.

www.morningstar.net Morningstar is a leading provider of mutual fund information. The site features much information and many links of interest to mutual fund investors. Items on the Web site include news, analysis, and columns by several Morningstar writers, and an interview with a fund manager. Past articles are available in an archive. The site also features sections dealing with learning, planning, and researching about mutual funds. A mutual fund screen allows users to find funds from Morningstar's database that meet certain investment category, return, rating, and volatility criteria.

www.mfmag.com The Web site of Mutual Funds Online is a subscription service offering fund price quotes, a variety of performance rankings, profiles on over 10,000 funds, and access to a variety of screens that help investors find the funds that best suit their needs.

www.ici.org The Investment Company Institute is a mutual fund trade organization. Visitors to their home page can view issues of their annual publication, *Mutual Fund Handbook*, learn mutual fund facts and figures, read ICI's newsletter, and get information about financial market and mutual fund regulation issues.

Summary

- There are two primary types of professional asset management companies. Management and advisory firms hold the assets of both individual and institutional investors in separate accounts, which allows for the possibility of managing each client's portfolio in a unique manner. Conversely, investment companies, such as closed- and open-end funds, are pools of assets that are managed collectively. Investors in these funds receive shares representing their proportional ownership in the underlying portfolio of stocks, bonds, or other securities. These fund shares can either be traded in the secondary market (closed-end) or sold directly back to the investment company (mutual fund) at the prevailing net asset value. A wide variety of funds are available, so you can find one to match almost any investment objective or combination of investment objectives.
- In recent years, the professional asset management industry has undergone considerable structural change. Most notably, there has been a trend toward consolidating assets under management (AUM) in large, multiproduct firms. This trend has had a beneficial effect for investors of reducing management fees, which are usually charged on a declining percentage of AUM. Investment companies also often charge fees for marketing their shares. These sales charges can take the form of front-end fees, annual 12b-1 fees, or back-end load fees. A substantial amount of publicly available information exists on mutual fund investment practices and performance to help investors make decisions that are appropriate for their circumstances.
- Issues of ethical behavior arise any time one person is hired to perform a service for another. The professional asset management industry protects investors through a series of government regulations and voluntary standards of practice imposed by trade associations on their members. The primary purpose of these regulations and standards is to ensure that managers deal with all investors fairly and equitably and that information about investment performance is accurately reported. Two areas of particular concern in the investment community involve manager compensation arrangements and the use of soft dollars.
- Numerous studies have examined the historical performance of mutual funds. Most found that less than half the funds matched the risk-adjusted net returns of the aggregate market. The results with gross returns generally indicated average risk-adjusted returns about equal to those of the market, with about half the funds (more than half for some studies) outperforming the market. Interestingly, some recent studies have found evidence of performance persistence.
- Although the returns received by the average individual investor on funds managed by investment companies will probably not be superior to the average results for a specific U.S. or international market, several other important services are provided by investment companies. Therefore, you should give serious consideration to these funds as an important alternative to investing in individual stocks and bonds in the United States or worldwide. For the vast majority of investors. the ideal way to invest internationally is through mutual funds for a country, a region, or a sector of the world (e.g., emerging markets).

Questions

1. What are the differences between a management and advisory firm and an investment company? Describe the approach toward portfolio management adopted by each organization.
2. It has been suggested that the professional asset management community is rapidly becoming dominated by a fairly small number of huge, multiproduct firms. Discuss whether the data presented in Table 26.1 support that view.
3. Closed-end funds generally invest in securities and financial instruments that are relatively illiquid whereas most mutual funds invest in widely traded stocks and bonds. Explain the difference between closed-end and open-end funds and why this liquidity distinction matters.
4. What two prices are provided for a closed-end investment company? What is the typical relationship between these prices?
5. What is the difference between a load fund and a no-load fund?
6. Discuss the risk–return differences between a common stock fund and a balanced fund.
7. Should you care about how well a mutual fund is diversified? Why or why not?

8. As an investigator evaluating how well mutual fund managers select undervalued stocks or project market returns, discuss whether net or gross returns are more relevant.
9. Based on the numerous tests of mutual fund performance, you believe that only about half the funds do better than a naive buy-and-hold policy. Does this mean you would forget about investing in investment companies? Why or why not?
10. You are told that Fund X experienced *above-average* performance over the past two years. Do you think it will continue over the next two years? Why or why not?
11. Most money managers have a portion of their compensation tied to the performance of the portfolios they manage. Explain how this arrangement can create an ethical dilemma for the manager.
12. What are soft dollar arrangements? Describe one potential way they can be used to transfer wealth from the investor to the manager.
13. You see advertisements for two mutual funds indicating that they have investment objectives that are consistent with yours.
    a. How would you get a quick view of these two funds' performance over the past two or three years?
    b. Where would you find longer-term and more in-depth information on the funds?

Problems

1. Suppose ABC Mutual fund had no liabilities and owned only four stocks as follows:

Stock	Shares	Price	Market Value
W	1,000	$12	$12,000
X	1,200	15	18,000
Y	1,500	22	33,000
Z	800	16	12,800
			$75,800

The fund began by selling $50,000 of stock at $8.00 per share. What is its NAV?

2. Suppose you are considering investing $1,000 in a load fund that charges a fee of 8 percent, and you expect your investment to earn 15 percent over the next year. Alternatively, you could invest in a no-load fund with similar risk that charges a 1 percent redemption fee. You estimate that this no-load fund will earn 12 percent. Given your expectations, which is the better investment and by how much?
3. Consider the recent performance of the Closed Fund, a closed-end fund devoted to finding undervalued, thinly traded stocks:

Period	NAV	Premium/Discount
0	$10.00	0.0%
1	11.25	−5.0
2	9.85	+2.3
3	10.50	−3.2
4	12.30	−7.0

Here price premiums and discounts are indicated by pluses and minuses, respectively, and period 0 represents Closed Fund's initiation date.

a. Calculate the average return per period for an investor who bought 100 shares of the Closed Fund at the initiation and then sold her position at the end of period 4.
b. What was the average periodic growth rate in NAV over that same period?
c. Calculate the periodic return for another investor who bought 100 shares of Closed Fund at the end of period 1 and sold his position at the end of period 2.
d. What was the periodic growth rate in NAV between periods 1 and 2?

4. CMD Asset Management has the following fee structure for clients in its equity fund:

1.00% of first $5 million invested
0.75% of next $5 million invested
0.60% of next $10 million invested
0.40% above $20 million

a. Calculate the annual dollar fees paid by Client 1, which has $27 million under management, and Client 2, which has $97 million under management.
b. Calculate the fees paid by both clients as a percentage of their assets under management.
c. What is the economic rationale for a fee schedule that declines (in percentage terms) with increases in assets under management?

CFA

5. *CFA Examination II (May 1997)*
Describe one potential conflict of interest that should be disclosed pursuant to AIMR's Code of Ethics and Standards of Professional Conduct in each of the following four situations:

I. An investment advisor serves on a company's board of directors.
II. A portfolio manager purchases initial public offerings for his own account.
III. A research analyst provides recommendations to investment management clients on a company for which her employer is the primary underwriter.
IV. A portfolio manager's investment management fee is based, in part, on performance of client accounts.

6. Suppose that at the start of the year, a no-load mutual fund has a net asset value of $27.15 per share. During the year, it pays its shareholders a capital gain and dividend distribution of $1.12 per share and finishes the year with an NAV of $30.34.
a. What is the return to an investor who holds 257.876 shares of this fund in his (nontaxable) retirement account?
b. What is the after-tax return for the same investor if these shares were held in an ordinary savings account? Assume that the investor is in the 30 percent tax bracket.
c. If the investment company allowed the investor to automatically reinvest his cash distribution in additional fund shares, how many additional shares could the investor acquire? Assume that the distribution occurred at year-end and that the proceeds from the distribution can be reinvested at the year-end NAV.

7. The Focus Fund is a mutual fund that holds long-term positions in a small number of non-dividend-paying stocks. Their holdings at the end of two recent years are as follows:

	YEAR 1		YEAR 2	
Stock	Shares	Price	Shares	Price
A	100,000	$45.25	100,000	$48.75
B	225,000	25.38	225,000	24.75
C	375,000	14.50	375,000	12.38
D	115,000	87.13	115,000	98.50
E	154,000	56.50	154,000	62.50
F	175,000	63.00	175,000	77.00
G	212,000	32.00	212,000	38.63
H	275,000	15.25	275,000	8.75
I	450,000	9.63	450,000	27.45
J	90,000	71.25	90,000	75.38
K	87,000	42.13	87,000	49.63
L	137,000	19.88	0	27.88
M	0	17.75	150,000	19.75
Cash		$3,542,000		$2,873,000
Expenses		$ 730,000		$ 830,000

At the end of both years, Focus Fund had 5,430,000 shares outstanding.

a. Calculate the net asset value for a share of the Focus Fund at the end of Year 1, being sure to include the cash position in the net total portfolio value.

b. Immediately after calculating its Year 1 NAV, Focus Fund sold its position in Stock L and purchased its position in Stock M (both transactions were done at Year 1 prices). Calculate the Year 2 NAV for Focus Fund and compute the growth rate in the fund share value on a percentage basis.

c. At the end of Year 2, how many fund shares of the Focus Fund could the manager redeem without having to liquidate her stock positions (i.e., using only the cash account)?

d. If immediately after calculating the Year 2 NAV the manager received investor redemption requests for 500,000 shares, how many shares of each stock would she have to sell in order to maintain the same proportional ownership position in each stock? Assume that she liquidates the entire cash position before she sells any stock holdings.

8. Mutual funds can effectively charge sales fees in one of three ways: front-end load fees, 12b-1 (i.e., annual) fees, or deferred (i.e., back-end) load fees. Assume that the SAS Fund offers its investors the choice of the following sales fee arrangements: (1) a 3 percent front-end load, (2) a 0.50 percent annual deduction, or (3) a 2 percent back-end load, paid at the liquidation of the investor's position. Also, assume that SAS Fund averages NAV growth of 12 percent per year.

   a. If you start with $100,000 in investment capital, calculate what an investment in SAS would be worth in three years under each of the proposed sales fee schemes. Which scheme would you choose?

   b. If your investment horizon were 10 years, would your answer in part a change? Demonstrate.

   c. Explain the relationship between the timing of the sales charge and your investment horizon. In general, if you intend to hold your position for a long time, which fee arrangement would you prefer?

CFA

9. *CFA Examination II (May 1995)*

   Clark & Kerns (C&K), a U.S. pension fund manager for more than 20 years, plans to establish offices in a European and a Pacific Rim country in order to manage pension funds located in those countries and invested in their local stock markets. Tony Clark, CFA, managing partner, learns that investment organizations and their affiliates in the European country perform three functions:

- consult with corporate pension sponsors on how the pension fund should be managed and by whom;
- manage their portfolios; and
- execute securities transactions as a broker for the funds.

Common practice in this country is to withhold disclosure of the ownership of business organizations. Clark believes that C&K must provide all three functions to compete effectively. He therefore decides to establish offices in Europe to offer all three services to prospective pension fund clients, through local organizations owned by C&K. The pension consulting organization will be Europension Group; the portfolio management firm will be C&K International; and the broker-dealer operation will be Alps Securities.

a. Briefly describe two AIMR Standards of Professional Conduct that apply to Clark, if C&K provides all three functions on a combined basis. Describe the specific duty Clark is required to perform to comply with these Standards.

Clark learns that a customary practice in the European country is to allocate at least 80 percent of pension fund assets to fixed-income securities.

b. Identify and briefly explain two AIMR Standards of Professional Conduct that apply to this situation.

Clark observes that portfolio managers in the Pacific Rim country frequently use insider information in their investment decisions. Because the pension fund management industry is performance oriented, Clark decides to adopt local investment practices as the only way to attract and retain local corporate clients in that country.

c. Identify and briefly explain two AIMR Standards of Professional Conduct that apply to this situation.

10. You have been asked to evaluate the investment performance of three different professional asset managers relative to each other and to the Standard and Poor's 500 index. After gathering quarterly return data over the past five years, you compute the following statistics:

Portfolio	Average Annual Return	Beta	Diversification Level
A	10.2%	0.82	86%
B	15.4	1.36	63
C	13.2	0.99	98
S&P	13.3	1.00	100

a. Based on this data, can you conclude that Manager A underperformed the market and Manager B outperformed the market? Why or why not?
b. What additional information do you think you would require in order to perform a compelling analysis of the investment performance of these managers?
c. What was the most likely investment objective followed by Portfolio Manager C? By Manager A?
d. What might explain the fact that Manager B's portfolio is so much less diversified than those run by Managers A and C?

References

Bekaert, Geert, and Michael S. Urias. "Diversification, Integration and Emerging Market Closed-End Funds." *Journal of Finance* 51, no. 3 (July 1996).

Bhatia, Sanjiv, ed. *Managing Endowment and Foundation Funds.* Charlottesville, Va.: Association for Investment Management and Research, 1996.

Brealey, Richard A. "How to Combine Active Management with Index Funds." *Journal of Portfolio Management* 12, no. 2 (winter 1986).

Carhart, Mark M. "On Persistence in Mutual Fund Performance." *Journal of Finance* 52, no. 1 (March 1997): 57–82.

Chordia, Tarun. "The Structure of Mutual Fund Charges." *Journal of Financial Economics* 41, no. 1 (May 1996): 3–39.

Ferson, Wayne E., and Rudi W. Schadt. "Measuring Fund Strategy and Performance in Changing Economic Conditions." *Journal of Finance* 51, no. 2 (June 1996).

Lakonishok, Josef, Andrei Shleifer, and Robert W. Vishny. "The Structure and Performance of the Money Management Industry." In *Brookings Papers on Economic Activity.* Washington, D.C.: Brookings Institute, 1992.

Peavy, John W. *Investment Counsel for Private Clients.* Charlottesville, Va.: Association for Investment Management and Research, 1993.

Pozen, Robert C. *The Mutual Fund Business.* Cambridge, Mass.: MIT Press, 1998.

Thaler, Richard. "Investor Sentiment and the Closed-End Fund Puzzle." *Journal of Finance* 46, no. 1 (March 1991).

Weiss, Kathleen. "The Post Offering Performance of Closed-End Funds." *Financial Management* 18, no. 3 (fall 1989).

Chapter 27 EVALUATION OF PORTFOLIO PERFORMANCE

After you read this chapter, you should be able to answer the following questions:

- What major requirements do clients expect from their portfolio managers?
- What can a portfolio manager do to attain superior performance?
- What is the peer group comparison method of evaluating an investor's performance?
- What is the Treynor portfolio performance measure?
- What is the Sharpe portfolio performance measure?
- What is the critical difference between the Treynor and Sharpe portfolio performance measures?
- What is the Jensen portfolio performance measure and how does it relate to the Treynor measure?
- What is the information ratio and how is it related to the other performance measures?
- When evaluating a sample of portfolios, how do you determine how well diversified they are?
- What is the bias found regarding the composite performance measures?
- What is the Fama portfolio performance measure and what information does it provide beyond other measures?
- What is attribution analysis and how can it be used to distinguish between a portfolio manager's market timing and security selection skills?
- What is the Roll benchmark error problem and what are the two factors that are affected when computing portfolio performance measures?
- What is the impact of global investing on the benchmark error problem?
- What are customized benchmarks?
- What are the important characteristics that any benchmark should possess?
- How do bond portfolio performance measures differ from equity portfolio performance measures?
- In the Wagner and Tito bond portfolio performance measure, what is the measure of risk used?
- What are the components of the Dietz, Fogler, and Hardy bond portfolio performance measure?
- What are the sources of return in the Fong, Pearson, and Vasicek bond portfolio performance measure?
- What are time-weighted and dollar-weighted returns and which should be reported under AIMR's Performance Presentation Standards?

Investors always are interested in evaluating the performance of their portfolios. It is both expensive and time consuming to analyze and select securities for a portfolio, so an individual, company, or institution must determine whether this effort is worth the time and money invested in it. Investors managing their own portfolios should evaluate their performance as should those who pay one or several professional money managers. In the latter case, it is imperative to determine whether the investment performance justifies the service's cost.

This chapter outlines the theory and practice of evaluating the performance of an investment portfolio. In the first section, we consider what is required of a portfolio manager. We pinpoint what to look for before we discuss techniques to evaluate portfolio managers.

In section two, we briefly discuss how performance was evaluated before portfolio theory and the CAPM were developed. The rest of the section contains a detailed discussion of four portfolio performance evaluation techniques (referred to as *composite performance measures*) that consider return and risk.

The third section applies these composite measures to gauge the performance of a selected sample of mutual funds. This demonstration analyzes how these measures relate to each other. Although some redundancy exists among the measures, each of them provides unique perspectives, so they are best viewed as complementary measures. We also consider a fifth measure that evaluates the components of performance. Because some observers have contended that these composite measures of performance are biased in favor of low-risk portfolios, we examine their arguments and the evidence for and against these contentions. The section concludes with an examination of attribution analysis, a measurement technique designed to establish the source of a portfolio manager's skill.

Section four identifies factors to consider when applying these measures. This includes the work of Roll, which questioned any evaluation technique that depends on the CAPM and a market portfolio. This controversy is referred to as the *benchmark problem.* We also discuss why this benchmark problem becomes larger when you begin investing globally. Notably, it affects both your measures of risk and your portfolio performance measures. The section concludes with a description of studies that have evaluated how reliable the composite measures are at predicting future performance.

In the fifth section, we discuss how factors that determine the performance of a bond portfolio differ from those that affect common stocks. Therefore, we consider several models developed to evaluate the performance of bond portfolios. Finally, we examine industry standards for calculating returns and reporting portfolio performance to investors.

WHAT IS REQUIRED OF A PORTFOLIO MANAGER?

There are two major requirements of a portfolio manager:

1. The ability to derive above-average returns for a given risk class
2. The ability to diversify the portfolio completely to eliminate all unsystematic risk

In terms of return, the first requirement is obvious, but the need to consider *risk* in this context was generally not apparent before the 1960s, when work in portfolio theory showed its significance. In modern theory, superior risk-adjusted returns can be derived through *either* superior timing or superior security selection.

An equity portfolio manager who can do a superior job of predicting the peaks or troughs of the equity market can adjust the portfolio's composition to anticipate market trends, holding a completely diversified portfolio of high-beta stocks through rising markets and favoring low-beta stocks and money market instruments during declining markets. Bigger gains in rising markets and smaller losses in declining markets give the portfolio manager above-average risk-adjusted returns.

A fixed-income portfolio manager with superior timing ability changes the portfolio's duration in anticipation of interest rate changes by increasing the duration of the portfolio in anticipation of failing interest rates and reducing the duration of the portfolio when rates are expected to rise. If properly executed, this bond portfolio management strategy likewise provides superior risk-adjusted returns.

As an alternative strategy, a portfolio manager and his or her analysts may try consistently to select undervalued stocks or bonds for a given risk class. Even without superior market timing, such a portfolio would likely experience above-average risk-adjusted returns.

The second factor to consider in evaluating a portfolio manager is the ability to diversify completely. As noted in Chapter 9, on average the market rewards investors only for bearing systematic (market) risk. Unsystematic risk is not considered when determining required returns because it can be eliminated in a diversified market portfolio. Because they can expect no reward for bearing this uncertainty, investors often want their portfolios completely diversified, which means they want the portfolio manager to eliminate most or all unsystematic risk. The level of diversification can be judged on the basis of the correlation between the portfolio returns and the returns for a market portfolio. A completely diversified portfolio is perfectly correlated with the fully diversified market portfolio.

These two requirements of a portfolio manager are important because some portfolio evaluation techniques take into account one requirement but not the other. Other techniques implicitly consider both factors, but do not differentiate between them.

COMPOSITE PORTFOLIO PERFORMANCE MEASURES

Portfolio Evaluation before 1960

At one time, investors evaluated portfolio performance almost entirely on the basis of the rate of return. They were aware of the concept of risk, but did not know how to quantify or measure it, so they could not consider it explicitly. Developments in portfolio theory in the early 1960s showed investors how to quantify and measure risk in terms of the variability of returns. Still, because no single measure combined both return and risk, the two factors had to be considered separately as researchers had done in several early studies.[1] Specifically, the investigators grouped portfolios into similar risk classes based on a measure of risk (such as the variance of return) and then compared the rates of return for alternative portfolios directly within these risk classes.

This section describes in detail the four major composite equity portfolio performance measures that combine risk and return performance into a single value. We describe each measure and its intent, and then demonstrate how to compute it and interpret the results. We also compare the measures and discuss how they differ and why they rank portfolios differently.

Peer Group Comparisons

Before examining measures of portfolio performance that adjust an investor's return for the level of investment risk, we first consider the concept of a **peer group comparison**. This method, which Kritzman describes as the most common manner of evaluating portfolio managers, collects the returns produced by a representative universe of investors over a specific period of time and displays them in a simple boxplot format.[2] To aid the comparison, the universe is typically divided into percentiles, which indicate the relative ranking of a given investor. For instance, a portfolio manager that produced a 1-year return of 12.4

---

[1]Irwin Friend, Marshall Blume, and Jean Crockett, *Mutual Funds and Other Institutional Investors* (New York: McGraw-Hill, 1970).

[2]See Mark P. Kritzman, "Quantitative Methods in Performance Measurement," in *Quantitative Methods for Financial Analysis,* 2d ed., ed. S. Brown and M. Kritzman (Homewood, Ill.: Dow Jones-Irwin, 1990).

percent would be in the 10th percentile if only nine other portfolios in a universe of 100 produced a higher return. Although these comparisons can get quite detailed, it is common for the boxplot graphic to include the maximum and minimum returns, as well as the returns falling at the 25th, 50th (i.e., the median), and 75th percentiles.

Figure 27.1 shows the returns from periods of varying length for a representative investor—labeled here as "U.S. Equity with Cash"—relative to its peer universe of other U.S. domestic equity managers.[3] Also included in the comparison are the periodic returns to three indexes of the overall market: Standard and Poor's 500, Russell 1000, and Russell 3000. The display shows return quartiles for investment periods ranging from 5 to 10 years, ending on June 30, 1996. In this example, the investor in question (indicated by the large dot) performed admirably, finishing above the median in each of the comparison periods. Indeed, the manager of this portfolio produced the largest 9-year return (16.5 percent), well above the median return of 13.0 percent. Notice, however, that although the investor's 10-year average return exceeds the 9-year level (16.6 percent), it falls below the fifth percentile, which, while still laudable, is no longer the best.

There are several potential problems with the peer group comparison method of evaluating an investor's performance. First, and foremost, the boxplots shown in Figure 27.1 do not make any explicit adjustment for the risk level of the portfolios in the universe. In fact, investment risk is only *implicitly* considered to the extent that all the portfolios in the universe have essentially the same level of volatility. This is not likely to be the case for any sizable peer group, particularly if the universe mixes portfolios with different investment styles. A second, related point is that it is almost impossible to form a truly comparable peer group that is large enough to make the percentile rankings valid and meaningful. Finally, by focusing on nothing more than relative returns, such a comparison loses sight of whether the investor in question—or any in the universe, for that matter—has accomplished his individual objectives and satisfied his investment constraints.

Treynor Portfolio Performance Measure

Treynor developed the first **composite measure** of portfolio performance that included risk.[4] He postulated two components of risk: (1) risk produced by general market fluctuations and (2) risk resulting from unique fluctuations in the portfolio securities. To identify risk due to market fluctuations, he introduced the *characteristic line,* which defines the relationship between the rates of return for a portfolio over time and the rates of return for an appropriate market portfolio, as we discussed in Chapter 9. He noted that the characteristic line's slope measures the *relative volatility* of the portfolio's returns in relation to returns for the aggregate market. As we also know from Chapter 9, this slope is the portfolio's beta coefficient. A higher slope (beta) characterizes a portfolio that is more sensitive to market returns and that has greater market risk.

Deviations from the characteristic line indicate unique returns for the portfolio relative to the market. These differences arise from the returns on individual stocks in the portfolio. In a completely diversified portfolio, these unique returns for individual stocks should cancel out. As the correlation of the portfolio with the market increases, unique risk declines and diversification improves. Because Treynor was not concerned about this aspect of portfolio performance, he gave no further consideration to the diversification measure.

---

[3]This example comes from Brian Singer, "Valuation of Portfolio Performance: Aggregate Return and Risk Analysis," *Journal of Performance Measurement* 1, no. 1 (fall 1996): 6–16, and was based on data from the Frank Russell Company.

[4]Jack L. Treynor, "How to Rate Management of Investment Funds," *Harvard Business Review* 43, no. 1 (January–February 1965): 63–75.

FIGURE 27.1 **AN ILLUSTRATIVE PEER GROUP COMPARISON**

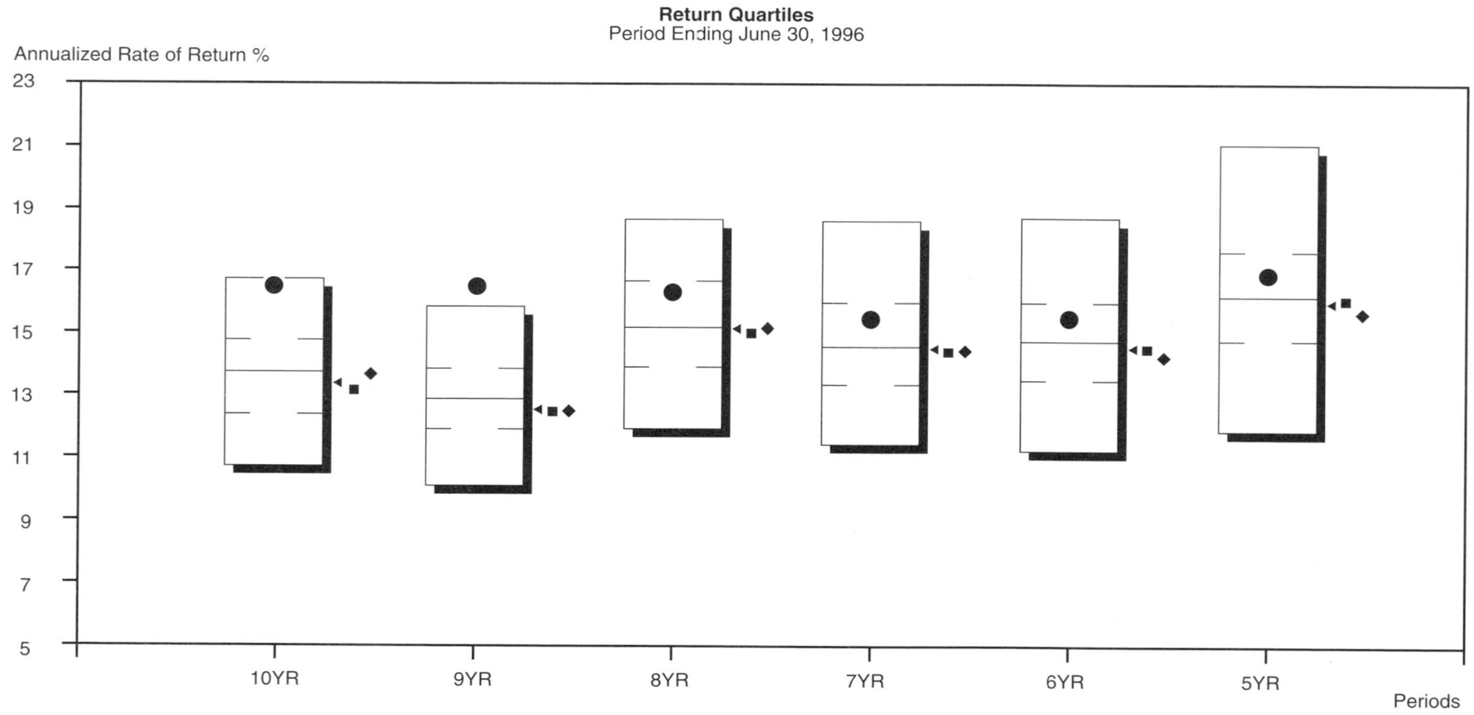

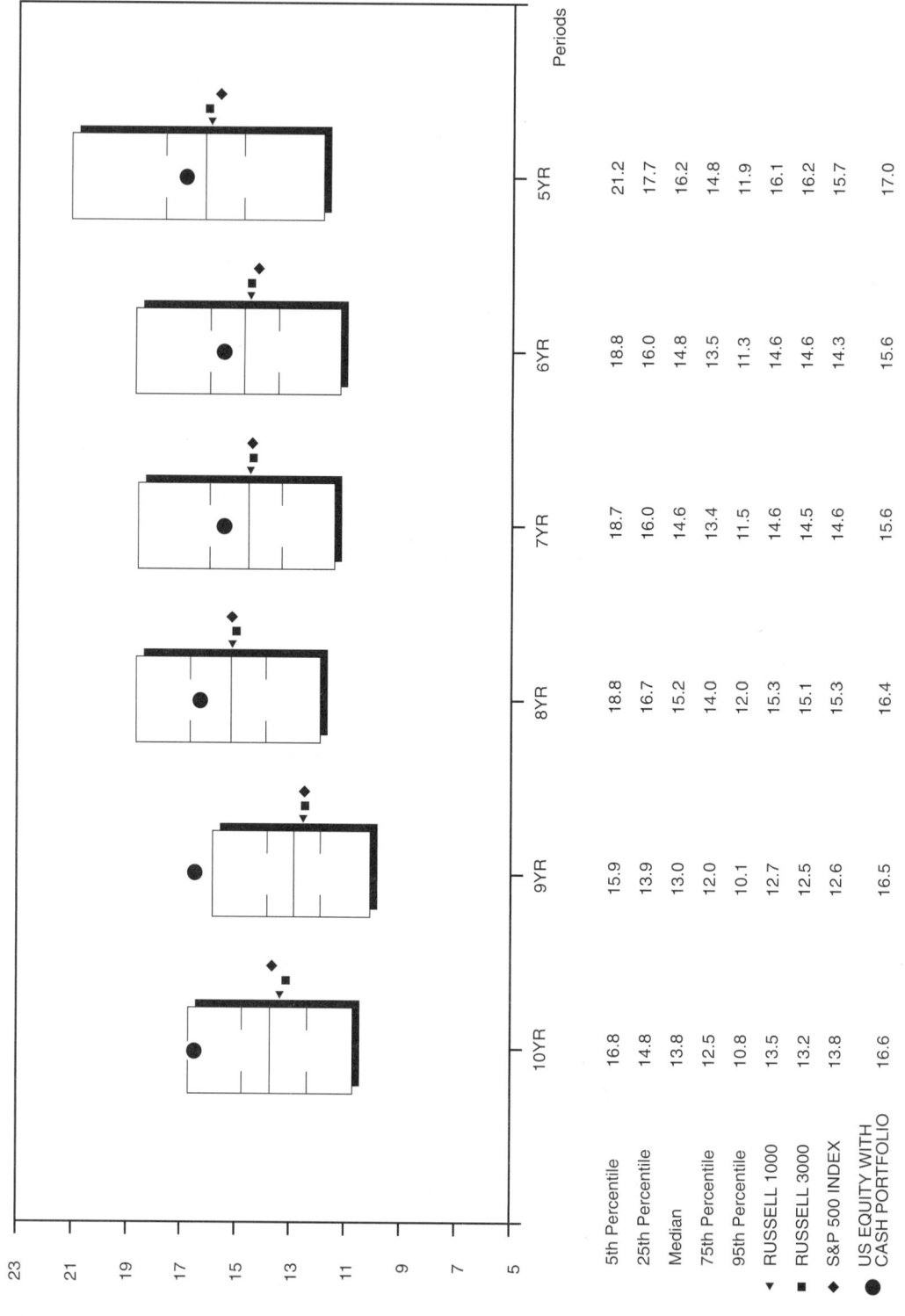

Return Quartiles
Period Ending June 30, 1996
Annualized Rate of Return %
23
21
19
17
15
13
11
9
7
5
10YR
9YR
8YR
7YR
6YR
5YR
Periods

	10YR	9YR	8YR	7YR	6YR	5YR
5th Percentile	16.8	15.9	18.8	18.7	18.8	21.2
25th Percentile	14.8	13.9	16.7	16.0	16.0	17.7
Median	13.8	13.0	15.2	14.6	14.8	16.2
75th Percentile	12.5	12.0	14.0	13.4	13.5	14.8
95th Percentile	10.8	10.1	12.0	11.5	11.3	11.9
◂ RUSSELL 1000	13.5	12.7	15.3	14.6	14.6	16.1
■ RUSSELL 3000	13.2	12.5	15.1	14.5	14.6	16.2
◆ S&P 500 INDEX	13.8	12.6	15.3	14.6	14.3	15.7
● US EQUITY WITH CASH PORTFOLIO	16.6	16.5	16.4	15.6	15.6	17.0

Source: Brian Singer, "Valuation of Portfolio Performance: Aggregate Return and Risk Analysis," *Journal of Performance Measurement* 1, no. 1 (fall 1996): 6–16.

TREYNOR'S COMPOSITE PERFORMANCE MEASURE Treynor was interested in a measure of performance that would apply to all investors—regardless of their risk preferences. Building on developments in capital market theory, he introduced a risk-free asset that could be combined with different portfolios to form a straight portfolio possibility line. He showed that rational, risk-averse investors would always prefer portfolio possibility lines with larger slopes because such high-slope lines would place investors on higher indifference curves. The slope of this portfolio possibility line (designated T) is equal to[5]

$$T = \frac{\bar{R}_i - \overline{RFR}}{\beta_i}$$

where:

$\bar{R}_i$ = the average rate of return for portfolio i during a specified time period
$\overline{RFR}$ = the average rate of return on a risk-free investment during the same time period
β_i = the slope of the fund's characteristic line during that time period (this indicates the portfolio's relative volatility)

As noted, a larger T value indicates a larger slope and a better portfolio for all investors (regardless of their risk preferences). Because the numerator of this ratio ($\bar{R}_i - \overline{RFR}$) is the *risk premium* and the denominator is a measure of risk, the total expression indicates the portfolio's *risk premium return per unit of risk.* All risk-averse investors would prefer to maximize this value. Note that the risk variable beta measures systematic risk and tells us nothing about the diversification of the portfolio. It *implicitly assumes* a completely diversified portfolio, which means that systematic risk is the relevant risk measure.

Comparing a portfolio's T value to a similar measure for the market portfolio indicates whether the portfolio would plot above the SML. Calculate the T value for the aggregate market as follows:

$$T_m = \frac{\bar{R}_m - \overline{RFR}}{\beta_m}$$

In this expression, β_m equals 1.0 (the market's beta) and indicates the slope of the SML. Therefore, a portfolio with a higher T value than the market portfolio plots above the SML, indicating superior risk-adjusted performance.

DEMONSTRATION OF COMPARATIVE TREYNOR MEASURES To understand how to use and interpret this measure of performance, suppose that during the most recent 10-year period, the average annual total rate of return (including dividends) on an aggregate market portfolio, such as the S&P 500, was 14 percent ($\bar{R}_m = 0.14$) and the average nominal rate of return on government T-bills was 8 percent ($\overline{RFR} = 0.08$). Assume that, as administrator of a large pension fund that has been divided among three money managers during the past 10 years, you must decide whether to renew your investment management contracts with all three managers. To do this, you must measure how they have performed.

Assume you are given the following results.

[5]The terms used in the formula differ from those used by Treynor but are consistent with our earlier discussion. Also, our discussion is concerned with general *portfolio* performance rather than being limited to mutual funds.

Investment Manager	Average Annual Rate of Return	Beta
W	0.12	0.90
X	0.16	1.05
Y	0.18	1.20

You can compute T values for the market portfolio and for each of the individual portfolio managers as follows:

$$T_M = \frac{0.14 - 0.08}{1.00} = 0.060$$

$$T_W = \frac{0.12 - 0.08}{0.90} = 0.044$$

$$T_X = \frac{0.16 - 0.08}{1.05} = 0.076$$

$$T_Y = \frac{0.18 - 0.08}{1.20} = 0.083$$

These results indicate that investment manager W not only ranked the lowest of the three managers, but did not perform as well as the aggregate market. In contrast, both X and Y beat the market portfolio, and manager Y performed somewhat better than manager X. In terms of the SML, both of their portfolios plotted above the line, as shown in Figure 27.2.

Very poor return performance or very good performance with very low risk may yield negative T values. An example of poor performance is a portfolio with both an average rate of return below the risk-free rate and a positive beta. For instance, in the preceding case assume that a fourth portfolio manager, Z, had a portfolio beta of 0.50, but an average rate of return of only 0.07. The T value would be

FIGURE 27.2 **PLOT OF PERFORMANCE ON SML (*T* MEASURE)**

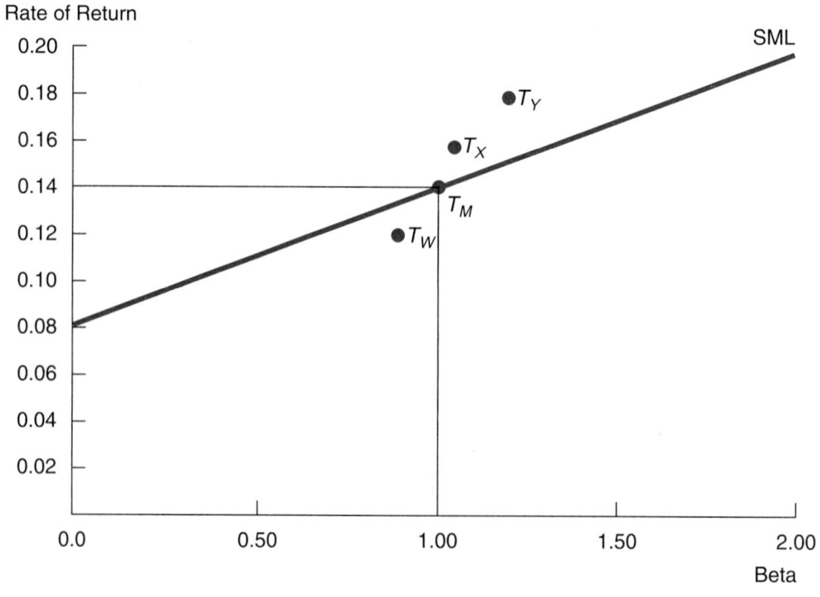
Rate of Return
0.20
0.18
0.16
0.14
0.12
0.10
0.08
0.06
0.04
0.02
SML
T_Y
T_X
T_M
T_W
0.0
0.50
1.00
1.50
2.00
Beta

$$T_Z = \frac{0.07 - 0.08}{0.50} = -0.02$$

Obviously, this performance would plot below the SML in Figure 27.2.

A portfolio with a *negative* beta and an average rate of return above the risk-free rate of return would likewise have a negative T value. In this case, however, it indicates exemplary performance. As an example, assume that portfolio manager G invested heavily in gold mining stocks during a period of great political and economic uncertainty. Because gold often has a negative correlation with most stocks, this portfolio's beta could be negative. If you were examining this portfolio after gold prices increased in value as a result of the uncertainty, you might find excellent returns. Assume that our gold portfolio G had a beta of −0.20 and yet experienced an average rate of return of 10 percent. The T value for this portfolio would then be

$$T_G = \frac{0.10 - 0.08}{-0.20} = -0.100$$

Although the T value is −0.100, if you plotted these results on a graph, it would indicate a position substantially above the SML in Figure 27.2.

Because negative betas can yield T values that give confusing results, it is preferable either to plot the portfolio on an SML graph or to compute the expected return for this portfolio using the SML equation and then compare this expected return to the actual return. This comparison will reveal whether the actual return was above or below expectations. In the preceding example for portfolio G, the expected return would be

$$\begin{aligned} E(R_G) &= RFR + \beta_i(R_m - RFR) \\ &= 0.08 + (-0.20)(0.06) \\ &= 0.08 - 0.012 \\ &= 0.068 \end{aligned}$$

Comparing this expected (required) rate of return of 6.8 percent to the actual return of 10 percent shows that portfolio manager G has done a superior job.

Sharpe Portfolio Performance Measure

Sharpe likewise conceived of a composite measure to evaluate the performance of mutual funds.[6] The measure followed closely his earlier work on the capital asset pricing model (CAPM), dealing specifically with the capital market line (CML).

The **Sharpe measure** of portfolio performance (designated S) is stated as follows:

$$S_i = \frac{\bar{R}_i - \overline{RFR}}{\sigma_i}$$

where:

$\bar{R}_i$ = the average rate of return for portfolio i during a specified time period
$\overline{RFR}$ = the average rate of return on risk-free assets during the same time period
σ_i = the standard deviation of the rate of return for portfolio i during the time period

[6] William F. Sharpe, "Mutual Fund Performance," *Journal of Business* 39, no. 1, part 2 (January 1966): 119–138. For a more recent interpretation of this measure, also see William F. Sharpe, "The Sharpe Ratio," *Journal of Portfolio Management* 21, no. 1 (fall 1994): 49–59.

This composite measure of portfolio performance clearly is similar to the Treynor measure; however, it seeks to measure the *total risk* of the portfolio by including the standard deviation of returns rather than considering only the systematic risk summarized by beta. Because the numerator is the portfolio's risk premium, this measure indicates the *risk premium return earned per unit of total risk.* In terms of capital market theory, this portfolio performance measure uses total risk to compare portfolios to the CML, whereas the Treynor measure examines portfolio performance in relation to the SML.

DEMONSTRATION OF COMPARATIVE SHARPE MEASURES The following examples use the Sharpe measure of performance. Again, assume that $\bar{R}_m = 0.14$ and $\overline{RFR} = 0.08$. Suppose you are told that the standard deviation of the annual rate of return for the market portfolio over the past 10 years was 20 percent ($\sigma_m = 0.20$). Now you want to examine the performance of the following portfolios:

Portfolio	Average Annual Rate of Return	Standard Deviation of Return
D	0.13	0.18
E	0.17	0.22
F	0.16	0.23

The Sharpe measures for these portfolios are as follows:

$$S_M = \frac{0.14 - 0.08}{0.20} = 0.300$$

$$S_D = \frac{0.13 - 0.08}{0.18} = 0.278$$

$$S_E = \frac{0.17 - 0.08}{0.22} = 0.409$$

$$S_F = \frac{0.16 - 0.08}{0.23} = 0.348$$

The D portfolio had the lowest risk premium return per unit of total risk, failing even to perform as well as the aggregate market portfolio. In contrast, portfolios E and F performed better than the aggregate market: portfolio E did better than portfolio F.

Given the market portfolio results during this period, it is possible to draw the CML. If we plot the results for portfolios D, E, and F on this graph, as shown in Figure 27.3, we see that portfolio D plots below the line, whereas the E and F portfolios are above the line, indicating superior risk-adjusted performance.

TREYNOR VERSUS SHARPE MEASURE The Sharpe portfolio performance measure uses the standard deviation of returns as the measure of risk, whereas the Treynor performance measure uses beta (systematic risk). The Sharpe measure, therefore, evaluates the portfolio manager on the basis of both rate of return performance and diversification.

For a completely diversified portfolio, one without any unsystematic risk, the two measures give identical rankings because the total variance of the completely diversified portfolio is its systematic variance. Alternatively, a poorly diversified portfolio could have a high ranking on the basis of the Treynor performance measure but a much lower ranking on the basis of the Sharpe performance measure. Any difference in rank would come directly from a difference in diversification.

FIGURE 27.3

PLOT OF PERFORMANCE ON CML (S MEASURE)

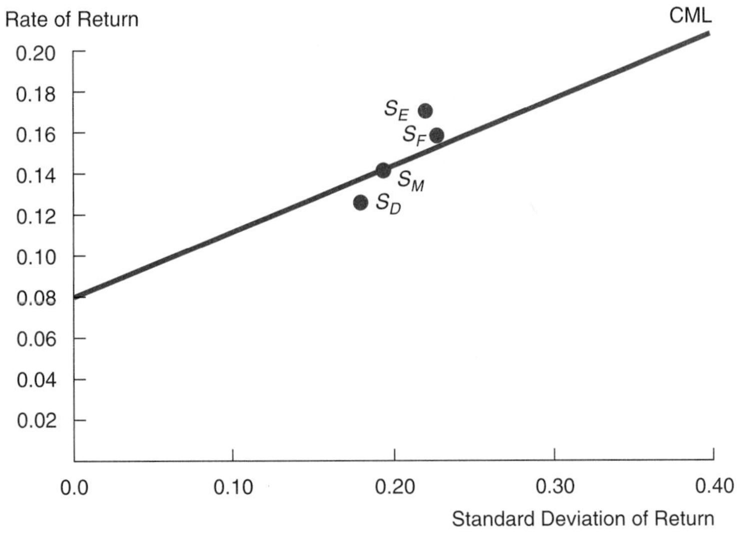
Rate of Return
CML
0.20
0.18
0.16
0.14
0.12
0.10
0.08
0.06
0.04
0.02
S_E
S_F
S_M
S_D
0.0
0.10
0.20
0.30
0.40
Standard Deviation of Return

Therefore, these two performance measures provide complementary yet different information, and both measures should be used. If you are dealing with a group of well-diversified portfolios, as many mutual funds are, the two measures provide similar rankings.

A disadvantage of the Treynor and Sharpe measures is that they produce relative, but not absolute, rankings of portfolio performance. That is, the Sharpe measures for portfolios E and F illustrated in Figure 27.3 show that both generated risk-adjusted returns above the market. Further, E's risk-adjusted performance measure is larger than F's. What we cannot say with certainty, however, is whether any of these differences are statistically significant.

JENSEN PORTFOLIO PERFORMANCE MEASURE

The **Jensen measure** is similar to the measures already discussed because it is based on the capital asset pricing model (CAPM).[7] All versions of the CAPM calculate the expected one-period return on any security or portfolio by the following expression:

$$E(R_j) = RFR + \beta_j[E(R_m) - RFR]$$

where:

$E(R_j)$ = the expected return on security or portfolio j
RFR = the one-period risk-free interest rate
β_j = the systematic risk (beta) for security or portfolio j
$E(R_m)$ = the expected return on the market portfolio of risky assets

The expected return and the risk-free return vary for different periods. Consequently, we are concerned with the time series of expected rates of return for security or portfolio *j*. Moreover, assuming the asset pricing model is empirically valid, you can express the expectations formula in terms of *realized* rates of return as follows:

[7]Michael C. Jensen, "The Performance of Mutual Funds in the Period 1945–1964," *Journal of Finance* 23, no. 2 (May 1968): 389–416.

$$R_{jt} = RFR_t + \beta_j[R_{mt} - RFR_t] + U_{jt}$$

This equation states that the realized rate of return on a security or portfolio during a given time period should be a linear function of the risk-free rate of return during the period, plus a risk premium that depends on the systematic risk of the security or portfolio during the period plus a random error term.

Subtracting the risk-free return from both sides, we have

$$R_{jt} - RFR_t = \beta_j[R_{mt} - RFR_t] + U_{jt}$$

This shows that the risk premium earned on the *j*th portfolio is equal to β_j times a market risk premium plus a random error term. In this form, an intercept for the regression is not expected if all assets and portfolios were in equilibrium.

Alternatively, superior portfolio managers who forecast market turns or consistently select undervalued securities earn higher risk premiums than those implied by this model. Specifically, superior portfolio managers have consistently positive random error terms because the actual returns for their portfolios consistently exceed the expected returns implied by this model. To detect and measure this superior performance, you must allow for an intercept (a nonzero constant) that measures any positive or negative difference from the model. Consistent positive differences cause a positive intercept, whereas consistent negative differences (inferior performance) cause a negative intercept. With an intercept or nonzero constant, the earlier equation becomes

$$R_{jt} - RFR_t = \alpha_j + \beta_j[R_{mt} - RFR_t] + U_{jt}$$

In this equation, the α_j value indicates whether the portfolio manager is superior or inferior in market timing and/or stock selection. A superior manager has a significant positive α (or "alpha") value because of the consistent positive residuals. In contrast, an inferior manager's returns consistently fall short of expectations based on the CAPM model giving consistently negative residuals. In such a case, α is a significant negative value.

The performance of a portfolio manager with no forecasting ability but not clearly inferior equals that of a naive buy-and-hold policy. In the equation, because the rate of return on such a portfolio typically matches the returns you expect on the basis of the CAPM, the residual returns generally are randomly positive and negative. This gives a constant term that differs insignificantly from zero, indicating that the portfolio manager basically matched the market on a risk-adjusted basis.

Therefore, the α represents how much of the rate of return on the portfolio is attributable to the manager's ability to derive above-average returns adjusted for risk. Superior risk-adjusted returns indicate that the manager is good at either predicting market turns, or selecting undervalued issues for the portfolio, or both.

APPLYING THE JENSEN MEASURE The Jensen measure of performance requires using a different *RFR* for each time interval during the sample period. For example, to examine the performance of a fund manager over a 10-year period using yearly intervals, you must examine the fund's annual returns less the return on risk-free assets for each year, and relate this to the annual return on the market portfolio less the same risk-free rate. This contrasts with the Treynor and Sharpe composite measures, which examine the *average* returns for the total period for all variables (the portfolio, the market, and the risk-free asset).

Also, like the Treynor measure, the Jensen measure does not directly consider the portfolio manager's ability to diversify because it calculates risk premiums in terms of systematic risk. As noted earlier, to evaluate the performance of a group of well-diversified portfolios such as mutual funds, this is likely to be a reasonable assumption. Jensen's analysis of mutual fund performance showed that complete diversification was a fairly reasonable assumption because the funds typically correlated with the market at rates above 0.90.

THE INFORMATION RATIO PERFORMANCE MEASURE

Closely related to the statistics just presented is another widely used performance measure: the **information ratio**. Also known as an *appraisal ratio,* this statistic measures a portfolio's average return in excess of that of a comparison, or **benchmark**, portfolio divided by the standard deviation of this excess return. Formally, the information ratio (*IR*) is calculated as:

$$IR_j = \frac{R_j - R_b}{\sigma_{ER}} = \frac{ER_j}{\sigma_{ER}}$$

where:

IR_j = the information ratio for portfolio j
R_j = the average return for portfolio j during the specified time period
R_b = the average return for the benchmark portfolio during the period
σ_{ER} = the standard deviation of the excess return during the period

To interpret *IR,* notice that the mean excess return in the numerator represents the investor's ability to use her talent and information to generate a portfolio return that differs from that of the benchmark against which her performance is being measured (e.g., the Standard and Poor's 500 index). Conversely, the denominator measures the amount of residual (unsystematic) risk that the investor incurred in pursuit of those excess returns. The coefficient σ_{ER} is sometimes called the *tracking error* of the investor's portfolio and it is a "cost" of active management in the sense that fluctuations in the periodic ER_j values represent random noise beyond an investor's control that could hurt performance. Thus, the *IR* can be viewed as a benefit-to-cost ratio that assesses the quality of the investor's information deflated by unsystematic risk generated by the investment process.

Goodwin has noted that the Sharpe ratio is a special case of the *IR* where the risk-free asset is the benchmark portfolio, despite the fact that this interpretation violates the spirit of a statistic that should have a value of zero for any passively managed portfolio.[8] More importantly, he also showed that if excess portfolio returns are estimated with historical data using the same single-factor regression equation used to compute Jensen's alpha, the *IR* simplifies to:

$$IR_j = \frac{\alpha_j}{\sigma_U}$$

where:

σ_U = the standard error of the regression[9]

Finally, he showed that one way an information ratio based on periodic returns measured T times per year could be annualized is as follows:

---

[8]See Thomas H. Goodwin, "The Information Ratio," *Financial Analysts Journal* 54, no. 4 (July–August 1998): 34–43.

[9]The development of this form of the information ratio is credited to Jack L. Treynor and Fischer Black, "How to Use Security Analysis to Improve Security Selection," *Journal of Business* 46, no. 1 (January 1973): 66–86.

$$\text{Annualized } IR = \frac{(T)\alpha_j}{\sqrt{T}\,\sigma_U} = \sqrt{T}\,(IR)$$

For instance, an investor that generated a quarterly ratio of 0.25 would have an annualized *IR* of 0.50 (= $\sqrt{4} \times 0.25$).

Grinold and Kahn have argued that reasonable information ratio levels should range from 0.50 to 1.00, with an investor having an *IR* of 0.50 being good and one with an *IR* of 1.00 being exceptional.[10] These, however, appear to be exceptionally difficult hurdles to clear. Goodwin studied the performance of more than 200 professional equity and fixed-income portfolio managers with various investment styles over a 10-year period. He found that the *IR* of the median manager in each style group was positive but that the ratio never exceeded 0.50. Thus, although the average manager appears to add value to investors—α (and hence *IR*) is greater than zero—she doesn't qualify as "good." Further, no style group had more than 3 percent of its managers deliver an *IR* in excess of 1.00. Information ratio histograms summarizing this research are shown in Figure 27.4.

APPLICATION OF PORTFOLIO PERFORMANCE MEASURES

To apply these measures, we selected 20 open-end mutual funds and used monthly data for the 5-year period from 1993 to 1997. The monthly rates of return for the first fund (Aim Constellation Fund) and the S&P 500 are contained in Table 27.1. The total rate of return for each month is computed as follows:

$$R_{it} = \frac{EP_{it} + Div_{it} + Cap.Dist._{it} - BP_{it}}{BP_{it}}$$

where:

R_{it} = **the total rate of return on fund *i* during month *t***
EP_{it} = **the ending price for fund *i* during month *t***
Div_{it} = **the dividend payments made by fund *i* during month *t***
$Cap.Dist._{it}$ = **the capital gain distributions made by fund *i* during month *t***
BP_{it} = **the beginning price for fund *i* during month *t***

These return computations do not take into account any sales charges by the funds. Given the monthly results for the fund and the aggregate market (as represented by the S&P 500), you can compute the composite measures presented in Table 27.1.

The arithmetic average annual rate of return for Aim Constellation Fund was 16.27 percent versus 19.13 percent for the market, and the fund's beta was greater than 1.00 (1.053). Using the average annual rate of T-bills of 4.57 percent as the $\overline{RFR}$, the Treynor measure for the Aim Constellation Fund (T_i) was substantially smaller than the comparable measure for the market (T_m) (11.109 versus 14.560). Likewise, the standard deviation of returns for Aim Constellation was greater than the market's (15.63 versus 10.58). Partly because of the higher standard deviation, the Sharpe measure for the fund (S_i) was smaller than the measure for the market (S_m) (0.748 versus 1.377).

Finally, a regression of the fund's annual risk premium ($R_{it} - RFR_t$) and the market's annual risk premium ($R_{mt} - RFR_t$) indicated a negative intercept (constant) value of −0.308,

[10] See Richard C. Grinold and Ronald N. Kahn, *Active Portfolio Management* (Chicago, Ill.: Probus Publishing, 1995).

FIGURE 27.4 **INFORMATION RATIOS FOR SIX INVESTMENT STYLES: 1986:Q1 TO 1995:Q4**

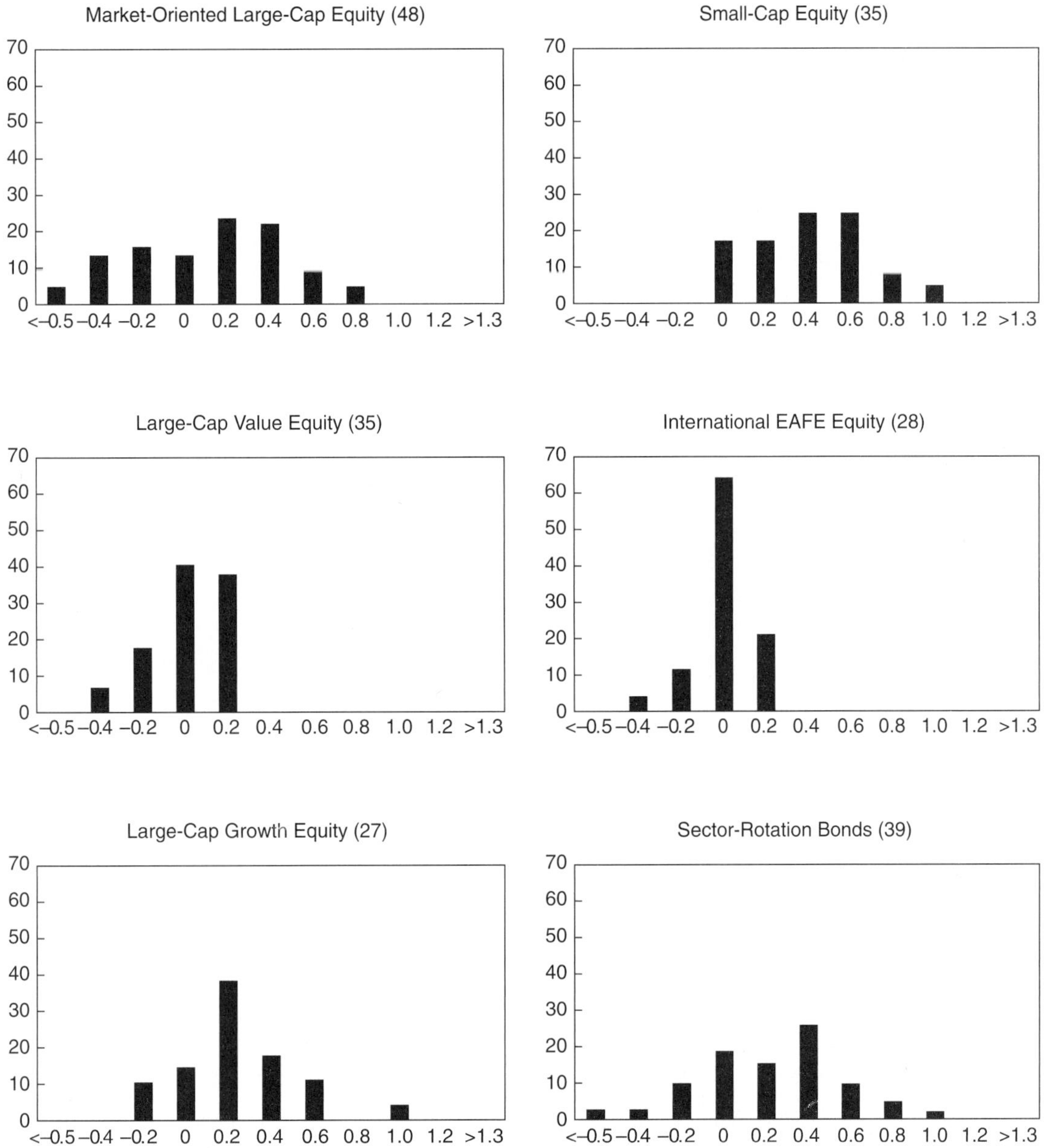
Market-Oriented Large-Cap Equity (48)
Small-Cap Equity (35)
Large-Cap Value Equity (35)
International EAFE Equity (28)
Large-Cap Growth Equity (27)
Sector-Rotation Bonds (39)
70
60
50
40
30
20
10
0
<-0.5 -0.4 -0.2 0 0.2 0.4 0.6 0.8 1.0 1.2 >1.3

Note: Midpoints of ranges. Information ratios are on the *x*-axes; relative frequencies, in percentages, are on the *y*-axes.

Source: Thomas H. Goodwin, "The Information Ratio," *Financial Analysts Journal* 54, no. 4 (July–August 1998): 34–43.

but was not statistically significant. If this intercept value had been significant, Aim Constellation's risk-adjusted annual rate of return would have averaged about 0.31 percent below the market on a reliable basis.

TOTAL SAMPLE RESULTS The overall results in Table 27.2 generally are consistent with the findings of earlier studies. Our sample was rather casually selected because

TABLE 27.1

EXAMPLE OF PORTFOLIO EVALUATION MEASURES COMPUTATION USING AIM CONSTELLATION FUND

	R_{it}	R_{mt}	RFR_t	$R_{it} - RFR_t$	$R_{mt} - RFR_t$
Jan. 1993	2.88	0.84	0.24	2.64	0.59
Feb. 1993	−6.06	1.36	0.25	−6.30	1.12
Mar. 1993	4.37	2.11	0.24	4.13	1.87
Apr. 1993	−3.59	−2.42	0.24	−3.83	−2.66
May 1993	7.51	2.67	0.26	7.26	2.41
Jun. 1993	1.60	0.29	0.25	1.35	0.04
Jul. 1993	−0.82	−0.40	0.25	−1.07	−0.66
Aug. 1993	4.64	3.79	0.25	4.39	3.54
Sep. 1993	3.47	−0.79	0.24	3.22	−1.03
Oct. 1993	0.12	2.07	0.25	−0.13	1.81
Nov. 1993	−1.82	−0.95	0.26	−2.08	−1.21
Dec. 1993	4.60	1.21	0.25	4.35	0.96
⋮	⋮	⋮	⋮	⋮	⋮
Jan. 1997	4.39	6.24	0.42	3.98	5.83
Feb. 1997	−4.40	0.79	0.43	−4.82	0.36
Mar. 1997	−6.35	−4.10	0.44	−6.78	−4.54
Apr. 1997	1.65	5.96	0.43	1.23	5.54
May 1997	10.08	6.08	0.40	9.68	5.68
Jun. 1997	3.29	4.48	0.42	2.88	4.06
Jul. 1997	10.70	7.95	0.43	10.27	7.53
Aug. 1997	−1.46	−5.60	0.42	−1.88	−6.02
Sep. 1997	4.90	5.47	0.41	4.49	5.06
Oct. 1997	−6.40	−3.34	0.42	−6.83	−3.76
Nov. 1997	−1.16	4.63	0.42	−1.59	4.20
Dec. 1997	−1.27	1.72	0.43	−1.71	1.28
Mean	16.27	19.13	4.57		
Standard Deviation	15.63	10.58	0.28		
Beta	1.053				
S_i	0.748				
S_m	1.377				
T_i	11.109				
T_m	14.560				
Jensen Intercept	−0.308				
R^2_{im}	0.506				

we intended it for demonstration purposes only. The mean annual return for all the funds was below the market return (17.23 versus 19.13). Considering only the rate of return, 2 of the 20 funds outperformed the market.

The R^2 for a portfolio with the market can serve as a measure of diversification. The closer the R^2 is to 1.00, the more completely diversified the portfolio. The average R^2 for our sample was not very high at 0.631, and the range was quite large, from 0.116 to 0.963. This indicates that many of the funds were not well diversified. Of the 20 funds, 11 had R^2 values less than 0.75.

The two risk measures (standard deviation and beta) also show a wide degree of dispersion, but generally are consistent with expectations. Specifically, 10 of the 20 funds had larger standard deviations than the market, and the mean standard deviation was larger (11.28 versus 10.58). Only three of the funds had a beta above 1.00; the average beta was 0.800.

TABLE 27.2 PERFORMANCE MEASURES FOR 20 SELECTED MUTUAL FUNDS

	Average Annual Rate of Return	Standard Deviation	Beta	R^2	Treynor		Sharpe		Jensen	
Aim Constellation A Fund	16.27	15.63	1.053	0.507	11.109	(18)	0.748	(17)	−0.308	(18)
Dean Witter Developing Growth B Fund	19.01	19.30	1.065	0.340	13.561	(15)	0.748	(16)	−0.096	(16)
Dreyfus Growth Opportunity Fund	11.68	12.35	0.943	0.652	7.532	(20)	0.575	(20)	−0.552	(20)
Fasciano Fund	16.91	10.04	0.563	0.352	21.906	(2)	1.229	(11)	0.350	(2)
Fidelity Magellan Fund	18.04	11.65	0.934	0.719	14.415	(12)	1.155	(13)	−0.016	(12)
Fidelity Puritan Fund	15.38	7.75	0.653	0.794	16.544	(7)	1.394	(5)	0.105	(7)
Gabelli Asset Fund	17.86	9.06	0.750	0.766	17.725	(4)	1.467	(4)	0.196	(5)
Guardian Park Avenue A Fund	20.72	10.75	0.923	0.824	17.497	(6)	1.502	(3)	0.224	(3)
IDS Mutual A Fund	12.83	6.85	0.584	0.814	14.128	(13)	1.205	(12)	−0.020	(13)
Income Fund of America	14.33	6.13	0.505	0.759	19.317	(3)	1.592	(2)	0.203	(4)
Investment Company of America Fund	16.85	9.13	0.847	0.963	14.493	(11)	1.345	(8)	−0.005	(11)
Janus Venture Fund	12.41	13.05	0.666	0.291	11.764	(17)	0.600	(19)	−0.155	(17)
Kemper Technology A Fund	18.70	20.05	1.298	0.469	10.882	(19)	0.705	(18)	−0.403	(19)
Lindner Dividend Fund	33.44	10.79	0.347	0.116	83.171	(1)	2.674	(1)	1.986[a]	(1)
Oppenheimer Growth A Fund	15.14	10.11	0.796	0.693	13.281	(16)	1.045	(14)	−0.081	(15)
Putnam Fund for Growth & Income A	17.71	9.46	0.858	0.919	15.315	(9)	1.389	(6)	0.053	(9)
Templeton World I Fund	17.95	10.65	0.763	0.574	17.533	(5)	1.256	(10)	0.181	(6)
T. Rowe Price Growth Stock Fund	17.72	9.92	0.870	0.862	15.099	(10)	1.325	(9)	0.037	(10)
Value Line Special Situations Fund	15.88	14.80	0.809	0.334	13.973	(14)	0.764	(15)	−0.040	(14)
Vanguard Wellington Fund	15.73	8.11	0.712	0.862	15.678	(8)	1.377	(7)	0.067	(8)
Mean	17.23	11.28	0.800	0.631	18.246		1.205		0.086	
S&P 500	19.13	10.58	1.000	1.000	14.560		1.377		0.000	
90-Day T-Bill Rate	4.57	0.28								

[a]Significant at the 0.05 level

Alternative measures ranked the performance of individual funds somewhat differently. Using the Treynor measure, 10 of the 20 funds had a value better than that of the market; only 7 funds had a Sharpe measure as large as that of the market. The Jensen measure indicated that 10 of the 20 had positive intercepts, but only one of these was statistically significant (none of the negative intercepts were significant). The mean values for the Sharpe and Treynor measures were smaller and greater, respectively, than the aggregate market figure. These results indicate that, on average, and without considering transaction costs, this sample of funds had essentially comparable risk-adjusted results to the market during this time period.

You should analyze the individual funds and consider each of the components: rate of return, risk (both standard deviation and beta), and the R^2 as a measure of diversification. One might expect the best performance by funds with low diversification because they apparently are attempting to beat the market by being unique in their selection or timing. This seems to be true for the top-performing funds, such as Lindner Dividend Fund and Fasciano Fund as well as some unsuccessful funds that had poor diversification but low returns, such as the Value Line Special Situations Fund.

Table 27.3 reports information ratios for these 20 funds. To interpret the display, consider that the Fasciano Fund had a monthly *IR* value of 0.148, which was calculated by dividing its alpha (0.350) by its regression standard error (2.37). This statistic is then annualized to 0.511 by multiplying the monthly *IR* by the square root of 12. Notice that 10 of the 20 funds had positive *IR* levels, which follows directly from the number of funds that had a positive value for Jensen's alpha measure. The mean annualized *IR* for the

TABLE 27.3 **INFORMATION RATIOS FOR 20 MUTUAL FUNDS**

	Alpha	Standard Error	*IR*	Annualized *IR*	Rank
Aim Constellation A Fund	−0.308	3.22	−0.095	−0.331	(19)
Dean Witter Developing Growth B Fund	−0.096	4.60	−0.021	−0.072	(14)
Dreyfus Growth Opportunity Fund	−0.552	2.14	−0.258	−0.894	(20)
Fasciano Fund	0.350	2.37	0.148	0.511	(5)
Fidelity Magellan Fund	−0.016	1.82	−0.009	−0.030	(11)
Fidelity Puritan Fund	0.105	1.05	0.100	0.347	(6)
Gabelli Asset Fund	0.196	1.29	0.152	0.525	(4)
Guardian Park Avenue A Fund	0.224	1.32	0.169	0.586	(3)
IDS Mutual A Fund	−0.020	0.88	−0.023	−0.080	(15)
Income Fund of America	0.203	0.88	0.230	0.798	(2)
Investment Company of America Fund	−0.005	0.52	−0.009	−0.033	(12)
Janus Venture Fund	−0.155	3.23	−0.048	−0.166	(16)
Kemper Technology A Fund	−0.403	4.29	−0.094	−0.326	(18)
Lindner Dividend Fund	1.986	2.99	0.665	2.304	(1)
Oppenheimer Growth A Fund	−0.081	1.64	−0.050	−0.172	(17)
Putnam Fund for Growth & Income A	0.053	0.79	0.067	0.234	(9)
Templeton World I Fund	0.181	2.05	0.088	0.306	(7)
T. Rowe Price Growth Stock Fund	0.037	1.08	0.035	0.120	(10)
Value Line Special Situations Fund	−0.040	3.55	−0.011	−0.039	(13)
Vanguard Wellington Fund	0.067	0.89	0.076	0.263	(8)
Mean:	0.086	2.029	0.056	0.193	
Median:	0.016	1.730	0.013	0.045	

sample was 0.193, well below the Grinold-Kahn standard for "good" performance of 0.500. Further, this average statistic is even biased upward because of the exceptional performance of one fund (Lindner Dividend Fund); the median annualized *IR* for the group was only 0.045. Thus, although this collection of funds added value, on average, to their investors, it did so modestly after accounting for tracking error costs.

POTENTIAL BIAS OF ONE-PARAMETER MEASURES Friend and Blume pointed out that, theoretically, the composite measures of performance should be independent of alternative measures of risk because they are *risk-adjusted* measures.[11] An analysis of the relationship between the composite measures of performance and two measures of risk (standard deviation and beta) for 200 random portfolios from the NYSE indicated a significant *inverse* relationship (the risk-adjusted performance of low-risk portfolios was better than the comparable performance for high-risk portfolios).

Subsequently, Klemkosky examined the relationship between composite performance measures and risk measures using actual mutual fund data in contrast to the random portfolio data used by Friend and Blume.[12] Beyond the preceding risk-adjusted performance measures, the author derived two statistics that computed the excess return above the risk-free rate relative to the semistandard deviation and relative to the mean absolute deviation as risk measures. The results indicated a positive bias—that is, a *positive* relationship between the composite performance measures and the risk involved. This was especially true

[11]Irwin Friend and Marshall Blume, "Measurement of Portfolio Performance under Uncertainty," *American Economic Review* 60, no. 4 (September 1970): 561–575.

[12]Robert C. Klemkosky, "The Bias in Composite Performance Measures," *Journal of Financial and Quantitative Analysis* 8, no. 3 (June 1973): 505–514.

for the Treynor and Jensen measures. The performance measures that used the mean absolute deviation and the semistandard deviation as risk proxies were less biased than the three standard performance measures. He concluded that although a bias might exist, one could not be certain of its direction. More recently, Leland has shown that alpha can be biased downward for those portfolios designed to limit downside risk.[13]

COMPONENTS OF INVESTMENT PERFORMANCE

Following the work of Treynor, Sharpe, and Jensen, Fama suggested a somewhat finer breakdown of performance.[14] The basic premise for Fama's technique is that *overall performance* of a portfolio, which is its return in excess of the risk-free rate, can be decomposed into measures of risk-taking and security selection skill. That is:

$$\text{Overall Performance} = \text{Excess Return} = (\text{Portfolio Risk}) + (\text{Selectivity})$$

Further, if there is a difference between the risk level specified by the investor and the actual risk level adopted by the portfolio manager (in cases where these are separate people), this calculation can be further refined to:

$$\text{Overall Performance} = [(\text{Investor's Risk}) + (\text{Manager's Risk})] + (\text{Selectivity})$$

Notice that the *selectivity* component represents the portion of the portfolio's actual return beyond that available to an unmanaged portfolio with identical systematic risk. Thus, this selectivity measure is used to assess the manager's investment prowess.

As with the preceding performance statistics, Fama's evaluation model assumes that returns to managed portfolios can be compared to those of naively selected portfolios with similar risk levels. The technique is based on the *ex ante* market line summarizing the equilibrium relationship between expected return and risk for portfolio j:

$$E(\hat{R}_j) = RFR + \left[\frac{E(\hat{R}_m) - RFR}{\sigma(\hat{R}_m)}\right]\frac{\text{Cov}(\hat{R}_j, \hat{R}_m)}{\sigma(\hat{R}_m)}$$

$\text{Cov}(R_j, R_m)$ is the covariance between the returns for portfolio j and the return on the market portfolio. This equation indicates that the expected return on portfolio j is the riskless rate of interest, RFR, plus a risk premium that is $[E(\tilde{R}_m) - RFR]/\sigma(\tilde{R}_m)$, called the *market price per unit of risk,* times the risk of asset j, which is $[\text{Cov}(\tilde{R}_j, \tilde{R}_m)]/\sigma(\tilde{R}_m)$.

If a portfolio manager believes that the market is not completely efficient and that she can make better judgments than the market, then an *ex post* version of this market line can provide a benchmark for the manager's performance. Given that the risk variable, $\text{Cov}(R_j, R_m)/\sigma(R_m)$, can be denoted β_x, the *ex post* market line is as follows:

$$R_x = RFR + \left(\frac{R_m - RFR}{\sigma(R_m)}\right)\beta_x$$

This *ex post* market line provides the benchmark used to evaluate managed portfolios in a sequence of more complex measures.

---

[13]Hayne E. Leland, "Beyond Mean-Variance: Performance Measurement in a Nonsymmetrical World," *Financial Analysts Journal* 55, no. 1 (January–February 1999): 27–36.

[14]Eugene F. Fama, "Components of Investment Performance," *Journal of Finance* 27, no. 3 (June 1972): 551–567.

FIGURE 27.5 **AN ILLUSTRATION OF THE PERFORMANCE MEASURES**

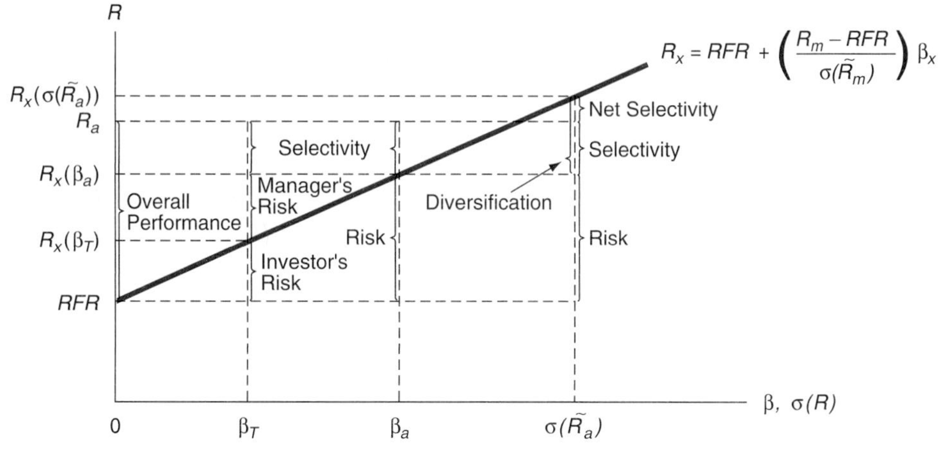

R
$R_x = RFR + \left(\frac{R_m - RFR}{\sigma(\tilde{R}_m)}\right)\beta_x$
$R_x(\sigma(\tilde{R}_a))$
R_a
$R_x(\beta_a)$
$R_x(\beta_T)$
RFR
Net Selectivity
Selectivity
Selectivity
Manager's Risk
Overall Performance
Diversification
Risk
Risk
Investor's Risk
0
β_T
β_a
$\sigma(\tilde{R}_a)$
$\beta, \sigma(R)$

Source: Eugene F. Fama, "Components of Investment Performance," *Journal of Finance* 27, no. 3 (June 1972): 588. Reprinted by permission.

EVALUATING SELECTIVITY Formally, you can measure the return due to selectivity as follows:

$$\text{Selectivity} = R_a - R_x(\beta_a)$$

where:

R_a = the actual return on the portfolio being evaluated
$R_x(\beta_a)$ = the return on the combination of the riskless asset and the market portfolio m that has risk β_x equal to β_a, the risk of the portfolio being evaluated

As shown in Figure 27.5, selectivity measures the vertical distance between the actual return and the *ex post* market line and is quite similar to Treynor's measure.

As noted above, you can examine overall performance in terms of selectivity and the returns from assuming risk as follows:

$$\underset{[R_a - RFR]}{\text{Overall Performance}} = \underset{[R_a - R_x(\beta_a)]}{\text{Selectivity}} + \underset{[R_x(\beta_a) - RFR]}{\text{Risk}}$$

Figure 27.5 shows that overall performance is the total return above the risk-free return and includes the return that *should* have been received for accepting the portfolio risk (β_a). This expected return for accepting risk (β_a) is equal to $[R_x(\beta_a) - RFR]$. Any excess over this expected return is due to selectivity.

EVALUATING DIVERSIFICATION This selectivity component can also be broken down into two parts. If a portfolio manager attempts to select undervalued stocks and in the process gives up some diversification, it is possible to measure the added return necessary to justify this diversification decision. The portfolio's *gross selectivity* is made up of *net selectivity* plus *diversification* as follows:

$$\underset{R_a - R_x(\beta_a)}{\text{Selectivity}} = \text{Net Selectivity} + \underset{[R_x(\sigma(R_a)) - R_x(\beta_a)]}{\text{Diversification}}$$

or

$$
\begin{aligned}
&\qquad\qquad\quad \text{Selectivity} \; - \; \text{Diversification} \\
\text{Net Selectivity} &= R_a - R_x(\beta_a) - [R_x(\sigma(R_a)) - R_x(\beta_a)] \\
&= R_a - R_x(\sigma(R_a))
\end{aligned}
$$

where:

$R_x(\sigma(R_a))$ = the return on the combination of the riskless asset and the market portfolio that has return dispersion equivalent to that of the portfolio being evaluated

Therefore, the diversification measure indicates the *added return* required to justify any loss of diversification in the portfolio. The term emphasizes that diversification is the elimination of all unsystematic variability. If the portfolio is completely diversified so that total risk (σ) is equal to systematic risk (β), then the $R_x(\sigma(R_a))$ would be the same as $R_x(\beta_a)$, and the diversification term would equal zero.

Because the diversification measure always is nonnegative, net selectivity will always be equal to or less than gross selectivity. The two will be equal when the portfolio is completely diversified. If the investor is not concerned with the diversification of the portfolio, this particular breakdown will not be important, and only selectivity will be considered.[15]

EVALUATING RISK Assuming the investor has a target level of risk for the portfolio equal to β_T, the portion of overall performance due to risk (the total return above the risk-free return) can be assessed as follows:

$$
\begin{aligned}
&\text{Risk} &&= \text{Manager's Risk} + \text{Investor's Risk} \\
&[R_x(\beta_a) - RFR] &&= [R_x(\beta_a) - R_x(\beta_T)] + [R_x(\beta_T) - RFR]
\end{aligned}
$$

where:

$R_x(\beta_T)$ = the return on the naively selected portfolio with the target level of market risk (β_T)

If the portfolio risk is equal to the target risk ($\beta_a = \beta_T$), then the manager's risk does not exist. If there is a difference between β_a and β_T, then the manager's risk is the return she must earn due to the decision to accept risk (β_a), which is different from the risk desired by the investor (β_T). The investor's risk is the return expected because the investor stipulated some positive level of risk. This evaluation is possible only if the client has specified a desired level of market risk, which is typical of pension funds and profit-sharing plans. Generally, it is not possible to compute this measure for *ex post* evaluations because the desired risk level is typically not available.

APPLICATION OF FAMA MEASURES Several of these performance components can be used in *ex post* evaluation, as shown in Table 27.4. Overall performance is the return derived above the risk-free return (i.e., the return above 4.57 percent as shown in Table 27.2). All of these mutual funds experienced positive overall performance. Next, determine how much the portfolio (fund) *should* receive for its systematic risk using the following expected return equation for this period (19.13 percent is the return on the S&P 500 during this period, as shown in Table 27.2):

---

[15]Franco Modigliani and Leah Modigliani, "Risk-Adjusted Performance," *Journal of Portfolio Management* 23, no. 2 (winter 1997): 45–54, presents a performance measure (dubbed M^2) that is a variation of both the Sharpe measure and Fama's $R_x[\sigma(R_a)]$ component.

TABLE 27.4 COMPONENTS OF PERFORMANCE FOR 20 SELECTED MUTUAL FUNDS

	Average Rate of Return	Standard Deviation	Beta	R^2	Overall Performance	Risk	Selectivity	Diversification	Net Selectivity
Aim Constellation A Fund	16.27	15.63	1.053	0.507	11.69	15.33	−3.63	6.20	−9.83 (16)
Dean Witter Developing Growth B Fund	19.01	19.30	1.065	0.340	14.44	15.50	−1.06	11.07	−12.14 (19)
Dreyfus Growth Opportunity Fund	11.68	12.35	0.943	0.652	7.10	13.73	−6.63	3.27	−9.90 (17)
Fasciano Fund	16.91	10.04	0.563	0.352	12.34	8.20	4.14	5.62	−1.48 (12)
Fidelity Magellan Fund	18.04	11.65	0.934	0.719	13.46	13.60	−0.14	2.44	−2.58 (13)
Fidelity Puritan Fund	15.38	7.75	0.653	0.794	10.80	9.51	1.30	1.16	0.13 (5)
Gabelli Asset Fund	17.86	9.06	0.750	0.766	13.29	10.92	2.37	1.55	0.82 (4)
Guardian Park Avenue A Fund	20.72	10.75	0.923	0.824	16.14	13.43	2.71	1.36	1.35 (2)
IDS Mutual A Fund	12.83	6.85	0.584	0.814	8.26	8.51	−0.25	0.92	−1.18 (10)
Income Fund of America	14.33	6.13	0.505	0.759	9.75	7.35	2.40	1.08	1.32 (3)
Investment Company of America Fund	16.85	9.13	0.847	0.963	12.28	12.34	−0.06	0.24	−0.29 (8)
Janus Venture Fund	12.41	13.05	0.666	0.291	7.83	9.69	−1.86	8.27	−10.13 (18)
Kemper Technology A Fund	18.70	20.05	1.298	0.469	14.13	18.90	−4.77	8.70	−13.47 (20)
Lindner Dividend Fund	33.44	10.79	0.347	0.116	28.87	5.05	23.81	9.81	14.00 (1)
Oppenheimer Growth A Fund	15.14	10.11	0.796	0.693	10.57	11.59	−1.02	2.34	−3.35 (14)
Putnam Fund for Growth & Income A	17.71	9.46	0.858	0.919	13.14	12.49	0.65	0.54	0.11 (6)
Templeton World I Fund	17.95	10.65	0.763	0.574	13.38	11.11	2.27	3.55	−1.29 (11)
T. Rowe Price Growth Stock Fund	17.72	9.92	0.870	0.862	13.14	12.67	0.47	0.98	−0.51 (9)
Value Line Special Situations Fund	15.88	14.80	0.809	0.334	11.31	11.78	−0.48	8.59	−9.07 (15)
Vanguard Wellington Fund	15.73	8.11	0.712	0.862	11.16	10.36	0.80	0.80	0.00 (7)
S&P 500	19.13	10.58							
90-Day T-Bill Rate	4.57	0.28							

$$E(R_i) = 4.57 + \beta_i(19.13 - 4.57)$$
$$= 4.57 + \beta_i(14.56)$$

The required return for risk simply is the latter term in this expression: $\beta_i(14.56)$. The required return for risk for Gabelli Asset Fund was 0.750(14.56) = 10.92 percent (its total required return is 4.57 + 10.92 = 15.49). The return for selectivity is the difference between overall performance (17.86 − 4.57 = 13.29) and the required return for risk (10.92). If the overall performance exceeds the required return for risk, the portfolio has experienced a positive return for selectivity. The results indicate that Gabelli Asset had an average annual return of 2.37 percent for selectivity (13.29 − 10.92). Ten funds had positive returns for selectivity. In contrast, several funds had positive overall performance, but their required return for risk exceeded this figure, giving them negative returns for selectivity (e.g., Kemper Technology Fund).

The next two columns in Table 27.4 indicate the effect of diversification on performance. The diversification term indicates the required return for not being completely diversified (i.e., having total risk above systematic risk). If a fund's total risk is equal to its systematic risk, then the ratio of its total risk to the market's total risk will equal its beta. If this is not the case, then the ratio of the fund's total risk for the fund relative to the market will be greater than its beta, which implies an added return required because of incomplete diversification. For Gabelli Asset, the ratio of total risk was

$$\frac{\sigma_i}{\sigma_m} = \frac{9.06}{10.58} = 0.856$$

This total risk ratio compares to the fund's beta of 0.750, indicating that the fund is not completely diversified, which is consistent with its R^2 of 0.766. The fund's required return, given its standard deviation, is

$$R_i = 4.57 + 0.856(14.56)$$
$$= 17.04$$

Recall that the fund's required return for systematic risk was 15.49 [= 4.57 + 0.75(14.56)]. The difference of 1.55 (= 17.04 − 15.49) is the added return required because of less than perfect diversification. This moderate required return for diversification is in contrast to Dean Witter Growth Fund, which has an R^2 with the market of 0.340 and a required return for diversification of 11.07 percent.

This required return for diversification is subtracted from the selectivity return to arrive at net selectivity. Gabelli Asset had a return for selectivity of 2.37 percent and net selectivity of 0.82 percent. This indicates that, even accounting for the added cost of incomplete diversification, the fund's performance was above the market line. Seven funds had non-negative net selectivity returns.

RELATIONSHIP AMONG PERFORMANCE MEASURES Table 27.5 contains the matrix of rank correlation coefficients among the Treynor, Sharpe, Jensen, Information Ratio, and Fama net selectivity measures. The striking feature of the display is that all of these statistics are highly positively correlated with one another, but not perfectly so. This suggests that although the measures provide a generally consistent assessment of portfolio performance when taken as a whole, they remain distinct at an individual level. This reinforces our earlier point that it is best to consider these composites collectively and that the user must understand what each means.

TABLE 27.5 CORRELATIONS AMONG ALTERNATIVE PORTFOLIO PERFORMANCE MEASURES

	Treynor	Sharpe	Jensen	Information Ratio	Net Selectivity
Treynor	—				
Sharpe	0.88	—			
Jensen	0.99	0.90	—		
Information Ratio	0.97	0.91	0.97	—	
Net Selectivity	0.83	0.98	0.86	0.86	—

PERFORMANCE ATTRIBUTION ANALYSIS

As noted earlier, portfolio managers can add value to their investors in either of two ways: selecting superior securities or demonstrating superior market timing skills by allocating funds to different asset classes or market segments. **Attribution analysis** attempts to distinguish which of these factors is the source of the portfolio's overall performance. Specifically, this method compares the total return to the manager's actual investment holdings to the return for a predetermined benchmark portfolio and decomposes the difference into an *allocation effect* and a *selection effect.* The most straightforward way to measure these two effects is as follows:

$$\text{Allocation Effect} = \Sigma_i\,[(w_{ai} - w_{pi}) \times (R_{pi} - R_p)]$$
$$\text{Selection Effect} = \Sigma_i\,[(w_{ai}) \times (R_{ai} - R_{pi})]$$

where:

w_{ai}, w_{pi} = the investment proportions given to the *i*th *market segment* (e.g., asset class, industry group) in the manager's actual portfolio and the benchmark portfolio, respectively

R_{ai}, R_{pi} = the investment return to the *i*th market segment in the manager's actual portfolio and the benchmark portfolio, respectively

R_p = the total return to the benchmark portfolio

Computed in this manner, the allocation effect measures the manager's decision to over- or underweight a particular market segment (i.e., $[w_{ai} - w_{pi}]$) in terms of that segment's return performance relative to the overall return to the benchmark (i.e., $[R_{pi} - R_p]$). Good timing skill is therefore a matter of investing more money in those market segments that end up producing greater than average returns. The selection effect measures the manager's ability to form specific market segment portfolios that generate superior returns relative to the way in which the comparable market segment is defined in the benchmark portfolio (i.e., $[R_{ai} - R_{pi}]$), weighted by the manager's actual market segment investment proportions. When constructed in this manner, the manager's total value-added performance is the sum of the allocation and selection effects.[16]

[16]Wainscott has argued that a better way to measure the selection effect is to multiply the market segment return differential by the benchmark for that segment, or $\Sigma_i[(w_{pi}) \times (R_{ai} - R_{pi})]$. A drawback of this approach, however, is that the allocation and selection effects no longer sum to the total value-added return. To balance the equation, he calculates an *interaction effect* as $\Sigma_i[(w_{ai} - w_{pi}) \times (R_{ai} - R_{pi})]$ to measure the residual performance. See Craig B. Wainscott, "Attribution Analysis for Equities," in *Performance Evaluation, Benchmarks, and Attribution Analysis,* ed. J. Squires (Charlottesville, Va.: Association for Investment Management and Research, 1995).

TABLE 27.6 **ASSET CLASS PERFORMANCE ATTRIBUTION ANALYSIS**

	Investment Weights			Returns		
Asset Class	Actual	Benchmark	Excess	Actual	Benchmark	Excess
Stock	0.50	0.60	−0.10	9.70%	8.60%	1.10%
Bonds	0.38	0.30	0.08	9.10%	9.20%	−0.10%
Cash	0.12	0.10	0.02	5.60%	5.40%	0.20%

ASSET CLASS ATTRIBUTION ANALYSIS: AN EXAMPLE

As an example of this process, consider an investor whose top-down portfolio strategy consists of two dimensions. First, he decides on a broad allocation of his investment dollars across three asset classes: U.S. stocks, U.S. long-term bonds, and cash equivalents, such as U.S. Treasury bills or certificates of deposit. Once this judgment is made, the investor's second general decision is choosing which stocks, bonds, and cash instruments to buy. As a benchmark, he selects a hypothetical portfolio with a 60 percent allocation to the Standard and Poor's 500 index, a 30 percent investment in the Lehman Corporate Long Bond index, and a 10 percent allocation to three-month Treasury bills.

Suppose that at the start of the investment period, the investor believes equity values are somewhat inflated and is not optimistic about the near-term performance of the stock market. Compared to the benchmark, he therefore decides to underweight stocks and overweight bonds and cash in his actual portfolio. The investment proportions he chooses are 50 percent in equity, 38 percent in bonds, and 12 percent in cash. Further, instead of selecting a broad portfolio of equities, he decides to concentrate on the interest rate–sensitive sectors, such as utilities and financial companies, while deemphasizing the technology and consumer durables sectors. Finally, he resolves to buy shorter duration bonds of a higher credit quality than are contained in the benchmark bond index and to buy commercial paper rather than Treasury bills.

In this example, the manager has made active investment decisions involving both the allocation of assets and the selection of individual securities. To determine if either (or both) of these decisions proved to be wise ones, at the end of the investment period he can calculate his overall and segment-specific performance. Table 27.6 summarizes these hypothetical returns for the investor's actual and benchmark asset class portfolios as well as the investment weightings for each. The overall actual and benchmark returns can be computed as follows:

$$\begin{aligned}\text{Overall Actual Return} &= (0.50 \times 0.097) + (0.38 \times 0.091) + (0.12 \times 0.056)\\ &= 8.98\%\end{aligned}$$

and

$$\begin{aligned}\text{Overall Benchmark Return} &= (0.60 \times 0.086) + (0.30 \times 0.092) + (0.10 \times 0.054)\\ &= 8.46\%\end{aligned}$$

Thus, the manager beat the benchmark by 52 basis points (= 0.0898 − 0.0846) over this particular investment horizon.

The goal of attribution analysis is to isolate the reason for this value-added performance. The manager's allocation effect can be computed by multiplying the excess asset class weight by that class's relative investment performance:

$$[(-0.10) \times (0.086 - 0.0846)] + [(0.08) \times (0.092 - 0.0846)] +$$
$$[(0.02) \times (0.054 - 0.0846)] = -0.02\%$$

This shows that if the investor had made just his market timing decisions and not picked different securities than those represented in the benchmark, his performance would have lagged the target return by two basis points. This total allocation effect can be broken down further into an equity allocation return of −2 basis points (= [(−0.10) × (0.086 − 0.0846)]), a bond allocation return of 6 basis points (= [(0.08) × (0.092 − 0.0846)]), and a cash allocation return of −6 basis points (= [(0.02) × (0.054 − 0.0846)]). Therefore, the decision to underweight stock and overweight cash (asset classes that generated returns above and below the benchmark, respectively) resulted in diminished performance that was more than enough to offset the benefit of emphasizing bonds.

Since the investor knows that he outperformed the benchmark overall, a negative allocation effect necessarily implies that he exhibited positive security selection skills. His selection effect can be computed as:

$$[(0.50) \times (0.097 - 0.086)] + [(0.38) \times (0.091 - 0.092)] + [(0.12) \times (0.056 - 0.054)] = 0.54\%$$

In this example, the investor formed superior stock and cash portfolios, although his bond selections did not perform quite as well as the Lehman Long Bond index. One important caveat in this analysis is that, because the returns are not risk-adjusted, it is possible that the asset class portfolios formed by the investor are riskier than their benchmark counterparts. If this is the case, which is almost certainly true for a cash portfolio that holds short-term corporate debt obligations instead of Treasury bills, the investor should expect a higher return that has nothing to do with his skill. Finally, notice that the investor's total incremental return of 52 basis points can be decomposed as:

$$\begin{aligned}\text{Total Value-Added} &= \text{Allocation Effect} + \text{Selection Effect}\\ &= (-0.02\%) + (0.54\%) = 0.52\%\end{aligned}$$

Using a procedure similar to the one just described, Brinson, Hood, and Beebower examined the return performance of a group of 91 large U.S. pension plans over the decade from 1974 to 1983.[17] They established that the mean annual return for this sample was 9.01 percent, compared to 10.11 percent for their benchmark. Thus, they documented that active management cost the average plan 110 basis points of return per year. This "value subtracted" return increment consisted of a −77 basis point allocation effect and a −33 basis point selection effect. Further, they concluded that a plan's initial strategic asset allocation choice, rather than any of its active management decisions, was the primary determinant of portfolio performance. In a follow-up study, Brinson, Singer, and Beebower reached a similar conclusion for a different group of 82 pension plans over the 1977–1987 period.[18] For this new sample, however, they showed that the total active return shortfall had fallen to −7 basis points, which was divided into an 18 basis point selection effect and a −25 basis point allocation effect.

Performance Attribution Extensions

Although the preceding example concentrated partly on an investor's ability to time broad asset class movements, the attribution methodology can be used to distinguish security selection skills from any of several other decisions that an investor might make. For instance, the manager of a broad-based, all-equity portfolio must decide what economic

[17]Gary P. Brinson, L. Randolph Hood, and Gilbert L. Beebower, "Determinants of Portfolio Performance," *Financial Analysts Journal* 42, no. 4 (July–August 1986): 39–44.

[18]Gary P. Brinson, Brian D. Singer, and Gilbert L. Beebower, "Determinants of Portfolio Performance II: An Update," *Financial Analysts Journal* 47, no. 3 (May–June 1991): 40–48.

TABLE 27.7 **MBA INVESTMENT FUND SECTOR PERFORMANCE ATTRIBUTION ANALYSIS**

	INVESTMENT WEIGHTS			EXCESS RETURNS
S&P 500 Sector	Actual	S&P 500	Excess	S&P Sector—Overall S&P
Basic materials	0.0331	0.0670	−0.0339	−15.15%
Capital equipment and technology	0.2544	0.1841	0.0703	−3.31
Consumer services	0.0208	0.0692	−0.0484	6.95
Consumer durables	0.0588	0.0353	0.0235	−21.34
Consumer nondurables	0.2752	0.2851	−0.0099	5.85
Energy	0.1170	0.0935	0.0235	−7.08
Financial	0.1619	0.1249	0.0370	7.15
Transportation	0.0199	0.0172	0.0027	−1.72
Utilities	0.0590	0.1000	−0.0410	1.91
Miscellaneous	0.0000	0.0242	−0.0242	−13.15

sectors (e.g., basic materials, consumer nondurables, transportation) to under- and overweight before she can choose her preferred companies in those sectors. In such cases, performance attribution analysis is still applicable, with a "sector rotation" effect replacing the market timing effect. To see how this might work, Table 27.7 summarizes the performance of The MBA Investment Fund, L.L.C., a privately funded investment portfolio managed by a group of graduate students at the University of Texas. During the time of this analysis, which covered the first full one-year period of the Fund's existence, the managers were restricted to investing in U.S.-traded equities and ADRs only. Because the Fund's investment mandate was to beat the return on the Standard and Poor's 500, the managers had two basic decisions to make: which sectors to emphasize and which individual stocks to buy within those sectors.

Over the course of the year, the overall returns to the S&P 500 and the Fund were 29.63 percent and 29.54 percent, respectively. The second and third columns of Table 27.7 document the actual and benchmark weights for the 10 economic sectors comprising the S&P 500 index, with the Fund's excess weightings (i.e., $[w_{ai} - w_{pi}]$) listed in the fourth column. The entries in the last column show the benchmark sector return relative to the overall S&P return (i.e., $[R_{pi} - R_p]$). Thus, the sector allocation effect can he calculated by summing the product of the entries in the last two columns:

$$[(-0.0339) \times (-0.1515)] + [(0.0703) \times (-0.0331)] \\ + \ldots + [(-0.0242) \times (-0.1315)] = -0.28\%$$

With an overall return difference of −9 basis points (= 0.2954 − 0.2963), this means that the Fund's managers generated a security selection effect of 19 basis points (= (−0.0009) − (−0.0028)). Consequently, although the student managers virtually matched the strong performance of the entire stock market, it appears they were better at picking stocks than forecasting broader economic trends.

This general attribution analysis methodology has been extended to other specific asset classes as well. Kuberek showed that producing fixed-income attributions for bond portfolio managers is quite straightforward once the relevant decision variables have been specified.[19] He noted that these decision variables might include allocations to different

[19]Robert C. Kuberek, "Attribution Analysis for Fixed Income," in *Performance Evaluation, Benchmarks, and Attribution Analysis,* ed. J. Squires (Charlottesville, Va.: Association for Investment Management and Research, 1995).

countries, foreign exchange effects, individual bond selections, and other risk factors, such as the portfolio's term structure positioning. Karnosky and Singer have developed a comprehensive, unified framework for attributing performance in a global asset management context.[20] In particular, they have added both active and hedged currency allocation returns to the single-currency attribution model of Brinson, Hood, and Beebower to allow for the intricacies of cross-border investing. In a comparison of the performance of one of their global investment portfolios relative to the MSCI World Equity Index during 1989, they demonstrated that the combined effect of the currency selection decision accounted for 563 basis points of the 7.66 percent return advantage that the portfolio enjoyed.

MEASURING MARKET TIMING SKILLS

As we saw in Chapter 22, tactical asset allocation (TAA) is a portfolio management strategy in which a manager attempts to produce active value-added returns solely through allocation decisions. Specifically, instead of trying to pick superior individual securities, TAA managers adjust their asset class exposures based on perceived changes in the relative valuations of those classes. A typical TAA fund shifts money between three asset classes—stocks, bonds, and cash equivalents—although many definitions of these categories (e.g., large cap versus small cap, long term versus short term) are used in practice. Of course, this means that the relevant performance measurement criterion for a TAA manager is how well he is able to time broad market movements. There are two reasons why attribution analysis is ill-suited for this task. First, by design, a TAA manager indexes his actual asset class investments and so the selection effect is not relevant. Second, a TAA approach to investing might entail dozens of changes to asset class weightings during an investment period, which could render meaningless an attribution effect computed on the average holdings. Because of these problems, many analysts consider a regression-based method for measuring timing skills to be a superior approach.

Weigel tested the market timing skills of a group of 17 U.S.-based managers using the TAA approach.[21] His methodology was motivated by the pioneering work of Merton and Hendriksson and assumed that perfect market timing ability was equivalent to owning a lookback call option that pays at expiration the return to the best-performing asset class.[22] That is, for any given investment period t, a manager with perfect market timing skills would have a return (R_{pt}) equal to:

$$R_{pt} = RFR_t + \max[R_{st} - RFR_t, R_{bt} - RFR_t, 0]$$

[20]Denis S. Karnosky and Brian D. Singer, *Global Asset Management and Performance Measurement* (Charlottesville, Va.: Research Foundation of the Institute of Chartered Financial Analysts, 1994). See also Ernest M. Ankrim and Chris R. Hensel, "Multicurrency Performance Attribution," *Financial Analysts Journal* 50, no. 2 (March–April 1994): 29–35.

[21]Eric J. Weigel, "The Performance of Tactical Asset Allocation," *Financial Analysts Journal* 47, no. 5 (September–October 1991): 63–70.

[22]Robert C. Merton, "On Market Timing and Investment Performance: An Equilibrium Theory of Value for Market Forecasts," *Journal of Business* 54, no. 3 (July 1981): 363–406, and Roy D. Hendriksson and Robert C. Merton, "On Market Timing and Investment Performance: Statistical Procedures for Evaluating Forecasting Skills," *Journal of Business* 54, no. 4 (October 1981): 513–534. See also Carl R. Chen, Anthony Chan, and Nancy J. Mohan, "Asset Allocation Managers' Investment Performance," *Journal of Fixed Income* 3, no. 3 (December 1993): 46–53, for another application of this methodology.

where R_{st} and R_{bt} are the period t returns to the stock and bond benchmark portfolios, respectively. Thus, controlling for stock and bond price movements in a manner comparable to Jensen's method, the following regression equation can be calculated:

$$(R_{pt} - RFR_t) = \alpha + \beta_b(R_{bt} - RFR_t) + \beta_s(R_{st} - RFR_t) \\ + \gamma\{\max[R_{st} - RFR_t, R_{bt} - RFR_t, 0]\} + U_t$$

Weigel showed that the samplewide average value for γ, which measures the proportion of the perfect timing option that the TAA managers were able to capture, was 0.30. This value was statistically significant, meaning that this group of managers had reliable, although not perfect, market timing skills. He also demonstrated that the average alpha was -0.5 percent per quarter, indicating that these same managers had negative nonmarket timing skills (e.g., hedging strategies).

Many other studies have examined the market timing ability of portfolio managers who are not exclusively TAA practitioners. Several investigations, as typified by Kon and Chang and Lewellen, concluded that mutual fund managers generally possess negative market timing skills.[23] Coggin, Fabozzi, and Rahman carried this analysis further by looking at both the timing and selectivity skills of a group of U.S. equity pension fund managers.[24] Using a regression-based model with monthly return data for an 8-year period ending in December 1990, they demonstrated that their sample of managers possessed positive, but small, selection skills and negative timing skills. From these studies, it is reasonable to conclude that only those managers explicitly trying to time market movements have a chance of doing so.

FACTORS THAT AFFECT USE OF PERFORMANCE MEASURES

All the performance measures just described are only as good as their data inputs. You must be careful when computing the rates of return to take proper account of all inflows and outflows. More importantly, you should use judgment and be patient in the evaluation process. It is not possible to evaluate a portfolio manager on the basis of a quarter or even a year. Your evaluation should extend over several years and cover at least a full market cycle. This will allow you to determine whether the manager's performance differs during rising and declining markets.[25] Beyond these general cautions, several specific factors should be considered when using these measures.

Although we discussed Roll's contentions regarding the measurement problem in Chapter 10, it is useful at this point to recall the problem, discuss the implications of a global capital market on this problem, and put it in perspective. With the exception of attribution analysis, all the equity portfolio performance measures we have discussed are derived from the CAPM. They assume the existence of a market portfolio at the point of tangency on the Markowitz efficient frontier. Theoretically, the market portfolio is an efficient, completely

---

[23]Stanley J. Kon, "The Market-Timing Performance of Mutual Fund Managers," *Journal of Business* 56, no. 3 (July 1983): 323–347; and Eric C. Chang and Wilbur G. Lewellen, "Market Timing and Mutual Fund Investment Performance," *Journal of Business* 57, no. 1 (1984): 57–72.

[24]T. Daniel Coggin, Frank J. Fabozzi, and Shafiqur Rahman, "The Investment Performance of U.S. Equity Pension Fund Managers: An Empirical Investigation," *Journal of Finance* 48, no. 3 (July 1993): 1039–1055.

[25]For a good discussion of how performance measurement can be affected by market cycles, see Wayne E. Ferson and Rudi W. Schadt, "Measuring Fund Strategy and Performance in Changing Economic Conditions," *Journal of Finance* 52, no. 2 (June 1996): 425–461.

diversified portfolio because it is on the efficient frontier. We also noted that this market portfolio must contain all risky assets in the economy, so that it will be completely diversified, and that all components are market-value weighted.

The problem arises in finding a realistic proxy for this theoretical market portfolio. As noted previously, analysts typically use the Standard and Poor's 500 Index as the proxy for the market portfolio because it contains a fairly diversified portfolio of stocks, and the sample is market-value weighted. Unfortunately, it does not represent the true composition of the market portfolio. Specifically, it includes only common stocks and most of them are listed on the NYSE. Notably, it excludes many other risky assets that theoretically should be considered, such as numerous AMEX and OTC stocks, foreign stocks, foreign and domestic bonds, real estate, coins, precious metals, stamps, and antiques.

This lack of completeness always has been recognized but was not highlighted until several articles by Roll detailed the problem with the market proxy and pointed out its implications for measuring portfolio performance.[26] Although a detailed discussion of Roll's critique will not be repeated here, we need to consider his major problem with the measurement of the market portfolio, which he refers to as a **benchmark error**.

When evaluating portfolio performance, various techniques use the market portfolio as the benchmark, and we use the market portfolio to derive our risk measures (betas). Roll showed that if the proxy for the market portfolio is not a truly efficient portfolio, then the SML using this proxy may not be the true SML—the true SML could have a higher slope. In such a case, a portfolio plotted above the SML and derived using a poor benchmark could actually plot below the SML that uses the true market portfolio. Also, the beta could differ from that computed using the true market portfolio. For example, if the true beta were larger than the beta computed using the proxy, the true position of the portfolio would shift to the right. In an empirical test, Brown and Brown documented a considerable amount of "ranking reversal" when the definition of the market portfolio was changed in a Jensen's alpha analysis of a sample of well-established mutual funds.[27] In efforts to address this problem, Grinblatt and Titman attempted to avoid the conflict altogether by introducing a performance measurement process that did not require benchmarks while Daniel, Grinblatt, Titman, and Wermers developed benchmarks based on the characteristics of the stock held, such as firm size and book-to-market ratios.[28]

Benchmark Errors and Global Investing

The concern with the benchmark error increases with global investing. The studies on international diversification discussed in Chapter 3 state clearly that adding non-U.S. securities to the portfolio universe almost certainly will move the efficient frontier to the left because including foreign securities reduces risk. You will recall that this reduction in risk continues as you add countries that have less economic interaction with the United States, such as some emerging market countries. Also, some of these additions increase the

[26]Richard Roll, "A Critique of the Asset Pricing Theory's Tests," *Journal of Financial Economics* 4, no. 4 (March 1977): 129–176; Richard Roll, "Ambiguity When Performance Is Measured by the Securities Market Line," *Journal of Finance* 33, no. 4 (September 1978): 1051–1069; Richard Roll, "Performance Evaluation and Benchmark Error I," *Journal of Portfolio Management* 6, no. 4 (summer 1980): 5–12; and Richard Roll, "Performance Evaluation and Benchmark Error II," *Journal of Portfolio Management* 7, no. 2 (winter 1981): 17–22.

[27]Keith C. Brown and Gregory D. Brown, "Does the Composition of the Market Portfolio Really Matter?" *Journal of Portfolio Management* 13, no. 2 (winter 1987): 26–32.

[28]See Mark Grinblatt and Sheridan Titman, "Performance Measurement without Benchmarks: An Examination of Mutual Fund Returns," *Journal of Business* 66, no. 1 (January 1993): 47–68; and Kent Daniel, Mark Grinblatt, Sheridan Titman, and Russ Wermers, "Measuring Mutual Fund Performance with Characteristic-Based Portfolios," *Journal of Finance* 52, no. 3 (July 1997): 1035–1058.

expected returns of the universe so that the efficient frontier moves up as well as leftward. The efficient frontier will almost certainly change when you invest in foreign securities.

The extent of the shift in the efficient frontier depends on the relationships among countries, and these relationships are changing dramatically. Because U.S. trade with European and Asian countries will continue its rapid growth from recent years, the interdependence of economies and the correlation of financial markets should increase. Also, individual European countries have become more interdependent after 1992, when numerous barriers to trade and travel in the European Economic Community were eliminated. Brinson and Fachler discuss the performance measurement problem for non-U.S. equities, while Brinson, Diermeier, and Schlarbaum describe a multiple markets index (MMI) that includes U.S. stocks and bonds, non-U.S. stocks, non-dollar bonds, venture capital, and real estate.[29]

A DEMONSTRATION OF THE GLOBAL BENCHMARK PROBLEM

To illustrate the impact of the benchmark problem in an environment of global capital markets, consider what happens to the individual measures of risk (beta) and the SML when the world equity market is employed. Table 27.8 contains the parameters of the characteristic line for the 30 stocks in the Dow Jones Industrial Average (DJIA) using the S&P 500, which is the typical proxy, and the Morgan Stanley Capital International (MSCI) World Stock Index, which is a market value–weighted index that contains stocks from around the world. These findings were calculated using monthly returns from the 5-year period from 1993–1998. The major differences are reflected in the betas and the R^2 of the regression lines. Specifically in the majority of cases, the beta was *smaller* when measured against the world index than against the S&P 500 index, and the average beta (0.996 versus 0.909) was about 10 percent lower. The impact also is reflected in the R^2, which was likewise often lower with the world index and had an average (0.292 versus 0.243) that was 17 percent smaller. These results imply a fairly significant impact on the individual measures of risk with a clear tendency for a decline in the measure. You will recall from the discussion in Chapter 9 that beta is equal to the covariance between an asset and the market portfolio divided by the variance of the market portfolio. It is shown that the world portfolio has a lower variance than the S&P 500 (as expected), but the covariance was lower still, which caused the decline in beta.

Reilly and Akhtar examined the effect of the choice of a benchmark on global performance measurement.[30] Their results are summarized in Figure 27.6, which plots the SMLs for six different indexes over three time horizons: 1983–1988, 1989–1994, and 1983–1994. Four country-specific benchmarks—the S&P 500 (United States), the Nikkei (Japan), the FT-All Shares (England), and the FAZ (Germany)—and two aggregate benchmarks—M-S World and Brinson GSMI—were used in the analysis. The results indicate that using

[29]Gary P. Brinson and Nimrod Fachler, "Measuring Non-U.S. Equity Portfolio Performance," *Journal of Portfolio Management* 11, no. 3 (spring 1985): 73–76 discusses the problems with developing an appropriate index and considers market selection (country) and stock selection within countries. The multiple markets index (MMI) is described in Gary P. Brinson, Jeffrey J. Diermeier, and G. G. Schlarbaum, "A Composite Portfolio Benchmark for Pension Plans," *Financial Analysts Journal* 42, no. 2 (March–April 1986): 15–24. See also Roger G. Ibbotson and Gary P. Brinson, *Global Investing* (New York: McGraw-Hill, 1993): 18–19.

[30]Frank K. Reilly and Rashid A. Akhtar, "The Benchmark Error Problem with Global Capital Markets," *Journal of Portfolio Management* 22, no. 1 (fall 1995): 33–52.

TABLE 27.8

PARAMETERS OF THE CHARACTERISTIC LINE FOR THE DOW JONES INDUSTRIALS, MONTHLY DATA: 1993–1998

	S&P 500				World		
Stock	Standard Deviation	Intercept	Beta	R^2	Intercept	Beta	R^2
Alcoa	0.071	0.002	0.833	0.189	0.005	0.823	0.179
Allied Signal Inc.	0.064	0.000	1.200	0.478	0.005	1.192	0.458
American Express	0.073	0.006	1.325	0.449	0.012	1.227	0.374
AT&T	0.072	0.002	0.906	0.217	0.007	0.717	0.132
Boeing	0.071	−0.002	0.851	0.195	0.000	0.969	0.245
Caterpillar	0.070	0.010	0.762	0.161	0.009	1.014	0.276
Chevron	0.046	0.007	0.582	0.221	0.009	0.621	0.245
Citigroup	0.130	−0.004	1.942	0.308	0.005	1.748	0.242
Coca-Cola	0.064	0.004	1.006	0.341	0.009	0.858	0.241
Disney	0.072	−0.002	1.038	0.284	0.003	0.926	0.220
Du Pont	0.063	0.004	0.756	0.195	0.006	0.825	0.226
Eastman Kodak	0.066	0.011	0.333	0.035	0.013	0.194	0.012
Exxon	0.038	0.007	0.623	0.377	0.009	0.580	0.318
General Electric	0.054	0.009	1.086	0.547	0.014	0.958	0.414
General Motors	0.075	0.003	0.894	0.194	0.006	0.980	0.226
Goodyear	0.062	−0.006	1.012	0.363	−0.003	1.031	0.366
Hewlett Packard	0.089	0.003	1.371	0.329	0.009	1.279	0.278
IBM	0.084	0.014	1.218	0.290	0.022	0.925	0.163
International Paper	0.074	−0.007	1.028	0.264	−0.001	0.881	0.189
J.P. Morgan	0.067	−0.006	1.180	0.428	−0.001	1.090	0.355
Johnson & Johnson	0.064	0.006	0.978	0.322	0.012	0.722	0.170
McDonald's	0.062	0.003	1.043	0.387	0.009	0.848	0.248
Merck	0.070	0.005	1.114	0.343	0.012	0.812	0.177
Minnesota M&M	0.057	0.000	0.647	0.178	0.002	0.604	0.151
Philip Morris	0.077	0.004	0.858	0.169	0.011	0.503	0.056
Procter & Gamble	0.061	0.006	0.943	0.329	0.012	0.743	0.198
Sears	0.085	0.002	1.182	0.264	0.006	1.194	0.261
Union Carbide	0.082	0.004	0.980	0.194	0.007	0.962	0.181
United Technologies	0.065	0.006	1.251	0.516	0.010	1.341	0.575
Wal-Mart	0.077	0.002	0.929	0.201	0.008	0.714	0.115
Mean	0.070	0.003	0.996	0.292	0.008	0.909	0.243

alternative market proxies for different countries or alternative composite series will generate SMLs that differ substantially during a given time period, and that these SMLs tend to be very unstable over time. For instance, the Nikkei SML goes from the largest risk premium during 1983–1988 to a negative risk premium during 1989–1994, which clearly is contrary to capital market theory. Notice, however, that this volatility would be masked by anyone looking at Japanese performance over the entire 1983–1994 period, during which the Nikkei SML assumed a more "normal" shape. Finally, the S&P 500 provided investors with the biggest performance hurdle over the whole sample period, which was mostly due to the high risk premiums in the United States during 1989–1994.

Implications of the Benchmark Problems

Several points are significant regarding this benchmark criticism. First, the benchmark problems noted by Roll, which are increased with global investing, do not negate the value of the CAPM as a *normative* model of equilibrium pricing; the theory is still viable. The problem is one of *measurement* when using the theory to evaluate portfolio performance.

FIGURE 27.6 **SECURITY MARKET LINES FOR S&P 500, NIKKEI, FT-ALL SHARES, FAZ, M-S WORLD, AND BRINSON GSMI INDEXES**

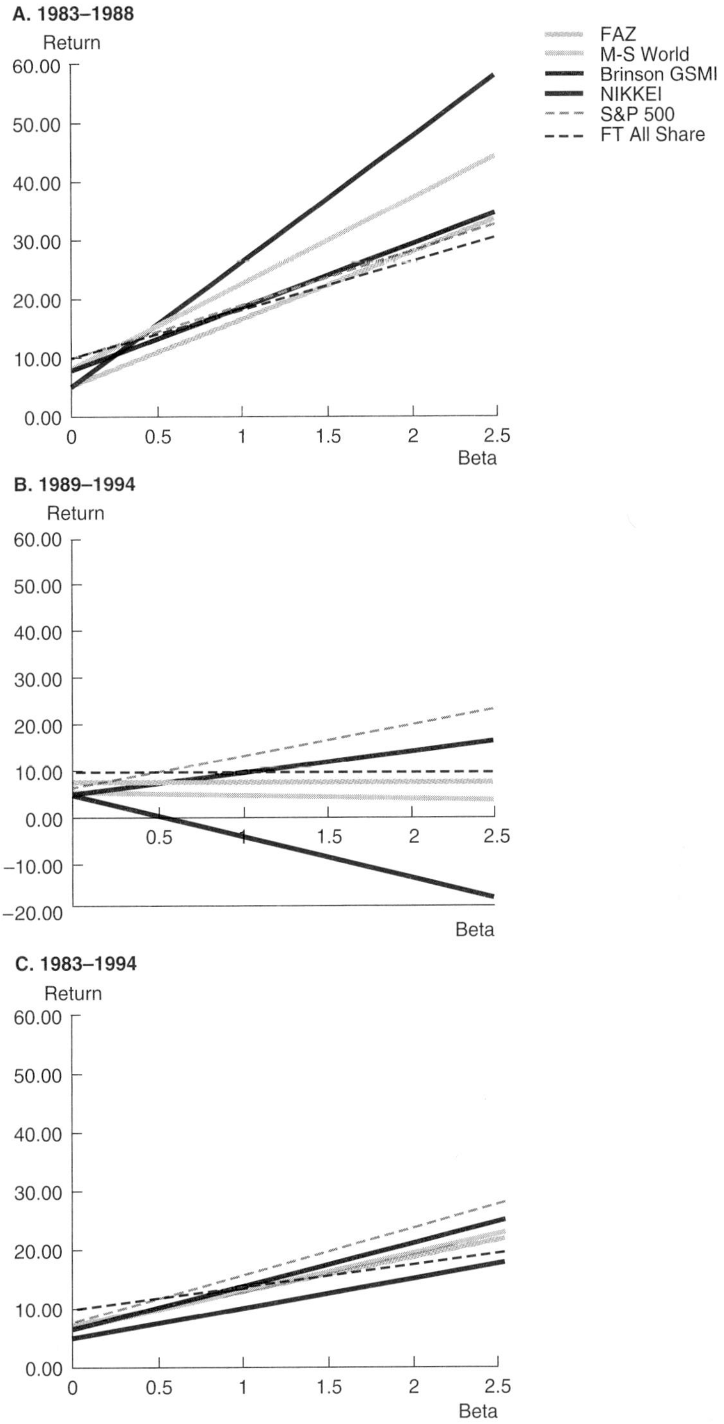
A. 1983–1988
Return
60.00
50.00
40.00
30.00
20.00
10.00
0.00
0
0.5
1
1.5
2
2.5
Beta
FAZ
M-S World
Brinson GSMI
NIKKEI
S&P 500
FT All Share
B. 1989–1994
Return
60.00
50.00
40.00
30.00
20.00
10.00
0.00
−10.00
−20.00
0.5
1
1.5
2
2.5
Beta
C. 1983–1994
Return
60.00
50.00
40.00
30.00
20.00
10.00
0.00
0
0.5
1
1.5
2
2.5
Beta

Source: Frank K. Reilly and Rashid A. Akhtar, "The Benchmark Error Problem with Global Capital Markets," *Journal of Portfolio Management* 22, no. 1 (fall 1995): 33–52.

You need to find a better proxy for the market portfolio or to adjust measured performance for benchmark errors. In fact, Roll made several suggestions to help overcome this problem.[31] From Chapter 5, we know that new comprehensive stock market and bond market series are being developed that will be available as market portfolio proxies. Finally, the multiple markets index (MMI), developed by Brinson, Diermeier, and Schlarbaum and maintained monthly by Brinson Partners, is a major step toward a truly comprehensive world market portfolio.

Alternatively, you might consider giving greater weight to the Sharpe portfolio performance measure because it does not depend heavily on the market portfolio. Recall that this measure relates excess return to the *standard deviation* of return—that is, to total risk. Although this evaluation process generally uses a benchmark portfolio as an example of an unmanaged portfolio for comparison purposes, the risk measure for the portfolio being evaluated does not directly depend on a market portfolio. Also, recall that the portfolio rank from the Sharpe measure typically correlates very highly with the ranks derived from alternative performance measures (see Table 27.5).

Required Characteristics of Benchmarks

The benchmark problem just discussed was described as being related to finding a proxy for the theoretical market portfolio, especially given the trend toward global capital markets. Concurrent with this search for a global market portfolio, there has also been a search for appropriate **normal portfolios**, which are customized benchmarks that reflect the specific styles of alternative managers. Bailey, Richards, and Tierney consider this a critical need of pension plans and endowments who hire multiple managers with widely divergent styles.[32] They point out that if a broad market index is used rather than a specific benchmark portfolio, it is implicitly assumed that the portfolio manager does not have an investment style, which is quite unrealistic. Also, it does not allow the plan sponsors to determine if the money manager is consistent with his or her stated investment style. The authors contend that any useful benchmark should have the following characteristics:

- *Unambiguous.* The names and weights of securities comprising the benchmark are clearly delineated.
- *Investable.* The option is available to forgo active management and simply hold the benchmark.
- *Measurable.* It is possible to calculate the return on the benchmark on a reasonably frequent basis.
- *Appropriate.* The benchmark is consistent with the manager's investment style or biases.
- *Reflective of current investment opinions.* The manager has current investment knowledge (be it positive, negative, or neutral) of the securities that make up the benchmark.
- *Specified in advance.* The benchmark is constructed prior to the start of an evaluation period.

If a benchmark does not possess all of these properties, it is considered flawed as an effective management tool. One example of a flawed benchmark is the use of the median man-

---

[31]Richard Roll, "Performance Evaluation and Benchmark Error II," *Journal of Portfolio Management* 7, no. 2 (winter 1981): 17–22. Also see Richard C. Grinold, "Are Benchmark Portfolios Efficient?" *Journal of Performance Management* 19, no. 1 (fall 1992): 34–40.

[32]Jeffrey V. Bailey, Thomas M. Richards, and David E. Tierney, "Benchmark Portfolios and the Manager/Plan Sponsor Relationship," *Current Topics in Investment Management* (New York: Harper & Row, 1990). See also Jeffrey Bailey and David E. Tierney, *Controlling Misfit Risk in Multiple-Manager Investment Programs* (Charlottesville, Va.: Research Foundation of the Institute of Chartered Financial Analysts, 1998).

ager from a broad universe of managers or even a limited universe of managers. This criticism is spelled out in detail by Bailey, who argues that the manager universe is inadequate on almost every characteristic.[33]

In summary, because of a growing desire to evaluate aggregate performance and identify what factors contribute to superior or inferior performance, benchmarks must be selected at two levels: (1) a *global* level that contains the broadest mix of risky assets available from around the world, and (2) a fairly specific level consistent with the management style of an individual money manager (i.e., a customized benchmark).

EVALUATION OF BOND PORTFOLIO PERFORMANCE

As discussed, the analysis of risk-adjusted performance for equity portfolios began in the late 1960s following the development of portfolio theory and the CAPM. The common stock risk measures have been fairly simple—either total risk (the standard deviation of returns) or systematic risk (betas). No such development has simplified analysis for the bond market, where numerous and complex factors can influence portfolio returns. One reason for this lack of development of bond portfolio performance measures was that prior to the 1970s most bond portfolio managers followed buy-and-hold strategies, so their performance probably did not differ much. In this era, interest rates were relatively stable, so one could gain little from the active management of bond portfolios.

The environment in the bond market changed considerably in the late 1970s and especially in the 1980s when interest rates increased dramatically and became more volatile. This created an incentive to trade bonds, and this trend toward more active management led to substantially more dispersed performance by bond portfolio managers. This dispersion in performance in turn created a demand for techniques that would help investors evaluate the performance of bond portfolio managers.

As with attribution analysis in the equity market, the critical questions are: (1) How did performance among portfolio managers compare to the overall bond market? and (2) What factors explain or contribute to superior or inferior bond portfolio performance? In this section, we present various attempts to develop bond portfolio performance evaluation systems that consider multiple-risk factors.[34]

A Bond Market Line

Wagner and Tito attempted to apply asset pricing techniques to the evaluation of bond portfolio performance.[35] A prime factor needed to evaluate performance properly is a measure of risk, such as the beta coefficient for equities. This is difficult to achieve because a bond's maturity and coupon have a significant effect on the volatility of its prices.

---

[33]Jeffrey V. Bailey, "Are Manager Universes Acceptable Performance Benchmarks?" *Journal of Portfolio Management* 18, no. 3 (spring 1992): 9–13. For a discussion of fixed-income benchmarks, see Chris P. Dialynas, "The Active Decisions in the Selection of Passive Management and Performance Bogeys," and Daralyn B. Peifer, "A Sponsor's View of Benchmark Portfolios," both in *The Handbook of Fixed-Income Securities,* 4th ed., ed. Frank J. Fabozzi and T. Dessa Fabozzi (Burr Ridge, Ill.: Irwin Professional Publishing, 1995).

[34]An overview of this area and a discussion of the historical development is contained in H. Gifford Fong, "Bond Management: Past, Current, and Future," in *The Handbook of Fixed-Income Securities,* 5th ed., ed. Frank J. Fabozzi (Chicago, Ill.: Irwin Professional Publishing, 1997).

[35]Wayne H. Wagner and Dennis A. Tito, "Definitive New Measures of Bond Performance and Risk," *Pension World* (May 1977): 17–26; and Dennis A. Tito and Wayne H. Wagner, "Is Your Bond Manager Skillful?" *Pension World* (June 1977): 10–16.

FIGURE 27.7 SPECIFICATION OF BOND MARKET LINE USING LEHMAN BROTHERS BOND INDEX

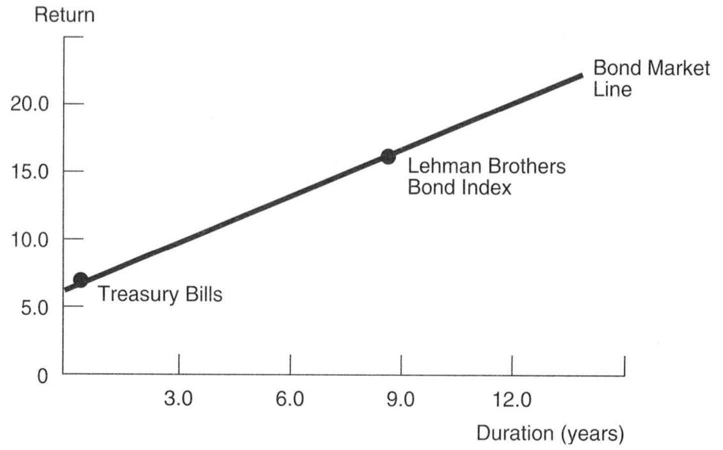
Return
20.0
15.0
10.0
5.0
0
Bond Market
Line
Lehman Brothers
Bond Index
Treasury Bills
3.0
6.0
9.0
12.0
Duration (years)

Source: Wayne H. Wagner and Dennis A. Tito, "Definitive New Measures of Bond Performance and Risk." *Pension World* (May 1977): 17–26. Reprinted with permission.

You know from our discussion in Chapter 16 that an appropriate composite risk measure indicates the relative price volatility for a bond compared to interest rate changes in the bond's *duration.* Using this as a measure of risk, the authors derived a bond market line much like the security market line used to evaluate equity performance. Duration simply replaces beta as the risk variable. The bond market line in Figure 27.7 is drawn from points defined by returns on Treasury bills to the Lehman Brothers Government-Corporate Bond Index rather than the S&P 500 index.[36] The Lehman Brothers Index gives the market's average annual rate of return during some common period, and the duration for the index is the value-weighted duration for the individual bonds in the index.

Given the bond market line, this technique divides the portfolio return that differs from the return on the Lehman Brothers Index into four components: (1) a **policy effect**, (2) a **rate anticipation effect**, (3) an **analysis effect**, and (4) a **trading effect**. When the latter three effects are combined, they are referred to as the **management effect**. These effects are portrayed in Figure 27.8.

The policy effect measures the difference in the expected return for a given portfolio because of a difference in policy regarding the duration of this portfolio compared to the duration of the Lehman Brothers Index. It is assumed that the duration of an unmanaged portfolio would be equal to the Lehman Brothers Index.[37] The duration of a portfolio being evaluated that differs from the index duration indicates a basic policy decision regarding relative risk (measured by duration), and there should be a difference in expected return consistent with that risk policy decision. For example, assume the duration and return for the Lehman Brothers Index is 9.0 years and 8.25 percent, respectively, If your portfolio has a duration of 9.5 years, according to the prevailing bond market line, your return should be

[36]We saw in Chapter 5 that it would be equally reasonable to use a comparable bond-market index series from Merrill Lynch, Salomon Brothers, or the Ryan Index.

[37]Notably, the duration of the various bond-market indexes has changed over time (i.e., the duration of the corporate bond series has declined, whereas the duration of the government bond series has increased slightly). For a presentation and discussion of this phenomenon, see Frank K. Reilly, Wenchi Kao, and David J. Wright, "Alternative Bond Market Indexes," *Financial Analysts Journal* 48, no. 3 (May–June 1992): 44–58.

FIGURE 27.8 **GRAPHIC DISPLAY OF BOND PORTFOLIO PERFORMANCE BREAKDOWN**

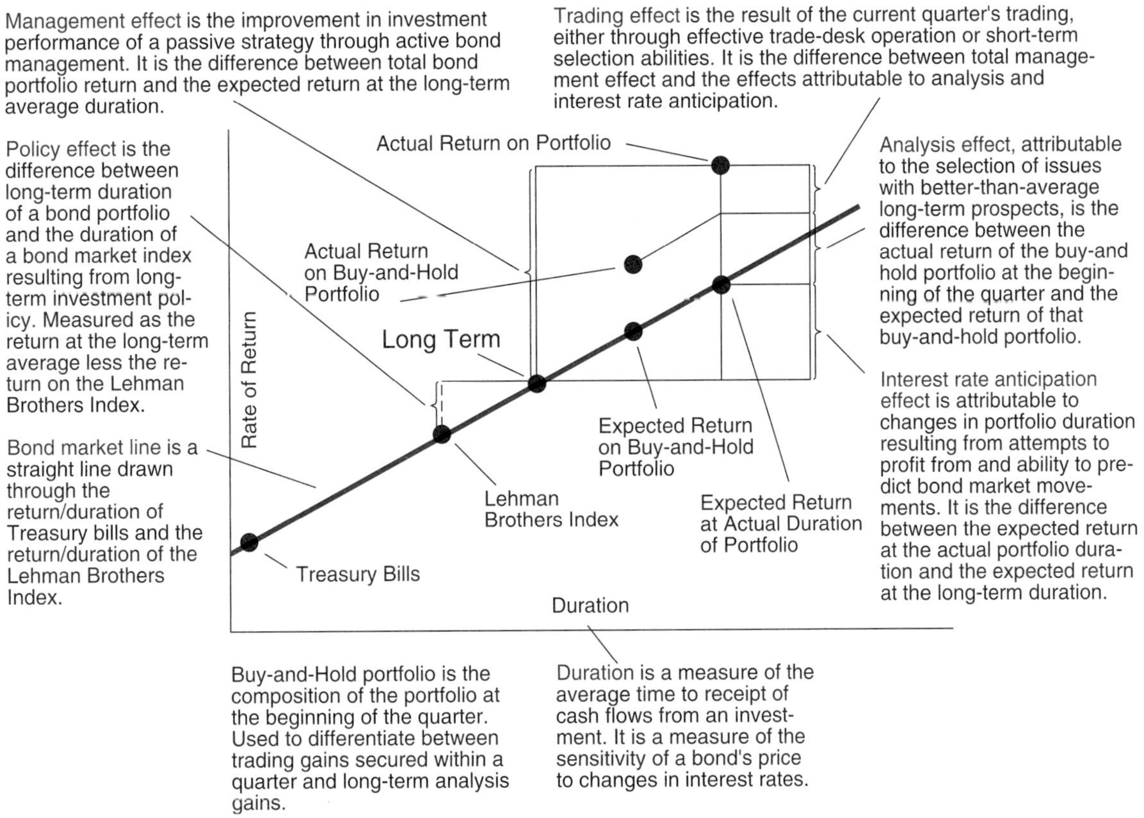
Management effect is the improvement in investment performance of a passive strategy through active bond management. It is the difference between total bond portfolio return and the expected return at the long-term average duration.
Trading effect is the result of the current quarter's trading, either through effective trade-desk operation or short-term selection abilities. It is the difference between total management effect and the effects attributable to analysis and interest rate anticipation.
Policy effect is the difference between long-term duration of a bond portfolio and the duration of a bond market index resulting from long-term investment policy. Measured as the return at the long-term average less the return on the Lehman Brothers Index.
Bond market line is a straight line drawn through the return/duration of Treasury bills and the return/duration of the Lehman Brothers Index.
Actual Return on Portfolio
Actual Return on Buy-and-Hold Portfolio
Long Term
Rate of Return
Expected Return on Buy-and-Hold Portfolio
Lehman Brothers Index
Expected Return at Actual Duration of Portfolio
Treasury Bills
Duration
Analysis effect, attributable to the selection of issues with better-than-average long-term prospects, is the difference between the actual return of the buy-and hold portfolio at the beginning of the quarter and the expected return of that buy-and-hold portfolio.
Interest rate anticipation effect is attributable to changes in portfolio duration resulting from attempts to profit from and ability to predict bond market movements. It is the difference between the expected return at the actual portfolio duration and the expected return at the long-term duration.
Buy-and-Hold portfolio is the composition of the portfolio at the beginning of the quarter. Used to differentiate between trading gains secured within a quarter and long-term analysis gains.
Duration is a measure of the average time to receipt of cash flows from an investment. It is a measure of the sensitivity of a bond's price to changes in interest rates.

Source: Wayne H. Wagner and Dennis A. Tito, "Definitive New Measures of Bond Performance and Risk," *Pension World* (May 1977): 17–26. Reprinted with permission.

about 8.60 percent. In this example, the policy effect is 0.5 year and 0.35 percent (35 basis points). Specifically, the higher duration implies that your portfolio should have a higher average return of 0.35 percent (this positive relationship assumes the typical upward-sloping yield curve).

Given the expected return and duration for this long-term portfolio, all deviations from the index portfolio are attributable to the remaining management effect components. The interest rate anticipation effect attempts to measure the differential return from changing the duration during this period compared to the portfolio's long-term duration. Hopefully, the manager would increase the duration of the portfolio during periods of declining interest rates to increase the price volatility (price appreciation) of your portfolio and reduce duration during periods of rising interest rates to minimize the price decline. Therefore, you would determine the duration of the actual portfolio during the period and compare this to the duration of the long-term portfolio. Then you would determine the difference in expected return for these portfolios and their two durations using the bond market line. For example, assume the duration for the long-term portfolio is 9.5 years, which implies an expected return of 8.60 percent, and that the prevailing duration for the portfolio being evaluated is 10.0 years, which implies an expected return of 9.00 percent using the bond market line. Therefore, the rate anticipation effect during this period is 0.40 percent (9.00 − 8.60).

The difference between this expected return based on the portfolio's duration and the actual return for the portfolio during this period is a combination of an analysis effect and a trading effect. The analysis effect is the differential return attributable to acquiring bonds that are temporarily mispriced relative to their risk level. To measure the analysis effect, compare the *expected* return for the portfolio held at the beginning of the period (using the bond market line) to the *actual* return of this same portfolio. If the actual return is greater than the expected return, it implies that the portfolio manager acquired some underpriced issues that became properly priced and thus provided excess returns during the period. For example, if the portfolio at the beginning of the period had a duration of 10 years, this might indicate that the portfolio's expected return was 9.00 percent for the period. In turn, if the actual return for this buy-and-hold portfolio was 9.40 percent, it would indicate an analysis effect of 40 basis points.

Finally, the trading effect occurs because of short-run changes in the portfolio during the period. It is measured as the residual after taking account of the analysis effect from the total excess return based on duration. For example, assume the total actual return is 10.50 percent with a duration of 10.0 years. The prevailing bond market line indicates an expected return of 9 percent for a portfolio with a 10-year duration. Thus, the combination of the analysis and trading effects is 1.50 percent (= 10.50 − 9.00). Previously, we determined that the analysis effect was 0.40 percent, so the trading effect must be 1.10 percent. In summary, for this portfolio manager, the actual return was 10.50 percent, compared to a return for the Lehman Brothers Index of 8.25 percent. This total excess of 2.25 percent would be divided as follows:

- 0.35 percent policy effect due to higher long-term duration
- 0.40 percent interest rate anticipation effect due to increasing the duration of the current portfolio above the long-term portfolio duration
- 0.40 percent analysis effect—the impact of superior selection of individual issues in the beginning portfolio
- 1.10 percent trading effect—the impact of trading the issues *during* the period

This technique breaks down the return based on the duration as a comprehensive risk measure. The only concern is that *it does not consider differences in the risk of default.* Specifically, the technique does not differentiate between an Aaa bond with a duration of 8 years and a Baa bond with the same duration. This could clearly affect the performance. A portfolio manager that invested in Baa bonds, for example, could experience a very positive analysis effect simply because the bonds were lower quality than the average quality implicit in the Lehman Brothers Index. The only way to avoid this would be to construct differential market lines for alternative ratings or construct a benchmark line that matches the quality makeup of the portfolio being evaluated.[38]

Decomposing Portfolio Returns

Dietz, Fogler, and Hardy developed a technique to decompose the bond portfolio returns into maturity, sector, and quality effects.[39] The total return for a bond during a period of time is composed of a known **income effect** (due to normal yield-to-maturity factors) and

[38]This problem is briefly discussed in Frank K. Reilly and Rupinder Sidhu, "The Many Uses of Bond Duration," *Financial Analysts Journal* 36, no. 4 (July–August 1980): 58–72. See also Arthur Gudikunst and Joseph McCarthy, "Determinants of Bond Mutual Fund Performance," *Journal of Fixed Income* 2, no. 1 (June 1992): 95–101.

[39]Peter O. Dietz, H. Russell Fogler, and Donald J. Hardy, "The Challenge of Analyzing Bond Portfolio Returns," *Journal of Portfolio Management* 6, no. 3 (spring 1980): 53–58.

an unknown **price change effect** (due to an interest rate effect, a sector/quality effect, and a residual effect). It is graphed as follows:

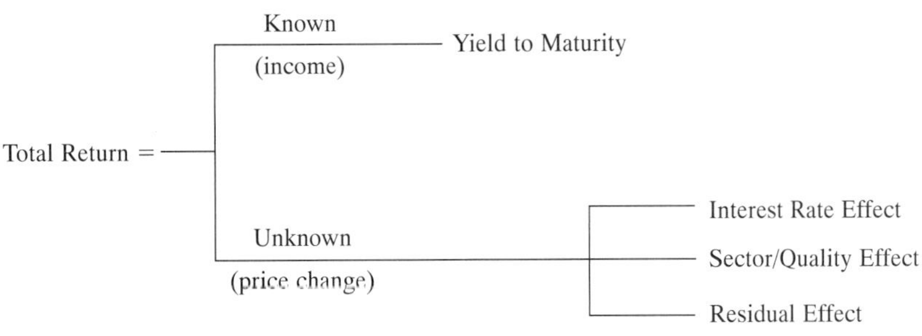
Known
(income)
Yield to Maturity
Total Return =
Unknown
(price change)
Interest Rate Effect
Sector/Quality Effect
Residual Effect

The yield-to-maturity (income) effect is the return an investor would receive if nothing had happened to the yield curve during the period. That is, the investor would receive the interest income, a price change relative to par, and any price change due to the passage of time and the shape of the yield curve.

The **interest rate effect** measures what happened to each issue because of changes in the term structure of interest rates during the period. Each bond is valued based on the Treasury yield curve at its maturity and takes account of its normal premium relative to Treasury yields. Assume a normal risk premium spread of 30 basis points and that yields on Treasury bonds with the maturity of your bond go from 8.50 percent to 9.25 percent. To determine the interest rate effect, you would compute the value of your bond at 8.80 percent (8.50 + 0.30) and at 9.55 percent (9.25 + 0.30) and then compute the price change. This is the price change caused by a change in market interest rates.

The **sector/quality effect** measures the expected impact on the returns because of the sector of the bonds (corporates, utilities, financial, GNMA, etc.) and also the quality of the bonds (Aaa, Aa, A, Baa). Given this breakdown, you can determine what happened to bonds in each sector after taking account of the yield to maturity and the interest rate effect. As an example, during a given period you might find that an average Aa utility had negative excess returns of −0.50 percent after taking account of the yield to maturity and the interest rate effect, whereas an A-rated corporate bond experienced a comparable positive excess return of 0.30 percent. Therefore, the sector/quality effect would be −0.50 and 0.30 for these sets of bonds.

The **residual effect** is what remains after taking account of the three prior factors—yield to maturity, interest rate effect, and the sector/quality effect. It is computed as follows:

$$\begin{matrix}\text{Total} \\ \text{Return}\end{matrix} - \begin{matrix}\text{Yield to} \\ \text{Maturity} \\ \text{Effect}\end{matrix} - \begin{matrix}\text{Interest} \\ \text{Rate Effect}\end{matrix} - \begin{matrix}\text{Sector/Quality} \\ \text{Effect}\end{matrix} = \text{Residual}$$

The presence of a consistently large positive residual would indicate superior bond selection capabilities. Specifically, a positive residual indicates that after taking account of all market effects from interest rate changes and sector/quality, it is still possible the bond manager has helped provide positive returns due to bond selection. Alternatively, large positive interest rate effects during periods of declining interest rates and small negative interest rate effects during periods of rising interest rates would indicate a bond manager with good skills at interest rate anticipation. Consistently positive sector/quality effects would indicate the ability to make proper allocations and to anticipate shifts in this area over time.

ANALYZING SOURCES OF RETURN

Fong, Pearson, and Vasicek proposed a performance evaluation technique that likewise divides the total returns into several components that affect bond returns.[40] Their intent was to measure total realized return and attribute the return to its sources (i.e., what factors contributed to the total return). The first breakdown divides the total return (R) between the effect of the external interest rate environment (I), which is beyond the control of the portfolio manager, and the contribution of the management process (C). Thus:

$$R = I + C$$

In turn, I is broken down into two parts. The first is the *expected* rate of return (E) on a portfolio of default-free securities, assuming no change in forward rates (i.e., no change in future one-period rates). This expected return also is referred to as the *market's implicit forecast.* The second component of I is U, the *unexpected* return on the Treasury index that is due to actual changes in forward rates. Thus:

$$I = E + U$$

For example, assume that at the beginning of a quarter, the expected annual return on a portfolio of Treasury bonds is 11 percent. (This expected return assumes no change in the term structure of bonds during this year.) At the end of the year, you determine that the actual return on this portfolio of Treasury bonds was 11.75 percent. This would imply an E of 11 percent and a U of 0.75 percent.

In turn, C (the management contribution) is composed of three factors:

- M = return from maturity management
- S = return from spread/quality management
- B = return attributable to the selection of specific securities

The return from *maturity management, M,* is determined by how well the portfolio manager changes maturity (duration) in anticipation of interest rate changes. The component is measured by computing the default-free price of every security (at the beginning and end of the period) based on the spot rate for its maturity, as indicated by the Treasury yield curve. The total return over the evaluation period is derived from these prices, while maintaining all actual trading activity. Given this total return based on maturity yields, subtract the actual return on the Treasury index (assumed earlier to be 11.75 percent) to arrive at the maturity return. For example, if the total return for the portfolio based on the pricing computations was 12.25 percent, the maturity management return would be 0.50 percent, assuming the Treasury index return of 11.75 percent.[41]

The *spread/quality management* component indicates the effect on return due to the manager's selection of bonds from various sectors and qualities. It is measured by pricing each bond at the beginning and end of the period using yields appropriate for its specific sector and quality and then computing the rate of return given these prices. This total return less the return for Treasury bonds, considering the maturity effect (assumed to be 12.25 percent), indicates the return attributable to sector/quality selection. If this sector/quality

[40]Gifford Fong, Charles Pearson, and Oldrich Vasicek, "Bond Performance: Analyzing Sources of Return," *Journal of Portfolio Management* 9, no. 3 (spring 1983): 46–50.

[41]A subsequent article suggests a possible refinement of the maturity management effect by considering the separate effects of duration, convexity, and yield curve "twist." See Gifford Fong, Charles Pearson, Oldrich Vasicek, and Theresa Conroy, "Fixed-Income Portfolio Performance: Analyzing Sources of Return," in *The Handbook of Fixed-Income Securities,* 3d ed., edited by Frank J. Fabozzi (Homewood, Ill.: Business One Irwin, 1991).

pricing indicates a total return of 12.0 percent, it would imply a negative 0.25 percent for sector/quality management (12.00 − 12.25).

The *selectivity component* (B) is the remaining return. It is attributable to the selection of specific bonds after considering the maturity and sector/quality decisions—specifically, what individual bonds were selected to carry out these decisions. It is measured as the difference between the actual total return on the portfolio and the prior total return that considered maturity and sector/quality. Continuing our example, if the actual total return on the portfolio was 13.00 percent, the selectivity component would be 1.00 percent because the return for maturity and sector/quality above was 12.00 percent. To summarize the results:

$$\begin{aligned} R &= \quad I \quad + \quad C \\ &= (E + U) + (M + S + B) \end{aligned}$$

where:

E = expected Treasury yield	**11.00**
U = unexpected Treasury yield	**0.75**
M = maturity management	**0.50**
S = spread/quality management	**(0.25)**
B = selectivity	**1.00**
Total return	**13.00**

This analysis indicates that the portfolio manager was quite good at maturity (duration) decisions and at selecting individual bonds but did not do well in terms of sector/quality decisions. As before, you should do a similar breakdown for some market index series as a basis of comparison to an unmanaged portfolio. Also, examine these components over time to determine any consistent strengths or weaknesses for the portfolio manager.

CONSISTENCY OF PERFORMANCE

Numerous investigators have documented performance inconsistency for managers of equity portfolios. Kritzman considered this question for bond managers by examining the ranking for 32 bond managers employed by AT&T.[42] He divided a 10-year period into two 5-year periods, determined each manager's percentile ranking in each period, and correlated the rankings. The results revealed *no relationship* between performance in the two periods. A further test also revealed *no relationship* between past and future performance even among the best and worst performers. Based on these results, Kritzman concluded that it would be necessary to examine something besides past performance to determine superior bond portfolio managers.

REPORTING INVESTMENT PERFORMANCE

The performance measures just described represent the essential elements of how any investor's performance should be evaluated. However, before the various composite statistics can be calculated, a more fundamental question must be addressed: How should the returns upon which the performance measures are based be reported to the investor? We conclude the chapter by exploring two dimensions of this problem. First, we consider the issue of how returns should be computed for a portfolio that experiences infusions and withdrawals of cash during the investment period. Second, we will briefly summarize the

[42]Mark Kritzman, "Can Bond Managers Perform Consistently?" *Journal of Portfolio Management* 9, no. 4 (summer 1983): 54–56.

performance presentation standards created by the Association for Investment Management and Research (AIMR), an international organization of over 35,000 investment practitioners and educators in more than 80 countries.

Time-Weighted and Dollar-Weighted Returns

As we saw in Chapter 1, the holding period yield (HPY) for any investment position was determined by that position's market value at the end of the period divided by its initial value:

$$\text{HPY} = \frac{\text{Ending Value of Investment}}{\text{Beginning Value of Investment}} - 1$$

For any security or portfolio of securities, we also saw that there are two basic reasons why the ending and beginning values could differ: the receipt of cash payments (e.g., dividends) or a change in price (e.g., capital gains) during the period. Thus, for most investment positions, calculating returns during any given time frame is a reasonably straightforward matter.

For professional money managers and management companies, however, there is another reason why the beginning and ending value of a portfolio can differ, and it has nothing to do with the manager's investment prowess. Specifically, if the investor either withdraws or adds to her initial investment capital during the period, the ending value of the position will reflect these changes. Of course, it would be unfair to credit the manager with having produced high returns that were due to additional capital commitments. Similarly, it would be equally unfair to penalize him for reductions in the ending value of the investment that were caused by the investor removing funds from her account. Consequently, an evaluation of the manager's true performance must take these contributions and withdrawals into account.

To see the potential problem more clearly, consider two portfolio managers (A and B) who have exactly identical investment styles and stock-picking abilities. Indeed, we will assume further that over a two-period investment horizon, they produce exactly the same capital gains with the investment capital entrusted to them: 25 percent in period 1 and 5 percent in period 2. Further, suppose that each manager receives from his respective investor $500,000 to invest. The difference is that manager A receives all of these funds immediately whereas manager B's investor commits only $250,000 initially and the remaining $250,000 at the end of the first period.

The immediate effect of this investment timing discrepancy can be seen by calculating the terminal (period 2) value of each portfolio:

$$\text{Portfolio A: } 500{,}000[(1 + 0.25)(1 + (0.05)] = \$656{,}250$$

and

$$\text{Portfolio B: } 250{,}000[(1 + 0.25)(1 + 0.05)] + 250{,}000(1 + 0.05) = \$590{,}625$$

Obviously, manager B's portfolio is worth less than manager A's, but this is a result of the way the investment funds were committed rather than of any real differences in the performance of the two managers. Accordingly, the managers' performance evaluation should not be affected by the investors' decisions concerning the timing of their capital commitments. In other words, manager B should not be held accountable for the fact that investor B did not have all of her funds invested during the high-return environment of the first period.

One common method of computing average returns that we have seen is to use a discounted cash flow approach to calculate an investment's internal rate of return. For the two managers in this example, these calculations generate the following returns:

$$\text{Manager A: } 500{,}000 = \frac{656{,}250}{(1 + r_{dA})^2}, \text{ or } r_{dA} = 14.56 \text{ percent}$$

and

$$\text{Manager B: } 250{,}000 = \frac{-250{,}000}{(1 + r_{dB})^1} + \frac{590{,}625}{(1 + r_{dB})^2}, \text{ or } r_{dB} = 11.63 \text{ percent}$$

These returns (r_{dA} and r_{dB}) are sometimes called *dollar-weighted* returns because they are the discount rates that set the present value of future cash flows (including future investment contributions and withdrawals) equal to the level of the initial investment. Unfortunately, in this case, dollar-weighted returns give an inaccurate impression of manager B's ability; he did not actually perform 2.93 percent (= 0.1456 − 0.1163) "worse" than manager A. Thus, while this internal rate of return method gives an accurate assessment of *investor* B's return, it is a misleading measure of *manager* B's talent.

A better way of evaluating a manager's performance would be to consider how well he did regardless of the size or timing of the investment funds involved. For both managers in this example, the *time-weighted* average return is simply the geometric average of (one plus) the periodic returns:

$$r_{tA} = r_{tB} = \sqrt[2]{(1 + 0.25)(1 + 0.05)} - 1 = 14.56\%$$

Notice that dollar-weighted and time-weighted returns are only the same when there are no interim investment contributions within the evaluation period. This was the case for manager A. For manager B, on the other hand, the dollar-weighted return understates the true (time-weighted) performance because of the way the investor deployed her funds. When there are contributions, Dietz has suggested a method for adjusting holding period yields:

$$\text{Adjusted HPY} = \frac{\text{Ending Value of Investment} - (1 - \text{DW})(\text{Contribution})}{\text{Beginning Value of Investment} + (\text{DW})(\text{Contribution})} - 1$$

where the contribution can be either positive (a new commitment) or negative (a withdrawal).[43] This adjustment process alters the initial and terminal values of the portfolios by the weighted amount of the contribution made during the holding period. In this calculation, the day-weight (DW) factor represents the portion of the period that the contribution is actually held in the account. For example, if a contribution were placed in the portfolio halfway through a 30-day month, DW would be 0.5 (= (30 − 15)/30).

PERFORMANCE PRESENTATION STANDARDS

The preceding example underscores the fact that there may not always be a single answer to a seemingly simple question. For instance, although portfolio B had an internal rate of return of 11.63 percent, its manager generated an average return of 14.56 percent. Which should be reported to the investor? Although Security and Exchange Commission regulations guard against the publication of outright fraudulent claims, only recently has the investment community begun to demand the adoption of a more rigorous set of reporting guidelines. In an effort to fulfill the call for uniform, accurate, and consistent performance reporting, AIMR has developed a comprehensive set of performance presentation standards (PPS). As the organization states its mission:

[43]Peter O. Dietz and Jeannette R. Kirschman, "Evaluating Portfolio Performance," in *Managing Investment Portfolios,* 2d ed., ed. J. Maginn and D. Tuttle (Boston: Warren, Gorham, & Lamont, 1990).

> The investment community's need for a common, accepted set of guidelines to promote fair representation and full disclosure in every firm's presentation of its performance results to clients and prospective clients has guided the development of the AIMR-PPS. The Standards are the manifestation of a set of guiding ethical principles and should be interpreted as *minimum* standards for presenting investment performance. The standards have been designed to meet the following four goals:
>
> - achieve greater uniformity and comparability among performance presentations;
> - improve the service offered to investment management clients;
> - enhance the professionalism of the industry;
> - bolster the notion of self-regulation.
>
> The Standards set expectations and provide an industry yardstick for evaluating fairness and accuracy in investment performance presentation.[44]

Introduced in 1987 and formally adopted in 1993, the AIMR-PPS have become the accepted practice within the investment management community. Although a detailed analysis of these standards is beyond our current scope, it is worth noting several of the fundamental principles on which the PPS are based:

- Total return, including realized and unrealized gains plus income, must be used when calculating investment performance.
- Time-weighted rates of return must be used.
- Portfolios must be valued at least quarterly, and periodic returns must be geometrically linked.
- If composite return performance is presented, this composite must contain all actual fee-paying accounts, including all terminated accounts for periods up through the last full reporting period the account was under management. Composite results may not link simulated or model portfolios with actual performance.
- Performance must be calculated after the deduction of trading expenses (e.g., broker commissions and SEC fees), if any.
- For taxable clients, taxes on income and realized capital gains must be recognized in the same period they were incurred and must be subtracted from results regardless of whether taxes are paid from assets outside the account.
- Annual returns for all years must be presented. Performance of less than one year must not be annualized. A 10-year performance record (or a record for the period since firm inception if less than 10 years) must be presented.
- Performance presentation must disclose whether performance results are calculated gross or net of investment management fees and what the firm's fee schedule is. Presentation should also disclose any use of leverage (including derivatives) and any material change in personnel responsible for investment management.

In addition to the preceding requirements, AIMR also encourages managers to disclose the volatility of the aggregate composite return and to identify benchmarks that parallel the risk or investment style the composite is expected to track. Figure 27.9 shows a checklist of many of the points necessary to ensure compliance with the PPS, while Figure 27.10 shows a sample performance presentation that is in compliance with the Standards.

---

[44]A complete discussion of these standards can be found in, *AIMR Performance Presentation Standards Handbook,* 2d ed. (Charlottesville, Va.: AIMR, 1997), as well as *Performance Reporting for Investment Managers* (Charlottesville, Va.: AIMR, 1991).

FIGURE 27.9 A CHECKLIST FOR AIMR'S PERFORMANCE PRESENTATION STANDARDS

This checklist for investment managers, their clients and prospects, and for consultants, is meant to assure proper conformance to the AIMR Performance Presentation Standards.

I. Performance calculations.

- ❑ A. Performance results have been calculated on a time-weighted basis.
- ❑ B. Returns combine income and current market valuations (thus, presenting so-called total returns).
- ❑ C. Manager fee levels have been disclosed along with performance records so that after-fee results can be measured.
- ❑ D. Performance results of broad security classes, such as equities or fixed-income, have been included with cash or substitute securities included. If cash has been excluded from the calculations, then returns with cash have been presented with the statement that AIMR Standards consider performance with cash to be most representative of managerial results and most representative for comparisons with other managers.
- ❑ E. All exclusions from performance calculations and presentation by the manager have been disclosed.
- ❑ F. The method of linking interim performance results (daily, monthly, quarterly) has been explained. AIMR Standard is for monthly linking.
- ❑ G. Balanced account performance.
  - ❑ 1. The manager has assigned cash and substitute securities to the specific asset category to which they belong, thereby allowing a clear division of the performance record for each asset managed.
  - ❑ 2. If cash and substitute securities are not assigned to a separate asset, comparisons should not be made against other managers' performance figures for assets where cash returns have been included.
  - ❑ 3. The manager has supplied information on risk, volatility, and/or other measures that allows for reasonable performance evaluation.
- ❑ H. Convertible securities have been consistently assigned to either equities or fixed-income, and have not been shifted without notice being given to clients concurrent or prior to such shift.
- ❑ I. Managers have provided the indexes against which their submitted performance records have normally been compared.
- ❑ J. If managers' assets have been leveraged, and performance returns calculated on this basis, results on an all-cash (unleveraged) basis have been provided.

II. Investment manager composites of performance results.

- ❑ A. The manager has submitted a composite of all accounts managed for each period submitted; the composite includes results from any and all accounts no longer clients of the firm.
- ❑ B. If a manager has separate composites, all have been submitted. A prospect should be able to account for the performance of all the manager's assets managed.
- ❑ C. Composites are not "survivors only" compilations; they include results of all accounts ever managed, including those of clients no longer with the firm.
- ❑ D. All performance results contained in the composite include cash and substitutable securities, as per I.D. above.
- ❑ E. All individual years and cumulative performance results for all periods have been supplied. The composite covers every year of the past 10 years, along with longer-term results if the manager has been in the business this long.
- ❑ F. Compound annualized returns have been provided for all periods.
- ❑ G. A clear statement from manager indicates that no selectivity of account results for partial periods exists.
- ❑ H. Composite or other data have not been altered for reasons of personnel changes or any other reasons.
- ❑ I. Composite results are:
  - ❑ 1. Weighted for the dollars under management (the AIMR Standard).
  - ❑ 2. Presented on a median (unweighted) basis (recommended only as additional information, not as the primary disclosure).
- ❑ J. Data includes:
  - ❑ 1. Number of client relationships in the composite.
  - ❑ 2. Assets under management for each period.
  - ❑ 3. Average and median size of accounts in the composite.
  - ❑ 4. Assets shown as a percentage of the manager's total accounts, which share very comparable investment guidelines and risks; and as a percentage of the manager's total funds under management. (All clients and related performance data for this asset type can be accounted for.)
- ❑ K. Fee information is clear, so that pre- and post-fee results can be determined.
- ❑ L. Composites include typical indexes against which the manager has been judged.
- ❑ M. Alpha, beta, standard deviation of returns, and other measures of risk, quality, variability, etc. within the composite for each year have been indicated.
- ❑ N. Other information provided.

III. Verification of performance data.

- ❑ A. Results have been audited by reputable auditors.
- ❑ B. Results are not audited, but include statements that calculations and presentation of individual accounts and composites conform to AIMR Standards.
- ❑ C. Neither A. nor B. above.

Source: *Performance Reporting for Investment Managers* (Charlottesville, Va.: Association for Investment Management and Research, 1991).

FIGURE 27.10 **A SAMPLE PERFORMANCE PRESENTATION**

XYZ INVESTMENT FIRM PERFORMANCE RESULTS: GROWTH-PLUS-INCOME BALANCED COMPOSITE, JANUARY 1, 1986, THROUGH DECEMBER 31, 1995

Year	Total Return (percent)	Benchmark Return[a] (percent)	Number of Portfolios	Composite Dispersion (percent)	Total Assets at End of Period ($ millions)	Percentage of Firm Assets
1986	12.1	9.4	6	3.2	$ 50	80
1987	24.2	26.4	10	5.4	85	82
1988	17.0	16.4	15	3.8	120	78
1989	−3.3	−1.7	14	1.2	100	80
1990	15.8	12.8	18	4.3	124	75
1991	16.0	14.1	26	4.5	165	70
1992	2.2	1.8	32	2.0	235	68
1993	22.4	24.1	38	5.7	344	65
1994	7.1	6.0	45	2.8	445	64
1995	8.5	8.0	48	3.1	520	62

[a]*Editor's note:* Presentation of benchmark returns is not required.

XYZ Investment Firm has prepared and presented this report in compliance with the Performance Presentation Standards of the Association for Investment Management and Research (AIMR-PPS™). AIMR has not been involved with the preparation or review of this report.

Notes:

1. XYZ Investment Firm is a balanced portfolio investment manager that invests solely in U.S.-based securities. XYZ Investment Firm is defined as an independent investment management firm that is not affiliated with any parent organization.
2. These results have been prepared and presented in compliance with the AIMR-PPS only for the period January 1, 1990, through December 31, 1995. The full period is not in compliance. Prior to January 1, 1990, not all fully discretionary portfolios were represented in appropriate composites. Composite results for the years 1986 through 1989 include the five largest institutional portfolios that were managed in accordance with the growth-plus-income strategy. These five accounts are consistently represented in the composite for the full period from 1986 through 1989.
3. Results for the full historical period are time weighted. From 1986 through 1992, results were calculated yearly and the composites were asset weighted by beginning-of-year asset values. Since January 1, 1993, composites have been valued quarterly and portfolio returns have been weighted by using beginning-of-quarter market values plus weighted cash flows.
4. The benchmark: 60 percent S&P 500 Index; 40 percent Lehman Intermediate Aggregate Index. Annualized compound composite return = 11.9 percent; annualized compound benchmark return = 11.4 percent.
5. None of XYZ Investment Firm's balanced portfolio segments are included in any single-asset composites for the firm, and cash has been allocated evenly among asset segments.
6. Standard deviation in annual composite returns = 8.24 percent versus a standard deviation in the yearly benchmark returns of 8.53 percent.
7. The dispersion of annual returns is measured by the range between the highest- and lowest-performing portfolios in the composite.
8. Performance results are presented before management and custodial fees. The management fee schedule is attached.
9. No alteration of composites as presented here has occurred because of changes in personnel or other reasons at any time.
10. Settlement-date accounting was used prior to 1992.
11. A complete list of firm composites and performance results is available upon request.

Source: *AIMR Performance Presentation Standards Handbook* (Charlottesville, Va.: Association for Investment Management and Research, 1997).

THE INTERNET *Investments Online*

Mutual fund performance is a matter of public knowledge, but performance for the vast variety of pension funds, endowments, insurance company portfolios, trust portfolios, and other private investment pools may not be public. Investors will have to use the tools discussed in this chapter to evaluate the performance of nonpublic portfolios. Many investor consultant and software firms have proprietary databases and products, and they try to sell their services to individual and institutional investors as a means of evaluating portfolio performance. Consultants who evaluate money managers for clients will not offer the proprietary results of that research for free on the Internet. Nonetheless, some sites are helpful in showing applications of the material covered in this chapter.

www.nelnet.com The Web site of the Nelson Investment Manager database calls itself the "World's Best Money Managers" page. Nelson has a database of over 2,500 investment managers. After registering at the site, users can specify investment categories and obtain ranking performance data in a variety of formats. The site offers links to industry analysis and news as well as to investment managers' home pages and to sites of institutional investment managers.

www.first-rate.com The First Rate, Inc., Web site offers sample portfolio evaluation reports that can be viewed online. Users will have to pay to receive actual reports.

www.styleadvisor.com Zephyr Associates, Inc.'s Web site features information about StyleADVISOR. StyleADVISOR is a returns-based style and performance analysis software package. It uses Sharpe's techniques of performance analysis and attribution. Pages offer visitors the chance to learn about StyleADVISOR and to view sample reports. Visitors can view past newsletters, which give analysis and insights into portfolio performance attribution issues.

www.fundstyle.com After visitors register for free, Advisor Software, Inc., offers free style analyses on over 9,000 mutual funds.

www.morningstar.net This site, mentioned in Chapter 21, allows users to obtain summary reports on funds. "Quicktake" reports offer information on returns, the Morningstar rating, graphs of fund performance versus a benchmark, and the sector weightings of a fund's investments. The report gives the fund's style, as well, using Morningstar's 3x3 style box.

www.valueline.com This site is mentioned again as subscribers can obtain useful mutual fund performance information, including charts, both absolute and relative-to-peer-group return performance, and the fund's style, using Value Line's style box.

www.aimr.org First mentioned in Chapter 2, the Association for Investment Management and Research's home page offers a link to information about the AIMR Performance Presentation Standards. These are a set of ethical principles and guidelines to help ensure fair representation, full disclosure, and comparability in reported portfolio performance results. The site provides links to resources for training and for library information on the standards.

Summary

- The first major goal of portfolio management is to derive rates of return that equal or exceed the returns on a naively selected portfolio with equal risk. The second goal is to attain complete diversification. Several techniques have been derived to evaluate equity portfolios in terms of both risk and return (composite measures) based on the CAPM. The Treynor measure considers the excess returns earned per unit of systematic risk. The Sharpe measure indicates the excess return per unit of total risk. The Jensen and Information Ratio measures likewise evaluate performance in terms of the systematic risk involved and show how to determine whether the difference in risk-adjusted performance (good or bad) is statistically significant. Additional work in equity portfolio evaluation has been concerned with models that indicate what components of the management process contributed to the results. A model by Fama divided the composite return into measures related to total risk, systematic risk, diversification, and selectivity, in addition to measuring overall performance. Finally, attribution analysis seeks to establish whether market timing or security selection skills (or both) are the source of a manager's performance.

- Roll challenged the validity of all techniques that assume a market portfolio that theoretically includes all risky assets when actually investigators use a proxy such as the S&P 500 that is limited to U.S. common stocks. This criticism does not invalidate the normative asset pricing model, only its application because of measurement problems related to the proxy for the market portfolio. It is demonstrated that the measurement problem is increased in an environment where global investing is the norm. The good news is that more comprehensive indexes are feasible and are currently being developed.
- Although the techniques for evaluating equity portfolio performance have been in existence for almost 35 years, comparable techniques for examining bond portfolio performance were initiated more recently. Notably, the evaluation models for bonds typically consider separately the several important decision variables related to bonds: the overall market factor, the impact of maturity-duration decisions, the influence of sector and quality factors, and the impact of individual bond selection. A study indicated a lack of consistency over time for a sample of bond managers similar to results for equity managers.
- In conclusion, investors need to evaluate their own performance and the performance of hired managers. The various techniques we discuss provide theoretically justifiable measures that differ slightly. Although there is high rank correlation among the alternative measures, *all the measures should be used* because they provide different insights regarding the performance of managers. Finally, an evaluation of a portfolio manager should be done many times over different market environments before a final judgment is reached regarding the strengths and weaknesses of a manager.

Questions

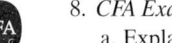

1. Describe two major factors that a portfolio manager should consider before designing an investment strategy. What types of decisions can a manager make to achieve these goals?
2. Compare and contrast four prominent approaches to measuring investment performance on a risk-adjusted basis. In developing your answer, comment on the conditions under which each measure will be most useful.
3. The Sharpe and Treynor performance measures both calculate a portfolio's average excess return per unit of risk. Under what circumstances would it make sense to use both measures to compare the performance of a given set of portfolios? What additional information is provided by a comparison of the rankings achieved using the two measures?
4. Describe how the Jensen measure of performance is calculated. Under what conditions should it give a similar set of portfolio rankings as the Sharpe and Treynor measures? Is it possible to adjust the Jensen measure so that a portfolio's alpha value is measured relative to an empirical form of the arbitrage pricing theory rather than the capital asset pricing model? Explain.
5. The Information Ratio (*IR*) has been described as a benefit-cost ratio. Explain how the *IR* measures portfolio performance and whether this analogy is appropriate.
6. A fund had an overall performance value of −0.50 percent using the Fama performance technique. Discuss whether the manager of this fund could have experienced a positive selectivity value and under what conditions that value might have occurred.
7. A portfolio has an R^2 with the market of 0.95 and a selectivity value of 2.5 percent. Would you expect this portfolio to have a positive or a negative net selectivity value? Explain.
8. CFA *CFA Examination I (June 1991)*
   a. Explain why the asset allocation decision is the primary determinant of total portfolio performance over time.
   b. Describe three reasons why successful implementation of asset allocation decisions is even more difficult in practice than in theory.
9. Performance attribution analysis is an attempt to divide a manager's "active" residual return into an allocation effect and a selection effect. Explain how these two effects are measured and why their sum must equal the total value-added return for the manager. Is this analysis valid if the actual portfolio in question is riskier than the benchmark portfolio to which it is being compared?

CFA

10. *CFA Examination III (June 1991)*
A number of different management "styles" are utilized by investment managers. Performance evaluation, however, is not standardized either within or across management styles. One development aimed at mitigating this problem is the emergence of the "benchmark portfolio" concept.
Against this background, comment on the role of benchmark portfolios in evaluating a manager's investment performance and contrast the suitability of benchmark portfolios for this purpose with that of the "median manager" approach often employed. Include *four* elements of comparison in your discussion.

CFA

11. *CFA Examination III (June 1981)*
Richard Roll, in an article on using the capital asset pricing model (CAPM) to evaluate portfolio performance, indicated that it may not be possible to evaluate portfolio management ability if there is error in the benchmark used.
   a. In evaluating portfolio performance, describe the general procedure, with emphasis on the benchmark employed.
   b. Explain what Roll meant by the benchmark error and identify the specific problem with this benchmark.
   c. Draw a graph that shows how a portfolio that has been judged as superior relative to a "measured" security market line (SML) can be inferior relative to the "true" SML.
   d. Assume that you are informed that a given portfolio manager has been evaluated as superior when compared to the DJIA, the S&P 500, and the NYSE Composite Index. Explain whether this consensus would make you feel more comfortable regarding the portfolio manager's true ability.
   e. While conceding the possible problem with benchmark errors as set forth by Roll, some contend this does not mean the CAPM is incorrect, but only that there is a measurement problem when implementing the theory. Others contend that because of benchmark errors, the whole technique should be scrapped. Take and defend one of these positions.
12. It has been contended that the derivation of an appropriate model for evaluating the performance of a bond manager is more difficult than an equity portfolio evaluation model because more decisions are required. Discuss some of the specific decisions that need to be considered when evaluating the performance of a bond portfolio manager.

CFA

13. *CFA Examination III (June 1982)*
During a quarterly review session, a client of Fixed Income Investors, a pension fund advisory firm, asks Fred Raymond, the portfolio manager for the company's account, if he could provide a more detailed analysis of their portfolio performance than simply total return. Specifically, the client had recently seen a copy of an article by Dietz, Fogler, and Hardy on the analysis of bond portfolio returns that attempted to decompose the total return into the following four components:
   a. Yield-to-maturity effect
   b. Interest rate effect
   c. Sector/quality effect
   d. Residual
Although he does not expect you to be able to provide such an analysis this year, he asks you to explain each of these components to him so he will be better prepared to understand such an analysis when you do it for his company's portfolio next year. Explain each of these components.

Problems

CFA

1. *CFA Examination III (June 1985)*
You have been asked to evaluate the performance of two portfolios: Good Samaritan Hospital's endowment assets and estate fund of the recently deceased Mrs. Mary Atkins, which has just been transferred in a bequest to Good Samaritan. The existing Good Samaritan endowment assets (excluding the Atkins estate) have been managed by an investment counseling firm with an income objective of approximately 5 percent annually. The returns from this portfolio and from Mrs. Atkins' portfolio are shown in the table below.

	Latest Fiscal Year Total Return	Beta
Good Samaritan existing endowment assets		
—equity only	11.8%	1.20
—total portfolio	8.4	
Mrs. Atkins' Portfolio		
—equity only	10.7%	1.05
—total portfolio	5.1	
S&P 500 Index	9.9%	
Lehman Bond Index	3.4	
90-day Treasury Bills	7.8	
Municipal Bond Index	1.4	

a. Calculate the risk-adjusted return of each of the two equity-only portfolios. Compare these returns to each other and to the S&P 500, and explain the significance of any differences.

b. List and briefly comment on three factors which could account for the difference in reported performance between Mrs. Atkins' and Good Samaritan's total portfolios.

2. The portfolios identified below are being considered for investment. During the period under consideration, $RFR = 0.07$.

Portfolio	Return	Beta	σ_i
P	0.15	1.0	0.05
Q	0.20	1.5	0.10
R	0.10	0.6	0.03
S	0.17	1.1	0.06
Market	0.13	1.0	0.04

a. Compute the Sharpe measure for each portfolio and the market portfolio.

b. Compute the Treynor measure for each portfolio and the market portfolio.

c. Rank the portfolios using each measure, explaining the cause for any differences you find in the rankings.

CFA

3. *CFA Examination I (June 1994)*

An analyst wants to evaluate Portfolio X, consisting entirely of U.S. common stocks, using both the Treynor and Sharpe measures of portfolio performance. The table below provides the average annual rate of return for Portfolio X, the market portfolio (as measured by the Standard and Poor's 500 Index), and U.S. Treasury bills (T-bills) during the past 8 years.

	Annual Average Rate of Return	Standard Deviation of Return	Beta
Portfolio X	10%	18%	0.60
S&P 500	12	13	1.00
T-bills	6	n/a	n/a

n/a = not applicable

a. Calculate both the Treynor measure and the Sharpe measure for both Portfolio X and the S&P 500. Briefly explain whether Portfolio X underperformed, equaled, or outperformed the S&P 500 on a risk-adjusted basis using both the Treynor measure and the Sharpe measure.

b. Based on the performance of Portfolio X relative to the S&P 500 calculated in Part a, briefly explain the reason for the conflicting results when using the Treynor measure versus the Sharpe measure.

4. You have been assigned the task of comparing the investment performance of five different pension fund managers. After gathering 60 months of excess returns (i.e., returns in excess of the monthly risk-free rate) on each fund as well as the monthly excess returns on the entire stock market, you perform the regressions of the form:

$$(R_{\text{fund}} - RFR)_t = \alpha + \beta(R_{\text{mkt}} - RFR)_t + U_t$$

You have prepared the following summary of the data, with the standard errors for each of the coefficients listed in parentheses.

	Regression Data:			$(R_{\text{FUND}} - RFR)$:	
Portfolio	α	β	R^2	**Mean**	σ
ABC	0.192 (0.11)	1.048 (0.10)	94.1%	1.022%	1.193%
DEF	−0.053 (0.19)	0.662 (0.09)	91.6	0.473	0.764
GHI	0.463 (0.19)	0.594 (0.07)	68.6	0.935	0.793
JKL	0.355 (0.22)	0.757 (0.08)	64.1	0.955	1.044
MNO	0.296 (0.14)	0.785 (0.12)	94.8	0.890	0.890

a. Which fund had the highest degree of diversification over the sample period? How is diversification measured in this statistical framework?

b. Rank these funds' performance according to the Sharpe, Treynor, and Jensen measures.

c. Since you know that according to the CAPM the intercept of these regressions (i.e., alpha) should be zero, this coefficient can be used as a measure of the value-added provided by the investment manager. Which funds have statistically outperformed and underperformed the market using a two-sided 95 percent confidence interval? (Note: The relevant t-statistic using 60 observations is 2.00.)

5. You have just gathered the following performance data for three different money managers, based on a regression of their excess returns relative to those for the S&P 500 index. Each manager's performance was measured over the same 3-year period, but the return period for each was different.

Manager	Alpha	Beta	Std. Error of Regression	Return Period
A	0.058%	0.95	0.533%	Weekly
B	0.115	1.12	5.884	Biweekly
C	0.250	0.78	2.165	Monthly

a. Calculate the information ratio for each manager, ignoring the difference in return reporting periods.

b. Calculate the annualized information ratio for each manager.

c. Rank the managers' performance according to your answers in parts a and b. Which manager performed the best? Explain.

6. You have decided to undertake an evaluation of the performance of the Cirrus International Fund (CIF) for your investment club. After collecting the following data:

$$R_a = 0.15$$
$$RFR = 0.05$$
$$\beta_a = 1.20$$
$$R_m = 0.10$$

a. Draw the security market line.
b. Calculate CIF's overall performance.
c. Calculate CIF's selectivity.
d. Calculate CIF's risk.

7. Consider the following historical performance data for two different portfolios, the Standard and Poor's 500, and the 90-day T-bill.

Investment Vehicle	Average Rate of Return	Standard Deviation	Beta	R^2
Fund 1	26.40%	20.67%	1.351	0.751
Fund 2	13.22	14.20	0.905	0.713
S&P 500	15.71	13.25		
90-day T-bill	6.20	0.50		

a. Calculate the Fama overall performance measure for both funds.
b. What is the return to risk for both funds?
c. For both funds, compute the measures of (i) selectivity, (ii) diversification, and (iii) net selectivity.
d. Explain the meaning of the net selectivity measure and how it helps you evaluate investor performance. Which fund had the best performance?

CFA

8. *CFA Examination III (June 1995)*

Your discussion with a client has turned to the measurement of investment performance, particularly with respect to international portfolios.

PERFORMANCE AND ATTRIBUTION DATA: ANNUALIZED RETURNS FOR 5 YEARS ENDED 12/31/94

International Manager/Index	Total Return	Country/Security Return	Currency Return
Manager A	−6.0%	2.0%	−8.0%
Manager B	−2.0	−1.0	−1.0
EAFE Index	−5.0	0.2	−5.2

a. Assume that the data in the above table for Manager A and Manager B accurately reflect their investment skills and that both managers actively manage currency exposure. Briefly describe one strength and one weakness for each manager.
b. Recommend and justify a strategy that would enable the Fund to take advantage of the strengths of each of the two managers while minimizing their weaknesses.

9. Consider the following performance data for two portfolio managers (A and B) and a common benchmark portfolio:

	BENCHMARK		**MANAGER A**		**MANAGER B**	
	Weight	**Return**	**Weight**	**Return**	**Weight**	**Return**
Stock	0.6	−5.0%	0.5	−4.0%	0.3	−5.0%
Bonds	0.3	−3.5	0.2	−2.5	0.4	−3.5
Cash	0.1	0.3	0.3	0.3	0.3	0.3

a. Calculate: (i) the overall return to the benchmark portfolio; (ii) the overall return to manager A's actual portfolio; and (iii) the overall return to manager B's actual portfolio. Briefly comment on whether these managers have under- or outperformed the benchmark fund.

b. Using attribution analysis, calculate (i) the *selection effect* for manager A, and (ii) the *allocation effect* for manager B. Using these numbers in conjunction with your results from part a, comment on whether these managers have added value through their selection skills, their allocation skills, or both.

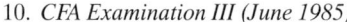

10. *CFA Examination III (June 1985)*

A U.S. pension plan hired two off-shore firms to manage the non-U.S. equity portion of its total portfolio. Each firm was free to own stocks in any country market included in Morgan Stanley/Capital International's Europe, Australia, and Far East Index (EAFE) and free to use any form of dollar and/or non-dollar cash or bonds as an equity substitute or reserve. After three years had elapsed, the records of the managers and the EAFE Index were as shown below:

SUMMARY: CONTRIBUTIONS TO RETURN

	Currency	Country Selection	Stock Selection	Cash/Bond Allocation	Total Return Recorded
Manager A	(9.0%)	19.7%	3.1%	0.6%	14.4%
Manager B	(7.4)	14.2	6.0	2.81	5.6
Composite of A & B	(8.2)	16.9	4.5	1.71	5.0
EAFE Index	(12.9)	19.9	—	—	7.0

You are a member of the plan sponsor's Pension Committee, which will soon meet with the plan's consultant to review manager performance. In preparation for this meeting, you go through the following analysis:

a. Briefly describe the strengths and weaknesses of each manager, relative to the EAFE Index data.

b. Briefly explain the meaning of the data in the "Currency" column.

11. Reggie Portmus has made a performance evaluation of his bond holdings. He has misplaced some of the values and has asked for your help in calculating the remaining ones. At present he holds 10-year AA, 5-year A, and 25-year B bonds, and the following information has been recovered:

I = external interest rate environment:	11.00
E = expected return:	10.00
U = unexpected return:	?
M = maturity:	0.2%/year in the first 5 years, 0.1%/year thereafter
S = spread/quality:	−0.2%/rank (AAA, AA, A, BBB, etc.)
B = specific selection:	0.25, 0.50, 075, respectively
C:	?
R:	?

CFA

12. *CFA Examination III (June 1994)*

To illustrate for the Investment Committee of the profit-sharing plan to which you are a consultant on some of the issues that arise in measuring performance, you have identified three U.S. fixed-income management firms whose investment approaches are representative of general practice. Each firm's approach is described below.

Firm A: An enhanced index fund manager that seeks to add value by superior security selection while maintaining portfolio duration and sector weights equal to the overall bond market.

Firm B: An active duration manager investing only in the government and corporate bond sectors. The firm uses futures to manage portfolio duration.

Firm C: An active manager seeking to add value by correctly anticipating changes in the shape of the yield curve, while maintaining portfolio duration and sector weights roughly equal to the overall bond market.

You have provided the Committee with the following additional information about these firms, derived from a consultant's database.

ANNUALIZED TOTAL RETURN DATA (PAST FIVE YEARS)

	Firm A	Firm B	Firm C
Reported Returns	9.2%	9.3%	9.0%

		Index Sectors			
	Aggregate Index	Governments	Corporates	Government/ Corporate	Mortgages
Index Return	8.7%	9.0%	9.8%	9.5%	8.3%

	Consultant's Manager Universe		
	All Managers	Managers Using the Aggregate Index as Their Benchmark	Managers Using the Govt./Corp. Sector as Their Benchmark
Return 5th percentile	6.0%	7.7%	8.4%
25th percentile	7.1	8.1	8.9
50th percentile	8.0	8.6	9.4
75th percentile	8.6	9.1	9.9
95th percentile	9.3	13.1	13.9

a. Evaluate the performance of each of these three firms relative to its appropriate Index and to the manager universe. Use only the data from the descriptions and the above table, even though other information would be required for a more complete and accurate appraisal.

To provide additional guidance to the Committee, you decide to do an attribution analysis on the returns produced by Firm A and Firm C and have prepared the following table:

PERFORMANCE ATTRIBUTION ANALYSIS
(PAST FIVE YEARS—ANNUALIZED TOTAL RETURNS)

	Total Return	=	Duration Decisions	+	Yield Curve Decisions	+	Sector Weighting Decisions	+	Security Selection Decisions & Residuals
			RETURN ATTRIBUTED TO						
Firm A									
Total Return	9.20%		8.00%		0.80%		0.00%		0.40%
Benchmark Index Return	8.70		7.00		0.50		0.70		0.50
Difference	0.50		1.00		0.30		−0.70		−0.10
Firm C									
Total Return	9.00%		7.03%		0.80%		0.71%		0.46%
Benchmark Index Return	8.70		7.00		0.50		0.70		0.50
Difference	0.30		0.03		0.30		0.01		−0.04

b. Evaluate the performance of Firm A and of Firm C based on all the information previously provided and your interpretation of the data in this new table.
c. Based solely on the attribution analysis you performed in Part b above, state which firm produced the better result and justify your conclusion.

13. For each of the last six quarters, managers L and M have provided you with the total dollar value of the funds they manage, along with the quarterly contributions or withdrawals made by their clients. (*Note:* Contributions are indicated by positive numbers, withdrawals by negative numbers.)

	MANAGER L		**MANAGER M**	
Quarter	Total Funds Under Management	Contributions/ Withdrawals	Total Funds Under Management	Contributions/ Withdrawals
Initial	$500,000	—	$700,000	—
1	527,000	12,000	692,000	−35,000
2	530,000	7,500	663,000	−35,000
3	555,000	13,500	621,000	−35,000
4	580,000	6,500	612,000	−35,000
5	625,000	10,000	625,000	−35,000

For each manager, calculate: (i) her dollar-weighted return; (ii) her time-weighted return; and (iii) estimates of her quarterly performance returns using the Dietz approximation method, assuming contributions/withdrawals are made exactly halfway through the quarter.

References

Brown, Stephen J., William Goetzmann, Roger G. Ibbottson, and Stephen A. Ross. "Survivorship Bias in Performance Studies." *Review of Financial Studies* 5, no. 4 (December 1992).

Dybvig, Philip H., and Stephen A. Ross. "The Analytics of Performance Measurement Using a Security Market Line." *Journal of Finance* 40, no. 2 (June 1985).

Elton, Edwin J., and Martin J. Gruber. *Modern Portfolio Theory and Investment Analysis.* 5th ed. New York: John Wiley & Sons, 1995.

Fabozzi, Frank J. *Bond Markets, Analysis and Strategies.* 3d ed. Upper Saddle River, N.J.: Prentice-Hall, 1996.

French, Dan W., and Glenn V. Henderson Jr. "How Well Does Performance Evaluation Perform?" *Journal of Portfolio Management* 11, no. 2 (winter 1985).

Grinblatt, Mark, and Sheridan Titman. "Performance Evaluation." In R. Jarrow et al., eds., *Handbook in Operations Research and Management Science.* New York: Elsevier Science B.V., 1995.

Maginn, John L., and Donald L. Tuttle, eds. *Managing Investment Portfolios: A Dynamic Process.* 2d ed. Boston, Mass.: Warren, Gorham, & Lamont, 1990.

Radcliffe, Robert, Robert Brooks, and Haim Levy. "Active Asset Allocation Decisions of Professional Equity Managers." *Review of Financial Services* 2, no. 1 (1992/1993).

Sharpe, William F. "Asset Allocation: Management Style and Performance Measurement." *Journal of Portfolio Management* 18, no. 2 (winter 1992).

Shulka, Ray, and Charles Trzcinka. "Performance Measurement of Managed Portfolios." In *Financial Markets, Institutions, and Investments* 1, no. 4. New York: New York University Salomon Center, 1992.

Squires, Jan, ed. *Performance Evaluation, Benchmarks, and Attribution Analysis.* Charlottesville, Va.: Association for Investment Management and Research, 1995.

APPENDIX A

HOW TO BECOME A CHARTERED FINANCIAL ANALYST

As mentioned in the section on career opportunities, the professional designation of Chartered Financial Analyst (CFA^{SM}) is becoming a significant requirement for a career in investment analysis and/or portfolio management. For that reason, this section presents the history and objectives of the Association for Investment Management and Research (AIMR) and general guidelines for acquiring the CFA designation. If you are interested in the program, you can write or email AIMR for more information.

The CFA examinations were first offered in 1963 by the Institute of Chartered Financial Analysts (ICFA) which was formed in 1959 to enhance the professionalism of those involved in various aspects of the investment decision-making process and to recognize those who achieve a high level of professionalism. The ICFA merged with the Financial Analysts Federation in 1991 to form AIMR.

The basic missions and purposes of AIMR are:

- To develop and keep current a "body of knowledge" applicable to the investment decision-making process. The principal components of this knowledge are financial accounting, economics, both debt and equity securities analysis, portfolio management, ethical and professional standards, and quantitative techniques.
- To administer a study and examination program for eligible candidates, the primary objectives of which are to assist the candidate in mastering and applying the body of knowledge and to test the candidate's competency in the knowledge gained.
- To award the professional CFA designation to those candidates who have passed three examination levels (encompassing a total of 18 hours of testing over a minimum of three years), who meet stipulated standards of professional conduct, and who otherwise are eligible for membership in AIMR.
- To provide a useful and informative program of continuing education through seminars, publications, and other formats that enable members, candidates, and others in the investment constituency to be more aware of and to better utilize the changing and expanding body of knowledge.
- To sponsor and enforce a Code of Ethics and Standards of Professional Conduct that apply to enrolled candidates and to all members.

To enter the CFA Program an applicant must have a bachelor's degree (or the equivalent work experience). An applicant must receive a bachelor's degree no later than September 30 of the current exam year in order to qualify for entrance. A candidate may sit for all three examinations without having had investment experience *per se* or having joined a member society or chapter of AIMR. However, after passing the three examination levels, the CFA Charter will not be awarded unless or until the candidate:

- has at least three years of experience as a financial analyst, which is defined as a person who has spent and/or is spending a substantial portion of his/her professional time collecting, evaluating, and applying financial, economic, and related data to the investment decision-making process; and
- has applied for membership or is a member of an affiliated member society or chapter of AIMR, if such a society/chapter exists within 50 miles of the candidate's principal place of business.

The curriculum of the CFA study program covers:

1. Ethical and Professional Standards
2. Quantitative Techniques
3. Economics
4. Financial Statement Analysis
5. Corporate Finance
6. Analysis of Debt Investments
7. Analysis of Equity Investments
8. Analysis and Application of Derivatives
9. Analysis of Alternative Investments
10. Portfolio Management
11. Performance Measurement and Portfolio Attribution Analysis

Source: Reprinted with permission from the Association for Investment Management and Research, Charlottesville, Virginia.

Members and candidates are typically employed in the investment field. From 1963 to August 1999, over 31,000 charters have been awarded. Nearly 60,000 individuals were registered in the 1999 CFA Candidate Program. If you are interested in learning more about the CFA Program, AIMR has a booklet that describes the program and includes an application form. The address is: AIMR, Attn: Information Central, PO Box 3668, Charlottesville, Virginia, 22903, USA. You may also request a booklet by email to info@aimr.org.

APPENDIX B

CODE OF ETHICS AND STANDARDS OF PROFESSIONAL CONDUCT

THE CODE OF ETHICS

Members of the Association for Investment Management and Research shall:
- Act with integrity, competence, dignity, and in an ethical manner when dealing with the public, clients, prospects, employers, employees, and fellow members.
- Practice and encourage others to practice in a professional and ethical manner that will reflect credit on members and their profession.
- Strive to maintain and improve their competence and the competence of others in the profession.
- Use reasonable care and exercise independent professional judgment.

STANDARDS OF PROFESSIONAL CONDUCT

Standard I: Fundamental Responsibilities
Members shall:
A. Maintain knowledge of and comply with all applicable laws, rules, and regulations (including AIMR's Code of Ethics and Standards of Professional Conduct) of any government, governmental agency, regulatory organization, licensing agency, or professional association governing the members' professional activities.
B. Not knowingly participate or assist in any violation of such laws, rules, or regulations.

Standard II: Relationships with and Responsibilities to the Profession
A. Use of Professional Designation.
1. AIMR members may reference their membership only in a dignified and judicious manner. The use of the reference may be accompanied by an accurate explanation of the requirements that have been met to obtain membership in these organizations.
2. Those who have earned the right to use the Chartered Financial Analyst designation may use the marks "Chartered Financial Analyst" or "CFA" and are encouraged to do so, but only in a proper, dignified, and judicious manner. The use of the designation may be accompanied by an accurate explanation of the requirements that have been met to obtain the right to use the designation.
3. Candidates in the CFA Program, as defined in the AIMR Bylaws, may reference their participation in the CFA Program, but the reference must clearly state that an individual is a candidate in the CFA Program and cannot imply that the candidate has achieved any type of partial designation.

B. Professional Misconduct.
1. Members shall not engage in any professional conduct involving dishonesty, fraud, deceit, or misrepresentation or commit any act that reflects adversely on their honesty, trustworthiness, or professional competence.
2. Members and candidates shall not engage in any conduct or commit any act that compromises the integrity of the CFA designation or the integrity or validity of the examinations leading to the award of the right to use the CFA designation.

C. Prohibition against Plagiarism. Members shall not copy or use, in substantially the same form as the original, material prepared by another without acknowledging and identifying the name of the author, publisher, or source of such material. Members may use, without acknowledgment, factual information published by recognized financial and statistical reporting services or similar sources.

Standard III: Relationships with and Responsibilities to the Employer
A. Obligation to Inform Employer of Code and Standards. Members shall:
1. Inform their employer in writing, through their direct supervisor, that they are obligated to comply with the Code and Standards and are subject to disciplinary sanctions for violations thereof.
2. Deliver a copy of the Code and Standards to their employer if the employer does not have a copy.

B. Duty to Employer. Members shall not undertake any independent practice that could result in compensation or other benefit in competition with their employer unless they obtain written consent from both their employer and the persons or entities for whom they undertake independent practice.

C. Disclosure of Conflicts to Employer. Members shall:
1. Disclose to their employer all matters, including beneficial ownership of securities or other investments, that reasonably could be expected to interfere with their duty to their employer or ability to make unbiased and objective recommendations.
2. Comply with any prohibitions on activities imposed by their employer if a conflict of interest exists.

D. Disclosure of Additional Compensation Arrangements. Members shall disclose to their employer in writing all monetary compensation or other benefits that they receive for their services that are in addition to compensation or benefits conferred by a member's employer.

E. Responsibilities of Supervisors. Members with supervisory responsibility, authority, or the ability to influence the conduct of others shall exercise reasonable supervision over those subject to their supervision or authority to prevent any violation of applicable statutes, regulations, or provisions of the Code and Standards. In so doing, members are entitled to rely on reasonable procedures designed to detect and prevent such violations.

Standard IV: Relationships with and Responsibilities to Clients and Prospects
A. Investment Process.
A.1 Reasonable Basis and Representations. Members shall:
a. Exercise diligence and thoroughness in making investment recommendations or in taking investment actions.
b. Have a reasonable and adequate basis, supported by appropriate research and investigation, for such recommendations or actions.
c. Make reasonable and diligent efforts to avoid any material misrepresentation in any research report or investment recommendation.
d. Maintain appropriate records to support the reasonableness of such recommendations or actions.

A.2 Research Reports. Members shall:
a. Use reasonable judgment regarding the inclusion or exclusion of relevant factors in research reports.
b. Distinguish between facts and opinions in research reports.
c. Indicate the basic characteristics of the investment involved when preparing for public distribution a research report that is not directly related to a specific portfolio or client.

A.3 Independence and Objectivity. Members shall use reasonable care and judgment to achieve and maintain independence and objectivity in making investment recommendations or taking investment action.

B. Interactions with Clients and Prospects.
B.1 Fiduciary Duties. In relationships with clients, members shall use particular care in determining applicable fiduciary duty and shall comply with such duty as to those persons and interests to whom the duty is owed. Members must act for the benefit of their clients and place their clients' interests before their own.

B.2 Portfolio Investment Recommendations and Actions. Members shall:
a. Make a reasonable inquiry into a client's financial situation, investment experience, and investment objectives prior to making any investment recommendations and shall update this information as necessary, but no less frequently than annually, to allow the members to adjust their investment recommendations to reflect changed circumstances.
b. Consider the appropriateness and suitability of investment recommendations or actions for each portfolio or client. In determining appropriateness and suitability, members shall consider applicable relevant factors, including the needs and circumstances of the portfolio or client, the basic characteristics of the investment involved, and the basic characteristics of the total portfolio. Members shall not make a recommendation unless they reasonably determine that the recommendation is suitable to the client's financial situation, investment experience, and investment objectives.
c. Distinguish between facts and opinions in the presentation of investment recommendations.
d. Disclose to clients and prospects the basic format and general principles of the investment processes by which securities are selected and portfolios are constructed and shall promptly disclose to clients and prospects any changes that might significantly affect those processes.

B.3 Fair Dealing. Members shall deal fairly and objectively with all clients and prospects when disseminating investment recommendations, disseminating material changes in prior investment recommendations, and taking investment action.

B.4 Priority of Transactions. Transactions for clients and employers shall have priority over transactions in securities or other investments of which a member is the beneficial owner so that such personal transactions do not operate adversely to their clients' or employer's interests. If members make a recommendation regarding the purchase or sale of a security or other investment, they shall give their clients and employer adequate opportunity to act on the recommendation before acting on their own behalf. For purposes of the Code and Standards, a member is a "beneficial owner" if the member has

---

Source: Reprinted with permission from the Association for Investment Management and Research, 560 Ray C. Hunt Drive, P.O. Box 3668, Charlottesville, Virginia 22903-0668. Amended and restated May 1999.

a. a direct or indirect pecuniary interest in the securities;
b. the power to vote or direct the voting of the shares of the securities or investments;
c. the power to dispose or direct the disposition of the security or investment.

B.5 Preservation of Confidentiality. Members shall preserve the confidentiality of information communicated by clients, prospects, or employers concerning matters within the scope of the client–member, prospect–member, or employer–member relationship unless the member receives information concerning illegal activities on the part of the client, prospect, or employer.

B.6 Prohibition against Misrepresentation. Members shall not make any statements, orally or in writing, that misrepresent
a. the services that they or their firms are capable of performing;
b. their qualifications or the qualifications of their firm;
c. the member's academic or professional credentials.

Members shall not make or imply, orally or in writing, any assurances or guarantees regarding any investment except to communicate accurate information regarding the terms of the investment instrument and the issuer's obligations under the instrument.

B.7 Disclosure of Conflicts to Clients and Prospects. Members shall disclose to their clients and prospects all matters, including beneficial ownership of securities or other investments, that reasonably could be expected to impair the member's ability to make unbiased and objective recommendations.

B.8 Disclosure of Referral Fees. Members shall disclose to clients and prospects any consideration or benefit received by the member or delivered to others for the recommendation of any services to the client or prospect.

Standard V: Relationships with and Responsibilities to the Investing Public

A. Prohibition against Use of Material Nonpublic Information. Members who possess material nonpublic information related to the value of a security shall not trade or cause others to trade in that security if such trading would breach a duty or if the information was misappropriated or relates to a tender offer. If members receive material nonpublic information in confidence, they shall not breach that confidence by trading or causing others to trade in securities to which such information relates. Members shall make reasonable efforts to achieve public dissemination of material nonpublic information disclosed in breach of a duty.

B. Performance Presentation.
1. Members shall not make any statements, orally or in writing, that misrepresent the investment performance that they or their firms have accomplished or can reasonably be expected to achieve.
2. If members communicate individual or firm performance information directly or indirectly to clients or prospective clients, or in a manner intended to be received by clients or prospective clients, members shall make every reasonable effort to assure that such performance information is a fair, accurate, and complete presentation of such performance.

Appendix C

Interest Tables

TABLE C.1 **Present Value of $1: PVIF = 1/(1 + k)^t**

Period	1%	2%	3%	4%	5%	6%	7%	8%	9%	10%	12%	14%	15%	16%	18%	20%	24%	28%	32%	36%
1	.9901	.9804	.9709	.9615	.9524	.9434	.9346	.9259	.9174	.9091	.8929	.8772	.8696	.8621	.8475	.8333	.8065	.7813	.7576	.7353
2	.9803	.9612	.9426	.9246	.9070	.8900	.8734	.8573	.8417	.8264	.7972	.7695	.7561	.7432	.7182	.6944	.6504	.6104	.5739	.5407
3	.9706	.9423	.9151	.8890	.8638	.8396	.8163	.7938	.7722	.7513	.7118	.6750	.6575	.6407	.6086	.5787	.5245	.4768	.4348	.3975
4	.9610	.9238	.8885	.8548	.8227	.7921	.7629	.7350	.7084	.6830	.6355	.5921	.5718	.5523	.5158	.4823	.4230	.3725	.3294	.2923
5	.9515	.9057	.8626	.8219	.7835	.7473	.7130	.6806	.6499	.6209	.5674	.5194	.4972	.4761	.4371	.4019	.3411	.2910	.2495	.2149
6	.9420	.8880	.8375	.7903	.7462	.7050	.6663	.6302	.5963	.5645	.5066	.4556	.4323	.4104	.3704	.3349	.2751	.2274	.1890	.1580
7	.9327	.8706	.8131	.7599	.7107	.6651	.6227	.5835	.5470	.5132	.4523	.3996	.3759	.3538	.3139	.2791	.2218	.1776	.1432	.1162
8	.9235	.8535	.7894	.7307	.6768	.6274	.5820	.5403	.5019	.4665	.4039	.3506	.3269	.3050	.2660	.2326	.1789	.1388	.1085	.0854
9	.9143	.8368	.7664	.7026	.6446	.5919	.5439	.5002	.4604	.4241	.3606	.3075	.2843	.2630	.2255	.1938	.1443	.1084	.0822	.0628
10	.9053	.8203	.7441	.6756	.6139	.5584	.5083	.4632	.4224	.3855	.3220	.2697	.2472	.2267	.1911	.1615	.1164	.0847	.0623	.0462
11	.8963	.8043	.7224	.6496	.5847	.5268	.4751	.4289	.3875	.3505	.2875	.2366	.2149	.1954	.1619	.1346	.0938	.0662	.0472	.0340
12	.8874	.7885	.7014	.6246	.5568	.4970	.4440	.3971	.3555	.3186	.2567	.2076	.1869	.1685	.1372	.1122	.0757	.0517	.0357	.0250
13	.8787	.7730	.6810	.6006	.5303	.4688	.4150	.3677	.3262	.2897	.2292	.1821	.1625	.1452	.1163	.0935	.0610	.0404	.0271	.0184
14	.8700	.7579	.6611	.5775	.5051	.4423	.3878	.3405	.2992	.2633	.2046	.1597	.1413	.1252	.0985	.0779	.0492	.0316	.0205	.0135
15	.8613	.7430	.6419	.5553	.4810	.4173	.3624	.3152	.2745	.2394	.1827	.1401	.1229	.1079	.0835	.0649	.0397	.0247	.0155	.0099
16	.8528	.7284	.6232	.5339	.4581	.3936	.3387	.2919	.2519	.2176	.1631	.1229	.1069	.0930	.0708	.0541	.0320	.0193	.0118	.0073
17	.8444	.7142	.6050	.5134	.4363	.3714	.3166	.2703	.2311	.1978	.1456	.1078	.0929	.0802	.0600	.0451	.0258	.0150	.0089	.0054
18	.8360	.7002	.5874	.4936	.4155	.3503	.2959	.2502	.2120	1799	.1300	.0946	.0808	.0691	.0508	.0376	.0208	.0118	.0068	.0039
19	.8277	.6864	.5703	.4746	.3957	.3305	.2765	.2317	.1945	1635	.1161	.0829	.0703	.0596	.0431	.0313	.0168	.0092	.0051	.0029
20	.8195	.6730	.5537	.4564	.3769	.3118	.2584	.2145	.1784	.1486	.1037	.0728	.0611	.0514	.0365	.0261	.0135	.0072	.0039	.0021
25	.7798	.6095	.4776	.3751	.2953	.2330	.1842	.1460	.1160	.0923	.0588	.0378	.0304	.0245	.0160	.0105	.0046	.0021	.0010	.0005
30	.7419	.5521	.4120	.3083	.2314	.1741	.1314	.0994	.0754	.0573	.0334	.0196	.0151	.0116	.0070	.0042	.0016	.0006	.0002	.0001
40	.6717	.4529	.3066	.2083	.1420	.0972	.0668	.0460	.0318	.0221	.0107	.0053	.0037	.0026	.0013	.0007	.0002	.0001	*	*
50	.6080	.3715	.2281	.1407	.0872	.0543	.0339	.0213	.0134	.0085	.0035	.0014	.0009	.0006	.0003	.0001	*	*	*	*
60	.5504	.3048	.1697	.0951	.0535	.0303	.0173	.0099	.0057	.0033	.0011	.0004	.0002	.0001	*	*	*	*	*	*

*The factor is zero to four decimal places.

TABLE C.2 Present Value of an Annuity of $1 Per Period for *n* Periods:

$$PVIFA = \sum_{t=1}^{n} \frac{1}{(1+k)^t} = \frac{1 - \frac{1}{(1+k)^n}}{k}$$

Number of Payments	1%	2%	3%	4%	5%	6%	7%	8%	9%	10%	12%	14%	15%	16%	18%	20%	24%	28%	32%
1	0.9901	0.9804	0.9709	0.9615	0.9524	0.9434	0.9346	0.9259	0.9174	0.9091	0.8929	0.8772	0.8696	0.8621	0.8475	0.8333	0.8065	0.7813	0.7576
2	1.9704	1.9416	1.9135	1.8861	1.8594	1.8334	1.8080	1.7833	1.7591	1.7355	1.6901	1.6467	1.6257	1.6052	1.5656	1.5278	1.4568	1.3916	1.3315
3	2.9410	2.8839	2.8286	2.7751	2.7232	2.6730	2.6243	2.5771	2.5313	2.4869	2.4018	2.3216	2.2832	2.2459	2.1743	2.1065	1.9813	1.8684	1.7663
4	3.9020	3.8077	3.7171	3.6299	3.5460	3.4651	3.3872	3.3121	3.2397	3.1699	3.0373	2.9137	2.8550	2.7982	2.6901	2.5887	2.4043	2.2410	2.0957
5	4.8534	4.7135	4.5797	4.4518	4.3295	4.2124	4.1002	3.9927	3.8897	3.7908	3.6048	3.4331	3.3522	3.2743	3.1272	2.9906	2.7454	2.5320	2.3452
6	5.7955	5.6014	5.4172	5.2421	5.0757	4.9173	4.7665	4.6229	4.4859	4.3553	4.1114	3.8887	3.7845	3.6847	3.4976	3.3255	3.0205	2.7594	2.5342
7	6.7282	6.4720	6.2303	6.0021	5.7864	5.5824	5.3893	5.2064	5.0330	4.8684	4.5638	4.2883	4.1604	4.0386	3.8115	3.6046	3.2423	2.9370	2.6775
8	7.6517	7.3255	7.0197	6.7327	6.4632	6.2098	5.9713	5.7466	5.5348	5.3349	4.9676	4.6389	4.4873	4.3436	4.0776	3.8372	3.4212	3.0758	2.7860
9	8.5660	8.1622	7.7861	7.4353	7.1078	6.8017	6.5152	6.2469	5.9952	5.7590	5.3282	4.9464	4.7716	4.6065	4.3030	4.0310	3.5655	3.1842	2.8681
10	9.4713	8.9826	8.5302	8.1109	7.7217	7.3601	7.0236	6.7101	6.4177	6.1446	5.6502	5.2161	5.0188	4.8332	4.4941	4.1925	3.6819	3.2689	2.9304
11	10.3676	9.7868	9.2526	8.7605	8.3064	7.8869	7.4987	7.1390	6.8052	6.4951	5.9377	5.4527	5.2337	5.0286	4.6560	4.3271	3.7757	3.3351	2.9776
12	11.2551	10.5753	9.9540	9.3851	8.8633	8.3838	7.9427	7.5361	7.1607	6.8137	6.1944	5.6603	5.4206	5.1971	4.7932	4.4392	3.8514	3.3868	3.0133
13	12.1337	11.3484	10.6350	9.9856	9.3936	8.8527	8.3577	7.9038	7.4869	7.1034	6.4235	5.8424	5.5831	5.3423	4.9095	4.5327	3.9124	3.4272	3.0404
14	13.0037	12.1062	11.2961	10.5631	9.8986	9.2950	8.7455	8.2442	7.7862	7.3667	6.6282	6.0021	5.7245	5.4675	5.0081	4.6106	3.9616	3.4587	3.0609
15	13.8651	12.8493	11.9379	11.1184	10.3797	9.7122	9.1079	8.5595	8.0607	7.6061	6.8109	6.1422	5.8474	5.5755	5.0916	4.6755	4.0013	3.4834	3.0764
16	14.7179	13.5777	12.5611	11.6523	10.8378	10.1059	9.4466	8.8514	8.3126	7.8237	6.9740	6.2651	5.9542	5.6685	5.1624	4.7296	4.0333	3.5026	3.0882
17	15.5623	14.2919	13.1661	12.1657	11.2741	10.4773	9.7632	9.1216	8.5436	8.0216	7.1196	6.3729	6.0472	5.7487	5.2223	4.7746	4.0591	3.5177	3.0971
18	16.3983	14.9920	13.7535	12.6593	11.6896	10.8276	10.0591	9.3719	8.7556	8.2014	7.2497	6.4674	6.1280	5.8178	5.2732	4.8122	4.0799	3.5294	3.1039
19	17.2260	15.6785	14.3238	13.1339	12.0853	11.1581	10.3356	9.6036	8.9501	8.3649	7.3658	6.5504	6.1982	5.8775	5.3162	4.8435	4.0967	3.5386	3.1090
20	18.0456	16.3514	14.8775	13.5903	12.4622	11.4699	10.5940	9.8181	9.1285	8.5136	7.4694	6.6231	6.2593	5.9288	5.3527	4.8696	4.1103	3.5458	3.1129
25	22.0232	19.5235	17.4131	15.6221	14.0939	12.7834	11.6536	10.6748	9.8226	9.0770	7.8431	6.8729	6.4641	6.0971	5.4669	4.9476	4.1474	3.5640	3.1220
30	25.8077	22.3965	19.6004	17.2920	15.3725	13.7648	12.4090	11.2578	10.2737	9.4269	8.0552	7.0027	6.5660	6.1772	5.5168	4.9789	4.1601	3.5693	3.1242
40	32.8347	27.3555	23.1148	19.7928	17.1591	15.0463	13.3317	11.9246	10.7574	9.7791	8.2438	7.1050	6.6418	6.2335	5.5482	4.9966	4.1659	3.5712	3.1250
50	39.1961	31.4236	25.7298	21.4822	18.2559	15.7619	13.8007	12.2335	10.9617	9.9148	8.3045	7.1327	6.6605	6.2463	5.5541	4.9995	4.1666	3.5714	3.1250
60	44.9550	34.7609	27.6756	22.6235	18.9293	16.1614	14.0392	12.3766	11.0480	9.9672	8.3240	7.1401	6.6651	6.2402	5.5553	4.9999	4.1667	3.5714	3.1250

TABLE C.3 **Future Value of $1 at the End of *n* Periods: $FVIF_{k,n} = (1 + k)^n$**

Period	1%	2%	3%	4%	5%	6%	7%	8%	9%	10%	12%	14%	15%	16%	18%	20%	24%	28%	32%	36%
1	1.0100	1.0200	1.0300	1.0400	1.0500	1.0600	1.0700	1.0800	1.0900	1.1000	1.1200	1.1400	1.1500	1.1600	1.1800	1.2000	1.2400	1.2800	1.3200	1.3600
2	1.0201	1.0404	1.0609	1.0816	1.1025	1.1236	1.1449	1.1664	1.1881	1.2100	1.2544	1.2996	1.3225	1.3456	1.3924	1.4400	1.5376	1.6384	1.7424	1.8496
3	1.0303	1.0612	1.0927	1.1249	1.1576	1.1910	1.2250	1.2597	1.2950	1.3310	1.4049	1.4815	1.5209	1.5609	1.6430	1.7280	1.9066	2.0972	2.3000	2.5155
4	1.0406	1.0824	1.1255	1.1699	1.2155	1.2625	1.3108	1.3605	1.4116	1.4641	1.5735	1.6890	1.7490	1.8106	1.9388	2.0736	2.3642	2.6844	3.0360	3.4210
5	1.0510	1.1041	1.1593	1.2167	1.2763	1.3382	1.4026	1.4693	1.5386	1.6105	1.7623	1.9254	2.0114	2.1003	2.2878	2.4883	2.9316	3.4360	4.0075	4.6526
6	1.0615	1.1262	1.1941	1.2653	1.3401	1.4185	1.5007	1.5869	1.6771	1.7716	1.9738	2.1950	2.3131	2.4364	2.6996	2.9860	3.6352	4.3980	5.2899	6.3275
7	1.0721	1.1487	1.2299	1.3159	1.4071	1.5036	1.6058	1.7138	1.8280	1.9487	2.2107	2.5023	2.6600	2.8262	3.1855	3.5832	4.5077	5.6295	6.9826	8.6054
8	1.0829	1.1717	1.2668	1.3686	1.4775	1.5938	1.7182	1.8509	1.9926	2.1436	2.4760	2.8526	3.0590	3.2784	3.7589	4.2998	5.5895	7.2058	9.2170	11.703
9	1.0937	1.1951	1.3048	1.4233	1.5513	1.6895	1.8385	1.9990	2.1719	2.3579	2.7731	3.2519	3.5179	3.8030	4.4355	5.1598	6.9310	9.2234	12.166	15.916
10	1.1046	1.2190	1.3439	1.4802	1.6289	1.7908	1.9672	2.1589	2.3674	2.5937	3.1058	3.7072	4.0456	4.4114	5.2338	6.1917	8.5944	11.805	16.059	21.646
11	1.1157	1.2434	1.3842	1.5395	1.7103	1.8983	2.1049	2.3316	2.5804	2.8531	3.4785	4.2262	4.6524	5.1173	6.1759	7.4301	10.657	15.111	21.198	29.439
12	1.1268	1.2682	1.4258	1.6010	1.7959	2.0122	2.2522	2.5182	2.8127	3.1384	3.8960	4.8179	5.3502	5.9360	7.2876	8.9161	13.214	19.342	27.982	40.037
13	1.1381	1.2936	1.4685	1.6651	1.8856	2.1329	2.4098	2.7196	3.0658	3.4523	4.3635	5.4924	6.1528	6.8858	8.5994	10.699	16.386	24.758	36.937	54.451
14	1.1495	1.3195	1.5126	1.7317	1.9799	2.2609	2.5785	2.9372	3.3417	3.7975	4.8871	6.2613	7.0757	7.9875	10.147	12.839	20.319	31.691	48.756	74.053
15	1.1610	1.3459	1.5580	1.8009	2.0789	2.3966	2.7590	3.1722	3.6425	4.1772	5.4736	7.1379	8.1371	9.2655	11.973	15.407	25.195	40.564	64.358	100.71
16	1.1726	1.3728	1.6047	1.8730	2.1829	2.5404	2.9522	3.4259	3.9703	4.5950	6.1304	8.1372	9.3576	10.748	14.129	18.488	31.242	51.923	84.953	136.96
17	1.1843	1.4002	1.6528	1.9479	2.2920	2.6928	3.1588	3.7000	4.3276	5.0545	6.8660	9.2765	10.761	12.467	16.672	22.186	38.740	66.461	112.13	186.27
18	1.1961	1.4282	1.7024	2.0258	2.4066	2.8543	3.3799	3.9960	4.7171	5.5599	7.6900	10.575	12.375	14.462	19.673	26.623	48.038	85.070	148.02	253.33
19	1.2081	1.4568	1.7535	2.1068	2.5270	3.0256	3.6165	4.3157	5.1417	6.1159	8.6128	12.055	14.231	16.776	23.214	31.948	59.567	108.89	195.39	344.53
20	1.2202	1.4859	1.8061	2.1911	2.6533	3.2071	3.8697	4.6610	5.6044	6.7275	9.6463	13.743	16.366	19.460	27.393	38.337	73.864	139.37	257.91	468.57
21	1.2324	1.5157	1.8603	2.2788	2.7860	3.3996	4.1406	5.0338	6.1088	7.4002	10.803	15.667	18.821	22.574	32.323	46.005	91.591	178.40	340.44	637.26
22	1.2447	1.5460	1.9161	2.3699	2.9253	3.6035	4.4304	5.4365	6.6586	8.1403	12.100	17.861	21.644	26.186	38.142	55.206	113.57	228.35	449.39	866.67
23	1.2572	1.5769	1.9736	2.4647	3.0715	3.8197	4.7405	5.8715	7.2579	8.9543	13.552	20.361	24.891	30.376	45.007	66.247	140.83	292.30	593.19	1178.6
24	1.2697	1.6084	2.0328	2.5633	3.2251	4.0489	5.0724	6.3412	7.9111	9.8497	15.178	23.212	28.625	35.236	53.108	79.496	174.63	374.14	783.02	1602.9
25	1.2824	1.6406	2.0938	2.6658	3.3864	4.2919	5.4274	6.8485	8.6231	10.834	17.000	26.461	32.918	40.874	62.668	95.396	216.54	478.90	1033.5	2180.0
26	1.2953	1.6734	2.1566	2.7725	3.5557	4.5494	5.8074	7.3964	9.3992	11.918	19.040	30.166	37.856	47.414	73.948	114.47	268.51	612.99	1364.3	2964.9
27	1.3082	1.7069	2.2213	2.8834	3.7335	4.8223	6.2139	7.9881	10.245	13.110	21.324	34.389	43.535	55.000	87.259	137.37	332.95	784.63	1800.9	4032.2
28	1.3213	1.7410	2.2879	2.9987	3.9201	5.1117	6.6488	8.6271	11.167	14.421	23.883	39.204	50.065	63.800	102.96	164.84	412.86	1004.3	2377.2	5483.8
29	1.3345	1.7758	2.3566	3.1187	4.1161	5.4184	7.1143	9.3173	12.172	15.863	26.749	44.693	57.575	74.008	121.50	197.81	511.95	1285.5	3137.9	7458.0
30	1.3478	1.8114	2.4273	3.2434	4.3219	5.7435	7.6123	10.062	13.267	17.449	29.959	50.950	66.211	85.849	143.37	237.37	634.81	1645.5	4142.0	10143.
40	1.4889	2.2080	3.2620	4.8010	7.0400	10.285	14.974	21.724	31.409	45.259	93.050	188.88	267.86	378.72	750.37	1469.7	5455.9	19426.	66520.	*
50	1.6446	2.6916	4.3839	7.1067	11.467	18.420	29.457	46.901	74.357	117.39	289.00	700.23	1083.6	1670.7	3927.3	9100.4	46890.	*	*	*
60	1.8167	3.2810	5.8916	10.519	18.679	32.987	57.946	101.25	176.03	304.48	897.59	2595.9	4383.9	7370.1	20555.	56347.	*	*	*	*

*FVIFA > 99.999

TABLE C.4

Sum of an Annuity of $1 Per Period for *n* Periods:

$$FVIFA_{k,n} = \sum_{t=1}^{n}(1 + k)^{t-1} = \frac{(1 + k)^{n-1}}{k}$$

Number of Periods	1%	2%	3%	4%	5%	6%	7%	8%	9%	10%	12%	14%	15%	16%	18%	20%	24%	28%	32%	36%
1	1.0000	1.0000	1.0000	1.0000	1.0000	1.0000	1.0000	1.0000	1.0000	1.0000	1.0000	1.0000	1.0000	1.0000	1.0000	1.0000	1.0000	1.0000	1.0000	1.0000
2	2.0100	2.0200	2.0300	2.0400	2.0500	2.0600	2.0700	2.0800	2.0900	2.1000	2.1200	2.1400	2.1500	2.1600	2.1800	2.2000	2.2400	2.2800	2.3200	2.3600
3	3.0301	3.0604	3.0909	3.1216	3.1525	3.1836	3.2149	3.2464	3.2781	3.3100	3.3744	3.4396	3.4725	3.5056	3.5724	3.6400	3.7776	3.9184	4.0624	4.2096
4	4.0604	4.1216	4.1836	4.2465	4.3101	4.3746	4.4399	4.5061	4.5731	4.6410	4.7793	4.9211	4.9934	5.0665	5.2154	5.3630	5.6842	6.0156	6.3624	6.7251
5	5.1010	5.2040	5.3091	5.4163	5.5256	5.6371	5.7507	5.8666	5.9847	6.1051	6.3528	6.6101	6.7424	6.8771	7.1542	7.4416	8.0484	8.6999	9.3983	10.146
6	6.1520	6.3081	6.4684	6.6330	6.8019	6.9753	7.1533	7.3359	7.5233	7.7156	8.1152	8.5355	8.7537	8.9775	9.4420	9.9299	10.980	12.135	13.405	14.798
7	7.2135	7.4343	7.6625	7.8983	8.1420	8.3938	8.6540	8.9228	9.2004	9.4872	10.089	10.730	11.066	11.413	12.141	12.915	14.615	16.533	18.695	21.126
8	8.2857	8.5830	8.8923	9.2142	9.5491	9.8975	10.259	10.636	11.028	11.435	12.299	13.232	13.726	14.240	15.327	16.499	19.122	22.163	25.678	29.731
9	9.3685	9.7546	10.159	10.582	11.026	11.491	11.978	12.487	13.021	13.579	14.775	16.085	16.785	17.518	19.085	20.798	24.712	29.369	34.895	41.435
10	10.462	10.949	11.463	12.006	12.577	13.180	13.816	14.486	15.192	15.937	17.548	19.337	20.303	21.321	23.521	25.958	31.643	38.592	47.061	57.351
11	11.566	12.168	12.807	13.486	14.206	14.971	15.783	16.645	17.560	18.531	20.654	23.044	24.349	25.732	28.755	32.150	40.237	50.398	63.121	78.998
12	12.682	13.412	14.192	15.025	15.917	16.869	17.888	18.977	20.140	21.384	24.133	27.270	29.001	30.850	34.931	39.580	50.894	65.510	84.320	108.43
13	13.809	14.680	15.617	16.626	17.713	18.882	20.140	21.495	22.953	24.522	28.029	32.088	34.351	36.786	42.218	48.496	64.109	84.852	112.30	148.47
14	14.947	15.973	17.086	18.291	19.598	21.015	22.550	24.214	26.019	27.975	32.392	37.581	40.504	43.672	50.818	59.195	80.496	109.61	149.23	202.92
15	16.096	17.293	18.598	20.023	21.578	23.276	25.129	27.152	29.360	31.772	37.279	43.842	47.580	51.659	60.965	72.035	100.81	141.30	197.99	276.97
16	17.257	18.639	20.156	21.824	23.657	25.672	27.888	30.324	33.003	35.949	42.753	50.980	55.717	60.925	72.939	87.442	126.01	181.86	262.35	377.69
17	18.430	20.012	21.761	23.697	25.840	28.212	30.840	33.750	36.973	40.544	48.883	59.117	65.075	71.673	87.068	105.93	157.25	233.79	347.30	514.66
18	19.614	21.412	23.414	25.645	28.132	30.905	33.999	37.450	41.301	45.599	55.749	68.394	75.836	84.140	103.74	128.11	195.99	300.25	459.44	700.93
19	20.810	22.840	25.116	27.671	30.539	33.760	37.379	41.446	46.018	51.159	63.439	78.969	88.211	98.603	123.41	154.74	244.03	385.32	607.47	954.27
20	22.019	24.297	26.870	29.778	33.066	36.785	40.995	45.762	51.160	57.275	72.052	91.024	102.44	115.37	146.62	186.68	303.60	494.21	802.86	1298.8
21	23.239	25.783	28.676	31.969	35.719	39.992	44.865	50.422	56.764	64.002	81.698	104.76	118.81	134.84	174.02	225.02	377.46	633.59	1060.7	1767.3
22	24.471	27.299	30.536	34.248	38.505	43.392	49.005	55.456	62.873	71.402	92.502	120.43	137.63	157.41	206.34	271.03	469.05	811.99	1401.2	2404.6
23	25.716	28.845	32.452	36.617	41.430	46.995	53.436	60.893	69.531	79.543	104.60	138.29	159.27	183.60	244.48	325.23	582.62	1040.3	1850.6	3271.3
24	26.973	30.421	34.426	39.082	44.502	50.815	58.176	66.764	76.789	88.497	118.15	158.65	184.16	213.97	289.49	392.48	723.46	1332.6	2443.8	4449.9
25	28.243	32.030	36.459	41.645	47.727	54.864	63.249	73.105	84.700	98.347	133.33	181.87	212.79	249.21	342.60	471.98	898.09	1706.8	3226.8	6052.9
26	29.525	33.670	38.553	44.311	51.113	59.156	68.676	79.954	93.323	109.18	150.33	208.33	245.71	290.08	405.27	567.37	1114.6	2185.7	4260.4	8233.0
27	30.820	35.344	40.709	47.084	54.669	63.705	74.483	87.350	102.72	121.09	169.37	238.49	283.56	337.50	479.22	681.85	1383.1	2798.7	5624.7	11197.9
28	32.129	37.051	42.930	49.967	58.402	68.528	80.697	95.338	112.96	134.20	190.69	272.88	327.10	392.50	566.48	819.22	1716.0	3583.3	7425.6	15230.2
29	33.450	38.792	45.218	52.966	62.322	73.639	87.346	103.96	124.13	148.63	214.58	312.09	377.16	456.30	669.44	984.06	2128.9	4587.6	9802.9	20714.1
30	34.784	40.568	47.575	56.084	66.438	79.058	94.460	113.28	136.30	164.49	241.33	356.78	434.74	530.31	790.94	1181.8	2640.9	5873.2	12940.	28172.2
40	48.886	60.402	75.401	95.025	120.79	154.76	199.63	259.05	337.88	442.59	767.09	1342.0	1779.0	2360.7	4163.2	7343.8	22728.	69377.	*	*
50	64.463	84.579	112.79	152.66	209.34	290.33	406.52	573.76	815.08	1163.9	2400.0	4994.5	7217.7	10435.	21813.	45497.	*	*	*	*
60	81.669	114.05	163.05	237.99	353.58	533.12	813.52	1253.2	1944.7	3034.8	7471.6	18535.	29219.	46057.	*	*	*	*	*	*

*FVIF > 99.999

APPENDIX D

STANDARD NORMAL PROBABILITIES

z	**0.00**	**0.01**	**0.02**	**0.03**	**0.04**	**0.05**	**0.06**	**0.07**	**0.08**	**0.09**
0.0	.5000	.5040	.5080	.5120	.5160	.5199	.5239	.5279	.5219	.5359
0.1	.5398	.5438	.5478	.5517	.5557	.5596	.5636	.5675	.5714	.5753
0.2	.5793	.5832	.5871	.5910	.5948	.5987	.6026	.6064	.6103	.6141
0.3	.6179	.6217	.6255	.6293	.6331	.6368	.6406	.6443	.6480	.6517
0.4	.6554	.6591	.6628	.6664	.6700	.6736	.6772	.6808	.6844	.6879
0.5	.6915	.6950	.6985	.7019	.7054	.7088	.7123	.7157	.7190	.7224
0.6	.7257	.7291	.7324	.7357	.7389	.7422	.7454	.7486	.7517	.7549
0.7	.7580	.7611	.7642	.7673	.7704	.7734	.7764	.7794	.7823	.7852
0.8	.7881	.7910	.7939	.7967	.7995	.8023	.8051	.8078	.8106	.8133
0.9	.8159	.8186	.8212	.8238	.8264	.8289	.8315	.8340	.8365	.8389
1.0	.8413	.8438	.8461	.8485	.8508	.8531	.8554	.8577	.8599	.8621
1.1	.8643	.8665	.8686	.8708	.8729	.8749	.8770	.8790	.8810	.8830
1.2	.8849	.8860	.8888	.8907	.8925	.8943	.8962	.8980	.8997	.9015
1.3	.9032	.9049	.9066	.9082	.9099	.9115	.9131	.9147	.9162	.9177
1.4	.9192	.9207	.9222	.9236	.9251	.9265	.9279	.9292	.9306	.9319
1.5	.9332	.9345	.9357	.9370	.9382	.9394	.9406	.9418	.9429	.9441
1.6	.9452	.9463	.9474	.9484	.9495	.9505	.9515	.9525	.9535	.9545
1.7	.9554	.9564	.9573	.9582	.9591	.9599	.9608	.9616	.9625	.9633
1.8	.9641	.9649	.9656	.9664	.9671	.9678	.9686	.9693	.9699	.9706
1.9	.9713	.9719	.9726	.9732	.9738	.9744	.9750	.9756	.9761	.9767
2.0	.9772	.9778	.9783	.9788	.9793	.9798	.9803	.9808	.9812	.9817
2.1	.9821	.9826	.9830	.9834	.9838	.9842	.9846	.9850	.9854	.9857
2.2	.9861	.9864	.9868	.9871	.9875	.9878	.9881	.9884	.9887	.9890
2.3	.9893	.9896	.9898	.9901	.9904	.9906	.9909	.9911	.9913	.9916
2.4	.9918	.9920	.9922	.9925	.9927	.9929	.9931	.9932	.9934	.9936
2.5	.9938	.9940	.9941	.9943	.9945	.9946	.9948	.9949	.9951	.9952
2.6	.9953	.9955	.9956	.9957	.9959	.9960	.9961	.9962	.9963	.9964
2.7	.9965	.9966	.9967	.9968	.9969	.9970	.9971	.9972	.9973	.9974
2.8	.9974	.9975	.9976	.9977	.9977	.9978	.9979	.9979	.9980	.9981
2.9	.9981	.9982	.9982	.9983	.9984	.9984	.9985	.9985	.9986	.9986
3.0	.9987	.9987	.9987	.9988	.9988	.9989	.9989	.9989	.9990	.9990

GLOSSARY

Abnormal rate of return The amount by which a security's return differs from the market's expected rate of return based on the market's rate of return and the security's relationship with the market.

Accumulation phase Phase in the investment life cycle during which individuals in the early-to-middle years of their working career attempt to accumulate assets to satisfy short-term needs and longer-term goals.

Actuarial rate of return The discount rate used to find the present value of a defined benefit pension plan's future obligations and thus determine the size of the firm's annual contribution to the plan.

American Depository Receipts (ADRs) Certificates of ownership issued by a U.S. bank that represent indirect ownership of a certain number of shares of a specific foreign firm. Shares are held on deposit in a bank in the firm's home country.

American option An option contract that can be exercised at any time until its expiration date.

Analysis effect The difference in performance of a bond portfolio from that of a chosen index due to acquisition of temporarily mispriced issues that then move to their correct prices.

Anomalies Security price relationships that appear to contradict a well-regarded hypothesis; in this case, the efficient market hypothesis.

Arbitrage A trading strategy designed to generate a guaranteed profit from a transaction that requires no capital commitment or risk bearing on the part of the trader. A simple example of an arbitrage trade would be the simultaneous purchase and sale of the same security in different markets at different prices.

Arbitrage pricing theory (APT) A theory concerned with deriving the expected or required rates of return on risky assets based on the asset's systematic relationship to several risk factors. This multifactor model is in contrast to the single-factor CAPM.

Arithmetic mean (AM) A measure of mean annual rates of return equal to the sum of annual holding period rates of return divided by the number of years.

Asset allocation The process of deciding how to distribute an investor's wealth among different asset classes for investment purposes.

Asset class Securities that have similar characteristics, attributes, and risk/return relationships.

Assets under management (AUM) The total market value of the assets managed by an investment firm.

At the money A special case of an option where the exercise price and the price of the underlying asset are identical.

Attribution analysis An assessment technique designed to establish whether a manager's performance relative to a benchmark resulted from market timing or security selection skills.

Average tax rate A person's total tax payment divided by their total income.

Autocorrelation test A test of the efficient market hypothesis that compares security price changes over time to check for predictable correlation patterns.

Backtest A method of testing a quantitative model in which computers are used to examine the composition and returns of portfolios based on historical data to determine if the selected strategy would have worked in the past.

Backwardated A situation in a futures market where the current contract price is greater than the current spot price for the underlying asset.

Balance sheet A financial statement that shows what assets the firm controls at a fixed point in time and how it has financed these assets.

Balanced fund A mutual fund with, generally, a three-part investment objective: (1) to conserve the investor's principal, (2) to pay current income, and (3) to increase both principal and income. The fund aims to achieve this by owning a mixture of bonds, preferred stocks, and common stocks.

Basis The difference between the spot price of the underlying asset and the futures contract price at any point in time (e.g., the *initial* basis at the time of contract origination, the *cover* basis at the time of contract termination).

Basis of an asset For tax purposes, the cost of an asset.

Basis risk The residual exposure to the price volatility of an underlying asset that results from a cross hedge transaction.

Bearer bond An unregistered bond for which ownership is determined by possession. The holder receives interest payments by clipping coupons attached to the security and sending them to the issuer for payment.

Benchmark error Situation where an inappropriate or incorrect benchmark is used to compare and assess portfolio returns and management.

Benchmark portfolio A comparison standard of risk and assets included in the policy statement and similar to the investor's risk preference and investment needs, which can be used to evaluate the investment performance of the portfolio manager.

Beta A standardized measure of systematic risk based upon an asset's covariance with the market portfolio.

Binomial option pricing model A valuation equation that assumes the price of the underlying asset changes through a series of discrete upward or downward movements.

Black-Scholes option pricing model A valuation equation that assumes the price of the underlying asset changes continuously through the option's expiration date by a statistical process known as *geometric Brownian motion.*

Bond price volatility The percentage changes in bond prices over time.

Bond swap An active bond portfolio management strategy that exchanges one position for another to take advantage of some difference between them.

Business risk The variability of operating income arising from the characteristics of the firm's industry. Two sources of business risk are sales variability and operating leverage.

Buy-and-hold strategy A passive bond portfolio management strategy in which bonds are bought and held to maturity.

Call market A market in which trading for individual stocks only takes place at specified times. All the bids and asks available at the time are combined and the market administrators specify a single price that will possibly clear the market at that time.

Call option Option to buy an asset within a certain period at a specified price called the *exercise price.*

Call premium Amount above par issuer must pay to bondholder for retiring the bond before its stated maturity.

Call provisions Specifies when and how a firm can issue a call for bonds outstanding prior to their maturity.

Cap agreement A contract that on each settlement date pays the holder the greater of the difference between the reference rate and the cap rate or zero; it is equivalent to a series of call options on the reference rate.

Capital appreciation A return objective in which the investor seeks to increase the portfolio value, primarily through capital gains, over time to meet a future need rather than dividend yield.

Capital asset pricing model (CAPM) A theory concerned with deriving the expected or required rates of return on risky assets based on the assets' systematic risk levels.

Capital market instruments Fixed-income or equity investments that trade in the secondary market.

Capital market line (CML) The line from the intercept point that represents the risk-free rate tangent to the original efficient frontier; it becomes the new efficient frontier since investments on this line dominate all the portfolios on the original Markowitz efficient frontier.

Capital preservation A return objective in which the investor seeks to minimize the risk of loss; generally a goal of the risk-averse investor.

Certificates of deposit (CDs) Instruments issued by banks and S&Ls that require minimum deposits for specified terms and that pay higher rates of interest than deposit accounts.

Characteristic line Regression line that indicates the systematic risk of a risky asset.

Closed-end investment company An investment company that issues only a limited number of shares, which it does not redeem (buy back). Instead, shares of a closed-end fund are traded in securities markets at prices determined by supply and demand.

Coefficient of variation (CV) A measure of relative variability that indicates risk per unit of return. It is equal to: standard deviation divided by the mean value. When used in investments, it is equal to: standard deviation of returns divided by the expected rate of return.

Coincident indicators A set of economic variables whose values reach peaks and troughs at about the same time as the aggregate economy.

Collateral trust bonds A mortgage bond wherein the assets backing the bond are financial assets like stocks and bonds.

Collateralized mortgage obligation (CMO) A debt security based on a pool of mortgage loans that provides a relatively stable stream of payments for a relatively predictable term.

Commission brokers Employees of a member firm who buy or sell securities for the customers of the firm.

Commodity swap A swap transaction in which one of the cash flows is tied to a fixed price for a commodity and the other is based on a fluctuating commodity index level.

Common size statements The normalization of balance sheet and income statement items to allow for more meaningful comparison of different-size firms. Balance sheet items are divided by total assets; income statement items are divided by total sales.

Common stock An equity investment that represents ownership of a firm, with full participation in its success or failure. The firm's directors must approve dividend payments.

Competitive environment The level of intensity of competition among firms in an industry, determined by an examination of five competitive forces.

Competitive strategy The search by a firm for a favorable competitive position within an industry, which affects evaluation of the industry's prospects.

Completely diversified portfolio A portfolio in which all unsystematic risk has been eliminated by diversification.

Completeness fund A specialized index used to form the basis of a passive portfolio whose purpose is to provide diversification to a client's total portfolio by excluding those segments in which the client's active managers invest.

Consolidation phase Phase in the investment life cycle during which individuals who are typically past the midpoint of their career have earnings that exceed expenses and invest them for future retirement or estate planning needs.

Contango A situation in a futures market where the current contract price is greater than the current spot price for the underlying asset.

Contingent deferred sales load A mutual fund that imposes a sales charge when the investor sells or redeems shares. Also referred to as *rear-end loads* or *redemption charges.*

Continuous market A market where stocks are priced and traded continuously by an auction process or by dealers when the market is open.

Contract price The transaction price specified in a forward or futures contract.

Convenience yield An adjustment made to the theoretical forward or futures contract delivery price to account for the preference that consumers have for holding spot positions in the underlying asset.

Conversion factors The adjustments made to Treasury bond futures contract terms to allow for the delivery of an instrument other than the standardized underlying asset.

Conversion parity price The price at which common stock can be obtained by surrendering the convertible instrument at par value.

Conversion premium The excess of the market value of the convertible security over its equity value if immediately converted into common stock. Typically expressed as a percentage of the equity value.

Conversion ratio The number of shares of common stock for which a convertible security may be exchanged.

Conversion value The value of the convertible security if converted into common stock at the stock's current market price

Convertible bonds A bond with the added feature that the bondholder has the option to turn the bond back to the firm in exchange for a specified number of common shares of the firm.

Convexity A measure of the degree to which a bond's price-yield curve departs from a straight line. This characteristic affects estimates of a bond's price volatility for a given change in yields.

Correlation coefficient A standardized measure of the relationship between two series that ranges from −1.00 to +1.00.

Cost of carry The net amount that would be required to store a commodity or security for future delivery, usually calculated as physical storage costs plus financial capital costs less dividends paid to the underlying asset.

Counterparty A participant to a derivative transaction.

Country risk Uncertainty due to the possibility of major political or economic change in the country where an investment is located. Also called *political risk.*

Coupon Indicates the interest payment on a debt security. It is the coupon rate times the par value that indicates the interest payments on a debt security.

Coupon reinvestment risk The component of interest rate risk due to the uncertainty of the rate at which coupon payments will be reinvested.

Covariance A measure of the degree to which two variables, such as rates of return for investment assets, move together over time relative to their individual mean returns.

Covered call A trading strategy in which a call option is sold as a supplement to a long position in an underlying asset or portfolio of assets.

Covered interest arbitrage A trading strategy involving borrowing money in one country and lending it to another designed to exploit price deviations from the interest rate parity model.

Credit analysis An active bond portfolio management strategy designed to identify bonds that are expected to experience changes in rating. This strategy is critical when investing in high-yield bonds.

Cross hedge A trading strategy in which the price volatility of a commodity or security position is hedged with a forward or futures contract based on a different underlying asset or different settlement terms.

Crossover price The price at which the yield to maturity equals the yield to call. Above this price, yield to call is the appropriate yield measure; below this price, yield to maturity is the appropriate yield measure.

Cross-sectional analysis An examination of a firm's performance in comparison to other firms in the industry with similar characteristics to the firm being studied.

Currency swap A swap transaction in which the cash flows, which can be either fixed or variable, are denominated in different currencies.

Current income A return objective in which the investor seeks to generate income rather than capital gains; generally a goal of an investor who wants to supplement earnings with income to meet living expenses.

Current yield A bond's yield as measured by its current income (coupon) as a percentage of its market price.

Cyclical change An economic trend arising from the ups and downs of the business cycle.

Cyclical company A firm whose earnings rise and fall with general economic activity.

Cyclical stock A stock with a high beta; its gains typically exceed those of a rising market and its losses typically exceed those of a falling market.

Debentures Bonds that promise payments of interest and principal but pledge no specific assets. Holders have first claim on the issuer's income and unpledged assets. Also known as *unsecured bonds.*

Declining trend channel The range defined by security prices as they move progressively lower.

Dedication A portfolio management technique in which the portfolio's cash flows are used to retire a set of liabilities over time.

Dedication with reinvestment A dedication strategy in which portfolio cash flows may precede their corresponding liabilities. Such cash flows can be reinvested to earn a return until the date the liability is due to be paid.

Defensive company Firms whose future earnings are likely to withstand an economic downturn.

Defensive competitive strategy Positioning the firm so that its capabilities provide the best means to deflect the effect of the competitive forces in the industry.

Defensive stock A stock whose return is not expected to decline as much as that of the overall market during a bear market.

Defined benefit pension plan A pension plan to which the company contributes a certain amount each year and that pays employees an income after they retire. The benefit size is based on factors such as workers' salary and time of employment.

Defined contribution pension plan A pension plan in which worker benefits are determined by the size of employees' contributions to the plan and the returns earned on the fund's investments.

Delta The change in the price of the option with respect to a one dollar change in the price of the underlying asset; this is the option's *hedge ratio,* or the number of units of the underlying asset that can be hedged by a single option contract.

Derivative security An instrument whose market value ultimately depends upon, or derives from, the value of a more fundamental investment vehicle called the underlying asset or security.

Diffusion index An indicator of the number of stocks rising during a specified period of time relative to the number of stocks declining and not changing price.

Discount A bond selling at a price below par value due to capital market conditions.

Dividend discount model (DDM) A technique for estimating the value of a stock issue as the present value of all future dividends.

Dollar-weighted return The discount rate that sets the present value of a future set of cash flows equal to the investment's current value; also known as the *internal rate of return.*

Downtick A price decline in a transaction price compared to the previous transaction price.

DuPont system A method of examining ROE by breaking it down into three component parts: (1) profit margin, (2) total asset turnover, and (3) financial leverage.

Duration A composite measure of the timing of a bond's cash flow characteristics taking into consideration its coupon and term to maturity.

Duration strategy A portfolio management strategy employed to reduce the interest rate risk of a bond portfolio by matching the modified duration of the portfolio with its investment horizon. For example, if the investment horizon is 10 years, the portfolio manager would construct a portfolio that has a modified duration of 10 years. This strategy is referred to as *immunization of the portfolio.*

Earnings momentum A strategy in which portfolios are constructed of stocks of firms with rising earnings.

Earnings multiplier Also known as the price/earnings ratio, it is a measurement of the relationship between a company's, or the aggregate stock market's, stock prices and earnings.

Earnings multiplier model A technique for estimating the value of a stock issue as a multiple of its earnings per share.

Earnings surprise A company announcement of earnings that differ from analysts' prevailing expectations.

Economic value added (EVA) Internal management performance measure that compares net operating profit to total cost of capital. Indicates how profitable company projects are as a sign of management performance.

Effective duration Direct measure of the interest rate sensitivity of a bond (or any financial instrument) based upon price changes derived from a pricing model.

Efficient capital market A market in which security prices rapidly reflect all information about securities.

Empirical duration Measures directly the interest rate sensitivity of an asset by examining the percentage price change for an asset in response to a change in yield during a specified period of time.

Ending-wealth value The total amount of money derived from investment in a bond until maturity, including principal, coupon payments, and income from reinvestment of coupon payments.

Equipment trust certificates Mortgage bonds that are secured by specific pieces of transportation equipment like boxcars and planes.

Equity swap A swap transaction in which one cash flow is tied to the return to an equity portfolio position, often an index such as the Standard and Poor's 500, while the other is based on a floating-rate index.

Estimated rate of return The rate of return an investor anticipates earning from a specific investment over a particular future holding period.

Eurobonds Bonds denominated in a currency not native to the country in which they are issued.

European option An option contract that can only be exercised on its expiration date.

Event study Research that examines the reaction of a security's price to a specific company, world event, or news announcement.

Exchange clearinghouse The functional unit attached to a futures exchange that guarantees contract performance, oversees delivery, serves as a bookkeeper, and calculates settlement transactions.

Exchange rate risk Uncertainty due to the denomination of an investment in a currency other than that of the investor's own country.

Exercise price The transaction price specified in an option contract; also known as the *strike* or *striking price.*

Exotic option Designed to have payoffs that differ from those of standard contract options. Three such nonstandard contracts are *Asian, lookback,* and *digital* options.

Expected rate of return The return that analysts' calculations suggest a security should provide, based on the market's rate of return during the period and the security's relationship to the market.

Expiry The expiration date of a derivative security.

External efficiency When prices reflect all available information about an asset, which implies that prices adjust quickly to new information regarding supply or demand. Also referred to as *informational efficiency.*

Fiduciary A person who supervises or oversees the investment portfolio of a third party, such as in a trust account, and makes investment decisions in accordance with the owner's wishes.

Filter rule A trading rule that recommends security transactions when price changes exceed a previously determined percentage.

Financial risk The variability of future income arising from the firm's fixed financing costs, for example, interest payments. The effect of fixed financial costs is to magnify the effect of changes in operating profit on net income or earnings per share.

Fixed-income investments Loans with contractually mandated payment schedules from investors to firms or governments.

Flat trend channel The range defined by security prices as they maintain a relatively steady level.

Floating rate note (FRN) Short- to intermediate-term bonds with regularly scheduled coupon payments linked to a variable interest rate, most often LIBOR.

Floor agreement A contract that on each settlement date pays the holder the greater of the difference between the floor rate and the reference rate or zero; it is equivalent to a series of put options on the reference rate.

Floor brokers Independent members of an exchange who act as brokers for other members.

Forward contract An agreement between two counterparties that requires the exchange of a commodity or security at a fixed time in the future at a predetermined price.

Forward discount A situation where, from the perspective of the domestic country, the spot exchange rate is smaller than the forward exchange rate with a foreign country.

Forward premium A situation where, from the perspective of the domestic country, the spot exchange rate is larger than the forward exchange rate with a foreign country.

Forward rate A short-term yield for a future holding period implied by the spot rates of two securities with different maturities.

Forward rate agreement (FRA) A transaction in which two counterparties agree to a single exchange of cash flows based on a fixed and floating rate, respectively.

Fourth market Direct trading of securities between owners, usually institutions, without any broker intermediation.

Franchise factor A firm's unique competitive advantage that makes it possible for a firm to earn excess returns (rates of return above a firm's cost of capital) on its capital projects. In turn, these excess returns and the franchise factor cause the firm's stock price to have a P/E ratio above its base P/E ratio that is equal to 1/k.

Free cash flow This cash flow measure equals cash flow from operations minus capital expenditures and dividends.

Full replication A technique for constructing a passive index portfolio in which all securities in an index are purchased in proportion to their weights in the index.

Fully taxable equivalent yield (FTEY) A yield on a tax-exempt bond that adjusts for its tax benefits to allow comparisons with taxable bonds.

Futures contract An agreement that provides for the future exchange of a particular asset at a specified delivery date in exchange for a specified payment at the time of delivery.

General obligation bond (GO) A municipal issue serviced from and guaranteed by the issuer's full taxing authority.

Generally accepted accounting principles (GAAP) Accounting principles formulated by the Financial Accounting Standards Board and used to construct financial statements.

Geometric mean (GM) The *n*th root of the product of the annual holding period returns for *n* years minus 1.

Gifting phase Phase in the investment life cycle during which individuals use excess assets to financially assist relatives or friends, establish charitable trusts, or construct trusts to minimize estate taxes.

Growth company A company that consistently has the opportunities and ability to invest in projects that provide rates of return that exceed the firm's cost of capital. Because of these investment opportunities, it retains a high proportion of earnings, and its earnings grow faster than those of average firms.

Growth stock A stock issue that generates a higher rate of return than other stocks in the market with similar risk characteristics.

Hedge A trading strategy in which derivative securities are used to reduce or completely offset a counterparty's risk exposure to an underlying asset.

Hedge ratio The number of derivative contracts that must be transacted to offset the price volatility of an underlying commodity or security position.

High-yield bond A bond rated below investment grade. Also referred to as *speculative-grade bonds* or *junk bonds.*

Holding period return (HPR) The total return from an investment, including all sources of income, for a given period of time. A value of 1.0 indicates no gain or loss.

Holding period yield (HPY) The total return from an investment for a given period of time stated as a percentage.

Immunization A bond portfolio management technique of matching modified duration to the investment horizon of the portfolio to eliminate interest rate risk.

Implied volatility The standard deviation of changes in the price of the underlying asset that can be inferred from an option's market price in relation to a specific valuation model.

In the money An option that has positive intrinsic value.

Income bonds Debentures that stipulate interest payments only if the issuer earns the income to make the payments by specified dates.

Income effect The known component of the total return for a bond during a period of time if the shape and position of the yield curve did not change.

Income statement A financial statement that shows the flow of the firm's sales, expenses, and earnings over a period of time.

Indenture The legal agreement that lists the obligations of the issuer of a bond to the bondholder, including payment schedules, call provisions, and sinking funds.

Indexing A passive bond portfolio management strategy that seeks to match the composition, and therefore the performance, of a selected market index.

Industry life cycle analysis An analysis that focuses on the industry's stage of development.

Information An attribute of a good market that includes providing buyers and sellers with timely, accurate information on the volume and prices of past transactions and on all currently outstanding bids and offers.

Information ratio Statistic used to measure a portfolio's average return in excess of a comparison, benchmark portfolio divided by the standard deviation of this excess return.

Informationally efficient market A more technical term for an efficient capital market that emphasizes the role of information in setting the market price.

Initial public offering (IPO) A new issue by a firm that has no existing public market.

Interest-on-interest Bond income from reinvestment of coupon payments.

Interest rate anticipation An active bond portfolio management strategy designed to preserve capital or take advantage of capital gains opportunities by predicting interest rates and their effects on bond prices.

Interest rate collar The combination of a long position in a cap agreement and a short position in a floor agreement, or vice versa; it is equivalent to a series of range forward positions.

Interest rate effect The return on a bond portfolio caused by changes in the term structure of interest rates during a period that affect both bond prices and reinvestment rates.

Interest rate parity The relationship that must exist in an efficient market between the spot and forward foreign exchange rates between two countries and the interest rates in those countries.

Interest rate risk The uncertainty of returns on an investment due to possible changes in interest rates over time.

Interest rate swap An agreement calling for the periodic exchange of cash flows, one based on an interest rate that remains fixed for the life of the contract and the other that is linked to a variable-rate index.

Internal liquidity (solvency) ratios Financial ratios that measure the ability of the firm to meet future short-term financial obligations.

Internal rate of return (IRR) The discount rate at which cash outflows of an investment equal cash inflows.

International domestic bonds Bonds issued by a foreign firm, denominated in the firm's native currency, and sold within its own country.

Intrinsic value The portion of a call option's total value equal to the greater of either zero or the difference between the current value of the underlying asset and the exercise price; for a put option, intrinsic value is the greater of either zero or the exercise price less the underlying asset price. For a stock, it is the value derived from fundamental analysis of the stock's expected returns or cash flows.

Investment The current commitment of dollars for a period of time in order to derive future payments that will compensate the investor for the time the funds are committed, the expected rate of inflation, and the uncertainty of future payments.

Investment company A firm that sells shares of the company and uses the proceeds to buy stock, bonds, or other financial instruments.

Investment decision process Estimation of value for comparison with market price to determine whether or not to invest.

Investment horizon The time period used for planning and forecasting purposes or the future time at which the investor requires the invested funds.

Investment management company A company separate from the investment company that manages the portfolio and performs administrative functions.

Jensen measure An absolute measure of a portfolio's risk-adjusted performance, computed as the intercept in a regression equation where the excess returns to a manager's portfolio and the market index are, respectively, the dependent and independent variables.

Lagging indicators A set of economic variables whose values reach peaks and troughs after the aggregate economy.

Leading indicators A set of economic variables whose values reach peaks and troughs in advance of the aggregate economy.

Limit order An order that lasts for a specified time to buy or sell a security when and if it trades at a specified price.

Liquid Term used to describe an asset that can be quickly converted to cash at a price close to fair market value.

Liquidity The ability to buy or sell an asset quickly and at a reasonable price.

Liquidity risk Uncertainty due to the ability to buy or sell an investment in the secondary market.

Long hedge A long position in a forward or futures contract used to offset the price volatility of a short position in the underlying asset.

Long position The buyer of a commodity or security or, for a forward contract, the counterparty who will be the eventual buyer of the underlying asset.

Long-term, high-priority goal A long-term financial investment goal of personal importance that typically includes achieving financial independence, such as being able to retire at a certain age.

Low-load fund A mutual fund that imposes a moderate front-end sales charge when the investor buys the fund, typically about 3 to 4 percent.

Lower-priority goal A financial investment goal of lesser personal importance, such as taking a luxurious vacation or buying a car every few years.

Macaulay duration A measure of the time flow of cash from a bond where cash flows are weighted by present values discounted by the yield to maturity.

Maintenance margin The required proportion that the investor's equity value must be to the total market value of the stock. If the proportion drops below this percent, the investor will receive a margin call.

Management and advisory firm A firm that provides a range of services from standard banking transactions (savings accounts, personal loans) to advising individual and institutional investors on structuring their portfolios and managing investment funds.

Management effect A combination of the interest rate anticipation effect, the analysis effect, and the trading effect.

Management fee The compensation an investment company pays to the investment management company for its services. The average annual fee is about 0.5 percent of fund assets.

Margin The percent of cost a buyer pays in cash for a security, borrowing the balance from the broker. This introduces leverage, which increases the risk of the transaction.

Margin account The collateral posted with the futures exchange clearinghouse by an outside counterparty to insure its eventual performance; the *initial* margin is the deposit required at contract origination while the *maintenance* margin is the minimum collateral necessary at all times.

Margin call A request by an investor's broker for additional capital for a security bought on margin if the investor's equity value declines below the required maintenance margin.

Marginal tax rate The part of each additional dollar in income that is paid as tax.

Marked to market The settlement process used to adjust the margin account of a futures contract for daily changes in the price of the underlying asset.

Market The means through which buyers and sellers are brought together to aid in the transfer of goods and/or services.

Market order An order to buy or sell a security immediately at the best price available.

Market portfolio The portfolio that includes all risky assets with relative weights equal to their proportional market values.

Market risk premium The amount of return above the risk-free rate that investors expect from the market in general as compensation for systematic risk.

Market value-added (MVA) External management performance measure to compare the market value of the company's debt and equity with the total capital invested in the firm.

Maturity strategy A portfolio management strategy employed to reduce the interest rate risk of a bond portfolio by matching the maturity of the portfolio with its investment horizon. For example, if the investment horizon is 10 years, the portfolio manager would construct a portfolio that will mature in 10 years.

Mean rates of return The average of an investment's returns over an extended period of time.

Modified duration A measure of Macaulay duration divided by yield maturity divided by the number of payments per year adjusted to help you estimate a bond's price volatility.

Money market The market for short-term debt securities with maturities of less than 1 year.

Money market funds Investment companies that hold portfolios of high-quality, short-term securities like T-bills. High liquidity and superior returns make them a good alternative to bank savings accounts.

Money market mutual fund A fund that invests in short-term securities sold in the money market. (Large companies, banks, and other institutions also invest their surplus cash in the money market for short periods of time.) In the entire investment spectrum, these are generally the safest, most stable securities available. They include Treasury bills, certificates of deposit of large banks, and commercial paper (short-term IOUs of large corporations).

Mortgage bonds Bonds that pledge specific assets such as buildings and equipment. The proceeds from the sale of these assets are used to pay off bondholders in case of bankruptcy.

Moving average The continually recalculating average of security prices for a period, often 200 days, to serve as an indication of the general trend of prices and also as a benchmark price.

Mutual fund An investment company that pools money from shareholders and invests in a variety of securities, including stocks, bonds, and money market securities. A mutual fund ordinarily stands ready to buy back (redeem) its shares at their current net asset value, which depends on the market value of the fund's portfolio of securities at the time. Mutual funds generally continuously offer new shares to investors.

National Association of Securities Dealers Automated Quotation (NASDAQ) system An electronic system for providing bid-ask quotes on OTC securities.

Near-term, high-priority goal A short-term financial investment goal of personal importance, such as accumulating funds for making a house down payment or buying a car.

Net asset value (NAV) per share The market value of an investment company's assets (securities, cash, and any accrued earnings) after deducting liabilities, divided by the number of shares outstanding.

New issue Common stocks or bonds offered by companies for public sale.

No-load fund A mutual fund that sells its shares at net asset value without adding sales charges.

Nominal yield A bond's yield as measured by its coupon rate.

Normal portfolio A specialized or customized benchmark constructed to evaluate a specific manager's investment style or philosophy.

Notes Intermediate-term debt securities with maturities longer than 1 year but less than 10 years.

Notional principal The principal value of a swap transaction, which is not exchanged but is used as a scale factor to translate interest rate differentials into cash settlement payments.

Objectives The investor's goals expressed in terms of risk and return and included in the policy statement.

Offensive competitive strategy A strategy whereby a firm attempts to use its strengths to affect the competitive forces in the industry and, in so doing, improves the firm's relative position in the industry.

Open-end investment company The more formal name for a mutual fund, which derives from the fact that it continuously offers new shares to investors and redeems them (buys them back) on demand.

Operating leverage The use of fixed-production costs in the firm's operating cost structure. The effect of fixed costs is to magnify the effect of a change in sales on operating profits.

Optimal portfolio The portfolio on the efficient frontier that has the highest utility for a given investor. It lies at the point of tangency between the efficient frontier and the curve with the investor's highest possible utility.

Option-adjusted spread A type of yield spread that considers changes in the term structure and alternative estimates of the volatility of interest rates.

Option clearing corporation (OCC) A company designed to guarantee, monitor margin accounts, and settle exchange-traded option transactions.

Option contract An agreement that grants the owner the right, but not the obligation, to make a future transaction in an underlying commodity or security at a fixed price and within a predetermined time in the future.

Option premium The initial price that the option buyer must pay to the option seller to acquire the contract.

Out of the money An option that has no intrinsic value.

Overfunded plan A defined benefit pension plan in which the present value of the pension liabilities is less than market value of the plan's assets.

Overweighted A condition in which a portfolio, for whatever reason, includes more of a class of securities than the relative market value alone would justify.

Payback The time required for the added income from the convertible relative to the stock to offset the conversion premium.

Peak The culmination of a bull market when prices stop rising and begin declining.

Peer group comparison A method of measuring portfolio performance by collecting the returns produced by a representative universe of investors over a specific period of time and displaying them in a simple boxplot format.

Performance presentation standards (PPS) A comprehensive set of reporting guidelines created by the Association for Investment Management and Research (AIMR), in an effort to fulfill the call for uniform, accurate, and consistent performance reporting.

Perpetuity An investment without any maturity date. It provides returns to its owner indefinitely.

Personal trust An amount of money set aside by a grantor and often managed by a third party, the trustee. Often constructed so one party receives income from the trust's investments and another party receives the residual value of the trust after the income beneficiaries' death.

Policy effect The difference in performance of a bond portfolio from that of a chosen index due to differences in duration, which result from a fund's investment policy.

Policy statement A statement in which the investor specifies investment goals, constraints, and risk preferences.

Portfolio A group of investments. Ideally, the investments should have different patterns of returns over time.

Preferred stock An equity investment that stipulates the dividend payment either as a coupon or a stated dollar amount. The firm's directors may withhold payments.

Premium A bond selling at a price above par value due to capital market conditions.

Price change effect The unknown component of the total return for a bond portfolio during a period of time due to the interest rate effect, sector/quality effect, and residual effect.

Price continuity A feature of a liquid market in which prices change little from one transaction to the next due to the depth of the market.

Price/earnings (P/E) ratio The number by which expected earnings per share is multiplied to estimate a stock's value; also called the *earnings multiplier.*

Price momentum A portfolio strategy in which you acquire stocks that have enjoyed above-market stock price increases.

Price risk The component of interest rate risk due to the uncertainty of the market price of a bond caused by possible changes in market interest rates.

Price-weighted series An indicator series calculated as an arithmetic average of the current prices of the sampled securities.

Primary market The market in which newly issued securities are sold by their issuers, who receive the proceeds.

Principal (par value) The original value of the debt underlying a bond that is payable at maturity.

Private placement A new issue sold directly to a small group of investors, usually institutions.

Promised yield to call (YTC) A bond's yield if held until the first available call date, with reinvestment of all coupon payments at the yield-to-call rate.

Promised yield to maturity (YTM) The most widely used measure of a bond's yield that states the fully compounded rate of return on a bond bought at market price and held to maturity with reinvestment of all coupon payments at the yield to maturity rate.

Protective put A trading strategy in which a put option is purchased as a supplement to a long position in an underlying asset or portfolio of assets; the most straightforward form of *portfolio insurance.*

Public bond A long-term, fixed-obligation debt security in a convenient, affordable denomination for sale to individuals and financial institutions.

Pure cash-matched dedicated portfolio A conservative dedicated portfolio management technique aimed at developing a bond portfolio that will provide payments exactly matching the specified liability schedules.

Put-call parity The relationship that must exist in an efficient market between the prices for put and call options having the same underlying asset, exercise price, and expiration date.

Put options Options to sell a firm's common stock within a certain period at a specified price.

Quadratic optimization A technique that relies on historical correlations in order to construct a portfolio that seeks to minimize tracking error with an index.

Range forward A trading strategy based on a variation of the put-call parity model where, for the same underlying asset but different exercise prices, a call option is purchased and a put option is sold (or vice versa).

Rate anticipation effect The difference in return because of changing the duration of the portfolio during a period as compared with the portfolio's long-term policy duration.

Real estate investment trusts (REITs) Investment funds that hold portfolios of real estate investments.

Real risk-free rate (RFR) The basic interest rate with no accommodation for inflation or uncertainty. The pure time value of money.

Realized capital gains Capital gains that result when an appreciated asset is sold; realized capital gains are taxable.

Realized yield The expected compounded yield on a bond that is sold before it matures assuming the reinvestment of all cash flows at an explicit rate. Also called *horizon yield* for the yield realized during an investment horizon period.

Refunding issue Bonds that provide funds to prematurely retire another bond issue. These bonds can be either a junior or senior issue.

Registered bond A bond for which ownership is registered with the issuer. The holder receives interest payments by check directly from the issuer.

Registered competitive market makers (RCMMs) Members of an exchange who are allowed to use their memberships to buy or sell for their own account within the specific trading obligations set down by the exchange.

Relative-strength (RS) ratio The ratio of a stock price or an industry index value to a market indicator series, indicating the stock's or the industry's performance relative to the overall market.

Required rate of return The return that compensates investors for their time, the expected rate of inflation, and the uncertainty of the return.

Residual effect The return on a bond portfolio after taking account of the three prior factors—yield to maturity, interest rate effect, and sector/quality effect.

Resistance level A price at which a technician would expect a substantial increase in the supply of a stock to reverse a rising trend.

Revenue bond A bond that is serviced by the income generated from specific revenue-producing projects of the municipality.

Rising trend channel The range defined by security prices as they move progressively higher.

Risk The uncertainty that an investment will earn its expected rate of return.

Risk averse The assumption about investors that they will choose the least risky alternative, all else being equal.

Risk-free asset An asset with returns that exhibit zero variance.

Risk premium (RP) The increase over the nominal risk-free rate that investors demand as compensation for an investment's uncertainty.

Risky asset An asset with uncertain future returns.

Runs test A test of the weak-form efficient market hypothesis that checks for trends that persist longer in terms of positive or negative price changes than one would expect for a random series.

Sampling A technique for constructing a passive index portfolio in which the portfolio manager buys a representative sample of stocks that comprise the benchmark index.

Secondary market The market in which outstanding securities are bought and sold by owners other than the issuers.

Sector/quality effect The return on a bond portfolio caused by changing yield spreads between bonds in different sectors and with different quality ratings.

Sector rotation strategy An active strategy that involves purchasing stocks in specific industries or stocks with specific characteristics (low P/E, growth, value) that are anticipated to rise in value more than the overall market.

Secured (senior) bond A bond backed by a legal claim on specified assets of the issuer.

Security-market indicator series An index created as a statistical measure of the performance of an entire market or segment of a market based on a sample of securities from the market or segment of a market.

Security market line (SML) The line that reflects the combination of risk and return of alternative investments. In CAPM risk is measured by systematic risk (beta).

Semistrong-form efficient market hypothesis The belief that security prices fully reflect all publicly available information, including information from security transactions and company, economic, and political news.

Separation theorem The proposition that the investment decision, which involves investing in the market portfolio on the capital market line, is separate from the financing decision, which targets a specific point on the CML based on the investor's risk preference.

Serial obligation bond A bond issue that has a series of maturity dates.

Settlement price The price determined by the exchange clearinghouse with which futures contract margin accounts are marked-to-market.

Sharpe measure A relative measure of a portfolio's benefit-to-risk ratio, calculated as its average return in excess of the risk-free rate divided by its standard deviation.

Short hedge A short position in a forward or futures contract used to offset the price volatility of a long position in the underlying asset.

Short position The seller of a commodity or security or, for a forward contract, the counterparty who will be the eventual seller of the underlying asset.

Short sale The sale of borrowed securities with the intention of repurchasing them later at a lower price and earning the difference.

Sinking fund Bond provision that requires the issuer to redeem some or all of the bond systematically over the term of the bond rather than in full at maturity.

Soft dollars A form of compensation to a money manager generated when the manager commits the investor to paying higher brokerage fees in exchange for the manager receiving additional services (e.g., stock research) from the broker.

Specialist The major market maker on U.S. stock exchanges who acts as a broker or dealer to ensure the liquidity and smooth functions of the secondary stock market.

Speculative company A firm with a great degree of business and/or financial risk, with commensurate high earnings potential.

Speculative stock A stock that appears to be highly overpriced compared to its reasonable valuation.

Spending phase Phase in the investment life cycle during which individuals' earning years end as they retire. They pay for expenses with income from social security and returns from prior investments and invest to protect against inflation.

Spread A trading strategy where long and short positions in two call (or two put) option contracts having the same underlying asset but different exercise prices or expiration dates are combined to create a customized return distribution.

Standard deviation A measure of variability equal to the square root of the variance.

Statement of cash flows A financial statement that shows the effects on the firm's cash flow of income flows and changes in its balance sheet.

Static yield spread Yield spreads that consider a spread over the total term structure.

Stock index arbitrage A trading strategy involving a long position in a stock portfolio and a short position in a stock index futures contract (or vice versa) designed to exploit a mispricing in the futures contract relative to the underlying index.

Straddle A trading strategy requiring the simultaneous purchase of a call option and a put option having the same exercise price, underlying asset, and expiration date. Variations of this theme include *strips, straps, strangles,* and *chooser options.*

Strong-form efficient market hypothesis The belief that security prices fully reflect all information from both public and private sources.

Structural change Economic trend occurring when the economy is undergoing a major change in organization or in how it functions.

Structured note A bond with an embedded derivative designed to create a payoff distribution that satisfies the needs of a specific investor clientele.

Style analysis An attempt to explain the variability in the observed returns to a security portfolio in terms of the movements in the returns to a series of benchmark portfolios designed to capture the essence of a particular security characteristic such as size, value, and growth.

Style grid A graph used to classify and display the investment style that best defines the nature of a security portfolio.

Subordinate (junior) bonds Debentures that, in case of default, entitle holders to claims on the issuer's assets only after the claims of holders of senior debentures and mortgage bonds are satisfied.

Support level A price at which a technician would expect a substantial increase in price and volume for a stock to reverse a declining trend that was due to profit taking.

Sustainable growth rate A measure of how fast a firm can grow using internal equity and debt financing and a constant capital structure. Equal to retention rate $\times$ ROE.

Swap spread A measure of the risk premium for an interest rate swap, calculated as the difference between the agreement's fixed rate and the yield on a Treasury bond with the same maturity.

Swaptions Also known as *swap options,* these contracts give the holder the right, but not the obligation, to enter into an interest rate or currency swap on prearranged terms.

SWOT analysis An examination of a firm's *S*trengths, *W*eaknesses, *O*pportunities, and *T*hreats. This analysis helps an analyst evaluate a firm's strategies to exploit its competitive advantages or defend against its weaknesses.

Systematic risk The variability of returns that is due to macroeconomic factors that affect all risky assets. Because it affects all risky assets, it cannot be eliminated by diversification.

Technical analysis Estimation of future security price movements based on past price and volume movements.

Term bond A bond that has a single maturity date.

Term structure of interest rates The relationship between term to maturity and yield to maturity for a sample of comparable bonds at a given time. Popularly known as the *yield curve.*

Term to maturity Specifies the date or the number of years before a bond matures or expires.

Third market Over-the-counter trading of securities listed on an exchange.

Tick The minimum price movement for the asset underlying a forward or futures contract; for Treasury bonds, one tick equals $\frac{1}{32}$ of 1 percent of par value.

Time premium The difference between an option's total market value and its intrinsic value.

Time-series analysis An examination of a firm's performance data over a period of time.

Time-weighted return The geometric average of (one plus) the *holding period yields* to an investment portfolio.

Total return A return objective in which the investor wants to increase the portfolio value to meet a future need by both capital gains and current income reinvestment.

Tracking error The difference between the return of a portfolio that is constructed to replicate an index and the return on the index itself.

Trading effect The difference in performance of a bond portfolio from that of a chosen index due to short-run changes in the composition of the portfolio.

Trading rule A formula for deciding on current transactions based on historical data.

Trading turnover The percentage of outstanding shares traded during a period of time.

Transaction cost The cost of executing a trade. Low costs characterize an operationally efficient market.

Treasury bill A negotiable U.S. government security with a maturity of less than 1 year that pays no periodic interest but yields the difference between its par value and its discounted purchase price.

Treasury bond A U.S. government security with a maturity of more than 10 years that pays interest periodically.

Treasury note A U.S. government security with maturities of 1 to 10 years that pays interest periodically.

Treynor measure A relative measure of a portfolio's benefit-to-risk ratio, calculated as its average return in excess of the risk-free rate divided by its beta coefficient.

Trough The culmination of a bear market at which prices stop declining and begin rising.

12b-1 fee A fee charged by some funds, named after the SEC rule that permits it. Such fees pay for distribution costs, such as advertising, or for brokers' commissions. The fund's prospectus details any 12b-1 charges that apply.

Underfunded plan A defined benefit pension plan in which the present value of the fund's liabilities to employees exceeds the value of the fund's assets.

Underweighted A condition in which a portfolio, for whatever reason, includes less of a class of securities than the relative market value alone would justify.

Unrealized capital gains Capital gains that reflect the price appreciation of currently held unsold assets; taxes on unrealized capital gains can be deferred indefinitely.

Unsecured bonds Bonds that promise payments of interest and principal but pledge no specific assets. Holders have first claim on the issuer's income and unpledged assets. Also known as *debentures.*

Unsystematic risk Risk that is unique to an asset, derived from its particular characteristics. It can be eliminated in a diversified portfolio.

Unweighted index An indicator series affected equally by the performance of each security in the sample regardless of price or market value. Also referred to as an *equal-weighted series.*

Unwind The negotiated termination of a forward or futures position before contract maturity.

Uptick An incremental movement upward in a transaction price over the previous transaction price.

Uptick-downtick ratio A ratio of the number of uptick block transactions (indicating buyers) to the number of downtick block transactions (indicating sellers of blocks). An indicator of institutional investor sentiment.

Valuation analysis An active bond portfolio management strategy designed to capitalize on expected price increases in temporarily undervalued issues.

Valuation process Part of the investment decision process in which you estimate the value of a security.

Value stocks Stocks that appear to be undervalued for reasons besides earnings growth potential. These stocks are usually identified based on high dividend yields, low P/E ratios, or low price-to-book ratios.

Value-weighted series An indicator series calculated as the total market value of the securities in the sample.

Variable-rate note A debt security for which the interest rate changes to follow some specified short-term rate, for example, the T-bill rate; see *floating rate note.*

Variance A measure of variability equal to the sum of the squares of a return's deviation from the mean, divided by n.

Warrant An instrument that allows the holder to purchase a specified number of shares of the firm's common stock from the firm at a specified price for a given period of time.

Weak-form efficient market hypothesis The belief that security prices fully reflect all security market information.

Yankee bonds Bonds sold in the United States and denominated in U.S. dollars but issued by a foreign firm or government.

Yield The promised rate of return on an investment under certain assumptions.

Yield illusion The erroneous expectation that a bond will provide its stated yield to maturity without recognizing the implicit reinvestment assumption related to coupon payments.

Yield spread The difference between the promised yields of alternative bond issues or market segments at a given time relative to yields on treasury issues of equal maturity.

Zero-coupon bond A bond that pays its par value at maturity, but no periodic interest payments. Its yield is determined by the difference between its par value and its discounted purchase price. Also called *original issue discount (OID) bonds.*

Name and Company Index

Subject Index

1223